FAMILYLIFE™
MARRIAGE
BIBLE

Betty J. Paul

PRESENTED TO

Gloria Renfro

BY

6 — 11 — 11

DATE

FAMILY
TREE
HUSBAND

HUSBAND
Ray W Paul Sr.

BROTHERS & SISTERS
John H Thomas
John W Thomas
Jerry Thomas
Leonard Thomas
Robert C Thomas
J L Thomas
Michael Thomas
John W

MOTHER
Mamie L
Luleym Adkins

BROTHERS & SISTERS
Billy Jean
Lois Shaw
Carolyn Thomas
Gloria Thomas
Carolyn

FATHER

BROTHERS & SISTERS

GRANDFATHER

BROTHERS & SISTERS

GRANDFATHER
Manuel Thomas

BROTHERS & SISTERS

GRANDMOTHER

BROTHERS & SISTERS

GRANDMOTHER

BROTHERS & SISTERS

GREAT GRANDFATHER

GREAT GRANDMOTHER

GREAT GRANDFATHER

GREAT GRANDMOTHER

GREAT GRANDFATHER

GREAT GRANDMOTHER

GREAT GRANDFATHER

GREAT GRANDMOTHER

FAMILY
TREE
WIFE

HUSBAND _____

BROTHERS & SISTERS _____
_____
_____
_____
_____
_____

MOTHER _____

BROTHERS & SISTERS _____
_____
_____
_____

FATHER _____

BROTHERS & SISTERS _____
_____
_____
_____

GRANDFATHER _____

BROTHERS & SISTERS _____
_____
_____

GRANDFATHER _____

BROTHERS & SISTERS _____
_____
_____

GRANDMOTHER _____

BROTHERS & SISTERS _____
_____
_____

GRANDMOTHER _____

BROTHERS & SISTERS _____
_____
_____

GREAT GRANDFATHER _____

GREAT GRANDMOTHER _____

GREAT GRANDFATHER _____

GREAT GRANDMOTHER _____

GREAT GRANDFATHER _____

GREAT GRANDMOTHER _____

GREAT GRANDFATHER _____

GREAT GRANDMOTHER _____

CERTIFICATE OF
MARRIAGE

THIS CERTIFIES THAT:

Gay Williard Paul

AND:

Betty J Paul

WERE UNITED IN:

HOLY MATRIMONY

ON *Aug 25,*   YEAR *193*

AT *5 PM*

Rev Hancock

OFFICIANT

WITNESS *Imogene Paul*

WITNESS

Births & Adoptions

O N _____

O N _____

O N _____

O N _____

O N _____

O N _____

O N _____

SPIRITUAL LANDMARKS

ON _____

_____

_____

_____

_____

_____

_____

_____

_____

_____

_____

_____

_____

_____

_____

_____

SPIRITUAL LANDMARKS

O N _____

_____

_____

_____

_____

_____

_____

_____

_____

_____

_____

_____

_____

_____

_____

_____

_____

SPIRITUAL LANDMARKS

O N

FAMILY LIFE™
MARRIAGE
BIBLE

equipping couples for life

FAMILYLIFE™
MARRIAGE BIBLE

Dennis & Barbara Rainey

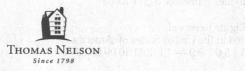

THOMAS NELSON
Since 1798

NASHVILLE   DALLAS   MEXICO CITY   RIO DE JANEIRO   BEIJING

FAMILYLIFE MARRIAGE BIBLE

IN ONE OF THE MOST FAMOUS sermons of all time, the Sermon on the Mount, Jesus concluded with a powerful illustration. He contrasted two kinds of houses. One house was built on an unstable, shifting foundation of sand, whereas the other house was anchored to bedrock.

Jesus asked His audience which of the two houses would be able to stand when the storms came. The answer was clear: the one that was built on the rock. The strength of the foundation determines whether a house will stand or fall in the storm.

This book is that foundation. The Bible promises to give us everything we need for life and for godliness (1 Pet. 1:3). The foundation your home needs.

The Bible is ultimately a book about relationships. It explains clearly how mankind's disobedience and pride separated us from our Creator. It shows us how God has taken the initiative to reconcile His relationship with us by offering His own Son as the sacrifice who took the punishment we deserved. Probably the best known verse in the Bible, John 3:16, teaches us that God so loved the world—or put another way, God is so committed to His relationship with us—that He gave His only begotten Son, that whoever believes in Him should not perish but have everlasting life.

The Bible also teaches us that God wants us to live in reconciled, harmonious, and loving relationships with each other. Jesus said that the greatest commandment is to love God with all our heart, soul, mind and strength. Then He quickly added the second great commandment, that we love our neighbor as ourselves (Matt. 22:36–40). Loving God and loving each other are at the top of God's priority list for us.

Marriage and family relationships provide us with the greatest test of our ability to love others as well as the greatest opportunity to know the joy of loving and being loved by another person. Nothing exposes our selfishness and pride like marriage and parenting. As we learn to love and serve each other in our marriage and as we love and lead our children toward adulthood, God is at work molding, shaping, and refining our character so that we become more like Jesus every day.

Our hope is that the articles and features we have included in this Bible will help you understand and apply God's truth in all your relationships—as couples, as parents, in your extended family, and in your relationships with friends, neighbors, and coworkers. We hope that you will make it a daily practice to spend time reading God's Word, and we have presented many opportunities for you to reflect on the passages you'll read. We hope that the introductions to the different books of the Bible will help provide you with an overview of what God wants to communicate to us in each particular book. And we hope that as you read, you'll be prayerfully asking the Lord to help you apply what you've read as you relate to one another each day.

You will notice that certain themes keep appearing in what we've written. Don't be surprised if you read something we've written and think to yourself, "They've touched on this subject in other articles in this Bible." We're not trying to be redundant, but we are very intentionally hoping to drive home certain principles. That's because we keep coming back to what have been the key concepts that have marked our marriage:

1. The lordship of Christ in all areas of life
2. Understanding marriage as a covenant commitment to one another
3. Working to keep communication alive
4. Being diligent to resolve conflict when it occurs
5. Husbands understanding and living out their responsibilities in a family
6. Wives understanding and living out their responsibilities in a family
7. Praying together as a couple
8. Learning how to grow stronger in seasons of suffering
9. Living by faith
10. Making romance in marriage a priority
11. Embracing a sense of mission for your life and for your family
12. Passing on a legacy of spiritual vitality to your children

We have found that checklist to be a good measuring stick by which we can gauge the health of our marriage and family. If we're experiencing challenges in our marriage (and we do . . . regularly!), we can usually trace the problem to one of these specific areas.

Since we helped launch FamilyLife in 1976, our desire has been to provide couples with practical, biblical help for their marriages and their families. We have done this through our daily radio program, FamilyLife Today, and at our Weekend to Remember marriage conferences for couples. Our website, **www.familylife.com**, was built to provide people with access to resources and information that can bring hope and help to every family. Our vision as a ministry is to see every home become a godly home. *The FamilyLife Marriage Bible* is perhaps the most significant resource we've helped create in support of that vision.

This is not just any book you're holding. The Bible promises to be a lamp that lights the path for us to help us keep from stumbling (Ps. 119:105). The Holy Spirit, who lives in each believer, is like an expert surgeon, and the Bible is His tool—His scalpel—for cutting away the cancer of sin in us and empowering us to fulfill what God has commanded. As you journey through the Bible over and over again throughout your life, you can count on God to renew your mind and transform your life.

One Home at a Time,

Dennis Rainey & *Barbara Rainey*

Dennis and Barbara Rainey

CONTENTS

FAMILY MANIFESTO
A DECLARATION OF TIMELESS VALUES

Preface

During the latter half of the twentieth century the American culture has suffered an unrelenting decline. Although scientific and technological advances have created an outer veneer of prosperity and progress, our inner moral values and convictions have rapidly crumbled. Once, most Americans based their sense of right and wrong on Judeo-Christian principles, which provided them with a solid, biblical foundation for life. Today, a growing number of Americans see morality and ethics as relative and subjective and have developed their own version of "morality" with little regard to absolute standards.

This idea of moral tolerance has been eroding the foundation of the American family and society. Many Americans today have little or no concept of how to maintain a successful marriage and how to raise children to become responsible adults. In addition, a growing number of educators, politicians, and members of the media are attacking and redefining the family, creating a vast amount of confusion about what a family is. Many people today proclaim that "family values" are important, but the gradual shift to moral relativism has led to a great debate about what "family values" ought to be.

Abraham Lincoln once said, "The strength of a nation lies in the homes of its people. "It is our conviction that the family is the backbone of the Christian church and of society as a whole. History shows that, if any society wants to survive, it must uphold, strengthen, and continue to build upon the biblical institutions of marriage and family.

The Bible begins in Genesis with the marriage of a man and a woman and ends in the Book of Revelation with the marriage of Christ and His bride, the Church. In between, God provides timeless blueprints for family life, which, if followed in a spirit of humility and obedience, provide us with the only true way to maintain healthy family relationships.

The following document affirms this biblical model and challenges us to consider how we should live within the walls of our own homes. It is offered in a spirit of love and humility, not of judgment or contention. Furthermore, it is not intended to be a comprehensive doctrinal statement about what the Bible says about marriage, family, and related subjects.

Unquestionably, this document attempts to face critical cultural issues. We invite response from anyone who wishes to affirm the truths of marriage and family from the Scriptures. It is our hope that this document will serve to accurately represent the truth God has revealed to us in Scripture, will provide insight into what a biblical family looks like, and will show how we can honor and glorify Him in our family relationships.

We freely acknowledge that we, like all people, have often denied the biblical truths of family life by the way we live. We desire, however, to live by God's grace in accordance with the principles stated herein and to pass these principles on to future generations so that He will be honored and glorified as our families reflect His character.

The Bible

We believe the Bible was written by men who were divinely inspired by God the Holy Spirit, and we believe it to be authoritative and errorless in its original autographs. We believe the Bible contains the blueprints for building solid marriage and family relationships. It teaches principles for marriage and family life that transcend time and culture. We are committed to communicating biblical truth in order to strengthen and give direction to a marriage and family. (2 Timothy 3:16; 2 Peter 1:20, 21; Hebrews 4:12)

Family

We believe God is the originator of the family. It was established by God in His inaugural act of the marriage between a man and a woman. The Bible further defines the family through God's instruction for married couples to have children, whether by birth or by adoption. We believe the purpose of the family is to glorify and honor God by forming the spiritual, emotional, physical, and economic foundation for individuals, the church, and any society.

It is at home that children see manhood and womanhood modeled. It is at home that moral values are taught by parents and placed into the hearts of their children. It is at home that people see the reality of a relationship with Jesus Christ modeled. It is at home that people learn to live out their convictions. Therefore, we are committed to upholding the concept of family as God's original and primary means of producing a godly offspring and passing on godly values from generation to generation. (Ephesians 3:14, 15; Genesis 1:26-28; Romans 8:15, 23; John 1:12; Galatians 3:29; Psalm 78:5-7; Deuteronomy 6:4-9)

Marriage

We believe God, not man, created marriage. We believe marriage was the first institution designed by God. We believe the Bible teaches that the covenant of marriage is sacred and life long. The Bible makes it clear that marriage is a legally binding public declaration of commitment and a private consummation between one man and one woman, never between the same sex. Therefore, we believe God gives a wife to a husband and a husband to a wife, and they are to receive one another as God's unique and personal provision to help meet their mutual needs.

We believe God created marriage for the purpose of couples glorifying God as one flesh, parenting godly children, and enjoying sexual pleasure. As iron sharpens iron, we believe God uses marriage to sharpen a man and woman into the image of Jesus Christ. Just as the Trinity reflects equal worth with differing roles, we believe God created a man and a woman with equal worth but with differing roles and responsibilities in marriage.

Finally, we declare the marriage commitment must be upheld in our culture as that sacred institution of God in which men and women can experience the truest sense of spiritual, emotional, and physical intimacy, so that the two can become one. (Genesis 2:18-25; Ephesians 5:30-32; 1 Corinthians 7:3; Matthew 19:4-6; Mark 10:6-9; 12:25; Proverbs 27:17; Romans 1:26, 27; 8:29; Hebrews 13:4; Matthew 22:30; Deuteronomy 24:5; Song of Solomon)

Husbands

We believe God has charged each husband to fulfill the responsibility of being the "head" (servant leader) of his wife. We believe God created a man incomplete, and as a husband, he needs his wife as his helper. We believe a husband will give account before God for how he has loved, served, and provided for his wife. We reject the notion that a husband is to dominate his wife. Likewise, we reject the notion that a husband is to abdicate his responsibilities to lead his wife. Rather, we believe his responsibility is to love his wife. This love is characterized by taking the initiative to serve her, care for her, and honor her as a gift from God. We believe his responsibility is to protect his wife and help provide for her physical, emotional, and spiritual needs.

We also believe a husband is to seek after and highly regard his wife's opinion and counsel and treat her as the equal partner she is in Christ. Therefore, we are committed to exhort and implore men not to abuse their God-given responsibilities as husbands, but rather to initiate a sacrificial love for their wives, in the same way Jesus Christ initiated sacrificial love and demonstrated it fully on the cross. (Genesis 2:18-25; Ephesians 5:22-33; Colossians 3:19; 1 Peter 3:7; 1 Timothy 5:8)

Wives

We believe God has charged each wife to fulfill the responsibility of being her husband's "helper." We believe a wife will give account to God for how she has loved, respected, and given support to her husband. We uphold the biblical truth that she is of equal value with her husband before God. We reject the notion that a wife should assume the leadership responsibilities of her husband. Likewise, we reject the notion that a wife should passively defer to the dominance of her husband. We believe that her responsibility is to willingly and intelligently affirm, respect, and submit to her husband as the leader in the relationship and in his vocational calling. Therefore, we are committed to exhorting a wife to be in support of her husband by accepting and excelling in her responsibility as his helper. (Genesis 2:18-25; Ephesians 5:22-33; Colossians 3:18; 1 Peter 3:1-6; Proverbs 31:10-12)

Sexual Union

We believe the Bible clearly states that marriage is the only context for sexual intimacy. We believe contemporary culture is pressing single people to engage prematurely in acts that are intended only for the context of marriage. Our culture has rejected God's plan for intimacy by promoting sexual promiscuity of various kinds and, as a consequence, has brought upon itself sexual diseases and relational dysfunctions. We believe in sexual purity and fidelity.

Therefore, we are committed to training parents to teach their children at an early age to respect their sexuality and to preserve their virginity and purity until marriage. We are committed to communicating the message to teenagers, single adults, and married couples that sexual intimacy is available only in the context of marriage. (Genesis 2:24, 25; Romans 1:24-27; 1 Thessalonians 4:3-8)

Fathers

We believe God has charged a father to execute the responsibilities of a family leader. He is accountable before God to lead his family by sacrificially loving his wife and children and by providing for their physical, spiritual, and emotional needs. We believe the greatest way a father can love his children is to love their mother. We believe children gain much of their concept of God from their fathers.

We believe a father should teach his children, by instruction and example, truth from the Bible and how to apply it practically in daily life. Therefore, a father should spend a quantity of time, as well as quality time, with each child. We believe a father should demonstrate godly character revealed in humility, tenderness, and patience toward his children. We believe a father should demonstrate love by practicing consistent discipline with each child. Therefore, we are committed to turning the hearts of fathers back to their children by emphasizing the importance of their role as "father." We are committed to exhorting every father to model a love for God and His Word, to model love for his wife, and to love his children. (Malachi 4:6; Ephesians 6:4; Colossians 3:20, 21; Deuteronomy 6:4-9; 1 Timothy 3:4, 5; 5:8)

Mothers

We believe God has uniquely designed women to be mothers. We believe the greatest way a mother can love her children is to love their father. We also believe God has created a woman with an innate and special ability to nurture and care for her children.

Therefore, we believe mothers are the primary people who execute the vital responsibilities of loving, nurturing, and mentoring children. We believe these responsibilities should be met before a mother contemplates any other duties. We believe our culture has devalued the role of a mother by placing greater significance on activities outside the home than on those inside the home.

We realize there are cases where a mother will find it necessary to work outside the home (e.g. financial distress, single parenthood); however, we also believe some couples have made career and lifestyle choices that result in de-emphasizing the mother's role as nurturer. Therefore, we are committed to presenting a biblical framework through which couples can rightly evaluate their priorities in light of a mother's role. We are committed to elevating motherhood by rightly assessing its exalted value in God's economy of the family. We are committed to exhorting mothers to model love for God and His Word, to model love for her husband, and to love her children. (Titus 2:4, 5; 1 Thessalonians 2:7; Proverbs 14:1; 31:1-31; Deuteronomy 6:6; 11:19; Ezekiel 16:44, 45)

Children

We believe children are the gifts of God and should be received and treated as such. We believe a child's life begins at conception. We believe children have a special responsibility to God in obeying and honoring their parents. We believe a child's identity and spiritual growth is either helped or hindered by his parents' devotion to God, to one another, and to him. Parents should see themselves as God's ambassadors, working to build strong character in the lives of their children through consistent godly living, nurturing, discipline, and teaching them right from wrong. We are committed to God's plan for passing His love down through the ages by encouraging parents to love their children "so the generations to come might know" the love and forgiveness of Christ. (Ephesians 6:1-3; Colossians 3:20; Psalms 78:5-8; 127:3-5; 139:13-16; Proverbs 4:1; 6:20)

Childless Couples

We believe God has allowed some couples to be without biological children according to His sovereign plan in their lives. We believe couples without children are of no less value before God than those with children. We believe in encouraging childless couples to consider adoption as a family alternative. We are committed to encouraging childless couples to pass on a godly legacy through involvement with children in their immediate families, churches, and communities. (Luke 1:6, 7; Romans 8:28, 29)

Grandparents

We believe grandparents are to be honored as valued family members. We believe their wisdom in living should be sought and passed on to their children and their children's children. We also believe that grandparents have the responsibility of teaching and modeling to their grandchildren how to know Jesus Christ and grow in a relationship with Him as well as passing along biblical principles for godly living. The Old Testament is filled with examples of grandfathers and grandmothers who excelled in their roles of grandparenting.

Therefore, we are committed to giving honor to grandparents by encouraging their children and grandchildren to listen to their voices of wisdom. We are also committed to exhorting grandparents to pray for and become actively involved with children and grandchildren whenever it is possible. (1 Timothy 5:4; Genesis 18:18, 19; Proverbs 17:6; Psalm 78)

Church

We believe the family and the church are interdependent. A primary responsibility of the church is to help build godly families, and godly families also help build the church. We believe the family supplies the relational rudiments of the local church. We believe the local church is the spiritual home where families should corporately worship God. It is the place where the knowledge and love of God may be communicated to fathers, mothers, and children.

Therefore, we are committed to exhorting families to support the local church through their involvement. We are also committed to exhorting the local church to uphold the priority of helping build godly marriages and families. (1 Timothy 3:15; Ephesians 5:22-33; Philemon 1:2; Colossians 4:15)

Divorce

We believe God's plan for marriage is that it be a lifelong commitment between one man and one woman. We believe God hates divorce. We believe divorce brings harm to every person involved. Therefore, reconciliation of a marriage should be encouraged and divorce discouraged. We also believe that God allows for divorce in certain situations, not because He wills it, but because of the hardness of people's hearts. We believe the Bible teaches that God allows for divorce in the case of adultery and in the case where an unbelieving spouse has chosen to abandon the commitment of marriage.

We believe, however, that it is God's priority that marital oneness be restored and that, through the power of the gospel of Jesus Christ, forgiveness and reconciliation be experienced. We believe that in the unfortunate cases of abuse and abandonment, God has provided protection for an abused spouse and provision for child support through the church, civil law, godly counselors, prayer, and other practical measures. We believe God can restore broken people and broken marriages by His grace, by the power of His Spirit, and by His practical truths found in the Bible. (Malachi 2:16; Matthew 5:31, 32; 19:3-9; Mark 10:6-12; Luke 16:18; Romans 7:1-3; Romans 13:1-5; 1 Corinthians 7:15)

Single Parents

We believe that, ideally, a child needs the influence of both a father and mother for healthy development in life and relationships. At the same time, we recognize that God's grace is sufficient and that He is a father to the fatherless and a husband to the husbandless. We also believe He is a guardian to children without a mother and a friend to a husband who has lost his wife.

We believe God, by His grace, can use the void left from a missing parent to accomplish His eternal purposes of building Christlike character in single parents and their children. We believe a single parent and his or her children are a family and that the Bible contains principles for them to grow as a family. We believe the local church should be a home for single parents, providing their children with godly people who serve as role models in place of the missing parent.

Therefore, we are committed to exhorting Christians within the local church to creatively help meet the needs associated with single-parent homes. We are committed to comforting and encouraging single-parent families by providing resources and developing biblical principles to assist those who struggle in the role of a single parent. (Psalm 68:5, 6; 1 Corinthians 7:32; James 1:27; 1 Timothy 5:3-16; Romans 8:28, 29; Luke 18:3-5)

Broken and Blended Families

We believe God has allowed men and women, either by circumstance or by choice, to endure difficult and painful consequences in their marriages and family relationships. We also believe God gives abundant grace to the broken, blended, and single-parent families.

Therefore, we believe He can and does enable them to carry out His functions and principles for healthy family life. We are committed to comforting, encouraging, and teaching these families God's principles of marriage and family life. We are also committed to exhorting the local church to help with the burden of the broken family. (James 1:27; 1 Timothy 5:16; Philippians 4:13)

Work and the Family

We believe work is an important and necessary aspect of one's service to God and one's responsibility to provide for the needs of the family. We also believe security and significance cannot be found through pursuing career goals or financial achievement apart from one's responsibility to God and one's spouse and family. Instead, we believe those needs are best met in the warmth of a home where parents and children are experiencing harmony in their relationships with each other and with Jesus Christ. Therefore, we are committed to challenging any person or couple to rearrange their priorities so that over the course of a lifetime they can be successful at home and not merely successful in their careers. (Revelation 3:14-22; Ephesians 6:7, 8; Matthew 6:33; 1 Timothy 5:8; 1 Thessalonians 4:10-12)

Mentors

We believe in the biblical admonition for older men and women to teach younger men and women. We believe younger couples today should seek out older couples for their wisdom and counsel in matters of marriage and family. We believe older couples should be taught and encouraged to mentor younger couples and we believe this is best accomplished through the local church. Therefore, we are committed to establishing a strategy for mentoring that the local church may implement and use to build strong marriages and families. (Titus 2:3-5)

Marriage Education

We believe single adults who choose to marry should be taught the biblical principles of marriage. We also believe the education of a married couple does not end after the wedding ceremony is over, but continues throughout life. Therefore, we believe that both premarital and post-marital education is helpful and essential in a couple's growth toward and in oneness. We are committed to elevating, establishing, and teaching the precepts of marriage by which single adults can rightly evaluate their relationships and equip themselves for marriage. We are committed to providing the teaching and training necessary to equip married couples to live a lifetime

together as one. Finally, we are committed to showing couples how their marriages can be used by God to give others the hope found only in Jesus Christ. (Titus 2; 2 Timothy 3:16, 17; Acts 16:31-34; John 4:53)

The Deceiver and Culture

We believe there is a living Devil who is God's enemy and whose nature and objective is to lie and deceive. We believe the Devil has attacked God's plan for the family from the beginning of man until now. We believe he uses the various aspects of the culture to promote personal independence, distort the differences between men and women, confuse their roles, and elevate personal rights over marital responsibilities. We believe the Devil seeks to persuade people to move away from God's plan for intimacy and oneness and toward isolation and divorce. (John 8:44; Genesis 3; Isaiah 14:12-14; Ezekiel 28:12-18; 1 Peter 5:8; Ephesians 6:12; 1 John 2:15)

God - the Creator of the Family

Father

We believe in the Fatherhood of God. The title "Father" implies that God is a relational being. The Bible reveals God has four primary relationships as Father: He is the Father of creation, of the nations, of the Lord Jesus Christ, and of all believers. We believe the Bible presents the title "Father" as one of the primary names Christians should use in addressing and relating to God. In doing so, Christians identify themselves as children who belong to the family of God. We are committed to proclaiming and demonstrating this truth about who God is and who we are, so that God will be glorified, and that He might use us to bring others into His family through a personal relationship with His Son. (John 1:12; Exodus 3:14, 15; Ephesians 3:16; Matthew 6:9; Romans 8:15; Acts 17:24-28)

Son

We believe God the Son, fully revealed in the person of Jesus Christ, was God's final sacrifice for the sins of man through the shedding of His blood on the cross and His resurrection from the dead. We believe He is the only way to know God the Father and to experience His plan for marriage and family. We are committed to introducing people to Jesus Christ in order that, by faith, they might personally receive Him, be born into the family of God, receive forgiveness and eternal life, and begin a relationship with God that is essential in marriage and family life. (John 1:4,12; 17:3; 1 John 2:23, 24; Ephesians 2:19-22; Colossians 1:13-18; Hebrews 1:1-4)

Holy Spirit

We believe God the Holy Spirit is the agent and teacher of a godly marriage and family. We believe when Christian couples and their children consistently yield to His control and power, they will experience harmony in their marriages and families. Therefore, we are committed to sharing the ministry of the Holy Spirit with people so they may know God better, make Him known to others, and appropriate His power in fulfilling their duties in marriage and family relationships. (John 14:26; 15:26; 16:5-15; Ephesians 5:18-21)

Preface to the
New King James Version®

Purpose

IN THE PREFACE to the 1611 edition, the translators of the Authorized Version, known popularly as the King James Bible, state that it was not their purpose "to make a new translation . . . but to make a good one better." Indebted to the earlier work of William Tyndale and others, they saw their best contribution to consist in revising and enhancing the excellence of the English versions which had sprung from the Reformation of the sixteenth century. In harmony with the purpose of the King James scholars, the translators and editors of the present work have not pursued a goal of innovation. They have perceived the Holy Bible, New King James Version, as a continuation of the labors of the earlier translators, thus unlocking for today's readers the spiritual treasures found especially in the Authorized Version of the Holy Scriptures.

A Living Legacy

For nearly four hundred years, and throughout several revisions of its English form, the King James Bible has been deeply revered among the English-speaking peoples of the world. The precision of translation for which it is historically renowned, and its majesty of style, have enabled that monumental version of the word of God to become the mainspring of the religion, language, and legal foundations of our civilization.

Although the Elizabethan period and our own era share in zeal for technical advance, the former period was more aggressively devoted to classical learning. Along with this awakened concern for the classics came a flourishing companion interest in the Scriptures, an interest that was enlivened by the conviction that the manuscripts were providentially handed down and were a trustworthy record of the inspired Word of God. The King James translators were committed to producing an English Bible that would be a precise translation, and by no means a paraphrase or a broadly approximate rendering. On the one hand, the scholars were almost as familiar with the original languages of the Bible as with their native English. On the other hand, their reverence for the divine Author and His Word assured a translation of the Scriptures in which only a principle of utmost accuracy could be accepted.

In 1786 Catholic scholar Alexander Geddes said of the King James Bible, "If accuracy and strictest attention to the letter of the text be supposed to constitute an excellent version, this is of all versions the most excellent." George Bernard Shaw became a literary legend in the twentieth century because of his severe and often humorous criticisms of our most cherished values. Surprisingly, however, Shaw pays the following tribute to the scholars commissioned by King James: "The translation was extraordinarily well done because to the translators what they were translating was not merely a curious collection of ancient books written by different authors in different stages of culture, but the Word of God divinely revealed through His chosen and expressly inspired scribes. In this conviction they carried out their work with boundless reverence and care and achieved a beautifully artistic result." History agrees with these estimates. Therefore, while seeking to unveil the excellent *form* of the traditional English Bible, special care has also been taken in the present edition to preserve the work of *precision* which is the legacy of the 1611 translators.

Complete Equivalence in Translation

Where new translation has been necessary in the New King James Version, the most complete representation of the original has been rendered by considering the history of usage and etymology of words in their contexts. This principle of complete equivalence seeks to preserve *all* of the information in the text, while presenting it in good literary form. Dynamic equivalence, a recent procedure in Bible translation, commonly results in paraphrasing where a more literal rendering is needed to reflect a specific and vital sense. For example, complete equivalence truly renders the original text in expressions such as "lifted her voice and wept" (Gen. 21:16); "I gave you cleanness of teeth" (Amos 4:6); "Jesus met them, saying, 'Rejoice!'" (Matt. 28:9); and "Woman, what does your concern have to do with Me?" (John 2:4). Complete equivalence translates fully, in order to provide an English text that is both accurate and readable.

In keeping with the principle of complete equivalence, it is the policy to translate interjections which are commonly omitted in modern language renderings of the Bible. As an example, the interjection *behold,* in the older King James editions, continues to have a place in English usage, especially in dramatically calling attention to a spectacular scene, or an event of profound importance such as the Immanuel prophecy of Isaiah 7:14. Consequently, *behold* is retained for these occasions in the present edition. However, the Hebrew and Greek originals for this word can be translated variously, depending on the circumstances in the passage. Therefore, in addition to *behold,* words such as *indeed, look, see,* and *surely* are also rendered to convey the appropriate sense suggested by the context in each case.

In faithfulness to God and to our readers, it was deemed appropriate that all participating scholars sign a statement affirming their belief in the verbal and plenary inspiration of Scripture, and in the inerrancy of the original autographs.

Devotional Quality

The King James scholars readily appreciated the intrinsic beauty of divine revelation. They accordingly disciplined their talents to render well-chosen English words of their time, as well as a graceful, often musical arrangement of language, which has stirred the hearts of Bible readers through the years. The translators, the committees, and the editors of the present edition, while sensitive to the late-twentieth-century English idiom, and while adhering faithfully to the Hebrew, Aramaic, and Greek texts, have sought to maintain those lyrical and devotional qualities that are so highly regarded in the Authorized Version. This devotional quality is especially apparent in the poetic and prophetic books, although even the relatively plain style of the Gospels and Epistles cannot strictly be likened, as sometimes suggested, to modern newspaper style. The Koine Greek of the New Testament is influenced by the Hebrew background of the writers, for whom even the gospel narratives were not merely flat utterance, but often song in various degrees of rhythm.

The Style

Students of the Bible applaud the timeless devotional character of our historic Bible. Yet it is also universally understood that our language, like all living languages, has undergone profound change since 1611. Subsequent revisions of the King James Bible have sought to keep abreast of changes in English speech. The present work is a further step toward this objective. Where obsolescence and other reading difficulties exist, present-day vocabulary, punctuation, and grammar have been carefully integrated. Words representing ancient objects, such as *chariot* and *phylactery,* have no modern substitutes and are therefore retained.

A special feature of the New King James Version is its conformity to the thought flow of the 1611 Bible. The reader discovers that the sequence and selection of words, phrases, and clauses of the new edition, while much clearer, are so close to the traditional that there is remarkable ease in listening to the reading of either edition while following with the other.

In the discipline of translating biblical and other ancient languages, a standard method of transliteration, that is, the English spelling of untranslated words, such as names of persons and places, has never been commonly adopted. In keeping with the design of the present work, the King James spelling of untranslated words is retained, although made uniform throughout. For example, instead of the spellings *Isaiah* and *Elijah* in the Old Testament, and *Esaias* and *Elias* in the New Testament, *Isaiah* and *Elijah* now appear in both Testaments.

King James doctrinal and theological terms, for example, *propitiation, justification,* and *sanctification,* are generally familiar to English-speaking peoples. Such terms have been retained except where the original language indicates need for a more precise translation.

Readers of the Authorized Version will immediately be struck by the absence of several pronouns: *thee, thou,* and *ye* are replaced by the simple *you,* while *your* and *yours* are substituted for *thy* and *thine* as applicable. *Thee, thou, thy* and *thine* were once forms of address to express a special relationship to human as well as divine persons. These pronouns are no longer part of our language. However, reverence for God in the present work is preserved by capitalizing pronouns, including *You, Your,* and *Yours,* which refer to Him. Additionally, capitalization of these pronouns benefits the reader by clearly distinguishing divine and human persons referred to in a passage. Without such capitalization the distinction is often obscure, because the antecedent of a pronoun is not always clear in the English translation.

In addition to the pronoun usages of the seventeenth century, the *-eth* and *-est* verb endings, so familiar in the earlier King James editions, are now obsolete. Unless a speaker is schooled in these verb endings, there is common difficulty in selecting the correct form to be used with a given subject of the verb in vocal prayer. That is, should we use *love, loveth,* or *lovest? do, doeth, doest,* or *dost? have, hath,* or *hast?* Because these forms are obsolete, contemporary English usage has been substituted for the previous verb endings.

In older editions of the King James Version, the frequency of the connective *and* far exceeded the limits of present English usage. Also, biblical linguists agree that the Hebrew and Greek original words for this conjunction may commonly be translated otherwise, depending on the immediate context. Therefore, instead of *and,* alternatives such as *also, but, however, now, so, then,* and *thus* are accordingly rendered in the present edition, when the original language permits.

The real character of the Authorized Version does not reside in its archaic pronouns or verbs or other grammatical forms of the seventeenth century, but rather in the care taken by its scholars to impart the letter and spirit of the original text in a majestic and reverent style.

The Format

The format of the New King James Version is designed to enhance the vividness and devotional quality of the Holy Scriptures:

• Subject headings assist the reader to identify topics and transitions in the biblical content.

• Words or phrases in *italics* indicate expressions in the original language which require clarification by additional English words, as also done throughout the history of the King James Bible.

• Oblique type in the New Testament indicates a quotation from the Old Testament.

- Prose is divided into paragraphs to indicate the structure of thought.
- Poetry is structured as contemporary verse to reflect the poetic form and beauty of the passage in the original language.
- The covenant name of God was usually translated from the Hebrew as LORD or GOD (using capital letters as shown) in the King James Old Testament. This tradition is maintained. In the present edition the name is so capitalized whenever the covenant name is quoted in the New Testament from a passage in the Old Testament.

The Old Testament Text

The Hebrew Bible has come down to us through the scrupulous care of ancient scribes who copied the original text in successive generations. By the sixth century A.D. the scribes were succeeded by a group known as the Masoretes, who continued to preserve the sacred Scriptures for another five hundred years in a form known as the Masoretic Text. Babylonia, Palestine, and Tiberias were the main centers of Masoretic activity; but by the tenth century A.D. the Masoretes of Tiberias, led by the family of ben Asher, gained the ascendancy. Through subsequent editions, the ben Asher text became in the twelfth century the only recognized form of the Hebrew Scriptures.

Daniel Bomberg printed the first Rabbinic Bible in 1516–17; that work was followed in 1524–25 by a second edition prepared by Jacob ben Chayyim and also published by Bomberg. The text of ben Chayyim was adopted in most subsequent Hebrew Bibles, including those used by the King James translators. The ben Chayyim text was also used for the first two editions of Rudolph Kittel's *Biblia Hebraica* of 1906 and 1912. In 1937 Paul Kahle published a third edition of *Biblia Hebraica*. This edition was based on the oldest dated manuscript of the ben Asher text, the Leningrad Manuscript B19a (A.D. 1008), which Kahle regarded as superior to that used by ben Chayyim.

For the New King James Version the text used was the 1967/1977 Stuttgart edition of the *Biblia Hebraica,* with frequent comparisons being made with the Bomberg edition of 1524–25. The Septuagint (Greek) Version of the Old Testament and the Latin Vulgate also were consulted. In addition to referring to a variety of ancient versions of the Hebrew Scriptures, the New King James Version draws on the resources of relevant manuscripts from the Dead Sea caves. In the few places where the Hebrew was so obscure that the 1611 King James was compelled to follow one of the versions, but where information is now available to resolve the problems, the New King James Version follows the Hebrew text. Significant variations are recorded in the New King James translators' notes.

The New Testament Text

There is more manuscript support for the New Testament than for any other body of ancient literature. Over five thousand Greek, eight thousand Latin, and many more manuscripts in other languages attest the integrity of the New Testament. There is only one basic New Testament used by Protestants, Roman Catholics, and Orthodox, by conservatives and liberals. Minor variations in hand copying have appeared through the centuries, before mechanical printing began about A.D. 1450.

Some variations exist in the spelling of Greek words, in word order, and in similar details. These ordinarily do not show up in translation and do not affect the sense of the text in any way.

Other manuscript differences such as omission or inclusion of a word or a clause, and two paragraphs in the Gospels, should not overshadow the overwhelming degree of *agreement* which exists among the ancient records. Bible readers may be assured that the most important differences in English New Testaments of today are due, not to manuscript divergence, but to the way in which translators view the task of translation: How literally should the text be rendered? How does the translator view the matter of biblical inspiration? Does the translator adopt a paraphrase when a literal rendering would be quite clear and more to the point? The New King James Version follows the historic precedent of the Authorized Version in maintaining a literal approach to translation, except where the idiom of the original language cannot be translated directly into our tongue.

The King James New Testament was based on the traditional text of the Greek-speaking churches, first published in 1516, and later called the Textus Receptus or Received Text. Although based on the relatively few available manuscripts, these were representative of many more which existed at the time but only became known later. In the late nineteenth century, B. Westcott and F. Hort taught that this text had been officially edited by the fourth-century church, but a total lack of historical evidence for this event has forced a revision of the theory. It is now widely held that the Byzantine Text that largely supports the Textus Receptus has as much right as the Alexandrian or any other tradition to be weighed in determining the text of the New Testament.

Since the 1880s most contemporary translations of the New Testament have relied upon a relatively few manuscripts discovered chiefly in the late nineteenth and early twentieth centuries. Such translations depend primarily on two manuscripts, Codex Vaticanus and Codex Sinaiticus, because of their greater age. The Greek text obtained by using these sources and the related papyri (our most ancient manuscripts) is known as the Alexandrian Text. However, some scholars have grounds for doubting the faithfulness of Vaticanus and Sinaiticus, since they often disagree with one another, and Sinaiticus exhibits excessive omission.

A third viewpoint of New Testament scholarship holds that the best text is based on the consensus of the majority of existing Greek manuscripts. This text is called the Majority Text. Most of these manuscripts are in substantial agreement. Even though many are late, and none is earlier than the fifth century, usually their readings are verified by papyri, ancient versions, quotations from the early church fathers, or a combination of these. The Majority Text is similar to the Textus Receptus, but it corrects those readings which have little or no support in the Greek manuscript tradition.

Today, scholars agree that the science of New Testament textual criticism is in a state of flux. Very few scholars still favor the Textus Receptus as such, and then often for its historical prestige as the text of Luther, Calvin, Tyndale, and the King James Version. For about a century most have followed a Critical Text (so called because it is edited according to specific principles of textual criticism) which depends heavily upon the Alexandrian type of text. More recently many have abandoned this Critical Text (which is quite similar to the one edited by Westcott and Hort) for one that is more eclectic. Finally, a small but growing number of scholars prefer the Majority Text, which is close to the traditional text except in the Revelation.

In light of these facts, and also because the New King James Version is the fifth revision of a historic document translated from specific Greek texts, the editors decided to retain the traditional text in the body of the New Testament and to indicate major Critical and Majority Text variant readings in the translators' notes. Although these variations are duly indicated in the translators' notes of the present edition, it is most important to emphasize that fully eighty-five percent of the New Testament text is the same in the Textus Receptus, the Alexandrian Text, and the Majority Text.

New King James Translators' Notes

Significant textual explanations, alternate translations, and New Testament citations of Old Testament passages are supplied in the New King James translators' notes.

Important textual variants in the Old Testament are identified in a standard form.

The textual notes in the present edition of the New Testament make no evaluation of readings, but do clearly indicate the manuscript sources of readings. They objectively present the facts without such tendentious remarks as "the best manuscripts omit" or "the most reliable manuscripts read." Such notes are value judgments that differ according to varying viewpoints on the text. By giving a clearly defined set of variants the New King James Version benefits readers of all textual persuasions.

Where significant variations occur in the New Testament Greek manuscripts, textual notes are classified as follows:

NU-Text

These variations from the traditional text generally represent the Alexandrian or Egyptian type of text described previously in "The New Testament Text." They are found in the Critical Text published in the twenty-seventh edition of the Nestle-Aland Greek New Testament (N) and in the United Bible Societies' fourth edition (U), hence the acronym, "NU-Text."

M-Text

This symbol indicates points of variation in the Majority Text from the traditional text, as also previously discussed in "The New Testament Text." It should be noted that M stands for whatever reading is printed in the published *Greek New Testament According to the Majority Text,* whether supported by overwhelming, strong, or only a divided majority textual tradition.

The textual notes reflect the scholarship of the past two centuries and will assist the reader to observe the variations between the different manuscript traditions of the New Testament. Such information is generally not available in English translations of the New Testament.

OLD TESTAMENT

GENESIS

GENESIS IS THE BOOK OF BEGINNINGS. It describes the origin of the physical world, the beginning of God's dealings with humankind, and the start of literally everything else. And that includes the family.

Once God set the planet to spinning and populated it with animals and plants of all kinds, He took special care to set apart the family as the first and most fundamental of all human institutions. Before He ordained human government, before He commissioned human courts, before He created human churches, He designed and ordained the human family. He brought one man, Adam, together with one woman, Eve, and so created the first marriage.

So long as Adam and Eve willingly kept God's commandments, they enjoyed a happy and harmonious home. This first human family enjoyed a perfect relationship with one another and with their God, thus precisely matching the perfect garden they called home. Their relationship, like everything else in Eden, could be termed "very good." No fights. No disappointments. No unhappy surprises. Just complete satisfaction and total contentment as they lived in an idyllic paradise.

But then chapter three comes along—and with it, the first human rebellion. No sooner have Adam and Eve sinned than they begin to experience the horrific impact of their revolt. Discord enters their marriage, where before they had known only unity. Blame-shifting mars their relationship. Pain and suffering sprout, both in their physical environment and under their own roof. From then on, life gets more difficult.

In the rest of the book, you see real people dealing with real (and often severe) family issues—marital conflict, children dishonoring parents, sibling rivalry, deception, jealousy, temptation, even murder. You also see beautiful evidence of God's grace in the lives of His people—from Noah and Abraham's remarkable faith, to Joseph's kindness and forgiveness of his scoundrel brothers. The Bible lays it all out for us, without any sugar coating. It does so in order that we may learn both from the mistakes His people make (and the consequences of those mistakes) and their successes (especially, how obedience leads to blessing).

The History of Creation

1 In the beginning God created the heavens and the earth. [2]The earth was without form, and void; and darkness *was*[a] on the face of the deep. And the Spirit of God was hovering over the face of the waters.

[3]Then God said, "Let there be light"; and there was light. [4]And God saw the light, that *it was* good; and God divided the light from the darkness. [5]God called the light Day, and the darkness He called Night. So the evening and the morning were the first day.

[6]Then God said, "Let there be a firmament in the midst of the waters, and let it divide the waters from the waters." [7]Thus God made the firmament, and divided the waters which *were* under the firmament from the waters which *were* above the firmament; and it was so. [8]And God called the firmament Heaven. So the evening and the morning were the second day.

[9]Then God said, "Let the waters under the heavens be gathered together into one place, and let the dry *land* appear"; and it was so. [10]And God called the dry *land* Earth, and the gathering together of the waters He called Seas. And God saw that *it was* good.

[11]Then God said, "Let the earth bring forth grass, the herb *that* yields seed, *and* the fruit tree *that* yields fruit according to its kind, whose seed *is* in itself, on the earth"; and it was so. [12]And the earth brought forth grass, the herb *that* yields seed according to its kind, and the tree *that* yields fruit, whose seed *is* in itself according to its kind. And God saw that *it was* good. [13]So the evening and the morning were the third day.

[14]Then God said, "Let there be lights in the firmament of the heavens to divide the day from the night; and let them be for signs and seasons, and for days and years; [15]and let them be for lights in the firmament of the heavens to give light on the earth"; and it was so. [16]Then God made two great lights: the greater light to rule the day, and the lesser light to rule the night. *He made* the stars also. [17]God set them in the firmament of the heavens to give light on the earth, [18]and to rule over the day and over the night, and to divide the light from the darkness. And God saw that *it was* good. [19]So the evening and the morning were the fourth day.

[20]Then God said, "Let the waters abound with an abundance of living creatures, and let birds fly above the earth across the face of the firmament of the heavens." [21]So God created great sea creatures and every living thing that moves, with which the waters

---

1:2 [a]Words in italic type have been added for clarity. They are not found in the original Hebrew or Aramaic.

The Essence of Goodness

Henry David Thoreau once said, "Goodness is the only investment that never fails."

"An investment?" you ask. That's right, an investment ... especially in your mate, your children, and your extended family.

Our grayish culture, void of absolutes, has bleached out the once colorful connotations to the word *good*. Today, if something is *good*, that usually means it's just okay. *Good* is third in line at Sears, just behind *better* and *best*. And we all know to steer clear of a *good* used car—it's probably been a rental, driven for 225,000 miles, and then used in a demolition derby!

To recover the once lofty meaning of *good*, recall God's consistent assessment of the world He made. I also think of the question Jesus put to the rich young ruler, "Why do you call Me good? No one is good but One, that is, God" (Matt. 19:17).

There's our clue! Only God is good. Merrill Unger writes of God's goodness, "It expresses the supreme benevolence, holiness, and excellence of the divine character, *the sum of all God's attributes*."

And God calls *your* marriage to be *good*! You have the opportunity to display "the excellence of the divine character"!

abounded, according to their kind, and every winged bird according to its kind. And God saw that *it was* good. ²²And God blessed them, saying, "Be fruitful and multiply, and fill the waters in the seas, and let birds multiply on the earth." ²³So the evening and the morning were the fifth day.

²⁴Then God said, "Let the earth bring forth the living creature according to its kind: cattle and creeping thing and beast of the earth, *each* according to its kind"; and it was so. ²⁵And God made the beast of the earth according to its kind, cattle according to its kind, and everything that creeps on the earth according to its kind. And God saw that *it was* good.

²⁶Then God said, "Let Us make man in Our image, according to Our likeness; let them have dominion over the fish of the sea, over the birds of the air, and over the cattle, over all[a] the earth and over every creeping thing that creeps on the earth." ²⁷So God created man in His *own* image; in the image of God He created him; male and female He created them. ²⁸Then God blessed them, and God said to them, "Be fruitful and multiply; fill the earth and subdue it; have dominion over the fish of the sea, over the birds of the air, and over every living thing that moves on the earth."

1:26 ªSyriac reads *all the wild animals of.*
2:4 ªHebrew *toledoth,* literally *generations*

²⁹And God said, "See, I have given you every herb *that* yields seed which *is* on the face of all the earth, and every tree whose fruit yields seed; to you it shall be for food. ³⁰Also, to every beast of the earth, to every bird of the air, and to everything that creeps on the earth, in which *there is* life, *I have given* every green herb for food"; and it was so. ³¹Then God saw everything that He had made, and indeed *it was* very good. So the evening and the morning were the sixth day.

2 Thus the heavens and the earth, and all the host of them, were finished. ²And on the seventh day God ended His work which He had done, and He rested on the seventh day from all His work which He had done. ³Then God blessed the seventh day and sanctified it, because in it He rested from all His work which God had created and made.

⁴This *is* the history[a] of the heavens and the earth when they were created, in the day that the LORD God made the earth and the heavens, ⁵before any plant of the field was in the earth and before any herb of the field had grown. For the LORD God had not caused it to rain on the earth, and *there was* no man to till the ground; ⁶but a mist went up from the earth and watered the whole face of the ground.

⁷And the LORD God formed man *of* the dust of the ground, and breathed into his

---

ROMANTIC QUOTES AND NOTES
Marriage Mirrors God's Image

After God created the earth and the animals, He said, "Let Us make man in Our image, according to Our likeness; let them have dominion over the fish of the sea, over the birds of the air, and over the cattle, over all the earth and over every creeping thing that creeps on the earth." The account then continues, "So God created man in His own image; in the image of God He created him; male and female He created them" (Gen. 1:26, 27).

God's first purpose for creating man and woman and joining them in marriage was to mirror His image on planet earth. Focus your attention on those words, *mirror His image.* The Hebrew word for *mirror* means to reflect God, to magnify, exalt, and glorify Him.

God intends for *your* marriage to reflect His image to a world that desperately needs to see who He is. That's why your mirror needs constant polishing in the light of His Word. Because *you* are created in the image of God, people who wouldn't otherwise know what God is like should be able to look at you and your relationship with your spouse and get a genuine, awe-inspiring glimpse of the divine.

Commanded to Multiply

GOD TOLD ADAM AND EVE to "be fruitful and multiply" (1:28). Later, the psalmist wrote, "Behold, children are a heritage from the LORD, the fruit of the womb is a reward ... Happy is the man who has his quiver full of them; they shall not be ashamed, but shall speak with their enemies in the gate" (Psalm 127:3, 5).

We believe it is very clear in Scripture that God wants—even commands— married couples to have children. Of course, there are extenuating circumstances that can cause couples to be childless, but the scriptural norm is for us to "be fruitful and multiply."

Why?

We don't believe we're commanded to have children just to have children. We believe God wants us to have children so that we can multiply a godly heritage, so that there will be new believers (and we are to make sure we do everything we can to encourage our children to fear and love God) to take the message of salvation to this world's next generation.

Children are a blessing to those who have made a lifetime commitment to marriage. But they are also messengers to a world that needs to hear God's message of love and salvation.

---

nostrils the breath of life; and man became a living being.

Life in God's Garden

8The LORD God planted a garden eastward in Eden, and there He put the man whom He had formed. 9And out of the ground the LORD God made every tree grow that is pleasant to the sight and good for food. The tree of life *was* also in the midst of the garden, and the tree of the knowledge of good and evil.

10Now a river went out of Eden to water the garden, and from there it parted and became four riverheads. 11The name of the first *is* Pishon; it *is* the one which skirts the whole land of Havilah, where *there is* gold. 12And the gold of that land *is* good. Bdellium and the onyx stone *are* there. 13The name of the second river *is* Gihon; it *is* the one which goes around the whole land of Cush. 14The name of the third river *is* Hiddekel;a it *is* the one which goes toward the east of Assyria. The fourth river *is* the Euphrates.

15Then the LORD God took the man and put him in the garden of Eden to tend and keep it. 16And the LORD God commanded the man, saying, "Of every tree of the garden you may freely eat; 17but of the tree of the knowledge of good and evil you shall not eat, for in the day that you eat of it you shall surely die."

18And the LORD God said, "It is not good that man should be alone; I will make him a helper comparable to him." 19Out of the ground the LORD God formed every beast of the field and every bird of the air, and brought *them* to Adam to see what he would call them. And whatever Adam called each living creature, that *was* its name. 20So Adam gave names to all cattle, to the birds of the air, and to every beast of the field. But for Adam there was not found a helper comparable to him.

21And the LORD God caused a deep sleep to fall on Adam, and he slept; and He took one of his ribs, and closed up the flesh in its place. 22Then the rib which the LORD God had taken from man He made into a woman, and He brought her to the man.

23And Adam said:

"This *is* now bone of my bones
And flesh of my flesh;
She shall be called Woman,
Because she was taken out of Man."

24Therefore a man shall leave his father and mother and be joined to his wife, and they shall become one flesh.

25And they were both naked, the man and his wife, and were not ashamed.

The Temptation and Fall of Man

3 Now the serpent was more cunning than any beast of the field which the LORD God had made. And he said to the

2:14 aOr *Tigris*

woman, "Has God indeed said, 'You shall not eat of every tree of the garden'?"

²And the woman said to the serpent, "We may eat the fruit of the trees of the garden; ³but of the fruit of the tree which *is* in the midst of the garden, God has said, 'You shall not eat it, nor shall you touch it, lest you die.'"

⁴Then the serpent said to the woman, "You will not surely die. ⁵For God knows that in the day you eat of it your eyes will be opened, and you will be like God, knowing good and evil."

⁶So when the woman saw that the tree *was* good for food, that it *was* pleasant to the eyes, and a tree desirable to make *one* wise, she took of its fruit and ate. She also gave to her husband with her, and he ate. ⁷Then the eyes of both of them were opened, and they knew that they *were* naked; and they sewed fig leaves together and made themselves coverings.

⁸And they heard the sound of the LORD God walking in the garden in the cool of the day, and Adam and his wife hid themselves from the presence of the LORD God among the trees of the garden. ⁹Then the LORD God called to Adam and said to him, "Where *are* you?"

¹⁰So he said, "I heard Your voice in the garden, and I was afraid because I was naked; and I hid myself."

¹¹And He said, "Who told you that you *were* naked? Have you eaten from the tree of which I commanded you that you should not eat?"

¹²Then the man said, "The woman whom You gave *to be* with me, she gave me of the tree, and I ate."

¹³And the LORD God said to the woman, "What *is* this you have done?"

The woman said, "The serpent deceived me, and I ate."

¹⁴So the LORD God said to the serpent:

"Because you have done this,
  You *are* cursed more than all
    cattle,
  And more than every beast of the
    field;
On your belly you shall go,
  And you shall eat dust
  All the days of your life.

BIBLICAL INSIGHTS • 2:18
A Comparable Helper

WHILE ALL OF US ARE CALLED to help others—"Bear one another's burdens, and so fulfill the law of Christ" (Gal. 6:2)—the Bible places a special emphasis on this responsibility for wives. It also tells us that God specially designed women to be the kinds of helpers that make them the ideal match for men as the two become one in marriage.

The very first book of God's Word tells us that part of God's plan of creation—including the creation of marriage—contained this declaration, "It is not good that man should be alone; I will make him a helper comparable to him" (Genesis 2:18).

It is interesting to note that the Hebrew word *helper* in this passage is found hereafter in the Bible only in reference to God as He helps us. The fact that God applies this same word to a wife signifies that women have been given tremendous power for good in the lives of their husbands.

This remarkable verse tells us that God has designed wives to be very much like their husbands—comparable—but also different in ways that complement or help their husbands become all that God intends them to be.

---

¹⁵ And I will put enmity
  Between you and the woman,
  And between your seed and her
    Seed;
  He shall bruise your head,
  And you shall bruise His heel."

¹⁶To the woman He said:

"I will greatly multiply your sorrow
  and your conception;
In pain you shall bring forth
  children;
Your desire *shall be* for your
  husband,

DEVOTIONS FOR COUPLES • 2:18
Marriage Fills Our Gaps

Genesis 2:18 clearly outlines one major purpose for marriage: for one spouse to complete the other. "It is not good that man should be alone," God declared. "I will make him a helper comparable to him."

Adam may have lived in the middle of a perfect garden, but he was alone. God created Eve to be his comparable helper and companion. The apostle Paul echoed this teaching when he wrote, "Nevertheless, neither is man independent of woman, nor woman independent of man, in the Lord" (1 Cor. 11:11). We really *do* need each other! As William Barclay's *Daily Study Bible* puts it, "In the Lord, woman is nothing without man nor man without woman."

Perhaps you saw the original *Rocky* film, before Sylvester Stallone started spinning off sequels. Do you remember the love relationship of Rocky and Adrian? She is the little wallflower who worked in the pet shop, the sister of Paulie, an insensitive goon who works at the meat house and who wants to become a debt collector for a loan shark. Paulie feels suspicious of Rocky's intentions toward Adrian. He asks the fighter one day, "What's the attraction? I don't see it."

I doubt that Sylvester Stallone, who wrote the script, has any idea that his words perfectly exemplify the principle for a suitable helper described in Genesis 2. Rocky declares, "I dunno—she fills gaps."

Paulie bristles. "What gaps?" he asks.

"She got gaps; I got gaps—together we fill the gaps."

In his simple but profound way, Rocky hits upon a great truth. He means that without him, Adrian has empty places in her life; and without her, he has empty places in his. But when the two of them get together, they fill those blank spots in one another.

That's exactly what God did when He fashioned a helpmate suitable for Adam. She filled his empty places and he filled hers.

I've never had any doubt that I need Barbara. I know she fills my gaps. I need her because she tells me the truth about myself, both the good, the bad, and the otherwise. I need Barbara to add a different perspective of life, of relationships, and of people. She also adds variety and spice to my life. She's an artist; I am not. Her pace is slower than mine. She helps me pull back on the throttle and helps me enjoy life. She has encouraged me, for instance, to read more—and I now actually *enjoy* it. That's what a helpmate does!

And he shall rule over you."

17Then to Adam He said, "Because you have heeded the voice of your wife, and have eaten from the tree of which I commanded you, saying, 'You shall not eat of it':

"Cursed *is* the ground for your sake;
In toil you shall eat *of* it
All the days of your life.
18 Both thorns and thistles it shall
    bring forth for you,
And you shall eat the herb of the
    field.
19 In the sweat of your face you shall
    eat bread
Till you return to the ground,
For out of it you were taken;

For dust you *are,*
And to dust you shall return."

20And Adam called his wife's name Eve, because she was the mother of all living.

21Also for Adam and his wife the LORD God made tunics of skin, and clothed them.

22Then the LORD God said, "Behold, the man has become like one of Us, to know good and evil. And now, lest he put out his hand and take also of the tree of life, and eat, and live forever"— 23therefore the LORD God sent him out of the garden of Eden to till the ground from which he was taken. 24So He drove out the man; and He placed cherubim at the east of the garden of Eden, and a flaming sword which turned every way, to guard the way to the tree of life.

Cain Murders Abel

4 Now Adam knew Eve his wife, and she conceived and bore Cain, and said, "I have acquired a man from the LORD." ²Then she bore again, this time his brother Abel. Now Abel was a keeper of sheep, but Cain was a tiller of the ground. ³And in the process of time it came to pass that Cain brought an offering of the fruit of the ground to the LORD. ⁴Abel also brought of the firstborn of his flock and of their fat. And the LORD respected Abel and his offering, ⁵but He did not respect Cain and his offering. And Cain was very angry, and his countenance fell.

⁶So the LORD said to Cain, "Why are you angry? And why has your countenance fallen? ⁷If you do well, will you not be accepted? And if you do not do well, sin lies at the door. And its desire *is* for you, but you should rule over it."

⁸Now Cain talked with Abel his brother;ᵃ and it came to pass, when they were in the field, that Cain rose up against Abel his brother and killed him.

⁹Then the LORD said to Cain, "Where *is* Abel your brother?"

He said, "I do not know. *Am* I my brother's keeper?"

4:8 ᵃSamaritan Pentateuch, Septuagint, Syriac, and Vulgate add *"Let us go out to the field."*
4:15 ᵃFollowing Masoretic Text and Targum; Septuagint, Syriac, and Vulgate read *Not so.*

¹⁰And He said, "What have you done? The voice of your brother's blood cries out to Me from the ground. ¹¹So now you *are* cursed from the earth, which has opened its mouth to receive your brother's blood from your hand. ¹²When you till the ground, it shall no longer yield its strength to you. A fugitive and a vagabond you shall be on the earth."

¹³And Cain said to the LORD, "My punishment *is* greater than I can bear! ¹⁴Surely You have driven me out this day from the face of the ground; I shall be hidden from Your face; I shall be a fugitive and a vagabond on the earth, and it will happen *that* anyone who finds me will kill me."

¹⁵And the LORD said to him, "Therefore,ᵃ whoever kills Cain, vengeance shall be taken on him sevenfold." And the LORD set a mark on Cain, lest anyone finding him should kill him.

The Family of Cain

¹⁶Then Cain went out from the presence of the LORD and dwelt in the land of Nod on the east of Eden. ¹⁷And Cain knew his wife, and she conceived and bore Enoch. And he built a city, and called the name of the city after the name of his son—Enoch. ¹⁸To Enoch was born Irad; and Irad begot Mehujael, and Mehujael begot Methushael, and Methushael begot Lamech.

¹⁹Then Lamech took for himself two

ROMANTIC QUOTES AND NOTES
You Married the Right Person

Everyone must adjust to qualities in a spouse that went unnoticed or got ignored during the dreamy days of dating. How many individuals have encountered a painful frustration in marriage and asked themselves, *Why did I do this? Did I marry the wrong person?*

When these questions arise, you need to confront them immediately. If you don't resolve these doubts promptly, they will hang around indefinitely, like a dark and distant cloud on the horizon of your relationship.

If you find yourself struggling with this question, go back to the admonition in Genesis 2:24, 25, where spouses are commanded to leave, cleave, become one flesh, and be completely transparent with each other. If such doubts bother you, face them by getting away alone for a weekend to seek out the Lord and pray for His peace on this matter.

Let me assure you that you *are* married to the right person. How do I know this? Because God hates divorce and He wants your marriage to last! You may have gone against some biblical admonitions in getting to where you are, but the Scripture is clear: You're not to try to undo a mistake and, in the process, make a second one.

BIBLICAL INSIGHTS • 2:25
Without Disguise or Covering

EFFECTIVE COMMUNICATION in any relationship begins with transparency. Transparency in marriage is described before the Fall, "And they were both naked, the man and his wife, and were not ashamed" (2:25).

Before Adam and Eve sinned against God, they wore no disguise or covering, had no mask. They were uncovered physically and had no need to cover up emotionally. They couldn't and wouldn't hide anything from one another. Adam and Eve were a picture of true transparency. They were *real* with one another, open to one another, and unafraid of rejection.

But this transparency totally changed after the Fall, "Then the eyes of both of them were opened, and they knew that they were naked; and they sewed fig leaves together and made themselves coverings" (3:7). Those famous fig leaf aprons were only part of their cover-up. Sin introduced a lot more than a need for modesty! It also brought deceit, lying, trickery, half-truths, manipulation, misrepresentation, distortion, hatred, jealousy, control, and many other vices, all prompting us to wear masks.

God's plan for marriage has always been transparency and openness. He never intended that couples engage in any kind of deceit, dishonesty, or any of the other problems that the Fall brought on the marriage relationship.

---

wives: the name of one *was* Adah, and the name of the second *was* Zillah. ²⁰And Adah bore Jabal. He was the father of those who dwell in tents and have livestock. ²¹His brother's name *was* Jubal. He was the father of all those who play the harp and flute. ²²And as for Zillah, she also bore Tubal-Cain, an instructor of every craftsman in bronze and iron. And the sister of Tubal-Cain *was* Naamah.

²³Then Lamech said to his wives:

"Adah and Zillah, hear my voice;
Wives of Lamech, listen to my speech!
For I have killed a man for wounding me,
Even a young man for hurting me.
²⁴   If Cain shall be avenged sevenfold,
Then Lamech seventy-sevenfold."

A New Son

²⁵And Adam knew his wife again, and she bore a son and named him Seth, "For God has appointed another seed for me instead of Abel, whom Cain killed." ²⁶And as for Seth, to him also a son was born; and he named him Enosh.ᵃ Then *men* began to call on the name of the LORD.

The Family of Adam

5 This is the book of the genealogy of Adam. In the day that God created man, He made him in the likeness of God. ²He created them male and female, and blessed them and called them Mankind in the day they were created. ³And Adam lived one hundred and thirty years, and begot *a son* in his own likeness, after his image, and named him Seth. ⁴After he begot Seth, the days of Adam were eight hundred years; and he had sons and daughters. ⁵So all the days that Adam lived were nine hundred and thirty years; and he died.

⁶Seth lived one hundred and five years, and begot Enosh. ⁷After he begot Enosh, Seth lived eight hundred and seven years, and had sons and daughters. ⁸So all the days of Seth were nine hundred and twelve years; and he died.

⁹Enosh lived ninety years, and begot Cainan.ᵃ ¹⁰After he begot Cainan, Enosh lived eight hundred and fifteen years, and had sons and daughters. ¹¹So all the days of Enosh were nine hundred and five years; and he died.

¹²Cainan lived seventy years, and begot Mahalalel. ¹³After he begot Mahalalel, Cainan lived eight hundred and forty years, and had sons and daughters. ¹⁴So all the days of Cainan were nine hundred and ten years; and he died.

4:26 ᵃGreek *Enos* 5:9 ᵃHebrew *Qenan*

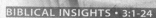

God's Purpose for Marriage

THE FIRST THREE CHAPTERS of Genesis provide us with a foundational understanding of God's purposes and plan for marriage:

- **1:27, 28** makes it clear that God made two sexes and that he made us with more than simple biological differences.
- **2:18–23** describes how God created the woman to be a companion and a helper to the man. Far from being a demeaning term, the word helper is a term God uses for Himself throughout the bible (see Psalm 54:4, Hos. 13:9, John 14:16).
- **2:24, 25** gives God's plan for marriage. A husband and wife must leave their parents, cleave to each other, and begin the process of becoming one in body, soul and spirit. They should be transparent with each other, naked and not ashamed.
- **3:1–24** reveals Satan's strategy for fostering rebellion against God and for dividing husbands and wives.
- **3:6** hints at the passivity of Adam who was with his wife while she was being tempted but who failed to lead by saying nothing. God holds Adam accountable for this first act of rebellion (3:9).
- **3:7–12** describes how Adam and Eve's disobedience led to feelings of shame, guilt and fear (v. 7–10) and blame-shifting (v. 12).
- **3:16** reveals that the consequences of Adam and Eve's rebellion include pain for mothers in bearing and raising children and a battle for control between a husband and his wife (v. 16). Men will experience suffering in their work because of the ground being cursed by God.

Like the first married couple in history, all of us are living out our marriages in the midst of a spiritual battle like the one Adam and Eve faced in Genesis 3. Your marriage is not taking place on a romantic balcony, but a spiritual battlefield. Only through a restored relationship with God through Christ can we begin to live out and enjoy God's original plan and purpose for marriage.

---

¹⁵Mahalalel lived sixty-five years, and begot Jared. ¹⁶After he begot Jared, Mahalalel lived eight hundred and thirty years, and had sons and daughters. ¹⁷So all the days of Mahalalel were eight hundred and ninety-five years; and he died.

¹⁸Jared lived one hundred and sixty-two years, and begot Enoch. ¹⁹After he begot Enoch, Jared lived eight hundred years, and had sons and daughters. ²⁰So all the days of Jared were nine hundred and sixty-two years; and he died.

²¹Enoch lived sixty-five years, and begot Methuselah. ²²After he begot Methuselah, Enoch walked with God three hundred years, and had sons and daughters. ²³So all the days of Enoch were three hundred and sixty-five years. ²⁴And Enoch walked with God; and he *was* not, for God took him.

²⁵Methuselah lived one hundred and eighty-seven years, and begot Lamech. ²⁶After he begot Lamech, Methuselah lived seven hundred and eighty-two years, and had sons and daughters. ²⁷So all the days of Methuselah were nine hundred and sixty-nine years; and he died.

²⁸Lamech lived one hundred and eighty-two years, and had a son. ²⁹And he called his name Noah, saying, "This *one* will comfort us concerning our work and the toil of our hands, because of the ground which the LORD has cursed." ³⁰After he begot Noah, Lamech lived five hundred and ninety-five years, and had sons and daughters. ³¹So all the days of Lamech were seven hundred and seventy-seven years; and he died.

³²And Noah was five hundred years old, and Noah begot Shem, Ham, and Japheth.

The Wickedness and Judgment of Man

6 Now it came to pass, when men began to multiply on the face of the earth, and daughters were born to them, ²that the sons of God saw the daughters of men, that they *were* beautiful; and they took wives for themselves of all whom they chose.

³And the LORD said, "My Spirit shall not strive[a] with man forever, for he *is* indeed flesh; yet his days shall be one hundred and twenty years." ⁴There were giants on the earth in those days, and also afterward, when the sons of God came in to the daughters of men and they bore *children* to them. Those *were* the mighty men who *were* of old, men of renown.

⁵Then the LORD[a] saw that the wickedness of man *was* great in the earth, and *that* every intent of the thoughts of his heart *was* only evil continually. ⁶And the LORD was sorry that He had made man on the earth, and He was grieved in His heart. ⁷So the LORD said, "I will destroy man whom I have created from the face of the earth, both man and beast, creeping thing and birds of the air, for I am sorry that I have made them." ⁸But Noah found grace in the eyes of the LORD.

Noah Pleases God

⁹This is the genealogy of Noah. Noah was a just man, perfect in his generations. Noah walked with God. ¹⁰And Noah begot three sons: Shem, Ham, and Japheth.

¹¹The earth also was corrupt before God, and the earth was filled with violence. ¹²So God looked upon the earth, and indeed it was corrupt; for all flesh had corrupted their way on the earth.

The Ark Prepared

¹³And God said to Noah, "The end of all flesh has come before Me, for the earth is filled with violence through them; and behold, I will destroy them with the earth. ¹⁴Make yourself an ark of gopherwood; make rooms in the ark, and cover it inside and outside with pitch. ¹⁵And this is how you shall make it: The length of the ark *shall be* three hundred cubits, its width fifty cubits, and its height thirty cubits. ¹⁶You shall make a window for the ark, and you shall finish it to a cubit from above; and set the door of the ark in its side. You shall make it *with* lower, second, and third *decks*. ¹⁷And behold, I Myself am bringing floodwaters on the earth, to destroy from under heaven all flesh in which *is* the breath of life; everything that *is* on the earth shall die. ¹⁸But I will establish My covenant with you; and you shall go into the ark—you, your sons, your wife, and your sons' wives with you. ¹⁹And of every living thing of all flesh you shall bring two of every *sort* into the ark, to keep *them* alive with you; they shall be male and female. ²⁰Of the birds after their kind, of animals after their kind, and of every creeping thing of the earth after its kind, two of every *kind* will come to you to keep *them* alive. ²¹And you shall take for yourself of all food that is eaten, and you shall gather *it* to yourself; and it shall be food for you and for them."

²²Thus Noah did; according to all that God commanded him, so he did.

The Great Flood

7 Then the LORD said to Noah, "Come into the ark, you and all your household, because I have seen *that* you *are* righteous before Me in this generation. ²You shall take with you seven each of every clean animal, a male and his female; two each of animals that *are* unclean, a male and his female; ³also seven each of

INTIMATE MOMENTS

Give your wife a small journal for recording her secret romantic wishes. When you present it to her, make sure she understands that it's a journal designed for you to read. You want to know what she really wants in the way of romance! Read it regularly . . . and then make her wishes come true!

6:3 [a]Septuagint, Syriac, Targum, and Vulgate read *abide.* **6:5** [a]Following Masoretic Text and Targum; Vulgate reads *God;* Septuagint reads LORD *God.*

birds of the air, male and female, to keep the species alive on the face of all the earth. ⁴For after seven more days I will cause it to rain on the earth forty days and forty nights, and I will destroy from the face of the earth all living things that I have made." ⁵And Noah did according to all that the LORD commanded him. ⁶Noah *was* six hundred years old when the floodwaters were on the earth.

⁷So Noah, with his sons, his wife, and his sons' wives, went into the ark because of the waters of the flood. ⁸Of clean animals, of animals that *are* unclean, of birds, and of everything that creeps on the earth, ⁹two by two they went into the ark to Noah, male and female, as God had commanded Noah. ¹⁰And it came to pass after seven days that the waters of the flood were on the earth. ¹¹In the six hundredth year of Noah's life, in the second month, the seventeenth day of the month, on that day all the fountains of the great deep were broken up, and the windows of heaven were opened. ¹²And the rain was on the earth forty days and forty nights.

¹³On the very same day Noah and Noah's sons, Shem, Ham, and Japheth, and Noah's wife and the three wives of his sons with them, entered the ark— ¹⁴they and every beast after its kind, all cattle after their kind, every creeping thing that creeps on the earth after its kind, and every bird after its kind, every bird of every sort. ¹⁵And they went into the ark to Noah, two by two, of all flesh in which *is* the breath of life. ¹⁶So those that entered, male and female of all flesh, went in as God had commanded him; and the LORD shut him in.

¹⁷Now the flood was on the earth forty days. The waters increased and lifted up the ark, and it rose high above the earth. ¹⁸The waters prevailed and greatly increased on the earth, and the ark moved about on the surface of the waters. ¹⁹And the waters prevailed exceedingly on the earth, and all the high hills under the whole heaven were covered. ²⁰The waters prevailed fifteen cubits upward, and the mountains were covered. ²¹And all flesh died that moved on the earth: birds and

BIBLICAL INSIGHTS • 5:1–32

Marriage Multiplies a Godly Legacy

A LINE OF GODLY DESCENDANTS—your children—will carry a reflection of God's character to the next generation, just as it did at the very beginning (5:1–32).

God's original plan called for the home to be a sort of greenhouse, a nurturing place where children learn godly character, values, and integrity. Too many couples raise their children without a sense of mission and direction. They never evaluate their lives in light of the Great Commission (Matt. 28:18–20).

Your assignment is to impart a sense of destiny to your children, to make your home a place where your children learn what it means to love and obey God. Your home should be a training center to equip your children to meet the needs of people and the world, even as Jesus did. If children do not embrace this spiritual mission as they grow up, they may live their entire lives without the privilege of God using them in a significant way.

Your marriage is far more important than you may have imagined. It affects God's reputation on this planet! That's why it's essential for you to set Jesus Christ apart as the Builder of your home.

cattle and beasts and every creeping thing that creeps on the earth, and every man. ²²All in whose nostrils *was* the breath of the spirit[a] of life, all that *was* on the dry *land,* died. ²³So He destroyed all living things which were on the face of the ground: both man and cattle, creeping thing and bird of the air. They were destroyed from the earth. Only Noah and those who *were* with him in the ark remained *alive.* ²⁴And the waters prevailed on the earth one hundred and fifty days.

Noah's Deliverance

8 Then God remembered Noah, and every living thing, and all the animals

that *were* with him in the ark. And God made a wind to pass over the earth, and the waters subsided. ²The fountains of the deep and the windows of heaven were also stopped, and the rain from heaven was restrained. ³And the waters receded continually from the earth. At the end of the hundred and fifty days the waters decreased. ⁴Then the ark rested in the seventh month, the seventeenth day of the month, on the mountains of Ararat. ⁵And the waters decreased continually until the tenth month. In the tenth *month,* on the first *day* of the month, the tops of the mountains were seen.

⁶So it came to pass, at the end of forty days, that Noah opened the window of the ark which he had made. ⁷Then he sent out a raven, which kept going to and fro until the waters had dried up from the earth. ⁸He also sent out from himself a dove, to see if the waters had receded from the face of the ground. ⁹But the dove found no resting place for the sole of her foot, and she returned into the ark to him, for the waters *were* on the face of the whole earth. So he put out his hand and took her, and drew her into the ark to himself. ¹⁰And he waited yet another seven days, and again he sent the dove out from the ark. ¹¹Then the dove came to him in the evening, and behold, a freshly plucked olive leaf *was* in her mouth; and Noah knew that the waters had receded from the earth. ¹²So he waited yet another seven days and sent out the dove, which did not return again to him anymore.

¹³And it came to pass in the six hundred and first year, in the first *month,* the first *day* of the month, that the waters were dried up from the earth; and Noah removed the covering of the ark and looked, and indeed the surface of the ground was dry. ¹⁴And in the second month, on the twenty-seventh day of the month, the earth was dried.

¹⁵Then God spoke to Noah, saying, ¹⁶"Go out of the ark, you and your wife, and your sons and your sons' wives with you. ¹⁷Bring out with you every living thing of all flesh that *is* with you: birds and cattle and every creeping thing that creeps on the earth, so that they may abound on the earth, and be fruitful and multiply on the earth." ¹⁸So Noah went out, and his sons and his wife and his sons' wives with him. ¹⁹Every animal, every creeping thing, every bird, *and* whatever creeps on the earth, according to their families, went out of the ark.

God's Covenant with Creation

²⁰Then Noah built an altar to the LORD, and took of every clean animal and of every clean bird, and offered burnt offerings on the altar. ²¹And the LORD smelled a soothing aroma. Then the LORD said in His heart, "I will never again curse the ground for man's sake, although the imagination of man's heart *is* evil from his youth; nor will I again destroy every living thing as I have done.

ROMANCE FAQ

Q: *What does it mean to have and to hold?*

When we declared our vows, most of us repeated the words, *to have and to hold,* till death do us part. But have you ever thought about what it means to *have* and *hold* your husband?

To have implies a possession. It means he belongs to you and she is no one else's. Are you fulfilling your sexual responsibility to him? For frequency? Creativity? Have you turned him down more often than you have invited his love? Do you put his needs *before* or *after* those of your children or your work?

To hold means to keep or bond, much like a magnet. A magnet has the power to pull a polar opposite to itself. Dennis and I are virtual opposites in nearly every way; it's what attracted us to each other in the first place. But I must continue to be a magnet to him if I am to cultivate my relationship with him. Dennis tells me that I am that magnet whenever I communicate, "I am available."

This may surprise you, but most men *really* want their wives to passionately desire them. And when you express sexual longing for him—whether verbally or nonverbally—most husbands are unlikely to refuse your magnetic power.

22 "While the earth remains,
      Seedtime and harvest,
      Cold and heat,
      Winter and summer,
      And day and night
      Shall not cease."

9 So God blessed Noah and his sons, and
    said to them: "Be fruitful and multiply,
and fill the earth.ᵃ ²And the fear of you
and the dread of you shall be on every
beast of the earth, on every bird of the air,
on all that move *on* the earth, and on all the
fish of the sea. They are given into your
hand. ³Every moving thing that lives shall
be food for you. I have given you all things,
even as the green herbs. ⁴But you shall not
eat flesh with its life, *that is,* its blood.
⁵Surely for your lifeblood I will demand *a
reckoning;* from the hand of every beast I
will require it, and from the hand of man.
From the hand of every man's brother I
will require the life of man.

6   "Whoever sheds man's blood,
      By man his blood shall be shed;

9:1 ᵃCompare Genesis 1:28 **9:9** ᵃLiterally *seed*

      For in the image of God
      He made man.
7   And as for you, be fruitful and
      multiply;
      Bring forth abundantly in the earth
      And multiply in it."

⁸Then God spoke to Noah and to his
sons with him, saying: ⁹"And as for Me,
behold, I establish My covenant with you
and with your descendantsᵃ after you,
¹⁰and with every living creature that *is*
with you: the birds, the cattle, and every
beast of the earth with you, of all that go
out of the ark, every beast of the earth.
¹¹Thus I establish My covenant with you:
Never again shall all flesh be cut off by the
waters of the flood; never again shall there
be a flood to destroy the earth."

¹²And God said: "This *is* the sign of the
covenant which I make between Me and
you, and every living creature that *is* with
you, for perpetual generations: ¹³I set My
rainbow in the cloud, and it shall be for the
sign of the covenant between Me and the
earth. ¹⁴It shall be, when I bring a cloud
over the earth, that the rainbow shall be
seen in the cloud; ¹⁵and I will remember

PARENTING MATTERS

Q: Why is it important to pray for our children?

Praying as a team for the needs of your children will make a big
difference in their lives.

   Over the years, we have been enriched when we pray and ask
God to work in our children's lives. We have prayed for each of our
children concerning every issue imaginable from the time they
were born on.

   Most parents' prayers for their children include:
   • safety and health issues
   • a growing understanding of God's love
   • an increasing ability to identify sin and differentiate right
      from wrong
   • the knowledge of God's forgiveness and salvation through a
      personal relationship with Jesus Christ
   • protection from the evil one and his influences
   • a growing knowledge of how to walk with God, hear His
      voice, and live according to the teachings of Scripture
   • good friends who will encourage them to walk on the right
      paths

   Of course, you should add your own petitions to this list. Praying
together fervently for your children (and grandchildren) will bring
innumerable blessings to your family now and provide a legacy
for generations to come.

My covenant which *is* between Me and you and every living creature of all flesh; the waters shall never again become a flood to destroy all flesh. ¹⁶The rainbow shall be in the cloud, and I will look on it to remember the everlasting covenant between God and every living creature of all flesh that *is* on the earth." ¹⁷And God said to Noah, "This *is* the sign of the covenant which I have established between Me and all flesh that *is* on the earth."

Noah and His Sons

¹⁸Now the sons of Noah who went out of the ark were Shem, Ham, and Japheth. And Ham *was* the father of Canaan. ¹⁹These three *were* the sons of Noah, and from these the whole earth was populated.

²⁰And Noah began *to be* a farmer, and he planted a vineyard. ²¹Then he drank of the wine and was drunk, and became uncovered in his tent. ²²And Ham, the father of Canaan, saw the nakedness of his father, and told his two brothers outside. ²³But Shem and Japheth took a garment, laid *it* on both their shoulders, and went backward and covered the nakedness of their father. Their faces *were* turned away, and they did not see their father's nakedness.

²⁴So Noah awoke from his wine, and knew what his younger son had done to him. ²⁵Then he said:

"Cursed *be* Canaan;
A servant of servants
He shall be to his brethren."

²⁶And he said:

"Blessed *be* the LORD,
The God of Shem,
And may Canaan be his servant.
²⁷   May God enlarge Japheth,
And may he dwell in the tents of
   Shem;
And may Canaan be his servant."

²⁸And Noah lived after the flood three hundred and fifty years. ²⁹So all the days of Noah were nine hundred and fifty years; and he died.

Nations Descended from Noah

10 Now this *is* the genealogy of the sons of Noah: Shem, Ham, and Japheth. And sons were born to them after the flood.

²The sons of Japheth *were* Gomer, Magog, Madai, Javan, Tubal, Meshech, and Tiras. ³The sons of Gomer *were* Ashkenaz, Riphath,^a and Togarmah. ⁴The sons of Javan *were* Elishah, Tarshish, Kittim, and Dodanim.^a ⁵From these the coastland *peoples* of the Gentiles were separated into their lands, everyone according to his language, according to their families, into their nations.

⁶The sons of Ham *were* Cush, Mizraim, Put,^a and Canaan. ⁷The sons of Cush *were* Seba, Havilah, Sabtah, Raamah, and Sabtechah; and the sons of Raamah *were* Sheba and Dedan.

⁸Cush begot Nimrod; he began to be a mighty one on the earth. ⁹He was a mighty hunter before the LORD; therefore it is said, "Like Nimrod the mighty hunter before the LORD." ¹⁰And the beginning of his kingdom was Babel, Erech, Accad, and Calneh, in the land of Shinar. ¹¹From that land he went to Assyria and built Nineveh, Rehoboth Ir, Calah, ¹²and Resen between Nineveh and Calah (that *is* the principal city).

¹³Mizraim begot Ludim, Anamim, Lehabim, Naphtuhim, ¹⁴Pathrusim, and Casluhim (from whom came the Philistines and Caphtorim).

¹⁵Canaan begot Sidon his firstborn, and Heth; ¹⁶the Jebusite, the Amorite, and the Girgashite; ¹⁷the Hivite, the Arkite, and the Sinite; ¹⁸the Arvadite, the Zemarite, and the Hamathite. Afterward the families of the Canaanites were dispersed. ¹⁹And the border of the Canaanites was from Sidon as you go toward Gerar, as far as Gaza; then as you go toward Sodom, Gomorrah, Admah, and Zeboiim, as far as Lasha. ²⁰These *were* the sons of Ham, according to their families, according to their languages, in their lands *and* in their nations.

²¹And *children* were born also to Shem, the father of all the children of Eber, the brother of Japheth the elder. ²²The sons of Shem *were* Elam, Asshur, Arphaxad, Lud, and Aram. ²³The sons of Aram *were* Uz,

---

10:3 ^aSpelled *Diphath* in 1 Chronicles 1:6
10:4 ^aSpelled *Rodanim* in Samaritan Pentateuch and 1 Chronicles 1:7 **10:6** ^aOr *Phut*

Hul, Gether, and Mash.ᵃ ²⁴Arphaxad begot Salah,ᵃ and Salah begot Eber. ²⁵To Eber were born two sons: the name of one *was* Peleg, for in his days the earth was divided; and his brother's name *was* Joktan. ²⁶Joktan begot Almodad, Sheleph, Hazarmaveth, Jerah, ²⁷Hadoram, Uzal, Diklah, ²⁸Obal,ᵃ Abimael, Sheba, ²⁹Ophir, Havilah, and Jobab. All these *were* the sons of Joktan. ³⁰And their dwelling place was from Mesha as you go toward Sephar, the mountain of the east. ³¹These *were* the sons of Shem, according to their families, according to their languages, in their lands, according to their nations.

³²These *were* the families of the sons of Noah, according to their generations, in their nations; and from these the nations were divided on the earth after the flood.

The Tower of Babel

11 Now the whole earth had one language and one speech. ²And it came to pass, as they journeyed from the east, that they found a plain in the land of Shinar, and they dwelt there. ³Then they said to one another, "Come, let us make bricks and bake *them* thoroughly." They had brick for stone, and they had asphalt for mortar. ⁴And they said, "Come, let us build ourselves a city, and a tower whose top *is* in the heavens; let us make a name for ourselves, lest we be scattered abroad over the face of the whole earth."

⁵But the LORD came down to see the city and the tower which the sons of men had built. ⁶And the LORD said, "Indeed the people *are* one and they all have one language, and this is what they begin to do; now nothing that they propose to do will be withheld from them. ⁷Come, let Us go down and there confuse their language, that they may not understand one another's speech." ⁸So the LORD scattered them abroad from there over the face of all the earth, and they ceased building the city. ⁹Therefore its name is called Babel, because there the LORD confused the language of all

---

10:23 ᵃCalled *Meshech* in Septuagint and 1 Chronicles 1:17 10:24 ᵃFollowing Masoretic Text, Vulgate, and Targum; Septuagint reads *Arphaxad begot Cainan, and Cainan begot Salah* (compare Luke 3:35, 36). 10:28 ᵃSpelled *Ebal* in 1 Chronicles 1:22

the earth; and from there the LORD scattered them abroad over the face of all the earth.

Shem's Descendants

¹⁰This *is* the genealogy of Shem: Shem *was* one hundred years old, and begot Arphaxad two years after the flood. ¹¹After he begot Arphaxad, Shem lived five hundred years, and begot sons and daughters.

¹²Arphaxad lived thirty-five years, and begot Salah. ¹³After he begot Salah, Arphaxad lived four hundred and three years, and begot sons and daughters.

¹⁴Salah lived thirty years, and begot Eber. ¹⁵After he begot Eber, Salah lived four hundred and three years, and begot sons and daughters.

¹⁶Eber lived thirty-four years, and begot Peleg. ¹⁷After he begot Peleg, Eber lived four hundred and thirty years, and begot sons and daughters.

¹⁸Peleg lived thirty years, and begot Reu. ¹⁹After he begot Reu, Peleg lived two hundred and nine years, and begot sons and daughters.

²⁰Reu lived thirty-two years, and begot Serug. ²¹After he begot Serug, Reu lived two hundred and seven years, and begot sons and daughters.

²²Serug lived thirty years, and begot Nahor. ²³After he begot Nahor, Serug lived two hundred years, and begot sons and daughters.

²⁴Nahor lived twenty-nine years, and begot Terah. ²⁵After he begot Terah, Nahor lived one hundred and nineteen years, and begot sons and daughters.

²⁶Now Terah lived seventy years, and begot Abram, Nahor, and Haran.

Terah's Descendants

²⁷This *is* the genealogy of Terah: Terah begot Abram, Nahor, and Haran. Haran begot Lot. ²⁸And Haran died before his father Terah in his native land, in Ur of the Chaldeans. ²⁹Then Abram and Nahor took wives: the name of Abram's wife *was* Sarai, and the name of Nahor's wife, Milcah, the daughter of Haran the father of Milcah and the father of Iscah. ³⁰But Sarai was barren; she had no child.

³¹And Terah took his son Abram and

his grandson Lot, the son of Haran, and his daughter-in-law Sarai, his son Abram's wife, and they went out with them from Ur of the Chaldeans to go to the land of Canaan; and they came to Haran and dwelt there. 32So the days of Terah were two hundred and five years, and Terah died in Haran.

Promises to Abram

12 Now the LORD had said to Abram:

"Get out of your country,
From your family
And from your father's house,
To a land that I will show you.
2 I will make you a great nation;
I will bless you
And make your name great;
And you shall be a blessing.
3 I will bless those who bless you,
And I will curse him who curses you;
And in you all the families of the
earth shall be blessed."

4So Abram departed as the LORD had spoken to him, and Lot went with him. And Abram *was* seventy-five years old when he departed from Haran. 5Then Abram took Sarai his wife and Lot his brother's son, and all their possessions that they had gathered, and the people whom they had acquired in Haran, and they departed to go to the land of Canaan. So they came to the land of Canaan. 6Abram passed through the land to the place of Shechem, as far as the terebinth tree of Moreh.a And the Canaanites *were* then in the land.

7Then the LORD appeared to Abram and said, "To your descendants I will give this land." And there he built an altar to the LORD, who had appeared to him. 8And he moved from there to the mountain east of Bethel, and he pitched his tent *with* Bethel on the west and Ai on the east; there he built an altar to the LORD and called on the name of the LORD. 9So Abram journeyed, going on still toward the South.a

Abram in Egypt

10Now there was a famine in the land, and Abram went down to Egypt to dwell there, for the famine *was* severe in the land. 11And it came to pass, when he was close to entering Egypt, that he said to Sarai his wife, "Indeed I know that you *are* a woman of beautiful countenance. 12Therefore it will happen, when the Egyptians see you, that they will say, 'This *is* his wife'; and they will kill me, but they will let you live. 13Please say you *are* my sister, that it may be well with me for your sake, and that Ia may live because of you."

14So it was, when Abram came into Egypt, that the Egyptians saw the woman, that she *was* very beautiful. 15The princes of Pharaoh also saw her and commended her to Pharaoh. And the woman was taken

---

12:6 aHebrew *Alon Moreh* **12:9** aHebrew *Negev*
12:13 aLiterally *my soul*

ROMANTIC QUOTES AND NOTES
A Real Storybook Finish

Do you want a marriage that both of you find fulfilling, satisfying, and sometimes thrilling? Then do in your marriage what the apostle Paul advises in Philippians 2:3, 4, "Esteem one another better than yourself, looking out not only for your own interests, but for the interests of your spouse." Imagine if Abraham had done this with Sarah, rather than forcing her to do something deceitful in an effort to save his own hide!

While looking out for the interests of another doesn't come naturally, couples who commit to self-sacrifice discover a whole new side to romance. Is this hard work? Absolutely! Is it worth the effort? You bet! After years of hard work, I have no question about the payoff: *Our love for each other and the romance we share are richer today than at any time in our marriage.*

Remember, marriage is not just about a grand beginning. It's about committing to a strong finish. It's weathering the storms of disappointment and the turbulence of life, never losing the ability to sing with Solomon, "How fair is your love . . . How much better than wine is your love" (Song 4:10). That kind of storybook finish can be yours.

to Pharaoh's house. ¹⁶He treated Abram well for her sake. He had sheep, oxen, male donkeys, male and female servants, female donkeys, and camels.

¹⁷But the LORD plagued Pharaoh and his house with great plagues because of Sarai, Abram's wife. ¹⁸And Pharaoh called Abram and said, "What *is* this you have done to me? Why did you not tell me that she *was* your wife? ¹⁹Why did you say, 'She *is* my sister'? I might have taken her as my wife. Now therefore, here is your wife; take *her* and go your way." ²⁰So Pharaoh commanded *his* men concerning him; and they sent him away, with his wife and all that he had.

Abram Inherits Canaan

13 Then Abram went up from Egypt, he and his wife and all that he had, and Lot with him, to the South.ᵃ ²Abram *was* very rich in livestock, in silver, and in gold. ³And he went on his journey from the South as far as Bethel, to the place where his tent had been at the beginning, between Bethel and Ai, ⁴to the place of the altar which he had made there at first. And there Abram called on the name of the LORD.

⁵Lot also, who went with Abram, had flocks and herds and tents. ⁶Now the land was not able to support them, that they might dwell together, for their possessions were so great that they could not dwell together. ⁷And there was strife between the herdsmen of Abram's livestock and the herdsmen of Lot's livestock. The Canaanites and the Perizzites then dwelt in the land.

⁸So Abram said to Lot, "Please let there be no strife between you and me, and between my herdsmen and your herdsmen; for we *are* brethren. ⁹Is not the whole land before you? Please separate from me. If *you take* the left, then I will go to the right; or, if *you go* to the right, then I will go to the left."

¹⁰And Lot lifted his eyes and saw all the plain of Jordan, that it *was* well watered everywhere (before the LORD destroyed Sodom and Gomorrah) like the garden of the LORD, like the land of Egypt as you go toward Zoar. ¹¹Then Lot chose for himself all the plain of Jordan, and Lot journeyed east. And they separated from each other. ¹²Abram dwelt in the land of Canaan, and Lot dwelt in the cities of the plain and pitched *his* tent even as far as Sodom. ¹³But the men of Sodom *were* exceedingly wicked and sinful against the LORD.

¹⁴And the LORD said to Abram, after Lot had separated from him: "Lift your eyes now and look from the place where you are—northward, southward, eastward, and westward; ¹⁵for all the land which you see I give to you and your descendantsᵃ forever. ¹⁶And I will make your descendants as the dust of the earth; so that if a man could number the dust of the earth, *then* your descendants also could be numbered. ¹⁷Arise, walk in the land through its length and its width, for I give it to you."

¹⁸Then Abram moved *his* tent, and went and dwelt by the terebinth trees of Mamre,ᵃ which *are* in Hebron, and built an altar there to the LORD.

Lot's Captivity and Rescue

14 And it came to pass in the days of Amraphel king of Shinar, Arioch king of Ellasar, Chedorlaomer king of Elam, and Tidal king of nations,ᵃ ²*that* they made war with Bera king of Sodom, Birsha king of Gomorrah, Shinab king of Admah, Shemeber king of Zeboiim, and the king of Bela (that is, Zoar). ³All these joined together in the Valley of Siddim (that is, the Salt Sea). ⁴Twelve years they served Chedorlaomer, and in the thirteenth year they rebelled.

⁵In the fourteenth year Chedorlaomer and the kings that *were* with him came and attacked the Rephaim in Ashteroth Karnaim, the Zuzim in Ham, the Emim in Shaveh Kiriathaim, ⁶and the Horites in their mountain of Seir, as far as El Paran, which *is* by the wilderness. ⁷Then they turned back and came to En Mishpat (that *is*, Kadesh), and attacked all the country of the Amalekites, and also the Amorites who dwelt in Hazezon Tamar.

⁸And the king of Sodom, the king of Gomorrah, the king of Admah, the king of Zeboiim, and the king of Bela (that *is*, Zoar) went out and joined together in battle in the

---

13:1 ᵃHebrew *Negev* **13:15** ᵃLiterally *seed,* and so throughout the book **13:18** ᵃHebrew *Alon Mamre* **14:1** ᵃHebrew *goyim*

Valley of Siddim ⁹against Chedorlaomer king of Elam, Tidal king of nations,ᵃ Amraphel king of Shinar, and Arioch king of Ellasar—four kings against five. ¹⁰Now the Valley of Siddim *was full of* asphalt pits; and the kings of Sodom and Gomorrah fled; *some* fell there, and the remainder fled to the mountains. ¹¹Then they took all the goods of Sodom and Gomorrah, and all their provisions, and went their way. ¹²They also took Lot, Abram's brother's son who dwelt in Sodom, and his goods, and departed.

¹³Then one who had escaped came and told Abram the Hebrew, for he dwelt by the terebinth trees of Mamreᵃ the Amorite, brother of Eshcol and brother of Aner; and they *were* allies with Abram. ¹⁴Now when Abram heard that his brother was taken captive, he armed his three hundred and eighteen trained *servants* who were born in his own house, and went in pursuit as far as Dan. ¹⁵He divided his forces against them by night, and he and his servants attacked them and pursued them as far as Hobah, which *is* north of Damascus. ¹⁶So he brought back all the goods, and also brought back his brother Lot and his goods, as well as the women and the people.

¹⁷And the king of Sodom went out to meet him at the Valley of Shaveh (that *is,* the King's Valley), after his return from the defeat of Chedorlaomer and the kings who *were* with him.

Abram and Melchizedek

¹⁸Then Melchizedek king of Salem brought out bread and wine; he *was* the priest of God Most High. ¹⁹And he blessed him and said:

"Blessed be Abram of God Most
   High,
   Possessor of heaven and earth;
20   And blessed be God Most High,
   Who has delivered your enemies into
   your hand."

And he gave him a tithe of all.
²¹Now the king of Sodom said to Abram, "Give me the persons, and take the goods for yourself."

²²But Abram said to the king of Sodom, "I have raised my hand to the LORD, God Most High, the Possessor of heaven and earth, ²³that I *will take* nothing, from a thread to a sandal strap, and that I will not take anything that *is* yours, lest you should say, 'I have made Abram rich'— ²⁴except only what the young men have eaten, and the portion of the men who went with me: Aner, Eshcol, and Mamre; let them take their portion."

God's Covenant with Abram

15 After these things the word of the LORD came to Abram in a vision, saying, "Do not be afraid, Abram. I *am* your shield, your exceedingly great reward."

²But Abram said, "Lord GOD, what will You give me, seeing I go childless, and the heir of my house *is* Eliezer of Damascus?" ³Then Abram said, "Look, You have given me no offspring; indeed one born in my house is my heir!"

⁴And behold, the word of the LORD *came* to him, saying, "This one shall not be your heir, but one who will come from your own body shall be your heir." ⁵Then He brought him outside and said, "Look now toward heaven, and count the stars if you are able to number them." And He said to him, "So shall your descendants be."

⁶And he believed in the LORD, and He accounted it to him for righteousness.
⁷Then He said to him, "I *am* the LORD,

INTIMATE MOMENTS

On Friday night, tell him he gets to sleep in late the next morning. Serve him breakfast in bed, taking care to load the tray with food he really likes. This is not the time to give him healthy fare that he detests! Make it a *special morning* that he'll remember for a long, long time. You might even consider presenting him with a menu on Friday, allowing him to make his own choices off of that menu.

14:9 ᵃHebrew *goyim* 14:13 ᵃHebrew *Alon Mamre*

who brought you out of Ur of the Chaldeans, to give you this land to inherit it."

⁸And he said, "Lord GOD, how shall I know that I will inherit it?"

⁹So He said to him, "Bring Me a three-year-old heifer, a three-year-old female goat, a three-year-old ram, a turtledove, and a young pigeon." ¹⁰Then he brought all these to Him and cut them in two, down the middle, and placed each piece opposite the other; but he did not cut the birds in two. ¹¹And when the vultures came down on the carcasses, Abram drove them away.

¹²Now when the sun was going down, a deep sleep fell upon Abram; and behold, horror *and* great darkness fell upon him. ¹³Then He said to Abram: "Know certainly that your descendants will be strangers in a land *that is* not theirs, and will serve them, and they will afflict them four hundred years. ¹⁴And also the nation whom they serve I will judge; afterward they shall come out with great possessions. ¹⁵Now as for you, you shall go to your fathers in peace; you shall be buried at a good old age. ¹⁶But in the fourth generation they shall return here, for the iniquity of the Amorites *is* not yet complete."

¹⁷And it came to pass, when the sun went down and it was dark, that behold, there appeared a smoking oven and a burning torch that passed between those pieces. ¹⁸On the same day the LORD made a covenant with Abram, saying:

"To your descendants I have given this land, from the river of Egypt to the great river, the River Euphrates— ¹⁹the Kenites, the Kenezzites, the Kadmonites, ²⁰the Hittites, the Perizzites, the Rephaim, ²¹the Amorites, the Canaanites, the Girgashites, and the Jebusites."

Hagar and Ishmael

16 Now Sarai, Abram's wife, had borne him no *children*. And she had an Egyptian maidservant whose name was Hagar. ²So Sarai said to Abram, "See now, the LORD has restrained me from bearing *children*. Please, go in to my maid; perhaps I shall obtain children by her." And Abram heeded the voice of Sarai. ³Then Sarai, Abram's wife, took Hagar her maid, the Egyptian, and gave her to her husband Abram to be his wife, after Abram had dwelt ten years in the land of Canaan. ⁴So he went in to Hagar, and she conceived. And when she saw that she had conceived, her mistress became despised in her eyes.

⁵Then Sarai said to Abram, "My wrong *be* upon you! I gave my maid into your embrace; and when she saw that she had conceived, I became despised in her eyes. The LORD judge between you and me."

⁶So Abram said to Sarai, "Indeed your maid *is* in your hand; do to her as you please." And when Sarai dealt harshly with her, she fled from her presence.

ROMANCE FAQ

Q: *Does God care how we relate to one another sexually?*

The Song of Songs, though full of spiritual meaning and application, provides an excellent description of God's intention for a husband and wife's sexual relationship. According to Solomon, the man has the freedom to enjoy his wife's body, and the woman has the freedom to enjoy his. This sensual book offers several key ideas on how to be a great lover.

First, Solomon readily praised his beloved. He told her how beautiful she was with vivid and picturesque language. I often ask the husbands at our Weekend to Remember marriage conferences, "When was the last time you wrote your wife a love letter that praised her and told her how beautiful she is?"

Second, Solomon was romantic. His poetic words describe his beloved's entire body as a source of delight. Few husbands have an easy time being romantically creative, but the rest of us need help in this area.

Third, Solomon's focus was physical. A wife may be tempted to resent her husband's sex drive and physical focus, but she should understand that a man is stimulated by sight *much* more than is a woman. God designed him this way deliberately!

7Now the Angel of the LORD found her by a spring of water in the wilderness, by the spring on the way to Shur. 8And He said, "Hagar, Sarai's maid, where have you come from, and where are you going?"

She said, "I am fleeing from the presence of my mistress Sarai."

9The Angel of the LORD said to her, "Return to your mistress, and submit yourself under her hand." 10Then the Angel of the LORD said to her, "I will multiply your descendants exceedingly, so that they shall not be counted for multitude." 11And the Angel of the LORD said to her:

"Behold, you *are* with child,
And you shall bear a son.
You shall call his name Ishmael,
Because the LORD has heard your
    affliction.
12   He shall be a wild man;
His hand *shall be* against every man,
And every man's hand against him.
And he shall dwell in the presence of
    all his brethren."

13Then she called the name of the LORD who spoke to her, You-Are-the-God-Who-Sees; for she said, "Have I also here seen Him who sees me?" 14Therefore the well was called Beer Lahai Roi;a observe, *it is* between Kadesh and Bered.

15So Hagar bore Abram a son; and Abram named his son, whom Hagar bore, Ishmael. 16Abram *was* eighty-six years old when Hagar bore Ishmael to Abram.

The Sign of the Covenant

17 When Abram was ninety-nine years old, the LORD appeared to Abram and said to him, "I *am* Almighty God; walk before Me and be blameless. 2And I will make My covenant between Me and you, and will multiply you exceedingly." 3Then Abram fell on his face, and God talked with him, saying: 4"As for Me, behold, My covenant is with you, and you shall be a father of many nations. 5No longer shall your name be called Abram, but your name shall be Abraham; for I have made you a father of many nations. 6I will make you exceedingly fruitful; and I will make nations of you, and kings shall come from you. 7And I will establish My covenant

between Me and you and your descendants after you in their generations, for an everlasting covenant, to be God to you and your descendants after you. 8Also I give to you and your descendants after you the land in which you are a stranger, all the land of Canaan, as an everlasting possession; and I will be their God."

9And God said to Abraham: "As for you, you shall keep My covenant, you and your descendants after you throughout their generations. 10This *is* My covenant which you shall keep, between Me and you and your descendants after you: Every male child among you shall be circumcised; 11and you shall be circumcised in the flesh of your foreskins, and it shall be a sign of the covenant between Me and you. 12He who is eight days old among you shall be circumcised, every male child in your generations, he who is born in your house or bought with money from any foreigner who is not your descendant. 13He who is born in your house and he who is bought with your money must be circumcised, and My covenant shall be in your flesh for an everlasting covenant. 14And the uncircumcised male child, who is not circumcised in the flesh of his foreskin, that person shall be cut off from his people; he has broken My covenant."

15Then God said to Abraham, "As for Sarai your wife, you shall not call her name Sarai, but Sarah *shall be* her name. 16And I will bless her and also give you a son by her; then I will bless her, and she shall be *a mother of* nations; kings of peoples shall be from her."

17Then Abraham fell on his face and laughed, and said in his heart, "Shall *a child* be born to a man who is one hundred years old? And shall Sarah, who is ninety years old, bear *a child?*" 18And Abraham said to God, "Oh, that Ishmael might live before You!"

19Then God said: "No, Sarah your wife shall bear you a son, and you shall call his name Isaac; I will establish My covenant with him for an everlasting covenant, *and* with his descendants after him. 20And as

---

16:14 aLiterally *Well of the One Who Lives and Sees Me*

for Ishmael, I have heard you. Behold, I have blessed him, and will make him fruitful, and will multiply him exceedingly. He shall beget twelve princes, and I will make him a great nation. ²¹But My covenant I will establish with Isaac, whom Sarah shall bear to you at this set time next year." ²²Then He finished talking with him, and God went up from Abraham.

²³So Abraham took Ishmael his son, all who were born in his house and all who were bought with his money, every male among the men of Abraham's house, and circumcised the flesh of their foreskins that very same day, as God had said to him. ²⁴Abraham *was* ninety-nine years old when he was circumcised in the flesh of his foreskin. ²⁵And Ishmael his son *was* thirteen years old when he was circumcised in the flesh of his foreskin. ²⁶That very same day Abraham was circumcised, and his son Ishmael; ²⁷and all the men of his house, born in the house or bought with money from a foreigner, were circumcised with him.

The Son of Promise

18 Then the LORD appeared to him by the terebinth trees of Mamre,ᵃ as he was sitting in the tent door in the heat of the day. ²So he lifted his eyes and looked, and behold, three men were standing by him; and when he saw *them,* he ran from the tent door to meet them, and bowed himself to the ground, ³and said, "My Lord, if I have now found favor in Your sight, do not pass on by Your servant. ⁴Please let a little water be brought, and wash your feet, and rest yourselves under the tree. ⁵And I will bring a morsel of bread, that you may refresh your hearts. After that you may pass by, inasmuch as you have come to your servant."

They said, "Do as you have said."

⁶So Abraham hurried into the tent to Sarah and said, "Quickly, make ready three measures of fine meal; knead *it* and make cakes." ⁷And Abraham ran to the herd, took a tender and good calf, gave *it* to a young man, and he hastened to prepare it. ⁸So he took butter and milk and the calf

18:1 ᵃHebrew *Alon Mamre*

BIBLICAL INSIGHTS • 18:12

Respect Your Husband

THE APOSTLE PETER calls special attention to the title Sarah used in addressing her husband, "my lord" (18:12; see 1 Peter 3:6). She used this title as a way to show Abraham her respect.

In a similar way, the apostle Paul writes, "Let the wife see that she respects her husband" (Eph. 5:33). When you respect your husband, you reverence him, notice him, regard him, honor him, prefer him, and esteem him. It means you value his opinion, admire his wisdom and character, appreciate his commitment to you, and consider his needs and values.

Husbands have many needs! One day Dennis gave me a list of what he considered to be some of the things that communicate respect to most men:

• Expressing confidence in him as a man
• Listening to him
• Being a friend and enjoying companionship
• Letting him know that he's needed

These are just a few of the many ways a wife can show that she respects her husband. To bolster Dennis's confidence, for example, I try to be his number one fan. Every husband wants his wife to be on his team and to coach him when necessary—but most of all, to be his cheerleader. A husband needs a wife who is behind him, believing in him, appreciating him, and cheering him on.

which he had prepared, and set *it* before them; and he stood by them under the tree as they ate.

⁹Then they said to him, "Where *is* Sarah your wife?"

So he said, "Here, in the tent."

¹⁰And He said, "I will certainly return to you according to the time of life, and behold, Sarah your wife shall have a son."

(Sarah was listening in the tent door which *was* behind him.) ¹¹Now Abraham and Sarah were old, well advanced in age; *and* Sarah had passed the age of childbearing.ᵃ ¹²Therefore Sarah laughed within herself, saying, "After I have grown old, shall I have pleasure, my lord being old also?"

¹³And the LORD said to Abraham, "Why did Sarah laugh, saying, 'Shall I surely bear *a child,* since I am old?' ¹⁴Is anything too hard for the LORD? At the appointed time I will return to you, according to the time of life, and Sarah shall have a son."

¹⁵But Sarah denied *it,* saying, "I did not laugh," for she was afraid.

And He said, "No, but you did laugh!"

Abraham Intercedes for Sodom

¹⁶Then the men rose from there and looked toward Sodom, and Abraham went with them to send them on the way. ¹⁷And the LORD said, "Shall I hide from Abraham what I am doing, ¹⁸since Abraham shall surely become a great and mighty nation, and all the nations of the earth shall be blessed in him? ¹⁹For I have known him, in order that he may command his children and his household after him, that they keep the way of the LORD, to do righteousness and justice, that the LORD may bring to Abraham what He has spoken to him."

²⁰And the LORD said, "Because the outcry against Sodom and Gomorrah is great, and because their sin is very grave, ²¹I will go down now and see whether they have done altogether according to the outcry against it that has come to Me; and if not, I will know."

²²Then the men turned away from there and went toward Sodom, but Abraham still stood before the LORD. ²³And Abraham came near and said, "Would You also destroy the righteous with the wicked? ²⁴Suppose there were fifty righteous within the city; would You also destroy the place and not spare *it* for the fifty righteous that were in it? ²⁵Far be it from You to do such a thing as this, to slay the righteous with the wicked, so that the righteous should be as the wicked; far be it from You! Shall not the Judge of all the earth do right?"

²⁶So the LORD said, "If I find in Sodom fifty righteous within the city, then I will spare all the place for their sakes."

²⁷Then Abraham answered and said, "Indeed now, I who *am but* dust and ashes

have taken it upon myself to speak to the Lord: ²⁸Suppose there were five less than the fifty righteous; would You destroy all of the city for *lack of* five?"

So He said, "If I find there forty-five, I will not destroy *it.*"

²⁹And he spoke to Him yet again and said, "Suppose there should be forty found there?"

So He said, "I will not do *it* for the sake of forty."

³⁰Then he said, "Let not the Lord be angry, and I will speak: Suppose thirty should be found there?"

So He said, "I will not do *it* if I find thirty there."

³¹And he said, "Indeed now, I have taken it upon myself to speak to the Lord: Suppose twenty should be found there?"

So He said, "I will not destroy *it* for the sake of twenty."

³²Then he said, "Let not the Lord be angry, and I will speak but once more: Suppose ten should be found there?"

And He said, "I will not destroy *it* for the sake of ten." ³³So the LORD went His way as soon as He had finished speaking with Abraham; and Abraham returned to his place.

Sodom's Depravity

19 Now the two angels came to Sodom in the evening, and Lot was sitting in the gate of Sodom. When Lot saw *them,* he rose to meet them, and he bowed himself with his face toward the ground. ²And he said, "Here now, my lords, please turn in to your servant's house and spend the night, and wash your feet; then you may rise early and go on your way."

And they said, "No, but we will spend the night in the open square."

³But he insisted strongly; so they turned in to him and entered his house. Then he made them a feast, and baked unleavened bread, and they ate.

⁴Now before they lay down, the men of the city, the men of Sodom, both old and young, all the people from every quarter, surrounded the house. ⁵And they called to

---

18:11 ᵃLiterally *the manner of women had ceased to be with Sarah*

Lot and said to him, "Where are the men who came to you tonight? Bring them out to us that we may know them *carnally.*"

⁶So Lot went out to them through the doorway, shut the door behind him, ⁷and said, "Please, my brethren, do not do so wickedly! ⁸See now, I have two daughters who have not known a man; please, let me bring them out to you, and you may do to them as you wish; only do nothing to these men, since this is the reason they have come under the shadow of my roof."

⁹And they said, "Stand back!" Then they said, "This one came in to stay *here,* and he keeps acting as a judge; now we will deal worse with you than with them." So they pressed hard against the man Lot, and came near to break down the door. ¹⁰But the men reached out their hands and pulled Lot into the house with them, and shut the door. ¹¹And they struck the men who *were* at the doorway of the house with blindness, both small and great, so that they became weary *trying* to find the door.

Sodom and Gomorrah Destroyed

¹²Then the men said to Lot, "Have you anyone else here? Son-in-law, your sons, your daughters, and whomever you have in the city—take *them* out of this place! ¹³For we will destroy this place, because the outcry against them has grown great before the face of the LORD, and the LORD has sent us to destroy it."

¹⁴So Lot went out and spoke to his sons-in-law, who had married his daughters, and said, "Get up, get out of this place; for the LORD will destroy this city!" But to his sons-in-law he seemed to be joking.

¹⁵When the morning dawned, the angels urged Lot to hurry, saying, "Arise, take your wife and your two daughters who are here, lest you be consumed in the punishment of the city." ¹⁶And while he lingered, the men took hold of his hand, his wife's hand, and the hands of his two daughters, the LORD being merciful to him, and they brought him out and set him outside the city. ¹⁷So it came to pass, when they had brought them outside, that he[a] said, "Escape for your life! Do not look

behind you nor stay anywhere in the plain. Escape to the mountains, lest you be destroyed."

¹⁸Then Lot said to them, "Please, no, my lords! ¹⁹Indeed now, your servant has found favor in your sight, and you have increased your mercy which you have shown me by saving my life; but I cannot escape to the mountains, lest some evil overtake me and I die. ²⁰See now, this city *is* near *enough* to flee to, and it *is* a little one; please let me escape there (*is* it not a little one?) and my soul shall live."

²¹And he said to him, "See, I have favored you concerning this thing also, in that I will not overthrow this city for which you have spoken. ²²Hurry, escape there. For I cannot do anything until you arrive there." Therefore the name of the city was called Zoar.

²³The sun had risen upon the earth when Lot entered Zoar. ²⁴Then the LORD rained brimstone and fire on Sodom and Gomorrah, from the LORD out of the heavens. ²⁵So He overthrew those cities, all the plain, all the inhabitants of the cities, and what grew on the ground. ²⁶But his wife looked back behind him, and she became a pillar of salt.

²⁷And Abraham went early in the morning to the place where he had stood before the LORD. ²⁸Then he looked toward Sodom and Gomorrah, and toward all the land of the plain; and he saw, and behold, the smoke of the land which went up like the smoke of a furnace. ²⁹And it came to pass, when God destroyed the cities of the plain, that God remembered Abraham, and sent Lot out of the midst of the overthrow, when He overthrew the cities in which Lot had dwelt.

The Descendants of Lot

³⁰Then Lot went up out of Zoar and dwelt in the mountains, and his two daughters were with him; for he was afraid to dwell in Zoar. And he and his two daughters dwelt in a cave. ³¹Now the firstborn said to the younger, "Our father *is* old, and *there is* no man on the earth to come in to us as is the custom of all the earth. ³²Come, let us make our father drink wine, and we will lie with him, that we may preserve the

---

19:17 [a]Septuagint, Syriac, and Vulgate read *they.*

lineage of our father." ³³So they made their father drink wine that night. And the first-born went in and lay with her father, and he did not know when she lay down or when she arose.

³⁴It happened on the next day that the firstborn said to the younger, "Indeed I lay with my father last night; let us make him drink wine tonight also, and you go in *and* lie with him, that we may preserve the lineage of our father." ³⁵Then they made their father drink wine that night also. And the younger arose and lay with him, and he did not know when she lay down or when she arose.

³⁶Thus both the daughters of Lot were with child by their father. ³⁷The firstborn bore a son and called his name Moab; he *is* the father of the Moabites to this day. ³⁸And the younger, she also bore a son and called his name Ben-Ammi; he *is* the father of the people of Ammon to this day.

Abraham and Abimelech

20 And Abraham journeyed from there to the South, and dwelt between Kadesh and Shur, and stayed in Gerar. ²Now Abraham said of Sarah his wife, "She *is* my sister." And Abimelech king of Gerar sent and took Sarah.

³But God came to Abimelech in a dream by night, and said to him, "Indeed you *are* a dead man because of the woman whom you have taken, for she *is* a man's wife."

⁴But Abimelech had not come near her; and he said, "Lord, will You slay a righteous nation also? ⁵Did he not say to me, 'She *is* my sister'? And she, even she herself said, 'He *is* my brother.' In the integrity of my heart and innocence of my hands I have done this."

⁶And God said to him in a dream, "Yes, I know that you did this in the integrity of your heart. For I also withheld you from sinning against Me; therefore I did not let you touch her. ⁷Now therefore, restore the man's wife; for he *is* a prophet, and he will pray for you and you shall live. But if you do not restore *her,* know that you shall surely die, you and all who *are* yours."

⁸So Abimelech rose early in the morning, called all his servants, and told all these things in their hearing; and the men were very much afraid. ⁹And Abimelech called Abraham and said to him, "What have you done to us? How have I offended you, that you have brought on me and on my kingdom a great sin? You have done deeds to me that ought not to be done." ¹⁰Then Abimelech said to Abraham, "What did you have in view, that you have done this thing?"

¹¹And Abraham said, "Because I thought, surely the fear of God *is* not in this place; and they will kill me on account of my wife. ¹²But indeed *she is* truly my sister. She *is* the daughter of my father, but not the daughter of my mother; and she became my wife. ¹³And it came to pass, when God caused me to wander from my father's house, that I

ROMANCE FAQ

Q: *What is wrong with looking at someone other than my spouse or thinking of this person in a sexual way?*

When we entertain sexual thoughts about strangers in the theater of our minds, *we give ourselves to those images.* When we invest our attention and sexual energy with others, we will have little or no sexual energy for our wives.

Lust can lead us down the pathway of poor choices, one compromising thought at a time, and ultimately to devastating consequences. The trouble with us men is that we underestimate our vulnerability in this area. We tend to think we're bulletproof. We forget the words of 1 Corinthians 10:12, which warn, "Let him who thinks he stands take heed lest he fall." We're seduced into believing that a little bit of porn . . . or lingering over the Victoria's Secret catalog . . . or visiting a marginal Internet site . . . is no big deal. We can control it.

We also underestimate the power of sin. Someone has said, "Sin would have fewer takers if its consequences occurred immediately." Sin and death are synonymous. Sin destroys romance and is deadly to marriage.

said to her, 'This *is* your kindness that you should do for me: in every place, wherever we go, say of me, "He *is* my brother."'"

¹⁴Then Abimelech took sheep, oxen, and male and female servants, and gave *them* to Abraham; and he restored Sarah his wife to him. ¹⁵And Abimelech said, "See, my land *is* before you; dwell where it pleases you." ¹⁶Then to Sarah he said, "Behold, I have given your brother a thousand *pieces* of silver; indeed this vindicates you[a] before all who *are* with you and before everybody." Thus she was rebuked.

¹⁷So Abraham prayed to God; and God healed Abimelech, his wife, and his female servants. Then they bore *children;* ¹⁸for the LORD had closed up all the wombs of the house of Abimelech because of Sarah, Abraham's wife.

Isaac Is Born

21 And the LORD visited Sarah as He had said, and the LORD did for Sarah as He had spoken. ²For Sarah conceived and bore Abraham a son in his old age, at the set time of which God had spoken to him. ³And Abraham called the name of his son who was born to him—whom Sarah bore to him—Isaac. ⁴Then Abraham circumcised his son Isaac when he was eight days old, as God had commanded him. ⁵Now Abraham was one hundred years old when his son Isaac was born to him. ⁶And Sarah said, "God has made me laugh, *and* all who hear will laugh with me." ⁷She also said, "Who would have said to Abraham that Sarah would nurse children? For I have borne *him* a son in his old age."

Hagar and Ishmael Depart

⁸So the child grew and was weaned. And Abraham made a great feast on the same day that Isaac was weaned. ⁹And Sarah saw the son of Hagar the Egyptian, whom she had borne to Abraham, scoffing. ¹⁰Therefore she said to Abraham, "Cast out this bondwoman and her son; for the son of this bondwoman shall not be heir with my son, *namely* with Isaac." ¹¹And the matter was very displeasing in Abraham's sight because of his son.

¹²But God said to Abraham, "Do not let it be displeasing in your sight because of the lad or because of your bondwoman. Whatever Sarah has said to you, listen to her voice; for in Isaac your seed shall be called. ¹³Yet I will also make a nation of the son of the bondwoman, because he *is* your seed."

¹⁴So Abraham rose early in the morning, and took bread and a skin of water; and putting *it* on her shoulder, he gave *it* and the boy to Hagar, and sent her away. Then she departed and wandered in the Wilderness of Beersheba. ¹⁵And the water in the skin was used up, and she placed the boy under one of the shrubs. ¹⁶Then she went and sat down across from *him* at a distance of about a bowshot; for she said to herself, "Let me not see the death of the boy." So she sat opposite *him,* and lifted her voice and wept.

¹⁷And God heard the voice of the lad. Then the angel of God called to Hagar out of heaven, and said to her, "What ails you, Hagar? Fear not, for God has heard the voice of the lad where he *is.* ¹⁸Arise, lift up the lad and hold him with your hand, for I will make him a great nation."

¹⁹Then God opened her eyes, and she saw a well of water. And she went and filled the skin with water, and gave the lad a drink. ²⁰So God was with the lad; and he grew and dwelt in the wilderness, and became an archer. ²¹He dwelt in the Wilderness of Paran; and his mother took a wife for him from the land of Egypt.

A Covenant with Abimelech

²²And it came to pass at that time that Abimelech and Phichol, the commander of his army, spoke to Abraham, saying, "God *is* with you in all that you do. ²³Now therefore, swear to me by God that you will not deal falsely with me, with my offspring, or with my posterity; but that according to the kindness that I have done to you, you will do to me and to the land in which you have dwelt."

²⁴And Abraham said, "I will swear." ²⁵Then Abraham rebuked Abimelech because of a well of water which Abimelech's servants had seized. ²⁶And Abimelech said, "I do not know who has done this

---

20:16 ª Literally *it is a covering of the eyes for you*

thing; you did not tell me, nor had I heard *of it* until today." ²⁷So Abraham took sheep and oxen and gave them to Abimelech, and the two of them made a covenant. ²⁸And Abraham set seven ewe lambs of the flock by themselves.

²⁹Then Abimelech asked Abraham, "What *is the meaning of* these seven ewe lambs which you have set by themselves?"

³⁰And he said, "You will take *these* seven ewe lambs from my hand, that they may be my witness that I have dug this well." ³¹Therefore he called that place Beersheba,ᵃ because the two of them swore an oath there.

³²Thus they made a covenant at Beersheba. So Abimelech rose with Phichol, the commander of his army, and they returned to the land of the Philistines. ³³Then *Abraham* planted a tamarisk tree in Beersheba, and there called on the name of the LORD, the Everlasting God. ³⁴And Abraham stayed in the land of the Philistines many days.

Abraham's Faith Confirmed

22 Now it came to pass after these things that God tested Abraham, and said to him, "Abraham!"

And he said, "Here I am."

²Then He said, "Take now your son, your only *son* Isaac, whom you love, and go to the land of Moriah, and offer him there as a burnt offering on one of the mountains of which I shall tell you."

³So Abraham rose early in the morning and saddled his donkey, and took two of his young men with him, and Isaac his son; and he split the wood for the burnt offering, and arose and went to the place of which God had told him. ⁴Then on the third day Abraham lifted his eyes and saw the place afar off. ⁵And Abraham said to his young men, "Stay here with the donkey; the ladᵃ and I will go yonder and worship, and we will come back to you."

⁶So Abraham took the wood of the burnt offering and laid *it* on Isaac his son; and he took the fire in his hand, and a knife, and the two of them went together. ⁷But Isaac spoke to Abraham his father and said, "My father!"

And he said, "Here I am, my son."

Then he said, "Look, the fire and the wood, but where *is* the lamb for a burnt offering?"

⁸And Abraham said, "My son, God will provide for Himself the lamb for a burnt offering." So the two of them went together.

⁹Then they came to the place of which God had told him. And Abraham built an altar there and placed the wood in order; and he bound Isaac his son and laid him on the altar, upon the wood. ¹⁰And Abraham stretched out his hand and took the knife to slay his son.

¹¹But the Angel of the LORD called to him from heaven and said, "Abraham, Abraham!"

So he said, "Here I am."

¹²And He said, "Do not lay your hand on the lad, or do anything to him; for now I know that you fear God, since you have not withheld your son, your only *son,* from Me."

¹³Then Abraham lifted his eyes and looked, and there behind *him was* a ram caught in a thicket by its horns. So Abraham went and took the ram, and offered it up for a burnt offering instead of his son. ¹⁴And Abraham called the name of the place, The-LORD-Will-Provide;ᵃ as it is said *to* this day, "In the Mount of the LORD it shall be provided."

¹⁵Then the Angel of the LORD called to Abraham a second time out of heaven, ¹⁶and said: "By Myself I have sworn, says the LORD, because you have done this thing, and have not withheld your son, your only *son*— ¹⁷blessing I will bless you, and multiplying I will multiply your descendants as the stars of the heaven and as the sand which *is* on the seashore; and your descendants shall possess the gate of their enemies. ¹⁸In your seed all the nations of the earth shall be blessed, because you have obeyed My voice." ¹⁹So Abraham returned to his young men, and they rose and went together to Beersheba; and Abraham dwelt at Beersheba.

The Family of Nahor

²⁰Now it came to pass after these things that it was told Abraham, saying, "Indeed

---

21:31 ᵃLiterally *Well of t5he Oath* or *Well of the Seven* **22:5** ᵃOr *young man* **22:14** ᵃHebrew *YHWH Yireh*

Milcah also has borne children to your brother Nahor: ²¹Huz his firstborn, Buz his brother, Kemuel the father of Aram, ²²Chesed, Hazo, Pildash, Jidlaph, and Bethuel." ²³And Bethuel begot Rebekah.^a These eight Milcah bore to Nahor, Abraham's brother. ²⁴His concubine, whose name was Reumah, also bore Tebah, Gaham, Thahash, and Maachah.

Sarah's Death and Burial

23 Sarah lived one hundred and twenty-seven years; *these were* the years of the life of Sarah. ²So Sarah died in Kirjath Arba (that *is,* Hebron) in the land of Canaan, and Abraham came to mourn for Sarah and to weep for her.

³Then Abraham stood up from before his dead, and spoke to the sons of Heth, saying, ⁴"I *am* a foreigner and a visitor among you. Give me property for a burial place among you, that I may bury my dead out of my sight."

⁵And the sons of Heth answered Abraham, saying to him, ⁶"Hear us, my lord: You *are* a mighty prince among us; bury your dead in the choicest of our burial places. None of us will withhold from you his burial place, that you may bury your dead."

⁷Then Abraham stood up and bowed himself to the people of the land, the sons of Heth. ⁸And he spoke with them, saying, "If it is your wish that I bury my dead out of my sight, hear me, and meet with Ephron the son of Zohar for me, ⁹that he may give me the cave of Machpelah which he has, which *is* at the end of his field. Let him give it to me at the full price, as property for a burial place among you."

¹⁰Now Ephron dwelt among the sons of Heth; and Ephron the Hittite answered Abraham in the presence of the sons of Heth, all who entered at the gate of his city, saying, ¹¹"No, my lord, hear me: I give you the field and the cave that *is* in it; I give it to you in the presence of the sons of my people. I give it to you. Bury your dead!"

¹²Then Abraham bowed himself down before the people of the land; ¹³and he spoke to Ephron in the hearing of the people of the land, saying, "If you *will give it,* please hear me. I will give you money for the field; take *it* from me and I will bury my dead there."

¹⁴And Ephron answered Abraham, saying to him, ¹⁵"My lord, listen to me; the land *is worth* four hundred shekels of silver. What *is* that between you and me? So bury your dead." ¹⁶And Abraham listened to Ephron; and Abraham weighed out the silver for Ephron which he had named in the hearing of the sons of Heth, four hundred shekels of silver, currency of the merchants.

¹⁷So the field of Ephron which *was* in Machpelah, which *was* before Mamre, the field and the cave which *was* in it, and all the trees that *were* in the field, which *were* within all the surrounding borders, were deeded ¹⁸to Abraham as a possession in the presence of the sons of Heth, before all who went in at the gate of his city.

¹⁹And after this, Abraham buried Sarah his wife in the cave of the field of Machpelah, before Mamre (that *is,* Hebron) in the land of Canaan. ²⁰So the field and the cave that *is* in it were deeded to Abraham by the sons of Heth as property for a burial place.

A Bride for Isaac

24 Now Abraham was old, well advanced in age; and the LORD had blessed Abraham in all things. ²So Abraham said to the oldest servant of his house, who ruled over all that he had, "Please, put your hand under my thigh, ³and I will make you swear by the LORD, the God of heaven and the God of the earth, that you will not take a wife for my son from the daughters of the Canaanites, among whom I dwell; ⁴but you shall go to my country and to my family, and take a wife for my son Isaac."

⁵And the servant said to him, "Perhaps the woman will not be willing to follow me to this land. Must I take your son back to the land from which you came?"

⁶But Abraham said to him, "Beware that you do not take my son back there. ⁷The LORD God of heaven, who took me from my father's house and from the land of my family, and who spoke to me and swore to me, saying, 'To your descendants^a

---

22:23 ^aSpelled *Rebecca* in Romans 9:10
24:7 ^aLiterally *seed*

BIBLICAL INSIGHTS • 24:67

A Wife's Ultimate Need

ISAAC, IT IS SAID, "took Rebekah and she became his wife, *and he loved her*" (24:67, italics added). Centuries later, that's still what a wife most wants out of marriage.

A wife wants her husband to love her, to cherish and care for her, to pursue her and continue to know who she is and who she is becoming. She wants her husband to seek a relationship with her. She wants him to seek to understand her. It's why on some occasions, our wives want to be intriguing and a challenge, not easily figured out.

When a woman sees her husband denying himself for her, she understands that it's because of love.

On the other hand, if a woman senses her husband is romancing her in order to meet his own personal needs, then she feels manipulated, or controlled, or less valued . . . used. She may begin to fear that she would be taken advantage of, taken for granted sexually, and unappreciated in all kinds of ways.

A wife's ultimate need is to be loved. No man will do that perfectly. But a husband seeking to become the man God wants him to be will learn how to better love his mate. The result is a wife who begins to feel and experience unconditional love—and a marriage of growing commitment, trust, and fulfillment.

I give this land,' He will send His angel before you, and you shall take a wife for my son from there. ⁸And if the woman is not willing to follow you, then you will be released from this oath; only do not take my son back there." ⁹So the servant put his hand under the thigh of Abraham his master, and swore to him concerning this matter.

¹⁰Then the servant took ten of his master's camels and departed, for all his master's goods *were in* his hand. And he arose and went to Mesopotamia, to the city of Nahor. ¹¹And he made his camels kneel down outside the city by a well of water at evening time, the time when women go out to draw *water.* ¹²Then he said, "O LORD God of my master Abraham, please give me success this day, and show kindness to my master Abraham. ¹³Behold, *here* I stand by the well of water, and the daughters of the men of the city are coming out to draw water. ¹⁴Now let it be that the young woman to whom I say, 'Please let down your pitcher that I may drink,' and she says, 'Drink, and I will also give your camels a drink'— *let* her *be the one* You have appointed for Your servant Isaac. And by this I will know that You have shown kindness to my master."

¹⁵And it happened, before he had finished speaking, that behold, Rebekah, who was born to Bethuel, son of Milcah, the wife of Nahor, Abraham's brother, came out with her pitcher on her shoulder. ¹⁶Now the young woman *was* very beautiful to behold, a virgin; no man had known her. And she went down to the well, filled her pitcher, and came up. ¹⁷And the servant ran to meet her and said, "Please let me drink a little water from your pitcher."

¹⁸So she said, "Drink, my lord." Then she quickly let her pitcher down to her hand, and gave him a drink. ¹⁹And when she had finished giving him a drink, she said, "I will draw *water* for your camels also, until they have finished drinking." ²⁰Then she quickly emptied her pitcher into the trough, ran back to the well to draw *water,* and drew for all his camels. ²¹And the man, wondering at her, remained silent so as to know whether the LORD had made his journey prosperous or not.

²²So it was, when the camels had finished drinking, that the man took a golden nose ring weighing half a shekel, and two bracelets for her wrists weighing ten *shekels* of gold, ²³and said, "Whose daughter *are* you? Tell me, please, is there room *in* your father's house for us to lodge?"

²⁴So she said to him, "I *am* the daughter of Bethuel, Milcah's son, whom she bore to Nahor." ²⁵Moreover she said to him, "We have both straw and feed enough, and room to lodge."

²⁶Then the man bowed down his head and worshiped the LORD. ²⁷And he said,

"Blessed *be* the LORD God of my master Abraham, who has not forsaken His mercy and His truth toward my master. As for me, being on the way, the LORD led me to the house of my master's brethren." ²⁸So the young woman ran and told her mother's household these things.

²⁹Now Rebekah had a brother whose name *was* Laban, and Laban ran out to the man by the well. ³⁰So it came to pass, when he saw the nose ring, and the bracelets on his sister's wrists, and when he heard the words of his sister Rebekah, saying, "Thus the man spoke to me," that he went to the man. And there he stood by the camels at the well. ³¹And he said, "Come in, O blessed of the LORD! Why do you stand outside? For I have prepared the house, and a place for the camels."

³²Then the man came to the house. And he unloaded the camels, and provided straw and feed for the camels, and water to wash his feet and the feet of the men who *were* with him. ³³*Food* was set before him to eat, but he said, "I will not eat until I have told about my errand."

And he said, "Speak on."

³⁴So he said, "I *am* Abraham's servant. ³⁵The LORD has blessed my master greatly, and he has become great; and He has given him flocks and herds, silver and gold, male and female servants, and camels and donkeys. ³⁶And Sarah my master's wife bore a son to my master when she was old; and to him he has given all that he has. ³⁷Now my master made me swear, saying, 'You shall not take a wife for my son from the daughters of the Canaanites, in whose land I dwell; ³⁸but you shall go to my father's house and to my family, and take a wife for my son.' ³⁹And I said to my master, 'Perhaps the woman will not follow me.' ⁴⁰But he said to me, 'The LORD, before whom I walk, will send His angel with you and prosper your way; and you shall take a wife for my son from my family and from my father's house. ⁴¹You will be clear from this oath when you arrive among my family; for if they will not give *her* to you, then you will be released from my oath.'

⁴²"And this day I came to the well and said, 'O LORD God of my master Abraham, if You will now prosper the way in which I go, ⁴³behold, I stand by the well of water; and it shall come to pass that when the virgin comes out to draw *water,* and I say to her, "Please give me a little water from your pitcher to drink," ⁴⁴and she says to me, "Drink, and I will draw for your camels also,"—*let* her *be* the woman whom the LORD has appointed for my master's son.'

⁴⁵"But before I had finished speaking in my heart, there was Rebekah, coming out with her pitcher on her shoulder; and she went down to the well and drew *water.* And I said to her, 'Please let me drink.' ⁴⁶And she made haste and let her pitcher down from her *shoulder,* and said, 'Drink, and I will give your camels a drink also.' So I drank, and she gave the camels a drink also. ⁴⁷Then I asked her, and said, 'Whose daughter *are* you?' And she said, 'The daughter of Bethuel, Nahor's son, whom Milcah bore to him.' So I put the nose ring on her nose and the bracelets on her wrists. ⁴⁸And I bowed my head and worshiped the LORD, and blessed the LORD God of my master Abraham, who had led me in the way of truth to take the daughter of my master's brother for his son. ⁴⁹Now if you will deal kindly and truly with my master, tell me. And if not, tell me, that I may turn to the right hand or to the left."

⁵⁰Then Laban and Bethuel answered and said, "The thing comes from the LORD; we cannot speak to you either bad or good. ⁵¹Here *is* Rebekah before you; take *her* and go, and let her be your master's son's wife, as the LORD has spoken."

⁵²And it came to pass, when Abraham's servant heard their words, that he worshiped the LORD, *bowing himself* to the earth. ⁵³Then the servant brought out jewelry of silver, jewelry of gold, and clothing, and gave *them* to Rebekah. He also gave precious things to her brother and to her mother.

⁵⁴And he and the men who *were* with him ate and drank and stayed all night. Then they arose in the morning, and he said, "Send me away to my master."

⁵⁵But her brother and her mother said, "Let the young woman stay with us *a few* days, at least ten; after that she may go."

⁵⁶And he said to them, "Do not hinder me, since the LORD has prospered my way;

send me away so that I may go to my master."

⁵⁷So they said, "We will call the young woman and ask her personally." ⁵⁸Then they called Rebekah and said to her, "Will you go with this man?"

And she said, "I will go."

⁵⁹So they sent away Rebekah their sister and her nurse, and Abraham's servant and his men. ⁶⁰And they blessed Rebekah and said to her:

"Our sister, *may* you *become*
  The mother of thousands of ten
    thousands;
And may your descendants possess
  The gates of those who hate them."

⁶¹Then Rebekah and her maids arose, and they rode on the camels and followed the man. So the servant took Rebekah and departed.

⁶²Now Isaac came from the way of Beer Lahai Roi, for he dwelt in the South. ⁶³And Isaac went out to meditate in the field in the evening; and he lifted his eyes and looked, and there, the camels *were* coming. ⁶⁴Then Rebekah lifted her eyes, and when she saw Isaac she dismounted from her camel; ⁶⁵for she had said to the servant, "Who *is* this man walking in the field to meet us?"

The servant said, "It *is* my master." So she took a veil and covered herself.

⁶⁶And the servant told Isaac all the things that he had done. ⁶⁷Then Isaac brought her into his mother Sarah's tent; and he took Rebekah and she became his wife, and he loved her. So Isaac was comforted after his mother's *death.*

Abraham and Keturah

25 Abraham again took a wife, and her name *was* Keturah. ²And she bore him Zimran, Jokshan, Medan, Midian, Ishbak, and Shuah. ³Jokshan begot Sheba and Dedan. And the sons of Dedan were Asshurim, Letushim, and Leummim. ⁴And the sons of Midian *were* Ephah, Epher, Hanoch, Abidah, and Eldaah. All these *were* the children of Keturah.

⁵And Abraham gave all that he had to Isaac. ⁶But Abraham gave gifts to the sons of the concubines which Abraham had; and while he was still living he sent them eastward, away from Isaac his son, to the country of the east.

Abraham's Death and Burial

⁷This *is* the sum of the years of Abraham's life which he lived: one hundred and seventy-five years. ⁸Then Abraham breathed his last and died in a good old age, an old man and full *of years,* and was gathered to his people. ⁹And his sons Isaac and Ishmael buried him in the cave of Machpelah, which *is* before Mamre, in the field of Ephron the son of Zohar the Hittite, ¹⁰the field which Abraham purchased from the sons of Heth. There Abraham was buried, and Sarah his wife. ¹¹And it came to pass, after the death of Abraham, that God blessed his son Isaac. And Isaac dwelt at Beer Lahai Roi.

The Families of Ishmael and Isaac

¹²Now this *is* the genealogy of Ishmael, Abraham's son, whom Hagar the Egyptian, Sarah's maidservant, bore to Abraham. ¹³And these *were* the names of the sons of Ishmael, by their names, according to their generations: The firstborn of Ishmael, Nebajoth; then Kedar, Adbeel, Mibsam, ¹⁴Mishma, Dumah, Massa, ¹⁵Hadar,[a] Tema, Jetur, Naphish, and Kedemah. ¹⁶These *were* the sons of Ishmael and these *were* their names, by their towns and their settlements, twelve princes according to their nations. ¹⁷These *were* the years of the life of Ishmael: one hundred and thirty-seven years; and he breathed his last and died, and was gathered to his people. ¹⁸(They dwelt from Havilah as far as Shur, which *is* east of Egypt as you go toward Assyria.) He died in the presence of all his brethren.

¹⁹This *is* the genealogy of Isaac, Abraham's son. Abraham begot Isaac. ²⁰Isaac was forty years old when he took Rebekah as wife, the daughter of Bethuel the Syrian of Padan Aram, the sister of Laban the Syrian. ²¹Now Isaac pleaded with the LORD for his wife, because she *was* barren; and the LORD granted his plea, and Rebekah his wife conceived. ²²But the children

---

25:15 [a]Masoretic Text reads *Hadad.*

struggled together within her; and she said, "If *all is* well, why *am I like* this?" So she went to inquire of the LORD.

²³And the LORD said to her:

"Two nations *are* in your womb,
Two peoples shall be separated from
    your body;
One people shall be stronger than the
    other,
And the older shall serve the
    younger."

²⁴So when her days were fulfilled *for her* to give birth, indeed *there were* twins in her womb. ²⁵And the first came out red. *He was* like a hairy garment all over; so they called his name Esau.ᵃ ²⁶Afterward his brother came out, and his hand took hold of Esau's heel; so his name was called Jacob.ᵃ Isaac *was* sixty years old when she bore them.

²⁷So the boys grew. And Esau was a skillful hunter, a man of the field; but Jacob was a mild man, dwelling in tents.

25:25 ᵃLiterally *Hairy* **25:26** ᵃLiterally *Supplanter*
25:30 ᵃLiterally *Red*

²⁸And Isaac loved Esau because he ate *of his* game, but Rebekah loved Jacob.

Esau Sells His Birthright

²⁹Now Jacob cooked a stew; and Esau came in from the field, and he *was* weary. ³⁰And Esau said to Jacob, "Please feed me with that same red *stew,* for I *am* weary." Therefore his name was called Edom.ᵃ ³¹But Jacob said, "Sell me your birthright as of this day."

³²And Esau said, "Look, I *am* about to die; so what *is* this birthright to me?" ³³Then Jacob said, "Swear to me as of this day."

So he swore to him, and sold his birthright to Jacob. ³⁴And Jacob gave Esau bread and stew of lentils; then he ate and drank, arose, and went his way. Thus Esau despised *his* birthright.

Isaac and Abimelech

26 There was a famine in the land, besides the first famine that was in the days of Abraham. And Isaac went to Abimelech king of the Philistines, in Gerar.

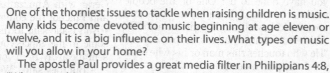

PARENTING MATTERS	**Q: How can we handle the issue of the music our children should and should not listen to?**

One of the thorniest issues to tackle when raising children is music. Many kids become devoted to music beginning at age eleven or twelve, and it is a big influence on their lives. What types of music will you allow in your home?

The apostle Paul provides a great media filter in Philippians 4:8, "Whatever things are true, whatever things are noble, whatever things are just, whatever things are pure, whatever things are lovely, whatever things are of good report, if there is any virtue and if there is anything praiseworthy—meditate on these things."

Parents should approach this issue shrewdly and wisely. Particularly as your child gets older, your ability to understand his taste in music is critical. You are a coach; you want him to understand for himself how different types of music will affect his emotions and moods, and especially how music can play a significant role in romantic relationships.

It's important to engage your children in ongoing discussions and to challenge their convictions with timely and thought-provoking questions that assist them in analyzing what they are doing and listening to. One of the most revealing things we've done with our teenagers is to read the lyrics to the music and talk about what values (or lack of values) are being promoted.

2Then the LORD appeared to him and said: "Do not go down to Egypt; live in the land of which I shall tell you. 3Dwell in this land, and I will be with you and bless you; for to you and your descendants I give all these lands, and I will perform the oath which I swore to Abraham your father. 4And I will make your descendants multiply as the stars of heaven; I will give to your descendants all these lands; and in your seed all the nations of the earth shall be blessed; 5because Abraham obeyed My voice and kept My charge, My commandments, My statutes, and My laws."

6So Isaac dwelt in Gerar. 7And the men of the place asked about his wife. And he said, "She *is* my sister"; for he was afraid to say, "*She is* my wife," *because he thought,* "lest the men of the place kill me for Rebekah, because she *is* beautiful to behold." 8Now it came to pass, when he had been there a long time, that Abimelech king of the Philistines looked through a window, and saw, and there was Isaac, showing endearment to Rebekah his wife. 9Then Abimelech called Isaac and said, "Quite obviously she *is* your wife; so how could you say, 'She *is* my sister'?"

Isaac said to him, "Because I said, 'Lest I die on account of her.' |"

10And Abimelech said, "What *is* this you have done to us? One of the people might soon have lain with your wife, and you would have brought guilt on us." 11So Abimelech charged all *his* people, saying, "He who touches this man or his wife shall surely be put to death."

12Then Isaac sowed in that land, and reaped in the same year a hundredfold; and the LORD blessed him. 13The man began to prosper, and continued prospering until he became very prosperous; 14for he had possessions of flocks and possessions of herds and a great number of servants. So the Philistines envied him. 15Now the Philistines had stopped up all the wells which his father's servants had dug in the days of Abraham his father, and they had filled them with earth. 16And Abimelech said to Isaac, "Go away from us, for you are much mightier than we."

17Then Isaac departed from there and pitched his tent in the Valley of Gerar, and dwelt there. 18And Isaac dug again the wells of water which they had dug in the days of Abraham his father, for the Philistines had stopped them up after the death of Abraham. He called them by the names which his father had called them.

19Also Isaac's servants dug in the valley, and found a well of running water there. 20But the herdsmen of Gerar quarreled with Isaac's herdsmen, saying, "The water *is* ours." So he called the name of the well Esek,a because they quarreled with him. 21Then they dug another well, and they quarreled over that *one* also. So he called its name Sitnah.a 22And he moved from there and dug another well, and they did not quarrel over it. So he called its name Rehoboth,a because he said, "For now the LORD has made room for us, and we shall be fruitful in the land."

23Then he went up from there to Beersheba. 24And the LORD appeared to him the same night and said, "I *am* the God of your father Abraham; do not fear, for I *am* with you. I will bless you and multiply your descendants for My servant Abraham's sake." 25So he built an altar there and called on the name of the LORD, and he pitched his tent there; and there Isaac's servants dug a well.

26Then Abimelech came to him from Gerar with Ahuzzath, one of his friends, and Phichol the commander of his army. 27And Isaac said to them, "Why have you come to me, since you hate me and have sent me away from you?"

28But they said, "We have certainly seen that the LORD is with you. So we said, 'Let there now be an oath between us, between you and us; and let us make a covenant with you, 29that you will do us no harm, since we have not touched you, and since we have done nothing to you but good and have sent you away in peace. You *are* now the blessed of the LORD.' "

30So he made them a feast, and they ate and drank. 31Then they arose early in the morning and swore an oath with one another; and Isaac sent them away, and they departed from him in peace.

26:20 aLiterally *Quarrel* **26:21** aLiterally *Enmity* **26:22** aLiterally *Spaciousness*

³²It came to pass the same day that Isaac's servants came and told him about the well which they had dug, and said to him, "We have found water." ³³So he called it Shebah.ᵃ Therefore the name of the city *is* Beershebaᵇ to this day.

³⁴When Esau was forty years old, he took as wives Judith the daughter of Beeri the Hittite, and Basemath the daughter of Elon the Hittite. ³⁵And they were a grief of mind to Isaac and Rebekah.

Isaac Blesses Jacob

27 Now it came to pass, when Isaac was old and his eyes were so dim that he could not see, that he called Esau his older son and said to him, "My son."

And he answered him, "Here I am."

²Then he said, "Behold now, I am old. I do not know the day of my death. ³Now therefore, please take your weapons, your quiver and your bow, and go out to the field and hunt game for me. ⁴And make me savory food, such as I love, and bring *it* to me that I may eat, that my soul may bless you before I die."

⁵Now Rebekah was listening when Isaac spoke to Esau his son. And Esau went to the field to hunt game and to bring *it*. ⁶So Rebekah spoke to Jacob her son, saying, "Indeed I heard your father speak to Esau your brother, saying, ⁷'Bring me game and make savory food for me, that I may eat it and bless you in the presence of the LORD before my death.' ⁸Now therefore, my son, obey my voice according to what I command you. ⁹Go now to the flock and bring me from there two choice kids of the goats, and I will make savory food from them for your father, such as he loves. ¹⁰Then you shall take *it* to your father, that he may eat *it,* and that he may bless you before his death."

¹¹And Jacob said to Rebekah his mother, "Look, Esau my brother *is* a hairy man, and I *am* a smooth-*skinned* man. ¹²Perhaps my father will feel me, and I shall seem to be a deceiver to him; and I shall bring a curse on myself and not a blessing."

¹³But his mother said to him, "*Let* your curse *be* on me, my son; only obey my voice, and go, get *them* for me." ¹⁴And he went and got *them* and brought *them* to his mother, and his mother made savory food, such as his father loved. ¹⁵Then Rebekah took the choice clothes of her elder son Esau, which *were* with her in the house, and put them on Jacob her younger son. ¹⁶And she put the skins of the kids of the goats on his hands and on the smooth part of his neck. ¹⁷Then she gave the savory food and the bread, which she had prepared, into the hand of her son Jacob.

¹⁸So he went to his father and said, "My father."

And he said, "Here I am. Who *are* you, my son?"

¹⁹Jacob said to his father, "I *am* Esau your firstborn; I have done just as you told me; please arise, sit and eat of my game, that your soul may bless me."

²⁰But Isaac said to his son, "How *is it* that you have found *it* so quickly, my son?"

And he said, "Because the LORD your God brought *it* to me."

²¹Isaac said to Jacob, "Please come near, that I may feel you, my son, whether you *are* really my son Esau or not." ²²So Jacob went near to Isaac his father, and he felt him and said, "The voice *is* Jacob's voice, but the hands *are* the hands of Esau." ²³And he did not recognize him, because his hands were hairy like his brother Esau's hands; so he blessed him.

²⁴Then he said, "*Are* you really my son Esau?"

He said, "I *am.*"

²⁵He said, "Bring *it* near to me, and I will eat of my son's game, so that my soul may bless you." So he brought *it* near to him, and he ate; and he brought him wine, and he drank. ²⁶Then his father Isaac said to him, "Come near now and kiss me, my son." ²⁷And he came near and kissed him; and he smelled the smell of his clothing, and blessed him and said:

> "Surely, the smell of my son
> *Is* like the smell of a field
> Which the LORD has blessed.
> 28 Therefore may God give you
> Of the dew of heaven,
> Of the fatness of the earth,
> And plenty of grain and wine.

26:33 ᵃLiterally *Oath* or *Seven* ᵇLiterally *Well of the Oath* or *Well of the Seven*

BIBLICAL INSIGHTS • 27:5

Fighting Conflict with Prayer

CAN YOU IMAGINE how the biblical record might be different if Isaac and Rebekah had learned to deal with their conflicts through prayer, rather than through deceit and manipulation (27:5–13)?

More to the point, would *you* like to do a better job of resolving conflict in your marriage? If so, then we encourage you to discover the power of praying together.

Even though praying in the middle of a conflict is just as important as praying during calm seas, most of us don't feel like praying with an opponent. But inviting the Prince of Peace into your boat in the middle of the storm is truly the answer.

For some of the best advice on how to resolve conflict in marriage, you have only to turn to Ephesians 4:25–27, "Therefore, putting away lying, 'Let each one of you speak truth with his neighbor,' for we are members of one another. 'Be angry, and do not sin': do not let the sun go down on your wrath, nor give place to the devil."

Note especially the phrase, "Do not let the sun go down on your wrath." If that single principle were observed, most marital conflicts would be resolved *much* sooner! The next time you have a conflict, instead of turning away to be angry, find a way to turn toward one another and God and pray together as a couple. Barbara and I have done this since 1972, and I can honestly say that this spiritual discipline of prayer has helped us resolve many conflicts.

29   Let peoples serve you,
And nations bow down to you.
Be master over your brethren,
And let your mother's sons bow
        down to you.
Cursed *be* everyone who curses you,
And blessed *be* those who bless you!"

Esau's Lost Hope

30Now it happened, as soon as Isaac had finished blessing Jacob, and Jacob had scarcely gone out from the presence of Isaac his father, that Esau his brother came in from his hunting. 31He also had made savory food, and brought it to his father, and said to his father, "Let my father arise and eat of his son's game, that your soul may bless me."

32And his father Isaac said to him, "Who *are* you?"

So he said, "I *am* your son, your firstborn, Esau."

33Then Isaac trembled exceedingly, and said, "Who? Where *is* the one who hunted game and brought *it* to me? I ate all *of it* before you came, and I have blessed him— *and* indeed he shall be blessed."

34When Esau heard the words of his father, he cried with an exceedingly great and bitter cry, and said to his father, "Bless me—me also, O my father!"

35But he said, "Your brother came with deceit and has taken away your blessing."

36And *Esau* said, "Is he not rightly named Jacob? For he has supplanted me these two times. He took away my birthright, and now look, he has taken away my blessing!" And he said, "Have you not reserved a blessing for me?"

37Then Isaac answered and said to Esau, "Indeed I have made him your master, and all his brethren I have given to him as servants; with grain and wine I have sustained him. What shall I do now for you, my son?"

38And Esau said to his father, "Have you only one blessing, my father? Bless me—me also, O my father!" And Esau lifted up his voice and wept.

39Then Isaac his father answered and said to him:

"Behold, your dwelling shall be of the
        fatness of the earth,
And of the dew of heaven from
        above.
40   By your sword you shall live,
And you shall serve your brother;
And it shall come to pass, when you
        become restless,
That you shall break his yoke from
        your neck."

DEVOTIONS FOR COUPLES • 28:1, 6-8
What Are Your Family's Values?

Although in many ways Jacob sired a messed-up family, in other ways his whole clan knew what he considered most important. They knew his values. They knew, for example, that he didn't want his sons marrying pagan women from among the Canaanites.

What's really valuable to *you*? What are *your* family's values? Jesus said, "Where your treasure is, there your heart will be also" (Matt. 6:21).

Working as a couple to establish a clear and concrete set of your own family values will strengthen your marriage and reduce stress in your relationship. And yielding to Jesus as Lord and Master—His life, teaching, death, and resurrection—must be our top priority (see 1 Cor. 15:3, 4). Beyond loving and obeying Christ, what we value may cover a wide range of possibilities.

Early in our marriage, Barbara and I determined that we needed to take the time to agree on our family's values; so we went away for a weekend together to discuss it. First, we separately listed our individual values and ranked them by priority. Then we prayerfully combined our lists and crafted a list of family values on which we could agree. Then, we ended up with our top five family values.

We discovered that while we shared some priorities, others were *very* different. On a typical summer Saturday, for example, Barbara could not wait to put on gloves and head for the flower garden, while my idea of a good time was for the whole family to head off for a day of fishing or an adventure.

Over the years we have learned that if our values aren't clear, we will live with more conflict than necessary, feel scattered or out of control, place unwise expectations on each other, and miss out on the peace that comes from prayerfully seeking to abide in God's will in every aspect of our lives. Prayerfully coming into agreement on your values is an essential component of your journey together.

If you have never hammered out your values together, we encourage you to begin praying and talking about it immediately. You may want to get away for a weekend like we did, or you could take a week and discuss a different topic each night. To more clearly define core values, brainstorm and write down your ideas. If needed, agree on a time when you will meet again to refine your list. Settling on your family's values will bring untold benefits to your marriage and family now and in years to come.

Jacob Escapes from Esau

[41]So Esau hated Jacob because of the blessing with which his father blessed him, and Esau said in his heart, "The days of mourning for my father are at hand; then I will kill my brother Jacob."

[42]And the words of Esau her older son were told to Rebekah. So she sent and called Jacob her younger son, and said to him, "Surely your brother Esau comforts himself concerning you *by intending* to kill you. [43]Now therefore, my son, obey my voice: arise, flee to my brother Laban in Haran. [44]And stay with him a few days, until your brother's fury turns away, [45]until your brother's anger turns away from you, and he forgets what you have done to him; then I will send and bring you from there. Why should I be bereaved also of you both in one day?"

[46]And Rebekah said to Isaac, "I am weary of my life because of the daughters of Heth; if Jacob takes a wife of the daughters of Heth, like these *who are* the daughters of the land, what good will my life be to me?"

28 Then Isaac called Jacob and blessed him, and charged him, and said to him: "You shall not take a wife from the daughters of Canaan. [2]Arise, go to Padan Aram, to the house of Bethuel your mother's father; and take yourself a wife from there of the daughters of Laban your mother's brother.

3   "May God Almighty bless you,
    And make you fruitful and multiply you,
    That you may be an assembly of peoples;
4   And give you the blessing of Abraham,
    To you and your descendants with you,
    That you may inherit the land
    In which you are a stranger,
    Which God gave to Abraham."

⁵So Isaac sent Jacob away, and he went to Padan Aram, to Laban the son of Bethuel the Syrian, the brother of Rebekah, the mother of Jacob and Esau.

Esau Marries Mahalath

⁶Esau saw that Isaac had blessed Jacob and sent him away to Padan Aram to take himself a wife from there, *and that* as he blessed him he gave him a charge, saying, "You shall not take a wife from the daughters of Canaan," ⁷and that Jacob had obeyed his father and his mother and had gone to Padan Aram. ⁸Also Esau saw that the daughters of Canaan did not please his father Isaac. ⁹So Esau went to Ishmael and took Mahalath the daughter of Ishmael, Abraham's son, the sister of Nebajoth, to be his wife in addition to the wives he had.

INTIMATE MOMENTS

Make a list of all the reasons why you love your wife. Spend some time with this! Take half an hour or so to really ponder all the ways she captures your heart. Come up with at least twenty reasons; don't stop at the first three or four! Then transfer these notes to sticky notes, one reason per note. Then hide them all around the house, some of them in places where it might take her days to find.

Jacob's Vow at Bethel

¹⁰Now Jacob went out from Beersheba and went toward Haran. ¹¹So he came to a certain place and stayed there all night, because the sun had set. And he took one of the stones of that place and put it at his head, and he lay down in that place to sleep. ¹²Then he dreamed, and behold, a ladder *was* set up on the earth, and its top reached to heaven; and there the angels of God were ascending and descending on it. ¹³And behold, the LORD stood above it and said: "I *am* the LORD God of Abraham your father and the God of Isaac; the land on which you lie I will give to you and your descendants. ¹⁴Also your descendants shall be as the dust of the earth; you shall spread abroad to the west and the east, to the north and the south; and in you and in your seed all the families of the earth shall be blessed. ¹⁵Behold, I *am* with you and will keep you wherever you go, and will bring you back to this land; for I will not leave you until I have done what I have spoken to you."

¹⁶Then Jacob awoke from his sleep and said, "Surely the LORD is in this place, and I did not know *it*." ¹⁷And he was afraid and said, "How awesome *is* this place! This *is* none other than the house of God, and this *is* the gate of heaven!"

¹⁸Then Jacob rose early in the morning, and took the stone that he had put at his head, set it up as a pillar, and poured oil on top of it. ¹⁹And he called the name of that place Bethel;ᵃ but the name of that city had been Luz previously. ²⁰Then Jacob made a vow, saying, "If God will be with me, and keep me in this way that I am going, and give me bread to eat and clothing to put on, ²¹so that I come back to my father's house in peace, then the LORD shall be my God. ²²And this stone which I have set as a pillar shall be God's house, and of all that You give me I will surely give a tenth to You."

Jacob Meets Rachel

29 So Jacob went on his journey and came to the land of the people of the East. ²And he looked, and saw a well in the field; and behold, there *were* three

---

28:19 ᵃLiterally *House of God*

flocks of sheep lying by it; for out of that well they watered the flocks. A large stone *was* on the well's mouth. ³Now all the flocks would be gathered there; and they would roll the stone from the well's mouth, water the sheep, and put the stone back in its place on the well's mouth.

⁴And Jacob said to them, "My brethren, where *are* you from?"

And they said, "We *are* from Haran."

⁵Then he said to them, "Do you know Laban the son of Nahor?"

And they said, "We know him."

⁶So he said to them, "Is he well?"

And they said, "*He is* well. And look, his daughter Rachel is coming with the sheep."

⁷Then he said, "Look, *it is* still high day; *it is* not time for the cattle to be gathered together. Water the sheep, and go and feed *them.*"

⁸But they said, "We cannot until all the flocks are gathered together, and they have rolled the stone from the well's mouth; then we water the sheep."

⁹Now while he was still speaking with them, Rachel came with her father's sheep, for she was a shepherdess. ¹⁰And it came to pass, when Jacob saw Rachel the daughter of Laban his mother's brother, and the sheep of Laban his mother's brother, that Jacob went near and rolled the stone from the well's mouth, and watered the flock of Laban his mother's brother. ¹¹Then Jacob kissed Rachel, and lifted up his voice and wept. ¹²And Jacob told Rachel that he *was* her father's relative and that he *was* Rebekah's son. So she ran and told her father.

¹³Then it came to pass, when Laban heard the report about Jacob his sister's son, that he ran to meet him, and embraced him and kissed him, and brought him to his house. So he told Laban all these things. ¹⁴And Laban said to him, "Surely you *are* my bone and my flesh." And he stayed with him for a month.

Jacob Marries Leah and Rachel

¹⁵Then Laban said to Jacob, "Because you *are* my relative, should you therefore serve me for nothing? Tell me, what *should*

your wages *be?*" ¹⁶Now Laban had two daughters: the name of the elder *was* Leah, and the name of the younger *was* Rachel. ¹⁷Leah's eyes *were* delicate, but Rachel was beautiful of form and appearance.

¹⁸Now Jacob loved Rachel; so he said, "I will serve you seven years for Rachel your younger daughter."

¹⁹And Laban said, "*It is* better that I give her to you than that I should give her to another man. Stay with me." ²⁰So Jacob served seven years for Rachel, and they seemed *only* a few days to him because of the love he had for her.

²¹Then Jacob said to Laban, "Give *me* my wife, for my days are fulfilled, that I may go in to her." ²²And Laban gathered together all the men of the place and made a feast. ²³Now it came to pass in the evening, that he took Leah his daughter and brought her to Jacob; and he went in to her. ²⁴And Laban gave his maid Zilpah to his daughter Leah *as* a maid. ²⁵So it came to pass in the morning, that behold, it *was* Leah. And he said to Laban, "What is this you have done to me? Was it not for Rachel that I served you? Why then have you deceived me?"

²⁶And Laban said, "It must not be done so in our country, to give the younger before the firstborn. ²⁷Fulfill her week, and we will give you this one also for the service which you will serve with me still another seven years."

²⁸Then Jacob did so and fulfilled her week. So he gave him his daughter Rachel as wife also. ²⁹And Laban gave his maid Bilhah to his daughter Rachel as a maid. ³⁰Then *Jacob* also went in to Rachel, and he also loved Rachel more than Leah. And he served with Laban still another seven years.

The Children of Jacob

³¹When the LORD saw that Leah *was* unloved, He opened her womb; but Rachel *was* barren. ³²So Leah conceived and bore a son, and she called his name Reuben;ᵃ for she said, "The LORD has surely looked on my affliction. Now therefore, my husband will love me." ³³Then she conceived again and bore a son, and said, "Because the LORD has heard that I *am* unloved, He has therefore given me this *son* also." And she called his name Simeon.ᵃ ³⁴She conceived

---

29:32 ᵃLiterally *See, a Son*   29:33 ᵃLiterally *Heard*

again and bore a son, and said, "Now this time my husband will become attached to me, because I have borne him three sons." Therefore his name was called Levi.[a] 35And she conceived again and bore a son, and said, "Now I will praise the LORD." Therefore she called his name Judah.[a] Then she stopped bearing.

30 Now when Rachel saw that she bore Jacob no children, Rachel envied her sister, and said to Jacob, "Give me children, or else I die!"

2And Jacob's anger was aroused against Rachel, and he said, "Am I in the place of God, who has withheld from you the fruit of the womb?"

3So she said, "Here is my maid Bilhah; go in to her, and she will bear a child on my knees, that I also may have children by her." 4Then she gave him Bilhah her maid as wife, and Jacob went in to her. 5And Bilhah conceived and bore Jacob a son. 6Then Rachel said, "God has judged my case; and He has also heard my voice and given me a son." Therefore she called his name Dan.[a] 7And Rachel's maid Bilhah conceived again and bore Jacob a second son. 8Then Rachel said, "With great wrestlings I have wrestled with my sister, and indeed I have prevailed." So she called his name Naphtali.[a]

9When Leah saw that she had stopped bearing, she took Zilpah her maid and gave her to Jacob as wife. 10And Leah's maid Zilpah bore Jacob a son. 11Then Leah said, "A troop comes!"[a] So she called his name Gad.[b] 12And Leah's maid Zilpah bore Jacob a second son. 13Then Leah said, "I am happy, for the daughters will call me blessed." So she called his name Asher.[a]

14Now Reuben went in the days of wheat harvest and found mandrakes in the field, and brought them to his mother Leah. Then Rachel said to Leah, "Please give me some of your son's mandrakes."

15But she said to her, "Is it a small matter that you have taken away my husband? Would you take away my son's mandrakes also?"

And Rachel said, "Therefore he will lie with you tonight for your son's mandrakes."

16When Jacob came out of the field in the evening, Leah went out to meet him and said, "You must come in to me, for I have surely hired you with my son's mandrakes." And he lay with her that night.

17And God listened to Leah, and she conceived and bore Jacob a fifth son. 18Leah said, "God has given me my wages, because I have given my maid to my husband." So she called his name Issachar.[a] 19Then Leah conceived again and bore Jacob a sixth son. 20And Leah said, "God has endowed me with a good endowment; now my husband will dwell with me, because I have borne him six sons." So she called his name Zebulun.[a] 21Afterward she bore a daughter, and called her name Dinah.

22Then God remembered Rachel, and God listened to her and opened her womb. 23And she conceived and bore a son, and said, "God has taken away my reproach." 24So she called his name Joseph,[a] and said, "The LORD shall add to me another son."

Jacob's Agreement with Laban

25And it came to pass, when Rachel had borne Joseph, that Jacob said to Laban, "Send me away, that I may go to my own place and to my country. 26Give me my wives and my children for whom I have served you, and let me go; for you know my service which I have done for you."

27And Laban said to him, "Please stay, if I have found favor in your eyes, for I have learned by experience that the LORD has blessed me for your sake." 28Then he said, "Name me your wages, and I will give it."

29So Jacob said to him, "You know how I have served you and how your livestock has been with me. 30For what you had before I came was little, and it has increased to a great amount; the LORD has blessed you since my coming. And now, when shall I also provide for my own house?"

31So he said, "What shall I give you?"

And Jacob said, "You shall not give me anything. If you will do this thing for me, I will again feed and keep your flocks: 32Let me pass through all your flock today,

29:34 aLiterally Attached 29:35 aLiterally Praise 30:6 aLiterally Judge 30:8 aLiterally My Wrestling 30:11 aFollowing Qere, Syriac, and Targum; Kethib, Septuagint, and Vulgate read in fortune. bLiterally Troop or Fortune 30:13 aLiterally Happy 30:18 aLiterally Wages 30:20 aLiterally Dwelling 30:24 aLiterally He Will Add

removing from there all the speckled and spotted sheep, and all the brown ones among the lambs, and the spotted and speckled among the goats; and *these* shall be my wages. ³³So my righteousness will answer for me in time to come, when the subject of my wages comes before you: every one that *is* not speckled and spotted among the goats, and brown among the lambs, will be considered stolen, if *it is* with me."

³⁴And Laban said, "Oh, that it were according to your word!" ³⁵So he removed that day the male goats that were speckled and spotted, all the female goats that were speckled and spotted, every one that had *some* white in it, and all the brown ones among the lambs, and gave *them* into the hand of his sons. ³⁶Then he put three days' journey between himself and Jacob, and Jacob fed the rest of Laban's flocks.

³⁷Now Jacob took for himself rods of green poplar and of the almond and chestnut trees, peeled white strips in them, and exposed the white which *was* in the rods. ³⁸And the rods which he had peeled, he set before the flocks in the gutters, in the watering troughs where the flocks came to drink, so that they should conceive when they came to drink. ³⁹So the flocks conceived before the rods, and the flocks brought forth streaked, speckled, and spotted. ⁴⁰Then Jacob separated the lambs, and made the flocks face toward the streaked and all the brown in the flock of Laban; but he put his own flocks by themselves and did not put them with Laban's flock.

⁴¹And it came to pass, whenever the stronger livestock conceived, that Jacob placed the rods before the eyes of the livestock in the gutters, that they might conceive among the rods. ⁴²But when the flocks were feeble, he did not put *them* in; so the feebler were Laban's and the stronger Jacob's. ⁴³Thus the man became exceedingly prosperous, and had large flocks, female and male servants, and camels and donkeys.

Jacob Flees from Laban

31 Now *Jacob* heard the words of Laban's sons, saying, "Jacob has taken away all that was our father's, and from what was our father's he has acquired all this wealth." ²And Jacob saw the countenance of Laban, and indeed it *was* not *favorable* toward him as before. ³Then the LORD said to Jacob, "Return to the land of your fathers and to your family, and I will be with you."

⁴So Jacob sent and called Rachel and Leah to the field, to his flock, ⁵and said to them, "I see your father's countenance, that it *is* not *favorable* toward me as before; but the God of my father has been with me. ⁶And you know that with all my might I have served your father. ⁷Yet your father has deceived me and changed my wages ten times, but God did not allow him to hurt me. ⁸If he said thus: 'The speckled shall be

---

ROMANCE FAQ

Q: *What is a woman's top need romantically?*

It might surprise you to read this, but a woman's most important romantic need *is for her husband to spiritually minister to her.*

Are you surprised that something to do with candy and flowers isn't number one? A woman wants her man to feel eager to be her protector, someone who cares not just about her security and physical needs but also (and even more importantly) about her spirituality, the well-being of her very soul.

A husband can be a spiritual protector and advocate for his wife by praying with her and for her every day. He can tenderly put his arms around her and say, "I want to ask God to bless you. I want to take any needs you have in your life right now to the Lord. And I'm going to pray for you throughout this day." A wise husband takes the lead in sharing Scripture and eagerly initiating conversation on spiritual issues.

A husband can contribute to his wife's spiritual well-being by giving her some time to pursue her spiritual growth. For example, he might watch their child while she attends an evening Bible study.

your wages,' then all the flocks bore speckled. And if he said thus: 'The streaked shall be your wages,' then all the flocks bore streaked. ⁹So God has taken away the livestock of your father and given *them* to me.

¹⁰"And it happened, at the time when the flocks conceived, that I lifted my eyes and saw in a dream, and behold, the rams which leaped upon the flocks *were* streaked, speckled, and gray-spotted. ¹¹Then the Angel of God spoke to me in a dream, saying, 'Jacob.' And I said, 'Here I am.' ¹²And He said, 'Lift your eyes now and see, all the rams which leap on the flocks *are* streaked, speckled, and gray-spotted; for I have seen all that Laban is doing to you. ¹³I *am* the God of Bethel, where you anointed the pillar *and* where you made a vow to Me. Now arise, get out of this land, and return to the land of your family.' "

¹⁴Then Rachel and Leah answered and said to him, "Is there still any portion or inheritance for us in our father's house? ¹⁵Are we not considered strangers by him? For he has sold us, and also completely consumed our money. ¹⁶For all these riches which God has taken from our father are *really* ours and our children's; now then, whatever God has said to you, do it."

¹⁷Then Jacob rose and set his sons and his wives on camels. ¹⁸And he carried away all his livestock and all his possessions which he had gained, his acquired livestock which he had gained in Padan Aram, to go to his father Isaac in the land of Canaan. ¹⁹Now Laban had gone to shear his sheep, and Rachel had stolen the household idols that were her father's. ²⁰And Jacob stole away, unknown to Laban the Syrian, in that he did not tell him that he intended to flee. ²¹So he fled with all that he had. He arose and crossed the river, and headed toward the mountains of Gilead.

Laban Pursues Jacob

²²And Laban was told on the third day that Jacob had fled. ²³Then he took his brethren with him and pursued him for seven days' journey, and he overtook him in the mountains of Gilead. ²⁴But God had come to Laban the Syrian in a dream by night, and said to him, "Be careful that you speak to Jacob neither good nor bad."

²⁵So Laban overtook Jacob. Now Jacob had pitched his tent in the mountains, and Laban with his brethren pitched in the mountains of Gilead.

²⁶And Laban said to Jacob: "What have you done, that you have stolen away unknown to me, and carried away my daughters like captives *taken* with the sword? ²⁷Why did you flee away secretly, and steal away from me, and not tell me; for I might have sent you away with joy and songs, with timbrel and harp? ²⁸And you did not allow me to kiss my sons and my daughters. Now you have done foolishly in *so* doing. ²⁹It is in my power to do you harm, but the God of your father spoke to me last night, saying, 'Be careful that you speak to Jacob neither good nor bad.' ³⁰And now you have surely gone because you greatly long for your father's house, *but* why did you steal my gods?"

³¹Then Jacob answered and said to Laban, "Because I was afraid, for I said, 'Perhaps you would take your daughters from me by force.' ³²With whomever you find your gods, do not let him live. In the presence of our brethren, identify what I have of yours and take *it* with you." For Jacob did not know that Rachel had stolen them.

³³And Laban went into Jacob's tent, into Leah's tent, and into the two maids' tents, but he did not find *them*. Then he went out of Leah's tent and entered Rachel's tent. ³⁴Now Rachel had taken the household idols, put them in the camel's saddle, and sat on them. And Laban searched all about the tent but did not find *them*. ³⁵And she said to her father, "Let it not displease my lord that I cannot rise before you, for the manner of women *is* with me." And he searched but did not find the household idols.

³⁶Then Jacob was angry and rebuked Laban, and Jacob answered and said to Laban: "What *is* my trespass? What *is* my sin, that you have so hotly pursued me? ³⁷Although you have searched all my things, what part of your household things have you found? Set *it* here before my brethren and your brethren, that they may judge between us both! ³⁸These twenty years I *have been* with you; your ewes and your female goats have not miscarried

their young, and I have not eaten the rams of your flock. ³⁹That which was torn *by beasts* I did not bring to you; I bore the loss of it. You required it from my hand, *whether* stolen by day or stolen by night. ⁴⁰*There* I was! In the day the drought consumed me, and the frost by night, and my sleep departed from my eyes. ⁴¹Thus I have been in your house twenty years; I served you fourteen years for your two daughters, and six years for your flock, and you have changed my wages ten times. ⁴²Unless the God of my father, the God of Abraham and the Fear of Isaac, had been with me, surely now you would have sent me away empty-handed. God has seen my affliction and the labor of my hands, and rebuked *you* last night."

Laban's Covenant with Jacob

⁴³And Laban answered and said to Jacob, "*These* daughters *are* my daughters, and *these* children *are* my children, and *this* flock *is* my flock; all that you see *is* mine. But what can I do this day to these my daughters or to their children whom they have borne? ⁴⁴Now therefore, come, let us make a covenant, you and I, and let it be a witness between you and me."

⁴⁵So Jacob took a stone and set it up *as* a pillar. ⁴⁶Then Jacob said to his brethren, "Gather stones." And they took stones and made a heap, and they ate there on the heap. ⁴⁷Laban called it Jegar Sahadutha,ᵃ but Jacob called it Galeed.ᵃ ⁴⁸And Laban said, "This heap *is* a witness between you and me this day." Therefore its name was called Galeed, ⁴⁹also Mizpah,ᵃ because he said, "May the LORD watch between you and me when we are absent one from another. ⁵⁰If you afflict my daughters, or if you take *other* wives besides my daughters, *although* no man *is* with us—see, God *is* witness between you and me!"

⁵¹Then Laban said to Jacob, "Here is this heap and here is *this* pillar, which I have placed between you and me. ⁵²This heap *is* a witness, and *this* pillar *is* a witness, that I will not pass beyond this heap

to you, and you will not pass beyond this heap and this pillar to me, for harm. ⁵³The God of Abraham, the God of Nahor, and the God of their father judge between us." And Jacob swore by the Fear of his father Isaac. ⁵⁴Then Jacob offered a sacrifice on the mountain, and called his brethren to eat bread. And they ate bread and stayed all night on the mountain. ⁵⁵And early in the morning Laban arose, and kissed his sons and daughters and blessed them. Then Laban departed and returned to his place.

Esau Comes to Meet Jacob

32 So Jacob went on his way, and the angels of God met him. ²When Jacob saw them, he said, "This *is* God's camp." And he called the name of that place Mahanaim.ᵃ

³Then Jacob sent messengers before him to Esau his brother in the land of Seir, the country of Edom. ⁴And he commanded them, saying, "Speak thus to my lord Esau, 'Thus your servant Jacob says: "I have dwelt with Laban and stayed there until now. ⁵I have oxen, donkeys, flocks, and male and female servants; and I have sent to tell my lord, that I may find favor in your sight." ' "

⁶Then the messengers returned to Jacob, saying, "We came to your brother Esau, and he also is coming to meet you, and four hundred men *are* with him." ⁷So Jacob was greatly afraid and distressed; and he divided the people that *were* with him, and the flocks and herds and camels, into two companies. ⁸And he said, "If Esau comes to the one company and attacks it, then the other company which is left will escape."

⁹Then Jacob said, "O God of my father Abraham and God of my father Isaac, the LORD who said to me, 'Return to your country and to your family, and I will deal well with you': ¹⁰I am not worthy of the least of all the mercies and of all the truth which You have shown Your servant; for I crossed over this Jordan with my staff, and now I have become two companies. ¹¹Deliver me, I pray, from the hand of my brother, from the hand of Esau; for I fear him, lest he come and attack me *and* the mother with the children. ¹²For You said, 'I

BIBLICAL INSIGHTS • 32:3-12

Is Digging Up the Past a Good Idea?

JACOB AND ESAU had a lot of baggage between them, a lot of hurt and resentment. Jacob so feared his brother, in fact, that he essentially bribed him with gifts to buy his own safety. Digging up the painful past was absolutely the *last* thing he wanted to do!

While it is true that those of us who have accepted salvation through Jesus have received a new nature (2 Cor. 5:17), the truth is that past sins have left us with scar tissue that affects how we respond to one another. There are enough challenges in marriage without saying, "We're not going to talk about those issues that have shaped our lives." You *must* get into those issues and create some level of understanding.

A marriage has to be built on a love-based commitment: "Perfect love casts out fear" (1 John 4:18). You can't risk hiding something important from your spouse, thinking, *If I share that, she'll reject me!* When you do that, your relationship is controlled by fear, not love—remember Esau?

When love encounters past mistakes in the loved one, it says, "I embrace you. I receive you. I accept you. I cherish you. And, yes, I forgive you."

---

will surely treat you well, and make your descendants as the sand of the sea, which cannot be numbered for multitude.' "

¹³So he lodged there that same night, and took what came to his hand as a present for Esau his brother: ¹⁴two hundred female goats and twenty male goats, two hundred ewes and twenty rams, ¹⁵thirty milk camels with their colts, forty cows and ten bulls, twenty female donkeys and ten foals. ¹⁶Then he delivered *them* to the hand of his servants, every drove by itself, and said to his servants, "Pass over before me, and put some distance between successive droves." ¹⁷And he commanded the first one, saying, "When Esau my brother meets you and asks you, saying, 'To whom do you belong, and where are you going? Whose *are* these in front of you?' ¹⁸then you shall say, 'They *are* your servant Jacob's. It *is* a present sent to my lord Esau; and behold, he also *is* behind us.' " ¹⁹So he commanded the second, the third, and all who followed the droves, saying, "In this manner you shall speak to Esau when you find him; ²⁰and also say, 'Behold, your servant Jacob *is* behind us.' " For he said, "I will appease him with the present that goes before me, and afterward I will see his face; perhaps he will accept me." ²¹So the present went on over before him, but he himself lodged that night in the camp.

Wrestling with God

²²And he arose that night and took his two wives, his two female servants, and his eleven sons, and crossed over the ford of Jabbok. ²³He took them, sent them over the brook, and sent over what he had. ²⁴Then Jacob was left alone; and a Man wrestled with him until the breaking of day. ²⁵Now when He saw that He did not prevail against him, He touched the socket of his hip; and the socket of Jacob's hip was out of joint as He wrestled with him. ²⁶And He said, "Let Me go, for the day breaks."

But he said, "I will not let You go unless You bless me!"

²⁷So He said to him, "What *is* your name?"

He said, "Jacob."

²⁸And He said, "Your name shall no longer be called Jacob, but Israel;ᵃ for you have struggled with God and with men, and have prevailed."

²⁹Then Jacob asked, saying, "Tell *me* Your name, I pray."

And He said, "Why *is* it *that* you ask about My name?" And He blessed him there.

³⁰So Jacob called the name of the place Peniel:ᵃ "For I have seen God face to face, and my life is preserved." ³¹Just as he crossed over Penuelᵃ the sun rose on him, and he limped on his hip. ³²Therefore to this day the children of Israel do not eat the

---

32:28 ᵃLiterally *Prince with God* **32:30** ᵃLiterally *Face of God* **32:31** ᵃSame as *Peniel*, verse 30

muscle that shrank, which *is* on the hip socket, because He touched the socket of Jacob's hip in the muscle that shrank.

Jacob and Esau Meet

33 Now Jacob lifted his eyes and looked, and there, Esau was coming, and with him were four hundred men. So he divided the children among Leah, Rachel, and the two maidservants. ²And he put the maidservants and their children in front, Leah and her children behind, and Rachel and Joseph last. ³Then he crossed over before them and bowed himself to the ground seven times, until he came near to his brother.

⁴But Esau ran to meet him, and embraced him, and fell on his neck and kissed him, and they wept. ⁵And he lifted his eyes and saw the women and children, and said, "Who *are* these with you?"

So he said, "The children whom God has graciously given your servant." ⁶Then the maidservants came near, they and their children, and bowed down. ⁷And Leah also came near with her children, and they bowed down. Afterward Joseph and Rachel came near, and they bowed down.

⁸Then Esau said, "What *do* you *mean by* all this company which I met?"

And he said, "*These are* to find favor in the sight of my lord."

⁹But Esau said, "I have enough, my brother; keep what you have for yourself."

¹⁰And Jacob said, "No, please, if I have now found favor in your sight, then receive my present from my hand, inasmuch as I have seen your face as though I had seen the face of God, and you were pleased with me. ¹¹Please, take my blessing that is brought to you, because God has dealt graciously with me, and because I have enough." So he urged him, and he took *it.*

¹²Then Esau said, "Let us take our journey; let us go, and I will go before you."

¹³But Jacob said to him, "My lord knows that the children *are* weak, and the flocks and herds which are nursing *are* with me. And if the men should drive them hard one day, all the flock will die. ¹⁴Please let my

lord go on ahead before his servant. I will lead on slowly at a pace which the livestock that go before me, and the children, are able to endure, until I come to my lord in Seir."

¹⁵And Esau said, "Now let me leave with you *some* of the people who *are* with me."

But he said, "What need is there? Let me find favor in the sight of my lord." ¹⁶So Esau returned that day on his way to Seir. ¹⁷And Jacob journeyed to Succoth, built himself a house, and made booths for his livestock. Therefore the name of the place is called Succoth.ᵃ

Jacob Comes to Canaan

¹⁸Then Jacob came safely to the city of Shechem, which *is* in the land of Canaan, when he came from Padan Aram; and he pitched his tent before the city. ¹⁹And he bought the parcel of land, where he had pitched his tent, from the children of Hamor, Shechem's father, for one hundred pieces of money. ²⁰Then he erected an altar there and called it El Elohe Israel.ᵃ

The Dinah Incident

34 Now Dinah the daughter of Leah, whom she had borne to Jacob, went out to see the daughters of the land. ²And when Shechem the son of Hamor the Hivite, prince of the country, saw her, he took her and lay with her, and violated her. ³His soul was strongly attracted to Dinah the daughter of Jacob, and he loved the young woman and spoke kindly to the young woman. ⁴So Shechem spoke to his father Hamor, saying, "Get me this young woman as a wife."

⁵And Jacob heard that he had defiled Dinah his daughter. Now his sons were with his livestock in the field; so Jacob held his peace until they came. ⁶Then Hamor the father of Shechem went out to Jacob to speak with him. ⁷And the sons of Jacob came in from the field when they heard *it;* and the men were grieved and very angry, because he had done a disgraceful thing in Israel by lying with Jacob's daughter, a thing which ought not to be done. ⁸But Hamor spoke with them, saying, "The soul of my son Shechem longs for your daughter. Please give her to him as a wife. ⁹And make marriages with us; give your daughters to us, and take our daughters to yourselves. ¹⁰So

33:17 ᵃLiterally *Booths* **33:20** ᵃLiterally *God, the God of Israel*

you shall dwell with us, and the land shall be before you. Dwell and trade in it, and acquire possessions for yourselves in it."

¹¹Then Shechem said to her father and her brothers, "Let me find favor in your eyes, and whatever you say to me I will give. ¹²Ask me ever so much dowry and gift, and I will give according to what you say to me; but give me the young woman as a wife."

¹³But the sons of Jacob answered Shechem and Hamor his father, and spoke deceitfully, because he had defiled Dinah their sister. ¹⁴And they said to them, "We cannot do this thing, to give our sister to one who is uncircumcised, for that *would be* a reproach to us. ¹⁵But on this *condition* we will consent to you: If you will become as we *are,* if every male of you is circumcised, ¹⁶then we will give our daughters to you, and we will take your daughters to us; and we will dwell with you, and we will become one people. ¹⁷But if you will not heed us and be circumcised, then we will take our daughter and be gone."

¹⁸And their words pleased Hamor and Shechem, Hamor's son. ¹⁹So the young man did not delay to do the thing, because he delighted in Jacob's daughter. He *was* more honorable than all the household of his father.

²⁰And Hamor and Shechem his son came to the gate of their city, and spoke with the men of their city, saying: ²¹"These men *are* at peace with us. Therefore let them dwell in the land and trade in it. For indeed the land *is* large enough for them. Let us take their daughters to us as wives, and let us give them our daughters. ²²Only on this *condition* will the men consent to dwell with us, to be one people: if every male among us is circumcised as they *are* circumcised. ²³*Will* not their livestock, their property, and every animal of theirs *be* ours? Only let us consent to them, and they will dwell with us." ²⁴And all who went out of the gate of his city heeded Hamor and Shechem his son; every male was circumcised, all who went out of the gate of his city.

²⁵Now it came to pass on the third day, when they were in pain, that two of the sons of Jacob, Simeon and Levi, Dinah's brothers, each took his sword and came boldly upon the city and killed all the males. ²⁶And they killed Hamor and Shechem his son with the edge of the sword, and took Dinah from Shechem's house, and went out. ²⁷The sons of Jacob came upon the slain, and plundered the city, because their sister had been defiled. ²⁸They took their sheep, their oxen, and their donkeys, what *was* in the city and what *was* in the field, ²⁹and all their wealth. All their little ones and their wives they took captive; and they plundered even all that *was* in the houses.

³⁰Then Jacob said to Simeon and Levi, "You have troubled me by making me obnoxious among the inhabitants of the land, among the Canaanites and the Perizzites; and since I *am* few in number, they will gather themselves together against me and kill me. I shall be destroyed, my household and I."

³¹But they said, "Should he treat our sister like a harlot?"

Jacob's Return to Bethel

35 Then God said to Jacob, "Arise, go up to Bethel and dwell there; and make an altar there to God, who appeared to you when you fled from the face of Esau your brother."

²And Jacob said to his household and to all who *were* with him, "Put away the foreign gods that *are* among you, purify yourselves, and change your garments. ³Then let us arise and go up to Bethel; and I will make an altar there to God, who answered me in the day of my distress and has been with me in the way which I have gone." ⁴So they gave Jacob all the foreign gods which *were* in their hands, and the earrings which *were* in their ears; and Jacob hid them under the terebinth tree which *was* by Shechem.

⁵And they journeyed, and the terror of God was upon the cities that *were* all around them, and they did not pursue the sons of Jacob. ⁶So Jacob came to Luz (that *is,* Bethel), which *is* in the land of Canaan, he and all the people who *were* with him. ⁷And he built an altar there and called the place El Bethel,[a] because there God appeared to him when he fled from the face of his brother.

35:7 [a]Literally *God of the House of God*

8Now Deborah, Rebekah's nurse, died, and she was buried below Bethel under the terebinth tree. So the name of it was called Allon Bachuth.a

9Then God appeared to Jacob again, when he came from Padan Aram, and blessed him. 10And God said to him, "Your name is Jacob; your name shall not be called Jacob anymore, but Israel shall be your name." So He called his name Israel. 11Also God said to him: "I am God Almighty. Be fruitful and multiply; a nation and a company of nations shall proceed from you, and kings shall come from your body. 12The land which I gave Abraham and Isaac I give to you; and to your descendants after you I give this land." 13Then God went up from him in the place where He talked with him. 14So Jacob set up a pillar in the place where He talked with him, a pillar of stone; and he poured a drink offering on it, and he poured oil on it. 15And Jacob called the name of the place where God spoke with him, Bethel.

Death of Rachel

16Then they journeyed from Bethel. And when there was but a little distance to go to Ephrath, Rachel labored in childbirth, and she had hard labor. 17Now it came to pass, when she was in hard labor, that the midwife said to her, "Do not fear; you will have this son also." 18And so it was, as her soul was departing (for she died), that she called his name Ben-Oni;a but his father called him Benjamin.b 19So Rachel died and was buried on the way to Ephrath (that is, Bethlehem). 20And Jacob set a pillar on her grave, which is the pillar of Rachel's grave to this day.

21Then Israel journeyed and pitched his tent beyond the tower of Eder. 22And it happened, when Israel dwelt in that land, that Reuben went and lay with Bilhah his father's concubine; and Israel heard about it.

Jacob's Twelve Sons

Now the sons of Jacob were twelve: 23the sons of Leah were Reuben, Jacob's firstborn, and Simeon, Levi, Judah, Issachar, and Zebulun; 24the sons of Rachel were Joseph and Benjamin; 25the sons of Bilhah, Rachel's maidservant, were Dan and Naphtali; 26and the sons of Zilpah, Leah's maidservant, were Gad and Asher. These were the sons of Jacob who were born to him in Padan Aram.

Death of Isaac

27Then Jacob came to his father Isaac at Mamre, or Kirjath Arbaa (that is, Hebron), where Abraham and Isaac had dwelt. 28Now the days of Isaac were one hundred and eighty years. 29So Isaac breathed his last and died, and was gathered to his people, being old and full of days. And his sons Esau and Jacob buried him.

The Family of Esau

36 Now this is the genealogy of Esau, who is Edom. 2Esau took his wives from the daughters of Canaan: Adah the daughter of Elon the Hittite; Aholibamah the daughter of Anah, the daughter of Zibeon the Hivite; 3and Basemath, Ishmael's daughter, sister of Nebajoth. 4Now Adah bore Eliphaz to Esau, and Basemath bore Reuel. 5And Aholibamah bore Jeush, Jaalam, and Korah. These were the sons of Esau who were born to him in the land of Canaan.

6Then Esau took his wives, his sons, his daughters, and all the persons of his household, his cattle and all his animals, and all his goods which he had gained in the land of Canaan, and went to a country away from the presence of his brother Jacob. 7For their possessions were too great for them to dwell together, and the land where they were strangers could not support them because of their livestock. 8So Esau dwelt in Mount Seir. Esau is Edom.

9And this is the genealogy of Esau the father of the Edomites in Mount Seir. 10These were the names of Esau's sons: Eliphaz the son of Adah the wife of Esau, and Reuel the son of Basemath the wife of Esau. 11And the sons of Eliphaz were Teman, Omar, Zepho,a Gatam, and Kenaz. 12Now Timna was the concubine of Eliphaz, Esau's son, and she bore Amalek to Eliphaz. These were the sons of Adah, Esau's wife.

35:8 aLiterally Terebinth of Weeping
35:18 aLiterally Son of My Sorrow bLiterally Son of the Right Hand **35:27** aLiterally Town of Arba
36:11 aSpelled Zephi in 1 Chronicles 1:36

¹³These *were* the sons of Reuel: Nathath, Zerah, Shammah, and Mizzah. These were the sons of Basemath, Esau's wife.

¹⁴These were the sons of Aholibamah, Esau's wife, the daughter of Anah, the daughter of Zibeon. And she bore to Esau: Jeush, Jaalam, and Korah.

The Chiefs of Edom

¹⁵These *were* the chiefs of the sons of Esau. The sons of Eliphaz, the firstborn *son* of Esau, were Chief Teman, Chief Omar, Chief Zepho, Chief Kenaz, ¹⁶Chief Korah,ᵃ Chief Gatam, *and* Chief Amalek. These *were* the chiefs of Eliphaz in the land of Edom. They *were* the sons of Adah.

¹⁷These *were* the sons of Reuel, Esau's son: Chief Nahath, Chief Zerah, Chief Shammah, and Chief Mizzah. These *were* the chiefs of Reuel in the land of Edom. These *were* the sons of Basemath, Esau's wife.

¹⁸And these *were* the sons of Aholibamah, Esau's wife: Chief Jeush, Chief Jaalam, and Chief Korah. These *were* the chiefs *who descended* from Aholibamah, Esau's wife, the daughter of Anah. ¹⁹These *were* the sons of Esau, who is Edom, and these *were* their chiefs.

The Sons of Seir

²⁰These *were* the sons of Seir the Horite who inhabited the land: Lotan, Shobal, Zibeon, Anah, ²¹Dishon, Ezer, and Dishan. These *were* the chiefs of the Horites, the sons of Seir, in the land of Edom.

²²And the sons of Lotan were Hori and Hemam.ᵃ Lotan's sister *was* Timna.

²³These *were* the sons of Shobal: Alvan,ᵃ Manahath, Ebal, Shepho,ᵇ and Onam.

²⁴These *were* the sons of Zibeon: both Ajah and Anah. This *was the* Anah who found the waterᵃ in the wilderness as he pastured the donkeys of his father Zibeon. ²⁵These *were* the children of Anah: Dishon and Aholibamah the daughter of Anah.

²⁶These *were* the sons of Dishon:ᵃ Hemdan,ᵇ Eshban, Ithran, and Cheran. ²⁷These *were* the sons of Ezer: Bilhan, Zaavan, and Akan.ᵃ ²⁸These *were* the sons of Dishan: Uz and Aran.

²⁹These *were* the chiefs of the Horites: Chief Lotan, Chief Shobal, Chief Zibeon, Chief Anah, ³⁰Chief Dishon, Chief Ezer, and Chief Dishan. These *were* the chiefs of the Horites, according to their chiefs in the land of Seir.

The Kings of Edom

³¹Now these *were* the kings who reigned in the land of Edom before any king reigned over the children of Israel: ³²Bela the son of Beor reigned in Edom, and the name of his city *was* Dinhabah. ³³And when Bela died, Jobab the son of Zerah of Bozrah reigned in his place. ³⁴When Jobab died, Husham of the land of the Temanites reigned in his place. ³⁵And when Husham died, Hadad the son of Bedad, who attacked Midian in the field of Moab, reigned in his place. And the name of his city *was* Avith. ³⁶When Hadad died, Samlah of Masrekah reigned in his place. ³⁷And when Samlah died, Saul of Rehoboth-*by*-the-River reigned in his place. ³⁸When Saul died, Baal-Hanan the son of Achbor reigned in his place. ³⁹And when Baal-Hanan the son of Achbor died, Hadarᵃ reigned in his place; and the name of his city *was* Pau.ᵇ His wife's name *was* Mehetabel, the daughter of Matred, the daughter of Mezahab.

The Chiefs of Esau

⁴⁰And these *were* the names of the chiefs of Esau, according to their families and their places, by their names: Chief Timnah, Chief Alvah,ᵃ Chief Jetheth, ⁴¹Chief Aholibamah, Chief Elah, Chief Pinon, ⁴²Chief Kenaz, Chief Teman, Chief Mibzar, ⁴³Chief Magdiel, and Chief Iram. These *were* the chiefs of Edom, according to their dwelling places in the land of their possession. Esau *was* the father of the Edomites.

36:16 ᵃSamaritan Pentateuch omits *Chief Korah.*
36:22 ᵃSpelled *Homam* in 1 Chronicles 1:39
36:23 ᵃSpelled *Alian* in 1 Chronicles 1:40 ᵇSpelled *Shephi* in 1 Chronicles 1:40 **36:24** ᵃFollowing Masoretic Text and Vulgate (*hot springs*); Septuagint reads *Jamin;* Targum reads *mighty men;* Talmud interprets as *mules.* **36:26** ᵃHebrew *Dishan* ᵇSpelled *Hamran* in 1 Chronicles 1:41 **36:27** ᵃSpelled *Jaakan* in 1 Chronicles 1:42 **36:39** ᵃSpelled *Hadad* in Samaritan Pentateuch, Syriac, and 1 Chronicles 1:50 ᵇSpelled *Pai* in 1 Chronicles 1:50 **36:40** ᵃSpelled *Aliah* in 1 Chronicles 1:51

Joseph Dreams of Greatness

37 Now Jacob dwelt in the land where his father was a stranger, in the land of Canaan. ²This *is* the history of Jacob.

Joseph, *being* seventeen years old, was feeding the flock with his brothers. And the lad *was* with the sons of Bilhah and the sons of Zilpah, his father's wives; and Joseph brought a bad report of them to his father.

³Now Israel loved Joseph more than all his children, because he *was* the son of his old age. Also he made him a tunic of *many* colors. ⁴But when his brothers saw that their father loved him more than all his brothers, they hated him and could not speak peaceably to him.

⁵Now Joseph had a dream, and he told *it* to his brothers; and they hated him even more. ⁶So he said to them, "Please hear this dream which I have dreamed: ⁷There we were, binding sheaves in the field. Then behold, my sheaf arose and also stood upright; and indeed your sheaves stood all around and bowed down to my sheaf."

⁸And his brothers said to him, "Shall you indeed reign over us? Or shall you indeed have dominion over us?" So they hated him even more for his dreams and for his words.

⁹Then he dreamed still another dream and told it to his brothers, and said, "Look, I have dreamed another dream. And this time, the sun, the moon, and the eleven stars bowed down to me."

¹⁰So he told *it* to his father and his brothers; and his father rebuked him and said to him, "What *is* this dream that you have dreamed? Shall your mother and I and your brothers indeed come to bow down to the earth before you?" ¹¹And his brothers envied him, but his father kept the matter *in mind.*

Joseph Sold by His Brothers

¹²Then his brothers went to feed their father's flock in Shechem. ¹³And Israel said to Joseph, "Are not your brothers feeding *the flock* in Shechem? Come, I will send you to them."

So he said to him, "Here I am."

¹⁴Then he said to him, "Please go and see if it is well with your brothers and well with the flocks, and bring back word to me." So he sent him out of the Valley of Hebron, and he went to Shechem.

¹⁵Now a certain man found him, and there he was, wandering in the field. And the man asked him, saying, "What are you seeking?"

¹⁶So he said, "I am seeking my brothers. Please tell me where they are feeding *their flocks.*"

¹⁷And the man said, "They have departed from here, for I heard them say, 'Let us go to Dothan.' " So Joseph went after his brothers and found them in Dothan.

¹⁸Now when they saw him afar off, even before he came near them, they conspired against him to kill him. ¹⁹Then they said to one another, "Look, this dreamer is coming! ²⁰Come therefore, let us now kill him and cast him into some pit; and we shall say, 'Some wild beast has devoured him.' We shall see what will become of his dreams!"

²¹But Reuben heard *it,* and he delivered him out of their hands, and said, "Let us not kill him." ²²And Reuben said to them, "Shed no blood, *but* cast him into this pit which *is* in the wilderness, and do not lay a hand on him"—that he might deliver him out of their hands, and bring him back to his father.

²³So it came to pass, when Joseph had come to his brothers, that they stripped Joseph *of* his tunic, the tunic of *many* colors that *was* on him. ²⁴Then they took him and cast him into a pit. And the pit *was* empty; *there was* no water in it.

²⁵And they sat down to eat a meal. Then they lifted their eyes and looked, and there was a company of Ishmaelites, coming from Gilead with their camels, bearing spices, balm, and myrrh, on their way to carry *them* down to Egypt. ²⁶So Judah said to his brothers, "What profit *is there* if we kill our brother and conceal his blood? ²⁷Come and let us sell him to the Ishmaelites, and let not our hand be upon him, for he *is* our brother *and* our flesh." And his brothers listened. ²⁸Then Midianite traders passed by; so *the brothers* pulled Joseph up and lifted him out of the pit, and sold him to the Ishmaelites for twenty *shekels* of silver. And they took Joseph to Egypt.

²⁹Then Reuben returned to the pit, and indeed Joseph *was* not in the pit; and he tore his clothes. ³⁰And he returned to his brothers and said, "The lad *is* no *more;* and I, where shall I go?"

³¹So they took Joseph's tunic, killed a kid of the goats, and dipped the tunic in the blood. ³²Then they sent the tunic of *many* colors, and they brought *it* to their father and said, "We have found this. Do you know whether it *is* your son's tunic or not?"

³³And he recognized it and said, "*It is* my son's tunic. A wild beast has devoured him. Without doubt Joseph is torn to pieces." ³⁴Then Jacob tore his clothes, put sackcloth on his waist, and mourned for his son many days. ³⁵And all his sons and all his daughters arose to comfort him; but he refused to be comforted, and he said, "For I shall go down into the grave to my son in mourning." Thus his father wept for him.

³⁶Now the Midianitesᵃ had sold him in Egypt to Potiphar, an officer of Pharaoh *and* captain of the guard.

Judah and Tamar

38 It came to pass at that time that Judah departed from his brothers, and visited a certain Adullamite whose name *was* Hirah. ²And Judah saw there a daughter of a certain Canaanite whose name *was* Shua, and he married her and went in to her. ³So she conceived and bore a son, and he called his name Er. ⁴She conceived again and bore a son, and she called his name Onan. ⁵And she conceived yet again and bore a son, and called his name Shelah. He was at Chezib when she bore him.

⁶Then Judah took a wife for Er his firstborn, and her name *was* Tamar. ⁷But Er, Judah's firstborn, was wicked in the sight of the LORD, and the LORD killed him. ⁸And Judah said to Onan, "Go in to your brother's wife and marry her, and raise up an heir to your brother." ⁹But Onan knew that the heir would not be his; and it came to pass, when he went in to his brother's wife, that he emitted on the ground, lest he should give an heir to his brother. ¹⁰And the thing which he did displeased the LORD; therefore He killed him also.

¹¹Then Judah said to Tamar his daughter-in-law, "Remain a widow in your father's house till my son Shelah is grown." For he said, "Lest he also die like his brothers." And Tamar went and dwelt in her father's house.

¹²Now in the process of time the daughter of Shua, Judah's wife, died; and Judah was comforted, and went up to his sheepshearers at Timnah, he and his friend Hirah the Adullamite. ¹³And it was told Tamar, saying, "Look, your father-in-law is going up to Timnah to shear his sheep." ¹⁴So she took off her widow's garments, covered *herself* with a veil and wrapped herself, and sat in an open place which *was* on the way to Timnah; for she saw that Shelah was grown, and she was not given to him as a wife. ¹⁵When Judah saw her, he thought she *was* a harlot, because she had covered her face. ¹⁶Then he turned to her by the way, and said, "Please let me come in to you"; for he did not know that she *was* his daughter-in-law.

So she said, "What will you give me, that you may come in to me?"

¹⁷And he said, "I will send a young goat from the flock."

So she said, "Will you give *me* a pledge till you send *it?*"

¹⁸Then he said, "What pledge shall I give you?"

So she said, "Your signet and cord, and your staff that *is* in your hand." Then he gave *them* to her, and went in to her, and she conceived by him. ¹⁹So she arose and went away, and laid aside her veil and put on the garments of her widowhood.

²⁰And Judah sent the young goat by the hand of his friend the Adullamite, to receive *his* pledge from the woman's hand, but he did not find her. ²¹Then he asked the men of that place, saying, "Where is the harlot who *was* openly by the roadside?"

And they said, "There was no harlot in this *place.*"

²²So he returned to Judah and said, "I cannot find her. Also, the men of the place said there was no harlot in this *place.*"

²³Then Judah said, "Let her take *them* for herself, lest we be shamed; for I sent this young goat and you have not found her."

²⁴And it came to pass, about three

37:36 ᵃMasoretic Text reads *Medanites.*

months after, that Judah was told, saying, "Tamar your daughter-in-law has played the harlot; furthermore she *is* with child by harlotry."

So Judah said, "Bring her out and let her be burned!"

25When she *was* brought out, she sent to her father-in-law, saying, "By the man to whom these belong, I *am* with child." And she said, "Please determine whose these *are*—the signet and cord, and staff."

26So Judah acknowledged *them* and said, "She has been more righteous than I, because I did not give her to Shelah my son." And he never knew her again.

27Now it came to pass, at the time for giving birth, that behold, twins *were* in her womb. 28And so it was, when she was giving birth, that *the one* put out *his* hand; and the midwife took a scarlet *thread* and bound it on his hand, saying, "This one came out first." 29Then it happened, as he drew back his hand, that his brother came out unexpectedly; and she said, "How did you break through? *This* breach *be* upon you!" Therefore his name was called Perez.a 30Afterward his brother came out who had the scarlet *thread* on his hand. And his name was called Zerah.

Joseph a Slave in Egypt

39 Now Joseph had been taken down to Egypt. And Potiphar, an officer of Pharaoh, captain of the guard, an Egyptian, bought him from the Ishmaelites who had taken him down there. 2The LORD was with Joseph, and he was a successful man; and he was in the house of his master the Egyptian. 3And his master saw that the LORD *was* with him and that the LORD made all he did to prosper in his hand. 4So Joseph found favor in his sight, and served him. Then he made him overseer of his house, and all *that* he had he put under his authority. 5So it was, from the time *that* he had made him overseer of his house and all that he had, that the LORD blessed the Egyptian's house for Joseph's sake; and the blessing of the LORD was on all that he had in the house and in the field. 6Thus he left all that he had in Joseph's hand, and he did

not know what he had except for the bread which he ate.

Now Joseph was handsome in form and appearance.

7And it came to pass after these things that his master's wife cast longing eyes on Joseph, and she said, "Lie with me."

8But he refused and said to his master's wife, "Look, my master does not know what *is* with me in the house, and he has committed all that he has to my hand. 9*There is* no one greater in this house than I, nor has he kept back anything from me but you, because you *are* his wife. How then can I do this great wickedness, and sin against God?"

10So it was, as she spoke to Joseph day by day, that he did not heed her, to lie with her *or* to be with her.

11But it happened about this time, when Joseph went into the house to do his work, and none of the men of the house *was* inside, 12that she caught him by his garment, saying, "Lie with me." But he left his garment in her hand, and fled and ran outside. 13And so it was, when she saw that he had left his garment in her hand and fled outside, 14that she called to the men of her house and spoke to them, saying, "See, he has brought in to us a Hebrew to mock us. He came in to me to lie with me, and I cried out with a loud voice. 15And it happened, when he heard that I lifted my voice and cried out, that he left his garment with me, and fled and went outside."

16So she kept his garment with her until his master came home. 17Then she spoke to him with words like these, saying, "The Hebrew servant whom you brought to us came in to me to mock me; 18so it happened, as I lifted my voice and cried out, that he left his garment with me and fled outside."

19So it was, when his master heard the words which his wife spoke to him, saying, "Your servant did to me after this manner," that his anger was aroused. 20Then Joseph's master took him and put him into the prison, a place where the king's prisoners *were* confined. And he was there in the prison. 21But the LORD was with Joseph and showed him mercy, and He gave him favor in the sight of the keeper of the prison. 22And the keeper of the prison committed

---

38:29 aLiterally *Breach* or *Breakthrough*

to Joseph's hand all the prisoners who *were* in the prison; whatever they did there, it was his doing. ²³The keeper of the prison did not look into anything *that was* under *Joseph's* authority,ᵃ because the LORD was with him; and whatever he did, the LORD made *it* prosper.

The Prisoners' Dreams

40 It came to pass after these things *that* the butler and the baker of the king of Egypt offended their lord, the king of Egypt. ²And Pharaoh was angry with his two officers, the chief butler and the chief baker. ³So he put them in custody in the house of the captain of the guard, in the prison, the place where Joseph *was* confined. ⁴And the captain of the guard charged Joseph with them, and he served them; so they were in custody for a while.

⁵Then the butler and the baker of the king of Egypt, who *were* confined in the prison, had a dream, both of them, each man's dream in one night *and* each man's dream with its *own* interpretation. ⁶And Joseph came in to them in the morning and looked at them, and saw that they *were* sad. ⁷So he asked Pharaoh's officers who *were* with him in the custody of his lord's house, saying, "Why do you look *so* sad today?"

⁸And they said to him, "We each have had a dream, and *there is* no interpreter of it."

So Joseph said to them, "Do not interpretations belong to God? Tell *them* to me, please."

⁹Then the chief butler told his dream to Joseph, and said to him, "Behold, in my dream a vine *was* before me, ¹⁰and in the vine *were* three branches; it *was* as though it budded, its blossoms shot forth, and its clusters brought forth ripe grapes. ¹¹Then Pharaoh's cup *was* in my hand; and I took the grapes and pressed them into Pharaoh's cup, and placed the cup in Pharaoh's hand."

¹²And Joseph said to him, "This *is* the interpretation of it: The three branches *are* three days. ¹³Now within three days Pharaoh will lift up your head and restore you to your place, and you will put Pharaoh's cup in his hand according to the former manner, when you were his butler.

¹⁴But remember me when it is well with you, and please show kindness to me; make mention of me to Pharaoh, and get me out of this house. ¹⁵For indeed I was stolen away from the land of the Hebrews; and also I have done nothing here that they should put me into the dungeon."

¹⁶When the chief baker saw that the interpretation was good, he said to Joseph, "I also *was* in my dream, and there *were* three white baskets on my head. ¹⁷In the uppermost basket *were* all kinds of baked goods for Pharaoh, and the birds ate them out of the basket on my head."

¹⁸So Joseph answered and said, "This *is* the interpretation of it: The three baskets *are* three days. ¹⁹Within three days Pharaoh will lift off your head from you and hang you on a tree; and the birds will eat your flesh from you."

²⁰Now it came to pass on the third day, *which was* Pharaoh's birthday, that he made a feast for all his servants; and he lifted up the head of the chief butler and of the chief baker among his servants. ²¹Then he restored the chief butler to his butlership again, and he placed the cup in Pharaoh's hand. ²²But he hanged the chief baker, as Joseph had interpreted to them. ²³Yet the chief butler did not remember Joseph, but forgot him.

Pharaoh's Dreams

41 Then it came to pass, at the end of two full years, that Pharaoh had a dream; and behold, he stood by the river. ²Suddenly there came up out of the river seven cows, fine looking and fat; and they fed in the meadow. ³Then behold, seven other cows came up after them out of the river, ugly and gaunt, and stood by the *other* cows on the bank of the river. ⁴And the ugly and gaunt cows ate up the seven fine looking and fat cows. So Pharaoh awoke. ⁵He slept and dreamed a second time; and suddenly seven heads of grain came up on one stalk, plump and good. ⁶Then behold, seven thin heads, blighted by the east wind, sprang up after them. ⁷And the seven thin heads devoured the seven plump and full heads. So Pharaoh awoke, and indeed, *it*

39:23 ᵃLiterally *his hand*

was a dream. [8]Now it came to pass in the morning that his spirit was troubled, and he sent and called for all the magicians of Egypt and all its wise men. And Pharaoh told them his dreams, but *there was* no one who could interpret them for Pharaoh.

[9]Then the chief butler spoke to Pharaoh, saying: "I remember my faults this day. [10]When Pharaoh was angry with his servants, and put me in custody in the house of the captain of the guard, *both* me and the chief baker, [11]we each had a dream in one night, he and I. Each of us dreamed according to the interpretation of his *own* dream. [12]Now there *was* a young Hebrew man with us there, a servant of the captain of the guard. And we told him, and he interpreted our dreams for us; to each man he interpreted according to his *own* dream. [13]And it came to pass, just as he interpreted for us, so it happened. He restored me to my office, and he hanged him."

[14]Then Pharaoh sent and called Joseph, and they brought him quickly out of the dungeon; and he shaved, changed his clothing, and came to Pharaoh. [15]And Pharaoh said to Joseph, "I have had a dream, and *there is* no one who can interpret it. But I have heard it said of you *that* you can understand a dream, to interpret it."

[16]So Joseph answered Pharaoh, saying, "*It is* not in me; God will give Pharaoh an answer of peace."

[17]Then Pharaoh said to Joseph: "Behold, in my dream I stood on the bank of the river. [18]Suddenly seven cows came up out of the river, fine looking and fat; and they fed in the meadow. [19]Then behold, seven other cows came up after them, poor and very ugly and gaunt, such ugliness as I have never seen in all the land of Egypt. [20]And the gaunt and ugly cows ate up the first seven, the fat cows. [21]When they had eaten them up, no one would have known that they had eaten them, for they *were* just as ugly as at the beginning. So I awoke. [22]Also I saw in my dream, and suddenly seven heads came up on one stalk, full and good. [23]Then behold, seven heads, withered, thin, *and* blighted by the east wind, sprang up after them. [24]And the thin heads devoured the seven good heads. So I told *this* to the magicians, but *there was* no one who could explain *it* to me."

[25]Then Joseph said to Pharaoh, "The dreams of Pharaoh *are* one; God has shown Pharaoh what He *is* about to do: [26]The seven good cows *are* seven years, and the seven good heads *are* seven years; the dreams *are* one. [27]And the seven thin and ugly cows which came up after them *are* seven years, and the seven empty heads blighted by the east wind are seven years of famine. [28]This *is* the thing which I have spoken to Pharaoh. God has shown Pharaoh what He *is* about to do. [29]Indeed seven years of great plenty will come throughout all the land of Egypt; [30]but after them seven years of famine will arise, and all the plenty will be forgotten in the land of Egypt; and the famine will deplete the land. [31]So the plenty will not be known in the land because of the famine following, for it *will be* very severe. [32]And the dream was repeated to Pharaoh twice because the thing *is* established by God, and God will shortly bring it to pass.

[33]"Now therefore, let Pharaoh select a discerning and wise man, and set him over the land of Egypt. [34]Let Pharaoh do *this,* and let him appoint officers over the land, to collect one-fifth *of the produce* of the land of Egypt in the seven plentiful years. [35]And let them gather all the food of those good years that are coming, and store up grain under the authority of Pharaoh, and let them keep food in the cities. [36]Then that food shall be as a reserve for the land for the seven years of famine which shall be in the land of Egypt, that the land may not perish during the famine."

Joseph's Rise to Power

[37]So the advice was good in the eyes of Pharaoh and in the eyes of all his servants. [38]And Pharaoh said to his servants, "Can we find *such a one* as this, a man in whom *is* the Spirit of God?"

[39]Then Pharaoh said to Joseph, "Inasmuch as God has shown you all this, *there is* no one as discerning and wise as you. [40]You shall be over my house, and all my people shall be ruled according to your word; only in regard to the throne will I be greater than you." [41]And Pharaoh said to Joseph, "See, I have set you over all the land of Egypt."

BIBLICAL INSIGHTS • 41:52
The Value of Suffering

THE PATRIARCH JOSEPH understood the value of suffering. He named his second son Ephraim, "For God has caused me to be fruitful in the land of my affliction" (41:52). And after being reunited with his estranged brothers, he told them, "You meant evil against me; but God meant it for good, in order to bring it about as it is this day, to save many people alive" (50:20).

Joseph's attitudes and actions toward those who hurt him reflect some simple truths we all need to understand in regard to the difficulties of living in a fallen world:

1. The pain of suffering pierces every heart.
2. God's timing and our timing seldom coincide.
3. The issue in any trial is faith and obedience, not freedom from pain.
4. Although it's natural to try to understand the reasons for suffering, no one will ever grasp all that God is up to.
5. God never meant for us to face trouble alone.
6. Humility and integrity are non-negotiables.
7. Forgive those who wound you.
8. God wants us to create holy scars. Charles Spurgeon says, "The Lord gets His best soldiers out of the highlands of affliction."
9. Every trial is ultimately about knowing God and glorifying Him.

The Scriptures clearly teach us that all suffering is purposeful and that we must ultimately trust God with whatever circumstances come our way. When it comes to troubling times, I'm reminded of the quote by Dr. Martin Lloyd Jones, "Faith is the refusal to panic."

---

⁴²Then Pharaoh took his signet ring off his hand and put it on Joseph's hand; and he clothed him in garments of fine linen and put a gold chain around his neck. ⁴³And he had him ride in the second chariot which he had; and they cried out before him, "Bow the knee!" So he set him over all the land of Egypt. ⁴⁴Pharaoh also said to Joseph, "I *am* Pharaoh, and without your consent no man may lift his hand or foot in all the land of Egypt." ⁴⁵And Pharaoh called Joseph's name Zaphnath-Paaneah. And he gave him as a wife Asenath, the daughter of Poti-Pherah priest of On. So Joseph went out over *all* the land of Egypt.

⁴⁶Joseph was thirty years old when he stood before Pharaoh king of Egypt. And Joseph went out from the presence of Pharaoh, and went throughout all the land of Egypt. ⁴⁷Now in the seven plentiful years the ground brought forth abundantly. ⁴⁸So he gathered up all the food of the seven years which were in the land of Egypt, and laid up the food in the cities; he laid up in every city the food of the fields which surrounded them. ⁴⁹Joseph gathered very much grain, as the sand of the sea, until he stopped counting, for *it was* immeasurable.

⁵⁰And to Joseph were born two sons before the years of famine came, whom Asenath, the daughter of Poti-Pherah priest of On, bore to him. ⁵¹Joseph called the name of the firstborn Manasseh:ᵃ "For God has made me forget all my toil and all my father's house." ⁵²And the name of the second he called Ephraim:ᵃ "For God has caused me to be fruitful in the land of my affliction."

⁵³Then the seven years of plenty which were in the land of Egypt ended, ⁵⁴and the seven years of famine began to come, as Joseph had said. The famine was in all lands, but in all the land of Egypt there was bread. ⁵⁵So when all the land of Egypt was famished, the people cried to Pharaoh for bread. Then Pharaoh said to all the Egyptians, "Go to Joseph; whatever he says to you, do." ⁵⁶The famine was over all the face of the earth, and Joseph opened all the storehousesᵃ and sold to the Egyptians. And the famine became severe in the land of Egypt. ⁵⁷So all countries came to Joseph in Egypt to buy *grain,* because the famine was severe in all lands.

41:51 ᵃLiterally *Making Forgetful* **41:52** ᵃLiterally *Fruitfulness* **41:56** ᵃLiterally *all that was in them*

Joseph's Brothers Go to Egypt

42 When Jacob saw that there was grain in Egypt, Jacob said to his sons, "Why do you look at one another?" ²And he said, "Indeed I have heard that there is grain in Egypt; go down to that place and buy for us there, that we may live and not die."

³So Joseph's ten brothers went down to buy grain in Egypt. ⁴But Jacob did not send Joseph's brother Benjamin with his brothers, for he said, "Lest some calamity befall him." ⁵And the sons of Israel went to buy *grain* among those who journeyed, for the famine was in the land of Canaan.

⁶Now Joseph *was* governor over the land; and it was he who sold to all the people of the land. And Joseph's brothers came and bowed down before him with *their* faces to the earth. ⁷Joseph saw his brothers and recognized them, but he acted as a stranger to them and spoke roughly to them. Then he said to them, "Where do you come from?"

And they said, "From the land of Canaan to buy food."

⁸So Joseph recognized his brothers, but they did not recognize him. ⁹Then Joseph remembered the dreams which he had dreamed about them, and said to them, "You *are* spies! You have come to see the nakedness of the land!"

¹⁰And they said to him, "No, my lord, but your servants have come to buy food. ¹¹We *are* all one man's sons; we *are* honest *men;* your servants are not spies."

¹²But he said to them, "No, but you have come to see the nakedness of the land."

¹³And they said, "Your servants *are* twelve brothers, the sons of one man in the land of Canaan; and in fact, the youngest *is* with our father today, and one *is* no more."

¹⁴But Joseph said to them, "It *is* as I spoke to you, saying, 'You *are* spies!' ¹⁵In this *manner* you shall be tested: By the life of Pharaoh, you shall not leave this place unless your youngest brother comes here. ¹⁶Send one of you, and let him bring your brother; and you shall be kept in prison, that your words may be tested to see whether *there is* any truth in you; or else, by the life of Pharaoh, surely you *are* spies!" ¹⁷So he put them all together in prison three days.

BIBLICAL INSIGHTS • 42:21

Be a Man, Not a Weasel

WHAT DOES IT TAKE for you to admit you're wrong? In the case of Joseph's brothers, it took what appeared to be an imminent disaster (42:21).

During the first years of our marriage, I struggled to admit I was wrong. Whenever I did so, I would often say, "*If* I was wrong when I did this, I'm sorry." An all-out confession was simply out of the question.

My attitude was childish, of course; but I couldn't see it then. It's amazing how many spouses behave like little kids who try to weasel out after getting caught with their hands in the cookie jar!

Over the years I've admitted to just about everyone in our family that I've been wrong; and of course, Barbara has heard me say it more than anyone. The first step is the hardest—admit you're wrong and ask forgiveness. Both sexes can have trouble with this one, but in most marriages, the edge goes to the men.

Nevertheless, it's liberating to admit you're wrong, and it's even more liberating when the other person forgives you and says, "That's okay—I know I've made mistakes, too." Seeking and granting forgiveness in marriage leads to oneness; ignoring these things leads to isolation.

---

¹⁸Then Joseph said to them the third day, "Do this and live, *for* I fear God: ¹⁹If you *are* honest *men,* let one of your brothers be confined to your prison house; but you, go and carry grain for the famine of your houses. ²⁰And bring your youngest brother to me; so your words will be verified, and you shall not die."

And they did so. ²¹Then they said to one another, "We *are* truly guilty concerning our brother, for we saw the anguish of his soul when he pleaded with us, and we would not hear; therefore this distress has come upon us."

²²And Reuben answered them, saying, "Did I not speak to you, saying, 'Do not sin

against the boy'; and you would not listen? Therefore behold, his blood is now required of us." ²³But they did not know that Joseph understood *them,* for he spoke to them through an interpreter. ²⁴And he turned himself away from them and wept. Then he returned to them again, and talked with them. And he took Simeon from them and bound him before their eyes.

The Brothers Return to Canaan

²⁵Then Joseph gave a command to fill their sacks with grain, to restore every man's money to his sack, and to give them provisions for the journey. Thus he did for them. ²⁶So they loaded their donkeys with the grain and departed from there. ²⁷But as one *of them* opened his sack to give his donkey feed at the encampment, he saw his money; and there it was, in the mouth of his sack. ²⁸So he said to his brothers, "My money has been restored, and there it is, in my sack!" Then their hearts failed *them* and they were afraid, saying to one another, "What *is* this *that* God has done to us?"

²⁹Then they went to Jacob their father in the land of Canaan and told him all that had happened to them, saying: ³⁰"The man *who is* lord of the land spoke roughly to us, and took us for spies of the country. ³¹But we said to him, 'We *are* honest *men;* we are not spies. ³²We *are* twelve brothers, sons of our father; one *is* no *more,* and the youngest *is* with our father this day in the land of Canaan.' ³³Then the man, the lord of the country, said to us, 'By this I will know that you *are* honest *men:* Leave one of your brothers *here* with me, take *food for* the famine of your households, and be gone. ³⁴And bring your youngest brother to me; so I shall know that you *are* not spies, but *that* you *are* honest *men.* I will grant your brother to you, and you may trade in the land.' "

³⁵Then it happened as they emptied their sacks, that surprisingly each man's bundle of money *was* in his sack; and when they and their father saw the bundles of money, they were afraid. ³⁶And Jacob their father said to them, "You have bereaved me: Joseph is no *more,* Simeon is no *more,* and you want to take Benjamin. All these things are against me."

The Law of Understanding

When Joseph's brothers came from Canaan to Egypt seeking food in the midst of the famine, they had to use an interpreter to communicate with their brother. There have been times in our marriage when Barbara and I have needed someone to interpret for us so we could truly understand each other! Understanding is not merely a transfer of information, but an empathy for the other person based on what he or she communicated with you. Barbara and I have found understanding to be essential in building each other's self-image. We are continually seeking to comprehend the context of each other's lives, the kind of context that helps to explain our self-image, our behavior, and our attitudes.

Applying the Law of Understanding will give you the right to be heard by your mate. If he or she senses that you truly understand—or at least *desire* to understand—then your suggestions and attempts to build into your mate will be better received.

The next time your mate expresses a concern, ask if he or she feels that you understand it. Practice listening with a sympathetic ear, and look beyond the response to its cause. What has occurred in your mate's life that contributes to this present attitude? Which pressures today may be crushing your mate's self-confidence?

Proverbs 24:3 reads, "Through wisdom a house is built, and by understanding it is established." And 1 Peter 3:7 teaches husbands to dwell with their wives with understanding. As we give each other the gift of understanding, we build a stronger, healthier marriage that endures.

³⁷Then Reuben spoke to his father, saying, "Kill my two sons if I do not bring him *back* to you; put him in my hands, and I will bring him back to you."

³⁸But he said, "My son shall not go down with you, for his brother is dead, and he is left alone. If any calamity should befall him along the way in which you go, then you would bring down my gray hair with sorrow to the grave."

Joseph's Brothers Return with Benjamin

43 Now the famine *was* severe in the land. ²And it came to pass, when they had eaten up the grain which they had brought from Egypt, that their father said to them, "Go back, buy us a little food."

³But Judah spoke to him, saying, "The man solemnly warned us, saying, 'You shall not see my face unless your brother *is* with you.' ⁴If you send our brother with us, we will go down and buy you food. ⁵But if you will not send *him,* we will not go down; for the man said to us, 'You shall not see my face unless your brother *is* with you.' "

⁶And Israel said, "Why did you deal *so* wrongfully with me *as* to tell the man whether you had still *another* brother?"

⁷But they said, "The man asked us pointedly about ourselves and our family, saying, 'Is your father still alive? Have you *another* brother?' And we told him according to these words. Could we possibly have known that he would say, 'Bring your brother down'?"

⁸Then Judah said to Israel his father, "Send the lad with me, and we will arise and go, that we may live and not die, both we and you *and* also our little ones. ⁹I myself will be surety for him; from my hand you shall require him. If I do not bring him *back* to you and set him before you, then let me bear the blame forever. ¹⁰For if we had not lingered, surely by now we would have returned this second time."

¹¹And their father Israel said to them, "If *it must be* so, then do this: Take some of the best fruits of the land in your vessels and carry down a present for the man—a little balm and a little honey, spices and myrrh, pistachio nuts and almonds. ¹²Take double money in your hand, and take back in your hand the money that was returned in the mouth of your sacks; perhaps it was

an oversight. ¹³Take your brother also, and arise, go back to the man. ¹⁴And may God Almighty give you mercy before the man, that he may release your other brother and Benjamin. If I am bereaved, I am bereaved!"

¹⁵So the men took that present and Benjamin, and they took double money in their hand, and arose and went down to Egypt; and they stood before Joseph. ¹⁶When Joseph saw Benjamin with them, he said to the steward of his house, "Take *these* men to my home, and slaughter an animal and make ready; for *these* men will dine with me at noon." ¹⁷Then the man did as Joseph ordered, and the man brought the men into Joseph's house.

¹⁸Now the men were afraid because they were brought into Joseph's house; and they said, "*It is* because of the money, which was returned in our sacks the first time, that we are brought in, so that he may make a case against us and seize us, to take us as slaves with our donkeys."

¹⁹When they drew near to the steward of Joseph's house, they talked with him at the door of the house, ²⁰and said, "O sir, we indeed came down the first time to buy food; ²¹but it happened, when we came to the encampment, that we opened our sacks, and there, *each* man's money *was* in the mouth of his sack, our money in full weight; so we have brought it back in our hand. ²²And we have brought down other money in our hands to buy food. We do not know who put our money in our sacks."

²³But he said, "Peace *be* with you, do not be afraid. Your God and the God of your father has given you treasure in your sacks; I had your money." Then he brought Simeon out to them.

²⁴So the man brought the men into Joseph's house and gave *them* water, and they washed their feet; and he gave their donkeys feed. ²⁵Then they made the present ready for Joseph's coming at noon, for they heard that they would eat bread there.

²⁶And when Joseph came home, they brought him the present which *was* in their hand into the house, and bowed down before him to the earth. ²⁷Then he asked them about *their* well-being, and said, "*Is* your father well, the old man of whom you spoke? *Is* he still alive?"

28And they answered, "Your servant our father *is* in good health; he *is* still alive." And they bowed their heads down and prostrated themselves.

29Then he lifted his eyes and saw his brother Benjamin, his mother's son, and said, "*Is* this your younger brother of whom you spoke to me?" And he said, "God be gracious to you, my son." 30Now his heart yearned for his brother; so Joseph made haste and sought *somewhere* to weep. And he went into *his* chamber and wept there. 31Then he washed his face and came out; and he restrained himself, and said, "Serve the bread."

32So they set him a place by himself, and them by themselves, and the Egyptians who ate with him by themselves; because the Egyptians could not eat food with the Hebrews, for that *is* an abomination to the Egyptians. 33And they sat before him, the firstborn according to his birthright and the youngest according to his youth; and the men looked in astonishment at one another. 34Then he took servings to them from before him, but Benjamin's serving was five times as much as any of theirs. So they drank and were merry with him.

Joseph's Cup

44 And he commanded the steward of his house, saying, "Fill the men's sacks with food, as much as they can carry, and put each man's money in the mouth of his sack. 2Also put my cup, the silver cup, in the mouth of the sack of the youngest, and his grain money." So he did according to the word that Joseph had spoken. 3As soon as the morning dawned, the men were sent away, they and their donkeys. 4When they had gone out of the city, *and* were not *yet* far off, Joseph said to his steward, "Get up, follow the men; and when you overtake them, say to them, 'Why have you repaid evil for good? 5*Is* not this *the one* from which my lord drinks, and with which he indeed practices divination? You have done evil in so doing.' "

6So he overtook them, and he spoke to them these same words. 7And they said to him, "Why does my lord say these words? Far be it from us that your servants should do such a thing. 8Look, we brought back to you from the land of Canaan the money which we found in the mouth of our sacks. How then could we steal silver or gold from your lord's house? 9With whomever of your servants it is found, let him die, and we also will be my lord's slaves."

10And he said, "Now also *let* it *be* according to your words; he with whom it is found shall be my slave, and you shall be blameless." 11Then each man speedily let down his sack to the ground, and each opened his sack. 12So he searched. He began with the oldest and left off with the youngest; and the cup was found in Benjamin's sack. 13Then they tore their clothes, and each man loaded his donkey and returned to the city.

14So Judah and his brothers came to Joseph's house, and he *was* still there; and they fell before him on the ground. 15And Joseph said to them, "What deed *is* this you have done? Did you not know that such a man as I can certainly practice divination?"

16Then Judah said, "What shall we say to my lord? What shall we speak? Or how shall we clear ourselves? God has found out the iniquity of your servants; here we are, my lord's slaves, both we and *he* also with whom the cup was found."

17But he said, "Far be it from me that I should do so; the man in whose hand the cup was found, he shall be my slave. And as for you, go up in peace to your father."

Judah Intercedes for Benjamin

18Then Judah came near to him and said: "O my lord, please let your servant speak a word in my lord's hearing, and do not let your anger burn against your servant; for you *are* even like Pharaoh. 19My lord asked his servants, saying, 'Have you a father or a brother?' 20And we said to my lord, 'We have a father, an old man, and a child of *his* old age, *who is* young; his brother is dead, and he alone is left of his mother's children, and his father loves him.' 21Then you said to your servants, 'Bring him down to me, that I may set my eyes on him.' 22And we said to my lord, 'The lad cannot leave his father, for *if* he should leave his father, *his father* would die.' 23But you said to your servants, 'Unless your youngest brother comes down with you, you shall see my face no more.'

²⁴"So it was, when we went up to your servant my father, that we told him the words of my lord. ²⁵And our father said, 'Go back *and* buy us a little food.' ²⁶But we said, 'We cannot go down; if our youngest brother is with us, then we will go down; for we may not see the man's face unless our youngest brother *is* with us.' ²⁷Then your servant my father said to us, 'You know that my wife bore me two sons; ²⁸and the one went out from me, and I said, "Surely he is torn to pieces"; and I have not seen him since. ²⁹But if you take this one also from me, and calamity befalls him, you shall bring down my gray hair with sorrow to the grave.'

³⁰"Now therefore, when I come to your servant my father, and the lad *is* not with us, since his life is bound up in the lad's life, ³¹it will happen, when he sees that the lad *is* not *with us,* that he will die. So your servants will bring down the gray hair of your servant our father with sorrow to the grave. ³²For your servant became surety for the lad to my father, saying, 'If I do not bring him *back* to you, then I shall bear the blame before my father forever.' ³³Now therefore, please let your servant remain instead of the lad as a slave to my lord, and let the lad go up with his brothers. ³⁴For how shall I go up to my father if the lad *is* not with me, lest perhaps I see the evil that would come upon my father?"

Joseph Revealed to His Brothers

45 Then Joseph could not restrain himself before all those who stood by him, and he cried out, "Make everyone go out from me!" So no one stood with him while Joseph made himself known to his brothers. ²And he wept aloud, and the Egyptians and the house of Pharaoh heard *it.*

³Then Joseph said to his brothers, "I *am* Joseph; does my father still live?" But his brothers could not answer him, for they were dismayed in his presence. ⁴And Joseph said to his brothers, "Please come near to me." So they came near. Then he said: "I *am* Joseph your brother, whom you sold into Egypt. ⁵But now, do not therefore be grieved or angry with yourselves because you sold me here; for God sent me before you to preserve life. ⁶For these two years the famine *has been* in the land, and *there are* still five years in which *there will be* neither plowing nor harvesting. ⁷And God sent me before you to preserve a posterity for you in the earth, and to save your lives by a great deliverance. ⁸So now *it was* not you *who* sent me here, but God; and He has made me a father to Pharaoh, and lord of all his house, and a ruler throughout all the land of Egypt.

⁹"Hurry and go up to my father, and say to him, 'Thus says your son Joseph: "God has made me lord of all Egypt; come down to me, do not tarry. ¹⁰You shall dwell in the land of Goshen, and you shall be near to me, you and your children, your children's children, your flocks and your herds, and all that you have. ¹¹There I will provide for you, lest you and your household, and all that you have, come to poverty; for *there are* still five years of famine."'

¹²"And behold, your eyes and the eyes of my brother Benjamin see that *it is* my mouth that speaks to you. ¹³So you shall tell my father of all my glory in Egypt, and of all that you have seen; and you shall hurry and bring my father down here."

¹⁴Then he fell on his brother Benjamin's neck and wept, and Benjamin wept on his neck. ¹⁵Moreover he kissed all his brothers and wept over them, and after that his brothers talked with him.

¹⁶Now the report of it was heard in Pharaoh's house, saying, "Joseph's brothers have come." So it pleased Pharaoh and his servants well. ¹⁷And Pharaoh said to Joseph, "Say to your brothers, 'Do this: Load your animals and depart; go to the land of

INTIMATE MOMENTS

Before your next day at the beach, prepare a special message in a bottle for your husband. Hide it in a place where the two of you will come across it as you lead him on a walk.

Canaan. ¹⁸Bring your father and your households and come to me; I will give you the best of the land of Egypt, and you will eat the fat of the land. ¹⁹Now you are commanded—do this: Take carts out of the land of Egypt for your little ones and your wives; bring your father and come. ²⁰Also do not be concerned about your goods, for the best of all the land of Egypt *is* yours.' "

²¹Then the sons of Israel did so; and Joseph gave them carts, according to the command of Pharaoh, and he gave them provisions for the journey. ²²He gave to all of them, to each man, changes of garments; but to Benjamin he gave three hundred *pieces* of silver and five changes of garments. ²³And he sent to his father these *things:* ten donkeys loaded with the good things of Egypt, and ten female donkeys loaded with grain, bread, and food for his father for the journey. ²⁴So he sent his brothers away, and they departed; and he said to them, "See that you do not become troubled along the way."

²⁵Then they went up out of Egypt, and came to the land of Canaan to Jacob their father. ²⁶And they told him, saying, "Joseph *is* still alive, and he *is* governor over all the land of Egypt." And Jacob's heart stood still, because he did not believe them. ²⁷But when they told him all the words which Joseph had said to them, and when he saw the carts which Joseph had sent to carry him, the spirit of Jacob their father revived. ²⁸Then Israel said, "*It is* enough. Joseph my son *is* still alive. I will go and see him before I die."

Jacob's Journey to Egypt

46 So Israel took his journey with all that he had, and came to Beersheba, and offered sacrifices to the God of his father Isaac. ²Then God spoke to Israel in the visions of the night, and said, "Jacob, Jacob!"

And he said, "Here I am."

³So He said, "I *am* God, the God of your father; do not fear to go down to Egypt, for I will make of you a great nation there. ⁴I will go down with you to Egypt, and I will also surely bring you up *again;* and Joseph will put his hand on your eyes."

⁵Then Jacob arose from Beersheba; and

the sons of Israel carried their father Jacob, their little ones, and their wives, in the carts which Pharaoh had sent to carry him. ⁶So they took their livestock and their goods, which they had acquired in the land of Canaan, and went to Egypt, Jacob and all his descendants with him. ⁷His sons and his sons' sons, his daughters and his sons' daughters, and all his descendants he brought with him to Egypt.

⁸Now these *were* the names of the children of Israel, Jacob and his sons, who went to Egypt: Reuben *was* Jacob's firstborn. ⁹The sons of Reuben *were* Hanoch, Pallu, Hezron, and Carmi. ¹⁰The sons of Simeon *were* Jemuel,ᵃ Jamin, Ohad, Jachin,ᵇ Zohar,ᶜ and Shaul, the son of a Canaanite woman. ¹¹The sons of Levi *were* Gershon, Kohath, and Merari. ¹²The sons of Judah *were* Er, Onan, Shelah, Perez, and Zerah (but Er and Onan died in the land of Canaan). The sons of Perez were Hezron and Hamul. ¹³The sons of Issachar *were* Tola, Puvah,ᵃ Job,ᵇ and Shimron. ¹⁴The sons of Zebulun *were* Sered, Elon, and Jahleel. ¹⁵These *were* the sons of Leah, whom she bore to Jacob in Padan Aram, with his daughter Dinah. All the persons, his sons and his daughters, *were* thirty-three.

¹⁶The sons of Gad *were* Ziphion,ᵃ Haggi, Shuni, Ezbon,ᵇ Eri, Arodi,ᶜ and Areli. ¹⁷The sons of Asher *were* Jimnah, Ishuah, Isui, Beriah, and Serah, their sister. And the sons of Beriah *were* Heber and Malchiel. ¹⁸These *were* the sons of Zilpah, whom Laban gave to Leah his daughter; and these she bore to Jacob: sixteen persons.

¹⁹The sons of Rachel, Jacob's wife, *were* Joseph and Benjamin. ²⁰And to Joseph in the land of Egypt were born Manasseh and Ephraim, whom Asenath, the daughter of Poti-Pherah priest of On, bore to him. ²¹The sons of Benjamin *were* Belah, Becher, Ashbel, Gera, Naaman, Ehi, Rosh, Muppim, Huppim,ᵃ and Ard. ²²These *were*

46:10 ᵃSpelled *Nemuel* in 1 Chronicles 4:24 ᵇCalled *Jarib* in 1 Chronicles 4:24 ᶜCalled *Zerah* in 1 Chronicles 4:24 **46:13** ᵃSpelled *Puah* in 1 Chronicles 7:1 ᵇSame as *Jashub* in Numbers 26:24 and 1 Chronicles 7:1 **46:16** ᵃSpelled *Zephon* in Samaritan Pentateuch, Septuagint, and Numbers 26:15 ᵇCalled *Ozni* in Numbers 26:16 ᶜSpelled *Arod* in Numbers 26:17 **46:21** ᵃCalled *Hupham* in Numbers 26:39

the sons of Rachel, who were born to Jacob: fourteen persons in all.

²³The son of Dan *was* Hushim.^a ²⁴The sons of Naphtali *were* Jahzeel,^a Guni, Jezer, and Shillem.^b ²⁵These *were* the sons of Bilhah, whom Laban gave to Rachel his daughter, and she bore these to Jacob: seven persons in all.

²⁶All the persons who went with Jacob to Egypt, who came from his body, besides Jacob's sons' wives, *were* sixty-six persons in all. ²⁷And the sons of Joseph who were born to him in Egypt *were* two persons. All the persons of the house of Jacob who went to Egypt were seventy.

Jacob Settles in Goshen

²⁸Then he sent Judah before him to Joseph, to point out before him *the way* to Goshen. And they came to the land of Goshen. ²⁹So Joseph made ready his chariot and went up to Goshen to meet his father Israel; and he presented himself to him, and fell on his neck and wept on his neck a good while.

³⁰And Israel said to Joseph, "Now let me

---

die, since I have seen your face, because you *are* still alive."

³¹Then Joseph said to his brothers and to his father's household, "I will go up and tell Pharaoh, and say to him, 'My brothers and those of my father's house, who *were* in the land of Canaan, have come to me. ³²And the men *are* shepherds, for their occupation has been to feed livestock; and they have brought their flocks, their herds, and all that they have.' ³³So it shall be, when Pharaoh calls you and says, 'What is your occupation?' ³⁴that you shall say, 'Your servants' occupation has been with livestock from our youth even till now, both we *and* also our fathers,' that you may dwell in the land of Goshen; for every shepherd *is* an abomination to the Egyptians."

47 Then Joseph went and told Pharaoh, and said, "My father and my brothers, their flocks and their herds and all that they possess, have come from the land of Canaan; and indeed they *are* in the land of Goshen." ²And he took five men from among his brothers and presented them to Pharaoh. ³Then Pharaoh said to his brothers, "What *is* your occupation?"

And they said to Pharaoh, "Your servants *are* shepherds, both we *and* also our fathers." ⁴And they said to Pharaoh, "We

---

46:23 ^aCalled *Shuham* in Numbers 26:42
46:24 ^aSpelled *Jahziel* in 1 Chronicles 7:13 ^bSpelled *Shallum* in 1 Chronicles 7:13

PARENTING MATTERS

Q: *What does it mean to be involved in our children's lives?*

Involvement means crawling inside your kid's head and heart and finding out what he's thinking and feeling. It means diving into the often-turbulent waves caused by emotions—both the child's and yours.

This can be scary and uncomfortable. And that's why so many parents run from involvement and withdraw to safer territory. The sobering truth is that you can be in the same house, but be clueless about what's really going on in your child's life.

Connecting with your teenager may be the most demanding challenge of your life, and you won't always see immediate results. But sometimes, connecting can be as simple as walking into your child's bedroom, sitting down and asking a few questions. Or taking your child out for hamburgers and letting her talk.

When you pursue real involvement in your child's life, you follow God's own example: "You have searched me and known me. You know my sitting down and my rising up; You understand my thought afar off. You comprehend my path and my lying down, and are acquainted with all my ways" (Psalm 139:1–3).

Wouldn't it be wonderful if our kids could say the same of us?

have come to dwell in the land, because your servants have no pasture for their flocks, for the famine *is* severe in the land of Canaan. Now therefore, please let your servants dwell in the land of Goshen."

⁵Then Pharaoh spoke to Joseph, saying, "Your father and your brothers have come to you. ⁶The land of Egypt *is* before you. Have your father and brothers dwell in the best of the land; let them dwell in the land of Goshen. And if you know *any* competent men among them, then make them chief herdsmen over my livestock."

⁷Then Joseph brought in his father Jacob and set him before Pharaoh; and Jacob blessed Pharaoh. ⁸Pharaoh said to Jacob, "How old *are* you?"

⁹And Jacob said to Pharaoh, "The days of the years of my pilgrimage *are* one hundred and thirty years; few and evil have been the days of the years of my life, and they have not attained to the days of the years of the life of my fathers in the days of their pilgrimage." ¹⁰So Jacob blessed Pharaoh, and went out from before Pharaoh.

¹¹And Joseph situated his father and his brothers, and gave them a possession in the land of Egypt, in the best of the land, in the land of Rameses, as Pharaoh had commanded. ¹²Then Joseph provided his father, his brothers, and all his father's household with bread, according to the number in *their* families.

Joseph Deals with the Famine

¹³Now *there was* no bread in all the land; for the famine *was* very severe, so that the land of Egypt and the land of Canaan languished because of the famine. ¹⁴And Joseph gathered up all the money that was found in the land of Egypt and in the land of Canaan, for the grain which they bought; and Joseph brought the money into Pharaoh's house.

¹⁵So when the money failed in the land of Egypt and in the land of Canaan, all the Egyptians came to Joseph and said, "Give us bread, for why should we die in your presence? For the money has failed."

¹⁶Then Joseph said, "Give your livestock, and I will give you *bread* for your livestock, if the money is gone." ¹⁷So they brought their livestock to Joseph, and Joseph gave

them bread *in exchange* for the horses, the flocks, the cattle of the herds, and for the donkeys. Thus he fed them with bread *in exchange* for all their livestock that year.

¹⁸When that year had ended, they came to him the next year and said to him, "We will not hide from my lord that our money is gone; my lord also has our herds of livestock. There is nothing left in the sight of my lord but our bodies and our lands. ¹⁹Why should we die before your eyes, both we and our land? Buy us and our land for bread, and we and our land will be servants of Pharaoh; give *us* seed, that we may live and not die, that the land may not be desolate."

²⁰Then Joseph bought all the land of Egypt for Pharaoh; for every man of the Egyptians sold his field, because the famine was severe upon them. So the land became Pharaoh's. ²¹And as for the people, he moved them into the cities,ᵃ from *one* end of the borders of Egypt to the *other* end. ²²Only the land of the priests he did not buy; for the priests had rations *allotted to them* by Pharaoh, and they ate their rations which Pharaoh gave them; therefore they did not sell their lands.

²³Then Joseph said to the people, "Indeed I have bought you and your land this day for Pharaoh. Look, *here is* seed for you, and you shall sow the land. ²⁴And it shall come to pass in the harvest that you shall give one-fifth to Pharaoh. Four-fifths shall be your own, as seed for the field and for your food, for those of your households and as food for your little ones."

²⁵So they said, "You have saved our lives; let us find favor in the sight of my lord, and we will be Pharaoh's servants." ²⁶And Joseph made it a law over the land of Egypt to this day, *that* Pharaoh should have one-fifth, except for the land of the priests only, *which* did not become Pharaoh's.

Joseph's Vow to Jacob

²⁷So Israel dwelt in the land of Egypt, in the country of Goshen; and they had

47:21 ᵃFollowing Masoretic Text and Targum; Samaritan Pentateuch, Septuagint, and Vulgate read *made the people virtual slaves.*

possessions there and grew and multiplied exceedingly. 28And Jacob lived in the land of Egypt seventeen years. So the length of Jacob's life was one hundred and forty-seven years. 29When the time drew near that Israel must die, he called his son Joseph and said to him, "Now if I have found favor in your sight, please put your hand under my thigh, and deal kindly and truly with me. Please do not bury me in Egypt, 30but let me lie with my fathers; you shall carry me out of Egypt and bury me in their burial place."

And he said, "I will do as you have said."

31Then he said, "Swear to me." And he swore to him. So Israel bowed himself on the head of the bed.

Jacob Blesses Joseph's Sons

48 Now it came to pass after these things that Joseph was told, "Indeed your father *is* sick"; and he took with him his two sons, Manasseh and Ephraim. 2And Jacob was told, "Look, your son Joseph is coming to you"; and Israel strengthened himself and sat up on the bed. 3Then Jacob said to Joseph: "God Almighty appeared to me at Luz in the land of Canaan and blessed me, 4and said to me, 'Behold, I will make you fruitful and multiply you, and I will make of you a multitude of people, and give this land to your descendants after you *as* an everlasting possession.' 5And now your two sons, Ephraim and Manasseh, who were born to you in the land of Egypt before I came to you in Egypt, *are* mine; as Reuben and Simeon, they shall be mine. 6Your offspring whom you beget after them shall be yours; they will be called by the name of their brothers in their inheritance. 7But as for me, when I came from Padan, Rachel died beside me in the land of Canaan on the way, when *there was* but a little distance to go to Ephrath; and I buried her there on the way to Ephrath (that is, Bethlehem)."

8Then Israel saw Joseph's sons, and said, "Who *are* these?"

9Joseph said to his father, "They *are* my sons, whom God has given me in this *place.*"

And he said, "Please bring them to me, and I will bless them." 10Now the eyes of Israel were dim with age, *so that* he could not see. Then Joseph brought them near him, and he kissed them and embraced them. 11And Israel said to Joseph, "I had not thought to see your face; but in fact, God has also shown me your offspring!"

12So Joseph brought them from beside his knees, and he bowed down with his face to the earth. 13And Joseph took them both, Ephraim with his right hand toward Israel's left hand, and Manasseh with his left hand toward Israel's right hand, and brought *them* near him. 14Then Israel stretched out his right hand and laid *it* on Ephraim's head, who *was* the younger, and his left hand on Manasseh's head, guiding his hands knowingly, for Manasseh *was* the firstborn. 15And he blessed Joseph, and said:

> "God, before whom my fathers
>   Abraham and Isaac walked,
>   The God who has fed me all my life
>   long to this day,
> 16 The Angel who has redeemed me
>   from all evil,
>   Bless the lads;
>   Let my name be named upon them,
>   And the name of my fathers
>   Abraham and Isaac;
>   And let them grow into a multitude
>   in the midst of the earth."

17Now when Joseph saw that his father laid his right hand on the head of Ephraim, it displeased him; so he took hold of his father's hand to remove it from Ephraim's head to Manasseh's head. 18And Joseph said to his father, "Not so, my father, for this *one is* the firstborn; put your right hand on his head."

19But his father refused and said, "I know, my son, I know. He also shall become a people, and he also shall be great; but truly his younger brother shall be greater than he, and his descendants shall become a multitude of nations."

20So he blessed them that day, saying, "By you Israel will bless, saying, 'May God make you as Ephraim and as Manasseh!' " And thus he set Ephraim before Manasseh.

21Then Israel said to Joseph, "Behold, I am dying, but God will be with you and bring you back to the land of your fathers. 22Moreover I have given to you one portion above your brothers, which I took from the hand of the Amorite with my sword and my bow."

Jacob's Last Words to His Sons

49 And Jacob called his sons and said, "Gather together, that I may tell you what shall befall you in the last days:

2 "Gather together and hear, you sons of Jacob,
And listen to Israel your father.

3 "Reuben, you are my firstborn,
My might and the beginning of my strength,
The excellency of dignity and the excellency of power.

4 Unstable as water, you shall not excel,
Because you went up to your father's bed;
Then you defiled *it*—
He went up to my couch.

5 "Simeon and Levi *are* brothers;
Instruments of cruelty *are in* their dwelling place.

6 Let not my soul enter their council;
Let not my honor be united to their assembly;
For in their anger they slew a man,
And in their self-will they hamstrung an ox.

7 Cursed *be* their anger, for *it is* fierce;
And their wrath, for it is cruel!
I will divide them in Jacob
And scatter them in Israel.

8 "Judah, you *are he* whom your brothers shall praise;
Your hand *shall be* on the neck of your enemies;
Your father's children shall bow down before you.

9 Judah *is* a lion's whelp;
From the prey, my son, you have gone up.
He bows down, he lies down as a lion;
And as a lion, who shall rouse him?

10 The scepter shall not depart from Judah,
Nor a lawgiver from between his feet,
Until Shiloh comes;
And to Him *shall be* the obedience of the people.

11 Binding his donkey to the vine,
And his donkey's colt to the choice vine,
He washed his garments in wine,
And his clothes in the blood of grapes.

12 His eyes *are* darker than wine,
And his teeth whiter than milk.

PARENTING MATTERS

Q: How can we encourage our children to serve God?

From their earliest days, Dennis and I let our children know that God had a special mission for their lives. Jesus' Great Commission to His disciples (see Matt. 28:19, 20) applies to them as much as it does to us.

God has gifted them with unique abilities, personalities, and qualities that He wants to use to help accomplish His plan. We want our children to know it would be better to be a garbage collector in the will of God than to be on the mission field merely to please their parents.

One great way to instill a service mindset in your child is to go together on a short-term mission trip. Besides the impact you will have for Christ, you will find that your child will change in significant ways as he moves out of his normal comfort zone and sees how much others also need Christ.

Your children will gain a far greater appreciation for what they enjoy in this country, and they will see firsthand what life is like for people in another land. And they will taste both the sacrifice and the joy of being a servant.

¹³ "Zebulun shall dwell by the haven of
the sea;
He *shall become* a haven for ships,
And his border shall adjoin Sidon.

¹⁴ "Issachar is a strong donkey,
Lying down between two burdens;
¹⁵ He saw that rest *was* good,
And that the land *was* pleasant;
He bowed his shoulder to bear *a
burden,*
And became a band of slaves.

¹⁶ "Dan shall judge his people
As one of the tribes of Israel.
¹⁷ Dan shall be a serpent by the way,
A viper by the path,
That bites the horse's heels
So that its rider shall fall backward.
¹⁸ I have waited for your salvation, O
LORD!

¹⁹ "Gad, a troop shall tramp upon him,
But he shall triumph at last.

²⁰ "Bread from Asher *shall be* rich,
And he shall yield royal dainties.

²¹ "Naphtali *is* a deer let loose;
He uses beautiful words.

²² "Joseph *is* a fruitful bough,
A fruitful bough by a well;
His branches run over the wall.
²³ The archers have bitterly grieved
him,
Shot *at him* and hated him.
²⁴ But his bow remained in strength,
And the arms of his hands were
made strong
By the hands of the Mighty *God* of
Jacob
(From there *is* the Shepherd, the
Stone of Israel),
²⁵ By the God of your father who will
help you,
And by the Almighty who will bless
you
With blessings of heaven above,
Blessings of the deep that lies
beneath,
Blessings of the breasts and of the
womb.
²⁶ The blessings of your father
Have excelled the blessings of my
ancestors,

Created for a Purpose

JUST BEFORE JACOB DIED, he gathered his sons around him to give them a stunning prophecy about their futures. He wanted them to know that God had created them all for a purpose.

"For we are His workmanship," Paul wrote, "created in Christ Jesus for good works, which God prepared beforehand that we should walk in them" (Eph. 2:10).

One of the most important things we need to know—and teach our children— is that God has a plan for each of us, and that we need to obediently and purposefully walk in the middle of that plan. God has given each of us unique abilities, personality traits, and other qualities to lead us to and to help us fulfill that plan.

Your children need to know that no matter where they end up professionally or vocationally, it can be in a place where God is able to use their talents and gifts to further His kingdom. Teach your children that God has a unique and special mission for their lives—and that the most fulfilling and blessed place for them to be is obediently and enthusiastically living and walking in a way that fulfills that mission.

Up to the utmost bound of the
everlasting hills.
They shall be on the head of Joseph,
And on the crown of the head of
him who was separate from his
brothers.

²⁷ "Benjamin is a ravenous wolf;
In the morning he shall devour the
prey,
And at night he shall divide the
spoil."

²⁸All these *are* the twelve tribes of Israel, and this *is* what their father spoke to them. And he blessed them; he blessed each one according to his own blessing.

Seek Forgiveness . . . Even If You Don't Feel Like It

Forgiveness is a necessary part of life, for the simple reason that "we all stumble in many things" (James 3:2). When Jacob died, all of Joseph's older brothers approached him with the plea to forgive their wicked treatment of him so many years before—even though Joseph had long ago forgiven them. They wanted to be *sure*.

In a similar way, without the cleansing power of forgiveness, at best marriage will be very hard duty. At worst it will be a disaster. No matter how hard two people try to love and please each other, they will fail. With failure comes hurt—and the only ultimate relief for hurt is the soothing salve of forgiveness.

The key to maintaining an open, intimate, and happy marriage is to ask for and grant forgiveness quickly. About the process of forgiveness, Jesus said, "For if you forgive men their trespasses, your heavenly Father will also forgive you. But if you do not forgive men their trespasses, neither will your Father forgive your trespasses" (Matt. 6:14, 15). His instruction is clear: God insists that we are to be forgivers, and

marriage—probably more than any other relationship—presents frequent opportunities to practice.

To forgive means to give up resentment against or relinquish the desire to punish. By an act of your will, you let the other person off the hook. As a Christian, you do not do this under duress, scratching and screaming in protest. Rather, you do it with a gentle spirit and love, as Paul urged, "Be kind to one another, tenderhearted, forgiving one another, even as God in Christ forgave you" (Eph. 4:32).

The real test of your ability to forgive comes on the battlefield when you and your spouse are ticked off and angry with each other. That is when you need the power of the Holy Spirit and must ask, "God, please help me here. I need to move to forgiveness, because You have commanded me to do so. Please empower me and enable me to give up the right of punishing my spouse and to forgive."

This took practice early in our marriage, but Barbara and I learned how to keep our relationship healthy most of the time by not burning excessive emotional energy on resentment. We grant forgiveness and ask for it freely—even when we don't feel like it.

Jacob's Death and Burial

²⁹Then he charged them and said to them: "I am to be gathered to my people; bury me with my fathers in the cave that *is* in the field of Ephron the Hittite, ³⁰in the cave that *is* in the field of Machpelah, which *is* before Mamre in the land of Canaan, which Abraham bought with the field of Ephron the Hittite as a possession for a burial place. ³¹There they buried Abraham and Sarah his wife, there they buried Isaac and Rebekah his wife, and there I buried Leah. ³²The field and the cave that *is* there *were* purchased from the sons of Heth." ³³And when Jacob had finished commanding his sons, he drew his feet up into the bed and breathed his last, and was gathered to his people.

50 Then Joseph fell on his father's face and wept over him, and kissed him. ²And Joseph commanded his servants the physicians to embalm his father. So the physicians embalmed Israel. ³Forty days were required for him, for such are the days required for those who are embalmed; and the Egyptians mourned for him seventy days.

⁴Now when the days of his mourning were past, Joseph spoke to the household of Pharaoh, saying, "If now I have found favor in your eyes, please speak in the hearing of Pharaoh, saying, ⁵'My father made me swear, saying, "Behold, I am dying; in my grave which I dug for myself in the land of Canaan, there you shall bury me." Now therefore, please let me go up and bury my father, and I will come back.' "

⁶And Pharaoh said, "Go up and bury your father, as he made you swear."

⁷So Joseph went up to bury his father; and with him went up all the servants of Pharaoh, the elders of his house, and all the elders of the land of Egypt, ⁸as well as all the house of Joseph, his brothers, and his father's house. Only their little ones, their flocks, and their herds they left in the land of Goshen. ⁹And there went up with him both chariots and horsemen, and it was a very great gathering.

¹⁰Then they came to the threshing floor of Atad, which *is* beyond the Jordan, and they mourned there with a great and very solemn lamentation. He observed seven days of mourning for his father. ¹¹And when the inhabitants of the land, the Canaanites, saw the mourning at the threshing floor of Atad, they said, "This *is* a deep mourning of the Egyptians." Therefore its name was called Abel Mizraim,ᵃ which *is* beyond the Jordan.

¹²So his sons did for him just as he had commanded them. ¹³For his sons carried him to the land of Canaan, and buried him in the cave of the field of Machpelah, before Mamre, which Abraham bought with the field from Ephron the Hittite as property for a burial place. ¹⁴And after he had buried his father, Joseph returned to Egypt, he and his brothers and all who went up with him to bury his father.

Joseph Reassures His Brothers

¹⁵When Joseph's brothers saw that their father was dead, they said, "Perhaps Joseph will hate us, and may actually repay us for all the evil which we did to him." ¹⁶So they sent *messengers* to Joseph, saying, "Before your father died he commanded, saying, ¹⁷'Thus you shall say to Joseph: "I beg you, please forgive the trespass of your brothers and their sin; for they did evil to you."' Now, please, forgive the trespass of the servants of the God of your father." And Joseph wept when they spoke to him. ¹⁸Then his brothers also went and fell down before his face, and they said, "Behold, we *are* your servants."

BIBLICAL INSIGHTS • 50:21

Speak Affirming Words

CAN YOU IMAGINE how relieved Joseph's brothers felt when their now-powerful younger sibling told them, "Do not be afraid; I will provide for you and your little ones"? And can you picture their body language when he "comforted them and spoke kindly to them" (50:21)? Joseph's words were powerful.

Our wives need the same kind of affirming words that create security and comfort. To encourage and bless your wife, affirm her consistently with pleasant, loving words. Let her know that you value, respect, and love her. Some evenings I come home, and I'm absolutely amazed at how busy Barbara has been for me and the children. Running errands, settling squabbles, fixing meals—the list is endless.

Occasionally, I'll miss my cue to encourage her and she'll say, "You know what I would like you to do? Just tell me you appreciate what I'm doing for you!" You can tell your wife how much you appreciate her through specific compliments:

- "I appreciate your efforts to keep my clothes clean and pressed. You're incredible!"
- "Thanks for looking so nice today."
- "I appreciate always being able to count on you to follow through, no matter what."
- "Thanks for being there—for always putting the children and me ahead of yourself."

¹⁹Joseph said to them, "Do not be afraid, for *am* I in the place of God? ²⁰But as for you, you meant evil against me; *but* God meant it for good, in order to bring it about as *it is* this day, to save many people alive. ²¹Now therefore, do not be afraid; I will provide for you and your little ones." And he comforted them and spoke kindly to them.

50:11 ᵃLiterally *Mourning of Egypt*

Death of Joseph

22So Joseph dwelt in Egypt, he and his father's household. And Joseph lived one hundred and ten years. 23Joseph saw Ephraim's children to the third *generation.* The children of Machir, the son of Manasseh, were also brought up on Joseph's knees.

24And Joseph said to his brethren, "I am dying; but God will surely visit you, and bring you out of this land to the land of which He swore to Abraham, to Isaac, and to Jacob." 25Then Joseph took an oath from the children of Israel, saying, "God will surely visit you, and you shall carry up my bones from here." 26So Joseph died, *being* one hundred and ten years old; and they embalmed him, and he was put in a coffin in Egypt.

EXODUS

THE CENTRAL THEME OF THE BOOK OF EXODUS is God's gracious deliverance of His people. It describes how the ancient Israelites, after spending generations in cruel bondage, are set free from their shackles by the power and love of God—and yet how, time and again, they respond with fickle hearts. How quickly they go from gratitude to grumbling, and even outright rebellion, when their journey from slavery to the land of promise gets difficult!

Sadly, we're not so different from them, are we? In Christ, God has delivered repentant men and women from slavery to sin—and yet we fall back into old sinful patterns and start grumbling when our journey gets hard! The Book of Exodus reminds us that human hardship does not equal divine abandonment, nor does following God always lead to comfort and ease. It does, however, always lead to God's best ... in the end. As the Lord told his people, "But if you indeed ... do all that I speak, then I will be an enemy to your enemies and an adversary to your adversaries ... I will fulfill the number of your days" (Ex. 23:22, 26).

At the very heart of this book you will find the Ten Commandments, given by God to Moses on Mt. Sinai. While the Lord ordered the people to keep their distance from the smoking mountain, Moses climbed to the summit and there met with God. After forty days, God finished speaking to Moses and gave him "two tablets of the Testimony, tablets of stone, written with the finger of God" (Ex. 31:18).

The holy words inscribed on those tablets "written with the finger of God" make it clear once more that the Lord expects His people to make marriage and family relationships a priority. In particular, the Fifth Commandment ("Honor your father and your mother.") and the Seventh Commandment ("You shall not commit adultery.") mandate respect for parents and faithfulness in marriage. God loves to bless obedience! And so He promises to bless those who give marriage and the family the place of honor they deserve.

Israel's Suffering in Egypt

1 Now these *are* the names of the children of Israel who came to Egypt; each man and his household came with Jacob: [2]Reuben, Simeon, Levi, and Judah; [3]Issachar, Zebulun, and Benjamin; [4]Dan, Naphtali, Gad, and Asher. [5]All those who were descendants[a] of Jacob were seventy[b] persons (for Joseph was in Egypt *already*). [6]And Joseph died, all his brothers, and all that generation. [7]But the children of Israel were fruitful and increased abundantly, multiplied and grew exceedingly mighty; and the land was filled with them.

[8]Now there arose a new king over Egypt, who did not know Joseph. [9]And he said to his people, "Look, the people of the children of Israel *are* more and mightier than we; [10]come, let us deal shrewdly with them, lest they multiply, and it happen, in the event of war, that they also join our enemies and fight against us, and *so* go up out of the land." [11]Therefore they set taskmasters over them to afflict them with their burdens. And they built for Pharaoh supply cities, Pithom and Raamses. [12]But the more they afflicted them, the more they multiplied and grew. And they were in dread of the children of Israel. [13]So the Egyptians made the children of Israel serve with rigor. [14]And they made their lives bitter with hard bondage—in mortar, in brick, and in all manner of service in the field. All their service in which they made them serve *was* with rigor.

[15]Then the king of Egypt spoke to the Hebrew midwives, of whom the name of one *was* Shiphrah and the name of the other Puah; [16]and he said, "When you do the duties of a midwife for the Hebrew women, and see *them* on the birthstools, if it *is* a son, then you shall kill him; but if it *is* a daughter, then she shall live." [17]But the midwives feared God, and did not do as the king of Egypt commanded them, but saved the male children alive. [18]So the king of Egypt called for the midwives and said to them, "Why have you done this thing, and saved the male children alive?"

1:5 [a]Literally *who came from the loins of* [b]Dead Sea Scrolls and Septuagint read *seventy-five* (compare Acts 7:14)

Help Your Mate Fulfill His/Her Purpose

Before you try to discover how you can love and serve God fully in your life and in your marriage, you must understand a few key truths. Without them, you would be like an old-time miner descending into a gold or silver mine to search for precious metals with no hard hat, pick, or flashlight.

First, God is intricately and ingeniously involved in creation. He knows the grains of sand in the ocean (Gen. 22:17), the names of all the stars (Ps. 147:4), the number of hairs on your head, and the very instant every little sparrow dies (Matt. 10:29, 30). If He knows the tiny details from the bottom of the ocean to the ends of the universe, then we can correctly assume that He knows everything that is going on in our lives as well.

Second, God is sovereign. He is fully in charge. He has a divine design for each life. God's overall plan, clearly, is to redeem humanity to Himself. Incredibly, He has chosen to use men and women like you and like us to execute His plan of influencing eternity.

Third, you are God's workmanship, and He created you to be part of fulfilling His plans for humanity (Eph. 2:10). God has woven a plan in every person's heart that is revealed over time. He wants us to help each other discover these passions and to have a vision for our lives. Discuss with your spouse what he or she is passionate about. What's his vision? What would she do if she knew she couldn't fail? You can be a human crowbar that dislodges dreams, goals, and unexpressed desires from inside your spouse's heart.

As you discuss together the greatness of God and the unspeakable privilege of being chosen by Him, you'll quickly discover what a privilege it is to have a part in serving Him and His kingdom.

He does have a plan for each person.

¹⁹And the midwives said to Pharaoh, "Because the Hebrew women *are* not like the Egyptian women; for they *are* lively and give birth before the midwives come to them."

²⁰Therefore God dealt well with the midwives, and the people multiplied and grew very mighty. ²¹And so it was, because the midwives feared God, that He provided households for them.

²²So Pharaoh commanded all his people, saying, "Every son who is bornᵃ you shall cast into the river, and every daughter you shall save alive."

Moses Is Born

2 And a man of the house of Levi went and took *as wife* a daughter of Levi. ²So the woman conceived and bore a son. And when she saw that he *was* a beautiful *child,* she hid him three months. ³But when she could no longer hide him, she took an ark of bulrushes for him, daubed it with asphalt and pitch, put the child in it, and laid *it* in the reeds by the river's bank. ⁴And his sister stood afar off, to know what would be done to him.

⁵Then the daughter of Pharaoh came down to bathe at the river. And her maidens walked along the riverside; and when she saw the ark among the reeds, she sent her maid to get it. ⁶And when she opened *it,* she saw the child, and behold, the baby wept. So she had compassion on him, and said, "This is one of the Hebrews' children."

⁷Then his sister said to Pharaoh's daughter, "Shall I go and call a nurse for you from the Hebrew women, that she may nurse the child for you?"

⁸And Pharaoh's daughter said to her, "Go." So the maiden went and called the child's mother. ⁹Then Pharaoh's daughter said to her, "Take this child away and nurse him for me, and I will give *you* your wages." So the woman took the child and nursed him. ¹⁰And the child grew, and she brought him to Pharaoh's daughter, and he became her son. So she called his name Moses,ᵃ saying, "Because I drew him out of the water."

Moses Flees to Midian

¹¹Now it came to pass in those days, when Moses was grown, that he went out to his brethren and looked at their burdens. And he saw an Egyptian beating a Hebrew, one of his brethren. ¹²So he looked this way and that way, and when he saw no one, he killed the Egyptian and hid him in the sand. ¹³And when he went out the second day, behold, two Hebrew men were fighting, and he said to the one who did the wrong, "Why are you striking your companion?"

¹⁴Then he said, "Who made you a prince and a judge over us? Do you intend to kill me as you killed the Egyptian?"

So Moses feared and said, "Surely this thing is known!" ¹⁵When Pharaoh heard of this matter, he sought to kill Moses. But Moses fled from the face of Pharaoh and dwelt in the land of Midian; and he sat down by a well.

¹⁶Now the priest of Midian had seven daughters. And they came and drew water, and they filled the troughs to water their father's flock. ¹⁷Then the shepherds came and drove them away; but Moses stood up and helped them, and watered their flock.

¹⁸When they came to Reuel their father, he said, "How *is it that* you have come so soon today?"

¹⁹And they said, "An Egyptian delivered us from the hand of the shepherds, and he also drew enough water for us and watered the flock."

²⁰So he said to his daughters, "And where *is* he? Why *is* it *that* you have left the man? Call him, that he may eat bread."

²¹Then Moses was content to live with the man, and he gave Zipporah his daughter to Moses. ²²And she bore *him* a son. He called his name Gershom,ᵃ for he said, "I have been a stranger in a foreign land."

²³Now it happened in the process of time that the king of Egypt died. Then the children of Israel groaned because of the bondage, and they cried out; and their cry came up to God because of the bondage. ²⁴So God heard their groaning, and God remembered His covenant with Abraham, with Isaac, and with Jacob. ²⁵And God looked upon the children of Israel, and God acknowledged *them.*

1:22 ᵃSamaritan Pentateuch, Septuagint, and Targum add *to the Hebrews.* **2:10** ᵃLiterally *Drawn Out*
2:22 ᵃLiterally *Stranger There*

DEVOTIONS FOR COUPLES • 3:1-22
An Anatomy of Failure

Exodus 3 begins with Moses in exile. He has just murdered an Egyptian and, fearing for his life, has fled from Pharaoh into the wilderness. The chapter is really a sober look at the anatomy of failure.

For forty years, Moses lived in the desert, hounded by a host of condemning voices. By the time God appeared to him in the burning bush, Moses was struggling with an identity problem—the result of failure and rejection. After forty years of exile in the desert, self-doubt filled his heart.

God told Moses that He was going to send him to free the Israelites, to which Moses responded, "Who am I?" God simply replied, "I will be with you." The ultimate solution for Moses' lack of confidence and doubt was God's reassuring presence. Without Him, Moses could never stand before Pharaoh. Left alone, he would certainly fail.

Moses' next question was, in effect, "Who are You? What is the name of the One who sends me?" God then gave Moses two signs of His divine presence. First, He transformed Moses' staff into a serpent. Second, he instantly afflicted Moses' hand with leprosy, and then immediately restored it. These two visual aids reminded Moses that God's presence was both powerful and transforming.

Yet despite these miraculous displays of God's omnipotence, Moses continued to focus and complain about his inadequacies. God graciously reminded Moses who made his mouth and told Moses that He would teach him what to say. Still, Moses essentially said, "I can't do what You've asked. Please choose someone else." Moses was like the little boy in the school play who had one line to deliver: "It is I; be not afraid." But on the night of the play, the frightened boy exclaimed, "It's me, and I'm scared!"

Only when Moses saw no way out did he submit to God's call. He felt so convinced of his own worthlessness that it took time for God to convince him otherwise.

Likewise, your mate may be plagued by failure and struggle with voices that whisper, "You're a big failure!" He or she may have a difficult time believing God and you.

God's solution to Moses' self-image problem was to provide a companion: Aaron. Undoubtedly, Aaron frequently reminded Moses of the truth that he really was God's man for the assignment, and that God would remain faithful to His promises.

That's God's role for you in your marriage. Just as Moses needed Aaron, so your mate needs you to remind him or her of the truth. Over the years, Barbara has used timely truthful words to refresh my memory and encourage me to keep fulfilling God's assignment for me. Never forget your words can be like a paintbrush, painting a picture, or like an ice pick, chipping away at your spouse. Fulfill your assignment in marriage carefully.

Moses at the Burning Bush

3 Now Moses was tending the flock of Jethro his father-in-law, the priest of Midian. And he led the flock to the back of the desert, and came to Horeb, the mountain of God. ²And the Angel of the LORD appeared to him in a flame of fire from the midst of a bush. So he looked, and behold, the bush was burning with fire, but the bush *was* not consumed. ³Then Moses said, "I will now turn aside and see this great sight, why the bush does not burn."

⁴So when the LORD saw that he turned aside to look, God called to him from the midst of the bush and said, "Moses, Moses!"

And he said, "Here I am."

⁵Then He said, "Do not draw near this place. Take your sandals off your feet, for the place where you stand *is* holy ground." ⁶Moreover He said, "I *am* the God of your

father—the God of Abraham, the God of Isaac, and the God of Jacob." And Moses hid his face, for he was afraid to look upon God.

7And the LORD said: "I have surely seen the oppression of My people who *are* in Egypt, and have heard their cry because of their taskmasters, for I know their sorrows. 8So I have come down to deliver them out of the hand of the Egyptians, and to bring them up from that land to a good and large land, to a land flowing with milk and honey, to the place of the Canaanites and the Hittites and the Amorites and the Perizzites and the Hivites and the Jebusites. 9Now therefore, behold, the cry of the children of Israel has come to Me, and I have also seen the oppression with which the Egyptians oppress them. 10Come now, therefore, and I will send you to Pharaoh that you may bring My people, the children of Israel, out of Egypt."

11But Moses said to God, "Who *am* I that I should go to Pharaoh, and that I should bring the children of Israel out of Egypt?"

12So He said, "I will certainly be with you. And this *shall be* a sign to you that I have sent you: When you have brought the people out of Egypt, you shall serve God on this mountain."

13Then Moses said to God, "Indeed, *when* I come to the children of Israel and say to them, 'The God of your fathers has sent me to you,' and they say to me, 'What *is* His name?' what shall I say to them?"

14And God said to Moses, "I AM WHO I AM." And He said, "Thus you shall say to the children of Israel, 'I AM has sent me to you.'" 15Moreover God said to Moses, "Thus you shall say to the children of Israel: 'The LORD God of your fathers, the God of Abraham, the God of Isaac, and the God of Jacob, has sent me to you. This *is* My name forever, and this *is* My memorial to all generations.' 16Go and gather the elders of Israel together, and say to them, 'The LORD God of your fathers, the God of Abraham, of Isaac, and of Jacob, appeared to me, saying, "I have surely visited you and *seen* what is done to you in Egypt; 17and I have said I will bring you up out of the affliction of Egypt to the land of the Canaanites and

the Hittites and the Amorites and the Perizzites and the Hivites and the Jebusites, to a land flowing with milk and honey." ' 18Then they will heed your voice; and you shall come, you and the elders of Israel, to the king of Egypt; and you shall say to him, 'The LORD God of the Hebrews has met with us; and now, please, let us go three days' journey into the wilderness, that we may sacrifice to the LORD our God.' 19But I am sure that the king of Egypt will not let you go, no, not even by a mighty hand. 20So I will stretch out My hand and strike Egypt with all My wonders which I will do in its midst; and after that he will let you go. 21And I will give this people favor in the sight of the Egyptians; and it shall be, when you go, that you shall not go empty-handed. 22But every woman shall ask of her neighbor, namely, of her who dwells near her house, articles of silver, articles of gold, and clothing; and you shall put *them* on your sons and on your daughters. So you shall plunder the Egyptians."

Miraculous Signs for Pharaoh

4 Then Moses answered and said, "But suppose they will not believe me or listen to my voice; suppose they say, 'The LORD has not appeared to you.'"

2So the LORD said to him, "What *is* that in your hand?"

He said, "A rod."

3And He said, "Cast it on the ground." So he cast it on the ground, and it became a serpent; and Moses fled from it. 4Then the LORD said to Moses, "Reach out your hand and take *it* by the tail" (and he reached out his hand and caught it, and it became a rod in his hand), 5"that they may believe that the LORD God of their fathers, the God of Abraham, the God of Isaac, and the God of Jacob, has appeared to you."

6Furthermore the LORD said to him, "Now put your hand in your bosom." And he put his hand in his bosom, and when he took it out, behold, his hand *was* leprous, like snow. 7And He said, "Put your hand in your bosom again." So he put his hand in his bosom again, and drew it out of his bosom, and behold, it was restored like his *other* flesh. 8"Then it will be, if they do not believe you, nor heed the message of the

BIBLICAL INSIGHTS • 4:14
Demonstrate Anger Appropriately

ANGER IS A GOD-GIVEN, God-created emotion that the Lord himself demonstrated on many occasions throughout human history, as He did with Moses, "So the anger of the LORD was kindled against Moses" (4:14).

Unfortunately, there is a big difference between God and us. While God is perfect in every way—including in how He experiences and demonstrates His anger—we are prone to experiencing and expressing our anger in inappropriate, sinful ways. Too often, our anger is not a righteous anger like God's is. God becomes angry at unrighteousness; we usually become angry when we don't get our own way or we feel slighted in some way.

If we want to have successful, satisfying marriages, if we want to be the kind of parents who teach their children to express themselves correctly, then we need to learn to distinguish between appropriate and inappropriate expressions of our anger, and we need to learn to express our anger appropriately.

Because many adults don't know how to properly handle their own anger, they respond in hurtful ways when their spouse or their children express anger inappropriately. So what may have begun as a child sinning devolves into two children sinning, one an adult child and the other an adolescent.

first sign, that they may believe the message of the latter sign. ⁹And it shall be, if they do not believe even these two signs, or listen to your voice, that you shall take water from the river[a] and pour *it* on the dry *land*. The water which you take from the river will become blood on the dry *land*."

¹⁰Then Moses said to the LORD, "O my Lord, I *am* not eloquent, neither before nor since You have spoken to Your servant; but I *am* slow of speech and slow of tongue."

¹¹So the LORD said to him, "Who has made man's mouth? Or who makes the mute, the deaf, the seeing, or the blind? *Have* not I, the LORD? ¹²Now therefore, go, and I will be with your mouth and teach you what you shall say."

¹³But he said, "O my Lord, please send by the hand of whomever *else* You may send."

¹⁴So the anger of the LORD was kindled against Moses, and He said: "Is not Aaron the Lemvite your brother? I know that he can speak well. And look, he is also coming out to meet you. When he sees you, he will be glad in his heart. ¹⁵Now you shall speak to him and put the words in his mouth. And I will be with your mouth and with his mouth, and I will teach you what you shall do. ¹⁶So he shall be your spokesman to the people. And he himself shall be as a mouth for you, and you shall be to him as God. ¹⁷And you shall take this rod in your hand, with which you shall do the signs."

Moses Goes to Egypt

¹⁸So Moses went and returned to Jethro his father-in-law, and said to him, "Please let me go and return to my brethren who *are* in Egypt, and see whether they are still alive."

And Jethro said to Moses, "Go in peace."

¹⁹Now the LORD said to Moses in Midian, "Go, return to Egypt; for all the men who sought your life are dead." ²⁰Then Moses took his wife and his sons and set them on a donkey, and he returned to the land of Egypt. And Moses took the rod of God in his hand.

²¹And the LORD said to Moses, "When you go back to Egypt, see that you do all those wonders before Pharaoh which I have put in your hand. But I will harden his heart, so that he will not let the people go. ²²Then you shall say to Pharaoh, 'Thus says the LORD: "Israel *is* My son, My firstborn. ²³So I say to you, let My son go that he may serve Me. But if you refuse to let him go, indeed I will kill your son, your firstborn."'"

²⁴And it came to pass on the way, at the encampment, that the LORD met him and sought to kill him. ²⁵Then Zipporah took a sharp stone and cut off the foreskin of her son and cast *it* at *Moses'*[a] feet, and said,

4:9 ᵃThat is, the Nile 4:25 ᵃLiterally *his*

"Surely you *are* a husband of blood to me!" ²⁶So He let him go. Then she said, "*You are* a husband of blood!"—because of the circumcision.

²⁷And the LORD said to Aaron, "Go into the wilderness to meet Moses." So he went and met him on the mountain of God, and kissed him. ²⁸So Moses told Aaron all the words of the LORD who had sent him, and all the signs which He had commanded him. ²⁹Then Moses and Aaron went and gathered together all the elders of the children of Israel. ³⁰And Aaron spoke all the words which the LORD had spoken to Moses. Then he did the signs in the sight of the people. ³¹So the people believed; and when they heard that the LORD had visited the children of Israel and that He had looked on their affliction, then they bowed their heads and worshiped.

First Encounter with Pharaoh

5 Afterward Moses and Aaron went in and told Pharaoh, "Thus says the LORD God of Israel: 'Let My people go, that they may hold a feast to Me in the wilderness.'"

²And Pharaoh said, "Who *is* the LORD, that I should obey His voice to let Israel go? I do not know the LORD, nor will I let Israel go."

³So they said, "The God of the Hebrews has met with us. Please, let us go three days' journey into the desert and sacrifice to the LORD our God, lest He fall upon us with pestilence or with the sword."

⁴Then the king of Egypt said to them, "Moses and Aaron, why do you take the people from their work? Get *back* to your labor." ⁵And Pharaoh said, "Look, the people of the land *are* many now, and you make them rest from their labor!"

⁶So the same day Pharaoh commanded the taskmasters of the people and their officers, saying, ⁷"You shall no longer give the people straw to make brick as before. Let them go and gather straw for themselves. ⁸And you shall lay on them the quota of bricks which they made before. You shall not reduce it. For they are idle; therefore they cry out, saying, 'Let us go *and* sacrifice to our God.' ⁹Let more work be laid on the men, that they may labor in it, and let them not regard false words."

¹⁰And the taskmasters of the people and their officers went out and spoke to the people, saying, "Thus says Pharaoh: 'I will not give you straw. ¹¹Go, get yourselves straw where you can find it; yet none of your work will be reduced.'" ¹²So the people were scattered abroad throughout all the land of Egypt to gather stubble instead of straw. ¹³And the taskmasters forced *them* to hurry, saying, "Fulfill your work, *your* daily quota, as when there was straw." ¹⁴Also the officers of the children of Israel, whom Pharaoh's taskmasters had set over them, were beaten *and* were asked, "Why have you not fulfilled your task in making brick both yesterday and today, as before?"

¹⁵Then the officers of the children of Israel came and cried out to Pharaoh, saying, "Why are you dealing thus with your servants? ¹⁶There is no straw given to your servants, and they say to us, 'Make brick!' And indeed your servants *are* beaten, but the fault *is* in your *own* people."

¹⁷But he said, "You *are* idle! Idle! Therefore you say, 'Let us go *and* sacrifice to the LORD.' ¹⁸Therefore go now *and* work; for no straw shall be given you, yet you shall deliver the quota of bricks." ¹⁹And the officers of the children of Israel saw *that* they *were* in trouble after it was said, "You shall not reduce *any* bricks from your daily quota."

²⁰Then, as they came out from Pharaoh, they met Moses and Aaron who stood there to meet them. ²¹And they said to them, "Let the LORD look on you and judge, because you have made us abhorrent in the sight of Pharaoh and in the sight of his servants, to put a sword in their hand to kill us."

Israel's Deliverance Assured

²²So Moses returned to the LORD and said, "Lord, why have You brought trouble on this people? Why *is* it You have sent me? ²³For since I came to Pharaoh to speak in Your name, he has done evil to this people; neither have You delivered Your people at all."

6 Then the LORD said to Moses, "Now you shall see what I will do to Pharaoh. For with a strong hand he will let them go, and with a strong hand he will drive them out of his land."

²And God spoke to Moses and said to him: "I *am* the LORD. ³I appeared to Abraham, to Isaac, and to Jacob, as God Almighty, but *by* My name LORD[a] I was not known to them. ⁴I have also established My covenant with them, to give them the land of Canaan, the land of their pilgrimage, in which they were strangers. ⁵And I have also heard the groaning of the children of Israel whom the Egyptians keep in bondage, and I have remembered My covenant. ⁶Therefore say to the children of Israel: 'I *am* the LORD; I will bring you out from under the burdens of the Egyptians, I will rescue you from their bondage, and I will redeem you with an outstretched arm and with great judgments. ⁷I will take you as My people, and I will be your God. Then you shall know that I *am* the LORD your God who brings you out from under the burdens of the Egyptians. ⁸And I will bring you into the land which I swore to give to Abraham, Isaac, and Jacob; and I will give it to you *as* a heritage: I *am* the LORD.'" ⁹So Moses spoke thus to the children of Israel; but they did not heed Moses, because of anguish of spirit and cruel bondage.

¹⁰And the LORD spoke to Moses, saying, ¹¹"Go in, tell Pharaoh king of Egypt to let the children of Israel go out of his land."

¹²And Moses spoke before the LORD, saying, "The children of Israel have not heeded me. How then shall Pharaoh heed me, for I *am* of uncircumcised lips?"

¹³Then the LORD spoke to Moses and Aaron, and gave them a command for the children of Israel and for Pharaoh king of Egypt, to bring the children of Israel out of the land of Egypt.

The Family of Moses and Aaron

¹⁴These *are* the heads of their fathers' houses: The sons of Reuben, the firstborn of Israel, *were* Hanoch, Pallu, Hezron, and Carmi. These are the families of Reuben. ¹⁵And the sons of Simeon *were* Jemuel,[a] Jamin, Ohad, Jachin, Zohar, and Shaul the son of a Canaanite woman. These *are* the families of Simeon. ¹⁶These *are* the names of the sons of Levi according to their generations: Gershon, Kohath, and Merari. And the years of the life of Levi *were* one hundred and thirty-seven. ¹⁷The sons of Gershon *were* Libni and Shimi according to their families. ¹⁸And the sons of Kohath *were* Amram, Izhar, Hembron, and Uzziel. And the years of the life of Kohath *were* one hundred and thirty-three. ¹⁹The sons of Merari *were* Mahli and Mushi. These *are* the families of Levi according to their generations.

²⁰Now Amram took for himself Jochebed, his father's sister, as wife; and she bore him Aaron and Moses. And the years of the life of Amram *were* one hundred and thirty-seven. ²¹The sons of Izhar *were* Korah, Nempheg, and Zichri. ²²And the sons of Uzziel *were* Mishael, Elzaphan, and Zithri. ²³Aaron took to himself Elisheba, daughter of Amminadab, sister of Nahshon, as wife; and she bore him Nadab, Abihu, Eleazar, and Ithamar. ²⁴And the sons of Korah *were* Assir, Elkanah, and Abiasaph. These are the families of the Korahites. ²⁵Eleazar, Aaron's son, took for himself one of the daughters of Putiel as wife; and she bore him Phinehas. These *are* the heads of the fathers' houses of the Levites according to their families.

²⁶These *are the same* Aaron and Moses to whom the LORD said, "Bring out the children of Israel from the land of Egypt according to their armies." ²⁷These *are* the ones who spoke to Pharaoh king of Egypt, to bring out the children of Israel from Egypt. These *are the same* Moses and Aaron.

INTIMATE MOMENTS

Write an endearing message to your husband on cardstock, and then cut it into five puzzle pieces. For four continuous days, mail him just one of the pieces. On the fifth day, reveal when and where he should meet you to get the final piece of the puzzle.

6:3 [a]Hebrew *YHWH*, traditionally *Jehovah*
6:15 [a]Spelled *Nemuel* in Numbers 26:12

Aaron Is Moses' Spokesman

[28]And it came to pass, on the day the LORD spoke to Moses in the land of Egypt, [29]that the LORD spoke to Moses, saying, "I *am* the LORD. Speak to Pharaoh king of Egypt all that I say to you."

[30]But Moses said before the LORD, "Behold, I *am* of uncircumcised lips, and how shall Pharaoh heed me?"

7 So the LORD said to Moses: "See, I have made you *as* God to Pharaoh, and Aaron your brother shall be your prophet. [2]You shall speak all that I command you. And Aaron your brother shall tell Pharaoh to send the children of Israel out of his land. [3]And I will harden Pharaoh's heart, and multiply My signs and My wonders in the land of Egypt. [4]But Pharaoh will not heed you, so that I may lay My hand on Egypt and bring My armies *and* My people, the children of Israel, out of the land of Egypt by great judgments. [5]And the Egyptians shall know that I *am* the LORD, when I stretch out My hand on Egypt and bring out the children of Israel from among them."

[6]Then Moses and Aaron did *so;* just as the LORD commanded them, so they did. [7]And Moses *was* eighty years old and Aaron eighty-three years old when they spoke to Pharaoh.

Aaron's Miraculous Rod

[8]Then the LORD spoke to Moses and Aaron, saying, [9]"When Pharaoh speaks to you, saying, 'Show a miracle for yourselves,' then you shall say to Aaron, 'Take your rod and cast *it* before Pharaoh, *and* let it become a serpent.'" [10]So Moses and Aaron went in to Pharaoh, and they did so, just as the LORD commanded. And Aaron cast down his rod before Pharaoh and before his servants, and it became a serpent. [11]But Pharaoh also called the wise men and the sorcerers; so the magicians of Egypt, they also did in like manner with their enchantments. [12]For every man threw down his rod, and they became serpents. But Aaron's rod swallowed up their rods. [13]And Pharaoh's heart grew hard, and he did not heed them, as the LORD had said.

The First Plague: Waters Become Blood

[14]So the LORD said to Moses: "Pharaoh's heart *is* hard; he refuses to let the people go. [15]Go to Pharaoh in the morning, when he goes out to the water, and you shall stand by the river's bank to meet him; and the rod which was turned to a serpent you shall take in your hand. [16]And you shall say to him, 'The LORD God of the Hebrews has sent me to you, saying, "Let My people go, that they may serve Me in the wilderness"; but indeed, until now you would not hear! [17]Thus says the LORD: "By this you shall know that I *am* the LORD. Behold, I will strike the waters which *are* in the river with the rod that *is* in my hand, and they shall be turned to blood. [18]And the fish that *are* in the river shall die, the river shall stink, and the Egyptians will loathe to drink the water of the river."'"

[19]Then the LORD spoke to Moses, "Say to Aaron, 'Take your rod and stretch out your hand over the waters of Egypt, over their streams, over their rivers, over their ponds, and over all their pools of water, that they may become blood. And there shall be blood throughout all the land of Egypt, both in *buckets of* wood and *pitchers of* stone.'" [20]And Moses and Aaron did so, just as the LORD commanded. So he lifted up the rod and struck the waters that *were* in the river, in the sight of Pharaoh and in the sight of his servants. And all the waters that *were* in the river were turned to blood. [21]The fish that *were* in the river died, the river stank, and the Egyptians could not drink the water of the river. So there was blood throughout all the land of Egypt.

[22]Then the magicians of Egypt did so with their enchantments; and Pharaoh's heart grew hard, and he did not heed them, as the LORD had said. [23]And Pharaoh turned and went into his house. Neither was his heart moved by this. [24]So all the Egyptians dug all around the river for water to drink, because they could not drink the water of the river. [25]And seven days passed after the LORD had struck the river.

The Second Plague: Frogs

8 And the LORD spoke to Moses, "Go to Pharaoh and say to him, 'Thus says

the LORD: "Let My people go, that they may serve Me. ²But if you refuse to let *them* go, behold, I will smite all your territory with frogs. ³So the river shall bring forth frogs abundantly, which shall go up and come into your house, into your bedroom, on your bed, into the houses of your servants, on your people, into your ovens, and into your kneading bowls. ⁴And the frogs shall come up on you, on your people, and on all your servants.""'

⁵Then the LORD spoke to Moses, "Say to Aaron, 'Stretch out your hand with your rod over the streams, over the rivers, and over the ponds, and cause frogs to come up on the land of Egypt.'" ⁶So Aaron stretched out his hand over the waters of Egypt, and the frogs came up and covered the land of Egypt. ⁷And the magicians did so with their enchantments, and brought up frogs on the land of Egypt.

⁸Then Pharaoh called for Moses and Aaron, and said, "Entreat the LORD that He may take away the frogs from me and from my people; and I will let the people go, that they may sacrifice to the LORD."

⁹And Moses said to Pharaoh, "Accept the honor of saying when I shall intercede for you, for your servants, and for your people, to destroy the frogs from you and your houses, *that* they may remain in the river only."

¹⁰So he said, "Tomorrow." And he said, "*Let it be* according to your word, that you may know that *there is* no one like the LORD our God. ¹¹And the frogs shall depart from you, from your houses, from your servants, and from your people. They shall remain in the river only."

¹²Then Moses and Aaron went out from Pharaoh. And Moses cried out to the LORD concerning the frogs which He had brought against Pharaoh. ¹³So the LORD did according to the word of Moses. And the frogs died out of the houses, out of the courtyards, and out of the fields. ¹⁴They gathered them together in heaps, and the land stank. ¹⁵But when Pharaoh saw that there was relief, he hardened his heart and did not heed them, as the LORD had said.

The Third Plague: Lice

¹⁶So the LORD said to Moses, "Say to Aaron, 'Stretch out your rod, and strike the dust of the land, so that it may become lice throughout all the land of Egypt.'" ¹⁷And they did so. For Aaron stretched out his hand with his rod and struck the dust of the earth, and it became lice on man and beast. All the dust of the land became lice throughout all the land of Egypt.

¹⁸Now the magicians so worked with their enchantments to bring forth lice, but they could not. So there were lice on man and beast. ¹⁹Then the magicians said to Pharaoh, "This *is* the finger of God." But Pharaoh's heart grew hard, and he did not heed them, just as the LORD had said.

The Fourth Plague: Flies

²⁰And the LORD said to Moses, "Rise early in the morning and stand before Pharaoh as he comes out to the water. Then say to him, 'Thus says the LORD: "Let My people go, that they may serve Me. ²¹Or else, if you will not let My people go, behold, I will send swarms *of flies* on you and your servants, on your people and into your houses. The houses of the Egyptians shall be full of swarms *of flies,* and also the ground on which they *stand.* ²²And in that day I will set apart the land of Goshen, in which My people dwell, that no swarms *of flies* shall be there, in order that you may know that I *am* the LORD in the midst of the land. ²³I will make a differenceª between My people and your people. Tomorrow this sign shall be."'" ²⁴And the LORD did so. Thick swarms *of flies* came into the house of Pharaoh, *into* his servants' houses, and into all the land of Egypt. The land was corrupted because of the swarms *of flies.*

²⁵Then Pharaoh called for Moses and Aaron, and said, "Go, sacrifice to your God in the land."

²⁶And Moses said, "It is not right to do so, for we would be sacrificing the abomination of the Egyptians to the LORD our God. If we sacrifice the abomination of the Egyptians before their eyes, then will they not stone us? ²⁷We will go three days' journey into the wilderness and sacrifice to the LORD our God as He will command us."

²⁸So Pharaoh said, "I will let you go,

8:23 ªLiterally *set a ransom* (compare Exodus 9:4 and 11:7) that you may sacrifice to the LORD your God in the wilderness; only you shall not go very far away. Intercede for me." ²⁹Then Moses said, "Indeed I am going out from you, and I will entreat the LORD, that the swarms *of flies* may depart tomorrow from Pharaoh, from his servants, and from his people. But let Pharaoh not deal deceitfully anymore in not letting the people go to sacrifice to the LORD."

³⁰So Moses went out from Pharaoh and entreated the LORD. ³¹And the LORD did according to the word of Moses; He removed the swarms *of flies* from Pharaoh, from his servants, and from his people. Not one remained. ³²But Pharaoh hardened his heart at this time also; neither would he let the people go.

The Fifth Plague: Livestock Diseased

9 Then the LORD said to Moses, "Go in to Pharaoh and tell him, 'Thus says the LORD God of the Hebrews: "Let My people go, that they may serve Me. ²For if you refuse to let *them* go, and still hold them, ³behold, the hand of the LORD will be on your cattle in the field, on the horses, on the donkeys, on the camels, on the oxen, and on the sheep—a very severe pestilence. ⁴And the LORD will make a difference between the livestock of Israel and the livestock of Egypt. So nothing shall die of all *that* belongs to the children of Israel." ' " ⁵Then the LORD appointed a set time, saying, "Tomorrow the LORD will do this thing in the land."

⁶So the LORD did this thing on the next day, and all the livestock of Egypt died; but of the livestock of the children of Israel, not one died. ⁷Then Pharaoh sent, and indeed, not even one of the livestock of the Israelites was dead. But the heart of Pharaoh became hard, and he did not let the people go.

The Sixth Plague: Boils

⁸So the LORD said to Moses and Aaron, "Take for yourselves handfuls of ashes from a furnace, and let Moses scatter it toward the heavens in the sight of Pharaoh. ⁹And it will become fine dust in all the land of Egypt, and it will cause boils that break out in sores on man and beast throughout all the land of Egypt." ¹⁰Then they took ashes from the furnace

and stood before Pharaoh, and Moses scattered *them* toward heaven. And *they* caused boils that break out in sores on man and beast. ¹¹And the magicians could not stand before Moses because of the boils, for the boils were on the magicians and on all the Egyptians. ¹²But the LORD hardened the heart of Pharaoh; and he did not heed them, just as the LORD had spoken to Moses.

The Seventh Plague: Hail

¹³Then the LORD said to Moses, "Rise early in the morning and stand before Pharaoh, and say to him, 'Thus says the LORD God of the Hebrews: "Let My people go, that they may serve Me, ¹⁴for at this time I will send all My plagues to your

---

ROMANCE FAQ

Q: How can couples learn to understand one another in the area of romance?

We continue to discover things about each other, and we've been married more than twenty-five years! Learning about one another is a lifetime process. The key is not to give up, not to lose heart, but instead to be encouraged and excited by the challenge of getting to know one another on an ever-deeper level.

Barbara and I were recently with a Christian leader and his wife who had just celebrated their 50th anniversary. I'll never forget his response when asked if he understood his mate. Speaking with the utmost love and respect for her, he said, "I'll never fully understand my wife—she's a woman; she's different. God made her that way."

In matters of the heart, the sexes speak different languages. Is God playing a cruel hoax on us by making us so different? I don't think so. As the years go by, we need to ask God to give us the ability to meet each other's needs. Every husband should seek to listen to truly understand his wife's language of love (and vice versa), and then begin finding creative ways of romancing her.

very heart, and on your servants and on your people, that you may know that *there is* none like Me in all the earth. ¹⁵Now if I had stretched out My hand and struck you and your people with pestilence, then you would have been cut off from the earth. ¹⁶But indeed for this *purpose* I have raised you up, that I may show My power *in* you, and that My name may be declared in all the earth. ¹⁷As yet you exalt yourself against My people in that you will not let them go. ¹⁸Behold, tomorrow about this time I will cause very heavy hail to rain down, such as has not been in Egypt since its founding until now. ¹⁹Therefore send now *and* gather your livestock and all that you have in the field, for the hail shall come down on every man and every animal which is found in the field and is not brought home; and they shall die.""

²⁰He who feared the word of the LORD among the servants of Pharaoh made his servants and his livestock flee to the houses. ²¹But he who did not regard the word of the LORD left his servants and his livestock in the field.

²²Then the LORD said to Moses, "Stretch out your hand toward heaven, that there may be hail in all the land of Egypt—on man, on beast, and on every herb of the field, throughout the land of Egypt." ²³And Moses stretched out his rod toward heaven; and the LORD sent thunder and hail, and fire darted to the ground. And the LORD rained hail on the land of Egypt. ²⁴So there was hail, and fire mingled with the hail, so very heavy that there was none like it in all the land of Egypt since it became a nation. ²⁵And the hail struck throughout the whole land of Egypt, all that *was* in the field, both man and beast; and the hail struck every herb of the field and broke every tree of the field. ²⁶Only in the land of Goshen, where the children of Israel *were,* there was no hail.

²⁷And Pharaoh sent and called for Moses and Aaron, and said to them, "I have sinned this time. The LORD *is* righteous, and my people and I *are* wicked. ²⁸Entreat the LORD, that there may be no *more* mighty thundering and hail, for *it is* enough. I will let you go, and you shall stay no longer."

PARENTING MATTERS

Q: *What do our teens need from us in order to grow up to become what God intends them to be?*

After years of managing the Rainey Zoo, Barbara and I have learned the following lessons:

Need #1: Your teenagers need you to prayerfully ask questions. Check up on them and ask them what they've been doing. Ask, "What's going on?" Listen carefully to what they say and to the things they don't say. Never forget that their ability to deceive you is greater than your ability to catch them!

Need #2: Your teens need you to persevere when they push you out. Teens tend to want their space, and they will often push you away. Give them some space, but don't give in to this dangerous game of isolation.

Need #3: Your teens need you to believe in them. The teenage years are clouded with self-doubt and insecurities. Your teens need you to create a harbor in the storms of puberty. Express your belief in them verbally and frequently.

Need #4: Your teen needs you to help him establish boundaries. God has given you an assignment of drawing boundaries—who he can hang out with, where he can go, etc.

Need #5: Your teen needs you to do battle over sin. Prayer is your most powerful weapon, and tough love is a close second. After you've prayed, don't hesitate to call sin what it really is and call them to the right standard.

²⁹So Moses said to him, "As soon as I have gone out of the city, I will spread out my hands to the LORD; the thunder will cease, and there will be no more hail, that you may know that the earth *is* the LORD's. ³⁰But as for you and your servants, I know that you will not yet fear the LORD God."

³¹Now the flax and the barley were struck, for the barley *was* in the head and the flax *was* in bud. ³²But the wheat and the spelt were not struck, for they *are* late crops.

³³So Moses went out of the city from Pharaoh and spread out his hands to the LORD; then the thunder and the hail ceased, and the rain was not poured on the earth. ³⁴And when Pharaoh saw that the rain, the hail, and the thunder had ceased, he sinned yet more; and he hardened his heart, he and his servants. ³⁵So the heart of Pharaoh was hard; neither would he let the children of Israel go, as the LORD had spoken by Moses.

The Eighth Plague: Locusts

10 Now the LORD said to Moses, "Go in to Pharaoh; for I have hardened his heart and the hearts of his servants, that I may show these signs of Mine before him, ²and that you may tell in the hearing of your son and your son's son the mighty things I have done in Egypt, and My signs which I have done among them, that you may know that I *am* the LORD."

³So Moses and Aaron came in to Pharaoh and said to him, "Thus says the LORD God of the Hebrews: 'How long will you refuse to humble yourself before Me? Let My people go, that they may serve Me. ⁴Or else, if you refuse to let My people go, behold, tomorrow I will bring locusts into your territory. ⁵And they shall cover the face of the earth, so that no one will be able to see the earth; and they shall eat the residue of what is left, which remains to you from the hail, and they shall eat every tree which grows up for you out of the field. ⁶They shall fill your houses, the houses of all your servants, and the houses of all the Egyptians—which neither your fathers nor your fathers' fathers have seen, since the day that they were on the earth to this day.'" And he turned and went out from Pharaoh.

⁷Then Pharaoh's servants said to him, "How long shall this man be a snare to us? Let the men go, that they may serve the LORD their God. Do you not yet know that Egypt is destroyed?"

⁸So Moses and Aaron were brought again to Pharaoh, and he said to them, "Go, serve the LORD your God. Who *are* the ones that are going?"

⁹And Moses said, "We will go with our young and our old; with our sons and our daughters, with our flocks and our herds we will go, for we must hold a feast to the LORD."

¹⁰Then he said to them, "The LORD had better be with you when I let you and your little ones go! Beware, for evil is ahead of you. ¹¹Not so! Go now, you *who are* men, and serve the LORD, for that is what you desired." And they were driven out from Pharaoh's presence.

¹²Then the LORD said to Moses, "Stretch out your hand over the land of Egypt for the locusts, that they may come upon the land of Egypt, and eat every herb of the land—all that the hail has left." ¹³So Moses stretched out his rod over the land of Egypt, and the LORD brought an east wind on the land all that day and all *that* night. When it was morning, the east wind brought the locusts. ¹⁴And the locusts went up over all the land of Egypt and rested on all the territory of Egypt. *They were* very severe; previously there had been no such locusts as they, nor shall there be such after them. ¹⁵For they covered the face of the whole earth, so that the land was darkened; and they ate every herb of the land and all the fruit of the trees which the hail had left. So there remained nothing green on the trees or on the plants of the field throughout all the land of Egypt.

¹⁶Then Pharaoh called for Moses and Aaron in haste, and said, "I have sinned against the LORD your God and against you. ¹⁷Now therefore, please forgive my sin only this once, and entreat the LORD your God, that He may take away from me this death only." ¹⁸So he went out from Pharaoh and entreated the LORD. ¹⁹And the LORD turned a very strong west wind, which took the locusts away and blew them into the Red Sea. There remained not one locust

in all the territory of Egypt. 20But the LORD hardened Pharaoh's heart, and he did not let the children of Israel go.

The Ninth Plague: Darkness

21Then the LORD said to Moses, "Stretch out your hand toward heaven, that there may be darkness over the land of Egypt, darkness *which* may even be felt." 22So Moses stretched out his hand toward heaven, and there was thick darkness in all the land of Egypt three days. 23They did not see one another; nor did anyone rise from his place for three days. But all the children of Israel had light in their dwellings.

24Then Pharaoh called to Moses and said, "Go, serve the LORD; only let your flocks and your herds be kept back. Let your little ones also go with you."

25But Moses said, "You must also give us sacrifices and burnt offerings, that we may sacrifice to the LORD our God. 26Our livestock also shall go with us; not a hoof shall be left behind. For we must take some of them to serve the LORD our God, and even we do not know with what we must serve the LORD until we arrive there."

27But the LORD hardened Pharaoh's heart, and he would not let them go. 28Then Pharaoh said to him, "Get away from me! Take heed to yourself and see my face no more! For in the day you see my face you shall die!"

29So Moses said, "You have spoken well. I will never see your face again."

Death of the Firstborn Announced

11 And the LORD said to Moses, "I will bring one more plague on Pharaoh and on Egypt. Afterward he will let you go from here. When he lets *you* go, he will surely drive you out of here altogether. 2Speak now in the hearing of the people, and let every man ask from his neighbor and every woman from her neighbor, articles of silver and articles of gold." 3And the LORD gave the people favor in the sight of the Egyptians. Moreover the man Moses *was* very great in the land of Egypt, in the sight of Pharaoh's servants and in the sight of the people.

4Then Moses said, "Thus says the LORD: 'About midnight I will go out into the midst of Egypt; 5and all the firstborn in the land of Egypt shall die, from the firstborn of Pharaoh who sits on his throne, even to the firstborn of the female servant who *is* behind the handmill, and all the firstborn of the animals. 6Then there shall be a great cry throughout all the land of Egypt, such as was not like it *before,* nor shall be like it again. 7But against none of the children of Israel shall a dog move its tongue, against man or beast, that you may know that the LORD does make a difference between the Egyptians and Israel.' 8And all these your servants shall come down to me and bow down to me, saying, 'Get out, and all the people who follow you!' After that I will go out." Then he went out from Pharaoh in great anger.

9But the LORD said to Moses, "Pharaoh will not heed you, so that My wonders may be multiplied in the land of Egypt." 10So Moses and Aaron did all these wonders before Pharaoh; and the LORD hardened Pharaoh's heart, and he did not let the children of Israel go out of his land.

The Passover Instituted

12 Now the LORD spoke to Moses and Aaron in the land of Egypt, saying, 2"This month *shall be* your beginning of months; it *shall be* the first month of the year to you. 3Speak to all the congregation of Israel, saying: 'On the tenth of this month every man shall take for himself a lamb, according to the house of *his* father, a lamb for a household. 4And if the household is too small for the lamb, let him and his neighbor next to his house take *it* according to the number of the persons; according to each man's need you shall make your count for the lamb. 5Your lamb shall be without blemish, a male of the first year. You may take *it* from the sheep or from the goats. 6Now you shall keep it until the fourteenth day of the same month. Then the whole assembly of the congregation of Israel shall kill it at twilight. 7And they shall take *some* of the blood and put *it* on the two doorposts and on the lintel of the houses where they eat it. 8Then they shall eat the flesh on that night; roasted in fire, with unleavened bread *and* with bitter *herbs* they shall eat it. 9Do not eat it raw, nor boiled at all with water, but roasted in fire—

its head with its legs and its entrails. ¹⁰You shall let none of it remain until morning, and what remains of it until morning you shall burn with fire. ¹¹And thus you shall eat it: *with* a belt on your waist, your sandals on your feet, and your staff in your hand. So you shall eat it in haste. It *is* the LORD's Passover.

¹²'For I will pass through the land of Egypt on that night, and will strike all the firstborn in the land of Egypt, both man and beast; and against all the gods of Egypt I will execute judgment: I *am* the LORD. ¹³Now the blood shall be a sign for you on the houses where you *are*. And when I see the blood, I will pass over you; and the plague shall not be on you to destroy *you* when I strike the land of Egypt.

¹⁴'So this day shall be to you a memorial; and you shall keep it as a feast to the LORD throughout your generations. You shall keep it as a feast by an everlasting ordinance. ¹⁵Seven days you shall eat unleavened bread. On the first day you shall remove leaven from your houses. For whoever eats leavened bread from the first day until the seventh day, that person shall be cut off from Israel. ¹⁶On the first day *there shall be* a holy convocation, and on the seventh day there shall be a holy convocation for you. No manner of work shall be done on them; but *that* which everyone must eat—that only may be prepared by you. ¹⁷So you shall observe *the Feast of* Unleavened Bread, for on this same day I will have brought your armies out of the land of Egypt. Therefore you shall observe this day throughout your generations as an everlasting ordinance. ¹⁸In the first *month,* on the fourteenth day of the month at evening, you shall eat unleavened bread, until the twenty-first day of the month at evening. ¹⁹For seven days no leaven shall be found in your houses, since whoever eats what is leavened, that same person shall be cut off from the congregation of Israel, whether *he is* a stranger or a native of the land. ²⁰You shall eat nothing leavened; in all your dwellings you shall eat unleavened bread.'"

²¹Then Moses called for all the elders of Israel and said to them, "Pick out and take lambs for yourselves according to your families, and kill the Passover *lamb.* ²²And you shall take a bunch of hyssop, dip *it* in the blood that *is* in the basin, and strike the lintel and the two doorposts with the blood that *is* in the basin. And none of you shall go out of the door of his house until morning. ²³For the LORD will pass through to strike the Egyptians; and when He sees the blood on the lintel and on the two doorposts, the LORD will pass over the door and not allow the destroyer to come into your houses to strike *you*. ²⁴And you shall observe this thing as an ordinance for you and your sons forever. ²⁵It will come to pass when you come to the land which the LORD will give you, just as He promised, that you shall keep this service. ²⁶And it shall be, when your children say to you, 'What do you mean by this service?' ²⁷that you shall say, 'It *is* the Passover sacrifice of the LORD, who passed over the houses of the children of Israel in Egypt when He struck the Egyptians and delivered our households.'" So the people bowed their heads and worshiped. ²⁸Then the children of Israel went away and did *so;* just as the LORD had commanded Moses and Aaron, so they did.

The Tenth Plague: Death of the Firstborn

²⁹And it came to pass at midnight that the LORD struck all the firstborn in the land of Egypt, from the firstborn of Pharaoh who sat on his throne to the firstborn of the captive who *was* in the dungeon, and all the firstborn of livestock. ³⁰So Pharaoh rose in the night, he, all his servants, and all the Egyptians; and there was a great cry in Egypt, for *there was* not a house where *there was* not one dead.

The Exodus

³¹Then he called for Moses and Aaron by night, and said, "Rise, go out from among my people, both you and the children of Israel. And go, serve the LORD as you have said. ³²Also take your flocks and your herds, as you have said, and be gone; and bless me also."

³³And the Egyptians urged the people, that they might send them out of the land in haste. For they said, "We *shall* all *be* dead." ³⁴So the people took their dough before it was leavened, having their

Focus on the Relationship

ONE DAY I ASKED the students in my sixth grade Sunday school class, "Do you guys know what a clean kitchen looks like?" They all started laughing and said, "Yeah, we know what it looks like."

"So" I said, "why don't you do it?"

They all replied, "We like to aggravate you guys. We like to get to you."

It is fascinating that by age twelve our children know what they ought to do, but they try to be obstinate. They may begin to look something like adults, but they're not. We have to remember we're raising children, so we shouldn't be surprised when they act childishly. They have to be taught the significance of important things (12:26), because they won't get it on their own.

First Corinthians 13:11 says that maturity involves putting away childish things. As parents, we need to first teach our children basic life skills, and then train them through demonstration and practice. If they get something wrong, we gently correct them. But if they are stubborn or rebellious, we may need to discipline them while making sure we are not provoking them to anger (Eph. 6:4).

When we assign chores and then follow up to make sure they've been completed, we need to *inspect* what we *expect*. We also want to make sure we don't lose our relationship with our child. If we get so angry that we begin to sever that relationship, then we, as the adults, need to remind ourselves of what's really important.

---

kneading bowls bound up in their clothes on their shoulders. 35Now the children of Israel had done according to the word of Moses, and they had asked from the Egyptians articles of silver, articles of gold, and clothing. 36And the LORD had given the people favor in the sight of the Egyptians, so that they granted them *what they*

requested. Thus they plundered the Egyptians.

37Then the children of Israel journeyed from Rameses to Succoth, about six hundred thousand men on foot, besides children. 38A mixed multitude went up with them also, and flocks and herds—a great deal of livestock. 39And they baked unleavened cakes of the dough which they had brought out of Egypt; for it was not leavened, because they were driven out of Egypt and could not wait, nor had they prepared provisions for themselves.

40Now the sojourn of the children of Israel who lived in Egypt[a] *was* four hundred and thirty years. 41And it came to pass at the end of the four hundred and thirty years—on that very same day—it came to pass that all the armies of the LORD went out from the land of Egypt. 42It *is* a night of solemn observance to the LORD for bringing them out of the land of Egypt. This *is* that night of the LORD, a solemn observance for all the children of Israel throughout their generations.

Passover Regulations

43And the LORD said to Moses and Aaron, "This *is* the ordinance of the Passover: No foreigner shall eat it. 44But every man's servant who is bought for money, when you have circumcised him, then he may eat it. 45A sojourner and a hired servant shall not eat it. 46In one house it shall be eaten; you shall not carry any of the flesh outside the house, nor shall you break one of its bones. 47All the congregation of Israel shall keep it. 48And when a stranger dwells with you *and wants* to keep the Passover to the LORD, let all his males be circumcised, and then let him come near and keep it; and he shall be as a native of the land. For no uncircumcised person shall eat it. 49One law shall be for the native-born and for the stranger who dwells among you."

50Thus all the children of Israel did; as the LORD commanded Moses and Aaron, so they did. 51And it came to pass, on that very same day, that the LORD brought the

---

12:40 [a]Samaritan Pentateuch and Septuagint read *Egypt and Canaan.*

children of Israel out of the land of Egypt according to their armies.

The Firstborn Consecrated

13 Then the LORD spoke to Moses, saying, 2"Consecrate to Me all the firstborn, whatever opens the womb among the children of Israel, *both* of man and beast; it is Mine."

The Feast of Unleavened Bread

3And Moses said to the people: "Remember this day in which you went out of Egypt, out of the house of bondage; for by strength of hand the LORD brought you out of this *place.* No leavened bread shall be eaten. 4On this day you are going out, in the month Abib. 5And it shall be, when the LORD brings you into the land of the Canaanites and the Hittites and the Amorites and the Hivites and the Jebusites, which He swore to your fathers to give you, a land flowing with milk and honey, that you shall keep this service in this month. 6Seven days you shall eat unleavened bread, and on the seventh day *there shall be* a feast to the LORD. 7Unleavened bread shall be eaten seven days. And no leavened bread shall be seen among you, nor shall leaven be seen among you in all your quarters. 8And you shall tell your son in that day, saying, '*This is done* because of what the LORD did for me when I came up from Egypt.' 9It shall be as a sign to you on your hand and as a memorial between your eyes, that the LORD's law may be in your mouth; for with a strong hand the LORD has brought you out of Egypt. 10You shall therefore keep this ordinance in its season from year to year.

The Law of the Firstborn

11"And it shall be, when the LORD brings you into the land of the Canaanites, as He swore to you and your fathers, and gives it to you, 12that you shall set apart to the LORD all that open the womb, that is, every firstborn that comes from an animal which you have; the males *shall be* the LORD's. 13But every firstborn of a donkey you shall redeem with a lamb; and if you will not redeem *it,* then you shall break its neck.

And all the firstborn of man among your sons you shall redeem. 14So it shall be, when your son asks you in time to come, saying, 'What *is* this?' that you shall say to him, 'By strength of hand the LORD brought us out of Egypt, out of the house of bondage. 15And it came to pass, when Pharaoh was stubborn about letting us go, that the LORD killed all the firstborn in the land of Egypt, both the firstborn of man and the firstborn of beast. Therefore I sacrifice to the LORD all males that open the womb, but all the firstborn of my sons I redeem.' 16It shall be as a sign on your hand and as frontlets between your eyes, for by strength of hand the LORD brought us out of Egypt."

The Wilderness Way

17Then it came to pass, when Pharaoh had let the people go, that God did not lead them *by* way of the land of the Philistines, although that *was* near; for God said, "Lest perhaps the people change their minds when they see war, and return to Egypt." 18So God led the people around *by* way of the wilderness of the Red Sea. And the children of Israel went up in orderly ranks out of the land of Egypt.

19And Moses took the bones of Joseph with him, for he had placed the children of Israel under solemn oath, saying, "God will surely visit you, and you shall carry up my bones from here with you."a

20So they took their journey from Succoth and camped in Etham at the edge of the wilderness. 21And the LORD went before them by day in a pillar of cloud to lead the way, and by night in a pillar of fire to give them light, so as to go by day and night. 22He did not take away the pillar of cloud by day or the pillar of fire by night *from* before the people.

The Red Sea Crossing

14 Now the LORD spoke to Moses, saying: 2"Speak to the children of Israel, that they turn and camp before Pi Hahiroth, between Migdol and the sea, opposite Baal Zephon; you shall camp before it by the sea. 3For Pharaoh will say of the children of Israel, 'They *are* bewildered by the land; the wilderness has closed

---

13:19 aGenesis 50:25

BIBLICAL INSIGHTS • 14:8
Do You Have Guts?

ONE OF THE LARGEST MUSCLE groups in the body is the stomach. In spiritual terms, your stomach is the place where courage resides. It is said of a courageous person, "He has guts."

But our society is guilty of flab in the waistline because of a lack of exercising spiritual courage. We don't want pain; we'd rather have comfort, thus the resulting bulge from our failure to be bold.

It is said that when the children of Israel, a motley and immature group of newly-released former slaves, marched out of Egypt, they did so "with boldness" (14:8). That's exactly the right spirit for men and women who call God "my Father."

Christians who lack guts sacrifice truth on the altar of love. Many lack the tough love to fearlessly confront a family member caught in the web of an addiction. They have a soft view of love that refuses to confront sin in someone else because they fear conflict, rejection, or loss of emotional comfort. So they don't broach painful subjects with those they love the most.

In fact, gutless believers are more concerned about *self* than they are about the wellbeing of others—unwilling to be hurt to see another healed. Don't forget Paul's words to Timothy, "For God has not given us a spirit of fear, but of power and of love and of a sound mind" (2 Tim. 1:7).

---

them in.' ⁴Then I will harden Pharaoh's heart, so that he will pursue them; and I will gain honor over Pharaoh and over all his army, that the Egyptians may know that I *am* the LORD." And they did so.

⁵Now it was told the king of Egypt that the people had fled, and the heart of Pharaoh and his servants was turned against the people; and they said, "Why have we done this, that we have let Israel go from serving us?" ⁶So he made ready his chariot and took his people with him.

⁷Also, he took six hundred choice chariots, and all the chariots of Egypt with captains over every one of them. ⁸And the LORD hardened the heart of Pharaoh king of Egypt, and he pursued the children of Israel; and the children of Israel went out with boldness. ⁹So the Egyptians pursued them, all the horses *and* chariots of Pharaoh, his horsemen and his army, and overtook them camping by the sea beside Pi Hahiroth, before Baal Zephon.

¹⁰And when Pharaoh drew near, the children of Israel lifted their eyes, and behold, the Egyptians marched after them. So they were very afraid, and the children of Israel cried out to the LORD. ¹¹Then they said to Moses, "Because *there were* no graves in Egypt, have you taken us away to die in the wilderness? Why have you so dealt with us, to bring us up out of Egypt? ¹²*Is* this not the word that we told you in Egypt, saying, 'Let us alone that we may serve the Egyptians'? For *it would have been* better for us to serve the Egyptians than that we should die in the wilderness."

¹³And Moses said to the people, "Do not be afraid. Stand still, and see the salvation of the LORD, which He will accomplish for you today. For the Egyptians whom you see today, you shall see again no more forever. ¹⁴The LORD will fight for you, and you shall hold your peace."

¹⁵And the LORD said to Moses, "Why do you cry to Me? Tell the children of Israel to go forward. ¹⁶But lift up your rod, and stretch out your hand over the sea and divide it. And the children of Israel shall go on dry *ground* through the midst of the sea. ¹⁷And I indeed will harden the hearts of the Egyptians, and they shall follow them. So I will gain honor over Pharaoh and over all his army, his chariots, and his horsemen. ¹⁸Then the Egyptians shall know that I *am* the LORD, when I have gained honor for Myself over Pharaoh, his chariots, and his horsemen."

¹⁹And the Angel of God, who went before the camp of Israel, moved and went behind them; and the pillar of cloud went from before them and stood behind them. ²⁰So it came between the camp of the Egyptians and the camp of Israel. Thus it was a cloud and darkness *to the one,* and it gave light by

night *to the other,* so that the one did not come near the other all that night.

²¹Then Moses stretched out his hand over the sea; and the Lᴏʀᴅ caused the sea to go *back* by a strong east wind all that night, and made the sea into dry *land,* and the waters were divided. ²²So the children of Israel went into the midst of the sea on the dry *ground,* and the waters *were* a wall to them on their right hand and on their left. ²³And the Egyptians pursued and went after them into the midst of the sea, all Pharaoh's horses, his chariots, and his horsemen.

²⁴Now it came to pass, in the morning watch, that the Lᴏʀᴅ looked down upon the army of the Egyptians through the pillar of fire and cloud, and He troubled the army of the Egyptians. ²⁵And He took off[a] their chariot wheels, so that they drove them with difficulty; and the Egyptians said, "Let us flee from the face of Israel, for the Lᴏʀᴅ fights for them against the Egyptians."

²⁶Then the Lᴏʀᴅ said to Moses, "Stretch out your hand over the sea, that the waters may come back upon the Egyptians, on their chariots, and on their horsemen."

14:25 [a]Samaritan Pentateuch, Septuagint, and Syriac read *bound.*

²⁷And Moses stretched out his hand over the sea; and when the morning appeared, the sea returned to its full depth, while the Egyptians were fleeing into it. So the Lᴏʀᴅ overthrew the Egyptians in the midst of the sea. ²⁸Then the waters returned and covered the chariots, the horsemen, *and* all the army of Pharaoh that came into the sea after them. Not so much as one of them remained. ²⁹But the children of Israel had walked on dry *land* in the midst of the sea, and the waters *were* a wall to them on their right hand and on their left.

³⁰So the Lᴏʀᴅ saved Israel that day out of the hand of the Egyptians, and Israel saw the Egyptians dead on the seashore. ³¹Thus Israel saw the great work which the Lᴏʀᴅ had done in Egypt; so the people feared the Lᴏʀᴅ, and believed the Lᴏʀᴅ and His servant Moses.

The Song of Moses

15 Then Moses and the children of Israel sang this song to the Lᴏʀᴅ, and spoke, saying:

"I will sing to the Lᴏʀᴅ,
For He has triumphed gloriously!
The horse and its rider
He has thrown into the sea!
2   The Lᴏʀᴅ *is* my strength and song,

ROMANTIC QUOTES AND NOTES
Reject Selfishness, Choose Harmony

TWO PEOPLE WHO BEGIN MARRIAGE by trying to go their own selfish, separate ways can never hope to experience the oneness of marriage as God intended.

The prophet Isaiah portrayed the problem accurately more than 2,500 years ago, "All of us like sheep have gone astray; we have turned, every one, to his own way" (Is. 53:6). Isaiah didn't know me, but his analysis sounds eerily familiar. I want to go my own way, do my own thing. I'm your basic, self-centered person. We all instinctively look out for number one.

Selfishness is possibly the most dangerous threat to oneness in marriage. Both partners enter marriage with all kinds of expectations, many of which go unmet because the other partner either doesn't know what is expected, is incapable of complying, or is unwilling to meet the expectation. Caught in this self-centered quagmire, many marriages end up stuck.

In our first years of marriage, I was more than a bit selfish. I was skilled at looking out for my own needs. But when I took Barbara as my wife, I assumed a new responsibility—loving Barbara as Christ loved the church. And that meant rejecting selfishness (repeatedly!) and instead seeking harmony. Marriage is one of God's primary tools that He has given the human race to finish the process of our growing up!

And He has become my salvation;
He *is* my God, and I will praise Him;
My father's God, and I will exalt Him.

3 The LORD *is* a man of war;
The LORD *is* His name.

4 Pharaoh's chariots and his army He
has cast into the sea;
His chosen captains also are
drowned in the Red Sea.

5 The depths have covered them;
They sank to the bottom like a stone.

6 "Your right hand, O LORD, has become
glorious in power;
Your right hand, O LORD, has dashed
the enemy in pieces.

7 And in the greatness of Your
excellence
You have overthrown those who rose
against You;
You sent forth Your wrath;
It consumed them like stubble.

8 And with the blast of Your nostrils
The waters were gathered together;
The floods stood upright like a heap;
The depths congealed in the heart of
the sea.

9 The enemy said, 'I will pursue,
I will overtake,
I will divide the spoil;
My desire shall be satisfied on them.
I will draw my sword,
My hand shall destroy them.'

10 You blew with Your wind,
The sea covered them;
They sank like lead in the mighty
waters.

11 "Who *is* like You, O LORD, among the
gods?
Who *is* like You, glorious in holiness,
Fearful in praises, doing wonders?

12 You stretched out Your right hand;
The earth swallowed them.

13 You in Your mercy have led forth
The people whom You have
redeemed;
You have guided *them* in Your
strength
To Your holy habitation.

14 "The people will hear *and* be afraid;
Sorrow will take hold of the
inhabitants of Philistia.

15 Then the chiefs of Edom will be
dismayed;
The mighty men of Moab,
Trembling will take hold of them;
All the inhabitants of Canaan will
melt away.

16 Fear and dread will fall on them;
By the greatness of Your arm
They will be *as* still as a stone,
Till Your people pass over, O LORD,
Till the people pass over
Whom You have purchased.

17 You will bring them in and plant them
In the mountain of Your inheritance,
In the place, O LORD, *which* You have
made
For Your own dwelling,
The sanctuary, O Lord, *which* Your
hands have established.

18 "The LORD shall reign forever and ever."

19For the horses of Pharaoh went with
his chariots and his horsemen into the sea,
and the LORD brought back the waters of
the sea upon them. But the children of Israel
went on dry *land* in the midst of the sea.

The Song of Miriam

20Then Miriam the prophetess, the sister of Aaron, took the timbrel in her hand;
and all the women went out after her with
timbrels and with dances. 21And Miriam
answered them:

"Sing to the LORD,
For He has triumphed gloriously!
The horse and its rider
He has thrown into the sea!"

Bitter Waters Made Sweet

22So Moses brought Israel from the Red
Sea; then they went out into the
Wilderness of Shur. And they went three
days in the wilderness and found no water.
23Now when they came to Marah, they
could not drink the waters of Marah, for
they *were* bitter. Therefore the name of it
was called Marah.[a] 24And the people complained against Moses, saying, "What
shall we drink?" 25So he cried out to the
LORD, and the LORD showed him a tree.

15:23 [a]Literally *Bitter*

87

EXODUS 16

When he cast *it* into the waters, the waters were made sweet.

There He made a statute and an ordinance for them, and there He tested them, ²⁶and said, "If you diligently heed the voice of the LORD your God and do what is right in His sight, give ear to His commandments and keep all His statutes, I will put none of the diseases on you which I have brought on the Egyptians. For I *am* the LORD who heals you."

²⁷Then they came to Elim, where there *were* twelve wells of water and seventy palm trees; so they camped there by the waters.

Bread from Heaven

16 And they journeyed from Elim, and all the congregation of the children of Israel came to the Wilderness of Sin, which is between Elim and Sinai, on the fifteenth day of the second month after they departed from the land of Egypt. ²Then the whole congregation of the children of Israel complained against Moses and Aaron in the wilderness. ³And the children of Israel said to them, "Oh, that we had died by the hand of the LORD in the land of Egypt, when we sat by the pots of meat *and* when we ate bread to the full! For you have brought us out into this wilderness to kill this whole assembly with hunger."

⁴Then the LORD said to Moses, "Behold, I will rain bread from heaven for you. And the people shall go out and gather a certain quota every day, that I may test them, whether they will walk in My law or not. ⁵And it shall be on the sixth day that they shall prepare what they bring in, and it shall be twice as much as they gather daily."

⁶Then Moses and Aaron said to all the children of Israel, "At evening you shall know that the LORD has brought you out of the land of Egypt. ⁷And in the morning you shall see the glory of the LORD; for He hears your complaints against the LORD. But what *are* we, that you complain against us?" ⁸Also Moses said, "*This shall be seen* when the LORD gives you meat to eat in the evening, and in the morning bread to the full; for the LORD hears your complaints which you make against Him. And what *are* we? Your complaints *are* not against us but against the LORD."

⁹Then Moses spoke to Aaron, "Say to all the congregation of the children of Israel, 'Come near before the LORD, for He has heard your complaints.'" ¹⁰Now it came to pass, as Aaron spoke to the whole congregation of the children of Israel, that they looked toward the wilderness, and behold, the glory of the LORD appeared in the cloud.

¹¹And the LORD spoke to Moses, saying, ¹²"I have heard the complaints of the children of Israel. Speak to them, saying, 'At twilight you shall eat meat, and in the morning you shall be filled with bread. And you shall know that I *am* the LORD your God.'"

¹³So it was that quails came up at evening and covered the camp, and in the morning the dew lay all around the camp. ¹⁴And when the layer of dew lifted, there, on the surface of the wilderness, was a small round substance, *as* fine as frost on the ground. ¹⁵So when the children of Israel saw *it,* they said to one another, "What is it?" For they did not know what it *was.*

And Moses said to them, "This *is* the bread which the LORD has given you to eat. ¹⁶This is the thing which the LORD has commanded: 'Let every man gather it according to each one's need, one omer for each person, *according to the* number of

INTIMATE MOMENTS
Let the Music Speak

MUSIC HAS A WAY OF SPEAKING directly to the heart that few, if any, other modes of expression can match. So what are some of her favorite love songs? If you don't know for sure, devise some sly ways of finding out. (Don't just blurt out, "Hey, Babe, could you write down for me your five all-time favorite songs? Thanks a bunch.") Once you have the list, record a love message to her—for her ears only, not for general broadcast!—and then pair it with those favorite love songs of hers. Then leave the whole package in the CD player of her car.

persons; let every man take for *those* who *are* in his tent.'"

¹⁷Then the children of Israel did so and gathered, some more, some less. ¹⁸So when they measured *it* by omers, he who gathered much had nothing left over, and he who gathered little had no lack. Every man had gathered according to each one's need. ¹⁹And Moses said, "Let no one leave any of it till morning." ²⁰Notwithstanding they did not heed Moses. But some of them left part of it until morning, and it bred worms and stank. And Moses was angry with them. ²¹So they gathered it every morning, every man according to his need. And when the sun became hot, it melted.

²²And so it was, on the sixth day, *that* they gathered twice as much bread, two omers for each one. And all the rulers of the congregation came and told Moses. ²³Then he said to them, "This *is what* the LORD has said: 'Tomorrow *is* a Sabbath rest, a holy Sabbath to the LORD. Bake what you will bake *today,* and boil what you will boil; and lay up for yourselves all that remains, to be kept until morning.'" ²⁴So they laid it up till morning, as Moses commanded; and it did not stink, nor were there any worms in it. ²⁵Then Moses said, "Eat that today, for today *is* a Sabbath to the LORD; today you will not find it in the field. ²⁶Six days you shall gather it, but on the seventh day, the Sabbath, there will be none."

²⁷Now it happened *that some* of the people went out on the seventh day to gather, but they found none. ²⁸And the LORD said to Moses, "How long do you refuse to keep My commandments and My laws? ²⁹See! For the LORD has given you the Sabbath; therefore He gives you on the sixth day bread for two days. Let every man remain in his place; let no man go out of his place on the seventh day." ³⁰So the people rested on the seventh day.

³¹And the house of Israel called its name Manna.[a] And it *was* like white coriander seed, and the taste of it *was* like wafers *made* with honey.

³²Then Moses said, "This *is* the thing which the LORD has commanded: 'Fill an omer with it, to be kept for your generations, that they may see the bread with which I fed you in the wilderness, when I brought you out of the land of Egypt.'" ³³And Moses said to Aaron, "Take a pot and put an omer of manna in it, and lay it up before the LORD, to be kept for your generations." ³⁴As the LORD commanded Moses, so Aaron laid it up before the Testimony, to be kept. ³⁵And the children of Israel ate manna forty years, until they came to an inhabited land; they ate manna until they came to the border of the land of Canaan. ³⁶Now an omer *is* one-tenth of an ephah.

Water from the Rock

17 Then all the congregation of the children of Israel set out on their journey from the Wilderness of Sin, according to the commandment of the LORD, and camped in Rephidim; but *there was* no water for the people to drink. ²Therefore the people contended with Moses, and said, "Give us water, that we may drink."

So Moses said to them, "Why do you contend with me? Why do you tempt the LORD?"

³And the people thirsted there for water, and the people complained against Moses, and said, "Why *is* it you have brought us up out of Egypt, to kill us and our children and our livestock with thirst?"

⁴So Moses cried out to the LORD, saying, "What shall I do with this people? They are almost ready to stone me!"

⁵And the LORD said to Moses, "Go on before the people, and take with you some of the elders of Israel. Also take in your hand your rod with which you struck the river, and go. ⁶Behold, I will stand before you there on the rock in Horeb; and you shall strike the rock, and water will come out of it, that the people may drink."

And Moses did so in the sight of the elders of Israel. ⁷So he called the name of the place Massah[a] and Meribah,[b] because of the contention of the children of Israel, and because they tempted the LORD, saying, "Is the LORD among us or not?"

Victory over the Amalekites

⁸Now Amalek came and fought with Israel in Rephidim. ⁹And Moses said to Joshua, "Choose us some men and go out,

---

16:31 [a]Literally *What?* (compare Exodus 16:15)
17:7 [a]Literally *Tempted* [b]Literally *Contention*

fight with Amalek. Tomorrow I will stand on the top of the hill with the rod of God in my hand." ¹⁰So Joshua did as Moses said to him, and fought with Amalek. And Moses, Aaron, and Hur went up to the top of the hill. ¹¹And so it was, when Moses held up his hand, that Israel prevailed; and when he let down his hand, Amalek prevailed. ¹²But Moses' hands *became* heavy; so they took a stone and put *it* under him, and he sat on it. And Aaron and Hur supported his hands, one on one side, and the other on the other side; and his hands were steady until the going down of the sun. ¹³So Joshua defeated Amalek and his people with the edge of the sword.

¹⁴Then the LORD said to Moses, "Write this *for* a memorial in the book and recount *it* in the hearing of Joshua, that I will utterly blot out the remembrance of Amalek from under heaven." ¹⁵And Moses built an altar and called its name, The-LORD-Is-My-Banner;ᵃ ¹⁶for he said, "Because the LORD has sworn: the LORD *will have* war with Amalek from generation to generation."

Jethro's Advice

18 And Jethro, the priest of Midian, Moses' father-in-law, heard of all that God had done for Moses and for Israel His people—that the LORD had brought Israel out of Egypt. ²Then Jethro, Moses' father-in-law, took Zipporah, Moses' wife, after he had sent her back, ³with her two sons, of whom the name of one *was* Gershom (for he said, "I have been a stranger in a foreign land")ᵃ ⁴and the name of the other *was* Eliezerᵃ (for *he said,* "The God of my father *was* my help, and delivered me from the sword of Pharaoh"); ⁵and Jethro, Moses' father-in-law, came with his sons and his wife to Moses in the wilderness, where he was encamped at the mountain of God. ⁶Now he had said to Moses, "I, your father-in-law Jethro, am coming to you with your wife and her two sons with her." ⁷So Moses went out to meet his father-in-law, bowed down, and kissed him. And

BIBLICAL INSIGHTS • 18:27
What Kind of Leaders?

ALL HUSBANDS AND FATHERS are called to be the spiritual leaders of their homes. But what makes a good leader? The Bible shows us that one prerequisite for spiritual leadership is a healthy fear of God.

Jethro, the father-in-law of Moses, knew that Moses needed help. The lawgiver of Israel was wearing out after leading the Hebrew nation out of Egyptian bondage, and Jethro exhorted him to start delegating some of his responsibilities to other leaders. And what kind of people should those leaders be? Here is the description Jethro gave, "Moreover you shall select from all the people able men, such as *fear God,* men of truth, hating covetousness; and place such over them to be rulers of thousands, rulers of hundreds, rulers of fifties, and rulers of tens" (18:21, italics added).

Jethro knew something that every family leader needs to understand: *those who don't fear God will not be the kind of men who can judge rightly and righteously.* On the other hand, those who fear God and live according to His laws and rules for living are *exactly* the kind of leaders every family needs.

Are you such a leader?

---

they asked each other about *their* well-being, and they went into the tent. ⁸And Moses told his father-in-law all that the LORD had done to Pharaoh and to the Egyptians for Israel's sake, all the hardship that had come upon them on the way, and *how* the LORD had delivered them. ⁹Then Jethro rejoiced for all the good which the LORD had done for Israel, whom He had delivered out of the hand of the Egyptians. ¹⁰And Jethro said, "Blessed *be* the LORD, who has delivered you out of the hand of the Egyptians and out of the hand of Pharaoh, *and* who has delivered the people from under the hand of the Egyptians.

17:15 ᵃHebrew *YHWH Nissi* **18:3** ᵃCompare Exodus 2:22 **18:4** ᵃLiterally *My God Is Help* **18:12** ᵃFollowing Masoretic Text and Septuagint; Syriac, Targum, and Vulgate read *offered.*

¹¹Now I know that the LORD *is* greater than all the gods; for in the very thing in which they behaved proudly, *He was* above them." ¹²Then Jethro, Moses' father-in-law, took^a a burnt offering and *other* sacrifices *to offer* to God. And Aaron came with all the elders of Israel to eat bread with Moses' father-in-law before God.

¹³And so it was, on the next day, that Moses sat to judge the people; and the people stood before Moses from morning until evening. ¹⁴So when Moses' father-in-law saw all that he did for the people, he said, "What *is* this thing that you are doing for the people? Why do you alone sit, and all the people stand before you from morning until evening?"

¹⁵And Moses said to his father-in-law, "Because the people come to me to inquire of God. ¹⁶When they have a difficulty, they come to me, and I judge between one and another; and I make known the statutes of God and His laws."

¹⁷So Moses' father-in-law said to him, "The thing that you do *is* not good. ¹⁸Both you and these people who *are* with you will surely wear yourselves out. For this thing *is* too much for you; you are not able to perform it by yourself. ¹⁹Listen now to my voice; I will give you counsel, and God will be with you: Stand before God for the people, so that you may bring the difficulties to God. ²⁰And you shall teach them the statutes and the laws, and show them the way in which they must walk and the work they must do. ²¹Moreover you shall select from all the people able men, such as fear God, men of truth, hating covetousness; and place *such* over them *to be* rulers of thousands, rulers of hundreds, rulers of fifties, and rulers of tens. ²²And let them judge the people at all times. Then it will be *that* every great matter they shall bring to you, but every small matter they themselves shall judge. So it will be easier for you, for they will bear *the burden* with you. ²³If you do this thing, and God *so* commands you, then you will be able to endure, and all this people will also go to their place in peace."

²⁴So Moses heeded the voice of his father-in-law and did all that he had said. ²⁵And Moses chose able men out of all Israel, and made them heads over the people: rulers of thousands, rulers of hundreds, rulers of fifties, and rulers of tens. ²⁶So they judged the people at all times; the hard cases they brought to Moses, but they judged every small case themselves.

²⁷Then Moses let his father-in-law depart, and he went his way to his own land.

Israel at Mount Sinai

19 In the third month after the children of Israel had gone out of the land of Egypt, on the same day, they came *to* the Wilderness of Sinai. ²For they had departed from Rephidim, had come *to* the Wilderness of Sinai, and camped in the wilderness. So Israel camped there before the mountain.

³And Moses went up to God, and the LORD called to him from the mountain, saying, "Thus you shall say to the house of Jacob, and tell the children of Israel: ⁴'You have seen what I did to the Egyptians, and *how* I bore you on eagles' wings and brought you to Myself. ⁵Now therefore, if you will indeed obey My voice and keep My covenant, then you shall be a special treasure to Me above all people; for all the earth *is* Mine. ⁶And you shall be to Me a kingdom of priests and a holy nation.' These *are* the words which you shall speak to the children of Israel."

⁷So Moses came and called for the elders of the people, and laid before them all these words which the LORD commanded him. ⁸Then all the people answered together and said, "All that the LORD has spoken we will do." So Moses brought back the words of the people to the LORD. ⁹And the LORD said to Moses, "Behold, I come to you in the thick cloud, that the people may hear when I speak with you, and believe you forever."

So Moses told the words of the people to the LORD.

¹⁰Then the LORD said to Moses, "Go to the people and consecrate them today and tomorrow, and let them wash their clothes. ¹¹And let them be ready for the third day. For on the third day the LORD will come down upon Mount Sinai in the sight of all the people. ¹²You shall set bounds for the people all around, saying, 'Take heed to yourselves *that* you do *not* go up to the mountain or touch its base. Whoever touches the mountain shall surely be put

to death. ¹³Not a hand shall touch him, but he shall surely be stoned or shot *with an arrow;* whether man or beast, he shall not live.' When the trumpet sounds long, they shall come near the mountain."

¹⁴So Moses went down from the mountain to the people and sanctified the people, and they washed their clothes. ¹⁵And he said to the people, "Be ready for the third day; do not come near *your* wives."

¹⁶Then it came to pass on the third day, in the morning, that there were thunderings and lightnings, and a thick cloud on the mountain; and the sound of the trumpet was very loud, so that all the people who *were* in the camp trembled. ¹⁷And Moses brought the people out of the camp to meet with God, and they stood at the foot of the mountain. ¹⁸Now Mount Sinai *was* completely in smoke, because the LORD descended upon it in fire. Its smoke ascended like the smoke of a furnace, and the whole mountain[a] quaked greatly. ¹⁹And when the blast of the trumpet sounded long and became louder and louder, Moses spoke, and God answered him by voice. ²⁰Then the LORD came down upon Mount Sinai, on the top of the mountain. And the LORD called Moses to the top of the mountain, and Moses went up.

²¹And the LORD said to Moses, "Go down and warn the people, lest they break through to gaze at the LORD, and many of them perish. ²²Also let the priests who come near the LORD consecrate themselves, lest the LORD break out against them."

²³But Moses said to the LORD, "The people cannot come up to Mount Sinai; for You warned us, saying, 'Set bounds around the mountain and consecrate it.'"

²⁴Then the LORD said to him, "Away! Get down and then come up, you and Aaron with you. But do not let the priests and the people break through to come up to the LORD, lest He break out against them." ²⁵So Moses went down to the people and spoke to them.

The Ten Commandments

20 And God spoke all these words, saying:

² "I *am* the LORD your God, who brought

19:18 [a]Septuagint reads *all the people.*

BIBLICAL INSIGHTS • 20:3

Your One and Only God

IN THE FIRST of the Ten Commandments, God said, "You shall have no other gods before Me" (20:3). The fact that it comes first suggests that we are prone to wandering toward false gods.

What false gods do we (and our children) tend to give our allegiance to the most? Here are the top three on our list:

1. *Self.* While everyone struggles with selfishness, teens often act like the world revolves around them. Our culture feeds the natural urge toward the big ME, and the hybrid youth culture encourages it even more. As adults, we struggle with pride as well. Alexander Solzenitzen said it best, "Pride grows on the human heart like lard on a pig."

2. *Popularity.* Everyone wants to be liked, and phenomenal pressure comes to bear on our kids to be people pleasers. Popularity can become a god, especially when we feel troubled or lonely or unloved at home.

3. *Success/achievement.* All of us look for approval, acceptance, adoration, and acclaim, and we can get sucked into making success—in sports, grades, work, hobbies, and other areas—a god and not just a goal.

The number one thing you can do to help yourself and your children experience true success and real joy in life is to create a home where the number one priority is to establish and cultivate a relationship with the one true God.

---

you out of the land of Egypt, out of the house of bondage.

³ "You shall have no other gods before Me.

⁴ "You shall not make for yourself a carved image—any likeness *of anything* that *is* in heaven above, or that *is* in the earth beneath, or that *is* in the water under the earth; ⁵you shall not bow down to them nor serve them. For I, the LORD

your God, *am* a jealous God, visiting the iniquity of the fathers upon the children to the third and fourth *generations* of those who hate Me, 6but showing mercy to thousands, to those who love Me and keep My commandments.

7 "You shall not take the name of the LORD your God in vain, for the LORD will not hold *him* guiltless who takes His name in vain.

8 "Remember the Sabbath day, to keep it holy. 9Six days you shall labor and do all your work, 10but the seventh day *is* the Sabbath of the LORD your God. *In it* you shall do no work: you, nor your son, nor your daughter, nor your male servant, nor your female servant, nor your cattle, nor your stranger who *is* within your gates. 11For *in* six days the LORD made the heavens and the earth, the sea, and all that *is* in them, and rested the seventh day. Therefore the LORD blessed the Sabbath day and hallowed it.

12 "Honor your father and your mother, that your days may be long upon the land which the LORD your God is giving you.

13 "You shall not murder.

14 "You shall not commit adultery.

15 "You shall not steal.

16 "You shall not bear false witness against your neighbor.

17 "You shall not covet your neighbor's house; you shall not covet your neighbor's wife, nor his male servant, nor his female servant, nor his ox, nor his donkey, nor anything that *is* your neighbor's."

The People Afraid of God's Presence

18Now all the people witnessed the thunderings, the lightning flashes, the sound of the trumpet, and the mountain smoking; and when the people saw *it,* they trembled and stood afar off. 19Then they said to Moses, "You speak with us, and we will hear; but let not God speak with us, lest we die."

20And Moses said to the people, "Do not fear; for God has come to test you, and that His fear may be before you, so that you may not sin." 21So the people stood afar off, but Moses drew near the thick darkness where God *was.*

The Law of the Altar

22Then the LORD said to Moses, "Thus you shall say to the children of Israel: 'You have seen that I have talked with you from heaven. 23You shall not make *anything to be* with Me—gods of silver or gods of gold you shall not make for yourselves. 24An altar of earth you shall make for Me, and

---

ROMANTIC QUOTES AND NOTES
Make Room for Sabbath Rest

ONE OF THE MOST NEGLECTED of the Ten Commandments is the Fourth Commandment: "Remember the Sabbath day, to keep it holy" (20:8). Dennis and I have found that one of the best ways to abide in Christ is to set aside a day of Sabbath rest (20:8–10).

Why is resting on the Sabbath so important? Because when we yield control of our lives to the Father, when we take a day to turn from our activity in order to abide more fully in Him, we receive strength for daily living throughout the coming week.

You might say a Sabbath rest is like a weekly tune-up for your soul. That's why this

courageous choice is so critical. Set aside one day in seven to rest from your work, to reengage your focus on the Lord, and to abide more fully in Him.

We're not necessarily suggesting that your Sabbath has to be on Sunday, although we think that's the best day. Pick your day. The key is to set aside one day in seven where you say no to the errands and the to-do list, where you step off the treadmill, catch your breath, and regain some margin. It's a day where you relax, pray, read Scripture, recreate, go fishing, take a walk, or take a nap.

you shall sacrifice on it your burnt offerings and your peace offerings, your sheep and your oxen. In every place where I record My name I will come to you, and I will bless you. ²⁵And if you make Me an altar of stone, you shall not build it of hewn stone; for if you use your tool on it, you have profaned it. ²⁶Nor shall you go up by steps to My altar, that your nakedness may not be exposed on it.'

The Law Concerning Servants

21 "Now these *are* the judgments which you shall set before them: ²If you buy a Hebrew servant, he shall serve six years; and in the seventh he shall go out free and pay nothing. ³If he comes in by himself, he shall go out by himself; if he *comes in* married, then his wife shall go out with him. ⁴If his master has given him a wife, and she has borne him sons or daughters, the wife and her children shall be her master's, and he shall go out by himself. ⁵But if the servant plainly says, 'I love my master, my wife, and my children; I will not go out free,' ⁶then his master shall bring him to the judges. He shall also bring him to the door, or to the doorpost, and his master shall pierce his ear with an awl; and he shall serve him forever.

⁷"And if a man sells his daughter to be a female slave, she shall not go out as the male slaves do. ⁸If she does not please her master, who has betrothed her to himself, then he shall let her be redeemed. He shall have no right to sell her to a foreign people, since he has dealt deceitfully with her. ⁹And if he has betrothed her to his son, he shall deal with her according to the custom of daughters. ¹⁰If he takes another *wife,* he shall not diminish her food, her clothing, and her marriage rights. ¹¹And if he does not do these three for her, then she shall go out free, without *paying* money.

The Law Concerning Violence

¹²"He who strikes a man so that he dies shall surely be put to death. ¹³However, if he did not lie in wait, but God delivered *him* into his hand, then I will appoint for you a place where he may flee.

¹⁴"But if a man acts with premeditation against his neighbor, to kill him by treachery, you shall take him from My altar, that he may die.

¹⁵"And he who strikes his father or his mother shall surely be put to death.

¹⁶"He who kidnaps a man and sells him, or if he is found in his hand, shall surely be put to death.

¹⁷"And he who curses his father or his mother shall surely be put to death.

¹⁸"If men contend with each other, and one strikes the other with a stone or with *his* fist, and he does not die but is confined to *his* bed, ¹⁹if he rises again and walks

ROMANTIC QUOTES AND NOTES
Honor Your Parents

GOD'S COMMAND TO HONOR OUR PARENTS (20:12) is radical in an age where we're encouraged to look back only to blame, throw stones, and find fault with them. Instead, the Lord wants us to appreciate and esteem our parents. How?

First, spend time with your parents on their agenda, not yours. That may mean visiting or calling them regularly.

Second, honor your parents through handwritten letters. In this junk-oriented world, nothing shows appreciation like taking the time to write out a lengthy letter—on paper, not e-mail.

Third, tell your parents, "I love you." Never underestimate the power of those three words! Your words of love are exactly what your mother or father needs to hear.

Finally, write and present a tribute. List the things you appreciate about your parents, including their admirable traits. When you're finished, type it, format it, and have it professionally framed. Then read it to them on a special occasion, such as a birthday, anniversary, or holiday.

DEVOTIONS FOR COUPLES • 20:14
Maintaining Emotional and Moral Fidelity

For too many people, Christians included, adultery is the first step out of a marriage. An emotional or sexual attachment to someone *other* than your spouse creates intense passions that sabotage trust and steal marital intimacy. For that reason, God stated emphatically in the Seventh Commandment, "You shall not commit adultery" (Ex. 20:14).

Adultery destroys homes and lives. Proverbs 6:27–29 details the consequences of playing with this kind of fire, "Can a man take fire to his bosom, and his clothes not be burned? Can one walk on hot coals, and his feet not be seared? So is he who goes in to his neighbor's wife; whoever touches her shall not be innocent."

Adultery, as alluring as it may seem, always fails to live up to its promises. It pledges excitement and fulfillment, and instead delivers pain and alienation. Peter Blichington, in his outstanding book *Sex Roles and the Christian Family*, cites a study by the Research Guild that measured sexual satisfaction. The guild found that "compared with the 67 percent of men and 55 percent of women who find marital sex very pleasurable, only 47 percent of the men and 37 percent of the women with extramarital experience rate its sexual aspect very pleasurable."

The grass is *not* greener on the other side of the fence!

The glistening highway of adultery is actually a rutted back road littered with loneliness, guilt, and broken hearts. Adultery supplants loyalty and trust with fear and suspicion. The consequences are enormous and last for a lifetime. As my colleague and friend Bob Lepine warns, "No sex outside of marriage is *that* good!"

Will you commit to emotional and moral fidelity to your spouse, no matter how much you struggle in your marriage? If so, three steps are critical:

First, *maintain a healthy sexual relationship.* Lovingly study your mate to learn what will keep him or her interested and satisfied in your sexual relationship. Cultivate the fine—and often forgotten—art of romance. Pursue your spouse with the same creativity and energy that characterized your dating relationship.

Second, *guard your heart in relation to the opposite sex.* According to Jesus, the eyes are the doorway to the heart (Matt. 6:22, 23). For this reason, restrict your gaze and refuse the temptation to look longingly at other men or women. Don't fantasize about someone else.

Proverbs 4:23 counsels, "Keep your heart with all diligence, for out of it spring the issues of life." Build boundaries around your heart by making yourself accountable to a friend for your secret thoughts.

Third, *be honest with your spouse about temptations.* One of the most important practices Barbara and I employed early in our marriage was that of sharing with each other when we experienced temptations. On more than one occasion I've asked her to pray for me because I was struggling with lust. Once, in our first year of marriage, Barbara shared with me that a certain man was being inappropriately friendly with her. These confessions can seem risky, but when a husband and wife are committed to each other, they actually help to nurture trust.

As partners in life, we need to protect our fidelity and trust ... all the days of our lives.

---

about outside with his staff, then he who struck *him* shall be acquitted. He shall only pay *for* the loss of his time, and shall provide *for him* to be thoroughly healed.

²⁰"And if a man beats his male or female servant with a rod, so that he dies under his hand, he shall surely be punished. ²¹Notwithstanding, if he remains alive a day or two, he shall not be punished; for he *is* his property.

²²"If men fight, and hurt a woman with child, so that she gives birth prematurely, yet no harm follows, he shall surely be punished accordingly as the woman's husband imposes on him; and he shall pay as the judges *determine.* ²³But if *any* harm follows, then you shall give life for life, ²⁴eye for eye, tooth for tooth, hand for hand, foot for foot, ²⁵burn for burn, wound for wound, stripe for stripe.

²⁶"If a man strikes the eye of his male or female servant, and destroys it, he shall let him go free for the sake of his eye. ²⁷And if he knocks out the tooth of his male or female servant, he shall let him go free for the sake of his tooth.

Animal Control Laws

²⁸"If an ox gores a man or a woman to death, then the ox shall surely be stoned, and its flesh shall not be eaten; but the owner of the ox *shall be* acquitted. ²⁹But if the ox tended to thrust with its horn in times past, and it has been made known to his owner, and he has not kept it confined, so that it has killed a man or a woman, the ox shall be stoned and its owner also shall be put to death. ³⁰If there is imposed on him a sum of money, then he shall pay to redeem his life, whatever is imposed on him. ³¹Whether it has gored a son or gored a daughter, according to this judgment it shall be done to him. ³²If the ox gores a male or female servant, he shall give to their master thirty shekels of silver, and the ox shall be stoned.

³³"And if a man opens a pit, or if a man digs a pit and does not cover it, and an ox or a donkey falls in it, ³⁴the owner of the pit shall make *it* good; he shall give money to their owner, but the dead *animal* shall be his.

³⁵"If one man's ox hurts another's, so that it dies, then they shall sell the live ox and divide the money from it; and the dead *ox* they shall also divide. ³⁶Or if it was known that the ox tended to thrust in time past, and its owner has not kept it confined, he shall surely pay ox for ox, and the dead animal shall be his own.

Responsibility for Property

22 "If a man steals an ox or a sheep, and slaughters it or sells it, he shall restore five oxen for an ox and four sheep for a sheep. ²If the thief is found breaking in, and he is struck so that he dies, *there shall be* no guilt for his bloodshed. ³If the sun has risen on him, *there shall be* guilt for his bloodshed. He should make full restitution; if he has nothing, then he shall be sold for his theft. ⁴If the theft is certainly found alive in his hand, whether it is an ox or donkey or sheep, he shall restore double.

⁵"If a man causes a field or vineyard to be grazed, and lets loose his animal, and it feeds in another man's field, he shall make restitution from the best of his own field and the best of his own vineyard.

⁶"If fire breaks out and catches in thorns, so that stacked grain, standing grain, or the field is consumed, he who kindled the fire shall surely make restitution.

⁷"If a man delivers to his neighbor money or articles to keep, and it is stolen out of the man's house, if the thief is found, he shall pay double. ⁸If the thief is not found, then the master of the house shall be brought to the judges *to see* whether he has put his hand into his neighbor's goods.

⁹"For any kind of trespass, *whether it concerns* an ox, a donkey, a sheep, or clothing, *or* for any kind of lost thing which *another* claims to be his, the cause of both parties shall come before the judges; *and* whomever the judges condemn shall pay double to his neighbor. ¹⁰If a man delivers to his neighbor a donkey, an ox, a sheep, or any animal to keep, and it dies, is hurt, or driven away, no one seeing *it,* ¹¹*then* an oath of the Lord shall be between them both, that he has not put his hand into his neighbor's goods; and the owner of it shall accept *that,* and he shall not make *it* good. ¹²But if, in fact, it is stolen from him, he shall make restitution to the owner of it. ¹³If it is torn to pieces *by a beast, then* he shall bring it as evidence, *and* he shall not make good what was torn.

¹⁴"And if a man borrows *anything* from his neighbor, and it becomes injured or dies, the owner of it not *being* with it, he shall surely make *it* good. ¹⁵If its owner *was* with it, he shall not make *it* good; if it *was* hired, it came for its hire.

Moral and Ceremonial Principles

¹⁶"If a man entices a virgin who is not betrothed, and lies with her, he shall surely pay the bride-price for her *to be* his wife. ¹⁷If her father utterly refuses to give her to him, he shall pay money according to the bride-price of virgins.

¹⁸"You shall not permit a sorceress to live.

¹⁹"Whoever lies with an animal shall surely be put to death.

²⁰"He who sacrifices to *any* god, except to the Lord only, he shall be utterly destroyed.

²¹"You shall neither mistreat a stranger nor oppress him, for you were strangers in the land of Egypt.

²²"You shall not afflict any widow or fatherless child. ²³If you afflict them in any way, *and* they cry at all to Me, I will surely hear their cry; ²⁴and My wrath will become hot, and I will kill you with the sword; your wives shall be widows, and your children fatherless.

²⁵"If you lend money to *any of* My people *who are* poor among you, you shall not

be like a moneylender to him; you shall not charge him interest. ²⁶If you ever take your neighbor's garment as a pledge, you shall return it to him before the sun goes down. ²⁷For that *is* his only covering, it *is* his garment for his skin. What will he sleep in? And it will be that when he cries to Me, I will hear, for I *am* gracious.

²⁸"You shall not revile God, nor curse a ruler of your people.

²⁹"You shall not delay *to offer* the first of your ripe produce and your juices. The first-born of your sons you shall give to Me. ³⁰Likewise you shall do with your oxen *and* your sheep. It shall be with its mother seven days; on the eighth day you shall give it to Me.

³¹"And you shall be holy men to Me: you shall not eat meat torn *by beasts* in the field; you shall throw it to the dogs.

Justice for All

23 "You shall not circulate a false report. Do not put your hand with the wicked to be an unrighteous witness. ²You shall not follow a crowd to do evil; nor shall you testify in a dispute so as to turn aside after many to pervert *justice.* ³You shall not show partiality to a poor man in his dispute.

⁴"If you meet your enemy's ox or his donkey going astray, you shall surely bring it back to him again. ⁵If you see the donkey of one who hates you lying under its burden, and you would refrain from helping it, you shall surely help him with it.

⁶"You shall not pervert the judgment of your poor in his dispute. ⁷Keep yourself far from a false matter; do not kill the innocent and righteous. For I will not justify the wicked. ⁸And you shall take no bribe, for a bribe blinds the discerning and perverts the words of the righteous.

⁹"Also you shall not oppress a stranger, for you know the heart of a stranger, because you were strangers in the land of Egypt.

The Law of Sabbaths

¹⁰"Six years you shall sow your land and gather in its produce, ¹¹but the seventh *year* you shall let it rest and lie fallow, that the poor of your people may eat; and what

---

ROMANCE FAQ

Q: *What is a biblical approach to contraception?*

1. God is the originator of life; therefore, all of life is sacred (Ps. 139; Job 31:15).

2. Human life was created in the image of God (Gen. 1:26).

3. Human life begins at conception (Ps. 139:13–16). Any method of contraception that interferes with the healthy development of a fertilized egg should be avoided.

4. God has given humankind authority, responsibility, and guardianship to protect human life (Gen. 1:26; Ex. 20:13).

5. Embrace a biblical view of children. While our culture sees children as a burden, the Bible considers them a gift.

6. The biblical command is to be fruitful and multiply (Gen. 1:28). Bearing children is one of God's purposes for marriage. Though some couples deal with infertility, nowhere does Scripture suggest that couples can choose on their own not to have children.

7. As a couple, you should seek wise counsel and prayerfully determine your contraceptive choices. Scripture gives no specific instruction about the size of a family (Rom. 12:1, 2).

8. Finally, don't use your convictions as a spiritual club on others. Be careful not to judge others who may view these issues from a perspective very different from your own.

they leave, the beasts of the field may eat. In like manner you shall do with your vineyard *and* your olive grove. [12]Six days you shall do your work, and on the seventh day you shall rest, that your ox and your donkey may rest, and the son of your female servant and the stranger may be refreshed.

[13]"And in all that I have said to you, be circumspect and make no mention of the name of other gods, nor let it be heard from your mouth.

Three Annual Feasts

[14]"Three times you shall keep a feast to Me in the year: [15]You shall keep the Feast of Unleavened Bread (you shall eat unleavened bread seven days, as I commanded you, at the time appointed in the month of Abib, for in it you came out of Egypt; none shall appear before Me empty); [16]and the Feast of Harvest, the firstfruits of your labors which you have sown in the field; and the Feast of Ingathering at the end of the year, when you have gathered in *the fruit of* your labors from the field.

[17]"Three times in the year all your males shall appear before the Lord God.[a]

[18]"You shall not offer the blood of My sacrifice with leavened bread; nor shall the fat of My sacrifice remain until morning. [19]The first of the firstfruits of your land you shall bring into the house of the LORD your God. You shall not boil a young goat in its mother's milk.

The Angel and the Promises

[20]"Behold, I send an Angel before you to keep you in the way and to bring you into the place which I have prepared. [21]Beware of Him and obey His voice; do not provoke Him, for He will not pardon your transgressions; for My name *is* in Him. [22]But if you indeed obey His voice and do all that I speak, then I will be an enemy to your enemies and an adversary to your adversaries. [23]For My Angel will go before you and bring you in to the Amorites and the Hittites and the Perizzites and the Canaanites and the Hivites and the Jebusites; and I will cut them off. [24]You shall not bow down to their gods,

nor serve them, nor do according to their works; but you shall utterly overthrow them and completely break down their *sacred* pillars.

[25]"So you shall serve the LORD your God, and He will bless your bread and your water. And I will take sickness away from the midst of you. [26]No one shall suffer miscarriage or be barren in your land; I will fulfill the number of your days.

[27]"I will send My fear before you, I will cause confusion among all the people to whom you come, and will make all your enemies turn *their* backs to you. [28]And I will send hornets before you, which shall drive out the Hivite, the Canaanite, and the Hittite from before you. [29]I will not drive them out from before you in one year, lest the land become desolate and the beasts of the field become too numerous for you. [30]Little by little I will drive them out from before you, until you have increased, and you inherit the land. [31]And I will set your bounds from the Red Sea to the sea, Philistia, and from the desert to the River.[a] For I will deliver the inhabitants of the land into your hand, and you shall drive them out before you. [32]You shall make no covenant with them, nor with their gods. [33]They shall not dwell in your land, lest they make you sin against Me. For *if* you serve their gods, it will surely be a snare to you."

Israel Affirms the Covenant

24 Now He said to Moses, "Come up to the LORD, you and Aaron, Nadab and Abihu, and seventy of the elders of Israel, and worship from afar. [2]And Moses alone shall come near the LORD, but they shall not come near; nor shall the people go up with him."

[3]So Moses came and told the people all the words of the LORD and all the judgments. And all the people answered with one voice and said, "All the words which the LORD has said we will do." [4]And Moses wrote all the words of the LORD. And he rose early in the morning, and built an altar at the foot of the mountain, and twelve pillars according to the twelve tribes of Israel. [5]Then he sent young men of the children of Israel, who offered burnt offerings and sacrificed peace offerings of oxen to the LORD.

23:17 [a]Hebrew *YHWH,* usually translated LORD
23:31 [a]Hebrew *Nahar,* the Euphrates

⁶And Moses took half the blood and put *it* in basins, and half the blood he sprinkled on the altar. ⁷Then he took the Book of the Covenant and read in the hearing of the people. And they said, "All that the LORD has said we will do, and be obedient." ⁸And Moses took the blood, sprinkled *it* on the people, and said, "This is the blood of the covenant which the LORD has made with you according to all these words."

On the Mountain with God

⁹Then Moses went up, also Aaron, Nadab, and Abihu, and seventy of the elders of Israel, ¹⁰and they saw the God of Israel. And *there was* under His feet as it were a paved work of sapphire stone, and it was like the very heavens in *its* clarity. ¹¹But on the nobles of the children of Israel He did not lay His hand. So they saw God, and they ate and drank.

¹²Then the LORD said to Moses, "Come up to Me on the mountain and be there; and I will give you tablets of stone, and the law and commandments which I have written, that you may teach them."

¹³So Moses arose with his assistant Joshua, and Moses went up to the mountain of God. ¹⁴And he said to the elders, "Wait here for us until we come back to you. Indeed, Aaron and Hur *are* with you. If any man has a difficulty, let him go to them." ¹⁵Then Moses went up into the mountain, and a cloud covered the mountain.

¹⁶Now the glory of the LORD rested on Mount Sinai, and the cloud covered it six days. And on the seventh day He called to Moses out of the midst of the cloud. ¹⁷The sight of the glory of the LORD *was* like a consuming fire on the top of the mountain in the eyes of the children of Israel. ¹⁸So Moses went into the midst of the cloud and went up into the mountain. And Moses was on the mountain forty days and forty nights.

Offerings for the Sanctuary

25 Then the LORD spoke to Moses, saying: ²"Speak to the children of Israel, that they bring Me an offering. From everyone who gives it willingly with his heart you shall take My offering. ³And this *is* the offering which you shall take from them: gold, silver, and bronze; ⁴blue, purple, and scarlet *thread,* fine linen, and goats' *hair;* ⁵ram skins dyed red, badger

---

| PARENTING MATTERS | **Q: *What benefits do our children receive from appropriate discipline?*** |

Parental discipline brings many benefits. Among them:

1. It gives wisdom. "The rod and rebuke give wisdom, but a child left to himself brings shame to his mother" (Prov. 29:15). God wants us to impart skill in everyday living to our kids.

2. It keeps a child from hell. "Do not withhold correction from a child, for if you beat him with a rod, he will not die. You shall beat him with a rod, and deliver his soul from hell" (Prov. 23:13, 14). This sounds harsh, but the consequences of a child's disobedience and uncurbed will can be eternal.

3. It prevents the ruin of a child's life. "Chasten your son while there is hope, and do not set your heart on his destruction" (Prov. 19:18). If your child doesn't learn about limits and boundaries from you, she will learn about them soon enough in less safe places.

4. It communicates love. "He who spares his rod hates his son, but he who loves him disciplines him promptly" (Prov. 13:24). You love your children when you install guard rails on their passions through appropriate discipline and boundaries.

5. It prevents the parents from being shamed. See Proverbs 29:15 above.

skins, and acacia wood; ⁶oil for the light, and spices for the anointing oil and for the sweet incense; ⁷onyx stones, and stones to be set in the ephod and in the breastplate. ⁸And let them make Me a sanctuary, that I may dwell among them. ⁹According to all that I show you, *that is,* the pattern of the tabernacle and the pattern of all its furnishings, just so you shall make *it.*

The Ark of the Testimony

¹⁰"And they shall make an ark of acacia wood; two and a half cubits *shall be* its length, a cubit and a half its width, and a cubit and a half its height. ¹¹And you shall overlay it with pure gold, inside and out you shall overlay it, and shall make on it a molding of gold all around. ¹²You shall cast four rings of gold for it, and put *them* in its four corners; two rings *shall be* on one side, and two rings on the other side. ¹³And you shall make poles *of* acacia wood, and overlay them with gold. ¹⁴You shall put the poles into the rings on the sides of the ark, that the ark may be carried by them. ¹⁵The poles shall be in the rings of the ark; they shall not be taken from it. ¹⁶And you shall put into the ark the Testimony which I will give you.

¹⁷"You shall make a mercy seat of pure gold; two and a half cubits *shall be* its length and a cubit and a half its width. ¹⁸And you shall make two cherubim of gold; of hammered work you shall make them at the two ends of the mercy seat. ¹⁹Make one cherub at one end, and the other cherub at the other end; you shall make the cherubim at the two ends of it *of one piece* with the mercy seat. ²⁰And the cherubim shall stretch out *their* wings above, covering the mercy seat with their wings, and they shall face one another; the faces of the cherubim *shall be* toward the mercy seat. ²¹You shall put the mercy seat on top of the ark, and in the ark you shall put the Testimony that I will give you. ²²And there I will meet with you, and I will speak with you from above the mercy seat, from between the two cherubim which *are* on the ark of the Testimony, about everything which I will give you in commandment to the children of Israel.

The Table for the Showbread

²³"You shall also make a table of acacia wood; two cubits *shall be* its length, a cubit its width, and a cubit and a half its height. ²⁴And you shall overlay it with pure gold, and make a molding of gold all around. ²⁵You shall make for it a frame of a handbreadth all around, and you shall make a gold molding for the frame all around. ²⁶And you shall make for it four rings of gold, and put the rings on the four corners that *are* at its four legs. ²⁷The rings shall be close to the frame, as holders for the poles to bear the table. ²⁸And you shall make the poles of acacia wood, and overlay them with gold, that the table may be carried with them. ²⁹You shall make its dishes, its pans, its pitchers, and its bowls for pouring. You shall make them of pure gold. ³⁰And you shall set the showbread on the table before Me always.

The Gold Lampstand

³¹"You shall also make a lampstand of pure gold; the lampstand shall be of hammered work. Its shaft, its branches, its bowls, its *ornamental* knobs, and flowers shall be *of one piece.* ³²And six branches shall come out of its sides: three branches of the lampstand out of one side, and three branches of the lampstand out of the other side. ³³Three bowls *shall be* made like almond *blossoms* on one branch, *with* an *ornamental* knob and a flower, and three bowls made like almond *blossoms* on the other branch, *with* an *ornamental* knob and a flower—and so for the six branches that come out of the lampstand. ³⁴On the lampstand itself four bowls *shall be* made like almond *blossoms, each with* its *ornamental* knob and flower. ³⁵And *there shall be* a knob under the *first* two branches of the same, a knob under the *second* two branches of the same, and a knob under the *third* two branches of the same, according to the six branches that extend from the lampstand. ³⁶Their knobs and their branches *shall be of one piece;* all of it *shall be* one hammered piece of pure gold. ³⁷You shall make seven lamps for it, and they shall arrange its lamps so that they give light in front of it. ³⁸And its wick-trimmers and

their trays *shall be* of pure gold. ³⁹It shall be made of a talent of pure gold, with all these utensils. ⁴⁰And see to it that you make *them* according to the pattern which was shown you on the mountain.

The Tabernacle

26 "Moreover you shall make the tabernacle *with* ten curtains *of* fine woven linen and blue, purple, and scarlet *thread;* with artistic designs of cherubim you shall weave them. ²The length of each curtain *shall be* twenty-eight cubits, and the width of each curtain four cubits. And every one of the curtains shall have the same measurements. ³Five curtains shall be coupled to one another, and *the other* five curtains *shall be* coupled to one another. ⁴And you shall make loops of blue *yarn* on the edge of the curtain on the selvedge of *one* set, and likewise you shall do on the outer edge of *the other* curtain of the second set. ⁵Fifty loops you shall make in the one curtain, and fifty loops you shall make on the edge of the curtain that *is* on the end of the second set, that the loops may be clasped to one another. ⁶And you shall make fifty clasps of gold, and couple the curtains together with the clasps, so that it may be one tabernacle.

⁷"You shall also make curtains of goats' *hair,* to be a tent over the tabernacle. You

shall make eleven curtains. ⁸The length of each curtain *shall be* thirty cubits, and the width of each curtain four cubits; and the eleven curtains shall all have the same measurements. ⁹And you shall couple five curtains by themselves and six curtains by themselves, and you shall double over the sixth curtain at the forefront of the tent. ¹⁰You shall make fifty loops on the edge of the curtain that is outermost in *one* set, and fifty loops on the edge of the curtain of the second set. ¹¹And you shall make fifty bronze clasps, put the clasps into the loops, and couple the tent together, that it may be one. ¹²The remnant that remains of the curtains of the tent, the half curtain that remains, shall hang over the back of the tabernacle. ¹³And a cubit on one side and a cubit on the other side, of what remains of the length of the curtains of the tent, shall hang over the sides of the tabernacle, on this side and on that side, to cover it.

¹⁴"You shall also make a covering of ram skins dyed red for the tent, and a covering of badger skins above that.

¹⁵"And for the tabernacle you shall make the boards of acacia wood, standing upright. ¹⁶Ten cubits *shall be* the length of a board, and a cubit and a half *shall be* the width of each board. ¹⁷Two tenons *shall be* in each board for binding one to another. Thus you shall make for all the boards of the tabernacle. ¹⁸And you shall make the boards for the tabernacle, twenty boards for the south side. ¹⁹You shall make forty sockets of silver under the twenty boards: two sockets under each of the boards for its two tenons. ²⁰And for the second side of the tabernacle, the north side, *there shall be* twenty boards ²¹and their forty sockets of silver: two sockets under each of the boards. ²²For the far side of the tabernacle, westward, you shall make six boards. ²³And you shall also make two boards for the two back corners of the tabernacle. ²⁴They shall be coupled together at the bottom and they shall be coupled together at the top by one ring. Thus it shall be for both of them. They shall be for the two corners. ²⁵So there shall be eight boards with their sockets of silver—sixteen sockets— two sockets under each of the boards. ²⁶"And you shall make bars of acacia

INTIMATE MOMENTS

Get into the habit of buying her silly souvenirs whenever you're out on a date. They don't have to be much—a little stuffed animal, a silk rose, a knick-knack, a sticker—anything that reminds her of your night together and that will bring a smile to her face. Purchase (or make) a special box where she can store all her keepsakes, and occasionally sneak a peak to remind yourself of all your special times together. And if she wants to talk about them, indulge her!

wood: five for the boards on one side of the tabernacle, ²⁷five bars for the boards on the other side of the tabernacle, and five bars for the boards of the side of the tabernacle, for the far side westward. ²⁸The middle bar shall pass through the midst of the boards from end to end. ²⁹You shall overlay the boards with gold, make their rings of gold *as* holders for the bars, and overlay the bars with gold. ³⁰And you shall raise up the tabernacle according to its pattern which you were shown on the mountain.

³¹"You shall make a veil woven of blue, purple, and scarlet *thread,* and fine woven linen. It shall be woven with an artistic design of cherubim. ³²You shall hang it upon the four pillars of acacia *wood* overlaid with gold. Their hooks *shall be* gold, upon four sockets of silver. ³³And you shall hang the veil from the clasps. Then you shall bring the ark of the Testimony in there, behind the veil. The veil shall be a divider for you between the holy *place* and the Most Holy. ³⁴You shall put the mercy seat upon the ark of the Testimony in the Most Holy. ³⁵You shall set the table outside the veil, and the lampstand across from the table on the side of the tabernacle toward the south; and you shall put the table on the north side.

³⁶"You shall make a screen for the door of the tabernacle, *woven of* blue, purple, and scarlet *thread,* and fine woven linen, made by a weaver. ³⁷And you shall make for the screen five pillars of acacia *wood,* and overlay them with gold; their hooks *shall be* gold, and you shall cast five sockets of bronze for them.

The Altar of Burnt Offering

27 "You shall make an altar of acacia wood, five cubits long and five cubits wide—the altar shall be square—and its height *shall be* three cubits. ²You shall make its horns on its four corners; its horns shall be of one piece with it. And you shall overlay it with bronze. ³Also you shall make its pans to receive its ashes, and its shovels and its basins and its forks and its firepans; you shall make all its utensils of bronze. ⁴You shall make a grate for it, a network of bronze; and on the network you shall make four bronze rings at its four corners. ⁵You

shall put it under the rim of the altar beneath, that the network may be midway up the altar. ⁶And you shall make poles for the altar, poles of acacia wood, and overlay them with bronze. ⁷The poles shall be put in the rings, and the poles shall be on the two sides of the altar to bear it. ⁸You shall make it hollow with boards; as it was shown you on the mountain, so shall they make *it.*

The Court of the Tabernacle

⁹"You shall also make the court of the tabernacle. For the south side *there shall be* hangings for the court *made of* fine woven linen, one hundred cubits long for one side. ¹⁰And its twenty pillars and their twenty sockets *shall be* bronze. The hooks of the pillars and their bands *shall be* silver. ¹¹Likewise along the length of the north side *there shall be* hangings one hundred *cubits* long, with its twenty pillars and their twenty sockets of bronze, and the hooks of the pillars and their bands of silver.

¹²"And along the width of the court on the west side *shall be* hangings of fifty cubits, with their ten pillars and their ten sockets. ¹³The width of the court on the east side *shall be* fifty cubits. ¹⁴The hangings on *one* side *of the gate shall be* fifteen cubits, *with* their three pillars and their three sockets. ¹⁵And on the other side *shall be* hangings of fifteen *cubits, with* their three pillars and their three sockets.

¹⁶"For the gate of the court *there shall be* a screen twenty cubits long, *woven of* blue, purple, and scarlet *thread,* and fine woven linen, made by a weaver. It *shall have* four pillars and four sockets. ¹⁷All the pillars around the court shall have bands of silver; their hooks *shall be* of silver and their sockets of bronze. ¹⁸The length of the court *shall be* one hundred cubits, the width fifty throughout, and the height five cubits, *made of* fine woven linen, and its sockets of bronze. ¹⁹All the utensils of the tabernacle for all its service, all its pegs, and all the pegs of the court, *shall be* of bronze.

The Care of the Lampstand

²⁰"And you shall command the children of Israel that they bring you pure oil of pressed olives for the light, to cause the lamp to burn continually. ²¹In the tabernacle

of meeting, outside the veil which *is* before the Testimony, Aaron and his sons shall tend it from evening until morning before the LORD. *It shall be* a statute forever to their generations on behalf of the children of Israel.

Garments for the Priesthood

28 "Now take Aaron your brother, and his sons with him, from among the children of Israel, that he may minister to Me as priest, Aaron *and* Aaron's sons: Nadab, Abihu, Eleazar, and Ithamar. ²And you shall make holy garments for Aaron your brother, for glory and for beauty. ³So you shall speak to all *who are* gifted artisans, whom I have filled with the spirit of wisdom, that they may make Aaron's garments, to consecrate him, that he may minister to Me as priest. ⁴And these *are* the garments which they shall make: a breastplate, an ephod,ᵃ a robe, a skillfully woven tunic, a turban, and a sash. So they shall make holy garments for Aaron your brother and his sons, that he may minister to Me as priest.

The Ephod

⁵"They shall take the gold, blue, purple, and scarlet *thread,* and the fine linen, ⁶and they shall make the ephod of gold, blue, purple, *and* scarlet *thread,* and fine woven linen, artistically worked. ⁷It shall have two shoulder straps joined at its two edges, and *so* it shall be joined together. ⁸And the intricately woven band of the ephod, which *is* on it, shall be of the same workmanship, *made of* gold, blue, purple, and scarlet *thread,* and fine woven linen.

⁹"Then you shall take two onyx stones and engrave on them the names of the sons of Israel: ¹⁰six of their names on one stone and six names on the other stone, in order of their birth. ¹¹With the work of an engraver in stone, *like* the engravings of a signet, you shall engrave the two stones with the names of the sons of Israel. You shall set them in settings of gold. ¹²And you shall put the two stones on the shoulders of the ephod *as* memorial stones for the sons of Israel. So Aaron shall bear their names before the LORD on his two shoulders as a memorial. ¹³You shall also make settings of gold, ¹⁴and you shall make two chains of pure gold like braided cords, and fasten the braided chains to the settings.

The Breastplate

¹⁵"You shall make the breastplate of judgment. Artistically woven according to the workmanship of the ephod you shall make it: of gold, blue, purple, and scarlet *thread,* and fine woven linen, you shall make it. ¹⁶It shall be doubled into a square: a span *shall be* its length, and a span *shall be* its width. ¹⁷And you shall put settings of stones in it, four rows of stones: *The first* row *shall be* a sardius, a topaz, and an emerald; *this shall be* the first row; ¹⁸the second row *shall be* a turquoise, a sapphire, and a diamond; ¹⁹the third row, a jacinth, an agate, and an amethyst; ²⁰and the fourth row, a beryl, an onyx, and a jasper. They shall be set in gold settings. ²¹And the stones shall have the names of the sons of Israel, twelve according to their names, *like* the engravings of a signet, each one with its own name; they shall be according to the twelve tribes.

²²"You shall make chains for the breastplate at the end, like braided cords of pure gold. ²³And you shall make two rings of gold for the breastplate, and put the two rings on the two ends of the breastplate. ²⁴Then you shall put the two braided *chains* of gold in the two rings which are on the ends of the breastplate; ²⁵and the *other* two ends of the two braided *chains* you shall fasten to the two settings, and put them on the shoulder straps of the ephod in the front.

²⁶"You shall make two rings of gold, and put them on the two ends of the breastplate, on the edge of it, which is on the inner side of the ephod. ²⁷And two *other* rings of gold you shall make, and put them on the two shoulder straps, underneath the ephod toward its front, right at the seam above the intricately woven band of the ephod. ²⁸They shall bind the breastplate by means of its rings to the rings of the ephod, using a blue cord, so that it is above the intricately woven band of the ephod, and so that the breastplate does not come loose from the ephod.

²⁹"So Aaron shall bear the names of the sons of Israel on the breastplate of judgment over his heart, when he goes into the

---

28:4 ᵃThat is, an ornamented vest

holy *place,* as a memorial before the LORD continually. [30]And you shall put in the breastplate of judgment the Urim and the Thummim,[a] and they shall be over Aaron's heart when he goes in before the LORD. So Aaron shall bear the judgment of the children of Israel over his heart before the LORD continually.

Other Priestly Garments

[31]"You shall make the robe of the ephod all of blue. [32]There shall be an opening for his head in the middle of it; it shall have a woven binding all around its opening, like the opening in a coat of mail, so that it does not tear. [33]And upon its hem you shall make pomegranates of blue, purple, and scarlet, all around its hem, and bells of gold between them all around: [34]a golden bell and a pomegranate, a golden bell and a pomegranate, upon the hem of the robe all around. [35]And it shall be upon Aaron when he ministers, and its sound will be heard when he goes into the holy *place* before the LORD and when he comes out, that he may not die.

[36]"You shall also make a plate of pure gold and engrave on it, *like* the engraving of a signet:

HOLINESS TO THE LORD.

[37]And you shall put it on a blue cord, that it may be on the turban; it shall be on the front of the turban. [38]So it shall be on Aaron's forehead, that Aaron may bear the iniquity of the holy things which the children of Israel hallow in all their holy gifts; and it shall always be on his forehead, that they may be accepted before the LORD.

[39]"You shall skillfully weave the tunic of fine linen *thread,* you shall make the turban of fine linen, and you shall make the sash of woven work.

[40]"For Aaron's sons you shall make tunics, and you shall make sashes for them. And you shall make hats for them, for glory and beauty. [41]So you shall put them on Aaron your brother and on his sons with him. You shall anoint them, consecrate them, and sanctify them, that they may

minister to Me as priests. [42]And you shall make for them linen trousers to cover their nakedness; they shall reach from the waist to the thighs. [43]They shall be on Aaron and on his sons when they come into the tabernacle of meeting, or when they come near the altar to minister in the holy *place,* that they do not incur iniquity and die. *It shall be* a statute forever to him and his descendants after him.

Aaron and His Sons Consecrated

29 "And this is what you shall do to them to hallow them for ministering to Me as priests: Take one young bull and two rams without blemish, [2]and unleavened bread, unleavened cakes mixed with oil, and unleavened wafers anointed with oil (you shall make them of wheat flour). [3]You shall put them in one basket and bring them in the basket, with the bull and the two rams.

[4]"And Aaron and his sons you shall bring to the door of the tabernacle of meeting, and you shall wash them with water. [5]Then you shall take the garments, put the tunic on Aaron, and the robe of the ephod, the ephod, and the breastplate, and gird him with the intricately woven band of the ephod. [6]You shall put the turban on his head, and put the holy crown on the turban. [7]And you shall take the anointing oil, pour *it* on his head, and anoint him. [8]Then you shall bring his sons and put tunics on them. [9]And you shall gird them with sashes, Aaron and his sons, and put the hats on them. The priesthood shall be theirs for a perpetual statute. So you shall consecrate Aaron and his sons.

[10]"You shall also have the bull brought before the tabernacle of meeting, and Aaron and his sons shall put their hands on the head of the bull. [11]Then you shall kill the bull before the LORD, *by* the door of the tabernacle of meeting. [12]You shall take *some* of the blood of the bull and put *it* on the horns of the altar with your finger, and pour all the blood beside the base of the altar. [13]And you shall take all the fat that covers the entrails, the fatty lobe *attached* to the liver, and the two kidneys and the fat that *is* on them, and burn *them* on the altar. [14]But the flesh of the bull, with its skin and

---

28:30 [a]Literally *the Lights and the Perfections* (compare Leviticus 8:8)

its offal, you shall burn with fire outside the camp. It *is* a sin offering.

15"You shall also take one ram, and Aaron and his sons shall put their hands on the head of the ram; 16and you shall kill the ram, and you shall take its blood and sprinkle *it* all around on the altar. 17Then you shall cut the ram in pieces, wash its entrails and its legs, and put *them* with its pieces and with its head. 18And you shall burn the whole ram on the altar. It *is* a burnt offering to the LORD; it *is* a sweet aroma, an offering made by fire to the LORD.

19"You shall also take the other ram, and Aaron and his sons shall put their hands on the head of the ram. 20Then you shall kill the ram, and take some of its blood and put *it* on the tip of the right ear of Aaron and on the tip of the right ear of his sons, on the thumb of their right hand and on the big toe of their right foot, and sprinkle the blood all around on the altar. 21And you shall take some of the blood that is on the altar, and some of the anointing oil, and sprinkle *it* on Aaron and on his garments, on his sons and on the garments of his sons with him; and he and his garments shall be hallowed, and his sons and his sons' garments with him.

22"Also you shall take the fat of the ram, the fat tail, the fat that covers the entrails, the fatty lobe *attached to* the liver, the two kidneys and the fat on them, the right thigh (for it *is* a ram of consecration), 23one loaf of bread, one cake *made with* oil, and one wafer from the basket of the unleavened bread that *is* before the LORD; 24and you shall put all these in the hands of Aaron and in the hands of his sons, and you shall wave them *as* a wave offering before the LORD. 25You shall receive them back from their hands and burn *them* on the altar as a burnt offering, as a sweet aroma before the LORD. It *is* an offering made by fire to the LORD.

26"Then you shall take the breast of the ram of Aaron's consecration and wave it *as* a wave offering before the LORD; and it shall be your portion. 27And from the ram of the consecration you shall consecrate the breast of the wave offering which is waved, and the thigh of the heave offering which is raised, of *that* which *is* for Aaron and of *that* which is for his sons. 28It shall be from the children of Israel *for* Aaron and his sons by a statute forever. For it is a heave offering; it shall be a heave offering from the children of Israel from the sacrifices of their peace offerings, *that is,* their heave offering to the LORD.

29"And the holy garments of Aaron shall

ROMANCE FAQ

Q: *How can a young couple best handle the inevitable challenges of the first five years of marriage?*

Some of the more common areas of conflict most couples face early on include: finances, in-laws, spiritual growth together, the roles of husband and wife, where to attend church, and conflict resolution. Consider a few pointers that will go a long way toward helping you and your spouse handle these challenges:

1. *During your first years of marriage, I'd strongly recommend that you ask a more mature couple to mentor you.* Habits are formed early in a marriage, so why not ask someone who's a bit further down the road to train both of you.

2. *When you married, you began a lifelong commitment to love and forgiveness.* Remain committed. Love always. Remember, "Love covers a multitude of sins" (1 Pet. 4:8).

3. *Your marriage won't grow without communication and understanding.* You'll know you understand your spouse when you can verbally express your mate's actual needs and desires, and he or she agrees with that expression. Guys, seek to understand your wives. Ladies, help him to understand you.

4. *Walk a mile in your mate's shoes.* Accept God's provision, knowing that He has an agenda for your life even through unmet expectations.

5. *Don't give up on your dreams.* While all the things you imagined your marriage to be may not come true, God may have a new dream for you. Talk about your dreams. Then dream together.

be his sons' after him, to be anointed in them and to be consecrated in them. ³⁰That son who becomes priest in his place shall put them on for seven days, when he enters the tabernacle of meeting to minister in the holy *place.*

³¹"And you shall take the ram of the consecration and boil its flesh in the holy place. ³²Then Aaron and his sons shall eat the flesh of the ram, and the bread that *is* in the basket, *by* the door of the tabernacle of meeting. ³³They shall eat those things with which the atonement was made, to consecrate *and* to sanctify them; but an outsider shall not eat *them,* because they *are* holy. ³⁴And if any of the flesh of the consecration offerings, or of the bread, remains until the morning, then you shall burn the remainder with fire. It shall not be eaten, because it *is* holy.

³⁵"Thus you shall do to Aaron and his sons, according to all that I have commanded you. Seven days you shall consecrate them. ³⁶And you shall offer a bull every day *as* a sin offering for atonement. You shall cleanse the altar when you make atonement for it, and you shall anoint it to sanctify it. ³⁷Seven days you shall make atonement for the altar and sanctify it. And the altar shall be most holy. Whatever touches the altar must be holy.ª

The Daily Offerings

³⁸"Now this *is* what you shall offer on the altar: two lambs of the first year, day by day continually. ³⁹One lamb you shall offer in the morning, and the other lamb you shall offer at twilight. ⁴⁰With the one lamb shall be one-tenth *of an ephah* of flour mixed with one-fourth of a hin of pressed oil, and one-fourth of a hin of wine *as* a drink offering. ⁴¹And the other lamb you shall offer at twilight; and you shall offer with it the grain offering and the drink offering, as in the morning, for a sweet aroma, an offering made by fire to the LORD. ⁴²*This shall be* a continual burnt offering throughout your generations *at* the door of the tabernacle of meeting before the LORD, where I will meet you to speak with you. ⁴³And there I will meet

with the children of Israel, and *the taber-nacle* shall be sanctified by My glory. ⁴⁴So I will consecrate the tabernacle of meeting and the altar. I will also consecrate both Aaron and his sons to minister to Me as priests. ⁴⁵I will dwell among the children of Israel and will be their God. ⁴⁶And they shall know that I *am* the LORD their God, who brought them up out of the land of Egypt, that I may dwell among them. I *am* the LORD their God.

The Altar of Incense

30 "You shall make an altar to burn incense on; you shall make it of acacia wood. ²A cubit *shall be* its length and a cubit its width—it shall be square—and two cubits *shall be* its height. Its horns *shall be* of one piece with it. ³And you shall overlay its top, its sides all around, and its horns with pure gold; and you shall make for it a molding of gold all around. ⁴Two gold rings you shall make for it, under the molding on both its sides. You shall place *them* on its two sides, and they will be holders for the poles with which to bear it. ⁵You shall make the poles of acacia wood, and overlay them with gold. ⁶And you shall put it before the veil that *is* before the ark of the Testimony, before the mercy seat that *is* over the Testimony, where I will meet with you.

⁷"Aaron shall burn on it sweet incense every morning; when he tends the lamps, he shall burn incense on it. ⁸And when Aaron lights the lamps at twilight, he shall burn incense on it, a perpetual incense before the LORD throughout your generations. ⁹You shall not offer strange incense on it, or a burnt offering, or a grain offering; nor shall you pour a drink offering on it. ¹⁰And Aaron shall make atonement upon its horns once a year with the blood of the sin offering of atonement; once a year he shall make atonement upon it throughout your generations. It *is* most holy to the LORD."

The Ransom Money

¹¹Then the LORD spoke to Moses, saying: ¹²"When you take the census of the children of Israel for their number, then every man shall give a ransom for himself to the LORD, when you number them, that there may be no plague among them when

---

29:37 ªCompare Numbers 4:15 and Haggai 2:11–13

you number them. [13]This is what everyone among those who are numbered shall give: half a shekel according to the shekel of the sanctuary (a shekel *is* twenty gerahs). The half-shekel *shall be* an offering to the LORD. [14]Everyone included among those who are numbered, from twenty years old and above, shall give an offering to the LORD. [15]The rich shall not give more and the poor shall not give less than half a shekel, when *you* give an offering to the LORD, to make atonement for yourselves. [16]And you shall take the atonement money of the children of Israel, and shall appoint it for the service of the tabernacle of meeting, that it may be a memorial for the children of Israel before the LORD, to make atonement for yourselves."

The Bronze Laver

[17]Then the LORD spoke to Moses, saying: [18]"You shall also make a laver of bronze, with its base also of bronze, for washing. You shall put it between the tabernacle of meeting and the altar. And you shall put water in it, [19]for Aaron and his sons shall wash their hands and their feet in water from it. [20]When they go into the tabernacle of meeting, or when they come near the altar to minister, to burn an offering made by fire to the LORD, they shall wash with water, lest they die. [21]So they shall wash their hands and their feet, lest they die. And it shall be a statute forever to them—to him and his descendants throughout their generations."

The Holy Anointing Oil

[22]Moreover the LORD spoke to Moses, saying: [23]"Also take for yourself quality spices—five hundred *shekels* of liquid myrrh, half as much sweet-smelling cinnamon (two hundred and fifty *shekels*), two hundred and fifty *shekels* of sweet-smelling cane, [24]five hundred *shekels* of cassia, according to the shekel of the sanctuary, and a hin of olive oil. [25]And you shall make from these a holy anointing oil, an ointment compounded according to the art of the perfumer. It shall be a holy anointing oil. [26]With it you shall anoint the tabernacle of meeting and the ark of the Testimony; [27]the table and all its utensils,

the lampstand and its utensils, and the altar of incense; [28]the altar of burnt offering with all its utensils, and the laver and its base. [29]You shall consecrate them, that they may be most holy; whatever touches them must be holy.[a] [30]And you shall anoint Aaron and his sons, and consecrate them, that *they* may minister to Me as priests.

[31]"And you shall speak to the children of Israel, saying: 'This shall be a holy anointing oil to Me throughout your generations. [32]It shall not be poured on man's flesh; nor shall you make *any other* like it, according to its composition. It *is* holy, *and* it shall be holy to you. [33]Whoever compounds *any* like it, or whoever puts *any* of it on an outsider, shall be cut off from his people.'"

The Incense

[34]And the LORD said to Moses: "Take sweet spices, stacte and onycha and galbanum, and pure frankincense with *these* sweet spices; there shall be equal amounts of each. [35]You shall make of these an incense, a compound according to the art of the perfumer, salted, pure, *and* holy. [36]And you shall beat *some* of it very fine, and put some of it before the Testimony in the tabernacle of meeting where I will meet with you. It shall be most holy to you. [37]But *as for* the incense which you shall make, you shall not make any for yourselves, according to its composition. It shall be to you holy for the LORD. [38]Whoever makes *any* like it, to smell it, he shall be cut off from his people."

Artisans for Building the Tabernacle

31 Then the LORD spoke to Moses, saying: [2]"See, I have called by name Bezalel the son of Uri, the son of Hur, of the tribe of Judah. [3]And I have filled him with the Spirit of God, in wisdom, in understanding, in knowledge, and in all *manner of* workmanship, [4]to design artistic works, to work in gold, in silver, in bronze, [5]in cutting jewels for setting, in carving wood, and to work in all *manner of* workmanship.

[6]"And I, indeed I, have appointed with him Aholiab the son of Ahisamach, of the

30:29 [a]Compare Numbers 4:15 and Haggai 2:11–13

tribe of Dan; and I have put wisdom in the hearts of all the gifted artisans, that they may make all that I have commanded you: 7the tabernacle of meeting, the ark of the Testimony and the mercy seat that *is* on it, and all the furniture of the tabernacle—8the table and its utensils, the pure *gold* lampstand with all its utensils, the altar of incense, 9the altar of burnt offering with all its utensils, and the laver and its base—10the garments of ministry,a the holy garments for Aaron the priest and the garments of his sons, to minister as priests, 11and the anointing oil and sweet incense for the holy *place.* According to all that I have commanded you they shall do."

The Sabbath Law

12And the LORD spoke to Moses, saying, 13"Speak also to the children of Israel, saying: 'Surely My Sabbaths you shall keep, for it *is* a sign between Me and you throughout your generations, that *you* may know that I *am* the LORD who sanctifies you. 14You shall keep the Sabbath, therefore, for *it is* holy to you. Everyone who profanes it shall surely be put to death; for whoever does *any* work on it, that person shall be cut off from among his people. 15Work shall be done for six days, but the seventh *is* the Sabbath of rest, holy to the LORD. Whoever does *any* work on the Sabbath day, he shall surely be put to death. 16Therefore the children of Israel shall keep the Sabbath, to observe the Sabbath throughout their generations *as* a perpetual covenant. 17It *is* a sign between Me and the children of Israel forever; for *in* six days the LORD made the heavens and the earth, and on the seventh day He rested and was refreshed.'"

18And when He had made an end of speaking with him on Mount Sinai, He gave Moses two tablets of the Testimony, tablets of stone, written with the finger of God.

The Gold Calf

32 Now when the people saw that Moses delayed coming down from the mountain, the people gathered together to Aaron, and said to him, "Come, make us gods that shall go before us; for *as for* this

Moses, the man who brought us up out of the land of Egypt, we do not know what has become of him."

2And Aaron said to them, "Break off the golden earrings which *are* in the ears of your wives, your sons, and your daughters, and bring *them* to me." 3So all the people broke off the golden earrings which *were* in their ears, and brought *them* to Aaron. 4And he received *the gold* from their hand, and he fashioned it with an engraving tool, and made a molded calf.

Then they said, "This *is* your god, O Israel, that brought you out of the land of Egypt!"

5So when Aaron saw *it,* he built an altar before it. And Aaron made a proclamation and said, "Tomorrow *is* a feast to the LORD." 6Then they rose early on the next day, offered burnt offerings, and brought peace offerings; and the people sat down to eat and drink, and rose up to play.

7And the LORD said to Moses, "Go, get down! For your people whom you brought out of the land of Egypt have corrupted *themselves.* 8They have turned aside quickly out of the way which I commanded them. They have made themselves a molded calf, and worshiped it and sacrificed to it, and said, 'This *is* your god, O Israel, that brought you out of the land of Egypt!'" 9And the LORD said to Moses, "I have seen this people, and indeed it *is* a stiff-necked people! 10Now therefore, let Me alone, that My wrath may burn hot against them and I may consume them. And I will make of you a great nation."

11Then Moses pleaded with the LORD his God, and said: "LORD, why does Your wrath burn hot against Your people whom You have brought out of the land of Egypt with great power and with a mighty hand? 12Why should the Egyptians speak, and say, 'He brought them out to harm them, to kill them in the mountains, and to consume them from the face of the earth'? Turn from Your fierce wrath, and relent from this harm to Your people. 13Remember Abraham, Isaac, and Israel, Your servants, to whom You swore by Your own self, and said to them, 'I will multiply your descendants as the stars of heaven; and all this land that I have spoken of I give to your descendants, and they shall inherit *it* forever.'"[a] ¹⁴So the LORD relented from the harm which He said He would do to His people.

¹⁵And Moses turned and went down from the mountain, and the two tablets of the Testimony *were* in his hand. The tablets *were* written on both sides; on the one *side* and on the other they were written. ¹⁶Now the tablets *were* the work of God, and the writing *was* the writing of God engraved on the tablets.

¹⁷And when Joshua heard the noise of the people as they shouted, he said to Moses, "*There is* a noise of war in the camp."

¹⁸But he said:

"*It is* not the noise of the shout of
    victory,
Nor the noise of the cry of defeat,
But the sound of singing I hear."

¹⁹So it was, as soon as he came near the camp, that he saw the calf *and* the dancing. So Moses' anger became hot, and he cast the tablets out of his hands and broke them at the foot of the mountain. ²⁰Then he took the calf which they had made, burned *it* in the fire, and ground *it* to powder; and he scattered *it* on the water and made the children of Israel drink *it*. ²¹And Moses said to Aaron, "What did this people do to you that you have brought *so* great a sin upon them?"

²²So Aaron said, "Do not let the anger of my lord become hot. You know the people, that they *are set* on evil. ²³For they said to me, 'Make us gods that shall go before us; *as for* this Moses, the man who brought us out of the land of Egypt, we do not know what has become of him.' ²⁴And I said to them, 'Whoever has any gold, let them break *it* off.' So they gave *it* to me, and I cast it into the fire, and this calf came out."

²⁵Now when Moses saw that the people *were* unrestrained (for Aaron had not restrained them, to *their* shame among their enemies), ²⁶then Moses stood in the entrance of the camp, and said, "Whoever *is* on the LORD's side—*come* to me!" And all the sons of Levi gathered themselves together to him. ²⁷And he said to them, "Thus says the LORD God of Israel: 'Let every man put his sword on his side, and go in and out from entrance to entrance throughout the camp, and let every man kill his brother, every man his companion, and every man his neighbor.'" ²⁸So the sons of Levi did according to the word of Moses. And about three thousand men of the people fell that day. ²⁹Then Moses said, "Consecrate yourselves today to the LORD, that He may bestow on you a blessing this day, for every man has opposed his son and his brother."

32:13 [a]Genesis 13:15 and 22:17

PARENTING MATTERS

Q: *How do we train our children to rightly resolve conflicts?*

The question for all families is not whether conflicts will occur, but when they will occur. Conflict will be a part of all families' lives, including the children's. As parents, we must teach our children to rightly resolve these conflicts. We do that by teaching them some of the basics:

Teach them to listen. Start by listening to what you children say. Then teach them how to listen carefully to what a wounded friend or sibling is talking about, without becoming defensive.

Teach them how to speak the truth in love. Children can be harsh with one another, so this takes training. And more training. And even more training!

Teach them to forgive. Teach your children what it means to forgive another person—that it involves giving up the right to payback and not holding what someone has done wrong against them. Teach them that forgiveness is a choice and that it means giving up the right to be angry. Instead, show them how to seek reconciliation. Teach them that God instructs us to seek forgiveness and to freely give it to others—even those who have hurt us badly.

[30]Now it came to pass on the next day that Moses said to the people, "You have committed a great sin. So now I will go up to the Lord; perhaps I can make atonement for your sin." [31]Then Moses returned to the Lord and said, "Oh, these people have committed a great sin, and have made for themselves a god of gold! [32]Yet now, if You will forgive their sin—but if not, I pray, blot me out of Your book which You have written." [33]And the Lord said to Moses, "Whoever has sinned against Me, I will blot him out of My book. [34]Now therefore, go, lead the people to *the place* of which I have spoken to you. Behold, My Angel shall go before you. Nevertheless, in the day when I visit for punishment, I will visit punishment upon them for their sin." [35]So the Lord plagued the people because of what they did with the calf which Aaron made.

The Command to Leave Sinai

33 Then the Lord said to Moses, "Depart *and* go up from here, you and the people whom you have brought out of the land of Egypt, to the land of which I swore to Abraham, Isaac, and Jacob, saying, 'To your descendants I will give it.' [2]And I will send *My* Angel before you, and I will drive out the Canaanite and the Amorite and the Hittite and the Perizzite and the Hivite and the Jebusite. [3]*Go up* to a land flowing with milk and honey; for I will not go up in your midst, lest I consume you on the way, for you *are* a stiff-necked people."

[4]And when the people heard this bad news, they mourned, and no one put on his ornaments. [5]For the Lord had said to Moses, "Say to the children of Israel, 'You *are* a stiff-necked people. I could come up into your midst in one moment and consume you. Now therefore, take off your ornaments, that I may know what to do to you.'" [6]So the children of Israel stripped themselves of their ornaments by Mount Horeb.

Moses Meets with the Lord

[7]Moses took his tent and pitched it outside the camp, far from the camp, and called it the tabernacle of meeting. And it came to pass *that* everyone who sought the Lord went out to the tabernacle of meeting which *was* outside the camp. [8]So it was, whenever Moses went out to the tabernacle, *that* all the people rose, and each man stood *at* his tent door and watched Moses until he had gone into the tabernacle. [9]And it came to pass, when Moses entered the tabernacle, that the pillar of cloud descended and stood *at* the door of the tabernacle, and *the Lord* talked with Moses. [10]All the people saw the pillar of cloud standing *at* the tabernacle door, and all the people rose and worshiped, each man *in* his tent door. [11]So the Lord spoke to Moses face to face, as a man speaks to his friend. And he would return to the camp, but his servant Joshua the son of Nun, a young man, did not depart from the tabernacle.

The Promise of God's Presence

[12]Then Moses said to the Lord, "See, You say to me, 'Bring up this people.' But You have not let me know whom You will send with me. Yet You have said, 'I know you by name, and you have also found grace in My sight.' [13]Now therefore, I pray, if I have found grace in Your sight, show me now Your way, that I may know You and that I may find grace in Your sight. And consider that this nation *is* Your people."

[14]And He said, "My Presence will go *with you,* and I will give you rest."

[15]Then he said to Him, "If Your Presence does not go *with us,* do not bring us up from here. [16]For how then will it be known that Your people and I have found grace in Your sight, except You go with us? So we shall be separate, Your people and I, from all the people who *are* upon the face of the earth."

[17]So the Lord said to Moses, "I will also do this thing that you have spoken; for you have found grace in My sight, and I know you by name."

[18]And he said, "Please, show me Your glory."

[19]Then He said, "I will make all My goodness pass before you, and I will proclaim the name of the Lord before you. I will be gracious to whom I will be gracious, and I will have compassion on whom I will have compassion." [20]But He said, "You cannot see My face; for no man shall see Me, and live." [21]And the Lord said, "Here is a place by Me, and you shall

Show Them Grace

DID YOU KNOW ONE GREAT WAY that we parents can exhibit the character of God to our kids? We can show them grace and forgiveness.

When Moses asked to see the glory of God, he heard the following words proclaimed in a loud voice: "The Lord, the Lord God, merciful and gracious, longsuffering, and abounding in goodness and truth" (34:6). That's a powerful word picture of who God really is!

While I think it's a good idea for children to have regular chores, such as making their beds every morning and keeping their rooms clean, I know very well that sometimes those chores won't get done. And while it's appropriate to discipline a child who ignores his chores, those occasions don't always require punishment! Those may be perfect times to show grace and forgiveness.

It's important that our children know we love them and will continue to love them, regardless of how they perform. That doesn't mean there won't be consequences if they fail to obey! But it does mean we will always accept them and love them. They need the security that comes from knowing that nothing they do can cause us to not love them anymore. They need to see how we model the grace and forgiveness of God as we relate to them and our spouse. That's an important key in raising children to maturity and helping them develop their understanding of what true grace and forgiveness are all about.

---

stand on the rock. ²²So it shall be, while My glory passes by, that I will put you in the cleft of the rock, and will cover you with My hand while I pass by. ²³Then I will take away My hand, and you shall see My back; but My face shall not be seen."

Moses Makes New Tablets

34 And the Lord said to Moses, "Cut two tablets of stone like the first *ones,* and I will write on *these* tablets the words that were on the first tablets which you broke. ²So be ready in the morning, and come up in the morning to Mount Sinai, and present yourself to Me there on the top of the mountain. ³And no man shall come up with you, and let no man be seen throughout all the mountain; let neither flocks nor herds feed before that mountain."

⁴So he cut two tablets of stone like the first *ones.* Then Moses rose early in the morning and went up Mount Sinai, as the Lord had commanded him; and he took in his hand the two tablets of stone.

⁵Now the Lord descended in the cloud and stood with him there, and proclaimed the name of the Lord. ⁶And the Lord passed before him and proclaimed, "The Lord, the Lord God, merciful and gracious, longsuffering, and abounding in goodness and truth, ⁷keeping mercy for thousands, forgiving iniquity and transgression and sin, by no means clearing *the guilty,* visiting the iniquity of the fathers upon the children and the children's children to the third and the fourth generation."

⁸So Moses made haste and bowed his head toward the earth, and worshiped. ⁹Then he said, "If now I have found grace in Your sight, O Lord, let my Lord, I pray, go among us, even though we *are* a stiffnecked people; and pardon our iniquity and our sin, and take us as Your inheritance."

The Covenant Renewed

¹⁰And He said: "Behold, I make a covenant. Before all your people I will do marvels such as have not been done in all the earth, nor in any nation; and all the people among whom you *are* shall see the work of the Lord. For it *is* an awesome thing that I will do with you. ¹¹Observe what I command you this day. Behold, I am driving out from before you the Amorite and the Canaanite and the Hittite and the Perizzite and the Hivite and the Jebusite. ¹²Take heed to yourself, lest you make a covenant with the inhabitants of the land

where you are going, lest it be a snare in your midst. ¹³But you shall destroy their altars, break their *sacred* pillars, and cut down their wooden images ¹⁴(for you shall worship no other god, for the LORD, whose name *is* Jealous, *is* a jealous God), ¹⁵lest you make a covenant with the inhabitants of the land, and they play the harlot with their gods and make sacrifice to their gods, and *one of them* invites you and you eat of his sacrifice, ¹⁶and you take of his daughters for your sons, and his daughters play the harlot with their gods and make your sons play the harlot with their gods.

¹⁷"You shall make no molded gods for yourselves.

¹⁸"The Feast of Unleavened Bread you shall keep. Seven days you shall eat unleavened bread, as I commanded you, in the appointed time of the month of Abib; for in the month of Abib you came out from Egypt.

¹⁹"All that open the womb *are* Mine, and every male firstborn among your livestock, *whether* ox or sheep. ²⁰But the firstborn of a donkey you shall redeem with a lamb. And if you will not redeem *him,* then you shall break his neck. All the firstborn of your sons you shall redeem.

"And none shall appear before Me empty-handed.

²¹"Six days you shall work, but on the seventh day you shall rest; in plowing time and in harvest you shall rest.

²²"And you shall observe the Feast of Weeks, of the firstfruits of wheat harvest, and the Feast of Ingathering at the year's end.

²³"Three times in the year all your men shall appear before the Lord, the LORD God of Israel. ²⁴For I will cast out the nations before you and enlarge your borders; neither will any man covet your land when you go up to appear before the LORD your God three times in the year.

²⁵"You shall not offer the blood of My sacrifice with leaven, nor shall the sacrifice of the Feast of the Passover be left until morning.

²⁶"The first of the firstfruits of your land you shall bring to the house of the LORD your God. You shall not boil a young goat in its mother's milk."

BIBLICAL INSIGHTS • 34:21
Don't Miss Out

ONE OF THE MOST PROFOUND and powerful principles in all of Scripture is that *spiritual rest precedes spiritual growth.* That's part of what the Sabbath is all about.

So, is Sunday any different from the other days of the week for you and your family? If not, you are missing out not only on physical refreshment, but also on spiritual restoration.

God knows that after six days of work, everyone needs a break. That's why He commanded, "Six days you shall work, but on the seventh day you shall rest" (34:21). That's the reason for the Sabbath—to give us regularly scheduled time to relax, reflect, think critically about life, and find a time of peace where we can clearly hear the voice of our Father. This is when parents can regroup and refocus on what needs to happen spiritually in their own lives and within their family.

In our culture, many people have to work on Sunday, including, of course, pastors and church staff who lead us in Sunday worship. But everyone needs a Sabbath—a time to rest and be refreshed, physically and spiritually. If you have to make your Sabbath a day other than Sunday, then do it. The key is to observe a day of rest and refreshment every week.

²⁷Then the LORD said to Moses, "Write these words, for according to the tenor of these words I have made a covenant with you and with Israel." ²⁸So he was there with the LORD forty days and forty nights; he neither ate bread nor drank water. And He wrote on the tablets the words of the covenant, the Ten Commandments.ᵃ

The Shining Face of Moses

²⁹Now it was so, when Moses came down from Mount Sinai (and the two tablets of

God's Solution for Schedule Stress

REPEATEDLY THROUGHOUT the Old Testament, God insists on the importance of the Sabbath. He said, for example, "Work shall be done for six days, but the seventh day shall be a holy day for you, a Sabbath of rest to the LORD" (35:2).

Among the Ten Commandments, God elaborated more on the Sabbath (the Fourth Commandment) than on any of the other nine. He told His people to "remember" it, to "keep it holy," to "do no work" on it. Why? "For in six days the LORD made the heavens and the earth, the sea, and all that is in them, and rested the seventh day. Therefore the LORD blessed the Sabbath day and hallowed it" (Ex. 20:8–11).

The New Covenant application to the Sabbath Law is this: Christians need to experience God's solution for the stress that comes from a crowded schedule. He thought so much of the idea that He modeled it for us during creation by taking the seventh day off.

Is Sunday any different around your home from other days of the week? If not, then you are missing out on a great personal and family benefit. God commands you to get some rest! In our hurried and harried culture, we need to create a Sabbath island of rest and restoration for ourselves and our families.

the Testimony *were* in Moses' hand when he came down from the mountain), that Moses did not know that the skin of his face shone while he talked with Him. ³⁰So when Aaron and all the children of Israel saw Moses, behold, the skin of his face shone, and they were afraid to come near him. ³¹Then Moses called to them, and Aaron and all the rulers of the congregation returned to him; and Moses talked with them. ³²Afterward all the children of Israel came near, and he gave them as commandments all that the LORD had spoken with him on Mount Sinai.

³³And when Moses had finished speaking with them, he put a veil on his face. ³⁴But whenever Moses went in before the LORD to speak with Him, he would take the veil off until he came out; and he would come out and speak to the children of Israel whatever he had been commanded. ³⁵And whenever the children of Israel saw the face of Moses, that the skin of Moses' face shone, then Moses would put the veil on his face again, until he went in to speak with Him.

Sabbath Regulations

35 Then Moses gathered all the congregation of the children of Israel together, and said to them, "These *are* the words which the LORD has commanded *you* to do: ²Work shall be done for six days, but the seventh day shall be a holy day for you, a Sabbath of rest to the LORD. Whoever does any work on it shall be put to death. ³You shall kindle no fire throughout your dwellings on the Sabbath day."

Offerings for the Tabernacle

⁴And Moses spoke to all the congregation of the children of Israel, saying, "This *is* the thing which the LORD commanded, saying: ⁵'Take from among you an offering to the LORD. Whoever *is* of a willing heart, let him bring it as an offering to the LORD: gold, silver, and bronze; ⁶blue, purple, and scarlet *thread*, fine linen, and goats' *hair;* ⁷ram skins dyed red, badger skins, and acacia wood; ⁸oil for the light, and spices for the anointing oil and for the sweet incense; ⁹onyx stones, and stones to be set in the ephod and in the breastplate.

Articles of the Tabernacle

¹⁰All *who are* gifted artisans among you shall come and make all that the LORD has commanded: ¹¹the tabernacle, its tent, its covering, its clasps, its boards, its bars, its pillars, and its sockets; ¹²the ark and its poles, *with* the mercy seat, and the veil of the covering; ¹³the table and its poles, all its utensils, and the showbread; ¹⁴also the lampstand for the light, its utensils, its lamps, and the oil for the light; ¹⁵the incense altar, its poles, the anointing oil, the sweet incense,

34:28 ᵃLiterally *Ten Words*

and the screen for the door at the entrance of the tabernacle; [16]the altar of burnt offering with its bronze grating, its poles, all its utensils, *and* the laver and its base; [17]the hangings of the court, its pillars, their sockets, and the screen for the gate of the court; [18]the pegs of the tabernacle, the pegs of the court, and their cords; [19]the garments of ministry,[a] for ministering in the holy *place*—the holy garments for Aaron the priest and the garments of his sons, to minister as priests.' "

The Tabernacle Offerings Presented

[20]And all the congregation of the children of Israel departed from the presence of Moses. [21]Then everyone came whose heart was stirred, and everyone whose spirit was willing, *and* they brought the LORD's offering for the work of the tabernacle of meeting, for all its service, and for the holy garments. [22]They came, both men and women, as many as had a willing heart, *and* brought earrings and nose rings, rings and necklaces, all jewelry of gold, that is, every man who *made* an offering of gold to the LORD. [23]And every man, with whom was found blue, purple, and scarlet *thread,* fine linen, goats' *hair,* red skins of rams, and badger skins, brought *them.* [24]Everyone who offered an offering of silver or bronze brought the LORD's offering. And everyone with whom was found acacia wood for any work of the service, brought *it.* [25]All the women *who were* gifted artisans spun yarn with their hands, and brought what they had spun, of blue, purple, *and* scarlet, and fine linen. [26]And all the women whose hearts stirred with wisdom spun yarn of goats' *hair.* [27]The rulers brought onyx stones, and the stones to be set in the ephod and in the breastplate, [28]and spices and oil for the light, for the anointing oil, and for the sweet incense. [29]The children of Israel brought a freewill offering to the LORD, all the men and women whose hearts were willing to bring *material* for all kinds of work which the LORD, by the hand of Moses, had commanded to be done.

The Artisans Called by God

[30]And Moses said to the children of Israel, "See, the LORD has called by name Bezalel the son of Uri, the son of Hur, of the tribe of Judah; [31]and He has filled him with the Spirit of God, in wisdom and understanding, in knowledge and all manner of workmanship, [32]to design artistic works, to work in gold and silver and bronze, [33]in cutting jewels for setting, in carving wood, and to work in all manner of artistic workmanship.

[34]"And He has put in his heart the ability to teach, *in* him and Aholiab the son of Ahisamach, of the tribe of Dan. [35]He has filled them with skill to do all manner of work of the engraver and the designer and the tapestry maker, in blue, purple, and scarlet *thread,* and fine linen, and of the weaver—those who do every work and those who design artistic works.

36 "And Bezalel and Aholiab, and every gifted artisan in whom the LORD has put wisdom and understanding, to know how to do all manner of work for the service of the sanctuary, shall do according to all that the LORD has commanded."

The People Give More than Enough

[2]Then Moses called Bezalel and Aholiab, and every gifted artisan in whose heart the LORD had put wisdom, everyone whose heart was stirred, to come and do the work. [3]And they received from Moses all the offering which the children of Israel had brought for the work of the service of making the sanctuary. So they continued bringing to him freewill offerings every morning. [4]Then all the craftsmen who were doing all the work of the sanctuary came, each from the work he was doing, [5]and they spoke to Moses, saying, "The people bring much more than enough for the service of the work which the LORD commanded *us* to do."

[6]So Moses gave a commandment, and they caused it to be proclaimed throughout the camp, saying, "Let neither man nor woman do any more work for the offering of the sanctuary." And the people were restrained from bringing, [7]for the material they had was sufficient for all the work to be done—indeed too much.

35:19 [a]Or *woven garments*

Add Empathy to Your Communication

THE DICTIONARY traditionally defines understanding as "the faculty of the human mind by which it . . . comprehends the ideas which others express and intend to communicate." Yet in the Bible, understanding is not just a transfer of information, but empathy for the other person.

Consider Exodus 36:1, which tells how two craftsmen named Bezalel and Aholiab were given divine wisdom and understanding, "to know how to do all manner of work for the service of the sanctuary," so that they could "do according to all that the LORD has commanded." This is a scriptural example of what the Bible refers to as "understanding." These men, and the other artisans working under their supervision, were given the divine ability not only to know how to work their magic with gold and silver and leather and beautiful fabrics and thread, but also how to communicate with one another in a way that would move their assignment forward.

Barbara and I have found that this kind of understanding—the kind that goes beyond mere facts to empathize with the other—is essential in building our relationship and family. When I know that she tries to understand some situation from my perspective (and vice versa), it's amazing how problems dissipate. As we make Jesus Christ the Builder of our homes (Psalm 127:1), we can begin to see our relationships reflect God's character.

Building the Tabernacle

8Then all the gifted artisans among them who worked on the tabernacle made ten curtains woven of fine linen, and of blue, purple, and scarlet *thread; with* artistic designs of cherubim they made them. 9The length of each curtain *was* twenty-eight cubits, and the width of each curtain four cubits; the curtains *were* all the same size. 10And he coupled five curtains to one another, and *the other* five curtains he coupled to one another. 11He made loops of blue *yarn* on the edge of the curtain on the selvedge of one set; likewise he did on the outer edge of *the other* curtain of the second set. 12Fifty loops he made on one curtain, and fifty loops he made on the edge of the curtain on the end of the second set; the loops held one *curtain* to another. 13And he made fifty clasps of gold, and coupled the curtains to one another with the clasps, that it might be one tabernacle.

14He made curtains of goats' *hair* for the tent over the tabernacle; he made eleven curtains. 15The length of each curtain *was* thirty cubits, and the width of each curtain four cubits; the eleven curtains *were* the same size. 16He coupled five curtains by themselves and six curtains by themselves. 17And he made fifty loops on the edge of the curtain that is outermost in one set, and fifty loops he made on the edge of the curtain of the second set. 18He also made fifty bronze clasps to couple the tent together, that it might be one. 19Then he made a covering for the tent of ram skins dyed red, and a covering of badger skins above *that*.

20For the tabernacle he made boards of acacia wood, standing upright. 21The length of each board *was* ten cubits, and the width of each board a cubit and a half. 22Each board had two tenons for binding one to another. Thus he made for all the boards of the tabernacle. 23And he made boards for the tabernacle, twenty boards for the south side. 24Forty sockets of silver he made to go under the twenty boards: two sockets under each of the boards for its two tenons. 25And for the other side of the tabernacle, the north side, he made twenty boards 26and their forty sockets of silver: two sockets under each of the boards. 27For the west side of the tabernacle he made six boards. 28He also made two boards for the two back corners of the tabernacle. 29And they were coupled at the bottom and coupled together at the top by one ring. Thus he made both of them for the two corners. 30So there were eight boards and their sockets—sixteen sockets of silver—two sockets under each of the boards.

³¹And he made bars of acacia wood: five for the boards on one side of the tabernacle, ³²five bars for the boards on the other side of the tabernacle, and five bars for the boards of the tabernacle on the far side westward. ³³And he made the middle bar to pass through the boards from one end to the other. ³⁴He overlaid the boards with gold, made their rings of gold *to be* holders for the bars, and overlaid the bars with gold.

³⁵And he made a veil of blue, purple, and scarlet *thread,* and fine woven linen; it was worked *with* an artistic design of cherubim. ³⁶He made for it four pillars of acacia *wood,* and overlaid them with gold, with their hooks of gold; and he cast four sockets of silver for them.

³⁷He also made a screen for the tabernacle door, of blue, purple, and scarlet *thread,* and fine woven linen, made by a weaver, ³⁸and its five pillars with their hooks. And he overlaid their capitals and their rings with gold, but their five sockets *were* bronze.

Making the Ark of the Testimony

37 Then Bezalel made the ark of acacia wood; two and a half cubits *was* its length, a cubit and a half its width, and a cubit and a half its height. ²He overlaid it with pure gold inside and outside, and made a molding of gold all around it. ³And he cast for it four rings of gold *to be set* in its four corners: two rings on one side, and two rings on the other side of it. ⁴He made poles of acacia wood, and overlaid them with gold. ⁵And he put the poles into the rings at the sides of the ark, to bear the ark. ⁶He also made the mercy seat of pure gold; two and a half cubits *was* its length and a cubit and a half its width. ⁷He made two cherubim of beaten gold; he made them of one piece at the two ends of the mercy seat: ⁸one cherub at one end on this side, and the other cherub at the *other* end on that side. He made the cherubim at the two ends *of one piece* with the mercy seat. ⁹The cherubim spread out *their* wings above, *and* covered the mercy seat with their wings. They faced one another; the faces of the cherubim were toward the mercy seat.

Making the Table for the Showbread

¹⁰He made the table of acacia wood; two cubits *was* its length, a cubit its width, and a cubit and a half its height. ¹¹And he overlaid it with pure gold, and made a molding of gold all around it. ¹²Also he made a frame of a handbreadth all around it, and made a molding of gold for the frame all around it. ¹³And he cast for it four rings of gold, and put the rings on the four corners that *were* at its four legs. ¹⁴The rings were close to the frame, as holders for the poles to bear the table. ¹⁵And he made the poles of acacia wood to bear the table, and overlaid them with gold. ¹⁶He made of pure gold the utensils which were on the table: its dishes, its cups, its bowls, and its pitchers for pouring.

Making the Gold Lampstand

¹⁷He also made the lampstand of pure gold; of hammered work he made the lampstand. Its shaft, its branches, its bowls, its *ornamental* knobs, and its flowers were of the same piece. ¹⁸And six branches came out of its sides: three branches of the lampstand out of one side, and three branches of the lampstand out of the other side. ¹⁹There were three bowls made like almond *blossoms* on one branch, with an *ornamental* knob and a flower, and three bowls made like almond *blossoms* on the other branch, with an *ornamental* knob and a flower— and so for the six branches coming out of the lampstand. ²⁰And on the lampstand itself *were* four bowls made like almond *blossoms, each with* its *ornamental* knob and flower. ²¹*There was* a knob under the *first* two branches of the same, a knob under the *second* two branches of the same, and a knob under the *third* two branches of the same, according to the six branches extending from it. ²²Their knobs and their branches were of one piece; all of it *was* one hammered piece of pure gold. ²³And he made its seven lamps, its wick-trimmers, and its trays of pure gold. ²⁴Of a talent of pure gold he made it, with all its utensils.

Making the Altar of Incense

²⁵He made the incense altar of acacia wood. Its length *was* a cubit and its width a cubit—*it was* square—and two cubits

was its height. Its horns were *of one piece* with it. 26And he overlaid it with pure gold: its top, its sides all around, and its horns. He also made for it a molding of gold all around it. 27He made two rings of gold for it under its molding, by its two corners on both sides, as holders for the poles with which to bear it. 28And he made the poles of acacia wood, and overlaid them with gold.

Making the Anointing Oil and the Incense

29He also made the holy anointing oil and the pure incense of sweet spices, according to the work of the perfumer.

Making the Altar of Burnt Offering

38 He made the altar of burnt offering of acacia wood; five cubits *was* its length and five cubits its width—*it was* square—and its height *was* three cubits. 2He made its horns on its four corners; the horns were *of one piece* with it. And he overlaid it with bronze. 3He made all the utensils for the altar: the pans, the shovels, the basins, the forks, and the firepans; all its utensils he made of bronze. 4And he made a grate of bronze network for the altar, under its rim, midway from the bottom. 5He cast four rings for the four corners of the bronze grating, *as* holders for the poles. 6And he made the poles of acacia wood, and overlaid them with bronze. 7Then he put the poles into the rings on the sides of the altar, with which to bear it. He made the altar hollow with boards.

Making the Bronze Laver

8He made the laver of bronze and its base of bronze, from the bronze mirrors of the serving women who assembled at the door of the tabernacle of meeting.

Making the Court of the Tabernacle

9Then he made the court on the south side; the hangings of the court *were of* fine woven linen, one hundred cubits long. 10There *were* twenty pillars for them, with twenty bronze sockets. The hooks of the pillars and their bands *were* silver. 11On the north side *the hangings were* one hundred cubits *long,* with twenty pillars and their twenty bronze sockets. The hooks of the

pillars and their bands *were* silver. 12And on the west side *there were* hangings of fifty cubits, with ten pillars and their ten sockets. The hooks of the pillars and their bands *were* silver. 13For the east side *the hangings were* fifty cubits. 14The hangings of one side *of the gate were* fifteen cubits *long, with* their three pillars and their three sockets, 15and the same for the other side of the court gate; on this side and that *were* hangings of fifteen cubits, *with* their three pillars and their three sockets. 16All the hangings of the court all around *were of* fine woven linen. 17The sockets for the pillars *were* bronze, the hooks of the pillars and their bands *were* silver, and the overlay of their capitals *was* silver; and all the pillars of the court had bands of silver. 18The screen for the gate of the court *was* woven of blue, purple, and scarlet *thread,* and of fine woven linen. The length *was* twenty cubits, and the height along its width *was* five cubits, corresponding to the hangings of the court. 19And *there were* four pillars *with* their four sockets of bronze; their hooks *were* silver, and the overlay of their capitals and their bands *was* silver. 20All the pegs of the tabernacle, and of the court all around, *were* bronze.

Materials of the Tabernacle

21This is the inventory of the tabernacle, the tabernacle of the Testimony, which was counted according to the commandment of Moses, for the service of the Levites, by the hand of Ithamar, son of Aaron the priest. 22Bezalel the son of Uri, the son of Hur, of the tribe of Judah, made all that the LORD had commanded Moses. 23And with him *was* Aholiab the son of Ahisamach, of the tribe of Dan, an engraver and designer, a weaver of blue, purple, and scarlet *thread,* and of fine linen.

24All the gold that was used in all the work of the holy *place,* that is, the gold of the offering, was twenty-nine talents and seven hundred and thirty shekels, according to the shekel of the sanctuary. 25And the silver from those who were numbered of the congregation *was* one hundred talents and one thousand seven hundred and seventy-five shekels, according to the shekel of the sanctuary: 26a bekah for each man (*that is,* half a shekel, according to the shekel of the sanctuary), for everyone included in the numbering from twenty years old and above, for six hundred and three thousand, five hundred and fifty *men.* 27And from the hundred talents of silver were cast the sockets of the sanctuary and the bases of the veil: one hundred sockets from the hundred talents, one talent for each socket. 28Then from the one thousand seven hundred and seventy-five *shekels* he made hooks for the pillars, overlaid their capitals, and made bands for them.

29The offering of bronze *was* seventy talents and two thousand four hundred shekels. 30And with it he made the sockets for the door of the tabernacle of meeting, the bronze altar, the bronze grating for it, and all the utensils for the altar, 31the sockets for the court all around, the bases for the court gate, all the pegs for the tabernacle, and all the pegs for the court all around.

Making the Garments of the Priesthood

39 Of the blue, purple, and scarlet *thread* they made garments of ministry,[a] for ministering in the holy *place,* and made the holy garments for Aaron, as the LORD had commanded Moses.

Making the Ephod

2He made the ephod of gold, blue, purple, and scarlet *thread,* and of fine woven linen. 3And they beat the gold into thin sheets and cut *it into* threads, to work *it* in *with* the blue, purple, and scarlet *thread,* and the fine linen, *into* artistic designs. 4They made shoulder straps for it to couple *it* together; it was coupled together at its two edges. 5And the intricately woven band of his ephod that *was* on it *was* of the same workmanship, *woven of* gold, blue, purple, and scarlet *thread,* and of fine woven linen, as the LORD had commanded Moses.

6And they set onyx stones, enclosed in settings of gold; they were engraved, as signets are engraved, with the names of the sons of Israel. 7He put them on the shoulders of the ephod *as* memorial stones for the sons of Israel, as the LORD had commanded Moses.

Making the Breastplate

8And he made the breastplate, artistically woven like the workmanship of the ephod, of gold, blue, purple, and scarlet *thread,* and of fine woven linen. 9They made the breastplate square by doubling it; a span *was* its length and a span its width when doubled. 10And they set in it four rows of stones: a row with a sardius, a topaz, and an emerald was the first row; 11the second row, a turquoise, a sapphire, and a diamond; 12the third row, a jacinth, an agate, and an amethyst; 13the fourth row, a beryl, an onyx, and a jasper. *They were* enclosed in settings of gold in their mountings. 14*There were* twelve stones according to the names of the sons of Israel: according to their names, *engraved like* a signet, each one with its own name according to the twelve tribes. 15And they made chains for the breastplate at the ends, like braided cords of pure gold. 16They also made two settings of gold and two gold rings, and put the two rings on the two ends of the breastplate. 17And they put the two braided *chains* of gold in the two rings on the ends of the breastplate. 18The two ends of the two braided *chains* they fastened in the two settings, and put them on the shoulder straps of the ephod in the front. 19And they made two rings of gold and put *them* on the two ends of the breastplate, on the edge of it, which *was* on the inward side of the ephod. 20They made two *other* gold rings and put them on the two shoulder straps, underneath the ephod toward its front, right at the seam above the intricately woven band of the ephod. 21And they bound the breastplate by means of its rings to the rings of the ephod with a blue cord, so that it would be above the intricately woven band of the ephod, and that the breastplate would not come loose from the ephod, as the LORD had commanded Moses.

Making the Other Priestly Garments

22He made the robe of the ephod of woven work, all of blue. 23And *there was* an opening in the middle of the robe, like the opening in a coat of mail, *with* a woven binding all around the opening, so that it would not tear. 24They made on the hem of

39:1 [a]Or *woven garments*

the robe pomegranates of blue, purple, and scarlet, and of fine woven *linen.* ²⁵And they made bells of pure gold, and put the bells between the pomegranates on the hem of the robe all around between the pomegranates: ²⁶a bell and a pomegranate, a bell and a pomegranate, all around the hem of the robe to minister in, as the LORD had commanded Moses.

²⁷They made tunics, artistically woven of fine linen, for Aaron and his sons, ²⁸a turban of fine linen, exquisite hats of fine linen, short trousers of fine woven linen, ²⁹and a sash of fine woven linen with blue, purple, and scarlet *thread,* made by a weaver, as the LORD had commanded Moses.

³⁰Then they made the plate of the holy crown of pure gold, and wrote on it an inscription *like* the engraving of a signet:

HOLINESS TO THE LORD.

³¹And they tied to it a blue cord, to fasten *it* above on the turban, as the LORD had commanded Moses.

The Work Completed

³²Thus all the work of the tabernacle of the tent of meeting was finished. And the children of Israel did according to all that the LORD had commanded Moses; so they did. ³³And they brought the tabernacle to Moses, the tent and all its furnishings: its clasps, its boards, its bars, its pillars, and its sockets; ³⁴the covering of ram skins dyed red, the covering of badger skins, and the veil of the covering; ³⁵the ark of the Testimony with its poles, and the mercy seat; ³⁶the table, all its utensils, and the showbread; ³⁷the pure *gold* lampstand with its lamps (the lamps set in order), all its utensils, and the oil for light; ³⁸the gold altar, the anointing oil, and the sweet incense; the screen for the tabernacle door; ³⁹the bronze altar, its grate of bronze, its poles, and all its utensils; the laver with its base; ⁴⁰the hangings of the court, its pillars and its sockets, the screen for the court gate, its cords, and its pegs; all the utensils for the service of the tabernacle, for the tent of meeting; ⁴¹and the garments of ministry,ᵃ to minister in the holy *place:* the holy garments for Aaron the priest, and his sons' garments, to minister as priests.

⁴²According to all that the LORD had commanded Moses, so the children of Israel did all the work. ⁴³Then Moses looked over all the work, and indeed they had done it; as the LORD had commanded, just so they had done it. And Moses blessed them.

The Tabernacle Erected and Arranged

40 Then the LORD spoke to Moses, saying: ²"On the first day of the first month you shall set up the tabernacle of the tent of meeting. ³You shall put in it the ark of the Testimony, and partition off the ark with the veil. ⁴You shall bring in the table and arrange the things that are to be set in order on it; and you shall bring in the lampstand and light its lamps. ⁵You shall also set the altar of gold for the incense before the ark of the Testimony, and put up the screen for the door of the tabernacle. ⁶Then you shall set the altar of the burnt offering before the door of the tabernacle of the tent of meeting. ⁷And you shall set the laver between the tabernacle of meeting and the altar, and put water in it. ⁸You shall set up the court all around, and hang up the screen at the court gate.

⁹"And you shall take the anointing oil, and anoint the tabernacle and all that *is* in it; and you shall hallow it and all its utensils, and it shall be holy. ¹⁰You shall anoint the altar of the burnt offering and all its utensils, and consecrate the altar. The altar shall be most holy. ¹¹And you shall anoint the laver and its base, and consecrate it.

¹²"Then you shall bring Aaron and his sons to the door of the tabernacle of meeting and wash them with water. ¹³You shall put the holy garments on Aaron, and anoint him and consecrate him, that he may minister to Me as priest. ¹⁴And you shall bring his sons and clothe them with tunics. ¹⁵You shall anoint them, as you anointed their father, that they may minister to Me as priests; for their anointing shall surely be an everlasting priesthood throughout their generations."

¹⁶Thus Moses did; according to all that the LORD had commanded him, so he did.

¹⁷And it came to pass in the first month

39:41 ᵃOr *woven garments*

of the second year, on the first *day* of the month, *that* the tabernacle was raised up. ¹⁸So Moses raised up the tabernacle, fastened its sockets, set up its boards, put in its bars, and raised up its pillars. ¹⁹And he spread out the tent over the tabernacle and put the covering of the tent on top of it, as the LORD had commanded Moses. ²⁰He took the Testimony and put *it* into the ark, inserted the poles through the rings of the ark, and put the mercy seat on top of the ark. ²¹And he brought the ark into the tabernacle, hung up the veil of the covering, and partitioned off the ark of the Testimony, as the LORD had commanded Moses.

²²He put the table in the tabernacle of meeting, on the north side of the tabernacle, outside the veil; ²³and he set the bread in order upon it before the LORD, as the LORD had commanded Moses. ²⁴He put the lampstand in the tabernacle of meeting, across from the table, on the south side of the tabernacle; ²⁵and he lit the lamps before the LORD, as the LORD had commanded Moses. ²⁶He put the gold altar in the tabernacle of meeting in front of the veil; ²⁷and he burned sweet incense on it, as the LORD had commanded Moses. ²⁸He hung up the screen *at* the door of the tabernacle. ²⁹And he put the altar of burnt offering *before* the door of the tabernacle

of the tent of meeting, and offered upon it the burnt offering and the grain offering, as the LORD had commanded Moses. ³⁰He set the laver between the tabernacle of meeting and the altar, and put water there for washing; ³¹and Moses, Aaron, and his sons would wash their hands and their feet *with water* from it. ³²Whenever they went into the tabernacle of meeting, and when they came near the altar, they washed, as the LORD had commanded Moses. ³³And he raised up the court all around the tabernacle and the altar, and hung up the screen of the court gate. So Moses finished the work.

The Cloud and the Glory

³⁴Then the cloud covered the tabernacle of meeting, and the glory of the LORD filled the tabernacle. ³⁵And Moses was not able to enter the tabernacle of meeting, because the cloud rested above it, and the glory of the LORD filled the tabernacle. ³⁶Whenever the cloud was taken up from above the tabernacle, the children of Israel would go onward in all their journeys. ³⁷But if the cloud was not taken up, then they did not journey till the day that it was taken up. ³⁸For the cloud of the LORD *was* above the tabernacle by day, and fire was over it by night, in the sight of all the house of Israel, throughout all their journeys.

LEVITICUS

ALL FAMILIES HAVE HOUSE RULES, a set of written or unwritten guidelines that describe how family members will function and support each other as they live out each day together. In one sense, much of what we find in the book of Leviticus is a record of the house rules for the nation of Israel.

God gave specific instructions to His people regarding worship (the ceremonial law) and conduct in society (the civil law). The totality of that law reflects and reveals the character of God and His standards for holiness and morality (the moral law). The detailed instructions of Leviticus—intended primarily for the priests of Moses' day, the men whom God had tabbed as the spiritual leaders of Israel—are designed to make it possible for a frequently wayward people to yet enjoy a living and dynamic relationship with the Holy One of Israel. The rules were designed to foster that relationship with God, not take its place. The rules pointed to something higher and better and richer than themselves.

Over time, your family will develop its own set of house rules that will govern how you live together in harmony and peace. These standards will undoubtedly reflect your family's values—the core convictions regarding what you believe is most important for each member of the family to live out, to practice, and to embrace. The Bible makes it clear that husbands are to serve as the spiritual leaders for their families, and in that capacity they must administer house rules as they encourage all members of their families to demonstrate grace, compassion, and love. House rules are not to take the place of relationships, whether in our homes or with God.

God's people today are no longer subject to the civil and ceremonial "house rules" given to the ancient nation of Israel. The reason is that Jesus Christ, through His sinless life, completely fulfilled the Old Testament law (see Matt. 5:17; Rom. 10:4). And when we place our faith in Him as the crucified and risen Lord, He applies His perfect record to our account. In Christ, therefore, we are free from the just penalty of violating God's law.

The Burnt Offering

1 Now the LORD called to Moses, and spoke to him from the tabernacle of meeting, saying, ²"Speak to the children of Israel, and say to them: 'When any one of you brings an offering to the LORD, you shall bring your offering of the livestock—of the herd and of the flock.

³'If his offering *is* a burnt sacrifice of the herd, let him offer a male without blemish; he shall offer it of his own free will at the door of the tabernacle of meeting before the LORD. ⁴Then he shall put his hand on the head of the burnt offering, and it will be accepted on his behalf to make atonement for him. ⁵He shall kill the bull before the LORD; and the priests, Aaron's sons, shall bring the blood and sprinkle the blood all around on the altar that *is by* the door of the tabernacle of meeting. ⁶And he shall skin the burnt offering and cut it into its pieces. ⁷The sons of Aaron the priest shall put fire on the altar, and lay the wood in order on the fire. ⁸Then the priests, Aaron's sons, shall lay the parts, the head, and the fat in order on the wood that *is* on the fire upon the altar; ⁹but he shall wash its entrails and its legs with water. And the priest shall burn all on the altar as a burnt sacrifice, an offering made by fire, a sweet aroma to the LORD.

¹⁰'If his offering *is* of the flocks—of the sheep or of the goats—as a burnt sacrifice, he shall bring a male without blemish. ¹¹He shall kill it on the north side of the altar before the LORD; and the priests, Aaron's sons, shall sprinkle its blood all around on the altar. ¹²And he shall cut it into its pieces, with its head and its fat; and the priest shall lay them in order on the wood that *is* on the fire upon the altar; ¹³but he shall wash the entrails and the legs with water. Then the priest shall bring *it* all and burn *it* on the altar; it *is* a burnt sacrifice, an offering made by fire, a sweet aroma to the LORD.

¹⁴'And if the burnt sacrifice of his offering to the LORD *is* of birds, then he shall bring his offering of turtledoves or young pigeons. ¹⁵The priest shall bring it to the altar, wring off its head, and burn *it* on the altar; its blood shall be drained out at the side of the altar. ¹⁶And he shall remove its crop with its feathers and cast it beside the altar on the east side, into the place for ashes. ¹⁷Then he shall split it at its wings, *but* shall not divide *it* completely; and the priest shall burn it on the altar, on the wood that *is* on the fire. It *is* a burnt sacrifice, an offering made by fire, a sweet aroma to the LORD.

INTIMATE MOMENTS

The next time your husband goes out of town, prepare a collection of sealed, handwritten notes designed especially for his encouragement, one for each day he will be gone. Tell him how much you love him, how much you miss him when he's gone, and how much you look forward to his return. Build anticipation in each note for his homecoming.

The Grain Offering

2 'When anyone offers a grain offering to the LORD, his offering shall be *of* fine flour. And he shall pour oil on it, and put frankincense on it. ²He shall bring it to Aaron's sons, the priests, one of whom shall take from it his handful of fine flour and oil with all the frankincense. And the priest shall burn *it as* a memorial on the altar, an offering made by fire, a sweet aroma to the LORD. ³The rest of the grain offering *shall be* Aaron's and his sons'. *It is* most holy of the offerings to the LORD made by fire.

⁴'And if you bring as an offering a grain offering baked in the oven, *it shall be* unleavened cakes of fine flour mixed with oil, or unleavened wafers anointed with oil. ⁵But if your offering *is* a grain offering *baked* in a pan, *it shall be of* fine flour, unleavened, mixed with oil. ⁶You shall break it in pieces and pour oil on it; it *is* a grain offering.

⁷'If your offering *is* a grain offering *baked* in a covered pan, it shall be made *of* fine flour with oil. ⁸You shall bring the grain offering that is made of these things to the LORD. And when it is presented to the priest, he shall bring it to the altar. ⁹Then the priest

shall take from the grain offering a memorial portion, and burn *it* on the altar. *It is* an offering made by fire, a sweet aroma to the LORD. ¹⁰And what is left of the grain offering *shall be* Aaron's and his sons'. *It is* most holy of the offerings to the LORD made by fire.

¹¹'No grain offering which you bring to the LORD shall be made with leaven, for you shall burn no leaven nor any honey in any offering to the LORD made by fire. ¹²As for the offering of the firstfruits, you shall offer them to the LORD, but they shall not be burned on the altar for a sweet aroma. ¹³And every offering of your grain offering you shall season with salt; you shall not allow the salt of the covenant of your God to be lacking from your grain offering. With all your offerings you shall offer salt.

¹⁴'If you offer a grain offering of your firstfruits to the LORD, you shall offer for the grain offering of your firstfruits green heads of grain roasted on the fire, grain beaten from full heads. ¹⁵And you shall put oil on it, and lay frankincense on it. It *is* a grain offering. ¹⁶Then the priest shall burn the memorial portion: *part* of its beaten grain and *part* of its oil, with all the frankincense, as an offering made by fire to the LORD.

The Peace Offering

3 'When his offering *is* a sacrifice of a peace offering, if he offers *it* of the herd, whether male or female, he shall offer it without blemish before the LORD. ²And he shall lay his hand on the head of his offering, and kill it *at* the door of the tabernacle of meeting; and Aaron's sons, the priests, shall sprinkle the blood all around on the altar. ³Then he shall offer from the sacrifice of the peace offering an offering made by fire to the LORD. The fat that covers the entrails and all the fat that *is* on the entrails, ⁴the two kidneys and the fat that *is* on them by the flanks, and the fatty lobe *attached* to the liver above the kidneys, he shall remove; ⁵and Aaron's sons shall burn it on the altar upon the burnt sacrifice, which *is* on the wood that *is* on the fire, *as* an offering made by fire, a sweet aroma to the LORD.

⁶'If his offering as a sacrifice of a peace offering to the LORD *is* of the flock, *whether* male or female, he shall offer it without blemish. ⁷If he offers a lamb as his offering, then he shall offer it before the LORD. ⁸And he shall lay his hand on the head of his offering, and kill it before the tabernacle of meeting; and Aaron's sons shall sprinkle its blood all around on the altar.

⁹'Then he shall offer from the sacrifice of the peace offering, as an offering made by fire to the LORD, its fat *and* the whole fat tail which he shall remove close to the backbone. And the fat that covers the entrails and all the fat that *is* on the entrails, ¹⁰the two kidneys and the fat that *is* on them by the flanks, and the fatty lobe *attached* to the liver above the kidneys, he shall remove; ¹¹and the priest shall burn *them* on the altar *as* food, an offering made by fire to the LORD.

¹²'And if his offering *is* a goat, then he shall offer it before the LORD. ¹³He shall lay his hand on its head and kill it before the tabernacle of meeting; and the sons of Aaron shall sprinkle its blood all around on the altar. ¹⁴Then he shall offer from it his offering, as an offering made by fire to the LORD. The fat that covers the entrails and all the fat that *is* on the entrails, ¹⁵the two kidneys and the fat that *is* on them by the flanks, and the fatty lobe *attached* to the liver above the kidneys, he shall remove; ¹⁶and the priest shall burn them on the altar *as* food, an offering made by fire for a sweet aroma; all the fat *is* the LORD's.

¹⁷'*This shall be* a perpetual statute throughout your generations in all your dwellings: you shall eat neither fat nor blood.' "

The Sin Offering

4 Now the LORD spoke to Moses, saying, ²"Speak to the children of Israel, saying: 'If a person sins unintentionally against any of the commandments of the LORD *in anything* which ought not to be done, and does any of them, ³if the anointed priest sins, bringing guilt on the people, then let him offer to the LORD for his sin which he has sinned a young bull without blemish as a sin offering. ⁴He shall bring the bull to the door of the tabernacle of meeting before the LORD, lay his hand on

the bull's head, and kill the bull before the LORD. ⁵Then the anointed priest shall take some of the bull's blood and bring it to the tabernacle of meeting. ⁶The priest shall dip his finger in the blood and sprinkle some of the blood seven times before the LORD, in front of the veil of the sanctuary. ⁷And the priest shall put some of the blood on the horns of the altar of sweet incense before the LORD, which is in the tabernacle of meeting; and he shall pour the remaining blood of the bull at the base of the altar of the burnt offering, which is at the door of the tabernacle of meeting. ⁸He shall take from it all the fat of the bull as the sin offering. The fat that covers the entrails and all the fat which *is* on the entrails, ⁹the two kidneys and the fat that *is* on them by the flanks, and the fatty lobe *attached* to the liver above the kidneys, he shall remove, ¹⁰as it was taken from the bull of the sacrifice of the peace offering; and the priest shall burn them on the altar of the burnt offering. ¹¹But the bull's hide and all its flesh, with its head and legs, its entrails and offal— ¹²the whole bull he shall carry outside the camp to a clean place, where the ashes are poured out, and burn it on wood with fire; where the ashes are poured out it shall be burned.

¹³'Now if the whole congregation of Israel sins unintentionally, and the thing is hidden from the eyes of the assembly, and they have done *something against* any of the commandments of the LORD *in anything* which should not be done, and are guilty; ¹⁴when the sin which they have committed becomes known, then the assembly shall offer a young bull for the sin, and bring it before the tabernacle of meeting. ¹⁵And the elders of the congregation shall lay their hands on the head of the bull before the LORD. Then the bull shall be killed before the LORD. ¹⁶The anointed priest shall bring some of the bull's blood to the tabernacle of meeting. ¹⁷Then the priest shall dip his finger in the blood and sprinkle *it* seven times before the LORD, in front of the veil. ¹⁸And he shall put *some* of the blood on the horns of the altar which *is* before the LORD, which *is* in the tabernacle of meeting; and he shall pour the remaining blood at the base of the altar of burnt offering, which is at the door of the tabernacle of meeting. ¹⁹He shall take all the fat from it and burn *it* on the altar. ²⁰And he shall do with the bull as he did with the bull as a sin offering; thus he shall do with it. So the priest shall make atonement for them, and it shall be forgiven them. ²¹Then he shall carry the bull outside the camp, and burn it as he burned the first bull. It *is* a sin offering for the assembly.

²²'When a ruler has sinned, and done *something* unintentionally *against* any of the commandments of the LORD his God *in*

ROMANTIC QUOTES AND NOTES
Your Home as a Greenhouse

Your marriage is far more important than you may have ever imagined. Why? Because it affects God's reputation on this planet. That's why it's essential for you to set Jesus Christ apart as the Builder of your home.

Your plans for children may still be in the future, but if God gives you a child, you will be in for an amazing adventure. Your children will carry a reflection of God's character to the next generation.

God's original plan called for the home to be a sort of greenhouse, a nurturing place where children grow up to learn godly character, values, and integrity. One of your most important assignments is to impart a sense of destiny, a spiritual mission, to your children. God calls you to make your home a place where your children learn the nitty-gritty of what it means to love and obey God.

Make your home into a training center that equips your children to look at the needs of those around them through the eyes of Jesus Christ. If your children do not embrace this spiritual mission as they grow up, they may live their entire lives without experiencing the privilege of God's using them in a significant way.

anything which should not be done, and is guilty, ²³or if his sin which he has committed comes to his knowledge, he shall bring as his offering a kid of the goats, a male without blemish. ²⁴And he shall lay his hand on the head of the goat, and kill it at the place where they kill the burnt offering before the LORD. It *is* a sin offering. ²⁵The priest shall take some of the blood of the sin offering with his finger, put *it* on the horns of the altar of burnt offering, and pour its blood at the base of the altar of burnt offering. ²⁶And he shall burn all its fat on the altar, like the fat of the sacrifice of the peace offering. So the priest shall make atonement for him concerning his sin, and it shall be forgiven him.

²⁷'If anyone of the common people sins unintentionally by doing *something against* any of the commandments of the LORD *in anything* which ought not to be done, and is guilty, ²⁸or if his sin which he has committed comes to his knowledge, then he shall bring as his offering a kid of the goats, a female without blemish, for his sin which he has committed. ²⁹And he shall lay his hand on the head of the sin offering, and kill the sin offering at the place of the burnt offering. ³⁰Then the priest shall take *some* of its blood with his finger, put *it* on the horns of the altar of burnt offering, and pour all *the remaining* blood at the base of the altar. ³¹He shall remove all its fat, as fat is removed from the sacrifice of the peace offering; and the priest shall burn it on the altar for a sweet aroma to the LORD. So the priest shall make atonement for him, and it shall be forgiven him.

³²'If he brings a lamb as his sin offering, he shall bring a female without blemish. ³³Then he shall lay his hand on the head of the sin offering, and kill it as a sin offering at the place where they kill the burnt offering. ³⁴The priest shall take *some* of the blood of the sin offering with his finger, put *it* on the horns of the altar of burnt offering, and pour all *the remaining* blood at the base of the altar. ³⁵He shall remove all its fat, as the fat of the lamb is removed from the sacrifice of the peace offering. Then the priest shall burn it on the altar, according to the offerings made by fire to the LORD. So the priest shall make atonement for his sin

that he has committed, and it shall be forgiven him.

The Trespass Offering

5 'If a person sins in hearing the utterance of an oath, and *is* a witness, whether he has seen or known *of the matter*—if he does not tell *it,* he bears guilt.

²'Or if a person touches any unclean thing, whether *it is* the carcass of an unclean beast, or the carcass of unclean livestock, or the carcass of unclean creeping things, and he is unaware of it, he also shall be unclean and guilty. ³Or if he touches human uncleanness—whatever uncleanness with which a man may be defiled, and he is unaware of it—when he realizes *it,* then he shall be guilty.

⁴'Or if a person swears, speaking thoughtlessly with *his* lips to do evil or to do good, whatever *it is* that a man may pronounce by an oath, and he is unaware of it—when he realizes *it,* then he shall be guilty in any of these *matters.*

⁵'And it shall be, when he is guilty in any of these *matters,* that he shall confess that he has sinned in that *thing;* ⁶and he shall bring his trespass offering to the LORD for his sin which he has committed, a female from the flock, a lamb or a kid of the goats as a sin offering. So the priest shall make atonement for him concerning his sin.

⁷'If he is not able to bring a lamb, then he shall bring to the LORD, for his trespass which he has committed, two turtledoves or two young pigeons: one as a sin offering and the other as a burnt offering. ⁸And he shall bring them to the priest, who shall offer *that* which *is* for the sin offering first, and wring off its head from its neck, but shall not divide *it* completely. ⁹Then he shall sprinkle *some* of the blood of the sin offering on the side of the altar, and the rest of the blood shall be drained out at the base of the altar. It *is* a sin offering. ¹⁰And he shall offer the second *as* a burnt offering according to the prescribed manner. So the priest shall make atonement on his behalf for his sin which he has committed, and it shall be forgiven him.

¹¹'But if he is not able to bring two turtledoves or two young pigeons, then he who sinned shall bring for his offering one-

tenth of an ephah of fine flour as a sin offering. He shall put no oil on it, nor shall he put frankincense on it, for it *is* a sin offering. ¹²Then he shall bring it to the priest, and the priest shall take his handful of it as a memorial portion, and burn *it* on the altar according to the offerings made by fire to the LORD. It *is* a sin offering. ¹³The priest shall make atonement for him, for his sin that he has committed in any of these matters; and it shall be forgiven him. *The rest* shall be the priest's as a grain offering.'"

Offerings with Restitution

¹⁴Then the LORD spoke to Moses, saying: ¹⁵"If a person commits a trespass, and sins unintentionally in regard to the holy things of the LORD, then he shall bring to the LORD as his trespass offering a ram without blemish from the flocks, with your valuation in shekels of silver according to the shekel of the sanctuary, as a trespass offering. ¹⁶And he shall make restitution for the harm that he has done in regard to the holy thing, and shall add one-fifth to it and give it to the priest. So the priest shall make atonement for him with the ram of the trespass offering, and it shall be forgiven him.

¹⁷"If a person sins, and commits any of these things which are forbidden to be done by the commandments of the LORD, though he does not know *it,* yet he is guilty and shall bear his iniquity. ¹⁸And he shall bring to the priest a ram without blemish from the flock, with your valuation, as a trespass offering. So the priest shall make atonement for him regarding his ignorance in which he erred and did not know *it,* and it shall be forgiven him. ¹⁹It is a trespass offering; he has certainly trespassed against the LORD."

6 And the LORD spoke to Moses, saying: ²"If a person sins and commits a trespass against the LORD by lying to his neighbor about what was delivered to him for safekeeping, or about a pledge, or about a robbery, or if he has extorted from his neighbor, ³or if he has found what was lost and lies concerning it, and swears falsely—in any one of these things that a man may do in which he sins: ⁴then it shall be, because he has sinned and is guilty, that he shall restore what he has stolen, or the thing which he has extorted, or what was delivered to him for safekeeping, or the lost thing which he found, ⁵or all that about which he has sworn falsely. He shall

---

| PARENTING MATTERS | **Q:** *Why can't we just give our kids the freedom to set their own standards?* |

We are amazed at how many moms and dads have never had a focused conversation on the specific boundaries and standards they will establish for their child during the preadolescent and teen years. We were regularly shocked in our sixth-grade Sunday school class by the choices children were making. One Sunday, over half the class of sixty eleven- and twelve-year-olds admitted they had viewed an R-rated movie in the last three months. Many watched the movies with their parents.

Have you and your spouse talked/discussed your convictions and boundaries about dating, driving, jobs, grades, curfews, friends, music, internet, movies, and after school activities? The list can seem endless. But we promise this: *If you don't nail down your own convictions ahead of time, your teenager and his peer group will establish their own!*

If you have not agreed as a couple upon guidelines, your child will soon hit you with the divide-and-conquer strategy. Children are experts on whether dad or mom is the easy touch on certain issues. Even when you know you should be united as a couple and clear on the rules, you may still stumble. Settle this ahead of time!

restore its full value, add one-fifth more to it, *and* give it to whomever it belongs, on the day of his trespass offering. ⁶And he shall bring his trespass offering to the LORD, a ram without blemish from the flock, with your valuation, as a trespass offering, to the priest. ⁷So the priest shall make atonement for him before the LORD, and he shall be forgiven for any one of these things that he may have done in which he trespasses."

The Law of the Burnt Offering

⁸Then the LORD spoke to Moses, saying, ⁹"Command Aaron and his sons, saying, 'This *is* the law of the burnt offering: The burnt offering *shall be* on the hearth upon the altar all night until morning, and the fire of the altar shall be kept burning on it. ¹⁰And the priest shall put on his linen garment, and his linen trousers he shall put on his body, and take up the ashes of the burnt offering which the fire has consumed on the altar, and he shall put them beside the altar. ¹¹Then he shall take off his garments, put on other garments, and carry the ashes outside the camp to a clean place. ¹²And the fire on the altar shall be kept burning on it; it shall not be put out. And the priest shall burn wood on it every morning, and lay the burnt offering in order on it; and he shall burn on it the fat of the peace offerings. ¹³A fire shall always be burning on the altar; it shall never go out.

The Law of the Grain Offering

¹⁴'This *is* the law of the grain offering: The sons of Aaron shall offer it on the altar before the LORD. ¹⁵He shall take from it his handful of the fine flour of the grain offering, with its oil, and all the frankincense which *is* on the grain offering, and shall burn *it* on the altar *for* a sweet aroma, as a memorial to the LORD. ¹⁶And the remainder of it Aaron and his sons shall eat; with unleavened bread it shall be eaten in a holy place; in the court of the tabernacle of meeting they shall eat it. ¹⁷It shall not be baked with leaven. I have given it *as* their portion of My offerings made by fire; it *is* most holy, like the sin offering and the trespass offering. ¹⁸All the males among the children of Aaron may eat it. *It shall be* a statute forever in your generations concerning the

offerings made by fire to the LORD. Everyone who touches them must be holy.' "ᵃ

¹⁹And the LORD spoke to Moses, saying, ²⁰"This *is* the offering of Aaron and his sons, which they shall offer to the LORD, *beginning* on the day when he is anointed: one-tenth of an ephah of fine flour as a daily grain offering, half of it in the morning and half of it at night. ²¹It shall be made in a pan with oil. *When it is* mixed, you shall bring it in. The baked pieces of the grain offering you shall offer *for* a sweet aroma to the LORD. ²²The priest from among his sons, who is anointed in his place, shall offer it. *It is* a statute forever to the LORD. It shall be wholly burned. ²³For every grain offering for the priest shall be wholly burned. It shall not be eaten."

The Law of the Sin Offering

²⁴Also the LORD spoke to Moses, saying, ²⁵"Speak to Aaron and to his sons, saying, 'This *is* the law of the sin offering: In the place where the burnt offering is killed, the sin offering shall be killed before the LORD. It *is* most holy. ²⁶The priest who offers it for sin shall eat it. In a holy place it shall be eaten, in the court of the tabernacle of meeting. ²⁷Everyone who touches its flesh must be holy.ᵃ And when its blood is sprinkled on any garment, you shall wash that on which it was sprinkled, in a holy place. ²⁸But the earthen vessel in which it is boiled shall be broken. And if it is boiled in a bronze pot, it shall be both scoured and rinsed in water. ²⁹All the males among the priests may eat it. It *is* most holy. ³⁰But no sin offering from which *any* of the blood is brought into the tabernacle of meeting, to make atonement in the holy *place,*ᵃ shall be eaten. It shall be burned in the fire.

The Law of the Trespass Offering

7 'Likewise this *is* the law of the trespass offering (it *is* most holy): ²In the place where they kill the burnt offering they shall kill the trespass offering. And its blood he shall sprinkle all around on the altar. ³And he shall offer from it all its fat.

6:18 ᵃCompare Numbers 4:15 and Haggai 2:11–13
6:27 ᵃCompare Numbers 4:15 and Haggai 2:11–13
6:30 ᵃThe Most Holy Place when capitalized

The fat tail and the fat that covers the entrails, 4the two kidneys and the fat that *is* on them by the flanks, and the fatty lobe *attached* to the liver above the kidneys, he shall remove; 5and the priest shall burn them on the altar *as* an offering made by fire to the LORD. It *is* a trespass offering. 6Every male among the priests may eat it. It shall be eaten in a holy place. It *is* most holy. 7The trespass offering *is* like the sin offering; *there is* one law for them both: the priest who makes atonement with it shall have *it*. 8And the priest who offers anyone's burnt offering, that priest shall have for himself the skin of the burnt offering which he has offered. 9Also every grain offering that is baked in the oven and all that is prepared in the covered pan, or in a pan, shall be the priest's who offers it. 10Every grain offering, *whether* mixed with oil or dry, shall belong to all the sons of Aaron, to one *as much as* the other.

The Law of Peace Offerings

11'This *is* the law of the sacrifice of peace offerings which he shall offer to the LORD: 12If he offers it for a thanksgiving, then he shall offer, with the sacrifice of thanksgiving, unleavened cakes mixed with oil, unleavened wafers anointed with oil, or cakes of blended flour mixed with oil. 13Besides the cakes, *as* his offering he shall offer leavened bread with the sacrifice of thanksgiving of his peace offering. 14And from it he shall offer one cake from each offering *as* a heave offering to the LORD. It shall belong to the priest who sprinkles the blood of the peace offering.

15'The flesh of the sacrifice of his peace offering for thanksgiving shall be eaten the same day it is offered. He shall not leave any of it until morning. 16But if the sacrifice of his offering *is* a vow or a voluntary offering, it shall be eaten the same day that he offers his sacrifice; but on the next day the remainder of it also may be eaten; 17the remainder of the flesh of the sacrifice on the third day must be burned with fire. 18And if *any* of the flesh of the sacrifice of

his peace offering is eaten at all on the third day, it shall not be accepted, nor shall it be imputed to him; it shall be an abomination *to* him who offers it, and the person who eats of it shall bear guilt.

19'The flesh that touches any unclean thing shall not be eaten. It shall be burned with fire. And as for the *clean* flesh, all who are clean may eat of it. 20But the person who eats the flesh of the sacrifice of the peace offering that *belongs* to the LORD, while he is unclean, that person shall be cut off from his people. 21Moreover the person who touches any unclean thing, *such as* human uncleanness, *an* unclean animal, or any abominable unclean thing,a and who eats the flesh of the sacrifice of the peace offering that *belongs* to the LORD, that person shall be cut off from his people.'"

Fat and Blood May Not Be Eaten

22And the LORD spoke to Moses, saying, 23"Speak to the children of Israel, saying: 'You shall not eat any fat, of ox or sheep or goat. 24And the fat of an animal that dies *naturally,* and the fat of what is torn by wild beasts, may be used in any other way; but you shall by no means eat it. 25For whoever eats the fat of the animal of which men offer an offering made by fire to the LORD, the person who eats *it* shall be cut off from his people. 26Moreover you shall not eat any blood in any of your dwellings, *whether* of bird or beast. 27Whoever eats any blood, that person shall be cut off from his people.'"

The Portion of Aaron and His Sons

28Then the LORD spoke to Moses, saying, 29"Speak to the children of Israel, saying: 'He who offers the sacrifice of his peace offering to the LORD shall bring his offering to the LORD from the sacrifice of his peace offering. 30His own hands shall bring the offerings made by fire to the LORD. The fat with the breast he shall bring, that the breast may be waved *as* a wave offering before the LORD. 31And the priest shall burn the fat on the altar, but the breast shall be Aaron's and his sons'. 32Also the right thigh you shall give to the priest *as* a heave offering from the sacrifices of your peace offerings. 33He among the sons of Aaron, who offers the blood of the peace offering and

---

7:21 aFollowing Masoretic Text, Septuagint, and Vulgate; Samaritan Pentateuch, Syriac, and Targum read *swarming thing* (compare 5:2).

the fat, shall have the right thigh for *his* part. ³⁴For the breast of the wave offering and the thigh of the heave offering I have taken from the children of Israel, from the sacrifices of their peace offerings, and I have given them to Aaron the priest and to his sons from the children of Israel by a statute forever.'"

³⁵This *is* the consecrated portion for Aaron and his sons, from the offerings made by fire to the LORD, on the day when *Moses* presented them to minister to the LORD as priests. ³⁶The LORD commanded this to be given to them by the children of Israel, on the day that He anointed them, *by* a statute forever throughout their generations.

³⁷This *is* the law of the burnt offering, the grain offering, the sin offering, the trespass offering, the consecrations, and the sacrifice of the peace offering, ³⁸which the LORD commanded Moses on Mount Sinai, on the day when He commanded the children of Israel to offer their offerings to the LORD in the Wilderness of Sinai.

Aaron and His Sons Consecrated

8 And the LORD spoke to Moses, saying: ²"Take Aaron and his sons with him, and the garments, the anointing oil, a bull as the sin offering, two rams, and a basket of unleavened bread; ³and gather all the congregation together at the door of the tabernacle of meeting."

⁴So Moses did as the LORD commanded him. And the congregation was gathered together at the door of the tabernacle of meeting. ⁵And Moses said to the congregation, "This *is* what the LORD commanded to be done."

⁶Then Moses brought Aaron and his sons and washed them with water. ⁷And he put the tunic on him, girded him with the sash, clothed him with the robe, and put the ephod on him; and he girded him with the intricately woven band of the ephod, and with it tied *the ephod* on him. ⁸Then he put the breastplate on him, and he put the Urim and the Thummimᵃ in the breastplate. ⁹And he put the turban on his head. Also on the turban, on its front, he put the golden plate, the holy crown, as the LORD had commanded Moses.

¹⁰Also Moses took the anointing oil, and anointed the tabernacle and all that *was* in it, and consecrated them. ¹¹He sprinkled

---

8:8 ᵃLiterally *the Lights and the Perfections* (compare Exodus 28:30)

Respectfully Leave Your Parents

You may have moved out of their house a long time ago, but have you *really* left your parents behind?

God did not mince words when He instructed a married couple to leave their parents. The Hebrew word that normally gets translated *leave* from Genesis 2:24 more fully means "to forsake dependence upon," "lose," "leave behind," "release," and "let go."

Centuries later, Jesus addressed this issue when He said that God never intended for *anybody*—not in-laws, not mother, not father, not children, not friends, not pastors, not employers—to come between a husband and a wife (Matt. 19:6). *No one!*

After our wedding ceremony, Barbara and I walked down the aisle together, symbolically proclaiming to all witnesses that we had left our parents. We had forsaken our dependence upon them for our livelihood and emotional support, and were turning now to each other—for the rest of our lives—as the most important persons in our universe. This public affirmation of our covenant to each other meant, "No relationship on earth, other than my relationship with Jesus Christ and God, is more important to me than the one with my spouse."

If you or your spouse has not fully left mother and father, begin to discuss how you have failed to leave and what you can do today to truly forsake dependence upon your parents and cleave to one another.

some of it on the altar seven times, anointed the altar and all its utensils, and the laver and its base, to consecrate them. ¹²And he poured some of the anointing oil on Aaron's head and anointed him, to consecrate him.

¹³Then Moses brought Aaron's sons and put tunics on them, girded them with sashes, and put hats on them, as the LORD had commanded Moses.

¹⁴And he brought the bull for the sin offering. Then Aaron and his sons laid their hands on the head of the bull for the sin offering, ¹⁵and Moses killed it. Then he took the blood, and put some on the horns of the altar all around with his finger, and purified the altar. And he poured the blood at the base of the altar, and consecrated it, to make atonement for it. ¹⁶Then he took all the fat that was on the entrails, the fatty lobe attached to the liver, and the two kidneys with their fat, and Moses burned them on the altar. ¹⁷But the bull, its hide, its flesh, and its offal, he burned with fire outside the camp, as the LORD had commanded Moses.

¹⁸Then he brought the ram as the burnt offering. And Aaron and his sons laid their hands on the head of the ram, ¹⁹and Moses killed it. Then he sprinkled the blood all around on the altar. ²⁰And he cut the ram into pieces; and Moses burned the head, the pieces, and the fat. ²¹Then he washed the entrails and the legs in water. And Moses burned the whole ram on the altar. It was a burnt sacrifice for a sweet aroma, an offering made by fire to the LORD, as the LORD had commanded Moses.

²²And he brought the second ram, the ram of consecration. Then Aaron and his sons laid their hands on the head of the ram, ²³and Moses killed it. Also he took some of its blood and put it on the tip of Aaron's right ear, on the thumb of his right hand, and on the big toe of his right foot. ²⁴Then he brought Aaron's sons. And Moses put some of the blood on the tips of their right ears, on the thumbs of their right hands, and on the big toes of their right feet. And Moses sprinkled the blood all around on the altar. ²⁵Then he took the fat and the fat tail, all the fat that was on the entrails, the fatty lobe attached to the liver, the two kidneys and their fat, and the right thigh; ²⁶and from the basket of unleavened bread that was before the LORD he took one unleavened cake, a cake of bread anointed with oil, and one wafer, and put them on the fat and on the right thigh; ²⁷and he put all these in Aaron's hands and in his sons' hands, and waved them as a wave offering before the LORD. ²⁸Then Moses took them from their hands and burned them on the altar, on the burnt offering. They were consecration offerings for a sweet aroma. That was an offering made by fire to the LORD. ²⁹And Moses took the breast and waved it as a wave offering before the LORD. It was Moses' part of the ram of consecration, as the LORD had commanded Moses.

³⁰Then Moses took some of the anointing oil and some of the blood which was on the altar, and sprinkled it on Aaron, on his garments, on his sons, and on the garments of his sons with him; and he consecrated Aaron, his garments, his sons, and the garments of his sons with him.

³¹And Moses said to Aaron and his sons, "Boil the flesh at the door of the tabernacle of meeting, and eat it there with the bread that is in the basket of consecration offerings, as I commanded, saying, 'Aaron and his sons shall eat it.' ³²What remains of the flesh and of the bread you shall burn with fire. ³³And you shall not go outside the door of the tabernacle of meeting for seven days, until the days of your consecration are ended. For seven days he shall consecrate you. ³⁴As he has done this day, so the LORD has commanded to do, to make atonement for you. ³⁵Therefore you shall stay at the door of the tabernacle of meeting day and night for seven days, and keep the charge of the LORD, so that you may not die; for so I have been commanded." ³⁶So Aaron and his sons did all the things that the LORD had commanded by the hand of Moses.

The Priestly Ministry Begins

9 It came to pass on the eighth day that Moses called Aaron and his sons and the elders of Israel. ²And he said to Aaron, "Take for yourself a young bull as a sin offering and a ram as a burnt offering, without blemish, and offer them before the LORD. ³And to the children of Israel you shall speak, saying, 'Take a kid of the goats as a sin offering, and a calf and a lamb, both of

the first year, without blemish, as a burnt offering, [4]also a bull and a ram as peace offerings, to sacrifice before the LORD, and a grain offering mixed with oil; for today the LORD will appear to you.'"

[5]So they brought what Moses commanded before the tabernacle of meeting. And all the congregation drew near and stood before the LORD. [6]Then Moses said, "This *is* the thing which the LORD commanded you to do, and the glory of the LORD will appear to you." [7]And Moses said to Aaron, "Go to the altar, offer your sin offering and your burnt offering, and make atonement for yourself and for the people. Offer the offering of the people, and make atonement for them, as the LORD commanded."

[8]Aaron therefore went to the altar and killed the calf of the sin offering, which *was* for himself. [9]Then the sons of Aaron brought the blood to him. And he dipped his finger in the blood, put *it* on the horns of the altar, and poured the blood at the base of the altar. [10]But the fat, the kidneys, and the fatty lobe from the liver of the sin offering he burned on the altar, as the LORD had commanded Moses. [11]The flesh and the hide he burned with fire outside the camp.

[12]And he killed the burnt offering; and Aaron's sons presented to him the blood, which he sprinkled all around on the altar. [13]Then they presented the burnt offering to him, with its pieces and head, and he burned *them* on the altar. [14]And he washed the entrails and the legs, and burned *them* with the burnt offering on the altar.

[15]Then he brought the people's offering, and took the goat, which *was* the sin offering for the people, and killed it and offered it for sin, like the first one. [16]And he brought the burnt offering and offered it according to the prescribed manner. [17]Then he brought the grain offering, took a handful of it, and burned *it* on the altar, besides the burnt sacrifice of the morning.

[18]He also killed the bull and the ram *as* sacrifices of peace offerings, which *were* for the people. And Aaron's sons presented to him the blood, which he sprinkled all around on the altar, [19]and the fat from the bull and the ram—the fatty tail, what covers *the entrails* and the kidneys, and the fatty lobe *attached to* the liver; [20]and they

put the fat on the breasts. Then he burned the fat on the altar; [21]but the breasts and the right thigh Aaron waved *as* a wave offering before the LORD, as Moses had commanded.

[22]Then Aaron lifted his hand toward the people, blessed them, and came down from offering the sin offering, the burnt offering, and peace offerings. [23]And Moses and Aaron went into the tabernacle of meeting, and came out and blessed the people. Then the glory of the LORD appeared to all the people, [24]and fire came out from before the LORD and consumed the burnt offering and the fat on the altar. When all the people saw *it,* they shouted and fell on their faces.

The Profane Fire of Nadab and Abihu

10 Then Nadab and Abihu, the sons of Aaron, each took his censer and put fire in it, put incense on it, and offered profane fire before the LORD, which He had not commanded them. [2]So fire went out from the LORD and devoured them, and they died before the LORD. [3]And Moses said to Aaron, "This is what the LORD spoke, saying:

' By those who come near Me
  I must be regarded as holy;
And before all the people
  I must be glorified.' "

So Aaron held his peace.

[4]Then Moses called Mishael and Elzaphan, the sons of Uzziel the uncle of Aaron, and said to them, "Come near, carry your brethren from before the sanctuary out of the camp." [5]So they went near and carried them by their tunics out of the camp, as Moses had said.

[6]And Moses said to Aaron, and to Elemazar and Ithamar, his sons, "Do not uncover your heads nor tear your clothes, lest you die, and wrath come upon all the people. But let your brethren, the whole house of Israel, bewail the burning which the LORD has kindled. [7]You shall not go out from the door of the tabernacle of meeting, lest you die, for the anointing oil of the LORD *is* upon you." And they did according to the word of Moses.

Conduct Prescribed for Priests

[8]Then the LORD spoke to Aaron, saying:
[9]"Do not drink wine or intoxicating drink,

you, nor your sons with you, when you go into the tabernacle of meeting, lest you die. *It shall be* a statute forever throughout your generations, [10]that you may distinguish between holy and unholy, and between unclean and clean, [11]and that you may teach the children of Israel all the statutes which the LORD has spoken to them by the hand of Moses."

[12]And Moses spoke to Aaron, and to Elemazar and Ithamar, his sons who were left: "Take the grain offering that remains of the offerings made by fire to the LORD, and eat it without leaven beside the altar; for it *is* most holy. [13]You shall eat it in a holy place, because it *is* your due and your sons' due, of the sacrifices made by fire to the LORD; for so I have been commanded. [14]The breast of the wave offering and the thigh of the heave offering you shall eat in a clean place, you, your sons, and your daughters with you; for *they are* your due and your sons' due, *which* are given from the sacrifices of peace offerings of the children of Israel. [15]The thigh of the heave offering and the breast of the wave offering they shall bring with the offerings of fat made by fire, to offer *as* a wave offering before the LORD. And it shall be yours and your sons' with you, by a statute forever, as the LORD has commanded."

[16]Then Moses made careful inquiry about the goat of the sin offering, and there it was—burned up. And he was angry with Elemazar and Ithamar, the sons of Aaron *who were* left, saying, [17]"Why have you not eaten the sin offering in a holy place, since it *is* most holy, and *God* has given it to you to bear the guilt of the congregation, to make atonement for them before the LORD? [18]See! Its blood was not brought inside the holy *place;*[a] indeed you should have eaten it in a holy *place,* as I commanded."

[19]And Aaron said to Moses, "Look, this day they have offered their sin offering and their burnt offering before the LORD, and such things have befallen me! *If* I had eaten the sin offering today, would it have been accepted in the sight of the LORD?" [20]So when Moses heard *that,* he was content.

10:18 [a]The Most Holy Place when capitalized

Foods Permitted and Forbidden

11 Now the LORD spoke to Moses and Aaron, saying to them, [2]"Speak to the children of Israel, saying, 'These *are* the animals which you may eat among all the animals that *are* on the earth: [3]Among the animals, whatever divides the hoof, having cloven hooves *and* chewing the cud—that

ROMANCE FAQ

Q: *How can we heal the isolation we've grown to feel toward one another?*

Isolation is the great killer of marriages. Many marriages continue for years in a state of armed truce. Competition replaces cooperation and ugly reality dashes dreams as conflict unravels the fabric of love and concern.

The choice to heal those rifts is yours. Every day, each partner makes choices that result in oneness or in isolation. Here are three important choices you need to make:

Choice #1: Resolve to pursue oneness with each other and repent of any isolation that already exists. Remember, you don't have to be married a long time to feel isolated.

Choice #2: Resolve to never go to bed angry with one another. Find a way to resolve your differences and move toward oneness. Resentment and oneness cannot coexist.

Choice #3: Resolve to take time to share intimately with each other. Allow your spouse into your life. Ask questions of your spouse and listen patiently. Learn the art of healthy, transparent communication.

Make the right choices and you'll know love, warmth, acceptance, and the freedom of true intimacy and genuine oneness. Make the wrong choices and you'll know the quiet desperation of living together but never really touching each other deeply. As a couple, resolve that you will not allow isolation to set up residence in your marriage.

you may eat. ⁴Nevertheless these you shall not eat among those that chew the cud or those that have cloven hooves: the camel, because it chews the cud but does not have cloven hooves, is unclean to you; ⁵the rock hyrax, because it chews the cud but does not have cloven hooves, *is* unclean to you; ⁶the hare, because it chews the cud but does not have cloven hooves, *is* unclean to you; ⁷and the swine, though it divides the hoof, having cloven hooves, yet does not chew the cud, *is* unclean to you. ⁸Their flesh you shall not eat, and their carcasses you shall not touch. They *are* unclean to you.

⁹"These you may eat of all that *are* in the water: whatever in the water has fins and scales, whether in the seas or in the rivers—that you may eat. ¹⁰But all in the seas or in the rivers that do not have fins and scales, all that move in the water or any living thing which *is* in the water, they *are* an abomination to you. ¹¹They shall be an abomination to you; you shall not eat their flesh, but you shall regard their carcasses as an abomination. ¹²Whatever in the water does not have fins or scales— that *shall be* an abomination to you.

¹³"And these you shall regard as an abomination among the birds; they shall not be eaten, they *are* an abomination: the eagle, the vulture, the buzzard, ¹⁴the kite, and the falcon after its kind; ¹⁵every raven after its kind, ¹⁶the ostrich, the short-eared owl, the sea gull, and the hawk after its kind; ¹⁷the little owl, the fisher owl, and the screech owl; ¹⁸the white owl, the jackdaw, and the carrion vulture; ¹⁹the stork, the heron after its kind, the hoopoe, and the bat.

²⁰"All flying insects that creep on *all* fours *shall be* an abomination to you. ²¹Yet these you may eat of every flying insect that creeps on *all* fours: those which have jointed legs above their feet with which to leap on the earth. ²²These you may eat: the locust after its kind, the destroying locust after its kind, the cricket after its kind, and the grasshopper after its kind. ²³But all *other* flying insects which have four feet *shall be* an abomination to you.

Unclean Animals

²⁴"By these you shall become unclean; whoever touches the carcass of any of them shall be unclean until evening; ²⁵whoever carries part of the carcass of any of them shall wash his clothes and be unclean until evening: ²⁶*The carcass* of any animal which divides the foot, but is not cloven-hoofed or does not chew the cud, *is* unclean to you. Everyone who touches it shall be unclean. ²⁷And whatever goes on its paws, among all kinds of animals that go on *all* fours, those *are* unclean to you. Whoever touches any such carcass shall be unclean until evening. ²⁸Whoever carries *any such* carcass shall wash his clothes and be unclean until evening. It *is* unclean to you.

²⁹"These also *shall be* unclean to you among the creeping things that creep on the earth: the mole, the mouse, and the large lizard after its kind; ³⁰the gecko, the monitor lizard, the sand reptile, the sand lizard, and the chameleon. ³¹These *are* unclean to you among all that creep. Whoever touches them when they are dead shall be unclean until evening. ³²Anything on which *any* of them falls, when they are dead shall be unclean, whether *it is* any item of wood or clothing or skin or sack, whatever item *it is,* in which *any* work is done, it must be put in water. And it shall be unclean until evening; then it shall be clean. ³³Any earthen vessel into which *any* of them falls you shall break; and whatever *is* in it shall be unclean: ³⁴in such a vessel, any edible food upon which water falls becomes unclean, and any drink that may be drunk from it becomes unclean. ³⁵And everything on which *a part* of *any such* carcass falls shall be unclean; *whether it is* an oven or cooking stove, it shall be broken down; *for* they *are* unclean, and shall be unclean to you. ³⁶Nevertheless a spring or a cistern, *in which there is* plenty of water, shall be clean, but whatever touches any such carcass becomes unclean. ³⁷And if a part of *any such* carcass falls on any planting seed which is to be sown, it *remains* clean. ³⁸But if water is put on the seed, and if *a part* of *any such* carcass falls on it, it *becomes* unclean to you.

³⁹"And if any animal which you may eat dies, he who touches its carcass shall be unclean until evening. ⁴⁰He who eats of its carcass shall wash his clothes and be

unclean until evening. He also who carries its carcass shall wash his clothes and be unclean until evening.

[41]'And every creeping thing that creeps on the earth *shall be* an abomination. It shall not be eaten. [42]Whatever crawls on its belly, whatever goes on *all* fours, or whatever has many feet among all creeping things that creep on the earth—these you shall not eat, for they *are* an abomination. [43]You shall not make yourselves abominable with any creeping thing that creeps; nor shall you make yourselves unclean with them, lest you be defiled by them. [44]For I *am* the LORD your God. You shall therefore consecrate yourselves, and you shall be holy; for I *am* holy. Neither shall you defile yourselves with any creeping thing that creeps on the earth. [45]For I *am* the LORD who brings you up out of the land of Egypt, to be your God. You shall therefore be holy, for I *am* holy.

[46]'This *is* the law of the animals and the birds and every living creature that moves in the waters, and of every creature that creeps on the earth, [47]to distinguish between the unclean and the clean, and between the animal that may be eaten and the animal that may not be eaten.'"

The Ritual After Childbirth

12 Then the LORD spoke to Moses, saying, [2]"Speak to the children of Israel, saying: 'If a woman has conceived, and borne a male child, then she shall be unclean seven days; as in the days of her customary impurity she shall be unclean. [3]And on the eighth day the flesh of his foreskin shall be circumcised. [4]She shall then continue in the blood of *her* purification thirty-three days. She shall not touch any hallowed thing, nor come into the sanctuary until the days of her purification are fulfilled.

[5]'But if she bears a female child, then she shall be unclean two weeks, as in her customary impurity, and she shall continue in the blood of *her* purification sixty-six days.

[6]'When the days of her purification are fulfilled, whether for a son or a daughter,

she shall bring to the priest a lamb of the first year as a burnt offering, and a young pigeon or a turtledove as a sin offering, to the door of the tabernacle of meeting. [7]Then he shall offer it before the LORD, and make atonement for her. And she shall be clean from the flow of her blood. This *is* the law for her who has borne a male or a female.

[8]'And if she is not able to bring a lamb, then she may bring two turtledoves or two young pigeons—one as a burnt offering and the other as a sin offering. So the priest shall make atonement for her, and she will be clean.'"

The Law Concerning Leprosy

13 And the LORD spoke to Moses and Aaron, saying: [2]"When a man has on the skin of his body a swelling, a scab, or a bright spot, and it becomes on the skin of his body *like* a leprous[a] sore, then he shall be brought to Aaron the priest or to one of his sons the priests. [3]The priest shall examine the sore on the skin of the body; and if the hair on the sore has turned white, and the sore appears *to be* deeper than the skin of his body, it *is* a leprous sore. Then the priest shall examine him, and pronounce him unclean. [4]But if the bright spot *is* white on the skin of his body, and does not appear *to be* deeper than the skin, and its hair has not turned white, then the priest shall isolate *the one who has* the sore seven days. [5]And the priest shall examine him on the seventh

INTIMATE MOMENTS

Get some dry-erase markers and, early in the morning, silently leave a love note for your sweetie on the bathroom mirror. Make it as long or as short as you want to, but make sure it expresses how much she means to you. Sign it with a little heart or some other token that captures how you feel about her—be as artistic as you dare. And remember this: the more effort you put into your message, the more it'll be remembered and appreciated.

13:2 [a]Hebrew *saraath,* disfiguring skin diseases, including leprosy, and so in verses 2–46 and 14:2–32

day; and indeed *if* the sore appears to be as it was, *and* the sore has not spread on the skin, then the priest shall isolate him another seven days. ⁶Then the priest shall examine him again on the seventh day; and indeed *if* the sore has faded, *and* the sore has not spread on the skin, then the priest shall pronounce him clean; it *is only* a scab, and he shall wash his clothes and be clean. ⁷But if the scab should at all spread over the skin, after he has been seen by the priest for his cleansing, he shall be seen by the priest again. ⁸And *if* the priest sees that the scab has indeed spread on the skin, then the priest shall pronounce him unclean. It *is* leprosy.

⁹"When the leprous sore is on a person, then he shall be brought to the priest. ¹⁰And the priest shall examine *him;* and indeed *if* the swelling on the skin *is* white, and it has turned the hair white, and *there is* a spot of raw flesh in the swelling, ¹¹it *is* an old leprosy on the skin of his body. The priest shall pronounce him unclean, and shall not isolate him, for he *is* unclean.

¹²"And if leprosy breaks out all over the skin, and the leprosy covers all the skin of *the one who has* the sore, from his head to his foot, wherever the priest looks, ¹³then the priest shall consider; and indeed *if* the leprosy has covered all his body, he shall pronounce *him* clean *who has* the sore. It has all turned white. He *is* clean. ¹⁴But when raw flesh appears on him, he shall be unclean. ¹⁵And the priest shall examine the raw flesh and pronounce him to be unclean; *for* the raw flesh *is* unclean. It *is* leprosy. ¹⁶Or if the raw flesh changes and turns white again, he shall come to the priest. ¹⁷And the priest shall examine him; and indeed *if* the sore has turned white, then the priest shall pronounce *him* clean *who has* the sore. He *is* clean.

¹⁸"If the body develops a boil in the skin, and it is healed, ¹⁹and in the place of the boil there comes a white swelling or a bright spot, reddish-white, then it shall be shown to the priest; ²⁰and *if,* when the priest sees it, it indeed appears deeper than the skin, and its hair has turned white, the priest shall pronounce him unclean. It *is* a leprous sore which has broken out of the boil. ²¹But if the priest

examines it, and indeed *there are* no white hairs in it, and it *is* not deeper than the skin, but has faded, then the priest shall isolate him seven days; ²²and if it should at all spread over the skin, then the priest shall pronounce him unclean. It *is* a leprous sore. ²³But if the bright spot stays in one place, *and* has not spread, it *is* the scar of the boil; and the priest shall pronounce him clean.

²⁴"Or if the body receives a burn on its skin by fire, and the raw *flesh* of the burn becomes a bright spot, reddish-white or white, ²⁵then the priest shall examine it; and indeed *if* the hair of the bright spot has turned white, and it appears deeper than the skin, it *is* leprosy broken out in the burn. Therefore the priest shall pronounce him unclean. It *is* a leprous sore. ²⁶But if the priest examines it, and indeed *there are* no white hairs in the bright spot, and it *is* not deeper than the skin, but has faded, then the priest shall isolate him seven days. ²⁷And the priest shall examine him on the seventh day. If it has at all spread over the skin, then the priest shall pronounce him unclean. It *is* a leprous sore. ²⁸But if the bright spot stays in one place, *and* has not spread on the skin, but has faded, it *is* a swelling from the burn. The priest shall pronounce him clean, for it *is* the scar from the burn.

²⁹"If a man or woman has a sore on the head or the beard, ³⁰then the priest shall examine the sore; and indeed if it appears deeper than the skin, *and there is* in it thin yellow hair, then the priest shall pronounce him unclean. It *is* a scaly leprosy of the head or beard. ³¹But if the priest examines the scaly sore, and indeed it does not appear deeper than the skin, and *there is* no black hair in it, then the priest shall isolate *the one who has* the scale seven days. ³²And on the seventh day the priest shall examine the sore; and indeed *if* the scale has not spread, and there is no yellow hair in it, and the scale does not appear deeper than the skin, ³³he shall shave himself, but the scale he shall not shave. And the priest shall isolate *the one who has* the scale another seven days. ³⁴On the seventh day the priest shall examine the scale; and indeed *if* the scale has not spread over the

skin, and does not appear deeper than the skin, then the priest shall pronounce him clean. He shall wash his clothes and be clean. [35]But if the scale should at all spread over the skin after his cleansing, [36]then the priest shall examine him; and indeed *if* the scale has spread over the skin, the priest need not seek for yellow hair. He *is* unclean. [37]But if the scale appears to be at a standstill, and there is black hair grown up in it, the scale has healed. He *is* clean, and the priest shall pronounce him clean.

[38]"If a man or a woman has bright spots on the skin of the body, *specifically* white bright spots, [39]then the priest shall look; and indeed *if* the bright spots on the skin of the body *are* dull white, it *is* a white spot *that* grows on the skin. He *is* clean.

[40]"As for the man whose hair has fallen from his head, he *is* bald, *but* he *is* clean. [41]He whose hair has fallen from his forehead, he *is* bald on the forehead, *but* he *is* clean. [42]And if there is on the bald head or bald forehead a reddish-white sore, it *is* leprosy breaking out on his bald head or his bald forehead. [43]Then the priest shall examine it; and indeed *if* the swelling of the sore *is* reddish-white on his bald head or on his bald forehead, as the appearance of leprosy on the skin of the body, [44]he is a leprous man. He *is* unclean. The priest shall surely pronounce him unclean; his sore *is* on his head.

[45]"Now the leper on whom the sore *is,* his clothes shall be torn and his head bare; and he shall cover his mustache, and cry, 'Unclean! Unclean!' [46]He shall be unclean. All the days he has the sore he shall be unclean. He *is* unclean, and he shall dwell alone; his dwelling *shall be* outside the camp.

The Law Concerning Leprous Garments

[47]"Also, if a garment has a leprous plague[a] in it, *whether it is* a woolen garment or a linen garment, [48]whether *it is* in the warp or woof of linen or wool, whether in leather or in anything made of leather, [49]and if the plague is greenish or reddish in the garment or in the leather, whether in the warp or in the woof, or in anything made of leather, it *is* a leprous plague and shall be shown to the priest. [50]The priest shall examine the plague and isolate *that which has* the plague seven days. [51]And he shall examine the plague on the seventh day. If the plague has spread in the garment, either in the warp or in the woof, in the leather *or* in anything made of leather, the plague *is* an active leprosy. It *is* unclean. [52]He shall therefore burn that garment in which is the plague, whether warp or woof, in wool or in linen, or anything of leather, for it *is* an active leprosy; *the garment* shall be burned in the fire.

[53]"But if the priest examines *it,* and indeed the plague has not spread in the garment, either in the warp or in the woof, or in anything made of leather, [54]then the priest shall command that they wash *the thing* in which *is* the plague; and he shall isolate it another seven days. [55]Then the priest shall examine the plague after it has been washed; and indeed *if* the plague has not changed its color, though the plague has not spread, it *is* unclean, and you shall burn it in the fire; it continues eating away, *whether* the damage *is* outside or inside. [56]If the priest examines *it,* and indeed the plague has faded after washing it, then he shall tear it out of the garment, whether out of the warp or out of the woof, or out of the leather. [57]But if it appears again in the garment, either in the warp or in the woof, or in anything made of leather, it *is* a spreading *plague;* you shall burn with fire that in which is the plague. [58]And if you wash the garment, either warp or woof, or whatever is made of leather, if the plague has disappeared from it, then it shall be washed a second time, and shall be clean.

[59]"This *is* the law of the leprous plague in a garment of wool or linen, either in the warp or woof, or in anything made of leather, to pronounce it clean or to pronounce it unclean."

The Ritual for Cleansing Healed Lepers

14 Then the LORD spoke to Moses, saying, [2]"This shall be the law of the leper for the day of his cleansing: He shall be brought to the priest. [3]And the priest shall go out of the camp, and the priest shall

---

13:47 [a]A mold, fungus, or similar infestation, and so in verses 47–59

examine *him;* and indeed, *if* the leprosy is healed in the leper, [4]then the priest shall command to take for him who is to be cleansed two living *and* clean birds, cedar wood, scarlet, and hyssop. [5]And the priest shall command that one of the birds be killed in an earthen vessel over running water. [6]As for the living bird, he shall take it, the cedar wood and the scarlet and the hyssop, and dip them and the living bird in the blood of the bird *that was* killed over the running water. [7]And he shall sprinkle it seven times on him who is to be cleansed from the leprosy, and shall pronounce him clean, and shall let the living bird loose in the open field. [8]He who is to be cleansed shall wash his clothes, shave off all his hair, and wash himself in water, that he may be clean. After that he shall come into the camp, and shall stay outside his tent seven days. [9]But on the seventh day he shall shave all the hair off his head and his beard and his eyebrows—all his hair he shall shave off. He shall wash his clothes and wash his body in water, and he shall be clean.

[10]"And on the eighth day he shall take two male lambs without blemish, one ewe lamb of the first year without blemish, three-tenths *of an ephah* of fine flour mixed with oil as a grain offering, and one log of oil. [11]Then the priest who makes *him* clean shall present the man who is to be made clean, and those things, before the LORD, *at* the door of the tabernacle of meeting. [12]And the priest shall take one male lamb and offer it as a trespass offering, and the log of oil, and wave them *as* a wave offering before the LORD. [13]Then he shall kill the lamb in the place where he kills the sin offering and the burnt offering, in a holy place; for as the sin offering *is* the priest's, so *is* the trespass offering. It *is* most holy. [14]The priest shall take *some* of the blood of the trespass offering, and the priest shall put *it* on the tip of the right ear of him who is to be cleansed, on the thumb of his right hand, and on the big toe of his right foot. [15]And the priest shall take *some* of the log of oil, and pour *it* into the palm of his own left hand. [16]Then the priest shall dip his right finger in the oil that *is* in his left hand, and shall sprinkle some of the oil with his finger seven times before the LORD. [17]And of the rest of the oil in his hand, the priest shall put *some* on the tip of the right ear of him who is to be cleansed, on the thumb of his right hand, and on the big toe of his right foot, on the blood of the trespass offering. [18]The rest of the oil that *is* in the priest's hand he shall put on the head of him who is to be cleansed. So the priest shall make atonement for him before the LORD.

[19]"Then the priest shall offer the sin

Talk Out Past Issues

Marriage has enough surprises without a spouse putting up a "No Trespassing" sign and saying, "I'm not going to talk about the issues from my past that have shaped my life." If you want to truly know your spouse, then you *must* get into those issues and so create a deeper level of understanding and compassion between the two of you. Then, when one of life's inevitable trials comes along, you'll already have put into place a deep level of trust in each other.

Every marriage must be built on love-based commitment. Remember 1 John 4:18— "Perfect love casts out fear." Is some guilty or shameful episode from your past tormenting you and saying, "Don't share *that*! She'll reject you"? If you are doing this, then your relationship is controlled by fear, not love. Don't risk hiding something important from your spouse, regardless of how painful it may feel.

When love encounters past mistakes in the loved one, it says, "I embrace you. I receive you. I accept you. I cherish you. And, yes, I forgive you."

The truth is, we have all fallen. All of us have done things we are tempted to hide. But Christ offers us grace, forgiveness, cleansing, and wholeness, all in plentiful supply.

offering, and make atonement for him who is to be cleansed from his uncleanness. Afterward he shall kill the burnt offering. 20And the priest shall offer the burnt offering and the grain offering on the altar. So the priest shall make atonement for him, and he shall be clean.

21"But if he *is* poor and cannot afford it, then he shall take one male lamb *as* a trespass offering to be waved, to make atonement for him, one-tenth *of an ephah* of fine flour mixed with oil as a grain offering, a log of oil, 22and two turtledoves or two young pigeons, such as he is able to afford: one shall be a sin offering and the other a burnt offering. 23He shall bring them to the priest on the eighth day for his cleansing, to the door of the tabernacle of meeting, before the LORD. 24And the priest shall take the lamb of the trespass offering and the log of oil, and the priest shall wave them *as* a wave offering before the LORD. 25Then he shall kill the lamb of the trespass offering, and the priest shall take *some* of the blood of the trespass offering and put *it* on the tip of the right ear of him who is to be cleansed, on the thumb of his right hand, and on the big toe of his right foot. 26And the priest shall pour some of the oil into the palm of his own left hand. 27Then the priest shall sprinkle with his right finger *some* of the oil that *is* in his left hand seven times before the LORD. 28And the priest shall put *some* of the oil that *is* in his hand on the tip of the right ear of him who is to be cleansed, on the thumb of the right hand, and on the big toe of his right foot, on the place of the blood of the trespass offering. 29The rest of the oil that *is* in the priest's hand he shall put on the head of him who is to be cleansed, to make atonement for him before the LORD. 30And he shall offer one of the turtledoves or young pigeons, such as he can afford— 31such as he is able to afford, the one *as* a sin offering and the other *as* a burnt offering, with the grain offering. So the priest shall make atonement for him who is to be cleansed before the LORD. 32This *is* the law *for one* who had

14:34 ªDecomposition by mildew, mold, dry rot, etc., and so in verses 34–53

a leprous sore, who cannot afford the usual cleansing."

The Law Concerning Leprous Houses

33And the LORD spoke to Moses and Aaron, saying: 34"When you have come into the land of Canaan, which I give you as a possession, and I put the leprous plagueª in a house in the land of your possession, 35and he who owns the house comes and tells the priest, saying, 'It seems to me that *there is* some plague in the house,' 36then the priest shall command that they empty the house, before the priest goes *into it* to examine the plague, that all that *is* in the house may not be made unclean; and afterward the priest shall go in to examine the house. 37And he shall examine the plague; and indeed *if* the plague *is* on the walls of the house with ingrained streaks, greenish or reddish, which appear to be deep in the wall, 38then the priest shall go out of the house, to the door of the house, and shut up the house seven days. 39And the priest shall come again on the seventh day and look; and indeed *if* the plague has spread on the walls of the house, 40then the priest shall command that they take away the stones in which *is* the plague, and they shall cast them into an unclean place outside the city. 41And he shall cause the house to be scraped inside, all around, and the dust that they scrape off they shall pour out in an unclean place outside the city. 42Then they shall take other stones and put *them* in the place of *those* stones, and he shall take other mortar and plaster the house.

43"Now if the plague comes back and breaks out in the house, after he has taken away the stones, after he has scraped the house, and after it is plastered, 44then the priest shall come and look; and indeed *if* the plague has spread in the house, it *is* an active leprosy in the house. It *is* unclean. 45And he shall break down the house, its stones, its timber, and all the plaster of the house, and he shall carry *them* outside the city to an unclean place. 46Moreover he who goes into the house at all while it is shut up shall be unclean until evening. 47And he who lies down in the house shall wash his clothes, and he who eats in the house shall wash his clothes.

48"But if the priest comes in and examines *it,* and indeed the plague has not spread in the house after the house was plastered, then the priest shall pronounce the house clean, because the plague is healed. 49And he shall take, to cleanse the house, two birds, cedar wood, scarlet, and hyssop. 50Then he shall kill one of the birds in an earthen vessel over running water; 51and he shall take the cedar wood, the hyssop, the scarlet, and the living bird, and dip them in the blood of the slain bird and in the running water, and sprinkle the house seven times. 52And he shall cleanse the house with the blood of the bird and the running water and the living bird, with the cedar wood, the hyssop, and the scarlet. 53Then he shall let the living bird loose outside the city in the open field, and make atonement for the house, and it shall be clean.

54"This *is* the law for any leprous sore and scale, 55for the leprosy of a garment and of a house, 56for a swelling and a scab and a bright spot, 57to teach when *it is* unclean and when *it is* clean. This *is* the law of leprosy."

The Law Concerning Bodily Discharges

15 And the LORD spoke to Moses and Aaron, saying, 2"Speak to the children of Israel, and say to them: 'When any man has a discharge from his body, his discharge *is* unclean. 3And this shall be his uncleanness in regard to his discharge— whether his body runs with his discharge, or his body is stopped up by his discharge, it *is* his uncleanness. 4Every bed is unclean on which he who has the discharge lies, and everything on which he sits shall be unclean. 5And whoever touches his bed shall wash his clothes and bathe in water, and be unclean until evening. 6He who sits on anything on which he who has the discharge sat shall wash his clothes and bathe in water, and be unclean until evening. 7And he who touches the body of him who has the discharge shall wash his clothes and bathe in water, and be unclean until evening. 8If he who has the discharge spits on him who is clean, then he shall

wash his clothes and bathe in water, and be unclean until evening. 9Any saddle on which he who has the discharge rides shall be unclean. 10Whoever touches anything that was under him shall be unclean until evening. He who carries *any of* those things shall wash his clothes and bathe in water, and be unclean until evening. 11And whomever the one who has the discharge touches, and has not rinsed his hands in water, he shall wash his clothes and bathe in water, and be unclean until evening. 12The vessel of earth that he who has the discharge touches shall be broken, and every vessel of wood shall be rinsed in water.

13'And when he who has a discharge is cleansed of his discharge, then he shall count for himself seven days for his cleansing, wash his clothes, and bathe his body in running water; then he shall be clean. 14On the eighth day he shall take for himself two turtledoves or two young pigeons, and come before the LORD, to the door of the tabernacle of meeting, and give them to the priest. 15Then the priest shall offer them, the one *as* a sin offering and the other *as* a burnt offering. So the priest shall make atonement for him before the LORD because of his discharge.

16'If any man has an emission of semen, then he shall wash all his body in water, and be unclean until evening. 17And any garment and any leather on which there is semen, it shall be washed with water, and be unclean until evening. 18Also, when a woman lies with a man, and *there is* an emission of semen, they shall bathe in water, and be unclean until evening.

19'If a woman has a discharge, *and* the discharge from her body is blood, she shall be set apart seven days; and whoever touches her shall be unclean until evening. 20Everything that she lies on during her impurity shall be unclean; also everything that she sits on shall be unclean. 21Whoever touches her bed shall wash his clothes and bathe in water, and be unclean until evening. 22And whoever touches anything that she sat on shall wash his clothes and bathe in water, and be unclean until evening. 23If *anything* is on *her* bed or on anything on which she sits, when he touches it, he shall be unclean until evening. 24And if any man lies with her at all, so that her impurity is on him, he shall be unclean seven days; and every bed on which he lies shall be unclean. ²⁵'If a woman has a discharge of blood for many days, other than at the time of her *customary* impurity, or if it runs beyond her *usual time of* impurity, all the days of her unclean discharge shall be as the days of her *customary* impurity. She *shall be* unclean. ²⁶Every bed on which she lies all the days of her discharge shall be to her as the bed of her impurity; and whatever she sits on shall be unclean, as the uncleanness of her impurity. ²⁷Whoever touches those things shall be unclean; he shall wash his clothes and bathe in water, and be unclean until evening.

²⁸'But if she is cleansed of her discharge, then she shall count for herself seven days, and after that she shall be clean. ²⁹And on the eighth day she shall take for herself two turtledoves or two young pigeons, and bring them to the priest, to the door of the tabernacle of meeting. ³⁰Then the priest shall offer the one *as* a sin offering and the other *as* a burnt offering, and the priest shall make atonement for her before the LORD for the discharge of her uncleanness.

³¹'Thus you shall separate the children of Israel from their uncleanness, lest they die in their uncleanness when they defile My tabernacle that *is* among them. ³²This *is* the law for one who has a discharge, and *for him* who emits semen and is unclean thereby, ³³and for her who is indisposed because of her *customary* impurity, and for one who has a discharge, either man or woman, and for him who lies with her who is unclean.'"

The Day of Atonement

16 Now the LORD spoke to Moses after the death of the two sons of Aaron, when they offered *profane fire* before the LORD, and died; ²and the LORD said to Moses: "Tell Aaron your brother not to come at *just* any time into the Holy *Place* inside the veil, before the mercy seat which *is* on the ark, lest he die; for I will appear in the cloud above the mercy seat.

³"Thus Aaron shall come into the Holy *Place:* with *the blood of* a young bull as a sin offering, and *of* a ram as a burnt offering. ⁴He shall put the holy linen tunic and the linen trousers on his body; he shall be girded with a linen sash, and with the linen turban he shall be attired. These *are* holy garments. Therefore he shall wash his body in water, and put them on. ⁵And he shall take from the congregation of the children

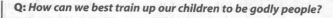

PARENTING MATTERS	**Q:** *How can we best train up our children to be godly people?*

We have found that effective training involves at least three parts.

First, parents need to clearly see the goal. They need to know what they are trying to achieve. Most parents have never written a mission statement for what they are trying to build into their children. It's no wonder so many parents feel like failures and don't really know if they've succeeded!

Second, effective training involves repetition. A Green Beret once told me, "As Green Berets, we train to learn what to do in every conceivable circumstance—over and over and over again. Then, in times of battle, we know what to do; it's just second nature to us." That is a picture of what parents should do. We train our children and instruct them in making the right choices in the circumstances they will face. And we do it over and over.

Finally, training involves accountability. One major mistake is giving our children too much freedom without appropriate oversight. This is especially true if a family has more than two children. We tend to over-control our firstborn child and release the younger children prematurely. Avoid that trap through accountability.

of Israel two kids of the goats as a sin offering, and one ram as a burnt offering.

6"Aaron shall offer the bull as a sin offering, which *is* for himself, and make atonement for himself and for his house. 7He shall take the two goats and present them before the LORD *at* the door of the tabernacle of meeting. 8Then Aaron shall cast lots for the two goats: one lot for the LORD and the other lot for the scapegoat. 9And Aaron shall bring the goat on which the LORD's lot fell, and offer it *as* a sin offering. 10But the goat on which the lot fell to be the scapegoat shall be presented alive before the LORD, to make atonement upon it, *and* to let it go as the scapegoat into the wilderness.

11"And Aaron shall bring the bull of the sin offering, which is for himself, and make atonement for himself and for his house, and shall kill the bull as the sin offering which *is* for himself. 12Then he shall take a censer full of burning coals of fire from the altar before the LORD, with his hands full of sweet incense beaten fine, and bring *it* inside the veil. 13And he shall put the incense on the fire before the LORD, that the cloud of incense may cover the mercy seat that *is* on the Testimony, lest he die. 14He shall take some of the blood of the bull and sprinkle *it* with his finger on the mercy seat on the east *side;* and before the mercy seat he shall sprinkle some of the blood with his finger seven times.

15"Then he shall kill the goat of the sin offering, which *is* for the people, bring its blood inside the veil, do with that blood as he did with the blood of the bull, and sprinkle it on the mercy seat and before the mercy seat. 16So he shall make atonement for the Holy *Place,* because of the uncleanness of the children of Israel, and because of their transgressions, for all their sins; and so he shall do for the tabernacle of meeting which remains among them in the midst of their uncleanness. 17There shall be no man in the tabernacle of meeting when he goes in to make atonement in the Holy *Place,* until he comes out, that he may make atonement for himself, for his household, and for all the assembly of Israel. 18And he shall go out to the altar that *is* before the LORD, and make atonement for it, and shall take some of the blood of the

bull and some of the blood of the goat, and put it on the horns of the altar all around. 19Then he shall sprinkle some of the blood on it with his finger seven times, cleanse it, and consecrate it from the uncleanness of the children of Israel.

20"And when he has made an end of atoning for the Holy *Place,* the tabernacle of meeting, and the altar, he shall bring the live goat. 21Aaron shall lay both his hands on the head of the live goat, confess over it all the iniquities of the children of Israel, and all their transgressions, concerning all their sins, putting them on the head of the goat, and shall send *it* away into the wilderness by the hand of a suitable man. 22The goat shall bear on itself all their iniquities to an uninhabited land; and he shall release the goat in the wilderness.

23"Then Aaron shall come into the tabernacle of meeting, shall take off the linen garments which he put on when he went into the Holy *Place,* and shall leave them there. 24And he shall wash his body with water in a holy place, put on his garments, come out and offer his burnt offering and the burnt offering of the people, and make atonement for himself and for the people. 25The fat of the sin offering he shall burn on the altar. 26And he who released the goat as the scapegoat shall wash his clothes and bathe his body in water, and afterward he may come into the camp. 27The bull *for* the sin offering and the goat *for* the sin offering, whose blood was brought in to make atonement in the Holy *Place,* shall be carried outside the camp. And they shall burn in the fire their skins, their flesh, and their offal. 28Then he who burns them shall wash his clothes and bathe his body in water, and afterward he may come into the camp.

29"*This* shall be a statute forever for you: In the seventh month, on the tenth *day* of the month, you shall afflict your souls, and do no work at all, *whether* a native of your own country or a stranger who dwells among you. 30For on that day *the priest* shall make atonement for you, to cleanse you, *that* you may be clean from all your sins before the LORD. 31It *is* a sabbath of solemn rest for you, and you shall afflict your souls. *It is* a statute forever. 32And the priest, who is anointed and consecrated to minister as priest in his father's place, shall make atonement, and put on the linen clothes, the holy garments; ³³then he shall make atonement for the Holy Sanctuary,ᵃ and he shall make atonement for the tabernacle of meeting and for the altar, and he shall make atonement for the priests and for all the people of the assembly. ³⁴This shall be an everlasting statute for you, to make atonement for the children of Israel, for all their sins, once a year." And he did as the LORD commanded Moses.

The Sanctity of Blood

17 And the LORD spoke to Moses, saying, ²"Speak to Aaron, to his sons, and to all the children of Israel, and say to them, 'This is the thing which the LORD has commanded, saying: ³"Whatever man of the house of Israel who kills an ox or lamb or goat in the camp, or who kills it outside the camp, ⁴and does not bring it to the door of the tabernacle of meeting to offer an offering to the LORD before the tabernacle of the LORD, the guilt of bloodshed shall be imputed to that man. He has shed blood; and that man shall be cut off from among his people, ⁵to the end that the children of Israel may bring their sacrifices which they offer in the open field, that they may bring them to the LORD at the door of the tabernacle of meeting, to the priest, and offer them as peace offerings to the LORD. ⁶And the priest shall sprinkle the blood on the altar of the LORD at the door of the tabernacle of meeting, and burn the fat for a sweet aroma to the LORD. ⁷They shall no more offer their sacrifices to demons, after whom they have played the harlot. This shall be a statute forever for them throughout their generations."'

⁸"Also you shall say to them: 'Whatever man of the house of Israel, or of the strangers who dwell among you, who offers a burnt offering or sacrifice, ⁹and does not bring it to the door of the tabernacle of meeting, to offer it to the LORD, that man shall be cut off from among his people.

¹⁰"And whatever man of the house of Israel, or of the strangers who dwell among you, who eats any blood, I will set My face against that person who eats blood, and will cut him off from among his people. ¹¹For the life of the flesh is in the blood, and I have given it to you upon the altar to make atonement for your souls; for it is the blood that makes atonement for the soul.' ¹²Therefore I said to the children of Israel, 'No one among you shall eat blood, nor shall any stranger who dwells among you eat blood.'

INTIMATE MOMENTS
Remember Your Vows

In your best handwriting, write out your wedding vows on a small card and sign your name to them. If you don't remember your exact words, get out your wedding video and take some notes. But do this on the sly—don't let her know you're doing it. Surprise is a big part of this gift! Once you have an accurate record of your vows, write out the card and either put it in a place she will see it every day, or have it framed and present it to her on some special occasion, such as a birthday or anniversary. Let her know that you think about those vows frequently and that, with God's help, you intend to keep them.

¹³"Whatever man of the children of Israel, or of the strangers who dwell among you, who hunts and catches any animal or bird that may be eaten, he shall pour out its blood and cover it with dust; ¹⁴for it is the life of all flesh. Its blood sustains its life. Therefore I said to the children of Israel, 'You shall not eat the blood of any flesh, for the life of all flesh is its blood. Whoever eats it shall be cut off.'

¹⁵"And every person who eats what died *naturally* or what was torn *by beasts,* whether he is a native of your own country or a stranger, he shall both wash his clothes and bathe in water, and be unclean until evening. Then he shall be clean. ¹⁶But if he does not wash *them* or bathe his body, then he shall bear his guilt."

16:33 ᵃThat is, the Most Holy Place

Laws of Sexual Morality

18 Then the LORD spoke to Moses, saying, ²"Speak to the children of Israel, and say to them: 'I am the LORD your God. ³According to the doings of the land of Egypt, where you dwelt, you shall not do; and according to the doings of the land of Canaan, where I am bringing you, you shall not do; nor shall you walk in their ordinances. ⁴You shall observe My judgments and keep My ordinances, to walk in them: I *am* the LORD your God. ⁵You shall therefore keep My statutes and My judgments, which if a man does, he shall live by them: I *am* the LORD.

⁶'None of you shall approach anyone who is near of kin to him, to uncover his nakedness: I *am* the LORD. ⁷The nakedness of your father or the nakedness of your mother you shall not uncover. She *is* your mother; you shall not uncover her nakedness. ⁸The nakedness of your father's wife you shall not uncover; it *is* your father's nakedness. ⁹The nakedness of your sister, the daughter of your father, or the daughter of your mother, *whether* born at home or elsewhere, their nakedness you shall not uncover. ¹⁰The nakedness of your son's daughter or your daughter's daughter, their nakedness you shall not uncover; for theirs *is* your own nakedness. ¹¹The nakedness of your father's wife's daughter, begotten by your father—she *is* your sister—you shall not uncover her nakedness. ¹²You shall not uncover the nakedness of your father's sister; she *is* near of kin to your father. ¹³You shall not uncover the nakedness of your mother's sister, for she *is* near of kin to your mother. ¹⁴You shall not uncover the nakedness of your father's brother. You shall not approach his wife; she *is* your aunt. ¹⁵You shall not uncover the nakedness of your daughter-in-law—she *is* your son's wife—you shall not uncover her nakedness. ¹⁶You shall not uncover the nakedness of your brother's wife; it *is* your brother's nakedness. ¹⁷You shall not uncover the nakedness of a woman and her daughter, nor shall you take her son's daughter or her daughter's daughter, to uncover her nakedness. They *are* near of kin to her. It *is* wickedness. ¹⁸Nor shall you take a woman as a rival to her sister, to uncover her nakedness while the other is alive.

¹⁹Also you shall not approach a woman to uncover her nakedness as long as she is in her *customary* impurity. ²⁰Moreover you shall not lie carnally with your neighbor's wife, to defile yourself with her. ²¹And you shall not let any of your descendants pass through *the fire* to Molech, nor shall you profane the name of your God: I *am* the LORD. ²²You shall not lie with a male as with a woman. It *is* an abomination. ²³Nor shall you mate with any animal, to defile yourself with it. Nor shall any woman stand before an animal to mate with it. It *is* perversion.

²⁴'Do not defile yourselves with any of these things; for by all these the nations are defiled, which I am casting out before you. ²⁵For the land is defiled; therefore I visit the punishment of its iniquity upon it, and the land vomits out its inhabitants. ²⁶You shall therefore keep My statutes and My judgments, and shall not commit *any* of these abominations, *either* any of your own nation or any stranger who dwells among you ²⁷(for all these abominations the men of the land have done, who *were* before you, and thus the land is defiled), ²⁸lest the land vomit you out also when you defile it, as it vomited out the nations that *were* before you. ²⁹For whoever commits any of these abominations, the persons who commit *them* shall be cut off from among their people.

³⁰'Therefore you shall keep My ordinance, so that *you* do not commit *any* of these abominable customs which were committed before you, and that you do not defile yourselves by them: I *am* the LORD your God.'"

Moral and Ceremonial Laws

19 And the LORD spoke to Moses, saying, ²"Speak to all the congregation of the children of Israel, and say to them: 'You shall be holy, for I the LORD your God *am* holy.

³'Every one of you shall revere his mother and his father, and keep My Sabbaths: I *am* the LORD your God.

⁴'Do not turn to idols, nor make for yourselves molded gods: I *am* the LORD your God.

⁵'And if you offer a sacrifice of a peace offering to the LORD, you shall offer it of your own free will. ⁶It shall be eaten the same day you offer *it*, and on the next day. And if any remains until the third day, it shall be burned in the fire. ⁷And if it is eaten at all on the third day, it *is* an abomination. It shall not be accepted. ⁸Therefore *everyone* who eats it shall bear his iniquity, because he has profaned the hallowed *offering* of the LORD; and that person shall be cut off from his people.

⁹'When you reap the harvest of your land, you shall not wholly reap the corners of your field, nor shall you gather the gleanings of your harvest. ¹⁰And you shall not glean your vineyard, nor shall you gather *every* grape of your vineyard; you shall leave them for the poor and the stranger: I *am* the LORD your God.

¹¹'You shall not steal, nor deal falsely, nor lie to one another. ¹²And you shall not swear by My name falsely, nor shall you profane the name of your God: I *am* the LORD.

¹³'You shall not cheat your neighbor, nor rob *him*. The wages of him who is hired shall not remain with you all night until morning. ¹⁴You shall not curse the deaf, nor put a stumbling block before the blind, but shall fear your God: I *am* the LORD.

¹⁵'You shall do no injustice in judgment. You shall not be partial to the poor, nor honor the person of the mighty. In righteousness you shall judge your neighbor. ¹⁶You shall not go about *as* a talebearer among your people; nor shall you take a stand against the life of your neighbor: I *am* the LORD.

¹⁷'You shall not hate your brother in your heart. You shall surely rebuke your neighbor, and not bear sin because of him. ¹⁸You shall not take vengeance, nor bear any grudge against the children of your people, but you shall love your neighbor as yourself: I *am* the LORD.

¹⁹'You shall keep My statutes. You shall not let your livestock breed with another kind. You shall not sow your field with mixed seed. Nor shall a garment of mixed linen and wool come upon you.

²⁰'Whoever lies carnally with a woman who *is* betrothed to a man as a concubine, and who has not at all been redeemed nor

BIBLICAL INSIGHTS · 19:3
Uniquely Designed to Be Mom

GOD HAS UNIQUELY designed women to be mothers, and the greatest way a mother can love her children is to love their father. The Bible teaches that God has created a woman with an innate and special ability to nurture and care for her family.

Therefore, mothers are the primary people whom God designed to love, nurture, and mentor children. Without question, this is one of the reasons why God so often insists that children are to honor their mothers. So Leviticus 19:3 declares, "Every one of you shall revere his mother."

We believe these crucial responsibilities of nurturing and caring for children should be met before a mother contemplates *any* other duties. This is more difficult today than it was a few decades ago, of course, because our culture has seriously devalued the role of a mother by placing greater significance on activities outside the home than on those inside the home.

Nevertheless, we ought to elevate motherhood to its rightfully high place by pointing out its exalted value in God's economy of the family. In our culture we ought to encourage mothers to model love for God and His Word, to love their husband, and to love their children. It's what they were designed for.

given her freedom, for this there shall be scourging; *but* they shall not be put to death, because she was not free. ²¹And he shall bring his trespass offering to the LORD, to the door of the tabernacle of meeting, a ram as a trespass offering. ²²The priest shall make atonement for him with the ram of the trespass offering before the LORD for his sin which he has committed. And the sin which he has committed shall be forgiven him.

²³'When you come into the land, and have planted all kinds of trees for food, then you shall count their fruit as uncircumcised.

Three Are Present

THE BIBLE HAS A LOT to say about the benefits of fearing God. Leviticus 19:14, for example, indicates that a healthy fear of God will motivate us to care for the needs of the disadvantaged with grace and kindness. Proverbs 22:4 tells us that fearing God leads us to life, while Proverbs 10:27 tells us that it prolongs life. And Psalm 145:19 says the Lord will fulfill the desires of those who fear Him.

In the New Testament, we see that the fear of God is the glue that holds our relationships—including our marriages—together. Ephesians 5:21 tells us that we should be "submitting to one another *in the fear of God"* (italics added).

I doubt there is any dispute or problem in marriage that can't be solved if both spouses properly fear the Lord and mutually honor and value each other out of that reverential respect for who God is. A marriage should be a relationship in which forgiveness and acceptance are freely expressed because we live our lives in His presence.

In a Christian marriage, three are present: the husband, the wife, and Jesus Christ. If the husband and wife share a mutual reverence and a holy desire to obey and serve Christ, God will use that healthy fear to draw the couple closer to each other and closer to Himself.

Three years it shall be as uncircumcised to you. *It* shall not be eaten. ²⁴But in the fourth year all its fruit shall be holy, a praise to the LORD. ²⁵And in the fifth year you may eat its fruit, that it may yield to you its increase: I *am* the LORD your God.

²⁶'You shall not eat *anything* with the blood, nor shall you practice divination or soothsaying. ²⁷You shall not shave around the sides of your head, nor shall you disfigure the edges of your beard. ²⁸You shall not make any cuttings in your flesh for the dead, nor tattoo any marks on you: I *am* the LORD.

²⁹'Do not prostitute your daughter, to cause her to be a harlot, lest the land fall into harlotry, and the land become full of wickedness.

³⁰'You shall keep My Sabbaths and reverence My sanctuary: I *am* the LORD.

³¹'Give no regard to mediums and familiar spirits; do not seek after them, to be defiled by them: I *am* the LORD your God.

³²'You shall rise before the gray headed and honor the presence of an old man, and fear your God: I *am* the LORD.

³³'And if a stranger dwells with you in your land, you shall not mistreat him. ³⁴The stranger who dwells among you shall be to you as one born among you, and you shall love him as yourself; for you were strangers in the land of Egypt: I *am* the LORD your God.

³⁵'You shall do no injustice in judgment, in measurement of length, weight, or volume. ³⁶You shall have honest scales, honest weights, an honest ephah, and an honest hin: I *am* the LORD your God, who brought you out of the land of Egypt.

³⁷'Therefore you shall observe all My statutes and all My judgments, and perform them: I *am* the LORD.' "

Penalties for Breaking the Law

20 Then the LORD spoke to Moses, saying, ²"Again, you shall say to the children of Israel: 'Whoever of the children of Israel, or of the strangers who dwell in Israel, who gives *any* of his descendants to Molech, he shall surely be put to death. The people of the land shall stone him with stones. ³I will set My face against that man, and will cut him off from his people, because he has given *some* of his descendants to Molech, to defile My sanctuary and profane My holy name. ⁴And if the people of the land should in any way hide their eyes from the man, when he gives *some* of his descendants to Molech, and they do not kill him, ⁵then I will set My face against that man and against his family; and I will cut him off from his people, and all who prostitute themselves with him to commit harlotry with Molech.

⁶'And the person who turns to mediums

and familiar spirits, to prostitute himself with them, I will set My face against that person and cut him off from his people. ⁷Consecrate yourselves therefore, and be holy, for I *am* the LORD your God. ⁸And you shall keep My statutes, and perform them: I *am* the LORD who sanctifies you.

⁹'For everyone who curses his father or his mother shall surely be put to death. He has cursed his father or his mother. His blood *shall be* upon him.

¹⁰'The man who commits adultery with *another* man's wife, *he* who commits adultery with his neighbor's wife, the adulterer and the adulteress, shall surely be put to death. ¹¹The man who lies with his father's wife has uncovered his father's nakedness; both of them shall surely be put to death. Their blood *shall be* upon them. ¹²If a man lies with his daughter-in-law, both of them shall surely be put to death. They have committed perversion. Their blood *shall be* upon them. ¹³If a man lies with a male as he lies with a woman, both of them have committed an abomination. They shall surely be put to death. Their blood *shall be* upon them. ¹⁴If a man marries a woman and her mother, it *is* wickedness. They shall be burned with fire, both he and they, that there may be no wickedness among you. ¹⁵If a man mates with an animal, he shall surely be put to death, and you shall kill the animal. ¹⁶If a woman approaches any animal and mates with it, you shall kill the woman and the animal. They shall surely be put to death. Their blood *is* upon them.

¹⁷'If a man takes his sister, his father's daughter or his mother's daughter, and sees her nakedness and she sees his nakedness, it *is* a wicked thing. And they shall be cut off in the sight of their people. He has uncovered his sister's nakedness. He shall bear his guilt. ¹⁸If a man lies with a woman during her sickness and uncovers her nakedness, he has exposed her flow, and she has uncovered the flow of her blood. Both of them shall be cut off from their people.

¹⁹'You shall not uncover the nakedness of your mother's sister nor of your father's sister, for that would uncover his near of kin. They shall bear their guilt. ²⁰If a man lies with his uncle's wife, he has uncovered his uncle's nakedness. They shall bear

BIBLICAL INSIGHTS • 20:10

The Glory of Repentance

DURING THE PAST TWO DECADES, I've counseled many people caught in adultery, many of whom have lied about it. One woman's story stands out as an example of the power of repentance.

She had been married nearly forty years when she told me of secret adulterous relationships that had occurred nearly a decade earlier. The more we talked about her infidelity, the more I became convinced that if her repentance and healing were to be complete, she must go to her husband and tell him what she had done. She had sinned against God and her mate (see Lev. 20:10). Their marriage would never be what God had intended if she kept this breach of trust a secret.

Long before I spoke with her, God had been working in her heart, burdening her with her deceit and unfaithfulness. Within several months her heart softened, and she agreed to tell her husband.

Broken and ashamed, she confessed her adultery to her husband. She came clean. She uncovered the decay that for years had polluted her heart and relationship with God and her husband. As a result, that couple wound up with a renewed commitment to one another and to the Lord.

Being honest and transparent with one another is an essential ingredient in a healthy marriage. We should be quick to confess when we have wronged our spouse and faithful to demonstrate the reality of our repentance. And when our spouse comes to us to confess, we should extend the kind of grace and forgiveness God has shown us in Christ (Eph. 4:32).

their sin; they shall die childless. ²¹If a man takes his brother's wife, it *is* an unclean thing. He has uncovered his brother's nakedness. They shall be childless.

²²'You shall therefore keep all My statutes and all My judgments, and perform them, that the land where I am bringing

you to dwell may not vomit you out. ²³And you shall not walk in the statutes of the nation which I am casting out before you; for they commit all these things, and therefore I abhor them. ²⁴But I have said to you, "You shall inherit their land, and I will give it to you to possess, a land flowing with milk and honey." I *am* the LORD your God, who has separated you from the peoples. ²⁵You shall therefore distinguish between clean animals and unclean, between unclean birds and clean, and you shall not make yourselves abominable by beast or by bird, or by any kind of living thing that creeps on the ground, which I have separated from you as unclean. ²⁶And you shall be holy to Me, for I the LORD *am* holy, and have separated you from the peoples, that you should be Mine.

²⁷'A man or a woman who is a medium, or who has familiar spirits, shall surely be put to death; they shall stone them with stones. Their blood *shall be* upon them.'"

Regulations for Conduct of Priests

21 And the LORD said to Moses, "Speak to the priests, the sons of Aaron, and say to them: 'None shall defile himself for the dead among his people, ²except for his relatives who are nearest to him: his mother, his father, his son, his daughter, and his brother; ³also his virgin sister who is near to him, who has had no husband, for her he may defile himself. ⁴*Otherwise* he shall not defile himself, *being* a chief man among his people, to profane himself.

⁵'They shall not make any bald *place* on their heads, nor shall they shave the edges of their beards nor make any cuttings in their flesh. ⁶They shall be holy to their God and not profane the name of their God, for they offer the offerings of the LORD made by fire, *and* the bread of their God; therefore they shall be holy. ⁷They shall not take a wife *who is* a harlot or a defiled woman, nor shall they take a woman divorced from her husband; for *the priest*ᵃ is holy to his God. ⁸Therefore you shall consecrate him, for he offers the bread of your God. He shall be holy to you, for I the LORD, who sanctify you, *am* holy. ⁹The daughter of any priest, if she profanes herself by playing

the harlot, she profanes her father. She shall be burned with fire.

¹⁰'*He who is* the high priest among his brethren, on whose head the anointing oil was poured and who is consecrated to wear the garments, shall not uncover his head nor tear his clothes; ¹¹nor shall he go near any dead body, nor defile himself for his father or his mother; ¹²nor shall he go out of the sanctuary, nor profane the sanctuary of his God; for the consecration of the anointing oil of his God *is* upon him: I *am* the LORD. ¹³And he shall take a wife in her virginity. ¹⁴A widow or a divorced woman or a defiled woman *or* a harlot— these he shall not marry; but he shall take a virgin of his own people as wife. ¹⁵Nor shall he profane his posterity among his people, for I the LORD sanctify him.'"

¹⁶And the LORD spoke to Moses, saying, ¹⁷"Speak to Aaron, saying: 'No man of your descendants in *succeeding* generations, who has *any* defect, may approach to offer the bread of his God. ¹⁸For any man who has a defect shall not approach: a man blind or lame, who has a marred *face* or any *limb* too long, ¹⁹a man who has a broken foot or broken hand, ²⁰or is a hunchback or a dwarf, or *a man* who has a defect in his eye, or eczema or scab, or is a eunuch. ²¹No man of the descendants of Aaron the priest, who has a defect, shall come near to offer the offerings made by fire to the LORD. He has a defect; he shall not come near to offer the bread of his God. ²²He may eat the bread of his God, *both* the most holy and the holy; ²³only he shall not go near the veil or approach the altar, because he has a defect, lest he profane My sanctuaries; for I the LORD sanctify them.'"

²⁴And Moses told *it* to Aaron and his sons, and to all the children of Israel.

22 Then the LORD spoke to Moses, saying, ²"Speak to Aaron and his sons, that they separate themselves from the holy things of the children of Israel, and that they do not profane My holy name *by* what they dedicate to Me: I *am* the LORD. ³Say to them: 'Whoever of all your descendants throughout your generations, who goes

---

21:7 ᵃLiterally *he*

near the holy things which the children of Israel dedicate to the LORD, while he has uncleanness upon him, that person shall be cut off from My presence: I *am* the LORD.

⁴'Whatever man of the descendants of Aaron, who *is* a leper or has a discharge, shall not eat the holy offerings until he is clean. And whoever touches anything made unclean *by* a corpse, or a man who has had an emission of semen, ⁵or whoever touches any creeping thing by which he would be made unclean, or any person by whom he would become unclean, whatever his uncleanness may be— ⁶the person who has touched any such thing shall be unclean until evening, and shall not eat the holy *offerings* unless he washes his body with water. ⁷And when the sun goes down he shall be clean; and afterward he may eat the holy *offerings,* because it *is* his food. ⁸Whatever dies *naturally* or is torn *by beasts* he shall not eat, to defile himself with it: I *am* the LORD.

⁹'They shall therefore keep My ordinance, lest they bear sin for it and die thereby, if they profane it: I the LORD sanctify them.

¹⁰'No outsider shall eat the holy *offering;* one who dwells with the priest, or a hired servant, shall not eat the holy thing. ¹¹But if the priest buys a person with his money, he may eat it; and one who is born in his house may eat his food. ¹²If the priest's daughter is married to an outsider, she may not eat of the holy offerings. ¹³But if the priest's daughter is a widow or divorced, and has no child, and has returned to her father's house as in her youth, she may eat her father's food; but no outsider shall eat it.

¹⁴'And if a man eats the holy *offering* unintentionally, then he shall restore a holy *offering* to the priest, and add one-fifth to it. ¹⁵They shall not profane the holy *offerings* of the children of Israel, which they offer to the LORD, ¹⁶or allow them to bear the guilt of trespass when they eat their holy *offerings;* for I the LORD sanctify them.'"

Offerings Accepted and Not Accepted

¹⁷And the LORD spoke to Moses, saying, ¹⁸"Speak to Aaron and his sons, and to all the children of Israel, and say to them: 'Whatever man of the house of Israel, or of the strangers in Israel, who offers his sacrifice for any of his vows or for any of his freewill offerings, which they offer to the LORD as a burnt offering— ¹⁹*you shall offer* of your own free will a male without blemish from the cattle, from the sheep, or from the goats. ²⁰Whatever has a defect, you shall not offer, for it shall not be acceptable on your behalf. ²¹And whoever offers a sacrifice of a peace offering to the LORD, to fulfill *his* vow, or a freewill offering from the cattle or the sheep, it must be perfect to be accepted; there shall be no defect in it. ²²Those *that are* blind or broken or maimed, or have an ulcer or eczema or scabs, you shall not offer to the LORD, nor make an

ROMANCE FAQ

Q: *How can I increase romance and intimacy in my marriage?*

A TV talk show host was interviewing one of Hollywood's biggest male stars, a man known for his prowess with the opposite sex. At one point, the host asked him, "What makes a great lover?"

"Two things," the actor replied. "First of all, it is a man who can satisfy one woman over a lifetime. And second, it is a man who can be satisfied with one woman for a lifetime."

What a great answer! The foundation of a strong, romantic marriage is a solid commitment of unconditional love. Romance is an outward expression of that love. It is the fire in the fireplace—the warm response of one spouse to another that says, "We may have struggles, but I love you, and everything is okay. Now, let's have some fun!"

The easiest way to increase the amount of true romance in your marriage is to build a lasting marriage of oneness and intimacy. And how do you accomplish that? You and your mate must commit to meet each other's physical and emotional needs. Do that, and you'll start to make romance an everyday part of your marriage.

offering by fire of them on the altar to the LORD. ²³Either a bull or a lamb that has any limb too long or too short you may offer *as* a freewill offering, but for a vow it shall not be accepted.

²⁴"You shall not offer to the LORD what is bruised or crushed, or torn or cut; nor shall you make *any offering of them* in your land. ²⁵Nor from a foreigner's hand shall you offer any of these as the bread of your God, because their corruption *is* in them, *and* defects *are* in them. They shall not be accepted on your behalf.'"

²⁶And the LORD spoke to Moses, saying: ²⁷"When a bull or a sheep or a goat is born, it shall be seven days with its mother; and from the eighth day and thereafter it shall be accepted as an offering made by fire to the LORD. ²⁸*Whether it is* a cow or ewe, do not kill both her and her young on the same day. ²⁹And when you offer a sacrifice of thanksgiving to the LORD, offer *it* of your own free will. ³⁰On the same day it shall be eaten; you shall leave none of it until morning: I *am* the LORD.

³¹"Therefore you shall keep My commandments, and perform them: I *am* the LORD. ³²You shall not profane My holy name, but I will be hallowed among the children of Israel. I *am* the LORD who sanctifies you, ³³who brought you out of the land of Egypt, to be your God: I *am* the LORD."

Feasts of the LORD

23 And the LORD spoke to Moses, saying, ²"Speak to the children of Israel, and say to them: 'The feasts of the LORD, which you shall proclaim *to be* holy convocations, these *are* My feasts.

The Sabbath

³'Six days shall work be done, but the seventh day *is* a Sabbath of solemn rest, a holy convocation. You shall do no work *on it;* it *is* the Sabbath of the LORD in all your dwellings.

The Passover and Unleavened Bread

⁴'These *are* the feasts of the LORD, holy convocations which you shall proclaim at their appointed times. ⁵On the fourteenth *day* of the first month at twilight *is* the LORD's Passover. ⁶And on the fifteenth day

of the same month *is* the Feast of Unleavened Bread to the LORD; seven days you must eat unleavened bread. ⁷On the first day you shall have a holy convocation; you shall do no customary work on it. ⁸But you shall offer an offering made by fire to the LORD for seven days. The seventh day *shall be* a holy convocation; you shall do no customary work *on it.*'"

The Feast of Firstfruits

⁹And the LORD spoke to Moses, saying, ¹⁰"Speak to the children of Israel, and say to them: 'When you come into the land which I give to you, and reap its harvest, then you shall bring a sheaf of the firstfruits of your harvest to the priest. ¹¹He shall wave the sheaf before the LORD, to be accepted on your behalf; on the day after the Sabbath the priest shall wave it. ¹²And you shall offer on that day, when you wave the sheaf, a male lamb of the first year, without blemish, as a burnt offering to the LORD. ¹³Its grain offering *shall be* two-tenths *of an ephah* of fine flour mixed with oil, an offering made by fire to the LORD, for a sweet aroma; and its drink offering *shall be* of wine, one-fourth of a hin. ¹⁴You shall eat neither bread nor parched grain nor fresh grain until the same day that you have brought an offering to your God; *it shall be* a statute forever throughout your generations in all your dwellings.

The Feast of Weeks

¹⁵'And you shall count for yourselves from the day after the Sabbath, from the day that you brought the sheaf of the wave offering: seven Sabbaths shall be completed. ¹⁶Count fifty days to the day after the seventh Sabbath; then you shall offer a new grain offering to the LORD. ¹⁷You shall bring from your dwellings two wave *loaves* of two-tenths *of an ephah.* They shall be of fine flour; they shall be baked with leaven. *They are* the firstfruits to the LORD. ¹⁸And you shall offer with the bread seven lambs of the first year, without blemish, one young bull, and two rams. They shall be *as* a burnt offering to the LORD, with their grain offering and their drink offerings, an offering made by fire for a sweet aroma to the LORD. ¹⁹Then you shall sacrifice one kid

of the goats as a sin offering, and two male lambs of the first year as a sacrifice of a peace offering. ²⁰The priest shall wave them with the bread of the firstfruits *as* a wave offering before the LORD, with the two lambs. They shall be holy to the LORD for the priest. ²¹And you shall proclaim on the same day *that* it is a holy convocation to you. You shall do no customary work *on it. It shall be* a statute forever in all your dwellings throughout your generations.

²²'When you reap the harvest of your land, you shall not wholly reap the corners of your field when you reap, nor shall you gather any gleaning from your harvest. You shall leave them for the poor and for the stranger: I *am* the LORD your God.' "

The Feast of Trumpets

²³Then the LORD spoke to Moses, saying, ²⁴"Speak to the children of Israel, saying: 'In the seventh month, on the first *day* of the month, you shall have a sabbath-*rest,* a memorial of blowing of trumpets, a holy convocation. ²⁵You shall do no customary work *on it;* and you shall offer an offering made by fire to the LORD.' "

The Day of Atonement

²⁶And the LORD spoke to Moses, saying: ²⁷"Also the tenth *day* of this seventh month *shall be* the Day of Atonement. It shall be a holy convocation for you; you shall afflict your souls, and offer an offering made by fire to the LORD. ²⁸And you shall do no work on that same day, for it *is* the Day of Atonement, to make atonement for you before the LORD your God. ²⁹For any person who is not afflicted *in soul* on that same day shall be cut off from his people. ³⁰And any person who does any work on that same day, that person I will destroy from among his people. ³¹You shall do no manner of work; *it shall be* a statute forever throughout your generations in all your dwellings. ³²It *shall be* to you a sabbath of *solemn* rest, and you shall afflict your souls; on the ninth *day* of the month at evening, from evening to evening, you shall celebrate your sabbath."

The Feast of Tabernacles

³³Then the LORD spoke to Moses, saying, ³⁴"Speak to the children of Israel, saying:

'The fifteenth day of this seventh month *shall be* the Feast of Tabernacles *for* seven days to the LORD. ³⁵On the first day *there shall be* a holy convocation. You shall do no customary work *on it.* ³⁶*For* seven days you shall offer an offering made by fire to the LORD. On the eighth day you shall have a holy convocation, and you shall offer an offering made by fire to the LORD. It *is* a sacred assembly, *and* you shall do no customary work *on it.*

³⁷'These *are* the feasts of the LORD which you shall proclaim *to be* holy convocations, to offer an offering made by fire to the LORD, a burnt offering and a grain offering, a sacrifice and drink offerings, everything on its day— ³⁸besides the Sabbaths of the LORD, besides your gifts, besides all your vows, and besides all your freewill offerings which you give to the LORD.

³⁹'Also on the fifteenth day of the seventh month, when you have gathered in the fruit of the land, you shall keep the feast of the LORD *for* seven days; on the first day *there shall be* a sabbath-*rest,* and on the eighth day a sabbath-*rest.* ⁴⁰And you shall take for yourselves on the first day the fruit of beautiful trees, branches of palm trees, the boughs of leafy trees, and willows of the brook; and you shall rejoice before the LORD your God for seven days. ⁴¹You shall keep it as a feast to the LORD for seven days in the year. *It shall be* a statute forever in your generations. You shall celebrate it in the seventh month. ⁴²You shall dwell in booths for seven days. All who are native Israelites shall dwell in booths, ⁴³that your generations may know that I made the children of Israel dwell in booths when I brought them out of the land of Egypt: I *am* the LORD your God.' "

⁴⁴So Moses declared to the children of Israel the feasts of the LORD.

Care of the Tabernacle Lamps

24 Then the LORD spoke to Moses, saying: ²"Command the children of Israel that they bring to you pure oil of pressed olives for the light, to make the lamps burn continually. ³Outside the veil of the Testimony, in the tabernacle of meeting, Aaron shall be in charge of it from evening until morning before the LORD

You Get What You Plant

ONE OF THE LAWS OF NATURE is that you never harvest one thing when you've planted something else. You don't get watermelons by planting cucumbers. Whatever seed you plant "grows of its own accord" (Lev. 25:5).

Marriage is a lot like that—we never get out of marriage what we do not put into it. One man confessed, "At work I concentrate on winning, and as a result, I am a winner. At home, however, I concentrate on just getting by."

It's no wonder he is losing. The seed he planted, neglect, grows of its own accord.

Americans normally think of themselves as winners. We are used to winning, but too many times, in the wrong places. As a result, we end up losing in the important places, such as at home. The late Vance Havner once said, "Americans know the price of everything, but the value of nothing."

If a business goes bankrupt, the president or the chairman of the board is to blame. Similarly, if our homes fail, you and I are to blame. We must master the ageless art of leadership and apply it to our families. If we ever hope to win at home, then we must consider what kind of harvest we want in the end. If we plant seeds of commitment to Christ and to one another, along with seeds of forgiveness and respect, we might well expect that God will grant us a great harvest.

---

continually; *it shall be* a statute forever in your generations. ⁴He shall be in charge of the lamps on the pure *gold* lampstand before the LORD continually.

The Bread of the Tabernacle

⁵"And you shall take fine flour and bake twelve cakes with it. Two-tenths *of an ephah* shall be in each cake. ⁶You shall set them in two rows, six in a row, on the pure *gold* table before the LORD. ⁷And you shall put pure frankincense on *each* row, that it may be on the bread for a memorial, an offering made by fire to the LORD. ⁸Every Sabbath he shall set it in order before the LORD continually, *being taken* from the children of Israel by an everlasting covenant. ⁹And it shall be for Aaron and his sons, and they shall eat it in a holy place; for it *is* most holy to him from the offerings of the LORD made by fire, by a perpetual statute."

The Penalty for Blasphemy

¹⁰Now the son of an Israelite woman, whose father *was* an Egyptian, went out among the children of Israel; and this Israelite *woman's* son and a man of Israel fought each other in the camp. ¹¹And the Israelite woman's son blasphemed the name *of the* LORD and cursed; and so they brought him to Moses. (His mother's name *was* Shelomith the daughter of Dibri, of the tribe of Dan.) ¹²Then they put him in custody, that the mind of the LORD might be shown to them.

¹³And the LORD spoke to Moses, saying, ¹⁴"Take outside the camp him who has cursed; then let all who heard *him* lay their hands on his head, and let all the congregation stone him.

¹⁵"Then you shall speak to the children of Israel, saying: 'Whoever curses his God shall bear his sin. ¹⁶And whoever blasphemes the name of the LORD shall surely be put to death. All the congregation shall certainly stone him, the stranger as well as him who is born in the land. When he blasphemes the name *of the* LORD, he shall be put to death.

¹⁷'Whoever kills any man shall surely be put to death. ¹⁸Whoever kills an animal shall make it good, animal for animal.

¹⁹'If a man causes disfigurement of his neighbor, as he has done, so shall it be done to him— ²⁰fracture for fracture, eye for eye, tooth for tooth; as he has caused disfigurement of a man, so shall it be done to him. ²¹And whoever kills an animal shall restore it; but whoever kills a man shall be put to death. ²²You shall have the same law for the stranger and for one from your own country; for I *am* the LORD your God.' "

²³Then Moses spoke to the children of Israel; and they took outside the camp him

who had cursed, and stoned him with stones. So the children of Israel did as the LORD commanded Moses.

The Sabbath of the Seventh Year

25 And the LORD spoke to Moses on Mount Sinai, saying, 2"Speak to the children of Israel, and say to them: 'When you come into the land which I give you, then the land shall keep a sabbath to the LORD. 3Six years you shall sow your field, and six years you shall prune your vineyard, and gather its fruit; 4but in the seventh year there shall be a sabbath of solemn rest for the land, a sabbath to the LORD. You shall neither sow your field nor prune your vineyard. 5What grows of its own accord of your harvest you shall not reap, nor gather the grapes of your untended vine, *for* it is a year of rest for the land. 6And the sabbath *produce* of the land shall be food for you: for you, your male and female servants, your hired man, and the stranger who dwells with you, 7for your livestock and the beasts that *are* in your land—all its produce shall be for food.

The Year of Jubilee

8"And you shall count seven sabbaths of years for yourself, seven times seven years; and the time of the seven sabbaths of years shall be to you forty-nine years. 9Then you shall cause the trumpet of the Jubilee to sound on the tenth *day* of the seventh month; on the Day of Atonement you shall make the trumpet to sound throughout all your land. 10And you shall consecrate the fiftieth year, and proclaim liberty throughout *all* the land to all its inhabitants. It shall be a Jubilee for you; and each of you shall return to his possession, and each of you shall return to his family. 11That fiftieth year shall be a Jubilee to you; in it you shall neither sow nor reap what grows of its own accord, nor gather *the grapes* of your untended vine. 12For it *is* the Jubilee; it shall be holy to you; you shall eat its produce from the field.

13"In this Year of Jubilee, each of you shall return to his possession. 14And if you sell anything to your neighbor or buy from your neighbor's hand, you shall not oppress one another. 15According to the number of years after the Jubilee you shall buy from your neighbor, and according to the number of years of crops he shall sell to you. 16According to the multitude of years you shall increase its price, and according to the fewer number of years you shall diminish its price; for he sells to you *according* to the number *of the years* of the crops. 17Therefore you shall not oppress one another, but you shall fear your God; for I *am* the LORD your God.

Provisions for the Seventh Year

18"So you shall observe My statutes and keep My judgments, and perform them; and you will dwell in the land in safety. 19Then the land will yield its fruit, and you will eat your fill, and dwell there in safety. 20And if you say, "What shall we eat in the seventh year, since we shall not sow nor gather in our produce?" 21Then I will command My blessing on you in the sixth year, and it will bring forth produce enough for three years. 22And you shall sow in the eighth year, and eat old produce until the ninth year; until its produce comes in, you shall eat *of* the old *harvest*.

Redemption of Property

23"The land shall not be sold permanently, for the land *is* Mine; for you *are* strangers and sojourners with Me. 24And in all the land of your possession you shall grant redemption of the land.

25"If one of your brethren becomes poor, and has sold *some* of his possession, and if his redeeming relative comes to redeem it, then he may redeem what his brother sold. 26Or if the man has no one to redeem it, but he himself becomes able to redeem it, 27then let him count the years since its sale, and restore the remainder to the man to whom he sold it, that he may return to his possession. 28But if he is not able to have *it* restored to himself, then what was sold shall remain in the hand of him who bought it until the Year of Jubilee; and in the Jubilee it shall be released, and he shall return to his possession.

29"If a man sells a house in a walled city, then he may redeem it within a whole year after it is sold; *within* a full year he may redeem it. 30But if it is not redeemed within the space of a full year, then the house in the walled city shall belong permanently to him who bought it, throughout his generations. It shall not be released in the Jubilee. 31However the houses of villages which have no wall around them shall be counted as the fields of the country. They may be redeemed, and they shall be released in the Jubilee. 32Nevertheless the cities of the Lemvites, *and* the houses in the cities of their possession, the Lemvites may redeem at any time. 33And if a man purchases a house from the Lemvites, then the house that was sold in the city of his possession shall be released in the Jubilee; for the houses in the cities of the Lemvites *are* their possession among the children of Israel. 34But the field of the common-land of their cities may not be sold, for it *is* their perpetual possession.

Lending to the Poor

35'If one of your brethren becomes poor, and falls into poverty among you, then you shall help him, like a stranger or a sojourner, that he may live with you. 36Take no usury or interest from him; but fear your God, that your brother may live with you. 37You shall not lend him your money for usury, nor lend him your food at a profit. 38I *am* the LORD your God, who brought you out of the land of Egypt, to give you the land of Canaan *and* to be your God.

The Law Concerning Slavery

39'And if *one of* your brethren *who dwells* by you becomes poor, and sells himself to you, you shall not compel him to serve as a slave. 40As a hired servant *and* a sojourner he shall be with you, *and* shall serve you until the Year of Jubilee. 41And *then* he shall depart from you—he and his children with him—and shall return to his own family. He shall return to the possession of his fathers. 42For they *are* My servants, whom I brought out of the land of Egypt; they shall not be sold as slaves. 43You shall not rule over him with rigor, but you shall fear your God. 44And as for your male and female slaves whom you may have—from the nations that are around you, from them you may buy male and female slaves. 45Moreover you may

buy the children of the strangers who dwell among you, and their families who are with you, which they beget in your land; and they shall become your property. 46And you may take them as an inheritance for your children after you, to inherit *them as* a possession; they shall be your permanent slaves. But regarding your brethren, the children of Israel, you shall not rule over one another with rigor.

47'Now if a sojourner or stranger close to you becomes rich, and *one of* your brethren *who dwells* by him becomes poor, and sells himself to the stranger *or* sojourner close to you, or to a member of the stranger's family, 48after he is sold he may be redeemed again. One of his brothers may redeem him; 49or his uncle or his uncle's son may redeem him; or *anyone* who is near of kin to him in his family may redeem him; or if he is able he may redeem himself. 50Thus he shall reckon with him who bought him: The price of his release shall be according to the number of years, from the year that he was sold to him until the Year of Jubilee; *it shall be* according to the time of a hired servant for him. 51If *there are* still many years *remaining,* according to them he shall repay the price of his redemption from the money with which he was bought. 52And if there remain but a few years until the Year of Jubilee, then he shall reckon with him, *and* according to his years he shall repay him the price of his redemption. 53He shall be with him as a yearly hired servant, and he shall not rule with rigor over him in your sight. 54And if he is not redeemed in these *years,* then he shall be released in the Year of Jubilee—he and his children with him. 55For the children of Israel *are* servants to Me; they *are* My servants whom I brought out of the land of Egypt: I *am* the LORD your God.

Promise of Blessing and Retribution

26 'You shall not make idols for yourselves;

neither a carved image nor a *sacred* pillar shall you rear up for yourselves;

nor shall you set up an engraved stone in your land, to bow down to it;

for I *am* the LORD your God.

2 You shall keep My Sabbaths and reverence My sanctuary:
I *am* the LORD.

3 'If you walk in My statutes and keep My commandments, and perform them,

4 then I will give you rain in its season, the land shall yield its produce, and the trees of the field shall yield their fruit.

5 Your threshing shall last till the time of vintage, and the vintage shall last till the time of sowing;
you shall eat your bread to the full, and dwell in your land safely.

6 I will give peace in the land, and you shall lie down, and none will make *you* afraid;
I will rid the land of evil beasts, and the sword will not go through your land.

7 You will chase your enemies, and they shall fall by the sword before you.

8 Five of you shall chase a hundred, and a hundred of you shall put ten thousand to flight;
your enemies shall fall by the sword before you.

9 'For I will look on you favorably and make you fruitful, multiply you and confirm My covenant with you.

10 You shall eat the old harvest, and clear out the old because of the new.

11 I will set My tabernacle among you, and My soul shall not abhor you.

12 I will walk among you and be your God, and you shall be My people.

13 I *am* the LORD your God, who brought you out of the land of Egypt, that *you* should not be their slaves;
I have broken the bands of your yoke and made you walk upright.

14 'But if you do not obey Me, and do not observe all these commandments,

15 and if you despise My statutes, or if your soul abhors My judgments, so that you do not perform all My commandments, *but* break My covenant,

BIBLICAL INSIGHTS • 26:6–9
Let's Get Some Leverage

THE BIBLE PROMISES SPIRITUAL leverage when we join other believers in battle. I think it's time for the body of Christ to experience the promise of Leviticus 26:6–9: "I will give you peace in the land, and you shall lie down, and none will make you afraid; I will rid the land of evil beasts, and the sword will not go through your land. You will chase your enemies, and they shall fall by the sword before you. Five of you shall chase a hundred, and a hundred of you shall put ten thousand to flight; your enemies shall fall by the sword before you. For I will look on you favorably and make you fruitful, multiply you, and confirm My covenant with you."

Mathematically speaking, 100 should cause only 2000 to flee. But with God's power, a group of united Christians has an exponential spiritual advantage that's five times more effective. What if just ten percent of the churches in your community shared resources and united in prayer for the family?

Before us is the opportunity of a lifetime! A generation of people are broken, lonely, and looking for help. And as God's people, we have the answers.

---

16 I also will do this to you:
I will even appoint terror over you, wasting disease and fever which shall consume the eyes and cause sorrow of heart.
And you shall sow your seed in vain, for your enemies shall eat it.

17 I will set My face against you, and you shall be defeated by your enemies.
Those who hate you shall reign over you, and you shall flee when no one pursues you.

18 'And after all this, if you do not obey Me, then I will punish you seven times more for your sins.

19 I will break the pride of your power;
I will make your heavens like iron and
your earth like bronze.

20 And your strength shall be spent in
vain;
for your land shall not yield its
produce, nor shall the trees of the
land yield their fruit.

21 'Then, if you walk contrary to Me, and
are not willing to obey Me, I will
bring on you seven times more
plagues, according to your sins.

22 I will also send wild beasts among
you, which shall rob you of your
children, destroy your livestock,
and make you few in number;
and your highways shall be desolate.

23 'And if by these things you are not
reformed by Me, but walk contrary to Me,

24 then I also will walk contrary to you,
and I will punish you yet seven
times for your sins.

25 And I will bring a sword against you
that will execute the vengeance of
the covenant;
when you are gathered together
within your cities I will send
pestilence among you;
and you shall be delivered into the
hand of the enemy.

26 When I have cut off your supply of
bread, ten women shall bake your
bread in one oven, and they shall
bring back your bread by weight,
and you shall eat and not be satisfied.

27 'And after all this, if you do not obey
Me, but walk contrary to Me,

28 then I also will walk contrary to you
in fury;
and I, even I, will chastise you seven
times for your sins.

29 You shall eat the flesh of your sons,
and you shall eat the flesh of your
daughters.

30 I will destroy your high places, cut
down your incense altars, and cast
your carcasses on the lifeless
forms of your idols;
and My soul shall abhor you.

31 I will lay your cities waste and bring
your sanctuaries to desolation, and
I will not smell the fragrance of
your sweet aromas.

32 I will bring the land to desolation, and
your enemies who dwell in it shall
be astonished at it.

33 I will scatter you among the nations
and draw out a sword after you;
your land shall be desolate and your
cities waste.

34 Then the land shall enjoy its sabbaths
as long as it lies desolate and you
are in your enemies' land;
then the land shall rest and enjoy its
sabbaths.

35 As long as *it* lies desolate it shall
rest—
for the time it did not rest on your
sabbaths when you dwelt in it.

36 'And as for those of you who are left,
I will send faintness into their
hearts in the lands of their enemies;
the sound of a shaken leaf shall
cause them to flee;
they shall flee as though fleeing from
a sword, and they shall fall when
no one pursues.

37 They shall stumble over one another,
as it were before a sword, when no
one pursues;
and you shall have no *power* to stand
before your enemies.

38 You shall perish among the nations,
and the land of your enemies shall
eat you up.

39 And those of you who are left shall
waste away in their iniquity in
your enemies' lands;
also in their fathers' iniquities, which
are with them, they shall waste
away.

40 'But if they confess their iniquity and
the iniquity of their fathers, with
their unfaithfulness in which they
were unfaithful to Me, and that
they also have walked contrary to
Me,

41 and *that* I also have walked contrary
to them and have brought them
into the land of their enemies;

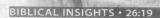

Why Pride Must Be Broken

Author, radio host and friend, Nancy Leigh DeMoss, once memorably contrasted proud people with broken people. Here's a portion of her remarkable list:

Proud People:	Broken People:
Focus on the failures of others	Overwhelmed with sense of their own spiritual need
Look down on others	Esteem others better than self
Independent/self-sufficient spirit	Dependent spirit/recognize need for others
Maintain control; must be my way	Surrender control
Have to prove that they are right	Willing to yield the right to be right
Desire to be served	Motivated to serve others
Desire to be a success	Desire to make others a success
Think of what they can do for God	Know that they have nothing to offer God
Quick to blame others	Accept personal responsibility
Defensive when criticized	Receive criticism with a humble, open heart
Concerned with being "respectable"	Concerned with being real
Concerned about what others think	All that matters is what God knows
Blind to their true heart condition	Walk in the light

Now, with this list in mind, listen to God's promise, "I will break the pride of your power; I will make your heavens like iron and your earth like bronze" (26:19). Ultimately when a person is filled with pride, he is saying to God, "I will be my own god, and You will not." Is there pride in your life that needs to be broken by God? Why not yield to Him right now and allow the Holy Spirit to do His work in your heart?

---

if their uncircumcised hearts are humbled, and they accept their guilt—

42 then I will remember My covenant with Jacob, and My covenant with Isaac and My covenant with Abraham I will remember; I will remember the land.

43 The land also shall be left empty by them, and will enjoy its sabbaths while it lies desolate without them; they will accept their guilt, because they despised My judgments and because their soul abhorred My statutes.

44 Yet for all that, when they are in the land of their enemies, I will not cast them away, nor shall I abhor them, to utterly destroy them and break My covenant with them; for I am the LORD their God.

45 But for their sake I will remember the covenant of their ancestors, whom I brought out of the land of Egypt in the sight of the nations, that I might be their God: I am the LORD.'"

46These are the statutes and judgments and laws which the LORD made between Himself and the children of Israel on Mount Sinai by the hand of Moses.

DEVOTIONS FOR COUPLES • 26:9
Live Out Your Marriage Covenant

Since most of us were married in a ceremony that did not emphasize the marriage covenant, consider five ideas that will make a covenantal commitment a reality in your marriage:

1. *Pray together every day as a couple.* When Barbara and I were first married, I asked a man I highly respected for his best counsel on marriage. He told me, "I've prayed every day with my Sara Jo for more than twenty-five years. Nothing has built our marriage more than our prayer time together."

Barbara and I usually pray together before going to sleep, but on some nights neither of us has felt like praying. The Lord has gently reminded me, *You need to pray with her.* And even though on occasion I haven't even wanted to *talk* to her, I have finally rolled over and said, "Let's pray." Our obedience to this spiritual discipline has reminded us of the real Source of strength in our marriage and has kept us connected and communicating.

2. *Never use the D word.* Marriage is tough, and at times every one of us probably has thought about giving up. The key word is *thought*. No matter how hopeless the situation seems or how lousy you feel, I urge you not to *say* the D word—divorce—in your home.

In Proverbs 18:21 we read, "Death and life are in the power of the tongue." Words have power. If you first think about divorce and then talk about it, before long what was once unthinkable becomes an option.

3. *Sign a marriage covenant.* Whether you are newlyweds or have been married for years, why not consider having a covenant-signing ceremony? You could do this with other couples at your church or in your home with witnesses from your family or close friends.

4. *Do what you promised.* It won't make any difference ultimately if you sign a piece of paper but later break your covenant. Don't let temptations and conflicts keep you from finishing strong in your marriage and family. Don't let go! Fulfill your vows.

5. *Urge others to keep their covenant.* We need to band together in the Christian community to stand for marital commitment and to fight divorce. We serve a God who has gone on record on this topic: "For the LORD God of Israel says that He hates divorce" (Mal. 2:16). We need to combat divorce in the most positive way—by honoring our covenants and encouraging others to do the same.

Redeeming Persons and Property Dedicated to God

27 Now the LORD spoke to Moses, saying, 2"Speak to the children of Israel, and say to them: 'When a man consecrates by a vow certain persons to the LORD, according to your valuation, 3if your valuation is of a male from twenty years old up to sixty years old, then your valuation shall be fifty shekels of silver, according to the shekel of the sanctuary. 4If it *is* a female, then your valuation shall be thirty shekels; 5and if from five years old up to twenty years old, then your valuation for a male shall be twenty shekels, and for a female ten shekels; 6and if from a month old up to five years old, then your valuation for a male shall be five shekels of silver, and for a female your valuation shall be three shekels of silver; 7and if from sixty years old and above, if *it is* a male, then your valuation shall be fifteen shekels, and for a female ten shekels.

8'But if he is too poor to pay your valuation, then he shall present himself before the priest, and the priest shall set a value for him; according to the ability of him who vowed, the priest shall value him.

9'If *it is* an animal that men may bring as an offering to the LORD, all that *anyone* gives to the LORD shall be holy. 10He shall not substitute it or exchange it, good for bad or bad for good; and if he at all exchanges animal for animal, then both it and the one exchanged for it shall be holy. [11]If *it is* an unclean animal which they do not offer as a sacrifice to the LORD, then he shall present the animal before the priest; [12]and the priest shall set a value for it, whether it is good or bad; as you, the priest, value it, so it shall be. [13]But if he *wants* at all *to* redeem it, then he must add one-fifth to your valuation.

[14]'And when a man dedicates his house *to be* holy to the LORD, then the priest shall set a value for it, whether it is good or bad; as the priest values it, so it shall stand. [15]If he who dedicated it *wants to* redeem his house, then he must add one-fifth of the money of your valuation to it, and it shall be his.

[16]'If a man dedicates to the LORD *part* of a field of his possession, then your valuation shall be according to the seed for it. A homer of barley seed *shall be valued* at fifty shekels of silver. [17]If he dedicates his field from the Year of Jubilee, according to your valuation it shall stand. [18]But if he dedicates his field after the Jubilee, then the priest shall reckon to him the money due according to the years that remain till the Year of Jubilee, and it shall be deducted from your valuation. [19]And if he who dedicates the field ever wishes to redeem it, then he must add one-fifth of the money of your valuation to it, and it shall belong to him. [20]But if he does not want to redeem the field, or if he has sold the field to another man, it shall not be redeemed anymore; [21]but the field, when it is released in the Jubilee, shall be holy to the LORD, as a devoted field; it shall be the possession of the priest.

[22]'And if a man dedicates to the LORD a field which he has bought, which is not the field of his possession, [23]then the priest shall reckon to him the worth of your valuation, up to the Year of Jubilee, and he shall give your valuation on that day *as* a holy *offering* to the LORD. [24]In the Year of Jubilee the field shall return to him from whom it was bought, to the one who *owned* the land as a possession. [25]And all your valuations shall be according to the shekel of the sanctuary: twenty gerahs to the shekel.

[26]'But the firstborn of the animals, which should be the LORD's firstborn, no man shall dedicate; whether *it is* an ox or sheep, it *is* the LORD's. [27]And if *it is* an unclean animal, then he shall redeem *it* according to your valuation, and shall add one-fifth to it; or if it is not redeemed, then it shall be sold according to your valuation.

[28]'Nevertheless no devoted *offering* that a man may devote to the LORD of all that he has, *both* man and beast, or the field of his possession, shall be sold or redeemed; every devoted *offering is* most holy to the LORD. [29]No person under the ban, who may become doomed to destruction among men, shall be redeemed, *but* shall surely be put to death. [30]And all the tithe of the land, *whether* of the seed of the land *or* of the fruit of the tree, *is* the LORD's. It *is* holy to the LORD. [31]If a man wants at all to redeem *any* of his tithes, he shall add one-fifth to it. [32]And concerning the tithe of the herd or the flock, of whatever passes under the rod, the tenth one shall be holy to the LORD. [33]He shall not inquire whether it is good or bad, nor shall he exchange it; and if he exchanges it at all, then both it and the one exchanged for it shall be holy; it shall not be redeemed.'"

[34]These *are* the commandments which the LORD commanded Moses for the children of Israel on Mount Sinai.

NUMBERS

THE BOOK OF NUMBERS focuses on the two generations of Israelites who lived during the thirty-nine years that the Hebrew nation spent in the wilderness before entering the Promised Land. The first generation had participated in the exodus, while the second generation had been born and grown up in the desert, with no direct memory of Egypt or of God's miraculous deliverance from slavery there. The whole Israelite nation had descended from the twelve sons of Jacob, and had mushroomed into a large nation during the time of Israel's captivity in Egypt.

God had miraculously delivered this large extended family, now almost 2.5 million strong, and had promised them a land flowing with milk and honey. But when God directed the nation to enter Canaan and subdue it, the people disobeyed. They doubted God's promise to help them overcome all enemy resistance, and by refusing to enter Canaan, they could not take hold of the good promises of God until they had finished their time of discipline in the wilderness.

The word *wilderness* appears forty-eight times in Numbers. The term refers to a geographical region where living things don't grow and where, because of a lack of rainfall, the land stubbornly resists cultivation. Our families probably will never spend forty years in an actual wilderness, but we *can* find ourselves in a spiritually dry place, the wilderness, as a result of our own disobedience. As you read through Numbers, ask yourself, "Am I committed to walking in faith and obedience to what God has commanded?" And, "In what ways has my resistance to God's will for me and for my family left us in a spiritually dry and barren place?"

Like the descendents of Jacob, you may have to live for some time with the consequences of your disobedience. But even there, in that difficult place, you can cooperate with God to get you to a much better place. And all the while you can find your delight and your supply for each day as you live committed to honoring God with your life and in your family.

The First Census of Israel

1 Now the LORD spoke to Moses in the Wilderness of Sinai, in the tabernacle of meeting, on the first *day* of the second month, in the second year after they had come out of the land of Egypt, saying: 2"Take a census of all the congregation of the children of Israel, by their families, by their fathers' houses, according to the number of names, every male individually, 3from twenty years old and above—all who *are able to* go to war in Israel. You and Aaron shall number them by their armies. 4And with you there shall be a man from every tribe, each one the head of his father's house.

5"These are the names of the men who shall stand with you: from Reuben, Elizur the son of Shedeur; 6from Simeon, Shelumiel the son of Zurishaddai; 7from Judah, Nahshon the son of Amminadab; 8from Issachar, Nethanel the son of Zuar; 9from Zebulun, Eliab the son of Helon; 10from the sons of Joseph: from Ephraim, Elishama the son of Ammihud; from Manasseh, Gamaliel the son of Pedahzur; 11from Benjamin, Abidan the son of Gideoni; 12from Dan, Ahiezer the son of Ammishaddai; 13from Asher, Pagiel the son of Ocran; 14from Gad, Eliasaph the son of Deuel;a 15from Naphtali, Ahira the son of Enan." 16These *were* chosen from the congregation, leaders of their fathers' tribes, heads of the divisions in Israel.

17Then Moses and Aaron took these men who had been mentioned by name, 18and they assembled all the congregation together on the first *day* of the second month; and they recited their ancestry by families, by their fathers' houses, according to the number of names, from twenty years old and above, each one individually. 19As the LORD commanded Moses, so he numbered them in the Wilderness of Sinai.

20Now the children of Reuben, Israel's oldest son, their genealogies by their families, by their fathers' house, according to the number of names, every male individually, from twenty years old and above, all who *were able to* go to war: 21those who were numbered of the tribe of Reuben *were* forty-six thousand five hundred.

22From the children of Simeon, their genealogies by their families, by their fathers' house, of those who were numbered, according to the number of names, every male individually, from twenty years old and above, all who *were able to* go to war: 23those who were numbered of the tribe of Simeon *were* fifty-nine thousand three hundred.

INTIMATE MOMENTS

A woman never tires of hearing how much her man loves her, so consider a unique way to express your affection. This one might sound a little odd, but the surprise is what makes it work. Leave a short love note for your wife on the toilet paper roll—a ballpoint pen works best. Make sure it's visible, right on top, so she's sure to see it the instant she looks.

24From the children of Gad, their genealogies by their families, by their fathers' house, according to the number of names, from twenty years old and above, all who *were able to* go to war: 25those who were numbered of the tribe of Gad *were* forty-five thousand six hundred and fifty.

26From the children of Judah, their genealogies by their families, by their fathers' house, according to the number of names, from twenty years old and above, all who *were able to* go to war: 27those who were numbered of the tribe of Judah *were* seventy-four thousand six hundred.

28From the children of Issachar, their genealogies by their families, by their fathers' house, according to the number of names, from twenty years old and above, all who *were able to* go to war: 29those who were numbered of the tribe of Issachar *were* fifty-four thousand four hundred.

30From the children of Zebulun, their genealogies by their families, by their fathers' house, according to the number of names, from twenty years old and above, all who *were able to* go to war: 31those who

1:14 aSpelled *Reuel* in 2:14

were numbered of the tribe of Zebulun *were* fifty-seven thousand four hundred.

³²From the sons of Joseph, the children of Ephraim, their genealogies by their families, by their fathers' house, according to the number of names, from twenty years old and above, all who *were able to* go to war: ³³those who were numbered of the tribe of Ephraim *were* forty thousand five hundred.

³⁴From the children of Manasseh, their genealogies by their families, by their fathers' house, according to the number of names, from twenty years old and above, all who *were able to* go to war: ³⁵those who were numbered of the tribe of Manasseh *were* thirty-two thousand two hundred.

³⁶From the children of Benjamin, their genealogies by their families, by their fathers' house, according to the number of names, from twenty years old and above, all who *were able to* go to war: ³⁷those who were numbered of the tribe of Benjamin *were* thirty-five thousand four hundred.

³⁸From the children of Dan, their genealogies by their families, by their fathers' house, according to the number of names, from twenty years old and above, all who *were able to* go to war: ³⁹those who were numbered of the tribe of Dan *were* sixty-two thousand seven hundred.

⁴⁰From the children of Asher, their genealogies by their families, by their fathers' house, according to the number of names, from twenty years old and above, all who *were able to* go to war: ⁴¹those who were numbered of the tribe of Asher *were* forty-one thousand five hundred.

⁴²From the children of Naphtali, their genealogies by their families, by their fathers' house, according to the number of names, from twenty years old and above, all who *were able to* go to war: ⁴³those who were numbered of the tribe of Naphtali *were* fifty-three thousand four hundred.

⁴⁴These are the ones who were numbered, whom Moses and Aaron numbered, with the leaders of Israel, twelve men, each one representing his father's house. ⁴⁵So all who were numbered of the children of Israel, by their fathers' houses, from twenty years old and above, all who *were able to* go to war in Israel— ⁴⁶all who

were numbered were six hundred and three thousand five hundred and fifty.

⁴⁷But the Levites were not numbered among them by their fathers' tribe; ⁴⁸for the LORD had spoken to Moses, saying: ⁴⁹"Only the tribe of Levi you shall not number, nor take a census of them among the children of Israel; ⁵⁰but you shall appoint the Levites over the tabernacle of the Testimony, over all its furnishings, and over all things that belong to it; they shall carry the tabernacle and all its furnishings; they shall attend to it and camp around the tabernacle. ⁵¹And when the tabernacle is to go forward, the Levites shall take it down; and when the tabernacle is to be set up, the Levites shall set it up. The outsider who comes near shall be put to death. ⁵²The children of Israel shall pitch their tents, everyone by his own camp, everyone by his own standard, according to their armies; ⁵³but the Levites shall camp around the tabernacle of the Testimony, that there may be no wrath on the congregation of the children of Israel; and the Levites shall keep charge of the tabernacle of the Testimony."

⁵⁴Thus the children of Israel did; according to all that the LORD commanded Moses, so they did.

The Tribes and Leaders by Armies

2 And the LORD spoke to Moses and Aaron, saying: ²"Everyone of the children of Israel shall camp by his own standard, beside the emblems of his father's house; they shall camp some distance from the tabernacle of meeting. ³On the east side, toward the rising of the sun, those of the standard of the forces with Judah shall camp according to their armies; and Nahshon the son of Amminadab *shall be* the leader of the children of Judah." ⁴And his army was numbered at seventy-four thousand six hundred.

⁵"Those who camp next to him *shall be* the tribe of Issachar, and Nethanel the son of Zuar *shall be* the leader of the children of Issachar." ⁶And his army was numbered at fifty-four thousand four hundred.

⁷"Then *comes* the tribe of Zebulun, and Eliab the son of Helon *shall be* the leader of the children of Zebulun." ⁸And his army

was numbered at fifty-seven thousand four hundred. 9"All who were numbered according to their armies of the forces with Judah, one hundred and eighty-six thousand four hundred—these shall break camp first.

10"On the south side *shall be* the standard of the forces with Reuben according to their armies, and the leader of the children of Reuben *shall be* Elizur the son of Shedeur." 11And his army was numbered at forty-six thousand five hundred.

12"Those who camp next to him *shall be* the tribe of Simeon, and the leader of the children of Simeon *shall be* Shelumiel the son of Zurishaddai." 13And his army was numbered at fifty-nine thousand three hundred.

14"Then *comes* the tribe of Gad, and the leader of the children of Gad *shall be* Eliasaph the son of Reuel."a 15And his army was numbered at forty-five thousand six hundred and fifty. 16"All who were numbered according to their armies of the forces with Reuben, one hundred and fifty-one thousand four hundred and fifty—they shall be the second to break camp.

17"And the tabernacle of meeting shall move out with the camp of the Levites in the middle of the camps; as they camp, so they shall move out, everyone in his place, by their standards.

18"On the west side *shall be* the standard of the forces with Ephraim according to their armies, and the leader of the children of Ephraim *shall be* Elishama the son of Ammihud." 19And his army was numbered at forty thousand five hundred.

20"Next to him *comes* the tribe of Manasseh, and the leader of the children of Manasseh *shall be* Gamaliel the son of Pedahzur." 21And his army was numbered at thirty-two thousand two hundred.

22"Then *comes* the tribe of Benjamin, and the leader of the children of Benjamin *shall be* Abidan the son of Gideoni." 23And his army was numbered at thirty-five thousand four hundred. 24"All who were numbered according to their armies of the forces with Ephraim, one hundred and eight thousand one hundred—they shall be the third to break camp.

25"The standard of the forces with Dan *shall be* on the north side according to their armies, and the leader of the children of Dan *shall be* Ahiezer the son of Ammishaddai." 26And his army was numbered at sixty-two thousand seven hundred.

27"Those who camp next to him *shall be* the tribe of Asher, and the leader of the children of Asher *shall be* Pagiel the son of Ocran." 28And his army was numbered at forty-one thousand five hundred.

29"Then *comes* the tribe of Naphtali, and the leader of the children of Naphtali *shall be* Ahira the son of Enan." 30And his army was numbered at fifty-three thousand four hundred. 31"All who were numbered of the forces with Dan, one hundred and fifty-seven thousand six hundred—they shall break camp last, with their standards."

32These *are* the ones who were numbered of the children of Israel by their fathers' houses. All who were numbered according to their armies of the forces *were* six hundred and three thousand five hundred and fifty. 33But the Levites were not numbered among the children of Israel, just as the LORD commanded Moses.

34Thus the children of Israel did according to all that the LORD commanded Moses; so they camped by their standards and so they broke camp, each one by his family, according to their fathers' houses.

The Sons of Aaron

3 Now these *are* the records of Aaron and Moses when the LORD spoke with Moses on Mount Sinai. 2And these *are* the names of the sons of Aaron: Nadab, the firstborn, and Abihu, Eleazar, and Ithamar. 3These *are* the names of the sons of Aaron, the anointed priests, whom he consecrated to minister as priests. 4Nadab and Abihu had died before the LORD when they offered profane fire before the LORD in the Wilderness of Sinai; and they had no children. So Eleazar and Ithamar ministered as priests in the presence of Aaron their father.

The Levites Serve in the Tabernacle

5And the LORD spoke to Moses, saying: 6"Bring the tribe of Levi near, and present them before Aaron the priest, that they may serve him. 7And they shall attend to his

2:14 aSpelled *Deuel* in 1:14 and 7:42

needs and the needs of the whole congregation before the tabernacle of meeting, to do the work of the tabernacle. [8]Also they shall attend to all the furnishings of the tabernacle of meeting, and to the needs of the children of Israel, to do the work of the tabernacle. [9]And you shall give the Levites to Aaron and his sons; they *are* given entirely to him[a] from among the children of Israel. [10]So you shall appoint Aaron and his sons, and they shall attend to their priesthood; but the outsider who comes near shall be put to death."

[11]Then the LORD spoke to Moses, saying: [12]"Now behold, I Myself have taken the Levites from among the children of Israel instead of every firstborn who opens the womb among the children of Israel. Therefore the Levites shall be Mine, [13]because all the firstborn *are* Mine. On the day that I struck all the firstborn in the land of Egypt, I sanctified to Myself all the firstborn in Israel, both man and beast. They shall be Mine: I *am* the LORD."

Census of the Levites Commanded

[14]Then the LORD spoke to Moses in the Wilderness of Sinai, saying: [15]"Number the children of Levi by their fathers' houses, by their families; you shall number every male from a month old and above."

[16]So Moses numbered them according to the word of the LORD, as he was commanded. [17]These were the sons of Levi by their names: Gershon, Kohath, and Merari. [18]And these *are* the names of the sons of Gershon by their families: Libni and Shimei. [19]And the sons of Kohath by their families: Amram, Izehar, Hebron, and Uzziel. [20]And the sons of Merari by their families: Mahli and Mushi. These *are* the families of the Levites by their fathers' houses.

[21]From Gershon *came* the family of the Libnites and the family of the Shimites; these *were* the families of the Gershonites. [22]Those who were numbered, according to the number of all the males from a month old and above—of those who were numbered *there were* seven thousand five hundred. [23]The families of the Gershonites were to camp behind the tabernacle westward. [24]And the leader of the father's house of the Gershonites *was* Eliasaph the son of Lael. [25]The duties of the children of Gershon in

the tabernacle of meeting *included* the tabernacle, the tent with its covering, the screen for the door of the tabernacle of meeting, [26]the screen for the door of the court, the hangings of the court which *are* around the tabernacle and the altar, and their cords, according to all the work relating to them.

[27]From Kohath *came* the family of the Amramites, the family of the Izharites, the family of the Hebronites, and the family of the Uzzielites; these *were* the families of the Kohathites. [28]According to the number of all the males, from a month old and above, *there were* eight thousand six[a] hundred keeping charge of the sanctuary. [29]The families of the children of Kohath were to camp on the south side of the tabernacle. [30]And the leader of the fathers' house of the families of the Kohathites *was* Elizaphan the son of Uzziel. [31]Their duty *included* the ark, the table, the lampstand, the altars, the utensils of the sanctuary with which they ministered, the screen, and all the work relating to them.

[32]And Eleazar the son of Aaron the priest *was to be* chief over the leaders of the Levites, *with* oversight of those who kept charge of the sanctuary.

[33]From Merari *came* the family of the Mahlites and the family of the Mushites; these *were* the families of Merari. [34]And those who were numbered, according to the number of all the males from a month old and above, *were* six thousand two hundred. [35]The leader of the fathers' house of the families of Merari *was* Zuriel the son of Abihail. These *were* to camp on the north side of the tabernacle. [36]And the appointed duty of the children of Merari *included* the boards of the tabernacle, its bars, its pillars, its sockets, its utensils, all the work relating to them, [37]and the pillars of the court all around, with their sockets, their pegs, and their cords.

[38]Moreover those who were to camp before the tabernacle on the east, before the tabernacle of meeting, *were* Moses, Aaron, and his sons, keeping charge of the sanctuary, to meet the needs of the children of Israel; but the outsider who came

---

3:9 [a]Samaritan Pentateuch and Septuagint read *Me.*
3:28 [a]Some manuscripts of the Septuagint read *three.*

near was to be put to death. ³⁹All who were numbered of the Levites, whom Moses and Aaron numbered at the command-ment of the LORD, by their families, all the males from a month old and above, *were* twenty-two thousand.

Levites Dedicated Instead of the Firstborn

⁴⁰Then the LORD said to Moses: "Number all the firstborn males of the children of Israel from a month old and above, and take the number of their names. ⁴¹And you shall take the Levites for Me—I *am* the LORD—instead of all the firstborn among the chil-dren of Israel, and the livestock of the Levites instead of all the firstborn among the livestock of the children of Israel." ⁴²So Moses numbered all the firstborn among the children of Israel, as the LORD com-manded him. ⁴³And all the firstborn males, according to the number of names from a month old and above, of those who were numbered of them, were twenty-two thou-sand two hundred and seventy-three.

⁴⁴Then the LORD spoke to Moses, say-ing: ⁴⁵"Take the Levites instead of all the firstborn among the children of Israel, and the livestock of the Levites instead of their livestock. The Levites shall be Mine: I *am*

the LORD. ⁴⁶And for the redemption of the two hundred and seventy-three of the firstborn of the children of Israel, who are more than the number of the Levites, ⁴⁷you shall take five shekels for each one individ-ually; you shall take *them* in the currency of the shekel of the sanctuary, the shekel of twenty gerahs. ⁴⁸And you shall give the money, with which the excess number of them is redeemed, to Aaron and his sons."

⁴⁹So Moses took the redemption money from those who were over and above those who were redeemed by the Levites. ⁵⁰From the firstborn of the children of Israel he took the money, one thousand three hun-dred and sixty-five *shekels,* according to the shekel of the sanctuary. ⁵¹And Moses gave their redemption money to Aaron and his sons, according to the word of the LORD, as the LORD commanded Moses.

Duties of the Sons of Kohath

4 Then the LORD spoke to Moses and Aaron, saying: ²"Take a census of the sons of Kohath from among the children of Levi, by their families, by their fathers' house, ³from thirty years old and above, even to fifty years old, all who enter the service to do the work in the tabernacle of meeting.

⁴"This *is* the service of the sons of

PARENTING MATTERS

Q: *How do we instill a sense of direction in our children?*

Christian parents should desire more than anything else to raise children who will grow up to love and walk with Jesus Christ. With that overall objective in mind, we have searched the Scriptures to discern what biblical goals we should aim for with our own chil-dren. The four qualities we developed give us four clear goals to pursue as we craft our children.

Identity: Every person is born with a unique, divinely-imprinted identity. If we want to properly guide our children to a healthy self-identity, we must acknowledge and support the Creator's design in three key areas: spiritual identity, emotional identity, and sexual identity.

Character: From Genesis to Revelation, character development is a major theme of God's work. Character is how your child responds to authority and life's circumstances.

Relationships: None of us was intended to make this journey through life alone. We need the strength, comfort, encourage-ment, resources, and power provided by God and others.

Mission: Every person needs a reason to live, a driving passion or calling that provides meaning and impact. This is a person's mis-sion, and it is necessary to instill in your child a sense of mission.

Kohath in the tabernacle of meeting, *relating to* the most holy things: [5]When the camp prepares to journey, Aaron and his sons shall come, and they shall take down the covering veil and cover the ark of the Testimony with it. [6]Then they shall put on it a covering of badger skins, and spread over *that* a cloth entirely of blue; and they shall insert its poles.

[7]"On the table of showbread they shall spread a blue cloth, and put on it the dishes, the pans, the bowls, and the pitchers for pouring; and the showbread[a] shall be on it. [8]They shall spread over them a scarlet cloth, and cover the same with a covering of badger skins; and they shall insert its poles. [9]And they shall take a blue cloth and cover the lampstand of the light, with its lamps, its wick-trimmers, its trays, and all its oil vessels, with which they service it. [10]Then they shall put it with all its utensils in a covering of badger skins, and put *it* on a carrying beam.

[11]"Over the golden altar they shall spread a blue cloth, and cover it with a covering of badger skins; and they shall insert its poles. [12]Then they shall take all the utensils of service with which they minister in the sanctuary, put *them* in a blue cloth, cover them with a covering of badger skins, and put *them* on a carrying beam. [13]Also they shall take away the ashes from the altar, and spread a purple cloth over it. [14]They shall put on it all its implements with which they minister there—the firepans, the forks, the shovels, the basins, and all the utensils of the altar—and they shall spread on it a covering of badger skins, and insert its poles. [15]And when Aaron and his sons have finished covering the sanctuary and all the furnishings of the sanctuary, when the camp is set to go, then the sons of Kohath shall come to carry *them;* but they shall not touch any holy thing, lest they die.

"These *are* the things in the tabernacle of meeting which the sons of Kohath are to carry.

[16]"The appointed duty of Eleazar the son of Aaron the priest *is* the oil for the light, the sweet incense, the daily grain offering, the anointing oil, the oversight of all the tabernacle, of all that *is* in it, with the sanctuary and its furnishings."

[17]Then the LORD spoke to Moses and Aaron, saying: [18]"Do not cut off the tribe of the families of the Kohathites from among the Levites; [19]but do this in regard to them, that they may live and not die when they approach the most holy things: Aaron and his sons shall go in and appoint each of them to his service and his task. [20]But they shall not go in to watch while the holy things are being covered, lest they die."

Duties of the Sons of Gershon

[21]Then the LORD spoke to Moses, saying: [22]"Also take a census of the sons of Gershon, by their fathers' house, by their families. [23]From thirty years old and above, even to fifty years old, you shall number them, all who enter to perform the service, to do the work in the tabernacle of meeting. [24]This *is* the service of the families of the Gershonites, in serving and carrying: [25]They shall carry the curtains of the tabernacle and the tabernacle of meeting *with* its covering, the covering of badger skins that *is* on it, the screen for the door of the tabernacle of meeting, [26]the screen for the door of the gate of the court, the hangings of the court which *are* around the tabernacle and altar, and their cords, all the furnishings for their service and all that is made for these things: so shall they serve.

[27]"Aaron and his sons shall assign all the service of the sons of the Gershonites, all their tasks and all their service. And you shall appoint to them all their tasks as their duty. [28]This *is* the service of the families of the sons of Gershon in the tabernacle of meeting. And their duties *shall be* under the authority[a] of Ithamar the son of Aaron the priest.

Duties of the Sons of Merari

[29]"*As for* the sons of Merari, you shall number them by their families and by their fathers' house. [30]From thirty years old and above, even to fifty years old, you shall number them, everyone who enters the service to do the work of the tabernacle of meeting. [31]And this *is* what they must carry as all their service for the tabernacle of meeting: the boards of the tabernacle,

---

4:7 [a]Literally *the continual bread* **4:28** [a]Literally *hand*

its bars, its pillars, its sockets, ³²and the pillars around the court with their sockets, pegs, and cords, with all their furnishings and all their service; and you shall assign *to each man* by name the items he must carry. ³³This *is* the service of the families of the sons of Merari, as all their service for the tabernacle of meeting, under the authority^a of Ithamar the son of Aaron the priest."

Census of the Levites

³⁴And Moses, Aaron, and the leaders of the congregation numbered the sons of the Kohathites by their families and by their fathers' house, ³⁵from thirty years old and above, even to fifty years old, everyone who entered the service for work in the tabernacle of meeting; ³⁶and those who were numbered by their families were two thousand seven hundred and fifty. ³⁷These *were* the ones who were numbered of the families of the Kohathites, all who might serve in the tabernacle of meeting, whom Moses and Aaron numbered according to the commandment of the LORD by the hand of Moses.

³⁸And those who were numbered of the sons of Gershon, by their families and by their fathers' house, ³⁹from thirty years old and above, even to fifty years old, everyone who entered the service for work in the tabernacle of meeting— ⁴⁰those who were numbered by their families, by their fathers' house, were two thousand six hundred and thirty. ⁴¹These *are* the ones who were numbered of the families of the sons of Gershon, of all who might serve in the tabernacle of meeting, whom Moses and Aaron numbered according to the commandment of the LORD.

⁴²Those of the families of the sons of Merari who were numbered, by their families, by their fathers' house, ⁴³from thirty years old and above, even to fifty years old, everyone who entered the service for work in the tabernacle of meeting— ⁴⁴those who were numbered by their families were three thousand two hundred. ⁴⁵These *are* the ones who were numbered of the families of the sons of Merari, whom Moses and Aaron numbered according to the word of the LORD by the hand of Moses.

⁴⁶All who were numbered of the Levites, whom Moses, Aaron, and the leaders of Israel numbered, by their families and by their fathers' houses, ⁴⁷from thirty years old and above, even to fifty years old, everyone who came to do the work of service and the work of bearing burdens in the tabernacle of meeting— ⁴⁸those who were numbered were eight thousand five hundred and eighty.

⁴⁹According to the commandment of the LORD they were numbered by the hand of Moses, each according to his service and according to his task; thus were they numbered by him, as the LORD commanded Moses.

Ceremonially Unclean Persons Isolated

5 And the LORD spoke to Moses, saying: ²"Command the children of Israel that they put out of the camp every leper, everyone who has a discharge, and whoever becomes defiled by a corpse. ³You shall put out both male and female; you shall put them outside the camp, that they may not defile their camps in the midst of which I dwell." ⁴And the children of Israel did so, and put them outside the camp; as the LORD spoke to Moses, so the children of Israel did.

Confession and Restitution

⁵Then the LORD spoke to Moses, saying, ⁶"Speak to the children of Israel: 'When a man or woman commits any sin that men commit in unfaithfulness against the LORD, and that person is guilty, ⁷then he shall confess the sin which he has committed. He shall make restitution for his trespass in full, plus one-fifth of it, and give *it* to the one he has wronged. ⁸But if the man has no relative to whom restitution may be made for the wrong, the restitution for the wrong *must go* to the LORD for the priest, in addition to the ram of the atonement with which atonement is made for him. ⁹Every offering of all the holy things of the children of Israel, which they bring to the priest, shall be his. ¹⁰And every man's holy things shall be his; whatever any man gives the priest shall be his.'"

Concerning Unfaithful Wives

¹¹And the LORD spoke to Moses, saying,

4:33 ^aLiterally *hand*

DEVOTIONS FOR COUPLES • 5:12
Avoid Emotional Adultery

From the very beginning, God warned His people about the dangers of going astray (5:12). It was a very real possibility then, and it remains so today. Know that when you find yourself connecting with another person who starts becoming, in even the smallest way, a substitute for your marital partner, you've already started to travel a dangerous road. Emotional adultery occurs when we reserve an inappropriate place in our hearts for any person other than our spouse.

So, how do you protect yourself and your marriage? Here are some principles many have found helpful:

1. *Know your boundaries.* Put fences around your heart and protect the sacred ground reserved only for your spouse. Barbara and I are careful to share our deepest feelings, needs, and difficulties *only* with each other. For us, this is a non-negotiable boundary.

2. *Realize the power of the eyes.* The eyes are the windows of your soul. Pull the shades down if you sense someone is pausing a little too long in front of those windows! Good eye contact may be necessary for effective communication, but you must reserve that deep type of look for your mate.

3. *Beware of isolation and concealment.*

One strategy of the enemy is to isolate you from your spouse by tempting you to keep secrets from your mate. Barbara and I both realize the danger of concealment in our marriage. We work hard at bringing things out into the open and discussing them. Our closets are empty.

4. *Extinguish any chemical reactions that may have begun.* You must quickly end any friendship with the opposite sex that seems to have begun meeting needs that your mate alone should be meeting. A simple rule of chemistry is this: to stop a chemical reaction, remove one of the elements. It may feel painful or embarrassing at first, but it doesn't inflict nearly the pain that comes when temptation gives birth to sin.

5. *Ask God to remind you how important it is to fear Him.* The fear of God has turned me from many a temptation. It's one thing to think a friend might learn that I had compromised my faith; it's quite another thing to realize that God's throne would have a knowledge of my disloyalty to Barbara faster than the speed of light.

It has been well said that, "a secret on earth is open scandal in heaven." My Heavenly Father and my earthly father are there right now—and the mere thought of disappointing either of them helps keep me pure.

12"Speak to the children of Israel, and say to them: 'If any man's wife goes astray and behaves unfaithfully toward him, 13and a man lies with her carnally, and it is hidden from the eyes of her husband, and it is concealed that she has defiled herself, and *there was* no witness against her, nor was she caught— 14if the spirit of jealousy comes upon him and he becomes jealous of his wife, who has defiled herself; or if the spirit of jealousy comes upon him and he becomes jealous of his wife, although she has not defiled herself— 15then the man shall bring his wife to the priest. He shall bring the offering required for her, one-tenth

of an ephah of barley meal; he shall pour no oil on it and put no frankincense on it, because it *is* a grain offering of jealousy, an offering for remembering, for bringing iniquity to remembrance.

16And the priest shall bring her near, and set her before the LORD. 17The priest shall take holy water in an earthen vessel, and take some of the dust that is on the floor of the tabernacle and put *it* into the water. 18Then the priest shall stand the woman before the LORD, uncover the woman's head, and put the offering for remembering in her hands, which *is* the grain offering of jealousy. And the priest shall have in his hand the bitter water that brings a curse. [19]And the priest shall put her under oath, and say to the woman, "If no man has lain with you, and if you have not gone astray to uncleanness *while* under your husband's *authority,* be free from this bitter water that brings a curse. [20]But if you have gone astray *while* under your husband's *authority,* and if you have defiled yourself and some man other than your husband has lain with you"— [21]then the priest shall put the woman under the oath of the curse, and he shall say to the woman—"the LORD make you a curse and an oath among your people, when the LORD makes your thigh rot and your belly swell; [22]and may this water that causes the curse go into your stomach, and make *your* belly swell and *your* thigh rot."

Then the woman shall say, "Amen, so be it."

[23]Then the priest shall write these curses in a book, and he shall scrape *them* off into the bitter water. [24]And he shall make the woman drink the bitter water that brings a curse, and the water that brings the curse shall enter her *to become* bitter. [25]Then the priest shall take the grain offering of jealousy from the woman's hand, shall wave the offering before the LORD, and bring it to the altar; [26]and the priest shall take a handful of the offering, as its memorial portion, burn *it* on the altar, and afterward make the woman drink the water. [27]When he has made her drink the water, then it shall be, if she has defiled herself and behaved unfaithfully toward her husband, that the water that brings a curse will enter her *and become* bitter, and her belly will swell, her thigh will rot, and the woman will become a curse among her people. [28]But if the woman has not defiled herself, and is clean, then she shall be free and may conceive children.

[29]'This *is* the law of jealousy, when a wife, *while* under her husband's *authority,* goes astray and defiles herself, [30]or when the spirit of jealousy comes upon a man, and he becomes jealous of his wife; then he shall stand the woman before the LORD, and the priest shall execute all this law upon her. [31]Then the man shall be free from iniquity, but that woman shall bear her guilt.'"

The Law of the Nazirite

6 Then the LORD spoke to Moses, saying, [2]"Speak to the children of Israel, and say to them: 'When either a man or woman consecrates an offering to take the vow of a Nazirite, to separate himself to the LORD, [3]he shall separate himself from wine and *similar* drink; he shall drink neither vinegar made from wine nor vinegar made from *similar* drink; neither shall he drink any grape juice, nor eat fresh grapes or raisins. [4]All the days of his separation he shall eat nothing that is produced by the grapevine, from seed to skin.

[5]'All the days of the vow of his separation no razor shall come upon his head; until the days are fulfilled for which he separated himself to the LORD, he shall be holy. *Then* he shall let the locks of the hair of his head grow. [6]All the days that he separates himself to the LORD he shall not go near a dead body. [7]He shall not make himself unclean even for his father or his mother, for his brother or his sister, when they die, because his separation to God *is* on his head. [8]All the days of his separation he shall be holy to the LORD.

[9]'And if anyone dies very suddenly beside him, and he defiles his consecrated head, then he shall shave his head on the day of his cleansing; on the seventh day he shall shave it. [10]Then on the eighth day he shall bring two turtledoves or two young pigeons to the priest, to the door of the tabernacle of meeting; [11]and the priest shall offer one as a sin offering and *the* other as a burnt offering, and make atonement for him, because he sinned in regard to the corpse; and he shall sanctify his head that same day. [12]He shall consecrate to the LORD the days of his separation, and bring a male lamb in its first year as a trespass offering; but the former days shall be lost, because his separation was defiled.

[13]'Now this *is* the law of the Nazirite: When the days of his separation are fulfilled, he shall be brought to the door of the tabernacle of meeting. [14]And he shall present his offering to the LORD: one male lamb in its first year without blemish as a burnt offering, one ewe lamb in its first year without blemish as a sin offering, one

ram without blemish as a peace offering, ¹⁵a basket of unleavened bread, cakes of fine flour mixed with oil, unleavened wafers anointed with oil, and their grain offering with their drink offerings.

¹⁶Then the priest shall bring *them* before the LORD and offer his sin offering and his burnt offering; ¹⁷and he shall offer the ram as a sacrifice of a peace offering to the LORD, with the basket of unleavened bread; the priest shall also offer its grain offering and its drink offering. ¹⁸Then the Nazirite shall shave his consecrated head *at* the door of the tabernacle of meeting, and shall take the hair from his consecrated head and put *it* on the fire which is under the sacrifice of the peace offering.

¹⁹And the priest shall take the boiled shoulder of the ram, one unleavened cake from the basket, and one unleavened wafer, and put *them* upon the hands of the Nazirite after he has shaved his consecrated *hair,* ²⁰and the priest shall wave them as a wave offering before the LORD; they *are* holy for the priest, together with the breast of the wave offering and the thigh of the heave offering. After that the Nazirite may drink wine.'

²¹"This is the law of the Nazirite who vows to the LORD the offering for his separation, and besides that, whatever else his hand is able to provide; according to the vow which he takes, so he must do according to the law of his separation."

The Priestly Blessing

²²And the LORD spoke to Moses, saying: ²³"Speak to Aaron and his sons, saying, 'This is the way you shall bless the children of Israel. Say to them:

²⁴   "The LORD bless you and keep you;
²⁵   The LORD make His face shine upon you,
       And be gracious to you;
²⁶   The LORD lift up His countenance upon you,
       And give you peace." '

²⁷"So they shall put My name on the children of Israel, and I will bless them."

Offerings of the Leaders

7 Now it came to pass, when Moses had finished setting up the tabernacle, that he anointed it and consecrated it and all its furnishings, and the altar and all its utensils; so he anointed them and consecrated them. ²Then the leaders of Israel, the heads of their fathers' houses, who *were* the leaders of the tribes and over those who were numbered, made an offering. ³And they brought their offering before the LORD, six covered

---

ROMANTIC QUOTES AND NOTES
The Power of Blessing Your Spouse

Even though God had promised to bless ancient Israel, He knew His people needed to hear that blessing spoken aloud and frequently. So God told Moses to say to Aaron, "This is the way you shall bless the children of Israel. Say to them: 'The LORD bless you and keep you; the LORD make His face shine upon you, and be gracious to you; the LORD lift up His countenance upon you, and give you peace.'" (6:23–26).

One of the most powerful truths for families found in the Old Testament is the power of blessing. The blessing in the Old Testament was never used flippantly, but in a deliberate act of prayer. Most of us have never considered how our words can be used to  bless our spouses and our children. When we bless another, we are setting them apart by invoking Almighty God's favor upon them.

As a husband and leader of your family, have you considered how you might formally bless your wife? Each child in your family? The blessing found in Numbers 6:24–26 is a profound way of consecrating those we love. Why not consider a time when you might ask your wife if you could bless her with this prayer, perhaps at the end of a date or at a special location that would set this time apart. Kneel beside her, place your hand on her shoulder and pray this blessing over her.

You may also want to consider how you would bless each of your children before sending them to college or getting married.

carts and twelve oxen, a cart for *every* two of the leaders, and for each one an ox; and they presented them before the tabernacle.

⁴Then the LORD spoke to Moses, saying, ⁵"Accept *these* from them, that they may be used in doing the work of the tabernacle of meeting; and you shall give them to the Levites, *to* every man according to his service." ⁶So Moses took the carts and the oxen, and gave them to the Levites. ⁷Two carts and four oxen he gave to the sons of Gershon, according to their service; ⁸and four carts and eight oxen he gave to the sons of Merari, according to their service, under the authorityª of Ithamar the son of Aaron the priest. ⁹But to the sons of Kohath he gave none, because theirs *was* the service of the holy things, *which* they carried on their shoulders.

¹⁰Now the leaders offered the dedication *offering* for the altar when it was anointed; so the leaders offered their offering before the altar. ¹¹For the LORD said to Moses, "They shall offer their offering, one leader each day, for the dedication of the altar."

¹²And the one who offered his offering on the first day *was* Nahshon the son of Amminadab, from the tribe of Judah. ¹³His offering *was* one silver platter, the weight of which *was* one hundred and thirty *shekels,* and one silver bowl of seventy shekels, according to the shekel of the sanctuary, both of them full of fine flour mixed with oil as a grain offering; ¹⁴one gold pan of ten *shekels,* full of incense; ¹⁵one young bull, one ram, and one male lamb in its first year, as a burnt offering; ¹⁶one kid of the goats as a sin offering; ¹⁷and for the sacrifice of peace offerings: two oxen, five rams, five male goats, and five male lambs in their first year. This *was* the offering of Nahshon the son of Amminadab.

¹⁸On the second day Nethanel the son of Zuar, leader of Issachar, presented *an offering.* ¹⁹For his offering he offered one silver platter, the weight of which *was* one hundred and thirty *shekels,* and one silver bowl of seventy shekels, according to the shekel of the sanctuary, both of them full of fine flour mixed with oil as a grain offering; ²⁰one gold pan of ten *shekels,* full of incense; ²¹one

young bull, one ram, and one male lamb in its first year, as a burnt offering; ²²one kid of the goats as a sin offering; ²³and as the sacrifice of peace offerings: two oxen, five rams, five male goats, and five male lambs in their first year. This *was* the offering of Nethanel the son of Zuar.

²⁴On the third day Eliab the son of Helon, leader of the children of Zebulun, *presented an offering.* ²⁵His offering *was* one silver platter, the weight of which *was* one hundred and thirty *shekels,* and one silver bowl of seventy shekels, according to the shekel of the sanctuary, both of them full of fine flour mixed with oil as a grain offering; ²⁶one gold pan of ten *shekels,* full of incense; ²⁷one young bull, one ram, and one male lamb in its first year, as a burnt offering; ²⁸one kid of the goats as a sin offering; ²⁹and for the sacrifice of peace offerings: two oxen, five rams, five male goats, and five male lambs in their first year. This *was* the offering of Eliab the son of Helon.

³⁰On the fourth day Elizur the son of Shedeur, leader of the children of Reuben, *presented an offering.* ³¹His offering *was* one silver platter, the weight of which *was* one hundred and thirty *shekels,* and one silver bowl of seventy shekels, according to the shekel of the sanctuary, both of them full of fine flour mixed with oil as a grain offering; ³²one gold pan of ten *shekels,* full of incense; ³³one young bull, one ram, and one male lamb in its first year, as a burnt offering; ³⁴one kid of the goats as a sin offering; ³⁵and as the sacrifice of peace offerings: two oxen, five rams, five male goats, and five male lambs in their first year. This *was* the offering of Elizur the son of Shedeur.

³⁶On the fifth day Shelumiel the son of Zurishaddai, leader of the children of Simeon, *presented an offering.* ³⁷His offering *was* one silver platter, the weight of which *was* one hundred and thirty *shekels,* and one silver bowl of seventy shekels, according to the shekel of the sanctuary, both of them full of fine flour mixed with oil as a grain offering; ³⁸one gold pan of ten *shekels,* full of incense; ³⁹one young bull, one ram, and one male lamb in its first year, as a burnt offering; ⁴⁰one kid of the goats

---

7:8 ªLiterally *hand*

as a sin offering; [41]and as the sacrifice of peace offerings: two oxen, five rams, five male goats, and five male lambs in their first year. This *was* the offering of Shelumiel the son of Zurishaddai.

[42]On the sixth day Eliasaph the son of Deuel,[a] leader of the children of Gad, *presented an offering.* [43]His offering *was* one silver platter, the weight of which *was* one hundred and thirty *shekels,* and one silver bowl of seventy shekels, according to the shekel of the sanctuary, both of them full of fine flour mixed with oil as a grain offering; [44]one gold pan of ten *shekels,* full of incense; [45]one young bull, one ram, and one male lamb in its first year, as a burnt offering; [46]one kid of the goats as a sin offering; [47]and as the sacrifice of peace offerings: two oxen, five rams, five male goats, and five male lambs in their first year. This *was* the offering of Eliasaph the son of Deuel.

[48]On the seventh day Elishama the son of Ammihud, leader of the children of Ephraim, *presented an offering.* [49]His offering *was* one silver platter, the weight of which *was* one hundred and thirty *shekels,* and one silver bowl of seventy shekels, according to the shekel of the sanctuary, both of them full of fine flour mixed with oil as a grain offering; [50]one gold pan of ten *shekels,* full of incense; [51]one young bull, one ram, and one male lamb in its first year, as a burnt offering; [52]one kid of the goats as a sin offering; [53]and as the sacrifice of peace offerings: two oxen, five rams, five male goats, and five male lambs in their first year. This *was* the offering of Elishama the son of Ammihud.

[54]On the eighth day Gamaliel the son of Pedahzur, leader of the children of Manasseh, *presented an offering.* [55]His offering *was* one silver platter, the weight of which *was* one hundred and thirty *shekels,* and one silver bowl of seventy shekels, according to the shekel of the sanctuary, both of them full of fine flour mixed with oil as a grain offering; [56]one gold pan of ten *shekels,* full of incense; [57]one young bull, one ram, and one male lamb in its first year, as a burnt offering; [58]one kid of the goats as a sin offering; [59]and as the sacrifice of peace offerings: two oxen, five rams, five male goats, and five male lambs in their

first year. This *was* the offering of Gamaliel the son of Pedahzur.

[60]On the ninth day Abidan the son of Gideoni, leader of the children of Benjamin, *presented an offering.* [61]His offering *was* one silver platter, the weight of which *was* one hundred and thirty *shekels,* and one silver bowl of seventy shekels, according to the shekel of the sanctuary, both of them full of fine flour mixed with oil as a grain offering; [62]one gold pan of ten *shekels,* full of incense; [63]one young bull, one ram, and one male lamb in its first year, as a burnt offering; [64]one kid of the goats as a sin offering; [65]and as the sacrifice of peace offerings: two oxen, five rams, five male goats, and five male lambs in their first year. This *was* the offering of Abidan the son of Gideoni.

[66]On the tenth day Ahiezer the son of Ammishaddai, leader of the children of Dan, *presented an offering.* [67]His offering *was* one silver platter, the weight of which *was* one hundred and thirty *shekels,* and one silver bowl of seventy shekels, according to the shekel of the sanctuary, both of them full of fine flour mixed with oil as a grain offering; [68]one gold pan of ten *shekels,* full of incense; [69]one young bull, one ram, and one male lamb in its first year, as a burnt offering; [70]one kid of the goats as a sin offering; [71]and as the sacrifice of peace offerings: two oxen, five rams, five male goats, and five male lambs in their first year. This *was* the offering of Ahiezer the son of Ammishaddai.

[72]On the eleventh day Pagiel the son of Ocran, leader of the children of Asher, *presented an offering.* [73]His offering *was* one silver platter, the weight of which *was* one hundred and thirty *shekels,* and one silver bowl of seventy shekels, according to the shekel of the sanctuary, both of them full of fine flour mixed with oil as a grain offering; [74]one gold pan of ten *shekels,* full of incense; [75]one young bull, one ram, and one male lamb in its first year, as a burnt offering; [76]one kid of the goats as a sin offering; [77]and as the sacrifice of peace offerings: two oxen, five rams, five male goats, and five male lambs in their first year. This *was* the offering of Pagiel the son of Ocran.

7:42 [a]Spelled *Reuel* in 2:14

⁷⁸On the twelfth day Ahira the son of Enan, leader of the children of Naphtali, *presented an offering.* ⁷⁹His offering *was* one silver platter, the weight of which *was* one hundred and thirty *shekels,* and one silver bowl of seventy shekels, according to the shekel of the sanctuary, both of them full of fine flour mixed with oil as a grain offering; ⁸⁰one gold pan of ten *shekels,* full of incense; ⁸¹one young bull, one ram, and one male lamb in its first year, as a burnt offering; ⁸²one kid of the goats as a sin offering; ⁸³and as the sacrifice of peace offerings: two oxen, five rams, five male goats, and five male lambs in their first year. This *was* the offering of Ahira the son of Enan.

⁸⁴This *was* the dedication *offering* for the altar from the leaders of Israel, when it was anointed: twelve silver platters, twelve silver bowls, and twelve gold pans. ⁸⁵Each silver platter *weighed* one hundred and thirty *shekels* and each bowl seventy *shekels.* All the silver of the vessels *weighed* two thousand four hundred *shekels,* according to the shekel of the sanctuary. ⁸⁶The twelve gold pans full of incense *weighed* ten *shekels* apiece, according to the shekel of the sanctuary; all the gold of the pans *weighed* one hundred and twenty *shekels.* ⁸⁷All the oxen for the burnt offering *were* twelve young bulls, the rams twelve, the male lambs in their first year twelve, with their grain offering, and the kids of the goats as a sin offering twelve. ⁸⁸And all the oxen for the sacrifice of peace offerings were twenty-four bulls, the rams sixty, the male goats sixty, and the lambs in their first year sixty. This *was* the dedication *offering* for the altar after it was anointed.

⁸⁹Now when Moses went into the tabernacle of meeting to speak with Him, he heard the voice of One speaking to him from above the mercy seat that *was* on the ark of the Testimony, from between the two cherubim; thus He spoke to him.

Arrangement of the Lamps

8 And the LORD spoke to Moses, saying: ²"Speak to Aaron, and say to him, 'When you arrange the lamps, the seven lamps shall give light in front of the lampstand.'" ³And Aaron did so; he arranged the lamps to face toward the front of the lampstand, as the LORD commanded Moses. ⁴Now this workmanship of the lampstand *was* hammered gold; from its shaft to its flowers it *was* hammered work. According to the pattern which the LORD had shown Moses, so he made the lampstand.

Cleansing and Dedication of the Levites

⁵Then the LORD spoke to Moses, saying: ⁶"Take the Levites from among the children of Israel and cleanse them *ceremonially.* ⁷Thus you shall do to them to cleanse them: Sprinkle water of purification on them, and let them shave all their body, and let them

---

The Pattern Fits

If you've ever sewn a dress, you know how a pattern works. When you begin, you don't have a garment, but only some scraps of cloth. When it's properly fitted together and made usable with buttons, a zipper, or snaps, however, these incomplete pieces make a whole dress.

Every pattern has pairs of parts: two sleeves, two bodice pieces, a front and back skirt; even the collar and facing pieces usually come in twos. That's how it is in marriage. God has designed a master pattern for husbands and wives that, when followed, will create a whole, usable, beautiful marriage.

I have experienced many frustrations in trying to fit in my part of the marriage pattern with my husband's. At times it felt too hard. Yet I know by faith, and am convinced by experience, that God's pattern for me as a wife is not meant to restrict my creativity in expressing who I am. If I trust the pattern, the finished product reflects the full beauty that its Creator intended. When this becomes a reality in my life, I experience oneness with God, oneness with my husband, and a real freedom to be all that God made me to be.

wash their clothes, and *so* make themselves clean. [8]Then let them take a young bull with its grain offering of fine flour mixed with oil, and you shall take another young bull as a sin offering. [9]And you shall bring the Levites before the tabernacle of meeting, and you shall gather together the whole congregation of the children of Israel. [10]So you shall bring the Levites before the LORD, and the children of Israel shall lay their hands on the Levites; [11]and Aaron shall offer the Levites before the LORD *like* a wave offering from the children of Israel, that they may perform the work of the LORD. [12]Then the Levites shall lay their hands on the heads of the young bulls, and you shall offer one as a sin offering and the other as a burnt offering to the LORD, to make atonement for the Levites.

[13]"And you shall stand the Levites before Aaron and his sons, and then offer them *like* a wave offering to the LORD. [14]Thus you shall separate the Levites from among the children of Israel, and the Levites shall be Mine. [15]After that the Levites shall go in to service the tabernacle of meeting. So you shall cleanse them and offer them *like* a wave offering. [16]For they *are* wholly given to Me from among the children of Israel; I have taken them for Myself instead of all who open the womb, the firstborn of all the children of Israel. [17]For all the firstborn among the children of Israel *are* Mine, *both* man and beast; on the day that I struck all the firstborn in the land of Egypt I sanctified them to Myself. [18]I have taken the Levites instead of all the firstborn of the children of Israel. [19]And I have given the Levites as a gift to Aaron and his sons from among the children of Israel, to do the work for the children of Israel in the tabernacle of meeting, and to make atonement for the children of Israel, that there be no plague among the children of Israel when the children of Israel come near the sanctuary."

[20]Thus Moses and Aaron and all the congregation of the children of Israel did to the Levites; according to all that the LORD commanded Moses concerning the Levites, so the children of Israel did to them. [21]And the Levites purified themselves and washed their clothes; then Aaron presented them *like* a wave offering before the LORD, and

Aaron made atonement for them to cleanse them. [22]After that the Levites went in to do their work in the tabernacle of meeting before Aaron and his sons; as the LORD commanded Moses concerning the Levites, so they did to them.

[23]Then the LORD spoke to Moses, saying, [24]"This *is* what *pertains* to the Levites: From twenty-five years old and above one may enter to perform service in the work of the tabernacle of meeting; [25]and at the age of fifty years they must cease performing this work, and shall work no more. [26]They may minister with their brethren in the tabernacle of meeting, to attend to needs, but they *themselves* shall do no work. Thus you shall do to the Levites regarding their duties."

The Second Passover

9 Now the LORD spoke to Moses in the Wilderness of Sinai, in the first month of the second year after they had come out of the land of Egypt, saying: [2]"Let the children of Israel keep the Passover at its appointed time. [3]On the fourteenth day of this month, at twilight, you shall keep it at its appointed time. According to all its rites and ceremonies you shall keep it." [4]So Moses told the children of Israel that they should keep the Passover. [5]And they kept the Passover on the fourteenth day of the first month, at twilight, in the Wilderness of Sinai; according to all that the LORD commanded Moses, so the children of Israel did.

[6]Now there were *certain* men who were defiled by a human corpse, so that they could not keep the Passover on that day; and they came before Moses and Aaron that day. [7]And those men said to him, "We *became* defiled by a human corpse. Why are we kept from presenting the offering of the LORD at its appointed time among the children of Israel?"

[8]And Moses said to them, "Stand still, that I may hear what the LORD will command concerning you."

[9]Then the LORD spoke to Moses, saying, [10]"Speak to the children of Israel, saying: 'If anyone of you or your posterity is unclean because of a corpse, or *is* far away on a journey, he may still keep the LORD's Passover. [11]On the fourteenth day of the second month, at twilight, they may keep it.

They shall eat it with unleavened bread and bitter herbs. [12]They shall leave none of it until morning, nor break one of its bones. According to all the ordinances of the Passover they shall keep it. [13]But the man who *is* clean and is not on a journey, and ceases to keep the Passover, that same person shall be cut off from among his people, because he did not bring the offering of the LORD at its appointed time; that man shall bear his sin.

[14]'And if a stranger dwells among you, and would keep the LORD's Passover, he must do so according to the rite of the Passover and according to its ceremony; you shall have one ordinance, both for the stranger and the native of the land.'"

The Cloud and the Fire

[15]Now on the day that the tabernacle was raised up, the cloud covered the tabernacle, the tent of the Testimony; from evening until morning it was above the tabernacle like the appearance of fire. [16]So it was always: the cloud covered it *by day*, and the appearance of fire by night. [17]Whenever the cloud was taken up from above the tabernacle, after that the children of Israel would journey; and in the place where the cloud settled, there the children of Israel would pitch their tents. [18]At the command of the LORD the children of Israel would journey, and at the command of the LORD they would camp; as long as the cloud stayed above the tabernacle they remained encamped. [19]Even when the cloud continued long, many days above the tabernacle, the children of Israel kept the charge of the LORD and did not journey. [20]So it was, when the cloud was above the tabernacle a few days: according to the command of the LORD they would remain encamped, and according to the command of the LORD they would journey. [21]So it was, when the cloud remained only from evening until morning: when the cloud was taken up in the morning, then they would journey; whether by day or by night, whenever the cloud was taken up, they would journey. [22]*Whether it was* two days, a month, or a year that the cloud remained above the tabernacle, the children of Israel would remain encamped and not journey; but when it was taken up, they

would journey. [23]At the command of the LORD they remained encamped, and at the command of the LORD they journeyed; they kept the charge of the LORD, at the command of the LORD by the hand of Moses.

Two Silver Trumpets

10 And the LORD spoke to Moses, saying: [2]"Make two silver trumpets for yourself; you shall make them of hammered work; you shall use them for calling the congregation and for directing the movement of the camps. [3]When they blow both of them, all the congregation shall gather before you at the door of the tabernacle of meeting. [4]But if they blow *only* one, then the leaders, the heads of the divisions of Israel, shall gather to you. [5]When you sound the advance, the camps that lie on the east side shall then begin their journey. [6]When you sound the advance the second time, then the camps that lie on the south side shall begin their journey; they shall sound the call for them to begin their journeys. [7]And when the assembly is to be gathered together, you shall blow, but not sound the advance. [8]The sons of Aaron, the priests, shall blow the trumpets; and these shall be to you as an ordinance forever throughout your generations.

[9]"When you go to war in your land against the enemy who oppresses you, then you shall sound an alarm with the trumpets, and you will be remembered before the LORD your God, and you will be saved from your enemies. [10]Also in the day of your gladness, in your appointed feasts, and at the beginning of your months, you shall blow the trumpets over your burnt offerings and over the sacrifices of your peace offerings; and they shall be a memorial for you before your God: I *am* the LORD your God."

Departure from Sinai

[11]Now it came to pass on the twentieth *day* of the second month, in the second year, that the cloud was taken up from above the tabernacle of the Testimony. [12]And the children of Israel set out from the Wilderness of Sinai on their journeys; then the cloud settled down in the Wilderness of Paran. [13]So they started out for the first

time according to the command of the LORD by the hand of Moses.

¹⁴The standard of the camp of the children of Judah set out first according to their armies; over their army was Nahshon the son of Amminadab. ¹⁵Over the army of the tribe of the children of Issachar *was* Nethanel the son of Zuar. ¹⁶And over the army of the tribe of the children of Zebulun *was* Eliab the son of Helon.

¹⁷Then the tabernacle was taken down; and the sons of Gershon and the sons of Merari set out, carrying the tabernacle.

¹⁸And the standard of the camp of Reuben set out according to their armies; over their army *was* Elizur the son of Shedeur. ¹⁹Over the army of the tribe of the children of Simeon *was* Shelumiel the son of Zurishaddai. ²⁰And over the army of the tribe of the children of Gad *was* Eliasaph the son of Deuel.

²¹Then the Kohathites set out, carrying the holy things. (The tabernacle would be prepared for their arrival.)

²²And the standard of the camp of the children of Ephraim set out according to their armies; over their army *was* Elishama the son of Ammihud. ²³Over the army of the tribe of the children of Manasseh *was* Gamaliel the son of Pedahzur. ²⁴And over the army of the tribe of the children of Benjamin *was* Abidan the son of Gideoni. ²⁵Then the standard of the camp of the children of Dan (the rear guard of all the camps) set out according to their armies; over their army *was* Ahiezer the son of Ammishaddai. ²⁶Over the army of the tribe of the children of Asher *was* Pagiel the son of Ocran. ²⁷And over the army of the tribe of the children of Naphtali *was* Ahira the son of Enan.

²⁸Thus *was* the order of march of the children of Israel, according to their armies, when they began their journey.

²⁹Now Moses said to Hobab the son of Reuelᵃ the Midianite, Moses' father-in-law, "We are setting out for the place of which the LORD said, 'I will give it to you.' Come with us, and we will treat you well; for the LORD has promised good things to Israel."

³⁰And he said to him, "I will not go, but I will depart to my *own* land and to my relatives."

³¹So *Moses* said, "Please do not leave, inasmuch as you know how we are to camp in the wilderness, and you can be our eyes. ³²And it shall be, if you go with us—indeed it shall be—that whatever good the LORD will do to us, the same we will do to you."

³³So they departed from the mountain of the LORD on a journey of three days; and the ark of the covenant of the LORD went before them for the three days' journey, to search out a resting place for them.

10:29 ᵃSeptuagint reads *Raguel* (compare Exodus 2:18).

ROMANTIC QUOTES AND NOTES
Don't Forget the Laughter

Did you know that laughter can cure the disease of self-importance? It's hard to puff yourself up to weather-balloon size if you deflate yourself with a good prick of self-directed humor!

How many laughs are you having—and how many at your own expense? God commanded His ancient people to enjoy a regular "day of … gladness" and sealed its importance with the reminder, "I am the LORD your God" (10:10). Before the wedding ceremony, couples should have a bold objective for their first year of marriage, "We will be found guilty of having too much fun rather than too little fun." That's not a bad objective for *any* year of marriage!

Courtship usually entails joy and romance and laughter, but this joy can quickly dry up after marriage. After we get married, our focus splinters in many directions, especially after children come *along. That's why we* need to make it a priority in marriage to find ways to participate in the fun, laugh-generating antics we did when we first dated. That requires us to flee from the television, telephone, and computer, in order to focus on each other. Find the time to laugh and seek to please each other!

³⁴And the cloud of the LORD *was* above them by day when they went out from the camp. ³⁵So it was, whenever the ark set out, that Moses said:

"Rise up, O LORD!
Let Your enemies be scattered,
And let those who hate You flee
before You."

³⁶And when it rested, he said:

"Return, O LORD,
To the many thousands of Israel."

The People Complain

11 Now *when* the people complained, it displeased the LORD; for the LORD heard *it,* and His anger was aroused. So the fire of the LORD burned among them, and consumed *some* in the outskirts of the camp. ²Then the people cried out to Moses, and when Moses prayed to the LORD, the fire was quenched. ³So he called the name of the place Taberah,ᵃ because the fire of the LORD had burned among them.

⁴Now the mixed multitude who were among them yielded to intense craving; so the children of Israel also wept again and said: "Who will give us meat to eat? ⁵We remember the fish which we ate freely in Egypt, the cucumbers, the melons, the leeks, the onions, and the garlic; ⁶but now our whole being *is* dried up; *there is* nothing at all except this manna *before* our eyes!"

⁷Now the manna *was* like coriander seed, and its color like the color of bdellium. ⁸The people went about and gathered *it,* ground *it* on millstones or beat *it* in the mortar, cooked *it* in pans, and made cakes of it; and its taste was like the taste of pastry prepared with oil. ⁹And when the dew fell on the camp in the night, the manna fell on it.

¹⁰Then Moses heard the people weeping throughout their families, everyone at the door of his tent; and the anger of the LORD was greatly aroused; Moses also was displeased. ¹¹So Moses said to the LORD, "Why have You afflicted Your servant? And why have I not found favor in Your sight, that You have laid the burden of all these people on me? ¹²Did I conceive all these people? Did I beget them, that You should say to me, 'Carry them in your bosom, as a guardian carries a nursing child,' to the land which You swore to their fathers? ¹³Where am I to get meat to give to all these people? For they weep all over me, saying, 'Give us meat, that we may eat.' ¹⁴I am not able to bear all these people alone, because the burden *is* too heavy for me. ¹⁵If You treat me like this, please kill me here and now—if I have found favor in Your sight—and do not let me see my wretchedness!"

The Seventy Elders

¹⁶So the LORD said to Moses: "Gather to Me seventy men of the elders of Israel, whom you know to be the elders of the people and officers over them; bring them to the tabernacle of meeting, that they may stand there with you. ¹⁷Then I will come down and talk with you there. I will take of the Spirit that *is* upon you and will put *the same* upon them; and they shall bear the burden of the people with you, that you may not bear *it* yourself alone. ¹⁸Then you shall say to the people, 'Consecrate yourselves for tomorrow, and you shall eat meat; for you have wept in the hearing of the LORD, saying, "Who will give us meat to eat? For *it was* well with us in Egypt." Therefore the LORD will give you meat, and you shall eat. ¹⁹You shall eat, not one day, nor two days, nor five days, nor ten days, nor twenty days, ²⁰but *for* a whole month, until it comes out of your nostrils and becomes loathsome to you, because you have despised the LORD who is among you, and have wept before Him, saying, "Why did we ever come up out of Egypt?" ' "

²¹And Moses said, "The people whom I *am* among *are* six hundred thousand men on foot; yet You have said, 'I will give them meat, that they may eat *for* a whole month.' ²²Shall flocks and herds be slaughtered for them, to provide enough for them? Or shall all the fish of the sea be gathered together for them, to provide enough for them?"

²³And the LORD said to Moses, "Has the LORD's arm been shortened? Now you shall see whether what I say will happen to you or not."

11:3 ᵃLiterally *Burning*

24So Moses went out and told the people the words of the LORD, and he gathered the seventy men of the elders of the people and placed them around the tabernacle. 25Then the LORD came down in the cloud, and spoke to him, and took of the Spirit that *was* upon him, and placed *the same* upon the seventy elders; and it happened, when the Spirit rested upon them, that they prophesied, although they never did *so* again.[a]

26But two men had remained in the camp: the name of one *was* Eldad, and the name of the other Medad. And the Spirit rested upon them. Now they *were* among those listed, but who had not gone out to the tabernacle; yet they prophesied in the camp. 27And a young man ran and told Moses, and said, "Eldad and Medad are prophesying in the camp."

28So Joshua the son of Nun, Moses' assistant, *one* of his choice men, answered and said, "Moses my lord, forbid them!" 29Then Moses said to him, "Are you zealous for my sake? Oh, that all the LORD's people were prophets *and* that the LORD would put His Spirit upon them!" 30And Moses returned to the camp, he and the elders of Israel.

The Lord Sends Quail

31Now a wind went out from the LORD, and it brought quail from the sea and left *them* fluttering near the camp, about a day's journey on this side and about a day's journey on the other side, all around the camp, and about two cubits above the surface of the ground. 32And the people stayed up all that day, all night, and all the next day, and gathered the quail (he who gathered least gathered ten homers); and they spread *them* out for themselves all around the camp. 33But while the meat *was* still between their teeth, before it was chewed, the wrath of the LORD was aroused against the people, and the LORD struck the people with a very great plague. 34So he called the name of that place Kibroth Hattaavah,[a] because there they buried the people who had yielded to craving.

35From Kibroth Hattaavah the people moved to Hazeroth, and camped at Hazeroth.

Dissension of Aaron and Miriam

12 Then Miriam and Aaron spoke against Moses because of the Ethiopian woman whom he had married; for he had married an Ethiopian woman. 2So they said, "Has the LORD indeed spoken only through Moses? Has He not spoken through us also?" And the LORD heard *it.* 3(Now the man Moses *was* very humble, more than all men who *were* on the face of the earth.)

4Suddenly the LORD said to Moses, Aaron, and Miriam, "Come out, you three, to the tabernacle of meeting!" So the three came out. 5Then the LORD came down in the pillar of cloud and stood *in* the door of the tabernacle, and called Aaron and Miriam. And they both went forward. 6Then He said,

"Hear now My words:
If there is a prophet among you,
I, the LORD, make Myself known to
    him in a vision;
I speak to him in a dream.
7   Not so with My servant Moses;
    He *is* faithful in all My house.
8   I speak with him face to face,
    Even plainly, and not in dark
        sayings;
    And he sees the form of the LORD.
    Why then were you not afraid
    To speak against My servant
        Moses?"

9So the anger of the LORD was aroused against them, and He departed. 10And when the cloud departed from above the tabernacle, suddenly Miriam *became* leprous, as *white as* snow. Then Aaron turned toward Miriam, and there she was, a leper. 11So Aaron said to Moses, "Oh, my lord! Please do not lay *this* sin on us, in which we have done foolishly and in which we have sinned. 12Please do not let her be as one dead, whose flesh is half consumed when he comes out of his mother's womb!"

13So Moses cried out to the LORD, saying, "Please heal her, O God, I pray!"

14Then the LORD said to Moses, "If her

11:25 [a]Targum and Vulgate read *did not cease.*
11:34 [a]Literally *Graves of Craving*

father had but spit in her face, would she not be shamed seven days? Let her be shut out of the camp seven days, and afterward she may be received *again.*" ¹⁵So Miriam was shut out of the camp seven days, and the people did not journey till Miriam was brought in *again.* ¹⁶And afterward the people moved from Hazeroth and camped in the Wilderness of Paran.

Spies Sent into Canaan

13 And the LORD spoke to Moses, saying, ²"Send men to spy out the land of Canaan, which I am giving to the children of Israel; from each tribe of their fathers you shall send a man, every one a leader among them."

³So Moses sent them from the Wilderness of Paran according to the command of the LORD, all of them men who *were* heads of the children of Israel. ⁴Now these *were* their names: from the tribe of Reuben, Shammua the son of Zaccur; ⁵from the tribe of Simeon, Shaphat the son of Hori; ⁶from the tribe of Judah, Caleb the son of Jephunneh; ⁷from the tribe of Issachar, Igal the son of Joseph; ⁸from the tribe of Ephraim, Hosheaᵃ the son of Nun; ⁹from the tribe of Benjamin, Palti the son of Raphu; ¹⁰from the tribe of Zebulun, Gaddiel the son of Sodi; ¹¹from the tribe of Joseph, *that is,* from the tribe of Manasseh, Gaddi the son of Susi; ¹²from the tribe of Dan, Ammiel the son of Gemalli; ¹³from the tribe of Asher, Sethur the son of Michael; ¹⁴from the tribe of Naphtali, Nahbi the son of Vophsi; ¹⁵from the tribe of Gad, Geuel the son of Machi.

¹⁶These *are* the names of the men whom Moses sent to spy out the land. And Moses called Hosheaᵃ the son of Nun, Joshua.

¹⁷Then Moses sent them to spy out the land of Canaan, and said to them, "Go up this *way* into the South, and go up to the mountains, ¹⁸and see what the land is like: whether the people who dwell in it *are* strong or weak, few or many; ¹⁹whether the land they dwell in *is* good or bad; whether the cities they inhabit *are* like

camps or strongholds; ²⁰whether the land *is* rich or poor; and whether there are forests there or not. Be of good courage. And bring some of the fruit of the land." Now the time *was* the season of the first ripe grapes.

²¹So they went up and spied out the land from the Wilderness of Zin as far as Rehob, near the entrance of Hamath. ²²And they went up through the South and came to Hebron; Ahiman, Sheshai, and Talmai, the descendants of Anak, *were* there. (Now Hebron was built seven years before Zoan in Egypt.) ²³Then they came to the Valley of Eshcol, and there cut down a branch with one cluster of grapes; they carried it between two of them on a pole. *They* also *brought* some of the pomegranates and figs. ²⁴The place was called the Valley of Eshcol,ᵃ because of the cluster which the men of Israel cut down there. ²⁵And they returned from spying out the land after forty days.

²⁶Now they departed and came back to Moses and Aaron and all the congregation of the children of Israel in the Wilderness of Paran, at Kadesh; they brought back word to them and to all the congregation, and showed them the fruit of the land. ²⁷Then they told him, and said: "We went to the land where you sent us. It truly flows with milk and honey, and this *is* its fruit. ²⁸Nevertheless the people who dwell in the land *are* strong; the cities *are* fortified *and* very large; moreover we saw the descendants of Anak there. ²⁹The Amalekites dwell in the land of the South; the Hittites, the Jebusites, and the Amorites dwell in the mountains; and the Canaanites dwell by the sea and along the banks of the Jordan."

³⁰Then Caleb quieted the people before Moses, and said, "Let us go up at once and take possession, for we are well able to overcome it."

³¹But the men who had gone up with him said, "We are not able to go up against the people, for they *are* stronger than we." ³²And they gave the children of Israel a bad report of the land which they had spied out, saying, "The land through which we have gone as spies *is* a land that devours its inhabitants, and all the people whom we saw in it *are* men of *great* stature. ³³There we saw the giantsᵃ (the descendants of

---

13:8 ᵃSeptuagint and Vulgate read *Oshea.*
13:16 ᵃSeptuagint and Vulgate read *Oshea.*
13:24 ᵃLiterally *Cluster* **13:33** ᵃHebrew *nephilim*

BIBLICAL INSIGHTS • 13:30
The Results of Belief

MY HEART RESONATES with Caleb. I want to be like him! In Numbers 13:30 we read, "Then Caleb quieted the people before Moses and said, 'Let us go up at once and take possession, for we are well able to overcome it.'"

Caleb believed the promises of God and he called the nation of Israel to take a step of faith. The Christian life is a faith adventure that we should embrace and call others to share with us.

I'm so convinced of the validity of the Scriptures and of God's promises that I will make this offer: I will renounce Christianity if any person can show me a better system on which to base my life. I have challenged hundreds with that offer, yet not one person has even suggested an alternative. It's not hard to see why. *There are none.*

Since I gave my life to Christ in 1969, I've attempted to live my life on what I know to be true. Here are some of those bedrock truths:

- Walking with God is an electrifying adventure. He is Sovereign.
- A life of faith brings a genuine and lasting sense of destiny and significance.
- It is a wonderful privilege to be used by God for His eternal purposes.
- His Holy Spirit empowers me to deny my selfishness and enables me to love people (some of whom I don't even like).
- When I obey God and walk with Him, I enjoy a sense of peace, well-being, and contentment.

Is there an area of your life for which you need to believe God's word and take a step of faith today? Be like Caleb. Step out and call your family to join you in the adventure of walking with God and being used by Him for His purposes.

Anak came from the giants); and we were like grasshoppers in our own sight, and so we were in their sight."

Israel Refuses to Enter Canaan

14 So all the congregation lifted up their voices and cried, and the people wept that night. ²And all the children of Israel complained against Moses and Aaron, and the whole congregation said to them, "If only we had died in the land of Egypt! Or if only we had died in this wilderness! ³Why has the LORD brought us to this land to fall by the sword, that our wives and children should become victims? Would it not be better for us to return to Egypt?" ⁴So they said to one another, "Let us select a leader and return to Egypt."

⁵Then Moses and Aaron fell on their faces before all the assembly of the congregation of the children of Israel.

⁶But Joshua the son of Nun and Caleb the son of Jephunneh, *who were* among those who had spied out the land, tore their clothes; ⁷and they spoke to all the congregation of the children of Israel, saying: "The land we passed through to spy out *is* an exceedingly good land. ⁸If the LORD delights in us, then He will bring us into this land and give it to us, 'a land which flows with milk and honey.'ᵃ ⁹Only do not rebel against the LORD, nor fear the people of the land, for they *are* our bread; their protection has departed from them, and the LORD *is* with us. Do not fear them."

¹⁰And all the congregation said to stone them with stones. Now the glory of the LORD appeared in the tabernacle of meeting before all the children of Israel.

Moses Intercedes for the People

¹¹Then the LORD said to Moses: "How long will these people reject Me? And how long will they not believe Me, with all the signs which I have performed among them? ¹²I will strike them with the pestilence and disinherit them, and I will make of you a nation greater and mightier than they."

¹³And Moses said to the LORD: "Then the Egyptians will hear *it*, for by Your might You brought these people up from among them, ¹⁴and they will tell *it* to the inhabitants of this land. They have heard that You, LORD, *are* among these people; that

14:8 ᵃExodus 3:8

You, LORD, are seen face to face and Your cloud stands above them, and You go before them in a pillar of cloud by day and in a pillar of fire by night. ¹⁵Now *if* You kill these people as one man, then the nations which have heard of Your fame will speak, saying, ¹⁶'Because the LORD was not able to bring this people to the land which He swore to give them, therefore He killed them in the wilderness.' ¹⁷And now, I pray, let the power of my Lord be great, just as You have spoken, saying, ¹⁸'The LORD is longsuffering and abundant in mercy, forgiving iniquity and transgression; but He by no means clears *the guilty,* visiting the iniquity of the fathers on the children to the third and fourth *generation.*'ᵃ ¹⁹Pardon the iniquity of this people, I pray, according to the greatness of Your mercy, just as You have forgiven this people, from Egypt even until now."

²⁰Then the LORD said: "I have pardoned, according to your word; ²¹but truly, as I live, all the earth shall be filled with the glory of the LORD— ²²because all these men who have seen My glory and the signs which I did in Egypt and in the wilderness, and have put Me to the test now these ten times, and have not heeded My voice, ²³they certainly shall not see the land of which I swore to their fathers, nor shall any of those who rejected Me see it. ²⁴But My servant Caleb, because he has a different spirit in him and has followed Me fully, I will bring into the land where he went, and his descendants shall inherit it. ²⁵Now the Amalekites and the Canaanites dwell in the valley; tomorrow turn and move out into the wilderness by the Way of the Red Sea."

Death Sentence on the Rebels

²⁶And the LORD spoke to Moses and Aaron, saying, ²⁷"How long *shall I bear with* this evil congregation who complain against Me? I have heard the complaints which the children of Israel make against Me. ²⁸Say to them, 'As I live,' says the LORD, 'just as you have spoken in My hearing, so I will do to you: ²⁹The carcasses of you who have complained against Me shall fall in this wilderness, all of you who were numbered,

14:18 ᵃExodus 34:6, 7

BIBLICAL INSIGHTS • 13:32
Where Is Your Focus?

AFTER EVERYTHING GOD had taken them through, the people of Israel just couldn't bring themselves to go that final step and claim what He had already promised them. The reason? Moses had sent twelve spies to check out the Land of Promise, and all but two of them came back to camp with a frightening report: "The land through which we have gone as spies is a land that devours its inhabitants, and all the people whom we saw in it are men of great stature. There we saw the giants ... and we were like grasshoppers in our own sight, and so we were in their sight" (13:32, 33).

Back in the early 70's when we were first beginning our ministry, I had a meeting with the President of Campus Crusade for Christ, Dr. Bill Bright. On his desk was an engraved plaque that read, "I'm No Grasshopper." Dr. Bright shared with me that he wanted to live his life as a man of faith, believing God for great things. As a young man, that message was engraved on my heart: Would I be a man of faith or would I become a grasshopper?

Focusing on the things that seem overwhelming can indeed make us feel small, like grasshoppers. But God has a better plan, and that is to keep our focus on Him, His promises, and His ability to do everything He says He'll do.

When you face a problem in your marriage or with your children, do you tend to focus more on how insurmountable the problem appears? Or do you respond in obedience and faith to the promises found in God's Word? Be courageous and trust God to take care of you and your family.

according to your entire number, from twenty years old and above. ³⁰Except for Caleb the son of Jephunneh and Joshua the son of Nun, you shall by no means enter the land which I swore I would make you dwell in.

Break Free

MOSES ONCE PRAYED for his wayward nation with a very specific request: "And now, I pray, let the power of my Lord be great, just as You have spoken, saying, 'The LORD is longsuffering and abundant in mercy, forgiving iniquity and transgression; but He by no means clears the guilty, visiting the iniquity of the fathers on the children to the third and fourth generation.' Pardon the iniquity of this people, I pray, according to the greatness of Your mercy, just as You have forgiven this people, from Egypt even until now" (14:17–19).

Too many people read this passage and others like it (see Deut. 5:9, 10) and wallow in guilt or fear, worrying that they are enslaved to their ancestors' wrong choices. They believe—wrongly—that they are permanently under the punishment of God because of the wicked things their forebears did.

You can stop the chain reaction through your repentance and confession. God in His grace stands ready to forgive you, to grant you His favor and to give you victory over your weaknesses. You can, by faith, stop even the most tyrannical control of some sin that has beset your family for generations by renouncing that sin and determining that you will begin a new chapter in your family's history (see Deut. 5:10).

---

³¹But your little ones, whom you said would be victims, I will bring in, and they shall know the land which you have despised. ³²But *as for* you, your carcasses shall fall in this wilderness. ³³And your sons shall be shepherds in the wilderness forty years, and bear the brunt of your infidelity, until your carcasses are consumed in the wilderness. ³⁴According to the number of the days in which you spied out the land, forty days, for each day you shall bear your guilt one year, *namely* forty years, and you shall know My

rejection. ³⁵I the LORD have spoken this. I will surely do so to all this evil congregation who are gathered together against Me. In this wilderness they shall be consumed, and there they shall die.'"

³⁶Now the men whom Moses sent to spy out the land, who returned and made all the congregation complain against him by bringing a bad report of the land, ³⁷those very men who brought the evil report about the land, died by the plague before the LORD. ³⁸But Joshua the son of Nun and Caleb the son of Jephunneh remained alive, of the men who went to spy out the land.

A Futile Invasion Attempt

³⁹Then Moses told these words to all the children of Israel, and the people mourned greatly. ⁴⁰And they rose early in the morning and went up to the top of the mountain, saying, "Here we are, and we will go up to the place which the LORD has promised, for we have sinned!"

⁴¹And Moses said, "Now why do you transgress the command of the LORD? For this will not succeed. ⁴²Do not go up, lest you be defeated by your enemies, for the LORD *is* not among you. ⁴³For the Amalekites and the Canaanites *are* there before you, and you shall fall by the sword; because you have turned away from the LORD, the LORD will not be with you."

⁴⁴But they presumed to go up to the mountaintop. Nevertheless, neither the ark of the covenant of the LORD nor Moses departed from the camp. ⁴⁵Then the Amalekites and the Canaanites who dwelt in that mountain came down and attacked them, and drove them back as far as Hormah.

Laws of Grain and Drink Offerings

15 And the LORD spoke to Moses, saying, ²"Speak to the children of Israel, and say to them: 'When you have come into the land you are to inhabit, which I am giving to you, ³and you make an offering by fire to the LORD, a burnt offering or a sacrifice, to fulfill a vow or as a freewill offering or in your appointed feasts, to make a sweet aroma to the LORD, from the herd or the flock, ⁴then he who presents his offering to the LORD shall bring a grain offering of

DEVOTIONS FOR COUPLES • 14:27
The Poison of Complaining

Few things steal the joy and harmony in a marriage than complaining and grumbling. Let's take a look at what God's Word says about complaining and why we need to avoid it.

1. *Realize that complaining is dangerous.* In recent days a number of Christian leaders have fallen into immorality—and I have wondered how many more Christians have been declared unusable by God because of their complaining. If the enemy of our soul can't derail us through lust or immorality, then he will seek a different bait for his trap. For many of us, that snare is the temptation to gripe, grumble, and complain against God (Num. 14:27; 1 Cor. 9:24—10:13). Illicit sex is not the only sin that puts Christians on the sidelines!

2. *Remember, God knows what He is doing.* The Old Testament hero Joseph is a great example for me. First, his brothers threw him into a pit and sold him into slavery. Then he's unjustly accused of fooling around with Potiphar's wife, thrown into prison, forgotten by a friend he had helped, and yet Scripture doesn't record a single complaint. He could've become bitter against his brothers. He didn't. He could've smashed his fist against the prison walls and complained about his unjust circumstances. He didn't.

What was the secret of his complaint-free life? The answer is found in Genesis 45:5–8, where we find Joseph, now the governor of Egypt, addressing his starving brothers, "And now do not be grieved or angry with yourselves ... because God has sent me before you to preserve life." Three times in four verses Joseph says, "*God* sent me here." Joseph grasped the truth that God is in control and that He knows what He is doing.

3. *Put away past complaints that may have turned bitter.* A grudge is an aging complaint, still actively held. The longer you carry a complaint, the greater the probability it will become a grudge too heavy to handle. If you have a complaint against a brother—or your spouse—go to him or her in private and clear the slate.

4. *Keep on giving thanks in all things (1 Thess. 5:18).* This is not just some power of positive thinking approach! No, we will never give thanks unless we see God as the Sovereign Ruler of the Universe, at work in our lives through our circumstances, even the ones we don't especially care for.

---

one-tenth *of an ephah* of fine flour mixed with one-fourth of a hin of oil; [5]and one-fourth of a hin of wine as a drink offering you shall prepare with the burnt offering or the sacrifice, for each lamb. [6]Or for a ram you shall prepare as a grain offering two-tenths *of an ephah* of fine flour mixed with one-third of a hin of oil; [7]and as a drink offering you shall offer one-third of a hin of wine as a sweet aroma to the LORD. [8]And when you prepare a young bull as a burnt offering, or as a sacrifice to fulfill a vow, or as a peace offering to the LORD, [9]then shall be offered with the young bull a grain offering of three-tenths *of an ephah* of fine flour mixed with half a hin of oil; [10]and you shall bring as the drink offering half a hin of wine as an offering made by fire, a sweet aroma to the LORD.

[11]Thus it shall be done for each young bull, for each ram, or for each lamb or young goat. [12]According to the number that you prepare, so you shall do with everyone according to their number. [13]All who are native-born shall do these things in this manner, in presenting an offering made by fire, a sweet aroma to the LORD. [14]And if a stranger dwells with you, or whoever *is* among you throughout your generations, and would present an offering made by fire, a sweet aroma to the LORD, just as you do, so shall he do. [15]One ordinance *shall be* for you of the assembly and for the stranger who dwells *with you,* an ordinance forever throughout your generations; as you are, so shall the stranger be before the LORD. [16]One law and one custom shall be for you and for the stranger who dwells with you.'"[a]

[17]Again the LORD spoke to Moses, saying,

15:16 [a]Compare Exodus 12:49

[18]"Speak to the children of Israel, and say to them: 'When you come into the land to which I bring you, [19]then it will be, when you eat of the bread of the land, that you shall offer up a heave offering to the LORD. [20]You shall offer up a cake of the first of your ground meal *as* a heave offering; as a heave offering of the threshing floor, so shall you offer it up. [21]Of the first of your ground meal you shall give to the LORD a heave offering throughout your generations.

Laws Concerning Unintentional Sin

[22]'If you sin unintentionally, and do not observe all these commandments which the LORD has spoken to Moses— [23]all that the LORD has commanded you by the hand of Moses, from the day the LORD gave commandment and onward throughout your generations— [24]then it will be, if it is unintentionally committed, without the knowledge of the congregation, that the whole congregation shall offer one young bull as a burnt offering, as a sweet aroma to the LORD, with its grain offering and its drink offering, according to the ordinance, and one kid of the goats as a sin offering. [25]So the priest shall make atonement for the whole congregation of the children of Israel, and it shall be forgiven them, for it was unintentional; they shall bring their offering, an offering made by fire to the LORD, and their sin offering before the LORD, for their unintended sin. [26]It shall be forgiven the whole congregation of the children of Israel and the stranger who dwells among them, because all the people *did it* unintentionally.

[27]'And if a person sins unintentionally, then he shall bring a female goat in its first year as a sin offering. [28]So the priest shall make atonement for the person who sins unintentionally, when he sins unintentionally before the LORD, to make atonement for him; and it shall be forgiven him. [29]You shall have one law for him who sins unintentionally, *for* him who is native-born among the children of Israel and for the stranger who dwells among them.

Law Concerning Presumptuous Sin

[30]'But the person who does *anything* presumptuously, *whether he is* native-born or a stranger, that one brings reproach on the LORD, and he shall be cut off from among his people. [31]Because he has despised the word of the LORD, and has broken His commandment, that person shall be completely cut off; his guilt *shall be* upon him.'"

Penalty for Violating the Sabbath

[32]Now while the children of Israel were in the wilderness, they found a man gathering sticks on the Sabbath day. [33]And those who found him gathering sticks brought him to Moses and Aaron, and to all the congregation. [34]They put him under guard, because it had not been explained what should be done to him.

[35]Then the LORD said to Moses, "The man must surely be put to death; all the congregation shall stone him with stones outside the camp." [36]So, as the LORD commanded Moses, all the congregation brought him outside the camp and stoned him with stones, and he died.

Tassels on Garments

[37]Again the LORD spoke to Moses, saying, [38]"Speak to the children of Israel: Tell them to make tassels on the corners of their garments throughout their generations, and to put a blue thread in the tassels of the corners. [39]And you shall have the tassel, that you may look upon it and remember all the commandments of the LORD and do them, and that you *may* not follow the harlotry to which your own heart and your own eyes are inclined, [40]and that you may remember and do all My commandments, and be holy for your God. [41]I *am* the LORD your God, who brought you out of the land of Egypt, to be your God: I *am* the LORD your God."

Rebellion Against Moses and Aaron

16 Now Korah the son of Izhar, the son of Kohath, the son of Levi, with Dathan and Abiram the sons of Eliab, and On the son of Peleth, sons of Reuben, took *men;* [2]and they rose up before Moses with some of the children of Israel, two hundred and fifty leaders of the congregation, representatives of the congregation, men of renown. [3]They gathered together against Moses and Aaron, and said to them, "*You*

take too much upon yourselves, for all the congregation *is* holy, every one of them, and the LORD *is* among them. Why then do you exalt yourselves above the assembly of the LORD?"

[4]So when Moses heard *it,* he fell on his face; [5]and he spoke to Korah and all his company, saying, "Tomorrow morning the LORD will show who *is* His and *who is* holy, and will cause *him* to come near to Him. That one whom He chooses He will cause to come near to Him. [6]Do this: Take censers, Korah and all your company; [7]put fire in them and put incense in them before the LORD tomorrow, and it shall be *that* the man whom the LORD chooses *is* the holy one. *You take* too much upon yourselves, you sons of Levi!"

[8]Then Moses said to Korah, "Hear now, you sons of Levi: [9]*Is it* a small thing to you that the God of Israel has separated you from the congregation of Israel, to bring you near to Himself, to do the work of the tabernacle of the LORD, and to stand before the congregation to serve them; [10]and that He has brought you near *to Himself,* you and all your brethren, the sons of Levi, with you? And are you seeking the priesthood also? [11]Therefore you and all your company *are* gathered together against the LORD. And what *is* Aaron that you complain against him?"

[12]And Moses sent to call Dathan and Abiram the sons of Eliab, but they said, "We will not come up! [13]*Is it* a small thing that you have brought us up out of a land flowing with milk and honey, to kill us in the wilderness, that you should keep acting like a prince over us? [14]Moreover you have not brought us into a land flowing with milk and honey, nor given us inheritance of fields and vineyards. Will you put out the eyes of these men? We will not come up!"

[15]Then Moses was very angry, and said to the LORD, "Do not respect their offering. I have not taken one donkey from them, nor have I hurt one of them."

[16]And Moses said to Korah, "Tomorrow, you and all your company be present before the LORD—you and they, as well as Aaron. [17]Let each take his censer and put incense in it, and each of you bring his censer before the LORD, two hundred and fifty censers;

BIBLICAL INSIGHTS • 16
The Power of Influencers

SO MUCH OF THE HARDSHIP that overtook the Israelites in the wilderness occurred because naïve people followed the lead of evil men. A wicked man named Korah, for example, was personally responsible for leading thousands of God's people to their deaths.

The Bible speaks pointedly on the power of your peers to influence us toward good behavior or bad. Paul wrote, "Do not be deceived: 'Evil company corrupts good habits'" (1 Cor. 15:33).

Peers—for good and bad—can tug on all of us, but will almost certainly tug at our teenagers. Outside the guidance we continue to have at home, nothing will influence our children as much as the choice of their friends.

The opposite is also true: good company guards against the development of bad habits. Many parents are so afraid of peer pressure they seldom use good peer pressure to their advantage.

As parents, we must prepare our children to combat the most insidious forms of peer pressure. This literally can be a life and death issue. Through choosing the right friends and developing and owning the right convictions, children can learn when it's okay to gallop with the herd and when it's better to graze alone.

both you and Aaron, each *with* his censer." [18]So every man took his censer, put fire in it, laid incense on it, and stood at the door of the tabernacle of meeting with Moses and Aaron. [19]And Korah gathered all the congregation against them at the door of the tabernacle of meeting. Then the glory of the LORD appeared to all the congregation.

[20]And the LORD spoke to Moses and Aaron, saying, [21]"Separate yourselves from among this congregation, that I may consume them in a moment."

[22]Then they fell on their faces, and said, "O God, the God of the spirits of all flesh,

shall one man sin, and You be angry with all the congregation?"

²³So the LORD spoke to Moses, saying, ²⁴"Speak to the congregation, saying, 'Get away from the tents of Korah, Dathan, and Abiram.'"

²⁵Then Moses rose and went to Dathan and Abiram, and the elders of Israel followed him. ²⁶And he spoke to the congregation, saying, "Depart now from the tents of these wicked men! Touch nothing of theirs, lest you be consumed in all their sins." ²⁷So they got away from around the tents of Korah, Dathan, and Abiram; and Dathan and Abiram came out and stood at the door of their tents, with their wives, their sons, and their little children.

²⁸And Moses said: "By this you shall know that the LORD has sent me to do all these works, for *I have* not *done them* of my own will. ²⁹If these men die naturally like all men, or if they are visited by the common fate of all men, *then* the LORD has not sent me. ³⁰But if the LORD creates a new thing, and the earth opens its mouth and swallows them up with all that belongs to them, and they go down alive into the pit, then you will understand that these men have rejected the LORD."

³¹Now it came to pass, as he finished speaking all these words, that the ground split apart under them, ³²and the earth opened its mouth and swallowed them up, with their households and all the men with Korah, with all *their* goods. ³³So they and all those with them went down alive into the pit; the earth closed over them, and they perished from among the assembly. ³⁴Then all Israel who *were* around them fled at their cry, for they said, "Lest the earth swallow us up *also!*"

³⁵And a fire came out from the LORD and consumed the two hundred and fifty men who were offering incense.

³⁶Then the LORD spoke to Moses, saying: ³⁷"Tell Eleazar, the son of Aaron the priest, to pick up the censers out of the blaze, for they are holy, and scatter the fire some distance away. ³⁸The censers of these men who sinned against their own souls, let them be made into hammered plates as a covering for the altar. Because they presented them before the LORD, therefore they are holy; and they shall be a sign to the children of Israel." ³⁹So Eleazar the priest took the bronze censers, which those who were burned up had presented, and they were hammered out as a covering on the altar,

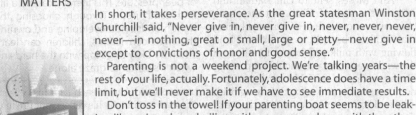

PARENTING MATTERS

Q: How do we handle rebellious or unresponsive children?

In short, it takes perseverance. As the great statesman Winston Churchill said, "Never give in, never give in, never, never, never, never—in nothing, great or small, large or petty—never give in except to convictions of honor and good sense."

Parenting is not a weekend project. We're talking years—the rest of your life, actually. Fortunately, adolescence does have a time limit, but we'll never make it if we have to see immediate results.

Don't toss in the towel! If your parenting boat seems to be leaking like a sieve, keep bailing with one arm and row with the other. Perseverance is the indispensable parenting quality that helps you keep doing all the other important things—praying, training, and setting standards.

You *will* get tired. You *will* suffer pain. Your heart *will* ache. The ones for whom you are sacrificing—your children—will sometimes say and do things that hurt you. They do that because they are children, and "Foolishness is bound up in the heart of a child" (Prov. 22:15).

At times you may have to endure even a broken heart, but you must not lose heart, "for in due time we shall reap if we do not grow weary" (Gal. 6:9).

⁴⁰*to be* a memorial to the children of Israel that no outsider, who *is* not a descendant of Aaron, should come near to offer incense before the LORD, that he might not become like Korah and his companions, just as the LORD had said to him through Moses.

Complaints of the People

⁴¹On the next day all the congregation of the children of Israel complained against Moses and Aaron, saying, "You have killed the people of the LORD." ⁴²Now it happened, when the congregation had gathered against Moses and Aaron, that they turned toward the tabernacle of meeting; and suddenly the cloud covered it, and the glory of the LORD appeared. ⁴³Then Moses and Aaron came before the tabernacle of meeting.

⁴⁴And the LORD spoke to Moses, saying, ⁴⁵"Get away from among this congregation, that I may consume them in a moment."

And they fell on their faces.

⁴⁶So Moses said to Aaron, "Take a censer and put fire in it from the altar, put incense *on it*, and take it quickly to the congregation and make atonement for them; for wrath has gone out from the LORD. The plague has begun." ⁴⁷Then Aaron took *it* as Moses commanded, and ran into the midst of the assembly; and already the plague had begun among the people. So he put in the incense and made atonement for the people. ⁴⁸And he stood between the dead and the living; so the plague was stopped. ⁴⁹Now those who died in the plague were fourteen thousand seven hundred, besides those who died in the Korah incident. ⁵⁰So Aaron returned to Moses at the door of the tabernacle of meeting, for the plague had stopped.

The Budding of Aaron's Rod

17 And the LORD spoke to Moses, saying: ²"Speak to the children of Israel, and get from them a rod from each father's house, all their leaders according to their fathers' houses—twelve rods. Write each man's name on his rod. ³And you shall write Aaron's name on the rod of Levi. For there shall be one rod for the head of *each* father's house. ⁴Then you shall place them in the tabernacle of meeting before the Testimony, where I meet with you. ⁵And it shall be *that*

the rod of the man whom I choose will blossom; thus I will rid Myself of the complaints of the children of Israel, which they make against you."

⁶So Moses spoke to the children of Israel, and each of their leaders gave him a rod apiece, for each leader according to their fathers' houses, twelve rods; and the rod of Aaron *was* among their rods. ⁷And Moses placed the rods before the LORD in the tabernacle of witness.

⁸Now it came to pass on the next day that Moses went into the tabernacle of witness, and behold, the rod of Aaron, of the house of Levi, had sprouted and put forth buds, had produced blossoms and yielded

---

ROMANCE FAQ

Q: *What can a woman do when her husband gains an unattractive amount of weight?*

An important ingredient of any marriage is the need for husbands and wives to please each other. Obviously, no husband can lose weight overnight; but if he is seeking to please his wife, then he can make an effort to look sharp and attractive.

Pray that the Lord would grant you opportunities to express how you feel in a gentle and supportive way. Ask if there is anything you can do to help. Ask God to help you avoid bitterness toward your husband. Don't become preoccupied with the negative, but give him some grace, and love him.

Remember as well that while weight does matter, other issues are more important than external appearance. Ask God to help you focus on the things that matter most—your husband's spiritual maturity and his leadership of the family and the marriage, character, faithfulness at work and at home.

If the relationship is healthy and he is meeting your needs and encouraging you and loving you, and you are focusing on what is most important, I think the old statement, "Love is blind," is true. Weight issues don't have to get in the way.

ripe almonds. ⁹Then Moses brought out all the rods from before the LORD to all the children of Israel; and they looked, and each man took his rod.

¹⁰And the LORD said to Moses, "Bring Aaron's rod back before the Testimony, to be kept as a sign against the rebels, that you may put their complaints away from Me, lest they die." ¹¹Thus did Moses; just as the LORD had commanded him, so he did.

¹²So the children of Israel spoke to Moses, saying, "Surely we die, we perish, we all perish! ¹³Whoever even comes near the tabernacle of the LORD must die. Shall we all utterly die?"

Duties of Priests and Levites

18 Then the LORD said to Aaron: "You and your sons and your father's house with you shall bear the iniquity *related to* the sanctuary, and you and your sons with you shall bear the iniquity *associated with* your priesthood. ²Also bring with you your brethren of the tribe of Levi, the tribe of your father, that they may be joined with you and serve you while you and your sons *are* with you before the tabernacle of witness. ³They shall attend to your needs and all the needs of the tabernacle; but they shall not come near the articles of the sanctuary and the altar, lest they die— they and you also. ⁴They shall be joined with you and attend to the needs of the tabernacle of meeting, for all the work of the tabernacle; but an outsider shall not come near you. ⁵And you shall attend to the duties of the sanctuary and the duties of the altar, that there *may* be no more wrath on the children of Israel. ⁶Behold, I Myself have taken your brethren the Levites from among the children of Israel; *they are* a gift to you, given by the LORD, to do the work of the tabernacle of meeting. ⁷Therefore you and your sons with you shall attend to your priesthood for everything at the altar and behind the veil; and you shall serve. I give your priesthood *to you* as a gift for service, but the outsider who comes near shall be put to death."

Offerings for Support of the Priests

⁸And the LORD spoke to Aaron: "Here, I Myself have also given you charge of My heave offerings, all the holy gifts of the children of Israel; I have given them as a portion to you and your sons, as an ordinance forever. ⁹This shall be yours of the most holy things *reserved* from the fire: every offering of theirs, every grain offering and every sin offering and every trespass offering which they render to Me, *shall be* most holy for you and your sons. ¹⁰In a most holy *place* you shall eat it; every male shall eat it. It shall be holy to you.

¹¹"This also *is* yours: the heave offering of their gift, with all the wave offerings of the children of Israel; I have given them to you, and your sons and daughters with you, as an ordinance forever. Everyone who is clean in your house may eat it.

¹²"All the best of the oil, all the best of the new wine and the grain, their firstfruits which they offer to the LORD, I have given them to you. ¹³Whatever first ripe fruit is in their land, which they bring to the LORD, shall be yours. Everyone who is clean in your house may eat it.

¹⁴"Every devoted thing in Israel shall be yours.

¹⁵"Everything that first opens the womb of all flesh, which they bring to the LORD, whether man or beast, shall be yours; nevertheless the firstborn of man you shall surely redeem, and the firstborn of unclean animals you shall redeem. ¹⁶And those redeemed of the devoted things you shall redeem when one month old, according to your valuation, for five shekels of silver, according to the shekel of the sanctuary, which *is* twenty gerahs. ¹⁷But the firstborn of a cow, the firstborn of a sheep, or the firstborn of a goat you shall not redeem; they *are* holy. You shall sprinkle their blood on the altar, and burn their fat *as* an offering made by fire for a sweet aroma to the LORD. ¹⁸And their flesh shall be yours, just as the wave breast and the right thigh are yours.

¹⁹"All the heave offerings of the holy things, which the children of Israel offer to the LORD, I have given to you and your sons and daughters with you as an ordinance forever; it *is* a covenant of salt forever before the LORD with you and your descendants with you."

²⁰Then the LORD said to Aaron: "You shall have no inheritance in their land, nor

shall you have any portion among them; I *am* your portion and your inheritance among the children of Israel.

Tithes for Support of the Levites

²¹"Behold, I have given the children of Levi all the tithes in Israel as an inheritance in return for the work which they perform, the work of the tabernacle of meeting. ²²Hereafter the children of Israel shall not come near the tabernacle of meeting, lest they bear sin and die. ²³But the Levites shall perform the work of the tabernacle of meeting, and they shall bear their iniquity; *it shall be* a statute forever, throughout your generations, that among the children of Israel they shall have no inheritance. ²⁴For the tithes of the children of Israel, which they offer up *as* a heave offering to the LORD, I have given to the Levites as an inheritance; therefore I have said to them, 'Among the children of Israel they shall have no inheritance.'"

The Tithe of the Levites

²⁵Then the LORD spoke to Moses, saying, ²⁶"Speak thus to the Levites, and say to them: 'When you take from the children of Israel the tithes which I have given you from them as your inheritance, then you shall offer up a heave offering of it to the LORD, a tenth of the tithe. ²⁷And your heave offering shall be reckoned to you as though *it were* the grain of the threshing floor and as the fullness of the winepress. ²⁸Thus you shall also offer a heave offering to the LORD from all your tithes which you receive from the children of Israel, and you shall give the LORD's heave offering from it to Aaron the priest. ²⁹Of all your gifts you shall offer up every heave offering due to the LORD, from all the best of them, the consecrated part of them.' ³⁰Therefore you shall say to them: 'When you have lifted up the best of it, then *the rest* shall be accounted to the Levites as the produce of the threshing floor and as the produce of the winepress. ³¹You may eat it in any place, you and your households, for it *is* your reward for your work in the tabernacle of meeting. ³²And you shall bear no sin because of it, when you have lifted up the

best of it. But you shall not profane the holy gifts of the children of Israel, lest you die.'"

Laws of Purification

19 Now the LORD spoke to Moses and Aaron, saying, ²"This *is* the ordinance of the law which the LORD has commanded, saying: 'Speak to the children of Israel, that they bring you a red heifer without blemish, in which there *is* no defect *and* on which a yoke has never come. ³You shall give it to Eleazar the priest, that he may take it outside the camp, and it shall be slaughtered before him; ⁴and Eleazar the priest shall take some of its blood with his finger, and sprinkle some of its blood seven times directly in front of the tabernacle of meeting. ⁵Then the heifer shall be burned in his sight: its hide, its flesh, its blood, and its offal shall be burned. ⁶And the priest shall take cedar wood and hyssop and scarlet, and cast *them* into the midst of the fire burning the heifer. ⁷Then the priest shall wash his clothes, he shall bathe in water, and afterward he shall come into the camp; the priest shall be unclean until evening. ⁸And the one who burns it shall wash his clothes in water, bathe in water, and shall be unclean until evening. ⁹Then a man *who is* clean shall gather up the ashes of the heifer, and store *them* outside the camp in a clean place; and they shall be kept for the congregation of the children of Israel for the water of purification;ᵃ it *is* for purifying from sin. ¹⁰And the one who gathers the ashes of the heifer shall wash his clothes, and be unclean until evening. It shall be a statute forever to the children of Israel and to the stranger who dwells among them.

¹¹'He who touches the dead body of anyone shall be unclean seven days. ¹²He shall purify himself with the water on the third day and on the seventh day; *then* he will be clean. But if he does not purify himself on the third day and on the seventh day, he will not be clean. ¹³Whoever touches the body of anyone who has died, and does not purify himself, defiles the tabernacle of the LORD. That person shall be cut off from Israel. He shall be unclean, because the water of purification was not sprinkled on him; his uncleanness *is* still on him.

¹⁴'This *is* the law when a man dies in a

19:9 ᵃLiterally *impurity*

tent: All who come into the tent and all who *are* in the tent shall be unclean seven days; [15]and every open vessel, which has no cover fastened on it, *is* unclean. [16]Whoever in the open field touches one who is slain by a sword or who has died, or a bone of a man, or a grave, shall be unclean seven days.

[17]And for an unclean *person* they shall take some of the ashes of the heifer burnt for purification from sin, and running water shall be put on them in a vessel. [18]A clean person shall take hyssop and dip *it* in the water, sprinkle *it* on the tent, on all the vessels, on the persons who were there, or on the one who touched a bone, the slain, the dead, or a grave. [19]The clean *person* shall sprinkle the unclean on the third day and on the seventh day; and on the seventh day he shall purify himself, wash his clothes, and bathe in water; and at evening he shall be clean.

[20]But the man who is unclean and does not purify himself, that person shall be cut off from among the assembly, because he has defiled the sanctuary of the LORD. The water of purification has not been sprinkled on him; he *is* unclean. [21]It shall be a perpetual statute for them. He who sprinkles the water of purification shall wash his clothes; and he who touches the water of purification shall be unclean until evening. [22]Whatever the unclean *person* touches shall be unclean; and the person who touches *it* shall be unclean until evening.' "

Moses' Error at Kadesh

20 Then the children of Israel, the whole congregation, came into the Wilderness of Zin in the first month, and the people stayed in Kadesh; and Miriam died there and was buried there.

[2]Now there was no water for the congregation; so they gathered together against Moses and Aaron. [3]And the people contended with Moses and spoke, saying: "If only we had died when our brethren died before the LORD! [4]Why have you brought up the assembly of the LORD into this wilderness, that we and our animals should die here? [5]And why have you made us come up out of Egypt, to bring us to this evil place? It *is* not a place of grain or figs or vines or pomegranates; nor *is* there

any water to drink." [6]So Moses and Aaron went from the presence of the assembly to the door of the tabernacle of meeting, and they fell on their faces. And the glory of the LORD appeared to them.

[7]Then the LORD spoke to Moses, saying, [8]"Take the rod; you and your brother Aaron gather the congregation together. Speak to the rock before their eyes, and it will yield its water; thus you shall bring water for them out of the rock, and give drink to the congregation and their animals." [9]So Moses took the rod from before the LORD as He commanded him.

[10]And Moses and Aaron gathered the assembly together before the rock; and he said to them, "Hear now, you rebels! Must we bring water for you out of this rock?" [11]Then Moses lifted his hand and struck the rock twice with his rod; and water came out abundantly, and the congregation and their animals drank.

[12]Then the LORD spoke to Moses and Aaron, "Because you did not believe Me, to hallow Me in the eyes of the children of Israel, therefore you shall not bring this assembly into the land which I have given them."

[13]This *was* the water of Meribah,[a] because the children of Israel contended with the LORD, and He was hallowed among them.

Passage Through Edom Refused

[14]Now Moses sent messengers from Kadesh to the king of Edom. "Thus says your brother Israel: 'You know all the hardship that has befallen us, [15]how our fathers went down to Egypt, and we dwelt in Egypt a long time, and the Egyptians afflicted us and our fathers. [16]When we cried out to the LORD, He heard our voice and sent the Angel and brought us up out of Egypt; now here we are in Kadesh, a city on the edge of your border. [17]Please let us pass through your country. We will not pass through fields or vineyards, nor will we drink water from wells; we will go along the King's Highway; we will not turn aside to the right hand or to the left until we have passed through your territory.' "

20:13 [a]Literally *Contention*

[18]Then Edom said to him, "You shall not pass through my *land,* lest I come out against you with the sword."

[19]So the children of Israel said to him, "We will go by the Highway, and if I or my livestock drink any of your water, then I will pay for it; let me only pass through on foot, nothing *more.*"

[20]Then he said, "You shall not pass through." So Edom came out against them with many men and with a strong hand. [21]Thus Edom refused to give Israel passage through his territory; so Israel turned away from him.

Death of Aaron

[22]Now the children of Israel, the whole congregation, journeyed from Kadesh and came to Mount Hor. [23]And the LORD spoke to Moses and Aaron in Mount Hor by the border of the land of Edom, saying: [24]"Aaron shall be gathered to his people, for he shall not enter the land which I have given to the children of Israel, because you rebelled against My word at the water of Meribah. [25]Take Aaron and Eleazar his son, and bring them up to Mount Hor; [26]and strip Aaron of his garments and put them on Eleazar his son; for Aaron shall be gathered *to his people* and die there." [27]So Moses did just as the LORD commanded, and they went up to Mount Hor in the sight of all the congregation. [28]Moses stripped Aaron of his garments and put them on Eleazar his son; and Aaron died there on the top of the mountain. Then Moses and Eleazar came down from the mountain. [29]Now when all the congregation saw that Aaron was dead, all the house of Israel mourned for Aaron thirty days.

Canaanites Defeated at Hormah

21 The king of Arad, the Canaanite, who dwelt in the South, heard that Israel was coming on the road to Atharim. Then he fought against Israel and took *some* of them prisoners. [2]So Israel made a vow to the LORD, and said, "If You will indeed deliver this people into my hand,

then I will utterly destroy their cities." [3]And the LORD listened to the voice of Israel and delivered up the Canaanites, and they utterly destroyed them and their cities. So the name of that place was called Hormah.[a]

The Bronze Serpent

[4]Then they journeyed from Mount Hor by the Way of the Red Sea, to go around the land of Edom; and the soul of the people became very discouraged on the way. [5]And the people spoke against God and against Moses: "Why have you brought us up out of Egypt to die in the wilderness? For *there is* no food and no water, and our soul loathes this worthless bread." [6]So the LORD sent fiery serpents among the people, and they bit the people; and many of the people of Israel died.

[7]Therefore the people came to Moses, and said, "We have sinned, for we have spoken against the LORD and against you; pray to the LORD that He take away the serpents from us." So Moses prayed for the people.

[8]Then the LORD said to Moses, "Make a fiery *serpent,* and set it on a pole; and it shall be that everyone who is bitten, when he looks at it, shall live." [9]So Moses made a bronze serpent, and put it on a pole; and so it was, if a serpent had bitten anyone, when he looked at the bronze serpent, he lived.

From Mount Hor to Moab

[10]Now the children of Israel moved on and camped in Oboth. [11]And they journeyed from Oboth and camped at Ije Abarim, in the wilderness which *is* east of Moab, toward the sunrise. [12]From there they moved and camped in the Valley of Zered. [13]From there they moved and camped on the other side of the Arnon, which *is* in the wilderness that extends from the border of the Amorites; for the Arnon *is* the border of Moab, between Moab and the Amorites. [14]Therefore it is said in the Book of the Wars of the LORD:

> "Waheb in Suphah,[a]
> The brooks of the Arnon,
15   And the slope of the brooks
> That reaches to the dwelling of Ar,
> And lies on the border of Moab."

21:3 [a]Literally *Utter Destruction*
21:14 [a]Ancient unknown places; Vulgate reads *What He did in the Red Sea.*

BIBLICAL INSIGHTS • 21:6

The Problem with Grumbling

IF YOU HAVE A PROBLEM with grumbling, you're not alone. The Old Testament book of Numbers could easily be renamed The Grumbler Chronicles.

The Israelites grumbled against Moses, Aaron, and God. They didn't like manna—so they complained, "Manna for breakfast. Manna for lunch. Manna for dinner! Is this all we get, this *manna*?" So God gave them quail. They had quail boiled and broiled, quail under glass, quail a la cactus, quail nuggets, and probably even McQuail burgers, until they were sick of it.

Can you empathize with them? We Americans are used to an almost limitless variety of culinary delights. We tend to think, *So what if they griped a little? A little complaining is understandable, isn't it?*

But the complaints of God's people weren't trivial, and God didn't view them lightly. Why not? In fact, they were complaining about the provision and will of God. Ungrateful human beings criticized and rejected His supernatural care. That explains God's severe response, "So the LORD sent fiery serpents among the people, and they bit the people; and many of the people of Israel died" (21:6).

The fact that the New Testament highlights this incident (1 Cor. 10:10) should get our attention. *Beware the sin of grumbling!* Instead, learn how to cultivate a grateful and contented heart in all circumstances (Phil 4:11–13).

---

¹⁶From there *they went* to Beer, which *is* the well where the LORD said to Moses, "Gather the people together, and I will give them water." ¹⁷Then Israel sang this song:

"Spring up, O well!
　All of you sing to it—
18　The well the leaders sank,
　Dug by the nation's nobles,
　By the lawgiver, with their staves."

And from the wilderness *they went* to Mattanah, ¹⁹from Mattanah to Nahaliel, from Nahaliel to Bamoth, ²⁰and from Bamoth, *in* the valley that *is* in the country of Moab, to the top of Pisgah which looks down on the wasteland.ᵃ

King Sihon Defeated

²¹Then Israel sent messengers to Sihon king of the Amorites, saying, ²²"Let me pass through your land. We will not turn aside into fields or vineyards; we will not drink water from wells. We will go by the King's Highway until we have passed through your territory." ²³But Sihon would not allow Israel to pass through his territory. So Sihon gathered all his people together and went out against Israel in the wilderness, and he came to Jahaz and fought against Israel. ²⁴Then Israel defeated him with the edge of the sword, and took possession of his land from the Arnon to the Jabbok, as far as the people of Ammon; for the border of the people of Ammon *was* fortified. ²⁵So Israel took all these cities, and Israel dwelt in all the cities of the Amorites, in Heshbon and in all its villages. ²⁶For Heshbon *was* the city of Sihon king of the Amorites, who had fought against the former king of Moab, and had taken all his land from his hand as far as the Arnon. ²⁷Therefore those who speak in proverbs say:

"Come to Heshbon, let it be built;
　Let the city of Sihon be repaired.

28　"For fire went out from Heshbon,
　A flame from the city of Sihon;
　It consumed Ar of Moab,
　The lords of the heights of the
　　Arnon.
29　Woe to you, Moab!
　You have perished, O people of
　　Chemosh!
　He has given his sons as fugitives,
　And his daughters into captivity,
　To Sihon king of the Amorites.
30　"But we have shot at them;
　Heshbon has perished as far as Dibon.
　Then we laid waste as far as Nophah,
　Which *reaches* to Medeba."

21:20 ᵃHebrew *Jeshimon*

³¹Thus Israel dwelt in the land of the Amorites. ³²Then Moses sent to spy out Jazer; and they took its villages and drove out the Amorites who *were* there.

King Og Defeated

³³And they turned and went up by the way to Bashan. So Og king of Bashan went out against them, he and all his people, to battle at Edrei. ³⁴Then the LORD said to Moses, "Do not fear him, for I have delivered him into your hand, with all his people and his land; and you shall do to him as you did to Sihon king of the Amorites, who dwelt at Heshbon." ³⁵So they defeated him, his sons, and all his people, until there was no survivor left him; and they took possession of his land.

Balak Sends for Balaam

22 Then the children of Israel moved, and camped in the plains of Moab on the side of the Jordan *across from* Jericho.

²Now Balak the son of Zippor saw all that Israel had done to the Amorites. ³And Moab was exceedingly afraid of the people because they *were* many, and Moab was sick with dread because of the children of Israel. ⁴So Moab said to the elders of Midian, "Now this company will lick up everything around us, as an ox licks up the grass of the field." And Balak the son of Zippor *was* king of the Moabites at that time. ⁵Then he sent messengers to Balaam the son of Beor at Pethor, which *is* near the River ᵃ in the land of the sons of his people, ᵇ to call him, saying: "Look, a people has come from Egypt. See, they cover the face of the earth, and are settling next to me! ⁶Therefore please come at once, curse this people for me, for they *are* too mighty for me. Perhaps I shall be able to defeat them and drive them out of the land, for I know that he whom you bless *is* blessed, and he whom you curse is cursed."

⁷So the elders of Moab and the elders of Midian departed with the diviner's fee in their hand, and they came to Balaam and spoke to him the words of Balak. ⁸And he said to them, "Lodge here tonight, and I will bring back word to you, as the LORD speaks

to me." So the princes of Moab stayed with Balaam.

⁹Then God came to Balaam and said, "Who *are* these men with you?"

¹⁰So Balaam said to God, "Balak the son of Zippor, king of Moab, has sent to me, *saying*, ¹¹'Look, a people has come out of Egypt, and they cover the face of the earth. Come now, curse them for me; perhaps I shall be able to overpower them and drive them out.'"

¹²And God said to Balaam, "You shall not go with them; you shall not curse the people, for they *are* blessed."

¹³So Balaam rose in the morning and said to the princes of Balak, "Go back to your land, for the LORD has refused to give me permission to go with you."

¹⁴And the princes of Moab rose and went to Balak, and said, "Balaam refuses to come with us."

¹⁵Then Balak again sent princes, more numerous and more honorable than they. ¹⁶And they came to Balaam and said to him, "Thus says Balak the son of Zippor: 'Please let nothing hinder you from coming to me; ¹⁷for I will certainly honor you greatly, and I will do whatever you say to me. Therefore please come, curse this people for me.'"

¹⁸Then Balaam answered and said to the servants of Balak, "Though Balak were to give me his house full of silver and gold, I could not go beyond the word of the LORD my God, to do less or more. ¹⁹Now therefore, please, you also stay here tonight, that I may know what more the LORD will say to me."

²⁰And God came to Balaam at night and said to him, "If the men come to call you, rise *and* go with them; but only the word which I speak to you—that you shall do." ²¹So Balaam rose in the morning, saddled his donkey, and went with the princes of Moab.

Balaam, the Donkey, and the Angel

²²Then God's anger was aroused because he went, and the Angel of the LORD took His stand in the way as an adversary against him. And he was riding on his donkey, and his two servants *were* with him. ²³Now the donkey saw the Angel of the LORD standing in the way with His drawn sword in His hand, and the donkey turned aside out of the way and went into the field. So Balaam

---

22:5 ᵃThat is, the Euphrates ᵇOr *the people of Amau*

BIBLICAL INSIGHTS • 22:28-30

Learn to Discern God's Will

IT IS IMPORTANT that we learn to discern God's will for our lives. As the apostle Paul wrote, "Therefore, do not be unwise, but understand what the will of the Lord is" (Eph. 5:17).

Repeatedly in the Old Testament we see men and women whom God placed in positions of responsibility. When they arrived at a fork in the road and had to make a key decision, however, many failed to ask God what they should do. Scripture teaches that a person who fails to consult God on decisions and directions is a fool.

Balaam may be one of the prime examples of this. Although the Lord truly did speak through him, he got sidetracked through a lust for money (see 2 Pet. 2:15). He wandered so far off track, in fact, that God resorted to speaking to him through his own donkey to restrain "the madness of the prophet" (2 Pet. 2:16).

God may test us with what looks like a small decision, but in reality it may be one of the most important choices of our lives. Do you want God's will in just the big decisions or in the little ones as well? The Christian life is composed of both! Cultivate the habit of seeking God's will through His word and in prayer in the decisions you face every day.

---

struck the donkey to turn her back onto the road. 24Then the Angel of the LORD stood in a narrow path between the vineyards, *with* a wall on this side and a wall on that side. 25And when the donkey saw the Angel of the LORD, she pushed herself against the wall and crushed Balaam's foot against the wall; so he struck her again. 26Then the Angel of the LORD went further, and stood in a narrow place where there *was* no way to turn either to the right hand or to the left. 27And when the donkey saw the Angel of the LORD, she lay down under Balaam; so Balaam's anger was aroused, and he struck the donkey with his staff.

28Then the LORD opened the mouth of the donkey, and she said to Balaam, "What have I done to you, that you have struck me these three times?"

29And Balaam said to the donkey, "Because you have abused me. I wish there were a sword in my hand, for now I would kill you!"

30So the donkey said to Balaam, "*Am* I not your donkey on which you have ridden, ever since *I became* yours, to this day? Was I ever disposed to do this to you?"

And he said, "No."

31Then the LORD opened Balaam's eyes, and he saw the Angel of the LORD standing in the way with His drawn sword in His hand; and he bowed his head and fell flat on his face. 32And the Angel of the LORD said to him, "Why have you struck your donkey these three times? Behold, I have come out to stand against you, because *your* way is perverse before Me. 33The donkey saw Me and turned aside from Me these three times. If she had not turned aside from Me, surely I would also have killed you by now, and let her live."

34And Balaam said to the Angel of the LORD, "I have sinned, for I did not know You stood in the way against me. Now therefore, if it displeases You, I will turn back."

35Then the Angel of the LORD said to Balaam, "Go with the men, but only the word that I speak to you, that you shall speak." So Balaam went with the princes of Balak.

36Now when Balak heard that Balaam was coming, he went out to meet him at the city of Moab, which *is* on the border at the Arnon, the boundary of the territory. 37Then Balak said to Balaam, "Did I not earnestly send to you, calling for you? Why did you not come to me? Am I not able to honor you?"

38And Balaam said to Balak, "Look, I have come to you! Now, have I any power at all to say anything? The word that God puts in my mouth, that I must speak." 39So Balaam went with Balak, and they came to Kirjath Huzoth. 40Then Balak offered oxen and sheep, and he sent *some* to Balaam and to the princes who *were* with him.

Balaam's First Prophecy

⁴¹So it was, the next day, that Balak took Balaam and brought him up to the high places of Baal, that from there he might observe the extent of the people.

23 Then Balaam said to Balak, "Build seven altars for me here, and prepare for me here seven bulls and seven rams."

²And Balak did just as Balaam had spoken, and Balak and Balaam offered a bull and a ram on *each* altar. ³Then Balaam said to Balak, "Stand by your burnt offering, and I will go; perhaps the LORD will come to meet me, and whatever He shows me I will tell you." So he went to a desolate height. ⁴And God met Balaam, and he said to Him, "I have prepared the seven altars, and I have offered on *each* altar a bull and a ram."

⁵Then the LORD put a word in Balaam's mouth, and said, "Return to Balak, and thus you shall speak." ⁶So he returned to him, and there he was, standing by his burnt offering, he and all the princes of Moab.

⁷And he took up his oracle and said:

"Balak the king of Moab has brought
      me from Aram,
   From the mountains of
      the east.
' Come, curse Jacob for me,
   And come, denounce Israel!'

8   "How shall I curse whom God has
         not cursed?
      And how shall I denounce *whom* the
         LORD has not denounced?
9   For from the top of the rocks I see
         him,
      And from the hills I behold him;
      There! A people dwelling alone,
      Not reckoning itself among the
         nations.
10 "Who can count the dustᵃ of Jacob,
      Or number one-fourth of Israel?
      Let me die the death of the
         righteous,
      And let my end be like his!"

¹¹Then Balak said to Balaam, "What have you done to me? I took you to curse my enemies, and look, you have blessed *them* bountifully!"

¹²So he answered and said, "Must I not take heed to speak what the LORD has put in my mouth?"

Balaam's Second Prophecy

¹³Then Balak said to him, "Please come with me to another place from which you may see them; you shall see only the outer part of them, and shall not see them all; curse them for me from there." ¹⁴So he brought him to the field of Zophim, to the top of Pisgah, and built seven altars, and offered a bull and a ram on *each* altar.

¹⁵And he said to Balak, "Stand here by your burnt offering while I meetᵃ *the LORD* over there."

¹⁶Then the LORD met Balaam, and put a word in his mouth, and said, "Go back to Balak, and thus you shall speak." ¹⁷So he came to him, and there he was, standing by his burnt offering, and the princes of Moab were with him. And Balak said to him, "What has the LORD spoken?"

¹⁸Then he took up his oracle and said:

"Rise up, Balak, and hear!
      Listen to me, son of Zippor!
19   "God *is* not a man, that He should lie,
      Nor a son of man, that He should
         repent.
      Has He said, and will He not do?
      Or has He spoken, and will He not
         make it good?
20   Behold, I have received *a command*
         to bless;
      He has blessed, and I cannot reverse it.

21   "He has not observed iniquity in
         Jacob,
      Nor has He seen wickedness in
         Israel.
      The LORD his God *is* with him,
      And the shout of a King *is* among
         them.
22   God brings them out of Egypt;
      He has strength like a wild ox.

23   "For *there is* no sorcery against Jacob,
      Nor any divination against Israel.
      It now must be said of Jacob
      And of Israel, 'Oh, what God has
         done!'

23:10 ᵃOr *dust cloud*   23:15 ᵃFollowing Masoretic Text, Targum, and Vulgate; Syriac reads *call;* Septuagint reads *go and ask God.*

BIBLICAL INSIGHTS • 23:19
Believe God, Not Your Circumstances

IN 1938 A MAN IN LONG ISLAND ordered a very expensive weather barometer. When he unwrapped it, he saw that the arrow indicating the current local weather seemed stuck at the bottom, pointing at *Hurricane*. So he slammed it down a few times, and when it didn't respond, he wrote a hot letter to the manufacturer and mailed it off. When he returned home from work, he found that the mailbox was gone. A hurricane *had* hit, and he no longer had a house to return to.

Sometimes we don't want to believe the truth. When life and Scripture collide, which one do you believe and trust? The deceiver wants you to believe the lie. Will you believe God? Numbers 23:19 says, "God is not a man, that He should lie, nor a son of man, that He should repent. Has He said, and will He not do? Or has He spoken, and will He not make it good?"

The Scriptures tell us that without faith it is impossible to please God (Heb. 11:6). Never forget that your adversary is the father of lies. He wants to destroy you, so he works to make you doubt God's promises—and then, before God, he accuses you of unbelief!

---

24 Look, a people rises like a lioness,
  And lifts itself up like a lion;
  It shall not lie down until it devours
    the prey,
  And drinks the blood of the slain."

25 Then Balak said to Balaam, "Neither curse them at all, nor bless them at all!" 26 So Balaam answered and said to Balak, "Did I not tell you, saying, 'All that the LORD speaks, that I must do'?"

Balaam's Third Prophecy

27 Then Balak said to Balaam, "Please come, I will take you to another place; perhaps it will please God that you may curse them for me from there." 28 So Balak took Balaam to the top of Peor, that overlooks the wasteland.[a] 29 Then Balaam said to Balak, "Build for me here seven altars, and prepare for me here seven bulls and seven rams." 30 And Balak did as Balaam had said, and offered a bull and a ram on *every* altar.

24 Now when Balaam saw that it pleased the LORD to bless Israel, he did not go as at other times, to seek to use sorcery, but he set his face toward the wilderness. 2 And Balaam raised his eyes, and saw Israel encamped according to their tribes; and the Spirit of God came upon him.

3 Then he took up his oracle and said:

"The utterance of Balaam the son of Beor,
  The utterance of the man whose eyes are opened,
4 The utterance of him who hears the words of God,
  Who sees the vision of the Almighty,
  Who falls down, with eyes wide open:

5 "How lovely are your tents, O Jacob!
  Your dwellings, O Israel!
6 Like valleys that stretch out,
  Like gardens by the riverside,
  Like aloes planted by the LORD,
  Like cedars beside the waters.
7 He shall pour water from his buckets,
  And his seed *shall be* in many waters.

"His king shall be higher than Agag,
  And his kingdom shall be exalted.

8 "God brings him out of Egypt;
  He has strength like a wild ox;
  He shall consume the nations, his enemies;
  He shall break their bones
  And pierce *them* with his arrows.
9 'He bows down, he lies down as a lion;
  And as a lion, who shall rouse him?'[a]

"Blessed *is* he who blesses you,
  And cursed *is* he who curses you."

10 Then Balak's anger was aroused against Balaam, and he struck his hands together; and Balak said to Balaam, "I called you to

---

23:28 [a]Hebrew *Jeshimon*   24:9 [a]Genesis 49:9

curse my enemies, and look, you have bountifully blessed *them* these three times! ¹¹Now
therefore, flee to your place. I said I would
greatly honor you, but in fact, the LORD has
kept you back from honor."

¹²So Balaam said to Balak, "Did I not
also speak to your messengers whom you
sent to me, saying, ¹³'If Balak were to give
me his house full of silver and gold, I could
not go beyond the word of the LORD, to do
good or bad of my own will. What the
LORD says, that I must speak'? ¹⁴And now,
indeed, I am going to my people. Come, I
will advise you what this people will do to
your people in the latter days."

Balaam's Fourth Prophecy

¹⁵So he took up his oracle and said:

"The utterance of Balaam the son of
     Beor,
   And the utterance of the man whose
     eyes are opened;
¹⁶ The utterance of him who hears the
     words of God,
   And has the knowledge of the Most
     High,
Who sees the vision of the Almighty,
Who falls down, with eyes wide open:

---

¹⁷ "I see Him, but not now;
   I behold Him, but not near;
   A Star shall come out of Jacob;
   A Scepter shall rise out of Israel,
   And batter the brow of Moab,
   And destroy all the sons of tumult.ᵃ
¹⁸ "And Edom shall be a possession;
   Seir also, his enemies, shall be a
     possession,
   While Israel does valiantly.
¹⁹ Out of Jacob One shall have dominion,
   And destroy the remains of the city."

²⁰Then he looked on Amalek, and he took
up his oracle and said:

"Amalek *was* first among the nations,
   But *shall be* last until he perishes."

²¹Then he looked on the Kenites, and he
took up his oracle and said:

"Firm is your dwelling place,
   And your nest is set in the rock;
²² Nevertheless Kain shall be burned.
   How long until Asshur carries you
     away captive?"

²³Then he took up his oracle and said:

"Alas! Who shall live when God does
     this?
²⁴ But ships *shall come* from the coasts
     of Cyprus,ᵃ

24:17 ᵃHebrew *Sheth* (compare Jeremiah 48:45)
24:24 ᵃHebrew *Kittim* ᵇLiterally *he* or *that one*

ROMANTIC QUOTES AND NOTES
A Strong Marriage Needs Knowledge

Every Sunday morning, thousands of preachers present polished gems—sermons
filled with outstanding biblical knowledge. But what do we usually do? After the message, we dutifully sing a song, listen to a prayer, and hustle out by noon.

Where do we take the time to assimilate what we've heard? Too often we gather up
the kids, grab a bite to eat, and launch into our Sunday afternoon routine.

Even Balaam, a non-Israelite prophet who apparently really did hear from God,
understood the importance of acquiring "the words of God, and . . . the knowledge of
the Most High" (24:16). Such knowledge is more than mere information—it's a knowledge that results in convictions and applications. It's a truly teachable spirit that
applies God's truth and blueprints amidst the raw realities of life.

Many of us need accountability in order to apply what we've
learned. We need someone who will break through our self-built
fences and our crowded loneliness and ask us if we are applying to
our marriages what we've learned from God's Word in our marriage
and family relationships. Do you have a friend who regularly checks
up on you?

Balaam, by the way, didn't have such an accountability partner—
and he wound up on the sharp side of a Hebrew sword (see Josh.
13:22). Learn from his mistake!

BIBLICAL INSIGHTS • 25:1

Are You Clean?

GOD TAKES SERIOUSLY our sexual lives. When some of God's ancient people "began to commit harlotry with the women of Moab" (25:1), the Lord responded swiftly and decisively. Thousands of years later, the apostle Paul remembered this sorry incident and wrote, "Nor let us commit sexual immorality, as some of them did, and in one day twenty-three thousand fell" (1 Cor. 10:8).

In a world where some of the grossest sexual sins no longer even turn heads, it seems almost passé to think about sexual immorality. But believers need to remember that God finds this kind of sin abhorrent.

So many have fallen to sexual sin in the community of faith, that we decided to make a point with the seventy couples who speak at our Weekend to Remember marriage conferences. When we meet each year for training, one of the ways we greet one another for the first time is to shake hands and look each other in the eye and ask, "Are you clean?" Typically, the response is "Yes. Are you clean?"

The point of our handshake and question is to challenge one another to guard our hearts against sin.

Ask yourself, "Am I clean?" If the answer is "yes," then you need to guard against outside immoral influences. And if the answer is "no," then you need to repent and do some housecleaning.

Don't be like the young man who fell into immorality by going after the harlot "as an ox goes to the slaughter" (Prov. 7:22). Instead, make sure that you are clean, both personally and in your home. That means being careful what you think about and look at, making sure to keep the right company.

Let's keep our homes free of even the hint of immorality (Eph. 5:3).

And they shall afflict Asshur and
   afflict Eber,
And so shall *Amalek*,[b] until he
   perishes."

²⁵So Balaam rose and departed and returned to his place; Balak also went his way.

Israel's Harlotry in Moab

25 Now Israel remained in Acacia Grove,[a] and the people began to commit harlotry with the women of Moab. ²They invited the people to the sacrifices of their gods, and the people ate and bowed down to their gods. ³So Israel was joined to Baal of Peor, and the anger of the LORD was aroused against Israel.

⁴Then the LORD said to Moses, "Take all the leaders of the people and hang the offenders before the LORD, out in the sun, that the fierce anger of the LORD may turn away from Israel."

⁵So Moses said to the judges of Israel, "Every one of you kill his men who were joined to Baal of Peor."

⁶And indeed, one of the children of Israel came and presented to his brethren a Midianite woman in the sight of Moses and in the sight of all the congregation of the children of Israel, who *were* weeping at the door of the tabernacle of meeting. ⁷Now when Phinehas the son of Eleazar, the son of Aaron the priest, saw *it*, he rose from among the congregation and took a javelin in his hand; ⁸and he went after the man of Israel into the tent and thrust both of them through, the man of Israel, and the woman through her body. So the plague was stopped among the children of Israel. ⁹And those who died in the plague were twenty-four thousand.

¹⁰Then the LORD spoke to Moses, saying: ¹¹"Phinehas the son of Eleazar, the son of Aaron the priest, has turned back My wrath from the children of Israel, because he was zealous with My zeal among them, so that I did not consume the children of Israel in My zeal. ¹²Therefore say, 'Behold, I give to him My covenant of peace; ¹³and it shall be to him and his descendants after him a covenant of an everlasting priesthood,

25:1 [a]Hebrew *Shittim*

because he was zealous for his God, and made atonement for the children of Israel.'"

¹⁴Now the name of the Israelite who was killed, who was killed with the Midianite woman, *was* Zimri the son of Salu, a leader of a father's house among the Simeonites. ¹⁵And the name of the Midianite woman who was killed *was* Cozbi the daughter of Zur; he *was* head of the people of a father's house in Midian.

¹⁶Then the LORD spoke to Moses, saying: ¹⁷"Harass the Midianites, and attack them; ¹⁸for they harassed you with their schemes by which they seduced you in the matter of Peor and in the matter of Cozbi, the daughter of a leader of Midian, their sister, who was killed in the day of the plague because of Peor."

The Second Census of Israel

26 And it came to pass, after the plague, that the LORD spoke to Moses and Eleazar the son of Aaron the priest, saying: ²"Take a census of all the congregation of the children of Israel from twenty years old and above, by their fathers' houses, all who are able to go to war in Israel." ³So Moses and Eleazar the priest spoke with them in the plains of Moab by the Jordan, *across from* Jericho, saying: ⁴"*Take a census of the people* from twenty years old and above, just as the LORD commanded Moses and the children of Israel who came out of the land of Egypt."

⁵Reuben *was* the firstborn of Israel. The children of Reuben *were: of* Hanoch, the family of the Hanochites; *of* Pallu, the family of the Palluites; ⁶*of* Hezron, the family of the Hezronites; *of* Carmi, the family of the Carmites. ⁷These *are* the families of the Reubenites: those who were numbered of them were forty-three thousand seven hundred and thirty. ⁸And the son of Pallu *was* Eliab. ⁹The sons of Eliab *were* Nemuel,

Dathan, and Abiram. These *are* the Dathan and Abiram, representatives of the congregation, who contended against Moses and Aaron in the company of Korah, when they contended against the LORD; ¹⁰and the earth opened its mouth and swallowed them up together with Korah when that company died, when the fire devoured two hundred and fifty men; and they became a sign. ¹¹Nevertheless the children of Korah did not die.

¹²The sons of Simeon according to their families *were: of* Nemuel,ᵃ the family of the Nemuelites; *of* Jamin, the family of the Jaminites; *of* Jachin,ᵇ the family of the Jachinites; ¹³*of* Zerah,ᵃ the family of the Zarhites; *of* Shaul, the family of the Shaulites. ¹⁴These *are* the families of the Simeonites: twenty-two thousand two hundred.

¹⁵The sons of Gad according to their families *were: of* Zephon,ᵃ the family of the Zephonites; *of* Haggi, the family of the Haggites; *of* Shuni, the family of the Shunites; ¹⁶*of* Ozni,ᵃ the family of the Oznites; *of* Eri, the family of the Erites; ¹⁷*of* Arod,ᵃ the family of the Arodites; *of* Areli, the family of the Arelites. ¹⁸These *are* the families of the sons of Gad according to those who were numbered of them: forty thousand five hundred.

¹⁹The sons of Judah *were* Er and Onan; and Er and Onan died in the land of Canaan. ²⁰And the sons of Judah according to their families were: *of* Shelah, the family of the Shelanites; *of* Perez, the family of the Parzites; *of* Zerah, the family of the Zarhites. ²¹And the sons of Perez were: *of* Hezron, the family of the Hezronites; *of* Hamul, the family of the Hamulites. ²²These *are* the families of Judah according to those who were numbered of them: seventy-six thousand five hundred.

²³The sons of Issachar according to their families *were: of* Tola, the family of the Tolaites; of Puah,ᵃ the family of the Punites;ᵇ ²⁴of Jashub, the family of the Jashubites; of Shimron, the family of the Shimronites. ²⁵These *are* the families of Issachar according to those who were numbered of them: sixty-four thousand three hundred.

²⁶The sons of Zebulun according to their families *were:* of Sered, the family of the Sardites; of Elon, the family of the Elonites;

26:12 ᵃSpelled *Jemuel* in Genesis 46:10 and Exodus 6:15 ᵇCalled *Jarib* in 1 Chronicles 4:24 26:13 ᵃCalled *Zohar* in Genesis 46:10 26:15 ᵃCalled *Ziphion* in Genesis 46:16 26:16 ᵃCalled *Ezbon* in Genesis 46:16 26:17 ᵃSpelled *Arodi* in Samaritan Pentateuch, Syriac, and Genesis 46:16 26:23 ᵃHebrew *Puvah* (compare Genesis 46:13 and 1 Chronicles 7:1); Samaritan Pentateuch, Septuagint, Syriac, and Vulgate read *Puah.* ᵇSamaritan Pentateuch, Septuagint, Syriac, and Vulgate read *Puaites.*

of Jahleel, the family of the Jahleelites. [27]These *are* the families of the Zebulunites according to those who were numbered of them: sixty thousand five hundred.

[28]The sons of Joseph according to their families, by Manasseh and Ephraim, *were:* [29]The sons of Manasseh: of Machir, the family of the Machirites; and Machir begot Gilead; of Gilead, the family of the Gileadites. [30]These *are* the sons of Gilead: *of* Jeezer,[a] the family of the Jeezerites; of Helek, the family of the Helekites; [31]*of* Asriel, the family of the Asrielites; *of* Shechem, the family of the Shechemites; [32]*of* Shemida, the family of the Shemidaites; *of* Hepher, the family of the Hepherites. [33]Now Zelophehad the son of Hepher had no sons, but daughters; and the names of the daughters of Zelophehad *were* Mahlah, Noah, Hoglah, Milcah, and Tirzah. [34]These *are* the families of Manasseh; and those who were numbered of them *were* fifty-two thousand seven hundred.

[35]These *are* the sons of Ephraim according to their families: of Shuthelah, the family of the Shuthalhites; of Becher,[a] the family of the Bachrites; of Tahan, the family of the Tahanites. [36]And these *are* the sons of Shuthelah: of Eran, the family of the Eranites. [37]These *are* the families of the sons of Ephraim according to those who were numbered of them: thirty-two thousand five hundred.

These *are* the sons of Joseph according to their families.

[38]The sons of Benjamin according to their families were: of Bela, the family of the Belaites; of Ashbel, the family of the Ashbelites; of Ahiram, the family of the Ahiramites; [39]of Shupham,[a] the family of the Shuphamites; of Hupham,[b] the family of the Huphamites. [40]And the sons of Bela were Ard[a] and Naaman: *of Ard,* the family of the Ardites; of Naaman, the family of the Naamites. [41]These *are* the sons of Benjamin according to their families; and those who were numbered of them *were* forty-five thousand six hundred.

[42]These *are* the sons of Dan according to their families: of Shuham,[a] the family of the Shuhamites. These *are* the families of Dan according to their families. [43]All the families of the Shuhamites, according to those who were numbered of them, *were* sixty-four thousand four hundred.

[44]The sons of Asher according to their families *were:* of Jimna, the family of the

---

ROMANCE FAQ

Q: *We seem to have lost much of our romantic fire. Why?*

What is it about marriage that seems to dull our romantic creativity? At some point in almost every marriage—usually within the first two years—a couple realizes that they just don't experience the same romantic feelings they once enjoyed. As one cynical person said, "The period of engagement is like an exciting introduction to a dull book."

Has this happened to you? If so, don't imagine that you're alone! In fact, it's a very common experience. The question is, what can you do about it?

One good place to begin: act on the counsel of Proverbs 5:18, 19, "Rejoice with the wife of your youth. As a loving deer and a graceful doe, let her breasts satisfy you at all times; and always be enraptured with her love."

That's a powerful image—to be *exhilarated* by your mate. This type of romance is part of what sets marriage apart from a mere friendship. While Barbara and I are friends, we also share a marriage bed and we dream thoughts and share intimacies that we share with nobody else. That's what God intended for the marriage relationship.

One of the reasons that a marriage can read like a dull book is that we stop investing in our relationship. We cease courting and allow boredom to set in. Add a little zest to your marriage (and invest in it!) by doing some of the things you did when you dated.

26:30 [a]Called *Abiezer* in Joshua 17:2
26:35 [a]Called *Bered* in 1 Chronicles 7:20
26:39 [a]Masoretic Text reads *Shephupham,* spelled *Shephuphan* in 1 Chronicles 8:5. [b]Called *Huppim* in Genesis 46:21 26:40 [a]Called *Addar* in 1 Chronicles 8:3 26:42 [a]Called *Hushim* in Genesis 46:23

Jimnites; of Jesui, the family of the Jesuites; of Beriah, the family of the Beriites. ⁴⁵Of the sons of Beriah: of Heber, the family of the Heberites; of Malchiel, the family of the Malchielites. ⁴⁶And the name of the daughter of Asher *was* Serah. ⁴⁷These *are* the families of the sons of Asher according to those who were numbered of them: fifty-three thousand four hundred.

⁴⁸The sons of Naphtali according to their families *were:* of Jahzeel,ᵃ the family of the Jahzeelites; of Guni, the family of the Gunites; ⁴⁹of Jezer, the family of the Jezerites; of Shillem, the family of the Shillemites. ⁵⁰These *are* the families of Naphtali according to their families; and those who were numbered of them *were* forty-five thousand four hundred.

⁵¹These *are* those who were numbered of the children of Israel: six hundred and one thousand seven hundred and thirty.

⁵²Then the LORD spoke to Moses, saying: ⁵³"To these the land shall be divided as an inheritance, according to the number of names. ⁵⁴To a large *tribe* you shall give a larger inheritance, and to a small *tribe* you shall give a smaller inheritance. Each shall be given its inheritance according to those who were numbered of them. ⁵⁵But the land shall be divided by lot; they shall inherit according to the names of the tribes of their fathers. ⁵⁶According to the lot their inheritance shall be divided between the larger and the smaller."

⁵⁷And these *are* those who were numbered of the Levites according to their families: of Gershon, the family of the Gershonites; of Kohath, the family of the Kohathites; of Merari, the family of the Merarites. ⁵⁸These *are* the families of the Levites: the family of the Libnites, the family of the Hebronites, the family of the Mahlites, the family of the Mushites, and the family of the Korathites. And Kohath begot Amram. ⁵⁹The name of Amram's wife *was* Jochebed the daughter of Levi, who was born to Levi in Egypt; and to Amram she bore Aaron and Moses and their sister Miriam. ⁶⁰To Aaron were born Nadab and Abihu, Eleazar and Ithamar. ⁶¹And Nadab and Abihu died when they offered profane fire before the LORD.

⁶²Now those who were numbered of them were twenty-three thousand, every male from a month old and above; for they were not numbered among the other children of Israel, because there was no inheritance given to them among the children of Israel.

⁶³These *are* those who were numbered by Moses and Eleazar the priest, who numbered the children of Israel in the plains of Moab by the Jordan, *across from* Jericho. ⁶⁴But among these there was not a man of those who were numbered by Moses and Aaron the priest when they numbered the children of Israel in the Wilderness of Sinai. ⁶⁵For the LORD had said of them, "They shall surely die in the wilderness." So there was not left a man of them, except Caleb the son of Jephunneh and Joshua the son of Nun.

Inheritance Laws

27 Then came the daughters of Zelophehad the son of Hepher, the son of Gilead, the son of Machir, the son of Manasseh, from the families of Manasseh the son of Joseph; and these *were* the names of his daughters: Mahlah, Noah, Hoglah, Milcah, and Tirzah. ²And they stood before Moses, before Eleazar the priest, and before the leaders and all the congregation, *by* the doorway of the tabernacle of meeting, saying: ³"Our father died in the wilderness; but he was not in the company of those who gathered together against the LORD, in company with Korah, but he died in his own sin; and he had no sons. ⁴Why should the name of our father be removed from among his family because he had no son? Give us a possession among our father's brothers."

⁵So Moses brought their case before the LORD.

⁶And the LORD spoke to Moses, saying: ⁷"The daughters of Zelophehad speak *what is* right; you shall surely give them a possession of inheritance among their father's brothers, and cause the inheritance of their father to pass to them. ⁸And you shall speak to the children of Israel, saying: 'If a man dies and has no son, then you shall cause his inheritance to pass to his daughter. ⁹If he has no daughter, then you shall give his inheritance to his brothers. ¹⁰If he has no brothers, then you shall give his inheritance to his

father's brothers. ¹¹And if his father has no brothers, then you shall give his inheritance to the relative closest to him in his family, and he shall possess it.'" And it shall be to the children of Israel a statute of judgment, just as the LORD commanded Moses.

Joshua the Next Leader of Israel

¹²Now the LORD said to Moses: "Go up into this Mount Abarim, and see the land which I have given to the children of Israel. ¹³And when you have seen it, you also shall be gathered to your people, as Aaron your brother was gathered. ¹⁴For in the Wilderness of Zin, during the strife of the congregation, you rebelled against My command to hallow Me at the waters before their eyes." (These *are* the waters of Meribah, at Kadesh in the Wilderness of Zin.)

¹⁵Then Moses spoke to the LORD, saying: ¹⁶"Let the LORD, the God of the spirits of all flesh, set a man over the congregation, ¹⁷who may go out before them and go in before them, who may lead them out and bring them in, that the congregation of the LORD may not be like sheep which have no shepherd."

¹⁸And the LORD said to Moses: "Take Joshua the son of Nun with you, a man in whom *is* the Spirit, and lay your hand on him; ¹⁹set him before Eleazar the priest and before all the congregation, and inaugurate him in their sight. ²⁰And you shall give *some* of your authority to him, that all the congregation of the children of Israel may be obedient. ²¹He shall stand before Eleazar the priest, who shall inquire before the LORD for him by the judgment of the Urim. At his word they shall go out, and at his word they shall come in, he and all the children of Israel with him—all the congregation."

²²So Moses did as the LORD commanded him. He took Joshua and set him before Eleazar the priest and before all the congregation. ²³And he laid his hands on him and inaugurated him, just as the LORD commanded by the hand of Moses.

Daily Offerings

28 Now the LORD spoke to Moses, saying, ²"Command the children of Israel, and say to them, 'My offering, My food for My offerings made by fire as a sweet aroma to Me, you shall be careful to offer to Me at their appointed time.'

³"And you shall say to them, 'This *is* the offering made by fire which you shall offer to the LORD: two male lambs in their first year without blemish, day by day, as a regular burnt offering. ⁴The one lamb you shall offer in the morning, the other lamb you shall offer in the evening, ⁵and one-tenth of an ephah of fine flour as a grain offering mixed with one-fourth of a hin of pressed oil. ⁶*It is* a regular burnt offering which was ordained at Mount Sinai for a sweet aroma, an offering made by fire to the LORD. ⁷And its drink offering *shall be* one-fourth of a hin for each lamb; in a holy *place* you shall pour out the drink to the LORD as an offering. ⁸The other lamb you shall offer in the evening; as the morning grain offering and its drink offering, you shall offer *it* as an offering made by fire, a sweet aroma to the LORD.

Sabbath Offerings

⁹"And on the Sabbath day two lambs in their first year, without blemish, and two-tenths *of an ephah* of fine flour as a grain offering, mixed with oil, with its drink offering— ¹⁰*this is* the burnt offering for every Sabbath, besides the regular burnt offering with its drink offering.

Monthly Offerings

¹¹'At the beginnings of your months you

INTIMATE MOMENTS

Send a bouquet of candies or cookies to his workplace with a sweet note. If you have a choice of sweets, try to make sure it's something he really likes. No sense sending him chocolate truffles when he really likes caramels, or a dozen snicker-doodles when he'd really prefer some old-fashioned sugar cookies! Play a little with the note, too; jazz it up for him a bit, to let him know you really *thought* about the sentiment.

shall present a burnt offering to the LORD: two young bulls, one ram, and seven lambs in their first year, without blemish; ¹²three-tenths *of an ephah* of fine flour as a grain offering, mixed with oil, for each bull; two-tenths *of an ephah* of fine flour as a grain offering, mixed with oil, for the one ram; ¹³and one-tenth *of an ephah* of fine flour, mixed with oil, as a grain offering for each lamb, as a burnt offering of sweet aroma, an offering made by fire to the LORD. ¹⁴Their drink offering shall be half a hin of wine for a bull, one-third of a hin for a ram, and one-fourth of a hin for a lamb; this *is* the burnt offering for each month throughout the months of the year. ¹⁵Also one kid of the goats as a sin offering to the LORD shall be offered, besides the regular burnt offering and its drink offering.

Offerings at Passover

¹⁶'On the fourteenth day of the first month *is* the Passover of the LORD. ¹⁷And on the fifteenth day of this month *is* the feast; unleavened bread shall be eaten for seven days. ¹⁸On the first day *you shall have* a holy convocation. You shall do no customary work. ¹⁹And you shall present an offering made by fire as a burnt offering to the LORD: two young bulls, one ram, and seven lambs in their first year. Be sure they are without blemish. ²⁰Their grain offering shall be of fine flour mixed with oil: three-tenths *of an ephah* you shall offer for a bull, and two-tenths for a ram; ²¹you shall offer one-tenth *of an ephah* for each of the seven lambs; ²²also one goat *as* a sin offering, to make atonement for you. ²³You shall offer these besides the burnt offering of the morning, which *is* for a regular burnt offering. ²⁴In this manner you shall offer the food of the offering made by fire daily for seven days, as a sweet aroma to the LORD; it shall be offered besides the regular burnt offering and its drink offering. ²⁵And on the seventh day you shall have a holy convocation. You shall do no customary work.

Offerings at the Feast of Weeks

²⁶'Also on the day of the firstfruits, when you bring a new grain offering to the LORD at your *Feast of* Weeks, you shall have a holy convocation. You shall do no customary work. ²⁷You shall present a burnt offering as a sweet aroma to the LORD: two young bulls, one ram, and seven lambs in their first year, ²⁸with their grain offering of fine flour mixed with oil: three-tenths *of an ephah* for each bull, two-tenths for the one ram, ²⁹and one-tenth for each of the seven lambs; ³⁰also one kid of the goats, to make atonement for you. ³¹Be sure they are without blemish. You shall present *them* with their drink offerings, besides the regular burnt offering with its grain offering.

Offerings at the Feast of Trumpets

29 'And in the seventh month, on the first *day* of the month, you shall have a holy convocation. You shall do no customary work. For you it is a day of blowing the trumpets. ²You shall offer a burnt offering as a sweet aroma to the LORD: one young bull, one ram, *and* seven lambs in their first year, without blemish. ³Their grain offering *shall be* fine flour mixed with oil: three-tenths *of an ephah* for the bull, two-tenths for the ram, ⁴and one-tenth for each of the seven lambs; ⁵also one kid of the goats as a sin offering, to make atonement for you; ⁶besides the burnt offering with its grain offering for the New Moon, the regular burnt offering with its grain offering, and their drink offerings, according to their ordinance, as a sweet aroma, an offering made by fire to the LORD.

Offerings on the Day of Atonement

⁷'On the tenth *day* of this seventh month you shall have a holy convocation. You shall afflict your souls; you shall not do any work. ⁸You shall present a burnt offering to the LORD *as* a sweet aroma: one young bull, one ram, *and* seven lambs in their first year. Be sure they are without blemish. ⁹Their grain offering *shall be of* fine flour mixed with oil: three-tenths *of an ephah* for the bull, two-tenths for the one ram, ¹⁰and one-tenth for each of the seven lambs; ¹¹also one kid of the goats *as* a sin offering, besides the sin offering for atonement, the regular burnt offering with its grain offering, and their drink offerings.

Offerings at the Feast of Tabernacles

¹²'On the fifteenth day of the seventh month you shall have a holy convocation. You shall do no customary work, and you shall keep a feast to the LORD seven days. ¹³You shall present a burnt offering, an offering made by fire as a sweet aroma to the LORD: thirteen young bulls, two rams, *and* fourteen lambs in their first year. They shall be without blemish. ¹⁴Their grain offering *shall be of* fine flour mixed with oil: three-tenths *of an ephah* for each of the thirteen bulls, two-tenths for each of the two rams, ¹⁵and one-tenth for each of the fourteen lambs; ¹⁶also one kid of the goats *as* a sin offering, besides the regular burnt offering, its grain offering, and its drink offering.

ROMANCE FAQ

Q: *How can I handle it when my child wants to invade my time with my mate?*

Many years ago I determined there was only one way Barbara and I could emerge intact from having six kids in ten years, and that was to protect our time as a couple. That means setting priorities that discriminate in favor of your marriage.

In addition to regularly scheduled date nights, on certain evenings we close the door to our room and say to our kids, "If this door is shut, don't come in. Mom and Dad need quiet time together." Now, we could tell when a child really needed us; but generally we held to this rule. Moms and dads need time to relate and talk to each other. The kids need to know that their parents' marriage is a priority.

It's especially important to do this when your kids are younger than eleven or twelve. When your kids move into the adolescent years, it's more difficult to *carve out time together because your* kids are staying up later at night. If you're not in the habit of spending time together, you'll *really* find it hard during the teenage years. Establish that pattern early on!

¹⁷'On the second day *present* twelve young bulls, two rams, fourteen lambs in their first year without blemish, ¹⁸and their grain offering and their drink offerings for the bulls, for the rams, and for the lambs, by their number, according to the ordinance; ¹⁹also one kid of the goats *as* a sin offering, besides the regular burnt offering with its grain offering, and their drink offerings.

²⁰'On the third day *present* eleven bulls, two rams, fourteen lambs in their first year without blemish, ²¹and their grain offering and their drink offerings for the bulls, for the rams, and for the lambs, by their number, according to the ordinance; ²²also one goat *as* a sin offering, besides the regular burnt offering, its grain offering, and its drink offering.

²³'On the fourth day *present* ten bulls, two rams, *and* fourteen lambs in their first year, without blemish, ²⁴and their grain offering and their drink offerings for the bulls, for the rams, and for the lambs, by their number, according to the ordinance; ²⁵also one kid of the goats *as* a sin offering, besides the regular burnt offering, its grain offering, and its drink offering.

²⁶'On the fifth day *present* nine bulls, two rams, *and* fourteen lambs in their first year without blemish, ²⁷and their grain offering and their drink offerings for the bulls, for the rams, and for the lambs, by their number, according to the ordinance; ²⁸also one goat *as* a sin offering, besides the regular burnt offering, its grain offering, and its drink offering.

²⁹'On the sixth day *present* eight bulls, two rams, *and* fourteen lambs in their first year without blemish, ³⁰and their grain offering and their drink offerings for the bulls, for the rams, and for the lambs, by their number, according to the ordinance; ³¹also one goat *as* a sin offering, besides the regular burnt offering, its grain offering, and its drink offering.

³²'On the seventh day *present* seven bulls, two rams, *and* fourteen lambs in their first year without blemish, ³³and their grain offering and their drink offerings for the bulls, for the rams, and for the lambs, by their number, according to the ordinance; ³⁴also one goat *as* a sin offering, besides the regular burnt offering, its grain offering, and its drink offering.

³⁵'On the eighth day you shall have a

sacred assembly. You shall do no customary work. ³⁶You shall present a burnt offering, an offering made by fire as a sweet aroma to the LORD: one bull, one ram, seven lambs in their first year without blemish, ³⁷and their grain offering and their drink offerings for the bull, for the ram, and for the lambs, by their number, according to the ordinance; ³⁸also one goat *as* a sin offering, besides the regular burnt offering, its grain offering, and its drink offering.

³⁹'These you shall present to the LORD at your appointed feasts (besides your vowed offerings and your freewill offerings) as your burnt offerings and your grain offerings, as your drink offerings and your peace offerings.' "

⁴⁰So Moses told the children of Israel everything, just as the LORD commanded Moses.

The Law Concerning Vows

30 Then Moses spoke to the heads of the tribes concerning the children of Israel, saying, "This *is* the thing which the LORD has commanded: ²If a man makes a vow to the LORD, or swears an oath to bind himself by some agreement, he shall not break his word; he shall do according to all that proceeds out of his mouth.

³"Or if a woman makes a vow to the LORD, and binds *herself* by some agreement while in her father's house in her youth, ⁴and her father hears her vow and the agreement by which she has bound herself, and her father holds his peace, then all her vows shall stand, and every agreement with which she has bound herself shall stand. ⁵But if her father overrules her on the day that he hears, then none of her vows nor her agreements by which she has bound herself shall stand; and the LORD will release her, because her father overruled her.

⁶"If indeed she takes a husband, while bound by her vows or by a rash utterance from her lips by which she bound herself, ⁷and her husband hears *it,* and makes no response to her on the day that he hears, then her vows shall stand, and her agreements by which she bound herself shall stand. ⁸But if her husband overrules her on the day that he hears *it,* he shall make void her vow which she took and what she

BIBLICAL INSIGHTS • 30:2
He Takes Vows Seriously

THE TRADITIONAL WEDDING vows used by most couples constitute a covenantal oath, not a two-party contract. The vows I shared with Barbara went like this: "I, Dennis, take you, Barbara, to be my lawful wedded wife. I promise and covenant, before God and these witnesses, to be your loving and faithful husband; to stand by you in riches and in poverty, in joy and in sorrow, in sickness and in health, forsaking all others, as long as we both shall live."

When we spoke these words, Barbara and I weren't agreeing to provide some personal services via a contract that could be terminated if either of us defaulted. Instead, we were entering into a covenant—the same type of sacred, binding obligation that God made with His children on several momentous occasions, such as with Noah after the flood.

Any covenant, including the marriage covenant, is a binding, weighty obligation. The Bible declares, "If a man makes a vow to the LORD, or swears an oath to bind himself by some agreement, he shall not break his word; he shall do according to all that proceeds out of his mouth" (30:2).

God takes the wedding covenant seriously, even when we do not. Your vows were more than just a promise NOT to divorce, but also a promise to love, honor, cherish and much more. Fulfill your vows.

uttered with her lips, by which she bound herself, and the LORD will release her.

⁹"Also any vow of a widow or a divorced woman, by which she has bound herself, shall stand against her.

¹⁰"If she vowed in her husband's house, or bound herself by an agreement with an oath, ¹¹and her husband heard *it,* and made no response to her *and* did not overrule her, then all her vows shall stand, and every agreement by which she bound herself shall

stand. ¹²But if her husband truly made them void on the day he heard *them,* then whatever proceeded from her lips concerning her vows or concerning the agreement binding her, it shall not stand; her husband has made them void, and the LORD will release her. ¹³Every vow and every binding oath to afflict her soul, her husband may confirm it, or her husband may make it void. ¹⁴Now if her husband makes no response whatever to her from day to day, then he confirms all her vows or all the agreements that bind her; he confirms them, because he made no response to her on the day that he heard *them.* ¹⁵But if he does make them void after he has heard *them,* then he shall bear her guilt."

¹⁶These *are* the statutes which the LORD commanded Moses, between a man and his wife, and between a father and his daughter in her youth in her father's house.

Vengeance on the Midianites

31 And the LORD spoke to Moses, saying: ²"Take vengeance on the Midianites for the children of Israel. Afterward you shall be gathered to your people."

³So Moses spoke to the people, saying, "Arm some of yourselves for war, and let them go against the Midianites to take vengeance for the LORD on Midian. ⁴A thousand from each tribe of all the tribes of Israel you shall send to the war."

⁵So there were recruited from the divisions of Israel one thousand from *each* tribe, twelve thousand armed for war. ⁶Then Moses sent them to the war, one thousand from *each* tribe; he sent them to the war with Phinehas the son of Eleazar the priest, with the holy articles and the signal trumpets in his hand. ⁷And they warred against the Midianites, just as the LORD commanded Moses, and they killed all the males. ⁸They killed the kings of Midian with *the rest of* those who were killed—Evi, Rekem, Zur, Hur, and Reba, the five kings of Midian. Balaam the son of Beor they also killed with the sword.

⁹And the children of Israel took the women of Midian captive, with their little ones, and took as spoil all their cattle, all their flocks, and all their goods. ¹⁰They also burned with fire all the cities where they dwelt, and all their forts. ¹¹And they took all the spoil and all the booty—of man and beast.

Return from the War

¹²Then they brought the captives, the booty, and the spoil to Moses, to Eleazar the priest, and to the congregation of the children of Israel, to the camp in the plains of Moab by the Jordan, *across from* Jericho. ¹³And Moses, Eleazar the priest, and all the leaders of the congregation, went to meet them outside the camp. ¹⁴But Moses was angry with the officers of the army, *with* the captains over thousands and captains over hundreds, who had come from the battle.

¹⁵And Moses said to them: "Have you kept all the women alive? ¹⁶Look, these *women* caused the children of Israel, through the counsel of Balaam, to trespass against the LORD in the incident of Peor, and there was a plague among the congregation of the LORD. ¹⁷Now therefore, kill every male among the little ones, and kill every woman who has known a man intimately. ¹⁸But keep alive for yourselves all the young girls who have not known a man intimately. ¹⁹And as for you, remain outside the camp seven days; whoever has killed any person, and whoever has touched any slain, purify yourselves and your captives on the third day and on the seventh day. ²⁰Purify every garment, everything made of leather, everything woven of goats' *hair,* and everything made of wood."

²¹Then Eleazar the priest said to the men of war who had gone to the battle, "This *is* the ordinance of the law which the LORD commanded Moses: ²²Only the gold, the silver, the bronze, the iron, the tin, and the lead, ²³everything that can endure fire, you shall put through the fire, and it shall be clean; and it shall be purified with the water of purification. But all that cannot endure fire you shall put through water. ²⁴And you shall wash your clothes on the seventh day and be clean, and afterward you may come into the camp."

Division of the Plunder

²⁵Now the LORD spoke to Moses, saying: ²⁶"Count up the plunder that was taken—of

man and beast—you and Eleazar the priest and the chief fathers of the congregation; ²⁷and divide the plunder into two parts, between those who took part in the war, who went out to battle, and all the congregation. ²⁸And levy a tribute for the LORD on the men of war who went out to battle: one of every five hundred of the persons, the cattle, the donkeys, and the sheep; ²⁹take *it* from their half, and give *it* to Eleazar the priest as a heave offering to the LORD. ³⁰And from the children of Israel's half you shall take one of every fifty, drawn from the persons, the cattle, the donkeys, and the sheep, from all the livestock, and give them to the Levites who keep charge of the tabernacle of the LORD." ³¹So Moses and Eleazar the priest did as the LORD commanded Moses.

³²The booty remaining from the plunder, which the men of war had taken, was six hundred and seventy-five thousand sheep, ³³seventy-two thousand cattle, ³⁴sixty-one thousand donkeys, ³⁵and thirty-two thousand persons in all, of women who had not known a man intimately. ³⁶And the half, the portion for those who had gone out to war, was in number three hundred and thirty-seven thousand five hundred sheep; ³⁷and the LORD's tribute of the sheep was six hundred and seventy-five. ³⁸The cattle *were* thirty-six thousand, of which the LORD's tribute *was* seventy-two. ³⁹The donkeys *were* thirty thousand five hundred, of which the LORD's tribute *was* sixty-one. ⁴⁰The persons *were* sixteen thousand, of which the LORD's tribute *was* thirty-two persons. ⁴¹So Moses gave the tribute *which was* the LORD's heave offering to Eleazar the priest, as the LORD commanded Moses.

⁴²And from the children of Israel's half, which Moses separated from the men who fought— ⁴³now the half belonging to the congregation was three hundred and thirty-seven thousand five hundred sheep, ⁴⁴thirty-six thousand cattle, ⁴⁵thirty thousand five hundred donkeys, ⁴⁶and sixteen thousand persons— ⁴⁷and from the children of Israel's half Moses took one of every fifty, drawn from man and beast, and gave them to the Levites, who kept charge of the tabernacle of the LORD, as the LORD commanded Moses.

⁴⁸Then the officers who *were* over thousands of the army, the captains of thousands and captains of hundreds, came near to Moses; ⁴⁹and they said to Moses, "Your servants have taken a count of the men of war who *are* under our command, and not a man of us is missing. ⁵⁰Therefore we have brought an offering for the LORD, what every man found of ornaments of gold: armlets and bracelets and signet rings and earrings and necklaces, to make atonement for ourselves before the LORD." ⁵¹So Moses and Eleazar the priest received the gold from them, all the fashioned ornaments. ⁵²And all the gold of the offering that they offered to the LORD, from the captains of thousands and captains of hundreds, was sixteen thousand seven hundred and fifty shekels. ⁵³(The men of war had taken spoil, every man for himself.) ⁵⁴And Moses and Eleazar the priest received the gold from the captains of thousands and of hundreds, and brought it into the tabernacle of meeting as a memorial for the children of Israel before the LORD.

The Tribes Settling East of the Jordan

32 Now the children of Reuben and the children of Gad had a very great multitude of livestock; and when they saw the land of Jazer and the land of Gilead, that indeed the region *was* a place for livestock, ²the children of Gad and the children of Reuben came and spoke to Moses, to Eleazar the priest, and to the leaders of the congregation, saying, ³"Ataroth, Dibon, Jazer, Nimrah, Heshbon, Elealeh, Shebam, Nebo, and Beon, ⁴the country which the LORD defeated before the congregation of Israel, *is* a land for livestock, and your servants have livestock." ⁵Therefore they said, "If we have found favor in your sight, let this land be given to your servants as a possession. Do not take us over the Jordan."

⁶And Moses said to the children of Gad and to the children of Reuben: "Shall your brethren go to war while you sit here? ⁷Now why will you discourage the heart of the children of Israel from going over into the land which the LORD has given them? ⁸Thus your fathers did when I sent them away from Kadesh Barnea to see the land. ⁹For when they went up to the Valley of Eshcol

BIBLICAL INSIGHTS • 32:11, 12

Good Friends Reinforce Your Efforts

WOULD YOU LIKE TO SEE your mate's self-perspective improve? If so, encourage him or her to spend time cultivating godly friendships. A godly friend will help your mate to see his or her good qualities and to better understand personal weaknesses. Such friends reflect your mate's true value, worth, significance, and importance. They give your mate a correct self-perspective and keep your spouse headed in the right direction.

It is no accident that Joshua and Caleb, alone of all the Israelites who left Egypt, made it finally into the Promised Land. These two friends encouraged each other to believe God's promises, and together they resisted the evil tug of the crowd. Could either have done so alone? Who knows? But with a godly friend, it becomes much easier.

Godly friends communicate to your mate that someone else also admires his or her ideas, thoughts, and character qualities. Your spouse may consider your opinion biased, but hearing positive things from a friend can really register. A friend—an objective third party—can encourage your mate by echoing the very things you've said. Over time your mate will begin to believe your affirming comments because another trusted person has spoken them, too.

and saw the land, they discouraged the heart of the children of Israel, so that they did not go into the land which the LORD had given them. ¹⁰So the LORD's anger was aroused on that day, and He swore an oath, saying, ¹¹"Surely none of the men who came up from Egypt, from twenty years old and above, shall see the land of which I swore to Abraham, Isaac, and Jacob, because they have not wholly followed Me, ¹²except Caleb the son of Jephunneh, the Kenizzite, and Joshua the son of Nun, for they have wholly followed the LORD.' ¹³So the LORD's anger

was aroused against Israel, and He made them wander in the wilderness forty years, until all the generation that had done evil in the sight of the LORD was gone. ¹⁴And look! You have risen in your fathers' place, a brood of sinful men, to increase still more the fierce anger of the LORD against Israel. ¹⁵For if you turn away from following Him, He will once again leave them in the wilderness, and you will destroy all these people."

¹⁶Then they came near to him and said: "We will build sheepfolds here for our livestock, and cities for our little ones, ¹⁷but we ourselves will be armed, ready *to go* before the children of Israel until we have brought them to their place; and our little ones will dwell in the fortified cities because of the inhabitants of the land. ¹⁸We will not return to our homes until every one of the children of Israel has received his inheritance. ¹⁹For we will not inherit with them on the other side of the Jordan and beyond, because our inheritance has fallen to us on this eastern side of the Jordan."

²⁰Then Moses said to them: "If you do this thing, if you arm yourselves before the LORD for the war, ²¹and all your armed men cross over the Jordan before the LORD until He has driven out His enemies from before Him, ²²and the land is subdued before the LORD, then afterward you may return and be blameless before the LORD and before Israel; and this land shall be your possession before the LORD. ²³But if you do not do so, then take note, you have sinned against the LORD; and be sure your sin will find you out. ²⁴Build cities for your little ones and folds for your sheep, and do what has proceeded out of your mouth."

²⁵And the children of Gad and the children of Reuben spoke to Moses, saying: "Your servants will do as my lord commands. ²⁶Our little ones, our wives, our flocks, and all our livestock will be there in the cities of Gilead; ²⁷but your servants will cross over, every man armed for war, before the LORD to battle, just as my lord says."

²⁸So Moses gave command concerning them to Eleazar the priest, to Joshua the son of Nun, and to the chief fathers of the tribes of the children of Israel. ²⁹And Moses said to them: "If the children of Gad and the children of Reuben cross over the Jordan with

you, every man armed for battle before the LORD, and the land is subdued before you, then you shall give them the land of Gilead as a possession. 30But if they do not cross over armed with you, they shall have possessions among you in the land of Canaan."

31Then the children of Gad and the children of Reuben answered, saying: "As the LORD has said to your servants, so we will do. 32We will cross over armed before the LORD into the land of Canaan, but the possession of our inheritance *shall remain* with us on this side of the Jordan."

33So Moses gave to the children of Gad, to the children of Reuben, and to half the tribe of Manasseh the son of Joseph, the kingdom of Sihon king of the Amorites and the kingdom of Og king of Bashan, the land with its cities within the borders, the cities of the surrounding country. 34And the children of Gad built Dibon and Ataroth and Aroer, 35Atroth and Shophan and Jazer and Jogbehah, 36Beth Nimrah and Beth Haran, fortified cities, and folds for sheep. 37And the children of Reuben built Heshbon and Elealeh and Kirjathaim, 38Nebo and Baal Meon (*their* names being changed) and Shibmah; and they gave *other* names to the cities which they built.

39And the children of Machir the son of Manasseh went to Gilead and took it, and dispossessed the Amorites who *were* in it. 40So Moses gave Gilead to Machir the son of Manasseh, and he dwelt in it. 41Also Jair the son of Manasseh went and took its small towns, and called them Havoth Jair.ᵃ 42Then Nobah went and took Kenath and its villages, and he called it Nobah, after his own name.

Israel's Journey from Egypt Reviewed

33 These *are* the journeys of the children of Israel, who went out of the land of Egypt by their armies under the hand of Moses and Aaron. 2Now Moses wrote down the starting points of their journeys at the command of the LORD. And these *are* their journeys according to their starting points:

3They departed from Rameses in the first month, on the fifteenth day of the first month; on the day after the Passover the children of Israel went out with boldness in the sight of all the Egyptians. 4For the Egyptians were burying all *their* firstborn, whom the LORD had killed among them. Also on their gods the LORD had executed judgments.

5Then the children of Israel moved from Rameses and camped at Succoth. 6They departed from Succoth and camped at Etham, which *is* on the edge of the wilderness. 7They moved from Etham and turned back to Pi Hahiroth, which *is* east of Baal Zephon; and they camped near Migdol. 8They departed from before Hahirothᵃ and passed through the midst of the sea into the wilderness, went three days' journey in the Wilderness of Etham, and camped at Marah. 9They moved from Marah and came to Elim. At Elim *were* twelve springs of water and seventy palm trees; so they camped there.

10They moved from Elim and camped by the Red Sea. 11They moved from the Red Sea and camped in the Wilderness of Sin. 12They journeyed from the Wilderness of Sin and camped at Dophkah. 13They departed from Dophkah and camped at Alush. 14They moved from Alush and camped at Rephidim, where there was no water for the people to drink.

15They departed from Rephidim and camped in the Wilderness of Sinai. 16They moved from the Wilderness of Sinai and camped at Kibroth Hattaavah. 17They departed from Kibroth Hattaavah and camped at Hazeroth. 18They departed from Hazeroth and camped at Rithmah. 19They departed from Rithmah and camped at Rimmon Perez. 20They departed from Rimmon Perez and camped at Libnah. 21They moved from Libnah and camped at Rissah. 22They journeyed from Rissah and camped at Kehelathah. 23They went from Kehelathah and camped at Mount Shepher. 24They moved from Mount Shepher and camped at Haradah. 25They moved from Haradah and camped at Makheloth. 26They moved from Makheloth and camped at Tahath. 27They departed from Tahath and camped at Terah. 28They moved from Terah

---

32:41 ᵃLiterally *Towns of Jair* 33:8 ᵃMany Hebrew manuscripts, Samaritan Pentateuch, Syriac, Targum, and Vulgate read *from Pi Hahiroth* (compare verse 7).

and camped at Mithkah. 29They went from Mithkah and camped at Hashmonah. 30They departed from Hashmonah and camped at Moseroth. 31They departed from Moseroth and camped at Bene Jaakan. 32They moved from Bene Jaakan and camped at Hor Hagidgad. 33They went from Hor Hagidgad and camped at Jotbathah. 34They moved from Jotbathah and camped at Abronah. 35They departed from Abronah and camped at Ezion Geber. 36They moved from Ezion Geber and camped in the Wilderness of Zin, which *is* Kadesh. 37They moved from Kadesh and camped at Mount Hor, on the boundary of the land of Edom.

38Then Aaron the priest went up to Mount Hor at the command of the LORD, and died there in the fortieth year after the children of Israel had come out of the land of Egypt, on the first *day* of the fifth month. 39Aaron *was* one hundred and twenty-three years old when he died on Mount Hor.

40Now the king of Arad, the Canaanite, who dwelt in the South in the land of Canaan, heard of the coming of the children of Israel.

41So they departed from Mount Hor and camped at Zalmonah. 42They departed from Zalmonah and camped at Punon. 43They departed from Punon and camped at Oboth. 44They departed from Oboth and camped at Ije Abarim, at the border of Moab. 45They departed from Ijima and camped at Dibon Gad. 46They moved from Dibon Gad and camped at Almon Diblathaim. 47They moved from Almon Diblathaim and camped in the mountains of Abarim, before Nebo. 48They departed from the mountains of Abarim and camped in the plains of Moab by the Jordan, *across from* Jericho. 49They camped by the Jordan, from Beth Jesimoth as far as the Abel Acacia Grovea in the plains of Moab.

Instructions for the Conquest of Canaan

50Now the LORD spoke to Moses in the plains of Moab by the Jordan, *across from* Jericho, saying, 51"Speak to the children of Israel, and say to them: 'When you have crossed the Jordan into the land of Canaan, 52then you shall drive out all the inhabitants of the land from before you, destroy all their engraved stones, destroy all their molded images, and demolish all their high places; 53you shall dispossess *the inhabitants of* the land and dwell in it, for I have given you the land to possess. 54And you shall divide the land by lot as an inheritance among your families; to the larger you shall give a larger inheritance, and to the smaller you shall give a smaller inheritance; there everyone's *inheritance* shall be whatever falls to him by lot. You shall inherit according to the tribes of your fathers. 55But if you do not drive out the inhabitants of the land from before you, then it shall be that those whom you let remain *shall be* irritants in your eyes and thorns in your sides, and they shall harass you in the land where you dwell. 56Moreover it shall be *that* I will do to you as I thought to do to them.'"

The Appointed Boundaries of Canaan

34 Then the LORD spoke to Moses, saying, 2"Command the children of Israel, and say to them: 'When you come into the land of Canaan, this *is* the land that shall fall to you as an inheritance—the land of Canaan to its boundaries. 3Your southern border shall be from the Wilderness of Zin along the border of Edom; then your southern border shall extend eastward to the end of the Salt Sea; 4your border shall turn from the southern side of the Ascent of Akrabbim, continue to Zin, and be on the south of Kadesh Barnea; then it shall go on to Hazar Addar, and continue to Azmon; 5the border shall turn from Azmon to the Brook of Egypt, and it shall end at the Sea.

6'As for the western border, you shall

INTIMATE MOMENTS

Scour the Internet for the perfect romantic e-card. If possible, pair it with a favorite tune or love song of hers and send it to your wife when she least expects it.

33:45 aSame as *Ije Abarim,* verse 44
33:49 aHebrew *Abel Shittim*

have the Great Sea for a border; this shall be your western border.

7"And this shall be your northern border: From the Great Sea you shall mark out your *border* line to Mount Hor; 8from Mount Hor you shall mark out *your border* to the entrance of Hamath; then the direction of the border shall be toward Zedad; 9the border shall proceed to Ziphron, and it shall end at Hazar Enan. This shall be your northern border.

10"You shall mark out your eastern border from Hazar Enan to Shepham; 11the border shall go down from Shepham to Riblah on the east side of Ain; the border shall go down and reach to the eastern side of the Sea of Chinnereth; 12the border shall go down along the Jordan, and it shall end at the Salt Sea. This shall be your land with its surrounding boundaries.'"

13Then Moses commanded the children of Israel, saying: "This *is* the land which you shall inherit by lot, which the LORD has commanded to give to the nine tribes and to the half-tribe. 14For the tribe of the children of Reuben according to the house of their fathers, and the tribe of the children of Gad according to the house of their fathers, have received *their inheritance;* and the half-tribe of Manasseh has received its inheritance. 15The two tribes and the half-tribe have received their inheritance on this side of the Jordan, *across from* Jericho eastward, toward the sunrise."

The Leaders Appointed to Divide the Land

16And the LORD spoke to Moses, saying, 17"These *are* the names of the men who shall divide the land among you as an inheritance: Eleazar the priest and Joshua the son of Nun. 18And you shall take one leader of every tribe to divide the land for the inheritance. 19These *are* the names of the men: from the tribe of Judah, Caleb the son of Jephunneh; 20from the tribe of the children of Simeon, Shemuel the son of Ammihud; 21from the tribe of Benjamin, Elidad the son of Chislon; 22a leader from the tribe of the children of Dan, Bukki the son of Jogli; 23from the sons of Joseph: a leader from the tribe of the children of Manasseh, Hanniel the son of Ephod, 24and a

leader from the tribe of the children of Ephraim, Kemuel the son of Shiphtan; 25a leader from the tribe of the children of Zebulun, Elizaphan the son of Parnach; 26a leader from the tribe of the children of Issachar, Paltiel the son of Azzan; 27a leader from the tribe of the children of Asher, Ahihud the son of Shelomi; 28and a leader from the tribe of the children of Naphtali, Pedahel the son of Ammihud."

29These *are* the ones the LORD commanded to divide the inheritance among the children of Israel in the land of Canaan.

Cities for the Levites

35 And the LORD spoke to Moses in the plains of Moab by the Jordan *across from* Jericho, saying: 2"Command the children of Israel that they give the Levites cities to dwell in from the inheritance of their possession, and you shall *also* give the Levites common-land around the cities. 3They shall have the cities to dwell in; and their common-land shall be for their cattle, for their herds, and for all their animals. 4The common-land of the cities which you will give the Levites *shall extend* from the wall of the city outward a thousand cubits all around. 5And you shall measure outside the city on the east side two thousand cubits, on the south side two thousand cubits, on the west side two thousand cubits, and on the north side two thousand cubits. The city *shall be* in the middle. This shall belong to them as common-land for the cities.

6"Now among the cities which you will give to the Levites *you shall appoint* six cities of refuge, to which a manslayer may flee. And to these you shall add forty-two cities. 7So all the cities you will give to the Levites *shall be* forty-eight; these *you shall give* with their common-land. 8And the cities which you will give *shall be* from the possession of the children of Israel; from the larger *tribe* you shall give many, from the smaller you shall give few. Each shall give some of its cities to the Levites, in proportion to the inheritance that each receives."

Cities of Refuge

9Then the LORD spoke to Moses, saying, 10"Speak to the children of Israel, and say to them: 'When you cross the Jordan into the land of Canaan, ¹¹then you shall appoint cities to be cities of refuge for you, that the manslayer who kills any person accidentally may flee there. ¹²They shall be cities of refuge for you from the avenger, that the manslayer may not die until he stands before the congregation in judgment. ¹³And of the cities which you give, you shall have six cities of refuge. ¹⁴You shall appoint three cities on this side of the Jordan, and three cities you shall appoint in the land of Canaan, *which* will be cities of refuge. ¹⁵These six cities shall be for refuge for the children of Israel, for the stranger, and for the sojourner among them, that anyone who kills a person accidentally may flee there.

¹⁶'But if he strikes him with an iron implement, so that he dies, he *is* a murderer; the murderer shall surely be put to death. ¹⁷And if he strikes him with a stone in the hand, by which one could die, and he does die, he *is* a murderer; the murderer shall surely be put to death. ¹⁸Or *if* he strikes him with a wooden hand weapon, by which one could die, and he does die, he *is* a murderer; the murderer shall surely be put to death. ¹⁹The avenger of blood himself shall put the murderer to death; when he meets him, he shall put him to death. ²⁰If he pushes him out of hatred or, while lying in wait, hurls something at him so that he dies, ²¹or in enmity he strikes him with his hand so that he dies, the one who struck *him* shall surely be put to death. He *is* a murderer. The avenger of blood shall put the murderer to death when he meets him.

²²'However, if he pushes him suddenly without enmity, or throws anything at him without lying in wait, ²³or uses a stone, by which a man could die, throwing *it* at him without seeing *him,* so that he dies, while he was not his enemy or seeking his harm, ²⁴then the congregation shall judge between the manslayer and the avenger of blood according to these judgments. ²⁵So the congregation shall deliver the manslayer from the hand of the avenger of blood, and the congregation shall return him to the city of refuge where he had fled, and he shall remain there until the death of the high priest who was anointed with the holy oil. ²⁶But if the manslayer at any time goes outside the limits of the city of refuge where he fled, ²⁷and the avenger of blood finds him outside the limits of his city of refuge, and the avenger of blood kills the manslayer, he shall not be guilty of blood, ²⁸because he should have remained in his city of refuge until the death of the high

---

PARENTING MATTERS

Q: *How can we be sure that our child is sticking to the convictions he/she is learning at home?*

Ask your child to tell you about some of the groups at school. What are they like, how do they act, who is their leader, what's their music, why are people attracted to them?

Be observant. If you see subtle (or not so subtle!) changes in dress or appearance, find out what's behind the new look.

As your child's freedom increases, don't be afraid to inspect what you expect. If you've given your child freedom to go get a pizza with friends, ask who went, what time your child left the pizza place, where did he go.

When failure occurs, make sure you talk through the situation and gently help the child articulate in his own words what went wrong. Your child will make some mistakes and succumb to peer pressure. When that happens, you can guide, correct, and instruct.

Applaud your child's good choices. When your child makes the right choice, acknowledge it.

Don't always try to rescue your child from loneliness. Don't give in to the temptation to think you're being too harsh by encouraging your child to stand alone against the herd.

priest. But after the death of the high priest the manslayer may return to the land of his possession.

²⁹'And these *things* shall be a statute of judgment to you throughout your generations in all your dwellings. ³⁰Whoever kills a person, the murderer shall be put to death on the testimony of witnesses; but one witness is not *sufficient* testimony against a person for the death *penalty.* ³¹Moreover you shall take no ransom for the life of a murderer who *is* guilty of death, but he shall surely be put to death. ³²And you shall take no ransom for him who has fled to his city of refuge, that he may return to dwell in the land before the death of the priest. ³³So you shall not pollute the land where you *are;* for blood defiles the land, and no atonement can be made for the land, for the blood that is shed on it, except by the blood of him who shed it. ³⁴Therefore do not defile the land which you inhabit, in the midst of which I dwell; for I the LORD dwell among the children of Israel.'"

Marriage of Female Heirs

36 Now the chief fathers of the families of the children of Gilead the son of Machir, the son of Manasseh, of the families of the sons of Joseph, came near and spoke before Moses and before the leaders, the chief fathers of the children of Israel. ²And they said: "The LORD commanded my lord *Moses* to give the land as an inheritance by lot to the children of Israel, and my lord was commanded by the LORD to give the inheritance of our brother Zelophehad to his daughters. ³Now if they are married to any of the sons of the *other* tribes of the children of Israel, then their inheritance will be taken from the inheritance of our fathers, and it will be added to the inheritance of the tribe into which they marry; so it will be

taken from the lot of our inheritance. ⁴And when the Jubilee of the children of Israel comes, then their inheritance will be added to the inheritance of the tribe into which they marry; so their inheritance will be taken away from the inheritance of the tribe of our fathers."

⁵Then Moses commanded the children of Israel according to the word of the LORD, saying: "What the tribe of the sons of Joseph speaks is right. ⁶This *is* what the LORD commands concerning the daughters of Zelophehad, saying, 'Let them marry whom they think best, but they may marry only within the family of their father's tribe.' ⁷So the inheritance of the children of Israel shall not change hands from tribe to tribe, for every one of the children of Israel shall keep the inheritance of the tribe of his fathers. ⁸And every daughter who possesses an inheritance in any tribe of the children of Israel shall be the wife of one of the family of her father's tribe, so that the children of Israel each may possess the inheritance of his fathers. ⁹Thus no inheritance shall change hands from *one* tribe to another, but every tribe of the children of Israel shall keep its own inheritance."

¹⁰Just as the LORD commanded Moses, so did the daughters of Zelophehad; ¹¹for Mahlah, Tirzah, Hoglah, Milcah, and Noah, the daughters of Zelophehad, were married to the sons of their father's brothers. ¹²They were married into the families of the children of Manasseh the son of Joseph, and their inheritance remained in the tribe of their father's family.

¹³These *are* the commandments and the judgments which the LORD commanded the children of Israel by the hand of Moses in the plains of Moab by the Jordan, *across from* Jericho.

DEUTERONOMY

THIS BOOK REFLECTS A SEASON OF COMING CHANGE for the descendents of Jacob, who have now become the nation of Israel. Deuteronomy is a collection of farewell speeches from the patriarch Moses as the Hebrew people prepare to enter the land without him. By the end of the book, Moses has entered in the final weeks of his life. And so Deuteronomy is like a long letter written from a great-grandfather to his children, grandchildren, and great-grandchildren, as they prepare for all that God has planned for them.

Moses reminds his kinsmen again of the Ten Commandments. He calls them to a total commitment to God in Deuteronomy 6:4, 5, one of the most famous passages in the Bible. He instructs parents to teach the things of God to their children in the flow of everyday life (6:6, 7). He reminds the nation not to forget God or to be enticed away from God by the false gods of other nations. He instructs the people on a wide variety of issues related to worship, leadership, living together in peace, settling disputes, and a host of other issues. He also reminds them that obedience consistently brings the blessing of God, while disobedience unavoidably brings God's chastening and discipline.

As you read Deuteronomy, read it as if it were a letter from an elderly, wise relative who has expressed a desire to pass on time-tested instructions for how to live rightly before God and with others. Notice in particular all the times you run into the words, *remember*, *promised*, *blessed*, and *cursed*. The presence of these words usually signals a special emphasis of the book and a firm priority of God.

You will also read some specific legal directives related to Hebrew society of this time, instructions that don't apply directly to Christian living today—for example, the commands regarding divorce and remarriage in Deuteronomy 24. Even so, the moral convictions that lie behind these detailed instructions will provide you with insight into the things that matter to God, for *all* people and for *all* times.

The Previous Command to Enter Canaan

1 These *are* the words which Moses spoke to all Israel on this side of the Jordan in the wilderness, in the plain[a] opposite Suph,[b] between Paran, Tophel, Laban, Hazeroth, and Dizahab. [2]*It is* eleven days' *journey* from Horeb by way of Mount Seir to Kadesh Barnea. [3]Now it came to pass in the fortieth year, in the eleventh month, on the first *day* of the month, *that* Moses spoke to the children of Israel according to all that the LORD had given him as commandments to them, [4]after he had killed Sihon king of the Amorites, who dwelt in Heshbon, and Og king of Bashan, who dwelt at Ashtaroth in[a] Edrei.

[5]On this side of the Jordan in the land of Moab, Moses began to explain this law, saying, [6]"The LORD our God spoke to us in Horeb, saying: 'You have dwelt long enough at this mountain. [7]Turn and take your journey, and go to the mountains of the Amorites, to all the neighboring *places* in the plain,[a] in the mountains and in the lowland, in the South and on the seacoast, to the land of the Canaanites and to Lebanon, as far as the great river, the River Euphrates. [8]See, I have set the land before you; go in and possess the land which the LORD swore to your fathers—to Abraham, Isaac, and Jacob—to give to them and their descendants after them.'

Tribal Leaders Appointed

[9]"And I spoke to you at that time, saying: 'I alone am not able to bear you. [10]The LORD your God has multiplied you, and here you *are* today, as the stars of heaven in multitude. [11]May the LORD God of your fathers make you a thousand times more numerous than you are, and bless you as He has promised you! [12]How can I alone bear your problems and your burdens and your complaints? [13]Choose wise, understanding, and knowledgeable men from among your tribes, and I will make them heads over you.' [14]And you answered me and said, 'The thing which you have told *us* to do *is* good.'

[15]So I took the heads of your tribes, wise and knowledgeable men, and made them heads over you, leaders of thousands, leaders of hundreds, leaders of fifties, leaders of tens, and officers for your tribes. [16]"Then I commanded your judges at that time, saying, 'Hear *the cases* between your brethren, and judge righteously between a man and his brother or the stranger who is with him. [17]You shall not show partiality in judgment; you shall hear the small as well as the great; you shall not be afraid in any man's presence, for the judgment *is* God's. The case that is too hard for you, bring to me, and I will hear it.' [18]And I commanded you at that time all the things which you should do.

Israel's Refusal to Enter the Land

[19]"So we departed from Horeb, and went through all that great and terrible wilderness which you saw on the way to the mountains of the Amorites, as the LORD our God had commanded us. Then we came to Kadesh Barnea. [20]And I said to you, 'You have come to the mountains of the Amorites, which the LORD our God is giving us. [21]Look, the LORD your God has set the land before you; go up *and* possess *it,* as the LORD God of your fathers has spoken to you; do not fear or be discouraged.'

INTIMATE MOMENTS

Tell your wife that you want to give her a hand or a foot massage. If she doesn't have time right at the moment, then schedule a time for later that you can play the role of masseuse. When the time is right, take at least fifteen minutes (although a half hour is better) to gently caress her hands or feet. As your hands work the tension and stress out of her body, softly express your appreciation for the various things she does with her hands and feet that show her love and care for others. Invite her to relax and soak it all in; no need to respond in kind. This time is just for her.

1:1 [a]Hebrew *arabah* [b]One manuscript of the Septuagint, also Targum and Vulgate, read *Red Sea*. **1:4** [a]Septuagint, Syriac, and Vulgate read *and* (compare Joshua 12:4). **1:7** [a]Hebrew *arabah*

²²"And every one of you came near to me and said, 'Let us send men before us, and let them search out the land for us, and bring back word to us of the way by which we should go up, and of the cities into which we shall come.'

²³"The plan pleased me well; so I took twelve of your men, one man from *each* tribe. ²⁴And they departed and went up into the mountains, and came to the Valley of Eshcol, and spied it out. ²⁵They also took *some* of the fruit of the land in their hands and brought *it* down to us; and they brought back word to us, saying, '*It is* a good land which the LORD our God is giving us.'

²⁶"Nevertheless you would not go up, but rebelled against the command of the LORD your God; ²⁷and you complained in your tents, and said, 'Because the LORD hates us, He has brought us out of the land of Egypt to deliver us into the hand of the Amorites, to destroy us. ²⁸Where can we go up? Our brethren have discouraged our hearts, saying, "The people *are* greater and taller than we; the cities *are* great and fortified up to heaven; moreover we have seen the sons of the Anakim there."'

²⁹"Then I said to you, 'Do not be terrified, or afraid of them. ³⁰The LORD your God, who goes before you, He will fight for you, according to all He did for you in Egypt before your eyes, ³¹and in the wilderness where you saw how the LORD your God carried you, as a man carries his son, in all the way that you went until you came to this place.' ³²Yet, for all that, you did not believe the LORD your God, ³³who went in the way before you to search out a place for you to pitch your tents, to show you the way you should go, in the fire by night and in the cloud by day.

The Penalty for Israel's Rebellion

³⁴"And the LORD heard the sound of your words, and was angry, and took an oath, saying, ³⁵'Surely not one of these men of this evil generation shall see that good land of which I swore to give to your fathers, ³⁶except Caleb the son of Jephunneh; he shall see it, and to him and his children I am giving the land on which he walked, because he wholly followed the LORD.' ³⁷The LORD was also angry with me for your sakes, saying, 'Even you shall not go in

there. ³⁸Joshua the son of Nun, who stands before you, he shall go in there. Encourage him, for he shall cause Israel to inherit it.

³⁹'Moreover your little ones and your children, who you say will be victims, who today have no knowledge of good and evil, they shall go in there; to them I will give it, and they shall possess it. ⁴⁰But *as for* you, turn and take your journey into the wilderness by the Way of the Red Sea.'

⁴¹"Then you answered and said to me, 'We have sinned against the LORD; we will go up and fight, just as the LORD our God commanded us.' And when everyone of you had girded on his weapons of war, you were ready to go up into the mountain.

⁴²"And the LORD said to me, 'Tell them, "Do not go up nor fight, for I *am* not among you; lest you be defeated before your enemies."' ⁴³So I spoke to you; yet you would not listen, but rebelled against the command of the LORD, and presumptuously went up into the mountain. ⁴⁴And the Amorites who dwelt in that mountain came out against you and chased you as bees do, and drove you back from Seir to Hormah. ⁴⁵Then you returned and wept before the LORD, but the LORD would not listen to your voice nor give ear to you.

⁴⁶"So you remained in Kadesh many days, according to the days that you spent *there*.

The Desert Years

2 "Then we turned and journeyed into the wilderness of the Way of the Red Sea, as the LORD spoke to me, and we skirted Mount Seir for many days.

²"And the LORD spoke to me, saying: ³'You have skirted this mountain long enough; turn northward. ⁴And command the people, saying, "You *are about to* pass through the territory of your brethren, the descendants of Esau, who live in Seir; and they will be afraid of you. Therefore watch yourselves carefully. ⁵Do not meddle with them, for I will not give you *any* of their land, no, not so much as one footstep, because I have given Mount Seir to Esau *as* a possession. ⁶You shall buy food from them with money, that you may eat; and you shall also buy water from them with money, that you may drink.

[7]"For the LORD your God has blessed you in all the work of your hand. He knows your trudging through this great wilderness. These forty years the LORD your God *has been* with you; you have lacked nothing.'"

[8]"And when we passed beyond our brethren, the descendants of Esau who dwell in Seir, away from the road of the plain, away from Elath and Ezion Geber, we turned and passed by way of the Wilderness of Moab. [9]Then the LORD said to me, 'Do not harass Moab, nor contend with them in battle, for I will not give you *any* of their land *as* a possession, because I have given Ar to the descendants of Lot *as* a possession.' "

[10](The Emim had dwelt there in times past, a people as great and numerous and tall as the Anakim. [11]They were also regarded as giants,[a] like the Anakim, but the Moabites call them Emim. [12]The Horites formerly dwelt in Seir, but the descendants of Esau dispossessed them and destroyed them from before them, and dwelt in their place, just as Israel did to the land of their possession which the LORD gave them.)

[13] 'Now rise and cross over the Valley of the Zered.' So we crossed over the Valley of the Zered. [14]And the time we took to come from Kadesh Barnea until we crossed over the Valley of the Zered *was* thirty-eight years, until all the generation of the men of war was consumed from the midst of the camp, just as the LORD had sworn to them. [15]For indeed the hand of the LORD was against them, to destroy them from the midst of the camp until they were consumed.

[16]"So it was, when all the men of war had finally perished from among the people, [17]that the LORD spoke to me, saying: [18]'This day you are to cross over at Ar, the boundary of Moab. [19]And *when* you come near the people of Ammon, do not harass them or meddle with them, for I will not give you *any* of the land of the people of Ammon *as* a possession, because I have given it to the descendants of Lot *as* a possession.' "

[20](That was also regarded as a land of giants;[a] giants formerly dwelt there. But the Ammonites call them Zamzummim, [21]a people as great and numerous and tall as the Anakim. But the LORD destroyed them before them, and they dispossessed them and dwelt in their place, [22]just as He had done for the descendants of Esau, who dwelt in Seir, when He destroyed the Horites from before them. They dispossessed them and dwelt in their place, even to this day. [23]And the Avim, who dwelt in villages as far as Gaza—the Caphtorim, who came from Caphtor, destroyed them and dwelt in their place.)

[24]" 'Rise, take your journey, and cross over the River Arnon. Look, I have given into your hand Sihon the Amorite, king of Heshbon, and his land. Begin to possess *it,* and engage him in battle. [25]This day I will begin to put the dread and fear of you upon the nations under the whole heaven, who shall hear the report of you, and shall tremble and be in anguish because of you.'

King Sihon Defeated

[26]"And I sent messengers from the Wilderness of Kedemoth to Sihon king of Heshbon, with words of peace, saying, [27]'Let me pass through your land; I will keep strictly to the road, and I will turn neither to the right nor to the left. [28]You shall sell me food for money, that I may eat, and give me water for money, that I may drink; only let me pass through on foot, [29]just as the descendants of Esau who dwell in Seir and the Moabites who dwell in Ar did for me, until I cross the Jordan to the land which the LORD our God is giving us.'

[30]"But Sihon king of Heshbon would not let us pass through, for the LORD your God hardened his spirit and made his heart obstinate, that He might deliver him into your hand, as *it is* this day. [31]"And the LORD said to me, 'See, I have begun to give Sihon and his land over to you. Begin to possess *it,* that you may inherit his land.' [32]Then Sihon and all his people came out against us to fight at Jahaz. [33]And the LORD our God delivered him over to us; so we defeated him, his sons, and all his people. [34]We took all his cities at that time, and we utterly destroyed the men, women, and little ones of every city; we left none remaining. [35]We took only

2:11 [a]Hebrew *rephaim* 2:20 [a]Hebrew *rephaim*

the livestock as plunder for ourselves, with the spoil of the cities which we took. [36]From Aroer, which *is* on the bank of the River Arnon, and *from* the city that *is* in the ravine, as far as Gilead, there was not one city too strong for us; the LORD our God delivered all to us. [37]Only you did not go near the land of the people of Ammon—anywhere along the River Jabbok, or to the cities of the mountains, or wherever the LORD our God had forbidden us.

King Og Defeated

3 "Then we turned and went up the road to Bashan; and Og king of Bashan came out against us, he and all his people, to battle at Edrei. [2]And the LORD said to me, 'Do not fear him, for I have delivered him and all his people and his land into your hand; you shall do to him as you did to Sihon king of the Amorites, who dwelt at Heshbon.'

[3]"So the LORD our God also delivered into our hands Og king of Bashan, with all his people, and we attacked him until he had no survivors remaining. [4]And we took all his cities at that time; there was not a city which we did not take from them: sixty cities, all the region of Argob, the kingdom of Og in Bashan. [5]All these cities *were* fortified with high walls, gates, and bars, besides a great many rural towns.

[6]And we utterly destroyed them, as we did to Sihon king of Heshbon, utterly destroying the men, women, and children of every city. [7]But all the livestock and the spoil of the cities we took as booty for ourselves.

[8]"And at that time we took the land from the hand of the two kings of the Amorites who *were* on this side of the Jordan, from the River Arnon to Mount Hermon [9](the Sidonians call Hermon Sirion, and the Amorites call it Senir), [10]all the cities of the plain, all Gilead, and all Bashan, as far as Salcah and Edrei, cities of the kingdom of Og in Bashan.

[11]"For only Og king of Bashan remained of the remnant of the giants.[a] Indeed his bedstead *was* an iron bedstead. (*Is* it not in Rabbah of the people of Ammon?) Nine cubits *is* its length and four cubits its width, according to the standard cubit.

The Land East of the Jordan Divided

[12]"And this land, *which* we possessed at that time, from Aroer, which *is* by the River Arnon, and half the mountains of Gilead and its cities, I gave to the Reubenites and the Gadites. [13]The rest of Gilead, and all Bashan, the kingdom of Og, I gave to half the tribe of Manasseh. (All the region of

---

3:11 [a]Hebrew *rephaim*

PARENTING MATTERS	**Q:** *How can we best teach our children about sexual purity?*

No matter what you teach your child, your model of purity will go farthest in protecting your child. He or she needs to see a commitment to purity in your life.

If anything can disqualify a parent from being able to talk to a son or daughter about sex, it is being involved in sexual sin, sexual addiction, an affair, or an affair of the heart. If any of these issues are ongoing in your life and you have not repented, your sin is not just personal; it *will* have an impact on your children, your grandchildren, and beyond. The Bible warns that *sin can be passed down to not one, but four generations* (Deut. 5:9). Repent and have your conscience cleansed by the forgiveness of Jesus Christ.

Trash the videos. Burn the literature. Turn off the TV when inappropriate programming comes on. Put an internet filter on your computer. Stop going to and renting suggestive movies. Cancel magazine or catalog subscriptions that bring suggestive material into your home. Break off a relationship with the opposite sex. You will not be able to instruct your child to keep out of the traps if you are not staying out of them yourself.

Argob, with all Bashan, was called the land of the giants.[a] [14]Jair the son of Manasseh took all the region of Argob, as far as the border of the Geshurites and the Maachathites, and called Bashan after his own name, Havoth Jair,[a] to this day.)

[15]"Also I gave Gilead to Machir. [16]And to the Reubenites and the Gadites I gave from Gilead as far as the River Arnon, the middle of the river as *the* border, as far as the River Jabbok, the border of the people of Ammon; [17]the plain also, with the Jordan as *the* border, from Chinnereth as far as the east side of the Sea of the Arabah (the Salt Sea), below the slopes of Pisgah.

[18]"Then I commanded you at that time, saying: 'The LORD your God has given you this land to possess. All you men of valor shall cross over armed before your brethren, the children of Israel. [19]But your wives, your little ones, and your livestock (I know that you have much livestock) shall stay in your cities which I have given you, [20]until the LORD has given rest to your brethren as to you, and they also possess the land which the LORD your God is giving them beyond the Jordan. Then each of you may return to his possession which I have given you.'

[21]"And I commanded Joshua at that time, saying, 'Your eyes have seen all that the LORD your God has done to these two kings; so will the LORD do to all the kingdoms through which you pass. [22]You must not fear them, for the LORD your God Himself fights for you.'

Moses Forbidden to Enter the Land

[23]"Then I pleaded with the LORD at that time, saying: [24]O Lord GOD, You have begun to show Your servant Your greatness and Your mighty hand, for what god *is there* in heaven or on earth who can do *anything* like Your works and Your mighty *deeds?* [25]I pray, let me cross over and see the good land beyond the Jordan, those pleasant mountains, and Lebanon.'

[26]"But the LORD was angry with me on your account, and would not listen to me. So the LORD said to me: 'Enough of that! Speak no more to Me of this matter. [27]Go up to the top of Pisgah, and lift your eyes

toward the west, the north, the south, and the east; behold *it* with your eyes, for you shall not cross over this Jordan. [28]But command Joshua, and encourage him and strengthen him; for he shall go over before this people, and he shall cause them to inherit the land which you will see.'

[29]"So we stayed in the valley opposite Beth Peor.

Moses Commands Obedience

4 "Now, O Israel, listen to the statutes and the judgments which I teach you to observe, that you may live, and go in and possess the land which the LORD God of your fathers is giving you. [2]You shall not add to the word which I command you, nor take from it, that you may keep the commandments of the LORD your God which I command you. [3]Your eyes have seen what the LORD did at Baal Peor; for the LORD your God has destroyed from among you all the men who followed Baal of Peor. [4]But you who held fast to the LORD your God *are* alive today, every one of you.

[5]"Surely I have taught you statutes and judgments, just as the LORD my God commanded me, that you should act according *to them* in the land which you go to possess. [6]Therefore be careful to observe *them;* for this *is* your wisdom and your understanding in the sight of the peoples who will hear all these statutes, and say, 'Surely this great nation *is* a wise and understanding people.'

[7]"For what great nation *is there* that has God *so* near to it, as the LORD our God *is* to us, for whatever *reason* we may call upon Him? [8]And what great nation *is there* that has *such* statutes and righteous judgments as are in all this law which I set before you this day? [9]Only take heed to yourself, and diligently keep yourself, lest you forget the things your eyes have seen, and lest they depart from your heart all the days of your life. And teach them to your children and your grandchildren, [10]*especially concerning* the day you stood before the LORD your God in Horeb, when the LORD said to me, 'Gather the people to Me, and I will let them hear My words, that they may learn to fear Me all the days they live on the earth, and *that* they may teach their children.'

[11]"Then you came near and stood at the

3:13 [a]Hebrew *rephaim* 3:14 [a]Literally *Towns of Jair*

foot of the mountain, and the mountain burned with fire to the midst of heaven, with darkness, cloud, and thick darkness. ¹²And the LORD spoke to you out of the midst of the fire. You heard the sound of the words, but saw no form; *you* only *heard* a voice. ¹³So He declared to you His covenant which He commanded you to perform, the Ten Commandments; and He wrote them on two tablets of stone. ¹⁴And the LORD commanded me at that time to teach you statutes and judgments, that you might observe them in the land which you cross over to possess.

Beware of Idolatry

¹⁵"Take careful heed to yourselves, for you saw no form when the LORD spoke to you at Horeb out of the midst of the fire, ¹⁶lest you act corruptly and make for yourselves a carved image in the form of any figure: the likeness of male or female, ¹⁷the likeness of any animal that *is* on the earth or the likeness of any winged bird that flies in the air, ¹⁸the likeness of anything that creeps on the ground or the likeness of any fish that *is* in the water beneath the earth. ¹⁹And *take heed,* lest you lift your eyes to heaven, and *when* you see the sun, the moon, and the stars, all the host of heaven, you feel driven to worship them and serve them, which the LORD your God has given to all the peoples under the whole heaven as a heritage. ²⁰But the LORD has taken you and brought you out of the iron furnace, out of Egypt, to be His people, an inheritance, as you are this day. ²¹Furthermore the LORD was angry with me for your sakes, and swore that I would not cross over the Jordan, and that I would not enter the good land which the LORD your God is giving you as an inheritance. ²²But I must die in this land, I must not cross over the Jordan; but you shall cross over and possess that good land. ²³Take heed to yourselves, lest you forget the covenant of the LORD your God which He made with you, and make for yourselves a carved image in the form of anything which the LORD your God has forbidden you. ²⁴For the LORD your God *is* a consuming fire, a jealous God.

²⁵"When you beget children and grandchildren and have grown old in the land, and act corruptly and make a carved image

in the form of anything, and do evil in the sight of the LORD your God to provoke Him to anger, ²⁶I call heaven and earth to witness against you this day, that you will soon utterly perish from the land which you cross over the Jordan to possess; you will not prolong *your* days in it, but will be utterly destroyed. ²⁷And the LORD will scatter you among the peoples, and you will be left few in number among the nations where the LORD will drive you. ²⁸And there you will serve gods, the work of men's hands, wood and stone, which neither see nor hear nor eat nor smell. ²⁹But from there you will seek the LORD your God, and you will find *Him* if you seek Him with all your heart and with all your soul. ³⁰When you are in distress, and all these things come upon you in the latter days, when you turn to the LORD your God and obey His voice ³¹(for the LORD your God *is* a merciful God), He will not forsake you nor destroy you, nor forget the covenant of your fathers which He swore to them.

³²"For ask now concerning the days that are past, which were before you, since the day that God created man on the earth, and *ask* from one end of heaven to the other, whether *any* great *thing* like this has happened, or *anything* like it has been heard. ³³Did *any* people *ever* hear the voice of God speaking out of the midst of the fire, as you have heard, and live? ³⁴Or did God *ever* try to go *and* take for Himself a nation from the midst of *another* nation, by trials, by signs, by wonders, by war, by a mighty hand and an outstretched arm, and by great terrors, according to all that the LORD your God did for you in Egypt before your eyes? ³⁵To you it was shown, that you might know that the LORD Himself *is* God; *there is* none other besides Him. ³⁶Out of heaven He let you hear His voice, that He might instruct you; on earth He showed you His great fire, and you heard His words out of the midst of the fire. ³⁷And because He loved your fathers, therefore He chose their descendants after them; and He brought you out of Egypt with His Presence, with His mighty power, ³⁸driving out from before you nations greater and mightier than you, to bring you in, to give you their land *as* an inheritance,

as *it is* this day. ³⁹Therefore know this day, and consider *it* in your heart, that the LORD Himself *is* God in heaven above and on the earth beneath; *there is* no other. ⁴⁰You shall therefore keep His statutes and His commandments which I command you today, that it may go well with you and with your children after you, and that you may prolong *your* days in the land which the LORD your God is giving you for all time."

Cities of Refuge East of the Jordan

⁴¹Then Moses set apart three cities on this side of the Jordan, toward the rising of the sun, ⁴²that the manslayer might flee there, who kills his neighbor unintentionally, without having hated him in time past, and that by fleeing to one of these cities he might live: ⁴³Bezer in the wilderness on the plateau for the Reubenites, Ramoth in Gilead for the Gadites, and Golan in Bashan for the Manassites.

Introduction to God's Law

⁴⁴Now this *is* the law which Moses set before the children of Israel. ⁴⁵These *are* the testimonies, the statutes, and the judgments which Moses spoke to the children of Israel after they came out of Egypt, ⁴⁶on this side of the Jordan, in the valley opposite Beth Peor, in the land of Sihon king of the Amorites, who dwelt at Heshbon, whom Moses and the children of Israel defeated after they came out of Egypt. ⁴⁷And they took possession of his land and the land of Og king of Bashan, two kings of the Amorites, who *were* on this side of the Jordan, toward the rising of the sun, ⁴⁸from Aroer, which *is* on the bank of the River Arnon, even to Mount Sion[a] (that is, Hermon), ⁴⁹and all the plain on the east side of the Jordan as far as the Sea of the Arabah, below the slopes of Pisgah.

The Ten Commandments Reviewed

5 And Moses called all Israel, and said to them: "Hear, O Israel, the statutes and judgments which I speak in your hearing today, that you may learn them and be careful to observe them. ²The LORD our

BIBLICAL INSIGHTS • 5:9

A Warning to Heed

DEUTERONOMY 5:9 SENDS cold shivers down the spines of some believers: "I . . . am a jealous God, visiting the iniquity of the fathers upon the children to the third and fourth generations of those who hate me."

What do you think this warning means? Is God trying to deliberately ruin the next generation? Why would God set up a system that inflicts one generation's flaws on three or four others?

I have a hunch that God is trying to tell us that the way we live is of supreme importance. Possibly, He's using a warning of future judgment on our descendants to keep us on the straight and narrow today.

Whether you like it or not, your children are becoming just like you. Their little eyes are watching to see how you relate to your mate, how you pray, how you walk with Christ every day. They hear your words and subconsciously mimic your attitudes, actions, and even your mannerisms.

And as time goes by, you'll find they've inherited some of the same tendencies toward sin that you learned from your own parents. And the time to stop that behavior is *now*.

God made a covenant with us in Horeb. ³The LORD did not make this covenant with our fathers, but with us, those who *are* here today, all of us who *are* alive. ⁴The LORD talked with you face to face on the mountain from the midst of the fire. ⁵I stood between the LORD and you at that time, to declare to you the word of the LORD; for you were afraid because of the fire, and you did not go up the mountain. *He* said:

⁶   ' I *am* the LORD your God who brought you out of the land of Egypt, out of the house of bondage.

⁷   ' You shall have no other gods before Me.

8 ' You shall not make for yourself a carved image—any likeness *of anything* that *is* in heaven above, or that *is* in the earth beneath, or that *is* in the water under the earth; ⁹you shall not bow down to them nor serve them. For I, the LORD your God, *am* a jealous God, visiting the iniquity of the fathers upon the children to the third and fourth *generations* of those who hate Me, ¹⁰but showing mercy to thousands, to those who love Me and keep My commandments.

11 ' You shall not take the name of the LORD your God in vain, for the LORD will not hold *him* guiltless who takes His name in vain.

12 ' Observe the Sabbath day, to keep it holy, as the LORD your God commanded you. ¹³Six days you shall labor and do all your work, ¹⁴but the seventh day *is* the Sabbath of the LORD your God. *In it* you shall do no work: you, nor your son, nor your daughter, nor your male servant, nor your female servant, nor your ox, nor your donkey, nor any of your cattle, nor your stranger who *is* within your gates, that your male servant and your female servant may rest as well as you. ¹⁵And remember that you were a slave in the land of Egypt, and the LORD your God brought you out from there by a mighty hand and by an outstretched arm; therefore the LORD your God commanded you to keep the Sabbath day.

16 ' Honor your father and your mother, as the LORD your God has commanded you, that your days may be long, and that it may be well with you in the land which the LORD your God is giving you.

17 ' You shall not murder.

18 ' You shall not commit adultery.

19 ' You shall not steal.

20 ' You shall not bear false witness against your neighbor.

21 ' You shall not covet your neighbor's wife; and you shall not desire your neighbor's house, his field, his male servant, his female servant, his ox, his donkey, or anything that *is* your neighbor's.'

²²"These words the LORD spoke to all your assembly, in the mountain from the midst of the fire, the cloud, and the thick darkness, with a loud voice; and He added no more. And He wrote them on two tablets of stone and gave them to me.

The People Afraid of God's Presence

²³"So it was, when you heard the voice from the midst of the darkness, while the mountain was burning with fire, that you came near to me, all the heads of your tribes and your elders. ²⁴And you said: 'Surely the LORD our God has shown us His glory and His greatness, and we have heard His voice from the midst of the fire. We have seen this day that God speaks with man; yet he *still* lives. ²⁵Now therefore, why should we die? For this great fire will consume us; if we hear the voice of the LORD our God anymore, then we shall die. ²⁶For who *is there* of all flesh who has heard the voice of the living God speaking from the midst of the fire, as we *have,* and lived? ²⁷You go near and hear all that the LORD our God may say, and tell us all that the LORD our God says to you, and we will hear and do *it.*'

²⁸"Then the LORD heard the voice of your words when you spoke to me, and the LORD said to me: 'I have heard the voice of the words of this people which they have spoken to you. They are right *in* all that they have spoken. ²⁹Oh, that they had such a heart in them that they would fear Me and always keep all My commandments, that it might be well with them and with their children forever! ³⁰Go and say to them, "Return to your tents." ³¹But as for you, stand here by Me, and I will speak to you all the commandments, the statutes, and the judgments which you shall teach them, that they may observe *them* in the land which I am giving them to possess.'

³²"Therefore you shall be careful to do as the LORD your God has commanded you; you shall not turn aside to the right hand or to the left. ³³You shall walk in all the ways which the LORD your God has commanded you, that you may live and

that it *may be* well with you, and *that* you may prolong *your* days in the land which you shall possess.

The Greatest Commandment

6 "Now this *is* the commandment, *and these are* the statutes and judgments which the LORD your God has commanded to teach you, that you may observe *them* in the land which you are crossing over to possess, [2]that you may fear the LORD your God, to keep all His statutes and His commandments which I command you, you and your son and your grandson, all the days of your life, and that your days may be prolonged. [3]Therefore hear, O Israel, and be careful to observe *it,* that it may be well with you, and that you may multiply greatly as the LORD God of your fathers has promised you—'a land flowing with milk and honey.'[a]

[4]"Hear, O Israel: The LORD our God, the LORD *is* one![a] [5]You shall love the LORD your God with all your heart, with all your soul, and with all your strength.

[6]"And these words which I command you today shall be in your heart. [7]You shall teach them diligently to your children, and shall talk of them when you sit in your house, when you walk by the way, when you lie down, and when you rise up. [8]You shall bind them as a sign on your hand, and they shall be as frontlets between your eyes. [9]You shall write them on the doorposts of your house and on your gates.

Caution Against Disobedience

[10]"So it shall be, when the LORD your God brings you into the land of which He swore to your fathers, to Abraham, Isaac, and Jacob, to give you large and beautiful cities which you did not build, [11]houses full of all good things, which you did not fill, hewn-out wells which you did not dig, vineyards and olive trees which you did not plant—when you have eaten and are full— [12]*then* beware, lest you forget the LORD who brought you out of the land of Egypt, from the house of bondage. [13]You shall fear the LORD your God and serve Him, and shall take oaths in His name. [14]You shall not go after other gods, the gods of the peoples who *are* all around you [15](for the LORD your God *is* a jealous God among you), lest the anger of the LORD your God be aroused against you and destroy you from the face of the earth.

[16]"You shall not tempt the LORD your God as you tempted *Him* in Massah. [17]You shall diligently keep the commandments of the LORD your God, His testimonies, and

6:3 [a]Exodus 3:8　6:4 [a]Or *The LORD is our God, the LORD alone* (that is, the only one)

Why We Are to Be Fruitful

Too many of us lack a true, biblical vision for children and parenting. In Deuteronomy 6 God reveals why He commands parents to be fruitful—not merely to have children, but to raise godly children *who will pass on a godly legacy as one generation connects to the next.*

The home is the best place for a child to learn about God. In a culture of weakening character and ethics, our best hope for spiritual renewal lies in the restoration of godly homes. God created the family circle to be the supreme conductor of Christianity to children and to the next generation. If you consider yourself a Christian parent who is following Christ, then it is a big part of your God-given responsibility and privilege to raise your children in a way that leaves them desiring the kind of relationship with God that you display day in and day out. Although it's sobering to bring children into a decadent society, your children will become His agents in advancing the Kingdom of God. It was Neil Postman who reminded us of the generational power of children. He said, "Our children are the living messengers we send to a time we will not see."

Let's recapture the biblical imperative that parenting is a sacred calling and that children are worth the effort! God has selected parents for a work the angels must envy—the stewardship of a child's soul.

BIBLICAL INSIGHTS • 6:6-9
Bring the Word into Your Home

THE BIBLE INSISTS that we are to make the Word of God a foundational part of our personal Christian lives as well as our home lives.

Thousands of years ago, God told His people, "And these words which I command you today shall be in your heart. You shall teach them diligently to your children, and shall talk of them when you sit in your house, when you walk by the way, when you lie down, and when you rise up. You shall bind them as a sign on your hand, and they shall be as frontlets between your eyes. You shall write them on the doorposts of your house and on your gates" (6:6–9).

This passage makes it clear that parents have the solemn responsibility—and the privilege—to spiritually instruct and train their children. The Scriptures declare that these words "shall be in your heart." This responsibility is to be a burden that is picked up and carried daily as we instruct the next generation. No one else can carry this burden. We can't delegate it to the Christian school our children attend or to Sunday school teachers. This is a weight we must decide to shoulder every day. It also strongly implies that this begins with some formal times set aside for that purpose.

For most of us, this is something of a process, starting with five minutes a day and working our way up. However you do it, it's important that you set aside time for the teaching and instruction of the Scriptures in your home.

His statutes which He has commanded you. [18]And you shall do *what is* right and good in the sight of the LORD, that it may be well with you, and that you may go in and possess the good land of which the LORD swore to your fathers, [19]to cast out all your enemies from before you, as the LORD has spoken.

[20]"When your son asks you in time to come, saying, 'What *is the meaning of* the testimonies, the statutes, and the judgments which the LORD our God has commanded you?' [21]then you shall say to your son: 'We were slaves of Pharaoh in Egypt, and the LORD brought us out of Egypt with a mighty hand; [22]and the LORD showed signs and wonders before our eyes, great and severe, against Egypt, Pharaoh, and all his household. [23]Then He brought us out from there, that He might bring us in, to give us the land of which He swore to our fathers. [24]And the LORD commanded us to observe all these statutes, to fear the LORD our God, for our good always, that He might preserve us alive, as *it is* this day. [25]Then it will be righteousness for us, if we are careful to observe all these commandments before the LORD our God, as He has commanded us.'

A Chosen People

7 "When the LORD your God brings you into the land which you go to possess, and has cast out many nations before you, the Hittites and the Girgashites and the Amorites and the Canaanites and the Perizzites and the Hivites and the Jebusites, seven nations greater and mightier than you, [2]and when the LORD your God delivers them over to you, you shall conquer them *and* utterly destroy them. You shall make no covenant with them nor show mercy to them. [3]Nor shall you make marriages with them. You shall not give your daughter to their son, nor take their daughter for your son. [4]For they will turn your sons away from following Me, to serve other gods; so the anger of the LORD will be aroused against you and destroy you suddenly. [5]But thus you shall deal with them: you shall destroy their altars, and break down their *sacred* pillars, and cut down their wooden images,[a] and burn their carved images with fire.

[6]"For you *are* a holy people to the LORD your God; the LORD your God has chosen you to be a people for Himself, a special treasure above all the peoples on the face of the earth. [7]The LORD did not set His love on you nor choose you because you were more in number than any other people, for you

7:5 [a]Hebrew *Asherim,* Canaanite deities

were the least of all peoples; [8]but because the LORD loves you, and because He would keep the oath which He swore to your fathers, the LORD has brought you out with a mighty hand, and redeemed you from the house of bondage, from the hand of Pharaoh king of Egypt.

[9]"Therefore know that the LORD your God, He *is* God, the faithful God who keeps covenant and mercy for a thousand generations with those who love Him and keep His commandments; [10]and He repays those who hate Him to their face, to destroy them. He will not be slack with him who hates Him; He will repay him to his face. [11]Therefore you shall keep the commandment, the statutes, and the judgments which I command you today, to observe them.

Blessings of Obedience

[12]"Then it shall come to pass, because you listen to these judgments, and keep and do them, that the LORD your God will keep with you the covenant and the mercy which He swore to your fathers. [13]And He will love you and bless you and multiply you; He will also bless the fruit of your womb and the fruit of your land, your grain and your new wine and your oil, the increase of your cattle and the offspring of your flock, in the land of which He swore to your fathers to give you. [14]You shall be blessed above all peoples; there shall not be a male or female barren among you or among your livestock. [15]And the LORD will take away from you all sickness, and will afflict you with none of the terrible diseases of Egypt which you have known, but will lay *them* on all those who hate you. [16]Also you shall destroy all the peoples whom the LORD your God delivers over to you; your eye shall have no pity on them; nor shall you serve their gods, for that *will be* a snare to you.

[17]"If you should say in your heart, 'These nations are greater than I; how can I dispossess them?'— [18]you shall not be afraid of them, *but* you shall remember well what the LORD your God did to Pharaoh and to all Egypt: [19]the great trials which your eyes saw, the signs and the wonders, the mighty hand and the outstretched arm, by which the LORD your God brought you out. So shall the LORD your God do to all the peoples of whom you are afraid. [20]Moreover the LORD your God will send the hornet among them until those who are left, who hide themselves from you, are destroyed. [21]You shall not be terrified of them; for the LORD your God, the great and awesome God, *is* among you. [22]And the LORD your God will drive out those nations before you little by little; you will be unable to destroy them at once, lest the beasts of the field become *too* numerous for you. [23]But the LORD your God will deliver them over to you, and will inflict defeat upon them until they are destroyed. [24]And He will deliver their kings into your hand, and you will destroy their name from under heaven; no one shall be able to stand against you until you have destroyed them. [25]You shall burn the carved images of their gods with fire; you shall not covet the silver or gold *that is* on them, nor take *it* for yourselves, lest you be snared by it; for it *is* an abomination to the LORD your God. [26]Nor shall you bring an abomination into your house, lest you be doomed to destruction like it. You shall utterly detest it and utterly abhor it, for it *is* an accursed thing.

Remember the LORD Your God

8 "Every commandment which I command you today you must be careful to observe, that you may live and multiply, and go in and possess the land of which the LORD swore to your fathers. [2]And you shall remember that the LORD your God led you all the way these forty years in the wilderness, to humble you *and* test you, to know what *was* in your heart, whether you would keep His commandments or not. [3]So He humbled you, allowed you to hunger, and fed you with manna which you did not know nor did your fathers know, that He might make you know that man shall not live by bread alone; but man lives by every *word* that proceeds from the mouth of the LORD. [4]Your garments did not wear out on you, nor did your foot swell these forty years. [5]You should know in your heart that as a man chastens his son, *so* the LORD your God chastens you.

[6]"Therefore you shall keep the commandments of the LORD your God, to walk in His ways and to fear Him. [7]For the LORD

your God is bringing you into a good land, a land of brooks of water, of fountains and springs, that flow out of valleys and hills; ⁸a land of wheat and barley, of vines and fig trees and pomegranates, a land of olive oil and honey; ⁹a land in which you will eat bread without scarcity, in which you will lack nothing; a land whose stones *are* iron and out of whose hills you can dig copper. ¹⁰When you have eaten and are full, then you shall bless the LORD your God for the good land which He has given you.

¹¹"Beware that you do not forget the LORD your God by not keeping His commandments, His judgments, and His statutes which I command you today, ¹²lest—*when*

ROMANCE FAQ

Q: How can we best choose priorities so that they enhance our relationship?

In a wonderful little booklet called *Tyranny of the Urgent*, Charles E. Hummel warned against letting the tyranny of urgent tasks rob us of what is really important. The most important relationship in a family, the marriage, is the easiest to ignore in the urgent demands of sick kids, diapers, ballgames, job deadlines, and a host of other daily life demands. Because I (Barbara) decided in the early years of our marriage to keep Dennis as top priority (after God), I refused to let the tenacious thief of the urgent consistently win in our relationship.

The tyranny of the urgent occurs when you plan a date with your husband, but your boss informs you some project must be done that evening, so you cancel your date. It occurs when a friend, a neighbor, or sister calls at the last minute, needing you to drop everything to watch a sick child so she can attend an important event.

Urgent needs always sound pressing, and sometimes you have no choice. But just as many times you can say, "No, I'm sorry, but I can't." Keep your marriage top priority!

you have eaten and are full, and have built beautiful houses and dwell *in them;* ¹³and *when* your herds and your flocks multiply, and your silver and your gold are multiplied, and all that you have is multiplied; ¹⁴when your heart is lifted up, and you forget the LORD your God who brought you out of the land of Egypt, from the house of bondage; ¹⁵who led you through that great and terrible wilderness, *in which were* fiery serpents and scorpions and thirsty land where there was no water; who brought water for you out of the flinty rock; ¹⁶who fed you in the wilderness with manna, which your fathers did not know, that He might humble you and that He might test you, to do you good in the end— ¹⁷then you say in your heart, 'My power and the might of my hand have gained me this wealth.'

¹⁸"And you shall remember the LORD your God, for *it is* He who gives you power to get wealth, that He may establish His covenant which He swore to your fathers, as *it is* this day. ¹⁹Then it shall be, if you by any means forget the LORD your God, and follow other gods, and serve them and worship them, I testify against you this day that you shall surely perish. ²⁰As the nations which the LORD destroys before you, so you shall perish, because you would not be obedient to the voice of the LORD your God.

Israel's Rebellions Reviewed

9 "Hear, O Israel: You *are* to cross over the Jordan today, and go in to dispossess nations greater and mightier than yourself, cities great and fortified up to heaven, ²a people great and tall, the descendants of the Anakim, whom you know, and *of whom* you heard *it said,* 'Who can stand before the descendants of Anak?' ³Therefore understand today that the LORD your God *is* He who goes over before you *as* a consuming fire. He will destroy them and bring them down before you; so you shall drive them out and destroy them quickly, as the LORD has said to you.

⁴"Do not think in your heart, after the LORD your God has cast them out before you, saying, 'Because of my righteousness the LORD has brought me in to possess this land'; but *it is* because of the wickedness of these nations *that* the LORD is driving them

out from before you. ⁵*It is* not because of your righteousness or the uprightness of your heart *that* you go in to possess their land, but because of the wickedness of these nations *that* the LORD your God drives them out from before you, and that He may fulfill the word which the LORD swore to your fathers, to Abraham, Isaac, and Jacob. ⁶Therefore understand that the LORD your God is not giving you this good land to possess because of your righteousness, for you *are* a stiff-necked people.

⁷"Remember! Do not forget how you provoked the LORD your God to wrath in the wilderness. From the day that you departed from the land of Egypt until you came to this place, you have been rebellious against the LORD. ⁸Also in Horeb you provoked the LORD to wrath, so that the LORD was angry *enough* with you to have destroyed you. ⁹When I went up into the mountain to receive the tablets of stone, the tablets of the covenant which the LORD made with you, then I stayed on the mountain forty days and forty nights. I neither ate bread nor drank water. ¹⁰Then the LORD delivered to me two tablets of stone written with the finger of God, and on them *were* all the words which the LORD had spoken to you on the mountain from the midst of the fire in the day of the assembly. ¹¹And it came to pass, at the end of forty days and forty nights, *that* the LORD gave me the two tablets of stone, the tablets of the covenant.

¹²"Then the LORD said to me, 'Arise, go down quickly from here, for your people whom you brought out of Egypt have acted corruptly; they have quickly turned aside from the way which I commanded them; they have made themselves a molded image.'

¹³"Furthermore the LORD spoke to me, saying, 'I have seen this people, and indeed they are a stiff-necked people. ¹⁴Let Me alone, that I may destroy them and blot out their name from under heaven; and I will make of you a nation mightier and greater than they.'

¹⁵"So I turned and came down from the mountain, and the mountain burned with fire; and the two tablets of the covenant *were* in my two hands. ¹⁶And I looked, and behold, you had sinned against the LORD your God—had made for yourselves a molded calf! You had turned aside quickly from the way which the LORD had commanded you. ¹⁷Then I took the two tablets and threw them out of my two hands and broke them before your eyes. ¹⁸And I fell down before the LORD, as at the first, forty days and forty nights; I neither ate bread nor drank water, because of all your sin which you committed in doing wickedly in the sight of the LORD, to provoke Him to anger. ¹⁹For I was afraid of the anger and hot displeasure with which the LORD was angry with you, to destroy you. But the LORD listened to me at that time also. ²⁰And the LORD was very angry with Aaron *and* would have destroyed him; so I prayed for Aaron also at the same time. ²¹Then I took your sin, the calf which you had made, and burned it with fire and crushed it *and* ground *it* very small, until it was as fine as dust; and I threw its dust into the brook that descended from the mountain.

²²"Also at Taberah and Massah and Kibroth Hattaavah you provoked the LORD to wrath. ²³Likewise, when the LORD sent you from Kadesh Barnea, saying, 'Go up and possess the land which I have given you,' then you rebelled against the commandment of the LORD your God, and you did not believe Him nor obey His voice. ²⁴You have been rebellious against the LORD from the day that I knew you.

²⁵"Thus I prostrated myself before the LORD; forty days and forty nights I kept prostrating myself, because the LORD had said He would destroy you. ²⁶Therefore I prayed to the LORD, and said: 'O Lord GOD, do not destroy Your people and Your inheritance whom You have redeemed through Your greatness, whom You have brought out of Egypt with a mighty hand. ²⁷Remember Your servants, Abraham, Isaac, and Jacob; do not look on the stubbornness of this people, or on their wickedness or their sin, ²⁸lest the land from which You brought us should say, "Because the LORD was not able to bring them to the land which He promised them, and because He hated them, He has brought them out to kill them in the wilderness." ²⁹Yet they *are* Your people and Your inheritance, whom You brought out by Your mighty power and by Your outstretched arm.'

Teaching Trust, Even When Things Aren't Fair

BARBARA AND I WANT our children to grow up realizing that while God won't give each of them the same share of earthly benefits, He will always deal with them in perfect judgment and according to His righteous character. Abraham spoke truly when he said, "The Judge of all the earth" will "do right" (Gen. 18:25).

That is the promise of Deuteronomy 10:17, "For the LORD your God is God of gods and Lord of lords, the great God, mighty and awesome, who shows no partiality nor takes a bribe."

We must trust that the Master, who owns everything, also knows what He is doing. God is the Sovereign Ruler of the universe and alone rules over all. He knows what He is doing, and He also loves us.

Everything that occurs in our children's lives will come either directly from God's hands or be gently sifted through His fingers. Everything is for the purpose of shaping their lives into His image. Circumstances, events, and problems may not always appear to be fair, but they all come from their loving Father.

Life isn't always fair. But I know the One who is just in all that He does and who has perfect judgment—and He can be trusted.

The Second Pair of Tablets

10 "At that time the LORD said to me, 'Hew for yourself two tablets of stone like the first, and come up to Me on the mountain and make yourself an ark of wood. ²And I will write on the tablets the words that were on the first tablets, which you broke; and you shall put them in the ark.'

³"So I made an ark of acacia wood, hewed two tablets of stone like the first, and went up the mountain, having the two tablets in my hand. ⁴And He wrote on the tablets according to the first writing, the Ten Commandments, which the LORD had spoken to you in the mountain from the midst of the fire in the day of the assembly; and the LORD gave them to me. ⁵Then I turned and came down from the mountain, and put the tablets in the ark which I had made; and there they are, just as the LORD commanded me."

⁶(Now the children of Israel journeyed from the wells of Bene Jaakan to Moserah, where Aaron died, and where he was buried; and Eleazar his son ministered as priest in his stead. ⁷From there they journeyed to Gudgodah, and from Gudgodah to Jotbathah, a land of rivers of water. ⁸At that time the LORD separated the tribe of Levi to bear the ark of the covenant of the LORD, to stand before the LORD to minister to Him and to bless in His name, to this day. ⁹Therefore Levi has no portion nor inheritance with his brethren; the LORD *is* his inheritance, just as the LORD your God promised him.)

¹⁰"As at the first time, I stayed in the mountain forty days and forty nights; the LORD also heard me at that time, *and* the LORD chose not to destroy you. ¹¹Then the LORD said to me, 'Arise, begin *your* journey before the people, that they may go in and possess the land which I swore to their fathers to give them.'

The Essence of the Law

¹²"And now, Israel, what does the LORD your God require of you, but to fear the LORD your God, to walk in all His ways and to love Him, to serve the LORD your God with all your heart and with all your soul, ¹³*and* to keep the commandments of the LORD and His statutes which I command you today for your good? ¹⁴Indeed heaven and the highest heavens belong to the LORD your God, *also* the earth with all that *is* in it. ¹⁵The LORD delighted only in your fathers, to love them; and He chose their descendants after them, you above all peoples, as *it is* this day. ¹⁶Therefore circumcise the foreskin of your heart, and be stiffnecked no longer. ¹⁷For the LORD your God *is* God of gods and Lord of lords, the great God, mighty and awesome, who shows no

partiality nor takes a bribe. [18]He administers justice for the fatherless and the widow, and loves the stranger, giving him food and clothing. [19]Therefore love the stranger, for you were strangers in the land of Egypt. [20]You shall fear the LORD your God; you shall serve Him, and to Him you shall hold fast, and take oaths in His name. [21]He *is* your praise, and He *is* your God, who has done for you these great and awesome things which your eyes have seen. [22]Your fathers went down to Egypt with seventy persons, and now the LORD your God has made you as the stars of heaven in multitude.

Love and Obedience Rewarded

11 "Therefore you shall love the LORD your God, and keep His charge, His statutes, His judgments, and His commandments always. [2]Know today that *I do* not *speak* with your children, who have not known and who have not seen the chastening of the LORD your God, His greatness and His mighty hand and His outstretched arm— [3]His signs and His acts which He did in the midst of Egypt, to Pharaoh king of Egypt, and to all his land; [4]what He did to the army of Egypt, to their horses and their chariots: how He made the waters of the Red Sea overflow them as they pursued you, and *how* the LORD has destroyed them to this day; [5]what He did for you in the wilderness until you came to this place; [6]and what He did to Dathan and Abiram the sons of Eliab, the son of Reuben: how the earth opened its mouth and swallowed them up, their households, their tents, and all the substance that *was* in their possession, in the midst of all Israel— [7]but your eyes have seen every great act of the LORD which He did.

[8]"Therefore you shall keep every commandment which I command you today, that you may be strong, and go in and possess the land which you cross over to possess, [9]and that you may prolong *your* days in the land which the LORD swore to give your fathers, to them and their descendants, 'a land flowing with milk and honey.'[a] [10]For the land which you go to possess *is* not like the land of Egypt from which you have

11:9 [a]Exodus 3:8

BIBLICAL INSIGHTS • 11:13
Peace for Your Soul

THE CHRISTIAN FAITH is not a bunch of rules and regulations, but rather a dynamic relationship with the living God made possible through the work of Jesus Christ. You are to "love the LORD your God and serve Him with all your heart and with all your soul" (11:13). When we fully grasp that fact, we are well on our way to living victoriously in every area of our lives, including marriage.

Loving God *fully* is the foundation of a great marriage. Loving God whole-heartedly means we obey Him, serve Him, and yield to Him. Totally. That's really the only hope that two imperfect people, a husband and a wife, have in truly experiencing all that God has for their lives, marriage and family. True success in life begins here and flows from this kind of relationship.

Let's face it—being married isn't always easy. There will be conflicts, illnesses, and external challenges. We need to learn how we fully love God and yield our wills to Him, knowing that He cares for us and that He is causing all things to work together for our good and for His glory (see Rom. 8:28; 1 Pet. 5:7).

The peace and assurance I need to be a good husband and father doesn't always come instantly; it's not like flipping on a switch. In the past, I've expected that Christ would *instantly* give me peace and strength to deal with my problems and needs and pressures. But I've learned that coming to Jesus with open hands is just the first step in a long process of learning from Him and receiving from Him.

come, where you sowed your seed and watered *it* by foot, as a vegetable garden; [11]but the land which you cross over to possess *is* a land of hills and valleys, which drinks water from the rain of heaven, [12]a land for which the LORD your God cares; the eyes of the LORD your God *are* always

BIBLICAL INSIGHTS • 11:27, 28
The Blessings of Obedience

OBEDIENCE TO GOD is one of the major themes of the Old Testament. God promised His people, through Moses, that they would receive a "blessing, if you obey the commandments of the LORD your God which I command you today" (11:27).

God gives spouses the responsibility of praying for each other. When we do that, we obey what God wants us to do and we call on Him to give our mates the strength it takes to walk and live in obedience.

James 5:16 says, "The effective, fervent prayer of a righteous man avails much." Effective prayer is asking God to do what He already wants to do in your mate's life. God delights in answering such prayer, because He wants you to know Him, to see Him work, and to continue to come to Him.

Come before God's throne on your mate's behalf, requesting that he or she will know God's love more fully and that God will develop a teachable, pure heart within him or her. Pray for an increased desire to obey and follow Christ. Ask God to give your mate a growing awareness of the benefits of walking with Him. Ask, too, that faithfulness, contentment, patience, self-control, discipline, and other godly virtues will be developed in the life of your loved one.

---

on it, from the beginning of the year to the very end of the year.

¹³'And it shall be that if you earnestly obey My commandments which I command you today, to love the LORD your God and serve Him with all your heart and with all your soul, ¹⁴then Iᵃ will give *you* the rain for your land in its season, the early rain and the latter rain, that you may gather in your grain, *your new wine, and your oil.* ¹⁵And I will send grass in your fields for your livestock, that you may eat and be filled.' ¹⁶Take heed to yourselves, lest your heart be deceived, and you turn aside and serve other gods and worship them, ¹⁷lest the LORD's anger be aroused against you, and He shut up the heavens so that there be no rain, and the land yield no produce, and you perish quickly from the good land which the LORD is giving you.

¹⁸"Therefore you shall lay up these words of mine in your heart and in your soul, and bind them as a sign on your hand, and they shall be as frontlets between your eyes. ¹⁹You shall teach them to your children, speaking of them when you sit in your house, when you walk by the way, when you lie down, and when you rise up. ²⁰And you shall write them on the doorposts of your house and on your gates, ²¹that your days and the days of your children may be multiplied in the land of which the LORD swore to your fathers to give them, like the days of the heavens above the earth.

²²"For if you carefully keep all these commandments which I command you to do—to love the LORD your God, to walk in all His ways, and to hold fast to Him— ²³then the LORD will drive out all these nations from before you, and you will dispossess greater and mightier nations than yourselves. ²⁴Every place on which the sole of your foot treads shall be yours: from the wilderness and Lebanon, from the river, the River Euphrates, even to the Western Sea,ᵃ shall be your territory. ²⁵No man shall be able to stand against you; the LORD your God will put the dread of you and the fear of you upon all the land where you tread, just as He has said to you.

²⁶"Behold, I set before you today a blessing and a curse: ²⁷the blessing, if you obey the commandments of the LORD your God which I command you today; ²⁸and the curse, if you do not obey the commandments of the LORD your God, but turn aside from the way which I command you today, to go after other gods which you have not known. ²⁹Now it shall be, when the LORD your God has brought you into the land which you go to possess, that you shall put the blessing on Mount Gerizim and the curse on Mount Ebal. ³⁰*Are* they not on the

---

11:14 ᵃFollowing Masoretic Text and Targum; Samaritan Pentateuch, Septuagint, and Vulgate read *He.* **11:24** ᵃThat is, the Mediterranean

other side of the Jordan, toward the setting sun, in the land of the Canaanites who dwell in the plain opposite Gilgal, beside the terebinth trees of Moreh? ³¹For you will cross over the Jordan and go in to possess the land which the LORD your God is giving you, and you will possess it and dwell in it. ³²And you shall be careful to observe all the statutes and judgments which I set before you today.

A Prescribed Place of Worship

12 "These *are* the statutes and judgments which you shall be careful to observe in the land which the LORD God of your fathers is giving you to possess, all the days that you live on the earth. ²You shall utterly destroy all the places where the nations which you shall dispossess served their gods, on the high mountains and on the hills and under every green tree. ³And you shall destroy their altars, break their *sacred* pillars, and burn their wooden images with fire; you shall cut down the carved images of their gods and destroy their names from that place. ⁴You shall not worship the LORD your God *with* such *things.*

⁵"But you shall seek the place where the LORD your God chooses, out of all your tribes, to put His name for His dwelling place; and there you shall go. ⁶There you shall take your burnt offerings, your sacrifices, your tithes, the heave offerings of your hand, your vowed offerings, your freewill offerings, and the firstborn of your herds and flocks. ⁷And there you shall eat before the LORD your God, and you shall rejoice in all to which you have put your hand, you and your households, in which the LORD your God has blessed you.

⁸"You shall not at all do as we are doing here today—every man doing whatever *is* right in his own eyes— ⁹for as yet you have not come to the rest and the inheritance which the LORD your God is giving you. ¹⁰But *when* you cross over the Jordan and dwell in the land which the LORD your God is giving you to inherit, and He gives you rest from all your enemies round about, so that you dwell in safety, ¹¹then there will be the place where the LORD your God chooses to make His name abide. There you shall bring all that I command

you: your burnt offerings, your sacrifices, your tithes, the heave offerings of your hand, and all your choice offerings which you vow to the LORD. ¹²And you shall rejoice before the LORD your God, you and your sons and your daughters, your male and female servants, and the Levite who *is* within your gates, since he has no portion nor inheritance with you. ¹³Take heed to yourself that you do not offer your burnt offerings in every place that you see; ¹⁴but in the place which the LORD chooses, in one of your tribes, there you shall offer your burnt offerings, and there you shall do all that I command you.

¹⁵"However, you may slaughter and eat meat within all your gates, whatever your heart desires, according to the blessing of the LORD your God which He has given you; the unclean and the clean may eat of it, of the gazelle and the deer alike. ¹⁶Only you shall not eat the blood; you shall pour it on the earth like water. ¹⁷You may not eat within your gates the tithe of your grain or your new wine or your oil, of the firstborn of your herd or your flock, of any of your offerings which you vow, of your freewill offerings, or of the heave offering of your hand. ¹⁸But you must eat them before the LORD your God in the place which the LORD your God chooses, you and your son and your daughter, your male servant and your female servant, and the Levite who *is* within your gates; and you shall rejoice before the LORD your God in all to which you put your hands. ¹⁹Take heed to yourself that you do not forsake the Levite as long as you live in your land.

²⁰"When the LORD your God enlarges your border as He has promised you, and you say, 'Let me eat meat,' because you long to eat meat, you may eat as much meat as your heart desires. ²¹If the place where the LORD your God chooses to put His name is too far from you, then you may slaughter from your herd and from your flock which the LORD has given you, just as I have commanded you, and you may eat within your gates as much as your heart desires. ²²Just as the gazelle and the deer are eaten, so you may eat them; the unclean and the clean alike may eat them. ²³Only be sure that you do not eat the blood, for the blood *is* the

life; you may not eat the life with the meat. ²⁴You shall not eat it; you shall pour it on the earth like water. ²⁵You shall not eat it, that it may go well with you and your children after you, when you do *what is* right in the sight of the LORD. ²⁶Only the holy things which you have, and your vowed offerings, you shall take and go to the place which the LORD chooses. ²⁷And you shall offer your burnt offerings, the meat and the blood, on the altar of the LORD your God; and the blood of your sacrifices shall be poured out on the altar of the LORD your God, and you shall eat the meat. ²⁸Observe and obey all these words which I command you, that it may go well with you and your children after you forever, when you do *what is* good and right in the sight of the LORD your God.

INTIMATE MOMENTS

When you're on the road together and it's safe to do so, slide over and sit next to your husband. Tussle his hair, or give him a soft neck massage. And make sure you're buckled up for safety!

Beware of False Gods

²⁹"When the LORD your God cuts off from before you the nations which you go to dispossess, and you displace them and dwell in their land, ³⁰take heed to yourself that you are not ensnared to follow them, after they are destroyed from before you, and that you do not inquire after their gods, saying, 'How did these nations serve their gods? I also will do likewise.' ³¹You shall not worship the LORD your God in that way; for every abomination to the LORD which He hates they have done to their gods; for they burn even their sons and daughters in the fire to their gods.

³²"Whatever I command you, be careful to observe it; you shall not add to it nor take away from it.

Punishment of Apostates

13 "If there arises among you a prophet or a dreamer of dreams, and he gives you a sign or a wonder, ²and the sign or the wonder comes to pass, of which he spoke to you, saying, 'Let us go after other gods'— which you have not known—'and let us serve them,' ³you shall not listen to the words of that prophet or that dreamer of dreams, for the LORD your God is testing you to know whether you love the LORD your God with all your heart and with all your soul. ⁴You shall walk after the LORD your God and fear Him, and keep His commandments and obey His voice; you shall serve Him and hold fast to Him. ⁵But that prophet or that dreamer of dreams shall be put to death, because he has spoken in order to turn *you* away from the LORD your God, who brought you out of the land of Egypt and redeemed you from the house of bondage, to entice you from the way in which the LORD your God commanded you to walk. So you shall put away the evil from your midst.

⁶"If your brother, the son of your mother, your son or your daughter, the wife of your bosom, or your friend who is as your own soul, secretly entices you, saying, 'Let us go and serve other gods,' which you have not known, neither you nor your fathers, ⁷of the gods of the people which *are* all around you, near to you or far off from you, from *one* end of the earth to the *other* end of the earth, ⁸you shall not consent to him or listen to him, nor shall your eye pity him, nor shall you spare him or conceal him; ⁹but you shall surely kill him; your hand shall be first against him to put him to death, and afterward the hand of all the people. ¹⁰And you shall stone him with stones until he dies, because he sought to entice you away from the LORD your God, who brought you out of the land of Egypt, from the house of bondage. ¹¹So all Israel shall hear and fear, and not again do such wickedness as this among you.

¹²"If you hear someone in one of your cities, which the LORD your God gives you to dwell in, saying, ¹³'Corrupt men have gone out from among you and enticed the inhabitants of their city, saying, "Let us go and serve other gods" '—which you have

not known— [14]then you shall inquire, search out, and ask diligently. And *if it is* indeed true *and* certain *that* such an abomination was committed among you, [15]you shall surely strike the inhabitants of that city with the edge of the sword, utterly destroying it, all that is in it and its livestock—with the edge of the sword. [16]And you shall gather all its plunder into the middle of the street, and completely burn with fire the city and all its plunder, for the LORD your God. It shall be a heap forever; it shall not be built again. [17]So none of the accursed things shall remain in your hand, that the LORD may turn from the fierceness of His anger and show you mercy, have compassion on you and multiply you, just as He swore to your fathers, [18]because you have listened to the voice of the LORD your God, to keep all His commandments which I command you today, to do *what is* right in the eyes of the LORD your God.

Improper Mourning

14 "You *are* the children of the LORD your God; you shall not cut yourselves nor shave the front of your head for the dead. [2]For you *are* a holy people to the LORD your God, and the LORD has chosen you to be a people for Himself, a special treasure above all the peoples who *are* on the face of the earth.

Clean and Unclean Meat

[3]"You shall not eat any detestable thing. [4]These *are* the animals which you may eat: the ox, the sheep, the goat, [5]the deer, the gazelle, the roe deer, the wild goat, the mountain goat,[a] the antelope, and the mountain sheep. [6]And you may eat every animal with cloven hooves, having the hoof split into two parts, *and that* chews the cud, among the animals. [7]Nevertheless, of those that chew the cud or have cloven hooves, you shall not eat, *such as* these: the camel, the hare, and the rock hyrax; for they chew the cud but do not have cloven hooves; they *are* unclean for you. [8]Also the swine is unclean for you, because it has cloven hooves, yet *does* not *chew* the cud; you shall not eat their flesh or touch their dead carcasses.

[9]"These you may eat of all that *are* in the waters: you may eat all that have fins and scales. [10]And whatever does not have fins and scales you shall not eat; it *is* unclean for you.

[11]"All clean birds you may eat. [12]But these you shall not eat: the eagle, the vulture, the buzzard, [13]the red kite, the falcon, and the kite after their kinds; [14]every raven after its kind; [15]the ostrich, the short-eared owl, the sea gull, and the hawk after their kinds; [16]the little owl, the screech owl, the white owl, [17]the jackdaw, the carrion vulture, the fisher owl, [18]the stork, the heron after its kind, and the hoopoe and the bat.

[19]"Also every creeping thing that flies is unclean for you; they shall not be eaten.

[20]"You may eat all clean birds.

[21]"You shall not eat anything that dies *of itself;* you may give it to the alien who *is* within your gates, that he may eat it, or you may sell it to a foreigner; for you *are* a holy people to the LORD your God.

"You shall not boil a young goat in its mother's milk.

Tithing Principles

[22]"You shall truly tithe all the increase of your grain that the field produces year by year. [23]And you shall eat before the LORD your God, in the place where He chooses to make His name abide, the tithe of your grain and your new wine and your oil, of the firstborn of your herds and your flocks, that you may learn to fear the LORD your God always. [24]But if the journey is too long for you, so that you are not able to carry *the tithe, or* if the place where the LORD your God chooses to put His name is too far from you, when the LORD your God has blessed you, [25]then you shall exchange *it* for money, take the money in your hand, and go to the place which the LORD your God chooses. [26]And you shall spend that money for whatever your heart desires: for oxen or sheep, for wine or similar drink, for whatever your heart desires; you shall eat there before the LORD your God, and you shall rejoice, you and your household. [27]You shall not forsake the Levite who *is* within your gates, for he has no part nor inheritance with you.

[28]"At the end of *every* third year you

14:5 [a]Or *addax*

shall bring out the tithe of your produce of that year and store *it* up within your gates. ²⁹And the Levite, because he has no portion nor inheritance with you, and the stranger and the fatherless and the widow who *are* within your gates, may come and eat and be satisfied, that the LORD your God may bless you in all the work of your hand which you do.

Debts Canceled Every Seven Years

15 "At the end of *every* seven years you shall grant a release *of debts*. ²And this *is* the form of the release: Every creditor who has lent *anything* to his neighbor shall release *it;* he shall not require *it* of his neighbor or his brother, because it is called the LORD's release. ³Of a foreigner you may require *it;* but you shall give up your claim to what is owed by your brother, ⁴except when there may be no poor among you; for the LORD will greatly bless you in the land which the LORD your God is giving you to possess *as* an inheritance— ⁵only if you carefully obey the voice of the LORD your God, to observe with care all these commandments which I command you today. ⁶For the LORD your God will bless you just as He promised you; you shall lend to many nations, but you shall not borrow; you shall reign over many nations, but they shall not reign over you.

Generosity to the Poor

⁷"If there is among you a poor man of your brethren, within any of the gates in your land which the LORD your God is giving you, you shall not harden your heart nor shut your hand from your poor brother, ⁸but you shall open your hand wide to him and willingly lend him sufficient for his need, whatever he needs. ⁹Beware lest there be a wicked thought in your heart, saying, 'The seventh year, the year of release, is at hand,' and your eye be evil against your poor brother and you give him nothing, and he cry out to the LORD against you, and it become sin among you. ¹⁰You shall surely give to him, and your heart should not be grieved when you give to him, because for this thing the LORD your God will bless you in all your works and in all to which you put your hand. ¹¹For the poor will never cease from the land; therefore I command you, saying, 'You shall open your hand wide to your brother, to your poor and your needy, in your land.'

The Law Concerning Bondservants

¹²"If your brother, a Hebrew man, or a Hebrew woman, is sold to you and serves you six years, then in the seventh year you shall let him go free from you. ¹³And when you send him away free from you, you shall not let him go away empty-handed; ¹⁴you shall supply him liberally from your

---

ROMANCE FAQ

Q: What practical steps can we take to make sure busyness doesn't take a toll on our romantic relationship?

First, be still and know that He is God (Ps. 46:10). Start by stopping. Begin by listening. Take time to pray and listen to God. And then spend time thinking and evaluating. Plan a date or two with your husband to reevaluate your schedules, your romance, and your marriage.

Second, decide what you value. God has made abundantly clear in His Word what He values. Make a priority list. What will you fight for, and what will both of you fight for?

Third, set important guidelines for yourself and your family.

Fourth, honestly evaluate your need for all the extra things in life. I know how easy it is to get busy with fixing my house, getting things for my kids, finding the best bargain. It's not wrong unless it leaves me stressed, exhausted, and unable to engage with my husband. It's a question of the important versus the urgent.

Stress and exhaustion in parenting are normal. While you can't eliminate them, they can be managed by evaluating your level of busyness and your lifestyle choices. Simplifying life is the best way to reduce these robbers of romance.

flock, from your threshing floor, and from your winepress. *From what* the LORD your God has blessed you with, you shall give to him. [15]You shall remember that you were a slave in the land of Egypt, and the LORD your God redeemed you; therefore I command you this thing today. [16]And if it happens that he says to you, 'I will not go away from you,' because he loves you and your house, since he prospers with you, [17]then you shall take an awl and thrust *it* through his ear to the door, and he shall be your servant forever. Also to your female servant you shall do likewise. [18]It shall not seem hard to you when you send him away free from you; for he has been worth a double hired servant in serving you six years. Then the LORD your God will bless you in all that you do.

The Law Concerning Firstborn Animals

[19]"All the firstborn males that come from your herd and your flock you shall sanctify to the LORD your God; you shall do no work with the firstborn of your herd, nor shear the firstborn of your flock. [20]You and your household shall eat *it* before the LORD your God year by year in the place which the LORD chooses. [21]But if there is a defect in it, *if it is* lame or blind *or has* any serious defect, you shall not sacrifice it to the LORD your God. [22]You may eat it within your gates; the unclean and the clean *person* alike *may eat it,* as *if it were* a gazelle or a deer. [23]Only you shall not eat its blood; you shall pour it on the ground like water.

The Passover Reviewed

16 "Observe the month of Abib, and keep the Passover to the LORD your God, for in the month of Abib the LORD your God brought you out of Egypt by night. [2]Therefore you shall sacrifice the Passover to the LORD your God, from the flock and the herd, in the place where the LORD chooses to put His name. [3]You shall eat no leavened bread with it; seven days you shall eat unleavened bread with it, *that is,* the bread of affliction (for you came out of the land of Egypt in haste), that you may remember the day in which you came out of the land of Egypt all the days of your life. [4]And no leaven shall be seen among you in all your territory for seven days, nor shall *any* of the meat which you sacrifice the first day at twilight remain overnight until morning.

[5]"You may not sacrifice the Passover within any of your gates which the LORD your God gives you; [6]but at the place where the LORD your God chooses to make His name abide, there you shall sacrifice the Passover at twilight, at the going down of the sun, at the time you came out of Egypt. [7]And you shall roast and eat *it* in the place which the LORD your God chooses, and in the morning you shall turn and go to your tents. [8]Six days you shall eat unleavened bread, and on the seventh day there *shall be* a sacred assembly to the LORD your God. You shall do no work *on it.*

The Feast of Weeks Reviewed

[9]"You shall count seven weeks for yourself; begin to count the seven weeks from *the time* you begin *to put* the sickle to the grain. [10]Then you shall keep the Feast of Weeks to the LORD your God with the tribute of a freewill offering from your hand, which you shall give as the LORD your God blesses you. [11]You shall rejoice before the LORD your God, you and your son and your daughter, your male servant and your female servant, the Levite who *is* within your gates, the stranger and the fatherless and the widow who *are* among you, at the place where the LORD your God chooses to make His name abide. [12]And you shall remember that you were a slave in Egypt, and you shall be careful to observe these statutes.

The Feast of Tabernacles Reviewed

[13]"You shall observe the Feast of Tabernacles seven days, when you have gathered from your threshing floor and from your winepress. [14]And you shall rejoice in your feast, you and your son and your daughter, your male servant and your female servant and the Levite, the stranger and the fatherless and the widow, who *are* within your gates. [15]Seven days you shall keep a sacred feast to the LORD your God in the place which the LORD chooses, because the LORD your God will bless you in all your produce and in all the work of your hands, so that you surely rejoice.

16"Three times a year all your males shall appear before the LORD your God in the place which He chooses: at the Feast of Unleavened Bread, at the Feast of Weeks, and at the Feast of Tabernacles; and they shall not appear before the LORD empty-handed. 17Every man *shall give* as he is able, according to the blessing of the LORD your God which He has given you.

Justice Must Be Administered

18"You shall appoint judges and officers in all your gates, which the LORD your God gives you, according to your tribes, and they shall judge the people with just judgment. 19You shall not pervert justice; you shall not show partiality, nor take a bribe, for a bribe blinds the eyes of the wise and twists the words of the righteous. 20You shall follow what is altogether just, that you may live and inherit the land which the LORD your God is giving you.

21"You shall not plant for yourself any tree, as a wooden image, near the altar which you build for yourself to the LORD your God.

22You shall not set up a *sacred* pillar, which the LORD your God hates.

17 "You shall not sacrifice to the LORD your God a bull or sheep which has any blemish *or* defect, for that *is* an abomination to the LORD your God.

2"If there is found among you, within any of your gates which the LORD your God gives you, a man or a woman who has been wicked in the sight of the LORD your God, in transgressing His covenant, 3who has gone and served other gods and worshiped them, either the sun or moon or any of the host of heaven, which I have not commanded, 4and it is told you, and you hear *of it*, then you shall inquire diligently. And if *it is* indeed true *and* certain that such an abomination has been committed in Israel, 5then you shall bring out to your gates that man or woman who has committed that wicked thing, and shall stone to death that man or woman with stones. 6Whoever is deserving of death shall be put to death on the testimony of two or three witnesses; he shall not be put to death on the testimony

---

PARENTING MATTERS

Q: *What benefits of sexual purity can we use to encourage our children to abstain from sex outside of marriage?*

The Bible clearly teaches that sex outside of marriage is a sin. God forbids fornication (1 Cor. 6:9, Matt. 15:19). Some believe only a cruel God would give teenagers a strong sex drive, and then order them not to act upon it until marriage; but whenever God forbids something, it is for our own good.

Use the following points to develop a clear, well-thought-out explanation on how God uses sexual purity for our good:

- You feel no guilt, no shame, and no emotional scars when you hold to a standard of sexual holiness. You don't hear any accusing voices in your conscience.
- You won't be tempted to compare your future spouse with a past lover.
- You have no risk of sexually-transmitted disease.
- You will not face the possibility of bearing a child out of wedlock.
- It gives you much needed training in self-control and self-denial.
- You please your heavenly Father.

Much of this information about God's view of sex can be discussed with your child in a formal setting as you look up Scriptures together. But also look for casual opportunities to communicate these truths.

of one witness. [7]The hands of the witnesses shall be the first against him to put him to death, and afterward the hands of all the people. So you shall put away the evil from among you.

[8]"If a matter arises which is too hard for you to judge, between degrees of guilt for bloodshed, between one judgment or another, or between one punishment or another, matters of controversy within your gates, then you shall arise and go up to the place which the LORD your God chooses. [9]And you shall come to the priests, the Levites, and to the judge *there* in those days, and inquire *of them;* they shall pronounce upon you the sentence of judgment. [10]You shall do according to the sentence which they pronounce upon you in that place which the LORD chooses. And you shall be careful to do according to all that they order you. [11]According to the sentence of the law in which they instruct you, according to the judgment which they tell you, you shall do; you shall not turn aside *to* the right hand or *to* the left from the sentence which they pronounce upon you. [12]Now the man who acts presumptuously and will not heed the priest who stands to minister there before the LORD your God, or the judge, that man shall die. So you shall put away the evil from Israel. [13]And all the people shall hear and fear, and no longer act presumptuously.

Principles Governing Kings

[14]"When you come to the land which the LORD your God is giving you, and possess it and dwell in it, and say, 'I will set a king over me like all the nations that *are* around me,' [15]you shall surely set a king over you whom the LORD your God chooses; *one* from among your brethren you shall set as king over you; you may not set a foreigner over you, who *is* not your brother. [16]But he shall not multiply horses for himself, nor cause the people to return to Egypt to multiply horses, for the LORD has said to you, 'You shall not return that way again.' [17]Neither shall he multiply wives for himself, lest his heart turn away; nor shall he greatly multiply silver and gold for himself.

[18]"Also it shall be, when he sits on the throne of his kingdom, that he shall write for himself a copy of this law in a book, from *the one* before the priests, the Levites. [19]And it shall be with him, and he shall read it all the days of his life, that he may learn to fear the LORD his God and be careful to observe all the words of this law and these statutes, [20]that his heart may not be lifted above his brethren, that he may not turn aside from the commandment *to* the right hand or *to* the left, and that he may prolong *his* days in his kingdom, he and his children in the midst of Israel.

The Portion of the Priests and Levites

18 "The priests, the Levites—all the tribe of Levi—shall have no part nor inheritance with Israel; they shall eat the offerings of the LORD made by fire, and His portion. [2]Therefore they shall have no inheritance among their brethren; the LORD is their inheritance, as He said to them.

[3]"And this shall be the priest's due from the people, from those who offer a sacrifice, whether *it is* bull or sheep: they shall give to the priest the shoulder, the cheeks, and the stomach. [4]The firstfruits of your grain and your new wine and your oil, and the first of the fleece of your sheep, you shall give him. [5]For the LORD your God has chosen him out of all your tribes to stand to minister in the name of the LORD, him and his sons forever.

[6]"So if a Levite comes from any of your gates, from where he dwells among all Israel, and comes with all the desire of his mind to the place which the LORD chooses, [7]then he may serve in the name of the LORD his God as all his brethren the Levites *do,* who stand there before the LORD. [8]They shall have equal portions to eat, besides what comes from the sale of his inheritance.

Avoid Wicked Customs

[9]"When you come into the land which the LORD your God is giving you, you shall not learn to follow the abominations of those nations. [10]There shall not be found among you *anyone* who makes his son or his daughter pass through the fire, *or one* who practices witchcraft, *or* a soothsayer, or one who interprets omens, or a sorcerer, [11]or one who conjures spells, or a medium, or a spiritist, or one who calls up the dead. [12]For all who do these things *are* an abomination to

the LORD, and because of these abominations the LORD your God drives them out from before you. ¹³You shall be blameless before the LORD your God. ¹⁴For these nations which you will dispossess listened to soothsayers and diviners; but as for you, the LORD your God has not appointed such for you.

INTIMATE MOMENTS

Take $10 to a dollar store and buy her ten fun gifts that remind you of her. Make sure these are *tender* things or *affectionate* things that bring her to your mind, and not utility items such as scouring pads or oven timers! Wrap each gift individually, and then, over dinner, give them to her one at a time. As she unwraps each one, tell her why you bought that item.

A New Prophet Like Moses

¹⁵"The LORD your God will raise up for you a Prophet like me from your midst, from your brethren. Him you shall hear, ¹⁶according to all you desired of the LORD your God in Horeb in the day of the assembly, saying, 'Let me not hear again the voice of the LORD my God, nor let me see this great fire anymore, lest I die.'

¹⁷"And the LORD said to me: 'What they have spoken is good. ¹⁸I will raise up for them a Prophet like you from among their brethren, and will put My words in His mouth, and He shall speak to them all that I command Him. ¹⁹And it shall be *that* whoever will not hear My words, which He speaks in My name, I will require *it* of him. ²⁰But the prophet who presumes to speak a word in My name, which I have not commanded him to speak, or who speaks in the name of other gods, that prophet shall die.' ²¹And if you say in your heart, 'How shall we know the word which the LORD has not spoken?'— ²²when a prophet speaks in the name of the LORD, if the thing does not happen or come to pass, that *is* the thing which the LORD has not spoken; the prophet has

spoken it presumptuously; you shall not be afraid of him.

Three Cities of Refuge

19 "When the LORD your God has cut off the nations whose land the LORD your God is giving you, and you dispossess them and dwell in their cities and in their houses, ²you shall separate three cities for yourself in the midst of your land which the LORD your God is giving you to possess. ³You shall prepare roads for yourself, and divide into three parts the territory of your land which the LORD your God is giving you to inherit, that any manslayer may flee there.

⁴"And this *is* the case of the manslayer who flees there, that he may live: Whoever kills his neighbor unintentionally, not having hated him in time past— ⁵as when *a man* goes to the woods with his neighbor to cut timber, and his hand swings a stroke with the ax to cut down the tree, and the head slips from the handle and strikes his neighbor so that he dies—he shall flee to one of these cities and live; ⁶lest the avenger of blood, while his anger is hot, pursue the manslayer and overtake him, because the way is long, and kill him, though he *was* not deserving of death, since he had not hated the victim in time past. ⁷Therefore I command you, saying, 'You shall separate three cities for yourself.'

⁸"Now if the LORD your God enlarges your territory, as He swore to your fathers, and gives you the land which He promised to give to your fathers, ⁹and if you keep all these commandments and do them, which I command you today, to love the LORD your God and to walk always in His ways, then you shall add three more cities for yourself besides these three, ¹⁰lest innocent blood be shed in the midst of your land which the LORD your God is giving you *as* an inheritance, and *thus* guilt of bloodshed be upon you.

¹¹"But if anyone hates his neighbor, lies in wait for him, rises against him and strikes him mortally, so that he dies, and he flees to one of these cities, ¹²then the elders of his city shall send and bring him from there, and deliver him over to the hand of the avenger of blood, that he may die. ¹³Your eye shall not pity him, but you shall put away

the guilt of innocent blood from Israel, that it may go well with you.

Property Boundaries

14"You shall not remove your neighbor's landmark, which the men of old have set, in your inheritance which you will inherit in the land that the LORD your God is giving you to possess.

The Law Concerning Witnesses

15"One witness shall not rise against a man concerning any iniquity or any sin that he commits; by the mouth of two or three witnesses the matter shall be established. 16If a false witness rises against any man to testify against him of wrongdoing, 17then both men in the controversy shall stand before the LORD, before the priests and the judges who serve in those days. 18And the judges shall make careful inquiry, and indeed, *if* the witness *is* a false witness, who has testified falsely against his brother, 19then you shall do to him as he thought to have done to his brother; so you shall put away the evil from among you. 20And those who remain shall hear and fear, and hereafter they shall not again commit such evil among you. 21Your eye shall not pity: life *shall be* for life, eye for eye, tooth for tooth, hand for hand, foot for foot.

Principles Governing Warfare

20 "When you go out to battle against your enemies, and see horses and chariots *and* people more numerous than you, do not be afraid of them; for the LORD your God *is* with you, who brought you up from the land of Egypt. 2So it shall be, when you are on the verge of battle, that the priest shall approach and speak to the people. 3And he shall say to them, 'Hear, O Israel: Today you are on the verge of battle with your enemies. Do not let your heart faint, do not be afraid, and do not tremble or be terrified because of them; 4for the LORD your God *is* He who goes with you, to fight for you against your enemies, to save you.'

5"Then the officers shall speak to the

people, saying: 'What man *is there* who has built a new house and has not dedicated it? Let him go and return to his house, lest he die in the battle and another man dedicate it. 6Also what man *is there* who has planted a vineyard and has not eaten of it? Let him go and return to his house, lest he die in the battle and another man eat of it. 7And what man *is there* who is betrothed to a woman and has not married her? Let him go and return to his house, lest he die in the battle and another man marry her.'

8"The officers shall speak further to the people, and say, 'What man *is there who is* fearful and fainthearted? Let him go and return to his house, lest the heart of his brethren faint[a] like his heart.' 9And so it shall be, when the officers have finished speaking to the people, that they shall make captains of the armies to lead the people.

10"When you go near a city to fight against it, then proclaim an offer of peace to it. 11And it shall be that if they accept your offer of peace, and open to you, then all the people *who are* found in it shall be placed under tribute to you, and serve you. 12Now if *the city* will not make peace with you, but war against you, then you shall besiege it. 13And when the LORD your God delivers it into your hands, you shall strike every male in it with the edge of the sword. 14But the women, the little ones, the livestock, and all that is in the city, all its spoil, you shall plunder for yourself; and you shall eat the enemies' plunder which the LORD your God gives you. 15Thus you shall do to all the cities *which are* very far from you, which *are* not of the cities of these nations.

16"But of the cities of these peoples which the LORD your God gives you *as* an inheritance, you shall let nothing that breathes remain alive, 17but you shall utterly destroy them: the Hittite and the Amorite and the Canaanite and the Perizzite and the Hivite and the Jebusite, just as the LORD your God has commanded you, 18lest they teach you to do according to all their abominations which they have done for their gods, and you sin against the LORD your God.

19"When you besiege a city for a long time, while making war against it to take it, you shall not destroy its trees by wielding

20:8 [a]Following Masoretic Text and Targum; Samaritan Pentateuch, Septuagint, Syriac, and Vulgate read *lest he make his brother's heart faint.*

DEVOTIONS FOR COUPLES • 21:05
Making Decisions Together

Early in our marriage, Barbara and I resolved that we would always make decisions together, and if at all possible, we would strive to agree with each other before making an important choice. The only exception would occur when we reached an impasse after much discussion and prayer. In that case, I would have the responsibility, as the head of our home, to decide the matter, and whatever happened as a result of following the course of action that I chose, I would assume full responsibility for the outcome.

Some husbands may think (erroneously) that it works best to pull rank with their headship and force their wives to submit to their decisions. This foolish attitude violates Scripture and it demeans a wife. God's blueprints for marriage teach that each spouse makes the other complete. Paul made this very clear, "Neither is man independent of woman, nor woman independent of man, in the Lord" (1 Cor. 11:11). We *need* each other.

Why would anyone knowingly choose to ignore the other in decision-making? Two heads really are better than one! It's important to realize that she may know something you don't. And when is it ever wise to ignore critical information?

On the other hand, some in the Christian community hold that there is no head of the home—a role-less marriage—and that a husband and a wife should share in all decisions equally. Yet there will be times when you won't agree, even after days of discussion, prayer, and carefully listening to each other. In a role-less marriage, who decides, especially on a major decision?

The structure of responsibility and authority established by God in the home addresses this dilemma. God's structure doesn't limit life for us, but enables us to experience life to the fullest, the way He designed it. As you will someday experience with your children, structure, boundaries, and rules provide the protection and security that bring freedom, not bondage.

Barbara and I make a lot of decisions every day. We have learned to consult each other on those decisions where we know that both of us need to talk before making a final determination. Rarely have I gone against her counsel, but on occasions I have had to make a tough call with which she disagreed. And in that case, as I said, I bear the responsibility for the decision, both the good and the bad.

---

an ax against them; if you can eat of them, do not cut them down to use in the siege, for the tree of the field *is* man's *food.* ²⁰Only the trees which you know *are* not trees for food you may destroy and cut down, to build siegeworks against the city that makes war with you, until it is subdued.

The Law Concerning Unsolved Murder

21 "If *anyone* is found slain, lying in the field in the land which the LORD your God is giving you to possess, *and* it is not known who killed him, ²then your elders and your judges shall go out and measure *the distance* from the slain man to the surrounding cities. ³And it shall be *that* the elders of the city nearest to the slain man will take a heifer which has not been worked *and* which has not pulled with a yoke. ⁴The elders of that city shall bring the heifer down to a valley with flowing water, which is neither plowed nor sown, and they shall break the heifer's neck there in the valley. ⁵Then the priests, the sons of Levi, shall come near, for the LORD your God has chosen them to minister to Him and to bless in the name of the LORD; by their word every controversy and every assault shall be *settled.* ⁶And all the elders of that city nearest to the slain *man* shall wash their hands over the heifer whose neck was broken in the valley. ⁷Then they shall answer and say, 'Our hands have not shed this blood, nor have our eyes seen *it.* ⁸Provide atonement, O LORD, for Your people Israel, whom You have redeemed, and do not lay innocent blood to

the charge of Your people Israel.' And atonement shall be provided on their behalf for the blood. ⁹So you shall put away the *guilt of* innocent blood from among you when you do *what is* right in the sight of the LORD.

Female Captives

¹⁰"When you go out to war against your enemies, and the LORD your God delivers them into your hand, and you take them captive, ¹¹and you see among the captives a beautiful woman, and desire her and would take her for your wife, ¹²then you shall bring her home to your house, and she shall shave her head and trim her nails. ¹³She shall put off the clothes of her captivity, remain in your house, and mourn her father and her mother a full month; after that you may go in to her and be her husband, and she shall be your wife. ¹⁴And it shall be, if you have no delight in her, then you shall set her free, but you certainly shall not sell her for money; you shall not treat her brutally, because you have humbled her.

Firstborn Inheritance Rights

¹⁵"If a man has two wives, one loved and the other unloved, and they have borne him children, *both* the loved and the unloved, and *if* the firstborn son is of her who is unloved, ¹⁶then it shall be, on the day he bequeaths his possessions to his sons, *that* he must not bestow firstborn status on the son of the loved wife in preference to the son of the unloved, the *true* firstborn. ¹⁷But he shall acknowledge the son of the unloved wife *as* the firstborn by giving him a double portion of all that he has, for he *is* the beginning of his strength; the right of the firstborn *is* his.

The Rebellious Son

¹⁸"If a man has a stubborn and rebellious son who will not obey the voice of his father or the voice of his mother, and *who,* when they have chastened him, will not heed them, ¹⁹then his father and his mother shall take hold of him and bring him out to the elders of his city, to the gate of his city. ²⁰And they shall say to the elders of his city, 'This son of ours is stubborn and rebellious; he will not obey our voice; he is a glutton and a drunkard.' ²¹Then all the men of his

city shall stone him to death with stones; so you shall put away the evil from among you, and all Israel shall hear and fear.

Miscellaneous Laws

²²"If a man has committed a sin deserving of death, and he is put to death, and you hang him on a tree, ²³his body shall not remain overnight on the tree, but you shall surely bury him that day, so that you do not defile the land which the LORD your God is giving you *as* an inheritance; for he who is hanged *is* accursed of God.

22 "You shall not see your brother's ox or his sheep going astray, and hide yourself from them; you shall certainly bring them back to your brother. ²And if your brother *is* not near you, or if you do not know him, then you shall bring it to your own house, and it shall remain with you until your brother seeks it; then you shall restore it to him. ³You shall do the same with his donkey, and so shall you do with his garment; with any lost thing of your brother's, which he has lost and you have found, you shall do likewise; you must not hide yourself.

⁴"You shall not see your brother's donkey or his ox fall down along the road, and hide yourself from them; you shall surely help him lift *them* up again.

⁵"A woman shall not wear anything that pertains to a man, nor shall a man put on a woman's garment, for all who do so *are* an abomination to the LORD your God.

⁶"If a bird's nest happens to be before you along the way, in any tree or on the ground, with young ones or eggs, with the mother sitting on the young or on the eggs, you shall not take the mother with the young; ⁷you shall surely let the mother go, and take the young for yourself, that it may be well with you and *that* you may prolong *your* days.

⁸"When you build a new house, then you shall make a parapet for your roof, that you may not bring guilt of bloodshed on your household if anyone falls from it.

⁹"You shall not sow your vineyard with different kinds of seed, lest the yield of the seed which you have sown and the fruit of your vineyard be defiled.

¹⁰"You shall not plow with an ox and a donkey together.

¹¹"You shall not wear a garment of different sorts, *such as* wool and linen mixed together.

¹²"You shall make tassels on the four corners of the clothing with which you cover *yourself.*

Laws of Sexual Morality

¹³"If any man takes a wife, and goes in to her, and detests her, ¹⁴and charges her with shameful conduct, and brings a bad name on her, and says, 'I took this woman, and when I came to her I found she *was* not a virgin,' ¹⁵then the father and mother of the young woman shall take and bring out *the evidence of* the young woman's virginity to the elders of the city at the gate. ¹⁶And the young woman's father shall say to the elders, 'I gave my daughter to this man as wife, and he detests her. ¹⁷Now he has charged her with shameful conduct, saying, "I found your daughter *was* not a virgin," and yet these *are the evidences of* my daughter's virginity.' And they shall spread the cloth before the elders of the city. ¹⁸Then the elders of that city shall take that man and punish him; ¹⁹and they shall fine him one hundred *shekels* of silver and give *them* to the father of the young woman, because he has brought a bad name on a virgin of Israel. And she shall be his wife; he cannot divorce her all his days.

²⁰"But if the thing is true, *and evidences of* virginity are not found for the young woman, ²¹then they shall bring out the young woman to the door of her father's house, and the men of her city shall stone her to death with stones, because she has done a disgraceful thing in Israel, to play the harlot in her father's house. So you shall put away the evil from among you.

²²"If a man is found lying with a woman married to a husband, then both of them shall die—the man that lay with the woman, and the woman; so you shall put away the evil from Israel.

²³"If a young woman *who is* a virgin is betrothed to a husband, and a man finds her in the city and lies with her, ²⁴then you shall bring them both out to the gate of that city, and you shall stone them to death with stones, the young woman because she did not cry out in the city, and the man because he humbled his neighbor's wife; so you shall put away the evil from among you.

²⁵"But if a man finds a betrothed young woman in the countryside, and the man forces her and lies with her, then only the man who lay with her shall die. ²⁶But you shall do nothing to the young woman; *there is* in the young woman no sin *deserving* of death, for just as when a man rises against his neighbor and kills him, even so *is* this matter. ²⁷For he found her in the countryside, *and* the betrothed young woman cried out, but *there was* no one to save her.

²⁸"If a man finds a young woman *who is* a virgin, who is not betrothed, and he seizes her and lies with her, and they are found out, ²⁹then the man who lay with her shall give to the young woman's father fifty *shekels* of silver, and she shall be his wife because he has humbled her; he shall not be permitted to divorce her all his days.

³⁰"A man shall not take his father's wife, nor uncover his father's bed.

Those Excluded from the Congregation

23 "He who is emasculated by crushing or mutilation shall not enter the assembly of the LORD.

²"One of illegitimate birth shall not enter the assembly of the LORD; even to the tenth generation none of his *descendants* shall enter the assembly of the LORD.

³"An Ammonite or Moabite shall not enter the assembly of the LORD; even to the tenth generation none of his *descendants* shall enter the assembly of the LORD forever, ⁴because they did not meet you with bread and water on the road when you came out of Egypt, and because they hired against you Balaam the son of Beor from Pethor of Mesopotamia,^a to curse you. ⁵Nevertheless the LORD your God would not listen to Balaam, but the LORD your God turned the curse into a blessing for you, because the LORD your God loves you. ⁶You shall not seek their peace nor their prosperity all your days forever.

⁷"You shall not abhor an Edomite, for he *is* your brother. You shall not abhor an Egyptian, because you were an alien in his land. ⁸The children of the third generation born to them may enter the assembly of the LORD.

Cleanliness of the Campsite

⁹"When the army goes out against your enemies, then keep yourself from every wicked thing. ¹⁰If there is any man among you who becomes unclean by some occurrence in the night, then he shall go outside the camp; he shall not come inside the camp. ¹¹But it shall be, when evening comes, that he shall wash with water; and when the sun sets, he may come into the camp.

¹²"Also you shall have a place outside the camp, where you may go out; ¹³and you shall have an implement among your equipment, and when you sit down outside, you shall dig with it and turn and cover your refuse. ¹⁴For the LORD your God walks in the midst of your camp, to deliver you and give your enemies over to you; therefore your camp shall be holy, that He may see no unclean thing among you, and turn away from you.

Miscellaneous Laws

¹⁵"You shall not give back to his master the slave who has escaped from his master to you. ¹⁶He may dwell with you in your midst, in the place which he chooses within one of your gates, where it seems best to him; you shall not oppress him.

¹⁷"There shall be no *ritual* harlot^a of the daughters of Israel, or a perverted^b one of the sons of Israel. ¹⁸You shall not bring the wages of a harlot or the price of a dog to the house of the LORD your God for any vowed offering, for both of these *are* an abomination to the LORD your God.

¹⁹"You shall not charge interest to your brother—interest on money *or* food *or* anything that is lent out at interest. ²⁰To a foreigner you may charge interest, but to your brother you shall not charge interest, that the LORD your God may bless you in all to which you set your hand in the land which you are entering to possess.

²¹"When you make a vow to the LORD your God, you shall not delay to pay it; for the LORD your God will surely require it of you, and it would be sin to you. ²²But if you abstain from vowing, it shall not be sin to you. ²³That which has gone from your lips you shall keep and perform, for you voluntarily vowed to the LORD your God what you have promised with your mouth.

²⁴"When you come into your neighbor's vineyard, you may eat your fill of grapes at your pleasure, but you shall not put *any* in your container. ²⁵When you come into your neighbor's standing grain, you may pluck the heads with your hand, but you

---

23:4 ^aHebrew *Aram Naharaim*
23:17 ^aHebrew *qedeshah,* feminine of *qadesh* (see note *b*) ^bHebrew *qadesh,* that is, one practicing sodomy and prostitution in religious rituals

shall not use a sickle on your neighbor's standing grain.

Law Concerning Divorce

24 "When a man takes a wife and marries her, and it happens that she finds no favor in his eyes because he has found some uncleanness in her, and he writes her a certificate of divorce, puts *it* in her hand, and sends her out of his house, ²when she has departed from his house, and goes and becomes another man's *wife*, ³if the latter husband detests her and writes her a certificate of divorce, puts *it* in her hand, and sends her out of his house, or if the latter husband dies who took her as his wife, ⁴*then* her former husband who divorced her must not take her back to be his wife after she has been defiled; for that *is* an abomination before the LORD, and you shall not bring sin on the land which the LORD your God is giving you *as* an inheritance.

Miscellaneous Laws

⁵"When a man has taken a new wife, he shall not go out to war or be charged with any business; he shall be free at home one year, and bring happiness to his wife whom he has taken.

⁶"No man shall take the lower or the upper millstone in pledge, for he takes *one's* living in pledge.

⁷"If a man is found kidnapping any of his brethren of the children of Israel, and mistreats him or sells him, then that kidnapper shall die; and you shall put away the evil from among you.

⁸"Take heed in an outbreak of leprosy, that you carefully observe and do according to all that the priests, the Levites, shall teach you; just as I commanded them, *so* you shall be careful to do. ⁹Remember what the LORD your God did to Miriam on the way when you came out of Egypt!

¹⁰"When you lend your brother anything, you shall not go into his house to get his pledge. ¹¹You shall stand outside, and the man to whom you lend shall bring the pledge out to you. ¹²And if the man *is* poor, you shall not keep his pledge overnight. ¹³You shall in any case return the pledge to him again when the sun goes down, that he may sleep in his own garment and bless you; and it shall be righteousness to you before the LORD your God.

¹⁴"You shall not oppress a hired servant *who is* poor and needy, *whether* one of your brethren or one of the aliens who *is* in your land within your gates. ¹⁵Each day you shall give *him* his wages, and not let the sun go down on it, for he *is* poor and has set his heart on it; lest he cry out against you to the LORD, and it be sin to you.

¹⁶"Fathers shall not be put to death for

ROMANTIC QUOTES AND NOTES
Marriage Is a Covenant

Marriage is not a private experiment, littered with prenuptial agreements and an attitude of "Try it! If it doesn't work, I can always bail out." Marriage is not a convenient relationship based upon "What's in it for me?" Marriage is not some kind of social contract, something you do only "for as long as you both shall love."

Marriage is a sacred, lifetime covenant between one man and one woman and their God. It is a public vow of how you will relate to your spouse as you form a new family unit. And any covenant, including the marriage covenant, is a *binding, weighty* obligation.

Deuteronomy 23:23 says, "That which has gone from your lips you shall keep and perform, for you have voluntarily vowed to the Lord your God what you have promised with your mouth." In Proverbs we read, "It is a snare for a man to devote rashly something as holy, and afterward to reconsider his vows" (20:25). Jesus said that, "every idle word that men may speak, they will give account of it in the day of judgment" (Matt. 12:36).

Our culture no longer takes marriage seriously, but these verses all proclaim the unchanging truth: God takes the wedding covenant and the vows that we make to one another very *seriously*.

their children, nor shall children be put to death for *their* fathers; a person shall be put to death for his own sin.

17"You shall not pervert justice due the stranger or the fatherless, nor take a widow's garment as a pledge. 18But you shall remember that you were a slave in Egypt, and the LORD your God redeemed you from there; therefore I command you to do this thing.

19"When you reap your harvest in your field, and forget a sheaf in the field, you shall not go back to get it; it shall be for the stranger, the fatherless, and the widow, that the LORD your God may bless you in all the work of your hands. 20When you beat your olive trees, you shall not go over the boughs again; it shall be for the stranger, the fatherless, and the widow. 21When you gather the grapes of your vineyard, you shall not glean *it* afterward; it shall be for the stranger, the fatherless, and the widow. 22And you shall remember that you were a slave in the land of Egypt; therefore I command you to do this thing.

25 "If there is a dispute between men, and they come to court, that *the judges* may judge them, and they justify the righteous and condemn the wicked, 2then it shall be, if the wicked man deserves to be beaten, that the judge will cause him to lie down and be beaten in his presence, according to his guilt, with a certain number of blows. 3Forty blows he may give him *and* no more, lest he should exceed this and beat him with many blows above these, and your brother be humiliated in your sight.

4"You shall not muzzle an ox while it treads out *the grain.*

Marriage Duty of the Surviving Brother

5"If brothers dwell together, and one of them dies and has no son, the widow of the dead man shall not be *married* to a stranger outside *the family;* her husband's brother shall go in to her, take her as his wife, and perform the duty of a husband's brother to her. 6And it shall be *that* the first-born son which she bears will succeed to the name of his dead brother, that his name

---

PARENTING MATTERS

Q: *At what age should we allow our teenager to start dating?*

As our teens approached what the culture calls "the dating years," we did everything we could to discourage intense dating relationships. Our junior high and high school age teens didn't date anyone exclusively. Our teens did not go out on a date every Friday and Saturday night.

Instead, we encouraged our children when they were still at home to focus on the friendship side of their relationships with members of the opposite sex. When our children did spend time with the opposite sex, it was primarily in a group setting, not one-on-one.

In light of our reformatted approach to dating, we had the following very general age guidelines for spending time with the opposite sex:

- Doing things together with an approved, mixed group of teens away from our home: Sometime after age fifteen if the child was mature enough to be trusted in those settings.

- Double dates or group dates: Usually at age seventeen, maybe earlier.

- Single dates: These are generally discouraged, but allowed in certain circumstances, like prom or special events.

Even with these guidelines, however, most of our teens had their first real date to the school prom in their junior year, at age seventeen. And for the most part, those first dates were all with friends, not with a romantic interest.

may not be blotted out of Israel. 7But if the man does not want to take his brother's wife, then let his brother's wife go up to the gate to the elders, and say, 'My husband's brother refuses to raise up a name to his brother in Israel; he will not perform the duty of my husband's brother.' 8Then the elders of his city shall call him and speak to him. But *if* he stands firm and says, 'I do not want to take her,' 9then his brother's wife shall come to him in the presence of the elders, remove his sandal from his foot, spit in his face, and answer and say, 'So shall it be done to the man who will not build up his brother's house.' 10And his name shall be called in Israel, 'The house of him who had his sandal removed.'

Miscellaneous Laws

11"If *two* men fight together, and the wife of one draws near to rescue her husband from the hand of the one attacking him, and puts out her hand and seizes him by the genitals, 12then you shall cut off her hand; your eye shall not pity *her.*

13"You shall not have in your bag differing weights, a heavy and a light. 14You shall not have in your house differing measures, a large and a small. 15You shall have a perfect and just weight, a perfect and just measure, that your days may be lengthened in the land which the LORD your God is giving you. 16For all who do such things,

all who behave unrighteously, *are* an abomination to the LORD your God.

Destroy the Amalekites

17"Remember what Amalek did to you on the way as you were coming out of Egypt, 18how he met you on the way and attacked your rear ranks, all the stragglers at your rear, when you *were* tired and weary; and he did not fear God. 19Therefore it shall be, when the LORD your God has given you rest from your enemies all around, in the land which the LORD your God is giving you to possess *as* an inheritance, *that* you will blot out the remembrance of Amalek from under heaven. You shall not forget.

Offerings of Firstfruits and Tithes

26 "And it shall be, when you come into the land which the LORD your God is giving you *as* an inheritance, and you possess it and dwell in it, 2that you shall take some of the first of all the produce of the ground, which you shall bring from your land that the LORD your God is giving you, and put *it* in a basket and go to the place where the LORD your God chooses to make His name abide. 3And you shall go to the one who is priest in those days, and say to him, 'I declare today to the LORD youra God

---

26:3 aSeptuagint reads *my.*

Learning to Adjust

Every marriage requires a time of adjustment. Since marriage involves the union of two people, each coming from different backgrounds and with their own set of values and expectations, it will take them time and effort to learn how to live together in harmony.

Even before Israel crossed over into the Promised Land, God highlighted this need for a time of marital adjustment. He commanded His people to give newly-married husbands one year off from military and commercial duties. Such a man "shall be free at home one year," God said, "and bring happiness to his wife whom he has taken" (24:5).

To have a grace-filled marriage means to selflessly give your partner room to be different, and then flexing on his or her behalf. It means putting his/her needs ahead of your own and it means allowing him/her to be who they are . . . even when that requires some unexpected adjustments.

God intended for marriage to be a picture of selfless giving, with both partners giving all they have to give for the good of the other. When we walk and live according to that model, we will be able to adjust to whatever our spouse brings to the table.

that I have come to the country which the LORD swore to our fathers to give us.'

4"Then the priest shall take the basket out of your hand and set it down before the altar of the LORD your God. 5And you shall answer and say before the LORD your God: 'My father *was* a Syrian,[a] about to perish, and he went down to Egypt and dwelt there, few in number; and there he became a nation, great, mighty, and populous. 6But the Egyptians mistreated us, afflicted us, and laid hard bondage on us. 7Then we cried out to the LORD God of our fathers, and the LORD heard our voice and looked on our affliction and our labor and our oppression. 8So the LORD brought us out of Egypt with a mighty hand and with an outstretched arm, with great terror and with signs and wonders. 9He has brought us to this place and has given us this land, "a land flowing with milk and honey";[a] 10and now, behold, I have brought the firstfruits of the land which you, O LORD, have given me.'

"Then you shall set it before the LORD your God, and worship before the LORD your God. 11So you shall rejoice in every good *thing* which the LORD your God has given to you and your house, you and the Levite and the stranger who *is* among you.

12"When you have finished laying aside all the tithe of your increase in the third year—the year of tithing—and have given *it* to the Levite, the stranger, the fatherless, and the widow, so that they may eat within your gates and be filled, 13then you shall say before the LORD your God: 'I have removed the holy *tithe* from *my* house, and also have given them to the Levite, the stranger, the fatherless, and the widow, according to all Your commandments which You have commanded me; I have not transgressed Your commandments, nor have I forgotten *them.* 14I have not eaten any of it when in mourning, nor have I removed *any* of it for an unclean *use,* nor given *any* of it for the dead. I have obeyed the voice of the LORD my God, and have done according to all that You have commanded me. 15Look down from Your holy habitation, from heaven, and bless Your people Israel and the land which

You have given us, just as You swore to our fathers, "a land flowing with milk and honey." '[a]

A Special People of God

16"This day the LORD your God commands you to observe these statutes and judgments; therefore you shall be careful to observe them with all your heart and with all your soul. 17Today you have proclaimed the LORD to be your God, and that you will walk in His ways and keep His statutes, His commandments, and His judgments, and that you will obey His voice. 18Also today the LORD has proclaimed you to be His special people, just as He promised you, that *you* should keep all His commandments, 19and that He will set you high above all nations which He has made, in praise, in name, and in honor, and that you may be a holy people to the LORD your God, just as He has spoken."

The Law Inscribed on Stones

27 Now Moses, with the elders of Israel, commanded the people, saying: "Keep all the commandments which I command you today. 2And it shall be, on the day when you cross over the Jordan to the land which the LORD your God is giving you, that you shall set up for yourselves large stones, and whitewash them with lime. 3You shall write on them all the words of this law, when you have crossed over, that you may enter the land which the LORD your God is giving you, 'a land flowing with milk and honey,'[a] just as the LORD God of your fathers promised you. 4Therefore it shall be, when you have crossed over the Jordan, *that* on Mount Ebal you shall set up these stones, which I command you today, and you shall whitewash them with lime. 5And there you shall build an altar to the LORD your God, an altar of stones; you shall not use an iron *tool* on them. 6You shall build with whole stones the altar of the LORD your God, and offer burnt offerings on it to the LORD your God. 7You shall offer peace offerings, and shall eat there, and rejoice before the LORD your God. 8And you shall write very plainly on the stones all the words of this law."

9Then Moses and the priests, the Levites, spoke to all Israel, saying, "Take heed and listen, O Israel: This day you have become the people of the LORD your God. ¹⁰Therefore you shall obey the voice of the LORD your God, and observe His commandments and His statutes which I command you today."

Curses Pronounced from Mount Ebal

¹¹And Moses commanded the people on the same day, saying, ¹²"These shall stand on Mount Gerizim to bless the people, when you have crossed over the Jordan: Simeon, Levi, Judah, Issachar, Joseph, and Benjamin; ¹³and these shall stand on Mount Ebal to curse: Reuben, Gad, Asher, Zebulun, Dan, and Naphtali.

¹⁴"And the Levites shall speak with a loud voice and say to all the men of Israel: ¹⁵'Cursed *is* the one who makes a carved or molded image, an abomination to the LORD, the work of the hands of the craftsman, and sets *it* up in secret.'

"And all the people shall answer and say, 'Amen!'

¹⁶'Cursed *is* the one who treats his father or his mother with contempt.'

"And all the people shall say, 'Amen!'

¹⁷'Cursed *is* the one who moves his neighbor's landmark.'

"And all the people shall say, 'Amen!'

¹⁸'Cursed *is* the one who makes the blind to wander off the road.'

"And all the people shall say, 'Amen!'

¹⁹'Cursed *is* the one who perverts the justice due the stranger, the fatherless, and widow.'

"And all the people shall say, 'Amen!'

²⁰'Cursed *is* the one who lies with his father's wife, because he has uncovered his father's bed.'

"And all the people shall say, 'Amen!'

²¹'Cursed *is* the one who lies with any kind of animal.'

"And all the people shall say, 'Amen!'

²²'Cursed *is* the one who lies with his sister, the daughter of his father or the daughter of his mother.'

"And all the people shall say, 'Amen!'

²³'Cursed *is* the one who lies with his mother-in-law.'

"And all the people shall say, 'Amen!'

²⁴'Cursed *is* the one who attacks his neighbor secretly.'

"And all the people shall say, 'Amen!'

²⁵'Cursed *is* the one who takes a bribe to slay an innocent person.'

"And all the people shall say, 'Amen!'

²⁶'Cursed *is* the one who does not confirm *all* the words of this law by observing them.'

"And all the people shall say, 'Amen!' "

Blessings on Obedience

28 "Now it shall come to pass, if you diligently obey the voice of the LORD your God, to observe carefully all His commandments which I command you today, that the LORD your God will set you high above all nations of the earth. ²And all these blessings shall come upon you and overtake you, because you obey the voice of the LORD your God:

³"Blessed *shall* you *be* in the city, and blessed *shall* you *be* in the country.

⁴"Blessed *shall be* the fruit of your body, the produce of your ground and the increase of your herds, the increase of your cattle and the offspring of your flocks.

⁵"Blessed *shall be* your basket and your kneading bowl.

⁶"Blessed *shall* you *be* when you come in, and blessed *shall* you *be* when you go out.

⁷"The LORD will cause your enemies who rise against you to be defeated before your face; they shall come out against you one way and flee before you seven ways.

⁸"The LORD will command the blessing on you in your storehouses and in all to which you set your hand, and He will bless you in the land which the LORD your God is giving you.

⁹"The LORD will establish you as a holy people to Himself, just as He has sworn to you, if you keep the commandments of the LORD your God and walk in His ways. ¹⁰Then all peoples of the earth shall see that you are called by the name of the LORD, and they shall be afraid of you. ¹¹And the LORD will grant you plenty of goods, in the fruit of your body, in the increase of your livestock, and in the produce of your ground, in the land of which the LORD swore to your fathers to give you. ¹²The LORD will open to you His good treasure, the heavens, to give the rain to your land in its season, and to bless all the work of your hand. You shall lend to many nations, but you shall not borrow. ¹³And the LORD will make you the

head and not the tail; you shall be above only, and not be beneath, if you heed the commandments of the LORD your God, which I command you today, and are careful to observe *them.* [14]So you shall not turn aside from any of the words which I command you this day, *to* the right or the left, to go after other gods to serve them.

Curses on Disobedience

[15]"But it shall come to pass, if you do not obey the voice of the LORD your God, to observe carefully all His commandments and His statutes which I command you today, that all these curses will come upon you and overtake you:

[16]"Cursed *shall* you *be* in the city, and cursed *shall* you *be* in the country.

[17]"Cursed *shall be* your basket and your kneading bowl.

[18]"Cursed *shall be* the fruit of your body and the produce of your land, the increase of your cattle and the offspring of your flocks.

[19]"Cursed *shall* you *be* when you come in, and cursed *shall* you *be* when you go out.

[20]"The LORD will send on you cursing, confusion, and rebuke in all that you set your hand to do, until you are destroyed and until you perish quickly, because of the wickedness of your doings in which you have forsaken Me. [21]The LORD will make the plague cling to you until He has consumed you from the land which you are going to possess. [22]The LORD will strike you with consumption, with fever, with inflammation, with severe burning fever, with the sword, with scorching, and with mildew; they shall pursue you until you perish. [23]And your heavens which *are* over your head shall be bronze, and the earth which is under you *shall be* iron. [24]The LORD will change the rain of your land to powder and dust; from the heaven it shall come down on you until you are destroyed.

[25]"The LORD will cause you to be defeated before your enemies; you shall go out one way against them and flee seven ways before them; and you shall become troublesome to all the kingdoms of the earth. [26]Your carcasses shall be food for all the birds of the air and the beasts of the earth, and no one shall frighten *them* away. [27]The LORD will strike you with the boils of Egypt, with tumors, with the scab, and with the itch, from which you cannot be healed. [28]The LORD will strike you with madness and blindness and confusion of heart. [29]And you shall grope at noonday, as a blind man gropes in darkness; you shall not prosper in your ways; you shall be only oppressed and plundered continually, and no one shall save *you.*

[30]"You shall betroth a wife, but another man shall lie with her; you shall build a house, but you shall not dwell in it; you shall plant a vineyard, but shall not gather its grapes. [31]Your ox *shall be* slaughtered before your eyes, but you shall not eat of it; your donkey *shall be* violently taken away from before you, and shall not be restored to you; your sheep *shall be* given to your enemies, and you shall have no one to rescue *them.* [32]Your sons and your daughters *shall be* given to another people, and your eyes shall look and fail *with longing* for them all day long; and *there shall be* no strength in your hand. [33]A nation whom you have not known shall eat the fruit of your land and the produce of your labor, and you shall be only oppressed and crushed continually. [34]So you shall be driven mad because of the sight which your eyes see. [35]The LORD will strike you in the knees and on the legs with severe boils which cannot be healed, and from the sole of your foot to the top of your head.

[36]"The LORD will bring you and the king whom you set over you to a nation which neither you nor your fathers have known, and there you shall serve other gods—wood and stone. [37]And you shall become an astonishment, a proverb, and a byword among all nations where the LORD will drive you.

[38]"You shall carry much seed out to the field but gather little in, for the locust shall consume it. [39]You shall plant vineyards and tend *them,* but you shall neither drink *of* the wine nor gather the *grapes;* for the worms shall eat them. [40]You shall have olive trees throughout all your territory, but you shall not anoint *yourself* with the oil; for your olives shall drop off. [41]You shall beget sons and daughters, but they shall not be yours; for they shall go into captivity. [42]Locusts shall consume all your trees and the produce of your land.

43"The alien who *is* among you shall rise higher and higher above you, and you shall come down lower and lower. 44He shall lend to you, but you shall not lend to him; he shall be the head, and you shall be the tail.

45"Moreover all these curses shall come upon you and pursue and overtake you, until you are destroyed, because you did not obey the voice of the LORD your God, to keep His commandments and His statutes which He commanded you. 46And they shall be upon you for a sign and a wonder, and on your descendants forever.

47"Because you did not serve the LORD your God with joy and gladness of heart, for the abundance of everything, 48therefore you shall serve your enemies, whom the LORD will send against you, in hunger, in thirst, in nakedness, and in need of everything; and He will put a yoke of iron on your neck until He has destroyed you. 49The LORD will bring a nation against you from afar, from the end of the earth, *as swift* as the eagle flies, a nation whose language you will not understand, 50a nation of fierce countenance, which does not respect the elderly nor show favor to the young. 51And they shall eat the increase of your livestock and the produce of your land, until you are destroyed; they shall not leave you grain or new wine or oil, *or* the increase of your cattle or the offspring of your flocks, until they have destroyed you.

52"They shall besiege you at all your gates until your high and fortified walls, in which you trust, come down throughout all your land; and they shall besiege you at all your gates throughout all your land which the LORD your God has given you. 53You shall eat the fruit of your own body, the flesh of your sons and your daughters whom the LORD your God has given you, in the siege and desperate straits in which your enemy shall distress you. 54The sensitive and very refined man among you will be hostile toward his brother, toward the wife of his bosom, and toward the rest of his children whom he leaves behind, 55so that he will not give any of them the flesh of his children whom he will eat, because he has nothing left in the siege and desperate straits in which your enemy shall distress you at all your gates. 56The tender and delicate woman among you, who would not venture to set the sole of her foot on the ground because of her delicateness and sensitivity, will refuse[a] to the husband of her bosom, and to her son and her daughter, 57her placenta which comes out from between her feet and her children whom she bears; for she will eat them secretly for lack of everything in the siege and desperate straits in which your enemy shall distress you at all your gates.

58"If you do not carefully observe all the words of this law that are written in this book, that you may fear this glorious and awesome name, THE LORD YOUR GOD, 59then the LORD will bring upon you and your descendants extraordinary plagues—great and prolonged plagues—and serious and prolonged sicknesses. 60Moreover He will bring back on you all the diseases of Egypt, of which you were afraid, and they shall cling to you. 61Also every sickness and every plague, which *is* not written in this Book of the Law, will the LORD bring upon you until you are destroyed. 62You shall be left few in number, whereas you were as the stars of heaven in multitude, because you would not obey the voice of the LORD your God. 63And it shall be, *that* just as the LORD rejoiced over you to do you good and multiply you, so the LORD will rejoice over you to destroy you and bring you to nothing; and you shall be plucked from off the land which you go to possess.

64"Then the LORD will scatter you among all peoples, from one end of the earth to the other, and there you shall serve other gods, which neither you nor your fathers have known—wood and stone. 65And among those nations you shall find no rest, nor shall the sole of your foot have a resting place; but there the LORD will give you a trembling heart, failing eyes, and anguish of soul. 66Your life shall hang in doubt before you; you shall fear day and night, and have no assurance of life. 67In the morning you shall say, 'Oh, that it were evening!' And at evening you shall say, 'Oh, that it were morning!' because of the fear which terrifies your heart, and because of the sight which your eyes see.

28:56 [a]Literally *her eye shall be evil toward*

68"And the LORD will take you back to Egypt in ships, by the way of which I said to you, 'You shall never see it again.' And there you shall be offered for sale to your enemies as male and female slaves, but no one will buy *you*."

The Covenant Renewed in Moab

29 These *are* the words of the covenant which the LORD commanded Moses to make with the children of Israel in the land of Moab, besides the covenant which He made with them in Horeb.

2Now Moses called all Israel and said to them: "You have seen all that the LORD did before your eyes in the land of Egypt, to Pharaoh and to all his servants and to all his land— 3the great trials which your eyes have seen, the signs, and those great wonders. 4Yet the LORD has not given you a heart to perceive and eyes to see and ears to hear, to this *very* day. 5And I have led you forty years in the wilderness. Your clothes have not worn out on you, and your sandals have not worn out on your feet. 6You have not eaten bread, nor have you drunk wine or *similar* drink, that you may know that I *am* the LORD your God. 7And when you came to this place, Sihon king of Heshbon and Og king of Bashan came out against us to battle, and we conquered them. 8We took their land and gave it as an inheritance to the Reubenites, to the Gadites, and to half the tribe of Manasseh. 9Therefore keep the words of this covenant, and do them, that you may prosper in all that you do.

10"All of you stand today before the LORD your God: your leaders and your tribes and your elders and your officers, all the men of Israel, 11your little ones and your wives— also the stranger who *is* in your camp, from the one who cuts your wood to the one who draws your water— 12that you may enter into covenant with the LORD your God, and into His oath, which the LORD your God makes with you today, 13that He may establish you today as a people for Himself, and *that* He may be God to you, just as He has spoken to you, and just as He has sworn to your fathers, to Abraham, Isaac, and Jacob.

14"I make this covenant and this oath, not with you alone, 15but with *him* who stands here with us today before the LORD our God, as well as with *him* who *is* not here with us today 16(for you know that we dwelt in the land of Egypt and that we came through the nations which you passed by, 17and you saw their abominations and their idols which *were* among them—wood and stone and silver and gold); 18so that there may not be among you man or woman or family or tribe, whose heart turns away today from the LORD our God, to go *and* serve the gods of these nations, and that there may not be among you a root bearing bitterness or wormwood; 19and so it may not happen, when he hears the words of this curse, that he blesses himself in his heart, saying, 'I shall have peace, even though I follow the dictatesa of my heart'—as though the drunkard could be included with the sober.

20"The LORD would not spare him; for then the anger of the LORD and His jealousy would burn against that man, and every curse that is written in this book would settle on him, and the LORD would blot out his name from under heaven. 21And the LORD would separate him from all the tribes of Israel for adversity, according to all the curses of the covenant that are written in this Book of the Law, 22so that the coming generation of your children who rise up after you, and the foreigner who comes from a far land, would say, when they see the plagues of that land and the sicknesses which the LORD has laid on it:

23"The whole land *is* brimstone, salt, and burning; it is not sown, nor does it bear, nor does any grass grow there, like the overthrow of Sodom and Gomorrah, Admah, and Zeboiim, which the LORD overthrew in His anger and His wrath.' 24All nations would say, 'Why has the LORD done so to this land? What does the heat of this great anger mean?' 25Then *people* would say: 'Because they have forsaken the covenant of the LORD God of their fathers, which He made with them when He brought them out of the land of Egypt; 26for they went and served other gods and worshiped them, gods that they did not know and that He had not given to them. 27Then the

---

29:19 aOr *stubbornness*

Never out of Reach

IF WE WANT TO WALK in God's ways and experience His love and power, then we need to obey His commands. "For this is the love of God," wrote John, "that we keep His commandments. And His commandments are not burdensome" (1 John 5:3).

Fortunately, God did not leave us powerless to obey His commandments! Deuteronomy 30:11 states, "For this commandment which I command you today is not too difficult for you, nor is it out of reach."

No human being in history, except for Jesus, has ever been able to obey the Ten Commandments perfectly. But He gave us the Holy Spirit, who gives us the power to obey Him: "If you love Me, you keep My commandments. And I will pray the Father, and He will give you another Helper, that He may abide with you forever—the Spirit of truth, whom the world cannot receive, because it neither sees Him nor knows Him, but you know Him because He dwells with you and will be in you" (John 14:15–17).

If you have received Christ as your Savior, God has given you His helper, the Holy Spirit, who can empower you to fulfill God's commandments. And when you are disobedient and blow it (and you will), remember that the message of the gospel is that by God's grace we can repent and we are forgiven. Turn away from your sin and simply admit (confess) your sins to God and thank Him for His forgiveness. Yield your will to Him and thank Him, by faith, that He will fill (empower) you again with the Holy Spirit.

---

anger of the LORD was aroused against this land, to bring on it every curse that is written in this book. ²⁸And the LORD uprooted them from their land in anger, in wrath, and in great indignation, and cast them into another land, as *it is* this day.'

²⁹"The secret *things belong* to the LORD our God, but those *things which are* revealed *belong* to us and to our children forever, that *we* may do all the words of this law.

The Blessing of Returning to God

30 "Now it shall come to pass, when all these things come upon you, the blessing and the curse which I have set before you, and you call *them* to mind among all the nations where the LORD your God drives you, ²and you return to the LORD your God and obey His voice, according to all that I command you today, you and your children, with all your heart and with all your soul, ³that the LORD your God will bring you back from captivity, and have compassion on you, and gather you again from all the nations where the LORD your God has scattered you. ⁴If *any* of you are driven out to the farthest *parts* under heaven, from there the LORD your God will gather you, and from there He will bring you. ⁵Then the LORD your God will bring you to the land which your fathers possessed, and you shall possess it. He will prosper you and multiply you more than your fathers. ⁶And the LORD your God will circumcise your heart and the heart of your descendants, to love the LORD your God with all your heart and with all your soul, that you may live.

⁷"Also the LORD your God will put all these curses on your enemies and on those who hate you, who persecuted you. ⁸And you will again obey the voice of the LORD and do all His commandments which I command you today. ⁹The LORD your God will make you abound in all the work of your hand, in the fruit of your body, in the increase of your livestock, and in the produce of your land for good. For the LORD will again rejoice over you for good as He rejoiced over your fathers, ¹⁰if you obey the voice of the LORD your God, to keep His commandments and His statutes which are written in this Book of the Law, *and* if you turn to the LORD your God with all your heart and with all your soul.

The Choice of Life or Death

¹¹"For this commandment which I command you today *is* not *too* mysterious for you, nor *is* it far off. ¹²It *is* not in heaven,

that you should say, 'Who will ascend into heaven for us and bring it to us, that we may hear it and do it?' ¹³Nor *is* it beyond the sea, that you should say, 'Who will go over the sea for us and bring it to us, that we may hear it and do it?' ¹⁴But the word *is* very near you, in your mouth and in your heart, that you may do it.

¹⁵"See, I have set before you today life and good, death and evil, ¹⁶in that I command you today to love the LORD your God, to walk in His ways, and to keep His commandments, His statutes, and His judgments, that you may live and multiply; and the LORD your God will bless you in the land which you go to possess. ¹⁷But if your heart turns away so that you do not hear, and are drawn away, and worship other gods and serve them, ¹⁸I announce to you today that you shall surely perish; you shall not prolong *your* days in the land which you cross over the Jordan to go in and possess. ¹⁹I call heaven and earth as witnesses today against you, *that* I have set before you life and death, blessing and cursing; therefore choose life, that both you and your descendants may live; ²⁰that you may love the LORD your God, that you may obey His voice, and that you may cling to Him, for He *is* your life and the length of your days; and that you may dwell in the land which the LORD swore to your fathers, to Abraham, Isaac, and Jacob, to give them."

Joshua the New Leader of Israel

31 Then Moses went and spoke these words to all Israel. ²And he said to them: "I *am* one hundred and twenty years old today. I can no longer go out and come in. Also the LORD has said to me, 'You shall not cross over this Jordan.' ³The LORD your God Himself crosses over before you; He will destroy these nations from before you, and you shall dispossess them. Joshua himself crosses over before you, just as the LORD has said. ⁴And the LORD will do to them as He did to Sihon and Og, the kings of the Amorites and their land, when He destroyed them. ⁵The LORD will give them over to you, that you may do to them according to every commandment which I have commanded you. ⁶Be strong and of good courage, do not fear nor be afraid of them; for the LORD your God, He *is* the One who goes with you. He will not leave you nor forsake you."

⁷Then Moses called Joshua and said to him in the sight of all Israel, "Be strong and of good courage, for you must go with this people to the land which the LORD has sworn to their fathers to give them, and you shall cause them to inherit it. ⁸And the LORD, He *is* the One who goes before you. He will be with you, He will not leave you nor forsake you; do not fear nor be dismayed."

The Law to Be Read Every Seven Years

⁹So Moses wrote this law and delivered it to the priests, the sons of Levi, who bore the ark of the covenant of the LORD, and to all the elders of Israel. ¹⁰And Moses commanded them, saying: "At the end of *every* seven years, at the appointed time in the year of release, at the Feast of Tabernacles, ¹¹when all Israel comes to appear before the LORD your God in the place which He chooses, you shall read this law before all Israel in their hearing. ¹²Gather the people together, men and women and little ones, and the stranger who *is* within your gates, that they may hear and that they may learn to fear the LORD your God and carefully observe all the words of this law, ¹³and *that* their children, who have not known it, may hear and learn to fear the LORD your God as long as you live in the land which you cross the Jordan to possess."

Prediction of Israel's Rebellion

¹⁴Then the LORD said to Moses, "Behold, the days approach when you must die; call Joshua, and present yourselves in the tabernacle of meeting, that I may inaugurate him."

So Moses and Joshua went and presented themselves in the tabernacle of meeting. ¹⁵Now the LORD appeared at the tabernacle in a pillar of cloud, and the pillar of cloud stood above the door of the tabernacle.

¹⁶And the LORD said to Moses: "Behold, you will rest with your fathers; and this people will rise and play the harlot with the gods of the foreigners of the land, where they go *to be* among them, and they will forsake Me and break My covenant

which I have made with them. ¹⁷Then My anger shall be aroused against them in that day, and I will forsake them, and I will hide My face from them, and they shall be devoured. And many evils and troubles shall befall them, so that they will say in that day, 'Have not these evils come upon us because our God *is* not among us?' ¹⁸And I will surely hide My face in that day because of all the evil which they have done, in that they have turned to other gods.

¹⁹"Now therefore, write down this song for yourselves, and teach it to the children of Israel; put it in their mouths, that this song may be a witness for Me against the children of Israel. ²⁰When I have brought them to the land flowing with milk and honey, of which I swore to their fathers, and they have eaten and filled themselves and grown fat, then they will turn to other gods and serve them; and they will provoke Me and break My covenant. ²¹Then it shall be, when many evils and troubles have come upon them, that this song will testify against them as a witness; for it will not be forgotten in the mouths of their descendants, for I know the inclination of their behavior today, even before I have brought them to the land of which I swore *to give them.*"

²²Therefore Moses wrote this song the same day, and taught it to the children of Israel. ²³Then He inaugurated Joshua the son of Nun, and said, "Be strong and of good courage; for you shall bring the children of Israel into the land of which I swore to them, and I will be with you."

²⁴So it was, when Moses had completed writing the words of this law in a book, when they were finished, ²⁵that Moses commanded the Levites, who bore the ark of the covenant of the LORD, saying: ²⁶"Take this Book of the Law, and put it beside the ark of the covenant of the LORD your God, that it may be there as a witness against you; ²⁷for I know your rebellion and your stiff neck. *If* today, while I am yet alive with you, you have been rebellious against the LORD, then how much more after my death? ²⁸Gather to me all the elders of your tribes, and your officers, that I may speak these words in their hearing and call heaven and earth to witness against them. ²⁹For I know that after my death you will become

utterly corrupt, and turn aside from the way which I have commanded you. And evil will befall you in the latter days, because you will do evil in the sight of the LORD, to provoke Him to anger through the work of your hands."

The Song of Moses

³⁰Then Moses spoke in the hearing of all the assembly of Israel the words of this song until they were ended:

32 "Give ear, O heavens, and I will speak;
   And hear, O earth, the words of my
      mouth.
2   Let my teaching drop as the rain,
   My speech distill as the dew,
   As raindrops on the tender herb,
   And as showers on the grass.
3   For I proclaim the name of the LORD:
   Ascribe greatness to our God.
4   *He is* the Rock, His work *is* perfect;
   For all His ways *are* justice,
   A God of truth and without injustice;
   Righteous and upright *is* He.

5   "They have corrupted themselves;
   They are not His children,
   Because of their blemish:
   A perverse and crooked generation.
6   Do you thus deal with the LORD,
   O foolish and unwise people?
   Is He not your Father, *who* bought
      you?
   Has He not made you and
      established you?

7   "Remember the days of old,
   Consider the years of many
      generations.
   Ask your father, and he will show you;
   Your elders, and they will tell you:
8   When the Most High divided their
      inheritance to the nations,
   When He separated the sons of Adam,
   He set the boundaries of the peoples
   According to the number of the
      children of Israel.
9   For the LORD's portion *is* His people;
   Jacob *is* the place of His inheritance.

10   "He found him in a desert land
   And in the wasteland, a howling
      wilderness;

He encircled him, He instructed him,
He kept him as the apple of His eye.
11 As an eagle stirs up its nest,
Hovers over its young,
Spreading out its wings, taking them
up,
Carrying them on its wings,
12 *So* the LORD alone led him,
And *there was* no foreign god with
him.

13 "He made him ride in the heights of
the earth,
That he might eat the produce of the
fields;
He made him draw honey from the
rock,
And oil from the flinty rock;
14 Curds from the cattle, and milk of
the flock,
With fat of lambs;
And rams of the breed of Bashan,
and goats,
With the choicest wheat;
And you drank wine, the blood of
the grapes.

15 "But Jeshurun grew fat and kicked;
You grew fat, you grew thick,
You are obese!
Then he forsook God *who* made
him,
And scornfully esteemed the Rock of
his salvation.
16 They provoked Him to jealousy with
foreign *gods;*
With abominations they provoked
Him to anger.
17 They sacrificed to demons, not to God,
To gods they did not know,
To new *gods,* new arrivals
That your fathers did not fear.
18 Of the Rock *who* begot you, you are
unmindful,
And have forgotten the God who
fathered you.

19 "And when the LORD saw *it,* He
spurned *them,*
Because of the provocation of His
sons and His daughters.
20 And He said: 'I will hide My face
from them,
I will see what their end *will be,*

For they *are* a perverse generation,
Children in whom *is* no faith.
21 They have provoked Me to jealousy
by *what* is not God;
They have moved Me to anger by
their foolish idols.
But I will provoke them to jealousy
by *those who are* not a nation;
I will move them to anger by a
foolish nation.
22 For a fire is kindled in My anger,
And shall burn to the lowest
hell;
It shall consume the earth with her
increase,
And set on fire the foundations of
the mountains.

23 'I will heap disasters on them;
I will spend My arrows on them.
24 *They shall be* wasted with hunger,
Devoured by pestilence and bitter
destruction;
I will also send against them the
teeth of beasts,
With the poison of serpents of the
dust.
25 The sword shall destroy outside;
There shall be terror within
For the young man and virgin,
The nursing child with the man of
gray hairs.
26 I would have said, "I will dash them
in pieces,
I will make the memory of them to
cease from among men,"
27 Had I not feared the wrath of the
enemy,
Lest their adversaries should
misunderstand,
Lest they should say, "Our hand *is*
high;
And it is not the LORD who has done
all this."'

28 "For they *are* a nation void of counsel,
Nor *is there any* understanding in
them.
29 Oh, that they were wise, *that* they
understood this,
That they would consider their latter
end!
30 How could one chase a thousand,
And two put ten thousand to flight,

Unless their Rock had sold them,
And the LORD had surrendered them?

31 For their rock *is* not like our Rock,
Even our enemies themselves *being*
judges.

32 For their vine *is* of the vine of Sodom
And of the fields of Gomorrah;
Their grapes *are* grapes of gall,
Their clusters *are* bitter.

33 Their wine *is* the poison of serpents,
And the cruel venom of cobras.

34 'Is this not laid up in store with Me,
Sealed up among My treasures?

35 Vengeance is Mine, and recompense;
Their foot shall slip in *due* time;
For the day of their calamity *is* at
hand,
And the things to come hasten upon
them.'

36 "For the LORD will judge His people
And have compassion on His servants,
When He sees that *their* power is gone,
And *there is* no one *remaining,* bond
or free.

37 He will say: 'Where *are* their gods,
The rock in which they sought
refuge?

38 Who ate the fat of their sacrifices,
And drank the wine of their drink
offering?
Let them rise and help you,
And be your refuge.

39 'Now see that I, *even* I, *am* He,
And *there is* no God besides Me;
I kill and I make alive;
I wound and I heal;
Nor *is there any* who can deliver
from My hand.

40 For I raise My hand to heaven,
And say, "*As* I live forever,

41 If I whet My glittering sword,
And My hand takes hold on
judgment,
I will render vengeance to My
enemies,
And repay those who hate Me.

42 I will make My arrows drunk with
blood,
And My sword shall devour flesh,
With the blood of the slain and the
captives,

From the heads of the leaders of the
enemy."'

43 "Rejoice, O Gentiles, *with* His people;[a]
For He will avenge the blood of His
servants,
And render vengeance to His
adversaries;
He will provide atonement for His
land *and* His people."

44 So Moses came with Joshua[a] the son of
Nun and spoke all the words of this song in
the hearing of the people. 45 Moses finished
speaking all these words to all Israel, 46 and
he said to them: "Set your hearts on all the
words which I testify among you today,
which you shall command your children to
be careful to observe—all the words of this
law. 47 For it *is* not a futile thing for you,
because it *is* your life, and by this word you
shall prolong *your* days in the land which
you cross over the Jordan to possess."

Moses to Die on Mount Nebo

48 Then the LORD spoke to Moses that
very same day, saying: 49 "Go up this mountain of the Abarim, Mount Nebo, which *is*
in the land of Moab, across from Jericho;
view the land of Canaan, which I give to
the children of Israel as a possession; 50 and
die on the mountain which you ascend, and
be gathered to your people, just as Aaron
your brother died on Mount Hor and was
gathered to his people; 51 because you trespassed against Me among the children of
Israel at the waters of Meribah Kadesh, in
the Wilderness of Zin, because you did not
hallow Me in the midst of the children of
Israel. 52 Yet you shall see the land before
you, though you shall not go there, into the
land which I am giving to the children of
Israel."

Moses' Final Blessing on Israel

33 Now this *is* the blessing with which
Moses the man of God blessed the
children of Israel before his death. 2 And he
said:

32:43 [a]A Dead Sea Scroll fragment adds *And let all
the gods (angels) worship Him* (compare Septuagint
and Hebrews 1:6). 32:44 [a]Hebrew *Hoshea* (compare
Numbers 13:8, 16)

"The LORD came from Sinai,
And dawned on them from Seir;
He shone forth from Mount Paran,
And He came with ten thousands of
   saints;
From His right hand
Came a fiery law for them.
3 Yes, He loves the people;
All His saints *are* in Your hand;
They sit down at Your feet;
Everyone receives Your words.
4 Moses commanded a law for us,
A heritage of the congregation of
   Jacob.
5 And He was King in Jeshurun,
When the leaders of the people were
   gathered,
All the tribes of Israel together.

6 "Let Reuben live, and not die,
Nor let his men be few."

7 And this he said of Judah:

"Hear, LORD, the voice of Judah,
And bring him to his people;
Let his hands be sufficient for him,
And may You be a help against his
   enemies."

8 And of Levi he said:

"*Let* Your Thummim and Your Urim
be with Your holy one,
Whom You tested at Massah,
And with whom You contended at
   the waters of Meribah,
9 Who says of his father and mother,
' I have not seen them';
Nor did he acknowledge his brothers,
Or know his own children;
For they have observed Your word
And kept Your covenant.
10 They shall teach Jacob Your
   judgments,
And Israel Your law.
They shall put incense before You,
And a whole burnt sacrifice on Your
   altar.
11 Bless his substance, LORD,
And accept the work of his hands;
Strike the loins of those who rise
   against him,
And of those who hate him, that
   they rise not again."

BIBLICAL INSIGHTS • 32:46, 47
A Biblical Approach to Manners

ONE OF THE GUESTS who have appeared on our radio program *FamilyLife Today* is an expert on manners. Her name is June Moore, and she sees manners as a lot more than social etiquette. Good manners have a biblical basis. Here is some of what she said during the radio interview:

Manners were God's idea. He gave us the Golden Rule, "Therefore, whatever you want men to do to you, do also to them, for this is the Law and the Prophets" (Matt. 7:12). And although Jesus was Christ the King, He humbled himself to serve others (John 13:3–5).

In a similar way, Deuteronomy 32:46, 47 instructs us to teach our children proper conduct. The first and best way to do that is by being good role models. Our children will imitate us, whether our actions are good or bad. We should model good behavior by doing kind things for others.

Scripture also tells us to "train up a child in the way he should go" (Prov. 22:6). One way to interpret "in the way" is to teach a child according to his or her natural bent. Some children learn best in role-playing activities, while others like to read and study the rules. Consider your child's learning style for a more pleasant teaching experience.

Social skills learned at home can produce the fruit of the Spirit: love, joy, peace, patience, kindness, goodness, faithfulness, gentleness, and self-control (see Gal. 5:22). Interpersonal skills such as listening, opening doors, saying "please," "thank you," "you're welcome," and sharing with others, reveal the good manners in our heart.

12 Of Benjamin he said:

"The beloved of the LORD shall dwell
   in safety by Him,
Who shelters him all the day long;
And he shall dwell between His
   shoulders."

13 And of Joseph he said:

"Blessed of the LORD *is* his land,
With the precious things of heaven,
    with the dew,
And the deep lying beneath,
14 With the precious fruits of the sun,
    With the precious produce of the
    months,
15 With the best things of the ancient
    mountains,
    With the precious things of the
    everlasting hills,
16 With the precious things of the earth
    and its fullness,
    And the favor of Him who dwelt in
    the bush.
    Let *the blessing* come 'on the head of
    Joseph,
    And on the crown of the head of
    him *who was* separate from his
    brothers.'ᵃ
17 His glory *is like* a firstborn bull,
    And his horns *like* the horns of the
    wild ox;
    Together with them
    He shall push the peoples
    To the ends of the earth;
    They *are* the ten thousands of
    Ephraim,
    And they *are* the thousands of
    Manasseh."
18 And of Zebulun he said:

"Rejoice, Zebulun, in your going out,
    And Issachar in your tents!
19 They shall call the peoples *to* the
    mountain;

There they shall offer sacrifices of
    righteousness;
For they shall partake *of* the
    abundance of the seas
And *of* treasures hidden in the sand."

20 And of Gad he said:

"Blessed *is* he who enlarges Gad;
    He dwells as a lion,
    And tears the arm and the crown of
    his head.
21 He provided the first *part* for himself,
    Because a lawgiver's portion was
    reserved there.
    He came *with* the heads of the people;
    He administered the justice of the
    LORD,
    And His judgments with Israel."

22 And of Dan he said:

"Dan *is* a lion's whelp;
    He shall leap from Bashan."

23 And of Naphtali he said:

"O Naphtali, satisfied with favor,
    And full of the blessing of the LORD,
    Possess the west and the south."

24 And of Asher he said:

"Asher *is* most blessed of sons;
    Let him be favored by his brothers,
    And let him dip his foot in oil.
25 Your sandals *shall be* iron and
    bronze;
    As your days, *so shall* your strength *be*.

26 "*There is* no one like the God of
    Jeshurun,
    Who rides the heavens to help you,
    And in His excellency on the clouds.
27 The eternal God *is your* refuge,
    And underneath *are* the everlasting
    arms;
    He will thrust out the enemy from
    before you,
    And will say, 'Destroy!'
28 Then Israel shall dwell in safety,
    The fountain of Jacob alone,
    In a land of grain and new wine;
    His heavens shall also drop dew.
29 Happy *are* you, O Israel!

**INTIMATE
MOMENTS**

Compose a love poem (or perhaps a haiku) for your husband. It doesn't have to rhyme . . . it just needs to be from the heart. Find a special time and place to read it to him. You might consider framing it and then hanging it in your bedroom.

33:16 ᵃGenesis 49:26

Who *is* like you, a people saved by
  the LORD,
The shield of your help
And the sword of your majesty!
Your enemies shall submit to you,
And you shall tread down their
  high places."

Moses Dies on Mount Nebo

34 Then Moses went up from the
plains of Moab to Mount Nebo, to
the top of Pisgah, which is across from
Jericho. And the LORD showed him all the
land of Gilead as far as Dan, [2]all Naphtali
and the land of Ephraim and Manasseh,
all the land of Judah as far as the Western
Sea,[a] [3]the South, and the plain of the
Valley of Jericho, the city of palm trees, as
far as Zoar. [4]Then the LORD said to him,
"This *is* the land of which I swore to give
Abraham, Isaac, and Jacob, saying, 'I will
give it to your descendants.' I have caused
you to see *it* with your eyes, but you shall
not cross over there."

[5]So Moses the servant of the LORD died
there in the land of Moab, according to the
word of the LORD. [6]And He buried him in
a valley in the land of Moab, opposite Beth
Peor; but no one knows his grave to this
day. [7]Moses *was* one hundred and twenty
years old when he died. His eyes were not
dim nor his natural vigor diminished.
[8]And the children of Israel wept for Moses
in the plains of Moab thirty days. So the
days of weeping *and* mourning for Moses
ended.

[9]Now Joshua the son of Nun was full of
the spirit of wisdom, for Moses had laid
his hands on him; so the children of Israel
heeded him, and did as the LORD had commanded Moses.

[10]But since then there has not arisen in
Israel a prophet like Moses, whom the
LORD knew face to face, [11]in all the signs
and wonders which the LORD sent him to
do in the land of Egypt, before Pharaoh,
before all his servants, and in all his land,
[12]and by all that mighty power and all the
great terror which Moses performed in the
sight of all Israel.

34:2 [a]That is, the Mediterranean

JOSHUA

GOD HAD RAISED UP MOSES TO LEAD the descendents of Jacob out of bondage in Egypt. But just as Israel became ready to enter and conquer the Promised Land, Moses passed from the scene, exactly as God had predicted. A new leader would have to take the Hebrew nation into the future God Himself had promised.

Joshua was that man. God raised up Joshua to lead His people into the rich and fertile territory that would become their homeland. You can imagine the emotional weight Joshua must have felt as he began to assume his new leadership responsibilities! It was a daunting task, to step into Moses' sandals—and that's why the book begins with God's charge to Joshua, "Be strong and of good courage" (1:6, 7, 9). God also promises to bless Joshua with success, to the extent that he daily meditates on and obeys God's Word (1:8).

The book of Joshua recounts God's miraculous involvement in the conquest of the Promised Land. You will read how God held back the waters of the Jordan River (chapter 3), how Israel won the battle of Jericho (chapter 6), and about the breathtaking day the sun stood still (10:12–15). You will meet Rahab, the pagan woman from Jericho who courageously protected the Jewish spies (chapter 2) and who later is commended for her faith (Hebrews 11:31). You will read about God's sobering judgment on disobedient Achan and his entire family when everyone in the family did what seemed best to them instead of obeying God's specific instructions (chapter 7).

The book of Joshua concludes with the well-known challenge from Joshua to his kinsmen: "And if it seems evil to you to serve the LORD, choose for yourselves this day whom you will serve, whether the gods which your fathers served that were on the other side of the River, or the gods of the Amorites, in whose land you dwell. But as for me and my house, we will serve the LORD" (24:15).

May each of us make the same bold declaration of firm commitment to God as we read and meditate on His Word!

God's Commission to Joshua

1 After the death of Moses the servant of the LORD, it came to pass that the LORD spoke to Joshua the son of Nun, Moses' assistant, saying: 2"Moses My servant is dead. Now therefore, arise, go over this Jordan, you and all this people, to the land which I am giving to them—the children of Israel. 3Every place that the sole of your foot will tread upon I have given you, as I said to Moses. 4From the wilderness and this Lebanon as far as the great river, the River Euphrates, all the land of the Hittites, and to the Great Sea toward the going down of the sun, shall be your territory. 5No man shall *be able to* stand before you all the days of your life; as I was with Moses, *so* I will be with you. I will not leave you nor forsake you. 6Be strong and of good courage, for to this people you shall divide as an inheritance the land which I swore to their fathers to give them. 7Only be strong and very courageous, that you may observe to do according to all the law which Moses My servant commanded you; do not turn from it to the right hand or to the left, that you may prosper wherever you go. 8This Book of the Law shall not depart from your mouth, but you shall meditate in it day and night, that you may observe to do according to all that is written in it. For then you will make your way prosperous, and then you will have good success. 9Have I not commanded you? Be strong and of good courage; do not be afraid, nor be dismayed, for the LORD your God *is* with you wherever you go."

The Order to Cross the Jordan

10Then Joshua commanded the officers of the people, saying, 11"Pass through the camp and command the people, saying, 'Prepare provisions for yourselves, for within three days you will cross over this Jordan, to go in to possess the land which the LORD your God is giving you to possess.' "

12And to the Reubenites, the Gadites, and half the tribe of Manasseh Joshua spoke, saying, 13"Remember the word which Moses the servant of the LORD commanded you, saying, 'The LORD your God is giving you rest and is giving you this land.' 14Your wives, your little ones, and your livestock shall remain in the land which Moses gave you on this side of the Jordan. But you shall pass before your brethren armed, all your mighty men of valor, and help them, 15until the LORD has given your brethren rest, as He *gave* you, and they also have taken possession of the land which the LORD your God is giving them. Then you shall return to the land of your possession and enjoy it, which Moses the LORD's servant gave you on this side of the Jordan toward the sunrise."

16So they answered Joshua, saying, "All that you command us we will do, and wherever you send us we will go. 17Just as we heeded Moses in all things, so we will heed

What Shapes Your Belief System?

One of the most important instructions God gave Joshua as he prepared to assume the mantle of leadership was to know and observe the Word of God: "This Book of the Law shall not depart from your mouth, but you shall meditate in it day and night, that you may observe to do according to all that is written in it. For then you will make your way prosperous, and then you will have good success" (1:8).

It is important that in your marriage you make the Word of God a top priority. Learn it well and apply it to every area of your married life! That is especially true if you're a parent, because it is the Word of God that is to shape your belief system.

As your children grow, their little radar units will lock in on you and your spouse. Your belief system may not seem tremendously important when your baby is in diapers, but not long thereafter, your deeply held values about life will influence your interactions with your children. Those beliefs will affect how you discipline, what kinds of TV shows and movies you allow your child to watch, who your child may date, and other values.

Turn on the Light Every Day

IT'S FASHIONABLE nowadays for Christians to complain that the Bible can't be read in public schools. But I think the more important issue is whether it's being read in our own homes. Too often, the honest answer to that question is "no."

The psalmist tells us that God gave us His Word as "a lamp to my feet and a light to my path" (119:105), to help us survive in a hostile world. The Word of God is the means by which He guides us and directs us in a dark and confused culture. But in order for it to change us as individuals and as families, we have to acknowledge we are lost and in need of direction. Only then can we seek the guidance we need from God's Word.

Someone once said, "A dusty Bible will lead to a dirty life." And although God calls His Word a light for our paths, the Bible can't give anyone light if we allow it to sit on an end table in the family room, collecting dust. We must commit ourselves to reading, studying, and meditating on the Bible every day, as God told Joshua, "You shall meditate in it day and night" (1:8). This is an integral part of our walk with Christ.

you. Only the LORD your God be with you, as He was with Moses. ¹⁸Whoever rebels against your command and does not heed your words, in all that you command him, shall be put to death. Only be strong and of good courage."

Rahab Hides the Spies

2 Now Joshua the son of Nun sent out two men from Acacia Grove[a] to spy secretly, saying, "Go, view the land, especially Jericho."

So they went, and came to the house of a harlot named Rahab, and lodged there. ²And it was told the king of Jericho, saying, "Behold, men have come here tonight from the children of Israel to search out the country."

³So the king of Jericho sent to Rahab, saying, "Bring out the men who have come to you, who have entered your house, for they have come to search out all the country."

⁴Then the woman took the two men and hid them. So she said, "Yes, the men came to me, but I did not know where they *were* from. ⁵And it happened as the gate was being shut, when it was dark, that the men went out. Where the men went I do not know; pursue them quickly, for you may overtake them." ⁶(But she had brought them up to the roof and hidden them with the stalks of flax, which she had laid in order on the roof.) ⁷Then the men pursued them by the road to the Jordan, to the fords. And as soon as those who pursued them had gone out, they shut the gate.

⁸Now before they lay down, she came up to them on the roof, ⁹and said to the men: "I know that the LORD has given you the land, that the terror of you has fallen on us, and that all the inhabitants of the land are fainthearted because of you. ¹⁰For we have heard how the LORD dried up the water of the Red Sea for you when you came out of Egypt, and what you did to the two kings of the Amorites who *were* on the other side of the Jordan, Sihon and Og, whom you utterly destroyed. ¹¹And as soon as we heard *these things,* our hearts melted; neither did there remain any more courage in anyone because of you, for the LORD your God, He *is* God in heaven above and on earth beneath. ¹²Now therefore, I beg you, swear to me by the LORD, since I have shown you kindness, that you also will show kindness to my father's house, and give me a true token, ¹³and spare my father, my mother, my brothers, my sisters, and all that they have, and deliver our lives from death."

¹⁴So the men answered her, "Our lives for yours, if none of you tell this business of ours. And it shall be, when the LORD has given us the land, that we will deal kindly and truly with you."

¹⁵Then she let them down by a rope through the window, for her house *was* on the city wall; she dwelt on the wall. ¹⁶And she said to them, "Get to the mountain, lest the pursuers meet you. Hide there three

2:1 ᵃHebrew *Shittim*

days, until the pursuers have returned. Afterward you may go your way."

¹⁷So the men said to her: "We *will be* blameless of this oath of yours which you have made us swear, ¹⁸unless, *when* we come into the land, you bind this line of scarlet cord in the window through which you let us down, and unless you bring your father, your mother, your brothers, and all your father's household to your own home. ¹⁹So it shall be *that* whoever goes outside the doors of your house into the street, his blood *shall be* on his own head, and we *will be* guiltless. And whoever is with you in the house, his blood *shall be* on our head if a hand is laid on him. ²⁰And if you tell this business of ours, then we will be free from your oath which you made us swear."

²¹Then she said, "According to your words, so *be* it." And she sent them away, and they departed. And she bound the scarlet cord in the window.

²²They departed and went to the mountain, and stayed there three days until the pursuers returned. The pursuers sought *them* all along the way, but did not find *them.* ²³So the two men returned, descended from the mountain, and crossed over; and they came to Joshua the son of Nun, and told him all that had befallen them. ²⁴And they said to Joshua, "Truly the LORD has delivered all the land into our hands, for indeed all the inhabitants of the country are fainthearted because of us."

Israel Crosses the Jordan

3 Then Joshua rose early in the morning; and they set out from Acacia Groveᵃ and came to the Jordan, he and all the children of Israel, and lodged there before they crossed over. ²So it was, after three days, that the officers went through the camp; ³and they commanded the people, saying, "When you see the ark of the covenant of the LORD your God, and the priests, the Levites, bearing it, then you shall set out from your place and go after it. ⁴Yet there shall be a space between you and it, about two thousand cubits by measure. Do not come near it, that you may know the way by which you must go, for you have not passed *this* way before."

⁵And Joshua said to the people, "Sanctify yourselves, for tomorrow the LORD will do wonders among you." ⁶Then Joshua spoke to the priests, saying, "Take up the ark of the covenant and cross over before the people."

So they took up the ark of the covenant and went before the people.

⁷And the LORD said to Joshua, "This day I will begin to exalt you in the sight of all Israel, that they may know that, as I was with Moses, *so* I will be with you. ⁸You shall command the priests who bear the ark of the covenant, saying, 'When you have come to the edge of the water of the Jordan, you shall stand in the Jordan.' "

⁹So Joshua said to the children of Israel, "Come here, and hear the words of the LORD your God." ¹⁰And Joshua said, "By this you shall know that the living God *is* among you, and *that* He will without fail drive out from before you the Canaanites and the Hittites and the Hivites and the Perizzites and the Girgashites and the Amorites and the Jebusites: ¹¹Behold, the ark of the covenant of the Lord of all the earth is crossing over before you into the Jordan. ¹²Now therefore, take for yourselves twelve men from the tribes of Israel, one man from every tribe. ¹³And it shall come to pass, as soon as the soles of the feet of the priests who bear the ark of the LORD, the Lord of all the earth, shall rest in the waters of Jordan, *that* the waters of the Jordan shall be cut off, the waters that come down from upstream, and they shall stand as a heap."

¹⁴So it was, when the people set out from their camp to cross over the Jordan, with the priests bearing the ark of the covenant before the people, ¹⁵and as those who bore the ark came to the Jordan, and the feet of the priests who bore the ark dipped in the edge of the water (for the Jordan overflows all its banks during the whole time of harvest), ¹⁶that the waters which came down from upstream stood *still, and* rose in a heap very far away at Adam, the city that *is* beside Zaretan. So the waters that went down into the Sea of the Arabah, the Salt Sea, failed, *and* were cut off; and the people crossed over opposite Jericho. ¹⁷Then the priests who bore the ark of the covenant of the LORD stood firm on dry ground in the midst of the Jordan; and all Israel crossed

3:1 ᵃHebrew *Shittim*

BIBLICAL INSIGHTS • 4:7
Create Some Spiritual Landmarks

THE FOURTH CHAPTER of Joshua records one of the most significant events in the history of Israel. It also gives us a potent example to follow and one of the most powerful spiritual principles in the Bible.

To commemorate Israel's crossing of the Jordan River, the Lord told His people to erect a monument of twelve stones, one stone for each tribe of Israel. Why would He give them such a command? Read His own rationale for its construction,"Then you shall answer them that the waters of the Jordan were cut off before the ark of the covenant of the LORD; when it crossed over the Jordan, the waters of the Jordan were cut off. And these stones shall be for a memorial to the children of Israel forever" (4:7).

Those dozen stones were meant to be a spiritual reminder to future generations of God's guidance and provision for His people. Most of us won't be crossing the Jordan any time soon, but we can still follow the example of the ancient Israelites. We are wise if we will find creative ways, as couples and families, to commemorate spiritual landmarks in our lives—events such as weddings, dedications or baptisms of our children, commitments we've made to the Lord individually and as families, or an instance in which God has clearly done something great in us or for us. Record these events in this Bible or find another visible means of collecting these memorial stones for the dull, drab days when doubt and fear have clouded your soul. You can record your spiritual milestones in the front section of this Bible.

2"Take for yourselves twelve men from the people, one man from every tribe, 3and command them, saying, 'Take for yourselves twelve stones from here, out of the midst of the Jordan, from the place where the priests' feet stood firm. You shall carry them over with you and leave them in the lodging place where you lodge tonight.' "

4Then Joshua called the twelve men whom he had appointed from the children of Israel, one man from every tribe; 5and Joshua said to them: "Cross over before the ark of the LORD your God into the midst of the Jordan, and each one of you take up a stone on his shoulder, according to the number of the tribes of the children of Israel, 6that this may be a sign among you when your children ask in time to come, saying, 'What do these stones *mean* to you?' 7Then you shall answer them that the waters of the Jordan were cut off before the ark of the covenant of the LORD; when it crossed over the Jordan, the waters of the Jordan were cut off. And these stones shall be for a memorial to the children of Israel forever."

8And the children of Israel did so, just as Joshua commanded, and took up twelve stones from the midst of the Jordan, as the LORD had spoken to Joshua, according to the number of the tribes of the children of Israel, and carried them over with them to the place where they lodged, and laid them down there. 9Then Joshua set up twelve stones in the midst of the Jordan, in the place where the feet of the priests who bore the ark of the covenant stood; and they are there to this day.

10So the priests who bore the ark stood in the midst of the Jordan until everything was finished that the LORD had commanded Joshua to speak to the people, according to all that Moses had commanded Joshua; and the people hurried and crossed over. 11Then it came to pass, when all the people had completely crossed over, that the ark of the LORD and the priests crossed over in the presence of the people. 12And the men of Reuben, the men of Gad, and half the tribe of Manasseh crossed over armed before the children of Israel, as Moses had spoken to them. 13About forty thousand prepared for war crossed over before the LORD for battle, to the plains of Jericho. 14On that day the

over on dry ground, until all the people had crossed completely over the Jordan.

The Memorial Stones

4 And it came to pass, when all the people had completely crossed over the Jordan, that the LORD spoke to Joshua, saying:

LORD exalted Joshua in the sight of all Israel; and they feared him, as they had feared Moses, all the days of his life.

15Then the LORD spoke to Joshua, saying, 16"Command the priests who bear the ark of the Testimony to come up from the Jordan." 17Joshua therefore commanded the priests, saying, "Come up from the Jordan." 18And it came to pass, when the priests who bore the ark of the covenant of the LORD had come from the midst of the Jordan, *and* the soles of the priests' feet touched the dry land, that the waters of the Jordan returned to their place and overflowed all its banks as before.

19Now the people came up from the Jordan on the tenth *day* of the first month, and they camped in Gilgal on the east border of Jericho. 20And those twelve stones which they took out of the Jordan, Joshua set up in Gilgal. 21Then he spoke to the children of Israel, saying: "When your children ask their fathers in time to come, saying, 'What *are* these stones?' 22then you shall let your children know, saying, 'Israel crossed over this Jordan on dry land'; 23for the LORD your God dried up the waters of the Jordan before you until you had crossed over, as the LORD your God did to the Red Sea, which He dried up before us until we had crossed over, 24that all the peoples of the earth may know the hand of the LORD, that it *is* mighty, that you may fear the LORD your God forever."

The Second Generation Circumcised

5 So it was, when all the kings of the Amorites who *were* on the west side of the Jordan, and all the kings of the Canaanites who *were* by the sea, heard that the LORD had dried up the waters of the Jordan from before the children of Israel until wea had crossed over, that their heart melted; and there was no spirit in them any longer because of the children of Israel.

2At that time the LORD said to Joshua, "Make flint knives for yourself, and circumcise the sons of Israel again the second time." 3So Joshua made flint knives for himself, and circumcised the sons of Israel

Spend Some Time

DID YOU KNOW that no other parents in the industrialized world spend less time with their children than American fathers and mothers? According to *The Wall Street Journal*, American parents spend, on average, "less than fifteen minutes a week in serious discussion with their children."

This lack of involvement is hastened by rising divorce rates, out-of-wedlock births, and working mothers. Parental abandonment, and, most notably, fatherlessness, tear like a fault-line at American culture. "Studies of young criminals have found," reports *Time* magazine, "that more than 70% of all juveniles in state reform institutions come from fatherless homes." Says David S. Murray, "Neighborhoods without fathers ... are seedbeds for predators. Without a female and a male who consider themselves responsible for children, the stable features of social continuity are not constructed."

God assumes that we *will* spend good chunks of quality time with our kids. That's why Joshua 4:21 says, "When your children ask their fathers in time to come." Not *if*, but *when*. The verse assumes a significant relationship that will give rise to significant conversations about deeply spiritual topics.

Are you creating this kind of home? Do you encourage your children to ask you significant questions? And are you ready to share with them the reality of your experience with God when they do ask?

at the hill of the foreskins.a 4And this *is* the reason why Joshua circumcised them: All the people who came out of Egypt *who were* males, all the men of war, had died in the wilderness on the way, after they had come out of Egypt. 5For all the people who came out had been circumcised, but all the people born in the wilderness, on the way as they came out of Egypt, had not been circumcised. 6For the children of Israel walked forty years in the wilderness, till all the people *who were* men of war, who came out of Egypt, were consumed, because they did not obey the voice of the LORD—to whom the LORD swore that He would not show them the land which the LORD had sworn to their fathers that He would give us, "a land flowing with milk and honey."ᵃ ⁷Then Joshua circumcised their sons *whom* He raised up in their place; for they were uncircumcised, because they had not been circumcised on the way.

⁸So it was, when they had finished circumcising all the people, that they stayed in their places in the camp till they were healed. ⁹Then the LORD said to Joshua, "This day I have rolled away the reproach of Egypt from you." Therefore the name of the place is called Gilgalᵃ to this day.

¹⁰Now the children of Israel camped in Gilgal, and kept the Passover on the fourteenth day of the month at twilight on the plains of Jericho. ¹¹And they ate of the produce of the land on the day after the Passover, unleavened bread and parched grain, on the very same day. ¹²Then the manna ceased on the day after they had eaten the produce of the land; and the children of Israel no longer had manna, but they ate the food of the land of Canaan that year.

The Commander of the Army of the LORD

¹³And it came to pass, when Joshua was by Jericho, that he lifted his eyes and looked, and behold, a Man stood opposite him with His sword drawn in His hand. And Joshua went to Him and said to Him, "*Are* You for us or for our adversaries?"

¹⁴So He said, "No, but *as* Commander of the army of the LORD I have now come."

And Joshua fell on his face to the earth and worshiped, and said to Him, "What does my Lord say to His servant?"

¹⁵Then the Commander of the LORD's army said to Joshua, "Take your sandal off your foot, for the place where you stand *is* holy." And Joshua did so.

The Destruction of Jericho

6 Now Jericho was securely shut up because of the children of Israel; none went out, and none came in. ²And the LORD said to Joshua: "See! I have given Jericho

into your hand, its king, *and* the mighty men of valor. ³You shall march around the city, all *you* men of war; you shall go all around the city once. This you shall do six days. ⁴And seven priests shall bear seven trumpets of rams' horns before the ark. But the seventh day you shall march around the city seven times, and the priests shall blow the trumpets. ⁵It shall come to pass, when they make a long *blast* with the ram's horn, *and* when you hear the sound of the trumpet, that all the people shall shout with a great shout; then the wall of the city will fall down flat. And the people shall go up every man straight before him."

⁶Then Joshua the son of Nun called the priests and said to them, "Take up the ark of the covenant, and let seven priests bear seven trumpets of rams' horns before the ark of the LORD." ⁷And he said to the people, "Proceed, and march around the city, and let him who is armed advance before the ark of the LORD."

⁸So it was, when Joshua had spoken to the people, that the seven priests bearing the seven trumpets of rams' horns before the LORD advanced and blew the trumpets, and the ark of the covenant of the LORD followed them. ⁹The armed men went before the priests who blew the trumpets, and the rear guard came after the ark, while *the priests* continued blowing the trumpets. ¹⁰Now Joshua had commanded the people, saying, "You shall not shout or make any noise with your voice, nor shall a word proceed out of your mouth, until the day I say to you, 'Shout!' Then you shall shout." ¹¹So he had the ark of the LORD circle the city, going around *it* once. Then they came into the camp and lodged in the camp.

¹²And Joshua rose early in the morning, and the priests took up the ark of the LORD. ¹³Then seven priests bearing seven trumpets of rams' horns before the ark of the LORD went on continually and blew with the trumpets. And the armed men went before them. But the rear guard came after the ark of the LORD, while *the priests* continued blowing the trumpets. ¹⁴And the second day they marched around the city once and returned to the camp. So they did six days.

5:6 ᵃExodus 3:8 **5:9** ᵃLiterally *Rolling*

¹⁵But it came to pass on the seventh day that they rose early, about the dawning of the day, and marched around the city seven times in the same manner. On that day only they marched around the city seven times. ¹⁶And the seventh time it happened, when the priests blew the trumpets, that Joshua said to the people: "Shout, for the LORD has given you the city! ¹⁷Now the city shall be doomed by the LORD to destruction, it and all who *are* in it. Only Rahab the harlot shall live, she and all who *are* with her in the house, because she hid the messengers that we sent. ¹⁸And you, by all means abstain from the accursed things, lest you become accursed when you take of the accursed things, and make the camp of Israel a curse, and trouble it. ¹⁹But all the silver and gold, and vessels of bronze and iron, *are* consecrated to the LORD; they shall come into the treasury of the LORD."

²⁰So the people shouted when *the priests* blew the trumpets. And it happened when the people heard the sound of the trumpet, and the people shouted with a great shout, that the wall fell down flat. Then the people went up into the city, every man straight before him, and they took the city. ²¹And they utterly destroyed all that *was* in the city, both man and woman, young and old, ox and sheep and donkey, with the edge of the sword.

²²But Joshua had said to the two men who had spied out the country, "Go into the harlot's house, and from there bring out the woman and all that she has, as you swore to her." ²³And the young men who had been spies went in and brought out Rahab, her father, her mother, her brothers, and all that she had. So they brought out all her relatives and left them outside the camp of Israel. ²⁴But they burned the city and all that *was* in it with fire. Only the silver and gold, and the vessels of bronze and iron, they put into the treasury of the house of the LORD. ²⁵And Joshua spared Rahab the harlot, her father's household, and all that she had. So she dwells in Israel to this day, because she hid the messengers whom Joshua sent to spy out Jericho.

²⁶Then Joshua charged *them* at that time, saying, "Cursed *be* the man before the LORD who rises up and builds this city Jericho; he shall lay its foundation with his firstborn, and with his youngest he shall set up its gates."

ROMANTIC QUOTES AND NOTES
How to Share Your Past with Your Mate

Scripture tells us that Rahab, the prostitute from Jericho who hid the Israelite spies (6:25), continued to live among God's people and eventually became an ancestor of Jesus Christ (see Matt. 1:5). You have to wonder: What did she tell her Hebrew husband about her past?

Any discussion of sensitive material from your past must occur between two people who understand and have experienced God's grace and forgiveness. If you are confident that you should proceed, consider some tips on how to confess information from your past:

1. *Explain why you are sharing this information now.* Make clear that you desire to deepen trust in your relationship.

2. *Give the big picture, not the details.* Don't provide specifics of how you sinned. And if you are receiving the information, do not ask probing questions merely to feed your morbid curiosity. Vivid images will haunt you more than general statements.

3. *Ask for and grant forgiveness.* Don't ever treat forgiveness flippantly, but ask for and grant forgiveness eagerly.

4. *Don't expect an immediate resolution.* Keep a leash on your expectations. Your spouse may not respond positively to your disclosure. That's okay. Give your mate time to process this new information.

Finally, as you discuss the past, if you get off in a ditch and can't get out, don't be ashamed to ask for some help. A trusted godly friend can be a great encouragement to both of you during these times.

27So the LORD was with Joshua, and his fame spread throughout all the country.

Defeat at Ai

7 But the children of Israel committed a trespass regarding the accursed things, for Achan the son of Carmi, the son of Zabdi,a the son of Zerah, of the tribe of Judah, took of the accursed things; so the anger of the LORD burned against the children of Israel.

2Now Joshua sent men from Jericho to Ai, which is beside Beth Aven, on the east side of Bethel, and spoke to them, saying, "Go up and spy out the country." So the men went up and spied out Ai. 3And they returned to Joshua and said to him, "Do not let all the people go up, but let about two or three thousand men go up and attack Ai. Do not weary all the people there, for the people of Ai are few." 4So about three thousand men went up there from the people, but they fled before the men of Ai. 5And the men of Ai struck down about thirty-six men, for they chased them from before the gate as far as Shebarim, and struck them down on the descent; therefore the hearts of the people melted and became like water.

6Then Joshua tore his clothes, and fell to the earth on his face before the ark of the LORD until evening, he and the elders of Israel; and they put dust on their heads. 7And Joshua said, "Alas, Lord GOD, why have You brought this people over the Jordan at all—to deliver us into the hand of the Amorites, to destroy us? Oh, that we had been content, and dwelt on the other side of the Jordan! 8O Lord, what shall I say when Israel turns its back before its enemies? 9For the Canaanites and all the inhabitants of the land will hear it, and surround us, and cut off our name from the earth. Then what will You do for Your great name?"

The Sin of Achan

10So the LORD said to Joshua: "Get up! Why do you lie thus on your face? 11Israel has sinned, and they have also transgressed My covenant which I commanded them. For they have even taken some of the accursed things, and have both stolen and deceived; and they have also put it among their own stuff. 12Therefore the children of Israel could not stand before their enemies, but turned their backs before their enemies, because they have become doomed to destruction. Neither will I be with you anymore, unless you destroy the accursed from among you. 13Get up, sanctify the people, and say, 'Sanctify yourselves for tomorrow, because thus says the LORD God of Israel: "There is an accursed thing in your midst, O Israel; you cannot stand before your enemies until you take away the accursed thing from among you." 14In the morning therefore you shall be brought according to your tribes. And it shall be that the tribe which the LORD takes shall come according to families; and the family which the LORD takes shall come by households; and the household which the LORD takes shall come man by man. 15Then it shall be that he who is taken with the accursed thing shall be burned with fire, he and all that he has, because he has transgressed the covenant of the LORD, and because he has done a disgraceful thing in Israel.' "

16So Joshua rose early in the morning and brought Israel by their tribes, and the tribe of Judah was taken. 17He brought the clan of Judah, and he took the family of the Zarhites; and he brought the family of the Zarhites man by man, and Zabdi was taken. 18Then he brought his household man by man, and Achan the son of Carmi, the son of Zabdi, the son of Zerah, of the tribe of Judah, was taken.

19Now Joshua said to Achan, "My son, I beg you, give glory to the LORD God of Israel, and make confession to Him, and tell me now what you have done; do not hide it from me."

20And Achan answered Joshua and said, "Indeed I have sinned against the LORD God of Israel, and this is what I have done: 21When I saw among the spoils a beautiful Babylonian garment, two hundred shekels of silver, and a wedge of gold weighing fifty shekels, I coveted them and took them. And there they are, hidden in the earth in the midst of my tent, with the silver under it."

22So Joshua sent messengers, and they ran to the tent; and there it was, hidden in

---

7:1 aCalled Zimri in 1 Chronicles 2:6

his tent, with the silver under it. ²³And they took them from the midst of the tent, brought them to Joshua and to all the children of Israel, and laid them out before the LORD. ²⁴Then Joshua, and all Israel with him, took Achan the son of Zerah, the silver, the garment, the wedge of gold, his sons, his daughters, his oxen, his donkeys, his sheep, his tent, and all that he had, and they brought them to the Valley of Achor. ²⁵And Joshua said, "Why have you troubled us? The LORD will trouble you this day." So all Israel stoned him with stones; and they burned them with fire after they had stoned them with stones.

²⁶Then they raised over him a great heap of stones, still there to this day. So the LORD turned from the fierceness of His anger. Therefore the name of that place has been called the Valley of Achor[a] to this day.

The Fall of Ai

8 Now the LORD said to Joshua: "Do not be afraid, nor be dismayed; take all the people of war with you, and arise, go up to Ai. See, I have given into your hand the king of Ai, his people, his city, and his land. ²And you shall do to Ai and its king as you did to Jericho and its king. Only its spoil and its cattle you shall take as booty for yourselves. Lay an ambush for the city behind it."

³So Joshua arose, and all the people of war, to go up against Ai; and Joshua chose thirty thousand mighty men of valor and sent them away by night. ⁴And he commanded them, saying: "Behold, you shall lie in ambush against the city, behind the city. Do not go very far from the city, but all of you be ready. ⁵Then I and all the people who *are* with me will approach the city; and it will come about, when they come out against us as at the first, that we shall flee before them. ⁶For they will come out after us till we have drawn them from the city, for they will say, 'They are fleeing before us as at the first.' Therefore we will flee before them. ⁷Then you shall rise from the ambush and seize the city, for the LORD your God will deliver it into your hand. ⁸And it will be, when you have taken the city, *that* you shall set the city on fire. According to

BIBLICAL INSIGHTS • 7:19, 20

The Serious Consequences of Sin

ONE EFFECTIVE WAY TO TEACH YOUR children a healthy fear of God is to study biblical characters and their encounters with Him. You can read, for example, about how Joshua, one of the greatest leaders in the history of the Jewish people, learned the fear of the Lord through the disobedience of a countryman.

An Israelite named Achan had directly disobeyed the commands of God, and the people of Israel unknowingly paid the price. Finally, God instructed Joshua to find out who had sinned and to deal with that person: "Now Joshua said to Achan, 'My son, I beg you, give glory to the LORD God of Israel, and make confession to Him, and tell me now what you have done; do not hide it from me.' And Achan answered Joshua and said, 'Indeed I have sinned against the LORD God of Israel, and this is what I have done'" (7:19, 20).

Achan paid a very steep price for his disobedience, because his sin had serious consequences for the whole nation. As we read the account of Achan's sin, we see that God takes sin very seriously—and so we learn the value of fearing Him and hating everything that offends Him.

the commandment of the LORD you shall do. See, I have commanded you."

⁹Joshua therefore sent them out; and they went to lie in ambush, and stayed between Bethel and Ai, on the west side of Ai; but Joshua lodged that night among the people. ¹⁰Then Joshua rose up early in the morning and mustered the people, and went up, he and the elders of Israel, before the people to Ai. ¹¹And all the people of war who *were* with him went up and drew near; and they came before the city and camped on the north side of Ai. Now a valley *lay* between them and Ai. ¹²So he took about five thousand men and set them in ambush between Bethel and Ai, on the west side of the city. ¹³And when they had set the people, all the

7:26 ªLiterally *Trouble*

army that *was* on the north of the city, and its rear guard on the west of the city, Joshua went that night into the midst of the valley.

¹⁴Now it happened, when the king of Ai saw *it*, that the men of the city hurried and rose early and went out against Israel to battle, he and all his people, at an appointed place before the plain. But he did not know that *there was* an ambush against him behind the city. ¹⁵And Joshua and all Israel made as if they were beaten before them, and fled by the way of the wilderness. ¹⁶So all the people who *were* in Ai were called together to pursue them. And they pursued Joshua and were drawn away from the city. ¹⁷There was not a man left in Ai or Bethel who did not go out after Israel. So they left the city open and pursued Israel.

¹⁸Then the LORD said to Joshua, "Stretch out the spear that *is* in your hand toward Ai, for I will give it into your hand." And Joshua stretched out the spear that *was* in his hand toward the city. ¹⁹So *those in* ambush arose quickly out of their place; they ran as soon as he had stretched out his hand, and they entered the city and took it, and hurried to set the city on fire. ²⁰And when the men of Ai looked behind them, they saw, and behold, the smoke of the city ascended to heaven. So they had no power to flee this way or that way, and the people who had fled to the wilderness turned back on the pursuers.

²¹Now when Joshua and all Israel saw that the ambush had taken the city and that the smoke of the city ascended, they turned back and struck down the men of Ai. ²²Then the others came out of the city against them; so they were *caught* in the midst of Israel, some on this side and some on that side. And they struck them down, so that they let none of them remain or escape. ²³But the king of Ai they took alive, and brought him to Joshua.

²⁴And it came to pass when Israel had made an end of slaying all the inhabitants of Ai in the field, in the wilderness where they pursued them, and when they all had fallen by the edge of the sword until they were consumed, that all the Israelites returned to Ai and struck it with the edge of the sword. ²⁵So it was *that* all who fell that day, both men and women, *were* twelve thousand—all the people of Ai. ²⁶For

Joshua did not draw back his hand, with which he stretched out the spear, until he had utterly destroyed all the inhabitants of Ai. ²⁷Only the livestock and the spoil of that city Israel took as booty for themselves, according to the word of the LORD which He had commanded Joshua. ²⁸So Joshua burned Ai and made it a heap forever, a desolation to this day. ²⁹And the king of Ai he hanged on a tree until evening. And as soon as the sun was down, Joshua commanded that they should take his corpse down from the tree, cast it at the entrance of the gate of the city, and raise over it a great heap of stones *that remains* to this day.

Joshua Renews the Covenant

³⁰Now Joshua built an altar to the LORD God of Israel in Mount Ebal, ³¹as Moses the servant of the LORD had commanded the children of Israel, as it is written in the Book of the Law of Moses: "an altar of whole stones over which no man has wielded an iron *tool*."ᵃ And they offered on it burnt offerings to the LORD, and sacrificed peace offerings. ³²And there, in the presence of the children of Israel, he wrote on the stones a copy of the law of Moses, which he had written. ³³Then all Israel, with their elders and officers and judges, stood on either side of the ark before the priests, the Levites, who bore the ark of the covenant of the LORD, the stranger as well as he who was born among them. Half of them *were* in front of Mount Gerizim and half of them in front of Mount Ebal, as Moses the servant of the LORD had commanded before, that they should bless the people of Israel. ³⁴And afterward he read all the words of the law, the blessings and the cursings, according to all that is written in the Book of the Law. ³⁵There was not a word of all that Moses had commanded which Joshua did not read before all the assembly of Israel, with the women, the little ones, and the strangers who were living among them.

The Treaty with the Gibeonites

9 And it came to pass when all the kings who *were* on this side of the Jordan, in the hills and in the lowland and in all the

---

8:31 ᵃDeuteronomy 27:5, 6

coasts of the Great Sea toward Lebanon—the Hittite, the Amorite, the Canaanite, the Perizzite, the Hivite, and the Jebusite—heard *about it,* ²that they gathered together to fight with Joshua and Israel with one accord.

³But when the inhabitants of Gibeon heard what Joshua had done to Jericho and Ai, ⁴they worked craftily, and went and pretended to be ambassadors. And they took old sacks on their donkeys, old wineskins torn and mended, ⁵old and patched sandals on their feet, and old garments on themselves; and all the bread of their provision was dry *and* moldy. ⁶And they went to Joshua, to the camp at Gilgal, and said to him and to the men of Israel, "We have come from a far country; now therefore, make a covenant with us."

⁷Then the men of Israel said to the Hivites, "Perhaps you dwell among us; so how can we make a covenant with you?"

⁸But they said to Joshua, "We *are* your servants."

And Joshua said to them, "Who *are* you, and where do you come from?"

⁹So they said to him: "From a very far country your servants have come, because of the name of the LORD your God; for we have heard of His fame, and all that He did in Egypt, ¹⁰and all that He did to the two kings of the Amorites who *were* beyond the Jordan—to Sihon king of Heshbon, and Og king of Bashan, who was at Ashtaroth. ¹¹Therefore our elders and all the inhabitants of our country spoke to us, saying, 'Take provisions with you for the journey, and go to meet them, and say to them, "We *are* your servants; now therefore, make a covenant with us."' ¹²This bread of ours we took hot *for* our provision from our houses on the day we departed to come to you. But now look, it is dry and moldy. ¹³And these wineskins which we filled *were* new, and see, they are torn; and these our garments and our sandals have become old because of the very long journey."

¹⁴Then the men of Israel took some of their provisions; but they did not ask counsel of the LORD. ¹⁵So Joshua made peace with them, and made a covenant with them to let them live; and the rulers of the congregation swore to them.

¹⁶And it happened at the end of three days, after they had made a covenant with them, that they heard that they *were* their neighbors who dwelt near them. ¹⁷Then the children of Israel journeyed and came to their cities on the third day. Now their cities *were* Gibeon, Chephirah, Beeroth, and Kirjath Jearim. ¹⁸But the children of Israel did not attack them, because the rulers of the congregation had sworn to them by the LORD God of Israel. And all the congregation complained against the rulers.

INTIMATE MOMENTS
Tickle Her Funny Bone

What makes your wife laugh? What does she consider funny? What shows make her smile, what jokes make her chuckle, what incidents in your own relationship bring laughter and fun to your home? Try to design an evening for the two of you in which laughter is the main goal. Don't settle for something easy, like taking her to a funny movie. That might be part of the date, but don't make it the main event. Spend some time figuring out how you can help your wife to really let loose and laugh, and then do your best to tickle her funny bone. Remember that the Bible insists "a merry heart does good, like medicine" (Prov. 17:22). Laughter makes any day better! So make this one better for both you and your spouse.

¹⁹Then all the rulers said to all the congregation, "We have sworn to them by the LORD God of Israel; now therefore, we may not touch them. ²⁰This we will do to them: We will let them live, lest wrath be upon us because of the oath which we swore to them." ²¹And the rulers said to them, "Let them live, but let them be woodcutters and water carriers for all the congregation, as the rulers had promised them."

²²Then Joshua called for them, and he spoke to them, saying, "Why have you deceived us, saying, 'We *are* very far from you,' when you dwell near us? ²³Now therefore, you *are* cursed, and none of you shall

DEVOTIONS FOR COUPLES • 10:25
Courageous Parenting

We live in urgent times, times that present tremendous challenges to us as parents, times when we need all the courage we can muster—all that God gives us—in order to raise our children to be the kind of people He calls them to be. One of the greatest needs of our day is parents who are willing to courageously follow Christ as they encounter opposition from the culture and raise their children to be spiritual warriors for their generation.

The Lord's words to Joshua apply to us parents today, "Do not be afraid, nor be dismayed; be strong and of good courage, for thus the LORD will do to all your enemies against whom you fight" (10:25). Courageous actions do cost us something, but encouraging words like these from our Father compel me to rise from my easy chair and march toward the action.

Are there ways to grow our courage? Yes! God will build moral fortitude into His children, regardless of our gene pools. Consider a few of the ways He does it:

First, we can begin fasting and praying more consistently. If you are burdened about the spiritual vitality of your life, marriage, and children, I invite you to join thousands who humbly seek God regularly. Ask God to show you the turf where you can engage the enemy.

Second, we can grow our courage by stepping out of our comfort zones and into divinely-ordered battle zones, those skirmishes, God brings our way. These brave acts may be both public confrontations, as well as family moments that count.

Third, we can adopt a war-time footing. War demands a personal sacrifice necessary for survival and victory. Consider Paul's words to Timothy, "You therefore must endure hardship as a good soldier of Jesus Christ. No one engaged in warfare entangles himself with the affairs of this life, that he may please the one who enlisted him as a soldier" (2 Tim. 2:3, 4). Barbara and I agreed early in our marriage that no other success could compensate for failure in our marriage and family. This war footing demanded personal sacrifices.

Next, if courage is to flourish, we must tenaciously persevere. With no moral consensus reinforcing Christian values, as a parent you must fight for the souls of your children, and expect little to no support from society. Paul wrote, "Let us not grow weary while doing good" (Gal. 6:9). Hang in there!

Finally, infect others with your courage. Courage is contagious. As I share stories of moms and dads, singles, and grandparents stepping into battle for families, others soon show a fierce desire to enter combat, too.

---

be freed from being slaves—woodcutters and water carriers for the house of my God."

24So they answered Joshua and said, "Because your servants were clearly told that the LORD your God commanded His servant Moses to give you all the land, and to destroy all the inhabitants of the land from before you; therefore we were very much afraid for our lives because of you, and have done this thing. 25And now, here we are, in your hands; do with us as it seems good and right to do to us." 26So he did to them, and delivered them out of the hand of the children of Israel, so that they did not kill them. 27And that day Joshua made them woodcutters and water carriers

for the congregation and for the altar of the LORD, in the place which He would choose, even to this day.

The Sun Stands Still

10 Now it came to pass when Adoni-Zedek king of Jerusalem heard how Joshua had taken Ai and had utterly destroyed it—as he had done to Jericho and its king, so he had done to Ai and its king—and how the inhabitants of Gibeon had made peace with Israel and were among them, 2that they feared greatly, because Gibeon *was* a great city, like one of the royal cities, and because it *was* greater than Ai, and all its men *were* mighty. 3Therefore

Adoni-Zedek king of Jerusalem sent to Hoham king of Hebron, Piram king of Jarmuth, Japhia king of Lachish, and Debir king of Eglon, saying, 4"Come up to me and help me, that we may attack Gibeon, for it has made peace with Joshua and with the children of Israel." 5Therefore the five kings of the Amorites, the king of Jerusalem, the king of Hebron, the king of Jarmuth, the king of Lachish, *and* the king of Eglon, gathered together and went up, they and all their armies, and camped before Gibeon and made war against it.

6And the men of Gibeon sent to Joshua at the camp at Gilgal, saying, "Do not forsake your servants; come up to us quickly, save us and help us, for all the kings of the Amorites who dwell in the mountains have gathered together against us."

7So Joshua ascended from Gilgal, he and all the people of war with him, and all the mighty men of valor. 8And the LORD said to Joshua, "Do not fear them, for I have delivered them into your hand; not a man of them shall stand before you." 9Joshua therefore came upon them suddenly, having marched all night from Gilgal. 10So the LORD routed them before Israel, killed them with a great slaughter at Gibeon, chased them along the road that goes to Beth Horon, and struck them down as far as Azekah and Makkedah. 11And it happened, as they fled before Israel *and* were on the descent of Beth Horon, that the LORD cast down large hailstones from heaven on them as far as Azekah, and they died. *There were* more who died from the hailstones than the children of Israel killed with the sword.

12Then Joshua spoke to the LORD in the day when the LORD delivered up the Amorites before the children of Israel, and he said in the sight of Israel:

"Sun, stand still over Gibeon;
And Moon, in the Valley of Aijalon."
13   So the sun stood still,
And the moon stopped,
Till the people had revenge
Upon their enemies.

Is this not written in the Book of Jasher? So the sun stood still in the midst of heaven, and did not hasten to go *down* for about a whole day. 14And there has been no day like that, before it or after it, that the LORD heeded the voice of a man; for the LORD fought for Israel.

15Then Joshua returned, and all Israel with him, to the camp at Gilgal.

The Amorite Kings Executed

16But these five kings had fled and hidden themselves in a cave at Makkedah. 17And it was told Joshua, saying, "The five kings have been found hidden in the cave at Makkedah."

18So Joshua said, "Roll large stones against the mouth of the cave, and set men by it to guard them. 19And do not stay *there* yourselves, *but* pursue your enemies, and attack their rear *guard*. Do not allow them to enter their cities, for the LORD your God has delivered them into your hand." 20Then it happened, while Joshua and the children of Israel made an end of slaying them with a very great slaughter, till they had finished, that those who escaped entered fortified cities. 21And all the people returned to the camp, to Joshua at Makkedah, in peace. No one moved his tongue against any of the children of Israel.

22Then Joshua said, "Open the mouth of the cave, and bring out those five kings to me from the cave." 23And they did so, and brought out those five kings to him from the cave: the king of Jerusalem, the king of Hebron, the king of Jarmuth, the king of Lachish, *and* the king of Eglon.

24So it was, when they brought out those kings to Joshua, that Joshua called for all the men of Israel, and said to the captains of the men of war who went with him, "Come near, put your feet on the necks of these kings." And they drew near and put their feet on their necks. 25Then Joshua said to them, "Do not be afraid, nor be dismayed; be strong and of good courage, for thus the LORD will do to all your enemies against whom you fight." 26And afterward Joshua struck them and killed them, and hanged them on five trees; and they were hanging on the trees until evening. 27So it was at the time of the going down of the sun *that* Joshua commanded, and they took them down from the trees, cast them into the cave where they had been hidden, and laid large stones against the cave's mouth, *which remain* until this very day.

Conquest of the Southland

²⁸On that day Joshua took Makkedah, and struck it and its king with the edge of the sword. He utterly destroyed them[a]—all the people who *were* in it. He let none remain. He also did to the king of Makkedah as he had done to the king of Jericho.

²⁹Then Joshua passed from Makkedah, and all Israel with him, to Libnah; and they fought against Libnah. ³⁰And the LORD also delivered it and its king into the hand of Israel; he struck it and all the people who *were* in it with the edge of the sword. He let none remain in it, but did to its king as he had done to the king of Jericho.

³¹Then Joshua passed from Libnah, and all Israel with him, to Lachish; and they encamped against it and fought against it. ³²And the LORD delivered Lachish into the hand of Israel, who took it on the second day, and struck it and all the people who *were* in it with the edge of the sword, according to all that he had done to Libnah. ³³Then Horam king of Gezer came up to help Lachish; and Joshua struck him and his people, until he left him none remaining.

³⁴From Lachish Joshua passed to Eglon, and all Israel with him; and they encamped against it and fought against it. ³⁵They took it on that day and struck it with the edge of the sword; all the people who *were* in it he utterly destroyed that day, according to all that he had done to Lachish.

³⁶So Joshua went up from Eglon, and all Israel with him, to Hebron; and they fought against it. ³⁷And they took it and struck it with the edge of the sword—its king, all its cities, and all the people who *were* in it; he left none remaining, according to all that he had done to Eglon, but utterly destroyed it and all the people who *were* in it.

³⁸Then Joshua returned, and all Israel with him, to Debir; and they fought against it. ³⁹And he took it and its king and all its cities; they struck them with the edge of the sword and utterly destroyed all the people who *were* in it. He left none remaining; as he had done to Hebron, so he did to Debir and its king, as he had done also to Libnah and its king.

⁴⁰So Joshua conquered all the land: the mountain country and the South[a] and the lowland and the wilderness slopes, and all their kings; he left none remaining, but utterly destroyed all that breathed, as the LORD God of Israel had commanded. ⁴¹And Joshua conquered them from Kadesh Barnea as far as Gaza, and all the country of Goshen, even as far as Gibeon. ⁴²All these kings and their land Joshua took at one time, because the LORD God of Israel fought for Israel. ⁴³Then Joshua returned, and all Israel with him, to the camp at Gilgal.

The Northern Conquest

11 And it came to pass, when Jabin king of Hazor heard *these things,* that he sent to Jobab king of Madon, to the king of Shimron, to the king of Achshaph, ²and to the kings who *were* from the north, in the mountains, in the plain south of Chinneroth, in the lowland, and in the heights of Dor on the west, ³to the Canaanites in the east and in the west, the Amorite, the Hittite, the Perizzite, the Jebusite in the mountains, and the Hivite below Hermon in the land of Mizpah. ⁴So they went out, they and all their armies with them, *as* many people *as* the sand that *is* on the seashore in multitude, with very many horses and chariots. ⁵And when all these kings had met together, they came and camped together at the waters of Merom to fight against Israel.

⁶But the LORD said to Joshua, "Do not be afraid because of them, for tomorrow about this time I will deliver all of them slain before Israel. You shall hamstring their horses and burn their chariots with fire." ⁷So Joshua and all the people of war with him came against them suddenly by the waters of Merom, and they attacked them. ⁸And the LORD delivered them into the hand of Israel, who defeated them and chased them to Greater Sidon, to the Brook Misrephoth,[a] and to the Valley of Mizpah eastward; they attacked them until they left none of them remaining. ⁹So Joshua did

---

10:28 [a]Following Masoretic Text and most authorities; many Hebrew manuscripts, some manuscripts of the Septuagint, and some manuscripts of the Targum read *it*. **10:40** [a]Hebrew *Negev,* and so throughout this book **11:8** [a]Hebrew *Misrephoth Maim*

to them as the LORD had told him: he hamstrung their horses and burned their chariots with fire.

[10]Joshua turned back at that time and took Hazor, and struck its king with the sword; for Hazor was formerly the head of all those kingdoms. [11]And they struck all the people who *were* in it with the edge of the sword, utterly destroying *them.* There was none left breathing. Then he burned Hazor with fire.

[12]So all the cities of those kings, and all their kings, Joshua took and struck with the edge of the sword. He utterly destroyed them, as Moses the servant of the LORD had commanded. [13]But *as for* the cities that stood on their mounds,[a] Israel burned none of them, except Hazor only, *which* Joshua burned. [14]And all the spoil of these cities and the livestock, the children of Israel took as booty for themselves; but they struck every man with the edge of the sword until they had destroyed them, and they left none breathing. [15]As the LORD had commanded Moses his servant, so Moses commanded Joshua, and so Joshua did. He left nothing undone of all that the LORD had commanded Moses.

Summary of Joshua's Conquests

[16]Thus Joshua took all this land: the mountain country, all the South, all the land of Goshen, the lowland, and the Jordan plain[a]—the mountains of Israel and its lowlands, [17]from Mount Halak and the ascent to Seir, even as far as Baal Gad in the Valley of Lebanon below Mount Hermon. He captured all their kings, and struck them down and killed them. [18]Joshua made war a long time with all those kings. [19]There was not a city that made peace with the children of Israel, except the Hivites, the inhabitants of Gibeon. All *the others* they took in battle. [20]For it was of the LORD to harden their hearts, that they should come against Israel in battle, that He might utterly destroy them, *and* that they might receive no mercy, but that He might destroy them, as the LORD had commanded Moses.

[21]And at that time Joshua came and cut off the Anakim from the mountains: from Hebron, from Debir, from Anab, from all the mountains of Judah, and from all the mountains of Israel; Joshua utterly destroyed them with their cities. [22]None of the Anakim were left in the land of the children of Israel; they remained only in Gaza, in Gath, and in Ashdod.

[23]So Joshua took the whole land, according to all that the LORD had said to Moses; and Joshua gave it as an inheritance to Israel according to their divisions by their tribes. Then the land rested from war.

ROMANCE FAQ

Q: *How can we become friends again after the children are gone?*

The most important thing you can do is to begin to develop some common interests, some things you enjoy doing together. Find something to share and make your relationship a priority. Rediscovering or even rebuilding the common basis that you lost during the years when he spent all day at work and you spent all day with the kids will take time and hard work.

One of you needs to take steps to participate in an activity that the other already is involved in or interested in, so that the relationship can have a chance to grow. The husband and wife need to reach a compromise, sacrificing their own rights and wishes for the ultimate good of the relationship.

You can also try to uncover a common cause, or a shared mission—some ministry that both of you can passionately support. Couples across the nation have found their common cause in mentoring younger couples. They are dedicating part of their lives to teaching others how to make marriages work and how to build godly homes through leading small groups in our HomeBuilders Couples Series®. These can be the best years of your life!

11:13 [a]Hebrew *tel,* a heap of successive city ruins
11:16 [a]Hebrew *arabah*

The Kings Conquered by Moses

12 These *are* the kings of the land whom the children of Israel defeated, and whose land they possessed on the other side of the Jordan toward the rising of the sun, from the River Arnon to Mount Hermon, and all the eastern Jordan plain: ²*One king was* Sihon king of the Amorites, who dwelt in Heshbon *and* ruled half of Gilead, from Aroer, which is on the bank of the River Arnon, from the middle of that river, even as far as the River Jabbok, *which is* the border of the Ammonites, ³and the eastern Jordan plain from the Sea of Chinneroth as far as the Sea of the Arabah (the Salt Sea), the road to Beth Jeshimoth, and southward below the slopes of Pisgah. ⁴*The other king was* Og king of Bashan and his territory, *who was* of the remnant of the giants, who dwelt at Ashtaroth and at Edrei, ⁵and reigned over Mount Hermon, over Salcah, over all Bashan, as far as the border of the Geshurites and the Maachathites, and over half of Gilead *to* the border of Sihon king of Heshbon.

⁶These Moses the servant of the LORD and the children of Israel had conquered; and Moses the servant of the LORD had given it *as* a possession to the Reubenites, the Gadites, and half the tribe of Manasseh.

The Kings Conquered by Joshua

⁷And these *are* the kings of the country which Joshua and the children of Israel conquered on this side of the Jordan, on the west, from Baal Gad in the Valley of Lebanon as far as Mount Halak and the ascent to Seir, which Joshua gave to the tribes of Israel *as* a possession according to their divisions, ⁸in the mountain country, in the lowlands, in the *Jordan* plain, in the slopes, in the wilderness, and in the South—the Hittites, the Amorites, the Canaanites, the Perizzites, the Hivites, and the Jebusites: ⁹the king of Jericho, one; the king of Ai, which *is* beside Bethel, one; ¹⁰the king of Jerusalem, one; the king of Hebron, one; ¹¹the king of Jarmuth, one; the king of Lachish, one; ¹²the king of Eglon, one; the king of Gezer, one; ¹³the king of Debir, one; the king of Geder, one; ¹⁴the king of Hormah, one; the king of Arad, one; ¹⁵the king of Libnah, one; the king of Adullam, one; ¹⁶the king of Makkedah, one; the king of Bethel, one; ¹⁷the king of Tappuah, one; the king of Hepher, one; ¹⁸the king of Aphek, one; the king of Lasharon, one; ¹⁹the king of Madon, one; the king of Hazor, one; ²⁰the king of Shimron Meron, one; the king of Achshaph, one; ²¹the king of Taanach, one; the king of Megiddo, one; ²²the king of Kedesh, one; the king of Jokneam in Carmel, one; ²³the king of Dor in the heights of Dor, one; the king of the people of Gilgal, one; ²⁴the king of Tirzah, one—all the kings, thirty-one.

Remaining Land to Be Conquered

13 Now Joshua was old, advanced in years. And the LORD said to him: "You are old, advanced in years, and there remains very much land yet to be possessed. ²This is the land that yet remains: all the territory of the Philistines and all *that of* the Geshurites, ³from Sihor, which *is* east of Egypt, as far as the border of Ekron northward (*which* is counted as Canaanite); the five lords of the Philistines—the Gazites, the Ashdodites, the Ashkelonites, the Gittites, and the Ekronites; also the Avites; ⁴from the south, all the land of the Canaanites, and Mearah that belongs to the Sidonians as far as Aphek, to the border of the Amorites; ⁵the land of the Gebalites,ᵃ and all Lebanon, toward the sunrise, from Baal Gad below Mount Hermon as far as the entrance to Hamath; ⁶all the inhabitants of the mountains from Lebanon as far as the Brook Misrephoth,ᵃ *and* all the Sidonians—them I will drive out from before the children of Israel; only divide it by lot to Israel as an inheritance, as I have commanded you. ⁷Now therefore, divide this land as an inheritance to the nine tribes and half the tribe of Manasseh."

The Land Divided East of the Jordan

⁸With the other half-tribe the Reubenites and the Gadites received their inheritance, which Moses had given them, beyond the Jordan eastward, as Moses the servant of the LORD had given them: ⁹from Aroer which *is* on the bank of the River Arnon, and the

13:5 ᵃOr *Giblites* **13:6** ᵃHebrew *Misrephoth Maim*

town that *is* in the midst of the ravine, and all the plain of Medeba as far as Dibon; [10]all the cities of Sihon king of the Amorites, who reigned in Heshbon, as far as the border of the children of Ammon; [11]Gilead, and the border of the Geshurites and Maachathites, all Mount Hermon, and all Bashan as far as Salcah; [12]all the kingdom of Og in Bashan, who reigned in Ashtaroth and Edrei, who remained of the remnant of the giants; for Moses had defeated and cast out these.

[13]Nevertheless the children of Israel did not drive out the Geshurites or the Maachathites, but the Geshurites and the Maachathites dwell among the Israelites until this day.

[14]Only to the tribe of Levi he had given no inheritance; the sacrifices of the LORD God of Israel made by fire *are* their inheritance, as He said to them.

The Land of Reuben

[15]And Moses had given to the tribe of the children of Reuben *an inheritance* according to their families. [16]Their territory was from Aroer, which *is* on the bank of the River Arnon, and the city that *is* in the midst of the ravine, and all the plain by Medeba; [17]Heshbon and all its cities that *are* in the plain: Dibon, Bamoth Baal, Beth Baal Meon, [18]Jahaza, Kedemoth, Mephaath, [19]Kirjathaim, Sibmah, Zereth Shahar on the mountain of the valley, [20]Beth Peor, the slopes of Pisgah, and Beth Jeshimoth— [21]all the cities of the plain and all the kingdom of Sihon king of the Amorites, who reigned in Heshbon, whom Moses had struck with the princes of Midian: Evi, Rekem, Zur, Hur, and Reba, who *were* princes of Sihon dwelling in the country. [22]The children of Israel also killed with the sword Balaam the son of Beor, the soothsayer, among those who were killed by them. [23]And the border of the children of Reuben was the bank of the Jordan. This *was* the inheritance of the children of Reuben according to their families, the cities and their villages.

The Land of Gad

[24]Moses also had given *an inheritance* to the tribe of Gad, to the children of Gad according to their families. [25]Their territory

was Jazer, and all the cities of Gilead, and half the land of the Ammonites as far as Aroer, which *is* before Rabbah, [26]and from Heshbon to Ramath Mizpah and Betonim, and from Mahanaim to the border of Debir, [27]and in the valley Beth Haram, Beth Nimrah, Succoth, and Zaphon, the rest of the kingdom of Sihon king of Heshbon, with the Jordan as *its* border, as far as the edge of the Sea of Chinnereth, on the other side of the Jordan eastward. [28]This *is* the inheritance of the children of Gad according to their families, the cities and their villages.

Half the Tribe of Manasseh (East)

[29]Moses also had given *an inheritance* to half the tribe of Manasseh; it was for half the tribe of the children of Manasseh according to their families: [30]Their territory was from Mahanaim, all Bashan, all the kingdom of Og king of Bashan, and all the towns of Jair which are in Bashan, sixty cities; [31]half of Gilead, and Ashtaroth and Edrei, cities of the kingdom of Og in Bashan, *were* for the children of Machir the son of Manasseh, for half of the children of Machir according to their families.

[32]These *are the areas* which Moses had distributed as an inheritance in the plains of Moab on the other side of the Jordan, by Jericho eastward. [33]But to the tribe of Levi Moses had given no inheritance; the LORD God of Israel *was* their inheritance, as He had said to them.

The Land Divided West of the Jordan

14 These *are the areas* which the children of Israel inherited in the land of Canaan, which Eleazar the priest, Joshua the son of Nun, and the heads of the fathers of the tribes of the children of Israel distributed as an inheritance to them. [2]Their inheritance *was* by lot, as the LORD had commanded by the hand of Moses, for the nine tribes and the half-tribe. [3]For Moses had given the inheritance of the two tribes and the half-tribe on the other side of the Jordan; but to the Levites he had given no inheritance among them. [4]For the children of Joseph were two tribes: Manasseh and Ephraim. And they gave no part to the Levites in the land, except cities

Best Friends Help Us Weather the Storms of Life

JOB CHANGES, FAILURES, and unexpected circumstances all can shake an otherwise settled self-image from its moorings. Life's ups and downs can spawn questions about one's self-worth and confidence. Self-doubt can spread quickly, almost overnight.

You'll more effectively handle *all* of life's changes—whether menopause, the birth of a child, the empty nest, a lost job, an illness, a midlife crisis, or difficulty with a teenager—with more than one person alongside you. And so will your mate.

I believe the best kind of friendships get formed in a bunker, during the battles of life. Those moments of trial, of testing, of difficulty, meld people together, just as they made Joshua and Caleb close friends and fellow soldiers for life (14:13).

No marriage takes place on a romantic balcony, but on a spiritual battlefield, where we are called to regain spiritual turf for Jesus Christ. We need friends who will stand by us in the bunker, Caleb-like friends who will take a stand for God.

A true friend can bring value and perspective when you or your mate has blown it. A good friend will hang in there when it seems the whole world has walked out—and so exhibit the unconditional love of God.

---

the land, and I brought back word to him as *it was* in my heart. ⁸Nevertheless my brethren who went up with me made the heart of the people melt, but I wholly followed the LORD my God. ⁹So Moses swore on that day, saying, 'Surely the land where your foot has trodden shall be your inheritance and your children's forever, because you have wholly followed the LORD my God.' ¹⁰And now, behold, the LORD has kept me alive, as He said, these forty-five years, ever since the LORD spoke this word to Moses while Israel wandered in the wilderness; and now, here I am this day, eighty-five years old. ¹¹As yet I *am as* strong this day as on the day that Moses sent me; just as my strength *was* then, so now *is* my strength for war, both for going out and for coming in. ¹²Now therefore, give me this mountain of which the LORD spoke in that day; for you heard in that day how the Anakim *were* there, and *that* the cities *were* great *and* fortified. It may be that the LORD *will be* with me, and I shall be able to drive them out as the LORD said."

¹³And Joshua blessed him, and gave Hebron to Caleb the son of Jephunneh as an inheritance. ¹⁴Hebron therefore became the inheritance of Caleb the son of Jephunneh the Kenizzite to this day, because he wholly followed the LORD God of Israel. ¹⁵And the name of Hebron formerly was Kirjath Arba (*Arba was* the greatest man among the Anakim).

Then the land had rest from war.

The Land of Judah

15 So *this* was the lot of the tribe of the children of Judah according to their families:

The border of Edom at the Wilderness of Zin southward *was* the extreme southern boundary. ²And their southern border began at the shore of the Salt Sea, from the bay that faces southward. ³Then it went out to the southern side of the Ascent of Akrabbim, passed along to Zin, ascended on the south side of Kadesh Barnea, passed along to Hezron, went up to Adar, and went around to Karkaa. ⁴*From there* it passed toward Azmon and went out to the Brook of Egypt; and the border ended at the sea. This shall be your southern border.

---

to dwell *in,* with their common-lands for their livestock and their property. ⁵As the LORD had commanded Moses, so the children of Israel did; and they divided the land.

Caleb Inherits Hebron

⁶Then the children of Judah came to Joshua in Gilgal. And Caleb the son of Jephunneh the Kenizzite said to him: "You know the word which the LORD said to Moses the man of God concerning you and me in Kadesh Barnea. ⁷I *was* forty years old when Moses the servant of the LORD sent me from Kadesh Barnea to spy out

⁵The east border *was* the Salt Sea as far as the mouth of the Jordan.

And the border on the northern quarter *began* at the bay of the sea at the mouth of the Jordan. ⁶The border went up to Beth Hoglah and passed north of Beth Arabah; and the border went up to the stone of Bohan the son of Reuben. ⁷Then the border went up toward Debir from the Valley of Achor, and it turned northward toward Gilgal, which *is* before the Ascent of Adummim, which *is* on the south side of the valley. The border continued toward the waters of En Shemesh and ended at En Rogel. ⁸And the border went up by the Valley of the Son of Hinnom to the southern slope of the Jebusite *city* (which *is* Jerusalem). The border went up to the top of the mountain that *lies* before the Valley of Hinnom westward, which *is* at the end of the Valley of Rephaim[a] northward. ⁹Then the border went around from the top of the hill to the fountain of the water of Nephtoah, and extended to the cities of Mount Ephron. And the border went around to Baalah (which *is* Kirjath Jearim). ¹⁰Then the border turned westward from Baalah to Mount Seir, passed along to the side of Mount Jearim on the north (which *is* Chesalon), went down to Beth Shemesh, and passed on to Timnah. ¹¹And the border went out to the side of Ekron northward. Then the border went around to Shicron, passed along to Mount Baalah, and extended to Jabneel; and the border ended at the sea.

¹²The west border *was* the coastline of the Great Sea. This *is* the boundary of the children of Judah all around according to their families.

Caleb Occupies Hebron and Debir

¹³Now to Caleb the son of Jephunneh he gave a share among the children of Judah, according to the commandment of the LORD to Joshua, *namely,* Kirjath Arba, which *is* Hebron (*Arba was* the father of Anak). ¹⁴Caleb drove out the three sons of Anak from there: Sheshai, Ahiman, and Talmai, the children of Anak. ¹⁵Then he went up from there to the inhabitants of Debir (formerly the name of Debir *was* Kirjath Sepher).

¹⁶And Caleb said, "He who attacks Kirjath Sepher and takes it, to him I will give Achsah my daughter as wife." ¹⁷So Othniel the son of Kenaz, the brother of Caleb, took it; and he gave him Achsah his daughter as wife. ¹⁸Now it was so, when she came *to him,* that she persuaded him to ask her father for a field. So she dismounted from *her* donkey, and Caleb said to her, "What do you wish?" ¹⁹She answered, "Give me a blessing; since you have given me land in the South, give me also springs of water." So he gave her the upper springs and the lower springs.

The Cities of Judah

²⁰This *was* the inheritance of the tribe of the children of Judah according to their families:

²¹The cities at the limits of the tribe of the children of Judah, toward the border of Edom in the South, were Kabzeel, Eder, Jagur, ²²Kinah, Dimonah, Adadah, ²³Kedesh, Hazor, Ithnan, ²⁴Ziph, Telem, Bealoth, ²⁵Hazor, Hadattah, Kerioth, Hezron (which *is* Hazor), ²⁶Amam, Shema, Moladah, ²⁷Hazar Gaddah, Heshmon, Beth Pelet, ²⁸Hazar Shual, Beersheba, Bizjothjah, ²⁹Baalah, Ijim, Ezem, ³⁰Eltolad, Chesil, Hormah, ³¹Ziklag, Madmannah, Sansannah, ³²Lebaoth, Shilhim, Ain, and Rimmon: all the cities *are* twenty-nine, with their villages.

³³In the lowland: Eshtaol, Zorah, Ashnah, ³⁴Zanoah, En Gannim, Tappuah, Enam, ³⁵Jarmuth, Adullam, Socoh, Azekah, ³⁶Sharaim, Adithaim, Gederah, and Gederothaim: fourteen cities with their villages; ³⁷Zenan, Hadashah, Migdal Gad, ³⁸Dilean, Mizpah, Joktheel, ³⁹Lachish, Bozkath, Eglon, ⁴⁰Cabbon, Lahmas,[a] Kithlish, ⁴¹Gederoth, Beth Dagon, Naamah, and Makkedah: sixteen cities with their villages; ⁴²Libnah, Ether, Ashan, ⁴³Jiphtah, Ashnah, Nezib, ⁴⁴Keilah, Achzib, and Mareshah: nine cities with their villages; ⁴⁵Ekron, with its towns and villages; ⁴⁶from Ekron to the sea, all that *lay* near Ashdod, with their villages; ⁴⁷Ashdod with its towns and villages, Gaza with its towns and villages—as far as the Brook of Egypt and the Great Sea with *its* coastline.

15:8 [a]Literally *Giants* **15:40** [a]Or *Lahmam*

⁴⁸And in the mountain country: Shamir, Jattir, Sochoh, ⁴⁹Dannah, Kirjath Sannah (which *is* Debir), ⁵⁰Anab, Eshtemoh, Anim, ⁵¹Goshen, Holon, and Giloh: eleven cities with their villages; ⁵²Arab, Dumah, Eshean, ⁵³Janum, Beth Tappuah, Aphekah, ⁵⁴Humtah, Kirjath Arba (which *is* Hebron), and Zior: nine cities with their villages; ⁵⁵Maon, Carmel, Ziph, Juttah, ⁵⁶Jezreel, Jokdeam, Zanoah, ⁵⁷Kain, Gibeah, and Timnah: ten cities with their villages; ⁵⁸Halhul, Beth Zur, Gedor, ⁵⁹Maarath, Beth Anoth, and Eltekon: six cities with their villages; ⁶⁰Kirjath Baal (which *is* Kirjath Jearim) and Rabbah: two cities with their villages.

⁶¹In the wilderness: Beth Arabah, Middin, Secacah, ⁶²Nibshan, the City of Salt, and En Gedi: six cities with their villages.

⁶³As for the Jebusites, the inhabitants of Jerusalem, the children of Judah could not drive them out; but the Jebusites dwell with the children of Judah at Jerusalem to this day.

Ephraim and West Manasseh

16 The lot fell to the children of Joseph from the Jordan, by Jericho, to the waters of Jericho on the east, to the wilderness that goes up from Jericho through the mountains to Bethel, ²then went out from Bethel to Luz,ᵃ passed along to the border of the Archites at Ataroth, ³and went down westward to the boundary of the Japhletites, as far as the boundary of Lower Beth Horon to Gezer; and it ended at the sea.

⁴So the children of Joseph, Manasseh and Ephraim, took their inheritance.

The Land of Ephraim

⁵The border of the children of Ephraim,

16:2 ᵃSeptuagint reads *Bethel* (that is, Luz).

PARENTING MATTERS

Q: How do we handle crises in a way that comforts and teaches our children?

In times of crisis, we must first lead by modeling, then lead our children back to the truths of God's Word, and finally coach them in how they should respond. During these times, many parents feel inadequate and fearful that their children will ask questions they don't know the answer to, but that is exactly why God has given us the Holy Spirit and the Scriptures. Step up to the challenge and begin leading your children to the truths outlined below.

Theme #1: *Give thanks in all things.* Giving thanks demonstrates our faith in the perfect character of God, that He knows what He is doing.

1 Thessalonians 5:16–18   Philippians 4:6

Theme #2: *God is sovereign.* God rules with absolute control and power. Nothing happens apart from what He allows or brings about.

2 Chronicles 2:5   Job 42:1–6
Psalm 115:3   1 Corinthians 15:54
1 Chronicles 29:11   Romans 8:28

Theme #3: *God is our redeemer, our Rock, and our personal refuge.* We can take comfort in our God through anything and everything.

2 Samuel 22:2, 3   Isaiah 33:15, 16
Psalm 46   Jeremiah 16:19, 20

Train your children in the basics of what they should do when they encounter various trials and challenging days. As our children grow up they need to know that suffering is not an optional course for followers of Christ. They will encounter difficulty. The question is: How will they respond?

according to their families, was *thus:* The border of their inheritance on the east side was Ataroth Addar as far as Upper Beth Horon.

6And the border went out toward the sea on the north side of Michmethath; then the border went around eastward to Taanath Shiloh, and passed by it on the east of Janohah. 7Then it went down from Janohah to Ataroth and Naarah,a reached to Jericho, and came out at the Jordan.

8The border went out from Tappuah westward to the Brook Kanah, and it ended at the sea. This *was* the inheritance of the tribe of the children of Ephraim according to their families. 9The separate cities for the children of Ephraim *were* among the inheritance of the children of Manasseh, all the cities with their villages.

10And they did not drive out the Canaanites who dwelt in Gezer; but the Canaanites dwell among the Ephraimites to this day and have become forced laborers.

The Other Half-Tribe of Manasseh (West)

17 There was also a lot for the tribe of Manasseh, for he *was* the firstborn of Joseph: *namely* for Machir the firstborn of Manasseh, the father of Gilead, because he was a man of war; therefore he was given Gilead and Bashan. 2And there was *a lot* for the rest of the children of Manasseh according to their families: for the children of Abiezer,a the children of Helek, the children of Asriel, the children of Shechem, the children of Hepher, and the children of Shemida; these *were* the male children of Manasseh the son of Joseph according to their families.

3But Zelophehad the son of Hepher, the son of Gilead, the son of Machir, the son of Manasseh, had no sons, but only daughters. And these *are* the names of his daughters: Mahlah, Noah, Hoglah, Milcah, and Tirzah. 4And they came near before Eleazar the priest, before Joshua the son of Nun, and before the rulers, saying, "The LORD commanded Moses to give us an inheritance among our brothers." Therefore, according to the commandment of the

LORD, he gave them an inheritance among their father's brothers. 5Ten shares fell to Manasseh, besides the land of Gilead and Bashan, which *were* on the other side of the Jordan, 6because the daughters of Manasseh received an inheritance among his sons; and the rest of Manasseh's sons had the land of Gilead.

7And the territory of Manasseh was from Asher to Michmethath, that *lies* east of Shechem; and the border went along

INTIMATE MOMENTS

Plan a romantic weekend for just your wife and you at a bed-and-breakfast. Make all of the arrangements yourself. Understand that bed-and-breakfasts vary tremendously in décor, style, amenities, and cost, so spend some time making sure that the one you pick is going to bring a smile to your wife's face. If she likes shopping at quirky little stores, then find a B&B that has plenty close by. It's not hard, but it does take time—so don't try to pull this one off at the last minute. Make it a getaway to remember!

south to the inhabitants of En Tappuah. 8Manasseh had the land of Tappuah, but Tappuah on the border of Manasseh *belonged* to the children of Ephraim. 9And the border descended to the Brook Kanah, southward to the brook. These cities of Ephraim *are* among the cities of Manasseh. The border of Manasseh *was* on the north side of the brook; and it ended at the sea.

10Southward *it was* Ephraim's, northward *it was* Manasseh's, and the sea was its border. Manasseh's territory was adjoining Asher on the north and Issachar on the east. 11And in Issachar and in Asher, Manasseh had Beth Shean and its towns, Ibleam and its towns, the inhabitants of Dor and its towns, the inhabitants of En Dor and its towns, the inhabitants of Taanach and its towns, and the inhabitants of Megiddo and its towns—three hilly regions. 12Yet the children of Manasseh

---

16:7 aOr *Naaran* (compare 1 Chronicles 7:28)
17:2 aCalled *Jeezer* in Numbers 26:30

could not drive out *the inhabitants of* those cities, but the Canaanites were determined to dwell in that land. ¹³And it happened, when the children of Israel grew strong, that they put the Canaanites to forced labor, but did not utterly drive them out.

More Land for Ephraim and Manasseh

¹⁴Then the children of Joseph spoke to Joshua, saying, "Why have you given us *only* one lot and one share to inherit, since we *are* a great people, inasmuch as the LORD has blessed us until now?"

¹⁵So Joshua answered them, "If you *are* a great people, *then* go up to the forest *country* and clear a place for yourself there in the land of the Perizzites and the giants, since the mountains of Ephraim are too confined for you."

¹⁶But the children of Joseph said, "The mountain country is not enough for us; and all the Canaanites who dwell in the land of the valley have chariots of iron, *both those* who *are* of Beth Shean and its towns and *those* who *are* of the Valley of Jezreel."

¹⁷And Joshua spoke to the house of Joseph—to Ephraim and Manasseh—saying, "You *are* a great people and have great power; you shall not have *only* one lot, ¹⁸but the mountain country shall be yours. Although it *is* wooded, you shall cut it down, and its farthest extent shall be yours; for you shall drive out the Canaanites, though they have iron chariots *and* are strong."

The Remainder of the Land Divided

18 Now the whole congregation of the children of Israel assembled together at Shiloh, and set up the tabernacle of meeting there. And the land was subdued before them. ²But there remained among the children of Israel seven tribes which had not yet received their inheritance.

³Then Joshua said to the children of Israel: "How long will you neglect to go and possess the land which the LORD God of your fathers has given you? ⁴Pick out from among you three men for *each* tribe, and I will send them; they shall rise and go through the land, survey it according to their inheritance, and come *back* to me. ⁵And they shall divide it into seven parts.

Judah shall remain in their territory on the south, and the house of Joseph shall remain in their territory on the north. ⁶You shall therefore survey the land in seven parts and bring *the survey* here to me, that I may cast lots for you here before the LORD our God. ⁷But the Levites have no part among you, for the priesthood of the LORD *is* their inheritance. And Gad, Reuben, and half the tribe of Manasseh have received their inheritance beyond the Jordan on the east, which Moses the servant of the LORD gave them."

⁸Then the men arose to go away; and Joshua charged those who went to survey the land, saying, "Go, walk through the land, survey it, and come back to me, that I may cast lots for you here before the LORD in Shiloh." ⁹So the men went, passed through the land, and wrote the survey in a book in seven parts by cities; and they came to Joshua at the camp in Shiloh. ¹⁰Then Joshua cast lots for them in Shiloh before the LORD, and there Joshua divided the land to the children of Israel according to their divisions.

The Land of Benjamin

¹¹Now the lot of the tribe of the children of Benjamin came up according to their families, and the territory of their lot came out between the children of Judah and the children of Joseph. ¹²Their border on the north side began at the Jordan, and the border went up to the side of Jericho on the north, and went up through the mountains westward; it ended at the Wilderness of Beth Aven. ¹³The border went over from there toward Luz, to the side of Luz (which *is* Bethel) southward; and the border descended to Ataroth Addar, near the hill that *lies* on the south side of Lower Beth Horon.

¹⁴Then the border extended around the west side to the south, from the hill that *lies* before Beth Horon southward; and it ended at Kirjath Baal (which *is* Kirjath Jearim), a city of the children of Judah. This *was* the west side.

¹⁵The south side *began* at the end of Kirjath Jearim, and the border extended on the west and went out to the spring of the waters of Nephtoah. ¹⁶Then the border

came down to the end of the mountain that *lies* before the Valley of the Son of Hinnom, which *is* in the Valley of the Rephaim[a] on the north, descended to the Valley of Hinnom, to the side of the Jebusite *city* on the south, and descended to En Rogel. [17]And it went around from the north, went out to En Shemesh, and extended toward Geliloth, which *is* before the Ascent of Adummim, and descended to the stone of Bohan the son of Reuben. [18]Then it passed along toward the north side of Arabah,[a] and went down to Arabah. [19]And the border passed along to the north side of Beth Hoglah; then the border ended at the north bay at the Salt Sea, at the south end of the Jordan. This *was* the southern boundary.

[20]The Jordan was its border on the east side. This *was* the inheritance of the children of Benjamin, according to its boundaries all around, according to their families.

[21]Now the cities of the tribe of the children of Benjamin, according to their families, were Jericho, Beth Hoglah, Emek Keziz, [22]Beth Arabah, Zemaraim, Bethel, [23]Avim, Parah, Ophrah, [24]Chephar Haammoni, Ophni, and Gaba: twelve cities with their villages; [25]Gibeon, Ramah, Beeroth, [26]Mizpah, Chephirah, Mozah, [27]Rekem, Irpeel, Taralah, [28]Zelah, Eleph, Jebus (which *is* Jerusalem), Gibeath, *and* Kirjath: fourteen cities with their villages. This was the inheritance of the children of Benjamin according to their families.

Simeon's Inheritance with Judah

19 The second lot came out for Simeon, for the tribe of the children of Simeon according to their families. And their inheritance was within the inheritance of the children of Judah. [2]They had in their inheritance Beersheba (Sheba), Moladah, [3]Hazar Shual, Balah, Ezem, [4]Eltolad, Bethul, Hormah, [5]Ziklag, Beth Marcaboth, Hazar Susah, [6]Beth Lebaoth, and Sharuhen: thirteen cities and their villages; [7]Ain, Rimmon, Ether, and Ashan: four cities and their villages; [8]and all the villages that *were* all around these cities as far as Baalath Beer, Ramah of the South. This *was* the inheritance of the tribe of the

children of Simeon according to their families.

[9]The inheritance of the children of Simeon *was included* in the share of the children of Judah, for the share of the children of Judah was too much for them. Therefore the children of Simeon had *their* inheritance within the inheritance of that people.

The Land of Zebulun

[10]The third lot came out for the children of Zebulun according to their families, and the border of their inheritance was as far as Sarid. [11]Their border went toward the west and to Maralah, went to Dabbasheth, and extended along the brook that is east of Jokneam. [12]Then from Sarid it went eastward toward the sunrise along the border of Chisloth Tabor, and went out toward Daberath, bypassing Japhia. [13]And from there it passed along on the east of Gath Hepher, toward Eth Kazin, and extended to Rimmon, which borders on Neah. [14]Then the border went around it on the north side of Hannathon, and it ended in the Valley of Jiphthah El. [15]Included were Kattath, Nahallal, Shimron, Idalah, and Bethlehem: twelve cities with their villages. [16]This *was* the inheritance of the children of Zebulun according to their families, these cities with their villages.

The Land of Issachar

[17]The fourth lot came out to Issachar, for the children of Issachar according to their families. [18]And their territory went to Jezreel, and *included* Chesulloth, Shunem, [19]Haphraim, Shion, Anaharath, [20]Rabbith, Kishion, Abez, [21]Remeth, En Gannim, En Haddah, and Beth Pazzez. [22]And the border reached to Tabor, Shahazimah, and Beth Shemesh; their border ended at the Jordan: sixteen cities with their villages. [23]This *was* the inheritance of the tribe of the children of Issachar according to their families, the cities and their villages.

The Land of Asher

[24]The fifth lot came out for the tribe of the children of Asher according to their families. [25]And their territory included Helkath, Hali, Beten, Achshaph, [26]Alammelech, Amad, and Mishal; it reached to

---

18:16 [a]Literally *Giants*
18:18 [a]Or *Beth Arabah* (compare 15:6 and 18:22)

Mount Carmel westward, along *the Brook* Shihor Libnath. [27]It turned toward the sunrise to Beth Dagon; and it reached to Zebulun and to the Valley of Jiphthah El, then northward beyond Beth Emek and Neiel, bypassing Cabul *which was* on the left, [28]including Ebron,[a] Rehob, Hammon, and Kanah, as far as Greater Sidon. [29]And the border turned to Ramah and to the fortified city of Tyre; then the border turned to Hosah, and ended at the sea by the region of Achzib. [30]Also Ummah, Aphek, and Rehob *were included:* twenty-two cities with their villages. [31]This *was* the inheritance of the tribe of the children of Asher according to their families, these cities with their villages.

The Land of Naphtali

[32]The sixth lot came out to the children of Naphtali, for the children of Naphtali according to their families. [33]And their border began at Heleph, enclosing the territory from the terebinth tree in Zaanannim, Adami Nekeb, and Jabneel, as far as Lakkum; it ended at the Jordan. [34]From Heleph the border extended westward to Aznoth Tabor, and went out from there toward Hukkok; it adjoined Zebulun on the south side and Asher on the west side, and ended at Judah by the Jordan toward the sunrise. [35]And the fortified cities *are* Ziddim, Zer, Hammath, Rakkath, Chinnereth, [36]Adamah, Ramah, Hazor, [37]Kedesh, Edrei, En Hazor, [38]Iron, Migdal El, Horem, Beth Anath, and Beth Shemesh: nineteen cities with their villages. [39]This *was* the inheritance of the tribe of the children of Naphtali according to their families, the cities and their villages.

The Land of Dan

[40]The seventh lot came out for the tribe of the children of Dan according to their families. [41]And the territory of their inheritance was Zorah, Eshtaol, Ir Shemesh, [42]Shaalabbin, Aijalon, Jethlah, [43]Elon, Timnah, Ekron, [44]Eltekeh, Gibbethon, Baalath, [45]Jehud, Bene Berak, Gath Rimmon, [46]Me Jarkon, and Rakkon, with the region near Joppa. [47]And the border of the children of Dan went beyond these, because the children of Dan went up to fight against Leshem and took it; and they struck it with the edge of the sword, took possession of it, and dwelt in it. They called Leshem, Dan, after the name of Dan their father. [48]This *is* the inheritance of the tribe of the children of Dan according to their families, these cities with their villages.

19:28 [a]Following Masoretic Text, Targum, and Vulgate; a few Hebrew manuscripts read *Abdon* (compare 21:30 and 1 Chronicles 6:74).

ROMANCE FAQ

Q: What questions can I ask to better connect emotionally with my spouse?

Here's a question I initially asked Barbara on a date night, "What is the most courageous thing you've ever done?" Try that question on a date night, and give her time to think about her answer. You also might consider sharing how *you* would answer the question.

Here are a dozen other questions to help you make the connection:

1. What is one of your earliest childhood memories?

2. What one thing from your past do you struggle with?

3. What was one of your proudest achievements before we met?

4. What was your relationship with your dad like? How about your mom?

5. When did you place your faith in Christ as your Savior? What were the circumstances?

6. What would you name as our best family vacation, and why?

7. What is your favorite book in the Bible? Hymn? Why?

8. If you could live anywhere in the world, where would you like to live?

9. What dreams do you have for our children?

10. What do you long to experience with me in our marriage?

11. What do you want to accomplish after the kids are grown?

12. What is your mission and purpose for life? If you could give your life for any cause, what would that cause be?

Joshua's Inheritance

⁴⁹When they had made an end of dividing the land as an inheritance according to their borders, the children of Israel gave an inheritance among them to Joshua the son of Nun. ⁵⁰According to the word of the LORD they gave him the city which he asked for, Timnath Serah in the mountains of Ephraim; and he built the city and dwelt in it.

⁵¹These *were* the inheritances which Eleazar the priest, Joshua the son of Nun, and the heads of the fathers of the tribes of the children of Israel divided as an inheritance by lot in Shiloh before the LORD, at the door of the tabernacle of meeting. So they made an end of dividing the country.

The Cities of Refuge

20 The LORD also spoke to Joshua, saying, ²"Speak to the children of Israel, saying: 'Appoint for yourselves cities of refuge, of which I spoke to you through Moses, ³that the slayer who kills a person accidentally *or* unintentionally may flee there; and they shall be your refuge from the avenger of blood. ⁴And when he flees to one of those cities, and stands at the entrance of the gate of the city, and declares his case in the hearing of the elders of that city, they shall take him into the city as one of them, and give him a place, that he may dwell among them. ⁵Then if the avenger of blood pursues him, they shall not deliver the slayer into his hand, because he struck his neighbor unintentionally, but did not hate him beforehand. ⁶And he shall dwell in that city until he stands before the congregation for judgment, *and* until the death of the one who is high priest in those days. Then the slayer may return and come to his own city and his own house, to the city from which he fled.' "

⁷So they appointed Kedesh in Galilee, in the mountains of Naphtali, Shechem in the mountains of Ephraim, and Kirjath Arba (which *is* Hebron) in the mountains of Judah. ⁸And on the other side of the Jordan, by Jericho eastward, they assigned Bezer in the wilderness on the plain, from the tribe of Reuben, Ramoth in Gilead, from the tribe of Gad, and Golan in Bashan, from the tribe of Manasseh. ⁹These were the cities appointed for all the children of Israel and for the stranger who dwelt among them, that whoever killed a person accidentally might flee there, and not die by the hand of the avenger of blood until he stood before the congregation.

Cities of the Levites

21 Then the heads of the fathers' *houses* of the Levites came near to Eleazar the priest, to Joshua the son of Nun, and to the heads of the fathers' *houses* of the tribes of the children of Israel. ²And they spoke to them at Shiloh in the land of Canaan, saying, "The LORD commanded through Moses to give us cities to dwell in, with their commonlands for our livestock." ³So the children of Israel gave to the Levites from their inheritance, at the commandment of the LORD, these cities and their common-lands:

⁴Now the lot came out for the families of the Kohathites. And the children of Aaron the priest, *who were* of the Levites, had thirteen cities by lot from the tribe of Judah, from the tribe of Simeon, and from the tribe of Benjamin. ⁵The rest of the children of Kohath had ten cities by lot from the families of the tribe of Ephraim, from the tribe of Dan, and from the half-tribe of Manasseh.

⁶And the children of Gershon had thirteen cities by lot from the families of the tribe of Issachar, from the tribe of Asher, from the tribe of Naphtali, and from the half-tribe of Manasseh in Bashan.

⁷The children of Merari according to their families had twelve cities from the tribe of Reuben, from the tribe of Gad, and from the tribe of Zebulun.

⁸And the children of Israel gave these cities with their common-lands by lot to the Levites, as the LORD had commanded by the hand of Moses.

⁹So they gave from the tribe of the children of Judah and from the tribe of the children of Simeon these cities which are designated by name, ¹⁰which were for the children of Aaron, one of the families of the Kohathites, *who were* of the children of Levi; for the lot was theirs first. ¹¹And they gave them Kirjath Arba (*Arba was* the father of Anak), which *is* Hebron, in the mountains of Judah, with the common-land

surrounding it. [12]But the fields of the city and its villages they gave to Caleb the son of Jephunneh as his possession.

[13]Thus to the children of Aaron the priest they gave Hebron with its common-land (a city of refuge for the slayer), Libnah with its common-land, [14]Jattir with its common-land, Eshtemoa with its common-land, [15]Holon with its common-land, Debir with its common-land, [16]Ain with its common-land, Juttah with its common-land, and Beth Shemesh with its common-land: nine cities from those two tribes; [17]and from the tribe of Benjamin, Gibeon with its common-land, Geba with its common-land, [18]Anathoth with its common-land, and Almon with its common-land: four cities. [19]All the cities of the children of Aaron, the priests, *were* thirteen cities with their common-lands.

[20]And the families of the children of Kohath, the Levites, the rest of the children of Kohath, even they had the cities of their lot from the tribe of Ephraim. [21]For they gave them Shechem with its common-land in the mountains of Ephraim (a city of refuge for the slayer), Gezer with its common-land, [22]Kibzaim with its common-land, and Beth Horon with its common-land: four cities; [23]and from the tribe of Dan, Eltekeh with its common-land, Gibbethon with its common-land, [24]Aijalon with its common-land, *and* Gath Rimmon with its common-land: four cities; [25]and from the half-tribe of Manasseh, Tanach with its common-land and Gath Rimmon with its common-land: two cities. [26]All the ten cities with their common-lands were for the rest of the families of the children of Kohath.

[27]Also to the children of Gershon, of the families of the Levites, from the *other* half-tribe of Manasseh, *they gave* Golan in Bashan with its common-land (a city of refuge for the slayer), and Be Eshterah with its common-land: two cities; [28]and from the tribe of Issachar, Kishion with its common-land, Daberath with its common-land, [29]Jarmuth with its common-land, *and* En Gannim with its common-land: four cities; [30]and from the tribe of Asher, Mishal with its common-land, Abdon with its common-land, [31]Helkath with its common-land, and Rehob with its common-land: four cities; [32]and from the tribe of

Naphtali, Kedesh in Galilee with its common-land (a city of refuge for the slayer), Hammoth Dor with its common-land, and Kartan with its common-land: three cities. [33]All the cities of the Gershonites according to their families *were* thirteen cities with their common-lands.

[34]And to the families of the children of Merari, the rest of the Levites, from the tribe of Zebulun, Jokneam with its common-land, Kartah with its common-land, [35]Dimnah with its common-land, *and* Nahalal with its common-land: four cities; [36]and from the tribe of Reuben, Bezer with its common-land, Jahaz with its common-land, [37]Kedemoth with its common-land, and Mephaath with its common-land: four cities;[a] [38]and from the tribe of Gad, Ramoth in Gilead with its common-land (a city of refuge for the slayer), Mahanaim with its common-land, [39]Heshbon with its common-land, *and* Jazer with its common-land: four cities in all. [40]So all the cities for the children of Merari according to their families, the rest of the families of the Levites, were *by* their lot twelve cities.

[41]All the cities of the Levites within the possession of the children of Israel *were* forty-eight cities with their common-lands. [42]Every one of these cities had its common-land surrounding it; thus *were* all these cities.

The Promise Fulfilled

[43]So the LORD gave to Israel all the land of which He had sworn to give to their fathers, and they took possession of it and dwelt in it. [44]The LORD gave them rest all around, according to all that He had sworn to their fathers. And not a man of all their enemies stood against them; the LORD delivered all their enemies into their hand. [45]Not a word failed of any good thing which the LORD had spoken to the house of Israel. All came to pass.

Eastern Tribes Return to Their Lands

22 Then Joshua called the Reubenites, the Gadites, and half the tribe of

---

21:37 [a]Following Septuagint and Vulgate (compare 1 Chronicles 6:78, 79); Masoretic Text, Bomberg, and Targum omit verses 36 and 37.

Manasseh, ²and said to them: "You have kept all that Moses the servant of the LORD commanded you, and have obeyed my voice in all that I commanded you. ³You have not left your brethren these many days, up to this day, but have kept the charge of the commandment of the LORD your God. ⁴And now the LORD your God has given rest to your brethren, as He promised them; now therefore, return and go to your tents *and* to the land of your possession, which Moses the servant of the LORD gave you on the other side of the Jordan. ⁵But take careful heed to do the commandment and the law which Moses the servant of the LORD commanded you, to love the LORD your God, to walk in all His ways, to keep His commandments, to hold fast to Him, and to serve Him with all your heart and with all your soul." ⁶So Joshua blessed them and sent them away, and they went to their tents.

⁷Now to half the tribe of Manasseh Moses had given a possession in Bashan, but to the *other* half of it Joshua gave *a possession* among their brethren on this side of the Jordan, westward. And indeed, when Joshua sent them away to their tents, he blessed them, ⁸and spoke to them, saying, "Return with much riches to your tents, with very much livestock, with silver, with gold, with bronze, with iron, and with very much clothing. Divide the spoil of your enemies with your brethren."

⁹So the children of Reuben, the children of Gad, and half the tribe of Manasseh returned, and departed from the children of Israel at Shiloh, which *is* in the land of Canaan, to go to the country of Gilead, to the land of their possession, which they had obtained according to the word of the LORD by the hand of Moses.

An Altar by the Jordan

¹⁰And when they came to the region of the Jordan which *is* in the land of Canaan, the children of Reuben, the children of Gad, and half the tribe of Manasseh built an altar there by the Jordan—a great, impressive altar. ¹¹Now the children of Israel heard *someone* say, "Behold, the children of Reuben, the children of Gad, and

---

PARENTING MATTERS

Q: How can we help our children get through a tragic incident?

Consider a few practical tips for helping your children through tragedy that may be on the national or local news:

For younger children:
- Recognize that some images may frighten them, so limit what they see on television.
- Talk with them about how they feel and why.
- Help them memorize helpful scriptures (Psalm 46:1; 56:3).
- Help them write a letter to the fire fighters and police officers involved in the rescue efforts.

For older children and teenagers:
- Recognize they may be concerned about their security and future; assure them that God is good (Psalm 25:8, Psalm 119:68).
- Ask them to express their feelings or write about their experiences, fears, and concerns in a journal.
- Remind them that suffering and pain are part of life.
- Help them think about these circumstances on a higher plane: "What would God have us do as Christians?" (2 Peter 3:11).
- Steer them back to God's Word.

Finally, let me encourage you to step up to the task before you. Your actions and words during a dramatic moment will have a lasting impact on the spiritual strength of the next generation. As a parent, you are important. Don't let the opportunity slip away!

half the tribe of Manasseh have built an altar on the frontier of the land of Canaan, in the region of the Jordan—on the children of Israel's side." 12And when the children of Israel heard *of it,* the whole congregation of the children of Israel gathered together at Shiloh to go to war against them.

13Then the children of Israel sent Phinehas the son of Eleazar the priest to the children of Reuben, to the children of Gad, and to half the tribe of Manasseh, into the land of Gilead, 14and with him ten rulers, one ruler each from the chief house of every tribe of Israel; and each one *was* the head of the house of his father among the divisionsa of Israel. 15Then they came to the children of Reuben, to the children of Gad, and to half the tribe of Manasseh, to the land of Gilead, and they spoke with them, saying, 16"Thus says the whole congregation of the LORD: 'What treachery *is* this that you have committed against the God of Israel, to turn away this day from following the LORD, in that you have built for yourselves an altar, that you might rebel this day against the LORD? 17*Is* the iniquity of Peor not enough for us, from which we are not cleansed till this day, although there was a plague in the congregation of the LORD, 18but that you must turn away this day from following the LORD? And it shall be, if you rebel today against the LORD, that tomorrow He will be angry with the whole congregation of Israel. 19Nevertheless, if the land of your possession *is* unclean, *then* cross over to the land of the possession of the LORD, where the LORD's tabernacle stands, and take possession among us; but do not rebel against the LORD, nor rebel against us, by building yourselves an altar besides the altar of the LORD our God. 20Did not Achan the son of Zerah commit a trespass in the accursed thing, and wrath fell on all the congregation of Israel? And that man did not perish alone in his iniquity.' "

21Then the children of Reuben, the children of Gad, and half the tribe of Manasseh answered and said to the heads of the divisionsa of Israel: 22"The LORD God of gods, the LORD God of gods, He knows, and let Israel itself know—if *it is* in rebellion, or if in treachery against the LORD, do not save us this day. 23If we have built ourselves an altar to turn from following the LORD, or if to offer on it burnt offerings or grain offerings, or if to offer peace offerings on it, let the LORD Himself require *an account.* 24But in fact we have done it for fear, for a reason, saying, 'In time to come your descendants may speak to our descendants, saying, "What have you to do with the LORD God of Israel? 25For the LORD has made the Jordan a border between you and us, *you* children of Reuben and children of Gad. You have no part in the LORD." So your descendants would make our descendants cease fearing the LORD.' 26Therefore we said, 'Let us now prepare to build ourselves an altar, not for burnt offering nor for sacrifice, 27but *that* it *may be* a witness between you and us and our generations after us, that we may perform the service of the LORD before Him with our burnt offerings, with our sacrifices, and with our peace offerings; that your descendants may not say to our descendants in time to come, "You have no part in the LORD." ' 28Therefore we said that it will be, when they say *this* to us or to our generations in time to come, that we may say, 'Here is the replica of the altar of the LORD which our fathers made, though not for burnt offerings nor for sacrifices; but it *is* a witness between us and us.' 29Far be it from us that we should rebel against the LORD, and turn from following the LORD this day, to build an altar for burnt offerings, for grain offerings, or for sacrifices, besides the altar of the LORD our God which *is* before His tabernacle."

30Now when Phinehas the priest and the rulers of the congregation, the heads of the divisionsa of Israel who *were* with him, heard the words that the children of Reuben, the children of Gad, and the children of Manasseh spoke, it pleased them. 31Then Phinehas the son of Eleazar the priest said to the children of Reuben, the children of Gad, and the children of Manasseh, "This day we perceive that the LORD *is* among us, because you have not committed this treachery against the LORD. Now you have delivered the children of Israel out of the hand of the LORD."

22:14 aLiterally *thousands* **22:21** aLiterally *thousands*
22:30 aLiterally *thousands*

³²And Phinehas the son of Eleazar the priest, and the rulers, returned from the children of Reuben and the children of Gad, from the land of Gilead to the land of Canaan, to the children of Israel, and brought back word to them. ³³So the thing pleased the children of Israel, and the children of Israel blessed God; they spoke no more of going against them in battle, to destroy the land where the children of Reuben and Gad dwelt.

³⁴The children of Reuben and the children of Gad^a called the altar, *Witness,* "For *it is* a witness between us that the LORD *is* God."

Joshua's Farewell Address

23 Now it came to pass, a long time after the LORD had given rest to Israel from all their enemies round about, that Joshua was old, advanced in age. ²And Joshua called for all Israel, for their elders, for their heads, for their judges, and for their officers, and said to them:

"I am old, advanced in age. ³You have seen all that the LORD your God has done to all these nations because of you, for the LORD your God *is* He who has fought for you. ⁴See, I have divided to you by lot these nations that remain, to be an inheritance for your tribes, from the Jordan, with all the nations that I have cut off, as far as the Great Sea westward. ⁵And the LORD your God will expel them from before you and drive them out of your sight. So you shall possess their land, as the LORD your God promised you. ⁶Therefore be very courageous to keep and to do all that is written in the Book of the Law of Moses, lest you turn aside from it to the right hand or to the left, ⁷*and* lest you go among these nations, these who remain among you. You shall not make mention of the name of their gods, nor cause *anyone* to swear *by them;* you shall not serve them nor bow down to them, ⁸but you shall hold fast to the LORD your God, as you have done to this day. ⁹For the LORD has driven out from before you great and strong nations; but *as for*

you, no one has been able to stand against you to this day. ¹⁰One man of you shall chase a thousand, for the LORD your God *is* He who fights for you, as He promised you. ¹¹Therefore take careful heed to yourselves, that you love the LORD your God. ¹²Or else, if indeed you do go back, and cling to the remnant of these nations—these that remain among you—and make marriages with them, and go in to them and they to you, ¹³know for certain that the LORD your God will no longer drive out these nations from before you. But they shall be snares and traps to you, and scourges on your sides and thorns in your eyes, until you perish from this good land which the LORD your God has given you.

¹⁴"Behold, this day I *am* going the way of all the earth. And you know in all your hearts and in all your souls that not one thing has failed of all the good things which the LORD your God spoke concerning you. All have come to pass for you; not one word of them has failed. ¹⁵Therefore it shall come to pass, that as all the good things have come upon you which the LORD your God promised you, so the LORD will bring upon you all harmful things, until He has destroyed you from this good land which the LORD your God has given you. ¹⁶When you have transgressed the covenant of the LORD your God, which He commanded you, and have gone and served other gods, and bowed down to them, then the anger of the LORD will burn against you, and you shall perish quickly from the good land which He has given you."

The Covenant at Shechem

24 Then Joshua gathered all the tribes of Israel to Shechem and called for the elders of Israel, for their heads, for their judges, and for their officers; and they presented themselves before God. ²And Joshua said to all the people, "Thus says the LORD God of Israel: 'Your fathers, *including* Terah, the father of Abraham and the father of Nahor, dwelt on the other side of the River^a in old times; and they served other gods. ³Then I took your father Abraham from the other side of the River, led him throughout all the land of Canaan,

---

22:34 ^aSeptuagint adds *and half the tribe of Manasseh.*
24:2 ^aHebrew *Nahar,* the Euphrates, and so in verses 3, 14, and 15

Give Your Children God's Vision

OUR ASSIGNMENT AS PARENTS is not only to impart to our kids our knowledge of God, but also to give them a vision for their world. That's what Joshua did, "Choose for yourselves this day whom you will serve, whether the gods which your fathers served that were on the other side of the River, or the gods of the Amorites, in whose land you dwell. But as for me and my house, we will serve the LORD" (24:15).

You do this just as Joshua did it. Pray for your children, that God's plan for their lives will be fulfilled. Also, give them a vision for the world. How? When you come home from work, tell them stories about how God showed up and is changing lives at your place of employment. When you go on family vacations, look for ways on the road to get them involved in God's kingdom work.

You and I are a part of a generational relay race in which we must make a good handoff to the next generation. Remember, your marriage and family are the headwaters of your legacy. What occurs downstream in history with your kids will flow only as strong as the source at home.

___

and multiplied his descendants and gave him Isaac. [4]To Isaac I gave Jacob and Esau. To Esau I gave the mountains of Seir to possess, but Jacob and his children went down to Egypt. [5]Also I sent Moses and Aaron, and I plagued Egypt, according to what I did among them. Afterward I brought you out.

[6]'Then I brought your fathers out of Egypt, and you came to the sea; and the Egyptians pursued your fathers with chariots and horsemen to the Red Sea. [7]So they cried out to the LORD; and He put darkness between you and the Egyptians, brought the sea upon them, and covered them. And your eyes saw what I did in Egypt. Then you dwelt in the wilderness a long time. [8]And I brought you into the land of the Amorites, who dwelt on the other side of the Jordan, and they fought with you. But I gave them into your hand, that you might possess their land, and I destroyed them from before you. [9]Then Balak the son of Zippor, king of Moab, arose to make war against Israel, and sent and called Balaam the son of Beor to curse you. [10]But I would not listen to Balaam; therefore he continued to bless you. So I delivered you out of his hand. [11]Then you went over the Jordan and came to Jericho. And the men of Jericho fought against you—*also* the Amorites, the Perizzites, the Canaanites, the Hittites, the Girgashites, the Hivites, and the Jebusites. But I delivered them into your hand. [12]I sent the hornet before you which drove them out from before you, *also* the two kings of the Amorites, *but* not with your sword or with your bow. [13]I have given you a land for which you did not labor, and cities which you did not build, and you dwell in them; you eat of the vineyards and olive groves which you did not plant.'

[14]"Now therefore, fear the LORD, serve Him in sincerity and in truth, and put away the gods which your fathers served on the other side of the River and in Egypt. Serve the LORD! [15]And if it seems evil to you to serve the LORD, choose for yourselves this day whom you will serve, whether the gods which your fathers served *that were* on the other side of the River, or the gods of the Amorites, in whose land you dwell. But as for me and my house, we will serve the LORD."

[16]So the people answered and said: "Far be it from us that we should forsake the LORD to serve other gods; [17]for the LORD our God *is* He who brought us and our fathers up out of the land of Egypt, from the house of bondage, who did those great signs in our sight, and preserved us in all the way that we went and among all the people through whom we passed. [18]And the LORD drove out from before us all the people, including the Amorites who dwelt in the land. We also will serve the LORD, for He *is* our God."

[19]But Joshua said to the people, "You cannot serve the LORD, for He *is* a holy God. He *is* a jealous God; He will not forgive your transgressions nor your sins. [20]If you forsake the LORD and serve foreign

gods, then He will turn and do you harm and consume you, after He has done you good."

²¹And the people said to Joshua, "No, but we will serve the LORD!"

²²So Joshua said to the people, "You *are* witnesses against yourselves that you have chosen the LORD for yourselves, to serve Him."

And they said, "*We are* witnesses!"

²³"Now therefore," *he said,* "put away the foreign gods which *are* among you, and incline your heart to the LORD God of Israel."

²⁴And the people said to Joshua, "The LORD our God we will serve, and His voice we will obey!"

²⁵So Joshua made a covenant with the people that day, and made for them a statute and an ordinance in Shechem.

²⁶Then Joshua wrote these words in the Book of the Law of God. And he took a large stone, and set it up there under the oak that *was* by the sanctuary of the LORD.

²⁷And Joshua said to all the people, "Behold, this stone shall be a witness to us, for it has heard all the words of the LORD which He spoke to us. It shall therefore be a witness to you, lest you deny your God."

²⁸So Joshua let the people depart, each to his own inheritance.

Death of Joshua and Eleazar

²⁹Now it came to pass after these things that Joshua the son of Nun, the servant of the LORD, died, *being* one hundred and ten years old. ³⁰And they buried him within the border of his inheritance at Timnath Serah, which *is* in the mountains of Ephraim, on the north side of Mount Gaash.

³¹Israel served the LORD all the days of Joshua, and all the days of the elders who outlived Joshua, who had known all the works of the LORD which He had done for Israel.

³²The bones of Joseph, which the children of Israel had brought up out of Egypt, they buried at Shechem, in the plot of ground which Jacob had bought from the sons of Hamor the father of Shechem for one hundred pieces of silver, and which had become an inheritance of the children of Joseph.

³³And Eleazar the son of Aaron died. They buried him in a hill *belonging to* Phinehas his son, which was given to him in the mountains of Ephraim.

JUDGES

FOR ABOUT 350 YEARS—from the time Joshua led the people into the Promised Land until Saul became the first king of Israel—God raised up fourteen unique leaders who served and protected His people. The book of Judges records how God worked through twelve of these fourteen judges of Israel to deliver the nation from its enemies.

Some of these judges bear familiar names: Deborah, Gideon, and Samson, for example. Most lack the fame of their better-known counterparts, but their stories have just as much to teach us. By reading the accounts of less famous judges such as Othniel, Ehud, Jephthah, and others, you will gain insight both into God's character and His deep concern for His people.

As you read these accounts—many of them bloody and even disheartening—you'll begin to see a pattern. During times of peace and prosperity, the Israelites forget or ignore God and so become disobedient and idolatrous. In response, God brings discipline to His people by allowing their enemies to conquer and enslave them. This prompts the people to repent and cry out to God for deliverance, and once more God graciously raises up a judge who leads the people to victory.

Too often during these days, God's people committed one of their worst compromises: They intermarried with their pagan neighbors, the Canaanites. Samson's story revolves around his lustful desire to marry a Canaanite wife, and the Bible does not shrink from showing us the disastrous consequences of his union. God's prohibition against intermarriage with the nations surrounding Israel was not based on racial differences, but on the essential spiritual differences between the two groups. The Israelites and the Canaanites worshiped and served totally different gods!

Accounts like these show us the tremendous wisdom behind the New Testament command that forbids a believer to be "unequally yoked together" with an unbeliever (2 Cor. 6:14, 15). Spiritual union is the foundation of every healthy and God-honoring marriage, and we can no more expect God to bless and delight in spiritually mixed marriages today than He did in the dark era of the judges.

The Continuing Conquest of Canaan

1 Now after the death of Joshua it came to pass that the children of Israel asked the LORD, saying, "Who shall be first to go up for us against the Canaanites to fight against them?"

²And the LORD said, "Judah shall go up. Indeed I have delivered the land into his hand."

³So Judah said to Simeon his brother, "Come up with me to my allotted territory, that we may fight against the Canaanites; and I will likewise go with you to your allotted territory." And Simeon went with him. ⁴Then Judah went up, and the LORD delivered the Canaanites and the Perizzites into their hand; and they killed ten thousand men at Bezek. ⁵And they found Adoni-Bezek in Bezek, and fought against him; and they defeated the Canaanites and the Perizzites. ⁶Then Adoni-Bezek fled, and they pursued him and caught him and cut off his thumbs and big toes. ⁷And Adoni-Bezek said, "Seventy kings with their thumbs and big toes cut off used to gather *scraps* under my table; as I have done, so God has repaid me." Then they brought him to Jerusalem, and there he died.

⁸Now the children of Judah fought against Jerusalem and took it; they struck it with the edge of the sword and set the city on fire. ⁹And afterward the children of Judah went down to fight against the Canaanites who dwelt in the mountains, in the South,ᵃ and in the lowland. ¹⁰Then Judah went against the Canaanites who dwelt in Hebron. (Now the name of Hebron *was* formerly Kirjath Arba.) And they killed Sheshai, Ahiman, and Talmai.

¹¹From there they went against the inhabitants of Debir. (The name of Debir *was* formerly Kirjath Sepher.) ¹²Then Caleb said, "Whoever attacks Kirjath Sepher and takes it, to him I will give my daughter Achsah as wife." ¹³And Othniel the son of Kenaz, Caleb's younger brother, took it; so he gave him his daughter Achsah as wife. ¹⁴Now it happened, when she came *to him,* that she urged himᵃ to ask her father for a field. And she dismounted

from *her* donkey, and Caleb said to her, "What do you wish?" ¹⁵So she said to him, "Give me a blessing; since you have given me land in the South, give me also springs of water."

INTIMATE MOMENTS

When the house is quiet, light some candles, play some soft music, and dance cheek-to-cheek with your husband. Clear off a place on the floor (you don't want him to go sprawling over a toy truck, poorly placed) and turn it into your own private dance studio. Make it a dance he will never forget!

And Caleb gave her the upper springs and the lower springs.

¹⁶Now the children of the Kenite, Moses' father-in-law, went up from the City of Palms with the children of Judah into the Wilderness of Judah, which *lies* in the South *near* Arad; and they went and dwelt among the people. ¹⁷And Judah went with his brother Simeon, and they attacked the Canaanites who inhabited Zephath, and utterly destroyed it. So the name of the city was called Hormah. ¹⁸Also Judah took Gaza with its territory, Ashkelon with its territory, and Ekron with its territory. ¹⁹So the LORD was with Judah. And they drove out the mountaineers, but they could not drive out the inhabitants of the lowland, because they had chariots of iron. ²⁰And they gave Hebron to Caleb, as Moses had said. Then he expelled from there the three sons of Anak. ²¹But the children of Benjamin did not drive out the Jebusites who inhabited Jerusalem; so the Jebusites dwell with the children of Benjamin in Jerusalem to this day.

²²And the house of Joseph also went up against Bethel, and the LORD *was* with them. ²³So the house of Joseph sent men to spy out Bethel. (The name of the city *was* formerly Luz.) ²⁴And when the spies saw a man coming out of the city, they said to him, "Please show us the entrance to the city, and

---

1:9 ᵃHebrew *Negev,* and so throughout this book
1:14 ᵃSeptuagint and Vulgate read *he urged her.*

we will show you mercy." 25So he showed them the entrance to the city, and they struck the city with the edge of the sword; but they let the man and all his family go. 26And the man went to the land of the Hittites, built a city, and called its name Luz, which *is* its name to this day.

Incomplete Conquest of the Land

27However, Manasseh did not drive out *the inhabitants of* Beth Shean and its villages, or Taanach and its villages, or the inhabitants of Dor and its villages, or the inhabitants of Ibleam and its villages, or the inhabitants of Megiddo and its villages; for the Canaanites were determined to dwell in that land. 28And it came to pass, when Israel was strong, that they put the Canaanites under tribute, but did not completely drive them out.

29Nor did Ephraim drive out the Canaanites who dwelt in Gezer; so the Canaanites dwelt in Gezer among them.

30Nor did Zebulun drive out the inhabitants of Kitron or the inhabitants of Nahalol; so the Canaanites dwelt among them, and were put under tribute.

31Nor did Asher drive out the inhabitants of Acco or the inhabitants of Sidon, or of Ahlab, Achzib, Helbah, Aphik, or Rehob. 32So the Asherites dwelt among the Canaanites, the inhabitants of the land; for they did not drive them out.

33Nor did Naphtali drive out the inhabitants of Beth Shemesh or the inhabitants of Beth Anath; but they dwelt among the Canaanites, the inhabitants of the land. Nevertheless the inhabitants of Beth Shemesh and Beth Anath were put under tribute to them.

34And the Amorites forced the children of Dan into the mountains, for they would not allow them to come down to the valley; 35and the Amorites were determined to dwell in Mount Heres, in Aijalon, and in Shaalbim;a yet when the strength of the house of Joseph became greater, they were put under tribute.

36Now the boundary of the Amorites *was* from the Ascent of Akrabbim, from Sela, and upward.

Israel's Disobedience

2 Then the Angel of the LORD came up from Gilgal to Bochim, and said: "I led you up from Egypt and brought you to the land of which I swore to your fathers; and I said, 'I will never break My covenant with you. 2And you shall make no covenant with the inhabitants of this land; you shall tear down their altars.' But you have not obeyed My voice. Why have you done this? 3Therefore I also said, 'I will not drive them out before you; but they shall be *thorns* in your

---

1:35 aSpelled *Shaalabbin* in Joshua 19:42

How to Rebuild a Culture

God established the family as His primary way for passing on the truth of His Word from one generation to the next. When parents don't pass a godly legacy to their children, the entire nation suffers. The whole book of Judges illustrates this ugly truth.

You may remember a time when our families and our nation were guided by biblical principles, a time when divorce was a disgrace, when the roles of men and women were much clearer, when fathers and mothers were more tuned-in to their children. Even most Americans who did not know Christ as Savior believed in a morality somehow based on the Bible.

At some point, the family began to deteriorate. Homes broke apart and more children grew up without a mom or dad. The biblical chain of one generation passing its godly values on to the next snapped, and soon the culture drifted from its moral moorings.

Why? Because, as my friend and pastor Dr. Robert Lewis states, "Family is culture." One family plus one family, multiplied exponentially, creates a culture. But if societies are destroyed one family at a time, they are rebuilt in the same way.

And that's *our* job as Christian parents.

side,[a] and their gods shall be a snare to you.' " [4]So it was, when the Angel of the LORD spoke these words to all the children of Israel, that the people lifted up their voices and wept.

[5]Then they called the name of that place Bochim;[a] and they sacrificed there to the LORD. [6]And when Joshua had dismissed the people, the children of Israel went each to his own inheritance to possess the land.

Death of Joshua

[7]So the people served the LORD all the days of Joshua, and all the days of the elders who outlived Joshua, who had seen all the great works of the LORD which He had done for Israel. [8]Now Joshua the son of Nun, the servant of the LORD, died *when he was* one hundred and ten years old. [9]And they buried him within the border of his inheritance at Timnath Heres, in the mountains of Ephraim, on the north side of Mount Gaash. [10]When all that generation had been gathered to their fathers, another generation arose after them who did not know the LORD nor the work which He had done for Israel.

Israel's Unfaithfulness

[11]Then the children of Israel did evil in the sight of the LORD, and served the Baals; [12]and they forsook the LORD God of their fathers, who had brought them out of the land of Egypt; and they followed other gods from *among* the gods of the people who *were* all around them, and they bowed down to them; and they provoked the LORD to anger. [13]They forsook the LORD and served Baal and the Ashtoreths.[a] [14]And the anger of the LORD was hot against Israel. So He delivered them into the hands of plunderers who despoiled them; and He sold them into the hands of their enemies all around, so that they could no longer stand before their enemies. [15]Wherever they went out, the hand of the LORD was against them for calamity, as the LORD had said, and as the LORD had sworn to them. And they were greatly distressed.

[16]Nevertheless, the LORD raised up judges

BIBLICAL INSIGHTS • 2:22, 23

This Is War

JUST AS THE NATION OF ISRAEL was called upon to fight its enemies in the Promised Land (2:22, 23), so are we called upon as parents to take on spiritual enemies on behalf of our children. Remember, when Israel refused to go on the offensive against her enemies, those enemies became a snare and a trap. Here are some suggestions:

- Realize that you and your family live on a spiritual battlefield.
- Your mate is not your enemy; go to war *alongside* your mate *against* your common enemy!
- Stand firm, remember you're on the winning side, and let God's Word be your guide (see Eph. 6:13–17).
- Pray without ceasing and give thanks in everything (see 1 Thess. 5:17, 18).
- Don't take temptation lightly; flee immorality (see 2 Tim. 2:22).
- Walk by faith, not by what you feel and see (see 2 Cor. 5:7).
- The body of Christ is mighty when we unite, so join forces with others in opposing evil.

Fighting the darkness is critical if we are to have spiritually strong families. Let's gear up and head to the battlefront, which for most of us is as close as the kitchen. For others, their battlefront may be confronting a family member who is in the process of making foolish decisions that will impact him adversely for the rest of his life.

who delivered them out of the hand of those who plundered them. [17]Yet they would not listen to their judges, but they played the harlot with other gods, and bowed down to them. They turned quickly from the way in which their fathers walked, in obeying the commandments of the LORD; they did not do so. [18]And when the LORD raised up judges for them, the LORD was

2:3 [a]Septuagint, Targum, and Vulgate read *enemies to you.* **2:5** [a]Literally *Weeping* **2:13** [a]Canaanite goddesses

with the judge and delivered them out of the hand of their enemies all the days of the judge; for the LORD was moved to pity by their groaning because of those who oppressed them and harassed them. [19]And it came to pass, when the judge was dead, that they reverted and behaved more corruptly than their fathers, by following other gods, to serve them and bow down to them. They did not cease from their own doings nor from their stubborn way.

[20]Then the anger of the LORD was hot against Israel; and He said, "Because this nation has transgressed My covenant which I commanded their fathers, and has not heeded My voice, [21]I also will no longer drive out before them any of the nations which Joshua left when he died, [22]so that through them I may test Israel, whether they will keep the ways of the LORD, to walk in them as their fathers kept *them,* or not." [23]Therefore the LORD left those nations, without driving them out immediately; nor did He deliver them into the hand of Joshua.

ROMANCE FAQ

Q: *I understand that being a good spiritual leader for my wife and family will enhance our romantic life. In what ways specifically can I lead?*

Here are some suggestions:

1. Pray daily with her.
2. Write a love letter that she'd like to receive.
3. Discover her top three needs and over the next twelve months, go all out to meet them.
4. Buy her a rose. Take her in your arms. Hold her face gently. Look into her eyes and say, "I'd marry you all over again!"
5. Take her on a weekend getaway.
6. Read the scriptures to her.
7. Replace the "D" word (divorce) with the "C" word (commitment)!
8. Court her.
9. Remain faithful to her.
10. Fulfill your marriage covenant (see p. 156).
11. Have a family time at least one night a week.
12. Use circumstances to teach your children to trust God.
13. Protect your family from evil.
14. Be involved in issues facing your teenager.
15. Set spiritual goals for your children.
16. Take one or two of your children on mission trips.
17. Catch your kids doing something right and cheer them on.
18. Date your daughters.
19. Inspect what you expect.
20. Do a Proverbs breakfast Bible study with your teens.

The Nations Remaining in the Land

3 Now these *are* the nations which the LORD left, that He might test Israel by them, *that is,* all who had not known any of the wars in Canaan [2](*this was* only so that the generations of the children of Israel might be taught to know war, at least those who had not formerly known it), [3]*namely,* five lords of the Philistines, all the Canaanites, the Sidonians, and the Hivites who dwelt in Mount Lebanon, from Mount Baal Hermon to the entrance of Hamath. [4]And they were *left, that He might* test Israel by them, to know whether they would obey the commandments of the LORD, which He had commanded their fathers by the hand of Moses.

[5]Thus the children of Israel dwelt among the Canaanites, the Hittites, the Amorites, the Perizzites, the Hivites, and the Jebusites. [6]And they took their daughters to be their wives, and gave their daughters to their sons; and they served their gods.

Othniel

[7]So the children of Israel did evil in the sight of the LORD. They forgot the LORD their God, and served the Baals and Asherahs.[a] [8]Therefore the anger of the LORD was hot against Israel, and He sold them into the hand of Cushan-Rishathaim king of Mesopotamia; and the children of Israel served Cushan-Rishathaim eight years. [9]When the children of Israel cried out to the

---

3:7 [a]Name or symbol for Canaanite goddesses

LORD, the LORD raised up a deliverer for the children of Israel, who delivered them: Othniel the son of Kenaz, Caleb's younger brother. [10]The Spirit of the LORD came upon him, and he judged Israel. He went out to war, and the LORD delivered Cushan-Rishathaim king of Mesopotamia into his hand; and his hand prevailed over Cushan-Rishathaim. [11]So the land had rest for forty years. Then Othniel the son of Kenaz died.

Ehud

[12]And the children of Israel again did evil in the sight of the LORD. So the LORD strengthened Eglon king of Moab against Israel, because they had done evil in the sight of the LORD. [13]Then he gathered to himself the people of Ammon and Amalek, went and defeated Israel, and took possession of the City of Palms. [14]So the children of Israel served Eglon king of Moab eighteen years.

[15]But when the children of Israel cried out to the LORD, the LORD raised up a deliverer for them: Ehud the son of Gera, the Benjamite, a left-handed man. By him the children of Israel sent tribute to Eglon king of Moab. [16]Now Ehud made himself a dagger (it was double-edged and a cubit in length) and fastened it under his clothes on his right thigh. [17]So he brought the tribute to Eglon king of Moab. (Now Eglon *was* a very fat man.) [18]And when he had finished presenting the tribute, he sent away the people who had carried the tribute. [19]But he himself turned back from the stone images that *were* at Gilgal, and said, "I have a secret message for you, O king."

He said, "Keep silence!" And all who attended him went out from him.

[20]So Ehud came to him (now he was sitting upstairs in his cool private chamber). Then Ehud said, "I have a message from God for you." So he arose from *his* seat. [21]Then Ehud reached with his left hand, took the dagger from his right thigh, and thrust it into his belly. [22]Even the hilt went in after the blade, and the fat closed over the blade, for he did not draw the dagger out of his belly; and his entrails came out. [23]Then Ehud went out through the porch and shut the doors of the upper room behind him and locked them.

[24]When he had gone out, *Eglon's*[a] servants came to look, and *to their* surprise, the doors of the upper room were locked. So they said, "He is probably attending to his needs in the cool chamber." [25]So they waited till they were embarrassed, and still he had not opened the doors of the upper room. Therefore they took the key and opened *them.* And there was their master, fallen dead on the floor.

[26]But Ehud had escaped while they delayed, and passed beyond the stone images and escaped to Seirah. [27]And it happened, when he arrived, that he blew the trumpet in the mountains of Ephraim, and the children of Israel went down with him from the mountains; and he led them. [28]Then he said to them, "Follow *me,* for the LORD has delivered your enemies the Moabites into your hand." So they went down after him, seized the fords of the Jordan leading to Moab, and did not allow anyone to cross over. [29]And at that time they killed about ten thousand men of Moab, all stout men of valor; not a man escaped. [30]So Moab was subdued that day under the hand of Israel. And the land had rest for eighty years.

Shamgar

[31]After him was Shamgar the son of Anath, who killed six hundred men of the Philistines with an ox goad; and he also delivered Israel.

Deborah

4 When Ehud was dead, the children of Israel again did evil in the sight of the LORD. [2]So the LORD sold them into the hand of Jabin king of Canaan, who reigned in Hazor. The commander of his army *was* Sisera, who dwelt in Harosheth Hagoyim. [3]And the children of Israel cried out to the LORD; for Jabin had nine hundred chariots of iron, and for twenty years he had harshly oppressed the children of Israel.

[4]Now Deborah, a prophetess, the wife of Lapidoth, was judging Israel at that time. [5]And she would sit under the palm tree of Deborah between Ramah and Bethel in the mountains of Ephraim. And the children of Israel came up to her for judgment.

3:24 [a]Literally *his*

⁶Then she sent and called for Barak the son of Abinoam from Kedesh in Naphtali, and said to him, "Has not the LORD God of Israel commanded, 'Go and deploy *troops* at Mount Tabor; take with you ten thousand men of the sons of Naphtali and of the sons of Zebulun; ⁷and against you I will deploy Sisera, the commander of Jabin's army, with his chariots and his multitude at the River Kishon; and I will deliver him into your hand'?"

⁸And Barak said to her, "If you will go with me, then I will go; but if you will not go with me, I will not go!"

⁹So she said, "I will surely go with you; nevertheless there will be no glory for you in the journey you are taking, for the LORD will sell Sisera into the hand of a woman." Then Deborah arose and went with Barak to Kedesh. ¹⁰And Barak called Zebulun and Naphtali to Kedesh; he went up with ten thousand men under his command,ᵃ and Deborah went up with him.

¹¹Now Heber the Kenite, of the children of Hobab the father-in-law of Moses, had separated himself from the Kenites and pitched his tent near the terebinth tree at Zaanaim, which *is* beside Kedesh.

¹²And they reported to Sisera that Barak the son of Abinoam had gone up to Mount Tabor. ¹³So Sisera gathered together all his chariots, nine hundred chariots of iron, and all the people who *were* with him, from Harosheth Hagoyim to the River Kishon.

¹⁴Then Deborah said to Barak, "Up! For this *is* the day in which the LORD has delivered Sisera into your hand. Has not the LORD gone out before you?" So Barak went down from Mount Tabor with ten thousand men following him. ¹⁵And the LORD routed Sisera and all *his* chariots and all *his* army with the edge of the sword before Barak; and Sisera alighted from *his* chariot and

4:10 ᵃLiterally *at his feet*

PARENTING MATTERS

Q: How should we administer discipline for our child's bad attitude?

Most, if not all, children will at some point demonstrate a bad attitude toward their parents—particularly as they edge toward adolescence. What follows is just an overview of how you can handle the bad attitudes:

1. *Affirm your love.* A child about to be corrected must be reminded that the parent's actions have good and right motivations.

3. *Speak the truth.* Be clear in your communication. Explain what has happened, why it is wrong, and make sure the child understands clearly the offense.

4. *Call for admission of guilt and repentance.* The purpose of your confrontation is to expose the problem and get it rectified. The child needs to acknowledge wrongdoing and appropriately express regret. The purpose of repentance is to take a new direction—not to repeat the same action.

5. *Assess a consequence (if necessary).* Examples of discipline for this age group include withholding of privileges, grounding, delaying the opportunity to double date (or single date), and so on.

6. *Reaffirm commitment and love.* Always end a discussion like this with a final reminder: "I love you; I want the best for you. I'm in your corner."

Be wise about the internet. Use filtering or monitoring software. Don't put computers in children's rooms; keep them out in the open where everyone can see what's on the screen. But remember your child will eventually have unfiltered internet access. Help him cultivate a desire for godliness in his life. Coach him on why the internet can be so dangerous.

fled away on foot. ¹⁶But Barak pursued the chariots and the army as far as Harosheth Hagoyim, and all the army of Sisera fell by the edge of the sword; not a man was left.

¹⁷However, Sisera had fled away on foot to the tent of Jael, the wife of Heber the Kenite; for *there was* peace between Jabin king of Hazor and the house of Heber the Kenite. ¹⁸And Jael went out to meet Sisera, and said to him, "Turn aside, my lord, turn aside to me; do not fear." And when he had turned aside with her into the tent, she covered him with a blanket.

¹⁹Then he said to her, "Please give me a little water to drink, for I am thirsty." So she opened a jug of milk, gave him a drink, and covered him. ²⁰And he said to her, "Stand at the door of the tent, and if any man comes and inquires of you, and says, 'Is there any man here?' you shall say, 'No.'"

²¹Then Jael, Heber's wife, took a tent peg and took a hammer in her hand, and went softly to him and drove the peg into his temple, and it went down into the ground; for he was fast asleep and weary. So he died. ²²And then, as Barak pursued Sisera, Jael came out to meet him, and said to him, "Come, I will show you the man whom you seek." And when he went into her *tent,* there lay Sisera, dead with the peg in his temple.

²³So on that day God subdued Jabin king of Canaan in the presence of the children of Israel. ²⁴And the hand of the children of Israel grew stronger and stronger against Jabin king of Canaan, until they had destroyed Jabin king of Canaan.

The Song of Deborah

5 Then Deborah and Barak the son of Abinoam sang on that day, saying:

2 "When leaders lead in Israel,
    When the people willingly offer
       themselves,
    Bless the LORD!

3 "Hear, O kings! Give ear, O princes!
    I, *even* I, will sing to the LORD;
    I will sing praise to the LORD God of
       Israel.

6 "LORD, when You went out from Seir,
    When You marched from the field of
       Edom,

The earth trembled and the heavens
    poured,
The clouds also poured water;
5 The mountains gushed before the
    LORD,
This Sinai, before the LORD God of
    Israel.

6 "In the days of Shamgar, son of Anath,
    In the days of Jael,
    The highways were deserted,
    And the travelers walked along the
       byways.
7 Village life ceased, it ceased in Israel,
    Until I, Deborah, arose,
    Arose a mother in Israel.
8 They chose new gods;
    Then *there was* war in the gates;
    Not a shield or spear was seen
       among forty thousand in Israel.
9 My heart *is* with the rulers of Israel
    Who offered themselves willingly
       with the people.
    Bless the LORD!

10 "Speak, you who ride on white
       donkeys,
    Who sit in judges' attire,
    And who walk along the road.
11 Far from the noise of the archers,
       among the watering places,
    There they shall recount the
       righteous acts of the LORD,
    The righteous acts *for* His villagers
       in Israel;
    Then the people of the LORD shall go
       down to the gates.

12 "Awake, awake, Deborah!
    Awake, awake, sing a song!
    Arise, Barak, and lead your captives
       away,
    O son of Abinoam!

13 "Then the survivors came down, the
       people against the nobles;
    The LORD came down for me against
       the mighty.
14 From Ephraim *were* those whose
       roots were in Amalek.
    After you, Benjamin, with your
       peoples,
    From Machir rulers came down,
    And from Zebulun those who bear
       the recruiter's staff.

15 And the princes of Issachar[a] *were*
with Deborah;
As Issachar, so *was* Barak
Sent into the valley under his
command;[b]
Among the divisions of Reuben
There were great resolves of heart.
16 Why did you sit among the
sheepfolds,
To hear the pipings for the flocks?
The divisions of Reuben have great
searchings of heart.
17 Gilead stayed beyond the Jordan,
And why did Dan remain on ships?[a]
Asher continued at the seashore,
And stayed by his inlets.
18 Zebulun *is* a people *who* jeopardized
their lives to the point of death,
Naphtali also, on the heights of the
battlefield.

19 "The kings came *and* fought,
Then the kings of Canaan fought
In Taanach, by the waters of
Megiddo;
They took no spoils of silver.
20 They fought from the heavens;
The stars from their courses fought
against Sisera.
21 The torrent of Kishon swept them
away,
That ancient torrent, the torrent of
Kishon.
O my soul, march on in strength!
22 Then the horses' hooves pounded,
The galloping, galloping of his
steeds.
23 'Curse Meroz,' said the angel[a] of the
LORD,
' Curse its inhabitants bitterly,
Because they did not come to the
help of the LORD,
To the help of the LORD against the
mighty.'

24 "Most blessed among women is Jael,
The wife of Heber the Kenite;
Blessed is she among women in tents.
25 He asked for water, she gave milk;
She brought out cream in a lordly
bowl.
26 She stretched her hand to the tent peg,
Her right hand to the workmen's
hammer;

She pounded Sisera, she pierced his
head,
She split and struck through his
temple.
27 At her feet he sank, he fell, he lay
still;
At her feet he sank, he fell;
Where he sank, there he fell dead.

28 "The mother of Sisera looked through
the window,
And cried out through the lattice,
' Why is his chariot *so* long in coming?
Why tarries the clatter of his
chariots?'
29 Her wisest ladies answered her,
Yes, she answered herself,
30 'Are they not finding and dividing the
spoil:
To every man a girl *or* two;
For Sisera, plunder of dyed
garments,
Plunder of garments embroidered
and dyed,
Two pieces of dyed embroidery for
the neck of the looter?'

31 "Thus let all Your enemies perish, O
LORD!
But *let* those who love Him *be* like
the sun
When it comes out in full strength."

So the land had rest for forty years.

Midianites Oppress Israel

6 Then the children of Israel did evil in the
sight of the LORD. So the LORD delivered
them into the hand of Midian for seven
years, [2]and the hand of Midian prevailed
against Israel. Because of the Midianites, the
children of Israel made for themselves the
dens, the caves, and the strongholds which
are in the mountains. [3]So it was, whenever
Israel had sown, Midianites would come up;
also Amalekites and the people of the East
would come up against them. [4]Then they
would encamp against them and destroy the
produce of the earth as far as Gaza, and
leave no sustenance for Israel, neither sheep

5:15 [a]Following Septuagint, Syriac, Targum, and
Vulgate; Masoretic Text reads *And my princes in
Issachar.* [b]Literally *at his feet* **5:17** [a]Or *at ease*
5:23 [a]Or *Angel*

Resolve Conflict through Loving Confrontation

Barbara and I manage our conflicts with a tool we call "loving confrontation." When either of us gets upset with the other, we try not to hide or deny what is making us see red; we get the hurt in the open through direct, but loving confrontation.

If you want to practice loving confrontation, you can't believe your mate is out to get you, nor can you be out to get your mate. Be willing to hear what God may be saying through your mate. Many of Barbara's best statements to me hurt a bit; but I need to hear them because they keep me on the right track. I want to hear what she is trying to say, instead of plotting how I will reply and defend myself.

Consider a few tips that Barbara and I have found useful in keeping a judgmental spirit out of confrontation:

Check your motivation. Will what you say help or hurt? Will bringing this up cause healing, wholeness, and oneness, or further conflict? Prayer is the best barometer of your motivation. When you take your situation to God and He shines His light on you and the problem, you usually see your motivation for what it is.

Check your attitude. A tender spirit expressed through loving confrontation says, "I care about you. I respect you, and I want you to respect me. I want to know how you feel." Don't hop on your bulldozer and run down your partner. Do you have a spirit of humility or pride?

Check the circumstances. The circumstances may include timing, location, and setting. Perhaps the most important is timing. Barbara should not confront me as I walk in the house after a hard day's work. I should not confront her as she's helping a sick child.

Check to determine what other pressures may be present. Be sensitive to where your mate is coming from. What's the context of your mate's life right now?

Check your readiness to take it as well as dish it out. Sometimes a confrontation can boomerang. Your mate may have some stuff saved on the other side of the fence that will suddenly come right back at you.

Check the emotional temperature. Call a time-out if the conflict escalates. Hot, emotionally charged words don't bring peace. Say to each other, "I'm not running away from our talk. I love you and want to work this out—but I need a little time to process before we continue our conversation."

How you handle conflict in your marriage and family will determine what kind of relationships you experience.

---

nor ox nor donkey. 5For they would come up with their livestock and their tents, coming in as numerous as locusts; both they and their camels were without number; and they would enter the land to destroy it. 6So Israel was greatly impoverished because of the Midianites, and the children of Israel cried out to the LORD.

7And it came to pass, when the children of Israel cried out to the LORD because of the Midianites, 8that the LORD sent a prophet to the children of Israel, who said to them, "Thus says the LORD God of Israel: 'I brought you up from Egypt and brought you out of the house of bondage; 9and I delivered you out of the hand of the Egyptians and out of the hand of all who oppressed you, and drove them out before you and gave you their land. 10Also I said to you, "I *am* the LORD your God; do not fear the gods of the Amorites, in whose land you dwell." But you have not obeyed My voice.' "

Gideon

11Now the Angel of the LORD came and sat under the terebinth tree which *was* in Ophrah, which *belonged* to Joash the Abiezrite, while his son Gideon threshed wheat in the winepress, in order to hide *it* from the Midianites. 12And the Angel of the LORD appeared to him, and said to him, "The LORD *is* with you, you mighty man of valor!"

[13]Gideon said to Him, "O my lord,[a] if the LORD is with us, why then has all this happened to us? And where *are* all His miracles which our fathers told us about, saying, 'Did not the LORD bring us up from Egypt?' But now the LORD has forsaken us and delivered us into the hands of the Midianites."

[14]Then the LORD turned to him and said, "Go in this might of yours, and you shall save Israel from the hand of the Midianites. Have I not sent you?"

[15]So he said to Him, "O my Lord,[a] how can I save Israel? Indeed my clan *is* the weakest in Manasseh, and I *am* the least in my father's house."

[16]And the LORD said to him, "Surely I will be with you, and you shall defeat the Midianites as one man."

[17]Then he said to Him, "If now I have found favor in Your sight, then show me a sign that it is You who talk with me. [18]Do not depart from here, I pray, until I come to You and bring out my offering and set *it* before You."

And He said, "I will wait until you come back."

[19]So Gideon went in and prepared a young goat, and unleavened bread from an ephah of flour. The meat he put in a basket, and he put the broth in a pot; and he brought *them* out to Him under the terebinth tree and presented *them.* [20]The Angel of God said to him, "Take the meat and the unleavened bread and lay *them* on this rock, and pour out the broth." And he did so.

[21]Then the Angel of the LORD put out the end of the staff that *was* in His hand, and touched the meat and the unleavened bread; and fire rose out of the rock and consumed the meat and the unleavened bread. And the Angel of the LORD departed out of his sight.

[22]Now Gideon perceived that He *was* the Angel of the LORD. So Gideon said, "Alas, O Lord GOD! For I have seen the Angel of the LORD face to face."

[23]Then the LORD said to him, "Peace *be* with you; do not fear, you shall not die." [24]So Gideon built an altar there to the LORD, and called it The-LORD-*Is*-Peace.[a] To this day it *is* still in Ophrah of the Abiezrites.

[25]Now it came to pass the same night that the LORD said to him, "Take your father's young bull, the second bull of seven years old, and tear down the altar of Baal that your father has, and cut down the wooden image[a] that *is* beside it; [26]and build an altar to the LORD your God on top of this rock in the proper arrangement, and take the second bull and offer a burnt sacrifice with the wood of the image which you shall cut down." [27]So Gideon took ten men from among his servants and did as the LORD had said to him. But because he feared his father's household and the men of the city too much to do *it* by day, he did *it* by night.

Gideon Destroys the Altar of Baal

[28]And when the men of the city arose early in the morning, there was the altar of Baal, torn down; and the wooden image that *was* beside it was cut down, and the second bull was being offered on the altar *which had been* built. [29]So they said to one another, "Who has done this thing?" And when they had inquired and asked, they said, "Gideon the son of Joash has done this thing." [30]Then the men of the city said to Joash, "Bring out your son, that he may die, because he has torn down the altar of Baal, and because he has cut down the wooden image that *was* beside it."

[31]But Joash said to all who stood against him, "Would you plead for Baal? Would you save him? Let the one who would plead for him be put to death by morning! If he *is* a god, let him plead for himself, because his altar has been torn down!" [32]Therefore on that day he called him Jerubbaal,[a] saying, "Let Baal plead against him, because he has torn down his altar."

[33]Then all the Midianites and Amalekites, the people of the East, gathered together; and they crossed over and encamped in the Valley of Jezreel. [34]But the Spirit of the LORD came upon Gideon; then he blew the trumpet, and the Abiezrites gathered behind him. [35]And he sent messengers throughout all Manasseh, who also gathered behind him.

6:13 [a]Hebrew *adoni,* used of man　6:15 [a]Hebrew *Adonai,* used of God　6:24 [a]Hebrew *YHWH Shalom*　6:25 [a]Hebrew *Asherah,* a Canaanite goddess　6:32 [a]Literally *Let Baal Plead*

He also sent messengers to Asher, Zebulun, and Naphtali; and they came up to meet them.

The Sign of the Fleece

³⁶So Gideon said to God, "If You will save Israel by my hand as You have said— ³⁷look, I shall put a fleece of wool on the threshing floor; if there is dew on the fleece only, and *it is* dry on all the ground, then I shall know that You will save Israel by my hand, as You have said." ³⁸And it was so. When he rose early the next morning and squeezed the fleece together, he wrung the dew out of the fleece, a bowlful of water. ³⁹Then Gideon said to God, "Do not be angry with me, but let me speak just once more: Let me test, I pray, just once more with the fleece; let it now be dry only on the fleece, but on all the ground let there be dew." ⁴⁰And God did so that night. It was dry on the fleece only, but there was dew on all the ground.

Gideon's Valiant Three Hundred

7 Then Jerubbaal (that *is,* Gideon) and all the people who *were* with him rose early and encamped beside the well of Harod, so that the camp of the Midianites was on the north side of them by the hill of Moreh in the valley.

²And the LORD said to Gideon, "The people who *are* with you *are* too many for Me to give the Midianites into their hands, lest Israel claim glory for itself against Me, saying, 'My own hand has saved me.' ³Now therefore, proclaim in the hearing of the people, saying, 'Whoever *is* fearful and afraid, let him turn and depart at once from Mount Gilead.' " And twenty-two thousand of the people returned, and ten thousand remained.

⁴But the LORD said to Gideon, "The people *are* still *too* many; bring them down to the water, and I will test them for you there. Then it will be, *that* of whom I say to you, 'This one shall go with you,' the same shall go with you; and of whomever I say to you, 'This one shall not go with you,' the same shall not go." ⁵So he brought the people down to the water. And the LORD said to Gideon, "Everyone who laps from the water with his tongue, as a dog laps, you

shall set apart by himself; likewise everyone who gets down on his knees to drink." ⁶And the number of those who lapped, *putting* their hand to their mouth, was three hundred men; but all the rest of the people got down on their knees to drink water. ⁷Then the LORD said to Gideon, "By the three hundred men who lapped I will save you, and deliver the Midianites into your hand. Let all the *other* people go, every man to his place." ⁸So the people took provisions and their trumpets in their hands. And he sent away all *the rest of* Israel, every man to his tent, and retained those three hundred men. Now the camp of Midian was below him in the valley.

⁹It happened on the same night that the LORD said to him, "Arise, go down against the camp, for I have delivered it into your hand. ¹⁰But if you are afraid to go down, go down to the camp with Purah your servant, ¹¹and you shall hear what they say; and afterward your hands shall be strengthened to go down against the camp." Then he went down with Purah his servant to the outpost of the armed men who *were* in the camp. ¹²Now the Midianites and Amalekites, all the people of the East, were lying in the valley as numerous as locusts; and their camels *were* without number, as the sand by the seashore in multitude.

¹³And when Gideon had come, there was a man telling a dream to his companion. He said, "I have had a dream: *To my* surprise, a loaf of barley bread tumbled into the camp of Midian; it came to a tent and struck it so that it fell and overturned, and the tent collapsed."

¹⁴Then his companion answered and said, "This *is* nothing else but the sword of Gideon the son of Joash, a man of Israel! Into his hand God has delivered Midian and the whole camp."

¹⁵And so it was, when Gideon heard the telling of the dream and its interpretation, that he worshiped. He returned to the camp of Israel, and said, "Arise, for the LORD has delivered the camp of Midian into your hand." ¹⁶Then he divided the three hundred men *into* three companies, and he put a trumpet into every man's hand, with empty pitchers, and torches inside the pitchers. ¹⁷And he said to them, "Look at me and do

likewise; watch, and when I come to the edge of the camp you shall do as I do: 18When I blow the trumpet, I and all who *are* with me, then you also blow the trumpets on every side of the whole camp, and say, '*The sword of* the LORD and of Gideon!' "

19So Gideon and the hundred men who *were* with him came to the outpost of the camp at the beginning of the middle watch, just as they had posted the watch; and they blew the trumpets and broke the pitchers that *were* in their hands. 20Then the three companies blew the trumpets and

INTIMATE MOMENTS

Get tickets for two (and that includes you!) to a chick flick she wants to see. Not sure which movie she's most interested in seeing? Read some current reviews to get a better idea, or talk to her closest friend, or just pick one and ask her, "Would you like to see this movie with me?" To make the evening especially enjoyable, take her out for a casual dinner before or after the film.

broke the pitchers—they held the torches in their left hands and the trumpets in their right hands for blowing—and they cried, "The sword of the LORD and of Gideon!" 21And every man stood in his place all around the camp; and the whole army ran and cried out and fled. 22When the three hundred blew the trumpets, the LORD set every man's sword against his companion throughout the whole camp; and the army fled to Beth Acacia,ª toward Zererah, as far as the border of Abel Meholah, by Tabbath. 23And the men of Israel gathered together from Naphtali, Asher, and all Manasseh, and pursued the Midianites.

24Then Gideon sent messengers throughout all the mountains of Ephraim, saying, "Come down against the Midianites, and seize from them the watering places as far as Beth Barah and the Jordan." Then all the men of Ephraim gathered together and seized the watering places as far as Beth

Barah and the Jordan. 25And they captured two princes of the Midianites, Oreb and Zeeb. They killed Oreb at the rock of Oreb, and Zeeb they killed at the winepress of Zeeb. They pursued Midian and brought the heads of Oreb and Zeeb to Gideon on the other side of the Jordan.

Gideon Subdues the Midianites

8 Now the men of Ephraim said to him, "Why have you done this to us by not calling us when you went to fight with the Midianites?" And they reprimanded him sharply.

2So he said to them, "What have I done now in comparison with you? *Is* not the gleaning *of the grapes* of Ephraim better than the vintage of Abiezer? 3God has delivered into your hands the princes of Midian, Oreb and Zeeb. And what was I able to do in comparison with you?" Then their anger toward him subsided when he said that.

4When Gideon came to the Jordan, he and the three hundred men who *were* with him crossed over, exhausted but still in pursuit. 5Then he said to the men of Succoth, "Please give loaves of bread to the people who follow me, for they are exhausted, and I am pursuing Zebah and Zalmunna, kings of Midian."

6And the leaders of Succoth said, "*Are* the hands of Zebah and Zalmunna now in your hand, that we should give bread to your army?"

7So Gideon said, "For this cause, when the LORD has delivered Zebah and Zalmunna into my hand, then I will tear your flesh with the thorns of the wilderness and with briers!" 8Then he went up from there to Penuel and spoke to them in the same way. And the men of Penuel answered him as the men of Succoth had answered. 9So he also spoke to the men of Penuel, saying, "When I come back in peace, I will tear down this tower!"

10Now Zebah and Zalmunna *were* at Karkor, and their armies with them, about fifteen thousand, all who were left of all the army of the people of the East; for one hundred and twenty thousand men who drew the sword had fallen. 11Then Gideon

7:22 ªHebrew *Beth Shittah*

went up by the road of those who dwell in tents on the east of Nobah and Jogbehah; and he attacked the army while the camp felt secure. ¹²When Zebah and Zalmunna fled, he pursued them; and he took the two kings of Midian, Zebah and Zalmunna, and routed the whole army.

¹³Then Gideon the son of Joash returned from battle, from the Ascent of Heres. ¹⁴And he caught a young man of the men of Succoth and interrogated him; and he wrote down for him the leaders of Succoth and its elders, seventy-seven men. ¹⁵Then he came to the men of Succoth and said, "Here are Zebah and Zalmunna, about whom you ridiculed me, saying, '*Are* the hands of Zebah and Zalmunna now in your hand, that we should give bread to your weary men?' " ¹⁶And he took the elders of the city, and thorns of the wilderness and briers, and with them he taught the men of Succoth. ¹⁷Then he tore down the tower of Penuel and killed the men of the city.

¹⁸And he said to Zebah and Zalmunna, "What kind of men *were they* whom you killed at Tabor?"

So they answered, "As you *are,* so *were* they; each one resembled the son of a king."

¹⁹Then he said, "They *were* my brothers, the sons of my mother. *As* the LORD lives, if you had let them live, I would not kill you." ²⁰And he said to Jether his firstborn, "Rise, kill them!" But the youth would not draw his sword; for he was afraid, because he *was* still a youth.

²¹So Zebah and Zalmunna said, "Rise yourself, and kill us; for as a man *is, so is* his strength." So Gideon arose and killed Zebah and Zalmunna, and took the crescent ornaments that *were* on their camels' necks.

Gideon's Ephod

²²Then the men of Israel said to Gideon, "Rule over us, both you and your son, and your grandson also; for you have delivered us from the hand of Midian."

²³But Gideon said to them, "I will not rule over you, nor shall my son rule over you; the LORD shall rule over you." ²⁴Then Gideon said to them, "I would like to make a request of you, that each of you would give me the earrings from his plunder." For

they had golden earrings, because they *were* Ishmaelites.

²⁵So they answered, "We will gladly give *them.*" And they spread out a garment, and each man threw into it the earrings from his plunder. ²⁶Now the weight of the gold earrings that he requested was one thousand seven hundred *shekels* of gold, besides the crescent ornaments, pendants, and purple robes which *were* on the kings of Midian, and besides the chains that *were* around their camels' necks. ²⁷Then Gideon made it into an ephod and set it up in his city, Ophrah. And all Israel played the harlot with it there. It became a snare to Gideon and to his house.

²⁸Thus Midian was subdued before the children of Israel, so that they lifted their heads no more. And the country was quiet for forty years in the days of Gideon.

Death of Gideon

²⁹Then Jerubbaal the son of Joash went and dwelt in his own house. ³⁰Gideon had seventy sons who were his own offspring, for he had many wives. ³¹And his concubine who *was* in Shechem also bore him a son, whose name he called Abimelech. ³²Now Gideon the son of Joash died at a good old age, and was buried in the tomb of Joash his father, in Ophrah of the Abiezrites.

³³So it was, as soon as Gideon was dead, that the children of Israel again played the harlot with the Baals, and made Baal-Berith their god. ³⁴Thus the children of Israel did not remember the LORD their God, who had delivered them from the hands of all their enemies on every side; ³⁵nor did they show kindness to the house of Jerubbaal (Gideon) in accordance with the good he had done for Israel.

Abimelech's Conspiracy

9 Then Abimelech the son of Jerubbaal went to Shechem, to his mother's brothers, and spoke with them and with all the family of the house of his mother's father, saying, ²"Please speak in the hearing of all the men of Shechem: 'Which is better for you, that all seventy of the sons of Jerubbaal reign over you, or that one reign over you?' Remember that I *am* your own flesh and bone."

³And his mother's brothers spoke all these words concerning him in the hearing of all the men of Shechem; and their heart was inclined to follow Abimelech, for they said, "He is our brother." ⁴So they gave him seventy *shekels* of silver from the temple of Baal-Berith, with which Abimelech hired worthless and reckless men; and they followed him. ⁵Then he went to his father's house at Ophrah and killed his brothers, the seventy sons of Jerubbaal, on one stone. But Jotham the youngest son of Jerubbaal was left, because he hid himself. ⁶And all the men of Shechem gathered together, all of Beth Millo, and they went and made Abimelech king beside the terebinth tree at the pillar that *was* in Shechem.

The Parable of the Trees

⁷Now when they told Jotham, he went and stood on top of Mount Gerizim, and lifted his voice and cried out. And he said to them:

"Listen to me, you men of Shechem,
　That God may listen to you!
8　"The trees once went forth to anoint a
　　king over them.
　And they said to the olive tree,
　' Reign over us!'
9　But the olive tree said to them,
　' Should I cease giving my oil,
　　With which they honor God and
　　　men,
　　And go to sway over trees?'
10　"Then the trees said to the fig tree,
　' You come *and* reign over us!'
11　But the fig tree said to them,
　' Should I cease my sweetness and my
　　　good fruit,
　　And go to sway over trees?'
12　"Then the trees said to the vine,
　' You come *and* reign over us!'
13　But the vine said to them,
　' Should I cease my new wine,
　　Which cheers *both* God and men,
　　And go to sway over trees?'
14　"Then all the trees said to the
　　bramble,
　' You come *and* reign over us!'
15　And the bramble said to the trees,
　' If in truth you anoint me as king
　　　over you,
　　Then come *and* take shelter in my
　　　shade;
　　But if not, let fire come out of the
　　　bramble
　　And devour the cedars of Lebanon!'

¹⁶"Now therefore, if you have acted in truth and sincerity in making Abimelech king, and if you have dealt well with Jerubbaal and his house, and have done to him as he deserves— ¹⁷for my father fought for you, risked his life, and delivered you out of the hand of Midian; ¹⁸but you have risen up against my father's house this

ROMANCE FAQ

Q: *How can I regain the respect I've lost for my husband?*

That's a difficult struggle, because Ephesians 5:33 makes it clear that wives are to respect their husbands. I suggest you make a real effort to think of things you can still respect about your husband. You have to choose to focus on the positive if you want to make your marriage last.

Pull back from the daily routine of life, look at him objectively, and say, "What is good about him? What did I respect in the first place?" Study him again and don't allow yourself to be blinded by his weaknesses and inadequacies, the things you don't like.

Some of these positive things may seem basic, but they really are important. In fact, it's easy for a wife to take some of these things for granted. The fact that a husband goes to work and provides for the family financially is worthy of respect. Maybe he plays ball with your son or daughter. That's worthy of respect.

You may wish he did more, but if you let him know how much you appreciate what he does, he will feel encouraged. Say, "I'm glad I'm married to a man who's faithful to provide for his family." Or write him a note expressing your appreciation and admiration.

day, and killed his seventy sons on one stone, and made Abimelech, the son of his female servant, king over the men of Shechem, because he is your brother— [19]if then you have acted in truth and sincerity with Jerubbaal and with his house this day, *then* rejoice in Abimelech, and let him also rejoice in you. [20]But if not, let fire come from Abimelech and devour the men of Shechem and Beth Millo; and let fire come from the men of Shechem and from Beth Millo and devour Abimelech!" [21]And Jotham ran away and fled; and he went to Beer and dwelt there, for fear of Abimelech his brother.

Downfall of Abimelech

[22]After Abimelech had reigned over Israel three years, [23]God sent a spirit of ill will between Abimelech and the men of Shechem; and the men of Shechem dealt treacherously with Abimelech, [24]that the crime *done* to the seventy sons of Jerubbaal might be settled and their blood be laid on Abimelech their brother, who killed them, and on the men of Shechem, who aided him in the killing of his brothers. [25]And the men of Shechem set men in ambush against him on the tops of the mountains, and they robbed all who passed by them along that way; and it was told Abimelech.

[26]Now Gaal the son of Ebed came with his brothers and went over to Shechem; and the men of Shechem put their confidence in him. [27]So they went out into the fields, and gathered *grapes* from their vineyards and trod *them,* and made merry. And they went into the house of their god, and ate and drank, and cursed Abimelech. [28]Then Gaal the son of Ebed said, "Who *is* Abimelech, and who *is* Shechem, that we should serve him? *Is he* not the son of Jerubbaal, and *is not* Zebul his officer? Serve the men of Hamor the father of Shechem; but why should we serve him? [29]If only this people were under my authority![a] Then I would remove Abimelech." So he[b] said to Abimelech, "Increase your army and come out!"

[30]When Zebul, the ruler of the city, heard the words of Gaal the son of Ebed, his anger was aroused. [31]And he sent messengers to Abimelech secretly, saying, "Take note! Gaal the son of Ebed and his brothers have come to Shechem; and here they are, fortifying the city against you. [32]Now therefore, get up by night, you and the people who *are* with you, and lie in wait in the field. [33]And it shall be, as soon as the sun is up in the morning, *that* you shall rise early and rush upon the city; and *when* he and the people who are with him come out against you, you may then do to them as you find opportunity."

[34]So Abimelech and all the people who *were* with him rose by night, and lay in wait against Shechem in four companies. [35]When Gaal the son of Ebed went out and stood in the entrance to the city gate, Abimelech and the people who *were* with him rose from lying in wait. [36]And when Gaal saw the people, he said to Zebul, "Look, people are coming down from the tops of the mountains!"

But Zebul said to him, "You see the shadows of the mountains as *if they were* men."

[37]So Gaal spoke again and said, "See, people are coming down from the center of the land, and another company is coming from the Diviners'[a] Terebinth Tree."

[38]Then Zebul said to him, "Where indeed *is* your mouth now, with which you said, 'Who is Abimelech, that we should serve him?' *Are* not these the people whom you despised? Go out, if you will, and fight with them now."

[39]So Gaal went out, leading the men of Shechem, and fought with Abimelech. [40]And Abimelech chased him, and he fled from him; and many fell wounded, to the *very* entrance of the gate. [41]Then Abimelech dwelt at Arumah, and Zebul drove out Gaal and his brothers, so that they would not dwell in Shechem.

[42]And it came about on the next day that the people went out into the field, and they told Abimelech. [43]So he took his people, divided them into three companies, and lay in wait in the field. And he looked, and there were the people, coming out of the city; and he rose against them and attacked them. [44]Then Abimelech and the company that *was* with him rushed forward and

---

9:29 [a]Literally *hand* [b]Following Masoretic Text and Targum; Dead Sea Scrolls read *they;* Septuagint reads *I.*
9:37 [a]Hebrew *Meonenim*

stood at the entrance of the gate of the city; and the *other* two companies rushed upon all who *were* in the fields and killed them. ⁴⁵So Abimelech fought against the city all that day; he took the city and killed the people who *were* in it; and he demolished the city and sowed it with salt.

⁴⁶Now when all the men of the tower of Shechem had heard *that,* they entered the stronghold of the temple of the god Berith. ⁴⁷And it was told Abimelech that all the men of the tower of Shechem were gathered together. ⁴⁸Then Abimelech went up to Mount Zalmon, he and all the people who *were* with him. And Abimelech took an ax in his hand and cut down a bough from the trees, and took it and laid *it* on his shoulder; then he said to the people who were with him, "What you have seen me do, make haste *and* do as I *have done.*" ⁴⁹So each of the people likewise cut down his own bough and followed Abimelech, put *them* against the stronghold, and set the stronghold on fire above them, so that all the people of the tower of Shechem died, about a thousand men and women.

⁵⁰Then Abimelech went to Thebez, and he encamped against Thebez and took it. ⁵¹But there was a strong tower in the city, and all the men and women—all the people of the city—fled there and shut themselves in; then they went up to the top of the tower. ⁵²So Abimelech came as far as the tower and fought against it; and he drew near the door of the tower to burn it with fire. ⁵³But a certain woman dropped an upper millstone on Abimelech's head and crushed his skull. ⁵⁴Then he called quickly to the young man, his armorbearer, and said to him, "Draw your sword and kill me, lest men say of me, 'A woman killed him.' " So his young man thrust him through, and he died. ⁵⁵And when the men of Israel saw that Abimelech was dead, they departed, every man to his place.

⁵⁶Thus God repaid the wickedness of Abimelech, which he had done to his father by killing his seventy brothers. ⁵⁷And all the evil of the men of Shechem God returned on their own heads, and on them came the curse of Jotham the son of Jerubbaal.

Tola

10 After Abimelech there arose to save Israel Tola the son of Puah, the son of Dodo, a man of Issachar; and he dwelt in Shamir in the mountains of Ephraim. ²He judged Israel twenty-three years; and he died and was buried in Shamir.

Jair

³After him arose Jair, a Gileadite; and he judged Israel twenty-two years. ⁴Now he had thirty sons who rode on thirty donkeys; they also had thirty towns, which are called "Havoth Jair"ᵃ to this day, which *are* in the land of Gilead. ⁵And Jair died and was buried in Camon.

Israel Oppressed Again

⁶Then the children of Israel again did evil in the sight of the LORD, and served the Baals and the Ashtoreths, the gods of Syria, the gods of Sidon, the gods of Moab, the gods of the people of Ammon, and the gods of the Philistines; and they forsook the LORD and did not serve Him. ⁷So the anger of the LORD was hot against Israel; and He sold them into the hands of the Philistines and into the hands of the people of Ammon. ⁸From that year they harassed and oppressed the children of Israel for eighteen years—all the children of Israel who *were* on the other side of the Jordan in the land of the Amorites, in Gilead. ⁹Moreover the people of Ammon crossed over the Jordan to fight against Judah also, against Benjamin, and against the house of Ephraim, so that Israel was severely distressed.

¹⁰And the children of Israel cried out to the LORD, saying, "We have sinned against You, because we have both forsaken our God and served the Baals!"

¹¹So the LORD said to the children of Israel, "*Did I* not *deliver you* from the Egyptians and from the Amorites and from the people of Ammon and from the Philistines? ¹²Also the Sidonians and Amalekites and Maonitesᵃ oppressed you; and you cried out to Me, and I delivered

---

10:4 ᵃLiterally *Towns of Jair* (compare Numbers 32:41 and Deuteronomy 3:14) **10:12** ᵃSome Septuagint manuscripts read *Midianites.*

you from their hand. ¹³Yet you have forsaken Me and served other gods. Therefore I will deliver you no more. ¹⁴Go and cry out to the gods which you have chosen; let them deliver you in your time of distress."

¹⁵And the children of Israel said to the LORD, "We have sinned! Do to us whatever seems best to You; only deliver us this day, we pray." ¹⁶So they put away the foreign gods from among them and served the LORD. And His soul could no longer endure the misery of Israel.

¹⁷Then the people of Ammon gathered together and encamped in Gilead. And the children of Israel assembled together and encamped in Mizpah. ¹⁸And the people, the leaders of Gilead, said to one another, "Who *is* the man who will begin the fight against the people of Ammon? He shall be head over all the inhabitants of Gilead."

Jephthah

11 Now Jephthah the Gileadite was a mighty man of valor, but he *was* the son of a harlot; and Gilead begot Jephthah. ²Gilead's wife bore sons; and when his wife's sons grew up, they drove Jephthah out, and said to him, "You shall have no inheritance in our father's house, for you *are* the son of another woman." ³Then Jephthah fled from his brothers and dwelt in the land of Tob; and worthless men banded together with Jephthah and went out *raiding* with him.

⁴It came to pass after a time that the people of Ammon made war against Israel. ⁵And so it was, when the people of Ammon made war against Israel, that the elders of Gilead went to get Jephthah from the land of Tob. ⁶Then they said to Jephthah, "Come and be our commander, that we may fight against the people of Ammon."

⁷So Jephthah said to the elders of Gilead, "Did you not hate me, and expel me from my father's house? Why have you come to me now when you are in distress?"

⁸And the elders of Gilead said to Jephthah, "That is why we have turned again to you now, that you may go with us and fight against the people of Ammon, and be our head over all the inhabitants of Gilead."

⁹So Jephthah said to the elders of Gilead, "If you take me back home to fight against the people of Ammon, and the LORD delivers them to me, shall I be your head?"

¹⁰And the elders of Gilead said to Jephthah, "The LORD will be a witness between

PARENTING MATTERS

Q: With so many media bombarding our child with negative sexual images, how can we monitor and control what he/she is seeing?

The media gives you a daily opportunity to observe and be involved in your child's choices and habits. Don't forget to ask our favorite question, "Have you been looking at or listening to something that's not good for you?" He may not like it, but you'll be surprised by the power of that simple question.

Here are some ideas for testing your child's convictions on the media trap:

Listen to his music. Regularly ask your child to play you a song or two from a favorite music group.

Be proactive in selecting reading material. Give your child some things to be looking for that might signal objectionable content. Each of you read one of the books and report back. Discuss what you find.

Do some interactive media together. Get on the Internet with your child and do some surfing. Show your child how to navigate toward acceptable materials and away from questionable websites. While still on the computer, play with your child some computer or video games that he enjoys. Discuss any messages or themes that are portrayed.

us, if we do not do according to your words." ¹¹Then Jephthah went with the elders of Gilead, and the people made him head and commander over them; and Jephthah spoke all his words before the LORD in Mizpah.

¹²Now Jephthah sent messengers to the king of the people of Ammon, saying, "What do you have against me, that you have come to fight against me in my land?"

¹³And the king of the people of Ammon answered the messengers of Jephthah, "Because Israel took away my land when they came up out of Egypt, from the Arnon as far as the Jabbok, and to the Jordan. Now therefore, restore those *lands* peaceably."

¹⁴So Jephthah again sent messengers to the king of the people of Ammon, ¹⁵and said to him, "Thus says Jephthah: 'Israel did not take away the land of Moab, nor the land of the people of Ammon; ¹⁶for when Israel came up from Egypt, they walked through the wilderness as far as the Red Sea and came to Kadesh. ¹⁷Then Israel sent messengers to the king of Edom, saying, "Please let me pass through your land." But the king of Edom would not heed. And in like manner they sent to the king of Moab, but he would not *consent.* So Israel remained in Kadesh. ¹⁸And they went along through the wilderness and bypassed the land of Edom and the land of Moab, came to the east side of the land of Moab, and encamped on the other side of the Arnon. But they did not enter the border of Moab, for the Arnon *was* the border of Moab. ¹⁹Then Israel sent messengers to Sihon king of the Amorites, king of Heshbon; and Israel said to him, "Please let us pass through your land into our place." ²⁰But Sihon did not trust Israel to pass through his territory. So Sihon gathered all his people together, encamped in Jahaz, and fought against Israel. ²¹And the LORD God of Israel delivered Sihon and all his people into the hand of Israel, and they defeated them. Thus Israel gained possession of all the land of the Amorites, who inhabited that country. ²²They took possession of all the territory of the Amorites, from the Arnon to the Jabbok and from the wilderness to the Jordan.

^{23t}And now the LORD God of Israel has dispossessed the Amorites from before His people Israel; should you then possess it? ²⁴Will you not possess whatever Chemosh your god gives you to possess? So whatever the LORD our God takes possession of before us, we will possess. ²⁵And now, *are* you any better than Balak the son of Zippor, king of Moab? Did he ever strive against Israel? Did he ever fight against them? ²⁶While Israel dwelt in Heshbon and its villages, in Aroer and its villages, and in all the cities along the banks of the Arnon, for three hundred years, why did you not recover *them* within that time? ²⁷Therefore I have not sinned against you, but you wronged me by fighting against me. May the LORD, the Judge, render judgment this day between the children of Israel and the people of Ammon.' " ²⁸However, the king of the people of Ammon did not heed the words which Jephthah sent him.

Jephthah's Vow and Victory

²⁹Then the Spirit of the LORD came upon Jephthah, and he passed through Gilead and Manasseh, and passed through Mizpah of Gilead; and from Mizpah of Gilead he advanced *toward* the people of Ammon. ³⁰And Jephthah made a vow to the LORD, and said, "If You will indeed deliver the people of Ammon into my hands, ³¹then it will be that whatever comes out of the doors of my house to meet me, when I return in peace from the people of Ammon, shall surely be the LORD's, and I will offer it up as a burnt offering."

³²So Jephthah advanced toward the people of Ammon to fight against them, and the LORD delivered them into his hands. ³³And he defeated them from Aroer as far as Minnith—twenty cities—and to Abel Keramim,^a with a very great slaughter. Thus the people of Ammon were subdued before the children of Israel.

Jephthah's Daughter

³⁴When Jephthah came to his house at Mizpah, there was his daughter, coming out to meet him with timbrels and dancing; and she *was his* only child. Besides her he had neither son nor daughter. ³⁵And it came to pass, when he saw her, that he tore his clothes, and

11:33 ^aLiterally *Plain of Vineyards*

said, "Alas, my daughter! You have brought me very low! You are among those who trouble me! For I have given my word to the LORD, and I cannot go back on it."

³⁶So she said to him, "My father, *if* you have given your word to the LORD, do to me according to what has gone out of your mouth, because the LORD has avenged you of your enemies, the people of Ammon." ³⁷Then she said to her father, "Let this thing be done for me: let me alone for two months, that I may go and wander on the mountains and bewail my virginity, my friends and I."

³⁸So he said, "Go." And he sent her away *for* two months; and she went with her friends, and bewailed her virginity on the mountains. ³⁹And it was so at the end of two months that she returned to her father, and he carried out his vow with her which he had vowed. She knew no man.

And it became a custom in Israel ⁴⁰*that* the daughters of Israel went four days each year to lament the daughter of Jephthah the Gileadite.

Jephthah's Conflict with Ephraim

12 Then the men of Ephraim gathered together, crossed over toward Zaphon, and said to Jephthah, "Why did you cross over to fight against the people of Ammon, and did not call us to go with you? We will burn your house down on you with fire!"

²And Jephthah said to them, "My people and I were in a great struggle with the people of Ammon; and when I called you, you did not deliver me out of their hands. ³So when I saw that you would not deliver *me*, I took my life in my hands and crossed over against the people of Ammon; and the LORD delivered them into my hand. Why then have you come up to me this day to fight against me?" ⁴Now Jephthah gathered together all the men of Gilead and fought against Ephraim. And the men of Gilead defeated Ephraim, because they said, "You Gileadites *are* fugitives of Ephraim among the Ephraimites *and* among the Manassites." ⁵The Gileadites seized the fords of the Jordan before the Ephraimites *arrived*. And when *any* Ephraimite who escaped said, "Let me cross over," the men of Gilead would say to him, "*Are* you an

Ephraimite?" If he said, "No," ⁶then they would say to him, "Then say, 'Shibboleth'!" And he would say, "Sibboleth," for he could not pronounce *it* right. Then they would take him and kill him at the fords of the Jordan. There fell at that time forty-two thousand Ephraimites.

⁷And Jephthah judged Israel six years. Then Jephthah the Gileadite died and was buried among the cities of Gilead.

Ibzan, Elon, and Abdon

⁸After him, Ibzan of Bethlehem judged Israel. ⁹He had thirty sons. And he gave away thirty daughters in marriage, and brought in thirty daughters from elsewhere for his sons. He judged Israel seven years. ¹⁰Then Ibzan died and was buried at Bethlehem.

¹¹After him, Elon the Zebulunite judged Israel. He judged Israel ten years. ¹²And Elon the Zebulunite died and was buried at Aijalon in the country of Zebulun.

¹³After him, Abdon the son of Hillel the Pirathonite judged Israel. ¹⁴He had forty sons and thirty grandsons, who rode on seventy young donkeys. He judged Israel eight years. ¹⁵Then Abdon the son of Hillel the Pirathonite died and was buried in Pirathon in the land of Ephraim, in the mountains of the Amalekites.

INTIMATE MOMENTS

The next time your husband is standing at the kitchen sink, walk up behind him and give him a really big hug. You don't have to say anything; just let him know that you're happy to be his wife, and to be with him at that moment.

The Birth of Samson

13 Again the children of Israel did evil in the sight of the LORD, and the LORD delivered them into the hand of the Philistines for forty years.

²Now there was a certain man from Zorah, of the family of the Danites, whose name *was* Manoah; and his wife *was* barren

and had no children. ³And the Angel of the LORD appeared to the woman and said to her, "Indeed now, you are barren and have borne no children, but you shall conceive and bear a son. ⁴Now therefore, please be careful not to drink wine or *similar* drink, and not to eat anything unclean. ⁵For behold, you shall conceive and bear a son. And no razor shall come upon his head, for the child shall be a Nazirite to God from the womb; and he shall begin to deliver Israel out of the hand of the Philistines."

⁶So the woman came and told her husband, saying, "A Man of God came to me, and His countenance *was* like the countenance of the Angel of God, very awesome; but I did not ask Him where He *was* from, and He did not tell me His name. ⁷And He said to me, 'Behold, you shall conceive and bear a son. Now drink no wine or *similar* drink, nor eat anything unclean, for the child shall be a Nazirite to God from the womb to the day of his death.' "

⁸Then Manoah prayed to the LORD, and said, "O my Lord, please let the Man of God whom You sent come to us again and teach us what we shall do for the child who will be born."

⁹And God listened to the voice of Manoah, and the Angel of God came to the woman again as she was sitting in the field; but Manoah her husband *was* not with her. ¹⁰Then the woman ran in haste and told her husband, and said to him, "Look, the Man who came to me the *other* day has just now appeared to me!"

¹¹So Manoah arose and followed his wife. When he came to the Man, he said to Him, "Are You the Man who spoke to this woman?"

And He said, "I *am*."

¹²Manoah said, "Now let Your words come *to pass!* What will be the boy's rule of life, and his work?"

¹³So the Angel of the LORD said to Manoah, "Of all that I said to the woman let her be careful. ¹⁴She may not eat anything that comes from the vine, nor may she drink wine or *similar* drink, nor eat anything unclean. All that I commanded her let her observe."

¹⁵Then Manoah said to the Angel of the LORD, "Please let us detain You, and we will prepare a young goat for You."

¹⁶And the Angel of the LORD said to Manoah, "Though you detain Me, I will not eat your food. But if you offer a burnt offering, you must offer it to the LORD." (For Manoah did not know He *was* the Angel of the LORD.)

¹⁷Then Manoah said to the Angel of the LORD, "What *is* Your name, that when Your words come *to pass* we may honor You?"

¹⁸And the Angel of the LORD said to him, "Why do you ask My name, seeing it *is* wonderful?"

¹⁹So Manoah took the young goat with

ROMANTIC QUOTES AND NOTES
Leave the Threats Behind

One of the Ten Commandments of Marriage should be, "Never threaten to leave." Threats create cracks in the commitment, erode the security of total acceptance, and fuel fear. In addition, threats rarely cause a person to change; they communicate only rejection.

Rather than threaten to leave, each of us should creatively express our commitment and acceptance to our mates. God gave us an example to follow. He didn't tell us only once that He loved us; He told us often and in many ways. He even sent His Son to demonstrate His love, and He gave us His Word. He continues to show us His love through the ongoing ministry of the Holy Spirit.

Our mates need to hear words of commitment and acceptance, not just once but many times. Tell your mate often how much you love her. Tell him that you accept him just as he is.

Each time a difficulty arises in your relationship—a misunderstanding, a difference, or a clash of wills—remind your mate that you intend to remain loyal. Assure him that your commitment will not change because of this unfortunate situation. Such infusions of truth will become the reinforcements you both need to work through any difficulties.

the grain offering, and offered it upon the rock to the LORD. And He did a wondrous thing while Manoah and his wife looked on— 20it happened as the flame went up toward heaven from the altar—the Angel of the LORD ascended in the flame of the altar! When Manoah and his wife saw *this,* they fell on their faces to the ground. 21When the Angel of the LORD appeared no more to Manoah and his wife, then Manoah knew that He *was* the Angel of the LORD.

22And Manoah said to his wife, "We shall surely die, because we have seen God!"

23But his wife said to him, "If the LORD had desired to kill us, He would not have accepted a burnt offering and a grain offering from our hands, nor would He have shown us all these *things,* nor would He have told us *such things* as these at this time."

24So the woman bore a son and called his name Samson; and the child grew, and the LORD blessed him. 25And the Spirit of the LORD began to move upon him at Mahaneh Dan[a] between Zorah and Eshtaol.

Samson's Philistine Wife

14 Now Samson went down to Timnah, and saw a woman in Timnah of the daughters of the Philistines. 2So he went up and told his father and mother, saying, "I have seen a woman in Timnah of the daughters of the Philistines; now therefore, get her for me as a wife."

3Then his father and mother said to him, "*Is there* no woman among the daughters of your brethren, or among all my people, that you must go and get a wife from the uncircumcised Philistines?"

And Samson said to his father, "Get her for me, for she pleases me well."

4But his father and mother did not know that it was of the LORD—that He was seeking an occasion to move against the Philistines. For at that time the Philistines had dominion over Israel.

5So Samson went down to Timnah with his father and mother, and came to the vineyards of Timnah.

Now *to his* surprise, a young lion *came* roaring against him. 6And the Spirit of the LORD came mightily upon him, and he tore

13:25 [a]Literally *Camp of Dan* (compare 18:12)

He Had a 'Tude

"HE'S GOT A 'TUDE." "His attitude stinks." "He'd better fix his attitude."

Did Samson's parents and friends ever say anything like this about him?

You remember Samson—the popular, affable, good-looking man's man who had everything going for him? Today Samson might have become an Olympic champion. He had the tools: athletic ability, physical strength, intelligence, courage, leadership qualities—even great hair!

Although he lived long before the arrival of arrogant trash-talkers, he definitely had a 'tude. Arrogant and proud, Samson thought that all he needed in life were his own strength and abilities. Weren't the rules designed only for weaker and less-gifted men?

He found out how wrong he was when he fell for a woman named Delilah. She plotted with Samson's enemies against him, and when Samson betrayed his lifelong covenant with his Lord, he learned quickly that his own strength was insufficient. His life collapsed.

God has His own words for what we call attitude: *rebellion* and *pride*. He despises them both. "Everyone proud in heart is an abomination to the LORD" (Prov. 16:5). Jesus said, "And whoever exalts himself will be humbled, and he who humbles himself will be exalted" (Matt. 23:12).

the lion apart as one would have torn apart a young goat, though *he had* nothing in his hand. But he did not tell his father or his mother what he had done.

7Then he went down and talked with the woman; and she pleased Samson well. 8After some time, when he returned to get her, he turned aside to see the carcass of the lion. And behold, a swarm of bees and honey *were* in the carcass of the lion. 9He took some of it in his hands and went along, eating. When he came to his father and mother, he gave *some* to them, and they also ate. But he did not tell them that he had taken the honey out of the carcass of the lion.

[10]So his father went down to the woman. And Samson gave a feast there, for young men used to do so. [11]And it happened, when they saw him, that they brought thirty companions to be with him.

[12]Then Samson said to them, "Let me pose a riddle to you. If you can correctly solve and explain it to me within the seven days of the feast, then I will give you thirty linen garments and thirty changes of clothing. [13]But if you cannot explain *it* to me, then you shall give me thirty linen garments and thirty changes of clothing."

And they said to him, "Pose your riddle, that we may hear it."

[14]So he said to them:

"Out of the eater came something to eat,
    And out of the strong came something sweet."

Now for three days they could not explain the riddle.

[15]But it came to pass on the seventh[a] day that they said to Samson's wife, "Entice your husband, that he may explain the riddle to us, or else we will burn you and your father's house with fire. Have you invited us in order to take what is ours? *Is that* not *so?*"

[16]Then Samson's wife wept on him, and said, "You only hate me! You do not love me! You have posed a riddle to the sons of my people, but you have not explained *it* to me."

And he said to her, "Look, I have not explained *it* to my father or my mother; so should I explain *it* to you?" [17]Now she had wept on him the seven days while their feast lasted. And it happened on the seventh day that he told her, because she pressed him so much. Then she explained the riddle to the sons of her people. [18]So the men of the city said to him on the seventh day before the sun went down:

"What *is* sweeter than honey?
    And what *is* stronger than a lion?"

And he said to them:

"If you had not plowed with my heifer,
    You would not have solved my riddle!"

[19]Then the Spirit of the LORD came upon him mightily, and he went down to Ashkelon and killed thirty of their men, took their apparel, and gave the changes *of clothing* to those who had explained the riddle. So his anger was aroused, and he went back up to his father's house. [20]And Samson's wife was *given* to his companion, who had been his best man.

Samson Defeats the Philistines

15 After a while, in the time of wheat harvest, it happened that Samson visited his wife with a young goat. And he said, "Let me go in to my wife, into *her* room." But her father would not permit him to go in.

[2]Her father said, "I really thought that you thoroughly hated her; therefore I gave her to your companion. *Is* not her younger sister better than she? Please, take her instead."

[3]And Samson said to them, "This time I shall be blameless regarding the Philistines if I harm them!" [4]Then Samson went and caught three hundred foxes; and he took torches, turned *the foxes* tail to tail, and put a torch between each pair of tails. [5]When he had set the torches on fire, he let *the foxes* go into the standing grain of the Philistines, and burned up both the shocks and the standing grain, as well as the vineyards *and* olive groves.

[6]Then the Philistines said, "Who has done this?"

And they answered, "Samson, the son-in-law of the Timnite, because he has taken his wife and given her to his companion." So the Philistines came up and burned her and her father with fire.

[7]Samson said to them, "Since you would do a thing like this, I will surely take revenge on you, and after that I will cease." [8]So he attacked them hip and thigh with a great slaughter; then he went down and dwelt in the cleft of the rock of Etam.

[9]Now the Philistines went up, encamped in Judah, and deployed themselves against Lehi. [10]And the men of Judah said, "Why have you come up against us?"

14:15 [a]Following Masoretic Text, Targum, and Vulgate; Septuagint and Syriac read *fourth.*

So they answered, "We have come up to arrest Samson, to do to him as he has done to us."

¹¹Then three thousand men of Judah went down to the cleft of the rock of Etam, and said to Samson, "Do you not know that the Philistines rule over us? What *is* this you have done to us?"

And he said to them, "As they did to me, so I have done to them."

¹²But they said to him, "We have come down to arrest you, that we may deliver you into the hand of the Philistines."

Then Samson said to them, "Swear to me that you will not kill me yourselves."

¹³So they spoke to him, saying, "No, but we will tie you securely and deliver you into their hand; but we will surely not kill you." And they bound him with two new ropes and brought him up from the rock.

¹⁴When he came to Lehi, the Philistines came shouting against him. Then the Spirit of the LORD came mightily upon him; and the ropes that *were* on his arms became like flax that is burned with fire, and his bonds broke loose from his hands. ¹⁵He found a fresh jawbone of a donkey, reached out his hand and took it, and killed a thousand men with it. ¹⁶Then Samson said:

"With the jawbone of a donkey,
    Heaps upon heaps,
With the jawbone of a donkey
    I have slain a thousand men!"

¹⁷And so it was, when he had finished speaking, that he threw the jawbone from his hand, and called that place Ramath Lehi.ᵃ

¹⁸Then he became very thirsty; so he cried out to the LORD and said, "You have given this great deliverance by the hand of Your servant; and now shall I die of thirst and fall into the hand of the uncircumcised?" ¹⁹So God split the hollow place that *is* in Lehi,ᵃ and water came out, and he drank; and his spirit returned, and he revived. Therefore he called its name En Hakkore,ᵇ which is in Lehi to this day. ²⁰And he judged Israel twenty years in the days of the Philistines.

15:17 ᵃLiterally *Jawbone Height* **15:19** ᵃLiterally *Jawbone* (compare verse 14) ᵇLiterally *Spring of the Caller*

BIBLICAL INSIGHTS • 16:4, 5

The Power of a Woman

THE STORY OF SAMSON AND DELILAH is a potent biblical example of what humankind has seen throughout history: the power of a woman for good or for evil in the life of a man. Samson could easily defeat an army of enemy warriors, but he surrendered meekly to the charms of one woman.

A woman's power over men has not lessened since biblical days. Today, the advertising industry exploits this power in order to sell everything from cars to toothpaste. Magazines, billboards, posters, and store windows use attractive women, seductive women, and blatant sexual images to catch a man's glance and capture his attention (and, they hope, his wallet).

Female attraction can be deadly. But death was not our Designer's intention! He designed feminine power to give life. He created Eve to complete her man, to nurture life in him and to create new life through bearing children.

Many wives do not understand how profound their feminine power is. God has blessed you with an extraordinary ability that you can use for great good in your husband's life. Your power can meet his aloneness and his companionship needs, affirm his sexual identity, protect him from temptation, and keep him for life. Use it well.

Samson and Delilah

16 Now Samson went to Gaza and saw a harlot there, and went in to her. ²*When* the Gazites *were told,* "Samson has come here!" they surrounded *the place* and lay in wait for him all night at the gate of the city. They were quiet all night, saying, "In the morning, when it is daylight, we will kill him." ³And Samson lay *low* till midnight; then he arose at midnight, took hold of the doors of the gate of the city and the two gateposts, pulled them up, bar and all, put *them* on his shoulders, and carried them to the top of the hill that faces Hebron.

⁴Afterward it happened that he loved a woman in the Valley of Sorek, whose name *was* Delilah. ⁵And the lords of the Philistines came up to her and said to her, "Entice him, and find out where his great strength *lies,* and by what *means* we may overpower him, that we may bind him to afflict him; and every one of us will give you eleven hundred *pieces* of silver."

⁶So Delilah said to Samson, "Please tell me where your great strength *lies,* and with what you may be bound to afflict you."

⁷And Samson said to her, "If they bind me with seven fresh bowstrings, not yet dried, then I shall become weak, and be like any *other* man."

⁸So the lords of the Philistines brought up to her seven fresh bowstrings, not yet dried, and she bound him with them. ⁹Now *men were* lying in wait, staying with her in the room. And she said to him, "The Philistines *are* upon you, Samson!" But he broke the bowstrings as a strand of yarn breaks when it touches fire. So the secret of his strength was not known.

¹⁰Then Delilah said to Samson, "Look, you have mocked me and told me lies. Now, please tell me what you may be bound with."

¹¹So he said to her, "If they bind me securely with new ropes that have never been used, then I shall become weak, and be like any *other* man."

¹²Therefore Delilah took new ropes and bound him with them, and said to him, "The Philistines *are* upon you, Samson!" And *men were* lying in wait, staying in the room. But he broke them off his arms like a thread.

¹³Delilah said to Samson, "Until now you have mocked me and told me lies. Tell me what you may be bound with."

And he said to her, "If you weave the seven locks of my head into the web of the loom"—

¹⁴So she wove *it* tightly with the batten of the loom, and said to him, "The Philistines *are* upon you, Samson!" But he awoke from his sleep, and pulled out the batten and the web from the loom.

¹⁵Then she said to him, "How can you say, 'I love you,' when your heart *is* not with me? You have mocked me these three times, and have not told me where your

great strength *lies.*" ¹⁶And it came to pass, when she pestered him daily with her words and pressed him, *so* that his soul was vexed to death, ¹⁷that he told her all his heart, and said to her, "No razor has ever come upon my head, for I *have been* a Nazirite to God from my mother's womb. If I am shaven, then my strength will leave me, and I shall become weak, and be like any *other* man."

¹⁸When Delilah saw that he had told her all his heart, she sent and called for the lords of the Philistines, saying, "Come up once more, for he has told me all his heart." So the lords of the Philistines came up to her and brought the money in their hand. ¹⁹Then she lulled him to sleep on her knees, and called for a man and had him shave off the seven locks of his head. Then she began to torment him,[a] and his strength left him. ²⁰And she said, "The Philistines *are* upon you, Samson!" So he awoke from his sleep, and said, "I will go out as before, at other times, and shake myself free!" But he did not know that the LORD had departed from him.

²¹Then the Philistines took him and put out his eyes, and brought him down to Gaza. They bound him with bronze fetters, and he became a grinder in the prison. ²²However, the hair of his head began to grow again after it had been shaven.

Samson Dies with the Philistines

²³Now the lords of the Philistines gathered together to offer a great sacrifice to Dagon their god, and to rejoice. And they said:

"Our god has delivered into our hands Samson our enemy!"

²⁴When the people saw him, they praised their god; for they said:

"Our god has delivered into our hands our enemy,
The destroyer of our land,
And the one who multiplied our dead."

16:19 [a]Following Masoretic Text, Targum, and Vulgate; Septuagint reads *he began to be weak.*

²⁵So it happened, when their hearts were merry, that they said, "Call for Samson, that he may perform for us." So they called for Samson from the prison, and he performed for them. And they stationed him between the pillars. ²⁶Then Samson said to the lad who held him by the hand, "Let me feel the pillars which support the temple, so that I can lean on them." ²⁷Now the temple was full of men and women. All the lords of the Philistines *were* there—about three thousand men and women on the roof watching while Samson performed.

²⁸Then Samson called to the LORD, saying, "O Lord GOD, remember me, I pray! Strengthen me, I pray, just this once, O God, that I may with one *blow* take vengeance on the Philistines for my two eyes!" ²⁹And Samson took hold of the two middle pillars which supported the temple, and he braced himself against them, one on his right and the other on his left. ³⁰Then Samson said, "Let me die with the Philistines!" And he pushed with *all his* might, and the temple fell on the lords and all the people who *were* in it. So the dead that he killed at his death were more than he had killed in his life.

³¹And his brothers and all his father's household came down and took him, and brought *him* up and buried him between Zorah and Eshtaol in the tomb of his father Manoah. He had judged Israel twenty years.

Micah's Idolatry

17 Now there was a man from the mountains of Ephraim, whose name *was* Micah. ²And he said to his mother, "The eleven hundred *shekels* of silver that were taken from you, and on which you put a curse, even saying it in my ears—here *is* the silver with me; I took it."

And his mother said, "*May you be* blessed by the LORD, my son!" ³So when he had returned the eleven hundred *shekels* of silver to his mother, his mother said, "I had wholly dedicated the silver from my hand to the LORD for my son, to make a carved image and a molded image; now therefore, I will return it to you." ⁴Thus he returned the silver to his mother. Then his mother took two hundred *shekels* of silver and gave

them to the silversmith, and he made it into a carved image and a molded image; and they were in the house of Micah.

⁵The man Micah had a shrine, and made an ephod and household idols;ᵃ and he consecrated one of his sons, who became his priest. ⁶In those days *there was* no king in Israel; everyone did *what was* right in his own eyes.

⁷Now there was a young man from Bethlehem in Judah, of the family of Judah; he *was* a Levite, and was staying there. ⁸The man departed from the city of Bethlehem in Judah to stay wherever he could find *a place*. Then he came to the mountains of Ephraim, to the house of Micah, as he journeyed. ⁹And Micah said to him, "Where do you come from?"

So he said to him, "I *am* a Levite from Bethlehem in Judah, and I am on my way to find *a place* to stay."

¹⁰Micah said to him, "Dwell with me, and be a father and a priest to me, and I will give you ten *shekels* of silver per year, a suit of clothes, and your sustenance." So the Levite went in. ¹¹Then the Levite was content to dwell with the man; and the young man became like one of his sons to him. ¹²So Micah consecrated the Levite, and the young man became his priest, and lived in the house of Micah. ¹³Then Micah said, "Now I know that the LORD will be good to me, since I have a Levite as priest!"

INTIMATE MOMENTS

After dinner, give the kitchen a thorough cleaning for her, without being asked.

The Danites Adopt Micah's Idolatry

18 In those days *there was* no king in Israel. And in those days the tribe of the Danites was seeking an inheritance for itself to dwell in; for until that day *their* inheritance among the tribes of Israel had not fallen to them. ²So the children of Dan sent five men of their family from their territory, men of valor from Zorah and

---

17:5 ᵃHebrew *teraphim*

Eshtaol, to spy out the land and search it. They said to them, "Go, search the land." So they went to the mountains of Ephraim, to the house of Micah, and lodged there. ³While they *were* at the house of Micah, they recognized the voice of the young Levite. They turned aside and said to him, "Who brought you here? What are you doing in this *place?* What do you have here?"

⁴He said to them, "Thus and so Micah did for me. He has hired me, and I have become his priest."

⁵So they said to him, "Please inquire of God, that we may know whether the journey on which we go will be prosperous."

⁶And the priest said to them, "Go in peace. The presence of the LORD *be* with you on your way."

⁷So the five men departed and went to Laish. They saw the people who *were* there, how they dwelt safely, in the manner of the Sidonians, quiet and secure. *There were* no rulers in the land who might put *them* to shame for anything. They *were* far from the Sidonians, and they had no ties with anyone.ᵃ

⁸Then *the spies* came back to their brethren at Zorah and Eshtaol, and their brethren said to them, "What *is* your report?"

⁹So they said, "Arise, let us go up against them. For we have seen the land, and indeed it *is* very good. *Would* you *do* nothing? Do not hesitate to go, *and* enter to possess the land. ¹⁰When you go, you will come to a secure people and a large land. For God has given it into your hands, a place where *there is* no lack of anything that *is* on the earth."

¹¹And six hundred men of the family of the Danites went from there, from Zorah and Eshtaol, armed with weapons of war. ¹²Then they went up and encamped in Kirjath Jearim in Judah. (Therefore they call that place Mahaneh Danᵃ to this day. There *it is,* west of Kirjath Jearim.) ¹³And they passed from there to the mountains of Ephraim, and came to the house of Micah.

¹⁴Then the five men who had gone to spy out the country of Laish answered and said to their brethren, "Do you know that there are in these houses an ephod, household idols, a carved image, and a molded image? Now therefore, consider what you should do." ¹⁵So they turned aside there, and came to the house of the young Levite man—to the house of Micah—and greeted him. ¹⁶The six hundred men armed with their weapons of war, who *were* of the children of Dan, stood by the entrance of the gate. ¹⁷Then the five men who had gone to spy out the land went up. Entering there, they took the carved image, the ephod, the household idols, and the molded image. The priest stood at the entrance of the gate with the six hundred men *who were* armed with weapons of war.

¹⁸When these went into Micah's house and took the carved image, the ephod, the household idols, and the molded image, the priest said to them, "What are you doing?"

¹⁹And they said to him, "Be quiet, put your hand over your mouth, and come with us; be a father and a priest to us. *Is it* better for you to be a priest to the household of one man, or that you be a priest to a tribe and a family in Israel?" ²⁰So the priest's heart was glad; and he took the ephod, the household idols, and the carved image, and took his place among the people.

²¹Then they turned and departed, and put the little ones, the livestock, and the goods in front of them. ²²When they were a good way from the house of Micah, the men who *were* in the houses near Micah's house gathered together and overtook the children of Dan. ²³And they called out to the children of Dan. So they turned around and said to Micah, "What ails you, that you have gathered such a company?"

²⁴So he said, "You have taken away my gods which I made, and the priest, and you have gone away. Now what more do I have? How can you say to me, 'What ails you?' "

²⁵And the children of Dan said to him, "Do not let your voice be heard among us, lest angry men fall upon you, and you lose your life, with the lives of your household!" ²⁶Then the children of Dan went their way. And when Micah saw that they *were* too strong for him, he turned and went back to his house.

18:7 ᵃFollowing Masoretic Text, Targum, and Vulgate; Septuagint reads *with Syria.*
18:12 ᵃLiterally *Camp of Dan*

Danites Settle in Laish

²⁷So they took *the things* Micah had made, and the priest who had belonged to him, and went to Laish, to a people quiet and secure; and they struck them with the edge of the sword and burned the city with fire. ²⁸*There was* no deliverer, because it *was* far from Sidon, and they had no ties with anyone. It was in the valley that belongs to Beth Rehob. So they rebuilt the city and dwelt there. ²⁹And they called the name of the city Dan, after the name of Dan their father, who was born to Israel. However, the name of the city formerly *was* Laish.

³⁰Then the children of Dan set up for themselves the carved image; and Jonathan the son of Gershom, the son of Manasseh,ᵃ and his sons were priests to the tribe of Dan until the day of the captivity of the land. ³¹So they set up for themselves Micah's carved image which he made, all the time that the house of God was in Shiloh.

The Levite's Concubine

19 And it came to pass in those days, when *there was* no king in Israel, that there was a certain Levite staying in the remote mountains of Ephraim. He took for himself a concubine from Bethlehem in Judah. ²But his concubine played the harlot against him, and went away from him to her father's house at Bethlehem in Judah, and was there four whole months. ³Then her husband arose and went after her, to speak kindly to her *and* bring her back, having his servant and a couple of donkeys with him. So she brought him into her father's house; and when the father of the young woman saw him, he was glad to meet him. ⁴Now his father-in-law, the young woman's father, detained him; and he stayed with him three days. So they ate and drank and lodged there.

⁵Then it came to pass on the fourth day that they arose early in the morning, and he stood to depart; but the young woman's father said to his son-in-law, "Refresh your heart with a morsel of bread, and afterward go your way."

⁶So they sat down, and the two of them ate and drank together. Then the young woman's father said to the man, "Please be content to stay all night, and let your heart be merry." ⁷And when the man stood to depart, his father-in-law urged him; so he lodged there again. ⁸Then he arose early in the morning on the fifth day to depart, but the young woman's father said, "Please refresh your heart." So they delayed until afternoon; and both of them ate.

⁹And when the man stood to depart—he and his concubine and his servant—his father-in-law, the young woman's father, said to him, "Look, the day is now drawing toward evening; please spend the night. See, the day is coming to an end; lodge here, that your heart may be merry. Tomorrow go your way early, so that you may get home."

¹⁰However, the man was not willing to spend that night; so he rose and departed, and came opposite Jebus (that *is,* Jerusalem). With him were the two saddled donkeys; his concubine *was* also with him. ¹¹They *were* near Jebus, and the day was far spent; and the servant said to his master, "Come, please, and let us turn aside into this city of the Jebusites and lodge in it."

¹²But his master said to him, "We will not turn aside here into a city of foreigners, who *are* not of the children of Israel; we will go on to Gibeah." ¹³So he said to his servant, "Come, let us draw near to one of these places, and spend the night in Gibeah or in Ramah." ¹⁴And they passed by and went their way; and the sun went down on them near Gibeah, which belongs to Benjamin. ¹⁵They turned aside there to go in to lodge in Gibeah. And when he went in, he sat down in the open square of the city, for no one would take them into *his* house to spend the night.

¹⁶Just then an old man came in from his work in the field at evening, who also *was* from the mountains of Ephraim; he was staying in Gibeah, whereas the men of the place *were* Benjamites. ¹⁷And when he raised his eyes, he saw the traveler in the open square of the city; and the old man said, "Where are you going, and where do you come from?"

¹⁸So he said to him, "We *are* passing from Bethlehem in Judah toward the remote mountains of Ephraim; I *am* from

---

18:30 ᵃSeptuagint and Vulgate read *Moses.*

The Pioneering Work of Thinking Right

TODAY WE DON'T LIKE TO THINK. It's too hard. It doesn't produce enough immediate results. We don't have time.

Quiet, reflective silence has become as endangered as the spotted owl. Yet if an unnamed Levite could confront his indifferent countrymen about a brutal attack with the words, "Consider it, confer, and speak up," (19:30), then shouldn't I learn how to reengage my brain? I'm learning the lost art of thinking right about life. Here are some of the questions I'm wrestling with:

• What do I really believe?
• Why am I doing what I do?
• What pressurizes my life?
• What drives me?
• What do I consider truly valuable?
• What are my values and does my schedule reflect my ultimate values?
• How will my present lifestyle affect my family in twenty years?
• What does God want me to do with my life, family, and possessions?
• What is my purpose?

I'm learning that thinking is gritty, lonesome work—if God isn't at the center. He has encouraged me that He's still in the business of creating original thoughts, life-changing ideas, and innovations that will shape the destiny of our homes.

I'm learning that real thinking is pioneering work.

there. I went to Bethlehem in Judah; *now* I am going to the house of the LORD. But there *is* no one who will take me into his house, 19although we have both straw and fodder for our donkeys, and bread and wine for myself, for your female servant, and for the young man *who is* with your servant; *there is* no lack of anything."

20And the old man said, "Peace *be* with you! However, *let* all your needs *be* my responsibility; only do not spend the night in the open square." 21So he brought him into his house, and gave fodder to the donkeys. And they washed their feet, and ate and drank.

Gibeah's Crime

22As they were enjoying themselves, suddenly certain men of the city, perverted men,[a] surrounded the house *and* beat on the door. They spoke to the master of the house, the old man, saying, "Bring out the man who came to your house, that we may know him *carnally!*"

23But the man, the master of the house, went out to them and said to them, "No, my brethren! I beg you, do not act *so* wickedly! Seeing this man has come into my house, do not commit this outrage. 24Look, *here is* my virgin daughter and *the man's*[a] concubine; let me bring them out now. Humble them, and do with them as you please; but to this man do not do such a vile thing!" 25But the men would not heed him. So the man took his concubine and brought *her* out to them. And they knew her and abused her all night until morning; and when the day began to break, they let her go.

26Then the woman came as the day was dawning, and fell down at the door of the man's house where her master *was,* till it was light.

27When her master arose in the morning, and opened the doors of the house and went out to go his way, there was his concubine, fallen *at* the door of the house with her hands on the threshold. 28And he said to her, "Get up and let us be going." But there was no answer. So the man lifted her onto the donkey; and the man got up and went to his place.

29When he entered his house he took a knife, laid hold of his concubine, and divided her into twelve pieces, limb by limb,[a] and sent her throughout all the territory of Israel. 30And so it was that all who saw it said, "No such deed has been done or seen from the day that the children of Israel came up from the land of Egypt until this day. Consider it, confer, and speak up!"

19:22 [a]Literally *sons of Belial*   19:24 [a]Literally *his*
19:29 [a]Literally *with her bones*

Israel's War with the Benjamites

20 So all the children of Israel came out, from Dan to Beersheba, as well as from the land of Gilead, and the congregation gathered together as one man before the LORD at Mizpah. ²And the leaders of all the people, all the tribes of Israel, presented themselves in the assembly of the people of God, four hundred thousand foot soldiers who drew the sword. ³(Now the children of Benjamin heard that the children of Israel had gone up to Mizpah.)

Then the children of Israel said, "Tell *us,* how did this wicked deed happen?"

⁴So the Levite, the husband of the woman who was murdered, answered and said, "My concubine and I went into Gibeah, which belongs to Benjamin, to spend the night. ⁵And the men of Gibeah rose against me, and surrounded the house at night because of me. They intended to kill me, but instead they ravished my concubine so that she died. ⁶So I took hold of my concubine, cut her in pieces, and sent her throughout all the territory of the inheritance of Israel, because they committed lewdness and outrage in Israel. ⁷Look! All of you *are* children of Israel; give your advice and counsel here and now!"

⁸So all the people arose as one man, saying, "None *of us* will go to his tent, nor will any turn back to his house; ⁹but now this *is* the thing which we will do to Gibeah: *We will go up* against it by lot. ¹⁰We will take ten men out of *every* hundred throughout all the tribes of Israel, a hundred out of *every* thousand, and a thousand out of *every* ten thousand, to make provisions for the people, that when they come to Gibeah in Benjamin, they may repay all the vileness that they have done in Israel." ¹¹So all the men of Israel were gathered against the city, united together as one man.

¹²Then the tribes of Israel sent men through all the tribe of Benjamin, saying, "What *is* this wickedness that has occurred among you? ¹³Now therefore, deliver up the men, the perverted men[a] who *are* in Gibeah, that we may put them to death and remove the evil from Israel!"

INTIMATE MOMENTS

Try It for a Week

Remember how much you and your wife talked when you were dating? Do you recall how polite you were, how respectful of her feelings, how eager to please and delight?

Why not try that for one week?

What kind of things did you talk about when you were dating? Probably not about diapers or budgets or household chores or the cost of groceries. Try to mentally reconstruct some of your most enjoyable conversations, and then use those topics for some freshly stimulating dialogues.

What did you do to show her you knew the meaning of *polite*? Did you open the car door for her? Invite her to go first? Allow her to finish a thought before you shared your own perspective? Make a list of all the things you did to show her what a gentleman you were, and do them again.

How did you get her to laugh? What especially pleased her? How did you demonstrate your concern for her feelings? Whatever you did, do it again, for a solid week … and then watch what happens.

But the children of Benjamin would not listen to the voice of their brethren, the children of Israel. ¹⁴Instead, the children of Benjamin gathered together from their cities to Gibeah, to go to battle against the children of Israel. ¹⁵And from their cities at that time the children of Benjamin numbered twenty-six thousand men who drew the sword, besides the inhabitants of Gibeah, who numbered seven hundred select men. ¹⁶Among all this people *were* seven hundred select men *who were* left-handed; every one could sling a stone at a hair's *breadth* and not miss. ¹⁷Now besides Benjamin, the men of Israel numbered four hundred thousand men who drew the sword; all of these *were* men of war.

¹⁸Then the children of Israel arose and went up to the house of God[a] to inquire of

20:13 ᵃLiterally *sons of Belial* **20:18** ᵃOr *Bethel*

God. They said, "Which of us shall go up first to battle against the children of Benjamin?"

The LORD said, "Judah first!"

19So the children of Israel rose in the morning and encamped against Gibeah. 20And the men of Israel went out to battle against Benjamin, and the men of Israel put themselves in battle array to fight against them at Gibeah. 21Then the children of Benjamin came out of Gibeah, and on that day cut down to the ground twenty-two thousand men of the Israelites. 22And the people, that is, the men of Israel, encouraged themselves and again formed the battle line at the place where they had put themselves in array on the first day. 23Then the children of Israel went up and wept before the LORD until evening, and asked counsel of the LORD, saying, "Shall I again draw near for battle against the children of my brother Benjamin?"

And the LORD said, "Go up against him."

24So the children of Israel approached the children of Benjamin on the second day. 25And Benjamin went out against them from Gibeah on the second day, and cut down to the ground eighteen thousand more of the children of Israel; all these drew the sword.

26Then all the children of Israel, that is, all the people, went up and came to the house of God[a] and wept. They sat there before the LORD and fasted that day until evening; and they offered burnt offerings and peace offerings before the LORD. 27So the children of Israel inquired of the LORD (the ark of the covenant of God was there in those days, 28and Phinehas the son of Eleazar, the son of Aaron, stood before it in those days), saying, "Shall I yet again go out to battle against the children of my brother Benjamin, or shall I cease?"

And the LORD said, "Go up, for tomorrow I will deliver them into your hand."

29Then Israel set men in ambush all around Gibeah. 30And the children of Israel went up against the children of Benjamin on the third day, and put themselves in battle array against Gibeah as at the other times. 31So the children of Benjamin went out against the people, and were drawn away from the city. They began to strike down and kill some of the people, as at the other times, in the highways (one of which goes up to Bethel and the other to Gibeah) and in the field, about thirty men of Israel. 32And the children of Benjamin said, "They are defeated before us, as at first."

But the children of Israel said, "Let us flee and draw them away from the city to the highways." 33So all the men of Israel rose from their place and put themselves in battle array at Baal Tamar. Then Israel's men in ambush burst forth from their position in the plain of Geba. 34And ten thousand select men from all Israel came against Gibeah, and the battle was fierce. But the Benjamites[a] did not know that disaster was upon them. 35The LORD defeated Benjamin before Israel. And the children of Israel destroyed that day twenty-five thousand one hundred Benjamites; all these drew the sword.

36So the children of Benjamin saw that they were defeated. The men of Israel had given ground to the Benjamites, because they relied on the men in ambush whom they had set against Gibeah. 37And the men in ambush quickly rushed upon Gibeah; the men in ambush spread out and struck the whole city with the edge of the sword. 38Now the appointed signal between the men of Israel and the men in ambush was that they would make a great cloud of smoke rise up from the city, 39whereupon the men of Israel would turn in battle. Now Benjamin had begun to strike and kill about thirty of the men of Israel. For they said, "Surely they are defeated before us, as in the first battle." 40But when the cloud began to rise from the city in a column of smoke, the Benjamites looked behind them, and there was the whole city going up in smoke to heaven. 41And when the men of Israel turned back, the men of Benjamin panicked, for they saw that disaster had come upon them. 42Therefore they turned their backs before the men of Israel in the direction of the wilderness; but the battle overtook them, and whoever came out of the cities they destroyed in their midst. 43They surrounded the Benjamites, chased them, and easily trampled them down as far as the front of Gibeah toward the east. 44And

20:26 [a]Or Bethel 20:34 [a]Literally they

eighteen thousand men of Benjamin fell; all these *were* men of valor. ⁴⁵Then they^a turned and fled toward the wilderness to the rock of Rimmon; and they cut down five thousand of them on the highways. Then they pursued them relentlessly up to Gidom, and killed two thousand of them. ⁴⁶So all who fell of Benjamin that day were twenty-five thousand men who drew the sword; all these *were* men of valor.

⁴⁷But six hundred men turned and fled toward the wilderness to the rock of Rimmon, and they stayed at the rock of Rimmon for four months. ⁴⁸And the men of Israel turned back against the children of Benjamin, and struck them down with the edge of the sword—from *every* city, men and beasts, all who were found. They also set fire to all the cities they came to.

Wives Provided for the Benjamites

21 Now the men of Israel had sworn an oath at Mizpah, saying, "None of us shall give his daughter to Benjamin as a wife." ²Then the people came to the house of God,^a and remained there before God till evening. They lifted up their voices and wept bitterly, ³and said, "O Lord God of Israel, why has this come to pass in Israel, that today there should be one tribe *missing* in Israel?"

⁴So it was, on the next morning, that the people rose early and built an altar there, and offered burnt offerings and peace offerings. ⁵The children of Israel said, "Who *is there* among all the tribes of Israel who did not come up with the assembly to the Lord?" For they had made a great oath concerning anyone who had not come up to the Lord at Mizpah, saying, "He shall surely be put to death." ⁶And the children of Israel grieved for Benjamin their brother, and said, "One tribe is cut off from Israel today. ⁷What shall we do for wives for those who remain, seeing we have sworn by the Lord that we will not give them our daughters as wives?"

⁸And they said, "What one *is there* from the tribes of Israel who did not come up to Mizpah to the Lord?" And, in fact, no one had come to the camp from Jabesh Gilead to

BIBLICAL INSIGHTS • 21:25
The Basis for Right Values

THE OLD TESTAMENT describes many difficult periods and dark days in the history of Israel. Of one particularly bad time, it was written, "In those days there was no king in Israel; everyone did what was right in his own eyes" (21:25).

That sounds very much like our culture today, doesn't it? We live in a time when there seems to be very little in the way of moral, spiritual, or social absolutes. Each person is free to define his or her own set of values and morals.

Our culture despises the idea of pushing one's own values on someone else. Even many Christians have adopted this attitude—which is tragic, because followers of Christ have been given the responsibility to broadcast the values of Scripture and the gospel of Christ. While room certainly exists for individuals to apply differing interpretations to some parts of the Bible, many scriptural values should be clear to all.

We need to ask ourselves, "Whose values are most important to us?" And "What are the values we ultimately embrace in our family?" If we answer with anything but those spelled out in the written Word of God, then it is past time for some personal reevaluation and change.

the assembly. ⁹For when the people were counted, indeed, not one of the inhabitants of Jabesh Gilead *was* there. ¹⁰So the congregation sent out there twelve thousand of their most valiant men, and commanded them, saying, "Go and strike the inhabitants of Jabesh Gilead with the edge of the sword, including the women and children. ¹¹And this *is* the thing that you shall do: You shall utterly destroy every male, and every woman who has known a man intimately." ¹²So they found among the inhabitants of Jabesh Gilead four hundred young virgins who had not known a man intimately; and they brought them to the camp at Shiloh, which is in the land of Canaan.

20:45 ^aSeptuagint reads *the rest.* **21:2** ^aOr *Bethel*

[13]Then the whole congregation sent *word* to the children of Benjamin who *were* at the rock of Rimmon, and announced peace to them. [14]So Benjamin came back at that time, and they gave them the women whom they had saved alive of the women of Jabesh Gilead; and yet they had not found enough for them.

[15]And the people grieved for Benjamin, because the LORD had made a void in the tribes of Israel.

[16]Then the elders of the congregation said, "What shall we do for wives for those who remain, since the women of Benjamin have been destroyed?" [17]And they said, "*There must be* an inheritance for the survivors of Benjamin, that a tribe may not be destroyed from Israel. [18]However, we cannot give them wives from our daughters, for the children of Israel have sworn an oath, saying, 'Cursed *be* the one who gives a wife to Benjamin.' " [19]Then they said, "In fact, *there is* a yearly feast of the LORD in Shiloh, which *is* north of Bethel, on the east side of the highway that goes up from Bethel to Shechem, and south of Lebonah."

[20]Therefore they instructed the children of Benjamin, saying, "Go, lie in wait in the vineyards, [21]and watch; and just when the daughters of Shiloh come out to perform their dances, then come out from the vineyards, and every man catch a wife for himself from the daughters of Shiloh; then go to the land of Benjamin. [22]Then it shall be, when their fathers or their brothers come to us to complain, that we will say to them, 'Be kind to them for our sakes, because we did not take a wife for any of them in the war; for *it is* not *as though* you have given the *women* to them at this time, making yourselves guilty of your oath.' "

[23]And the children of Benjamin did so; they took enough wives for their number from those who danced, whom they caught. Then they went and returned to their inheritance, and they rebuilt the cities and dwelt in them. [24]So the children of Israel departed from there at that time, every man to his tribe and family; they went out from there, every man to his inheritance.

[25]In those days *there was* no king in Israel; everyone did *what was* right in his own eyes.

RUTH

THE BOOK OF RUTH memorably recalls God's kindness and providence in the life of two widows: Naomi, a Hebrew, and her daughter-in-law, Ruth. Although no Israelite blood flowed in Ruth's veins, she had become a believer in the God of Israel, probably by observing the godly (and attractive!) lifestyle of Naomi. In time, these two poverty-stricken women find the favor of a wealthy Hebrew farmer named Boaz, who falls in love with and marries Ruth.

The book of Ruth paints a remarkable portrait of a woman who, despite growing up in a pagan culture, learned to honor God through her stellar character and her deep humility. Boaz commends her as "a virtuous woman" (3:11)—and there is much that mothers and daughters today can learn from her example. Boaz also provides us with a wonderful example of a godly man who kindly cares for these widows in their distress (as James 1:27 instructs all of us to do).

Ruth and Boaz together comprise a major branch in the family tree of Jesus, who lived 1,100 years after His ancestors died. Their godly relationship stunningly pictures God's redeeming work, just as all marriage illustrates the unique relationship between Christ and His church (Eph. 5:31, 32).

Modern readers of the book not only delight in the love story it tells, they also frequently quote one of its verses at weddings: "Whither thou goest, I will go; and where thou lodgest, I will lodge: thy people *shall be* my people, and thy God my God" (1:16, KJV). While many of us use that solemn declaration as a part of our covenant promise to one another as husband and wife, we should remember that Ruth first spoke it to her mother-in-law after they both became widows. Ruth felt so compelled by the piety and character of Naomi, that she refused to stay in the land of her birth, but rather chose to accompany and support this dear woman, who had become her spiritual mentor. And so Ruth became one of a select handful of non-Israelites to gain an honored place in the lineage of Jesus Christ.

Elimelech's Family Goes to Moab

1 Now it came to pass, in the days when the judges ruled, that there was a famine in the land. And a certain man of Bethlehem, Judah, went to dwell in the country of Moab, he and his wife and his two sons. ²The name of the man *was* Elimelech, the name of his wife *was* Naomi, and the names of his two sons *were* Mahlon and Chilion—Ephrathites of Bethlehem, Judah. And they went to the country of Moab and remained there. ³Then Elimelech, Naomi's husband, died; and she was left, and her two sons. ⁴Now they took wives of the women of Moab: the name of the one *was* Orpah, and the name of the other Ruth. And they dwelt there about ten years. ⁵Then both Mahlon and Chilion also died; so the woman survived her two sons and her husband.

Naomi Returns with Ruth

⁶Then she arose with her daughters-in-law that she might return from the country of Moab, for she had heard in the country of Moab that the LORD had visited His people by giving them bread. ⁷Therefore she went out from the place where she was, and her two daughters-in-law with her; and they went on the way to return to the land of Judah. ⁸And Naomi said to her two daughters-in-law, "Go, return each to her mother's house. The LORD deal kindly with you, as you have dealt with the dead and with me. ⁹The LORD grant that you may find rest, each in the house of her husband."

So she kissed them, and they lifted up their voices and wept. ¹⁰And they said to her, "Surely we will return with you to your people."

¹¹But Naomi said, "Turn back, my daughters; why will you go with me? *Are* there still sons in my womb, that they may be your husbands? ¹²Turn back, my daughters, go—for I am too old to have a husband. If I should say I have hope, *if* I should have a husband tonight and should also bear sons, ¹³would you wait for them till they were grown? Would you restrain yourselves from having husbands? No, my daughters; for it grieves me very much for your sakes that the hand of the LORD has gone out against me!"

¹⁴Then they lifted up their voices and wept again; and Orpah kissed her mother-in-law, but Ruth clung to her.

¹⁵And she said, "Look, your sister-in-law has gone back to her people and to her gods; return after your sister-in-law."

¹⁶But Ruth said:

"Entreat me not to leave you,
Or to turn back from following
   after you;
For wherever you go, I will go;
And wherever you lodge, I will lodge;
Your people *shall be* my people,
And your God, my God.
17 Where you die, I will die,
And there will I be buried.
The LORD do so to me, and more
   also,
If *anything but* death parts you
   and me."

¹⁸When she saw that she was determined to go with her, she stopped speaking to her.

¹⁹Now the two of them went until they came to Bethlehem. And it happened, when they had come to Bethlehem, that all the city was excited because of them; and the women said, "*Is* this Naomi?"

²⁰But she said to them, "Do not call me Naomi;ᵃ call me Mara,ᵇ for the Almighty has dealt very bitterly with me. ²¹I went out full, and the LORD has brought me home again empty. Why do you call me Naomi, since the LORD has testified against me, and the Almighty has afflicted me?"

²²So Naomi returned, and Ruth the Moabitess her daughter-in-law with her, who returned from the country of Moab. Now they came to Bethlehem at the beginning of barley harvest.

Ruth Meets Boaz

2 There was a relative of Naomi's husband, a man of great wealth, of the family of Elimelech. His name *was* Boaz. ²So Ruth the Moabitess said to Naomi, "Please let me go to the field, and glean heads of grain after *him* in whose sight I may find favor."

And she said to her, "Go, my daughter." ³Then she left, and went and gleaned in

---

1:20 ᵃLiterally *Pleasant* ᵇLiterally *Bitter*

the field after the reapers. And she happened to come to the part of the field *belonging* to Boaz, who *was* of the family of Elimelech.

⁴Now behold, Boaz came from Bethlehem, and said to the reapers, "The LORD *be* with you!"

And they answered him, "The LORD bless you!"

⁵Then Boaz said to his servant who was in charge of the reapers, "Whose young woman *is* this?"

⁶So the servant who was in charge of the reapers answered and said, "It *is* the young Moabite woman who came back with Naomi from the country of Moab. ⁷And she said, 'Please let me glean and gather after the reapers among the sheaves.' So she came and has continued from morning until now, though she rested a little in the house."

⁸Then Boaz said to Ruth, "You will listen, my daughter, will you not? Do not go to glean in another field, nor go from here, but stay close by my young women. ⁹*Let* your eyes *be* on the field which they reap, and go after them. Have I not commanded the young men not to touch you? And when you are thirsty, go to the vessels and drink from what the young men have drawn."

¹⁰So she fell on her face, bowed down to the ground, and said to him, "Why have I found favor in your eyes, that you should take notice of me, since I *am* a foreigner?"

¹¹And Boaz answered and said to her, "It has been fully reported to me, all that you have done for your mother-in-law since the death of your husband, and *how* you have left your father and your mother and the land of your birth, and have come to a people whom you did not know before. ¹²The LORD repay your work, and a full reward be given you by the LORD God of Israel, under whose wings you have come for refuge."

¹³Then she said, "Let me find favor in your sight, my lord; for you have comforted me, and have spoken kindly to your maidservant, though I am not like one of your maidservants."

¹⁴Now Boaz said to her at mealtime, "Come here, and eat of the bread, and dip your piece of bread in the vinegar." So she sat beside the reapers, and he passed

BIBLICAL INSIGHTS • 1:6–16

The Power of Godly Character

RUTH'S EXTRAORDINARY LOYALTY to Naomi is one of the greatest examples of family commitment in the Bible. How many people do you know who, upon losing a spouse, would continue showing such honor and dedication to an in-law?

Reading through the book of Ruth, it seems evident that this loyalty was unusual in those times as well. In this passage, Naomi urges her daughters-in-law to return to their own families after their husbands have died, and is surprised when they say they want to remain with her. "Turn back, my daughters," she says. "Why will you go with me? Are there still sons in my womb, that they may be your husbands?" (1:11) When Orpah decides to return to her home and Ruth refuses, Naomi tries again to persuade her to leave.

Word of Ruth's devotion to Naomi apparently spread among the people of Israel. In the next chapter Ruth asks Boaz, "Why have I found favor in your eyes, that you should take notice of me, since I am a foreigner?" He replies, "It has been fully reported to me, all that you have done for your mother-in-law since the death of your husband, and how you have left your father and your mother and the land of your birth, and have come to a people whom you did not know before. The LORD repay your work, and a full reward be given you by the LORD God of Israel, under whose wings you have come for refuge" (2:10–12).

What a wonderful story of the power of godly character!

parched *grain* to her; and she ate and was satisfied, and kept some back. ¹⁵And when she rose up to glean, Boaz commanded his young men, saying, "Let her glean even among the sheaves, and do not reproach her. ¹⁶Also let *grain* from the bundles fall purposely for her; leave *it* that she may glean, and do not rebuke her."

¹⁷So she gleaned in the field until evening, and beat out what she had gleaned, and it was about an ephah of barley. ¹⁸Then she took *it* up and went into the city, and her mother-in-law saw what she had gleaned. So she brought out and gave to her what she had kept back after she had been satisfied.

¹⁹And her mother-in-law said to her, "Where have you gleaned today? And where did you work? Blessed be the one who took notice of you."

So she told her mother-in-law with whom she had worked, and said, "The man's name with whom I worked today *is* Boaz."

²⁰Then Naomi said to her daughter-in-law, "Blessed *be* he of the LORD, who has not forsaken His kindness to the living and the dead!" And Naomi said to her, "This man *is* a relation of ours, one of our close relatives."

²¹Ruth the Moabitess said, "He also said to me, 'You shall stay close by my young men until they have finished all my harvest.' "

²²And Naomi said to Ruth her daughter-in-law, "*It is* good, my daughter, that you go out with his young women, and that people do not meet you in any other field."

²³So she stayed close by the young women of Boaz, to glean until the end of barley harvest and wheat harvest; and she dwelt with her mother-in-law.

Ruth's Redemption Assured

3 Then Naomi her mother-in-law said to her, "My daughter, shall I not seek security for you, that it may be well with you? ²Now Boaz, whose young women you were with, *is he* not our relative? In fact, he is winnowing barley tonight at the threshing floor. ³Therefore wash yourself and anoint yourself, put on your *best* garment and go down to the threshing floor; *but* do not make yourself known to the man until he has finished eating and drinking. ⁴Then it shall be, when he lies down, that you shall notice the place where he lies; and you shall go in, uncover his feet, and lie down; and he will tell you what you should do."

⁵And she said to her, "All that you say to me I will do."

⁶So she went down to the threshing floor and did according to all that her mother-in-law instructed her. ⁷And after Boaz had eaten and drunk, and his heart was cheerful, he went to lie down at the end of the heap of grain; and she came softly, uncovered his feet, and lay down.

⁸Now it happened at midnight that the man was startled, and turned himself; and there, a woman was lying at his feet. ⁹And he said, "Who *are* you?"

So she answered, "I *am* Ruth, your maidservant. Take your maidservant under your wing,ᵃ for you are a close relative."

¹⁰Then he said, "Blessed *are* you of the LORD, my daughter! For you have shown more kindness at the end than at the beginning, in that you did not go after young men, whether poor or rich. ¹¹And now, my daughter, do not fear. I will do for you all that you request, for all the people of my town know that you *are* a virtuous woman. ¹²Now it is true that I *am* a close relative; however, there is a relative closer than I. ¹³Stay this night, and in the morning it shall be *that* if he will perform the duty of a close relative for you—good; let him do it. But if he does not want to perform the

INTIMATE MOMENTS

Don't Forget the Feet

Just as feet played a key role in the courtship of Ruth and Boaz (see 3:8), so they can play a fun role in your relationship with your husband. Don't merely uncover his feet, however; pamper those tootsies with a relaxing foot massage. All you need is a warm basin of water, some soap, a towel, some lotion—and a genuine desire to make him feel great. And who knows? You might even get the same response Ruth got from her man: "Blessed are you of the LORD! For you have shown more kindness at the end than at the beginning" (see 3:10).

3:9 ᵃOr *Spread the corner of your garment over your maidservant*

duty for you, then I will perform the duty for you, *as* the LORD lives! Lie down until morning."

[14]So she lay at his feet until morning, and she arose before one could recognize another. Then he said, "Do not let it be known that the woman came to the threshing floor." [15]Also he said, "Bring the shawl that *is* on you and hold it." And when she held it, he measured six *ephahs* of barley, and laid *it* on her. Then she[a] went into the city.

[16]When she came to her mother-in-law, she said, "*Is* that you, my daughter?"

Then she told her all that the man had done for her. [17]And she said, "These six *ephahs* of barley he gave me; for he said to me, 'Do not go empty-handed to your mother-in-law.' "

[18]Then she said, "Sit still, my daughter, until you know how the matter will turn out; for the man will not rest until he has concluded the matter this day."

Boaz Redeems Ruth

4 Now Boaz went up to the gate and sat down there; and behold, the close relative of whom Boaz had spoken came by. So Boaz said, "Come aside, friend,[a] sit down here." So he came aside and sat down. [2]And he took ten men of the elders of the city, and said, "Sit down here." So they sat down. [3]Then he said to the close relative, "Naomi, who has come back from the country of Moab, sold the piece of land which *belonged* to our brother Elimelech. [4]And I thought to inform you, saying, 'Buy *it* back in the presence of the inhabitants and the elders of my people. If you will redeem *it*, redeem *it*; but if you[a] will not redeem *it*, *then* tell me, that I may know; for *there is* no one but you to redeem *it*, and I *am* next after you.' "

And he said, "I will redeem *it*."

[5]Then Boaz said, "On the day you buy the field from the hand of Naomi, you must also buy *it* from Ruth the Moabitess,

BIBLICAL INSIGHTS • 3:18
The Man Will Not Rest

AS A STRANGER in a strange land, Ruth could not have known much about life in Israel. So at the beginning of her short courtship with Boaz, she had little idea of what to expect. She must have felt unsure, uneasy, and more than a little frightened.

Yet from the very beginning, Boaz demonstrated himself to be a godly man of strong character who would certainly keep his word, whatever it was. When marriage to him became a distinct possibility, it must have reassured her to hear Naomi say, "The man will not rest until he has concluded the matter this day" (3:18). What Boaz said he would do, he would most certainly do.

A woman needs to feel her husband's covenantal commitment to stay married and to love her and accept her. Then she feels safe to give him the gift of who she is. Every wife needs to know that romantic intimacy is just between her and her husband, and that he will not share any personal details with his friends. Apparently that described Ruth, for after watching Boaz in many contexts, she could marry this man with a strong sense of both contentment and security.

the wife of the dead, to perpetuate[a] the name of the dead through his inheritance."

[6]And the close relative said, "I cannot redeem *it* for myself, lest I ruin my own inheritance. You redeem my right of redemption for yourself, for I cannot redeem *it*."

[7]Now this *was the custom* in former times in Israel concerning redeeming and exchanging, to confirm anything: one man took off his sandal and gave *it* to the other, and this *was* a confirmation in Israel.

[8]Therefore the close relative said to Boaz, "Buy *it* for yourself." So he took off his sandal. [9]And Boaz said to the elders and all the people, "You *are* witnesses this

---

3:15 [a]Many Hebrew manuscripts, Syriac, and Vulgate read *she;* Masoretic Text, Septuagint, and Targum read *he.* **4:1** [a]Hebrew *peloni almoni;* literally *so and so* **4:4** [a]Following many Hebrew manuscripts, Septuagint, Syriac, Targum, and Vulgate; Masoretic Text reads *he.* **4:5** [a]Literally *raise up*

day that I have bought all that was Elimelech's, and all that *was* Chilion's and Mahlon's, from the hand of Naomi. [10]Moreover, Ruth the Moabitess, the widow of Mahlon, I have acquired as my wife, to perpetuate the name of the dead through his inheritance, that the name of the dead may not be cut off from among his brethren and from his position at the gate.[a] You *are* witnesses this day."

[11]And all the people who *were* at the gate, and the elders, said, "*We are* witnesses. The LORD make the woman who is coming to your house like Rachel and Leah, the two who built the house of Israel; and may you prosper in Ephrathah and be famous in Bethlehem. [12]May your house be like the house of Perez, whom Tamar bore to Judah, because of the offspring which the LORD will give you from this young woman."

Descendants of Boaz and Ruth

[13]So Boaz took Ruth and she became his wife; and when he went in to her, the LORD gave her conception, and she bore a son. [14]Then the women said to Naomi, "Blessed *be* the LORD, who has not left you this day without a close relative; and may his name be famous in Israel! [15]And may he be to you a restorer of life and a nourisher of your old age; for your daughter-in-law, who loves you, who is better to you than seven sons, has borne him." [16]Then Naomi took the child and laid him on her bosom, and became a nurse to him. [17]Also the neighbor women gave him a name, saying, "There is a son born to Naomi." And they called his name Obed. He *is* the father of Jesse, the father of David.

[18]Now this *is* the genealogy of Perez: Perez begot Hezron; [19]Hezron begot Ram, and Ram begot Amminadab; [20]Amminadab begot Nahshon, and Nahshon begot Salmon;[a] [21]Salmon begot Boaz, and Boaz begot Obed; [22]Obed begot Jesse, and Jesse begot David.

4:10 [a]Probably his civic office **4:20** [a]Hebrew *Salmah*

1 SAMUEL

FIRST SAMUEL IS THE FIRST OF SIX BIBLICAL BOOKS that outline the history of Israel, following the 350 years of the judges. At this time, God's people lived in the Promised Land as twelve distinct family groups, or tribes. This book describes how the nation became a united political entity, living under the rule of a king.

First Samuel gives special attention to three primary characters: Samuel the prophet, Saul the first king, and David the second king and "sweet psalmist of Israel" (2 Sam. 23:1). The famous account of David's battle with the Philistine giant Goliath is found in 1 Samuel 17.

You can gain a tremendous amount of wisdom by carefully considering the lives of the men and women profiled in 1 Samuel. The book also contains a number of marriage and family-related accounts that illustrate key biblical principles taught in other parts of the Bible.

The story begins with the heartbreak of a godly and faithful woman named Hannah, who had been unable to conceive a child. To her great joy, the Lord answers her prayers late in life and gives her a son named Samuel, who would become the last judge of Israel. Her life demonstrates that it is God who opens and closes the womb (Isaiah 66:9).

You also read the tragic account of the wicked sons of Eli the prophet, who show us clearly that our children must choose for themselves whether they will honor God and experience His blessing, or dishonor Him with their lives and suffer His judgment.

The poignant account of Samuel's anointing of Jesse's youngest son, David, as the person set apart by God to replace Saul as king, provides a great reminder that God has a plan for each of our lives—even the youngest member of a family. The book of Acts puts a capstone on this idea when it tells us that David "served his own generation by the will of God" (Acts 13:36). If David could do so, then there is every reason to think that you, too, can serve your own generation "by the will of God."

The Family of Elkanah

1 Now there was a certain man of Ramathaim Zophim, of the mountains of Ephraim, and his name *was* Elkanah the son of Jeroham, the son of Elihu,[a] the son of Tohu,[b] the son of Zuph, an Ephraimite. ²And he had two wives: the name of one *was* Hannah, and the name of the other Peninnah. Peninnah had children, but Hannah had no children. ³This man went up from his city yearly to worship and sacrifice to the LORD of hosts in Shiloh. Also the two sons of Eli, Hophni and Phinehas, the priests of the LORD, *were* there. ⁴And whenever the time came for Elkanah to make an offering, he would give portions to Peninnah his wife and to all her sons and daughters. ⁵But to Hannah he would give a double portion, for he loved Hannah, although the LORD had closed her womb. ⁶And her rival also provoked her severely, to make her miserable, because the LORD had closed her womb. ⁷So it was, year by year, when she went up to the house of the LORD, that she provoked her; therefore she wept and did not eat.

Hannah's Vow

⁸Then Elkanah her husband said to her, "Hannah, why do you weep? Why do you not eat? And why is your heart grieved? *Am* I not better to you than ten sons?"

⁹So Hannah arose after they had finished eating and drinking in Shiloh. Now Eli the priest was sitting on the seat by the doorpost of the tabernacle[a] of the LORD. ¹⁰And she *was* in bitterness of soul, and prayed to the LORD and wept in anguish. ¹¹Then she made a vow and said, "O LORD of hosts, if You will indeed look on the affliction of Your maidservant and remember me, and not forget Your maidservant, but will give Your maidservant a male child, then I will give him to the LORD all the days of his life, and no razor shall come upon his head."

¹²And it happened, as she continued praying before the LORD, that Eli watched her mouth. ¹³Now Hannah spoke in her heart; only her lips moved, but her voice was not heard. Therefore Eli thought she was drunk. ¹⁴So Eli said to her, "How long will you be drunk? Put your wine away from you!"

¹⁵But Hannah answered and said, "No, my lord, I *am* a woman of sorrowful spirit. I have drunk neither wine nor intoxicating drink, but have poured out my soul before the LORD. ¹⁶Do not consider your maidservant a wicked woman,[a] for out of the abundance of my complaint and grief I have spoken until now."

¹⁷Then Eli answered and said, "Go in peace, and the God of Israel grant your petition which you have asked of Him."

¹⁸And she said, "Let your maidservant find favor in your sight." So the woman went her way and ate, and her face was no longer *sad.*

Samuel Is Born and Dedicated

¹⁹Then they rose early in the morning and worshiped before the LORD, and returned and came to their house at Ramah. And Elkanah knew Hannah his wife, and the LORD remembered her. ²⁰So it came to pass in the process of time that Hannah conceived and bore a son, and called his name Samuel,[a] *saying,* "Because I have asked for him from the LORD."

²¹Now the man Elkanah and all his house went up to offer to the LORD the yearly sacrifice and his vow. ²²But Hannah did not go up, for she said to her husband, "*Not* until the child is weaned; then I will take him, that he may appear before the LORD and remain there forever."

²³So Elkanah her husband said to her, "Do what seems best to you; wait until you have weaned him. Only let the LORD establish His[a] word." Then the woman stayed and nursed her son until she had weaned him.

²⁴Now when she had weaned him, she took him up with her, with three bulls,[a] one ephah of flour, and a skin of wine, and brought him to the house of the LORD in Shiloh. And the child *was* young. ²⁵Then they slaughtered a bull, and brought the child to Eli. ²⁶And she said, "O my lord! As

---

1:1 [a]Spelled *Eliel* in 1 Chronicles 6:34 [b]Spelled *Toah* in 1 Chronicles 6:34 **1:9** [a]Hebrew *heykal,* palace or temple **1:16** [a]Literally *daughter of Belial* **1:20** [a]Literally *Heard by God* **1:23** [a]Following Masoretic Text, Targum, and Vulgate; Dead Sea Scrolls, Septuagint, and Syriac read *your.* **1:24** [a]Dead Sea Scrolls, Septuagint, and Syriac read *a three-year-old bull.*

your soul lives, my lord, I *am* the woman who stood by you here, praying to the LORD. [27]For this child I prayed, and the LORD has granted me my petition which I asked of Him. [28]Therefore I also have lent him to the LORD; as long as he lives he shall be lent to the LORD." So they worshiped the LORD there.

Hannah's Prayer

2 And Hannah prayed and said:

My heart rejoices in the LORD;
My horn[a] is exalted in the LORD.
I smile at my enemies,
Because I rejoice in Your salvation.

2 "No one is holy like the LORD,
For *there is* none besides You,
Nor *is there* any rock like our God.

3 "Talk no more so very proudly;
Let no arrogance come from your mouth,
For the LORD *is* the God of knowledge;
And by Him actions are weighed.

4 "The bows of the mighty men *are* broken,
And those who stumbled are girded with strength.

5 *Those who were* full have hired themselves out for bread,
And the hungry have ceased *to hunger.*
Even the barren has borne seven,
And she who has many children has become feeble.

6 "The LORD kills and makes alive;
He brings down to the grave and brings up.

7 The LORD makes poor and makes rich;
He brings low and lifts up.

8 He raises the poor from the dust
And lifts the beggar from the ash heap,
To set *them* among princes
And make them inherit the throne of glory.

"For the pillars of the earth *are* the LORD's,

2:1 [a]That is, strength

BIBLICAL INSIGHTS • 1:24-28
A Fitting Dedication

EVERY INDIVIDUAL BORN into this world must settle for himself what he will do with God's offer of salvation through faith in Jesus Christ. That is a decision that no one but the individual can make—but as Christian parents, we should follow the example that Hannah set for us and make sure that we bring our children (God's most wonderful gift to us, outside of eternal salvation and the gift of our spouse) to Him and dedicate them to His service.

Hannah fully understood, more than many of us, perhaps, what a gift her son really was. For years she had suffered the kind of emotional pain that no one can fully grasp other than another woman who also desperately wants to have children, but has been unable to conceive. Once the Lord answered Hannah's prayer and gave her a son, she intended to make sure that this delightful gift would bring praise and honor to the One who made it all possible.

So with joyful tears Hannah told Eli the priest, "For this child I prayed, and the LORD has granted me my petition which I asked of Him. Therefore I also have lent him to the LORD; as long as he lives he shall be lent to the LORD" (1:27, 28).

When we dedicate our children to God, it is much more than a public declaration of intent in a church service. Dedication is a *setting apart* or a *commitment* to equip, train and nurture a child with a heart for God and His work. I often wonder when I watch baby dedications at church if these young couples realize the importance of their public declaration. This is a solemn responsibility that demands prayer, hard work, and perseverance all the days that God gives us with our children. Then, it demands truly letting go when your children steps out of the nest to engage in spiritual battle. We are mere stewards of children for a season. Children are ultimately His.

And He has set the world upon them.
9   He will guard the feet of His saints,
     But the wicked shall be silent in
       darkness.

     "For by strength no man shall prevail.
10   The adversaries of the LORD shall be
       broken in pieces;
     From heaven He will thunder against
       them.
     The LORD will judge the ends of the
       earth.

     "He will give strength to His king,
     And exalt the horn of His anointed."

¹¹Then Elkanah went to his house at Ramah. But the child ministered to the LORD before Eli the priest.

The Wicked Sons of Eli

¹²Now the sons of Eli *were* corrupt;[a] they did not know the LORD. ¹³And the priests' custom with the people *was that* when any man offered a sacrifice, the priest's servant would come with a three-pronged fleshhook in his hand while the meat was boiling. ¹⁴Then he would thrust *it* into the pan, or kettle, or caldron, or pot; and the priest would take for himself all that the fleshhook brought up. So they did in Shiloh to all the Israelites who came there. ¹⁵Also, before they burned the fat, the priest's servant would come and say to the man who sacrificed, "Give meat for roasting to the priest, for he will not take boiled meat from you, but raw."

¹⁶And *if* the man said to him, "They should really burn the fat first; *then* you may take *as much* as your heart desires," he would then answer him, "*No,* but you must give *it* now; and if not, I will take *it* by force."

¹⁷Therefore the sin of the young men was very great before the LORD, for men abhorred the offering of the LORD.

Samuel's Childhood Ministry

¹⁸But Samuel ministered before the LORD, *even as* a child, wearing a linen ephod. ¹⁹Moreover his mother used to make him a little robe, and bring *it* to him year by year when she came up with her husband to offer the yearly sacrifice. ²⁰And Eli would bless Elkanah and his wife, and say, "The LORD give you descendants from this woman for the loan that was given to the LORD." Then they would go to their own home.

²¹And the LORD visited Hannah, so that she conceived and bore three sons and two daughters. Meanwhile the child Samuel grew before the LORD.

2:12 ᵃLiterally *sons of Belial*

ROMANTIC QUOTES AND NOTES
Know and Feel God's Pleasure

The sad story of Eli declares that God is pleased with those who obey Him but opposed to those who defy Him. This is an all-important principle for every couple! We can testify that a couple walking closely with God *knows* and *feels* God's pleasure. You were created to know God and to enjoy Him!

When you and your mate experience God, you experience life at its fullest. But when you allow yourselves to drift away from a close walk with Him, life becomes empty and purposeless.

Note how the Bible characterizes the ungodly sons of Eli, "Now the sons of Eli were corrupt; they did not know the LORD" (2:12). These young men—quite religious, but spiritually bankrupt—badly abused their priestly role: "The sin of the young men was very great before the LORD, for men abhorred the offering of the LORD" (v. 17). The word *abhorred* means "to scorn, feel disgust toward, hate, loathe, abhor, laugh at." The flagrantly rebellious lifestyle of Eli's sons became infectious.

But here is what God says, "Those who honor Me I will honor, and those who despise Me shall be lightly esteemed" (2:30). Honor God if you want to experience true joy in life and in your marriage.

Prophecy Against Eli's Household

22Now Eli was very old; and he heard everything his sons did to all Israel,a and how they lay with the women who assembled at the door of the tabernacle of meeting. 23So he said to them, "Why do you do such things? For I hear of your evil dealings from all the people. 24No, my sons! For *it is* not a good report that I hear. You make the LORD's people transgress. 25If one man sins against another, God will judge him. But if a man sins against the LORD, who will intercede for him?" Nevertheless they did not heed the voice of their father, because the LORD desired to kill them.

26And the child Samuel grew in stature, and in favor both with the LORD and men.

27Then a man of God came to Eli and said to him, "Thus says the LORD: 'Did I not clearly reveal Myself to the house of your father when they were in Egypt in Pharaoh's house? 28Did I not choose him out of all the tribes of Israel *to be* My priest, to offer upon My altar, to burn incense, and to wear an ephod before Me? And did I not give to the house of your father all the offerings of the children of Israel made by fire? 29Why do you kick at My sacrifice and My offering which I have commanded *in My* dwelling place, and honor your sons more than Me, to make yourselves fat with the best of all the offerings of Israel My people?' 30Therefore the LORD God of Israel says: 'I said indeed *that* your house and the house of your father would walk before Me forever.' But now the LORD says: 'Far be it from Me; for those who honor Me I will honor, and those who despise Me shall be lightly esteemed. 31Behold, the days are coming that I will cut off your arm and the arm of your father's house, so that there will not be an old man in your house. 32And you will see an enemy *in My* dwelling place, *despite* all the good which God does for Israel. And there shall not be an old man in your house forever. 33But any of your men *whom* I do not cut off from My altar shall consume your eyes and grieve your heart. And all

the descendants of your house shall die in the flower of their age. 34Now this *shall be* a sign to you that will come upon your two sons, on Hophni and Phinehas: in one day they shall die, both of them. 35Then I will raise up for Myself a faithful priest *who* shall do according to what *is* in My heart and in My mind. I will build him a sure house, and he shall walk before My anointed forever. 36And it shall come to pass that everyone who is left in your house will come *and* bow down to him for a piece of silver and a morsel of bread, and say, "Please, put me in one of the priestly positions, that I may eat a piece of bread." ' "

Samuel's First Prophecy

3 Now the boy Samuel ministered to the LORD before Eli. And the word of the LORD was rare in those days; *there was* no widespread revelation. 2And it came to pass at that time, while Eli *was* lying down in his place, and when his eyes had begun to grow so dim that he could not see, 3and before the lamp of God went out in the tabernaclea of the LORD where the ark of God *was,* and while Samuel was lying down, 4that the LORD called Samuel. And he answered, "Here I am!" 5So he ran to Eli and said, "Here I am, for you called me."

And he said, "I did not call; lie down again." And he went and lay down.

6Then the LORD called yet again, "Samuel!"

So Samuel arose and went to Eli, and said, "Here I am, for you called me." He answered, "I did not call, my son; lie down again." 7(Now Samuel did not yet know the LORD, nor was the word of the LORD yet revealed to him.)

8And the LORD called Samuel again the third time. So he arose and went to Eli, and said, "Here I am, for you did call me."

Then Eli perceived that the LORD had called the boy. 9Therefore Eli said to Samuel, "Go, lie down; and it shall be, if He calls you, that you must say, 'Speak, LORD, for Your servant hears.' " So Samuel went and lay down in his place.

10Now the LORD came and stood and called as at other times, "Samuel! Samuel!"

And Samuel answered, "Speak, for Your servant hears."

2:22 aFollowing Masoretic Text, Targum, and Vulgate; Dead Sea Scrolls and Septuagint omit the rest of this verse. 3:3 aHebrew *heykal,* palace or temple

BIBLICAL INSIGHTS • 3:9

Learning to Hear

IF YOU'RE GOING TO SERVE GOD in your marriage and in your family, then you must learn to be still and listen to what He has to say.

The Old Testament prophet Samuel had to learn this lesson while still a young boy. Three times the Lord called out to him, but Samuel did not yet recognize His voice; he mistakenly thought that his mentor, the old prophet Eli, had called him. When Eli realized what was happening, he instructed Samuel to answer, "Speak, Lord, for Your servant hears" (3:9). Note that Samuel had to *learn* to hear the voice of God. The text says, "Now Samuel did not yet know the Lord, nor was the word of the Lord yet revealed to him" (3:7).

How many of us can hear God calling us above all the background noise that threatens to drown out His voice? Any number of media vie for our attention— the television, the internet, music, etc. If we want a vibrant, growing relationship with God, however—and if we want Him to direct and guide us—then we must learn to slow down, get in a quiet place, open God's Word, and say, as did Samuel, "Speak, Lord, for Your servant hears."

C.S. Lewis called this kind of hearing "spiritual receptivity." It's being in tune with God so we can hear Him and also obey Him. Cultivate a teachable heart that can hear God, not only in your life but in the lives of your children.

---

¹¹Then the LORD said to Samuel: "Behold, I will do something in Israel at which both ears of everyone who hears it will tingle. ¹²In that day I will perform against Eli all that I have spoken concerning his house, from beginning to end. ¹³For I have told him that I will judge his house forever for the iniquity which he knows, because his sons made themselves vile, and he did not restrain them. ¹⁴And therefore I have

sworn to the house of Eli that the iniquity of Eli's house shall not be atoned for by sacrifice or offering forever."

¹⁵So Samuel lay down until morning,ᵃ and opened the doors of the house of the LORD. And Samuel was afraid to tell Eli the vision. ¹⁶Then Eli called Samuel and said, "Samuel, my son!"

He answered, "Here I am."

¹⁷And he said, "What *is* the word that *the LORD* spoke to you? Please do not hide *it* from me. God do so to you, and more also, if you hide anything from me of all the things that He said to you." ¹⁸Then Samuel told him everything, and hid nothing from him. And he said, "It *is* the LORD. Let Him do what seems good to Him."

¹⁹So Samuel grew, and the LORD was with him and let none of his words fall to the ground. ²⁰And all Israel from Dan to Beersheba knew that Samuel *had been* established as a prophet of the LORD. ²¹Then the LORD appeared again in Shiloh. For the LORD revealed Himself to Samuel in Shiloh by the word of the LORD.

4 And the word of Samuel came to all Israel.ᵃ

The Ark of God Captured

Now Israel went out to battle against the Philistines, and encamped beside Ebenezer; and the Philistines encamped in Aphek. ²Then the Philistines put themselves in battle array against Israel. And when they joined battle, Israel was defeated by the Philistines, who killed about four thousand men of the army in the field. ³And when the people had come into the camp, the elders of Israel said, "Why has the LORD defeated us today before the Philistines? Let us bring the ark of the covenant of the LORD from Shiloh to us, that when it comes among us it may save us from the hand of our enemies." ⁴So the people sent to Shiloh, that they might bring from there the ark of the covenant of the LORD of hosts, who dwells *between* the

---

3:15 ᵃFollowing Masoretic Text, Targum, and Vulgate; Septuagint adds *and he arose in the morning.* **4:1** ᵃFollowing Masoretic Text and Targum; Septuagint and Vulgate add *And it came to pass in those days that the Philistines gathered themselves together to fight;* Septuagint adds further *against Israel.*

cherubim. And the two sons of Eli, Hophni and Phinehas, *were* there with the ark of the covenant of God.

5And when the ark of the covenant of the LORD came into the camp, all Israel shouted so loudly that the earth shook. 6Now when the Philistines heard the noise of the shout, they said, "What *does* the sound of this great shout in the camp of the Hebrews *mean?*" Then they understood that the ark of the LORD had come into the camp. 7So the Philistines were afraid, for they said, "God has come into the camp!" And they said, "Woe to us! For such a thing has never happened before. 8Woe to us! Who will deliver us from the hand of these mighty gods? These *are* the gods who struck the Egyptians with all the plagues in the wilderness. 9Be strong and conduct yourselves like men, you Philistines, that you do not become servants of the Hebrews, as they have been to you. Conduct yourselves like men, and fight!"

10So the Philistines fought, and Israel was defeated, and every man fled to his tent. There was a very great slaughter, and there fell of Israel thirty thousand foot soldiers. 11Also the ark of God was captured; and the two sons of Eli, Hophni and Phinehas, died.

Death of Eli

12Then a man of Benjamin ran from the battle line the same day, and came to Shiloh with his clothes torn and dirt on his head. 13Now when he came, there was Eli, sitting on a seat by the wayside watching,a for his heart trembled for the ark of God. And when the man came into the city and told *it,* all the city cried out. 14When Eli heard the noise of the outcry, he said, "What *does* the sound of this tumult *mean?*" And the man came quickly and told Eli. 15Eli was ninety-eight years old, and his eyes were so dim that he could not see.

16Then the man said to Eli, "I *am* he who came from the battle. And I fled today from the battle line."

And he said, "What happened, my son?" 17So the messenger answered and said,

"Israel has fled before the Philistines, and there has been a great slaughter among the people. Also your two sons, Hophni and Phinehas, are dead; and the ark of God has been captured."

18Then it happened, when he made mention of the ark of God, that Eli fell off the seat backward by the side of the gate; and his neck was broken and he died, for the man was old and heavy. And he had judged Israel forty years.

INTIMATE MOMENTS

On some chilly night, cuddle under a blanket with your husband and watch a movie (his choice). Pop some popcorn and enjoy the flick with him, even if you don't particularly care for aliens dropping from the sky or big explosions ripping through the night air. Make only positive comments about his choice of film—and then surprise him with a little kiss on the lips or a nip on the neck.

Ichabod

19Now his daughter-in-law, Phinehas' wife, was with child, *due* to be delivered; and when she heard the news that the ark of God was captured, and that her father-in-law and her husband were dead, she bowed herself and gave birth, for her labor pains came upon her. 20And about the time of her death the women who stood by her said to her, "Do not fear, for you have borne a son." But she did not answer, nor did she regard *it.* 21Then she named the child Ichabod,a saying, "The glory has departed from Israel!" because the ark of God had been captured and because of her father-in-law and her husband. 22And she said, "The glory has departed from Israel, for the ark of God has been captured."

The Philistines and the Ark

5 Then the Philistines took the ark of God and brought it from Ebenezer to Ashdod. 2When the Philistines took the ark of God, they brought it into the house of

---

4:13 aFollowing Masoretic Text and Vulgate; Septuagint reads *beside the gate watching the road.* 4:21 aLiterally *Inglorious* 5:2 aA Philistine idol

Dagon[a] and set it by Dagon. [3]And when the people of Ashdod arose early in the morning, there was Dagon, fallen on its face to the earth before the ark of the LORD. So they took Dagon and set it in its place again. [4]And when they arose early the next morning, there was Dagon, fallen on its face to the ground before the ark of the LORD. The head of Dagon and both the palms of its hands *were* broken off on the threshold; only Dagon's *torso*[a] was left of it. [5]Therefore neither the priests of Dagon nor any who come into Dagon's house tread on the threshold of Dagon in Ashdod to this day.

[6]But the hand of the LORD was heavy on the people of Ashdod, and He ravaged them and struck them with tumors,[a] *both* Ashdod and its territory. [7]And when the men of Ashdod saw how *it was,* they said, "The ark of the God of Israel must not remain with us, for His hand is harsh toward us and Dagon our god." [8]Therefore they sent and gathered to themselves all the lords of the Philistines, and said, "What shall we do with the ark of the God of Israel?"

And they answered, "Let the ark of the God of Israel be carried away to Gath." So they carried the ark of the God of Israel away. [9]So it was, after they had carried it away, that the hand of the LORD was against the city with a very great destruction; and He struck the men of the city, both small and great, and tumors broke out on them.

[10]Therefore they sent the ark of God to Ekron. So it was, as the ark of God came to Ekron, that the Ekronites cried out, saying, "They have brought the ark of the God of Israel to us, to kill us and our people!" [11]So they sent and gathered together all the lords of the Philistines, and said, "Send away the ark of the God of Israel, and let it go back to its own place, so that it does not kill us and our people." For there was a deadly destruction throughout all the city; the hand of God was very heavy there. [12]And the men who did not die were stricken with the tumors, and the cry of the city went up to heaven.

The Ark Returned to Israel

6 Now the ark of the LORD was in the country of the Philistines seven months. [2]And the Philistines called for the priests and the diviners, saying, "What shall we do with the ark of the LORD? Tell us how we should send it to its place."

[3]So they said, "If you send away the ark of the God of Israel, do not send it empty; but by all means return *it* to Him *with* a trespass offering. Then you will be healed, and it will be known to you why His hand is not removed from you."

[4]Then they said, "What *is* the trespass offering which we shall return to Him?"

They answered, "Five golden tumors and five golden rats, *according to* the number of the lords of the Philistines. For the same plague *was* on all of you and on your lords. [5]Therefore you shall make images of your tumors and images of your rats that ravage the land, and you shall give glory to the God of Israel; perhaps He will lighten His hand from you, from your gods, and from your land. [6]Why then do you harden your hearts as the Egyptians and Pharaoh hardened their hearts? When He did mighty things among them, did they not let the people go, that they might depart? [7]Now therefore, make a new cart, take two milk cows which have never been yoked, and hitch the cows to the cart; and take their calves home, away from them. [8]Then take the ark of the LORD and set it on the cart; and put the articles of gold which you are returning to Him *as* a trespass offering in a chest by its side. Then send it away, and let it go. [9]And watch: if it goes up the road to its own territory, to Beth Shemesh, *then* He has done us this great evil. But if not, then we shall know that *it is* not His hand *that* struck us—it happened to us by chance."

[10]Then the men did so; they took two milk cows and hitched them to the cart, and shut up their calves at home. [11]And they set the ark of the LORD on the cart, and the chest with the gold rats and the images of their tumors. [12]Then the cows headed straight for the road to Beth Shemesh, *and* went along the highway, lowing as they went, and did not turn aside to the right hand or the left. And the lords of the Philistines went after them to the border of Beth Shemesh.

5:4 [a]Following Septuagint, Syriac, Targum, and Vulgate; Masoretic Text reads *Dagon.* **5:6** [a]Probably bubonic plague. Septuagint and Vulgate add here *And in the midst of their land rats sprang up, and there was a great death panic in the city.*

¹³Now *the people of* Beth Shemesh *were* reaping their wheat harvest in the valley; and they lifted their eyes and saw the ark, and rejoiced to see *it*. ¹⁴Then the cart came into the field of Joshua of Beth Shemesh, and stood there; a large stone *was* there. So they split the wood of the cart and offered the cows as a burnt offering to the LORD. ¹⁵The Levites took down the ark of the LORD and the chest that *was* with it, in which *were* the articles of gold, and put *them* on the large stone. Then the men of Beth Shemesh offered burnt offerings and made sacrifices the same day to the LORD. ¹⁶So when the five lords of the Philistines had seen *it*, they returned to Ekron the same day.

¹⁷These *are* the golden tumors which the Philistines returned *as* a trespass offering to the LORD: one for Ashdod, one for Gaza, one for Ashkelon, one for Gath, one for Ekron; ¹⁸and the golden rats, *according to* the number of all the cities of the Philistines *belonging* to the five lords, *both* fortified cities and country villages, even as far as the large *stone of* Abel on which they set the ark of the LORD, *which stone remains* to this day in the field of Joshua of Beth Shemesh.

¹⁹Then He struck the men of Beth Shemesh, because they had looked into the ark of the LORD. He struck fifty thousand and seventy menª of the people, and the people lamented because the LORD had struck the people with a great slaughter.

The Ark at Kirjath Jearim

²⁰And the men of Beth Shemesh said, "Who is able to stand before this holy LORD God? And to whom shall it go up from us?" ²¹So they sent messengers to the inhabitants of Kirjath Jearim, saying, "The Philistines have brought back the ark of the LORD; come down *and* take it up with you."

7 Then the men of Kirjath Jearim came and took the ark of the LORD, and brought it into the house of Abinadab on the hill, and consecrated Eleazar his son to keep the ark of the LORD.

6:19 ªOr *He struck seventy men of the people and fifty oxen of a man*　**7:3** ªCanaanite goddesses
7:4 ªCanaanite goddesses　**7:12** ªLiterally *Stone of Help*

BIBLICAL INSIGHTS • 7:6

Make It Real

I'D BE WILLING TO GUESS that one of the greatest reasons the church is not having more of an effect on our nation and on our families is that we in the church struggle with being real. We want others to believe everything is okay, so we hide our flaws and our mistakes and our sin and refuse to admit the truth, namely, that we need help.

We could stand a giant helping of confession.

Confession is what healed a family I counseled years ago. The confession brought surprise and tears and momentary anger, but there was also forgiveness, real forgiveness from God and from the erring woman's husband. A spiritual housecleaning took place, and God broke through in their lives.

This couple isn't just playing church anymore. Now God is real. God's grace and mercy are real. God's Word is real. And their relationship is real.

To experience this kind of sweeping transformation in our diseased culture, Christians must come clean. We must confess the truth. Our families, churches and culture will once again start having an impact for God when we cry out, as did the children of Israel, "We have sinned against the LORD" (7:6).

Samuel Judges Israel

²So it was that the ark remained in Kirjath Jearim a long time; it was there twenty years. And all the house of Israel lamented after the LORD.

³Then Samuel spoke to all the house of Israel, saying, "If you return to the LORD with all your hearts, *then* put away the foreign gods and the Ashtorethsª from among you, and prepare your hearts for the LORD, and serve Him only; and He will deliver you from the hand of the Philistines." ⁴So the children of Israel put away the Baals and the Ashtoreths,ª and served the LORD only.

⁵And Samuel said, "Gather all Israel to Mizpah, and I will pray to the LORD for you." ⁶So they gathered together at Mizpah, drew water, and poured *it* out before the LORD. And they fasted that day, and said there, "We have sinned against the LORD." And Samuel judged the children of Israel at Mizpah.

⁷Now when the Philistines heard that the children of Israel had gathered together at Mizpah, the lords of the Philistines went up against Israel. And when the children of Israel heard *of it*, they were afraid of the Philistines. ⁸So the children of Israel said to Samuel, "Do not cease to cry out to the LORD our God for us, that He may save us from the hand of the Philistines."

⁹And Samuel took a suckling lamb and offered *it as* a whole burnt offering to the LORD. Then Samuel cried out to the LORD for Israel, and the LORD answered him. ¹⁰Now as Samuel was offering up the burnt offering, the Philistines drew near to battle against Israel. But the LORD thundered with a loud thunder upon the Philistines that day, and so confused them that they were overcome before Israel. ¹¹And the men of Israel went out of Mizpah and pursued the Philistines, and drove them back as far as below Beth Car. ¹²Then Samuel took a stone and set *it* up between Mizpah and Shen, and called its name Ebenezer,ᵃ saying, "Thus far the LORD has helped us."

¹³So the Philistines were subdued, and they did not come anymore into the territory of Israel. And the hand of the LORD was against the Philistines all the days of Samuel. ¹⁴Then the cities which the Philistines had taken from Israel were restored to Israel, from Ekron to Gath; and Israel recovered its territory from the hands of the Philistines. Also there was peace between Israel and the Amorites.

¹⁵And Samuel judged Israel all the days of his life. ¹⁶He went from year to year on a circuit to Bethel, Gilgal, and Mizpah, and judged Israel in all those places. ¹⁷But he always returned to Ramah, for his home *was* there. There he judged Israel, and there he built an altar to the LORD.

Israel Demands a King

8 Now it came to pass when Samuel was old that he made his sons judges over Israel. ²The name of his firstborn was Joel, and the name of his second, Abijah; *they were* judges in Beersheba. ³But his sons did not walk in his ways; they turned aside after dishonest gain, took bribes, and perverted justice.

⁴Then all the elders of Israel gathered together and came to Samuel at Ramah, ⁵and said to him, "Look, you are old, and your sons do not walk in your ways. Now make us a king to judge us like all the nations."

⁶But the thing displeased Samuel when they said, "Give us a king to judge us." So Samuel prayed to the LORD. ⁷And the LORD said to Samuel, "Heed the voice of the people in all that they say to you; for they have not rejected you, but they have rejected Me, that

---

ROMANCE FAQ

Q: *What does my husband most need from me to know that my love for him is real?*

Two words: **unconditional acceptance.**

I remember when I first realized Dennis was not like my father.

My dad was Mr. Fix-it. He was in charge of maintenance at a large steel plant, and at home he could do *anything.* He loved making repairs, painting, tinkering on the car.

Dennis, on the other hand, declared that, "If you can't fix something with baling wire and gray tape, you should throw it away and get a new one." He preferred to spend his spare time watching sports.

In those early days, Dennis would plop in his easy chair in front of the television, and I would circle him like a vulture, hinting how I felt he could better use his time.

Dennis and I have come a long way. He's still not Mr. Fix-it, but he tries. And somewhere along the way he learned to enjoy gardening so he could spend time with me.

I've learned an important lesson—the importance of loving my husband unconditionally. I need to receive Dennis as a gift from God. And I need to remember that God is working in his life.

I should not reign over them. [8]According to all the works which they have done since the day that I brought them up out of Egypt, even to this day—with which they have forsaken Me and served other gods—so they are doing to you also. [9]Now therefore, heed their voice. However, you shall solemnly forewarn them, and show them the behavior of the king who will reign over them."

[10]So Samuel told all the words of the LORD to the people who asked him for a king. [11]And he said, "This will be the behavior of the king who will reign over you: He will take your sons and appoint *them* for his own chariots and *to be* his horsemen, and *some* will run before his chariots. [12]He will appoint captains over his thousands and captains over his fifties, *will set some* to plow his ground and reap his harvest, and *some* to make his weapons of war and equipment for his chariots. [13]He will take your daughters *to be* perfumers, cooks, and bakers. [14]And he will take the best of your fields, your vineyards, and your olive groves, and give *them* to his servants. [15]He will take a tenth of your grain and your vintage, and give it to his officers and servants. [16]And he will take your male servants, your female servants, your finest young men,[a] and your donkeys, and put *them* to his work. [17]He will take a tenth of your sheep. And you will be his servants. [18]And you will cry out in that day because of your king whom you have chosen for yourselves, and the LORD will not hear you in that day."

[19]Nevertheless the people refused to obey the voice of Samuel; and they said, "No, but we will have a king over us, [20]that we also may be like all the nations, and that our king may judge us and go out before us and fight our battles."

[21]And Samuel heard all the words of the people, and he repeated them in the hearing of the LORD. [22]So the LORD said to Samuel, "Heed their voice, and make them a king."

And Samuel said to the men of Israel, "Every man go to his city."

Saul Chosen to Be King

9 There was a man of Benjamin whose name *was* Kish the son of Abiel, the son

of Zeror, the son of Bechorath, the son of Aphiah, a Benjamite, a mighty man of power. [2]And he had a choice and handsome son whose name *was* Saul. *There was* not a more handsome person than he among the children of Israel. From his shoulders upward *he was* taller than any of the people.

[3]Now the donkeys of Kish, Saul's father, were lost. And Kish said to his son Saul, "Please take one of the servants with you, and arise, go and look for the donkeys." [4]So he passed through the mountains of Ephraim and through the land of Shalisha, but they did not find *them*. Then they passed through the land of Shaalim, and *they were* not *there*. Then he passed through the land of the Benjamites, but they did not find *them*.

[5]When they had come to the land of Zuph, Saul said to his servant who *was* with him, "Come, let us return, lest my father cease *caring* about the donkeys and become worried about us."

[6]And he said to him, "Look now, *there is* in this city a man of God, and *he is* an honorable man; all that he says surely comes to pass. So let us go there; perhaps he can show us the way that we should go."

[7]Then Saul said to his servant, "But look, *if* we go, what shall we bring the man? For the bread in our vessels is all gone, and *there is* no present to bring to the man of God. What do we have?"

[8]And the servant answered Saul again and said, "Look, I have here at hand one-fourth of a shekel of silver. I will give *that* to the man of God, to tell us our way." [9](Formerly in Israel, when a man went to inquire of God, he spoke thus: "Come, let us go to the seer"; for *he who is* now *called* a prophet was formerly called a seer.)

[10]Then Saul said to his servant, "Well said; come, let us go." So they went to the city where the man of God *was*.

[11]As they went up the hill to the city, they met some young women going out to draw water, and said to them, "Is the seer here?"

[12]And they answered them and said, "Yes, there he is, just ahead of you. Hurry now; for today he came to this city, because there is a sacrifice of the people today on the high place. [13]As soon as you come into the city, you will surely find him before he

---

8:16 [a]Septuagint reads *cattle*.

Stop Your Worrying

WHO AMONG US DOESN'T WORRY? Ever since the fall, worrying has been a human pastime. Saul's father did it (10:2), I do it, and no doubt you do it, too.

Let me share a helpful lesson that came to me out my study about worry: *Declare verbally to God and then to other people what the Bible says about your circumstances and affirm that you're not going to worry about that issue anymore.*

Since many of my fears lurk on the inside of my soul, I never get clear perspective on them. They're buried deep inside, and from there they continue to mug me and hold me captive.

Several years ago I had a running battle with worry over what my boss thought of me. Finally I just confessed it all to the Lord and said, "Lord, I want to affirm to You, right now by faith, that You're going to enable me not to worry any longer about this situation. If You're for me, what can man do to me?"

Does something frequently trouble you, or are you worrying about something right now? If so, what do the Scriptures say about your situations? Philippians 4:6, 7, tell us "Be anxious for nothing, but in everything, by prayer and supplication, with thanksgiving, let your requests be made known to God; and the peace of God, which surpasses all understanding, will guard your hearts and minds through Christ Jesus." Embrace the truth of what God says. Then go to the Lord and affirm that you're just not going to remain fearful about that. As an act of faith, continue to confess your affirmation and walk by faith with Him.

goes up to the high place to eat. For the people will not eat until he comes, because he must bless the sacrifice; afterward those who are invited will eat. Now therefore, go up, for about this time you will find him." ¹⁴So they went up to the city. As they were coming into the city, there was Samuel, coming out toward them on his way up to the high place.

¹⁵Now the LORD had told Samuel in his ear the day before Saul came, saying, ¹⁶"Tomorrow about this time I will send you a man from the land of Benjamin, and you shall anoint him commander over My people Israel, that he may save My people from the hand of the Philistines; for I have looked upon My people, because their cry has come to Me."

¹⁷So when Samuel saw Saul, the LORD said to him, "There he is, the man of whom I spoke to you. This one shall reign over My people." ¹⁸Then Saul drew near to Samuel in the gate, and said, "Please tell me, where *is* the seer's house?"

¹⁹Samuel answered Saul and said, "I *am* the seer. Go up before me to the high place, for you shall eat with me today; and tomorrow I will let you go and will tell you all that *is* in your heart. ²⁰But as for your donkeys that were lost three days ago, do not be anxious about them, for they have been found. And on whom *is* all the desire of Israel? *Is it* not on you and on all your father's house?"

²¹And Saul answered and said, "*Am* I not a Benjamite, of the smallest of the tribes of Israel, and my family the least of all the families of the tribeª of Benjamin? Why then do you speak like this to me?"

²²Now Samuel took Saul and his servant and brought them into the hall, and had them sit in the place of honor among those who were invited; there *were* about thirty persons. ²³And Samuel said to the cook, "Bring the portion which I gave you, of which I said to you, 'Set it apart.'" ²⁴So the cook took up the thigh with its upper part and set *it* before Saul. And *Samuel* said, "Here it is, what was kept back. *It* was set apart for you. Eat; for until this time it has been kept for you, since I said I invited the people." So Saul ate with Samuel that day.

²⁵When they had come down from the high place into the city, *Samuel* spoke with Saul on the top of the house.ª ²⁶They arose

9:21 ªLiterally *tribes* 9:25 ªFollowing Masoretic Text and Targum; Septuagint omits *He spoke with Saul on the top of the house;* Septuagint and Vulgate add *And he prepared a bed for Saul on the top of the house, and he slept.*

early; and it was about the dawning of the day that Samuel called to Saul on the top of the house, saying, "Get up, that I may send you on your way." And Saul arose, and both of them went outside, he and Samuel.

Saul Anointed King

27As they were going down to the outskirts of the city, Samuel said to Saul, "Tell the servant to go on ahead of us." And he went on. "But you stand here awhile, that I may announce to you the word of God."

10 Then Samuel took a flask of oil and poured *it* on his head, and kissed him and said: "*Is it* not because the LORD has anointed you commander over His inheritance?a 2When you have departed from me today, you will find two men by Rachel's tomb in the territory of Benjamin at Zelzah; and they will say to you, 'The donkeys which you went to look for have been found. And now your father has ceased caring about the donkeys and is worrying about you, saying, "What shall I do about my son?"' 3Then you shall go on forward from there and come to the terebinth tree of Tabor. There three men going up to God at Bethel will meet you, one carrying three young goats, another carrying three loaves of bread, and another carrying a skin of wine. 4And they will greet you and give you two *loaves* of bread, which you shall receive from their hands. 5After that you shall come to the hill of God where the Philistine garrison *is*. And it will happen, when you have come there to the city, that you will meet a group of prophets coming down from the high place with a stringed instrument, a tambourine, a flute, and a harp before them; and they will be prophesying. 6Then the Spirit of the LORD will come upon you, and you will prophesy with them and be turned into another man. 7And let it be, when these signs come to you, *that* you do as the occasion demands; for God *is* with you. 8You shall go down before me to Gilgal; and

surely I will come down to you to offer burnt offerings *and* make sacrifices of peace offerings. Seven days you shall wait, till I come to you and show you what you should do."

9So it was, when he had turned his back to go from Samuel, that God gave him another heart; and all those signs came to pass that day. 10When they came there to the hill, there was a group of prophets to meet him; then the Spirit of God came upon him, and he prophesied among them. 11And it happened, when all who knew him formerly saw that he indeed prophesied among the prophets, that the people said to one another, "What *is* this *that* has come upon the son of Kish? *Is* Saul also among the prophets?" 12Then a man from there answered and said, "But who *is* their father?" Therefore it became a proverb: "*Is* Saul also among the prophets?" 13And when he had finished prophesying, he went to the high place.

14Then Saul's uncle said to him and his servant, "Where did you go?"

So he said, "To look for the donkeys. When we saw that *they were* nowhere *to be found,* we went to Samuel."

15And Saul's uncle said, "Tell me, please, what Samuel said to you."

16So Saul said to his uncle, "He told us plainly that the donkeys had been found." But about the matter of the kingdom, he did not tell him what Samuel had said.

Saul Proclaimed King

17Then Samuel called the people together to the LORD at Mizpah, 18and said to the children of Israel, "Thus says the LORD God of Israel: 'I brought up Israel out of Egypt, and delivered you from the hand of the Egyptians *and* from the hand of all kingdoms and from those who oppressed you.' 19But you have today rejected your God, who Himself saved you from all your adversities and your tribulations; and you have said to Him, 'No, set a king over us!' Now therefore, present yourselves before the LORD by your tribes and by your clans."a

20And when Samuel had caused all the tribes of Israel to come near, the tribe of Benjamin was chosen. 21When he had caused the tribe of Benjamin to come near by their families, the family of Matri was chosen. And Saul the son of Kish was chosen.

10:1 aFollowing Masoretic Text, Targum, and Vulgate; Septuagint reads *His people Israel; and you shall rule the people of the Lord;* Septuagint and Vulgate add *And you shall deliver His people from the hands of their enemies all around them. And this shall be a sign to you, that God has anointed you to be a prince.* 10:19 aLiterally *thousands*

But when they sought him, he could not be found. ²²Therefore they inquired of the LORD further, "Has the man come here yet?"

And the LORD answered, "There he is, hidden among the equipment."

²³So they ran and brought him from there; and when he stood among the people, he was taller than any of the people from his shoulders upward. ²⁴And Samuel said to all the people, "Do you see him whom the LORD has chosen, that *there is* no one like him among all the people?"

So all the people shouted and said, "Long live the king!"

²⁵Then Samuel explained to the people the behavior of royalty, and wrote *it* in a book and laid *it* up before the LORD. And Samuel sent all the people away, every man to his house. ²⁶And Saul also went home to Gibeah; and valiant *men* went with him, whose hearts God had touched. ²⁷But some rebels said, "How can this man save us?" So they despised him, and brought him no presents. But he held his peace.

Saul Saves Jabesh Gilead

11 Then Nahash the Ammonite came up and encamped against Jabesh Gilead; and all the men of Jabesh said to Nahash, "Make a covenant with us, and we will serve you."

²And Nahash the Ammonite answered them, "On this *condition* I will make *a covenant* with you, that I may put out all your right eyes, and bring reproach on all Israel."

³Then the elders of Jabesh said to him, "Hold off for seven days, that we may send messengers to all the territory of Israel. And then, if *there is* no one to save us, we will come out to you."

⁴So the messengers came to Gibeah of Saul and told the news in the hearing of the people. And all the people lifted up their voices and wept. ⁵Now there was Saul, coming behind the herd from the field; and Saul said, "What *troubles* the people, that they weep?" And they told him the words of the men of Jabesh. ⁶Then the Spirit of God came upon Saul when he heard this news, and his anger was greatly aroused. ⁷So he took a yoke of oxen and cut them in pieces, and sent *them* throughout all the territory of Israel by the hands of messengers, saying, "Whoever does not go out with Saul and Samuel to battle, so it shall be done to his oxen."

And the fear of the LORD fell on the people, and they came out with one consent. ⁸When he numbered them in Bezek, the children of Israel were three hundred thousand, and the men of Judah thirty thousand. ⁹And they said to the messengers who came, "Thus you shall say to the men of Jabesh Gilead: 'Tomorrow, by *the time* the sun is hot, you shall have help.'" Then the messengers came and reported *it* to the men of Jabesh, and they were glad. ¹⁰Therefore the men of Jabesh said, "Tomorrow we will come out to you, and you may do with us whatever seems good to you."

¹¹So it was, on the next day, that Saul put the people in three companies; and they came into the midst of the camp in the morning watch, and killed Ammonites until the heat of the day. And it happened that those who survived were scattered, so that no two of them were left together.

¹²Then the people said to Samuel, "Who *is* he who said, 'Shall Saul reign over us?' Bring the men, that we may put them to death."

¹³But Saul said, "Not a man shall be put to death this day, for today the LORD has accomplished salvation in Israel."

¹⁴Then Samuel said to the people, "Come, let us go to Gilgal and renew the kingdom there." ¹⁵So all the people went to Gilgal, and there they made Saul king before the LORD in Gilgal. There they made sacrifices of peace offerings before the LORD, and there Saul and all the men of Israel rejoiced greatly.

Samuel's Address at Saul's Coronation

12 Now Samuel said to all Israel: "Indeed I have heeded your voice in all that you said to me, and have made a king over you. ²And now here is the king, walking before you; and I am old and gray-headed, and look, my sons *are* with you. I have walked before you from my childhood to this day. ³Here I am. Witness against me before the LORD and before His anointed: Whose ox have I taken, or whose donkey have I taken, or whom have I cheated? Whom have I oppressed, or from whose

hand have I received *any* bribe with which to blind my eyes? I will restore *it* to you."

⁴And they said, "You have not cheated us or oppressed us, nor have you taken anything from any man's hand."

⁵Then he said to them, "The LORD *is* witness against you, and His anointed *is* witness this day, that you have not found anything in my hand."

And they answered, "*He is* witness."

⁶Then Samuel said to the people, "*It is* the LORD who raised up Moses and Aaron, and who brought your fathers up from the land of Egypt. ⁷Now therefore, stand still, that I may reason with you before the LORD concerning all the righteous acts of the LORD which He did to you and your fathers: ⁸When Jacob had gone into Egypt,ᵃ and your fathers cried out to the LORD, then the LORD sent Moses and Aaron, who brought your fathers out of Egypt and made them dwell in this place. ⁹And when they forgot the LORD their God, He sold them into the hand of Sisera, commander of the army of Hazor, into the hand of the Philistines, and into the hand of the king of Moab; and they fought against them. ¹⁰Then they cried out to the LORD, and said, 'We have sinned, because we have forsaken the LORD and served the Baals and Ashtoreths;ᵃ but now deliver us from the hand of our enemies, and we will serve You.' ¹¹And the LORD sent Jerubbaal,ᵃ Bedan,ᵇ Jephthah, and Samuel,ᶜ and delivered you out of the hand of your enemies on every side; and you dwelt in safety. ¹²And when you saw that Nahash king of the Ammonites came against you, you said to me, 'No, but a king shall reign over us,' when the LORD your God *was* your king.

¹³"Now therefore, here is the king whom you have chosen *and* whom you have desired. And take note, the LORD has set a king over you. ¹⁴If you fear the LORD and serve Him and obey His voice, and do not rebel against the commandment of the LORD, then both you and the king who reigns over you will continue following the LORD your God. ¹⁵However, if you do not obey the voice of the LORD, but rebel against the commandment of the LORD, then the hand of the LORD will be against you, as *it was* against your fathers.

¹⁶"Now therefore, stand and see this great thing which the LORD will do before your eyes: ¹⁷*Is* today not the wheat harvest? I will call to the LORD, and He will send thunder and rain, that you may perceive and see that your wickedness *is* great, which you have done in the sight of the LORD, in asking a king for yourselves."

¹⁸So Samuel called to the LORD, and the LORD sent thunder and rain that day; and all the people greatly feared the LORD and Samuel.

¹⁹And all the people said to Samuel, "Pray for your servants to the LORD your God, that we may not die; for we have added to all our sins the evil of asking a king for ourselves."

²⁰Then Samuel said to the people, "Do not fear. You have done all this wickedness; yet do not turn aside from following the LORD, but serve the LORD with all your heart. ²¹And do not turn aside; for *then you would go* after empty things which cannot profit or deliver, for they *are* nothing. ²²For the LORD will not forsake His people, for His great name's sake, because it has pleased the LORD to make you His people. ²³Moreover, as for me, far be it from me that I should sin against the LORD in ceasing to pray for you; but I will teach you the good and the right way. ²⁴Only fear the LORD, and serve Him in truth with all your heart; for consider what great things He has done for you. ²⁵But if you still do wickedly, you shall be swept away, both you and your king."

Saul's Unlawful Sacrifice

13 Saul reigned one year; and when he had reigned two years over Israel,ᵃ ²Saul chose for himself three thousand *men* of Israel. Two thousand were with Saul in Michmash and in the mountains of Bethel, and a thousand were with Jonathan in Gibeah of Benjamin. The rest of the people he sent away, every man to his tent.

³And Jonathan attacked the garrison of

12:8 ᵃFollowing Masoretic Text, Targum, and Vulgate; Septuagint adds *and the Egyptians afflicted them.* 12:10 ᵃCanaanite goddesses 12:11 ᵃSyriac reads *Deborah;* Targum reads *Gideon.* ᵇSeptuagint and Syriac read *Barak;* Targum reads *Simson.* ᶜSyriac reads *Simson.* 13:1 ᵃThe Hebrew is difficult (compare 2 Samuel 5:4; 2 Kings 14:2; see also 2 Samuel 2:10; Acts 13:21).

the Philistines that *was* in Geba, and the Philistines heard *of it*. Then Saul blew the trumpet throughout all the land, saying, "Let the Hebrews hear!" [4]Now all Israel heard it said *that* Saul had attacked a garrison of the Philistines, and *that* Israel had also become an abomination to the Philistines. And the people were called together to Saul at Gilgal.

INTIMATE MOMENTS

Without telling her why you're asking the question, ask your wife to identify what animal you most remind her of. Have some fun discussing why she chose that particular animal, and then move on to some other topic. But in the next day or so, purchase a stuffed version of the animal and present it to her.

[5]Then the Philistines gathered together to fight with Israel, thirty[a] thousand chariots and six thousand horsemen, and people as the sand which *is* on the seashore in multitude. And they came up and encamped in Michmash, to the east of Beth Aven. [6]When the men of Israel saw that they were in danger (for the people were distressed), then the people hid in caves, in thickets, in rocks, in holes, and in pits. [7]And *some of* the Hebrews crossed over the Jordan to the land of Gad and Gilead.

As for Saul, he *was* still in Gilgal, and all the people followed him trembling. [8]Then he waited seven days, according to the time set by Samuel. But Samuel did not come to Gilgal; and the people were scattered from him. [9]So Saul said, "Bring a burnt offering and peace offerings here to me." And he offered the burnt offering. [10]Now it happened, as soon as he had finished presenting the burnt offering, that Samuel came; and Saul went out to meet him, that he might greet him.

[11]And Samuel said, "What have you done?"

Saul said, "When I saw that the people

were scattered from me, and *that* you did not come within the days appointed, and *that* the Philistines gathered together at Michmash, [12]then I said, 'The Philistines will now come down on me at Gilgal, and I have not made supplication to the LORD.' Therefore I felt compelled, and offered a burnt offering."

[13]And Samuel said to Saul, "You have done foolishly. You have not kept the commandment of the LORD your God, which He commanded you. For now the LORD would have established your kingdom over Israel forever. [14]But now your kingdom shall not continue. The LORD has sought for Himself a man after His own heart, and the LORD has commanded him *to be* commander over His people, because you have not kept what the LORD commanded you."

[15]Then Samuel arose and went up from Gilgal to Gibeah of Benjamin.[a] And Saul numbered the people present with him, about six hundred men.

No Weapons for the Army

[16]Saul, Jonathan his son, and the people present with them remained in Gibeah of Benjamin. But the Philistines encamped in Michmash. [17]Then raiders came out of the camp of the Philistines in three companies. One company turned onto the road to Ophrah, to the land of Shual, [18]another company turned to the road *to* Beth Horon, and another company turned *to* the road of the border that overlooks the Valley of Zeboim toward the wilderness.

[19]Now there was no blacksmith to be found throughout all the land of Israel, for the Philistines said, "Lest the Hebrews make swords or spears." [20]But all the Israelites would go down to the Philistines to sharpen each man's plowshare, his mattock, his ax, and his sickle; [21]and the charge for a sharpening was a pim[a] for the plowshares, the mattocks, the forks, and the axes, and to set the points of the goads. [22]So it came about, on the day of battle, that there was neither

13:5 [a]Following Masoretic Text, Septuagint, Targum, and Vulgate; Syriac and some manuscripts of the Septuagint read *three*. **13:15** [a]Following Masoretic Text and Targum; Septuagint and Vulgate add *And the rest of the people went up after Saul to meet the people who fought against them, going from Gilgal to Gibeah in the hill of Benjamin*. **13:21** [a]About two-thirds shekel weight

sword nor spear found in the hand of any of the people who *were* with Saul and Jonathan. But they were found with Saul and Jonathan his son.

²³And the garrison of the Philistines went out to the pass of Michmash.

Jonathan Defeats the Philistines

14 Now it happened one day that Jonathan the son of Saul said to the young man who bore his armor, "Come, let us go over to the Philistines' garrison that *is* on the other side." But he did not tell his father. ²And Saul was sitting in the outskirts of Gibeah under a pomegranate tree which *is* in Migron. The people who *were* with him *were* about six hundred men. ³Ahijah the son of Ahitub, Ichabod's brother, the son of Phinehas, the son of Eli, the LORD's priest in Shiloh, was wearing an ephod. But the people did not know that Jonathan had gone.

⁴Between the passes, by which Jonathan sought to go over to the Philistines' garrison, *there was* a sharp rock on one side and a sharp rock on the other side. And the name of one *was* Bozez, and the name of the other Seneh. ⁵The front of one faced northward opposite Michmash, and the other southward opposite Gibeah.

⁶Then Jonathan said to the young man who bore his armor, "Come, let us go over to the garrison of these uncircumcised; it may be that the LORD will work for us. For nothing restrains the LORD from saving by many or by few."

⁷So his armorbearer said to him, "Do all that is in your heart. Go then; here I am with you, according to your heart."

⁸Then Jonathan said, "Very well, let us cross over to *these* men, and we will show ourselves to them. ⁹If they say thus to us, 'Wait until we come to you,' then we will stand still in our place and not go up to them. ¹⁰But if they say thus, 'Come up to us,' then we will go up. For the LORD has delivered them into our hand, and this *will be* a sign to us."

¹¹So both of them showed themselves to the garrison of the Philistines. And the Philistines said, "Look, the Hebrews are coming out of the holes where they have hidden." ¹²Then the men of the garrison called to Jonathan and his armorbearer, and said, "Come up to us, and we will show you something."

Jonathan said to his armorbearer, "Come up after me, for the LORD has delivered them into the hand of Israel." ¹³And Jonathan climbed up on his hands and knees with his armorbearer after him; and they fell before Jonathan. And as he came after him, his armorbearer killed them. ¹⁴That first slaughter which Jonathan and his armorbearer made was about twenty men within about half an acre of land.ᵃ

¹⁵And there was trembling in the camp, in the field, and among all the people. The garrison and the raiders also trembled; and the earth quaked, so that it was a very great trembling. ¹⁶Now the watchmen of Saul in Gibeah of Benjamin looked, and *there* was the multitude, melting away; and they went here and there. ¹⁷Then Saul said to the people who *were* with him, "Now call the roll and see who has gone from us." And when they had called the roll, surprisingly, Jonathan and his armorbearer *were* not *there.* ¹⁸And Saul said to Ahijah, "Bring the arkᵃ of God here" (for at that time the arkᵇ of God was with the children of Israel). ¹⁹Now it happened, while Saul talked to the priest, that the noise which *was* in the camp of the Philistines continued to increase; so Saul said to the priest, "Withdraw your hand." ²⁰Then Saul and all the people who *were* with him assembled, and they went to the battle; and indeed every man's sword was against his neighbor, *and there was* very great confusion. ²¹Moreover the Hebrews *who* were with the Philistines before that time, who went up with them into the camp *from the* surrounding *country,* they also joined the Israelites who *were* with Saul and Jonathan. ²²Likewise all the men of Israel who had hidden in the mountains of Ephraim, *when* they heard that the Philistines fled, they also followed hard after them in the battle. ²³So the LORD saved Israel that day, and the battle shifted to Beth Aven.

14:14 ᵃLiterally *half the area plowed by a yoke* (of oxen in a day) **14:18** ᵃFollowing Masoretic Text, Targum, and Vulgate; Septuagint reads *ephod.*
ᵇFollowing Masoretic Text, Targum, and Vulgate; Septuagint reads *ephod.*

Saul's Rash Oath

24And the men of Israel were distressed that day, for Saul had placed the people under oath, saying, "Cursed *is* the man who eats *any* food until evening, before I have taken vengeance on my enemies." So none of the people tasted food. 25Now all *the people* of the land came to a forest; and there was honey on the ground. 26And when the people had come into the woods, there was the honey, dripping; but no one put his hand to his mouth, for the people feared the oath. 27But Jonathan had not heard his father charge the people with the oath; therefore he stretched out the end of the rod that *was* in his hand and dipped it in a honeycomb, and put his hand to his mouth; and his countenance brightened. 28Then one of the people said, "Your father strictly charged the people with an oath, saying, 'Cursed *is* the man who eats food this day.' " And the people were faint.

29But Jonathan said, "My father has troubled the land. Look now, how my countenance has brightened because I tasted a little of this honey. 30How much better if the people had eaten freely today of the spoil of their enemies which they found! For now would there not have been a much greater slaughter among the Philistines?"

31Now they had driven back the Philistines that day from Michmash to Aijalon. So the people were very faint. 32And the people rushed on the spoil, and took sheep, oxen, and calves, and slaughtered *them* on the ground; and the people ate *them* with the blood. 33Then they told Saul, saying, "Look, the people are sinning against the LORD by eating with the blood!"

So he said, "You have dealt treacherously; roll a large stone to me this day." 34Then Saul said, "Disperse yourselves among the people, and say to them, 'Bring me here every man's ox and every man's sheep, slaughter *them* here, and eat; and do not sin against the LORD by eating with the blood.' " So every one of the people brought his ox with him that night, and slaughtered *it* there. 35Then Saul built an altar to the LORD. This was the first altar that he built to the LORD.

36Now Saul said, "Let us go down after the Philistines by night, and plunder them until the morning light; and let us not leave a man of them."

And they said, "Do whatever seems good to you."

Then the priest said, "Let us draw near to God here."

37So Saul asked counsel of God, "Shall I go down after the Philistines? Will You deliver them into the hand of Israel?" But He did not answer him that day. 38And Saul said, "Come over here, all you chiefs of the people, and know and see what this sin was today. 39For *as* the LORD lives, who saves Israel, though it be in Jonathan my son, he shall surely die." But not a man among all the people answered him. 40Then he said to all Israel, "You be on one side, and my son Jonathan and I will be on the other side."

And the people said to Saul, "Do what seems good to you."

41Therefore Saul said to the LORD God of Israel, "Give a perfect *lot*."a So Saul and Jonathan were taken, but the people escaped. 42And Saul said, "Cast *lots* between my son Jonathan and me." So Jonathan was taken. 43Then Saul said to Jonathan, "Tell me what you have done."

And Jonathan told him, and said, "I only tasted a little honey with the end of the rod that *was* in my hand. So now I must die!"

44Saul answered, "God do so and more also; for you shall surely die, Jonathan."

45But the people said to Saul, "Shall Jonathan die, who has accomplished this great deliverance in Israel? Certainly not! *As* the LORD lives, not one hair of his head shall fall to the ground, for he has worked with God this day." So the people rescued Jonathan, and he did not die.

46Then Saul returned from pursuing the Philistines, and the Philistines went to their own place.

Saul's Continuing Wars

47So Saul established his sovereignty over Israel, and fought against all his enemies on

14:41 aFollowing Masoretic Text and Targum; Septuagint and Vulgate read *Why do You not answer Your servant today? If the injustice is with me or Jonathan my son, O LORD God of Israel, give proof; and if You say it is with Your people Israel, give holiness.*

every side, against Moab, against the people of Ammon, against Edom, against the kings of Zobah, and against the Philistines. Wherever he turned, he harassed *them.*[a] [48]And he gathered an army and attacked the Amalekites, and delivered Israel from the hands of those who plundered them.

[49]The sons of Saul were Jonathan, Jishui,[a] and Malchishua. And the names of his two daughters *were these:* the name of the firstborn Merab, and the name of the younger Michal. [50]The name of Saul's wife *was* Ahinoam the daughter of Ahimaaz. And the name of the commander of his army *was* Abner the son of Ner, Saul's uncle. [51]Kish *was* the father of Saul, and Ner the father of Abner *was* the son of Abiel.

[52]Now there was fierce war with the Philistines all the days of Saul. And when Saul saw any strong man or any valiant man, he took him for himself.

Saul Spares King Agag

15 Samuel also said to Saul, "The LORD sent me to anoint you king over His people, over Israel. Now therefore, heed the voice of the words of the LORD. [2]Thus says the LORD of hosts: 'I will punish Amalek *for* what he did to Israel, how he ambushed him on the way when he came up from Egypt. [3]Now go and attack Amalek, and utterly destroy all that they have, and do not spare them. But kill both man and woman, infant and nursing child, ox and sheep, camel and donkey.' "

[4]So Saul gathered the people together and numbered them in Telaim, two hundred thousand foot soldiers and ten thousand men of Judah. [5]And Saul came to a city of Amalek, and lay in wait in the valley.

[6]Then Saul said to the Kenites, "Go, depart, get down from among the Amalekites, lest I destroy you with them. For you showed kindness to all the children of Israel when they came up out of Egypt." So the Kenites departed from among the Amalekites. [7]And Saul attacked the Amalekites, from Havilah all the way to Shur, which is east of Egypt. [8]He also took Agag king of the Amalekites alive, and

utterly destroyed all the people with the edge of the sword. [9]But Saul and the people spared Agag and the best of the sheep, the oxen, the fatlings, the lambs, and all *that was* good, and were unwilling to utterly destroy them. But everything despised and worthless, that they utterly destroyed.

Saul Rejected as King

[10]Now the word of the LORD came to Samuel, saying, [11]"I greatly regret that I have set up Saul *as* king, for he has turned back from following Me, and has not performed My commandments." And it grieved Samuel, and he cried out to the LORD all night. [12]So when Samuel rose early in the morning to meet Saul, it was told Samuel, saying, "Saul went to Carmel, and indeed, he set up a monument for himself; and he has gone on around, passed by, and gone down to Gilgal." [13]Then Samuel went to Saul, and Saul said to him, "Blessed *are* you of the LORD! I have performed the commandment of the LORD."

[14]But Samuel said, "What then *is* this bleating of the sheep in my ears, and the lowing of the oxen which I hear?"

[15]And Saul said, "They have brought them from the Amalekites; for the people spared the best of the sheep and the oxen, to sacrifice to the LORD your God; and the rest we have utterly destroyed."

[16]Then Samuel said to Saul, "Be quiet! And I will tell you what the LORD said to me last night."

And he said to him, "Speak on."

[17]So Samuel said, "When you *were* little in your own eyes, *were* you not head of the tribes of Israel? And did not the LORD anoint you king over Israel? [18]Now the LORD sent you on a mission, and said, 'Go, and utterly destroy the sinners, the Amalekites, and fight against them until they are consumed.' [19]Why then did you not obey the voice of the LORD? Why did you swoop down on the spoil, and do evil in the sight of the LORD?"

[20]And Saul said to Samuel, "But I have obeyed the voice of the LORD, and gone on the mission on which the LORD sent me, and brought back Agag king of Amalek; I have utterly destroyed the Amalekites. [21]But the people took of the plunder, sheep and oxen, the best of the things which should have

---

14:47 [a]Septuagint and Vulgate read *prospered.*
14:49 [a]Called *Abinadab* in 1 Chronicles 8:33 and 9:39

DEVOTIONS FOR COUPLES • 15:22
Learning Obedience

Can you name all of the Ten Command-ments? If not, pull out Exodus 20, read it, and discuss the commandments at din-ner tonight. I'll give you a head start by discussing four of them.

1. You shall have no other gods before me. One of modern Christianity's worst forms of idolatry is our worship of *things.* Barbara and I constantly struggle to stay out of this quicksand. We never want to leave a lega-cy of materialism to our kids. Another form of idolatry is our worship of self-fulfillment and personal happiness. The personal rights movement has sired our attitudes about divorce, our general preoccupation with "what's in it for me," as well as career choices and the number of children we decide to have.

2. You shall not take the name of the Lord your God in vain. Taking God's name in vain is more than just using it as a curse word. It means to take His name to mean nothing. God is holy and sacred . . . a God to be feared. If we are to have a godly family, then each of its members must hold His name in highest respect.

3. You shall not commit adultery. I was stunned by a poll I saw in a local newspa-per. The pollster asked, "Would you cheat on your spouse if you knew you would never get caught?" How do you think the people of Arkansas— people who live just a few miles from the buckle of the Bible belt—answered that question? Can you believe that *seventy-four* percent said they would cheat! I immediately wondered about the national response: eighty, eighty-five, maybe a horrid ninety percent?

We need an epidemic of moral, godly adults and teenagers. How about talking about the value of virginity and fidelity with your pre-teen or teenagers at dinner tonight?

4. You shall not steal. A good business-man or businesswoman obeys God in his dealings with his employer, employees, and clients. He reports all of his income at income tax time. Why would he rob his children by failing to spend time with them? I think of what the prophet Samuel told a disobedient King Saul, "Has the LORD as great delight in burnt offerings and sac-rifices, as in obeying the voice of the LORD? Behold, to obey is better than sacrifice, and to heed than the fat of rams" (1 Sam. 15:22).

---

been utterly destroyed, to sacrifice to the LORD your God in Gilgal."

²²So Samuel said:

"Has the LORD *as great* delight in
    burnt offerings and sacrifices,
As in obeying the voice of the LORD?
Behold, to obey is better than sacrifice,
And to heed than the fat of rams.
23   For rebellion *is as* the sin of
        witchcraft,
    And stubbornness *is as* iniquity and
        idolatry.
    Because you have rejected the word
        of the LORD,
    He also has rejected you from *being*
        king."

²⁴Then Saul said to Samuel, "I have sinned, for I have transgressed the commandment of the LORD and your words, because I feared the people and obeyed their voice. ²⁵Now therefore, please pardon my sin, and return with me, that I may worship the LORD."

²⁶But Samuel said to Saul, "I will not return with you, for you have rejected the word of the LORD, and the LORD has reject-ed you from being king over Israel." ²⁷And as Samuel turned around to go away, *Saul* seized the edge of his robe, and it tore. ²⁸So Samuel said to him, "The LORD has torn the kingdom of Israel from you today, and has given it to a neighbor of yours, *who is* better than you. ²⁹And also the Strength of Israel will not lie nor relent. For He *is* not a man, that He should relent." ³⁰Then he said, "I have sinned; *yet* honor me now, please, before the elders of my peo-ple and before Israel, and return with me, that I may worship the LORD your God."

[31]So Samuel turned back after Saul, and Saul worshiped the LORD.

[32]Then Samuel said, "Bring Agag king of the Amalekites here to me." So Agag came to him cautiously.

And Agag said, "Surely the bitterness of death is past."

[33]But Samuel said, "As your sword has made women childless, so shall your mother be childless among women." And Samuel hacked Agag in pieces before the LORD in Gilgal.

[34]Then Samuel went to Ramah, and Saul went up to his house at Gibeah of Saul. [35]And Samuel went no more to see Saul until the day of his death. Nevertheless Samuel mourned for Saul, and the LORD regretted that He had made Saul king over Israel.

David Anointed King

16 Now the LORD said to Samuel, "How long will you mourn for Saul, seeing I have rejected him from reigning over Israel? Fill your horn with oil, and go; I am sending you to Jesse the Bethlehemite. For I have provided Myself a king among his sons."

[2]And Samuel said, "How can I go? If Saul hears *it,* he will kill me."

But the LORD said, "Take a heifer with you, and say, 'I have come to sacrifice to the LORD.' [3]Then invite Jesse to the sacrifice, and I will show you what you shall do; you shall anoint for Me the one I name to you."

[4]So Samuel did what the LORD said, and went to Bethlehem. And the elders of the town trembled at his coming, and said, "Do you come peaceably?"

[5]And he said, "Peaceably; I have come to sacrifice to the LORD. Sanctify yourselves, and come with me to the sacrifice." Then he consecrated Jesse and his sons, and invited them to the sacrifice.

[6]So it was, when they came, that he looked at Eliab and said, "Surely the LORD's anointed *is* before Him!"

[7]But the LORD said to Samuel, "Do not look at his appearance or at his physical stature, because I have refused him. For *the LORD does* not *see* as man sees;[a] for man looks at the outward appearance, but the LORD looks at the heart."

[8]So Jesse called Abinadab, and made him pass before Samuel. And he said, "Neither has the LORD chosen this one." [9]Then Jesse made Shammah pass by. And he said, "Neither has the LORD chosen this one." [10]Thus Jesse made seven of his sons pass before Samuel. And Samuel said to Jesse, "The LORD has not chosen these." [11]And Samuel said to Jesse, "Are all the young men here?" Then he said, "There remains yet the youngest, and there he is, keeping the sheep."

And Samuel said to Jesse, "Send and bring him. For we will not sit down[a] till he comes here." [12]So he sent and brought him in. Now he *was* ruddy, with bright eyes, and good-looking. And the LORD said, "Arise, anoint him; for this *is* the one!" [13]Then Samuel took the horn of oil and anointed him in the midst of his brothers; and the Spirit of the LORD came upon David from that day forward. So Samuel arose and went to Ramah.

A Distressing Spirit Troubles Saul

[14]But the Spirit of the LORD departed from Saul, and a distressing spirit from the LORD troubled him. [15]And Saul's servants said to him, "Surely, a distressing spirit from God is troubling you. [16]Let our master now command your servants, *who are* before you, to seek out a man *who is* a skillful player on the harp. And it shall be that he will play it with his hand when the distressing spirit from God is upon you, and you shall be well."

[17]So Saul said to his servants, "Provide me now a man who can play well, and bring *him* to me."

[18]Then one of the servants answered and said, "Look, I have seen a son of Jesse the Bethlehemite, *who is* skillful in playing, a mighty man of valor, a man of war, prudent in speech, and a handsome person; and the LORD *is* with him."

[19]Therefore Saul sent messengers to Jesse, and said, "Send me your son David, who *is* with the sheep." [20]And Jesse took a

---

16:7 [a]Septuagint reads *For God does not see as man sees;* Targum reads *It is not by the appearance of a man;* Vulgate reads *Nor do I judge according to the looks of a man.* **16:11** [a]Following Septuagint and Vulgate; Masoretic Text reads *turn around;* Targum and Syriac read *turn away.*

donkey *loaded with* bread, a skin of wine, and a young goat, and sent *them* by his son David to Saul. 21So David came to Saul and stood before him. And he loved him greatly, and he became his armorbearer. 22Then Saul sent to Jesse, saying, "Please let David stand before me, for he has found favor in my sight." 23And so it was, whenever the spirit from God was upon Saul, that David would take a harp and play *it* with his hand. Then Saul would become refreshed and well, and the distressing spirit would depart from him.

David and Goliath

17 Now the Philistines gathered their armies together to battle, and were gathered at Sochoh, which *belongs* to Judah; they encamped between Sochoh and Azekah, in Ephes Dammim. 2And Saul and the men of Israel were gathered together, and they encamped in the Valley of Elah, and drew up in battle array against the Philistines. 3The Philistines stood on a mountain on one side, and Israel stood on a mountain on the other side, with a valley between them.

4And a champion went out from the camp of the Philistines, named Goliath, from Gath, whose height *was* six cubits and a span. 5*He had* a bronze helmet on his head, and he *was* armed with a coat of mail, and the weight of the coat *was* five thousand shekels of bronze. 6And *he had* bronze armor on his legs and a bronze javelin between his shoulders. 7Now the staff of his spear *was* like a weaver's beam, and his iron spearhead *weighed* six hundred shekels; and a shield-bearer went before him. 8Then he stood and cried out to the armies of Israel, and said to them, "Why have you come out to line up for battle? *Am* I not a Philistine, and you the servants of Saul? Choose a man for yourselves, and let him come down to me. 9If he is able to fight with me and kill me, then we will be your servants. But if I prevail against him and kill him, then you shall be our servants and serve us." 10And the Philistine said, "I defy the armies of Israel this day; give me a man, that we may fight together." 11When Saul and all Israel heard these words of the Philistine, they were dismayed and greatly afraid.

12Now David *was* the son of that Ephrathite of Bethlehem Judah, whose name *was* Jesse, and who had eight sons. And the man was old, advanced *in years*, in the days of Saul. 13The three oldest sons of Jesse had gone to follow Saul to the battle. The names of his three sons who went to the battle *were* Eliab the firstborn, next to him Abinadab, and the third Shammah. 14David *was* the youngest. And the three oldest followed Saul. 15But David occasionally went and returned from Saul to feed his father's sheep at Bethlehem.

16And the Philistine drew near and presented himself forty days, morning and evening.

17Then Jesse said to his son David, "Take now for your brothers an ephah of this dried *grain* and these ten loaves, and run to your brothers at the camp. 18And carry these ten cheeses to the captain of *their* thousand, and see how your brothers fare, and bring back news of them." 19Now Saul and they and all the men of Israel *were* in the Valley of Elah, fighting with the Philistines.

20So David rose early in the morning, left the sheep with a keeper, and took *the things* and went as Jesse had commanded him. And he came to the camp as the army was going out to the fight and shouting for the battle. 21For Israel and the Philistines had drawn up in battle array, army against army. 22And David left his supplies in the hand of the supply keeper, ran to the army, and came and greeted his brothers. 23Then as he talked with them, there was the champion, the Philistine of Gath, Goliath by name, coming up from the armies of the Philistines; and he spoke according to the same words. So David heard *them*. 24And all the men of Israel, when they saw the man, fled from him and were dreadfully afraid. 25So the men of Israel said, "Have you seen this man who has come up? Surely he has come up to defy Israel; and it shall be *that* the man who kills him the king will enrich with great riches, will give him his daughter, and give his father's house exemption *from taxes* in Israel."

26Then David spoke to the men who stood by him, saying, "What shall be done for the man who kills this Philistine and takes away the reproach from Israel? For who *is* this uncircumcised Philistine, that he should defy the armies of the living God?"

27And the people answered him in this manner, saying, "So shall it be done for the man who kills him."

28Now Eliab his oldest brother heard when he spoke to the men; and Eliab's anger was aroused against David, and he said, "Why did you come down here? And with whom have you left those few sheep in the wilderness? I know your pride and the insolence of your heart, for you have come down to see the battle."

29And David said, "What have I done now? *Is there* not a cause?" 30Then he turned from him toward another and said the same thing; and these people answered him as the first ones *did*.

31Now when the words which David spoke were heard, they reported *them* to Saul; and he sent for him. 32Then David said to Saul, "Let no man's heart fail because of him; your servant will go and fight with this Philistine."

33And Saul said to David, "You are not able to go against this Philistine to fight with him; for you *are* a youth, and he a man of war from his youth."

34But David said to Saul, "Your servant used to keep his father's sheep, and when a lion or a bear came and took a lamb out of the flock, 35I went out after it and struck it, and delivered *the lamb* from its mouth; and when it arose against me, I caught *it* by its beard, and struck and killed it. 36Your servant has killed both lion and bear; and this uncircumcised Philistine will be like one of them, seeing he has defied the armies of the living God." 37Moreover David said, "The LORD, who delivered me from the paw of the lion and from the paw of the bear, He will deliver me from the hand of this Philistine."

And Saul said to David, "Go, and the LORD be with you!"

38So Saul clothed David with his armor, and he put a bronze helmet on his head; he also clothed him with a coat of mail. 39David fastened his sword to his armor and tried to walk, for he had not tested *them*. And David said to Saul, "I cannot walk with these, for I have not tested *them*." So David took them off.

40Then he took his staff in his hand; and

BIBLICAL INSIGHTS • 17:45
Faith . . . In the Right Spot

WE HAVE TO PLACE OUR FAITH in the right spot. The trick is in knowing where that spot is! Fortunately, the victory of a young shepherd boy named David over a giant named Goliath demonstrated where to find that spot.

The belligerent Goliath taunted the soldiers of Israel, none of whom had the courage to stand up to him. He then taunted David himself when the boy had the nerve to confront him in the name of his God.

With the stirring words David confidently answered the giant, "You come to me with a sword, with a spear, and with a javelin. But I come to you in the name of the LORD of hosts, the God of the armies of Israel, whom you have defied. This day the LORD will deliver you into my hand, and I will strike you and take your head from you" (17:45, 46). David's courage—and the victory that followed—grew out of his faith. He focused on God and His promises, not on his circumstances.

What are you facing today that looms large in your marriage? What are the giants that threaten your family? Part of faith is the courage to have confidence in God's Word, even when it seems that the odds against us are overwhelming. That is exactly the kind of faith we need in our marriages and in our homes. Why not bow in prayer right now and ask God to give you the courage to slay your giants?

he chose for himself five smooth stones from the brook, and put them in a shepherd's bag, in a pouch which he had, and his sling was in his hand. And he drew near to the Philistine. 41So the Philistine came, and began drawing near to David, and the man who bore the shield *went* before him. 42And when the Philistine looked about and saw David, he disdained him; for he was *only* a youth, ruddy and good-looking. 43So the

Philistine said to David, "*Am* I a dog, that you come to me with sticks?" And the Philistine cursed David by his gods. ⁴⁴And the Philistine said to David, "Come to me, and I will give your flesh to the birds of the air and the beasts of the field!"

⁴⁵Then David said to the Philistine, "You come to me with a sword, with a spear, and with a javelin. But I come to you in the name of the LORD of hosts, the God of the armies of Israel, whom you have defied. ⁴⁶This day the LORD will deliver you into my hand, and I will strike you and take your head from you. And this day I will give the carcasses of the camp of the Philistines to the birds of the air and the wild beasts of the earth, that all the earth may know that there is a God in Israel. ⁴⁷Then all this assembly shall know that the LORD does not save with sword and spear; for the battle *is* the LORD's, and He will give you into our hands."

⁴⁸So it was, when the Philistine arose and came and drew near to meet David, that David hurried and ran toward the army to meet the Philistine. ⁴⁹Then David put his hand in his bag and took out a stone; and he slung *it* and struck the Philistine in his forehead, so that the stone sank into his forehead, and he fell on his face to the earth. ⁵⁰So David prevailed over the Philistine with a sling and a stone, and struck the Philistine and killed him. But *there was* no sword in the hand of David. ⁵¹Therefore David ran and stood over the Philistine, took his sword and drew it out of its sheath and killed him, and cut off his head with it.

And when the Philistines saw that their champion was dead, they fled. ⁵²Now the men of Israel and Judah arose and shouted, and pursued the Philistines as far as the entrance of the valley^a and to the gates of Ekron. And the wounded of the Philistines fell along the road to Shaaraim, even as far as Gath and Ekron. ⁵³Then the children of Israel returned from chasing the Philistines, and they plundered their tents. ⁵⁴And David took the head of the Philistine and brought it to Jerusalem, but he put his armor in his tent.

⁵⁵When Saul saw David going out against the Philistine, he said to Abner, the commander of the army, "Abner, whose son *is* this youth?"

And Abner said, "As your soul lives, O king, I do not know."

⁵⁶So the king said, "Inquire whose son this young man *is.*"

⁵⁷Then, as David returned from the slaughter of the Philistine, Abner took him and brought him before Saul with the head of the Philistine in his hand. ⁵⁸And Saul said to him, "Whose son *are* you, young man?"

So David answered, "*I am* the son of your servant Jesse the Bethlehemite."

Saul Resents David

18 Now when he had finished speaking to Saul, the soul of Jonathan was knit to the soul of David, and Jonathan loved him as his own soul. ²Saul took him that day, and would not let him go home to his father's house anymore. ³Then Jonathan and David made a covenant, because he loved him as his own soul. ⁴And Jonathan took off the robe that *was* on him and gave it to David, with his armor, even to his sword and his bow and his belt.

⁵So David went out wherever Saul sent him, *and* behaved wisely. And Saul set him over the men of war, and he was accepted in the sight of all the people and also in the sight of Saul's servants. ⁶Now it had happened as they were coming *home,* when David was returning from the slaughter of the Philistine, that the women had come out of all the cities of Israel, singing and dancing, to meet King Saul, with tambourines, with joy, and with musical instruments. ⁷So the women sang as they danced, and said:

"Saul has slain his thousands,
    And David his ten thousands."

⁸Then Saul was very angry, and the saying displeased him; and he said, "They have ascribed to David ten thousands, and to me they have ascribed *only* thousands. Now *what* more can he have but the kingdom?" ⁹So Saul eyed David from that day forward.

¹⁰And it happened on the next day that the distressing spirit from God came upon Saul, and he prophesied inside the house. So David played *music* with his hand, as at

---

17:52 ^aFollowing Masoretic Text, Syriac, Targum, and Vulgate; Septuagint reads *Gath.*

other times; but *there was* a spear in Saul's hand. ¹¹And Saul cast the spear, for he said, "I will pin David to the wall!" But David escaped his presence twice.

¹²Now Saul was afraid of David, because the LORD was with him, but had departed from Saul. ¹³Therefore Saul removed him from his presence, and made him his captain over a thousand; and he went out and came in before the people. ¹⁴And David behaved wisely in all his ways, and the LORD *was* with him. ¹⁵Therefore, when Saul saw that he behaved very wisely, he was afraid of him. ¹⁶But all Israel and Judah loved David, because he went out and came in before them.

David Marries Michal

¹⁷Then Saul said to David, "Here is my older daughter Merab; I will give her to you as a wife. Only be valiant for me, and fight the LORD's battles." For Saul thought, "Let my hand not be against him, but let the hand of the Philistines be against him."

¹⁸So David said to Saul, "Who *am* I, and what *is* my life *or* my father's family in Israel, that I should be son-in-law to the king?" ¹⁹But it happened at the time when Merab, Saul's daughter, should have been given to David, that she was given to Adriel the Meholathite as a wife.

²⁰Now Michal, Saul's daughter, loved David. And they told Saul, and the thing pleased him. ²¹So Saul said, "I will give her to him, that she may be a snare to him, and that the hand of the Philistines may be against him." Therefore Saul said to David a second time, "You shall be my son-in-law today."

²²And Saul commanded his servants, "Communicate with David secretly, and say, 'Look, the king has delight in you, and all his servants love you. Now therefore, become the king's son-in-law.' "

²³So Saul's servants spoke those words in the hearing of David. And David said, "Does it seem to you *a* light *thing* to be a king's son-in-law, seeing I *am* a poor and lightly esteemed man?" ²⁴And the servants of Saul told him, saying, "In this manner David spoke."

²⁵Then Saul said, "Thus you shall say to David: 'The king does not desire any dowry but one hundred foreskins of the Philistines, to take vengeance on the king's enemies.' " But Saul thought to make David fall by the hand of the Philistines. ²⁶So when his servants told David these words, it pleased David well to become the king's son-in-law. Now the days had not expired; ²⁷therefore David arose and went, he and his men, and killed two hundred men of the Philistines. And David brought their foreskins, and they gave them in full count to the king, that he might become the king's son-in-law. Then Saul gave him Michal his daughter as a wife.

²⁸Thus Saul saw and knew that the LORD *was* with David, and *that* Michal, Saul's daughter, loved him; ²⁹and Saul was still more afraid of David. So Saul became David's enemy continually. ³⁰Then the princes of the Philistines went out *to war.* And so it was, whenever they went out, *that* David behaved more wisely than all the servants of Saul, so that his name became highly esteemed.

Saul Persecutes David

19 Now Saul spoke to Jonathan his son and to all his servants, that they should kill David; but Jonathan, Saul's son, delighted greatly in David. ²So Jonathan told David, saying, "My father Saul seeks to kill you. Therefore please be on your guard until morning, and stay in a secret *place* and hide. ³And I will go out and stand beside my father in the field where you *are,* and I will speak with my father about you. Then what I observe, I will tell you."

⁴Thus Jonathan spoke well of David to Saul his father, and said to him, "Let not the king sin against his servant, against David, because he has not sinned against you, and because his works *have been* very good toward you. ⁵For he took his life in his hands and killed the Philistine, and the LORD brought about a great deliverance for all Israel. You saw *it* and rejoiced. Why then will you sin against innocent blood, to kill David without a cause?"

⁶So Saul heeded the voice of Jonathan, and Saul swore, "*As* the LORD lives, he shall not be killed." ⁷Then Jonathan called David, and Jonathan told him all these things. So

Jonathan brought David to Saul, and he was in his presence as in times past.

⁸And there was war again; and David went out and fought with the Philistines, and struck them with a mighty blow, and they fled from him.

⁹Now the distressing spirit from the LORD came upon Saul as he sat in his house with his spear in his hand. And David was playing *music* with *his* hand. ¹⁰Then Saul sought to pin David to the wall with the spear, but he slipped away from Saul's presence; and he drove the spear into the wall. So David fled and escaped that night.

¹¹Saul also sent messengers to David's house to watch him and to kill him in the morning. And Michal, David's wife, told him, saying, "If you do not save your life tonight, tomorrow you will be killed." ¹²So Michal let David down through a window. And he went and fled and escaped. ¹³And Michal took an image and laid *it* in the bed, put a cover of goats' *hair* for his head, and covered *it* with clothes. ¹⁴So when Saul sent messengers to take David, she said, "He *is* sick."

¹⁵Then Saul sent the messengers *back* to see David, saying, "Bring him up to me in the bed, that I may kill him." ¹⁶And when the messengers had come in, there was the image in the bed, with a cover of goats' *hair* for his head. ¹⁷Then Saul said to Michal, "Why have you deceived me like this, and sent my enemy away, so that he has escaped?"

And Michal answered Saul, "He said to me, 'Let me go! Why should I kill you?' "

¹⁸So David fled and escaped, and went to Samuel at Ramah, and told him all that Saul had done to him. And he and Samuel went and stayed in Naioth. ¹⁹Now it was told Saul, saying, "Take note, David *is* at Naioth in Ramah!" ²⁰Then Saul sent messengers to take David. And when they saw the group of prophets prophesying, and Samuel standing *as* leader over them, the Spirit of God came upon the messengers of Saul, and they also prophesied. ²¹And when Saul was told, he sent other messengers, and they prophesied likewise. Then Saul sent messengers again the third time, and they prophesied also. ²²Then he also went to Ramah, and came to the great well that *is* at Sechu. So he asked, and said, "Where *are* Samuel and David?"

And *someone* said, "Indeed *they are* at

PARENTING MATTERS

Q: How can we best model godly expressions of anger for our children?

Since most of us are still learning how to properly handle our own anger, we often end up getting inappropriately angry with our inappropriately angry child. So an incident that started out as one child sinning ends up with two children sinning—one of them an adult.

Correcting wrong ideas and habits related to the expression of anger takes time, humility, and the work of the Holy Spirit. Some of our saved-up anger is buried so deep that we may have to dig to uncover the source. Or we may have labeled our rotting anger with softer words like *frustration* or *stressed out* that we use to deny what we're really feeling.

We need to work at modeling appropriate expressions of anger:
- Not acting or speaking unless emotions are under control (being "quick to hear, slow to speak and slow to anger," James 1:19).
- Keep it from getting personal: Direct your anger at the specific cause rather than spraying anger at your spouse, children, or other people.
- Seeking resolution and reconciliation, not payback.

Remember that children are like little radar units, watching how we will react. Not only that, they will often begin reacting to certain situations the same way they see Mom and Dad reacting.

Naioth in Ramah." [23]So he went there to Naioth in Ramah. Then the Spirit of God was upon him also, and he went on and prophesied until he came to Naioth in Ramah. [24]And he also stripped off his clothes and prophesied before Samuel in like manner, and lay down naked all that day and all that night. Therefore they say, "Is Saul also among the prophets?"[a]

Jonathan's Loyalty to David

20 Then David fled from Naioth in Ramah, and went and said to Jonathan, "What have I done? What *is* my iniquity, and what *is* my sin before your father, that he seeks my life?"

[2]So Jonathan said to him, "By no means! You shall not die! Indeed, my father will do nothing either great or small without first telling me. And why should my father hide this thing from me? It *is* not *so!*"

[3]Then David took an oath again, and said, "Your father certainly knows that I have found favor in your eyes, and he has said, 'Do not let Jonathan know this, lest he be grieved.' But truly, *as* the LORD lives and *as* your soul lives, *there is* but a step between me and death."

[4]So Jonathan said to David, "Whatever you yourself desire, I will do *it* for you."

[5]And David said to Jonathan, "Indeed tomorrow *is* the New Moon, and I should not fail to sit with the king to eat. But let me go, that I may hide in the field until the third *day* at evening. [6]If your father misses me at all, then say, 'David earnestly asked *permission* of me that he might run over to Bethlehem, his city, for *there is* a yearly sacrifice there for all the family.' [7]If he says thus: '*It is* well,' your servant will be safe. But if he is very angry, be sure that evil is determined by him. [8]Therefore you shall deal kindly with your servant, for you have brought your servant into a covenant of the LORD with you. Nevertheless, if there is iniquity in me, kill me yourself, for why should you bring me to your father?"

[9]But Jonathan said, "Far be it from you! For if I knew certainly that evil was determined by my father to come upon you, then would I not tell you?"

[10]Then David said to Jonathan, "Who will tell me, or what *if* your father answers you roughly?"

[11]And Jonathan said to David, "Come, let us go out into the field." So both of them went out into the field. [12]Then Jonathan said to David: "The LORD God of Israel *is witness!* When I have sounded out my father sometime tomorrow, *or* the third *day,* and indeed *there is* good toward David, and I do not send to you and tell you, [13]may the LORD do so and much more to Jonathan. But if it pleases my father *to do* you evil, then I will report it to you and send you away, that you may go in safety. And the LORD be with you

19:24 [a]Compare 1 Samuel 10:12

Friendship: Spokes on the Wheel

Marriage is like the hub of a wheel. It provides a point of strength, and as such should provide each spouse with an assurance of total acceptance. In marriage, we find a haven from others' rejection and disapproval.

But God never intended for a husband or a wife to bear the total responsibility for building self-esteem in a spouse! That would be an enormous weight for one person to  carry. Instead, both partners need to reach out from the hub and extend spokes of friendship to strengthen each of them. These spokes do not threaten the security and strength of the hub. Instead, the presence of a few stout and loyal friends enhances and strengthens the marriage.

You may be thinking, *My mate and I like each other—we don't need anyone else.* But no matter how good a marriage you have, you still need friends. A married couple with no outside friends will be unable to achieve a healthy, balanced relationship. Mature believers recognize their need for friends outside the marriage—close confidants with whom they can be real, unaffected, and natural.

as He has been with my father. ¹⁴And you shall not only show me the kindness of the LORD while I still live, that I may not die; ¹⁵but you shall not cut off your kindness from my house forever, no, not when the LORD has cut off every one of the enemies of David from the face of the earth." ¹⁶So Jonathan made *a covenant* with the house of David, *saying,* "Let the LORD require *it* at the hand of David's enemies."

¹⁷Now Jonathan again caused David to vow, because he loved him; for he loved him as he loved his own soul. ¹⁸Then Jonathan said to David, "Tomorrow *is* the New Moon; and you will be missed, because your seat will be empty. ¹⁹And *when* you have stayed three days, go down quickly and come to the place where you hid on the day of the deed; and remain by the stone Ezel. ²⁰Then I will shoot three arrows to the side, as though I shot at a target; ²¹and there I will send a lad, *saying,* 'Go, find the arrows.' If I expressly say to the lad, 'Look, the arrows *are* on this side of you; get them and come'—then, as the LORD lives, *there is* safety for you and no harm. ²²But if I say thus to the young man, 'Look, the arrows *are* beyond you'—go your way, for the LORD has sent you away. ²³And as for the matter which you and I have spoken of, indeed the LORD *be* between you and me forever."

²⁴Then David hid in the field. And when the New Moon had come, the king sat down to eat the feast. ²⁵Now the king sat on his seat, as at other times, on a seat by the wall. And Jonathan arose,ᵃ and Abner sat by Saul's side, but David's place was empty. ²⁶Nevertheless Saul did not say anything that day, for he thought, "Something has happened to him; he *is* unclean, surely he *is* unclean." ²⁷And it happened the next day, the second *day* of the month, that David's place was empty. And Saul said to Jonathan his son, "Why has the son of Jesse not come to eat, either yesterday or today?"

²⁸So Jonathan answered Saul, "David earnestly asked *permission* of me *to go* to Bethlehem. ²⁹And he said, 'Please let me go, for our family has a sacrifice in the city, and my brother has commanded me *to be there.* And now, if I have found favor in your eyes, please let me get away and see

my brothers.' Therefore he has not come to the king's table."

³⁰Then Saul's anger was aroused against Jonathan, and he said to him, "You son of a perverse, rebellious *woman!* Do I not know that you have chosen the son of Jesse to your own shame and to the shame of your mother's nakedness? ³¹For as long as the son of Jesse lives on the earth, you shall not be established, nor your kingdom. Now therefore, send and bring him to me, for he shall surely die."

³²And Jonathan answered Saul his father, and said to him, "Why should he be killed? What has he done?" ³³Then Saul cast a spear at him to kill him, by which Jonathan knew that it was determined by his father to kill David.

³⁴So Jonathan arose from the table in fierce anger, and ate no food the second day of the month, for he was grieved for David, because his father had treated him shamefully.

³⁵And so it was, in the morning, that Jonathan went out into the field at the time appointed with David, and a little lad *was* with him. ³⁶Then he said to his lad, "Now run, find the arrows which I shoot." As the lad ran, he shot an arrow beyond him. ³⁷When the lad had come to the place where the arrow was which Jonathan had shot, Jonathan cried out after the lad and said, "*Is* not the arrow beyond you?" ³⁸And Jonathan cried out after the lad, "Make haste, hurry, do not delay!" So Jonathan's lad gathered up the arrows and came back to his master. ³⁹But the lad did not know anything. Only Jonathan and David knew of the matter. ⁴⁰Then Jonathan gave his weapons to his lad, and said to him, "Go, carry *them* to the city."

⁴¹As soon as the lad had gone, David arose from *a place* toward the south, fell on his face to the ground, and bowed down three times. And they kissed one another; and they wept together, but David more so. ⁴²Then Jonathan said to David, "Go in peace, since we have both sworn in the name of the LORD, saying, 'May the LORD be between you and me, and between your descendants and my descendants, forever.' "

20:25 ᵃFollowing Masoretic Text, Syriac, Targum, and Vulgate; Septuagint reads *he sat across from Jonathan.*

So he arose and departed, and Jonathan went into the city.

David and the Holy Bread

21 Now David came to Nob, to Ahimelech the priest. And Ahimelech was afraid when he met David, and said to him, "Why *are* you alone, and no one is with you?"

²So David said to Ahimelech the priest, "The king has ordered me on some business, and said to me, 'Do not let anyone know anything about the business on which I send you, or what I have commanded you.' And I have directed *my* young men to such and such a place. ³Now therefore, what have you on hand? Give *me* five *loaves of* bread in my hand, or whatever can be found."

⁴And the priest answered David and said, "*There is* no common bread on hand; but there is holy bread, if the young men have at least kept themselves from women."

⁵Then David answered the priest, and said to him, "Truly, women *have been* kept from us about three days since I came out. And the vessels of the young men are holy, and *the bread is* in effect common, even though it was consecrated in the vessel this day."

⁶So the priest gave him holy *bread;* for there was no bread there but the showbread which had been taken from before the LORD, in order to put hot bread *in its place* on the day when it was taken away.

⁷Now a certain man of the servants of Saul *was* there that day, detained before the LORD. And his name *was* Doeg, an Edomite, the chief of the herdsmen who *belonged* to Saul.

⁸And David said to Ahimelech, "Is there not here on hand a spear or a sword? For I have brought neither my sword nor my weapons with me, because the king's business required haste."

⁹So the priest said, "The sword of Goliath the Philistine, whom you killed in the Valley of Elah, there it is, wrapped in a cloth behind the ephod. If you will take that, take *it.* For *there is* no other except that one here."

And David said, "*There is* none like it; give it to me."

21:11 ᵃCompare 1 Samuel 18:7

BIBLICAL INSIGHTS • 22:3

An Example of Honor

WE FONDLY REMEMBER DAVID as a shepherd boy, a fierce warrior, and a godly king. But how many of us remember that he also went out of his way to safeguard and honor his aged parents?

Before he became king, David gathered a group of would-be warriors to help his countrymen, suffering under Philistine oppression. He lived with danger, and so he took his parents to a safer neighborhood. "Please let my father and mother come here with you," he said to the ruler, "till I know what God will do for me" (22:3). David teaches us to *aggressively honor our parents.* Honoring parents gives you and your mate a sense of well-being

As your parents age, they need to see that you and your mate have compassion for them. They need you to care. They need affirming words. They need to be hugged and appreciated. They need you and your mate to see them as people who have needs and struggles. Just as a parent will hug a child and bandage his skinned knee, so you and your mate can come alongside both sets of parents and stand with them.

If your parents are still living, why not pull out a sheet of paper right now and take an inventory of what their needs might be? Then write out a couple of practical ways that you can honor them.

David Flees to Gath

¹⁰Then David arose and fled that day from before Saul, and went to Achish the king of Gath. ¹¹And the servants of Achish said to him, "*Is* this not David the king of the land? Did they not sing of him to one another in dances, saying:

' Saul has slain his thousands,
And David his ten thousands'?"ᵃ

¹²Now David took these words to heart, and was very much afraid of Achish the king of Gath. ¹³So he changed his behavior

before them, pretended madness in their hands, scratched on the doors of the gate, and let his saliva fall down on his beard. ¹⁴Then Achish said to his servants, "Look, you see the man is insane. Why have you brought him to me? ¹⁵Have I need of madmen, that you have brought this *fellow* to play the madman in my presence? Shall this *fellow* come into my house?"

David's Four Hundred Men

22 David therefore departed from there and escaped to the cave of Adullam. So when his brothers and all his father's house heard *it,* they went down there to him. ²And everyone *who was* in distress, everyone who *was* in debt, and everyone *who was* discontented gathered to him. So he became captain over them. And there were about four hundred men with him.

³Then David went from there to Mizpah of Moab; and he said to the king of Moab, "Please let my father and mother come here with you, till I know what God will do for me." ⁴So he brought them before the king of Moab, and they dwelt with him all the time that David was in the stronghold.

⁵Now the prophet Gad said to David, "Do not stay in the stronghold; depart, and go to the land of Judah." So David departed and went into the forest of Hereth.

Saul Murders the Priests

⁶When Saul heard that David and the men who *were* with him had been discovered—now Saul was staying in Gibeah under a tamarisk tree in Ramah, with his spear in his hand, and all his servants standing about him— ⁷then Saul said to his servants who stood about him, "Hear now, you Benjamites! Will the son of Jesse give every one of you fields and vineyards, *and* make you all captains of thousands and captains of hundreds? ⁸All of you have conspired against me, and *there is* no one who reveals to me that my son has made a covenant with the son of Jesse; and *there is* not one of you who is sorry for me or reveals to me that my son has stirred up my servant against me, to lie in wait, as *it is* this day."

⁹Then answered Doeg the Edomite, who was set over the servants of Saul, and said, "I saw the son of Jesse going to Nob, to Ahimelech the son of Ahitub. ¹⁰And he inquired of the LORD for him, gave him provisions, and gave him the sword of Goliath the Philistine."

¹¹So the king sent to call Ahimelech the priest, the son of Ahitub, and all his father's house, the priests who *were* in Nob. And they all came to the king. ¹²And Saul said, "Hear now, son of Ahitub!"

He answered, "Here I am, my lord."

¹³Then Saul said to him, "Why have you conspired against me, you and the son of Jesse, in that you have given him bread and a sword, and have inquired of God for him, that he should rise against me, to lie in wait, as it is this day?"

¹⁴So Ahimelech answered the king and said, "And who among all your servants *is as* faithful as David, who is the king's son-in-law, who goes at your bidding, and is honorable in your house? ¹⁵Did I then begin to inquire of God for him? Far be it from me! Let not the king impute anything to his servant, *or* to any in the house of my father. For your servant knew nothing of all this, little or much."

¹⁶And the king said, "You shall surely die, Ahimelech, you and all your father's house!" ¹⁷Then the king said to the guards who stood about him, "Turn and kill the priests of the LORD, because their hand also *is* with David, and because they knew when he fled and did not tell it to me." But the servants of the king would not lift their hands to strike the priests of the LORD. ¹⁸And the king said to Doeg, "You turn and kill the priests!" So Doeg the Edomite turned and struck the priests, and killed on that day eighty-five men who wore a linen ephod. ¹⁹Also Nob, the city of the priests, he struck with the edge of the sword, both men and women, children and nursing infants, oxen and donkeys and sheep—with the edge of the sword.

²⁰Now one of the sons of Ahimelech the son of Ahitub, named Abiathar, escaped and fled after David. ²¹And Abiathar told David that Saul had killed the LORD's priests. ²²So David said to Abiathar, "I knew that day, when Doeg the Edomite *was* there, that he would surely tell Saul. I have caused *the death* of all the persons of your father's house. ²³Stay with me; do not fear. For he

who seeks my life seeks your life, but with me you *shall be* safe."

David Saves the City of Keilah

23 Then they told David, saying, "Look, the Philistines are fighting against Keilah, and they are robbing the threshing floors."

[2]Therefore David inquired of the Lord, saying, "Shall I go and attack these Philistines?"

And the Lord said to David, "Go and attack the Philistines, and save Keilah."

[3]But David's men said to him, "Look, we are afraid here in Judah. How much more then if we go to Keilah against the armies of the Philistines?" [4]Then David inquired of the Lord once again.

And the Lord answered him and said, "Arise, go down to Keilah. For I will deliver the Philistines into your hand." [5]And David and his men went to Keilah and fought with the Philistines, struck them with a mighty blow, and took away their livestock. So David saved the inhabitants of Keilah.

[6]Now it happened, when Abiathar the son of Ahimelech fled to David at Keilah, *that* he went down *with* an ephod in his hand.

[7]And Saul was told that David had gone to Keilah. So Saul said, "God has delivered him into my hand, for he has shut himself in by entering a town that has gates and bars." [8]Then Saul called all the people together for war, to go down to Keilah to besiege David and his men.

[9]When David knew that Saul plotted evil against him, he said to Abiathar the priest, "Bring the ephod here." [10]Then David said, "O Lord God of Israel, Your servant has certainly heard that Saul seeks to come to Keilah to destroy the city for my sake. [11]Will the men of Keilah deliver me into his hand? Will Saul come down, as Your servant has heard? O Lord God of Israel, I pray, tell Your servant."

And the Lord said, "He will come down."

[12]Then David said, "Will the men of Keilah deliver me and my men into the hand of Saul?"

And the Lord said, "They will deliver *you.*"

[13]So David and his men, about six hundred, arose and departed from Keilah and went wherever they could go. Then it was told Saul that David had escaped from Keilah; so he halted the expedition.

David in Wilderness Strongholds

[14]And David stayed in strongholds in the wilderness, and remained in the mountains in the Wilderness of Ziph. Saul sought him every day, but God did not deliver him into his hand. [15]So David saw that Saul had come out to seek his life. And David *was* in the Wilderness of Ziph in a forest.[a] [16]Then Jonathan, Saul's son, arose and went to David in the woods and strengthened his hand in God. [17]And he said to him, "Do not fear, for the hand of Saul my father shall not find you. You shall be king over Israel, and I shall be next to you. Even my father Saul knows that." [18]So the two of them made a covenant before the Lord. And David stayed in the woods, and Jonathan went to his own house.

[19]Then the Ziphites came up to Saul at Gibeah, saying, "Is David not hiding with us in strongholds in the woods, in the hill of Hachilah, which *is* on the south of Jeshimon? [20]Now therefore, O king, come down according to all the desire of your soul to come down; and our part *shall be* to deliver him into the king's hand."

[21]And Saul said, "Blessed *are* you of the Lord, for you have compassion on me. [22]Please go and find out for sure, and see the place where his hideout is, *and* who has seen him there. For I am told he is very crafty. [23]See therefore, and take knowledge of all the lurking places where he hides; and come back to me with certainty, and I will go with you. And it shall be, if he is in the land, that I will search for him throughout all the clans[a] of Judah."

[24]So they arose and went to Ziph before Saul. But David and his men *were* in the Wilderness of Maon, in the plain on the south of Jeshimon. [25]When Saul and his men went to seek *him,* they told David. Therefore he went down to the rock, and stayed in the Wilderness of Maon. And when Saul heard *that,* he pursued David in

---

23:15 [a]Or *in Horesh* **23:23** [a]Literally *thousands*

the Wilderness of Maon. ²⁶Then Saul went on one side of the mountain, and David and his men on the other side of the mountain. So David made haste to get away from Saul, for Saul and his men were encircling David and his men to take them.

²⁷But a messenger came to Saul, saying, "Hurry and come, for the Philistines have invaded the land!" ²⁸Therefore Saul returned from pursuing David, and went against the Philistines; so they called that place the Rock of Escape.ᵃ ²⁹Then David went up from there and dwelt in strongholds at En Gedi.

David Spares Saul

24 Now it happened, when Saul had returned from following the Philistines, that it was told him, saying, "Take note! David *is* in the Wilderness of En Gedi." ²Then Saul took three thousand chosen men from all Israel, and went to seek David and his men on the Rocks of the Wild Goats. ³So he came to the sheepfolds by the road, where there *was* a cave; and Saul went in to attend to his needs. (David and his men were staying in the recesses of the cave.) ⁴Then the men of David said to him, "This is the day of which the LORD said to you, 'Behold, I will deliver your enemy into your hand, that you may do to him as it seems good to you.' " And David arose and secretly cut off a corner of Saul's robe. ⁵Now it happened afterward that David's heart troubled him because he had cut Saul's robe. ⁶And he said to his men, "The LORD forbid that I should do this thing to my master, the LORD's anointed, to stretch out my hand against him, seeing he *is* the anointed of the LORD." ⁷So David restrained his servants with *these* words, and did not allow them to rise against Saul. And Saul got up from the cave and went on *his* way.

⁸David also arose afterward, went out of the cave, and called out to Saul, saying, "My lord the king!" And when Saul looked behind him, David stooped with his face to the earth, and bowed down. ⁹And David said to Saul: "Why do you listen to the words of men who say, 'Indeed David seeks your harm'? ¹⁰Look, this day your eyes have seen that the LORD delivered you today into my hand in the cave, and *someone* urged *me* to kill you. But *my eye* spared you, and I said, 'I will not stretch out my hand against my lord, for he *is* the LORD's anointed.' ¹¹Moreover, my father, see! Yes, see the corner of your robe in my hand! For in that I cut off the corner of your robe, and did not kill you, know and see that *there is* neither evil nor rebellion in my hand, and I have not sinned against you. Yet you hunt my life to take it. ¹²Let the LORD judge between you and me, and let the LORD avenge me on you. But my hand shall not be against you. ¹³As the proverb of the ancients says, 'Wickedness proceeds from the wicked.' But my hand shall not be against you. ¹⁴After whom has the king of Israel come out? Whom do you pursue? A dead dog? A flea? ¹⁵Therefore let the LORD be judge, and judge between you and me, and see and plead my case, and deliver me out of your hand."

INTIMATE MOMENTS
Give Her a Day Off

Your wife does a lot for you and your family, and while kind words can go a long way toward telling her, "thank you," kind actions can be even more thoughtful.

Think for a bit about an ordinary day in the life of your spouse. What does she do? A list like the following is probably swirling around in her head, even now: *Bathe the kids. Clean the kitchen. Fold the laundry. Make the bed. Fix lunch, then dinner. Get groceries. Call the doctor. Send thank you notes. Retrieve the mail. Prepare Sunday school lesson. Vacuum the carpet. Straighten the living room. Dust the family room. Wash the dog. Pay the electric bill.*

And that's just getting started! To show how much you appreciate all she does, arrange for a day to do whatever it is she normally does. And tell her to *relax.* I promise you, at the end of that day, you *will* have a greater appreciation of your wife.

¹⁶So it was, when David had finished speaking these words to Saul, that Saul said, "Is this your voice, my son David?" And Saul lifted up his voice and wept. ¹⁷Then he said to David: "You *are* more righteous than I; for you have rewarded me with good, whereas I have rewarded you with evil. ¹⁸And you have shown this day how you have dealt well with me; for when the LORD delivered me into your hand, you did not kill me. ¹⁹For if a man finds his enemy, will he let him get away safely? Therefore may the LORD reward you with good for what you have done to me this day. ²⁰And now I know indeed that you shall surely be king, and that the kingdom of Israel shall be established in your hand. ²¹Therefore swear now to me by the LORD that you will not cut off my descendants after me, and that you will not destroy my name from my father's house."

²²So David swore to Saul. And Saul went home, but David and his men went up to the stronghold.

Death of Samuel

25 Then Samuel died; and the Israelites gathered together and lamented for him, and buried him at his home in Ramah. And David arose and went down to the Wilderness of Paran.ᵃ

David and the Wife of Nabal

²Now *there was* a man in Maon whose business *was* in Carmel, and the man *was* very rich. He had three thousand sheep and a thousand goats. And he was shearing his sheep in Carmel. ³The name of the man *was* Nabal, and the name of his wife Abigail. And *she was* a woman of good understanding and beautiful appearance; but the man *was* harsh and evil in *his* doings. He *was of the house of* Caleb.

⁴When David heard in the wilderness that Nabal was shearing his sheep, ⁵David sent ten young men; and David said to the young men, "Go up to Carmel, go to Nabal, and greet him in my name. ⁶And thus you shall say to him who lives *in prosperity:*

'Peace *be* to you, peace to your house, and peace to all that you have! ⁷Now I have heard that you have shearers. Your shepherds were with us, and we did not hurt them, nor was there anything missing from them all the while they were in Carmel. ⁸Ask your young men, and they will tell you. Therefore let *my* young men find favor in your eyes, for we come on a feast day. Please give whatever comes to your hand to your servants and to your son David.' "

⁹So when David's young men came, they spoke to Nabal according to all these words in the name of David, and waited.

¹⁰Then Nabal answered David's servants, and said, "Who *is* David, and who *is* the son of Jesse? There are many servants nowadays who break away each one from his master. ¹¹Shall I then take my bread and my water and my meat that I have killed for my shearers, and give *it* to men when I do not know where they *are* from?"

¹²So David's young men turned on their heels and went back; and they came and told him all these words. ¹³Then David said to his men, "Every man gird on his sword." So every man girded on his sword, and David also girded on his sword. And about four hundred men went with David, and two hundred stayed with the supplies.

¹⁴Now one of the young men told Abigail, Nabal's wife, saying, "Look, David sent messengers from the wilderness to greet our master; and he reviled them. ¹⁵But the men *were* very good to us, and we were not hurt, nor did we miss anything as long as we accompanied them, when we were in the fields. ¹⁶They were a wall to us both by night and day, all the time we were with them keeping the sheep. ¹⁷Now therefore, know and consider what you will do, for harm is determined against our master and against all his household. For he *is such* a scoundrelᵃ that *one* cannot speak to him."

¹⁸Then Abigail made haste and took two hundred *loaves* of bread, two skins of wine, five sheep already dressed, five seahs of roasted *grain,* one hundred clusters of raisins, and two hundred cakes of figs, and loaded *them* on donkeys. ¹⁹And she said to her servants, "Go on before me; see, I am coming after you." But she did not tell her husband Nabal.

25:1 ᵃFollowing Masoretic Text, Syriac, Targum, and Vulgate; Septuagint reads *Maon.* 25:17 ᵃLiterally *son of Belial*

A Loving Leader Is a Servant

ABIGAIL SAW HERSELF AS A SERVANT—even the servant of servants—even though she was about to become the wife of David (25:41). Still, you never get the sense that she saw herself as weak or inferior. In fact, she was a terrific leader.

Christ, the Head of the church, took on the very nature of a servant when He came to earth (Phil. 2:7). Jesus didn't just *talk* about serving; He even washed His disciples' feet (John 13:1–17). I've washed Barbara's feet as a statement to her that I want to nourish and cherish her and meet her needs. If you've never washed your wife's feet to show that you want to serve her, then think of a special time when you could perform this symbolic ceremony.

I've also found that there is no better way to serve your wife than to understand her needs and try to meet them. If you haven't asked her recently, find out what her top three needs are. If she works outside the home, do you help with meals and household chores? Does she have time to exercise and visit with her girlfriends? What does she like to do for a night out? Have you found a way to serve her lately?

If you're a young husband, I advise you to find an older husband you respect and ask him to mentor you in becoming a servant-leader. If I had my first years of marriage to do over again, I'd go to school with a seasoned veteran husband.

---

²⁰So it was, *as* she rode on the donkey, that she went down under cover of the hill; and there were David and his men, coming down toward her, and she met them. ²¹Now David had said, "Surely in vain I have protected all that this *fellow* has in the wilderness, so that nothing was missed of all that *belongs* to him. And he has repaid me evil for good. ²²May God do so, and more also, to the enemies of David, if I leave one male of all who *belong* to him by morning light."

²³Now when Abigail saw David, she dismounted quickly from the donkey, fell on her face before David, and bowed down to the ground. ²⁴So she fell at his feet and said: "On me, my lord, *on me let* this iniquity *be!* And please let your maidservant speak in your ears, and hear the words of your maidservant. ²⁵Please, let not my lord regard this scoundrel Nabal. For as his name *is,* so *is* he: Nabalᵃ *is* his name, and folly *is* with him! But I, your maidservant, did not see the young men of my lord whom you sent. ²⁶Now therefore, my lord, *as* the LORD lives and *as* your soul lives, since the LORD has held you back from coming to bloodshed and from avenging yourself with your own hand, now then, let your enemies and those who seek harm for my lord be as Nabal. ²⁷And now this present which your maidservant has brought to my lord, let it be given to the young men who follow my lord. ²⁸Please forgive the trespass of your maidservant. For the LORD will certainly make for my lord an enduring house, because my lord fights the battles of the LORD, and evil is not found in you throughout your days. ²⁹Yet a man has risen to pursue you and seek your life, but the life of my lord shall be bound in the bundle of the living with the LORD your God; and the lives of your enemies He shall sling out, *as from* the pocket of a sling. ³⁰And it shall come to pass, when the LORD has done for my lord according to all the good that He has spoken concerning you, and has appointed you ruler over Israel, ³¹that this will be no grief to you, nor offense of heart to my lord, either that you have shed blood without cause, or that my lord has avenged himself. But when the LORD has dealt well with my lord, then remember your maidservant."

³²Then David said to Abigail: "Blessed *is* the LORD God of Israel, who sent you this day to meet me! ³³And blessed *is* your advice and blessed *are* you, because you have kept me this day from coming to bloodshed and from avenging myself with my own hand. ³⁴For indeed, *as* the LORD God of Israel lives, who has kept me back from hurting you, unless you had hurried and come to meet me, surely by morning light no males would have been left to Nabal!" ³⁵So David received

25:25 ᵃLiterally *Fool*

from her hand what she had brought him, and said to her, "Go up in peace to your house. See, I have heeded your voice and respected your person."

³⁶Now Abigail went to Nabal, and there he was, holding a feast in his house, like the feast of a king. And Nabal's heart *was* merry within him, for he *was* very drunk; therefore she told him nothing, little or much, until morning light. ³⁷So it was, in the morning, when the wine had gone from Nabal, and his wife had told him these things, that his heart died within him, and he became *like* a stone. ³⁸Then it happened, *after* about ten days, that the LORD struck Nabal, and he died.

³⁹So when David heard that Nabal was dead, he said, "Blessed *be* the LORD, who has pleaded the cause of my reproach from the hand of Nabal, and has kept His servant from evil! For the LORD has returned the wickedness of Nabal on his own head."

And David sent and proposed to Abigail, to take her as his wife. ⁴⁰When the servants of David had come to Abigail at Carmel, they spoke to her saying, "David sent us to you, to ask you to become his wife."

⁴¹Then she arose, bowed her face to the earth, and said, "Here is your maidservant, a servant to wash the feet of the servants of my lord." ⁴²So Abigail rose in haste and rode on a donkey, attended by five of her maidens; and she followed the messengers of David, and became his wife. ⁴³David also took Ahinoam of Jezreel, and so both of them were his wives.

⁴⁴But Saul had given Michal his daughter, David's wife, to Palti[a] the son of Laish, who *was* from Gallim.

David Spares Saul a Second Time

26 Now the Ziphites came to Saul at Gibeah, saying, "Is David not hiding in the hill of Hachilah, opposite Jeshimon?" ²Then Saul arose and went down to the Wilderness of Ziph, having three thousand chosen men of Israel with him, to seek David in the Wilderness of Ziph. ³And Saul encamped in the hill of Hachilah, which *is* opposite Jeshimon, by the road. But David stayed in the wilderness,

and he saw that Saul came after him into the wilderness. ⁴David therefore sent out spies, and understood that Saul had indeed come.

⁵So David arose and came to the place where Saul had encamped. And David saw the place where Saul lay, and Abner the son of Ner, the commander of his army. Now Saul lay within the camp, with the people encamped all around him. ⁶Then David answered, and said to Ahimelech the Hittite and to Abishai the son of Zeruiah, brother of Joab, saying, "Who will go down with me to Saul in the camp?"

And Abishai said, "I will go down with you."

⁷So David and Abishai came to the people by night; and there Saul lay sleeping within the camp, with his spear stuck in the ground by his head. And Abner and the people lay all around him. ⁸Then Abishai said to David, "God has delivered your enemy into your hand this day. Now therefore, please, let me strike him at once with the spear, right to the earth; and I will not *have to strike* him a second time!"

⁹But David said to Abishai, "Do not destroy him; for who can stretch out his hand against the LORD's anointed, and be guiltless?" ¹⁰David said furthermore, "*As* the LORD lives, the LORD shall strike him, or his day shall come to die, or he shall go out to battle and perish. ¹¹The LORD forbid that I should stretch out my hand against the LORD's anointed. But please, take now the spear and the jug of water that *are* by his head, and let us go." ¹²So David took the spear and the jug of water *by* Saul's head, and they got away; and no man saw or knew *it* or awoke. For they *were* all asleep, because a deep sleep from the LORD had fallen on them.

¹³Now David went over to the other side, and stood on the top of a hill afar off, a great distance *being* between them. ¹⁴And David called out to the people and to Abner the son of Ner, saying, "Do you not answer, Abner?"

Then Abner answered and said, "Who *are* you, calling out to the king?"

¹⁵So David said to Abner, "*Are* you not a man? And who *is* like you in Israel? Why then have you not guarded your lord the

^{25:44} [a]Spelled *Paltiel* in 2 Samuel 3:15

king? For one of the people came in to destroy your lord the king. [16]This thing that you have done *is* not good. *As* the LORD lives, you deserve to die, because you have not guarded your master, the LORD's anointed. And now see where the king's spear *is,* and the jug of water that *was* by his head."

[17]Then Saul knew David's voice, and said, "*Is* that your voice, my son David?"

David said, "*It is* my voice, my lord, O king." [18]And he said, "Why does my lord thus pursue his servant? For what have I done, or what evil *is* in my hand? [19]Now therefore, please, let my lord the king hear the words of his servant: If the LORD has stirred you up against me, let Him accept

---

ROMANCE FAQ

Q: What steps can a man take to keep romance alive?

Nowhere in marriage are the differences between men and women more evident than on the romance side of the ledger. Women generally spell romance: r-e-l-a-t-i-o-n-s-h-i-p. Men spell it a different way: S-E-X.

Typically, a man's focus is physical while a woman's focus is relational. That's why we married men need to learn how to communicate with our wives in a language that clearly speaks the relational aspect of love and romance. If you don't know what this is, *find out.*

One thing is certain: You need to cultivate romance if it is going to grow in your marriage. It is easy for a man, after he's been married for a time, to become complacent, to think that he doesn't have to compete for his wife or need to communicate his love for her in both words and actions, that he no longer needs to romance her. You could hardly make a bigger mistake!

What would communicate love to your wife? A love letter? Then write one. A hug and a kiss that says I love you? Do it! Helping her at home with the children and household duties? Go the extra mile!

---

an offering. But if *it is* the children of men, *may* they *be* cursed before the LORD, for they have driven me out this day from sharing in the inheritance of the LORD, saying, 'Go, serve other gods.' [20]So now, do not let my blood fall to the earth before the face of the LORD. For the king of Israel has come out to seek a flea, as when one hunts a partridge in the mountains."

[21]Then Saul said, "I have sinned. Return, my son David. For I will harm you no more, because my life was precious in your eyes this day. Indeed I have played the fool and erred exceedingly."

[22]And David answered and said, "Here is the king's spear. Let one of the young men come over and get it. [23]May the LORD repay every man *for* his righteousness and his faithfulness; for the LORD delivered you into *my* hand today, but I would not stretch out my hand against the LORD's anointed. [24]And indeed, as your life was valued much this day in my eyes, so let my life be valued much in the eyes of the LORD, and let Him deliver me out of all tribulation."

[25]Then Saul said to David, "*May* you *be* blessed, my son David! You shall both do great things and also still prevail."

So David went on his way, and Saul returned to his place.

David Allied with the Philistines

27 And David said in his heart, "Now I shall perish someday by the hand of Saul. *There is* nothing better for me than that I should speedily escape to the land of the Philistines; and Saul will despair of me, to seek me anymore in any part of Israel. So I shall escape out of his hand." [2]Then David arose and went over with the six hundred men who *were* with him to Achish the son of Maoch, king of Gath. [3]So David dwelt with Achish at Gath, he and his men, each man with his household, *and* David with his two wives, Ahinoam the Jezreelitess, and Abigail the Carmelitess, Nabal's widow. [4]And it was told Saul that David had fled to Gath; so he sought him no more.

[5]Then David said to Achish, "If I have now found favor in your eyes, let them give me a place in some town in the country, that I may dwell there. For why should your

servant dwell in the royal city with you?" [6]So Achish gave him Ziklag that day. Therefore Ziklag has belonged to the kings of Judah to this day. [7]Now the time that David dwelt in the country of the Philistines was one full year and four months.

[8]And David and his men went up and raided the Geshurites, the Girzites,[a] and the Amalekites. For those *nations* were the inhabitants of the land from of old, as you go to Shur, even as far as the land of Egypt. [9]Whenever David attacked the land, he left neither man nor woman alive, but took away the sheep, the oxen, the donkeys, the camels, and the apparel, and returned and came to Achish. [10]Then Achish would say, "Where have you made a raid today?" And David would say, "Against the southern *area* of Judah, or against the southern *area* of the Jerahmeelites, or against the southern *area* of the Kenites." [11]David would save neither man nor woman alive, to bring *news* to Gath, saying, "Lest they should inform on us, saying, 'Thus David did.'" And thus *was* his behavior all the time he dwelt in the country of the Philistines. [12]So Achish believed David, saying, "He has made his people Israel utterly abhor him; therefore he will be my servant forever."

28 Now it happened in those days that the Philistines gathered their armies together for war, to fight with Israel. And Achish said to David, "You assuredly know that you will go out with me to battle, you and your men."

[2]So David said to Achish, "Surely you know what your servant can do."

And Achish said to David, "Therefore I will make you one of my chief guardians forever."

Saul Consults a Medium

[3]Now Samuel had died, and all Israel had lamented for him and buried him in Ramah, in his own city. And Saul had put the mediums and the spiritists out of the land.

[4]Then the Philistines gathered together, and came and encamped at Shunem. So Saul gathered all Israel together, and they encamped at Gilboa. [5]When Saul saw the army of the Philistines, he was afraid, and

his heart trembled greatly. [6]And when Saul inquired of the LORD, the LORD did not answer him, either by dreams or by Urim or by the prophets.

[7]Then Saul said to his servants, "Find me a woman who is a medium, that I may go to her and inquire of her."

And his servants said to him, "In fact, *there is* a woman who is a medium at En Dor."

[8]So Saul disguised himself and put on other clothes, and he went, and two men with him; and they came to the woman by night. And he said, "Please conduct a séance for me, and bring up for me the one I shall name to you."

[9]Then the woman said to him, "Look, you know what Saul has done, how he has cut off the mediums and the spiritists from the land. Why then do you lay a snare for my life, to cause me to die?"

[10]And Saul swore to her by the LORD, saying, "*As* the LORD lives, no punishment shall come upon you for this thing."

[11]Then the woman said, "Whom shall I bring up for you?"

And he said, "Bring up Samuel for me."

[12]When the woman saw Samuel, she cried out with a loud voice. And the woman spoke to Saul, saying, "Why have you deceived me? For you *are* Saul!"

[13]And the king said to her, "Do not be afraid. What did you see?"

And the woman said to Saul, "I saw a spirit[a] ascending out of the earth."

[14]So he said to her, "What *is* his form?"

And she said, "An old man is coming up, and he *is* covered with a mantle." And Saul perceived that it *was* Samuel, and he stooped with *his* face to the ground and bowed down.

[15]Now Samuel said to Saul, "Why have you disturbed me by bringing me up?"

And Saul answered, "I am deeply distressed; for the Philistines make war against me, and God has departed from me and does not answer me anymore, neither by prophets nor by dreams. Therefore I have called you, that you may reveal to me what I should do."

[16]Then Samuel said: "So why do you ask me, seeing the LORD has departed from you and has become your enemy? [17]And the

---

27:8 [a]Or *Gezrites*   **28:13** [a]Hebrew *elohim*

LORD has done for Himself[a] as He spoke by me. For the LORD has torn the kingdom out of your hand and given it to your neighbor, David. [18]Because you did not obey the voice of the LORD nor execute His fierce wrath upon Amalek, therefore the LORD has done this thing to you this day. [19]Moreover the LORD will also deliver Israel with you into the hand of the Philistines. And tomorrow you and your sons *will be* with me. The LORD will also deliver the army of Israel into the hand of the Philistines."

[20]Immediately Saul fell full length on the ground, and was dreadfully afraid because of the words of Samuel. And there was no strength in him, for he had eaten no food all day or all night.

[21]And the woman came to Saul and saw that he was severely troubled, and said to him, "Look, your maidservant has obeyed your voice, and I have put my life in my hands and heeded the words which you spoke to me. [22]Now therefore, please, heed also the voice of your maidservant, and let me set a piece of bread before you; and eat, that you may have strength when you go on *your* way."

[23]But he refused and said, "I will not eat." So his servants, together with the woman, urged him; and he heeded their voice. Then he arose from the ground and sat on the bed. [24]Now the woman had a fatted calf in the house, and she hastened to kill it. And she took flour and kneaded *it,* and baked unleavened bread from it. [25]So she brought *it* before Saul and his servants, and they ate. Then they rose and went away that night.

The Philistines Reject David

29 Then the Philistines gathered together all their armies at Aphek, and the Israelites encamped by a fountain which *is* in Jezreel. [2]And the lords of the Philistines passed in review by hundreds and by thousands, but David and his men passed in review at the rear with Achish. [3]Then the princes of the Philistines said, "What *are* these Hebrews *doing here?*"

And Achish said to the princes of the Philistines, "*Is* this not David, the servant of Saul king of Israel, who has been with me these days, or these years? And to this day I have found no fault in him since he defected *to me.*"

[4]But the princes of the Philistines were angry with him; so the princes of the Philistines said to him, "Make this fellow

---

28:17 [a]Or *him,* that is, David

return, that he may go back to the place which you have appointed for him, and do not let him go down with us to battle, lest in the battle he become our adversary. For with what could he reconcile himself to his master, if not with the heads of these men? [5]*Is* this not David, of whom they sang to one another in dances, saying:

‘ Saul has slain his thousands,
    And David his ten thousands’?”[a]

[6]Then Achish called David and said to him, “Surely, *as* the LORD lives, you have been upright, and your going out and your coming in with me in the army *is* good in my sight. For to this day I have not found evil in you since the day of your coming to me. Nevertheless the lords do not favor you. [7]Therefore return now, and go in peace, that you may not displease the lords of the Philistines.”

[8]So David said to Achish, “But what have I done? And to this day what have you found in your servant as long as I have been with you, that I may not go and fight against the enemies of my lord the king?”

[9]Then Achish answered and said to David, “I know that you *are* as good in my sight as an angel of God; nevertheless the princes of the Philistines have said, ‘He shall not go up with us to the battle.’ [10]Now therefore, rise early in the morning with your master’s servants who have come with you.[a] And as soon as you are up early in the morning and have light, depart.”

[11]So David and his men rose early to depart in the morning, to return to the land of the Philistines. And the Philistines went up to Jezreel.

David’s Conflict with the Amalekites

30 Now it happened, when David and his men came to Ziklag, on the third day, that the Amalekites had invaded the South and Ziklag, attacked Ziklag and burned it with fire, [2]and had taken captive the women and those who *were* there, from small to great; they did not kill anyone, but carried *them* away and went their way. [3]So David and his men came to the city, and there it was, burned with fire; and their wives, their sons, and their daughters had been taken captive. [4]Then David and the people who *were* with him lifted up their voices and wept, until they had no more power to weep. [5]And David’s two wives, Ahinoam the Jezreelitess, and Abigail the widow of Nabal the Carmelite, had been taken captive. [6]Now David was greatly distressed, for the people spoke of stoning him, because the soul of all the people was grieved, every man for his sons and his daughters. But David strengthened himself in the LORD his God.

[7]Then David said to Abiathar the priest, Ahimelech’s son, “Please bring the ephod here to me.” And Abiathar brought the ephod to David. [8]So David inquired of the LORD, saying, “Shall I pursue this troop? Shall I overtake them?”

And He answered him, “Pursue, for you shall surely overtake *them* and without fail recover *all*.”

[9]So David went, he and the six hundred men who *were* with him, and came to the Brook Besor, where those stayed who were left behind. [10]But David pursued, he and four hundred men; for two hundred stayed *behind*, who were so weary that they could not cross the Brook Besor.

[11]Then they found an Egyptian in the field, and brought him to David; and they gave him bread and he ate, and they let him drink water. [12]And they gave him a piece of a cake of figs and two clusters of raisins. So when he had eaten, his strength came back to him; for he had eaten no bread nor drunk water for three days and three nights. [13]Then David said to him, “To whom do you *belong,* and where *are* you from?”

And he said, “I *am* a young man from Egypt, servant of an Amalekite; and my master left me behind, because three days ago I fell sick. [14]We made an invasion of the southern *area* of the Cherethites, in the *territory* which *belongs* to Judah, and of the southern *area* of Caleb; and we burned Ziklag with fire.”

[15]And David said to him, “Can you take me down to this troop?”

So he said, “Swear to me by God that you

29:5 [a]Compare 1 Samuel 18:7 **29:10** [a]Following Masoretic Text, Targum, and Vulgate; Septuagint adds *and go to the place which I have selected for you there; and set no bothersome word in your heart, for you are good before me. And rise on your way.*

will neither kill me nor deliver me into the hands of my master, and I will take you down to this troop."

¹⁶And when he had brought him down, there they were, spread out over all the land, eating and drinking and dancing, because of all the great spoil which they had taken from the land of the Philistines and from the land of Judah. ¹⁷Then David attacked them from twilight until the evening of the next day. Not a man of them escaped, except four hundred young men who rode on camels and fled. ¹⁸So David recovered all that the Amalekites had carried away, and David rescued his two wives. ¹⁹And nothing of theirs was lacking, either small or great, sons or daughters, spoil or anything which they had taken from them; David recovered all. ²⁰Then David took all the flocks and herds they had driven before those *other* livestock, and said, "This *is* David's spoil."

²¹Now David came to the two hundred men who had been so weary that they could not follow David, whom they also had made to stay at the Brook Besor. So they went out

INTIMATE MOMENTS

Get up a few minutes earlier than usual, brush your teeth, then get back in bed and wake up your husband with a kiss.

to meet David and to meet the people who *were* with him. And when David came near the people, he greeted them. ²²Then all the wicked and worthless menª of those who went with David answered and said, "Because they did not go with us, we will not give them *any* of the spoil that we have recovered, except for every man's wife and children, that they may lead *them* away and depart."

²³But David said, "My brethren, you shall not do so with what the LORD has given us, who has preserved us and delivered into our hand the troop that came against us. ²⁴For who will heed you in this matter? But as his part *is* who goes down to the battle, so *shall* his part *be* who stays by the supplies; they shall share alike." ²⁵So it was, from that day forward; he made it a statute and an ordinance for Israel to this day.

²⁶Now when David came to Ziklag, he sent *some* of the spoil to the elders of Judah, to his friends, saying, "Here is a present for you from the spoil of the enemies of the LORD"— ²⁷to *those* who *were* in Bethel, *those* who *were* in Ramoth of the South, *those* who *were* in Jattir, ²⁸*those* who *were* in Aroer, *those* who *were* in Siphmoth, *those* who *were* in Eshtemoa, ²⁹*those* who *were* in Rachal, *those* who *were* in the cities of the Jerahmeelites, *those* who *were* in the cities of the Kenites, ³⁰*those* who *were* in Hormah, *those* who *were* in Chorashan,ª *those* who *were* in Athach, ³¹*those* who *were* in Hebron, and to all the places where David himself and his men were accustomed to rove.

The Tragic End of Saul and His Sons

31 Now the Philistines fought against Israel; and the men of Israel fled from before the Philistines, and fell slain on Mount Gilboa. ²Then the Philistines followed hard after Saul and his sons. And the Philistines killed Jonathan, Abinadab, and Malchishua, Saul's sons. ³The battle became fierce against Saul. The archers hit him, and he was severely wounded by the archers.

⁴Then Saul said to his armorbearer, "Draw your sword, and thrust me through with it, lest these uncircumcised men come and thrust me through and abuse me."

But his armorbearer would not, for he was greatly afraid. Therefore Saul took a sword and fell on it. ⁵And when his armorbearer saw that Saul was dead, he also fell on his sword, and died with him. ⁶So Saul, his three sons, his armorbearer, and all his men died together that same day.

⁷And when the men of Israel who *were* on the other side of the valley, and *those* who *were* on the other side of the Jordan, saw that the men of Israel had fled and that Saul and his sons were dead, they forsook the cities and fled; and the Philistines came and dwelt in them. ⁸So it happened

30:22 ªLiterally *men of Belial* 30:30 ªOr *Borashan*

the next day, when the Philistines came to strip the slain, that they found Saul and his three sons fallen on Mount Gilboa. [9]And they cut off his head and stripped off his armor, and sent *word* throughout the land of the Philistines, to proclaim *it in* the temple of their idols and among the people. [10]Then they put his armor in the temple of the Ashtoreths, and they fastened his body to the wall of Beth Shan.[a]

[11]Now when the inhabitants of Jabesh Gilead heard what the Philistines had done to Saul, [12]all the valiant men arose and traveled all night, and took the body of Saul and the bodies of his sons from the wall of Beth Shan; and they came to Jabesh and burned them there. [13]Then they took their bones and buried *them* under the tamarisk tree at Jabesh, and fasted seven days.

31:10 [a]Spelled *Beth Shean* in Joshua 17:11 and elsewhere

2 SAMUEL

THE BOOKS OF 1 AND 2 SAMUEL originally comprised a single book. Together they record the history of Israel from about 1100 BC until David's death in 971 BC. Second Samuel begins with the events that lead up to David's inauguration as Israel's new king.

While the nation of Israel prospered under David's reign, David's personal life suffered a few serious bumps along the way. Second Samuel unflinchingly records David's sins of adultery with Bathsheba and his machinations behind the scenes to orchestrate the murder of her husband. You also will read the tragic account of David's daughter Tamar being raped by her half-brother Amnon, followed by the murder of Amnon by David's son Absalom. Absalom ultimately rebels against his father, seeking to take his place on the throne. When his revolt fails, Absalom dies at the hand of Joab, David's military commander.

These honest accounts provide us with a stark reminder that someone can be a person after God's own heart—as David was (1 Sam. 13:14)—and still be drawn into temptation and terrible sin. Even a godly parent can raise children who make devastating personal choices. David's life reminds us that each of us must remain constantly on the alert against the sins that would so easily entangle us (Heb. 12:2). What happened to his family warns us against neglecting the discipline that all children need, as David refused to discipline his sons (see 1 Kings 1:6). We must diligently pray for our children and teach them to honor God with *all* of their lives.

Although David brought trauma upon his own family, his reign as king provided a time of great peace and prosperity for Israel. In later years, the Jewish people would look back upon the reign of David and wish for God to send another king like him, one who would sit on David's throne. As you read about David's life, pay particular attention to the ways in which he provides a picture of Jesus, the man the Gospels often call "the Son of David"—and therefore the Great King of Israel.

The Report of Saul's Death

1 Now it came to pass after the death of Saul, when David had returned from the slaughter of the Amalekites, and David had stayed two days in Ziklag, ²on the third day, behold, it happened that a man came from Saul's camp with his clothes torn and dust on his head. So it was, when he came to David, that he fell to the ground and prostrated himself.

³And David said to him, "Where have you come from?"

So he said to him, "I have escaped from the camp of Israel."

⁴Then David said to him, "How did the matter go? Please tell me."

And he answered, "The people have fled from the battle, many of the people are fallen and dead, and Saul and Jonathan his son are dead also."

⁵So David said to the young man who told him, "How do you know that Saul and Jonathan his son are dead?"

⁶Then the young man who told him said, "As I happened by chance *to be* on Mount Gilboa, there was Saul, leaning on his spear; and indeed the chariots and horsemen followed hard after him. ⁷Now when he looked behind him, he saw me and called to me. And I answered, 'Here I am.' ⁸And he said to me, 'Who *are* you?' So I answered him, 'I *am* an Amalekite.' ⁹He said to me again, 'Please stand over me and kill me, for anguish has come upon me, but my life still *remains* in me.' ¹⁰So I stood over him and killed him, because I was sure that he could not live after he had fallen. And I took the crown that *was* on his head and the bracelet that *was* on his arm, and have brought them here to my lord."

¹¹Therefore David took hold of his own clothes and tore them, and *so did* all the men who *were* with him. ¹²And they mourned and wept and fasted until evening for Saul and for Jonathan his son, for the people of the LORD and for the house of Israel, because they had fallen by the sword.

¹³Then David said to the young man who told him, "Where *are* you from?"

And he answered, "I *am* the son of an alien, an Amalekite."

¹⁴So David said to him, "How was it you were not afraid to put forth your hand to destroy the LORD's anointed?" ¹⁵Then David called one of the young men and said, "Go near, *and* execute him!" And he struck him so that he died. ¹⁶So David said to him, "Your blood *is* on your own head, for your own mouth has testified against you, saying, 'I have killed the LORD's anointed.'"

The Song of the Bow

¹⁷Then David lamented with this lamentation over Saul and over Jonathan his son, ¹⁸and he told *them* to teach the children of Judah *the Song of* the Bow; indeed *it is* written in the Book of Jasher:

INTIMATE MOMENTS

Make your husband a book of coupons that are good for things he especially likes: his favorite dessert, a special meal, and you.

19   "The beauty of Israel is slain on your
      high places!
  How the mighty have fallen!
20   Tell *it* not in Gath,
  Proclaim *it* not in the streets of
      Ashkelon—
  Lest the daughters of the Philistines
      rejoice,
  Lest the daughters of the
      uncircumcised triumph.

21   "O mountains of Gilboa,
  Let there be no dew nor rain upon you,
  Nor fields of offerings.
  For the shield of the mighty is cast
      away there!
  The shield of Saul, not anointed with
      oil.
22   From the blood of the slain,
  From the fat of the mighty,
  The bow of Jonathan did not turn
      back,
  And the sword of Saul did not
      return empty.

23   "Saul and Jonathan *were* beloved and
      pleasant in their lives,

And in their death they were not
divided;
They were swifter than eagles,
They were stronger than lions.

24 "O daughters of Israel, weep over Saul,
Who clothed you in scarlet, with
luxury;
Who put ornaments of gold on your
apparel.

25 "How the mighty have fallen in the
midst of the battle!
Jonathan *was* slain in your high
places.

26 I am distressed for you, my brother
Jonathan;
You have been very pleasant to me;
Your love to me was wonderful,
Surpassing the love of women.

27 "How the mighty have fallen,
And the weapons of war perished!"

David Anointed King of Judah

2 It happened after this that David
inquired of the LORD, saying, "Shall I
go up to any of the cities of Judah?"

And the LORD said to him, "Go up."

David said, "Where shall I go up?"

And He said, "To Hebron."

2So David went up there, and his two
wives also, Ahinoam the Jezreelitess, and
Abigail the widow of Nabal the Carmelite.
3And David brought up the men who *were*
with him, every man with his household.
So they dwelt in the cities of Hebron.

4Then the men of Judah came, and there
they anointed David king over the house of
Judah. And they told David, saying, "The
men of Jabesh Gilead *were the ones* who
buried Saul." 5So David sent messengers to
the men of Jabesh Gilead, and said to them,
"You *are* blessed of the LORD, for you have
shown this kindness to your lord, to Saul,
and have buried him. 6And now may the
LORD show kindness and truth to you. I
also will repay you this kindness, because
you have done this thing. 7Now therefore,
let your hands be strengthened, and be
valiant; for your master Saul is dead, and
also the house of Judah has anointed me
king over them."

Ishbosheth Made King of Israel

8But Abner the son of Ner, commander
of Saul's army, took Ishbosheth[a] the son of
Saul and brought him over to Mahanaim;
9and he made him king over Gilead, over the
Ashurites, over Jezreel, over Ephraim, over
Benjamin, and over all Israel. 10Ishbosheth,
Saul's son, *was* forty years old when he
began to reign over Israel, and he reigned
two years. Only the house of Judah followed
David. 11And the time that David was king
in Hebron over the house of Judah was
seven years and six months.

Israel and Judah at War

12Now Abner the son of Ner, and the servants of Ishbosheth the son of Saul, went
out from Mahanaim to Gibeon. 13And Joab
the son of Zeruiah, and the servants of
David, went out and met them by the pool
of Gibeon. So they sat down, one on one
side of the pool and the other on the other
side of the pool. 14Then Abner said to Joab,
"Let the young men now arise and compete
before us."

And Joab said, "Let them arise."

15So they arose and went over by number,
twelve from Benjamin, *followers* of
Ishbosheth the son of Saul, and twelve from
the servants of David. 16And each one
grasped his opponent by the head and
thrust his sword in his opponent's side; so
they fell down together. Therefore that place
was called the Field of Sharp Swords,[a]
which *is* in Gibeon. 17So there was a very
fierce battle that day, and Abner and the
men of Israel were beaten before the servants of David.

18Now the three sons of Zeruiah were
there: Joab and Abishai and Asahel. And
Asahel *was as* fleet of foot as a wild gazelle.
19So Asahel pursued Abner, and in going he
did not turn to the right hand or to the left
from following Abner.

20Then Abner looked behind him and
said, "*Are* you Asahel?"

He answered, "I *am.*"

21And Abner said to him, "Turn aside to
your right hand or to your left, and lay hold
on one of the young men and take his

2:8 [a]Called *Esh-Baal* in 1 Chronicles 8:33 and 9:39
2:16 [a]Hebrew *Helkath Hazzurim*

armor for yourself." But Asahel would not turn aside from following him. ²²So Abner said again to Asahel, "Turn aside from following me. Why should I strike you to the ground? How then could I face your brother Joab?" ²³However, he refused to turn aside. Therefore Abner struck him in the stomach with the blunt end of the spear, so that the spear came out of his back; and he fell down there and died on the spot. So it was *that* as many as came to the place where Asahel fell down and died, stood still.

²⁴Joab and Abishai also pursued Abner. And the sun was going down when they came to the hill of Ammah, which *is* before Giah by the road to the Wilderness of Gibeon. ²⁵Now the children of Benjamin gathered together behind Abner and became a unit, and took their stand on top of a hill. ²⁶Then Abner called to Joab and said, "Shall the sword devour forever? Do you not know that it will be bitter in the latter end? How long will it be then until you tell the people to return from pursuing their brethren?"

²⁷And Joab said, "*As* God lives, unless you had spoken, surely then by morning all the people would have given up pursuing their brethren." ²⁸So Joab blew a trumpet; and all the people stood still and did not pursue Israel anymore, nor did they fight anymore. ²⁹Then Abner and his men went on all that night through the plain, crossed over the Jordan, and went through all Bithron; and they came to Mahanaim.

³⁰So Joab returned from pursuing Abner. And when he had gathered all the people together, there were missing of David's servants nineteen men and Asahel. ³¹But the servants of David had struck down, of Benjamin and Abner's men, three hundred and sixty men who died. ³²Then they took up Asahel and buried him in his father's tomb, which *was in* Bethlehem. And Joab and his men went all night, and they came to Hebron at daybreak.

3 Now there was a long war between the house of Saul and the house of David. But David grew stronger and stronger, and the house of Saul grew weaker and weaker.

Sons of David

²Sons were born to David in Hebron: His firstborn was Amnon by Ahinoam the Jezreelitess; ³his second, Chileab, by Abigail the widow of Nabal the Carmelite; the third, Absalom the son of Maacah, the daughter of Talmai, king of Geshur; ⁴the fourth, Adonijah the son of Haggith; the fifth, Shephatiah the son of Abital; ⁵and the sixth, Ithream, by David's wife Eglah. These were born to David in Hebron.

Abner Joins Forces with David

⁶Now it was so, while there was war between the house of Saul and the house of David, that Abner was strengthening *his hold* on the house of Saul.

⁷And Saul had a concubine, whose name *was* Rizpah, the daughter of Aiah. So *Ishbosheth* said to Abner, "Why have you gone in to my father's concubine?"

⁸Then Abner became very angry at the words of Ishbosheth, and said, "*Am* I a dog's head that belongs to Judah? Today I show loyalty to the house of Saul your father, to his brothers, and to his friends, and have not delivered you into the hand of David; and you charge me today with a fault concerning this woman? ⁹May God do so to Abner, and more also, if I do not do for David as the LORD has sworn to him— ¹⁰to transfer the kingdom from the house of Saul, and set up the throne of David over Israel and over Judah, from Dan to Beersheba." ¹¹And he could not answer Abner another word, because he feared him.

¹²Then Abner sent messengers on his behalf to David, saying, "Whose *is* the land?" saying *also,* "Make your covenant with me, and indeed my hand *shall be* with you to bring all Israel to you."

¹³And *David* said, "Good, I will make a covenant with you. But one thing I require of you: you shall not see my face unless you first bring Michal, Saul's daughter, when you come to see my face." ¹⁴So David sent messengers to Ishbosheth, Saul's son, saying, "Give *me* my wife Michal, whom I betrothed to myself for a hundred foreskins of the Philistines." ¹⁵And Ishbosheth sent and took her from *her* husband, from Paltielᵃ the son of Laish. ¹⁶Then her husband went

BIBLICAL INSIGHTS • 3:13
A Three-Legged Race

WHEN AN ANGRY GENERAL, Abner, abandoned the family of Saul to support David as the new king of Israel, he told David, "Make your covenant with me, and indeed my hand shall be with you to bring all Israel to you" (3:12). David readily agreed, because he knew he could use all the help he could get.

So can you, especially in your marriage. To be successful in marriage, ultimately both of you must agree to head in the same direction. The Roman philosopher Seneca said, "You must know for which harbor you are headed if you are to catch the right wind to take you there."

Among some of my most valued childhood memories are the family picnics we held every summer. These were no small get-togethers, but gatherings of all my aunts and uncles along with what seemed like dozens of cousins. I played all kinds of games with my cousins, including the three-legged race, which was everyone's favorite. Locked arm in arm and stepping in unison, contestants made rapid progress toward the finish line. They might stumble and fall, but they always got there faster and more efficiently than if they had been paired facing opposite ways (which we also did sometimes, just for fun).

Marriage is a lot like a three-legged race. You can run it facing in the same direction, locking arms and trying to stay in step with your partner, or you can run the race facing in totally different directions and constantly stumble and fall. The main question is: Do you want to win? If so, determine what the real finish line is, lock your arms together, match strides with each other, and run the race as one.

were seeking for David *to be* king over you. [18]Now then, do *it!* For the LORD has spoken of David, saying, 'By the hand of My servant David, I[a] will save My people Israel from the hand of the Philistines and the hand of all their enemies.' " [19]And Abner also spoke in the hearing of Benjamin. Then Abner also went to speak in the hearing of David in Hebron all that seemed good to Israel and the whole house of Benjamin.

[20]So Abner and twenty men with him came to David at Hebron. And David made a feast for Abner and the men who *were* with him. [21]Then Abner said to David, "I will arise and go, and gather all Israel to my lord the king, that they may make a covenant with you, and that you may reign over all that your heart desires." So David sent Abner away, and he went in peace.

Joab Murders Abner

[22]At that moment the servants of David and Joab came from a raid and brought much spoil with them. But Abner *was* not with David in Hebron, for he had sent him away, and he had gone in peace. [23]When Joab and all the troops that *were* with him had come, they told Joab, saying, "Abner the son of Ner came to the king, and he sent him away, and he has gone in peace." [24]Then Joab came to the king and said, "What have you done? Look, Abner came to you; why *is* it *that* you sent him away, and he has already gone? [25]Surely you realize that Abner the son of Ner came to deceive you, to know your going out and your coming in, and to know all that you are doing."

[26]And when Joab had gone from David's presence, he sent messengers after Abner, who brought him back from the well of Sirah. But David did not know *it.* [27]Now when Abner had returned to Hebron, Joab took him aside in the gate to speak with him privately, and there stabbed him in the stomach, so that he died for the blood of Asahel his brother.

[28]Afterward, when David heard *it,* he said, "My kingdom and I *are* guiltless before the LORD forever of the blood of Abner the son of Ner. [29]Let it rest on the head of Joab

along with her to Bahurim, weeping behind her. So Abner said to him, "Go, return!" And he returned.

[17]Now Abner had communicated with the elders of Israel, saying, "In time past you

---

3:18 [a]Following many Hebrew manuscripts, Septuagint, Syriac, and Targum; Masoretic Text reads *he.*

and on all his father's house; and let there never fail to be in the house of Joab one who has a discharge or is a leper, who leans on a staff or falls by the sword, or who lacks bread." [30]So Joab and Abishai his brother killed Abner, because he had killed their brother Asahel at Gibeon in the battle.

David's Mourning for Abner

[31]Then David said to Joab and to all the people who were with him, "Tear your clothes, gird yourselves with sackcloth, and mourn for Abner." And King David followed the coffin. [32]So they buried Abner in Hebron; and the king lifted up his voice and wept at the grave of Abner, and all the people wept. [33]And the king sang *a lament* over Abner and said:

"Should Abner die as a fool dies?
[34] Your hands were not bound
Nor your feet put into fetters;
As a man falls before wicked men,
so you fell."

Then all the people wept over him again.

[35]And when all the people came to persuade David to eat food while it was still day, David took an oath, saying, "God do so to me, and more also, if I taste bread or anything else till the sun goes down!" [36]Now all the people took note *of it,* and it pleased them, since whatever the king did pleased all the people. [37]For all the people and all Israel understood that day that it had not been the king's *intent* to kill Abner the son of Ner. [38]Then the king said to his servants, "Do you not know that a prince and a great man has fallen this day in Israel? [39]And I *am* weak today, though anointed king; and these men, the sons of Zeruiah, *are* too harsh for me. The LORD shall repay the evildoer according to his wickedness."

Ishbosheth Is Murdered

4 When Saul's son[a] heard that Abner had died in Hebron, he lost heart, and all Israel was troubled. [2]Now Saul's son *had* two men *who were* captains of troops. The name of one *was* Baanah and the name of the other Rechab, the sons of Rimmon the Beerothite, of the children of Benjamin. (For Beeroth also was *part* of Benjamin, [3]because the Beerothites fled to Gittaim and have been sojourners there until this day.)

[4]Jonathan, Saul's son, had a son *who was* lame in *his* feet. He was five years old when the news about Saul and Jonathan came from Jezreel; and his nurse took him up and fled. And it happened, as she made haste to flee, that he fell and became lame. His name *was* Mephibosheth.[a]

[5]Then the sons of Rimmon the Beerothite, Rechab and Baanah, set out and came at about the heat of the day to the house of Ishbosheth, who was lying on his bed at noon. [6]And they came there, all the way into the house, *as though* to get wheat, and they stabbed him in the stomach. Then Rechab and Baanah his brother escaped. [7]For when they came into the house, he was lying on his bed in his bedroom; then they struck him and killed him, beheaded him and took his head, and were all night escaping through the plain. [8]And they brought the head of Ishbosheth to David at Hebron, and said to the king, "Here is the head of Ishbosheth, the son of Saul your enemy, who sought your life; and the LORD has avenged my lord the king this day of Saul and his descendants."

[9]But David answered Rechab and Baanah his brother, the sons of Rimmon the Beerothite, and said to them, "*As* the LORD lives, who has redeemed my life from all adversity, [10]when someone told me, saying, 'Look, Saul is dead,' thinking to have brought good news, I arrested him and had him executed in Ziklag—the one who *thought* I would give him a reward for *his* news. [11]How much more, when wicked men have killed a righteous person in his own house on his bed? Therefore, shall I not now require his blood at your hand and remove you from the earth?" [12]So David commanded his young men, and they executed them, cut off their hands and feet, and hanged *them* by the pool in Hebron. But they took the head of Ishbosheth and buried *it* in the tomb of Abner in Hebron.

David Reigns over All Israel

5 Then all the tribes of Israel came to David at Hebron and spoke, saying, "Indeed we *are* your bone and your flesh.

4:1 [a]That is, Ishbosheth 4:4 [a]Called *Merib-Baal* in 1 Chronicles 8:34 and 9:40

²Also, in time past, when Saul was king over us, you were the one who led Israel out and brought them in; and the LORD said to you, 'You shall shepherd My people Israel, and be ruler over Israel.' " ³Therefore all the elders of Israel came to the king at Hebron, and King David made a covenant with them at Hebron before the LORD. And they anointed David king over Israel. ⁴David *was* thirty years old when he began to reign, *and* he reigned forty years. ⁵In Hebron he reigned over Judah seven years and six months, and in Jerusalem he reigned thirty-three years over all Israel and Judah.

The Conquest of Jerusalem

⁶And the king and his men went to Jerusalem against the Jebusites, the inhabitants of the land, who spoke to David, saying, "You shall not come in here; but the blind and the lame will repel you," thinking, "David cannot come in here." ⁷Nevertheless David took the stronghold of Zion (that *is,* the City of David).

⁸Now David said on that day, "Whoever climbs up by way of the water shaft and defeats the Jebusites (the lame and the blind, *who are* hated by David's soul), *he shall be chief and captain.*"ᵃ Therefore they say, "The blind and the lame shall not come into the house."

⁹Then David dwelt in the stronghold,

5:8 ᵃCompare 1 Chronicles 11:6

PARENTING MATTERS	**Q: How can we help shape our children's dress and appearance standards?**

The process of shaping convictions in this area needs to begin early. Talk with your preteen child about the issues he'll face as he moves into the teenage years. Help him begin to think about how he will draw some boundaries that will protect him as a teenager.

Here's a checklist of what we talked about with our sons and daughters.

Our sons:
- Modesty
- Masculinity
- Saggy, sloppy, or grunge clothing
- T-shirts with inappropriate messages
- Clothing with holes in it, especially in inappropriate places

Our daughters:
- Modesty
- Femininity
- Swimsuits
- Body piercing and tattoos
- Halter tops and other skimpy clothing
- Length of dresses, skirts, and shorts.

In each of these areas, we pressed our children to tell us their convictions. If necessary, we would gently attempt to steer them in a new direction—and on some of these topics, it took months and even years of hammering away.

Dads can help their daughters by teaching them how a young man thinks when he sees a young lady who is dressed immodestly, and moms can talk to their sons about why girls appreciate boys who know how to dress appropriately and attractively.

One word of advice: In each of these areas, determine where YOUR non-negotiables are for your teens while they are living at home. Caution: Not every issue listed above is a hill to die upon as a parent. Pick your hills carefully.

and called it the City of David. And David built all around from the Millo[a] and inward. [10]So David went on and became great, and the LORD God of hosts *was* with him.

[11]Then Hiram king of Tyre sent messengers to David, and cedar trees, and carpenters and masons. And they built David a house. [12]So David knew that the LORD had established him as king over Israel, and that He had exalted His kingdom for the sake of His people Israel.

[13]And David took more concubines and wives from Jerusalem, after he had come from Hebron. Also more sons and daughters were born to David. [14]Now these *are* the names of those who were born to him in Jerusalem: Shammua,[a] Shobab, Nathan, Solomon, [15]Ibhar, Elishua,[a] Nepheg, Japhia, [16]Elishama, Eliada, and Eliphelet.

The Philistines Defeated

[17]Now when the Philistines heard that they had anointed David king over Israel, all the Philistines went up to search for David. And David heard *of it* and went down to the stronghold. [18]The Philistines also went and deployed themselves in the Valley of Rephaim. [19]So David inquired of the LORD, saying, "Shall I go up against the Philistines? Will You deliver them into my hand?"

And the LORD said to David, "Go up, for I will doubtless deliver the Philistines into your hand."

[20]So David went to Baal Perazim, and David defeated them there; and he said, "The LORD has broken through my enemies before me, like a breakthrough of water." Therefore he called the name of that place Baal Perazim.[a] [21]And they left their images there, and David and his men carried them away.

[22]Then the Philistines went up once again and deployed themselves in the Valley of Rephaim. [23]Therefore David inquired of the LORD, and He said, "You shall not go up; circle around behind them, and come upon them in front of the mulberry trees. [24]And it shall be, when you hear the sound of marching in the tops of the mulberry trees, then you shall advance quickly. For then the LORD will go out before you to strike the camp of the Philistines." [25]And David did so, as the LORD commanded him; and he drove back the Philistines from Geba[a] as far as Gezer.

The Ark Brought to Jerusalem

6 Again David gathered all *the* choice *men* of Israel, thirty thousand. [2]And David arose and went with all the people who *were* with him from Baale Judah to bring up from there the ark of God, whose name is called by the Name,[a] the LORD of Hosts, who dwells *between* the cherubim. [3]So they set the ark of God on a new cart, and brought it out of the house of Abinadab, which *was* on the hill; and Uzzah and Ahio, the sons of Abinadab, drove the new cart.[a] [4]And they brought it out of the house of Abinadab, which *was* on the hill, accompanying the ark of God; and Ahio went before the ark. [5]Then David and all the house of Israel played *music* before the LORD on all kinds of *instruments of* fir wood, on harps, on stringed instruments, on tambourines, on sistrums, and on cymbals.

[6]And when they came to Nachon's threshing floor, Uzzah put out *his hand* to the ark of God and took hold of it, for the oxen stumbled. [7]Then the anger of the LORD was aroused against Uzzah, and God struck him there for *his* error; and he died there by the ark of God. [8]And David became angry because of the LORD's outbreak against Uzzah; and he called the name of the place Perez Uzzah[a] to this day.

[9]David was afraid of the LORD that day; and he said, "How can the ark of the LORD come to me?" [10]So David would not move the ark of the LORD with him into the City of David; but David took it aside into the house of Obed-Edom the Gittite. [11]The ark of the LORD remained in the house of Obed-Edom the Gittite three months. And the LORD blessed Obed-Edom and all his household.

[12]Now it was told King David, saying, "The LORD has blessed the house of Obed-Edom and all that *belongs* to him, because of

---

5:9 [a]Literally *The Landfill* **5:14** [a]Spelled *Shimea* in 1 Chronicles 3:5 **5:15** [a]Spelled *Elishama* in 1 Chronicles 3:6 **5:20** [a]Literally *Master of Breakthroughs* **5:25** [a]Following Masoretic Text, Targum, and Vulgate; Septuagint reads *Gibeon.* **6:2** [a]Septuagint, Targum, and Vulgate omit *by the Name;* many Hebrew manuscripts and Syriac read *there.* **6:3** [a]Septuagint adds *with the ark.* **6:8** [a]Literally *Outburst Against Uzzah*

DEVOTIONS FOR COUPLES • 6:23
Give Up, Give In, Give All

Why did "Michal the daughter of Saul [have] no children to the day of her death" (6:23)? She remained childless because her selfish agenda prompted her to publicly scorn her husband David, who reacted by shutting her out. In essence, their marriage died.

Our sin and selfishness focuses us on our own agendas like a sharpshooter locking a target in the crosshairs of his rifle. Left to ourselves, we will go for what we want every time. And when two spouses focus only on what they want, all hope for peace vanishes.

Jesus shows us that instead of insisting on being first, we must be willing to be last. Instead of wanting to be served, we must serve. Instead of trying to save our lives, we must lose them. We must love our spouses as much as we love ourselves. In short, if we want to defeat selfishness, we must give up, give in, and give all.

To experience oneness, you must give up your will for the will of another. But to do this, you must first give up your will to Christ—only then will you find it possible to give up your will for that of your mate.

---

the ark of God." So David went and brought up the ark of God from the house of Obed-Edom to the City of David with gladness. 13And so it was, when those bearing the ark of the LORD had gone six paces, that he sacrificed oxen and fatted sheep. 14Then David danced before the LORD with all *his* might; and David *was* wearing a linen ephod. 15So David and all the house of Israel brought up the ark of the LORD with shouting and with the sound of the trumpet.

16Now as the ark of the LORD came into the City of David, Michal, Saul's daughter, looked through a window and saw King David leaping and whirling before the LORD; and she despised him in her heart. 17So they brought the ark of the LORD, and set it in its place in the midst of the tabernacle that David had erected for it. Then David offered burnt offerings and peace offerings before the LORD. 18And when David had finished offering burnt offerings and peace offerings, he blessed the people in the name of the LORD of hosts. 19Then he distributed among all the people, among the whole multitude of Israel, both the women and the men, to everyone a loaf of bread, a piece *of meat,* and a cake of raisins. So all the people departed, everyone to his house.

20Then David returned to bless his household. And Michal the daughter of Saul came out to meet David, and said, "How glorious was the king of Israel today, uncovering himself today in the eyes of the maids of his servants, as one of the base fellows shamelessly uncovers himself!"

21So David said to Michal, "*It was* before the LORD, who chose me instead of your father and all his house, to appoint me ruler over the people of the LORD, over Israel. Therefore I will play *music* before the LORD. 22And I will be even more undignified than this, and will be humble in my own sight. But as for the maidservants of whom you have spoken, by them I will be held in honor."

23Therefore Michal the daughter of Saul had no children to the day of her death.

God's Covenant with David

7 Now it came to pass when the king was dwelling in his house, and the LORD had given him rest from all his enemies all around, 2that the king said to Nathan the prophet, "See now, I dwell in a house of cedar, but the ark of God dwells inside tent curtains."

3Then Nathan said to the king, "Go, do all that *is* in your heart, for the LORD *is* with you."

4But it happened that night that the word of the LORD came to Nathan, saying, 5"Go and tell My servant David, 'Thus says the LORD: "Would you build a house for Me to dwell in? 6For I have not dwelt in a house since the time that I brought the children of Israel up from Egypt, even to this day, but have moved about in a tent and in a tabernacle. ⁷Wherever I have moved about with all the children of Israel, have I ever spoken a word to anyone from the tribes of Israel, whom I commanded to shepherd My people Israel, saying, 'Why have you not built Me a house of cedar?' " ⁸Now therefore, thus shall you say to My servant David, 'Thus says the LORD of hosts: "I took you from the sheepfold, from following the sheep, to be ruler over My people, over Israel. ⁹And I have been with you wherever you have gone, and have cut off all your enemies from before you, and have made you a great name, like the name of the great men who *are* on the earth. ¹⁰Moreover I will appoint a place for My people Israel, and will plant them, that they may dwell in a place of their own and move no more; nor shall the sons of wickedness oppress them anymore, as previously, ¹¹since the time that I commanded judges *to be* over My people Israel, and have caused you to rest from all your enemies. Also the LORD tells you that He will make you a house.ᵃ

¹²"When your days are fulfilled and you rest with your fathers, I will set up your seed after you, who will come from your body, and I will establish his kingdom. ¹³He shall build a house for My name, and I will establish the throne of his kingdom forever. ¹⁴I will be his Father, and he shall be My son. If he commits iniquity, I will chasten him with the rod of men and with the blows of the sons of men. ¹⁵But My mercy shall not depart from him, as I took *it* from Saul, whom I removed from before you. ¹⁶And your house and your kingdom shall be established forever before you.ᵃ Your throne shall be established forever." ' "

¹⁷According to all these words and according to all this vision, so Nathan spoke to David.

David's Thanksgiving to God

¹⁸Then King David went in and sat before the LORD; and he said: "Who *am* I, O Lord GOD? And what is my house, that You have brought me this far? ¹⁹And yet this was a small thing in Your sight, O

BIBLICAL INSIGHTS • 7:14

A Godly Legacy

IF YOU'RE A MOTHER or a father, one of your top concerns must be to focus on the kind of legacy you are leaving behind. Are you diligently working to raise your children to love and fear God and walk with Him?

Speaking through the prophet Nathan, God gave David an amazing word picture of his legacy. The Lord said of David's son, Solomon, "I will be his Father, and he shall be My son … your house and your kingdom shall be established forever before you. Your throne shall be established forever" (7:14, 16).

Our culture stands in desperate need of reformation, and that can happen only when godly individuals begin doing what they must do in order to leave behind a godly legacy. This has to start with each of us determining what type of legacy we want to pass on to our children.

How will your children remember you? Will they remember you as a man or woman preoccupied with the things of this world? Or will they recall their parents as committed children of God who modeled a life-changing faith in Jesus Christ?

Legacies are comprised of the choices we make. Someone has said, "The doors of opportunity swing on the little hinges of obedience." The opportunity you have to impact your children is found as you faithfully obey Jesus Christ:

- Telling the truth
- Loving those who don't love you
- Being faithful in the little things
- Submitting to Him in the midst of challenging days
- Sending your treasure on ahead—investing in His work
- Ultimately being His bond slave, serving the Master and having no rights

If you could look ahead in time twenty, thirty, even forty years, *how will your children remember you?*

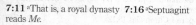

7:11 ᵃThat is, a royal dynasty **7:16** ᵃSeptuagint reads *Me*.

Lord GOD; and You have also spoken of Your servant's house for a great while to come. *Is* this the manner of man, O Lord GOD? [20]Now what more can David say to You? For You, Lord GOD, know Your servant. [21]For Your word's sake, and according to Your own heart, You have done all these great things, to make Your servant know *them.* [22]Therefore You are great, O Lord GOD.[a] For *there is* none like You, nor *is there any* God besides You, according to all that we have heard with our ears. [23]And who *is* like Your people, like Israel, the one nation on the earth whom God went to redeem for Himself as a people, to make for Himself a name—and to do for Yourself great and awesome deeds for Your land—before Your people whom You redeemed for Yourself from Egypt, the nations, and their gods? [24]For You have made Your people Israel Your very own people forever; and You, LORD, have become their God.

[25]"Now, O LORD God, the word which You have spoken concerning Your servant and concerning his house, establish *it* forever and do as You have said. [26]So let Your name be magnified forever, saying, 'The LORD of hosts *is* the God over Israel.' And let the house of Your servant David be established before You. [27]For You, O LORD of hosts, God of Israel, have revealed *this* to Your servant, saying, 'I will build you a house.' Therefore Your servant has found it in his heart to pray this prayer to You.

[28]"And now, O Lord GOD, You are God, and Your words are true, and You have promised this goodness to Your servant. [29]Now therefore, let it please You to bless the house of Your servant, that it may continue before You forever; for You, O Lord GOD, have spoken *it,* and with Your blessing let the house of Your servant be blessed forever."

David's Further Conquests

8 After this it came to pass that David attacked the Philistines and subdued them. And David took Metheg Ammah from the hand of the Philistines.

[2]Then he defeated Moab. Forcing them down to the ground, he measured them off with a line. With two lines he measured off those to be put to death, and with one full line those to be kept alive. So the Moabites became David's servants, *and* brought tribute.

[3]David also defeated Hadadezer the son of Rehob, king of Zobah, as he went to recover his territory at the River Euphrates. [4]David took from him one thousand *chariots,* seven hundred[a] horsemen, and twenty thousand foot soldiers. Also David hamstrung all the chariot *horses,* except that he spared *enough* of them for one hundred chariots.

[5]When the Syrians of Damascus came to help Hadadezer king of Zobah, David killed twenty-two thousand of the Syrians. [6]Then David put garrisons in Syria of Damascus; and the Syrians became David's servants, *and* brought tribute. So the LORD preserved David wherever he went. [7]And David took the shields of gold that had belonged to the servants of Hadadezer, and brought them to Jerusalem. [8]Also from Betah[a] and from Berothai, cities of Hadadezer, King David took a large amount of bronze.

[9]When Toi[a] king of Hamath heard that David had defeated all the army of Hadadezer, [10]then Toi sent Joram[a] his son to King David, to greet him and bless him, because he had fought against Hadadezer and defeated him (for Hadadezer had been at war with Toi); and *Joram* brought with him articles of silver, articles of gold, and articles of bronze. [11]King David also dedicated these to the LORD, along with the silver and gold that he had dedicated from all the nations which he had subdued— [12]from Syria,[a] from Moab, from the people of Ammon, from the Philistines, from Amalek, and from the spoil of Hadadezer the son of Rehob, king of Zobah.

[13]And David made *himself* a name when he returned from killing eighteen thousand Syrians[a] in the Valley of Salt. [14]He also put garrisons in Edom; throughout all Edom he put garrisons, and all the Edomites became

7:22 [a]Targum and Syriac read *O LORD God.* **8:4** [a]Or *seven thousand* (compare 1 Chronicles 18:4) **8:8** [a]Spelled *Tibhath* in 1 Chronicles 18:8 **8:9** [a]Spelled *Tou* in 1 Chronicles 18:9 **8:10** [a]Spelled *Hadoram* in 1 Chronicles 18:10 **8:12** [a]Septuagint, Syriac, and some Hebrew manuscripts read *Edom.* **8:13** [a]Septuagint, Syriac, and some Hebrew manuscripts read *Edomites* (compare 1 Chronicles 18:12).

David's servants. And the LORD preserved David wherever he went.

David's Administration

[15]So David reigned over all Israel; and David administered judgment and justice to all his people. [16]Joab the son of Zeruiah *was* over the army; Jehoshaphat the son of Ahilud *was* recorder; [17]Zadok the son of Ahitub and Ahimelech the son of Abiathar *were* the priests; Seraiah[a] *was* the scribe; [18]Benaiah the son of Jehoiada *was over* both the Cherethites and the Pelethites; and David's sons were chief ministers.

David's Kindness to Mephibosheth

9 Now David said, "Is there still anyone who is left of the house of Saul, that I may show him kindness for Jonathan's sake?"

[2]And *there was* a servant of the house of Saul whose name *was* Ziba. So when they had called him to David, the king said to him, "*Are* you Ziba?"

He said, "At your service!"

[3]Then the king said, "*Is* there not still someone of the house of Saul, to whom I may show the kindness of God?"

And Ziba said to the king, "There is still a son of Jonathan *who is* lame in *his* feet."

[4]So the king said to him, "Where *is* he?"

And Ziba said to the king, "Indeed he *is* in the house of Machir the son of Ammiel, in Lo Debar."

[5]Then King David sent and brought him out of the house of Machir the son of Ammiel, from Lo Debar.

[6]Now when Mephibosheth the son of Jonathan, the son of Saul, had come to David, he fell on his face and prostrated himself. Then David said, "Mephibosheth?"

And he answered, "Here is your servant!"

[7]So David said to him, "Do not fear, for I will surely show you kindness for Jonathan your father's sake, and will restore to you all the land of Saul your grandfather; and you shall eat bread at my table continually."

[8]Then he bowed himself, and said, "What *is* your servant, that you should look upon such a dead dog as I?"

[9]And the king called to Ziba, Saul's servant, and said to him, "I have given to your master's son all that belonged to Saul and to all his house. [10]You therefore, and your sons and your servants, shall work the land for him, and you shall bring in *the harvest,* that your master's son may have food to eat. But Mephibosheth your master's son shall eat bread at my table always." Now Ziba had fifteen sons and twenty servants.

[11]Then Ziba said to the king, "According to all that my lord the king has commanded his servant, so will your servant do."

"As for Mephibosheth," *said the king,* "he shall eat at my table[a] like one of the king's sons." [12]Mephibosheth had a young son

---

ROMANCE FAQ

Q: *How can I best find out what my wife's real needs are?*

I have an assignment for you: Take your wife out on a date or a retreat, where you ask her the following questions:

- What can I do to help you feel more loved, honored, and cherished?
- What can I do to illustrate the fact that I respect you, your ideas, and your role as my wife?
- What can I do to assure you that I hear and understand your heart's desires?
- What can I do to ensure that you have confidence and joy in our future direction?
- What attribute or practice would you like to see me improve or develop?
- What attribute would you most like to develop in yourself?
- What would indicate to you my desire to be more like Christ?
- What mutual goal would you like to see us accomplish together?

I got these questions from a friend of mine, Tom Elliff, who poses them to his wife every year. He takes notes as his wife talks, and then writes out a clear statement of his intentions in response to each of these issues. Last, he signs a pledge. I can promise you—his wife feels loved and cared for!

8:17 [a]Spelled *Shavsha* in 1 Chronicles 18:16
9:11 [a]Septuagint reads *David's table.*

whose name *was* Micha. And all who dwelt in the house of Ziba *were* servants of Mephibosheth. ¹³So Mephibosheth dwelt in Jerusalem, for he ate continually at the king's table. And he was lame in both his feet.

The Ammonites and Syrians Defeated

10 It happened after this that the king of the people of Ammon died, and Hanun his son reigned in his place. ²Then David said, "I will show kindness to Hanun the son of Nahash, as his father showed kindness to me."

So David sent by the hand of his servants to comfort him concerning his father. And David's servants came into the land of the people of Ammon. ³And the princes of the people of Ammon said to Hanun their lord, "Do you think that David really honors your father because he has sent comforters to you? Has David not *rather* sent his servants to you to search the city, to spy it out, and to overthrow it?"

⁴Therefore Hanun took David's servants, shaved off half of their beards, cut off their garments in the middle, at their buttocks, and sent them away. ⁵When they told David, he sent to meet them, because the men were greatly ashamed. And the king said, "Wait at Jericho until your beards have grown, and *then* return."

⁶When the people of Ammon saw that they had made themselves repulsive to David, the people of Ammon sent and hired the Syrians of Beth Rehob and the Syrians of Zoba, twenty thousand foot soldiers; and from the king of Maacah one thousand men, and from Ish-Tob twelve thousand men. ⁷Now when David heard *of it,* he sent Joab and all the army of the mighty men. ⁸Then the people of Ammon came out and put themselves in battle array at the entrance of the gate. And the Syrians of Zoba, Beth Rehob, Ish-Tob, and Maacah *were* by themselves in the field.

⁹When Joab saw that the battle line was against him before and behind, he chose some of Israel's best and put *them* in battle array against the Syrians. ¹⁰And the rest of the people he put under the command of Abishai his brother, that he might set *them* in battle array against the people of Ammon. ¹¹Then he said, "If the Syrians are too strong for me, then you shall help me; but if the people of Ammon are too strong for you, then I will come and help you. ¹²Be of good courage, and let us be strong for our people and for the cities of our God. And may the LORD do *what is* good in His sight."

¹³So Joab and the people who *were* with him drew near for the battle against the Syrians, and they fled before him. ¹⁴When the people of Ammon saw that the Syrians were fleeing, they also fled before Abishai, and entered the city. So Joab returned from the people of Ammon and went to Jerusalem.

¹⁵When the Syrians saw that they had been defeated by Israel, they gathered together. ¹⁶Then Hadadezer[a] sent and brought out the Syrians who *were* beyond the River,[b] and they came to Helam. And Shobach the commander of Hadadezer's army *went* before them. ¹⁷When it was told David, he gathered all Israel, crossed over the Jordan, and came to Helam. And the Syrians set themselves in battle array against David and fought with him. ¹⁸Then the Syrians fled before Israel; and David killed seven hundred charioteers and forty thousand horsemen of the Syrians, and struck Shobach the commander of their army, who died there. ¹⁹And when all the kings *who were* servants to Hadadezer[a] saw that they were defeated by Israel, they made peace with Israel and served them. So the Syrians were afraid to help the people of Ammon anymore.

David, Bathsheba, and Uriah

11 It happened in the spring of the year, at the time when kings go out *to battle,* that David sent Joab and his servants with him, and all Israel; and they destroyed the people of Ammon and besieged Rabbah. But David remained at Jerusalem.

²Then it happened one evening that David arose from his bed and walked on the roof of the king's house. And from the roof he saw a woman bathing, and the woman *was* very beautiful to behold. ³So David sent and inquired about the woman. And *someone* said, "*Is* this not Bathsheba, the daughter of Eliam, the wife of Uriah the Hittite?" ⁴Then David sent messengers,

---

10:16 ᵃHebrew *Hadarezer* ᵇThat is, the Euphrates
10:19 ᵃHebrew *Hadarezer*

and took her; and she came to him, and he lay with her, for she was cleansed from her impurity; and she returned to her house. 5And the woman conceived; so she sent and told David, and said, "I *am* with child."

6Then David sent to Joab, *saying,* "Send me Uriah the Hittite." And Joab sent Uriah to David. 7When Uriah had come to him, David asked how Joab was doing, and how the people were doing, and how the war prospered. 8And David said to Uriah, "Go down to your house and wash your feet." So Uriah departed from the king's house, and a gift *of food* from the king followed him. 9But Uriah slept at the door of the king's house with all the servants of his lord, and did not go down to his house. 10So when they told David, saying, "Uriah did not go down to his house," David said to Uriah, "Did you not come from a journey? Why did you not go down to your house?"

11And Uriah said to David, "The ark and Israel and Judah are dwelling in tents, and my lord Joab and the servants of my lord are encamped in the open fields. Shall I then go to my house to eat and drink, and to lie with my wife? *As* you live, and *as* your soul lives, I will not do this thing."

12Then David said to Uriah, "Wait here today also, and tomorrow I will let you depart." So Uriah remained in Jerusalem that day and the next. 13Now when David called him, he ate and drank before him; and he made him drunk. And at evening he went out to lie on his bed with the servants of his lord, but he did not go down to his house.

14In the morning it happened that David wrote a letter to Joab and sent *it* by the hand of Uriah. 15And he wrote in the letter, saying, "Set Uriah in the forefront of the hottest battle, and retreat from him, that he may be struck down and die." 16So it was, while Joab besieged the city, that he assigned Uriah to a place where he knew there *were* valiant men. 17Then the men of the city came out and fought with Joab. And *some* of the people of the servants of David fell; and Uriah the Hittite died also.

18Then Joab sent and told David all the things concerning the war, 19and charged the messenger, saying, "When you have finished telling the matters of the war to the king, 20if it happens that the king's wrath rises, and he says to you: 'Why did you approach so near to the city when you fought? Did you not know that they would shoot from the wall? 21Who struck Abimelech the son of Jerubbesheth?a Was it not

---

11:21 aSame as *Jerubbaal* (Gideon), Judges 6:32ff

A Chemistry Lesson

High school chemistry taught me a very valuable lesson: When certain substances come into close contact, they can cause a chemical reaction. I proved that fact during my senior year of high school, when I dropped a jar full of pure sodium into a river and nearly blew up a bridge below!

I've learned since then that many people don't respect the laws of chemistry, any more than I did as a teenager. They mix volatile ingredients without giving much thought to the consequences—just as David did in the sordid account of Bathsheba. Just the mere sight of her caused him to start a slide down a very slippery slope. It can be that simple. I've discovered that many married people don't understand that a chemical reaction can occur with someone other than their mates.

Don't misunderstand—I'm not talking merely about sexual attraction. I'm referring to a reaction of two hearts, the chemistry of two souls. This is emotional adultery—an intimacy with the opposite sex outside of marriage. When two people begin discussing intimate struggles, doubts or feelings, they may be sharing their souls in a way that God intended exclusively for marriage partners. Emotional adultery is friendship with the opposite sex that progresses too far. In most cases, adulterous relationships start as casual relationships at work, school, even church.

So guard your heart!

BIBLICAL INSIGHTS • 12:07

Let Someone Sharpen You

DAVID GOT SET UP.

Just as David had set up Uriah the Hittite, so Nathan the prophet had set up King David—not to kill him, but to confront him with his ugly sin. Nathan told the king a moving story, precisely so David would confess when the prophet pointed his long finger at him and declared, "You are the man!" (12:7).

God has given us fellow believers to hold us accountable for our actions and to encourage us in our pursuit of godliness. If you can catch the importance of submitting to another person for personal accountability, then you will begin to catch the fear of the Lord—and your pursuit of godliness will take a giant leap forward.

One of my adult children called me recently, disheartened at yet another casualty of sin—a soldier in the King's army who had been compromising for years. I listened as my child shared how a half-dozen people who had been influential in his life had been caught in moral compromise. As we talked, I shared how earlier in my life I had come to a similar point of being discouraged over the compromises of men I thought were godly. We talked about accountability and how we must seek to be accountable to others. I shared with him, "I'm convinced that no one can force you to be accountable. *You* must decide that you *will* be accountable to others."

The bottom line: We all need others who have access to our lives.

I'm reminded of what Martin Luther once wrote, "Without confrontation, faith stagnates." I do not know a single person who does not need to be confronted from time to time. We all need it to be sharpened, to grow, to avoid mediocrity and becoming lukewarm, to be spurred on to greatness and not settle for a life of mere existence. If you want to accomplish great things in your family, then it starts with becoming a great person—and that will not happen unless you submit yourself to another person in a relationship of accountability.

---

a woman who cast a piece of a millstone on him from the wall, so that he died in Thebez? Why did you go near the wall?'—then you shall say, 'Your servant Uriah the Hittite is dead also.'"

²²So the messenger went, and came and told David all that Joab had sent by him. ²³And the messenger said to David, "Surely the men prevailed against us and came out to us in the field; then we drove them back as far as the entrance of the gate. ²⁴The archers shot from the wall at your servants; and *some* of the king's servants are dead, and your servant Uriah the Hittite is dead also."

²⁵Then David said to the messenger, "Thus you shall say to Joab: 'Do not let this thing displease you, for the sword devours one as well as another. Strengthen your attack against the city, and overthrow it.' So encourage him."

²⁶When the wife of Uriah heard that Uriah her husband was dead, she mourned for her husband. ²⁷And when her mourning was over, David sent and brought her to his house, and she became his wife and bore him a son. But the thing that David had done displeased the LORD.

Nathan's Parable and David's Confession

12 Then the LORD sent Nathan to David. And he came to him, and said to him: "There were two men in one city, one rich and the other poor. ²The rich *man* had exceedingly many flocks and herds. ³But the poor *man* had nothing, except one little ewe lamb which he had bought and nourished; and it grew up together with him and with his children. It ate of his own food and drank from his own cup and lay in his bosom; and it was like a daughter to him. [4]And a traveler came to the rich man, who refused to take from his own flock and from his own herd to prepare one for the wayfaring man who had come to him; but he took the poor man's lamb and prepared it for the man who had come to him."

[5]So David's anger was greatly aroused against the man, and he said to Nathan, "*As* the LORD lives, the man who has done this shall surely die! [6]And he shall restore fourfold for the lamb, because he did this thing and because he had no pity."

[7]Then Nathan said to David, "You *are* the man! Thus says the LORD God of Israel: 'I anointed you king over Israel, and I delivered you from the hand of Saul. [8]I gave you your master's house and your master's wives into your keeping, and gave you the house of Israel and Judah. And if *that had been* too little, I also would have given you much more! [9]Why have you despised the commandment of the LORD, to do evil in His sight? You have killed Uriah the Hittite with the sword; you have taken his wife *to be* your wife, and have killed him with the sword of the people of Ammon. [10]Now therefore, the sword shall never depart from your house, because you have despised Me, and have taken the wife of Uriah the Hittite to be your wife.' [11]Thus says the LORD: 'Behold, I will raise up adversity against you from your own house; and I will take your wives before your eyes and give *them* to your neighbor, and he shall lie with your wives in the sight of this sun. [12]For you did *it* secretly, but I will do this thing before all Israel, before the sun.' "

[13]So David said to Nathan, "I have sinned against the LORD."

And Nathan said to David, "The LORD also has put away your sin; you shall not die. [14]However, because by this deed you have given great occasion to the enemies of the LORD to blaspheme, the child also *who is* born to you shall surely die." [15]Then Nathan departed to his house.

The Death of David's Son

And the LORD struck the child that Uriah's wife bore to David, and it became ill. [16]David therefore pleaded with God for the child, and David fasted and went in and lay all night on the ground. [17]So the elders of his house arose *and went* to him, to raise him up from the ground. But he would not, nor did he eat food with them. [18]Then on the seventh day it came to pass that the child died. And the servants of David were afraid to tell him that the child was dead. For they said, "Indeed, while the child was alive, we spoke to him, and he would not heed our voice. How can we tell him that the child is dead? He may do some harm!"

[19]When David saw that his servants were whispering, David perceived that the child was dead. Therefore David said to his servants, "Is the child dead?"

And they said, "He is dead."

[20]So David arose from the ground, washed and anointed himself, and changed his clothes; and he went into the house of the LORD and worshiped. Then he went to his own house; and when he requested, they set food before him, and he ate. [21]Then his servants said to him, "What *is* this that you have done? You fasted and wept for the child *while he was* alive, but when the child died, you arose and ate food."

[22]And he said, "While the child was alive, I fasted and wept; for I said, 'Who can tell *whether* the LORD[a] will be gracious to me, that the child may live?' [23]But now he is dead; why should I fast? Can I bring him back again? I shall go to him, but he shall not return to me."

Solomon Is Born

[24]Then David comforted Bathsheba his wife, and went in to her and lay with her. So she bore a son, and he[a] called his name Solomon. Now the LORD loved him, [25]and He sent *word* by the hand of Nathan the prophet: So he[a] called his name Jedidiah,[b] because of the LORD.

12:22 [a]A few Hebrew manuscripts and Syriac read *God*. 12:24 [a]Following Kethib, Septuagint, and Vulgate; Qere, a few Hebrew manuscripts, Syriac, and Targum read *she*. 12:25 [a]Qere, some Hebrew manuscripts, Syriac, and Targum read *she*. [b]Literally *Beloved of the LORD*

Rabbah Is Captured

²⁶Now Joab fought against Rabbah of the people of Ammon, and took the royal city. ²⁷And Joab sent messengers to David, and said, "I have fought against Rabbah, and I have taken the city's water *supply*. ²⁸Now therefore, gather the rest of the people together and encamp against the city and take it, lest I take the city and it be called after my name." ²⁹So David gathered all the people together and went to Rabbah, fought against it, and took it. ³⁰Then he took their king's crown from his head. Its weight *was* a talent of gold, with precious stones. And it was *set* on David's head. Also he brought out the spoil of the city in great abundance. ³¹And he brought out the people who *were* in it, and put *them to work* with saws and iron picks and iron axes, and made them cross over to the brick works. So he did to all the cities of the people of Ammon. Then David and all the people returned to Jerusalem.

INTIMATE MOMENTS
Bring the Bling

We know of very few women who don't like jewelry, even though tastes can vary tremendously. What one woman sees as a gorgeous pendant, another may consider a gaudy trinket.

What kind of jewelry does your wife like? Small and elegant, or large and bold? Does she prefer her birthstone, or a gem of a different color? Does she like to wear gold, silver, platinum, or something else? If you don't know for sure, find out.

Then go out and splurge on a special piece of jewelry. It doesn't necessarily have to be expensive, but it should be something she is sure to enjoy. Make it even more personal by having a romantic message engraved somewhere on the piece. Present it to her as a surprise, whether at home or on a date night. Make it an event to remember!

Amnon and Tamar

13 After this Absalom the son of David had a lovely sister, whose name *was* Tamar; and Amnon the son of David loved her. ²Amnon was so distressed over his sister Tamar that he became sick; for she *was* a virgin. And it was improper for Amnon to do anything to her. ³But Amnon had a friend whose name *was* Jonadab the son of Shimeah, David's brother. Now Jonadab *was* a very crafty man. ⁴And he said to him, "Why *are* you, the king's son, becoming thinner day after day? Will you not tell me?"

Amnon said to him, "I love Tamar, my brother Absalom's sister."

⁵So Jonadab said to him, "Lie down on your bed and pretend to be ill. And when your father comes to see you, say to him, 'Please let my sister Tamar come and give me food, and prepare the food in my sight, that I may see *it* and eat it from her hand.'" ⁶Then Amnon lay down and pretended to be ill; and when the king came to see him, Amnon said to the king, "Please let Tamar my sister come and make a couple of cakes for me in my sight, that I may eat from her hand."

⁷And David sent home to Tamar, saying, "Now go to your brother Amnon's house, and prepare food for him." ⁸So Tamar went to her brother Amnon's house; and he was lying down. Then she took flour and kneaded *it*, made cakes in his sight, and baked the cakes. ⁹And she took the pan and placed *them* out before him, but he refused to eat. Then Amnon said, "Have everyone go out from me." And they all went out from him. ¹⁰Then Amnon said to Tamar, "Bring the food into the bedroom, that I may eat from your hand." And Tamar took the cakes which she had made, and brought *them* to Amnon her brother in the bedroom. ¹¹Now when she had brought *them* to him to eat, he took hold of her and said to her, "Come, lie with me, my sister."

¹²But she answered him, "No, my brother, do not force me, for no such thing should be done in Israel. Do not do this disgraceful thing! ¹³And I, where could I take my shame? And as for you, you would be like one of the fools in Israel. Now therefore, please speak to the king; for he will not withhold me from

you." ¹⁴However, he would not heed her voice; and being stronger than she, he forced her and lay with her.

¹⁵Then Amnon hated her exceedingly, so that the hatred with which he hated her *was* greater than the love with which he had loved her. And Amnon said to her, "Arise, be gone!"

¹⁶So she said to him, "No, indeed! This evil of sending me away *is* worse than the other that you did to me."

But he would not listen to her. ¹⁷Then he called his servant who attended him, and said, "Here! Put this *woman* out, away from me, and bolt the door behind her." ¹⁸Now she had on a robe of many colors, for the king's virgin daughters wore such apparel. And his servant put her out and bolted the door behind her.

¹⁹Then Tamar put ashes on her head, and tore her robe of many colors that *was* on her, and laid her hand on her head and went away crying bitterly. ²⁰And Absalom her brother said to her, "Has Amnon your brother been with you? But now hold your peace, my sister. He *is* your brother; do not take this thing to heart." So Tamar remained desolate in her brother Absalom's house.

²¹But when King David heard of all these things, he was very angry. ²²And Absalom spoke to his brother Amnon neither good nor bad. For Absalom hated Amnon, because he had forced his sister Tamar.

Absalom Murders Amnon

²³And it came to pass, after two full years, that Absalom had sheepshearers in Baal Hazor, which *is* near Ephraim; so Absalom invited all the king's sons. ²⁴Then Absalom came to the king and said, "Kindly note, your servant has sheepshearers; please, let the king and his servants go with your servant." ²⁵But the king said to Absalom, "No, my son, let us not all go now, lest we be a burden

to you." Then he urged him, but he would not go; and he blessed him.

²⁶Then Absalom said, "If not, please let my brother Amnon go with us."

And the king said to him, "Why should he go with you?" ²⁷But Absalom urged him; so he let Amnon and all the king's sons go with him.

²⁸Now Absalom had commanded his servants, saying, "Watch now, when Amnon's heart is merry with wine, and when I say to you, 'Strike Amnon!' then kill him. Do not be afraid. Have I not commanded you? Be courageous and valiant." ²⁹So the servants of Absalom did to Amnon as Absalom had commanded. Then all the king's sons arose, and each one got on his mule and fled.

³⁰And it came to pass, while they were on the way, that news came to David, saying, "Absalom has killed all the king's sons, and not one of them is left!" ³¹So the king arose and tore his garments and lay on the ground, and all his servants stood by with their clothes torn. ³²Then Jonadab the son of Shimeah, David's brother, answered and said, "Let not my lord suppose *they have* killed all the young men, the king's sons, for only Amnon is dead. For by the command of Absalom this has been determined from the day that he forced his sister Tamar. ³³Now therefore, let not my lord the king take the thing to his heart, to think that all the king's sons are dead. For only Amnon is dead."

Absalom Flees to Geshur

³⁴Then Absalom fled. And the young man who was keeping watch lifted his eyes and looked, and there, many people were coming from the road on the hillside behind him.ᵃ ³⁵And Jonadab said to the king, "Look, the king's sons are coming; as your servant said, so it is." ³⁶So it was, as soon as he had finished speaking, that the king's sons indeed came, and they lifted up their voice and wept. Also the king and all his servants wept very bitterly.

³⁷But Absalom fled and went to Talmai the son of Ammihud, king of Geshur. And *David* mourned for his son every day. ³⁸So Absalom fled and went to Geshur, and was there three years. ³⁹And King Davidᵃ longed to go toᵇ Absalom. For he had been comforted concerning Amnon, because he was dead.

13:34 ᵃSeptuagint adds *And the watchman went and told the king, and said, "I see men from the way of Horonaim, from the regions of the mountains."*
13:39 ᵃFollowing Masoretic Text, Syriac, and Vulgate; Septuagint reads *the spirit of the king;* Targum reads *the soul of King David.* ᵇFollowing Masoretic Text and Targum; Septuagint and Vulgate read *ceased to pursue after.*

Absalom Returns to Jerusalem

14 So Joab the son of Zeruiah perceived that the king's heart *was* concerned about Absalom. [2]And Joab sent to Tekoa and brought from there a wise woman, and said to her, "Please pretend to be a mourner, and put on mourning apparel; do not anoint yourself with oil, but act like a woman who has been mourning a long time for the dead. [3]Go to the king and speak to him in this manner." So Joab put the words in her mouth.

[4]And when the woman of Tekoa spoke[a] to the king, she fell on her face to the ground and prostrated herself, and said, "Help, O king!"

[5]Then the king said to her, "What troubles you?"

And she answered, "Indeed I *am* a widow, my husband is dead. [6]Now your maidservant had two sons; and the two fought with each other in the field, and *there was* no one to part them, but the one struck the other and killed him. [7]And now the whole family has risen up against your maidservant, and they said, 'Deliver him who struck his brother, that we may execute him for the life of his brother whom he killed; and we will destroy the heir also.' So they would extinguish my ember that is left, and leave to my husband *neither* name nor remnant on the earth."

[8]Then the king said to the woman, "Go to your house, and I will give orders concerning you."

[9]And the woman of Tekoa said to the king, "My lord, O king, *let* the iniquity *be* on me and on my father's house, and the king and his throne *be* guiltless."

[10]So the king said, "Whoever says *anything* to you, bring him to me, and he shall not touch you anymore."

[11]Then she said, "Please let the king remember the LORD your God, and do not permit the avenger of blood to destroy anymore, lest they destroy my son."

And he said, "*As* the LORD lives, not one hair of your son shall fall to the ground."

[12]Therefore the woman said, "Please, let your maidservant speak *another* word to my lord the king."

And he said, "Say on."

[13]So the woman said: "Why then have you schemed such a thing against the people of God? For the king speaks this thing as one who is guilty, *in that* the king does not bring his banished one home again. [14]For we will surely die and *become* like water spilled on the ground, which cannot be gathered up again. Yet God does not take away a life; but He devises means, so that His banished ones are not expelled from Him. [15]Now therefore, I have come to speak of this thing to my lord the king because the people have made me afraid. And your maidservant said, 'I will now speak to the king; it may be that the king will perform the request of his maidservant. [16]For the king will hear and deliver his maidservant from the hand of the man *who would* destroy me and my son together from the inheritance of God.' [17]Your maidservant said, 'The word of my lord the king will now be comforting; for as the angel of God, so *is* my lord the king in discerning good and evil. And may the LORD your God be with you.' "

[18]Then the king answered and said to the woman, "Please do not hide from me anything that I ask you."

And the woman said, "Please, let my lord the king speak."

[19]So the king said, "*Is* the hand of Joab with you in all this?" And the woman answered and said, "*As* you live, my lord the king, no one can turn to the right hand or to the left from anything that my lord the king has spoken. For your servant Joab commanded me, and he put all these words in the mouth of your maidservant. [20]To bring about this change of affairs your servant Joab has done this thing; but my lord *is* wise, according to the wisdom of the angel of God, to know everything that *is* in the earth."

[21]And the king said to Joab, "All right, I have granted this thing. Go therefore, bring back the young man Absalom."

[22]Then Joab fell to the ground on his face and bowed himself, and thanked the king. And Joab said, "Today your servant knows that I have found favor in your sight, my lord, O king, in that the king has fulfilled the request of his servant." [23]So Joab arose and went to Geshur, and brought Absalom

---

14:4 [a]Many Hebrew manuscripts, Septuagint, Syriac, and Vulgate read *came.*

to Jerusalem. 24And the king said, "Let him return to his own house, but do not let him see my face." So Absalom returned to his own house, but did not see the king's face.

David Forgives Absalom

25Now in all Israel there was no one who was praised as much as Absalom for his good looks. From the sole of his foot to the crown of his head there was no blemish in him. 26And when he cut the hair of his head—at the end of every year he cut it because it was heavy on him—when he cut it, he weighed the hair of his head at two hundred shekels according to the king's standard. 27To Absalom were born three sons, and one daughter whose name was Tamar. She was a woman of beautiful appearance.

28And Absalom dwelt two full years in Jerusalem, but did not see the king's face. 29Therefore Absalom sent for Joab, to send him to the king, but he would not come to him. And when he sent again the second time, he would not come. 30So he said to his servants, "See, Joab's field is near mine, and he has barley there; go and set it on fire." And Absalom's servants set the field on fire.

31Then Joab arose and came to Absalom's house, and said to him, "Why have your servants set my field on fire?"

32And Absalom answered Joab, "Look, I sent to you, saying, 'Come here, so that I may send you to the king, to say, "Why have I come from Geshur? It would be better for me to be there still."' Now therefore, let me see the king's face; but if there is iniquity in me, let him execute me."

33So Joab went to the king and told him. And when he had called for Absalom, he came to the king and bowed himself on his face to the ground before the king. Then the king kissed Absalom.

Absalom's Treason

15 After this it happened that Absalom provided himself with chariots and horses, and fifty men to run before him. 2Now Absalom would rise early and stand beside the way to the gate. So it was, whenever anyone who had a lawsuit came to the

king for a decision, that Absalom would call to him and say, "What city are you from?" And he would say, "Your servant is from such and such a tribe of Israel." 3Then Absalom would say to him, "Look, your case is good and right; but there is no deputy of the king to hear you." 4Moreover Absalom would say, "Oh, that I were made judge in the land, and everyone who has any suit or cause would come to me; then I would give him justice." 5And so it was, whenever anyone came near to bow down to him, that he would put out his hand and take him and kiss him. 6In this manner Absalom acted toward all Israel who came to the king for judgment. So Absalom stole the hearts of the men of Israel.

7Now it came to pass after forty[a] years that Absalom said to the king, "Please, let me go to Hebron and pay the vow which I made to the LORD. 8For your servant took a vow while I dwelt at Geshur in Syria, saying, 'If the LORD indeed brings me back to Jerusalem, then I will serve the LORD.' "

9And the king said to him, "Go in peace." So he arose and went to Hebron.

10Then Absalom sent spies throughout all the tribes of Israel, saying, "As soon as you hear the sound of the trumpet, then you shall say, 'Absalom reigns in Hebron!' "

11And with Absalom went two hundred men invited from Jerusalem, and they went along innocently and did not know anything. 12Then Absalom sent for Ahithophel the Gilonite, David's counselor, from his city—from Giloh—while he offered sacrifices. And the conspiracy grew strong, for the people with Absalom continually increased in number.

David Escapes from Jerusalem

13Now a messenger came to David, saying, "The hearts of the men of Israel are with Absalom."

14So David said to all his servants who were with him at Jerusalem, "Arise, and let us flee, or we shall not escape from Absalom. Make haste to depart, lest he overtake us suddenly and bring disaster upon us, and strike the city with the edge of the sword."

15And the king's servants said to the king, "We are your servants, ready to do

---

15:7 aSeptuagint manuscripts, Syriac, and Josephus read four.

Keep Your Vows

BOTH CHURCHES AND INDIVIDUALS have a holy responsibility to take radical measures to restore meaning to the covenant of marriage. Churches, for example, could:

- Refuse to marry couples that will not take a church-prescribed marriage preparation course.
- Refuse to marry couples that will not sign and be held accountable to a written marriage covenant.
- Assign a mentoring couple to all newlyweds.

  Likewise, engaged couples could:

- Refuse to sign any type of prenuptial agreement.
- Pledge to each other, to their family, and to the community, never to divorce but to solemnly fulfill the marriage vows.

By no means is this a comprehensive list, nor will it eliminate failure; but it does give us a proactive starting point. We are already far too like Absalom, who even while contemplating the overthrow of King David, said, "Please, let me go to Hebron and pay the vow which I made to the LORD. For your servant took a vow while I dwelt at Geshur in Syria, saying, 'If the LORD indeed brings me back to Jerusalem, then I will serve the LORD'" (15:7, 8). He had no more intention of fulfilling that vow than many married couples have of fulfilling theirs.

And this kind of flippant attitude toward our marriage vows must stop. As individuals and as a society, we must recapture the sacred nature of the marriage covenant.

whatever my lord the king commands." [16]Then the king went out with all his household after him. But the king left ten women, concubines, to keep the house. [17]And the king went out with all the people after him, and stopped at the outskirts. [18]Then all his servants passed before him; and all the Cherethites, all the Pelethites, and all the Gittites, six hundred men who had followed him from Gath, passed before the king.

[19]Then the king said to Ittai the Gittite, "Why are you also going with us? Return and remain with the king. For you *are* a foreigner and also an exile from your own place. [20]In fact, you came *only* yesterday. Should I make you wander up and down with us today, since I go I know not where? Return, and take your brethren back. Mercy and truth *be* with you."

[21]But Ittai answered the king and said, "*As* the LORD lives, and *as* my lord the king lives, surely in whatever place my lord the king shall be, whether in death or life, even there also your servant will be." [22]So David said to Ittai, "Go, and cross over." Then Ittai the Gittite and all his men and all the little ones who *were* with him crossed over. [23]And all the country wept with a loud voice, and all the people crossed over. The king himself also crossed over the Brook Kidron, and all the people crossed over toward the way of the wilderness.

[24]There was Zadok also, and all the Levites with him, bearing the ark of the covenant of God. And they set down the ark of God, and Abiathar went up until all the people had finished crossing over from the city. [25]Then the king said to Zadok, "Carry the ark of God back into the city. If I find favor in the eyes of the LORD, He will bring me back and show me *both* it and His dwelling place. [26]But if He says thus: 'I have no delight in you,' here I am, let Him do to me as seems good to Him." [27]The king also said to Zadok the priest, "*Are* you *not* a seer? Return to the city in peace, and your two sons with you, Ahimaaz your son, and Jonathan the son of Abiathar. [28]See, I will wait in the plains of the wilderness until word comes from you to inform me." [29]Therefore Zadok and Abiathar carried the ark of God back to Jerusalem. And they remained there.

[30]So David went up by the Ascent of the *Mount of* Olives, and wept as he went up; and he had his head covered and went barefoot. And all the people who *were* with him covered their heads and went up, weeping as they went up. [31]Then *someone* told David, saying, "Ahithophel *is* among the conspirators with Absalom." And David said, "O

LORD, I pray, turn the counsel of Ahithophel into foolishness!"

[32]Now it happened when David had come to the top *of the mountain,* where he worshiped God—there was Hushai the Archite coming to meet him with his robe torn and dust on his head. [33]David said to him, "If you go on with me, then you will become a burden to me. [34]But if you return to the city, and say to Absalom, 'I will be your servant, O king; *as* I *was* your father's servant previously, so I *will* now also *be* your servant,' then you may defeat the counsel of Ahithophel for me. [35]And *do* you not *have* Zadok and Abiathar the priests with you there? Therefore it will be *that* whatever you hear from the king's house, you shall tell to Zadok and Abiathar the priests. [36]Indeed *they have* there with them their two sons, Ahimaaz, Zadok's *son,* and Jonathan, Abiathar's *son;* and by them you shall send me everything you hear."

[37]So Hushai, David's friend, went into the city. And Absalom came into Jerusalem.

Mephibosheth's Servant

16 When David was a little past the top *of the mountain,* there was Ziba the servant of Mephibosheth, who met him with a couple of saddled donkeys, and on them two hundred *loaves* of bread, one hundred clusters of raisins, one hundred summer fruits, and a skin of wine. [2]And the king said to Ziba, "What do you mean to do with these?"

So Ziba said, "The donkeys *are* for the king's household to ride on, the bread and summer fruit for the young men to eat, and the wine for those who are faint in the wilderness to drink."

[3]Then the king said, "And where *is* your master's son?"

And Ziba said to the king, "Indeed he is staying in Jerusalem, for he said, 'Today the house of Israel will restore the kingdom of my father to me.' "

[4]So the king said to Ziba, "Here, all that *belongs* to Mephibosheth *is* yours."

And Ziba said, "I humbly bow before you, *that* I may find favor in your sight, my lord, O king!"

Shimei Curses David

[5]Now when King David came to Bahurim, there was a man from the family of the house of Saul, whose name *was* Shimei the son of Gera, coming from there. He came out, cursing continuously as he came. [6]And he threw stones at David and at all the servants of King David. And all the people and all the mighty men *were* on his right hand and on his left. [7]Also Shimei said thus when he cursed: "Come out! Come out! You bloodthirsty man, you rogue! [8]The LORD has brought upon you all the blood of the house of Saul, in whose place you have reigned; and the LORD has delivered the kingdom into the hand of Absalom your son. So now you *are caught* in your own evil, because you are a bloodthirsty man!"

[9]Then Abishai the son of Zeruiah said to the king, "Why should this dead dog curse my lord the king? Please, let me go over and take off his head!"

[10]But the king said, "What have I to do with you, you sons of Zeruiah? So let him curse, because the LORD has said to him, 'Curse David.' Who then shall say, 'Why have you done so?' "

[11]And David said to Abishai and all his servants, "See how my son who came from my own body seeks my life. How much more now *may this* Benjamite? Let him alone, and let him curse; for so the LORD has ordered him. [12]It may be that the LORD will look on my affliction,[a] and that the LORD will repay me with good for his cursing this day." [13]And as David and his men went along the road, Shimei went along the hillside opposite him and cursed as he went, threw stones at him and kicked up dust. [14]Now the king and all the people who *were* with him became weary; so they refreshed themselves there.

The Advice of Ahithophel

[15]Meanwhile Absalom and all the people, the men of Israel, came to Jerusalem; and Ahithophel *was* with him. [16]And so it was, when Hushai the Archite, David's friend,

---

16:12 [a]Following Kethib, Septuagint, Syriac, and Vulgate; Qere reads *my eyes;* Targum reads *tears of my eyes.*

came to Absalom, that Hushai said to Absalom, "*Long* live the king! *Long* live the king!"

17So Absalom said to Hushai, "*Is* this your loyalty to your friend? Why did you not go with your friend?"

18And Hushai said to Absalom, "No, but whom the LORD and this people and all the men of Israel choose, his I will be, and with him I will remain. 19Furthermore, whom should I serve? *Should I* not *serve* in the presence of his son? As I have served in your father's presence, so will I be in your presence."

INTIMATE MOMENTS

This one will take a little pre-planning on your part, but send your wife an invitation to a night of romance. You can either describe the evening in detail, or simply keep her in suspense. But for the *piece de resistance*, get the envelope postmarked from Romance, Arkansas. (You do that by sending the envelope to be mailed to your sweetie inside another envelope, addressed to: Postmaster Romance, AR, Re-mailing, Romance, AR, 72136.)

20Then Absalom said to Ahithophel, "Give advice as to what we should do."

21And Ahithophel said to Absalom, "Go in to your father's concubines, whom he has left to keep the house; and all Israel will hear that you are abhorred by your father. Then the hands of all who are with you will be strong." 22So they pitched a tent for Absalom on the top of the house, and Absalom went in to his father's concubines in the sight of all Israel.

23Now the advice of Ahithophel, which he gave in those days, *was* as if one had inquired *at the oracle of God*. So *was* all the advice of Ahithophel both with David and with Absalom.

17 Moreover Ahithophel said to Absalom, "Now let me choose twelve thousand men, and I will arise and pursue David tonight. 2I will come upon him while he *is* weary and weak, and make him afraid. And all the people who *are* with him will flee, and I will strike only the king. 3Then I will bring back all the people to you. When all return except the man whom you seek, all the people will be at peace." 4And the saying pleased Absalom and all the elders of Israel.

The Advice of Hushai

5Then Absalom said, "Now call Hushai the Archite also, and let us hear what he says too." 6And when Hushai came to Absalom, Absalom spoke to him, saying, "Ahithophel has spoken in this manner. Shall we do as he says? If not, speak up."

7So Hushai said to Absalom: "The advice that Ahithophel has given *is* not good at this time. 8For," said Hushai, "you know your father and his men, that they *are* mighty men, and they *are* enraged in their minds, like a bear robbed of her cubs in the field; and your father *is* a man of war, and will not camp with the people. 9Surely by now he is hidden in some pit, or in some *other* place. And it will be, when some of them are overthrown at the first, that whoever hears *it* will say, 'There is a slaughter among the people who follow Absalom.' 10And even he *who is* valiant, whose heart *is* like the heart of a lion, will melt completely. For all Israel knows that your father *is* a mighty man, and *those* who *are* with him *are* valiant men. 11Therefore I advise that all Israel be fully gathered to you, from Dan to Beersheba, like the sand that *is* by the sea for multitude, and that you go to battle in person. 12So we will come upon him in some place where he may be found, and we will fall on him as the dew falls on the ground. And of him and all the men who *are* with him there shall not be left so much as one. 13Moreover, if he has withdrawn into a city, then all Israel shall bring ropes to that city; and we will pull it into the river, until there is not one small stone found there."

14So Absalom and all the men of Israel said, "The advice of Hushai the Archite *is* better than the advice of Ahithophel." For the LORD had purposed to defeat the good advice of Ahithophel, to the intent that the LORD might bring disaster on Absalom.

Hushai Warns David to Escape

[15]Then Hushai said to Zadok and Abiathar the priests, "Thus and so Ahithophel advised Absalom and the elders of Israel, and thus and so I have advised. [16]Now therefore, send quickly and tell David, saying, 'Do not spend this night in the plains of the wilderness, but speedily cross over, lest the king and all the people who *are* with him be swallowed up.' " [17]Now Jonathan and Ahimaaz stayed at En Rogel, for they dared not be seen coming into the city; so a female servant would come and tell them, and they would go and tell King David. [18]Nevertheless a lad saw them, and told Absalom. But both of them went away quickly and came to a man's house in Bahurim, who had a well in his court; and they went down into it. [19]Then the woman took and spread a covering over the well's mouth, and spread ground grain on it; and the thing was not known. [20]And when Absalom's servants came to the woman at the house, they said, "Where *are* Ahimaaz and Jonathan?"

So the woman said to them, "They have gone over the water brook."

And when they had searched and could not find *them,* they returned to Jerusalem. [21]Now it came to pass, after they had departed, that they came up out of the well and went and told King David, and said to David, "Arise and cross over the water quickly. For thus has Ahithophel advised against you." [22]So David and all the people who *were* with him arose and crossed over the Jordan. By morning light not one of them was left who had not gone over the Jordan.

[23]Now when Ahithophel saw that his advice was not followed, he saddled a donkey, and arose and went home to his house, to his city. Then he put his household in order, and hanged himself, and died; and he was buried in his father's tomb.

[24]Then David went to Mahanaim. And Absalom crossed over the Jordan, he and all the men of Israel with him. [25]And Absalom made Amasa captain of the army instead of Joab. This Amasa *was* the son of a man whose name *was* Jithra,[a] an Israelite,[b] who had gone in to Abigail the daughter of Nahash, sister of Zeruiah, Joab's mother. [26]So Israel and Absalom encamped in the land of Gilead.

[27]Now it happened, when David had come to Mahanaim, that Shobi the son of Nahash from Rabbah of the people of Ammon, Machir the son of Ammiel from Lo Debar, and Barzillai the Gileadite from Rogelim, [28]brought beds and basins, earthen vessels and wheat, barley and flour, parched *grain* and beans, lentils and parched *seeds,* [29]honey and curds, sheep and cheese of the herd, for David and the people who *were* with him to eat. For they said, "The people are hungry and weary and thirsty in the wilderness."

Absalom's Defeat and Death

18 And David numbered the people who *were* with him, and set captains of thousands and captains of hundreds over them. [2]Then David sent out one third of the people under the hand of Joab, one third under the hand of Abishai the son of Zeruiah, Joab's brother, and one third under the hand of Ittai the Gittite. And the king said to the people, "I also will surely go out with you myself."

[3]But the people answered, "You shall not go out! For if we flee away, they will not care about us; nor if half of us die, will they care about us. But *you are* worth ten thousand of us now. For you are now more help to us in the city."

[4]Then the king said to them, "Whatever seems best to you I will do." So the king stood beside the gate, and all the people went out by hundreds and by thousands. [5]Now the king had commanded Joab, Abishai, and Ittai, saying, "*Deal* gently for my sake with the young man Absalom." And all the people heard when the king gave all the captains orders concerning Absalom.

[6]So the people went out into the field of battle against Israel. And the battle was in

17:25 [a]Spelled *Jether* in 1 Chronicles 2:17 and elsewhere [b]Following Masoretic Text, some manuscripts of the Septuagint, and Targum; some manuscripts of the Septuagint read *Ishmaelite* (compare 1 Chronicles 2:17); Vulgate reads *of Jezrael.*

the woods of Ephraim. [7]The people of Israel were overthrown there before the servants of David, and a great slaughter of twenty thousand took place there that day. [8]For the battle there was scattered over the face of the whole countryside, and the woods devoured more people that day than the sword devoured.

[9]Then Absalom met the servants of David. Absalom rode on a mule. The mule went under the thick boughs of a great terebinth tree, and his head caught in the terebinth; so he was left hanging between heaven and earth. And the mule which *was* under him went on. [10]Now a certain man saw *it* and told Joab, and said, "I just saw Absalom hanging in a terebinth tree!"

[11]So Joab said to the man who told him, "You just saw *him!* And why did you not strike him there to the ground? I would have given you ten *shekels* of silver and a belt."

[12]But the man said to Joab, "Though I were to receive a thousand *shekels* of silver in my hand, I would not raise my hand against the king's son. For in our hearing the king commanded you and Abishai and Ittai, saying, 'Beware lest anyone *touch* the young man Absalom!'[a] [13]Otherwise I would have dealt falsely against my own life. For there is nothing hidden from the king, and you yourself would have set yourself against *me.*"

[14]Then Joab said, "I cannot linger with you." And he took three spears in his hand and thrust them through Absalom's heart, while he was *still* alive in the midst of the terebinth tree. [15]And ten young men who bore Joab's armor surrounded Absalom, and struck and killed him.

[16]So Joab blew the trumpet, and the people returned from pursuing Israel. For Joab held back the people. [17]And they took Absalom and cast him into a large pit in the woods, and laid a very large heap of stones over him. Then all Israel fled, everyone to his tent.

[18]Now Absalom in his lifetime had taken and set up a pillar for himself, which *is* in the King's Valley. For he said, "I have no son to keep my name in remembrance." He called the pillar after his own name. And to this day it is called Absalom's Monument.

David Hears of Absalom's Death

[19]Then Ahimaaz the son of Zadok said, "Let me run now and take the news to the king, how the LORD has avenged him of his enemies."

[20]And Joab said to him, "You shall not take the news this day, for you shall take the news another day. But today you shall take no news, because the king's son is dead." [21]Then Joab said to the Cushite, "Go, tell the king what you have seen." So the Cushite bowed himself to Joab and ran.

18:12 [a]The ancient versions read *'Protect the young man Absalom for me!'*

ROMANCE FAQ

Q: *How specifically can I build up my spouse —especially when I feel critical?*

I often look to Proverbs 18:21 as a good reminder of the power of words. It says, "Death and life are in the power of the tongue, and those who love it will eat its fruit." It's a simple choice—you can either choose to give life with your words, or give death. This is especially true when it comes to your spouse.

Sometimes it's easy, even automatic, to pick out wrong things your spouse does. But how about this instead? The next time you start to criticize your spouse for doing something wrong, think about the last time you praised him or her for something he or she did *right*.

One word of caution: don't falsely flatter your spouse, or insincerely attempt to compliment him or her. It is better to find two or three things that you honestly admire than to lavish praise that is undeserved.

We all need someone on our team, someone who's pulling for us during the tough times. There's a special comfort and security in knowing your spouse will cheer for you, even when the world is dragging you down.

²²And Ahimaaz the son of Zadok said again to Joab, "But whatever happens, please let me also run after the Cushite."

So Joab said, "Why will you run, my son, since you have no news ready?"

²³"But whatever happens," *he said,* "let me run."

So he said to him, "Run." Then Ahimaaz ran by way of the plain, and outran the Cushite.

²⁴Now David was sitting between the two gates. And the watchman went up to the roof over the gate, to the wall, lifted his eyes and looked, and there was a man, running alone. ²⁵Then the watchman cried out and told the king. And the king said, "If he *is* alone, *there is* news in his mouth." And he came rapidly and drew near.

²⁶Then the watchman saw *another* man running, and the watchman called to the gatekeeper and said, "There is *another* man, running alone!"

And the king said, "He also brings news."

²⁷So the watchman said, "I think the running of the first is like the running of Ahimaaz the son of Zadok."

And the king said, "He *is* a good man, and comes with good news."

²⁸So Ahimaaz called out and said to the king, "All is well!" Then he bowed down with his face to the earth before the king, and said, "Blessed *be* the Lord your God, who has delivered up the men who raised their hand against my lord the king!"

²⁹The king said, "Is the young man Absalom safe?"

Ahimaaz answered, "When Joab sent the king's servant and *me* your servant, I saw a great tumult, but I did not know what *it was about.*"

³⁰And the king said, "Turn aside *and* stand here." So he turned aside and stood still.

³¹Just then the Cushite came, and the Cushite said, "There is good news, my lord the king! For the Lord has avenged you this day of all those who rose against you."

³²And the king said to the Cushite, "Is the young man Absalom safe?"

So the Cushite answered, "May the enemies of my lord the king, and all who rise against you to do harm, be like *that* young man!"

David's Mourning for Absalom

³³Then the king was deeply moved, and went up to the chamber over the gate, and wept. And as he went, he said thus: "O my son Absalom—my son, my son Absalom—if only I had died in your place! O Absalom my son, my son!"

19 And Joab was told, "Behold, the king is weeping and mourning for Absalom." ²So the victory that day was *turned* into mourning for all the people. For the people heard it said that day, "The king is grieved for his son." ³And the people stole back into the city that day, as people who are ashamed steal away when they flee in battle. ⁴But the king covered his face, and the king cried out with a loud voice, "O my son Absalom! O Absalom, my son, my son!"

⁵Then Joab came into the house to the king, and said, "Today you have disgraced all your servants who today have saved your life, the lives of your sons and daughters, the lives of your wives and the lives of your concubines, ⁶in that you love your enemies and hate your friends. For you have declared today that you regard neither princes nor servants; for today I perceive that if Absalom had lived and all of us had died today, then it would have pleased you well. ⁷Now therefore, arise, go out and speak comfort to your servants. For I swear by the Lord, if you do not go out, not one will stay with you this night. And that will be worse for you than all the evil that has befallen you from your youth until now." ⁸Then the king arose and sat in the gate. And they told all the people, saying, "There is the king, sitting in the gate." So all the people came before the king.

For everyone of Israel had fled to his tent.

David Returns to Jerusalem

⁹Now all the people were in a dispute throughout all the tribes of Israel, saying, "The king saved us from the hand of our enemies, he delivered us from the hand of the Philistines, and now he has fled from the land because of Absalom. ¹⁰But Absalom,

whom we anointed over us, has died in battle. Now therefore, why do you say nothing about bringing back the king?"

¹¹So King David sent to Zadok and Abiathar the priests, saying, "Speak to the elders of Judah, saying, 'Why are you the last to bring the king back to his house, since the words of all Israel have come to the king, to his *very* house? ¹²You *are* my brethren, you *are* my bone and my flesh. Why then are you the last to bring back the king?' ¹³And say to Amasa, 'Are you not my bone and my flesh? God do so to me, and more also, if you are not commander of the army before me continually in place of Joab.' " ¹⁴So he swayed the hearts of all the men of Judah, just as *the heart of* one man, so that they sent *this word* to the king: "Return, you and all your servants!"

¹⁵Then the king returned and came to the Jordan. And Judah came to Gilgal, to go to meet the king, to escort the king across the Jordan. ¹⁶And Shimei the son of Gera, a Benjamite, who *was* from Bahurim, hurried and came down with the men of Judah to meet King David. ¹⁷*There were* a thousand men of Benjamin with him, and Ziba the servant of the house of Saul, and his fifteen sons and his twenty servants with him; and they went over the Jordan before the king. ¹⁸Then a ferryboat went across to carry over the king's household, and to do what he thought good.

David's Mercy to Shimei

Now Shimei the son of Gera fell down before the king when he had crossed the Jordan. ¹⁹Then he said to the king, "Do not let my lord impute iniquity to me, or remember what wrong your servant did on the day that my lord the king left Jerusalem, that the king should take *it* to heart. ²⁰For I, your servant, know that I have sinned. Therefore here I am, the first to come today of all the house of Joseph to go down to meet my lord the king."

²¹But Abishai the son of Zeruiah answered and said, "Shall not Shimei be put to death for this, because he cursed the Lord's anointed?"

²²And David said, "What have I to do with you, you sons of Zeruiah, that you should be adversaries to me today? Shall

any man be put to death today in Israel? For do I not know that today I *am* king over Israel?" ²³Therefore the king said to Shimei, "You shall not die." And the king swore to him.

David and Mephibosheth Meet

²⁴Now Mephibosheth the son of Saul came down to meet the king. And he had not cared for his feet, nor trimmed his mustache, nor washed his clothes, from the day the king departed until the day he returned in peace. ²⁵So it was, when he had come to Jerusalem to meet the king, that the king said to him, "Why did you not go with me, Mephibosheth?"

²⁶And he answered, "My lord, O king, my servant deceived me. For your servant said, 'I will saddle a donkey for myself, that I may ride on it and go to the king,' because your servant *is* lame. ²⁷And he has slandered your servant to my lord the king, but my lord the king *is* like the angel of God. Therefore do *what is* good in your eyes. ²⁸For all my father's house were but dead men before my lord the king. Yet you set your servant among those who eat at your own table. Therefore what right have I still to cry out anymore to the king?"

²⁹So the king said to him, "Why do you speak anymore of your matters? I have said, 'You and Ziba divide the land.' "

³⁰Then Mephibosheth said to the king, "Rather, let him take it all, inasmuch as my lord the king has come back in peace to his own house."

David's Kindness to Barzillai

³¹And Barzillai the Gileadite came down from Rogelim and went across the Jordan with the king, to escort him across the Jordan. ³²Now Barzillai was a very aged man, eighty years old. And he had provided the king with supplies while he stayed at Mahanaim, for he *was* a very rich man. ³³And the king said to Barzillai, "Come across with me, and I will provide for you while you are with me in Jerusalem."

³⁴But Barzillai said to the king, "How long have I to live, that I should go up with the king to Jerusalem? ³⁵I *am* today eighty years old. Can I discern between the good and bad? Can your servant taste what I eat

or what I drink? Can I hear any longer the voice of singing men and singing women? Why then should your servant be a further burden to my lord the king? ³⁶Your servant will go a little way across the Jordan with the king. And why should the king repay me *with* such a reward? ³⁷Please let your servant turn back again, that I may die in my own city, near the grave of my father and mother. But here is your servant Chimham; let him cross over with my lord the king, and do for him what seems good to you."

³⁸And the king answered, "Chimham shall cross over with me, and I will do for him what seems good to you. Now whatever you request of me, I will do for you." ³⁹Then all the people went over the Jordan. And when the king had crossed over, the king kissed Barzillai and blessed him, and he returned to his own place.

The Quarrel About the King

⁴⁰Now the king went on to Gilgal, and Chimham[a] went on with him. And all the people of Judah escorted the king, and also half the people of Israel. ⁴¹Just then all the men of Israel came to the king, and said to the king, "Why have our brethren, the men of Judah, stolen you away and brought the king, his household, and all David's men with him across the Jordan?"

⁴²So all the men of Judah answered the men of Israel, "Because the king *is* a close relative of ours. Why then are you angry over this matter? Have we ever eaten at the king's *expense?* Or has he given us any gift?"

⁴³And the men of Israel answered the men of Judah, and said, "We have ten shares in the king; therefore we also have more *right* to David than you. Why then do you despise us—were we not the first to advise bringing back our king?"

Yet the words of the men of Judah were fiercer than the words of the men of Israel.

The Rebellion of Sheba

20 And there happened to be there a rebel,[a] whose name *was* Sheba the son of Bichri, a Benjamite. And he blew a trumpet, and said:

"We have no share in David,
  Nor do we have inheritance in the
    son of Jesse;
  Every man to his tents, O Israel!"

²So every man of Israel deserted David, *and* followed Sheba the son of Bichri. But the men of Judah, from the Jordan as far as Jerusalem, remained loyal to their king.

³Now David came to his house at Jerusalem. And the king took the ten women, his concubines whom he had left to keep the house, and put them in seclusion and supported them, but did not go in to them. So they were shut up to the day of their death, living in widowhood.

⁴And the king said to Amasa, "Assemble the men of Judah for me within three days, and be present here yourself." ⁵So Amasa went to assemble *the men of* Judah. But he delayed longer than the set time which David had appointed him. ⁶And David said to Abishai, "Now Sheba the son of Bichri will do us more harm than Absalom. Take your lord's servants and pursue him, lest he find for himself fortified cities, and escape us." ⁷So Joab's men, with the Cherethites, the Pelethites, and all the mighty men, went out after him. And they went out of Jerusalem to pursue Sheba the son of Bichri. ⁸When they *were* at the large stone which *is* in Gibeon, Amasa came before them. Now Joab was dressed in battle armor; on it was a belt *with* a sword fastened in its sheath at his hips; and as he was going forward, it fell out. ⁹Then Joab said to Amasa, "*Are* you in health, my brother?" And Joab took Amasa by the beard with his right hand to kiss him. ¹⁰But Amasa did not notice the sword that *was* in Joab's hand. And he struck him with it in the stomach, and his entrails poured out on the ground; and he did not *strike* him again. Thus he died.

Then Joab and Abishai his brother pursued Sheba the son of Bichri. ¹¹Meanwhile one of Joab's men stood near Amasa, and said, "Whoever favors Joab and whoever *is* for David—follow Joab!" ¹²But Amasa wallowed in *his* blood in the middle of the highway. And when the man saw that all the people stood still, he moved Amasa from

---

19:40 ªMasoretic Text reads *Chimham*. **20:1**
ªLiterally *man of Belial*

the highway to the field and threw a garment over him, when he saw that everyone who came upon him halted. ¹³When he was removed from the highway, all the people went on after Joab to pursue Sheba the son of Bichri.

¹⁴And he went through all the tribes of Israel to Abel and Beth Maachah and all the Berites. So they were gathered together and also went after *Sheba*.ᵃ ¹⁵Then they came and besieged him in Abel of Beth Maachah; and they cast up a siege mound against the city, and it stood by the rampart. And all the people who *were* with Joab battered the wall to throw it down.

¹⁶Then a wise woman cried out from the city, "Hear, hear! Please say to Joab, 'Come nearby, that I may speak with you.' " ¹⁷When he had come near to her, the woman said, "*Are* you Joab?"

He answered, "I *am*."

Then she said to him, "Hear the words of your maidservant."

And he answered, "I am listening."

¹⁸So she spoke, saying, "They used to talk in former times, saying, 'They shall surely seek *guidance* at Abel,' and so they would end *disputes*. ¹⁹I *am among the* peaceable *and* faithful in Israel. You seek to destroy a city and a mother in Israel. Why would you swallow up the inheritance of the LORD?"

²⁰And Joab answered and said, "Far be it, far be it from me, that I should swallow up or destroy! ²¹That *is* not so. But a man from the mountains of Ephraim, Sheba the son of Bichri by name, has raised his hand against the king, against David. Deliver him only, and I will depart from the city."

So the woman said to Joab, "Watch, his head will be thrown to you over the wall." ²²Then the woman in her wisdom went to all the people. And they cut off the head of Sheba the son of Bichri, and threw *it* out to Joab. Then he blew a trumpet, and they withdrew from the city, every man to his tent. So Joab returned to the king at Jerusalem.

20:14 ᵃLiterally *him*

PARENTING MATTERS

Q: *How can we test our children's dress and appearance convictions?*

Here are some ways to test your preadolescent or teenager on his journey through the appearance traps.

Ask questions. Ask your child what he thinks about his appearance. Is he satisfied with his clothes, haircut, etc.? Why or why not?

Encourage your child to observe others. Without becoming critical, help your child or teen observe what others wear and the impression that clothing styles give. Ask him or her to share with you what their appearance communicates about them. What message are they sending to their peers? One good place to do this is while you're at a mall or a sporting event that attracts a large crowd.

Organize a panel discussion. If you are involved in your child's Sunday school class or youth group, suggest a panel discussion on the subject of dress. You will need a strong person to moderate the questions and discussion to keep it focused. Have the guys talk about what they feel when girls wear clothing that calls attention to their bodies. Likewise, have the girls tell the guys what they find attractive in the way a guy dresses. We have found that peers in these settings really can make observations and say things that you can't as a parent!

Always be ready to applaud. On the issue of appearance, the big deal is to applaud and compliment like crazy when your child makes good choices. Realize that their choices likely cost them more than you could ever understand.

David's Government Officers

[23]And Joab *was* over all the army of Israel; Benaiah the son of Jehoiada *was* over the Cherethites and the Pelethites; [24]Adoram *was* in charge of revenue; Jehoshaphat the son of Ahilud *was* recorder; [25]Sheva *was* scribe; Zadok and Abiathar *were* the priests; [26]and Ira the Jairite was a chief minister under David.

David Avenges the Gibeonites

21 Now there was a famine in the days of David for three years, year after year; and David inquired of the LORD. And the LORD answered, "*It is* because of Saul and *his* bloodthirsty house, because he killed the Gibeonites." [2]So the king called the Gibeonites and spoke to them. Now the Gibeonites *were* not of the children of Israel, but of the remnant of the Amorites; the children of Israel had sworn protection to them, but Saul had sought to kill them in his zeal for the children of Israel and Judah.

[3]Therefore David said to the Gibeonites, "What shall I do for you? And with what shall I make atonement, that you may bless the inheritance of the LORD?"

[4]And the Gibeonites said to him, "We will have no silver or gold from Saul or from his house, nor shall you kill any man in Israel for us."

So he said, "Whatever you say, I will do for you."

[5]Then they answered the king, "As for the man who consumed us and plotted against us, *that* we should be destroyed from remaining in any of the territories of Israel, [6]let seven men of his descendants be delivered to us, and we will hang them before the LORD in Gibeah of Saul, *whom* the LORD chose."

And the king said, "I will give *them.*"

[7]But the king spared Mephibosheth the son of Jonathan, the son of Saul, because of the LORD's oath that *was* between them, between David and Jonathan the son of Saul. [8]So the king took Armoni and Mephibosheth, the two sons of Rizpah the daughter of Aiah, whom she bore to Saul, and the five sons of Michal[a] the daughter of Saul, whom she brought up for Adriel the son of Barzillai the Meholathite; [9]and he delivered them into the hands of the Gibeonites, and they hanged them on the hill before the LORD. So they fell, *all* seven together, and were put to death in the days of harvest, in the first *days,* in the beginning of barley harvest.

[10]Now Rizpah the daughter of Aiah took sackcloth and spread it for herself on the rock, from the beginning of harvest until the late rains poured on them from heaven. And she did not allow the birds of the air to rest on them by day nor the beasts of the field by night.

[11]And David was told what Rizpah the daughter of Aiah, the concubine of Saul, had done. [12]Then David went and took the bones of Saul, and the bones of Jonathan his son, from the men of Jabesh Gilead who had stolen them from the street of Beth Shan,[a] where the Philistines had hung them up, after the Philistines had struck down Saul in Gilboa. [13]So he brought up the bones of Saul and the bones of Jonathan his son from there; and they gathered the bones of those who had been hanged. [14]They buried the bones of Saul and Jonathan his son in the country of Benjamin in Zelah, in the tomb of Kish his father. So they performed all that the king commanded. And after that God heeded the prayer for the land.

Philistine Giants Destroyed

[15]When the Philistines were at war again with Israel, David and his servants with him went down and fought against the Philistines; and David grew faint. [16]Then Ishbi-Benob, who *was* one of the sons of the giant, the weight of whose bronze spear *was* three hundred *shekels,* who was bearing a new *sword,* thought he could kill David. [17]But Abishai the son of Zeruiah came to his aid, and struck the Philistine and killed him. Then the men of David swore to him, saying, "You shall go out no more with us to battle, lest you quench the lamp of Israel."

[18]Now it happened afterward that there was again a battle with the Philistines at Gob. Then Sibbechai the Hushathite killed

21:8 [a]Or *Merab* (compare 1 Samuel 18:19 and 25:44; 2 Samuel 3:14 and 6:23) **21:12** [a]Spelled *Beth Shean* in Joshua 17:11 and elsewhere

Saph,ᵃ who *was* one of the sons of the giant. ¹⁹Again there was war at Gob with the Philistines, where Elhanan the son of Jaare-Oregimᵃ the Bethlehemite killed *the brother of* Goliath the Gittite, the shaft of whose spear *was* like a weaver's beam.

²⁰Yet again there was war at Gath, where there was a man of *great* stature, who had six fingers on each hand and six toes on each foot, twenty-four in number; and he also was born to the giant. ²¹So when he defied Israel, Jonathan the son of Shimea,ᵃ David's brother, killed him.

²²These four were born to the giant in Gath, and fell by the hand of David and by the hand of his servants.

Praise for God's Deliverance

22 Then David spoke to the LORD the words of this song, on the day when the LORD had delivered him from the hand of all his enemies, and from the hand of Saul. ²And he said:ᵃ

"The LORD *is* my rock and my fortress and my deliverer;
3　The God of my strength, in whom I will trust;
　My shield and the horn of my salvation,
　My stronghold and my refuge;
　My Savior, You save me from violence.
4　I will call upon the LORD, *who is worthy* to be praised;
　So shall I be saved from my enemies.

5　"When the waves of death surrounded me,
　The floods of ungodliness made me afraid.
6　The sorrows of Sheol surrounded me;
　The snares of death confronted me.
7　In my distress I called upon the LORD,
　And cried out to my God;
　He heard my voice from His temple,
　And my cry *entered* His ears.

8　"Then the earth shook and trembled;
　The foundations of heavenᵃ quaked and were shaken,
　Because He was angry.

9　Smoke went up from His nostrils,
　And devouring fire from His mouth;
　Coals were kindled by it.
10　He bowed the heavens also, and came down
　With darkness under His feet.
11　He rode upon a cherub, and flew;
　And He was seenᵃ upon the wings of the wind.
12　He made darkness canopies around Him,
　Dark waters *and* thick clouds of the skies.
13　From the brightness before Him
　Coals of fire were kindled.

14　"The LORD thundered from heaven,
　And the Most High uttered His voice.
15　He sent out arrows and scattered them;
　Lightning bolts, and He vanquished them.
16　Then the channels of the sea were seen,
　The foundations of the world were uncovered,
　At the rebuke of the LORD,
　At the blast of the breath of His nostrils.

17　"He sent from above, He took me,
　He drew me out of many waters.
18　He delivered me from my strong enemy,
　From those who hated me;
　For they were too strong for me.
19　They confronted me in the day of my calamity,
　But the LORD was my support.
20　He also brought me out into a broad place;
　He delivered me because He delighted in me.

21　"The LORD rewarded me according to my righteousness;

21:18 ᵃSpelled *Sippai* in 1 Chronicles 20:4　**21:19** ᵃSpelled *Jair* in 1 Chronicles 20:5　**21:21** ᵃSpelled *Shammah* in 1 Samuel 16:9 and elsewhere　**22:2** ᵃCompare Psalm 18　**22:8** ᵃFollowing Masoretic Text, Septuagint, and Targum; Syriac and Vulgate read *hills* (compare Psalm 18:7).　**22:11** ᵃFollowing Masoretic Text and Septuagint; many Hebrew manuscripts, Syriac, and Vulgate read *He flew* (compare Psalm 18:10); Targum reads *He spoke with power*.

According to the cleanness of my
  hands
He has recompensed me.

22 For I have kept the ways of the
  LORD,
And have not wickedly departed
  from my God.

23 For all His judgments *were* before
  me;
And *as for* His statutes, I did not
  depart from them.

24 I was also blameless before Him,
And I kept myself from my iniquity.

25 Therefore the LORD has recompensed
  me according to my
  righteousness,
According to my cleanness in His
  eyes.[a]

26 "With the merciful You will show
  Yourself merciful;
With a blameless man You will show
  Yourself blameless;

27 With the pure You will show
  Yourself pure;
And with the devious You will show
  Yourself shrewd.

28 You will save the humble people;
But Your eyes *are* on the haughty,
  that You may bring *them* down.

29 "For You *are* my lamp, O LORD;
The LORD shall enlighten my
  darkness.

30 For by You I can run against a troop;
By my God I can leap over a wall.

31 *As for* God, His way *is* perfect;
The word of the LORD *is* proven;
He *is* a shield to all who trust in Him.

32 "For who *is* God, except the LORD?
And who *is* a rock, except our God?

33 God *is* my strength *and* power,[a]
And He makes my[b] way perfect.

34 He makes my[a] feet like the *feet* of deer,
And sets me on my high places.

35 He teaches my hands to make war,
So that my arms can bend a bow of
  bronze.

36 "You have also given me the shield of
  Your salvation;
Your gentleness has made me great.

37 You enlarged my path under me;
So my feet did not slip.

38 "I have pursued my enemies and
  destroyed them;
Neither did I turn back again till
  they were destroyed.

39 And I have destroyed them and
  wounded them,
So that they could not rise;
They have fallen under my feet.

40 For You have armed me with
  strength for the battle;
You have subdued under me those
  who rose against me.

41 You have also given me the necks of
  my enemies,
So that I destroyed those who hated
  me.

42 They looked, but *there was* none to
  save;
Even to the LORD, but He did not
  answer them.

43 Then I beat them as fine as the dust
  of the earth;
I trod them like dirt in the streets,
And I spread them out.

44 "You have also delivered me from the
  strivings of my people;
You have kept me as the head of the
  nations.
A people I have not known shall
  serve me.

45 The foreigners submit to me;
As soon as they hear, they obey me.

46 The foreigners fade away,
And come frightened[a] from their
  hideouts.

47 "The LORD lives!
Blessed *be* my Rock!
Let God be exalted,
The Rock of my salvation!

22:25 [a]Septuagint, Syriac, and Vulgate read *the cleanness of my hands in His sight* (compare Psalm 18:24); Targum reads *my cleanness before His word.* **22:33** [a]Dead Sea Scrolls, Septuagint, Syriac, and Vulgate read *It is God who arms me with strength* (compare Psalm 18:32); Targum reads *It is God who sustains me with strength.* [b]Following Qere, Septuagint, Syriac, Targum, and Vulgate (compare Psalm 18:32); Kethib reads *His.* **22:34** [a]Following Qere, Septuagint, Syriac, Targum, and Vulgate (compare Psalm 18:33); Kethib reads *His.* **22:46** [a]Following Septuagint, Targum, and Vulgate (compare Psalm 18:45); Masoretic Text reads *gird themselves.*

He Saves the Humble

IN JULY OF 1995, Barbara and I traveled to Fort Collins, Colorado, for the U.S. Staff Conference of Campus Crusade for Christ. More than 3,000 staff members and volunteers made the pilgrimage from campuses, cities, and homes across America and from abroad to join forces and celebrate the cause of Christ.

Our first three days together were memorable.

The last three were unforgettable.

On the fourth day of the conference, Nancy Leigh DeMoss gave a message that ignited a fire. She spoke of our desperate need to turn from pride to humility, our need for spiritual brokenness and confession. Nancy vividly described the stark differences between proud people and broken people. Perhaps the greatest difference between the two is the one noted by David, the sweet singer of Israel, "You will save the humble people; but Your eyes are on the haughty, that You may bring them down" (22:28).

It is humility—a deep recognition and glad appreciation of the infinite gulf that yawns between us and Almighty God—that is the foundation of a right relationship with our Creator. God resists the proud, but gives grace to the humble (James 4:6; 1 Pet. 5:5).

48 *It is* God who avenges me,
And subdues the peoples
under me;

49 He delivers me from my enemies.
You also lift me up above those who
rise against me;
You have delivered me from the
violent man.

50 Therefore I will give thanks to You,
O LORD, among the Gentiles,
And sing praises to Your name.

51 *He is* the tower of salvation to His
king,

And shows mercy to His anointed,
To David and his descendants
forevermore."

David's Last Words

23 Now these *are* the last words of David.

Thus says David the son of Jesse;
Thus says the man raised up on high,
The anointed of the God of Jacob,
And the sweet psalmist of Israel:

2 "The Spirit of the LORD spoke by me,
And His word *was* on my tongue.

3 The God of Israel said,
The Rock of Israel spoke to me:
'He who rules over men *must be* just,
Ruling in the fear of God.

4 And *he shall be* like the light of the
morning *when* the sun rises,
A morning without clouds,
Like the tender grass *springing* out
of the earth,
By clear shining after rain.'

5 "Although my house *is* not so with God,
Yet He has made with me an
everlasting covenant,
Ordered in all *things* and secure.
For *this is* all my salvation and all
my desire;
Will He not make *it* increase?

6 But *the sons* of rebellion *shall* all *be*
as thorns thrust away,
Because they cannot be taken with
hands.

7 But the man *who* touches them
Must be armed with iron and the
shaft of a spear,
And they shall be utterly burned
with fire in *their* place."

David's Mighty Men

8 These *are* the names of the mighty men whom David had: Josheb-Basshebeth[a] the Tachmonite, chief among the captains.[b] He was called Adino the Eznite, because he had killed eight hundred men at one time. 9 And after him *was* Eleazar the son of Dodo,[a] the

---

23:8 [a]Literally *One Who Sits in the Seat* (compare 1 Chronicles 11:11) [b]Following Masoretic Text and Targum; Septuagint and Vulgate read *the three*. **23:9** [a]Spelled *Dodai* in 1 Chronicles 27:4

Ahohite, *one* of the three mighty men with David when they defied the Philistines *who* were gathered there for battle, and the men of Israel had retreated. [10]He arose and attacked the Philistines until his hand was weary, and his hand stuck to the sword. The LORD brought about a great victory that day; and the people returned after him only to plunder. [11]And after him *was* Shammah the son of Agee the Hararite. The Philistines had gathered together into a troop where there was a piece of ground full of lentils. So the people fled from the Philistines. [12]But he stationed himself in the middle of the field, defended it, and killed the Philistines. So the LORD brought about a great victory.

[13]Then three of the thirty chief men went down at harvest time and came to David at the cave of Adullam. And the troop of Philistines encamped in the Valley of Rephaim. [14]David *was* then in the stronghold, and the garrison of the Philistines *was* then *in* Bethlehem. [15]And David said with longing, "Oh, that someone would give me a drink of the water from the well of Bethlehem, which *is* by the gate!" [16]So the three mighty men broke through the camp of the Philistines, drew water from the well of Bethlehem that *was* by the gate, and took it and brought *it* to David. Nevertheless he would not drink it, but poured it out to the LORD. [17]And he said, "Far be it from me, O LORD, that I should do this! Is *this not* the blood of the men who went in *jeopardy of* their lives?" Therefore he would not drink it.

These things were done by the three mighty men.

[18]Now Abishai the brother of Joab, the son of Zeruiah, was chief of *another* three.[a] He lifted his spear against three hundred *men,* killed *them,* and won a name among *these* three. [19]Was he not the most honored of three? Therefore he became their captain. However, he did not attain to the *first* three.

[20]Benaiah *was* the son of Jehoiada, the son of a valiant man from Kabzeel, who had done many deeds. He had killed two lion-like heroes of Moab. He also had gone down and killed a lion in the midst of a pit on a snowy day. [21]And he killed an Egyptian, a spectacular man. The Egyptian *had* a spear in his hand; so he went down to him with a staff, wrested the spear out of the Egyptian's hand, and killed him with his own spear. [22]These *things* Benaiah the son of Jehoiada did, and won a name among three mighty men. [23]He was more honored than the thirty, but he did not attain to the *first* three. And David appointed him over his guard.

INTIMATE MOMENTS

Bring him a surprise from the grocery store—a magazine, a candy bar, or whatever else will let him know you were thinking about him.

[24]Asahel the brother of Joab *was* one of the thirty; Elhanan the son of Dodo of Bethlehem, [25]Shammah the Harodite, Elika the Harodite, [26]Helez the Paltite, Ira the son of Ikkesh the Tekoite, [27]Abiezer the Anathothite, Mebunnai the Hushathite, [28]Zalmon the Ahohite, Maharai the Netophathite, [29]Heleb the son of Baanah (the Netophathite), Ittai the son of Ribai from Gibeah of the children of Benjamin, [30]Benaiah a Pirathonite, Hiddai from the brooks of Gaash, [31]Abi-Albon the Arbathite, Azmaveth the Barhumite, [32]Eliahba the Shaalbonite (of the sons of Jashen), Jonathan, [33]Shammah the Hararite, Ahiam the son of Sharar the Hararite, [34]Eliphelet the son of Ahasbai, the son of the Maachathite, Eliam the son of Ahithophel the Gilonite, [35]Hezrai[a] the Carmelite, Paarai the Arbite, [36]Igal the son of Nathan of Zobah, Bani the Gadite, [37]Zelek the Ammonite, Naharai the Beerothite (armorbearer of Joab the son of Zeruiah), [38]Ira the Ithrite, Gareb the Ithrite, [39]*and* Uriah the Hittite: thirty-seven in all.

David's Census of Israel and Judah

24 Again the anger of the LORD was aroused against Israel, and He

---

23:18 [a]Following Masoretic Text, Septuagint, and Vulgate; some Hebrew manuscripts and Syriac read *thirty;* Targum reads *the mighty men.* **23:35** [a]Spelled *Hezro* in 1 Chronicles 11:37

Embody God's Grace and Mercy

AS THE YEARS ROLL ON, I want to increasingly exhibit both the grace and the mercy of God. In His grace, God *gives us something good* that we do not deserve. In His mercy, He *withholds something bad* that we do deserve. We must learn to demonstrate both.

When someone in your family comes to you consumed with guilt, and you truly shower that individual with both grace and mercy, at that moment you may be the best picture of God that your loved one will ever get.

Some time ago the Lord enabled me to act like this toward two men who had deeply hurt me. Both said to me, "I cannot *believe* that you can give me such grace." In this particular circumstance, God gave me such a unique love for both men that I could say, "I love you. It does not matter. And if your heart is repentant, it does not matter to God."

David's only source of comfort after his own sin was God's grace and mercy when, after his own sin, he told the prophet Gad, "Please let us fall into the hand of the LORD, for His mercies are great" (24:14). David *knew*. Make sure your family knows, too.

Do you practice grace and mercy at home, where it counts?

---

moved David against them to say, "Go, number Israel and Judah."

2So the king said to Joab the commander of the army who *was* with him, "Now go throughout all the tribes of Israel, from Dan to Beersheba, and count the people, that I may know the number of the people."

3And Joab said to the king, "Now may the LORD your God add to the people a hundred times more than there are, and may the eyes of my lord the king see *it.* But why does my lord the king desire this thing?" 4Nevertheless the king's word prevailed against Joab and against the captains of the army. Therefore Joab and the captains of the army went out from the presence of the king to count the people of Israel.

5And they crossed over the Jordan and camped in Aroer, on the right side of the town which *is* in the midst of the ravine of Gad, and toward Jazer. 6Then they came to Gilead and to the land of Tahtim Hodshi; they came to Dan Jaan and around to Sidon; 7and they came to the stronghold of Tyre and to all the cities of the Hivites and the Canaanites. Then they went out to South Judah *as far as* Beersheba. 8So when they had gone through all the land, they came to Jerusalem at the end of nine months and twenty days. 9Then Joab gave the sum of the number of the people to the king. And there were in Israel eight hundred thousand valiant men who drew the sword, and the men of Judah were five hundred thousand men.

The Judgment on David's Sin

10And David's heart condemned him after he had numbered the people. So David said to the LORD, "I have sinned greatly in what I have done; but now, I pray, O LORD, take away the iniquity of Your servant, for I have done very foolishly."

11Now when David arose in the morning, the word of the LORD came to the prophet Gad, David's seer, saying, 12"Go and tell David, 'Thus says the LORD: "I offer you three *things;* choose one of them for yourself, that I may do *it* to you."' " 13So Gad came to David and told him; and he said to him, "Shall sevena years of famine come to you in your land? Or shall you flee three months before your enemies, while they pursue you? Or shall there be three days' plague in your land? Now consider and see what answer I should take back to Him who sent me."

14And David said to Gad, "I am in great distress. Please let us fall into the hand of the LORD, for His mercies *are* great; but do not let me fall into the hand of man."

15So the LORD sent a plague upon Israel

24:13 aFollowing Masoretic Text, Syriac, Targum, and Vulgate; Septuagint reads *three* (compare 1 Chronicles 21:12).

from the morning till the appointed time. From Dan to Beersheba seventy thousand men of the people died. [16]And when the angel[a] stretched out His hand over Jerusalem to destroy it, the LORD relented from the destruction, and said to the angel who was destroying the people, "It is enough; now restrain your hand." And the angel of the LORD was by the threshing floor of Araunah[b] the Jebusite.

[17]Then David spoke to the LORD when he saw the angel who was striking the people, and said, "Surely I have sinned, and I have done wickedly; but these sheep, what have they done? Let Your hand, I pray, be against me and against my father's house."

The Altar on the Threshing Floor

[18]And Gad came that day to David and said to him, "Go up, erect an altar to the LORD on the threshing floor of Araunah the Jebusite." [19]So David, according to the word of Gad, went up as the LORD commanded. [20]Now Araunah looked, and saw the king and his servants coming toward him. So

Araunah went out and bowed before the king with his face to the ground.

[21]Then Araunah said, "Why has my lord the king come to his servant?"

And David said, "To buy the threshing floor from you, to build an altar to the LORD, that the plague may be withdrawn from the people."

[22]Now Araunah said to David, "Let my lord the king take and offer up whatever *seems* good to him. Look, *here are* oxen for burnt sacrifice, and threshing implements and the yokes of the oxen for wood. [23]All these, O king, Araunah has given to the king."

And Araunah said to the king, "May the LORD your God accept you."

[24]Then the king said to Araunah, "No, but I will surely buy *it* from you for a price; nor will I offer burnt offerings to the LORD my God with that which costs me nothing." So David bought the threshing floor and the oxen for fifty shekels of silver. [25]And David built there an altar to the LORD, and offered burnt offerings and peace offerings. So the LORD heeded the prayers for the land, and the plague was withdrawn from Israel.

24:16 [a]Or *Angel* [b]Spelled *Ornan* in 1 Chronicles 21:15

1 KINGS

THE BOOK OF 1 KINGS PICKS UP where 2 Samuel leaves off, following the death of King David. Together with 2 Kings, these books provide us with a full account of the history of Israel, from the time of Solomon all the way until the nation enters a seventy-year period of captivity in Babylon.

Solomon's reign begins with promise and ends with division. In chapter 3, God invites Solomon to ask for whatever he wants. Solomon asks for wisdom, which pleases the Lord. Over the years, however, Solomon gradually goes his own way. He marries 700 foreign wives and takes 300 concubines—in direct disobedience to God's Word (see Deut. 17:17)—and these pagan women turn his heart away from the Lord (11:3). By the end of his reign, the single nation of Israel is ready to divide into the northern and southern kingdoms. The tribes of Judah and Benjamin live in and around Jerusalem, while the remaining ten tribes comprise the northern kingdom, living scattered throughout Galilee.

Solomon wrote three books of the Bible (Ecclesiastes, the Song of Solomon, and most of Proverbs), all three of which illustrate his great wisdom. Yet they also illustrate that even great wisdom, divorced from a living and dynamic walk with God, will always end badly. His life provides us with a stern reminder to raise our children with both wisdom and character in mind. The two must go hand-in-hand. To overemphasize the pursuit of knowledge, as some Christian parents do, without working to cultivate character in a child's life, is a major mistake. We must take care not to forget one of Solomon's wisest sayings (as he himself apparently did), "The fear of the Lord is the beginning of knowledge" (Prov. 1:7).

First Kings also recounts the ministry of one of the first and most influential prophets of Israel, Elijah. His famed confrontation with the priests of Baal on Mt. Carmel is recounted in 1 Kings 18. We could scarcely do better than to teach our children to speak as did Elijah so often, "As the Lord of hosts lives, before whom I stand."

Adonijah Presumes to Be King

1 Now King David was old, advanced in years; and they put covers on him, but he could not get warm. ²Therefore his servants said to him, "Let a young woman, a virgin, be sought for our lord the king, and let her stand before the king, and let her care for him; and let her lie in your bosom, that our lord the king may be warm." ³So they sought for a lovely young woman throughout all the territory of Israel, and found Abishag the Shunammite, and brought her to the king. ⁴The young woman *was* very lovely; and she cared for the king, and served him; but the king did not know her.

⁵Then Adonijah the son of Haggith exalted himself, saying, "I will be king"; and he prepared for himself chariots and horsemen, and fifty men to run before him. ⁶(And his father had not rebuked him at any time by saying, "Why have you done so?" He *was* also very good-looking. *His mother* had borne him after Absalom.) ⁷Then he conferred with Joab the son of Zeruiah and with Abiathar the priest, and they followed and helped Adonijah. ⁸But Zadok the priest, Benaiah the son of Jehoiada, Nathan the prophet, Shimei, Rei, and the mighty men who *belonged* to David were not with Adonijah.

⁹And Adonijah sacrificed sheep and oxen and fattened cattle by the stone of Zoheleth, which *is* by En Rogel; he also invited all his brothers, the king's sons, and all the men of Judah, the king's servants. ¹⁰But he did not invite Nathan the prophet, Benaiah, the mighty men, or Solomon his brother.

¹¹So Nathan spoke to Bathsheba the mother of Solomon, saying, "Have you not heard that Adonijah the son of Haggith has become king, and David our lord does not know *it?* ¹²Come, please, let me now give you advice, that you may save your own life and the life of your son Solomon. ¹³Go immediately to King David and say to him, 'Did you not, my lord, O king, swear to your maidservant, saying, "Assuredly your son Solomon shall reign after me, and he shall sit on my throne"? Why then has Adonijah become king?' ¹⁴Then, while you are still

talking there with the king, I also will come in after you and confirm your words."

¹⁵So Bathsheba went into the chamber to the king. (Now the king was very old, and Abishag the Shunammite was serving the king.) ¹⁶And Bathsheba bowed and did homage to the king. Then the king said, "What is your wish?"

¹⁷Then she said to him, "My lord, you swore by the LORD your God to your maidservant, *saying*, 'Assuredly Solomon your son shall reign after me, and he shall sit on my throne.' ¹⁸So now, look! Adonijah has become king; and now, my lord the king, you do not know about *it*. ¹⁹He has sacrificed oxen and fattened cattle and sheep in abundance, and has invited all the sons of the king, Abiathar the priest, and Joab the commander of the army; but Solomon your servant he has not invited. ²⁰And as for you, my lord, O king, the eyes of all Israel *are* on you, that you should tell them who will sit on the throne of my lord the king after him. ²¹Otherwise it will happen, when my lord the king rests with his fathers, that I and my son Solomon will be counted as offenders."

INTIMATE MOMENTS

What kinds of games does your husband like to play? Cards? Board games? Sports? Play his favorite one, and concentrate on having as much fun as possible.

²²And just then, while she was still talking with the king, Nathan the prophet also came in. ²³So they told the king, saying, "Here is Nathan the prophet." And when he came in before the king, he bowed down before the king with his face to the ground. ²⁴And Nathan said, "My lord, O king, have you said, 'Adonijah shall reign after me, and he shall sit on my throne'? ²⁵For he has gone down today, and has sacrificed oxen and fattened cattle and sheep in abundance, and has invited all the king's sons, and the commanders of the army, and Abiathar the priest; and look! They are eating and drinking before him; and they say, '*Long* live King

Adonijah!" 26But he has not invited me—me your servant—nor Zadok the priest, nor Benaiah the son of Jehoiada, nor your servant Solomon. 27Has this thing been done by my lord the king, and you have not told your servant who should sit on the throne of my lord the king after him?"

David Proclaims Solomon King

28Then King David answered and said, "Call Bathsheba to me." So she came into the king's presence and stood before the king. 29And the king took an oath and said, "*As* the LORD lives, who has redeemed my life from every distress, 30just as I swore to you by the LORD God of Israel, saying, 'Assuredly Solomon your son shall be king after me, and he shall sit on my throne in my place,' so I certainly will do this day."

31Then Bathsheba bowed with *her* face to the earth, and paid homage to the king, and said, "Let my lord King David live forever!"

32And King David said, "Call to me Zadok the priest, Nathan the prophet, and Benaiah the son of Jehoiada." So they came before the king. 33The king also said to them, "Take with you the servants of your lord, and have Solomon my son ride on my own mule, and take him down to Gihon. 34There let Zadok the priest and Nathan the prophet anoint him king over Israel; and blow the horn, and say, '*Long* live King Solomon!' 35Then you shall come up after him, and he shall come and sit on my throne, and he shall be king in my place. For I have appointed him to be ruler over Israel and Judah."

36Benaiah the son of Jehoiada answered the king and said, "Amen! May the LORD God of my lord the king say so *too.* 37As the LORD has been with my lord the king, even so may He be with Solomon, and make his throne greater than the throne of my lord King David."

38So Zadok the priest, Nathan the prophet, Benaiah the son of Jehoiada, the Cherethites, and the Pelethites went down and had Solomon ride on King David's mule, and took him to Gihon. 39Then Zadok the priest took a horn of oil from the tabernacle and anointed Solomon. And they blew the horn, and all the people said, "*Long* live King Solomon!" 40And all the people went up after him; and the people played the flutes and rejoiced with great joy, so that the earth *seemed to* split with their sound.

41Now Adonijah and all the guests who *were* with him heard *it* as they finished eating. And when Joab heard the sound of the horn, he said, "Why *is* the city in such a noisy uproar?" 42While he was still speaking, there came Jonathan, the son of Abiathar the priest. And Adonijah said to him, "Come in, for you *are* a prominent man, and bring good news."

43Then Jonathan answered and said to Adonijah, "No! Our lord King David has made Solomon king. 44The king has sent with him Zadok the priest, Nathan the prophet, Benaiah the son of Jehoiada, the Cherethites, and the Pelethites; and they have made him ride on the king's mule. 45So Zadok the priest and Nathan the prophet have anointed him king at Gihon; and they have gone up from there rejoicing, so that the city is in an uproar. This *is* the noise that you have heard. 46Also Solomon sits on the throne of the kingdom. 47And moreover the king's servants have gone to bless our lord King David, saying, 'May God make the name of Solomon better than your name, and may He make his throne greater than your throne.' Then the king bowed himself on the bed. 48Also the king said thus, 'Blessed *be* the LORD God of Israel, who has given *one* to sit on my throne this day, while my eyes see *it!*'"

49So all the guests who were with Adonijah were afraid, and arose, and each one went his way.

50Now Adonijah was afraid of Solomon; so he arose, and went and took hold of the horns of the altar. 51And it was told Solomon, saying, "Indeed Adonijah is afraid of King Solomon; for look, he has taken hold of the horns of the altar, saying, 'Let King Solomon swear to me today that he will not put his servant to death with the sword.'"

52Then Solomon said, "If he proves himself a worthy man, not one hair of him shall fall to the earth; but if wickedness is found in him, he shall die." 53So King Solomon sent them to bring him down from the altar. And he came and fell down before King Solomon; and Solomon said to him, "Go to your house."

David's Instructions to Solomon

2 Now the days of David drew near that he should die, and he charged Solomon his son, saying: [2]"I go the way of all the earth; be strong, therefore, and prove yourself a man. [3]And keep the charge of the LORD your God: to walk in His ways, to keep His statutes, His commandments, His judgments, and His testimonies, as it is written in the Law of Moses, that you may prosper in all that you do and wherever you turn; [4]that the LORD may fulfill His word which He spoke concerning me, saying, 'If your sons take heed to their way, to walk before Me in truth with all their heart and with all their soul,' He said, 'you shall not lack a man on the throne of Israel.'

[5]"Moreover you know also what Joab the son of Zeruiah did to me, *and* what he did to the two commanders of the armies of Israel, to Abner the son of Ner and Amasa the son of Jether, whom he killed. And he shed the blood of war in peacetime, and put the blood of war on his belt that *was* around his waist, and on his sandals that *were* on his feet. [6]Therefore do according to your wisdom, and do not let his gray hair go down to the grave in peace.

[7]"But show kindness to the sons of Barzillai the Gileadite, and let them be among those who eat at your table, for so they came to me when I fled from Absalom your brother.

[8]"And see, *you have* with you Shimei the son of Gera, a Benjamite from Bahurim, who cursed me with a malicious curse in the day when I went to Mahanaim. But he came down to meet me at the Jordan, and I swore to him by the LORD, saying, 'I will not put you to death with the sword.' [9]Now therefore, do not hold him guiltless, for you *are* a wise man and know what you ought to do to him; but bring his gray hair down to the grave with blood."

Death of David

[10]So David rested with his fathers, and was buried in the City of David. [11]The period that David reigned over Israel *was* forty years; seven years he reigned in Hebron, and in Jerusalem he reigned thirty-three years. [12]Then Solomon sat on the throne of his father David; and his kingdom was firmly established.

Solomon Executes Adonijah

[13]Now Adonijah the son of Haggith came to Bathsheba the mother of Solomon. So she said, "Do you come peaceably?"

And he said, "Peaceably." [14]Moreover he said, "I have something *to say* to you."

And she said, "Say it."

[15]Then he said, "You know that the kingdom was mine, and all Israel had set their expectations on me, that I should reign. However, the kingdom has been turned over, and has become my brother's; for it was his from the LORD. [16]Now I ask one petition of you; do not deny me."

And she said to him, "Say it."

[17]Then he said, "Please speak to King Solomon, for he will not refuse you, that he may give me Abishag the Shunammite as wife."

[18]So Bathsheba said, "Very well, I will speak for you to the king."

[19]Bathsheba therefore went to King Solomon, to speak to him for Adonijah. And the king rose up to meet her and bowed down to her, and sat down on his throne and had a throne set for the king's mother; so she sat at his right hand. [20]Then she said, "I desire one small petition of you; do not refuse me."

And the king said to her, "Ask it, my mother, for I will not refuse you."

[21]So she said, "Let Abishag the Shunammite be given to Adonijah your brother as wife."

[22]And King Solomon answered and said to his mother, "Now why do you ask Abishag the Shunammite for Adonijah? Ask for him the kingdom also—for he *is* my older brother—for him, and for Abiathar the priest, and for Joab the son of Zeruiah." [23]Then King Solomon swore by the LORD, saying, "May God do so to me, and more also, if Adonijah has not spoken this word against his own life! [24]Now therefore, *as* the LORD lives, who has confirmed me and set me on the throne of David my father, and who has established a house[a] for me, as He promised, Adonijah shall be put to death today!"

2:24 [a]That is, a royal dynasty

²⁵So King Solomon sent by the hand of Benaiah the son of Jehoiada; and he struck him down, and he died.

Abiathar Exiled, Joab Executed

²⁶And to Abiathar the priest the king said, "Go to Anathoth, to your own fields, for you *are* deserving of death; but I will not put you to death at this time, because you carried the ark of the Lord GOD before my father David, and because you were afflicted every time my father was afflicted." ²⁷So Solomon removed Abiathar from being priest to the LORD, that he might fulfill the word of the LORD which He spoke concerning the house of Eli at Shiloh.

²⁸Then news came to Joab, for Joab had defected to Adonijah, though he had not defected to Absalom. So Joab fled to the tabernacle of the LORD, and took hold of the horns of the altar. ²⁹And King Solomon was told, "Joab has fled to the tabernacle of the LORD; there *he is,* by the altar." Then Solomon sent Benaiah the son of Jehoiada, saying, "Go, strike him down." ³⁰So Benaiah went to the tabernacle of the LORD, and said to him, "Thus says the king, 'Come out!'"

And he said, "No, but I will die here." And Benaiah brought back word to the king, saying, "Thus said Joab, and thus he answered me."

³¹Then the king said to him, "Do as he has said, and strike him down and bury him, that you may take away from me and from the house of my father the innocent blood which Joab shed. ³²So the LORD will return his blood on his head, because he struck down two men more righteous and better than he, and killed them with the sword—Abner the son of Ner, the commander of the army of Israel, and Amasa the son of Jether, the commander of the army of Judah—though my father David did not know *it.* ³³Their blood shall therefore return upon the head of Joab and upon the head of his descendants forever. But upon David and his descendants, upon his house and his throne, there shall be peace forever from the LORD."

³⁴So Benaiah the son of Jehoiada went up and struck and killed him; and he was buried in his own house in the wilderness. ³⁵The king put Benaiah the son of Jehoiada in his place over the army, and the king put Zadok the priest in the place of Abiathar.

Shimei Executed

³⁶Then the king sent and called for Shimei, and said to him, "Build yourself a house in Jerusalem and dwell there, and do not go out from there anywhere. ³⁷For it shall be, on the day you go out and cross the Brook Kidron, know for certain you shall surely die; your blood shall be on your own head."

³⁸And Shimei said to the king, "The saying *is* good. As my lord the king has said, so your servant will do." So Shimei dwelt in Jerusalem many days.

³⁹Now it happened at the end of three years, that two slaves of Shimei ran away to Achish the son of Maachah, king of Gath. And they told Shimei, saying, "Look, your slaves *are* in Gath!" ⁴⁰So Shimei arose, saddled his donkey, and went to Achish at Gath to seek his slaves. And Shimei went and brought his slaves from Gath. ⁴¹And Solomon was told that Shimei had gone from Jerusalem to Gath and had come back. ⁴²Then the king sent and called for Shimei, and said to him, "Did I not make you swear by the LORD, and warn you, saying, 'Know for certain that on the day you go out and travel anywhere, you shall surely die'? And you said to me, 'The word I have heard *is* good.' ⁴³Why then have you not kept the oath of the LORD and the commandment that I gave you?" ⁴⁴The king said moreover to Shimei, "You know, as your heart acknowledges, all the wickedness that you did to my father David; therefore the LORD will return your wickedness on your own head. ⁴⁵But King Solomon *shall be* blessed, and the throne of David shall be established before the LORD forever."

⁴⁶So the king commanded Benaiah the son of Jehoiada; and he went out and struck him down, and he died. Thus the kingdom was established in the hand of Solomon.

Solomon Requests Wisdom

3 Now Solomon made a treaty with Pharaoh king of Egypt, and married Pharaoh's daughter; then he brought her to the City of David until he had finished building his own house, and the house of the LORD, and the wall all around Jerusalem.

²Meanwhile the people sacrificed at the high places, because there was no house built for the name of the LORD until those days. ³And Solomon loved the LORD, walking in the statutes of his father David, except that he sacrificed and burned incense at the high places.

⁴Now the king went to Gibeon to sacrifice there, for that *was* the great high place: Solomon offered a thousand burnt offerings on that altar. ⁵At Gibeon the LORD appeared to Solomon in a dream by night; and God said, "Ask! What shall I give you?"

⁶And Solomon said: "You have shown great mercy to Your servant David my father, because he walked before You in truth, in righteousness, and in uprightness of heart with You; You have continued this great kindness for him, and You have given him a son to sit on his throne, as *it is* this day. ⁷Now, O LORD my God, You have made Your servant king instead of my father David, but I *am* a little child; I do not know *how* to go out or come in. ⁸And Your servant *is* in the midst of Your people whom You have chosen, a great people, too numerous to be numbered or counted. ⁹Therefore give to Your servant an understanding heart to judge Your people, that I may discern between good and evil. For who is able to judge this great people of Yours?"

¹⁰The speech pleased the Lord, that Solomon had asked this thing. ¹¹Then God said to him: "Because you have asked this thing, and have not asked long life for yourself, nor have asked riches for yourself, nor have asked the life of your enemies, but have asked for yourself understanding to discern justice, ¹²behold, I have done according to your words; see, I have given you a wise and understanding heart, so that there has not been anyone like you before you, nor shall any like you arise after you. ¹³And I have also given you what you have not asked: both riches and honor, so that there shall not be anyone like you among the kings all your days. ¹⁴So if you walk in My ways, to keep My statutes and My commandments, as your father David walked, then I will lengthen your days."

¹⁵Then Solomon awoke; and indeed it had been a dream. And he came to Jerusalem and stood before the ark of the covenant of the

LORD, offered up burnt offerings, offered peace offerings, and made a feast for all his servants.

Solomon's Wise Judgment

¹⁶Now two women *who were* harlots came to the king, and stood before him. ¹⁷And one woman said, "O my lord, this woman and I dwell in the same house; and I gave birth while she *was* in the house.

18Then it happened, the third day after I had given birth, that this woman also gave birth. And we *were* together; no one *was* with us in the house, except the two of us in the house. 19And this woman's son died in the night, because she lay on him. 20So she arose in the middle of the night and took my son from my side, while your maidservant slept, and laid him in her bosom, and laid her dead

ROMANCE FAQ

Q: *How can a woman encourage her husband to be a spiritual leader?*

When we first married, it never occurred to me that Dennis didn't know how to provide spiritual leadership. I didn't know that for most husbands this has to be learned in marriage.

It may take years for a man to grow spiritually so that he can lead his wife. Many never had a good model of spiritual leadership as they grew up. It's important to realize there are different ways to give spiritual leadership in the home.

My big mistake early on was thinking that spiritual leadership meant you have daily devotions. I didn't realize that a man can give spiritual leadership in all kinds of other ways. If he points his children to Christ and to the Scripture, then he is giving spiritual leadership. It doesn't have to be in a formal Bible study.

Pray that God will give your husband a heart to lead your family spiritually. Be grateful for any kind of spiritual leadership he displays. Be patient, because it may not come as quickly as you would like. Find a good resource (devotional) for your family to use and set him up to win with your family by scheduling the time and encouraging him to lead. Finally, affirm your husband for what he does right. Even if it is as little as praying over meals, thank him for the spiritual leadership that he initiates.

One caution: Whatever you do, do not nag. There are ways to encourage him to be the spiritual leader without constantly nagging him.

child in my bosom. 21And when I rose in the morning to nurse my son, there he was, dead. But when I had examined him in the morning, indeed, he was not my son whom I had borne."

22Then the other woman said, "No! But the living one *is* my son, and the dead one *is* your son."

And the first woman said, "No! But the dead one *is* your son, and the living one *is* my son."

Thus they spoke before the king.

23And the king said, "The one says, 'This *is* my son, who lives, and your son *is* the dead one'; and the other says, 'No! But your son *is* the dead one, and my son *is* the living one.'" 24Then the king said, "Bring me a sword." So they brought a sword before the king. 25And the king said, "Divide the living child in two, and give half to one, and half to the other."

26Then the woman whose son *was* living spoke to the king, for she yearned with compassion for her son; and she said, "O my lord, give her the living child, and by no means kill him!"

But the other said, "Let him be neither mine nor yours, *but* divide *him*."

27So the king answered and said, "Give the first woman the living child, and by no means kill him; she *is* his mother."

28And all Israel heard of the judgment which the king had rendered; and they feared the king, for they saw that the wisdom of God *was* in him to administer justice.

Solomon's Administration

4 So King Solomon was king over all Israel. 2And these *were* his officials: Azariah the son of Zadok, the priest; 3Elihoreph and Ahijah, the sons of Shisha, scribes; Jehoshaphat the son of Ahilud, the recorder; 4Benaiah the son of Jehoiada, over the army; Zadok and Abiathar, the priests; 5Azariah the son of Nathan, over the officers; Zabud the son of Nathan, a priest *and* the king's friend; 6Ahishar, over the household; and Adoniram the son of Abda, over the labor force.

7And Solomon had twelve governors over all Israel, who provided food for the king and his household; each one made provision for one month of the year. 8These *are* their names: Ben-Hur,[a] in the mountains of Ephraim; [9]Ben-Deker,[a] in Makaz, Shaalbim, Beth Shemesh, and Elon Beth Hanan; [10]Ben-Hesed,[a] in Arubboth; to him *belonged* Sochoh and all the land of Hepher; [11]Ben-Abinadab,[a] *in* all the regions of Dor; he had Taphath the daughter of Solomon as wife; [12]Baana the son of Ahilud, *in* Taanach, Megiddo, and all Beth Shean, which *is* beside Zaretan below Jezreel, from Beth Shean to Abel Meholah, as far as the other side of Jokneam; [13]Ben-Geber,[a] in Ramoth Gilead; to him *belonged* the towns of Jair the son of Manasseh, in Gilead; to him *also belonged* the region of Argob in Bashan—sixty large cities with walls and bronze gate-bars; [14]Ahinadab the son of Iddo, *in* Mahanaim; [15]Ahimaaz, in Naphtali; he also took Basemath the daughter of Solomon as wife; [16]Baanah the son of Hushai, in Asher and Aloth; [17]Jehoshaphat the son of Paruah, in Issachar; [18]Shimei the son of Elah, in Benjamin; [19]Geber the son of Uri, in the land of Gilead, *in* the country of Sihon king of the Amorites, and of Og king of Bashan. *He was* the only governor who *was* in the land.

Prosperity and Wisdom of Solomon's Reign

[20]Judah and Israel *were* as numerous as the sand by the sea in multitude, eating and drinking and rejoicing. [21]So Solomon reigned over all kingdoms from the River[a] *to* the land of the Philistines, as far as the border of Egypt. *They* brought tribute and served Solomon all the days of his life.

[22]Now Solomon's provision for one day was thirty kors of fine flour, sixty kors of meal, [23]ten fatted oxen, twenty oxen from the pastures, and one hundred sheep, besides deer, gazelles, roebucks, and fatted fowl.

[24]For he had dominion over all *the region* on this side of the River[a] from Tiphsah even to Gaza, namely over all the kings on

this side of the River; and he had peace on every side all around him. [25]And Judah and Israel dwelt safely, each man under his vine and his fig tree, from Dan as far as Beersheba, all the days of Solomon.

[26]Solomon had forty[a] thousand stalls of horses for his chariots, and twelve thousand horsemen. [27]And these governors, each man in his month, provided food for King Solomon and for all who came to King Solomon's table. There was no lack in their supply. [28]They also brought barley and straw to the proper place, for the horses and steeds, each man according to his charge.

[29]And God gave Solomon wisdom and exceedingly great understanding, and largeness of heart like the sand on the seashore. [30]Thus Solomon's wisdom excelled the wisdom of all the men of the East and all the wisdom of Egypt. [31]For he was wiser than all men—than Ethan the Ezrahite, and Heman, Chalcol, and Darda, the sons of Mahol; and his fame was in all the surrounding nations. [32]He spoke three thousand proverbs, and his songs were one thousand and five. [33]Also he spoke of trees, from the cedar tree of Lebanon even to the hyssop that springs out of the wall; he spoke also of animals, of birds, of creeping things, and of fish. [34]And men of all nations, from all the kings of the earth who had heard of his wisdom, came to hear the wisdom of Solomon.

Solomon Prepares to Build the Temple

5 Now Hiram king of Tyre sent his servants to Solomon, because he heard that they had anointed him king in place of his father, for Hiram had always loved David. [2]Then Solomon sent to Hiram, saying:

3　　You know how my father David could not build a house for the name of the LORD his God because of the wars which were fought against him on every side, until the LORD put *his* foes[a] under the soles of his feet.

4　　But now the LORD my God has given me rest on every side; *there is* neither adversary nor evil occurrence.

5　　And behold, I propose to build a house for the name of the LORD my God, as the LORD spoke to my father David, saying, "Your son, whom I

4:8 [a]Literally *Son of Hur*　**4:9** [a]Literally *Son of Deker*　**4:10** [a]Literally *Son of Hesed*　**4:11** [a]Literally *Son of Abinadab*　**4:13** [a]Literally *Son of Geber*　**4:21** [a]That is, the Euphrates　**4:24** [a]That is, the Euphrates　**4:26** [a]Following Masoretic Text and most other authorities; some manuscripts of the Septuagint read *four* (compare 2 Chronicles 9:25).　**5:3** [a]Literally *them*

will set on your throne in your place, he shall build the house for My name."

6   Now therefore, command that they cut down cedars for me from Lebanon; and my servants will be with your servants, and I will pay you wages for your servants according to whatever you say. For you know *there is* none among us who has skill to cut timber like the Sidonians.

7So it was, when Hiram heard the words of Solomon, that he rejoiced greatly and said,

Blessed *be* the LORD this day, for He has given David a wise son over this great people!

8Then Hiram sent to Solomon, saying:

I have considered *the message* which you sent me, *and* I will do all you desire concerning the cedar and cypress logs.

9   My servants shall bring *them* down from Lebanon to the sea; I will float them in rafts by sea to the place you indicate to me, and will have them broken apart there; then you can take *them* away. And you shall fulfill my desire by giving food for my household.

10Then Hiram gave Solomon cedar and cypress logs *according to* all his desire. 11And Solomon gave Hiram twenty thousand kors of wheat *as* food for his household, and twentya kors of pressed oil. Thus Solomon gave to Hiram year by year.

12So the LORD gave Solomon wisdom, as He had promised him; and there was peace between Hiram and Solomon, and the two of them made a treaty together.

13Then King Solomon raised up a labor force out of all Israel; and the labor force was thirty thousand men. 14And he sent them to Lebanon, ten thousand a month in shifts: they were one month in Lebanon *and* two months at home; Adoniram *was* in charge of the labor force. 15Solomon had seventy thousand who carried burdens, and eighty thousand who quarried *stone* in the mountains, 16besides three thousand three hundreda from the chiefs of Solomon's deputies, who supervised the people who labored in the work. 17And the king commanded them to quarry large stones, costly stones, *and* hewn stones, to lay the foundation of the temple.a 18So Solomon's builders, Hiram's builders, and the Gebalites quarried *them;* and they prepared timber and stones to build the temple.

Solomon Builds the Temple

6 And it came to pass in the four hundred and eightietha year after the children of Israel had come out of the land of Egypt, in the fourth year of Solomon's reign over Israel, in the month of Ziv, which *is* the second month, that he began to build the house of the LORD. 2Now the house which King Solomon built for the LORD, its length *was* sixty cubits, its width twenty, and its height thirty cubits. 3The vestibule in front of the sanctuarya of the house *was* twenty cubits long across the width of the house, *and* the width of *the vestibule*b *extended* ten cubits from the front of the house. 4And he made for the house windows with beveled frames.

5Against the wall of the temple he built chambers all around, *against* the walls of the temple, all around the sanctuary and the inner sanctuary.a Thus he made side chambers all around it. 6The lowest chamber *was* five cubits wide, the middle *was* six cubits wide, and the third *was* seven cubits wide; for he made narrow ledges around the outside of the temple, so that *the support beams* would not be fastened into the walls of the temple. 7And the temple, when it was being built, was built with stone finished at the quarry, so that no hammer or chisel *or* any iron tool was heard in the temple while it was being built. 8The doorway for the

---

5:11 aFollowing Masoretic Text, Targum, and Vulgate; Septuagint and Syriac read *twenty thousand.* **5:16** aFollowing Masoretic Text, Targum, and Vulgate; Septuagint reads *three thousand six hundred.* **5:17** aLiterally *house,* and so frequently throughout this book **6:1** aFollowing Masoretic Text, Targum, and Vulgate; Septuagint reads *fortieth.* **6:3** aHebrew *heykal;* here the main room of the temple, elsewhere called the holy place (compare Exodus 26:33 and Ezekiel 41:1) bLiterally *it* **6:5** aHebrew *debir;* here the inner room of the temple, elsewhere called the Most Holy Place (compare verse 16)

middle story[a] *was* on the right side of the temple. They went up by stairs to the middle *story,* and from the middle to the third.

⁹So he built the temple and finished it, and he paneled the temple with beams and boards of cedar. ¹⁰And he built side chambers against the entire temple, each five cubits high; they were attached to the temple with cedar beams.

¹¹Then the word of the LORD came to Solomon, saying: ¹²*"Concerning* this temple which you are building, if you walk in My statutes, execute My judgments, keep all My commandments, and walk in them, then I will perform My word with you, which I spoke to your father David. ¹³And I will dwell among the children of Israel, and will not forsake My people Israel."

¹⁴So Solomon built the temple and finished it. ¹⁵And he built the inside walls of the temple with cedar boards; from the floor of the temple to the ceiling he paneled the inside with wood; and he covered the floor

---

6:8 [a]Following Masoretic Text and Vulgate; Septuagint reads *upper story;* Targum reads *ground story.*

of the temple with planks of cypress. ¹⁶Then he built the twenty-cubit room at the rear of the temple, from floor to ceiling, with cedar boards; he built *it* inside as the inner sanctuary, as the Most Holy *Place.* ¹⁷And in front of it the temple sanctuary was forty cubits *long.* ¹⁸The inside of the temple was cedar, carved with ornamental buds and open flowers. All *was* cedar; there was no stone *to be* seen.

¹⁹And he prepared the inner sanctuary inside the temple, to set the ark of the covenant of the LORD there. ²⁰The inner sanctuary *was* twenty cubits long, twenty cubits wide, and twenty cubits high. He overlaid it with pure gold, and overlaid the altar of cedar. ²¹So Solomon overlaid the inside of the temple with pure gold. He stretched gold chains across the front of the inner sanctuary, and overlaid it with gold. ²²The whole temple he overlaid with gold, until he had finished all the temple; also he overlaid with gold the entire altar that *was* by the inner sanctuary.

²³Inside the inner sanctuary he made two cherubim *of* olive wood, *each* ten cubits

---

PARENTING MATTERS

Q: *How can we convince our children of the rightness of always speaking the truth?*

Nobody ever had to teach a child how to lie. It comes naturally, just as it did to you! But if your child sees you speaking the truth as a way of life, it will be much easier for him or her. Teach your child to tell the truth in two ways:

First, teach him about Jesus Christ. Jesus said, "I am the way, *the truth*, and the life" (John 14:6, italics added). You expose your child to the truth as you teach about Jesus Christ's life, His mission, and His teachings. He is the incarnation of the truth. And as your child understands what a straight line looks like, he'll be able to spot the deceitful line.

Second, teach him the Scripture. Diligently teach the truth of God's Word through Scripture-memory programs, family Bible study, and Bible-verse reminders of what it looks like to obey God when life and truth collide.

Third, when he lies, discipline and instruct him. All six of our children lied. Some lied habitually. Use these times as an opportunity to illustrate to your child that there are consequences for deceitful behavior.

Help your child develop his convictions by contrasting the results of being deceitful with those of telling the truth. When we train our children to know the truth of God's Word, Scripture will help him guard their hearts from deceit, evil, and destruction.

high. 24One wing of the cherub *was* five cubits, and the other wing of the cherub five cubits: ten cubits from the tip of one wing to the tip of the other. 25And the other cherub *was* ten cubits; both cherubim *were* of the same size and shape. 26The height of one cherub *was* ten cubits, and so *was* the other cherub. 27Then he set the cherubim inside the inner room;[a] and they stretched out the wings of the cherubim so that the wing of the one touched *one* wall, and the wing of the other cherub touched the other wall. And their wings touched each other in the middle of the room. 28Also he overlaid the cherubim with gold.

29Then he carved all the walls of the temple all around, both the inner and outer *sanctuaries,* with carved figures of cherubim, palm trees, and open flowers. 30And the floor of the temple he overlaid with gold, both the inner and outer *sanctuaries.*

31For the entrance of the inner sanctuary he made doors *of* olive wood; the lintel *and* doorposts *were* one-fifth *of the wall.* 32The two doors *were of* olive wood; and he carved on them figures of cherubim, palm trees, and open flowers, and overlaid *them* with gold; and he spread gold on the cherubim and on the palm trees. 33So for the door of the sanctuary he also made doorposts *of* olive wood, one-fourth *of the wall.* 34And the two doors *were of* cypress wood; two panels *comprised* one folding door, and two panels *comprised* the other folding door. 35Then he carved cherubim, palm trees, and open flowers *on them,* and overlaid *them* with gold applied evenly on the carved work.

36And he built the inner court with three rows of hewn stone and a row of cedar beams.

37In the fourth year the foundation of the house of the LORD was laid, in the month of Ziv. 38And in the eleventh year, in the month of Bul, which is the eighth month, the house was finished in all its details and according to all its plans. So he was seven years in building it.

Solomon's Other Buildings

7 But Solomon took thirteen years to build his own house; so he finished all his house.

2He also built the House of the Forest of Lebanon; its length *was* one hundred cubits, its width fifty cubits, and its height thirty cubits, with four rows of cedar pillars, and cedar beams on the pillars. 3And *it was* paneled with cedar above the beams that *were* on forty-five pillars, fifteen *to* a row. 4*There were* windows *with beveled frames in* three rows, and window *was* opposite window *in* three tiers. 5And all the doorways and doorposts *had* rectangular frames; and window *was* opposite window *in* three tiers.

6He also made the Hall of Pillars: its length *was* fifty cubits, and its width thirty cubits; and in front of them *was* a portico with pillars, and a canopy *was* in front of them.

7Then he made a hall for the throne, the Hall of Judgment, where he might judge; and *it was* paneled with cedar from floor to ceiling.[a]

8And the house where he dwelt *had* another court inside the hall, of like workmanship. Solomon also made a house like this hall for Pharaoh's daughter, whom he had taken *as wife.*

9All these *were of* costly stones cut to size, trimmed with saws, inside and out, from the foundation to the eaves, and also on the outside to the great court. 10The foundation *was of* costly stones, large stones, some ten cubits and some eight cubits. 11And above *were* costly stones, hewn to size, and cedar wood. 12The great court *was* enclosed with three rows of hewn stones and a row of cedar beams. So were the inner court of the house of the LORD and the vestibule of the temple.

Hiram the Craftsman

13Now King Solomon sent and brought Huram[a] from Tyre. 14He *was* the son of a widow from the tribe of Naphtali, and his father *was* a man of Tyre, a bronze worker; he was filled with wisdom and understanding and skill in working with all kinds of bronze work. So he came to King Solomon and did all his work.

The Bronze Pillars for the Temple

15And he cast two pillars of bronze, each

6:27 [a]Literally *house* 7:7 [a]Literally *floor,* that is, of the upper level 7:13 [a]Hebrew *Hiram* (compare 2 Chronicles 2:13, 14)

one eighteen cubits high, and a line of twelve cubits measured the circumference of each. [16]Then he made two capitals *of* cast bronze, to set on the tops of the pillars. The height of one capital *was* five cubits, and the height of the other capital *was* five cubits. [17]*He made* a lattice network, with wreaths of chainwork, for the capitals which *were* on top of the pillars: seven chains for one capital and seven for the other capital. [18]So he made the pillars, and two rows of pomegranates above the network all around to cover the capitals that *were* on top; and thus he did for the other capital.

[19]The capitals which *were* on top of the pillars in the hall *were* in the shape of lilies, four cubits. [20]The capitals on the two pillars also *had pomegranates* above, by the convex surface which *was* next to the network; and there *were* two hundred such pomegranates in rows on each of the capitals all around.

[21]Then he set up the pillars by the vestibule of the temple; he set up the pillar on the right and called its name Jachin, and he set up the pillar on the left and called its name Boaz. [22]The tops of the pillars were in the shape of lilies. So the work of the pillars was finished.

The Sea and the Oxen

[23]And he made the Sea of cast bronze, ten cubits from one brim to the other; *it was* completely round. Its height *was* five cubits, and a line of thirty cubits measured its circumference.

[24]Below its brim *were* ornamental buds encircling it all around, ten to a cubit, all the way around the Sea. The ornamental buds *were* cast in two rows when it was cast. [25]It stood on twelve oxen: three looking toward the north, three looking toward the west, three looking toward the south, and three looking toward the east; the Sea *was set* upon them, and all their back parts *pointed* inward. [26]It *was* a handbreadth thick; and its brim was shaped like the brim of a cup, *like* a lily blossom. It contained two thousand[a] baths.

The Carts and the Lavers

[27]He also made ten carts of bronze; four cubits *was* the length of each cart, four cubits its width, and three cubits its height. [28]And this *was* the design of the carts: They had panels, and the panels *were* between frames; [29]on the panels that *were* between the frames *were* lions, oxen, and cherubim. And on the frames *was* a pedestal on top. Below the lions and oxen *were* wreaths of plaited work. [30]Every cart had four bronze wheels and axles of bronze, and its four feet had supports. Under the laver *were* supports of cast *bronze* beside each wreath. [31]Its opening inside the crown at the top *was* one cubit in diameter; and the opening *was* round, shaped *like* a pedestal, one and a half cubits in outside diameter; and also on the opening *were* engravings, but the panels were square, not round. [32]Under the panels *were* the four wheels, and the axles of the wheels *were joined* to the cart. The height of a wheel *was* one and a half cubits. [33]The workmanship of the wheels *was* like the workmanship of a chariot wheel; their axle pins, their rims, their spokes, and their hubs *were* all of cast *bronze*. [34]And *there were* four supports at the four corners of each cart; its supports *were* part of the cart itself. [35]On the top of the cart, at the height of half a cubit, *it was* perfectly round. And on the top of the cart, its flanges and its panels *were* of the same casting. [36]On the plates of its flanges and on its panels he engraved cherubim, lions, and palm trees, wherever there was a clear space on each, with wreaths all around. [37]Thus he made the ten carts. All of them were of the same mold, one measure, *and* one shape.

[38]Then he made ten lavers of bronze; each laver contained forty baths, *and* each laver *was* four cubits. On each of the ten carts *was* a laver. [39]And he put five carts on the right side of the house, and five on the left side of the house. He set the Sea on the right side of the house, toward the southeast.

Furnishings of the Temple

[40]Huram[a] made the lavers and the shovels and the bowls. So Huram finished doing all the work that he was to do for King

---

7:26 [a]Or *three thousand* (compare 2 Chronicles 4:5)
7:40 [a]Hebrew *Hiram* (compare 2 Chronicles 2:13, 14)

Solomon *for* the house of the LORD: [41]the two pillars, the *two* bowl-shaped capitals that *were* on top of the two pillars; the two networks covering the two bowl-shaped capitals which *were* on top of the pillars; [42]four hundred pomegranates for the two networks (two rows of pomegranates for each network, to cover the two bowl-shaped capitals that *were* on top of the pillars); [43]the ten carts, and ten lavers on the carts; [44]one Sea, and twelve oxen under the Sea; [45]the pots, the shovels, and the bowls.

All these articles which Huram[a] made for King Solomon *for* the house of the LORD *were of* burnished bronze. [46]In the plain of Jordan the king had them cast in clay molds, between Succoth and Zaretan. [47]And Solomon did not weigh all the articles, because *there were* so many; the weight of the bronze was not determined.

INTIMATE MOMENTS

Secretly buy her tickets to a special event that you know she'll love. Plan a lunch/ dinner date on the day of the event. After dessert, give her the tickets.

[48]Thus Solomon had all the furnishings made for the house of the LORD: the altar of gold, and the table of gold on which *was* the showbread; [49]the lampstands of pure gold, five on the right *side* and five on the left in front of the inner sanctuary, with the flowers and the lamps and the wick-trimmers of gold; [50]the basins, the trimmers, the bowls, the ladles, and the censers of pure gold; and the hinges of gold, *both* for the doors of the inner room (the Most Holy *Place*) *and* for the doors of the main hall of the temple.

[51]So all the work that King Solomon had done for the house of the LORD was finished; and Solomon brought in the things which his father David had dedicated: the silver and the gold and the furnishings. He put them in the treasuries of the house of the LORD.

The Ark Brought into the Temple

8 Now Solomon assembled the elders of Israel and all the heads of the tribes, the chief fathers of the children of Israel, to King Solomon in Jerusalem, that they might bring up the ark of the covenant of the LORD from the City of David, which *is* Zion. [2]Therefore all the men of Israel assembled with King Solomon at the feast in the month of Ethanim, which *is* the seventh month. [3]So all the elders of Israel came, and the priests took up the ark. [4]Then they brought up the ark of the LORD, the tabernacle of meeting, and all the holy furnishings that *were* in the tabernacle. The priests and the Levites brought them up. [5]Also King Solomon, and all the congregation of Israel who were assembled with him, *were* with him before the ark, sacrificing sheep and oxen that could not be counted or numbered for multitude. [6]Then the priests brought in the ark of the covenant of the LORD to its place, into the inner sanctuary of the temple, to the Most Holy *Place,* under the wings of the cherubim. [7]For the cherubim spread *their* two wings over the place of the ark, and the cherubim overshadowed the ark and its poles. [8]The poles extended so that the ends of the poles could be seen from the holy *place,* in front of the inner sanctuary; but they could not be seen from outside. And they are there to this day. [9]Nothing *was* in the ark except the two tablets of stone which Moses put there at Horeb, when the LORD made *a covenant* with the children of Israel, when they came out of the land of Egypt.

[10]And it came to pass, when the priests came out of the holy *place,* that the cloud filled the house of the LORD, [11]so that the priests could not continue ministering because of the cloud; for the glory of the LORD filled the house of the LORD.

[12]Then Solomon spoke:

"The LORD said He would dwell in the dark cloud.
[13]   I have surely built You an exalted house,
   And a place for You to dwell in forever."

7:45 [a]Hebrew *Hiram* (compare 2 Chronicles 2:13, 14)

Solomon's Speech at Completion of the Work

¹⁴Then the king turned around and blessed the whole assembly of Israel, while all the assembly of Israel was standing. ¹⁵And he said: "Blessed *be* the Lᴏʀᴅ God of Israel, who spoke with His mouth to my father David, and with His hand has fulfilled *it,* saying, ¹⁶'Since the day that I brought My people Israel out of Egypt, I have chosen no city from any tribe of Israel *in which* to build a house, that My name might be there; but I chose David to be over My people Israel.' ¹⁷Now it was in the heart of my father David to build a templeᵃ for the name of the Lᴏʀᴅ God of Israel. ¹⁸But the Lᴏʀᴅ said to my father David, 'Whereas it was in your heart to build a temple for My name, you did well that it was in your heart. ¹⁹Nevertheless you shall not build the temple, but your son who will come from your body, he shall build the temple for My name.' ²⁰So the Lᴏʀᴅ has fulfilled His word which He spoke; and I have filled the position of my father David, and sit on the throne of Israel, as the Lᴏʀᴅ promised; and I have built a temple for the name of the Lᴏʀᴅ God of Israel. ²¹And there I have made a place for the ark, in which *is* the covenant of the Lᴏʀᴅ which He made with our fathers, when He brought them out of the land of Egypt."

Solomon's Prayer of Dedication

²²Then Solomon stood before the altar of the Lᴏʀᴅ in the presence of all the assembly of Israel, and spread out his hands toward heaven; ²³and he said: "Lᴏʀᴅ God of Israel, *there is* no God in heaven above or on earth below like You, who keep *Your* covenant and mercy with Your servants who walk before You with all their hearts. ²⁴You have kept what You promised Your servant David my father; You have both spoken with Your mouth and fulfilled *it* with Your hand, as *it is* this day. ²⁵Therefore, Lᴏʀᴅ God of Israel, now keep what You promised Your servant David my father, saying, 'You shall not fail to have a man sit before Me on the throne of Israel, only if your sons take heed to their way, that they walk before Me

as you have walked before Me.' ²⁶And now I pray, O God of Israel, let Your word come true, which You have spoken to Your servant David my father.

²⁷"But will God indeed dwell on the earth? Behold, heaven and the heaven of heavens cannot contain You. How much less this temple which I have built! ²⁸Yet regard the prayer of Your servant and his supplication, O Lᴏʀᴅ my God, and listen to the cry and the prayer which Your servant is praying before You today: ²⁹that Your eyes may be open toward this temple night and day, toward the place of which You said, 'My name shall be there,' that You may hear the prayer which Your servant makes toward this place. ³⁰And may You hear the supplication of Your servant and of Your people Israel, when they pray toward this place. Hear in heaven Your dwelling place; and when You hear, forgive.

³¹"When anyone sins against his neighbor, and is forced to take an oath, and comes *and* takes an oath before Your altar in this temple, ³²then hear in heaven, and act, and judge Your servants, condemning the wicked, bringing his way on his head, and justifying the righteous by giving him according to his righteousness.

³³"When Your people Israel are defeated before an enemy because they have sinned against You, and when they turn back to You and confess Your name, and pray and make supplication to You in this temple, ³⁴then hear in heaven, and forgive the sin of Your people Israel, and bring them back to the land which You gave to their fathers.

³⁵"When the heavens are shut up and there is no rain because they have sinned against You, when they pray toward this place and confess Your name, and turn from their sin because You afflict them, ³⁶then hear in heaven, and forgive the sin of Your servants, Your people Israel, that You may teach them the good way in which they should walk; and send rain on Your land which You have given to Your people as an inheritance.

³⁷"When there is famine in the land, pestilence *or* blight *or* mildew, locusts *or* grasshoppers; when their enemy besieges them in the land of their cities; whatever plague *or* whatever sickness *there is;*

8:17 ᵃLiterally *house,* and so in verses 18–20

³⁸whatever prayer, whatever supplication is made by anyone, *or* by all Your people Israel, when each one knows the plague of his own heart, and spreads out his hands toward this temple: ³⁹then hear in heaven Your dwelling place, and forgive, and act, and give to everyone according to all his ways, whose heart You know (for You alone know the hearts of all the sons of men), ⁴⁰that they may fear You all the days that they live in the land which You gave to our fathers.

⁴¹"Moreover, concerning a foreigner, who *is* not of Your people Israel, but has come from a far country for Your name's sake ⁴²(for they will hear of Your great name and Your strong hand and Your outstretched arm), when he comes and prays toward this temple, ⁴³hear in heaven Your dwelling place, and do according to all for which the foreigner calls to You, that all peoples of the earth may know Your name and fear You, as *do* Your people Israel, and that they may know that this temple which I have built is called by Your name.

⁴⁴"When Your people go out to battle against their enemy, wherever You send them, and when they pray to the LORD toward the city which You have chosen and the temple which I have built for Your name, ⁴⁵then hear in heaven their prayer and their supplication, and maintain their cause.

⁴⁶"When they sin against You (for *there is* no one who does not sin), and You become angry with them and deliver them to the enemy, and they take them captive to the land of the enemy, far or near; ⁴⁷*yet* when they come to themselves in the land where they were carried captive, and repent, and make supplication to You in the land of those who took them captive, saying, 'We have sinned and done wrong, we have committed wickedness'; ⁴⁸and *when* they return to You with all their heart and with all their soul in the land of their enemies who led them away captive, and pray to You toward their land which You gave to their fathers, the city which You have chosen and the temple which I have built for Your name: ⁴⁹then hear in heaven Your dwelling place their prayer and their supplication, and maintain their cause, ⁵⁰and forgive Your people who have

sinned against You, and all their transgressions which they have transgressed against You; and grant them compassion before those who took them captive, that they may have compassion on them ⁵¹(for they *are* Your people and Your inheritance, whom You brought out of Egypt, out of the iron furnace), ⁵²that Your eyes may be open to the supplication of Your servant and the supplication of Your people Israel, to listen to them whenever they call to You. ⁵³For You separated them from among all the peoples of the earth *to be* Your inheritance, as You spoke by Your servant Moses, when You brought our fathers out of Egypt, O Lord GOD."

Solomon Blesses the Assembly

⁵⁴And so it was, when Solomon had finished praying all this prayer and supplication to the LORD, that he arose from before the altar of the LORD, from kneeling on his knees with his hands spread up to heaven. ⁵⁵Then he stood and blessed all the assembly of Israel with a loud voice, saying: ⁵⁶"Blessed *be* the LORD, who has given rest to His people Israel, according to all that He promised. There has not failed one word of all His good promise, which He promised through His servant Moses. ⁵⁷May the LORD our God be with us, as He was with our fathers. May He not leave us nor forsake us, ⁵⁸that He may incline our hearts to Himself, to walk in all His ways, and to keep His commandments and His statutes and His judgments, which He commanded our fathers. ⁵⁹And may these words of mine, with which I have made supplication before the LORD, be near the LORD our God day and night, that He may maintain the cause of His servant and the cause of His people Israel, as each day may require, ⁶⁰that all the peoples of the earth may know that the LORD *is* God; *there is* no other. ⁶¹Let your heart therefore be loyal to the LORD our God, to walk in His statutes and keep His commandments, as at this day."

Solomon Dedicates the Temple

⁶²Then the king and all Israel with him offered sacrifices before the LORD. ⁶³And Solomon offered a sacrifice of peace offerings, which he offered to the LORD, twenty-two thousand bulls and one hundred and

twenty thousand sheep. So the king and all the children of Israel dedicated the house of the LORD. ⁶⁴On the same day the king consecrated the middle of the court that *was* in front of the house of the LORD; for there he offered burnt offerings, grain offerings, and the fat of the peace offerings, because the bronze altar that *was* before the LORD *was* too small to receive the burnt offerings, the grain offerings, and the fat of the peace offerings.

⁶⁵At that time Solomon held a feast, and all Israel with him, a great assembly from the entrance of Hamath to the Brook of Egypt, before the LORD our God, seven days and seven *more* days—fourteen days. ⁶⁶On the eighth day he sent the people away; and they blessed the king, and went to their tents joyful and glad of heart for all the good that the LORD had done for His servant David, and for Israel His people.

God's Second Appearance to Solomon

9 And it came to pass, when Solomon had finished building the house of the LORD and the king's house, and all Solomon's desire which he wanted to do, ²that the LORD appeared to Solomon the second time, as He had appeared to him at Gibeon. ³And the LORD said to him: "I have heard your prayer and your supplication that you have made before Me; I have consecrated this house which you have built to put My name there forever, and My eyes and My heart will be there perpetually. ⁴Now if you walk before Me as your father David walked, in integrity of heart and in uprightness, to do according to all that I have commanded you, *and* if you keep My statutes and My judgments, ⁵then I will establish the throne of your kingdom over Israel forever, as I promised David your father, saying, 'You shall not fail to have a man on the throne of Israel.' ⁶*But* if you or your sons at all turn from following Me, and do not keep My commandments *and* My statutes which I have set before you, but go and serve other gods and worship them, ⁷then I will cut off Israel from the land which I have given them; and this house which I have consecrated for My name I will cast out of My sight. Israel will be a proverb and a byword among all peoples. ⁸And *as for* this house, *which* is exalted, everyone who passes by it will be astonished and will hiss, and say, 'Why has the LORD done thus to this land and to this house?' ⁹Then they will answer, 'Because they forsook the LORD their God, who brought their fathers out of the land of Egypt, and have embraced other gods, and worshiped them and served them; therefore the LORD has brought all this calamity on them.'"

ROMANTIC QUOTES AND NOTES
Dealing with Disappointment

The reality of disappointment surprises most couples. In the flush of new love, most think *their* relationship will be different. They believe their love will stay strong and fresh despite all odds.

Love is demanding, however, and once the honeymoon ends, young husbands and wives usually start seeing defects in their mates that they hadn't noticed before. The result? Disappointment.

They end up feeling like King Hiram, who eagerly visited some cities that a friend had given to him—but once there, "they did not please him. So he said, 'What kind of cities are these which you have given me, my brother?' And he called them the land of Cabul [which in Hebrew sounds like, 'good-for-nothing']" (9:12, 13).

As the experience of disappointed love becomes a daily lifestyle, couples fight, retreat to separate corners, and walk on eggshells. "When I got married," someone once said, "I was looking for the ideal. But it soon became an ordeal. Now I want a new deal."

God is waiting to give you understanding, compassion, and His love for your mate. He wants you to see that you can't iron out the wrinkles on your own. Only He can provide the kind of love you are looking for.

Solomon and Hiram Exchange Gifts

[10]Now it happened at the end of twenty years, when Solomon had built the two houses, the house of the LORD and the king's house [11](Hiram the king of Tyre had supplied Solomon with cedar and cypress and gold, as much as he desired), *that* King Solomon then gave Hiram twenty cities in the land of Galilee. [12]Then Hiram went from Tyre to see the cities which Solomon had given him, but they did not please him. [13]So he said, "What *kind of* cities *are* these which you have given me, my brother?" And he called them the land of Cabul,[a] as they are to this day. [14]Then Hiram sent the king one hundred and twenty talents of gold.

Solomon's Additional Achievements

[15]And this *is* the reason for the labor force which King Solomon raised: to build the house of the LORD, his own house, the Millo,[a] the wall of Jerusalem, Hazor, Megiddo, and Gezer. [16](Pharaoh king of Egypt had gone up and taken Gezer and burned it with fire, had killed the Canaanites who dwelt in the city, and had given it *as* a dowry to his daughter, Solomon's wife.) [17]And Solomon built Gezer, Lower Beth Horon, [18]Baalath, and Tadmor in the wilderness, in the land *of Judah,* [19]all the storage cities that Solomon had, cities for his chariots and cities for his cavalry, and whatever Solomon desired to build in Jerusalem, in Lebanon, and in all the land of his dominion.

[20]All the people *who were* left of the Amorites, Hittites, Perizzites, Hivites, and Jebusites, who *were* not of the children of Israel— [21]that is, their descendants who were left in the land after them, whom the children of Israel had not been able to destroy completely—from these Solomon raised forced labor, as it is to this day. [22]But of the children of Israel Solomon made no forced laborers, because they *were* men of war and his servants: his officers, his captains, commanders of his chariots, and his cavalry.

[23]Others *were* chiefs of the officials who *were* over Solomon's work: five hundred and fifty, who ruled over the people who did the work.

[24]But Pharaoh's daughter came up from the City of David to her house which Solomon[a] had built for her. Then he built the Millo.

[25]Now three times a year Solomon offered burnt offerings and peace offerings on the altar which he had built for the LORD, and he burned incense with them *on the altar* that *was* before the LORD. So he finished the temple.

[26]King Solomon also built a fleet of ships at Ezion Geber, which *is* near Elath[a] on the shore of the Red Sea, in the land of Edom. [27]Then Hiram sent his servants with the fleet, seamen who knew the sea, to work with the servants of Solomon. [28]And they went to Ophir, and acquired four hundred and twenty talents of gold from there, and brought *it* to King Solomon.

The Queen of Sheba's Praise of Solomon

10 Now when the queen of Sheba heard of the fame of Solomon concerning the name of the LORD, she came to test him with hard questions. [2]She came to Jerusalem with a very great retinue, with camels that bore spices, very much gold, and precious stones; and when she came to Solomon, she spoke with him about all that was in her heart. [3]So Solomon answered all her questions; there was nothing so difficult for the king that he could not explain *it* to her. [4]And when the queen of Sheba had seen all the wisdom of Solomon, the house that he had built, [5]the food on his table, the seating of his servants, the service of his waiters and their apparel, his cupbearers, and his entryway by which he went up to the house of the LORD, there was no more spirit in her. [6]Then she said to the king: "It was a true report which I heard in my own land about your words and your wisdom. [7]However I did not believe the words until I came and saw with my own eyes; and indeed the half was not told me. Your wisdom and prosperity exceed the fame of which I heard. [8]Happy *are* your men and happy *are* these

---

9:13 [a]Literally *Good for Nothing* **9:15** [a]Literally *The Landfill* **9:24** [a]Literally *he* (compare 2 Chronicles 8:11) **9:26** [a]Hebrew *Eloth* (compare 2 Kings 14:22)

BIBLICAL INSIGHTS • 10:21

The Folly of Acquiring Stuff

OUR CULTURE APPLAUDS DRIVEN men and women who excel in their chosen career paths. We subconsciously regard these people as having arrived. We tend to view them as significant individuals, when, in reality, many have trashed their marriages, their children, and their friendships, merely to juggle the inhuman pressures necessary for their success.

It's not worth it.

The wealthiest man of his era, Solomon, he had it all. He accumulated unimaginable riches—servants, forests, vineyards, and much more. In fact, "All King Solomon's drinking vessels were gold, and all the vessels of the House of the Forest of Lebanon were pure gold. Not one was silver, for this was accounted as nothing in the days of Solomon" (10:21).

Our culture would insist that Solomon had arrived. Big time! Yet at the end of his life, he characterized his own success as utterly meaningless (Eccl. 1:2).

Over the years, one of the more stimulating conversations with our teenagers regarded what Barbara and I did with our royalties. Early in our ministry we decided that we would donate 100 percent of our royalties from books to FamilyLife. As our children got older they began to understand what this meant. Stating it another way, they began to estimate the numbers and decided that with each book we wrote, we were giving away the possibility of better cars for them!

While I do not think there is anything wrong with authors taking their royalties, for us it became one of the statements of what's important to our children. There's no question those royalties could have taken some pressure off of us financially, but our prayer was that our children got the picture of what is truly important.

Bill Bright, founder and president of Campus Crusade for Christ once challenged me, "Wear the cloak of materialism loosely." As I have gotten older, I now understand his exhortation and how many of those who attempt to follow Christ in America are weigh down by things and material wealth.

Jesus taught us to give to those in need, because, "It is more blessed to give than to receive" (Acts 20:35). If you put acquiring stuff at the top of your agenda, you will end up a fool. Lasting significance comes when you align yourself with the heart of God and make His agenda your agenda.

---

your servants, who stand continually before you *and* hear your wisdom! ⁹Blessed be the LORD your God, who delighted in you, setting you on the throne of Israel! Because the LORD has loved Israel forever, therefore He made you king, to do justice and righteousness."

¹⁰Then she gave the king one hundred and twenty talents of gold, spices in great quantity, and precious stones. There never again came such abundance of spices as the queen of Sheba gave to King Solomon. ¹¹Also, the ships of Hiram, which brought

gold from Ophir, brought great quantities of almug^a wood and precious stones from Ophir. ¹²And the king made steps of the almug wood for the house of the LORD and for the king's house, also harps and stringed instruments for singers. There never again came such almug wood, nor has the like been seen to this day.

¹³Now King Solomon gave the queen of Sheba all she desired, whatever she asked, besides what Solomon had given her according to the royal generosity. So she turned and went to her own country, she and her servants.

10:11 ªOr *algum* (compare 2 Chronicles 9:10, 11)

Solomon's Great Wealth

¹⁴The weight of gold that came to Solomon yearly was six hundred and sixty-six talents of gold, ¹⁵besides *that* from the traveling merchants, from the income of traders, from all the kings of Arabia, and from the governors of the country.

¹⁶And King Solomon made two hundred large shields *of* hammered gold; six hundred *shekels* of gold went into each shield. ¹⁷He also *made* three hundred shields *of* hammered gold; three minas of gold went into each shield. The king put them in the House of the Forest of Lebanon.

¹⁸Moreover the king made a great throne of ivory, and overlaid it with pure gold. ¹⁹The throne had six steps, and the top of the throne *was* round at the back; *there were* armrests on either side of the place of the seat, and two lions stood beside the armrests. ²⁰Twelve lions stood there, one on each side of the six steps; nothing like *this* had been made for any *other* kingdom.

²¹All King Solomon's drinking vessels *were* gold, and all the vessels of the House of the Forest of Lebanon *were* pure gold. Not *one was* silver, for this was accounted as nothing in the days of Solomon. ²²For the king had merchant ships^a at sea with the fleet of Hiram. Once every three years the merchant ships came bringing gold, silver, ivory, apes, and monkeys.^b ²³So King Solomon surpassed all the kings of the earth in riches and wisdom.

²⁴Now all the earth sought the presence of Solomon to hear his wisdom, which God had put in his heart. ²⁵Each man brought his present: articles of silver and gold, garments, armor, spices, horses, and mules, at a set rate year by year.

²⁶And Solomon gathered chariots and horsemen; he had one thousand four hundred chariots and twelve thousand horsemen, whom he stationed^a in the chariot cities and with the king at Jerusalem. ²⁷The king made silver *as common* in Jerusalem as stones, and he made cedar trees as abundant as the sycamores which *are* in the lowland.

²⁸Also Solomon had horses imported from Egypt and Keveh; the king's merchants bought them in Keveh at the *current* price. ²⁹Now a chariot that was imported from Egypt cost six hundred *shekels* of silver, and a horse one hundred and fifty; and thus, through their agents,^a they exported *them* to all the kings of the Hittites and the kings of Syria.

Solomon's Heart Turns from the LORD

11 But King Solomon loved many foreign women, as well as the daughter of Pharaoh: women of the Moabites, Ammonites, Edomites, Sidonians, *and* Hittites— ²from the nations of whom the LORD had said to the children of Israel, "You shall not intermarry with them, nor they with you. Surely they will turn away your hearts after their gods." Solomon clung to these in love. ³And he had seven hundred wives, princesses, and three hundred concubines; and his wives turned away his heart. ⁴For it was so, when Solomon was old, that his wives turned his heart after other gods; and his heart was not loyal to the LORD his God, as *was* the heart of his father David. ⁵For Solomon went after Ashtoreth the goddess of the Sidonians, and after Milcom the abomination of the Ammonites. ⁶Solomon did evil in the sight of the LORD, and did not fully follow the LORD, as *did* his father David. ⁷Then Solomon built a high place for Chemosh the abomination of Moab, on the hill that *is* east of Jerusalem, and for Molech the abomination of the people of Ammon. ⁸And he did likewise for all his foreign wives, who burned incense and sacrificed to their gods.

⁹So the LORD became angry with Solomon, because his heart had turned from the LORD God of Israel, who had appeared to him twice, ¹⁰and had commanded him concerning this thing, that he should not go after other gods; but he did not keep what the LORD had commanded. ¹¹Therefore the LORD said to Solomon, "Because you have done this, and have not kept My covenant and My statutes, which I have commanded you, I will surely tear the kingdom away from you and give it to your servant. ¹²Nevertheless I will not do it in your days,

10:22 ^aLiterally *ships of Tarshish,* deep-sea vessels ^bOr *peacocks* **10:26** ^aFollowing Septuagint, Syriac, Targum, and Vulgate (compare 2 Chronicles 9:25); Masoretic Text reads *led.* **10:29** ^aLiterally *by their hands*

for the sake of your father David; I will tear it out of the hand of your son. ¹³However I will not tear away the whole kingdom; I will give one tribe to your son for the sake of My servant David, and for the sake of Jerusalem which I have chosen."

Adversaries of Solomon

¹⁴Now the LORD raised up an adversary against Solomon, Hadad the Edomite; he *was* a descendant of the king in Edom. ¹⁵For it happened, when David was in Edom, and Joab the commander of the army had gone up to bury the slain, after he had killed every male in Edom ¹⁶(because for six months Joab remained there with all Israel, until he had cut down every male in Edom), ¹⁷that Hadad fled to go to Egypt, he and certain Edomites of his father's servants with him. Hadad *was* still a little child. ¹⁸Then they arose from Midian and came to Paran; and they took men with them from Paran and came to Egypt, to Pharaoh king of Egypt, who gave him a house, apportioned food for him, and gave him land. ¹⁹And Hadad found great favor in the sight of Pharaoh, so that he gave him as wife the sister of his own wife, that is, the sister of Queen Tahpenes. ²⁰Then the sister of Tahpenes bore him Genubath his son, whom Tahpenes weaned in Pharaoh's house. And Genubath was in Pharaoh's household among the sons of Pharaoh.

²¹So when Hadad heard in Egypt that David rested with his fathers, and that Joab the commander of the army was dead, Hadad said to Pharaoh, "Let me depart, that I may go to my own country."

²²Then Pharaoh said to him, "But what have you lacked with me, that suddenly you seek to go to your own country?"

So he answered, "Nothing, but do let me go anyway."

²³And God raised up *another* adversary against him, Rezon the son of Eliadah, who had fled from his lord, Hadadezer king of Zobah. ²⁴So he gathered men to him and became captain over a band *of raiders,* when David killed those *of Zobah.* And they went to Damascus and dwelt there, and

reigned in Damascus. ²⁵He was an adversary of Israel all the days of Solomon (besides the trouble that Hadad *caused*); and he abhorred Israel, and reigned over Syria.

Jeroboam's Rebellion

²⁶Then Solomon's servant, Jeroboam the son of Nebat, an Ephraimite from Zereda, whose mother's name *was* Zeruah, a widow, also rebelled against the king. ²⁷And this *is* what caused him to rebel against the king: Solomon had built the Millo *and* repaired the damages to the City of David his father. ²⁸The man Jeroboam *was* a mighty man of valor; and Solomon, seeing that the young man was industrious, made him the officer over all the labor force of the house of Joseph.

²⁹Now it happened at that time, when Jeroboam went out of Jerusalem, that the prophet Ahijah the Shilonite met him on the way; and he had clothed himself with a new garment, and the two *were* alone in the field. ³⁰Then Ahijah took hold of the new garment that *was* on him, and tore it *into* twelve pieces. ³¹And he said to Jeroboam, "Take for yourself ten pieces, for thus says the LORD, the God of Israel: 'Behold, I will tear the kingdom out of the hand of Solomon and will give ten tribes to you ³²(but he shall have one tribe for the sake of My servant David, and for the sake of Jerusalem, the city which I have chosen out of all the tribes of Israel), ³³because they have[a] forsaken Me, and worshiped Ashtoreth the goddess of the Sidonians, Chemosh the god of the Moabites, and Milcom the god of the people of Ammon, and have not walked in My ways to do *what is* right in My eyes and *keep* My statutes and My judgments, as *did* his father David. ³⁴However I will not take the whole kingdom out of his hand, because I have made him ruler all the days of his life for the sake of My servant David, whom I chose because he kept My commandments and My statutes. ³⁵But I will take the kingdom out of his son's hand and give it to you—ten tribes. ³⁶And to his son I will give one tribe, that My servant David may always have a lamp before Me in Jerusalem, the city which I have chosen for Myself, to put My name there. ³⁷So I will take you, and you shall reign over all your heart desires, and you shall be king over Israel. ³⁸Then it shall be, if

---

11:33 ᵃFollowing Masoretic Text and Targum; Septuagint, Syriac, and Vulgate read *he has.*

Adolescents Gone Bad

A REPORT FROM THE CARNEGIE COUNCIL on Adolescent Development sounded an alarm about parents who—through ignorance, selfishness, or fear—fail to remain involved in the lives of their children after they reach early adolescence.

"Barely out of childhood, young people ages ten to fourteen are today experiencing more freedom, autonomy, and choice than ever at a time when they still need special nurturing, protection, and guidance. Without the sustained involvement of parents and other adults in safeguarding their welfare, young adolescents are at risk of harming themselves and others ... Many reach adulthood ill-equipped to participate responsibly in our democratic society." Writer James Lincoln Collier says that America's abandonment of parental responsibility is "unmatched in human history."

We can't abandon one generation of children without altering the social, moral, and spiritual landscape of the next generation—but this is precisely what too many parents have been doing now for thirty years.

I can't help but wonder if that isn't what happened with Rehoboam, Solomon's son, and his buddies. Apparently their parents spent so little time with them that they rejected the wisdom of their elders—and their subsequent recklessness split the nation of Israel in two.

Teenagers will often act as if they don't need our help, our counsel, our wisdom, or our involvement in their lives. Don't let your teenager push you out. He needs you along side him as he walks through his teen years, whether he knows it or not.

---

you heed all that I command you, walk in My ways, and do *what is* right in My sight, to keep My statutes and My commandments, as My servant David did, then I will be with you and build for you an enduring house, as I built for David, and will give Israel to you. ³⁹And I will afflict the descendants of David because of this, but not forever.'"

⁴⁰Solomon therefore sought to kill Jeroboam. But Jeroboam arose and fled to Egypt, to Shishak king of Egypt, and was in Egypt until the death of Solomon.

Death of Solomon

⁴¹Now the rest of the acts of Solomon, all that he did, and his wisdom, *are* they not written in the book of the acts of Solomon? ⁴²And the period that Solomon reigned in Jerusalem over all Israel *was* forty years. ⁴³Then Solomon rested with his fathers, and was buried in the City of David his father. And Rehoboam his son reigned in his place.

The Revolt Against Rehoboam

12 And Rehoboam went to Shechem, for all Israel had gone to Shechem to make him king. ²So it happened, when Jeroboam the son of Nebat heard *it* (he was still in Egypt, for he had fled from the presence of King Solomon and had been dwelling in Egypt), ³that they sent and called him. Then Jeroboam and the whole assembly of Israel came and spoke to Rehoboam, saying, ⁴"Your father made our yoke heavy; now therefore, lighten the burdensome service of your father, and his heavy yoke which he put on us, and we will serve you."

⁵So he said to them, "Depart *for* three days, then come back to me." And the people departed.

⁶Then King Rehoboam consulted the elders who stood before his father Solomon while he still lived, and he said, "How do you advise *me* to answer these people?"

⁷And they spoke to him, saying, "If you will be a servant to these people today, and serve them, and answer them, and speak good words to them, then they will be your servants forever."

⁸But he rejected the advice which the elders had given him, and consulted the young men who had grown up with him, who stood before him. ⁹And he said to them, "What advice do you give? How should we answer this people who have spoken to me, saying, 'Lighten the yoke which your father put on us'?"

¹⁰Then the young men who had grown

up with him spoke to him, saying, "Thus you should speak to this people who have spoken to you, saying, 'Your father made our yoke heavy, but you make *it* lighter on us'—thus you shall say to them: 'My little *finger* shall be thicker than my father's waist! ¹¹And now, whereas my father put a heavy yoke on you, I will add to your yoke; my father chastised you with whips, but I will chastise you with scourges!' "ᵃ

¹²So Jeroboam and all the people came to Rehoboam the third day, as the king had directed, saying, "Come back to me the third day." ¹³Then the king answered the people roughly, and rejected the advice which the elders had given him; ¹⁴and he spoke to them according to the advice of the young men, saying, "My father made your yoke heavy, but I will add to your yoke; my father chastised you with whips, but I will chastise you with scourges!"ᵃ ¹⁵So the king did not listen to the people; for the turn *of events* was from the LORD, that He might fulfill His word, which the LORD had spoken by Ahijah the Shilonite to Jeroboam the son of Nebat.

¹⁶Now when all Israel saw that the king did not listen to them, the people answered the king, saying:

"What share have we in David?
    We have no inheritance in the son of
        Jesse.
To your tents, O Israel!
Now, see to your own house, O David!"

So Israel departed to their tents. ¹⁷But Rehoboam reigned over the children of Israel who dwelt in the cities of Judah.

¹⁸Then King Rehoboam sent Adoram, who *was* in charge of the revenue; but all Israel stoned him with stones, and he died. Therefore King Rehoboam mounted his chariot in haste to flee to Jerusalem. ¹⁹So Israel has been in rebellion against the house of David to this day.

²⁰Now it came to pass when all Israel heard that Jeroboam had come back, they sent for him and called him to the congregation, and made him king over all Israel. There was none who followed the house of David, but the tribe of Judah only.

²¹And when Rehoboam came to Jerusalem, he assembled all the house of Judah with the tribe of Benjamin, one hundred and eighty thousand chosen *men* who were warriors, to fight against the house of Israel, that he might restore the kingdom to Rehoboam the son of Solomon. ²²But the word of God came to Shemaiah the man of God, saying, ²³"Speak to Rehoboam the son of Solomon, king of Judah, to all the house of Judah and Benjamin, and to the rest of the people, saying, ²⁴'Thus says the LORD: "You shall not go up nor fight against your brethren the children of Israel. Let every man return to his house, for this thing is from Me." '" Therefore they obeyed the word of the LORD, and turned back, according to the word of the LORD.

Jeroboam's Gold Calves

²⁵Then Jeroboam built Shechem in the mountains of Ephraim, and dwelt there. Also he went out from there and built Penuel. ²⁶And Jeroboam said in his heart, "Now the kingdom may return to the house of David: ²⁷If these people go up to offer sacrifices in the house of the LORD at Jerusalem, then the heart of this people will turn back to their lord, Rehoboam king of Judah, and they will kill me and go back to Rehoboam king of Judah."

²⁸Therefore the king asked advice, made two calves of gold, and said to the people, "It is too much for you to go up to Jerusalem. Here are your gods, O Israel, which brought you up from the land of Egypt!" ²⁹And he set up one in Bethel, and the other he put in Dan. ³⁰Now this thing became a sin, for the people went *to worship* before the one as far as Dan. ³¹He made shrinesᵃ on the high places, and made priests from every class of people, who were not of the sons of Levi.

³²Jeroboam ordained a feast on the fifteenth day of the eighth month, like the feast that *was* in Judah, and offered sacrifices on the altar. So he did at Bethel, sacrificing to the calves that he had made. And at Bethel he installed the priests of the high places which he had made. ³³So he made offerings on the altar which he had made at Bethel on the fifteenth day of the eighth month, in the month which he had devised in his own heart. And he ordained a feast

---

12:11 ᵃLiterally *scorpions* **12:14** ᵃLiterally *scorpions*
12:31 ᵃLiterally *a house*

Let's Turn the Corner

ALTHOUGH A YOUNG KING REHOBOAM acted foolishly when his harsh edict split Israel into two kingdoms, he at least avoided a bloody civil war by listening (finally!) to a genuine word from God (12:22).

In a similar way today, while families across this nation are struggling, we can turn the corner if once more we will begin listening to what God says in His Word.

By knowing, applying, experiencing, embracing, and proclaiming God's truth about marriage and family, we can stop the unraveling of our nation's greatest natural resource. The culture promotes countless ideas about values, morality, marriage, family, and parenting, which usually collide head-on with the unchanging truth of Scripture. The problem is that too few Christians know how to understand and apply what the Bible teaches in these critical areas. As a result, many of our marriage and family problems can be traced to biblical illiteracy.

Applying God's truth requires following God's blueprint for your own life and family relationships. We apply God's truth to our lives when we measure our attitudes and actions against the yardstick of God's Word. We believe God's ways are absolute, unchanging, and always best for us. This belief demands application, a strong step of faith and obedience—believing that God's Word is more trustworthy than our feelings or opinions.

As parents we must not only take these steps of faith ourselves, but also train our children to do the same. The words of Judges 2:10 grimly warn us of the consequences of failing in this assignment, "When all that generation had been gathered to their fathers, another generation arose after them who did not know the LORD nor the work which He had done for Israel."

for the children of Israel, and offered sacrifices on the altar and burned incense.

The Message of the Man of God

13 And behold, a man of God went from Judah to Bethel by the word of the LORD, and Jeroboam stood by the altar to burn incense. ²Then he cried out against the altar by the word of the LORD, and said, "O altar, altar! Thus says the LORD: 'Behold, a child, Josiah by name, shall be born to the house of David; and on you he shall sacrifice the priests of the high places who burn incense on you, and men's bones shall be burned on you.'" ³And he gave a sign the same day, saying, "This *is* the sign which the LORD has spoken: Surely the altar shall split apart, and the ashes on it shall be poured out."

⁴So it came to pass when King Jeroboam heard the saying of the man of God, who cried out against the altar in Bethel, that he stretched out his hand from the altar, saying, "Arrest him!" Then his hand, which he stretched out toward him, withered, so that he could not pull it back to himself. ⁵The altar also was split apart, and the ashes poured out from the altar, according to the sign which the man of God had given by the word of the LORD. ⁶Then the king answered and said to the man of God, "Please entreat the favor of the LORD your God, and pray for me, that my hand may be restored to me."

So the man of God entreated the LORD, and the king's hand was restored to him, and became as before. ⁷Then the king said to the man of God, "Come home with me and refresh yourself, and I will give you a reward."

⁸But the man of God said to the king, "If you were to give me half your house, I would not go in with you; nor would I eat bread nor drink water in this place. ⁹For so it was commanded me by the word of the LORD, saying, 'You shall not eat bread, nor drink water, nor return by the same way you came.'" ¹⁰So he went another way and did not return by the way he came to Bethel.

Death of the Man of God

¹¹Now an old prophet dwelt in Bethel, and his sons came and told him all the

DEVOTIONS FOR COUPLES • 13:6
Pray As a Couple for Your Children

When God blessed us with six children over a ten-year period, I gave thanks and at the same time trembled! Raising children is a sobering task. We have no ultimate control over how they will turn out. God must break through in their lives so that they will choose the narrow gate, "which leads to life," and not the wide gate "that leads to destruction" (Matt. 7:14). We generally begin to see what kind of choices a child is going to make as they approach the teenage years and adulthood. If other experiences in life have not shown us how much we depend on God, then parenting a preadolescent or teenager will.

Once we give up the naive idea that we can somehow dictate the choices our children will make, then we are ready to slip on the knee pads and get serious about prayer.

What have we learned about prayer for our children as they prepare for and enter adolescence?

Pray regularly. Bring every concern, dream, or desire about your child to God in fervent, persistent prayer. Luke 18:1–8 contains a great parable on persistent prayer that must have been written for parents of teenagers.

Pray offensively. Before your child hits adolescence, pray for his peer group, that he will have at least one strong Christian buddy for the teenage years. Ask God to protect your child daily from others who would have an evil influence.

Pray defensively. From time to time, we have felt that one of our teens might be deceiving us, but we could never be absolutely certain. In those situations, we have asked God to help us catch him if he's doing something wrong.

Pray intensely. One of the most misunderstood spiritual disciplines of the Christian life is prayer accompanied with fasting. Although fasting does not earn points with God, He nonetheless assumes in Scripture that we will fast and pray (see Matt. 6:16–18), and He works through this spiritual discipline and promises if we do it with the right heart.

Pray with your child. It's easy for prayer to become an exclusive dialogue—you and God. But why not try praying *with* your child, and not just for him or her? We conducted a survey of the community of faith and found that 35% of us pray *for* our children and less than 10% of us pray *with* our children.

Pray together as a couple. No spiritual discipline has protected our marriage and family more than this time of daily communion together with God.

Three of our six children have made it through adolescence. With that behind us, you might think we are tempted to coast to the finish line. Hardly! We've been humbled so many times as parents that we know how impossible it is for a mom or a dad to ultimately shape the hearts of their children and their response to God. Even now, when our children are grown, we pray more than ever for them.

---

works that the man of God had done that day in Bethel; they also told their father the words which he had spoken to the king. [12]And their father said to them, "Which way did he go?" For his sons had seen[a] which way the man of God went who came from Judah. [13]Then he said to his sons, "Saddle the donkey for me." So they saddled the donkey for him; and he rode on it, [14]and went after the man of God, and found him sitting under an oak. Then he said to him, "*Are* you the man of God who came from Judah?"

And he said, "I *am.*"

[15]Then he said to him, "Come home with me and eat bread."

[16]And he said, "I cannot return with you nor go in with you; neither can I eat bread nor drink water with you in this place. [17]For

13:12 [a]Septuagint, Syriac, Targum, and Vulgate read *showed him.*

I have been told by the word of the LORD, 'You shall not eat bread nor drink water there, nor return by going the way you came.'"

¹⁸He said to him, "I too *am* a prophet as you *are,* and an angel spoke to me by the word of the LORD, saying, 'Bring him back with you to your house, that he may eat bread and drink water.'" (He was lying to him.)

¹⁹So he went back with him, and ate bread in his house, and drank water.

²⁰Now it happened, as they sat at the table, that the word of the LORD came to the prophet who had brought him back; ²¹and he cried out to the man of God who came from Judah, saying, "Thus says the LORD: 'Because you have disobeyed the word of the LORD, and have not kept the commandment which the LORD your God commanded you, ²²but you came back, ate bread, and drank water in the place of which *the LORD* said to you, "Eat no bread and drink no water," your corpse shall not come to the tomb of your fathers.'"

²³So it was, after he had eaten bread and after he had drunk, that he saddled the donkey for him, the prophet whom he had brought back. ²⁴When he was gone, a lion met him on the road and killed him. And his corpse was thrown on the road, and the donkey stood by it. The lion also stood by the corpse. ²⁵And there, men passed by and saw the corpse thrown on the road, and the lion standing by the corpse. Then they went and told *it* in the city where the old prophet dwelt.

²⁶Now when the prophet who had brought him back from the way heard *it,* he said, "It *is* the man of God who was disobedient to the word of the LORD. Therefore the LORD has delivered him to the lion, which has torn him and killed him, according to the word of the LORD which He spoke to him." ²⁷And he spoke to his sons, saying, "Saddle the donkey for me." So they saddled *it.* ²⁸Then he went and found his corpse thrown on the road, and the donkey and the lion standing by the corpse. The lion had not eaten the corpse nor torn the donkey. ²⁹And the prophet took up the corpse of the man of God, laid it on the donkey, and

brought it back. So the old prophet came to the city to mourn, and to bury him. ³⁰Then he laid the corpse in his own tomb; and they mourned over him, *saying,* "Alas, my brother!" ³¹So it was, after he had buried him, that he spoke to his sons, saying, "When I am dead, then bury me in the tomb where the man of God *is* buried; lay my bones beside his bones. ³²For the saying which he cried out by the word of the LORD against the altar in Bethel, and against all the shrinesᵃ on the high places which *are* in the cities of Samaria, will surely come to pass."

³³After this event Jeroboam did not turn from his evil way, but again he made priests from every class of people for the high places; whoever wished, he consecrated him, and he became *one* of the priests of the high places. ³⁴And this thing was the sin of the house of Jeroboam, so as to exterminate and destroy *it* from the face of the earth.

Judgment on the House of Jeroboam

14 At that time Abijah the son of Jeroboam became sick. ²And Jeroboam said to his wife, "Please arise, and disguise yourself, that they may not recognize you as the wife of Jeroboam, and go to Shiloh. Indeed, Ahijah the prophet *is* there, who told me that I *would be* king over this people. ³Also take with you ten loaves, *some* cakes, and a jar of honey, and go to him; he will tell you what will become of the child." ⁴And Jeroboam's wife did so; she arose and went to Shiloh, and came to the house of Ahijah. But Ahijah could not see, for his eyes were glazed by reason of his age.

⁵Now the LORD had said to Ahijah, "Here is the wife of Jeroboam, coming to ask you something about her son, for he *is* sick. Thus and thus you shall say to her; for it will be, when she comes in, that she will pretend *to be* another *woman.*"

⁶And so it was, when Ahijah heard the sound of her footsteps as she came through the door, he said, "Come in, wife of Jeroboam. Why do you pretend *to be* another *person?* For I *have been* sent to you *with* bad *news.* ⁷Go, tell Jeroboam, 'Thus says the LORD God of Israel: "Because I exalted

13:32 ᵃLiterally *houses*

you from among the people, and made you ruler over My people Israel, ⁸and tore the kingdom away from the house of David, and gave it to you; and *yet* you have not been as My servant David, who kept My commandments and who followed Me with all his heart, to do only *what was* right in My eyes; ⁹but you have done more evil than all who were before you, for you have gone and made for yourself other gods and molded images to provoke Me to anger, and have cast Me behind your back— ¹⁰therefore behold! I will bring disaster on the house of Jeroboam, and will cut off from Jeroboam every male in Israel, bond and free; I will take away the remnant of the house of Jeroboam, as one takes away refuse until it is all gone. ¹¹The dogs shall eat whoever belongs to Jeroboam and dies in the city, and the birds of the air shall eat whoever dies in the field; for the LORD has spoken!"' ¹²Arise therefore, go to your own house. When your feet enter the city, the child shall die. ¹³And all Israel shall mourn for him and bury him, for he is the only one of Jeroboam who shall come to the grave, because in him there is found something good toward the LORD God of Israel in the house of Jeroboam.

¹⁴"Moreover the LORD will raise up for Himself a king over Israel who shall cut off the house of Jeroboam; this is the day. What? Even now! ¹⁵For the LORD will strike Israel, as a reed is shaken in the water. He will uproot Israel from this good land which He gave to their fathers, and will scatter them beyond the River,ᵃ because they have made their wooden images,ᵇ provoking the LORD to anger. ¹⁶And He will give Israel up because of the sins of Jeroboam, who sinned and who made Israel sin."

¹⁷Then Jeroboam's wife arose and departed, and came to Tirzah. When she came to the threshold of the house, the child died. ¹⁸And they buried him; and all Israel mourned for him, according to the word of the LORD which He spoke through His servant Ahijah the prophet.

Death of Jeroboam

¹⁹Now the rest of the acts of Jeroboam, how he made war and how he reigned, indeed they *are* written in the book of the chronicles of the kings of Israel. ²⁰The period that Jeroboam reigned *was* twenty-two years. So he rested with his fathers. Then Nadab his son reigned in his place.

Rehoboam Reigns in Judah

²¹And Rehoboam the son of Solomon reigned in Judah. Rehoboam *was* forty-one years old when he became king. He reigned seventeen years in Jerusalem, the city which the LORD had chosen out of all the tribes of Israel, to put His name there. His mother's name *was* Naamah, an Ammonitess. ²²Now Judah did evil in the sight of the LORD, and they provoked Him to jealousy with their sins which they committed, more than all that their fathers had done. ²³For they also built for themselves high places, *sacred* pillars, and wooden images on every high hill and under every green tree. ²⁴And there were also perverted personsᵃ in the land. They did according to all the abominations of the nations which the LORD had cast out before the children of Israel.

²⁵It happened in the fifth year of King Rehoboam *that* Shishak king of Egypt came up against Jerusalem. ²⁶And he took away the treasures of the house of the LORD and the treasures of the king's house; he took away everything. He also took away all the gold shields which Solomon had made. ²⁷Then King Rehoboam made bronze shields in their place, and committed *them* to the hands of the captains of the guard, who guarded the doorway of the king's house. ²⁸And whenever the king entered the house of the LORD, the guards carried them, then brought them back into the guardroom.

²⁹Now the rest of the acts of Rehoboam, and all that he did, *are* they not written in the book of the chronicles of the kings of Judah? ³⁰And there was war between Rehoboam and Jeroboam all *their* days. ³¹So Rehoboam rested with his fathers, and was buried with his fathers in the City of David. His mother's name *was* Naamah, an Ammonitess. Then Abijamᵃ his son reigned in his place.

14:15 ᵃThat is, the Euphrates ᵇHebrew *Asherim*, Canaanite deities **14:24** ᵃHebrew *qadesh*, that is, one practicing sodomy and prostitution in religious rituals **14:31** ᵃSpelled *Abijah* in 2 Chronicles 12:16ff

Abijam Reigns in Judah

15 In the eighteenth year of King Jeroboam the son of Nebat, Abijam became king over Judah. ²He reigned three years in Jerusalem. His mother's name *was* Maachah the granddaughter of Abishalom. ³And he walked in all the sins of his father, which he had done before

ROMANCE FAQ

Q: What steps can we take to build a foundation for a successful marriage?

Here are our top five secrets for having a successful marriage:

#1 Settle the issue of ownership. Who is going to be Lord of your life and family? What we give to God is minor compared to what God has given us. He has established us exceedingly abundantly beyond all that we could ask or think. He owns it all!

#2 Secure your commitment to one another. Marriage is ultimately a relationship that is established with a promise, your marriage covenant. Affirm your vows by doing what you promised.

#3 Pray with your spouse every day. I received this secret shortly after Barbara and I were first married. It has been the cement of our marriage! The spiritual discipline of praying together has forced us to resolve our conflicts before we go to bed.

#4 Maintain a teachable heart that seeks and grants forgiveness. All communication is the result of trust. If you're entertaining bitterness, anger, or unforgiveness in your heart, you can't communicate on an intimate level.

#5 Follow a biblical blueprint for marriage. One reason our conferences help so many couples, whether they're engaged or have been married for years, is that both the man and woman leave having heard the same set of biblical principles—blueprints that allow God to be build that marriage and family.

him; his heart was not loyal to the LORD his God, as was the heart of his father David. ⁴Nevertheless for David's sake the LORD his God gave him a lamp in Jerusalem, by setting up his son after him and by establishing Jerusalem; ⁵because David did *what was* right in the eyes of the LORD, and had not turned aside from anything that He commanded him all the days of his life, except in the matter of Uriah the Hittite. ⁶And there was war between Rehoboam[a] and Jeroboam all the days of his life. ⁷Now the rest of the acts of Abijam, and all that he did, *are* they not written in the book of the chronicles of the kings of Judah? And there was war between Abijam and Jeroboam.

⁸So Abijam rested with his fathers, and they buried him in the City of David. Then Asa his son reigned in his place.

Asa Reigns in Judah

⁹In the twentieth year of Jeroboam king of Israel, Asa became king over Judah. ¹⁰And he reigned forty-one years in Jerusalem. His grandmother's name *was* Maachah the granddaughter of Abishalom. ¹¹Asa did *what was* right in the eyes of the LORD, as *did* his father David. ¹²And he banished the perverted persons[a] from the land, and removed all the idols that his fathers had made. ¹³Also he removed Maachah his grandmother from *being* queen mother, because she had made an obscene image of Asherah.[a] And Asa cut down her obscene image and burned *it* by the Brook Kidron. ¹⁴But the high places were not removed. Nevertheless Asa's heart was loyal to the LORD all his days. ¹⁵He also brought into the house of the LORD the things which his father had dedicated, and the things which he himself had dedicated: silver and gold and utensils.

¹⁶Now there was war between Asa and Baasha king of Israel all their days. ¹⁷And Baasha king of Israel came up against Judah, and built Ramah, that he might let none go out or come in to Asa king of Judah.

15:6 [a]Following Masoretic Text, Septuagint, Targum, and Vulgate; some Hebrew manuscripts and Syriac read *Abijam*. **15:12** [a]Hebrew *qedeshim*, that is, those practicing sodomy and prostitution in religious rituals **15:13** [a]A Canaanite goddess

¹⁸Then Asa took all the silver and gold *that was* left in the treasuries of the house of the LORD and the treasuries of the king's house, and delivered them into the hand of his servants. And King Asa sent them to Ben-Hadad the son of Tabrimmon, the son of Hezion, king of Syria, who dwelt in Damascus, saying, ¹⁹*"Let there be* a treaty between you and me, as there was between my father and your father. See, I have sent you a present of silver and gold. Come and break your treaty with Baasha king of Israel, so that he will withdraw from me."

²⁰So Ben-Hadad heeded King Asa, and sent the captains of his armies against the cities of Israel. He attacked Ijon, Dan, Abel Beth Maachah, and all Chinneroth, with all the land of Naphtali. ²¹Now it happened, when Baasha heard *it,* that he stopped building Ramah, and remained in Tirzah. ²²Then King Asa made a proclamation throughout all Judah; none *was* exempted. And they took away the stones and timber of Ramah, which Baasha had used for building; and with them King Asa built Geba of Benjamin, and Mizpah.

²³The rest of all the acts of Asa, all his might, all that he did, and the cities which he built, *are* they not written in the book of the chronicles of the kings of Judah? But in the time of his old age he was diseased in his feet. ²⁴So Asa rested with his fathers, and was buried with his fathers in the City of David his father. Then Jehoshaphat his son reigned in his place.

Nadab Reigns in Israel

²⁵Now Nadab the son of Jeroboam became king over Israel in the second year of Asa king of Judah, and he reigned over Israel two years. ²⁶And he did evil in the sight of the LORD, and walked in the way of his father, and in his sin by which he had made Israel sin.

²⁷Then Baasha the son of Ahijah, of the house of Issachar, conspired against him. And Baasha killed him at Gibbethon, which *belonged* to the Philistines, while Nadab and all Israel laid siege to Gibbethon. ²⁸Baasha killed him in the third year of Asa king of Judah, and reigned in his place. ²⁹And it was so, when he became king, *that* he killed all the house of Jeroboam. He did not leave to Jeroboam anyone that breathed, until he had destroyed him, according to the word of the LORD which He had spoken by His servant Ahijah the Shilonite, ³⁰because of the sins of Jeroboam, which he had sinned and by which he had made Israel sin, because of his provocation with which he had provoked the LORD God of Israel to anger.

³¹Now the rest of the acts of Nadab, and all that he did, *are* they not written in the book of the chronicles of the kings of Israel? ³²And there was war between Asa and Baasha king of Israel all their days.

Baasha Reigns in Israel

³³In the third year of Asa king of Judah, Baasha the son of Ahijah became king over all Israel in Tirzah, and *reigned* twenty-four years. ³⁴He did evil in the sight of the LORD, and walked in the way of Jeroboam, and in his sin by which he had made Israel sin.

16 Then the word of the LORD came to Jehu the son of Hanani, against Baasha, saying: ²"Inasmuch as I lifted you out of the dust and made you ruler over My people Israel, and you have walked in the way of Jeroboam, and have made My people Israel sin, to provoke Me to anger with their sins, ³surely I will take away the posterity of Baasha and the posterity of his house, and I will make your house like the house of Jeroboam the son of Nebat. ⁴The dogs shall eat whoever belongs to Baasha and dies in the city, and the birds of the air shall eat whoever dies in the fields."

⁵Now the rest of the acts of Baasha, what he did, and his might, *are* they not written in the book of the chronicles of the kings of Israel? ⁶So Baasha rested with his fathers and was buried in Tirzah. Then Elah his son reigned in his place.

⁷And also the word of the LORD came by the prophet Jehu the son of Hanani against Baasha and his house, because of all the evil that he did in the sight of the LORD in provoking Him to anger with the work of his hands, in being like the house of Jeroboam, and because he killed them.

Elah Reigns in Israel

⁸In the twenty-sixth year of Asa king of Judah, Elah the son of Baasha became king over Israel, *and reigned* two years in Tirzah.

⁹Now his servant Zimri, commander of half *his* chariots, conspired against him as he was in Tirzah drinking himself drunk in the house of Arza, steward of *his* house in Tirzah. ¹⁰And Zimri went in and struck him and killed him in the twenty-seventh year of Asa king of Judah, and reigned in his place.

¹¹Then it came to pass, when he began to reign, as soon as he was seated on his throne, *that* he killed all the household of Baasha; he did not leave him one male, neither of his relatives nor of his friends. ¹²Thus Zimri destroyed all the household of Baasha, according to the word of the LORD, which He spoke against Baasha by Jehu the prophet, ¹³for all the sins of Baasha and the sins of Elah his son, by which they had sinned and by which they had made Israel sin, in provoking the LORD God of Israel to anger with their idols.

¹⁴Now the rest of the acts of Elah, and all that he did, *are* they not written in the book of the chronicles of the kings of Israel?

Zimri Reigns in Israel

¹⁵In the twenty-seventh year of Asa king of Judah, Zimri had reigned in Tirzah seven days. And the people *were* encamped against Gibbethon, which *belonged* to the Philistines. ¹⁶Now the people *who were* encamped heard it said, "Zimri has conspired and also has killed the king." So all Israel made Omri, the commander of the army, king over Israel that day in the camp. ¹⁷Then Omri and all Israel with him went up from Gibbethon, and they besieged Tirzah. ¹⁸And it happened, when Zimri saw that the city was taken, that he went into the citadel of the king's house and burned the king's house down upon himself with fire, and died, ¹⁹because of the sins which he had committed in doing evil in the sight of the LORD, in walking in the way of Jeroboam, and in his sin which he had committed to make Israel sin.

²⁰Now the rest of the acts of Zimri, and the treason he committed, *are* they not written in the book of the chronicles of the kings of Israel?

Omri Reigns in Israel

²¹Then the people of Israel were divided into two parts: half of the people followed Tibni the son of Ginath, to make him king, and half followed Omri. ²²But the people who followed Omri prevailed over the people who followed Tibni the son of Ginath. So Tibni died and Omri reigned. ²³In the thirty-first year of Asa king of Judah, Omri became king over Israel, *and reigned* twelve years. Six years he reigned in Tirzah. ²⁴And he bought the hill of Samaria from Shemer for two talents of silver; then he built on the hill, and called the name of the city which he built, Samaria, after the name of Shemer, owner of the hill. ²⁵Omri did evil in the eyes of the LORD, and did worse than all who *were* before him. ²⁶For he walked in all the ways of Jeroboam the son of Nebat, and in his sin by which he had made Israel sin, provoking the LORD God of Israel to anger with their idols.

²⁷Now the rest of the acts of Omri which he did, and the might that he showed, *are* they not written in the book of the chronicles of the kings of Israel?

²⁸So Omri rested with his fathers and was buried in Samaria. Then Ahab his son reigned in his place.

Ahab Reigns in Israel

²⁹In the thirty-eighth year of Asa king of Judah, Ahab the son of Omri became king over Israel; and Ahab the son of Omri reigned over Israel in Samaria twenty-two years. ³⁰Now Ahab the son of Omri did evil in the sight of the LORD, more than all who *were* before him. ³¹And it came to pass, as though it had been a trivial thing for him to walk in the sins of Jeroboam the son of Nebat, that he took as wife Jezebel the daughter of Ethbaal, king of the Sidonians; and he went and served Baal and worshiped him. ³²Then he set up an altar for Baal in the temple of Baal, which he had built in Samaria. ³³And Ahab made a wooden image.ᵃ Ahab did more to provoke the LORD God of Israel to anger than all the kings of Israel who were before him. ³⁴In his days Hiel of Bethel built Jericho. He laid its foundation with Abiram his firstborn, and with his youngest *son* Segub he set up its gates, according to the word of the LORD, which He had spoken through Joshua the son of Nun.ᵃ

16:33 ᵃHebrew *Asherah,* a Canaanite goddess
16:34 ᵃCompare Joshua 6:26

Elijah Proclaims a Drought

17 And Elijah the Tishbite, of the inhabitants of Gilead, said to Ahab, "As the LORD God of Israel lives, before whom I stand, there shall not be dew nor rain these years, except at my word."

²Then the word of the LORD came to him, saying, ³"Get away from here and turn eastward, and hide by the Brook Cherith, which flows into the Jordan. ⁴And it will be *that* you shall drink from the brook, and I have commanded the ravens to feed you there."

⁵So he went and did according to the word of the LORD, for he went and stayed by the Brook Cherith, which flows into the Jordan. ⁶The ravens brought him bread and meat in the morning, and bread and meat in the evening; and he drank from the brook. ⁷And it happened after a while that the brook dried up, because there had been no rain in the land.

Elijah and the Widow

⁸Then the word of the LORD came to him, saying, ⁹"Arise, go to Zarephath, which *belongs* to Sidon, and dwell there. See, I have commanded a widow there to provide for you." ¹⁰So he arose and went to Zarephath. And when he came to the gate of the city, indeed a widow *was* there gathering sticks. And he called to her and said, "Please bring me a little water in a cup, that I may drink." ¹¹And as she was going to get *it*, he called to her and said, "Please bring me a morsel of bread in your hand."

¹²So she said, "As the LORD your God lives, I do not have bread, only a handful of flour in a bin, and a little oil in a jar; and see, I *am* gathering a couple of sticks that I may go in and prepare it for myself and my son, that we may eat it, and die."

¹³And Elijah said to her, "Do not fear; go *and* do as you have said, but make me a small cake from it first, and bring *it* to me; and afterward make *some* for yourself and your son. ¹⁴For thus says the LORD God of Israel: 'The bin of flour shall not be used up, nor shall the jar of oil run dry, until the day the LORD sends rain on the earth.'"

¹⁵So she went away and did according to the word of Elijah; and she and he and her household ate for *many* days. ¹⁶The bin

ROMANTIC QUOTES AND NOTES
A Divine Partnership

Do you want to be a terrific spouse? If so, God wants to partner with you—and a big part of that partnership is praying for your mate.

Effective prayer is asking God to do what He already wants to do in your mate's life. God delights in answering such prayer, because He wants you both to know Him, to see Him work, and to continue to come to Him.

What would you like to see happen in your relationship? The Scriptures tell us, "You do not have because you do not ask" (James 4:2). "But I'm nobody!" you say. James would answer, "Elijah was a man with a nature like ours" (5:17), and yet his prayers made a drought last for three years (1 Kings 17:1). Go to God repeatedly with your needs and requests, expecting Him to act for your benefit!

One of my habits when I pray over my lunch (whether she's with me or not) is to also pray for Barbara. I regularly pray that she will experience God as she goes through the remaining part of her day and that she will grow in faith. On other occasions, such as before I leave for work, I'll take her by the hand and bring her and one of her burdens to God in prayer.

Come before God's throne on your mate's behalf, requesting a deeper knowledge of God's love. Pray for an increased desire to obey and follow Christ. Ask God to give your mate a growing awareness of the benefits of walking with Him and that faithfulness, contentment, patience, self-control, discipline, and other godly virtues will continue to grown.

Pray for your mate. They need the prayer. And you and I need the practice.

of flour was not used up, nor did the jar of oil run dry, according to the word of the LORD which He spoke by Elijah.

Elijah Revives the Widow's Son

17Now it happened after these things *that* the son of the woman who owned the house became sick. And his sickness was so serious that there was no breath left in him. 18So she said to Elijah, "What have I to do with you, O man of God? Have you come to me to bring my sin to remembrance, and to kill my son?"

19And he said to her, "Give me your son." So he took him out of her arms and carried him to the upper room where he was staying, and laid him on his own bed. 20Then he cried out to the LORD and said, "O LORD my God, have You also brought tragedy on the widow with whom I lodge, by killing her son?" 21And he stretched himself out on the child three times, and cried out to the LORD and said, "O LORD my God, I pray, let this child's soul come back to him." 22Then the LORD heard the voice of Elijah; and the soul of the child came back to him, and he revived. 23And Elijah took the child and brought him down from the upper room into the house, and gave him to his mother. And Elijah said, "See, your son lives!"

24Then the woman said to Elijah, "Now by this I know that you *are* a man of God, *and* that the word of the LORD in your mouth *is* the truth."

Elijah's Message to Ahab

18 And it came to pass *after* many days that the word of the LORD came to Elijah, in the third year, saying, "Go, present yourself to Ahab, and I will send rain on the earth."

2So Elijah went to present himself to Ahab; and *there was* a severe famine in Samaria. 3And Ahab had called Obadiah, who *was* in charge of *his* house. (Now Obadiah feared the LORD greatly. 4For so it was, while Jezebel massacred the prophets of the LORD, that Obadiah had taken one hundred prophets and hidden them, fifty to a cave, and had fed them with bread and water.) 5And Ahab had said to Obadiah, "Go into the land to all the springs of water and to all the brooks; perhaps we may find grass to keep the horses and mules alive, so that we will not have to kill any livestock." 6So they divided the land between them to explore it; Ahab went one way by himself, and Obadiah went another way by himself.

7Now as Obadiah was on his way, suddenly Elijah met him; and he recognized

---

ROMANTIC QUOTES AND NOTES
Believe the Truth

Some women experience a power outage in marriage because they believe the wrong things. Fairy-tale wishes, celebrity fantasies, magazine psychologists, book authorities, videos, and talk show hosts offer advice on adding sizzle to your marriage. Some of it is good; much of it is not. A lot of it is simply untrue.

What lies do women believe about romance?

Lie #1: I deserve Prince Charming and a happily-ever-after life.

Lie #2: Love is a feeling. No feelings = no love.

Lie #3: Romance should be easy, like falling off a log.

Lie #4: It's *his* fault that I feel this way. If only he'd talk more; if only he'd lose weight; if only he were more romantic.

Lie #5: Romance is *his* responsibility, not mine.

Lies, lies, and more lies!

Turn off the lies and learn to think as did the relieved mother found in 1 Kings 17:24, who told Elijah, "I know that you are a man of God, and that the word of the LORD in your mouth is the truth."

What lies do you believe? And how do they influence your thinking about your husband's need for your romance and affirmation and blessing of his sexuality? Knowing the truth allows you to affirm and act on the truth to meet your husband's needs.

him, and fell on his face, and said, "*Is that you, my lord Elijah?*"

[8]And he answered him, "*It is I. Go, tell your master, 'Elijah is here.'*"

[9]So he said, "How have I sinned, that you are delivering your servant into the hand of Ahab, to kill me? [10]*As* the LORD your God lives, there is no nation or kingdom where my master has not sent someone to hunt for you; and when they said, '*He is* not *here*,' he took an oath from the kingdom or nation that they could not find you. [11]And now you say, 'Go, tell your master, "Elijah *is here*"'! [12]And it shall come to pass, *as soon as* I am gone from you, that the Spirit of the LORD will carry you to a place I do not know; so when I go and tell Ahab, and he cannot find you, he will kill me. But I your servant have feared the LORD from my youth. [13]Was it not reported to my lord what I did when Jezebel killed the prophets of the LORD, how I hid one hundred men of the LORD's prophets, fifty to a cave, and fed them with bread and water? [14]And now you say, 'Go, tell your master, "Elijah *is here*."' He will kill me!"

[15]Then Elijah said, "*As* the LORD of hosts lives, before whom I stand, I will surely present myself to him today."

[16]So Obadiah went to meet Ahab, and told him; and Ahab went to meet Elijah.

[17]Then it happened, when Ahab saw Elijah, that Ahab said to him, "*Is that* you, O troubler of Israel?"

[18]And he answered, "I have not troubled Israel, but you and your father's house *have,* in that you have forsaken the commandments of the LORD and have followed the Baals. [19]Now therefore, send *and* gather all Israel to me on Mount Carmel, the four hundred and fifty prophets of Baal, and the four hundred prophets of Asherah,[a] who eat at Jezebel's table."

Elijah's Mount Carmel Victory

[20]So Ahab sent for all the children of Israel, and gathered the prophets together on Mount Carmel. [21]And Elijah came to all the people, and said, "How long will you falter between two opinions? If the LORD *is* God, follow Him; but if Baal, follow him." But the people answered him not a word.

18:19 [a]A Canaanite goddess

BIBLICAL INSIGHTS • 18:3

Fear God, Not Men

OUR GOD, THE LORD ALMIGHTY, IS HOLY. When I think of the awesome power He wields, I can't help but fear Him and hold Him in reverential awe.

The fear of the Lord keeps us from evil and sin. A.W. Tozer writes, "It is impossible to keep our moral practices sound and our inward attitudes right while our idea of God is erroneous or inadequate." When we lose the fear of God and don't respect Him and His commandments, we will live without accountability to God and one another, which triggers any number of devastating sins. Tozer goes on to say, "The most important thing about us is what we think about God." Our understanding of who God is determines how we live.

The fear of God is what enabled many heroic men throughout history to stand up to tyrants. I think of Obadiah, faithfully serving God despite King Ahab's wretched rule, "And Ahab had called Obadiah, who was in charge of his house. (Now Obadiah feared the LORD greatly)" (18:3).

Do you care more about what men think of you than God? Then learn to fear God, and you will become so preoccupied in walking in His presence that you will cease to care what others think. You will begin to live in light of eternity, and the fleeting views of men simply won't matter anymore.

---

[22]Then Elijah said to the people, "I alone am left a prophet of the LORD; but Baal's prophets *are* four hundred and fifty men. [23]Therefore let them give us two bulls; and let them choose one bull for themselves, cut it in pieces, and lay *it* on the wood, but put no fire *under it;* and I will prepare the other bull, and lay *it* on the wood, but put no fire *under it.* [24]Then you call on the name of your gods, and I will call on the name of the LORD; and the God who answers by fire, He is God."

So all the people answered and said, "It is well spoken."

²⁵Now Elijah said to the prophets of Baal, "Choose one bull for yourselves and prepare it first, for you are many; and call on the name of your god, but put no fire under it."

²⁶So they took the bull which was given them, and they prepared it, and called on the name of Baal from morning even till noon, saying, "O Baal, hear us!" But there was no voice; no one answered. Then they leaped about the altar which they had made.

²⁷And so it was, at noon, that Elijah mocked them and said, "Cry aloud, for he is a god; either he is meditating, or he is busy, or he is on a journey, or perhaps he is sleeping and must be awakened." ²⁸So they cried aloud, and cut themselves, as was their custom, with knives and lances, until the blood gushed out on them. ²⁹And when midday was past, they prophesied until the time of the offering of the evening sacrifice. But there was no voice; no one answered, no one paid attention.

³⁰Then Elijah said to all the people, "Come near to me." So all the people came near to him. And he repaired the altar of the LORD that was broken down. ³¹And Elijah took twelve stones, according to the number of the tribes of the sons of Jacob, to whom the word of the LORD had come, saying, "Israel shall be your name."ᵃ ³²Then with the stones he built an altar in the name of the LORD; and he made a trench around the altar large enough to hold two seahs of seed. ³³And he put the wood in order, cut the bull in pieces, and laid it on the wood, and said, "Fill four waterpots with water, and pour it on the burnt sacrifice and on the wood." ³⁴Then he said, "Do it a second time," and they did it a second time; and he said, "Do it a third time," and they did it a third time. ³⁵So the water ran all around the altar; and he also filled the trench with water.

³⁶And it came to pass, at the time of the offering of the evening sacrifice, that Elijah the prophet came near and said, "LORD God of Abraham, Isaac, and Israel, let it be known this day that You are God in Israel and I am Your servant, and that I have done all these things at Your word. ³⁷Hear me, O LORD, hear me, that this people may know that You are the LORD God, and that You have turned their hearts back to You again."

³⁸Then the fire of the LORD fell and consumed the burnt sacrifice, and the wood and the stones and the dust, and it licked up the water that was in the trench. ³⁹Now when all the people saw it, they fell on their faces; and they said, "The LORD, He is God! The LORD, He is God!"

⁴⁰And Elijah said to them, "Seize the prophets of Baal! Do not let one of them escape!" So they seized them; and Elijah brought them down to the Brook Kishon and executed them there.

The Drought Ends

⁴¹Then Elijah said to Ahab, "Go up, eat and drink; for there is the sound of abundance of rain." ⁴²So Ahab went up to eat and drink. And Elijah went up to the top of Carmel; then he bowed down on the ground, and put his face between his knees, ⁴³and said to his servant, "Go up now, look toward the sea."

So he went up and looked, and said, "There is nothing." And seven times he said, "Go again."

⁴⁴Then it came to pass the seventh time, that he said, "There is a cloud, as small as a man's hand, rising out of the sea!" So he said, "Go up, say to Ahab, 'Prepare your chariot, and go down before the rain stops you.'"

⁴⁵Now it happened in the meantime that the sky became black with clouds and wind, and there was a heavy rain. So Ahab rode away and went to Jezreel. ⁴⁶Then the hand of the LORD came upon Elijah; and he girded up his loins and ran ahead of Ahab to the entrance of Jezreel.

Elijah Escapes from Jezebel

19 And Ahab told Jezebel all that Elijah had done, also how he had executed all the prophets with the sword. ²Then Jezebel sent a messenger to Elijah, saying, "So let the gods do to me, and more also, if I do not make your life as the life of one of them by tomorrow about this time." ³And when he saw that, he arose and ran for his life, and went to Beersheba, which belongs to Judah, and left his servant there.

18:31 ᵃGenesis 32:28

⁴But he himself went a day's journey into the wilderness, and came and sat down under a broom tree. And he prayed that he might die, and said, "It is enough! Now, LORD, take my life, for I *am* no better than my fathers!"

⁵Then as he lay and slept under a broom tree, suddenly an angel[a] touched him, and said to him, "Arise *and* eat." ⁶Then he looked, and there by his head *was* a cake baked on coals, and a jar of water. So he ate and drank, and lay down again. ⁷And the angel[a] of the LORD came back the second time, and touched him, and said, "Arise *and* eat, because the journey *is* too great for you." ⁸So he arose, and ate and drank; and he went in the strength of that food forty days and forty nights as far as Horeb, the mountain of God.

⁹And there he went into a cave, and spent the night in that place; and behold, the word of the LORD *came* to him, and He said to him, "What are you doing here, Elijah?"

¹⁰So he said, "I have been very zealous for the LORD God of hosts; for the children of Israel have forsaken Your covenant, torn down Your altars, and killed Your prophets with the sword. I alone am left; and they seek to take my life."

God's Revelation to Elijah

¹¹Then He said, "Go out, and stand on the mountain before the LORD." And behold, the LORD passed by, and a great and strong wind tore into the mountains and broke the rocks in pieces before the LORD, *but* the LORD *was* not in the wind; and after the wind an earthquake, *but* the LORD *was* not in the earthquake; ¹²and after the earthquake a fire, *but* the LORD *was* not in the fire; and after the fire a still small voice.

¹³So it was, when Elijah heard *it,* that he wrapped his face in his mantle and went out and stood in the entrance of the cave. Suddenly a voice *came* to him, and said, "What are you doing here, Elijah?"

¹⁴And he said, "I have been very zealous for the LORD God of hosts; because the children of Israel have forsaken Your covenant, torn down Your altars, and killed Your prophets with the sword. I alone am left; and they seek to take my life."

¹⁵Then the LORD said to him: "Go, return on your way to the Wilderness of Damascus; and when you arrive, anoint Hazael *as* king over Syria. ¹⁶Also you shall anoint Jehu the son of Nimshi *as* king over Israel. And Elisha the son of Shaphat of Abel Meholah you shall anoint *as* prophet in your place. ¹⁷It shall be *that* whoever escapes the sword of Hazael, Jehu will kill; and whoever escapes the sword of Jehu, Elisha will kill. ¹⁸Yet I have reserved seven thousand in Israel, all whose knees have not bowed to Baal, and every mouth that has not kissed him."

Elisha Follows Elijah

¹⁹So he departed from there, and found Elisha the son of Shaphat, who *was* plowing *with* twelve yoke *of oxen* before him, and he was with the twelfth. Then Elijah passed by him and threw his mantle on him. ²⁰And he left the oxen and ran after Elijah, and said, "Please let me kiss my father and my mother, and *then* I will follow you."

And he said to him, "Go back again, for what have I done to you?"

²¹So *Elisha* turned back from him, and took a yoke of oxen and slaughtered them and boiled their flesh, using the oxen's equipment, and gave it to the people, and they ate. Then he arose and followed Elijah, and became his servant.

Ahab Defeats the Syrians

20 Now Ben-Hadad the king of Syria gathered all his forces together; thirty-two kings *were* with him, with horses and chariots. And he went up and besieged Samaria, and made war against it. ²Then he sent messengers into the city to Ahab king of Israel, and said to him, "Thus says Ben-Hadad: ³'Your silver and your gold *are* mine; your loveliest wives and children are mine.'"

⁴And the king of Israel answered and said, "My lord, O king, just as you say, I and all that I have *are* yours."

⁵Then the messengers came back and said, "Thus speaks Ben-Hadad, saying, 'Indeed I have sent to you, saying, "You shall deliver to me your silver and your gold, your wives and your children"; ⁶but I will send my servants to you tomorrow about this time, and they shall search your house and

---

19:5 ᵃOr *Angel* **19:7** ᵃOr *Angel*

Not a Safe Place to Be

THE ENEMY OF OUR SOULS likes us to remain isolated. He wants us to make major decisions—like choosing a mate or choosing a vocation—without asking for the counsel of other mature believers.

If you do not appreciate the power of isolation, then let me point to some memorable biblical examples. Each of these men were alone when Satan tempted them:

- Joseph was alone when Potiphar's wife propositioned him.
- David was alone when he gawked at Bathsheba.
- Peter was alone when he denied Christ.

Elijah was also alone after he won a great victory over the prophets of Baal, and in his isolation, a wicked queen froze his heart with a deadly threat (19:2, 3). He actually ran away—the same man who had called down fire from heaven on his adversaries! (see 1 Kings 1:10, 12)—and asked to resign from active prophetic duty. God responded to his funk by telling him, "I have reserved seven thousand in Israel, all whose knees have not bowed to Baal" (19:18). Elijah was not alone at all, but as long as he remained isolated, he caved in to depression.

Don't remain isolated! It's not a safe place to be. Instead, seek wise counsel from other godly men and women who can give you perspective and courage when you need it. And if you are isolated emotionally, spiritually, or physically from your spouse, do what it takes to come near and become one.

to me for my wives, my children, my silver, and my gold; and I did not deny him."

⁸And all the elders and all the people said to him, "Do not listen or consent."

⁹Therefore he said to the messengers of Ben-Hadad, "Tell my lord the king, 'All that you sent for to your servant the first time I will do, but this thing I cannot do.'"

And the messengers departed and brought back word to him.

¹⁰Then Ben-Hadad sent to him and said, "The gods do so to me, and more also, if enough dust is left of Samaria for a handful for each of the people who follow me."

¹¹So the king of Israel answered and said, "Tell *him,* 'Let not the one who puts on *his armor* boast like the one who takes *it off.*'"

¹²And it happened when *Ben-Hadad* heard this message, as he and the kings *were* drinking at the command post, that he said to his servants, "Get ready." And they got ready to attack the city.

¹³Suddenly a prophet approached Ahab king of Israel, saying, "Thus says the LORD: 'Have you seen all this great multitude? Behold, I will deliver it into your hand today, and you shall know that I *am* the LORD.'"

¹⁴So Ahab said, "By whom?"

And he said, "Thus says the LORD: 'By the young leaders of the provinces.'"

Then he said, "Who will set the battle in order?"

And he answered, "You."

¹⁵Then he mustered the young leaders of the provinces, and there were two hundred and thirty-two; and after them he mustered all the people, all the children of Israel—seven thousand.

¹⁶So they went out at noon. Meanwhile Ben-Hadad and the thirty-two kings helping him were getting drunk at the command post. ¹⁷The young leaders of the provinces went out first. And Ben-Hadad sent out *a patrol,* and they told him, saying, "Men are coming out of Samaria!" ¹⁸So he said, "If they have come out for peace, take them alive; and if they have come out for war, take them alive."

¹⁹Then these young leaders of the provinces went out of the city with the army which followed them. ²⁰And each one killed his man; so the Syrians fled, and Israel pursued them; and Ben-Hadad the king of Syria

the houses of your servants. And it shall be, *that* whatever is pleasant in your eyes, they will put *it* in their hands and take *it.*'"

⁷So the king of Israel called all the elders of the land, and said, "Notice, please, and see how this *man* seeks trouble, for he sent

escaped on a horse with the cavalry. ²¹Then the king of Israel went out and attacked the horses and chariots, and killed the Syrians with a great slaughter.

²²And the prophet came to the king of Israel and said to him, "Go, strengthen yourself; take note, and see what you should do, for in the spring of the year the king of Syria will come up against you."

The Syrians Again Defeated

²³Then the servants of the king of Syria said to him, "Their gods *are* gods of the hills. Therefore they were stronger than we; but if we fight against them in the plain, surely we will be stronger than they. ²⁴So do this thing: Dismiss the kings, each from his position, and put captains in their places; ²⁵and you shall muster an army like the army that you have lost, horse for horse and chariot for chariot. Then we will fight against them in the plain; surely we will be stronger than they."

And he listened to their voice and did so.

²⁶So it was, in the spring of the year, that Ben-Hadad mustered the Syrians and went up to Aphek to fight against Israel. ²⁷And the children of Israel were mustered and given provisions, and they went against them. Now the children of Israel encamped before them like two little flocks of goats, while the Syrians filled the countryside.

²⁸Then a man of God came and spoke to the king of Israel, and said, "Thus says the LORD: 'Because the Syrians have said, "The LORD *is* God of the hills, but He *is* not God of the valleys," therefore I will deliver all this great multitude into your hand, and you shall know that I *am* the LORD.'" ²⁹And they encamped opposite each other for seven days. So it was that on the seventh day the battle was joined; and the children of Israel killed one hundred thousand foot soldiers *of* the Syrians in one day. ³⁰But the rest fled to Aphek, into the city; then a wall fell on twenty-seven thousand of the men *who were* left.

And Ben-Hadad fled and went into the city, into an inner chamber.

Ahab's Treaty with Ben-Hadad

³¹Then his servants said to him, "Look now, we have heard that the kings of the house of Israel *are* merciful kings. Please, let us put sackcloth around our waists and ropes around our heads, and go out to the king of Israel; perhaps he will spare your life." ³²So they wore sackcloth around their waists and *put* ropes around their heads, and came to the king of Israel and said, "Your servant Ben-Hadad says, 'Please let me live.'"

And he said, "*Is* he still alive? He *is* my brother."

INTIMATE MOMENTS
You Make a Deal

Have you ever seen the TV show, "Let's Make a Deal"? No big deal if you haven't, but it might make the following game a little more fun for your wife if you have.

Buy your wife three gifts, all very different from each other. Wrap them separately and then put them away. When just the two of you are together, bring them all out and let her choose *only one* to open. But don't just hand her the gift when she states her preference! No, have some fun trying to change her mind (if you watch the show, you can get some ideas here). Once she chooses a gift and sticks with her choice, put the other two gifts away for later—and go through the whole, fun process again.

³³Now the men were watching closely to see whether *any sign of mercy would come* from him; and they quickly grasped *at this word* and said, "Your brother Ben-Hadad."

So he said, "Go, bring him." Then Ben-Hadad came out to him; and he had him come up into the chariot.

³⁴So *Ben-Hadad* said to him, "The cities which my father took from your father I will restore; and you may set up market-places for yourself in Damascus, as my father did in Samaria."

Then *Ahab said,* "I will send you away with this treaty." So he made a treaty with him and sent him away.

Ahab Condemned

35Now a certain man of the sons of the prophets said to his neighbor by the word of the LORD, "Strike me, please." And the man refused to strike him. 36Then he said to him, "Because you have not obeyed the voice of the LORD, surely, as soon as you depart from me, a lion shall kill you." And as soon as he left him, a lion found him and killed him.

37And he found another man, and said, "Strike me, please." So the man struck him, inflicting a wound. 38Then the prophet departed and waited for the king by the road, and disguised himself with a bandage over his eyes. 39Now as the king passed by, he cried out to the king and said, "Your servant went out into the midst of the battle; and there, a man came over and brought a man to me, and said, 'Guard this man; if by any means he is missing, your life shall be for his life, or else you shall pay a talent of silver.' 40While your servant was busy here and there, he was gone."

Then the king of Israel said to him, "So *shall* your judgment *be;* you yourself have decided *it.*"

41And he hastened to take the bandage away from his eyes; and the king of Israel recognized him as one of the prophets. 42Then he said to him, "Thus says the LORD: 'Because you have let slip out of *your* hand a man whom I appointed to utter destruction, therefore your life shall go for his life, and your people for his people.'"

43So the king of Israel went to his house sullen and displeased, and came to Samaria.

Naboth Is Murdered for His Vineyard

21 And it came to pass after these things *that* Naboth the Jezreelite had a vineyard which *was* in Jezreel, next to the palace of Ahab king of Samaria. 2So Ahab spoke to Naboth, saying, "Give me your vineyard, that I may have it for a vegetable garden, because it *is* near, next to my house; and for it I will give you a vineyard better than it. *Or,* if it seems good to you, I will give you its worth in money."

3But Naboth said to Ahab, "The LORD forbid that I should give the inheritance of my fathers to you!"

4So Ahab went into his house sullen and displeased because of the word which Naboth the Jezreelite had spoken to him; for he had said, "I will not give you the inheritance of my fathers." And he lay down on his bed, and turned away his face, and would eat no food. 5But Jezebel his wife came to him, and said to him, "Why is your spirit so sullen that you eat no food?"

6He said to her, "Because I spoke to Naboth the Jezreelite, and said to him, 'Give me your vineyard for money; or else, if it pleases you, I will give you *another* vineyard for it.' And he answered, 'I will not give you my vineyard.'"

7Then Jezebel his wife said to him, "You now exercise authority over Israel! Arise, eat food, and let your heart be cheerful; I will give you the vineyard of Naboth the Jezreelite."

8And she wrote letters in Ahab's name, sealed *them* with his seal, and sent the letters to the elders and the nobles who *were* dwelling in the city with Naboth. 9She wrote in the letters, saying,

Proclaim a fast, and seat Naboth with high honor among the people; 10and seat two men, scoundrels, before him to bear witness against him, saying, "You have blasphemed God and the king." *Then* take him out, and stone him, that he may die.

11So the men of his city, the elders and nobles who were inhabitants of his city, did as Jezebel had sent to them, as it *was* written in the letters which she had sent to them. 12They proclaimed a fast, and seated Naboth with high honor among the people. 13And two men, scoundrels, came in and sat before him; and the scoundrels witnessed against him, against Naboth, in the presence of the people, saying, "Naboth has blasphemed God and the king!" Then they took him outside the city and stoned him with stones, so that he died. 14Then they sent to Jezebel, saying, "Naboth has been stoned and is dead."

15And it came to pass, when Jezebel heard that Naboth had been stoned and was dead, that Jezebel said to Ahab, "Arise, take possession of the vineyard of Naboth the Jezreelite, which he refused to give you for money; for Naboth is not alive, but dead." 16So it was, when Ahab heard that Naboth was dead, that Ahab got up and went down to take possession of the vineyard of Naboth the Jezreelite.

The LORD Condemns Ahab

[17]Then the word of the LORD came to Elijah the Tishbite, saying, [18]"Arise, go down to meet Ahab king of Israel, who *lives* in Samaria. There *he is,* in the vineyard of Naboth, where he has gone down to take possession of it. [19]You shall speak to him, saying, 'Thus says the LORD: "Have you murdered and also taken possession?"' And you shall speak to him, saying, 'Thus says the LORD: "In the place where dogs licked the blood of Naboth, dogs shall lick your blood, even yours."'"

[20]So Ahab said to Elijah, "Have you found me, O my enemy?"

21:23 [a]Following Masoretic Text and Septuagint; some Hebrew manuscripts, Syriac, Targum, and Vulgate read *plot of ground* (compare 2 Kings 9:36).

And he answered, "I have found *you,* because you have sold yourself to do evil in the sight of the LORD: [21]Behold, I will bring calamity on you. I will take away your posterity, and will cut off from Ahab every male in Israel, both bond and free. [22]I will make your house like the house of Jeroboam the son of Nebat, and like the house of Baasha the son of Ahijah, because of the provocation with which you have provoked *Me* to anger, and made Israel sin.' [23]And concerning Jezebel the LORD also spoke, saying, 'The dogs shall eat Jezebel by the wall[a] of Jezreel.' [24]The dogs shall eat whoever belongs to Ahab and dies in the city, and the birds of the air shall eat whoever dies in the field."

[25]But there was no one like Ahab who sold himself to do wickedness in the sight of the LORD, because Jezebel his wife stirred him up. [26]And he behaved very abominably in following idols, according to all *that* the

---

PARENTING MATTERS

Q: How can we keep from raising spoiled children?

This is a great question. Families today are raising what is likely the most privileged generation in the history of mankind. Far too many families are child-centric, revolving around the needs, wants and desires of children. We find an illustration of what happens when a child constantly gets his way in the Book of Kings.

The Old Testament describes a young man named Adonijah, who grew up extremely privileged as King David's son. Yet he became an arrogant and rebellious young man. In modern terms, he was spoiled rotten.

First Kings 1:6 gives us a clue about Adonijah's character deficit, "And his father had not rebuked him at any time by saying, 'Why have you done so?'" Another translation says that David had never "crossed" Adonijah, which literally means he had never "pained" him.

The problem with Adonijah was that David wasn't involved in shaping his son's character or disciplining him in any way, and as a result, Adonijah grew up into a man with little conscience and no humility, feeling like he was entitled to privilege and happiness.

The dangers of this culture are clear. It is difficult for a child to develop positive character traits, such as humility or generosity, on his or her own. God uses parents, the Scriptures, and the local church to teach a child about the importance of good character. If you want to make sure your children don't grow up to be spoiled rotten, then make sure they have lots and lots of all three—parents, the Scriptures, and church—in their lives, from the time they are born. And pray that your children will put their faith in Christ, the One who can transform a selfish, spoiled child into someone whose life displays godly character.

Amorites had done, whom the LORD had cast out before the children of Israel.

27So it was, when Ahab heard those words, that he tore his clothes and put sackcloth on his body, and fasted and lay in sackcloth, and went about mourning.

28And the word of the LORD came to Elijah the Tishbite, saying, 29"See how Ahab has humbled himself before Me? Because he has humbled himself before Me, I will not bring the calamity in his days. In the days of his son I will bring the calamity on his house."

Micaiah Warns Ahab

22 Now three years passed without war between Syria and Israel. 2Then it came to pass, in the third year, that Jehoshaphat the king of Judah went down to *visit* the king of Israel.

3And the king of Israel said to his servants, "Do you know that Ramoth in Gilead *is* ours, but we hesitate to take it out of the hand of the king of Syria?" 4So he said to Jehoshaphat, "Will you go with me to fight at Ramoth Gilead?"

Jehoshaphat said to the king of Israel, "I *am* as you *are*, my people as your people, my horses as your horses." 5Also Jehoshaphat said to the king of Israel, "Please inquire for the word of the LORD today."

6Then the king of Israel gathered the prophets together, about four hundred men, and said to them, "Shall I go against Ramoth Gilead to fight, or shall I refrain?"

So they said, "Go up, for the Lord will deliver *it* into the hand of the king."

7And Jehoshaphat said, "*Is there* not still a prophet of the LORD here, that we may inquire of Him?"a

8So the king of Israel said to Jehoshaphat, "*There is* still one man, Micaiah the son of Imlah, by whom we may inquire of the LORD; but I hate him, because he does not prophesy good concerning me, but evil."

And Jehoshaphat said, "Let not the king say such things!"

9Then the king of Israel called an officer and said, "Bring Micaiah the son of Imlah quickly!"

10The king of Israel and Jehoshaphat the king of Judah, having put on *their* robes, sat each on his throne, at a threshing floor at the entrance of the gate of Samaria; and all the prophets prophesied before them. 11Now Zedekiah the son of Chenaanah had made horns of iron for himself; and he said, "Thus says the LORD: 'With these you shall gore the Syrians until they are destroyed.'" 12And all the prophets prophesied so, saying, "Go up to Ramoth Gilead and prosper, for the LORD will deliver *it* into the king's hand."

13Then the messenger who had gone to call Micaiah spoke to him, saying, "Now listen, the words of the prophets with one accord encourage the king. Please, let your word be like the word of one of them, and speak encouragement."

14And Micaiah said, "*As* the LORD lives, whatever the LORD says to me, that I will speak."

15Then he came to the king; and the king said to him, "Micaiah, shall we go to war against Ramoth Gilead, or shall we refrain?"

And he answered him, "Go and prosper, for the LORD will deliver *it* into the hand of the king!"

16So the king said to him, "How many times shall I make you swear that you tell me nothing but the truth in the name of the LORD?"

17Then he said, "I saw all Israel scattered on the mountains, as sheep that have no shepherd. And the LORD said, 'These have no master. Let each return to his house in peace.'"

18And the king of Israel said to Jehoshaphat, "Did I not tell you he would not prophesy good concerning me, but evil?"

19Then *Micaiah* said, "Therefore hear the word of the LORD: I saw the LORD sitting on His throne, and all the host of heaven standing by, on His right hand and on His left. 20And the LORD said, 'Who will persuade Ahab to go up, that he may fall at Ramoth Gilead?' So one spoke in this manner, and another spoke in that manner. 21Then a spirit came forward and stood before the LORD, and said, 'I will persuade him.' 22The LORD said to him, 'In what way?' So he said, 'I will go out and be a lying spirit in the mouth of all his prophets.' And the LORD said, 'You shall persuade *him*, and also prevail. Go out and do so.' 23Therefore look! The LORD has

22:7 aOr *him*

put a lying spirit in the mouth of all these prophets of yours, and the LORD has declared disaster against you."

²⁴Now Zedekiah the son of Chenaanah went near and struck Micaiah on the cheek, and said, "Which way did the spirit from the LORD go from me to speak to you?"

²⁵And Micaiah said, "Indeed, you shall see on that day when you go into an inner chamber to hide!"

²⁶So the king of Israel said, "Take Micaiah, and return him to Amon the governor of the city and to Joash the king's son; ²⁷and say, 'Thus says the king: "Put this *fellow* in prison, and feed him with bread of affliction and water of affliction, until I come in peace."'"

²⁸But Micaiah said, "If you ever return in peace, the LORD has not spoken by me." And he said, "Take heed, all you people!"

Ahab Dies in Battle

²⁹So the king of Israel and Jehoshaphat the king of Judah went up to Ramoth Gilead. ³⁰And the king of Israel said to Jehoshaphat, "I will disguise myself and go into battle; but you put on your robes." So the king of Israel disguised himself and went into battle.

³¹Now the king of Syria had commanded the thirty-two captains of his chariots, saying, "Fight with no one small or great, but only with the king of Israel." ³²So it was, when the captains of the chariots saw Jehoshaphat, that they said, "Surely it *is* the king of Israel!" Therefore they turned aside to fight against him, and Jehoshaphat cried out. ³³And it happened, when the captains of the chariots saw that it *was* not the king of Israel, that they turned back from pursuing him. ³⁴Now a *certain* man drew a bow at random, and struck the king of Israel between the joints of his armor. So he said to the driver of his chariot, "Turn around and take me out of the battle, for I am wounded."

³⁵The battle increased that day; and the king was propped up in his chariot, facing the Syrians, and died at evening. The blood ran out from the wound onto the floor of the chariot. ³⁶Then, as the sun was going down, a shout went throughout the army, saying,

BIBLICAL INSIGHTS • 22:14
Stick With the Truth

LIFE HAS A WAY OF EDITING THE TRUTH of Scripture. Imagine what happens, for example, when a daughter says through tears that her Christian husband is verbally abusing her and her children.

"Daddy," she sobs, "I don't know how much longer I can take this!" At that moment we would do anything to free her from her pain. "After all," we conclude, "wouldn't peace be better for the kids than hostility?"

If we react only with our hearts, however, we may forget about God's Word and resort to the world's solution—divorce. It's in these real life situations that the truth of Scripture can too easily be set aside for immediate peace and the expediency of life. If we let it, life can indeed edit Scripture.

The prophet Micaiah refused to cave in like this. He insisted on speaking the truth of God, regardless of how much pain it caused him. "As the LORD lives," he declared, "whatever the LORD says to me, that I will speak" (22:4).

I'm not trying to dismiss this problem by giving a cut-and-dried theological answer. I believe parents can and should seek help from law enforcement officials if a son or daughter is in physical danger. We can encourage our married children to seek godly counsel for a troubled marriage. But we must not rush to accept the world's solutions and ignore truth of God's Word. His counsel is sure and life giving. Our compassion and advice must be informed and guided by *all* the truth of Scripture.

"Every man to his city, and every man to his own country!"

³⁷So the king died, and was brought to Samaria. And they buried the king in Samaria. ³⁸Then *someone* washed the chariot at a pool in Samaria, and the dogs licked up his blood while the harlots bathed,ᵃ according to the word of the LORD which He had spoken.

22:38 ᵃSyriac and Targum read *they washed his armor.*

³⁹Now the rest of the acts of Ahab, and all that he did, the ivory house which he built and all the cities that he built, *are* they not written in the book of the chronicles of the kings of Israel? ⁴⁰So Ahab rested with his fathers. Then Ahaziah his son reigned in his place.

Jehoshaphat Reigns in Judah

⁴¹Jehoshaphat the son of Asa had become king over Judah in the fourth year of Ahab king of Israel. ⁴²Jehoshaphat *was* thirty-five years old when he became king, and he reigned twenty-five years in Jerusalem. His mother's name *was* Azubah the daughter of Shilhi. ⁴³And he walked in all the ways of his father Asa. He did not turn aside from them, doing *what was* right in the eyes of the LORD. Nevertheless the high places were not taken away, *for* the people offered sacrifices and burned incense on the high places. ⁴⁴Also Jehoshaphat made peace with the king of Israel.

⁴⁵Now the rest of the acts of Jehoshaphat, the might that he showed, and how he made war, *are* they not written in the book of the chronicles of the kings of Judah? ⁴⁶And the rest of the perverted persons,ᵃ who remained in the days of his father Asa, he banished from the land. ⁴⁷*There was* then no king in Edom, only a deputy of the king.

⁴⁸Jehoshaphat made merchant shipsᵃ to go to Ophir for gold; but they never sailed, for the ships were wrecked at Ezion Geber. ⁴⁹Then Ahaziah the son of Ahab said to Jehoshaphat, "Let my servants go with your servants in the ships." But Jehoshaphat would not.

⁵⁰And Jehoshaphat rested with his fathers, and was buried with his fathers in the City of David his father. Then Jehoram his son reigned in his place.

Ahaziah Reigns in Israel

⁵¹Ahaziah the son of Ahab became king over Israel in Samaria in the seventeenth year of Jehoshaphat king of Judah, and reigned two years over Israel. ⁵²He did evil in the sight of the LORD, and walked in the way of his father and in the way of his mother and in the way of Jeroboam the son of Nebat, who had made Israel sin; ⁵³for he served Baal and worshiped him, and provoked the LORD God of Israel to anger, according to all that his father had done.

22:46 ᵃHebrew *qadesh,* that is, one practicing sodomy and prostitution in religious rituals **22:48** ᵃOr *ships of Tarshish*

2 KINGS

THIS BOOK IS "PART TWO" of the 400-year history of the Hebrew people from the time of Solomon until the Babylonian conquest and capture of the Israelites living in the southern kingdom (the people of the northern kingdom had been conquered and taken into captivity by the Assyrians about 135 years before Judah went into exile). First and Second Kings should be considered as a single book of history. It was originally divided into two parts in order to fit more easily onto scrolls.

Second Kings begins with the death of Elijah the prophet and the rise of his protégé, Elisha. God validated Elisha's ministry by working miracles through him—exactly twice as many as Elijah, in precise fulfillment of the prophecy stated in 1 Kings 2:9, 10. Through Elisha, a widow gets her financial needs met when the contents of a single jar of oil provides her with an abundant supply—enough to satisfy the large debts incurred by her husband, and yet still provide for her family. An older woman who had been unable to have children shows kindness to Elisha, and gets rewarded with the miraculous conception and birth of a son. A foreign army commander hears of the powerful ministry of Elisha, and after he gets healed of a loathsome skin disease, he returns to his own land, a firm believer in the God of Israel.

With a few notable exceptions, the kings of both the northern and southern kingdoms refuse to honor the word of God or pay attention to the prophets of God. They thus ignore the counsel of King David: "He who rules over men must be just, ruling in the fear of God" (2 Samuel 23:3). Most of the kings you will read about in this book had little time for God. In fact, the most common epitaph inscribed on their gravestones is the very sad note, "But [King X] did evil in the eyes of the LORD." Their failure to rule in the fear of God would lead the Israelites into one of the darkest chapters in their national history.

God Judges Ahaziah

1 Moab rebelled against Israel after the death of Ahab.

2Now Ahaziah fell through the lattice of his upper room in Samaria, and was injured; so he sent messengers and said to them, "Go, inquire of Baal-Zebub, the god of Ekron, whether I shall recover from this injury." 3But the angela of the LORD said to Elijah the Tishbite, "Arise, go up to meet the messengers of the king of Samaria, and say to them, 'Is it because *there is* no God in Israel *that* you are going to inquire of Baal-Zebub, the god of Ekron?' 4Now therefore, thus says the LORD: 'You shall not come down from the bed to which you have gone up, but you shall surely die.'" So Elijah departed.

5And when the messengers returned to him, he said to them, "Why have you come back?"

6So they said to him, "A man came up to meet us, and said to us, 'Go, return to the king who sent you, and say to him, "Thus says the LORD: 'Is it because *there is* no God in Israel *that* you are sending to inquire of Baal-Zebub, the god of Ekron? Therefore you shall not come down from the bed to which you have gone up, but you shall surely die.'"'"

7Then he said to them, "What kind of man *was it* who came up to meet you and told you these words?"

8So they answered him, "A hairy man wearing a leather belt around his waist."

And he said, "It *is* Elijah the Tishbite."

9Then the king sent to him a captain of fifty with his fifty men. So he went up to him; and there he was, sitting on the top of a hill. And he spoke to him: "Man of God, the king has said, 'Come down!'"

10So Elijah answered and said to the captain of fifty, "If I *am* a man of God, then let fire come down from heaven and consume you and your fifty men." And fire came down from heaven and consumed him and his fifty. 11Then he sent to him another captain of fifty with his fifty men.

And he answered and said to him: "Man of God, thus has the king said, 'Come down quickly!'"

12So Elijah answered and said to them, "If I *am* a man of God, let fire come down from heaven and consume you and your fifty men." And the fire of God came down from heaven and consumed him and his fifty.

13Again, he sent a third captain of fifty with his fifty men. And the third captain of fifty went up, and came and fell on his knees before Elijah, and pleaded with him, and said to him: "Man of God, please let my life and the life of these fifty servants of yours be precious in your sight. 14Look, fire has come down from heaven and burned up the first two captains of fifties with their fifties. But let my life now be precious in your sight."

15And the angela of the LORD said to Elijah, "Go down with him; do not be afraid of him." So he arose and went down with him to the king. 16Then he said to him, "Thus says the LORD: 'Because you have sent messengers to inquire of Baal-Zebub, the god of Ekron, *is it* because *there is* no God in Israel to inquire of His word? Therefore you shall not come down from

---

INTIMATE MOMENTS

Frame It

Does your husband have a recent, professionally done photo of you? If not, call a professional photographer and schedule a shoot with you. Most areas have a number of such businesses, and most of them have specials throughout the year that you could take advantage of.

Decide before the session what you'd like to wear, but be sure to consult with the photographer ahead of time to avoid any difficulties with specific colors, patterns, or fabrics. You want to make this photo really sing! Usually you will have your pick of several poses. Choose your favorite pose, put it in a nice frame, and give it to your husband. You might want to pick a frame that can be either hung on a wall or stand up on a desk.

1:3 aOr *Angel*   1:15 aOr *Angel*

the bed to which you have gone up, but you shall surely die.'"

[17]So *Ahaziah* died according to the word of the LORD which Elijah had spoken. Because he had no son, Jehoram[a] became king in his place, in the second year of Jehoram the son of Jehoshaphat, king of Judah.

[18]Now the rest of the acts of Ahaziah which he did, *are* they not written in the book of the chronicles of the kings of Israel?

Elijah Ascends to Heaven

2 And it came to pass, when the LORD was about to take up Elijah into heaven by a whirlwind, that Elijah went with Elisha from Gilgal. [2]Then Elijah said to Elisha, "Stay here, please, for the LORD has sent me on to Bethel."

But Elisha said, "*As* the LORD lives, and *as* your soul lives, I will not leave you!" So they went down to Bethel.

[3]Now the sons of the prophets who *were* at Bethel came out to Elisha, and said to him, "Do you know that the LORD will take away your master from over you today?"

And he said, "Yes, I know; keep silent!"

[4]Then Elijah said to him, "Elisha, stay here, please, for the LORD has sent me on to Jericho."

But he said, "*As* the LORD lives, and *as* your soul lives, I will not leave you!" So they came to Jericho.

[5]Now the sons of the prophets who *were* at Jericho came to Elisha and said to him, "Do you know that the LORD will take away your master from over you today?"

So he answered, "Yes, I know; keep silent!"

[6]Then Elijah said to him, "Stay here, please, for the LORD has sent me on to the Jordan."

But he said, "*As* the LORD lives, and *as* your soul lives, I will not leave you!" So the two of them went on. [7]And fifty men of the sons of the prophets went and stood facing *them* at a distance, while the two of them stood by the Jordan. [8]Now Elijah took his mantle, rolled *it* up, and struck the water; and it was divided this way and that, so that the two of them crossed over on dry ground.

---

[9]And so it was, when they had crossed over, that Elijah said to Elisha, "Ask! What may I do for you, before I am taken away from you?"

Elisha said, "Please let a double portion of your spirit be upon me."

[10]So he said, "You have asked a hard thing. *Nevertheless,* if you see me *when I am* taken from you, it shall be so for you; but if not, it shall not be *so.*" [11]Then it happened, as they continued on and talked, that suddenly a chariot of fire *appeared* with horses of fire, and separated the two of them; and Elijah went up by a whirlwind into heaven.

[12]And Elisha saw *it,* and he cried out, "My father, my father, the chariot of Israel and its horsemen!" So he saw him no more. And he took hold of his own clothes and tore them into two pieces. [13]He also took up the mantle of Elijah that had fallen from him, and went back and stood by the bank of the Jordan. [14]Then he took the mantle of Elijah that had fallen from him, and struck the water, and said, "Where *is* the LORD God of Elijah?" And when he also had struck the water, it was divided this way and that; and Elisha crossed over.

[15]Now when the sons of the prophets who *were* from Jericho saw him, they said, "The spirit of Elijah rests on Elisha." And they came to meet him, and bowed to the ground before him. [16]Then they said to him, "Look now, there are fifty strong men with your servants. Please let them go and search for your master, lest perhaps the Spirit of the LORD has taken him up and cast him upon some mountain or into some valley."

And he said, "You shall not send anyone."

[17]But when they urged him till he was ashamed, he said, "Send *them!*" Therefore they sent fifty men, and they searched for three days but did not find him. [18]And when they came back to him, for he had stayed in Jericho, he said to them, "Did I not say to you, 'Do not go'?"

Elisha Performs Miracles

[19]Then the men of the city said to Elisha, "Please notice, the situation of this city *is* pleasant, as my lord sees; but the water *is* bad, and the ground barren."

1:17 [a]The son of Ahab king of Israel (compare 3:1)

²⁰And he said, "Bring me a new bowl, and put salt in it." So they brought *it* to him. ²¹Then he went out to the source of the water, and cast in the salt there, and said, "Thus says the LORD: 'I have healed this water; from it there shall be no more death or barrenness.'" ²²So the water remains healed to this day, according to the word of Elisha which he spoke.

²³Then he went up from there to Bethel; and as he was going up the road, some youths came from the city and mocked him, and said to him, "Go up, you baldhead! Go up, you baldhead!"

²⁴So he turned around and looked at them, and pronounced a curse on them in the name of the LORD. And two female bears came out of the woods and mauled forty-two of the youths.

²⁵Then he went from there to Mount Carmel, and from there he returned to Samaria.

Moab Rebels Against Israel

3 Now Jehoram the son of Ahab became king over Israel at Samaria in the eighteenth year of Jehoshaphat king of Judah, and reigned twelve years. ²And he did evil in the sight of the LORD, but not like his father and mother; for he put away the *sacred* pillar of Baal that his father had made. ³Nevertheless he persisted in the sins of Jeroboam the son of Nebat, who had made Israel sin; he did not depart from them.

⁴Now Mesha king of Moab was a sheep-breeder, and he regularly paid the king of Israel one hundred thousand lambs and the wool of one hundred thousand rams. ⁵But it happened, when Ahab died, that the king of Moab rebelled against the king of Israel.

⁶So King Jehoram went out of Samaria at that time and mustered all Israel. ⁷Then he went and sent to Jehoshaphat king of Judah, saying, "The king of Moab has rebelled against me. Will you go with me to fight against Moab?"

And he said, "I will go up; I *am* as you *are*, my people as your people, my horses as your horses." ⁸Then he said, "Which way shall we go up?"

And he answered, "By way of the Wilderness of Edom."

⁹So the king of Israel went with the king of Judah and the king of Edom, and they marched on that roundabout route seven days; and there was no water for the army, nor for the animals that followed them. ¹⁰And the king of Israel said, "Alas! For the LORD has called these three kings together to deliver them into the hand of Moab."

¹¹But Jehoshaphat said, "*Is there* no prophet of the LORD here, that we may inquire of the LORD by him?"

So one of the servants of the king of

ROMANCE FAQ

Q: What simple things can we do to make sure neither of us strays?

Here are seven exhortations to affair-proof your marriage:

1. *Make your marriage bed your priority.* Exhaustion is the great zapper of passion. Make your sexual relationship a priority in your married life.

2. *Talk about what pleases one another.* Describe what would truly please you, and encourage him/her to do the same.

3. *Fan the flames of romance.* Find out what setting sparks or even ignites your love for your mate.

4. *Have fun with one another, but not at each other's expense.* Grins, giggles, and laughter ought to occasionally drift out of our bedrooms.

5. *Add the element of surprise to your marriage bed.* If the sexual area of your marriage has been a struggle, then ask permission before cooking up something you think is wonderful that your spouse might not appreciate (Rom. 15:1–7).

6. *Be patient with your mate.* Married love demands that we continually grow and learn about one another (see 1 Thess. 5:14, 15).

7. *Beware of bitterness.* Bitterness quenches the fires of romance. Keep short accounts and ask forgiveness when you fail or if you have become bitter (Eph. 4:26, 27).

Israel answered and said, "Elisha the son of Shaphat *is* here, who poured water on the hands of Elijah."

¹²And Jehoshaphat said, "The word of the LORD is with him." So the king of Israel and Jehoshaphat and the king of Edom went down to him.

¹³Then Elisha said to the king of Israel, "What have I to do with you? Go to the prophets of your father and the prophets of your mother."

But the king of Israel said to him, "No, for the LORD has called these three kings *together* to deliver them into the hand of Moab."

¹⁴And Elisha said, "*As* the LORD of hosts lives, before whom I stand, surely were it not that I regard the presence of Jehoshaphat king of Judah, I would not look at you, nor see you. ¹⁵But now bring me a musician."

Then it happened, when the musician played, that the hand of the LORD came upon him. ¹⁶And he said, "Thus says the LORD: 'Make this valley full of ditches.' ¹⁷For thus says the LORD: 'You shall not see wind, nor shall you see rain; yet that valley shall be filled with water, so that you, your cattle, and your animals may drink.' ¹⁸And this is a simple matter in the sight of the LORD; He will also deliver the Moabites into your hand. ¹⁹Also you shall attack every fortified city and every choice city, and shall cut down every good tree, and stop up every spring of water, and ruin every good piece of land with stones."

²⁰Now it happened in the morning, when the grain offering was offered, that

---

| PARENTING MATTERS | **Q: How can we deter or discourage our children from using drugs or alcohol?** |

First, model a rich love relationship with Jesus Christ. That, we believe, will draw your child away from a desire for any false high. This is the key to fighting off a host of temptations, not just drugs and alcohol.

Our Creator placed within our souls deep longings for happiness and satisfaction that God alone can satisfy. He alone is the source of complete and unending pleasure: "In Your presence is fullness of joy; at Your right hand there are pleasures forevermore" (Ps. 16:11).

Second, present a model of personal behavior that minimizes your child's opportunity to have any excuse to use or abuse substances. The following words of King David express well the desire we have to not cause our children to stumble by what they see us doing: "My eyes shall be upon the faithful of the land, that they may dwell with me; he who walks in a blameless way, he shall sever me" (Ps. 101:6).

Next, talk with your children while they are preteens about their convictions and standards. Shape their thoughts and attitudes in advance of their facing the temptation. The ages of 10–12 can be a tremendous time of instructing your child on various issues they will face later as adolescents and in adulthood. Role-play with them what they would do when a friend pressures them to drink, do drugs, or get in the car with someone who is under the influence of a substance.

Finally, stay emotionally connected to your child, offering generous attention, acceptance, affection—that means love. That will encourage him or her toward proper behavior. Let them know that if they fail, you will respond with grace and forgiveness. They need to know that their relationship with you is secure.

suddenly water came by way of Edom, and the land was filled with water.

21And when all the Moabites heard that the kings had come up to fight against them, all who were able to bear arms and older were gathered; and they stood at the border. 22Then they rose up early in the morning, and the sun was shining on the water; and the Moabites saw the water on the other side *as* red as blood. 23And they said, "This is blood; the kings have surely struck swords and have killed one another; now therefore, Moab, to the spoil!"

24So when they came to the camp of Israel, Israel rose up and attacked the Moabites, so that they fled before them; and they entered *their* land, killing the Moabites. 25Then they destroyed the cities, and each man threw a stone on every good piece of land and filled it; and they stopped up all the springs of water and cut down all the good trees. But they left the stones of Kir Haraseth *intact.* However the slingers surrounded and attacked it.

26And when the king of Moab saw that the battle was too fierce for him, he took with him seven hundred men who drew swords, to break through to the king of Edom, but they could not. 27Then he took his eldest son who would have reigned in his place, and offered him *as* a burnt offering upon the wall; and there was great indignation against Israel. So they departed from him and returned to *their own* land.

Elisha and the Widow's Oil

4 A certain woman of the wives of the sons of the prophets cried out to Elisha, saying, "Your servant my husband is dead, and you know that your servant feared the LORD. And the creditor is coming to take my two sons to be his slaves."

2So Elisha said to her, "What shall I do for you? Tell me, what do you have in the house?" And she said, "Your maidservant has nothing in the house but a jar of oil."

3Then he said, "Go, borrow vessels from everywhere, from all your neighbors— empty vessels; do not gather just a few. 4And when you have come in, you shall shut the door behind you and your sons; then pour it into all those vessels, and set aside the full ones."

5So she went from him and shut the door behind her and her sons, who brought *the vessels* to her; and she poured *it* out. 6Now it came to pass, when the vessels were full, that she said to her son, "Bring me another vessel."

And he said to her, "*There is* not another vessel." So the oil ceased. 7Then she came and told the man of God. And he said, "Go, sell the oil and pay your debt; and you *and* your sons live on the rest."

Elisha Raises the Shunammite's Son

8Now it happened one day that Elisha went to Shunem, where there *was* a notable woman, and she persuaded him to eat some food. So it was, as often as he passed by, he would turn in there to eat some food. 9And she said to her husband, "Look now, I know that this *is* a holy man of God, who passes by us regularly. 10Please, let us make a small upper room on the wall; and let us put a bed for him there, and a table and a chair and a lampstand; so it will be, whenever he comes to us, he can turn in there."

11And it happened one day that he came there, and he turned in to the upper room and lay down there. 12Then he said to Gehazi his servant, "Call this Shunammite woman." When he had called her, she stood before him. 13And he said to him, "Say now to her, 'Look, you have been concerned for us with all this care. What *can I* do for you? Do you want me to speak on your behalf to the king or to the commander of the army?'"

She answered, "I dwell among my own people."

14So he said, "What then *is* to be done for her?"

And Gehazi answered, "Actually, she has no son, and her husband is old."

15So he said, "Call her." When he had called her, she stood in the doorway. 16Then he said, "About this time next year you shall embrace a son."

And she said, "No, my lord. Man of God, do not lie to your maidservant!"

17But the woman conceived, and bore a son when the appointed time had come, of which Elisha had told her.

18And the child grew. Now it happened one day that he went out to his father, to the reapers. ¹⁹And he said to his father, "My head, my head!"

So he said to a servant, "Carry him to his mother." ²⁰When he had taken him and brought him to his mother, he sat on her knees till noon, and *then* died. ²¹And she went up and laid him on the bed of the man of God, shut *the door* upon him, and went out. ²²Then she called to her husband, and said, "Please send me one of the young men and one of the donkeys, that I may run to the man of God and come back."

²³So he said, "Why are you going to him today? *It is* neither the New Moon nor the Sabbath."

And she said, "*It is* well." ²⁴Then she saddled a donkey, and said to her servant, "Drive, and go forward; do not slacken the pace for me unless I tell you." ²⁵And so she departed, and went to the man of God at Mount Carmel.

So it was, when the man of God saw her afar off, that he said to his servant Gehazi, "Look, the Shunammite woman! ²⁶Please run now to meet her, and say to her, 'Is it well with you? *Is it* well with your husband? *Is it* well with the child?'"

And she answered, "*It is* well." ²⁷Now when she came to the man of God at the hill, she caught him by the feet, but Gehazi came near to push her away. But the man of God said, "Let her alone; for her soul *is* in deep distress, and the LORD has hidden *it* from me, and has not told me."

²⁸So she said, "Did I ask a son of my lord? Did I not say, 'Do not deceive me'?"

²⁹Then he said to Gehazi, "Get yourself ready, and take my staff in your hand, and be on your way. If you meet anyone, do not greet him; and if anyone greets you, do not answer him; but lay my staff on the face of the child."

³⁰And the mother of the child said, "*As* the LORD lives, and *as* your soul lives, I will not leave you." So he arose and followed her. ³¹Now Gehazi went on ahead of them, and laid the staff on the face of the child; but *there was* neither voice nor hearing. Therefore he went back to meet him, and told him, saying, "The child has not awakened."

³²When Elisha came into the house, there was the child, lying dead on his bed.

³³He went in therefore, shut the door behind the two of them, and prayed to the LORD. ³⁴And he went up and lay on the child, and put his mouth on his mouth, his eyes on his eyes, and his hands on his hands; and he stretched himself out on the child, and the flesh of the child became warm. ³⁵He returned and walked back and forth in the house, and again went up and stretched himself out on him; then the child sneezed seven times, and the child opened his eyes. ³⁶And he called Gehazi and said, "Call this Shunammite woman." So he called her. And when she came in to him, he said, "Pick up your son." ³⁷So she went in, fell at his feet, and bowed to the ground; then she picked up her son and went out.

Elisha Purifies the Pot of Stew

³⁸And Elisha returned to Gilgal, and *there was* a famine in the land. Now the sons of the prophets *were* sitting before him; and he said to his servant, "Put on the large pot, and boil stew for the sons of the prophets." ³⁹So one went out into the field to gather herbs, and found a wild vine, and gathered from it a lapful of wild gourds, and came and sliced *them* into the pot of stew, though they did not know *what they were.* ⁴⁰Then they served it to the men to eat. Now it happened, as they were eating the stew, that they cried out and said, "Man of God, *there is* death in the pot!" And they could not eat *it.*

⁴¹So he said, "Then bring some flour." And he put *it* into the pot, and said, "Serve *it* to the people, that they may eat." And there was nothing harmful in the pot.

Elisha Feeds One Hundred Men

⁴²Then a man came from Baal Shalisha, and brought the man of God bread of the firstfruits, twenty loaves of barley bread, and newly ripened grain in his knapsack. And he said, "Give *it* to the people, that they may eat."

⁴³But his servant said, "What? Shall I set this before one hundred men?"

He said again, "Give it to the people, that they may eat; for thus says the LORD: 'They shall eat and have *some* left over.'" ⁴⁴So he set *it* before them; and they ate and had *some* left over, according to the word of the LORD.

DEVOTIONS FOR COUPLES • 5:18

Granting Forgiveness Is Tough

As difficult as it is to ask for forgiveness, it can be even more difficult at times to grant forgiveness to someone who has wronged you. And this is every bit as true in marriage—maybe even more so—than it is in any other relationship.

I often advise married couples to take out a joint membership in the Seventy Times Seven Club. This club began when Peter asked Jesus how many times we must forgive one another. Peter wondered if seven times would be enough? Christ answered, "I do not say to you, up to seven times, but up to seventy times seven" (Matt. 18:22). In other words, forgive an infinite number of times, not just when you feel like it.

You can tell whether you have forgiven your spouse by asking yourself one simple question: *Have I given up my desire to punish my mate?* When you lay aside that desire and no longer seek revenge, you free your spouse and yourself from the bonds of your anger.

Forgiveness cannot be conditional. Once you forgive, that's it. Feelings may still be raw, and it is not hypocritical to feel as though you don't want to forgive your spouse. If someone has hurt you, you can choose to forgive immediately, but still be processing feelings of disappointment or rejection. Forgiveness is a choice, an act of the will—not an emotion. It may take a while for your feelings to catch up with your will. But your will needs to respond to the scriptural mandate to forgive your spouse.

If you're not careful, you may dilute the power of forgiveness. How many times have you heard someone say, "I'm sorry I offended you; will you forgive me?" And the other person quickly says without apparent reflection, "Sure, I forgive you!" The two people move on, but then the offender offends again, and the scenario repeats, perhaps many times.

Such behavior mocks authentic forgiveness. I believe tough love must break this cycle by saying, "You know, if you are really serious about being sorry, your actions need to show some believable repentance."

While a mate can administer this "love with teeth," outside help may also be needed, particularly in the early years of marriage. Most churches offer counseling to couples experiencing marital stresses. Or you may ask an older couple to serve as marriage mentors. If problems persist and forgiveness is absent, tell someone. Seek help!

Forgiveness is one of the disciplines in marriage that must be practiced for a lifetime. No marriage can be all that God intended without it.

Naaman's Leprosy Healed

5 Now Naaman, commander of the army of the king of Syria, was a great and honorable man in the eyes of his master, because by him the LORD had given victory to Syria. He was also a mighty man of valor, *but* a leper. ²And the Syrians had gone out on raids, and had brought back captive a young girl from the land of Israel. She waited on Naaman's wife. ³Then she said to her mistress, "If only my master *were* with the prophet who *is* in Samaria! For he would heal him of his leprosy." ⁴And *Naaman* went in and told his master, saying, "Thus and thus said the girl who *is* from the land of Israel."

⁵Then the king of Syria said, "Go now, and I will send a letter to the king of Israel."

So he departed and took with him ten talents of silver, six thousand *shekels* of gold, and ten changes of clothing. ⁶Then he brought the letter to the king of Israel, which said,

> Now be advised, when this letter comes to you, that I have sent Naaman my servant to you, that you may heal him of his leprosy.

⁷And it happened, when the king of Israel read the letter, that he tore his clothes and said, "*Am* I God, to kill and make alive, that

this man sends a man to me to heal him of his leprosy? Therefore please consider, and see how he seeks a quarrel with me."

8So it was, when Elisha the man of God heard that the king of Israel had torn his clothes, that he sent to the king, saying, "Why have you torn your clothes? Please let him come to me, and he shall know that there is a prophet in Israel."

9Then Naaman went with his horses and chariot, and he stood at the door of Elisha's house. 10And Elisha sent a messenger to him, saying, "Go and wash in the Jordan seven times, and your flesh shall be restored to you, and *you shall* be clean." 11But Naaman became furious, and went away and said, "Indeed, I said to myself, 'He will surely come out *to me,* and stand and call on the name of the LORD his God, and wave his hand over the place, and heal the leprosy.' 12*Are* not the Abanah[a] and the Pharpar, the rivers of Damascus, better than all the waters of Israel? Could I not wash in them and be clean?" So he turned and went away in a rage. 13And his servants came near and spoke to him, and said, "My father, *if* the prophet had told you *to do* something great, would you not have done *it?* How much more then, when he says to you, 'Wash, and be clean'?" 14So he went down and dipped seven times in the Jordan, according to the saying of the man of God; and his flesh was restored like the flesh of a little child, and he was clean.

15And he returned to the man of God, he and all his aides, and came and stood before him; and he said, "Indeed, now I know that *there is* no God in all the earth, except in Israel; now therefore, please take a gift from your servant."

16But he said, "*As* the LORD lives, before whom I stand, I will receive nothing." And he urged him to take *it,* but he refused.

17So Naaman said, "Then, if not, please let your servant be given two mule-loads of earth; for your servant will no longer offer either burnt offering or sacrifice to other gods, but to the LORD. 18Yet in this thing may the LORD pardon your servant: when my master goes into the temple of Rimmon

to worship there, and he leans on my hand, and I bow down in the temple of Rimmon— when I bow down in the temple of Rimmon, may the LORD please pardon your servant in this thing."

19Then he said to him, "Go in peace." So he departed from him a short distance.

Gehazi's Greed

20But Gehazi, the servant of Elisha the man of God, said, "Look, my master has spared Naaman this Syrian, while not receiving from his hands what he brought; but *as* the LORD lives, I will run after him and take something from him." 21So Gehazi pursued Naaman. When Naaman saw *him* running after him, he got down from the chariot to meet him, and said, "*Is* all well?"

22And he said, "All *is* well. My master has sent me, saying, 'Indeed, just now two young men of the sons of the prophets have come to me from the mountains of Ephraim. Please give them a talent of silver and two changes of garments.'"

23So Naaman said, "Please, take two talents." And he urged him, and bound two talents of silver in two bags, with two changes of garments, and handed *them* to two of his servants; and they carried *them* on ahead of him. 24When he came to the citadel, he took *them* from their hand, and stored *them* away in the house; then he let the men go, and they departed. 25Now he went in and stood before his master. Elisha said to him, "Where *did you go,* Gehazi?"

And he said, "Your servant did not go anywhere."

26Then he said to him, "Did not my heart go *with you* when the man turned back from his chariot to meet you? *Is it* time to receive money and to receive clothing, olive groves and vineyards, sheep and oxen, male and female servants? 27Therefore the leprosy of Naaman shall cling to you and your descendants forever." And he went out from his presence leprous, *as white* as snow.

The Floating Ax Head

6 And the sons of the prophets said to Elisha, "See now, the place where we dwell with you is too small for us. 2Please, let us go to the Jordan, and let every man

---

5:12 [a]Following Kethib, Septuagint, and Vulgate; Qere, Syriac, and Targum read *Amanah.*

BIBLICAL INSIGHTS • 5:26
The Test of Money

SOMETHING MEMORABLE HAPPENS to almost all newlyweds. A husband or wife assembles a pile of bills and receipts, looks at the checkbook balance—and then breaks into a cold sweat! If the differing expectations and value systems present in every new home have not collided before now, they are about to.

There's no question that differing ways of handling money cause stress in most marriages. While most of us want to believe that our only real money problem is not having enough, deep down, we all know a lack of money is not the real issue. We need the knowledge and discipline to use wisely the money we already have.

God uses money to test us. He certainly did this with Gehazi, the servant of Elisha—a man who failed the test and who paid dearly for it (5:26). God tests us to see whether we are going to trust Him to supply our needs.

We need to remember some of what the Scripture teaches about money:

#1 We are stewards, not owners, of money (Matt. 25:14–29). All our wealth comes from God and we need to acknowledge that He has given us money to manage wisely.

#2 Our use of money is a measure of where our hearts are. If you want to know your *real* values, study your checkbook records and see where you spend money.

#3 Giving is not optional. Most understand that the Scriptures teach us to tithe. That's a good beginning point. As a husband and wife, you should frequently reassess where you are investing. The Bible is clear that investing in God's work is imperishable.

Money is part of life, not its essence or goal. If we keep our attention on God and His objectives, then we will walk in obedience and help build His kingdom, and He will richly supply our needs (1 Tim. 6:17, 18).

take a beam from there, and let us make there a place where we may dwell."

So he answered, "Go."

³Then one said, "Please consent to go with your servants."

And he answered, "I will go." ⁴So he went with them. And when they came to the Jordan, they cut down trees. ⁵But as one was cutting down a tree, the iron *ax head* fell into the water; and he cried out and said, "Alas, master! For it was borrowed."

⁶So the man of God said, "Where did it fall?" And he showed him the place. So he cut off a stick, and threw *it* in there; and he made the iron float. ⁷Therefore he said, "Pick *it* up for yourself." So he reached out his hand and took it.

The Blinded Syrians Captured

⁸Now the king of Syria was making war against Israel; and he consulted with his servants, saying, "My camp *will be* in such and such a place." ⁹And the man of God sent to the king of Israel, saying, "Beware that you do not pass this place, for the Syrians are coming down there." ¹⁰Then the king of Israel sent *someone* to the place of which the man of God had told him. Thus he warned him, and he was watchful there, not just once or twice.

¹¹Therefore the heart of the king of Syria was greatly troubled by this thing; and he called his servants and said to them, "Will you not show me which of us *is* for the king of Israel?"

¹²And one of his servants said, "None, my lord, O king; but Elisha, the prophet who *is* in Israel, tells the king of Israel the words that you speak in your bedroom."

¹³So he said, "Go and see where he *is*, that I may send and get him."

And it was told him, saying, "Surely *he is* in Dothan."

¹⁴Therefore he sent horses and chariots and a great army there, and they came by night and surrounded the city. ¹⁵And when the servant of the man of God arose early and went out, there was an army, surrounding the city with horses and chariots. And his servant said to him, "Alas, my master! What shall we do?"

¹⁶So he answered, "Do not fear, for those who *are* with us *are* more than those who

are with them." ¹⁷And Elisha prayed, and said, "LORD, I pray, open his eyes that he may see." Then the LORD opened the eyes of the young man, and he saw. And behold, the mountain *was* full of horses and chariots of fire all around Elisha. ¹⁸So when *the Syrians* came down to him, Elisha prayed to the LORD, and said, "Strike this people, I pray, with blindness." And He struck them with blindness according to the word of Elisha.

¹⁹Now Elisha said to them, "This *is* not the way, nor *is* this the city. Follow me, and I will bring you to the man whom you seek." But he led them to Samaria.

²⁰So it was, when they had come to Samaria, that Elisha said, "LORD, open the eyes of these *men*, that they may see." And the LORD opened their eyes, and they saw; and there *they were*, inside Samaria!

²¹Now when the king of Israel saw them, he said to Elisha, "My father, shall I kill *them*? Shall I kill *them*?"

²²But he answered, "You shall not kill *them*. Would you kill those whom you have taken captive with your sword and your bow? Set food and water before them, that they may eat and drink and go to their master." ²³Then he prepared a great feast for them; and after they ate and drank, he sent them away and they went to their master. So the bands of Syrian *raiders* came no more into the land of Israel.

Syria Besieges Samaria in Famine

²⁴And it happened after this that Ben-Hadad king of Syria gathered all his army, and went up and besieged Samaria. ²⁵And there was a great famine in Samaria; and indeed they besieged it until a donkey's head was *sold* for eighty *shekels* of silver, and one-fourth of a kab of dove droppings for five *shekels* of silver.

²⁶Then, as the king of Israel was passing by on the wall, a woman cried out to him, saying, "Help, my lord, O king!"

²⁷And he said, "If the LORD does not help you, where can I find help for you? From the threshing floor or from the winepress?" ²⁸Then the king said to her, "What is troubling you?"

And she answered, "This woman said to me, 'Give your son, that we may eat him today, and we will eat my son tomorrow.'

BIBLICAL INSIGHTS • 6:16
Overcoming Your Mate's Fear

THERE ARE 365 "FEAR NOTS" in the Scripture. It's clear that we fear a host of things, yet for many of us, the greatest fear is the fear of rejection. Perhaps you or your mate fears failure or appearing stupid, forgetful, or insensitive. All of these can become grounds for rejection.

The more fears your mate has, the less open he or she will be in relationships. If the words *withdrawn* and *unexpressive* describe your mate, then recognize it as a possible clue to actual or perceived rejections of the past. And remember Elisha's word to his fearful servant: "Do not fear, for those who are with us are more than those who are with them" (6:16). Fear dissipates when someone who is fearful knows that significant people in his life (people like you!) are *with* him.

Be careful of communicating rejection to your mate in any way. Instead, seek to understand your mate. Ask yourself, *Why is my mate fearful?* You may need to ask forgiveness for adding to the problem.

A fearful person needs to be received gently in love. He or she needs to be heard. Those fears are real, no matter how inconsequential they may seem to you. To be ignored can make your spouse feel uncared for and unimportant. First John 4:18 promises us, "There is no fear in love; but perfect love casts out fear, because fear involves torment. But he who fears has not been made perfect in love." Choose to love, and see how God will use your love to help your spouse overcome her fears!

²⁹So we boiled my son, and ate him. And I said to her on the next day, 'Give your son, that we may eat him'; but she has hidden her son."

³⁰Now it happened, when the king heard the words of the woman, that he tore his clothes; and as he passed by on the wall, the people looked, and there underneath *he had* sackcloth on his body. ³¹Then he said,

"God do so to me and more also, if the head of Elisha the son of Shaphat remains on him today!"

³²But Elisha was sitting in his house, and the elders were sitting with him. And *the king* sent a man ahead of him, but before the messenger came to him, he said to the elders, "Do you see how this son of a murderer has sent someone to take away my head? Look, when the messenger comes, shut the door, and hold him fast at the door. *Is* not the sound of his master's feet behind him?" ³³And while he was still talking with them, there was the messenger, coming down to him; and then *the king* said, "Surely this calamity *is* from the LORD; why should I wait for the LORD any longer?"

7 Then Elisha said, "Hear the word of the LORD. Thus says the LORD: 'Tomorrow about this time a seah of fine flour *shall be sold* for a shekel, and two seahs of barley for a shekel, at the gate of Samaria.'"

²So an officer on whose hand the king leaned answered the man of God and said, "Look, *if* the LORD would make windows in heaven, could this thing be?"

And he said, "In fact, you shall see *it* with your eyes, but you shall not eat of it."

The Syrians Flee

³Now there were four leprous men at the entrance of the gate; and they said to one another, "Why are we sitting here until we die? ⁴If we say, 'We will enter the city,' the famine *is* in the city, and we shall die there.

And if we sit here, we die also. Now therefore, come, let us surrender to the army of the Syrians. If they keep us alive, we shall live; and if they kill us, we shall only die." ⁵And they rose at twilight to go to the camp of the Syrians; and when they had come to the outskirts of the Syrian camp, to their surprise no one *was* there. ⁶For the Lord had caused the army of the Syrians to hear the noise of chariots and the noise of horses—the noise of a great army; so they said to one another, "Look, the king of Israel has hired against us the kings of the Hittites and the kings of the Egyptians to attack us!" ⁷Therefore they arose and fled at twilight, and left the camp intact—their tents, their horses, and their donkeys— and they fled for their lives. ⁸And when these lepers came to the outskirts of the camp, they went into one tent and ate and drank, and carried from it silver and gold and clothing, and went and hid *them;* then they came back and entered another tent, and carried *some* from there *also,* and went and hid *it.*

⁹Then they said to one another, "We are not doing right. This day *is* a day of good news, and we remain silent. If we wait until morning light, some punishment will come upon us. Now therefore, come, let us go and tell the king's household." ¹⁰So they went and called to the gatekeepers of the city, and told them, saying, "We went to the Syrian camp, and surprisingly no one *was* there, not a human sound—only horses and donkeys tied, and the tents intact." ¹¹And the gatekeepers called out, and they told *it* to the king's household inside.

¹²So the king arose in the night and said to his servants, "Let me now tell you what the Syrians have done to us. They know that we *are* hungry; therefore they have gone out of the camp to hide themselves in the field, saying, 'When they come out of the city, we shall catch them alive, and get into the city.'"

¹³And one of his servants answered and said, "Please, let several *men* take five of the remaining horses which are left in the city. Look, they *may either become* like all the multitude of Israel that are left in it; or indeed, *I say,* they *may become* like all the multitude of Israel left from those who are consumed; so let us send them and see."

INTIMATE MOMENTS

If your husband is a collector of coins, baseball cards, etc., buy him something that adds to his collection. Then ask him to tell any stories that might be behind either his whole collection or any particular piece in the collection. Make it the focal point of a fun discussion that centers around a part of his life that he considers important.

¹⁴Therefore they took two chariots with horses; and the king sent them in the direction of the Syrian army, saying, "Go and see." ¹⁵And they went after them to the Jordan; and indeed all the road *was* full of garments and weapons which the Syrians had thrown away in their haste. So the messengers returned and told the king. ¹⁶Then the people went out and plundered the tents of the Syrians. So a seah of fine flour was *sold* for a shekel, and two seahs of barley for a shekel, according to the word of the LORD.

¹⁷Now the king had appointed the officer on whose hand he leaned to have charge of the gate. But the people trampled him in the gate, and he died, just as the man of God had said, who spoke when the king came down to him. ¹⁸So it happened just as the man of God had spoken to the king, saying, "Two seahs of barley for a shekel, and a seah of fine flour for a shekel, shall be *sold* tomorrow about this time in the gate of Samaria."

¹⁹Then that officer had answered the man of God, and said, "Now look, *if* the LORD would make windows in heaven, could such a thing be?"

And he had said, "In fact, you shall see *it* with your eyes, but you shall not eat of it." ²⁰And so it happened to him, for the people trampled him in the gate, and he died.

The King Restores the Shunammite's Land

8 Then Elisha spoke to the woman whose son he had restored to life, saying, "Arise and go, you and your household, and stay wherever you can; for the LORD has called for a famine, and furthermore, it will come upon the land for seven years." ²So the woman arose and did according to the saying of the man of God, and she went with her household and dwelt in the land of the Philistines seven years.

³It came to pass, at the end of seven years, that the woman returned from the land of the Philistines; and she went to make an appeal to the king for her house and for her land. ⁴Then the king talked with Gehazi, the servant of the man of God, saying, "Tell me, please, all the great things Elisha has done." ⁵Now it happened, as he was telling the king how he had restored the dead to life, that there was the woman whose son he had restored to life, appealing to the king for her house and for her land. And Gehazi said, "My lord, O king, this *is* the woman, and this *is* her son whom Elisha restored to life." ⁶And when the king asked the woman, she told him.

So the king appointed a certain officer for her, saying, "Restore all that *was* hers, and all the proceeds of the field from the day that she left the land until now."

Death of Ben-Hadad

⁷Then Elisha went to Damascus, and Ben-Hadad king of Syria was sick; and it was told him, saying, "The man of God has come here." ⁸And the king said to Hazael, "Take a present in your hand, and go to meet the man of God, and inquire of the LORD by him, saying, 'Shall I recover from this disease?'" ⁹So Hazael went to meet him and took a present with him, of every good thing of Damascus, forty camel-loads; and he came and stood before him, and said, "Your son Ben-Hadad king of Syria has sent me to you, saying, 'Shall I recover from this disease?'"

¹⁰And Elisha said to him, "Go, say to him, 'You shall certainly recover.' However the LORD has shown me that he will really die." ¹¹Then he set his countenance in a stare until he was ashamed; and the man of God wept. ¹²And Hazael said, "Why is my lord weeping?"

He answered, "Because I know the evil that you will do to the children of Israel: Their strongholds you will set on fire, and their young men you will kill with the sword; and you will dash their children, and rip open their women with child."

¹³So Hazael said, "But what *is* your servant—a dog, that he should do this gross thing?"

And Elisha answered, "The LORD has shown me that you *will become* king over Syria."

¹⁴Then he departed from Elisha, and came to his master, who said to him, "What did Elisha say to you?" And he answered, "He told me you would surely recover." ¹⁵But it happened on the next day that he took a thick cloth and dipped *it* in water, and spread *it* over his face so that he died; and Hazael reigned in his place.

Jehoram Reigns in Judah

16Now in the fifth year of Joram the son of Ahab, king of Israel, Jehoshaphat *having been* king of Judah, Jehoram the son of Jehoshaphat began to reign as king of Judah. 17He was thirty-two years old when he became king, and he reigned eight years in Jerusalem. 18And he walked in the way of the kings of Israel, just as the house of Ahab had done, for the daughter of Ahab was his wife; and he did evil in the sight of the LORD. 19Yet the LORD would not destroy Judah, for the sake of His servant David, as He promised him to give a lamp to him *and* his sons forever.

20In his days Edom revolted against Judah's authority, and made a king over themselves. 21So Jorama went to Zair, and all his chariots with him. Then he rose by night and attacked the Edomites who had surrounded him and the captains of the chariots; and the troops fled to their tents. 22Thus Edom has been in revolt against Judah's authority to this day. And Libnah revolted at that time.

23Now the rest of the acts of Joram, and all that he did, *are* they not written in the book of the chronicles of the kings of Judah? 24So Joram rested with his fathers, and was buried with his fathers in the City of David. Then Ahaziah his son reigned in his place.

Ahaziah Reigns in Judah

25In the twelfth year of Joram the son of Ahab, king of Israel, Ahaziah the son of Jehoram, king of Judah, began to reign. 26Ahaziah *was* twenty-two years old when he became king, and he reigned one year in Jerusalem. His mother's name *was* Athaliah the granddaughter of Omri, king of Israel. 27And he walked in the way of the house of Ahab, and did evil in the sight of the LORD, like the house of Ahab, for he *was* the son-in-law of the house of Ahab.

28Now he went with Joram the son of Ahab to war against Hazael king of Syria at Ramoth Gilead; and the Syrians wounded Joram. 29Then King Joram went back to Jezreel to recover from the wounds which the Syrians had inflicted on him at Ramah, when he fought against Hazael king of Syria. And Ahaziah the son of Jehoram, king of Judah, went down to see Joram the son of Ahab in Jezreel, because he was sick.

8:21 aSpelled *Jehoram* in verse 16

PARENTING MATTERS

Q: What part should community play in rearing children?

Humorist Garrison Keillor has said, "Adults no longer dare to influence other people's children. You should be able to discipline another person's child, up to a point. Children are supposed to be raised by all sorts of people."

Keillor uses a key phrase—*adults no longer dare.* In our age of tolerance, we have developed the philosophy that we have no right to tell another parent about a concern we have about his child. And our children suffer from our failure to be involved in the lives of others.

We've called parents about behavior we have observed in their children and had them tell us they "didn't want to hear it." They didn't want to know. One parent angrily chewed me out for calling about something his son had done that was clearly wrong.

We need to drop our defensiveness and fear and encourage others to offer observations to us about how our children are doing when we're not there to see for ourselves. Take the initiative by telling the parents of friends of your child, "If you see my teenager doing anything questionable, you have the freedom to tell me. I want to know." Then when they do come and share something with you, resist the urge to become defensive and thank them for caring enough about your children to come to you.

Jehu Anointed King of Israel

9 And Elisha the prophet called one of the sons of the prophets, and said to him, "Get yourself ready, take this flask of oil in your hand, and go to Ramoth Gilead. ²Now when you arrive at that place, look there for Jehu the son of Jehoshaphat, the son of Nimshi, and go in and make him rise up from among his associates, and take him to an inner room. ³Then take the flask of oil, and pour *it* on his head, and say, 'Thus says the LORD: "I have anointed you king over Israel."' Then open the door and flee, and do not delay."

⁴So the young man, the servant of the prophet, went to Ramoth Gilead. ⁵And when he arrived, there *were* the captains of the army sitting; and he said, "I have a message for you, Commander."

Jehu said, "For which *one* of us?"

And he said, "For you, Commander." ⁶Then he arose and went into the house. And he poured the oil on his head, and said to him, "Thus says the LORD God of Israel: 'I have anointed you king over the people of the LORD, over Israel. ⁷You shall strike down the house of Ahab your master, that I may avenge the blood of My servants the prophets, and the blood of all the servants of the LORD, at the hand of Jezebel. ⁸For the whole house of Ahab shall perish; and I will cut off from Ahab all the males in Israel, both bond and free. ⁹So I will make the house of Ahab like the house of Jeroboam the son of Nebat, and like the house of Baasha the son of Ahijah. ¹⁰The dogs shall eat Jezebel on the plot *of ground* at Jezreel, and *there shall be* none to bury *her.*'" And he opened the door and fled.

¹¹Then Jehu came out to the servants of his master, and *one* said to him, "*Is* all well? Why did this madman come to you?"

And he said to them, "You know the man and his babble."

¹²And they said, "A lie! Tell us now."

So he said, "Thus and thus he spoke to me, saying, 'Thus says the LORD: "I have anointed you king over Israel."'"

¹³Then each man hastened to take his garment and put *it* under him on the top of the steps; and they blew trumpets, saying, "Jehu is king!"

Joram of Israel Killed

¹⁴So Jehu the son of Jehoshaphat, the son of Nimshi, conspired against Joram. (Now Joram had been defending Ramoth Gilead, he and all Israel, against Hazael king of Syria. ¹⁵But King Joram had returned to Jezreel to recover from the wounds which the Syrians had inflicted on him when he fought with Hazael king of Syria.) And Jehu said, "If you are so minded, let no one leave *or* escape from the city to go and tell *it* in Jezreel." ¹⁶So Jehu rode in a chariot and went to Jezreel, for Joram was laid up there; and Ahaziah king of Judah had come down to see Joram.

¹⁷Now a watchman stood on the tower in Jezreel, and he saw the company of Jehu as he came, and said, "I see a company of men."

And Joram said, "Get a horseman and send him to meet them, and let him say, '*Is it* peace?'"

¹⁸So the horseman went to meet him, and said, "Thus says the king: '*Is it* peace?'"

And Jehu said, "What have you to do with peace? Turn around and follow me."

So the watchman reported, saying, "The messenger went to them, but is not coming back."

¹⁹Then he sent out a second horseman who came to them, and said, "Thus says the king: '*Is it* peace?'"

And Jehu answered, "What have you to do with peace? Turn around and follow me."

²⁰So the watchman reported, saying, "He went up to them and is not coming back; and the driving *is* like the driving of Jehu the son of Nimshi, for he drives furiously!"

²¹Then Joram said, "Make ready." And his chariot was made ready. Then Joram king of Israel and Ahaziah king of Judah went out, each in his chariot; and they went out to meet Jehu, and met him on the property of Naboth the Jezreelite. ²²Now it happened, when Joram saw Jehu, that he said, "*Is it* peace, Jehu?"

So he answered, "What peace, as long as the harlotries of your mother Jezebel and her witchcraft *are so* many?"

²³Then Joram turned around and fled, and said to Ahaziah, "Treachery, Ahaziah!" ²⁴Now Jehu drew his bow with full strength

and shot Jehoram between his arms; and the arrow came out at his heart, and he sank down in his chariot. 25Then *Jehu* said to Bidkar his captain, "Pick *him* up, *and* throw him into the tract of the field of Naboth the Jezreelite; for remember, when you and I were riding together behind Ahab his father, that the LORD laid this burden upon him: 26'Surely I saw yesterday the blood of Naboth and the blood of his sons,' says the LORD, 'and I will repay you in this plot,' says the LORD. Now therefore, take *and* throw him on the plot *of ground,* according to the word of the LORD."

Ahaziah of Judah Killed

27But when Ahaziah king of Judah saw *this,* he fled by the road to Beth Haggan.[a] So Jehu pursued him, and said, "Shoot him also in the chariot." *And they shot him* at the Ascent of Gur, which is by Ibleam. Then he fled to Megiddo, and died there. 28And his servants carried him in the chariot to Jerusalem, and buried him in his tomb with his fathers in the City of David. 29In the eleventh year of Joram the son of Ahab, Ahaziah had become king over Judah.

Jezebel's Violent Death

30Now when Jehu had come to Jezreel, Jezebel heard *of it;* and she put paint on her eyes and adorned her head, and looked through a window. 31Then, as Jehu entered at the gate, she said, "*Is it* peace, Zimri, murderer of your master?"

32And he looked up at the window, and said, "Who *is* on my side? Who?" So two *or* three eunuchs looked out at him. 33Then he said, "Throw her down." So they threw her down, and *some* of her blood spattered on

the wall and on the horses; and he trampled her underfoot. 34And when he had gone in, he ate and drank. Then he said, "Go now, see to this accursed *woman,* and bury her, for she was a king's daughter." 35So they went to bury her, but they found no more of her than the skull and the feet and the palms of *her* hands. 36Therefore they came back and told him. And he said, "This *is* the word of the LORD, which He spoke by His servant Elijah the Tishbite, saying, 'On the plot *of ground* at Jezreel dogs shall eat the flesh of Jezebel;[a] 37and the corpse of Jezebel shall be as refuse on the surface of the field, in the plot at Jezreel, so that they shall not say, "Here *lies* Jezebel." ' "

Ahab's Seventy Sons Killed

10 Now Ahab had seventy sons in Samaria. And Jehu wrote and sent letters to Samaria, to the rulers of Jezreel,[a] to the elders, and to those who reared Ahab's *sons,* saying:

2   Now as soon as this letter comes to you, since your master's sons *are* with you, and you have chariots and horses, a fortified city also, and weapons, 3choose the best qualified of your master's sons, set *him* on his father's throne, and fight for your master's house.

4But they were exceedingly afraid, and said, "Look, two kings could not stand up to him; how then can we stand?" 5And he who *was* in charge of the house, and he who *was* in charge of the city, the elders also, and those who reared *the sons,* sent to Jehu, saying, "We *are* your servants, we will do all you tell us; but we will not make anyone king. Do *what is* good in your sight." 6Then he wrote a second letter to them, saying:

If you *are* for me and will obey my voice, take the heads of the men, your master's sons, and come to me at Jezreel by this time tomorrow.

Now the king's sons, seventy persons, *were* with the great men of the city, *who*

INTIMATE MOMENTS

Sign up as a couple for dancing lessons— and let her choose the style: ballroom, swing, square dance, etc. Focus on having fun, rather than on how well you're mastering the particular steps.

9:27 [a]Literally *The Garden House* **9:36** [a]1 Kings 21:23 **10:1** [a]Following Masoretic Text, Syriac, and Targum; Septuagint reads *Samaria;* Vulgate reads *city.*

were rearing them. 7So it was, when the letter came to them, that they took the king's sons and slaughtered seventy persons, put their heads in baskets and sent *them* to him at Jezreel.

8Then a messenger came and told him, saying, "They have brought the heads of the king's sons."

And he said, "Lay them in two heaps at the entrance of the gate until morning."

9So it was, in the morning, that he went out and stood, and said to all the people, "You *are* righteous. Indeed I conspired against my master and killed him; but who killed all these? 10Know now that nothing shall fall to the earth of the word of the LORD which the LORD spoke concerning the house of Ahab; for the LORD has done what He spoke by His servant Elijah." 11So Jehu killed all who remained of the house of Ahab in Jezreel, and all his great men and his close acquaintances and his priests, until he left him none remaining.

Ahaziah's Forty-two Brothers Killed

12And he arose and departed and went to Samaria. On the way, at Beth Ekeda of the Shepherds, 13Jehu met with the brothers of Ahaziah king of Judah, and said, "Who *are* you?"

So they answered, "We *are* the brothers of Ahaziah; we have come down to greet the sons of the king and the sons of the queen mother."

14And he said, "Take them alive!" So they took them alive, and killed them at the well of Beth Eked, forty-two men; and he left none of them.

The Rest of Ahab's Family Killed

15Now when he departed from there, he met Jehonadab the son of Rechab, *coming* to meet him; and he greeted him and said to him, "Is your heart right, as my heart *is* toward your heart?"

And Jehonadab answered, "It is."

Jehu said, "If it is, give *me* your hand." So he gave *him* his hand, and he took him up to him into the chariot. 16Then he said,

"Come with me, and see my zeal for the LORD." So they had him ride in his chariot. 17And when he came to Samaria, he killed all who remained to Ahab in Samaria, till he had destroyed them, according to the word of the LORD which He spoke to Elijah.

Worshipers of Baal Killed

18Then Jehu gathered all the people together, and said to them, "Ahab served Baal a little, Jehu will serve him much. 19Now therefore, call to me all the prophets of Baal, all his servants, and all his priests. Let no one be missing, for I have a great sacrifice for Baal. Whoever is missing shall not live." But Jehu acted deceptively, with the intent of destroying the worshipers of Baal. 20And Jehu said, "Proclaim a solemn assembly for Baal." So they proclaimed *it.* 21Then Jehu sent throughout all Israel; and all the worshipers of Baal came, so that there was not a man left who did not come. So they came into the templea of Baal, and °the temple of Baal was full from one end to the other. 22And he said to the one in charge of the wardrobe, "Bring out vestments for all the worshipers of Baal." So he brought out vestments for them. 23Then Jehu and Jehonadab the son of Rechab went into the temple of Baal, and said to the worshipers of Baal, "Search and see that no servants of the LORD are here with you, but only the worshipers of Baal." 24So they went in to offer sacrifices and burnt offerings. Now Jehu had appointed for himself eighty men on the outside, and had said, "*If* any of the men whom I have brought into your hands escapes, *whoever lets him escape, it shall be* his life for the life of the other."

25Now it happened, as soon as he had made an end of offering the burnt offering, that Jehu said to the guard and to the captains, "Go in *and* kill them; let no one come out!" And they killed them with the edge of the sword; then the guards and the officers threw *them* out, and went into the inner room of the temple of Baal. 26And they brought the *sacred* pillars out of the temple of Baal and burned them. 27Then they broke down the *sacred* pillar of Baal, and tore down the temple of Baal and made it a refuse dump to this day. 28Thus Jehu destroyed Baal from Israel.

10:12 aOr *The Shearing House* **10:21** aLiterally *house,* and so elsewhere in this chapter

[29]However Jehu did not turn away from the sins of Jeroboam the son of Nebat, who had made Israel sin, *that is,* from the golden calves that *were* at Bethel and Dan. [30]And the LORD said to Jehu, "Because you have done well in doing *what is* right in My sight, *and* have done to the house of Ahab all that *was* in My heart, your sons shall sit on the throne of Israel to the fourth *generation.*" [31]But Jehu took no heed to walk in the law of the LORD God of Israel with all his heart; for he did not depart from the sins of Jeroboam, who had made Israel sin.

Death of Jehu

[32]In those days the LORD began to cut off *parts* of Israel; and Hazael conquered them in all the territory of Israel [33]from the Jordan eastward: all the land of Gilead— Gad, Reuben, and Manasseh—from Aroer, which *is* by the River Arnon, including Gilead and Bashan.

[34]Now the rest of the acts of Jehu, all that he did, and all his might, *are* they not written in the book of the chronicles of the kings of Israel? [35]So Jehu rested with his fathers, and they buried him in Samaria. Then Jehoahaz his son reigned in his place. [36]And the period that Jehu reigned over Israel in Samaria *was* twenty-eight years.

Athaliah Reigns in Judah

11 When Athaliah the mother of Ahaziah saw that her son was dead, she arose and destroyed all the royal heirs. [2]But Jehosheba, the daughter of King Joram, sister of Ahaziah, took Joash the son of Ahaziah, and stole him away from among the king's sons *who were* being murdered; and they hid him and his nurse in the bedroom, from Athaliah, so that he was not killed. [3]So he was hidden with her in the house of the LORD for six years, while Athaliah reigned over the land.

Joash Crowned King of Judah

[4]In the seventh year Jehoiada sent and brought the captains of hundreds—of the bodyguards and the escorts—and brought them into the house of the LORD to him. And he made a covenant with them and took an oath from them in the house of the LORD, and showed them the king's son.

[5]Then he commanded them, saying, "This *is* what you shall do: One-third of you who come on duty on the Sabbath shall be keeping watch over the king's house, [6]one-third *shall be* at the gate of Sur, and one-third at the gate behind the escorts. You shall keep the watch of the house, lest it be broken down. [7]The two contingents of you who go off duty on the Sabbath shall keep the watch of the house of the LORD for the king. [8]But you shall surround the king on all sides, every man with his weapons in his hand; and whoever comes within range, let him be put to death. You are to be with the king as he goes out and as he comes in."

[9]So the captains of the hundreds did according to all that Jehoiada the priest commanded. Each of them took his men who were to be on duty on the Sabbath, with those who were going off duty on the Sabbath, and came to Jehoiada the priest. [10]And the priest gave the captains of hundreds the spears and shields which *had belonged* to King David, that were in the temple of the LORD. [11]Then the escorts stood, every man with his weapons in his hand, all around the king, from the right side of the temple to the left side of the temple, by the altar and the house. [12]And he brought out the king's son, put the crown on him, and *gave him* the Testimony;[a] they made him king and anointed him, and they clapped their hands and said, "Long live the king!"

Death of Athaliah

[13]Now when Athaliah heard the noise of the escorts *and* the people, she came to the people *in* the temple of the LORD. [14]When she looked, there was the king standing by a pillar according to custom; and the leaders and the trumpeters were by the king. All the people of the land were rejoicing and blowing trumpets. So Athaliah tore her clothes and cried out, "Treason! Treason!"

[15]And Jehoiada the priest commanded the captains of the hundreds, the officers of the army, and said to them, "Take her outside under guard, and slay with the sword whoever follows her." For the priest had said, "Do not let her be killed in the

---

11:12 [a]That is, the Law (compare Exodus 25:16, 21 and Deuteronomy 31:9)

house of the Lord." ¹⁶So they seized her; and she went by way of the horses' entrance *into* the king's house, and there she was killed.

¹⁷Then Jehoiada made a covenant between the Lord, the king, and the people, that they should be the Lord's people, and *also* between the king and the people. ¹⁸And all the people of the land went to the temple of Baal, and tore it down. They thoroughly broke in pieces its altars and images, and killed Mattan the priest of Baal before the altars. And the priest appointed officers over the house of the Lord. ¹⁹Then he took the captains of hundreds, the bodyguards, the escorts, and all the people of the land; and they brought the king down from the house of the Lord, and went by way of the gate of the escorts to the king's house. Then he sat on the throne of the kings. ²⁰So all the people of the land rejoiced; and the city was quiet, for they had slain Athaliah with the sword *in* the king's house. ²¹Jehoash *was* seven years old when he became king.

Jehoash Repairs the Temple

12 In the seventh year of Jehu, Jehoash[a] became king, and he reigned forty years in Jerusalem. His mother's name *was* Zibiah of Beersheba. ²Jehoash did *what was* right in the sight of the Lord all the days in which Jehoiada the priest instructed him. ³But the high places were not taken away; the people still sacrificed and burned incense on the high places.

⁴And Jehoash said to the priests, "All the money of the dedicated gifts that are brought into the house of the Lord—each man's census money, each man's assessment money[a]—*and* all the money that a man purposes in his heart to bring into the house of the Lord, ⁵let the priests take *it* themselves, each from his constituency; and let them repair the damages of the temple, wherever any dilapidation is found."

⁶Now it was so, by the twenty-third year of King Jehoash, *that* the priests had not repaired the damages of the temple. ⁷So King Jehoash called Jehoiada the priest and the *other* priests, and said to them, "Why

Whose Money Is It?

THE TRUTHS OF SCRIPTURE should influence our attitude about money. We should not take pride in the money we make, for example, because it all comes from God. In Psalm 50:10 He tells us, "For every beast of the forest is Mine, the cattle on a thousand hills."

We also should avoid giving our devotion to money. So 1 Timothy 6:10 declares, "the love of money is a root of all sorts of evil, and some by longing for it have wandered away from the faith and pierced themselves with many griefs."

Biblical truths about money also should influence our actions. Ultimately, our stewardship—what we do with what God gives us—will reflect whether Christ truly is or is not Lord of our lives. King Jehoash spoke of "all the money that a man purposes in his heart to bring into the house of the Lord" (12:4), speaking of the funds given to the work of the Lord, above and beyond any tithes. Such gifts speak volumes about what lies in the heart that gave them. God wants us to set aside the first part of our paycheck for the work of His kingdom. When we do, we show where our real priorities, and our hearts, lie.

have you not repaired the damages of the temple? Now therefore, do not take *more* money from your constituency, but deliver it for repairing the damages of the temple." ⁸And the priests agreed that they would neither receive *more* money from the people, nor repair the damages of the temple.

⁹Then Jehoiada the priest took a chest, bored a hole in its lid, and set it beside the altar, on the right side as one comes into the house of the Lord; and the priests who kept the door put there all the money brought into the house of the Lord. ¹⁰So it was, whenever they saw that *there was* much money in the chest, that the king's scribe and the high priest came up and put

it in bags, and counted the money that was found in the house of the LORD. ¹¹Then they gave the money, which had been apportioned, into the hands of those who did the work, who had the oversight of the house of the LORD; and they paid it out to the carpenters and builders who worked on the house of the LORD, ¹²and to masons and stonecutters, and for buying timber and hewn stone, to repair the damage of the house of the LORD, and for all that was paid out to repair the temple. ¹³However there were not made for the house of the LORD basins of silver, trimmers, sprinkling-bowls, trumpets, any articles of gold or articles of silver, from the money brought into the house of the LORD. ¹⁴But they gave that to the workmen, and they repaired the house of the LORD with it. ¹⁵Moreover they did not require an account from the men into whose hand they delivered the money to be paid to workmen, for they dealt faithfully. ¹⁶The money from the trespass offerings and the money from the sin offerings was not brought into the house of the LORD. It belonged to the priests.

Hazael Threatens Jerusalem

¹⁷Hazael king of Syria went up and fought against Gath, and took it; then Hazael set his face to go up to Jerusalem. ¹⁸And Jehoash king of Judah took all the sacred things that his fathers, Jehoshaphat and Jehoram and Ahaziah, kings of Judah, had dedicated, and his own sacred things, and all the gold found in the treasuries of the house of the LORD and in the king's house, and sent *them* to Hazael king of Syria. Then he went away from Jerusalem.

Death of Joash

¹⁹Now the rest of the acts of Joash,ᵃ and all that he did, *are* they not written in the book of the chronicles of the kings of Judah?
²⁰And his servants arose and formed a conspiracy, and killed Joash in the house of the Millo,ᵃ which goes down to Silla. ²¹For Jozacharᵃ the son of Shimeath and Jehozabad the son of Shomer,ᵇ his servants, struck him. So he died, and they buried him with his fathers in the City of David. Then Amaziah his son reigned in his place.

Jehoahaz Reigns in Israel

13 In the twenty-third year of Joashᵃ the son of Ahaziah, king of Judah, Jehoahaz the son of Jehu became king over Israel in Samaria, *and reigned* seventeen years. ²And he did evil in the sight of the LORD, and followed the sins of Jeroboam the son of Nebat, who had made Israel sin. He did not depart from them.

³Then the anger of the LORD was aroused against Israel, and He delivered them into the hand of Hazael king of Syria, and into the hand of Ben-Hadad the son of Hazael, all *their* days. ⁴So Jehoahaz pleaded with the LORD, and the LORD listened to him; for He saw the oppression of Israel, because the king of Syria oppressed them. ⁵Then the LORD gave Israel a deliverer, so that they escaped from under the hand of the Syrians; and the children of Israel dwelt in their tents as before. ⁶Nevertheless they did not depart from the sins of the house of Jeroboam, who had made Israel sin, *but* walked in them; and the wooden imageᵃ also remained in Samaria. ⁷For He left of the army of Jehoahaz only fifty horsemen, ten chariots, and ten thousand foot soldiers; for the king of Syria had destroyed them and made them like the dust at threshing.

⁸Now the rest of the acts of Jehoahaz, all that he did, and his might, *are* they not written in the book of the chronicles of the kings of Israel? ⁹So Jehoahaz rested with his fathers, and they buried him in Samaria. Then Joash his son reigned in his place.

Jehoash Reigns in Israel

¹⁰In the thirty-seventh year of Joash king of Judah, Jehoashᵃ the son of Jehoahaz became king over Israel in Samaria, *and reigned* sixteen years. ¹¹And he did evil in the sight of the LORD. He did not depart from all the sins of Jeroboam the son of Nebat, who made Israel sin, *but* walked in them.

¹²Now the rest of the acts of Joash, all that he did, and his might with which he

---

12:19 ᵃSpelled *Jehoash* in 12:1ff **12:20** ᵃLiterally *The Landfill* **12:21** ᵃCalled *Zabad* in 2 Chronicles 24:26 ᵇCalled *Shimrith* in 2 Chronicles 24:26 **13:1** ᵃSpelled *Jehoash* in 12:1ff **13:6** ᵃHebrew *Asherah,* a Canaanite goddess **13:10** ᵃSpelled *Joash* in verse 9

fought against Amaziah king of Judah, *are* they not written in the book of the chronicles of the kings of Israel? 13So Joash rested with his fathers. Then Jeroboam sat on his throne. And Joash was buried in Samaria with the kings of Israel.

Death of Elisha

14Elisha had become sick with the illness of which he would die. Then Joash the king of Israel came down to him, and wept over his face, and said, "O my father, my father, the chariots of Israel and their horsemen!"

15And Elisha said to him, "Take a bow and some arrows." So he took himself a bow and some arrows. 16Then he said to the king of Israel, "Put your hand on the bow." So he put his hand *on it,* and Elisha put his hands on the king's hands. 17And he said, "Open the east window"; and he opened *it.* Then Elisha said, "Shoot"; and he shot. And he said, "The arrow of the LORD's deliverance and the arrow of deliverance from Syria; for you must strike the Syrians at Aphek till you have destroyed *them.*" 18Then he said, "Take the arrows"; so he took *them.* And he said to the king of Israel, "Strike the ground"; so he struck three times, and stopped. 19And the man of God was angry with him, and said, "You should have struck five or six times; then you would have struck Syria till you had destroyed *it!* But now you will strike Syria *only* three times."

20Then Elisha died, and they buried him. And the *raiding* bands from Moab invaded the land in the spring of the year. 21So it was, as they were burying a man, that suddenly they spied a band *of raiders;* and they put the man in the tomb of Elisha; and when the man was let down and touched the bones of Elisha, he revived and stood on his feet.

Israel Recaptures Cities from Syria

22And Hazael king of Syria oppressed Israel all the days of Jehoahaz. 23But the LORD was gracious to them, had compassion on them, and regarded them, because

of His covenant with Abraham, Isaac, and Jacob, and would not yet destroy them or cast them from His presence.

24Now Hazael king of Syria died. Then Ben-Hadad his son reigned in his place. 25And Jehoash[a] the son of Jehoahaz recaptured from the hand of Ben-Hadad, the son of Hazael, the cities which he had taken out of the hand of Jehoahaz his father by war. Three times Joash defeated him and recaptured the cities of Israel.

Amaziah Reigns in Judah

14 In the second year of Joash the son of Jehoahaz, king of Israel, Amaziah the son of Joash, king of Judah, became king. 2He was twenty-five years old when he became king, and he reigned twenty-nine years in Jerusalem. His mother's name was Jehoaddan of Jerusalem. 3And he did *what was* right in the sight of the LORD, yet not like his father David; he did everything as his father Joash had done. 4However the high places were not taken away, and the people still sacrificed and burned incense on the high places.

5Now it happened, as soon as the kingdom was established in his hand, that he executed his servants who had murdered his father the king. 6But the children of the murderers he did not execute, according to what is written in the Book of the Law of Moses, in which the LORD commanded, saying, "Fathers shall not be put to death for their children, nor shall children be put to death for their fathers; but a person shall be put to death for his own sin."[a]

7He killed ten thousand Edomites in the Valley of Salt, and took Sela by war, and called its name Joktheel to this day.

8Then Amaziah sent messengers to Jehoash[a] the son of Jehoahaz, the son of Jehu, king of Israel, saying, "Come, let us face one another *in battle.*" 9And Jehoash king of Israel sent to Amaziah king of Judah, saying, "The thistle that *was* in Lebanon sent to the cedar that *was* in Lebanon, saying, 'Give your daughter to my son as wife'; and a wild beast that *was* in Lebanon passed by and trampled the thistle. 10You have indeed defeated Edom, and your heart has lifted you up. Glory *in that,* and stay at home; for why should you meddle with trouble so that you fall—you and Judah with you?"

¹¹But Amaziah would not heed. Therefore Jehoash king of Israel went out; so he and Amaziah king of Judah faced one another at Beth Shemesh, which *belongs* to Judah. ¹²And Judah was defeated by Israel, and every man fled to his tent. ¹³Then Jehoash king of Israel captured Amaziah king of Judah, the son of Jehoash, the son of Ahaziah, at Beth Shemesh; and he went to Jerusalem, and broke down the wall of Jerusalem from the Gate of Ephraim to the Corner Gate—four hundred cubits. ¹⁴And he took all the gold and silver, all the articles that were found in the house of the LORD and in the treasuries of the king's house, and hostages, and returned to Samaria.

INTIMATE MOMENTS

Purchase a piece of clothing for yourself that you know he will especially like. Then pick a special time and place to wear it.

¹⁵Now the rest of the acts of Jehoash which he did—his might, and how he fought with Amaziah king of Judah—*are* they not written in the book of the chronicles of the kings of Israel? ¹⁶So Jehoash rested with his fathers, and was buried in Samaria with the kings of Israel. Then Jeroboam his son reigned in his place.

¹⁷Amaziah the son of Joash, king of Judah, lived fifteen years after the death of Jehoash the son of Jehoahaz, king of Israel. ¹⁸Now the rest of the acts of Amaziah, *are* they not written in the book of the chronicles of the kings of Judah? ¹⁹And they formed a conspiracy against him in Jerusalem, and he fled to Lachish; but they sent after him to Lachish and killed him there. ²⁰Then they brought him on horses, and he was buried at Jerusalem with his fathers in the City of David.

²¹And all the people of Judah took Azariah,ᵃ who *was* sixteen years old, and

made him king instead of his father Amaziah. ²²He built Elath and restored it to Judah, after the king rested with his fathers.

Jeroboam II Reigns in Israel

²³In the fifteenth year of Amaziah the son of Joash, king of Judah, Jeroboam the son of Joash, king of Israel, became king in Samaria, *and reigned* forty-one years. ²⁴And he did evil in the sight of the LORD; he did not depart from all the sins of Jeroboam the son of Nebat, who had made Israel sin. ²⁵He restored the territory of Israel from the entrance of Hamath to the Sea of the Arabah, according to the word of the LORD God of Israel, which He had spoken through His servant Jonah the son of Amittai, the prophet who *was* from Gath Hepher. ²⁶For the LORD saw *that* the affliction of Israel *was* very bitter; and whether bond or free, there was no helper for Israel. ²⁷And the LORD did not say that He would blot out the name of Israel from under heaven; but He saved them by the hand of Jeroboam the son of Joash.

²⁸Now the rest of the acts of Jeroboam, and all that he did—his might, how he made war, and how he recaptured for Israel, from Damascus and Hamath, *what had belonged* to Judah—*are* they not written in the book of the chronicles of the kings of Israel? ²⁹So Jeroboam rested with his fathers, the kings of Israel. Then Zechariah his son reigned in his place.

Azariah Reigns in Judah

15 In the twenty-seventh year of Jeroboam king of Israel, Azariah the son of Amaziah, king of Judah, became king. ²He was sixteen years old when he became king, and he reigned fifty-two years in Jerusalem. His mother's name *was* Jecholiah of Jerusalem. ³And he did *what was* right in the sight of the LORD, according to all that his father Amaziah had done, ⁴except that the high places were not removed; the people still sacrificed and burned incense on the high places. ⁵Then the LORD struck the king, so that he was a

---

14:21 ᵃCalled *Uzziah* in 2 Chronicles 26:1ff, Isaiah 6:1, and elsewhere

leper until the day of his death; so he dwelt in an isolated house. And Jotham the king's son *was* over the *royal* house, judging the people of the land.

[6]Now the rest of the acts of Azariah, and all that he did, *are* they not written in the book of the chronicles of the kings of Judah? [7]So Azariah rested with his fathers, and they buried him with his fathers in the City of David. Then Jotham his son reigned in his place.

Zechariah Reigns in Israel

[8]In the thirty-eighth year of Azariah king of Judah, Zechariah the son of Jeroboam reigned over Israel in Samaria six months. [9]And he did evil in the sight of the LORD, as his fathers had done; he did not depart from the sins of Jeroboam the son of Nebat, who had made Israel sin. [10]Then Shallum the son of Jabesh conspired against him, and struck and killed him in front of the people; and he reigned in his place.

[11]Now the rest of the acts of Zechariah, indeed they *are* written in the book of the chronicles of the kings of Israel.

[12]This *was* the word of the LORD which He spoke to Jehu, saying, "Your sons shall sit on the throne of Israel to the fourth *generation*."[a] And so it was.

Shallum Reigns in Israel

[13]Shallum the son of Jabesh became king in the thirty-ninth year of Uzziah[a] king of Judah; and he reigned a full month in Samaria. [14]For Menahem the son of Gadi went up from Tirzah, came to Samaria, and struck Shallum the son of Jabesh in Samaria and killed him; and he reigned in his place.

[15]Now the rest of the acts of Shallum, and the conspiracy which he led, indeed they *are* written in the book of the chronicles of the kings of Israel. [16]Then from Tirzah, Menahem attacked Tiphsah, all who *were* there, and its territory. Because they did not surrender, therefore he attacked *it.* All the women there who were with child he ripped open.

Menahem Reigns in Israel

[17]In the thirty-ninth year of Azariah king of Judah, Menahem the son of Gadi became king over Israel, *and reigned* ten years in Samaria. [18]And he did evil in the sight of the LORD; he did not depart all his days from the sins of Jeroboam the son of Nebat, who had made Israel sin. [19]Pul[a] king of Assyria came against the land; and Menahem gave Pul a thousand talents of silver, that his hand might be with him to strengthen the kingdom under his control. [20]And Menahem exacted the money from Israel, from all the very wealthy, from each man fifty shekels of silver, to give to the king of Assyria. So the king of Assyria turned back, and did not stay there in the land.

[21]Now the rest of the acts of Menahem, and all that he did, *are* they not written in the book of the chronicles of the kings of Israel? [22]So Menahem rested with his fathers. Then Pekahiah his son reigned in his place.

Pekahiah Reigns in Israel

[23]In the fiftieth year of Azariah king of Judah, Pekahiah the son of Menahem became king over Israel in Samaria, *and reigned* two years. [24]And he did evil in the sight of the LORD; he did not depart from the sins of Jeroboam the son of Nebat, who had made Israel sin. [25]Then Pekah the son of Remaliah, an officer of his, conspired against him and killed him in Samaria, in the citadel of the king's house, along with Argob and Arieh; and with him were fifty men of Gilead. He killed him and reigned in his place.

[26]Now the rest of the acts of Pekahiah, and all that he did, indeed they *are* written in the book of the chronicles of the kings of Israel.

Pekah Reigns in Israel

[27]In the fifty-second year of Azariah king of Judah, Pekah the son of Remaliah became king over Israel in Samaria, *and reigned* twenty years. [28]And he did evil in the sight of the LORD; he did not depart from the sins of Jeroboam the son of Nebat, who had made Israel sin. [29]In the

---

15:12 [a]2 Kings 10:30 **15:13** [a]Called *Azariah* in 14:21ff and 15:1ff **15:19** [a]That is, Tiglath-Pileser III (compare verse 29)

days of Pekah king of Israel, Tiglath-Pileser king of Assyria came and took Ijon, Abel Beth Maachah, Janoah, Kedesh, Hazor, Gilead, and Galilee, all the land of Naphtali; and he carried them captive to Assyria. 30Then Hoshea the son of Elah led a conspiracy against Pekah the son of Remaliah, and struck and killed him; so he reigned in his place in the twentieth year of Jotham the son of Uzziah.

31Now the rest of the acts of Pekah, and all that he did, indeed they *are* written in the book of the chronicles of the kings of Israel.

Jotham Reigns in Judah

32In the second year of Pekah the son of Remaliah, king of Israel, Jotham the son of Uzziah, king of Judah, began to reign. 33He was twenty-five years old when he became king, and he reigned sixteen years in Jerusalem. His mother's name *was* Jerusha[a] the daughter of Zadok. 34And he did *what was* right in the sight of the LORD; he did according to all that his father Uzziah had done. 35However the high places were not removed; the people still sacrificed and burned incense on the high places. He built the Upper Gate of the house of the LORD.

36Now the rest of the acts of Jotham, and all that he did, *are* they not written in the book of the chronicles of the kings of Judah? 37In those days the LORD began to send Rezin king of Syria and Pekah the son of Remaliah against Judah. 38So Jotham

rested with his fathers, and was buried with his fathers in the City of David his father. Then Ahaz his son reigned in his place.

Ahaz Reigns in Judah

16 In the seventeenth year of Pekah the son of Remaliah, Ahaz the son of Jotham, king of Judah, began to reign. 2Ahaz *was* twenty years old when he became king, and he reigned sixteen years in Jerusalem; and he did not do *what was* right in the sight of the LORD his God, as his father David *had done*. 3But he walked in the way of the kings of Israel; indeed he made his son pass through the fire, according to the abominations of the nations whom the LORD had cast out from before the children of Israel. 4And he sacrificed and burned incense on the high places, on the hills, and under every green tree.

5Then Rezin king of Syria and Pekah the son of Remaliah, king of Israel, came up to Jerusalem to *make* war; and they besieged Ahaz but could not overcome *him*. 6At that time Rezin king of Syria captured Elath for Syria, and drove the men of Judah from Elath. Then the Edomites[a] went to Elath, and dwell there to this day.

7So Ahaz sent messengers to Tiglath-Pileser king of Assyria, saying, "I *am* your servant and your son. Come up and save

15:33 [a]Spelled *Jerushah* in 2 Chronicles 27:1
16:6 [a]Some ancient authorities read *Syrians*.

ROMANTIC QUOTES AND NOTES
Put Your Spouse First

Have you made the decision that, no matter what, your spouse is number one (obviously, after Jesus Christ)? You married each other for life. You are not guaranteed how long that life together will be. Putting your spouse first says, in effect, "I choose to make the most of whatever time we will share on this earth."

At one level, this means making sure your mutual needs for romance and physical oneness get met. At another level, it means choosing to give each other the gift of mutually pleasing one another however you can.

Do you have a heart for your spouse and his or her needs? Do you show appreciation for your mate's efforts to remain pure in thinking and faithful to you in your marriage? Do you value how God designed him or her and show it with any kind of admiration and gratitude?

It's been said that less than 20 percent of all married couples have conversations about sex. Is that true of you? Do the two of you talk about what you like and don't like? Do you know what would please your mate? You can't enflame your romance if you don't know each other's needs and what would communicate love to your spouse.

me from the hand of the king of Syria and from the hand of the king of Israel, who rise up against me." ⁸And Ahaz took the silver and gold that was found in the house of the LORD, and in the treasuries of the king's house, and sent *it as* a present to the king of Assyria. ⁹So the king of Assyria heeded him; for the king of Assyria went up against Damascus and took it, carried *its people* captive to Kir, and killed Rezin.

¹⁰Now King Ahaz went to Damascus to meet Tiglath-Pileser king of Assyria, and saw an altar that *was* at Damascus; and King Ahaz sent to Urijah the priest the design of the altar and its pattern, according to all its workmanship. ¹¹Then Urijah the priest built an altar according to all that King Ahaz had sent from Damascus. So Urijah the priest made *it* before King Ahaz came back from Damascus. ¹²And when the king came back from Damascus, the king saw the altar; and the king approached the altar and made offerings on it. ¹³So he burned his burnt offering and his grain offering; and he poured his drink offering and sprinkled the blood of his peace offerings on the altar. ¹⁴He also brought the bronze altar which *was* before the LORD, from the front of the temple— from between the *new* altar and the house of the LORD—and put it on the north side of the *new* altar. ¹⁵Then King Ahaz commanded Urijah the priest, saying, "On the great *new* altar burn the morning burnt offering, the evening grain offering, the king's burnt sacrifice, and his grain offering, with the burnt offering of all the people of the land, their grain offering, and their drink offerings; and sprinkle on it all the blood of the burnt offering and all the blood of the sacrifice. And the bronze altar shall be for me to inquire *by*." ¹⁶Thus did Urijah the priest, according to all that King Ahaz commanded.

¹⁷And King Ahaz cut off the panels of the carts, and removed the lavers from them; and he took down the Sea from the bronze oxen that *were* under it, and put it on a pavement of stones. ¹⁸Also he removed the Sabbath pavilion which they had built in the temple, and he removed the king's

17:10 ᵃHebrew *Asherim,* Canaanite deities

outer entrance from the house of the LORD, on account of the king of Assyria.

¹⁹Now the rest of the acts of Ahaz which he did, *are* they not written in the book of the chronicles of the kings of Judah? ²⁰So Ahaz rested with his fathers, and was buried with his fathers in the City of David. Then Hezekiah his son reigned in his place.

Hoshea Reigns in Israel

17 In the twelfth year of Ahaz king of Judah, Hoshea the son of Elah became king of Israel in Samaria, *and he reigned* nine years. ²And he did evil in the sight of the LORD, but not as the kings of Israel who were before him. ³Shalmaneser king of Assyria came up against him; and Hoshea became his vassal, and paid him tribute money. ⁴And the king of Assyria uncovered a conspiracy by Hoshea; for he had sent messengers to So, king of Egypt, and brought no tribute to the king of Assyria, as *he had done* year by year. Therefore the king of Assyria shut him up, and bound him in prison.

Israel Carried Captive to Assyria

⁵Now the king of Assyria went throughout all the land, and went up to Samaria and besieged it for three years. ⁶In the ninth year of Hoshea, the king of Assyria took Samaria and carried Israel away to Assyria, and placed them in Halah and by the Habor, the River of Gozan, and in the cities of the Medes.

⁷For so it was that the children of Israel had sinned against the LORD their God, who had brought them up out of the land of Egypt, from under the hand of Pharaoh king of Egypt; and they had feared other gods, ⁸and had walked in the statutes of the nations whom the LORD had cast out from before the children of Israel, and of the kings of Israel, which they had made. ⁹Also the children of Israel secretly did against the LORD their God things that *were* not right, and they built for themselves high places in all their cities, from watchtower to fortified city. ¹⁰They set up for themselves *sacred* pillars and wooden imagesᵃ on every high hill and under every green tree. ¹¹There they burned incense on all the high places, like the nations whom

the LORD had carried away before them; and they did wicked things to provoke the LORD to anger, ¹²for they served idols, of which the LORD had said to them, "You shall not do this thing."

¹³Yet the LORD testified against Israel and against Judah, by all of His prophets, every seer, saying, "Turn from your evil ways, and keep My commandments *and* My statutes, according to all the law which I commanded your fathers, and which I sent to you by My servants the prophets." ¹⁴Nevertheless they would not hear, but stiffened their necks, like the necks of their fathers, who did not believe in the LORD their God. ¹⁵And they rejected His statutes and His covenant that He had made with their fathers, and His testimonies which He had testified against them; they followed idols, became idolaters, and *went* after the nations who *were* all around them, *concerning* whom the LORD had charged them that they should not do like them. ¹⁶So they left all the commandments of the LORD their God, made for themselves a molded image *and* two calves, made a wooden image and worshiped all the host of heaven, and served Baal. ¹⁷And they caused their sons and daughters to pass through the fire, practiced witchcraft and soothsaying, and sold themselves to do evil in the sight of the LORD, to provoke Him to anger. ¹⁸Therefore the LORD was very angry with Israel, and removed them from His sight; there was none left but the tribe of Judah alone.

¹⁹Also Judah did not keep the commandments of the LORD their God, but walked in the statutes of Israel which they made. ²⁰And the LORD rejected all the descendants of Israel, afflicted them, and delivered them into the hand of plunderers, until He had cast them from His sight. ²¹For He tore Israel from the house of David, and they made Jeroboam the son of Nebat king. Then Jeroboam drove Israel from following the LORD, and made them commit a great sin. ²²For the children of Israel walked in all the sins of Jeroboam which he did; they did not depart from them, ²³until the LORD removed Israel out of His sight, as He had said by all His servants the prophets. So Israel was carried away from their own land to Assyria, *as it is* to this day.

Assyria Resettles Samaria

²⁴Then the king of Assyria brought *people* from Babylon, Cuthah, Ava, Hamath, and from Sepharvaim, and placed *them* in the cities of Samaria instead of the children of Israel; and they took possession of Samaria and dwelt in its cities. ²⁵And it was so, at the beginning of their dwelling there, *that* they did not fear the LORD; therefore the LORD sent lions among them, which killed *some* of them. ²⁶So they spoke to the king of Assyria, saying, "The nations whom you have removed and placed in the cities of Samaria do not know the rituals of the God of the land; therefore He has sent lions among them, and indeed, they are killing them because they do not know the rituals of the God of the land." ²⁷Then the king of Assyria commanded, saying, "Send there one of the priests whom you brought from there; let him go and dwell there, and let him teach them the rituals of the God of the land." ²⁸Then one of the priests whom they had carried away from Samaria came and dwelt in Bethel, and taught them how they should fear the LORD.

²⁹However every nation continued to make gods of its own, and put *them* in the shrines on the high places which the Samaritans had made, *every* nation in the cities where they dwelt. ³⁰The men of Babylon made Succoth Benoth, the men of Cuth made Nergal, the men of Hamath made Ashima, ³¹and the Avites made Nibhaz and Tartak; and the Sepharvites burned their children in fire to Adrammelech and Anammelech, the gods of Sepharvaim. ³²So they feared the LORD, and from every class they appointed for themselves priests of the high places, who sacrificed for them in the shrines of the high places. ³³They feared the LORD, yet served their own gods— according to the rituals of the nations from among whom they were carried away.

³⁴To this day they continue practicing the former rituals; they do not fear the LORD, nor do they follow their statutes or their ordinances, or the law and commandment which the LORD had commanded the children of Jacob, whom He named Israel, ³⁵with whom the LORD had made a covenant and charged them, saying: "You shall not fear other gods,

nor bow down to them nor serve them nor sacrifice to them; [36]but the LORD, who brought you up from the land of Egypt with great power and an outstretched arm, Him you shall fear, Him you shall worship, and to Him you shall offer sacrifice. [37]And the statutes, the ordinances, the law, and the commandment which He wrote for you, you shall be careful to observe forever; you shall not fear other gods. [38]And the covenant that I have made with you, you shall not forget, nor shall you fear other gods. [39]But the LORD your God you shall fear; and He will deliver you from the hand of all your enemies." [40]However they did not obey, but they followed their former rituals. [41]So these nations feared the LORD, yet served their carved images; also their children and their children's children have continued doing as their fathers did, even to this day.

Hezekiah Reigns in Judah

18 Now it came to pass in the third year of Hoshea the son of Elah, king of Israel, *that* Hezekiah the son of Ahaz, king of Judah, began to reign. [2]He was twenty-five years old when he became king, and he reigned twenty-nine years in Jerusalem. His mother's name *was* Abi[a] the daughter of Zechariah. [3]And he did *what was* right in the sight of the LORD, according to all that his father David had done.

[4]He removed the high places and broke the *sacred* pillars, cut down the wooden image[a] and broke in pieces the bronze serpent that Moses had made; for until those days the children of Israel burned incense to it, and called it Nehushtan.[b] [5]He trusted in the LORD God of Israel, so that after him was none like him among all the kings of Judah, nor who were before him. [6]For he held fast to the LORD; he did not depart from following Him, but kept His commandments, which the LORD had commanded Moses. [7]The LORD was with him; he prospered wherever he went. And he rebelled against the king of Assyria and did not serve him. [8]He subdued the Philistines, as far as Gaza and its territory, from watchtower to fortified city.

18:2 [a]Called *Abijah* in 2 Chronicles 29:1ff
18:4 [a]Hebrew *Asherah*, a Canaanite goddess
[b]Literally *Bronze Thing*

BIBLICAL INSIGHTS • 17:27
Only the Humble Learn

THE BIBLE REPEATEDLY TEACHES that growth cannot occur without a teachable heart. A teachable spirit is one of the most important components in any marriage.

A growing desire to learn requires the ability to freely admit fault and to ask forgiveness. Ultimately, it means a willingness to do what is right and what God wants, regardless of the personal sacrifice or cost. At the heart of teachability lies humility.

The foreigners who settled the towns vacated by the exiled Israelites had to humble themselves and learn what God required of those who would inhabit His land. Many of them died because they did not fear the Lord (17:24–27).

It is imperative in our relationships to retain our ability to say, "I have not arrived," "I have more to learn," and "Please help me develop in this area." Regularly ask God to give you and your mate teachable hearts willing to do all He has commanded.

"But my mate is not teachable!" you object. Then begin to pray now that he or she will hunger and thirst for progress and not get satisfied with mediocrity. Also, model a teachable heart. Teachability can be contagious! You may be the best example of this humble virtue your mate ever sees.

[9]Now it came to pass in the fourth year of King Hezekiah, which *was* the seventh year of Hoshea the son of Elah, king of Israel, *that* Shalmaneser king of Assyria came up against Samaria and besieged it. [10]And at the end of three years they took it. In the sixth year of Hezekiah, that *is,* the ninth year of Hoshea king of Israel, Samaria was taken. [11]Then the king of Assyria carried Israel away captive to Assyria, and put them in Halah and by the Habor, the River of Gozan, and in the cities of the Medes, [12]because they did not obey the voice of the LORD their God, but transgressed His

covenant *and* all that Moses the servant of the LORD had commanded; and they would neither hear nor do *them.*

¹³And in the fourteenth year of King Hezekiah, Sennacherib king of Assyria came up against all the fortified cities of Judah and took them. ¹⁴Then Hezekiah king of Judah sent to the king of Assyria at Lachish, saying, "I have done wrong; turn away from me; whatever you impose on me I will pay." And the king of Assyria assessed Hezekiah king of Judah three hundred talents of silver and thirty talents of gold. ¹⁵So Hezekiah gave *him* all the silver that was found in the house of the LORD and in the treasuries of the king's house. ¹⁶At that time Hezekiah stripped *the gold from* the doors of the temple of the LORD, and *from* the pillars which Hezekiah king of Judah had overlaid, and gave it to the king of Assyria.

Sennacherib Boasts Against the LORD

¹⁷Then the king of Assyria sent *the* Tartan,ᵃ *the* Rabsaris,ᵇ *and the* Rabshakehᶜ from Lachish, with a great army against Jerusalem, to King Hezekiah. And they went up and came to Jerusalem. When they had come up, they went and stood by the aqueduct from the upper pool, which *was* on the highway to the Fuller's Field. ¹⁸And when they had called to the king, Eliakim the son of Hilkiah, who *was* over the household, Shebna the scribe, and Joah the son of Asaph, the recorder, came out to them. ¹⁹Then *the* Rabshakeh said to them, "Say now to Hezekiah, 'Thus says the great king, the king of Assyria: "What confidence *is* this in which you trust? ²⁰You speak of *having* plans and power for war; but *they are* mere words. And in whom do you trust, that you rebel against me? ²¹Now look! You are trusting in the staff of this broken reed, Egypt, on which if a man leans, it will go into his hand and pierce it. So *is* Pharaoh king of Egypt to all who trust in him. ²²But if you say to me, 'We trust in the LORD our God,' *is* it not He whose high places and whose altars Hezekiah has taken away, and said to Judah and Jerusalem, 'You shall

18:17 ᵃA title, probably *Commander in Chief* ᵇA title, probably *Chief Officer* ᶜA title, probably *Chief of Staff* or *Governor*

ROMANTIC QUOTES AND NOTES
Talking . . . Face to Face

If you want to touch your wife deeply, look into her soul through her eyes. She's longing for intimate conversation! Touching base by phone is fine, but for a woman, that's like watching an old black-and-white TV.

One of her top romantic needs is to be heard and understood by her man. She longs for openness, a sharing of dreams, hopes, desires, and even disappointments, through focused conversation.

You might be thinking, *Time out, Dennis! A conversationalist? I'm a man of few words.*

Funny, that's what Moses said when God asked him to be His spokesman: "Moses said to the LORD, 'O Lord, I have never been eloquent, neither in the past nor since you have spoken to your servant. I am slow of speech and tongue" (Ex. 4:10). And what did the Lord tell him? "Who gave man his mouth? Who makes him deaf or mute? . . . Now go; I will help you speak and will teach you what to say" (vv. 11, 12).

You may say, "Now that's fine for Moses leading the nation of Israel, but will God give me words to better communicate with your wife?" My answer: Absolutely. He cares about your wife and your marriage. The Holy Spirit still guides men (and women) in what they need to say.

Are you wondering how this is going to work? It's easier than you may think. Start by praying and asking God to help you. Then practice answering your wife's questions *with more than one sentence.* It's okay if there's silence for a while, but work on really sharing with her on an intimate level what you are thinking and feeling. And if you don't know, keep on praying and asking God to help you. He will. And He may use your wife to do it!

worship before this altar in Jerusalem'?"' ²³Now therefore, I urge you, give a pledge to my master the king of Assyria, and I will give you two thousand horses—if you are able on your part to put riders on them! ²⁴How then will you repel one captain of the least of my master's servants, and put your trust in Egypt for chariots and horsemen? ²⁵Have I now come up without the LORD against this place to destroy it? The LORD said to me, 'Go up against this land, and destroy it.'"

²⁶Then Eliakim the son of Hilkiah, Shebna, and Joah said to *the* Rabshakeh, "Please speak to your servants in Aramaic, for we understand *it;* and do not speak to us in Hebrewᵃ in the hearing of the people who *are* on the wall."

²⁷But *the* Rabshakeh said to them, "Has my master sent me to your master and to you to speak these words, and not to the men who sit on the wall, who will eat and drink their own waste with you?"

²⁸Then *the* Rabshakeh stood and called out with a loud voice in Hebrew, and spoke, saying, "Hear the word of the great king, the king of Assyria! ²⁹Thus says the king: 'Do not let Hezekiah deceive you, for he shall not be able to deliver you from his hand; ³⁰nor let Hezekiah make you trust in the LORD, saying, "The LORD will surely deliver us; this city shall not be given into the hand of the king of Assyria."' ³¹Do not listen to Hezekiah; for thus says the king of Assyria: 'Make *peace* with me by a present and come out to me; and every one of you eat from his own vine and every one from his own fig tree, and every one of you drink the waters of his own cistern; ³²until I come and take you away to a land like your own land, a land of grain and new wine, a land of bread and vineyards, a land of olive groves and honey, that you may live and not die. But do not listen to Hezekiah, lest he persuade you, saying, "The LORD will deliver us." ³³Has any of the gods of the nations at all delivered its land from the hand of the king of Assyria? ³⁴Where *are* the gods of Hamath and Arpad? Where *are* the gods of Sepharvaim and Hena and Ivah? Indeed, have they delivered Samaria

from my hand? ³⁵Who among all the gods of the lands have delivered their countries from my hand, that the LORD should deliver Jerusalem from my hand?'"

³⁶But the people held their peace and answered him not a word; for the king's commandment was, "Do not answer him." ³⁷Then Eliakim the son of Hilkiah, who *was* over the household, Shebna the scribe, and Joah the son of Asaph, the recorder, came to Hezekiah with *their* clothes torn, and told him the words of *the* Rabshakeh.

Isaiah Assures Deliverance

19 And so it was, when King Hezekiah heard *it,* that he tore his clothes, covered himself with sackcloth, and went into the house of the LORD. ²Then he sent Eliakim, who *was* over the household, Shebna the scribe, and the elders of the priests, covered with sackcloth, to Isaiah the prophet, the son of Amoz. ³And they said to him, "Thus says Hezekiah: 'This day *is* a day of trouble, and rebuke, and blasphemy; for the children have come to birth, but *there is* no strength to bring them forth. ⁴It may be that the LORD your God will hear all the words of *the* Rabshakeh, whom his master the king of Assyria has sent to reproach the living God, and will rebuke the words which the LORD your God has heard. Therefore lift up *your* prayer for the remnant that is left.'"

⁵So the servants of King Hezekiah came to Isaiah. ⁶And Isaiah said to them, "Thus you shall say to your master, 'Thus says the LORD: "Do not be afraid of the words which you have heard, with which the servants of the king of Assyria have blasphemed Me. ⁷Surely I will send a spirit upon him, and he shall hear a rumor and return to his own land; and I will cause him to fall by the sword in his own land."'"

Sennacherib's Threat and Hezekiah's Prayer

⁸Then *the* Rabshakeh returned and found the king of Assyria warring against Libnah, for he heard that he had departed from Lachish. ⁹And the king heard concerning Tirhakah king of Ethiopia, "Look, he has come out to make war with you." So he again sent messengers to Hezekiah, saying, ¹⁰"Thus you shall speak to Hezekiah

---

18:26 ᵃLiterally *Judean*

Face Down Your Difficulties

YOUR COVENANT OF COMMITMENT to God and each other is what remains after reality has edited what you *thought* marriage would be. Think back to your wedding. You stood before God at the altar and promised never to leave or forsake your spouse, in sickness and in health, for better or for worse. When you stare "worse" in the face, you have a choice.

Will you honor that commitment?

At this crossroads, you can reject your vows, believing there is no hope; or you can trust God, believing that He is able to help you rekindle the smoldering ashes and transform them into something vibrant.

When King Hezekiah faced disaster at the hands of the invading Assyrians, he humbly turned to God for rescue—and God erased the Assyrian threat. The same thing can happen in your marriage! As some dear friends said to us when we reached a very difficult time of testing in our family, "What an awesome opportunity to see God work!"

Your marriages will face some challenging seasons. All marriages do. When you trust God to renew your commitment to one another and to rekindle your romance, you set your marriage on a course to experience the season of mature, committed love. This season is well worth the work! We know. We've experienced it.

---

king of Judah, saying: 'Do not let your God in whom you trust deceive you, saying, "Jerusalem shall not be given into the hand of the king of Assyria." ¹¹Look! You have heard what the kings of Assyria have done to all lands by utterly destroying them; and shall you be delivered? ¹²Have the gods of the nations delivered those whom my fathers have destroyed, Gozan and Haran and Rezeph, and the people of Eden who *were* in Telassar? ¹³Where *is* the king of Hamath, the king of Arpad, and the king of the city of Sepharvaim, Hena, and Ivah?'"

¹⁴And Hezekiah received the letter from the hand of the messengers, and read it; and Hezekiah went up to the house of the LORD, and spread it before the LORD. ¹⁵Then Hezekiah prayed before the LORD, and said: "O LORD God of Israel, *the One* who dwells *between* the cherubim, You are God, You alone, of all the kingdoms of the earth. You have made heaven and earth. ¹⁶Incline Your ear, O LORD, and hear; open Your eyes, O LORD, and see; and hear the words of Sennacherib, which he has sent to reproach the living God. ¹⁷Truly, LORD, the kings of Assyria have laid waste the nations and their lands, ¹⁸and have cast their gods into the fire; for they *were* not gods, but the work of men's hands—wood and stone. Therefore they destroyed them. ¹⁹Now therefore, O LORD our God, I pray, save us from his hand, that all the kingdoms of the earth may know that You *are* the LORD God, You alone."

The Word of the LORD Concerning Sennacherib

²⁰Then Isaiah the son of Amoz sent to Hezekiah, saying, "Thus says the LORD God of Israel: 'Because you have prayed to Me against Sennacherib king of Assyria, I have heard.' ²¹This *is* the word which the LORD has spoken concerning him:

'The virgin, the daughter of Zion,
  Has despised you, laughed you to
    scorn;
  The daughter of Jerusalem
  Has shaken *her* head behind your
    back!

²² 'Whom have you reproached and
    blasphemed?
  Against whom have you raised *your*
    voice,
  And lifted up your eyes on high?
  Against the Holy *One* of Israel.
²³ By your messengers you have
    reproached the Lord,
  And said: "By the multitude of my
    chariots
  I have come up to the height of the
    mountains,
  To the limits of Lebanon;
  I will cut down its tall cedars
  And its choice cypress trees;

I will enter the extremity of its
    borders,
To its fruitful forest.
24 I have dug and drunk strange water,
    And with the soles of my feet I have
        dried up
    All the brooks of defense."

25 'Did you not hear long ago
    How I made it,
    From ancient times that I formed it?
    Now I have brought it to pass,
    That you should be
    For crushing fortified cities *into*
        heaps of ruins.
26 Therefore their inhabitants had little
        power;
    They were dismayed and confounded;
    They were *as* the grass of the field
    And the green herb,
    As the grass on the housetops
    And *grain* blighted before it is grown.

27 'But I know your dwelling place,
    Your going out and your coming in,
    And your rage against Me.
28 Because your rage against Me and
        your tumult
    Have come up to My ears,
    Therefore I will put My hook in your
        nose
    And My bridle in your lips,
    And I will turn you back
    By the way which you came.

29 'This *shall be* a sign to you:

    You shall eat this year such as grows
        of itself,
    And in the second year what springs
        from the same;
    Also in the third year sow and reap,
    Plant vineyards and eat the fruit of
        them.
30 And the remnant who have escaped
        of the house of Judah
    Shall again take root downward,
    And bear fruit upward.
31 For out of Jerusalem shall go a
        remnant,
    And those who escape from Mount
        Zion.

    The zeal of the LORD of hosts[a] will
        do this.'

32 "Therefore thus says the LORD concerning the king of Assyria:

    'He shall not come into this city,
    Nor shoot an arrow there,
    Nor come before it with shield,
    Nor build a siege mound against it.
33 By the way that he came,
    By the same shall he return;
    And he shall not come into this city,'
    Says the LORD.
34 'For I will defend this city, to save it
    For My own sake and for My servant
        David's sake.'"

Sennacherib's Defeat and Death

35 And it came to pass on a certain night
that the angel[a] of the LORD went out, and
killed in the camp of the Assyrians one hundred and eighty-five thousand; and when
people arose early in the morning, there were
the corpses—all dead. 36 So Sennacherib
king of Assyria departed and went away,
returned *home,* and remained at Nineveh.
37 Now it came to pass, as he was worshiping
in the temple of Nisroch his god, that his
sons Adrammelech and Sharezer struck
him down with the sword; and they escaped
into the land of Ararat. Then Esarhaddon
his son reigned in his place.

Hezekiah's Life Extended

20 In those days Hezekiah was sick and
near death. And Isaiah the prophet,
the son of Amoz, went to him and said to
him, "Thus says the LORD: 'Set your house
in order, for you shall die, and not live.'"
2 Then he turned his face toward the wall,
and prayed to the LORD, saying, 3 "Remember now, O LORD, I pray, how I have walked
before You in truth and with a loyal heart,
and have done *what was* good in Your
sight." And Hezekiah wept bitterly.
4 And it happened, before Isaiah had gone
out into the middle court, that the word of
the LORD came to him, saying, 5 "Return and
tell Hezekiah the leader of My people, 'Thus
says the LORD, the God of David your
father: "I have heard your prayer, I have
seen your tears; surely I will heal you. On
the third day you shall go up to the house of

19:31 [a]Following many Hebrew manuscripts and
ancient versions (compare Isaiah 37:32); Masoretic
Text omits *of hosts.* **19:35** [a]Or *Angel*

the LORD. ⁶And I will add to your days fifteen years. I will deliver you and this city
from the hand of the king of Assyria; and I
will defend this city for My own sake, and
for the sake of My servant David.'"

⁷Then Isaiah said, "Take a lump of figs."
So they took and laid *it* on the boil, and he
recovered.

⁸And Hezekiah said to Isaiah, "What *is*
the sign that the LORD will heal me, and that
I shall go up to the house of the LORD the
third day?"

⁹Then Isaiah said, "This is the sign to
you from the LORD, that the LORD will do
the thing which He has spoken: *shall* the
shadow go forward ten degrees or go backward ten degrees?"

¹⁰And Hezekiah answered, "It is an easy
thing for the shadow to go down ten
degrees; no, but let the shadow go backward ten degrees."

¹¹So Isaiah the prophet cried out to the
LORD, and He brought the shadow ten degrees backward, by which it had gone down
on the sundial of Ahaz.

The Babylonian Envoys

¹²At that time Berodach-Baladanᵃ the
son of Baladan, king of Babylon, sent letters and a present to Hezekiah, for he heard
that Hezekiah had been sick. ¹³And Hezekiah was attentive to them, and showed
them all the house of his treasures—the
silver and gold, the spices and precious
ointment, and allᵃ his armory—all that
was found among his treasures. There was
nothing in his house or in all his dominion
that Hezekiah did not show them.

¹⁴Then Isaiah the prophet went to King
Hezekiah, and said to him, "What did
these men say, and from where did they
come to you?"

So Hezekiah said, "They came from a far
country, from Babylon."

¹⁵And he said, "What have they seen in
your house?"

So Hezekiah answered, "They have
seen all that *is* in my house; there is nothing among my treasures that I have not
shown them."

¹⁶Then Isaiah said to Hezekiah, "Hear
the word of the LORD: ¹⁷'Behold, the days
are coming when all that *is* in your house,

and what your fathers have accumulated
until this day, shall be carried to Babylon;
nothing shall be left,' says the LORD. ¹⁸'And
they shall take away some of your sons
who will descend from you, whom you will
beget; and they shall be eunuchs in the
palace of the king of Babylon.'"

¹⁹So Hezekiah said to Isaiah, "The word
of the LORD which you have spoken *is*
good!" For he said, "Will there not be peace
and truth at least in my days?"

Death of Hezekiah

²⁰Now the rest of the acts of Hezekiah—
all his might, and how he made a pool and
a tunnel and brought water into the city—
are they not written in the book of the
chronicles of the kings of Judah? ²¹So Hezekiah rested with his fathers. Then Manasseh
his son reigned in his place.

Manasseh Reigns in Judah

21 Manasseh *was* twelve years old when
he became king, and he reigned fifty-
five years in Jerusalem. His mother's name
was Hephzibah. ²And he did evil in the
sight of the LORD, according to the abominations of the nations whom the LORD had
cast out before the children of Israel. ³For
he rebuilt the high places which Hezekiah
his father had destroyed; he raised up altars
for Baal, and made a wooden image,ᵃ as
Ahab king of Israel had done; and he worshiped all the host of heavenᵇ and served
them. ⁴He also built altars in the house of
the LORD, of which the LORD had said, "In
Jerusalem I will put My name." ⁵And he
built altars for all the host of heaven in the
two courts of the house of the LORD. ⁶Also
he made his son pass through the fire, practiced soothsaying, used witchcraft, and consulted spiritists and mediums. He did much
evil in the sight of the LORD, to provoke
Him to anger. ⁷He even set a carved image
of Asherahᵃ that he had made, in the
house of which the LORD had said to David
and to Solomon his son, "In this house and

20:12 ᵃSpelled *Merodach-Baladan* in Isaiah 39:1
20:13 ᵃFollowing many Hebrew manuscripts, Syriac,
and Targum; Masoretic Text omits *all*. **21:3** ᵃHebrew
Asherah, a Canaanite goddess ᵇThe gods of the
Assyrians **21:7** ᵃA Canaanite goddess

in Jerusalem, which I have chosen out of all the tribes of Israel, I will put My name forever; 8and I will not make the feet of Israel wander anymore from the land which I gave their fathers—only if they are careful to do according to all that I have commanded them, and according to all the law that My servant Moses commanded them." 9But they paid no attention, and Manasseh seduced them to do more evil than the nations whom the LORD had destroyed before the children of Israel.

10And the LORD spoke by His servants the prophets, saying, 11"Because Manasseh king of Judah has done these abominations (he has acted more wickedly than all the Amorites who *were* before him, and has also made Judah sin with his idols), 12therefore thus says the LORD God of Israel: 'Behold, *I* am bringing *such* calamity upon Jerusalem and Judah, that whoever hears of it, both his ears will tingle. 13And I will stretch over Jerusalem the measuring line of Samaria and the plummet of the house of Ahab; I will wipe Jerusalem as *one* wipes a dish, wiping *it* and turning *it* upside down. 14So I will forsake the remnant of My inheritance and deliver them into the hand of their enemies; and they shall become victims of plunder to all their enemies, 15because they have done evil in My sight, and have provoked Me to anger since the day their fathers came out of Egypt, even to this day.' "

16Moreover Manasseh shed very much innocent blood, till he had filled Jerusalem from one end to another, besides his sin by which he made Judah sin, in doing evil in the sight of the LORD.

17Now the rest of the acts of Manasseh—all that he did, and the sin that he committed—*are* they not written in the book of the chronicles of the kings of Judah? 18So Manasseh rested with his fathers, and was buried in the garden of his own house, in the garden of Uzza. Then his son Amon reigned in his place.

Amon's Reign and Death

19Amon *was* twenty-two years old when he became king, and he reigned two years in Jerusalem. His mother's name *was* Meshullemeth the daughter of Haruz of Jotbah. 20And he did evil in the sight of the LORD, as his father Manasseh had done. 21So he walked in all the ways that his father had walked; and he served the idols that his father had served, and worshiped them. 22He forsook the LORD God of his fathers, and did not walk in the way of the LORD.

23Then the servants of Amon conspired against him, and killed the king in his own house. 24But the people of the land executed all those who had conspired against King Amon. Then the people of the land made his son Josiah king in his place.

25Now the rest of the acts of Amon which he did, *are* they not written in the book of the chronicles of the kings of Judah? 26And he was buried in his tomb in the garden of Uzza. Then Josiah his son reigned in his place.

Josiah Reigns in Judah

22 Josiah *was* eight years old when he became king, and he reigned thirty-one years in Jerusalem. His mother's name *was* Jedidah the daughter of Adaiah of Bozkath. 2And he did *what was* right in the sight of the LORD, and walked in all the ways of his father David; he did not turn aside to the right hand or to the left.

Hilkiah Finds the Book of the Law

3Now it came to pass, in the eighteenth year of King Josiah, *that* the king sent Shaphan the scribe, the son of Azaliah, the son of Meshullam, to the house of the LORD, saying: 4"Go up to Hilkiah the high priest, that he may count the money which has been brought into the house of the LORD, which the doorkeepers have gathered from the people. 5And let them deliver it into the hand of those doing the work, who are the overseers in the house of the LORD; let them give it to those who *are* in the house of the LORD doing the work, to repair the damages of the house— 6to carpenters and builders and masons—and to buy timber and hewn stone to repair the house. 7However there need be no accounting made with them of the money delivered into their hand, because they deal faithfully."

8Then Hilkiah the high priest said to Shaphan the scribe, "I have found the Book of the Law in the house of the LORD." And Hilkiah gave the book to Shaphan, and he

BIBLICAL INSIGHTS • 22:19

Hope Even in the Darkness

REGARDLESS OF HOW GRIM your situation may look—either in your own family or in your community—repentance and faith in God, powered by confidence in His Word, can bring hope to the darkest of days. That is the lesson of King Josiah (22:19).

You experience God's truth in your family as you apply His Word repeatedly. When God blesses your faith and obedience, in both trials and triumphs, you will see changes in your family. Following Christ will not be some sacred theory or once-a-week tradition, but a day-by-day experience with the living Creator of the Universe. What could be more thrilling than praying for needs as a family and then watching those prayers get answered?

And when you make choices and decisions based on the absolute standard of Scripture, there will be benefits: Peace, harmony, and hope. When you embrace and proclaim God's truth, your convictions take root and emerge. When someone proclaims publicly that which he embraces privately, he takes a huge step toward maturity and godliness. No longer is he satisfied with seeing God work in his life and family; now he becomes a soldier for truth, a conduit of love, grace, and life change in others.

What challenge are you facing today that demands that you embrace God's Word, step out, and proclaim publicly what you believe?

read it. ⁹So Shaphan the scribe went to the king, bringing the king word, saying, "Your servants have gathered the money that was found in the house, and have delivered it into the hand of those who do the work, who oversee the house of the LORD." ¹⁰Then Shaphan the scribe showed the king, saying, "Hilkiah the priest has given me a book." And Shaphan read it before the king. ¹¹Now it happened, when the king heard the words of the Book of the Law, that he

tore his clothes. ¹²Then the king commanded Hilkiah the priest, Ahikam the son of Shaphan, Achborᵃ the son of Michaiah, Shaphan the scribe, and Asaiah a servant of the king, saying, ¹³"Go, inquire of the LORD for me, for the people and for all Judah, concerning the words of this book that has been found; for great *is* the wrath of the LORD that is aroused against us, because our fathers have not obeyed the words of this book, to do according to all that is written concerning us."

¹⁴So Hilkiah the priest, Ahikam, Achbor, Shaphan, and Asaiah went to Huldah the prophetess, the wife of Shallum the son of Tikvah, the son of Harhas, keeper of the wardrobe. (She dwelt in Jerusalem in the Second Quarter.) And they spoke with her. ¹⁵Then she said to them, "Thus says the LORD God of Israel, 'Tell the man who sent you to Me, ¹⁶"Thus says the LORD: 'Behold, I will bring calamity on this place and on its inhabitants—all the words of the book which the king of Judah has read— ¹⁷because they have forsaken Me and burned incense to other gods, that they might provoke Me to anger with all the works of their hands. Therefore My wrath shall be aroused against this place and shall not be quenched.'"' ¹⁸But as for the king of Judah, who sent you to inquire of the LORD, in this manner you shall speak to him, 'Thus says the LORD God of Israel: "*Concerning* the words which you have heard— ¹⁹because your heart was tender, and you humbled yourself before the LORD when you heard what I spoke against this place and against its inhabitants, that they would become a desolation and a curse, and you tore your clothes and wept before Me, I also have heard *you*," says the LORD. ²⁰"Surely, therefore, I will gather you to your fathers, and you shall be gathered to your grave in peace; and your eyes shall not see all the calamity which I will bring on this place."'" So they brought back word to the king.

Josiah Restores True Worship

23 Now the king sent them to gather all the elders of Judah and Jerusalem to him. ²The king went up to the house of

---

22:12 ᵃ*Abdon the son of Micah* in 2 Chronicles 34:20

the LORD with all the men of Judah, and with him all the inhabitants of Jerusalem— the priests and the prophets and all the people, both small and great. And he read in their hearing all the words of the Book of the Covenant which had been found in the house of the LORD.

³Then the king stood by a pillar and made a covenant before the LORD, to follow the LORD and to keep His commandments and His testimonies and His statutes, with all *his* heart and all *his* soul, to perform the words of this covenant that were written in this book. And all the people took a stand for the covenant. ⁴And the king command- ed Hilkiah the high priest, the priests of the second order, and the doorkeepers, to bring out of the temple of the LORD all the articles that were made for Baal, for Asherah,ᵃ and for all the host of heaven;ᵇ and he burned them outside Jerusalem in the fields of Kidron, and carried their ashes to Bethel. ⁵Then he removed the idolatrous priests whom the kings of Judah had ordained to burn incense on the high places in the cities of Judah and in the places all around Jeru- salem, and those who burned incense to

Baal, to the sun, to the moon, to the constel- lations, and to all the host of heaven. ⁶And he brought out the wooden imageᵃ from the house of the LORD, to the Brook Kidron out- side Jerusalem, burned it at the Brook Kidron and ground *it* to ashes, and threw its ashes on the graves of the common people. ⁷Then he tore down the *ritual* booths of the perverted personsᵃ that *were* in the house of the LORD, where the women wove hangings for the wooden image. ⁸And he brought all the priests from the cities of Judah, and defiled the high places where the priests had burned incense, from Geba to Beer- sheba; also he broke down the high places at the gates which *were* at the entrance of the Gate of Joshua the governor of the city, which *were* to the left of the city gate. ⁹Nevertheless the priests of the high places did not come up to the altar of the LORD in Jerusalem, but they ate unleavened bread among their brethren.

¹⁰And he defiled Topheth, which *is* in the Valley of the Sonᵃ of Hinnom, that no man might make his son or his daughter pass through the fire to Molech. ¹¹Then he removed the horses that the kings of Judah had dedicated to the sun, at the entrance to the house of the LORD, by the chamber of Nathan-Melech, the officer who *was* in the court; and he burned the chariots of the sun with fire. ¹²The altars that *were* on the roof,

---

23:4 ᵃA Canaanite goddess ᵇThe gods of the Assyrians **23:6** ᵃHebrew *Asherah,* a Canaanite god- dess **23:7** ᵃHebrew *qedeshim,* that is, those practic- ing sodomy and prostitution in religious rituals **23:10** ᵃKethib reads *Sons.*

Live By the Blueprint

Marriages and families are like the pieces of a puzzle. Even when the pieces are all there, we need something to help us bring order out of chaos. We need a box top or a blueprint if we are to fit our lives, marriages, and families together in a purposeful design.

Unfortunately, some Christians never stop to evaluate what they are building. Many give in to the temptation simply to increase the speed at which they jam the pieces of life together. They rush to get married, raise kids, and assemble their picture of success, only to find at life's end that they were using a flawed blueprint—a counterfeit image of life.

Others measure success in the size of the puzzle or number of its pieces, but not in the value of the picture itself. So they sacrifice order for quantity—and the result is discord and disarray, isolation and loneliness, and a picture that never quite comes together.

Consider for a moment what *you* are building:

Are you building off the right blueprint? Are decisions that you make about your marriage and family made by using the biblical blueprints?

I'm not asking if you have a perfect marriage or are raising perfect children—only if you are using the blueprint of the Bible and daily consulting the Maker of families as you build your home.

the upper chamber of Ahaz, which the kings of Judah had made, and the altars which Manasseh had made in the two courts of the house of the LORD, the king broke down and pulverized there, and threw their dust into the Brook Kidron. 13Then the king defiled the high places that *were* east of Jerusalem, which *were* on the south of the Mount of Corruption, which Solomon king of Israel had built for Ashtoreth the abomination of the Sidonians, for Chemosh the abomination of the Moabites, and for Milcom the abomination of the people of Ammon. 14And he broke in pieces the *sacred* pillars and cut down the wooden images, and filled their places with the bones of men.

15Moreover the altar that *was* at Bethel, *and* the high place which Jeroboam the son of Nebat, who made Israel sin, had made, both that altar and the high place he broke down; and he burned the high place *and* crushed *it* to powder, and burned the wooden image. 16As Josiah turned, he saw the tombs that *were* there on the mountain. And he sent and took the bones out of the tombs and burned *them* on the altar, and defiled it according to the word of the LORD which the man of God proclaimed, who proclaimed these words. 17Then he said, "What gravestone *is* this that I see?"

So the men of the city told him, "*It is* the tomb of the man of God who came from Judah and proclaimed these things which you have done against the altar of Bethel."

18And he said, "Let him alone; let no one move his bones." So they let his bones alone, with the bones of the prophet who came from Samaria.

19Now Josiah also took away all the shrines of the high places that *were* in the cities of Samaria, which the kings of Israel had made to provoke the LORDa to anger; and he did to them according to all the deeds he had done in Bethel. 20He executed all the priests of the high places who *were* there, on the altars, and burned men's bones on them; and he returned to Jerusalem.

21Then the king commanded all the people, saying, "Keep the Passover to the LORD your God, as *it is* written in this Book of the Covenant." 22Such a Passover surely had never been held since the days of the judges who judged Israel, nor in all the days of the kings of Israel and the kings of Judah. 23But in the eighteenth year of King Josiah this Passover was held before the LORD in Jerusalem. 24Moreover Josiah put away those who consulted mediums and spiritists, the household gods and idols, all the abominations that were seen in the land of Judah and in Jerusalem, that he might perform the words of the law which were written in the book that Hilkiah the priest found in the house of the LORD. 25Now before him there was no king like him, who turned to the LORD with all his heart, with all his soul, and with all his might, according to all the Law of Moses; nor after him did *any* arise like him.

Impending Judgment on Judah

26Nevertheless the LORD did not turn from the fierceness of His great wrath, with which His anger was aroused against Judah, because of all the provocations with which Manasseh had provoked Him. 27And the LORD said, "I will also remove Judah from My sight, as I have removed Israel, and will cast off this city Jerusalem which I have chosen, and the house of which I said, 'My name shall be there.'"a

Josiah Dies in Battle

28Now the rest of the acts of Josiah, and all that he did, *are* they not written in the book of the chronicles of the kings of Judah? 29In his days Pharaoh Necho king of Egypt went to the aid of the king of Assyria, to the River Euphrates; and King Josiah went against him. And *Pharaoh Necho* killed him at Megiddo when he confronted him. 30Then his servants moved his body in a chariot from Megiddo, brought him to Jerusalem, and buried him in his own tomb. And the people of the land took Jehoahaz the son of Josiah, anointed him, and made him king in his father's place.

The Reign and Captivity of Jehoahaz

31Jehoahaz *was* twenty-three years old when he became king, and he reigned three months in Jerusalem. His mother's name

23:19 aFollowing Septuagint, Syriac, and Vulgate; Masoretic Text and Targum omit *the LORD*.
23:27 a1 Kings 8:29

was Hamutal the daughter of Jeremiah of Libnah. ³²And he did evil in the sight of the LORD, according to all that his fathers had done. ³³Now Pharaoh Necho put him in prison at Riblah in the land of Hamath, that he might not reign in Jerusalem; and he imposed on the land a tribute of one hundred talents of silver and a talent of gold. ³⁴Then Pharaoh Necho made Eliakim the son of Josiah king in place of his father Josiah, and changed his name to Jehoiakim. And *Pharaoh* took Jehoahaz and went to Egypt, and heᵃ died there.

Jehoiakim Reigns in Judah

³⁵So Jehoiakim gave the silver and gold to Pharaoh; but he taxed the land to give money according to the command of Pharaoh; he exacted the silver and gold from the people of the land, from every one according to his assessment, to give *it* to Pharaoh Necho. ³⁶Jehoiakim *was* twenty-five years old when he became king, and he reigned eleven years in Jerusalem. His mother's name *was* Zebudah the daughter of Pedaiah of Rumah. ³⁷And he did evil in the sight of the LORD, according to all that his fathers had done.

Judah Overrun by Enemies

24 In his days Nebuchadnezzar king of Babylon came up, and Jehoiakim became his vassal *for* three years. Then he turned and rebelled against him. ²And the LORD sent against him *raiding* bands of Chaldeans, bands of Syrians, bands of Moabites, and bands of the people of Ammon; He sent them against Judah to destroy it, according to the word of the LORD which He had spoken by His servants the prophets. ³Surely at the commandment of the LORD *this* came upon Judah, to remove *them* from His sight because of the sins of Manasseh, according to all that he had done, ⁴and also because of the innocent blood that he had shed; for he had filled Jerusalem with innocent blood, which the LORD would not pardon.

⁵Now the rest of the acts of Jehoiakim, and all that he did, *are* they not written in the book of the chronicles of the kings of Judah? ⁶So Jehoiakim rested with his fathers. Then Jehoiachin his son reigned in his place.

⁷And the king of Egypt did not come out of his land anymore, for the king of Babylon had taken all that belonged to the king of Egypt from the Brook of Egypt to the River Euphrates.

The Reign and Captivity of Jehoiachin

⁸Jehoiachin *was* eighteen years old when he became king, and he reigned in Jerusalem three months. His mother's name *was* Nehushta the daughter of Elnathan of Jerusalem. ⁹And he did evil in the sight of the LORD, according to all that his father had done.

¹⁰At that time the servants of Nebuchadnezzar king of Babylon came up against Jerusalem, and the city was besieged. ¹¹And Nebuchadnezzar king of Babylon came against the city, as his servants were besieging it. ¹²Then Jehoiachin king of Judah, his mother, his servants, his princes, and his officers went out to the king of Babylon; and the king of Babylon, in the eighth year of his reign, took him prisoner.

The Captivity of Jerusalem

¹³And he carried out from there all the treasures of the house of the LORD and the treasures of the king's house, and he cut in pieces all the articles of gold which Solomon king of Israel had made in the temple of the LORD, as the LORD had said. ¹⁴Also he carried into captivity all Jerusalem: all the captains and all the mighty men of valor, ten thousand captives, and all the craftsmen and smiths. None remained except the poorest people of the land. ¹⁵And he carried Jehoiachin captive to Babylon. The king's mother, the king's wives, his officers, and the mighty of the land he carried into captivity from Jerusalem to Babylon. ¹⁶All the valiant men, seven thousand, and craftsmen and smiths, one thousand, all *who were* strong *and* fit for war, these the king of Babylon brought captive to Babylon.

Zedekiah Reigns in Judah

¹⁷Then the king of Babylon made Mattaniah, *Jehoiachin's*ᵃ uncle, king in his place, and changed his name to Zedekiah.

23:34 ᵃThat is, Jehoahaz **24:17** ᵃLiterally *his*

BIBLICAL INSIGHTS • 25:28

If Evil-Merodach Can Do It . . .

THE BIBLE IS AMAZING. It can use even the actions of a proud, pagan king to instruct us on how to treat our wives with respect. I see this in 2 Kings 25:28, which describes how the Babylonian ruler Evil-Merodach treated the captive King Jehoiachin: "He spoke kindly to him, and gave him a more prominent seat than those of the kings who were with him in Babylon." This foreign ruler was not required to speak to and treat King Jehoiachin with such respect. But he did.

Do you speak kindly to your spouse? Do you speak with respect? Without careful attention, your tongue can become caustic, searing, and accusing. I work hard in this area, because I know that honor begins with attitude. I also know that when I am under pressure, I can become curt and snippy.

I've learned that I must protect my wife from others who speak disrespectfully to her. When our children talked back to Barbara, they knew that were going to have to deal with me. Our children were great, but they tried to mug her on numerous occasions. She was outnumbered! That's why I did my best not to let them get away with speaking to her disrespectfully.

In addition, do you give your wife a prominent seat higher than others? If your wife works outside the home, she may need you to supply a free evening once or twice a week, when you volunteer to do it all: put the children to bed, clean the kitchen, do the laundry, etc. Hey, if Evil-Merodach can do it for a captive king, why can't you treat your partner for life even better?

---

¹⁸Zedekiah *was* twenty-one years old when he became king, and he reigned eleven years in Jerusalem. His mother's name *was* Hamutal the daughter of Jeremiah of Libnah. ¹⁹He also did evil in the sight of the LORD, according to all that Jehoiakim had done. ²⁰For because of the anger of the LORD *this* happened in Jerusalem and Judah, that He finally cast them out from His presence. Then Zedekiah rebelled against the king of Babylon.

The Fall and Captivity of Judah

25 Now it came to pass in the ninth year of his reign, in the tenth month, on the tenth *day* of the month, *that* Nebuchadnezzar king of Babylon and all his army came against Jerusalem and encamped against it; and they built a siege wall against it all around. ²So the city was besieged until the eleventh year of King Zedekiah. ³By the ninth *day* of the *fourth* month the famine had become so severe in the city that there was no food for the people of the land.

⁴Then the city wall was broken through, and all the men of war *fled* at night by way of the gate between two walls, which was by the king's garden, even though the Chaldeans *were* still encamped all around against the city. And *the king*ᵃ went by way of the plain.ᵇ ⁵But the army of the Chaldeans pursued the king, and they overtook him in the plains of Jericho. All his army was scattered from him. ⁶So they took the king and brought him up to the king of Babylon at Riblah, and they pronounced judgment on him. ⁷Then they killed the sons of Zedekiah before his eyes, put out the eyes of Zedekiah, bound him with bronze fetters, and took him to Babylon.

⁸And in the fifth month, on the seventh *day* of the month (which *was* the nineteenth year of King Nebuchadnezzar king of Babylon), Nebuzaradan the captain of the guard, a servant of the king of Babylon, came to Jerusalem. ⁹He burned the house of the LORD and the king's house; all the houses of Jerusalem, that is, all the houses of the great, he burned with fire. ¹⁰And all the army of the Chaldeans who *were with* the captain of the guard broke down the walls of Jerusalem all around.

¹¹Then Nebuzaradan the captain of the guard carried away captive the rest of the people *who* remained in the city and the defectors who had deserted to the king of

---

25:4 ᵃLiterally *he* ᵇOr *Arabah,* that is, the Jordan Valley

Babylon, with the rest of the multitude. [12]But the captain of the guard left *some* of the poor of the land as vinedressers and farmers. [13]The bronze pillars that *were* in the house of the Lord, and the carts and the bronze Sea that *were* in the house of the Lord, the Chaldeans broke in pieces, and carried their bronze to Babylon. [14]They also took away the pots, the shovels, the trimmers, the spoons, and all the bronze utensils with which the priests ministered. [15]The firepans and the basins, the things of solid gold and solid silver, the captain of the guard took away. [16]The two pillars, one Sea, and the carts, which Solomon had made for the house of the Lord, the bronze of all these articles was beyond measure. [17]The height of one pillar *was* eighteen cubits, and the capital on it *was* of bronze. The height of the capital was three cubits, and the network and pomegranates all around the capital were all of bronze. The second pillar was the same, with a network.

[18]And the captain of the guard took Seraiah the chief priest, Zephaniah the second priest, and the three doorkeepers. [19]He also took out of the city an officer who had charge of the men of war, five men of the king's close associates who were found in the city, the chief recruiting officer of the army, who mustered the people of the land, and sixty men of the people of the land *who were* found in the city. [20]So Nebuzaradan, captain of the guard, took these and brought them to the king of Babylon at Riblah. [21]Then the king of Babylon struck them and put them to death at Riblah in the land of Hamath. Thus Judah was carried away captive from its own land.

Gedaliah Made Governor of Judah

[22]Then he made Gedaliah the son of Ahikam, the son of Shaphan, governor over the people who remained in the land of Judah, whom Nebuchadnezzar king of Babylon had left. [23]Now when all the captains of the armies, they and *their* men, heard that the king of Babylon had made Gedaliah governor, they came to Gedaliah at Mizpah—Ishmael the son of Nethaniah, Johanan the son of Careah, Seraiah the son of Tanhumeth the Netophathite, and Jaazaniah[a] the son of a Maachathite, they and their men. [24]And Gedaliah took an oath before them and their men, and said to them, "Do not be afraid of the servants of the Chaldeans. Dwell in the land and serve the king of Babylon, and it shall be well with you."

[25]But it happened in the seventh month that Ishmael the son of Nethaniah, the son of Elishama, of the royal family, came with ten men and struck and killed Gedaliah, the Jews, as well as the Chaldeans who were with him at Mizpah. [26]And all the people, small and great, and the captains of the armies, arose and went to Egypt; for they were afraid of the Chaldeans.

INTIMATE MOMENTS

Practice good hygiene. Brush your teeth, take a shower, and put on clean clothes before you romance your sweetie. Use the perfume or cologne you wore when you dated!

Jehoiachin Released from Prison

[27]Now it came to pass in the thirty-seventh year of the captivity of Jehoiachin king of Judah, in the twelfth month, on the twenty-seventh *day* of the month, *that* Evil-Merodach[a] king of Babylon, in the year that he began to reign, released Jehoiachin king of Judah from prison. [28]He spoke kindly to him, and gave him a more prominent seat than those of the kings who *were* with him in Babylon. [29]So Jehoiachin changed from his prison garments, and he ate bread regularly before the king all the days of his life. [30]And as for his provisions, *there was* a regular ration given him by the king, a portion for each day, all the days of his life.

25:23 [a]Spelled *Jezaniah* in Jeremiah 40:8
25:27 [a]Literally *Man of Marduk*

1 CHRONICLES

INTRODUCTION

THE FOUR BOOKS THAT PRECEDE 1 AND 2 CHRONICLES record the history of the Hebrew people from the time just before Saul becomes the first king of Israel through the period when the once-powerful nation has been taken into captivity by the Babylonians. First and 2 Chronicles provide additional historical material for that era, from a slightly different perspective, designed to fill in some of the gaps that exist in the previous books. In fact, the early Greek translation of the Old Testament (the Septuagint) called 1 and 2 Chronicles "The Books of *Paralipomenon*," which means, "things omitted" or "supplements."

Of course, 1 and 2 Chronicles do much more than fill in missing details from the other historical books! Together they offer another divinely-inspired account of a significant period in the history of the Israelite people, from which we can gain many helpful insights. Like 1 and 2 Samuel and 1 and 2 Kings, 1 and 2 Chronicles originally made up a single book that scribes halved in order to make it more easily copied onto scrolls.

The first ten chapters of 1 Chronicles provide us with an extended family tree, tracing the history of humankind from Adam to Noah, from Noah's son Shem to Abraham, Isaac and Jacob, to the twelve tribes of Israel. The writer of 1 Chronicles (Jewish tradition suggests that Ezra the scribe wrote 1 and 2 Chronicles, as well as Nehemiah) pays particular interest to the family tree as it grows toward King David and beyond. Details about David's life and reign occupy the rest of 1 Chronicles.

First Chronicles probably was written after the Jewish people had been freed from captivity in Babylon by King Cyrus, around 517 B.C. After seventy years in captivity, the nation returned to rebuild a devastated Jerusalem. Part of the rebuilding process involved the recording of a written genealogy that firmly demonstrates God's faithfulness.

Every family can benefit from recalling God's faithfulness as it has unfolded uniquely for its members throughout the years. Perhaps you should begin keeping your own Chronicles for your own family!

The Family of Adam—Seth to Abraham

1 Adam, Seth, Enosh, [2]Cainan,[a] Mahalalel, Jared, [3]Enoch, Methuselah, Lamech, [4]Noah,[a] Shem, Ham, and Japheth.

[5]The sons of Japheth *were* Gomer, Magog, Madai, Javan, Tubal, Meshech, and Tiras. [6]The sons of Gomer *were* Ashkenaz, Diphath,[a] and Togarmah. [7]The sons of Javan *were* Elishah, Tarshishah,[a] Kittim, and Rodanim.[b]

[8]The sons of Ham *were* Cush, Mizraim, Put, and Canaan. [9]The sons of Cush *were* Seba, Havilah, Sabta,[a] Raama,[b] and Sabtecha. The sons of Raama *were* Sheba and Dedan. [10]Cush begot Nimrod; he began to be a mighty one on the earth. [11]Mizraim begot Ludim, Anamim, Lehabim, Naphtuhim, [12]Pathrusim, Casluhim (from whom came the Philistines and the Caphtorim). [13]Canaan begot Sidon, his firstborn, and Heth; [14]the Jebusite, the Amorite, and the Girgashite; [15]the Hivite, the Arkite, and the Sinite; [16]the Arvadite, the Zemarite, and the Hamathite.

[17]The sons of Shem *were* Elam, Asshur, Arphaxad, Lud, Aram, Uz, Hul, Gether, and Meshech.[a] [18]Arphaxad begot Shelah, and Shelah begot Eber. [19]To Eber were born two sons: the name of one *was* Peleg,[a] for in his days the earth was divided; and his brother's name *was* Joktan. [20]Joktan begot Almodad, Sheleph, Hazarmaveth, Jerah, [21]Hadoram, Uzal, Diklah, [22]Ebal,[a] Abimael, Sheba, [23]Ophir, Havilah, and Jobab. All these *were* the sons of Joktan.

[24]Shem, Arphaxad, Shelah, [25]Eber, Peleg, Reu, [26]Serug, Nahor, Terah, [27]and Abram, who *is* Abraham. [28]The sons of Abraham *were* Isaac and Ishmael.

The Family of Ishmael

[29]These *are* their genealogies: The firstborn of Ishmael *was* Nebajoth; then Kedar, Adbeel, Mibsam, [30]Mishma, Dumah, Massa, Hadad,[a] Tema, [31]Jetur, Naphish, and Kedemah. These *were* the sons of Ishmael.

The Family of Keturah

[32]Now the sons born to Keturah, Abraham's concubine, *were* Zimran, Jokshan, Medan, Midian, Ishbak, and Shuah. The sons of Jokshan *were* Sheba and Dedan. [33]The sons of Midian *were* Ephah, Epher, Hanoch, Abida, and Eldaah. All these were the children of Keturah.

The Family of Isaac

[34]And Abraham begot Isaac. The sons of Isaac *were* Esau and Israel. [35]The sons of Esau *were* Eliphaz, Reuel, Jeush, Jaalam, and Korah. [36]And the sons of Eliphaz *were* Teman, Omar, Zephi,[a] Gatam, *and* Kenaz; and *by* Timna,[b] Amalek. [37]The sons of Reuel *were* Nahath, Zerah, Shammah, and Mizzah.

The Family of Seir

[38]The sons of Seir *were* Lotan, Shobal, Zibeon, Anah, Dishon, Ezer, and Dishan. [39]And the sons of Lotan *were* Hori and Homam; Lotan's sister *was* Timna. [40]The sons of Shobal *were* Alian,[a] Manahath, Ebal, Shephi,[b] and Onam. The sons of Zibeon *were* Ajah and Anah. [41]The son of Anah *was* Dishon. The sons of Dishon *were* Hamran,[a] Eshban, Ithran, and Cheran. [42]The sons of Ezer *were* Bilhan, Zaavan, *and* Jaakan.[a] The sons of Dishan *were* Uz and Aran.

The Kings of Edom

[43]Now these *were* the kings who reigned in the land of Edom before a king reigned over the children of Israel: Bela the son of Beor, and the name of his city was Dinhabah. [44]And when Bela died, Jobab the son of Zerah of Bozrah reigned in his place. [45]When Jobab died, Husham of the land of the Temanites reigned in his place. [46]And when Husham died, Hadad the son of Bedad, who attacked Midian in the field of Moab, reigned in his place. The name of his city *was* Avith. [47]When Hadad died, Samlah of Masrekah reigned in his place. [48]And when Samlah died, Saul of Rehoboth-by-the-River reigned in his place. [49]When Saul

---

1:2 [a]Hebrew *Qenan* 1:4 [a]Following Masoretic Text and Vulgate; Septuagint adds *the sons of Noah.* 1:6 [a]Spelled *Riphath* in Genesis 10:3 1:7 [a]Spelled *Tarshish* in Genesis 10:4 [b]Spelled *Dodanim* in Genesis 10:4 1:9 [a]Spelled *Sabtah* in Genesis 10:7 [b]Spelled *Raamah* in Genesis 10:7 1:17 [a]Spelled *Mash* in Genesis 10:23 1:19 [a]Literally *Division* 1:22 [a]Spelled *Obal* in Genesis 10:28 1:30 [a]Spelled *Hadar* in Genesis 25:15 1:36 [a]Spelled *Zepho* in Genesis 36:11 [b]Compare Genesis 36:12 1:40 [a]Spelled *Alvan* in Genesis 36:23 [b]Spelled *Shepho* in Genesis 36:23 1:41 [a]Spelled *Hemdan* in Genesis 36:26 1:42 [a]Spelled *Akan* in Genesis 36:27

died, Baal-Hanan the son of Achbor reigned in his place. ⁵⁰And when Baal-Hanan died, Hadadᵃ reigned in his place; and the name of his city was Pai.ᵇ His wife's name was Mehetabel the daughter of Matred, the daughter of Mezahab. ⁵¹Hadad died also. And the chiefs of Edom were Chief Timnah, Chief Aliah,ᵃ Chief Jetheth, ⁵²Chief Aholibamah, Chief Elah, Chief Pinon, ⁵³Chief Kenaz, Chief Teman, Chief Mibzar, ⁵⁴Chief Magdiel, and Chief Iram. These *were* the chiefs of Edom.

INTIMATE MOMENTS

When you see your wife after work, kiss her. Not just a peck on the cheek. *Really* kiss her. Make her feel like a desirable woman. Make her believe that you really would marry her all over again. Hey, if simple pictures are worth a thousand words, then how much could a heartfelt kiss from you be worth to her?

The Family of Israel

2 These *were* the sons of Israel: Reuben, Simeon, Levi, Judah, Issachar, Zebulun, ²Dan, Joseph, Benjamin, Naphtali, Gad, and Asher.

From Judah to David

³The sons of Judah *were* Er, Onan, and Shelah. *These* three were born to him by the daughter of Shua, the Canaanitess. Er, the firstborn of Judah, was wicked in the sight of the LORD; so He killed him. ⁴And Tamar, his daughter-in-law, bore him Perez and Zerah. All the sons of Judah *were* five. ⁵The sons of Perez *were* Hezron and Hamul. ⁶The sons of Zerah *were* Zimri, Ethan, Heman, Calcol, and Dara—five of them in all. ⁷The son of Carmi *was* Achar,ᵃ the troubler of Israel, who transgressed in the accursed thing. ⁸The son of Ethan *was* Azariah. ⁹Also the sons of Hezron who were born

to him *were* Jerahmeel, Ram, and Chelubai.ᵃ ¹⁰Ram begot Amminadab, and Amminadab begot Nahshon, leader of the children of Judah; ¹¹Nahshon begot Salma,ᵃ and Salma begot Boaz; ¹²Boaz begot Obed, and Obed begot Jesse; ¹³Jesse begot Eliab his firstborn, Abinadab the second, Shimeaᵃ the third, ¹⁴Nethanel the fourth, Raddai the fifth, ¹⁵Ozem the sixth, *and* David the seventh. ¹⁶Now their sisters *were* Zeruiah and Abigail. And the sons of Zeruiah *were* Abishai, Joab, and Asahel—three. ¹⁷Abigail bore Amasa; and the father of Amasa *was* Jether the Ishmaelite.ᵃ

The Family of Hezron

¹⁸Caleb the son of Hezron had children by Azubah, *his* wife, and by Jerioth. Now these were her sons: Jesher, Shobab, and Ardon. ¹⁹When Azubah died, Caleb took Ephrathᵃ as his wife, who bore him Hur. ²⁰And Hur begot Uri, and Uri begot Bezalel. ²¹Now afterward Hezron went in to the daughter of Machir the father of Gilead, whom he married when he *was* sixty years old; and she bore him Segub. ²²Segub begot Jair, who had twenty-three cities in the land of Gilead. ²³(Geshur and Syria took from them the towns of Jair, with Kenath and its towns—sixty towns.) All these *belonged to* the sons of Machir the father of Gilead. ²⁴After Hezron died in Caleb Ephrathah, Hezron's wife Abijah bore him Ashhur the father of Tekoa.

The Family of Jerahmeel

²⁵The sons of Jerahmeel, the firstborn of Hezron, *were* Ram, the firstborn, and Bunah, Oren, Ozem, *and* Ahijah. ²⁶Jerahmeel had another wife, whose name was Atarah; she was the mother of Onam. ²⁷The sons of Ram, the firstborn of Jerahmeel, were Maaz, Jamin, and Eker. ²⁸The sons of Onam were Shammai and Jada. The sons of Shammai *were* Nadab and Abishur. ²⁹And the name of the wife of Abishur

---

1:50 ᵃSpelled *Hadar* in Genesis 36:39 ᵇSpelled *Pau* in Genesis 36:39 **1:51** ᵃSpelled *Alvah* in Genesis 36:40 **2:7** ᵃSpelled *Achan* in Joshua 7:1 and elsewhere **2:9** ᵃSpelled *Caleb* in 2:18, 42 **2:11** ᵃSpelled *Salmon* in Ruth 4:21 and Luke 3:32 **2:13** ᵃSpelled *Shammah* in 1 Samuel 16:9 and elsewhere **2:17** ᵃCompare 2 Samuel 17:25 **2:19** ᵃSpelled *Ephrathah* elsewhere

DEVOTIONS FOR COUPLES • 3:4
Five Things
Every Parent Needs

Barbara and I believe that every parent needs five things to successfully raise children:

1. Understand the Times. Paul wrote, "Therefore, be careful how you walk, not as unwise men, but as wise, making the most of your time, because the days are evil" (Eph. 5:15, 16). As you raise your children in this decaying culture, you need a community of faith, a church that will help you succeed as parents. You need to be able to ask questions of other like-minded parents who are somewhat ahead of you in the family cycle.

2. A Sacred Commitment to Each Other. Your kids need to see your vows lived out, in every circumstance, in times of peace and conflict. I will never forget when I was about age six, my mom and dad had a quarrel. I remember thinking, *Are my parents going to get a divorce?* Divorce was never even discussed back then. But if I had such anxious feelings years ago, what does the average first grader today feel?

3. Know What You Believe. You don't need a list of 101 values; choose a half dozen or so that represent your unshakable convictions about how you will raise your child. Here are a few of ours:

- We will first and foremost train our children in the Scriptures to love, obey, and experience God and His mission for their lives.
- We will train our children to relate to others with respect; when they fail, they will ask one another for forgiveness.
- We will attempt to impart God's heart for the world and train them to be part of the Great Commission.

4. Maintain God's Perspective on Children. God's perspective on children has three aspects: (1) Children are a gift from God; (2) raising your children is a privilege and responsibility He has given to no one else; and; (3) raise your children for the glory of God.

5. Possess a Purpose and a Goal for Your Children. Most parents have a life plan for their children, but too often it doesn't go far enough. On the spiritual side, their plan usually doesn't go much further than making sure their children live a good life, go to church and (they hope) receive Christ. Don't settle for a vision of your child's destiny that is less than what God has in mind!

---

was Abihail, and she bore him Ahban and Molid. ³⁰The sons of Nadab *were* Seled and Appaim; Seled died without children. ³¹The son of Appaim *was* Ishi, the son of Ishi *was* Sheshan, and Sheshan's son *was* Ahlai. ³²The sons of Jada, the brother of Shammai, *were* Jether and Jonathan; Jether died without children. ³³The sons of Jonathan *were* Peleth and Zaza. These were the sons of Jerahmeel.

³⁴Now Sheshan had no sons, only daughters. And Sheshan had an Egyptian servant whose name *was* Jarha. ³⁵Sheshan gave his daughter to Jarha his servant as wife, and she bore him Attai. ³⁶Attai begot Nathan, and Nathan begot Zabad; ³⁷Zabad begot Ephlal, and Ephlal begot Obed; ³⁸Obed begot Jehu, and Jehu begot Azariah; ³⁹Azariah begot Helez, and Helez begot Eleasah; ⁴⁰Eleasah begot Sismai, and Sismai begot Shallum; ⁴¹Shallum begot Jekamiah, and Jekamiah begot Elishama.

The Family of Caleb

⁴²The descendants of Caleb the brother of Jerahmeel *were* Mesha, his firstborn, who was the father of Ziph, and the sons of Mareshah the father of Hebron. ⁴³The sons of Hebron *were* Korah, Tappuah, Rekem, and Shema. ⁴⁴Shema begot Raham the father of Jorkoam, and Rekem begot Shammai. ⁴⁵And the son of Shammai *was* Maon, and Maon *was* the father of Beth Zur.

⁴⁶Ephah, Caleb's concubine, bore Haran, Moza, and Gazez; and Haran begot Gazez. ⁴⁷And the sons of Jahdai *were* Regem, Jotham, Geshan, Pelet, Ephah, and Shaaph.

⁴⁸Maachah, Caleb's concubine, bore

Sheber and Tirhanah. ⁴⁹She also bore Shaaph the father of Madmannah, Sheva the father of Machbenah and the father of Gibea. And the daughter of Caleb *was* Achsah.

⁵⁰These were the descendants of Caleb: The sons of Hur, the firstborn of Ephrathah, *were* Shobal the father of Kirjath Jearim, ⁵¹Salma the father of Bethlehem, *and* Hareph the father of Beth Gader.

⁵²And Shobal the father of Kirjath Jearim had descendants: Haroeh, *and* half of the *families of* Manuhoth.ᵃ ⁵³The families of Kirjath Jearim *were* the Ithrites, the Puthites, the Shumathites, and the Mishraites. From these came the Zorathites and the Eshtaolites.

⁵⁴The sons of Salma *were* Bethlehem, the Netophathites, Atroth Beth Joab, half of the Manahethites, and the Zorites.

⁵⁵And the families of the scribes who dwelt at Jabez *were* the Tirathites, the Shimeathites, *and* the Suchathites. These *were* the Kenites who came from Hammath, the father of the house of Rechab.

The Family of David

3 Now these were the sons of David who were born to him in Hebron: The firstborn *was* Amnon, by Ahinoam the Jezreelitess; the second, Daniel,ᵃ by Abigail the Carmelitess; ²the third, Absalom the son of Maacah, the daughter of Talmai, king of Geshur; the fourth, Adonijah the son of Haggith; ³the fifth, Shephatiah, by Abital; the sixth, Ithream, by his wife Eglah.

⁴*These* six were born to him in Hebron. There he reigned seven years and six months, and in Jerusalem he reigned thirty-three years. ⁵And these were born to him in Jerusalem: Shimea,ᵃ Shobab, Nathan, and Solomon—four by Bathshuaᵇ the daughter of Ammiel.ᶜ ⁶Also *there* were Ibhar, Elishama,ᵃ Eliphelet,ᵇ ⁷Nogah, Nepheg, Japhia, ⁸Elishama, Eliada,ᵃ and Eliphelet—nine *in all.* ⁹*These were* all the sons of David, besides the sons of the concubines, and Tamar their sister.

The Family of Solomon

¹⁰Solomon's son *was* Rehoboam; Abijahᵃ *was* his son, Asa his son, Jehoshaphat his son, ¹¹Joramᵃ his son, Ahaziah his son, Joashᵇ his son, ¹²Amaziah his son, Azariahᵃ

his son, Jotham his son, ¹³Ahaz his son, Hezekiah his son, Manasseh his son, ¹⁴Amon his son, *and* Josiah his son. ¹⁵The sons of Josiah *were* Johanan the firstborn, the second Jehoiakim, the third Zedekiah, and the fourth Shallum.ᵃ ¹⁶The sons of Jehoiakim *were* Jeconiah his son *and* Zedekiahᵃ his son.

The Family of Jeconiah

¹⁷And the sons of Jeconiahᵃ *were* Assir,ᵇ Shealtiel his son, ¹⁸*and* Malchiram, Pedaiah, Shenazzar, Jecamiah, Hoshama, and Nedabiah. ¹⁹The sons of Pedaiah *were* Zerubbabel and Shimei. The sons of Zerubbabel *were* Meshullam, Hananiah, Shelomith their sister, ²⁰and Hashubah, Ohel, Berechiah, Hasadiah, and Jushab-Hesed—five *in all.*

²¹The sons of Hananiah *were* Pelatiah and Jeshaiah, the sons of Rephaiah, the sons of Arnan, the sons of Obadiah, and the sons of Shechaniah. ²²The son of Shechaniah was Shemaiah. The sons of Shemaiah *were* Hattush, Igal, Bariah, Neariah, and Shaphat—six *in all.* ²³The sons of Neariah *were* Elioenai, Hezekiah, and Azrikam—three *in all.* ²⁴The sons of Elioenai *were* Hodaviah, Eliashib, Pelaiah, Akkub, Johanan, Delaiah, and Anani—seven *in all.*

The Family of Judah

4 The sons of Judah *were* Perez, Hezron, Carmi, Hur, and Shobal. ²And Reaiah the son of Shobal begot Jahath, and Jahath begot Ahumai and Lahad. These *were* the families of the Zorathites. ³These *were the sons of* the father of Etam: Jezreel, Ishma, and Idbash; and the name of their sister *was* Hazelelponi; ⁴and Penuel *was* the father of Gedor, and Ezer *was the* father of Hushah.

2:52 ᵃSame as *the Manahethites,* verse 54 **3:1** ᵃCalled *Chileab* in 2 Samuel 3:3 **3:5** ᵃSpelled *Shammua* in 14:4 and 2 Samuel 5:14 ᵇSpelled *Bathsheba* in 2 Samuel 11:3 ᵃCalled *Eliam* in 2 Samuel 11:3 **3:6** ᵃSpelled *Elishua* in 14:5 and 2 Samuel 5:15 ᵇSpelled *Elpelet* in 14:5 **3:8** ᵃSpelled *Beeliada* in 14:7 **3:10** ᵃSpelled *Abijam* in 1 Kings 15:1 **3:11** ᵃSpelled *Jehoram* in 2 Kings 1:17 and 8:16 ᵇSpelled *Jehoash* in 2 Kings 12:1 **3:12** ᵃCalled *Uzziah* in Isaiah 6:1 **3:15** ᵃCalled *Jehoahaz* in 2 Kings 23:31 **3:16** ᵃCompare 2 Kings 24:17 **3:17** ᵃAlso called *Coniah* in Jeremiah 22:24 and *Jehoiachin* in 2 Kings 24:8 ᵇOr *Jeconiah the captive were*

These *were* the sons of Hur, the firstborn of Ephrathah the father of Bethlehem.

⁵And Ashhur the father of Tekoa had two wives, Helah and Naarah. ⁶Naarah bore him Ahuzzam, Hepher, Temeni, and Haahashtari. These *were* the sons of Naarah. ⁷The sons of Helah *were* Zereth, Zohar, and Ethnan; ⁸and Koz begot Anub, Zobebah, and the families of Aharhel the son of Harum.

⁹Now Jabez was more honorable than his brothers, and his mother called his name Jabez,ᵃ saying, "Because I bore *him* in pain." ¹⁰And Jabez called on the God of Israel saying, "Oh, that You would bless me indeed, and enlarge my territory, that Your hand would be with me, and that You would keep *me* from evil, that I may not cause pain!" So God granted him what he requested.

¹¹Chelub the brother of Shuhah begot Mehir, who *was* the father of Eshton. ¹²And Eshton begot Beth-Rapha, Paseah, and Tehinnah the father of Ir-Nahash. These *were* the men of Rechah.

¹³The sons of Kenaz *were* Othniel and Seraiah. The sons of Othniel *were* Hathath,ᵃ ¹⁴and Meonothai *who* begot Ophrah. Seraiah begot Joab the father of Ge Harashim,ᵃ for they were craftsmen. ¹⁵The sons of Caleb the son of Jephunneh *were* Iru, Elah, and Naam. The son of Elah *was* Kenaz. ¹⁶The sons of Jehallelel *were* Ziph, Ziphah, Tiria, and Asarel. ¹⁷The sons of Ezrah *were* Jether, Mered, Epher, and Jalon. And *Mered's wife*ᵃ bore Miriam, Shammai, and Ishbah the father of Eshtemoa. ¹⁸(His wife Jehudijahᵃ bore Jered the father of Gedor, Heber the father of Sochoh, and Jekuthiel the father of Zanoah.) And these were the sons of Bithiah the daughter of Pharaoh, whom Mered took.

¹⁹The sons of Hodiah's wife, the sister of Naham, *were* the fathers of Keilah the Garmite and of Eshtemoa the Maachathite. ²⁰And the sons of Shimon *were* Amnon, Rinnah, Ben-Hanan, and Tilon. And the sons of Ishi *were* Zoheth and Ben-Zoheth.

²¹The sons of Shelah the son of Judah *were* Er the father of Lecah, Laadah the father of Mareshah, and the families of the

A Model Prayer for Couples

IF COUPLES SHOULD PRAY for one thing consistently, it is that God will use them to accomplish His purposes. That is the theme of a biblical prayer by an obscure man named Jabez, whom the Bible describes as "more honorable than his brothers" (4:9).

Jabez prayed, "Oh, that You would bless me indeed, and enlarge my territory, that Your hand would be with me, and that You would keep me from evil, that I may not cause pain!" And note what happened, "So God granted him what he requested" (4:10).

Jabez asked God to do several things, and every one is something that all married couples can and should ask for. First, he asked that God bless him and "enlarge his territory"—meaning, give him new turf and enlarge his sphere of influence so that he could more widely influence others for God.

He also asked God to keep him from evil so that he wouldn't cause pain to others through his own sin—in other words, that God would keep him from temptation.

The prayer of Jabez should not be a mantra recited in hopes that saying these particular words will unlock some spiritual blessing. This prayer reflects the righteous desires of a godly man. Do you desire that God would provide you with greater influence for His kingdom and would keep you from sin? Then make the prayer of Jabez a model for how you pray together as a couple today.

---

house of the linen workers of the house of Ashbea; ²²also Jokim, the men of Chozeba, and Joash; Saraph, who ruled in Moab, and Jashubi-Lehem. Now the records are ancient. ²³These *were* the potters and those who dwell at Netaimᵃ and Gederah;ᵇ there they dwelt with the king for his work.

4:9 ᵃLiterally *He Will Cause Pain*
4:13 ᵃSeptuagint and Vulgate add *and Meonothai.*
4:14 ᵃLiterally *Valley of Craftsmen*   **4:17** ᵃLiterally *she*   **4:18** ᵃOr *His Judean wife*   **4:23** ᵃLiterally *Plants*
ᵇLiterally *Hedges*

The Family of Simeon

24The sons of Simeon *were* Nemuel, Jamin, Jarib,a Zerah,b *and* Shaul, 25Shallum his son, Mibsam his son, and Mishma his son. 26And the sons of Mishma *were* Hamuel his son, Zacchur his son, and Shimei his son. 27Shimei had sixteen sons and six daughters; but his brothers did not have many children, nor did any of their families multiply as much as the children of Judah.

28They dwelt at Beersheba, Moladah, Hazar Shual, 29Bilhah, Ezem, Tolad, 30Bethuel, Hormah, Ziklag, 31Beth Marcaboth, Hazar Susim, Beth Biri, and at Shaaraim. These *were* their cities until the reign of David. 32And their villages *were* Etam, Ain, Rimmon, Tochen, and Ashan—five cities— 33and all the villages that *were* around these cities as far as Baal.a These *were* their dwelling places, and they maintained their genealogy: 34Meshobab, Jamlech, and Joshah the son of Amaziah; 35Joel, and Jehu the son of Joshibiah, the son of Seraiah, the son of Asiel; 36Elioenai, Jaakobah, Jeshohaiah, Asaiah, Adiel, Jesimiel, and Benaiah; 37Ziza the son of Shiphi, the son of Allon, the son of Jedaiah, the son of Shimri, the son of Shemaiah— 38these mentioned by name *were* leaders in their families, and their father's house increased greatly.

39So they went to the entrance of Gedor, as far as the east side of the valley, to seek pasture for their flocks. 40And they found rich, good pasture, and the land *was* broad, quiet, and peaceful; for some Hamites formerly lived there.

41These recorded by name came in the days of Hezekiah king of Judah; and they attacked their tents and the Meunites who were found there, and utterly destroyed them, as it is to this day. So they dwelt in their place, because *there was* pasture for their flocks there. 42Now *some* of them, five hundred men of the sons of Simeon, went to Mount Seir, having as their captains Pelatiah, Neariah, Rephaiah, and Uzziel, the sons of Ishi. 43And they defeated the rest of the Amalekites who had escaped. They have dwelt there to this day.

The Family of Reuben

5 Now the sons of Reuben the firstborn of Israel—he *was* indeed the firstborn, but because he defiled his father's bed, his birthright was given to the sons of Joseph, the son of Israel, so that the genealogy is not listed according to the birthright; 2yet Judah prevailed over his brothers, and from him *came* a ruler, although the birthright

4:24 aCalled *Jachin* in Genesis 46:10 bCalled *Zohar* in Genesis 46:10 4:33 aOr *Baalath Beer* (compare Joshua 19:8)

was Joseph's— ³the sons of Reuben the firstborn of Israel were Hanoch, Pallu, Hezron, and Carmi.

⁴The sons of Joel *were* Shemaiah his son, Gog his son, Shimei his son, ⁵Micah his son, Reaiah his son, Baal his son, ⁶and Beerah his son, whom Tiglath-Pileser[a] king of Assyria carried into captivity. He *was* leader of the Reubenites. ⁷And his brethren by their families, when the genealogy of their generations was registered: the chief, Jeiel, and Zechariah, ⁸and Bela the son of Azaz, the son of Shema, the son of Joel, who dwelt in Aroer, as far as Nebo and Baal Meon. ⁹Eastward they settled as far as the entrance of the wilderness this side of the River Euphrates, because their cattle had multiplied in the land of Gilead.

¹⁰Now in the days of Saul they made war with the Hagrites, who fell by their hand; and they dwelt in their tents throughout the entire *area* east of Gilead.

The Family of Gad

¹¹And the children of Gad dwelt next to them in the land of Bashan as far as Salcah: ¹²Joel *was* the chief, Shapham the next, then Jaanai and Shaphat in Bashan, ¹³and their brethren of their father's house: Michael, Meshullam, Sheba, Jorai, Jachan, Zia, and Eber—seven *in all.* ¹⁴These *were* the children of Abihail the son of Huri, the son of Jaroah, the son of Gilead, the son of Michael, the son of Jeshishai, the son of Jahdo, the son of Buz; ¹⁵Ahi the son of Abdiel, the son of Guni, *was* chief of their father's house. ¹⁶And *the Gadites* dwelt in Gilead, in Bashan and in its villages, and in all the commonlands of Sharon within their borders. ¹⁷All these were registered by genealogies in the days of Jotham king of Judah, and in the days of Jeroboam king of Israel.

¹⁸The sons of Reuben, the Gadites, and half the tribe of Manasseh *had* forty-four thousand seven hundred and sixty valiant men, men able to bear shield and sword, to shoot with the bow, and skillful in war, who went to war. ¹⁹They made war with the Hagrites, Jetur, Naphish, and Nodab. ²⁰And they were helped against them, and the Hagrites were delivered into their hand, and all who *were* with them, for they cried out to God in the battle. He heeded their prayer, because they put their trust in Him. ²¹Then they took away their livestock—fifty thousand of their camels, two hundred and fifty thousand of their sheep, and two thousand of their donkeys—also one hundred thousand of their men; ²²for many fell dead, because the war *was* God's. And they dwelt in their place until the captivity.

The Family of Manasseh (East)

²³So the children of the half-tribe of Manasseh dwelt in the land. Their *numbers* increased from Bashan to Baal Hermon, that is, to Senir, or Mount Hermon. ²⁴These *were* the heads of their fathers' houses: Epher, Ishi, Eliel, Azriel, Jeremiah, Hodaviah, and Jahdiel. They were mighty men of valor, famous men, *and* heads of their fathers' houses.

²⁵And they were unfaithful to the God of their fathers, and played the harlot after the gods of the peoples of the land, whom God had destroyed before them. ²⁶So the God of Israel stirred up the spirit of Pul king of Assyria, that is, Tiglath-Pileser[a] king of Assyria. He carried the Reubenites, the Gadites, and the half-tribe of Manasseh into captivity. He took them to Halah, Habor, Hara, and the river of Gozan to this day.

The Family of Levi

6 The sons of Levi *were* Gershon, Kohath, and Merari. ²The sons of Kohath *were* Amram, Izhar, Hebron, and Uzziel. ³The children of Amram *were* Aaron, Moses, and Miriam. And the sons of Aaron *were* Nadab, Abihu, Eleazar, and Ithamar. ⁴Eleazar begot Phinehas, *and* Phinehas begot Abishua; ⁵Abishua begot Bukki, and Bukki begot Uzzi; ⁶Uzzi begot Zerahiah, and Zerahiah begot Meraioth; ⁷Meraioth begot Amariah, and Amariah begot Ahitub; ⁸Ahitub begot Zadok, and Zadok begot Ahimaaz; ⁹Ahimaaz begot Azariah, and Azariah begot Johanan; ¹⁰Johanan begot Azariah (it was he who ministered as priest in the temple that Solomon built in Jerusalem); ¹¹Azariah begot Amariah, and Amariah begot Ahitub; ¹²Ahitub begot Zadok, and Zadok begot

---

5:6 ᵃHebrew *Tilgath-Pilneser*
5:26 ᵃHebrew *Tilgath-Pilneser*

Shallum; [13]Shallum begot Hilkiah, and Hilkiah begot Azariah; [14]Azariah begot Seraiah, and Seraiah begot Jehozadak. [15]Jehozadak went *into captivity* when the LORD carried Judah and Jerusalem into captivity by the hand of Nebuchadnezzar.

[16]The sons of Levi *were* Gershon,[a] Kohath, and Merari. [17]These are the names of the sons of Gershon: Libni and Shimei. [18]The sons of Kohath *were* Amram, Izhar, Hebron, and Uzziel. [19]The sons of Merari *were* Mahli and Mushi. Now these *are* the families of the Levites according to their fathers: [20]Of Gershon *were* Libni his son, Jahath his son, Zimmah his son, [21]Joah his son, Iddo his son, Zerah his son, *and* Jeatherai his son. [22]The sons of Kohath *were* Amminadab his son, Korah his son, Assir his son, [23]Elkanah his son, Ebiasaph his son, Assir his son, [24]Tahath his son, Uriel his son, Uzziah his son, and Shaul his son. [25]The sons of Elkanah *were* Amasai and Ahimoth. [26]*As for* Elkanah,[a] the sons of Elkanah *were* Zophai[b] his son, Nahath[c] his son, [27]Eliab[a] his son, Jeroham his son, *and* Elkanah his son. [28]The sons of Samuel *were* Joel[a] the firstborn, and Abijah the second.[b] [29]The sons of Merari *were* Mahli, Libni his son, Shimei his son, Uzzah his son, [30]Shimea his son, Haggiah his son, *and* Asaiah his son.

Musicians in the House of the LORD

[31]Now these are the men whom David appointed over the service of song in the house of the LORD, after the ark came to rest. [32]They were ministering with music before the dwelling place of the tabernacle of meeting, until Solomon had built the house of the LORD in Jerusalem, and they served in their office according to their order.

[33]And these *are* the ones who ministered with their sons: Of the sons of the Kohathites *were* Heman the singer, the son of Joel, the son of Samuel, [34]the son of Elkanah, the son of Jeroham, the son of Eliel,[a] the son of Toah,[b] [35]the son of Zuph, the son of Elkanah, the son of Mahath, the son of Amasai, [36]the son of Elkanah, the son of Joel, the son of Azariah, the son of Zephaniah, [37]the son of Tahath, the son of Assir, the son of Ebiasaph, the son of Korah, [38]the son of Izhar, the son of Kohath, the son of Levi, the son of Israel. [39]And his

brother Asaph, who stood at his right hand, *was* Asaph the son of Berachiah, the son of Shimea, [40]the son of Michael, the son of Baaseiah, the son of Malchijah, [41]the son of Ethni, the son of Zerah, the son of Adaiah, [42]the son of Ethan, the son of Zimmah, the son of Shimei, [43]the son of Jahath, the son of Gershon, the son of Levi.

[44]Their brethren, the sons of Merari, on the left hand, *were* Ethan the son of Kishi, the son of Abdi, the son of Malluch, [45]the son of Hashabiah, the son of Amaziah, the son of Hilkiah, [46]the son of Amzi, the son of Bani, the son of Shamer, [47]the son of Mahli, the son of Mushi, the son of Merari, the son of Levi.

[48]And their brethren, the Levites, *were* appointed to every kind of service of the tabernacle of the house of God.

The Family of Aaron

[49]But Aaron and his sons offered sacrifices on the altar of burnt offering and on the altar of incense, for all the work of the Most Holy *Place,* and to make atonement for Israel, according to all that Moses the servant of God had commanded. [50]Now these *are* the sons of Aaron: Eleazar his son, Phinehas his son, Abishua his son, [51]Bukki his son, Uzzi his son, Zerahiah his son, [52]Meraioth his son, Amariah his son, Ahitub his son, [53]Zadok his son, *and* Ahimaaz his son.

Dwelling Places of the Levites

[54]Now these *are* their dwelling places throughout their settlements in their territory, for they were *given* by lot to the sons of Aaron, of the family of the Kohathites: [55]They gave them Hebron in the land of Judah, with its surrounding common-lands. [56]But the fields of the city and its villages they gave to Caleb the son of Jephunneh. [57]And to the sons of Aaron they gave *one of* the cities of refuge, Hebron; also Libnah with its common-lands, Jattir, Eshtemoa

---

6:16 [a]Hebrew *Gershom* (alternate spelling of *Gershon,* as in verses 1, 17, 20, 43, 62, and 71) **6:26** [a]Compare verse 35 [b]Spelled *Zuph* in verse 35 and 1 Samuel 1:1 [c]Compare verse 34 **6:27** [a]Compare verse 34
6:28 [a]Following Septuagint, Syriac, and Arabic (compare verse 33 and 1 Samuel 8:2) [b]Hebrew *Vasheni*
6:34 [a]Spelled *Elihu* in 1 Samuel 1:1 [b]Spelled *Tohu* in 1 Samuel 1:1

with its common-lands, ⁵⁸Hilen^a with its common-lands, Debir with its common-lands, ⁵⁹Ashan^a with its common-lands, and Beth Shemesh with its common-lands. ⁶⁰And from the tribe of Benjamin: Geba with its common-lands, Alemeth^a with its common-lands, and Anathoth with its common-lands. All their cities among their families *were* thirteen.

⁶¹To the rest of the family of the tribe of the Kohathites *they gave* by lot ten cities from half the tribe of Manasseh. ⁶²And to the sons of Gershon, throughout their families, *they gave* thirteen cities from the tribe of Issachar, from the tribe of Asher, from the tribe of Naphtali, and from the tribe of Manasseh in Bashan. ⁶³To the sons of Merari, throughout their families, *they gave* twelve cities from the tribe of Reuben, from the tribe of Gad, and from the tribe of Zebulun. ⁶⁴So the children of Israel gave *these* cities with their common-lands to the Levites. ⁶⁵And they gave by lot from the tribe of the children of Judah, from the tribe of the children of Simeon, and from the tribe of the children of Benjamin these cities which are called by *their* names.

⁶⁶Now some of the families of the sons of Kohath *were given* cities as their territory from the tribe of Ephraim. ⁶⁷And they gave them *one of* the cities of refuge, Shechem with its common-lands, in the mountains of Ephraim, also Gezer with its common-lands, ⁶⁸Jokmeam with its common-lands, Beth Horon with its common-lands, ⁶⁹Aijalon with its common-lands, and Gath Rimmon with its common-lands. ⁷⁰And from the half-tribe of Manasseh: Aner with its common-lands and Bileam with its common-lands, for the rest of the family of the sons of Kohath.

⁷¹From the family of the half-tribe of Manasseh the sons of Gershon *were given* Golan in Bashan with its common-lands and Ashtaroth with its common-lands. ⁷²And from the tribe of Issachar: Kedesh with its common-lands, Daberath with its common-lands, ⁷³Ramoth with its common-lands, and Anem with its common-lands. ⁷⁴And from the tribe of Asher: Mashal with its common-lands, Abdon with its common-lands, ⁷⁵Hukok with its common-lands, and Rehob with its common-lands. ⁷⁶And from the tribe of Naphtali: Kedesh in Galilee with its common-lands, Hammon with its common-lands, and Kirjathaim with its common-lands.

⁷⁷From the tribe of Zebulun the rest of

6:58 ^aSpelled *Holon* in Joshua 21:15
6:59 ^aSpelled *Ain* in Joshua 21:16
6:60 ^aSpelled *Almon* in Joshua 21:18

PARENTING MATTERS

Q: *How can we best influence and even control our child's relationships that may be undesirable?*

Maintaining control of those who influence your children is within the bounds of your authority as a parent. As friendships begin to take shape, steer your children in the direction of positive peer pressure. We have made it difficult for our children to spend time with friends who do not provide the kind of influence we desire. In certain cases, we've even declared certain friends off limits. You need to carefully choose the orchard where your children will do their picking.

We have encouraged our children to invite their friends over, to *make our home the place to be*. We particularly encourage our children to invite those friends that we know are good influences. If all the apples are hanging out at your house, you can check out the quality of the fruit. Also, get to know the friend's parents in order to gain some idea of their values, beliefs, and convictions.

Be especially careful about where you allow your child to spend the night. That's one setting where peer pressure can be intense—to participate in ungodly conversation, for example, or to watch movies or play games that do not meet your standards.

the children of Merari *were given* Rimmon[a] with its common-lands and Tabor with its common-lands. [78]And on the other side of the Jordan, across from Jericho, on the east side of the Jordan, *they were given* from the tribe of Reuben: Bezer in the wilderness with its common-lands, Jahzah with its common-lands, [79]Kedemoth with its common-lands, and Mephaath with its common-lands. [80]And from the tribe of Gad: Ramoth in Gilead with its common-lands, Mahanaim with its common-lands, [81]Heshbon with its common-lands, and Jazer with its common-lands.

The Family of Issachar

7 The sons of Issachar *were* Tola, Puah,[a] Jashub, and Shimron—four *in all.* [2]The sons of Tola *were* Uzzi, Rephaiah, Jeriel, Jahmai, Jibsam, and Shemuel, heads of their father's house. *The sons* of Tola *were* mighty men of valor in their generations; their number in the days of David *was* twenty-two thousand six hundred. [3]The son of Uzzi *was* Izrahiah, and the sons of Izrahiah *were* Michael, Obadiah, Joel, and Ishiah. All five of them *were* chief men. [4]And with them, by their generations, according to their fathers' houses, *were* thirty-six thousand troops ready for war; for they had many wives and sons.

[5]Now their brethren among all the families of Issachar *were* mighty men of valor, listed by their genealogies, eighty-seven thousand in all.

The Family of Benjamin

[6]*The sons* of Benjamin *were* Bela, Becher, and Jediael—three *in all.* [7]The sons of Bela *were* Ezbon, Uzzi, Uzziel, Jerimoth, and Iri—five *in all.* They *were* heads of *their* fathers' houses, and they were listed by their genealogies, twenty-two thousand and thirty-four mighty men of valor.

[8]The sons of Becher *were* Zemirah, Joash, Eliezer, Elioenai, Omri, Jerimoth, Abijah, Anathoth, and Alemeth. All these *are* the sons of Becher. [9]And they were recorded by genealogy according to their generations, heads of their fathers' houses, twenty thousand two hundred mighty men of valor. [10]The son of Jediael *was* Bilhan, and the sons of Bilhan *were* Jeush, Benjamin, Ehud, Chenaanah, Zethan, Tharshish, and Ahishahar.

[11]All these sons of Jediael *were* heads of their fathers' houses; *there were* seventeen thousand two hundred mighty men of valor fit to go out for war *and* battle. [12]Shuppim and Huppim[a] *were* the sons of Ir, *and* Hushim *was* the son of Aher.

The Family of Naphtali

[13]The sons of Naphtali *were* Jahziel,[a] Guni, Jezer, and Shallum,[b] the sons of Bilhah.

The Family of Manasseh (West)

[14]The descendants of Manasseh: his Syrian concubine bore him Machir the father of Gilead, the father of Asriel.[a] [15]Machir took as his wife *the sister* of Huppim and Shuppim,[a] whose name *was* Maachah. The name of *Gilead's* grandson[b] *was* Zelophehad,[c] but Zelophehad begot only daughters. [16](Maachah the wife of Machir bore a son, and she called his name Peresh. The name of his brother *was* Sheresh, and his sons *were* Ulam and Rakem. [17]The son of Ulam *was* Bedan.) These *were* the descendants of Gilead the son of Machir, the son of Manasseh.

[18]His sister Hammoleketh bore Ishhod, Abiezer, and Mahlah.

[19]And the sons of Shemida *were* Ahian, Shechem, Likhi, and Aniam.

The Family of Ephraim

[20]The sons of Ephraim *were* Shuthelah, Bered his son, Tahath his son, Eladah his son, Tahath his son, [21]Zabad his son, Shuthelah his son, and Ezer and Elead. The men of Gath who were born in *that* land killed *them* because they came down to take away their cattle. [22]Then Ephraim their father mourned many days, and his brethren came to comfort him.

[23]And when he went in to his wife, she conceived and bore a son; and he called his

---

6:77 [a]Hebrew *Rimmono,* alternate spelling of *Rimmon;* see 4:32 **7:1** [a]Spelled *Puvah* in Genesis 46:13 **7:12** [a]Called *Hupham* in Numbers 26:39 **7:13** [a]Spelled *Jahzeel* in Genesis 46:24 [b]Spelled *Shillem* in Genesis 46:24 **7:14** [a]The son of Gilead (compare Numbers 26:30, 31) **7:15** [a]Compare verse 12 [b]Literally *the second* [c]Compare Numbers 26:30–33 name Beriah,[a] because tragedy had come upon his house. [24]Now his daughter *was* Sheerah, who built Lower and Upper Beth Horon and Uzzen Sheerah; [25]and Rephah *was* his son, *as well* as Resheph, and Telah his son, Tahan his son, [26]Laadan his son, Ammihud his son, Elishama his son, [27]Nun[a] his son, and Joshua his son.

[28]Now their possessions and dwelling places *were* Bethel and its towns: to the east Naaran, to the west Gezer and its towns, and Shechem and its towns, as far as Ayyah[a] and its towns; [29]and by the borders of the children of Manasseh *were* Beth Shean and its towns, Taanach and its towns, Megiddo and its towns, Dor and its towns. In these dwelt the children of Joseph, the son of Israel.

The Family of Asher

[30]The sons of Asher *were* Imnah, Ishvah, Ishvi, Beriah, and their sister Serah. [31]The sons of Beriah *were* Heber and Malchiel, who was the father of Birzaith.[a] [32]And Heber begot Japhlet, Shomer,[a] Hotham,[b] and their sister Shua. [33]The sons of Japhlet *were* Pasach, Bimhal, and Ashvath. These *were* the children of Japhlet. [34]The sons of Shemer *were* Ahi, Rohgah, Jehubbah, and Aram. [35]And the sons of his brother Helem *were* Zophah, Imna, Shelesh, and Amal. [36]The sons of Zophah *were* Suah, Harnepher, Shual, Beri, Imrah, [37]Bezer, Hod, Shamma, Shilshah, Jithran,[a] and Beera. [38]The sons of Jether *were* Jephunneh, Pispah, and Ara. [39]The sons of Ulla *were* Arah, Haniel, and Rizia.

[40]All these *were* the children of Asher, heads of *their* fathers' houses, choice men, mighty men of valor, chief leaders. And they were recorded by genealogies among the army fit for battle; their number *was* twenty-six thousand.

The Family Tree of King Saul of Benjamin

8 Now Benjamin begot Bela his first-born, Ashbel the second, Aharah[a] the third, [2]Nohah the fourth, and Rapha the fifth. [3]The sons of Bela *were* Addar,[a] Gera, Abihud, [4]Abishua, Naaman, Ahoah, [5]Gera, Shephuphan, and Huram.

[6]These *are* the sons of Ehud, who were the heads of the fathers' *houses* of the inhabitants of Geba, and who forced them to move to Manahath: [7]Naaman, Ahijah, and Gera who forced them to move. He begot Uzza and Ahihud.

[8]Also Shaharaim had children in the country of Moab, after he had sent away Hushim and Baara his wives. [9]By Hodesh his wife he begot Jobab, Zibia, Mesha, Malcam, [10]Jeuz, Sachiah, and Mirmah. These *were* his sons, heads of their fathers' *houses*.

[11]And by Hushim he begot Abitub and Elpaal. [12]The sons of Elpaal *were* Eber, Misham, and Shemed, who built Ono and Lod with its towns; [13]and Beriah and Shema, who *were* heads of their fathers' *houses* of the inhabitants of Aijalon, who drove out the inhabitants of Gath. [14]Ahio, Shashak, Jeremoth, [15]Zebadiah, Arad, Eder, [16]Michael, Ispah, and Joha *were* the sons of Beriah. [17]Zebadiah, Meshullam, Hizki, Heber, [18]Ishmerai, Jizliah, and Jobab *were* the sons of Elpaal. [19]Jakim, Zichri, Zabdi, [20]Elienai, Zillethai, Eliel, [21]Adaiah, Beraiah, and Shimrath *were* the sons of Shimei. [22]Ishpan, Eber, Eliel, [23]Abdon, Zichri, Hanan, [24]Hananiah, Elam, Antothijah, [25]Iphdeiah, and Penuel *were* the sons of Shashak. [26]Shamsherai, Shehariah, Athaliah, [27]Jaareshiah, Elijah, and Zichri *were* the sons of Jeroham.

[28]These *were* heads of the fathers' *houses* by their generations, chief men. These dwelt in Jerusalem.

[29]Now the father of Gibeon, whose wife's name *was* Maacah, dwelt at Gibeon. [30]And his firstborn son *was* Abdon, then Zur, Kish, Baal, Nadab, [31]Gedor, Ahio, Zecher, [32]and Mikloth, *who* begot Shimeah.[a] They also dwelt alongside their relatives in Jerusalem, with their brethren. [33]Ner[a] begot Kish, Kish begot Saul, and Saul begot Jonathan, Malchishua, Abinadab,[b] and Esh-Baal.[c] [34]The son of Jonathan *was* Merib-Baal,[a] and

---

7:23 [a]Literally *In Tragedy* **7:27** [a]Hebrew *Non*
7:28 [a]Many Hebrew manuscripts, Bomberg, Septuagint, Targum, and Vulgate read *Gazza*. **7:31** [a]Or *Birzavith* or *Birzoth* **7:32** [a]Spelled *Shemer* in verse 34 [b]Spelled *Helem* in verse 35 **7:37** [a]Spelled *Jether* in verse 38 **8:1** [a]Spelled *Ahiram* in Numbers 26:38 **8:3** [a]Called *Ard* in Numbers 26:40 **8:32** [a]Spelled *Shimeam* in 9:38 **8:33** [a]Also the son of Gibeon (compare 9:36, 39) [b]Called *Jishui* in 1 Samuel 14:49 [c]Called *Ishbosheth* in 2 Samuel 2:8 and elsewhere **8:34** [a]Called *Mephibosheth* in 2 Samuel 4:4

Merib-Baal begot Micah. [35]The sons of Micah *were* Pithon, Melech, Tarea, and Ahaz. [36]And Ahaz begot Jehoaddah;[a] Jehoaddah begot Alemeth, Azmaveth, and Zimri; and Zimri begot Moza. [37]Moza begot Binea, Raphah[a] his son, Eleasah his son, *and* Azel his son.

[38]Azel had six sons whose names *were* these: Azrikam, Bocheru, Ishmael, Sheariah, Obadiah, and Hanan. All these *were* the sons of Azel. [39]And the sons of Eshek his brother *were* Ulam his firstborn, Jeush the second, and Eliphelet the third.

[40]The sons of Ulam were mighty men of valor—archers. *They* had many sons and grandsons, one hundred and fifty *in all.* These *were* all sons of Benjamin.

9 So all Israel was recorded by genealogies, and indeed, they *were* inscribed in the book of the kings of Israel. But Judah was carried away captive to Babylon because of their unfaithfulness. [2]And the first inhabitants who *dwelt* in their possessions in their cities *were* Israelites, priests, Levites, and the Nethinim.

Dwellers in Jerusalem

[3]Now in Jerusalem the children of Judah dwelt, and some of the children of Benjamin, and of the children of Ephraim and Manasseh: [4]Uthai the son of Ammihud, the son of Omri, the son of Imri, the son of Bani, of the descendants of Perez, the son of Judah. [5]Of the Shilonites: Asaiah the

firstborn and his sons. [6]Of the sons of Zerah: Jeuel, and their brethren—six hundred and ninety. [7]Of the sons of Benjamin: Sallu the son of Meshullam, the son of Hodaviah, the son of Hassenuah; [8]Ibneiah the son of Jeroham; Elah the son of Uzzi, the son of Michri; Meshullam the son of Shephatiah, the son of Reuel, the son of Ibnijah; [9]and their brethren, according to their generations—nine hundred and fifty-six. All these men *were* heads of a father's *house* in their fathers' houses.

The Priests at Jerusalem

[10]Of the priests: Jedaiah, Jehoiarib, and Jachin; [11]Azariah the son of Hilkiah, the son of Meshullam, the son of Zadok, the son of Meraioth, the son of Ahitub, the officer over the house of God; [12]Adaiah the son of Jeroham, the son of Pashur, the son of Malchijah; Maasai the son of Adiel, the son of Jahzerah, the son of Meshullam, the son of Meshillemith, the son of Immer; [13]and their brethren, heads of their fathers' houses—one thousand seven hundred and sixty. *They were* very able men for the work of the service of the house of God.

The Levites at Jerusalem

[14]Of the Levites: Shemaiah the son of Hasshub, the son of Azrikam, the son of

---

8:36 [a]Spelled *Jarah* in 9:42
8:37 [a]Spelled *Rephaiah* in 9:43

The Price of Greatness

Would you like to have a great marriage? Would you like to look back on your fiftieth anniversary and say, "That was *great*"? If so, you should listen to Winston Churchill.

"The price of greatness," he once said, "is responsibility."

Great marriages don't just happen. They are not the automatic result of two well-matched people coming together. Good marriages are the product of two people who take full responsibility for the quality of their union.

As you aim for greatness in your marriage, you'll come face to face with great responsibilities—and with that comes pressure. You can either let that pressure move you into greatness, or allow it to blast your union apart.

I like how Abraham Lincoln responded to these two truths. Abe earned his greatness by taking responsibility and handling pressure. While locked in conflict with the congress, he once looked out his window at the Capitol building and said "I have been told I was on the road to hell, but I had no idea that it was just a mile down the road with a dome on it."

Who said serious had to mean grim?

Hashabiah, of the sons of Merari; [15]Bakbak-kar, Heresh, Galal, and Mattaniah the son of Micah, the son of Zichri, the son of Asaph; [16]Obadiah the son of Shemaiah, the son of Galal, the son of Jeduthun; and Berechiah the son of Asa, the son of Elkanah, who lived in the villages of the Netophathites.

The Levite Gatekeepers

[17]And the gatekeepers *were* Shallum, Akkub, Talmon, Ahiman, and their brethren. Shallum *was* the chief. [18]Until then *they had been* gatekeepers for the camps of the children of Levi at the King's Gate on the east.

[19]Shallum the son of Kore, the son of Ebiasaph, the son of Korah, and his brethren, from his father's house, the Korahites, *were* in charge of the work of the service, gatekeepers of the tabernacle. Their fathers had been keepers of the entrance to the camp of the LORD. [20]And Phinehas the son of Eleazar had been the officer over them in time past; the LORD *was* with him. [21]Zechariah the son of Meshelemiah *was* keeper of the door of the tabernacle of meeting.

[22]All those chosen as gatekeepers *were* two hundred and twelve. They were recorded by their genealogy, in their villages. David and Samuel the seer had appointed them to their trusted office. [23]So they and their children *were* in charge of the gates of the house of the LORD, the house of the tabernacle, by assignment. [24]The gatekeepers were assigned to the four directions: the east, west, north, and south. [25]And their brethren in their villages *had* to come with them from time to time for seven days. [26]For in this trusted office *were* four chief gatekeepers; they were Levites. And they had charge over the chambers and treasuries of the house of God. [27]And they lodged *all* around the house of God because they *had* the responsibility, and they *were* in charge of opening *it* every morning.

Other Levite Responsibilities

[28]Now *some* of them were in charge of the serving vessels, for they brought them in and took them out by count. [29]*Some* of them *were* appointed over the furnishings and over all the implements of the sanctuary, and over the fine flour and the wine and the oil and the incense and the spices. [30]And *some* of the sons of the priests made the ointment of the spices.

[31]Mattithiah of the Levites, the first-born of Shallum the Korahite, had the trusted office over the things that were baked in the pans. [32]And some of their brethren of the sons of the Kohathites *were* in charge of preparing the show-bread for every Sabbath.

[33]These are the singers, heads of the fathers' *houses* of the Levites, *who lodged* in the chambers, *and were* free *from other duties;* for they were employed in *that* work day and night. [34]These heads of the fathers' *houses* of the Levites *were* heads throughout their generations. They dwelt at Jerusalem.

The Family of King Saul

[35]Jeiel the father of Gibeon, whose wife's name *was* Maacah, dwelt at Gibeon. [36]His firstborn son *was* Abdon, then Zur, Kish, Baal, Ner, Nadab, [37]Gedor, Ahio, Zechariah,[a] and Mikloth. [38]And Mikloth begot Shim-eam.[a] They also dwelt alongside their relatives in Jerusalem, with their brethren. [39]Ner begot Kish, Kish begot Saul, and Saul begot Jonathan, Malchishua, Abinadab, and Esh-Baal. [40]The son of Jonathan *was* Merib-Baal, and Merib-Baal begot Micah. [41]The sons of Micah *were* Pithon, Melech, Tahrea,[a] and Ahaz.[b] [42]And Ahaz begot Jarah;[a] Jarah begot Alemeth, Azmaveth, and Zimri; and Zimri begot Moza; [43]Moza begot Binea, Rephaiah[a] his son, Eleasah his son, and Azel his son.

[44]And Azel had six sons whose names *were* these: Azrikam, Bocheru, Ishmael, Sheariah, Obadiah, and Hanan; these *were* the sons of Azel.

Tragic End of Saul and His Sons

10 Now the Philistines fought against Israel; and the men of Israel fled from before the Philistines, and fell slain on

9:37 [a]Called *Zecher* in 8:31 9:38 [a]Spelled *Shimeah* in 8:32 9:41 [a]Spelled *Tarea* in 8:35 [b]Following Arabic, Syriac, Targum, and Vulgate (compare 8:35); Masoretic Text and Septuagint omit *and Ahaz.* 9:42 [a]Spelled *Jehoaddah* in 8:36 9:43 [a]Spelled *Raphah* in 8:37

Mount Gilboa. ²Then the Philistines followed hard after Saul and his sons. And the Philistines killed Jonathan, Abinadab, and Malchishua, Saul's sons. ³The battle became fierce against Saul. The archers hit him, and he was wounded by the archers. ⁴Then Saul said to his armorbearer, "Draw your sword, and thrust me through with it, lest these uncircumcised men come and abuse me." But his armorbearer would not, for he was greatly afraid. Therefore Saul took a sword and fell on it. ⁵And when his armorbearer saw that Saul was dead, he also fell on his sword and died. ⁶So Saul and his house died together, and all his house died together. ⁷And when all the men of Israel who *were* in the valley saw that they had fled and that Saul and his sons were dead, they forsook their cities and fled; then the Philistines came and dwelt in them.

⁸So it happened the next day, when the Philistines came to strip the slain, that they found Saul and his sons fallen on Mount Gilboa. ⁹And they stripped him and took his head and his armor, and sent word throughout the land of the Philistines to proclaim the news *in the temple* of their idols and among the people. ¹⁰Then they put his armor in the temple of their gods, and fastened his head in the temple of Dagon.

¹¹And when all Jabesh Gilead heard all that the Philistines had done to Saul, ¹²all the valiant men arose and took the body of Saul and the bodies of his sons; and they brought them to Jabesh, and buried their bones under the tamarisk tree at Jabesh, and fasted seven days.

¹³So Saul died for his unfaithfulness which he had committed against the LORD, because he did not keep the word of the LORD, and also because he consulted a medium for guidance. ¹⁴But *he* did not inquire of the LORD; therefore He killed him, and turned the kingdom over to David the son of Jesse.

David Made King over All Israel

11 Then all Israel came together to David at Hebron, saying, "Indeed we *are* your bone and your flesh. ²Also, in time past, even when Saul was king, you *were* the one who led Israel out and brought them in; and the LORD your God said to you, 'You shall shepherd My people Israel, and be ruler over My people Israel.'" ³Therefore all the elders of Israel came to the king at Hebron, and David made a covenant with them at Hebron before the LORD. And they anointed David king over Israel, according to the word of the LORD by Samuel.

The City of David

⁴And David and all Israel went to Jerusalem, which is Jebus, where the Jebusites *were,* the inhabitants of the land. ⁵But the inhabitants of Jebus said to David, "You shall not come in here!" Nevertheless David took the stronghold of Zion (that is, the City of David). ⁶Now David said, "Whoever attacks the Jebusites first shall be chief and captain." And Joab the son of Zeruiah went up first, and became chief. ⁷Then David dwelt in the stronghold; therefore they called it the City of David. ⁸And he built the city around it, from the Milloᵃ to the surrounding area. Joab repaired the rest of the city. ⁹So David went on and became great, and the LORD of hosts *was* with him.

The Mighty Men of David

¹⁰Now these *were* the heads of the mighty men whom David had, who strengthened themselves with him in his kingdom, with all Israel, to make him king, according to the word of the LORD concerning Israel.

¹¹And this *is* the number of the mighty men whom David had: Jashobeam the son of a Hachmonite, chief of the captains;ᵃ he had lifted up his spear against three hundred, killed *by him* at one time.

¹²After him *was* Eleazar the son of Dodo, the Ahohite, who *was one* of the three mighty men. ¹³He was with David at Pasdammim. Now there the Philistines were gathered for battle, and there was a piece of ground full of barley. So the people fled from the Philistines. ¹⁴But they stationed themselves in the middle of *that* field, defended it, and killed the Philistines. So the LORD brought about a great victory.

¹⁵Now three of the thirty chief men went down to the rock to David, into the cave of Adullam; and the army of the Philistines

---

11:8 ᵃLiterally *The Landfill* **11:11** ᵃFollowing Qere; Kethib, Septuagint, and Vulgate read *the thirty* (compare 2 Samuel 23:8).

encamped in the Valley of Rephaim. [16]David *was* then in the stronghold, and the garrison of the Philistines *was* then in Bethlehem. [17]And David said with longing, "Oh, that someone would give me a drink of water from the well of Bethlehem, which is by the gate!" [18]So the three broke through the camp of the Philistines, drew water from the well of Bethlehem that *was* by the gate, and took *it* and brought *it* to David. Nevertheless David would not drink it, but poured it out to the LORD. [19]And he said, "Far be it from me, O my God, that I should do this! Shall I drink the blood of these men *who have put* their lives *in jeopardy?* For at the risk of their lives they brought it." Therefore he would not drink it. These things were done by the three mighty men.

[20]Abishai the brother of Joab was chief of *another* three.[a] He had lifted up his spear against three hundred *men,* killed *them,* and won a name among *these* three. [21]Of the three he was more honored than the other two men. Therefore he became their captain. However he did not attain to the *first* three.

[22]Benaiah was the son of Jehoiada, the son of a valiant man from Kabzeel, who had done many deeds. He had killed two lion-like heroes of Moab. He also had gone down and killed a lion in the midst of a pit on a snowy day. [23]And he killed an Egyptian, a man of *great* height, five cubits tall. In the Egytian's hand *there was* a spear like a weaver's beam; and he went down to him with a staff, wrested the spear out of the Egyptian's hand, and killed him with his own spear. [24]These *things* Benaiah the son of Jehoiada did, and won a name among three mighty men. [25]Indeed he was more honored than the thirty, but he did not attain to the *first* three. And David appointed him over his guard.

[26]Also the mighty warriors *were* Asahel the brother of Joab, Elhanan the son of Dodo of Bethlehem, [27]Shammoth the Harorite,[a] Helez the Pelonite,[b] [28]Ira the son of Ikkesh the Tekoite, Abiezer the Anathothite, [29]Sibbechai the Hushathite, Ilai the Ahohite, [30]Maharai the Netophathite, Heled[a] the son of Baanah the Netophathite, [31]Ithai[a] the son of Ribai of Gibeah, of the sons of Benjamin, Benaiah the Pirathonite, [32]Hurai[a] of the brooks of Gaash, Abiel[b] the Arbathite, [33]Azmaveth the Baharumite,[a] Eliahba the Shaalbonite, [34]the sons of Hashem the Gizonite, Jonathan the son of Shageh the Hararite, [35]Ahiam the son of Sacar the Hararite, Eliphal the son of Ur, [36]Hepher the Mecherathite, Ahijah the Pelonite, [37]Hezro the Carmelite, Naarai the son of Ezbai, [38]Joel the brother of Nathan, Mibhar the son of Hagri, [39]Zelek the Ammonite, Naharai the Berothite[a] (the armorbearer of Joab the son of Zeruiah), [40]Ira the Ithrite, Gareb the Ithrite, [41]Uriah the Hittite, Zabad the son of Ahlai, [42]Adina the son of Shiza the Reubenite (a chief of the Reubenites) and thirty with him, [43]Hanan the son of Maachah, Joshaphat the Mithnite, [44]Uzzia the Ashteratite, Shama and Jeiel the sons of Hotham the Aroerite, [45]Jediael the son of Shimri, and Joha his brother, the Tizite, [46]Eliel the Mahavite, Jeribai and Joshaviah the sons of Elnaam, Ithmah the Moabite, [47]Eliel, Obed, and Jaasiel the Mezobaite.

The Growth of David's Army

12 Now these *were* the men who came to David at Ziklag while he was still a fugitive from Saul the son of Kish; and they *were* among the mighty men, helpers in the war, [2]armed with bows, using both the right hand and the left in *hurling* stones and *shooting* arrows with the bow. *They were* of Benjamin, Saul's brethren.

[3]The chief *was* Ahiezer, then Joash, the sons of Shemaah the Gibeathite; Jeziel and Pelet the sons of Azmaveth; Berachah, and Jehu the Anathothite; [4]Ishmaiah the Gibeonite, a mighty man among the thirty, and over the thirty; Jeremiah, Jahaziel, Johanan, and Jozabad the Gederathite; [5]Eluzai, Jerimoth, Bealiah, Shemariah, and Shephatiah the Haruphite; [6]Elkanah, Jisshiah, Azarel, Joezer, and Jashobeam, the Korahites; [7]and Joelah and Zebadiah the sons of Jeroham of Gedor.

11:20 [a]Following Masoretic Text, Septuagint, and Vulgate; Syriac reads *thirty.* **11:27** [a]Spelled *Harodite* in 2 Samuel 23:25 [b]Called *Paltite* in 2 Samuel 23:26 **11:30** [a]Spelled *Heleb* in 2 Samuel 23:29 and *Heldai* in 1 Chronicles 27:15 **11:31** [a]Spelled *Ittai* in 2 Samuel 23:29 **11:32** [a]Spelled *Hiddai* in 2 Samuel 23:30 [b]Spelled *Abi-Albon* in 2 Samuel 23:31 **11:33** [a]Spelled *Barhumite* in 2 Samuel 23:31 **11:39** [a]Spelled *Beerothite* in 2 Samuel 23:37

What to Do Next?

IN A WORLD THAT CONSTANTLY URGES young people to take the wrong turn and make the bad choice, Christian parents need the kind of wisdom that shows them what to do next. The Bible describes a group of people who had exactly that kind of wisdom, "The sons of Issachar, who had understanding of the times, to know what Israel ought to do" (12:32).

Leading your home does not mean you must have all the answers. It simply means that you know what to do *next*. That means having an understanding of the times and making wise use of your time, "See then that you walk circumspectly, not as fools but as wise, redeeming the time, because the days are evil" (Eph. 5:15, 16). It also means valuing what the Scriptures have to say about the priorities for your family, rather than the input of our materialistic, anything-goes culture (see 2 Pet. 2:1–4).

Moms and dads need to pray daily for wisdom. Understanding the times and knowing what to do next is absolutely critical as you make your decisions about where you will educate your children, how you will prepare your preteen for the issues of adolescence, and how you train and launch your son or daughter into adulthood.

All believers need to be wise these days, especially parents. If we are going to bring our children up to fear and love God, then we need to understand the times in which we live and understand how God's Word directs us to live for him in the midst of a "crooked and perverse generation" (Phil. 2:15).

Do you know what the number one struggle is for each of your children right now? Do you know what to do?

8*Some* Gadites joined David at the stronghold in the wilderness, mighty men of valor, men trained for battle, who could handle shield and spear, whose faces *were* like the faces of lions, and *were* as swift as gazelles on the mountains: 9Ezer the first, Obadiah the second, Eliab the third, 10Mishmannah the fourth, Jeremiah the fifth, 11Attai the sixth, Eliel the seventh, 12Johanan the eighth, Elzabad the ninth, 13Jeremiah the tenth, and Machbanai the eleventh. 14These *were* from the sons of Gad, captains of the army; the least was over a hundred, and the greatest was over a thousand. 15These *are* the ones who crossed the Jordan in the first month, when it had overflowed all its banks; and they put to flight all *those* in the valleys, to the east and to the west.

16Then some of the sons of Benjamin and Judah came to David at the stronghold. 17And David went out to meet them, and answered and said to them, "If you have come peaceably to me to help me, my heart will be united with you; but if to betray me to my enemies, since *there is* no wrong in my hands, may the God of our fathers look and bring judgment." 18Then the Spirit came upon Amasai, chief of the captains, *and he said:*

"*We are* yours, O David;
We *are* on your side, O son of Jesse!
Peace, peace to you,
And peace to your helpers!
For your God helps you."

So David received them, and made them captains of the troop.

19And *some* from Manasseh defected to David when he was going with the Philistines to battle against Saul; but they did not help them, for the lords of the Philistines sent him away by agreement, saying, "He may defect to his master Saul *and endanger* our heads." 20When he went to Ziklag, those of Manasseh who defected to him were Adnah, Jozabad, Jediael, Michael, Jozabad, Elihu, and Zillethai, captains of the thousands who *were* from Manasseh. 21And they helped David against the bands *of raiders,* for they *were* all mighty men of valor, and they were captains in the army. 22For at *that* time they came to David day by day to help him, until *it was* a great army, like the army of God.

David's Army at Hebron

23Now these *were* the numbers of the divisions *that were* equipped for war, *and* came to David at Hebron to turn *over* the kingdom of Saul to him, according to the word of the LORD: ²⁴of the sons of Judah bearing shield and spear, six thousand eight hundred armed for war; ²⁵of the sons of Simeon, mighty men of valor fit for war, seven thousand one hundred; ²⁶of the sons of Levi four thousand six hundred; ²⁷Jehoiada, the leader of the Aaronites, and with him three thousand seven hundred; ²⁸Zadok, a young man, a valiant warrior, and from his father's house twenty-two captains; ²⁹of the sons of Benjamin, relatives of Saul, three thousand (until then the greatest part of them had remained loyal to the house of Saul); ³⁰of the sons of Ephraim twenty thousand eight hundred, mighty men of valor, famous men throughout their father's house; ³¹of the half-tribe of Manasseh eighteen thousand, who were designated by name to come and make David king; ³²of the sons of Issachar who had understanding of the times, to know what Israel ought to do, their chiefs were two hundred; and all their brethren were at their command; ³³of Zebulun there were fifty thousand who went out to battle, expert in war with all weapons of war, stouthearted men who could keep ranks; ³⁴of Naphtali one thousand captains, and with them thirty-seven thousand with shield and spear; ³⁵of the Danites who could keep battle formation, twenty-eight thousand six hundred; ³⁶of Asher, those who could go out to war, able to keep battle formation, forty thousand; ³⁷of the Reubenites and the Gadites and the half-tribe of Manasseh, from the other side of the Jordan, one hundred and twenty thousand armed for battle with every *kind* of weapon of war.

³⁸All these men of war, who could keep ranks, came to Hebron with a loyal heart, to make David king over all Israel; and all the rest of Israel *were* of one mind to make David king. ³⁹And they were there with David three days, eating and drinking, for their brethren had prepared for them. ⁴⁰Moreover those who were near to them, from as far away as Issachar and Zebulun

and Naphtali, were bringing food on donkeys and camels, on mules and oxen—provisions of flour and cakes of figs and cakes of raisins, wine and oil and oxen and sheep abundantly, for *there was* joy in Israel.

The Ark Brought from Kirjath Jearim

13 Then David consulted with the captains of thousands and hundreds, *and* with every leader. ²And David said to all the assembly of Israel, "If *it seems* good to you, and if it is of the LORD our God, let us send out to our brethren everywhere *who are* left in all the land of Israel, and with them to the priests and Levites *who are* in their cities *and* their common-lands, that they may gather together to us; ³and let us bring the ark of our God back to us, for we have not inquired at it since the days of Saul." ⁴Then all the assembly said that they would do so, for the thing was right in the eyes of all the people.

⁵So David gathered all Israel together, from Shihor in Egypt to as far as the entrance of Hamath, to bring the ark of God from Kirjath Jearim. ⁶And David and all Israel went up to Baalah,ᵃ to Kirjath Jearim, which belonged to Judah, to bring up from there the ark of God the LORD, who dwells *between* the cherubim, where *His* name is proclaimed. ⁷So they carried the ark of God on a new cart from the house of Abinadab, and Uzza and Ahio drove the cart. ⁸Then David and all Israel played *music* before God with all *their* might, with singing, on harps, on stringed instruments, on tambourines, on cymbals, and with trumpets.

⁹And when they came to Chidon'sᵃ threshing floor, Uzza put out his hand to hold the ark, for the oxen stumbled. ¹⁰Then the anger of the LORD was aroused against Uzza, and He struck him because he put his hand to the ark; and he died there before God. ¹¹And David became angry because of the LORD's outbreak against Uzza; therefore that place is called Perez Uzzaᵃ to this day. ¹²David was afraid of God that day, saying, "How can I bring the ark of God to me?"

¹³So David would not move the ark with him into the City of David, but took it aside into the house of Obed-Edom the Gittite. ¹⁴The ark of God remained with the family

13:6 ᵃCalled *Baale Judah* in 2 Samuel 6:2 **13:9** ᵃCalled *Nachon* in 2 Samuel 6:6 **13:11** ᵃLiterally *Outburst Against Uzza*

of Obed-Edom in his house three months. And the LORD blessed the house of Obed-Edom and all that he had.

David Established at Jerusalem

14 Now Hiram king of Tyre sent messengers to David, and cedar trees, with masons and carpenters, to build him a house. ²So David knew that the LORD had established him as king over Israel, for his kingdom was highly exalted for the sake of His people Israel.

³Then David took more wives in Jerusalem, and David begot more sons and daughters. ⁴And these are the names of his children whom he had in Jerusalem: Shammua,ᵃ Shobab, Nathan, Solomon, ⁵Ibhar, Elishua,ᵃ Elpelet,ᵇ ⁶Nogah, Nepheg, Japhia, ⁷Elishama, Beeliada,ᵃ and Eliphelet.

The Philistines Defeated

⁸Now when the Philistines heard that David had been anointed king over all Israel, all the Philistines went up to search for David. And David heard *of it* and went out against them. ⁹Then the Philistines went and made a raid on the Valley of Rephaim. ¹⁰And David inquired of God, saying, "Shall I go up against the Philistines? Will You deliver them into my hand?"

The LORD said to him, "Go up, for I will deliver them into your hand."

¹¹So they went up to Baal Perazim, and David defeated them there. Then David said, "God has broken through my enemies by my hand like a breakthrough of water." Therefore they called the name of that place Baal Perazim.ᵃ ¹²And when they left their gods there, David gave a commandment, and they were burned with fire.

¹³Then the Philistines once again made a raid on the valley. ¹⁴Therefore David inquired again of God, and God said to him, "You shall not go up after them; circle around them, and come upon them in front of the mulberry trees. ¹⁵And it shall be, when you hear a sound of marching in the tops of the mulberry trees, then you shall go out to battle, for God has gone out before you to strike the camp of the Philistines." ¹⁶So David did as God commanded him, and they drove back the army of the Philistines from

Gibeon as far as Gezer. ¹⁷Then the fame of David went out into all lands, and the LORD brought the fear of him upon all nations.

The Ark Brought to Jerusalem

15 *David* built houses for himself in the City of David; and he prepared a place for the ark of God, and pitched a tent for it. ²Then David said, "No one may carry the ark of God but the Levites, for the LORD has chosen them to carry the ark of God and to minister before Him forever." ³And David gathered all Israel together at Jerusalem, to bring up the ark of the LORD to its place, which he had prepared for it. ⁴Then David assembled the children of Aaron and the Levites: ⁵of the sons of Kohath, Uriel the chief, and one hundred and twenty of his brethren; ⁶of the sons of Merari, Asaiah the chief, and two hundred and twenty of his brethren; ⁷of the sons of Gershom, Joel the chief, and one hundred and thirty of his brethren; ⁸of the sons of Elizaphan, Shemaiah the chief, and two hundred of his brethren; ⁹of the sons of Hebron, Eliel the chief, and eighty of his brethren; ¹⁰of the sons of Uzziel, Amminadab the chief, and one hundred and twelve of his brethren.

¹¹And David called for Zadok and Abiathar the priests, and for the Levites: for Uriel, Asaiah, Joel, Shemaiah, Eliel, and Amminadab. ¹²He said to them, "You *are* the heads of the fathers' *houses* of the Levites; sanctify yourselves, you and your brethren, that you may bring up the ark of the LORD God of Israel to *the place* I have prepared for it. ¹³For because you *did* not *do it* the first *time*, the LORD our God broke out against us, because we did not consult Him about the proper order."

¹⁴So the priests and the Levites sanctified themselves to bring up the ark of the LORD God of Israel. ¹⁵And the children of the Levites bore the ark of God on their shoulders, by its poles, as Moses had commanded according to the word of the LORD.

¹⁶Then David spoke to the leaders of the Levites to appoint their brethren *to be* the

---

14:4 ᵃSpelled *Shimea* in 3:5 14:5 ᵃSpelled *Elishama* in 3:6 ᵇSpelled *Eliphelet* in 3:6 14:7 ᵃSpelled *Eliada* in 3:8 14:11 ᵃLiterally *Master of Breakthroughs*

singers accompanied by instruments of music, stringed instruments, harps, and cymbals, by raising the voice with resounding joy. [17]So the Levites appointed Heman the son of Joel; and of his brethren, Asaph the son of Berechiah; and of their brethren, the sons of Merari, Ethan the son of Kushaiah; [18]and with them their brethren of the second *rank:* Zechariah, Ben,[a] Jaaziel, Shemiramoth, Jehiel, Unni, Eliab, Benaiah, Maaseiah, Mattithiah, Elipheleh, Mikneiah, Obed-Edom, and Jeiel, the gatekeepers; [19]the singers, Heman, Asaph, and Ethan, *were* to sound the cymbals of bronze; [20]Zechariah, Aziel, Shemiramoth, Jehiel, Unni, Eliab, Maaseiah, and Benaiah, with strings according to Alamoth; [21]Mattithiah, Elipheleh, Mikneiah, Obed-Edom, Jeiel, and Azaziah, to direct with harps on the Sheminith; [22]Chenaniah, leader of the Levites, was instructor *in charge of* the music, because he *was* skillful; [23]Berechiah and Elkanah *were* doorkeepers for the ark; [24]Shebaniah, Joshaphat, Nethanel, Amasai, Zechariah, Benaiah, and Eliezer, the priests, were to blow the trumpets before the ark of God; and Obed-Edom and Jehiah, doorkeepers for the ark.

[25]So David, the elders of Israel, and the captains over thousands went to bring up the ark of the covenant of the LORD from the house of Obed-Edom with joy. [26]And so it was, when God helped the Levites who bore the ark of the covenant of the LORD, that they offered seven bulls and seven rams. [27]David was clothed with a robe of fine linen, as were all the Levites who bore the ark, the singers, and Chenaniah the music master *with* the singers. David also wore a linen ephod. [28]Thus all Israel brought up the ark of the covenant of the LORD with shouting and with the sound of the horn, with trumpets and with cymbals, making music with stringed instruments and harps.

[29]And it happened, *as* the ark of the covenant of the LORD came to the City of David, that Michal, Saul's daughter, looked through a window and saw King David whirling and playing music; and she despised him in her heart.

15:18 [a]Following Masoretic Text and Vulgate; Septuagint omits *Ben.*

The Ark Placed in the Tabernacle

16 So they brought the ark of God, and set it in the midst of the tabernacle that David had erected for it. Then they offered burnt offerings and peace offerings before God. [2]And when David had finished offering the burnt offerings and the peace offerings, he blessed the people in the name of the LORD. [3]Then he distributed to everyone of Israel, both man and woman, to everyone a loaf of bread, a piece *of meat,* and a cake of raisins.

[4]And he appointed some of the Levites to minister before the ark of the LORD, to commemorate, to thank, and to praise the LORD God of Israel: [5]Asaph the chief, and next to him Zechariah, *then* Jeiel, Shemiramoth, Jehiel, Mattithiah, Eliab, Benaiah, and Obed-Edom: Jeiel with stringed instruments and harps, but Asaph made music with cymbals; [6]Benaiah and Jahaziel the priests regularly *blew* the trumpets before the ark of the covenant of God.

David's Song of Thanksgiving

[7]On that day David first delivered *this psalm* into the hand of Asaph and his brethren, to thank the LORD:

8   Oh, give thanks to the LORD!
    Call upon His name;
    Make known His deeds among the peoples!

9   Sing to Him, sing psalms to Him;
    Talk of all His wondrous works!

10   Glory in His holy name;
    Let the hearts of those rejoice who seek the LORD!

11   Seek the LORD and His strength;
    Seek His face evermore!

12   Remember His marvelous works which He has done,
    His wonders, and the judgments of His mouth,

13   O seed of Israel His servant,
    You children of Jacob, His chosen ones!

14   He *is* the LORD our God;
    His judgments *are* in all the earth.

15   Remember His covenant forever,
    The word which He commanded, for a thousand generations,

Giving Thanks in Times of Trouble

DURING TIMES OF TROUBLE, Barbara and I have learned a simple, four-word principle for handling problems, "In everything give thanks" (1 Thess. 5:18). King David expressed the same principle centuries before when he wrote, "Save us, O God of our salvation; gather us together, and deliver us from the Gentiles, to give thanks to Your holy name, to triumph in Your praise" (16:35).

This isn't a simplistic excuse to put your head in the sand and ignore reality. On the contrary, I believe it's a step of faith in dealing with the storms of life—and that includes the little things as well as the big challenges.

Giving thanks in everything means that you have to ask yourself, "Is God really involved in the details of my life?" Could God possibly want to teach you something through a flat tire, a kid's runny nose, or a Lego-covered floor? Does He really want to be part of every moment of your day, or is He willing to settle for the 9:30 to noon slot on Sunday morning?

So the next time you face an interruption or things are unraveling at a high rate of speed, try giving thanks to God in all things. Those four little words express our belief that God knows what He is doing and that He can be trusted.

---

16   *The covenant which* He made with Abraham,
And His oath to Isaac,

17   And confirmed it to Jacob for a statute,
To Israel *for* an everlasting covenant,

18   Saying, "To you I will give the land of Canaan
As the allotment of your inheritance,"

19   When you were few in number,
Indeed very few, and strangers in it.

20   When they went from one nation to another,

And from *one* kingdom to another people,

21   He permitted no man to do them wrong;
Yes, He rebuked kings for their sakes,

22   *Saying,* "Do not touch My anointed ones,
And do My prophets no harm."[a]

23   Sing to the LORD, all the earth;
Proclaim the good news of His salvation from day to day.

24   Declare His glory among the nations,
His wonders among all peoples.

25   For the LORD *is* great and greatly to be praised;
He *is* also to be feared above all gods.

26   For all the gods of the peoples *are* idols,
But the LORD made the heavens.

27   Honor and majesty *are* before Him;
Strength and gladness are in His place.

28   Give to the LORD, O families of the peoples,
Give to the LORD glory and strength.

29   Give to the LORD the glory *due* His name;
Bring an offering, and come before Him.
Oh, worship the LORD in the beauty of holiness!

30   Tremble before Him, all the earth.
The world also is firmly established,
It shall not be moved.

31   Let the heavens rejoice, and let the earth be glad;
And let them say among the nations,
"The LORD reigns."

32   Let the sea roar, and all its fullness;
Let the field rejoice, and all that *is* in it.

33   Then the trees of the woods shall rejoice before the LORD,
For He is coming to judge the earth.[a]

34   Oh, give thanks to the LORD, for *He is* good!
For His mercy *endures* forever.[a]

16:22 [a]Compare verses 8–22 with Psalm 105:1–15
16:33 [a]Compare verses 23–33 with Psalm 96:1–13
16:34 [a]Compare verse 34 with Psalm 106:1

35 And say, "Save us, O God of our
      salvation;
   Gather us together, and deliver us
      from the Gentiles,
   To give thanks to Your holy name,
   To triumph in Your praise."

36 Blessed *be* the LORD God of Israel
   From everlasting to everlasting!a

And all the people said, "Amen!" and
praised the LORD.

Regular Worship Maintained

37So he left Asaph and his brothers
there before the ark of the covenant of the
LORD to minister before the ark regularly, as
every day's work required; 38and Obed-
Edom with his sixty-eight brethren, including Obed-Edom the son of Jeduthun, and
Hosah, *to be* gatekeepers; 39and Zadok the
priest and his brethren the priests, before
the tabernacle of the LORD at the high
place that *was* at Gibeon, 40to offer burnt
offerings to the LORD on the altar of burnt
offering regularly morning and evening,
and *to do* according to all that is written in
the Law of the LORD which He commanded
Israel; 41and with them Heman and Jeduthun and the rest who were chosen, who
were designated by name, to give thanks to
the LORD, because His mercy *endures* forever; 42and with them Heman and Jeduthun,
to sound aloud with trumpets and cymbals
and the musical instruments of God. Now
the sons of Jeduthun *were* gatekeepers.

43Then all the people departed, every
man to his house; and David returned to
bless his house.

God's Covenant with David

17 Now it came to pass, when David
was dwelling in his house, that
David said to Nathan the prophet, "See
now, I dwell in a house of cedar, but the
ark of the covenant of the LORD *is* under
tent curtains."

2Then Nathan said to David, "Do all that
is in your heart, for God *is* with you."

3But it happened that night that the
word of God came to Nathan, saying, 4"Go

and tell My servant David, 'Thus says the
LORD: "You shall not build Me a house to
dwell in. 5For I have not dwelt in a house
since the time that I brought up Israel,
even to this day, but have gone from tent to
tent, and from *one* tabernacle *to another.*
6Wherever I have moved about with all
Israel, have I ever spoken a word to any of
the judges of Israel, whom I commanded
to shepherd My people, saying, 'Why have
you not built Me a house of cedar?'"' 7Now
therefore, thus shall you say to My servant
David, 'Thus says the LORD of hosts: "I
took you from the sheepfold, from following the sheep, to be ruler over My people
Israel. 8And I have been with you wherever you have gone, and have cut off all your
enemies from before you, and have made
you a name like the name of the great men
who *are* on the earth. 9Moreover I will
appoint a place for My people Israel, and
will plant them, that they may dwell in a
place of their own and move no more; nor
shall the sons of wickedness oppress them
anymore, as previously, 10since the time that
I commanded judges *to be* over My people
Israel. Also I will subdue all your enemies.
Furthermore I tell you that the LORD will
build you a house.a 11And it shall be, when
your days are fulfilled, when you must go
to be with your fathers, that I will set up
your seed after you, who will be of your
sons; and I will establish his kingdom. 12He
shall build Me a house, and I will establish
his throne forever. 13I will be his Father,
and he shall be My son; and I will not take
My mercy away from him, as I took *it* from
him who was before you. 14And I will
establish him in My house and in My kingdom forever; and his throne shall be established forever."'"

15According to all these words and
according to all this vision, so Nathan
spoke to David.

16Then King David went in and sat
before the LORD; and he said: "Who *am* I, O
LORD God? And what is my house, that You
have brought me this far? 17And *yet* this
was a small thing in Your sight, O God; and
You have *also* spoken of Your servant's
house for a great while to come, and have
regarded me according to the rank of a
man of high degree, O LORD God. 18What

16:36 aCompare verses 35, 36 with Psalm 106:47, 48
17:10 aThat is, a royal dynasty

more can David *say* to You for the honor of Your servant? For You know Your servant. ¹⁹O LORD, for Your servant's sake, and according to Your own heart, You have done all this greatness, in making known all these great things. ²⁰O LORD, *there is* none like You, nor *is there any* God besides You, according to all that we have heard with our ears. ²¹And who *is* like Your people Israel, the one nation on the earth whom God went to redeem for Himself *as* a people—to make for Yourself a name by great and awesome deeds, by driving out nations from before Your people whom You redeemed from Egypt? ²²For You have made Your people Israel Your very own people forever; and You, LORD, have become their God.

²³"And now, O LORD, the word which You have spoken concerning Your servant and concerning his house, *let it* be established forever, and do as You have said. ²⁴So let it be established, that Your name may be magnified forever, saying, 'The LORD of hosts, the God of Israel, *is* Israel's God.' And let the house of Your servant David be established before You. ²⁵For You, O my God, have revealed to Your servant that You will build him a house. Therefore Your servant has found it *in his heart* to pray before You. ²⁶And now, LORD, You are God, and have promised this goodness to Your servant. ²⁷Now You have been pleased to bless the house of Your servant, that it may continue before You forever; for You have blessed it, O LORD, and *it shall be* blessed forever."

David's Further Conquests

18 After this it came to pass that David attacked the Philistines, subdued them, and took Gath and its towns from the hand of the Philistines. ²Then he defeated Moab, and the Moabites became David's servants, *and* brought tribute.

³And David defeated Hadadezer[a] king of Zobah *as far as* Hamath, as he went to establish his power by the River Euphrates. ⁴David took from him one thousand chariots, seven thousand[a] horsemen, and twenty thousand foot soldiers. Also David hamstrung all the chariot *horses,* except that he spared enough of them for one hundred chariots.

⁵When the Syrians of Damascus came to help Hadadezer king of Zobah, David killed twenty-two thousand of the Syrians. ⁶Then David put *garrisons* in Syria of Damascus; and the Syrians became David's servants, *and* brought tribute. So the LORD preserved David wherever he went. ⁷And David took the shields of gold that were on the servants of Hadadezer, and brought them to Jerusalem. ⁸Also from Tibhath[a] and from Chun, cities of Hadadezer, David brought a large amount of bronze, with which Solomon made the bronze Sea, the pillars, and the articles of bronze.

⁹Now when Tou[a] king of Hamath heard that David had defeated all the army of Hadadezer king of Zobah, ¹⁰he sent Hadoram[a] his son to King David, to greet him and bless him, because he had fought against Hadadezer and defeated him (for Hadadezer had been at war with Tou); and *Hadoram brought with him* all kinds of articles of gold, silver, and bronze. ¹¹King David also dedicated these to the LORD, along with the silver and gold that he had brought from all *these* nations—from Edom, from Moab, from the people of Ammon, from the Philistines, and from Amalek.

¹²Moreover Abishai the son of Zeruiah killed eighteen thousand Edomites[a] in the Valley of Salt. ¹³He also put garrisons in Edom, and all the Edomites became David's servants. And the LORD preserved David wherever he went.

INTIMATE MOMENTS

Handwrite his favorite Bible verse on parchment. After laminating it, surprise him by tucking it inside his Bible.

18:3 ªHebrew *Hadarezer,* and so throughout chapters 18 and 19 **18:4** ªOr *seven hundred* (compare 2 Samuel 8:4) **18:8** ªSpelled *Betah* in 2 Samuel 8:8 **18:9** ªSpelled *Toi* in 2 Samuel 8:9, 10 **18:10** ªSpelled *Joram* in 2 Samuel 8:10 **18:12** ªOr *Syrians* (compare 2 Samuel 8:13)

David's Administration

14So David reigned over all Israel, and administered judgment and justice to all his people. 15Joab the son of Zeruiah *was* over the army; Jehoshaphat the son of Ahilud *was* recorder; 16Zadok the son of Ahitub and Abimelech the son of Abiathar *were* the priests; Shavsha[a] *was* the scribe; 17Benaiah the son of Jehoiada *was* over the Cherethites and the Pelethites; and David's sons *were* chief ministers at the king's side.

The Ammonites and Syrians Defeated

19 It happened after this that Nahash the king of the people of Ammon died, and his son reigned in his place. 2Then David said, "I will show kindness to Hanun the son of Nahash, because his father showed kindness to me." So David sent messengers to comfort him concerning his father. And David's servants came to Hanun in the land of the people of Ammon to comfort him.

3And the princes of the people of Ammon said to Hanun, "Do you think that David really honors your father because he has sent comforters to you? Did his servants not come to you to search and to overthrow and to spy out the land?" 4Therefore Hanun took David's servants, shaved them, and cut off their garments in the middle, at their buttocks, and sent them away. 5Then *some* went and told David about the men; and he sent to meet them, because the men were greatly ashamed. And the king said, "Wait at Jericho until your beards have grown, and *then* return."

6When the people of Ammon saw that they had made themselves repulsive to David, Hanun and the people of Ammon sent a thousand talents of silver to hire for themselves chariots and horsemen from Mesopotamia,[a] from Syrian Maacah, and from Zobah.[b] 7So they hired for themselves thirty-two thousand chariots, with the king of Maacah and his people, who came and encamped before Medeba. Also the people of Ammon gathered together from their cities, and came to battle.

8Now when David heard *of it,* he sent Joab and all the army of the mighty men. 9Then the people of Ammon came out and put themselves in battle array before the gate of the city, and the kings who had come *were* by themselves in the field.

10When Joab saw that the battle line was against him before and behind, he chose some of Israel's best, and put *them* in battle array against the Syrians. 11And the rest of the people he put under the command of Abishai his brother, and they set *themselves* in battle array against the people of Ammon. 12Then he said, "If the

---

ROMANCE FAQ

Q: *My wife feels mentally and physically drained by our children. What can we do?*

A lot of young moms face this problem. By the end of the day, they don't feel they have anything left for their husbands.

Tips for wives: First, set aside the time you need with your husband to develop your marriage. Ask yourself if you *want* to improve your sexual relationship. All this spells, "Time."

Second, make sure you are getting the physical and spiritual rest that you need. Take a nap in the afternoon if necessary. Take advantage of weekends to catch up on sleep.

Tips for husbands: First, reaffirm your commitment to your wife. Make sure she knows you are her top priority, after the Lord.

Second, demonstrate this commitment by seeking to understand her emotional, spiritual, and physical needs. Remember, your wife longs for real intimacy with you! This may mean making a greater effort to help her out around the house. Some men never clean the kitchen or help put the kids to bed—and then they expect their wives to meet their sexual needs at the end of the day, even though they've done nothing to meet their mate's needs.

18:16 [a]Spelled *Seraiah* in 2 Samuel 8:17
19:6 [a]Hebrew *Aram Naharaim* [b]Spelled *Zoba* in 2 Samuel 10:6

Syrians are too strong for me, then you shall help me; but if the people of Ammon are too strong for you, then I will help you. [13]Be of good courage, and let us be strong for our people and for the cities of our God. And may the LORD do *what is* good in His sight."

[14]So Joab and the people who *were* with him drew near for the battle against the Syrians, and they fled before him. [15]When the people of Ammon saw that the Syrians were fleeing, they also fled before Abishai his brother, and entered the city. So Joab went to Jerusalem.

[16]Now when the Syrians saw that they had been defeated by Israel, they sent messengers and brought the Syrians who were beyond the River,[a] and Shophach[b] the commander of Hadadezer's army *went* before them. [17]When it was told David, he gathered all Israel, crossed over the Jordan and came upon them, and set up in *battle* array against them. So when David had set up in battle array against the Syrians, they fought with him. [18]Then the Syrians fled before Israel; and David killed seven thousand[a] charioteers and forty thousand foot soldiers[b] of the Syrians, and killed Shophach the commander of the army. [19]And when the servants of Hadadezer saw that they were defeated by Israel, they made peace with David and became his servants. So the Syrians were not willing to help the people of Ammon anymore.

Rabbah Is Conquered

20 It happened in the spring of the year, at the time kings go out *to battle,* that Joab led out the armed forces and ravaged the country of the people of Ammon, and came and besieged Rabbah. But David stayed at Jerusalem. And Joab defeated Rabbah and overthrew it. [2]Then David took their king's crown from his head, and found it to weigh a talent of gold, and *there were* precious stones in it. And it was set on David's head. Also he brought out the spoil of the city in great abundance. [3]And he brought out the people who *were* in it, and put *them* to work[a] with saws, with iron picks, and with axes. So David did to all the cities of the people

of Ammon. Then David and all the people returned *to* Jerusalem.

Philistine Giants Destroyed

[4]Now it happened afterward that war broke out at Gezer with the Philistines, at which time Sibbechai the Hushathite killed Sippai,[a] *who was one* of the sons of the giant. And they were subdued.

[5]Again there was war with the Philistines, and Elhanan the son of Jair[a] killed Lahmi the brother of Goliath the Gittite, the shaft of whose spear *was* like a weaver's beam.

[6]Yet again there was war at Gath, where there was a man of *great* stature, with twenty-four fingers and toes, six *on each hand* and six *on each foot;* and he also was born to the giant. [7]So when he defied Israel, Jonathan the son of Shimea,[a] David's brother, killed him.

[8]These were born to the giant in Gath, and they fell by the hand of David and by the hand of his servants.

The Census of Israel and Judah

21 Now Satan stood up against Israel, and moved David to number Israel. [2]So David said to Joab and to the leaders of the people, "Go, number Israel from Beersheba to Dan, and bring the number of them to me that I may know *it.*"

[3]And Joab answered, "May the LORD make His people a hundred times more than they are. But, my lord the king, *are* they not all my lord's servants? Why then does my lord require this thing? Why should he be a cause of guilt in Israel?"

[4]Nevertheless the king's word prevailed against Joab. Therefore Joab departed and went throughout all Israel and came to Jerusalem. [5]Then Joab gave the sum of the number of the people to David. All Israel *had* one million one hundred thousand men who drew the sword, and Judah *had* four hundred and seventy thousand men

19:16 [a]That is, the Euphrates [b]Spelled *Shobach* in 2 Samuel 10:16 **19:18** [a]Or *seven hundred* (compare 2 Samuel 10:18) [b]Or *horsemen* (compare 2 Samuel 10:18) **20:3** [a]Septuagint reads *cut them.* **20:4** [a]Spelled *Saph* in 2 Samuel 21:18 **20:5** [a]Spelled *Jaare-Oregim* in 2 Samuel 21:19 **20:7** [a]Spelled *Shimeah* in 2 Samuel 21:21 and *Shammah* in 1 Samuel 16:9

who drew the sword. [6]But he did not count Levi and Benjamin among them, for the king's word was abominable to Joab.

[7]And God was displeased with this thing; therefore He struck Israel. [8]So David said to God, "I have sinned greatly, because I have done this thing; but now, I pray, take away the iniquity of Your servant, for I have done very foolishly."

[9]Then the LORD spoke to Gad, David's seer, saying, [10]"Go and tell David, saying, 'Thus says the LORD: "I offer you three *things;* choose one of them for yourself, that I may do *it* to you."'"

[11]So Gad came to David and said to him, "Thus says the LORD: 'Choose for yourself, [12]either three[a] years of famine, or three months to be defeated by your foes with the sword of your enemies overtaking *you,* or else for three days the sword of the LORD—the plague in the land, with the angel[b] of the LORD destroying throughout all the territory of Israel.' Now consider what answer I should take back to Him who sent me."

[13]And David said to Gad, "I am in great distress. Please let me fall into the hand of the LORD, for His mercies *are* very great; but do not let me fall into the hand of man."

21:12 [a]Or *seven* (compare 2 Samuel 24:13) [b]Or *Angel,* and so elsewhere in this chapter **21:15** [a]Or *He* [b]Or *Your* [c]Spelled *Araunah* in 2 Samuel 24:16

[14]So the LORD sent a plague upon Israel, and seventy thousand men of Israel fell. [15]And God sent an angel to Jerusalem to destroy it. As he[a] was destroying, the LORD looked and relented of the disaster, and said to the angel who was destroying, "It is enough; now restrain your[b] hand." And the angel of the LORD stood by the threshing floor of Ornan[a] the Jebusite.

[16]Then David lifted his eyes and saw the angel of the LORD standing between earth and heaven, having in his hand a drawn sword stretched out over Jerusalem. So David and the elders, clothed in sackcloth, fell on their faces. [17]And David said to God, "Was it not I who commanded the people to be numbered? I am the one who has sinned and done evil indeed; but these sheep, what have they done? Let Your hand, I pray, O LORD my God, be against me and my father's house, but not against Your people that they should be plagued."

[18]Therefore, the angel of the LORD commanded Gad to say to David that David should go and erect an altar to the LORD on the threshing floor of Ornan the Jebusite. [19]So David went up at the word of Gad, which he had spoken in the name of the LORD. [20]Now Ornan turned and saw the angel; and his four sons *who were* with him hid themselves, but Ornan continued threshing wheat. [21]So David came to Ornan,

---

PARENTING MATTERS

Q: *In a culture that makes it hard to raise godly children, how do we keep from burning out or losing heart?*

Many parents grow weary of holding on to their moral beliefs, boundaries, and commitments. So, little by little in this tug-of-war, they drop their guard and loosen their grip. But you don't have to!

First, realize you are not holding the rope alone. Romans 8:31 tells us, "What then shall we say to these things? If God is for us, who can be against us?" If God is for you, what does it matter who is against you? He is for you and He does not grow weary.

Second, understand why you feel weary. Take an inventory of all the areas you are pulling against. Curfews, dress, language, limits in dating, language, knowing peers, magazines, music, media, telephones, and other cultural heavyweights. You can't eliminate all your tug-of-war opponents, but you can get rid of some.

Third, recruit some other parents and join with them in the tug-of-war. Look out for somebody else's child and not just your own. This may mean talking with other parents and agreeing to call each other if you observe inappropriate behavior in any of your children.

and Ornan looked and saw David. And he went out from the threshing floor, and bowed before David with *his* face to the ground. ²²Then David said to Ornan, "Grant me the place of *this* threshing floor, that I may build an altar on it to the LORD. You shall grant it to me at the full price, that the plague may be withdrawn from the people."

²³But Ornan said to David, "Take *it* to yourself, and let my lord the king do *what is* good in his eyes. Look, I *also* give *you* the oxen for burnt offerings, the threshing implements for wood, and the wheat for the grain offering; I give *it* all."

²⁴Then King David said to Ornan, "No, but I will surely buy *it* for the full price, for I will not take what is yours for the LORD, nor offer burnt offerings with *that which* costs *me* nothing." ²⁵So David gave Ornan six hundred shekels of gold by weight for the place. ²⁶And David built there an altar to the LORD, and offered burnt offerings and peace offerings, and called on the LORD; and He answered him from heaven by fire on the altar of burnt offering.

²⁷So the LORD commanded the angel, and he returned his sword to its sheath.

²⁸At that time, when David saw that the LORD had answered him on the threshing floor of Ornan the Jebusite, he sacrificed there. ²⁹For the tabernacle of the LORD and the altar of the burnt offering, which Moses had made in the wilderness, *were* at that time at the high place in Gibeon. ³⁰But David could not go before it to inquire of God, for he was afraid of the sword of the angel of the LORD.

David Prepares to Build the Temple

22 Then David said, "This *is* the house of the LORD God, and this *is* the altar of burnt offering for Israel." ²So David commanded to gather the aliens who *were* in the land of Israel; and he appointed masons to cut hewn stones to build the house of God. ³And David prepared iron in abundance for the nails of the doors of the gates and for the joints, and bronze in abundance beyond measure, ⁴and cedar trees in abundance; for the Sidonians and those from Tyre brought much cedar wood to David.

⁵Now David said, "Solomon my son *is* young and inexperienced, and the house to be built for the LORD *must be* exceedingly magnificent, famous and glorious throughout all countries. I will now make preparation for it." So David made abundant preparations before his death.

⁶Then he called for his son Solomon, and charged him to build a house for the LORD God of Israel. ⁷And David said to Solomon: "My son, as for me, it was in my mind to build a house to the name of the LORD my God; ⁸but the word of the LORD came to me, saying, 'You have shed much blood and have made great wars; you shall not build a house for My name, because you have shed much blood on the earth in My sight. ⁹Behold, a son shall be born to you, who shall be a man of rest; and I will give him rest from all his enemies all around. His name shall be Solomon,ᵃ for I will give peace and quietness to Israel in his days. ¹⁰He shall build a house for My name, and he shall be My son, and I *will be* his Father; and I will establish the throne of his kingdom over Israel forever.' ¹¹Now, my son, may the LORD be with you; and may you prosper, and build the house of the LORD your God, as He has said to you. ¹²Only may the LORD give you wisdom and understanding, and give you charge concerning Israel, that you may keep the law of the LORD your God. ¹³Then you will prosper, if you take care to fulfill the statutes and judgments with which the LORD charged Moses concerning Israel. Be strong and of good courage; do not fear nor be dismayed. ¹⁴Indeed I have taken much trouble to prepare for the house of the LORD one hundred thousand talents of gold and one million talents of silver, and bronze and iron beyond measure, for it is so abundant. I have prepared timber and stone also, and you may add to them. ¹⁵Moreover *there are* workmen with you in abundance: woodsmen and stonecutters, and all types of skillful men for every kind of work. ¹⁶Of gold and silver and bronze and iron *there is* no limit. Arise and begin working, and the LORD be with you."

¹⁷David also commanded all the leaders of Israel to help Solomon his son, *saying,* ¹⁸"*Is* not the LORD your God with you? And

22:9 ᵃLiterally *Peaceful*

has He *not* given you rest on every side? For He has given the inhabitants of the land into my hand, and the land is subdued before the LORD and before His people. ¹⁹Now set your heart and your soul to seek the LORD your God. Therefore arise and build the sanctuary of the LORD God, to bring the ark of the covenant of the LORD and the holy articles of God into the house that is to be built for the name of the LORD."

The Divisions of the Levites

23 So when David was old and full of days, he made his son Solomon king over Israel.

²And he gathered together all the leaders of Israel, with the priests and the Levites. ³Now the Levites were numbered from the age of thirty years and above; and the number of individual males was thirty-eight thousand. ⁴Of these, twenty-four thousand *were* to look after the work of the house of the LORD, six thousand *were* officers and judges, ⁵four thousand *were* gatekeepers, and four thousand praised the LORD with *musical* instruments, "which I made," *said David,* "for giving praise."

⁶Also David separated them into divisions among the sons of Levi: Gershon, Kohath, and Merari.

⁷Of the Gershonites: Laadan[a] and Shimei. ⁸The sons of Laadan: the first Jehiel, then Zetham and Joel—three *in all.* ⁹The sons of Shimei: Shelomith, Haziel, and Haran—three *in all.* These were the heads of the fathers' *houses* of Laadan. ¹⁰And the sons of Shimei: Jahath, Zina,[a] Jeush, and Beriah. These *were* the four sons of Shimei. ¹¹Jahath was the first and Zizah the second. But Jeush and Beriah did not have many sons; therefore they were assigned as one father's house.

¹²The sons of Kohath: Amram, Izhar, Hebron, and Uzziel—four *in all.* ¹³The sons of Amram: Aaron and Moses; and Aaron was set apart, he and his sons forever, that he should sanctify the most holy things, to burn incense before the LORD, to minister to

Him, and to give the blessing in His name forever. ¹⁴Now the sons of Moses the man of God were reckoned to the tribe of Levi. ¹⁵The sons of Moses *were* Gershon[a] and Eliezer. ¹⁶Of the sons of Gershon, Shebuel[a] *was* the first. ¹⁷Of the descendants of Eliezer, Rehabiah was the first. And Eliezer had no other sons, but the sons of Rehabiah were very many. ¹⁸Of the sons of Izhar, Shelomith *was* the first. ¹⁹Of the sons of Hebron, Jeriah *was* the first, Amariah the second, Jahaziel the third, and Jekameam the fourth. ²⁰Of the sons of Uzziel, Micah *was* the first and Jesshiah the second.

²¹The sons of Merari *were* Mahli and Mushi. The sons of Mahli *were* Eleazar and Kish. ²²And Eleazar died, and had no sons, but only daughters; and their brethren, the sons of Kish, took them *as wives.* ²³The sons of Mushi *were* Mahli, Eder, and Jeremoth—three *in all.*

INTIMATE MOMENTS

Leave one of your wife's dress shoes in the front seat of the car. Tuck a note inside it, telling her that she is your Cinderella and that she is to meet you at a certain time and place so that you can buy her a new pair of shoes.

²⁴These *were* the sons of Levi by their fathers' houses—the heads of the fathers' *houses* as they were counted individually by the number of their names, who did the work for the service of the house of the LORD, from the age of twenty years and above.

²⁵For David said, "The LORD God of Israel has given rest to His people, that they may dwell in Jerusalem forever"; ²⁶and also to the Levites, "They shall no longer carry the tabernacle, or any of the articles for its service." ²⁷For by the last words of David the Levites *were* numbered from twenty years old and above; ²⁸because their duty *was* to help the sons of Aaron in the service of the house of the LORD, in the

---

23:7 ᵃSpelled *Libni* in Exodus 6:17
23:10 ᵃSeptuagint and Vulgate read *Zizah* (compare verse 11). 23:15 ᵃHebrew *Gershom* (compare 6:16)
23:16 ᵃSpelled *Shubael* in 24:20

courts and in the chambers, in the purifying of all holy things and the work of the service of the house of God, 29both with the showbread and the fine flour for the grain offering, with the unleavened cakes and *what is baked in* the pan, with what is mixed and with all kinds of measures and sizes; 30to stand every morning to thank and praise the LORD, and likewise at evening; 31and at every presentation of a burnt offering to the LORD on the Sabbaths and on the New Moons and on the set feasts, by number according to the ordinance governing them, regularly before the LORD; 32and that they should attend to the needs of the tabernacle of meeting, the needs of the holy *place,* and the needs of the sons of Aaron their brethren in the work of the house of the LORD.

The Divisions of the Priests

24 Now *these are* the divisions of the sons of Aaron. The sons of Aaron *were* Nadab, Abihu, Eleazar, and Ithamar. 2And Nadab and Abihu died before their father, and had no children; therefore Eleazar and Ithamar ministered as priests. 3Then David with Zadok of the sons of Eleazar, and Ahimelech of the sons of Ithamar, divided them according to the schedule of their service.

4There were more leaders found of the sons of Eleazar than of the sons of Ithamar, and *thus* they were divided. Among the sons of Eleazar *were* sixteen heads of *their* fathers' houses, and eight heads of their fathers' houses among the sons of Ithamar. 5Thus they were divided by lot, one group as another, for there were officials of the sanctuary and officials *of the house* of God, from the sons of Eleazar and from the sons of Ithamar. 6And the scribe, Shemaiah the son of Nethanel, *one of* the Levites, wrote them down before the king, the leaders, Zadok the priest, Ahimelech the son of Abiathar, and the heads of the fathers' *houses* of the priests and Levites, one father's house taken for Eleazar and *one* for Ithamar.

7Now the first lot fell to Jehoiarib, the second to Jedaiah, 8the third to Harim, the fourth to Seorim, 9the fifth to Malchijah, the sixth to Mijamin, 10the seventh to Hakkoz, the eighth to Abijah, 11the ninth to Jeshua, the tenth to Shecaniah, 12the eleventh to Eliashib, the twelfth to Jakim, 13the thirteenth to Huppah, the fourteenth to Jeshebeab, 14the fifteenth to Bilgah, the sixteenth to Immer, 15the seventeenth to Hezir, the eighteenth to Happizzez,a 16the nineteenth to Pethahiah, the twentieth to Jehezekel,a 17the twenty-first to Jachin, the twenty-second to Gamul, 18the twenty-third to Delaiah, the twenty-fourth to Maaziah.

19This *was* the schedule of their service for coming into the house of the LORD according to their ordinance by the hand of Aaron their father, as the LORD God of Israel had commanded him.

Other Levites

20And the rest of the sons of Levi: of the sons of Amram, Shubael;a of the sons of Shubael, Jehdeiah. 21Concerning Rehabiah, of the sons of Rehabiah, the first *was* Isshiah. 22Of the Izharites, Shelomoth;a of the sons of Shelomoth, Jahath. 23Of the sons *of Hebron,*a Jeriah *was the first,*b Amariah the second, Jahaziel the third, *and* Jekameam the fourth. 24*Of* the sons of Uzziel, Michah; of the sons of Michah, Shamir. 25The brother of Michah, Isshiah; of the sons of Isshiah, Zechariah. 26The sons of Merari *were* Mahli and Mushi; the son of Jaaziah, Beno. 27The sons of Merari by Jaaziah *were* Beno, Shoham, Zaccur, and Ibri. 28Of Mahli: Eleazar, who had no sons. 29Of Kish: the son of Kish, Jerahmeel.

30Also the sons of Mushi *were* Mahli, Eder, and Jerimoth. These *were* the sons of the Levites according to their fathers' houses.

31These also cast lots just as their brothers the sons of Aaron did, in the presence of King David, Zadok, Ahimelech, and the heads of the fathers' *houses* of the priests and Levites. The chief fathers *did* just as their younger brethren.

24:15 aSeptuagint and Vulgate read *Aphses.*
24:16 aMasoretic Text reads *Jehezkel.* **24:20** aSpelled *Shebuel* in 23:16 **24:22** aSpelled *Shelomith* in 23:18
24:23 aSupplied from 23:19 (following some Hebrew manuscripts and Septuagint manuscripts) bSupplied from 23:19 (following some Hebrew manuscripts and Septuagint manuscripts)

The Musicians

25 Moreover David and the captains of the army separated for the service *some* of the sons of Asaph, of Heman, and of Jeduthun, who *should* prophesy with harps, stringed instruments, and cymbals. And the number of the skilled men performing their service was: [2]Of the sons of Asaph: Zaccur, Joseph, Nethaniah, and Asharelah;[a] the sons of Asaph *were* under the direction of Asaph, who prophesied according to the order of the king. [3]Of Jeduthun, the sons of Jeduthun: Gedaliah, Zeri,[a] Jeshaiah, *Shimei,* Hashabiah, and Mattithiah, six,[b] under the direction of their father Jeduthun, who prophesied with a harp to give thanks and to praise the LORD. [4]Of Heman, the sons of Heman: Bukkiah, Mattaniah, Uzziel,[a] Shebuel,[b] Jerimoth,[c] Hananiah, Hanani, Eliathah, Giddalti, Romamti-Ezer, Joshbekashah, Mallothi, Hothir, *and* Mahazioth. [5]All these *were* the sons of Heman the king's seer in the words of God, to exalt his horn.[a] For God gave Heman fourteen sons and three daughters.

[6]All these *were* under the direction of their father for the music *in* the house of the LORD, with cymbals, stringed instruments, and harps, for the service of the house of God. Asaph, Jeduthun, and Heman *were* under the authority of the king. [7]So the number of them, with their brethren who were instructed in the songs of the LORD, all who were skillful, *was* two hundred and eighty-eight.

[8]And they cast lots for their duty, the small as well as the great, the teacher with the student.

[9]Now the first lot for Asaph came out for Joseph; the second for Gedaliah, him with his brethren and sons, twelve; [10]the third for Zaccur, his sons and his brethren, twelve; [11]the fourth for Jizri,[a] his sons and his brethren, twelve; [12]the fifth for Nethaniah, his sons and his brethren, twelve; [13]the sixth for Bukkiah, his sons and his brethren, twelve; [14]the seventh for Jesharelah,[a] his sons and his brethren, twelve; [15]the eighth for Jeshaiah, his sons and his brethren, twelve; [16]the ninth for Mattaniah, his sons and his brethren, twelve; [17]the tenth for Shimei, his sons and his brethren, twelve; [18]the eleventh for Azarel,[a] his sons and his brethren, twelve; [19]the twelfth for Hashabiah, his sons and his brethren,

---

25:2 [a]Spelled *Jesharelah* in verse 14 **25:3** [a]Spelled *Jizri* in verse 11 [b]*Shimei*, appearing in one Hebrew and several Septuagint manuscripts, completes the total of six sons (compare verse 17). **25:4** [a]Spelled *Azarel* in verse 18 [b]Spelled *Shubael* in verse 20 [c]Spelled *Jeremoth* in verse 22 **25:5** [a]That is, to increase his power or influence **25:11** [a]Spelled *Zeri* in verse 3 **25:14** [a]Spelled *Asharelah* in verse 2 **25:18** [a]Spelled *Uzziel* in verse 4

ROMANCE FAQ

Q: *What are some specific ways to please my husband?*

All of us need an occasional cue card to help us to reach out. Here are a few ideas:

1. Put a love note in his lunchbox or briefcase.

2. Prepare his favorite meal.

3. Arrange an evening out for just the two of you.

4. Wear his favorite dress with your hair done the way he likes it.

5. Purchase something small and frivolous for him that he won't buy himself.

6. Give him a nicely framed picture of yourself—or of you and the children—for his office.

7. Surprise him with an all-expenses-paid trip to do something he likes, such as golf, fishing, or hunting.

8. Put the children to bed early and prepare a candlelight dinner.

9. Do something that especially pleased him when you were dating.

10. Read Scriptures and pray with him regularly.

11. Wear his favorite negligee or buy a new nightgown to add sizzle to your evening attire.

12. Clean out the car for him.

Sometimes the smallest gestures can make the biggest difference. Pick out something you haven't tried before; don't give complacency a foothold in your marriage.

twelve; [20]the thirteenth for Shubael,[a] his sons and his brethren, twelve; [21]the fourteenth for Mattithiah, his sons and his brethren, twelve; [22]the fifteenth for Jeremoth,[a] his sons and his brethren, twelve; [23]the sixteenth for Hananiah, his sons and his brethren, twelve; [24]the seventeenth for Joshbekashah, his sons and his brethren, twelve; [25]the eighteenth for Hanani, his sons and his brethren, twelve; [26]the nineteenth for Mallothi, his sons and his brethren, twelve; [27]the twentieth for Eliathah, his sons and his brethren, twelve; [28]the twenty-first for Hothir, his sons and his brethren, twelve; [29]the twenty-second for Giddalti, his sons and his brethren, twelve; [30]the twenty-third for Mahazioth, his sons and his brethren, twelve; [31]the twenty-fourth for Romamti-Ezer, his sons and his brethren, twelve.

The Gatekeepers

26 Concerning the divisions of the gatekeepers: of the Korahites, Meshelemiah the son of Kore, of the sons of Asaph. [2]And the sons of Meshelemiah were Zechariah the firstborn, Jediael the second, Zebadiah the third, Jathniel the fourth, [3]Elam the fifth, Jehohanan the sixth, Eliehoenai the seventh.

[4]Moreover the sons of Obed-Edom were Shemaiah the firstborn, Jehozabad the second, Joah the third, Sacar the fourth, Nethanel the fifth, [5]Ammiel the sixth, Issachar the seventh, Peulthai the eighth; for God blessed him.

[6]Also to Shemaiah his son were sons born who governed their fathers' houses, because they were men of great ability. [7]The sons of Shemaiah were Othni, Rephael, Obed, and Elzabad, whose brothers Elihu and Semachiah were able men.

[8]All these were of the sons of Obed-Edom, they and their sons and their brethren, able men with strength for the work: sixty-two of Obed-Edom.

[9]And Meshelemiah had sons and brethren, eighteen able men.

[10]Also Hosah, of the children of Merari, had sons: Shimri the first (for though he was not the firstborn, his father made him the first), [11]Hilkiah the second, Tebaliah

the third, Zechariah the fourth; all the sons and brethren of Hosah were thirteen.

[12]Among these were the divisions of the gatekeepers, among the chief men, having duties just like their brethren, to serve in the house of the LORD. [13]And they cast lots for each gate, the small as well as the great, according to their father's house. [14]The lot for the East Gate fell to Shelemiah. Then they cast lots for his son Zechariah, a wise counselor, and his lot came out for the North Gate; [15]to Obed-Edom the South Gate, and to his sons the storehouse.[a] [16]To Shuppim and Hosah the lot came out for the West Gate, with the Shallecheth Gate on the ascending highway—watchman opposite watchman. [17]On the east were six Levites, on the north four each day, on the south four each day, and for the storehouse[a] two by two. [18]As for the Parbar[a] on the west, there were four on the highway and two at the Parbar. [19]These were the divisions of the gatekeepers among the sons of Korah and among the sons of Merari.

The Treasuries and Other Duties

[20]Of the Levites, Ahijah was over the treasuries of the house of God and over the treasuries of the dedicated things. [21]The sons of Laadan, the descendants of the Gershonites of Laadan, heads of their fathers' houses, of Laadan the Gershonite: Jehieli. [22]The sons of Jehieli, Zetham and Joel his brother, were over the treasuries of the house of the LORD. [23]Of the Amramites, the Izharites, the Hebronites, and the Uzzielites: [24]Shebuel the son of Gershom, the son of Moses, was overseer of the treasuries. [25]And his brethren by Eliezer were Rehabiah his son, Jeshaiah his son, Joram his son, Zichri his son, and Shelomith his son.

[26]This Shelomith and his brethren were over all the treasuries of the dedicated things which King David and the heads of fathers' houses, the captains over thousands and hundreds, and the captains of

25:20 [a]Spelled *Shebuel* in verse 4 **25:22** [a]Spelled *Jerimoth* in verse 4 **26:15** [a]Hebrew *asuppim*
26:17 [a]Hebrew *asuppim* **26:18** [a]Probably a court or colonnade extending west of the temple

the army, had dedicated. ²⁷Some of the spoils won in battles they dedicated to maintain the house of the LORD. ²⁸And all that Samuel the seer, Saul the son of Kish, Abner the son of Ner, and Joab the son of Zeruiah had dedicated, every dedicated *thing,* was under the hand of Shelomith and his brethren.

²⁹Of the Izharites, Chenaniah and his sons *performed* duties as officials and judges over Israel outside Jerusalem.

³⁰Of the Hebronites, Hashabiah and his brethren, one thousand seven hundred able men, had the oversight of Israel on the west side of the Jordan for all the business of the LORD, and in the service of the king. ³¹Among the Hebronites, Jerijah *was* head of the Hebronites according to his genealogy of the fathers. In the fortieth year of the reign of David they were sought, and there were found among them capable men at Jazer of Gilead. ³²And his brethren *were* two thousand seven hundred able men, heads of fathers' *houses,* whom King David made officials over the Reubenites, the Gadites, and the half-tribe of Manasseh, for every matter pertaining to God and the affairs of the king.

The Military Divisions

27 And the children of Israel, according to their number, the heads of fathers' *houses,* the captains of thousands and hundreds and their officers, served the king in every matter of the *military* divisions. *These divisions* came in and went out month by month throughout all the months of the year, each division *having* twenty-four thousand.

²Over the first division for the first month *was* Jashobeam the son of Zabdiel, and in his division *were* twenty-four thousand; ³he *was* of the children of Perez, and the chief of all the captains of the army for the first month. ⁴Over the division of the second month *was* Dodai[a] an Ahohite, and of his division Mikloth also *was* the leader; in his division *were* twenty-four thousand.

⁵The third captain of the army for the third month *was* Benaiah, the son of Jehoiada the priest, who was chief; in his division *were* twenty-four thousand. ⁶This was the Benaiah *who was* mighty *among* the thirty, and was over the thirty; in his division *was* Ammizabad his son. ⁷The fourth *captain* for the fourth month *was* Asahel the brother of Joab, and Zebadiah his son after him; in his division *were* twenty-four thousand. ⁸The fifth captain for the fifth month *was* Shamhuth[a] the Izrahite; in his division were twenty-four thousand. ⁹The sixth *captain* for the sixth month *was* Ira the son of Ikkesh the Tekoite; in his division *were* twenty-four thousand. ¹⁰The seventh *captain* for the seventh month *was* Helez the Pelonite, of the children of Ephraim; in his division *were* twenty-four thousand. ¹¹The eighth *captain* for the eighth month *was* Sibbechai the Hushathite, of the Zarhites; in his division *were* twenty-four thousand. ¹²The ninth *captain* for the ninth month *was* Abiezer the Anathothite, of the Benjamites; in his division *were* twenty-four thousand. ¹³The tenth *captain* for the tenth month *was* Maharai the Netophathite, of the Zarhites; in his division *were* twenty-four thousand. ¹⁴The eleventh *captain* for the eleventh month *was* Benaiah the Pirathonite, of the children of Ephraim; in his division *were* twenty-four thousand. ¹⁵The twelfth *captain* for the twelfth month *was* Heldai[a] the Netophathite, of Othniel; in his division *were* twenty-four thousand.

Leaders of Tribes

¹⁶Furthermore, over the tribes of Israel: the officer over the Reubenites *was* Eliezer the son of Zichri; over the Simeonites, Shephatiah the son of Maachah; ¹⁷over the Levites, Hashabiah the son of Kemuel; over the Aaronites, Zadok; ¹⁸over Judah, Elihu, *one* of David's brothers; *over* Issachar, Omri the son of Michael; ¹⁹over Zebulun, Ishmaiah the son of Obadiah; *over* Naphtali, Jerimoth the son of Azriel; ²⁰over the children of Ephraim, Hoshea the son of Azaziah; *over* the half-tribe of Manasseh, Joel the son of Pedaiah; ²¹over the half-*tribe* of Manasseh in Gilead, Iddo the son of Zechariah; *over* Benjamin, Jaasiel the son of Abner; ²²over Dan, Azarel the son of

---

27:4 [a]Hebrew *Dodai,* usually spelled *Dodo* (compare 2 Samuel 23:9) **27:8** [a]Spelled *Shammoth* in 11:27 and *Shammah* in 2 Samuel 23:11 **27:15** [a]Spelled *Heled* in 11:30 and *Heleb* in 2 Samuel 23:29

Jeroham. These *were* the leaders of the tribes of Israel.

²³But David did not take the number of those twenty years old and under, because the LORD had said He would multiply Israel like the stars of the heavens. ²⁴Joab the son of Zeruiah began a census, but he did not finish, for wrath came upon Israel because of this census; nor was the number recorded in the account of the chronicles of King David.

Other State Officials

²⁵And Azmaveth the son of Adiel *was* over the king's treasuries; and Jehonathan the son of Uzziah was over the storehouses in the field, in the cities, in the villages, and in the fortresses. ²⁶Ezri the son of Chelub was over those who did the work of the field for tilling the ground. ²⁷And Shimei the Ramathite *was* over the vineyards, and Zabdi the Shiphmite was over the produce of the vineyards for the supply of wine. ²⁸Baal-Hanan the Gederite was over the olive trees and the sycamore trees that *were* in the lowlands, and Joash *was* over the store of oil. ²⁹And Shitrai the Sharonite *was* over the herds that fed in Sharon, and Shaphat the son of Adlai was over the herds *that were* in the valleys. ³⁰Obil the Ishmaelite *was* over the camels, Jehdeiah the Meronothite *was* over the donkeys, ³¹and Jaziz the Hagrite *was* over the flocks. All these *were* the officials over King David's property.

³²Also Jehonathan, David's uncle, *was* a counselor, a wise man, and a scribe; and Jehiel the son of Hachmoni *was* with the king's sons. ³³Ahithophel *was* the king's counselor, and Hushai the Archite *was* the king's companion. ³⁴After Ahithophel *was* Jehoiada the son of Benaiah, then Abiathar. And the general of the king's army *was* Joab.

Solomon Instructed to Build the Temple

28 Now David assembled at Jerusalem all the leaders of Israel: the officers of the tribes and the captains of the divisions who served the king, the captains over thousands and captains over hundreds, and the stewards over all the substance and possessions of the king and of his sons, with the officials, the valiant men, and all the mighty men of valor.

²Then King David rose to his feet and said, "Hear me, my brethren and my people: I *had* it in my heart to build a house of rest for the ark of the covenant of the LORD, and for the footstool of our God, and had made preparations to build it. ³But God said to me, 'You shall not build a house for My name, because you *have been* a man of war and have shed blood.' ⁴However, the LORD God of Israel chose me above all the house of my father to be king over Israel forever, for He has chosen Judah *to be* the ruler. And of the house of Judah, the house of my father, and among the sons of my father, He was pleased with me to make *me* king over all Israel. ⁵And of all my sons (for the LORD has given me many sons) He has chosen my son Solomon to sit on the throne of the kingdom of the LORD over Israel. ⁶Now He said to me, 'It is your

INTIMATE MOMENTS

The Best Gift of All?

Do you think that it's possible you might spend hours and hours searching for that special something that you just *know* your husband will love, only to discover it's not really on his radar screen at all? It's not only possible, we're sure it happens all the time.

And yet there's a gift we absolutely *guarantee* that he'll love.

You won't find it at the department store. It's not for sale in the athletic shop. You won't pick it off the shelf in the automotive parts store, secure it in the athletic club, spot it at the bowling alley, or purchase it at your local big box megahemoth shopping center.

Actually, you already have it … you just have to give it. So would you like to know what it is? We really think it might be the best gift of all. And here it is:

Refrain from saying, "I told you so."

son Solomon *who* shall build My house and My courts; for I have chosen him *to be* My son, and I will be his Father. [7]Moreover I will establish his kingdom forever, if he is steadfast to observe My commandments and My judgments, as it is this day.' [8]Now therefore, in the sight of all Israel, the assembly of the LORD, and in the hearing of our God, be careful to seek out all the commandments of the LORD your God, that you may possess this good land, and leave *it* as an inheritance for your children after you forever.

[9]"As for you, my son Solomon, know the God of your father, and serve Him with a loyal heart and with a willing mind; for the LORD searches all hearts and understands all the intent of the thoughts. If you seek Him, He will be found by you; but if you forsake Him, He will cast you off forever. [10]Consider now, for the LORD has chosen you to build a house for the sanctuary; be strong, and do it."

[11]Then David gave his son Solomon the plans for the vestibule, its houses, its treasuries, its upper chambers, its inner chambers, and the place of the mercy seat; [12]and the plans for all that he had by the Spirit, of the courts of the house of the LORD, of all the chambers all around, of the treasuries of the house of God, and of the treasuries for the dedicated things; [13]also for the division of the priests and the Levites, for all the work of the service of the house of the LORD, and for all the articles of service in the house of the LORD. [14]*He gave* gold by weight for *things* of gold, for all articles used in every kind of service; also *silver* for all articles of silver by weight, for all articles used in every kind of service; [15]the weight for the lampstands of gold, and their lamps of gold, by weight for each lampstand and its lamps; for the lampstands of silver by weight, for the lampstand and its lamps, according to the use of each lampstand. [16]And by weight *he gave* gold for the tables of the showbread, for each table, and silver for the tables of silver; [17]also pure gold for the forks, the basins, the pitchers of pure gold, and the golden bowls—*he gave* gold by weight for

every bowl; and for the silver bowls, *silver* by weight for every bowl; [18]and refined gold by weight for the altar of incense, and for the construction of the chariot, that is, the gold cherubim that spread *their wings* and overshadowed the ark of the covenant of the LORD. [19]"All *this*," said *David*, "the LORD made me understand in writing, by *His* hand upon me, all the works of these plans."

[20]And David said to his son Solomon, "Be strong and of good courage, and do *it*; do not fear nor be dismayed, for the LORD God—my God—*will be* with you. He will not leave you nor forsake you, until you have finished all the work for the service of the house of the LORD. [21]*Here are* the divisions of the priests and the Levites for all the service of the house of God; and every willing craftsman *will be* with you for all manner of workmanship, for every kind of service; also the leaders and all the people *will be* completely at your command."

Offerings for Building the Temple

29 Furthermore King David said to all the assembly: "My son Solomon, whom alone God has chosen, *is* young and inexperienced; and the work *is* great, because the temple[a] *is* not for man but for the LORD God. [2]Now for the house of my God I have prepared with all my might: gold for *things to be made of* gold, silver for *things of* silver, bronze for *things of* bronze, iron for *things of* iron, wood for *things of* wood, onyx stones, *stones* to be set, glistening stones of various colors, all kinds of precious stones, and marble slabs in abundance. [3]Moreover, because I have set my affection on the house of my God, I have given to the house of my God, over and above all that I have prepared for the holy house, my own special treasure of gold and silver: [4]three thousand talents of gold, of the gold of Ophir, and seven thousand talents of refined silver, to overlay the walls of the houses; [5]the gold for *things of* gold and the silver for *things of* silver, and for all kinds of work *to be done* by the hands of craftsmen. Who *then* is willing to consecrate himself this day to the LORD?"

[6]Then the leaders of the fathers' *houses*, leaders of the tribes of Israel, the captains

---

29:1 [a]Literally *palace*

Remember Who Is in Control

WE HAVE HAD SOME difficult experiences with our children that have reminded us of several important things we must do in order to stand strong when a storm hits—the most crucial of which is using times of trial and suffering as opportunities to draw close to God.

Nothing happens in our lives apart from what God allows or ordains. As 1 Chron. 29:11 tells us, "Yours, O LORD, is the greatness, the power and the glory, the victory and the majesty; for all that is in heaven and in earth is Yours; yours is the kingdom, O LORD, and You are exalted as head over all."

A friend of mine gave me a customized framed quote for my office. I guess he must have felt that I needed it. It read:

Dennis:

Trust Me. I have everything under control.

Jesus

I've read that quote on more than one occasion when I needed to be reminded of the truth—He is in control.

Yet this same sovereign Lord seeks a close relationship with us. As the following two passages tell us, He is our Comforter during times of distress and suffering:

- "The LORD is near to the brokenhearted and saves those who are crushed in spirit" (Ps. 34:18).
- "Fear not, for I am with you, be not dismayed, for I am your God; I will strengthen you, I will help you, I will uphold you with my victorious right hand" (Is. 41:10).

When you remember Who is in control, you will realize that your life is never really out of control.

---

bronze, and one hundred thousand talents of iron. [8]And whoever had *precious* stones gave *them* to the treasury of the house of the LORD, into the hand of Jehiel[a] the Gershonite. [9]Then the people rejoiced, for they had offered willingly, because with a loyal heart they had offered willingly to the LORD; and King David also rejoiced greatly.

David's Praise to God

[10]Therefore David blessed the LORD before all the assembly; and David said:

"Blessed are You, LORD God of Israel,
    our Father, forever and ever.
[11]   Yours, O LORD, *is* the greatness,
    The power and the glory,
    The victory and the majesty;
    For all *that is* in heaven and in earth
        is Yours;
    Yours *is* the kingdom, O LORD,
    And You are exalted as head over all.
[12]   Both riches and honor *come* from You,
    And You reign over all.
    In Your hand *is* power and might;
    In Your hand *it is* to make great
    And to give strength to all.

[13] "Now therefore, our God,
    We thank You
    And praise Your glorious name.
[14]   But who *am* I, and who *are* my
        people,
    That we should be able to offer so
        willingly as this?
    For all things *come* from You,
    And of Your own we have given You.
[15]   For we *are* aliens and pilgrims before
        You,
    As *were* all our fathers;
    Our days on earth *are* as a shadow,
    And without hope.

[16]"O LORD our God, all this abundance that we have prepared to build You a house for Your holy name is from Your hand, and *is* all Your own. [17]I know also, my God, that You test the heart and have pleasure in uprightness. As for me, in the uprightness of my heart I have willingly offered all these *things;* and now with joy I have seen Your people, who are present here to offer

---

of thousands and of hundreds, with the officers over the king's work, offered willingly. [7]They gave for the work of the house of God five thousand talents and ten thousand darics of gold, ten thousand talents of silver, eighteen thousand talents of

29:8 [a]Possibly the same as *Jehieli* (compare 26:21, 22)

willingly to You. ¹⁸O LORD God of Abraham, Isaac, and Israel, our fathers, keep this forever in the intent of the thoughts of the heart of Your people, and fix their heart toward You. ¹⁹And give my son Solomon a loyal heart to keep Your commandments and Your testimonies and Your statutes, to do all *these things,* and to build the temple^a for which I have made provision."

²⁰Then David said to all the assembly, "Now bless the LORD your God." So all the assembly blessed the LORD God of their fathers, and bowed their heads and prostrated themselves before the LORD and the king.

Solomon Anointed King

²¹And they made sacrifices to the LORD and offered burnt offerings to the LORD on the next day: a thousand bulls, a thousand rams, a thousand lambs, with their drink offerings, and sacrifices in abundance for all Israel. ²²So they ate and drank before the LORD with great gladness on that day. And they made Solomon the son of David king the second time, and anointed *him* before the LORD *to be* the leader, and Zadok *to be* priest. ²³Then Solomon sat on the throne of the LORD as king instead of David his father, and prospered; and all Israel obeyed him. ²⁴All the leaders and the mighty men, and also all the sons of King David, submitted themselves to King Solomon. ²⁵So the LORD exalted Solomon exceedingly in the sight of all Israel, and bestowed on him *such* royal majesty as had not been on any king before him in Israel.

The Close of David's Reign

²⁶Thus David the son of Jesse reigned over all Israel. ²⁷And the period that he reigned over Israel *was* forty years; seven years he reigned in Hebron, and thirty-three *years* he reigned in Jerusalem. ²⁸So he died in a good old age, full of days and riches and

BIBLICAL INSIGHTS • 29:17

The Look of Character

NEAR THE CLOSE OF HIS REIGN, King David prayed, "I know also, my God, that You test the heart and have pleasure in uprightness. As for me, in the uprightness of my heart I have willingly offered all these things; and now with joy I have seen Your people, who are present here to offer willingly to You" (29:17).

When King David used the word "uprightness" in his prayer, he was talking about what we often call character—godly character—which we can define as doing what is right simply because it is the right thing to do.

Character helps keep us within our budget.

Character leads us to turn to God in a time of hardship and pain.

Character helps us pursue our mates to resolve a major conflict in a loving manner.

Character enables us to make that extra phone call or work that extra hour to do our jobs right.

Character directs us in times of material prosperity and in a financial crisis.

And character gives us the strength to keep our minds and bodies pure when everyone in the world and everything within us says, "Just give in to that temptation. It won't hurt you."

honor; and Solomon his son reigned in his place. ²⁹Now the acts of King David, first and last, indeed they *are* written in the book of Samuel the seer, in the book of Nathan the prophet, and in the book of Gad the seer, ³⁰with all his reign and his might, and the events that happened to him, to Israel, and to all the kingdoms of the lands.

2 CHRONICLES

THIS SECOND HALF OF THE ALTERNATE BIBLICAL ACCOUNT of God's faithfulness to His people, covering a period from the time of Solomon to the end of the seventy-year Babylonian exile, provides us with additional insights into how the Lord deals with His much-loved but frequently fickle people. The writer (the same person who wrote 1 Chronicles, probably Ezra the Scribe) fills in details not found in 1 and 2 Samuel or 1 and 2 Kings about the history of the Israelites throughout the era of the divided kingdom. He pays particular attention to the building of the temple (chapters 3—7) and the activities of the priests.

The writer wants to present his readers with more than just the facts. He often assumes his readers know the details of the accounts he is recording and instead focuses on interpreting those facts in such a way that his readers can see God's hand at work in the life of God's people. At the end of 2 Chronicles, for example, the writer provides an explanation for the calamity brought on Israel by the Babylonians, "And the LORD God of their fathers sent warnings to them by His messengers, rising up early and sending them, because He had compassion on His people and on His dwelling place. But they mocked the messengers of God, despised His words, and scoffed at His prophets, until the wrath of the LORD arose against His people, till there was no remedy" (36:15, 16). But he is also quick to say that God restored His people after the seventy years of captivity prophesied by Jeremiah the prophet, a time ordained to give the land the Sabbath rest its people had long neglected (36:21).

If Ezra is the writer of 1 and 2 Chronicles, then his original readers likely would have been the very people involved in rebuilding the temple and reestablishing the priesthood. The Chronicler wants to draw his readers' attention to how God works through godly men to govern His people—surely chastened, but certainly still His—and how they are to respond to and honor Him in worship.

Solomon Requests Wisdom

1 Now Solomon the son of David was strengthened in his kingdom, and the LORD his God *was* with him and exalted him exceedingly.

2And Solomon spoke to all Israel, to the captains of thousands and of hundreds, to the judges, and to every leader in all Israel, the heads of the fathers' *houses*. 3Then Solomon, and all the assembly with him, went to the high place that *was* at Gibeon; for the tabernacle of meeting with God was there, which Moses the servant of the LORD had made in the wilderness. 4But David had brought up the ark of God from Kirjath Jearim to *the place* David had prepared for it, for he had pitched a tent for it at Jerusalem. 5Now the bronze altar that Bezalel the son of Uri, the son of Hur, had made, he puta before the tabernacle of the LORD; Solomon and the assembly sought Him *there*. 6And Solomon went up there to the bronze altar before the LORD, which *was* at the tabernacle of meeting, and offered a thousand burnt offerings on it.

7On that night God appeared to Solomon, and said to him, "Ask! What shall I give you?"

8And Solomon said to God: "You have shown great mercy to David my father, and have made me king in his place. 9Now, O LORD God, let Your promise to David my father be established, for You have made me king over a people like the dust of the earth in multitude. 10Now give me wisdom and knowledge, that I may go out and come in before this people; for who can judge this great people of Yours?"

11Then God said to Solomon: "Because this was in your heart, and you have not asked riches or wealth or honor or the life of your enemies, nor have you asked long life—but have asked wisdom and knowledge for yourself, that you may judge My people over whom I have made you king— 12wisdom and knowledge *are* granted to you; and I will give you riches and wealth and honor, such as none of the kings have

had who *were* before you, nor shall any after you have the like."

Solomon's Military and Economic Power

13So Solomon came to Jerusalem from the high place that *was* at Gibeon, from before the tabernacle of meeting, and reigned over Israel. 14And Solomon gathered chariots and horsemen; he had one thousand four hundred chariots and twelve thousand horsemen, whom he stationed in the chariot cities and with the king in Jerusalem. 15Also the king made silver and gold as common in Jerusalem as stones, and he made cedars as abundant as the sycamores which *are* in the lowland. 16And Solomon had horses imported from Egypt and Keveh; the king's merchants bought them in Keveh at the *current* price. 17They also acquired and imported from Egypt a chariot for six hundred *shekels* of silver, and a horse for one hundred and fifty; thus, through their agents,a they exported them to all the kings of the Hittites and the kings of Syria.

Solomon Prepares to Build the Temple

2 Then Solomon determined to build a temple for the name of the LORD, and a royal house for himself. 2Solomon selected seventy thousand men to bear burdens, eighty thousand to quarry *stone* in the mountains, and three thousand six hundred to oversee them.

3Then Solomon sent to Hirama king of Tyre, saying:

As you have dealt with David my father, and sent him cedars to build himself a house to dwell in, *so deal with me.* 4Behold, I am building a temple for the name of the LORD my God, to dedicate *it* to Him, to burn before Him sweet incense, for the continual showbread, for the burnt offerings morning and evening, on the Sabbaths, on the New Moons, and on the set feasts of the LORD our God. This *is an ordinance* forever to Israel.

5 And the temple which I build *will be* great, for our God is greater than all gods. 6But who is able to build Him a temple, since heaven and the heaven

---

1:5 aSome authorities read *it was there.*
1:17 aLiterally *by their hands*
2:3 aHebrew *Huram* (compare 1 Kings 5:1)

of heavens cannot contain Him? Who *am* I then, that I should build Him a temple, except to burn sacrifice before Him?

7 Therefore send me at once a man skillful to work in gold and silver, in bronze and iron, in purple and crimson and blue, who has skill to engrave with the skillful men who are with me in Judah and Jerusalem, whom David my father provided. 8 Also send me cedar and cypress and algum logs from Lebanon, for I know that your servants have skill to cut timber in Lebanon; and indeed my servants *will be* with your servants, 9 to prepare timber for me in abundance,

---

ROMANCE FAQ

Q: My husband just made a big mistake. How should I handle it?

In our first month of marriage, Dennis took the initiative to make a small financial investment, and we ended up losing money. As we talked it over and I shared my disappointment, it was obvious Dennis knew he had made a poor choice.

At that point I faced a choice of my own: Would I accept him as my husband, or would I nag him and make him feel like a failure even more?

I realized that God had a plan for Dennis. He wanted to use this mistake to teach Dennis how to depend on Christ and be a better husband. I needed to get out of God's way and let Him work in my husband's life.

At times like this, a wife learns that love is not all feelings. This is where you honor your wedding vows and say, "I'm committed to you, no matter what." That's what real love is, and that's what a husband most needs from his wife—especially when he makes a big mistake. He *knows* he's failed; what he doesn't know is if you'll still accept him and respect him. Make sure you do!

for the temple which I am about to build *shall be* great and wonderful.

10 And indeed I will give to your servants, the woodsmen who cut timber, twenty thousand kors of ground wheat, twenty thousand kors of barley, twenty thousand baths of wine, and twenty thousand baths of oil.

11 Then Hiram king of Tyre answered in writing, which he sent to Solomon:

Because the LORD loves His people, He has made you king over them.

12 Hiram[a] also said:

Blessed *be* the LORD God of Israel, who made heaven and earth, for He has given King David a wise son, endowed with prudence and understanding, who will build a temple for the LORD and a royal house for himself!

13 And now I have sent a skillful man, endowed with understanding, Huram[a] my master[b] *craftsman* 14 (the son of a woman of the daughters of Dan, and his father was a man of Tyre), skilled to work in gold and silver, bronze and iron, stone and wood, purple and blue, fine linen and crimson, and to make any engraving and to accomplish any plan which may be given to him, with your skillful men and with the skillful men of my lord David your father.

15 Now therefore, the wheat, the barley, the oil, and the wine which my lord has spoken of, let him send to his servants. 16 And we will cut wood from Lebanon, as much as you need; we will bring it to you in rafts by sea to Joppa, and you will carry it up to Jerusalem.

17 Then Solomon numbered all the aliens who *were* in the land of Israel, after the census in which David his father had numbered them; and there were found to be one hundred and fifty-three thousand six

---

2:12 [a]Hebrew *Huram* (compare 1 Kings 5:1)
2:13 [a]Spelled *Hiram* in 1 Kings 7:13 [b]Literally *father* (compare 1 Kings 7:13, 14)

hundred. [18]And he made seventy thousand of them bearers of burdens, eighty thousand stonecutters in the mountain, and three thousand six hundred overseers to make the people work.

Solomon Builds the Temple

3 Now Solomon began to build the house of the LORD at Jerusalem on Mount Moriah, where *the LORD*[a] had appeared to his father David, at the place that David had prepared on the threshing floor of Ornan[b] the Jebusite. [2]And he began to build on the second *day* of the second month in the fourth year of his reign.

[3]This is the foundation which Solomon laid for building the house of God: The length *was* sixty cubits (by cubits according to the former measure) and the width twenty cubits. [4]And the vestibule that *was* in front *of the sanctuary*[a] was twenty cubits long across the width of the house, and the height *was* one hundred and[b] twenty. He overlaid the inside with pure gold. [5]The larger room[a] he paneled with cypress which he overlaid with fine gold, and he carved palm trees and chainwork on it. [6]And he decorated the house with precious stones for beauty, and the gold *was* gold from Parvaim. [7]He also overlaid the house—the beams and doorposts, its walls and doors—with gold; and he carved cherubim on the walls.

[8]And he made the Most Holy Place. Its length was according to the width of the house, twenty cubits, and its width twenty cubits. He overlaid it with six hundred talents of fine gold. [9]The weight of the nails *was* fifty shekels of gold; and he overlaid the upper area with gold. [10]In the Most Holy Place he made two cherubim, fashioned by carving, and overlaid them with gold. [11]The wings of the cherubim *were* twenty cubits in *overall* length: one wing *of the one cherub was* five cubits, touching the wall of the room, and the other wing *was* five cubits,

touching the wing of the other cherub; [12]*one* wing of the other cherub *was* five cubits, touching the wall of the room, and the other wing *also was* five cubits, touching the wing of the other cherub. [13]The wings of these cherubim spanned twenty cubits overall. They stood on their feet, and they faced inward. [14]And he made the veil of blue, purple, crimson, and fine linen, and wove cherubim into it.

[15]Also he made in front of the temple[a] two pillars thirty-five[b] cubits high, and the capital that *was* on the top of each of *them* was five cubits. [16]He made wreaths of chainwork, as in the inner sanctuary, and put *them* on top of the pillars; and he made one hundred pomegranates, and put *them* on the wreaths of chainwork. [17]Then he set up the pillars before the temple, one on the right hand and the other on the left; he called the name of the one on the right hand Jachin, and the name of the one on the left Boaz.

Furnishings of the Temple

4 Moreover he made a bronze altar: twenty cubits was its length, twenty cubits its width, and ten cubits its height.

INTIMATE MOMENTS
Create Your Own Drive-In

There aren't a lot of drive-in theaters across America any more, but so what? You can create your own.

Scout around for a romantic, remote location. Make sure it's safe. You want a place that you can transform it into your own drive-in movie location. And just to be sure, double check that your presence there at night won't cause any problems.

Then on the night you choose (probably best if it's dry, warm, and all around pleasant), take your wife in the car and drive to your chosen spot. Set up a portable DVD player in the front seat of the car, while you and your wife snuggle in the back seat and enjoy the tasty snacks and beverages you brought along.

3:1 [a]Literally *He,* following Masoretic Text and Vulgate; Septuagint reads *the LORD;* Targum reads *the Angel of the LORD.* [b]Spelled *Araunah* in 2 Samuel 24:16ff   **3:4** [a]The main room of the temple; elsewhere called the holy place (compare 1 Kings 6:3) [b]Following Masoretic Text, Septuagint, and Vulgate; Arabic, some manuscripts of the Septuagint, and Syriac omit *one hundred and.*   **3:5** [a]Literally *house* **3:15** [a]Literally *house* [b]Or *eighteen* (compare 1 Kings 7:15; 2 Kings 25:17; and Jeremiah 52:21)

²Then he made the Sea of cast *bronze,* ten cubits from one brim to the other; *it was* completely round. Its height *was* five cubits, and a line of thirty cubits measured its circumference. ³And under it *was* the likeness of oxen encircling it all around, ten to a cubit, all the way around the Sea. The oxen *were* cast in two rows, when it was cast. ⁴It stood on twelve oxen: three looking toward the north, three looking toward the west, three looking toward the south, and three looking toward the east; the Sea *was set* upon them, and all their back parts *pointed* inward. ⁵It *was* a handbreadth thick; and its brim was shaped like the brim of a cup, *like* a lily blossom. It contained three thousandᵃ baths.

⁶He also made ten lavers, and put five on the right side and five on the left, to wash in them; such things as they offered for the burnt offering they would wash in them, but the Sea *was* for the priests to wash in. ⁷And he made ten lampstands of gold according to their design, and set *them* in the temple, five on the right side and five on the left. ⁸He also made ten tables, and placed *them* in the temple, five on the right side and five on the left. And he made one hundred bowls of gold.

⁹Furthermore he made the court of the priests, and the great court and doors for the court; and he overlaid these doors with bronze. ¹⁰He set the Sea on the right side, toward the southeast.

¹¹Then Huram made the pots and the shovels and the bowls. So Huram finished doing the work that he was to do for King Solomon for the house of God: ¹²the two pillars and the bowl-shaped capitals *that were* on top of the two pillars; the two networks covering the two bowl-shaped capitals which *were* on top of the pillars; ¹³four hundred pomegranates for the two networks (two rows of pomegranates for each network, to cover the two bowl-shaped capitals that *were* on the pillars); ¹⁴he also made carts and the lavers on the carts; ¹⁵one Sea and twelve oxen under it; ¹⁶also the pots, the shovels, the forks—and all their articles Huram his masterᵃ *craftsman* made of burnished bronze for King Solomon for the house of the LORD.

¹⁷In the plain of Jordan the king had them cast in clay molds, between Succoth and Zeredah.ᵃ ¹⁸And Solomon had all these articles made in such great abundance that the weight of the bronze was not determined.

¹⁹Thus Solomon had all the furnishings made for the house of God: the altar of gold and the tables on which *was* the showbread; ²⁰the lampstands with their lamps of pure gold, to burn in the prescribed manner in front of the inner sanctuary, ²¹with the flowers and the lamps and the wick-trimmers of gold, of purest gold; ²²the trimmers, the bowls, the ladles, and the censers of pure gold. As for the entry of the sanctuary, its inner doors to the Most Holy *Place,* and the doors of the main hall of the temple, *were* gold.

5 So all the work that Solomon had done for the house of the LORD was finished; and Solomon brought in the things which his father David had dedicated: the silver and the gold and all the furnishings. And he put *them* in the treasuries of the house of God.

The Ark Brought into the Temple

²Now Solomon assembled the elders of Israel and all the heads of the tribes, the chief fathers of the children of Israel, in Jerusalem, that they might bring the ark of the covenant of the LORD up from the City of David, which *is* Zion. ³Therefore all the men of Israel assembled with the king at the feast, which *was* in the seventh month. ⁴So all the elders of Israel came, and the Levites took up the ark. ⁵Then they brought up the ark, the tabernacle of meeting, and all the holy furnishings that *were* in the tabernacle. The priests and the Levites brought them up. ⁶Also King Solomon, and all the congregation of Israel who were assembled with him before the ark, were sacrificing sheep and oxen that could not be counted or numbered for multitude. ⁷Then the priests brought in the ark of the covenant of the LORD to its place, into the inner sanctuary of the temple,ᵃ to the Most Holy *Place,* under the wings of the cherubim. ⁸For the cherubim spread *their* wings over the place

---

4:5 ᵃOr *two thousand* (compare 1 Kings 7:26)
4:16 ᵃLiterally *father* **4:17** ᵃSpelled *Zaretan* in 1 Kings 7:46 **5:7** ᵃLiterally *house*

of the ark, and the cherubim overshadowed the ark and its poles. [9]The poles extended so that the ends of the poles of the ark could be seen from *the holy place,* in front of the inner sanctuary; but they could not be seen from outside. And they are there to this day. [10]Nothing was in the ark except the two tablets which Moses put *there* at Horeb, when the LORD made *a covenant* with the children of Israel, when they had come out of Egypt.

[11]And it came to pass when the priests came out of the *Most* Holy *Place* (for all the priests who *were* present had sanctified themselves, without keeping to their divisions), [12]and the Levites *who were* the singers, all those of Asaph and Heman and Jeduthun, with their sons and their brethren, stood at the east end of the altar, clothed in white linen, having cymbals, stringed instruments and harps, and with them one hundred and twenty priests sounding with trumpets— [13]indeed it came to pass, when the trumpeters and singers *were* as one, to make one sound to be heard in praising and thanking the LORD, and when they lifted up their voice with the trumpets and cymbals and instruments of music, and praised the LORD, *saying:*

"*For He is* good,
   For His mercy *endures* forever,"[a]

that the house, the house of the LORD, was filled with a cloud, [14]so that the priests could not continue ministering because of the cloud; for the glory of the LORD filled the house of God.

6 Then Solomon spoke:

"The LORD said He would dwell in the dark cloud.
[2]   I have surely built You an exalted house,
   And a place for You to dwell in forever."

Solomon's Speech upon Completion of the Work

[3]Then the king turned around and blessed the whole assembly of Israel, while all the assembly of Israel was standing. [4]And he said: "Blessed *be* the LORD God of Israel, who has fulfilled with His hands *what* He spoke with His mouth to my father David, saying, [5]'Since the day that I brought My people out of the land of Egypt, I have chosen no city from any tribe of Israel *in which* to build a house, that My name might be there, nor did I choose any man to be a ruler over My people Israel. [6]Yet I have chosen Jerusalem, that My name may be there, and I have chosen David to be over My people Israel.' [7]Now it was in the heart of my father David to build a temple[a] for the name of the LORD God of Israel. [8]But the LORD said to my father David, 'Whereas it was in your heart to build a temple for My name, you did well in that it was in your heart. [9]Nevertheless you shall not build the temple, but your son who will come from your body, he shall build the temple for My name.' [10]So the LORD has fulfilled His word which He spoke, and I have filled the position of my father David, and sit on the throne of Israel, as the LORD promised; and I have built the temple for the name of the LORD God of Israel. [11]And there I have put the ark, in which *is* the covenant of the LORD which He made with the children of Israel."

Solomon's Prayer of Dedication

[12]Then *Solomon*[a] stood before the altar of the LORD in the presence of all the assembly of Israel, and spread out his hands [13](for Solomon had made a bronze platform five cubits long, five cubits wide, and three cubits high, and had set it in the midst of the court; and he stood on it, knelt down on his knees before all the assembly of Israel, and spread out his hands toward heaven); [14]and he said: "LORD God of Israel, *there is* no God in heaven or on earth like You, who keep *Your* covenant and mercy with Your servants who walk before You with all their hearts. [15]You have kept what You promised Your servant David my father; You have both spoken with Your mouth and fulfilled *it* with Your hand, as *it is* this day. [16]Therefore, LORD God of Israel, now keep what You promised Your servant David my father, saying, 'You shall not fail to have a man sit before Me on the throne of Israel,

---

5:13 [a]Compare Psalm 106:1 **6:7** [a]Literally *house,* and so in verses 8–10 **6:12** [a]Literally *he* (compare 1 Kings 8:22)

BIBLICAL INSIGHTS • 6:37

From out There to in Here

GOD MUST WORK *IN* US before he can work *through* us. We must allow Him to touch us in the deepest part of our hearts before we can expect Him to use us to positively affect the world around us. This means that we must change our mindset from out there to in here.

That was a main point of King Solomon's great prayer as he stood before the people to dedicate the Temple. He imagined a time in the future when Israel as a nation had wandered away from God, and declared only a single remedy for their troubles, that "they come to themselves in the land where they were carried captive" (6:37). The New International Version translates the phrase, "come to themselves" as "change of heart."

I deeply appreciate the work of the Spirit of God in my heart, for He makes the real issues of my life crystal clear. I realize that the beginning, the flash point, for any kind of transformation in a family is individual and personal repentance, which is an intensely personal matter. Prompted by the Holy Spirit, I repent, and in doing so I acknowledge that any spiritual renovation in our family needs to begin as a spiritual change in my own heart.

Do you want to have a marriage and family that is all God intended it to be, that is spiritually alive, and that truly represents Jesus Christ? This is where it begins—in your heart.

---

only if your sons take heed to their way, that they walk in My law as you have walked before Me.' [17]And now, O LORD God of Israel, let Your word come true, which You have spoken to Your servant David.

[18]"But will God indeed dwell with men on the earth? Behold, heaven and the heaven of heavens cannot contain You. How much less this temple[a] which I have built! [19]Yet regard the prayer of Your servant and his supplication, O LORD my God, and listen to the cry and the prayer which Your servant is praying before You: [20]that Your eyes may be open toward this temple day and night, toward the place where *You* said *You would* put Your name, that You may hear the prayer which Your servant makes toward this place. [21]And may You hear the supplications of Your servant and of Your people Israel, when they pray toward this place. Hear from heaven Your dwelling place, and when You hear, forgive.

[22]"If anyone sins against his neighbor, and is forced to take an oath, and comes *and* takes an oath before Your altar in this temple, [23]then hear from heaven, and act, and judge Your servants, bringing retribution on the wicked by bringing his way on his own head, and justifying the righteous by giving him according to his righteousness.

[24]"Or if Your people Israel are defeated before an enemy because they have sinned against You, and return and confess Your name, and pray and make supplication before You in this temple, [25]then hear from heaven and forgive the sin of Your people Israel, and bring them back to the land which You gave to them and their fathers.

[26]"When the heavens are shut up and there is no rain because they have sinned against You, when they pray toward this place and confess Your name, and turn from their sin because You afflict them, [27]then hear *in* heaven, and forgive the sin of Your servants, Your people Israel, that You may teach them the good way in which they should walk; and send rain on Your land which You have given to Your people as an inheritance.

[28]"When there is famine in the land, pestilence or blight or mildew, locusts or grasshoppers; when their enemies besiege them in the land of their cities; whatever plague or whatever sickness *there is;* [29]whatever prayer, whatever supplication is *made* by anyone, or by all Your people Israel, when each one knows his own burden and his own grief, and spreads out his hands to this temple: [30]then hear from heaven Your dwelling place, and forgive, and give to everyone according to all his ways, whose heart You know (for You alone know the hearts of the sons of men), [31]that they may

---

6:18 [a]Literally *house*

fear You, to walk in Your ways as long as they live in the land which You gave to our fathers.

³²"Moreover, concerning a foreigner, who is not of Your people Israel, but has come from a far country for the sake of Your great name and Your mighty hand and Your outstretched arm, when they come and pray in this temple; ³³then hear from heaven Your dwelling place, and do according to all for which the foreigner calls to You, that all peoples of the earth may know Your name and fear You, as *do* Your people Israel, and that they may know that this temple which I have built is called by Your name.

³⁴"When Your people go out to battle against their enemies, wherever You send them, and when they pray to You toward this city which You have chosen and the temple which I have built for Your name, ³⁵then hear from heaven their prayer and their supplication, and maintain their cause.

³⁶"When they sin against You (for *there is* no one who does not sin), and You become angry with them and deliver them to the enemy, and they take them captive to a land far or near; ³⁷yet when they come to themselves in the land where they were carried captive, and repent, and make supplication to You in the land of their captivity, saying, 'We have sinned, we have done wrong, and have committed wickedness'; ³⁸and *when* they return to You with all their heart and with all their soul in the land of their captivity, where they have been carried captive, and pray toward their land which You gave to their fathers, the city which You have chosen, and toward the temple which I have built for Your name: ³⁹then hear from heaven Your dwelling place their prayer and their supplications, and maintain their cause, and forgive Your people who have sinned against You. ⁴⁰Now, my God, I pray, let Your eyes be open and *let* Your ears *be* attentive to the prayer *made* in this place.

⁴¹ "Now therefore,
Arise, O Lord God, to Your resting place,
You and the ark of Your strength.

Let Your priests, O Lord God, be
clothed with salvation,
And let Your saints rejoice in
goodness.

⁴² "O Lord God, do not turn away the
face of Your Anointed;
Remember the mercies of Your
servant David."^a

Solomon Dedicates the Temple

7 When Solomon had finished praying, fire came down from heaven and consumed the burnt offering and the sacrifices; and the glory of the Lord filled the temple.^a ²And the priests could not enter the house of the Lord, because the glory of the Lord had filled the Lord's house. ³When all the children of Israel saw how the fire came down, and the glory of the Lord on the temple, they bowed their faces to the ground on the pavement, and worshiped and praised the Lord, *saying:*

"For *He is* good,
For His mercy *endures* forever."^a

⁴Then the king and all the people offered sacrifices before the Lord. ⁵King Solomon offered a sacrifice of twenty-two thousand bulls and one hundred and twenty thousand sheep. So the king and all the people dedicated the house of God. ⁶And the priests attended to their services; the Levites also with instruments of the music of the Lord, which King David had made to praise the Lord, saying, "For His mercy *endures* forever,"^a whenever David offered praise by their ministry. The priests sounded trumpets opposite them, while all Israel stood.

⁷Furthermore Solomon consecrated the middle of the court that *was* in front of the house of the Lord; for there he offered burnt offerings and the fat of the peace offerings, because the bronze altar which Solomon had made was not able to receive the burnt offerings, the grain offerings, and the fat.

⁸At that time Solomon kept the feast seven days, and all Israel with him, a very great assembly from the entrance of Hamath to the Brook of Egypt.^a ⁹And on the eighth day they held a sacred assembly, for they observed the dedication of the altar seven

---

6:42 ^aCompare Psalm 132:8–10 **7:1** ^aLiterally *house*
7:3 ^aCompare Psalm 106:1 **7:6** ^aCompare Psalm 106:1
7:8 ^aThat is, the Shihor (compare 1 Chronicles 13:5)

BIBLICAL INSIGHTS • 7:14
Healing Begins at Home

THE WELL-KNOWN promise of 2 Chronicles 7:14 is what we call a conditional promise, meaning that God has told us that in order to receive the blessing, we need to do something. In this case, God asked His people to humble themselves, pray, seek Him, and turn from their sins with a heart of repentance. If they would do those things, He promised to hear them, forgive them and heal their land.

True reformation and revival will never come to any nation until we finally admit we are helpless and hopeless, confess our sins, and join together in pleading with God to defend us. If we don't repent, and if God doesn't heal our land, then I fear for my children as they get married and raise their children.

As individuals and as couples, we need to ask God to expose the sin, evil, and wickedness first in our homes, and then in the world around us. Then we need to ask Him to heal our homes, our neighborhoods, our cities, and our nation of its sin, sickness, and violence. He wants to do it—He is simply waiting for us to want it, too.

---

days, and the feast seven days. ¹⁰On the twenty-third day of the seventh month he sent the people away to their tents, joyful and glad of heart for the good that the LORD had done for David, for Solomon, and for His people Israel. ¹¹Thus Solomon finished the house of the LORD and the king's house; and Solomon successfully accomplished all that came into his heart to make in the house of the LORD and in his own house.

God's Second Appearance to Solomon

¹²Then the LORD appeared to Solomon by night, and said to him: "I have heard your prayer, and have chosen this place for Myself as a house of sacrifice. ¹³When I shut up heaven and there is no rain, or command the locusts to devour the land, or send pestilence among My people, ¹⁴if My people who are called by My name will humble themselves, and pray and seek My face, and turn from their wicked ways, then I will hear from heaven, and will forgive their sin and heal their land. ¹⁵Now My eyes will be open and My ears attentive to prayer *made* in this place. ¹⁶For now I have chosen and sanctified this house, that My name may be there forever; and My eyes and My heart will be there perpetually. ¹⁷As for you, if you walk before Me as your father David walked, and do according to all that I have commanded you, and if you keep My statutes and My judgments, ¹⁸then I will establish the throne of your kingdom, as I covenanted with David your father, saying, 'You shall not fail *to have* a man as ruler in Israel.'

¹⁹"But if you turn away and forsake My statutes and My commandments which I have set before you, and go and serve other gods, and worship them, ²⁰then I will uproot them from My land which I have given them; and this house which I have sanctified for My name I will cast out of My sight, and will make it a proverb and a byword among all peoples.

²¹"And *as for* this house, which is exalted, everyone who passes by it will be astonished and say, 'Why has the LORD done thus to this land and this house?' ²²Then they will answer, 'Because they forsook the LORD God of their fathers, who brought them out of the land of Egypt, and embraced other gods, and worshiped them and served them; therefore He has brought all this calamity on them.'"

Solomon's Additional Achievements

8 It came to pass at the end of twenty years, when Solomon had built the house of the LORD and his own house, ²that the cities which Hiramᵃ had given to Solomon, Solomon built them; and he settled the children of Israel there. ³And Solomon went to Hamath Zobah and seized it. ⁴He also built Tadmor in the wilderness, and all the storage cities which he built in Hamath. ⁵He built Upper Beth Horon and Lower Beth Horon, fortified cities *with* walls,

---

8:2 ᵃHebrew *Huram* (compare 2 Chronicles 2:3)

gates, and bars, [6]also Baalath and all the storage cities that Solomon had, and all the chariot cities and the cities of the cavalry, and all that Solomon desired to build in Jerusalem, in Lebanon, and in all the land of his dominion.

[7]All the people *who were* left of the Hittites, Amorites, Perizzites, Hivites, and Jebusites, who *were* not of Israel— [8]that is, their descendants who were left in the land after them, whom the children of Israel did not destroy—from these Solomon raised forced labor, as it is to this day. [9]But Solomon did not make the children of Israel servants for his work. Some *were* men of war, captains of his officers, captains of his chariots, and his cavalry. [10]And others *were* chiefs of the officials of King Solomon: two hundred and fifty, who ruled over the people.

[11]Now Solomon brought the daughter of Pharaoh up from the City of David to the house he had built for her, for he said, "My wife shall not dwell in the house of David king of Israel, because *the places* to which the ark of the LORD has come are holy."

[12]Then Solomon offered burnt offerings to the LORD on the altar of the LORD which he had built before the vestibule, [13]according to the daily rate, offering according to the commandment of Moses, for the Sabbaths, the New Moons, and the three appointed yearly feasts—the Feast of Unleavened Bread, the Feast of Weeks, and the Feast of Tabernacles. [14]And, according to the order of David his father, he appointed the divisions of the priests for their service, the Levites for their duties (to praise and serve before the priests) as the duty of each day required, and the gatekeepers by their divisions at each gate; for so David the man of God had commanded. [15]They did not depart from the command of the king to the priests and Levites concerning any matter or concerning the treasuries.

[16]Now all the work of Solomon was well-ordered from[a] the day of the foundation of the house of the LORD until it was finished. So the house of the LORD was completed.

[17]Then Solomon went to Ezion Geber and Elath[a] on the seacoast, in the land of Edom. [18]And Hiram sent him ships by the hand of his servants, and servants who knew the sea. They went with the servants of Solomon to Ophir, and acquired four hundred and fifty talents of gold from there, and brought it to King Solomon.

INTIMATE MOMENTS

For a significant anniversary, buy him a handsome gold watch. Engrave it with a romantic phrase such as, "I'll always have time for you." Present it to him in a beautifully-wrapped box, and then make sure that you have time for him *right then.*

The Queen of Sheba's Praise of Solomon

9 Now when the queen of Sheba heard of the fame of Solomon, she came to Jerusalem to test Solomon with hard questions, *having* a very great retinue, camels that bore spices, gold in abundance, and precious stones; and when she came to Solomon, she spoke with him about all that was in her heart. [2]So Solomon answered all her questions; there was nothing so difficult for Solomon that he could not explain it to her. [3]And when the queen of Sheba had seen the wisdom of Solomon, the house that he had built, [4]the food on his table, the seating of his servants, the service of his waiters and their apparel, his cupbearers and their apparel, and his entryway by which he went up to the house of the LORD, there was no more spirit in her.

[5]Then she said to the king: "*It was* a true report which I heard in my own land about your words and your wisdom. [6]However I did not believe their words until I came and saw with my own eyes; and indeed the half of the greatness of your wisdom was not told me. You exceed the fame of which I heard. [7]Happy *are* your men and happy *are* these your servants, who stand continually before you and hear your wisdom! [8]Blessed be the LORD your God, who delighted in you, setting you on His throne *to be* king

---

8:16 [a]Following Septuagint, Syriac, and Vulgate; Masoretic Text reads *as far as.* **8:17** [a]Hebrew *Eloth* (compare 2 Kings 14:22)

for the LORD your God! Because your God has loved Israel, to establish them forever, therefore He made you king over them, to do justice and righteousness."

⁹And she gave the king one hundred and twenty talents of gold, spices in great abundance, and precious stones; there never were any spices such as those the queen of Sheba gave to King Solomon.

¹⁰Also, the servants of Hiram and the servants of Solomon, who brought gold from Ophir, brought algumᵃ wood and precious stones. ¹¹And the king made walkways *of* the algumᵃ wood for the house of the LORD and for the king's house, also harps and stringed instruments for singers; and there were none such *as these* seen before in the land of Judah.

¹²Now King Solomon gave to the queen of Sheba all she desired, whatever she asked, *much more* than she had brought to the king. So she turned and went to her own country, she and her servants.

Solomon's Great Wealth

¹³The weight of gold that came to Solomon yearly was six hundred and sixty-six talents of gold, ¹⁴besides *what* the traveling merchants and traders brought. And all the kings of Arabia and governors of the country brought gold and silver to Solomon. ¹⁵And King Solomon made two hundred large shields of hammered gold; six hundred *shekels* of hammered gold went into each shield. ¹⁶He also *made* three hundred shields of hammered gold; three hundred *shekels*ᵃ of gold went into each shield. The king put them in the House of the Forest of Lebanon.

¹⁷Moreover the king made a great throne of ivory, and overlaid it with pure gold. ¹⁸The throne *had* six steps, with a footstool of gold, *which were* fastened to the throne; there were armrests on either side of the place of the seat, and two lions stood beside the armrests. ¹⁹Twelve lions stood there, one on each side of the six steps; nothing like *this* had been made for any *other* kingdom.

²⁰All King Solomon's drinking vessels *were* gold, and all the vessels of the House of the Forest of Lebanon *were* pure gold. Not *one was* silver, for this was accounted

as nothing in the days of Solomon. ²¹For the king's ships went to Tarshish with the servants of Hiram.ᵃ Once every three years the merchant shipsᵇ came, bringing gold, silver, ivory, apes, and monkeys.ᶜ

²²So King Solomon surpassed all the kings of the earth in riches and wisdom. ²³And all the kings of the earth sought the presence of Solomon to hear his wisdom, which God had put in his heart. ²⁴Each man brought his present: articles of silver and gold, garments, armor, spices, horses, and mules, at a set rate year by year.

²⁵Solomon had four thousand stalls for horses and chariots, and twelve thousand horsemen whom he stationed in the chariot cities and with the king at Jerusalem.

²⁶So he reigned over all the kings from the Riverᵃ to the land of the Philistines, as far as the border of Egypt. ²⁷The king made silver *as common* in Jerusalem as stones, and he made cedar trees as abundant as the sycamores which *are* in the lowland. ²⁸And they brought horses to Solomon from Egypt and from all lands.

Death of Solomon

²⁹Now the rest of the acts of Solomon, first and last, *are* they not written in the book of Nathan the prophet, in the prophecy of Ahijah the Shilonite, and in the visions of Iddo the seer concerning Jeroboam the son of Nebat? ³⁰Solomon reigned in Jerusalem over all Israel forty years. ³¹Then Solomon rested with his fathers, and was buried in the City of David his father. And Rehoboam his son reigned in his place.

The Revolt Against Rehoboam

10 And Rehoboam went to Shechem, for all Israel had gone to Shechem to make him king. ²So it happened, when Jeroboam the son of Nebat heard *it* (he was in Egypt, where he had fled from the presence of King Solomon), that Jeroboam returned from Egypt. ³Then they sent for him and called him. And Jeroboam and all

---

9:10 ᵃOr *almug* (compare 1 Kings 10:11, 12)
9:11 ᵃOr *almug* (compare 1 Kings 10:11, 12)
9:16 ᵃOr *three minas* (compare 1 Kings 10:17)
9:21 ᵃHebrew *Huram* (compare 1 Kings 10:22)
 ᵇLiterally *ships of Tarshish* (deep-sea vessels)
 ᶜOr *peacocks* **9:26** ᵃThat is, the Euphrates

Israel came and spoke to Rehoboam, saying, [4]"Your father made our yoke heavy; now therefore, lighten the burdensome service of your father and his heavy yoke which he put on us, and we will serve you."

[5]So he said to them, "Come back to me after three days." And the people departed.

[6]Then King Rehoboam consulted the elders who stood before his father Solomon while he still lived, saying, "How do you advise me to answer these people?"

[7]And they spoke to him, saying, "If you are kind to these people, and please them, and speak good words to them, they will be your servants forever."

[8]But he rejected the advice which the elders had given him, and consulted the young men who had grown up with him, who stood before him. [9]And he said to them, "What advice do you give? How should we answer this people who have spoken to me, saying, 'Lighten the yoke which your father put on us'?"

[10]Then the young men who had grown up with him spoke to him, saying, "Thus you should speak to the people who have spoken to you, saying, 'Your father made our yoke heavy, but you make it lighter on us'—thus you shall say to them: 'My little finger shall be thicker than my father's waist! [11]And now, whereas my father put a heavy yoke on you, I will add to your yoke; my father chastised you with whips, but I will chastise you with scourges!' "[a]

[12]So Jeroboam and all the people came to Rehoboam on the third day, as the king had directed, saying, "Come back to me the third day." [13]Then the king answered them roughly. King Rehoboam rejected the advice of the elders, [14]and he spoke to them according to the advice of the young men, saying, "My father[a] made your yoke heavy, but I will add to it; my father chastised you with whips, but I will chastise you with scourges!"[b] [15]So the king did not listen to the people; for the turn of events was from God, that the LORD might fulfill His word, which

---

10:11 [a]Literally *scorpions* 10:14 [a]Following many Hebrew manuscripts, Septuagint, Syriac, and Vulgate (compare verse 10 and 1 Kings 12:14); Masoretic Text reads *I*. [b]Literally *scorpions*

PARENTING MATTERS

Q: *What does it mean to set boundaries for our children?*

Setting boundaries takes courage—you certainly won't win any popularity contests with your children. But your children don't need buddies or chums; they need spiritual and moral leaders, parents who love them enough to occasionally cramp their style.

So how do you set boundaries? I would begin by prayerfully discussing what *your* boundaries will be. Most parents don't fully realize how their choices reflect their values . . . until they have children! As a couple, discuss and decide what your boundaries will be around the following topics:

- What are we going to drink?
- What magazines and books are we going to read?
- What movies and television shows will we view?
- What music will we listen to?
- Will we allow profanity in our home?
- Are we going to obey the law? Speed limits?

At this point I can hear you saying, "Hold it...why do you keep saying 'we'? I thought you were going to help me with my children!" I just did.

One problem in Christian families today is that many parents fail to establish limits in their own lives. You need to set standards for your kids that you will keep yourself. Otherwise, your children ask, "Why should I live by a standard that you ignore?" Boundaries begin with you—with *your* choices and *your* limits.

He had spoken by the hand of Ahijah the Shilonite to Jeroboam the son of Nebat.

[16]Now when all Israel *saw* that the king did not listen to them, the people answered the king, saying:

"What share have we in David?
We have no inheritance in the son of Jesse.
Every man to your tents, O Israel!
Now see to your own house,
O David!"

So all Israel departed to their tents. [17]But Rehoboam reigned over the children of Israel who dwelt in the cities of Judah.

[18]Then King Rehoboam sent Hadoram, who *was* in charge of revenue; but the children of Israel stoned him with stones, and he died. Therefore King Rehoboam mounted *his* chariot in haste to flee to Jerusalem. [19]So Israel has been in rebellion against the house of David to this day.

11 Now when Rehoboam came to Jerusalem, he assembled from the house of Judah and Benjamin one hundred and eighty thousand chosen *men* who were warriors, to fight against Israel, that he might restore the kingdom to Rehoboam.

[2]But the word of the LORD came to Shemaiah the man of God, saying, [3]"Speak to Rehoboam the son of Solomon, king of Judah, and to all Israel in Judah and Benjamin, saying, [4]'Thus says the LORD: "You shall not go up or fight against your brethren! Let every man return to his house, for this thing is from Me."'" Therefore they obeyed the words of the LORD, and turned back from attacking Jeroboam.

Rehoboam Fortifies the Cities

[5]So Rehoboam dwelt in Jerusalem, and built cities for defense in Judah. [6]And he built Bethlehem, Etam, Tekoa, [7]Beth Zur, Sochoh, Adullam, [8]Gath, Mareshah, Ziph, [9]Adoraim, Lachish, Azekah, [10]Zorah, Aijalon, and Hebron, which are in Judah and Benjamin, fortified cities. [11]And he fortified the strongholds, and put captains in them, and stores of food, oil, and wine. [12]Also in every city *he put* shields and spears, and made them very strong, having Judah and Benjamin on his side.

Priests and Levites Move to Judah

[13]And from all their territories the priests and the Levites who *were* in all Israel took their stand with him. [14]For the Levites left their common-lands and their possessions and came to Judah and Jerusalem, for Jeroboam and his sons had rejected them from serving as priests to the LORD. [15]Then he appointed for himself priests for the high places, for the demons, and the calf idols which he had made. [16]And after *the Levites left,*[a] those from all the tribes of Israel, such as set their heart to seek the LORD God of Israel, came to Jerusalem to sacrifice to the LORD God of their fathers. [17]So they strengthened the kingdom of Judah, and made Rehoboam the son of Solomon strong for three years, because they walked in the way of David and Solomon for three years.

The Family of Rehoboam

[18]Then Rehoboam took for himself as wife Mahalath the daughter of Jerimoth the son of David, *and of* Abihail the daughter of Eliah the son of Jesse. [19]And she bore him children: Jeush, Shamariah, and Zaham. [20]After her he took Maachah the granddaughter[a] of Absalom; and she bore him Abijah, Attai, Ziza, and Shelomith. [21]Now Rehoboam loved Maachah the granddaughter of Absalom more than all his wives and his concubines; for he took eighteen wives and sixty concubines, and begot twenty-eight sons and sixty daughters. [22]And Rehoboam appointed Abijah the son of Maachah as chief, *to be* leader among his brothers; for

INTIMATE MOMENTS

Develop a special sign or secret word— just for her—that communicates your love.

he *intended* to make him king. ²³He dealt wisely, and dispersed some of his sons throughout all the territories of Judah and Benjamin, to every fortified city; and he gave them provisions in abundance. He also sought many wives *for them.*

Egypt Attacks Judah

12 Now it came to pass, when Rehoboam had established the kingdom and had strengthened himself, that he forsook the law of the LORD, and all Israel along with him. ²And it happened in the fifth year of King Rehoboam *that* Shishak king of Egypt came up against Jerusalem, because they had transgressed against the LORD, ³with twelve hundred chariots, sixty thousand horsemen, and people without number who came with him out of Egypt— the Lubim and the Sukkiim and the Ethiopians. ⁴And he took the fortified cities of Judah and came to Jerusalem.

⁵Then Shemaiah the prophet came to Rehoboam and the leaders of Judah, who were gathered together in Jerusalem because of Shishak, and said to them, "Thus says the LORD: 'You have forsaken Me, and therefore I also have left you in the hand of Shishak.'"

⁶So the leaders of Israel and the king humbled themselves; and they said, "The LORD *is* righteous."

⁷Now when the LORD saw that they humbled themselves, the word of the LORD came to Shemaiah, saying, "They have humbled themselves; *therefore* I will not destroy them, but I will grant them some deliverance. My wrath shall not be poured out on Jerusalem by the hand of Shishak. ⁸Nevertheless they will be his servants, that they may distinguish My service from the service of the kingdoms of the nations."

⁹So Shishak king of Egypt came up against Jerusalem, and took away the treasures of the house of the LORD and the treasures of the king's house; he took everything. He also carried away the gold shields which Solomon had made. ¹⁰Then King Rehoboam made bronze shields in their place, and committed *them* to the hands of the captains of the guard, who guarded the doorway of the king's house. ¹¹And whenever the king entered the house of the LORD, the guard would go and bring them out; then they would take them back into the guardroom. ¹²When he humbled himself, the wrath of the LORD turned from him, so as not to destroy *him* completely; and things also went well in Judah.

The End of Rehoboam's Reign

¹³Thus King Rehoboam strengthened himself in Jerusalem and reigned. Now Rehoboam *was* forty-one years old when he became king; and he reigned seventeen years in Jerusalem, the city which the LORD had chosen out of all the tribes of Israel, to put His name there. His mother's name *was* Naamah, an Ammonitess. ¹⁴And he did evil, because he did not prepare his heart to seek the LORD.

¹⁵The acts of Rehoboam, first and last, *are* they not written in the book of Shemaiah the prophet, and of Iddo the seer concerning genealogies? And *there were*

wars between Rehoboam and Jeroboam all their days. [16]So Rehoboam rested with his fathers, and was buried in the City of David. Then Abijah[a] his son reigned in his place.

Abijah Reigns in Judah

13 In the eighteenth year of King Jeroboam, Abijah became king over Judah. [2]He reigned three years in Jerusalem. His mother's name *was* Michaiah[a] the daughter of Uriel of Gibeah.

And there was war between Abijah and Jeroboam. [3]Abijah set the battle in order with an army of valiant warriors, four hundred thousand choice men. Jeroboam also drew up in battle formation against him with eight hundred thousand choice men, mighty men of valor.

[4]Then Abijah stood on Mount Zemaraim, which *is* in the mountains of Ephraim, and said, "Hear me, Jeroboam and all Israel: [5]Should you not know that the LORD God of Israel gave the dominion over Israel to David forever, to him and his sons, by a covenant of salt? [6]Yet Jeroboam the son of Nebat, the servant of Solomon the son of David, rose up and rebelled against his lord. [7]Then worthless rogues gathered to him, and strengthened themselves against Rehoboam the son of Solomon, when Rehoboam was young and inexperienced and could not withstand them. [8]And now you think to withstand the kingdom of the LORD, which is in the hand of the sons of David; and you *are* a great multitude, and with you are the gold calves which Jeroboam made for you as gods. [9]Have you not cast out the priests of the LORD, the sons of Aaron, and the Levites, and made for yourselves priests, like the peoples of *other* lands, so that whoever comes to consecrate himself with a young bull and seven rams may be a priest of *things that are* not gods? [10]But as for us, the LORD *is* our God, and we have not forsaken Him; and the priests who minister to the LORD *are* the sons of Aaron, and the Levites *attend* to *their* duties. [11]And they burn to the LORD every morning and every evening burnt sacrifices and sweet incense; *they* also *set* the showbread *in order on* the pure *gold* table, and the lampstand of gold with its lamps to burn every evening; for we keep the command of the LORD our God, but you have forsaken Him. [12]Now look, God Himself is with us as *our* head, and His priests with sounding trumpets to sound the alarm against you. O children of Israel, do not fight against the LORD God of your fathers, for you shall not prosper!"

[13]But Jeroboam caused an ambush to go around behind them; so they were in front of Judah, and the ambush *was* behind them. [14]And when Judah looked around, to their surprise the battle line *was* at both front and rear; and they cried out to the LORD, and the priests sounded the trumpets. [15]Then the men of Judah gave a shout; and as the men of Judah shouted, it happened that God struck Jeroboam and all Israel before Abijah and Judah. [16]And the children of Israel fled before Judah, and God delivered them into their hand. [17]Then Abijah and his people struck them with a great slaughter; so five hundred thousand choice men of Israel fell slain. [18]Thus the children of Israel were subdued at that time; and the children of Judah prevailed, because they relied on the LORD God of their fathers.

[19]And Abijah pursued Jeroboam and took cities from him: Bethel with its villages, Jeshanah with its villages, and Ephrain[a] with its villages. [20]So Jeroboam did not recover strength again in the days of Abijah; and the LORD struck him, and he died.

[21]But Abijah grew mighty, married fourteen wives, and begot twenty-two sons and sixteen daughters. [22]Now the rest of the acts of Abijah, his ways, and his sayings *are* written in the annals of the prophet Iddo.

14 So Abijah rested with his fathers, and they buried him in the City of David. Then Asa his son reigned in his place. In his days the land was quiet for ten years.

Asa Reigns in Judah

[2]Asa did *what was* good and right in the eyes of the LORD his God, [3]for he removed

---

12:16 [a]Spelled *Abijam* in 1 Kings 14:31
13:2 [a]Spelled *Maachah* in 11:20, 21 and 1 Kings 15:2
13:19 [a]Or *Ephron*

the altars of the foreign *gods* and the high places, and broke down the *sacred* pillars and cut down the wooden images. ⁴He commanded Judah to seek the LORD God of their fathers, and to observe the law and the commandment. ⁵He also removed the high places and the incense altars from all the cities of Judah, and the kingdom was quiet under him. ⁶And he built fortified cities in Judah, for the land had rest; he had no war in those years, because the LORD had given him rest. ⁷Therefore he said to Judah, "Let us build these cities and make walls around *them,* and towers, gates, and bars, *while* the land *is* yet before us, because we have sought the LORD our God; we have sought *Him,* and He has given us rest on every side." So they built and prospered. ⁸And Asa had an army of three hundred thousand from Judah who carried shields and spears, and from Benjamin two hundred and eighty thousand men who carried shields and drew bows; all these *were* mighty men of valor.

⁹Then Zerah the Ethiopian came out against them with an army of a million men and three hundred chariots, and he came to Mareshah. ¹⁰So Asa went out against him, and they set the troops in battle array in the Valley of Zephathah at Mareshah. ¹¹And Asa cried out to the LORD his God, and said, "LORD, *it is* nothing for You to help, whether with many or with those who have no power; help us, O LORD our God, for we rest on You, and in Your name we go against this multitude. O LORD, You *are* our God; do not let man prevail against You!"

¹²So the LORD struck the Ethiopians before Asa and Judah, and the Ethiopians fled. ¹³And Asa and the people who *were* with him pursued them to Gerar. So the Ethiopians were overthrown, and they could not recover, for they were broken before the LORD and His army. And they carried away very much spoil. ¹⁴Then they defeated all the cities around Gerar, for the fear of the LORD came upon them; and they plundered all the cities, for there was exceedingly

much spoil in them. ¹⁵They also attacked the livestock enclosures, and carried off sheep and camels in abundance, and returned to Jerusalem.

The Reforms of Asa

15 Now the Spirit of God came upon Azariah the son of Oded. ²And he went out to meet Asa, and said to him: "Hear me, Asa, and all Judah and Benjamin. The LORD *is* with you while you are with Him. If you seek Him, He will be found by you; but if you forsake Him, He will forsake you. ³For a long time Israel *has been* without the true God, without a teaching priest, and without law; ⁴but when in their trouble they turned to the LORD God of Israel, and sought Him, He was found by them. ⁵And in those times *there was* no peace to the one who went out, nor to the one who came in, but great turmoil *was* on all the inhabitants of the lands. ⁶So nation was destroyed by nation, and city by city, for God troubled them with every adversity. ⁷But you, be strong and do not let your hands be weak, for your work shall be rewarded!"

⁸And when Asa heard these words and the prophecy of Oded[a] the prophet, he took courage, and removed the abominable idols from all the land of Judah and Benjamin and from the cities which he had taken in the mountains of Ephraim; and he restored the altar of the LORD that *was* before the vestibule of the LORD. ⁹Then he gathered all Judah and Benjamin, and those who dwelt with them from Ephraim, Manasseh, and Simeon, for they came over to him in great numbers from Israel when they saw that the LORD his God was with him.

¹⁰So they gathered together at Jerusalem in the third month, in the fifteenth year of the reign of Asa. ¹¹And they offered to the LORD at that time seven hundred bulls and seven thousand sheep from the spoil they had brought. ¹²Then they entered into a covenant to seek the LORD God of their fathers with all their heart and with all their soul; ¹³and whoever would not seek the LORD God of Israel was to be put to death, whether small or great, whether man or woman. ¹⁴Then they took an oath before the LORD with a loud voice, with

15:8 [a]Following Masoretic Text and Septuagint; Syriac and Vulgate read *Azariah the son of Oded* (compare verse 1).

shouting and trumpets and rams' horns. [15]And all Judah rejoiced at the oath, for they had sworn with all their heart and sought Him with all their soul; and He was found by them, and the LORD gave them rest all around.

[16]Also he removed Maachah, the mother of Asa the king, from *being* queen mother, because she had made an obscene image of Asherah;[a] and Asa cut down her obscene image, then crushed and burned *it* by the Brook Kidron. [17]But the high places were not removed from Israel. Nevertheless the heart of Asa was loyal all his days.

[18]He also brought into the house of God the things that his father had dedicated and that he himself had dedicated: silver and gold and utensils. [19]And there was no war until the thirty-fifth year of the reign of Asa.

Asa's Treaty with Syria

16 In the thirty-sixth year of the reign of Asa, Baasha king of Israel came up against Judah and built Ramah, that he might let none go out or come in to Asa king of Judah. [2]Then Asa brought silver and gold from the treasuries of the house of the LORD and of the king's house, and sent to Ben-Hadad king of Syria, who dwelt in Damascus, saying, [3]"*Let there be* a treaty between you and me, as there was between my father and your father. See, I have sent you silver and gold; come, break your treaty with Baasha king of Israel, so that he will withdraw from me."

[4]So Ben-Hadad heeded King Asa, and sent the captains of his armies against the cities of Israel. They attacked Ijon, Dan, Abel Maim, and all the storage cities of Naphtali. [5]Now it happened, when Baasha heard *it,* that he stopped building Ramah and ceased his work. [6]Then King Asa took all Judah, and they carried away the stones and timber of Ramah, which Baasha had used for building; and with them he built Geba and Mizpah.

Hanani's Message to Asa

[7]And at that time Hanani the seer came to Asa king of Judah, and said to him: "Because you have relied on the king of Syria, and have not relied on the LORD your God, therefore the army of the king of Syria has escaped from your hand. [8]Were the Ethiopians and the Lubim not a huge army with very many chariots and horsemen? Yet, because you relied on the LORD, He delivered them into your hand. [9]For the eyes of the LORD run to and fro throughout the whole earth, to show Himself strong on behalf of *those* whose heart *is* loyal to Him. In this you have done foolishly; therefore from now on you shall have wars." [10]Then Asa was angry with the seer, and put him in prison, for *he was* enraged at him because

---

ROMANCE FAQ

Q: *What kinds of thoughts go through my husband's mind when he initiates physical intimacy?*

There is more going though a typical husband's mind at that moment than many women may realize! Consider a few of the questions he may be asking himself:

1. Do you want me? Will you welcome me? There is no other person I can go to who will affirm this side of me.

2. Will you trust me with your body? Or will you pull away?

3. Do you really want to please me? Do you have any idea how important this is to me? Am I important enough in your life to focus on what I need sexually as a man?

4. How did I do? Did I do just okay, or did I really bring great pleasure to you? I gain my greatest satisfaction from knowing that you have received and enjoyed pleasure.

The sexual fulfillment of your husband is directly related to how his wife communicates her sexual love to him. How do you communicate that you need him? Do you usually wait for him, or do you initiate? Do you respond, or do you resist? Your attitude and actions are essential parts of the experience.

15:16 [a]A Canaanite deity

of this. And Asa oppressed *some* of the people at that time.

Illness and Death of Asa

[11]Note that the acts of Asa, first and last, are indeed written in the book of the kings of Judah and Israel. [12]And in the thirty-ninth year of his reign, Asa became diseased in his feet, and his malady was severe; yet in his disease he did not seek the LORD, but the physicians.

[13]So Asa rested with his fathers; he died in the forty-first year of his reign. [14]They buried him in his own tomb, which he had made for himself in the City of David; and they laid him in the bed which was filled with spices and various ingredients prepared in a mixture of ointments. They made a very great burning for him.

Jehoshaphat Reigns in Judah

17 Then Jehoshaphat his son reigned in his place, and strengthened himself against Israel. [2]And he placed troops in all the fortified cities of Judah, and set garrisons in the land of Judah and in the cities of Ephraim which Asa his father had taken. [3]Now the LORD was with Jehoshaphat, because he walked in the former ways of his father David; he did not seek the Baals, [4]but sought the God[a] of his father, and walked in His commandments and not according to the acts of Israel. [5]Therefore the LORD established the kingdom in his hand; and all Judah gave presents to Jehoshaphat, and he had riches and honor in abundance. [6]And his heart took delight in the ways of the LORD; moreover he removed the high places and wooden images from Judah.

[7]Also in the third year of his reign he sent his leaders, Ben-Hail, Obadiah, Zechariah, Nethanel, and Michaiah, to teach in the cities of Judah. [8]And with them *he sent* Levites: Shemaiah, Nethaniah, Zebadiah, Asahel, Shemiramoth, Jehonathan, Adonijah, Tobijah, and Tobadonijah—the Levites; and with them Elishama and Jehoram, the priests. [9]So they taught in Judah, and *had* the Book of the Law of the LORD with them; they went throughout all the cities of Judah and taught the people.

[10]And the fear of the LORD fell on all the kingdoms of the lands that *were* around Judah, so that they did not make war against Jehoshaphat. [11]Also *some* of the Philistines brought Jehoshaphat presents and silver as tribute; and the Arabians brought him flocks, seven thousand seven hundred rams and seven thousand seven hundred male goats.

[12]So Jehoshaphat became increasingly powerful, and he built fortresses and storage cities in Judah. [13]He had much property in the cities of Judah; and the men of war, mighty men of valor, *were* in Jerusalem.

[14]These *are* their numbers, according to their fathers' houses. Of Judah, the captains of thousands: Adnah the captain, and with him three hundred thousand mighty men of valor; [15]and next to him *was* Jehohanan the captain, and with him two hundred and eighty thousand; [16]and next to him *was* Amasiah the son of Zichri, who willingly offered himself to the LORD, and with him two hundred thousand mighty men of valor. [17]Of Benjamin: Eliada a mighty man of valor, and with him two hundred thousand men armed with bow and shield; [18]and next to him *was* Jehozabad, and with him one hundred and eighty thousand prepared for war. [19]These served the king, besides those the king put in the fortified cities throughout all Judah.

Micaiah Warns Ahab

18 Jehoshaphat had riches and honor in abundance; and by marriage he allied himself with Ahab. [2]After some years he went down to *visit* Ahab in Samaria; and Ahab killed sheep and oxen in abundance for him and the people who were with him, and persuaded him to go up *with him* to Ramoth Gilead. [3]So Ahab king of Israel said to Jehoshaphat king of Judah, "Will you go with me *against* Ramoth Gilead?"

And he answered him, "I *am* as you *are*, and my people as your people; *we will be* with you in the war."

[4]Also Jehoshaphat said to the king of Israel, "Please inquire for the word of the LORD today."

[5]Then the king of Israel gathered the prophets together, four hundred men, and

---

17:4 [a]Septuagint reads LORD God.

said to them, "Shall we go to war against Ramoth Gilead, or shall I refrain?"

So they said, "Go up, for God will deliver it into the king's hand."

[6]But Jehoshaphat said, "*Is there* not still a prophet of the LORD here, that we may inquire of Him?"[a]

[7]So the king of Israel said to Jehoshaphat, "*There is* still one man by whom we may inquire of the LORD; but I hate him, because he never prophesies good concerning me, but always evil. He *is* Micaiah the son of Imla."

And Jehoshaphat said, "Let not the king say such things!"

[8]Then the king of Israel called one *of his* officers and said, "Bring Micaiah the son of Imla quickly!"

[9]The king of Israel and Jehoshaphat king of Judah, clothed in *their* robes, sat each on his throne; and they sat at a threshing floor at the entrance of the gate of Samaria; and all the prophets prophesied before them. [10]Now Zedekiah the son of Chenaanah had made horns of iron for himself; and he said, "Thus says the LORD: 'With these you shall gore the Syrians until they are destroyed.'"

[11]And all the prophets prophesied so, saying, "Go up to Ramoth Gilead and prosper, for the LORD will deliver *it* into the king's hand."

[12]Then the messenger who had gone to call Micaiah spoke to him, saying, "Now listen, the words of the prophets with one accord encourage the king. Therefore please let your word be like *the word of* one of them, and speak encouragement."

[13]And Micaiah said, "*As* the LORD lives, whatever my God says, that I will speak."

[14]Then he came to the king; and the king said to him, "Micaiah, shall we go to war against Ramoth Gilead, or shall I refrain?"

And he said, "Go and prosper, and they shall be delivered into your hand!"

[15]So the king said to him, "How many times shall I make you swear that you tell me nothing but the truth in the name of the LORD?"

[16]Then he said, "I saw all Israel scattered on the mountains, as sheep that have no shepherd. And the LORD said, 'These have no master. Let each return to his house in peace.'"

[17]And the king of Israel said to Jehoshaphat, "Did I not tell you he would not prophesy good concerning me, but evil?"

[18]Then *Micaiah* said, "Therefore hear the word of the LORD: I saw the LORD sitting on His throne, and all the host of heaven standing on His right hand and His left. [19]And the LORD said, 'Who will persuade Ahab king of Israel to go up, that he may fall at Ramoth Gilead?' So one spoke in this manner, and another spoke in that manner. [20]Then a spirit came forward and stood before the LORD, and said, 'I will persuade him.' The LORD said to him, 'In what way?' [21]So he said, 'I will go out and be a lying spirit in the mouth of all his prophets.' And *the LORD* said, 'You shall persuade *him* and also prevail; go out and do so.' [22]Therefore look! The LORD has put a lying spirit in the mouth of these prophets of yours, and the LORD has declared disaster against you."

[23]Then Zedekiah the son of Chenaanah went near and struck Micaiah on the cheek, and said, "Which way did the spirit from the LORD go from me to speak to you?"

[24]And Micaiah said, "Indeed you shall see on that day when you go into an inner chamber to hide!"

[25]Then the king of Israel said, "Take Micaiah, and return him to Amon the governor of the city and to Joash the king's son; [26]and say, 'Thus says the king: "Put this *fellow* in prison, and feed him with bread of affliction and water of affliction, until I return in peace."'"

[27]But Micaiah said, "If you ever return in peace, the LORD has not spoken by me." And he said, "Take heed, all you people!"

Ahab Dies in Battle

[28]So the king of Israel and Jehoshaphat the king of Judah went up to Ramoth Gilead. [29]And the king of Israel said to Jehoshaphat, "I will disguise myself and go into battle; but you put on your robes." So the king of Israel disguised himself, and they went into battle.

[30]Now the king of Syria had commanded

18:6 [a]Or *him*

the captains of the chariots who *were* with him, saying, "Fight with no one small or great, but only with the king of Israel."

³¹So it was, when the captains of the chariots saw Jehoshaphat, that they said, "It *is* the king of Israel!" Therefore they surrounded him to attack; but Jehoshaphat cried out, and the LORD helped him, and God diverted them from him. ³²For so it was, when the captains of the chariots saw that it was not the king of Israel, that they turned back from pursuing him. ³³Now a certain man drew a bow at random, and struck the king of Israel between the joints of his armor. So he said to the driver of his chariot, "Turn around and take me out of the battle, for I am wounded." ³⁴The battle increased that day, and the king of Israel propped *himself* up in *his* chariot facing the Syrians until evening; and about the time of sunset he died.

19 Then Jehoshaphat the king of Judah returned safely to his house in Jerusalem. ²And Jehu the son of Hanani the seer went out to meet him, and said to King Jehoshaphat, "Should you help the wicked and love those who hate the LORD? Therefore the wrath of the LORD *is* upon you. ³Nevertheless good things are found in you, in that you have removed the wooden images from the land, and have prepared your heart to seek God."

The Reforms of Jehoshaphat

⁴So Jehoshaphat dwelt at Jerusalem; and he went out again among the people from Beersheba to the mountains of Ephraim, and brought them back to the LORD God of their fathers. ⁵Then he set judges in the land throughout all the fortified cities of Judah, city by city, ⁶and said to the judges, "Take heed to what you are doing, for you do not judge for man but for the LORD, who *is* with you in the judgment. ⁷Now therefore, let the fear of the LORD be upon you; take care and do *it,* for *there is* no iniquity with the LORD our God, no partiality, nor taking of bribes."

⁸Moreover in Jerusalem, for the judgment of the LORD and for controversies, Jehoshaphat appointed some of the Levites and priests, and some of the chief fathers of Israel, when they returned to Jerusalem.^a ⁹And he commanded them, saying, "Thus you shall act in the fear of the LORD, faithfully and with a loyal heart: ¹⁰Whatever case comes to you from your brethren who dwell in their cities, whether of bloodshed or offenses against law or commandment, against statutes or ordinances, you shall warn them, lest they trespass against the LORD and wrath come upon you and your brethren. Do this, and you will not be guilty. ¹¹And take notice: Amariah the chief priest *is* over you in all matters of the LORD; and Zebadiah the son of Ishmael, the ruler of the house of Judah, for all the king's matters; also the Levites *will be* officials before you. Behave courageously, and the LORD will be with the good."

INTIMATE MOMENTS

Save your spare change in a large, clear jar. Put it somewhere he can easily see it, and let him know you are saving up to buy him something special. As the coins start piling up, ask him what he might like to have—but make it clear that the gift will be a surprise, from your heart to his.

Ammon, Moab, and Mount Seir Defeated

20 It happened after this *that* the people of Moab with the people of Ammon, and *others* with them besides the Ammonites,^a came to battle against Jehoshaphat. ²Then some came and told Jehoshaphat, saying, "A great multitude is coming against you from beyond the sea, from Syria;^a and they are in Hazazon Tamar" (which *is* En Gedi). ³And Jehoshaphat feared, and set himself to seek the LORD, and proclaimed a fast throughout all Judah. ⁴So Judah gathered together to ask *help* from the LORD; and from all the cities of Judah they came to seek the LORD.

19:8 ^aSeptuagint and Vulgate read *for the inhabitants of Jerusalem.* **20:1** ^aFollowing Masoretic Text and Vulgate; Septuagint reads *Meunites* (compare 26:7). **20:2** ^aFollowing Masoretic Text, Septuagint, and Vulgate; some Hebrew manuscripts and Old Latin read *Edom.*

Why Fast?

KING JEHOSHAPHAT KNEW HE WAS IN trouble. A massive army had gathered to topple his kingdom and he was fresh out of options. So, he "proclaimed a fast throughout all Judah" (20:3).

Jehoshaphat had in essence humbled—even humiliated—himself before God, asking the Lord for help. "For we have no power against this great multitude that is coming against us," he said, "nor do we know what to do, but our eyes are upon You" (20:12).

The Bible contains many references to the spiritual discipline of fasting. Several Old Testament characters fasted, and Jesus Himself fasted—once for forty days, following His baptism.

But why fast today? There is something about going without food for a set period of time that demonstrates your seriousness before God as you go to Him in prayer. It's as if you are saying to Him, "Lord, you are worth going hungry for."

When our family was younger we wanted to teach them a dimension of fasting and sacrifice for child hunger. We decided to sponsor a child, and to symbolize that sponsorship we decided to serve a meal of only rice. Although this was not a true fast, that act of giving up food and ending our meal a little hungry served its purposes. We prayed for the child and discussed how it was likely that this child and millions of others would only have rice to eat today and every day. Although at the time those attempts to teach our children about fasting, prayer, and sacrifice for others didn't seem very successful, looking back I regret that we didn't employ something similar more often.

When you face a serious issue and you need answers—for some trial that has come your way or over some issue of God's discipline—it is a good idea to mix fasting with your prayer. This lets God and you alike know that you're serious about seeking God and that you want His answers.

---

⁵Then Jehoshaphat stood in the assembly of Judah and Jerusalem, in the house of the LORD, before the new court, ⁶and said: "O LORD God of our fathers, *are* You not God in heaven, and do You *not* rule over all the kingdoms of the nations, and in Your hand *is there not* power and might, so that no one is able to withstand You? ⁷*Are* You not our God, *who* drove out the inhabitants of this land before Your people Israel, and gave it to the descendants of Abraham Your friend forever? ⁸And they dwell in it, and have built You a sanctuary in it for Your name, saying, ⁹'If disaster comes upon us—sword, judgment, pestilence, or famine—we will stand before this temple and in Your presence (for Your name *is* in this temple), and cry out to You in our affliction, and You will hear and save.' ¹⁰And now, here are the people of Ammon, Moab,

and Mount Seir—whom You would not let Israel invade when they came out of the land of Egypt, but they turned from them and did not destroy them— ¹¹here they are, rewarding us by coming to throw us out of Your possession which You have given us to inherit. ¹²O our God, will You not judge them? For we have no power against this great multitude that is coming against us; nor do we know what to do, but our eyes *are* upon You."

¹³Now all Judah, with their little ones, their wives, and their children, stood before the LORD.

¹⁴Then the Spirit of the LORD came upon Jahaziel the son of Zechariah, the son of Benaiah, the son of Jeiel, the son of Mattaniah, a Levite of the sons of Asaph, in the midst of the assembly. ¹⁵And he said, "Listen, all you of Judah and you inhabitants of

Jerusalem, and you, King Jehoshaphat! Thus says the LORD to you: 'Do not be afraid nor dismayed because of this great multitude, for the battle *is* not yours, but God's. ¹⁶Tomorrow go down against them. They will surely come up by the Ascent of Ziz, and you will find them at the end of the brook before the Wilderness of Jeruel. ¹⁷You will not *need* to fight in this *battle.* Position yourselves, stand still and see the salvation of the LORD, who is with you, O Judah and Jerusalem!' Do not fear or be dismayed; tomorrow go out against them, for the LORD *is* with you."

¹⁸And Jehoshaphat bowed his head with *his* face to the ground, and all Judah and the inhabitants of Jerusalem bowed before the LORD, worshiping the LORD. ¹⁹Then the Levites of the children of the Kohathites and of the children of the Korahites stood up to praise the LORD God of Israel with voices loud and high.

²⁰So they rose early in the morning and went out into the Wilderness of Tekoa; and as they went out, Jehoshaphat stood and said, "Hear me, O Judah and you inhabitants of Jerusalem: Believe in the LORD your God, and you shall be established; believe His prophets, and you shall prosper." ²¹And when he had consulted with the people, he appointed those who should sing to the LORD, and who should praise the beauty of holiness, as they went out before the army and were saying:

"Praise the LORD,
   For His mercy *endures* forever."ᵃ

²²Now when they began to sing and to praise, the LORD set ambushes against the people of Ammon, Moab, and Mount Seir, who had come against Judah; and they were defeated. ²³For the people of Ammon and Moab stood up against the inhabitants of Mount Seir to utterly kill and destroy *them.* And when they had made an end of the inhabitants of Seir, they helped to destroy one another.

²⁴So when Judah came to a place overlooking the wilderness, they looked toward

BIBLICAL INSIGHTS • 20:13
Pray for Your Children

Children need the prayers of their parents. Why does it so often take a crisis, like the one that faced ancient Judah, for us to come before the Lord? "Now all Judah, with their little ones, their wives, and their children, stood before the LORD" (20:13).

We must not allow ourselves to be deterred or discouraged in this process. Here are two suggestions to help you pray for your children with both effectiveness and power.

1. *Acknowledge that your children belong first to God, then to you.* Acknowledge that His love for them is even greater than your love for them. Acknowledge that He can and does influence them more than you do. Acknowledge your own dependence upon Him to fulfill the calling He's given you as a parent (see John 15:5).

2. *Be an example of Christian integrity for your children.* Don't be their excuse for not living as they ought. Be available to pray *with,* and not just *for,* your children. Be trustworthy as a model of Christ-likeness. Recall what Paul said in 1 Corinthians 11:1, "Imitate me, just as I also imitate Christ." Your divine calling is to be what you desire *them* to be.

the multitude; and there *were* their dead bodies, fallen on the earth. No one had escaped.

²⁵When Jehoshaphat and his people came to take away their spoil, they found among them an abundance of valuables on the dead bodies,ᵃ and precious jewelry, which they stripped off for themselves, more than they could carry away; and they were three days gathering the spoil because there was so much. ²⁶And on the fourth day they assembled in the Valley of Berachah, for there they blessed the LORD; therefore the name of that place was called The Valley of Berachahᵃ until this day. ²⁷Then they returned, every man of Judah and Jerusalem, with Jehoshaphat in front

---

20:21 ᵃCompare Psalm 106:1   **20:25** ᵃA few Hebrew manuscripts, Old Latin, and Vulgate read *garments;* Septuagint reads *armor.*   **20:26** ᵃLiterally *Blessing*

DEVOTIONS FOR COUPLES • 20:15
Overcoming Discouragement

We all face times of discouragement in our marriages and families. So what do we need to overcome discouragement? What should we do?

First, *be truthful with God.* I've found that I never fool God through my lofty prayers for the missionaries in Africa, when deep inside I'm hurting. God is able to handle your emotions of disappointment and being disheartened. Be honest!

Are you discouraged about a child who rarely reaches your expectations? Tell God about it. Disheartened about your mate and an unresolved issue that habitually occurs? God knows about it already, but pour it out. Disillusioned with a friend? Then pray. Are you questioning God—His fairness, your circumstances, or your unanswered prayers? Get alone and share your grief with the One who knows you best. It's normal to get discouraged, but it's not acceptable to *stay* discouraged.

Second, *find the source of your discouragement.* Sometimes it's a goal that you didn't attain ...*again.* Or the problem may be a cutting remark of a friend, the feeling that you're carrying this heavy burden alone, or the lack of approval by an important person in your life.

By isolating the source of my discouragement, many times I've found that I had placed my hope in the wrong person or in the wrong place. On other occasions, I've judged my response to be quite normal—and because I can't quit, I've need to work through my all-too-human desire to lose hope and give up.

Third, *with a heart of faith, look beyond your circumstances and your emotions to a God who will renew you day by day.* Realize that God uses hardship to perfect your faith (Rom. 5:1–10). And recall what He told a disheartened group of Israelites, "Do not be afraid nor dismayed because of this great multitude [or in your case, this great challenge], for the battle is not yours, but God's" (2 Chron. 20:15).

My friend, the tomb is empty! Jesus Christ is alive! And He is the One who can lift up your heavy hands or your burdened heart.

Barbara and I have concluded that God has given us a life that will bring occasional times of discouragement and disappointment. We love the way Philip Yancey puts it, "The alternative to disappointment with God seems to be disappointment without God." You can handle the uncertainty of life only through a tough, resilient faith in a God who knows what He is doing.

---

of them, to go back to Jerusalem with joy, for the LORD had made them rejoice over their enemies. ²⁸So they came to Jerusalem, with stringed instruments and harps and trumpets, to the house of the LORD. ²⁹And the fear of God was on all the kingdoms of *those* countries when they heard that the LORD had fought against the enemies of Israel. ³⁰Then the realm of Jehoshaphat was quiet, for his God gave him rest all around.

The End of Jehoshaphat's Reign

³¹So Jehoshaphat was king over Judah. *He was* thirty-five years old when he became king, and he reigned twenty-five years in Jerusalem. His mother's name *was* Azubah the daughter of Shilhi. ³²And he

walked in the way of his father Asa, and did not turn aside from it, doing *what was* right in the sight of the LORD. ³³Nevertheless the high places were not taken away, for as yet the people had not directed their hearts to the God of their fathers.

³⁴Now the rest of the acts of Jehoshaphat, first and last, indeed they *are* written in the book of Jehu the son of Hanani, which *is* mentioned in the book of the kings of Israel.

³⁵After this Jehoshaphat king of Judah allied himself with Ahaziah king of Israel, who acted very wickedly. ³⁶And he allied himself with him to make ships to go to Tarshish, and they made the ships in Ezion Geber. ³⁷But Eliezer the son of Dodavah of Mareshah prophesied against Jehoshaphat,

saying, "Because you have allied yourself with Ahaziah, the LORD has destroyed your works." Then the ships were wrecked, so that they were not able to go to Tarshish.

Jehoram Reigns in Judah

21 And Jehoshaphat rested with his fathers, and was buried with his fathers in the City of David. Then Jehoram his son reigned in his place. ²He had brothers, the sons of Jehoshaphat: Azariah, Jehiel, Zechariah, Azaryahu, Michael, and Shephatiah; all these *were* the sons of Jehoshaphat king of Israel. ³Their father gave them great gifts of silver and gold and precious things, with fortified cities in Judah; but he gave the kingdom to Jehoram, because he *was* the firstborn.

⁴Now when Jehoram was established over the kingdom of his father, he strengthened himself and killed all his brothers with the sword, and also *others* of the princes of Israel.

⁵Jehoram *was* thirty-two years old when he became king, and he reigned eight years in Jerusalem. ⁶And he walked in the way of the kings of Israel, just as the house of Ahab had done, for he had the daughter of Ahab as a wife; and he did evil in the sight of the LORD. ⁷Yet the LORD would not destroy the house of David, because of the covenant that He had made with David, and since He had promised to give a lamp to him and to his sons forever.

⁸In his days Edom revolted against Judah's authority, and made a king over themselves. ⁹So Jehoram went out with his officers, and all his chariots with him. And he rose by night and attacked the Edomites who had surrounded him and the captains of the chariots. ¹⁰Thus Edom has been in revolt against Judah's authority to this day. At that time Libnah revolted against his rule, because he had forsaken the LORD God of his fathers. ¹¹Moreover he made high places in the mountains of Judah, and caused the inhabitants of Jerusalem to commit harlotry, and led Judah astray.

¹²And a letter came to him from Elijah the prophet, saying,

> Thus says the LORD God of your father David:
> Because you have not walked in the ways of Jehoshaphat your father, or in the ways of Asa king of Judah, ¹³but have walked in the way of the kings of Israel, and have made Judah and the inhabitants of Jerusalem to

---

ROMANTIC QUOTES AND NOTES
You Need Your Spouse

Beware of living independently of one another! Sure, you're both busy. Sometimes, however, busy people build their lives around activities, only to find themselves, years later, all alone. Such people are so imprisoned by selfishness and a failure to take risks, they live independently of the person whom God has sovereignly given them to share life with.

So what can you do today? Well, how about a project for you and your mate to complete after dinner tonight?

List on a clean sheet of paper, five to ten specific ways you need your mate. C'mon now, work at this! Don't list any of the "vanilla" stuff—laundry, paycheck, meals, and, oh yes, sex (unless that would *really* surprise your mate!).

Once you do that, here are two ways to express your need of your husband or wife (feel free to creatively move beyond these two suggestions). Using your list, compose a letter expressing your need of your mate. Or, take a long walk and use the time to share the ways you need him or her.

Above all, do it *right*—don't just read your list! A tender touch and eye-to-eye expression of this will make it more meaningful. Hold her hand as your read your letter to her.

You really *do* need your mate.

play the harlot like the harlotry of the house of Ahab, and also have killed your brothers, those of your father's household, *who were* better than yourself, [14]behold, the LORD will strike your people with a serious affliction—your children, your wives, and all your possessions; [15]and you *will become* very sick with a disease of your intestines, until your intestines come out by reason of the sickness, day by day.

[16]Moreover the LORD stirred up against Jehoram the spirit of the Philistines and the Arabians who *were* near the Ethiopians. [17]And they came up into Judah and invaded it, and carried away all the possessions that were found in the king's house, and also his sons and his wives, so that there was not a son left to him except Jehoahaz,[a] the youngest of his sons.

[18]After all this the LORD struck him in his intestines with an incurable disease. [19]Then it happened in the course of time, after the end of two years, that his intestines came out because of his sickness; so he died in severe pain. And his people made no burning for him, like the burning for his fathers.

[20]He was thirty-two years old when he became king. He reigned in Jerusalem eight years and, to no one's sorrow, departed. However they buried him in the City of David, but not in the tombs of the kings.

Ahaziah Reigns in Judah

22 Then the inhabitants of Jerusalem made Ahaziah his youngest son king in his place, for the raiders who came with the Arabians into the camp had killed all the older *sons.* So Ahaziah the son of Jehoram, king of Judah, reigned. [2]Ahaziah

was forty-two[a] years old when he became king, and he reigned one year in Jerusalem. His mother's name *was* Athaliah the grand-daughter of Omri. [3]He also walked in the ways of the house of Ahab, for his mother advised him to do wickedly. [4]Therefore he did evil in the sight of the LORD, like the house of Ahab; for they were his counselors after the death of his father, to his destruction. [5]He also followed their advice, and went with Jehoram[a] the son of Ahab king of Israel to war against Hazael king of Syria at Ramoth Gilead; and the Syrians wounded Joram. [6]Then he returned to Jezreel to recover from the wounds which he had received at Ramah, when he fought against Hazael king of Syria. And Azariah[a] the son of Jehoram, king of Judah, went down to see Jehoram the son of Ahab in Jezreel, because he was sick.

[7]His going to Joram was God's occasion for Ahaziah's downfall; for when he arrived, he went out with Jehoram against Jehu the son of Nimshi, whom the LORD had anointed to cut off the house of Ahab. [8]And it happened, when Jehu was executing judgment on the house of Ahab, and found the princes of Judah and the sons of Ahaziah's brothers who served Ahaziah, that he killed them. [9]Then he searched for Ahaziah; and they caught him (he was hiding in Samaria), and brought him to Jehu. When they had killed him, they buried him, "because," they said, "he is the son of Jehoshaphat, who sought the LORD with all his heart."

So the house of Ahaziah had no one to assume power over the kingdom.

Athaliah Reigns in Judah

[10]Now when Athaliah the mother of Ahaziah saw that her son was dead, she arose and destroyed all the royal heirs of the house of Judah. [11]But Jehoshabeath,[a] the daughter of the king, took Joash the son of Ahaziah, and stole him away from among the king's sons who were being murdered,

INTIMATE MOMENTS

Leave roses in the front seat of her vehicle—just because.

21:17 [a]Elsewhere called *Ahaziah* (compare 2 Chronicles 22:1) **22:2** [a]Or *twenty-two* (compare 2 Kings 8:26) **22:5** [a]Also spelled *Joram* (compare verses 5 and 7; 2 Kings 8:28; and elsewhere) **22:6** [a]Some Hebrew manuscripts, Septuagint, Syriac, Vulgate, and 2 Kings 8:29 read *Ahaziah.* **22:11** [a]Spelled *Jehosheba* in 2 Kings 11:2

and put him and his nurse in a bedroom. So Jehoshabeath, the daughter of King Jehoram, the wife of Jehoiada the priest (for she was the sister of Ahaziah), hid him from Athaliah so that she did not kill him. ¹²And he was hidden with them in the house of God for six years, while Athaliah reigned over the land.

Joash Crowned King of Judah

23 In the seventh year Jehoiada strengthened himself, *and made a* covenant with the captains of hundreds: Azariah the son of Jeroham, Ishmael the son of Jehohanan, Azariah the son of Obed, Maaseiah the son of Adaiah, and Elishaphat the son of Zichri. ²And they went throughout Judah and gathered the Levites from all the cities of Judah, and the chief fathers of Israel, and they came to Jerusalem.

³Then all the assembly made a covenant with the king in the house of God. And he said to them, "Behold, the king's son shall reign, as the LORD has said of the sons of David. ⁴This *is* what you shall do: One-third of you entering on the Sabbath, of the priests and the Levites, *shall be* keeping watch over the doors; ⁵one-third *shall be* at the king's house; and one-third at the Gate of the Foundation. All the people *shall be* in the courts of the house of the LORD. ⁶But let no one come into the house of the LORD except the priests and those of the Levites who serve. They may go in, for they *are* holy; but all the people shall keep the watch of the LORD. ⁷And the Levites shall surround the king on all sides, every man with his weapons in his hand; and whoever comes into the house, let him be put to death. You are to be with the king when he comes in and when he goes out."

⁸So the Levites and all Judah did according to all that Jehoiada the priest commanded. And each man took his men who were to be on duty on the Sabbath, with those who were going *off duty* on the Sabbath; for Jehoiada the priest had not dismissed the divisions. ⁹And Jehoiada the priest gave to the captains of hundreds the spears and the large and small shields

which *had belonged* to King David, that *were* in the temple of God. ¹⁰Then he set all the people, every man with his weapon in his hand, from the right side of the temple to the left side of the temple, along by the altar and by the temple, all around the king. ¹¹And they brought out the king's son, put the crown on him, *gave him* the Testimony,ᵃ and made him king. Then Jehoiada and his sons anointed him, and said, "*Long* live the king!"

Death of Athaliah

¹²Now when Athaliah heard the noise of the people running and praising the king, she came to the people *in* the temple of the LORD. ¹³*When* she looked, there was the king standing by his pillar at the entrance; and the leaders and the trumpeters *were* by the king. All the people of the land were rejoicing and blowing trumpets, also the singers with musical instruments, and those who led in praise. So Athaliah tore her clothes and said, "Treason! Treason!"

¹⁴And Jehoiada the priest brought out the captains of hundreds who were set over the army, and said to them, "Take her outside under guard, and slay with the sword whoever follows her." For the priest had said, "Do not kill her in the house of the LORD."

¹⁵So they seized her; and she went by way of the entrance of the Horse Gate *into* the king's house, and they killed her there.

¹⁶Then Jehoiada made a covenant between himself, the people, and the king, that they should be the LORD's people. ¹⁷And all the people went to the templeᵃ of Baal, and tore it down. They broke in pieces its altars and images, and killed Mattan the priest of Baal before the altars. ¹⁸Also Jehoiada appointed the oversight of the house of the LORD to the hand of the priests, the Levites, whom David had assigned in the house of the LORD, to offer the burnt offerings of the LORD, as *it is* written in the Law of Moses, with rejoicing and with singing, *as it was established* by David. ¹⁹And he set the gatekeepers at the gates of the house of the LORD, so that no one *who was* in any way unclean should enter.

²⁰Then he took the captains of hundreds, the nobles, the governors of the people, and all the people of the land, and brought

---

23:11 ᵃThat is, the Law (compare Exodus 25:16, 21; 31:18) **23:17** ᵃLiterally *house*

the king down from the house of the LORD; and they went through the Upper Gate to the king's house, and set the king on the throne of the kingdom. 21So all the people of the land rejoiced; and the city was quiet, for they had slain Athaliah with the sword.

Joash Repairs the Temple

24 Joash *was* seven years old when he became king, and he reigned forty years in Jerusalem. His mother's name *was* Zibiah of Beersheba. 2Joash did *what was* right in the sight of the LORD all the days of Jehoiada the priest. 3And Jehoiada took two wives for him, and he had sons and daughters.

4Now it happened after this *that* Joash set his heart on repairing the house of the LORD. 5Then he gathered the priests and the Levites, and said to them, "Go out to the cities of Judah, and gather from all Israel money to repair the house of your God from year to year, and see that you do it quickly." However the Levites did not do it quickly. 6So the king called Jehoiada the chief *priest,* and said to him, "Why have you not required the Levites to bring in from Judah and from Jerusalem the collection, *according to the commandment* of Moses the servant of the LORD and of the assembly of Israel, for the tabernacle of witness?" 7For the sons of Athaliah, that wicked woman, had broken into the house of God, and had also presented all the dedicated things of the house of the LORD to the Baals.

8Then at the king's command they made a chest, and set it outside at the gate of the house of the LORD. 9And they made a proclamation throughout Judah and Jerusalem to bring to the LORD the collection *that* Moses the servant of God *had imposed* on Israel in the wilderness. 10Then all the leaders and all the people rejoiced, brought their contributions, and put *them* into the chest until all had given. 11So it was, at that time, when the chest was brought to the king's official by the hand of the Levites, and when they saw that *there was* much money, that the king's scribe and the high priest's officer came and emptied the chest, and took it and returned it to its place. Thus they did day by day, and gathered money in abundance. 12The king and Jehoiada gave it to those

who did the work of the service of the house of the LORD; and they hired masons and carpenters to repair the house of the LORD, and also those who worked in iron and bronze to restore the house of the LORD. 13So the workmen labored, and the work was completed by them; they restored the house of God to its original condition and reinforced it. 14When they had finished, they brought the rest of the money before the king and Jehoiada; they made from it articles for the house of the LORD, articles for serving and offering, spoons and vessels of gold and silver. And they offered burnt offerings in the house of the LORD continually all the days of Jehoiada.

Apostasy of Joash

15But Jehoiada grew old and was full of days, and he died; *he was* one hundred and thirty years old when he died. 16And they buried him in the City of David among the kings, because he had done good in Israel, both toward God and His house.

17Now after the death of Jehoiada the leaders of Judah came and bowed down to the king. And the king listened to them. 18Therefore they left the house of the LORD God of their fathers, and served wooden images and idols; and wrath came upon Judah and Jerusalem because of their trespass. 19Yet He sent prophets to them, to bring them back to the LORD; and they testified against them, but they would not listen. 20Then the Spirit of God came upon Zechariah the son of Jehoiada the priest, who stood above the people, and said to them, "Thus says God: 'Why do you transgress the commandments of the LORD, so that you cannot prosper? Because you have forsaken the LORD, He also has forsaken you.'" 21So they conspired against him, and at the command of the king they stoned him with stones in the court of the house of the LORD. 22Thus Joash the king did not remember the kindness which Jehoiada his father had done to him, but killed his son; and as he died, he said, "The LORD look on *it,* and repay!"

Death of Joash

23So it happened in the spring of the year *that* the army of Syria came up against him; and they came to Judah and Jerusalem, and destroyed all the leaders of the people from among the people, and sent all their spoil to the king of Damascus. [24]For the army of the Syrians came with a small company of men; but the LORD delivered a very great army into their hand, because they had forsaken the LORD God of their fathers. So they executed judgment against Joash. [25]And when they had withdrawn from him (for they left him severely wounded), his own servants conspired against him because of the blood of the sons[a] of Jehoiada the priest, and killed him on his bed. So he died. And they buried him in the City of David, but they did not bury him in the tombs of the kings.

[26]These are the ones who conspired against him: Zabad[a] the son of Shimeath the Ammonitess, and Jehozabad the son of Shimrith[b] the Moabitess. [27]Now *concerning* his sons, and the many oracles about him, and the repairing of the house of God, indeed they *are* written in the annals of the book of the kings. Then Amaziah his son reigned in his place.

24:25 [a]Septuagint and Vulgate read *son* (compare verses 20–22). 24:26 [a]Or *Jozachar* (compare 2 Kings 12:21) [b]Or *Shomer* (compare 2 Kings 12:21) 25:4 [a]Deuteronomy 24:16

Amaziah Reigns in Judah

25 Amaziah *was* twenty-five years old *when* he became king, and he reigned twenty-nine years in Jerusalem. His mother's name *was* Jehoaddan of Jerusalem. [2]And he did *what was* right in the sight of the LORD, but not with a loyal heart.

[3]Now it happened, as soon as the kingdom was established for him, that he executed his servants who had murdered his father the king. [4]However he did not execute their children, but *did* as *it is* written in the Law in the Book of Moses, where the LORD commanded, saying, "The fathers shall not be put to death for their children, nor shall the children be put to death for their fathers; but a person shall die for his own sin."[a]

The War Against Edom

[5]Moreover Amaziah gathered Judah together and set over them captains of thousands and captains of hundreds, according to *their* fathers' houses, throughout all Judah and Benjamin; and he numbered them from twenty years old and above, and found them to be three hundred thousand choice *men, able* to go to war, who could handle spear and shield. [6]He also hired one hundred thousand mighty men of valor from

---

PARENTING MATTERS	**Q: How can we develop a strong conscience in our child?**

Being a parent can become wearisome because if you're doing it right, then you're going to be "interfering" and being a "pain" to your children. That's why the early years of childhood development are so important. You are your children's conscience—calling them, training them, prodding them to a higher good and refusing evil.

This is why it is absolutely imperative that you start at an early age (no later than eighteen months) with limits that interfere with your child's tendency to go his own way. When he chooses wrong rather than right, you interrupt his life with consequences—pain. When you repeat this training over the years, a child learns that lies and deceit will destroy him, that hurting other people will ruin her relationships, that God sets good and evil before us so that we might choose life and not death.

Barbara and I haven't done it perfectly, but we have sought to shape our children's conscience by not letting them get away with doing wrong. As they grow up, they become attuned to listening to God as He speaks to them, convicting them of wrong and giving them discernment between good and evil.

Israel for one hundred talents of silver. ⁷But a man of God came to him, saying, "O king, do not let the army of Israel go with you, for the LORD *is* not with Israel—*not with* any of the children of Ephraim. ⁸But if you go, be gone! Be strong in battle! *Even so,* God shall make you fall before the enemy; for God has power to help and to overthrow."

⁹Then Amaziah said to the man of God, "But what *shall we* do about the hundred talents which I have given to the troops of Israel?"

And the man of God answered, "The LORD is able to give you much more than this." ¹⁰So Amaziah discharged the troops that had come to him from Ephraim, to go back home. Therefore their anger was greatly aroused against Judah, and they returned home in great anger.

¹¹Then Amaziah strengthened himself, and leading his people, he went to the Valley of Salt and killed ten thousand of the people of Seir. ¹²Also the children of Judah took captive ten thousand alive, brought them to the top of the rock, and cast them down from the top of the rock, so that they all were dashed in pieces.

¹³But as for the soldiers of the army which Amaziah had discharged, so that they would not go with him to battle, they raided the cities of Judah from Samaria to Beth Horon, killed three thousand in them, and took much spoil.

¹⁴Now it was so, after Amaziah came from the slaughter of the Edomites, that he brought the gods of the people of Seir, set them up *to be* his gods, and bowed down before them and burned incense to them. ¹⁵Therefore the anger of the LORD was aroused against Amaziah, and He sent him a prophet who said to him, "Why have you sought the gods of the people, which could not rescue their own people from your hand?"

¹⁶So it was, as he talked with him, that *the king* said to him, "Have we made you the king's counselor? Cease! Why should you be killed?"

Then the prophet ceased, and said, "I know that God has determined to destroy you, because you have done this and have not heeded my advice."

Israel Defeats Judah

¹⁷Now Amaziah king of Judah asked advice and sent to Joash[a] the son of Jehoahaz, the son of Jehu, king of Israel, saying, "Come, let us face one another *in battle.*"

¹⁸And Joash king of Israel sent to Amaziah king of Judah, saying, "The thistle that *was* in Lebanon sent to the cedar that was in Lebanon, saying, 'Give your daughter to my son as wife'; and a wild beast that *was* in Lebanon passed by and trampled the thistle. ¹⁹Indeed you say that you have defeated the Edomites, and your heart is lifted up to boast. Stay at home now; why should you meddle with trouble, that you should fall—you and Judah with you?"

²⁰But Amaziah would not heed, for it *came* from God, that He might give them into the hand *of their enemies,* because they sought the gods of Edom. ²¹So Joash king of Israel went out; and he and Amaziah king of Judah faced one another at Beth Shemesh, which *belongs* to Judah. ²²And Judah was defeated by Israel, and every man fled to his tent. ²³Then Joash the king of Israel captured Amaziah king of Judah, the son of Joash, the son of Jehoahaz, at Beth Shemesh; and he brought him to Jerusalem, and broke down the wall of Jerusalem from the Gate of Ephraim to the Corner Gate—four hundred cubits. ²⁴And *he took* all the gold and silver, all the articles that were found in the house of God with Obed-Edom, the treasures of the king's house, and hostages, and returned to Samaria.

Death of Amaziah

²⁵Amaziah the son of Joash, king of Judah, lived fifteen years after the death of Joash the son of Jehoahaz, king of Israel. ²⁶Now the rest of the acts of Amaziah, from first to last, indeed *are* they not written in the book of the kings of Judah and Israel? ²⁷After the time that Amaziah turned away from following the LORD, they made a conspiracy against him in Jerusalem, and he fled to Lachish; but they sent after him to Lachish and killed him there. ²⁸Then they brought him on horses and buried him with his fathers in the City of Judah.

25:17 ªSpelled *Jehoash* in 2 Kings 14:8ff

Uzziah Reigns in Judah

26 Now all the people of Judah took Uzziah,[a] who *was* sixteen years old, and made him king instead of his father Amaziah. [2]He built Elath[a] and restored it to Judah, after the king rested with his fathers.

[3]Uzziah *was* sixteen years old when he became king, and he reigned fifty-two years in Jerusalem. His mother's name was Jecholiah of Jerusalem. [4]And he did *what was* right in the sight of the LORD, according to all that his father Amaziah had done. [5]He sought God in the days of Zechariah, who had understanding in the visions[a] of God; and as long as he sought the LORD, God made him prosper.

[6]Now he went out and made war against the Philistines, and broke down the wall of Gath, the wall of Jabneh, and the wall of Ashdod; and he built cities *around* Ashdod and among the Philistines. [7]God helped him against the Philistines, against the Arabians who lived in Gur Baal, and against the Meunites. [8]Also the Ammonites brought tribute to Uzziah. His fame spread as far as the entrance of Egypt, for he became exceedingly strong.

[9]And Uzziah built towers in Jerusalem at the Corner Gate, at the Valley Gate, and at the corner buttress of the wall; then he fortified them. [10]Also he built towers in the desert. He dug many wells, for he had much livestock, both in the lowlands and in the plains; *he also had* farmers and vine-dressers in the mountains and in Carmel, for he loved the soil.

[11]Moreover Uzziah had an army of fighting men who went out to war by companies, according to the number on their roll as prepared by Jeiel the scribe and Maaseiah the officer, under the hand of Hananiah, *one* of the king's captains. [12]The total number of chief officers[a] of the mighty men of valor *was* two thousand six hundred. [13]And under their authority *was* an army of three hundred and seven thousand five hundred, that made war with mighty power, to help the king against the enemy. [14]Then Uzziah prepared for them, for the entire army, shields, spears, helmets, body armor, bows, and slings *to cast* stones. [15]And he made devices in Jerusalem, invented by skillful men, to be on the towers and the corners, to shoot arrows and large stones. So his fame spread far and wide, for he was marvelously helped till he became strong.

The Penalty for Uzziah's Pride

[16]But when he was strong his heart was lifted up, to *his* destruction, for he transgressed against the LORD his God by entering the temple of the LORD to burn incense on the altar of incense. [17]So Azariah the priest went in after him, and with him were eighty priests of the LORD—valiant men. [18]And they withstood King Uzziah, and said to him, "*It is* not for you, Uzziah, to burn incense to the LORD, but for the priests, the sons of Aaron, who are consecrated to burn incense. Get out of the sanctuary, for you have trespassed! You *shall have* no honor from the LORD God."

[19]Then Uzziah became furious; and he *had* a censer in his hand to burn incense. And while he was angry with the priests, leprosy broke out on his forehead, before the priests in the house of the LORD, beside the incense altar. [20]And Azariah the chief priest and all the priests looked at him, and there, on his forehead, he *was* leprous; so they thrust him out of that place. Indeed he also hurried to get out, because the LORD had struck him.

[21]King Uzziah was a leper until the day of his death. He dwelt in an isolated house, because he was a leper; for he was cut off from the house of the LORD. Then Jotham his son *was* over the king's house, judging the people of the land.

[22]Now the rest of the acts of Uzziah, from first to last, the prophet Isaiah the son of Amoz wrote. [23]So Uzziah rested with his fathers, and they buried him with his fathers in the field of burial which *belonged* to the kings, for they said, "He is a leper." Then Jotham his son reigned in his place.

Jotham Reigns in Judah

27 Jotham *was* twenty-five years old when he became king, and he

---

26:1 [a]Called *Azariah* in 2 Kings 14:21ff 26:2 [a]Hebrew *Eloth* 26:5 [a]Several Hebrew manuscripts, Septuagint, Syriac, Targum, and Arabic read *fear.* 26:12 [a]Literally *chief fathers*

reigned sixteen years in Jerusalem. His mother's name *was* Jerushah[a] the daughter of Zadok. [2]And he did *what was* right in the sight of the LORD, according to all that his father Uzziah had done (although he did not enter the temple of the LORD). But still the people acted corruptly.

[3]He built the Upper Gate of the house of the LORD, and he built extensively on the wall of Ophel. [4]Moreover he built cities in the mountains of Judah, and in the forests he built fortresses and towers. [5]He also fought with the king of the Ammonites and defeated them. And the people of Ammon gave him in that year one hundred talents of silver, ten thousand kors of wheat, and ten thousand of barley. The people of Ammon paid this to him in the second and third years also. [6]So Jotham became mighty, because he prepared his ways before the LORD his God.

[7]Now the rest of the acts of Jotham, and all his wars and his ways, indeed they *are* written in the book of the kings of Israel and Judah. [8]He was twenty-five years old when he became king, and he reigned sixteen years in Jerusalem. [9]So Jotham rested with his fathers, and they buried him in the City of David. Then Ahaz his son reigned in his place.

Ahaz Reigns in Judah

28 Ahaz *was* twenty years old when he became king, and he reigned sixteen years in Jerusalem; and he did not do *what was* right in the sight of the LORD, as his father David *had done*. [2]For he walked in the ways of the kings of Israel, and made molded images for the Baals. [3]He burned incense in the Valley of the Son of Hinnom, and burned his children in the fire, according to the abominations of the nations whom the LORD had cast out before the children of Israel. [4]And he sacrificed and burned incense on the high places, on the hills, and under every green tree.

Syria and Israel Defeat Judah

[5]Therefore the LORD his God delivered him into the hand of the king of Syria. They defeated him, and carried away a great multitude of them as captives, and brought *them* to Damascus. Then he was also delivered into the hand of the king of Israel, who defeated him with a great slaughter. [6]For Pekah the son of Remaliah killed one hundred and twenty thousand in Judah in one day, all valiant men, because they had forsaken the LORD God of their fathers. [7]Zichri, a mighty man of Ephraim, killed Maaseiah the king's son, Azrikam the officer over the house, and Elkanah *who was* second to the king. [8]And the children of Israel carried away captive of their brethren two hundred thousand women, sons, and daughters; and they also took away much spoil from them, and brought the spoil to Samaria.

Israel Returns the Captives

[9]But a prophet of the LORD was there, whose name *was* Oded; and he went out before the army that came to Samaria, and said to them: "Look, because the LORD God of your fathers was angry with Judah, He has delivered them into your hand; but you have killed them in a rage *that* reaches up to heaven. [10]And now you propose to force the children of Judah and Jerusalem to be your male and female slaves; *but are* you not also guilty before the LORD your God? [11]Now hear me, therefore, and return the captives, whom you have taken captive from your brethren, for the fierce wrath of the LORD *is* upon you."

[12]Then some of the heads of the children of Ephraim, Azariah the son of Johanan, Berechiah the son of Meshillemoth, Jehizkiah the son of Shallum, and Amasa the son of Hadlai, stood up against those who came from the war, [13]and said to them, "You shall not bring the captives here, for we *already* have offended the LORD. You intend to add to our sins and to our guilt; for our guilt is great, and *there is* fierce wrath against Israel." [14]So the armed men left the captives

INTIMATE MOMENTS

Serve him his favorite dessert or gourmet coffee—by candlelight.

27:1 [a]Spelled *Jerusha* in 2 Kings 15:33

and the spoil before the leaders and all the assembly. ¹⁵Then the men who were designated by name rose up and took the captives, and from the spoil they clothed all who were naked among them, dressed them and gave them sandals, gave them food and drink, and anointed them; and they let all the feeble ones ride on donkeys. So they brought them to their brethren at Jericho, the city of palm trees. Then they returned to Samaria.

Assyria Refuses to Help Judah

¹⁶At the same time King Ahaz sent to the kings[a] of Assyria to help him. ¹⁷For again the Edomites had come, attacked Judah, and carried away captives. ¹⁸The Philistines also had invaded the cities of the lowland and of the South of Judah, and had taken Beth Shemesh, Aijalon, Gederoth, Sochoh with its villages, Timnah with its villages, and Gimzo with its villages; and they dwelt there. ¹⁹For the LORD brought Judah low because of Ahaz king of Israel, for he had encouraged moral decline in Judah and had been continually unfaithful to the LORD. ²⁰Also Tiglath-Pileser[a] king of Assyria came to him and distressed him, and did not assist him. ²¹For Ahaz took part *of the treasures* from the house of the LORD, from the house of the king, and from the leaders, and he gave *it* to the king of Assyria; but he did not help him.

Apostasy and Death of Ahaz

²²Now in the time of his distress King Ahaz became increasingly unfaithful to the LORD. This *is that* King Ahaz. ²³For he sacrificed to the gods of Damascus which had defeated him, saying, "Because the gods of the kings of Syria help them, I will sacrifice to them that they may help me." But they were the ruin of him and of all Israel. ²⁴So Ahaz gathered the articles of the house of God, cut in pieces the articles of the house of God, shut up the doors of the house of the LORD, and made for himself altars in every corner of Jerusalem. ²⁵And in every single city of Judah he made high places to burn incense to other gods, and provoked to anger the LORD God of his fathers.

²⁶Now the rest of his acts and all his ways, from first to last, indeed they *are* written in the book of the kings of Judah and Israel. ²⁷So Ahaz rested with his fathers, and they buried him in the city, in Jerusalem; but they did not bring him into the tombs of the kings of Israel. Then Hezekiah his son reigned in his place.

Hezekiah Reigns in Judah

29 Hezekiah became king *when he was* twenty-five years old, and he reigned twenty-nine years in Jerusalem. His mother's name *was* Abijah[a] the daughter of Zechariah. ²And he did *what was* right in the sight of the LORD, according to all that his father David had done.

Hezekiah Cleanses the Temple

³In the first year of his reign, in the first month, he opened the doors of the house of the LORD and repaired them. ⁴Then he brought in the priests and the Levites, and gathered them in the East Square, ⁵and said to them: "Hear me, Levites! Now sanctify yourselves, sanctify the house of the LORD God of your fathers, and carry out the rubbish from the holy *place.* ⁶For our fathers have trespassed and done evil in the eyes of the LORD our God; they have forsaken Him, have turned their faces away from the dwelling place of the LORD, and turned *their* backs *on Him.* ⁷They have also shut up the doors of the vestibule, put out the lamps, and have not burned incense or offered burnt offerings in the holy *place* to the God of Israel. ⁸Therefore the wrath of the LORD fell upon Judah and Jerusalem, and He has given them up to trouble, to desolation, and to jeering, as you see with your eyes. ⁹For indeed, because of this our fathers have fallen by the sword; and our sons, our daughters, and our wives *are* in captivity.

¹⁰"Now *it is* in my heart to make a covenant with the LORD God of Israel, that His fierce wrath may turn away from us. ¹¹My sons, do not be negligent now, for the LORD has chosen you to stand before Him, to serve Him, and that you should minister to Him and burn incense."

¹²Then these Levites arose: Mahath the son of Amasai and Joel the son of Azariah, of the sons of the Kohathites; of the sons of

BIBLICAL INSIGHTS • 30:6

You Return, He Returns

THE MESSAGE of King Hezekiah to his wandering people is the very same message we need to hear today in America, "Return to the LORD God of Abraham, Isaac, and Israel; then He will return to ... you" (30:6).

These days I am burdened daily with my responsibility to pray for my wife and children, to read and instruct them in the Scriptures, to protect them from evil. I'm continually challenged to be the man of God they need me to be.

I have also been convicted to practice regularly the spiritual disciplines of prayer and fasting. I confess that I'm just a beginner at fasting, one of the more important (yet neglected) aspects of the Christian life. God is using these disciplines to strip away layer after layer of selfishness in my life.

It is fascinating to see what happens as we give up food and experience hunger for several meals. I am amazed at how much of my life revolves around food and the kind of food that I am going to eat to satisfy my hunger. Even sunrise until sundown is a great opportunity to deny your own desires for food and use your hunger pangs to prompt you to pray about an issue where you need to see God work.

It is clear that a return to God alone is our only hope. The psalmist says it best, "Unless the LORD builds the house, they labor in vain who build it" (Ps. 127:1). There are no solutions to our family problems until our individual relationships with Jesus Christ are set right and our lives come under the control of the Holy Spirit.

Merari, Kish the son of Abdi and Azariah the son of Jehallelel; of the Gershonites, Joah the son of Zimmah and Eden the son of Joah; ¹³of the sons of Elizaphan, Shimri and Jeiel; of the sons of Asaph, Zechariah and Mattaniah; ¹⁴of the sons of Heman, Jehiel and Shimei; and of the sons of Jeduthun, Shemaiah and Uzziel.

¹⁵And they gathered their brethren, sanctified themselves, and went according to the commandment of the king, at the words of the LORD, to cleanse the house of the LORD. ¹⁶Then the priests went into the inner part of the house of the LORD to cleanse *it,* and brought out all the debris that they found in the temple of the LORD to the court of the house of the LORD. And the Levites took *it* out and carried *it* to the Brook Kidron.

¹⁷Now they began to sanctify on the first *day* of the first month, and on the eighth day of the month they came to the vestibule of the LORD. So they sanctified the house of the LORD in eight days, and on the sixteenth day of the first month they finished.

¹⁸Then they went in to King Hezekiah and said, "We have cleansed all the house of the LORD, the altar of burnt offerings with all its articles, and the table of the showbread with all its articles. ¹⁹Moreover all the articles which King Ahaz in his reign had cast aside in his transgression we have prepared and sanctified; and there they *are,* before the altar of the LORD."

Hezekiah Restores Temple Worship

²⁰Then King Hezekiah rose early, gathered the rulers of the city, and went up to the house of the LORD. ²¹And they brought seven bulls, seven rams, seven lambs, and seven male goats for a sin offering for the kingdom, for the sanctuary, and for Judah. Then he commanded the priests, the sons of Aaron, to offer *them* on the altar of the LORD. ²²So they killed the bulls, and the priests received the blood and sprinkled *it* on the altar. Likewise they killed the rams and sprinkled the blood on the altar. They also killed the lambs and sprinkled the blood on the altar. ²³Then they brought out the male goats *for* the sin offering before the king and the assembly, and they laid their hands on them. ²⁴And the priests killed them; and they presented their blood on the altar as a sin offering to make an atonement for all Israel, for the king commanded *that* the burnt offering and the sin offering *be made* for all Israel.

²⁵And he stationed the Levites in the house of the LORD with cymbals, with stringed instruments, and with harps, according to the commandment of David,

of Gad the king's seer, and of Nathan the prophet; for thus *was* the commandment of the LORD by His prophets. [26]The Levites stood with the instruments of David, and the priests with the trumpets. [27]Then Hezekiah commanded *them* to offer the burnt offering on the altar. And when the burnt offering began, the song of the LORD *also* began, with the trumpets and with the instruments of David king of Israel. [28]So all the assembly worshiped, the singers sang, and the trumpeters sounded; all *this continued* until the burnt offering was finished. [29]And when they had finished offering, the king and all who were present with him bowed and worshiped. [30]Moreover King Hezekiah and the leaders commanded the Levites to sing praise to the LORD with the words of David and of Asaph the seer. So they sang praises with gladness, and they bowed their heads and worshiped.

[31]Then Hezekiah answered and said, "Now *that* you have consecrated yourselves to the LORD, come near, and bring sacrifices and thank offerings into the house of the LORD." So the assembly brought in sacrifices and thank offerings, and as many as were of a willing heart *brought* burnt offerings. [32]And the number of the burnt offerings which the assembly brought was seventy bulls, one hundred rams, *and* two hundred lambs; all these *were* for a burnt offering to the LORD. [33]The consecrated things *were* six hundred bulls and three thousand sheep. [34]But the priests were too few, so that they could not skin all the burnt offerings; therefore their brethren the Levites helped them until the work was ended and until the *other* priests had sanctified themselves, for the Levites were more diligent in sanctifying themselves than the priests. [35]Also the burnt offerings *were* in abundance, with the fat of the peace offerings and *with* the drink offerings for *every* burnt offering.

So the service of the house of the LORD was set in order. [36]Then Hezekiah and all the people rejoiced that God had prepared the people, since the events took place so suddenly.

30:3 [a]That is, the first month (compare Leviticus 23:5); literally *at that time*

BIBLICAL INSIGHTS • 30:8
Curing a Stiff Neck

DID YOU KNOW that a lot of neck problems are actually heart problems? It's true! Whenever you see someone called "stiff-necked" in the Bible (30:8), the underlying problem is always a hard heart.

So what's the best way to loosen a stiff neck? The biblical answer is submission.

We can all better submit to God when we voluntarily submit ourselves to a relationship of accountability. This submission says to another believer, "I will give you the key to some private rooms in my life."

Being accountable does not mean, of course, that you give this person the key to *every* room. At first, you might give him the key to only one very small closet in the basement. After you experience the freedom that comes from opening that closet, you'll find that you will want to turn over even more of those keys.

Submission provides protection. String may hold a kite down, but that very string also allows it to soar. A kite that breaks away from the string might experience freedom for a short while, but soon it comes crashing to earth.

Submission in the body of Christ works the same way. By submitting your life to another to hold you up and to hold you down, you will experience one of the great protections available in the body of Christ

Hezekiah Keeps the Passover

30 And Hezekiah sent to all Israel and Judah, and also wrote letters to Ephraim and Manasseh, that they should come to the house of the LORD at Jerusalem, to keep the Passover to the LORD God of Israel. [2]For the king and his leaders and all the assembly in Jerusalem had agreed to keep the Passover in the second month. [3]For they could not keep it at the regular time,[a] because a sufficient number of priests had not consecrated themselves, nor had the people gathered together at Jerusalem. ⁴And the matter pleased the king and all the assembly. ⁵So they resolved to make a proclamation throughout all Israel, from Beersheba to Dan, that they should come to keep the Passover to the LORD God of Israel at Jerusalem, since they had not done *it* for a long *time* in the *prescribed* manner.

⁶Then the runners went throughout all Israel and Judah with the letters from the king and his leaders, and spoke according to the command of the king: "Children of Israel, return to the LORD God of Abraham, Isaac, and Israel; then He will return to the remnant of you who have escaped from the hand of the kings of Assyria. ⁷And do not be like your fathers and your brethren, who trespassed against the LORD God of their fathers, so that He gave them up to desolation, as you see. ⁸Now do not be stiff-necked, as your fathers *were, but* yield yourselves to the LORD; and enter His sanctuary, which He has sanctified forever, and serve the LORD your God, that the fierceness of His wrath may turn away from you. ⁹For if you return to the LORD, your brethren and your children *will be treated* with compassion by those who lead them captive, so that they may come back to this land; for the LORD your God *is* gracious and merciful, and will not turn *His* face from you if you return to Him."

¹⁰So the runners passed from city to city

through the country of Ephraim and Manasseh, as far as Zebulun; but they laughed at them and mocked them. ¹¹Nevertheless some from Asher, Manasseh, and Zebulun humbled themselves and came to Jerusalem. ¹²Also the hand of God was on Judah to give them singleness of heart to obey the command of the king and the leaders, at the word of the LORD.

¹³Now many people, a very great assembly, gathered at Jerusalem to keep the Feast of Unleavened Bread in the second month. ¹⁴They arose and took away the altars that *were* in Jerusalem, and they took away all the incense altars and cast *them* into the Brook Kidron. ¹⁵Then they slaughtered the Passover *lambs* on the fourteenth *day* of the second month. The priests and the Levites were ashamed, and sanctified themselves, and brought the burnt offerings to the house of the LORD. ¹⁶They stood in their place according to their custom, according to the Law of Moses the man of God; the priests sprinkled the blood *received* from the hand of the Levites. ¹⁷For *there were* many in the assembly who had not sanctified themselves; therefore the Levites had charge of the slaughter of the Passover *lambs* for everyone *who was* not clean, to sanctify *them* to the LORD. ¹⁸For a multitude of the people, many from Ephraim, Manasseh, Issachar, and Zebulun, had not cleansed

Understand and Appreciate Your Differences

A handsome thirty-something husband and wife team told me how they finally understood how their differences complemented one another. The husband explained, "My wife is a prosecuting attorney. I felt like she prosecuted from eight to five and persecuted from five to eight!

"In the year and a half we have been married, I found out she is a strong woman. I had hoped I could pressure her to change—if I persevered, I might be able to beat her down. But I have finally understood that I don't *have* to compete with her. I can let her be who she is, and not feel insecure about who I am."

That husband has come to understand how he and his wife balance each other. He realizes he can lead her, even though at times she might challenge him, but that even this is good for him.

Understanding your mate from God's perspective results in acceptance of his or her differences and beginning to learn how God made that person to complement you. Understanding produces compassion for your partner. It will give you insight to lead wisely or to follow prudently. Understanding builds oneness by establishing the relationship on a foundation of common insight.

themselves, yet they ate the Passover contrary to what was written. But Hezekiah prayed for them, saying, "May the good LORD provide atonement for everyone ¹⁹*who* prepares his heart to seek God, the LORD God of his fathers, though *he is* not *cleansed* according to the purification of the sanctuary." ²⁰And the LORD listened to Hezekiah and healed the people.

²¹So the children of Israel who were present at Jerusalem kept the Feast of Unleavened Bread seven days with great gladness; and the Levites and the priests praised the LORD day by day, *singing* to the LORD, accompanied by loud instruments. ²²And Hezekiah gave encouragement to all the Levites who taught the good knowledge of the LORD; and they ate throughout the feast seven days, offering peace offerings and making confession to the LORD God of their fathers.

²³Then the whole assembly agreed to keep *the feast* another seven days, and they kept it *another* seven days with gladness. ²⁴For Hezekiah king of Judah gave to the assembly a thousand bulls and seven thousand sheep, and the leaders gave to the assembly a thousand bulls and ten thousand sheep; and a great number of priests sanctified themselves. ²⁵The whole assembly of Judah rejoiced, also the priests and Levites, all the assembly that came from Israel, the sojourners who came from the land of Israel, and those who dwelt in Judah. ²⁶So there was great joy in Jerusalem, for since the time of Solomon the son of David, king of Israel, *there had* been nothing like this in Jerusalem. ²⁷Then the priests, the Levites, arose and blessed the people, and their voice was heard; and their prayer came *up* to His holy dwelling place, to heaven.

The Reforms of Hezekiah

31 Now when all this was finished, all Israel who were present went out to the cities of Judah and broke the *sacred* pillars in pieces, cut down the wooden images, and threw down the high places and the altars—from all Judah, Benjamin, Ephraim, and Manasseh—until they had

utterly destroyed them all. Then all the children of Israel returned to their own cities, every man to his possession.

²And Hezekiah appointed the divisions of the priests and the Levites according to their divisions, each man according to his service, the priests and Levites for burnt offerings and peace offerings, to serve, to give thanks, and to praise in the gates of the camp^a of the LORD. ³The king also *appointed* a portion of his possessions for the burnt offerings: for the morning and evening burnt offerings, the burnt offerings for the Sabbaths and the New Moons and the set feasts, as *it is* written in the Law of the LORD.

⁴Moreover he commanded the people who dwelt in Jerusalem to contribute support for the priests and the Levites, that they might devote themselves to the Law of the LORD.

⁵As soon as the commandment was circulated, the children of Israel brought in abundance the firstfruits of grain and wine, oil and honey, and of all the produce of the field; and they brought in abundantly the tithe of everything. ⁶And the children of Israel and Judah, who dwelt in the cities of Judah, brought the tithe of oxen and sheep; also the tithe of holy things which were consecrated to the LORD their God they laid in heaps.

⁷In the third month they began laying them in heaps, and they finished in the seventh month. ⁸And when Hezekiah and the leaders came and saw the heaps, they blessed the LORD and His people Israel. ⁹Then Hezekiah questioned the priests and the Levites concerning the heaps. ¹⁰And Azariah the chief priest, from the house of Zadok, answered him and said, "Since *the people* began to bring the offerings into the house of the LORD, we have had enough to eat and have plenty left, for the LORD has blessed His people; and what is left *is* this great abundance."

¹¹Now Hezekiah commanded *them* to prepare rooms in the house of the LORD, and they prepared them. ¹²Then they faithfully brought in the offerings, the tithes, and the dedicated things; Cononiah the Levite had charge of them, and Shimei his brother *was* the next. ¹³Jehiel, Azaziah,

31:2 ^aThat is, the temple

Nahath, Asahel, Jerimoth, Jozabad, Eliel, Ismachiah, Mahath, and Benaiah *were* overseers under the hand of Cononiah and Shimei his brother, at the commandment of Hezekiah the king and Azariah the ruler of the house of God. [14]Kore the son of Imnah the Levite, the keeper of the East Gate, *was* over the freewill offerings to God, to distribute the offerings of the LORD and the most holy things. [15]And under him *were* Eden, Miniamin, Jeshua, Shemaiah, Amariah, and Shecaniah, *his* faithful assistants in the cities of the priests, to distribute allotments to their brethren by divisions, to the great as well as the small.

[16]Besides those males from three years old and up who were written in the genealogy, they distributed to everyone who entered the house of the LORD his daily portion for the work of his service, by his division, [17]and to the priests who were written in the genealogy according to their father's house, and to the Levites from twenty years old and up according to their work, by their divisions, [18]and to all who were written in the genealogy—their little ones and their wives, their sons and daughters, the whole company of them—for in their faithfulness they sanctified themselves in holiness.

[19]Also for the sons of Aaron the priests, *who were* in the fields of the common-lands of their cities, in every single city, *there were* men who were designated by name to distribute portions to all the males among the priests and to all who were listed by genealogies among the Levites.

[20]Thus Hezekiah did throughout all Judah, and he did what *was* good and right and true before the LORD his God. [21]And in every work that he began in the service of the house of God, in the law and in the commandment, to seek his God, he did *it* with all his heart. So he prospered.

Sennacherib Boasts Against the LORD

32 After these deeds of faithfulness, Sennacherib king of Assyria came and entered Judah; he encamped against the fortified cities, thinking to win them over to himself. [2]And when Hezekiah saw that Sennacherib had come, and that his purpose was to make war against Jerusalem, [3]he consulted with his leaders and commanders[a] to stop the water from the springs which *were* outside the city; and they helped him. [4]Thus many people gathered together who stopped all the springs and the brook that ran through the land, saying, "Why should the kings[a] of Assyria come and find much water?" [5]And he strengthened himself, built up all the wall that was broken, raised *it* up to the towers, and *built* another wall outside; also he repaired the Millo[a] *in* the City of David, and made weapons and shields in abundance. [6]Then he set military captains over the people, gathered them together to him in the open square of the city gate, and gave them encouragement, saying, [7]"Be strong and courageous; do not be afraid nor dismayed before the king of Assyria, nor before all the multitude that *is* with him; for *there are* more with us than with him. [8]With him *is* an arm of flesh; but with us *is* the LORD our God, to help us and to fight our battles." And the people were strengthened by the words of Hezekiah king of Judah.

[9]After this Sennacherib king of Assyria sent his servants to Jerusalem (but he and all the forces with him *laid siege* against Lachish), to Hezekiah king of Judah, and to all Judah who *were* in Jerusalem, saying, [10]"Thus says Sennacherib king of Assyria: 'In what do you trust, that you remain under siege in Jerusalem? [11]Does not Hezekiah persuade you to give yourselves over to die by famine and by thirst, saying, "The LORD our God will deliver us from the hand of the king of Assyria"? [12]Has not the same Hezekiah taken away His high places and His altars, and commanded Judah and Jerusalem, saying, "You shall worship before one altar and burn incense on it"? [13]Do you not know what I and my fathers have done to all the peoples of *other* lands? Were the gods of the nations of those lands in any way able to deliver their lands out of my hand? [14]Who *was there* among all the gods of those nations that my fathers

---

32:3 [a]Literally *mighty men* **32:4** [a]Following Masoretic Text and Vulgate; Arabic, Septuagint, and Syriac read *king*. **32:5** [a]Literally *The Landfill*

utterly destroyed that could deliver his people from my hand, that your God should be able to deliver you from my hand? [15]Now therefore, do not let Hezekiah deceive you or persuade you like this, and do not believe him; for no god of any nation or kingdom was able to deliver his people from my hand or the hand of my fathers. How much less will your God deliver you from my hand?'"

[16]Furthermore, his servants spoke against the LORD God and against His servant Hezekiah.

[17]He also wrote letters to revile the LORD God of Israel, and to speak against Him, saying, "As the gods of the nations of *other* lands have not delivered their people from my hand, so the God of Hezekiah will not deliver His people from my hand." [18]Then they called out with a loud voice in Hebrew[a] to the people of Jerusalem who *were* on the wall, to frighten them and trouble them, that they might take the city. [19]And they spoke against the God of Jerusalem, as against the gods of the people of the earth—the work of men's hands.

Sennacherib's Defeat and Death

[20]Now because of this King Hezekiah and the prophet Isaiah, the son of Amoz, prayed and cried out to heaven. [21]Then the LORD sent an angel who cut down every mighty man of valor, leader, and captain in the camp of the king of Assyria. So he returned shamefaced to his own land. And when he had gone into the temple of his god, some of his own offspring struck him down with the sword there.

[22]Thus the LORD saved Hezekiah and the inhabitants of Jerusalem from the hand of Sennacherib the king of Assyria, and from the hand of all *others*, and guided them[a] on every side. [23]And many brought gifts to the LORD at Jerusalem, and presents to Hezekiah king of Judah, so that he was exalted in the sight of all nations thereafter.

Hezekiah Humbles Himself

[24]In those days Hezekiah was sick and near death, and he prayed to the LORD; and He spoke to him and gave him a sign. [25]But

---

32:18 [a]Literally *Judean*   **32:22** [a]Septuagint reads *gave them rest;* Vulgate reads *gave them treasures.*

BIBLICAL INSIGHTS • 32:26
Death to Your Pride

I'VE BEEN GRAZING recently in the book of 2 Chronicles, where I've found ample acreage to browse and plenty to chew on. The theme of pride caught my attention, "Then Hezekiah humbled himself for the pride of his heart, he and the inhabitants of Jerusalem, so that the wrath of the LORD did not come upon them in the days of Hezekiah" (32:26).

"Pride," said Soviet dissident Alexander Solzhenitsyn, "grows in the human heart like lard on a pig." Pride is one of the few things that can grow in the human heart without any outside sustenance. The human race is prone to be proud.

Pride has many faces. It can try to demand control: "I want to be my own god, run my own show, and submit to no one." It can be seen in stubbornness, what the Scriptures call "stiff-necked" or "hard of heart." Pride refuses to be corrected and never asks for forgiveness when wounding another person. And it is most easily detected in those who carry themselves in an arrogant manner.

Daily I attempt to put self to death and ask that Jesus Christ might have unhindered access to every area of my life. Then, as I feel tempted to get angry when things don't go my way, I'm reminded that to give in to pride is to submit to death.

Hezekiah did not repay according to the favor *shown* him, for his heart was lifted up; therefore wrath was looming over him and over Judah and Jerusalem. [26]Then Hezekiah humbled himself for the pride of his heart, he and the inhabitants of Jerusalem, so that the wrath of the LORD did not come upon them in the days of Hezekiah.

Hezekiah's Wealth and Honor

[27]Hezekiah had very great riches and honor. And he made himself treasuries for silver, for gold, for precious stones, for

spices, for shields, and for all kinds of desirable items; ²⁸storehouses for the harvest of grain, wine, and oil; and stalls for all kinds of livestock, and folds for flocks.ᵃ ²⁹Moreover he provided cities for himself, and possessions of flocks and herds in abundance; for God had given him very much property. ³⁰This same Hezekiah also stopped the water outlet of Upper Gihon, and brought the water by tunnelᵃ to the west side of the City of David. Hezekiah prospered in all his works.

³¹However, *regarding* the ambassadors of the princes of Babylon, whom they sent to him to inquire about the wonder that was *done* in the land, God withdrew from him, in order to test him, that He might know all *that was* in his heart.

Death of Hezekiah

³²Now the rest of the acts of Hezekiah, and his goodness, indeed they *are* written in the vision of Isaiah the prophet, the son of Amoz, *and* in the book of the kings of Judah and Israel. ³³So Hezekiah rested with his fathers, and they buried him in the upper tombs of the sons of David; and all Judah and the inhabitants of Jerusalem honored him at his death. Then Manasseh his son reigned in his place.

Manasseh Reigns in Judah

33 Manasseh *was* twelve years old when he became king, and he reigned fifty-five years in Jerusalem. ²But he did evil in the sight of the LORD, according to the abominations of the nations whom the LORD had cast out before the children of Israel. ³For he rebuilt the high places which Hezekiah his father had broken down; he raised up altars for the Baals, and made wooden images; and he worshiped all the host of heavenᵃ and served them. ⁴He also built altars in the house of the LORD, of which the LORD had said, "In Jerusalem shall My name be forever." ⁵And he built altars for all the host of heaven in the two courts of the house of the LORD. ⁶Also he caused his sons to pass through the fire in the Valley of the Son of Hinnom; he practiced soothsaying, used witchcraft and sorcery, and consulted mediums and spiritists. He did much evil in the sight of

the LORD, to provoke Him to anger. ⁷He even set a carved image, the idol which he had made, in the house of God, of which God had said to David and to Solomon his son, "In this house and in Jerusalem, which I have chosen out of all the tribes of Israel, I will put My name forever; ⁸and I will not again remove the foot of Israel from the land which I have appointed for your fathers—only if they are careful to do all that I have commanded them, according to the whole law and the statutes and the ordinances by the hand of Moses." ⁹So Manasseh seduced Judah and the inhabitants of Jerusalem to do more evil than the nations whom the LORD had destroyed before the children of Israel.

Manasseh Restored After Repentance

¹⁰And the LORD spoke to Manasseh and his people, but they would not listen. ¹¹Therefore the LORD brought upon them the captains of the army of the king of Assyria, who took Manasseh with hooks,ᵃ bound him with bronze *fetters,* and carried him off to Babylon. ¹²Now when he was in affliction, he implored the LORD his God, and humbled himself greatly before the God of his fathers, ¹³and prayed to Him; and He received his entreaty, heard his supplication, and brought him back to Jerusalem into his kingdom. Then Manasseh knew that the LORD *was* God.

¹⁴After this he built a wall outside the City of David on the west side of Gihon, in the valley, as far as the entrance of the Fish Gate; and *it* enclosed Ophel, and he raised it to a very great height. Then he put military captains in all the fortified cities of Judah. ¹⁵He took away the foreign gods and the idol from the house of the LORD, and all the altars that he had built in the mount of the house of the LORD and in Jerusalem; and he cast *them* out of the city. ¹⁶He also repaired the altar of the LORD, sacrificed peace offerings and thank offerings on it, and commanded Judah to serve

---

32:28 ᵃFollowing Septuagint and Vulgate; Arabic and Syriac omit *folds for flocks;* Masoretic Text reads *flocks for sheepfolds.* **32:30** ᵃLiterally *brought it straight* (compare 2 Kings 20:20) **33:3** ᵃThe gods of the Assyrians **33:11** ᵃThat is, nose hooks (compare 2 Kings 19:28)

the LORD God of Israel. [17]Nevertheless the people still sacrificed on the high places, *but* only to the LORD their God.

Death of Manasseh

[18]Now the rest of the acts of Manasseh, his prayer to his God, and the words of the seers who spoke to him in the name of the LORD God of Israel, indeed they *are written* in the book[a] of the kings of Israel. [19]Also his prayer and *how God* received his entreaty, and all his sin and trespass, and the sites where he built high places and set up wooden images and carved images, before he was humbled, indeed they *are* written among the sayings of Hozai.[a] [20]So Manasseh rested with his fathers, and they buried him in his own house. Then his son Amon reigned in his place.

Amon's Reign and Death

[21]Amon *was* twenty-two years old when he became king, and he reigned two years in Jerusalem. [22]But he did evil in the sight of the LORD, as his father Manasseh had done; for Amon sacrificed to all the carved images which his father Manasseh had made, and served them. [23]And he did not humble himself before the LORD, as his father Manasseh had humbled himself; but Amon trespassed more and more.

[24]Then his servants conspired against him, and killed him in his own house. [25]But the people of the land executed all those who had conspired against King Amon. Then the people of the land made his son Josiah king in his place.

Josiah Reigns in Judah

34 Josiah *was* eight years old when he became king, and he reigned thirty-one years in Jerusalem. [2]And he did *what was* right in the sight of the LORD, and walked in the ways of his father David; *he* did *not* turn aside to the right hand or to the left.

[3]For in the eighth year of his reign, while he was still young, he began to seek the God of his father David; and in the twelfth year he began to purge Judah and Jerusalem of the high places, the wooden images, the carved images, and the molded images. [4]They broke down the altars of the Baals in his presence, and the incense altars which *were* above them he cut down; and the wooden images, the carved images, and the molded images he broke in pieces, and made dust of them and scattered *it* on the graves of those who had sacrificed to them. [5]He also burned the bones of the priests on their altars, and cleansed Judah and Jerusalem. [6]And *so he did* in the cities of Manasseh, Ephraim, and Simeon, as far as Naphtali and all around, with axes.[a] [7]When he had broken down the altars and the wooden images, had beaten the carved images into powder, and cut down all the incense altars throughout all the land of Israel, he returned to Jerusalem.

INTIMATE MOMENTS

Feed your wife chocolate-covered strawberries that you prepared yourself. Go to the supermarket and pick out some fresh, sweet strawberries, along with some chocolate chips. When you bring both items home, first wash and dry the strawberries. Then pour the chocolate chips into a pan and melt them over low heat. Last, dip the strawberries (pointy end down!) into the melted chocolate and put the finished product on a sheet of waxed paper. Clean yourself up, put the newly-created confections on a nice plate or serving dish, and enjoy with your honey.

Hilkiah Finds the Book of the Law

[8]In the eighteenth year of his reign, when he had purged the land and the temple,[a] he sent Shaphan the son of Azaliah, Maaseiah the governor of the city, and Joah the son of Joahaz the recorder, to repair the house of the LORD his God. [9]When they came to Hilkiah the high priest, they delivered the money that was brought into the house of God, which the

---

33:18 [a]Literally *words*   **33:19** [a]Septuagint reads *the seers.*   **34:6** [a]Literally *swords*   **34:8** [a]Literally *house*

Levites who kept the doors had gathered from the hand of Manasseh and Ephraim, from all the remnant of Israel, from all Judah and Benjamin, and *which* they had brought back to Jerusalem. [10]Then they put *it* in the hand of the foremen who had the oversight of the house of the LORD; and they gave it to the workmen who worked in the house of the LORD, to repair and restore the house. [11]They gave *it* to the craftsmen and builders to buy hewn stone and timber for beams, and to floor the houses which the kings of Judah had destroyed. [12]And the men did the work faithfully. Their overseers *were* Jahath and Obadiah the Levites, of the sons of Merari, and Zechariah and Meshullam, of the sons of the Kohathites, to supervise. *Others of* the Levites, all of whom were skillful with instruments of music, [13]*were* over the burden bearers and *were* overseers of all who did work in any kind of service. And *some* of the Levites *were* scribes, officers, and gatekeepers.

[14]Now when they brought out the money that was brought into the house of the LORD, Hilkiah the priest found the Book of the Law of the LORD *given* by Moses. [15]Then Hilkiah answered and said to Shaphan the scribe, "I have found the Book of the Law in the house of the LORD." And Hilkiah gave the book to Shaphan. [16]So Shaphan carried the book to the king, bringing the king word, saying, "All that was committed to your servants they are doing. [17]And they have gathered the money that was found in the house of the LORD, and have delivered it into the hand of the overseers and the workmen." [18]Then Shaphan the scribe told the king, saying, "Hilkiah the priest has given me a book." And Shaphan read it before the king.

[19]Thus it happened, when the king heard the words of the Law, that he tore his clothes. [20]Then the king commanded Hilkiah, Ahikam the son of Shaphan, Abdon[a] the son of Micah, Shaphan the scribe, and Asaiah a servant of the king, saying, [21]"Go, inquire of the LORD for me, and for those who are left in Israel and Judah, concerning the words of the book that is found; for great *is* the wrath of the LORD that is poured out on us, because our fathers have not kept the word of the LORD, to do according to all that is written in this book."

[22]So Hilkiah and those the king *had appointed* went to Huldah the prophetess, the wife of Shallum the son of Tokhath,[a] the son of Hasrah,[b] keeper of the wardrobe. (She dwelt in Jerusalem in the Second Quarter.) And they spoke to her to that *effect.*

[23]Then she answered them, "Thus says the LORD God of Israel, 'Tell the man who sent you to Me, [24]"Thus says the LORD: 'Behold, I will bring calamity on this place and on its inhabitants, all the curses that are written in the book which they have read before the king of Judah, [25]because they have forsaken Me and burned incense to other gods, that they might provoke Me to anger with all the works of their hands. Therefore My wrath will be poured out on this place, and not be quenched.' " [26]But as for the king of Judah, who sent you to inquire of the LORD, in this manner you shall speak to him, 'Thus says the LORD God of Israel: "*Concerning* the words which you have heard— [27]because your heart was tender, and you humbled yourself before God when you heard His words against this place and against its inhabitants, and you humbled yourself before Me, and you tore your clothes and wept before Me, I also have heard *you,*" says the LORD. [28]"Surely I will gather you to your fathers, and you shall be gathered to your grave in peace; and your eyes shall not see all the calamity which I will bring on this place and its inhabitants." ' " So they brought back word to the king.

Josiah Restores True Worship

[29]Then the king sent and gathered all the elders of Judah and Jerusalem. [30]The king went up to the house of the LORD, with all the men of Judah and the inhabitants of Jerusalem—the priests and the Levites, and all the people, great and small. And he read in their hearing all the words of the Book of the Covenant which had been found in the house of the LORD.

34:20 [a]*Achbor the son of Michaiah* in 2 Kings 22:12
34:22 [a]Spelled *Tikvah* in 2 Kings 22:14 [b]Spelled *Harhas* in 2 Kings 22:14

³¹Then the king stood in his place and made a covenant before the Lord, to follow the Lord, and to keep His commandments and His testimonies and His statutes with all his heart and all his soul, to perform the words of the covenant that were written in this book. ³²And he made all who were present in Jerusalem and Benjamin take a stand. So the inhabitants of Jerusalem did according to the covenant of God, the God of their fathers. ³³Thus Josiah removed all the abominations from all the country that *belonged* to the children of Israel, and made all who were present in Israel diligently serve the Lord their God. All his days they did not depart from following the Lord God of their fathers.

Josiah Keeps the Passover

35 Now Josiah kept a Passover to the Lord in Jerusalem, and they slaughtered the Passover *lambs* on the fourteenth *day* of the first month. ²And he set the priests in their duties and encouraged them for the service of the house of the Lord. ³Then he said to the Levites who taught all Israel, who were holy to the Lord: "Put the holy ark in the house which Solomon the son of David, king of Israel, built. *It shall* no longer *be* a burden on *your* shoulders. Now serve the Lord your God and His people Israel. ⁴Prepare *yourselves* according to your fathers' houses, according to your divisions, following the written instruction of David king of Israel and the written instruction of Solomon his son. ⁵And stand in the holy *place* according to the divisions of the fathers' houses of your brethren the *lay* people, and *according to* the division of the father's house of the Levites. ⁶So slaughter the Passover *offerings,* consecrate yourselves, and prepare *them* for your brethren, that *they* may do according to the word of the Lord by the hand of Moses."

⁷Then Josiah gave the *lay* people lambs and young goats from the flock, all for Passover *offerings* for all who were present, to the number of thirty thousand, as well as three thousand cattle; these *were* from the king's possessions. ⁸And his leaders gave willingly to the people, to the priests, and to the Levites. Hilkiah, Zechariah, and Jehiel, rulers of the house of God, gave to the priests for the Passover *offerings* two thousand six hundred *from the flock,* and three hundred cattle. ⁹Also Conaniah, his brothers Shemaiah and Nethanel, and Hashabiah and Jeiel and Jozabad, chief of the Levites, gave to the Levites for Passover *offerings* five thousand *from the flock* and five hundred cattle.

¹⁰So the service was prepared, and the priests stood in their places, and the Levites in their divisions, according to the king's command. ¹¹And they slaughtered the Passover *offerings;* and the priests sprinkled *the blood* with their hands, while the Levites skinned *the animals.* ¹²Then they removed the burnt offerings that *they* might give them to the divisions of the fathers' houses of the *lay* people, to offer to the Lord, as *it is* written in the Book of Moses. And so *they did* with the cattle. ¹³Also they roasted the Passover *offerings* with fire according to the ordinance; but the *other* holy *offerings* they boiled in pots, in caldrons, and in pans, and divided *them* quickly among all the *lay* people. ¹⁴Then afterward they prepared portions for themselves and for the priests, because the priests, the sons of Aaron, *were busy* in offering burnt offerings and fat until night; therefore the Levites prepared portions for themselves and for the priests, the sons of Aaron. ¹⁵And the singers, the sons of Asaph, *were* in their places, according to the command of David, Asaph, Heman, and Jeduthun the king's seer. Also the gatekeepers were at each gate; they did not have to leave their position, because their brethren the Levites prepared portions for them.

¹⁶So all the service of the Lord was prepared the same day, to keep the Passover and to offer burnt offerings on the altar of the Lord, according to the command of King Josiah. ¹⁷And the children of Israel who were present kept the Passover at that time, and the Feast of Unleavened Bread for seven days. ¹⁸There had been no Passover kept in Israel like that since the days of Samuel the prophet; and none of the kings of Israel had kept such a Passover as Josiah kept, with the priests and the Levites, all Judah and Israel who were present, and the inhabitants of

The Sweet Fruit of Repentance

YOUNG KING ZEDEKIAH HAD A CHANCE to save his nation. He could have led his people to a time of spiritual renewal. But instead, "He stiffened his neck and hardened his heart against turning to the LORD God of Israel" (36:13).

It's no accident that he was the last king of Judah.

Repentance involves a turn *from* sin and a pursuit *of* righteousness. We do not argue with God; we admit our wickedness, turn away from it, and endeavor to live wholly for Him. Author J. I. Packer once wrote, "The repentance that Christ requires of His people consists in a settled refusal to set any limit to the claims which He may make on their lives."

Several years ago at a national Christian conference, God orchestrated what became three days of holy introspection, confession, and cleansing. Individuals streamed to the platform, publicly asking God to forgive them. Hundreds of others sought forgiveness face-to-face and prayed for healing and reconciliation. That cavernous building became a temple filled with the presence of God. And God began a work in that place that is still bearing fruit in my own heart years later.

Repentance is never easy, but the resulting fruit is sweet. Husbands and wives forgive one another. Children regain loving, attentive parents. The guilty find relief and freedom. And a true family reformation begins where it matters most, in your home.

Jerusalem. ¹⁹In the eighteenth year of the reign of Josiah this Passover was kept.

Josiah Dies in Battle

²⁰After all this, when Josiah had prepared the temple, Necho king of Egypt came up to fight against Carchemish by the Euphrates; and Josiah went out against him. ²¹But he sent messengers to him, saying, "What have I to do with you, king of Judah? *I have* not *come* against you this day, but against the house with which I have war; for God commanded me to make haste. Refrain *from meddling with* God, who *is* with me, lest He destroy you." ²²Nevertheless Josiah would not turn his face from him, but disguised himself so that he might fight with him, and did not heed the words of Necho from the mouth of God. So he came to fight in the Valley of Megiddo.

²³And the archers shot King Josiah; and the king said to his servants, "Take me away, for I am severely wounded." ²⁴His servants therefore took him out of that chariot and put him in the second chariot that he had, and they brought him to Jerusalem. So he died, and was buried in *one of* the tombs of his fathers. And all Judah and Jerusalem mourned for Josiah.

²⁵Jeremiah also lamented for Josiah. And to this day all the singing men and the singing women speak of Josiah in their lamentations. They made it a custom in Israel; and indeed they *are* written in the Laments.

²⁶Now the rest of the acts of Josiah and his goodness, according to *what was* written in the Law of the LORD, ²⁷and his deeds from first to last, indeed they *are* written in the book of the kings of Israel and Judah.

The Reign and Captivity of Jehoahaz

36 Then the people of the land took Jehoahaz the son of Josiah, and made him king in his father's place in Jerusalem. ²Jehoahazᵃ *was* twenty-three years old when he became king, and he reigned three months in Jerusalem. ³Now the king of Egypt deposed him at Jerusalem; and he imposed on the land a tribute of one hundred talents of silver and a talent of gold. ⁴Then the king of Egypt made *Jehoahaz's*ᵃ brother Eliakim king over Judah and Jerusalem, and changed his name to Jehoiakim. And Necho took Jehoahazᵇ his brother and carried him off to Egypt.

The Reign and Captivity of Jehoiakim

⁵Jehoiakim *was* twenty-five years old

36:2 ᵃMasoretic Text reads *Joahaz*.
36:4 ᵃLiterally *his* ᵇMasoretic Text reads *Joahaz*.

when he became king, and he reigned eleven years in Jerusalem. And he did evil in the sight of the LORD his God. ⁶Nebuchadnezzar king of Babylon came up against him, and bound him in bronze *fetters* to carry him off to Babylon. ⁷Nebuchadnezzar also carried off *some* of the articles from the house of the LORD to Babylon, and put them in his temple at Babylon. ⁸Now the rest of the acts of Jehoiakim, the abominations which he did, and what was found against him, indeed they *are* written in the book of the kings of Israel and Judah. Then Jehoiachin his son reigned in his place.

The Reign and Captivity of Jehoiachin

⁹Jehoiachin *was* eight^a years old when he became king, and he reigned in Jerusalem three months and ten days. And he did evil in the sight of the LORD. ¹⁰At the turn of the year King Nebuchadnezzar summoned *him* and took him to Babylon, with the costly articles from the house of the LORD, and made Zedekiah, *Jehoiakim's*^a brother, king over Judah and Jerusalem.

Zedekiah Reigns in Judah

¹¹Zedekiah *was* twenty-one years old when he became king, and he reigned eleven years in Jerusalem. ¹²He did evil in the sight of the LORD his God, *and* did not humble himself before Jeremiah the prophet, *who spoke* from the mouth of the LORD. ¹³And he also rebelled against King Nebuchadnezzar, who had made him swear *an oath* by God; but he stiffened his neck and hardened his heart against turning to the LORD God of Israel. ¹⁴Moreover all the leaders of the priests and the people transgressed more and more, *according* to all the abominations of the nations, and defiled the house of the LORD which He had consecrated in Jerusalem.

The Fall of Jerusalem

¹⁵And the LORD God of their fathers sent *warnings* to them by His messengers, rising up early and sending *them,* because He had compassion on His people and on His dwelling place. ¹⁶But they mocked the messengers of God, despised His words, and scoffed at His prophets, until the wrath of the LORD arose against His people, till *there was* no remedy.

¹⁷Therefore He brought against them the king of the Chaldeans, who killed their young men with the sword in the house of their sanctuary, and had no compassion on young man or virgin, on the aged or the weak; He gave *them* all into his hand. ¹⁸And all the articles from the house of God, great and small, the treasures of the house of the LORD, and the treasures of the king and of his leaders, all *these* he took to Babylon. ¹⁹Then they burned the house of God, broke down the wall of Jerusalem, burned all its palaces with fire, and destroyed all its precious possessions. ²⁰And those who escaped from the sword he carried away to Babylon, where they became servants to him and his sons until the rule of the kingdom of Persia, ²¹to fulfill the word of the LORD by the mouth of Jeremiah, until the land had enjoyed her Sabbaths. As long as she lay desolate she kept Sabbath, to fulfill seventy years.

The Proclamation of Cyrus

²²Now in the first year of Cyrus king of Persia, that the word of the LORD by the mouth of Jeremiah might be fulfilled, the LORD stirred up the spirit of Cyrus king of Persia, so that he made a proclamation throughout all his kingdom, and also *put it* in writing, saying,

²³ Thus says Cyrus king of Persia:
All the kingdoms of the earth the LORD God of heaven has given me. And He has commanded me to build Him a house at Jerusalem which is in Judah. Who *is* among you of all His people? May the LORD his God *be* with him, and let him go up!

36:9 ^aSome Hebrew manuscripts, Septuagint, Syriac, and 2 Kings 24:8 read *eighteen.*
36:10 ^aLiterally *his* (compare 2 Kings 24:17)

EZRA

TOGETHER WITH THE BOOK OF NEHEMIAH, Ezra gives an account of the end of the seventy years of Hebrew captivity in Babylon, and the return to Jerusalem of two groups of faithful Jews. Chapters 1—6 tell how the first group of more than 40,000 people left Babylon immediately after being freed by King Cyrus. Over the next twenty years, they re-inhabited the city of Jerusalem and rebuilt the temple (a much smaller and less ornate structure than the one built by Solomon). Two generations later, Ezra led a second group of Jews from Babylon to Jerusalem (chapters 7—10).

The books of Ezra and Nehemiah originally appeared as a single work and so ought to be studied together. Ezra picks up where 2 Chronicles leaves off; in fact, the last two verses of 2 Chronicles are identical to the first two verses in Ezra. Regardless of whether Ezra wrote all four books, a clear link exists between them.

God had ordained the seven decades of captivity in Babylon as chastening for the stubborn disobedience of His people. They had ignored the warnings of the prophet Jeremiah (Jer. 2:14–25) and had continued to worship foreign gods and pagan idols. Yet even while God was disciplining His erring people, He was also working miraculously through a pagan king, Cyrus, to set His people free. God's actions demonstrate that the heart of the king—whether righteous or wicked, Jew or Gentile—is in the hand of the Lord, who turns it wherever He wills (Prov. 21:1). Ezra reminds us that God rules over the affairs of men to accomplish His own divine purposes.

Families play a crucial role in the rebuilding of Jerusalem and of the temple. Ezra is careful to tell us that families worked together to begin the reconstruction of the house of God (3:9), and that families celebrated its dedication (6:16). He describes in detail the families that accompanied him to Jerusalem from Babylon (8:1–36), and he even tells of a prayer for traveling mercies that he offered "for us and our little ones and all our possessions" (8:21).

End of the Babylonian Captivity

1 Now in the first year of Cyrus king of Persia, that the word of the LORD by the mouth of Jeremiah might be fulfilled, the LORD stirred up the spirit of Cyrus king of Persia, so that he made a proclamation throughout all his kingdom, and also *put it* in writing, saying,

2   Thus says Cyrus king of Persia:
      All the kingdoms of the earth the
      LORD God of heaven has given me.
      And He has commanded me to build
      Him a house at Jerusalem which *is* in
      Judah. ³Who *is* among you of all His
      people? May his God be with him,
      and let him go up to Jerusalem which
      is in Judah, and build the house of
      the LORD God of Israel (He *is* God),
      which *is* in Jerusalem. ⁴And whoever
      is left in any place where he dwells,
      let the men of his place help him
      with silver and gold, with goods and
      livestock, besides the freewill
      offerings for the house of God which
      is in Jerusalem.

⁵Then the heads of the fathers' *houses* of Judah and Benjamin, and the priests and the Levites, with all whose spirits God had moved, arose to go up and build the house of the LORD which *is* in Jerusalem. ⁶And all those who *were* around them encouraged them with articles of silver and gold, with goods and livestock, and with precious things, besides all *that* was willingly offered.

⁷King Cyrus also brought out the articles of the house of the LORD, which Nebuchadnezzar had taken from Jerusalem and put in the temple of his gods; ⁸and Cyrus king of Persia brought them out by the hand of Mithredath the treasurer, and counted them out to Sheshbazzar the prince of Judah. ⁹This *is* the number of them: thirty gold platters, one thousand silver platters, twenty-nine knives, ¹⁰thirty gold basins, four hundred and ten silver basins of a similar *kind, and* one thousand other articles. ¹¹All the articles of gold and silver *were* five thousand

four hundred. All *these* Sheshbazzar took with the captives who were brought from Babylon to Jerusalem.

The Captives Who Returned to Jerusalem

2 Now[a] these *are* the people of the province who came back from the captivity, of those who had been carried away, whom Nebuchadnezzar the king of Babylon had carried away to Babylon, and who returned to Jerusalem and Judah, everyone to his *own* city.

ROMANCE FAQ

Q: What is God's real purpose for sex?

The Designer of sex, God, has made numerous statements in His Word that describe His purpose for the sexual aspect of marriage.

First, sex is the process He gave us to multiply a godly heritage. He commanded us to "be fruitful and multiply, and fill the earth, and subdue it" (Gen. 1:28). Some have joked that this is the *only* divine command that humankind has ever faithfully obeyed! This, however, overlooks the truth that God isn't interested merely in a planet full of humans; what He's after is a godly heritage, boys and girls who grow up in godly homes who love to worship and serve their Creator.

Second, God designed sex for our pleasure. In fact, Scripture talks significantly more about enjoying the pleasures of sex than it does about being fruitful and multiplying. Do you think it is mere accident that our bodies have such huge numbers of pleasure receptors on and around the sexual organs? God *designed* us this way.

Third, in some profound way, the physical act of two becoming one is meant to echo the eternal and infinite fellowship that the members of the Godhead have always enjoyed with one another.

2:1 [a]Compare this chapter with Nehemiah 7:6–73.

²*Those* who came with Zerubbabel *were* Jeshua, Nehemiah, Seraiah, Reelaiah, Mordecai, Bilshan, Mispar,ᵃ Bigvai, Rehum,ᵇ *and* Baanah. The number of the men of the people of Israel: ³the people of Parosh, two thousand one hundred and seventy-two; ⁴the people of Shephatiah, three hundred and seventy-two; ⁵the people of Arah, seven hundred and seventy-five; ⁶the people of Pahath-Moab, of the people of Jeshua *and* Joab, two thousand eight hundred and twelve; ⁷the people of Elam, one thousand two hundred and fifty-four; ⁸the people of Zattu, nine hundred and forty-five; ⁹the people of Zaccai, seven hundred and sixty; ¹⁰the people of Bani,ᵃ six hundred and forty-two; ¹¹the people of Bebai, six hundred and twenty-three; ¹²the people of Azgad, one thousand two hundred and twenty-two; ¹³the people of Adonikam, six hundred and sixty-six; ¹⁴the people of Bigvai, two thousand and fifty-six; ¹⁵the people of Adin, four hundred and fifty-four; ¹⁶the people of Ater of Hezekiah, ninety-eight; ¹⁷the people of Bezai, three hundred and twenty-three; ¹⁸the people of Jorah,ᵃ one hundred and twelve; ¹⁹the people of Hashum, two hundred and twenty-three; ²⁰the people of Gibbar,ᵃ ninety-five; ²¹the people of Bethlehem, one hundred and twenty-three; ²²the men of Netophah, fifty-six; ²³the men of Anathoth, one hundred and twenty-eight; ²⁴the people of Azmaveth,ᵃ forty-two; ²⁵the people of Kirjath Arim,ᵃ Chephirah, and Beeroth, seven hundred and forty-three; ²⁶the people of Ramah and Geba, six hundred and twenty-one; ²⁷the men of Michmas, one hundred and twenty-two; ²⁸the men of Bethel and Ai, two hundred and twenty-three; ²⁹the people of Nebo, fifty-two; ³⁰the people of Magbish, one hundred and fifty-six; ³¹the people of the other Elam, one thousand two hundred and fifty-four; ³²the people of Harim, three hundred and twenty; ³³the people of Lod, Hadid, and Ono, seven hundred and twenty-five; ³⁴the people of Jericho, three hundred and forty-five; ³⁵the people of Senaah, three thousand six hundred and thirty.

³⁶The priests: the sons of Jedaiah, of the house of Jeshua, nine hundred and seventy-three; ³⁷the sons of Immer, one thousand and fifty-two; ³⁸the sons of Pashhur, one thousand two hundred and forty-seven; ³⁹the sons of Harim, one thousand and seventeen.

⁴⁰The Levites: the sons of Jeshua and Kadmiel, of the sons of Hodaviah,ᵃ seventy-four.

⁴¹The singers: the sons of Asaph, one hundred and twenty-eight.

⁴²The sons of the gatekeepers: the sons of Shallum, the sons of Ater, the sons of Talmon, the sons of Akkub, the sons of Hatita, and the sons of Shobai, one hundred and thirty-nine *in* all.

⁴³The Nethinim: the sons of Ziha, the sons of Hasupha, the sons of Tabbaoth, ⁴⁴the sons of Keros, the sons of Siaha,ᵃ the sons of Padon, ⁴⁵the sons of Lebanah, the sons of Hagabah, the sons of Akkub, ⁴⁶the sons of Hagab, the sons of Shalmai, the sons of Hanan, ⁴⁷the sons of Giddel, the sons of Gahar, the sons of Reaiah, ⁴⁸the sons of Rezin, the sons of Nekoda, the sons of Gazzam, ⁴⁹the sons of Uzza, the sons of Paseah, the sons of Besai, ⁵⁰the sons of Asnah, the sons of Meunim, the sons of Nephusim,ᵃ ⁵¹the sons of Bakbuk, the sons of Hakupha, the sons of Harhur, ⁵²the sons of Bazluth,ᵃ the sons of Mehida, the sons of Harsha, ⁵³the sons of Barkos, the sons of Sisera, the sons of Tamah, ⁵⁴the sons of Neziah, and the sons of Hatipha.

⁵⁵The sons of Solomon's servants: the sons of Sotai, the sons of Sophereth, the sons of Peruda,ᵃ ⁵⁶the sons of Jaala, the sons of Darkon, the sons of Giddel, ⁵⁷the sons of Shephatiah, the sons of Hattil, the sons of Pochereth of Zebaim, and the sons of Ami.ᵃ ⁵⁸All the Nethinim and the children of Solomon's servants were three hundred and ninety-two.

⁵⁹And these *were* the ones who came up from Tel Melah, Tel Harsha, Cherub,

---

2:2 ᵃSpelled *Mispereth* in Nehemiah 7:7 ᵇSpelled *Nehum* in Nehemiah 7:7 **2:10** ᵃSpelled *Binnui* in Nehemiah 7:15 **2:18** ᵃCalled *Hariph* in Nehemiah 7:24 **2:20** ᵃCalled *Gibeon* in Nehemiah 7:25 **2:24** ᵃCalled *Beth Azmaveth* in Nehemiah 7:28 **2:25** ᵃCalled *Kirjath Jearim* in Nehemiah 7:29 **2:40** ᵃSpelled *Hodevah* in Nehemiah 7:43 **2:44** ᵃSpelled *Sia* in Nehemiah 7:47 **2:50** ᵃSpelled *Nephishesim* in Nehemiah 7:52 **2:52** ᵃSpelled *Bazlith* in Nehemiah 7:54 **2:55** ᵃSpelled *Perida* in Nehemiah 7:57 **2:57** ᵃSpelled *Amon* in Nehemiah 7:59

Addan,[a] and Immer; but they could not identify their father's house or their genealogy,[b] whether they *were* of Israel: [60]the sons of Delaiah, the sons of Tobiah, and the sons of Nekoda, six hundred and fifty-two; [61]and of the sons of the priests: the sons of Habaiah, the sons of Koz,[a] and the sons of Barzillai, who took a wife of the daughters of Barzillai the Gileadite, and was called by their name. [62]These sought their listing *among* those who were registered by genealogy, but they were not found; therefore they *were excluded* from the priesthood as defiled. [63]And the governor[a] said to them that they should not eat of the most holy things till a priest could consult with the Urim and Thummim.

[64]The whole assembly together *was* forty-two thousand three hundred *and* sixty, [65]besides their male and female servants, of whom *there were* seven thousand three hundred and thirty-seven; and they had two hundred men and women singers. [66]Their horses *were* seven hundred and thirty-six, their mules two hundred and forty-five, [67]their camels four hundred and thirty-five, and *their* donkeys six thousand seven hundred and twenty.

[68]*Some* of the heads of the fathers' *houses,* when they came to the house of the LORD which *is* in Jerusalem, offered freely for the house of God, to erect it in its place: [69]According to their ability, they gave to the treasury for the work sixty-one thousand gold drachmas, five thousand minas of silver, and one hundred priestly garments.

[70]So the priests and the Levites, *some* of the people, the singers, the gatekeepers, and the Nethinim, dwelt in their cities, and all Israel in their cities.

Worship Restored at Jerusalem

3 And when the seventh month had come, and the children of Israel *were* in the cities, the people gathered together as one man to Jerusalem. [2]Then Jeshua the son of Jozadak[a] and his brethren the

BIBLICAL INSIGHTS • 3:11
Claim What's Yours

ALL OF US HAVE MADE BAD CHOICES and taken wrong turns. Some of them earned us a spanking, while others may have cost us our innocence, our virginity, or even our basic human dignity.

No matter the error or who is responsible, your sin can hang around in the form of shame and guilt. And even knowing that your sins are forgiven does not prevent the accuser, Satan, from reminding and accusing you of past failures.

Ultimately, you must both receive and claim God's forgiveness. Claiming it can sometimes be tough when your feelings shout that God could never forgive you, that your sin is beyond God's forgiveness. If you struggle with this, focus on the truth of God's Word regarding forgiveness:

• As far as the east is the west, so far has He removed our transgressions from us. (Ps. 103:12)

• If we confess our sins, He is faithful and just to forgive us our sins and to cleanse us from all unrighteousness. (1 John 1:9)

Memorize these verses (and others like them), and when doubts or negative feelings arise, repeat the Scriptures. As a precious child of God, you can find great comfort in the certainty that you have been forgiven. And go ahead and proclaim it, "His mercy endures forever!" (3:11).

---

priests, and Zerubbabel the son of Shealtiel and his brethren, arose and built the altar of the God of Israel, to offer burnt offerings on it, as *it is* written in the Law of Moses the man of God. [3]Though fear *had come* upon them because of the people of those countries, they set the altar on its bases; and they offered burnt offerings on it to the LORD, *both* the morning and evening burnt offerings. [4]They also

---

2:59 [a]Spelled *Addon* in Nehemiah 7:61   [b]Literally *seed*
2:61 [a]Or *Hakkoz*   2:63 [a]Hebrew *Tirshatha*
3:2 [a]Spelled *Jehozadak* in 1 Chronicles 6:14
3:8 [a]Spelled *Jehozadak* in 1 Chronicles 6:14

kept the Feast of Tabernacles, as *it is* written, and *offered* the daily burnt offerings in the number required by ordinance for each day. [5]Afterwards *they offered* the regular burnt offering, and *those* for New Moons and for all the appointed feasts of the LORD that were consecrated, and *those* of everyone who willingly offered a freewill offering to the LORD. [6]From the first day of the seventh month they began to offer burnt offerings to the LORD, although the foundation of the temple of the LORD had not been laid. [7]They also gave money to the masons and the carpenters, and food, drink, and oil to the people of Sidon and Tyre to bring cedar logs from Lebanon to the sea, to Joppa, according to the permission which they had from Cyrus king of Persia.

Restoration of the Temple Begins

[8]Now in the second month of the second year of their coming to the house of God at Jerusalem, Zerubbabel the son of Shealtiel, Jeshua the son of Jozadak,[a] and the rest of their brethren the priests and the Levites, and all those who had come out of the captivity to Jerusalem, began *work* and appointed the Levites from twenty years old and above to oversee the work of the house of the LORD. [9]Then Jeshua *with* his sons and brothers, Kadmiel *with* his sons, and the sons of Judah,[a] arose as one to oversee those working on the house of God: the sons of Henadad *with* their sons and their brethren the Levites.

[10]When the builders laid the foundation of the temple of the LORD, the priests stood[a] in their apparel with trumpets, and the Levites, the sons of Asaph, with cymbals, to praise the LORD, according to the ordinance of David king of Israel. [11]And they sang responsively, praising and giving thanks to the LORD:

"For *He is* good,
    For His mercy *endures* forever
        toward Israel."[a]

Then all the people shouted with a great shout, when they praised the LORD, because the foundation of the house of the LORD was laid.

[12]But many of the priests and Levites and heads of the fathers' *houses,* old men who had seen the first temple, wept with a loud voice when the foundation of this temple was laid before their eyes. Yet many shouted aloud for joy, [13]so that the people could not discern the noise of the shout of joy from the noise of the weeping of the people, for the people shouted with a loud shout, and the sound was heard afar off.

Resistance to Rebuilding the Temple

4 Now when the adversaries of Judah and Benjamin heard that the descendants of the captivity were building the temple of the LORD God of Israel, [2]they came to Zerubbabel and the heads of the fathers' *houses,* and said to them, "Let us build with you, for we seek your God as you *do;* and we have sacrificed to Him since the days of Esarhaddon king of Assyria, who brought us here." [3]But Zerubbabel and Jeshua and the rest of the heads of the fathers' *houses* of Israel said to them, "You may do nothing with us to build a house for our God; but we alone will build to the LORD God of Israel, as King Cyrus the king of Persia has commanded us." [4]Then the people of the land tried to discourage the people of Judah. They troubled them in building, [5]and hired counselors against them to frustrate their purpose all the days of Cyrus king of Persia, even until the reign of Darius king of Persia.

Rebuilding of Jerusalem Opposed

[6]In the reign of Ahasuerus, in the beginning of his reign, they wrote an accusation against the inhabitants of Judah and Jerusalem.

[7]In the days of Artaxerxes also, Bishlam, Mithredath, Tabel, and the rest of their companions wrote to Artaxerxes king of Persia; and the letter *was* written in Aramaic script, and translated into the Aramaic language. [8]Rehum[a] the commander and Shimshai the scribe wrote a letter against Jerusalem to King Artaxerxes in this fashion:

3:9 [a]Or *Hodaviah* (compare 2:40) **3:10** [a]Following Septuagint, Syriac, and Vulgate; Masoretic Text reads *they stationed the priests.* **3:11** [a]Compare Psalm 136:1 **4:8** [a]The original language of Ezra 4:8 through 6:18 is Aramaic.

9 From[a] Rehum the commander, Shimshai the scribe, and the rest of their companions—*representatives* of the Dinaites, the Apharsathchites, the Tarpelites, the people of Persia and Erech and Babylon and Shushan,[b] the Dehavites, the Elamites, 10and the rest of the nations whom the great and noble Osnapper took captive and settled in the cities of Samaria and the remainder beyond the River[a]—and so forth.[b]

11(This *is* a copy of the letter that they sent him)

To King Artaxerxes from your servants, the men *of the region* beyond the River, and so forth:[a]

12 Let it be known to the king that the Jews who came up from you have come to us at Jerusalem, and are building the rebellious and evil city, and are finishing *its* walls and repairing the foundations. 13Let it now be known to the king that, if this city is built and the walls completed, they will not pay tax, tribute, or custom, and the king's treasury will be diminished. 14Now because we receive support from the palace, it was not proper for us to see the king's dishonor; therefore we have sent and informed the king, 15that search may be made in the book of the records of your fathers. And you will find in the book of the records and know that this city *is* a rebellious city, harmful to kings and provinces, and that they have incited sedition within the city in former times, for which cause this city was destroyed.

16 We inform the king that if this city is rebuilt and its walls are completed, the result will be that you will have no dominion beyond the River.

17The king sent an answer:

To Rehum the commander, *to* Shimshai the scribe, *to* the rest of their companions who dwell in Samaria, and *to* the remainder beyond the River:

Peace, and so forth.[a]

18 The letter which you sent to us has been clearly read before me. 19And I gave the command, and a search has been made, and it was found that this city in former times has revolted against kings, and rebellion and sedition have been fostered in it. 20There have also been mighty kings over Jerusalem, who have ruled over all *the region* beyond the River; and tax, tribute, and custom were paid to them. 21Now give the command to make these men cease, that this city may not be built until the command is given by me.

22 Take heed now that you do not fail to do this. Why should damage increase to the hurt of the kings?

23Now when the copy of King Artaxerxes' letter *was* read before Rehum, Shimshai the scribe, and their companions, they went up in haste to Jerusalem against the Jews, and by force of arms made them cease. 24Thus the work of the house of God which *is* at Jerusalem ceased, and it was discontinued until the second year of the reign of Darius king of Persia.

Restoration of the Temple Resumed

5 Then the prophet Haggai and Zechariah the son of Iddo, prophets, prophesied to the Jews who *were* in Judah and Jerusalem, in the name of the God of Israel, *who was* over them. 2So Zerubbabel the son of Shealtiel and Jeshua the son of Jozadak[a] rose up and began to build the house of God which *is* in Jerusalem; and the prophets of God *were* with them, helping them.

3At the same time Tattenai the governor of *the region* beyond the River[a] and Shethar-Boznai and their companions came to them and spoke thus to them: "Who has

---

4:9 [a]Literally *Then* [b]Or *Susa* 4:10 [a]That is, the Euphrates [b]Literally *and now* 4:11 [a]Literally *and now* 4:17 [a]Literally *and now* 5:2 [a]Spelled *Jehozadak* in 1 Chronicles 6:14 5:3 [a]That is, the Euphrates

commanded you to build this temple and finish this wall?" ⁴Then, accordingly, we told them the names of the men who were constructing this building. ⁵But the eye of their God was upon the elders of the Jews, so that they could not make them cease till a report could go to Darius. Then a written answer was returned concerning this *matter.* ⁶This is a copy of the letter that Tattenai sent:

The governor of *the region* beyond the River, and Shethar-Boznai, and his companions, the Persians who *were in the region* beyond the River, to Darius the king.

⁷(They sent a letter to him, in which was written thus)

To Darius the king:

All peace.

⁸ Let it be known to the king that we went into the province of Judea, to the temple of the great God, which is being built with heavy stones, and timber is being laid in the walls; and this work goes on diligently and prospers in their hands.

9 Then we asked those elders, *and* spoke thus to them: "Who commanded you to build this temple and to finish these walls?" ¹⁰We also asked them their names to inform you, that we might write the names of the men who *were* chief among them.

11 And thus they returned us an answer, saying: "We are the servants of the God of heaven and earth, and we are rebuilding the temple that was built many years ago, which a great king of Israel built and completed. ¹²But because our fathers provoked the God of heaven to wrath, He gave them into the hand of Nebuchadnezzar king of Babylon, the Chaldean, *who* destroyed this temple and carried the people away to Babylon. ¹³However, in the first

---

year of Cyrus king of Babylon, King Cyrus issued a decree to build this house of God. ¹⁴Also, the gold and silver articles of the house of God, which Nebuchadnezzar had taken from the temple that *was* in Jerusalem and carried into the temple of Babylon—those King Cyrus took from the temple of Babylon, and they were given to one named Sheshbazzar, whom he had made governor. ¹⁵And he said to him, 'Take these articles; go, carry them to the temple *site* that *is* in Jerusalem, and let the house of God be rebuilt on its former site.' ¹⁶Then the same Sheshbazzar came *and* laid the foundation of the house of God which *is* in Jerusalem; but from that time even until now it has been under construction, and it is not finished."

¹⁷ Now therefore, if *it seems* good to the king, let a search be made in the king's treasure house, which *is* there in Babylon, whether it is *so* that a decree was issued by King Cyrus to build this house of God at Jerusalem, and let the king send us his pleasure concerning this *matter.*

The Decree of Darius

6 Then King Darius issued a decree, and a search was made in the archives,ª where the treasures were stored in Babylon. ²And at Achmetha,ª in the palace that *is* in the province of Media, a scroll was found, and in it a record *was* written thus:

³ In the first year of King Cyrus, King Cyrus issued a decree *concerning* the house of God at Jerusalem: "Let the house be rebuilt, the place where they offered sacrifices; and let the foundations of it be firmly laid, its height sixty cubits *and* its width sixty cubits, ⁴*with* three rows of heavy stones and one row of new timber. Let the expenses be paid from the king's treasury. ⁵Also let the

gold and silver articles of the house of God, which Nebuchadnezzar took from the temple which *is* in Jerusalem and brought to Babylon, be restored and taken back to the temple which *is* in Jerusalem, *each* to its place; and deposit *them* in the house of God"—

⁶ Now *therefore,* Tattenai, governor of *the region* beyond the River, and Shethar-Boznai, and your companions the Persians who *are* beyond the River, keep yourselves far from there. ⁷Let the work of this house of God alone; let the governor of the Jews and the elders of the Jews build this house of God on its site.

⁸ Moreover I issue a decree *as to* what you shall do for the elders of these Jews, for the building of this house of God: Let the cost be paid at the king's expense from taxes *on the region* beyond the River; this is to be given immediately to these men, so that they are not hindered. ⁹And whatever they need—young bulls, rams, and lambs for the burnt offerings of the God of heaven, wheat, salt, wine, and oil, according to the request of the priests who *are* in Jerusalem—let it be given them day by day without fail, ¹⁰that they may offer sacrifices of sweet aroma to the God of heaven, and pray for the life of the king and his sons.

¹¹ Also I issue a decree that whoever alters this edict, let a timber be pulled from his house and erected, and let him be hanged on it; and let his house be made a refuse heap because of this. ¹²And may the God who causes His name to dwell there destroy any king or people who put their hand to alter it, or to destroy this house of God which is in Jerusalem. I Darius issue a decree; let it be done diligently.

The Temple Completed and Dedicated

¹³Then Tattenai, governor of *the region* beyond the River, Shethar-Boznai, and

---

6:1 ªLiterally *house of the scrolls*
6:2 ªProbably *Ecbatana,* the ancient capital of Media

their companions diligently did according to what King Darius had sent. [14]So the elders of the Jews built, and they prospered through the prophesying of Haggai the prophet and Zechariah the son of Iddo. And they built and finished *it,* according to the commandment of the God of Israel, and according to the command of Cyrus, Darius, and Artaxerxes king of Persia. [15]Now the temple was finished on the third day of the month of Adar, which was in the sixth year of the reign of King Darius. [16]Then the children of Israel, the priests and the Levites and the rest of the descendants of the captivity, celebrated the dedication of this house of God with joy. [17]And they offered sacrifices at the dedication of this house of God, one hundred bulls, two hundred rams, four hundred lambs, and as a sin offering for all Israel twelve male goats, according to the number of the tribes of Israel. [18]They assigned the priests to their divisions and the Levites to their divisions, over the service of God in Jerusalem, as it is written in the Book of Moses.

The Passover Celebrated

[19]And the descendants of the captivity kept the Passover on the fourteenth *day* of the first month. [20]For the priests and the Levites had purified themselves; all of them *were ritually* clean. And they slaughtered the Passover *lambs* for all the descendants of the captivity, for their brethren the priests, and for themselves. [21]Then the children of Israel who had returned from the captivity ate together with all who had separated themselves from the filth of the nations of the land in order to seek the LORD God of Israel. [22]And they kept the Feast of Unleavened Bread seven days with joy; for the LORD made them joyful, and turned the heart of the king of Assyria toward them, to strengthen their hands in the work of the house of God, the God of Israel.

The Arrival of Ezra

7 Now after these things, in the reign of Artaxerxes king of Persia, Ezra the son of Seraiah, the son of Azariah, the son of Hilkiah, [2]the son of Shallum, the son of Zadok, the son of Ahitub, [3]the son of Amariah, the son of Azariah, the son of Meraioth, [4]the son of Zerahiah, the son of Uzzi, the son of Bukki, [5]the son of Abishua, the son of Phinehas, the son of Eleazar, the son of Aaron the chief priest— [6]this Ezra came up from Babylon; and he *was* a skilled scribe in the Law of Moses, which the LORD God of Israel had given. The king granted him all his request, according to the hand of the LORD his God upon him. [7]*Some* of the children of Israel, the priests, the Levites, the singers, the gatekeepers, and the Nethinim came up to Jerusalem in the seventh year of King Artaxerxes. [8]And Ezra came to Jerusalem in the fifth month, which *was* in the seventh year of the king. [9]On the first *day* of the first month he began *his* journey from Babylon, and on the first *day* of the fifth month he came to Jerusalem, according to the good hand of his God upon him. [10]For Ezra had prepared his heart to seek the Law of the LORD, and to do *it,* and to teach statutes and ordinances in Israel.

The Letter of Artaxerxes to Ezra

[11]This *is* a copy of the letter that King Artaxerxes gave Ezra the priest, the scribe, expert in the words of the commandments of the LORD, and of His statutes to Israel:

12   Artaxerxes,[a] king of kings,

To Ezra the priest, a scribe of the Law of the God of heaven:

Perfect *peace,* and so forth.[b]

13   I issue a decree that all those of the people of Israel and the priests and Levites in my realm, who volunteer to go up to Jerusalem, may go with you. [14]And whereas you are being sent by the king and his seven counselors to inquire concerning Judah and Jerusalem, with regard to the Law of your God which *is* in your hand; [15]and *whereas you are* to carry the silver and gold which the

---

7:12 [a]The original language of Ezra 7:12–26 is Aramaic. [b]Literally *and now*

DEVOTIONS FOR COUPLES • 7
Study Your Spouse

Would you like to know the best elixir of romance ever invented? Having it can spell the difference between disappointment and satisfaction. Here it is:

Knowledge.

If you want to know how to best romance your wife, then become a student of her. Find out what she likes and dislikes, discover her strengths and weaknesses, know her fears and hopes. What does she consider romantic? What does she consider a turn-off? What really revs her engine? What places make her dreamy-eyed? What aromas make her heart beat faster?

Make it a point to *really* get to know your wife. This will take work! You can't just hand her a questionnaire and ask her to fill it out. You'll need to listen to her, observe her, ask questions—in other words, study her. It will take time, but it will be worth it. Your diligent studies and the knowledge you gain of her will enable you to produce the most potent elixir of love available.

---

king and his counselors have freely offered to the God of Israel, whose dwelling *is* in Jerusalem; 16and *whereas* all the silver and gold that you may find in all the province of Babylon, along with the freewill offering of the people and the priests, *are to be* freely offered for the house of their God in Jerusalem— 17now therefore, be careful to buy with this money bulls, rams, and lambs, with their grain offerings and their drink offerings, and offer them on the altar of the house of your God in Jerusalem.

18 And whatever seems good to you and your brethren to do with the rest of the silver and the gold, do it according to the will of your God. 19Also the articles that are given to you for the service of the house of your God, deliver in full before the God of Jerusalem. 20And whatever more may be needed for the house of your God, which you may have occasion to provide, pay *for it* from the king's treasury.

21 And I, *even* I, Artaxerxes the king, issue a decree to all the treasurers who *are in the region* beyond the River, that whatever Ezra the priest, the scribe of the Law of the God of heaven, may require of you, let it be done diligently, 22up to one hundred talents of silver, one hundred kors of wheat, one hundred baths of wine, one hundred baths of oil, and salt without prescribed limit. 23Whatever is commanded by the God of heaven, let it diligently be done for the house of the God of heaven. For why should there be wrath against the realm of the king and his sons?

24 Also we inform you that it shall not be lawful to impose tax, tribute, or custom on any of the priests, Levites, singers, gatekeepers, Nethinim, or servants of this house of God. 25And you, Ezra, according to your God-given wisdom, set magistrates and judges who may judge all the people who *are in the region* beyond the River, all such as know the laws of your God; and teach those who do not know *them.* 26Whoever will not observe the law of your God and the law of the king, let judgment be executed speedily on him, whether *it be* death, or banishment, or confiscation of goods, or imprisonment.

27Blessed *be* the LORD God of our fathers, who has put *such a thing* as this in the king's heart, to beautify the house of the LORD which *is* in Jerusalem, 28and has extended mercy to me before the king and his counselors, and before all the king's mighty princes.

So I was encouraged, as the hand of the LORD my God *was* upon me; and I gathered leading men of Israel to go up with me.

Heads of Families Who Returned with Ezra

8 These *are* the heads of their fathers' *houses,* and *this is* the genealogy of those who went up with me from Babylon, in the reign of King Artaxerxes: ²of the sons of Phinehas, Gershom; of the sons of Ithamar, Daniel; of the sons of David, Hattush; ³of the sons of Shecaniah, of the sons of Parosh, Zechariah; and registered with him *were* one hundred and fifty males; ⁴of the sons of Pahath-Moab, Eliehoenai the son of Zerahiah, and with him two hundred males; ⁵of the sons of Shechaniah,ᵃ Ben-Jahaziel, and with him three hundred males; ⁶of the sons of Adin, Ebed the son of Jonathan, and with him fifty males; ⁷of the sons of Elam, Jeshaiah the son of Athaliah, and with him seventy males; ⁸of the sons of Shephatiah, Zebadiah the son of Michael, and with him eighty males; ⁹of the sons of Joab, Obadiah the son of Jehiel, and with him two hundred and eighteen males; ¹⁰of the sons of Shelomith,ᵃ Ben-Josiphiah, and with him one hundred and sixty males; ¹¹of the sons of Bebai, Zechariah the son of Bebai, and with him twenty-eight males; ¹²of the sons of Azgad, Johanan the son of Hakkatan, and with him one hundred and ten males; ¹³of the last sons of Adonikam,

whose names *are* these—Eliphelet, Jeiel, and Shemaiah—and with them sixty males; ¹⁴also of the sons of Bigvai, Uthai and Zabbud, and with them seventy males.

Servants for the Temple

¹⁵Now I gathered them by the river that flows to Ahava, and we camped there three days. And I looked among the people and the priests, and found none of the sons of Levi there. ¹⁶Then I sent for Eliezer, Ariel, Shemaiah, Elnathan, Jarib, Elnathan, Nathan, Zechariah, and Meshullam, leaders; also for Joiarib and Elnathan, men of understanding. ¹⁷And I gave them a command for Iddo the chief man at the place Casiphia, and I told them what they should say to Iddo *and* his brethrenᵃ the Nethinim at the place Casiphia—that they should bring us servants for the house of our God. ¹⁸Then, by the good hand of our God upon us, they brought us a man of understanding, of the sons of Mahli the son of Levi, the son of Israel, namely Sherebiah, with his sons and brothers, eighteen men; ¹⁹and Hashabiah, and with him Jeshaiah of the sons of Merari, his brothers and their sons, twenty men; ²⁰also of the Nethinim, whom David and the lead-

8:5 ᵃFollowing Masoretic Text and Vulgate; Septuagint reads *the sons of Zatho, Shechaniah.*
8:10 ᵃFollowing Masoretic Text and Vulgate; Septuagint reads *the sons of Banni, Shelomith.*
8:17 ᵃFollowing Vulgate; Masoretic Text reads *to Iddo his brother;* Septuagint reads *to their brethren.*

ROMANTIC QUOTES AND NOTES
No Prayer Too Small or Too Big

Even though you know God invites you to bring all your concerns to Him in prayer (see Phil. 4:6), do you sometimes hold back, fearing that they just might not be spiritual enough? Maybe you have a secret desire, or maybe it's something as mundane as requesting traveling mercies for your family.

We have a friend who used to secretly scoff whenever he heard someone pray for traveling mercies. He expected the next request to be trite or trivial.

And then he read Ezra 8:21. Listen to the old scribe as he recalls his preparations for a family move to Jerusalem, "Then I proclaimed a fast there at the river of Ahava, that we might humble ourselves before our God, to seek from Him the right way for us and our little ones and all our possessions."

It couldn't get much clearer, could it? That's a prayer for traveling mercies if there ever were one—and God enshrined it in the Bible to encourage us to bring *all* our concerns to Him, no matter how small or large. He cares for our families more than we do!

ers had appointed for the service of the Levites, two hundred and twenty Nethinim. All of them were designated by name.

Fasting and Prayer for Protection

21Then I proclaimed a fast there at the river of Ahava, that we might humble ourselves before our God, to seek from Him the right way for us and our little ones and all our possessions. 22For I was ashamed to request of the king an escort of soldiers and horsemen to help us against the enemy on the road, because we had spoken to the king, saying, "The hand of our God *is* upon all those for good who seek Him, but His power and His wrath *are* against all those who forsake Him." 23So we fasted and entreated our God for this, and He answered our prayer.

Gifts for the Temple

24And I separated twelve of the leaders of the priests—Sherebiah, Hashabiah, and ten of their brethren with them— 25and weighed out to them the silver, the gold, and the articles, the offering for the house of our God which the king and his counselors and his princes, and all Israel *who were* present, had offered. 26I weighed into their hand six hundred and fifty talents of silver, silver articles *weighing* one hundred talents, one hundred talents of gold, 27twenty gold basins *worth* a thousand drachmas, and two vessels of fine polished bronze, precious as gold. 28And I said to them, "You *are* holy to the LORD; the articles *are* holy also; and the silver and the gold *are* a freewill offering to the LORD God of your fathers. 29Watch and keep *them* until you weigh *them* before the leaders of the priests and the Levites and heads of the fathers' *houses* of Israel in Jerusalem, *in* the chambers of the house of the LORD." 30So the priests and the Levites received the silver and the gold and the articles by weight, to bring *them* to Jerusalem to the house of our God.

The Return to Jerusalem

31Then we departed from the river of Ahava on the twelfth *day* of the first month, to go to Jerusalem. And the hand of our God was upon us, and He delivered us

from the hand of the enemy and from ambush along the road. 32So we came to Jerusalem, and stayed there three days.

33Now on the fourth day the silver and the gold and the articles were weighed in the house of our God by the hand of Meremoth the son of Uriah the priest, and with him *was* Eleazar the son of Phinehas; with them *were* the Levites, Jozabad the son of Jeshua and Noadiah the son of Binnui, 34with the number *and* weight of everything. All the weight was written down at that time.

35The children of those who had been carried away captive, who had come from the captivity, offered burnt offerings to the God of Israel: twelve bulls for all Israel, ninety-six rams, seventy-seven lambs, and twelve male goats *as* a sin offering. All *this was* a burnt offering to the LORD.

36And they delivered the king's orders to the king's satraps and the governors *in the region* beyond the River. So they gave support to the people and the house of God.

Intermarriage with Pagans

9 When these things were done, the leaders came to me, saying, "The people of Israel and the priests and the Levites have not separated themselves from the peoples of the lands, with respect to the abominations of the Canaanites, the Hittites, the Perizzites, the Jebusites, the Ammonites, the Moabites, the Egyptians, and the Amorites. 2For they have taken some of their daughters *as wives* for themselves and their sons, so that the holy seed is mixed with the peoples of *those* lands. Indeed, the hand of the leaders and rulers has been foremost in this trespass." 3So when I heard this thing, I tore my garment and my robe, and plucked out some of the hair of my head and beard, and sat down astonished. 4Then everyone who trembled at the words of the God of Israel assembled to me, because of the transgression of those who had been carried away captive, and I sat astonished until the evening sacrifice.

5At the evening sacrifice I arose from my fasting; and having torn my garment and my robe, I fell on my knees and spread out my hands to the LORD my God. 6And I said: "O my God, I am too ashamed and

BIBLICAL INSIGHTS • 10:2
The Need of the Hour

HOWARD HENDRICKS, A FRIEND and spiritual mentor, tells a compelling story of how a spiritual and family reformation began long ago in one local church: "Richard Baxter was a great man of God who took a very wealthy and sophisticated parish. For three years he preached with all the passion of his heart without any visible response. Finally, he cried out, 'O God, You must do something with these people or I'll die!'

"He said, 'It was as if God spoke to me audibly, "Baxter, you are working in the wrong place. You're expecting revival to come through the church. Try the home."'

Richard Baxter went out and called on home after home. He spent entire evenings in homes helping parents set up family worship times with their children. He moved from one home to another. Finally, the Spirit of God started to light fires all over until they swept through the congregation and made it the great church that it became."

The book of Ezra also teaches us that national revival begins with change in the home (10:2). We must humble ourselves and make our families a visible priority. And when that occurs, we can say with Shecaniah, "Yet now there is hope."

and give us a measure of revival in our bondage. [9]For we *were* slaves. Yet our God did not forsake us in our bondage; but He extended mercy to us in the sight of the kings of Persia, to revive us, to repair the house of our God, to rebuild its ruins, and to give us a wall in Judah and Jerusalem. [10]And now, O our God, what shall we say after this? For we have forsaken Your commandments, [11]which You commanded by Your servants the prophets, saying, 'The land which you are entering to possess is an unclean land, with the uncleanness of the peoples of the lands, with their abominations which have filled it from one end to another with their impurity. [12]Now therefore, do not give your daughters as wives for their sons, nor take their daughters to your sons; and never seek their peace or prosperity, that you may be strong and eat the good of the land, and leave *it* as an inheritance to your children forever.' [13]And after all that has come upon us for our evil deeds and for our great guilt, since You our God have punished us less than our iniquities *deserve,* and have given us *such* deliverance as this, [14]should we again break Your commandments, and join in marriage with the people *committing* these abominations? Would You not be angry with us until You had consumed *us,* so that *there would be* no remnant or survivor? [15]O LORD God of Israel, You *are* righteous, for we are left as a remnant, as *it is* this day. Here we *are* before You, in our guilt, though no one can stand before You because of this!"

Confession of Improper Marriages

10 Now while Ezra was praying, and while he was confessing, weeping, and bowing down before the house of God, a very large assembly of men, women, and children gathered to him from Israel; for the people wept very bitterly. [2]And Shecaniah the son of Jehiel, *one* of the sons of Elam, spoke up and said to Ezra, "We have trespassed against our God, and have taken pagan wives from the peoples of the land; yet now there is hope in Israel in spite of this. [3]Now therefore, let us make a covenant with our God to put away all these wives and those who have been born

humiliated to lift up my face to You, my God; for our iniquities have risen higher than *our* heads, and our guilt has grown up to the heavens. [7]Since the days of our fathers to this day we *have been* very guilty, and for our iniquities we, our kings, *and* our priests have been delivered into the hand of the kings of the lands, to the sword, to captivity, to plunder, and to humiliation, as *it is* this day. [8]And now for a little while grace has been *shown* from the LORD our God, to leave us a remnant to escape, and to give us a peg in His holy place, that our God may enlighten our eyes

to them, according to the advice of my master and of those who tremble at the commandment of our God; and let it be done according to the law. [4]Arise, for *this* matter *is* your *responsibility.* We also *are* with you. Be of good courage, and do *it.*"

[5]Then Ezra arose, and made the leaders of the priests, the Levites, and all Israel swear an oath that they would do according to this word. So they swore an oath. [6]Then Ezra rose up from before the house of God, and went into the chamber of Jehohanan the son of Eliashib; and *when* he came there, he ate no bread and drank no water, for he mourned because of the guilt of those from the captivity.

[7]And they issued a proclamation throughout Judah and Jerusalem to all the descendants of the captivity, that they must gather at Jerusalem, [8]and that whoever would not come within three days, according to the instructions of the leaders and elders, all his property would be confiscated, and he himself would be separated from the assembly of those from the captivity.

[9]So all the men of Judah and Benjamin gathered at Jerusalem within three days. It *was* the ninth month, on the twentieth of the month; and all the people sat in the open square of the house of God, trembling because of *this* matter and because of heavy rain. [10]Then Ezra the priest stood up and said to them, "You have transgressed and have taken pagan wives, adding to the guilt of Israel. [11]Now therefore, make confession to the LORD God of your fathers, and do His will; separate yourselves from the peoples of the land, and from the pagan wives."

[12]Then all the assembly answered and said with a loud voice, "Yes! As you have said, so we must do. [13]But *there are* many people; *it is* the season for heavy rain, and we are not able to stand outside. Nor *is this* the work of one or two days, for *there are* many of us who have transgressed in this matter. [14]Please, let the leaders of our entire assembly stand; and let all those in our cities who have taken pagan wives come at appointed times, together with the elders and judges of their cities, until the fierce wrath of our God is turned away from us in this matter." [15]Only Jonathan the son of Asahel and Jahaziah the son of Tikvah opposed this, and Meshullam and Shabbethai the Levite gave them support.

[16]Then the descendants of the captivity did so. And Ezra the priest, *with* certain heads of the fathers' *households,* were set apart by the fathers' households, each of them by name; and they sat down on the first day of the tenth month to examine the matter. [17]By the first day of the first month they finished *questioning* all the men who had taken pagan wives.

Pagan Wives Put Away

[18]And among the sons of the priests who had taken pagan wives *the following* were found of the sons of Jeshua the son of Jozadak,[a] and his brothers: Maaseiah, Eliezer, Jarib, and Gedaliah. [19]And they gave their promise that they would put away their wives; and *being* guilty, *they presented* a ram of the flock as their trespass offering.

[20]Also of the sons of Immer: Hanani and Zebadiah; [21]of the sons of Harim: Maaseiah, Elijah, Shemaiah, Jehiel, and Uzziah; [22]of the sons of Pashhur: Elioenai, Maaseiah, Ishmael, Nethanel, Jozabad, and Elasah.

[23]Also of the Levites: Jozabad, Shimei, Kelaiah (the same *is* Kelita), Pethahiah, Judah, and Eliezer.

[24]Also of the singers: Eliashib; and of the gatekeepers: Shallum, Telem, and Uri.

[25]And others of Israel: of the sons of Parosh: Ramiah, Jeziah, Malchiah, Mijamin, Eleazar, Malchijah, and Benaiah; [26]of the sons of Elam: Mattaniah, Zechariah, Jehiel, Abdi, Jeremoth, and Eliah; [27]of the sons of Zattu: Elioenai, Eliashib, Mattaniah, Jeremoth, Zabad, and Aziza; [28]of the sons of Bebai: Jehohanan, Hananiah, Zabbai, *and* Athlai; [29]of the sons of Bani: Meshullam, Malluch, Adaiah, Jashub, Sheal, *and* Ramoth;[a] [30]of the sons of Pahath-Moab: Adna, Chelal, Benaiah, Maaseiah, Mattaniah, Bezalel, Binnui, and Manasseh; [31]*of* the sons of Harim: Eliezer, Ishijah, Malchijah, Shemaiah, Shimeon, [32]Benjamin,

---

10:18 [a]Spelled *Jehozadak* in 1 Chronicles 6:14
10:29 [a]Or *Jeremoth*

Malluch, *and* Shemariah; 33of the sons of Hashum: Mattenai, Mattattah, Zabad, Eliphelet, Jeremai, Manasseh, *and* Shimei; 34of the sons of Bani: Maadai, Amram, Uel, 35Benaiah, Bedeiah, Cheluh,a 36Vaniah, Meremoth, Eliashib, 37Mattaniah, Mattenai, Jaasai,a 38Bani, Binnui, Shimei, 39Shelemiah, Nathan, Adaiah, 40Machnadebai, Shashai, Sharai, 41Azarel, Shelemiah, Shemariah, 42Shallum, Amariah, *and* Joseph; 43of the sons of Nebo: Jeiel, Mattithiah, Zabad, Zebina, Jaddai,a Joel, *and* Benaiah.

44All these had taken pagan wives, and *some* of them had wives *by whom* they had children.

10:35 aOr *Cheluhi,* or *Cheluhu*
10:37 aOr *Jaasu*
10:43 aOr *Jaddu*

NEHEMIAH

ORIGINALLY TITLED "SECOND EZRA" and probably written by Ezra, the book of Nehemiah continues the account of the return of God's people to Jerusalem following their seventy years of exile in Babylon. When King Cyrus of Persia liberated the Jewish captives in 539 B.C., Zerubbabel led the first group of Jews back to Jerusalem (Ezra 1—6). Sometime around 458 B.C., Ezra led a second group of Jews back to the Promised Land (Ezra 7—10). Then, thirteen years later, in 445 B.C., Nehemiah led a third group of God's people to Jerusalem (Nehemiah 1—6).

As the book begins, we see Nehemiah serving the king of Persia as his trusted cupbearer. When Nehemiah learns that his countrymen who have returned to Jerusalem have not rebuilt the city's walls, he asks the king for permission to return to Jerusalem so that he might lead the charge to re-establish the city's security. The king agrees, and once he reaches Israel, Nehemiah rallies his countrymen, oversees the reconstruction effort—it takes a mere fifty-two days—and the whole nation comes together for a day to hear Ezra read and explain the Law.

His work done, Nehemiah returns to Persia. But when he hears reports that leaders of the Jewish remnant have not continued the spiritual reforms he initiated, he rides back to Jerusalem, where he serves a second term as governor of the city.

Nehemiah displays a great many strong leadership traits, but one of his key strategies calls for familes to rebuild the portion of the city wall that lies closest to their own homes. He knows that no one wants his house to adjoin the weakest part of the wall, since that is where enemies would most likely attack.

In the same way, each of us must ensure that the spiritual walls of protection around our own homes remain strong (1 Cor. 16:13). And how can we best do this? Once more, Nehemiah has a great strategy. Nehemiah fasted and prayed; he had the resources needed to rebuild the wall, and he called the people to action. The key is to trust God in *all* the details of life and then to obey His Word with both expectation and joy.

BIBLICAL INSIGHTS • 1:5-7
Repentance Starts from Within

WE FIND AN AMAZING prayer of repentance in the book of Nehemiah. When Nehemiah, a high official in the court of the Persian King Artaxerxes, heard about the terrible condition of the repatriated Jews living in Judah and in the city of Jerusalem, he sat down to weep and mourn. At the end of many days, he began to "confess the sins of the children of Israel which we have sinned against You. Both my father's house and I have sinned. We have acted very corruptly against You, and have not kept the commandments, the statutes, nor the ordinances which You commanded Your servant Moses" (1:6, 7).

We see no false piety in Nehemiah's life or words, no pointing of fingers at others. He didn't merely confess the sins of the nation, but he also freely admitted his own unrighteousness. Nehemiah had heard the Word of God concerning his people's sin, and he knew that the first place to make changes was within himself.

God calls believing couples and believing families to be the starting points for national reformation and revival. That begins only when we look first at ourselves and then do whatever it takes to get our own houses clean.

Nehemiah Prays for His People

1 The words of Nehemiah the son of Hachaliah.

It came to pass in the month of Chislev, *in* the twentieth year, as I was in Shushan[a] the citadel, [2]that Hanani one of my brethren came with men from Judah; and I asked them concerning the Jews who had escaped, who had survived the captivity, and concerning Jerusalem. [3]And they said to me, "The survivors who are left from the captivity in the province *are* there in great distress and reproach. The wall of Jerusalem *is* also broken down, and its gates are burned with fire."

[4]So it was, when I heard these words, that I sat down and wept, and mourned *for many* days; I was fasting and praying before the God of heaven.

[5]And I said: "I pray, LORD God of heaven, O great and awesome God, *You* who keep *Your* covenant and mercy with those who love You[a] and observe Your[b] commandments, [6]please let Your ear be attentive and Your eyes open, that You may hear the prayer of Your servant which I pray before You now, day and night, for the children of Israel Your servants, and confess the sins of the children of Israel which we have sinned against You. Both my father's house and I have sinned. [7]We have acted very corruptly against You, and have not kept the commandments, the statutes, nor the ordinances which You commanded Your servant Moses. [8]Remember, I pray, the word that You commanded Your servant Moses, saying, 'If you are unfaithful, I will scatter you among the nations;[a] [9]but *if* you return to Me, and keep My commandments and do them, though some of you were cast out to the farthest part of the heavens, *yet* I will gather them from there, and bring them to the place which I have chosen as a dwelling for My name.'[a] [10]Now these *are* Your servants and Your people, whom You have redeemed by Your great power, and by Your strong hand. [11]O Lord, I pray, please let Your ear be attentive to the prayer of Your servant, and to the prayer of Your servants who desire to fear Your name; and let Your servant prosper this day, I pray, and grant him mercy in the sight of this man."

For I was the king's cupbearer.

Nehemiah Sent to Judah

2 And it came to pass in the month of Nisan, in the twentieth year of King Artaxerxes, *when* wine *was* before him, that I took the wine and gave it to the king. Now I had never been sad in his presence before. [2]Therefore the king said to me, "Why *is* your face sad, since you *are* not sick? This *is* nothing but sorrow of heart."

1:1 [a]Or *Susa* 1:5 [a]Literally *Him* [b]Literally *His*
1:8 [a]Leviticus 26:33 1:9 [a]Deuteronomy 30:2–5

So I became dreadfully afraid, [3]and said to the king, "May the king live forever! Why should my face not be sad, when the city, the place of my fathers' tombs, *lies* waste, and its gates are burned with fire?"

[4]Then the king said to me, "What do you request?"

So I prayed to the God of heaven. [5]And I said to the king, "If it pleases the king, and if your servant has found favor in your sight, I ask that you send me to Judah, to the city of my fathers' tombs, that I may rebuild it."

[6]Then the king said to me (the queen also sitting beside him), "How long will your journey be? And when will you return?" So it pleased the king to send me; and I set him a time.

[7]Furthermore I said to the king, "If it pleases the king, let letters be given to me for the governors *of the region* beyond the River,[a] that they must permit me to pass through till I come to Judah, [8]and a letter to Asaph the keeper of the king's forest, that he must give me timber to make beams for the gates of the citadel which *pertains* to the temple,[a] for the city wall, and for the house that I will occupy." And the king

granted *them* to me according to the good hand of my God upon me.

[9]Then I went to the governors *in the region* beyond the River, and gave them the king's letters. Now the king had sent captains of the army and horsemen with me. [10]When Sanballat the Horonite and Tobiah the Ammonite official[a] heard *of it,* they were deeply disturbed that a man had come to seek the well-being of the children of Israel.

Nehemiah Views the Wall of Jerusalem

[11]So I came to Jerusalem and was there three days. [12]Then I arose in the night, I and a few men with me; I told no one what my God had put in my heart to do at Jerusalem; nor was there any animal with me, except the one on which I rode. [13]And I went out by night through the Valley Gate to the Serpent Well and the Refuse Gate, and viewed the walls of Jerusalem which were broken down and its gates which were burned with fire. [14]Then I went on to the Fountain Gate and to the King's Pool, but *there was* no room for the animal under me to pass. [15]So I went up in the night by the valley, and viewed the wall; then I turned back and entered by the Valley Gate, and so returned. [16]And the officials did not know where I had gone or what I had done; I had not yet told the

---

2:7 [a]That is, the Euphrates, and so elsewhere in this book **2:8** [a]Literally *house* **2:10** [a]Literally *servant,* and so elsewhere in this book

---

Let Us Rise Up and Build

In his Pulitzer Prize winning book, *Profiles in Courage*, John F. Kennedy wrote, "Some men showed courage throughout their lives; others sailed with the wind until the decisive moment when their conscience and events propelled them into the center of the storm." Twenty-five hundred years ago in the land of Persia, the terrible plight of his people propelled a man named Nehemiah into the center of the storm.

Nehemiah risked his life by sharing his burden with his boss, a powerful, pagan king. When asked to state his objective, Nehemiah replied, "Send me to Judah, to the city of my fathers' tombs, that I may rebuild it" (2:5). The king granted his bold request.

Weeks later, when Nehemiah stood before the forlorn inhabitants of Jerusalem, he cried out, "You see the distress that we are in, how Jerusalem lies waste and its gates are burned with fire. Come and let us build the wall of Jerusalem, that we may no longer be a reproach." And the people responded heartily, "Let us rise up and build" (2:17, 18).

Are the walls of your marriage lying waste or burned with fire? Does anything about your union feel like a reproach? If so, take of Nehemiah's courage, rise up, and *rebuild those walls!*

Building a Family Reformation

TWO THINGS GRIP ME about this story. First is the determination and courage of Nehemiah. The masses were paralyzed. Their wall was in total ruin. Nehemiah looked and saw an opportunity to ask God Almighty for deliverance. And he risked his life by approaching a powerful ruler to share his burden and request permission to rebuild the wall.

Second, I'm captivated by the strategy employed to rebuild the wall. Successful construction begins with a strategic plan: The Jews were organized into teams and shared construction of different projects (3:1–8), and many rebuilt the section of the wall *in front of their own homes* (3:10, 23, 28–30).

What an ingenious strategy! Where were the people *most* motivated to rebuild the wall? Near their homes!

Where are *you* most motivated to rebuild the wall? Obviously, around *your* home, *your* neighborhood, and *your* community.

That's where a family reformation must begin.

Jews, the priests, the nobles, the officials, or the others who did the work.

[17]Then I said to them, "You see the distress that we *are* in, how Jerusalem *lies* waste, and its gates are burned with fire. Come and let us build the wall of Jerusalem, that we may no longer be a reproach." [18]And I told them of the hand of my God which had been good upon me, and also of the king's words that he had spoken to me.

So they said, "Let us rise up and build." Then they set their hands to *this* good *work*.

[19]But when Sanballat the Horonite, Tobiah the Ammonite official, and Geshem the Arab heard *of it*, they laughed at us and despised us, and said, "What *is* this thing that you are doing? Will you rebel against the king?"

[20]So I answered them, and said to them, "The God of heaven Himself will prosper us; therefore we His servants will arise and build, but you have no heritage or right or memorial in Jerusalem."

Rebuilding the Wall

3 Then Eliashib the high priest rose up with his brethren the priests and built the Sheep Gate; they consecrated it and hung its doors. They built as far as the Tower of the Hundred,[a] *and* consecrated it, then as far as the Tower of Hananel. [2]Next to *Eliashib*[a] the men of Jericho built. And next to them Zaccur the son of Imri built.

[3]Also the sons of Hassenaah built the Fish Gate; they laid its beams and hung its doors with its bolts and bars. [4]And next to them Meremoth the son of Urijah, the son of Koz,[a] made repairs. Next to them Meshullam the son of Berechiah, the son of Meshezabel, made repairs. Next to them Zadok the son of Baana made repairs. [5]Next to them the Tekoites made repairs; but their nobles did not put their shoulders[a] to the work of their Lord.

[6]Moreover Jehoiada the son of Paseah and Meshullam the son of Besodeiah repaired the Old Gate; they laid its beams and hung its doors, with its bolts and bars. [7]And next to them Melatiah the Gibeonite, Jadon the Meronothite, the men of Gibeon and Mizpah, repaired the residence[a] of the governor *of the region* beyond the River. [8]Next to him Uzziel the son of Harhaiah, one of the goldsmiths, made repairs. Also next to him Hananiah, one[a] of the perfumers, made repairs; and they fortified Jerusalem as far as the Broad Wall. [9]And next to them Rephaiah the son of Hur, leader of half the district of Jerusalem, made repairs. [10]Next to them Jedaiah the son of Harumaph made repairs in front of his house. And next to him Hattush the son of Hashabniah made repairs.

[11]Malchijah the son of Harim and Hashub the son of Pahath-Moab repaired another section, as well as the Tower of the Ovens. [12]And next to him was Shallum

3:1 [a]Hebrew *Hammeah*, also at 12:39 **3:2** [a]Literally *On his hand* **3:4** [a]Or *Hakkoz* **3:5** [a]Literally *necks* **3:7** [a]Literally *throne* **3:8** [a]Literally *the son*

the son of Hallohesh, leader of half the district of Jerusalem; he and his daughters made repairs.

13Hanun and the inhabitants of Zanoah repaired the Valley Gate. They built it, hung its doors with its bolts and bars, and *repaired* a thousand cubits of the wall as far as the Refuse Gate.

14Malchijah the son of Rechab, leader of the district of Beth Haccerem, repaired the Refuse Gate; he built it and hung its doors with its bolts and bars.

15Shallun the son of Col-Hozeh, leader of the district of Mizpah, repaired the Fountain Gate; he built it, covered it, hung its doors with its bolts and bars, and repaired the wall of the Pool of Shelah by the King's Garden, as far as the stairs that go down from the City of David. 16After him Nehemiah the son of Azbuk, leader of half the district of Beth Zur, made repairs as far as *the place* in front of the tombsᵃ of David, to the man-made pool, and as far as the House of the Mighty.

17After him the Levites, *under* Rehum the son of Bani, made repairs. Next to him Hashabiah, leader of half the district of Keilah, made repairs for his district. 18After him their brethren, *under* Bavaiᵃ the son of Henadad, leader of the *other* half of the district of Keilah, made repairs. 19And next to him Ezer the son of Jeshua, the leader of Mizpah, repaired another section in front of the Ascent to the Armory at the buttress. 20After him Baruch the son of Zabbaiᵃ carefully repaired the other section, from the buttress to the door of the house of Eliashib the high priest. 21After him Meremoth the son of Urijah, the son of Koz,ᵃ repaired another section, from the door of the house of Eliashib to the end of the house of Eliashib.

22And after him the priests, the men of the plain, made repairs. 23After him Benjamin and Hasshub made repairs opposite their house. After them Azariah the son of Maaseiah, the son of Ananiah, made repairs by his house. 24After him Binnui the son of Henadad repaired another section, from the house of Azariah to the buttress, even as far as the corner. 25Palal the son of Uzai *made repairs* opposite the buttress, and on the tower which projects from the king's upper house that *was* by the court of the prison. After him Pedaiah the son of Parosh *made repairs*.

26Moreover the Nethinim who dwelt in Ophel *made repairs* as far as *the place* in front of the Water Gate toward the east, and on the projecting tower. 27After them the Tekoites repaired another section, next to the great projecting tower, and as far as the wall of Ophel.

28Beyond the Horse Gate the priests made repairs, each in front of his *own* house. 29After them Zadok the son of Immer made repairs in front of his *own* house. After him Shemaiah the son of Shechaniah, the keeper of the East Gate, made repairs. 30After him Hananiah the son of Shelemiah, and Hanun, the sixth son of Zalaph, repaired another section. After him Meshullam the son of Berechiah made repairs in front of his dwelling. 31After him Malchijah, one of the goldsmiths, made repairs as far as the house of the Nethinim and of the merchants, in front of the Miphkadᵃ Gate, and as far as the upper room at the corner. 32And between the upper room at the corner, as far as the Sheep Gate, the goldsmiths and the merchants made repairs.

The Wall Defended Against Enemies

4 But it so happened, when Sanballat heard that we were rebuilding the wall, that he was furious and very indignant, and mocked the Jews. 2And he spoke before his brethren and the army of Samaria, and said, "What are these feeble Jews doing? Will they fortify themselves? Will they offer sacrifices? Will they complete it in a day? Will they revive the stones from the heaps of rubbish—*stones* that are burned?"

3Now Tobiah the Ammonite *was* beside him, and he said, "Whatever they build, if even a fox goes up *on it,* he will break down their stone wall."

4Hear, O our God, for we are despised; turn their reproach on their own heads,

---

3:16 ᵃSeptuagint, Syriac, and Vulgate read *tomb.*
3:18 ᵃFollowing Masoretic Text and Vulgate; some Hebrew manuscripts, Septuagint, and Syriac read *Binnui* (compare verse 24). **3:20** ᵃA few Hebrew manuscripts, Syriac, and Vulgate read *Zaccai.*
3:21 ᵃOr *Hakkoz* **3:31** ᵃLiterally *Inspection* or *Recruiting*

DEVOTIONS FOR COUPLES • 4:2
Building Your Mate during the Storm

The storms of life are coming, and believe us, they will affect you and your mate differently. So how can you turn toward one another instead of away from each other? There are many ways to do this:

First, recognize that suffering will come. James 1:2 says, "Count it all joy when you fall into various trials." The passage doesn't say *if* you encounter trials, but *when* you encounter them. Anticipate possible challenges and freely share your feelings about suffering. If you have a plan and know biblically how to view adversity, then it won't cause you to go to war with one another. Indeed, you can turn troubles and trials into something purposeful, meaningful, and an opportunity for growth.

Second, give your mate the freedom to process what's going on in his life. Don't expect him or her to flip a switch and just deal with the problem and move on. It's not usually that easy. If your mate's suffering doesn't diminish after a reasonable time, resist the temptation to make such statements as, "Snap out of it and trust God!" or, "Quit acting like a big baby!" or, "We've spent enough time talking about this. I think it's time we just put the whole matter to rest." We become like Christ only by going through a lifelong process. Trials and tragedies should force us to turn to God, but one person may take longer than another to come to that point.

Third, find out what your mate needs. Often it is best simply to say, "I want to meet your needs and be the best possible partner I can be, but at times I don't know how. Would you tell me how you want me to love and encourage you in this situation?" Talk about your feelings and give your spouse the freedom to feel *whatever*.

Fourth, build your marital foundation on Christ. Jesus said, "Therefore whoever hears these sayings of Mine, and does them, I will liken him to a wise man who built his house on the rock: and the rain descended, the floods came, and the winds blew and beat on that house; and it did not fall, for it was founded on the rock" (Matt. 7:24, 25). When you build your home on Christ, you place it on the only foundation that can withstand trouble, trials, and tribulation.

---

and give them as plunder to a land of captivity! ⁵Do not cover their iniquity, and do not let their sin be blotted out from before You; for they have provoked *You* to anger before the builders.

⁶So we built the wall, and the entire wall was joined together up to half its *height,* for the people had a mind to work.

⁷Now it happened, when Sanballat, Tobiah, the Arabs, the Ammonites, and the Ashdodites heard that the walls of Jerusalem were being restored and the gaps were beginning to be closed, that they became very angry, ⁸and all of them conspired together to come *and* attack Jerusalem and create confusion. ⁹Nevertheless we made our prayer to our God, and because of them we set a watch against them day and night.

¹⁰Then Judah said, "The strength of the laborers is failing, and *there is* so much rubbish that we are not able to build the wall."

¹¹And our adversaries said, "They will neither know nor see anything, till we come into their midst and kill them and cause the work to cease."

¹²So it was, when the Jews who dwelt near them came, that they told us ten times, "From whatever place you turn, *they will be* upon us."

¹³Therefore I positioned *men* behind the lower parts of the wall, at the openings; and I set the people according to their families, with their swords, their spears, and their bows. ¹⁴And I looked, and arose and said to the nobles, to the leaders, and to the rest of the people, "Do not be afraid of them. Remember the Lord, great and awesome

and fight for your brethren, your sons, your daughters, your wives, and your houses."

[15]And it happened, when our enemies heard that it was known to us, and *that* God had brought their plot to nothing, that all of us returned to the wall, everyone to his work. [16]So it was, from that time on, *that* half of my servants worked at construction, while the other half held the spears, the shields, the bows, and *wore* armor; and the leaders *were* behind all the house of Judah. [17]Those who built on the wall, and those who carried burdens, loaded themselves so that with one hand they worked at construction, and with the other held a weapon. [18]Every one of the builders had his sword girded at his side as he built. And the one who sounded the trumpet *was* beside me.

[19]Then I said to the nobles, the rulers, and the rest of the people, "The work *is* great and extensive, and we are separated far from one another on the wall. [20]Wherever you hear the sound of the trumpet, rally to us there. Our God will fight for us."

[21]So we labored in the work, and half of *the men*[a] held the spears from daybreak until the stars appeared. [22]At the same time I also said to the people, "Let each man and his servant stay at night in Jerusalem, that they may be our guard by night and a working party by day." [23]So neither I, my brethren, my servants, nor the men of the guard who followed me took off our clothes, *except* that everyone took them off for washing.

Nehemiah Deals with Oppression

5 And there was a great outcry of the people and their wives against their Jewish brethren. [2]For there were those who said, "We, our sons, and our daughters *are* many; therefore let us get grain, that we may eat and live."

[3]There were also *some* who said, "We have mortgaged our lands and vineyards and houses, that we might buy grain because of the famine."

[4]There were also those who said, "We have borrowed money for the king's tax *on* our lands and vineyards. [5]Yet now our flesh *is* as the flesh of our brethren, our children as their children; and indeed we are forcing our sons and our daughters to be slaves, and *some* of our daughters have been brought into slavery. *It is* not in our power *to redeem them,* for other men have our lands and vineyards."

[6]And I became very angry when I heard their outcry and these words. [7]After serious thought, I rebuked the nobles and rulers, and said to them, "Each of you is exacting usury from his brother." So I called a great assembly against them. [8]And I said to them, "According to our ability we have redeemed our Jewish brethren who were sold to the nations. Now indeed, will you even sell your brethren? Or should they be sold to us?"

Then they were silenced and found nothing *to say.* [9]Then I said, "What you are doing *is* not good. Should you not walk in the fear of our God because of the reproach of the nations, our enemies? [10]I also, *with* my brethren and my servants, am lending them money and grain. Please, let us stop this usury! [11]Restore now to them, even this day, their lands, their vineyards, their olive groves, and their houses, also a hundredth of the money and the grain, the new wine and the oil, that you have charged them."

[12]So they said, "We will restore *it,* and will require nothing from them; we will do as you say."

Then I called the priests, and required an oath from them that they would do according to this promise. [13]Then I shook out the fold of my garment[a] and said, "So may God shake out each man from his house, and from his property, who does not perform this promise. Even thus may he be shaken out and emptied."

And all the assembly said, "Amen!" and praised the LORD. Then the people did according to this promise.

The Generosity of Nehemiah

[14]Moreover, from the time that I was appointed to be their governor in the land of Judah, from the twentieth year until the

---

4:21 [a]Literally *them* 5:13 [a]Literally *my lap*

thirty-second year of King Artaxerxes, twelve years, neither I nor my brothers ate the governor's provisions. ¹⁵But the former governors who *were* before me laid burdens on the people, and took from them bread and wine, besides forty shekels of silver. Yes, even their servants bore rule over the people, but I did not do so, because of the fear of God. ¹⁶Indeed, I also continued the work on this wall, and we[a] did not buy any land. All my servants *were* gathered there for the work.

¹⁷And at my table *were* one hundred and fifty Jews and rulers, besides those who came to us from the nations around us. ¹⁸Now *that* which was prepared daily *was* one ox *and* six choice sheep. Also fowl were prepared for me, and once every ten days an abundance of all kinds of wine. Yet in spite of this I did not demand the governor's provisions, because the bondage was heavy on this people.

¹⁹Remember me, my God, for good, *according to* all that I have done for this people.

INTIMATE MOMENTS

When your wife comments on something she would really like to have, make a note of it and keep the note in a secure place (somewhere you won't forget it!). When Christmas time rolls around, get out your list and purchase that gift for her.

Conspiracy Against Nehemiah

6 Now it happened when Sanballat, Tobiah, Geshem the Arab, and the rest of our enemies heard that I had rebuilt the wall, and *that* there were no breaks left in it (though at that time I had not hung the doors in the gates), ²that Sanballat and Geshem sent to me, saying, "Come, let us meet together among the villages in the plain of Ono." But they thought to do me harm.

³So I sent messengers to them, saying, "I *am* doing a great work, so that I cannot come down. Why should the work cease while I leave it and go down to you?"

⁴But they sent me this message four times, and I answered them in the same manner.

⁵Then Sanballat sent his servant to me as before, the fifth time, with an open letter in his hand. ⁶In it *was* written:

It is reported among the nations, and Geshem[a] says, *that* you and the Jews plan to rebel; therefore, according to these rumors, you are rebuilding the wall, that you may be their king. ⁷And you have also appointed prophets to proclaim concerning you at Jerusalem, saying, "*There is* a king in Judah!" Now these matters will be reported to the king. So come, therefore, and let us consult together.

⁸Then I sent to him, saying, "No such things as you say are being done, but you invent them in your own heart."

⁹For they all *were trying to* make us afraid, saying, "Their hands will be weakened in the work, and it will not be done." Now therefore, *O God,* strengthen my hands.

¹⁰Afterward I came to the house of Shemaiah the son of Delaiah, the son of Mehetabel, who *was* a secret informer; and he said, "Let us meet together in the house of God, within the temple, and let us close the doors of the temple, for they are coming to kill you; indeed, at night they will come to kill you."

¹¹And I said, "Should such a man as I flee? And who *is there* such as I who would go into the temple to save his life? I will not go in!" ¹²Then I perceived that God had not sent him at all, but that he pronounced *this* prophecy against me because Tobiah and Sanballat had hired him. ¹³For this reason he *was* hired, that I should be afraid and act that way and sin, so *that* they might have *cause* for an evil report, that they might reproach me.

¹⁴My God, remember Tobiah and Sanballat, according to these their works, and the prophetess Noadiah and the rest of

---

5:16 [a]Following Masoretic Text; Septuagint, Syriac, and Vulgate read *I.* **6:6** [a]Hebrew *Gashmu*

the prophets who would have made me afraid.

The Wall Completed

15So the wall was finished on the twenty-fifth *day* of Elul, in fifty-two days. 16And it happened, when all our enemies heard *of it,* and all the nations around us saw *these things,* that they were very disheartened in their own eyes; for they perceived that this work was done by our God.

17Also in those days the nobles of Judah sent many letters to Tobiah, and *the letters of* Tobiah came to them. 18For many in Judah were pledged to him, because he was the son-in-law of Shechaniah the son of Arah, and his son Jehohanan had married the daughter of Meshullam the son of Berechiah. 19Also they reported his good deeds before me, and reported my words to him. Tobiah sent letters to frighten me.

7 Then it was, when the wall was built and I had hung the doors, when the gatekeepers, the singers, and the Levites had been appointed, 2that I gave the charge of Jerusalem to my brother Hanani, and Hananiah the leader of the citadel, for he *was* a faithful man and feared God more than many.

3And I said to them, "Do not let the gates of Jerusalem be opened until the sun is hot; and while they stand *guard,* let them shut and bar the doors; and appoint guards from among the inhabitants of Jerusalem, one at his watch station and another in front of his own house."

The Captives Who Returned to Jerusalem

4Now the city *was* large and spacious, but the people in it *were* few, and the houses *were* not rebuilt. 5Then my God put it into my heart to gather the nobles, the rulers, and the people, that they might be registered by genealogy. And I found a register of the genealogy of those who had come up in the first *return,* and found written in it:

6 Thesea *are* the people of the province who came back from the captivity, of those who had been carried away, whom Nebuchadnezzar the king of Babylon had carried away, and who returned to Jerusalem and Judah, everyone to his city.

7 Those who came with Zerubbabel *were* Jeshua, Nehemiah, Azariah, Raamiah, Nahamani, Mordecai, Bilshan, Mispereth,a Bigvai, Nehum, and Baanah.

The number of the men of the people of Israel: 8the sons of Parosh, two thousand one hundred and seventy-two;
9the sons of Shephatiah, three hundred and seventy-two;
10the sons of Arah, six hundred and fifty-two;
11the sons of Pahath-Moab, of the sons of Jeshua and Joab, two thousand eight hundred and eighteen;
12the sons of Elam, one thousand two hundred and fifty-four;
13the sons of Zattu, eight hundred and forty-five;
14the sons of Zaccai, seven hundred and sixty;
15the sons of Binnui,a six hundred and forty-eight;
16the sons of Bebai, six hundred and twenty-eight;
17the sons of Azgad, two thousand three hundred and twenty-two;
18the sons of Adonikam, six hundred and sixty-seven;
19the sons of Bigvai, two thousand and sixty-seven;
20the sons of Adin, six hundred and fifty-five;
21the sons of Ater of Hezekiah, ninety-eight;
22the sons of Hashum, three hundred and twenty-eight;
23the sons of Bezai, three hundred and twenty-four;
24the sons of Hariph,a one hundred and twelve;
25the sons of Gibeon,a ninety-five;
26the men of Bethlehem and

7:6 aCompare verses 6–72 with Ezra 2:1–70
7:7 aSpelled *Mispar* in Ezra 2:2 7:15 aSpelled *Bani* in Ezra 2:10 7:24 aCalled *Jorah* in Ezra 2:18
7:25 aCalled *Gibbar* in Ezra 2:20

Netophah, one hundred and eighty-eight;

²⁷the men of Anathoth, one hundred and twenty-eight;

²⁸the men of Beth Azmaveth,^a forty-two;

²⁹the men of Kirjath Jearim, Chephirah, and Beeroth, seven hundred and forty-three;

³⁰the men of Ramah and Geba, six hundred and twenty-one;

³¹the men of Michmas, one hundred and twenty-two;

³²the men of Bethel and Ai, one hundred and twenty-three;

³³the men of the other Nebo, fifty-two;

³⁴the sons of the other Elam, one thousand two hundred and fifty-four;

³⁵the sons of Harim, three hundred and twenty;

³⁶the sons of Jericho, three hundred and forty-five;

³⁷the sons of Lod, Hadid, and Ono, seven hundred and twenty-one;

³⁸the sons of Senaah, three thousand nine hundred and thirty.

³⁹ The priests: the sons of Jedaiah, of the house of Jeshua, nine hundred and seventy-three;

⁴⁰the sons of Immer, one thousand and fifty-two;

⁴¹the sons of Pashhur, one thousand two hundred and forty-seven;

⁴²the sons of Harim, one thousand and seventeen.

⁴³ The Levites: the sons of Jeshua, of Kadmiel, *and* of the sons of Hodevah,^a seventy-four.

⁴⁴ The singers: the sons of Asaph, one hundred and forty-eight.

⁴⁵ The gatekeepers: the sons of Shallum, the sons of Ater, the sons of Talmon, the sons of Akkub, the sons of Hatita, the sons of Shobai, one hundred and thirty-eight.

⁴⁶ The Nethinim: the sons of Ziha, the sons of Hasupha,

the sons of Tabbaoth,

⁴⁷the sons of Keros, the sons of Sia,^a the sons of Padon,

⁴⁸the sons of Lebana,^a the sons of Hagaba,^b the sons of Salmai,^c

⁴⁹the sons of Hanan, the sons of Giddel, the sons of Gahar,

⁵⁰the sons of Reaiah, the sons of Rezin, the sons of Nekoda,

⁵¹the sons of Gazzam, the sons of Uzza, the sons of Paseah,

⁵²the sons of Besai, the sons of Meunim, the sons of Nephishesim,^a

⁵³the sons of Bakbuk, the sons of Hakupha, the sons of Harhur,

⁵⁴the sons of Bazlith,^a the sons of Mehida, the sons of Harsha,

⁵⁵the sons of Barkos, the sons of Sisera, the sons of Tamah,

⁵⁶the sons of Neziah, and the sons of Hatipha.

⁵⁷ The sons of Solomon's servants: the sons of Sotai, the sons of Sophereth, the sons of Perida,^a

⁵⁸the sons of Jaala, the sons of Darkon, the sons of Giddel,

⁵⁹the sons of Shephatiah, the sons of Hattil, the sons of Pochereth of Zebaim, and the sons of Amon.^a

⁶⁰All the Nethinim, and the sons of Solomon's servants, *were* three hundred and ninety-two.

⁶¹ And these *were* the ones who came

7:28 ^aCalled *Azmaveth* in Ezra 2:24 **7:43** ^aSpelled *Hodaviah* in Ezra 2:40 **7:47** ^aSpelled *Siaha* in Ezra 2:44 **7:48** ^aMasoretic Text reads *Lebanah.* ^bMasoretic Text reads *Hogabah.* ^cOr *Shalmai,* or *Shamlai* **7:52** ^aSpelled *Nephusim* in Ezra 2:50 **7:54** ^aSpelled *Bazluth* in Ezra 2:52 **7:57** ^aSpelled *Peruda* in Ezra 2:55 **7:59** ^aSpelled *Ami* in Ezra 2:57

up from Tel Melah, Tel Harsha, Cherub, Addon,[a] and Immer, but they could not identify their father's house nor their lineage, whether they *were* of Israel: [62]the sons of Delaiah, the sons of Tobiah, the sons of Nekoda, six hundred and forty-two;

[63]and of the priests: the sons of Habaiah, the sons of Koz,[a] the sons of Barzillai, who took a wife of the daughters of Barzillai the Gileadite, and was called by their name.

[64]These sought their listing *among* those who were registered by genealogy, but it was not found; therefore they were excluded from the priesthood as defiled. [65]And the governor[a] said to them that they should not eat of the most holy things till a priest could consult with the Urim and Thummim.

[66] Altogether the whole assembly *was* forty-two thousand three hundred and sixty, [67]besides their male and female servants, of whom *there were* seven thousand three hundred and thirty-seven; and they had two hundred and forty-five men and women singers. [68]Their horses were seven hundred and thirty-six, their mules two hundred and forty-five, [69]*their* camels four hundred and thirty-five, *and* donkeys six thousand seven hundred and twenty.

[70] And some of the heads of the fathers' *houses* gave to the work. The governor[a] gave to the treasury one thousand gold drachmas, fifty basins, and five hundred and thirty priestly garments. [71]Some of the heads of the fathers' *houses* gave to the treasury of the work twenty thousand gold drachmas, and two thousand two hundred silver minas. [72]And that which the rest of the people gave *was* twenty thousand gold drachmas, two thousand silver minas, and sixty-seven priestly garments.

[73]So the priests, the Levites, the gatekeepers, the singers, *some* of the people, the Nethinim, and all Israel dwelt in their cities.

Ezra Reads the Law

When the seventh month came, the children of Israel *were* in their cities.

8 Now all the people gathered together as one man in the open square that *was* in front of the Water Gate; and they told Ezra the scribe to bring the Book of the Law of Moses, which the LORD had commanded Israel. [2]So Ezra the priest brought the Law before the assembly of men and women and all who *could* hear with understanding on the first day of the seventh month. [3]Then he read from it in the open square that *was* in front of the Water Gate from morning until midday, before the men and women and those who could understand; and the ears of all the people *were attentive* to the Book of the Law.

[4]So Ezra the scribe stood on a platform of wood which they had made for the purpose; and beside him, at his right hand, stood Mattithiah, Shema, Anaiah, Urijah, Hilkiah, and Maaseiah; and at his left hand Pedaiah, Mishael, Malchijah, Hashum, Hashbadana, Zechariah, *and* Meshullam. [5]And Ezra opened the book in the sight of all the people, for he was *standing* above all the people; and when he opened it, all the people stood up. [6]And Ezra blessed the LORD, the great God.

Then all the people answered, "Amen, Amen!" while lifting up their hands. And they bowed their heads and worshiped the LORD with *their* faces to the ground.

[7]Also Jeshua, Bani, Sherebiah, Jamin, Akkub, Shabbethai, Hodijah, Maaseiah, Kelita, Azariah, Jozabad, Hanan, Pelaiah, and the Levites, helped the people to understand the Law; and the people *stood* in their place. [8]So they read distinctly from the book, in the Law of God; and they gave the sense, and helped *them* to understand the reading.

7:61 [a]Spelled *Addan* in Ezra 2:59 **7:63** [a]Or *Hakkoz*
7:65 [a]Hebrew *Tirshatha* **7:70** [a]Hebrew *Tirshatha*

BIBLICAL INSIGHTS • 8:8
Make the Meaning Clear

A VERSE FROM NEHEMIAH really hit me the other day, "So they read distinctly from the book, in the Law of God; and they gave the sense, and helped them to understand the reading" (8:8). It occurred to me that when we read the Bible to our families, we need to do so in a way so that we understand what we have just read, *and* that our children also grasp the meaning.

It is so easy to stick with the text of the Scripture and read it word for word, flying by words like *reproach* and *exhortation*—lofty words that may (or may not) be clear to us, but which leave our kids with blank looks on their faces.

When you read the Bible to your children, take the time to stop and explain the words and ideas they may have difficulty grasping. If needed, try paraphrasing the text to give them a down-home explanation of what it's saying. Give them the freedom to stop you and ask what something means if they feel confused or stuck.

Reading and studying the Bible as a family can be a source of great blessing. But we need to make sure we aren't just reading through it as quickly as possible, without helping everyone to understand what's being read.

⁹And Nehemiah, who *was* the governor,ᵃ Ezra the priest *and* scribe, and the Levites who taught the people said to all the people, "This day *is* holy to the LORD your God; do not mourn nor weep." For all the people wept, when they heard the words of the Law.

¹⁰Then he said to them, "Go your way, eat the fat, drink the sweet, and send portions to those for whom nothing is prepared; for *this* day *is* holy to our Lord. Do not sorrow, for the joy of the LORD is your strength."

¹¹So the Levites quieted all the people, saying, "Be still, for the day *is* holy; do not be grieved." ¹²And all the people went their way to eat and drink, to send portions and rejoice greatly, because they understood the words that were declared to them.

The Feast of Tabernacles

¹³Now on the second day the heads of the fathers' *houses* of all the people, with the priests and Levites, were gathered to Ezra the scribe, in order to understand the words of the Law. ¹⁴And they found written in the Law, which the LORD had commanded by Moses, that the children of Israel should dwell in booths during the feast of the seventh month, ¹⁵and that they should announce and proclaim in all their cities and in Jerusalem, saying, "Go out to the mountain, and bring olive branches, branches of oil trees, myrtle branches, palm branches, and branches of leafy trees, to make booths, as *it is* written."

¹⁶Then the people went out and brought *them* and made themselves booths, each one on the roof of his house, or in their courtyards or the courts of the house of God, and in the open square of the Water Gate and in the open square of the Gate of Ephraim. ¹⁷So the whole assembly of those who had returned from the captivity made booths and sat under the booths; for since the days of Joshua the son of Nun until that day the children of Israel had not done so. And there was very great gladness. ¹⁸Also day by day, from the first day until the last day, he read from the Book of the Law of God. And they kept the feast seven days; and on the eighth day *there was* a sacred assembly, according to the *prescribed* manner.

The People Confess Their Sins

9 Now on the twenty-fourth day of this month the children of Israel were assembled with fasting, in sackcloth, and with dust on their heads.ᵃ ²Then those of Israelite lineage separated themselves from all foreigners; and they stood and confessed their sins and the iniquities of their fathers. ³And they stood up in their place and read from the Book of the Law of the LORD their God *for one*-fourth of the

8:9 ᵃHebrew *Tirshatha* **9:1** ᵃLiterally *earth on them*

day; and *for another* fourth they confessed and worshiped the LORD their God.

⁴Then Jeshua, Bani, Kadmiel, Shebaniah, Bunni, Sherebiah, Bani, *and* Chenani stood on the stairs of the Levites and cried out with a loud voice to the LORD their God. ⁵And the Levites, Jeshua, Kadmiel, Bani, Hashabniah, Sherebiah, Hodijah, Shebaniah, *and* Pethahiah, said:

"Stand up *and* bless the LORD your
      God
   Forever and ever!

"Blessed be Your glorious name,
   Which is exalted above all blessing
      and praise!
⁶ You alone *are* the LORD;
   You have made heaven,
   The heaven of heavens, with all their
      host,
   The earth and everything on it,
   The seas and all that is in them,
   And You preserve them all.
   The host of heaven worships You.

⁷ "You *are* the LORD God,
   Who chose Abram,
   And brought him out of Ur of the
      Chaldeans,
   And gave him the name Abraham;
⁸ You found his heart faithful before
      You,
   And made a covenant with him
   To give the land of the Canaanites,
   The Hittites, the Amorites,
   The Perizzites, the Jebusites,
   And the Girgashites—
   To give *it* to his descendants.
   You have performed Your words,
   For You *are* righteous.

⁹ "You saw the affliction of our fathers
      in Egypt,
   And heard their cry by the Red Sea.
¹⁰ You showed signs and wonders
      against Pharaoh,
   Against all his servants,
   And against all the people of his land.
   For You knew that they acted
      proudly against them.
   So You made a name for Yourself, as
      it is this day.
¹¹ And You divided the sea before
      them,

BIBLICAL INSIGHTS • 9:16, 17

The Importance of Confession

HOW'S THE FOLLOWING for an honest confession?

"But they and our fathers acted proudly, hardened their necks, and did not heed Your commandments. They refused to obey, and they were not mindful of Your wonders that You did among them. But they hardened their necks, and in their rebellion they appointed a leader to return to their bondage" (9:16, 17).

Nehemiah recorded this prayer by some of the spiritual leaders of Israel, and their confessions read like a laundry list of the sins God has repeatedly warned His people to avoid: pride, arrogance, closed ears, failing to remember God's works, and general disobedience.

These ancient people understood what we must understand, and that's the importance of being willing to confess sin whenever it comes to our attention. That is especially important to those of us who have children, because our sins and shortcomings affect not only us, but also our children.

Good news comes in the next line of the prayer, "But You are God, ready to pardon, gracious and merciful, slow to anger, abundant in kindness, and did not forsake them" (9:17). What a great promise! God is faithful, even when we aren't! What better reason to come to Him in humble obedience?

So that they went through the midst
      of the sea on the dry land;
   And their persecutors You threw into
      the deep,
   As a stone into the mighty waters.
¹² Moreover You led them by day with
      a cloudy pillar,
   And by night with a pillar of fire,
   To give them light on the road
   Which they should travel.

¹³ "You came down also on Mount Sinai,

And spoke with them from heaven,
And gave them just ordinances and
true laws,
Good statutes and commandments.
14 You made known to them Your holy
Sabbath,
And commanded them precepts,
statutes and laws,
By the hand of Moses Your servant.
15 You gave them bread from heaven
for their hunger,
And brought them water out of the
rock for their thirst,
And told them to go in to possess
the land
Which You had sworn to
give them.

16 "But they and our fathers acted
proudly,
Hardened their necks,
And did not heed Your
commandments.
17 They refused to obey,
And they were not mindful of
Your wonders
That You did among them.
But they hardened their necks,
And in their rebellion[a]
They appointed a leader
To return to their bondage.
But You *are* God,
Ready to pardon,
Gracious and merciful,
Slow to anger,
Abundant in kindness,
And did not forsake them.
18 "Even when they made a molded calf
for themselves,
And said, 'This *is* your god
That brought you up out of Egypt,'
And worked great provocations,
19 Yet in Your manifold mercies
You did not forsake them in the
wilderness.
The pillar of the cloud did not
depart from them by day,
To lead them on the road;
Nor the pillar of fire by night,
To show them light,
And the way they should go.
20 You also gave Your good Spirit to
instruct them,

And did not withhold Your manna
from their mouth,
And gave them water for their thirst.
21 Forty years You sustained them in
the wilderness;
They lacked nothing;
Their clothes did not wear out[a]
And their feet did not swell.

22 "Moreover You gave them kingdoms
and nations,
And divided them into districts.[a]
So they took possession of the land
of Sihon,
The land of[b] the king of Heshbon,
And the land of Og king of Bashan.
23 You also multiplied their children as
the stars of heaven,
And brought them into the land
Which You had told their fathers
To go in and possess.
24 So the people went in
And possessed the land;
You subdued before them the
inhabitants of the land,
The Canaanites,
And gave them into their hands,
With their kings
And the people of the land,
That they might do with them as
they wished.
25 And they took strong cities and a
rich land,
And possessed houses full of all
goods,
Cisterns *already* dug, vineyards, olive
groves,
And fruit trees in abundance.
So they ate and were filled and grew
fat,
And delighted themselves in Your
great goodness.

26 "Nevertheless they were
disobedient
And rebelled against You,
Cast Your law behind their backs
And killed Your prophets, who
testified against them

9:17 [a]Following Masoretic Text and Vulgate;
Septuagint reads *in Egypt.* **9:21** [a]Compare
Deuteronomy 29:5 **9:22** [a]Literally *corners* [b]Following
Masoretic Text and Vulgate; Septuagint omits
The land of.

To turn them to Yourself;
And they worked great provocations.

27 Therefore You delivered them into
the hand of their enemies,
Who oppressed them;
And in the time of their trouble,
When they cried to You,
You heard from heaven;
And according to Your abundant
mercies
You gave them deliverers who saved
them
From the hand of their enemies.

28 "But after they had rest,
They again did evil before You.
Therefore You left them in the hand
of their enemies,
So that they had dominion over
them;
Yet when they returned and cried out
to You,
You heard from heaven;
And many times You delivered them
according to Your mercies,

29 And testified against them,
That You might bring them back to
Your law.
Yet they acted proudly,
And did not heed Your
commandments,
But sinned against Your
judgments,
'Which if a man does, he shall live by
them.'a
And they shrugged their shoulders,
Stiffened their necks,
And would not hear.

30 Yet for many years You had patience
with them,
And testified against them by Your
Spirit in Your prophets.
Yet they would not listen;
Therefore You gave them into the
hand of the peoples of the lands.

31 Nevertheless in Your great mercy
You did not utterly consume them
nor forsake them;
For You are God, gracious and
merciful.

32 "Now therefore, our God,

The great, the mighty, and awesome
God,
Who keeps covenant and mercy:
Do not let all the trouble seem small
before You
That has come upon us,
Our kings and our princes,
Our priests and our prophets,
Our fathers and on all Your people,
From the days of the kings of
Assyria until this day.

33 However You are just in all that has
befallen us;
For You have dealt faithfully,
But we have done wickedly.

34 Neither our kings nor our princes,
Our priests nor our fathers,
Have kept Your law,
Nor heeded Your commandments
and Your testimonies,
With which You testified against
them.

35 For they have not served You in their
kingdom,
Or in the many good things that You
gave them,
Or in the large and rich land which
You set before them;
Nor did they turn from their wicked
works.

36 "Here we are, servants today!
And the land that You gave to our
fathers,
To eat its fruit and its bounty,
Here we are, servants in it!

37 And it yields much increase to the
kings
You have set over us,
Because of our sins;
Also they have dominion over our
bodies and our cattle
At their pleasure;
And we are in great distress.

38 "And because of all this,
We make a sure covenant and write it;
Our leaders, our Levites, and our
priests seal it."

The People Who Sealed the Covenant

10 Now those who placed their seal on
the document were:
Nehemiah the governor, the son of

9:29 aLeviticus 18:5

Hacaliah, and Zedekiah, ²Seraiah, Azariah, Jeremiah, ³Pashhur, Amariah, Malchijah, ⁴Hattush, Shebaniah, Malluch, ⁵Harim, Meremoth, Obadiah, ⁶Daniel, Ginnethon, Baruch, ⁷Meshullam, Abijah, Mijamin, ⁸Maaziah, Bilgai, *and* Shemaiah. These *were* the priests.

⁹The Levites: Jeshua the son of Azaniah, Binnui of the sons of Henadad, *and* Kadmiel.

¹⁰Their brethren: Shebaniah, Hodijah, Kelita, Pelaiah, Hanan, ¹¹Micha, Rehob, Hashabiah, ¹²Zaccur, Sherebiah, Shebaniah, ¹³Hodijah, Bani, *and* Beninu.

¹⁴The leaders of the people: Parosh, Pahath-Moab, Elam, Zattu, Bani, ¹⁵Bunni, Azgad, Bebai, ¹⁶Adonijah, Bigvai, Adin, ¹⁷Ater, Hezekiah, Azzur, ¹⁸Hodijah, Hashum, Bezai, ¹⁹Hariph, Anathoth, Nebai, ²⁰Magpiash, Meshullam, Hezir, ²¹Meshezabel, Zadok, Jaddua, ²²Pelatiah, Hanan, Anaiah, ²³Hoshea, Hananiah, Hasshub, ²⁴Hallohesh, Pilha, Shobek, ²⁵Rehum, Hashabnah, Maaseiah, ²⁶Ahijah, Hanan, Anan, ²⁷Malluch, Harim, *and* Baanah.

The Covenant That Was Sealed

²⁸Now the rest of the people—the priests, the Levites, the gatekeepers, the singers, the Nethinim, and all those who had separated themselves from the peoples of the lands to the Law of God, their wives, their sons, and their daughters, everyone who had knowledge and understanding— ²⁹these joined with their brethren, their nobles, and entered into a curse and an oath to walk in God's Law, which was given by Moses the servant of God, and to observe and do all the commandments of the LORD our Lord, and His ordinances and His statutes: ³⁰We would not give our daughters as wives to the peoples of the land, nor take their daughters for our sons; ³¹*if* the peoples of the land brought wares or any grain to sell on the Sabbath day, we would not buy it from them on the Sabbath, or on a holy day; and we would forego the seventh year's *produce* and the exacting of every debt.

³²Also we made ordinances for ourselves, to exact from ourselves yearly one-third of a shekel for the service of the house of our God: ³³for the showbread, for the regular grain offering, for the regular burnt offering of the Sabbaths, the New Moons, and the set feasts; for the holy things, for the sin offerings to make atonement for Israel, and all the work of the house of our God. ³⁴We cast lots among the priests, the Levites, and the people, for bringing the wood offering into the house of our God, according to our fathers' houses, at the appointed times year by year, to burn on the altar of the LORD our God as *it is* written in the Law.

³⁵And *we made ordinances* to bring the firstfruits of our ground and the firstfruits of all fruit of all trees, year by year, to the house of the LORD; ³⁶to bring the firstborn of our sons and our cattle, as *it is* written in the Law, and the firstborn of our herds and our flocks, to the house of our God, to the priests who minister in the house of our God; ³⁷to bring the firstfruits of our dough, our offerings, the fruit from all kinds of trees, *the* new wine and oil, to the priests, to the storerooms of the house of our God; and to bring the tithes of our land to the Levites, for the Levites should receive the tithes in all our farming communities. ³⁸And the priest, the descendant of Aaron, shall be with the Levites when the Levites receive tithes; and the Levites shall bring up a tenth of the tithes to the house of our God, to the rooms of the storehouse.

³⁹For the children of Israel and the children of Levi shall bring the offering of the grain, of the new wine and the oil, to the storerooms where the articles of the sanctuary *are, where* the priests who minister and the gatekeepers and the singers *are;* and we will not neglect the house of our God.

The People Dwelling in Jerusalem

11 Now the leaders of the people dwelt at Jerusalem; the rest of the people cast lots to bring one out of ten to dwell in Jerusalem, the holy city, and nine-tenths *were to dwell* in *other* cities. ²And the people blessed all the men who willingly offered themselves to dwell at Jerusalem.

³These *are* the heads of the province who dwelt in Jerusalem. (But in the cities of Judah everyone dwelt in his own possession in their cities—Israelites, priests, Levites, Nethinim, and descendants of Solomon's

servants.) ⁴Also in Jerusalem dwelt *some* of the children of Judah and of the children of Benjamin.

The children of Judah: Athaiah the son of Uzziah, the son of Zechariah, the son of Amariah, the son of Shephatiah, the son of Mahalalel, of the children of Perez; ⁵and Maaseiah the son of Baruch, the son of Col-Hozeh, the son of Hazaiah, the son of Adaiah, the son of Joiarib, the son of Zechariah, the son of Shiloni. ⁶All the sons of Perez who dwelt at Jerusalem *were* four hundred and sixty-eight valiant men.

⁷And these are the sons of Benjamin: Sallu the son of Meshullam, the son of Joed, the son of Pedaiah, the son of Kolaiah, the son of Maaseiah, the son of Ithiel, the son of Jeshaiah; ⁸and after him Gabbai *and* Sallai, nine hundred and twenty-eight. ⁹Joel the son of Zichri *was* their overseer, and Judah the son of Senuahª *was* second over the city.

¹⁰Of the priests: Jedaiah the son of Joiarib, and Jachin; ¹¹Seraiah the son of Hilkiah, the son of Meshullam, the son of Zadok, the son of Meraioth, the son of Ahitub, *was* the leader of the house of God. ¹²Their brethren who did the work of the house *were* eight hundred and twenty-two; and Adaiah the son of Jeroham, the son of Pelaliah, the son of Amzi, the son of Zechariah, the son of Pashhur, the son of Malchijah, ¹³and his brethren, heads of the fathers' *houses,* were two hundred and forty-two; and Amashai the son of Azarel, the son of Ahzai, the son of Meshillemoth, the son of Immer, ¹⁴and their brethren, mighty men of valor, *were* one hundred and twenty-eight. Their overseer *was* Zabdiel the son of *one of* the great men.ª

¹⁵Also of the Levites: Shemaiah the son of Hasshub, the son of Azrikam, the son of Hashabiah, the son of Bunni; ¹⁶Shabbethai and Jozabad, of the heads of the Levites, *had* the oversight of the business outside of the house of God; ¹⁷Mattaniah the son of Micha,ª the son of Zabdi, the son of Asaph, the leader *who* began the thanksgiving with prayer; Bakbukiah, the second among his brethren; and Abda the son of

Shammua, the son of Galal, the son of Jeduthun. ¹⁸All the Levites in the holy city *were* two hundred and eighty-four.

¹⁹Moreover the gatekeepers, Akkub, Talmon, and their brethren who kept the gates, *were* one hundred and seventy-two.

²⁰And the rest of Israel, of the priests *and* Levites, *were* in all the cities of Judah, everyone in his inheritance. ²¹But the Nethinim dwelt in Ophel. And Ziha and Gishpa *were* over the Nethinim.

INTIMATE MOMENTS
Wink, but Don't Tell

Anticipation is a great tool for awakening romance. So to get your hubby's mind going, get a small map—one that you can tape to the refrigerator—and then circle and star a location on that map. When he asks what it means, just smile and wink—but don't tell him a thing.

Then, on the appointed day, drive him to the location—a place you've scouted out previously, so you know what to expect—and either have a picnic or just kiss and hug. Your choice! (Or maybe his choice, once you get there.)

²²Also the overseer of the Levites at Jerusalem *was* Uzzi the son of Bani, the son of Hashabiah, the son of Mattaniah, the son of Micha, of the sons of Asaph, the singers in charge of the service of the house of God. ²³For *it was* the king's command concerning them that a certain portion should be for the singers, a quota day by day. ²⁴Pethahiah the son of Meshezabel, of the children of Zerah the son of Judah, *was* the king's deputyª in all matters concerning the people.

The People Dwelling Outside Jerusalem

²⁵And as for the villages with their fields, *some* of the children of Judah dwelt in Kirjath Arba and its villages, Dibon and its villages, Jekabzeel and its villages; ²⁶in Jeshua, Moladah, Beth Pelet, ²⁷Hazar Shual,

---

11:9 ªOr *Hassenuah*　**11:14** ªOr *the son of Haggedolim*
11:17 ªOr *Michah*　**11:24** ªLiterally *at the king's hand*

and Beersheba and its villages; [28]in Ziklag and Meconah and its villages; [29]in En Rimmon, Zorah, Jarmuth, [30]Zanoah, Adullam, and their villages; in Lachish and its fields; in Azekah and its villages. They dwelt from Beersheba to the Valley of Hinnom.

[31]Also the children of Benjamin from Geba *dwelt* in Michmash, Aija, and Bethel, and their villages; [32]in Anathoth, Nob, Ananiah; [33]in Hazor, Ramah, Gittaim; [34]in Hadid, Zeboim, Neballat; [35]in Lod, Ono, *and* the Valley of Craftsmen. [36]Some of the Judean divisions of Levites *were* in Benjamin.

The Priests and Levites

12 Now these *are* the priests and the Levites who came up with Zerubbabel the son of Shealtiel, and Jeshua: Seraiah, Jeremiah, Ezra, [2]Amariah, Malluch, Hattush, [3]Shechaniah, Rehum, Meremoth, [4]Iddo, Ginnethoi,[a] Abijah, [5]Mijamin, Maadiah, Bilgah, [6]Shemaiah, Joiarib, Jedaiah, [7]Sallu, Amok, Hilkiah, *and* Jedaiah. These *were* the heads of the priests and their brethren in the days of Jeshua.

[8]Moreover the Levites *were* Jeshua, Binnui, Kadmiel, Sherebiah, Judah, *and* Mattaniah *who led* the thanksgiving *psalms,* he and his brethren. [9]Also Bakbukiah and Unni, their brethren, *stood* across from them in *their* duties.

[10]Jeshua begot Joiakim, Joiakim begot Eliashib, Eliashib begot Joiada, [11]Joiada begot Jonathan, and Jonathan begot Jaddua.

[12]Now in the days of Joiakim, the priests, the heads of the fathers' *houses were:* of Seraiah, Meraiah; of Jeremiah, Hananiah; [13]of Ezra, Meshullam; of Amariah, Jehohanan; [14]of Melichu,[a] Jonathan; of Shebaniah,[b] Joseph; [15]of Harim,[a] Adna; of Meraioth,[b] Helkai; [16]of Iddo, Zechariah; of Ginnethon, Meshullam; [17]of Abijah, Zichri; *the son* of Minjamin;[a] of Moadiah,[b] Piltai; [18]of Bilgah, Shammua; of Shemaiah, Jehonathan; [19]of Joiarib, Mattenai; of Jedaiah, Uzzi; [20]of Sallai,[a] Kallai; of Amok, Eber; [21]of Hilkiah, Hashabiah; *and* of Jedaiah, Nethanel.

[22]During the reign of Darius the Persian, a record *was also kept* of the Levites and priests *who had been* heads of their fathers' *houses* in the days of Eliashib, Joiada, Johanan, and Jaddua. [23]The sons of Levi, the heads of the fathers' *houses* until the days of Johanan the son of Eliashib, *were* written in the book of the chronicles.

[24]And the heads of the Levites *were* Hashabiah, Sherebiah, and Jeshua the son of Kadmiel, with their brothers across from them, to praise *and* give thanks, group alternating with group, according to the command of David the man of God. [25]Mattaniah, Bakbukiah, Obadiah, Meshullam, Talmon, and Akkub *were* gatekeepers keeping the watch at the storerooms of the gates. [26]These *lived* in the days of Joiakim the son of Jeshua, the son of Jozadak,[a] and in the days of Nehemiah the governor, and of Ezra the priest, the scribe.

Nehemiah Dedicates the Wall

[27]Now at the dedication of the wall of Jerusalem they sought out the Levites in all their places, to bring them to Jerusalem to celebrate the dedication with gladness, both with thanksgivings and singing, *with* cymbals and stringed instruments and harps. [28]And the sons of the singers gathered together from the countryside around Jerusalem, from the villages of the Netophathites, [29]from the house of Gilgal, and from the fields of Geba and Azmaveth; for the singers had built themselves villages all around Jerusalem. [30]Then the priests and Levites purified themselves, and purified the people, the gates, and the wall.

[31]So I brought the leaders of Judah up on the wall, and appointed two large thanksgiving choirs. *One* went to the right hand on the wall toward the Refuse Gate. [32]After them went Hoshaiah and half of the leaders of Judah, [33]and Azariah, Ezra, Meshullam, [34]Judah, Benjamin, Shemaiah, Jeremiah, [35]and some of the priests' sons with trumpets—Zechariah the son of Jonathan, the son of Shemaiah, the son of Mattaniah, the son of Michaiah, the son of Zaccur, the son of Asaph, [36]and his brethren, Shemaiah, Azarel, Milalai, Gilalai,

---

12:4 [a]Or *Ginnethon* (compare verse 16)
12:14 [a]Or *Malluch* (compare verse 2) [b]Or *Shechaniah* (compare verse 3) 12:15 [a]Or *Rehum* (compare verse 3) [b]Or *Meremoth* (compare verse 3) 12:17 [a]Or *Mijamin* (compare verse 5) [b]Or *Maadiah* (compare verse 5)
12:20 [a]Or *Sallu* (compare verse 7)
12:26 [a]Spelled *Jehozadak* in 1 Chronicles 6:14

Maai, Nethanel, Judah, *and* Hanani, with the musical instruments of David the man of God. And Ezra the scribe *went* before them. [37]By the Fountain Gate, in front of them, they went up the stairs of the City of David, on the stairway of the wall, beyond the house of David, as far as the Water Gate eastward.

[38]The other thanksgiving choir went the opposite *way*, and I *was* behind them with half of the people on the wall, going past the Tower of the Ovens as far as the Broad Wall, [39]and above the Gate of Ephraim, above the Old Gate, above the Fish Gate, the Tower of Hananel, the Tower of the Hundred, as far as the Sheep Gate; and they stopped by the Gate of the Prison.

[40]So the two thanksgiving choirs stood in the house of God, likewise I and the half of the rulers with me; [41]and the priests, Eliakim, Maaseiah, Minjamin,[a] Michaiah, Elioenai, Zechariah, *and* Hananiah, with trumpets; [42]also Maaseiah, Shemaiah, Eleazar, Uzzi, Jehohanan, Malchijah, Elam, and Ezer. The singers sang loudly with Jezrahiah the director.

[43]Also that day they offered great sacrifices, and rejoiced, for God had made them rejoice with great joy; the women and the children also rejoiced, so that the joy of Jerusalem was heard afar off.

Temple Responsibilities

[44]And at the same time some were appointed over the rooms of the storehouse for the offerings, the firstfruits, and the tithes, to gather into them from the fields of the cities the portions specified by the Law for the priests and Levites; for Judah rejoiced over the priests and Levites who ministered. [45]Both the singers and the gatekeepers kept the charge of their God and the charge of the purification, according to the command of David *and* Solomon his son. [46]For in the days of David and Asaph of old *there were* chiefs of the singers, and songs of praise and thanksgiving to God. [47]In the days of Zerubbabel and in the days of Nehemiah all Israel gave the portions for the singers and the gatekeepers, a portion for each day. They

also consecrated *holy things* for the Levites, and the Levites consecrated *them* for the children of Aaron.

Principles of Separation

13 On that day they read from the Book of Moses in the hearing of the people, and in it was found written that no Ammonite or Moabite should ever come into the assembly of God, [2]because they had not met the children of Israel with bread and water, but hired Balaam against them to curse them. However, our God turned the curse into a blessing. [3]So it was, when they had heard the Law, that they separated all the mixed multitude from Israel.

ROMANCE FAQ

Q: What are a man's most important romantic needs?

Show your husband the following list of needs and ask him if they are true for him. If so, ask him to prioritize them in order of importance.

1. He needs his wife to respect and celebrate who he is as a man and how God made him sexually. A critical wife can create an impotent man.

2. He needs his wife to make his romantic needs (frequency and creativity) a priority in their relationship.

3. He needs his wife to desire and make him feel wanted. He needs his wife to be unashamed of her passion for him.

4. He needs his wife to be adventuresome, fun, and sexually imaginative. He needs his wife to be unafraid about using her sexual power as a woman.

5. He needs his wife to let him know that he is a great lover. That he brings his wife great pleasure.

Romantic love is part of God's character. He made us in His image and He gave us emotions. Just as He woos us to follow after Him and express our love for Him, so a husband and wife should attempt to win each other's affections.

12:41 [a]Or *Mijamin* (compare verse 5)

The Reforms of Nehemiah

⁴Now before this, Eliashib the priest, having authority over the storerooms of the house of our God, *was* allied with Tobiah. ⁵And he had prepared for him a large room, where previously they had stored the grain offerings, the frankincense, the articles, the tithes of grain, the new wine and oil, which were commanded *to be given* to the Levites and singers and gatekeepers, and the offerings for the priests. ⁶But during all this I was not in Jerusalem, for in the thirty-second year of Artaxerxes king of Babylon I had returned to the king. Then after certain days I obtained leave from the king, ⁷and I came to Jerusalem and discovered the evil that Eliashib had done for Tobiah, in preparing a room for him in the courts of the house of God. ⁸And it grieved me bitterly; therefore I threw all the household goods of Tobiah out of the room. ⁹Then I commanded them to cleanse the rooms; and I brought back into them the articles of the house of God, with the grain offering and the frankincense.

¹⁰I also realized that the portions for the Levites had not been given *them;* for each of the Levites and the singers who did the work had gone back to his field. ¹¹So I contended with the rulers, and said, "Why is the house of God forsaken?" And I gathered them together and set them in their place. ¹²Then all Judah brought the tithe of the grain and the new wine and the oil to the storehouse. ¹³And I appointed as treasurers over the storehouse Shelemiah the priest and Zadok the scribe, and of the Levites, Pedaiah; and next to them *was* Hanan the son of Zaccur, the son of Mattaniah; for they were considered faithful, and their task *was* to distribute to their brethren.

¹⁴Remember me, O my God, concerning this, and do not wipe out my good deeds that I have done for the house of my God, and for its services!

¹⁵In those days I saw *people* in Judah treading winepresses on the Sabbath, and bringing in sheaves, and loading donkeys with wine, grapes, figs, and all *kinds of* burdens, which they brought into Jerusalem on the Sabbath day. And I warned *them* about the day on which they were selling provisions. ¹⁶Men of Tyre dwelt there also, who brought in fish and all kinds of goods, and sold *them* on the Sabbath to the children of Judah, and in Jerusalem.

¹⁷Then I contended with the nobles of Judah, and said to them, "What evil thing *is* this that you do, by which you profane the Sabbath day? ¹⁸Did not your fathers do

---

PARENTING MATTERS

Q: *How can we constructively and enjoyably use our time with our children on long road trips?*

Early on, we realized we needed to plan our time in the car as well as we planned the activities at our destinations. Kids—especially young ones—have no concept of time or distance. All they know is that they're stuck in a car, and they're bored. That's why you need a game plan for your vacation. Here are a few suggestions:

1. *Bring along plenty of special activities for the kids.* I kept a box full of books, puzzles, coloring books, and travel games and brought it out only for our trips.

2. *Listen to prerecorded CD's.* Our favorites are narrations of C.S. Lewis's *The Chronicles of Narnia* series. We listened to these over and over to keep our minds off the endless miles. The kids were mesmerized by these stories and they sparked some great spiritual discussions.

3. *Remember to use your time to build relationships.* Play games. Sing songs. Ask fun questions. Observe cool things along the way. Enjoy each other.

Remember that your vacation begins when you start your drive—not when you arrive at your destination. Use that time wisely.

thus, and did not our God bring all this disaster on us and on this city? Yet you bring added wrath on Israel by profaning the Sabbath."

[19]So it was, at the gates of Jerusalem, as it began to be dark before the Sabbath, that I commanded the gates to be shut, and charged that they must not be opened till after the Sabbath. Then I posted *some* of my servants at the gates, *so that* no burdens would be brought in on the Sabbath day. [20]Now the merchants and sellers of all kinds of wares lodged outside Jerusalem once or twice. [21]Then I warned them, and said to them, "Why do you spend the night around the wall? If you do *so* again, I will lay hands on you!" From that time on they came no *more* on the Sabbath. [22]And I commanded the Levites that they should cleanse themselves, and that they should go and guard the gates, to sanctify the Sabbath day.

Remember me, O my God, *concerning* this also, and spare me according to the greatness of Your mercy!

[23]In those days I also saw Jews *who* had married women of Ashdod, Ammon, *and* Moab. [24]And half of their children spoke the language of Ashdod, and could not speak the language of Judah, but spoke according to the language of one or the other people.

[25]So I contended with them and cursed them, struck some of them and pulled out their hair, and made them swear by God, *saying,* "You shall not give your daughters as wives to their sons, nor take their daughters for your sons or yourselves. [26]Did not Solomon king of Israel sin by these things? Yet among many nations there was no king like him, who was beloved of his God; and God made him king over all Israel. Nevertheless pagan women caused even him to sin. [27]Should we then hear of your doing all this great evil, transgressing against our God by marrying pagan women?"

[28]And *one* of the sons of Joiada, the son of Eliashib the high priest, *was* a son-in-law of Sanballat the Horonite; therefore I drove him from me.

[29]Remember them, O my God, because they have defiled the priesthood and the covenant of the priesthood and the Levites.

[30]Thus I cleansed them of everything pagan. I also assigned duties to the priests and the Levites, each to his service, [31]and *to bringing* the wood offering and the firstfruits at appointed times.

Remember me, O my God, for good!

ESTHER

THIS BOOK DESCRIBES HOW GOD USES a young Jewish girl living in the Persian city of Shushan (Susa) to foil a plot that might have led to the extermination of God's people. Many devout Jews remain very familiar with these events, since the story is a vital part of the annual celebration of the feast of Purim.

The Book of Esther explains how the Persian King Xerxes I (known to the Jews by his Hebrew name Ahasuerus) took a beautiful young Jewish woman named Esther (in Hebrew, Hadassah) as his wife and queen. At the same time, a courtier to the king named Haman got very angry when a Jew named Mordecai—Esther's older cousin, who reared her when her own parents died—refused to bow down to him. Seeking vengeance, Haman convinced the king to approve an edict that gives him the power to round up and kill all the Jews living in the Persian Empire. When Mordecai learns of Haman's despicable plot, he convinced Esther, at the risk of her own life, to ask the king to spare the Jews. Esther cleverly played to the king's sympathies, Haman was eventually exposed and hanged, and Mordecai became the king's prime minister.

Like no other book in Scripture, Esther illustrates God's providential care for His people—even though the book nowhere mentions the name of the Lord. For this very reason, some ancient scholars recommended that the book be excluded from the canon. Wiser heads prevailed, however, maintaining in essence that, "although God's face is seen nowhere, His fingerprints appear everywhere." That is often the way it is with God's providence: He remains busy at work behind the scenes, even when it may seem and especially feel as though He has left the building.

Esther's famous remark at the end of chapter four can serve as a great discussion point for modern families who find themselves living in a culture antagonistic to their faith. When faith calls for courage and risk, remind your children of Esther's words, "I will go to the king, which is against the law; and if I perish, I perish!" (v. 16).

The King Dethrones Queen Vashti

1 Now it came to pass in the days of Ahasuerus[a] (this *was* the Ahasuerus who reigned over one hundred and twenty-seven provinces, from India to Ethiopia), [2]in those days when King Ahasuerus sat on the throne of his kingdom, which *was* in Shushan[a] the citadel, [3]that in the third year of his reign he made a feast for all his officials and servants—the powers of Persia and Media, the nobles, and the princes of the provinces *being* before him— [4]when he showed the riches of his glorious kingdom and the splendor of his excellent majesty for many days, one hundred and eighty days *in all*.

[5]And when these days were completed, the king made a feast lasting seven days for all the people who were present in Shushan the citadel, from great to small, in the court of the garden of the king's palace. [6]*There were* white and blue linen *curtains* fastened with cords of fine linen and purple on silver rods and marble pillars; *and the* couches *were* of gold and silver on a *mosaic* pavement of alabaster, turquoise, and white and black marble. [7]And they served drinks in golden vessels, each vessel being different from the other, with royal wine in abundance, according to the generosity of the king. [8]In accordance with the law, the drinking was not compulsory; for so the king had ordered all the officers of his household, that they should do according to each man's pleasure.

[9]Queen Vashti also made a feast for the women *in* the royal palace which *belonged* to King Ahasuerus.

[10]On the seventh day, when the heart of the king was merry with wine, he commanded Mehuman, Biztha, Harbona, Bigtha, Abagtha, Zethar, and Carcas, seven eunuchs who served in the presence of King Ahasuerus, [11]to bring Queen Vashti before the king, *wearing* her royal crown, in order to show her beauty to the people and the officials, for she *was* beautiful to behold. [12]But Queen Vashti refused to come at the king's command *brought* by *his*

eunuchs; therefore the king was furious, and his anger burned within him.

[13]Then the king said to the wise men who understood the times (for this *was* the king's manner toward all who knew law and justice, [14]those closest to him *being* Carshena, Shethar, Admatha, Tarshish, Meres, Marsena, and Memucan, the seven princes of Persia and Media, who had access to the king's presence, *and* who ranked highest in the kingdom): [15]"What *shall we* do to Queen Vashti, according to law, because she did not obey the command of King Ahasuerus *brought to her* by the eunuchs?"

INTIMATE MOMENTS

Learn from Esther

Queen Esther showed herself to be a master of romance by the clever way she piqued her husband's curiosity and then honored him the kinds of things he really liked. Take a cue from her and celebrate your wife by arranging for a bubble bath once a month.

Vary the routine each month so it never gets predictable, but you might try lighting various kinds of candles, filling the room with different beautiful scents, arranging for a variety of musical backgrounds. Then carefully prepare a bath, warm a towel, and serve her favorite beverage.

[16]And Memucan answered before the king and the princes: "Queen Vashti has not only wronged the king, but also all the princes, and all the people who *are* in all the provinces of King Ahasuerus. [17]For the queen's behavior will become known to all women, so that they will despise their husbands in their eyes, when they report, 'King Ahasuerus commanded Queen Vashti to be brought in before him, but she did not come.' [18]This very day the *noble* ladies of Persia and Media will say to all the king's officials that they have heard of

---

1:1 [a]Generally identified with Xerxes I (485–464 B.C.)
1:2 [a]Or *Susa,* and so throughout this book

the behavior of the queen. Thus *there will be* excessive contempt and wrath. [19]If it pleases the king, let a royal decree go out from him, and let it be recorded in the laws of the Persians and the Medes, so that it will not be altered, that Vashti shall come no more before King Ahasuerus; and let the king give her royal position to another who is better than she. [20]When the king's decree which he will make is proclaimed throughout all his empire (for it is great), all wives will honor their husbands, both great and small."

[21]And the reply pleased the king and the princes, and the king did according to the word of Memucan. [22]Then he sent letters to all the king's provinces, to each province in its own script, and to every people in their own language, that each man should be master in his own house, and speak in the language of his own people.

Esther Becomes Queen

2 After these things, when the wrath of King Ahasuerus subsided, he remembered Vashti, what she had done, and what had been decreed against her. [2]Then the king's servants who attended him said: "Let beautiful young virgins be sought for the king; [3]and let the king appoint officers in all the provinces of his kingdom, that they may gather all the beautiful young virgins to Shushan the citadel, into the women's quarters, under the custody of Hegai[a] the king's eunuch, custodian of the women. And let beauty preparations be given *them.* [4]Then let the young woman who pleases the king be queen instead of Vashti."

This thing pleased the king, and he did so.

[5]In Shushan the citadel there was a certain Jew whose name *was* Mordecai the son of Jair, the son of Shimei, the son of Kish, a Benjamite. [6]*Kish*[a] had been carried away from Jerusalem with the captives who had been captured with Jeconiah[b] king of Judah, whom Nebuchadnezzar the king of Babylon had carried away. [7]And *Mordecai* had brought up Hadassah, that *is,* Esther, his uncle's daughter, for she had neither father nor mother. The young woman *was* lovely and beautiful. When her father and mother died, Mordecai took her as his own daughter.

[8]So it was, when the king's command and decree were heard, and when many young women were gathered at Shushan the citadel, *under* the custody of Hegai, that Esther also was taken to the king's palace, into the care of Hegai the custodian of the women. [9]Now the young woman pleased him, and she obtained his favor; so he readily gave beauty preparations to her, besides her allowance. Then seven choice maidservants were provided for her from the king's palace, and he moved her and her maidservants to the best *place* in the house of the women.

[10]Esther had not revealed her people or family, for Mordecai had charged her not to reveal *it.* [11]And every day Mordecai paced in front of the court of the women's quarters, to learn of Esther's welfare and what was happening to her.

[12]Each young woman's turn came to go in to King Ahasuerus after she had completed twelve months' preparation, according to the regulations for the women, for thus were the days of their preparation apportioned: six months with oil of myrrh, and six months with perfumes and preparations for beautifying women. [13]Thus *prepared, each* young woman went to the king, and she was given whatever she desired to take with her from the women's quarters to the king's palace. [14]In the evening she went, and in the morning she returned to the second house of the women, to the custody of Shaashgaz, the king's eunuch who kept the concubines. She would not go in to the king again unless the king delighted in her and called for her by name.

[15]Now when the turn came for Esther the daughter of Abihail the uncle of Mordecai, who had taken her as his daughter, to go in to the king, she requested nothing but what Hegai the king's eunuch, the custodian of the women, advised. And Esther obtained favor in the sight of all who saw her. [16]So Esther was taken to King Ahasuerus, into his royal palace, in the tenth month, which *is* the month of Tebeth, in the seventh year of his reign.

2:3 [a]Hebrew *Hege* 2:6 [a]Literally *Who* [b]Same as *Jehoiachin,* 2 Kings 24:6 and elsewhere

DEVOTIONS FOR COUPLES • 2:1-23
Meet a Worthy Queen

How did a nice Jewish girl become queen of the entire Persian Empire? That's the story of the book of Esther. We learn that while Esther was selected from among the most beautiful women of the kingdom to be the queen, she was far more than a beautiful young woman. Her worthy character reveals itself as this romantic tale suddenly changes into a serious drama.

When Mordecai, the cousin of Queen Esther, informs her of a plot to destroy all the Jews living in the kingdom, he urges her to go to the king and plead with him on behalf of her people. But this request presents the young queen with a tough decision. She knows that the rules and laws of the palace dictate that *no one* can approach the king without being summoned ... and she knows that the queen before her was removed from her position for her insolence. But because of the urgency of the moment, she decides to risk her position for a higher good. And in that decision, Esther reveals several things about her relationship with the king:

First, she was not presumptuous. She came before him as his queen, wearing her royal robes, but she came humbly, standing and waiting for him to notice her. She didn't barge into the throne room. Even though she had a relationship with the king, she didn't abuse that privilege. God, in turn, honored her.

Second, Esther respected her husband and his position as king. As she reached the throne, she touched his golden scepter, demonstrating that she recognized his authority and power.

Third, Esther began her reply to her husband, "If it please the king." In the other two recorded conversations between this king and queen, the same statement prefaces her remarks. This was *not* just an official formality, but a genuine expression to Ahasuerus of her overall commitment, respect, and submission to him as her husband and her authority. Although my husband, Dennis, is not a king like Ahasuerus, he is worthy of my respect.

Before I present my case to Dennis, I also try to assure him of my respectful loyalty to him as my partner and authority. At times I speak frankly about his weaknesses and how they affect me, but when I do, he is much more able to hear my words because of my loyalty and frequent verbal reassurances. He knows that even if *nothing* changes, I will still remain committed to him.

What I learn from Queen Esther and how I respected her husband reminds me of the advice shared by a good friend of ours who was married for nearly 50 years. Speaking with a small group of women, she said, "Ladies, if you crown him king, he will treat you like a queen!"

---

[17]The king loved Esther more than all the *other* women, and she obtained grace and favor in his sight more than all the virgins; so he set the royal crown upon her head and made her queen instead of Vashti. [18]Then the king made a great feast, the Feast of Esther, for all his officials and servants; and he proclaimed a holiday in the provinces and gave gifts according to the generosity of a king.

Mordecai Discovers a Plot

[19]When virgins were gathered together a second time, Mordecai sat within the king's gate. [20]*Now* Esther had not revealed her family and her people, just as Mordecai had charged her, for Esther obeyed the command of Mordecai as when she was brought up by him.

[21]In those days, while Mordecai sat within the king's gate, two of the king's eunuchs, Bigthan and Teresh, doorkeepers, became furious and sought to lay hands on King Ahasuerus. [22]So the matter became known to Mordecai, who told Queen Esther, and Esther informed the king in Mordecai's name. [23]And when an inquiry was made into the matter, it was

confirmed, and both were hanged on a gallows; and it was written in the book of the chronicles in the presence of the king.

Haman's Conspiracy Against the Jews

3 After these things King Ahasuerus promoted Haman, the son of Hammedatha the Agagite, and advanced him and set his seat above all the princes who *were* with him. ²And all the king's servants who *were* within the king's gate bowed and paid homage to Haman, for so the king had commanded concerning him. But Mordecai would not bow or pay homage. ³Then the king's servants who *were* within the king's gate said to Mordecai, "Why do you transgress the king's command?" ⁴Now it happened, when they spoke to him daily and he would not listen to them, that they told *it* to Haman, to see whether Mordecai's words would stand; for *Mordecai* had told them that he *was* a Jew. ⁵When Haman saw that Mordecai did not bow or pay him homage, Haman was filled with wrath. ⁶But he disdained to lay hands on Mordecai alone, for they had told him of the people of Mordecai. Instead, Haman sought to destroy all the Jews who *were* throughout the whole kingdom of Ahasuerus—the people of Mordecai.

⁷In the first month, which is the month of Nisan, in the twelfth year of King Ahasuerus, they cast Pur (that *is*, the lot), before Haman to determine the day and the month,ᵃ until *it fell on the* twelfth *month*,ᵃ which *is* the month of Adar. ⁸Then Haman said to King Ahasuerus, "There is a certain people scattered and dispersed among the people in all the provinces of your kingdom; their laws *are* different from all *other* people's, and they do not keep the king's laws. Therefore it *is* not fitting for the king to let them remain. ⁹If it pleases the king, let *a decree* be written that they be destroyed, and I will pay ten thousand talents of silver into the hands of those who do the work, to bring *it* into the king's treasuries."

¹⁰So the king took his signet ring from his hand and gave it to Haman, the son of Hammedatha the Agagite, the enemy of the Jews. ¹¹And the king said to Haman,

"The money and the people *are* given to you, to do with them as seems good to you."

¹²Then the king's scribes were called on the thirteenth day of the first month, and *a decree* was written according to all that Haman commanded—to the king's satraps, to the governors who *were* over each province, to the officials of all people, to every province according to its script, and to every people in their language. In the name of King Ahasuerus it was written, and sealed with the king's signet ring. ¹³And the letters were sent by couriers into all the king's provinces, to destroy, to kill, and to annihilate all the Jews, both young and old, little children and women, in one day, on the thirteenth *day* of the twelfth month, which *is* the month of Adar, and to plunder their possessions.ᵃ ¹⁴A copy of the document was to be issued as law in every province, being published for all people, that they should be ready for that day. ¹⁵The couriers went out, hastened by the king's command; and the decree was proclaimed in Shushan the citadel. So the king and Haman sat down to drink, but the city of Shushan was perplexed.

Esther Agrees to Help the Jews

4 When Mordecai learned all that had happened, he tore his clothes and put on sackcloth and ashes, and went out into the midst of the city. He cried out with a loud and bitter cry. ²He went as far as the front of the king's gate, for no one *might* enter the king's gate clothed with sackcloth. ³And in every province where the king's command and decree arrived, *there was* great mourning among the Jews, with fasting, weeping, and wailing; and many lay in sackcloth and ashes.

⁴So Esther's maids and eunuchs came and told her, and the queen was deeply distressed. Then she sent garments to clothe Mordecai and take his sackcloth away from him, but he would not accept *them*. ⁵Then Esther called Hathach, *one* of the king's

<hr/>

3:7 ᵃSeptuagint adds *to destroy the people of Mordecai in one day;* Vulgate adds *the nation of the Jews should be destroyed.* ᵇFollowing Masoretic Text and Vulgate; Septuagint reads *and the lot fell on the fourteenth of the month.*
3:13 ᵃSeptuagint adds the text of the letter here.

eunuchs whom he had appointed to attend her, and she gave him a command concerning Mordecai, to learn what and why this *was*. ⁶So Hathach went out to Mordecai in the city square that *was* in front of the king's gate. ⁷And Mordecai told him all that had happened to him, and the sum of money that Haman had promised to pay into the king's treasuries to destroy the Jews. ⁸He also gave him a copy of the written decree for their destruction, which was given at Shushan, that he might show it to Esther and explain it to her, and that he might command her to go in to the king to make supplication to him and plead before him for her people. ⁹So Hathach returned and told Esther the words of Mordecai.

¹⁰Then Esther spoke to Hathach, and gave him a command for Mordecai: ¹¹"All the king's servants and the people of the king's provinces know that any man or woman who goes into the inner court to the king, who has not been called, *he has* but one law: put *all* to death, except the one to whom the king holds out the golden scepter, that he may live. Yet I myself have not been called to go in to the king these thirty days." ¹²So they told Mordecai Esther's words.

¹³And Mordecai told *them* to answer Esther: "Do not think in your heart that you will escape in the king's palace any more than all the other Jews. ¹⁴For if you remain completely silent at this time, relief and deliverance will arise for the Jews from another place, but you and your father's house will perish. Yet who knows whether you have come to the kingdom for *such* a time as this?"

¹⁵Then Esther told *them* to reply to Mordecai: ¹⁶"Go, gather all the Jews who are present in Shushan, and fast for me; neither eat nor drink for three days, night or day. My maids and I will fast likewise. And so I will go to the king, which *is* against the law; and if I perish, I perish!"

¹⁷So Mordecai went his way and did according to all that Esther commanded him.ᵃ

4:17 ᵃSeptuagint adds a prayer of Mordecai here.
5:1 ᵃSeptuagint adds many extra details in verses 1 and 2.

BIBLICAL INSIGHTS • 4:13
You Can Do Something

HAVE YOU TAKEN A COLD, hard look at the world around you? A mindset of entitlement and a thirst for self-fulfillment have stripped away much of what used to be good in our culture. You may feel powerless to fix crime, welfare, health care, education, politics, the economy, the media, or the environment—but you *can* do something about your own family.

Centuries ago, Esther faced an enormous, culture-wide problem that seemed far too big for her to tackle. Apparently she felt tempted to sit this one out. That is, until her cousin Mordecai reminded her, "Do not think in your heart that you will escape in the king's palace any more than all the other Jews. For if you remain completely silent . . . you and your father's house will perish" (4:13, 14). Mordecai challenged Esther to take action, beginning in her own family. As a result, not only did she save her own family, but many others. Esther's courageous faith teaches us that we never know when our actions will be used by God to do something much larger than ourselves.

In fact, our real problem is not *out there*, but *in here*. I'm thinking about my family. And yours. The time has come to confront our own indifference, lethargy, pride, and disobedience. It's time to do something. It's time to join together in a family reformation.

What are you facing today that demands courageous faith and obedience?

Esther's Banquet

5 Now it happened on the third day that Esther put on *her* royal *robes* and stood in the inner court of the king's palace, across from the king's house, while the king sat on his royal throne in the royal house, facing the entrance of the house.ᵃ ²So it was, when the king saw Queen Esther standing in the court, *that* she found favor in his sight, and the king held out to Esther the golden scepter that *was* in his hand. Then Esther went near and touched the top of the scepter.

³And the king said to her, "What do you wish, Queen Esther? What *is* your request? It shall be given to you—up to half the kingdom!"

⁴So Esther answered, "If it pleases the king, let the king and Haman come today to the banquet that I have prepared for him."

⁵Then the king said, "Bring Haman quickly, that he may do as Esther has said." So the king and Haman went to the banquet that Esther had prepared.

⁶At the banquet of wine the king said to Esther, "What *is* your petition? It shall be granted you. What *is* your request, up to half the kingdom? It shall be done!"

⁷Then Esther answered and said, "My petition and request *is this:* ⁸If I have found favor in the sight of the king, and if it pleases the king to grant my petition and fulfill my request, then let the king and Haman come to the banquet which I will prepare for them, and tomorrow I will do as the king has said."

Haman's Plot Against Mordecai

⁹So Haman went out that day joyful and with a glad heart; but when Haman saw Mordecai in the king's gate, and that he did not stand or tremble before him, he was filled with indignation against Mordecai. ¹⁰Nevertheless Haman restrained himself and went home, and he sent and called for his friends and his wife Zeresh. ¹¹Then Haman told them of his great riches, the multitude of his children, everything in which the king had promoted him, and how he had advanced him above the officials and servants of the king.

¹²Moreover Haman said, "Besides, Queen Esther invited no one but me to come in with the king to the banquet that she prepared; and tomorrow I am again invited by her, along with the king. ¹³Yet all this avails me nothing, so long as I see Mordecai the Jew sitting at the king's gate."

¹⁴Then his wife Zeresh and all his friends said to him, "Let a gallows be made, fifty cubits high, and in the morning suggest to the king that Mordecai be hanged on it; then go merrily with the king to the banquet."

And the thing pleased Haman; so he had the gallows made.

The King Honors Mordecai

6 That night the king could not sleep. So one was commanded to bring the book of the records of the chronicles; and they were read before the king. ²And it was

found written that Mordecai had told of Bigthana and Teresh, two of the king's eunuchs, the doorkeepers who had sought to lay hands on King Ahasuerus. ³Then the king said, "What honor or dignity has been bestowed on Mordecai for this?"

And the king's servants who attended him said, "Nothing has been done for him."

⁴So the king said, "Who *is* in the court?" Now Haman had *just* entered the outer court of the king's palace to suggest that the king hang Mordecai on the gallows that he had prepared for him.

⁵The king's servants said to him, "Haman is there, standing in the court."

And the king said, "Let him come in."

⁶So Haman came in, and the king asked him, "What shall be done for the man whom the king delights to honor?"

Now Haman thought in his heart, "Whom would the king delight to honor more than me?" ⁷And Haman answered the king, "*For* the man whom the king delights to honor, ⁸let a royal robe be brought which the king has worn, and a horse on which the king has ridden, which has a royal crest placed on its head. ⁹Then let this robe and horse be delivered to the hand of one of the king's most noble princes, that he may array the man whom the king delights to honor. Then parade him on horseback through the city square, and proclaim before him: 'Thus shall it be done to the man whom the king delights to honor!'"

¹⁰Then the king said to Haman, "Hurry, take the robe and the horse, as you have suggested, and do so for Mordecai the Jew who sits within the king's gate! Leave nothing undone of all that you have spoken."

¹¹So Haman took the robe and the horse, arrayed Mordecai and led him on horseback through the city square, and proclaimed before him, "Thus shall it be done to the man whom the king delights to honor!"

¹²Afterward Mordecai went back to the king's gate. But Haman hurried to his house, mourning and with his head covered. ¹³When Haman told his wife Zeresh and all his friends everything that had happened to him, his wise men and his wife Zeresh said to him, "If Mordecai, before whom you have begun to fall, is of Jewish descent, you will not prevail against him but will surely fall before him."

¹⁴While they *were* still talking with him, the king's eunuchs came, and hastened to bring Haman to the banquet which Esther had prepared.

Haman Hanged Instead of Mordecai

7 So the king and Haman went to dine with Queen Esther. ²And on the second day, at the banquet of wine, the king again said to Esther, "What *is* your petition, Queen Esther? It shall be granted you. And what *is* your request, up to half the kingdom? It shall be done!"

³Then Queen Esther answered and said, "If I have found favor in your sight, O king, and if it pleases the king, let my life be given me at my petition, and my people at my request. ⁴For we have been sold, my people and I, to be destroyed, to be killed, and to be annihilated. Had we been sold as male and female slaves, I would have held my tongue, although the enemy could never compensate for the king's loss."

⁵So King Ahasuerus answered and said to Queen Esther, "Who is he, and where is he, who would dare presume in his heart to do such a thing?"

⁶And Esther said, "The adversary and enemy *is* this wicked Haman!"

So Haman was terrified before the king and queen.

⁷Then the king arose in his wrath from the banquet of wine *and went* into the palace garden; but Haman stood before Queen Esther, pleading for his life, for he saw that evil was determined against him by the king. ⁸When the king returned from the palace garden to the place of the banquet of wine, Haman had fallen across the couch where Esther *was*. Then the king said, "Will he also assault the queen while I *am* in the house?"

As the word left the king's mouth, they covered Haman's face. ⁹Now Harbonah, one of the eunuchs, said to the king, "Look! The gallows, fifty cubits high, which Haman made for Mordecai, who spoke good on the king's behalf, is standing at the house of Haman."

Then the king said, "Hang him on it!"

¹⁰So they hanged Haman on the gallows

that he had prepared for Mordecai. Then the king's wrath subsided.

Esther Saves the Jews

8 On that day King Ahasuerus gave Queen Esther the house of Haman, the enemy of the Jews. And Mordecai came before the king, for Esther had told how he *was related* to her. [2]So the king took off his signet ring, which he had taken from Haman, and gave it to Mordecai; and Esther appointed Mordecai over the house of Haman.

[3]Now Esther spoke again to the king, fell down at his feet, and implored him with tears to counteract the evil of Haman the Agagite, and the scheme which he had devised against the Jews. [4]And the king held out the golden scepter toward Esther. So Esther arose and stood before the king, [5]and said, "If it pleases the king, and if I have found favor in his sight and the thing *seems* right to the king and I am pleasing in his eyes, let it be written to revoke the letters devised by Haman, the son of Hammedatha the Agagite, which he wrote to annihilate the Jews who *are* in all the king's provinces. [6]For how can I endure to see the evil that will come to my people? Or how can I endure to see the destruction of my countrymen?"

[7]Then King Ahasuerus said to Queen Esther and Mordecai the Jew, "Indeed, I have given Esther the house of Haman, and they have hanged him on the gallows because he *tried to* lay his hand on the Jews. [8]You yourselves write *a decree* concerning the Jews, as you please, in the king's name, and seal *it* with the king's signet ring; for whatever is written in the king's name and sealed with the king's signet ring no one can revoke."

[9]So the king's scribes were called at that time, in the third month, which *is* the month of Sivan, on the twenty-third *day;* and it was written, according to all that Mordecai commanded, to the Jews, the satraps, the governors, and the princes of the provinces from India to Ethiopia, one hundred and twenty-seven provinces *in all,* to every province in its own script, to every people in their own language, and to the Jews in their own script and language.

[10]And he wrote in the name of King Ahasuerus, sealed *it* with the king's signet ring, and sent letters by couriers on horseback, riding on royal horses bred from swift steeds.[a]

[11]By these letters the king permitted the Jews who *were* in every city to gather together and protect their lives—to destroy, kill, and annihilate all the forces of any people or province that would assault them, *both* little children and women, and to plunder their possessions, [12]on one day in all the provinces of King Ahasuerus, on the thirteenth *day* of the twelfth month, which *is* the month of Adar.[a] [13]A copy of the document was to be issued as a decree in every province and published for all people, so that the Jews would be ready on that day to avenge themselves on their enemies. [14]The couriers who rode on royal horses went out, hastened and pressed on by the king's command. And the decree was issued in Shushan the citadel.

[15]So Mordecai went out from the presence of the king in royal apparel of blue and white, with a great crown of gold and a garment of fine linen and purple; and the city of Shushan rejoiced and was glad. [16]The Jews had light and gladness, joy and honor. [17]And in every province and city, wherever the king's command and decree came, the Jews had joy and gladness, a feast and a holiday. Then many of the people of the land became Jews, because fear of the Jews fell upon them.

The Jews Destroy Their Tormentors

9 Now in the twelfth month, that *is,* the month of Adar, on the thirteenth day, *the time* came for the king's command and his decree to be executed. On the day that the enemies of the Jews had hoped to overpower them, the opposite occurred, in that the Jews themselves overpowered those who hated them. [2]The Jews gathered together in their cities throughout all the provinces of King Ahasuerus to lay hands on those who sought their harm. And no one could withstand them, because fear of them fell upon all people. [3]And all the officials of

---

8:10 [a]Literally *sons of the swift horses*
8:12 [a]Septuagint adds the text of the letter here.

he provinces, the satraps, the governors, and all those doing the king's work, helped the Jews, because the fear of Mordecai fell upon them. [4]For Mordecai *was* great in the king's palace, and his fame spread throughout all the provinces; for this man Mordecai became increasingly prominent. [5]Thus the Jews defeated all their enemies with the stroke of the sword, with slaughter and destruction, and did what they pleased with those who hated them.

[6]And in Shushan the citadel the Jews killed and destroyed five hundred men. Also Parshandatha, Dalphon, Aspatha, Poratha, Adalia, Aridatha, [9]Parmashta, Arisai, Aridai, and Vajezatha— [10]the ten sons of Haman the son of Hammedatha, the enemy of the Jews—they killed; but they did not lay a hand on the plunder.

[11]On that day the number of those who were killed in Shushan the citadel was brought to the king. [12]And the king said to Queen Esther, "The Jews have killed and destroyed five hundred men in Shushan the citadel, and the ten sons of Haman. What have they done in the rest of the king's provinces? Now what *is* your petition? It shall be granted to you. Or what *is* your further request? It shall be done."

[13]Then Esther said, "If it pleases the king, let it be granted to the Jews who *are* in Shushan to do again tomorrow according to today's decree, and let Haman's ten sons be hanged on the gallows."

[14]So the king commanded this to be done; the decree was issued in Shushan, and they hanged Haman's ten sons.

[15]And the Jews who *were* in Shushan gathered together again on the fourteenth day of the month of Adar and killed three hundred men at Shushan; but they did not lay a hand on the plunder.

[16]The remainder of the Jews in the king's provinces gathered together and protected their lives, had rest from their enemies, and killed seventy-five thousand of their enemies; but they did not lay a hand on the plunder. [17]*This was* on the thirteenth day of the month of Adar. And on the fourteenth of *the month*[a] they rested and made it a day of feasting and gladness.

The Feast of Purim

[18]But the Jews who *were* at Shushan assembled together on the thirteenth *day,* as well as on the fourteenth; and on the fifteenth of *the month*[a] they rested, and made it a day of feasting and gladness. [19]Therefore the Jews of the villages who dwelt in the unwalled towns celebrated the fourteenth day of the month of Adar *with* gladness and feasting, as a holiday, and for sending presents to one another.

[20]And Mordecai wrote these things and sent letters to all the Jews, near and far, who *were* in all the provinces of King Ahasuerus, [21]to establish among them that they should celebrate yearly the fourteenth and fifteenth days of the month of Adar, [22]as the days on which the Jews had rest from their enemies, as the month which was turned from sorrow to joy for them, and from mourning to a holiday; that they should make them days of feasting and joy, of sending presents to one another and gifts to the poor. [23]So the Jews accepted the custom which they had begun, as Mordecai had written to them, [24]because Haman, the son of Hammedatha the Agagite, the enemy of all the Jews, had plotted against the Jews to annihilate them, and had cast Pur (that *is,* the lot), to consume them and destroy them; [25]but when *Esther*[a] came before the king, he commanded by letter that this[b] wicked plot which *Haman* had devised against the Jews should return on his own head, and that he and his sons should be hanged on the gallows.

[26]So they called these days Purim, after the name Pur. Therefore, because of all the words of this letter, what they had seen concerning this matter, and what had happened to them, [27]the Jews established and imposed it upon themselves and their descendants and all who would join them, that without fail they should celebrate these two days every year, according to the written *instructions* and according to the *prescribed* time, [28]*that* these days *should be* remembered and kept throughout every generation, every family, every province, and every city, that these days of Purim

---

9:17 [a]Literally *it* 9:18 [a]Literally *it* 9:25 [a]Literally *he* or *it* [b]Literally *his*

should not fail *to be observed* among the Jews, and *that* the memory of them should not perish among their descendants.

[29]Then Queen Esther, the daughter of Abihail, with Mordecai the Jew, wrote with full authority to confirm this second letter about Purim. [30]And *Mordecai* sent letters to all the Jews, to the one hundred and twenty-seven provinces of the kingdom of Ahasuerus, *with* words of peace and truth, [31]to confirm these days of Purim at their *appointed* time, as Mordecai the Jew and Queen Esther had prescribed for them, and as they had decreed for themselves and their descendants concerning matters of their fasting and lamenting. [32]So the decree of Esther confirmed these matters of Purim, and it was written in the book.

Mordecai's Advancement

10 And King Ahasuerus imposed tribute on the land and *on* the islands of the sea. [2]Now all the acts of his power and his might, and the account of the greatness of Mordecai, to which the king advanced him, *are* they not written in the book of the chronicles of the kings of Media and Persia? [3]For Mordecai the Jew *was* second to King Ahasuerus, and was great among the Jews and well received by the multitude of his brethren, seeking the good of his people and speaking peace to all his countrymen.[a]

10:3 [a]Literally *seed.* Septuagint and Vulgate add a dream of Mordecai here; Vulgate adds six more chapters.

JOB

WHY WOULD AN ALL-POWERFUL, loving God allow evil to exist? That's one of the oldest questions facing humankind, and the question lying at the heart of the book of Job.

Ezekiel links the man Job with Daniel and Noah as examples of righteous men who face calamity and who are ultimately delivered by God's grace. Job lived in "the land of Uz," a region likely near Midian, where Moses lived for forty years. A number of factors lead us to believe that Job lived after the flood but before the time of Abraham.

In the prologue of the book, Satan comes before God to suggest that Job worships God only because of His kindness to him. Satan implies that if God were to remove His blessings from Job's life, the man would renounce his faith and denounce God. So God allows Satan to put Job to the test. In a single day, Job's livestock, his servants, and his sons and daughters all die. In addition, sores break out all over Job's body. Job's wife tells her husband to "curse God and die" (2:9), but Job responds with the profound question, "Shall we indeed accept good from God, and shall we not accept adversity?" (2:10).

Three friends eventually come by to offer Job a variety of explanations for his personal tragedy; these conversations make up the majority of the book. Finally, God speaks directly to Job (37:1), showing him that the best way to face tragic events is with faith. A kind and loving God remains in control, working out His plan for our good and His glory.

When modern families face tragedies—a critical illness, the death of a loved one, financial hardship—we must remember that a sovereign God remains in control. We may never understand His purposes in this life, but we can trust Him. As Job said, "For I know that my Redeemer lives, and He shall stand at last on the earth; and after my skin is destroyed, this I know, that in my flesh I shall see God" (19:25, 26).

Be On Guard

EACH OF US LIVES IN THE MIDDLE of an unseen spiritual world. Just as God is accomplishing His work on earth, so Satan is seeking to undermine God's work in you and your mate.

That is precisely what the devil had in mind when he brought Job to God's attention. He intended to destroy this righteous man's faith and prove that no one would follow God unless they enjoyed an unending stream of physical blessings.

Centuries later Peter wrote, "Be sober, be vigilant; because your adversary the devil walks about like a roaring lion, seeking whom he may devour." (1 Pet. 5:8). Lions prey upon the weak, the unsuspecting, the unprotected, and the stragglers. Similarly, Satan looks for marriages with weak spots, mates with unprotected self-esteem issues, and spouses who live independently of each other. Be advised, and be on the alert.

"Be strong in the Lord and in the power of His might," Paul writes. "Put on the whole armor of God, that you may be able to stand against the wiles of the devil" (Eph. 6:10, 11). Standing firm in Christ means living obediently and believing that what God says is true, regardless of how you feel.

Job and His Family in Uz

1 There was a man in the land of Uz, whose name *was* Job; and that man was blameless and upright, and one who feared God and shunned evil. ²And seven sons and three daughters were born to him. ³Also, his possessions were seven thousand sheep, three thousand camels, five hundred yoke of oxen, five hundred female donkeys, and a very large household, so that this man was the greatest of all the people of the East.

⁴And his sons would go and feast *in* their houses, each on his *appointed* day, and would send and invite their three sisters to eat and drink with them. ⁵So it was, when the days of feasting had run their course, that Job would send and sanctify them, and he would rise early in the morning and offer burnt offerings *according to* the number of them all. For Job said, "It may be that my sons have sinned and cursedᵃ God in their hearts." Thus Job did regularly.

Satan Attacks Job's Character

⁶Now there was a day when the sons of God came to present themselves before the LORD, and Satanᵃ also came among them. ⁷And the LORD said to Satan, "From where do you come?"

So Satan answered the LORD and said, "From going to and fro on the earth, and from walking back and forth on it."

⁸Then the LORD said to Satan, "Have you considered My servant Job, that *there is* none like him on the earth, a blameless and upright man, one who fears God and shuns evil?"

⁹So Satan answered the LORD and said, "Does Job fear God for nothing? ¹⁰Have You not made a hedge around him, around his household, and around all that he has on every side? You have blessed the work of his hands, and his possessions have increased in the land. ¹¹But now, stretch out Your hand and touch all that he has, and he will surely curse You to Your face!"

¹²And the LORD said to Satan, "Behold, all that he has *is* in your power; only do not lay a hand on his *person.*"

So Satan went out from the presence of the LORD.

Job Loses His Property and Children

¹³Now there was a day when his sons and daughters *were* eating and drinking wine in their oldest brother's house; ¹⁴and a messenger came to Job and said, "The oxen were plowing and the donkeys feeding beside them, ¹⁵when the Sabeansᵃ raided *them* and took them away—indeed they have killed

1:5 ᵃLiterally *blessed,* but used here in the evil sense, and so in verse 11 and 2:5, 9   1:6 ᵃLiterally *the Adversary,* and so throughout this book
1:15 ᵃLiterally *Sheba* (compare 6:19)

the servants with the edge of the sword; and I alone have escaped to tell you!"

¹⁶While he *was* still speaking, another also came and said, "The fire of God fell from heaven and burned up the sheep and the servants, and consumed them; and I alone have escaped to tell you!"

¹⁷While he *was* still speaking, another also came and said, "The Chaldeans formed three bands, raided the camels and took them away, yes, and killed the servants with the edge of the sword; and I alone have escaped to tell you!"

¹⁸While he *was* still speaking, another also came and said, "Your sons and daughters *were* eating and drinking wine in their oldest brother's house, ¹⁹and suddenly a great wind came from across[a] the wilderness and struck the four corners of the house, and it fell on the young people, and they are dead; and I alone have escaped to tell you!"

²⁰Then Job arose, tore his robe, and shaved his head; and he fell to the ground and worshiped. ²¹And he said:

"Naked I came from my mother's
        womb,
    And naked shall I return there.
    The LORD gave, and the LORD has
        taken away;
    Blessed be the name of the LORD."

²²In all this Job did not sin nor charge God with wrong.

Satan Attacks Job's Health

2 Again there was a day when the sons of God came to present themselves before the LORD, and Satan came also among them to present himself before the LORD. ²And the LORD said to Satan, "From where do you come?"

Satan answered the LORD and said, "From going to and fro on the earth, and from walking back and forth on it."

³Then the LORD said to Satan, "Have you considered My servant Job, that *there is* none like him on the earth, a blameless and upright man, one who fears God and shuns evil? And still he holds fast to his integrity, although you incited Me against him, to destroy him without cause."

BIBLICAL INSIGHTS • 1:8

A Reward for Righteousness

ONE OF THE BENEFITS of righteousness is that God sees from His throne in heaven and expresses His pleasure when we do what honors Him.

In the book of Job, He even points out to Satan, the enemy of our souls, that one man stood out among all others as one who feared Him and avoided evil: "Then the LORD said to Satan, 'Have you considered My servant Job, that there *is* none like him on the earth, a blameless and upright man, one who fears God and shuns evil?'" (Job 1:8).

At some point in his or her life, every Christian needs to come to an understanding that God's approval is infinitely more rewarding than the approval of any human being. First Peter 3:14–17 tells us, "But even if you should suffer for righteousness' sake, you are blessed. '*And do not be afraid of their threats, nor be troubled.*' But sanctify the Lord God in your hearts . . . For it is better, if it is the will of God, to suffer for doing good than for doing evil."

Those are the tremendous benefits of obedience—the eternal rewards of being willing to stand out in a crowd for doing what is right.

⁴So Satan answered the LORD and said, "Skin for skin! Yes, all that a man has he will give for his life. ⁵But stretch out Your hand now, and touch his bone and his flesh, and he will surely curse You to Your face!"

⁶And the LORD said to Satan, "Behold, he *is* in your hand, but spare his life."

⁷So Satan went out from the presence of the LORD, and struck Job with painful boils from the sole of his foot to the crown of his head. ⁸And he took for himself a potsherd with which to scrape himself while he sat in the midst of the ashes.

⁹Then his wife said to him, "Do you still

1:19 [a]Septuagint omits *across*.

BIBLICAL INSIGHTS • 2:8, 9
The Gift of Compassion

WHEN JOB LOST NEARLY EVERYTHING he had—his children, his possessions, his reputation, and his health—that's when he needed his wife to step in and give him her unconditional support. But this is what he got: "Then his wife said to him, 'Do you still hold fast to your integrity? Curse God and die!'" (2:8, 9). These were obviously not the words Job needed to hear from his wife.

Don't leave your spouse alone to deal with his own personal tragedies. Whatever he's facing, he needs you to face it with him. He needs your compassionate, consistent, and tireless belief in him. It's in these moments when you will experience what Proverbs 18:21 teaches, "Death and life are in the power of the tongue." Your words have enormous power in the life of your spouse. Find ways to use your words to encourage his faith, not his unbelief.

Talk about the context of his life and together gain an understanding of what has shaped him. The more you fully grasp the context of your mate's journey to adulthood—and express compassion for where he has been—the more freedom he will feel to pour out his heart. Remember that parents, coaches, teachers, peers, siblings, and other significant people gave him a personal heritage of either success or failure.

Tell him that you are unlike those who have rejected him; your commitment is unwavering and your love is consistent. In this climate of compassion and patience, he will begin to feel free to take risks and to move ahead without fear of rejection.

---

hold fast to your integrity? Curse God and die!"

[10]But he said to her, "You speak as one of the foolish women speaks. Shall we indeed accept good from God, and shall we not accept adversity?" In all this Job did not sin with his lips.

Job's Three Friends

[11]Now when Job's three friends heard of all this adversity that had come upon him, each one came from his own place—Eliphaz the Temanite, Bildad the Shuhite, and Zophar the Naamathite. For they had made an appointment together to come and mourn with him, and to comfort him. [12]And when they raised their eyes from afar, and did not recognize him, they lifted their voices and wept; and each one tore his robe and sprinkled dust on his head toward heaven. [13]So they sat down with him on the ground seven days and seven nights, and no one spoke a word to him, for they saw that *his* grief was very great.

Job Deplores His Birth

3 After this Job opened his mouth and cursed the day of his *birth*. [2]And Job spoke, and said:

3   "May the day perish on which I was
       born,
      And the night *in which* it was said,
 ' A male child is conceived.'
4   May that day be darkness;
      May God above not seek it,
      Nor the light shine upon it.
5   May darkness and the shadow of
       death claim it;
      May a cloud settle on it;
      May the blackness of the day
       terrify it.
6   *As for* that night, may darkness
       seize it;
      May it not rejoice[a] among the days of
       the year,
      May it not come into the number of
       the months.
7   Oh, may that night be barren!
      May no joyful shout come into it!
8   May those curse it who curse the day,
      Those who are ready to arouse
       Leviathan.
9   May the stars of its morning
       be dark;
      May it look for light, but *have* none,
      And not see the dawning of
       the day;

3:6 [a]Septuagint, Syriac, Targum, and Vulgate read *be joined*.

10 Because it did not shut up the doors
    of my *mother's* womb,
    Nor hide sorrow from my eyes.

11 "Why did I not die at birth?
    Why did I *not* perish when I came
      from the womb?
12 Why did the knees receive me?
    Or why the breasts, that I should
      nurse?
13 For now I would have lain still and
      been quiet,
    I would have been asleep;
    Then I would have been at rest
14 With kings and counselors of the
      earth,
    Who built ruins for themselves,
15 Or with princes who had gold,
    Who filled their houses *with* silver;
16 Or *why* was I not hidden like a
      stillborn child,
    Like infants who never saw light?
17 There the wicked cease *from*
      troubling,
    And there the weary are at rest.
18 *There* the prisoners rest together;
    They do not hear the voice of the
      oppressor.
19 The small and great are there,

3:24 [a]Literally *my bread*

And the servant *is* free from his
    master.
20 "Why is light given to him who is in
      misery,
    And life to the bitter of soul,
21 Who long for death, but it does not
      come,
    And search for it more than hidden
      treasures;
22 Who rejoice exceedingly,
    And are glad when they can find the
      grave?
23 *Why is light given* to a man whose
      way is hidden,
    And whom God has hedged in?
24 For my sighing comes before I eat,[a]
    And my groanings pour out like
      water.
25 For the thing I greatly feared has
      come upon me,
    And what I dreaded has happened
      to me.
26 I am not at ease, nor am I quiet;
    I have no rest, for trouble comes."

Eliphaz: Job Has Sinned

4 Then Eliphaz the Temanite answered
and said:

2 "If one attempts a word with you, will
    you become weary?

ROMANTIC QUOTES AND NOTES
Closeting Your Disappointment

We know all too well the mindset that prompted Job to cry out, "May the day perish on which I was born, and the night in which it was said, 'A male child is conceived'" (3:3).

Both Barbara and I have on occasion closeted our discouragement. Instead of working out the dark emotions, we try to tuck it all away, like a box full of Christmas ornaments in an obscure closet. The problem is that unresolved discouragement and disillusionment can easily replace faith and expectancy. We've found that it's much healthier, spiritually speaking, if we open the closet door, bring them out and discuss our disappointment. With God first, but also with one another.

Do you closet your own disappointment with God? Do you ever become dishonest with God and put on an external spiritual veneer that says, "All is well"?

Unprocessed discouragement results in mistrust—and at this critical point the enemy of our souls has us exactly where he wants us. Paralyzed in unbelief from the neck down, our eyes see and our minds know what we ought to believe, but the faith of our hearts lies frozen. And a subtle mistrust of God sets in.

Dealing with "Why did God allow that?" is never easy. But in a relationship where expectations have gone unmet and discouragement has taken up residence, it is essential that the problem be processed.

But who can withhold himself from
   speaking?

3 Surely you have instructed many,
   And you have strengthened weak
     hands.

4 Your words have upheld him who
     was stumbling,
   And you have strengthened the
     feeble knees;

5 But now it comes upon you, and you
     are weary;
   It touches you, and you are troubled.

6 *Is* not your reverence your
     confidence?
   And the integrity of your ways your
     hope?

7 "Remember now, who *ever* perished
     being innocent?
   Or where were the upright *ever* cut
     off?

8 Even as I have seen,
   Those who plow iniquity
   And sow trouble reap the same.

9 By the blast of God they perish,
   And by the breath of His anger they
     are consumed.

10 The roaring of the lion,
   The voice of the fierce lion,
   And the teeth of the young lions are
     broken.

11 The old lion perishes for lack of
     prey,
   And the cubs of the lioness are
     scattered.

12 "Now a word was secretly brought to
     me,
   And my ear received a whisper of it.

13 In disquieting thoughts from the
     visions of the night,
   When deep sleep falls on men,

14 Fear came upon me, and trembling,
   Which made all my bones shake.

15 Then a spirit passed before my face;
   The hair on my body stood up.

16 It stood still,
   But I could not discern its
     appearance.
   A form *was* before my eyes;
   There was silence;
   Then I heard a voice *saying:*

17 'Can a mortal be more righteous than
     God?

Can a man be more pure than his
     Maker?

18 If He puts no trust in His servants,
   If He charges His angels with error,

19 How much more those who dwell in
     houses of clay,
   Whose foundation is in the dust,
   Who are crushed before a moth?

20 They are broken in pieces from
     morning till evening;
   They perish forever, with no one
     regarding.

21 Does not their own excellence go
     away?
   They die, even without wisdom.'

Eliphaz: Job Is Chastened by God

5 "Call out now;
   Is there anyone who will answer you?
   And to which of the holy ones will
     you turn?

2 For wrath kills a foolish man,
   And envy slays a simple one.

3 I have seen the foolish taking root,
   But suddenly I cursed his dwelling
     place.

4 His sons are far from safety,
   They are crushed in the gate,
   And *there is* no deliverer.

5 Because the hungry eat up his
     harvest,
   Taking it even from the thorns,[a]
   And a snare snatches their substance.[b]

6 For affliction does not come from the
     dust,
   Nor does trouble spring from the
     ground;

7 Yet man is born to trouble,
   As the sparks fly upward.

8 "But as for me, I would seek God,
   And to God I would commit my
     cause—

9 Who does great things, and
     unsearchable,
   Marvelous things without number.

10 He gives rain on the earth,
   And sends waters on the fields.

5:5 [a]Septuagint reads *They shall not be taken from
evil men;* Vulgate reads *And the armed man shall
take him by violence.* [b]Septuagint reads *The might
shall draw them off;* Vulgate reads *And the thirsty
shall drink up their riches.*

11 He sets on high those who are lowly,
And those who mourn are lifted to safety.
12 He frustrates the devices of the crafty,
So that their hands cannot carry out their plans.
13 He catches the wise in their own craftiness,
And the counsel of the cunning comes quickly upon them.
14 They meet with darkness in the daytime,
And grope at noontime as in the night.
15 But He saves the needy from the sword,
From the mouth of the mighty,
And from their hand.
16 So the poor have hope,
And injustice shuts her mouth.

17 "Behold, happy *is* the man whom God corrects;
Therefore do not despise the chastening of the Almighty.
18 For He bruises, but He binds up;
He wounds, but His hands make whole.
19 He shall deliver you in six troubles,
Yes, in seven no evil shall touch you.
20 In famine He shall redeem you from death,
And in war from the power of the sword.
21 You shall be hidden from the scourge of the tongue,
And you shall not be afraid of destruction when it comes.
22 You shall laugh at destruction and famine,
And you shall not be afraid of the beasts of the earth.
23 For you shall have a covenant with the stones of the field,
And the beasts of the field shall be at peace with you.
24 You shall know that your tent *is* in peace;
You shall visit your dwelling and find nothing amiss.
25 You shall also know that your descendants *shall be* many,

BIBLICAL INSIGHTS • 5:11
Humility: Seeing Yourself in Relation to God

IN THE MIDST OF unspeakable suffering, the Old Testament character Job listened as his friend Eliphaz stated, "He [God] sets on high those who are lowly, and those who mourn are lifted to safety" (Job 5:11).

In other words, God lifts up those who are humble and comforts those who are suffering. That was good for Job to know, and it's also good for us to know today.

In order to enjoy success in any relationship—with our God, with our spouse, with our family, and with our friends—we need humility, which comes as we see what the Bible teaches about the holiness and righteousness of God and about our need to be forgiven and redeemed.

Philips Brooks once said, "The true way to be humble is not to stoop until you are smaller than yourself, but to stand at your real height against some higher nature that will show you what the real smallness of your greatness is."

My pride wants to say, "I don't need God; I'm perfectly happy without Him." But real happiness comes only when I'm willing to humble myself and with my life do what He wills. The process may be painful, but it also brings deep joy in the midst of challenging days.

And your offspring like the grass of the earth.
26 You shall come to the grave at a full age,
As a sheaf of grain ripens in its season.
27 Behold, this we have searched out;
It *is* true.
Hear it, and know for yourself."

Job: My Complaint Is Just

6 Then Job answered and said:

2 "Oh, that my grief were fully weighed,

And my calamity laid with it on the scales!

3 For then it would be heavier than the sand of the sea—
Therefore my words have been rash.

4 For the arrows of the Almighty *are* within me;
My spirit drinks in their poison;
The terrors of God are arrayed against me.

5 Does the wild donkey bray when it has grass,
Or does the ox low over its fodder?

6 Can flavorless food be eaten without salt?
Or is there *any* taste in the white of an egg?

7 My soul refuses to touch them;
They *are* as loathsome food to me.

8 "Oh, that I might have my request,
That God would grant *me* the thing that I long for!

9 That it would please God to crush me,
That He would loose His hand and cut me off!

10 Then I would still have comfort;
Though in anguish I would exult,
He will not spare;
For I have not concealed the words of the Holy One.

11 "What strength do I have, that I should hope?
And what *is* my end, that I should prolong my life?

12 *Is* my strength the strength of stones?
Or is my flesh bronze?

13 *Is* my help not within me?
And is success driven from me?

14 "To him who is afflicted, kindness *should be shown* by his friend,
Even though he forsakes the fear of the Almighty.

15 My brothers have dealt deceitfully like a brook,
Like the streams of the brooks that pass away,

16 Which are dark because of the ice,
And into which the snow vanishes.

17 When it is warm, they cease to flow;
When it is hot, they vanish from their place.

18 The paths of their way turn aside,
They go nowhere and perish.

19 The caravans of Tema look,
The travelers of Sheba hope for them.

20 They are disappointed because they were confident;
They come there and are confused.

21 For now you are nothing,
You see terror and are afraid.

22 Did I ever say, 'Bring *something* to me'?
Or, 'Offer a bribe for me from your wealth'?

23 Or, 'Deliver me from the enemy's hand'?
Or, 'Redeem me from the hand of oppressors'?

24 "Teach me, and I will hold my tongue;
Cause me to understand wherein I have erred.

25 How forceful are right words!
But what does your arguing prove?

26 Do you intend to rebuke *my* words,
And the speeches of a desperate one, *which are* as wind?

27 Yes, you overwhelm the fatherless,
And you undermine your friend.

28 Now therefore, be pleased to look at me;
For I would never lie to your face.

29 Yield now, let there be no injustice!
Yes, concede, my righteousness still stands!

30 Is there injustice on my tongue?
Cannot my taste discern the unsavory?

Job: My Suffering Is Comfortless

7 "*Is there* not a time of hard service for man on earth?
Are not his days also like the days of a hired man?

2 Like a servant who earnestly desires the shade,
And like a hired man who eagerly looks for his wages,

3 So I have been allotted months of futility,
And wearisome nights have been appointed to me.

4 When I lie down, I say, 'When shall I arise,

And the night be ended?'
For I have had my fill of tossing till
      dawn.
5   My flesh is caked with worms and
         dust,
    My skin is cracked and breaks out
         afresh.
6   "My days are swifter than a weaver's
         shuttle,
    And are spent without hope.
7   Oh, remember that my life *is* a
         breath!
    My eye will never again see good.
8   The eye of him who sees me will see
         me no *more;*
    While your eyes *are* upon me, I shall
         no longer *be.*
9   *As* the cloud disappears and
         vanishes away,
    So he who goes down to the grave
         does not come up.
10 He shall never return to his house,
    Nor shall his place know him
         anymore.

11 "Therefore I will not restrain my
         mouth;
    I will speak in the anguish of my
         spirit;
    I will complain in the bitterness of
         my soul.
12 *Am* I a sea, or a sea serpent,
    That You set a guard over me?
13 When I say, 'My bed will comfort me,
    My couch will ease my complaint,'
14 Then You scare me with dreams
    And terrify me with visions,
15 So that my soul chooses strangling
    And death rather than my body.[a]
16 I loathe *my life;*
    I would not live forever.
    Let me alone,
    For my days *are but* a breath.

17 "What *is* man, that You should exalt
         him,
    That You should set Your heart on
         him,
18 That You should visit him every
         morning,

And test him every moment?
19 How long?
    Will You not look away from me,
    And let me alone till I swallow my
         saliva?
20 Have I sinned?
    What have I done to You, O watcher
         of men?
    Why have You set me as Your target,
    So that I am a burden to myself?[a]
21 Why then do You not pardon my
         transgression,
    And take away my iniquity?
    For now I will lie down in the dust,
    And You will seek me diligently,
    But I *will* no longer *be.*"

Bildad: Job Should Repent

8 Then Bildad the Shuhite answered and
   said:

2   "How long will you speak these *things,*
    And the words of your mouth *be like*
         a strong wind?
3   Does God subvert judgment?
    Or does the Almighty pervert
         justice?
4   If your sons have sinned against Him,
    He has cast them away for their
         transgression.
5   If you would earnestly seek God
    And make your supplication to the
         Almighty,
6   If you *were* pure and upright,
    Surely now He would awake for you,
    And prosper your rightful dwelling
         place.
7   Though your beginning was small,
    Yet your latter end would increase
         abundantly.

8   "For inquire, please, of the former
         age,
    And consider the things discovered
         by their fathers;
9   For we *were born* yesterday, and
         know nothing,
    Because our days on earth *are* a
         shadow.
10 Will they not teach you and tell you,
    And utter words from their heart?

11 "Can the papyrus grow up without a
         marsh?

7:15 [a]Literally *my bones*   7:20 [a]Following Masoretic
Text, Targum, and Vulgate; Septuagint and Jewish
tradition read *to You.*

DEVOTIONS FOR COUPLES • 8:21
Take Time to Laugh

Bildad the Shuhite didn't get many things right in his conversation with Job, but he did make at least one accurate statement. He told Job that God "will yet fill your mouth with laughing, and your lips with rejoicing" (8:21). Laughter is crucial for building a close relationship, and that's as true in marriage as it is anywhere. Consider a few ideas on how to bring a smile to your mate:

•*Become a student of what pleases your mate.* What brings a smile to the face? What tickles the funny bone? Keep a list filled with ideas on what makes your partner happy.

•*What made your spouse laugh in the first place?* You don't always need new material! This "audience of one" will appreciate the old gags, expressions, and words that first sparked laughter in your relationship.

•*Do something absolutely unplanned and positively spontaneous.* Marriage has robbed many a relationship of its fun. We forget what it's like to drop everything and do something for the sheer fun of it.

•*Relive the times you have enjoyed the most pleasure and fun together.* Some of the great laughs came about spontaneously because you were together doing fun stuff.

•*Learn the art of not taking each other or life too seriously.* Life has a way of becoming heavy and weighing you down. If you're not careful, you will lose the sheer joy of being together.

•*Spend focused, regularly scheduled time together.* Barbara and I have a Sunday night date. Often we do the same things we did while dating. Because we are together, away from the usual distractions and pressures, there's a good chance we will have some fun.

•*Read your spouse a funny story.* Call from work to share a humorous situation. Don't be guilty of always dumping heavy emotional loads on your spouse! Liberally sprinkle the dust of comic relief.

•*Do something frivolous with your spouse.* When was the last time you did something really silly with your wife or husband—something that couldn't help but provoke laughter? You took those risks when you dated. Why not try them again?

Laughter is a gift that helps keep life in balance and put some frosting on the joy God has promised us even in the middle of difficult times. Ecclesiastes says there is an appointed time for everything—and that includes a time to laugh (3:4).

Can the reeds flourish without
    water?
12 While it *is* yet green *and* not cut
    down,
It withers before any *other* plant.
13 So *are* the paths of all who forget
    God;
And the hope of the hypocrite shall
    perish,
14 Whose confidence shall be cut off,
And whose trust *is* a spider's web.
15 He leans on his house, but it does not
    stand.
He holds it fast, but it does not
    endure.
16 He grows green in the sun,
And his branches spread out in his
    garden.

17 His roots wrap around the
    rock heap,
And look for a place in the
    stones.
18 If he is destroyed from his
    place,
Then *it* will deny him, *saying,*
    'I have not seen you.'

19 "Behold, this is the joy of His way,
And out of the earth others will
    grow.
20 Behold, God will not cast away the
    blameless,
Nor will He uphold the evildoers.
21 He will yet fill your mouth with
    laughing,
And your lips with rejoicing.

22 Those who hate you will be clothed
with shame,
And the dwelling place of the
wicked will come to nothing."ᵃ

Job: There Is No Mediator

9 Then Job answered and said:

2 "Truly I know *it is* so,
But how can a man be righteous
before God?
3 If one wished to contend with Him,
He could not answer Him one time
out of a thousand.
4 *God is* wise in heart and mighty in
strength.
Who has hardened *himself* against
Him and prospered?
5 He removes the mountains, and they
do not know
When He overturns them in His anger;
6 He shakes the earth out of its place,
And its pillars tremble;
7 He commands the sun, and it does
not rise;
He seals off the stars;
8 He alone spreads out the heavens,
And treads on the waves of the sea;
9 He made the Bear, Orion, and the
Pleiades,
And the chambers of the south;
10 He does great things past finding out,
Yes, wonders without number.
11 If He goes by me, I do not see *Him;*
If He moves past, I do not perceive
Him;
12 If He takes away, who can hinder
Him?
Who can say to Him, 'What are You
doing?'
13 God will not withdraw His anger,
The allies of the proudᵃ lie prostrate
beneath Him.

14 "How then can I answer Him,
And choose my words *to reason* with
Him?
15 For though I were righteous, I could
not answer Him;
I would beg mercy of my Judge.

16 If I called and He answered me,
I would not believe that He was
listening to my voice.
17 For He crushes me with a tempest,
And multiplies my wounds without
cause.
18 He will not allow me to catch my
breath,
But fills me with bitterness.
19 If *it is a matter* of strength, indeed
He is strong;
And if of justice, who will appoint
my day *in court?*
20 Though I were righteous, my own
mouth would condemn me;
Though I *were* blameless, it would
prove me perverse.

21 "I am blameless, yet I do not know
myself;
I despise my life.
22 It *is* all one *thing;*
Therefore I say, 'He destroys the
blameless and the wicked.'
23 If the scourge slays suddenly,
He laughs at the plight of the
innocent.
24 The earth is given into the hand of
the wicked.
He covers the faces of its judges.
If it is not *He,* who else could it be?

25 "Now my days are swifter than a
runner;
They flee away, they see no good.
26 They pass by like swift ships,
Like an eagle swooping on its prey.
27 If I say, 'I will forget my complaint,
I will put off my sad face and wear a
smile,'
28 I am afraid of all my sufferings;
I know that You will not hold me
innocent.
29 *If* I am condemned,
Why then do I labor in vain?
30 If I wash myself with snow water,
And cleanse my hands with soap,
31 Yet You will plunge me into the pit,
And my own clothes will abhor me.

32 "For *He is* not a man, as I *am,*
That I may answer Him,
And that we should go to court
together.

8:22 ᵃLiterally *will not be*
9:13 ᵃHebrew *rahab*

33 Nor is there any mediator between us,
  Who may lay his hand on us both.
34 Let Him take His rod away from me,
  And do not let dread of Him terrify
    me.
35 *Then* I would speak and not fear Him,
  But it is not so with me.

Job: I Would Plead with God

10 "My soul loathes my life;
  I will give free course to my
    complaint,
  I will speak in the bitterness of my
    soul.
2 I will say to God, 'Do not condemn me;
  Show me why You contend with me.
3 *Does it* seem good to You that You
    should oppress,
  That You should despise the work of
    Your hands,
  And smile on the counsel of the
    wicked?
4 Do You have eyes of flesh?
  Or do You see as man sees?
5 *Are* Your days like the days of a
    mortal man?
  Are Your years like the days of a
    mighty man,
6 That You should seek for my iniquity
  And search out my sin,
7 Although You know that I am not
    wicked,
  And *there is* no one who can deliver
    from Your hand?
8 'Your hands have made me and
    fashioned me,
  An intricate unity;
  Yet You would destroy me.
9 Remember, I pray, that You have
    made me like clay.
  And will You turn me into dust
    again?
10 Did You not pour me out like milk,
  And curdle me like cheese,
11 Clothe me with skin and flesh,
  And knit me together with bones and
    sinews?
12 You have granted me life and favor,
  And Your care has preserved my
    spirit.
13 'And these *things* You have hidden in
    Your heart;

I know that this *was* with You:
14 If I sin, then You mark me,
  And will not acquit me of my
    iniquity.
15 If I am wicked, woe to me;
  Even *if* I am righteous, I cannot lift
    up my head.
  I am full of disgrace;
  See my misery!
16 If *my head* is exalted,
  You hunt me like a fierce lion,
  And again You show Yourself
    awesome against me.
17 You renew Your witnesses against
    me,
  And increase Your indignation
    toward me;
  Changes and war are *ever* with me.
18 'Why then have You brought me out
    of the womb?
  Oh, that I had perished and no eye
    had seen me!
19 I would have been as though I had
    not been.
  I would have been carried from the
    womb to the grave.
20 Are not my days few?
  Cease! Leave me alone, that I may
    take a little comfort,
21 Before I go *to the place from which* I
    shall not return,
  To the land of darkness and the
    shadow of death,
22 A land as dark as darkness *itself,*
  As the shadow of death, without any
    order,
  Where even the light *is* like
    darkness.' "

Zophar Urges Job to Repent

11 Then Zophar the Naamathite answered and said:

2 "Should not the multitude of words
    be answered?
  And should a man full of talk be
    vindicated?
3 Should your empty talk make men
    hold their peace?
  And when you mock, should no one
    rebuke you?
4 For you have said,
  'My doctrine *is* pure,

And I am clean in your eyes.'
5 But oh, that God would speak,
And open His lips against you,
6 That He would show you the secrets
of wisdom!
For *they would* double *your* prudence.
Know therefore that God exacts from
you
Less than your iniquity *deserves.*

7 "Can you search out the deep things
of God?
Can you find out the limits of the
Almighty?
8 *They are* higher than heaven— what
can you do?
Deeper than Sheol— what can you
know?
9 Their measure *is* longer than the
earth
And broader than the sea.

10 "If He passes by, imprisons, and
gathers *to judgment,*
Then who can hinder Him?
11 For He knows deceitful men;
He sees wickedness also.
Will He not then consider *it?*
12 For an empty-headed man will be
wise,
When a wild donkey's colt is born a
man.

13 "If you would prepare your heart,
And stretch out your hands toward
Him;
14 If iniquity *were* in your hand, *and
you* put it far away,
And would not let wickedness dwell
in your tents;
15 Then surely you could lift up your
face without spot;
Yes, you could be steadfast, and not
fear;
16 Because you would forget *your*
misery,
And remember *it* as waters *that have*
passed away,
17 And *your* life would be brighter than
noonday.
Though you were dark, you would be
like the morning.

18 And you would be secure, because
there is hope;
Yes, you would dig *around you, and*
take your rest in safety.
19 You would also lie down, and no one
would make *you* afraid;
Yes, many would court your favor.
20 But the eyes of the wicked will fail,
And they shall not escape,
And their hope—loss of life!"

**INTIMATE
MOMENTS**

Never underestimate the power of positive words! Make it a practice to compliment your wife in front of others—
especially your kids. And work equally
hard at avoiding criticizing her in front
of others.

Job Answers His Critics

12 Then Job answered and said:
2 "No doubt you *are* the people,
And wisdom will die with you!
3 But I have understanding as well as
you;
I *am* not inferior to you.
Indeed, who does not *know* such
things as these?

4 "I am one mocked by his friends,
Who called on God, and He answered
him,
The just and blameless *who is*
ridiculed.
5 A lamp[a] is despised in the thought of
one who is at ease;
It is made ready for those whose feet
slip.
6 The tents of robbers prosper,
And those who provoke God are
secure—
In what God provides by His hand.

7 "But now ask the beasts, and they
will teach you;
And the birds of the air, and they
will tell you;

12:5 [a]Or *disaster*

8 Or speak to the earth, and it will teach you;
And the fish of the sea will explain to you.
9 Who among all these does not know
That the hand of the LORD has done this,
10 In whose hand *is* the life of every living thing,
And the breath of all mankind?
11 Does not the ear test words
And the mouth taste its food?
12 Wisdom *is* with aged men,
And with length of days, understanding.

13 "With Him *are* wisdom and strength,
He has counsel and understanding.
14 If He breaks *a thing* down, it cannot be rebuilt;
If He imprisons a man, there can be no release.
15 If He withholds the waters, they dry up;
If He sends them out, they overwhelm the earth.
16 With Him *are* strength and prudence.
The deceived and the deceiver *are* His.
17 He leads counselors away plundered,
And makes fools of the judges.
18 He loosens the bonds of kings,
And binds their waist with a belt.
19 He leads princes[a] away plundered,
And overthrows the mighty.
20 He deprives the trusted ones of speech,
And takes away the discernment of the elders.
21 He pours contempt on princes,
And disarms the mighty.
22 He uncovers deep things out of darkness,
And brings the shadow of death to light.
23 He makes nations great, and destroys them;
He enlarges nations, and guides them.
24 He takes away the understanding[a] of the chiefs of the people of the earth,
And makes them wander in a pathless wilderness.
25 They grope in the dark without light,
And He makes them stagger like a drunken *man.*

13 "Behold, my eye has seen all *this,* My ear has heard and understood it.
2 What you know, I also know;
I *am* not inferior to you.
3 But I would speak to the Almighty,
And I desire to reason with God.
4 But you forgers of lies,
You *are* all worthless physicians.
5 Oh, that you would be silent,
And it would be your wisdom!
6 Now hear my reasoning,
And heed the pleadings of my lips.
7 Will you speak wickedly for God,
And talk deceitfully for Him?
8 Will you show partiality for Him?
Will you contend for God?
9 Will it be well when He searches you out?
Or can you mock Him as one mocks a man?
10 He will surely rebuke you
If you secretly show partiality.
11 Will not His excellence make you afraid,
And the dread of Him fall upon you?
12 Your platitudes *are* proverbs of ashes,
Your defenses are defenses of clay.

13 "Hold your peace with me, and let me speak,
Then let come on me what *may!*
14 Why do I take my flesh in my teeth,
And put my life in my hands?
15 Though He slay me, yet will I trust Him.
Even so, I will defend my own ways before Him.
16 He also *shall* be my salvation,
For a hypocrite could not come before Him.
17 Listen carefully to my speech,
And to my declaration with your ears.
18 See now, I have prepared *my* case,
I know that I shall be vindicated.
19 Who *is* he *who* will contend with me?
If now I hold my tongue, I perish.

12:19 [a]Literally *priests,* but not in a technical sense
12:24 [a]Literally *heart*

Job's Despondent Prayer

20 "Only two *things* do not do to me,
   Then I will not hide myself from You:
21 Withdraw Your hand far from me,
   And let not the dread of You make
      me afraid.
22 Then call, and I will answer;
   Or let me speak, then You respond to
      me.
23 How many *are* my iniquities and sins?
   Make me know my transgression
      and my sin.
24 Why do You hide Your face,
   And regard me as Your enemy?
25 Will You frighten a leaf driven to
      and fro?
   And will You pursue dry stubble?
26 For You write bitter things against
      me,
   And make me inherit the iniquities of
      my youth.
27 You put my feet in the stocks,
   And watch closely all my paths.
   You set a limit[a] for the soles of my
      feet.

28 "*Man*[a] decays like a rotten thing,
   Like a garment that is moth-eaten.

14 "Man *who is* born of woman
   Is of few days and full of trouble.
2 He comes forth like a flower and
      fades away;

He flees like a shadow and does not
      continue.
3 And do You open Your eyes on such
      a one,
   And bring me[a] to judgment with
      Yourself?
4 Who can bring a clean *thing* out of
      an unclean?
   No one!
5 Since his days *are* determined,
   The number of his months *is* with
      You;
   You have appointed his limits, so
      that he cannot pass.
6 Look away from him that he may rest,
   Till like a hired man he finishes his
      day.

7 "For there is hope for a tree,
   If it is cut down, that it will sprout
      again,
   And that its tender shoots will not
      cease.
8 Though its root may grow old in the
      earth,
   And its stump may die in the
      ground,
9 *Yet* at the scent of water it will bud
   And bring forth branches like a
      plant.
10 But man dies and is laid away;
   Indeed he breathes his last
   And where *is* he?
11 *As* water disappears from the
      sea,

13:27 [a]Literally *inscribe a print* **13:28** [a]Literally *He*
14:3 [a]Septuagint, Syriac, and Vulgate read *him.*

And a river becomes parched and
    dries up,
12 So man lies down and does not rise.
    Till the heavens *are* no more,
    They will not awake
    Nor be roused from their sleep.

13 "Oh, that You would hide me in the
    grave,
    That You would conceal me until
    Your wrath is past,
    That You would appoint me a set
    time, and remember me!
14 If a man dies, shall he live *again?*
    All the days of my hard service I
    will wait,
    Till my change comes.
15 You shall call, and I will answer You;
    You shall desire the work of Your
    hands.
16 For now You number my steps,
    But do not watch over my sin.
17 My transgression *is* sealed up in a
    bag,
    And You cover[a] my iniquity.

18 "But *as* a mountain falls *and*
    crumbles away,
    And *as* a rock is moved from its
    place;
19 *As* water wears away stones,
    And as torrents wash away the soil
    of the earth;
    So You destroy the hope of man.
20 You prevail forever against him, and
    he passes on;
    You change his countenance and
    send him away.
21 His sons come to honor, and he does
    not know *it;*
    They are brought low, and he does
    not perceive *it.*
22 But his flesh will be in pain over it,
    And his soul will mourn over it."

Eliphaz Accuses Job of Folly

15 Then Eliphaz the Temanite answered
and said:

2 "Should a wise man answer with
    empty knowledge,
    And fill himself with the east wind?
3 Should he reason with unprofitable
    talk,

Or by speeches with which he can do
    no good?
4 Yes, you cast off fear,
    And restrain prayer before God.
5 For your iniquity teaches your
    mouth,
    And you choose the tongue of the
    crafty.
6 Your own mouth condemns you, and
    not I;
    Yes, your own lips testify against you.

7 "*Are* you the first man *who* was born?
    Or were you made before the hills?
8 Have you heard the counsel of God?
    Do you limit wisdom to yourself?
9 What do you know that we do not
    know?
    What do you understand that *is* not
    in us?
10 Both the gray-haired and the aged
    are among us,
    Much older than your father.
11 *Are* the consolations of God too
    small for you,
    And the word *spoken* gently[a] with
    you?
12 Why does your heart carry you
    away,
    And what do your eyes wink at,
13 That you turn your spirit against
    God,
    And let *such* words go out of your
    mouth?

14 "What *is* man, that he could be pure?
    And *he who is* born of a woman,
    that he could be righteous?
15 If *God* puts no trust in His saints,
    And the heavens are not pure in His
    sight,
16 How much less man, *who is*
    abominable and filthy,
    Who drinks iniquity like water!

17 "I will tell you, hear me;
    What I have seen I will declare,
18 What wise men have told,
    Not hiding *anything received* from
    their fathers,
19 To whom alone the land was given,
    And no alien passed among them:

14:17 [a]Literally *plaster over*
15:11 [a]Septuagint reads *a secret thing.*

²⁰ The wicked man writhes with pain
all *his* days,
And the number of years is hidden
from the oppressor.
²¹ Dreadful sounds *are* in his ears;
In prosperity the destroyer comes
upon him.
²² He does not believe that he will
return from darkness,
For a sword is waiting for him.
²³ He wanders about for bread, *saying,*
'Where *is it?*'
He knows that a day of darkness is
ready at his hand.
²⁴ Trouble and anguish make him
afraid;
They overpower him, like a king
ready for battle.
²⁵ For he stretches out his hand against
God,
And acts defiantly against the
Almighty,
²⁶ Running stubbornly against Him
With his strong, embossed shield.

²⁷ "Though he has covered his face with
his fatness,
And made *his* waist heavy with fat,
²⁸ He dwells in desolate cities,
In houses which no one inhabits,
Which are destined to become ruins.
²⁹ He will not be rich,
Nor will his wealth continue,
Nor will his possessions overspread
the earth.
³⁰ He will not depart from darkness;
The flame will dry out his branches,
And by the breath of His mouth he
will go away.
³¹ Let him not trust in futile *things,*
deceiving himself,
For futility will be his reward.
³² It will be accomplished before his
time,
And his branch will not be green.
³³ He will shake off his unripe grape
like a vine,
And cast off his blossom like an
olive tree.
³⁴ For the company of hypocrites *will
be* barren,

And fire will consume the tents of
bribery.
³⁵ They conceive trouble and bring
forth futility;
Their womb prepares deceit."

Job Reproaches His Pitiless Friends

16 Then Job answered and said:

² "I have heard many such things;
Miserable comforters *are* you all!
³ Shall words of wind have an end?
Or what provokes you that you
answer?
⁴ I also could speak as you *do,*
If your soul were in my soul's place.
I could heap up words against you,
And shake my head at you;
⁵ *But* I would strengthen you with my
mouth,
And the comfort of my lips would
relieve *your grief.*

⁶ "Though I speak, my grief is not
relieved;
And *if* I remain silent, how am I eased?
⁷ But now He has worn me out;
You have made desolate all my
company.
⁸ You have shriveled me up,
And it is a witness *against me;*
My leanness rises up against me
And bears witness to my face.
⁹ He tears *me* in His wrath, and hates
me;
He gnashes at me with His teeth;
My adversary sharpens His gaze on
me.
¹⁰ They gape at me with their mouth,
They strike me reproachfully on the
cheek,
They gather together against me.
¹¹ God has delivered me to the ungodly,
And turned me over to the hands of
the wicked.
¹² I was at ease, but He has shattered
me;
He also has taken *me* by my neck,
and shaken me to pieces;
He has set me up for His target,
¹³ His archers surround me.
He pierces my heart[a] and does not
pity;

16:13 [a]Literally *kidneys*

He pours out my gall on the ground.
14 He breaks me with wound upon
    wound;
    He runs at me like a warrior.[a]

15 "I have sewn sackcloth over my skin,
    And laid my head[a] in the dust.
16 My face is flushed from weeping,
    And on my eyelids *is* the shadow of
    death;
17 Although no violence *is* in my hands,
    And my prayer *is* pure.

18 "O earth, do not cover my blood,
    And let my cry have no *resting* place!
19 Surely even now my witness *is* in
    heaven,
    And my evidence *is* on high.
20 My friends scorn me;
    My eyes pour out *tears* to God.
21 Oh, that one might plead for a man
    with God,
    As a man *pleads* for his neighbor!
22 For when a few years are finished,
    I shall go the way of no return.

Job Prays for Relief

17 "My spirit is broken,
    My days are extinguished,
    The grave *is ready* for me.
2 *Are* not mockers with me?
    And does not my eye dwell on their
    provocation?

3 "Now put down a pledge for me with
    Yourself.
    Who *is* he *who* will shake hands with
    me?
4 For You have hidden their heart from
    understanding;
    Therefore You will not exalt *them*.
5 He who speaks flattery to *his* friends,
    Even the eyes of his children will
    fail.

6 "But He has made me a byword of
    the people,
    And I have become one in whose face
    men spit.
7 My eye has also grown dim because
    of sorrow,
    And all my members *are* like
    shadows.
8 Upright *men* are astonished at this,
    And the innocent stirs himself up
    against the hypocrite.
9 Yet the righteous will hold to his
    way,
    And he who has clean hands will be
    stronger and stronger.

10 "But please, come back again, all of
    you,[a]

ROMANCE FAQ

**Q: How do husbands
and wives differ regarding
the sexual relationship?**

Sex is a beautiful, God-given desire that
in many ways measures the depth of a
marital relationship. It often indicates the
level of commitment and intimacy in
other areas of the marriage.

For sex to be truly satisfying to both
partners, each has to risk being totally
open and vulnerable to the other. Each
person in the marriage should feel needed,
wanted, accepted, and loved sacrificially.
One key to building this type of relationship is understanding the general differences between men and women in how
they view sex.

Most men tend to focus on the physical
aspects of a relationship. They are stimulated, drawn, and captivated by the sight
of their wives. Sight, smell, and the body
stimulate a man. A man needs respect,
admiration, and to be needed physically.
Generally, men put a much higher priority
on sex than women do.

Women have a different orientation
that demands a different approach. Most
women are more oriented to the relationship. The woman desires emotional oneness. Touch, attitudes, actions, words, and
the whole person stimulate the woman.
The woman needs understanding, love, to
be needed emotionally, and time to warm
up to the sexual act.

16:14 [a]Vulgate reads *giant*. 16:15 [a]Literally *horn*
17:10 [a]Following some Hebrew manuscripts,
Septuagint, Syriac, and Vulgate; Masoretic Text and
Targum read *all of them*.

For I shall not find *one* wise *man*
    among you.

11 My days are past,
    My purposes are broken off,
    Even the thoughts of my heart.

12 They change the night into day;
    'The light *is* near,' *they say,* in the face
      of darkness.

13 If I wait *for* the grave *as* my house,
    If I make my bed in the darkness,

14 If I say to corruption, 'You *are* my
      father,'
    And to the worm, 'You *are* my
      mother and my sister,'

15 Where then *is* my hope?
    As for my hope, who can see it?

16 *Will* they go down to the gates of
      Sheol?
    Shall *we have* rest together in the
      dust?"

Bildad: The Wicked Are Punished

18 Then Bildad the Shuhite answered
and said:

2 "How long *till* you put an end to
      words?
    Gain understanding, and afterward
      we will speak.

3 Why are we counted as beasts,
    And regarded as stupid in your
      sight?

4 You who tear yourself in anger,
    Shall the earth be forsaken for you?
    Or shall the rock be removed from its
      place?

5 "The light of the wicked indeed goes
      out,
    And the flame of his fire does not
      shine.

6 The light is dark in his tent,
    And his lamp beside him is put out.

7 The steps of his strength are
      shortened,
    And his own counsel casts him
      down.

8 For he is cast into a net by his own
      feet,
    And he walks into a snare.

9 The net takes *him* by the heel,
    And a snare lays hold of him.

10 A noose *is* hidden for him on the
      ground,
    And a trap for him in the road.

11 Terrors frighten him on every side,
    And drive him to his feet.

12 His strength is starved,
    And destruction *is* ready at his side.

13 It devours patches of his skin;
    The firstborn of death devours his
      limbs.

14 He is uprooted from the shelter of
      his tent,
    And they parade him before the king
      of terrors.

15 They dwell in his tent *who are* none
      of his;
    Brimstone is scattered on his
      dwelling.

16 His roots are dried out below,
    And his branch withers above.

17 The memory of him perishes from
      the earth,
    And he has no name among the
      renowned.[a]

18 He is driven from light into darkness,
    And chased out of the world.

19 He has neither son nor posterity
      among his people,
    Nor any remaining in his dwellings.

20 Those in the west are astonished at
      his day,
    As those in the east are frightened.

21 Surely such *are* the dwellings of the
      wicked,
    And this *is* the place *of him who*
      does not know God."

Job Trusts in His Redeemer

19 Then Job answered and said:

2 "How long will you torment my soul,
    And break me in pieces with words?

3 These ten times you have reproached
      me;
    You are not ashamed *that* you have
      wronged me.[a]

4 And if indeed I have erred,
    My error remains with me.

5 If indeed you exalt *yourselves*
      against me,
    And plead my disgrace against me,

18:17 [a]Literally *before the outside,* meaning distinguished, famous **19:3** [a]A Jewish tradition reads *make yourselves strange to me.*

6 Know then that God has wronged
   me,
   And has surrounded me with His
   net.

7 "If I cry out concerning wrong, I am
   not heard.
   If I cry aloud, *there is* no justice.

8 He has fenced up my way, so that I
   cannot pass;
   And He has set darkness in my paths.

9 He has stripped me of my glory,
   And taken the crown *from* my head.

10 He breaks me down on every side,
    And I am gone;
    My hope He has uprooted like a tree.

11 He has also kindled His wrath
    against me,
    And He counts me as *one of* His
    enemies.

12 His troops come together
    And build up their road against me;
    They encamp all around my tent.

INTIMATE MOMENTS

Wrap up a skeleton key in a box with a note to your wife that says, "You hold the key to my heart."

13 "He has removed my brothers far
    from me,
    And my acquaintances are
    completely estranged from me.

14 My relatives have failed,
    And my close friends have forgotten
    me.

15 Those who dwell in my house, and
    my maidservants,
    Count me as a stranger;
    I am an alien in their sight.

16 I call my servant, but he gives no
    answer;
    I beg him with my mouth.

17 My breath is offensive to my wife,
    And I am repulsive to the children of
    my own body.

18 Even young children despise me;
    I arise, and they speak against me.

19 All my close friends abhor me,
    And those whom I love have turned
    against me.

20 My bone clings to my skin and to my
    flesh,
    And I have escaped by the skin of
    my teeth.

21 "Have pity on me, have pity on me, O
    you my friends,
    For the hand of God has struck me!

22 Why do you persecute me as God
    does,
    And are not satisfied with my flesh?

23 "Oh, that my words were written!
    Oh, that they were inscribed in a
    book!

24 That they were engraved on a rock
    With an iron pen and lead, forever!

25 For I know *that* my Redeemer lives,
    And He shall stand at last on the
    earth;

26 And after my skin is destroyed, this *I
    know,*
    That in my flesh I shall see God,

27 Whom I shall see for myself,
    And my eyes shall behold, and not
    another.
    How my heart yearns within me!

28 If you should say, 'How shall we
    persecute him?'—
    Since the root of the matter is found
    in me,

29 Be afraid of the sword for
    yourselves;
    For wrath *brings* the punishment of
    the sword,
    That you may know *there is* a
    judgment."

Zophar's Sermon on the Wicked Man

20 Then Zophar the Naamathite
    answered and said:

2 "Therefore my anxious thoughts
   make me answer,
   Because of the turmoil within me.

3 I have heard the rebuke that
   reproaches me,
   And the spirit of my understanding
   causes me to answer.

4 "Do you *not* know this of old,
Since man was placed on earth,

5 That the triumphing of the wicked is
short,
And the joy of the hypocrite is *but*
for a moment?

6 Though his haughtiness mounts up
to the heavens,
And his head reaches to the clouds,

7 *Yet* he will perish forever like his
own refuse;
Those who have seen him will say,
'Where is he?'

8 He will fly away like a dream, and
not be found;
Yes, he will be chased away like a
vision of the night.

9 The eye *that* saw him will *see him* no
more,
Nor will his place behold him
anymore.

10 His children will seek the favor of
the poor,
And his hands will restore his wealth.

11 His bones are full of his youthful
vigor,
But it will lie down with him in the
dust.

12 "Though evil is sweet in his mouth,
And he hides it under his tongue,

13 *Though* he spares it and does not
forsake it,
But still keeps it in his mouth,

14 *Yet* his food in his stomach turns sour;
It becomes cobra venom within him.

15 He swallows down riches
And vomits them up again;
God casts them out of his belly.

16 He will suck the poison of cobras;
The viper's tongue will slay him.

17 He will not see the streams,
The rivers flowing with honey and
cream.

18 He will restore that for which he
labored,
And will not swallow *it* down;
From the proceeds of business
He will get no enjoyment.

19 For he has oppressed *and* forsaken
the poor,

He has violently seized a house
which he did not build.

20 "Because he knows no quietness in
his heart,[a]
He will not save anything he desires.

21 Nothing is left for him to eat;
Therefore his well-being will not last.

22 In his self-sufficiency he will be in
distress;
Every hand of misery will come
against him.

23 *When* he is about to fill his stomach,
God will cast on him the fury of His
wrath,
And will rain *it* on him while he is
eating.

24 He will flee from the iron weapon;
A bronze bow will pierce him
through.

25 It is drawn, and comes out of the
body;
Yes, the glittering *point comes* out of
his gall.
Terrors *come* upon him;

26 Total darkness *is* reserved for his
treasures.
An unfanned fire will consume him;
It shall go ill with him who is left in
his tent.

27 The heavens will reveal his iniquity,
And the earth will rise up against
him.

28 The increase of his house will depart,
And his goods will flow away in the
day of His wrath.

29 This *is* the portion from God for a
wicked man,
The heritage appointed to him by
God."

Job's Discourse on the Wicked

21 Then Job answered and said:

2 "Listen carefully to my speech,
And let this be your consolation.

3 Bear with me that I may speak,
And after I have spoken, keep
mocking.

4 "As for me, *is* my complaint against
man?
And if *it were,* why should I not be
impatient?

20:20 [a]Literally *belly*

5 Look at me and be astonished;
   Put *your* hand over *your* mouth.
6 Even when I remember I am terrified,
   And trembling takes hold of my
   flesh.
7 Why do the wicked live *and* become
   old,
   Yes, become mighty in power?
8 Their descendants are established
   with them in their sight,
   And their offspring before their eyes.
9 Their houses *are* safe from fear,
   Neither *is* the rod of God upon them.
10 Their bull breeds without failure;
   Their cow calves without
   miscarriage.
11 They send forth their little ones like
   a flock,
   And their children dance.
12 They sing to the tambourine and
   harp,
   And rejoice to the sound of the flute.
13 They spend their days in wealth,
   And in a moment go down to the
   grave.ᵃ
14 Yet they say to God, 'Depart from us,
   For we do not desire the knowledge
   of Your ways.
15 Who *is* the Almighty, that we should
   serve Him?
   And what profit do we have if we
   pray to Him?'
16 Indeed their prosperity *is* not in their
   hand;
   The counsel of the wicked is far
   from me.

17 "How often is the lamp of the wicked
   put out?
   How often does their destruction
   come upon them,
   The sorrows *God* distributes in His
   anger?
18 They are like straw before the wind,
   And like chaff that a storm carries
   away.
19 *They say,* 'God lays up one'sᵃ iniquity
   for his children';
   Let Him recompense him, that he
   may know *it.*
20 Let his eyes see his destruction,
   And let him drink of the wrath of
   the Almighty.

21 For what does he care about his
   household after him,
   When the number of his months is
   cut in half?

22 "Can *anyone* teach God knowledge,
   Since He judges those on high?
23 One dies in his full strength,
   Being wholly at ease and secure;
24 His pailsᵃ are full of milk,
   And the marrow of his bones is moist.
25 Another man dies in the bitterness of
   his soul,
   Never having eaten with pleasure.
26 They lie down alike in the dust,
   And worms cover them.

27 "Look, I know your thoughts,
   And the schemes *with which* you
   would wrong me.
28 For you say,
   'Where *is* the house of the prince?
   And where *is* the tent,ᵃ
   The dwelling place of the wicked?'
29 Have you not asked those who travel
   the road?
   And do you not know their signs?
30 For the wicked are reserved for the
   day of doom;
   They shall be brought out on the day
   of wrath.
31 Who condemns his way to his face?
   And who repays him *for what* he has
   done?
32 Yet he shall be brought to the grave,
   And a vigil kept over the tomb.
33 The clods of the valley shall be
   sweet to him;
   Everyone shall follow him,
   As countless *have gone* before him.
34 How then can you comfort me with
   empty words,
   Since falsehood remains in your
   answers?"

Eliphaz Accuses Job of Wickedness

22 Then Eliphaz the Temanite answered
   and said:

2 "Can a man be profitable to God,

21:13 ᵃOr *Sheol* 21:19 ᵃLiterally *his*
21:24 ᵃSeptuagint and Vulgate read *bowels;* Syriac
reads *sides;* Targum reads *breasts.* 21:28 ᵃVulgate
omits *the tent.*

Though he who is wise may be
  profitable to himself?
3 *Is it* any pleasure to the Almighty
  that you are righteous?
  Or *is it* gain *to Him* that you make
    your ways blameless?

4 "Is it because of your fear of Him
    that He corrects you,
  And enters into judgment with you?
5 *Is* not your wickedness great,
  And your iniquity without end?
6 For you have taken pledges from
    your brother for no reason,
  And stripped the naked of their
    clothing.
7 You have not given the weary water
    to drink,
  And you have withheld bread from
    the hungry.
8 But the mighty man possessed the
    land,
  And the honorable man dwelt in it.
9 You have sent widows away empty,
  And the strength of the fatherless
    was crushed.
10 Therefore snares *are* all around you,
  And sudden fear troubles you,
11 Or darkness *so that* you cannot see;
  And an abundance of water covers
    you.

12 "Is not God in the height of heaven?
  And see the highest stars, how lofty
    they are!
13 And you say, 'What does God know?
  Can He judge through the deep
    darkness?
14 Thick clouds cover Him, so that He
    cannot see,
  And He walks above the circle of
    heaven.'
15 Will you keep to the old way
  Which wicked men have trod,
16 Who were cut down before their time,
  Whose foundations were swept away
    by a flood?
17 They said to God, 'Depart from us!
  What can the Almighty do to them?'[a]

18 Yet He filled their houses with good
    things;
  But the counsel of the wicked is far
    from me.

19 "The righteous see *it* and are glad,
  And the innocent laugh at them:
20 'Surely our adversaries[a] are
    cut down,
  And the fire consumes their remnant.'

21 "Now acquaint yourself with Him,
    and be at peace;
  Thereby good will come to you.
22 Receive, please, instruction from His
    mouth,
  And lay up His words in your heart.
23 If you return to the Almighty, you
    will be built up;
  You will remove iniquity far from
    your tents.
24 Then you will lay your gold in the
    dust,
  And the *gold* of Ophir among the
    stones of the brooks.
25 Yes, the Almighty will be your gold[a]
  And your precious silver;
26 For then you will have your delight
    in the Almighty,
  And lift up your face to God.
27 You will make your prayer to Him,
    He will hear you,
  And you will pay your vows.
28 You will also declare a thing,
  And it will be established for you;
  So light will shine on your ways.
29 When they cast *you* down, and you
    say, 'Exaltation *will come!*'
  Then He will save the humble
    person.
30 He will *even* deliver one who is not
    innocent;
  Yes, he will be delivered by the
    purity of your hands."

Job Proclaims God's Righteous Judgments

23 Then Job answered and said:

2 "Even today my complaint is bitter;
  My[a] hand is listless because of my
    groaning.
3 Oh, that I knew where I might find
    Him,

22:17 [a]Septuagint and Syriac read *us.*
22:20 [a]Septuagint reads *substance.* **22:25** [a]The
ancient versions suggest *defense;* Hebrew reads *gold*
as in verse 24. **23:2** [a]Following Masoretic Text,
Targum, and Vulgate; Septuagint and Syriac read *His.*

BIBLICAL INSIGHTS • 23:2
The Antidote for Complaining

I WONDER WHAT WE WOULD find if we could do a little open-heart surgery on a complainer? I think it would show that grumbling can be a form of heart disease—rebellion against authority. When Job said, "Even today my complaint is bitter," immediately he added, "Oh, that I knew where I might find Him [God], that I might come to His seat"—in order to complain about the injustices done to him (23:2, 3).

I have a confession: I struggle with complaining. Over the years, God has taught me a few things about this problem.

Usually, I've found, complaining is a loss of perspective, a failure to remember who is in control. Such a person wonders, "Does God really know what's best for me?"

Generally a grumbler feels dissatisfied with his lot in life, with the circumstances God has allowed to come his way. Israel's grumbling in the desert was symptomatic of a far more fatal disease: unbelief, a lack of faith that God knew what He was doing.

So what's God's prescription for this heart problem? "Do all things without complaining and disputing," Paul writes, "that you may become blameless and harmless, children of God without fault in the midst of a crooked and perverse generation, among whom you shine as lights in the world" (Phil. 2:14, 15). Are you guilty of grumbling, or does *your* light shine in your marriage and family?

It may be that you will want to memorize this verse, then lead your family in the same assignment. I did. And it helped!

That I might come to His seat!
4 I would present *my* case before Him,
And fill my mouth with arguments.
5 I would know the words *which* He would answer me,
And understand what He would say to me.

6 Would He contend with me in His great power?
No! But He would take *note* of me.
7 There the upright could reason with Him,
And I would be delivered forever from my Judge.

8 "Look, I go forward, but He is not *there,*
And backward, but I cannot perceive Him;
9 When He works on the left hand, I cannot behold *Him;*
When He turns to the right hand, I cannot see *Him.*
10 But He knows the way that I take;
When He has tested me, I shall come forth as gold.
11 My foot has held fast to His steps;
I have kept His way and not turned aside.
12 I have not departed from the commandment of His lips;
I have treasured the words of His mouth
More than my necessary *food.*

13 "But He *is* unique, and who can make Him change?
And *whatever* His soul desires, *that* He does.
14 For He performs *what is* appointed for me,
And many such *things are* with Him.
15 Therefore I am terrified at His presence;
When I consider *this,* I am afraid of Him.
16 For God made my heart weak,
And the Almighty terrifies me;
17 Because I was not cut off from the presence of darkness,
And He did *not* hide deep darkness from my face.

Job Complains of Violence on the Earth

24 "*Since* times are not hidden from the Almighty,
Why do those who know Him see not His days?

2 "*Some* remove landmarks;
They seize flocks violently and feed *on them;*

3 They drive away the donkey of the
fatherless;
They take the widow's ox as a pledge.
4 They push the needy off the road;
All the poor of the land are forced to
hide.
5 Indeed, *like* wild donkeys in the
desert,
They go out to their work, searching
for food.
The wilderness *yields* food for them
and for *their* children.
6 They gather their fodder in the field
And glean in the vineyard of the
wicked.
7 They spend the night naked, without
clothing,
And have no covering in the cold.
8 They are wet with the showers of
the mountains,
And huddle around the rock for want
of shelter.

9 "*Some* snatch the fatherless from the
breast,
And take a pledge from the poor.
10 They cause *the poor* to go naked,
without clothing;
And they take away the sheaves
from the hungry.
11 They press out oil within their walls,
And tread winepresses, yet suffer
thirst.
12 The dying groan in the city,
And the souls of the wounded cry out;
Yet God does not charge *them* with
wrong.

13 "There are those who rebel against
the light;
They do not know its ways
Nor abide in its paths.
14 The murderer rises with the light;
He kills the poor and needy;
And in the night he is like a thief.
15 The eye of the adulterer waits for
the twilight,
Saying, 'No eye will see me';
And he disguises *his* face.
16 In the dark they break into houses
Which they marked for themselves
in the daytime;

They do not know the light.
17 For the morning is the same to them
as the shadow of death;
If *someone* recognizes *them*,
They are in the terrors of the
shadow of death.

18 "They *should be* swift on the face of
the waters,
Their portion *should be* cursed in the
earth,
So that no *one would* turn into the
way of their vineyards.
19 As drought and heat consume the
snow waters,
So the grave[a] *consumes those who
have sinned.*
20 The womb *should* forget him,
The worm *should* feed sweetly on
him;
He *should* be remembered no more,
And wickedness *should* be broken
like a tree.
21 For he preys on the barren *who* do
not bear,
And does no good for the widow.

22 "But *God* draws the mighty away
with His power;
He rises up, but no *man* is sure of
life.
23 He gives them security, and they rely
on it;
Yet His eyes *are* on their ways.
24 They are exalted for a little while,
Then they are gone.
They are brought low;
They are taken out of the way like
all *others;*
They dry out like the heads of grain.
25 "Now if *it is* not *so,* who will prove me
a liar,
And make my speech worth
nothing?"

Bildad: How Can Man Be Righteous?

25 Then Bildad the Shuhite answered
and said:

2 "Dominion and fear *belong* to Him;
He makes peace in His high places.
3 Is there any number to His armies?
Upon whom does His light not rise?

24:19 [a]Or *Sheol*

4   How then can man be righteous
        before God?
     Or how can he be pure *who is* born
        of a woman?
5   If even the moon does not shine,
     And the stars are not pure in His
        sight,
6   How much less man, *who is* a
        maggot,
     And a son of man, *who is* a worm?"

Job: Man's Frailty and God's Majesty

26 But Job answered and said:

2   "How have you helped *him who is*
        without power?
     How have you saved the arm *that
        has* no strength?
3   How have you counseled *one who
        has* no wisdom?
     And *how* have you declared sound
        advice to many?
4   To whom have you uttered words?
     And whose spirit came from you?

5   "The dead tremble,
     Those under the waters and those
        inhabiting them.
6   Sheol *is* naked before Him,
     And Destruction has no covering.
7   He stretches out the north over
        empty space;

He hangs the earth on nothing.
8   He binds up the water in His thick
        clouds,
     Yet the clouds are not broken under it.
9   He covers the face of *His* throne,
     And spreads His cloud over it.
10   He drew a circular horizon on the
        face of the waters,
     At the boundary of light and
        darkness.
11   The pillars of heaven tremble,
     And are astonished at His rebuke.
12   He stirs up the sea with His
        power,
     And by His understanding He breaks
        up the storm.
13   By His Spirit He adorned the
        heavens;
     His hand pierced the fleeing serpent.
14   Indeed these *are* the mere edges of
        His ways,
     And how small a whisper we hear of
        Him!
     But the thunder of His power who
        can understand?"

Job Maintains His Integrity

27 Moreover Job continued his discourse, and said:

2   "*As* God lives, *who* has taken away
        my justice,

PARENTING MATTERS

Q: *How do we train our children to respect and honor the dignity of others?*

Training your child to respect the dignity of others means teaching them to be humble. That's what the apostle Paul meant when he wrote, "Be of the same mind toward one another. Do not set your mind on high things, but associate with the humble. Do not be wise in your own opinion" (Rom. 12:16).

Respect has become an afterthought in our culture. People no longer respect God or authority, and they don't show one another proper respect. If we will not fear God whom we cannot see, then why would we have any respect for a person made in His image whom we can see? When we lose our fear of God, we lose our respect for others.

If you want your children to be "salt and light" in this area, it's a good idea to teach them what the Scriptures say about the value God places on each human being as His unique creation. Teach them that all humans are of immeasurable worth to God—no matter what station they have in life and no matter where they are spiritually.

And the Almighty, *who* has made my
soul bitter,

3 As long as my breath *is* in me,
And the breath of God in my
nostrils,

4 My lips will not speak wickedness,
Nor my tongue utter deceit.

5 Far be it from me
That I should say you are right;
Till I die I will not put away my
integrity from me.

6 My righteousness I hold fast, and
will not let it go;
My heart shall not reproach *me* as
long as I live.

7 "May my enemy be like the wicked,
And he who rises up against me like
the unrighteous.

8 For what is the hope of the
hypocrite,
Though he may gain *much,*
If God takes away his life?

9 Will God hear his cry
When trouble comes upon him?

10 Will he delight himself in the
Almighty?
Will he always call on God?

11 "I will teach you about the hand of
God;
What *is* with the Almighty I will not
conceal.

12 Surely all of you have seen *it;*
Why then do you behave with
complete nonsense?

13 "This is the portion of a wicked man
with God,
And the heritage of oppressors,
received from the Almighty:

14 If his children are multiplied, *it is* for
the sword;
And his offspring shall not be
satisfied with bread.

15 Those who survive him shall be
buried in death,

16 And their[a] widows shall not weep,
Though he heaps up silver like dust,
And piles up clothing like clay—

17 He may pile *it* up, but the just will
wear *it,*
And the innocent will divide the
silver.

18 He builds his house like a moth,[a]
Like a booth *which* a watchman
makes.

19 The rich man will lie down,
But not be gathered *up;*[a]
He opens his eyes,
And he *is* no more.

20 Terrors overtake him like a flood;
A tempest steals him away in the
night.

21 The east wind carries him away, and
he is gone;
It sweeps him out of his place.

22 It hurls against him and does not
spare;
He flees desperately from its power.

23 *Men* shall clap their hands at him,
And shall hiss him out of his place.

Job's Discourse on Wisdom

28 "Surely there is a mine for silver,
And a place *where* gold is refined.

2 Iron is taken from the earth,
And copper *is* smelted *from* ore.

3 *Man* puts an end to darkness,
And searches every recess
For ore in the darkness and the
shadow of death.

4 He breaks open a shaft away from
people;
In places forgotten by feet
They hang far away from men;
They swing to and fro.

5 *As for* the earth, from it comes bread,
But underneath it is turned up as by
fire;

6 Its stones *are* the source of sapphires,
And it contains gold dust.

7 *That* path no bird knows,
Nor has the falcon's eye seen it.

8 The proud lions[a] have not trodden it,
Nor has the fierce lion passed over it.

9 He puts his hand on the flint;
He overturns the mountains at the
roots.

10 He cuts out channels in the rocks,

27:15 [a]Literally *his*   **27:18** [a]Following Masoretic
Text and Vulgate; Septuagint and Syriac read *spider*
(compare 8:14); Targum reads *decay.*
27:19 [a]Following Masoretic Text and Targum;
Septuagint and Syriac read *But shall not add* (that is,
do it again); Vulgate reads *But take away nothing.*
28:8 [a]Literally *sons of pride,* figurative of the
great lions

And his eye sees every precious thing.

11 He dams up the streams from trickling;
What is hidden he brings forth to light.

12 "But where can wisdom be found?
And where *is* the place of understanding?

13 Man does not know its value,
Nor is it found in the land of the living.

14 The deep says, *'It is* not in me';
And the sea says, *'It is* not with me.'

15 It cannot be purchased for gold,
Nor can silver be weighed *for* its price.

16 It cannot be valued in the gold of Ophir,
In precious onyx or sapphire.

17 Neither gold nor crystal can equal it,
Nor can it be exchanged for jewelry of fine gold.

18 No mention shall be made of coral or quartz,
For the price of wisdom *is* above rubies.

19 The topaz of Ethiopia cannot equal it,
Nor can it be valued in pure gold.

20 "From where then does wisdom come?
And where *is* the place of understanding?

21 It is hidden from the eyes of all living,
And concealed from the birds of the air.

22 Destruction and Death say,
'We have heard a report about it with our ears.'

23 God understands its way,
And He knows its place.

24 For He looks to the ends of the earth,
And sees under the whole heavens,

25 To establish a weight for the wind,
And apportion the waters by measure.

26 When He made a law for the rain,
And a path for the thunderbolt,

27 Then He saw *wisdom*ᵃ and declared it;
He prepared it, indeed, He searched it out.

28 And to man He said,
'Behold, the fear of the Lord, that *is* wisdom,
And to depart from evil *is* understanding.' "

Job's Summary Defense

29 Job further continued his discourse, and said:

2 "Oh, that I were as *in* months past,
As *in* the days *when* God watched over me;

3 When His lamp shone upon my head,
And when by His light I walked *through* darkness;

4 Just as I was in the days of my prime,
When the friendly counsel of God *was* over my tent;

5 When the Almighty *was* yet with me,
When my children *were* around me;

6 When my steps were bathed with cream,ᵃ
And the rock poured out rivers of oil for me!

7 "When I went out to the gate by the city,
When I took my seat in the open square,

8 The young men saw me and hid,
And the aged arose *and* stood;

9 The princes refrained from talking,
And put *their* hand on their mouth;

10 The voice of nobles was hushed,
And their tongue stuck to the roof of their mouth.

11 When the ear heard, then it blessed me,
And when the eye saw, then it approved me;

12 Because I delivered the poor who cried out,
The fatherless and *the one who* had no helper.

13 The blessing of a perishing *man* came upon me,

28:27 ᵃLiterally *it* 29:6 ᵃMasoretic Text reads *wrath;* ancient versions and some Hebrew manuscripts read *cream* (compare 20:17).

Facing Trials

IT IS EASY TO IDENTIFY with Job in chapter 29 as he speaks of his former life, "when the friendly counsel of God was over my tent" (v. 4). But one lesson from Job's life should be that hardships and suffering are inevitable in life. If you haven't already faced significant trials as a couple, you will eventually.

Here's what we've learned during these times:

First, we need to use times of suffering *as an opportunity to draw close to God*. Nothing happens in our lives apart from what He allows or ordains. As Psalm 24:3 tells us, "Yea, though I walk through the valley of the shadow of death, I will fear no evil; for You *are* with me; Your rod and Your staff, they comfort me."

Second, *we need to be there for each other*. A husband and wife must be involved with each other during a crisis. When our teenage son, Samuel, was diagnosed with muscular dystrophy, I remember it took a deliberate act of my will to move toward Barbara and the pain she was experiencing because I wasn't at the same place she was. I wasn't as ready to talk about it as she was and she needed to talk about it. So I took the initiative to talk with her.

Third, *we need to make our marriage a priority*. We know that if our marriage remains on solid ground, our children will feel stronger and more secure as well.

Fourth, we've learned that *we need to allow the body of Christ to minister to us*. The biggest way our friends helped during the situation with Samuel was in writing letters. These letters really broadened Samuel's perspective of the body of Christ. I don't think he had any idea that people cared like they do.

Finally, we have learned to *hold to the truth of God's Word no matter what our emotions told us*. We can't deny our emotions, but we can't allow them to control our responses, either. You've got to hang on to the truth of Scripture and let that be the foundation of your home.

Even when we don't feel God loves us, we know from Scripture that *He* does. When we don't feel any good can come out of a trial or calamity, we *know* from Romans 8:28 that all things really do "work together for good to those who love God, to those who are called according to His purpose."

Through the experience with Samuel, we saw that our son was learning to trust God even when he didn't understand His plan. I remember one evening a few months after the diagnosis, when he and I were driving home from the grocery. We had been talking about his limitations, and I shared how God has always used people regardless of their situation. My feeble efforts to comfort him seemed shallow. A moment of silence filled the car.

Then Samuel turned from looking out the window and said resolutely "Well, Dad, I guess you don't need legs to serve God."

Tears filled my eyes. My son was teaching me a lesson on trust. And as I drove home I prayed silently, "Lord, increase my faith and use our son for Your purposes."

And I caused the widow's heart to
  sing for joy.
14 I put on righteousness, and it clothed
    me;
  My justice *was* like a robe and a
    turban.

15 I *was* eyes to the blind,
  And I *was* feet to the lame.
16 I *was* a father to the poor,
  And I searched out the case *that* I
    did not know.
17 I broke the fangs of the wicked,

And plucked the victim from his teeth.

18 "Then I said, 'I shall die in my nest,
And multiply *my* days as the sand.
19 My root *is* spread out to the waters,
And the dew lies all night on my
branch.
20 My glory *is* fresh within me,
And my bow is renewed in my hand.'

21 "*Men* listened to me and waited,
And kept silence for my counsel.
22 After my words they did not speak
again,
And my speech settled on them *as
dew.*
23 They waited for me *as* for the rain,
And they opened their mouth wide
as for the spring rain.
24 *If* I mocked at them, they did not
believe *it,*
And the light of my countenance
they did not cast down.
25 I chose the way for them, and sat as
chief;
So I dwelt as a king in the army,
As one *who* comforts mourners.

30 "But now they mock at me, *men*
younger than I,
Whose fathers I disdained to put
with the dogs of my flock.
2 Indeed, what *profit* is the strength of
their hands to me?
Their vigor has perished.
3 *They are* gaunt from want and
famine,
Fleeing late to the wilderness,
desolate and waste,
4 Who pluck mallow by the bushes,
And broom tree roots *for* their food.
5 They were driven out from among
men,
They shouted at them *as at* a thief.
6 *They had* to live in the clefts of the
valleys,
In caves of the earth and the rocks.
7 Among the bushes they brayed,
Under the nettles they nestled.
8 *They were* sons of fools,
Yes, sons of vile men;
They were scourged from the land.

9 "And now I am their taunting song;
Yes, I am their byword.

10 They abhor me, they keep far from
me;
They do not hesitate to spit in my face.
11 Because He has loosed my[a]
bowstring and afflicted me,
They have cast off restraint before
me.
12 At *my* right *hand* the rabble arises;
They push away my feet,
And they raise against me their
ways of destruction.
13 They break up my path,
They promote my calamity;
They have no helper.
14 They come as broad breakers;
Under the ruinous storm they roll
along.
15 Terrors are turned upon me;
They pursue my honor as the wind,
And my prosperity has passed like a
cloud.

16 "And now my soul is poured out
because of my *plight;*
The days of affliction take hold of me.
17 My bones are pierced in me at night,
And my gnawing pains take no rest.
18 By great force my garment is
disfigured;
It binds me about as the collar of my
coat.
19 He has cast me into the mire,
And I have become like dust and
ashes.

20 "I cry out to You, but You do not
answer me;
I stand up, and You regard me.
21 *But* You have become cruel to me;
With the strength of Your hand You
oppose me.
22 You lift me up to the wind and cause
me to ride *on it;*
You spoil my success.
23 For I know *that* You will bring me *to*
death,
And *to* the house appointed for all
living.

24 "Surely He would not stretch out *His*
hand against a heap of ruins,
If they cry out when He destroys *it.*

30:11 [a]Following Masoretic Text, Syriac, and
Targum; Septuagint and Vulgate read *His.*

25 Have I not wept for him who was in
     trouble?
   Has *not* my soul grieved for the
     poor?
26 But when I looked for good, evil
     came *to me;*
   And when I waited for light, then
     came darkness.
27 My heart is in turmoil and cannot
     rest;
   Days of affliction confront me.
28 I go about mourning, but not in the
     sun;
   I stand up in the assembly *and* cry
     out for help.
29 I am a brother of jackals,
   And a companion of ostriches.
30 My skin grows black and falls from
     me;
   My bones burn with fever.
31 My harp is *turned* to mourning,
   And my flute to the voice of those
     who weep.

31 "I have made a covenant with my
       eyes;
   Why then should I look upon a
     young woman?
2 For what *is* the allotment of God
     from above,
   And the inheritance of the Almighty
     from on high?
3 *Is* it not destruction for the wicked,
   And disaster for the workers of
     iniquity?
4 Does He not see my ways,
   And count all my steps?
5 "If I have walked with falsehood,
   Or if my foot has hastened to deceit,
6 Let me be weighed on honest scales,
   That God may know my integrity.
7 If my step has turned from the way,
   Or my heart walked after my eyes,
   Or if any spot adheres to my hands,
8 *Then* let me sow, and another eat;
   Yes, let my harvest be rooted out.
9 "If my heart has been enticed by a
     woman,
   Or *if* I have lurked at my neighbor's
     door,

10 *Then* let my wife grind for another,
   And let others bow down over her.
11 For that *would be* wickedness;
   Yes, it *would be* iniquity *deserving of*
     judgment.
12 For that *would be* a fire *that*
     consumes to destruction,
   And would root out all my increase.
13 "If I have despised the cause of my
     male or female servant
   When they complained against me,
14 What then shall I do when God rises
     up?
   When He punishes, how shall I
     answer Him?
15 Did not He who made me in the
     womb make them?
   Did not the same One fashion us in
     the womb?

INTIMATE MOMENTS

Wash and vacuum his car. And the final
touch—top off his gas tank, too!

16 "If I have kept the poor from *their*
     desire,
   Or caused the eyes of the widow to
     fail,
17 Or eaten my morsel by myself,
   So that the fatherless could not eat of
     it
18 (But from my youth I reared him as a
     father,
   And from my mother's womb I
     guided *the widow*[a]);
19 If I have seen anyone perish for lack
     of clothing,
   Or any poor *man* without covering;
20 If his heart[a] has not blessed me,
   And *if* he was *not* warmed with the
     fleece of my sheep;
21 If I have raised my hand against the
     fatherless,
   When I saw I had help in the gate;
22 *Then* let my arm fall from my
     shoulder,
   Let my arm be torn from the socket.

31:18 [a]Literally *her* (compare verse 16)
31:20 [a]Literally *loins*

23 For destruction *from* God *is* a terror
    to me,
    And because of His magnificence I
    cannot endure.

24 "If I have made gold my hope,
    Or said to fine gold, '*You are* my
    confidence';
25 If I have rejoiced because my wealth
    was great,
    And because my hand had gained
    much;
26 If I have observed the sun[a] when it
    shines,
    Or the moon moving *in* brightness,
27 So that my heart has been secretly
    enticed,
    And my mouth has kissed my hand;
28 This also *would be* an iniquity
    deserving of judgment,
    For I would have denied God *who is*
    above.

29 "If I have rejoiced at the destruction
    of him who hated me,
    Or lifted myself up when evil found
    him
30 (Indeed I have not allowed my mouth
    to sin
    By asking for a curse on his soul);
31 If the men of my tent have not said,
    'Who is there that has not been
    satisfied with his meat?'
32 (*But* no sojourner had to lodge in the
    street,
    For I have opened my doors to the
    traveler[a]);
33 If I have covered my transgressions
    as Adam,
    By hiding my iniquity in my bosom,
34 Because I feared the great multitude,
    And dreaded the contempt of
    families,
    So that I kept silence
    And did not go out of the door—
35 Oh, that I had one to hear me!
    Here is my mark.
    Oh, that the Almighty would answer
    me,
    That my Prosecutor had written a
    book!
36 Surely I would carry it on my
    shoulder,
    And bind it on me *like* a crown;

37 I would declare to Him the number of
    my steps;
    Like a prince I would approach Him.

38 "If my land cries out against me,
    And its furrows weep together;
39 If I have eaten its fruit[a] without
    money,
    Or caused its owners to lose their
    lives;
40 *Then* let thistles grow instead of
    wheat,
    And weeds instead of barley."

The words of Job are ended.

Elihu Contradicts Job's Friends

32 So these three men ceased answering Job, because he *was* righteous in his own eyes. ²Then the wrath of Elihu, the son of Barachel the Buzite, of the family of Ram, was aroused against Job; his wrath was aroused because he justified himself rather than God. ³Also against his three friends his wrath was aroused, because they had found no answer, and *yet* had condemned Job.

⁴Now because they *were* years older than he, Elihu had waited to speak to Job.[a] ⁵When Elihu saw that *there was* no answer in the mouth of these three men, his wrath was aroused.

⁶So Elihu, the son of Barachel the Buzite, answered and said:

"I *am* young in years, and you *are*
    very old;
    Therefore I was afraid,
    And dared not declare my opinion to
    you.
7 I said, 'Age[a] should speak,
    And multitude of years should teach
    wisdom.'
8 But *there is* a spirit in man,
    And the breath of the Almighty
    gives him understanding.
9 Great men[a] are not *always* wise,
    Nor do the aged *always* understand
    justice.

31:26 [a]Literally *light* **31:32** [a]Following Septuagint, Syriac, Targum, and Vulgate; Masoretic Text reads *road.* **31:39** [a]Literally *its strength* **32:4** [a]Vulgate reads *till Job had spoken.* **32:7** [a]Literally *Days,* that is, years **32:9** [a]Or *Men of many years*

10 "Therefore I say, 'Listen to me,
    I also will declare my opinion.'
11 Indeed I waited for your words,
    I listened to your reasonings, while
        you searched out what to say.
12 I paid close attention to you;
    And surely not one of you convinced
        Job,
    Or answered his words—
13 Lest you say,
    'We have found wisdom';
    God will vanquish him, not man.
14 Now he has not directed *his* words
        against me;
    So I will not answer him with your
        words.

15 "They are dismayed and answer no
        more;
    Words escape them.
16 And I have waited, because they did
        not speak,
    Because they stood still *and*
        answered no more.
17 I also will answer my part,
    I too will declare my opinion.
18 For I am full of words;
    The spirit within me compels me.
19 Indeed my belly *is* like wine *that* has
        no vent;
    It is ready to burst like new wineskins.
20 I will speak, that I may find relief;
    I must open my lips and answer.
21 Let me not, I pray, show partiality to
        anyone;
    Nor let me flatter any man.
22 For I do not know how to flatter,
    Else my Maker would soon take me
        away.

Elihu Contradicts Job

33 "But please, Job, hear my speech,
    And listen to all my words.
2 Now, I open my mouth;
    My tongue speaks in my mouth.
3 My words *come* from my upright
        heart;
    My lips utter pure knowledge.
4 The Spirit of God has made me,
    And the breath of the Almighty
        gives me life.

5 If you can answer me,
    Set *your words* in order before me;
    Take your stand.
6 Truly I *am* as your spokesman[a]
        before God;
    I also have been formed out of clay.
7 Surely no fear of me will terrify you,
    Nor will my hand be heavy on you.

8 "Surely you have spoken in my
        hearing,
    And I have heard the sound of *your*
        words, *saying,*

33:6 [a]Literally *as your mouth*

ROMANCE FAQ

Q: *How are forgiveness and romance related?*

There's nothing worse than lying in the darkness, back-to-back, and fuming about some petty argument. Satan is out to destroy marriages, and one of his best tools is *unresolved conflict.* No wonder Paul urged believers: "Be kind to one another, tender-hearted, forgiving one another, even as God in Christ forgave you" (Eph. 4:32).

How did Christ forgive us? By laying down His life. He didn't wait until we apologized. He took the initiative to forgive. I should do the same, even when I feel my husband is clearly in the wrong. Sometimes it's much easier for me to see only *what he did wrong* than it is for me to admit my part in the conflict.

When conflict arises, I must resist my tendency to *run from* a confrontation and, instead, *run toward* forgiveness. I must choose to listen, to imagine how my husband feels, and to pray for wisdom, understanding, and God's help to work it all out.

Seek help from a Christian counselor if needed. But for the sake of your marriage, forgive "not . . . up to seven times, but up to seventy times seven" (Matt. 18:22). Allow Christ to use His resurrection power to heal and restore your marriage.

Forgiveness guards our hearts from bitterness and creates fertile soil in which romance and love can grow.

9 'I *am* pure, without transgression;
   I *am* innocent, and *there is* no
      iniquity in me.
10 Yet He finds occasions against me,
   He counts me as His enemy;
11 He puts my feet in the stocks,
   He watches all my paths.'

12 "Look, *in* this you are not righteous.
   I will answer you,
   For God is greater than man.
13 Why do you contend with Him?
   For He does not give an accounting
      of any of His words.
14 For God may speak in one way, or in
      another,
   Yet man does not perceive it.
15 In a dream, in a vision of the night,
   When deep sleep falls upon men,
   While slumbering on their beds,
16 Then He opens the ears of men,
   And seals their instruction.
17 In order to turn man *from his* deed,
   And conceal pride from man,
18 He keeps back his soul from the Pit,
   And his life from perishing by the
      sword.

19 "*Man* is also chastened with pain on
      his bed,
   And with strong *pain* in many of his
      bones,
20 So that his life abhors bread,
   And his soul succulent food.
21 His flesh wastes away from sight,
   And his bones stick out *which once*
      were not seen.
22 Yes, his soul draws near the Pit,
   And his life to the executioners.

23 "If there is a messenger for him,
   A mediator, one among a thousand,
   To show man His uprightness,
24 Then He is gracious to him, and
      says,
   ' Deliver him from going down to the
      Pit;
   I have found a ransom';
25 His flesh shall be young like a child's,
   He shall return to the days of his
      youth.
26 He shall pray to God, and He will
      delight in him,
   He shall see His face with joy,

For He restores to man His
   righteousness.
27 Then he looks at men and says,
   ' I have sinned, and perverted *what
      was* right,
   And it did not profit me.'
28 He will redeem his[a] soul from going
      down to the Pit,
   And his[b] life shall see the light.

29 "Behold, God works all these *things,*
   Twice, *in fact,* three *times* with a man,
30 To bring back his soul from the Pit,
   That he may be enlightened with the
      light of life.

31 "Give ear, Job, listen to me;
   Hold your peace, and I will speak.
32 If you have anything to say, answer
      me;
   Speak, for I desire to justify you.
33 If not, listen to me;
   Hold your peace, and I will teach you
      wisdom."

Elihu Proclaims God's Justice

34 Elihu further answered and said:

2 "Hear my words, you wise *men;*
   Give ear to me, you who have
      knowledge.
3 For the ear tests words
   As the palate tastes food.
4 Let us choose justice for ourselves;
   Let us know among ourselves what
      is good.

5 "For Job has said, 'I am righteous,
   But God has taken away my justice;
6 Should I lie concerning my right?
   My wound *is* incurable, *though I am*
      without transgression.'
7 What man *is* like Job,
   Who drinks scorn like water,
8 Who goes in company with the
      workers of iniquity,
   And walks with wicked men?
9 For he has said, 'It profits a man
      nothing
   That he should delight in God.'

10 "Therefore listen to me, you men of
      understanding:

33:28 [a]Or *my* (Kethib) [b]Or *my* (Kethib)

Far be it from God *to do* wickedness,
And *from* the Almighty to *commit*
　　iniquity.
11 For He repays man *according to* his
　　work,
And makes man to find a reward
　　according to *his* way.
12 Surely God will never do wickedly,
Nor will the Almighty pervert
　　justice.
13 Who gave Him charge over the
　　earth?
Or who appointed *Him over* the
　　whole world?
14 If He should set His heart on it,
If He should gather to Himself His
　　Spirit and His breath,
15 All flesh would perish together,
And man would return to dust.

16 "If *you have* understanding, hear this;
Listen to the sound of my words:
17 Should one who hates justice govern?
Will you condemn *Him who is* most
　　just?
18 *Is it fitting* to say to a king, '*You are*
　　worthless,'
And to nobles, '*You are* wicked'?
19 Yet He is not partial to princes,
Nor does He regard the rich more
　　than the poor;
For they *are* all the work of His
　　hands.
20 In a moment they die, in the middle
　　of the night;
The people are shaken and pass
　　away;
The mighty are taken away without
　　a hand.
21 "For His eyes *are* on the ways of man,
And He sees all his steps.
22 There is no darkness nor shadow of
　　death
Where the workers of iniquity may
　　hide themselves.
23 For He need not further consider a
　　man,
That he should go before God in
　　judgment.
24 He breaks in pieces mighty men
　　without inquiry,
And sets others in their place.
25 Therefore He knows their works;

He overthrows *them* in the night,
And they are crushed.
26 He strikes them as wicked *men*
In the open sight of others,
27 Because they turned back from Him,
And would not consider any of His
　　ways,
28 So that they caused the cry of the
　　poor to come to Him;
For He hears the cry of the afflicted.
29 When He gives quietness, who then
　　can make trouble?
And when He hides *His* face, who
　　then can see Him,
Whether *it is* against a nation or a
　　man alone?—
30 That the hypocrite should not reign,
Lest the people be ensnared.

31 "For has *anyone* said to God,
'I have borne *chastening*;
I will offend no more;
32 Teach me *what* I do not see;
If I have done iniquity, I will do no
　　more'?
33 Should He repay *it* according to your
　　terms,
Just because you disavow it?
You must choose, and not I;
Therefore speak what you know.

34 "Men of understanding say to me,
Wise men who listen to me:
35 'Job speaks without knowledge,
His words *are* without wisdom.'
36 Oh, that Job were tried to the utmost,
Because *his* answers *are like* those of
　　wicked men!
37 For he adds rebellion to his sin;
He claps *his hands* among us,
And multiplies his words against
　　God."

Elihu Condemns Self-Righteousness

35 Moreover Elihu answered and said:

2 "Do you think this is right?
Do you say,
'My righteousness is more than
　　God's'?
3 For you say,
'What advantage will it be to You?
What profit shall I have, more than *if*
　　I had sinned?'

4   "I will answer you,
And your companions with you.

5   Look to the heavens and see;
And behold the clouds—
They are higher than you.

6   If you sin, what do you accomplish
against Him?
Or, *if* your transgressions are
multiplied, what do you do to
Him?

7   If you are righteous, what do you
give Him?
Or what does He receive from your
hand?

8   Your wickedness affects a man such
as you,
And your righteousness a son of
man.

9   "Because of the multitude of
oppressions they cry out;
They cry out for help because of the
arm of the mighty.

10   But no one says, 'Where *is* God my
Maker,
Who gives songs in the night,

11   Who teaches us more than the beasts
of the earth,
And makes us wiser than the birds
of heaven?'

12   There they cry out, but He does not
answer,
Because of the pride of evil men.

13   Surely God will not listen to empty
talk,
Nor will the Almighty regard it.

14   Although you say you do not see
Him,
Yet justice *is* before Him, and you
must wait for Him.

15   And now, because He has not
punished in His anger,
Nor taken much notice of folly,

16   Therefore Job opens his mouth in
vain;
He multiplies words without
knowledge."

Elihu Proclaims God's Goodness

36 Elihu also proceeded and said:

2   "Bear with me a little, and I will show
you
That *there are* yet words to speak on
God's behalf.

3   I will fetch my knowledge from afar;
I will ascribe righteousness to my
Maker.

4   For truly my words *are* not false;

PARENTING MATTERS

Q: How can we give our children a sense of a divinely-appointed spiritual mission?

One of our assignments as parents is to impart not just our knowledge of God, but a vision for the world. Begin to do this by praying for your children. Pray that God's plan and will for their lives will be fulfilled.

Give them a vision for the world by making them a part of your own ministry (you do have one, you know). Share stories of how God is at work when you come home to your family. Take them with you on trips and give them a responsibility in your ministry. You and I are a part of a generational relay race in which we must make a good handoff to the next generation.

Psalm 112:1–3 declares, "Blessed is the man who fears the LORD, who delights greatly in His commandments. His descendants will be mighty on earth; the generation of the upright will be blessed. Wealth and riches will be in his house, and his righteousness endures forever."

Remember, your marriage and family are the headwaters of your legacy. Your legacy begins at home. What occurs downstream in your ministry will be only as deep as the source at home.

One who is perfect in knowledge *is*
with you.

5 "Behold, God *is* mighty, but despises
no one;
He *is* mighty in strength of
understanding.

6 He does not preserve the life of the
wicked,
But gives justice to the oppressed.

7 He does not withdraw His eyes from
the righteous;
But *they are* on the throne with
kings,
For He has seated them forever,
And they are exalted.

8 And if *they are* bound in fetters,
Held in the cords of affliction,

9 Then He tells them their work and
their transgressions—
That they have acted defiantly.

10 He also opens their ear to
instruction,
And commands that they turn from
iniquity.

11 If they obey and serve *Him,*
They shall spend their days in
prosperity,
And their years in pleasures.

12 But if they do not obey,
They shall perish by the sword,
And they shall die without
knowledge.[a]

13 "But the hypocrites in heart store up
wrath;
They do not cry for help when He
binds them.

14 They die in youth,
And their life *ends* among the
perverted persons.[a]

15 He delivers the poor in their
affliction,
And opens their ears in oppression.

16 "Indeed He would have brought you
out of dire distress,
Into a broad place where *there is* no
restraint;
And what is set on your table *would
be* full of richness.

17 But you are filled with the judgment
due the wicked;
Judgment and justice take hold *of you.*

18 Because *there is* wrath, *beware* lest
He take you away with *one* blow;
For a large ransom would not help
you avoid *it.*

19 Will your riches,
Or all the mighty forces,
Keep you from distress?

20 Do not desire the night,
When people are cut off in their place.

21 Take heed, do not turn to iniquity,
For you have chosen this rather than
affliction.

22 "Behold, God is exalted by His power;
Who teaches like Him?

23 Who has assigned Him His way,
Or who has said, 'You have done
wrong'?

Elihu Proclaims God's Majesty

24 "Remember to magnify His work,
Of which men have sung.

25 Everyone has seen it;
Man looks on *it* from afar.

26 "Behold, God *is* great, and we do not
know *Him;*
Nor can the number of His years *be*
discovered.

27 For He draws up drops of water,
Which distill as rain from the mist,

28 Which the clouds drop down
And pour abundantly on man.

29 Indeed, can *anyone* understand the
spreading of clouds,
The thunder from His canopy?

30 Look, He scatters His light upon it,
And covers the depths of the sea.

31 For by these He judges the peoples;
He gives food in abundance.

32 He covers *His* hands with lightning,
And commands it to strike.

33 His thunder declares it,
The cattle also, concerning the rising
storm.

37 "At this also my heart trembles,
And leaps from its place.

2 Hear attentively the thunder of His
voice,
And the rumbling *that* comes from
His mouth.

36:12 [a]Masoretic Text reads *as one without knowledge.* **36:14** [a]Hebrew *qedeshim,* that is, those practicing sodomy and prostitution in religious rituals

3   He sends it forth under the whole
        heaven,
     His lightning to the ends of the
        earth.
4   After it a voice roars;
     He thunders with His majestic voice,
     And He does not restrain them when
        His voice is heard.
5   God thunders marvelously with His
        voice;
     He does great things which we
        cannot comprehend.
6   For He says to the snow, 'Fall *on* the
        earth';
     Likewise to the gentle rain and the
        heavy rain of His strength.
7   He seals the hand of every man,
     That all men may know His work.
8   The beasts go into dens,
     And remain in their lairs.
9   From the chamber *of the south*
        comes the whirlwind,
     And cold from the scattering winds
        of the north.
10   By the breath of God ice is given,
     And the broad waters are frozen.
11   Also with moisture He saturates the
        thick clouds;
     He scatters His bright clouds.
12   And they swirl about, being turned
        by His guidance,
     That they may do whatever He
        commands them
     On the face of the whole earth.ᵃ
13   He causes it to come,
     Whether for correction,
     Or for His land,
     Or for mercy.
14   "Listen to this, O Job;
     Stand still and consider the
        wondrous works of God.
15   Do you know when God dispatches
        them,
     And causes the light of His cloud to
        shine?
16   Do you know how the clouds are
        balanced,
     Those wondrous works of Him who
        is perfect in knowledge?
17   Why *are* your garments hot,
     When He quiets the earth by the
        south *wind?*

18   With Him, have you spread out the
        skies,
     Strong as a cast metal mirror?
19   "Teach us what we should say to Him,
     For we can prepare nothing because
        of the darkness.
20   Should He be told that I *wish to*
        speak?
     If a man were to speak, surely he
        would be swallowed up.
21   Even now *men* cannot look at the
        light *when it is* bright in the skies,
     When the wind has passed and
        cleared them.
22   He comes from the north *as* golden
        splendor;
     With God *is* awesome majesty.
23   *As for* the Almighty, we cannot find
        Him;
     He is excellent in power,
     In judgment and abundant justice;
     He does not oppress.
24   Therefore men fear Him;
     He shows no partiality to any *who
        are* wise of heart."

The LORD Reveals His Omnipotence to Job

38 Then the LORD answered Job out of
   the whirlwind, and said:

2   "Who *is* this who darkens counsel
     By words without knowledge?
3   Now prepare yourself like a man;
     I will question you, and you shall
        answer Me.

4   "Where were you when I laid the
        foundations of the earth?
     Tell *Me,* if you have understanding.
5   Who determined its measurements?
     Surely you know!
     Or who stretched the line upon it?
6   To what were its foundations
        fastened?
     Or who laid its cornerstone,
7   When the morning stars sang
        together,
     And all the sons of God shouted for
        joy?
8   "Or *who* shut in the sea with doors,

37:12 ᵃLiterally *the world of the earth*

When it burst forth *and* issued from
   the womb;
9 When I made the clouds its garment,
   And thick darkness its swaddling
   band;
10 When I fixed My limit for it,
   And set bars and doors;
11 When I said,
   ' This far you may come, but no
   farther,
   And here your proud waves must
   stop!'

12 "Have you commanded the morning
   since your days *began,*
   And caused the dawn to know its
   place,
13 That it might take hold of the ends
   of the earth,
   And the wicked be shaken out of it?
14 It takes on form like clay *under* a seal,
   And stands out like a garment.
15 From the wicked their light is
   withheld,
   And the upraised arm is broken.

16 "Have you entered the springs of the
   sea?
   Or have you walked in search of the
   depths?
17 Have the gates of death been
   revealed to you?
   Or have you seen the doors of the
   shadow of death?
18 Have you comprehended the breadth
   of the earth?
   Tell *Me,* if you know all this.

19 "Where *is* the way *to* the dwelling of
   light?
   And darkness, where *is* its place,
20 That you may take it to its territory,
   That you may know the paths *to* its
   home?
21 Do you know *it,* because you were
   born then,
   Or *because* the number of your days
   is great?

22 "Have you entered the treasury of
   snow,
   Or have you seen the treasury of hail,
23 Which I have reserved for the time of
   trouble,
   For the day of battle and war?

BIBLICAL INSIGHTS • 38:1–41

Hard Questions

WHEN GOD FINALLY ANSWERED Job out of the whirlwind, He answered the man's questions with some much harder questions of His own. In the spirit of hard questions, I have a few I'd like to ask of the contemporary church:

Why is the divorce rate inside the church nearly identical to the divorce rate outside the church?

Why do so many Christian men perform aggressively at work and remain so disengaged and passive at home?

Why are so many Christian parents negative about having and rearing children?

Why do so many Christians say their secular job is their ministry, but then show so little fruit for their efforts?

Why do Christians talk about family values while their lifestyles are virtually identical to the average non-Christian?

Why have so many Christians in full-time ministry washed out because of immorality and impurity?

Why is the fifth commandment—to honor our parents—neglected by large numbers of Christians?

Why do less than 10 percent of all Christians regularly tell others about God's forgiveness and the new life found in Christ?

If Jesus Christ changes lives, then why do 50 million Americans claiming to be born again have such a marginal impact on society?

I believe the answer to each of these questions can be tied to a failure to obey and take seriously the lordship of Christ in our lives. When we learn to humbly trust and obey God, He brings personal transformation. And that's how cultures are changed—one person and one home at a time.

24 By what way is light diffused,
   Or the east wind scattered over the
   earth?

25 "Who has divided a channel for the
     overflowing *water*,
     Or a path for the thunderbolt,
26 To cause it to rain on a land *where
     there is* no one,
     A wilderness in which *there is* no
     man;
27 To satisfy the desolate waste,
     And cause to spring forth the growth
     of tender grass?
28 Has the rain a father?
     Or who has begotten the drops of
     dew?
29 From whose womb comes the ice?
     And the frost of heaven, who gives it
     birth?
30 The waters harden like stone,
     And the surface of the deep is
     frozen.

31 "Can you bind the cluster of the
     Pleiades,
     Or loose the belt of Orion?
32 Can you bring out Mazzaroth[a] in its
     season?
     Or can you guide the Great Bear
     with its cubs?
33 Do you know the ordinances of the
     heavens?
     Can you set their dominion over the
     earth?

34 "Can you lift up your voice to the
     clouds,
     That an abundance of water may
     cover you?
35 Can you send out lightnings, that
     they may go,
     And say to you, 'Here we *are!*'?
36 Who has put wisdom in the mind?[a]
     Or who has given understanding to
     the heart?
37 Who can number the clouds by
     wisdom?
     Or who can pour out the bottles of
     heaven,
38 When the dust hardens in clumps,
     And the clods cling together?

39 "Can you hunt the prey for the lion,
     Or satisfy the appetite of the young
     lions,
40 When they crouch in *their* dens,
     Or lurk in their lairs to lie in wait?

41 Who provides food for the raven,
     When its young ones cry to God,
     And wander about for lack of food?

39 "Do you know the time when the
     wild mountain goats bear young?
     Or can you mark when the deer
     gives birth?
2 Can you number the months *that*
     they fulfill?
     Or do you know the time when they
     bear young?
3 They bow down,
     They bring forth their young,
     They deliver their offspring.[a]
4 Their young ones are healthy,
     They grow strong with grain;
     They depart and do not return to
     them.

5 "Who set the wild donkey free?
     Who loosed the bonds of the onager,
6 Whose home I have made the
     wilderness,
     And the barren land his dwelling?
7 He scorns the tumult of the city;
     He does not heed the shouts of the
     driver.
8 The range of the mountains *is* his
     pasture,
     And he searches after every green
     thing.

9 "Will the wild ox be willing to serve
     you?
     Will he bed by your manger?
10 Can you bind the wild ox in the
     furrow with ropes?
     Or will he plow the valleys behind
     you?
11 Will you trust him because his
     strength *is* great?
     Or will you leave your labor to him?
12 Will you trust him to bring home
     your grain,
     And gather it to your threshing floor?

13 "The wings of the ostrich wave
     proudly,
     But are her wings and pinions *like
     the* kindly stork's?

38:32 [a]Literally *Constellations*
38:36 [a]Literally *inward parts*
39:3 [a]Literally *pangs,* figurative of offspring

14 For she leaves her eggs on the
ground,
And warms them in the dust;
15 She forgets that a foot may crush
them,
Or that a wild beast may break them.
16 She treats her young harshly, as
though *they were* not hers;
Her labor is in vain, without concern,
17 Because God deprived her of
wisdom,
And did not endow her with
understanding.
18 When she lifts herself on high,
She scorns the horse and its rider.

19 "Have you given the horse strength?
Have you clothed his neck with
thunder?ᵃ
20 Can you frighten him like a locust?
His majestic snorting strikes terror.
21 He paws in the valley, and rejoices in
his strength;
He gallops into the clash of arms.
22 He mocks at fear, and is not
frightened;
Nor does he turn back from the
sword.
23 The quiver rattles against him,
The glittering spear and javelin.
24 He devours the distance with
fierceness and rage;
Nor does he come to a halt because
the trumpet *has* sounded.
25 At *the blast of* the trumpet he says,
'Aha!'
He smells the battle from afar,
The thunder of captains and
shouting.

26 "Does the hawk fly by your wisdom,
And spread its wings toward the
south?
27 Does the eagle mount up at your
command,
And make its nest on high?
28 On the rock it dwells and resides,
On the crag of the rock and the
stronghold.
29 From there it spies out the prey;
Its eyes observe from afar.

30 Its young ones suck up blood;
And where the slain *are,* there it *is.*"

40 Moreover the LORD answered Job,
and said:

2 "Shall the one who contends with the
Almighty correct *Him?*
He who rebukes God, let him answer
it."

Job's Response to God

3 Then Job answered the LORD and said:

4 "Behold, I am vile;
What shall I answer You?
I lay my hand over my mouth.
5 Once I have spoken, but I will not
answer;
Yes, twice, but I will proceed no
further."

God's Challenge to Job

6 Then the LORD answered Job out of the
whirlwind, and said:

7 "Now prepare yourself like a man;
I will question you, and you shall
answer Me:

8 "Would you indeed annul My
judgment?
Would you condemn Me that you
may be justified?
9 Have you an arm like God?
Or can you thunder with a voice like
His?
10 Then adorn yourself *with* majesty
and splendor,
And array yourself with glory and
beauty.
11 Disperse the rage of your wrath;
Look on everyone *who is* proud, and
humble him.
12 Look on everyone *who is* proud, *and*
bring him low;
Tread down the wicked in their place.
13 Hide them in the dust together,
Bind their faces in hidden *darkness.*
14 Then I will also confess to you
That your own right hand can save
you.

15 "Look now at the behemoth,ᵃ which I
made *along* with you;
He eats grass like an ox.

39:19 ᵃOr *a mane*
40:15 ᵃA large animal, exact identity unknown

16 See now, his strength *is* in his hips,
And his power *is* in his stomach
muscles.

17 He moves his tail like a cedar;
The sinews of his thighs are tightly
knit.

18 His bones *are like* beams of bronze,
His ribs like bars of iron.

19 He *is* the first of the ways of God;
Only He who made him can bring
near His sword.

20 Surely the mountains yield food for
him,
And all the beasts of the field play
there.

21 He lies under the lotus trees,
In a covert of reeds and marsh.

22 The lotus trees cover him *with* their
shade;
The willows by the brook surround
him.

23 Indeed the river may rage,
Yet he is not disturbed;
He is confident, though the Jordan
gushes into his mouth,

24 *Though* he takes it in his eyes,
Or one pierces *his* nose with a snare.

41 "Can you draw out Leviathanᵃ with
a hook,
Or *snare* his tongue with a line *which*
you lower?

2 Can you put a reed through his nose,
Or pierce his jaw with a hook?

3 Will he make many supplications to
you?
Will he speak softly to you?

4 Will he make a covenant with you?
Will you take him as a servant forever?

5 Will you play with him as *with* a
bird,
Or will you leash him for your
maidens?

6 Will *your* companions make a
banquetᵃ of him?
Will they apportion him among the
merchants?

7 Can you fill his skin with harpoons,
Or his head with fishing spears?

8 *Lay your hand* on him;
Remember the battle—
Never do it again!

9 Indeed, *any* hope of *overcoming* him
is false;

Shall *one not* be overwhelmed at the
sight of him?

10 No one *is so* fierce that he would dare
stir him up.
Who then is able to stand against
Me?

11 Who has preceded Me, that I should
pay *him?*
Everything under heaven is Mine.

12 "I will not concealᵃ his limbs,
His mighty power, or his graceful
proportions.

13 Who can remove his outer coat?
Who can approach *him* with a
double bridle?

14 Who can open the doors of his face,
With his terrible teeth all around?

15 *His* rows of scales are *his* pride,
Shut up tightly *as with* a seal;

16 One is so near another
That no air can come between them;

17 They are joined one to another,
They stick together and cannot be
parted.

18 His sneezings flash forth light,
And his eyes *are* like the eyelids of
the morning.

19 Out of his mouth go burning lights;
Sparks of fire shoot out.

20 Smoke goes out of his nostrils,
As *from* a boiling pot and burning
rushes.

21 His breath kindles coals,
And a flame goes out of his mouth.

22 Strength dwells in his neck,
And sorrow dances before him.

23 The folds of his flesh are joined
together;
They are firm on him and cannot be
moved.

24 His heart is as hard as stone,
Even as hard as the lower *millstone.*

25 When he raises himself up, the
mighty are afraid;
Because of his crashings they are
besideᵃ themselves.

26 *Though* the sword reaches him, it
cannot avail;
Nor does spear, dart, or javelin.

41:1 ᵃA large sea creature, exact identity unknown
41:6 ᵃOr *bargain over him* 41:12 ᵃLiterally *keep
silent about* 41:25 ᵃOr *purify themselves*

27 He regards iron as straw,
   And bronze as rotten wood.
28 The arrow cannot make him flee;
   Slingstones become like stubble to
   him.
29 Darts are regarded as straw;
   He laughs at the threat of javelins.
30 His undersides *are* like sharp
   potsherds;
   He spreads pointed *marks* in the
   mire.
31 He makes the deep boil like a pot;
   He makes the sea like a pot of
   ointment.
32 He leaves a shining wake behind
   him;
   One would think the deep had white
   hair.
33 On earth there is nothing like him,
   Which is made without fear.
34 He beholds every high *thing;*
   He *is* king over all the children of
   pride."

Job's Repentance and Restoration

42 Then Job answered the LORD and
   said:

2 "I know that You can do everything,
   And that no purpose *of Yours* can be
   withheld from You.
3 *You asked,* 'Who *is* this who hides
   counsel without knowledge?'
   Therefore I have uttered what I did
   not understand,
   Things too wonderful for me, which
   I did not know.
4 Listen, please, and let me speak;
   You said, 'I will question you, and
   you shall answer Me.'
5 "I have heard of You by the hearing
   of the ear,
   But now my eye sees You.
6 Therefore I abhor *myself,*
   And repent in dust and ashes."

7 And so it was, after the LORD had spoken these words to Job, that the LORD said
to Eliphaz the Temanite, "My wrath is
aroused against you and your two friends,
for you have not spoken of Me *what is*

right, as My servant Job *has.* 8Now therefore, take for yourselves seven bulls and
seven rams, go to My servant Job, and offer
up for yourselves a burnt offering; and My
servant Job shall pray for you. For I will
accept him, lest I deal with you *according
to your* folly; because you have not spoken
of Me *what is* right, as My servant Job *has.*"
9So Eliphaz the Temanite and Bildad
the Shuhite *and* Zophar the Naamathite
went and did as the LORD commanded
them; for the LORD had accepted Job. 10And
the LORD restored Job's lossesa when he
prayed for his friends. Indeed the LORD
gave Job twice as much as he had before.
11Then all his brothers, all his sisters, and
all those who had been his acquaintances
before, came to him and ate food with him
in his house; and they consoled him and
comforted him for all the adversity that the
LORD had brought upon him. Each one
gave him a piece of silver and each a ring
of gold.

INTIMATE MOMENTS

Have your lady write down on small slips
of paper her five favorite things to do.
Fold them and place them in a bowl. Let
her draw one out and read it—then do it
together. Save the others for later.

12Now the LORD blessed the latter *days*
of Job more than his beginning; for he had
fourteen thousand sheep, six thousand
camels, one thousand yoke of oxen, and
one thousand female donkeys. 13He also
had seven sons and three daughters. 14And
he called the name of the first Jemimah,
the name of the second Keziah, and the
name of the third Keren-Happuch. 15In all
the land were found no women *so* beautiful
as the daughters of Job; and their father
gave them an inheritance among their
brothers.
16After this Job lived one hundred and
forty years, and saw his children and
grandchildren *for* four generations. 17So
Job died, old and full of days.

42:10 aLiterally *Job's captivity,* that is, what was captured from Job

PSALMS

THE RABBIS GAVE THIS BOOK THE TITLE *The Book of Praises*. The name *Psalms* comes from a Greek word that refers to plucking a string. Psalms is the God-breathed hymnal for ancient Israel, collected over a period of 900 years. King David wrote most of the psalms, but we also find selections by Moses, Solomon, Asaph, and the sons of Korah. About a third of the book is anonymous.

These ancient hymns take the full range of human experience and emotions and point us to lives of joyful dependence on God. The Psalms teach us that in every aspect of our lives, from times of trouble and turmoil to times of triumph, joy, and celebration, we can and should give voice to our trust and confidence in God and in how He is working out His sovereign will for us.

Many types of psalms make up this book. Some psalms emphasize living with godly wisdom. Others express the sorrow and pain connected with daily life. The writers of some psalms confess their sins and seek God's forgiveness. Many psalms center on thanking and praising God for graciously delivering His people from calamity and destruction, or celebrate His rule and majesty as the King and Ruler over the whole world.

Naturally, many psalms speak to the joys and blessings of marriage and family. Psalm 45, for example, is a royal wedding song in which a young bride-to-be looks forward to her wedding day. Psalm 78 talks about the need for one generation to pass along the truth about God to the next generation. Psalm 127 begins with a charge to families to make sure they build their houses on a solid spiritual foundation. And Psalm 128 shows how the fear of the Lord supplies the basis for a healthy marriage and family.

Whatever circumstance you face today and whatever emotion you're experiencing, you are likely to find a psalm that resonates with your heart and that directs your thinking back to God and His care for you. Great comfort and encouragement awaits your soul in the Psalms!

Book One: Psalms 1—41

PSALM 1

The Way of the Righteous and the End of the Ungodly

1 Blessed *is* the man
Who walks not in the counsel of the ungodly,
Nor stands in the path of sinners,
Nor sits in the seat of the scornful;

2 But his delight *is* in the law of the LORD,
And in His law he meditates day and night.

3 He shall be like a tree
Planted by the rivers of water,
That brings forth its fruit in its season,
Whose leaf also shall not wither;
And whatever he does shall prosper.

4 The ungodly *are* not so,
But *are* like the chaff which the wind drives away.

5 Therefore the ungodly shall not stand in the judgment,
Nor sinners in the congregation of the righteous.

6 For the LORD knows the way of the righteous,
But the way of the ungodly shall perish.

PSALM 2

The Messiah's Triumph and Kingdom

1 Why do the nations rage,
And the people plot a vain thing?

2 The kings of the earth set themselves,
And the rulers take counsel together,
Against the LORD and against His Anointed, *saying,*

3 "Let us break Their bonds in pieces
And cast away Their cords from us."

4 He who sits in the heavens shall laugh;
The Lord shall hold them in derision.

5 Then He shall speak to them in His wrath,
And distress them in His deep displeasure:

6 "Yet I have set My King
On My holy hill of Zion."

7 "I will declare the decree:
The LORD has said to Me,
'You *are* My Son,
Today I have begotten You.

8 Ask of Me, and I will give *You*
The nations *for* Your inheritance,
And the ends of the earth *for* Your possession.

9 You shall break[a] them with a rod of iron;
You shall dash them to pieces like a potter's vessel.' "

10 Now therefore, be wise, O kings;
Be instructed, you judges of the earth.

11 Serve the LORD with fear,
And rejoice with trembling.

12 Kiss the Son,[a] lest He[b] be angry,
And you perish *in* the way,
When His wrath is kindled but a little.
Blessed *are* all those who put their trust in Him.

PSALM 3

The LORD Helps His Troubled People

A Psalm of David
when he fled from Absalom his son.

1 LORD, how they have increased who trouble me!
Many *are* they who rise up against me.

INTIMATE MOMENTS

Admit when you're wrong and be willing to say to your wife, "I'm sorry, will you forgive me?"

2:9 [a]Following Masoretic Text and Targum; Septuagint, Syriac, and Vulgate read *rule* (compare Revelation 2:27). **2:12** [a]Septuagint and Vulgate read *Embrace discipline;* Targum reads *Receive instruction.* [b]Septuagint reads *the LORD.*

2 Many *are* they who say of me,
   "*There is* no help for him in God."
                                    Selah

3 But You, O LORD, *are* a shield for me,
   My glory and the One who lifts up
      my head.
4 I cried to the LORD with my voice,
   And He heard me from His holy hill.
                                    Selah

5 I lay down and slept;
   I awoke, for the LORD sustained me.
6 I will not be afraid of ten thousands
      of people
   Who have set *themselves* against me
      all around.

7 Arise, O LORD;
   Save me, O my God!
   For You have struck all my enemies
      on the cheekbone;
   You have broken the teeth of the
      ungodly.
8 Salvation *belongs* to the LORD.
   Your blessing *is* upon Your people.
                                    Selah

PSALM 4

The Safety of the Faithful

To the Chief Musician.
With stringed instruments. A Psalm of David.

1 Hear me when I call, O God of my
      righteousness!
   You have relieved me in *my* distress;
   Have mercy on me, and hear my
      prayer.

2 How long, O you sons of men,
   Will you turn my glory to shame?
   How long will you love
      worthlessness
   And seek falsehood?   Selah
3 But know that the LORD has set
      apart[a] for Himself him who is
      godly;
   The LORD will hear when I call to Him.

4 Be angry, and do not sin.
   Meditate within your heart on your
      bed, and be still.   Selah
5 Offer the sacrifices of righteousness,
   And put your trust in the LORD.

6 *There are* many who say,
   "Who will show us *any* good?"
   LORD, lift up the light of Your
      countenance upon us.
7 You have put gladness in my heart,
   More than in the season that their
      grain and wine increased.
8 I will both lie down in peace, and
      sleep;
   For You alone, O LORD, make me
      dwell in safety.

PSALM 5

A Prayer for Guidance

To the Chief Musician.
With flutes.[a] A Psalm of David.

1 Give ear to my words, O LORD,
   Consider my meditation.
2 Give heed to the voice of my cry,
   My King and my God,
   For to You I will pray.
3 My voice You shall hear in the
      morning, O LORD;
   In the morning I will direct *it*
      to You,
   And I will look up.

4 For You *are* not a God who takes
      pleasure in wickedness,
   Nor shall evil dwell with You.
5 The boastful shall not stand in Your
      sight;
   You hate all workers of iniquity.
6 You shall destroy those who speak
      falsehood;
   The LORD abhors the bloodthirsty
      and deceitful man.

7 But as for me, I will come into Your
      house in the multitude of Your
      mercy;
   In fear of You I will worship toward
      Your holy temple.
8 Lead me, O LORD, in Your
      righteousness because of my
      enemies;
   Make Your way straight before my
      face.

4:3 [a]Many Hebrew manuscripts, Septuagint, Targum,
and Vulgate read *made wonderful.*
5:title [a]Hebrew *nehiloth*

9 For *there is* no faithfulness in their
   mouth;
   Their inward part *is* destruction;
   Their throat *is* an open tomb;
   They flatter with their tongue.
10 Pronounce them guilty, O God!
   Let them fall by their own counsels;
   Cast them out in the multitude of
   their transgressions,
   For they have rebelled against You.
11 But let all those rejoice who put their
   trust in You;
   Let them ever shout for joy, because
   You defend them;
   Let those also who love Your name
   Be joyful in You.
12 For You, O LORD, will bless the
   righteous;
   With favor You will surround him as
   with a shield.

PSALM 6

A Prayer of Faith in Time of Distress

To the Chief Musician.
With stringed instruments.
On an eight-stringed harp.[a] A Psalm of David.

1 O LORD, do not rebuke me in Your
   anger,
   Nor chasten me in Your hot
   displeasure.
2 Have mercy on me, O LORD, for I *am*
   weak;
   O LORD, heal me, for my bones are
   troubled.
3 My soul also is greatly troubled;
   But You, O LORD—how long?

4 Return, O LORD, deliver me!
   Oh, save me for Your mercies' sake!
5 For in death *there is* no remembrance
   of You;
   In the grave who will give You
   thanks?

6 I am weary with my groaning;
   All night I make my bed swim;
   I drench my couch with my tears.
7 My eye wastes away because of
   grief;

It grows old because of all my
   enemies.
8 Depart from me, all you workers of
   iniquity;
   For the LORD has heard the voice of
   my weeping.
9 The LORD has heard my supplication;
   The LORD will receive my prayer.
10 Let all my enemies be ashamed and
   greatly troubled;
   Let them turn back *and* be ashamed
   suddenly.

PSALM 7

Prayer and Praise for Deliverance from Enemies

A Meditation[a] of David, which he sang
to the LORD concerning the words of Cush,
a Benjamite.

1 O LORD my God, in You I put my
   trust;
   Save me from all those who
   persecute me;
   And deliver me,
2 Lest they tear me like a lion,
   Rending *me* in pieces, while *there is*
   none to deliver.

3 O LORD my God, if I have done this:
   If there is iniquity in my hands,
4 If I have repaid evil to him who was
   at peace with me,
   Or have plundered my enemy
   without cause,
5 Let the enemy pursue me and
   overtake *me;*
   Yes, let him trample my life to the
   earth,
   And lay my honor in the dust. Selah

6 Arise, O LORD, in Your anger;
   Lift Yourself up because of the rage
   of my enemies;
   Rise up for me[a] *to* the judgment You
   have commanded!
7 So the congregation of the peoples
   shall surround You;
   For their sakes, therefore, return on
   high.
8 The LORD shall judge the peoples;
   Judge me, O LORD, according to my
   righteousness,

6:title [a]Hebrew *sheminith* 7:title [a]Hebrew *Shiggaion*
7:6 [a]Following Masoretic Text, Targum, and Vulgate;
Septuagint reads *O LORD my God.*

And according to my integrity
    within me.

9   Oh, let the wickedness of the wicked
    come to an end,
But establish the just;
For the righteous God tests the
    hearts and minds.

10   My defense *is* of God,
Who saves the upright in heart.

11   God *is* a just judge,
And God is angry *with the wicked*
    every day.

12   If he does not turn back,
He will sharpen His sword;
He bends His bow and makes it
    ready.

13   He also prepares for Himself
    instruments of death;
He makes His arrows into fiery shafts.

14   Behold, *the wicked* brings forth
    iniquity;
Yes, he conceives trouble and brings
    forth falsehood.

15   He made a pit and dug it out,
And has fallen into the ditch *which*
    he made.

16   His trouble shall return upon his
    own head,
And his violent dealing shall come
    down on his own crown.

17   I will praise the LORD according to
    His righteousness,

And will sing praise to the name of
    the LORD Most High.

PSALM 8

The Glory of the LORD in Creation

To the Chief Musician.
On the instrument of Gath.[a] A Psalm of David.

1   O LORD, our Lord,
How excellent *is* Your name in all the
    earth,
Who have set Your glory above the
    heavens!

2   Out of the mouth of babes and
    nursing infants
You have ordained strength,
Because of Your enemies,
That You may silence the enemy and
    the avenger.

3   When I consider Your heavens, the
    work of Your fingers,
The moon and the stars, which You
    have ordained,

4   What is man that You are mindful of
    him,
And the son of man that You visit
    him?

5   For You have made him a little lower
    than the angels,[a]

8:title [a]Hebrew *Al Gittith*   **8:5** [a]Hebrew *Elohim, God;*
Septuagint, Syriac, Targum, and Jewish tradition
translate as *angels.*

ROMANTIC QUOTES AND NOTES
Your God-Given Worth

Helen Keller once said, "So much has been given to me, I have no time to ponder over that which has been denied."

This blind and deaf woman looked beyond limiting circumstances to see that which couldn't be taken away. She knew God had given her worth and value. Fashioned in His image, she saw herself as the pinnacle of His creation. And she knew that, as Psalm 8:5 says, she was crowned with "glory and honor."

You and your mate also have great worth. God has given you both *assigned worth.* He gave value to all people as His creation, and to Christians as His children. Just as John F. Kennedy was born into the Kennedy family and thus received a certain type of worth, those who are born again into God's family (through faith in Christ) have been assigned worth. It is a gift—part of our birthright—when we trust in Christ and ask Him to forgive our sins.

Especially when times get hard, help each other remember that you are children of the King! Remind each other of the benefits that are yours by virtue of the new birth (see Eph. 1:3–14).

And You have crowned him with
glory and honor.

6 You have made him to have
dominion over the works of Your
hands;
You have put all *things* under his feet,

7 All sheep and oxen—
Even the beasts of the field,

8 The birds of the air,
And the fish of the sea
That pass through the paths of the
seas.

9 O LORD, our Lord,
How excellent *is* Your name in all the
earth!

PSALM 9

Prayer and Thanksgiving for the LORD's Righteous Judgments

To the Chief Musician.
To *the tune of* "Death of the Son."ᵃ
A Psalm of David.

1 I will praise *You*, O LORD, with my
whole heart;
I will tell of all Your marvelous
works.

2 I will be glad and rejoice in You;
I will sing praise to Your name, O
Most High.

3 When my enemies turn back,
They shall fall and perish at Your
presence.

4 For You have maintained my right
and my cause;
You sat on the throne judging in
righteousness.

5 You have rebuked the nations,
You have destroyed the wicked;
You have blotted out their name
forever and ever.

6 O enemy, destructions are finished
forever!
And you have destroyed cities;
Even their memory has perished.

7 But the LORD shall endure
forever;
He has prepared His throne for
judgment.

8 He shall judge the world in
righteousness,
And He shall administer judgment
for the peoples in uprightness.

9 The LORD also will be a refuge for
the oppressed,
A refuge in times of trouble.

10 And those who know Your name will
put their trust in You;
For You, LORD, have not forsaken
those who seek You.

11 Sing praises to the LORD, who dwells
in Zion!
Declare His deeds among
the people.

12 When He avenges blood, He
remembers them;
He does not forget the cry of the
humble.

13 Have mercy on me, O LORD!
Consider my trouble from those who
hate me,
You who lift me up from the gates of
death,

14 That I may tell of all Your praise
In the gates of the daughter of Zion.
I will rejoice in Your salvation.

15 The nations have sunk down in the
pit *which* they made;
In the net which they hid, their own
foot is caught.

16 The LORD is known *by* the judgment
He executes;
The wicked is snared in the work of
his own hands.
                        Meditation.ᵃ   Selah

17 The wicked shall be turned into hell,
And all the nations that forget God.

18 For the needy shall not always be
forgotten;
The expectation of the poor shall *not*
perish forever.

19 Arise, O LORD,
Do not let man prevail;
Let the nations be judged in Your
sight.

20 Put them in fear, O LORD,
That the nations may know
themselves *to be but* men.   Selah

9:title ᵃHebrew *Muth Labben*   9:16 ᵃHebrew *Higgaion*

PSALM 10

A Song of Confidence in God's Triumph over Evil

1 Why do You stand afar off, O LORD?
  Why do You hide in times of trouble?
2 The wicked in *his* pride persecutes
    the poor;
  Let them be caught in the plots
    which they have devised.

3 For the wicked boasts of his heart's
    desire;
  He blesses the greedy *and* renounces
    the LORD.
4 The wicked in his proud countenance
    does not seek *God;*
  God *is* in none of his thoughts.

5 His ways are always prospering;
  Your judgments *are* far above, out of
    his sight;
  As for all his enemies, he sneers at
    them.
6 He has said in his heart, "I shall not
    be moved;
  I shall never be in adversity."

7 His mouth is full of cursing and
    deceit and oppression;
  Under his tongue *is* trouble and
    iniquity.
8 He sits in the lurking places of the
    villages;
  In the secret places he murders the
    innocent;
  His eyes are secretly fixed on the
    helpless.
9 He lies in wait secretly, as a lion in
    his den;
  He lies in wait to catch the poor;
  He catches the poor when he draws
    him into his net.

10 So he crouches, he lies low,
   That the helpless may fall by his
     strength.
11 He has said in his heart,
  "God has forgotten;
   He hides His face;
   He will never see."

12 Arise, O LORD!
   O God, lift up Your hand!
   Do not forget the humble.
13 Why do the wicked renounce God?
   He has said in his heart,
  "You will not require *an account.*"

14 But You have seen, for You observe
     trouble and grief,
   To repay *it* by Your hand.
   The helpless commits himself to You;
   You are the helper of the fatherless.
15 Break the arm of the wicked and the
     evil *man;*
   Seek out his wickedness *until* You
     find none.

16 The LORD *is* King forever and ever;
   The nations have perished out of His
     land.
17 LORD, You have heard the desire of
     the humble;
   You will prepare their heart;
   You will cause Your ear to hear,
18 To do justice to the fatherless and the
     oppressed,
   That the man of the earth may
     oppress no more.

PSALM 11

Faith in the LORD's Righteousness

To the Chief Musician. *A Psalm* of David.

1 In the LORD I put my trust;
  How can you say to my soul,
  "Flee *as* a bird to your mountain"?
2 For look! The wicked bend *their* bow,
  They make ready their arrow on the
    string,
  That they may shoot secretly at the
    upright in heart.
3 If the foundations are destroyed,
  What can the righteous do?

4 The LORD *is* in His holy temple,
  The LORD's throne *is* in heaven;

INTIMATE MOMENTS

Give him a break from his weekend chores either by mowing the lawn or arranging for it to be done.

His eyes behold,
His eyelids test the sons of men.
5 The LORD tests the righteous,
But the wicked and the one who
    loves violence His soul hates.
6 Upon the wicked He will rain coals;
Fire and brimstone and a burning
    wind
Shall be the portion of their cup.

7 For the LORD *is* righteous,
He loves righteousness;
His countenance beholds the upright.[a]

PSALM 12

Man's Treachery and God's Constancy

To the Chief Musician.
On an eight-stringed harp.[a] A Psalm of David.

1 Help, LORD, for the godly man ceases!
For the faithful disappear from
    among the sons of men.
2 They speak idly everyone with his
    neighbor;
With flattering lips *and* a double
    heart they speak.

3 May the LORD cut off all flattering lips,
And the tongue that speaks proud
    things,
4 Who have said,
"With our tongue we will prevail;
Our lips *are* our own;
Who *is* lord over us?"

5 "For the oppression of the poor, for
    the sighing of the needy,
Now I will arise," says the LORD;
"I will set *him* in the safety for which
    he yearns."

6 The words of the LORD *are* pure
    words,
Like silver tried in a furnace of earth,
Purified seven times.
7 You shall keep them, O LORD,
You shall preserve them from this
    generation forever.

8 The wicked prowl on every side,
When vileness is exalted among the
    sons of men.

PSALM 13

Trust in the Salvation of the LORD

To the Chief Musician. A Psalm of David.

1 How long, O LORD? Will You forget
    me forever?
How long will You hide Your face
    from me?
2 How long shall I take counsel in my
    soul,
Having sorrow in my heart daily?
How long will my enemy be exalted
    over me?

3 Consider *and* hear me, O LORD my
    God;
Enlighten my eyes,
Lest I sleep the *sleep of* death;
4 Lest my enemy say,
"I have prevailed against him";
Lest those who trouble me rejoice
    when I am moved.

5 But I have trusted in Your mercy;
My heart shall rejoice in Your
    salvation.
6 I will sing to the LORD,
Because He has dealt bountifully
    with me.

PSALM 14

Folly of the Godless, and God's Final Triumph

To the Chief Musician. *A Psalm* of David.

1 The fool has said in his heart,
"*There is* no God."
They are corrupt,
They have done abominable works,
There is none who does good.

2 The LORD looks down from heaven
    upon the children of men,
To see if there are any who
    understand, who seek God.
3 They have all turned aside,
They have together become corrupt;
There is none who does good,
No, not one.

4 Have all the workers of iniquity no
    knowledge,
Who eat up my people *as* they eat
    bread,
And do not call on the LORD?

11:7 [a]Or *The upright beholds His countenance*
12:title [a]Hebrew *sheminith*

BIBLICAL INSIGHTS • 15:1, 2

Uncovering Deceit

KING DAVID TOLD US why we should passionately long to banish deceit from our homes. He posed the question, "LORD, who may abide in Your tabernacle? Who may dwell in Your holy hill?" (Psalm 15:1). In other words, "Who gets the privilege of being near you, Lord?"

The answer is, "He who walks uprightly, and works righteousness, and speaks the truth in his heart" (15:2).

Honesty is vitally important to God. That is why it is crucial for us as couples to be honest with each other, and for parents to work to raise a generation of young people who gladly turn away from lies, who eagerly dwell near God, and who wholeheartedly pursue righteousness all their days.

Pray for wisdom and opportunities to uncover deceit and deal with it. God wants to help you with your children more than you can imagine. Perhaps your son is hanging around with some new friends and you feel unsettled. Or possibly you sense your daughter is hiding something or not being entirely truthful. Maybe there's nothing outwardly wrong; you just feel bothered.

Ask God for wisdom and insight into the situation. He loves to respond to the prayers of helpless parents! We have seen God orchestrate circumstances to enable parents to get an errant child back on the right track.

5   There they are in great fear,
       For God *is* with the generation of the
          righteous.
6   You shame the counsel of the poor,
       But the LORD *is* his refuge.

7   Oh, that the salvation of Israel *would
          come* out of Zion!
       When the LORD brings back the
          captivity of His people,
       Let Jacob rejoice *and* Israel be glad.

PSALM 15

The Character of Those Who May Dwell with the LORD

A Psalm of David.

1   LORD, who may abide in Your
          tabernacle?
       Who may dwell in Your holy hill?

2   He who walks uprightly,
       And works righteousness,
       And speaks the truth in his heart;

3   He *who* does not backbite with his
          tongue,
       Nor does evil to his neighbor,
       Nor does he take up a reproach
          against his friend;

4   In whose eyes a vile person is
          despised,
       But he honors those who fear the
          LORD;
       He *who* swears to his own hurt and
          does not change;

5   He *who* does not put out his money
          at usury,
       Nor does he take a bribe against
          the innocent.

       He who does these *things* shall never
          be moved.

PSALM 16

The Hope of the Faithful, and the Messiah's Victory

A Michtam of David.

1   Preserve me, O God, for in You I put
          my trust.

2   *O my soul,* you have said to the LORD,
       "You *are* my Lord,
       My goodness is nothing apart from
          You."

3   As for the saints who *are* on the earth,
       "They are the excellent ones, in whom
          is all my delight."

4   Their sorrows shall be multiplied
          who hasten *after* another *god;*
       Their drink offerings of blood I will
          not offer,
       Nor take up their names on my lips.

5   O LORD, *You are* the portion of my
          inheritance and my cup;

You maintain my lot.
6   The lines have fallen to me in
        pleasant *places;*
    Yes, I have a good inheritance.

7   I will bless the LORD who has given
        me counsel;
    My heart also instructs me in the
        night seasons.
8   I have set the LORD always before me;
    Because *He is* at my right hand I
        shall not be moved.

9   Therefore my heart is glad, and my
        glory rejoices;
    My flesh also will rest in hope.
10 For You will not leave my soul in
        Sheol,
    Nor will You allow Your Holy One to
        see corruption.
11 You will show me the path of life;
    In Your presence *is* fullness of joy;
    At Your right hand *are* pleasures
        forevermore.

PSALM 17

Prayer with Confidence in Final Salvation

A Prayer of David.

1   Hear a just cause, O LORD,
    Attend to my cry;
    Give ear to my prayer *which is* not
        from deceitful lips.
2   Let my vindication come from Your
        presence;
    Let Your eyes look on the things that
        are upright.

3   You have tested my heart;
    You have visited *me* in the night;
    You have tried me and have found
        nothing;
    I have purposed that my mouth shall
        not transgress.
4   Concerning the works of men,
    By the word of Your lips,
    I have kept away from the paths of
        the destroyer.
5   Uphold my steps in Your paths,
    That my footsteps may not slip.

6   I have called upon You, for You will
        hear me, O God;

Incline Your ear to me, *and* hear my
        speech.
7   Show Your marvelous
        lovingkindness by Your right
        hand,
    O You who save those who trust *in
        You*
    From those who rise up *against them.*
8   Keep me as the apple of Your eye;
    Hide me under the shadow of Your
        wings,
9   From the wicked who oppress me,
    From my deadly enemies who
        surround me.

10 They have closed up their fat *hearts;*
    With their mouths they speak proudly.
11 They have now surrounded us in our
        steps;
    They have set their eyes, crouching
        down to the earth,
12 As a lion is eager to tear his prey,
    And like a young lion lurking in
        secret places.

13 Arise, O LORD,
    Confront him, cast him down;
    Deliver my life from the wicked with
        Your sword,
14 With Your hand from men, O LORD,
    From men of the world *who have*
        their portion in *this* life,
    And whose belly You fill with Your
        hidden treasure.
    They are satisfied with children,
    And leave the rest of their *possession*
        for their babes.

15 As for me, I will see Your face in
        righteousness;
    I shall be satisfied when I awake in
        Your likeness.

PSALM 18

God the Sovereign Savior

To the Chief Musician. *A Psalm* of David the
servant of the LORD, who spoke to the LORD the
words of this song on the day that the LORD
delivered him from the hand of all his enemies
and from the hand of Saul. And he said:

1   I will love You, O LORD, my strength.
2   The LORD is my rock and my fortress
        and my deliverer;

My God, my strength, in whom I will
trust;
My shield and the horn of my
salvation, my stronghold.

3 I will call upon the LORD, *who is
worthy* to be praised;
So shall I be saved from my enemies.

4 The pangs of death surrounded me,
And the floods of ungodliness made
me afraid.

5 The sorrows of Sheol surrounded
me;
The snares of death confronted me.

6 In my distress I called upon the
LORD,
And cried out to my God;
He heard my voice from His temple,
And my cry came before Him, *even*
to His ears.

7 Then the earth shook and trembled;
The foundations of the hills also
quaked and were shaken,
Because He was angry.

8 Smoke went up from His nostrils,
And devouring fire from His mouth;
Coals were kindled by it.

9 He bowed the heavens also, and
came down
With darkness under His feet.

10 And He rode upon a cherub, and
flew;
He flew upon the wings of the wind.

11 He made darkness His secret place;
His canopy around Him *was* dark
waters
And thick clouds of the skies.

12 From the brightness before Him,
His thick clouds passed with
hailstones and coals of fire.

13 The LORD thundered from heaven,
And the Most High uttered His voice,
Hailstones and coals of fire.[a]

14 He sent out His arrows and scattered
the foe,
Lightnings in abundance, and He
vanquished them.

15 Then the channels of the sea were
seen,
The foundations of the world were
uncovered
At Your rebuke, O LORD,

At the blast of the breath of Your
nostrils.

16 He sent from above, He took me;
He drew me out of many waters.

17 He delivered me from my strong
enemy,
From those who hated me,
For they were too strong for me.

18 They confronted me in the day of
my calamity,
But the LORD was my support.

19 He also brought me out into a broad
place;
He delivered me because He
delighted in me.

20 The LORD rewarded me according to
my righteousness;
According to the cleanness of my
hands
He has recompensed me.

21 For I have kept the ways of the LORD,
And have not wickedly departed
from my God.

22 For all His judgments *were* before
me,
And I did not put away His statutes
from me.

23 I was also blameless before Him,
And I kept myself from my iniquity.

24 Therefore the LORD has recompensed
me according to my
righteousness,
According to the cleanness of my
hands in His sight.

25 With the merciful You will show
Yourself merciful;
With a blameless man You will show
Yourself blameless;

26 With the pure You will show
Yourself pure;
And with the devious You will show
Yourself shrewd.

27 For You will save the humble people,
But will bring down haughty looks.

28 For You will light my lamp;
The LORD my God will enlighten my
darkness.

18:13 [a]Following Masoretic Text, Targum, and
Vulgate; a few Hebrew manuscripts and Septuagint
omit *Hailstones and coals of fire.*

29 For by You I can run against a troop,
By my God I can leap over a wall.

30 *As for* God, His way *is* perfect;
The word of the LORD is proven;
He *is* a shield to all who trust in Him.

31 For who *is* God, except the LORD?
And who *is* a rock, except our God?

32 *It is* God who arms me with strength,
And makes my way perfect.

33 He makes my feet like the *feet of*
deer,
And sets me on my high places.

34 He teaches my hands to make war,
So that my arms can bend a bow of
bronze.

35 You have also given me the shield of
Your salvation;
Your right hand has held me up,
Your gentleness has made
me great.

36 You enlarged my path under me,
So my feet did not slip.

37 I have pursued my enemies and
overtaken them;
Neither did I turn back again till
they were destroyed.

38 I have wounded them,
So that they could not rise;
They have fallen under my feet.

39 For You have armed me with
strength for the battle;
You have subdued under me those
who rose up against me.

40 You have also given me the necks of
my enemies,
So that I destroyed those who hated
me.

41 They cried out, but *there was* none to
save;
Even to the LORD, but He did not
answer them.

42 Then I beat them as fine as the dust
before the wind;
I cast them out like dirt in the streets.

43 You have delivered me from the
strivings of the people;
You have made me the head of the
nations;

A people I have not known shall
serve me.

44 As soon as they hear of me they
obey me;
The foreigners submit to me.

45 The foreigners fade away,
And come frightened from their
hideouts.

46 The LORD lives!
Blessed *be* my Rock!
Let the God of my salvation be
exalted.

47 *It is* God who avenges me,
And subdues the peoples under me;

48 He delivers me from my enemies.
You also lift me up above those who
rise against me;
You have delivered me from the
violent man.

49 Therefore I will give thanks to You,
O LORD, among the Gentiles,
And sing praises to Your name.

50 Great deliverance He gives to His
king,
And shows mercy to His anointed,
To David and his descendants
forevermore.

PSALM 19

The Perfect Revelation of the LORD

To the Chief Musician. A Psalm of David.

1 The heavens declare the glory of
God;
And the firmament shows His
handiwork.

2 Day unto day utters speech,
And night unto night reveals
knowledge.

3 *There is* no speech nor language
Where their voice is not heard.

4 Their line[a] has gone out through all
the earth,
And their words to the end of the
world.

In them He has set a tabernacle for
the sun,

5 Which *is* like a bridegroom coming
out of his chamber,
And rejoices like a strong man to run
its race.

19:4 [a]Septuagint, Syriac, and Vulgate read *sound;*
Targum reads *business.*

6   Its rising *is* from one end of heaven,
     And its circuit to the other end;
     And there is nothing hidden from its
         heat.

7   The law of the LORD *is* perfect,
         converting the soul;
     The testimony of the LORD *is* sure,
         making wise the simple;

8   The statutes of the LORD *are* right,
         rejoicing the heart;
     The commandment of the LORD *is*
         pure, enlightening the eyes;

ROMANCE FAQ

**Q: *How important
is intimate conversation?***

According to an article I read recently, the typical couple spends only four minutes a day in meaningful conversation with each other. Four minutes! That's less time than the commercial breaks during a half-hour TV program.

A lot of us husbands don't realize that in order for our wives to consider us romantic, we must first of all be great friends and conversationalists. Grunts and one-word answers just won't cut it! Too many women feel that their husbands don't really need them—and bare-bones conversation confirms their sense of low personal value.

Many men who once were accomplished at deep conversation during courtship, seem to lose this talent later. You can rediscover the groove! Make a commitment to learn to make intimate conversation a priority with your wife. You need to talk and fill her in on the details of your life—not just facts, but *feelings*.

When a husband sincerely shows his desire for conversation and a deepening relationship—emotional intimacy—he will find that his wife is much more interested in sexual intimacy. Her dreams, hopes, desires, and disappointments are no longer divorced from the marriage bed, but are a part of it.

9   The fear of the LORD *is* clean,
         enduring forever;
     The judgments of the LORD *are* true
         and righteous altogether.

10   More to be desired *are they* than gold,
     Yea, than much fine gold;
     Sweeter also than honey and the
         honeycomb.

11   Moreover by them Your servant is
         warned,
     And in keeping them *there is* great
         reward.

12   Who can understand *his* errors?
     Cleanse me from secret *faults.*

13   Keep back Your servant also from
         presumptuous *sins;*
     Let them not have dominion over me.
     Then I shall be blameless,
     And I shall be innocent of great
         transgression.

14   Let the words of my mouth and the
         meditation of my heart
     Be acceptable in Your sight,
     O LORD, my strength and my
         Redeemer.

PSALM 20

The Assurance of God's Saving Work

To the Chief Musician. A Psalm of David.

1   May the LORD answer you in the day
         of trouble;
     May the name of the God of Jacob
         defend you;

2   May He send you help from the
         sanctuary,
     And strengthen you out of Zion;

3   May He remember all your offerings,
     And accept your burnt sacrifice.
                                    Selah

4   May He grant you according to your
         heart's *desire,*
     And fulfill all your purpose.

5   We will rejoice in your salvation,
     And in the name of our God we will
         set up *our* banners!
     May the LORD fulfill all your
         petitions.

6   Now I know that the LORD saves His
         anointed;

He will answer him from His holy
  heaven
With the saving strength of His right
  hand.

7 Some *trust* in chariots, and some in
  horses;
But we will remember the name of
  the LORD our God.

8 They have bowed down and fallen;
But we have risen and stand upright.

9 Save, LORD!
May the King answer us when we
  call.

PSALM 21

Joy in the Salvation of the LORD

To the Chief Musician. A Psalm of David.

1 The king shall have joy in Your
  strength, O LORD;
And in Your salvation how greatly
  shall he rejoice!

2 You have given him his heart's
  desire,
And have not withheld the request of
  his lips.   Selah

3 For You meet him with the blessings
  of goodness;
You set a crown of pure gold upon
  his head.

4 He asked life from You, *and* You gave
  it to him—
Length of days forever and ever.

5 His glory *is* great in Your salvation;
Honor and majesty You have placed
  upon him.

6 For You have made him most blessed
  forever;
You have made him exceedingly glad
  with Your presence.

7 For the king trusts in the LORD,
And through the mercy of the Most
  High he shall not be moved.

8 Your hand will find all Your enemies;
Your right hand will find those who
  hate You.

9 You shall make them as a fiery oven
  in the time of Your anger;

The LORD shall swallow them up in
  His wrath,
And the fire shall devour them.

10 Their offspring You shall destroy
  from the earth,
And their descendants from among
  the sons of men.

11 For they intended evil against You;
They devised a plot *which* they are
  not able *to perform.*

12 Therefore You will make them turn
  their back;
You will make ready *Your arrows* on
  Your string toward their faces.

13 Be exalted, O LORD, in Your own
  strength!
We will sing and praise Your power.

PSALM 22

The Suffering, Praise, and Posterity of the Messiah

To the Chief Musician. Set to
"The Deer of the Dawn."[a] A Psalm of David.

1 My God, My God, why have You
  forsaken Me?
Why are You so far from helping Me,
And from the words of My groaning?

2 O My God, I cry in the daytime, but
  You do not hear;
And in the night season, and am not
  silent.

3 But You *are* holy,
Enthroned in the praises of Israel.

4 Our fathers trusted in You;
They trusted, and You delivered
  them.

5 They cried to You, and were
  delivered;
They trusted in You, and were not
  ashamed.

6 But I *am* a worm, and no man;
A reproach of men, and despised by
  the people.

7 All those who see Me ridicule Me;
They shoot out the lip, they shake
  the head, *saying,*

8 "He trusted[a] in the LORD, let Him
  rescue Him;
Let Him deliver Him, since He
  delights in Him!"

22:title [a]Hebrew *Aijeleth Hashahar*

⁹ But You *are* He who took Me out of
the womb;
You made Me trust *while* on My
mother's breasts.
¹⁰ I was cast upon You from birth.
From My mother's womb
You *have been* My God.
¹¹ Be not far from Me,
For trouble *is* near;
For *there is* none to help.

¹² Many bulls have surrounded Me;
Strong *bulls* of Bashan have
encircled Me.
¹³ They gape at Me *with* their mouths,
Like a raging and roaring lion.

¹⁴ I am poured out like water,
And all My bones are out of joint;
My heart is like wax;
It has melted within Me.
¹⁵ My strength is dried up like a
potsherd,
And My tongue clings to My jaws;
You have brought Me to the dust of
death.

¹⁶ For dogs have surrounded Me;
The congregation of the wicked has
enclosed Me.
They pierced^a My hands and My feet;
¹⁷ I can count all My bones.
They look *and* stare at Me.
¹⁸ They divide My garments among
them,
And for My clothing they cast lots.
¹⁹ But You, O LORD, do not be far from
Me;
O My Strength, hasten to help Me!
²⁰ Deliver Me from the sword,
My precious *life* from the power of
the dog.
²¹ Save Me from the lion's mouth
And from the horns of the
wild oxen!

You have answered Me.

²² I will declare Your name to My
brethren;
In the midst of the assembly I will
praise You.
²³ You who fear the LORD, praise Him!
All you descendants of Jacob, glorify
Him,

And fear Him, all you offspring of
Israel!
²⁴ For He has not despised nor
abhorred the affliction of the
afflicted;
Nor has He hidden His face from Him;
But when He cried to Him, He heard.

²⁵ My praise *shall be* of You in the
great assembly;
I will pay My vows before those who
fear Him.
²⁶ The poor shall eat and be satisfied;
Those who seek Him will praise the
LORD.
Let your heart live forever!

²⁷ All the ends of the world
Shall remember and turn to the
LORD,
And all the families of the nations
Shall worship before You.^a
²⁸ For the kingdom *is* the LORD's,
And He rules over the nations.

²⁹ All the prosperous of the earth
Shall eat and worship;
All those who go down to the dust
Shall bow before Him,
Even he who cannot keep himself
alive.

³⁰ A posterity shall serve Him.
It will be recounted of the Lord to
the *next* generation,
³¹ They will come and declare His
righteousness to a people who
will be born,
That He has done *this*.

PSALM 23

The LORD the Shepherd of His People

A Psalm of David.

¹ The LORD *is* my shepherd;
I shall not want.
² He makes me to lie down in green
pastures;

22:8 ^aSeptuagint, Syriac, and Vulgate read *hoped;*
Targum reads *praised.* **22:16** ^aFollowing some
Hebrew manuscripts, Septuagint, Syriac, Vulgate;
Masoretic Text reads *Like a lion.* **22:27** ^aFollowing
Masoretic Text, Septuagint, and Targum; Arabic,
Syriac, and Vulgate read *Him.*

He leads me beside the still waters.
3 He restores my soul;
He leads me in the paths of
righteousness
For His name's sake.

4 Yea, though I walk through the
valley of the shadow of death,
I will fear no evil;
For You *are* with me;
Your rod and Your staff, they
comfort me.

5 You prepare a table before me in the
presence of my enemies;
You anoint my head with oil;
My cup runs over.

6 Surely goodness and mercy shall
follow me
All the days of my life;
And I will dwell[a] in the house of the
LORD
Forever.

PSALM 24

The King of Glory and His Kingdom

A Psalm of David.

1 The earth *is* the LORD's, and all its
fullness,
The world and those who dwell
therein.

2 For He has founded it upon the seas,
And established it upon the waters.

3 Who may ascend into the hill of the
LORD?
Or who may stand in His holy place?

4 He who has clean hands and a pure
heart,
Who has not lifted up his soul to an
idol,
Nor sworn deceitfully.

5 He shall receive blessing from the
LORD,
And righteousness from the God of
his salvation.

6 This *is* Jacob, the generation of those
who seek Him,
Who seek Your face.   Selah

7 Lift up your heads, O you gates!

And be lifted up, you everlasting
doors!
And the King of glory shall come in.

8 Who *is* this King of glory?
The LORD strong and mighty,
The LORD mighty in battle.

9 Lift up your heads, O you gates!
Lift up, you everlasting doors!
And the King of glory shall come in.

10 Who is this King of glory?
The LORD of hosts,
He *is* the King of glory.   Selah

PSALM 25

A Plea for Deliverance and Forgiveness

A Psalm of David.

1 To You, O LORD, I lift up my soul.

2 O my God, I trust in You;
Let me not be ashamed;
Let not my enemies triumph over me.

3 Indeed, let no one who waits on You
be ashamed;
Let those be ashamed who deal
treacherously without cause.

4 Show me Your ways, O LORD;
Teach me Your paths.

5 Lead me in Your truth and teach me,
For You *are* the God of my salvation;
On You I wait all the day.

6 Remember, O LORD, Your tender
mercies and Your
lovingkindnesses,
For they *are* from of old.

7 Do not remember the sins of my
youth, nor my transgressions;
According to Your mercy remember
me,
For Your goodness' sake, O LORD.

8 Good and upright *is* the LORD;
Therefore He teaches sinners in the
way.

9 The humble He guides in justice,
And the humble He teaches His way.

10 All the paths of the LORD *are* mercy
and truth,
To such as keep His covenant and
His testimonies.

11 For Your name's sake, O LORD,
Pardon my iniquity, for it
is great.

23:6 [a]Following Septuagint, Syriac, Targum, and
Vulgate; Masoretic Text reads *return*.

12 Who *is* the man that fears the LORD?
Him shall He[a] teach in the way He[b]
chooses.
13 He himself shall dwell in prosperity,
And his descendants shall inherit the
earth.
14 The secret of the LORD *is* with those
who fear Him,
And He will show them His
covenant.
15 My eyes *are* ever toward the LORD,
For He shall pluck my feet out of the
net.

16 Turn Yourself to me, and have
mercy on me,
For I *am* desolate and afflicted.
17 The troubles of my heart have
enlarged;
Bring me out of my distresses!
18 Look on my affliction and my pain,
And forgive all my sins.
19 Consider my enemies, for they are
many;
And they hate me with cruel hatred.
20 Keep my soul, and deliver me;
Let me not be ashamed, for I put my
trust in You.
21 Let integrity and uprightness
preserve me,
For I wait for You.

22 Redeem Israel, O God,
Out of all their troubles!

PSALM 26

A Prayer for Divine Scrutiny and Redemption

A Psalm of David.

1 Vindicate me, O LORD,
For I have walked in my integrity.
I have also trusted in the LORD;
I shall not slip.
2 Examine me, O LORD, and prove me;
Try my mind and my heart.
3 For Your lovingkindness *is* before
my eyes,
And I have walked in Your truth.
4 I have not sat with idolatrous mortals,
Nor will I go in with hypocrites.
5 I have hated the assembly of
evildoers,
And will not sit with the wicked.

6 I will wash my hands in innocence;
So I will go about Your altar, O LORD,
7 That I may proclaim with the voice
of thanksgiving,
And tell of all Your wondrous works.
8 LORD, I have loved the habitation of
Your house,
And the place where Your glory
dwells.

9 Do not gather my soul with sinners,
Nor my life with bloodthirsty men,

25:12 [a]Or *he* [b]Or *he*

A Prayer for Victory

The Bible features many prayers that I find both useful and appropriate for those who want to enjoy a successful, blessed marriage and family life. King David uttered one of those prayers: "O my God, I trust in You; let me not be ashamed; let not my enemies triumph over me" (25:2).

That is the kind of prayer we need for our lives as spouses and as parents! We need to give such a prayer a prominent place in our regular arsenal. Wartime calls for warfare prayers! We also need to pray this way for our teenagers as they move into the enemy territory of adolescence.

Married couples, parents, pre-adolescents and teens all face a world full of landmines, a world growing ever more hostile toward the principles of godly marriage and parenthood. For that reason, we need the kind of faith the psalmist prayed for, so that we might rely on God to give us the strength and direction to live in a way that glorifies Him and encourages others. Armed with faith and shielded by such prayers, we can be victorious over the enemies who would come against what we are trying to accomplish as Christian families.

10 In whose hands *is* a sinister scheme,
And whose right hand is full of
     bribes.

11 But as for me, I will walk in my
     integrity;
Redeem me and be merciful to me.

12 My foot stands in an even place;
In the congregations I will bless the
     LORD.

PSALM 27

An Exuberant Declaration of Faith

A Psalm of David.

1 The LORD *is* my light and my
     salvation;
Whom shall I fear?
The LORD *is* the strength of my life;
Of whom shall I be afraid?

2 When the wicked came against me
To eat up my flesh,
My enemies and foes,
They stumbled and fell.

3 Though an army may encamp
     against me,
My heart shall not fear;
Though war may rise against me,
In this I *will be* confident.

4 One *thing* I have desired of the LORD,
That will I seek:
That I may dwell in the house of the
     LORD
All the days of my life,
To behold the beauty of the LORD,
And to inquire in His temple.

5 For in the time of trouble
He shall hide me in His pavilion;
In the secret place of His tabernacle
He shall hide me;
He shall set me high upon a rock.

6 And now my head shall be lifted up
     above my enemies all around me;
Therefore I will offer sacrifices of joy
     in His tabernacle;
I will sing, yes, I will sing praises to
     the LORD.

7 Hear, O LORD, *when* I cry with my
     voice!
Have mercy also upon me, and
     answer me.

8 *When You said,* "Seek My face,"
My heart said to You, "Your face,
     LORD, I will seek."

9 Do not hide Your face from me;
Do not turn Your servant away in
     anger;
You have been my help;
Do not leave me nor forsake me,
O God of my salvation.

10 When my father and my mother
     forsake me,
Then the LORD will take care of me.

11 Teach me Your way, O LORD,
And lead me in a smooth path,
     because of my enemies.

12 Do not deliver me to the will of my
     adversaries;
For false witnesses have risen
     against me,
And such as breathe out violence.

13 *I would have lost heart,* unless I had
     believed
That I would see the goodness of the
     LORD
In the land of the living.

14 Wait on the LORD;
Be of good courage,
And He shall strengthen your heart;
Wait, I say, on the LORD!

PSALM 28

Rejoicing in Answered Prayer

A Psalm of David.

1 To You I will cry, O LORD my Rock:
Do not be silent to me,
Lest, if You *are* silent to me,
I become like those who go down to
     the pit.

2 Hear the voice of my supplications
When I cry to You,
When I lift up my hands toward
     Your holy sanctuary.

3 Do not take me away with the
     wicked
And with the workers of iniquity,
Who speak peace to their neighbors,
But evil *is* in their hearts.

4 Give them according to their deeds,
And according to the wickedness of
     their endeavors;

Give them according to the work of
their hands;
Render to them what they deserve.
5 Because they do not regard the
works of the LORD,
Nor the operation of His hands,
He shall destroy them
And not build them up.

6 Blessed *be* the LORD,
Because He has heard the voice of
my supplications!
7 The LORD *is* my strength and my
shield;
My heart trusted in Him, and I am
helped;
Therefore my heart greatly rejoices,
And with my song I will praise Him.

8 The LORD *is* their strength,[a]
And He *is* the saving refuge of His
anointed.
9 Save Your people,
And bless Your inheritance;
Shepherd them also,
And bear them up forever.

PSALM 29

Praise to God in His Holiness and Majesty

A Psalm of David.

1 Give unto the LORD, O you mighty
ones,
Give unto the LORD glory and
strength.
2 Give unto the LORD the glory due to
His name;
Worship the LORD in the beauty of
holiness.
3 The voice of the LORD *is* over the
waters;
The God of glory thunders;
The LORD *is* over many waters.
4 The voice of the LORD *is* powerful;
The voice of the LORD *is* full of
majesty.
5 The voice of the LORD breaks the
cedars,
Yes, the LORD splinters the cedars of
Lebanon.
6 He makes them also skip like a calf,

Lebanon and Sirion like a young
wild ox.
7 The voice of the LORD divides the
flames of fire.
8 The voice of the LORD shakes the
wilderness;
The LORD shakes the Wilderness of
Kadesh.
9 The voice of the LORD makes the
deer give birth,
And strips the forests bare;
And in His temple everyone says,
"Glory!"

10 The LORD sat *enthroned* at the Flood,
And the LORD sits as King forever.
11 The LORD will give strength to His
people;
The LORD will bless His people with
peace.

PSALM 30

The Blessedness of Answered Prayer

A Psalm. A Song at the dedication of the
house of David.

1 I will extol You, O LORD, for You
have lifted me up,
And have not let my foes rejoice over
me.
2 O LORD my God, I cried out to You,
And You healed me.
3 O LORD, You brought my soul up
from the grave;
You have kept me alive, that I should
not go down to the pit.[a]

4 Sing praise to the LORD, you saints of
His,
And give thanks at the remembrance
of His holy name.[a]
5 For His anger *is but for* a moment,
His favor *is for* life;
Weeping may endure for a night,
But joy *comes* in the morning.

6 Now in my prosperity I said,
"I shall never be moved."

28:8 [a]Following Masoretic Text and Targum;
Septuagint, Syriac, and Vulgate read *the strength of
His people*. **30:3** [a]Following Qere and Targum;
Kethib, Septuagint, Syriac, and Vulgate read *from
those who descend to the pit*. **30:4** [a]Or *His holiness*

LORD, by Your favor You have made
   my mountain stand strong;
You hid Your face, *and* I was
   troubled.

I cried out to You, O LORD;
And to the LORD I made supplication:
"What profit *is there* in my blood,
When I go down to the pit?
Will the dust praise You?
Will it declare Your truth?
⁰ Hear, O LORD, and have mercy on me;
LORD, be my helper!"

¹ You have turned for me my
     mourning into dancing;
You have put off my sackcloth and
   clothed me with gladness,
² To the end that *my* glory may sing
   praise to You and not be silent.
O LORD my God, I will give thanks to
   You forever.

PSALM 31

The LORD a Fortress in Adversity

To the Chief Musician. A Psalm of David.

¹ In You, O LORD, I put my trust;
Let me never be ashamed;
Deliver me in Your righteousness.
² Bow down Your ear to me,
Deliver me speedily;
Be my rock of refuge,
A fortress of defense to save me.

³ For You *are* my rock and my
     fortress;
Therefore, for Your name's sake,
Lead me and guide me.
⁴ Pull me out of the net which they
     have secretly laid for me,
For You *are* my strength.
⁵ Into Your hand I commit my spirit;
You have redeemed me, O LORD God
   of truth.

⁶ I have hated those who regard
     useless idols;
But I trust in the LORD.
⁷ I will be glad and rejoice in Your
     mercy,
For You have considered my trouble;
You have known my soul in
   adversities,

⁸ And have not shut me up into the
     hand of the enemy;
You have set my feet in a wide place.

⁹ Have mercy on me, O LORD, for I am
     in trouble;
My eye wastes away with grief,
Yes, my soul and my body!
¹⁰ For my life is spent with grief,
And my years with sighing;
My strength fails because of my
   iniquity,
And my bones waste away.
¹¹ I am a reproach among all my
     enemies,
But especially among my neighbors,
And *am* repulsive to my
   acquaintances;
Those who see me outside flee from
   me.
¹² I am forgotten like a dead man, out
   of mind;
I am like a broken vessel.
¹³ For I hear the slander of many;
Fear *is* on every side;
While they take counsel together
     against me,
They scheme to take away my life.

¹⁴ But as for me, I trust in You, O LORD;
I say, "You *are* my God."
¹⁵ My times *are* in Your hand;
Deliver me from the hand of my
     enemies,
And from those who persecute me.
¹⁶ Make Your face shine upon Your
     servant;
Save me for Your mercies' sake.
¹⁷ Do not let me be ashamed, O LORD,
     for I have called upon You;
Let the wicked be ashamed;
Let them be silent in the grave.
¹⁸ Let the lying lips be put to silence,
Which speak insolent things proudly
     and contemptuously against the
     righteous.

¹⁹ Oh, how great *is* Your goodness,
Which You have laid up for those
     who fear You,
Which You have prepared for those
     who trust in You
In the presence of the sons
     of men!

Confess Your Sin

WHEN YOU TRY TO KEEP some sin secret, your spirit becomes increasingly troubled. That was certainly the experience of King David, "When I kept silent, my bones grew old through my groaning all the day long. For day and night Your hand was heavy upon me; my vitality was turned into the drought of summer" (32:3, 4).

David realized he could not go on until he confessed his sin to God, "I acknowledged my sin to You, and my iniquity I have not hidden. I said, 'I will confess my transgressions to the LORD,' and You forgave the iniquity of my sin" (32:5).

Repentance means *to turn around and go the other way*. When you indulge a sinful habit, it is like getting in a car and driving away from God. When you repent, you stop moving away from God and turn around to face Him, and through His power start moving toward Him again. Genuine repentance brings a sorrow that comes from realizing that you have offended the very holiness of God.

How does God respond when you come to Him, broken and repentant? He offers complete forgiveness and cleansing—and He'll free you from the crushing weight of guilt and shame.

20 You shall hide them in the secret
    place of Your presence
From the plots of man;
You shall keep them secretly in a
    pavilion
From the strife of tongues.
21 Blessed *be* the LORD,
For He has shown me His marvelous
    kindness in a strong city!
22 For I said in my haste,
"I am cut off from before Your
    eyes";
Nevertheless You heard the voice of
    my supplications
When I cried out to You.

23 Oh, love the LORD, all you His saints!
For the LORD preserves the faithful,
And fully repays the proud person.
24 Be of good courage,
And He shall strengthen your heart,
All you who hope in the LORD.

PSALM 32

The Joy of Forgiveness

A Psalm of David. A Contemplation.[a]

1 Blessed *is he whose* transgression *is*
    forgiven,
Whose sin *is* covered.
2 Blessed *is* the man to whom the LORD
    does not impute iniquity,
And in whose spirit *there is* no deceit.

3 When I kept silent, my bones grew old
Through my groaning all the day
    long.
4 For day and night Your hand was
    heavy upon me;
My vitality was turned into the
    drought of summer.   Selah
5 I acknowledged my sin to You,
And my iniquity I have not hidden.
I said, "I will confess my
    transgressions to the LORD,"
And You forgave the iniquity of my
    sin.   Selah

6 For this cause everyone who is godly
    shall pray to You
In a time when You may be found;
Surely in a flood of great waters
They shall not come near him.
7 You *are* my hiding place;
You shall preserve me from trouble;
You shall surround me with songs of
    deliverance.   Selah

8 I will instruct you and teach you in
    the way you should go;
I will guide you with My eye.
9 Do not be like the horse *or* like the
    mule,
Which have no understanding,
Which must be harnessed with bit
    and bridle,
Else they will not come near you.
10 Many sorrows *shall be* to the wicked;

32:title [a]Hebrew *Maschil*

DEVOTIONS FOR COUPLES • 32:6
Reasons to Pray Together

Scripture gives several compelling reasons for couples to faithfully and regularly pray together. Barbara and I have found that the more we put these into practice, the closer we come to one another and to the Lord.

First, we are commanded to pray. Psalm 32:6 says, "everyone who is godly shall pray to You in a time when you may be found." Jesus said we are to pray at all times and "not lose heart" (Luke 18:1). Paul told us to "pray without ceasing" (1 Thess. 5:17). If you are a believer in Christ, then prayer should define your life.

Second, through prayer we meet with God and build a relationship with him. What an unspeakable honor to come boldly into the presence of the Creator of the universe! The Scriptures tell us that God inhabits the praises of His people (see Psalm 22:3, KJV). God delights in hearing us acknowledge His goodness, character, and kindness; and when we pray, He comes to dwell in the middle of our marriage and our family. One wife told us, "Prayer together helps keep God in the center." Through prayer, God comes to dwell in the middle of your marriage and family!

Third, in prayer we have the opportunity to confess (and repent of) our sins to God and receive a clean conscience in return. In 1 John 1:9 we learn, "If we confess our sins, He is faithful and righteous to forgive us our sins and to cleanse us from all unrighteousness."

Fourth, prayer is how we receive answers and wisdom from the Lord. If any of you lacks wisdom, let him ask of God, who gives to all liberally and without reproach, and it will be given to him" (James 1:5). Prayer reveals God's wisdom to us. God delights in giving you the insights you need to handle the problems you face. There's nothing quite like crying out to God together as a couple, asking Him for wisdom from above to be able to handle life's challenges here.

Finally, prayer lightens our load. Jesus said, "Come to Me, all who labor and are heavy laden, and I will give you rest" (Matt. 11:28). Prayer is a very practical way to exchange your worries for peace, "Be anxious for nothing, but in everything by prayer and supplication, with thanksgiving, let your requests be made known to God; and the peace of God, which surpasses all understanding, will guard your hearts and minds through Christ Jesus" (Phil. 4:6, 7).

Praying together as a couple is a spiritual experience, simple but profound. As you grow in this spiritual discipline, you'll unlock many other benefits to experiencing God through prayer.

But he who trusts in the LORD, mercy
    shall surround him.
11 Be glad in the LORD and rejoice, you
    righteous;
And shout for joy, all *you* upright in
    heart!

PSALM 33

The Sovereignty of the LORD in Creation and History

1 Rejoice in the LORD, O you righteous!
    For praise from the upright is
      beautiful.
2 Praise the LORD with the harp;

Make melody to Him with an
    instrument of ten strings.
3 Sing to Him a new song;
Play skillfully with a shout
    of joy.

4 For the word of the LORD *is* right,
And all His work *is done* in truth.
5 He loves righteousness and
    justice;
The earth is full of the goodness of
    the LORD.

6 By the word of the LORD the heavens
    were made,
And all the host of them by the
    breath of His mouth.

DEVOTIONS FOR COUPLES · 33:6, 9
Verbally Plant Good Seeds

When God created the universe, he used a unique vehicle—words. The psalmist records how God created all that we see: "By the *word* of the Lord the heavens were made ... For He *spoke*, and it was done; He *commanded*, and it stood fast" (Psalm 33:6, 9, italics added).

When God wanted to free Israel from brutal slavery in Egypt, again He used words: "He *spoke*, and there came swarms of flies, and lice in all their territory . . . He *spoke*, and locust came, young locusts without number" (Psalm 105:31,34, italics added).

God conceived human life in His mind and gave it birth through His words. He could have fashioned creation gently in His hands—yet He chose to use words. He spoke, and it "stood fast."

In a similar way, the words you use can be powerful and even life-giving to your spouse. One of the most important things about a married couple is what they say to each other. When positive words flow, the relationship grows robust and flourishes. But if the lines of understanding and positive communication go down permanently, it is only a matter of time before that marriage dies. You can create life in your mate with your positive words, or you can inflict destruction with negative or neglectful words.

During World War II many factories in the United States were converted into manufacturing firms producing ammunition, ships, and other wartime resources. Posted throughout those factories were little signs with these words, "Loose lips sink ships." Today, we need little signs in our homes that read, "Loose lips sink partnerships."

Proverbs 12:25 is clear, "Anxiety in the heart of man causes depression, but a good word makes it glad." Notice the impact of a "good word." Gladness comes not from a sentence or a paragraph or from an entire message. Gladness comes from just *one* well-placed, positive word!

Be sure to appreciate the power of words. They can assault your mate or honor him or her as a valuable person who has God-given worth and assets. Your efforts to give unconditional acceptance will go for naught if you sow pessimistic, critical, or unsympathetic words into the heart of your mate.

---

7   He gathers the waters of the sea
       together as a heap;[a]
    He lays up the deep in storehouses.

8   Let all the earth fear the LORD;
    Let all the inhabitants of the world
       stand in awe of Him.

9   For He spoke, and it was *done;*
    He commanded, and it stood fast.

10 The LORD brings the counsel of the
       nations to nothing;
    He makes the plans of the peoples of
       no effect.

11 The counsel of the LORD stands
       forever,
    The plans of His heart to all
       generations.

12 Blessed *is* the nation whose God *is*
       the LORD,
    The people He has chosen as His
       own inheritance.

13 The LORD looks from heaven;
    He sees all the sons of men.

14 From the place of His dwelling He
       looks
    On all the inhabitants of the earth;

15 He fashions their hearts individually;
    He considers all their works.

16 No king *is* saved by the multitude of
       an army;
    A mighty man is not delivered by
       great strength.

17 A horse *is* a vain hope for safety;
    Neither shall it deliver *any* by its
       great strength.

18 Behold, the eye of the LORD *is* on
       those who fear Him,
    On those who hope in His mercy,

33:7 [a]Septuagint, Targum, and Vulgate read *in a vessel.*

¹⁹ To deliver their soul from death,
And to keep them alive in famine.

²⁰ Our soul waits for the LORD;
He *is* our help and our shield.

²¹ For our heart shall rejoice in Him,
Because we have trusted in His holy
name.

²² Let Your mercy, O LORD, be upon us,
Just as we hope in You.

PSALM 34

The Happiness of Those Who Trust in God

A Psalm of David when he pretended madness before Abimelech, who drove him away, and he departed.

¹ I will bless the LORD at all times;
His praise *shall* continually *be* in my
mouth.

² My soul shall make its boast in the
LORD;
The humble shall hear *of it* and be
glad.

³ Oh, magnify the LORD with me,
And let us exalt His name together.

⁴ I sought the LORD, and He heard me,
And delivered me from all my fears.

⁵ They looked to Him and were
radiant,
And their faces were not ashamed.

⁶ This poor man cried out, and the
LORD heard *him,*
And saved him out of all his
troubles.

⁷ The angel[a] of the LORD encamps all
around those who fear Him,
And delivers them.

⁸ Oh, taste and see that the LORD *is*
good;
Blessed *is* the man *who* trusts in
Him!

⁹ Oh, fear the LORD, you His saints!
There is no want to those who fear
Him.

¹⁰ The young lions lack and suffer
hunger;
But those who seek the LORD shall
not lack any good *thing.*

34:7 [a]Or *Angel*

BIBLICAL INSIGHTS • 34:4

Assassinate Fear through Faith in a Great God

AS MENTIONED EARLIER in the Book of Joshua, the phrase "fear not" appears 365 times in the Bible. Like a daily vitamin, God has provided just what we need to conquer our daily dreads.

Faith in Jesus Christ and the promises of His Word will cause fear to flee. Instead of feeling terrorized, paralyzed, and hypnotized by our fears, faith galvanizes our character with courage. Why not commit one or more of the following verses to memory?

- "I sought the LORD, and He heard me, and delivered me from all my fears" (Ps. 34:4).

- "Whenever I am afraid, I will trust in You" (Ps. 56:3).

- "Be strong and courageous; do not be afraid nor dismayed before the king of Assyria, nor before all the multitude that is with him; for there are more with us than with him. With him is an arm of flesh; but with us is the LORD our God, to help us and to fight our battles" (2 Chron. 32:7, 8).

- "You will keep him in perfect peace, whose mind is stayed on You" (Isaiah 26:3).

If you struggle with fear in your marriage and family, take those fears to a God who not only tells you not to fear, but who also gives you reason *not* to fear. He is the One Who can deliver you from your fears and replace them with peace, comfort, and courage.

¹¹ Come, you children, listen to me;
I will teach you the fear of the LORD.

¹² Who *is* the man *who* desires life,
And loves *many* days, that he may
see good?

¹³ Keep your tongue from evil,
And your lips from speaking deceit.

¹⁴ Depart from evil and do good;
Seek peace and pursue it.

15 The eyes of the LORD *are* on the
righteous,
And His ears *are open* to their cry.
16 The face of the LORD *is* against those
who do evil,
To cut off the remembrance of them
from the earth.
17 *The righteous* cry out, and the LORD
hears,
And delivers them out of all their
troubles.
18 The LORD *is* near to those who have a
broken heart,
And saves such as have a contrite
spirit.
19 Many *are* the afflictions of the
righteous,
But the LORD delivers him out of
them all.
20 He guards all his bones;
Not one of them is broken.
21 Evil shall slay the wicked,
And those who hate the righteous
shall be condemned.
22 The LORD redeems the soul of His
servants,
And none of those who trust in Him
shall be condemned.

PSALM 35

The LORD the Avenger of His People

A Psalm of David.

1 Plead *my cause,* O LORD, with those
who strive with me;
Fight against those who fight
against me.
2 Take hold of shield and buckler,
And stand up for my help.
3 Also draw out the spear,
And stop those who pursue me.
Say to my soul,
"I *am* your salvation."

4 Let those be put to shame and
brought to dishonor
Who seek after my life;
Let those be turned back and
brought to confusion
Who plot my hurt.
5 Let them be like chaff before the
wind,

And let the angel[a] of the LORD chase
them.
6 Let their way be dark and slippery,
And let the angel of the LORD pursue
them.
7 For without cause they have hidden
their net for me *in* a pit,
Which they have dug without cause
for my life.
8 Let destruction come upon him
unexpectedly,
And let his net that he has hidden
catch himself;
Into that very destruction let him fall.

9 And my soul shall be joyful in the
LORD;
It shall rejoice in His salvation.
10 All my bones shall say,
"LORD, who *is* like You,
Delivering the poor from him who is
too strong for him,
Yes, the poor and the needy from
him who plunders him?"

11 Fierce witnesses rise up;
They ask me *things* that I do not
know.
12 They reward me evil for good,
To the sorrow of my soul.
13 But as for me, when they were sick,
My clothing *was* sackcloth;
I humbled myself with fasting;
And my prayer would return to my
own heart.
14 I paced about as though *he were* my
friend *or* brother;
I bowed down heavily, as one who
mourns *for his* mother.

15 But in my adversity they rejoiced
And gathered together;
Attackers gathered against me,
And I did not know *it;*
They tore *at* me and did not cease;
16 With ungodly mockers at feasts
They gnashed at me with their teeth.

17 Lord, how long will You look on?
Rescue me from their destructions,
My precious *life* from the lions.
18 I will give You thanks in the great
assembly;

35:5 [a]Or *Angel*

I will praise You among many
    people.
19 Let them not rejoice over me who are
    wrongfully my enemies;
    Nor let them wink with the eye who
    hate me without a cause.
20 For they do not speak peace,
    But they devise deceitful matters
    Against *the* quiet ones in the land.
21 They also opened their mouth wide
    against me,
    And said, "Aha, aha!
    Our eyes have seen *it.*"
22 *This* You have seen, O LORD;
    Do not keep silence.
    O Lord, do not be far from me.
23 Stir up Yourself, and awake to my
    vindication,
    To my cause, my God and my Lord.
24 Vindicate me, O LORD my God,
    according to Your righteousness;
    And let them not rejoice over me.
25 Let them not say in their hearts, "Ah,
    so we would have it!"
    Let them not say, "We have
    swallowed him up."
26 Let them be ashamed and brought to
    mutual confusion
    Who rejoice at my hurt;
    Let them be clothed with shame and
    dishonor
    Who exalt themselves against me.

27 Let them shout for joy and be glad,
    Who favor my righteous cause;
    And let them say continually,
   "Let the LORD be magnified,
    Who has pleasure in the prosperity
    of His servant."
28 And my tongue shall speak of Your
    righteousness
    And of Your praise all the day long.

PSALM 36

Man's Wickedness and God's Perfections

To the Chief Musician. *A Psalm* of David the
    servant of the LORD.

1 An oracle within my heart
    concerning the transgression of
    the wicked:
    There is no fear of God before his
    eyes.
2 For he flatters himself in his own
    eyes,
    When he finds out his iniquity *and*
    when he hates.
3 The words of his mouth *are*
    wickedness and deceit;
    He has ceased to be wise *and* to do
    good.
4 He devises wickedness on his bed;
    He sets himself in a way *that is* not
    good;
    He does not abhor evil.

PARENTING MATTERS

Q: How do we balance teaching our children to be truthful with knowing they will face the consequences of confessing their mistakes?

First of all, it is important to teach your children to be honest and truthful, regardless of the severity of the consequences they may face. In many (if not most) cases, people lie and deceive in an attempt to avoid the responsibility for consequences of their mistakes, or to maintain illegitimate control.

One reason lying is an affront to God is that it displays a lack of trust in Him. You must teach your child that it's better to tell the truth and trust in God's control of his life. When a child does make a right choice, like admitting a mistake or telling the truth when it might get him in trouble, make sure you let him know what a great thing he has done.

Parents often reward their children for good things that are not eternal—like good grades on a report card. But how about rewards for progress in living honestly?

5 Your mercy, O LORD, *is* in the heavens;
  Your faithfulness *reaches* to the
    clouds.
6 Your righteousness *is* like the great
    mountains;
  Your judgments *are* a great deep;
  O LORD, You preserve man and beast.

7 How precious *is* Your
    lovingkindness, O God!
  Therefore the children of men put
    their trust under the shadow of
    Your wings.
8 They are abundantly satisfied with
    the fullness of Your house,
  And You give them drink from the
    river of Your pleasures.
9 For with You *is* the fountain of life;
  In Your light we see light.

10 Oh, continue Your lovingkindness to
    those who know You,
  And Your righteousness to the
    upright in heart.
11 Let not the foot of pride come
    against me,
  And let not the hand of the wicked
    drive me away.
12 There the workers of iniquity have
    fallen;
  They have been cast down and are
    not able to rise.

PSALM 37

The Heritage of the Righteous and the Calamity of the Wicked

A Psalm of David.

1 Do not fret because of evildoers,
  Nor be envious of the workers of
    iniquity.
2 For they shall soon be cut down like
    the grass,
  And wither as the green herb.

3 Trust in the LORD, and do good;
  Dwell in the land, and feed on His
    faithfulness.
4 Delight yourself also in the LORD,
  And He shall give you the desires of
    your heart.
5 Commit your way to the LORD,
  Trust also in Him,

And He shall bring *it* to pass.
6 He shall bring forth your
    righteousness as the light,
  And your justice as the noonday.

7 Rest in the LORD, and wait patiently
    for Him;
  Do not fret because of him who
    prospers in his way,
  Because of the man who brings
    wicked schemes to pass.
8 Cease from anger, and forsake wrath;
  Do not fret—*it* only *causes* harm.
9 For evildoers shall be cut off;
  But those who wait on the LORD,
  They shall inherit the earth.
10 For yet a little while and the wicked
    shall be no *more;*
  Indeed, you will look carefully for his
    place,
  But it *shall be* no *more.*
11 But the meek shall inherit the earth,
  And shall delight themselves in the
    abundance of peace.

12 The wicked plots against the just,
  And gnashes at him with his teeth.
13 The Lord laughs at him,
  For He sees that his day is coming.
14 The wicked have drawn the sword
  And have bent their bow,
  To cast down the poor and needy,
  To slay those who are of upright
    conduct.
15 Their sword shall enter their own
    heart,
  And their bows shall be broken.

16 A little that a righteous man has
  Is better than the riches of many
    wicked.
17 For the arms of the wicked shall be
    broken,
  But the LORD upholds the righteous.
18 The LORD knows the days of the
    upright,
  And their inheritance shall be forever.
19 They shall not be ashamed in the
    evil time,
  And in the days of famine they shall
    be satisfied.
20 But the wicked shall perish;
  And the enemies of the LORD,

Like the splendor of the meadows,
    shall vanish.
Into smoke they shall vanish away.

21 The wicked borrows and does not
    repay,
But the righteous shows mercy and
    gives.

22 For *those* blessed by Him shall
    inherit the earth,
But *those* cursed by Him shall be cut
    off.

23 The steps of a *good* man are ordered
    by the LORD,
And He delights in his way.

24 Though he fall, he shall not be
    utterly cast down;
For the LORD upholds *him with* His
    hand.

25 I have been young, and *now* am old;
Yet I have not seen the righteous
    forsaken,
Nor his descendants begging bread.

26 *He is* ever merciful, and lends;
And his descendants *are* blessed.

27 Depart from evil, and do good;
And dwell forevermore.

28 For the LORD loves justice,
And does not forsake His saints;
They are preserved forever,
But the descendants of the wicked
    shall be cut off.

29 The righteous shall inherit the land,
And dwell in it forever.

30 The mouth of the righteous speaks
    wisdom,
And his tongue talks of justice.

31 The law of his God *is* in his heart;
None of his steps shall slide.

32 The wicked watches the righteous,
And seeks to slay him.

33 The LORD will not leave him in his
    hand,
Nor condemn him when he is judged.

34 Wait on the LORD,
And keep His way,
And He shall exalt you to inherit the
    land;

When the wicked are cut off, you
    shall see *it.*

35 I have seen the wicked in great power,
And spreading himself like a native
    green tree.

36 Yet he passed away,[a] and behold, he
    was no *more;*
Indeed I sought him, but he could
    not be found.

37 Mark the blameless *man,* and
    observe the upright;
For the future of *that* man *is* peace.

38 But the transgressors shall be
    destroyed together;
The future of the wicked shall be cut
    off.

39 But the salvation of the righteous *is*
    from the LORD;
He is their strength in the time of
    trouble.

40 And the LORD shall help them and
    deliver them;
He shall deliver them from the
    wicked,
And save them,
Because they trust in Him.

PSALM 38

Prayer in Time of Chastening

A Psalm of David. To bring to remembrance.

1 O LORD, do not rebuke me in Your
    wrath,
Nor chasten me in Your hot
    displeasure!

2 For Your arrows pierce me deeply,
And Your hand presses me down.

3 *There is* no soundness in my flesh
Because of Your anger,
Nor *any* health in my bones
Because of my sin.

4 For my iniquities have gone over my
    head;
Like a heavy burden they are too
    heavy for me.

5 My wounds are foul *and* festering
Because of my foolishness.

6 I am troubled, I am bowed down
    greatly;
I go mourning all the day long.

37:36 [a]Following Masoretic Text, Septuagint, and
Targum; Syriac and Vulgate read *I passed by.*

7 For my loins are full of
  inflammation,
  And *there is* no soundness in my
  flesh.
8 I am feeble and severely broken;
  I groan because of the turmoil of my
  heart.
9 Lord, all my desire *is* before You;
  And my sighing is not hidden from
  You.
10 My heart pants, my strength fails
  me;
  As for the light of my eyes, it also
  has gone from me.
11 My loved ones and my friends stand
  aloof from my plague,
  And my relatives stand afar off.
12 Those also who seek my life lay
  snares *for me;*
  Those who seek my hurt speak of
  destruction,
  And plan deception all the day long.
13 But I, like a deaf *man,* do not hear;
  And *I am* like a mute *who* does not
  open his mouth.
14 Thus I am like a man who does not
  hear,
  And in whose mouth *is* no response.
15 For in You, O LORD, I hope;
  You will hear, O Lord my God.
16 For I said, *"Hear me,* lest they rejoice
  over me,
  Lest, when my foot slips, they exalt
  themselves against me."
17 For I *am* ready to fall,
  And my sorrow *is* continually before
  me.
18 For I will declare my iniquity;
  I will be in anguish over my sin.
19 But my enemies *are* vigorous, *and*
  they are strong;
  And those who hate me wrongfully
  have multiplied.
20 Those also who render evil for good,
  They are my adversaries, because I
  follow *what is* good.
21 Do not forsake me, O LORD;
  O my God, be not far from me!
22 Make haste to help me,
  O Lord, my salvation!

PSALM 39

Prayer for Wisdom and Forgiveness

To the Chief Musician. To Jeduthun.
A Psalm of David.

1 I said, "I will guard my ways,
  Lest I sin with my tongue;
  I will restrain my mouth with a
  muzzle,
  While the wicked are before me."
2 I was mute with silence,
  I held my peace *even* from good;
  And my sorrow was stirred up.
3 My heart was hot within me;
  While I was musing, the fire burned.
  Then I spoke with my tongue:
4 "LORD, make me to know my end,
  And what *is* the measure of my
  days,
  That I may know how frail I *am.*
5 Indeed, You have made my days *as*
  handbreadths,
  And my age *is* as nothing before
  You;
  Certainly every man at his best state
  is but vapor.   Selah
6 Surely every man walks about like a
  shadow;
  Surely they busy themselves in vain;
  He heaps up *riches,*
  And does not know who will gather
  them.
7 "And now, Lord, what do I wait for?
  My hope *is* in You.
8 Deliver me from all my
  transgressions;
  Do not make me the reproach of the
  foolish.
9 I was mute, I did not open my
  mouth,
  Because it was You who did *it.*
10 Remove Your plague from me;
  I am consumed by the blow of Your
  hand.
11 When with rebukes You correct man
  for iniquity,
  You make his beauty melt away like
  a moth;
  Surely every man *is* vapor.   Selah
12 "Hear my prayer, O LORD,
  And give ear to my cry;

Do not be silent at my tears;
For I *am* a stranger with You,
A sojourner, as all my fathers *were*.
13 Remove Your gaze from me, that I
   may regain strength,
   Before I go away and am no more."

PSALM 40

Faith Persevering in Trial

To the Chief Musician. A Psalm of David.

1 I waited patiently for the LORD;
  And He inclined to me,
  And heard my cry.
2 He also brought me up out of a
  horrible pit,
  Out of the miry clay,
  And set my feet upon a rock,
  And established my steps.
3 He has put a new song in my
  mouth—
  Praise to our God;
  Many will see *it* and fear,
  And will trust in the LORD.

4 Blessed *is* that man who makes the
  LORD his trust,
  And does not respect the proud, nor
  such as turn aside to lies.
5 Many, O LORD my God, *are* Your
  wonderful works
  Which You have done;
  And Your thoughts toward us
  Cannot be recounted to You in order;
  If I would declare and speak *of them,*
  They are more than can be
  numbered.

6 Sacrifice and offering You did not
  desire;
  My ears You have opened.
  Burnt offering and sin offering You
  did not require.
7 Then I said, "Behold, I come;
  In the scroll of the book *it is* written
  of me.
8 I delight to do Your will, O my God,
  And Your law *is* within my heart."

9 I have proclaimed the good news of
  righteousness
  In the great assembly;
  Indeed, I do not restrain my lips,
  O LORD, You Yourself know.

10 I have not hidden Your righteousness
   within my heart;
   I have declared Your faithfulness and
   Your salvation;
   I have not concealed Your
   lovingkindness and Your truth
   From the great assembly.

11 Do not withhold Your tender mercies
   from me, O LORD;
   Let Your lovingkindness and Your
   truth continually preserve me.
12 For innumerable evils have
   surrounded me;
   My iniquities have overtaken me, so
   that I am not able to look up;
   They are more than the hairs of my
   head;
   Therefore my heart fails me.

13 Be pleased, O LORD, to deliver me;
   O LORD, make haste to help me!
14 Let them be ashamed and brought to
   mutual confusion
   Who seek to destroy my life;
   Let them be driven backward and
   brought to dishonor
   Who wish me evil.
15 Let them be confounded because of
   their shame,
   Who say to me, "Aha, aha!"

16 Let all those who seek You rejoice
   and be glad in You;
   Let such as love Your salvation say
   continually,
   "The LORD be magnified!"
17 But I *am* poor and needy;
   Yet the LORD thinks upon me.
   You *are* my help and my deliverer;
   Do not delay, O my God.

PSALM 41

The Blessing and Suffering of the Godly

To the Chief Musician. A Psalm of David.

1 Blessed *is* he who considers the poor;
  The LORD will deliver him in time of
  trouble.
2 The LORD will preserve him and keep
  him alive,
  And he will be blessed on the earth;
  You will not deliver him to the will of
  his enemies.

3 The LORD will strengthen him on his
   bed of illness;
   You will sustain him on his sickbed.

4 I said, "LORD, be merciful to me;
   Heal my soul, for I have sinned
   against You."

5 My enemies speak evil of me:
   "When will he die, and his name
   perish?"

6 And if he comes to see *me,* he
   speaks lies;
   His heart gathers iniquity to itself;
   When he goes out, he tells *it.*

7 All who hate me whisper together
   against me;
   Against me they devise my hurt.

8 "An evil disease," *they say,* "clings to
   him.
   And *now* that he lies down, he will
   rise up no more."

9 Even my own familiar friend in
   whom I trusted,
   Who ate my bread,
   Has lifted up *his* heel against me.

10 But You, O LORD, be merciful to me,
   and raise me up,
   That I may repay them.

11 By this I know that You are well
   pleased with me,
   Because my enemy does not triumph
   over me.

12 As for me, You uphold me in my
   integrity,
   And set me before Your face forever.

13 Blessed *be* the LORD God of Israel
   From everlasting to everlasting!
   Amen and Amen.

Book Two: Psalms 42—72

PSALM 42

Yearning for God in the Midst of Distresses

To the Chief Musician. A Contemplation[a] of
the sons of Korah.

1 As the deer pants for the water
   brooks,
   So pants my soul for You,
   O God.

2 My soul thirsts for God, for the
   living God.
   When shall I come and appear before
   God?[a]

3 My tears have been my food day and
   night,
   While they continually say to me,
   "Where *is* your God?"

4 When I remember these *things,*
   I pour out my soul within me.
   For I used to go with the multitude;
   I went with them to the house of
   God,
   With the voice of joy and praise,
   With a multitude that kept a pilgrim
   feast.

5 Why are you cast down, O my soul?
   And *why* are you disquieted within
   me?
   Hope in God, for I shall yet praise Him
   For the help of His countenance.[a]

6 O my God,[a] my soul is cast down
   within me;
   Therefore I will remember You from
   the land of the Jordan,
   And from the heights of Hermon,
   From the Hill Mizar.

7 Deep calls unto deep at the noise of
   Your waterfalls;
   All Your waves and billows have
   gone over me.

8 The LORD will command His
   lovingkindness in the daytime,
   And in the night His song *shall be*
   with me—
   A prayer to the God of my life.

9 I will say to God my Rock,
   "Why have You forgotten me?
   Why do I go mourning because of
   the oppression of the enemy?"

10 *As* with a breaking of my bones,
   My enemies reproach me,

42:title [a]Hebrew *Maschil* **42:2** [a]Following Masoretic
Text and Vulgate; some Hebrew manuscripts,
Septuagint, Syriac, and Targum read *I see the face of
God.* **42:5** [a]Following Masoretic Text and Targum; a
few Hebrew manuscripts, Septuagint, Syriac, and
Vulgate read *The help of my countenance, my God.*
42:6 [a]Following Masoretic Text and Targum; a few
Hebrew manuscripts, Septuagint, Syriac, and Vulgate
put *my God* at the end of verse 5.

While they say to me all day long,
"Where *is* your God?"

11 Why are you cast down, O my soul?
And why are you disquieted within
me?
Hope in God;
For I shall yet praise Him,
The help of my countenance and my
God.

PSALM 43

Prayer to God in Time of Trouble

1 Vindicate me, O God,
And plead my cause against an
ungodly nation;
Oh, deliver me from the deceitful and
unjust man!
2 For You *are* the God of my strength;
Why do You cast me off?
Why do I go mourning because of
the oppression of the enemy?

3 Oh, send out Your light and Your
truth!
Let them lead me;
Let them bring me to Your holy hill
And to Your tabernacle.
4 Then I will go to the altar of God,
To God my exceeding joy;
And on the harp I will praise You,
O God, my God.

5 Why are you cast down, O my soul?
And why are you disquieted within
me?
Hope in God;
For I shall yet praise Him,
The help of my countenance and my
God.

PSALM 44

Redemption Remembered in Present Dishonor

To the Chief Musician. A Contemplation[a] of
the sons of Korah.

1 We have heard with our ears, O God,
Our fathers have told us,

The deeds You did in their days,
In days of old:
2 You drove out the nations with Your
hand,
But them You planted;
You afflicted the peoples, and cast
them out.
3 For they did not gain possession of
the land by their own sword,
Nor did their own arm save them;
But it was Your right hand, Your
arm, and the light of Your
countenance,
Because You favored them.

4 You are my King, O God;[a]
Command[b] victories for Jacob.
5 Through You we will push down our
enemies;
Through Your name we will trample
those who rise up against us.
6 For I will not trust in my bow,
Nor shall my sword save me.
7 But You have saved us from our
enemies,
And have put to shame those who
hated us.
8 In God we boast all day long,
And praise Your name forever. Selah

9 But You have cast *us* off and put us
to shame,
And You do not go out with our
armies.
10 You make us turn back from the
enemy,
And those who hate us have taken
spoil for themselves.
11 You have given us up like sheep
intended for food,
And have scattered us among the
nations.
12 You sell Your people for *next to*
nothing,
And are not enriched by selling them.
13 You make us a reproach to our
neighbors,
A scorn and a derision to those all
around us.
14 You make us a byword among the
nations,
A shaking of the head among the
peoples.

44:title [a]Hebrew *Maschil* **44:4** [a]Following Masoretic
Text and Targum; Septuagint and Vulgate read *and
my God.* [b]Following Masoretic Text and Targum;
Septuagint, Syriac, and Vulgate read *Who commands.*

15 My dishonor *is* continually before me,
And the shame of my face has
covered me,
16 Because of the voice of him who
reproaches and reviles,
Because of the enemy and the
avenger.

17 All this has come upon us;
But we have not forgotten You,
Nor have we dealt falsely with Your
covenant.
18 Our heart has not turned back,
Nor have our steps departed from
Your way;
19 But You have severely broken us in
the place of jackals,
And covered us with the shadow of
death.

20 If we had forgotten the name of our
God,
Or stretched out our hands to a
foreign god,
21 Would not God search this out?
For He knows the secrets of the
heart.
22 Yet for Your sake we are killed all
day long;
We are accounted as sheep for the
slaughter.

23 Awake! Why do You sleep, O Lord?
Arise! Do not cast *us* off forever.
24 Why do You hide Your face,
And forget our affliction and our
oppression?
25 For our soul is bowed down to the
dust;
Our body clings to the ground.
26 Arise for our help,
And redeem us for Your mercies' sake.

PSALM 45

The Glories of the Messiah and His Bride

To the Chief Musician. Set to "The Lilies."[a]
A Contemplation[b] of the sons of Korah.
A Song of Love.

1 My heart is overflowing with a good
theme;
I recite my composition concerning
the King;
My tongue *is* the pen of a ready
writer.

2 You are fairer than the sons of men;
Grace is poured upon Your lips;
Therefore God has blessed You
forever.
3 Gird Your sword upon *Your* thigh, O
Mighty One,
With Your glory and Your majesty.
4 And in Your majesty ride
prosperously because of truth,
humility, *and* righteousness;
And Your right hand shall teach You
awesome things.
5 Your arrows *are* sharp in the heart of
the King's enemies;
The peoples fall under You.

6 Your throne, O God, *is* forever and
ever;
A scepter of righteousness *is* the
scepter of Your kingdom.
7 You love righteousness and hate
wickedness;
Therefore God, Your God, has
anointed You
With the oil of gladness more than
Your companions.
8 All Your garments *are scented* with
myrrh and aloes *and* cassia,
Out of the ivory palaces, by which
they have made You glad.
9 Kings' daughters *are* among Your
honorable women;
At Your right hand stands the queen
in gold from Ophir.

10 Listen, O daughter,
Consider and incline your ear;
Forget your own people also, and
your father's house;
11 So the King will greatly desire your
beauty;
Because He *is* your Lord, worship Him.
12 And the daughter of Tyre *will come*
with a gift;
The rich among the people will seek
your favor.

13 The royal daughter *is* all glorious
within *the palace;*
Her clothing *is* woven with gold.

45:title [a]Hebrew *Shoshannim* [b]Hebrew *Maschil*

14 She shall be brought to the King in
    robes of many colors;
  The virgins, her companions who
    follow her, shall be brought to
    You.
15 With gladness and rejoicing they
    shall be brought;
  They shall enter the King's palace.
16 Instead of Your fathers shall be Your
    sons,
  Whom You shall make princes in all
    the earth.
17 I will make Your name to be
    remembered in all generations;
  Therefore the people shall praise You
    forever and ever.

PSALM 46

God the Refuge of His People and Conqueror of the Nations

To the Chief Musician. *A Psalm* of the sons of
  Korah. A Song for Alamoth.

1 God *is* our refuge and strength,
  A very present help in trouble.
2 Therefore we will not fear,
  Even though the earth be removed,
  And though the mountains be
    carried into the midst of the sea;
3 *Though* its waters roar *and* be
    troubled,

Though the mountains shake with its
    swelling.   Selah
4 *There is* a river whose streams shall
    make glad the city of God,
  The holy *place* of the tabernacle of
    the Most High.
5 God *is* in the midst of her, she shall
    not be moved;
  God shall help her, just at the break
    of dawn.
6 The nations raged, the kingdoms
    were moved;
  He uttered His voice, the earth
    melted.
7 The LORD of hosts *is* with us;
  The God of Jacob *is* our refuge. Selah
8 Come, behold the works of the LORD,
  Who has made desolations in the
    earth.
9 He makes wars cease to the end of
    the earth;
  He breaks the bow and cuts the
    spear in two;
  He burns the chariot in the fire.
10 Be still, and know that I *am* God;
  I will be exalted among the nations,
  I will be exalted in the earth!
11 The LORD of hosts *is* with us;
  The God of Jacob *is* our refuge. Selah

ROMANTIC QUOTES AND NOTES
Be Still

God tells us in His Word to "Be still, and know that I am God" (46:10). This instruction suggests that silence is a far better medium to hear from God than is frenetic activity. Yet sadly, in too many homes—including Christian ones—the frenzy of day-to-day life makes it difficult, if not impossible, to "be still."

Do *you* know how to be still? Does your spouse? Does your child? We fear that many Christians struggle to hear God speak to them because they have never learned to rest and to listen for His voice in the silence. Instead, they seem addicted to activity and external stimuli.

As spouses and as parents, we need to set the course for our homes (especially while we still control our children's schedules), knowing that at a time just around the corner, the activity monster will barge through our front doors and eat our time and resources.

We encourage you to formulate a mission statement on activities that will set boundaries for the well-being of everyone in your family—and that includes Mom and Dad! Such a mission statement should spell out how you can set aside some unhurried time to "be still" before God.

PSALM 47

Praise to God, the Ruler of the Earth

To the Chief Musician.
A Psalm of the sons of Korah.

1   Oh, clap your hands, all you peoples!
    Shout to God with the voice of
        triumph!
2   For the Lord Most High *is* awesome;
    He is a great King over all the earth.
3   He will subdue the peoples under us,
    And the nations under our feet.
4   He will choose our inheritance for us,
    The excellence of Jacob whom He
        loves.   Selah

5   God has gone up with a shout,
    The Lord with the sound of a
        trumpet.
6   Sing praises to God, sing praises!
    Sing praises to our King, sing
        praises!
7   For God *is* the King of all the earth;
    Sing praises with understanding.

8   God reigns over the nations;
    God sits on His holy throne.
9   The princes of the people have
        gathered together,
    The people of the God of Abraham.
    For the shields of the earth *belong* to
        God;
    He is greatly exalted.

PSALM 48

The Glory of God in Zion

A Song. A Psalm of the sons of Korah.

1   Great *is* the Lord, and greatly to be
        praised
    In the city of our God,
    In His holy mountain.
2   Beautiful in elevation,
    The joy of the whole earth,
    Is Mount Zion *on* the sides of the
        north,
    The city of the great King.
3   God *is* in her palaces;
    He is known as her refuge.
4   For behold, the kings assembled,
    They passed by together.
5   They saw *it, and* so they marveled;

They were troubled, they hastened
    away.
6   Fear took hold of them there,
    And pain, as of a woman in birth
        pangs,
7   *As when* You break the ships of
        Tarshish
    With an east wind.
8   As we have heard,
    So we have seen
    In the city of the Lord of hosts,
    In the city of our God:
    God will establish it forever.   Selah

9   We have thought, O God, on Your
        lovingkindness,
    In the midst of Your temple.
10 According to Your name, O God,
    So *is* Your praise to the ends of the
        earth;
    Your right hand is full of
        righteousness.
11 Let Mount Zion rejoice,
    Let the daughters of Judah be glad,
    Because of Your judgments.

12 Walk about Zion,
    And go all around her.
    Count her towers;
13 Mark well her bulwarks;
    Consider her palaces;
    That you may tell *it* to the generation
        following.
14 For this *is* God,
    Our God forever and ever;
    He will be our guide
    Even to death.[a]

PSALM 49

The Confidence of the Foolish

To the Chief Musician.
A Psalm of the sons of Korah.

1   Hear this, all peoples;
    Give ear, all inhabitants of the world,
2   Both low and high,
    Rich and poor together.
3   My mouth shall speak wisdom,
    And the meditation of my heart *shall*
        give understanding.

48:14 [a]Following Masoretic Text and Syriac;
Septuagint and Vulgate read *Forever.*

4 I will incline my ear to a proverb;
I will disclose my dark saying on the harp.

5 Why should I fear in the days of evil,
When the iniquity at my heels surrounds me?

6 Those who trust in their wealth
And boast in the multitude of their riches,

7 None *of them* can by any means redeem *his* brother,
Nor give to God a ransom for him—

8 For the redemption of their souls *is* costly,
And it shall cease forever—

9 That he should continue to live eternally,
And not see the Pit.

10 For he sees wise men die;
Likewise the fool and the senseless person perish,
And leave their wealth to others.

11 Their inner thought *is that* their houses *will last* forever,[a]
Their dwelling places to all generations;
They call *their* lands after their own names.

12 Nevertheless man, *though* in honor, does not remain;[a]
He is like the beasts *that* perish.

13 This is the way of those who *are* foolish,
And of their posterity who approve their sayings.   Selah

14 Like sheep they are laid in the grave;
Death shall feed on them;
The upright shall have dominion over them in the morning;
And their beauty shall be consumed in the grave, far from their dwelling.

15 But God will redeem my soul from the power of the grave,
For He shall receive me.   Selah

16 Do not be afraid when one becomes rich,
When the glory of his house is increased;

17 For when he dies he shall carry nothing away;
His glory shall not descend after him.

18 Though while he lives he blesses himself
(For *men* will praise you when you do well for yourself),

19 He shall go to the generation of his fathers;
They shall never see light.

20 A man *who is* in honor, yet does not understand,
Is like the beasts *that* perish.

PSALM 50

God the Righteous Judge

A Psalm of Asaph.

1 The Mighty One, God the LORD,
Has spoken and called the earth
From the rising of the sun to its going down.

2 Out of Zion, the perfection of beauty,
God will shine forth.

3 Our God shall come, and shall not keep silent;
A fire shall devour before Him,
And it shall be very tempestuous all around Him.

4 He shall call to the heavens from above,
And to the earth, that He may judge His people:

5 "Gather My saints together to Me,
Those who have made a covenant with Me by sacrifice."

6 Let the heavens declare His righteousness,
For God Himself *is* Judge.   Selah

7 "Hear, O My people, and I will speak,
O Israel, and I will testify against you;
I *am* God, your God!

8 I will not rebuke you for your sacrifices
Or your burnt offerings,
Which are continually before Me.

49:11 [a]Septuagint, Syriac, Targum, and Vulgate read *Their graves shall be their houses forever.*
49:12 [a]Following Masoretic Text and Targum; Septuagint, Syriac, and Vulgate read *understand* (compare verse 20).

9   I will not take a bull from your
         house,
      Nor goats out of your folds.
10   For every beast of the forest *is* Mine,
      And the cattle on a thousand hills.
11   I know all the birds of the
         mountains,
      And the wild beasts of the field *are*
         Mine.
12   "If I were hungry, I would not tell
         you;
      For the world *is* Mine, and all its
         fullness.
13   Will I eat the flesh of bulls,
      Or drink the blood of goats?
14   Offer to God thanksgiving,
      And pay your vows to the Most
         High.
15   Call upon Me in the day of trouble;
      I will deliver you, and you shall
         glorify Me."

16   But to the wicked God says:
      "What *right* have you to declare My
         statutes,
      Or take My covenant in your mouth,
17   Seeing you hate instruction
      And cast My words behind you?
18   When you saw a thief, you
         consented[a] with him,
      And have been a partaker with
         adulterers.
19   You give your mouth to evil,
      And your tongue frames deceit.
20   You sit *and* speak against your
         brother;
      You slander your own mother's son.
21   These *things* you have done, and I
         kept silent;
      You thought that I was altogether
         like you;
      But I will rebuke you,
      And set *them* in order before your
         eyes.

22   "Now consider this, you who forget
         God,
      Lest I tear *you* in pieces,
      And *there be* none to deliver:
23   Whoever offers praise glorifies Me;
      And to him who orders *his* conduct
         aright
      I will show the salvation of God."

PSALM 51

A Prayer of Repentance

To the Chief Musician. A Psalm of David
when Nathan the prophet went to him, after he
had gone in to Bathsheba.

1   Have mercy upon me, O God,
      According to Your lovingkindness;
      According to the multitude of Your
         tender mercies,
      Blot out my transgressions.
2   Wash me thoroughly from my
         iniquity,
      And cleanse me from my sin.

3   For I acknowledge my
         transgressions,
      And my sin *is* always before me.
4   Against You, You only, have I sinned,
      And done *this* evil in Your sight—
      That You may be found just when
         You speak,[a]
      And blameless when You judge.

5   Behold, I was brought forth in
         iniquity,
      And in sin my mother conceived me.
6   Behold, You desire truth in the
         inward parts,
      And in the hidden *part* You will
         make me to know wisdom.

7   Purge me with hyssop, and I shall be
         clean;
      Wash me, and I shall be whiter than
         snow.
8   Make me hear joy and gladness,
      That the bones You have broken may
         rejoice.
9   Hide Your face from my sins,
      And blot out all my iniquities.

10   Create in me a clean heart, O God,
      And renew a steadfast spirit within
         me.
11   Do not cast me away from Your
         presence,
      And do not take Your Holy Spirit
         from me.
12   Restore to me the joy of Your
         salvation,

50:18 [a]Septuagint, Syriac, Targum, and Vulgate read
ran. 51:4 [a]Septuagint, Targum, and Vulgate read *in
Your words.*

And uphold me *by Your* generous
   Spirit.
13 *Then* I will teach transgressors Your
      ways,
   And sinners shall be converted to You.

14 Deliver me from the guilt of
      bloodshed, O God,
   The God of my salvation,
   And my tongue shall sing aloud of
      Your righteousness.
15 O Lord, open my lips,
   And my mouth shall show forth
      Your praise.
16 For You do not desire sacrifice, or
      else I would give *it;*
   You do not delight in burnt offering.
17 The sacrifices of God *are* a broken
      spirit,
   A broken and a contrite heart—
   These, O God, You will not despise.

18 Do good in Your good pleasure to
      Zion;
   Build the walls of Jerusalem.
19 Then You shall be pleased with the
      sacrifices of righteousness,
   With burnt offering and whole burnt
      offering;
   Then they shall offer bulls on Your
      altar.

PSALM 52

The End of the Wicked and the Peace of the Godly

To the Chief Musician. A Contemplation[a]
of David when Doeg the Edomite went and
told Saul, and said to him, "David has gone
to the house of Ahimelech."

1 Why do you boast in evil, O mighty
      man?
   The goodness of God *endures*
      continually.
2 Your tongue devises destruction,
   Like a sharp razor, working
      deceitfully.
3 You love evil more than good,
   Lying rather than speaking
      righteousness.   Selah
4 You love all devouring words,
   You deceitful tongue.

5 God shall likewise destroy you forever;
   He shall take you away, and pluck
      you out of *your* dwelling place,
   And uproot you from the land of the
      living.   Selah
6 The righteous also shall see and fear,
   And shall laugh at him, *saying,*
7 "Here is the man *who* did not make
      God his strength,
   But trusted in the abundance of his
      riches,
   And strengthened himself in his
      wickedness."

8 But I *am* like a green olive tree in the
      house of God;
   I trust in the mercy of God forever
      and ever.
9 I will praise You forever,
   Because You have done *it;*
   And in the presence of Your saints
   I will wait on Your name, for *it is*
      good.

PSALM 53

Folly of the Godless, and the Restoration of Israel

To the Chief Musician. Set to "Mahalath."
   A Contemplation[a] of David.

1 The fool has said in his heart,
   "*There is* no God."
   They are corrupt, and have done
      abominable iniquity;
   There is none who does good.

2 God looks down from heaven upon
      the children of men,
   To see if there are *any* who
      understand, who seek God.
3 Every one of them has turned aside;
   They have together become corrupt;
   There is none who does good,
   No, not one.

4 Have the workers of iniquity no
      knowledge,
   Who eat up my people *as* they eat
      bread,
   And do not call upon God?
5 There they are in great fear
   Where no fear was,
   For God has scattered the bones of
      him who encamps against you;

52:title [a]Hebrew *Maschil*   **53:title** [a]Hebrew *Maschil*

You have put *them* to shame,
Because God has despised them.

6 Oh, that the salvation of Israel
     would come out of Zion!
When God brings back the captivity
     of His people,
Let Jacob rejoice *and* Israel be glad.

PSALM 54

Answered Prayer for Deliverance from Adversaries

To the Chief Musician. With stringed instruments.[a] A Contemplation[b] of David when the Ziphites went and said to Saul, "Is David not hiding with us?"

1 Save me, O God, by Your name,
And vindicate me by Your strength.
2 Hear my prayer, O God;
Give ear to the words of my mouth.
3 For strangers have risen up against
     me,
And oppressors have sought after
     my life;
They have not set God before them.
                     Selah

4 Behold, God *is* my helper;
The Lord *is* with those who uphold
     my life.
5 He will repay my enemies for their
     evil.
Cut them off in Your truth.

6 I will freely sacrifice to You;
I will praise Your name, O LORD, for
     it is good.
7 For He has delivered me out of all
     trouble;
And my eye has seen *its desire* upon
     my enemies.

PSALM 55

Trust in God Concerning the Treachery of Friends

To the Chief Musician.
With stringed instruments.[a]
A Contemplation[b] of David.

1 Give ear to my prayer, O God,
And do not hide Yourself from my
     supplication.
2 Attend to me, and hear me;

I am restless in my complaint, and
     moan noisily,
3 Because of the voice of the enemy,
Because of the oppression of the
     wicked;
For they bring down trouble upon me,
And in wrath they hate me.

4 My heart is severely pained within
     me,
And the terrors of death have fallen
     upon me.
5 Fearfulness and trembling have come
     upon me,
And horror has overwhelmed me.
6 So I said, "Oh, that I had wings like a
     dove!
I would fly away and be at rest.
7 Indeed, I would wander far off,
And remain in the wilderness.   Selah
8 I would hasten my escape
From the windy storm *and* tempest."

9 Destroy, O Lord, *and* divide their
     tongues,
For I have seen violence and strife in
     the city.
10 Day and night they go around it on
     its walls;
Iniquity and trouble *are* also in the
     midst of it.
11 Destruction *is* in its midst;
Oppression and deceit do not depart
     from its streets.

12 For *it is* not an enemy *who*
     reproaches me;
Then I could bear *it.*
Nor *is it* one *who* hates me who has
     exalted *himself* against me;
Then I could hide from him.
13 But *it was* you, a man my equal,
My companion and my
     acquaintance.
14 We took sweet counsel together,
And walked to the house of God in
     the throng.

15 Let death seize them;
Let them go down alive into hell,
For wickedness *is* in their dwellings
     and among them.

54:title [a]Hebrew *neginoth*   [b]Hebrew *Maschil*
55:title [a]Hebrew *neginoth*   [b]Hebrew *Maschil*

16 As for me, I will call upon God,
   And the LORD shall save me.
17 Evening and morning and at noon
   I will pray, and cry aloud,
   And He shall hear my voice.
18 He has redeemed my soul in peace
      from the battle *that was* against
      me,
   For there were many against me.
19 God will hear, and afflict them,
   Even He who abides from of old.
                                    Selah
   Because they do not change,
   Therefore they do not fear God.

20 He has put forth his hands against
      those who were at peace with him;
   He has broken his covenant.
21 *The words* of his mouth were
      smoother than butter,
   But war *was* in his heart;
   His words were softer than oil,
   Yet they *were* drawn swords.

22 Cast your burden on the LORD,
   And He shall sustain you;
   He shall never permit the righteous
      to be moved.

23 But You, O God, shall bring them
      down to the pit of destruction;
   Bloodthirsty and deceitful men shall
      not live out half their days;
   But I will trust in You.

PSALM 56

Prayer for Relief from Tormentors

To the Chief Musician.
Set to "The Silent Dove in Distant Lands."[a]
A Michtam of David when the Philistines
captured him in Gath.

1 Be merciful to me, O God, for man
      would swallow me up;
   Fighting all day he oppresses me.
2 My enemies would hound *me* all day,
   For *there are* many who fight against
      me, O Most High.

3 Whenever I am afraid,
   I will trust in You.
4 In God (I will praise His word),
   In God I have put my trust;

   I will not fear.
   What can flesh do to me?

5 All day they twist my words;
   All their thoughts *are* against me for
      evil.
6 They gather together,
   They hide, they mark my steps,
   When they lie in wait for my life.
7 Shall they escape by iniquity?
   In anger cast down the peoples, O
      God!

ROMANCE FAQ

Q: *How can a husband best voice his acceptance of his wife, including in her appearance?*

Every man should take a page from the Song of Solomon. Solomon knew the importance of elevating his wife's beauty, her appearance, her dignity, her worth, and her value as a woman. He carefully chose *his words* to communicate how beautiful she was to him. Every women needs to hear such praise and affirmation. Acceptance begins with *an understanding of what your wife is feeling about herself.*

Does she feel good about the way she looks? Her hair? Her clothes and shoes? Her weight? Her skin tone? Her body image? Her teeth? Her overall attractiveness?

Chances are good that she compares herself to the airbrushed models of perfection she sees every day. From the covers of the magazines in the checkout line to the advertisements she watches on television, your wife is constantly made to feel inferior, unworthy, and unacceptable.

Solomon recognized his wife's need for affirmation and didn't hesitate to go beyond mere acceptance. He lavished praise on her. He said, "I have compared you, my love, to my filly among Pharaoh's chariots" (1:9). Solomon used poetic language to tell his wife that she was *magnificent.*

56:title [a]Hebrew *Jonath Elem Rechokim*

8   You number my wanderings;
    Put my tears into Your bottle;
    Are they not in Your book?
9   When I cry out *to You,*
    Then my enemies will turn back;
    This I know, because God *is* for me.
10   In God (I will praise *His* word),
    In the LORD (I will praise *His* word),
11   In God I have put my trust;
    I will not be afraid.
    What can man do to me?

12   Vows *made* to You *are binding* upon
     me, O God;
    I will render praises to You,
13   For You have delivered my soul from
     death.
    Have You not *kept* my feet from
     falling,
    That I may walk before God
    In the light of the living?

PSALM 57

Prayer for Safety from Enemies

To the Chief Musician.
Set to "Do Not Destroy."[a] A Michtam of David
when he fled from Saul into the cave.

1   Be merciful to me, O God, be
     merciful to me!
    For my soul trusts in You;
    And in the shadow of Your wings I
     will make my refuge,
    Until *these* calamities have passed
     by.
2   I will cry out to God Most High,
    To God who performs *all things* for
     me.
3   He shall send from heaven and save
     me;
    He reproaches the one who would
     swallow me up.   Selah
    God shall send forth His mercy and
     His truth.
4   My soul *is* among lions;
    I lie *among* the sons of men
    Who are set on fire,
    Whose teeth *are* spears and arrows,
    And their tongue a sharp sword.
5   Be exalted, O God, above the
     heavens;
    Let Your glory *be* above all the earth.

6   They have prepared a net for my
     steps;
    My soul is bowed down;
    They have dug a pit before me;
    Into the midst of it they *themselves*
    have fallen.   Selah

7   My heart is steadfast, O God, my
     heart is steadfast;
    I will sing and give praise.
8   Awake, my glory!
    Awake, lute and harp!
    I will awaken the dawn.
9   I will praise You, O Lord, among the
     peoples;
    I will sing to You among the nations.
10   For Your mercy reaches unto the
     heavens,
    And Your truth unto the clouds.
11   Be exalted, O God, above the
     heavens;
    Let Your glory *be* above all the earth.

PSALM 58

The Just Judgment of the Wicked

To the Chief Musician. Set to "Do Not
Destroy."[a] A Michtam of David.

1   Do you indeed speak righteousness,
     you silent ones?
    Do you judge uprightly, you sons of
     men?
2   No, in heart you work wickedness;
    You weigh out the violence of your
     hands in the earth.

3   The wicked are estranged from the
     womb;
    They go astray as soon as they are
     born, speaking lies.
4   Their poison *is* like the poison of a
     serpent;
    They are like the deaf cobra *that*
     stops its ear,
5   Which will not heed the voice of
     charmers,
    Charming ever so skillfully.

6   Break their teeth in their mouth, O
     God!

57:title [a]Hebrew *Al Tashcheth*
58:title [a]Hebrew *Al Tashcheth*

Break out the fangs of the young
    lions, O LORD!
7 Let them flow away as waters *which*
    run continually;
    When he bends *his bow,*
    Let his arrows be as if cut in pieces.
8 *Let them be* like a snail which melts
    away as it goes,
    Like a stillborn child of a woman,
    that they may not see the sun.

9 Before your pots can feel *the burning*
    thorns,
    He shall take them away as with a
    whirlwind,
    As in His living and burning wrath.
10 The righteous shall rejoice when he
    sees the vengeance;
    He shall wash his feet in the blood of
    the wicked,
11 So that men will say,
    "Surely *there is* a reward for the
    righteous;
    Surely He is God who judges in the
    earth."

PSALM 59

The Assured Judgment of the Wicked

To the Chief Musician.
Set to "Do Not Destroy."[a] A Michtam of David
when Saul sent men, and they watched the
house in order to kill him.

1 Deliver me from my enemies, O my
    God;
    Defend me from those who rise up
    against me.
2 Deliver me from the workers of
    iniquity,
    And save me from bloodthirsty men.

3 For look, they lie in wait for my life;
    The mighty gather against me,
    Not *for* my transgression nor *for* my
    sin, O LORD.

59:title [a]Hebrew *Al Tashcheth* **59:9** [a]Following
Masoretic Text and Syriac; some Hebrew manu-
scripts, Septuagint, Targum, and Vulgate read *my
Strength.* **59:10** [a]Following Qere; some Hebrew man-
uscripts, Septuagint, and Vulgate read *My God, His
mercy;* Kethib, some Hebrew manuscripts and
Targum read *O God, my mercy;* Syriac reads *O God,
Your mercy.* **59:15** [a]Following Septuagint and
Vulgate; Masoretic Text, Syriac, and Targum read
spend the night.

4 They run and prepare themselves
    through no fault *of mine.*

    Awake to help me, and behold!
5 You therefore, O LORD God of hosts,
    the God of Israel,
    Awake to punish all the nations;
    Do not be merciful to any wicked
    transgressors.   Selah

6 At evening they return,
    They growl like a dog,
    And go all around the city.
7 Indeed, they belch with their mouth;
    Swords *are* in their lips;
    For *they say,* "Who hears?"

8 But You, O LORD, shall laugh at them;
    You shall have all the nations in
    derision.
9 I will wait for You, O You his
    Strength;[a]
    For God *is* my defense.
10 My God of mercy[a] shall come to
    meet me;
    God shall let me see *my desire* on my
    enemies.

11 Do not slay them, lest my people
    forget;
    Scatter them by Your power,
    And bring them down,
    O Lord our shield.
12 *For* the sin of their mouth *and* the
    words of their lips,
    Let them even be taken in their pride,
    And for the cursing and lying *which*
    they speak.
13 Consume *them* in wrath, consume
    them,
    That they *may* not *be;*
    And let them know that God rules in
    Jacob
    To the ends of the earth.   Selah

14 And at evening they return,
    They growl like a dog,
    And go all around the city.
15 They wander up and down for food,
    And howl[a] if they are not satisfied.

16 But I will sing of Your power;
    Yes, I will sing aloud of Your mercy
    in the morning;
    For You have been my defense
    And refuge in the day of my trouble.

17   To You, O my Strength, I will sing
          praises;
      For God *is* my defense,
      My God of mercy.

PSALM 60

Urgent Prayer for the Restored Favor of God

To the Chief Musician. Set to "Lily of the
Testimony."[a] A Michtam of David. For
teaching. When he fought against
Mesopotamia and Syria of Zobah, and Joab
returned and killed twelve thousand Edomites
in the Valley of Salt.

1   O God, You have cast us off;
      You have broken us down;
      You have been displeased;
      Oh, restore us again!
2   You have made the earth tremble;
      You have broken it;
      Heal its breaches, for it is shaking.
3   You have shown Your people hard
          things;
      You have made us drink the wine of
          confusion.

4   You have given a banner to those
          who fear You,
      That it may be displayed because of
          the truth.   Selah
5   That Your beloved may be delivered,
      Save *with* Your right hand, and hear
          me.

6   God has spoken in His holiness:
      "I will rejoice;
      I will divide Shechem
      And measure out the Valley of
          Succoth.
7   Gilead *is* Mine, and Manasseh *is* Mine;
      Ephraim also *is* the helmet for My
          head;
      Judah *is* My lawgiver.
8   Moab *is* My washpot;
      Over Edom I will cast My shoe;
      Philistia, shout in triumph because of
          Me."

9   Who will bring me *to* the strong city?
      Who will lead me to Edom?
10   *Is it* not You, O God, *who* cast us off?
      And You, O God, *who* did not go out
          with our armies?

11   Give us help from trouble,
      For the help of man *is* useless.
12   Through God we will do valiantly,
      For *it is* He *who* shall tread down our
          enemies.[a]

PSALM 61

Assurance of God's Eternal Protection

To the Chief Musician.
On a stringed instrument.[a] *A Psalm* of David.

1   Hear my cry, O God;
      Attend to my prayer.
2   From the end of the earth I will cry
          to You,
      When my heart is overwhelmed;
      Lead me to the rock that is higher
          than I.
3   For You have been a shelter for me,
      A strong tower from the enemy.
4   I will abide in Your tabernacle
          forever;
      I will trust in the shelter of Your
          wings.   Selah

5   For You, O God, have heard my
          vows;
      You have given *me* the heritage of
          those who fear Your name.
6   You will prolong the king's life,
      His years as many generations.
7   He shall abide before God forever.
      Oh, prepare mercy and truth, *which*
          may preserve him!

8   So I will sing praise to Your name
          forever,
      That I may daily perform my vows.

PSALM 62

A Calm Resolve to Wait for the Salvation of God

To the Chief Musician.
To Jeduthun. A Psalm of David.

1   Truly my soul silently *waits* for God;
      From Him *comes* my salvation.
2   He only *is* my rock and my salvation;
      He is my defense;
      I shall not be greatly moved.

60:title [a]Hebrew *Shushan Eduth* **60:12** [a]Compare
verses 5–12 with 108:6–13 **61:title** [a]Hebrew *neginah*

3 How long will you attack a man?
You shall be slain, all of you,
Like a leaning wall and a tottering
   fence.
4 They only consult to cast *him* down
   from his high position;
They delight in lies;
They bless with their mouth,
But they curse inwardly.   Selah

5 My soul, wait silently for God alone,
For my expectation *is* from Him.
6 He only *is* my rock and my salvation;
He is my defense;
I shall not be moved.
7 In God *is* my salvation and my glory;
The rock of my strength,
And my refuge, *is* in God.

8 Trust in Him at all times, you people;
Pour out your heart before Him;
God *is* a refuge for us.   Selah

9 Surely men of low degree *are* a
   vapor,
Men of high degree *are* a lie;
If they are weighed on the scales,
They *are* altogether *lighter* than vapor.
10 Do not trust in oppression,
Nor vainly hope in robbery;
If riches increase,
Do not set *your* heart *on them.*

11 God has spoken once,
Twice I have heard this:
That power *belongs* to God.
12 Also to You, O Lord, *belongs* mercy;
For You render to each one according
   to his work.

PSALM 63

Joy in the Fellowship of God

A Psalm of David when he was in the
wilderness of Judah.

1 O God, You *are* my God;
Early will I seek You;
My soul thirsts for You;
My flesh longs for You
In a dry and thirsty land
Where there is no water.
2 So I have looked for You in the
   sanctuary,
To see Your power and Your glory.

3 Because Your lovingkindness *is*
   better than life,
My lips shall praise You.
4 Thus I will bless You while I live;
I will lift up my hands in Your name.
5 My soul shall be satisfied as with
   marrow and fatness,
And my mouth shall praise *You* with
   joyful lips.

6 When I remember You on my bed,
I meditate on You in the *night*
   watches.
7 Because You have been my help,
Therefore in the shadow of Your
   wings I will rejoice.
8 My soul follows close behind You;
Your right hand upholds me.

9 But those *who* seek my life, to
   destroy *it,*
Shall go into the lower parts of the
   earth.
10 They shall fall by the sword;
They shall be a portion for jackals.

11 But the king shall rejoice in God;
Everyone who swears by Him shall
   glory;
But the mouth of those who speak
   lies shall be stopped.

PSALM 64

Oppressed by the Wicked but Rejoicing in the LORD

To the Chief Musician.
A Psalm of David.

1 Hear my voice, O God, in my
   meditation;
Preserve my life from fear of the
   enemy.
2 Hide me from the secret plots of the
   wicked,
From the rebellion of the workers of
   iniquity,
3 Who sharpen their tongue like a
   sword,
And bend *their bows to shoot* their
   arrows—bitter words,
4 That they may shoot in secret at the
   blameless;
Suddenly they shoot at him and do
   not fear.

5 They encourage themselves *in* an
   evil matter;
   They talk of laying snares secretly;
   They say, "Who will see them?"
6 They devise iniquities:
   "We have perfected a shrewd scheme."
   Both the inward thought and the
   heart of man are deep.

7 But God shall shoot at them *with* an
   arrow;
   Suddenly they shall be wounded.
8 So He will make them stumble over
   their own tongue;
   All who see them shall flee away.
9 All men shall fear,
   And shall declare the work of God;
   For they shall wisely consider His
   doing.

10 The righteous shall be glad in the
   LORD, and trust in Him.
   And all the upright in heart shall
   glory.

PSALM 65

Praise to God for His Salvation and Providence

To the Chief Musician.
A Psalm of David. A Song.

1 Praise is awaiting You, O God, in Zion;
   And to You the vow shall be
   performed.
2 O You who hear prayer,
   To You all flesh will come.
3 Iniquities prevail against me;
   As for our transgressions,
   You will provide atonement for them.

4 Blessed *is the man* You choose,

And cause to approach *You,*
That he may dwell in Your courts.
We shall be satisfied with the
   goodness of Your house,
Of Your holy temple.

5 *By* awesome deeds in righteousness
   You will answer us,
   O God of our salvation,
   You who are the confidence of all the
   ends of the earth,
   And of the far-off seas;
6 Who established the mountains by
   His strength,
   Being clothed with power;
7 You who still the noise of the seas,
   The noise of their waves,
   And the tumult of the peoples.
8 They also who dwell in the farthest
   parts are afraid of Your signs;
   You make the outgoings of the
   morning and evening rejoice.

9 You visit the earth and water it,
   You greatly enrich it;
   The river of God is full of water;
   You provide their grain,
   For so You have prepared it.
10 You water its ridges abundantly,
   You settle its furrows;
   You make it soft with showers,
   You bless its growth.

11 You crown the year with Your
   goodness,
   And Your paths drip *with*
   abundance.
12 They drop *on* the pastures of the
   wilderness,
   And the little hills rejoice on every
   side.
13 The pastures are clothed with flocks;
   The valleys also are covered with
   grain;
   They shout for joy, they also sing.

PSALM 66

Praise to God for His Awesome Works

To the Chief Musician. A Song. A Psalm.

1 Make a joyful shout to God, all the
   earth!
2 Sing out the honor of His name;
   Make His praise glorious.

INTIMATE MOMENTS

Enjoy a second, third, or fourth honeymoon. Make reservations to spend the night at a nice hotel in your area. If money is tight, start saving $5 or $10 per week until you have enough.

3   Say to God,
    "How awesome are Your works!
    Through the greatness of Your power
    Your enemies shall submit
        themselves to You.
4   All the earth shall worship You
    And sing praises to You;
    They shall sing praises *to* Your
        name."   Selah

5   Come and see the works of God;
    He is awesome *in His* doing toward
        the sons of men.
6   He turned the sea into dry *land;*
    They went through the river on foot.
    There we will rejoice in Him.
7   He rules by His power forever;
    His eyes observe the nations;
    Do not let the rebellious exalt
        themselves.   Selah

8   Oh, bless our God, you peoples!
    And make the voice of His praise to
        be heard,
9   Who keeps our soul among the living,
    And does not allow our feet to be
        moved.
10 For You, O God, have tested us;
    You have refined us as silver is
        refined.
11 You brought us into the net;
    You laid affliction on our backs.
12 You have caused men to ride over
        our heads;
    We went through fire and through
        water;
    But You brought us out to rich
        fulfillment.

13 I will go into Your house with burnt
        offerings;
    I will pay You my vows,
14 Which my lips have uttered
    And my mouth has spoken when I
        was in trouble.
15 I will offer You burnt sacrifices of fat
        animals,
    With the sweet aroma of rams;
    I will offer bulls with goats.   Selah

16 Come *and* hear, all you who fear God,
    And I will declare what He has done
        for my soul.

17 I cried to Him with my mouth,
    And He was extolled with my
        tongue.
18 If I regard iniquity in my heart,
    The Lord will not hear.
19 *But* certainly God has heard *me;*
    He has attended to the voice of my
        prayer.
20 Blessed *be* God,
    Who has not turned away my prayer,
    Nor His mercy from me!

PSALM 67

An Invocation and a Doxology

To the Chief Musician. On stringed
instruments.[a] A Psalm. A Song.

1   God be merciful to us and bless us,
    And cause His face to shine upon us,
                                 Selah
2   That Your way may be known on
        earth,
    Your salvation among all nations.
3   Let the peoples praise You, O God;
    Let all the peoples praise You.
4   Oh, let the nations be glad and sing
        for joy!
    For You shall judge the people
        righteously,
    And govern the nations on earth.
                                 Selah
5   Let the peoples praise You, O God;
    Let all the peoples praise You.
6   *Then* the earth shall yield her
        increase;
    God, our own God, shall bless us.
7   God shall bless us,
    And all the ends of the earth shall
        fear Him.

PSALM 68

The Glory of God in His Goodness to Israel

To the Chief Musician.
A Psalm of David. A Song.

1   Let God arise,
    Let His enemies be scattered;
    Let those also who hate Him flee
        before Him.

67:title [a]Hebrew *neginoth*

2 As smoke is driven away,
So drive *them* away;
As wax melts before the fire,
So let the wicked perish at the
presence of God.

3 But let the righteous be glad;
Let them rejoice before God;
Yes, let them rejoice exceedingly.

4 Sing to God, sing praises to His name;
Extol Him who rides on the clouds,[a]
By His name YAH,
And rejoice before Him.

5 A father of the fatherless, a defender
of widows,
Is God in His holy habitation.

6 God sets the solitary in families;
He brings out those who are bound
into prosperity;
But the rebellious dwell in a dry
land.

7 O God, when You went out before
Your people,
When You marched through the
wilderness,   Selah

8 The earth shook;
The heavens also dropped *rain* at the
presence of God;
Sinai itself *was moved* at the
presence of God, the God of
Israel.

9 You, O God, sent a plentiful rain,
Whereby You confirmed Your
inheritance,
When it was weary.

10 Your congregation dwelt in it;
You, O God, provided from Your
goodness for the poor.

11 The Lord gave the word;
Great *was* the company of those who
proclaimed *it:*

12 "Kings of armies flee, they flee,
And she who remains at home
divides the spoil.

13 Though you lie down among the
sheepfolds,
You will be like the wings of a dove
covered with silver,
And her feathers with yellow gold."

14 When the Almighty scattered kings
in it,
It was *white* as snow in Zalmon.

15 A mountain of God *is* the mountain
of Bashan;
A mountain *of many* peaks *is* the
mountain of Bashan.

16 Why do you fume with envy, you
mountains of *many* peaks?

68:4 [a]Masoretic Text reads *deserts;* Targum reads
heavens (compare verse 34 and Isaiah 19:1).

PARENTING MATTERS

Q: How can we decide whether or not to have children?

Fears over having children can feel overwhelming. Paralysis can set in. Years can pass. In making this decision, I offer one important piece of advice: *Look* at children through the eyes of God, *feel* about children with the heart of God, and *think* about children with the mind of God.

First, realize that God commands us to have children. In the very beginning, God explained His desires when He commanded Adam and Eve to, "Be fruitful and multiply; fill the earth and subdue it; have dominion over the fish of the sea, over the birds of the air, and over every living thing that moves on the earth" (Gen. 1:28). For those who can have children, the command is clear, "Be fruitful." Children aren't optional equipment for a married couple!

Many couples who want children, however, are unable to get pregnant. And infertility can create a profound sense of loss in a marriage. I urge you, though, if God does not allow you to bear your own children, consider adoption. Giving a child a "forever family" is certainly a noble response to Jesus' comment that when we help one in need, we help Him (Matt. 25:40).

This is the mountain *which* God
desires to dwell in;
Yes, the LORD will dwell *in it* forever.

17 The chariots of God *are* twenty
thousand,
Even thousands of thousands;
The Lord is among them *as in* Sinai,
in the Holy *Place.*

18 You have ascended on high,
You have led captivity captive;
You have received gifts among men,
Even *from* the rebellious,
That the LORD God might dwell *there.*

19 Blessed *be* the Lord,
Who daily loads us *with benefits,*
The God of our salvation!   Selah

20 Our God *is* the God of salvation;
And to GOD the Lord *belong* escapes
from death.

21 But God will wound the head of His
enemies,
The hairy scalp of the one who still
goes on in his trespasses.

22 The Lord said, "I will bring back
from Bashan,
I will bring *them* back from the
depths of the sea,

23 That your foot may crush *them*ᵃ in
blood,
And the tongues of your dogs *may
have* their portion from *your*
enemies."

24 They have seen Your procession, O
God,
The procession of my God, my King,
into the sanctuary.

25 The singers went before, the players
on instruments *followed* after;
Among *them were* the maidens
playing timbrels.

26 Bless God in the congregations,
The Lord, from the fountain of
Israel.

27 There *is* little Benjamin, their leader,
The princes of Judah *and* their
company,

The princes of Zebulun *and the*
princes of Naphtali.

28 Your God has commandedᵃ your
strength;
Strengthen, O God, what You have
done for us.

29 Because of Your temple at
Jerusalem,
Kings will bring presents to You.

30 Rebuke the beasts of the reeds,
The herd of bulls with the calves of
the peoples,
Till everyone submits himself with
pieces of silver.
Scatter the peoples *who* delight in
war.

31 Envoys will come out of Egypt;
Ethiopia will quickly stretch out her
hands to God.

32 Sing to God, you kingdoms of the
earth;
Oh, sing praises to the Lord,   Selah

33 To Him who rides on the heaven of
heavens, *which were* of old!
Indeed, He sends out His voice, a
mighty voice.

34 Ascribe strength to God;
His excellence *is* over Israel,
And His strength *is* in the clouds.

35 O God, *You are* more awesome than
Your holy places.
The God of Israel *is* He who gives
strength and power to *His* people.

Blessed *be* God!

PSALM 69

An Urgent Plea for Help in Trouble

To the Chief Musician.
Set to "The Lilies."ᵃ *A Psalm* of David.

1 Save me, O God!
For the waters have come up to *my*
neck.

2 I sink in deep mire,
Where *there is* no standing;
I have come into deep waters,
Where the floods overflow me.

3 I am weary with my crying;
My throat is dry;
My eyes fail while I wait for
my God.

68:23 ᵃSeptuagint, Syriac, Targum, and Vulgate read
you may dip your foot. 68:28 ᵃSeptuagint, Syriac,
Targum, and Vulgate read *Command, O God.*
69:title ᵃHebrew *Shoshannim*

4 Those who hate me without a cause
Are more than the hairs of my head;
They are mighty who would destroy me,
Being my enemies wrongfully;
Though I have stolen nothing,
I *still* must restore *it.*

5 O God, You know my foolishness;
And my sins are not hidden from You.

6 Let not those who wait for You, O Lord GOD of hosts, be ashamed because of me;
Let not those who seek You be confounded because of me, O God of Israel.

7 Because for Your sake I have borne reproach;
Shame has covered my face.

8 I have become a stranger to my brothers,
And an alien to my mother's children;

9 Because zeal for Your house has eaten me up,
And the reproaches of those who reproach You have fallen on me.

10 When I wept *and chastened* my soul with fasting,
That became my reproach.

11 I also made sackcloth my garment;
I became a byword to them.

12 Those who sit in the gate speak against me,
And I *am* the song of the drunkards.

13 But as for me, my prayer *is* to You, O LORD, *in* the acceptable time;
O God, in the multitude of Your mercy,
Hear me in the truth of Your salvation.

14 Deliver me out of the mire,
And let me not sink;
Let me be delivered from those who hate me,
And out of the deep waters.

15 Let not the floodwater overflow me,
Nor let the deep swallow me up;
And let not the pit shut its mouth on me.

16 Hear me, O LORD, for Your lovingkindness *is* good;
Turn to me according to the multitude of Your tender mercies.

17 And do not hide Your face from Your servant,
For I am in trouble;
Hear me speedily.

18 Draw near to my soul, *and* redeem it;
Deliver me because of my enemies.

19 You know my reproach, my shame, and my dishonor;
My adversaries *are* all before You.

20 Reproach has broken my heart,
And I am full of heaviness;
I looked *for someone* to take pity, but *there was* none;
And for comforters, but I found none.

21 They also gave me gall for my food,
And for my thirst they gave me vinegar to drink.

22 Let their table become a snare before them,
And their well-being a trap.

23 Let their eyes be darkened, so that they do not see;
And make their loins shake continually.

24 Pour out Your indignation upon them,
And let Your wrathful anger take hold of them.

25 Let their dwelling place be desolate;
Let no one live in their tents.

26 For they persecute the *ones* You have struck,
And talk of the grief of those You have wounded.

27 Add iniquity to their iniquity,
And let them not come into Your righteousness.

28 Let them be blotted out of the book of the living,
And not be written with the righteous.

29 But I *am* poor and sorrowful;
Let Your salvation, O God, set me up on high.

30 I will praise the name of God with a song,
And will magnify Him with thanksgiving.

31 *This* also shall please the Lord better
    than an ox *or* bull,
    Which has horns and hooves.
32 The humble shall see *this and* be
    glad;
    And you who seek God, your hearts
    shall live.
33 For the Lord hears the poor,
    And does not despise His prisoners.

34 Let heaven and earth praise Him,
    The seas and everything that moves
    in them.
35 For God will save Zion
    And build the cities of Judah,
    That they may dwell there and
    possess it.
36 Also, the descendants of His
    servants shall inherit it,
    And those who love His name shall
    dwell in it.

PSALM 70

Prayer for Relief from Adversaries

To the Chief Musician.
A Psalm of David. To bring to remembrance.

1 *Make haste,* O God, to deliver me!
    Make haste to help me, O Lord!

2 Let them be ashamed and
    confounded
    Who seek my life;
    Let them be turned back[a] and
    confused
    Who desire my hurt.
3 Let them be turned back because of
    their shame,
    Who say, "Aha, aha!"

4 Let all those who seek You rejoice
    and be glad in You;
    And let those who love Your
    salvation say continually,
    "Let God be magnified!"

5 But I *am* poor and needy;
    Make haste to me, O God!
    You *are* my help and my deliverer;
    O Lord, do not delay.

70:2 [a]Following Masoretic Text, Septuagint, Targum, and Vulgate; some Hebrew manuscripts and Syriac read *be appalled* (compare 40:15).

PSALM 71

God the Rock of Salvation

1 In You, O Lord, I put my trust;
    Let me never be put to shame.
2 Deliver me in Your righteousness,
    and cause me to escape;
    Incline Your ear to me, and save me.
3 Be my strong refuge,
    To which I may resort continually;
    You have given the commandment to
    save me,
    For You *are* my rock and my fortress.

4 Deliver me, O my God, out of the
    hand of the wicked,
    Out of the hand of the unrighteous
    and cruel man.
5 For You are my hope, O Lord God;
    You are my trust from my youth.
6 By You I have been upheld from
    birth;
    You are He who took me out of my
    mother's womb.
    My praise *shall be* continually of You.

7 I have become as a wonder to many,
    But You *are* my strong refuge.
8 Let my mouth be filled *with* Your
    praise
    And with Your glory all the day.

INTIMATE MOMENTS

Host a party for him and his friends to watch their favorite sporting event on TV.

9 Do not cast me off in the time of old
    age;
    Do not forsake me when my strength
    fails.
10 For my enemies speak against me;
    And those who lie in wait for my life
    take counsel together,
11 Saying, "God has forsaken him;
    Pursue and take him, for *there is*
    none to deliver *him.*"

12 O God, do not be far from me;
    O my God, make haste to help me!

13 Let them be confounded *and* consumed
Who are adversaries of my life;
Let them be covered *with* reproach
and dishonor
Who seek my hurt.

14 But I will hope continually,
And will praise You yet more and
more.

15 My mouth shall tell of Your
righteousness
And Your salvation all the day,
For I do not know *their* limits.

16 I will go in the strength of the Lord
GOD;
I will make mention of Your
righteousness, of Yours only.

17 O God, You have taught me from my
youth;
And to this *day* I declare Your
wondrous works.

18 Now also when *I am* old and
grayheaded,
O God, do not forsake me,
Until I declare Your strength to *this*
generation,
Your power to everyone *who* is to
come.

19 Also Your righteousness, O God, *is*
very high,
You who have done great things;
O God, who *is* like You?

20 *You,* who have shown me great and
severe troubles,
Shall revive me again,
And bring me up again from the
depths of the earth.

21 You shall increase my greatness,
And comfort me on every side.

22 Also with the lute I will praise You—
And Your faithfulness, O my God!
To You I will sing with the harp,
O Holy One of Israel.

23 My lips shall greatly rejoice when I
sing to You,
And my soul, which You have
redeemed.

24 My tongue also shall talk of Your
righteousness all the day long;
For they are confounded,
For they are brought to shame
Who seek my hurt.

PSALM 72

Glory and Universality of the Messiah's Reign

A Psalm of Solomon.

1 Give the king Your judgments, O
God,
And Your righteousness to the king's
Son.

2 He will judge Your people with
righteousness,
And Your poor with justice.

3 The mountains will bring peace to
the people,
And the little hills, by righteousness.

4 He will bring justice to the poor of
the people;
He will save the children of the
needy,
And will break in pieces the
oppressor.

5 They shall fear You[a]
As long as the sun and moon endure,
Throughout all generations.

6 He shall come down like rain upon
the grass before mowing,
Like showers *that* water the earth.

7 In His days the righteous shall
flourish,
And abundance of peace,
Until the moon is no more.

8 He shall have dominion also from sea
to sea,
And from the River to the ends of
the earth.

9 Those who dwell in the wilderness
will bow before Him,
And His enemies will lick the dust.

10 The kings of Tarshish and of the
isles
Will bring presents;
The kings of Sheba and Seba
Will offer gifts.

11 Yes, all kings shall fall down before
Him;
All nations shall serve Him.

12 For He will deliver the needy when
he cries,

72:5 [a]Following Masoretic Text and Targum;
Septuagint and Vulgate read *They shall continue.*

The poor also, and *him* who has no
  helper.

13 He will spare the poor and needy,
   And will save the souls of the needy.

14 He will redeem their life from
     oppression and violence;
   And precious shall be their blood in
     His sight.

15 And He shall live;
   And the gold of Sheba will be given
     to Him;
   Prayer also will be made for Him
     continually,
   And daily He shall be praised.

16 There will be an abundance of grain
     in the earth,
   On the top of the mountains;
   Its fruit shall wave like Lebanon;
   And *those* of the city shall flourish
     like grass of the earth.

17 His name shall endure forever;
   His name shall continue as long as
     the sun.
   And *men* shall be blessed in Him;
   All nations shall call Him blessed.

18 Blessed *be* the LORD God, the God of
     Israel,
   Who only does wondrous things!

19 And blessed *be* His glorious name
     forever!
   And let the whole earth be filled *with*
     His glory.
   Amen and Amen.

20 The prayers of David the son of
     Jesse are ended.

Book Three: Psalms 73—89

PSALM 73

The Tragedy of the Wicked, and the Blessedness of Trust in God

A Psalm of Asaph.

1 Truly God *is* good to Israel,
   To such as are pure in heart.

2 But as for me, my feet had almost
     stumbled;

3 My steps had nearly slipped.
   For I *was* envious of the boastful,
   When I saw the prosperity of the
     wicked.

4 For *there are* no pangs in their death,
   But their strength *is* firm.

5 They *are* not in trouble *as other* men,
   Nor are they plagued like *other* men.

6 Therefore pride serves as their
     necklace;
   Violence covers them *like* a garment.

7 Their eyes bulge[a] with abundance;
   They have more than heart could
     wish.

8 They scoff and speak wickedly
     concerning oppression;
   They speak loftily.

9 They set their mouth against the
     heavens,
   And their tongue walks through the
     earth.

10 Therefore his people return here,
   And waters of a full *cup* are drained
     by them.

11 And they say, "How does God know?
   And is there knowledge in the Most
     High?"

12 Behold, these *are* the ungodly,
   Who are always at ease;
   They increase *in* riches.

13 Surely I have cleansed my heart *in*
     vain,
   And washed my hands in innocence.

14 For all day long I have been plagued,
   And chastened every morning.

15 If I had said, "I will speak thus,"
   Behold, I would have been untrue to
     the generation of Your children.

16 When I thought *how* to understand
     this,
   It *was* too painful for me—

17 Until I went into the sanctuary of
     God;
   Then I understood their end.

18 Surely You set them in slippery
     places;
   You cast them down to destruction.

19 Oh, how they are *brought* to
     desolation, as in a moment!
   They are utterly consumed with
     terrors.

73:7 [a]Targum reads *face bulges;* Septuagint, Syriac,
and Vulgate read *iniquity bulges.*

20 As a dream when *one* awakes,
　　So, Lord, when You awake,
　　You shall despise their image.

21 Thus my heart was grieved,
　　And I was vexed in my mind.
22 I *was* so foolish and ignorant;
　　I was *like* a beast before You.
23 Nevertheless I *am* continually with
　　　　You;
　　You hold *me* by my right hand.
24 You will guide me with Your
　　　　counsel,
　　And afterward receive me *to* glory.

25 Whom have I in heaven *but You?*
　　And *there is* none upon earth *that* I
　　　　desire besides You.
26 My flesh and my heart fail;
　　But God *is* the strength of my heart
　　　　and my portion forever.

27 For indeed, those who are far from
　　　　You shall perish;
　　You have destroyed all those who
　　　　desert You for harlotry.
28 But *it is* good for me to draw near to
　　　　God;
　　I have put my trust in the Lord GOD,
　　That I may declare all Your works.

PSALM 74

A Plea for Relief from Oppressors

A Contemplation[a] of Asaph.

1 O God, why have You cast *us* off
　　　　forever?
　　Why does Your anger smoke against
　　　　the sheep of Your pasture?
2 Remember Your congregation, *which*
　　　　You have purchased of old,
　　The tribe of Your inheritance, *which*
　　　　You have redeemed—
　　This Mount Zion where You have
　　　　dwelt.
3 Lift up Your feet to the perpetual
　　　　desolations.
　　The enemy has damaged everything
　　　　in the sanctuary.
4 Your enemies roar in the midst of
　　　　Your meeting place;
　　They set up their banners *for* signs.
5 They seem like men who lift up
　　Axes among the thick trees.

6 And now they break down its carved
　　　　work, all at once,
　　With axes and hammers.
7 They have set fire to Your sanctuary;
　　They have defiled the dwelling place
　　　　of Your name to the ground.
8 They said in their hearts,
　　"Let us destroy them altogether."
　　They have burned up all the meeting
　　　　places of God in the land.

9 We do not see our signs;
　　There is no longer any prophet;
　　Nor *is there* any among us who
　　　　knows how long.
10 O God, how long will the adversary
　　　　reproach?
　　Will the enemy blaspheme Your
　　　　name forever?
11 Why do You withdraw Your hand,
　　　　even Your right hand?
　　Take it out of Your bosom and
　　　　destroy *them.*
12 For God *is* my King from of old,
　　Working salvation in the midst of
　　　　the earth.
13 You divided the sea by Your strength;
　　You broke the heads of the sea
　　　　serpents in the waters.
14 You broke the heads of Leviathan in
　　　　pieces,
　　And gave him *as* food to the people
　　　　inhabiting the wilderness.
15 You broke open the fountain and the
　　　　flood;
　　You dried up mighty rivers.
16 The day *is* Yours, the night also *is*
　　　　Yours;
　　You have prepared the light and the
　　　　sun.
17 You have set all the borders of the
　　　　earth;
　　You have made summer and winter.

18 Remember this, *that* the enemy has
　　　　reproached, O LORD,
　　And *that* a foolish people has
　　　　blasphemed Your name.
19 Oh, do not deliver the life of Your
　　　　turtledove to the wild beast!
　　Do not forget the life of Your poor
　　　　forever.

74:title [a]Hebrew *Maschil*

20 Have respect to the covenant;
For the dark places of the earth are
full of the haunts of cruelty.
21 Oh, do not let the oppressed return
ashamed!
Let the poor and needy praise Your
name.
22 Arise, O God, plead Your own cause;
Remember how the foolish man
reproaches You daily.
23 Do not forget the voice of Your
enemies;
The tumult of those who rise up
against You increases continually.

PSALM 75

Thanksgiving for God's Righteous Judgment

To the Chief Musician.
Set to "Do Not Destroy."[a]
A Psalm of Asaph. A Song.

1 We give thanks to You, O God, we
give thanks!
For Your wondrous works declare
that Your name is near.

2 "When I choose the proper time,
I will judge uprightly.
3 The earth and all its inhabitants are
dissolved;
I set up its pillars firmly.   Selah

4 "I said to the boastful, 'Do not deal
boastfully,'
And to the wicked, 'Do not lift up the
horn.
5 Do not lift up your horn on high;
Do *not* speak with a stiff neck.' "

6 For exaltation *comes* neither from the
east
Nor from the west nor from the
south.
7 But God *is* the Judge:
He puts down one,
And exalts another.
8 For in the hand of the LORD *there is* a
cup,
And the wine is red;
It is fully mixed, and He pours it out;

Surely its dregs shall all the wicked
of the earth
Drain *and* drink down.
9 But I will declare forever,
I will sing praises to the God of
Jacob.
10 "All the horns of the wicked I will
also cut off,
But the horns of the righteous shall
be exalted."

PSALM 76

The Majesty of God in Judgment

To the Chief Musician.
On stringed instruments.[a]
A Psalm of Asaph. A Song.

1 In Judah God *is* known;
His name *is* great in Israel.
2 In Salem[a] also is His tabernacle,
And His dwelling place in Zion.
3 There He broke the arrows of the
bow,
The shield and sword of battle.
Selah

4 You *are* more glorious and excellent
Than the mountains of prey.
5 The stouthearted were plundered;
They have sunk into their sleep;
And none of the mighty men have
found the use of their hands.
6 At Your rebuke, O God of Jacob,
Both the chariot and horse were cast
into a dead sleep.

7 You, Yourself, *are* to be feared;
And who may stand in Your presence
When once You are angry?
8 You caused judgment to be heard
from heaven;
The earth feared and was still,
9 When God arose to judgment,
To deliver all the oppressed of the
earth.   Selah

10 Surely the wrath of man shall praise
You;
With the remainder of wrath You
shall gird Yourself.
11 Make vows to the LORD your God,
and pay *them*;

75:title [a]Hebrew *Al Tashcheth* **76:title** [a]Hebrew *neginoth* **76:2** [a]That is, Jerusalem

Let all who are around Him bring
    presents to Him who ought to be
    feared.
12 He shall cut off the spirit of princes;
    He is awesome to the kings of the
    earth.

PSALM 77

The Consoling Memory of God's Redemptive Works

To the Chief Musician.
To Jeduthun. A Psalm of Asaph.

1 I cried out to God with my voice—
    To God with my voice;
    And He gave ear to me.
2 In the day of my trouble I sought the
    Lord;
    My hand was stretched out in the
    night without ceasing;
    My soul refused to be comforted.
3 I remembered God, and was
    troubled;
    I complained, and my spirit was
    overwhelmed.   Selah

4 You hold my eyelids *open;*
    I am so troubled that I cannot speak.
5 I have considered the days of old,
    The years of ancient times.
6 I call to remembrance my song in the
    night;
    I meditate within my heart,
    And my spirit makes diligent search.

7 Will the Lord cast off forever?
    And will He be favorable no more?
8 Has His mercy ceased forever?
    Has *His* promise failed forevermore?
9 Has God forgotten to be gracious?
    Has He in anger shut up His tender
    mercies?   Selah

10 And I said, "This *is* my anguish;
    But I will remember the years of the
    right hand of the Most High."
11 I will remember the works of the
    LORD;
    Surely I will remember Your wonders
    of old.
12 I will also meditate on all Your work,
    And talk of Your deeds.
13 Your way, O God, *is* in the sanctuary;
    Who *is* so great a God as *our* God?

14 You *are* the God who does wonders;
    You have declared Your strength
    among the peoples.
15 You have with *Your* arm redeemed
    Your people,
    The sons of Jacob and Joseph. Selah

16 The waters saw You, O God;
    The waters saw You, they were
    afraid;
    The depths also trembled.
17 The clouds poured out water;
    The skies sent out a sound;
    Your arrows also flashed about.
18 The voice of Your thunder *was* in the
    whirlwind;
    The lightnings lit up the world;
    The earth trembled and shook.
19 Your way *was* in the sea,
    Your path in the great waters,
    And Your footsteps were not known.
20 You led Your people like a flock
    By the hand of Moses and Aaron.

PSALM 78

God's Kindness to Rebellious Israel

A Contemplation[a] of Asaph.

1 Give ear, O my people, *to* my law;
    Incline your ears to the words of my
    mouth.
2 I will open my mouth in a parable;
    I will utter dark sayings of old,
3 Which we have heard and known,
    And our fathers have told us.
4 We will not hide *them* from their
    children,
    Telling to the generation to come the
    praises of the LORD,
    And His strength and His wonderful
    works that He has done.

5 For He established a testimony in
    Jacob,
    And appointed a law in Israel,
    Which He commanded our fathers,
    That they should make them known
    to their children;
6 That the generation to come might
    know *them,*
    The children *who* would be born,

78:title [a]Hebrew *Maschil*

That they may arise and declare
    them to their children,
7 That they may set their hope in God,
    And not forget the works of God,
    But keep His commandments;
8 And may not be like their fathers,
    A stubborn and rebellious
      generation,
    A generation *that* did not set its
      heart aright,
    And whose spirit was not faithful to
      God.

9 The children of Ephraim, *being*
    armed *and* carrying bows,
    Turned back in the day of battle.
10 They did not keep the covenant of
    God;
    They refused to walk in His law,
11 And forgot His works
    And His wonders that He had shown
      them.

12 Marvelous things He did in the sight
    of their fathers,
    In the land of Egypt, *in* the field of
      Zoan.
13 He divided the sea and caused them
    to pass through;
    And He made the waters stand up
      like a heap.
14 In the daytime also He led them with
    the cloud,
    And all the night with a light of fire.
15 He split the rocks in the wilderness,
    And gave *them* drink in abundance
      like the depths.
16 He also brought streams out of the
    rock,
    And caused waters to run down like
      rivers.

17 But they sinned even more against
    Him
    By rebelling against the Most High
      in the wilderness.
18 And they tested God in their heart
    By asking for the food of their fancy.
19 Yes, they spoke against God:
    They said, "Can God prepare a table
      in the wilderness?
20 Behold, He struck the rock,
    So that the waters gushed out,
    And the streams overflowed.

BIBLICAL INSIGHTS • 78:1–8

Teach Your Children Well

WHAT AN AWESOME RESPONSIBILITY and privilege we have in these last days to be a parent! Psalm 78 shows us the importance of leaving a godly heritage by making sure our children know of the wonderful works of God and His faithfulness to us, "For He [The Lord] established a testimony in Jacob, and appointed a law in Israel, which He commanded our fathers, that they should make them known to their children; that the generation to come might know them, the children who would be born, that they may arise and declare them to their children" (vv. 5, 6).

Why are parents to teach their children the wonderful works that God has done? We are to do so that our children "may set their hope in God, and not forget the works of God, but keep His commandments" (78:7).

If anything makes a family distinctively Christian, it's that the mother and father remain committed to the Great Commandment, which is to love God with all their heart, soul, mind, and strength (Mark 12:30), and to the Great Commission, which is, "Go therefore and make disciples of all the nations" (Matt. 28:19). When we build obedience to these two commandments into the lives of our children, we leave them with a great heritage indeed.

Why not use your next dinner together as a couple or a family to compile a list of what God has done in your lives and family? Keep the list active and live, adding to it on a regular basis.

Can He give bread also?
    Can He provide meat for His people?"

21 Therefore the LORD heard *this* and
    was furious;
    So a fire was kindled against Jacob,
    And anger also came up against
      Israel,

22 Because they did not believe in God,
And did not trust in His salvation.
23 Yet He had commanded the clouds above,
And opened the doors of heaven,
24 Had rained down manna on them to eat,
And given them of the bread of heaven.
25 Men ate angels' food;
He sent them food to the full.
26 He caused an east wind to blow in the heavens;
And by His power He brought in the south wind.
27 He also rained meat on them like the dust,
Feathered fowl like the sand of the seas;
28 And He let *them* fall in the midst of their camp,
All around their dwellings.
29 So they ate and were well filled,
For He gave them their own desire.
30 They were not deprived of their craving;
But while their food *was* still in their mouths,

31 The wrath of God came against them,
And slew the stoutest of them,
And struck down the choice *men* of Israel.
32 In spite of this they still sinned,
And did not believe in His wondrous works.
33 Therefore their days He consumed in futility,
And their years in fear.
34 When He slew them, then they sought Him;
And they returned and sought earnestly for God.
35 Then they remembered that God *was* their rock,
And the Most High God their Redeemer.
36 Nevertheless they flattered Him with their mouth,
And they lied to Him with their tongue;
37 For their heart was not steadfast with Him,
Nor were they faithful in His covenant.
38 But He, *being* full of compassion, forgave *their* iniquity,

ROMANTIC QUOTES AND NOTES
Are You a Good Shepherd?

If you're a parent, then you're a shepherd. The only real question is, are you a good one or a bad one?

A good shepherd has integrity of heart. It is said of David, "So he shepherded them according to the integrity of his heart, and guided them by the skillfulness of his hands" (78:72).

Are you a man or woman of integrity? Do you do what you say you're going to do? Are you the same person in public that you are in private?

A good shepherd also has skillful hands—such a leader knows the sheep in his or her care, as well as their needs. And good shepherds don't lead any faster than their sheep can follow.

Good shepherds also protect their sheep from predators. It's the job of all parents! God calls you to protect your family in a world gone crazy. For example, guard your  children from the major negative influencers in their lives: media and peers. Know what they are watching (pornography on the Internet? Movies full of sex and violence?) and who they are spending time with.

A good shepherd anticipates danger and counts it a privilege to care for the real needs of the sheep. Being a good parent doesn't mean you do everything or that you do it perfectly, but it does require constant diligence and perseverance.

Are you a good shepherd?

And did not destroy *them.*
Yes, many a time He turned His
anger away,
And did not stir up all His wrath;

39 For He remembered that they *were
but* flesh,
A breath that passes away and does
not come again.

40 How often they provoked Him in the
wilderness,
And grieved Him in the desert!

41 Yes, again and again they tempted
God,
And limited the Holy One of Israel.

42 They did not remember His power:
The day when He redeemed them
from the enemy,

43 When He worked His signs in
Egypt,
And His wonders in the field of
Zoan;

44 Turned their rivers into blood,
And their streams, that they could
not drink.

45 He sent swarms of flies among them,
which devoured them,
And frogs, which destroyed them.

46 He also gave their crops to the
caterpillar,
And their labor to the locust.

47 He destroyed their vines with hail,
And their sycamore trees with frost.

48 He also gave up their cattle to the
hail,
And their flocks to fiery lightning.

49 He cast on them the fierceness of His
anger,
Wrath, indignation, and trouble,
By sending angels of destruction
among them.

50 He made a path for His anger;
He did not spare their soul from
death,
But gave their life over to the plague,

51 And destroyed all the firstborn in
Egypt,
The first of *their* strength in the
tents of Ham.

52 But He made His own people go
forth like sheep,
And guided them in the wilderness
like a flock;

53 And He led them on safely, so that
they did not fear;
But the sea overwhelmed their
enemies.

54 And He brought them to His holy
border,
This mountain *which* His right hand
had acquired.

55 He also drove out the nations before
them,
Allotted them an inheritance by
survey,
And made the tribes of Israel dwell
in their tents.

56 Yet they tested and provoked the
Most High God,
And did not keep His testimonies,

57 But turned back and acted
unfaithfully like their fathers;
They were turned aside like a
deceitful bow.

58 For they provoked Him to anger with
their high places,
And moved Him to jealousy with
their carved images.

59 When God heard *this,* He was
furious,
And greatly abhorred Israel,

60 So that He forsook the tabernacle of
Shiloh,
The tent He had placed among men,

61 And delivered His strength into
captivity,
And His glory into the enemy's hand.

62 He also gave His people over to the
sword,
And was furious with His
inheritance.

63 The fire consumed their young men,
And their maidens were not given in
marriage.

64 Their priests fell by the sword,
And their widows made no
lamentation.

65 Then the Lord awoke as *from* sleep,
Like a mighty man who shouts
because of wine.

66 And He beat back His enemies;
He put them to a perpetual reproach.

67 Moreover He rejected the tent of
Joseph,

From Mud to Marble

PLAYWRIGHT EUGENE O'NEILL SAID, "You do not build a marble tower out of a mixture of mud and manure." His words remind us that we would do well to begin *now* the process of becoming the men our family will someday look up to.

I'm comforted by the fact that a man's character is shaped by his relationship with God. That's where my hope lies. God hasn't given up on me! He's still squeezing the mud and manure out of my life, building a strong, enduring marble tower instead, "Help us, O God of our salvation, for the glory of Your name; and deliver us, and provide atonement for our sins, for Your name's sake!" (79:9)

Do you see the reason we can have any hope at all that we can become the kind of men who will one day deserve to be remembered fondly? It doesn't depend on us. It doesn't depend on our cleverness or our resources or even our dogged determination. No! In fact, God has staked His very name and reputation on what He will do in us. For *His own sake* He will transform us into people who look increasingly like Jesus Christ (Rom. 8:29).

And did not choose the tribe of
      Ephraim,
68 But chose the tribe of Judah,
      Mount Zion which He loved.
69 And He built His sanctuary like the
      heights,
      Like the earth which He has
      established forever.
70 He also chose David His servant,
      And took him from the sheepfolds;
71 From following the ewes that had
      young He brought him,
      To shepherd Jacob His people,
      And Israel His inheritance.
72 So he shepherded them according to
      the integrity of his heart,
      And guided them by the skillfulness
      of his hands.

PSALM 79

A Dirge and a Prayer for Israel, Destroyed by Enemies

A Psalm of Asaph.

1 O God, the nations have come into
      Your inheritance;
      Your holy temple they have defiled;
      They have laid Jerusalem in heaps.
2 The dead bodies of Your servants
      They have given *as* food for the
      birds of the heavens,
      The flesh of Your saints to the
      beasts of the earth.
3 Their blood they have shed like
      water all around Jerusalem,
      And *there was* no one to bury *them.*
4 We have become a reproach to our
      neighbors,
      A scorn and derision to those who
      are around us.

5 How long, LORD?
      Will You be angry forever?
      Will Your jealousy burn like fire?
6 Pour out Your wrath on the nations
      that do not know You,
      And on the kingdoms that do not call
      on Your name.
7 For they have devoured Jacob,
      And laid waste his dwelling place.

8 Oh, do not remember former
      iniquities against us!
      Let Your tender mercies come
      speedily to meet us,
      For we have been brought very
      low.
9 Help us, O God of our salvation,
      For the glory of Your name;
      And deliver us, and provide
      atonement for our sins,
      For Your name's sake!
10 Why should the nations say,
   "Where *is* their God?"
      Let there be known among the
      nations in our sight
      The avenging of the blood of Your
      servants *which has been* shed.

11 Let the groaning of the prisoner
      come before You;
      According to the greatness of Your
      power

Preserve those who are appointed to
    die;

12 And return to our neighbors
        sevenfold into their bosom
    Their reproach with which they have
        reproached You, O Lord.

13 So we, Your people and sheep of
        Your pasture,
    Will give You thanks forever;
    We will show forth Your praise to all
        generations.

PSALM 80

Prayer for Israel's Restoration

To the Chief Musician. Set to "The Lilies."[a]
A Testimony[b] of Asaph. A Psalm.

1 Give ear, O Shepherd of Israel,
    You who lead Joseph like a flock;
    You who dwell *between* the
        cherubim, shine forth!

2 Before Ephraim, Benjamin, and
        Manasseh,
    Stir up Your strength,
    And come *and* save us!

3 Restore us, O God;
    Cause Your face to shine,
    And we shall be saved!

4 O LORD God of hosts,
    How long will You be angry
    Against the prayer of Your people?

5 You have fed them with the bread of
        tears,
    And given them tears to drink in
        great measure.

6 You have made us a strife to our
        neighbors,
    And our enemies laugh among
        themselves.

7 Restore us, O God of hosts;
    Cause Your face to shine,
    And we shall be saved!

8 You have brought a vine out of Egypt;
    You have cast out the nations, and
        planted it.

9 You prepared *room* for it,

And caused it to take deep root,
    And it filled the land.

10 The hills were covered with its
        shadow,
    And the mighty cedars with its
        boughs.

11 She sent out her boughs to the Sea,[a]
    And her branches to the River.[b]

12 Why have You broken down her
        hedges,
    So that all who pass by the way
        pluck her *fruit?*

13 The boar out of the woods
        uproots it,
    And the wild beast of the field
        devours it.

14 Return, we beseech You, O God of
        hosts;
    Look down from heaven and see,
    And visit this vine

15 And the vineyard which Your right
        hand has planted,
    And the branch *that* You made
        strong for Yourself.

16 *It is* burned with fire, *it is* cut down;
    They perish at the rebuke of Your
        countenance.

17 Let Your hand be upon the man of
        Your right hand,
    Upon the son of man *whom* You
        made strong for Yourself.

18 Then we will not turn back from You;
    Revive us, and we will call upon
        Your name.

19 Restore us, O LORD God of hosts;
    Cause Your face to shine,
    And we shall be saved!

PSALM 81

An Appeal for Israel's Repentance

To the Chief Musician. On an instrument of
Gath.[a] *A Psalm* of Asaph.

1 Sing aloud to God our strength;
    Make a joyful shout to the God of
        Jacob.

2 Raise a song and strike the timbrel,
    The pleasant harp with the lute.

3 Blow the trumpet at the time of the
        New Moon,

80:title [a]Hebrew *Shoshannim* [b]Hebrew *Eduth*
80:11 [a]That is, the Mediterranean [b]That is, the
Euphrates **81:title** [a]Hebrew *Al Gittith*

At the full moon, on our solemn feast
day.
4 For this *is* a statute for Israel,
A law of the God of Jacob.
5 This He established in Joseph *as* a
testimony,
When He went throughout the land
of Egypt,
Where I heard a language I did not
understand.

6 "I removed his shoulder from the
burden;
His hands were freed from the baskets.

ROMANCE FAQ

**Q: How important
are tender touch
and gentle words?**

Before marriage, two people in love can
hardly keep their hands off each other.
They find the touch of their beloved
thrilling. But what happens after the wedding? After just a few years of marriage,
some couples would consider a firm
handshake a wildly intimate encounter.

This should not be the case! There is
great power in tender touch, even if it's
just a long, full-body hug or a lingering
kiss. Or the touch may be a gentle caress
of her face that has no secret motive to
make sexual demands but instead communicates, "I love you, Sweetheart, and I
care for you tenderly."

Gentle words have similar power.
Consider the following list of some
things any husband could use in complimenting and praising his wife: charm;
femininity; faithfulness (to God, to you, to
your children); hard work; beauty; personality; her love (including her receptivity and responsiveness to you as a man);
her advice and counsel; character; desir-
ability; friendship. And that's just a start!

What wife wouldn't respond to a husband who praises her regularly with gentle words for all these wonderful qualities?
Why don't you try it, and find out for
yourself?

7 You called in trouble, and I delivered
you;
I answered you in the secret place of
thunder;
I tested you at the waters of Meribah.
Selah

8 "Hear, O My people, and I will
admonish you!
O Israel, if you will listen to Me!
9 There shall be no foreign god among
you;
Nor shall you worship any foreign
god.
10 I *am* the LORD your God,
Who brought you out of the land of
Egypt;
Open your mouth wide, and I will
fill it.

11 "But My people would not heed My
voice,
And Israel would *have* none of Me.
12 So I gave them over to their own
stubborn heart,
To walk in their own counsels.

13 "Oh, that My people would listen to
Me,
That Israel would walk in My ways!
14 I would soon subdue their enemies,
And turn My hand against their
adversaries.
15 The haters of the LORD would
pretend submission to Him,
But their fate would endure forever.
16 He would have fed them also with
the finest of wheat;
And with honey from the rock I
would have satisfied you."

PSALM 82

A Plea for Justice

A Psalm of Asaph.

1 God stands in the congregation of
the mighty;
He judges among the gods.[a]
2 How long will you judge unjustly,
And show partiality to the wicked?
Selah
3 Defend the poor and fatherless;

82:1 [a]Hebrew *elohim, mighty ones;* that is, the judges

Do justice to the afflicted and needy.

4 Deliver the poor and needy;
   Free *them* from the hand of the
      wicked.

5 They do not know, nor do they
      understand;
   They walk about in darkness;
   All the foundations of the earth are
      unstable.

6 I said, "You *are* gods,ᵃ
   And all of you *are* children of the
      Most High.

7 But you shall die like men,
   And fall like one of the princes."

8 Arise, O God, judge the earth;
   For You shall inherit all nations.

PSALM 83

Prayer to Frustrate Conspiracy Against Israel

A Song. A Psalm of Asaph.

1 Do not keep silent, O God!
   Do not hold Your peace,
   And do not be still, O God!

2 For behold, Your enemies make a
      tumult;
   And those who hate You have lifted
      up their head.

3 They have taken crafty counsel
      against Your people,
   And consulted together against Your
      sheltered ones.

4 They have said, "Come, and let us
      cut them off from *being* a nation,
   That the name of Israel may be
      remembered no more."

5 For they have consulted together
      with one consent;
   They form a confederacy against You:

6 The tents of Edom and the
      Ishmaelites;
   Moab and the Hagrites;

7 Gebal, Ammon, and Amalek;
   Philistia with the inhabitants of Tyre;

8 Assyria also has joined with them;
   They have helped the children of
      Lot.   Selah

9 Deal with them as *with* Midian,
   As *with* Sisera,
   As *with* Jabin at the Brook Kishon,

10 Who perished at En Dor,
   Who became *as* refuse on the earth.

11 Make their nobles like Oreb and like
      Zeeb,
   Yes, all their princes like Zebah and
      Zalmunna,

12 Who said, "Let us take for ourselves
   The pastures of God for a
      possession."

13 O my God, make them like the
      whirling dust,
   Like the chaff before the wind!

14 As the fire burns the woods,
   And as the flame sets the mountains
      on fire,

15 So pursue them with Your tempest,
   And frighten them with Your storm.

16 Fill their faces with shame,
   That they may seek Your name, O
      LORD.

17 Let them be confounded and
      dismayed forever;
   Yes, let them be put to shame and
      perish,

18 That they may know that You,
   whose name alone *is* the LORD,
   Are the Most High over all the earth.

PSALM 84

The Blessedness of Dwelling in the House of God

To the Chief Musician. On an instrument of
Gath.ᵃ A Psalm of the sons of Korah.

1 How lovely *is* Your tabernacle,
   O LORD of hosts!

2 My soul longs, yes, even faints
   For the courts of the LORD;
   My heart and my flesh cry out for
      the living God.

3 Even the sparrow has found a home,
   And the swallow a nest for herself,
   Where she may lay her young—
   Even Your altars, O LORD of hosts,
   My King and my God.

4 Blessed *are* those who dwell in Your
      house;
   They will still be praising You.   Selah

82:6 ᵃHebrew *elohim, mighty ones;* that is, the judges
84:title ᵃHebrew *Al Gittith*

5 Blessed *is* the man whose strength *is*
in You,
Whose heart *is* set on pilgrimage.
6 *As they* pass through the Valley of
Baca,
They make it a spring;
The rain also covers it with pools.
7 They go from strength to strength;
Each one appears before God in
Zion.[a]

8 O LORD God of hosts, hear my prayer;
Give ear, O God of Jacob!   Selah
9 O God, behold our shield,
And look upon the face of Your
anointed.

10 For a day in Your courts *is* better
than a thousand.
I would rather be a doorkeeper in the
house of my God
Than dwell in the tents of
wickedness.
11 For the LORD God *is* a sun and shield;
The LORD will give grace and glory;
No good *thing* will He withhold
From those who walk uprightly.

12 O LORD of hosts,
Blessed *is* the man who trusts in You!

PSALM 85

Prayer that the LORD Will Restore Favor to the Land

To the Chief Musician.
A Psalm of the sons of Korah.

1 LORD, You have been favorable to
Your land;
You have brought back the captivity
of Jacob.
2 You have forgiven the iniquity of
Your people;
You have covered all their sin. Selah
3 You have taken away all Your wrath;
You have turned from the fierceness
of Your anger.

4 Restore us, O God of our salvation,
And cause Your anger toward us to
cease.
5 Will You be angry with us forever?
Will You prolong Your anger to all
generations?

6 Will You not revive us again,
That Your people may rejoice in You?
7 Show us Your mercy, LORD,
And grant us Your salvation.

8 I will hear what God the LORD will
speak,
For He will speak peace
To His people and to His saints;
But let them not turn back to folly.
9 Surely His salvation *is* near to those
who fear Him,
That glory may dwell in our land.

10 Mercy and truth have met together;
Righteousness and peace have
kissed.
11 Truth shall spring out of the earth,
And righteousness shall look down
from heaven.
12 Yes, the LORD will give *what is* good;
And our land will yield its increase.
13 Righteousness will go before Him,
And shall make His footsteps *our*
pathway.

PSALM 86

Prayer for Mercy, with Meditation on the Excellencies of the LORD

A Prayer of David.

1 Bow down Your ear, O LORD, hear me;
For I *am* poor and needy.
2 Preserve my life, for I *am* holy;
You are my God;
Save Your servant who trusts in You!
3 Be merciful to me, O Lord,
For I cry to You all day long.
4 Rejoice the soul of Your servant,
For to You, O Lord, I lift up my soul.
5 For You, Lord, *are* good, and ready to
forgive,
And abundant in mercy to all those
who call upon You.

6 Give ear, O LORD, to my prayer;
And attend to the voice of my
supplications.
7 In the day of my trouble I will call
upon You,
For You will answer me.

84:7 [a]Septuagint, Syriac, and Vulgate read *The God of gods shall be seen.*

8   Among the gods *there is* none like
You, O Lord;
Nor *are there any works* like Your
works.

9   All nations whom You have made
Shall come and worship before You,
O Lord,
And shall glorify Your name.

10   For You *are* great, and do wondrous
things;
You alone *are* God.

11   Teach me Your way, O LORD;
I will walk in Your truth;
Unite my heart to fear Your name.

12   I will praise You, O Lord my God,
with all my heart,
And I will glorify Your name
forevermore.

13   For great *is* Your mercy toward me,
And You have delivered my soul
from the depths of Sheol.

14   O God, the proud have risen against
me,
And a mob of violent *men* have
sought my life,
And have not set You before them.

15   But You, O Lord, *are* a God full of
compassion, and gracious,
Longsuffering and abundant in
mercy and truth.

16   Oh, turn to me, and have mercy on
me!
Give Your strength to Your servant,
And save the son of Your
maidservant.

17   Show me a sign for good,
That those who hate me may see *it*
and be ashamed,
Because You, LORD, have helped me
and comforted me.

PSALM 87

The Glories of the City of God

A Psalm of the sons of Korah. A Song.

1   His foundation *is* in the holy
mountains.

2   The LORD loves the gates of Zion
More than all the dwellings of Jacob.

3   Glorious things are spoken of you,
O city of God!   Selah

4   "I will make mention of Rahab and
Babylon to those who know Me;
Behold, O Philistia and Tyre, with
Ethiopia:
'   This *one* was born there.' "

5   And of Zion it will be said,
"This *one* and that *one* were born in
her;
And the Most High Himself shall
establish her."

6   The LORD will record,
When He registers the peoples:
"This *one* was born there."   Selah

7   Both the singers and the players on
instruments *say,*
"All my springs *are* in you."

PSALM 88

A Prayer for Help in Despondency

A Song. A Psalm of the sons of Korah. To the
Chief Musician. Set to "Mahalath Leannoth." A
Contemplation[a] of Heman the Ezrahite.

1   O LORD, God of my salvation,
I have cried out day and night before
You.

2   Let my prayer come before You;
Incline Your ear to my cry.

3   For my soul is full of troubles,
And my life draws near to the grave.

4   I am counted with those who go
down to the pit;
I am like a man *who has* no strength,

5   Adrift among the dead,
Like the slain who lie in the grave,
Whom You remember no more,
And who are cut off from Your hand.

INTIMATE MOMENTS

The next time your favorite team (or show) is on TV, skip it and take her shopping or out to dinner. Let her know that she is more important than what you're giving up.

88:title [a]Hebrew *Maschil*

6 You have laid me in the lowest pit,
In darkness, in the depths.

7 Your wrath lies heavy upon me,
And You have afflicted *me* with all
Your waves.   Selah

8 You have put away my
acquaintances far from me;
You have made me an abomination
to them;
I am shut up, and I cannot get out;

9 My eye wastes away because of
affliction.

LORD, I have called daily upon You;
I have stretched out my hands to You.

10 Will You work wonders for the dead?
Shall the dead arise *and* praise You?
                    Selah

11 Shall Your lovingkindness be
declared in the grave?
Or Your faithfulness in the place of
destruction?

12 Shall Your wonders be known in the
dark?
And Your righteousness in the land
of forgetfulness?

13 But to You I have cried out, O LORD,
And in the morning my prayer
comes before You.

14 LORD, why do You cast off my soul?
Why do You hide Your face from me?

15 I *have been* afflicted and ready to die
from *my* youth;
I suffer Your terrors;
I am distraught.

16 Your fierce wrath has gone over me;
Your terrors have cut me off.

17 They came around me all day long
like water;
They engulfed me altogether.

18 Loved one and friend You have put
far from me,
And my acquaintances into
darkness.

PSALM 89

Remembering the Covenant with David, and Sorrow for Lost Blessings

A Contemplation[a] of Ethan the Ezrahite.

1 I will sing of the mercies of the LORD
forever;

With my mouth will I make known
Your faithfulness to all
generations.

2 For I have said, "Mercy shall be built
up forever;
Your faithfulness You shall establish
in the very heavens."

3 "I have made a covenant with My
chosen,
I have sworn to My servant David:

4 'Your seed I will establish forever,
And build up your throne to all
generations.' "   Selah

5 And the heavens will praise Your
wonders, O LORD;
Your faithfulness also in the
assembly of the saints.

6 For who in the heavens can be
compared to the LORD?
Who among the sons of the mighty
can be likened to the LORD?

7 God is greatly to be feared in the
assembly of the saints,
And to be held in reverence by all
those around Him.

8 O LORD God of hosts,
Who *is* mighty like You, O LORD?
Your faithfulness also surrounds
You.

9 You rule the raging of the sea;
When its waves rise, You still them.

10 You have broken Rahab in pieces, as
one who is slain;
You have scattered Your enemies
with Your mighty arm.

11 The heavens *are* Yours, the earth
also *is* Yours;
The world and all its fullness, You
have founded them.

12 The north and the south, You have
created them;
Tabor and Hermon rejoice in Your
name.

13 You have a mighty arm;
Strong is Your hand, *and* high is
Your right hand.

14 Righteousness and justice *are* the
foundation of Your throne;
Mercy and truth go before Your face.

89:title [a] Hebrew *Maschil*

15 Blessed *are* the people who know the
     joyful sound!
   They walk, O LORD, in the light of
     Your countenance.
16 In Your name they rejoice all day
     long,
   And in Your righteousness they are
     exalted.
17 For You *are* the glory of their
     strength,
   And in Your favor our horn is
     exalted.
18 For our shield *belongs* to the LORD,
   And our king to the Holy One of
     Israel.

19 Then You spoke in a vision to Your
     holy one,[a]
   And said: "I have given help to *one
     who is* mighty;
   I have exalted one chosen from the
     people.
20 I have found My servant David;
   With My holy oil I have anointed him,
21 With whom My hand shall be
     established;
   Also My arm shall strengthen him.
22 The enemy shall not outwit him,
   Nor the son of wickedness afflict
     him.
23 I will beat down his foes before his
     face,
   And plague those who hate him.

24 "But My faithfulness and My mercy
     shall be with him,
   And in My name his horn shall be
     exalted.
25 Also I will set his hand over the sea,
   And his right hand over the rivers.
26 He shall cry to Me, 'You *are* my
     Father,
   My God, and the rock of my
     salvation.'
27 Also I will make him *My* firstborn,
   The highest of the kings of the
     earth.
28 My mercy I will keep for him forever,
   And My covenant shall stand firm
     with him.

29 His seed also I will make *to endure*
     forever,
   And his throne as the days of heaven.

30 "If his sons forsake My law
   And do not walk in My judgments,
31 If they break My statutes
   And do not keep My commandments,
32 Then I will punish their
     transgression with the rod,
   And their iniquity with stripes.
33 Nevertheless My lovingkindness I
     will not utterly take from him,
   Nor allow My faithfulness to fail.
34 My covenant I will not break,
   Nor alter the word that has gone out
     of My lips.
35 Once I have sworn by My holiness;
   I will not lie to David:
36 His seed shall endure forever,
   And his throne as the sun before Me;
37 It shall be established forever like the
     moon,
   Even *like* the faithful witness in the
     sky."   Selah

38 But You have cast off and abhorred,
   You have been furious with Your
     anointed.
39 You have renounced the covenant of
     Your servant;
   You have profaned his crown *by
     casting it* to the ground.
40 You have broken down all his hedges;
   You have brought his strongholds to
     ruin.
41 All who pass by the way plunder
     him;
   He is a reproach to his neighbors.
42 You have exalted the right hand of
     his adversaries;
   You have made all his enemies
     rejoice.
43 You have also turned back the edge
     of his sword,
   And have not sustained him in the
     battle.
44 You have made his glory cease,
   And cast his throne down to the
     ground.
45 The days of his youth You have
     shortened;
   You have covered him with shame.
                                       Selah

89:19 [a]Following many Hebrew manuscripts;
Masoretic Text, Septuagint, Targum, and Vulgate
read *holy ones*.

46 How long, LORD?
   Will You hide Yourself forever?
   Will Your wrath burn like fire?
47 Remember how short my time is;
   For what futility have You created all
      the children of men?
48 What man can live and not see
      death?
   Can he deliver his life from the power
      of the grave?   Selah
49 Lord, where *are* Your former
      lovingkindnesses,
   Which You swore to David in Your
      truth?
50 Remember, Lord, the reproach of
      Your servants—
   How I bear in my bosom *the
      reproach of* all the many peoples,
51 With which Your enemies have
      reproached, O LORD,
   With which they have reproached the
      footsteps of Your anointed.

52 Blessed *be* the LORD forevermore!
   Amen and Amen.

Book Four: Psalms 90—106

PSALM 90

The Eternity of God, and Man's Frailty

A Prayer of Moses the man of God.

1 Lord, You have been our dwelling
      place[a] in all generations.
2 Before the mountains were brought
      forth,
   Or ever You had formed the earth
      and the world,
   Even from everlasting to everlasting,
      You *are* God.
3 You turn man to destruction,
   And say, "Return, O children
      of men."
4 For a thousand years in Your sight
   Are like yesterday when it is past,
   And *like* a watch in the night.
5 You carry them away *like* a flood;
   They are like a sleep.
   In the morning they are like grass
      which grows up:
6 In the morning it flourishes and
      grows up;

In the evening it is cut down and
   withers.
7 For we have been consumed by Your
      anger,
   And by Your wrath we are terrified.
8 You have set our iniquities before You,
   Our secret *sins* in the light of Your
      countenance.
9 For all our days have passed away in
      Your wrath;
   We finish our years like a sigh.
10 The days of our lives *are* seventy
      years;
   And if by reason of strength *they
      are* eighty years,
   Yet their boast *is* only labor and
      sorrow;
   For it is soon cut off, and we fly away.
11 Who knows the power of Your anger?
   For as the fear of You, *so is* Your
      wrath.
12 So teach *us* to number our days,
   That we may gain a heart of wisdom.
13 Return, O LORD!
   How long?
   And have compassion on Your
      servants.
14 Oh, satisfy us early with Your mercy,
   That we may rejoice and be glad all
      our days!
15 Make us glad according to the days
   in which You have afflicted us,
   The years *in which* we have seen evil.
16 Let Your work appear to Your
      servants,
   And Your glory to their children.
17 And let the beauty of the LORD our
      God be upon us,
   And establish the work of our hands
      for us;
   Yes, establish the work of our hands.

PSALM 91

Safety of Abiding in the Presence of God

1 He who dwells in the secret place of
      the Most High
   Shall abide under the shadow of the
      Almighty.

90:1 [a]Septuagint, Targum, and Vulgate read *refuge.*

2   I will say of the LORD, "He is my
      refuge and my fortress;
     My God, in Him I will trust."

3   Surely He shall deliver you from the
      snare of the fowler[a]
     And from the perilous pestilence.
4   He shall cover you with His feathers,
     And under His wings you shall take
      refuge;
     His truth *shall be your* shield and
      buckler.
5   You shall not be afraid of the terror
      by night,
     Nor of the arrow *that* flies by day,
6   *Nor* of the pestilence *that* walks in
      darkness,
     Nor of the destruction *that* lays
      waste at noonday.

7   A thousand may fall at your side,
     And ten thousand at your right
      hand;
     But it shall not come near you.
8   Only with your eyes shall you look,
     And see the reward of the wicked.

9   Because you have made the LORD,
      who is my refuge,
     Even the Most High, your dwelling
      place,
10   No evil shall befall you,
     Nor shall any plague come near your
      dwelling;
11   For He shall give His angels charge
      over you,
     To keep you in all your ways.
12   In *their* hands they shall bear you up,
     Lest you dash your foot against a
      stone.
13   You shall tread upon the lion and the
      cobra,
     The young lion and the serpent you
      shall trample underfoot.

14   "Because he has set his love upon Me,
      therefore I will deliver him;
     I will set him on high, because he has
      known My name.
15   He shall call upon Me, and I will
      answer him;
     I *will be* with him in trouble;
     I will deliver him and honor him.

91:3 [a]That is, one who catches birds in a trap or snare

16   With long life I will satisfy him,
     And show him My salvation."

PSALM 92

Praise to the LORD for His Love and Faithfulness

A Psalm. A Song for the Sabbath day.

1   *It is* good to give thanks to the LORD,
     And to sing praises to Your name, O
      Most High;
2   To declare Your lovingkindness in
      the morning,
     And Your faithfulness every night,
3   On an instrument of ten strings,
     On the lute,
     And on the harp,
     With harmonious sound.
4   For You, LORD, have made me glad
      through Your work;
     I will triumph in the works of Your
      hands.

5   O LORD, how great are Your works!
     Your thoughts are very deep.
6   A senseless man does not know,
     Nor does a fool understand this.
7   When the wicked spring up like grass,
     And when all the workers of iniquity
      flourish,
     It is that they may be destroyed
      forever.

8   But You, LORD, *are* on high
      forevermore.
9   For behold, Your enemies, O LORD,
     For behold, Your enemies shall
      perish;
     All the workers of iniquity shall be
      scattered.

10   But my horn You have exalted like a
      wild ox;
     I have been anointed with fresh oil.
11   My eye also has seen *my desire* on
      my enemies;
     My ears hear *my desire* on the
      wicked
     Who rise up against me.

12   The righteous shall flourish like a
      palm tree,
     He shall grow like a cedar in
      Lebanon.

Old but Still Green

AS OUR SONS AND DAUGHTERS mature and eventually leave the nest, our role as parents gradually changes, as does our day-to-day purpose and level of involvement. But we should *never* buy into the world's view that our impact diminishes as we age! In fact, God wants us to stay intimately connected to our children's lives, regardless of how old they (or we) grow.

I'll never forget leading a Bible study with a group of a dozen men, most of whom had been married for more than 50 years. As we talked about their involvement in their adult children's lives, most of these men expressed that they felt like their influence was over. What a tragedy—for their children and for these patriarchs. At a time when they had the most wisdom and time to invest, they no longer felt needed.

But the psalmist wrote, "The righteous shall flourish like a palm tree, he shall grow like a cedar in Lebanon. Those who are planted in the house of the LORD shall flourish in the courts of our God. They shall still bear fruit in old age; they shall be fresh and flourishing" (92:12–14).

The Divine Gardener cultivates a different perspective of old age.

God wants you to flourish, to be a sap-filled and green tree even when you get old! But do you know the only way that will happen? You need to grow *today* so that you'll enjoy a green *tomorrow*.

Embrace this truth as the years pass: You play a vital role as mentor and spiritual leader of your family. We parents have the awesome, joyful privilege of sowing godly seed—not just in the generation of our children, but also in the generation of our children's children.

13 Those who are planted in the house
of the LORD
Shall flourish in the courts of our
God.

14 They shall still bear fruit in old age;
They shall be fresh and flourishing,
15 To declare that the LORD is upright;
He is my rock, and *there is* no
unrighteousness in Him.

PSALM 93

The Eternal Reign of the LORD

1 The LORD reigns, He is clothed with
majesty;
The LORD is clothed,
He has girded Himself with strength.
Surely the world is established, so
that it cannot be moved.
2 Your throne *is* established from of old;
You *are* from everlasting.

3 The floods have lifted up, O LORD,
The floods have lifted up their voice;
The floods lift up their waves.
4 The LORD on high *is* mightier
Than the noise of many waters,
Than the mighty waves of the sea.

5 Your testimonies are very sure;
Holiness adorns Your house,
O LORD, forever.

PSALM 94

God the Refuge of the Righteous

1 O LORD God, to whom vengeance
belongs—
O God, to whom vengeance belongs,
shine forth!
2 Rise up, O Judge of the earth;
Render punishment to the proud.
3 LORD, how long will the wicked,
How long will the wicked triumph?
4 They utter speech, *and* speak
insolent things;
All the workers of iniquity boast in
themselves.
5 They break in pieces Your people, O
LORD,
And afflict Your heritage.
6 They slay the widow and the stranger,
And murder the fatherless.
7 Yet they say, "The LORD does not
see,
Nor does the God of Jacob
understand."

8 Understand, you senseless among
the people;
And *you* fools, when will you be wise?
9 He who planted the ear, shall He not
hear?
He who formed the eye, shall He not
see?
10 He who instructs the nations, shall
He not correct,
He who teaches man knowledge?
11 The LORD knows the thoughts of man,
That they *are* futile.

12 Blessed *is* the man whom You
instruct, O LORD,
And teach out of Your law,
13 That You may give him rest from the
days of adversity,
Until the pit is dug for the wicked.
14 For the LORD will not cast off His
people,
Nor will He forsake His inheritance.
15 But judgment will return to
righteousness,
And all the upright in heart will
follow it.

16 Who will rise up for me against the
evildoers?
Who will stand up for me against the
workers of iniquity?
17 Unless the LORD *had been* my help,
My soul would soon have settled in
silence.
18 If I say, "My foot slips,"
Your mercy, O LORD, will hold me up.
19 In the multitude of my anxieties
within me,
Your comforts delight my soul.

20 Shall the throne of iniquity, which
devises evil by law,
Have fellowship with You?
21 They gather together against the life
of the righteous,
And condemn innocent blood.
22 But the LORD has been my defense,
And my God the rock of my refuge.
23 He has brought on them their own
iniquity,
And shall cut them off in their own
wickedness;
The LORD our God shall cut them off.

95:8 [a] Or *Meribah* [b] Or *Massah*

PSALM 95

A Call to Worship and Obedience

1 Oh come, let us sing to the LORD!
Let us shout joyfully to the Rock of
our salvation.
2 Let us come before His presence with
thanksgiving;
Let us shout joyfully to Him with
psalms.
3 For the LORD *is* the great God,
And the great King above all gods.
4 In His hand *are* the deep places of
the earth;
The heights of the hills *are* His also.
5 The sea *is* His, for He made it;
And His hands formed the dry *land.*

6 Oh come, let us worship and bow
down;
Let us kneel before the LORD our
Maker.
7 For He *is* our God,
And we *are* the people of His pasture,
And the sheep of His hand.

Today, if you will hear His voice:
8 "Do not harden your hearts, as in the
rebellion,[a]
As *in* the day of trial[b] in the
wilderness,
9 When your fathers tested Me;
They tried Me, though they saw My
work.
10 For forty years I was grieved with
that generation,
And said, 'It *is* a people who go
astray in their hearts,
And they do not know My ways.'
11 So I swore in My wrath,
'They shall not enter My rest.' "

PSALM 96

A Song of Praise to God Coming in Judgment

1 Oh, sing to the LORD a new song!
Sing to the LORD, all the earth.
2 Sing to the LORD, bless
His name;
Proclaim the good news of His
salvation from day to day.
3 Declare His glory among the nations,
His wonders among all peoples.

4 For the LORD *is* great and greatly to
    be praised;
    He *is* to be feared above all gods.
5 For all the gods of the peoples *are*
    idols,
    But the LORD made the heavens.
6 Honor and majesty *are* before Him;
    Strength and beauty *are* in His
    sanctuary.

7 Give to the LORD, O families of the
    peoples,
    Give to the LORD glory and strength.
8 Give to the LORD the glory *due* His
    name;
    Bring an offering, and come into His
    courts.
9 Oh, worship the LORD in the beauty
    of holiness!
    Tremble before Him, all the earth.

10 Say among the nations, "The LORD
    reigns;
    The world also is firmly established,
    It shall not be moved;
    He shall judge the peoples
    righteously."

11 Let the heavens rejoice, and let
    the earth be glad;
    Let the sea roar, and all its fullness;
12 Let the field be joyful, and all
    that *is* in it.
    Then all the trees of the woods
    will rejoice before the LORD.
13 For He is coming, for He is coming
    to judge the earth.
    He shall judge the world with
    righteousness,
    And the peoples with His truth.

PSALM 97

A Song of Praise to the Sovereign LORD

1 The LORD reigns;
    Let the earth rejoice;
    Let the multitude of isles be glad!

2 Clouds and darkness surround
    Him;
    Righteousness and justice *are* the
    foundation of His throne.
3 A fire goes before Him,
    And burns up His enemies round
    about.

4 His lightnings light the world;
    The earth sees and trembles.
5 The mountains melt like wax at the
    presence of the LORD,
    At the presence of the Lord of the
    whole earth.
6 The heavens declare His
    righteousness,
    And all the peoples see His glory.

7 Let all be put to shame who serve
    carved images,
    Who boast of idols.
    Worship Him, all *you* gods.
8 Zion hears and is glad,
    And the daughters of Judah rejoice
    Because of Your judgments,
    O LORD.
9 For You, LORD, *are* most high above
    all the earth;
    You are exalted far above all gods.

10 You who love the LORD, hate evil!
    He preserves the souls of His saints;
    He delivers them out of the hand of
    the wicked.
11 Light is sown for the righteous,
    And gladness for the upright in
    heart.
12 Rejoice in the LORD, you righteous,
    And give thanks at the remembrance
    of His holy name.[a]

PSALM 98

A Song of Praise to the LORD for His Salvation and Judgment

A Psalm.

1 Oh, sing to the LORD a new song!
    For He has done marvelous things;
    His right hand and His holy arm
    have gained Him the victory.
2 The LORD has made known His
    salvation;
    His righteousness He has revealed in
    the sight of the nations.
3 He has remembered His mercy and
    His faithfulness to the house of
    Israel;
    All the ends of the earth have seen
    the salvation of our God.

97:12 [a]Or *His holiness*

4 Shout joyfully to the LORD, all the earth;
Break forth in song, rejoice, and sing praises.
5 Sing to the LORD with the harp,
With the harp and the sound of a psalm,
6 With trumpets and the sound of a horn;
Shout joyfully before the LORD, the King.

7 Let the sea roar, and all its fullness,
The world and those who dwell in it;
8 Let the rivers clap *their* hands;
Let the hills be joyful together before the LORD,
9 For He is coming to judge the earth.
With righteousness He shall judge the world,
And the peoples with equity.

PSALM 99

Praise to the LORD for His Holiness

1 The LORD reigns;
Let the peoples tremble!
He dwells *between* the cherubim;
Let the earth be moved!
2 The LORD *is* great in Zion,
And He *is* high above all the peoples.
3 Let them praise Your great and awesome name—
He *is* holy.

4 The King's strength also loves justice;
You have established equity;
You have executed justice and righteousness in Jacob.
5 Exalt the LORD our God,
And worship at His footstool—
He *is* holy.

6 Moses and Aaron were among His priests,

PARENTING MATTERS

Q: How should we teach our children to resolve a conflict between us?

As you build and maintain a relationship with your youngster, you must admit that you will hurt and disappoint each other. Breaches of trust will take place, demanding that you know how to resolve conflict.

Here's how you might work through a conflict:

Communication: Tell your child that something he/she has done or his/her attitude is unacceptable to you and that it has caused you pain. Your child may not receive that information in the way you'd hoped, but it's important to speak honestly about what has happened, "speaking the truth in love" (Eph. 4:15). Let your child know that the door to forgiveness and reconciliation always open.

Forgiveness: When your child is ready to move to the next step, model forgiveness in action. When your child tells you that he or she is sorry, you need to sincerely offer forgiveness and be ready to move on to the next step. It's important for a parent to communicate what forgiveness really means. Forgiveness gives up the right to emotionally punish another. Helping your child understand this now will yield many benefits later as they develop their relationships.

Reconciliation: Now your child needs to understand that if he/she has disobeyed or hurt another person, just saying "I'm sorry" doesn't get him/her completely off the hook. Making things right in the relationship will often mean accepting the consequences for the hurtful actions, making restitution, and showing the reality of his repentance by changing future behavior.

BIBLICAL INSIGHTS • 101:2–4

A Life They Can Trust

THE PSALMIST SPEAKS of the power of a life of integrity, "I will behave wisely in a perfect way. Oh, when will You come to me? I will walk within my house with a perfect heart. I will set nothing wicked before my eyes; I hate the work of those who fall away; it shall not cling to me. A perverse heart shall depart from me; I will not know wickedness" (101:2–4).

Scripture insists that *how we live in private does matter,* because God sees all. If you want to build godly character into another person's life—especially into the lives of your children—then you need the powerful foundation that a life of integrity provides.

Look at your life. Do you see any persistent deceit there? If so, you will not make much headway in trying to root out deceit in your child. Watch for the subtle deceptions we adults are so prone to—giving phony reasons for not taking phone calls, failing to keep promises to our children, offering excuses to get out of commitments. Face up to the areas where you may be failing and ask God to work in your heart so that you model a life of integrity.

And Samuel was among those who
    called upon His name;
They called upon the LORD, and He
    answered them.
7 He spoke to them in the cloudy
    pillar;
They kept His testimonies and the
    ordinance He gave them.

8 You answered them, O LORD our God;
You were to them God-Who-
    Forgives,
Though You took vengeance on their
    deeds.
9 Exalt the LORD our God,
And worship at His holy hill;
For the LORD our God *is* holy.

PSALM 100

A Song of Praise for the Faithfulness to His People

A Psalm of Thanksgiving.

1 Make a joyful shout to the LORD, all
    you lands!
2 Serve the LORD with gladness;
Come before His presence with
    singing.
3 Know that the LORD, He *is* God;
It is He *who* has made us, and not we
    ourselves;[a]
We are His people and the sheep of
    His pasture.

4 Enter into His gates with
    thanksgiving,
And into His courts with praise.
Be thankful to Him, *and* bless His
    name.
5 For the LORD *is* good;
His mercy *is* everlasting,
And His truth *endures* to all
    generations.

PSALM 101

Promised Faithfulness to the LORD

A Psalm of David.

1 I will sing of mercy and justice;
To You, O LORD, I will sing praises.

2 I will behave wisely in a perfect way.
Oh, when will You come to me?
I will walk within my house with a
    perfect heart.

3 I will set nothing wicked before my
    eyes;
I hate the work of those who fall
    away;
It shall not cling to me.
4 A perverse heart shall depart from me;
I will not know wickedness.

5 Whoever secretly slanders his
    neighbor,
Him I will destroy;
The one who has a haughty look and
    a proud heart,
Him I will not endure.

100:3 [a]Following Kethib, Septuagint, and Vulgate; Qere, many Hebrew manuscripts, and Targum read *we are His.*

6 My eyes *shall be* on the faithful of
      the land,
   That they may dwell with me;
   He who walks in a perfect way,
   He shall serve me.
7 He who works deceit shall not dwell
      within my house;
   He who tells lies shall not continue in
      my presence.
8 Early I will destroy all the wicked of
      the land,
   That I may cut off all the evildoers
      from the city of the LORD.

PSALM 102

The LORD's Eternal Love

A Prayer of the afflicted, when he is
overwhelmed and pours out his complaint
before the LORD.

1 Hear my prayer, O LORD,
   And let my cry come to You.
2 Do not hide Your face from me in the
      day of my trouble;
   Incline Your ear to me;
   In the day that I call, answer me
      speedily.
3 For my days are consumed like
      smoke,
   And my bones are burned like a
      hearth.
4 My heart is stricken and withered
      like grass,
   So that I forget to eat my bread.
5 Because of the sound of my
      groaning
   My bones cling to my skin.
6 I am like a pelican of the wilderness;
   I am like an owl of the desert.
7 I lie awake,
   And am like a sparrow alone on the
      housetop.
8 My enemies reproach me all
      day long;
   Those who deride me swear an
      oath against me.
9 For I have eaten ashes like bread,
   And mingled my drink with
      weeping,
10 Because of Your indignation and
   Your wrath;

For You have lifted me up and cast
   me away.
11 My days *are* like a shadow that
      lengthens,
   And I wither away like grass.
12 But You, O LORD, shall endure
      forever,
   And the remembrance of Your name
      to all generations.
13 You will arise *and* have mercy on
      Zion;
   For the time to favor her,
   Yes, the set time, has come.
14 For Your servants take pleasure in
      her stones,
   And show favor to her dust.
15 So the nations shall fear the name of
      the LORD,
   And all the kings of the earth Your
      glory.
16 For the LORD shall build up Zion;
   He shall appear in His glory.
17 He shall regard the prayer of the
      destitute,
   And shall not despise their prayer.
18 This will be written for the
      generation to come,
   That a people yet to be created may
      praise the LORD.
19 For He looked down from the height
      of His sanctuary;
   From heaven the LORD viewed the
      earth,
20 To hear the groaning of the prisoner,
   To release those appointed to death,
21 To declare the name of the LORD in
      Zion,
   And His praise in Jerusalem,
22 When the peoples are gathered
      together,
   And the kingdoms, to serve the LORD.
23 He weakened my strength in the
      way;
   He shortened my days.
24 I said, "O my God,
   Do not take me away in the midst of
      my days;
   Your years *are* throughout all
      generations.
25 Of old You laid the foundation of the
      earth,

BIBLICAL INSIGHTS • 103:12
They Really Won't Ever Meet

IN A DAY LONG BEFORE the existence of supersonic transports, instant messaging, and video conferencing, Rudyard Kipling wrote, "East is East/ And West is West/ And never the twain shall meet."

While many significant cultural differences still keep parts of the west at arm's length from the east, much of the power of this little verse has evaporated in the new realities of the information age. In fact, east meets west all the time, and both sides are learning how to make a tidy little profit off of the interchange.

Still, while many things have changed radically since those poetic lines first took shape, at least one thing continues to walk in lockstep with the sentiment of the old poem. And it just happens to be another set of poetic lines, "As far as the east is from the west, so far has He [God] removed our transgressions from us" (103:12).

Do you realize what an advantage this is to your lives, marriage, and family? Regardless of what you've done, you don't have to carry around a load of guilt that will sabotage your family life. Give it all to God! And He'll make sure that east and west *never* meet.

And the heavens *are* the work of
    Your hands.
26 They will perish, but You will
    endure;
    Yes, they will all grow old like a
    garment;
    Like a cloak You will change them,
    And they will be changed.
27 But You *are* the same,
    And Your years will have no end.
28 The children of Your servants will
    continue,
    And their descendants will be
    established before You."

PSALM 103

Praise for the LORD's Mercies

A Psalm of David.

1 Bless the LORD, O my soul;
    And all that is within me, *bless* His
      holy name!
2 Bless the LORD, O my soul,
    And forget not all His benefits:
3 Who forgives all your iniquities,
    Who heals all your diseases,
4 Who redeems your life from
      destruction,
    Who crowns you with lovingkindness
      and tender mercies,
5 Who satisfies your mouth with good
      things,
    So that your youth is renewed like
      the eagle's.

6 The LORD executes righteousness
    And justice for all who are oppressed.
7 He made known His ways to Moses,
    His acts to the children of Israel.
8 The LORD *is* merciful and gracious,
    Slow to anger, and abounding in
      mercy.
9 He will not always strive *with us,*
    Nor will He keep *His anger* forever.
10 He has not dealt with us according to
      our sins,
    Nor punished us according to our
      iniquities.
11 For as the heavens are high above
      the earth,
    So great is His mercy toward those
      who fear Him;
12 As far as the east is from the west,
    So far has He removed our
      transgressions from us.
13 As a father pities *his* children,
    So the LORD pities those who fear Him.
14 For He knows our frame;
    He remembers that we *are* dust.

15 *As for* man, his days *are* like grass;
    As a flower of the field, so he
      flourishes.
16 For the wind passes over it, and it is
      gone,
    And its place remembers it no more.[a]

103:16 [a]Compare Job 7:10

17 But the mercy of the LORD *is* from
    everlasting to everlasting
On those who fear Him,
And His righteousness to children's
    children,
18 To such as keep His covenant,
And to those who remember His
    commandments to do them.

19 The LORD has established His throne
    in heaven,
And His kingdom rules over all.

20 Bless the LORD, you His angels,
Who excel in strength, who do His
    word,
Heeding the voice of His word.
21 Bless the LORD, all *you* His hosts,
You ministers of His, who do His
    pleasure.
22 Bless the LORD, all His works,
In all places of His dominion.

Bless the LORD, O my soul!

PSALM 104

Praise to the Sovereign LORD for His Creation and Providence

1 Bless the LORD, O my soul!

O LORD my God, You are very great:
You are clothed with honor and
    majesty,
2 Who cover *Yourself* with light as
    with a garment,
Who stretch out the heavens like a
    curtain.
3 He lays the beams of His upper
    chambers in the waters,
Who makes the clouds His chariot,
Who walks on the wings of the wind,
4 Who makes His angels spirits,
His ministers a flame of fire.

5 *You who* laid the foundations of the
    earth,
So *that* it should not be moved
    forever,
6 You covered it with the deep as *with*
    a garment;
The waters stood above the
    mountains.

7 At Your rebuke they fled;
At the voice of Your thunder they
    hastened away.
8 They went up over the mountains;
They went down into the valleys,
To the place which You founded for
    them.
9 You have set a boundary that they
    may not pass over,
That they may not return to cover
    the earth.

10 He sends the springs into the valleys;
They flow among the hills.
11 They give drink to every beast of
    the field;
The wild donkeys quench their
    thirst.
12 By them the birds of the heavens
    have their home;
They sing among the branches.
13 He waters the hills from His upper
    chambers;
The earth is satisfied with the fruit
    of Your works.

14 He causes the grass to grow for the
    cattle,
And vegetation for the service of
    man,
That he may bring forth food from
    the earth,
15 And wine *that* makes glad the heart
    of man,
Oil to make *his* face shine,
And bread *which* strengthens man's
    heart.
16 The trees of the LORD are full *of sap,*
The cedars of Lebanon which He
    planted,
17 Where the birds make their nests;
The stork has her home in the fir
    trees.
18 The high hills *are* for the wild goats;
The cliffs are a refuge for the rock
    badgers.[a]

19 He appointed the moon for seasons;
The sun knows its going down.
20 You make darkness, and it is night,
In which all the beasts of the forest
    creep about.
21 The young lions roar after their prey,
And seek their food from God.

104:18 [a]Or *rock hyrax* (compare Leviticus 11:5)

22 *When* the sun rises, they gather
    together
    And lie down in their dens.
23 Man goes out to his work
    And to his labor until the evening.

24 O LORD, how manifold are Your
    works!
    In wisdom You have made them all.
    The earth is full of Your
    possessions—
25 This great and wide sea,
    In which *are* innumerable teeming
    things,
    Living things both small and
    great.
26 There the ships sail about;
    There is that Leviathan
    Which You have made to play
    there.

27 These all wait for You,
    That You may give *them* their food
    in due season.
28 *What* You give them they gather in;
    You open Your hand, they are filled
    with good.
29 You hide Your face, they are
    troubled;
    You take away their breath, they die
    and return to their dust.
30 You send forth Your Spirit, they are
    created;
    And You renew the face of the earth.

31 May the glory of the LORD endure
    forever;
    May the LORD rejoice in His works.
32 He looks on the earth, and it
    trembles;
    He touches the hills, and they smoke.

33 I will sing to the LORD as long as I
    live;
    I will sing praise to my God while I
    have my being.
34 May my meditation be sweet to Him;
    I will be glad in the LORD.
35 May sinners be consumed from the
    earth,
    And the wicked be no more.

    Bless the LORD, O my soul!
    Praise the LORD!

PSALM 105

The Eternal Faithfulness of the LORD

1 Oh, give thanks to the LORD!
    Call upon His name;
    Make known His deeds among the
    peoples!
2 Sing to Him, sing psalms to Him;
    Talk of all His wondrous works!
3 Glory in His holy name;
    Let the hearts of those rejoice who
    seek the LORD!
4 Seek the LORD and His strength;
    Seek His face evermore!
5 Remember His marvelous works
    which He has done,
    His wonders, and the judgments of
    His mouth,
6 O seed of Abraham His servant,
    You children of Jacob, His chosen
    ones!

7 He *is* the LORD our God;
    His judgments *are* in all the earth.
8 He remembers His covenant forever,
    The word *which* He commanded, for
    a thousand generations,
9 *The covenant* which He made with
    Abraham,
    And His oath to Isaac,
10 And confirmed it to Jacob for a
    statute,
    To Israel *as* an everlasting covenant,
11 Saying, "To you I will give the land
    of Canaan
    As the allotment of your inheritance,"
12 When they were few in number,
    Indeed very few, and strangers in it.
13 When they went from one nation to
    another,
    From *one* kingdom to another people,
14 He permitted no one to do them
    wrong;
    Yes, He rebuked kings for their
    sakes,
15 *Saying,* "Do not touch My anointed
    ones,
    And do My prophets no harm."

16 Moreover He called for a famine in
    the land;
    He destroyed all the provision of
    bread.

17 He sent a man before them—
Joseph—*who* was sold as a slave.
18 They hurt his feet with fetters,
He was laid in irons.
19 Until the time that his word came to
pass,
The word of the LORD tested him.
20 The king sent and released him,
The ruler of the people let him go
free.
21 He made him lord of his house,
And ruler of all his possessions,
22 To bind his princes at his pleasure,
And teach his elders wisdom.
23 Israel also came into Egypt,
And Jacob dwelt in the land of Ham.
24 He increased His people greatly,
And made them stronger than their
enemies.
25 He turned their heart to hate His
people,
To deal craftily with His servants.
26 He sent Moses His servant,
And Aaron whom He had chosen.
27 They performed His signs among
them,
And wonders in the land of Ham.
28 He sent darkness, and made *it* dark;
And they did not rebel against His
word.
29 He turned their waters into blood,
And killed their fish.
30 Their land abounded with frogs,
Even in the chambers of their kings.
31 He spoke, and there came swarms of
flies,
And lice in all their territory.
32 He gave them hail for rain,
And flaming fire in their land.
33 He struck their vines also, and their
fig trees,
And splintered the trees of their
territory.
34 He spoke, and locusts came,
Young locusts without number,
35 And ate up all the vegetation in their
land,
And devoured the fruit of their
ground.

36 He also destroyed all the firstborn in
their land,
The first of all their strength.
37 He also brought them out with silver
and gold,
And *there was* none feeble among
His tribes.
38 Egypt was glad when they departed,
For the fear of them had fallen upon
them.
39 He spread a cloud for a covering,
And fire to give light in the night.
40 *The people* asked, and He brought
quail,
And satisfied them with the bread of
heaven.
41 He opened the rock, and water
gushed out;
It ran in the dry places *like* a river.
42 For He remembered His holy promise,
And Abraham His servant.
43 He brought out His people with joy,
His chosen ones with gladness.
44 He gave them the lands of the
Gentiles,
And they inherited the labor of the
nations,
45 That they might observe His statutes
And keep His laws.

Praise the LORD!

PSALM 106

Joy in Forgiveness of Israel's Sins

1 Praise the LORD!

Oh, give thanks to the LORD, for *He
is* good!
For His mercy *endures* forever.

2 Who can utter the mighty acts of the
LORD?
Who can declare all His praise?
3 Blessed *are* those who keep justice,
And he who does[a] righteousness at
all times!

4 Remember me, O LORD, with the
favor *You have toward* Your
people.
Oh, visit me with Your salvation,
5 That I may see the benefit of Your
chosen ones,

106:3 [a]Septuagint, Syriac, Targum, and Vulgate read
those who do.

BIBLICAL INSIGHTS • 106:25
Keep a God Focus Instead of a Self Focus

GOD REPEATEDLY REMINDED the Israelites what a special people they were. The Hebrews knew God had set them apart to make a unique contribution to humankind. And while that helped to build national unity, what they chose to believe about their individual relationship with God made a big difference in their *personal* participation in God's plan.

Many Israelites grumbled in their tents (106:25). They fussed, complained, and felt sorry for themselves. Through their complaining, they eventually convinced themselves that God had forgotten them—and soon they lost their sense of national destiny.

Griping and complaining ultimately reveal a lack of faith. When we tell ourselves that God has forgotten us, or that He doesn't know what He's doing, then we, too, are grumbling in our tents. Even if we never grumble out loud, our internal conversations can express discontent and dissatisfaction with the present.

We can decide to replace grumbling with a different kind of speech. We can counsel our own hearts with the truth of God's Word and choose to believe what He has said (Ps. 42:5). And we can teach our children to do the same. For example, when our children grow afraid, we can remind them of what is true: that Dad and Mom love them and will protect them and that Jesus loves them and will protect them. Then we remind them of a song or a verse in the Bible, or we pray with them. We encourage them to *believe* the truth.

That I may rejoice in the gladness of
   Your nation,
That I may glory with Your
   inheritance.

6 We have sinned with our fathers,
We have committed iniquity,

We have done wickedly.
7 Our fathers in Egypt did not
   understand Your wonders;
They did not remember the
   multitude of Your mercies,
But rebelled by the sea—the Red
   Sea.
8 Nevertheless He saved them for His
   name's sake,
That He might make His mighty
   power known.
9 He rebuked the Red Sea also, and it
   dried up;
So He led them through the depths,
As through the wilderness.
10 He saved them from the hand of him
   who hated *them*,
And redeemed them from the hand
   of the enemy.
11 The waters covered their enemies;
There was not one of them left.
12 Then they believed His words;
They sang His praise.
13 They soon forgot His works;
They did not wait for His counsel,
14 But lusted exceedingly in the
   wilderness,
And tested God in the desert.
15 And He gave them their request,
But sent leanness into their soul.
16 When they envied Moses in the
   camp,
And Aaron the saint of the LORD,
17 The earth opened up and swallowed
   Dathan,
And covered the faction of Abiram.
18 A fire was kindled in their company;
The flame burned up the wicked.
19 They made a calf in Horeb,
And worshiped the molded image.
20 Thus they changed their glory
Into the image of an ox that eats
   grass.
21 They forgot God their Savior,
Who had done great things in Egypt,
22 Wondrous works in the land of Ham,
Awesome things by the Red Sea.
23 Therefore He said that He would
   destroy them,
Had not Moses His chosen one stood
   before Him in the breach,

To turn away His wrath, lest He
    destroy *them*.

24 Then they despised the pleasant land;
    They did not believe His word,
25 But complained in their tents,
    And did not heed the voice of the
      LORD.
26 Therefore He raised His hand *in an*
    oath against them,
    To overthrow them in the wilderness,
27 To overthrow their descendants
    among the nations,
    And to scatter them in the lands.
28 They joined themselves also to Baal
    of Peor,
    And ate sacrifices made to the dead.
29 Thus they provoked *Him* to anger
    with their deeds,
    And the plague broke out among
    them.
30 Then Phinehas stood up and
    intervened,
    And the plague was stopped.
31 And that was accounted to him for
    righteousness
    To all generations forevermore.

32 They angered *Him* also at the waters
    of strife,[a]
    So that it went ill with Moses on
    account of them;
33 Because they rebelled against His
    Spirit,
    So that he spoke rashly with his lips.

34 They did not destroy the peoples,
    Concerning whom the LORD had
    commanded them,
35 But they mingled with the Gentiles
    And learned their works;
36 They served their idols,
    Which became a snare to them.
37 They even sacrificed their sons
    And their daughters to demons,
38 And shed innocent blood,
    The blood of their sons and
    daughters,
    Whom they sacrificed to the idols of
    Canaan;
    And the land was polluted with
    blood.

39 Thus they were defiled by their own
    works,
    And played the harlot by their own
    deeds.
40 Therefore the wrath of the LORD was
    kindled against His people,
    So that He abhorred His own
    inheritance.
41 And He gave them into the hand of
    the Gentiles,
    And those who hated them ruled
    over them.
42 Their enemies also oppressed them,
    And they were brought into
    subjection under their hand.
43 Many times He delivered them;
    But they rebelled in their counsel,
    And were brought low for their
    iniquity.

44 Nevertheless He regarded their
    affliction,
    When He heard their cry;
45 And for their sake He remembered
    His covenant,
    And relented according to the
    multitude of His mercies.
46 He also made them to be pitied
    By all those who carried them away
    captive.

47 Save us, O LORD our God,
    And gather us from among the
    Gentiles,
    To give thanks to Your holy name,
    To triumph in Your praise.

48 Blessed *be* the LORD God of Israel
    From everlasting to everlasting!
    And let all the people say, "Amen!"

    Praise the LORD!

    Book Five: Psalms 107—150

PSALM 107

Thanksgiving to the LORD for His Great Works of Deliverance

1 Oh, give thanks to the LORD, for *He*
    is good!
    For His mercy *endures* forever.
2 Let the redeemed of the LORD
    say *so*,

106:32 [a] Or *Meribah*

DEVOTIONS FOR COUPLES • 107:1
Give Thanks Always

Some time ago a couple told us, "It is as important to pray thankfully during times of thanksgiving as it is during times of pain or when begging God for help. God blesses a joyful heart!"

Yes, giving thanks to God in all things is an important spiritual practice. So Psalm 107:1 counsels us, "Oh, give thanks to the LORD, for He is good! For His mercy endures forever." And in 1 Thessalonians 5:18 we learn to give thanks in *everything*, "for this is the will of God in Christ Jesus for you." We have learned to give thanks for:

- Good days and bad
- Good health and runny noses
- Problems at work, with a child, with a parent, or with a neighbor
- Flat tires, umpires with seemingly poor vision at little league games, teenage attitudes, and vacation days gone awry.

When we give thanks in all things, we see more clearly how God is involved in every part of our lives. We are also reminded that He is in control. And as Barbara and I have practiced giving thanks continually over the years, it has become easier and easier.

Ponder three reasons why God wants us to be thankful through all circumstances and conditions:

First, giving thanks expresses faith—faith in our God, who is competent and never makes a mistake. He can be trusted!

Second, when we determine to be thankful in all things, we quickly begin to exhibit more of the fruits of righteousness (see Gal. 5:22, 23). No one is naturally thankful. In fact, if guided by our natural tendencies, we are so self-oriented that we tend to think life revolves around our needs and wishes. But as we yield to His Spirit, we become more and more of what the Bible calls a spiritual person (see 1 Cor. 2:14, 15).

Third, because He has big stuff for us to do on His behalf, God wants us to move beyond the small stuff. If we spend our lives overwhelmed with the details of daily existence, how will we ever become warriors for the big causes of Jesus Christ?

Learning the art of giving thanks as a twosome is one of the most rewarding experiences of praying together. You can begin doing that by individually writing down a list of things you are thankful for, exchanging the completed lists, then giving thanks in prayer for those things.

Whom He has redeemed from the hand of the enemy,
3 And gathered out of the lands,
From the east and from the west,
From the north and from the south.

4 They wandered in the wilderness in a desolate way;
They found no city to dwell in.
5 Hungry and thirsty,
Their soul fainted in them.
6 Then they cried out to the LORD in their trouble,
And He delivered them out of their distresses.
7 And He led them forth by the right way,
That they might go to a city for a dwelling place.

8 Oh, that *men* would give thanks to the LORD *for* His goodness,
And *for* His wonderful works to the children of men!
9 For He satisfies the longing soul,
And fills the hungry soul with goodness.

10 Those who sat in darkness and in the shadow of death,
Bound in affliction and irons—
11 Because they rebelled against the words of God,
And despised the counsel of the Most High,
12 Therefore He brought down their heart with labor;
They fell down, and *there was* none to help.

13 Then they cried out to the LORD in
their trouble,
And He saved them out of their
distresses.

14 He brought them out of darkness
and the shadow of death,
And broke their chains in pieces.

15 Oh, that *men* would give thanks to
the LORD *for* His goodness,
And *for* His wonderful works to the
children of men!

16 For He has broken the gates of
bronze,
And cut the bars of iron in two.

17 Fools, because of their transgression,
And because of their iniquities, were
afflicted.

18 Their soul abhorred all manner of
food,
And they drew near to the gates of
death.

19 Then they cried out to the LORD in
their trouble,
And He saved them out of their
distresses.

20 He sent His word and healed them,
And delivered *them* from their
destructions.

21 Oh, that *men* would give thanks to
the LORD *for* His goodness,
And *for* His wonderful works to the
children of men!

22 Let them sacrifice the sacrifices of
thanksgiving,
And declare His works with
rejoicing.

23 Those who go down to the sea in
ships,
Who do business on great waters,

24 They see the works of the LORD,
And His wonders in the deep.

25 For He commands and raises the
stormy wind,
Which lifts up the waves of the sea.

26 They mount up to the heavens,
They go down again to the depths;
Their soul melts because of trouble.

27 They reel to and fro, and stagger like
a drunken man,
And are at their wits' end.

28 Then they cry out to the LORD in
their trouble,

And He brings them out of their
distresses.

29 He calms the storm,
So that its waves are still.

30 Then they are glad because they are
quiet;
So He guides them to their desired
haven.

31 Oh, that *men* would give thanks to
the LORD *for* His goodness,
And *for* His wonderful works to the
children of men!

32 Let them exalt Him also in the
assembly of the people,
And praise Him in the company of
the elders.

33 He turns rivers into a wilderness,
And the watersprings into dry
ground;

34 A fruitful land into barrenness,
For the wickedness of those who
dwell in it.

35 He turns a wilderness into pools of
water,
And dry land into watersprings.

36 There He makes the hungry dwell,
That they may establish a city for a
dwelling place,

37 And sow fields and plant vineyards,
That they may yield a fruitful
harvest.

38 He also blesses them, and they
multiply greatly;
And He does not let their cattle
decrease.

39 When they are diminished and
brought low
Through oppression, affliction, and
sorrow,

40 He pours contempt on princes,
And causes them to wander in the
wilderness *where there is* no way;

41 Yet He sets the poor on high, far
from affliction,
And makes *their* families like a flock.

42 The righteous see *it* and rejoice,
And all iniquity stops its mouth.

43 Whoever *is* wise will observe these
things,
And they will understand the
lovingkindness of the LORD.

PSALM 108

Assurance of God's Victory over Enemies

A Song. A Psalm of David.

1   O God, my heart is steadfast;
     I will sing and give praise, even with my glory.
2   Awake, lute and harp!
     I will awaken the dawn.
3   I will praise You, O LORD, among the peoples,
     And I will sing praises to You among the nations.
4   For Your mercy *is* great above the heavens,
     And Your truth *reaches* to the clouds.

5   Be exalted, O God, above the heavens,
     And Your glory above all the earth;
6   That Your beloved may be delivered,
     Save *with* Your right hand, and hear me.

7   God has spoken in His holiness:
   "I will rejoice;
     I will divide Shechem
     And measure out the Valley of Succoth.
8   Gilead *is* Mine; Manasseh *is* Mine;
     Ephraim also *is* the helmet for My head;
     Judah *is* My lawgiver.
9   Moab *is* My washpot;
     Over Edom I will cast My shoe;
     Over Philistia I will triumph."

10   Who will bring me *into* the strong city?
11   *Is it* not You, O God, *who* cast us off?
     And *You,* O God, *who* did not go out with our armies?
12   Give us help from trouble,
     For the help of man is useless.
13   Through God we will do valiantly,
     For *it is* He *who* shall tread down our enemies.[a]

PSALM 109

Plea for Judgment of False Accusers

To the Chief Musician. A Psalm of David.

1   Do not keep silent,
     O God of my praise!
2   For the mouth of the wicked and the mouth of the deceitful
     Have opened against me;
     They have spoken against me with a lying tongue.
3   They have also surrounded me with words of hatred,
     And fought against me without a cause.
4   In return for my love they are my accusers,
     But I *give myself to* prayer.
5   Thus they have rewarded me evil for good,
     And hatred for my love.

6   Set a wicked man over him,
     And let an accuser[a] stand at his right hand.
7   When he is judged, let him be found guilty,
     And let his prayer become sin.
8   Let his days be few,
     And let another take his office.
9   Let his children be fatherless,
     And his wife a widow.
10   Let his children continually be vagabonds, and beg;
     Let them seek *their bread*[a] also from their desolate places.
11   Let the creditor seize all that he has,
     And let strangers plunder his labor.

INTIMATE MOMENTS

Surprise your husband with a special spa treatment after he's had a long, hard day at work. Draw him a bath and create a soothing environment—scented candles, bubbles, music, refreshing beverages, etc.

108:13 [a] Compare verses 6–13 with 60:5–12
109:6 [a] Hebrew *satan*   **109:10** [a] Following Masoretic Text and Targum; Septuagint and Vulgate read *be cast out.*

¹² Let there be none to extend mercy to
        him,
    Nor let there be any to favor his
        fatherless children.
¹³ Let his posterity be cut off,
    And in the generation following let
        their name be blotted out.
¹⁴ Let the iniquity of his fathers be
        remembered before the LORD,
    And let not the sin of his mother be
        blotted out.
¹⁵ Let them be continually before the
        LORD,
    That He may cut off the memory of
        them from the earth;
¹⁶ Because he did not remember to
        show mercy,
    But persecuted the poor and needy
        man,
    That he might even slay the broken
        in heart.
¹⁷ As he loved cursing, so let it come to
        him;
    As he did not delight in blessing, so
        let it be far from him.
¹⁸ As he clothed himself with cursing
        as with his garment,
    So let it enter his body like water,
    And like oil into his bones.
¹⁹ Let it be to him like the garment
        which covers him,
    And for a belt with which he girds
        himself continually.
²⁰ *Let* this *be* the LORD's reward to my
        accusers,
    And to those who speak evil against
        my person.

²¹ But You, O GOD the Lord,
    Deal with me for Your name's sake;
    Because Your mercy *is* good, deliver
        me.
²² For I *am* poor and needy,
    And my heart is wounded within me.
²³ I am gone like a shadow when it
        lengthens;
    I am shaken off like a locust.
²⁴ My knees are weak through fasting,
    And my flesh is feeble from lack of
        fatness.
²⁵ I also have become a reproach to them;
    When they look at me, they shake
        their heads.

²⁶ Help me, O LORD my God!
    Oh, save me according to Your
        mercy,
²⁷ That they may know that this *is*
        Your hand—
    That You, LORD, have done it!

ROMANCE FAQ

Q: *How can husbands and wives please one another more consistently?*

As you seek to learn what pleases your mate, consider the following top fives provided by Dr. Willard Harley in his book *His Needs, Her Needs*:

Top Five Ways for a Man to Please His Wife

1. Have a strong commitment to your family; make it a priority.

2. Provide security: emotional, financial, personal protection, etc.

3. Be willing to be her partner, to share life with her in honest, open relationship.

4. Talk with her in complete sentences; take time to discuss subjects with her.

5. Provide nonsexual affection: hugging, touching, tenderness, closeness that doesn't demand a sexual response.

Top Five Ways for a Woman to Please Her Husband

1. Show your mate admiration and respect through verbal praise.

2. Provide domestic support—help to keep the home in order.

3. Be attractive; he wants to be proud of you.

4. Offer recreational companionship.

5. Help him to pleasure you through an exciting, satisfying sexual union.

Paul wrote, "Let each of us please his neighbor for his good, leading to edification" (Rom. 15:2). Well, who is more your "neighbor" than your spouse, with whom you spend so many hours together every day?

28 Let them curse, but You bless;
When they arise, let them be
ashamed,
But let Your servant rejoice.
29 Let my accusers be clothed with
shame,
And let them cover themselves with
their own disgrace as with a
mantle.

30 I will greatly praise the LORD with
my mouth;
Yes, I will praise Him among the
multitude.
31 For He shall stand at the right hand
of the poor,
To save *him* from those who
condemn him.

PSALM 110

Announcement of the Messiah's Reign

A Psalm of David.

1 The LORD said to my Lord,
"Sit at My right hand,
Till I make Your enemies Your
footstool."
2 The LORD shall send the rod of Your
strength out of Zion.
Rule in the midst of Your enemies!
3 Your people *shall be* volunteers
In the day of Your power;
In the beauties of holiness, from the
womb of the morning,
You have the dew of Your youth.
4 The LORD has sworn
And will not relent,
"You *are* a priest forever
According to the order of
Melchizedek."

5 The Lord *is* at Your right hand;
He shall execute kings in the day of
His wrath.
6 He shall judge among the nations,
He shall fill *the places* with dead
bodies,
He shall execute the heads of many
countries.
7 He shall drink of the brook by the
wayside;
Therefore He shall lift up the head.

PSALM 111

Praise to God for His Faithfulness and Justice

1 Praise the LORD!

I will praise the LORD with *my* whole
heart,
In the assembly of the upright and
in the congregation.
2 The works of the LORD *are* great,
Studied by all who have pleasure in
them.
3 His work *is* honorable and glorious,
And His righteousness endures
forever.
4 He has made His wonderful works to
be remembered;
The LORD *is* gracious and full of
compassion.
5 He has given food to those who fear
Him;
He will ever be mindful of His
covenant.
6 He has declared to His people the
power of His works,
In giving them the heritage of the
nations.
7 The works of His hands *are* verity
and justice;
All His precepts *are* sure.
8 They stand fast forever and ever,
And are done in truth and
uprightness.
9 He has sent redemption to His people;
He has commanded His covenant
forever:
Holy and awesome *is* His name.

10 The fear of the LORD *is* the
beginning of wisdom;
A good understanding have all those
who do *His commandments.*
His praise endures forever.

PSALM 112

The Blessed State of the Righteous

1 Praise the LORD!

Blessed *is* the man *who* fears the LORD,
Who delights greatly in His
commandments.

DEVOTIONS FOR COUPLES • 112:1, 2
Five Essentials for Leaving a Legacy

One primary reason why God established marriage was so that people could leave a godly legacy. Consider five ways you can leave a legacy that will outlive you.

1. Fear the Lord and obey Him. Your legacy begins in your heart, in your relationship with God. Psalm 112:1, 2 reads, "Blessed is the man who fears the LORD, who delights greatly in His commandments. His descendants will be mighty on earth; the generation of the upright will be blessed."

On our first Christmas together, we gave a gift to God—the title deeds to our lives, to our marriage, to our family, to our relationships, to whatever ministry God gave us. We gave Him *everything.* More than 17 years later, I took my title deed out of the safety deposit box and considered all that God had done for us. He has wonderfully blessed us! Now, more than 35 years since that first Christmas, we marvel at all that He has accomplished in our lives and family. If you haven't ever done it, give God what is truly His: you! And your family!

2. Recognize the world's needs and respond with compassion and action. Matthew 9:36 says, "But when He [Jesus] saw the multitudes, He was moved with compassion for them." You and your mate can leave a legacy by being committed to doing something positive about our world. Act with courage to reach out to those in need.

3. Pray as a couple that God will use you to accomplish His purposes. An Old Testament saint named Jabez prayed, "Oh, that You would bless me indeed, and enlarge my territory, that Your hand would be with me, and that You would keep me from evil" (1 Chron. 4:10).

Jabez asked God to bless him by giving him new turf and enlarging his sphere of influence. He asked to be kept from temptation and that God would stay with him. His prayer reflects the heart of a man who greatly desired that God would use him for kingdom purposes. Our prayers ought to have the same focus.

4. Help your mate be a better steward of his gifts and abilities. Help him or her recognize how God has already used his or her gifts and abilities. Together, become actively involved in a local church that teaches God's Word faithfully and has a vision for the community.

5. Ask God to give your children a sense of purpose, direction, and mission. The challenge here is to leave your children the heritage of a vision, not just an inheritance. Remember what Neil Postman said, "Our children are messengers we send to a time we will not see."

---

2   His descendants will be mighty on
    earth;
  The generation of the upright will be
    blessed.
3   Wealth and riches *will be* in his house,
  And his righteousness endures
    forever.
4   Unto the upright there arises light in
    the darkness;
  He is gracious, and full of
    compassion, and righteous.
5   A good man deals graciously and
    lends;
  He will guide his affairs with
    discretion.
6   Surely he will never be shaken;

  The righteous will be in everlasting
    remembrance.
7   He will not be afraid of evil tidings;
  His heart is steadfast, trusting in the
    LORD.
8   His heart *is* established;
  He will not be afraid,
  Until he sees *his desire* upon his
    enemies.
9   He has dispersed abroad,
  He has given to the poor;
  His righteousness endures forever;
  His horn will be exalted with honor.
10 The wicked will see *it* and be grieved;
  He will gnash his teeth and melt away;
  The desire of the wicked shall perish.

Mothering As Your Career

IN ORDER TO BE A MOTHER of influence, a mom needs to give her primary attention to her children. We mothers must rise above the mentality of merely providing for our children's physical needs and wants to reach our higher calling of preparing them for life. That's the way to become "a joyful mother of children" (113:9).

Today, a majority of mothers now work outside the home, which can severely limit the number of hours they can devote to their children. I realize that many reasons exist for this outside-the-home employment—from sheer survival to a desire for extra income to support a variety of choices—but I want to help you think objectively for a few moments about your situation.

Consider Titus 2:4, 5, which says that young women are to "love their husbands, to love their children, to be discreet, chaste, homemakers, good, obedient to their own husbands."

Notice the priority of commitment: first to their husbands, and then to their children. Paul describes their character as discreet, chaste, and good. And, then there is that little word, "homemakers." Whatever choices a couple may make about a wife working outside the home, God wants a mom's highest priority to be her family and her home.

PSALM 113

The Majesty and Condescension of God

1   Praise the LORD!

Praise, O servants of the LORD,
Praise the name of the LORD!

2   Blessed be the name of the LORD
From this time forth and forevermore!

3   From the rising of the sun to its
        going down
The LORD's name *is* to be praised.

4   The LORD *is* high above all nations,

His glory above the heavens.

5   Who *is* like the LORD our God,
Who dwells on high,

6   Who humbles Himself to behold
The things that are in the heavens
        and in the earth?

7   He raises the poor out of the dust,
And lifts the needy out of the ash
        heap,

8   That He may seat *him* with
        princes—
With the princes of His people.

9   He grants the barren woman a home,
Like a joyful mother of children.

Praise the LORD!

PSALM 114

The Power of God in His Deliverance of Israel

1   When Israel went out of Egypt,
The house of Jacob from a people of
        strange language,

2   Judah became His sanctuary,
And Israel His dominion.

3   The sea saw *it* and fled;
Jordan turned back.

4   The mountains skipped like rams,
The little hills like lambs.

5   What ails you, O sea, that you fled?
O Jordan, *that* you turned back?

6   O mountains, *that* you skipped like
        rams?
O little hills, like lambs?

7   Tremble, O earth, at the presence of
        the Lord,
At the presence of the God of Jacob,

8   Who turned the rock *into* a pool of
        water,
The flint into a fountain of waters.

PSALM 115

The Futility of Idols and the Trustworthiness of God

1   Not unto us, O LORD, not unto us,
But to Your name give glory,
Because of Your mercy,
Because of Your truth.

2   Why should the Gentiles say,
"So where *is* their God?"

³ But our God *is* in heaven;
He does whatever He pleases.

⁴ Their idols *are* silver and gold,
The work of men's hands.

⁵ They have mouths, but they do not
speak;
Eyes they have, but they do not see;

⁶ They have ears, but they do not
hear;
Noses they have, but they do not
smell;

⁷ They have hands, but they do not
handle;
Feet they have, but they do
not walk;
Nor do they mutter through their
throat.

⁸ Those who make them are like them;
So is everyone who trusts in them.

⁹ O Israel, trust in the LORD;
He *is* their help and their shield.

¹⁰ O house of Aaron, trust in
the LORD;
He *is* their help and their shield.

¹¹ You who fear the LORD, trust in the
LORD;
He *is* their help and their shield.

¹² The LORD has been mindful of *us;*
He will bless us;
He will bless the house of Israel;
He will bless the house of Aaron.

¹³ He will bless those who fear the
LORD,
Both small and great.

¹⁴ May the LORD give you increase more
and more,
You and your children.

¹⁵ *May* you *be* blessed by the LORD,
Who made heaven and earth.

¹⁶ The heaven, *even* the heavens, *are*
the LORD's;
But the earth He has given to the
children of men.

¹⁷ The dead do not praise the LORD,
Nor any who go down into silence.

¹⁸ But we will bless the LORD
From this time forth and
forevermore.

Praise the LORD!

PSALM 116

Thanksgiving for Deliverance from Death

¹ I love the LORD, because He has
heard
My voice *and* my supplications.

² Because He has inclined His ear to
me,
Therefore I will call *upon Him* as
long as I live.

³ The pains of death surrounded me,
And the pangs of Sheol laid hold of
me;
I found trouble and sorrow.

⁴ Then I called upon the name of the
LORD:
"O LORD, I implore You, deliver my
soul!"

⁵ Gracious *is* the LORD, and righteous;
Yes, our God *is* merciful.

⁶ The LORD preserves the simple;
I was brought low, and He saved me.

⁷ Return to your rest, O my soul,
For the LORD has dealt bountifully
with you.

⁸ For You have delivered my soul from
death,
My eyes from tears,
And my feet from falling.

⁹ I will walk before the LORD
In the land of the living.

¹⁰ I believed, therefore I spoke,
"I am greatly afflicted."

¹¹ I said in my haste,
"All men *are* liars."

¹² What shall I render to the LORD
For all His benefits toward me?

¹³ I will take up the cup of salvation,
And call upon the name of the LORD.

¹⁴ I will pay my vows to the LORD
Now in the presence of all His people.

¹⁵ Precious in the sight of the LORD
Is the death of His saints.

¹⁶ O LORD, truly I *am* Your servant;
I *am* Your servant, the son of Your
maidservant;
You have loosed my bonds.

¹⁷ I will offer to You the sacrifice of
thanksgiving,

And will call upon the name of the
LORD.

18 I will pay my vows to the LORD
Now in the presence of all His people,

19 In the courts of the LORD's house,
In the midst of you, O Jerusalem.

Praise the LORD!

PSALM 117

Let All Peoples Praise the LORD

1 Praise the LORD, all you Gentiles!
Laud Him, all you peoples!

2 For His merciful kindness is great
toward us,
And the truth of the LORD *endures*
forever.

Praise the LORD!

PSALM 118

Praise to God for His Everlasting Mercy

1 Oh, give thanks to the LORD, for *He
is* good!
For His mercy *endures* forever.

2 Let Israel now say,
"His mercy *endures* forever."

3 Let the house of Aaron now say,
"His mercy *endures* forever."

4 Let those who fear the LORD now say,
"His mercy *endures* forever."

5 I called on the LORD in distress;
The LORD answered me *and set me* in
a broad place.

6 The LORD *is* on my side;
I will not fear.
What can man do to me?

7 The LORD is for me among those who
help me;
Therefore I shall see *my desire* on
those who hate me.

8 *It is* better to trust in the LORD
Than to put confidence in man.

9 *It is* better to trust in the LORD
Than to put confidence in princes.

10 All nations surrounded me,
But in the name of the LORD I will
destroy them.

11 They surrounded me,
Yes, they surrounded me;
But in the name of the LORD I will
destroy them.

12 They surrounded me like bees;
They were quenched like a fire of
thorns;

PARENTING MATTERS

Q: How can we make long road trips bearable for everyone in the car?

If you haven't yet heard the unending question, "Are we there yet?" you will. It's inevitable. You asked it, and so will your kids.

As the parents of six active kids, we discovered very quickly that we had better come prepared to make a long road trip into something other than a marathon endurance run. So consider two of our own little tricks for making the journey both fun and productive.

1. *Bring along a "complaint jar."* We would fill a jar with dimes (or quarters, when the kids grew older) and set it on the dashboard. If a child began to complain too much, we would remove a coin from the jar. At the end of the trip (or the day, if the driving times was especially long), we would let the kids spend the remaining money as they pleased. This little device did wonders to instantly lower the complaint level. (We even took dimes out to the jar when they complained about our taking a dime out of the jar!)

2. *Have kids keep vacation scrapbooks.* These can include drawings, postcards, and souvenirs. This can help keep the kids busy at your vacation spot as well. Years later, these simple journals are absolutely priceless.

A little planning can go a long way, especially on a long trip!

For in the name of the LORD I will
   destroy them.
13 You pushed me violently, that I
   might fall,
But the LORD helped me.
14 The LORD *is* my strength and song,
And He has become my salvation.[a]

15 The voice of rejoicing and salvation
Is in the tents of the righteous;
The right hand of the LORD does
   valiantly.
16 The right hand of the LORD is
   exalted;
The right hand of the LORD does
   valiantly.
17 I shall not die, but live,
And declare the works of the LORD.
18 The LORD has chastened me severely,
But He has not given me over to
   death.

19 Open to me the gates of
   righteousness;
I will go through them,
And I will praise the LORD.
20 This is the gate of the LORD,
Through which the righteous shall
   enter.

21 I will praise You,
For You have answered me,
And have become my salvation.

22 The stone *which* the builders rejected
Has become the chief cornerstone.
23 This was the LORD's doing;
It *is* marvelous in our eyes.
24 This *is* the day the LORD has made;
We will rejoice and be glad in it.

25 Save now, I pray, O LORD;
O LORD, I pray, send now prosperity.
26 Blessed *is* he who comes in the name
   of the LORD!
We have blessed you from the house
   of the LORD.
27 God *is* the LORD,
And He has given us light;
Bind the sacrifice with cords to the
   horns of the altar.
28 You *are* my God, and I will praise You;
You are my God, I will exalt You.

29 Oh, give thanks to the LORD, for *He
   is* good!
For His mercy *endures* forever.

PSALM 119

Meditations on the Excellencies of the Word of God

א   ALEPH

1 Blessed *are* the undefiled in the way,
Who walk in the law of the LORD!
2 Blessed *are* those who keep His
   testimonies,
Who seek Him with the whole heart!
3 They also do no iniquity;
They walk in His ways.
4 You have commanded *us*
To keep Your precepts diligently.
5 Oh, that my ways were directed
To keep Your statutes!
6 Then I would not be ashamed,
When I look into all Your
   commandments.
7 I will praise You with uprightness of
   heart,
When I learn Your righteous
   judgments.
8 I will keep Your statutes;
Oh, do not forsake me utterly!

ב   BETH

9 How can a young man cleanse his
   way?
By taking heed according to Your
   word.
10 With my whole heart I have sought
   You;
Oh, let me not wander from Your
   commandments!
11 Your word I have hidden in my
   heart,
That I might not sin against You.
12 Blessed *are* You, O LORD!
Teach me Your statutes.
13 With my lips I have declared
All the judgments of Your mouth.
14 I have rejoiced in the way of Your
   testimonies,
As *much as* in all riches.
15 I will meditate on Your precepts,
And contemplate Your ways.

118:14 [a]Compare Exodus 15:2

Obedience Is a Blessing

GOD BLESSES THOSE who honor and obey His Word, and that includes His directives regarding marriage. When a man and woman enter into a holy, lifelong commitment to God and to one another, when they raise a family in accordance with the wise principles outlined in the Bible, they are sure to receive the Lord's blessings.

The psalmist wrote, "Blessed are those who keep His testimonies, who seek Him with the whole heart! They also do no iniquity; they walk in His ways" (119:2, 3). To "walk in His ways" means to joyfully obey His commands and to go where and how He directs us to go.

Does this mean that godly men and women never have problems? Does it mean they won't have conflicts between themselves and with their children? Of course not! We are all soldiers fighting battles in enemy territory against a fierce opponent. And just because we're Christians doesn't mean that we and our spouses and families won't sometimes take hits from the enemy.

But when we do things God's way, our setbacks are temporary. In the bigger picture of our marriages and families, we will enjoy His blessings and avoid many of the problems that plague so many other families.

16   I will delight myself in Your statutes;
    I will not forget Your word.

ℷ   GIMEL

17   Deal bountifully with Your servant,
    That I may live and keep Your word.
18   Open my eyes, that I may see
    Wondrous things from Your law.
19   I *am* a stranger in the earth;
    Do not hide Your commandments
       from me.
20   My soul breaks with longing
    For Your judgments at all times.

21   You rebuke the proud—the cursed,
    Who stray from Your
       commandments.
22   Remove from me reproach and
       contempt,
    For I have kept Your testimonies.
23   Princes also sit *and* speak against
       me,
    But Your servant meditates on Your
       statutes.
24   Your testimonies also *are* my delight
    And my counselors.

ד   DALETH

25   My soul clings to the dust;
    Revive me according to Your
       word.
26   I have declared my ways, and You
       answered me;
    Teach me Your statutes.
27   Make me understand the way of
       Your precepts;
    So shall I meditate on Your
       wonderful works.
28   My soul melts from heaviness;
    Strengthen me according to Your
       word.
29   Remove from me the way of lying,
    And grant me Your law graciously.
30   I have chosen the way of truth;
    Your judgments I have laid *before*
       me.
31   I cling to Your testimonies;
    O LORD, do not put me to shame!
32   I will run the course of Your
       commandments,
    For You shall enlarge my heart.

ה   HE

33   Teach me, O LORD, the way of Your
       statutes,
    And I shall keep it *to* the end.
34   Give me understanding, and I shall
       keep Your law;
    Indeed, I shall observe it with *my*
       whole heart.
35   Make me walk in the path of Your
       commandments,
    For I delight in it.
36   Incline my heart to Your
       testimonies,
    And not to covetousness.

37 Turn away my eyes from looking at
     worthless things,
     And revive me in Your way.[a]
38 Establish Your word to Your servant,
     Who *is devoted* to fearing You.
39 Turn away my reproach which I
     dread,
     For Your judgments *are* good.
40 Behold, I long for Your precepts;
     Revive me in Your righteousness.

ו   WAW

41 Let Your mercies come also to me, O
     LORD—
     Your salvation according to Your
     word.
42 So shall I have an answer for him
     who reproaches me,
     For I trust in Your word.
43 And take not the word of truth
     utterly out of my mouth,
     For I have hoped in Your ordinances.
44 So shall I keep Your law
     continually,
     Forever and ever.
45 And I will walk at liberty,
     For I seek Your precepts.
46 I will speak of Your testimonies also
     before kings,
     And will not be ashamed.
47 And I will delight myself in Your
     commandments,
     Which I love.
48 My hands also I will lift up to Your
     commandments,
     Which I love,
     And I will meditate on Your statutes.

ז   ZAYIN

49 Remember the word to Your servant,
     Upon which You have caused me to
     hope.
50 This *is* my comfort in my affliction,
     For Your word has given me life.
51 The proud have me in great derision,
     Yet I do not turn aside from Your
     law.
52 I remembered Your judgments of
     old, O LORD,

BIBLICAL INSIGHTS • 119:36
Spoiled Rotten?

I'M CONVINCED THAT, for the most part, we women in America have become pampered to the point of being spoiled rotten. We have heard hundreds of thousands of messages over the past 40 years that say in various ways, "Stand up for your rights," "Have it YOUR way," "Don't let him run over you," and on and on.

Almost all advertising, most book promotions, radio and TV programming, and nearly all retail business are aimed at women. Our affluence is feverishly feeding every woman's obsession with self, and our culture may be promoting and encouraging women to be more self-focused today than at any time since the days of the Roman Empire (see Ps. 119:36). And has all this self-focus made us happier, more content, more satisfied? Hardly.

The antidote for selfishness is found in sacrificially serving others. Sacrifice is the language of romance, and it's how you build a great marriage. Having the marriage you once dreamed of is impossible without self-denial. Remember Philippians 2:4, "Let each of you look out not only for his own interests, but also for the interests of others." Take your eyes off yourself, and take an appreciative look at your husband. Take a good, hard, look. Notice what he does for you and your kids—and then thank him for it.

     And have comforted myself.
53 Indignation has taken hold of me
     Because of the wicked, who forsake
     Your law.
54 Your statutes have been my songs
     In the house of my pilgrimage.
55 I remember Your name in the night,
     O LORD,
     And I keep Your law.
56 This has become mine,
     Because I kept Your precepts.

119:37 [a]Following Masoretic Text, Septuagint, and Vulgate; Targum reads *Your words*.

ח HETH

57 *You are* my portion, O LORD;
  I have said that I would keep Your
    words.
58 I entreated Your favor with *my* whole
    heart;
  Be merciful to me according to Your
    word.
59 I thought about my ways,
  And turned my feet to Your
    testimonies.
60 I made haste, and did not delay
  To keep Your commandments.
61 The cords of the wicked have bound
    me,
  But I have not forgotten Your law.
62 At midnight I will rise to give thanks
    to You,
  Because of Your righteous
    judgments.
63 I *am* a companion of all who fear You,
  And of those who keep Your
    precepts.
64 The earth, O LORD, is full of Your
    mercy;
  Teach me Your statutes.

ט TETH

65 You have dealt well with Your
    servant,
  O LORD, according to Your word.
66 Teach me good judgment and
    knowledge,
  For I believe Your commandments.
67 Before I was afflicted I went astray,
  But now I keep Your word.
68 You *are* good, and do good;
  Teach me Your statutes.
69 The proud have forged a lie against
    me,
  But I will keep Your precepts with
    my whole heart.
70 Their heart is as fat as grease,
  But I delight in Your law.
71 *It is* good for me that I have been
    afflicted,
  That I may learn Your statutes.
72 The law of Your mouth *is* better to
    me
  Than thousands of *coins of* gold and
    silver.

י YOD

73 Your hands have made me and
    fashioned me;
  Give me understanding, that I may
    learn Your commandments.
74 Those who fear You will be glad
    when they see me,
  Because I have hoped in Your word.
75 I know, O LORD, that Your judgments
    are right,
  And *that* in faithfulness You have
    afflicted me.
76 Let, I pray, Your merciful kindness be
    for my comfort,
  According to Your word to Your
    servant.
77 Let Your tender mercies come to me,
    that I may live;
  For Your law *is* my delight.
78 Let the proud be ashamed,
  For they treated me wrongfully with
    falsehood;
  But I will meditate on Your precepts.
79 Let those who fear You turn to me,
  Those who know Your testimonies.
80 Let my heart be blameless regarding
    Your statutes,
  That I may not be ashamed.

כ KAPH

81 My soul faints for Your salvation,
  But I hope in Your word.
82 My eyes fail *from searching* Your
    word,
  Saying, "When will You comfort
    me?"
83 For I have become like a wineskin in
    smoke,
  Yet I do not forget Your statutes.
84 How many *are* the days of Your
    servant?
  When will You execute judgment on
    those who persecute me?
85 The proud have dug pits for me,
  Which *is* not according to Your law.
86 All Your commandments *are* faithful;
  They persecute me wrongfully;
  Help me!
87 They almost made an end of me on
    earth,
  But I did not forsake Your precepts.

88 Revive me according to Your
lovingkindness,
So that I may keep the testimony of
Your mouth.

ל LAMED

89 Forever, O LORD,
Your word is settled in heaven.
90 Your faithfulness *endures* to all
generations;
You established the earth, and it
abides.
91 They continue this day according to
Your ordinances,
For all *are* Your servants.
92 Unless Your law *had been* my
delight,
I would then have perished in my
affliction.
93 I will never forget Your precepts,
For by them You have given me life.
94 I *am* Yours, save me;
For I have sought Your precepts.
95 The wicked wait for me to destroy
me,
But I will consider Your testimonies.
96 I have seen the consummation of all
perfection,
But Your commandment *is*
exceedingly broad.

מ MEM

97 Oh, how I love Your law!
It *is* my meditation all the day.
98 You, through Your commandments,
make me wiser than my enemies;
For they *are* ever with me.
99 I have more understanding than all
my teachers,
For Your testimonies *are* my
meditation.
100 I understand more than the ancients,
Because I keep Your precepts.
101 I have restrained my feet from every
evil way,
That I may keep Your word.
102 I have not departed from Your
judgments,
For You Yourself have taught me.
103 How sweet are Your words to my
taste,
Sweeter than honey to my mouth!

104 Through Your precepts I get
understanding;
Therefore I hate every false way.

נ NUN

105 Your word *is* a lamp to my feet
And a light to my path.
106 I have sworn and confirmed
That I will keep Your righteous
judgments.
107 I am afflicted very much;
Revive me, O LORD, according to
Your word.
108 Accept, I pray, the freewill offerings
of my mouth, O LORD,
And teach me Your judgments.
109 My life *is* continually in my hand,
Yet I do not forget Your law.
110 The wicked have laid a snare for me,
Yet I have not strayed from Your
precepts.
111 Your testimonies I have taken as a
heritage forever,
For they *are* the rejoicing of my heart.
112 I have inclined my heart to perform
Your statutes
Forever, to the very end.

ס SAMEK

113 I hate the double-minded,
But I love Your law.
114 You *are* my hiding place and my
shield;
I hope in Your word.
115 Depart from me, you evildoers,
For I will keep the commandments of
my God!
116 Uphold me according to Your word,
that I may live;
And do not let me be ashamed of my
hope.
117 Hold me up, and I shall be safe,
And I shall observe Your statutes
continually.
118 You reject all those who stray from
Your statutes,
For their deceit *is* falsehood.
119 You put away all the wicked of the
earth *like* dross;
Therefore I love Your testimonies.
120 My flesh trembles for fear of You,
And I am afraid of Your judgments.

ע AYIN

121 I have done justice and
  righteousness;
  Do not leave me to my oppressors.
122 Be surety for Your servant
  for good;
  Do not let the proud oppress me.
123 My eyes fail *from seeking* Your
  salvation
  And Your righteous word.
124 Deal with Your servant according to
  Your mercy,
  And teach me Your statutes.
125 I *am* Your servant;
  Give me understanding,
  That I may know Your testimonies.
126 *It is* time for *You* to act, O LORD,
  For they have regarded Your law as
  void.
127 Therefore I love Your
  commandments
  More than gold, yes, than fine gold!
128 Therefore all *Your* precepts
  concerning all *things*
  I consider *to be* right;
  I hate every false way.

פ PE

129 Your testimonies are wonderful;
  Therefore my soul keeps them.
130 The entrance of Your words gives
  light;
  It gives understanding to the simple.
131 I opened my mouth and panted,
  For I longed for Your
  commandments.
132 Look upon me and be merciful to me,
  As Your custom *is* toward those who
  love Your name.
133 Direct my steps by Your word,
  And let no iniquity have dominion
  over me.
134 Redeem me from the oppression of
  man,
  That I may keep Your precepts.
135 Make Your face shine upon Your
  servant,
  And teach me Your statutes.
136 Rivers of water run down from my
  eyes,
  Because *men* do not keep Your law.

צ TSADDE

137 Righteous *are* You, O LORD,
  And upright *are* Your judgments.
138 Your testimonies, *which* You have
  commanded,
  Are righteous and very faithful.
139 My zeal has consumed me,
  Because my enemies have forgotten
  Your words.
140 Your word *is* very pure;
  Therefore Your servant loves it.
141 I *am* small and despised,
  Yet I do not forget Your precepts.
142 Your righteousness *is* an everlasting
  righteousness,
  And Your law *is* truth.
143 Trouble and anguish have overtaken
  me,
  Yet Your commandments *are* my
  delights.
144 The righteousness of Your
  testimonies *is* everlasting;
  Give me understanding, and I shall
  live.

ק QOPH

145 I cry out with *my* whole heart;
  Hear me, O LORD!
  I will keep Your statutes.
146 I cry out to You;
  Save me, and I will keep Your
  testimonies.
147 I rise before the dawning of the
  morning,
  And cry for help;
  I hope in Your word.
148 My eyes are awake through the *night*
  watches,
  That I may meditate on Your word.
149 Hear my voice according to Your
  lovingkindness;
  O LORD, revive me according to Your
  justice.
150 They draw near who follow after
  wickedness;
  They are far from Your law.
151 You *are* near, O LORD,
  And all Your commandments *are*
  truth.
152 Concerning Your testimonies,
  I have known of old that You have
  founded them forever.

ר RESH

153 Consider my affliction and deliver me,
For I do not forget Your law.
154 Plead my cause and redeem me;
Revive me according to Your word.
155 Salvation *is* far from the wicked,
For they do not seek Your statutes.
156 Great *are* Your tender mercies, O
LORD;
Revive me according to Your
judgments.
157 Many *are* my persecutors and my
enemies,
Yet I do not turn from Your
testimonies.
158 I see the treacherous, and am
disgusted,
Because they do not keep Your word.
159 Consider how I love Your precepts;
Revive me, O LORD, according to
Your lovingkindness.
160 The entirety of Your word *is* truth,
And every one of Your righteous
judgments *endures* forever.

ש SHIN

161 Princes persecute me without a cause,
But my heart stands in awe of Your
word.
162 I rejoice at Your word
As one who finds great treasure.
163 I hate and abhor lying,
But I love Your law.
164 Seven times a day I praise You,
Because of Your righteous
judgments.
165 Great peace have those who love
Your law,
And nothing causes them to stumble.
166 LORD, I hope for Your salvation,
And I do Your commandments.
167 My soul keeps Your testimonies,
And I love them exceedingly.
168 I keep Your precepts and Your
testimonies,
For all my ways *are* before You.

ת TAU

169 Let my cry come before You, O LORD;
Give me understanding according to
Your word.

170 Let my supplication come before You;
Deliver me according to Your word.
171 My lips shall utter praise,
For You teach me Your statutes.
172 My tongue shall speak of Your word,
For all Your commandments *are*
righteousness.
173 Let Your hand become my help,
For I have chosen Your precepts.
174 I long for Your salvation, O LORD,
And Your law *is* my delight.
175 Let my soul live, and it shall praise
You;
And let Your judgments help me.
176 I have gone astray like a lost sheep;
Seek Your servant,
For I do not forget Your
commandments.

PSALM 120

Plea for Relief from Bitter Foes

A Song of Ascents.

1 In my distress I cried to the LORD,
And He heard me.
2 Deliver my soul, O LORD, from lying
lips
And from a deceitful tongue.

3 What shall be given to you,
Or what shall be done to you,
You false tongue?
4 Sharp arrows of the warrior,
With coals of the broom tree!

5 Woe is me, that I dwell in Meshech,
That I dwell among the tents of
Kedar!
6 My soul has dwelt too long
With one who hates peace.
7 I *am for* peace;
But when I speak, they *are* for war.

PSALM 121

God the Help of Those Who Seek Him

A Song of Ascents.

1 I will lift up my eyes to the hills—
From whence comes my help?
2 My help *comes* from the LORD,
Who made heaven and earth.

3 He will not allow your foot to be
moved;

He who keeps you will not slumber.
4 Behold, He who keeps Israel
Shall neither slumber nor sleep.

5 The LORD *is* your keeper;
The LORD *is* your shade at your right
hand.
6 The sun shall not strike you by day,
Nor the moon by night.

7 The LORD shall preserve you from all
evil;
He shall preserve your soul.
8 The LORD shall preserve your going
out and your coming in
From this time forth, and even
forevermore.

PSALM 122

The Joy of Going to the House of the LORD

A Song of Ascents. Of David.

1 I was glad when they said to me,
"Let us go into the house of the
LORD."
2 Our feet have been standing
Within your gates, O Jerusalem!

3 Jerusalem is built
As a city that is compact together,
4 Where the tribes go up,
The tribes of the LORD,
To the Testimony of Israel,
To give thanks to the name of the
LORD.
5 For thrones are set there for judgment,
The thrones of the house of David.

6 Pray for the peace of Jerusalem:
"May they prosper who love you.

7 Peace be within your walls,
Prosperity within your palaces."
8 For the sake of my brethren and
companions,
I will now say, "Peace *be* within you."
9 Because of the house of the LORD
our God
I will seek your good.

PSALM 123

Prayer for Relief from Contempt

A Song of Ascents.

1 Unto You I lift up my eyes,
O You who dwell in the heavens.
2 Behold, as the eyes of servants *look*
to the hand of their masters,
As the eyes of a maid to the hand of
her mistress,
So our eyes *look* to the LORD
our God,
Until He has mercy on us.

3 Have mercy on us, O LORD, have
mercy on us!
For we are exceedingly filled with
contempt.
4 Our soul is exceedingly filled
With the scorn of those who are at
ease,
With the contempt of the proud.

PSALM 124

The LORD the Defense of His People

A Song of Ascents. Of David.

1 "If it had not been the LORD who was
on our side,"
Let Israel now say—
2 "If it had not been the LORD who was
on our side,
When men rose up against us,
3 Then they would have swallowed us
alive,
When their wrath was kindled
against us;
4 Then the waters would have
overwhelmed us,
The stream would have gone over
our soul;
5 Then the swollen waters
Would have gone over our soul."

INTIMATE MOMENTS

Ask your wife to write down three things
she'd like you to start doing, three things
she'd like you to stop doing, and three
things she'd like you to keep doing. Read
the list and do it.

6 Blessed *be* the LORD,
Who has not given us *as* prey to
their teeth.
7 Our soul has escaped as a bird from
the snare of the fowlers;[a]
The snare is broken, and we have
escaped.
8 Our help *is* in the name of
the LORD,
Who made heaven and earth.

PSALM 125

The LORD the Strength of His People

A Song of Ascents.

1 Those who trust in the LORD
Are like Mount Zion,
Which cannot be moved, *but* abides
forever.
2 As the mountains surround
Jerusalem,
So the LORD surrounds His people
From this time forth and forever.
3 For the scepter of wickedness shall
not rest
On the land allotted to the righteous,
Lest the righteous reach out their
hands to iniquity.

4 Do good, O LORD, to *those who are*
good,
And to *those who are* upright in their
hearts.
5 As for such as turn aside to their
crooked ways,
The LORD shall lead them away
With the workers of iniquity.

Peace *be* upon Israel!

PSALM 126

A Joyful Return to Zion

A Song of Ascents.

1 When the LORD brought back the
captivity of Zion,
We were like those who dream.
2 Then our mouth was filled with
laughter,

124:7 [a]That is, persons who catch birds in a trap or snare

BIBLICAL INSIGHTS • 126:1–3
For Those Who Dream

WHEN YOU DREAM, do you dream about the things of God, the truly permanent? Or do you fantasize about the things of the world, the truly perishable? What injustice causes you to pound the table and weep?

A godly vision will be fueled by what could be and what should be. It is an earnest quest for God's alternative, a desire to fulfill what He wants to accomplish in and through your lives, marriage, and family. And remember, a godly vision for your life will rock boats—our Savior was crucified because He shook up the system.

Does your family have a vision that will affect the present and the eternal? Are you teaching your children that they have a divinely ordered destiny? Are you adding fuel to their dreams and visions by encouraging their faith and steps of courage? Are you helping them see the eternal in the midst of time?

Do you want your family to follow you? Remember, no one follows an insignificant person with trivial goals.

And our tongue with singing.
Then they said among the nations,
"The LORD has done great things for
them."
3 The LORD has done great things for
us,
And we are glad.

4 Bring back our captivity, O LORD,
As the streams in the South.

5 Those who sow in tears
Shall reap in joy.
6 He who continually goes forth
weeping,
Bearing seed for sowing,
Shall doubtless come again with
rejoicing,
Bringing his sheaves *with him*.

PSALM 127

Laboring and Prospering with the LORD

A Song of Ascents. Of Solomon.

1 Unless the LORD builds the house,
They labor in vain who build it;
Unless the LORD guards the city,
The watchman stays awake in vain.

2 *It is* vain for you to rise up early,
To sit up late,
To eat the bread of sorrows;
For so He gives His beloved sleep.

3 Behold, children *are* a heritage from
the LORD,
The fruit of the womb *is* a reward.

4 Like arrows in the hand of a warrior,
So *are* the children of one's youth.

5 Happy *is* the man who has his quiver
full of them;
They shall not be ashamed,
But shall speak with their enemies in
the gate.

PSALM 128

Blessings of Those Who Fear the LORD

A Song of Ascents.

1 Blessed *is* every one who fears the
LORD,
Who walks in His ways.

2 When you eat the labor of your
hands,
You *shall be* happy, and *it shall be*
well with you.

3 Your wife *shall be* like a fruitful vine
In the very heart of your house,
Your children like olive plants
All around your table.

4 Behold, thus shall the man be
blessed
Who fears the LORD.

5 The LORD bless you out of Zion,
And may you see the good of
Jerusalem
All the days of your life.

6 Yes, may you see your children's
children.

Peace *be* upon Israel!

PSALM 129

Song of Victory over Zion's Enemies

A Song of Ascents.

1 "Many a time they have afflicted me
from my youth,"
Let Israel now say—

2 "Many a time they have afflicted me
from my youth;
Yet they have not prevailed against
me.

ROMANTIC QUOTES AND NOTES
It's All about God's Grace

Being a spouse and a parent brings big responsibilities and difficult burdens into our lives that we would never have to deal with otherwise. But since these are God-given responsibilities and burdens, they are the kind of responsibilities that cause us to rely on Him, to go to Him with open hands seeking His grace and mercy to make us into the kind of people He calls us to be.

The Psalmist wrote, "Unless the LORD builds the house, they labor in vain who build it" (127:1). I believe this verse is meant to bring us to a point of total dependence on God, knowing that without His direction and enabling, we have no chance of doing the things He has called us to do, or of becoming the people He has called us to be. In the words of Jesus Himself, "Without Me you can do nothing" (John 15:5).

We have learned that it is all about the grace of God. So we have built our marriage, our home, and our parenthood on His grace, knowing that without Him empowering us, guiding us, and giving us wisdom, we could have accomplished none of it. His grace gives imperfect people the way of relating to each other successfully so that they can truly build a home that honors God.

Build your home on the grace of God!

3   The plowers plowed on my
       back;
       They made their furrows long."
4   The LORD *is* righteous;
       He has cut in pieces the cords of the
       wicked.

5   Let all those who hate Zion
       Be put to shame and turned back.
6   Let them be as the grass *on* the
       housetops,
       Which withers before it grows up,
7   With which the reaper does not fill
       his hand,
       Nor he who binds sheaves, his arms.
8   Neither let those who pass by them
       say,
   "The blessing of the LORD *be* upon
       you;
       We bless you in the name of the
       LORD!"

PSALM 130

Waiting for the Redemption of the LORD

A Song of Ascents.

1   Out of the depths I have cried to
       You, O LORD;
2   Lord, hear my voice!
       Let Your ears be attentive
       To the voice of my supplications.

3   If You, LORD, should mark
       iniquities,
       O Lord, who could stand?
4   But *there is* forgiveness with You,
       That You may be feared.

5   I wait for the LORD, my soul waits,
       And in His word I do hope.
6   My soul *waits* for the Lord
       More than those who watch for the
       morning—
       Yes, more than those who watch for
       the morning.

7   O Israel, hope in the LORD;
       For with the LORD *there is* mercy,
       And with Him *is* abundant
       redemption.
8   And He shall redeem Israel
       From all his iniquities.

BIBLICAL INSIGHTS • 127:3
God's Perspective on Children

GOD IS BIG ON KIDS! "Behold, children are a heritage from the LORD," declares Psalm 127:3; "the fruit of the womb is a reward."

In Genesis 1:22, God commands parents to "Be fruitful and multiply." In other places in Scripture He calls children a blessing, a privilege, and a responsibility.

I think it's time for a heart-check about children in the Christian community. Do we truly have God's heart for children? Do we really have His perspective and believe children are a blessing? Or have we ever so slightly begun to adopt the world's view of children?

During the past few decades, the size of American families has steadily decreased because most parents are choosing to have fewer children. Many people believe that it's somehow wrong to have more than two or three children. If your family grows beyond these limits, someone will undoubtedly express great concern, "Don't you know how much kids cost? Can you afford to send them to college?"

Have you stopped to consider what a strange statement of values this is—that parents might actually decide not to have more children because they might not be able to afford their college expenses?

Do we *really* believe children are a gift from God? A blessing? How does the Bible affect your view of children? It's time for the community of faith to embrace God's view of children—that they really are a reward, a gift, and they represent the next generation who will take our places representing Christ to their generation.

PSALM 131

Simple Trust in the LORD

A Song of Ascents. Of David.

1   LORD, my heart is not haughty,
       Nor my eyes lofty.
       Neither do I concern myself with
       great matters,

Arrows in Your Hand

IT HAS BEEN SAID that a child is a parent's heart walking around outside his body.

In Psalm 127:4, God compares children to "arrows in the hand of warrior." Arrows are not designed to stay in the quiver. Arrows are created for flight, to rush toward God's target. They're meant for battle. And from the time you bring them home from the hospital, those little arrows must be shaped, sharpened, and honed for God's intended purpose.

Every archer worth his salt can tell you there is pain in launching an arrow. As the archer lets go, his left forearm can be painfully stung with the slap of the string. The same is true of a parent's heart. While the arrow is enjoying the flight he was made for, the heart of a parent feels the sting of the release.

Releasing is also scary. Will they fly straight? Will they get blown off course? Will they fall short of the God's intended destination for their lives?

You'll never know if you don't release them. You'll never know what God has intended specifically for each one. In fact, they'll never grow up at all if you keep them safe in your quiver, away from the battlefield. At the appropriate time, take careful aim. Pull back slowly and deliberately launch your arrow. Then resist the urge to pull that arrow back and into the quiver where it's safe.

We've launched six and trust me, it got tougher to let go with each arrow! But we've learned that we must let go if our children are to fly toward the target that God has for them.

Nor with things too profound for me.

2   Surely I have calmed and quieted my soul,
Like a weaned child with his mother;
Like a weaned child *is* my soul
within me.

3   O Israel, hope in the LORD
From this time forth and forever.

PSALM 132

The Eternal Dwelling of God in Zion

A Song of Ascents.

1   LORD, remember David
And all his afflictions;
2   How he swore to the LORD,
And vowed to the Mighty One of
Jacob:
3   "Surely I will not go into the chamber
of my house,
Or go up to the comfort of my bed;
4   I will not give sleep to my eyes
Or slumber to my eyelids,
5   Until I find a place for the LORD,
A dwelling place for the Mighty One
of Jacob."

6   Behold, we heard of it in Ephrathah;
We found it in the fields of the
woods.[a]
7   Let us go into His tabernacle;
Let us worship at His footstool.
8   Arise, O LORD, to Your resting place,
You and the ark of Your strength.
9   Let Your priests be clothed with
righteousness,
And let Your saints shout for joy.

10 For Your servant David's sake,
Do not turn away the face of Your
Anointed.

11 The LORD has sworn *in* truth to
David;
He will not turn from it:
"I will set upon your throne the fruit
of your body.
12 If your sons will keep My covenant
And My testimony which I shall
teach them,
Their sons also shall sit upon your
throne forevermore."

13 For the LORD has chosen Zion;
He has desired *it* for His dwelling
place:
14 "This *is* My resting place forever;
Here I will dwell, for I have desired it.

132:6 [a]Hebrew *Jaar*

15 I will abundantly bless her
  provision;
  I will satisfy her poor with bread.
16 I will also clothe her priests with
  salvation,
  And her saints shall shout aloud for
  joy.
17 There I will make the horn of David
  grow;
  I will prepare a lamp for My
  Anointed.
18 His enemies I will clothe with shame,
  But upon Himself His crown shall
  flourish."

PSALM 133

Blessed Unity of the People of God

A Song of Ascents. Of David.

1 Behold, how good and how pleasant
  it is
  For brethren to dwell together in
  unity!
2 *It is* like the precious oil upon the
  head,
  Running down on the beard,
  The beard of Aaron,
  Running down on the edge of his
  garments.
3 *It is* like the dew of Hermon,
  Descending upon the mountains of
  Zion;
  For there the LORD commanded the
  blessing—
  Life forevermore.

PSALM 134

Praising the LORD in His House at Night

A Song of Ascents.

1 Behold, bless the LORD,
  All *you* servants of the LORD,
  Who by night stand in the house of
  the LORD!
2 Lift up your hands *in* the sanctuary,
  And bless the LORD.

3 The LORD who made heaven and
  earth
  Bless you from Zion!

PSALM 135

Praise to God in Creation and Redemption

1 Praise the LORD!

  Praise the name of the LORD;
  Praise *Him,* O you servants of the
  LORD!
2 You who stand in the house of the
  LORD,
  In the courts of the house of our God,
3 Praise the LORD, for the LORD *is* good;
  Sing praises to His name, for *it is*
  pleasant.

ROMANCE FAQ

Q: How important is verbally complimenting my wife?

One important way to connect emotionally is to verbally *compliment your wife.* Proverbs offers this pointer: "Pleasant words are like a honeycomb, sweetness to the soul and health to the bones" (16:24). How often do you praise your wife for what she does? Consider a few of these compliments to brighten her day:

- "Dinner was great! Thank you for always making creative meals, even when you're tired of cooking."
- "I love the way you read books to our kids. That's so much better for them than watching TV."
- "I'm grateful that you carefully budget our paycheck each month."
- "I admire the way you handled yourself with that rude salesman—you have such a winsome approach."

As you study your wife and learn how and when to build security, acceptance, and emotional connection into your relationship through well-chosen, affirming words, you will become an irresistible man. And let me make one last practical suggestion: When you come home from work, here are four of the most romantic words *ever* to say to your wife: "How can I help?" Why not try it—and mean it—tonight?

4 For the LORD has chosen Jacob for
   Himself,
   Israel for His special treasure.

5 For I know that the LORD *is* great,
   And our Lord *is* above all gods.
6 Whatever the LORD pleases He does,
   In heaven and in earth,
   In the seas and in all deep places.
7 He causes the vapors to ascend from
   the ends of the earth;
   He makes lightning for the rain;
   He brings the wind out of His
   treasuries.

8 He destroyed the firstborn of Egypt,
   Both of man and beast.
9 He sent signs and wonders into the
   midst of you, O Egypt,
   Upon Pharaoh and all his servants.
10 He defeated many nations
   And slew mighty kings—
11 Sihon king of the Amorites,
   Og king of Bashan,
   And all the kingdoms of Canaan—
12 And gave their land *as* a heritage,
   A heritage to Israel His people.

13 Your name, O LORD, *endures* forever,
   Your fame, O LORD, throughout all
   generations.
14 For the LORD will judge His people,
   And He will have compassion on His
   servants.

15 The idols of the nations *are* silver
   and gold,
   The work of men's hands.
16 They have mouths, but they do not
   speak;
   Eyes they have, but they do not see;
17 They have ears, but they do not hear;
   Nor is there *any* breath in their
   mouths.
18 Those who make them are like them;
   So is everyone who trusts in them.

19 Bless the LORD, O house of Israel!
   Bless the LORD, O house of Aaron!
20 Bless the LORD, O house of Levi!
   You who fear the LORD, bless the
   LORD!
21 Blessed be the LORD out of Zion,
   Who dwells in Jerusalem!

   Praise the LORD!

PSALM 136

Thanksgiving to God for His Enduring Mercy

1 Oh, give thanks to the LORD, for *He
   is* good!
   For His mercy *endures* forever.
2 Oh, give thanks to the God of gods!
   For His mercy *endures* forever.
3 Oh, give thanks to the Lord of lords!
   For His mercy *endures* forever:

4 To Him who alone does great
   wonders,
   For His mercy *endures* forever;
5 To Him who by wisdom made the
   heavens,
   For His mercy *endures* forever;
6 To Him who laid out the earth above
   the waters,
   For His mercy *endures* forever;
7 To Him who made great lights,
   For His mercy *endures* forever—
8 The sun to rule by day,
   For His mercy *endures* forever;
9 The moon and stars to rule by night,
   For His mercy *endures* forever.

10 To Him who struck Egypt in their
   firstborn,
   For His mercy *endures* forever;
11 And brought out Israel from among
   them,
   For His mercy *endures* forever;
12 With a strong hand, and with an
   outstretched arm,
   For His mercy *endures* forever;
13 To Him who divided the Red Sea in
   two,
   For His mercy *endures* forever;
14 And made Israel pass through the
   midst of it,
   For His mercy *endures* forever;
15 But overthrew Pharaoh and his army
   in the Red Sea,
   For His mercy *endures* forever;
16 To Him who led His people through
   the wilderness,
   For His mercy *endures* forever;
17 To Him who struck down great
   kings,
   For His mercy *endures* forever;
18 And slew famous kings,
   For His mercy *endures* forever—

19 Sihon king of the Amorites,
   For His mercy *endures* forever;
20 And Og king of Bashan,
   For His mercy *endures* forever—
21 And gave their land as a heritage,
   For His mercy *endures* forever;
22 A heritage to Israel His servant,
   For His mercy *endures* forever.

23 Who remembered us in our lowly
       state,
   For His mercy *endures* forever;
24 And rescued us from our enemies,
   For His mercy *endures* forever;
25 Who gives food to all flesh,
   For His mercy *endures* forever.

26 Oh, give thanks to the God of heaven!
   For His mercy *endures* forever.

PSALM 137

Longing for Zion in a Foreign Land

1 By the rivers of Babylon,
   There we sat down, yea, we wept
   When we remembered Zion.
2 We hung our harps
   Upon the willows in the midst of it.
3 For there those who carried us away
       captive asked of us a song,
   And those who plundered us
       requested mirth,
   Saying, "Sing us *one* of the songs of
       Zion!"

4 How shall we sing the LORD's song
   In a foreign land?
5 If I forget you, O Jerusalem,
   Let my right hand forget *its skill!*
6 If I do not remember you,
   Let my tongue cling to the roof of
       my mouth—
   If I do not exalt Jerusalem
   Above my chief joy.

7 Remember, O LORD, against the sons
       of Edom
   The day of Jerusalem,
   Who said, "Raze *it,* raze *it,*
   To its very foundation!"

8 O daughter of Babylon, who are to
       be destroyed,
   Happy the one who repays you as
       you have served us!

9 Happy the one who takes and dashes
   Your little ones against the rock!

PSALM 138

The LORD's Goodness to the Faithful

A Psalm of David.

1 I will praise You with my whole heart;
   Before the gods I will sing praises to
       You.
2 I will worship toward Your holy
       temple,
   And praise Your name
   For Your lovingkindness and Your
       truth;
   For You have magnified Your word
       above all Your name.
3 In the day when I cried out, You
       answered me,
   And made me bold *with* strength in
       my soul.

4 All the kings of the earth shall
       praise You, O LORD,
   When they hear the words of Your
       mouth.
5 Yes, they shall sing of the ways of
       the LORD,
   For great *is* the glory of the LORD.
6 Though the LORD *is* on high,
   Yet He regards the lowly;
   But the proud He knows from afar.

7 Though I walk in the midst of
       trouble, You will revive me;
   You will stretch out Your hand
   Against the wrath of my enemies,
   And Your right hand will save me.
8 The LORD will perfect *that which*
       concerns me;
   Your mercy, O LORD, *endures* forever;
   Do not forsake the works of Your
       hands.

PSALM 139

God's Perfect Knowledge of Man

For the Chief Musician. A Psalm of David.

1 O LORD, You have searched me and
       known *me.*
2 You know my sitting down and my
       rising up;
   You understand my thought afar off.

3   You comprehend my path and my
         lying down,
     And are acquainted with all my ways.

4   For *there is* not a word on my
         tongue,
     But behold, O LORD, You know it
         altogether.

5   You have hedged me behind and
         before,
     And laid Your hand upon me.

6   *Such* knowledge *is* too wonderful for
         me;
     It is high, I cannot *attain* it.

7   Where can I go from Your Spirit?
     Or where can I flee from Your
         presence?

8   If I ascend into heaven, You *are* there;
     If I make my bed in hell, behold, You
         are there.

9   *If* I take the wings of the morning,
     And dwell in the uttermost parts of
         the sea,

10   Even there Your hand shall lead me,
     And Your right hand shall hold me.

11   If I say, "Surely the darkness shall
         fall[a] on me,"
     Even the night shall be light about
         me;

12   Indeed, the darkness shall not hide
         from You,
     But the night shines as the day;

The darkness and the light *are* both
     alike *to* You.

13   For You formed my inward parts;
     You covered me in my mother's
         womb.

14   I will praise You, for I am fearfully
         and wonderfully made;[a]
     Marvelous are Your works,
     And *that* my soul knows very well.

15   My frame was not hidden from You,
     When I was made in secret,
     And skillfully wrought in the lowest
         parts of the earth.

16   Your eyes saw my substance, being
         yet unformed.
     And in Your book they all were
         written,
     The days fashioned for me,
     When *as yet there were* none of
         them.

17   How precious also are Your thoughts
         to me, O God!
     How great is the sum of them!

18   *If* I should count them, they would be
         more in number than the sand;
     When I awake, I am still with You.

139:11 [a]Vulgate and Symmachus read *cover.*
139:14 [a]Following Masoretic Text and Targum;
Septuagint, Syriac, and Vulgate read *You are fearfully
wonderful.*

**PARENTING
MATTERS**

Q: *How do we handle sassiness in our young children?*

It's not uncommon for young children to try their parents with
sassiness. That can include reactions such as rolling the eyes, a sigh,
a grunt, or saying things like, "Who cares?" or "Whatever!" when their
parents tell them to do something.

When children say things like that—or even demonstrate those
attitudes—it needs to be dealt with swiftly, because the underlying
tone is, "I'm in charge, and you're not."

I would start by taking the child in my lap, hugging and loving on
him/her, and then saying, "You're a terrific person, but we want you
to know that you are being disrespectful when you talk like that.
Your attitude isn't pleasing to God, is it? God wants you to be
respectful of Mommy and me."

Such words of love and correction should be followed with a
clear warning of the consequences, should the negative attitude
continue. We believe it is important to warn our children, because
in the Scripture God repeatedly warned His children. He told them
what would happen if they disobeyed. Our kids need to know the
limits and what will happen if they disobey.

19 Oh, that You would slay the wicked,
      O God!
   Depart from me, therefore, you
      bloodthirsty men.
20 For they speak against You wickedly;
   Your enemies take *Your name* in
      vain.ᵃ
21 Do I not hate them, O LORD, who
      hate You?
   And do I not loathe those who rise
      up against You?
22 I hate them with perfect hatred;
   I count them my enemies.
23 Search me, O God, and know my
      heart;
   Try me, and know my anxieties;
24 And see if *there is any* wicked way
      in me,
   And lead me in the way everlasting.

PSALM 140

Prayer for Deliverance from Evil Men

To the Chief Musician. A Psalm of David.

1 Deliver me, O LORD, from evil men;
   Preserve me from violent men,
2 Who plan evil things in *their* hearts;
   They continually gather together *for*
      war.
3 They sharpen their tongues like a
      serpent;
   The poison of asps *is* under their
      lips.   Selah
4 Keep me, O LORD, from the hands of
      the wicked;
   Preserve me from violent men,
   Who have purposed to make my
      steps stumble.
5 The proud have hidden a snare for
      me, and cords;
   They have spread a net by the
      wayside;
   They have set traps for me.   Selah
6 I said to the LORD: "You *are* my God;
   Hear the voice of my supplications,
      O LORD.
7 O GOD the Lord, the strength of my
      salvation,

   You have covered my head in the day
      of battle.
8 Do not grant, O LORD, the desires of
      the wicked;
   Do not further his *wicked* scheme,
   Lest they be exalted.   Selah
9 "*As for* the head of those who
      surround me,
   Let the evil of their lips cover them;
10 Let burning coals fall upon them;
   Let them be cast into the fire,
   Into deep pits, that they rise not up
      again.
11 Let not a slanderer be established in
      the earth;
   Let evil hunt the violent man to
      overthrow *him.*"
12 I know that the LORD will maintain
   The cause of the afflicted,
   And justice for the poor.
13 Surely the righteous shall give
      thanks to Your name;
   The upright shall dwell in Your
      presence.

PSALM 141

Prayer for Safekeeping from Wickedness

A Psalm of David.

1 LORD, I cry out to You;
   Make haste to me!
   Give ear to my voice when I cry out
      to You.
2 Let my prayer be set before You *as*
      incense,
   The lifting up of my hands *as* the
      evening sacrifice.
3 Set a guard, O LORD, over my mouth;
   Keep watch over the door of my lips.
4 Do not incline my heart to any evil
      thing,
   To practice wicked works
   With men who work iniquity;
   And do not let me eat of their
      delicacies.
5 Let the righteous strike me;
   It shall be a kindness.
   And let him rebuke me;
   It shall be as excellent oil;
   Let my head not refuse it.

139:20 ᵃSeptuagint and Vulgate read *They take your cities in vain.*

For still my prayer *is* against the
deeds of the wicked.

6 Their judges are overthrown by the
sides of the cliff,
And they hear my words, for they
are sweet.

7 Our bones are scattered at the mouth
of the grave,
As when one plows and breaks up
the earth.

8 But my eyes *are* upon You, O GOD
the Lord;
In You I take refuge;
Do not leave my soul destitute.

9 Keep me from the snares they have
laid for me,
And from the traps of the workers of
iniquity.

10 Let the wicked fall into their own
nets,
While I escape safely.

PSALM 142

A Plea for Relief from Persecutors

A Contemplation[a] of David.
A Prayer when he was in the cave.

1 I cry out to the LORD with my voice;
With my voice to the LORD I make
my supplication.

2 I pour out my complaint before Him;
I declare before Him my trouble.

3 When my spirit was overwhelmed
within me,
Then You knew my path.
In the way in which I walk
They have secretly set a snare for
me.

4 Look on *my* right hand and see,
For *there is* no one who
acknowledges me;
Refuge has failed me;
No one cares for my soul.

5 I cried out to You, O LORD:
I said, "You *are* my refuge,
My portion in the land of the living.

6 Attend to my cry,
For I am brought very low;
Deliver me from my persecutors,
For they are stronger than I.

7 Bring my soul out of prison,

That I may praise Your name;
The righteous shall surround me,
For You shall deal bountifully with
me."

PSALM 143

An Earnest Appeal for Guidance and Deliverance

A Psalm of David.

1 Hear my prayer, O LORD,
Give ear to my supplications!
In Your faithfulness answer me,
And in Your righteousness.

2 Do not enter into judgment with
Your servant,
For in Your sight no one living is
righteous.

3 For the enemy has persecuted my
soul;
He has crushed my life to the
ground;
He has made me dwell in darkness,
Like those who have long been dead.

4 Therefore my spirit is overwhelmed
within me;
My heart within me is distressed.

5 I remember the days of old;
I meditate on all Your works;
I muse on the work of Your hands.

6 I spread out my hands to You;
My soul *longs* for You like a thirsty
land.   Selah

7 Answer me speedily, O LORD;
My spirit fails!
Do not hide Your face from me,
Lest I be like those who go down into
the pit.

8 Cause me to hear Your
lovingkindness in the morning,
For in You do I trust;
Cause me to know the way in which
I should walk,
For I lift up my soul to You.

9 Deliver me, O LORD, from my
enemies;
In You I take shelter.[a]

10 Teach me to do Your will,

142:title [a]Hebrew *Maschil*
143:9 [a]Septuagint and Vulgate read *To You I flee.*

For You *are* my God;
Your Spirit *is* good.
Lead me in the land of uprightness.

11 Revive me, O LORD, for Your name's
   sake!
   For Your righteousness' sake bring
   my soul out of trouble.

12 In Your mercy cut off my enemies,
   And destroy all those who afflict my
   soul;
   For I *am* Your servant.

PSALM 144

A Song to the LORD Who Preserves and Prospers His People

A Psalm of David.

1 Blessed *be* the LORD my Rock,
  Who trains my hands for war,
  And my fingers for battle—
2 My lovingkindness and my fortress,
  My high tower and my deliverer,
  My shield and *the One* in whom I
  take refuge,
  Who subdues my people[a] under me.

3 LORD, what *is* man, that You take
  knowledge of him?
  Or the son of man, that You are
  mindful of him?
4 Man is like a breath;
  His days *are* like a passing shadow.

5 Bow down Your heavens, O LORD,
  and come down;
  Touch the mountains, and they shall
  smoke.
6 Flash forth lightning and scatter them;
  Shoot out Your arrows and destroy
  them.
7 Stretch out Your hand from above;
  Rescue me and deliver me out of
  great waters,
  From the hand of foreigners,
8 Whose mouth speaks lying words,
  And whose right hand *is* a right
  hand of falsehood.

9 I will sing a new song to You, O God;
  On a harp of ten strings I will sing
  praises to You,
10 *The One* who gives salvation to
   kings,
   Who delivers David His servant
   From the deadly sword.

11 Rescue me and deliver me from the
   hand of foreigners,
   Whose mouth speaks lying words,
   And whose right hand *is* a right
   hand of falsehood—
12 That our sons *may be* as plants
   grown up in their youth;
   That our daughters *may be* as
   pillars,
   Sculptured in palace style;
13 *That* our barns *may be* full,
   Supplying all kinds of produce;
   That our sheep may bring forth
   thousands
   And ten thousands in our fields;
14 *That* our oxen *may be* well laden;
   That there be no breaking in, or
   going out;
   That there be no outcry in our
   streets.
15 Happy *are* the people who are in
   such a state;
   Happy *are* the people whose God *is*
   the LORD!

PSALM 145

A Song of God's Majesty and Love

A Praise of David.

1 I will extol You, my God, O King;
  And I will bless Your name forever
  and ever.
2 Every day I will bless You,
  And I will praise Your name forever
  and ever.
3 Great *is* the LORD, and greatly to be
  praised;
  And His greatness *is* unsearchable.

4 One generation shall praise Your
  works to another,
  And shall declare Your mighty acts.
5 I[a] will meditate on the glorious
  splendor of Your majesty,
  And on Your wondrous works.[b]

144:2 [a]Following Masoretic Text, Septuagint, and
Vulgate; Syriac and Targum read *the peoples* (compare 18:47). **145:5** [a]Following Masoretic Text and
Targum; Dead Sea Scrolls, Septuagint, Syriac, and
Vulgate read *They.* [b]Literally *on the words of Your
wondrous works*

6   *Men* shall speak of the might of
Your awesome acts,
And I will declare Your
greatness.
7   They shall utter the memory of
Your great goodness,
And shall sing of Your
righteousness.

8   The LORD *is* gracious and full of
compassion,
Slow to anger and great in mercy.
9   The LORD *is* good to all,
And His tender mercies *are* over all
His works.

10   All Your works shall praise You,
O LORD,
And Your saints shall bless You.
11   They shall speak of the glory of
Your kingdom,
And talk of Your power,
12   To make known to the sons of men
His mighty acts,
And the glorious majesty of His
kingdom.
13   Your kingdom *is* an everlasting
kingdom,
And Your dominion *endures*
throughout all generations.[a]

14   The LORD upholds all who fall,
And raises up all *who are* bowed
down.
15   The eyes of all look expectantly to
You,
And You give them their food in
due season.
16   You open Your hand
And satisfy the desire of every
living thing.

17   The LORD *is* righteous in all His
ways,
Gracious in all His works.
18   The LORD *is* near to all who call
upon Him,
To all who call upon Him in truth.
19   He will fulfill the desire of those
who fear Him;
He also will hear their cry and save
them.
20   The LORD preserves all who love
Him,
But all the wicked He will destroy.

21   My mouth shall speak the praise of
the LORD,
And all flesh shall bless His holy
name
Forever and ever.

PSALM 146

The Happiness of Those Whose Help Is the LORD

1   Praise the LORD!

Praise the LORD, O my soul!
2   While I live I will praise the LORD;
I will sing praises to my God while I
have my being.

3   Do not put your trust in princes,
Nor in a son of man, in whom *there
is* no help.
4   His spirit departs, he returns to his
earth;
In that very day his plans perish.

5   Happy *is* he who *has* the God of
Jacob for his help,
Whose hope *is* in the LORD his God,
6   Who made heaven and earth,
The sea, and all that *is* in them;
Who keeps truth forever,
7   Who executes justice for the
oppressed,
Who gives food to the hungry.
The LORD gives freedom to the
prisoners.

8   The LORD opens *the eyes of* the blind;
The LORD raises those who are
bowed down;
The LORD loves the righteous.
9   The LORD watches over the
strangers;
He relieves the fatherless and widow;
But the way of the wicked He turns
upside down.

10   The LORD shall reign forever—
Your God, O Zion, to all generations.

Praise the LORD!

145:13 [a]Following Masoretic Text and Targum;
Dead Sea Scrolls, Septuagint, Syriac, and Vulgate add
*The LORD is faithful in all His words, And holy in all
His works.*

PSALM 147

Praise to God for His Word and Providence

1   Praise the LORD!
    For *it is* good to sing praises to our
        God;
    For *it is* pleasant, *and* praise is
        beautiful.
2   The LORD builds up Jerusalem;
    He gathers together the outcasts of
        Israel.
3   He heals the brokenhearted
    And binds up their wounds.
4   He counts the number of the stars;
    He calls them all by name.
5   Great *is* our Lord, and mighty in
        power;
    His understanding *is* infinite.
6   The LORD lifts up the humble;
    He casts the wicked down to the
        ground.

7   Sing to the LORD with thanksgiving;
    Sing praises on the harp to our God,
8   Who covers the heavens with clouds,
    Who prepares rain for the earth,
    Who makes grass to grow on the
        mountains.
9   He gives to the beast its food,
    And to the young ravens that cry.

10 He does not delight in the strength of
        the horse;
    He takes no pleasure in the legs of a
        man.
11 The LORD takes pleasure in those
        who fear Him,
    In those who hope in His mercy.

12 Praise the LORD, O Jerusalem!
    Praise your God, O Zion!
13 For He has strengthened the bars of
        your gates;
    He has blessed your children within
        you.
14 He makes peace *in* your borders,
    And fills you with the finest wheat.

15 He sends out His command *to the*
        earth;
    His word runs very swiftly.
16 He gives snow like wool;
    He scatters the frost like ashes;

BIBLICAL INSIGHTS • 147:1

Praising God in Difficulties

NO MATTER WHAT CIRCUMSTANCES you face as a couple, nothing will refresh and energize your communication with God like praising Him. A few of the many Scriptures that praise God also encourage us to express our adoration of Him. Consider the following psalms:

- And my tongue shall speak of Your righteousness and of Your praise all the day long. (35:28)
- Enter into His gates with thanksgiving, and into His courts with praise. (100:4)
- Praise the LORD! For it is good to sing praises to our God; for it is pleasant, and praise is beautiful. (147:1)

Over the years, we've learned to praise Him for:

- Who He is—He is God almighty!
- What he's done for us in the past, calling to mind in prayer His acts on our behalf.
- What He has promised us in Scripture, including His pledge to never leave nor forsake us.

When we acknowledge God's greatness in our lives, we remember who He really is and His great love for us. We like what one couple told us: "We've learned to praise God in the hard times and to call to Him and lift His name high even when the circumstances look impossible or difficult." As a result, we've learned that praising God lifts us out of our challenges and realigns our hearts with His.

The next time you face a difficult circumstance, pause and begin to praise God for what you are facing. Ask Him to fill you with His Spirit and honor Him in the midst of your difficulty.

17 He casts out His hail like morsels;
    Who can stand before His cold?
18 He sends out His word and melts
        them;

He causes His wind to blow, *and* the
waters flow.

19 He declares His word to Jacob,
His statutes and His judgments to
Israel.

20 He has not dealt thus with any nation;
And *as for His* judgments, they have
not known them.

Praise the LORD!

PSALM 148

Praise to the LORD from Creation

1 Praise the LORD!

Praise the LORD from the heavens;
Praise Him in the heights!

2 Praise Him, all His angels;
Praise Him, all His hosts!

3 Praise Him, sun and moon;
Praise Him, all you stars of light!

4 Praise Him, you heavens of heavens,
And you waters above the heavens!

5 Let them praise the name of the LORD,
For He commanded and they were
created.

6 He also established them forever and
ever;
He made a decree which shall not
pass away.

7 Praise the LORD from the earth,
You great sea creatures and all the
depths;

8 Fire and hail, snow and clouds;
Stormy wind, fulfilling His word;

9 Mountains and all hills;
Fruitful trees and all cedars;

10 Beasts and all cattle;
Creeping things and flying fowl;

11 Kings of the earth and all peoples;
Princes and all judges of the earth;

12 Both young men and maidens;
Old men and children.

13 Let them praise the name of the
LORD,
For His name alone is exalted;
His glory *is* above the earth and
heaven.

14 And He has exalted the horn of His
people,
The praise of all His saints—

Of the children of Israel,
A people near to Him.

Praise the LORD!

PSALM 149

Praise to God for His Salvation and Judgment

1 Praise the LORD!

Sing to the LORD a new song,
And His praise in the assembly of
saints.

2 Let Israel rejoice in their Maker;
Let the children of Zion be joyful in
their King.

3 Let them praise His name with the
dance;
Let them sing praises to Him with
the timbrel and harp.

4 For the LORD takes pleasure in His
people;
He will beautify the humble with
salvation.

5 Let the saints be joyful in glory;
Let them sing aloud on their beds.

6 *Let* the high praises of God *be* in
their mouth,
And a two-edged sword in their hand,

7 To execute vengeance on the nations,
And punishments on the peoples;

8 To bind their kings with chains,
And their nobles with fetters of iron;

9 To execute on them the written
judgment—
This honor have all His saints.

Praise the LORD!

PSALM 150

Let All Things Praise the LORD

1 Praise the LORD!

Praise God in His sanctuary;
Praise Him in His mighty firmament!

2 Praise Him for His mighty acts;
Praise Him according to His excellent
greatness!

3 Praise Him with the sound of the
trumpet;
Praise Him with the lute and harp!

4   Praise Him with the timbrel and
         dance;
     Praise Him with stringed
         instruments and flutes!
5   Praise Him with loud cymbals;

     Praise Him with clashing cymbals!
6   Let everything that has breath praise
         the LORD.

     Praise the LORD!

PROVERBS

NOT FAR INTO THE BOOK OF PROVERBS, you come across this statement, "My son, hear the instruction of your father, and do not forsake the law of your mother" (1:8). It's clear that one of the primary objectives of the book is to equip parents to pass along wisdom, godly skill for everyday living, to their children. Proverbs teaches that "foolishness is bound up in the heart of a child" (22:15). This foolishness must be addressed and corrected, even through the use of corporal punishment—a measured amount of physical pain, never applied in anger—to teach a child obedience and wisdom (see 13:24; 22:15; 23:13, 14). This book is loaded with practical counsel to help us raise wise sons and daughters who grow to become men and women of character.

Proverbs is a divinely inspired tool for equipping this generation and the next to make wise decisions. The call to pursue wisdom (2:1–10) is contrasted repeatedly with listening to the evil influences of those who are fools (2:11–22). Wisdom is acquired as we make it a lifetime pursuit.

And it's not only wisdom for parents to pass along to their children! Proverbs has much to say to husbands and wives about marriage and how to raise a godly family. Chapters five through seven, for example, contain very honest and direct counsel about how a husband should guard against the temptations of an adulterous woman. Proverbs warns wives against being contentious and quarrelsome (21:9; 21:19; 25:24; 27:15).

One of the Bible's best-known chapters is found in Proverbs 31. There we get some wise counsel regarding the kind of woman to look for as a wife. The chapter details the character of a "virtuous wife" and even today it provides a helpful model for wives and mothers who want to make choices that honor God and their families.

Many people read a chapter of Proverbs each day; its 31 chapters match the number of days in most months. When our children were teenagers, I used to take them out for breakfast once a week, before school, and we would read a chapter from Proverbs and talk about the godly wisdom it offers. Those times remain among the highlights of all the time I spent with our children during their teen years.

Each time you read Proverbs, have a highlighter handy so you can mark and memorize verses that address the critical issues you or your children face. Proverbs will indeed equip you with a godly skill in everyday living.

The Beginning of Knowledge

1 The proverbs of Solomon the son of David, king of Israel:

2 To know wisdom and instruction,
To perceive the words of understanding,
3 To receive the instruction of wisdom,
Justice, judgment, and equity;
4 To give prudence to the simple,
To the young man knowledge and discretion—
5 A wise *man* will hear and increase learning,
And a man of understanding will attain wise counsel,
6 To understand a proverb and an enigma,
The words of the wise and their riddles.

7 The fear of the LORD *is* the beginning of knowledge,
But fools despise wisdom and instruction.

Shun Evil Counsel

8 My son, hear the instruction of your father,
And do not forsake the law of your mother;
9 For they *will be* a graceful ornament on your head,
And chains about your neck.

10 My son, if sinners entice you,
Do not consent.
11 If they say, "Come with us,
Let us lie in wait to *shed* blood;
Let us lurk secretly for the innocent without cause;
12 Let us swallow them alive like Sheol,[a]
And whole, like those who go down to the Pit;
13 We shall find all *kinds* of precious possessions,
We shall fill our houses with spoil;
14 Cast in your lot among us,
Let us all have one purse"—

15 My son, do not walk in the way with them,
Keep your foot from their path;
16 For their feet run to evil,
And they make haste to shed blood.
17 Surely, in vain the net is spread
In the sight of any bird;
18 But they lie in wait for their *own* blood,
They lurk secretly for their *own* lives.
19 So *are* the ways of everyone who is greedy for gain;
It takes away the life of its owners.

The Call of Wisdom

20 Wisdom calls aloud outside;
She raises her voice in the open squares.
21 She cries out in the chief concourses,[a]
At the openings of the gates in the city
She speaks her words:
22 "How long, you simple ones, will you love simplicity?
For scorners delight in their scorning,
And fools hate knowledge.
23 Turn at my rebuke;
Surely I will pour out my spirit on you;
I will make my words known to you.
24 Because I have called and you refused,
I have stretched out my hand and no one regarded,
25 Because you disdained all my counsel,
And would have none of my rebuke,
26 I also will laugh at your calamity;
I will mock when your terror comes,
27 When your terror comes like a storm,
And your destruction comes like a whirlwind,
When distress and anguish come upon you.

28 "Then they will call on me, but I will not answer;
They will seek me diligently, but they will not find me.
29 Because they hated knowledge
And did not choose the fear of the LORD,

1:12 [a]Or *the grave*
1:21 [a]Septuagint, Syriac, and Targum read *top of the walls;* Vulgate reads *the head of multitudes.*

DEVOTIONS FOR COUPLES • 2:2
Get Understanding

The book of Proverbs is one of my favorites in the entire Bible because it contains such practical wisdom about everyday life. One theme that constantly pops up is the tremendous value of becoming a person of understanding. Take some time to read and consider the teaching of each of the following verses:

Apply your heart to understanding. (2:2)

Understanding will watch over you. (2:11)

Call understanding your nearest kin. (7:4)

A man [or woman] of understanding walks upright. (15:21)

Understanding is a wellspring of life to him [or her] who has it. (16:22)

Understanding is never an end in itself; it is merely a vehicle to wisdom, direction, and to life. A person of understanding views life and people from God's own perspective. Understanding enables you to feel for another person, to identify with his or her struggles and difficulties, and to know what to say and what not to say.

Oh, how we need understanding in our marriages!

In the husband-wife relationship, your level of understanding often determines your level of acceptance. Having God's perspective of your spouse and how He designed him to complement you is essential if you are truly going to love him.

At a FamilyLife Weekend to Remember marriage conference a few years ago, I talked to several women who described various problems in their marriages. One woman resented her husband's schedule. Another disagreed with her husband regarding how to discipline their children. A third spoke of how jealous her husband was of the time she spent with her sister.

I gave essentially the same advice to all of these women: Seek to understand *why* your husband is feeling or acting this way. Focus on better understanding *him*, not on the negative circumstances and how *you* are affected. By his unwanted actions, is he communicating some unmet need for affirmation, commitment, or loyalty?

Even if you don't totally understand your mate, give him or her your complete acceptance. It may be necessary to ask God to help you accept your mate. Many are living in circumstances that are very difficult and they need God's guidance and power to be able to love their spouses well.

Why is understanding so important? Because without it, your spouse will feel that you are pressuring him or her to become something he or she is not. With it, your spouse will sense that you love him or her for who he or she is today, and not for what you hope he or she will become tomorrow.

---

30 They would have none of my counsel
    And despised my every rebuke.
31 Therefore they shall eat the fruit of
    their own way,
    And be filled to the full with their
    own fancies.
32 For the turning away of the simple
    will slay them,
    And the complacency of fools will
    destroy them;
33 But whoever listens to me will dwell
    safely,
    And will be secure, without fear of
    evil."

The Value of Wisdom

2 My son, if you receive my words,
   And treasure my commands within
       you,
2 So that you incline your ear to
       wisdom,
   And apply your heart to
       understanding;
3 Yes, if you cry out for discernment,
   And lift up your voice for
       understanding,
4 If you seek her as silver,
   And search for her as *for* hidden
       treasures;

5 Then you will understand the fear of
the LORD,
And find the knowledge of God.
6 For the LORD gives wisdom;
From His mouth *come* knowledge
and understanding;
7 He stores up sound wisdom for the
upright;
He is a shield to those who walk
uprightly;
8 He guards the paths of justice,
And preserves the way of His saints.
9 Then you will understand
righteousness and justice,
Equity *and* every good path.

10 When wisdom enters your heart,
And knowledge is pleasant to your
soul,
11 Discretion will preserve you;
Understanding will keep you,
12 To deliver you from the way of evil,
From the man who speaks perverse
things,
13 From those who leave the paths of
uprightness
To walk in the ways of darkness;
14 Who rejoice in doing evil,
And delight in the perversity of the
wicked;
15 Whose ways *are* crooked,
And *who are* devious in their paths;
16 To deliver you from the immoral
woman,
From the seductress *who* flatters
with her words,
17 Who forsakes the companion of her
youth,
And forgets the covenant of her God.
18 For her house leads down to death,
And her paths to the dead;
19 None who go to her return,
Nor do they regain the paths of
life—
20 So you may walk in the way of
goodness,
And keep *to* the paths of
righteousness.
21 For the upright will dwell in the land,
And the blameless will remain in it;

22 But the wicked will be cut off from
the earth,
And the unfaithful will be uprooted
from it.

Guidance for the Young

3 My son, do not forget my law,
But let your heart keep my
commands;
2 For length of days and long life
And peace they will add to you.

3 Let not mercy and truth forsake you;
Bind them around your neck,
Write them on the tablet of your
heart,
4 *And* so find favor and high esteem
In the sight of God and man.

5 Trust in the LORD with all your heart,
And lean not on your own
understanding;
6 In all your ways acknowledge Him,
And He shall direct[a] your paths.

7 Do not be wise in your own eyes;
Fear the LORD and depart from evil.
8 It will be health to your flesh,[a]
And strength[b] to your bones.

9 Honor the LORD with your
possessions,
And with the firstfruits of all your
increase;
10 So your barns will be filled with
plenty,
And your vats will overflow with
new wine.

11 My son, do not despise the
chastening of the LORD,
Nor detest His correction;
12 For whom the LORD loves He
corrects,
Just as a father the son *in whom* he
delights.

13 Happy *is* the man *who* finds wisdom,
And the man *who* gains
understanding;
14 For her proceeds *are* better than the
profits of silver,
And her gain than fine gold.
15 She *is* more precious than rubies,
And all the things you may desire
cannot compare with her.

3:6 [a]Or *make smooth* or *straight* **3:8** [a]Literally *navel,*
figurative of the body [b]Literally *drink* or *refreshment*

16 Length of days *is* in her right hand,
In her left hand riches and honor.
17 Her ways *are* ways of pleasantness,
And all her paths *are* peace.
18 She *is* a tree of life to those who take
hold of her,
And happy *are all* who retain her.

19 The LORD by wisdom founded the
earth;
By understanding He established the
heavens;
20 By His knowledge the depths were
broken up,
And clouds drop down the dew.

21 My son, let them not depart from
your eyes—
Keep sound wisdom and discretion;
22 So they will be life to your soul
And grace to your neck.
23 Then you will walk safely in your way,
And your foot will not stumble.
24 When you lie down, you will not be
afraid;
Yes, you will lie down and your sleep
will be sweet.
25 Do not be afraid of sudden terror,
Nor of trouble from the wicked when
it comes;
26 For the LORD will be your confidence,
And will keep your foot from being
caught.

27 Do not withhold good from those to
whom it is due,
When it is in the power of your hand
to do *so*.
28 Do not say to your neighbor,
"Go, and come back,
And tomorrow I will give *it*,"
When you have it with you.
29 Do not devise evil against your
neighbor,
For he dwells by you for safety's sake.
30 Do not strive with a man without
cause,
If he has done you no harm.
31 Do not envy the oppressor,
And choose none of his ways;
32 For the perverse *person is* an
abomination to the LORD,
But His secret counsel *is* with the
upright.

33 The curse of the LORD *is* on the
house of the wicked,
But He blesses the home of the just.
34 Surely He scorns the scornful,
But gives grace to the humble.
35 The wise shall inherit glory,
But shame shall be the legacy of fools.

Security in Wisdom

4 Hear, *my* children, the instruction of
a father,
And give attention to know
understanding;
2 For I give you good doctrine:
Do not forsake my law.
3 When I was my father's son,
Tender and the only one in the
sight of my mother,
4 He also taught me, and said
to me:
"Let your heart retain my words;
Keep my commands, and live.
5 Get wisdom! Get understanding!
Do not forget, nor turn away from
the words of my mouth.
6 Do not forsake her, and she will
preserve you;
Love her, and she will keep you.
7 Wisdom *is* the principal thing;
Therefore get wisdom.
And in all your getting, get
understanding.
8 Exalt her, and she will promote you;
She will bring you honor, when you
embrace her.
9 She will place on your head an
ornament of grace;
A crown of glory she will deliver to
you."

10 Hear, my son, and receive my sayings,
And the years of your life will be
many.
11 I have taught you in the way of
wisdom;
I have led you in right paths.
12 When you walk, your steps will not
be hindered,
And when you run, you will not
stumble.
13 Take firm hold of instruction, do not
let go;
Keep her, for she *is* your life.

14 Do not enter the path of the wicked,
And do not walk in the way of evil.
15 Avoid it, do not travel on it;
Turn away from it and pass on.
16 For they do not sleep unless they
have done evil;
And their sleep is taken away unless
they make *someone* fall.
17 For they eat the bread of
wickedness,
And drink the wine of violence.

18 But the path of the just *is* like the
shining sun,[a]
That shines ever brighter unto the
perfect day.
19 The way of the wicked *is* like
darkness;
They do not know what makes
them stumble.

20 My son, give attention to my
words;
Incline your ear to my sayings.
21 Do not let them depart from your
eyes;
Keep them in the midst of your
heart;
22 For they *are* life to those who find
them,
And health to all their flesh.
23 Keep your heart with all diligence,
For out of it *spring* the issues of
life.
24 Put away from you a deceitful
mouth,
And put perverse lips far from you.
25 Let your eyes look straight ahead,
And your eyelids look right before you.
26 Ponder the path of your feet,
And let all your ways be established.
27 Do not turn to the right or the left;
Remove your foot from evil.

The Peril of Adultery

5 My son, pay attention to my wisdom;
Lend your ear to my understanding,
2 That you may preserve discretion,
And your lips may keep knowledge.

4:18 [a]Literally *light*
5:5 [a]Or *Sheol*

BIBLICAL INSIGHTS • 4:1, 2
Call Him "Spiritual Leader"

ACCORDING TO PROVERBS 4:1, 2, it is Dad's job as the family minister-shepherd to bear the weight of transferring God's truth to his children. Children need their father to lead them spiritually.

Dad, you can take advantage of daily opportunities to equip your children spiritually. First, get clearly in your mind what you want to teach your children. Early in the lives of my own children, I started carrying around a list I called, "Twenty-five Things I Am Teaching My Kids." This list always faced my daily "To Do" list. On this page, Barbara and I listed things such as "Being faithful in little things," "Becoming a man of character," and "Becoming a woman who has a gentle and quiet spirit." It reminded me of what is important, beyond my daily tasks.

Over the years, that list grew to more than 50 items! I still carry the list with me, even though our children are grown. There are still important lessons I'm learning that I can pass along to my adult children, not as a parent, but as an adult peer.

God designed the family to be a spiritual garden. It is the single most important place where faith gets planted and hope is nurtured. This garden must survive weeds from previous generations, present-day droughts, and future attacks from the enemy of our souls. Yet when all else in the culture perishes, the family that is committed to Jesus Christ and embraces His skill (wisdom) in everyday living stands strong and enjoys sweet rewards, both now and for generations to come.

3 For the lips of an immoral woman
drip honey,
And her mouth *is* smoother than oil;
4 But in the end she is bitter as
wormwood,
Sharp as a two-edged sword.
5 Her feet go down to death,
Her steps lay hold of hell.[a]

6 Lest you ponder *her* path of life—
Her ways are unstable;
You do not know *them*.

7 Therefore hear me now, *my* children,
And do not depart from the words of
my mouth.

8 Remove your way far from her,
And do not go near the door of her
house,

9 Lest you give your honor to others,
And your years to the cruel *one;*

10 Lest aliens be filled with your
wealth,

ROMANCE FAQ

**Q: *Marriage has
seemed to dull our
romantic creativity—
what should we do?***

At some point in almost every marriage, a couple realizes that they just don't experience the same romantic feelings they once enjoyed.

Romance is the sugar and spice of marriage. It is the fire in the fireplace—the warm response of one spouse to another that says, "We may have struggles, but I love you, and everything is okay." We can enjoy the warmth of our love for one another, even in the midst of the chilling winds of difficult times.

Romance should be a part of our everyday marriage experience. Proverbs 5:18, 19, tells husbands, "Rejoice with the wife of your youth, as a loving deer and a graceful doe, let her breasts satisfy you at all times. And always be enraptured with her love."

That's a powerful image— literally, to be *enraptured* with your mate. This type of romance is part of what sets a marriage apart from just a friendship. Barbara is my friend, but a side of our relationship goes way beyond that. We share a marriage bed and we dream thoughts and share intimacies that are reserved only for us!

God designed the marriage relationship to experience exhilaration with your most intimate of friends, your spouse. Don't settle for less.

And your labors *go* to the house of a
foreigner;

11 And you mourn at last,
When your flesh and your body are
consumed,

12 And say:
"How I have hated instruction,
And my heart despised correction!

13 I have not obeyed the voice of my
teachers,
Nor inclined my ear to those who
instructed me!

14 I was on the verge of total ruin,
In the midst of the assembly and
congregation."

15 Drink water from your own cistern,
And running water from your own
well.

16 Should your fountains be dispersed
abroad,
Streams of water in the streets?

17 Let them be only your own,
And not for strangers with you.

18 Let your fountain be blessed,
And rejoice with the wife of your
youth.

19 As *a* loving deer and a graceful doe,
Let her breasts satisfy you at all
times;
And always be enraptured with her
love.

20 For why should you, my son, be
enraptured by an immoral
woman,
And be embraced in the arms of a
seductress?

21 For the ways of man *are* before the
eyes of the LORD,
And He ponders all his paths.

22 His own iniquities entrap the wicked
man,
And he is caught in the cords of his
sin.

23 He shall die for lack of instruction,
And in the greatness of his folly he
shall go astray.

Dangerous Promises

6 My son, if you become surety for
your friend,
If you have shaken hands in pledge
for a stranger,

2   You are snared by the words of your
       mouth;
     You are taken by the words of your
       mouth.
3   So do this, my son, and deliver
       yourself;
     For you have come into the hand of
       your friend:
     Go and humble yourself;
     Plead with your friend.
4   Give no sleep to your eyes,
     Nor slumber to your eyelids.
5   Deliver yourself like a gazelle from
       the hand *of the hunter,*
     And like a bird from the hand of the
       fowler.[a]

The Folly of Indolence

6   Go to the ant, you sluggard!
     Consider her ways and be wise,
7   Which, having no captain,
     Overseer or ruler,
8   Provides her supplies in the summer,
     And gathers her food in the harvest.
9   How long will you slumber, O
       sluggard?
     When will you rise from your sleep?
10   A little sleep, a little slumber,
     A little folding of the hands to
       sleep—

6:5 [a]That is, one who catches birds in a trap or snare

11   So shall your poverty come on you
       like a prowler,
     And your need like an armed man.

The Wicked Man

12   A worthless person, a wicked man,
     Walks with a perverse mouth;
13   He winks with his eyes,
     He shuffles his feet,
     He points with his fingers;
14   Perversity *is* in his heart,
     He devises evil continually,
     He sows discord.
15   Therefore his calamity shall come
       suddenly;
     Suddenly he shall be broken without
       remedy.
16   These six *things* the Lord hates,
     Yes, seven *are* an abomination to Him:
17   A proud look,
     A lying tongue,
     Hands that shed innocent blood,
18   A heart that devises wicked plans,
     Feet that are swift in running to evil,
19   A false witness *who* speaks lies,
     And one who sows discord among
       brethren.

Beware of Adultery

20   My son, keep your father's
       command,

And do not forsake the law of your
  mother.
21 Bind them continually upon your
  heart;
  Tie them around your neck.
22 When you roam, they[a] will lead you;
  When you sleep, they will keep you;
  And *when* you awake, they will
  speak with you.
23 For the commandment *is* a lamp,
  And the law a light;
  Reproofs of instruction *are* the way
  of life,
24 To keep you from the evil woman,
  From the flattering tongue of a
  seductress.
25 Do not lust after her beauty in your
  heart,
  Nor let her allure you with her eyelids.
26 For by means of a harlot
  A man is reduced to a crust of
  bread;
  And an adulteress[a] will prey upon
  his precious life.
27 Can a man take fire to his bosom,
  And his clothes not be burned?
28 Can one walk on hot coals,
  And his feet not be seared?
29 So *is* he who goes in to his neighbor's
  wife;
  Whoever touches her shall not be
  innocent.
30 *People* do not despise a thief
  If he steals to satisfy himself when
  he is starving.
31 Yet *when* he is found, he must restore
  sevenfold;
  He may have to give up all the
  substance of his house.
32 Whoever commits adultery with a
  woman lacks understanding;
  He *who* does so destroys his own
  soul.
33 Wounds and dishonor he will get,
  And his reproach will not be wiped
  away.
34 For jealousy *is* a husband's fury;
  Therefore he will not spare in the
  day of vengeance.
35 He will accept no recompense,
  Nor will he be appeased though you
  give many gifts.

7 My son, keep my words,
  And treasure my commands within
  you.
2 Keep my commands and live,
  And my law as the apple of your eye.
3 Bind them on your fingers;
  Write them on the tablet of your heart.
4 Say to wisdom, "You *are* my sister,"
  And call understanding *your* nearest
  kin,
5 That they may keep you from the
  immoral woman,
  From the seductress *who* flatters
  with her words.

The Crafty Harlot

6 For at the window of my house
  I looked through my lattice,
7 And saw among the simple,
  I perceived among the youths,
  A young man devoid of
  understanding,
8 Passing along the street near her
  corner;
  And he took the path to her house
9 In the twilight, in the evening,
  In the black and dark night.

10 And there a woman met him,
  With the attire of a harlot, and a
  crafty heart.
11 She *was* loud and rebellious,
  Her feet would not stay at home.
12 At times *she was* outside, at times in
  the open square,
  Lurking at every corner.
13 So she caught him and kissed him;
  With an impudent face she said to
  him:
14 "*I have* peace offerings with me;
  Today I have paid my vows.
15 So I came out to meet you,
  Diligently to seek your face,
  And I have found you.
16 I have spread my bed with tapestry,
  Colored coverings of Egyptian linen.
17 I have perfumed my bed
  With myrrh, aloes, and cinnamon.
18 Come, let us take our fill of love until
  morning;

6:22 [a]Literally *it*
6:26 [a]Literally *a man's wife*, that is, of another

Let us delight ourselves with love.
19 For my husband *is* not at home;
He has gone on a long journey;
20 He has taken a bag of money with
him,
And will come home on the
appointed day."

21 With her enticing speech she caused
him to yield,
With her flattering lips she seduced
him.
22 Immediately he went after her, as an
ox goes to the slaughter,
Or as a fool to the correction of the
stocks,[a]
23 Till an arrow struck his liver.
As a bird hastens to the snare,
He did not know it *would cost*
his life.

24 Now therefore, listen to me, *my*
children;
Pay attention to the words of my
mouth:
25 Do not let your heart turn aside to
her ways,
Do not stray into her paths;
26 For she has cast down many
wounded,
And all who were slain by her were
strong *men.*
27 Her house *is* the way to hell,[a]
Descending to the chambers of
death.

The Excellence of Wisdom

8 Does not wisdom cry out,
And understanding lift up her voice?
2 She takes her stand on the top of the
high hill,
Beside the way, where the paths
meet.
3 She cries out by the gates, at the
entry of the city,
At the entrance of the doors:
4 "To you, O men, I call,
And my voice *is* to the sons of men.

5 O you simple ones, understand
prudence,
And you fools, be of an
understanding heart.
6 Listen, for I will speak of excellent
things,
And from the opening of my lips
will come right things;
7 For my mouth will speak truth;
Wickedness *is* an abomination to my
lips.
8 All the words of my mouth *are* with
righteousness;
Nothing crooked or perverse *is* in
them.
9 They *are* all plain to him who
understands,
And right to those who find
knowledge.
10 Receive my instruction, and not silver,
And knowledge rather than choice
gold;
11 For wisdom *is* better than rubies,
And all the things one may desire
cannot be compared with her.

12 "I, wisdom, dwell with prudence,
And find out knowledge *and*
discretion.
13 The fear of the LORD *is* to hate evil;
Pride and arrogance and the evil way
And the perverse mouth I hate.
14 Counsel *is* mine, and sound wisdom;
I *am* understanding, I have strength.
15 By me kings reign,
And rulers decree justice.
16 By me princes rule, and nobles,
All the judges of the earth.[a]
17 I love those who love me,
And those who seek me diligently
will find me.
18 Riches and honor *are* with me,
Enduring riches and righteousness.
19 My fruit *is* better than gold, yes, than
fine gold,
And my revenue than choice silver.
20 I traverse the way of righteousness,
In the midst of the paths of justice,
21 That I may cause those who love me
to inherit wealth,
That I may fill their treasuries.

22 "The LORD possessed me at the
beginning of His way,

7:22 [a]Septuagint, Syriac, and Targum read *as a dog
to bonds;* Vulgate reads *as a lamb . . . to bonds.*
7:27 [a]Or *Sheol*
8:16 [a]Masoretic Text, Syriac, Targum, and Vulgate
read *righteousness;* Septuagint, Bomberg, and some
manuscripts and editions read *earth.*

Before His works of old.

23 I have been established from everlasting,
From the beginning, before there was ever an earth.

24 When *there were* no depths I was brought forth,
When *there were* no fountains abounding with water.

25 Before the mountains were settled,
Before the hills, I was brought forth;

26 While as yet He had not made the earth or the fields,
Or the primal dust of the world.

27 When He prepared the heavens, I *was* there,
When He drew a circle on the face of the deep,

28 When He established the clouds above,
When He strengthened the fountains of the deep,

29 When He assigned to the sea its limit,
So that the waters would not transgress His command,
When He marked out the foundations of the earth,

30 Then I was beside Him *as* a master craftsman;[a]
And I was daily *His* delight,
Rejoicing always before Him,

31 Rejoicing in His inhabited world,
And my delight *was* with the sons of men.

32 "Now therefore, listen to me, *my* children,
For blessed *are those who* keep my ways.

33 Hear instruction and be wise,
And do not disdain *it*.

34 Blessed is the man who listens to me,
Watching daily at my gates,
Waiting at the posts of my doors.

35 For whoever finds me finds life,
And obtains favor from the LORD;

36 But he who sins against me wrongs his own soul;
All those who hate me love death."

The Way of Wisdom

9 Wisdom has built her house,
She has hewn out her seven pillars;

2 She has slaughtered her meat,
She has mixed her wine,
She has also furnished her table.

3 She has sent out her maidens,
She cries out from the highest places of the city,

4 "Whoever *is* simple, let him turn in here!"
As for him who lacks understanding, she says to him,

5 "Come, eat of my bread
And drink of the wine I have mixed.

6 Forsake foolishness and live,
And go in the way of understanding.

7 "He who corrects a scoffer gets shame for himself,
And he who rebukes a wicked *man* only harms himself.

8 Do not correct a scoffer, lest he hate you;
Rebuke a wise *man,* and he will love you.

9 Give *instruction* to a wise *man,* and he will be still wiser;
Teach a just *man,* and he will increase in learning.

10 "The fear of the LORD *is* the beginning of wisdom,
And the knowledge of the Holy One *is* understanding.

11 For by me your days will be multiplied,
And years of life will be added to you.

12 If you are wise, you are wise for yourself,
And *if* you scoff, you will bear *it* alone."

INTIMATE MOMENTS

Do something active together: Take a class, play tennis, start a walking program, remodel a room, or plant a vegetable garden. Just do it *together*.

8:30 [a] A Jewish tradition reads *one brought up.*

The Way of Folly

13 A foolish woman is clamorous;
She is simple, and knows nothing.
14 For she sits at the door of her house,
On a seat *by* the highest places of
the city,
15 To call to those who pass by,
Who go straight on their way:
16 "Whoever *is* simple, let him turn in
here";
And *as for* him who lacks
understanding, she says to him,
17 "Stolen water is sweet,
And bread *eaten* in secret is
pleasant."
18 But he does not know that the dead
are there,
That her guests *are* in the depths of
hell.[a]

Wise Sayings of Solomon

10 The proverbs of Solomon:

A wise son makes a glad father,
But a foolish son *is* the grief of his
mother.

2 Treasures of wickedness profit
nothing,

But righteousness delivers from
death.
3 The LORD will not allow the
righteous soul to famish,
But He casts away the desire of the
wicked.
4 He who has a slack hand becomes
poor,
But the hand of the diligent makes
rich.
5 He who gathers in summer *is* a wise
son;
He who sleeps in harvest *is* a son
who causes shame.
6 Blessings *are* on the head of the
righteous,
But violence covers the mouth of the
wicked.
7 The memory of the righteous *is*
blessed,
But the name of the wicked will rot.
8 The wise in heart will receive
commands,
But a prating fool will fall.
9 He who walks with integrity walks
securely,
But he who perverts his ways will
become known.

9:18 [a] Or *Sheol*

PARENTING
MATTERS

Q: How can we start teaching our child that it is always best to be truthful?

You can start by instilling in him the conviction that deceit is dangerous and will lead him down an evil path. Shaping your child's convictions about deceit begins as you *teach him to fear God.* Proverbs 14:27 encourages us, "The fear of the LORD is a fountain of life, to turn one away from the snares of death." And Proverbs 16:6 says, "In mercy and truth atonement is provided for iniquity; and by the fear of the LORD one departs from evil."

Teach your child to fear God by teaching him who He really is. He is truth. Love. Holy. Sovereign. Omnipotent. Omnipresent. And much more! As your child begins to learn about who God is and sees you practicing the presence of God in your life, he will grow in the understanding that God sees all and that He is to be feared.

In addition, teach your child about his own tendency to deceive and to lie. We are all just one step away from being ensnared by this trap! You can do this by sharing situations from your life where you stepped into a deceitful snare. Talk about the consequences of those choices.

10   He who winks with the eye causes
      trouble,
    But a prating fool will fall.

11   The mouth of the righteous *is* a well
      of life,
    But violence covers the mouth of the
      wicked.

12   Hatred stirs up strife,
    But love covers all sins.

13   Wisdom is found on the lips of him
      who has understanding,
    But a rod *is* for the back of him who
      is devoid of understanding.

14   Wise *people* store up knowledge,
    But the mouth of the foolish *is* near
      destruction.

15   The rich man's wealth *is* his strong
      city;
    The destruction of the poor *is* their
      poverty.

16   The labor of the righteous *leads* to
      life,
    The wages of the wicked to sin.

17   He who keeps instruction *is in* the
      way of life,
    But he who refuses correction goes
      astray.

18   Whoever hides hatred *has* lying lips,
    And whoever spreads slander *is* a
      fool.

19   In the multitude of words sin is not
      lacking,
    But he who restrains his lips *is* wise.

20   The tongue of the righteous *is* choice
      silver;
    The heart of the wicked *is worth*
      little.

21   The lips of the righteous feed many,
    But fools die for lack of wisdom.[a]

22   The blessing of the LORD makes *one*
      rich,
    And He adds no sorrow with it.

23   To do evil *is* like sport to a fool,
    But a man of understanding has
      wisdom.

24   The fear of the wicked will come
      upon him,
    And the desire of the righteous will
      be granted.

25   When the whirlwind passes by, the
      wicked *is* no *more*,
    But the righteous *has* an everlasting
      foundation.

26   As vinegar to the teeth and smoke to
      the eyes,
    So *is* the lazy *man* to those who send
      him.

27   The fear of the LORD prolongs days,
    But the years of the wicked will be
      shortened.

28   The hope of the righteous *will be*
      gladness,
    But the expectation of the wicked
      will perish.

29   The way of the LORD *is* strength for
      the upright,
    But destruction *will come* to the
      workers of iniquity.

30   The righteous will never be
      removed,
    But the wicked will not inhabit
      the earth.

31   The mouth of the righteous brings
      forth wisdom,
    But the perverse tongue will be cut
      out.

32   The lips of the righteous know what
      is acceptable,
    But the mouth of the wicked *what is*
      perverse.

11   Dishonest scales *are* an
      abomination to the LORD,
    But a just weight *is* His delight.

2   When pride comes, then comes
      shame;
    But with the humble *is* wisdom.

3   The integrity of the upright will
      guide them,
    But the perversity of the unfaithful
      will destroy them.

4   Riches do not profit in the day of
      wrath,
    But righteousness delivers from
      death.

10:21 [a]Literally *heart*

5   The righteousness of the blameless
        will direct[a] his way aright,
    But the wicked will fall by his own
        wickedness.
6   The righteousness of the upright
        will deliver them,
    But the unfaithful will be caught by
        their lust.

7   When a wicked man dies, *his*
        expectation will perish,
    And the hope of the unjust perishes.
8   The righteous is delivered from
        trouble,
    And it comes to the wicked instead.
9   The hypocrite with *his* mouth
        destroys his neighbor,
    But through knowledge the righteous
        will be delivered.
10 When it goes well with the righteous,
        the city rejoices;
    And when the wicked perish, *there
        is* jubilation.
11 By the blessing of the upright the
        city is exalted,
    But it is overthrown by the mouth of
        the wicked.

12 He who is devoid of wisdom
        despises his neighbor,
    But a man of understanding holds
        his peace.

13 A talebearer reveals secrets,
    But he who is of a faithful spirit
        conceals a matter.

14 Where *there is* no counsel, the people
        fall;
    But in the multitude of counselors
        there is safety.

15 He who is surety for a stranger will
        suffer,
    But one who hates being surety is
        secure.

16 A gracious woman retains honor,
    But ruthless *men* retain riches.
17 The merciful man does good for his
        own soul,
    But *he who is* cruel troubles his own
        flesh.

18 The wicked *man* does deceptive work,
    But he who sows righteousness *will
        have* a sure reward.
19 As righteousness *leads* to life,
    So he who pursues evil *pursues it* to
        his own death.
20 Those who are of a perverse heart
        are an abomination to the LORD,
    But *the* blameless in their ways *are*
        His delight.
21 *Though they* join forces,[a] the wicked
        will not go unpunished;
    But the posterity of the righteous
        will be delivered.

22 *As* a ring of gold in a swine's
        snout,
    So is a lovely woman who lacks
        discretion.

23 The desire of the righteous *is* only
        good,
    But the expectation of the wicked
        is wrath.

24 There is *one* who scatters, yet
        increases more;
    And there is *one* who withholds
        more than is right,
    But it *leads* to poverty.
25 The generous soul will be
        made rich,
    And he who waters will also be
        watered himself.
26 The people will curse him who
        withholds grain,
    But blessing *will be* on the head of
        him who sells *it.*

27 He who earnestly seeks good finds
        favor,
    But trouble will come to him who
        seeks *evil.*

28 He who trusts in his riches will fall,
    But the righteous will flourish like
        foliage.

29 He who troubles his own house will
        inherit the wind,
    And the fool *will be* servant to the
        wise of heart.

30 The fruit of the righteous *is a* tree of
        life,
    And he who wins souls *is* wise.

11:5 [a]Or *make smooth* or *straight*
11:21 [a]Literally *hand to hand*

31 If the righteous will be recompensed
on the earth,
How much more the ungodly and the
sinner.

12 Whoever loves instruction loves
knowledge,
But he who hates correction *is* stupid.

2 A good *man* obtains favor from the
LORD,
But a man of wicked intentions He
will condemn.

3 A man is not established by
wickedness,
But the root of the righteous cannot
be moved.

4 An excellent[a] wife *is* the crown of
her husband,
But she who causes shame *is* like
rottenness in his bones.

5 The thoughts of the righteous *are*
right,
But the counsels of the wicked *are*
deceitful.

6 The words of the wicked *are,* "Lie in
wait for blood,"
But the mouth of the upright will
deliver them.

7 The wicked are overthrown and *are*
no more,
But the house of the righteous will
stand.

8 A man will be commended according
to his wisdom,
But he who is of a perverse heart
will be despised.

9 Better *is the one* who is slighted but
has a servant,
Than he who honors himself but
lacks bread.

10 A righteous *man* regards the life of
his animal,
But the tender mercies of the wicked
are cruel.

11 He who tills his land will be satisfied
with bread,
But he who follows frivolity *is* devoid
of understanding.[a]

12 The wicked covet the catch of evil
men,
But the root of the righteous yields
fruit.

13 The wicked is ensnared by the
transgression of *his* lips,
But the righteous will come through
trouble.

14 A man will be satisfied with good by
the fruit of *his* mouth,
And the recompense of a man's
hands will be rendered to him.

15 The way of a fool *is* right in his own
eyes,
But he who heeds counsel *is* wise.

16 A fool's wrath is known at once,
But a prudent *man* covers shame.

17 He *who* speaks truth declares
righteousness,
But a false witness, deceit.

18 There is one who speaks like the
piercings of a sword,
But the tongue of the wise *promotes*
health.

19 The truthful lip shall be established
forever,
But a lying tongue *is* but for a
moment.

20 Deceit is in the heart of those who
devise evil,
But counselors of peace have joy.

21 No grave trouble will overtake the
righteous,
But the wicked shall be filled with
evil.

22 Lying lips *are* an abomination to the
LORD,
But those who deal truthfully *are* His
delight.

23 A prudent man conceals knowledge,
But the heart of fools proclaims
foolishness.

24 The hand of the diligent will rule,
But the lazy *man* will be put to
forced labor.

25 Anxiety in the heart of man causes
depression,
But a good word makes it glad.

12:4 [a]Literally *A wife of valor* **12:11** [a]Literally *heart*

26 The righteous should choose his
friends carefully,
For the way of the wicked leads
them astray.

27 The lazy *man* does not roast what he
took in hunting,
But diligence *is* man's precious
possession.

28 In the way of righteousness *is* life,
And in *its* pathway *there is* no death.

13

A wise son *heeds* his father's
instruction,
But a scoffer does not listen to
rebuke.

2 A man shall eat well by the fruit of
his mouth,
But the soul of the unfaithful feeds
on violence.

3 He who guards his mouth preserves
his life,
But he who opens wide his lips shall
have destruction.

4 The soul of a lazy *man* desires, and
has nothing;
But the soul of the diligent shall be
made rich.

5 A righteous *man* hates lying,
But a wicked *man* is loathsome and
comes to shame.

6 Righteousness guards *him whose*
way is blameless,
But wickedness overthrows the
sinner.

7 There is one who makes himself
rich, yet *has* nothing;
And one who makes himself poor,
yet *has* great riches.

8 The ransom of a man's life *is* his
riches,
But the poor does not hear rebuke.

9 The light of the righteous rejoices,
But the lamp of the wicked will be
put out.

10 By pride comes nothing but strife,
But with the well-advised *is* wisdom.

11 Wealth *gained by* dishonesty will be
diminished,
But he who gathers by labor will
increase.

12 Hope deferred makes the heart sick,
But *when* the desire comes, *it is* a
tree of life.

13 He who despises the word will be
destroyed,
But he who fears the commandment
will be rewarded.

14 The law of the wise *is* a fountain of
life,
To turn *one* away from the snares of
death.

15 Good understanding gains favor,
But the way of the unfaithful *is* hard.

16 Every prudent *man* acts with
knowledge,
But a fool lays open *his* folly.

17 A wicked messenger falls into trouble,
But a faithful ambassador *brings*
health.

18 Poverty and shame *will come* to him
who disdains correction,
But he who regards a rebuke will be
honored.

19 A desire accomplished is sweet to the
soul,
But *it is* an abomination to fools to
depart from evil.

20 He who walks with wise *men* will be
wise,
But the companion of fools will be
destroyed.

21 Evil pursues sinners,
But to the righteous, good shall be
repaid.

22 A good *man* leaves an inheritance to
his children's children,
But the wealth of the sinner is stored
up for the righteous.

23 Much food *is in* the fallow *ground* of
the poor,
And for lack of justice there is
waste.[a]

24 He who spares his rod hates his son,

13:23 [a]Literally *what is swept away*

BIBLICAL INSIGHTS • 14:1

Will You Build Up or Pull Down?

EVERY WIFE HAS THE POWER to create or destroy her relationship with her husband, "The wise woman builds her house, but the foolish pulls it down with her hands" (14:1).

Remember that God is in control and you can trust Him. Also remember that you have to choose to obey God through honoring and respecting your husband. Every man needs his wife's respect; it's one of his deepest needs. He has others, but your respect—or lack thereof—impacts his whole life.

Respecting your husband includes really listening to him, not simply hearing the words that come out of his mouth. Take seriously what he says! When Barbara listens to me when I express something that I consider important for the family—and then acts on what I have said—she demonstrates respect. On more than one occasion, her respect has empowered me to lead. Not only does she benefit, but so does the entire family. Some wives do not realize how powerful they can be in their husband's life when they truly respect their man.

A husband should never try to force his wife to respect him. Instead, he should seek to be a man worthy of respect by demonstrating godly character and sacrificial love. And a wife should look for ways to affirm and respond to her husband's leadership. It starts by praising him for those areas in which he deserves genuine respect.

> But he who loves him disciplines him promptly.

25 The righteous eats to the satisfying of his soul,
But the stomach of the wicked shall be in want.

14
The wise woman builds her house,
But the foolish pulls it down with her hands.

2 He who walks in his uprightness fears the LORD,
But *he who is* perverse in his ways despises Him.

3 In the mouth of a fool *is* a rod of pride,
But the lips of the wise will preserve them.

4 Where no oxen *are*, the trough *is* clean;
But much increase *comes* by the strength of an ox.

5 A faithful witness does not lie,
But a false witness will utter lies.

6 A scoffer seeks wisdom and does not *find it*,
But knowledge *is* easy to him who understands.

7 Go from the presence of a foolish man,
When you do not perceive *in him* the lips of knowledge.

8 The wisdom of the prudent *is to* understand his way,
But the folly of fools *is* deceit.

9 Fools mock at sin,
But among the upright *there is* favor.

10 The heart knows its own bitterness,
And a stranger does not share its joy.

11 The house of the wicked will be overthrown,
But the tent of the upright will flourish.

12 There is a way *that seems* right to a man,
But its end *is* the way of death.

13 Even in laughter the heart may sorrow,
And the end of mirth *may be* grief.

14 The backslider in heart will be filled with his own ways,
But a good man *will be satisfied* from above.[a]

15 The simple believes every word,
But the prudent considers well his steps.

14:14 [a]Literally *from above himself*

16 A wise *man* fears and departs from
   evil,
   But a fool rages and is self-confident.
17 A quick-tempered *man* acts foolishly,
   And a man of wicked intentions is
   hated.
18 The simple inherit folly,
   But the prudent are crowned with
   knowledge.
19 The evil will bow before the good,
   And the wicked at the gates of the
   righteous.

20 The poor *man* is hated even by his
   own neighbor,
   But the rich *has* many friends.
21 He who despises his neighbor sins;
   But he who has mercy on the poor,
   happy *is* he.

22 Do they not go astray who devise evil?
   But mercy and truth *belong* to those
   who devise good.

23 In all labor there is profit,
   But idle chatter[a] *leads* only to
   poverty.

24 The crown of the wise is their riches,
   But the foolishness of fools *is* folly.

25 A true witness delivers souls,
   But a deceitful *witness* speaks lies.

26 In the fear of the LORD *there is*
   strong confidence,
   And His children will have a place of
   refuge.
27 The fear of the LORD *is* a fountain of
   life,
   To turn *one* away from the snares of
   death.

28 In a multitude of people *is* a king's
   honor,
   But in the lack of people *is* the
   downfall of a prince.

29 *He who is* slow to wrath has great
   understanding,
   But *he who is* impulsive[a] exalts folly.

30 A sound heart *is* life to the body,
   But envy *is* rottenness to the bones.

BIBLICAL INSIGHTS • 14:26, 27

A Place of Refuge

WOULD YOU LIKE YOUR FAMILY to exhibit strong courage in this fear-ridden world? Would you like your children to have a place of refuge in the midst of trouble? Would you like them to drink from a fountain of life and be able to escape the death traps that ensnare so many others?

Here is where that kind of courage and character begins, "In the fear of the LORD there is strong confidence, and His children will have a place of refuge. The fear of the LORD is a fountain of life, to turn one away from the snares of death" (14:26, 27).

To fear God means that you practice the presence of God in the midst of everyday choices. This means that if you are to teach your children to fear God, then you must choose to live a life that seeks to please Him in all respects. If *you* have the fear of the Lord, then you can infect your children with the same life-giving disease.

Those who fear the Lord apply the Scriptures to effectively meet whatever challenges come their way. They aren't perfect, but as they depend on God for strength, they will find that His power can equip them to meet every challenge they face.

This is why the fear of the Lord is described as the beginning of wisdom—godly skill in every-day living.

31 He who oppresses the poor
   reproaches his Maker,
   But he who honors Him has mercy
   on the needy.

32 The wicked is banished in his
   wickedness,
   But the righteous has a refuge in his
   death.

33 Wisdom rests in the heart of him
   who has understanding,
   But *what is* in the heart of fools is
   made known.

14:23 [a]Literally *talk of the lips*
14:29 [a]Literally *short of spirit*

34 Righteousness exalts a nation,
But sin *is* a reproach to *any* people.

35 The king's favor *is* toward a wise
servant,
But his wrath *is against* him who
causes shame.

15 A soft answer turns away wrath,
But a harsh word stirs up anger.

2 The tongue of the wise uses
knowledge rightly,
But the mouth of fools pours forth
foolishness.

3 The eyes of the LORD *are* in every
place,
Keeping watch on the evil and the
good.

4 A wholesome tongue *is* a tree of life,
But perverseness in it breaks the
spirit.

5 A fool despises his father's
instruction,
But he who receives correction is
prudent.

6 *In* the house of the righteous *there
is* much treasure,
But in the revenue of the wicked is
trouble.

7 The lips of the wise disperse
knowledge,
But the heart of the fool *does* not
do so.

8 The sacrifice of the wicked *is* an
abomination to the LORD,
But the prayer of the upright *is* His
delight.

9 The way of the wicked *is* an
abomination to the LORD,
But He loves him who follows
righteousness.

10 Harsh discipline *is* for him who
forsakes the way,
And he who hates correction
will die.

11 Hell[a] and Destruction[a] *are* before the
LORD;
So how much more the hearts of the
sons of men.

12 A scoffer does not love one who
corrects him,
Nor will he go to the wise.

13 A merry heart makes a cheerful
countenance,
But by sorrow of the heart the spirit
is broken.

14 The heart of him who has
understanding seeks knowledge,
But the mouth of fools feeds on
foolishness.

15 All the days of the afflicted *are* evil,
But he who is of a merry heart *has* a
continual feast.

16 Better *is* a little with the fear of the
LORD,
Than great treasure with trouble.

17 Better *is* a dinner of herbs[a] where
love is,
Than a fatted calf with hatred.

18 A wrathful man stirs up strife,
But *he who is* slow to anger allays
contention.

19 The way of the lazy *man is* like a
hedge of thorns,
But the way of the upright *is* a
highway.

20 A wise son makes a father glad,
But a foolish man despises his
mother.

21 Folly *is* joy *to him who is* destitute of
discernment,
But a man of understanding walks
uprightly.

22 Without counsel, plans go awry,
But in the multitude of counselors
they are established.

23 A man has joy by the answer of his
mouth,
And a word *spoken* in due season,
how good *it is!*

24 The way of life *winds* upward for the
wise,
That he may turn away from hell[a]
below.

15:11 [a]Or *Sheol* [b]Hebrew *Abaddon*
15:17 [a]Or *vegetables* 15:24 [a]Or *Sheol*

25 The LORD will destroy the house of
the proud,
But He will establish the boundary of
the widow.

26 The thoughts of the wicked *are* an
abomination to the LORD,
But the words of the pure *are*
pleasant.

27 He who is greedy for gain troubles
his own house,
But he who hates bribes will live.

28 The heart of the righteous studies
how to answer,
But the mouth of the wicked pours
forth evil.

29 The LORD *is* far from the wicked,
But He hears the prayer of the
righteous.

30 The light of the eyes rejoices the heart,
And a good report makes the bones
healthy.ᵃ

31 The ear that hears the rebukes of life
Will abide among the wise.

32 He who disdains instruction despises
his own soul,
But he who heeds rebuke gets
understanding.

33 The fear of the LORD *is* the
instruction of wisdom,
And before honor *is* humility.

16 The preparations of the heart
belong to man,
But the answer of the tongue *is* from
the LORD.

2 All the ways of a man *are* pure in
his own eyes,
But the LORD weighs the spirits.

3 Commit your works to the LORD,
And your thoughts will be
established.

4 The LORD has made all for Himself,
Yes, even the wicked for the day of
doom.

5 Everyone proud in heart *is* an
abomination to the LORD;

15:30 ᵃLiterally *fat* 16:5 ᵃLiterally *hand to hand*

BIBLICAL INSIGHTS • 15:1
Don't Climb in the Mud Pit

IF YOU LIVE in a family setting, then times
will surely come when you must deal with
someone's anger, and sometimes that
anger will get expressed in an unhealthy
or inappropriate way.

We've learned that people—especially
children—who express anger wrongly are
like mud wrestlers. They make a mess of
themselves and of everyone around them!
For that reason, a parent with an angry,
irrational child must stay outside the mud
pit, remaining as objective and loving as
possible. When a parent joins the out-of-
control child in slinging mud, he or she
immediately becomes just another mud
wrestler. And a child knows that when he
has engaged his mom or dad in mud
wrestling, most of the time, he's won!

So how are we to respond to a mud
wrestler? As Solomon so wisely said, "A
soft answer turns away wrath, but a harsh
word stirs up anger" (15:1). In other
words, it is not wise, when dealing with
an angry child, to say or do things to
make him or her even angrier. Parents
must be careful not to provoke our children to anger (Eph. 6:4). It's important for
a parent to invite the child out of the
mud pit. One of the ways you can do this
is to give your child or teenager some
time to cool off, or to gently remind that
child to choose his or her words carefully!

Remember, you are the parent and in
order to train your child to handle his
emotions properly, you need to be able
to control your emotions too!

Though they join forces,ᵃ none will
go unpunished.

6 In mercy and truth
Atonement is provided for iniquity;
And by the fear of the LORD *one*
departs from evil.

7 When a man's ways please the LORD,

BIBLICAL INSIGHTS • 16:24

Choose the Honeycomb

HUSBAND, ARE YOU LOOKING for a good way to connect emotionally with your wife? If so, Proverbs offers this pointer, "Pleasant words are like a honeycomb, sweetness to the soul and health to the bones" (16:24).

How often do you praise your wife? Consider a few compliments to brighten her day:

- "Dinner was great! Thank you for always making creative meals, even when you're tired of cooking."
- "I love the way you read books to our kids. That's so much better for them than watching TV."
- "I'm grateful that you carefully budget our paycheck each month."
- "I admire the way you handled yourself with that rude salesman—you have such a winsome approach."
- "The flowers you planted make our home so much more inviting. I appreciate your hard work."

Speaking pleasant words to your spouse helps to establish and strengthen emotional connections. As you work to make a genuine connection with your words, go below the surface to the real issues of life. Share with her, for example, what goes on at work. Most women love hearing all of the details. You'll also discover that she can provide wise counsel on the issues you face.

He makes even his enemies to be at peace with him.

8 Better *is* a little with righteousness,
Than vast revenues without justice.

9 A man's heart plans his way,
But the LORD directs his steps.

10 Divination *is* on the lips of the king;
His mouth must not transgress in judgment.

11 Honest weights and scales *are* the LORD's;
All the weights in the bag *are* His work.

12 *It is* an abomination for kings to commit wickedness,
For a throne is established by righteousness.

13 Righteous lips *are* the delight of kings,
And they love him who speaks *what is* right.

14 As messengers of death *is* the king's wrath,
But a wise man will appease it.

15 In the light of the king's face *is* life,
And his favor *is* like a cloud of the latter rain.

16 How much better to get wisdom than gold!
And to get understanding is to be chosen rather than silver.

17 The highway of the upright *is* to depart from evil;
He who keeps his way preserves his soul.

18 Pride *goes* before destruction,
And a haughty spirit before a fall.

19 Better *to be* of a humble spirit with the lowly,
Than to divide the spoil with the proud.

20 He who heeds the word wisely will find good,
And whoever trusts in the LORD, happy *is* he.

21 The wise in heart will be called prudent,
And sweetness of the lips increases learning.

22 Understanding *is* a wellspring of life to him who has it.
But the correction of fools *is* folly.

23 The heart of the wise teaches his mouth,
And adds learning to his lips.

24 Pleasant words *are like* a honeycomb,
Sweetness to the soul and health to the bones.

25 There is a way *that seems* right to a
man,
But its end *is* the way of death.

26 The person who labors, labors for
himself,
For his *hungry* mouth drives him *on.*

27 An ungodly man digs up evil,
And *it is* on his lips like a burning
fire.

28 A perverse man sows strife,
And a whisperer separates the best
of friends.

29 A violent man entices his neighbor,
And leads him in a way *that is* not
good.

30 He winks his eye to devise perverse
things;
He purses his lips *and* brings about
evil.

31 The silver-haired head *is* a crown of
glory,
If it is found in the way of
righteousness.

32 *He who is* slow to anger *is* better
than the mighty,
And he who rules his spirit than he
who takes a city.

33 The lot is cast into the lap,
But its every decision *is* from the
LORD.

17 Better *is* a dry morsel with
quietness,
Than a house full of feasting[a] *with*
strife.

2 A wise servant will rule over a son
who causes shame,
And will share an inheritance among
the brothers.

3 The refining pot *is* for silver and the
furnace for gold,
But the LORD tests the hearts.

4 An evildoer gives heed to false lips;
A liar listens eagerly to a spiteful
tongue.

5 He who mocks the poor reproaches
his Maker;

He who is glad at calamity will not
go unpunished.

6 Children's children *are* the crown of
old men,
And the glory of children *is* their
father.

7 Excellent speech is not becoming to
a fool,
Much less lying lips to a prince.

8 A present *is* a precious stone in the
eyes of its possessor;
Wherever he turns, he prospers.

9 He who covers a transgression seeks
love,
But he who repeats a matter
separates friends.

10 Rebuke is more effective for a wise
man
Than a hundred blows on a fool.

11 An evil *man* seeks only rebellion;
Therefore a cruel messenger will be
sent against him.

12 Let a man meet a bear robbed of her
cubs,
Rather than a fool in his folly.

13 Whoever rewards evil for good,
Evil will not depart from his house.

14 The beginning of strife *is like*
releasing water;
Therefore stop contention before a
quarrel starts.

15 He who justifies the wicked, and he
who condemns the just,
Both of them alike *are* an
abomination to the LORD.

16 Why *is there* in the hand of a fool
the purchase price of wisdom,
Since *he has* no heart *for it?*

17 A friend loves at all times,
And a brother is born for adversity.

18 A man devoid of understanding
shakes hands in a pledge,
And becomes surety for his friend.

19 He who loves transgression loves
strife,
And he who exalts his gate seeks
destruction.

17:1 [a]Or *sacrificial meals*

20 He who has a deceitful heart finds no
    good,
    And he who has a perverse tongue
    falls into evil.

21 He who begets a scoffer *does so* to
    his sorrow,
    And the father of a fool has no joy.

22 A merry heart does good, *like
    medicine,*ᵃ
    But a broken spirit dries the bones.

23 A wicked *man* accepts a bribe
    behind the backᵃ
    To pervert the ways of justice.

24 Wisdom *is* in the sight of him who
    has understanding,
    But the eyes of a fool *are* on the ends
    of the earth.

25 A foolish son *is* a grief to his father,
    And bitterness to her who bore him.

26 Also, to punish the righteous *is* not
    good,
    Nor to strike princes for *their*
    uprightness.

27 He who has knowledge spares his
    words,
    And a man of understanding is of a
    calm spirit.

28 Even a fool is counted wise when he
    holds his peace;
    When he shuts his lips, *he is
    considered* perceptive.

18 A man who isolates himself seeks
    his own desire;
    He rages against all wise judgment.

2 A fool has no delight in
    understanding,
    But in expressing his own heart.

3 When the wicked comes, contempt
    comes also;
    And with dishonor *comes* reproach.

4 The words of a man's mouth *are*
    deep waters;
    The wellspring of wisdom *is* a
    flowing brook.

5 *It is* not good to show partiality to
    the wicked,

    Or to overthrow the righteous in
    judgment.

6 A fool's lips enter into contention,
    And his mouth calls for blows.

7 A fool's mouth *is* his destruction,
    And his lips *are* the snare of his soul.

8 The words of a talebearer *are* like
    tasty trifles,ᵃ
    And they go down into the inmost
    body.

9 He who is slothful in his work
    Is a brother to him who is a great
    destroyer.

10 The name of the LORD *is* a strong
    tower;
    The righteous run to it and are safe.

11 The rich man's wealth *is* his strong
    city,
    And like a high wall in his own
    esteem.

12 Before destruction the heart of a
    man is haughty,
    And before honor *is* humility.

13 He who answers a matter before he
    hears *it,*
    It *is* folly and shame to him.

14 The spirit of a man will sustain him
    in sickness,
    But who can bear a broken spirit?

15 The heart of the prudent acquires
    knowledge,
    And the ear of the wise seeks
    knowledge.

16 A man's gift makes room for him,
    And brings him before great men.

17 The first *one* to plead his cause
    seems right,
    Until his neighbor comes and
    examines him.

18 Casting lots causes contentions to
    cease,
    And keeps the mighty apart.

19 A brother offended *is harder to win*
    than a strong city,

17:22 ᵃOr *makes medicine even better*
17:23 ᵃLiterally *from the bosom*
18:8 ᵃA Jewish tradition reads *wounds.*

And contentions *are* like the bars of
a castle.

20 A man's stomach shall be satisfied
from the fruit of his mouth;
From the produce of his lips he shall
be filled.

21 Death and life *are* in the power of
the tongue,
And those who love it will eat its fruit.

22 *He who* finds a wife finds a good
thing,
And obtains favor from the LORD.

23 The poor *man* uses entreaties,
But the rich answers roughly.

24 A man *who has* friends must himself
be friendly,[a]
But there is a friend *who* sticks closer
than a brother.

19 Better *is* the poor who walks in his
integrity
Than *one who is* perverse in his lips,
and is a fool.

2 Also it is not good *for* a soul *to be*
without knowledge,
And he sins who hastens with *his*
feet.

3 The foolishness of a man twists his
way,
And his heart frets against the LORD.

4 Wealth makes many friends,
But the poor is separated from his
friend.

5 A false witness will not go
unpunished,
And *he who* speaks lies will not
escape.

6 Many entreat the favor of the
nobility,
And every man *is* a friend to one
who gives gifts.

7 All the brothers of the poor hate
him;
How much more do his friends go far
from him!
He may pursue *them with* words, *yet*
they abandon *him.*

8 He who gets wisdom loves his own
soul;
He who keeps understanding will
find good.

9 A false witness will not go
unpunished,
And *he who* speaks lies shall perish.

10 Luxury is not fitting for a fool,
Much less for a servant to rule over
princes.

11 The discretion of a man makes him
slow to anger,
And his glory *is* to overlook a
transgression.

12 The king's wrath *is* like the roaring
of a lion,
But his favor *is* like dew on the
grass.

13 A foolish son *is* the ruin of his
father,
And the contentions of a wife *are* a
continual dripping.

14 Houses and riches *are* an inheritance
from fathers,
But a prudent wife *is* from the LORD.

15 Laziness casts *one* into a deep sleep,
And an idle person will suffer
hunger.

16 He who keeps the commandment
keeps his soul,
But he who is careless[a] of his ways
will die.

17 He who has pity on the poor lends to
the LORD,
And He will pay back what he has
given.

18 Chasten your son while there is hope,
And do not set your heart on his
destruction.[a]

19 *A man of* great wrath will suffer
punishment;
For if you rescue *him,* you will have
to do it again.

18:24 [a]Following Greek manuscripts, Syriac,
Targum, and Vulgate; Masoretic Text reads *may come
to ruin.* 19:16 [a]Literally *despises,* figurative of recklessness or carelessness 19:18 [a]Literally *to put him
to death;* a Jewish tradition reads *on his crying*

The Meaning of *Covenant*

ANY COVENANT—including the marriage covenant—is a binding, weighty obligation. In Proverbs 20:25, we read, "It is a snare for a man to devote rashly something as holy, and afterward to reconsider his vows."

When couples speak their vows to each other during the wedding ceremony, they are pledging to faithfully enter the estate of *holy* matrimony. It's holy because God has set it apart and blessed it. The Old Testament declares, "For the LORD God of Israel says that He hates divorce" (Mal. 2:16), and in the New Testament, Jesus proclaims, "Therefore what God has joined together, let not man separate" (Matt. 19:6). As others have so rightly pointed out, the Lord didn't stutter when He spoke these words!

It is time for us to embrace and proclaim God's sacred view of marriage, as well as His holy hatred for divorce. We can best do that by first committing our marriages to the Lord. God wants to demonstrate to the world through our marriages that He is indeed alive and active in this most important of all human relationships. Second, we can help others succeed at marriage. We live in a culture of divorce which not only accepts divorce, but also expects it. Why not try to come alongside friends or family members who are having difficulty in their marriages? Too many marriages are dissolved far too quickly over what ultimately are insignificant matters. We all need cheerleaders and coaches! Why not become one?

20 Listen to counsel and receive instruction,
That you may be wise in your latter days.

21 There are many plans in a man's heart,
Nevertheless the LORD's counsel—
that will stand.

22 What is desired in a man is kindness,
And a poor man is better than a liar.

23 The fear of the LORD *leads* to life,
And *he who has it* will abide in satisfaction;
He will not be visited with evil.

24 A lazy *man* buries his hand in the bowl,[a]
And will not so much as bring it to his mouth again.

25 Strike a scoffer, and the simple will become wary;
Rebuke one who has understanding, *and* he will discern knowledge.

26 He who mistreats *his* father *and* chases away *his* mother
Is a son who causes shame and brings reproach.

27 Cease listening to instruction, my son,
And you will stray from the words of knowledge.

28 A disreputable witness scorns justice,
And the mouth of the wicked devours iniquity.

29 Judgments are prepared for scoffers,
And beatings for the backs of fools.

20 Wine *is* a mocker,
Strong drink *is* a brawler,
And whoever is led astray by it is not wise.

2 The wrath[a] of a king *is* like the roaring of a lion;
Whoever provokes him to anger sins *against* his own life.

3 *It is* honorable for a man to stop striving,
Since any fool can start a quarrel.

4 The lazy *man* will not plow because of winter;
He will beg during harvest and *have* nothing.

19:24 [a]Septuagint and Syriac read *bosom;* Targum and Vulgate read *armpit.* 20:2 [a]Literally *fear* or *terror* which is produced by the king's wrath

5 Counsel in the heart of man *is like* deep water,
But a man of understanding will draw it out.

6 Most men will proclaim each his own goodness,
But who can find a faithful man?

7 The righteous *man* walks in his integrity;
His children *are* blessed after him.

8 A king who sits on the throne of judgment
Scatters all evil with his eyes.

9 Who can say, "I have made my heart clean,
I am pure from my sin"?

10 Diverse weights *and* diverse measures,
They *are* both alike, an abomination to the LORD.

11 Even a child is known by his deeds,
Whether what he does *is* pure and right.

12 The hearing ear and the seeing eye,
The LORD has made them both.

13 Do not love sleep, lest you come to poverty;
Open your eyes, *and* you will be satisfied with bread.

14 "*It is* good for nothing,"[a] cries the buyer;
But when he has gone his way, then he boasts.

15 There is gold and a multitude of rubies,
But the lips of knowledge *are* a precious jewel.

16 Take the garment of one who is surety *for* a stranger,
And hold it as a pledge *when it* is for a seductress.

17 Bread gained by deceit *is* sweet to a man,
But afterward his mouth will be filled with gravel.

18 Plans are established by counsel;
By wise counsel wage war.

19 He who goes about *as* a talebearer reveals secrets;
Therefore do not associate with one who flatters with his lips.

20 Whoever curses his father or his mother,
His lamp will be put out in deep darkness.

21 An inheritance gained hastily at the beginning
Will not be blessed at the end.

22 Do not say, "I will recompense evil";
Wait for the LORD, and He will save you.

23 Diverse weights *are* an abomination to the LORD,
And dishonest scales *are* not good.

24 A man's steps *are* of the LORD;
How then can a man understand his own way?

25 *It is* a snare for a man to devote rashly *something as* holy,
And afterward to reconsider *his* vows.

26 A wise king sifts out the wicked,
And brings the threshing wheel over them.

27 The spirit of a man *is* the lamp of the LORD,
Searching all the inner depths of his heart.[a]

28 Mercy and truth preserve the king,
And by lovingkindness he upholds his throne.

29 The glory of young men *is* their strength,
And the splendor of old men *is* their gray head.

30 Blows that hurt cleanse away evil,
As *do* stripes the inner depths of the heart.[a]

21 The king's heart *is* in the hand of the LORD,
Like the rivers of water;
He turns it wherever He wishes.

20:14 [a]Literally *evil, evil* **20:27** [a]Literally *the rooms of the belly* **20:30** [a]Literally *the rooms of the belly*

2   Every way of a man *is* right in his
     own eyes,
     But the LORD weighs the hearts.

3   To do righteousness and justice
     Is more acceptable to the LORD than
     sacrifice.

4   A haughty look, a proud heart,
     And the plowing[a] of the wicked *are*
     sin.

5   The plans of the diligent *lead* surely
     to plenty,
     But *those of* everyone *who is* hasty,
     surely to poverty.

6   Getting treasures by a lying tongue
     Is the fleeting fantasy of those who
     seek death.[a]

7   The violence of the wicked will
     destroy them,[a]
     Because they refuse to do justice.

8   The way of a guilty man *is* perverse;[a]
     But *as for* the pure, his work *is* right.

9   Better to dwell in a corner of a
     housetop,
     Than in a house shared with a
     contentious woman.

10   The soul of the wicked desires evil;
     His neighbor finds no favor in his
     eyes.

11   When the scoffer is punished, the
     simple is made wise;
     But when the wise is instructed, he
     receives knowledge.

12   The righteous *God* wisely considers
     the house of the wicked,
     Overthrowing the wicked for *their*
     wickedness.

13   Whoever shuts his ears to the cry of
     the poor
     Will also cry himself and not be
     heard.

14   A gift in secret pacifies anger,
     And a bribe behind the back,[a] strong
     wrath.

15   *It is* a joy for the just to do justice,
     But destruction *will come* to the
     workers of iniquity.

16   A man who wanders from the way of
     understanding
     Will rest in the assembly of the dead.

17   He who loves pleasure *will be* a poor
     man;
     He who loves wine and oil will not be
     rich.

18   The wicked *shall be* a ransom for the
     righteous,
     And the unfaithful for the upright.

19   Better to dwell in the wilderness,
     Than with a contentious and angry
     woman.

20   *There is* desirable treasure,
     And oil in the dwelling of the wise,
     But a foolish man squanders it.

21   He who follows righteousness and
     mercy
     Finds life, righteousness, and honor.

22   A wise *man* scales the city of the
     mighty,
     And brings down the trusted
     stronghold.

23   Whoever guards his mouth and
     tongue
     Keeps his soul from troubles.

24   A proud *and* haughty *man*—
     "Scoffer" *is* his name;
     He acts with arrogant pride.

25   The desire of the lazy *man* kills him,
     For his hands refuse to labor.

26   He covets greedily all day long,
     But the righteous gives and does not
     spare.

27   The sacrifice of the wicked *is* an
     abomination;
     How much more *when* he brings it
     with wicked intent!

28   A false witness shall perish,
     But the man who hears *him* will
     speak endlessly.

21:4 [a]Or *lamp* **21:6** [a]Septuagint reads *Pursue vanity
on the snares of death;* Vulgate reads *Is vain and
foolish, and shall stumble on the snares of death;*
Targum reads *They shall be destroyed, and they shall
fall who seek death.* **21:7** [a]Literally *drag them away*
21:8 [a]Or *The way of a man is perverse and strange*
21:14 [a]Literally *in the bosom*

²⁹ A wicked man hardens his face,
But *as for* the upright, he
establishes[a] his way.

³⁰ *There is* no wisdom or understanding
Or counsel against the LORD.

³¹ The horse *is* prepared for the day of
battle,
But deliverance *is* of the LORD.

22 A *good* name is to be chosen rather
than great riches,
Loving favor rather than silver and
gold.

² The rich and the poor have this in
common,
The LORD *is* the maker of them all.

³ A prudent *man* foresees evil and
hides himself,
But the simple pass on and are
punished.

⁴ By humility *and* the fear of the LORD
Are riches and honor and life.

⁵ Thorns *and* snares *are* in the way of
the perverse;
He who guards his soul will be far
from them.

⁶ Train up a child in the way he
should go,
And when he is old he will not
depart from it.

⁷ The rich rules over the poor,
And the borrower *is* servant to the
lender.

⁸ He who sows iniquity will reap
sorrow,
And the rod of his anger will fail.

⁹ He who has a generous eye will be
blessed,
For he gives of his bread to the poor.

¹⁰ Cast out the scoffer, and contention
will leave;
Yes, strife and reproach will cease.

¹¹ He who loves purity of heart
And has grace on his lips,
The king *will be* his friend.

¹² The eyes of the LORD preserve
knowledge,
But He overthrows the words of the
faithless.

¹³ The lazy *man* says, "*There is* a lion
outside!
I shall be slain in the streets!"

¹⁴ The mouth of an immoral woman *is*
a deep pit;
He who is abhorred by the LORD will
fall there.

¹⁵ Foolishness *is* bound up in the heart
of a child;
The rod of correction will drive it far
from him.

¹⁶ He who oppresses the poor to
increase his *riches,*
And he who gives to the rich, *will*
surely *come* to poverty.

Sayings of the Wise

¹⁷ Incline your ear and hear the words
of the wise,
And apply your heart to my
knowledge;

¹⁸ For *it is* a pleasant thing if you keep
them within you;
Let them all be fixed upon your lips,

¹⁹ So that your trust may be in the LORD;
I have instructed you today, even you.

²⁰ Have I not written to you excellent
things
Of counsels and knowledge,

²¹ That I may make you know the
certainty of the words of truth,
That you may answer words of truth
To those who send to you?

²² Do not rob the poor because he *is*
poor,
Nor oppress the afflicted at the gate;

**INTIMATE
MOMENTS**

The next time you and your spouse
attend a wedding—tell him, "If I had to
do it all over again, I'd marry you again."

---

23 For the LORD will plead their cause,
And plunder the soul of those who
plunder them.

24 Make no friendship with an angry
man,
And with a furious man do not go,

25 Lest you learn his ways
And set a snare for your soul.

26 Do not be one of those who shakes
hands in a pledge,
One of those who is surety for debts;

27 If you have nothing *with which* to pay,
Why should he take away your bed
from under you?

28 Do not remove the ancient landmark
Which your fathers have set.

29 Do you see a man *who* excels in his
work?
He will stand before kings;
He will not stand before unknown
men.

23 When you sit down to eat with
a ruler,
Consider carefully what *is* before you;

2 And put a knife to your throat
If you *are* a man given to appetite.

3 Do not desire his delicacies,
For they *are* deceptive food.

4 Do not overwork to be rich;
Because of your own understanding,
cease!

5 Will you set your eyes on that which
is not?
For *riches* certainly make themselves
wings;
They fly away like an eagle *toward*
heaven.

6 Do not eat the bread of a miser,[a]
Nor desire his delicacies;

7 For as he thinks in his heart, so *is* he.
"Eat and drink!" he says to you,
But his heart is not with you.

8 The morsel you have eaten, you will
vomit up,
And waste your pleasant words.

9 Do not speak in the hearing of a fool,
For he will despise the wisdom of
your words.

10 Do not remove the ancient landmark,
Nor enter the fields of the fatherless;

11 For their Redeemer *is* mighty;
He will plead their cause against you.

12 Apply your heart to instruction,
And your ears to words of knowledge.

13 Do not withhold correction from a
child,
For *if* you beat him with a rod, he
will not die.

14 You shall beat him with a rod,
And deliver his soul from hell.[a]

15 My son, if your heart is wise,
My heart will rejoice—indeed, I
myself;

16 Yes, my inmost being will rejoice
When your lips speak right things.

17 Do not let your heart envy sinners,
But *be zealous* for the fear of the
LORD all the day;

18 For surely there is a hereafter,
And your hope will not be cut off.

19 Hear, my son, and be wise;
And guide your heart in the way.

20 Do not mix with winebibbers,
Or with gluttonous eaters of meat;

21 For the drunkard and the glutton
will come to poverty,
And drowsiness will clothe *a man*
with rags.

22 Listen to your father who begot you,
And do not despise your mother
when she is old.

23 Buy the truth, and do not sell *it,*
Also wisdom and instruction and
understanding.

24 The father of the righteous will
greatly rejoice,
And he who begets a wise *child* will
delight in him.

25 Let your father and your mother be
glad,
And let her who bore you rejoice.

26 My son, give me your heart,
And let your eyes observe my ways.

27 For a harlot *is* a deep pit,

23:6 [a]Literally *one who has an evil eye*
23:14 [a]Or *Sheol*

DEVOTIONS FOR COUPLES • 24:3, 4
Choose a *Oneness Marriage*

What is a *Oneness Marriage*? A *Oneness Marriage* is a husband and wife who are working to craft intimacy, trust, and understanding with one another. It's a couple that is chiseling out a common direction, common purpose, and common plan for their lives.

A *Oneness Marriage* demands a lifetime process of relying on God and forging an enduring relationship according to His design. It's more than a mere mingling of two humans; it's a tender merger of body, soul, and spirit.

Every *Oneness Marriage* features three foundational components. King Solomon spoke of the mortar of the marriage merger in Proverbs 24:3, 4, "Through *wisdom* a house is built, and by *understanding* it is established; by *knowledge* the rooms are filled with all precious and pleasant riches."

1. A Oneness Marriage needs wisdom. Wisdom is skill in everyday living. It means that we respond to circumstances according to God's design. A wise home-builder recognizes God as the architect and builder of marriages. As we ask God for wisdom and search the Scriptures, He supplies the skill to build our homes. King David warns, "Unless the LORD builds the house, they labor in vain who build" (Psalm 127:1). For many the architect and builder of their marriage is *self*, so it's no wonder so many marriages fail.

2. A Oneness Marriage needs understanding. Understanding means responding to life's circumstances with insight, a perspective that looks at life through God's eyes. Understanding your mate from God's perspective results in acceptance of your differences and beginning to learn how God uses your mate to complement you. Understanding produces compassion for your partner. It will give you insight to lead wisely or to follow prudently.

3. A Oneness Marriage needs knowledge. We live in an information age. Our culture practically worships information, but information without application is an empty and powerless deity.

A godly kind of knowledge fills homes with "all precious and pleasant riches." It's more than mere information; it's a knowledge that results in deep convictions and habitual application. It's a true teachable spirit that applies God's blueprints amidst the raw realities of life.

What do many of us need in order to apply to our marriage what we've learned? Accountability. We need someone who will break through the fences we build and our crowded loneliness and ask us if we are applying in our marriages what we're learning.

And a seductress *is* a narrow well.
28   She also lies in wait as *for* a victim,
     And increases the unfaithful among
         men.

29   Who has woe?
     Who has sorrow?
     Who has contentions?
     Who has complaints?
     Who has wounds without cause?
     Who has redness of eyes?
30   Those who linger long at the wine,
     Those who go in search of mixed
         wine.
31   Do not look on the wine when it is red,
     When it sparkles in the cup,

     When it swirls around smoothly;
32   At the last it bites like a serpent,
     And stings like a viper.
33   Your eyes will see strange things,
     And your heart will utter perverse
         things.
34   Yes, you will be like one who lies
         down in the midst of the sea,
     Or like one who lies at the top of the
         mast, *saying:*
35   "They have struck me, *but* I was not
         hurt;
     They have beaten me, but I did not
         feel *it.*
     When shall I awake, that I may seek
         another *drink?*"

24
Do not be envious of evil men,
Nor desire to be with them;

2 For their heart devises violence,
And their lips talk of troublemaking.

3 Through wisdom a house is built,
And by understanding it is established;

4 By knowledge the rooms are filled
With all precious and pleasant riches.

5 A wise man *is* strong,
Yes, a man of knowledge increases
strength;

6 For by wise counsel you will wage
your own war,
And in a multitude of counselors
there is safety.

7 Wisdom *is* too lofty for a fool;
He does not open his mouth in the
gate.

8 He who plots to do evil
Will be called a schemer.

9 The devising of foolishness *is* sin,
And the scoffer *is* an abomination to
men.

10 *If* you faint in the day of adversity,
Your strength *is* small.

11 Deliver *those who* are drawn toward
death,
And hold back *those* stumbling to
the slaughter.

12 If you say, "Surely we did not know
this,"
Does not He who weighs the hearts
consider *it*?
He who keeps your soul, does He *not*
know *it*?
And will He *not* render to *each* man
according to his deeds?

13 My son, eat honey because *it is* good,
And the honeycomb *which is* sweet to
your taste;

14 So *shall* the knowledge of wisdom
be to your soul;
If you have found *it*, there is a
prospect,
And your hope will not be cut off.

15 Do not lie in wait, O wicked *man*,
against the dwelling of the
righteous;
Do not plunder his resting place;

16 For a righteous *man* may fall seven
times
And rise again,
But the wicked shall fall by calamity.

17 Do not rejoice when your enemy falls,
And do not let your heart be glad
when he stumbles;

18 Lest the LORD see *it*, and it displease
Him,
And He turn away His wrath from
him.

19 Do not fret because of evildoers,
Nor be envious of the wicked;

20 For there will be no prospect for the
evil *man*;
The lamp of the wicked will be put
out.

21 My son, fear the LORD and the king;
Do not associate with those given to
change;

22 For their calamity will rise suddenly,
And who knows the ruin those two
can bring?

Further Sayings of the Wise

23 These *things* also *belong* to the wise:

It is not good to show partiality in
judgment.

24 He who says to the wicked, "You *are*
righteous,"
Him the people will curse;
Nations will abhor him.

25 But those who rebuke *the wicked* will
have delight,
And a good blessing will come upon
them.

26 He who gives a right answer kisses
the lips.

27 Prepare your outside work,
Make it fit for yourself in the field;
And afterward build your house.

28 Do not be a witness against your
neighbor without cause,
For would you deceive[a] with your lips?

29 Do not say, "I will do to him just as
he has done to me;
I will render to the man according to
his work."

24:28 [a]Septuagint and Vulgate read *Do not deceive.*

30 I went by the field of the lazy *man,*
And by the vineyard of the man
    devoid of understanding;
31 And there it was, all overgrown with
    thorns;
Its surface was covered with nettles;
Its stone wall was broken down.
32 When I saw *it,* I considered *it* well;
I looked on *it and* received instruction:
33 A little sleep, a little slumber,
A little folding of the hands to rest;
34 So shall your poverty come *like* a
    prowler,
And your need like an armed man.

Further Wise Sayings of Solomon

25 These also *are* proverbs of Solomon
which the men of Hezekiah king of
Judah copied:

2 *It is* the glory of God to conceal a
    matter,
But the glory of kings *is* to search
    out a matter.

3 *As* the heavens for height and the
    earth for depth,
So the heart of kings *is* unsearchable.

4 Take away the dross from silver,
And it will go to the silversmith *for*
    jewelry.

5 Take away the wicked from before
    the king,
And his throne will be established in
    righteousness.

6 Do not exalt yourself in the presence
    of the king,
And do not stand in the place of the
    great;

7 For *it is* better that he say to you,
"Come up here,"
Than that you should be put lower in
    the presence of the prince,
Whom your eyes have seen.

8 Do not go hastily to court;
For what will you do in the end,
When your neighbor has put you to
    shame?

9 Debate your case with your
    neighbor,
And do not disclose the secret to
    another;

BIBLICAL INSIGHTS • 24:21

**Teach Your Children the Fear of
God**

AS JOSHUA WAS ABOUT TO TAKE the
mantle of leadership from Moses, he was
instructed to continue the practice of
teaching God's law so "that their children,
who have not known it, may hear and
learn to fear the LORD your God as long as
you live in the land which you cross the
Jordan to possess" (31:13).

One of our most important missions is
to teach our children what it means to
fear God. John Witherspoon said, "It is
only the fear of God that can deliver us
from the fear of men." And Proverbs 16:6
tells us, "By the fear of the LORD one
departs from evil."

If your child develops a reverential awe
of God, then he or she will desire to
please Him in every way. That will go a
long way in helping him or her overcome
the peer pressure and temptations this
world is sure to bring. He or she will be
more concerned with what God thinks
than what anyone else thinks.

I suggest three ways to teach your children to fear God:

1. Practice His presence in how you
   relate to others and the respectful
   words you use in relating to your
   family.

2. Talk about God with reverence.
   Explain who He is, His character, attributes, etc. When you impart who He is,
   children will learn there is none like
   Him.

3. Share with your children how the
   fear of God has turned you away
   from evil and temptation.

Accomplishing these goals will require
you to pursue a vital relationship with
your child. The most important ingredient in helping your kids handle peer
pressure is a contagious relationship
with you.

10   Lest he who hears *it* expose your shame,
     And your reputation be ruined.

11   A word fitly spoken *is like* apples of gold
     In settings of silver.

12   *Like* an earring of gold and an ornament of fine gold
     Is a wise rebuker to an obedient ear.

13   Like the cold of snow in time of harvest
     Is a faithful messenger to those who send him,
     For he refreshes the soul of his masters.

14   Whoever falsely boasts of giving
     Is like clouds and wind without rain.

15   By long forbearance a ruler is persuaded,
     And a gentle tongue breaks a bone.

16   Have you found honey?
     Eat only as much as you need,
     Lest you be filled with it and vomit.

17   Seldom set foot in your neighbor's house,
     Lest he become weary of you and hate you.

18   A man who bears false witness against his neighbor
     Is like a club, a sword, and a sharp arrow.

19   Confidence in an unfaithful *man* in time of trouble
     Is like a bad tooth and a foot out of joint.

20   *Like* one who takes away a garment in cold weather,
     And like vinegar on soda,
     Is one who sings songs to a heavy heart.

21   If your enemy is hungry, give him bread to eat;
     And if he is thirsty, give him water to drink;

22   For *so* you will heap coals of fire on his head,
     And the LORD will reward you.

23   The north wind brings forth rain,
     And a backbiting tongue an angry countenance.

24   *It is* better to dwell in a corner of a housetop,
     Than in a house shared with a contentious woman.

25   *As* cold water to a weary soul,
     So *is* good news from a far country.

26   A righteous *man* who falters before the wicked
     Is like a murky spring and a polluted well.

27   *It is* not good to eat much honey;
     So to seek one's own glory *is not* glory.

28   Whoever *has* no rule over his own spirit
     Is like a city broken down, without walls.

26

1   As snow in summer and rain in harvest,
     So honor is not fitting for a fool.

2   Like a flitting sparrow, like a flying swallow,
     So a curse without cause shall not alight.

3   A whip for the horse,
     A bridle for the donkey,
     And a rod for the fool's back.

4   Do not answer a fool according to his folly,
     Lest you also be like him.

5   Answer a fool according to his folly,
     Lest he be wise in his own eyes.

6   He who sends a message by the hand of a fool
     Cuts off *his own* feet *and* drinks violence.

7   *Like* the legs of the lame that hang limp
     Is a proverb in the mouth of fools.

8   Like one who binds a stone in a sling
     Is he who gives honor to a fool.

9   *Like* a thorn *that* goes into the hand of a drunkard
     Is a proverb in the mouth of fools.

10   The great *God* who formed everything

Gives the fool *his* hire and the
transgressor *his* wages.[a]

11 As a dog returns to his own vomit,
So a fool repeats his folly.

12 Do you see a man wise in his own
eyes?
There is more hope for a fool than
for him.

13 The lazy *man* says, "*There is* a lion
in the road!
A fierce lion *is* in the streets!"

14 *As* a door turns on its hinges,
So *does* the lazy *man* on his bed.

15 The lazy *man* buries his hand in the
bowl;[a]
It wearies him to bring it back to his
mouth.

16 The lazy *man is* wiser in his
own eyes

26:10 [a]The Hebrew is difficult; ancient and modern
translators differ greatly. 26:15 [a]Compare 19:24

Than seven men who can answer
sensibly.

17 He who passes by *and* meddles in a
quarrel not his own
Is like one who takes a dog by the ears.

18 Like a madman who throws
firebrands, arrows, and death,

19 *Is* the man *who* deceives his neighbor,
And says, "I was only joking!"

20 Where *there is* no wood, the fire goes
out;
And where *there is* no talebearer,
strife ceases.

21 *As* charcoal *is* to burning coals, and
wood to fire,
So *is* a contentious man to kindle
strife.

22 The words of a talebearer *are* like
tasty trifles,
And they go down into the inmost
body.

PARENTING MATTERS

Q: *How do I decide when to spank or discipline my child?*

The Bible is a practical, working guide for parents who want to hear what the Lord says about discipline. Barbara and I built our own philosophy of spanking from Proverbs 6:16, 17, "There are six things which the LORD hates, yes seven, which are an abomination to Him." From those verses, here's a list of what I call the "dirty half-dozen," the characteristics God finds most displeasing and that, as a result, we should bring appropriate discipline to our children:

1. *A proud look.* Sassiness or disrespectful speaking or gestures.

2. *Hands that shed innocent blood.* This is when a child hurts someone else—physically or verbally—because he's angry and doesn't like what's happening.

3. *A heart that devises wicked plans.* In this situation, a child thinks up a devious plan or is deceitfully planning ahead as to how to con someone.

4. *Feet that are swift in running to evil.* This describes a child who has a propensity to always do something wrong.

5. *A false witness.* Lies need to be dealt with swiftly and judicially.

6. *One who sows discord among brethren.* Conflict is one thing, but a child who continually stirs up brother against brother needs discipline that corrects and instructs in how healthy relationships flourish.

It's not a bad idea to sit down with your children when they're very young, as soon as they can begin to understand what you're saying, and go through these verses with them. Clearly establish boundaries and punishment for disobedience that you and your spouse agree upon for your family. It's never too early to start talking about these problems and how we can honor God in our relationships.

23   Fervent lips with a wicked heart
     Are like earthenware covered with
     silver dross.

24   He who hates, disguises *it* with his
     lips,
     And lays up deceit within himself;
25   When he speaks kindly, do not
     believe him,
     For *there are* seven abominations in
     his heart;
26   *Though his* hatred is covered by deceit,
     His wickedness will be revealed
     before the assembly.

27   Whoever digs a pit will fall into it,
     And he who rolls a stone will have it
     roll back on him.

28   A lying tongue hates *those who are*
     crushed by it,
     And a flattering mouth works ruin.

27 Do not boast about tomorrow,
     For you do not know what a day
     may bring forth.

2   Let another man praise you, and not
     your own mouth;
     A stranger, and not your own lips.

3   A stone *is* heavy and sand *is* weighty,
     But a fool's wrath *is* heavier than
     both of them.

4   Wrath *is* cruel and anger a torrent,
     But who *is* able to stand before
     jealousy?

5   Open rebuke *is* better
     Than love carefully concealed.

6   Faithful *are* the wounds of a friend,
     But the kisses of an enemy *are*
     deceitful.

7   A satisfied soul loathes the
     honeycomb,
     But to a hungry soul every bitter
     thing *is* sweet.

8   Like a bird that wanders from its nest
     Is a man who wanders from his place.

9   Ointment and perfume delight the
     heart,
     And the sweetness of a man's friend
     gives delight by hearty counsel.

10   Do not forsake your own friend or
     your father's friend,
     Nor go to your brother's house in the
     day of your calamity;
     Better *is* a neighbor nearby than a
     brother far away.

11   My son, be wise, and make my heart
     glad,
     That I may answer him who
     reproaches me.

12   A prudent *man* foresees evil *and*
     hides himself;
     The simple pass on *and* are
     punished.

13   Take the garment of him who is
     surety for a stranger,
     And hold it in pledge *when* he is
     surety for a seductress.

14   He who blesses his friend with a loud
     voice, rising early in the morning,
     It will be counted a curse to him.

15   A continual dripping on a very rainy
     day
     And a contentious woman are alike;
16   Whoever restrains her restrains the
     wind,
     And grasps oil with his right hand.

17   *As* iron sharpens iron,
     So a man sharpens the countenance
     of his friend.

18   Whoever keeps the fig tree will eat
     its fruit;
     So he who waits on his master will
     be honored.

19   As in water face *reflects* face,
     So a man's heart *reveals* the man.

20   Hell[a] and Destruction[b] are never full;
     So the eyes of man are never satisfied.

21   The refining pot *is* for silver and the
     furnace for gold,
     And a man *is valued* by what others
     say of him.

22   Though you grind a fool in a mortar
     with a pestle along with crushed
     grain,

27:20 [a]Or *Sheol* [b]Hebrew *Abaddon*

Yet his foolishness will not depart
    from him.

23 Be diligent to know the state of your
    flocks,
    And attend to your herds;
24 For riches *are* not forever,
    Nor does a crown *endure* to all
    generations.
25 *When* the hay is removed, and the
    tender grass shows itself,
    And the herbs of the mountains are
    gathered in,
26 The lambs *will provide* your
    clothing,
    And the goats the price of a field;
27 *You shall have* enough goats' milk
    for your food,
    For the food of your household,
    And the nourishment of your
    maidservants.

28

The wicked flee when no one
    pursues,
But the righteous are bold as a lion.

2 Because of the transgression of a
    land, many *are* its princes;
    But by a man of understanding *and*
    knowledge
    Right will be prolonged.

3 A poor man who oppresses the poor
    Is like a driving rain which leaves no
    food.

4 Those who forsake the law praise the
    wicked,
    But such as keep the law contend
    with them.

5 Evil men do not understand justice,
    But those who seek the LORD
    understand all.

6 Better *is* the poor who walks in his
    integrity
    Than one perverse *in his* ways,
    though he *be* rich.

7 Whoever keeps the law *is* a
    discerning son,
    But a companion of gluttons shames
    his father.

8 One who increases his possessions
    by usury and extortion

    Gathers it for him who will pity the
    poor.

9 One who turns away his ear from
    hearing the law,
    Even his prayer *is* an abomination.

10 Whoever causes the upright to go
    astray in an evil way,
    He himself will fall into his own pit;
    But the blameless will inherit good.

11 The rich man *is* wise in his own eyes,
    But the poor who has understanding
    searches him out.

12 When the righteous rejoice, *there is*
    great glory;
    But when the wicked arise, men hide
    themselves.

13 He who covers his sins will not
    prosper,
    But whoever confesses and forsakes
    them will have mercy.

14 Happy *is* the man who is always
    reverent,
    But he who hardens his heart will
    fall into calamity.

15 *Like* a roaring lion and a charging
    bear
    Is a wicked ruler over poor people.

16 A ruler who lacks understanding *is* a
    great oppressor,
    But he who hates covetousness will
    prolong *his* days.

17 A man burdened with bloodshed will
    flee into a pit;
    Let no one help him.

18 Whoever walks blamelessly will be
    saved,
    But *he who is* perverse *in his* ways
    will suddenly fall.

19 He who tills his land will have plenty
    of bread,
    But he who follows frivolity will
    have poverty enough!

20 A faithful man will abound with
    blessings,
    But he who hastens to be rich will
    not go unpunished.

21 To show partiality *is* not good,
Because for a piece of bread a man
will transgress.

22 A man with an evil eye hastens after
riches,
And does not consider that poverty
will come upon him.

23 He who rebukes a man will find
more favor afterward
Than he who flatters with the tongue.

24 Whoever robs his father or his
mother,
And says, "*It is* no transgression,"
The same *is* companion to a
destroyer.

25 He who is of a proud heart stirs up
strife,
But he who trusts in the Lord will be
prospered.

26 He who trusts in his own heart is a
fool,
But whoever walks wisely will be
delivered.

27 He who gives to the poor will not
lack,
But he who hides his eyes will have
many curses.

28 When the wicked arise, men hide
themselves;
But when they perish, the righteous
increase.

29 He who is often rebuked, *and*
hardens *his* neck,
Will suddenly be destroyed, and that
without remedy.

2 When the righteous are in authority,
the people rejoice;
But when a wicked *man* rules, the
people groan.

3 Whoever loves wisdom makes his
father rejoice,
But a companion of harlots wastes
his wealth.

4 The king establishes the land by
justice,
But he who receives bribes
overthrows it.

5 A man who flatters his neighbor
Spreads a net for his feet.

6 By transgression an evil man is
snared,
But the righteous sings and rejoices.

7 The righteous considers the cause of
the poor,
But the wicked does not understand
such knowledge.

8 Scoffers set a city aflame,
But wise *men* turn away wrath.

9 *If* a wise man contends with a foolish
man,
Whether *the fool* rages or laughs,
there is no peace.

10 The bloodthirsty hate the blameless,
But the upright seek his well-being.[a]

11 A fool vents all his feelings,[a]
But a wise *man* holds them back.

12 If a ruler pays attention to lies,
All his servants *become* wicked.

13 The poor *man* and the oppressor
have this in common:
The Lord gives light to the eyes of
both.

14 The king who judges the poor with
truth,
His throne will be established
forever.

15 The rod and rebuke give wisdom,
But a child left *to himself* brings
shame to his mother.

16 When the wicked are multiplied,
transgression increases;
But the righteous will see their fall.

17 Correct your son, and he will give
you rest;
Yes, he will give delight to your soul.

18 Where *there is* no revelation,[a] the
people cast off restraint;
But happy *is* he who keeps the law.

19 A servant will not be corrected by
mere words;

29:10 [a]Literally *soul* 29:11 [a]Literally *spirit*
29:18 [a]Or *prophetic vision*

For though he understands, he will
 not respond.

20 Do you see a man hasty in his words?
 There is more hope for a fool than
  for him.

21 He who pampers his servant from
  childhood
 Will have him as a son in the end.

22 An angry man stirs up strife,
 And a furious man abounds in
  transgression.

23 A man's pride will bring him low,
 But the humble in spirit will retain
  honor.

24 Whoever is a partner with a thief
  hates his own life;
 He swears to tell the truth,[a] but
  reveals nothing.

25 The fear of man brings a snare,
 But whoever trusts in the LORD shall
  be safe.

26 Many seek the ruler's favor,
 But justice for man *comes* from
  the LORD.

27 An unjust man *is* an abomination to
  the righteous,
 And *he who is* upright in the way *is*
  an abomination to the wicked.

The Wisdom of Agur

30 The words of Agur the son of Jakeh,
his utterance. This man declared to
Ithiel—to Ithiel and Ucal:

2 Surely I *am* more stupid than *any* man,
 And do not have the understanding
  of a man.

3 I neither learned wisdom
 Nor have knowledge of the Holy One.

4 Who has ascended into heaven, or
  descended?
 Who has gathered the wind in His
  fists?
 Who has bound the waters in a
  garment?
 Who has established all the ends of
  the earth?

29:24 [a] Literally *hears the adjuration*

What *is* His name, and what *is* His
 Son's name,
If you know?

5 Every word of God *is* pure;
 He *is* a shield to those who put their
  trust in Him.

6 Do not add to His words,
 Lest He rebuke you, and you be
  found a liar.

7 Two *things* I request of You
 (Deprive me not before I die):

8 Remove falsehood and lies far from
  me;
 Give me neither poverty nor riches—
 Feed me with the food allotted to me;

9 Lest I be full and deny *You,*
 And say, "Who *is* the LORD?"
 Or lest I be poor and steal,
 And profane the name of my God.

INTIMATE MOMENTS

Secretly buy her tickets to a special event
(concert, game, exhibit). Plan a lunch or
dinner date on the day of the event. After
dessert, give her the tickets.

---

10 Do not malign a servant to his master,
 Lest he curse you, and you be found
  guilty.

11 *There is* a generation *that* curses its
  father,
 And does not bless its mother.

12 *There is* a generation *that is* pure in
  its own eyes,
 Yet is not washed from its filthiness.

13 *There is* a generation—oh, how lofty
  are their eyes!
 And their eyelids are lifted up.

14 *There is* a generation whose teeth
  are like swords,
 And whose fangs *are like* knives,
 To devour the poor from off the earth,
 And the needy from *among* men.

15 The leech has two daughters—
 Give *and* Give!

There are three *things that* are never
satisfied,
Four never say, "Enough!":
16   The grave,[a]
The barren womb,
The earth *that* is not satisfied with
water—
And the fire never says, "Enough!"

17   The eye *that* mocks *his* father,
And scorns obedience to *his* mother,
The ravens of the valley will pick it
out,
And the young eagles will eat it.

18   There are three *things which* are too
wonderful for me,
Yes, four *which* I do not understand:
19   The way of an eagle in the air,
The way of a serpent on a rock,
The way of a ship in the midst of
the sea,
And the way of a man with a virgin.

20   This *is* the way of an adulterous
woman:
She eats and wipes her mouth,
And says, "I have done no
wickedness."

21   For three *things* the earth is perturbed,
Yes, for four it cannot bear up:
22   For a servant when he reigns,
A fool when he is filled with food,
23   A hateful *woman* when she is married,
And a maidservant who succeeds
her mistress.

24   There are four *things which* are little
on the earth,
But they *are* exceedingly wise:
25   The ants *are* a people not strong,
Yet they prepare their food in the
summer;
26   The rock badgers[a] are a feeble folk,
Yet they make their homes in the
crags;
27   The locusts have no king,
Yet they all advance in ranks;
28   The spider[a] skillfully grasps with its
hands,
And it is in kings' palaces.

29   There are three *things which* are
majestic in pace,
Yes, four *which* are stately in walk:

30   A lion, *which is* mighty among
beasts
And does not turn away from any;
31   A greyhound,[a]
A male goat also,
And a king *whose* troops *are* with
him.[b]

32   If you have been foolish in exalting
yourself,
Or if you have devised evil, *put your*
hand on *your* mouth.
33   For *as* the churning of milk produces
butter,
And wringing the nose produces
blood,
So the forcing of wrath produces
strife.

The Words of King Lemuel's Mother

31   The words of King Lemuel, the utterance which his mother taught him:

2   What, my son?
And what, son of my womb?
And what, son of my vows?
3   Do not give your strength to
women,
Nor your ways to that which
destroys kings.

4   *It is* not for kings, O Lemuel,
It is not for kings to drink wine,
Nor for princes intoxicating drink;
5   Lest they drink and forget the law,
And pervert the justice of all the
afflicted.
6   Give strong drink to him who is
perishing,
And wine to those who are bitter of
heart.
7   Let him drink and forget his poverty,
And remember his misery no more.

8   Open your mouth for the speechless,
In the cause of all *who are* appointed
to die.[a]
9   Open your mouth, judge righteously,
And plead the cause of the poor and
needy.

30:16 [a]Or *Sheol* **30:26** [a]Or *hyraxes* **30:28** [a]Or *lizard*
30:31 [a]Exact identity unknown [b]A Jewish tradition
reads *a king against whom there is no uprising*
31:8 [a]Literally *sons of passing away*

The Virtuous Wife

10 Who[a] can find a virtuous[b] wife?
  For her worth *is* far above rubies.
11 The heart of her husband safely
    trusts her;
  So he will have no lack of gain.
12 She does him good and not evil
  All the days of her life.
13 She seeks wool and flax,
  And willingly works with her hands.
14 She is like the merchant ships,
  She brings her food from afar.
15 She also rises while it is yet night,
  And provides food for her household,
  And a portion for her maidservants.
16 She considers a field and buys it;
  From her profits she plants a
    vineyard.
17 She girds herself with strength,
  And strengthens her arms.
18 She perceives that her merchandise *is*
    good,
  And her lamp does not go out by
    night.
19 She stretches out her hands to the
    distaff,
  And her hand holds the spindle.
20 She extends her hand to the poor,
  Yes, she reaches out her hands to the
    needy.

31:10 [a]Verses 10 through 31 are an alphabetic acrostic in Hebrew (compare Psalm 119). [b]Literally *a wife of valor,* in the sense of all forms of excellence

21 She is not afraid of snow for her
    household,
  For all her household *is* clothed with
    scarlet.
22 She makes tapestry for herself;
  Her clothing *is* fine linen and purple.
23 Her husband is known in the gates,
  When he sits among the elders of
    the land.
24 She makes linen garments and sells
    them,
  And supplies sashes for the
    merchants.
25 Strength and honor *are* her clothing;
  She shall rejoice in time to come.
26 She opens her mouth with wisdom,
  And on her tongue *is* the law of
    kindness.
27 She watches over the ways of her
    household,
  And does not eat the bread of
    idleness.
28 Her children rise up and call her
    blessed;
  Her husband *also,* and he praises her:
29 "Many daughters have done well,
  But you excel them all."
30 Charm *is* deceitful and beauty *is*
    passing,
  But a woman *who* fears the LORD, she
    shall be praised.
31 Give her of the fruit of her hands,
  And let her own works praise her in
    the gates.

ECCLESIASTES

THE BOOK OF ECCLESIASTES can feel like a confusing book for many readers, especially those who have never read it before. It contains the musings of an elderly (and even cynical) King Solomon about the meaning and purpose of life. The first two chapters address the futility of life lived apart from God. Solomon says that living apart from a relationship with God and an understanding of His plan for us (life lived "under the sun") is fleeting, meaningless, and incomprehensible. The remaining chapters grapple with the issues we face every day as we try to make sense of confusing and difficult-to-understand events.

Even though Solomon began his rule with honor and distinction, in later life he turned his back on God's Word and fruitlessly sought to find meaning and purpose from materialism, hedonism, and intellectualism. As he neared the end of his days, Solomon hoped that others could benefit from his gross mistakes. A weary Solomon declared that we find real life only when we "fear God and keep His commandments" (12:13).

Reading Ecclesiastes can feel like spending time with a pessimist. Consider this verse about marriage, "Live joyfully with the wife whom you love all the days of your vain life which He has given you under the sun, all your days of vanity; for that is your portion in life, and in the labor which you perform under the sun" (9:9). Pretty depressing, isn't it? Ecclesiastes offers such wisdom about the value of companionship both within and outside of marriage (4:9–12). Yet the book continually drives home the central theme that a life lived apart from God will be empty and meaningless, while a life of obedience to God will produce joy, even in the midst of confusion and hardships.

Solomon has much to say about many issues: politics and power, wealth, the problem of evil and the sovereignty of God, old age and impending death. At times, he sounds like a modern existentialist. At other points, he sounds like a skeptic. Ultimately, Ecclesiastes trumpets the truth that we find ultimate purpose and meaning for life only in a growing relationship with God.

The Vanity of Life

1 The words of the Preacher, the son of David, king in Jerusalem.

2 "Vanity[a] of vanities," says the
   Preacher;
"Vanity of vanities, all *is* vanity."

3 What profit has a man from all his
   labor
In which he toils under the sun?
4 *One* generation passes away, and
   another generation comes;
But the earth abides forever.
5 The sun also rises, and the sun goes
   down,
And hastens to the place where it
   arose.
6 The wind goes toward the south,
And turns around to the north;
The wind whirls about continually,
And comes again on its circuit.
7 All the rivers run into the sea,
Yet the sea *is* not full;
To the place from which the rivers
   come,
There they return again.
8 All things *are* full of labor;
Man cannot express *it.*
The eye is not satisfied with seeing,
Nor the ear filled with hearing.

9 That which has been *is* what will be,
That which *is* done is what will be
   done,
And *there is* nothing new under the
   sun.
10 Is there anything of which it may be
   said,
"See, this *is* new"?
It has already been in ancient times
   before us.
11 *There is* no remembrance of former
   things,
Nor will there be any remembrance
   of *things* that are to come
By *those* who will come after.

The Grief of Wisdom

12 I, the Preacher, was king over Israel in Jerusalem. 13 And I set my heart to seek and

BIBLICAL INSIGHTS • 1:1–2:26

Think!

DO YOU FIND YOURSELF traveling through life but stuck in some deeply dug ruts? In the book of Ecclesiastes, Solomon challenges us to examine our ruts and realize the impact they have on us and on those around us. He wants us to stop, climb out of the ruts, and consider carefully where we're headed. He dares us to *think.* To think about God and His purposes for our lives.

In the first two chapters, Solomon reflects on all the ways he has tried to seek satisfaction. He looked for life in knowledge and intelligence (1:12–18), in sensual pleasure (2:1–3), in a strong work ethic (2:4), in hobbies (2:5, 6), in activity and possessions (2:7, 8), and in a lofty life position (2:9). All of it counted for precisely *nothing.* Solomon called it vanity and concluded that all is vanity when you leave God out.

What a conclusion to reach at the end of a celebrated life! Think of it! Years wasted in a fruitless quest for happiness, unsuccessfully trying to quench a raging thirst for significance and meaning.

But like a shaft of light breaking into Solomon's dark prison of despair, come these words, "Then I turned myself to consider wisdom" (2:12). Finally, Solomon stopped *pursuing* and started *thinking.* He began to think about life from God's perspective—and once you do that, you break free from your ruts and the journey begins to make sense.

search out by wisdom concerning all that is done under heaven; this burdensome task God has given to the sons of man, by which they may be exercised. 14 I have seen all the works that are done under the sun; and indeed, all *is* vanity and grasping for the wind.

15 *What is* crooked cannot be made
   straight,
And what is lacking cannot be
   numbered.

1:2 [a] Or *Absurdity, Frustration, Futility, Nonsense;* and so throughout this book

¹⁶I communed with my heart, saying, "Look, I have attained greatness, and have gained more wisdom than all who were before me in Jerusalem. My heart has understood great wisdom and knowledge." ¹⁷And I set my heart to know wisdom and to know madness and folly. I perceived that this also is grasping for the wind.

18   For in much wisdom *is* much grief,
      And he who increases knowledge
            increases sorrow.

The Vanity of Pleasure

2 I said in my heart, "Come now, I will test you with mirth; therefore enjoy pleasure"; but surely, this also *was* vanity. ²I said of laughter—"Madness!"; and of mirth, "What does it accomplish?" ³I searched in my heart *how* to gratify my flesh with wine, while guiding my heart with wisdom, and how to lay hold on folly, till I might see what *was* good for the sons of men to do under heaven all the days of their lives.

⁴I made my works great, I built myself houses, and planted myself vineyards. ⁵I made myself gardens and orchards, and I planted all *kinds* of fruit trees in them. ⁶I made myself water pools from which to water the growing trees of the grove. ⁷I acquired male and female servants, and had servants born in my house. Yes, I had greater possessions of herds and flocks than all who were in Jerusalem before me. ⁸I also gathered for myself silver and gold and the special treasures of kings and of the provinces. I acquired male and female

singers, the delights of the sons of men, *and* musical instruments[a] of all kinds.

⁹So I became great and excelled more than all who were before me in Jerusalem. Also my wisdom remained with me.

10   Whatever my eyes desired I did not
            keep from them.
      I did not withhold my heart from any
            pleasure,
      For my heart rejoiced in all my labor;
      And this was my reward from all my
            labor.
11   Then I looked on all the works that
            my hands had done
      And on the labor in which I had toiled;
      And indeed all *was* vanity and
            grasping for the wind.
      There was no profit under the sun.

The End of the Wise and the Fool

12   Then I turned myself to consider
            wisdom and madness and folly;
      For what *can* the man *do* who
            succeeds the king?—
      Only what he has already done.
13   Then I saw that wisdom excels folly
      As light excels darkness.
14   The wise man's eyes *are* in his head,
      But the fool walks in darkness.
      Yet I myself perceived
      That the same event happens to
            them all.

15   So I said in my heart,
      "As it happens to the fool,
      It also happens to me,
      And why was I then more wise?"
      Then I said in my heart,
      "This also *is* vanity."
16   For *there is* no more remembrance of
            the wise than of the fool forever,
      Since all that now *is* will be forgotten
            in the days to come.
      And how does a wise *man* die?
      As the fool!

¹⁷Therefore I hated life because the work that was done under the sun *was* distressing to me, for all *is* vanity and grasping for the wind. ¹⁸Then I hated all my labor in which I

INTIMATE MOMENTS

Arrange a date with your wife at least once a month. Mark it on your calendar and take the initiative to make it happen! Put some effort into the date and make it a day or an evening that she will not soon forget.

2:8 [a]Exact meaning unknown

had toiled under the sun, because I must leave it to the man who will come after me. ¹⁹And who knows whether he will be wise or a fool? Yet he will rule over all my labor in which I toiled and in which I have shown myself wise under the sun. This also *is* vanity. ²⁰Therefore I turned my heart and despaired of all the labor in which I had toiled under the sun. ²¹For there is a man whose labor *is* with wisdom, knowledge, and skill; yet he must leave his heritage to a man who has not labored for it. This also *is* vanity and a great evil. ²²For what has man for all his labor, and for the striving of his heart with which he has toiled under the sun? ²³For all his days *are* sorrowful, and his work burdensome; even in the night his heart takes no rest. This also is vanity.

²⁴Nothing *is* better for a man *than* that he should eat and drink, and *that* his soul should enjoy good in his labor. This also, I saw, was from the hand of God. ²⁵For who can eat, or who can have enjoyment, more than I?[a] ²⁶For *God* gives wisdom and knowledge and joy to a man who *is* good in His sight; but to the sinner He gives the work of gathering and collecting, that he may give to *him who is* good before God. This also *is* vanity and grasping for the wind.

Everything Has Its Time

3 To everything *there is* a season,
A time for every purpose under heaven:

² A time to be born,
And a time to die;
A time to plant,
And a time to pluck *what is* planted;

³ A time to kill,
And a time to heal;
A time to break down,
And a time to build up;

⁴ A time to weep,
And a time to laugh;
A time to mourn,
And a time to dance;

⁵ A time to cast away stones,
And a time to gather stones;

A time to embrace,
And a time to refrain from embracing;

⁶ A time to gain,
And a time to lose;
A time to keep,
And a time to throw away;

⁷ A time to tear,
And a time to sew;
A time to keep silence,
And a time to speak;

⁸ A time to love,
And a time to hate;
A time of war,
And a time of peace.

The God-Given Task

⁹What profit has the worker from that in which he labors? ¹⁰I have seen the God-given task with which the sons of men are to be occupied. ¹¹He has made everything beautiful in its time. Also He has put eternity in their hearts, except that no one can find out the work that God does from beginning to end.

¹²I know that nothing *is* better for them than to rejoice, and to do good in their lives, ¹³and also that every man should eat and drink and enjoy the good of all his labor—it *is* the gift of God.

¹⁴ I know that whatever God does,
It shall be forever.
Nothing can be added to it,
And nothing taken from it.
God does *it*, that men should fear before Him.

¹⁵ That which is has already been,
And what is to be has already been;
And God requires an account of what is past.

Injustice Seems to Prevail

¹⁶Moreover I saw under the sun:

In the place of judgment,
Wickedness *was* there;
And *in* the place of righteousness,
Iniquity *was* there.

¹⁷I said in my heart,

"God shall judge the righteous and the wicked,

2:25 ᵃFollowing Masoretic Text, Targum, and Vulgate; some Hebrew manuscripts, Septuagint, and Syriac read *without Him.*

DEVOTIONS FOR COUPLES • 4:9, 10
Be Accountable to Your Spouse

The wise preacher declared, "Two are better than one because ... For if they fall, one will lift up his companion. But woe to him who is alone when he falls, for he has no one to help him up" (4:9, 10). That Scripture shouts the value of accountability in marriage.

Consider a few areas where Barbara and I have learned to practice accountability in our own marriage:

1. *Spiritual health.* In order to remain on track, every marriage must involve daily communication with and dependence on God. Most of us are prone to laziness or distraction in the daily maintenance of our spiritual needs. A loving spouse who has permission to encourage us in our devotion to Christ can help by asking open-ended questions such as, "What has God been teaching you lately?"

2. *Emotional and sexual fidelity.* This is a potentially sensitive but critical area in any Christian marriage. The way in which you handle the issues of temptation and moral struggles will largely chart the course for your relationship. Neither you nor your spouse can risk opening the door to inappropriate intimacy with someone of the opposite sex. Be open and honest about temptations that you are struggling with.

3. *Schedules.* We try to help each other make good decisions by monitoring each other's workload and schedules. Making good decisions means saying yes to some good things and no to others. This is one of the biggest struggles that Barbara and I have faced in our marriage and family. Schedules are ultimately a statement of our *true* priorities.

4. *Money and values.* Nothing in our marriage created the need for accountability more than the checkbook! Early on it became a fork in the road as to what each of us felt was most important. I recall some early accountability tests. Would I listen to her? Would I consider her advice? Would she trust me with a final decision? These were all natural opportunities to practice godly, caring accountability in each other's life.

5. *Parenting practice.* When Barbara and I had our first child, we began the lifelong process of being accountable to each other for our performance as parents. Early on we interacted and sharpened each other on our parenting styles. We all tend to draw on the parenting techniques modeled for us by our parents. When Barbara and I noticed a good or bad tendency, we would either encourage or help the other improve.

6. *No secrets.* Secrets are one of Satan's primary tools to divide couples. Accountability between husband and wife is a superb way to keep them from messing with your marriage.

One of the greatest challenges to any marriage is the access we give one another to our lives on a daily basis. Accountability is an honest, practical submission of your life to your spouse that says, "I have no secrets that I will withhold from you."

For *there is* a time there for every purpose and for every work."

[18]I said in my heart, "Concerning the condition of the sons of men, God tests them, that they may see that they themselves are *like* animals." [19]For what happens to the sons of men also happens to animals; one thing befalls them: as one dies, so dies the other. Surely, they all have one breath; man has no advantage over animals, for all *is* vanity. [20]All go to one place: all are from the dust, and all return to dust. [21]Who knows the spirit of the sons of men, which goes upward, and the spirit of the animal, which goes down to the earth?[a] [22]So I perceived that nothing *is* better than that a man should rejoice in his own works, for that *is* his heritage. For who can bring him to see what will happen after him?

4 Then I returned and considered all the oppression that is done under the sun:

And look! The tears of the
oppressed,

3:21 [a]Septuagint, Syriac, Targum, and Vulgate read *Who knows whether the spirit . . . goes upward, and whether . . . goes downward to the earth?*

But they have no comforter—
On the side of their oppressors *there
is* power,
But they have no comforter.

2 Therefore I praised the dead who
were already dead,
More than the living who are still
alive.

3 Yet, better than both *is he* who has
never existed,
Who has not seen the evil work that
is done under the sun.

The Vanity of Selfish Toil

4 Again, I saw that for all toil and every
skillful work a man is envied by his neighbor. This also *is* vanity and grasping for
the wind.

5 The fool folds his hands
And consumes his own flesh.

6 Better a handful *with* quietness
Than both hands full, *together with*
toil and grasping for the wind.

7 Then I returned, and I saw vanity
under the sun:

8 There is one alone, without
companion:
He has neither son nor brother.
Yet *there is* no end to all his labors,

Nor is his eye satisfied with riches.
But he never asks,
"For whom do I toil and deprive
myself of good?"
This also *is* vanity and a grave
misfortune.

The Value of a Friend

9 Two *are* better than one,
Because they have a good reward for
their labor.

10 For if they fall, one will lift up his
companion.
But woe to him *who is* alone when he
falls,
For *he has* no one to help him up.

11 Again, if two lie down together, they
will keep warm;
But how can one be warm *alone?*

12 Though one may be overpowered by
another, two can withstand him.
And a threefold cord is not quickly
broken.

Popularity Passes Away

13 Better a poor and wise youth
Than an old and foolish king who
will be admonished no more.

14 For he comes out of prison to be king,
Although he was born poor in his
kingdom.

The Grass Suffers

An African proverb says, "When the elephants fight, it's the grass that suffers."

Do you have any idea what your children—your grass—are seeing in your marriage when you have a conflict? What kind of model for the husband/wife relationship is beginning to emerge in their minds? Do they see it as a union of peace and harmony and joy, or of strife and discord and disappointment?

We have often seen Ecclesiastes 4:9, 10 as a beautiful example of godly parenting. When two parents are on the same page—which is God's ideal—then they support one another and give their children a sense of security and consistency. In that case, the grass beneath them grows verdant, beautiful, and attractive.

But there is more, "Again, if two lie down together, they will keep warm; but how can one be warm alone? Though one may be over-powered by another, two can withstand him. And a threefold cord is not quickly broken" (4:11, 12).

Christian marriage is a cord of three strands—a husband, a wife, and a third party, Jesus Christ. Those three strands, bound together, are not easily broken. And they work together in unity to nurture the healthiest kind of grass on the planet. Protect the strength of that unity. Your oneness gives security and comfort to your children.

15 I saw all the living who walk under the sun;
They were with the second youth who stands in his place.

16 *There was* no end of all the people over whom he was made king;
Yet those who come afterward will not rejoice in him.
Surely this also *is* vanity and grasping for the wind.

Fear God, Keep Your Vows

5 Walk prudently when you go to the house of God; and draw near to hear rather than to give the sacrifice of fools, for they do not know that they do evil.

2 Do not be rash with your mouth,
And let not your heart utter anything hastily before God.
For God *is* in heaven, and you on earth;
Therefore let your words be few.

3 For a dream comes through much activity,
And a fool's voice *is known* by *his* many words.

4 When you make a vow to God, do not delay to pay it;
For *He has* no pleasure in fools.
Pay what you have vowed—

5 Better not to vow than to vow and not pay.

6 Do not let your mouth cause your flesh to sin, nor say before the messenger *of God* that it *was* an error. Why should God be angry at your excuse[a] and destroy the work of your hands? 7 For in the multitude of dreams and many words *there is* also vanity. But fear God.

The Vanity of Gain and Honor

8 If you see the oppression of the poor, and the violent perversion of justice and righteousness in a province, do not marvel at the matter; for high official watches over high official, and higher officials are over them.

9 Moreover the profit of the land is for all; *even* the king is served from the field.

10 He who loves silver will not be satisfied with silver;
Nor he who loves abundance, with increase.
This also *is* vanity.

11 When goods increase,
They increase who eat them;
So what profit have the owners
Except to see *them* with their eyes?

12 The sleep of a laboring man *is* sweet,
Whether he eats little or much;
But the abundance of the rich will not permit him to sleep.

13 There is a severe evil *which* I have seen under the sun:
Riches kept for their owner to his hurt.

14 But those riches perish through misfortune;
When he begets a son, *there is* nothing in his hand.

15 As he came from his mother's womb, naked shall he return,
To go as he came;
And he shall take nothing from his labor
Which he may carry away in his hand.

16 And this also *is* a severe evil—
Just exactly as he came, so shall he go.
And what profit has he who has labored for the wind?

17 All his days he also eats in darkness,
And *he has* much sorrow and sickness and anger.

18 Here is what I have seen: *It is* good and fitting *for one* to eat and drink, and to enjoy the good of all his labor in which he toils under the sun all the days of his life which God gives him; for it *is* his heritage. 19 As for every man to whom God has given riches and wealth, and given him power to eat of it, to receive his heritage and rejoice in his labor—this *is* the gift of God. 20 For he will not dwell unduly on the days of his life, because God keeps *him* busy with the joy of his heart.

5:6 [a]Literally *voice*

6 There is an evil which I have seen under the sun, and it *is* common among men: ²A man to whom God has given riches and wealth and honor, so that he lacks nothing for himself of all he desires; yet God does not give him power to eat of it, but a foreigner consumes it. This *is* vanity, and it *is* an evil affliction.

³If a man begets a hundred *children* and lives many years, so that the days of his years are many, but his soul is not satisfied with goodness, or indeed he has no burial, I say *that* a stillborn child *is* better than he— ⁴for it comes in vanity and departs in darkness, and its name is covered with darkness. ⁵Though it has not seen the sun or known *anything,* this has more rest than that man, ⁶even if he lives a thousand years twice—but has not seen goodness. Do not all go to one place?

⁷ All the labor of man *is* for his mouth,
And yet the soul is not satisfied.

⁸ For what more has the wise *man*
    than the fool?
What does the poor man have,
Who knows *how* to walk before the
    living?

⁹ Better *is* the sight of the eyes than
    the wandering of desire.
This also *is* vanity and grasping for
    the wind.

¹⁰ Whatever one is, he has been named
    already,
For it is known that he *is* man;
And he cannot contend with Him
    who is mightier than he.

¹¹ Since there are many things that
    increase vanity,
How *is* man the better?

¹²For who knows what *is* good for man in life, all the days of his vain life which he passes like a shadow? Who can tell a man what will happen after him under the sun?

The Value of Practical Wisdom

7 A good name *is* better than precious ointment,
And the day of death than the day of
    one's birth;

² Better to go to the house of mourning
Than to go to the house of feasting,

For that *is* the end of all men;
And the living will take *it* to heart.

³ Sorrow *is* better than laughter,
For by a sad countenance the heart is
    made better.

⁴ The heart of the wise *is* in the house
    of mourning,
But the heart of fools *is* in the house
    of mirth.

⁵ *It is* better to hear the rebuke of the
    wise
Than for a man to hear the song of
    fools.

⁶ For like the crackling of thorns
    under a pot,
So *is* the laughter of the fool.
This also is vanity.

⁷ Surely oppression destroys a wise
    man's reason,
And a bribe debases the heart.

⁸ The end of a thing *is* better than its
    beginning;
The patient in spirit *is* better than
    the proud in spirit.

⁹ Do not hasten in your spirit to be
    angry,
For anger rests in the bosom of fools.

¹⁰ Do not say,
"Why were the former days better
    than these?"
For you do not inquire wisely
    concerning this.

¹¹ Wisdom *is* good with an inheritance,
And profitable to those who see the
    sun.

¹² For wisdom *is* a defense *as* money *is*
    a defense,
But the excellence of knowledge *is*
    that wisdom gives life to those
    who have it.

INTIMATE MOMENTS

Think of a couple of things that your honey does for you and the family (he is a good provider, he can fix things, etc.) and let him know how much you appreciate him.

13 Consider the work of God;
For who can make straight what He
has made crooked?
14 In the day of prosperity be joyful,
But in the day of adversity consider:
Surely God has appointed the one as
well as the other,
So that man can find out nothing
that will come after him.

15 I have seen everything in my days of
vanity:

There is a just *man* who perishes in
his righteousness,
And there is a wicked *man* who
prolongs *life* in his wickedness.

16 Do not be overly righteous,
Nor be overly wise:
Why should you destroy yourself?
17 Do not be overly wicked,
Nor be foolish:
Why should you die before your
time?
18 *It is* good that you grasp this,

And also not remove your hand from
the other;
For he who fears God will escape
them all.

19 Wisdom strengthens the wise
More than ten rulers of the city.
20 For *there is* not a just man on earth
who does good
And does not sin.

21 Also do not take to heart everything
people say,
Lest you hear your servant cursing
you.
22 For many times, also, your own heart
has known
That even you have cursed others.

23 All this I have proved by wisdom.
I said, "I will be wise";
But it *was* far from me.
24 As for that which is far off and
exceedingly deep,
Who can find it out?
25 I applied my heart to know,

| PARENTING MATTERS | **Q: *How can we cultivate healthy and deep communication with our children?*** |

Tom and Jeannie Elliff, are friends and co-laborers in strengthening marriages and families. In their book *Letters to Lovers*, they highlight the importance of asking questions. Here is a list of ten questions parents could ask their children to cultivate communication:

1. How well do you feel we are getting along together?
2. What do you think we could do to improve our relationship?
3. Do you believe that I really care about who you are as an individual, or just how you behave?
4. Have I ever made a promise to you that I didn't keep?
5. Do you feel that I respect you? Do you respect me?
6. Is there something you would enjoy doing with me? What would keep us from doing this together?
7. Is there some secret you are keeping from me, out of fear that I would love you less?
8. What can I do to show you that I want to be more like Christ?
9. Is there something I do that annoys you, or embarrasses you?
10. How could I best express to you just how much I love you, and how honored I feel to be your parent?

Why not schedule a special time with your son or daughter to ask two or three of these questions? Don't be discouraged if your child doesn't give you much of an answer; be patient and keep listening.

To search and seek out wisdom and
    the reason *of things,*
To know the wickedness of folly,
Even of foolishness *and* madness.

26 And I find more bitter than death
    The woman whose heart *is* snares
    and nets,
Whose hands *are* fetters.
He who pleases God shall escape
    from her,
But the sinner shall be trapped by
    her.

27 "Here is what I have found," says the
    Preacher,
"*Adding* one thing to the other to find
    out the reason,

28 Which my soul still seeks but I
    cannot find:
One man among a thousand I have
    found,
But a woman among all these I have
    not found.

29 Truly, this only I have found:
That God made man upright,
But they have sought out many
    schemes."

8

Who *is* like a wise *man?*
And who knows the interpretation
    of a thing?
A man's wisdom makes his face
    shine,
And the sternness of his face is
    changed.

Obey Authorities for God's Sake

2 I *say,* "Keep the king's commandment
for the sake of your oath to God. 3 Do not
be hasty to go from his presence. Do not
take your stand for an evil thing, for he
does whatever pleases him."

4 Where the word of a king *is, there is*
    power;
And who may say to him, "What are
    you doing?"

5 He who keeps his command will
    experience nothing harmful;
And a wise man's heart discerns
    both time and judgment,

6 Because for every matter there is a
    time and judgment,
Though the misery of man increases
    greatly.

7 For he does not know what will
    happen;
So who can tell him when it will
    occur?

8 No one has power over the spirit to
    retain the spirit,
And no one has power in the day of
    death.
There is no release from that war,
And wickedness will not deliver
    those who are given to it.

9 All this I have seen, and applied my
heart to every work that is done under the
sun: *There is* a time in which one man
rules over another to his own hurt.

Death Comes to All

10 Then I saw the wicked buried, who had
come and gone from the place of holiness,
and they were forgotten[a] in the city where
they had so done. This also *is* vanity.
11 Because the sentence against an evil work
is not executed speedily, therefore the heart
of the sons of men is fully set in them to do
evil. 12 Though a sinner does evil a hundred
times, and his *days* are prolonged, yet I
surely know that it will be well with those
who fear God, who fear before Him. 13 But it
will not be well with the wicked; nor will he
prolong *his* days, *which are* as a shadow,
because he does not fear before God.

14 There is a vanity which occurs on
earth, that there are just *men* to whom it
happens according to the work of the
wicked; again, there are wicked *men* to
whom it happens according to the work of
the righteous. I said that this also *is* vanity.

15 So I commended enjoyment, because a
man has nothing better under the sun than
to eat, drink, and be merry; for this will
remain with him in his labor *all* the days of
his life which God gives him under the sun.

16 When I applied my heart to know wisdom and to see the business that is done on
earth, even though one sees no sleep day or
night, 17 then I saw all the work of God, that
a man cannot find out the work that is done
under the sun. For though a man labors to

8:10 [a]Some Hebrew manuscripts, Septuagint, and
Vulgate read *praised.*

discover *it,* yet he will not find *it;* moreover, though a wise *man* attempts to know *it,* he will not be able to find *it.*

9 For I considered all this in my heart, so that I could declare it all: that the righteous and the wise and their works *are* in the hand of God. People know neither love nor hatred *by* anything *they see* before them. ²All things *come* alike to all:

> One event *happens* to the righteous
>   and the wicked;
> To the good,ᵃ the clean, and the
>   unclean;
> To him who sacrifices and him who
>   does not sacrifice.
> As is the good, so *is* the sinner;
> He who takes an oath as *he* who
>   fears an oath.

INTIMATE MOMENTS

Plan a vacation together—permanently, in ink.

³This *is* an evil in all that is done under the sun: that one thing *happens* to all. Truly the hearts of the sons of men are full of evil; madness *is* in their hearts while they live, and after that *they go* to the dead. ⁴But for him who is joined to all the living there is hope, for a living dog is better than a dead lion.

5 For the living know that they will
        die;
    But the dead know nothing,
    And they have no more reward,
    For the memory of them is forgotten.
6 Also their love, their hatred, and
        their envy have now perished;
    Nevermore will they have a share
    In anything done under the sun.

7 Go, eat your bread with joy,
    And drink your wine with a merry
        heart;
    For God has already accepted your
        works.

8 Let your garments always be white,
    And let your head lack no oil.

⁹Live joyfully with the wife whom you love all the days of your vain life which He has given you under the sun, all your days of vanity; for that *is* your portion in life, and in the labor which you perform under the sun.

¹⁰Whatever your hand finds to do, do *it* with your might; for *there is* no work or device or knowledge or wisdom in the grave where you are going.

¹¹I returned and saw under the sun that—

> The race *is* not to the swift,
> Nor the battle to the strong,
> Nor bread to the wise,
> Nor riches to men of understanding,
> Nor favor to men of skill;
> But time and chance happen to them
>   all.
12 For man also does not know his time:
    Like fish taken in a cruel net,
    Like birds caught in a snare,
    So the sons of men *are* snared in an
        evil time,
    When it falls suddenly upon them.

Wisdom Superior to Folly

¹³This wisdom I have also seen under the sun, and it *seemed* great to me: ¹⁴*There was* a little city with few men in it; and a great king came against it, besieged it, and built great snaresᵃ around it. ¹⁵Now there was found in it a poor wise man, and he by his wisdom delivered the city. Yet no one remembered that same poor man.

¹⁶Then I said:

> "Wisdom *is* better than strength.
>   Nevertheless the poor man's wisdom
>   *is* despised,
>   And his words are not heard.
17 Words of the wise, *spoken* quietly,
        should be heard
    Rather than the shout of a ruler of
        fools.
18 Wisdom *is* better than weapons of
        war;
    But one sinner destroys much good."

9:2 ᵃSeptuagint, Syriac, and Vulgate read *good and bad.* **9:14** ᵃSeptuagint, Syriac, and Vulgate read *bulwarks.*

10 Dead flies putrefy[a] the perfumer's ointment,
And cause it to give off a foul odor;
So does a little folly to one respected for wisdom *and* honor.

2 A wise man's heart *is* at his right hand,
But a fool's heart at his left.

3 Even when a fool walks along the way,
He lacks wisdom,
And he shows everyone *that* he *is* a fool.

4 If the spirit of the ruler rises against you,
Do not leave your post;
For conciliation pacifies great offenses.

5 There is an evil I have seen under the sun,
As an error proceeding from the ruler:

6 Folly is set in great dignity,
While the rich sit in a lowly place.

7 I have seen servants on horses,
While princes walk on the ground like servants.

8 He who digs a pit will fall into it,
And whoever breaks through a wall will be bitten by a serpent.

9 He who quarries stones may be hurt by them,
And he who splits wood may be endangered by it.

10 If the ax is dull,
And one does not sharpen the edge,
Then he must use more strength;
But wisdom brings success.

11 A serpent may bite when *it is* not charmed;
The babbler is no different.

12 The words of a wise man's mouth *are* gracious,
But the lips of a fool shall swallow him up;

13 The words of his mouth begin with foolishness,
And the end of his talk *is* raving madness.

14 A fool also multiplies words.
No man knows what is to be;
Who can tell him what will be after him?

15 The labor of fools wearies them,
For they do not even know how to go to the city!

16 Woe to you, O land, when your king *is* a child,
And your princes feast in the morning!

17 Blessed *are* you, O land, when your king *is* the son of nobles,
And your princes feast at the proper time—
For strength and not for drunkenness!

18 Because of laziness the building decays,
And through idleness of hands the house leaks.

19 A feast is made for laughter,
And wine makes merry;
But money answers everything.

20 Do not curse the king, even in your thought;
Do not curse the rich, even in your bedroom;
For a bird of the air may carry your voice,
And a bird in flight may tell the matter.

The Value of Diligence

11 Cast your bread upon the waters,
For you will find it after many days.

2 Give a serving to seven, and also to eight,
For you do not know what evil will be on the earth.

3 If the clouds are full of rain,
They empty *themselves* upon the earth;
And if a tree falls to the south or the north,
In the place where the tree falls, there it shall lie.

4 He who observes the wind will not sow,
And he who regards the clouds will not reap.

10:1 [a]Targum and Vulgate omit *putrefy.*

Give Them a Sense of Mission

GOD CALLS YOU TO LIVE before your family according to His agenda. That means He wants you to build your life around the great commandment (to love God with all that you are) and the Great Commission (to preach the gospel to the world around you). Our words and our actions ought to reflect these twin directives as our top priorities.

You and I truly do impart a sense of mission with our words. That is what Solomon meant when he wrote that "the words of a wise man are like goads and the words of scholars are like well-driven nails" (12:11). Like goads, words can push your audience in a particular direction; like nails, they help to solidify and make permanent their sense of purpose in life.

Your spouse needs words that can direct as he makes important decisions. Never forget that you possess a unique responsibility as you use words to encourage him to do good, instead of evil. Reminding him of the truth about God, himself, and life can help him secure a well lived life.

Your words can also create a godly direction for your children, prodding them toward good things. And with six billion people on this planet, children today desperately need a sense of mission! They *must* have a sense of God's imprint on their lives, encouraging and prompting them to do His work throughout their lives.

And here's the great news: *You* have the tremendous privilege of marking their lives with a divine imprint through your well-chosen words. Don't nag or preach—just keep on being a truth speaker and using your words to direct those you love.

5　As you do not know what *is* the way of the wind,[a]
　　Or how the bones *grow* in the womb of her who is with child,

So you do not know the works of God who makes everything.
6　In the morning sow your seed,
　　And in the evening do not withhold your hand;
　　For you do not know which will prosper,
　　Either this or that,
　　Or whether both alike *will be* good.

7　Truly the light is sweet,
　　And *it is* pleasant for the eyes to behold the sun;
8　But if a man lives many years
　　And rejoices in them all,
　　Yet let him remember the days of darkness,
　　For they will be many.
　　All that is coming *is* vanity.

Seek God in Early Life

9　Rejoice, O young man, in your youth,
　　And let your heart cheer you in the days of your youth;
　　Walk in the ways of your heart,
　　And in the sight of your eyes;
　　But know that for all these
　　God will bring you into judgment.
10　Therefore remove sorrow from your heart,
　　And put away evil from your flesh,
　　For childhood and youth *are* vanity.

12 Remember now your Creator in the days of your youth,
　　Before the difficult days come,
　　And the years draw near when you say,
　　"I have no pleasure in them":
2　While the sun and the light,
　　The moon and the stars,
　　Are not darkened,
　　And the clouds do not return after the rain;
3　In the day when the keepers of the house tremble,
　　And the strong men bow down;
　　When the grinders cease because they are few,
　　And those that look through the windows grow dim;

11:5 [a]Or *spirit*

4 When the doors are shut in the
     streets,
And the sound of grinding is low;
When one rises up at the sound of a
     bird,
And all the daughters of music are
     brought low.
5 Also they are afraid of height,
And of terrors in the way;
When the almond tree blossoms,
The grasshopper is a burden,
And desire fails.
For man goes to his eternal home,
And the mourners go about the
     streets.

6 *Remember your Creator* before the
     silver cord is loosed,ª
Or the golden bowl is broken,
Or the pitcher shattered at the
     fountain,
Or the wheel broken at the well.
7 Then the dust will return to the
     earth as it was,
And the spirit will return to God
     who gave it.

8 "Vanity of vanities," says the
     Preacher,
"All *is* vanity."

12:6 ªFollowing Qere and Targum; Kethib reads
removed; Septuagint and Vulgate read *broken.*
12:11 ªLiterally *masters of the assemblies*

The Whole Duty of Man

9 And moreover, because the Preacher
was wise, he still taught the people knowledge; yes, he pondered and sought out *and*
set in order many proverbs. 10 The Preacher
sought to find acceptable words; and *what
was* written *was* upright—words of truth.
11 The words of the wise are like goads,
and the words of scholarsª are like well-
driven nails, given by one Shepherd. 12 And
further, my son, be admonished by these.
Of making many books *there is* no end,
and much study *is* wearisome to the flesh.

13 Let us hear the conclusion of the
whole matter:

Fear God and keep His
     commandments,
For this is man's all.
14 For God will bring every work into
     judgment,
Including every secret thing,
Whether good or evil.

INTIMATE
MOMENTS

Take turns sharing your favorite romantic
moments with one another. Talk about
what made those moments so memorable.

SONG OF SOLOMON

THE BIBLE SAYS THAT KING SOLOMON WROTE more than 1,000 songs (1 Kings 4:32). This sizzling book of poetry contains his finest songwriting accomplishment—hence its name, the Song of Songs. It's a beautiful, passionate, even erotic love song written for his wife, referred to as his "beloved" or as "the Shulamite."

To understand the Song of Solomon, you must recognize that several individuals have parts in the song. The Shulamite and Solomon sing back and forth to each other, describing their relationship and celebrating their love. At various times, their song gets interrupted by a chorus of "the daughters of Jerusalem," or by the brothers of the Shulamite. Although the original text does not indicate who is speaking, the New King James version includes notations about who is likely speaking the various lines.

Many Bible scholars throughout history have understood this book as an allegory, either expressing God's love for Israel, or describing the love of Christ for His church. But nothing in the text supports such a view. In fact, the song never even mentions God by name! It is best understood for what it is—an inspired love song that expresses the blessings of God on the romantic and sexual love enjoyed by a husband and his wife.

Professor Howard Hendricks at Dallas Seminary used to say, "We should not be ashamed to discuss what God was not ashamed to create." Sex was God's idea! The Song of Solomon can help us cultivate a healthy perspective on marital love, romance, and passion in today's hyper-sexualized culture. It provides instruction for couples on how to express their love for each other, how to resolve marital conflicts, and how to enjoy one another's body in marriage. It even has a helpful warning for teenagers and single adults, not to "stir up or awaken love" until marriage (8:4). This is a great book for husbands and wives to read out loud to each other as part of night-time devotions!

DEVOTIONS FOR COUPLES • 1:1–4
A Biblical Look at Sex

We live in a culture today in which sexual sin is both rampant and accepted. The best way to respond to the cultural attitudes about sex is to remember what the Bible has to say about sex and to make that instruction a part of your marital life and family teaching.

Here is the truth about sex:

God created sex. Not Hugh Hefner, not Dr. Phil or Dr. Ruth. Genesis 1:27 tells us, "So God created man in His own image, in the image of God He created him; male and female He created them." The Creator of the universe stamped and embedded His image within us in a way that is somehow mysteriously tied to our sexuality.

Christians often get portrayed as backward, narrow-minded prudes. But sexual intercourse in marriage glorifies God. God felt no embarrassment when Adam and Eve had intercourse in the garden. He didn't put His hand over his eyes and shame them with a curt, "Now, cut it out! I didn't create you to do *that!*" No, God designed the equipment and He blessed the union.

When God made them male and female, He called it "very good" (Gen. 1:31).

Sex is for procreation in marriage. God created sex so that we can reproduce after our own kind. Genesis 1:28 tells us that God blessed the man and the woman and commanded them to be fruitful and multiply and fill the earth.

Sex is for intimacy in marriage. Genesis 4:1 says, "Now Adam knew Eve his wife, and she conceived and bore Cain." When it says that Adam "knew" Eve, it doesn't mean he shook her hand. He had sexual relations with his wife, and she conceived. God intended us to become one flesh to draw us together. It's a wonderful aspect of sex.

Sex is for pleasure in marriage. God approves of appropriate gestures of love, romance, and pleasure within marriage. Consider Proverbs 5:19: "As a loving hind and a graceful doe, let her breasts satisfy you at all times; be exhilarated always with her love." *God* said it. He also wrote an entire book of the Bible about sexual love in marriage, the Song of Solomon.

Obviously, God is not down on sexual pleasure in marriage. On the contrary, that is the only kind of sexual pleasure He sees as good and blesses!

1

The song of songs, which *is* Solomon's.

The Banquet

THE SHULAMITE[a]

2 Let him kiss me with the kisses of
     his mouth—
   For your[b] love *is* better than wine.
3 Because of the fragrance of your
     good ointments,
   Your name *is* ointment poured forth;
   Therefore the virgins love you.
4 Draw me away!

THE DAUGHTERS OF JERUSALEM

   We will run after you.[a]

THE SHULAMITE

   The king has brought me into his
     chambers.

THE DAUGHTERS OF JERUSALEM

   We will be glad and rejoice in you.[b]

   We will remember your[c] love more
     than wine.

THE SHULAMITE

   Rightly do they love you.[d]

5 I *am* dark, but lovely,
   O daughters of Jerusalem,
   Like the tents of Kedar,
   Like the curtains of Solomon.
6 Do not look upon me, because I *am*
     dark,

1:2 [a]A Palestinian young woman (compare 6:13). The speaker and audience are identified according to the number, gender, and person of the Hebrew words. Occasionally the identity is not certain. [b]Masculine singular, that is, the Beloved **1:4** [a]Masculine singular, that is, the Beloved [b]Feminine singular, that is, the Shulamite [c]Masculine singular, that is, the Beloved [d]Masculine singular, that is, the Beloved

BIBLICAL INSIGHTS • 1:1–11

Real Romance

THIS BOOK WASTES NO TIME in establishing its theme—in verse two the Shulamite woman says, "Let him kiss me with the kisses of his mouth—for your love is better than wine." The word *love* here means sexual love; it is mentioned four times in the book and two times in the first four verses. The idea here is that sexual love is better than any earthly celebration, any earthly party, any earthly drink, anything you can partake of. Sensual, erotic, sexual love is divinely designed to be celebrated between the husband and his wife and in a way where they are not ashamed that they can delight in that pleasure.

Two other significant themes appear in these first few verses. First, the woman says, "Your name is ointment poured forth, therefore the virgins love you" (v. 3). What she's saying is that he had a name that was above reproach in the marketplace. All the women knew Solomon. They respected and admired him. I think a man needs to know that his character is crucial if he is interested in seeing his wife respond to him sexually. As you become a man who is devoted to pursuing God, you become a man who is attractive to your wife.

For example, at the heart of godly character is humility. This means being teachable, responsive to God, and quick to admit to mistake and error and ask for forgiveness. A husband who is the opposite—arrogant, stubborn, rebellious—will not be attractive to his wife.

A second lesson appears in verse nine, when Solomon recognizes his bride's need for affirmation and doesn't hesitate to go beyond mere acceptance. He lavishes stunning praise on her, "I have compared you, my love, to my filly among Pharaoh's chariots."

Now, before you try that line on your wife, keep in mind the context! Solomon carefully painted a picture of his finest mare, most likely an Arabian beauty, a dark creature of unquestioned magnificence, the finest horse that money could buy. This exotic creature would have turned heads, maybe even caused a stampede, because of her exquisite beauty.

In other words, Solomon skillfully uses evocative poetic language to tell his wife how magnificent she is. But that's not all! He quickly adds, "Your cheeks are lovely with ornaments, your neck with chains of gold" (v. 10). He not only accepts her and sees her as a woman of great loveliness, but he lavishes jewelry on her to accentuate her beauty.

Husband, when did you last spring for a new bracelet? A necklace? A ring? Like Solomon, you married someone extraordinary. Let her know how greatly you esteem her!

Because the sun has tanned me.
My mother's sons were angry with me;
They made me the keeper of the vineyards,
But my own vineyard I have not kept.

(To Her Beloved)

7   Tell me, O you whom I love,
Where you feed *your flock,*
Where you make *it* rest at noon.

For why should I be as one who veils herself[a]
By the flocks of your companions?

The Beloved

8   If you do not know, O fairest among women,
Follow in the footsteps of the flock,
And feed your little goats
Beside the shepherds' tents.

1:7 [a]Septuagint, Syriac, and Vulgate read *wanders.*

9   I have compared you, my love,
    To my filly among Pharaoh's chariots.
10   Your cheeks are lovely with ornaments,
    Your neck with chains *of gold.*

THE DAUGHTERS OF JERUSALEM

11   We will make youª ornaments of gold
    With studs of silver.

THE SHULAMITE

12   While the king *is* at his table,
    My spikenard sends forth its
    fragrance.
13   A bundle of myrrh *is* my beloved to
    me,
    That lies all night between my breasts.
14   My beloved *is* to me a cluster of
    henna *blooms*
    In the vineyards of En Gedi.

THE BELOVED

15   Behold, you *are* fair, my love!
    Behold, you *are* fair!
    You *have* dove's eyes.

THE SHULAMITE

16   Behold, you *are* handsome, my beloved!
    Yes, pleasant!
    Also our bed *is* green.
17   The beams of our houses *are* cedar,
    And our rafters of fir.

2   I *am* the rose of Sharon,
    And the lily of the valleys.

THE BELOVED

2   Like a lily among thorns,
    So is my love among the daughters.

THE SHULAMITE

3   Like an apple tree among the trees of
    the woods,
    So *is* my beloved among the sons.
    I sat down in his shade with great
    delight,
    And his fruit *was* sweet to my taste.

**THE SHULAMITE TO THE DAUGHTERS OF
JERUSALEM**

4   He brought me to the banqueting
    house,
    And his banner over me *was* love.

1:11 ªFeminine singular, that is, the Shulamite

BIBLICAL INSIGHTS • 2:8–14

The Power of Anticipation

LOOK AT HOW THE WOMAN describes her husband, "Behold, he comes leaping upon the mountains, skipping upon the hills. My beloved is like a gazelle or a young stag" (2:9). Can you sense the power of this love, the anticipation she feels as she scans the horizon? Her soul is longing to catch a glimpse of him.

And in verses 10–14 you begin to see how Solomon has cultivated this power of anticipation. He woos her with descriptions of flowers and springtime and secret places where they will go.

The wise husband will take a page out of Solomon's songbook and court his wife. He will realize she wants special time away with him—away from newspapers, televisions, radio, telephone, kids. She wants him to sweep her off her feet.

As I look back on the times of passion and romance and love that Barbara and I have most enjoyed, they have happened when we plan something special and build in the element of surprise. It might be a special date, a surprise picnic, a weekend away at a cabin in the wood … anything that sparks the imagination and builds a sense of anticipation. It's one of the greatest secrets to keeping the romantic fires burning in your marriage.

5   Sustain me with cakes of raisins,
    Refresh me with apples,
    For I *am* lovesick.
6   His left hand *is* under my head,
    And his right hand embraces me.
7   I charge you, O daughters of
    Jerusalem,
    By the gazelles or by the does of the
    field,
    Do not stir up nor awaken love
    Until it pleases.

The Beloved's Request

THE SHULAMITE

8   The voice of my beloved!
     Behold, he comes
     Leaping upon the mountains,
     Skipping upon the hills.
9   My beloved is like a gazelle or a
          young stag.
     Behold, he stands behind our wall;
     He is looking through the windows,
     Gazing through the lattice.
10   My beloved spoke, and said to me:
     "Rise up, my love, my fair one,
       And come away.

ROMANCE FAQ

Q: How can I protect my marriage from the things that would rob it of romance?

The Bible suggests an appropriate name for romance robbers. After the bride of King Solomon described him in endearing, poetic terms, her brothers said, "Catch us the foxes, the little foxes that spoil the vines, for our vines have tender grapes" (2:15).

In those days, a wise gardener would protect his vineyard from foxes. The nocturnal bandits would sneak in during the dead of the night and eat the most tender parts of the vine, rendering them fruitless and useless.

The vineyard is like your marriage. The foxes are the things that sneak up on you and snatch the fruit of passion before it can bloom. And they can be *anything*: television, cell phones, household chores, hobbies—you name it. Even children can be foxes! The terrible thing is that these sly creatures are *relentless*. Drop your guard, and they'll reduce the vineyard of your marriage to a barren, lifeless place where romance shrivels on the vine.

Don't let it happen to you! Catch those little foxes and keep them out of your garden. If you don't know what they are, then observe carefully. You'll spot them if you look for them!

11   For lo, the winter is past,
     The rain is over *and* gone.
12   The flowers appear on the earth;
     The time of singing has come,
     And the voice of the turtledove
     Is heard in our land.
13   The fig tree puts forth her green figs,
     And the vines *with* the tender grapes
     Give a *good* smell.
     Rise up, my love, my fair one,
     And come away!
14   "O my dove, in the clefts of the rock,
     In the secret *places* of the cliff,
     Let me see your face,
     Let me hear your voice;
     For your voice *is* sweet,
     And your face *is* lovely."

HER BROTHERS

15   Catch us the foxes,
     The little foxes that spoil the vines,
     For our vines *have* tender grapes.

THE SHULAMITE

16   My beloved *is* mine, and I *am* his.
     He feeds *his flock* among the lilies.

(TO HER BELOVED)

17   Until the day breaks
     And the shadows flee away,
     Turn, my beloved,
     And be like a gazelle
     Or a young stag
     Upon the mountains of Bether.[a]

A Troubled Night

THE SHULAMITE

3   By night on my bed I sought
          the one I love;
     I sought him, but I did not find him.
2   "I will rise now," *I said,*
     "And go about the city;
     In the streets and in the squares
     I will seek the one I love."
     I sought him, but I did not find him.
3   The watchmen who go about the city
          found me;
     I said,
     "Have you seen the one I love?"

2:17 [a]Literally *Separation*

4 Scarcely had I passed by them,
   When I found the one I love.
   I held him and would not let him go,
   Until I had brought him to the house
       of my mother,
   And into the chamber of her who
       conceived me.

5 I charge you, O daughters of
       Jerusalem,
   By the gazelles or by the does of the
       field,
   Do not stir up nor awaken love
   Until it pleases.

The Coming of Solomon

THE SHULAMITE

6 Who *is* this coming out of the
       wilderness
   Like pillars of smoke,
   Perfumed with myrrh and
       frankincense,
   With all the merchant's fragrant
       powders?

7 Behold, it *is* Solomon's couch,
   With sixty valiant men around it,
   Of the valiant of Israel.

8 They all hold swords,
   Being expert in war.
   Every man *has* his sword on his thigh
   Because of fear in the night.

9 Of the wood of Lebanon
   Solomon the King
   Made himself a palanquin:[a]

10 He made its pillars *of* silver,
   Its support *of* gold,
   Its seat *of* purple,
   Its interior paved *with* love
   By the daughters of Jerusalem.

11 Go forth, O daughters of Zion,
   And see King Solomon with the crown
   With which his mother crowned him
   On the day of his wedding,
   The day of the gladness of his heart.

The Bridegroom Praises the Bride

THE BELOVED

4 Behold, you *are* fair, my love!
   Behold, you *are* fair!

You *have* dove's eyes behind your veil.
Your hair *is* like a flock of goats,
Going down from Mount Gilead.

2 Your teeth *are* like a flock of shorn
       sheep
   Which have come up from the
       washing,
   Every one of which bears twins,
   And none *is* barren among them.

3 Your lips *are* like a strand of scarlet,
   And your mouth is lovely.
   Your temples behind your veil
   Are like a piece of pomegranate.

4 Your neck *is* like the tower of David,
   Built for an armory,
   On which hang a thousand bucklers,
   All shields of mighty men.

5 Your two breasts *are* like two fawns,
   Twins of a gazelle,
   Which feed among the lilies.

6 Until the day breaks
   And the shadows flee away,
   I will go my way to the mountain of
       myrrh
   And to the hill of frankincense.

7 You *are* all fair, my love,
   And *there is* no spot in you.

8 Come with me from Lebanon, *my*
       spouse,
   With me from Lebanon.
   Look from the top of Amana,
   From the top of Senir and Hermon,
   From the lions' dens,
   From the mountains of the
       leopards.

9 You have ravished my heart,
   My sister, *my* spouse;
   You have ravished my heart
   With one *look* of your eyes,
   With one link of your necklace.

3:9 [a] A portable enclosed chair

INTIMATE MOMENTS

As he heads out for work, give him a passionate kiss. If he wants to know what it was for, tell him it's the appetizer for tonight's menu.

DEVOTIONS FOR COUPLES • 5:1
God, Prayer, and Sexual Intimacy

Would it surprise you to see the words *prayer* and *lovemaking* in the same sentence? In fact, they go together quite well.

Making love in the marriage bed is both fantastic and beautiful. Real, passionate, and intimate love is exactly what should occur between two unashamed married lovers: "Drink, yes, drink deeply, O beloved ones!" (5:1).

So what role does prayer play? Praying together will always draw a couple closer. In fact, as your prayer life grows, you will become better lovers. Since marital intimacy was God's idea, He wants you to experience it to the fullest. As with all other important spiritual endeavors, you and I need His Spirit's power for true success. Vonette Bright, the wife of the late Bill Bright, said this about sex, "It's just as important to be filled with the Holy Spirit in bed as it is in witnessing to another about Jesus Christ."

That's why you should pray for one another before you go to bed. Ask Him to make you the finest lovers. Here are a few ideas to help keep lovemaking fresh.

1. *Praying together builds respect and attraction.* Husbands, did you know that initiating prayer with your wife makes you more desirable?

2. *Ask God to bless your spouse through your time together.* Husbands, what a privilege to pray for your wife before initiating intimacy! Wives, did you know that expressing admiration and respect for your husband in prayer will minister to him?

3. *If you've struggled as a couple with sex, ask God to bless your time and give you understanding for one another.* We have prayed over this area of our marriage, and He has answered.

4. *Pray for patience with one another.* There's nothing quite like asking God to help you be more gentle and kind with your spouse in lovemaking.

5. *Pray during lovemaking!* Yes, we're serious. Hold your spouse and give thanks for him or her and your time together. You'll see what we mean.

6. *Thank God for the gift of intimacy and pleasure in your marriage.* A husband and wife wrote to us, "It is special to pray together after having made love. Since God invented this beautiful expression, why should we be afraid to pray together afterward? What a way to celebrate having come to each other in purity."

Amen! We urge you to pray together ... and turn out the lights early tonight!

---

10 How fair is your love,
My sister, *my* spouse!
How much better than wine is your love,
And the scent of your perfumes
Than all spices!

11 Your lips, O *my* spouse,
Drip as the honeycomb;
Honey and milk *are* under your tongue;
And the fragrance of your garments
Is like the fragrance of Lebanon.

12 A garden enclosed
Is my sister, *my* spouse,
A spring shut up,
A fountain sealed.

13 Your plants *are* an orchard of pomegranates
With pleasant fruits,
Fragrant henna with spikenard,

14 Spikenard and saffron,
Calamus and cinnamon,
With all trees of frankincense,
Myrrh and aloes,
With all the chief spices—

15 A fountain of gardens,
A well of living waters,
And streams from Lebanon.

THE SHULAMITE

16 Awake, O north *wind,*
And come, O south!
Blow upon my garden,
That its spices may flow out.
Let my beloved come to his garden
And eat its pleasant fruits.

THE BELOVED

5 I have come to my garden, my sister,
    my spouse;
I have gathered my myrrh with my
    spice;
I have eaten my honeycomb with my
    honey;
I have drunk my wine with my milk.

(TO HIS FRIENDS)

Eat, O friends!
Drink, yes, drink deeply,
O beloved ones!

The Shulamite's Troubled Evening

THE SHULAMITE

2   I sleep, but my heart is awake;
     It is the voice of my beloved!
     He knocks, *saying,*
     "Open for me, my sister, my love,
     My dove, my perfect one;
     For my head is covered with dew,
     My locks with the drops of the
         night."

3   I have taken off my robe;
     How can I put it on *again?*
     I have washed my feet;
     How can I defile them?

4   My beloved put his hand
     By the latch *of the door,*
     And my heart yearned for him.

5   I arose to open for my beloved,
     And my hands dripped *with* myrrh,
     My fingers with liquid myrrh,
     On the handles of the lock.

6   I opened for my beloved,
     But my beloved had turned away
         and was gone.
     My heart leaped up when he spoke.
     I sought him, but I could not find
         him;
     I called him, but he gave me no
         answer.

7   The watchmen who went about the
         city found me.
     They struck me, they wounded me;
     The keepers of the walls
     Took my veil away from me.

8   I charge you, O daughters of
         Jerusalem,

If you find my beloved,
That you tell him I *am* lovesick!

THE DAUGHTERS OF JERUSALEM

9   What *is* your beloved
     More than *another* beloved,
     O fairest among women?
     What *is* your beloved
     More than *another* beloved,
     That you so charge us?

ROMANCE FAQ

Q: What does it take to become the romantic man of my wife's dreams?

The key is learning to become fluent in her romantic love language.

•*A romantic man* engages his wife in a living and growing relationship without losing sight that physical intimacy is an important part of that relationship.

•*A romantic man* commits to learning nonsexual ways to love his lover while nurturing in her the freedom to be sexually responsive.

•*A romantic man* can kiss, hug, touch, and cuddle without a sexual agenda, while helping his wife embrace the joy of sex at the right time.

•*A romantic man* connects to his wife's world, supports, listens, and shares his heart, while being confidently aware that sexual intimacy is vital to the survival of his marriage.

•*A romantic man* will do all of these things *even when his spouse is sexually unresponsive,* knowing that in due time he will reap what he sows.

You can learn to speak your wife's language of romantic love and still be fully a man, with all the sexual desire God put there. Remember, there is no shame, no condemnation, and no apology for being a real man.

THE SHULAMITE

10 My beloved *is* white and ruddy,
    Chief among ten thousand.
11 His head *is like* the finest gold;
    His locks *are* wavy,
    And black as a raven.
12 His eyes *are* like doves
    By the rivers of waters,
    Washed with milk,
    And fitly set.
13 His cheeks *are* like a bed of spices,
    Banks of scented herbs.
    His lips *are* lilies,
    Dripping liquid myrrh.
14 His hands *are* rods of gold
    Set with beryl.
    His body *is* carved ivory
    Inlaid *with* sapphires.
15 His legs *are* pillars of marble
    Set on bases of fine gold.
    His countenance *is* like Lebanon,
    Excellent as the cedars.
16 His mouth *is* most sweet,
    Yes, he *is* altogether lovely.
    This *is* my beloved,
    And this *is* my friend,
    O daughters of Jerusalem!

THE DAUGHTERS OF JERUSALEM

6 Where has your beloved gone,
   O fairest among women?
   Where has your beloved turned
       aside,
   That we may seek him with you?

THE SHULAMITE

2 My beloved has gone to his garden,
   To the beds of spices,
   To feed *his flock* in the gardens,
   And to gather lilies.

3 I *am* my beloved's,
   And my beloved *is* mine.
   He feeds *his flock* among the lilies.

Praise of the Shulamite's Beauty

THE BELOVED

4 O my love, you *are as* beautiful as
       Tirzah,
   Lovely as Jerusalem,
   Awesome as *an army* with banners!
5 Turn your eyes away from me,
   For they have overcome me.
   Your hair *is* like a flock of goats
   Going down from Gilead.
6 Your teeth *are* like a flock of sheep
   Which have come up from the
       washing;
   Every one bears twins,
   And none *is* barren among them.
7 Like a piece of pomegranate
   Are your temples behind your veil.

8 There are sixty queens
   And eighty concubines,
   And virgins without number.
9 My dove, my perfect one,
   Is the only one,
   The only one of her mother,
   The favorite of the one who
       bore her.
   The daughters saw her
   And called her blessed,
   The queens and the concubines,
   And they praised her.

10 Who is she who looks forth as the
       morning,
    Fair as the moon,
    Clear as the sun,
    Awesome as *an army* with
       banners?

THE SHULAMITE

11 I went down to the garden of nuts
    To see the verdure of the valley,
    To see whether the vine had budded
    And the pomegranates had bloomed.
12 Before I was even aware,
    My soul had made me
    As the chariots of my noble
       people.[a]

6:12 [a]Hebrew *Ammi Nadib*

INTIMATE MOMENTS

Make foreplay the focus. Take your time.
Focus on her: play with her hair, caress her
face, and gently stroke her arms and legs.
Let things build slowly.

THE BELOVED AND HIS FRIENDS

13   Return, return, O Shulamite;
      Return, return, that we may look
          upon you!

THE SHULAMITE

      What would you see in the
          Shulamite—
      As it were, the dance of the two
          camps?a

Expressions of Praise

THE BELOVED

7   How beautiful are your feet in sandals,
         O prince's daughter!
      The curves of your thighs *are* like
          jewels,
      The work of the hands of a skillful
          workman.
2   Your navel *is* a rounded goblet;
      It lacks no blended beverage.
      Your waist *is* a heap of wheat
      Set about with lilies.
3   Your two breasts *are* like two fawns,
      Twins of a gazelle.
4   Your neck *is* like an ivory tower,
      Your eyes *like* the pools in Heshbon
      By the gate of Bath Rabbim.
      Your nose *is* like the tower of
          Lebanon
      Which looks toward Damascus.
5   Your head *crowns* you like *Mount*
          Carmel,
      And the hair of your head *is* like
          purple;
      A king *is* held captive by *your* tresses.

6   How fair and how pleasant you are,
      O love, with your delights!
7   This stature of yours is like a palm
          tree,
      And your breasts *like* its clusters.
8   I said, "I will go up to the palm tree,
      I will take hold of its branches."
      Let now your breasts be like clusters
          of the vine,
      The fragrance of your breath like
          apples,
9   And the roof of your mouth like the
          best wine.

THE SHULAMITE

      *The wine goes *down* smoothly for
          my beloved,
      Moving gently the lips of sleepers.a
10   I *am* my beloved's,
      And his desire *is* toward me.

11   Come, my beloved,
      Let us go forth to the field;
      Let us lodge in the villages.
12   Let us get up early to the vineyards;
      Let us see if the vine has budded,
      Whether the grape blossoms are
          open,
      And the pomegranates are in bloom.
      There I will give you my love.
13   The mandrakes give off a fragrance,
      And at our gates *are* pleasant *fruits,*
      All manner, new and old,
      Which I have laid up for you, my
          beloved.

8   Oh, that you were like my brother,
      Who nursed at my mother's breasts!
      If I should find you outside,
      I would kiss you;
      I would not be despised.
2   I would lead you *and* bring you
      Into the house of my mother,
      She *who* used to instruct me.
      I would cause you to drink of spiced
          wine,
      Of the juice of my pomegranate.

(TO THE DAUGHTERS OF JERUSALEM)

3   His left hand *is* under my head,
      And his right hand embraces me.
4   I charge you, O daughters of
          Jerusalem,
      Do not stir up nor awaken love
      Until it pleases.

6:13 aHebrew *Mahanaim*   **7:9** aSeptuagint, Syriac,
and Vulgate read *lips and teeth.*

INTIMATE MOMENTS

Treat your hardworking honey to a back-rub.

BIBLICAL INSIGHTS • 7:10–13
Time to Enjoy One Another

EVERY WOMAN NEEDS TO FEEL safe and secure with her husband. She needs to feel his commitment to stay married, his commitment to love her and accept her so that she can feel it is safe to give him this gift of who she is in the marriage relationship. In chapter 7, the Shulamite woman says, "I am my beloved's, and his desire is toward me" (v. 10). Can you feel her sense of contentment and security?

And then note one of the ways that a husband can foster this sense of security in his wife—by going away with her for a special time away from normal responsibilities. "Come, my beloved," she says, "let us go forth to the field; let us lodge in the villages. Let us get up early to the vineyards …There I will give you my love" (vv. 11, 12). She invites him to go into a secluded spot, and there they are going to have a picnic and enjoy physical food that satisfies hunger and sexual food that satisfied their souls.

This passage demonstrates the power of a romantic getaway. For a husband to meet his wife's needs, and vice versa, they need to give each other *time*. Time to pursue each other, set each other apart, stay up late talking without having to get up the next morning. Time just to enjoy one another.

Barbara and I have committed to going on getaways like this at least a couple of times each year. We have three purposes for these weekends away. The first is to spend time together with one another and with God—just a quiet time to listen to the Lord, to pray together, to sit and be quiet. A good portion of a weekend getaway might be just sitting by a fire with our feet propped up. We don't go anywhere, don't answer phones …we just sit quietly and talk if we feel like it, or we read a book. Or we might take a long walk and talk about whatever we want.

A second purpose for our getaways is planning. We pull out the calendar and we talk about where we're headed for the next week, the next month, the next six months, and the next year. We talk about vacations, work trips, family reunions, anything we need to talk about.

And then the third purpose is romance and pure pleasure. Just an opportunity to reconnect, soul to soul, heart to heart, and yes, body to body.

Getaways like these are a good time to get away and enjoy romance and a refreshing of our relationship with one another.

Love Renewed in Lebanon

A RELATIVE

5   Who *is* this coming up from the
         wilderness,
      Leaning upon her beloved?

      I awakened you under the apple tree.
      There your mother brought you forth;
      There she *who* bore you brought *you*
         forth.

THE SHULAMITE TO HER BELOVED

6   Set me as a seal upon your heart,
      As a seal upon your arm;
      For love *is as* strong as death,

      Jealousy *as* cruel as the grave;[a]
      Its flames *are* flames of fire,
      A most vehement flame.[b]

7   Many waters cannot quench love,
      Nor can the floods drown it.
      If a man would give for love
      All the wealth of his house,
      It would be utterly despised.

THE SHULAMITE'S BROTHERS

8   We have a little sister,
      And she has no breasts.
      What shall we do for our sister

8:6 [a]Or *Sheol* [b]Literally *A flame of YAH* (a poetic form of *YHWH, the LORD*)

In the day when she is spoken for?

9 If she *is* a wall,
We will build upon her
A battlement of silver;
And if she *is* a door,
We will enclose her
With boards of cedar.

THE SHULAMITE

10 I *am* a wall,
And my breasts like towers;
Then I became in his eyes
As one who found peace.

11 Solomon had a vineyard at Baal
    Hamon;
He leased the vineyard to keepers;
Everyone was to bring for its fruit
A thousand silver *coins.*

(TO SOLOMON)

12 My own vineyard *is* before me.
You, O Solomon, *may have* a
    thousand,
And those who tend its fruit two
    hundred.

SHE BELOVED

13 You who dwell in the gardens,
The companions listen for your
    voice—
Let me hear it!

THE SHULAMITE

14 Make haste, my beloved,
And be like a gazelle
Or a young stag
On the mountains of spices.

ISAIAH

SOMEONE ONCE ASKED WINSTON CHURCHILL to give the personal qualifications needed for success in politics. He replied, "A politician needs the ability to foretell what is going to happen tomorrow, next week, next month, and next year. And to have the ability afterwards to explain why it didn't happen."

God raised up the prophet Isaiah to speak to the political and spiritual leaders of Judah and Israel. He ministered for forty years, during the reigns of Jotham, Ahaz, and Hezekiah. According to tradition, Isaiah was a citizen of Jerusalem and born into nobility; therefore he had access to the royal courts and to the priests. He was married to a woman known simply as "the prophetess" (8:3). They had two sons, each given a name with a prophetic meaning. Isaiah began to speak out as a prophet around 739 BC the year King Uzziah died.

Chapters 1—39 of his book address various issues facing the southern kingdom between 740–700 BC while chapters 40—66 describe how God will care for His people during the coming Babylonian captivity. Because Isaiah spoke with such pinpoint accuracy about future events, many scholars have presumed that chapters 40—66 were written decades after the prophet's death. The New Testament, however, assumes Isaiah wrote the whole book (e.g., Matt. 3:3; Mark 1:2; Luke 3:4; 4:17; John 12:38).

Isaiah pleads with his people to return to the true worship of God. His favorite name for God is "the Holy One of Israel," a phrase he uses twenty-five times (it appears only five times in the rest of the Old Testament). He repeatedly warns the kings of Judah to get their foreign policy in sync with God's will.

Isaiah also prophesies a great deal about Jesus Christ and His ministry. Chapters 40—66 are filled with allusion to the coming of God's Messiah. One of his four "Servant Songs" about Jesus (52:13—53:12) is quoted or alluded to nearly forty times in the New Testament. In addition, Isaiah prophesied about the birth of Christ (7:14; 9:6) and about the ministry of John the Baptist (40:1–6). Jesus Himself read from Isaiah 61 as He began His public ministry. Some have called the book of Isaiah "The Old Testament Gospel."

1 The vision of Isaiah the son of Amoz, which he saw concerning Judah and Jerusalem in the days of Uzziah, Jotham, Ahaz, *and* Hezekiah, kings of Judah.

The Wickedness of Judah

2 Hear, O heavens, and give ear,
   O earth!
   For the LORD has spoken:
   "I have nourished and brought up
      children,
   And they have rebelled against Me;
3 The ox knows its owner
   And the donkey its master's crib;
   But Israel does not know,
   My people do not consider."

4 Alas, sinful nation,
   A people laden with iniquity,
   A brood of evildoers,
   Children who are corrupters!
   They have forsaken the LORD,
   They have provoked to anger
   The Holy One of Israel,
   They have turned away backward.

5 Why should you be stricken again?
   You will revolt more and more.
   The whole head is sick,
   And the whole heart faints.
6 From the sole of the foot even to the
      head,
   There is no soundness in it,
   But wounds and bruises and
      putrefying sores;
   They have not been closed or bound
      up,
   Or soothed with ointment.

7 Your country *is* desolate,
   Your cities *are* burned with fire;
   Strangers devour your land in your
      presence;
   And *it is* desolate, as overthrown by
      strangers.
8 So the daughter of Zion is left as a
      booth in a vineyard,
   As a hut in a garden of cucumbers,
   As a besieged city.
9 Unless the LORD of hosts
   Had left to us a very small remnant,
   We would have become like Sodom,
   We would have been made like
      Gomorrah.

10 Hear the word of the LORD,
   You rulers of Sodom;
   Give ear to the law of our God,
   You people of Gomorrah:
11 "To what purpose *is* the multitude of
      your sacrifices to Me?"
   Says the LORD.
   "I have had enough of burnt offerings
      of rams
   And the fat of fed cattle.
   I do not delight in the blood of bulls,
   Or of lambs or goats.

12 "When you come to appear before Me,
   Who has required this from your hand,
   To trample My courts?
13 Bring no more futile sacrifices;
   Incense is an abomination to Me.
   The New Moons, the Sabbaths, and
      the calling of assemblies—
   I cannot endure iniquity and the
      sacred meeting.
14 Your New Moons and your
      appointed feasts
   My soul hates;
   They are a trouble to Me,
   I am weary of bearing *them.*
15 When you spread out your hands,
   I will hide My eyes from you;
   Even though you make many prayers,
   I will not hear.
   Your hands are full of blood.

16 "Wash yourselves, make yourselves
      clean;
   Put away the evil of your doings
      from before My eyes.
   Cease to do evil,
17 Learn to do good;
   Seek justice,
   Rebuke the oppressor;[a]
   Defend the fatherless,
   Plead for the widow.

18 "Come now, and let us reason together,"
   Says the LORD,
   "Though your sins are like scarlet,
   They shall be as white as snow;
   Though they are red like crimson,
   They shall be as wool.
19 If you are willing and obedient,
   You shall eat the good of the land;

1:17 [a]Some ancient versions read *the oppressed.*

20 But if you refuse and rebel,
You shall be devoured by the sword";
For the mouth of the LORD has
   spoken.

The Degenerate City

21 How the faithful city has become a
   harlot!
It was full of justice;
Righteousness lodged in it,
But now murderers.
22 Your silver has become dross,
Your wine mixed with water.
23 Your princes *are* rebellious,
And companions of thieves;
Everyone loves bribes,
And follows after rewards.
They do not defend the fatherless,
Nor does the cause of the widow
   come before them.

24 Therefore the Lord says,
The LORD of hosts, the Mighty One
   of Israel,
"Ah, I will rid Myself of My
   adversaries,
And take vengeance on My enemies.
25 I will turn My hand against you,
And thoroughly purge away your
   dross,
And take away all your alloy.
26 I will restore your judges as at the
   first,
And your counselors as at the
   beginning.
Afterward you shall be called the
   city of righteousness, the faithful
   city."

27 Zion shall be redeemed with justice,
And her penitents with
   righteousness.
28 The destruction of transgressors
   and of sinners *shall be* together,
And those who forsake the LORD
   shall be consumed.
29 For they[a] shall be ashamed of the
   terebinth trees
Which you have desired;
And you shall be embarrassed
   because of the gardens
Which you have chosen.
30 For you shall be as a terebinth whose
   leaf fades,

And as a garden that has no water.
31 The strong shall be as tinder,
And the work of it as a spark;
Both will burn together,
And no one shall quench *them.*

The Future House of God

2 The word that Isaiah the son of Amoz
saw concerning Judah and Jerusalem.

2 Now it shall come to pass in the
   latter days
That the mountain of the LORD's
   house
Shall be established on the top of the
   mountains,
And shall be exalted above the hills;
And all nations shall flow to it.
3 Many people shall come and say,
"Come, and let us go up to the
   mountain of the LORD,
To the house of the God of Jacob;
He will teach us His ways,
And we shall walk in His paths."
For out of Zion shall go forth the law,
And the word of the LORD from
   Jerusalem.
4 He shall judge between the nations,
And rebuke many people;
They shall beat their swords into
   plowshares,
And their spears into pruning hooks;
Nation shall not lift up sword against
   nation,
Neither shall they learn war
   anymore.

The Day of the LORD

5 O house of Jacob, come and let us
   walk
In the light of the LORD.

6 For You have forsaken Your people,
   the house of Jacob,
Because they are filled with eastern
   ways;
They *are* soothsayers like the
   Philistines,
And they are pleased with the
   children of foreigners.

1:29 [a]Following Masoretic Text, Septuagint, and
Vulgate; some Hebrew manuscripts and Targum
read *you.*

7   Their land is also full of silver and
       gold,
    And there is no end to their
       treasures;
    Their land is also full of horses,
    And there is no end to their chariots.
8   Their land is also full of idols;
    They worship the work of their own
       hands,
    That which their own fingers have
       made.
9   People bow down,
    And each man humbles himself;
    Therefore do not forgive them.

10 Enter into the rock, and hide in the
       dust,
    From the terror of the LORD
    And the glory of His majesty.
11 The lofty looks of man shall be
       humbled,
    The haughtiness of men shall be
       bowed down,
    And the LORD alone shall be exalted
       in that day.

12 For the day of the LORD of hosts
    Shall come upon everything proud
       and lofty,
    Upon everything lifted up—
    And it shall be brought low—
13 Upon all the cedars of Lebanon *that
       are* high and lifted up,
    And upon all the oaks of Bashan;
14 Upon all the high mountains,
    And upon all the hills *that are* lifted
       up;
15 Upon every high tower,
    And upon every fortified wall;
16 Upon all the ships of Tarshish,
    And upon all the beautiful sloops.
17 The loftiness of man shall be bowed
       down,
    And the haughtiness of men shall be
       brought low;
    The LORD alone will be exalted in
       that day,
18 But the idols He shall utterly abolish.

19 They shall go into the holes of the
       rocks,
    And into the caves of the earth,
    From the terror of the LORD
    And the glory of His majesty,
    When He arises to shake the earth
       mightily.
20 In that day a man will cast away his
       idols of silver
    And his idols of gold,
    Which they made, *each* for himself
       to worship,
    To the moles and bats,
21 To go into the clefts of the rocks,
    And into the crags of the rugged
       rocks,
    From the terror of the LORD
    And the glory of His majesty,
    When He arises to shake the earth
       mightily.

22 Sever yourselves from such a man,
    Whose breath *is* in his nostrils;
    For of what account is he?

Judgment on Judah and Jerusalem

3   For behold, the Lord, the LORD
       of hosts,
    Takes away from Jerusalem and
       from Judah
    The stock and the store,
    The whole supply of bread and the
       whole supply of water;
2   The mighty man and the man of war,
    The judge and the prophet,
    And the diviner and the elder;
3   The captain of fifty and the
       honorable man,
    The counselor and the skillful
       artisan,
    And the expert enchanter.

4   "I will give children *to be* their
       princes,
    And babes shall rule over them.
5   The people will be oppressed,
    Every one by another and every one
       by his neighbor;

INTIMATE MOMENTS

Remember, your wife is God's gift to *you*.
Thank Him for her, and then tell her you
did so.

The child will be insolent toward the elder,
And the base toward the honorable."

6 When a man takes hold of his brother
In the house of his father, *saying,*
"You have clothing;
You be our ruler,
And *let* these ruins *be* under your power,"[a]

7 In that day he will protest, saying,
"I cannot cure *your* ills,
For in my house *is* neither food nor clothing;
Do not make me a ruler of the people."

8 For Jerusalem stumbled,
And Judah is fallen,
Because their tongue and their doings
Are against the LORD,
To provoke the eyes of His glory.

9 The look on their countenance witnesses against them,
And they declare their sin as Sodom;
They do not hide *it.*
Woe to their soul!
For they have brought evil upon themselves.

10 "Say to the righteous that *it shall be* well *with them,*
For they shall eat the fruit of their doings.

11 Woe to the wicked! *It shall be* ill *with him,*
For the reward of his hands shall be given him.

12 *As for* My people, children *are* their oppressors,
And women rule over them.
O My people! Those who lead you cause *you* to err,
And destroy the way of your paths."

Oppression and Luxury Condemned

13 The LORD stands up to plead,
And stands to judge the people.

14 The LORD will enter into judgment
With the elders of His people
And His princes:
"For you have eaten up the vineyard;
The plunder of the poor *is* in your houses.

15 What do you mean by crushing My people
And grinding the faces of the poor?"
Says the Lord GOD of hosts.

16 Moreover the LORD says:

"Because the daughters of Zion are haughty,
And walk with outstretched necks
And wanton eyes,
Walking and mincing *as* they go,
Making a jingling with their feet,

17 Therefore the Lord will strike with a scab
The crown of the head of the daughters of Zion,
And the LORD will uncover their secret parts."

18 In that day the Lord will take away the finery:
The jingling anklets, the scarves, and the crescents;

19 The pendants, the bracelets, and the veils;

20 The headdresses, the leg ornaments, and the headbands;
The perfume boxes, the charms, and the rings;

21

22 The nose jewels,
the festal apparel, and the mantles;
The outer garments, the purses,

23 and the mirrors;
The fine linen, the turbans, and the robes.

24 And so it shall be:

Instead of a sweet smell there will be a stench;
Instead of a sash, a rope;
Instead of well-set hair, baldness;
Instead of a rich robe, a girding of sackcloth;
And branding instead of beauty.

25 Your men shall fall by the sword,
And your mighty in the war.

26 Her gates shall lament and mourn,
And she *being* desolate shall sit on the ground.

3:6 [a]Literally *hand*

4 And in that day seven women shall
   take hold of one man, saying,
"We will eat our own food and wear
   our own apparel;
Only let us be called by your name,
To take away our reproach."

The Renewal of Zion

2   In that day the Branch of the LORD
      shall be beautiful and glorious;
   And the fruit of the earth *shall be*
      excellent and appealing
   For those of Israel who have
      escaped.

³And it shall come to pass that *he who
is* left in Zion and remains in Jerusalem will
be called holy—everyone who is recorded
among the living in Jerusalem. ⁴When the
Lord has washed away the filth of the
daughters of Zion, and purged the blood of
Jerusalem from her midst, by the spirit of
judgment and by the spirit of burning,
⁵then the LORD will create above every
dwelling place of Mount Zion, and above
her assemblies, a cloud and smoke by day
and the shining of a flaming fire by night.
For over all the glory there *will be* a covering. ⁶And there will be a tabernacle for
shade in the daytime from the heat, for a
place of refuge, and for a shelter from
storm and rain.

God's Disappointing Vineyard

5 Now let me sing to my Well-beloved
   A song of my Beloved regarding His
      vineyard:

   My Well-beloved has a vineyard
   On a very fruitful hill.
2 He dug it up and cleared out its
      stones,
   And planted it with the choicest
      vine.
   He built a tower in its midst,
   And also made a winepress in it;
   So He expected *it* to bring forth *good*
      grapes,
   But it brought forth wild grapes.

3 "And now, O inhabitants of Jerusalem
      and men of Judah,
   Judge, please, between Me and My
      vineyard.

4 What more could have been done to
      My vineyard
   That I have not done in it?
   Why then, when I expected *it* to
      bring forth *good* grapes,
   Did it bring forth wild grapes?

5 And now, please let Me tell you what
      I will do to My vineyard:
   I will take away its hedge, and it
      shall be burned;
   And break down its wall, and it shall
      be trampled down.
6 I will lay it waste;
   It shall not be pruned or dug,
   But there shall come up briers and
      thorns.
   I will also command the clouds
   That they rain no rain on it."

7 For the vineyard of the LORD of
      hosts *is* the house of Israel,
   And the men of Judah are His
      pleasant plant.
   He looked for justice, but behold,
      oppression;
   For righteousness, but behold, a cry
      for help.

Impending Judgment on Excesses

8 Woe to those who join house to
      house;
   They add field to field,
   Till *there is* no place
   Where they may dwell alone in the
      midst of the land!

9 In my hearing the LORD of hosts
      said,
   "Truly, many houses shall be desolate,
   Great and beautiful ones, without
      inhabitant.
10 For ten acres of vineyard shall yield
      one bath,
   And a homer of seed shall yield one
      ephah."

11 Woe to those who rise early in the
      morning,
   That they may follow intoxicating
      drink;
   Who continue until night, *till* wine
      inflames them!
12 The harp and the strings,
   The tambourine and flute,
   And wine are in their feasts;

But they do not regard the work of
the LORD,
Nor consider the operation of His
hands.

13 Therefore my people have gone into
captivity,
Because *they have* no knowledge;
Their honorable men *are* famished,
And their multitude dried up with
thirst.

14 Therefore Sheol has enlarged itself
And opened its mouth beyond
measure;
Their glory and their multitude and
their pomp,
And he who is jubilant, shall descend
into it.

15 People shall be brought down,
Each man shall be humbled,
And the eyes of the lofty shall be
humbled.

16 But the LORD of hosts shall be
exalted in judgment,
And God who is holy shall be
hallowed in righteousness.

17 Then the lambs shall feed in their
pasture,
And in the waste places of the fat
ones strangers shall eat.

18 Woe to those who draw iniquity with
cords of vanity,
And sin as if with a cart rope;

19 That say, "Let Him make speed *and*
hasten His work,
That we may see *it;*
And let the counsel of the Holy One
of Israel draw near and come,
That we may know *it.*"

20 Woe to those who call evil good, and
good evil;
Who put darkness for light, and light
for darkness;
Who put bitter for sweet, and sweet
for bitter!

21 Woe to *those who are* wise in their
own eyes,
And prudent in their own sight!

22 Woe to men mighty at drinking wine,
Woe to men valiant for mixing
intoxicating drink,

23 Who justify the wicked for a bribe,
And take away justice from the
righteous man!

24 Therefore, as the fire devours the
stubble,
And the flame consumes the chaff,
So their root will be as rottenness,
And their blossom will ascend like
dust;
Because they have rejected the law of
the LORD of hosts,
And despised the word of the Holy
One of Israel.

25 Therefore the anger of the LORD is
aroused against His people;
He has stretched out His hand
against them
And stricken them,
And the hills trembled.
Their carcasses *were* as refuse in the
midst of the streets.

For all this His anger is not turned
away,
But His hand *is* stretched out still.

26 He will lift up a banner to the nations
from afar,
And will whistle to them from the
end of the earth;
Surely they shall come with speed,
swiftly.

27 No one will be weary or stumble
among them,
No one will slumber or sleep;
Nor will the belt on their loins be
loosed,
Nor the strap of their sandals be
broken;

28 Whose arrows *are* sharp,
And all their bows bent;
Their horses' hooves will seem like
flint,
And their wheels like a whirlwind.

29 Their roaring *will be* like a lion,
They will roar like young lions;
Yes, they will roar
And lay hold of the prey;
They will carry *it* away safely,
And no one will deliver.

30 In that day they will roar against
them
Like the roaring of the sea.

And if *one* looks to the land,
Behold, darkness *and* sorrow;
And the light is darkened by the
  clouds.

Isaiah Called to Be a Prophet

6 In the year that King Uzziah died, I saw the Lord sitting on a throne, high and lifted up, and the train of His *robe* filled the temple. ²Above it stood seraphim; each one had six wings: with two he covered his face, with two he covered his feet, and with two he flew. ³And one cried to another and said:

"Holy, holy, holy *is* the LORD of hosts;
  The whole earth *is* full of His glory!"

⁴And the posts of the door were shaken by the voice of him who cried out, and the house was filled with smoke.
⁵So I said:

"Woe *is* me, for I am undone!
Because I *am* a man of unclean lips,
And I dwell in the midst of a people
  of unclean lips;
For my eyes have seen the King,
  The LORD of hosts."

⁶Then one of the seraphim flew to me, having in his hand a live coal *which* he had taken with the tongs from the altar. ⁷And he touched my mouth *with it,* and said:

"Behold, this has touched your lips;
Your iniquity is taken away,
And your sin purged."

⁸Also I heard the voice of the Lord, saying:

"Whom shall I send,
And who will go for Us?"

Then I said, "Here *am* I! Send me."
⁹And He said, "Go, and tell this people:

' Keep on hearing, but do not
  understand;
Keep on seeing, but do not perceive.'

¹⁰ "Make the heart of this people dull,
And their ears heavy,
And shut their eyes;
Lest they see with their eyes,

And hear with their ears,
And understand with their heart,
And return and be healed."

¹¹Then I said, "Lord, how long?"
And He answered:

"Until the cities are laid waste and
  without inhabitant,
The houses are without a man,
The land is utterly desolate,
¹² The LORD has removed men far
  away,
And the forsaken places *are* many in
  the midst of the land.
¹³ But yet a tenth *will be* in it,
And will return and be for
  consuming,
As a terebinth tree or as an oak,
Whose stump *remains* when it is cut
  down.
So the holy seed *shall be* its stump."

Isaiah Sent to King Ahaz

7 Now it came to pass in the days of Ahaz the son of Jotham, the son of Uzziah, king of Judah, *that* Rezin king of Syria and Pekah the son of Remaliah, king of Israel, went up to Jerusalem to *make* war against it, but could not prevail against it. ²And it was told to the house of David, saying, "Syria's forces are deployed in Ephraim." So his heart and the heart of his people were moved as the trees of the woods are moved with the wind.

³Then the LORD said to Isaiah, "Go out now to meet Ahaz, you and Shear-Jashub[a] your son, at the end of the aqueduct from the upper pool, on the highway to the Fuller's Field, ⁴and say to him: 'Take heed, and be quiet; do not fear or be fainthearted for these two stubs of smoking firebrands, for the fierce anger of Rezin and Syria, and the son of Remaliah. ⁵Because Syria, Ephraim, and the son of Remaliah have plotted evil against you, saying, ⁶"Let us go up against Judah and trouble it, and let us make a gap in its wall for ourselves, and set a king over them, the son of Tabel"— ⁷thus says the Lord GOD:

"It shall not stand,
Nor shall it come to pass.
⁸ For the head of Syria *is* Damascus,

7:3 ªLiterally *A Remnant Shall Return*

You have increased the nation;
Behold, the king and someone
And the nations increased by the
People

BIBLICAL INSIGHTS • 6:8
Total Surrender

WHEN GOD CALLED OUT, "Whom shall I send, and who will go for Us?" (6:8), Isaiah had a clear choice to make. Would he remain committed to his own petty concerns, or would he submit himself totally to his Lord? The prophet made his choice when he replied, "Here am I! Send me."

Isaiah understood that God was the master and he was the servant. He knew that situation called for total surrender, without reservation. While many see this type of service as lowly—and it *is* humbling—we should consider it a privilege to serve such a loving Lord in every area of our lives ... including our marriages.

In 1972, the first year of our marriage, Barbara and I decided that before we would give anything to each other, we would surrender our lives, totally and completely, in writing, to Jesus Christ. We gave Him everything we ever dreamed of having. We offered it all up and handed over to Him the title deed to our lives. Today those two title deeds are among the most important papers we have.

That first Christmas together, Barbara sat down in our kitchen, and I went to our sparsely furnished living room and took a seat on the hand-me-down sofa. There we sat contemplating giving God all that we had and everything we hoped to have as a couple and as a family. She made her list. I made mine.

What we gave God was what we felt was most important on that day. I gave Him my desires for a successful ministry, nice furniture and things, plenty of money, staying healthy, and some nice ski equipment. Barbara's list was similar—a house with a fireplace and a bay window, children (at least one boy and one girl) who would honor God, her rights to be settled and stable.

Looking back, what we signed over to God on that day seems so trivial now compared to what He has given us. In many instances what He gave us was far more than we ever dreamed or imagined. I see that we gave Him what was already His: our lives. In return, He has given us "exceedingly abundantly above all that we ask or think" (Eph. 3:20). As human beings we mistakenly think that surrendering our lives to the God of the universe is the loss of our lives. In reality, total surrender to God brings not total defeat, but total victory!

And the head of Damascus *is* Rezin.
Within sixty-five years Ephraim will
    be broken,
So that it will not *be* a people.
9   The head of Ephraim *is* Samaria,
And the head of Samaria *is*
    Remaliah's son.
If you will not believe,
Surely you shall not be established."'"

The Immanuel Prophecy

¹⁰Moreover the LORD spoke again to Ahaz, saying, ¹¹"Ask a sign for yourself from the LORD your God; ask it either in the depth or in the height above."

¹²But Ahaz said, "I will not ask, nor will I test the LORD!"

¹³Then he said, "Hear now, O house of David! *Is it* a small thing for you to weary men, but will you weary my God also? ¹⁴Therefore the Lord Himself will give you a sign: Behold, the virgin shall conceive and bear a Son, and shall call His name Immanuel.ᵃ ¹⁵Curds and honey He shall eat, that He may know to refuse the evil and choose the good. ¹⁶For before the Child shall know to refuse the evil and choose the good, the land that you dread will be forsaken by both her kings. ¹⁷The LORD will bring the king of Assyria upon you and your people and your father's house—days that have not come since the day that Ephraim departed from Judah."

7:14 ᵃLiterally *God-With-Us*

18 And it shall come to pass in that day
   That the Lord will whistle for the fly
   That *is* in the farthest part of the
      rivers of Egypt,
   And for the bee that *is* in the land of
      Assyria.
19 They will come, and all of them will
      rest
   In the desolate valleys and in the
      clefts of the rocks,
   And on all thorns and in all pastures.

20 In the same day the Lord will shave
      with a hired razor,
   With those from beyond the River,[a]
      with the king of Assyria,
   The head and the hair of the legs,
   And will also remove the beard.

21 It shall be in that day
   That a man will keep alive a young
      cow and two sheep;
22 So it shall be, from the abundance of
      milk they give,
   That he will eat curds;
   For curds and honey everyone will
      eat who is left in the land.

23 It shall happen in that day,
   That wherever there could be a
      thousand vines
   Worth a thousand *shekels* of
      silver,
   It will be for briers and thorns.
24 With arrows and bows men will
      come there,
   Because all the land will become
      briers and thorns.

25 And to any hill which could be dug
      with the hoe,
   You will not go there for fear of
      briers and thorns;
   But it will become a range for oxen
   And a place for sheep to roam.

Assyria Will Invade the Land

8 Moreover the Lord said to me, "Take a
   large scroll, and write on it with a
man's pen concerning Maher-Shalal-Hash-
Baz.[a] 2And I will take for Myself faithful

witnesses to record, Uriah the priest and
Zechariah the son of Jeberechiah."
   3Then I went to the prophetess, and she
conceived and bore a son. Then the Lord
said to me, "Call his name Maher-Shalal-
Hash-Baz; 4for before the child shall have
knowledge to cry 'My father' and 'My mother,' the riches of Damascus and the spoil of
Samaria will be taken away before the
king of Assyria."
   5The Lord also spoke to me again, saying:

6 "Inasmuch as these people refused
      The waters of Shiloah that flow softly,
      And rejoice in Rezin and in
         Remaliah's son;
7 Now therefore, behold, the Lord
      brings up over them
   The waters of the River,[a] strong and
      mighty—
   The king of Assyria and all his glory;
   He will go up over all his channels
   And go over all his banks.
8 He will pass through Judah,
   He will overflow and pass over,
   He will reach up to the neck;
   And the stretching out of his wings
   Will fill the breadth of Your land, O
      Immanuel.[a]

9 "Be shattered, O you peoples, and be
      broken in pieces!
   Give ear, all you from far countries.
   Gird yourselves, but be broken in
      pieces;
   Gird yourselves, but be broken in
      pieces.
10 Take counsel together, but it will
      come to nothing;
   Speak the word, but it will not stand,
   For God *is* with us."[a]

Fear God, Heed His Word

11For the Lord spoke thus to me with a
strong hand, and instructed me that I
should not walk in the way of this people,
saying:

12 "Do not say, 'A conspiracy,'
   Concerning all that this people call a
      conspiracy,
   Nor be afraid of their threats, nor be
      troubled.

7:20 [a]That is, the Euphrates **8:1** [a]Literally *Speed the Spoil, Hasten the Booty* **8:7** [a]That is, the Euphrates **8:8** [a]Literally *God-With-Us* **8:10** [a]Hebrew *Immanuel*

The Right Kind of Fear

FEAR CAN PROMPT US TO DO all sorts of foolish and hurtful things. When you let it pile up in your marriage, it can cause an avalanche of trouble.

For example, how would you respond to your wife if you feared she didn't respect you, didn't love you, and thought you were a sorry excuse for a husband?

How would you respond to your husband if you feared he considered you little more than an old piece of luggage and didn't value you or your opinion?

How would you respond to your in-laws if you feared they thought of you as a poor choice of spouse?

Fears—most of them irrational—can creep into your home in a thousand ways. If that's the case for you, Isaiah has a good word for you, "The LORD of hosts, Him you shall hallow; let Him be your fear, and let Him be your dread" (8:13). When we truly fear the Lord, all other fears pale into nothingness. A healthy fear of God calms our nerves and helps us to see the universe as it truly is—safe and secure in His very competent hands. The fear of God can deliver you from the fear of man. And since the fear of the Lord is the beginning of wisdom (Ps. 111:10), no home can be built successfully without it.

13 The LORD of hosts, Him you shall
        hallow;
     Let Him *be* your fear,
     And *let* Him *be* your dread.
14 He will be as a sanctuary,
     But a stone of stumbling and a rock
        of offense
     To both the houses of Israel,
     As a trap and a snare to the
        inhabitants of Jerusalem.
15 And many among them shall
        stumble;
     They shall fall and be broken,
     Be snared and taken."

16 Bind up the testimony,
     Seal the law among my disciples.
17 And I will wait on the LORD,
     Who hides His face from the house
        of Jacob;
     And I will hope in Him.
18 Here am I and the children whom the
        LORD has given me!
     We are for signs and wonders in Israel
     From the LORD of hosts,
     Who dwells in Mount Zion.

19And when they say to you, "Seek those who are mediums and wizards, who whisper and mutter," should not a people seek their God? *Should they seek* the dead on behalf of the living? 20To the law and to the testimony! If they do not speak according to this word, *it is* because *there is* no light in them.

21They will pass through it hard-pressed and hungry; and it shall happen, when they are hungry, that they will be enraged and curse their king and their God, and look upward. 22Then they will look to the earth, and see trouble and darkness, gloom of anguish; and *they will be* driven into darkness.

The Government of the Promised Son

9 Nevertheless the gloom *will* not *be*
        upon her who *is* distressed,
     As when at first He lightly esteemed
     The land of Zebulun and the land of
        Naphtali,
     And afterward more heavily
        oppressed *her,*
     By the way of the sea, beyond the
        Jordan,
     In Galilee of the Gentiles.
2   The people who walked in
        darkness
     Have seen a great light;
     Those who dwelt in the land of the
        shadow of death,
     Upon them a light has shined.

3   You have multiplied the nation
     And increased its joy;ª
     They rejoice before You

9:3 ªFollowing Qere and Targum; Kethib and Vulgate read *not increased joy;* Septuagint reads *Most of the people You brought down in Your joy.*

According to the joy of harvest,
As *men* rejoice when they divide the
    spoil.
4 For You have broken the yoke of his
        burden
And the staff of his shoulder,
The rod of his oppressor,
As in the day of Midian.
5 For every warrior's sandal from the
        noisy battle,
And garments rolled in blood,
Will be used for burning *and* fuel of
    fire.

6 For unto us a Child is born,
Unto us a Son is given;
And the government will be upon
    His shoulder.
And His name will be called
Wonderful, Counselor, Mighty God,
Everlasting Father, Prince of Peace.
7 Of the increase of *His* government
        and peace
There will be no end,
Upon the throne of David and over
    His kingdom,
To order it and establish it with
    judgment and justice
From that time forward, even forever.
The zeal of the Lord of hosts will
    perform this.

The Punishment of Samaria

8 The Lord sent a word against Jacob,
And it has fallen on Israel.
9 All the people will know—
Ephraim and the inhabitant of
    Samaria—
Who say in pride and arrogance of
    heart:
10 "The bricks have fallen down,
But we will rebuild with hewn
    stones;
The sycamores are cut down,
But we will replace *them* with cedars."
11 Therefore the LORD shall set up
The adversaries of Rezin
        against him,
And spur his enemies on,
12 The Syrians before and the
        Philistines behind;
And they shall devour Israel with an
    open mouth.

For all this His anger is not turned
    away,
But His hand *is* stretched out still.

13 For the people do not turn to Him
        who strikes them,
Nor do they seek the LORD of hosts.
14 Therefore the LORD will cut off head
        and tail from Israel,
Palm branch and bulrush in one day.
15 The elder and honorable, he *is* the
        head;
The prophet who teaches lies, he *is*
        the tail.
16 For the leaders of this people cause
        them to err,
And *those who are* led by them are
    destroyed.
17 Therefore the Lord will have no joy
        in their young men,
Nor have mercy on their fatherless
    and widows;
For everyone *is* a hypocrite and an
    evildoer,
And every mouth speaks folly.

For all this His anger is not turned
    away,
But His hand *is* stretched out still.

18 For wickedness burns as the fire;
It shall devour the briers and thorns,
And kindle in the thickets of the
    forest;
They shall mount up *like* rising
    smoke.
19 Through the wrath of the LORD of
        hosts
The land is burned up,
And the people shall be as fuel for
    the fire;
No man shall spare his brother.
20 And he shall snatch on the right hand
And be hungry;
He shall devour on the left hand
And not be satisfied;
Every man shall eat the flesh of his
    own arm.
21 Manasseh *shall devour* Ephraim, and
        Ephraim Manasseh;
Together they *shall be* against Judah.

For all this His anger is not turned
    away,
But His hand *is* stretched out still.

10
"Woe to those who decree
unrighteous decrees,
Who write misfortune,
Which they have prescribed

2 To rob the needy of justice,
And to take what is right from the
poor of My people,
That widows may be their prey,
And *that* they may rob the fatherless.

3 What will you do in the day of
punishment,
And in the desolation *which* will
come from afar?
To whom will you flee for help?
And where will you leave your
glory?

4 Without Me they shall bow down
among the prisoners,
And they shall fall among the slain."

For all this His anger is not turned
away,
But His hand *is* stretched out still.

Arrogant Assyria Also Judged

5 "Woe to Assyria, the rod of My anger
And the staff in whose hand is My
indignation.

6 I will send him against an ungodly
nation,
And against the people of My wrath
I will give him charge,
To seize the spoil, to take the prey,
And to tread them down like the
mire of the streets.

7 Yet he does not mean so,
Nor does his heart think so;
But *it is* in his heart to destroy,
And cut off not a few nations.

8 For he says,
'*Are* not my princes altogether kings?

9 *Is* not Calno like Carchemish?
Is not Hamath like Arpad?
Is not Samaria like Damascus?

10 As my hand has found the kingdoms
of the idols,
Whose carved images excelled those
of Jerusalem and Samaria,

11 As I have done to Samaria and her
idols,
Shall I not do also to Jerusalem and
her idols?'"

12 Therefore it shall come to pass, when
the Lord has performed all His work on
Mount Zion and on Jerusalem, *that He will
say,* "I will punish the fruit of the arrogant
heart of the king of Assyria, and the glory
of his haughty looks."

13 For he says:

"By the strength of my hand I have
done *it,*
And by my wisdom, for I am
prudent;
Also I have removed the boundaries
of the people,
And have robbed their treasuries;
So I have put down the inhabitants
like a valiant *man.*

14 My hand has found like a nest the
riches of the people,
And as one gathers eggs *that are*
left,
I have gathered all the earth;
And there was no one who moved *his*
wing,
Nor opened *his* mouth with even a
peep."

15 Shall the ax boast itself against him
who chops with it?
Or shall the saw exalt itself against
him who saws with it?
As if a rod could wield *itself* against
those who lift it up,
Or as if a staff could lift up, *as if it
were* not wood!

16 Therefore the Lord, the Lord[a] of
hosts,
Will send leanness among his fat ones;
And under his glory
He will kindle a burning
Like the burning of a fire.

17 So the Light of Israel will be for a
fire,
And his Holy One for a flame;
It will burn and devour
His thorns and his briers in one day.

18 And it will consume the glory of his
forest and of his fruitful field,
Both soul and body;
And they will be as when a sick man
wastes away.

10:16 [a]Following Bomberg; Masoretic Text and Dead
Sea Scrolls read *YHWH* (*the* Lord).

19 Then the rest of the trees of his forest
Will be so few in number
That a child may write them.

The Returning Remnant of Israel

20 And it shall come to pass in that day
That the remnant of Israel,
And such as have escaped of the
house of Jacob,
Will never again depend on him who
defeated them,
But will depend on the LORD, the
Holy One of Israel, in truth.
21 The remnant will return, the
remnant of Jacob,
To the Mighty God.
22 For though your people, O Israel, be
as the sand of the sea,
A remnant of them will return;
The destruction decreed shall
overflow with righteousness.
23 For the Lord GOD of hosts
Will make a determined end
In the midst of all the land.

24Therefore thus says the Lord GOD of hosts: "O My people, who dwell in Zion, do not be afraid of the Assyrian. He shall strike you with a rod and lift up his staff against you, in the manner of Egypt. 25For yet a very little while and the indignation will cease, as will My anger in their destruction." 26And the LORD of hosts will stir up a scourge for him like the slaughter of Midian at the rock of Oreb; *as* His rod was on the sea, so will He lift it up in the manner of Egypt.

27 It shall come to pass in that day
That his burden will be taken away
from your shoulder,
And his yoke from your neck,
And the yoke will be destroyed
because of the anointing oil.
28 He has come to Aiath,
He has passed Migron;
At Michmash he has attended to his
equipment.
29 They have gone along the ridge,
They have taken up lodging at Geba.
Ramah is afraid,

Gibeah of Saul has fled.
30 Lift up your voice,
O daughter of Gallim!
Cause it to be heard as far as Laish—
O poor Anathoth![a]
31 Madmenah has fled,
The inhabitants of Gebim seek
refuge.
32 As yet he will remain at Nob that day;
He will shake his fist at the mount of
the daughter of Zion,
The hill of Jerusalem.

33 Behold, the Lord,
The LORD of hosts,
Will lop off the bough with terror;
Those of high stature *will be* hewn
down,
And the haughty will be humbled.
34 He will cut down the thickets of the
forest with iron,
And Lebanon will fall by the Mighty
One.

The Reign of Jesse's Offspring

11 There shall come forth a Rod from
the stem of Jesse,
And a Branch shall grow out of his
roots.
2 The Spirit of the LORD shall rest
upon Him,
The Spirit of wisdom and
understanding,
The Spirit of counsel and might,
The Spirit of knowledge and of the
fear of the LORD.

3 His delight *is* in the fear of the LORD,
And He shall not judge by the sight
of His eyes,
Nor decide by the hearing of His
ears;
4 But with righteousness He shall
judge the poor,
And decide with equity for the meek
of the earth;
He shall strike the earth with the rod
of His mouth,
And with the breath of His lips He
shall slay the wicked.
5 Righteousness shall be the belt of
His loins,
And faithfulness the belt of His
waist.

10:30 [a]Following Masoretic Text, Targum, and Vulgate; Septuagint and Syriac read *Listen to her, O Anathoth.*

6 "The wolf also shall dwell with the
    lamb,
  The leopard shall lie down with the
    young goat,
  The calf and the young lion and the
    fatling together;
  And a little child shall lead them.
7 The cow and the bear shall graze;
  Their young ones shall lie down
    together;
  And the lion shall eat straw like the
    ox.
8 The nursing child shall play by the
    cobra's hole,
  And the weaned child shall put his
    hand in the viper's den.
9 They shall not hurt nor destroy in all
    My holy mountain,
  For the earth shall be full of the
    knowledge of the LORD
  As the waters cover the sea.

10 "And in that day there shall be a Root
    of Jesse,
  Who shall stand as a banner to the
    people;
  For the Gentiles shall seek Him,
  And His resting place shall be
    glorious."

11 It shall come to pass in that day

That the Lord shall set His hand
  again the second time
To recover the remnant of His people
  who are left,
From Assyria and Egypt,
From Pathros and Cush,
From Elam and Shinar,
From Hamath and the islands of the
  sea.
12 He will set up a banner for the nations,
  And will assemble the outcasts of
    Israel,
  And gather together the dispersed of
    Judah
  From the four corners of the earth.
13 Also the envy of Ephraim shall
    depart,
  And the adversaries of Judah shall
    be cut off;
  Ephraim shall not envy Judah,
  And Judah shall not harass Ephraim.
14 But they shall fly down upon the
    shoulder of the Philistines toward
    the west;
  Together they shall plunder the
    people of the East;
  They shall lay their hand on Edom
    and Moab;
  And the people of Ammon shall
    obey them.

PARENTING MATTERS

Q: *How can I best create a loving relationship between brothers who are three years apart in age?*

We had to work really hard on this with our two boys. When they were young, their interests were different, their personalities were different, they looked different, they acted different in school. One thing they did have in common, however, was that both were very competitive, so they tended to butt heads!

Before our oldest left for college, our boys developed a common interest: hunting with Dennis. It was something they shared without competing. That helped to forge their friendship.

I also tried to cast a vision for our boys. I've reminded them, "Someday you are both going to be grown. You will always be brothers. You may not always have these other guys as friends, but you will always have each other. You can choose to be friends or you can choose to be enemies. You can choose to try to be kind to one another, or you can choose to be mean, tacky, and ugly."

I know they didn't fully see the big picture at the time, but I have seen them grow closer as they've become adults. You may think your children will never get along, but keep planting good seeds and let the Lord work in their heart.

15 The LORD will utterly destroy[a] the
   tongue of the Sea of Egypt;
   With His mighty wind He will shake
   His fist over the River,[b]
   And strike it in the seven streams,
   And make *men* cross over dryshod.
16 There will be a highway for the
   remnant of His people
   Who will be left from Assyria,
   As it was for Israel
   In the day that he came up from the
   land of Egypt.

A Hymn of Praise

12 And in that day you will say:

   "O LORD, I will praise You;
   Though You were angry with me,
   Your anger is turned away, and You
   comfort me.
2 Behold, God *is* my salvation,
   I will trust and not be afraid;
   'For YAH, the LORD, *is* my strength
   and song;
   He also has become my salvation.'"[a]

3 Therefore with joy you will draw
   water
   From the wells of salvation.

4 And in that day you will say:

   "Praise the LORD, call upon His name;
   Declare His deeds among the peoples,
   Make mention that His name is
   exalted.
5 Sing to the LORD,
   For He has done excellent things;
   This *is* known in all the earth.
6 Cry out and shout, O inhabitant of
   Zion,
   For great *is* the Holy One of Israel in
   your midst!"

Proclamation Against Babylon

13 The burden against Babylon which
   Isaiah the son of Amoz saw.
2 "Lift up a banner on the high
   mountain,
   Raise your voice to them;

   Wave your hand, that they may enter
   the gates of the nobles.
3 I have commanded My sanctified
   ones;
   I have also called My mighty ones
   for My anger—
   Those who rejoice in My exaltation."

4 The noise of a multitude in the
   mountains,
   Like that of many people!
   A tumultuous noise of the kingdoms
   of nations gathered together!
   The LORD of hosts musters
   The army for battle.
5 They come from a far country,
   From the end of heaven—
   The LORD and His weapons of
   indignation,
   To destroy the whole land.

6 Wail, for the day of the LORD *is* at
   hand!
   It will come as destruction from the
   Almighty.
7 Therefore all hands will be limp,
   Every man's heart will melt,
8 And they will be afraid.
   Pangs and sorrows will take hold of
   them;
   They will be in pain as a woman in
   childbirth;
   They will be amazed at one another;
   Their faces *will be like* flames.

9 Behold, the day of the LORD comes,
   Cruel, with both wrath and fierce
   anger,
   To lay the land desolate;
   And He will destroy its sinners
   from it.
10 For the stars of heaven and their
   constellations
   Will not give their light;
   The sun will be darkened in its going
   forth,
   And the moon will not cause its light
   to shine.

11 "I will punish the world for *its* evil,
   And the wicked for their iniquity;
   I will halt the arrogance of the
   proud,
   And will lay low the haughtiness of
   the terrible.

11:15 [a]Following Masoretic Text and Vulgate;
Septuagint, Syriac, and Targum read *dry up.* [b]That
is, the Euphrates **12:2** [a]Exodus 15:2

12 I will make a mortal more rare than
    fine gold,
A man more than the golden wedge
    of Ophir.
13 Therefore I will shake the heavens,
And the earth will move out of her
    place,
In the wrath of the LORD of hosts
And in the day of His fierce anger.
14 It shall be as the hunted gazelle,
And as a sheep that no man takes up;
Every man will turn to his own
    people,
And everyone will flee to his own
    land.
15 Everyone who is found will be thrust
    through,
And everyone who is captured will
    fall by the sword.
16 Their children also will be dashed to
    pieces before their eyes;
Their houses will be plundered
And their wives ravished.

**INTIMATE
MOMENTS**

Offer to wash his car or clean out his
closet.

17 "Behold, I will stir up the Medes
    against them,
Who will not regard silver;
And as for gold, they will not delight
    in it.
18 Also their bows will dash the young
    men to pieces,
And they will have no pity on the
    fruit of the womb;
Their eye will not spare children.
19 And Babylon, the glory of kingdoms,
The beauty of the Chaldeans' pride,
Will be as when God overthrew
    Sodom and Gomorrah.
20 It will never be inhabited,
Nor will it be settled from generation
    to generation;
Nor will the Arabian pitch tents
    there,

Nor will the shepherds make their
    sheepfolds there.
21 But wild beasts of the desert will lie
    there,
And their houses will be full of owls;
Ostriches will dwell there,
And wild goats will caper there.
22 The hyenas will howl in their
    citadels,
And jackals in their pleasant palaces.
Her time is near to come,
And her days will not be prolonged."

Mercy on Jacob

14 For the LORD will have mercy on
Jacob, and will still choose Israel,
and settle them in their own land. The
strangers will be joined with them, and
they will cling to the house of Jacob. 2Then
people will take them and bring them to
their place, and the house of Israel will
possess them for servants and maids in
the land of the LORD; they will take them
captive whose captives they were, and rule
over their oppressors.

Fall of the King of Babylon

3It shall come to pass in the day the
LORD gives you rest from your sorrow, and
from your fear and the hard bondage in
which you were made to serve, 4that you
will take up this proverb against the king
of Babylon, and say:

"How the oppressor has ceased,
    The goldena city ceased!
5 The LORD has broken the staff of the
    wicked,
The scepter of the rulers;
6 He who struck the people in wrath
    with a continual stroke,
He who ruled the nations in anger,
Is persecuted and no one hinders.
7 The whole earth is at rest and quiet;
They break forth into singing.
8 Indeed the cypress trees rejoice over
    you,
And the cedars of Lebanon,
Saying, 'Since you were cut down,
No woodsman has come up against
    us.'

14:4 aOr insolent

9 "Hell from beneath is excited about
   you,
　To meet *you* at your coming;
　It stirs up the dead for you,
　All the chief ones of the earth;
　It has raised up from their thrones
　All the kings of the nations.
10 They all shall speak and say to you:
　' Have you also become as weak as we?
　Have you become like us?
11 Your pomp is brought down to Sheol,
　And the sound of your stringed
　　instruments;
　The maggot is spread under you,
　And worms cover you.'

The Fall of Lucifer

12 "How you are fallen from heaven,
　O Lucifer,[a] son of the morning!
　How you are cut down to the ground,
　You who weakened the nations!
13 For you have said in your heart:
　'I will ascend into heaven,
　I will exalt my throne above the stars
　　of God;
　I will also sit on the mount of the
　　congregation
　On the farthest sides of the north;
14 I will ascend above the heights of the
　　clouds,
　I will be like the Most High.'
15 Yet you shall be brought down to
　　Sheol,
　To the lowest depths of the Pit.

16 "Those who see you will gaze at you,
　And consider you, *saying:*
　'*Is* this the man who made the earth
　　tremble,
　Who shook kingdoms,
17 Who made the world as a wilderness
　And destroyed its cities,
　Who did not open the house of his
　　prisoners?'

18 "All the kings of the nations,
　All of them, sleep in glory,
　Everyone in his own house;
19 But you are cast out of your grave
　Like an abominable branch,
　Like the garment of those who are
　　slain,

Thrust through with a sword,
Who go down to the stones of the pit,
Like a corpse trodden underfoot.
20 You will not be joined with them in
　　burial,
　Because you have destroyed your land
　And slain your people.
　The brood of evildoers shall never be
　　named.
21 Prepare slaughter for his children
　Because of the iniquity of their
　　fathers,
　Lest they rise up and possess the
　　land,
　And fill the face of the world with
　　cities."

Babylon Destroyed

22 "For I will rise up against them," says
　　the Lord of hosts,
　"And cut off from Babylon the name
　　and remnant,
　And offspring and posterity," says
　　the Lord.
23 "I will also make it a possession for
　　the porcupine,
　And marshes of muddy water;
　I will sweep it with the broom of
　　destruction," says the Lord of
　　hosts.

Assyria Destroyed

24 The Lord of hosts has sworn, saying,
　"Surely, as I have thought, so it shall
　　come to pass,
　And as I have purposed, *so* it shall
　　stand:
25 That I will break the Assyrian in My
　　land,
　And on My mountains tread him
　　underfoot.
　Then his yoke shall be removed from
　　them,
　And his burden removed from their
　　shoulders.
26 This *is* the purpose that is purposed
　　against the whole earth,
　And this *is* the hand that is stretched
　　out over all the nations.
27 For the Lord of hosts has purposed,
　And who will annul *it?*
　His hand *is* stretched out,
　And who will turn it back?"

14:12 [a]Literally *Day Star*

Philistia Destroyed

[28]This is the burden which came in the year that King Ahaz died.

[29] "Do not rejoice, all you of Philistia,
      Because the rod that struck you is
          broken;
      For out of the serpent's roots will
          come forth a viper,
      And its offspring *will be* a fiery
          flying serpent.
[30] The firstborn of the poor will feed,
      And the needy will lie down in safety;
      I will kill your roots with famine,
      And it will slay your remnant.
[31] Wail, O gate! Cry, O city!
      All you of Philistia *are* dissolved;
      For smoke will come from the north,
      And no one *will be* alone in his
          appointed times."

[32] What will they answer the
          messengers of the nation?
      That the LORD has founded Zion,

ROMANCE FAQ

**Q: *How can I best
respect my husband?***

When you respect your husband—something that God commands wives to do in Ephesians 5:33— you notice him, regard him, honor him, prefer him, and esteem him. Respecting him means valuing his opinion, admiring his wisdom and character, appreciating his commitment to you, and considering his values and needs— and our husbands have many needs!

I believe that meeting these needs is what respecting your husband is all about. To bolster Dennis's confidence, for example, I try to be his number one fan. Every husband wants his wife to be on his team, to coach him when necessary— but most of all, to be his cheerleader. The macho man who is self-contained, independent, and invulnerable is a myth. Your husband needs a wife who is behind him, believing in him, appreciating him, and cheering him on as he goes out into the world every day.

And the poor of His people shall
    take refuge in it.

Proclamation Against Moab

15 The burden against Moab.

      Because in the night Ar of Moab is
          laid waste
      And destroyed,
      Because in the night Kir of Moab is
          laid waste
      And destroyed,
[2]   He has gone up to the temple[a] and
          Dibon,
      To the high places to weep.
      Moab will wail over Nebo and over
          Medeba;
      On all their heads *will be* baldness,
      And every beard cut off.
[3]   In their streets they will clothe
          themselves with sackcloth;
      On the tops of their houses
      And in their streets
      Everyone will wail, weeping bitterly.
[4]   Heshbon and Elealeh will cry out,
      Their voice shall be heard as far as
          Jahaz;
      Therefore the armed soldiers[a] of
          Moab will cry out;
      His life will be burdensome to him.

[5]   "My heart will cry out for Moab;
      His fugitives *shall flee* to Zoar,
      Like a three-year-old heifer.[a]
      For by the Ascent of Luhith
      They will go up with weeping;
      For in the way of Horonaim
      They will raise up a cry of
          destruction,
[6]   For the waters of Nimrim will be
          desolate,
      For the green grass has withered
          away;
      The grass fails, there is nothing green.
[7]   Therefore the abundance they have
          gained,
      And what they have laid up,
      They will carry away to the Brook of
          the Willows.

15:2 [a]Hebrew *bayith,* literally *house*
15:4 [a]Following Masoretic Text, Targum, and Vulgate; Septuagint and Syriac read *loins.*
15:5 [a]Or *The Third Eglath,* an unknown city (compare Jeremiah 48:34)

8 For the cry has gone all around the
        borders of Moab,
    Its wailing to Eglaim
    And its wailing to Beer Elim.
9 For the waters of Dimon[a] will be full
        of blood;
    Because I will bring more upon
        Dimon,[a]
    Lions upon him who escapes from
        Moab,
    And on the remnant of the land."

Moab Destroyed

16 Send the lamb to the ruler of the
        land,
    From Sela to the wilderness,
    To the mount of the daughter of Zion.
2 For it shall be as a wandering bird
        thrown out of the nest;
    So shall be the daughters of Moab at
        the fords of the Arnon.

3 "Take counsel, execute judgment;
    Make your shadow like the night in
        the middle of the day;
    Hide the outcasts,
    Do not betray him who escapes.
4 Let My outcasts dwell with you, O
        Moab;
    Be a shelter to them from the face of
        the spoiler.
    For the extortioner is at an end,
    Devastation ceases,
    The oppressors are consumed out of
        the land.
5 In mercy the throne will be
        established;
    And One will sit on it in truth, in the
        tabernacle of David,
    Judging and seeking justice and
        hastening righteousness."

6 We have heard of the pride of Moab—
    He is very proud—
    Of his haughtiness and his pride and
        his wrath;
    But his lies *shall* not *be* so.
7 Therefore Moab shall wail for Moab;
    Everyone shall wail.

For the foundations of Kir Hareseth
    you shall mourn;
Surely *they are* stricken.

8 For the fields of Heshbon languish,
    And the vine of Sibmah;
    The lords of the nations have broken
        down its choice plants,
    Which have reached to Jazer
    And wandered through the
        wilderness.
    Her branches are stretched out,
    They are gone over the sea.
9 Therefore I will bewail the vine of
        Sibmah,
    With the weeping of Jazer;
    I will drench you with my tears,
    O Heshbon and Elealeh;
    For battle cries have fallen
    Over your summer fruits and your
        harvest.

10 Gladness is taken away,
    And joy from the plentiful field;
    In the vineyards there will be no
        singing,
    Nor will there be shouting;
    No treaders will tread out wine in the
        presses;
    I have made their shouting cease.
11 Therefore my heart shall resound
        like a harp for Moab,
    And my inner being for Kir Heres.

12 And it shall come to pass,
    When it is seen that Moab is weary
        on the high place,
    That he will come to his sanctuary to
        pray;
    But he will not prevail.

13 This *is* the word which the LORD has
spoken concerning Moab since that time.
14 But now the LORD has spoken, saying,
"Within three years, as the years of a hired
man, the glory of Moab will be despised
with all that great multitude, and the remnant *will be* very small *and* feeble."

Proclamation Against Syria and Israel

17 The burden against Damascus.

    "Behold, Damascus will cease from
        being a city,
    And it will be a ruinous heap.

15:9 [a]Following Masoretic Text and Targum; Dead
Sea Scrolls and Vulgate read *Dibon;* Septuagint reads
Rimon. [b]Following Masoretic Text and Targum; Dead
Sea Scrolls and Vulgate read *Dibon;* Septuagint reads
Rimon.

2 The cities of Aroer *are* forsaken;[a]
They will be for flocks
Which lie down, and no one will
 make *them* afraid.
3 The fortress also will cease from
 Ephraim,
The kingdom from Damascus,
And the remnant of Syria;
They will be as the glory of the
 children of Israel,"
Says the LORD of hosts.

4 "In that day it shall come to pass
That the glory of Jacob will wane,
And the fatness of his flesh grow
 lean.
5 It shall be as when the harvester
 gathers the grain,
And reaps the heads with his arm;
It shall be as he who gathers heads
 of grain
In the Valley of Rephaim.
6 Yet gleaning grapes will be left in it,
Like the shaking of an olive tree,
Two *or* three olives at the top of the
 uppermost bough,
Four *or* five in its most fruitful
 branches,"
Says the LORD God of Israel.

7 In that day a man will look to his
 Maker,
And his eyes will have respect for
 the Holy One of Israel.
8 He will not look to the altars,
The work of his hands;
He will not respect what his fingers
 have made,
Nor the wooden images[a] nor the
 incense altars.

9 In that day his strong cities will be
 as a forsaken bough[a]
And an uppermost branch,[b]
Which they left because of the
 children of Israel;
And there will be desolation.

10 Because you have forgotten the God
 of your salvation,
And have not been mindful of the
 Rock of your stronghold,
Therefore you will plant pleasant
 plants
And set out foreign seedlings;

11 In the day you will make your plant
 to grow,
And in the morning you will make
 your seed to flourish;
But the harvest *will be* a heap of ruins
In the day of grief and desperate
 sorrow.

12 Woe to the multitude of many people
Who make a noise like the roar of
 the seas,
And to the rushing of nations
That make a rushing like the
 rushing of mighty waters!
13 The nations will rush like the
 rushing of many waters;
But *God* will rebuke them and they
 will flee far away,
And be chased like the chaff of the
 mountains before the wind,
Like a rolling thing before the
 whirlwind.
14 Then behold, at eventide, trouble!
And before the morning, he *is* no
 more.
This *is* the portion of those who
 plunder us,
And the lot of those who rob us.

Proclamation Against Ethiopia

18 Woe to the land shadowed with
 buzzing wings,
Which *is* beyond the rivers of
 Ethiopia,
2 Which sends ambassadors by sea,
Even in vessels of reed on the
 waters, *saying,*
"Go, swift messengers, to a nation tall
 and smooth *of skin,*
To a people terrible from their
 beginning onward,
A nation powerful and treading
 down,
Whose land the rivers divide."

3 All inhabitants of the world and
 dwellers on the earth:

17:2 [a]Following Masoretic Text and Vulgate;
Septuagint reads *It shall be forsaken forever;* Targum
reads *Its cities shall be forsaken and desolate.*
17:8 [a]Hebrew *Asherim,* Canaanite deities
17:9 [a]Septuagint reads *Hivites;* Targum reads *laid
waste;* Vulgate reads *as the plows.* [b]Septuagint reads
Amorites; Targum reads *in ruins;* Vulgate reads *corn.*

When he lifts up a banner on the
mountains, you see *it;*
And when he blows a trumpet, you
hear *it.*
4 For so the LORD said to me,
"I will take My rest,
And I will look from My dwelling
place
Like clear heat in sunshine,
Like a cloud of dew in the heat of
harvest."
5 For before the harvest, when the bud
is perfect
And the sour grape is ripening in the
flower,
He will both cut off the sprigs with
pruning hooks
And take away *and* cut down the
branches.
6 They will be left together for the
mountain birds of prey
And for the beasts of the earth;
The birds of prey will summer on
them,
And all the beasts of the earth will
winter on them.

7 In that time a present will be brought
to the LORD of hosts
From[a] a people tall and smooth *of
skin,*
And from a people terrible from their
beginning onward,
A nation powerful and treading down,
Whose land the rivers divide—
To the place of the name of the LORD
of hosts,
To Mount Zion.

Proclamation Against Egypt

19 The burden against Egypt.

Behold, the LORD rides on a swift
cloud,
And will come into Egypt;
The idols of Egypt will totter at His
presence,
And the heart of Egypt will melt in
its midst.

2 "I will set Egyptians against Egyptians;
Everyone will fight against his
brother,
And everyone against his neighbor,
City against city, kingdom against
kingdom.
3 The spirit of Egypt will fail in its
midst;
I will destroy their counsel,
And they will consult the idols and
the charmers,
The mediums and the sorcerers.
4 And the Egyptians I will give
Into the hand of a cruel master,
And a fierce king will rule over
them,"
Says the Lord, the LORD of hosts.

5 The waters will fail from the sea,
And the river will be wasted and
dried up.
6 The rivers will turn foul;
The brooks of defense will be
emptied and dried up;
The reeds and rushes will wither.
7 The papyrus reeds by the River,[a] by
the mouth of the River,
And everything sown by the River,
Will wither, be driven away, and be
no more.
8 The fishermen also will mourn;
All those will lament who cast hooks
into the River,
And they will languish who spread
nets on the waters.
9 Moreover those who work in fine flax
And those who weave fine fabric will
be ashamed;
10 And its foundations will be broken.
All who make wages *will be* troubled
of soul.

11 Surely the princes of Zoan *are* fools;
Pharaoh's wise counselors give
foolish counsel.
How do you say to Pharaoh, "I *am*
the son of the wise,
The son of ancient kings?"
12 Where *are* they?
Where are your wise men?
Let them tell you now,
And let them know what the LORD of
hosts has purposed against
Egypt.

18:7 [a]Following Dead Sea Scrolls, Septuagint, and
Vulgate; Masoretic Text omits *From;* Targum
reads *To.*   19:7 [a]That is, the Nile

13 The princes of Zoan have become
        fools;
    The princes of Noph[a] are deceived;
    They have also deluded Egypt,
    Those who are the mainstay of its
        tribes.
14 The LORD has mingled a perverse
        spirit in her midst;
    And they have caused Egypt to err
        in all her work,
    As a drunken man staggers in his
        vomit.
15 Neither will there be *any* work for
        Egypt,
    Which the head or tail,
    Palm branch or bulrush, may do.[a]

16In that day Egypt will be like women, and will be afraid and fear because of the waving of the hand of the LORD of hosts, which He waves over it. 17And the land of Judah will be a terror to Egypt; everyone who makes mention of it will be afraid in himself, because of the counsel of the LORD of hosts which He has determined against it.

Egypt, Assyria, and Israel Blessed

18In that day five cities in the land of Egypt will speak the language of Canaan and swear by the LORD of hosts; one will be called the City of Destruction.[a]

19In that day there will be an altar to the LORD in the midst of the land of Egypt, and a pillar to the LORD at its border. 20And it will be for a sign and for a witness to the LORD of hosts in the land of Egypt; for they will cry to the LORD because of the oppressors, and He will send them a Savior and a Mighty One, and He will deliver them. 21Then the LORD will be known to Egypt, and the Egyptians will know the LORD in that day, and will make sacrifice and offering; yes, they will make a vow to the LORD and perform *it.* 22And the LORD will strike Egypt, He will strike and heal *it;* they will return to the LORD, and He will be entreated by them and heal them.

23In that day there will be a highway from Egypt to Assyria, and the Assyrian will come into Egypt and the Egyptian into Assyria, and the Egyptians will serve with the Assyrians.

24In that day Israel will be one of three with Egypt and Assyria—a blessing in the midst of the land, 25whom the LORD of hosts shall bless, saying, "Blessed *is* Egypt My people, and Assyria the work of My hands, and Israel My inheritance."

The Sign Against Egypt and Ethiopia

20 In the year that Tartan[a] came to Ashdod, when Sargon the king of Assyria sent him, and he fought against Ashdod and took it, 2at the same time the LORD spoke by Isaiah the son of Amoz, saying, "Go, and remove the sackcloth from your body, and take your sandals off your feet." And he did so, walking naked and barefoot.

3Then the LORD said, "Just as My servant Isaiah has walked naked and barefoot three years *for* a sign and a wonder against Egypt and Ethiopia, 4so shall the king of Assyria lead away the Egyptians as prisoners and the Ethiopians as captives, young and old, naked and barefoot, with their buttocks uncovered, to the shame of Egypt. 5Then they shall be afraid and ashamed of Ethiopia their expectation and Egypt their glory. 6And the inhabitant of this territory will say in that day, 'Surely such *is* our expectation, wherever we flee for help to be delivered from the king of Assyria; and how shall we escape?'"

The Fall of Babylon Proclaimed

21 The burden against the Wilderness of the Sea.

    As whirlwinds in the South pass
        through,
    So it comes from the desert, from a
        terrible land.
2   A distressing vision is declared to me;
    The treacherous dealer deals
        treacherously,
    And the plunderer plunders.
    Go up, O Elam!
    Besiege, O Media!

19:13 [a]That is, ancient Memphis
19:15 [a]Compare Isaiah 9:14–16
19:18 [a]Some Hebrew manuscripts, Arabic, Dead Sea Scrolls, Targum, and Vulgate read *Sun;* Septuagint reads *Asedek* (literally *Righteousness*).
20:1 [a]Or *the Commander in Chief*

All its sighing I have made to cease.

3 Therefore my loins are filled with pain;
Pangs have taken hold of me, like
the pangs of a woman in labor.
I was distressed when *I* heard *it;*
I was dismayed when *I* saw *it.*
4 My heart wavered, fearfulness
frightened me;
The night for which I longed He
turned into fear for me.
5 Prepare the table,
Set a watchman in the tower,
Eat and drink.
Arise, you princes,
Anoint the shield!

6 For thus has the Lord said to me:
"Go, set a watchman,
Let him declare what he sees."
7 And he saw a chariot *with* a pair of
horsemen,
A chariot of donkeys, *and* a chariot
of camels,
And he listened earnestly with great
care.
8 Then he cried, "A lion,[a] my Lord!
I stand continually on the
watchtower in the daytime;
I have sat at my post every night.
9 And look, here comes a chariot of
men *with* a pair of horsemen!"

Then he answered and said,
"Babylon is fallen, is fallen!
And all the carved images of her
gods
He has broken to the ground."

10 Oh, my threshing and the grain of
my floor!
That which I have heard from the
LORD of hosts,
The God of Israel,
I have declared to you.

Proclamation Against Edom

11 The burden against Dumah.

He calls to me out of Seir,
"Watchman, what of the night?
Watchman, what of the night?"
12 The watchman said,
"The morning comes, and also the
night.
If you will inquire, inquire;
Return! Come back!"

Proclamation Against Arabia

13 The burden against Arabia.

In the forest in Arabia you will lodge,
O you traveling companies of
Dedanites.
14 O inhabitants of the land of Tema,
Bring water to him who is thirsty;
With their bread they met him who
fled.

21:8 [a]Dead Sea Scrolls read *Then the observer cried.*

PARENTING MATTERS

Q: *When is it appropriate to stop bathing my son and daughter together?*

Bath time is a good time for kids to play together. Usually they like to play with soap bubbles and bath toys and have fun while getting clean. While they are still little, I would allow them to bathe together as long as they feel comfortable doing it.

As they get to be around four or five, however, one of the children will probably begin to feel a sense of personal modesty and will want to have some privacy. Respect that child's development and give him that privacy.

Your child will tell you when it is inappropriate for him to be bathing with his brother or sister, and he'll tell you when he feels uncomfortable with you in the bathroom while he bathes. At that point, affirm the child and respect his modesty. I wouldn't worry much about a lack of modesty in children before they reach age eight or nine. At that point, though, a child is approaching pre-adolescence and needs to start practicing modesty.

15 For they fled from the swords, from
the drawn sword,
From the bent bow, and from the
distress of war.

16For thus the LORD has said to me:
"Within a year, according to the year of a
hired man, all the glory of Kedar will fail;
17and the remainder of the number of
archers, the mighty men of the people of
Kedar, will be diminished; for the LORD
God of Israel has spoken *it*."

Proclamation Against Jerusalem

22 The burden against the Valley of
Vision.

What ails you now, that you have all
gone up to the housetops,
2 You who are full of noise,
A tumultuous city, a joyous city?
Your slain *men are* not slain with the
sword,
Nor dead in battle.
3 All your rulers have fled together;
They are captured by the archers.
All who are found in you are bound
together;
They have fled from afar.
4 Therefore I said, "Look away from me,
I will weep bitterly;
Do not labor to comfort me
Because of the plundering of the
daughter of my people."

5 For *it is* a day of trouble and
treading down and perplexity
By the Lord GOD of hosts
In the Valley of Vision—
Breaking down the walls
And of crying to the mountain.
6 Elam bore the quiver
With chariots of men *and* horsemen,
And Kir uncovered the shield.
7 It shall come to pass *that* your
choicest valleys
Shall be full of chariots,
And the horsemen shall set
themselves in array at the gate.

8 He removed the protection of Judah.
You looked in that day to the armor
of the House of the Forest;
9 You also saw the damage to the city
of David,

That it was great;
And you gathered together the
waters of the lower pool.
10 You numbered the houses of
Jerusalem,
And the houses you broke down
To fortify the wall.
11 You also made a reservoir between
the two walls
For the water of the old pool.
But you did not look to its
Maker,
Nor did you have respect for Him
who fashioned it long ago.

12 And in that day the Lord GOD of
hosts
Called for weeping and for
mourning,
For baldness and for girding with
sackcloth.
13 But instead, joy and gladness,
Slaying oxen and killing sheep,
Eating meat and drinking wine:
"Let us eat and drink, for tomorrow
we die!"

14 Then it was revealed in my hearing
by the LORD of hosts,
"Surely for this iniquity there will be
no atonement for you,
Even to your death," says the Lord
GOD of hosts.

The Judgment on Shebna

15Thus says the Lord GOD of hosts:

"Go, proceed to this steward,
To Shebna, who *is* over the house,
and say:
16 'What have you here, and whom have
you here,
That you have hewn a sepulcher
here,
As he who hews himself a sepulcher
on high,
Who carves a tomb for himself in a
rock?
17 Indeed, the LORD will throw you
away violently,
O mighty man,
And will surely seize you.
18 He will surely turn violently and toss
you like a ball

Into a large country;
There you shall die, and there your
    glorious chariots
Shall be the shame of your master's
    house.
19 So I will drive you out of your office,
And from your position he will pull
    you down.ᵃ

20 'Then it shall be in that day,
That I will call My servant Eliakim
    the son of Hilkiah;
21 I will clothe him with your robe
And strengthen him with your belt;
I will commit your responsibility into
    his hand.
He shall be a father to the
    inhabitants of Jerusalem
And to the house of Judah.
22 The key of the house of David
I will lay on his shoulder;
So he shall open, and no one shall shut;
And he shall shut, and no one shall
    open.
23 I will fasten him *as* a peg in a secure
    place,
And he will become a glorious throne
    to his father's house.

24'They will hang on him all the glory of his father's house, the offspring and the posterity, all vessels of small quantity, from the cups to all the pitchers. 25In that day,' says the LORD of hosts, 'the peg that is fastened in the secure place will be removed and be cut down and fall, and the burden that *was* on it will be cut off; for the LORD has spoken.'"

Proclamation Against Tyre

23 The burden against Tyre.

Wail, you ships of Tarshish!
For it is laid waste,
So that there is no house, no harbor;
From the land of Cyprusᵃ it is
    revealed to them.

2 Be still, you inhabitants of the
    coastland,
You merchants of Sidon,
Whom those who cross the sea have
    filled.ᵃ
3 And on great waters the grain of
    Shihor,
The harvest of the River,ᵃ *is* her
    revenue;
And she is a marketplace for the
    nations.

4 Be ashamed, O Sidon;
For the sea has spoken,
The strength of the sea, saying,
"I do not labor, nor bring forth
    children;
Neither do I rear young men,
Nor bring up virgins."
5 When the report *reaches* Egypt,
They also will be in agony at the
    report of Tyre.

INTIMATE MOMENTS

Women view romance differently from men. Ask your wife to describe what's romantic to her. Don't be surprised when her ideas sound very different from yours.

6 Cross over to Tarshish;
Wail, you inhabitants of the
    coastland!
7 *Is* this your joyous *city,*
Whose antiquity *is* from ancient
    days,
Whose feet carried her far off to
    dwell?
8 Who has taken this counsel against
    Tyre, the crowning *city,*
Whose merchants *are* princes,
Whose traders *are* the honorable of
    the earth?
9 The LORD of hosts has purposed
    it,
To bring to dishonor the pride of all
    glory,
To bring into contempt all the
    honorable of the earth.

22:19 ᵃSeptuagint omits *he will pull you down;* Syriac, Targum, and Vulgate read *I will pull you down.* **23:1** ᵃHebrew *Kittim,* western lands, especially Cyprus **23:2** ᵃFollowing Masoretic Text and Vulgate; Septuagint and Targum read *Passing over the water;* Dead Sea Scrolls read *Your messengers passing over the sea.* **23:3** ᵃThat is, the Nile

10 Overflow through your land like the
       River,[a]
    O daughter of Tarshish;
    There is no more strength.
11 He stretched out His hand over the
       sea,
    He shook the kingdoms;
    The LORD has given a commandment
       against Canaan
    To destroy its strongholds.
12 And He said, "You will rejoice no
       more,
    O you oppressed virgin daughter of
       Sidon.
    Arise, cross over to Cyprus;
    There also you will have no rest."

13 Behold, the land of the Chaldeans,
    This people *which* was not;
    Assyria founded it for wild beasts of
       the desert.
    They set up its towers,
    They raised up its palaces,
    And brought it to ruin.

14 Wail, you ships of Tarshish!
    For your strength is laid waste.

15Now it shall come to pass in that day
that Tyre will be forgotten seventy years,
according to the days of one king. At the
end of seventy years it will happen to Tyre
as *in* the song of the harlot:

16 "Take a harp, go about the city,
    You forgotten harlot;
    Make sweet melody, sing many songs,
    That you may be remembered."

17And it shall be, at the end of seventy
years, that the LORD will deal with Tyre.
She will return to her hire, and commit fornication with all the kingdoms of the
world on the face of the earth. 18Her gain
and her pay will be set apart for the LORD;
it will not be treasured nor laid up, for her
gain will be for those who dwell before the
LORD, to eat sufficiently, and for fine clothing.

Impending Judgment on the Earth

24 Behold, the LORD makes the earth
    empty and makes it waste,
    Distorts its surface
    And scatters abroad its inhabitants.

2 And it shall be:
    As with the people, so with the priest;
    As with the servant, so with his
       master;
    As with the maid, so with her
       mistress;
    As with the buyer, so with the seller;
    As with the lender, so with the
       borrower;
    As with the creditor, so with the
       debtor.
3 The land shall be entirely emptied
       and utterly plundered,
    For the LORD has spoken this word.

4 The earth mourns *and* fades away,
    The world languishes *and* fades away;
    The haughty people of the earth
       languish.
5 The earth is also defiled under its
       inhabitants,
    Because they have transgressed the
       laws,
    Changed the ordinance,
    Broken the everlasting covenant.
6 Therefore the curse has devoured the
       earth,
    And those who dwell in it are
       desolate.
    Therefore the inhabitants of the
       earth are burned,
    And few men *are* left.
7 The new wine fails, the vine
       languishes,
    All the merry-hearted sigh.
8 The mirth of the tambourine ceases,
    The noise of the jubilant ends,
    The joy of the harp ceases.
9 They shall not drink wine with a
       song;
    Strong drink is bitter to those who
       drink it.
10 The city of confusion is broken down;
    Every house is shut up, so that none
       may go in.
11 *There is* a cry for wine in the streets,
    All joy is darkened,
    The mirth of the land is gone.
12 In the city desolation is left,
    And the gate is stricken with
       destruction.

23:10 [a]That is, the Nile

13 When it shall be thus in the midst of
   the land among the people,
   It shall be like the shaking of an
   olive tree,
   Like the gleaning of grapes when
   the vintage is done.

14 They shall lift up their voice, they
   shall sing;
   For the majesty of the LORD
   They shall cry aloud from the sea.

15 Therefore glorify the LORD in the
   dawning light,
   The name of the LORD God of Israel
   in the coastlands of the sea.

16 From the ends of the earth we have
   heard songs:
   "Glory to the righteous!"
   But I said, "I am ruined, ruined!
   Woe to me!
   The treacherous dealers have dealt
   treacherously,
   Indeed, the treacherous dealers have
   dealt very treacherously."

17 Fear and the pit and the snare
   Are upon you, O inhabitant of the
   earth.

18 And it shall be
   That he who flees from the noise of
   the fear
   Shall fall into the pit,
   And he who comes up from the
   midst of the pit
   Shall be caught in the snare;
   For the windows from on high are
   open,
   And the foundations of the earth are
   shaken.

19 The earth is violently broken,
   The earth is split open,
   The earth is shaken exceedingly.

20 The earth shall reel to and fro like a
   drunkard,
   And shall totter like a hut;
   Its transgression shall be heavy
   upon it,
   And it will fall, and not rise again.

21 It shall come to pass in that day
   That the LORD will punish on high
   the host of exalted ones,
   And on the earth the kings of the
   earth.

22 They will be gathered together,
   As prisoners are gathered in the pit,
   And will be shut up in the prison;
   After many days they will be
   punished.

23 Then the moon will be disgraced
   And the sun ashamed;
   For the LORD of hosts will reign
   On Mount Zion and in Jerusalem
   And before His elders, gloriously.

Praise to God

25 O LORD, You *are* my God.
   I will exalt You,
   I will praise Your name,
   For You have done wonderful *things;*
   Your counsels of old *are* faithfulness
   and truth.

2 For You have made a city a ruin,
   A fortified city a ruin,
   A palace of foreigners to be a city no
   more;
   It will never be rebuilt.

3 Therefore the strong people will
   glorify You;
   The city of the terrible nations will
   fear You.

4 For You have been a strength to the
   poor,
   A strength to the needy in his distress,
   A refuge from the storm,
   A shade from the heat;
   For the blast of the terrible ones *is* as
   a storm *against* the wall.

5 You will reduce the noise of aliens,
   As heat in a dry place;
   As heat in the shadow of a cloud,
   The song of the terrible ones will be
   diminished.

6 And in this mountain
   The LORD of hosts will make for all
   people
   A feast of choice pieces,
   A feast of wines on the lees,
   Of fat things full of marrow,
   Of well-refined wines on the lees.

7 And He will destroy on this
   mountain
   The surface of the covering cast over
   all people,
   And the veil that is spread over all
   nations.

God's Peace Overcomes Fear

A BATTLE RAGES within each of us, especially those who attempt to build godly marriages and families in a culture that stands against nearly everything God has to say about love, marriage, and family. It's a battle to overcome fear with faith.

The world sees fear and anxiety as normal, but God's Word tells us to allow His peace to take up residence in our hearts: "You will keep him in perfect peace, whose mind is stayed on You, because he trusts in You" (26:3). Notice the sequence: *We* put our trust in God; *we* focus on the truth of God and His Word; and *He* keeps us in "perfect peace."

Those who put their faith in God— who make their faith a way of thinking, acting, and being—get to live and walk in God's peace. And that's the only perfect peace any of us can ever know.

While fear urges us to worry about tomorrow, faith encourages us to trust God for issues in our marriage and family, such as:

- whether your husband will ever become the spiritual leader in your marriage and family
- a child who is not making wise choices
- resolving debt and paying the bills

Fear wants us to fret about what lies ahead, but faith calls us to cast all our cares upon our heavenly Father. Faith trumps fear ... so long as it's faith in Almighty God.

---

8 He will swallow up death forever,
   And the Lord GOD will wipe away
      tears from all faces;
   The rebuke of His people
   He will take away from all the earth;
   For the LORD has spoken.

9 And it will be said in that day:
   "Behold, this *is* our God;
   We have waited for Him, and He will
      save us.

This *is* the LORD;
We have waited for Him;
We will be glad and rejoice in His
   salvation."

10 For on this mountain the hand of the
      LORD will rest,
   And Moab shall be trampled down
      under Him,
   As straw is trampled down for the
      refuse heap.

11 And He will spread out His hands in
      their midst
   As a swimmer reaches out to swim,
   And He will bring down their pride
   Together with the trickery of their
      hands.

12 The fortress of the high fort of your
      walls
   He will bring down, lay low,
   And bring to the ground, down to
      the dust.

A Song of Salvation

26 In that day this song will be sung in the land of Judah:

"We have a strong city;
   God will appoint salvation *for* walls
      and bulwarks.

2 Open the gates,
   That the righteous nation which
      keeps the truth may enter in.

3 You will keep *him* in perfect peace,
   Whose mind *is* stayed *on You,*
   Because he trusts in You.

4 Trust in the LORD forever,
   For in YAH, the LORD, *is* everlasting
      strength.[a]

5 For He brings down those who dwell
      on high,
   The lofty city;
   He lays it low,
   He lays it low to the ground,
   He brings it down to the dust.

6 The foot shall tread it down—
   The feet of the poor
   And the steps of the needy."

7 The way of the just *is* uprightness;
   O Most Upright,
   You weigh the path of the just.

26:4 ªOr *Rock of Ages*

8 Yes, in the way of Your judgments,
O LORD, we have waited for You;
The desire of *our* soul *is* for Your name
And for the remembrance of You.
9 With my soul I have desired You in
the night,
Yes, by my spirit within me I will
seek You early;
For when Your judgments *are* in the
earth,
The inhabitants of the world will
learn righteousness.
10 Let grace be shown to the wicked,
Yet he will not learn righteousness;
In the land of uprightness he will
deal unjustly,
And will not behold the majesty of
the LORD.
11 LORD, *when* Your hand is lifted up,
they will not see.
But they will see and be ashamed
For *their* envy of people;
Yes, the fire of Your enemies shall
devour them.
12 LORD, You will establish peace for us,
For You have also done all our works
in us.
13 O LORD our God, masters besides You
Have had dominion over us;
But by You only we make mention of
Your name.
14 *They are* dead, they will not live;
They are deceased, they will not rise.
Therefore You have punished and
destroyed them,
And made all their memory to perish.
15 You have increased the nation,
O LORD,
You have increased the nation;
You are glorified;
You have expanded all the borders of
the land.
16 LORD, in trouble they have visited You,
They poured out a prayer *when* Your
chastening *was* upon them.

17 As a woman with child
Is in pain and cries out in her pangs,
When she draws near the time of her
delivery,
So have we been in Your sight,
O LORD.
18 We have been with child, we have
been in pain;
We have, as it were, brought forth
wind;
We have not accomplished any
deliverance in the earth,
Nor have the inhabitants of the
world fallen.
19 Your dead shall live;
Together with my dead body[a] they
shall arise.
Awake and sing, you who dwell in
dust;
For your dew *is like* the dew of herbs,
And the earth shall cast out the dead.

Take Refuge from the Coming Judgment

20 Come, my people, enter your
chambers,
And shut your doors behind you;
Hide yourself, as it were, for a little
moment,
Until the indignation is past.
21 For behold, the LORD comes out of
His place
To punish the inhabitants of the
earth for their iniquity;
The earth will also disclose her blood,
And will no more cover her slain.

27 In that day the LORD with His
severe sword, great and strong,
Will punish Leviathan the fleeing
serpent,
Leviathan that twisted serpent;
And He will slay the reptile that *is* in
the sea.

The Restoration of Israel

2 In that day sing to her,
"A vineyard of red wine![a]
3 I, the LORD, keep it,
I water it every moment;
Lest any hurt it,
I keep it night and day.

26:19 [a]Following Masoretic Text and Vulgate; Syriac
and Targum read *their dead bodies;* Septuagint reads
those in the tombs. **27:2** [a]Following Masoretic Text
(Kittel's *Biblia Hebraica*), Bomberg, and Vulgate;
Masoretic Text (*Biblia Hebraica Stuttgartensia*), some
Hebrew manuscripts, and Septuagint read *delight;*
Targum reads *choice vineyard.*

DEVOTIONS FOR COUPLES • 27:6
Help Each Other Grow up in Faith

Do you want to grow up in your faith? Do you and your spouse desire to know the deep joy that comes from maturing in your relationship with God? If so, I have an insider's secret that will help. For centuries followers of Jesus have recognized the critical importance of *discipline*. While I have no interest in a lifeless list of legalistic tasks that will turn the Christian life into a graceless, joyless religion based on works, I know that certain basic exercises will change a flabby, weak faith into a strong one. Consider a few of the most important:

- *Prayer*. Prayer is the way we communicate with God. Pray both as individuals and as a couple. Perhaps the two of you can pray together briefly before you go to sleep at night.

- *Bible study*. In God's Word we learn everything we need to know about God, His promises, and what He wants from us. Make use of commute time or an exercise session by carrying a pocket-sized Bible or listening to the Bible on CD or your MP3 player.

- *Worship*. If you are not worshiping God, you are probably worshiping something else. Find a vibrant, Christ-worshiping, Bible-believing church, and commit to regular worship there.

- *Giving*. We own nothing; we are simply stewards of resources, on loan from God. Regular tithing (giving 10 percent of your income) to your local church and generous giving to other Christian causes is a great way to strengthen your heart for God's work (see Matt. 6:21).

- *Fellowship*. We need others and they need us to accomplish the work of the kingdom. How about building relationships with others by joining or offering to lead a small group Bible study at your church?

- *Service*. In every local church, there is a need for people to use their spiritual gifts and natural abilities to serve others. And there are ministries in every community that need volunteers to feed the hungry and help the poor. Seek one out!

- *Witness*. Jesus has entrusted to us the task of reconciling men and women to God. Cultivate friendships with neighbors, plant seeds by sharing your testimony along with insights from God's Word, and extend an invitation for them to receive Christ. Let the light of Jesus shine out of your life.

The apostle Paul instructed Timothy to exercise himself for godliness. When you practice these important spiritual disciplines, you'll be getting the kind of workout that makes you spiritually strong.

---

4   Fury *is* not in Me.
Who would set briers *and* thorns
   Against Me in battle?
I would go through them,
I would burn them together.

5   Or let him take hold of My strength,
   That he may make peace with Me;
   And he shall make peace with Me."

6   Those who come He shall cause to
      take root in Jacob;
   Israel shall blossom and bud,
   And fill the face of the world with
      fruit.

7   Has He struck Israel as He struck
      those who struck him?
   Or has He been slain according to
      the slaughter of those who were
      slain by Him?

8   In measure, by sending it away,
   You contended with it.
   He removes *it* by His rough
      wind
   In the day of the east wind.

9   Therefore by this the iniquity of
      Jacob will be covered;
   And this *is* all the fruit of taking
      away his sin:

When he makes all the stones of the
altar
Like chalkstones that are beaten to
dust,
Wooden images[a] and incense altars
shall not stand.

10 Yet the fortified city *will be* desolate,
The habitation forsaken and left like
a wilderness;
There the calf will feed, and there it
will lie down
And consume its branches.

11 When its boughs are withered, they
will be broken off;
The women come *and* set them on
fire.
For it *is* a people of no
understanding;
Therefore He who made them will
not have mercy on them,
And He who formed them will show
them no favor.

12 And it shall come to pass in that day
That the LORD will thresh,
From the channel of the River[a] to the
Brook of Egypt;
And you will be gathered one by one,
O you children of Israel.

13 So it shall be in that day:
The great trumpet will be blown;
They will come, who are about to
perish in the land of Assyria,
And they who are outcasts in the
land of Egypt,
And shall worship the LORD in the
holy mount at Jerusalem.

Woe to Ephraim and Jerusalem

28 Woe to the crown of pride, to the
drunkards of Ephraim,
Whose glorious beauty *is* a fading
flower
Which *is* at the head of the verdant
valleys,
To those who are overcome with wine!

2 Behold, the Lord has a mighty and
strong one,
Like a tempest of hail and a
destroying storm,

Like a flood of mighty waters
overflowing,
Who will bring *them* down to the
earth with *His* hand.

3 The crown of pride, the drunkards
of Ephraim,
Will be trampled underfoot;

4 And the glorious beauty is a fading
flower
Which *is* at the head of the verdant
valley,
Like the first fruit before the summer,
Which an observer sees;
He eats it up while it is still in his
hand.

5 In that day the LORD of hosts will be
For a crown of glory and a diadem
of beauty
To the remnant of His people,

6 For a spirit of justice to him who sits
in judgment,
And for strength to those who turn
back the battle at the gate.

7 But they also have erred through wine,
And through intoxicating drink are
out of the way;
The priest and the prophet have
erred through intoxicating drink,
They are swallowed up by wine,
They are out of the way through
intoxicating drink;
They err in vision, they stumble *in*
judgment.

8 For all tables are full of vomit *and*
filth;
No place *is clean.*

9 "Whom will he teach knowledge?
And whom will he make to
understand the message?
Those *just* weaned from milk?
Those *just* drawn from the breasts?

10 For precept *must be* upon precept,
precept upon precept,
Line upon line, line upon line,
Here a little, there a little."

11 For with stammering lips and
another tongue
He will speak to this people,

12 To whom He said, "This *is* the rest
with which
You may cause the weary to rest,"

27:9 [a]Hebrew *Asherim*, Canaanite deities
27:12 [a]That is, the Euphrates

And, "This *is* the refreshing";
Yet they would not hear.
13 But the word of the LORD was to them,
"Precept upon precept, precept upon
precept,
Line upon line, line upon line,
Here a little, there a little,"
That they might go and fall
backward, and be broken
And snared and caught.

14 Therefore hear the word of the LORD,
you scornful men,
Who rule this people who *are* in
Jerusalem,
15 Because you have said, "We have
made a covenant with death,
And with Sheol we are in agreement.
When the overflowing scourge
passes through,
It will not come to us,
For we have made lies our refuge,
And under falsehood we have hidden
ourselves."

A Cornerstone in Zion

16Therefore thus says the Lord GOD:

"Behold, I lay in Zion a stone for a
foundation,
A tried stone, a precious cornerstone,
a sure foundation;
Whoever believes will not act
hastily.
17 Also I will make justice the
measuring line,
And righteousness the plummet;
The hail will sweep away the refuge
of lies,
And the waters will overflow the
hiding place.
18 Your covenant with death will be
annulled,
And your agreement with Sheol will
not stand;
When the overflowing scourge
passes through,
Then you will be trampled down by it.
19 As often as it goes out it will take you;
For morning by morning it will pass
over,
And by day and by night;
It will be a terror just to understand
the report."

20 For the bed is too short to stretch out
on,
And the covering so narrow that one
cannot wrap himself *in it.*
21 For the LORD will rise up as *at* Mount
Perazim,
He will be angry as in the Valley of
Gibeon—
That He may do His work, His
awesome work,
And bring to pass His act, His
unusual act.
22 Now therefore, do not be mockers,
Lest your bonds be made strong;
For I have heard from the Lord GOD
of hosts,
A destruction determined even upon
the whole earth.

Listen to the Teaching of God

23 Give ear and hear my voice,
Listen and hear my speech.
24 Does the plowman keep plowing all
day to sow?
Does he keep turning his soil and
breaking the clods?
25 When he has leveled its surface,
Does he not sow the black cummin
And scatter the cummin,
Plant the wheat in rows,
The barley in the appointed place,
And the spelt in its place?
26 For He instructs him in right
judgment,
His God teaches him.

27 For the black cummin is not threshed
with a threshing sledge,
Nor is a cartwheel rolled over the
cummin;
But the black cummin is beaten out
with a stick,
And the cummin with a rod.
28 Bread *flour* must be ground;
Therefore he does not thresh it
forever,
Break *it with* his cartwheel,
Or crush *it with* his horsemen.
29 This also comes from the LORD of
hosts,
Who is wonderful in counsel *and*
excellent in guidance.

Woe to Jerusalem

29 "Woe to Ariel,[a] to Ariel, the city
where David dwelt!
Add year to year;
Let feasts come around.

2 Yet I will distress Ariel;
There shall be heaviness and sorrow,
And it shall be to Me as Ariel.

3 I will encamp against you all around,
I will lay siege against you with a
    mound,
And I will raise siegeworks against
    you.

4 You shall be brought down,
You shall speak out of the ground;
Your speech shall be low, out of the
    dust;
Your voice shall be like a medium's,
    out of the ground;
And your speech shall whisper out
    of the dust.

5 "Moreover the multitude of your foes
Shall be like fine dust,
And the multitude of the terrible
    ones
Like chaff that passes away;
Yes, it shall be in an instant,
    suddenly.

6 You will be punished by the LORD of
    hosts
With thunder and earthquake and
    great noise,
With storm and tempest
And the flame of devouring fire.

7 The multitude of all the nations who
    fight against Ariel,
Even all who fight against her and
    her fortress,
And distress her,
Shall be as a dream of a night vision.

8 It shall even be as when a hungry
    man dreams,
And look—he eats;
But he awakes, and his soul is still
    empty;
Or as when a thirsty man dreams,
And look—he drinks;
But he awakes, and indeed *he is*
    faint,
And his soul still craves:

So the multitude of all the nations
    shall be,
Who fight against Mount Zion."

The Blindness of Disobedience

9 Pause and wonder!
Blind yourselves and be blind!
They are drunk, but not with wine;
They stagger, but not with
    intoxicating drink.

10 For the LORD has poured out on you
The spirit of deep sleep,
And has closed your eyes, namely,
    the prophets;
And He has covered your heads,
    namely, the seers.

11 The whole vision has become to you
like the words of a book that is sealed,
which *men* deliver to one who is literate,
saying, "Read this, please."
And he says, "I cannot, for it *is* sealed."
12 Then the book is delivered to one who
is illiterate, saying, "Read this, please."
And he says, "I am not literate."
13 Therefore the Lord said:

"Inasmuch as these people draw near
    with their mouths
And honor Me with their lips,
But have removed their hearts far
    from Me,
And their fear toward Me is taught
    by the commandment of men,

14 Therefore, behold, I will again do a
    marvelous work
Among this people,
A marvelous work and a wonder;
For the wisdom of their wise *men*
    shall perish,
And the understanding of their
    prudent *men* shall be hidden."

15 Woe to those who seek deep to hide
    their counsel far from the LORD,
And their works are in the dark;
They say, "Who sees us?" and, "Who
    knows us?"

16 Surely you have things turned
    around!
Shall the potter be esteemed as the
    clay;
For shall the thing made say of him
    who made it,

29:1 [a] That is, Jerusalem

"He did not make me"?
Or shall the thing formed say of him
who formed it,
"He has no understanding"?

Future Recovery of Wisdom

17 Is it not yet a very little while
Till Lebanon shall be turned into a
fruitful field,
And the fruitful field be esteemed as
a forest?
18 In that day the deaf shall hear the
words of the book,
And the eyes of the blind shall see
out of obscurity and out of
darkness.
19 The humble also shall increase *their*
joy in the LORD,
And the poor among men shall rejoice
In the Holy One of Israel.
20 For the terrible one is brought to
nothing,
The scornful one is consumed,
And all who watch for iniquity are
cut off—
21 Who make a man an offender by a
word,
And lay a snare for him who
reproves in the gate,
And turn aside the just by empty
words.

22Therefore thus says the LORD, who
redeemed Abraham, concerning the house
of Jacob:

"Jacob shall not now be ashamed,
Nor shall his face now grow pale;
23 But when he sees his children,
The work of My hands, in his midst,
They will hallow My name,
And hallow the Holy One of Jacob,
And fear the God of Israel.
24 These also who erred in spirit will
come to understanding,
And those who complained will learn
doctrine."

Futile Confidence in Egypt

30 "Woe to the rebellious children,"
says the LORD,
"Who take counsel, but not of Me,
And who devise plans, but not of
My Spirit,

That they may add sin to sin;
2 Who walk to go down to Egypt,
And have not asked My advice,
To strengthen themselves in the
strength of Pharaoh,
And to trust in the shadow of Egypt
3 Therefore the strength of Pharaoh
Shall be your shame,
And trust in the shadow of Egypt
Shall be *your* humiliation.
4 For his princes were at Zoan,
And his ambassadors came to Hanes
5 They were all ashamed of a people
who could not benefit them,
Or be help or benefit,
But a shame and also a reproach."

6The burden against the beasts of the
South.

Through a land of trouble and
anguish,
From which *came* the lioness and
lion,
The viper and fiery flying serpent,
They will carry their riches on the
backs of young donkeys,
And their treasures on the humps of
camels,
To a people *who* shall not profit;
7 For the Egyptians shall help in vain
and to no purpose.
Therefore I have called her
Rahab-Hem-Shebeth.[a]

A Rebellious People

8 Now go, write it before them on a
tablet,
And note it on a scroll,
That it may be for time to come,
Forever and ever:
9 That this *is* a rebellious people,
Lying children,
Children *who* will not hear the law of
the LORD;
10 Who say to the seers, "Do not see,"
And to the prophets, "Do not
prophesy to us right things;
Speak to us smooth things, prophesy
deceits.
11 Get out of the way,
Turn aside from the path,

30:7 [a]Literally *Rahab Sits Idle*

Cause the Holy One of Israel
To cease from before us."

¹²Therefore thus says the Holy One of Israel:

"Because you despise this word,
And trust in oppression and
perversity,
And rely on them,
¹³ Therefore this iniquity shall be to
you
Like a breach ready to fall,
A bulge in a high wall,
Whose breaking comes suddenly, in
an instant.
¹⁴ And He shall break it like the
breaking of the potter's vessel,
Which is broken in pieces;
He shall not spare.
So there shall not be found among its
fragments
A shard to take fire from the hearth,
Or to take water from the cistern."

¹⁵For thus says the Lord GOD, the Holy One of Israel:

"In returning and rest you shall be
saved;
In quietness and confidence shall be
your strength."
But you would not,
¹⁶ And you said, "No, for we will flee on
horses"—
Therefore you shall flee!
And, "We will ride on swift *horses*"—
Therefore those who pursue you
shall be swift!

¹⁷ One thousand *shall flee* at the threat
of one,
At the threat of five you shall flee,
Till you are left as a pole on top of a
mountain
And as a banner on a hill.

God Will Be Gracious

¹⁸ Therefore the LORD will wait, that He
may be gracious to you;
And therefore He will be exalted,
that He may have mercy on you.
For the LORD *is* a God of justice;
Blessed *are* all those who wait for
Him.

BIBLICAL INSIGHTS • 30:15
Be Willing to Rest

SOME OF US NEED TO STOP complaining about the pressure in our lives. We need to quit grumbling, as Isaiah 30:15 says, "In returning and rest you shall be saved; in quietness and confidence shall be your strength." Yet to this good instruction, too many of us give a foolish reply, "No, for we will flee on horses" (30:16). In other words, instead of looking to God for our solutions, we place our hope in our ability to escape the problem.

Jesus did not die on a cross so that we could grumble and complain about our circumstances for the rest of our lives! He didn't die for our sins so that we could become self sufficient. We need to lay all that aside and learn to *rest in Him*.

Whether the difficulty is a person you don't get along with, a disobedient child, or disappointment at work, God gives you the strength to handle the pressure. Jesus said, "Come to Me, all you who labor and are heavy laden, and I will give you rest. Take My yoke upon you and learn from Me, for I am gentle and lowly in heart, and you will find rest for your souls" (Matt. 11:28, 29). Don't forget who offers to step into the yoke with you! Jesus wants to be your partner—and He always pulls at the right speed, in the right direction, at the right pace, and at the right time.

Want peace? Don't flee. Come to Jesus, the Author and Maker of your soul.

¹⁹ For the people shall dwell in Zion at
Jerusalem;
You shall weep no more.
He will be very gracious to you at
the sound of your cry;
When He hears it, He will answer you.
²⁰ And *though* the Lord gives you
The bread of adversity and the
water of affliction,
Yet your teachers will not be moved
into a corner anymore,
But your eyes shall see your teachers.

21 Your ears shall hear a word behind
  you, saying,
  "This *is* the way, walk in it,"
  Whenever you turn to the right
  hand
  Or whenever you turn to the left.
22 You will also defile the covering of
  your images of silver,
  And the ornament of your molded
  images of gold.
  You will throw them away as an
  unclean thing;
  You will say to them, "Get away!"

23 Then He will give the rain for your
  seed
  With which you sow the ground,
  And bread of the increase of the
  earth;
  It will be fat and plentiful.
  In that day your cattle will feed
  In large pastures.
24 Likewise the oxen and the young
  donkeys that work the ground
  Will eat cured fodder,
  Which has been winnowed with the
  shovel and fan.
25 There will be on every high
  mountain
  And on every high hill
  Rivers *and* streams of waters,
  In the day of the great slaughter,
  When the towers fall.
26 Moreover the light of the moon will
  be as the light of the sun,
  And the light of the sun will be
  sevenfold,
  As the light of seven days,
  In the day that the LORD binds up the
  bruise of His people
  And heals the stroke of their wound.

Judgment on Assyria

27 Behold, the name of the LORD comes
  from afar,
  Burning *with* His anger,
  And *His* burden *is* heavy;
  His lips are full of indignation,
  And His tongue like a devouring
  fire.
28 His breath is like an overflowing
  stream,
  Which reaches up to the neck,

To sift the nations with the sieve of
  futility;
  And *there shall be* a bridle in the
  jaws of the people,
  Causing *them* to err.

29 You shall have a song
  As in the night *when* a holy festival
  is kept,
  And gladness of heart as when one
  goes with a flute,
  To come into the mountain of the
  LORD,
  To the Mighty One of Israel.
30 The LORD will cause His glorious
  voice to be heard,
  And show the descent of His arm,
  With the indignation of *His* anger
  And the flame of a devouring fire,
  With scattering, tempest, and
  hailstones.
31 For through the voice of the LORD
  Assyria will be beaten down,
  As He strikes with the rod.
32 And *in* every place where the staff
  of punishment passes,
  Which the LORD lays on him,
  It will be with tambourines and
  harps;
  And in battles of brandishing He
  will fight with it.
33 For Tophet *was* established of old,
  Yes, for the king it is prepared.
  He has made *it* deep and large;
  Its pyre *is* fire with much wood;
  The breath of the LORD, like a
  stream of brimstone,
  Kindles it.

The Folly of Not Trusting God

31 Woe to those who go down to
  Egypt for help,
  And rely on horses,
  Who trust in chariots because *they*
  are many,
  And in horsemen because they are
  very strong,
  But who do not look to the Holy One
  of Israel,
  Nor seek the LORD!
2 Yet He also *is* wise and will bring
  disaster,
  And will not call back His words,

But will arise against the house of
   evildoers,
And against the help of those who
   work iniquity.
3 Now the Egyptians *are* men, and not
   God;
And their horses are flesh, and not
   spirit.
When the LORD stretches out His
   hand,
Both he who helps will fall,
And he who is helped will fall down;
They all will perish together.

God Will Deliver Jerusalem

4For thus the LORD has spoken to me:

"As a lion roars,
   And a young lion over his prey
(When a multitude of shepherds is
   summoned against him,
He will not be afraid of their voice
Nor be disturbed by their noise),
So the LORD of hosts will come down
To fight for Mount Zion and for its
   hill.
5 Like birds flying about,
So will the LORD of hosts defend
   Jerusalem.
Defending, He will also deliver *it;*
Passing over, He will preserve *it.*"

6Return *to Him* against whom the children of Israel have deeply revolted. 7For in
that day every man shall throw away his
idols of silver and his idols of gold—sin,
which your own hands have made for
yourselves.

8 "Then Assyria shall fall by a sword
   not of man,
And a sword not of mankind shall
   devour him.
But he shall flee from the sword,
And his young men shall become
   forced labor.
9 He shall cross over to his stronghold
   for fear,
And his princes shall be afraid of the
   banner,"
Says the LORD,
Whose fire *is* in Zion
And whose furnace *is* in Jerusalem.

A Reign of Righteousness

32 Behold, a king will reign in
   righteousness,
And princes will rule with justice.
2 A man will be as a hiding place from
   the wind,
And a cover from the tempest,
As rivers of water in a dry place,
As the shadow of a great rock in a
   weary land.
3 The eyes of those who see will not
   be dim,
And the ears of those who hear will
   listen.
4 Also the heart of the rash will
   understand knowledge,
And the tongue of the stammerers
   will be ready to speak plainly.
5 The foolish person will no longer be
   called generous,
Nor the miser said *to be* bountiful;
6 For the foolish person will speak
   foolishness,
And his heart will work iniquity:
To practice ungodliness,
To utter error against the LORD,
To keep the hungry unsatisfied,
And he will cause the drink of the
   thirsty to fail.
7 Also the schemes of the schemer *are*
   evil;
He devises wicked plans
To destroy the poor with lying words,
Even when the needy speaks justice.
8 But a generous man devises
   generous things,
And by generosity he shall stand.

Consequences of Complacency

9 Rise up, you women who are at ease,
Hear my voice;
You complacent daughters,
Give ear to my speech.
10 In a year and *some* days
You will be troubled, you complacent
   women;
For the vintage will fail,
The gathering will not come.
11 Tremble, you *women* who are at ease;
Be troubled, you complacent ones;
Strip yourselves, make yourselves bare,
And gird *sackcloth* on *your* waists.

12 People shall mourn upon their breasts
For the pleasant fields, for the
fruitful vine.
13 On the land of my people will come
up thorns *and* briers,
Yes, on all the happy homes *in* the
joyous city;
14 Because the palaces will be forsaken,
The bustling city will be deserted.
The forts and towers will become
lairs forever,
A joy of wild donkeys, a pasture of
flocks—
15 Until the Spirit is poured upon us
from on high,
And the wilderness becomes a
fruitful field,
And the fruitful field is counted as a
forest.

The Peace of God's Reign

16 Then justice will dwell in the
wilderness,
And righteousness remain in the
fruitful field.
17 The work of righteousness will be
peace,
And the effect of righteousness,
quietness and assurance forever.
18 My people will dwell in a peaceful
habitation,
In secure dwellings, and in quiet
resting places,
19 Though hail comes down on the forest,
And the city is brought low in
humiliation.
20 Blessed *are* you who sow beside all
waters,
Who send out freely the feet of the
ox and the donkey.

A Prayer in Deep Distress

33 Woe to you who plunder, though
you *have* not *been* plundered;
And you who deal treacherously,
though they have not dealt
treacherously with you!
When you cease plundering,
You will be plundered;
When you make an end of dealing
treacherously,
They will deal treacherously with you.

2 O LORD, be gracious to us;
We have waited for You.
Be their[a] arm every morning,
Our salvation also in the time of
trouble.
3 At the noise of the tumult the people
shall flee;
When You lift Yourself up, the
nations shall be scattered;
4 And Your plunder shall be gathered
Like the gathering of the caterpillar;
As the running to and fro of locusts,
He shall run upon them.

5 The LORD is exalted, for He dwells on
high;
He has filled Zion with justice and
righteousness.
6 Wisdom and knowledge will be the
stability of your times,
And the strength of salvation;
The fear of the LORD *is* His treasure.

7 Surely their valiant ones shall cry
outside,
The ambassadors of peace shall
weep bitterly.
8 The highways lie waste,
The traveling man ceases.
He has broken the covenant,
He has despised the cities,[a]
He regards no man.
9 The earth mourns *and* languishes,
Lebanon is shamed *and* shriveled;
Sharon is like a wilderness,
And Bashan and Carmel shake off
their fruits.

Impending Judgment on Zion

10 "Now I will rise," says the LORD;
"Now I will be exalted,
Now I will lift Myself up.
11 You shall conceive chaff,
You shall bring forth stubble;
Your breath, *as* fire, shall devour you.
12 And the people shall be *like* the
burnings of lime;
Like thorns cut up they shall be
burned in the fire.

33:2 [a]Septuagint omits *their;* Syriac, Targum, and
Vulgate read *our.* **33:8** [a]Following Masoretic Text
and Vulgate; Dead Sea Scrolls read *witnesses;*
Septuagint omits *cities;* Targum reads *They have been
removed from their cities.*

13 Hear, you *who are* afar off, what I
   have done;
   And you *who are* near, acknowledge
   My might."

14 The sinners in Zion are afraid;
   Fearfulness has seized the
   hypocrites:
   "Who among us shall dwell with the
   devouring fire?
   Who among us shall dwell with
   everlasting burnings?"

15 He who walks righteously and
   speaks uprightly,
   He who despises the gain of
   oppressions,
   Who gestures with his hands,
   refusing bribes,
   Who stops his ears from hearing of
   bloodshed,
   And shuts his eyes from seeing evil:

16 He will dwell on high;
   His place of defense *will be* the
   fortress of rocks;
   Bread will be given him,
   His water *will be* sure.

The Land of the Majestic King

17 Your eyes will see the King in His
   beauty;
   They will see the land that is very
   far off.

18 Your heart will meditate on terror:
   "Where *is* the scribe?
   Where *is* he who weighs?
   Where *is* he who counts the towers?"

19 You will not see a fierce people,
   A people of obscure speech, beyond
   perception,
   Of a stammering tongue *that you*
   cannot understand.

20 Look upon Zion, the city of our
   appointed feasts;
   Your eyes will see Jerusalem, a quiet
   home,
   A tabernacle *that* will not be taken
   down;
   Not one of its stakes will ever be
   removed,
   Nor will any of its cords be broken.

21 But there the majestic LORD *will be*
   for us
   A place of broad rivers *and* streams,

In which no galley with oars will sail,
Nor majestic ships pass by

22 (For the LORD *is* our Judge,
   The LORD *is* our Lawgiver,
   The LORD *is* our King;
   He will save us);

23 Your tackle is loosed,
   They could not strengthen their mast,
   They could not spread the sail.

   Then the prey of great plunder is
   divided;
   The lame take the prey.

ROMANCE FAQ

Q: *What does it mean to focus on my wife?*

Focus means giving someone your undivided attention. I win in my relationship with Barbara when I turn from my list of priorities in order to zero in on her. I win when I listen to her without staring at the television or going through the mail. I win when I respond thoughtfully to what she has said. Sometimes that means ignoring the cell phone while she's trying to bare her soul. I've learned that there are times when she wants my attention, even if we aren't saying anything!

A great way to focus on your wife is to enjoy a regular date night. (Sunday night was our standard time to get away and talk.) Or consider heading to bed early and asking her how her day was. Focus fosters communication and a deeper connection.

Focus also understands her needs for romance. Do you recall how she spells it? R-e-l-a-t-i-o-n-s-h-i-p. Spend energy prayerfully thinking about how you can meet her needs for romance. Craft a highly romantic day and evening *just for her*. On paper, spell out the specifics of how you are going to focus on her—a love letter, a gift, flowers, a walk, a picnic or a nice meal, a drawn bubble bath, scented candles and a massage. Make sure you are speaking her love language, not your own.

24 And the inhabitant will not say, "I am sick";
The people who dwell in it *will be* forgiven *their* iniquity.

Judgment on the Nations

34 Come near, you nations, to hear;
And heed, you people!
Let the earth hear, and all that is in it,
The world and all things that come forth from it.
2 For the indignation of the LORD *is* against all nations,
And *His* fury against all their armies;
He has utterly destroyed them,
He has given them over to the slaughter.
3 Also their slain shall be thrown out;
Their stench shall rise from their corpses,
And the mountains shall be melted with their blood.
4 All the host of heaven shall be dissolved,
And the heavens shall be rolled up like a scroll;
All their host shall fall down
As the leaf falls from the vine,
And as *fruit* falling from a fig tree.

5 "For My sword shall be bathed in heaven;
Indeed it shall come down on Edom,
And on the people of My curse, for judgment.
6 The sword of the LORD is filled with blood,
It is made overflowing with fatness,
With the blood of lambs and goats,
With the fat of the kidneys of rams.
For the LORD has a sacrifice in Bozrah,
And a great slaughter in the land of Edom.
7 The wild oxen shall come down with them,
And the young bulls with the mighty bulls;
Their land shall be soaked with blood,
And their dust saturated with fatness."

8 For *it is* the day of the LORD's vengeance,
The year of recompense for the cause of Zion.

9 Its streams shall be turned into pitch,
And its dust into brimstone;
Its land shall become burning pitch.
10 It shall not be quenched night or day;
Its smoke shall ascend forever.
From generation to generation it shall lie waste;
No one shall pass through it forever and ever.
11 But the pelican and the porcupine shall possess it,
Also the owl and the raven shall dwell in it.
And He shall stretch out over it
The line of confusion and the stones of emptiness.
12 They shall call its nobles to the kingdom,
But none *shall be* there, and all its princes shall be nothing.
13 And thorns shall come up in its palaces,
Nettles and brambles in its fortresses;
It shall be a habitation of jackals,
A courtyard for ostriches.
14 The wild beasts of the desert shall also meet with the jackals,
And the wild goat shall bleat to its companion;
Also the night creature shall rest there,
And find for herself a place of rest.
15 There the arrow snake shall make her nest and lay *eggs*
And hatch, and gather *them* under her shadow;
There also shall the hawks be gathered,
Every one with her mate.

16 "Search from the book of the LORD, and read:
Not one of these shall fail;
Not one shall lack her mate.
For My mouth has commanded it,
and His Spirit has gathered them.
17 He has cast the lot for them,
And His hand has divided it among them with a measuring line.
They shall possess it forever;
From generation to generation they shall dwell in it."

BIBLICAL INSIGHTS • 35:4
Freedom from Crippling Fear

HOW DOES FEAR SHAPE YOUR response to life's difficult moments, especially in the family?

Fear pushes some to procrastinate and put off decisions they know they should make. Others erect barriers to keep anyone from truly knowing them. Still others are controlled by a fear of failure. Finally, fear drives people away from God. Some men and women refuse to surrender to God and His will, fearing what He might require of them.

So what is the best antidote to this kind of crippling fear? Hear what Isaiah says, "Say to those who are fearful-hearted, 'Be strong, do not fear! Behold, your God will come with vengeance, with the recompense of God; He will come and save you'" (35:4). The best antidote to crippling fear is prayer and total surrender of your will to Jesus Christ.

How many things do you *really* need to worry about? None. Instead, you should entrust your situation to a loving and almighty God. Your Lord wants you to approach Him with an attitude of gratefulness for who He is, what He has done, and what He will do. As you pray and yield your life, marriage, and family to God, and as you learn to "be anxious for nothing" (Phil. 4:6) and begin "casting all your cares upon Him" (1 Pet. 5:7), God will begin to replace your fears with faith.

The Future Glory of Zion

35 The wilderness and the wasteland
shall be glad for them,
And the desert shall rejoice and
blossom as the rose;

2 It shall blossom abundantly and
rejoice,
Even with joy and singing.
The glory of Lebanon shall be given
to it,
The excellence of Carmel and
Sharon.
They shall see the glory of the LORD,
The excellency of our God.

3 Strengthen the weak hands,
And make firm the feeble knees.

4 Say to those *who are* fearful-hearted,
"Be strong, do not fear!
Behold, your God will come *with*
vengeance,
With the recompense of God;
He will come and save you."

5 Then the eyes of the blind shall be
opened,
And the ears of the deaf shall be
unstopped.

6 Then the lame shall leap like a deer,
And the tongue of the dumb sing.
For waters shall burst forth in the
wilderness,
And streams in the desert.

7 The parched ground shall become a
pool,
And the thirsty land springs of
water;
In the habitation of jackals, where
each lay,
There shall be grass with reeds and
rushes.

8 A highway shall be there, and a
road,
And it shall be called the Highway of
Holiness.
The unclean shall not pass over it,
But it *shall be* for others.
Whoever walks the road, although a
fool,
Shall not go astray.

9 No lion shall be there,
Nor shall *any* ravenous beast go up
on it;
It shall not be found there.
But the redeemed shall walk *there,*

10 And the ransomed of the LORD shall
   return,
   And come to Zion with singing,
   With everlasting joy on their heads.
   They shall obtain joy and gladness,
   And sorrow and sighing shall flee
   away.

Sennacherib Boasts Against the LORD

36 Now it came to pass in the fourteenth year of King Hezekiah *that* Sennacherib king of Assyria came up against all the fortified cities of Judah and took them. ²Then the king of Assyria sent *the* Rabshakeh[a] with a great army from Lachish to King Hezekiah at Jerusalem. And he stood by the aqueduct from the upper pool, on the highway to the Fuller's Field. ³And Eliakim the son of Hilkiah, who was over the household, Shebna the scribe, and Joah the son of Asaph, the recorder, came out to him.

⁴Then *the* Rabshakeh said to them, "Say now to Hezekiah, 'Thus says the great king, the king of Assyria: "What confidence is this in which you trust? ⁵I say you speak of having plans and power for war; but *they are* mere words. Now in whom do you trust, that you rebel against me? ⁶Look! You are trusting in the staff of this broken reed, Egypt, on which if a man leans, it will go into his hand and pierce it. So *is* Pharaoh king of Egypt to all who trust in him.

⁷"But if you say to me, 'We trust in the LORD our God,' *is it* not He whose high places and whose altars Hezekiah has taken away, and said to Judah and Jerusalem, 'You shall worship before this altar'?" ⁸Now therefore, I urge you, give a pledge to my master the king of Assyria, and I will give you two thousand horses— if you are able on your part to put riders on them! ⁹How then will you repel one captain of the least of my master's servants, and put your trust in Egypt for chariots and horsemen? ¹⁰Have I now come up without the LORD against this land to destroy it? The LORD said to me, 'Go up against this land, and destroy it.'"

¹¹Then Eliakim, Shebna, and Joah said to *the* Rabshakeh, "Please speak to your servants in Aramaic, for we understand *it;* and do not speak to us in Hebrew[a] in the hearing of the people who *are* on the wall."

¹²But *the* Rabshakeh said, "Has my master sent me to your master and to you to speak these words, and not to the men who sit on the wall, who will eat and drink their own waste with you?"

¹³Then *the* Rabshakeh stood and called out with a loud voice in Hebrew, and said, "Hear the words of the great king, the king of Assyria! ¹⁴Thus says the king: 'Do not let Hezekiah deceive you, for he will not be able to deliver you; ¹⁵nor let Hezekiah make you trust in the LORD, saying, "The LORD will surely deliver us; this city will not be given into the hand of the king of Assyria."' ¹⁶Do not listen to Hezekiah; for thus says the king of Assyria: 'Make *peace* with me *by a* present and come out to me; and every one of you eat from his own vine and every one from his own fig tree, and every one of you drink the waters of his own cistern; ¹⁷until I come and take you away to a land like your own land, a land of grain and new wine, a land of bread and vineyards. ¹⁸*Beware* lest Hezekiah persuade you, saying, "The LORD will deliver us." Has any one of the gods of the nations delivered its land from the hand of the king of Assyria? ¹⁹Where *are* the gods of Hamath and Arpad? Where *are* the gods of Sepharvaim? Indeed, have they delivered Samaria from my hand? ²⁰Who among all the gods of these lands have delivered their countries from my hand, that the LORD should deliver Jerusalem from my hand?'"

²¹But they held their peace and answered him not a word; for the king's commandment was, "Do not answer him." ²²Then Eliakim the son of Hilkiah, who *was* over the household, Shebna the scribe, and Joah the son of Asaph, the recorder, came to Hezekiah with *their* clothes torn, and told him the words of *the* Rabshakeh.

Isaiah Assures Deliverance

37 And so it was, when King Hezekiah heard *it,* that he tore his clothes, covered himself with sackcloth, and went into the house of the LORD. ²Then he sent

---

36:2 [a]A title, probably *Chief of Staff* or *Governor*
36:11 [a]Literally *Judean*

Eliakim, who *was* over the household, Shebna the scribe, and the elders of the priests, covered with sackcloth, to Isaiah the prophet, the son of Amoz. ³And they said to him, "Thus says Hezekiah: 'This day *is* a day of trouble and rebuke and blasphemy; for the children have come to birth, but *there is* no strength to bring them forth. ⁴It may be that the LORD your God will hear the words of *the* Rabshakeh, whom his master the king of Assyria has sent to reproach the living God, and will rebuke the words which the LORD your God has heard. Therefore lift up *your* prayer for the remnant that is left.'"

⁵So the servants of King Hezekiah came to Isaiah. ⁶And Isaiah said to them, "Thus you shall say to your master, 'Thus says the LORD: "Do not be afraid of the words which you have heard, with which the servants of the king of Assyria have blasphemed Me. ⁷Surely I will send a spirit upon him, and he shall hear a rumor and return to his own land; and I will cause him to fall by the sword in his own land."'"

Sennacherib's Threat and Hezekiah's Prayer

⁸Then *the* Rabshakeh returned, and found the king of Assyria warring against Libnah, for he heard that he had departed from Lachish. ⁹And the king heard concerning Tirhakah king of Ethiopia, "He has come out to make war with you." So when he heard *it,* he sent messengers to Hezekiah, saying, ¹⁰"Thus you shall speak to Hezekiah king of Judah, saying: 'Do not let your God in whom you trust deceive you, saying, "Jerusalem shall not be given into the hand of the king of Assyria." ¹¹Look! You have heard what the kings of Assyria have done to all lands by utterly destroying them; and shall you be delivered? ¹²Have the gods of the nations delivered those whom my fathers have destroyed, Gozan and Haran and Rezeph, and the people of Eden who *were* in Telassar? ¹³Where *is* the king of Hamath, the king of Arpad, and the king of the city of Sepharvaim, Hena, and Ivah?'"

¹⁴And Hezekiah received the letter from the hand of the messengers, and read it;

and Hezekiah went up to the house of the LORD, and spread it before the LORD. ¹⁵Then Hezekiah prayed to the LORD, saying: ¹⁶"O LORD of hosts, God of Israel, *the One* who dwells *between* the cherubim, You *are* God, You alone, of all the kingdoms of the earth. You have made heaven and earth. ¹⁷Incline Your ear, O LORD, and hear; open Your eyes, O LORD, and see; and hear all the words of Sennacherib, which he has sent to reproach the living God. ¹⁸Truly, LORD, the kings of Assyria have laid waste all the nations and their lands, ¹⁹and have cast their gods into the fire; for they *were* not gods, but the work of men's hands—wood and stone. Therefore they destroyed them. ²⁰Now therefore, O LORD our God, save us from his hand, that all the kingdoms of the earth may know that You *are* the LORD, You alone."

The Word of the LORD Concerning Sennacherib

²¹Then Isaiah the son of Amoz sent to Hezekiah, saying, "Thus says the LORD God of Israel, 'Because you have prayed to Me against Sennacherib king of Assyria, ²²this *is* the word which the LORD has spoken concerning him:

"The virgin, the daughter of Zion,
    Has despised you, laughed you to
        scorn;
    The daughter of Jerusalem
    Has shaken *her* head behind your
        back!

23 "Whom have you reproached and
        blasphemed?
    Against whom have you raised *your*
        voice,
    And lifted up your eyes on high?
    Against the Holy One of Israel.
24 By your servants you have
        reproached the Lord,
    And said, 'By the multitude of my
        chariots
    I have come up to the height of the
        mountains,
    To the limits of Lebanon;
    I will cut down its tall cedars
    And its choice cypress trees;
    I will enter its farthest height,
    To its fruitful forest.

25   I have dug and drunk water,
     And with the soles of my feet I have
          dried up
     All the brooks of defense.'

26   "Did you not hear long ago
     How I made it,
     From ancient times that I formed it?
     Now I have brought it to pass,
     That you should be
     For crushing fortified cities *into*
          heaps of ruins.

27   Therefore their inhabitants *had* little
          power;
     They were dismayed and confounded;
     They were *as* the grass of the field
     And the green herb,
     As the grass on the housetops
     And grain blighted before it is
          grown.

28   "But I know your dwelling place,
     Your going out and your coming in,
     And your rage against Me.

29   Because your rage against Me and
          your tumult
     Have come up to My ears,
     Therefore I will put My hook in your
          nose
     And My bridle in your lips,
     And I will turn you back
     By the way which you came."'

30"This *shall be* a sign to you:

     You shall eat this year such as grows
          of itself,
     And the second year what springs
          from the same;
     Also in the third year sow and reap,
     Plant vineyards and eat the fruit of
          them.

31   And the remnant who have escaped
          of the house of Judah
     Shall again take root downward,
     And bear fruit upward.

32   For out of Jerusalem shall go a
          remnant,
     And those who escape from Mount
          Zion.
     The zeal of the LORD of hosts will do
          this.

33"Therefore thus says the LORD concerning the king of Assyria:

     'He shall not come into this city,
     Nor shoot an arrow there,
     Nor come before it with shield,
     Nor build a siege mound against it.

34   By the way that he came,
     By the same shall he return;
     And he shall not come into this city,'
     Says the LORD.

35   'For I will defend this city, to save it
     For My own sake and for My servant
          David's sake.'"

Sennacherib's Defeat and Death

36Then the angel[a] of the LORD went out,
and killed in the camp of the Assyrians
one hundred and eighty-five thousand; and
when *people* arose early in the morning,
there were the corpses—all dead. 37So
Sennacherib king of Assyria departed and
went away, returned *home,* and remained
at Nineveh. 38Now it came to pass, as he
was worshiping in the house of Nisroch
his god, that his sons Adrammelech and
Sharezer struck him down with the sword;
and they escaped into the land of Ararat.
Then Esarhaddon his son reigned in his
place.

Hezekiah's Life Extended

38 In those days Hezekiah was sick and
near death. And Isaiah the prophet,
the son of Amoz, went to him and said to
him, "Thus says the LORD: 'Set your house
in order, for you shall die and not live.'"

2Then Hezekiah turned his face toward
the wall, and prayed to the LORD, 3and said,
"Remember now, O LORD, I pray, how I
have walked before You in truth and with a
loyal heart, and have done *what is* good in
Your sight." And Hezekiah wept bitterly.

4And the word of the LORD came to
Isaiah, saying, 5"Go and tell Hezekiah,
'Thus says the LORD, the God of David
your father: "I have heard your prayer, I
have seen your tears; surely I will add to
your days fifteen years. 6I will deliver you
and this city from the hand of the king of
Assyria, and I will defend this city."' 7And
this *is* the sign to you from the LORD, that
the LORD will do this thing which He has
spoken: 8Behold, I will bring the shadow

37:36 [a]Or *Angel*

on the sundial, which has gone down with the sun on the sundial of Ahaz, ten degrees backward." So the sun returned ten degrees on the dial by which it had gone down.

⁹This is the writing of Hezekiah king of Judah, when he had been sick and had recovered from his sickness:

¹⁰ I said,
   "In the prime of my life
   I shall go to the gates of Sheol;
   I am deprived of the remainder of
      my years."
¹¹ I said,
   "I shall not see YAH,
   The LORDᵃ in the land of the living;
   I shall observe man no more among
      the inhabitants of the world.ᵇ
¹² My life span is gone,
   Taken from me like a shepherd's tent;
   I have cut off my life like a weaver.
   He cuts me off from the loom;
   From day until night You make an
      end of me.

¹³ I have considered until morning—
   Like a lion,
   So He breaks all my bones;
   From day until night You make an
      end of me.
¹⁴ Like a crane or a swallow, so I
      chattered;
   I mourned like a dove;
   My eyes fail from looking upward.
   O LORD,ᵃ I am oppressed;
   Undertake for me!
¹⁵ "What shall I say?
   He has both spoken to me,ᵃ
   And He Himself has done it.
   I shall walk carefully all my years
   In the bitterness of my soul.
¹⁶ O Lord, by these things men live;
   And in all these things is the life of
      my spirit;
   So You will restore me and make me
      live.
¹⁷ Indeed it was for my own peace
   That I had great bitterness;
   But You have lovingly delivered my
      soul from the pit of corruption,
   For You have cast all my sins behind
      Your back.
¹⁸ For Sheol cannot thank You,
   Death cannot praise You;
   Those who go down to the pit cannot
      hope for Your truth.

38:11 ᵃHebrew YAH, YAH ᵇFollowing some Hebrew manuscripts; Masoretic Text and Vulgate read rest; Septuagint omits among the inhabitants of the world; Targum reads land. **38:14** ᵃFollowing Bomberg; Masoretic Text and Dead Sea Scrolls read Lord. **38:15** ᵃFollowing Masoretic Text and Vulgate; Dead Sea Scrolls and Targum read And shall I say to Him; Septuagint omits first half of this verse.

ROMANTIC QUOTES AND NOTES
The Trouble with the 50/50 Plan

All husbands and wives have expectations of how the relationship should work. Often, they assume, "My spouse will meet me halfway." Over the years we've heard couples talk about having a 50/50 marriage. "You do your part," the thinking goes, "and I'll do mine." But while this concept sounds logical, couples who try to live it out are destined for disappointment. One reason why is that we focus more on what the other person is giving than on what we are doing. So we withhold love until the other person meets our expectations. Of course, it's impossible to know if a person has ever met you halfway. As Thomas Fuller said, "Every horse thinks its own pack heaviest."

Early in our marriage, we tried this plan. I would give affection to Barbara only when I felt she had earned it. Barbara would show me affection and praise only when she thought I had held up my end of things.

Contrast this with the type of love God shows for us. No matter what we do, He gives us 100 percent. He gives us love even when we don't deserve it!

So I propose that couples adopt the 100/100 Plan in marriage. Under this plan, each person gives 100 percent . . . no matter what the other person does.

BIBLICAL INSIGHTS • 39
Collect the Right Stuff

IS SOMETHING INNATELY a part of human nature that drives us to collect stuff? People collect all kinds of things: oil paintings, sculptures, political campaign buttons, guns, stamps, coins. I'll never forget riding on a train in England and meeting a man who collected hotel keys, thousands of them. The world has seen some pretty strange collections.

In Isaiah 39, we read of the treasures accumulated by Judah's kings—"silver and gold, the spices and precious ointment, and all his [Hezekiah's] armory" (39:2)—that Hezekiah showed off to some visitors from far-off Babylon. He wanted to impress his guests—and indeed he did. Isaiah prophesied that everything the king had shown to the Babylonians, would one day wind up in the hands of his descendants' enemies.

Taking pride in stuff is just plain foolish. And yet, like the kings of Juday, we line in a culture in which many people measure their own worth by totaling the value of their stuff!

By contrast, 1 Timothy 6:18 tells us to "be rich in good works." That's the only type of collection that lasts—the type you give away. Think of Dorcas, the woman who made her own collection of garments for the poor. It became not only her treasure in heaven, but also her story has become the heritage of millions (see Acts 9:36–43).

What kind of collection are *you* acquiring? Is it of things that will decay or be destroyed? Or are you focusing on eternal treasures (Matt. 6:19, 20). In the end, the stuff you do to love and serve others will be worth much more than the stuff you collect.

Pray that God will help you collect good deeds, and so store up for the future.

---

19 The living, the living man, he shall praise You,
As I *do* this day;
The father shall make known Your truth to the children.

20 "The LORD *was ready* to save me;
Therefore we will sing my songs
with stringed instruments
All the days of our life, in the house of the LORD."

21Now Isaiah had said, "Let them take a lump of figs, and apply *it* as a poultice on the boil, and he shall recover."

22And Hezekiah had said, "What *is* the sign that I shall go up to the house of the LORD?"

The Babylonian Envoys

39 At that time Merodach-Baladan[a] the son of Baladan, king of Babylon, sent letters and a present to Hezekiah, for he heard that he had been sick and had recovered. 2And Hezekiah was pleased with them, and showed them the house of his treasures—the silver and gold, the spices and precious ointment, and all his armory—all that was found among his treasures. There was nothing in his house or in all his dominion that Hezekiah did not show them.

3Then Isaiah the prophet went to King Hezekiah, and said to him, "What did these men say, and from where did they come to you?"

So Hezekiah said, "They came to me from a far country, from Babylon."

4And he said, "What have they seen in your house?"

So Hezekiah answered, "They have seen all that *is* in my house; there is nothing among my treasures that I have not shown them."

39:1 aSpelled *Berodach-Baladan* in 2 Kings 20:12

⁵Then Isaiah said to Hezekiah, "Hear the word of the LORD of hosts: ⁶'Behold, the days are coming when all that *is* in your house, and what your fathers have accumulated until this day, shall be carried to Babylon; nothing shall be left,' says the LORD. ⁷'And they shall take away *some* of your sons who will descend from you, whom you will beget; and they shall be eunuchs in the palace of the king of Babylon.'"

⁸So Hezekiah said to Isaiah, "The word of the LORD which you have spoken *is* good!" For he said, "At least there will be peace and truth in my days."

God's People Are Comforted

40 "Comfort, yes, comfort My people!"
Says your God.
2 "Speak comfort to Jerusalem, and cry
out to her,
That her warfare is ended,
That her iniquity is pardoned;
For she has received from the LORD's
hand
Double for all her sins."

3 The voice of one crying in the
wilderness:
"Prepare the way of the LORD;
Make straight in the desertᵃ
A highway for our God.
4 Every valley shall be exalted
And every mountain and hill
brought low;
The crooked places shall be made
straight
And the rough places smooth;
5 The glory of the LORD shall be
revealed,
And all flesh shall see *it* together;
For the mouth of the LORD has
spoken."

6 The voice said, "Cry out!"
And heᵃ said, "What shall I
cry?"

"All flesh *is* grass,
And all its loveliness *is* like the
flower of the field.
7 The grass withers, the flower fades,
Because the breath of the LORD
blows upon it;
Surely the people *are* grass.
8 The grass withers, the flower fades,
But the word of our God stands
forever."

9 O Zion,
You who bring good tidings,
Get up into the high mountain;
O Jerusalem,
You who bring good tidings,
Lift up your voice with strength,
Lift *it* up, be not afraid;
Say to the cities of Judah, "Behold
your God!"

10 Behold, the Lord GOD shall come
with a strong *hand,*
And His arm shall rule for Him;
Behold, His reward *is* with Him,
And His work before Him.
11 He will feed His flock like a
shepherd;
He will gather the lambs with His arm,
And carry *them* in His bosom,
And gently lead those who are with
young.

12 Who has measured the watersᵃ in the
hollow of His hand,
Measured heaven with a span
And calculated the dust of the earth
in a measure?
Weighed the mountains in scales
And the hills in a balance?
13 Who has directed the Spirit of the
LORD,
Or *as* His counselor has taught Him?
14 With whom did He take counsel, and
who instructed Him,
And taught Him in the path of
justice?
Who taught Him knowledge,
And showed Him the way of
understanding?

15 Behold, the nations *are* as a drop in a
bucket,
And are counted as the small dust on
the scales;

40:3 ᵃFollowing Masoretic Text, Targum, and Vulgate; Septuagint omits *in the desert.*
40:6 ᵃFollowing Masoretic Text and Targum; Dead Sea Scrolls, Septuagint, and Vulgate read *I.*
40:12 ᵃFollowing Masoretic Text, Septuagint, and Vulgate; Dead Sea Scrolls read *waters of the sea;* Targum reads *waters of the world.*

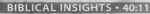

Trust In a Sovereign God

HOW DO YOU RESPOND when tragedy strikes your family? I had to grapple with that question when our thirteen-year-old son Samuel was diagnosed with a rare neurological disorder that took away his ability to run. Barbara and I grieved for our son and his loss. It's in these moments that what you truly know about God will determine how you process circumstances that make no sense. At various points in our lives we will likely face difficult experiences that leave us with thorny questions, questions that remain unanswered.

Why would God allow a child we know to be sexually molested?

Why do so many couples who desperately want children, find themselves infertile?

Why do some spouses who have every reason to remain faithful, suddenly abandon their families?

Why would God seemingly take a good young person to heaven and leave an evil old person here?

While Scripture rarely provides simple answers to such questions, it does invite us to trust the God who in the midst of adversity promises to be our Great Shepherd, gathering us in His arms and carrying us close to His heart (40:11). When the Bible asserts that God is in control, it invites us to believe that evil does not have the last word. A loving, sovereign God can be trusted to overwhelm present evils.

In our own situation, a hint of how God is using adversity to mold our character came one evening when Samuel and I were driving home from the grocery store. As we talked about his limitations, Samuel turned from gazing out the window, looked at me, and said resolutely, "Well, Dad, I guess you don't need legs to serve God."

The Scriptures never promise that Christians will be kept from adversity. But God does promise to provide grace to face the challenges and to use trials to make us more like Jesus Christ.

Look, He lifts up the isles as a very little thing.

16 And Lebanon *is* not sufficient to burn,
Nor its beasts sufficient for a burnt offering.

17 All nations before Him *are* as nothing,
And they are counted by Him less than nothing and worthless.

18 To whom then will you liken God?
Or what likeness will you compare to Him?

19 The workman molds an image,
The goldsmith overspreads it with gold,
And the silversmith casts silver chains.

20 Whoever *is* too impoverished for *such* a contribution
Chooses a tree *that* will not rot;
He seeks for himself a skillful workman
To prepare a carved image *that* will not totter.

21 Have you not known?
Have you not heard?
Has it not been told you from the beginning?
Have you not understood from the foundations of the earth?

22 *It is* He who sits above the circle of the earth,
And its inhabitants *are* like grasshoppers,
Who stretches out the heavens like a curtain,
And spreads them out like a tent to dwell in.

23 He brings the princes to nothing;

He makes the judges of the earth
useless.

24 Scarcely shall they be planted,
Scarcely shall they be sown,
Scarcely shall their stock take root in
the earth,
When He will also blow on them,
And they will wither,
And the whirlwind will take them
away like stubble.

25 "To whom then will you liken Me,
Or *to whom* shall I be equal?" says
the Holy One.

26 Lift up your eyes on high,
And see who has created these *things,*
Who brings out their host by number;
He calls them all by name,
By the greatness of His might
And the strength of *His* power;
Not one is missing.

27 Why do you say, O Jacob,
And speak, O Israel:
"My way is hidden from the LORD,
And my just claim is passed over by
my God"?

28 Have you not known?
Have you not heard?
The everlasting God, the LORD,
The Creator of the ends of the earth,
Neither faints nor is weary.
His understanding is unsearchable.

29 He gives power to the weak,
And to *those who have* no might He
increases strength.

30 Even the youths shall faint and be
weary,
And the young men shall utterly fall,

31 But those who wait on the LORD
Shall renew *their* strength;
They shall mount up with wings like
eagles,
They shall run and not be weary,
They shall walk and not faint.

Israel Assured of God's Help

41 "Keep silence before Me,
O coastlands,
And let the people renew *their*
strength!
Let them come near, then let them
speak;

Let us come near together for
judgment.

2 "Who raised up one from the east?
Who in righteousness called him to
His feet?
Who gave the nations before him,
And made *him* rule over kings?
Who gave *them* as the dust *to* his
sword,
As driven stubble to his bow?

3 Who pursued them, *and* passed safely
By the way *that* he had not gone
with his feet?

4 Who has performed and done *it,*
Calling the generations from the
beginning?
' I, the LORD, am the first;
And with the last I *am* He.' "

5 The coastlands saw *it* and feared,
The ends of the earth were afraid;
They drew near and came.

6 Everyone helped his neighbor,
And said to his brother,
"Be of good courage!"

7 So the craftsman encouraged the
goldsmith;
He who smooths *with* the hammer
inspired him who strikes the anvil,
Saying, "It *is* ready for the soldering";
Then he fastened it with pegs,
That it might not totter.

8 "But you, Israel, *are* My servant,
Jacob whom I have chosen,
The descendants of Abraham My
friend.

9 *You* whom I have taken from the
ends of the earth,
And called from its farthest regions,
And said to you,
' You *are* My servant,
I have chosen you and have not cast
you away:

10 Fear not, for I *am* with you;
Be not dismayed, for I *am* your God.
I will strengthen you,
Yes, I will help you,
I will uphold you with My righteous
right hand.'

11 "Behold, all those who were incensed
against you
Shall be ashamed and disgraced;

They shall be as nothing,
And those who strive with you shall
    perish.

12 You shall seek them and not find
        them—
Those who contended with you.
Those who war against you
Shall be as nothing,
As a nonexistent thing.

13 For I, the LORD your God, will hold
        your right hand,
Saying to you, 'Fear not, I will help
        you.'

14 "Fear not, you worm Jacob,
You men of Israel!
I will help you," says the LORD
And your Redeemer, the Holy One of
    Israel.

15 "Behold, I will make you into a new
        threshing sledge with sharp teeth;
You shall thresh the mountains and
        beat *them* small,
And make the hills like chaff.

16 You shall winnow them, the wind
        shall carry them away,
And the whirlwind shall scatter
        them;
You shall rejoice in the LORD,
And glory in the Holy One of Israel.

17 "The poor and needy seek water, but
        there is none,
Their tongues fail for thirst.
I, the LORD, will hear them;
I, the God of Israel, will not forsake
        them.

18 I will open rivers in desolate heights,
And fountains in the midst of the
        valleys;
I will make the wilderness a pool of
        water,
And the dry land springs of water.

19 I will plant in the wilderness the
        cedar and the acacia tree,
The myrtle and the oil tree;
I will set in the desert the cypress
        tree *and* the pine
And the box tree together,

20 That they may see and know,
And consider and understand
        together,
That the hand of the LORD has done
        this,
And the Holy One of Israel has
        created it.

The Futility of Idols

21 "Present your case," says the LORD.
"Bring forth your strong *reasons*,"
        says the King of Jacob.

ROMANTIC QUOTES AND NOTES
It's a Matter of Who (and Whose) We Are

Most of our problems—marital and otherwise—can be summed up in two things:

1. We forget who God is.
2. We forget who we are in Christ.

When we lose sight of who God is and of our identity as Christians, when we forget that we are children of the King, for whom nothing is impossible, we set ourselves up for failure in the very areas in which God has called us to succeed. This is particularly true in the home.

When God calls us to marriage and parenthood, He doesn't promise us that it will always be easy. What He *does* promise, however, is that He will strengthen us, help us,

and uphold us through anything that comes our way. Speaking through the Old Testament prophet Isaiah, God lovingly tells His people, "You are My servant, I have chosen you and have not cast you away: Fear not, for I am with you; be not dismayed, for I am your God. I will strengthen you, yes, I will help you, I will uphold you with My righteous right hand'" (41:9, 10).

Are you struggling with some difficulty in your home right now? If so, remember that you belong to the Creator of the universe, and that you belong to Him. Fear not!

Take Him at His word ... He promised to uphold you.

22 "Let them bring forth and show us
     what will happen;
  Let them show the former things,
     what they *were,*
  That we may consider them,
  And know the latter end of them;
  Or declare to us things to come.
23 Show the things that are to come
     hereafter,
  That we may know that you *are* gods;
  Yes, do good or do evil,
  That we may be dismayed and
     see *it* together.
24 Indeed you *are* nothing,
  And your work *is* nothing;
  He who chooses you *is* an
     abomination.

25 "I have raised up one from the north,
  And he shall come;
  From the rising of the sun he shall
     call on My name;
  And he shall come against princes
     as *though* mortar,
  As the potter treads clay.
26 Who has declared from the
     beginning, that we may know?
  And former times, that we may say,
     'He *is* righteous'?
  Surely *there is* no one who shows,
  Surely *there is* no one who declares,
  Surely *there is* no one who hears
     your words.
27 The first time *I said* to Zion,
 'Look, there they are!'
  And I will give to Jerusalem one who
     brings good tidings.
28 For I looked, and *there was* no man;
  I looked among them, but *there was*
     no counselor,
  Who, when I asked of them, could
     answer a word.
29 Indeed they *are* all worthless;[a]
  Their works *are* nothing;
  Their molded images *are* wind and
     confusion.

The Servant of the LORD

42 "Behold! My Servant whom I
   uphold,

41:29 [a]Following Masoretic Text and Vulgate; Dead
Sea Scrolls, Syriac, and Targum read *nothing;*
Septuagint omits the first line.

My Elect One *in whom* My soul
     delights!
  I have put My Spirit upon Him;
  He will bring forth justice to the
     Gentiles.
2 He will not cry out, nor raise *His voice,*
  Nor cause His voice to be heard in
     the street.
3 A bruised reed He will not break,
  And smoking flax He will not quench;
  He will bring forth justice for truth.
4 He will not fail nor be discouraged,
  Till He has established justice in the
     earth;
  And the coastlands shall wait for His
     law."

5 Thus says God the LORD,
  Who created the heavens and
     stretched them out,
  Who spread forth the earth and that
     which comes from it,
  Who gives breath to the people on it,
  And spirit to those who walk on it:
6 "I, the LORD, have called You in
     righteousness,
  And will hold Your hand;
  I will keep You and give You as a
     covenant to the people,
  As a light to the Gentiles,
7 To open blind eyes,
  To bring out prisoners from the
     prison,
  Those who sit in darkness from the
     prison house.
8 I *am* the LORD, that *is* My name;
  And My glory I will not give to
     another,
  Nor My praise to carved images.
9 Behold, the former things have come
     to pass,
  And new things I declare;
  Before they spring forth I tell you of
     them."

Praise to the LORD

10 Sing to the LORD a new song,
  And His praise from the ends of the
     earth,
  You who go down to the sea, and all
     that is in it,
  You coastlands and you inhabitants
     of them!

11 Let the wilderness and its cities lift
       up *their voice*,
    The villages *that* Kedar inhabits.
    Let the inhabitants of Sela sing,
    Let them shout from the top of the
       mountains.
12 Let them give glory to the LORD,
    And declare His praise in the
       coastlands.
13 The LORD shall go forth like a
       mighty man;
    He shall stir up *His* zeal like a man
       of war.
    He shall cry out, yes, shout aloud;
    He shall prevail against His enemies.

Promise of the LORD's Help

14 "I have held My peace a long time,
    I have been still and restrained
       Myself.
    Now I will cry like a woman in labor,
    I will pant and gasp at once.
15 I will lay waste the mountains and
       hills,
    And dry up all their vegetation;
    I will make the rivers coastlands,
    And I will dry up the pools.
16 I will bring the blind by a way they
       did not know;
    I will lead them in paths they have
       not known.
    I will make darkness light before
       them,
    And crooked places straight.
    These things I will do for them,
    And not forsake them.
17 They shall be turned back,
    They shall be greatly ashamed,
    Who trust in carved images,
    Who say to the molded images,
    ' You *are* our gods.'

18 "Hear, you deaf;
    And look, you blind, that you may see.
19 Who *is* blind but My servant,
    Or deaf as My messenger *whom* I
       send?
    Who *is* blind as *he who is* perfect,
    And blind as the LORD's servant?
20 Seeing many things, but you do not
       observe;
    Opening the ears, but he does not
       hear."

Israel's Obstinate Disobedience

21 The LORD is well pleased for His
       righteousness' sake;
    He will exalt the law and make *it*
       honorable.
22 But this *is* a people robbed and
       plundered;
    All of them are snared in holes,
    And they are hidden in prison houses;
    They are for prey, and no one delivers;
    For plunder, and no one says,
    "Restore!"

23 Who among you will give ear to this?
    Who will listen and hear for the time
       to come?
24 Who gave Jacob for plunder, and
       Israel to the robbers?
    Was it not the LORD,
    He against whom we have sinned?
    For they would not walk in His ways,
    Nor were they obedient to His law.
25 Therefore He has poured on him the
       fury of His anger
    And the strength of battle;
    It has set him on fire all around,
    Yet he did not know;
    And it burned him,
    Yet he did not take *it* to heart.

The Redeemer of Israel

43 But now, thus says the LORD,
       who created you, O Jacob,
    And He who formed you, O Israel:
    "Fear not, for I have redeemed you;
    I have called *you* by your name;
    You *are* Mine.
2   When you pass through the waters, I
       will be with you;
    And through the rivers, they shall
       not overflow you.
    When you walk through the fire, you
       shall not be burned,
    Nor shall the flame scorch you.
3   For I *am* the LORD your God,
    The Holy One of Israel, your Savior;
    I gave Egypt for your ransom,
    Ethiopia and Seba in your place.
4   Since you were precious in My sight,
    You have been honored,
    And I have loved you;
    Therefore I will give men for you,
    And people for your life.

5 Fear not, for I *am* with you;
I will bring your descendants from
the east,
And gather you from the west;
6 I will say to the north, 'Give them up!'
And to the south, 'Do not keep them
back!'
Bring My sons from afar,
And My daughters from the ends of
the earth—
7 Everyone who is called by My name,
Whom I have created for My glory;
I have formed him, yes, I have made
him."

8 Bring out the blind people who have
eyes,
And the deaf who have ears.
9 Let all the nations be gathered
together,
And let the people be assembled.
Who among them can declare this,
And show us former things?
Let them bring out their witnesses,
that they may be justified;
Or let them hear and say, "*It is* truth."
10 "You *are* My witnesses," says the LORD,
"And My servant whom I have chosen,
That you may know and believe Me,
And understand that I *am* He.
Before Me there was no God formed,
Nor shall there be after Me.
11 I, *even* I, *am* the LORD,
And besides Me *there is* no savior.
12 I have declared and saved,
I have proclaimed,
And *there was* no foreign *god* among
you;
Therefore you *are* My witnesses,"
Says the LORD, "that I *am* God.
13 Indeed before the day *was,* I *am* He;
And *there is* no one who can deliver
out of My hand;
I work, and who will reverse it?"

14 Thus says the LORD, your Redeemer,
The Holy One of Israel:
"For your sake I will send to Babylon,
And bring them all down as
fugitives—
The Chaldeans, who rejoice in their
ships.
15 I *am* the LORD, your Holy One,
The Creator of Israel, your King."

BIBLICAL INSIGHTS • 43:18, 19
Look Toward the Future

ARE YOU OR YOUR SPOUSE weighed down or burdened by events from your past? I think some Christians are living life like someone who is trying to drive a car but can't take his eyes off the rearview mirror. In your own family, you may need to help your mate understand that he or she has no business dwelling on things God has already forgotten.

One woman I know had been in an ungodly dating relationship that she finally broke off. During the next year, Isaiah 43:18, 19 became very real to her, "Do not remember the former things, nor consider the things of old. Behold, I will do a new thing, now it shall spring forth; shall you not know it? I will even make a road in the wilderness and rivers in the desert." What a promise! If you or your spouse struggles over foolish choices in the past, may I encourage you to dwell upon the promise of this passage?

Along the same lines, Paul writes, "forgetting those things which are behind and reaching forward to those things which are ahead, I press toward the goal for the prize of the upward call of God in Christ Jesus" (Phil. 3:13, 14). Paul refused to focus on his rearview mirror. He resolutely looked forward—at the Person of Christ. Help your mate do the same. Encourage your children to learn to deal with their failures and receive God's grace.

16 Thus says the LORD, who makes a
way in the sea
And a path through the mighty waters,
17 Who brings forth the chariot and
horse,
The army and the power
(They shall lie down together, they
shall not rise;
They are extinguished, they are
quenched like a wick):
18 "Do not remember the former things,
Nor consider the things of old.

DEVOTIONS FOR COUPLES • 43:19
Adjusting to One Another

In marriage, God brings together two people of differing backgrounds, tastes, and outlooks—and that means issues of adjustment. I'm sure you've noticed! But you may not have realized that the key to making these necessary adjustments in your relationship is for both of you to see each other and your marriage as more important than your individual values and desires. In fact, if you insist on holding on tightly to what *you* want, you'll never develop the kind of relationship you really want.

Keep some critical points in mind as you learn to make adjustments in your relationship:

1. *Recognize that adjustments are inevitable.*

Every married couple has to deal with grains of sand in their shoes. Remember what James wrote, "My brethren, count it all joy when you fall into various trials" (James 1:2). He said *when* you encounter trials, not *if* you encounter them. As you begin to accept the fact that you will have to make changes in your behavior and learn how to receive your mate as a gift from God, even with his or her frustrating traits, you'll be heading in the direction of oneness in marriage.

2. *Understand that adjustments have a divine purpose.*

God uses such issues to combine two unique people into something new called "Us." He uses adjustments to teach us how to love another dramatically different, imperfect human being. At prime moments, God will use your marriage to show you how to love the unlovely.

3. *Ask God for wisdom on how to live with this person who's so different from you.*

Instead of trying to change your spouse and correct all the bad habits, either accept the situation or adjust yourself. Barbara recalls, "I had to realize that God had to change Dennis. I couldn't." Martin Luther said, "Marriage may be an institution, but it isn't a reformatory!"

4. *Be more concerned about your own rough spots than those of your spouse.*

Jesus instructed us to take the log out of our own eye before trying to take a speck out of someone else's eye (Matt. 7:3–5). That's truly advice made for marriage. If I'm not willing to make changes, how can I expect Barbara to change?

5. *Make a commitment to work through the inevitable adjustments together.*

The apostle Paul provided guidelines for handling adjustment rhubarbs, "Let nothing be done through selfish ambition or conceit, but in lowliness of mind, let each esteem others better than himself" (Phil. 2:3). That's a description of a grace-filled marriage—giving your partner room to be different and flexing on his or her behalf.

Look over my list of five adjustments and pick one that you'd like to implement for your spouse.

---

19 Behold, I will do a new thing,
Now it shall spring forth;
Shall you not know it?
I will even make a road in the
    wilderness
And rivers in the desert.

20 The beast of the field will honor Me,
The jackals and the ostriches,
Because I give waters in the
    wilderness
And rivers in the desert,
To give drink to My people, My
    chosen.

21 This people I have formed for
    Myself;
They shall declare My praise.

Pleading with Unfaithful Israel

22 "But you have not called upon Me, O
    Jacob;
And you have been weary of Me, O
    Israel.

23 You have not brought Me the sheep
    for your burnt offerings,
Nor have you honored Me with your
    sacrifices.

I have not caused you to serve with
grain offerings,
Nor wearied you with incense.

24 You have bought Me no sweet cane
with money,
Nor have you satisfied Me with the
fat of your sacrifices;
But you have burdened Me with your
sins,
You have wearied Me with your
iniquities.

25 "I, *even* I, *am* He who blots out your
transgressions for My own sake;
And I will not remember your sins.

26 Put Me in remembrance;
Let us contend together;
State your *case,* that you may be
acquitted.

27 Your first father sinned,
And your mediators have
transgressed against Me.

28 Therefore I will profane the princes
of the sanctuary;
I will give Jacob to the curse,
And Israel to reproaches.

God's Blessing on Israel

44 "Yet hear me now, O Jacob
My servant,
And Israel whom I have chosen.

2 Thus says the LORD who made you
And formed you from the womb,
who will help you:
' Fear not, O Jacob My servant;
And you, Jeshurun, whom I have
chosen.

3 For I will pour water on him who is
thirsty,
And floods on the dry ground;
I will pour My Spirit on your
descendants,
And My blessing on your offspring;

4 They will spring up among the grass
Like willows by the watercourses.'

5 One will say, 'I *am* the LORD's';
Another will call *himself* by the name
of Jacob;
Another will write *with* his hand,
'The LORD's,'
And name *himself* by the name of
Israel.

There Is No Other God

6 "Thus says the LORD, the King of
Israel,
And his Redeemer, the LORD of hosts:
' I *am* the First and I *am* the Last;
Besides Me *there is* no God.

7 And who can proclaim as I do?
Then let him declare it and set it in
order for Me,
Since I appointed the ancient people.
And the things that are coming and
shall come,
Let them show these to them.

8 Do not fear, nor be afraid;
Have I not told you from that time,
and declared *it?*
You *are* My witnesses.
Is there a God besides Me?
Indeed *there is* no other Rock;
I know not *one.*' "

Idolatry Is Foolishness

9 Those who make an image, all of
them *are* useless,
And their precious things shall not
profit;
They *are* their own witnesses;
They neither see nor know, that they
may be ashamed.

10 Who would form a god or mold an
image
That profits him nothing?

11 Surely all his companions would be
ashamed;
And the workmen, they *are* mere men.
Let them all be gathered together,
Let them stand up;
Yet they shall fear,
They shall be ashamed together.

12 The blacksmith with the tongs
works one in the coals,
Fashions it with hammers,
And works it with the strength of
his arms.
Even so, he is hungry, and his
strength fails;
He drinks no water and is faint.

13 The craftsman stretches out *his* rule,
He marks one out with chalk;
He fashions it with a plane,
He marks it out with the compass,

And makes it like the figure of a man,
According to the beauty of a man,
   that it may remain in the house.
14 He cuts down cedars for himself,
And takes the cypress and the oak;
He secures *it* for himself among the
   trees of the forest.
He plants a pine, and the rain
   nourishes *it*.
15 Then it shall be for a man to burn,
For he will take some of it and warm
   himself;
Yes, he kindles *it* and bakes bread;
Indeed he makes a god and worships
   it;
He makes it a carved image, and falls
   down to it.
16 He burns half of it in the fire;
With this half he eats meat;
He roasts a roast, and is satisfied.
He even warms *himself* and says,
"Ah! I am warm,
I have seen the fire."
17 And the rest of it he makes into a
   god,
His carved image.
He falls down before it and worships
   it,
Prays to it and says,
"Deliver me, for you *are* my god!"

18 They do not know nor understand;
For He has shut their eyes, so that
   they cannot see,
And their hearts, so that they cannot
   understand.
19 And no one considers in his heart,
Nor *is there* knowledge nor
   understanding to say,
"I have burned half of it in the fire,
Yes, I have also baked bread on its
   coals;
I have roasted meat and eaten *it;*
And shall I make the rest of it an
   abomination?
Shall I fall down before a block of
   wood?"
20 He feeds on ashes;
A deceived heart has turned him
   aside;
And he cannot deliver his soul,
Nor say, "*Is there* not a lie in my
   right hand?"

Israel Is Not Forgotten

21 "Remember these, O Jacob,
And Israel, for you *are* My servant;
I have formed you, you *are* My
   servant;
O Israel, you will not be forgotten by
   Me!
22 I have blotted out, like a thick cloud,
   your transgressions,
And like a cloud, your sins.
Return to Me, for I have redeemed
   you."

23 Sing, O heavens, for the LORD has
   done *it!*
Shout, you lower parts of the earth;
Break forth into singing, you
   mountains,
O forest, and every tree in it!
For the LORD has redeemed Jacob,
And glorified Himself in Israel.

Judah Will Be Restored

24 Thus says the LORD, your Redeemer,
And He who formed you from the
   womb:
"I *am* the LORD, who makes all *things,*
Who stretches out the heavens all
   alone,
Who spreads abroad the earth by
   Myself;
25 Who frustrates the signs of the
   babblers,
And drives diviners mad;
Who turns wise men backward,
And makes their knowledge
   foolishness;
26 Who confirms the word of His
   servant,
And performs the counsel of His
   messengers;
Who says to Jerusalem, 'You shall be
   inhabited,'
To the cities of Judah, 'You shall be
   built,'
And I will raise up her waste places;
27 Who says to the deep, 'Be dry!
And I will dry up your rivers';
28 Who says of Cyrus, '*He is* My
   shepherd,
And he shall perform all My pleasure,
Saying to Jerusalem, "You shall be
   built,"

And to the temple, "Your foundation
   shall be laid." '

Cyrus, God's Instrument

45 "Thus says the LORD to His
         anointed,
   To Cyrus, whose right hand I have
      held—
   To subdue nations before him
   And loose the armor of kings,
   To open before him the double doors,
   So that the gates will not be shut:
2 'I will go before you
   And make the crooked places[a]
      straight;
   I will break in pieces the gates of
      bronze
   And cut the bars of iron.
3 I will give you the treasures of
      darkness
   And hidden riches of secret places,
   That you may know that I, the LORD,
   Who call *you* by your name,
   Am the God of Israel.
4 For Jacob My servant's sake,
   And Israel My elect,
   I have even called you by your name;
   I have named you, though you have
      not known Me.
5 I *am* the LORD, and *there is* no other;
   There is no God besides Me.
   I will gird you, though you have not
      known Me,
6 That they may know from the rising
      of the sun to its setting
   That *there is* none besides Me.
   I *am* the LORD, and *there is* no other;
7 I form the light and create darkness,
   I make peace and create calamity;
   I, the LORD, do all these *things.*'

8 "Rain down, you heavens, from above,
   And let the skies pour down
      righteousness;
   Let the earth open, let them bring
      forth salvation,
   And let righteousness spring up
      together.
   I, the LORD, have created it.

9 "Woe to him who strives with his
      Maker!
   Let the potsherd *strive* with the
      potsherds of the earth!
   Shall the clay say to him who forms
      it, 'What are you making?'
   Or shall your handiwork *say,* 'He has
      no hands'?
10 Woe to him who says to *his* father,
      'What are you begetting?'
   Or to the woman, 'What have you
      brought forth?'"

11 Thus says the LORD,
   The Holy One of Israel, and his
      Maker:
   "Ask Me of things to come
      concerning My sons;
   And concerning the work of My
      hands, you command Me.
12 I have made the earth,
   And created man on it.
   I—My hands—stretched out the
      heavens,
   And all their host I have commanded.
13 I have raised him up in righteousness,
   And I will direct all his ways;
   He shall build My city
   And let My exiles go free,
   Not for price nor reward,"
   Says the LORD of hosts.

The LORD, the Only Savior

14 Thus says the LORD:

   "The labor of Egypt and merchandise
      of Cush
   And of the Sabeans, men of stature,
   Shall come over to you, and they
      shall be yours;
   They shall walk behind you,
   They shall come over in chains;
   And they shall bow down to you.
   They will make supplication to you,
      saying, 'Surely God *is* in you,
   And *there is* no other;
   There is no other God.'"

15 Truly You *are* God, who hide Yourself,
   O God of Israel, the Savior!
16 They shall be ashamed
   And also disgraced, all of them;
   They shall go in confusion together,
   Who are makers of idols.

45:2 [a]Dead Sea Scrolls and Septuagint read *mountains;* Targum reads *I will trample down the walls;* Vulgate reads *I will humble the great ones of the earth.*

17 *But* Israel shall be saved by the LORD
With an everlasting salvation;
You shall not be ashamed or
disgraced
Forever and ever.

18 For thus says the LORD,
Who created the heavens,
Who is God,
Who formed the earth and made it,
Who has established it,
Who did not create it in vain,
Who formed it to be inhabited:
"I *am* the LORD, and *there is* no other.

19 I have not spoken in secret,
In a dark place of the earth;
I did not say to the seed of Jacob,
'Seek Me in vain';
I, the LORD, speak righteousness,
I declare things that are right.

20 "Assemble yourselves and come;
Draw near together,
You *who have* escaped from the
nations.
They have no knowledge,
Who carry the wood of their carved
image,
And pray to a god *that* cannot save.

21 Tell and bring forth *your case;*
Yes, let them take counsel together.
Who has declared this from ancient
time?
Who has told it from that time?
Have not I, the LORD?
And *there is* no other God besides Me,
A just God and a Savior;
There is none besides Me.

22 "Look to Me, and be saved,
All you ends of the earth!
For I *am* God, and *there is* no other.

23 I have sworn by Myself;
The word has gone out of My mouth
in righteousness,
And shall not return,
That to Me every knee shall bow,
Every tongue shall take an oath.

24 He shall say,
'Surely in the LORD I have
righteousness and strength.
To Him *men* shall come,
And all shall be ashamed
Who are incensed against Him.

25 In the LORD all the descendants of
Israel
Shall be justified, and shall glory.'"

Dead Idols and the Living God

46 Bel bows down, Nebo stoops;
Their idols were on the beasts
and on the cattle.
Your carriages *were* heavily loaded,
A burden to the weary *beast.*

2 They stoop, they bow down together;
They could not deliver the burden,
But have themselves gone into
captivity.

3 "Listen to Me, O house of Jacob,
And all the remnant of the house of
Israel,
Who have been upheld *by Me* from
birth,
Who have been carried from the
womb:

4 Even to *your* old age, I *am* He,
And *even* to gray hairs I will carry
you!
I have made, and I will bear;
Even I will carry, and will deliver *you.*

5 "To whom will you liken Me, and
make *Me* equal
And compare Me, that we should be
alike?

6 They lavish gold out of the bag,
And weigh silver on the scales;
They hire a goldsmith, and he makes
it a god;
They prostrate themselves, yes, they
worship.

7 They bear it on the shoulder, they
carry it
And set it in its place, and it stands;
From its place it shall not move.
Though *one* cries out to it, yet it
cannot answer
Nor save him out of his trouble.

8 "Remember this, and show yourselves
men;
Recall to mind, O you transgressors.

9 Remember the former things of old,
For I *am* God, and *there is* no other;
I *am* God, and *there is* none like Me,

10 Declaring the end from the
beginning,

And from ancient times *things* that
are not *yet* done,
Saying, 'My counsel shall stand,
And I will do all My pleasure,'
11 Calling a bird of prey from the east,
The man who executes My counsel,
from a far country.
Indeed I have spoken *it;*
I will also bring it to pass.
I have purposed *it;*
I will also do it.

12 "Listen to Me, you stubborn-hearted,
Who *are* far from righteousness:
13 I bring My righteousness near, it
shall not be far off;
My salvation shall not linger.
And I will place salvation in Zion,
For Israel My glory.

The Humiliation of Babylon

47 "Come down and sit in the dust,
O virgin daughter of Babylon;
Sit on the ground without a throne,
O daughter of the Chaldeans!
For you shall no more be called
Tender and delicate.
2 Take the millstones and grind meal.
Remove your veil,
Take off the skirt,
Uncover the thigh,
Pass through the rivers.
3 Your nakedness shall be uncovered,
Yes, your shame will be seen;
I will take vengeance,
And I will not arbitrate with a man."

4 *As for* our Redeemer, the LORD of
hosts *is* His name,
The Holy One of Israel.

5 "Sit in silence, and go into
darkness,
O daughter of the Chaldeans;
For you shall no longer be called
The Lady of Kingdoms.
6 I was angry with My people;
I have profaned My inheritance,
And given them into your hand.
You showed them no mercy;
On the elderly you laid your yoke
very heavily.
7 And you said, 'I shall be a lady
forever,'

So that you did not take these *things*
to heart,
Nor remember the latter end of them.

8 "Therefore hear this now, *you who are*
given to pleasures,
Who dwell securely,
Who say in your heart, 'I *am,* and
there is no one else besides me;
I shall not sit *as* a widow,
Nor shall I know the loss of
children';
9 But these two *things* shall come to
you
In a moment, in one day:
The loss of children, and
widowhood.
They shall come upon you in their
fullness
Because of the multitude of your
sorceries,
For the great abundance of your
enchantments.

10 "For you have trusted in your
wickedness;
You have said, 'No one sees me';
Your wisdom and your knowledge
have warped you;
And you have said in your heart,
'I *am,* and *there is* no one else besides
me.'
11 Therefore evil shall come upon you;
You shall not know from where it
arises.
And trouble shall fall upon you;
You will not be able to put it off.
And desolation shall come upon you
suddenly,
Which you shall not know.

12 "Stand now with your enchantments
And the multitude of your sorceries,
In which you have labored from your
youth—
Perhaps you will be able to profit,
Perhaps you will prevail.
13 You are wearied in the multitude of
your counsels;
Let now the astrologers, the
stargazers,
And the monthly prognosticators
Stand up and save you
From what shall come upon you.

14 Behold, they shall be as stubble,
The fire shall burn them;
They shall not deliver themselves
From the power of the flame;
It shall not *be* a coal to be warmed by,
Nor a fire to sit before!

15 Thus shall they be to you
With whom you have labored,
Your merchants from your youth;
They shall wander each one to his
quarter.
No one shall save you.

Israel Refined for God's Glory

48 "Hear this, O house of Jacob,

Who are called by the name of
Israel,
And have come forth from the
wellsprings of Judah;
Who swear by the name of the LORD,
And make mention of the God of
Israel,
But not in truth or in righteousness;

2 For they call themselves after the
holy city,
And lean on the God of Israel;
The LORD of hosts *is* His name:

3 "I have declared the former things
from the beginning;
They went forth from My mouth,
and I caused them to hear it.
Suddenly I did *them,* and they came
to pass.

4 Because I knew that you *were*
obstinate,
And your neck *was* an iron sinew,
And your brow bronze,

5 Even from the beginning I have
declared *it* to you;
Before it came to pass I proclaimed *it*
to you,
Lest you should say, 'My idol has
done them,
And my carved image and my
molded image
Have commanded them.'

6 "You have heard;
See all this.
And will you not declare *it?*
I have made you hear new things
from this time,

Even hidden things, and you did not
know them.

7 They are created now and not from
the beginning;
And before this day you have not
heard them,
Lest you should say, 'Of course I
knew them.'

8 Surely you did not hear,
Surely you did not know;
Surely from long ago your ear was
not opened.
For I knew that you would deal very
treacherously,
And were called a transgressor from
the womb.

9 "For My name's sake I will defer My
anger,
And *for* My praise I will restrain it
from you,
So that I do not cut you off.

10 Behold, I have refined you, but not as
silver;
I have tested you in the furnace of
affliction.

11 For My own sake, for My own sake, I
will do *it;*
For how should *My name* be
profaned?
And I will not give My glory to
another.

God's Ancient Plan to Redeem Israel

12 "Listen to Me, O Jacob,
And Israel, My called:
I *am* He, I *am* the First,
I *am* also the Last.

13 Indeed My hand has laid the
foundation of the earth,
And My right hand has stretched out
the heavens;
When I call to them,
They stand up together.

14 "All of you, assemble yourselves, and
hear!
Who among them has declared these
things?
The LORD loves him;
He shall do His pleasure on
Babylon,
And His arm *shall be against*
the Chaldeans.

15   I, *even* I, have spoken;
      Yes, I have called him,
      I have brought him, and his way will
          prosper.

16   "Come near to Me, hear this:
      I have not spoken in secret from the
          beginning;
      From the time that it was, I *was*
          there.
      And now the Lord GOD and His
          Spirit
      Have[a] sent Me."

17   Thus says the LORD, your Redeemer,
      The Holy One of Israel:
      "I *am* the LORD your God,
      Who teaches you to profit,
      Who leads you by the way you
          should go.

18   Oh, that you had heeded My
          commandments!
      Then your peace would have been
          like a river,
      And your righteousness like the
          waves of the sea.

19   Your descendants also would have
          been like the sand,
      And the offspring of your body like
          the grains of sand;
      His name would not have been cut
          off
      Nor destroyed from before Me."

20   Go forth from Babylon!
      Flee from the Chaldeans!
      With a voice of singing,
      Declare, proclaim this,
      Utter it to the end of the earth;
      Say, "The LORD has redeemed
      His servant Jacob!"

21   And they did not thirst
      When He led them through the
          deserts;
      He caused the waters to flow from
          the rock for them;
      He also split the rock, and the waters
          gushed out.

22   "*There is* no peace," says the LORD,
      "for the wicked."

The Servant, the Light to the Gentiles

49   "Listen, O coastlands, to Me,
          And take heed, you peoples from
          afar!
      The LORD has called Me from the
          womb;
      From the matrix of My mother He
          has made mention of My name.
2   And He has made My mouth like a
          sharp sword;
      In the shadow of His hand He has
          hidden Me,
      And made Me a polished shaft;
      In His quiver He has hidden Me."

3   "And He said to me,
      ' You *are* My servant, O Israel,
      In whom I will be glorified.'
4   Then I said, 'I have labored in vain,
      I have spent my strength for nothing
          and in vain;
      Yet surely my just reward *is* with the
          LORD,
      And my work with my God.'"

5   "And now the LORD says,
      Who formed Me from the womb *to
          be* His Servant,
      To bring Jacob back to Him,
      So that Israel is gathered to Him[a]
      (For I shall be glorious in the eyes of
          the LORD,
      And My God shall be My strength),
6   Indeed He says,
      'It is too small a thing that You
          should be My Servant
      To raise up the tribes of Jacob,
      And to restore the preserved ones of
          Israel;
      I will also give You as a light to the
          Gentiles,
      That You should be My salvation to
          the ends of the earth.'"

7   Thus says the LORD,
      The Redeemer of Israel, their Holy
          One,
      To Him whom man despises,
      To Him whom the nation abhors,
      To the Servant of rulers:
      "Kings shall see and arise,
      Princes also shall worship,
      Because of the LORD who is faithful,
      The Holy One of Israel;
      And He has chosen You."

48:16 [a] The Hebrew verb is singular.
49:5 [a] Qere, Dead Sea Scrolls, and Septuagint read *is gathered to Him*; Kethib reads *is not gathered.*

BIBLICAL INSIGHTS • 49:15

Prepare Them for What's Ahead

AS THE PROPHET ISAIAH speaks to God's people about His covenant love for them, he asks the rhetorical question, "Can a woman forget her nursing child, and not have compassion on the son of her womb?" (49:15).

The obvious answer, of course, is "No." God made women with a capacity to love their children with unending devotion.

But beyond the initial love affair a mother usually feels for her newborns, what keeps a mother lovingly devoted to her children for a *lifetime*? I think it's her awareness that raising and releasing her children is the ultimate mission of motherhood. Her love and care for her children helps give them the security they will need to serve God throughout their lives.

Every mother needs to see into the future—to envision the finish line—because she knows God has called her to prepare her children for a life independent of their mother's love. A wise mother knows that present difficulties, though unpleasant, are often the schoolroom for building character.

Lady Bird Johnson, the wife of former U.S. President Lyndon Johnson, was speaking to all mothers when she said, "Sometimes the greatest bravery of all is simply to get up in the morning and go about your business." I remember a lot of mornings when I felt the exact same way! But remembering my assignment from the Lord to pour my life into the lives of our six children provided the motivation I needed.

---

⁸Thus says the Lord:

"In an acceptable time I have heard You,
And in the day of salvation I have
    helped You;
I will preserve You and give You
As a covenant to the people,
To restore the earth,

To cause them to inherit the desolate
    heritages;
⁹ That You may say to the prisoners,
    'Go forth,'
To those who *are* in darkness, 'Show
    yourselves.'

"They shall feed along the roads,
And their pastures *shall be* on all
    desolate heights.
¹⁰ They shall neither hunger nor thirst,
Neither heat nor sun shall strike
    them;
For He who has mercy on them will
    lead them,
Even by the springs of water He will
    guide them.
¹¹ I will make each of My mountains a
    road,
And My highways shall be elevated.
¹² Surely these shall come from afar;
Look! Those from the north and the
    west,
And these from the land of Sinim."

¹³ Sing, O heavens!
Be joyful, O earth!
And break out in singing, O
    mountains!
For the Lord has comforted His
    people,
And will have mercy on His afflicted.

God Will Remember Zion

¹⁴ But Zion said, "The Lord has
    forsaken me,
And my Lord has forgotten me."

¹⁵ "Can a woman forget her nursing
    child,
And not have compassion on the son
    of her womb?
Surely they may forget,
Yet I will not forget you.
¹⁶ See, I have inscribed you on the
    palms *of My hands;*
Your walls *are* continually before
    Me.
¹⁷ Your sonsᵃ shall make haste;
Your destroyers and those who laid
    you waste
Shall go away from you.

49:17 ᵃDead Sea Scrolls, Septuagint, Targum, and Vulgate read *builders*.

18   Lift up your eyes, look around and
          see;
       All these gather together *and* come
          to you.
       As I live," says the LORD,
       "You shall surely clothe yourselves
          with them all as an ornament,
       And bind them *on you* as a bride
          does.

19   "For your waste and desolate places,
       And the land of your destruction,
       Will even now be too small for the
          inhabitants;
       And those who swallowed you up
          will be far away.

20   The children you will have,
       After you have lost the others,
       Will say again in your ears,
     ' The place *is* too small for me;
       Give me a place where I may
          dwell.'

21   Then you will say in your heart,
     ' Who has begotten these for me,
       Since I have lost my children and am
          desolate,
       A captive, and wandering to and fro?
       And who has brought these up?
       There I was, left alone;
       But these, where *were* they?'"

22Thus says the Lord GOD:

       "Behold, I will lift My hand in an oath
          to the nations,
       And set up My standard for the
          peoples;
       They shall bring your sons in *their*
          arms,
       And your daughters shall be carried
          on *their* shoulders;

23   Kings shall be your foster fathers,
       And their queens your nursing
          mothers;
       They shall bow down to you with
          their faces to the earth,
       And lick up the dust of your feet.
       Then you will know that I *am* the
          LORD,
       For they shall not be ashamed who
          wait for Me."

24   Shall the prey be taken from the
          mighty,
       Or the captives of the righteous[a] be
          delivered?

25But thus says the LORD:

       "Even the captives of the mighty
          shall be taken away,
       And the prey of the terrible be
          delivered;
       For I will contend with him who
          contends with you,
       And I will save your children.

26   I will feed those who oppress you
          with their own flesh,
       And they shall be drunk with their
          own blood as with sweet wine.
       All flesh shall know
       That I, the LORD, *am* your Savior,
       And your Redeemer, the Mighty One
          of Jacob."

The Servant, Israel's Hope

50   Thus says the LORD:

       "Where *is* the certificate of your
          mother's divorce,
       Whom I have put away?
       Or which of My creditors *is it* to
          whom I have sold you?
       For your iniquities you have sold
          yourselves,
       And for your transgressions your
          mother has been put away.

2   Why, when I came, *was there* no man?
       Why, when I called, *was there* none to
          answer?
       Is My hand shortened at all that it
          cannot redeem?
       Or have I no power to deliver?
       Indeed with My rebuke I dry up the
          sea,
       I make the rivers a wilderness;
       Their fish stink because *there is* no
          water,
       And die of thirst.

3   I clothe the heavens with blackness,
       And I make sackcloth their covering."

4   "The Lord GOD has given Me
       The tongue of the learned,
       That I should know how to speak
       A word in season to *him who is* weary.

49:24 aFollowing Masoretic Text and Targum; Dead
Sea Scrolls, Syriac, and Vulgate read *the mighty;*
Septuagint reads *unjustly.*

He awakens Me morning by morning,
He awakens My ear
To hear as the learned.

5 The Lord GOD has opened My ear;
And I was not rebellious,
Nor did I turn away.

6 I gave My back to those who struck
Me,
And My cheeks to those who
plucked out the beard;
I did not hide My face from shame
and spitting.

7 "For the Lord GOD will help Me;
Therefore I will not be disgraced;
Therefore I have set My face like a
flint,
And I know that I will not be
ashamed.

8 *He is* near who justifies Me;
Who will contend with Me?
Let us stand together.
Who *is* My adversary?
Let him come near Me.

9 Surely the Lord GOD will help Me;
Who *is* he *who* will condemn Me?
Indeed they will all grow old like a
garment;
The moth will eat them up.

10 "Who among you fears the LORD?
Who obeys the voice of His Servant?
Who walks in darkness
And has no light?
Let him trust in the name of the LORD
And rely upon his God.

11 Look, all you who kindle a fire,
Who encircle *yourselves* with sparks:
Walk in the light of your fire and in
the sparks you have kindled—
This you shall have from My hand:
You shall lie down in torment.

The LORD Comforts Zion

51 "Listen to Me, you who follow after
righteousness,
You who seek the LORD:
Look to the rock *from which* you
were hewn,
And to the hole of the pit *from which*
you were dug.

2 Look to Abraham your father,
And to Sarah *who* bore you;
For I called him alone,

And blessed him and increased him."

3 For the LORD will comfort Zion,
He will comfort all her waste places;
He will make her wilderness like
Eden,
And her desert like the garden of the
LORD;
Joy and gladness will be found in it,
Thanksgiving and the voice of
melody.

4 "Listen to Me, My people;
And give ear to Me, O My nation:
For law will proceed from Me,
And I will make My justice rest
As a light of the peoples.

5 My righteousness *is* near,
My salvation has gone forth,
And My arms will judge the peoples;
The coastlands will wait upon Me,
And on My arm they will trust.

6 Lift up your eyes to the heavens,
And look on the earth beneath.
For the heavens will vanish away
like smoke,
The earth will grow old like a
garment,
And those who dwell in it will die in
like manner;
But My salvation will be forever,
And My righteousness will not be
abolished.

7 "Listen to Me, you who know
righteousness,
You people in whose heart *is* My law:
Do not fear the reproach of men,
Nor be afraid of their insults.

8 For the moth will eat them up like a
garment,
And the worm will eat them like wool;
But My righteousness will be forever,
And My salvation from generation to
generation."

9 Awake, awake, put on strength,
O arm of the LORD!
Awake as in the ancient days,
In the generations of old.
Are You not *the arm* that cut Rahab
apart,
And wounded the serpent?

10 *Are* You not *the One* who dried up
the sea,

The waters of the great deep;
That made the depths of the sea a
   road
For the redeemed to cross over?
11 So the ransomed of the LORD shall
   return,
And come to Zion with singing,
With everlasting joy on their heads.
They shall obtain joy and gladness;
Sorrow and sighing shall flee away.

12 "I, *even* I, *am* He who comforts you.
Who *are* you that you should be afraid
Of a man *who* will die,
And of the son of a man *who* will be
   made like grass?
13 And you forget the LORD your Maker,
Who stretched out the heavens
And laid the foundations of the earth;
You have feared continually every day
Because of the fury of the oppressor,
When *he has* prepared to destroy.
And where *is* the fury of the
   oppressor?
14 The captive exile hastens, that he
   may be loosed,
That he should not die in the pit,
And that his bread should not fail.
15 But I *am* the LORD your God,
Who divided the sea whose waves
   roared—
The LORD of hosts *is* His name.
16 And I have put My words in your
   mouth;
I have covered you with the shadow
   of My hand,
That I may plant the heavens,
Lay the foundations of the earth,
And say to Zion, 'You *are* My people.'"

God's Fury Removed

17 Awake, awake!
Stand up, O Jerusalem,
You who have drunk at the hand of
   the LORD
The cup of His fury;
You have drunk the dregs of the cup
   of trembling,
And drained *it* out.
18 *There is* no one to guide her
Among all the sons she has brought
   forth;

Nor *is there any* who takes her by
   the hand
Among all the sons she has brought
   up.
19 These two *things* have come to you;
Who will be sorry for you?—
Desolation and destruction, famine
   and sword—
By whom will I comfort you?
20 Your sons have fainted,
They lie at the head of all the
   streets,
Like an antelope in a net;
They are full of the fury of the LORD,
The rebuke of your God.

21 Therefore please hear this, you
   afflicted,
And drunk but not with wine.
22 Thus says your Lord,
The LORD and your God,
Who pleads the cause of His people:
"See, I have taken out of your hand
The cup of trembling,
The dregs of the cup of My fury;
You shall no longer drink it.
23 But I will put it into the hand of
   those who afflict you,
Who have said to you,[a]
' Lie down, that we may walk over you.'
And you have laid your body like the
   ground,
And as the street, for those who
   walk over."

God Redeems Jerusalem

52 Awake, awake!
Put on your strength, O Zion;
Put on your beautiful garments,
O Jerusalem, the holy city!
For the uncircumcised and the
   unclean
Shall no longer come to you.
2 Shake yourself from the dust, arise;
Sit down, O Jerusalem!
Loose yourself from the bonds of
   your neck,
O captive daughter of Zion!

3 For thus says the LORD:

"You have sold yourselves for nothing,
And you shall be redeemed without
   money."

51:23 [a]Literally *your soul*

⁴For thus says the Lord GOD:

"My people went down at first
Into Egypt to dwell there;
Then the Assyrian oppressed them
    without cause.
5 Now therefore, what have I here,"
    says the LORD,
"That My people are taken away for
    nothing?
Those who rule over them
Make them wail,"ᵃ says the LORD,
"And My name is blasphemed
    continually every day.
6 Therefore My people shall know My
    name;
Therefore they shall know in that day
That I am He who speaks:
'Behold, it is I.'"

7 How beautiful upon the mountains
Are the feet of him who brings good
    news,
Who proclaims peace,
Who brings glad tidings of good
    things,
Who proclaims salvation,
Who says to Zion,
"Your God reigns!"
8 Your watchmen shall lift up their
    voices,
With their voices they shall sing
    together;
For they shall see eye to eye
When the LORD brings back Zion.
9 Break forth into joy, sing together,
You waste places of Jerusalem!
For the LORD has comforted His
    people,
He has redeemed Jerusalem.
10 The LORD has made bare His holy
    arm
In the eyes of all the nations;
And all the ends of the earth shall
    see
The salvation of our God.

11 Depart! Depart! Go out from there,
Touch no unclean thing;
Go out from the midst of her,
Be clean,
You who bear the vessels of the LORD.
12 For you shall not go out with haste,
Nor go by flight;

For the LORD will go before you,
And the God of Israel will be your
    rear guard.

The Sin-Bearing Servant

13 Behold, My Servant shall deal
    prudently;
He shall be exalted and extolled and
    be very high.
14 Just as many were astonished at you,
So His visage was marred more than
    any man,
And His form more than the sons of
    men;
15 So shall He sprinkleᵃ many nations.
Kings shall shut their mouths at
    Him;
For what had not been told them
    they shall see,
And what they had not heard they
    shall consider.

53 Who has believed our report?
And to whom has the arm of the
    LORD been revealed?
2 For He shall grow up before Him as
    a tender plant,
And as a root out of dry ground.
He has no form or comeliness;
And when we see Him,
There is no beauty that we should
    desire Him.
3 He is despised and rejected by men,
A Man of sorrows and acquainted
    with grief.
And we hid, as it were, our faces
    from Him;
He was despised, and we did not
    esteem Him.

4 Surely He has borne our griefs
And carried our sorrows;
Yet we esteemed Him stricken,
Smitten by God, and afflicted.
5 But He was wounded for our
    transgressions,
He was bruised for our iniquities;
The chastisement for our peace was
    upon Him,
And by His stripes we are healed.

52:5 ᵃDead Sea Scrolls read Mock; Septuagint reads
Marvel and wail; Targum reads Boast themselves;
Vulgate reads Treat them unjustly. 52:15 ᵃOr startle

BIBLICAL INSIGHTS • 53:6

A Bird Dog Like Me

DO YOU KNOW WHY ALL OF US struggle in obeying God? It's because we all have a will contrary to His will. Isaiah pictures our stubborn disobedience and rebellion with these famous words: "All we like sheep have gone astray; we have turned, every one, to his own way" (53:6).

Sheep are not the only creatures that remind me of our selfish bent. Dogs do, too. I can see my own stiff-necked response to God mirrored in the training of bird dogs known as retrievers. While all breeds must be trained to fetch, each type of retriever responds differently to training.

For the strong-willed Chesapeake Bay retriever, trainers must use a club to teach the dogs to obey the commands of their master. For the black Labrador, only the sting of a freshly cut switch is required. And the golden retriever is the most sensitive of all: a trainer needs only his voice to train these eager-to-please dogs.

I wonder, what does God have to use to train you? Does He need a club, a switch, or just the sound of His voice?

There have been times when He's had to use all three on me. I can tell you from experience which is the least painful!

When Isaiah spoke of our being sheep, he used a well-known animal of his day. Today, we may not be familiar with sheep, but there is plenty of evidence that we still do want to go our own way. Why run from the One who loves you the most? Why not go His way?

---

6   All we like sheep have gone astray;
     We have turned, every one, to his
        own way;
     And the LORD has laid on Him the
        iniquity of us all.

7   He was oppressed and He was
        afflicted,
     Yet He opened not His mouth;
     He was led as a lamb to the
        slaughter,
     And as a sheep before its shearers is
        silent,
     So He opened not His mouth.

8   He was taken from prison and from
        judgment,
     And who will declare His generation?
     For He was cut off from the land of
        the living;
     For the transgressions of My people
        He was stricken.

9   And they[a] made His grave with the
        wicked—
     But with the rich at His death,

Because He had done no violence,
     Nor *was any* deceit in His mouth.

10 Yet it pleased the LORD to bruise Him;
     He has put *Him* to grief.
     When You make His soul an offering
        for sin,
     He shall see *His* seed, He shall
        prolong *His* days,
     And the pleasure of the LORD shall
        prosper in His hand.

11 He shall see the labor of His soul,[a]
        and be satisfied.
     By His knowledge My righteous
        Servant shall justify many,
     For He shall bear their iniquities.

12 Therefore I will divide Him a portion
        with the great,
     And He shall divide the spoil with
        the strong,
     Because He poured out His soul unto
        death,
     And He was numbered with the
        transgressors,
     And He bore the sin of many,
     And made intercession for the
        transgressors.

53:9 [a]Literally *he* or *He*
53:11 [a]Following Masoretic Text, Targum, and Vulgate; Dead Sea Scrolls and Septuagint read *From the labor of His soul He shall see light.*

A Perpetual Covenant of Peace

54 "Sing, O barren,
You *who* have not borne!
Break forth into singing, and cry aloud,
You *who* have not labored with child!
For more *are* the children of the desolate
Than the children of the married woman," says the LORD.

2 "Enlarge the place of your tent,
And let them stretch out the curtains of your dwellings;
Do not spare;
Lengthen your cords,
And strengthen your stakes.

3 For you shall expand to the right and to the left,
And your descendants will inherit the nations,
And make the desolate cities inhabited.

4 "Do not fear, for you will not be ashamed;
Neither be disgraced, for you will not be put to shame;
For you will forget the shame of your youth,
And will not remember the reproach of your widowhood anymore.

5 For your Maker *is* your husband,
The LORD of hosts *is* His name;
And your Redeemer *is* the Holy One of Israel;

He is called the God of the whole earth.

6 For the LORD has called you
Like a woman forsaken and grieved in spirit,
Like a youthful wife when you were refused,"
Says your God.

7 "For a mere moment I have forsaken you,
But with great mercies I will gather you.

8 With a little wrath I hid My face from you for a moment;
But with everlasting kindness I will have mercy on you,"
Says the LORD, your Redeemer.

9 "For this *is* like the waters of Noah to Me;
For as I have sworn
That the waters of Noah would no longer cover the earth,
So have I sworn
That I would not be angry with you, nor rebuke you.

10 For the mountains shall depart
And the hills be removed,
But My kindness shall not depart from you,
Nor shall My covenant of peace be removed,"
Says the LORD, who has mercy on you.

ROMANTIC QUOTES AND NOTES
Create Some Safety

Although we've been married since 1972, Barbara and I are still learning how to love one another in a way that casts out fear and keeps it from having a grip on our lives. So, for example, instead of getting irritated or resentful when Barbara sometimes feels reluctant to share her feelings, I recognize that my behavior can feel intimidating to her, and that's a form of fear. Since I don't want her to fear me (or my reaction to her), I need to change my behavior.

We both know that we are totally committed to each other, and I want to be more sensitive to her disposition, which is so different from my own. I've also sought ways to gently encourage Barbara to open up, and she's learning to take more risks as well. I want to embody God's words: "Do not fear, for you will not be ashamed; neither be disgraced, for you will not be put to shame" (54:4).

How are you different from your mate? How can you handle these differences in a way that makes your relationship totally safe for each other? Pray that you can grow as a couple to trust each other completely and so feel completely safe with one another.

11 "O you afflicted one,
   Tossed with tempest, *and* not
      comforted,
   Behold, I will lay your stones with
      colorful gems,
   And lay your foundations with
      sapphires.
12 I will make your pinnacles of rubies,
   Your gates of crystal,
   And all your walls of precious
      stones.
13 All your children *shall be* taught by
      the LORD,
   And great *shall be* the peace of your
      children.
14 In righteousness you shall be
      established;
   You shall be far from oppression, for
      you shall not fear;
   And from terror, for it shall not come
      near you.
15 Indeed they shall surely assemble,
      but not because of Me.
   Whoever assembles against you
      shall fall for your sake.

16 "Behold, I have created the blacksmith
   Who blows the coals in the fire,
   Who brings forth an instrument for
      his work;
   And I have created the spoiler to
      destroy.
17 No weapon formed against you shall
      prosper,
   And every tongue *which* rises against
      you in judgment
   You shall condemn.
   This *is* the heritage of the servants
      of the LORD,
   And their righteousness *is* from Me,"
   Says the LORD.

An Invitation to Abundant Life

55 "Ho! Everyone who thirsts,
   Come to the waters;
   And you who have no money,
   Come, buy and eat.
   Yes, come, buy wine and milk
   Without money and without price.
2 Why do you spend money for *what is*
      not bread,
   And your wages for *what* does not
      satisfy?

   Listen carefully to Me, and eat *what
      is* good,
   And let your soul delight itself in
      abundance.
3 Incline your ear, and come to Me.
   Hear, and your soul shall live;
   And I will make an everlasting
      covenant with you—
   The sure mercies of David.
4 Indeed I have given him *as* a witness
      to the people,
   A leader and commander for the
      people.
5 Surely you shall call a nation you do
      not know,
   And nations *who* do not know you
      shall run to you,
   Because of the LORD your God,
   And the Holy One of Israel;
   For He has glorified you."

6 Seek the LORD while He may be found,
   Call upon Him while He is near.
7 Let the wicked forsake his way,
   And the unrighteous man his
      thoughts;
   Let him return to the LORD,
   And He will have mercy on him;
   And to our God,
   For He will abundantly pardon.

8 "For My thoughts *are* not your
      thoughts,
   Nor *are* your ways My ways," says
      the LORD.
9 "For *as* the heavens are higher than
      the earth,
   So are My ways higher than your
      ways,
   And My thoughts than your thoughts.
10 "For as the rain comes down, and the
      snow from heaven,
   And do not return there,
   But water the earth,
   And make it bring forth and bud,
   That it may give seed to the sower
   And bread to the eater,
11 So shall My word be that goes forth
      from My mouth;
   It shall not return to Me void,
   But it shall accomplish what I please,
   And it shall prosper *in the thing* for
      which I sent it.

BIBLICAL INSIGHTS • 55:8, 9
Listen, Learn, and Live

ALTHOUGH I'VE NEVER HEARD anyone actually ask the question, there are times when I know couples wonder, "What was God *thinking* when He brought the two of us together?"

Actually, I encourage spouses to pursue this line of thought. If they do, they might find some relief for their marital troubles. And I'm not kidding!

God says through Isaiah, "'For My thoughts are not your thoughts, nor are your ways My ways,' says the Lord. 'For as the heavens are higher than the earth, so are My ways higher than your ways, and My thoughts than your thoughts'" (55:8, 9).

God's thoughts and ways are different from yours, but He wants to make them accessible to you—for your benefit and His glory. So if you're wondering, "*What was God thinking?*", then I encourage you to labor to find out. God wants you to learn to think His thoughts after Him, to discover and to walk in His ways.

"But how do I do *that?*" you wonder.

It's simple, really. You train yourself to *listen* to God in His Word, "Oh, that My people would listen to Me, that Israel would walk in My ways!" (Ps. 81:13). That's it! Listen, learn, and live. In the process, you just may better understand what God was *thinking* when he brought you and your mate together! His ways are not our ways.

---

12 "For you shall go out with joy,
   And be led out with peace;
   The mountains and the hills
   Shall break forth into singing before
      you,
   And all the trees of the field shall
      clap *their* hands.
13 Instead of the thorn shall come up
      the cypress tree,
   And instead of the brier shall come
      up the myrtle tree;
   And it shall be to the LORD for a name,

For an everlasting sign *that* shall not
   be cut off."

Salvation for the Gentiles

56 Thus says the LORD:

"Keep justice, and do righteousness,
For My salvation *is* about to come,
And My righteousness to be
   revealed.
2 Blessed *is* the man *who* does this,
   And the son of man *who* lays hold
      on it;
   Who keeps from defiling the Sabbath,
   And keeps his hand from doing any
      evil."

3 Do not let the son of the foreigner
   Who has joined himself to the LORD
   Speak, saying,
   "The LORD has utterly separated me
      from His people";
   Nor let the eunuch say,
   "Here I am, a dry tree."
4 For thus says the LORD:
   "To the eunuchs who keep My
      Sabbaths,
   And choose what pleases Me,
   And hold fast My covenant,
5 Even to them I will give in My house
   And within My walls a place and a
      name
   Better than that of sons and
      daughters;
   I will give them[a] an everlasting name
   That shall not be cut off.

6 "Also the sons of the foreigner
   Who join themselves to the LORD, to
      serve Him,
   And to love the name of the LORD, to
      be His servants—
   Everyone who keeps from defiling
      the Sabbath,
   And holds fast My covenant—
7 Even them I will bring to My holy
      mountain,
   And make them joyful in My house
      of prayer.
   Their burnt offerings and their
      sacrifices
   Will be accepted on My altar;

56:5 [a]Literally *him*

For My house shall be called a house
of prayer for all nations."

8 The Lord GOD, who gathers the
outcasts of Israel, says,
"Yet I will gather to him
Others besides those who are
gathered to him."

Israel's Irresponsible Leaders

9 All you beasts of the field, come to
devour,
All you beasts in the forest.

10 His watchmen *are* blind,
They are all ignorant;
They *are* all dumb dogs,
They cannot bark;
Sleeping, lying down, loving to
slumber.

11 Yes, *they are* greedy dogs
Which never have enough.
And they *are* shepherds
Who cannot understand;
They all look to their own way,
Every one for his own gain,
From his *own* territory.

12 "Come," *one says,* "I will bring wine,
And we will fill ourselves with
intoxicating drink;
Tomorrow will be as today,
And much more abundant."

Israel's Futile Idolatry

57 The righteous perishes,
And no man takes *it* to heart;
Merciful men *are* taken away,
While no one considers
That the righteous is taken away
from evil.

2 He shall enter into peace;
They shall rest in their beds,
Each one walking *in* his uprightness.

3 "But come here,
You sons of the sorceress,
You offspring of the adulterer and
the harlot!

4 Whom do you ridicule?
Against whom do you make a wide
mouth
And stick out the tongue?
Are you not children of transgression,

Offspring of falsehood,

5 Inflaming yourselves with gods
under every green tree,
Slaying the children in the valleys,
Under the clefts of the rocks?

6 Among the smooth *stones* of the
stream
Is your portion;
They, they, *are* your lot!
Even to them you have poured a
drink offering,
You have offered a grain offering.
Should I receive comfort in these?

INTIMATE MOMENTS

Plan a weekend away for the two of you.
Cater to his desires and his needs.

7 "On a lofty and high mountain
You have set your bed;
Even there you went up
To offer sacrifice.

8 Also behind the doors and their
posts
You have set up your remembrance;
For you have uncovered yourself *to
those other* than Me,
And have gone up to them;
You have enlarged your bed
And made *a covenant* with them;
You have loved their bed,
Where you saw *their* nudity.ᵃ

9 You went to the king with ointment,
And increased your perfumes;
You sent your messengers far off,
And *even* descended to Sheol.

10 You are wearied in the length of
your way;
Yet you did not say, 'There is no
hope.'
You have found the life of your hand;
Therefore you were not grieved.

11 "And of whom have you been afraid,
or feared,
That you have lied
And not remembered Me,

57:8 ᵃLiterally *hand,* a euphemism

Nor taken *it* to your heart?
Is it not because I have held My
    peace from of old
That you do not fear Me?
12 I will declare your righteousness
And your works,
For they will not profit you.
13 When you cry out,
Let your collection *of idols* deliver you.
But the wind will carry them all
    away,
A breath will take *them.*
But he who puts his trust in Me shall
    possess the land,
And shall inherit My holy
    mountain."

Healing for the Backslider

14 And one shall say,
    "Heap it up! Heap it up!
    Prepare the way,
    Take the stumbling block out of the
      way of My people."

15 For thus says the High and Lofty
    One
Who inhabits eternity, whose name *is*
    Holy:
"I dwell in the high and holy *place,*
With him *who* has a contrite and
    humble spirit,
To revive the spirit of the humble,
And to revive the heart of the
    contrite ones.
16 For I will not contend forever,
Nor will I always be angry;
For the spirit would fail before Me,
And the souls *which* I have made.
17 For the iniquity of his covetousness
I was angry and struck him;
I hid and was angry,
And he went on backsliding in the
    way of his heart.
18 I have seen his ways, and will heal
    him;
I will also lead him,
And restore comforts to him
And to his mourners.
19 "I create the fruit of the lips:
Peace, peace to *him who is* far off
    and to *him who is* near,"
Says the LORD,
"And I will heal him."

20 But the wicked *are* like the troubled
    sea,
When it cannot rest,
Whose waters cast up mire and dirt.
21 "*There is* no peace,"
Says my God, "for the wicked."

Fasting that Pleases God

58 "Cry aloud, spare not;
    Lift up your voice like a trumpet;
Tell My people their transgression,
And the house of Jacob their sins.
2 Yet they seek Me daily,
And delight to know My ways,
As a nation that did righteousness,
And did not forsake the ordinance of
    their God.
They ask of Me the ordinances of
    justice;
They take delight in approaching
    God.
3 'Why have we fasted,' *they say,* 'and
    You have not seen?
Why have we afflicted our souls, and
    You take no notice?'

"In fact, in the day of your fast you
    find pleasure,
And exploit all your laborers.
4 Indeed you fast for strife and
    debate,
And to strike with the fist of
    wickedness.
You will not fast as *you do* this day,
To make your voice heard on high.
5 Is it a fast that I have chosen,
A day for a man to afflict his soul?
Is it to bow down his head like a
    bulrush,
And to spread out sackcloth and
    ashes?
Would you call this a fast,
And an acceptable day to the LORD?

6 "*Is* this not the fast that I have chosen:
To loose the bonds of wickedness,
To undo the heavy burdens,
To let the oppressed go free,
And that you break every yoke?
7 *Is it* not to share your bread with the
    hungry,
And that you bring to your house the
    poor who are cast out;

When you see the naked, that you
  cover him,
And not hide yourself from your
  own flesh?
8 Then your light shall break forth like
  the morning,
Your healing shall spring forth
  speedily,
And your righteousness shall go
  before you;
The glory of the LORD shall be your
  rear guard.
9 Then you shall call, and the LORD
  will answer;
You shall cry, and He will say, 'Here I
  am.'

"If you take away the yoke from your
  midst,
The pointing of the finger, and
  speaking wickedness,
10 *If* you extend your soul to the
  hungry
And satisfy the afflicted soul,
Then your light shall dawn in the
  darkness,
And your darkness shall *be* as the
  noonday.

11 The LORD will guide you continually,
And satisfy your soul in drought,
And strengthen your bones;
You shall be like a watered garden,
And like a spring of water, whose
  waters do not fail.
12 Those from among you
Shall build the old waste places;
You shall raise up the foundations of
  many generations;
And you shall be called the Repairer
  of the Breach,
The Restorer of Streets to Dwell In.

13 "If you turn away your foot from the
  Sabbath,
From doing your pleasure on My
  holy day,
And call the Sabbath a delight,
The holy *day* of the LORD honorable,
And shall honor Him, not doing your
  own ways,
Nor finding your own pleasure,
Nor speaking *your own* words,
14 Then you shall delight yourself in
  the LORD;
And I will cause you to ride on the
  high hills of the earth,

PARENTING MATTERS

Q: *Does my presence as a father make a difference in my son's life?*

Yes! In fact, a father's involvement is a key social issue today. It's a much bigger deal than the national debt. The major problem facing America isn't in Washington, D.C.; it is in the hearts of American fathers.

A boy needs at least one man who pays attention to him, spends time with him, and admires him. A boy needs a role model, a man whom he can regard as a mentor. Boys need to be able to spend time with mature men who can help guide them on their own path to manhood. That's one of the key roles a father plays in his son's life.

Being the kind of father your son needs you to be requires courage, not perfection. We can't be perfect dads. So what can we do? We have to learn how to reserve energy so that we don't come home from work so emotionally exhausted that we have nothing left for our kids.

Ask yourself, "When I'm with my children, am I present, not just physically, but emotionally, relationally, and spiritually? Am I really *there* with my kids?" You will answer these questions differently depending on how old your kids are, what's happening with your career, and what's going on with your marriage. But they are important diagnostic questions to ask yourself from time to time!

And feed you with the heritage of
    Jacob your father.
The mouth of the LORD has spoken."

Separated from God

59 Behold, the LORD's hand is not
    shortened,
    That it cannot save;
    Nor His ear heavy,
    That it cannot hear.
2   But your iniquities have separated
    you from your God;
    And your sins have hidden *His* face
    from you,
    So that He will not hear.
3   For your hands are defiled with
    blood,
    And your fingers with iniquity;
    Your lips have spoken lies,
    Your tongue has muttered perversity.

4   No one calls for justice,
    Nor does *any* plead for truth.
    They trust in empty words and
    speak lies;
    They conceive evil and bring forth
    iniquity.
5   They hatch vipers' eggs and weave
    the spider's web;
    He who eats of their eggs dies,
    And *from* that which is crushed a
    viper breaks out.

6   Their webs will not become
    garments,
    Nor will they cover themselves with
    their works;
    Their works *are* works of iniquity,
    And the act of violence *is* in their
    hands.
7   Their feet run to evil,
    And they make haste to shed
    innocent blood;
    Their thoughts *are* thoughts of
    iniquity;
    Wasting and destruction *are* in their
    paths.
8   The way of peace they have not
    known,
    And *there is* no justice in their ways;
    They have made themselves crooked
    paths;
    Whoever takes that way shall not
    know peace.

Sin Confessed

9   Therefore justice is far from us,
    Nor does righteousness overtake us;
    We look for light, but there is
    darkness!
    For brightness, *but* we walk in
    blackness!
10   We grope for the wall like the blind,
    And we grope as if *we had* no eyes;
    We stumble at noonday as at
    twilight;
    We are as dead *men* in desolate
    places.
11   We all growl like bears,
    And moan sadly like doves;
    We look for justice, but *there is* none;
    For salvation, *but* it is far from us.
12   For our transgressions are multiplied
    before You,
    And our sins testify against us;
    For our transgressions *are* with us,
    And *as for* our iniquities, we know
    them:
13   In transgressing and lying against
    the LORD,
    And departing from our God,
    Speaking oppression and revolt,
    Conceiving and uttering from the
    heart words of falsehood.
14   Justice is turned back,
    And righteousness stands afar off;
    For truth is fallen in the street,
    And equity cannot enter.
15   So truth fails,
    And he *who* departs from evil makes
    himself a prey.

The Redeemer of Zion

    Then the LORD saw *it,* and it
    displeased Him
    That *there was* no justice.
16   He saw that *there was* no man,
    And wondered that *there was* no
    intercessor;
    Therefore His own arm brought
    salvation for Him;
    And His own righteousness, it
    sustained Him.
17   For He put on righteousness as a
    breastplate,
    And a helmet of salvation on His
    head;

He put on the garments of
vengeance for clothing,
And was clad with zeal as a cloak.
18 According to *their* deeds, accordingly
He will repay,
Fury to His adversaries,
Recompense to His enemies;
The coastlands He will fully repay.
19 So shall they fear
The name of the LORD from the west,
And His glory from the rising of the
sun;
When the enemy comes in like a
flood,
The Spirit of the LORD will lift up a
standard against him.
20 "The Redeemer will come to Zion,
And to those who turn from
transgression in Jacob,"
Says the LORD.

21"As for Me," says the LORD, "this *is* My
covenant with them: My Spirit who *is* upon
you, and My words which I have put in
your mouth, shall not depart from your
mouth, nor from the mouth of your
descendants, nor from the mouth of your
descendants' descendants," says the LORD,
"from this time and forevermore."

The Gentiles Bless Zion

60 Arise, shine;
For your light has come!
And the glory of the LORD is risen
upon you.
2 For behold, the darkness shall cover
the earth,
And deep darkness the people;
But the LORD will arise over you,
And His glory will be seen upon you.
3 The Gentiles shall come to your light,
And kings to the brightness of your
rising.

4 "Lift up your eyes all around, and see:
They all gather together, they come
to you;
Your sons shall come from afar,
And your daughters shall be nursed
at *your* side.
5 Then you shall see and become
radiant,
And your heart shall swell with joy;

Because the abundance of the sea
shall be turned to you,
The wealth of the Gentiles shall
come to you.
6 The multitude of camels shall cover
your *land*,
The dromedaries of Midian and
Ephah;

ROMANCE FAQ

**Q: *What can I do to
rekindle my wife's
desire for romance?***

Use the following top ten list as a place
to start.

10. *Hold hands.* Hold hands while driving, walking, sitting in church, or talking in bed.

9. *Give her a massage.* Give foot rubs,
back rubs, neck rubs, or a body massage.

8. *Serve her.* Remember the common
courtesies: opening the door, pulling
out a chair for her, etc.

7. *Give her a kiss.* Nibble on the back of
her ear or her neck, or just kiss her
before leaving for work.

6. *Walk together.* As a couple, go for a
walk in the early morning, after dinner, or as the sun sets.

5. *Write something romantic.* Leave
notes, letters, poems, cards, and
other romantic written messages
where she'll find them.

4. *Go out on a date.* A weekly date without the kids can be a lifesaver.

3. *Prepare a meal.* Have a quiet meal
together with candlelight, linger
over breakfast, or go on a picnic.

2. *Touch her tenderly.* Use nonsexual
touch: hold her, hug her, cuddle with
her, or place an arm around her in
public.

1. *Give her flowers.* Deliver, hand-pick, or
bring home a single rose. Tulips are a
great second choice!

All those from Sheba shall come;
They shall bring gold and incense,
And they shall proclaim the praises
   of the LORD.

7 All the flocks of Kedar shall be
      gathered together to you,
   The rams of Nebaioth shall minister
      to you;
   They shall ascend with acceptance
      on My altar,
   And I will glorify the house of My
      glory.

8 "Who *are* these *who* fly like a cloud,
   And like doves to their roosts?
9 Surely the coastlands shall wait for Me;
   And the ships of Tarshish *will come*
      first,
   To bring your sons from afar,
   Their silver and their gold with them,
   To the name of the LORD your God,
   And to the Holy One of Israel,
   Because He has glorified you.

10 "The sons of foreigners shall build up
      your walls,
   And their kings shall minister to you;
   For in My wrath I struck you,
   But in My favor I have had mercy on
      you.
11 Therefore your gates shall be open
      continually;
   They shall not be shut day or night,
   That *men* may bring to you the
      wealth of the Gentiles,
   And their kings in procession.
12 For the nation and kingdom which
      will not serve you shall perish,
   And *those* nations shall be utterly
      ruined.

13 "The glory of Lebanon shall come to
      you,
   The cypress, the pine, and the box
      tree together,
   To beautify the place of My sanctuary;
   And I will make the place of My feet
      glorious.
14 Also the sons of those who afflicted
      you
   Shall come bowing to you,
   And all those who despised you shall
      fall prostrate at the soles of your
      feet;

And they shall call you The City of
   the LORD,
Zion of the Holy One of Israel.

15 "Whereas you have been forsaken and
      hated,
   So that no one went through *you,*
   I will make you an eternal excellence,
   A joy of many generations.
16 You shall drink the milk of the
      Gentiles,
   And milk the breast of kings;
   You shall know that I, the LORD, *am*
      your Savior
   And your Redeemer, the Mighty One
      of Jacob.

17 "Instead of bronze I will bring gold,
   Instead of iron I will bring silver,
   Instead of wood, bronze,
   And instead of stones, iron.
   I will also make your officers peace,
   And your magistrates righteousness.
18 Violence shall no longer be heard in
      your land,
   Neither wasting nor destruction
      within your borders;
   But you shall call your walls
      Salvation,
   And your gates Praise.

God the Glory of His People

19 "The sun shall no longer be your light
      by day,
   Nor for brightness shall the moon
      give light to you;
   But the LORD will be to you an
      everlasting light,
   And your God your glory.
20 Your sun shall no longer go down,
   Nor shall your moon withdraw itself;
   For the LORD will be your everlasting
      light,
   And the days of your mourning
      shall be ended.
21 Also your people *shall* all *be*
      righteous;
   They shall inherit the land forever,
   The branch of My planting,
   The work of My hands,
   That I may be glorified.
22 A little one shall become a thousand,
   And a small one a strong nation.
   I, the LORD, will hasten it in its time."

The Good News of Salvation

61 "The Spirit of the Lord GOD *is*
upon Me,
Because the LORD has anointed Me
To preach good tidings to the poor;
He has sent Me to heal the
brokenhearted,
To proclaim liberty to the captives,
And the opening of the prison to
those who are bound;
2 To proclaim the acceptable year of
the LORD,
And the day of vengeance of our God;
To comfort all who mourn,
3 To console those who mourn in Zion,
To give them beauty for ashes,
The oil of joy for mourning,
The garment of praise for the spirit
of heaviness;
That they may be called trees of
righteousness,
The planting of the LORD, that He
may be glorified."

4 And they shall rebuild the old ruins,
They shall raise up the former
desolations,
And they shall repair the ruined cities,
The desolations of many generations.

5 Strangers shall stand and feed your
flocks,
And the sons of the foreigner
Shall be your plowmen and your
vinedressers.
6 But you shall be named the priests of
the LORD,
They shall call you the servants of
our God.
You shall eat the riches of the
Gentiles,
And in their glory you shall boast.
7 Instead of your shame *you shall have*
double *honor,*
And *instead of* confusion they shall
rejoice in their portion.
Therefore in their land they shall
possess double;
Everlasting joy shall be theirs.

8 "For I, the LORD, love justice;
I hate robbery for burnt offering;
I will direct their work in truth,
And will make with them an
everlasting covenant.
9 Their descendants shall be known
among the Gentiles,
And their offspring among the
people.

How Do You Spell *Important*?

What's most important to you? You and your mate would greatly benefit from spending some time singling out what you value the most.

At one season in our marriage, as Barbara and I were prayerfully discussing our individual core values, we made a profound discovery. We had different priorities! One of Barbara's top 5 values was teaching our children a good work ethic. I didn't even list that value in my top 10! Nor did she have one of my top 5 core values, teaching our children to develop healthy relationships, down on her sheet.

Suddenly it became clear why our weekend schedule sometimes felt like a battlefield. Barbara wanted to use our Saturdays to work on the house or in the yard, while I preferred to build memories in a boat on the lake. Neither value was wrong, they were just different.

Each of us spends our time on the things we feel are most important. Barbara and I ultimately settled on core values for our family that included the Great Commandment, cultivating compassion for others, developing a strong work ethic, healthy relationships, and the Great Commission.

And because most of us never get around to defining our core values, we end up living scattered and hectic lives, driven by unreal expectations or comparing ourselves with others.

Know what's most important to you both, and as a couple establish your own set of your five most important core values.

All who see them shall acknowledge
  them,
That they *are* the posterity *whom* the
  LORD has blessed."

10 I will greatly rejoice in the LORD,
My soul shall be joyful in my God;
For He has clothed me with the
  garments of salvation,
He has covered me with the robe of
  righteousness,
As a bridegroom decks *himself* with
  ornaments,
And as a bride adorns *herself* with
  her jewels.
11 For as the earth brings forth its bud,
As the garden causes the things that
  are sown in it to spring forth,
So the Lord GOD will cause
  righteousness and praise to
  spring forth before all the nations.

Assurance of Zion's Salvation

62 For Zion's sake I will not hold
  My peace,
And for Jerusalem's sake I will not
  rest,
Until her righteousness goes forth as
  brightness,
And her salvation as a lamp *that*
  burns.
2 The Gentiles shall see your
  righteousness,
And all kings your glory.
You shall be called by a new name,
Which the mouth of the LORD will
  name.
3 You shall also be a crown of glory
In the hand of the LORD,
And a royal diadem
In the hand of your God.
4 You shall no longer be termed
  Forsaken,
Nor shall your land any more be
  termed Desolate;
But you shall be called Hephzibah,[a]
  and your land Beulah;[a]
For the LORD delights in you,
And your land shall be married.
5 For *as* a young man marries a virgin,
So shall your sons marry you;
And *as* the bridegroom rejoices over
  the bride,

So shall your God rejoice over you.
6 I have set watchmen on your walls,
  O Jerusalem;
They shall never hold their peace
  day or night.
You who make mention of the LORD,
  do not keep silent,
7 And give Him no rest till He
  establishes
And till He makes Jerusalem a praise
  in the earth.

8 The LORD has sworn by His right
  hand
And by the arm of His strength:
"Surely I will no longer give your grain
As food for your enemies;
And the sons of the foreigner shall
  not drink your new wine,
For which you have labored.
9 But those who have gathered it shall
  eat it,
And praise the LORD;
Those who have brought it together
  shall drink it in My holy courts."

10 Go through,
Go through the gates!
Prepare the way for the people;
Build up,
Build up the highway!
Take out the stones,
Lift up a banner for the peoples!

11 Indeed the LORD has proclaimed
To the end of the world:
"Say to the daughter of Zion,
' Surely your salvation is coming;
Behold, His reward *is* with Him,
And His work before Him.' "
12 And they shall call them The Holy
  People,
The Redeemed of the LORD;
And you shall be called Sought Out,
A City Not Forsaken.

The LORD in Judgment and Salvation

63 Who *is* this who comes from Edom,
  With dyed garments from Bozrah,
This *One who is* glorious in His
  apparel,

62:4 [a]Literally *My Delight Is in Her* [b]Literally
Married

Traveling in the greatness of His
    strength?—

"I who speak in righteousness,
    mighty to save."

2 Why *is* Your apparel red,
    And Your garments like one who
      treads in the winepress?

3 "I have trodden the winepress alone,
    And from the peoples no one *was*
      with Me.
    For I have trodden them in My anger,
    And trampled them in My fury;
    Their blood is sprinkled upon My
      garments,
    And I have stained all My robes.
4 For the day of vengeance *is* in My
      heart,
    And the year of My redeemed has
      come.
5 I looked, but *there was* no one to
      help,
    And I wondered
    That *there was* no one to uphold;
    Therefore My own arm brought
      salvation for Me;
    And My own fury, it sustained Me.
6 I have trodden down the peoples in
      My anger,
    Made them drunk in My fury,
    And brought down their strength to
      the earth."

God's Mercy Remembered

7 I will mention the lovingkindnesses
      of the LORD
    And the praises of the LORD,
    According to all that the LORD has
      bestowed on us,
    And the great goodness toward the
      house of Israel,
    Which He has bestowed on them
      according to His mercies,
    According to the multitude of His
      lovingkindnesses.
8 For He said, "Surely they *are* My
      people,
    Children *who* will not lie."
    So He became their Savior.
9 In all their affliction He was afflicted,
    And the Angel of His Presence saved
      them;

In His love and in His pity He
    redeemed them;
    And He bore them and carried them
    All the days of old.
10 But they rebelled and grieved His
      Holy Spirit;
    So He turned Himself against them
      as an enemy,
    And He fought against them.

11 Then he remembered the days of old,
    Moses *and* his people, *saying:*
    "Where *is* He who brought them up
      out of the sea
    With the shepherd of His flock?
    Where *is* He who put His Holy Spirit
      within them,
12 Who led *them* by the right hand of
      Moses,
    With His glorious arm,
    Dividing the water before them
    To make for Himself an everlasting
      name,
13 Who led them through the deep,
    As a horse in the wilderness,
    That they might not stumble?"

14 As a beast goes down into the valley,
    And the Spirit of the LORD causes
      him to rest,
    So You lead Your people,
    To make Yourself a glorious name.

A Prayer of Penitence

15 Look down from heaven,
    And see from Your habitation, holy
      and glorious.
    Where *are* Your zeal and Your
      strength,
    The yearning of Your heart and
      Your mercies toward me?
    Are they restrained?
16 Doubtless You *are* our Father,
    Though Abraham was ignorant of us,
    And Israel does not acknowledge us.
    You, O LORD, *are* our Father;
    Our Redeemer from Everlasting *is*
      Your name.
17 O LORD, why have You made us stray
      from Your ways,
    And hardened our heart from Your
      fear?
    Return for Your servants' sake,
    The tribes of Your inheritance.

18 Your holy people have possessed *it*
        but a little while;
    Our adversaries have trodden down
        Your sanctuary.
19 We have become *like* those of old,
        over whom You never ruled,
    Those who were never called by
        Your name.

64 Oh, that You would rend
            the heavens!
    That You would come down!
    That the mountains might shake at
        Your presence—
2   As fire burns brushwood,
    As fire causes water to boil—
    To make Your name known to Your
        adversaries,
    That the nations may tremble at
        Your presence!
3   When You did awesome things *for*
        which we did not look,
    You came down,
    The mountains shook at Your presence.
4   For since the beginning of the world
    Men have not heard nor perceived by
        the ear,
    Nor has the eye seen any God
        besides You,

    Who acts for the one who waits for
        Him.
5   You meet him who rejoices and does
        righteousness,
    Who remembers You in Your ways.
    You are indeed angry, for we have
        sinned—
    In these ways we continue;
    And we need to be saved.
6   But we are all like an unclean *thing,*
    And all our righteousnesses *are* like
        filthy rags;
    We all fade as a leaf,
    And our iniquities, like the wind,
    Have taken us away.
7   And *there is* no one who calls on
        Your name,
    Who stirs himself up to take hold of
        You;
    For You have hidden Your face from
        us,
    And have consumed us because of
        our iniquities.
8   But now, O LORD,
    You *are* our Father;
    We *are* the clay, and You our potter;
    And all we *are* the work of Your
        hand.

PARENTING MATTERS

Q: *How can we build memories with our children?*

Decide now that your family is going to be guilty of having too much fun, rather than too little. Carve time out of your schedule for that to happen! You must purposefully sacrifice your time, because treasured memories rarely get built by default. These memories are more than just fun; through building treasured memories, you are laying an important foundation for the future in your child's life.

Vacations are great memory makers because they provide a time to get away and recharge your batteries. Holiday times are also important seasons in which lasting family memories are made. While the romance of a marriage can grow through romantic getaways, the romance of a relationship with your child is a rich heritage of shared family experiences. One of the most important ways to build memories is to practice the lost art of storytelling. Begin by telling your children how you met as a couple. Through the years, I kept a family scrapbook, and every New Year's Day while we cooked our dinner over a campfire, the whole family gathered around the scrapbook and we relived the year together. It's important for us to build a sense of connectedness to the past, because the lessons of life are often found in our past choices.

9 Do not be furious, O LORD,
Nor remember iniquity forever;
Indeed, please look—we all *are* Your
people!
10 Your holy cities are a wilderness,
Zion is a wilderness,
Jerusalem a desolation.
11 Our holy and beautiful temple,
Where our fathers praised You,
Is burned up with fire;
And all our pleasant things are laid
waste.
12 Will You restrain Yourself because of
these *things*, O LORD?
Will You hold Your peace, and afflict
us very severely?

The Righteousness of God's Judgment

65 "I was sought by *those who* did
not ask *for Me;*
I was found by *those who* did not
seek Me.
I said, 'Here I am, here I am,'
To a nation *that* was not called by
My name.
2 I have stretched out My hands all
day long to a rebellious people,
Who walk in a way *that is* not good,
According to their own thoughts;
3 A people who provoke Me to anger
continually to My face;
Who sacrifice in gardens,
And burn incense on altars of brick;
4 Who sit among the graves,
And spend the night in the tombs;
Who eat swine's flesh,
And the broth of abominable things
is *in* their vessels;
5 Who say, 'Keep to yourself,
Do not come near me,
For I am holier than you!'
These *are* smoke in My nostrils,
A fire that burns all the day.

6 "Behold, *it is* written before Me:
I will not keep silence, but will
repay—
Even repay into their bosom—
7 Your iniquities and the iniquities of
your fathers together,"
Says the LORD,

"Who have burned incense on the
mountains
And blasphemed Me on the hills;
Therefore I will measure their former
work into their bosom."

8 Thus says the LORD:

"As the new wine is found in the
cluster,
And *one* says, 'Do not destroy it,
For a blessing *is* in it,'
So will I do for My servants' sake,
That I may not destroy them all.
9 I will bring forth descendants from
Jacob,
And from Judah an heir of My
mountains;
My elect shall inherit it,
And My servants shall dwell there.
10 Sharon shall be a fold of flocks,
And the Valley of Achor a place for
herds to lie down,
For My people who have sought Me.

11 "But you *are* those who forsake the
LORD,
Who forget My holy mountain,
Who prepare a table for Gad,[a]
And who furnish a drink offering for
Meni.[b]
12 Therefore I will number you for the
sword,
And you shall all bow down to the
slaughter;
Because, when I called, you did not
answer;
When I spoke, you did not hear,
But did evil before My eyes,
And chose *that* in which I do not
delight."

13 Therefore thus says the Lord GOD:

"Behold, My servants shall eat,
But you shall be hungry;
Behold, My servants shall drink,
But you shall be thirsty;
Behold, My servants shall rejoice,
But you shall be ashamed;
14 Behold, My servants shall sing for
joy of heart,
But you shall cry for sorrow of
heart,
And wail for grief of spirit.

65:11 [a]Literally *Troop* or *Fortune,* a pagan deity
[b]Literally *Number* or *Destiny,* a pagan deity

15 You shall leave your name as a curse
    to My chosen;
For the Lord GOD will slay you,
And call His servants by another
    name;
16 So that he who blesses himself in the
    earth
Shall bless himself in the God of
    truth;
And he who swears in the earth
Shall swear by the God of truth;
Because the former troubles are
    forgotten,
And because they are hidden from
    My eyes.

The Glorious New Creation

17 "For behold, I create new heavens and
    a new earth;
And the former shall not be
    remembered or come to mind.
18 But be glad and rejoice forever in
    what I create;
For behold, I create Jerusalem *as a*
    rejoicing,
And her people a joy.
19 I will rejoice in Jerusalem,
And joy in My people;
The voice of weeping shall no longer
    be heard in her,
Nor the voice of crying.

20 "No more shall an infant from there
    live but a few days,
Nor an old man who has not fulfilled
    his days;
For the child shall die one hundred
    years old,
But the sinner *being* one hundred
    years old shall be accursed.
21 They shall build houses and inhabit
    them;
They shall plant vineyards and eat
    their fruit.
22 They shall not build and another
    inhabit;
They shall not plant and another eat;
For as the days of a tree, *so shall be*
    the days of My people,
And My elect shall long enjoy the
    work of their hands.
23 They shall not labor in vain,
Nor bring forth children for trouble;

For they *shall be* the descendants of
    the blessed of the LORD,
And their offspring with them.
24 "It shall come to pass
That before they call, I will answer;
And while they are still speaking, I
    will hear.
25 The wolf and the lamb shall feed
    together,
The lion shall eat straw like the ox,
And dust *shall be* the serpent's food.
They shall not hurt nor destroy in all
    My holy mountain,"
Says the LORD.

True Worship and False

66 Thus says the LORD:

"Heaven *is* My throne,
    And earth *is* My footstool.
Where *is* the house that you will
    build Me?
And where *is* the place of My rest?
2 For all those *things* My hand has
    made,
And all those *things* exist,"
Says the LORD.
"But on this *one* will I look:
On *him who is* poor and of a contrite
    spirit,
And who trembles at My word.

3 "He who kills a bull *is as if* he slays a
    man;
He who sacrifices a lamb, *as if* he
    breaks a dog's neck;
He who offers a grain offering, *as if
    he offers* swine's blood;
He who burns incense, *as if* he
    blesses an idol.
Just as they have chosen their own
    ways,
And their soul delights in their
    abominations,
4 So will I choose their delusions,
And bring their fears on them;
Because, when I called, no one
    answered,
When I spoke they did not hear;
But they did evil before My eyes,
And chose *that* in which I do not
    delight."

The Lord Vindicates Zion

5   Hear the word of the Lord,
    You who tremble at His word:
    "Your brethren who hated you,
    Who cast you out for My name's
        sake, said,
    ' Let the Lord be glorified,
    That we may see your joy.'
    But they shall be ashamed."

6   The sound of noise from the city!
    A voice from the temple!
    The voice of the Lord,
    Who fully repays His enemies!

7   "Before she was in labor, she gave
        birth;
    Before her pain came,
    She delivered a male child.

8   Who has heard such a thing?
    Who has seen such things?
    Shall the earth be made to give birth
        in one day?
    Or shall a nation be born at once?
    For as soon as Zion was in labor,
    She gave birth to her children.

9   Shall I bring to the time of birth, and
        not cause delivery?" says the Lord.
    "Shall I who cause delivery shut up
    the womb?" says your God.

10 "Rejoice with Jerusalem,
    And be glad with her, all you who
        love her;
    Rejoice for joy with her, all you who
        mourn for her;

11 That you may feed and be satisfied
    With the consolation of her bosom,
    That you may drink deeply and be
        delighted
    With the abundance of her glory."

12 For thus says the Lord:

    "Behold, I will extend peace to her
        like a river,
    And the glory of the Gentiles like a
        flowing stream.
    Then you shall feed;
    On *her* sides shall you be carried,
    And be dandled on *her* knees.

13 As one whom his mother comforts,
    So I will comfort you;
    And you shall be comforted in
        Jerusalem."

BIBLICAL INSIGHTS • 66:2

In Search of a Neck Machine

PERHAPS YOU'VE BEEN TO A GYM that has all those new machines so you can work out. I went to one that had about 25 different machines—each one of them dedicated to a different muscle group. I wish I had a machine that worked on the spiritual muscles of the neck. It would increase my flexibility whenever I become stiff-necked, especially when I grow too proud to admit mistakes, too stubborn to ask for forgiveness, or too arrogant to admit I need to depend upon God.

This machine would demand that I get on my knees, with my neck bent downward in prayer. To help work out the kinks, a vigorous massage with certain scriptures would be useful:

•God resists the proud, but gives grace to the humble. (James 4:6)

•On this one will I look: on him who is poor and of a contrite spirit, and who trembles at My word. (Is. 66:2)

•Therefore humble yourselves under the mighty hand of God, that He may exalt you in due time. (1 Pet. 5:6)

Being teachable with God and others would increase as the muscles of humility began to develop in my neck area. As I became more willing to hear the truth, admit failures, and take responsibility for wrong actions, a genuine joy would begin to move from my neck to my face.

Got any stiffness in *your* neck? Then consider for a minute that God is "full of compassion, and gracious, longsuffering and abundant in mercy and truth" (Ps. 86:15). His ways *are* higher—and better—than yours!

The Reign and Indignation of God

14 When you see *this,* your heart shall
        rejoice,
    And your bones shall flourish like
        grass;

The hand of the LORD shall be
known to His servants,
And *His* indignation to His enemies.
15 For behold, the LORD will come with
fire
And with His chariots, like a
whirlwind,
To render His anger with fury,
And His rebuke with flames of fire.
16 For by fire and by His sword
The LORD will judge all flesh;
And the slain of the LORD shall be
many.

17 "Those who sanctify themselves and
purify themselves,
To go to the gardens
After an *idol* in the midst,
Eating swine's flesh and the
abomination and the mouse,
Shall be consumed together," says
the LORD.

18"For I *know* their works and their
thoughts. It shall be that I will gather all
nations and tongues; and they shall come
and see My glory. 19I will set a sign among
them; and those among them who escape I
will send to the nations: *to* Tarshish and
Pul[a] and Lud, who draw the bow, and
Tubal and Javan, *to* the coastlands afar off
who have not heard My fame nor seen My
glory. And they shall declare My glory
among the Gentiles. 20Then they shall
bring all your brethren for an offering to
the LORD out of all nations, on horses and
in chariots and in litters, on mules and on
camels, to My holy mountain Jerusalem,"
says the LORD, "as the children of Israel
bring an offering in a clean vessel into the
house of the LORD. 21And I will also take
some of them for priests *and* Levites,"
says the LORD.

22 "For as the new heavens and the new
earth
Which I will make shall remain
before Me," says the LORD,
"So shall your descendants and your
name remain.
23 And it shall come to pass
That from one New Moon to another,
And from one Sabbath to another,
All flesh shall come to worship
before Me," says the LORD.

24 "And they shall go forth and look
Upon the corpses of the men
Who have transgressed against Me.
For their worm does not die,
And their fire is not quenched.
They shall be an abhorrence to all
flesh."

66:19 [a]Following Masoretic Text and Targum;
Septuagint reads *Put* (compare Jeremiah 46:9).

JEREMIAH

ABOUT SEVENTY YEARS AFTER ISAIAH, God raised up another man to speak out for Him to the people of Judah. Jeremiah was the son of a priest (and may have been a priest himself) who began his ministry in 627 B.C., during the reign of King Josiah (640–609 B.C.). He continued to speak on God's behalf for four decades, during the reigns of the last kings of Judah (Jehoahaz, 609; Jehoiakim, 609–597; Jehoiachin, 597; Zedekiah, 597–587).

In Jeremiah's day, the people regularly and openly practiced idol worship, including the horrific practice of child sacrifice. Although King Josiah sought to implement spiritual reforms, the spiritual revival soon fizzled and the people drifted right back into pagan practices.

Jeremiah had a hard life as a prophet. God called him to singleness (16:1–4) and he was threatened, put on trial for his life, put in stocks, forced to flee, and was publicly ridiculed by a false prophet. We know him as the "weeping prophet," not because of these hardships, but because of his deep desire to see God's people repent and avoid the coming devastation at the hands of the Babylonians.

The Book of Jeremiah does not follow a strict chronological order. The first 29 chapters describe the prophet's call and his dire warnings about the imminent invasion. Chapters 30—33 provide hope for the nation's restoration, following its time of captivity. Chapters 34—45 provide historical data about the Babylonian conquest of Judah and Jerusalem. The remaining chapters feature warnings from God to the pagan nations around Judah.

Although Jeremiah never gained popularity among his people, the beleaguered prophet never caved into intense pressure to change his message. He cared more about faithfulness to God than the esteem of men. He provides our children and us with a model as we seek to stand for God and His ways in an increasingly hostile culture. His message speaks to us today, calling us to turn from pride, rebellion against God, and spiritual lethargy. He also offers words of hope and encouragement to those who seek to be faithful and live obediently before God.

1 The words of Jeremiah the son of Hilkiah, of the priests who *were* in Anathoth in the land of Benjamin, ²to whom the word of the LORD came in the days of Josiah the son of Amon, king of Judah, in the thirteenth year of his reign. ³It came also in the days of Jehoiakim the son of Josiah, king of Judah, until the end of the eleventh year of Zedekiah the son of Josiah, king of Judah, until the carrying away of Jerusalem captive in the fifth month.

INTIMATE MOMENTS

Hold her hand whenever you are in public together. Open her door. Pull out her chair and allow her to be seated first.

The Prophet Is Called

⁴Then the word of the LORD came to me, saying:

5 "Before I formed you in the womb I
        knew you;
    Before you were born I sanctified
        you;
    I ordained you a prophet to the
        nations."

⁶Then said I:

"Ah, Lord GOD!
    Behold, I cannot speak, for I *am* a
        youth."

⁷But the LORD said to me:

"Do not say, 'I *am* a youth,'
    For you shall go to all to whom I
        send you,
    And whatever I command you, you
        shall speak.
8   Do not be afraid of their faces,
    For I *am* with you to deliver you,"
        says the LORD.

⁹Then the LORD put forth His hand and touched my mouth, and the LORD said to me:

"Behold, I have put My words in your
    mouth.

10 See, I have this day set you over the
        nations and over the kingdoms,
    To root out and to pull down,
    To destroy and to throw down,
    To build and to plant."

¹¹Moreover the word of the LORD came to me, saying, "Jeremiah, what do you see?"

And I said, "I see a branch of an almond tree."

¹²Then the LORD said to me, "You have seen well, for I am ready to perform My word."

¹³And the word of the LORD came to me the second time, saying, "What do you see?"

And I said, "I see a boiling pot, and it is facing away from the north."

¹⁴Then the LORD said to me:

"Out of the north calamity shall
        break forth
    On all the inhabitants of the land.
15   For behold, I am calling
    All the families of the kingdoms of
        the north," says the LORD;

"They shall come and each one set his
        throne
    At the entrance of the gates of
        Jerusalem,
    Against all its walls all around,
    And against all the cities of Judah.
16   I will utter My judgments
    Against them concerning all their
        wickedness,
    Because they have forsaken Me,
    Burned incense to other gods,
    And worshiped the works of their
        own hands.

17   "Therefore prepare yourself and arise,
    And speak to them all that I
        command you.
    Do not be dismayed before their
        faces,
    Lest I dismay you before them.
18   For behold, I have made you this day
    A fortified city and an iron pillar,
    And bronze walls against the whole
        land—
    Against the kings of Judah,
    Against its princes,
    Against its priests,
    And against the people of the land.

19   They will fight against you,
 But they shall not prevail against you.
 For I *am* with you," says the LORD,
  "to deliver you."

God's Case Against Israel

2 Moreover the word of the LORD came to me, saying, [2]"Go and cry in the hearing of Jerusalem, saying, 'Thus says the LORD:

 "I remember you,
 The kindness of your youth,
 The love of your betrothal,
 When you went after Me in the
  wilderness,
 In a land not sown.
3   Israel *was* holiness to the LORD,
 The firstfruits of His increase.
 All that devour him will offend;
 Disaster will come upon them," says
  the LORD.'"

[4]Hear the word of the LORD, O house of Jacob and all the families of the house of Israel. [5]Thus says the LORD:

 "What injustice have your fathers
  found in Me,
 That they have gone far from Me,
 Have followed idols,
 And have become idolaters?
6   Neither did they say, 'Where *is* the
  LORD,
 Who brought us up out of the land
  of Egypt,
 Who led us through the wilderness,
 Through a land of deserts and pits,
 Through a land of drought and the
  shadow of death,
 Through a land that no one crossed
 And where no one dwelt?'
7   I brought you into a bountiful country,
 To eat its fruit and its goodness.
 But when you entered, you defiled
  My land
 And made My heritage an
  abomination.
8   The priests did not say, 'Where *is* the
  LORD?'

 And those who handle the law did
  not know Me;
 The rulers also transgressed against
  Me;
 The prophets prophesied by Baal,
 And walked after *things that* do not
  profit.

9   "Therefore I will yet bring charges
  against you," says the LORD,
 "And against your children's children
  I will bring charges.
10   For pass beyond the coasts of
  Cyprus[a] and see,
 Send to Kedar[b] and consider diligently,
 And see if there has been such *a*
  thing.
11   Has a nation changed *its* gods,
 Which *are* not gods?
 But My people have changed their
  Glory
 For *what* does not profit.
12   Be astonished, O heavens, at this,
 And be horribly afraid;
 Be very desolate," says the LORD.
13   "For My people have committed two
  evils:
 They have forsaken Me, the fountain
  of living waters,
 And hewn themselves cisterns—
  broken cisterns that can hold no
  water.

14   "*Is* Israel a servant?
 Is he a homeborn *slave?*
 Why is he plundered?
15   The young lions roared at him, *and*
  growled;
 They made his land waste;
 His cities are burned, without
  inhabitant.
16   Also the people of Noph[a] and
  Tahpanhes
 Have broken the crown of your head.
17   Have you not brought this on
  yourself,
 In that you have forsaken the LORD
  your God
 When He led you in the way?
18   And now why take the road to
  Egypt,
 To drink the waters of Sihor?
 Or why take the road to Assyria,
 To drink the waters of the River?[a]

2:10 [a]Hebrew *Kittim,* western lands, especially Cyprus [b]In the northern Arabian desert, representative of the eastern cultures **2:16** [a]That is, Memphis in ancient Egypt **2:18** [a]That is, the Euphrates

19 Your own wickedness will correct you,
And your backslidings will rebuke you.
Know therefore and see that *it is* an
   evil and bitter *thing*
That you have forsaken the LORD
   your God,
And the fear of Me *is* not in you,"
Says the Lord GOD of hosts.

20 "For of old I have broken your yoke
   and burst your bonds;
And you said, 'I will not transgress,'
When on every high hill and under
   every green tree
You lay down, playing the harlot.

ROMANCE FAQ

Q: *How can I set my wife apart and put her on a pedestal?*

It may sound like a cliché, but a wife wants her husband to sweep her off her feet, carry her away to the castle, look deeply into her eyes and say, "Let's spend some time together." To a woman, that kind of focused attention is like precious gold.

One time Barbara and I had a little unresolved argument over a weekend. A couple of days later, we went on our weekly date, a custom for us. On that date we finally had enough time and a suitable environment where we could fully discuss and resolve our differences. We just needed several hours away from phones, papers and bills, and the needs of our children. And you need it just as much as we do!

Even when you and your wife have no conflicts or problems to work out, however, your better half craves such focused attention from you. Don't deprive her! The Song of Songs has taught me a great deal about living joyfully with Barbara, but maybe the most important truth I have found there is that *a relationship needs time for romance,* for two people to connect deeply, to understand each other, to enjoy each other's company, and to build mutual trust.

---

21 Yet I had planted you a noble vine, a
   seed of highest quality.
How then have you turned before Me
Into the degenerate plant of an alien
   vine?
22 For though you wash yourself with
   lye, and use much soap,
Yet your iniquity is marked before
   Me," says the Lord GOD.

23 "How can you say, 'I am not polluted,
I have not gone after the Baals'?
See your way in the valley;
Know what you have done:
You are a swift dromedary breaking
   loose in her ways,
24 A wild donkey used to the wilderness,
That sniffs at the wind in her desire;
In her time of mating, who can turn
   her away?
All those who seek her will not
   weary themselves;
In her month they will find her.
25 Withhold your foot from being
   unshod, and your throat from
   thirst.
But you said, 'There is no hope.
No! For I have loved aliens, and after
   them I will go.'

26 "As the thief is ashamed when he is
   found out,
So is the house of Israel ashamed;
They and their kings and their
   princes, and their priests and their
   prophets,
27 Saying to a tree, 'You *are* my father,'
And to a stone, 'You gave birth to me.'
For they have turned *their* back to
   Me, and not *their* face.
But in the time of their trouble
They will say, 'Arise and save us.'
28 But where *are* your gods that you
   have made for yourselves?
Let them arise,
If they can save you in the time of
   your trouble;
For *according to* the number of your
   cities
Are your gods, O Judah.

29 "Why will you plead with Me?
You all have transgressed against
   Me," says the LORD.

30 "In vain I have chastened your children;
     They received no correction.
   Your sword has devoured your
          prophets
     Like a destroying lion.

31 "O generation, see the word of the
          LORD!
   Have I been a wilderness to Israel,
   Or a land of darkness?
   Why do My people say, 'We are lords;
   We will come no more to You'?

32 Can a virgin forget her ornaments,
   Or a bride her attire?
   Yet My people have forgotten Me
          days without number.

33 "Why do you beautify your way to
          seek love?
   Therefore you have also taught
   The wicked women your ways.

34 Also on your skirts is found
   The blood of the lives of the poor
          innocents.
   I have not found it by secret search,
   But plainly on all these things.

35 Yet you say, 'Because I am innocent,
   Surely His anger shall turn from me.'
   Behold, I will plead My case against
          you,
   Because you say, 'I have not sinned.'

36 Why do you gad about so much to
          change your way?
   Also you shall be ashamed of Egypt
          as you were ashamed of Assyria.

37 Indeed you will go forth from him
   With your hands on your head;
   For the LORD has rejected your
          trusted allies,
   And you will not prosper by them.

Israel Is Shameless

3 "They say, 'If a man divorces his wife,
     And she goes from him
     And becomes another man's,
   May he return to her again?'
   Would not that land be greatly
          polluted?
   But you have played the harlot with
          many lovers;
   Yet return to Me," says the LORD.

2 "Lift up your eyes to the desolate
          heights and see:

Where have you not lain *with men*?
   By the road you have sat for them
   Like an Arabian in the wilderness;
   And you have polluted the land
   With your harlotries and your
          wickedness.

3 Therefore the showers have been
          withheld,
   And there has been no latter rain.
   You have had a harlot's forehead;
   You refuse to be ashamed.

4 Will you not from this time cry to Me,
   ' My Father, You *are* the guide of
          my youth?

5 Will He remain angry forever?
   Will He keep it to the end?'
   Behold, you have spoken and done
          evil things,
   As you were able."

A Call to Repentance

6 The LORD said also to me in the days of
Josiah the king: "Have you seen what backsliding Israel has done? She has gone up
on every high mountain and under every
green tree, and there played the harlot.
7 And I said, after she had done all these
things, 'Return to Me.' But she did not
return. And her treacherous sister Judah
saw it. 8 Then I saw that for all the causes
for which backsliding Israel had committed adultery, I had put her away and given
her a certificate of divorce; yet her treacherous sister Judah did not fear, but went
and played the harlot also. 9 So it came to
pass, through her casual harlotry, that she
defiled the land and committed adultery
with stones and trees. 10 And yet for all this
her treacherous sister Judah has not
turned to Me with her whole heart, but in
pretense," says the LORD.

11 Then the LORD said to me,
"Backsliding Israel has shown herself
more righteous than treacherous Judah.
12 Go and proclaim these words toward the
north, and say:

'Return, backsliding Israel,' says the
          LORD;
   'I will not cause My anger to fall on
          you.
   For I *am* merciful,' says the LORD;
   'I will not remain angry forever.

BIBLICAL INSIGHTS • 3:15

Train Them to Walk With God

WE'VE SURVEYED HUNDREDS of parents at FamilyLife's Weekend to Remember® marriage conferences on numerous issues, and the number-one need of parents is *learning how to effectively train their children to walk with God*. We want our children to have good jobs and healthy marriages and families, but what matters most is that they each have a vital relationship with Christ.

We have the unique privilege of shepherding our children's hearts so that as they grow older, they will desire to remain close to the heart of God. It is a profound responsibility, "And I will give you shepherds according to My heart, who will feed you with knowledge and understanding" (3:15).

In order for your children to embrace their God-given identity, they need to understand who God is and that knowing Him is the key to what life is all about. Some key concepts about God for you to share with your children are:

• God alone is Lord—there is no other.

• God is eternal.

• God is sovereign and has absolute authority.

• God has personality—mind, emotions, and will.

• God is love—He made human beings for relationships, both with Himself and with each other.

• God created us in His image—we are made to reflect God's love to others.

• God loves us—each of us is a person of value.

As our children learn these basic attributes of God, they will begin to see He is the One who gives their lives ultimate purpose and meaning. A. W. Tozer's statement is worth repeating, "The most important thing you think is what you think about God."

Ultimately, it's not who our children or even what family they come from that matters. It's what they think about God and who they are in Him.

---

13 Only acknowledge your iniquity,
   That you have transgressed against
      the LORD your God,
   And have scattered your charms
   To alien deities under every green
      tree,
   And you have not obeyed My voice,'
      says the LORD.

14"Return, O backsliding children," says the LORD; "for I am married to you. I will take you, one from a city and two from a family, and I will bring you to Zion. 15And I will give you shepherds according to My heart, who will feed you with knowledge and understanding.

16"Then it shall come to pass, when you are multiplied and increased in the land in those days," says the LORD, "that they will say no more, 'The ark of the covenant of the LORD.' It shall not come to mind, nor shall they remember it, nor shall they visit *it,* nor shall it be made anymore.

17"At that time Jerusalem shall be called The Throne of the LORD, and all the nations shall be gathered to it, to the name of the LORD, to Jerusalem. No more shall they follow the dictates of their evil hearts.

18"In those days the house of Judah shall walk with the house of Israel, and they shall come together out of the land of the north to the land that I have given as an inheritance to your fathers.

19"But I said:

   'How can I put you among the children
   And give you a pleasant land,
   A beautiful heritage of the hosts of
      nations?'

"And I said:

'You shall call Me, "My Father,"
And not turn away from Me.'
20 Surely, *as* a wife treacherously
      departs from her husband,
So have you dealt treacherously
      with Me,
O house of Israel," says the LORD.

21 A voice was heard on the desolate
      heights,
Weeping *and* supplications of the
      children of Israel.
For they have perverted their way;
They have forgotten the LORD their
      God.

22 "Return, you backsliding children,
    And I will heal your backslidings."

"Indeed we do come to You,
For You are the LORD our God.
23 Truly, in vain *is salvation hoped for*
      from the hills,
And from the multitude of
      mountains;
Truly, in the LORD our God
Is the salvation of Israel.
24 For shame has devoured
The labor of our fathers from our
      youth—
Their flocks and their herds,
Their sons and their daughters.
25 We lie down in our shame,
And our reproach covers us.
For we have sinned against the LORD
      our God,
We and our fathers,
From our youth even to this day,
And have not obeyed the voice of the
      LORD our God."

4 "If you will return, O Israel,"
   says the LORD,
"Return to Me;
And if you will put away your
      abominations out of My sight,
Then you shall not be moved.
2 And you shall swear, 'The LORD lives,'
In truth, in judgment, and in
      righteousness;
The nations shall bless themselves in
      Him,
And in Him they shall glory."

BIBLICAL INSIGHTS • 4:2
Work "As The Lord Lives"

WE HAVE NOTICED a great imbalance in the Christian community in regard to work. Either it drives us and we become too focused on it, or we suffer from poor work habits that result in mediocre performance.

We need to train our children in a thoroughly biblical approach to work.

The Bible insists that we do not work merely for men, but for the glory of God. The apostle Paul wrote, "Whatever you do, do it heartily, as to the Lord and not to men, knowing that from the Lord you will receive the reward of the inheritance; for you serve the Lord Christ" (Col. 3:23, 24).

Our children need to know that sliding along and getting by with as little as possible will not fool anybody indefinitely. More important, it will not fool God—the One who ultimately will determine if a person can be used for His purposes.

We need to teach our children to strive for excellence in everything they do. We should challenge every child, within his or her God-given capabilities, to rise above the crowd, seek higher standards of achievement, and become all that God has gifted them to be.

Our children need to be trained and instructed that God has work for them to do. However noble that work may be, they need to be warned that they are not to worship work or become addicted to it. God designed work so that we would trust Him and honor Him in the process, not so that work would become an idol.

This means that as parents, we must model a healthy approach to work. We must work "as the Lord lives," demonstrating to our children how a true follower of Jesus Christ keeps Him at the center of our lives, not our vocational pursuits.

³For thus says the LORD to the men of Judah and Jerusalem:

"Break up your fallow ground,
And do not sow among thorns.
4 Circumcise yourselves to the LORD,
And take away the foreskins of your hearts,
You men of Judah and inhabitants of Jerusalem,
Lest My fury come forth like fire,
And burn so that no one can quench *it*,
Because of the evil of your doings."

An Imminent Invasion

⁵Declare in Judah and proclaim in Jerusalem, and say:

"Blow the trumpet in the land;
Cry, 'Gather together,'
And say, 'Assemble yourselves,
And let us go into the fortified cities.'
6 Set up the standard toward Zion.
Take refuge! Do not delay!
For I will bring disaster from the north,
And great destruction."

7 The lion has come up from his thicket,
And the destroyer of nations is on his way.
He has gone forth from his place
To make your land desolate.
Your cities will be laid waste,
Without inhabitant.
8 For this, clothe yourself with sackcloth,
Lament and wail.
For the fierce anger of the LORD
Has not turned back from us.

9 "And it shall come to pass in that day," says the LORD,
"*That* the heart of the king shall perish,
And the heart of the princes;
The priests shall be astonished,
And the prophets shall wonder."

10 Then I said, "Ah, Lord GOD!
Surely You have greatly deceived this people and Jerusalem,
Saying, 'You shall have peace,'
Whereas the sword reaches to the heart."

11 At that time it will be said
To this people and to Jerusalem,
"A dry wind of the desolate heights *blows* in the wilderness
Toward the daughter of My people—
Not to fan or to cleanse—
12 A wind too strong for these will come for Me;
Now I will also speak judgment against them."

13 "Behold, he shall come up like clouds,
And his chariots like a whirlwind.
His horses are swifter than eagles.
Woe to us, for we are plundered!"

14 O Jerusalem, wash your heart from wickedness,
That you may be saved.
How long shall your evil thoughts lodge within you?
15 For a voice declares from Dan
And proclaims affliction from Mount Ephraim:
16 "Make mention to the nations,
Yes, proclaim against Jerusalem,
That watchers come from a far country
And raise their voice against the cities of Judah.
17 Like keepers of a field they are against her all around,
Because she has been rebellious against Me," says the LORD.
18 "Your ways and your doings
Have procured these *things* for you.
This *is* your wickedness,
Because it is bitter,
Because it reaches to your heart."

Sorrow for the Doomed Nation

19 O my soul, my soul!
I am pained in my very heart!
My heart makes a noise in me;
I cannot hold my peace,
Because you have heard, O my soul,
The sound of the trumpet,
The alarm of war.
20 Destruction upon destruction is cried,
For the whole land is plundered.
Suddenly my tents are plundered,
And my curtains in a moment.

21 How long will I see the standard,
   And hear the sound of the trumpet?

22 "For My people *are* foolish,
   They have not known Me.
   They *are* silly children,
   And they have no understanding.
   They *are* wise to do evil,
   But to do good they have no
     knowledge."

23 I beheld the earth, and indeed *it was*
     without form, and void;
   And the heavens, they *had* no light.
24 I beheld the mountains, and indeed
     they trembled,
   And all the hills moved back and
     forth.
25 I beheld, and indeed *there was* no man,
   And all the birds of the heavens had
     fled.
26 I beheld, and indeed the fruitful land
     was a wilderness,
   And all its cities were broken down
   At the presence of the LORD,
   By His fierce anger.

27 For thus says the LORD:

   "The whole land shall be desolate;
   Yet I will not make a full end.
28 For this shall the earth mourn,
   And the heavens above be black,
   Because I have spoken.
   I have purposed and will not relent,
   Nor will I turn back from it.
29 The whole city shall flee from the
     noise of the horsemen and
     bowmen.
   They shall go into thickets and climb
     up on the rocks.
   Every city *shall be* forsaken,
   And not a man shall dwell in it.

30 "And *when* you *are* plundered,
   What will you do?
   Though you clothe yourself with
     crimson,
   Though you adorn *yourself* with
     ornaments of gold,
   Though you enlarge your eyes with
     paint,
   In vain you will make yourself fair;
   Your lovers will despise you;
   They will seek your life.

31 "For I have heard a voice as of a
     woman in labor,
   The anguish as of her who brings
     forth her first child,
   The voice of the daughter of Zion
     bewailing herself;
   She spreads her hands, *saying,*
   ' Woe *is* me now, for my soul is weary
   Because of murderers!'

The Justice of God's Judgment

5 "Run to and fro through the streets
     of Jerusalem;
   See now and know;
   And seek in her open places
   If you can find a man,
   If there is *anyone* who executes
     judgment,
   Who seeks the truth,
   And I will pardon her.
2 Though they say, 'As the LORD lives,'
   Surely they swear falsely."

3 O LORD, *are* not Your eyes on the
     truth?
   You have stricken them,
   But they have not grieved;
   You have consumed them,
   But they have refused to receive
     correction.
   They have made their faces harder
     than rock;
   They have refused to return.

4 Therefore I said, "Surely these *are*
     poor.
   They are foolish;
   For they do not know the way of the
     LORD,
   The judgment of their God.
5 I will go to the great men and speak
     to them,
   For they have known the way of the
     LORD,
   The judgment of their God."

   But these have altogether broken the
     yoke
   And burst the bonds.
6 Therefore a lion from the forest shall
     slay them,
   A wolf of the deserts shall destroy
     them;
   A leopard will watch over their cities.

Everyone who goes out from there
 shall be torn in pieces,
Because their transgressions are
 many;
 Their backslidings have increased.

7 "How shall I pardon you for this?
 Your children have forsaken Me
 And sworn by *those that are* not gods.
 When I had fed them to the full,
 Then they committed adultery
 And assembled themselves by troops
  in the harlots' houses.

8 They were *like* well-fed lusty stallions;
 Every one neighed after his
  neighbor's wife.

9 Shall I not punish *them* for these
  things?" says the LORD.
 "And shall I not avenge Myself on
  such a nation as this?

10 "Go up on her walls and destroy,
 But do not make a complete end.
 Take away her branches,
 For they *are* not the LORD's.

11 For the house of Israel and the house
  of Judah
 Have dealt very treacherously with
  Me," says the LORD.

12 They have lied about the LORD,
 And said, "*It is* not He.
 Neither will evil come upon us,
 Nor shall we see sword or famine.

13 And the prophets become wind,
 For the word *is* not in them.
 Thus shall it be done to them."

14 Therefore thus says the LORD God of
hosts:

"Because you speak this word,
 Behold, I will make My words in
  your mouth fire,
 And this people wood,
 And it shall devour them.

15 Behold, I will bring a nation against
  you from afar,
 O house of Israel," says the LORD.
 "It *is* a mighty nation,
 It *is* an ancient nation,
 A nation whose language you do not
  know,
 Nor can you understand what they
  say.

16 Their quiver *is* like an open tomb;
 They *are* all mighty men.

17 And they shall eat up your harvest
  and your bread,
 Which your sons and daughters
  should eat.
 They shall eat up your flocks and
  your herds;
 They shall eat up your vines and
  your fig trees;
 They shall destroy your fortified
  cities,
 In which you trust, with the sword.

18 "Nevertheless in those days," says the
LORD, "I will not make a complete end of
you. 19 And it will be when you say, 'Why
does the LORD our God do all these *things*
to us?' then you shall answer them, 'Just as
you have forsaken Me and served foreign
gods in your land, so you shall serve aliens
in a land *that is* not yours.'

20 "Declare this in the house of Jacob
 And proclaim it in Judah, saying,

21 'Hear this now, O foolish people,
 Without understanding,
 Who have eyes and see not,
 And who have ears and hear not:

22 Do you not fear Me?' says the LORD.
 'Will you not tremble at My presence,
 Who have placed the sand as the
  bound of the sea,
 By a perpetual decree, that it cannot
  pass beyond it?
 And though its waves toss to and
  fro,
 Yet they cannot prevail;
 Though they roar, yet they cannot
  pass over it.

23 But this people has a defiant and
  rebellious heart;
 They have revolted and departed.

24 They do not say in their heart,
 "Let us now fear the LORD our God,
 Who gives rain, both the former and
  the latter, in its season.
 He reserves for us the appointed
  weeks of the harvest."

25 Your iniquities have turned these
  things away,
 And your sins have withheld good
  from you.

26 'For among My people are found
      wicked *men;*
   They lie in wait as one who sets
      snares;
   They set a trap;
   They catch men.
27 As a cage is full of birds,
   So their houses *are* full of deceit.
   Therefore they have become great
      and grown rich.
28 They have grown fat, they are sleek;
   Yes, they surpass the deeds of the
      wicked;
   They do not plead the cause,
   The cause of the fatherless;
   Yet they prosper,
   And the right of the needy they do
      not defend.
29 Shall I not punish *them* for these
      things? says the LORD.
   'Shall I not avenge Myself on such a
      nation as this?'
30 "An astonishing and horrible thing
   Has been committed in the land:
31 The prophets prophesy falsely,

And the priests rule by their *own*
   power;
And My people love *to have it* so.
But what will you do in the end?

Impending Destruction from the North

6 "O you children of Benjamin,
   Gather yourselves to flee from the
      midst of Jerusalem!
   Blow the trumpet in Tekoa,
   And set up a signal-fire in Beth
      Haccerem;
   For disaster appears out of the
      north,
   And great destruction.
2 I have likened the daughter of Zion
   To a lovely and delicate woman.
3 The shepherds with their flocks shall
      come to her.
   They shall pitch *their* tents against
      her all around.
   Each one shall pasture in his own
      place."

4 "Prepare war against her;
   Arise, and let us go up at noon.

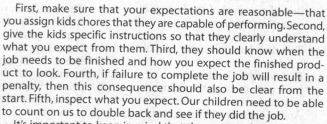

PARENTING MATTERS

Q: We have a hard time getting our kids to do their chores. Usually they refuse to obey us. Then, after we threaten them, they give in; but they do a sloppy job with a terrible attitude. How should we handle assigning chores and disciplining when they're not done?

First, make sure that your expectations are reasonable—that you assign kids chores that they are capable of performing. Second, give the kids specific instructions so that they clearly understand what you expect from them. Third, they should know when the job needs to be finished and how you expect the finished product to look. Fourth, if failure to complete the job will result in a penalty, then this consequence should also be clear from the start. Fifth, inspect what you expect. Our children need to be able to count on us to double back and see if they did the job.

It's important to keep in mind that the purpose behind assigning kids chores is to teach them responsibility and maturity. Sometimes we get so caught up in the task we that we miss a great opportunity to teach them an important lesson. If the child's character is shaping up and he is learning responsibility, I think that is more important than whether his room is perfectly clean. If I were dealing with a child with a rebellious attitude, however—and if that messy room were a statement of rebellion—then I would not let that situation continue.

The key is to stay focused on the end goals; and in light of that, there is a time for grace.

Woe to us, for the day goes away,
For the shadows of the evening are
lengthening.
5 Arise, and let us go by night,
And let us destroy her palaces."

6For thus has the LORD of hosts said:

"Cut down trees,
And build a mound against Jerusalem.
This *is* the city to be punished.
She *is* full of oppression in her midst.
7 As a fountain wells up with water,
So she wells up with her wickedness.
Violence and plundering are heard in
her.
Before Me continually *are* grief and
wounds.
8 Be instructed, O Jerusalem,
Lest My soul depart from you;
Lest I make you desolate,
A land not inhabited."

9Thus says the LORD of hosts:

"They shall thoroughly glean as a
vine the remnant of Israel;
As a grape-gatherer, put your hand
back into the branches."

10 To whom shall I speak and give
warning,
That they may hear?
Indeed their ear *is* uncircumcised,
And they cannot give heed.
Behold, the word of the LORD is a
reproach to them;
They have no delight in it.
11 Therefore I am full of the fury of the
LORD.
I am weary of holding *it* in.
"I will pour it out on the children
outside,
And on the assembly of young men
together;
For even the husband shall be taken
with the wife,
The aged with *him who is* full of
days.
12 And their houses shall be turned
over to others,
Fields and wives together;
For I will stretch out My hand
Against the inhabitants of the land,"
says the LORD.

13 "Because from the least of them even
to the greatest of them,
Everyone *is* given to covetousness;
And from the prophet even to the
priest,
Everyone deals falsely.
14 They have also healed the hurt of
My people slightly,
Saying, 'Peace, peace!'
When *there is* no peace.
15 Were they ashamed when they had
committed abomination?
No! They were not at all ashamed;
Nor did they know how to blush.
Therefore they shall fall among those
who fall;
At the time I punish them,
They shall be cast down," says the
LORD.

16Thus says the LORD:

"Stand in the ways and see,
And ask for the old paths, where the
good way *is,*
And walk in it;
Then you will find rest for your
souls.
But they said, 'We will not walk *in
it.*'
17 Also, I set watchmen over you,
saying,
'Listen to the sound of the trumpet!'
But they said, 'We will not listen.'
18 Therefore hear, you nations,
And know, O congregation, what *is*
among them.
19 Hear, O earth!
Behold, I will certainly bring
calamity on this people—
The fruit of their thoughts,
Because they have not heeded My
words
Nor My law, but rejected it.
20 For what purpose to Me
Comes frankincense from Sheba,
And sweet cane from a far country?
Your burnt offerings *are* not
acceptable,
Nor your sacrifices sweet to Me."

21Therefore thus says the LORD:

"Behold, I will lay stumbling blocks
before this people,

> And the fathers and the sons
> together shall fall on them.
> The neighbor and his friend shall
> perish."

²²Thus says the LORD:

> "Behold, a people comes from the
> north country,
> And a great nation will be raised
> from the farthest parts of the
> earth.
>
> 23 They will lay hold on bow and spear;
> They *are* cruel and have no mercy;
> Their voice roars like the sea;
> And they ride on horses,
> As men of war set in array against
> you, O daughter of Zion."
>
> 24 We have heard the report of it;
> Our hands grow feeble.
> Anguish has taken hold of us,
> Pain as of a woman in labor.
> 25 Do not go out into the field,
> Nor walk by the way.
> Because of the sword of the enemy,
> Fear *is* on every side.
> 26 O daughter of my people,
> Dress in sackcloth
> And roll about in ashes!
> Make mourning *as for* an only son,
> most bitter lamentation;
> For the plunderer will suddenly come
> upon us.
>
> 27 "I have set you *as* an assayer *and* a
> fortress among My people,
> That you may know and test their
> way.
> 28 They *are* all stubborn rebels,
> walking as slanderers.
> *They are* bronze and iron,
> *They are* all corrupters;
> 29 The bellows blow fiercely,
> The lead is consumed by the fire;
> The smelter refines in vain,
> For the wicked are not drawn off.
> 30 *People* will call them rejected silver,
> Because the LORD has rejected them."

Trusting in Lying Words

7 The word that came to Jeremiah from the LORD, saying, ²"Stand in the gate of the LORD's house, and proclaim there this word, and say, 'Hear the word of the LORD,

Only One Solution

YOU CAN'T READ THE BOOK OF JEREMIAH without realizing how often the prophet returns again and again to the only solution for Israel's problems: repentance. So God says in Jeremiah 7:3, "Amend your ways and your doings, and I will cause you to dwell in this place."

Today, however, spiritual decay is not always so easy to recognize in the church. Because we're good at God-talk and playing church, we can mask an unrepentant heart without much effort. Yet as Jerry White so perceptively points out, "No one is so empty as the man who has stopped walking with God and doesn't know it. He smiles at church, serves on boards, even teaches the Bible, but he is an empty shell. He lives on past knowledge and correct doctrine. He says and does the right things. But there is a hollow ring to his life. No one really notices, however, because there are so many other hollow rings around him."

Are there any areas of your life where God is calling you to "amend your ways" right now? At this very moment, is the Spirit pricking your conscience about some phase of your walk with God that's been slipping?

There have been periods when God has been at work on an issue in my life. This is the convicting and sanctifying work of the Holy Spirit. He wants to shape your life and character to look more and more like Jesus Christ. As we submit to the Holy Spirit and His work, the image of Christ will emerge in your life.

But, like the nation of Israel in Jeremiah's day, the only solution for your spiritual stagnation is to confess your sin to God and to reengage your relationship with Him. That begins with repentance, a 180-degree turn from your sin and back toward God.

all *you of* Judah who enter in at these gates to worship the LORD!'" ³Thus says the LORD of hosts, the God of Israel: "Amend your ways and your doings, and I will cause you to dwell in this place. ⁴Do not trust in these lying words, saying, 'The temple of the LORD, the temple of the LORD, the temple of the LORD *are* these.'

⁵"For if you thoroughly amend your ways and your doings, if you thoroughly execute judgment between a man and his neighbor, ⁶if you do not oppress the stranger, the fatherless, and the widow, and do not shed innocent blood in this place, or walk after other gods to your hurt, ⁷then I will cause you to dwell in this place, in the land that I gave to your fathers forever and ever.

⁸"Behold, you trust in lying words that cannot profit. ⁹Will you steal, murder, commit adultery, swear falsely, burn incense to Baal, and walk after other gods whom you do not know, ¹⁰and *then* come and stand before Me in this house which is called by My name, and say, 'We are delivered to do all these abominations'? ¹¹Has this house, which is called by My name, become a den of thieves in your eyes? Behold, I, even I, have seen *it,*" says the LORD.

¹²"But go now to My place which *was* in Shiloh, where I set My name at the first, and see what I did to it because of the wickedness of My people Israel. ¹³And now, because you have done all these works," says the LORD, "and I spoke to you, rising up early and speaking, but you did not hear, and I called you, but you did not answer, ¹⁴therefore I will do to the house which is called by My name, in which you trust, and to this place which I gave to you and your fathers, as I have done to Shiloh. ¹⁵And I will cast you out of My sight, as I have cast out all your brethren—the whole posterity of Ephraim.

¹⁶"Therefore do not pray for this people, nor lift up a cry or prayer for them, nor make intercession to Me; for I will not hear you. ¹⁷Do you not see what they do in the cities of Judah and in the streets of Jerusalem? ¹⁸The children gather wood, the fathers kindle the fire, and the women knead dough, to make cakes for the queen of heaven; and *they* pour out drink offerings to other gods, that they may provoke Me to anger. ¹⁹Do they provoke Me to anger?" says the LORD. "*Do they* not *provoke* themselves, to the shame of their own faces?"

²⁰Therefore thus says the Lord GOD: "Behold, My anger and My fury will be poured out on this place—on man and on beast, on the trees of the field and on the fruit of the ground. And it will burn and not be quenched."

²¹Thus says the LORD of hosts, the God of Israel: "Add your burnt offerings to your sacrifices and eat meat. ²²For I did not speak to your fathers, or command them in the day that I brought them out of the land of Egypt, concerning burnt offerings or sacrifices. ²³But this is what I commanded them, saying, 'Obey My voice, and I will be your God, and you shall be My people. And walk in all the ways that I have commanded you, that it may be well with you.' ²⁴Yet they did not obey or incline their ear, but followed the counsels *and* the dictates of their evil hearts, and went backward and not forward. ²⁵Since the day that your fathers came out of the land of Egypt until this day, I have even sent to you all My servants the prophets, daily rising up early and sending *them.* ²⁶Yet they did not obey Me or incline their ear, but stiffened their neck. They did worse than their fathers.

²⁷"Therefore you shall speak all these words to them, but they will not obey you. You shall also call to them, but they will not answer you.

Judgment on Obscene Religion

²⁸"So you shall say to them, 'This *is* a nation that does not obey the voice of the LORD their God nor receive correction. Truth has perished and has been cut off from their mouth. ²⁹Cut off your hair and cast *it* away, and take up a lamentation on the desolate heights; for the LORD has rejected and forsaken the generation of His wrath.' ³⁰For the children of Judah have done evil in My sight," says the LORD. "They have set their abominations in the house which is called by My name, to pollute it. ³¹And they have built the high places of Tophet, which *is* in the Valley of the Son of Hinnom, to burn their sons and their daughters in the fire, which I did not command, nor did it come into My heart.

³²"Therefore behold, the days are coming," says the LORD, "when it will no more be called Tophet, or the Valley of the Son of Hinnom, but the Valley of Slaughter; for they will bury in Tophet until there is no room. ³³The corpses of this people will be food for the birds of the heaven and for the beasts of the earth. And no one will frighten *them away.* ³⁴Then I will cause to cease from the cities of Judah and from the streets of Jerusalem the voice of mirth and the voice of gladness, the voice of the bridegroom and the voice of the bride. For the land shall be desolate.

8 "At that time," says the LORD, "they shall bring out the bones of the kings of Judah, and the bones of its princes, and the bones of the priests, and the bones of the prophets, and the bones of the inhabitants of Jerusalem, out of their graves. ²They shall spread them before the sun and the moon and all the host of heaven, which they have loved and which they have served and after which they have walked, which they have sought and which they have worshiped. They shall not be gathered nor buried; they shall be like refuse on the face of the earth. ³Then death shall be chosen rather than life by all the residue of those who remain of this evil family, who remain in all the places where I have driven them," says the LORD of hosts.

The Peril of False Teaching

⁴"Moreover you shall say to them, 'Thus says the LORD:

"Will they fall and not rise?
   Will one turn away and not return?
5 Why has this people slidden back,
   Jerusalem, in a perpetual
      backsliding?
   They hold fast to deceit,
   They refuse to return.
6 I listened and heard,
   But they do not speak aright.
   No man repented of his wickedness,
   Saying, 'What have I done?'
   Everyone turned to his own course,
   As the horse rushes into the battle.

7 "Even the stork in the heavens
   Knows her appointed times;

BIBLICAL INSIGHTS • 7:9, 10

Saved to Do Right

THE MAN WE KNOW AS "the weeping prophet" had a lot to weep about. He saw his people had "evil hearts" (3:17) that lusted after idols (2:5). Incredibly, as their evils mounted, these people of God "refused to be ashamed" (3:3) and had even forgotten "how to blush" (6:15). Their spiritual leaders ignored the truth of God's Word and ruled by their own authority (5:30, 31). And just like in our own generation, these deceived, distracted "believers" sat contentedly in the house of God, week after week, listening to the teaching of Scripture but refusing to repent and seek personal purity.

In one of the most scathing condemnations in all of the Bible, Jeremiah relays God's thoughts on all of this, "Will you steal, murder, commit adultery, swear falsely, burn incense to Baal, and walk after other gods whom you do not know, and then come and stand before Me in this house which is called by My name, and say, 'We are delivered to do all these abominations'?" (7:9, 10).

God does not save us so that we might sin with impunity; He saves us so that we might live for Him and reflect His holiness in our own lives. Is your life characterized more by the good fruit of godliness or the corrupt fruit of sin? In the same way that a tree is known by its fruit (Luke 6:44), the reality of our walk with God is seen as we live lives that are transformed by His power and His grace. We need to be reminded that this transformation is the work of the Holy Spirit in our lives. He is the One who will empower you to be delivered from besetting sins.

The question is, will you yield to Him and His work in your life?

And the turtledove, the swift, and the
      swallow
   Observe the time of their coming.
   But My people do not know the
      judgment of the LORD.

8   "How can you say, 'We *are* wise,
     And the law of the LORD *is* with us'?
     Look, the false pen of the scribe
        certainly works falsehood.
9   The wise men are ashamed,
     They are dismayed and taken.
     Behold, they have rejected the word
        of the LORD;
     So what wisdom do they have?
10   Therefore I will give their wives to
        others,
     And their fields to those who will
        inherit *them;*
     Because from the least even to the
        greatest
     Everyone is given to covetousness;
     From the prophet even to the priest
     Everyone deals falsely.
11   For they have healed the hurt of the
        daughter of My people slightly,
     Saying, 'Peace, peace!'
     When *there is* no peace.
12   Were they ashamed when they had
        committed abomination?
     No! They were not at all ashamed,
     Nor did they know how to blush.
     Therefore they shall fall among those
        who fall;
     In the time of their punishment
     They shall be cast down," says the
        LORD.

13   "I will surely consume them," says the
        LORD.
     "No grapes *shall be* on the vine,
     Nor figs on the fig tree,
     And the leaf shall fade;
     And *the things* I have given them
        shall pass away from them.'"'

14   "Why do we sit still?
     Assemble yourselves,
     And let us enter the fortified cities,
     And let us be silent there.
     For the LORD our God has put us to
        silence
     And given us water of gall to drink,
     Because we have sinned against the
        LORD.
15   "*We* looked for peace, but no good
        came;
     And for a time of health, and there
        was trouble!

16   The snorting of His horses was
        heard from Dan.
     The whole land trembled at the
        sound of the neighing of His
        strong ones;
     For they have come and devoured the
        land and all that is in it,
     The city and those who dwell in it."

17   "For behold, I will send serpents
        among you,
     Vipers which cannot be charmed,
     And they shall bite you," says the
        LORD.

The Prophet Mourns for the People

18   I would comfort myself in sorrow;
     My heart *is* faint in me.
19   Listen! The voice,
     The cry of the daughter of my
        people
     From a far country:
     "*Is* not the LORD in Zion?
     Is not her King in her?"

     "Why have they provoked Me to
        anger
     With their carved images—
     With foreign idols?"

20   "The harvest is past,
     The summer is ended,
     And we are not saved!"

21   For the hurt of the daughter of my
        people I am hurt.
     I am mourning;
     Astonishment has taken hold of me.
22   *Is there* no balm in Gilead,
     Is there no physician there?
     Why then is there no recovery
     For the health of the daughter of my
        people?

9   Oh, that my head were waters,
     And my eyes a fountain of tears,
     That I might weep day and night
     For the slain of the daughter of my
        people!
2   Oh, that I had in the wilderness
     A lodging place for travelers;
     That I might leave my people,
     And go from them!
     For they *are* all adulterers,
     An assembly of treacherous men.

3 "And *like* their bow they have bent
       their tongues *for* lies.
   They are not valiant for the truth on
       the earth.
   For they proceed from evil to evil,
   And they do not know Me," says the
       LORD.
4 "Everyone take heed to his neighbor,
   And do not trust any brother;
   For every brother will utterly supplant,
   And every neighbor will walk with
       slanderers.
5 Everyone will deceive his neighbor,
   And will not speak the truth;
   They have taught their tongue to
       speak lies;
   They weary themselves to commit
       iniquity.
6 Your dwelling place *is* in the midst of
       deceit;
   Through deceit they refuse to know
       Me," says the LORD.

7 Therefore thus says the LORD of hosts:

   "Behold, I will refine them and try
       them;
   For how shall I deal with the
       daughter of My people?
8 Their tongue *is* an arrow shot out;
   It speaks deceit;
   One speaks peaceably to his
       neighbor with his mouth,
   But in his heart he lies in wait.
9 Shall I not punish them for these
       things?" says the LORD.
   "Shall I not avenge Myself on such a
       nation as this?"

10 I will take up a weeping and wailing
       for the mountains,
   And for the dwelling places of the
       wilderness a lamentation,
   Because they are burned up,
   So *that* no one can pass through;
   Nor can *men* hear the voice of the
       cattle.
   Both the birds of the heavens and
       the beasts have fled;
   They are gone.
11 "I will make Jerusalem a heap of
       ruins, a den of jackals.
   I will make the cities of Judah
       desolate, without an inhabitant."

12 Who *is* the wise man who may understand this? And *who is he* to whom the
mouth of the LORD has spoken, that he
may declare it? Why does the land perish
and burn up like a wilderness, so that no
one can pass through?
13 And the LORD said, "Because they
have forsaken My law which I set before
them, and have not obeyed My voice, nor
walked according to it, 14 but they have
walked according to the dictates of their
own hearts and after the Baals, which their
fathers taught them," 15 therefore thus says
the LORD of hosts, the God of Israel:
"Behold, I will feed them, this people, with
wormwood, and give them water of gall to
drink. 16 I will scatter them also among the
Gentiles, whom neither they nor their
fathers have known. And I will send a
sword after them until I have consumed
them."

The People Mourn in Judgment

17 Thus says the LORD of hosts:

   "Consider and call for the mourning
       women,
   That they may come;
   And send for skillful *wailing*
       women,
   That they may come.
18 Let them make haste
   And take up a wailing for us,
   That our eyes may run with tears,
   And our eyelids gush with water.
19 For a voice of wailing is heard from
       Zion:
   'How we are plundered!
   We are greatly ashamed,
   Because we have forsaken the land,
   Because we have been cast out of
       our dwellings.'"
20 Yet hear the word of the LORD, O
       women,
   And let your ear receive the word of
       His mouth;
   Teach your daughters wailing,
   And everyone her neighbor a
       lamentation.
21 For death has come through our
       windows,
   Has entered our palaces,

BIBLICAL INSIGHTS • 9:24

Knowledge before Conviction

NO ONE CAN BUILD a strong marriage without spending time cultivating a relationship with God. But to develop genuine faith, you need knowledge. Knowledge comes before conviction, and an accurate knowledge of God comes as we spend time in the Scriptures.

How well do you know God? Did you know that God praises the individual who "understands and knows Me, that I am the LORD, exercising lovingkindness, judgment, and righteousness in the earth. For in these I delight" (9:24)? How well do you understand and know God?

Early in my life I went through a period where I thought I had a terminal disease. I was honestly shocked at how poorly I handled my apparent crisis. I couldn't sleep. I was preoccupied with my condition. My faith was rocked.

The crisis passed and it was determined that I didn't have the disease. The whole event ended up being a wake-up call for me by revealing that I needed to know more about God and understand His love and plan for my life.

That experience showed me that my faith is only as good as its object. It is confidence, a firm conviction that God and His Word are true.

If we are to trust God with our lives, we need to know that our heavenly Father loves us. How can we trust that which we do not know? How can we exhibit faith in God if we don't know Him?

So again, *how well do you know God?* How much time have you spent with Him lately? Pray that God would give you a deeper knowledge of Him and that you and your spouse will grow in the grace and knowledge of the Lord Jesus Christ.

To kill off the children—*no longer to be* outside!
And the young men—*no longer* on the streets!

22 Speak, "Thus says the LORD:

'Even the carcasses of men shall fall
　　as refuse on the open field,
Like cuttings after the harvester,
　　And no one shall gather *them*.'"

23 Thus says the LORD:

"Let not the wise *man* glory in his
　　wisdom,
Let not the mighty *man* glory in his
　　might,
Nor let the rich *man* glory in his
　　riches;
24 But let him who glories glory in this,
That he understands and knows Me,
That I *am* the LORD, exercising
　　lovingkindness, judgment, and
　　righteousness in the earth.
For in these I delight," says the LORD.

25 "Behold, the days are coming," says the LORD, "that I will punish all *who are* circumcised with the uncircumcised— 26 Egypt, Judah, Edom, the people of Ammon, Moab, and all *who are* in the farthest corners, who dwell in the wilderness. For all *these* nations *are* uncircumcised, and all the house of Israel *are* uncircumcised in the heart."

Idols and the True God

10 Hear the word which the LORD speaks to you, O house of Israel. 2 Thus says the LORD:

"Do not learn the way of the Gentiles;
Do not be dismayed at the signs of
　　heaven,
For the Gentiles are dismayed at them.
3 For the customs of the peoples *are*
　　futile;
For *one* cuts a tree from the forest,
The work of the hands of the
　　workman, with the ax.
4 They decorate it with silver and
　　gold;
They fasten it with nails and
　　hammers
So that it will not topple.
5 They *are* upright, like a palm tree,
And they cannot speak;
They must be carried,
Because they cannot go *by themselves*.

Do not be afraid of them,
For they cannot do evil,
Nor can they do any good."

6 Inasmuch as *there is* none like You, O
LORD
(You *are* great, and Your name *is*
great in might),
7 Who would not fear You, O King of
the nations?
For this is Your rightful due.
For among all the wise *men* of the
nations,
And in all their kingdoms,
There is none like You.
8 But they are altogether dull-hearted
and foolish;
A wooden idol *is* a worthless
doctrine.
9 Silver is beaten into plates;
It is brought from Tarshish,
And gold from Uphaz,
The work of the craftsman
And of the hands of the metalsmith;
Blue and purple *are* their clothing;
They *are* all the work of skillful
men.
10 But the LORD *is* the true God;
He *is* the living God and the
everlasting King.
At His wrath the earth will tremble,
And the nations will not be able to
endure His indignation.

11 Thus you shall say to them: "The gods
that have not made the heavens and the
earth shall perish from the earth and from
under these heavens."

12 He has made the earth by His power,
He has established the world by His
wisdom,
And has stretched out the heavens at
His discretion.
13 When He utters His voice,
There is a multitude of waters in the
heavens:
"And He causes the vapors to ascend
from the ends of the earth.
He makes lightning for the rain,
He brings the wind out of His
treasuries."[a]

14 Everyone is dull-hearted, without
knowledge;
Every metalsmith is put to shame by
an image;
For his molded image *is* falsehood,
And *there is* no breath in them.
15 They *are* futile, a work of errors;
In the time of their punishment they
shall perish.
16 The Portion of Jacob *is* not like
them,
For He *is* the Maker of all *things,*
And Israel *is* the tribe of His
inheritance;
The LORD of hosts *is* His name.

The Coming Captivity of Judah

17 Gather up your wares from the land,
O inhabitant of the fortress!

18 For thus says the LORD:

"Behold, I will throw out at this time
The inhabitants of the land,
And will distress them,
That they may find *it so.*"

19 Woe is me for my hurt!
My wound is severe.
But I say, "Truly this *is* an infirmity,
And I must bear it."
20 My tent is plundered,
And all my cords are broken;
My children have gone from me,
And they *are* no more.
There is no one to pitch my tent
anymore,
Or set up my curtains.
21 For the shepherds have become dull-
hearted,
And have not sought the LORD;
Therefore they shall not prosper,
And all their flocks shall be scattered.
22 Behold, the noise of the report has
come,
And a great commotion out of the
north country,
To make the cities of Judah desolate,
a den of jackals.

23 O LORD, I know the way of man *is*
not in himself;
It is not in man who walks to direct
his own steps.

10:13 [a] Psalm 135:7

24 O LORD, correct me, but with justice;
    Not in Your anger, lest You bring me
      to nothing.
25 Pour out Your fury on the Gentiles,
      who do not know You,
    And on the families who do not call
      on Your name;

ROMANCE FAQ

**Q: *What danger
signs should I look
for in relationships
with the opposite sex?***

Whenever you develop an in-depth relationship with someone of the opposite
sex—at *any* level—certain forces come
into play that can result in a potent chemical reaction that can cause considerable
trouble. Some signs that this reaction is
beginning to occur include the following:

- You have a need that you feel your
  mate isn't meeting—for attention,
  approval, affection—and that other
  person begins meeting your need.

- You find it easier to unwind with
  someone other than your spouse by
  dissecting the day's difficulties over
  lunch, coffee, or during a ride home.

- You begin to talk about problems
  you are having with your spouse.

- You rationalize the relationship by
  saying that surely it must be God's
  will to talk so openly and honestly
  with a fellow Christian. You become
  defensive about the relationship and
  protective of it.

- You look forward to being with this
  person more than with your own
  mate.

- You wonder what you'd do if you did-
  n't have this friend to talk to.

- You hide the relationship from your
  mate.

If you see any of these warning signs,
take action immediately. Your friendship
with this other person must end, even if
it means taking drastic measures. Don't
put your marriage at risk!

For they have eaten up Jacob,
Devoured him and consumed him,
And made his dwelling place
  desolate.

The Broken Covenant

11 The word that came to Jeremiah
from the LORD, saying, [2]"Hear the
words of this covenant, and speak to the
men of Judah and to the inhabitants of
Jerusalem; [3]and say to them, 'Thus says the
LORD God of Israel: "Cursed *is* the man
who does not obey the words of this
covenant [4]which I commanded your fathers
in the day I brought them out of the land of
Egypt, from the iron furnace, saying, 'Obey
My voice, and do according to all that I
command you; so shall you be My people,
and I will be your God,' [5]that I may establish the oath which I have sworn to your
fathers, to give them 'a land flowing with
milk and honey,'[a] as *it is* this day.' " "

And I answered and said, "So be it,
LORD."

[6]Then the LORD said to me, "Proclaim
all these words in the cities of Judah and in
the streets of Jerusalem, saying: 'Hear the
words of this covenant and do them. [7]For I
earnestly exhorted your fathers in the day I
brought them up out of the land of Egypt,
until this day, rising early and exhorting,
saying, "Obey My voice." [8]Yet they did not
obey or incline their ear, but everyone followed the dictates of his evil heart; therefore I will bring upon them all the words of
this covenant, which I commanded *them* to
do, but *which* they have not done.' "

[9]And the LORD said to me, "A conspiracy has been found among the men of
Judah and among the inhabitants of
Jerusalem. [10]They have turned back to the
iniquities of their forefathers who refused
to hear My words, and they have gone
after other gods to serve them; the house of
Israel and the house of Judah have broken
My covenant which I made with their
fathers."

[11]Therefore thus says the LORD: "Behold,
I will surely bring calamity on them which
they will not be able to escape; and though
they cry out to Me, I will not listen to them.

11:5 [a]Exodus 3:8

12Then the cities of Judah and the inhabitants of Jerusalem will go and cry out to the gods to whom they offer incense, but they will not save them at all in the time of their trouble. 13For *according to* the number of your cities were your gods, O Judah; and *according to* the number of the streets of Jerusalem you have set up altars to *that* shameful thing, altars to burn incense to Baal.

14"So do not pray for this people, or lift up a cry or prayer for them; for I will not hear *them* in the time that they cry out to Me because of their trouble.

15 "What has My beloved to do in My
      house,
   Having done lewd deeds with
      many?
   And the holy flesh has passed
      from you.
   When you do evil, then you rejoice.
16 The Lord called your name,
   Green Olive Tree, Lovely *and* of
      Good Fruit.
   With the noise of a great tumult
   He has kindled fire on it,
   And its branches are broken.

17"For the Lord of hosts, who planted you, has pronounced doom against you for the evil of the house of Israel and of the house of Judah, which they have done against themselves to provoke Me to anger in offering incense to Baal."

Jeremiah's Life Threatened

18Now the Lord gave me knowledge *of it,* and I know *it;* for You showed me their doings. 19But I *was* like a docile lamb brought to the slaughter; and I did not know that they had devised schemes against me, *saying,* "Let us destroy the tree with its fruit, and let us cut him off from the land of the living, that his name may be remembered no more."

20 But, O Lord of hosts,
   You who judge righteously,
   Testing the mind and the heart,
   Let me see Your vengeance on them,
   For to You I have revealed my cause.

21"Therefore thus says the Lord concerning the men of Anathoth who seek your life, saying, 'Do not prophesy in the name of the Lord, lest you die by our hand'— 22therefore thus says the Lord of hosts: 'Behold, I will punish them. The young men shall die by the sword, their sons and their daughters shall die by famine; 23and there shall be no remnant of them, for I will bring catastrophe on the men of Anathoth, *even* the year of their punishment.'"

Jeremiah's Question

12 Righteous *are* You, O Lord, when
      I plead with You;
   Yet let me talk with You about *Your*
      judgments.
   Why does the way of the wicked
      prosper?
   Why are those happy who deal so
      treacherously?
2 You have planted them, yes, they
      have taken root;
   They grow, yes, they bear fruit.
   You *are* near in their mouth
   But far from their mind.
3 But You, O Lord, know me;
   You have seen me,
   And You have tested my heart
      toward You.
   Pull them out like sheep for the
      slaughter,
   And prepare them for the day of
      slaughter.
4 How long will the land mourn,
   And the herbs of every field wither?
   The beasts and birds are consumed,
   For the wickedness of those who
      dwell there,
   Because they said, "He will not see
      our final end."

The Lord Answers Jeremiah

5 "If you have run with the footmen,
      and they have wearied you,
   Then how can you contend with
      horses?
   And *if* in the land of peace,
   In which you trusted, *they wearied you,*
   Then how will you do in the
      floodplaina of the Jordan?

12:5 aOr *thicket*

BIBLICAL INSIGHTS • 12:5

A Pilgrim on a Journey

WHEN I WAS YOUNGER, I used to try to run three miles at least three times each week. When I started out, I could barely run downhill for one mile. I had to build up quite a bit of stamina to reach three miles a day.

God gives us hills so that our legs can grow stronger. At the beginning of his prophetic career, Jeremiah sucked so much wind that God asked him, "If you have run with the footmen, and they have wearied you, then how can you contend with horses?" (12:5). Just like us, Jeremiah had to learn endurance, how to draw on God's strength in the hard times when he felt like packing it in.

As you run your race and persevere through life, you can count on God's grace to empower those tired muscles. And if you are following the Lord, your walk is really taking you somewhere! You're not just a sweating sufferer on a treadmill; you're a pilgrim on a journey. You have the promise of God, "Blessed is the man who endures temptation; for when he has been approved, he will receive the crown of life which the Lord has promised to those who love him" (James 1:12).

---

6   For even your brothers, the house of
         your father,
     Even they have dealt treacherously
         with you;
     Yes, they have called a multitude
         after you.
     Do not believe them,
     Even though they speak smooth
         words to you.
7   "I have forsaken My house, I have left
         My heritage;
     I have given the dearly beloved of My
         soul into the hand of her enemies.
8   My heritage is to Me like a lion in the
         forest;
     It cries out against Me;

Therefore I have hated it.
9   My heritage *is* to Me *like* a speckled
         vulture;
     The vultures all around *are* against
         her.
     Come, assemble all the beasts of the
         field,
     Bring them to devour!

10   "Many rulers[a] have destroyed My
         vineyard,
     They have trodden My portion
         underfoot;
     They have made My pleasant
         portion a desolate wilderness.
11   They have made it desolate;
     Desolate, it mourns to Me;
     The whole land is made desolate,
     Because no one takes *it* to heart.
12   The plunderers have come
     On all the desolate heights in the
         wilderness,
     For the sword of the LORD shall
         devour
     From *one* end of the land to the *other*
         end of the land;
     No flesh shall have peace.
13   They have sown wheat but reaped
         thorns;
     They have put themselves to pain
         but do not profit.
     But be ashamed of your harvest
     Because of the fierce anger of the
         LORD."

14Thus says the LORD: "Against all My evil neighbors who touch the inheritance which I have caused My people Israel to inherit—behold, I will pluck them out of their land and pluck out the house of Judah from among them. 15Then it shall be, after I have plucked them out, that I will return and have compassion on them and bring them back, everyone to his heritage and everyone to his land. 16And it shall be, if they will learn carefully the ways of My people, to swear by My name, 'As the LORD lives,' as they taught My people to swear by Baal, then they shall be established in the midst of My people. 17But if they do not obey, I will utterly pluck up and destroy that nation," says the LORD.

12:10 aLiterally *shepherds* or *pastors*

Symbol of the Linen Sash

13 Thus the LORD said to me: "Go and get yourself a linen sash, and put it around your waist, but do not put it in water." [2]So I got a sash according to the word of the LORD, and put *it* around my waist.

[3]And the word of the LORD came to me the second time, saying, [4]"Take the sash that you acquired, which *is* around your waist, and arise, go to the Euphrates,[a] and hide it there in a hole in the rock." [5]So I went and hid it by the Euphrates, as the LORD commanded me.

[6]Now it came to pass after many days that the LORD said to me, "Arise, go to the Euphrates, and take from there the sash which I commanded you to hide there." [7]Then I went to the Euphrates and dug, and I took the sash from the place where I had hidden it; and there was the sash, ruined. It was profitable for nothing.

[8]Then the word of the LORD came to me, saying, [9]"Thus says the LORD: 'In this manner I will ruin the pride of Judah and the great pride of Jerusalem. [10]This evil people, who refuse to hear My words, who follow the dictates of their hearts, and walk after other gods to serve them and worship them, shall be just like this sash which is profitable for nothing. [11]For as the sash clings to the waist of a man, so I have caused the whole house of Israel and the whole house of Judah to cling to Me,' says the LORD, 'that they may become My people, for renown, for praise, and for glory; but they would not hear.'

Symbol of the Wine Bottles

[12]"Therefore you shall speak to them this word: 'Thus says the LORD God of Israel: "Every bottle shall be filled with wine."'

"And they will say to you, 'Do we not certainly know that every bottle will be filled with wine?'

[13]"Then you shall say to them, 'Thus says the LORD: "Behold, I will fill all the inhabitants of this land—even the kings who sit on David's throne, the priests, the prophets, and all the inhabitants of

Jerusalem—with drunkenness! [14]And I will dash them one against another, even the fathers and the sons together," says the LORD. "I will not pity nor spare nor have mercy, but will destroy them."'"

Pride Precedes Captivity

[15] Hear and give ear:
Do not be proud,
For the LORD has spoken.
[16] Give glory to the LORD your God
Before He causes darkness,
And before your feet stumble
On the dark mountains,
And while you are looking for light,
He turns it into the shadow of death
And makes *it* dense darkness.
[17] But if you will not hear it,
My soul will weep in secret for *your* pride;
My eyes will weep bitterly
And run down with tears,
Because the LORD's flock has been taken captive.

[18] Say to the king and to the queen mother,
"Humble yourselves;
Sit down,
For your rule shall collapse, the crown of your glory."
[19] The cities of the South shall be shut up,
And no one shall open *them;*
Judah shall be carried away captive, all of it;
It shall be wholly carried away captive.

[20] Lift up your eyes and see
Those who come from the north.
Where *is* the flock *that* was given to you,
Your beautiful sheep?
[21] What will you say when He punishes you?
For you have taught them
To be chieftains, to be head over you.
Will not pangs seize you,
Like a woman in labor?
[22] And if you say in your heart,
"Why have these things come upon me?"
For the greatness of your iniquity

13:4 [a]Hebrew *Perath*

Break the Back of Procrastination

I SUPPOSE PROCRASTINATION IS as old as death itself. It's interesting how we tend to procrastinate on some of the most important decisions of our lives:

- Saying words of encouragement, appreciation, and love to our mates
- Giving our loved ones a hug
- Playing with our children
- Writing that letter of appreciation to our parents for all their hard work in raising us right
- Committing our lives fully to Christ as Lord and Savior
- Living for eternity instead of for the moment

Procrastination moves us steadily, slowly, and methodically toward a life of destruction. Its companions are mediocrity, compromise, laziness, lies, broken vows and promises, escapism, and daydreaming. Perhaps we need to heed Jeremiah's warning: "Give glory to the LORD your God before He causes darkness, and before your feet stumble on the dark mountains, and while you are looking for light, He turns it into the shadow of death and makes it dense darkness" (13:16).

What are you putting off doing today, thinking you'll do it tomorrow? If you or your mate tend to procrastinate, what can you do to help each other to break this destructive habit? One final question: How can you and your spouse train your children to do what they need to do and not practice the habit of procrastination?

Your skirts have been uncovered,
Your heels made bare.
23 Can the Ethiopian change his skin or
the leopard its spots?
Then may you also do good who are
accustomed to do evil.

24 "Therefore I will scatter them like
stubble
That passes away by the wind of the
wilderness.
25 This is your lot,
The portion of your measures from
Me," says the LORD,
"Because you have forgotten Me
And trusted in falsehood.
26 Therefore I will uncover your skirts
over your face,
That your shame may appear.
27 I have seen your adulteries
And your *lustful* neighings,
The lewdness of your harlotry,
Your abominations on the hills in the
fields.
Woe to you, O Jerusalem!
Will you still not be made clean?"

Sword, Famine, and Pestilence

14 The word of the LORD that came to Jeremiah concerning the droughts.

2 "Judah mourns,
And her gates languish;
They mourn for the land,
And the cry of Jerusalem has gone up.
3 Their nobles have sent their lads for
water;
They went to the cisterns *and* found
no water.
They returned with their vessels
empty;
They were ashamed and confounded
And covered their heads.
4 Because the ground is parched,
For there was no rain in the land,
The plowmen were ashamed;
They covered their heads.
5 Yes, the deer also gave birth in the
field,
But left because there was no grass.
6 And the wild donkeys stood in the
desolate heights;
They sniffed at the wind like jackals;
Their eyes failed because *there was*
no grass."

7 O LORD, though our iniquities testify
against us,
Do it for Your name's sake;
For our backslidings are many,
We have sinned against You.

8 O the Hope of Israel, his Savior in
    time of trouble,
Why should You be like a stranger in
    the land,
And like a traveler *who* turns aside
    to tarry for a night?
9 Why should You be like a man
    astonished,
Like a mighty one *who* cannot save?
Yet You, O LORD, *are* in our midst,
And we are called by Your name;
    Do not leave us!

10Thus says the LORD to this people:

"Thus they have loved to wander;
    They have not restrained their feet.
Therefore the LORD does not accept
    them;
He will remember their iniquity now,
    And punish their sins."

11Then the LORD said to me, "Do not
pray for this people, for *their* good. 12When
they fast, I will not hear their cry; and
when they offer burnt offering and grain
offering, I will not accept them. But I will
consume them by the sword, by the
famine, and by the pestilence."

13Then I said, "Ah, Lord GOD! Behold,
the prophets say to them, 'You shall not see
the sword, nor shall you have famine, but I
will give you assured peace in this place.'"

14And the LORD said to me, "The
prophets prophesy lies in My name. I have
not sent them, commanded them, nor spoken to them; they prophesy to you a false
vision, divination, a worthless thing, and
the deceit of their heart. 15Therefore thus
says the LORD concerning the prophets who
prophesy in My name, whom I did not
send, and who say, 'Sword and famine shall
not be in this land'—'By sword and famine
those prophets shall be consumed! 16And
the people to whom they prophesy shall be
cast out in the streets of Jerusalem because
of the famine and the sword; they will have
no one to bury them—them nor their
wives, their sons nor their daughters—for I
will pour their wickedness on them.'

17"Therefore you shall say this word to
them:

'Let my eyes flow with tears night
    and day,

And let them not cease;
For the virgin daughter of my people
Has been broken with a mighty
    stroke, with a very severe blow.
18 If I go out to the field,
Then behold, those slain with the
    sword!
And if I enter the city,
Then behold, those sick from famine!
Yes, both prophet and priest go about
    in a land they do not know.'"

The People Plead for Mercy

19 Have You utterly rejected Judah?
Has Your soul loathed Zion?
Why have You stricken us so that
    there is no healing for us?
We looked for peace, but *there was*
    no good;
And for the time of healing, and
    there was trouble.
20 We acknowledge, O LORD, our
    wickedness
And the iniquity of our fathers,
For we have sinned against You.
21 Do not abhor *us,* for Your name's sake;
Do not disgrace the throne of Your
    glory.
Remember, do not break Your
    covenant with us.
22 Are there any among the idols of the
    nations that can cause rain?
Or can the heavens give showers?
Are You not He, O LORD our God?
Therefore we will wait for You,
Since You have made all these.

The LORD Will Not Relent

15 Then the LORD said to me, "*Even* if
Moses and Samuel stood before Me,
My mind *would* not *be* favorable toward
this people. Cast *them* out of My sight, and
let them go forth. 2And it shall be, if they
say to you, 'Where should we go?' then you
shall tell them, 'Thus says the LORD:

"Such as *are* for death, to death;
And such as *are* for the sword, to the
    sword;
And such as *are* for the famine, to
    the famine;
And such as *are* for the captivity, to
    the captivity."'

3"And I will appoint over them four forms *of destruction*," says the LORD: "the sword to slay, the dogs to drag, the birds of the heavens and the beasts of the earth to devour and destroy. 4I will hand them over to trouble, to all kingdoms of the earth, because of Manasseh the son of Hezekiah, king of Judah, for what he did in Jerusalem.

5 "For who will have pity on you, O
    Jerusalem?
  Or who will bemoan you?
  Or who will turn aside to ask how
    you are doing?
6 You have forsaken Me," says the LORD,
  "You have gone backward.
  Therefore I will stretch out My hand
    against you and destroy you;
  I am weary of relenting!
7 And I will winnow them with a
    winnowing fan in the gates of the
    land;
  I will bereave *them* of children;
  I will destroy My people,
  Since they do not return from their
    ways.

8 Their widows will be increased to
    Me more than the sand of the
    seas;
  I will bring against them,
  Against the mother of the young men,
  A plunderer at noonday;
  I will cause anguish and terror to fall
    on them suddenly.

9 "She languishes who has borne seven;
  She has breathed her last;
  Her sun has gone down
  While *it was* yet day;
  She has been ashamed and
    confounded.
  And the remnant of them I will
    deliver to the sword
  Before their enemies," says the LORD.

Jeremiah's Dejection

10 Woe is me, my mother,
  That you have borne me,
  A man of strife and a man of
    contention to the whole earth!
  I have neither lent for interest,
  Nor have men lent to me for interest.
  Every one of them curses me.

PARENTING MATTERS

Q: *How do we respond to our adolescent child's anger when we reprimand her or make rules? Should we allow her to express her anger toward us?*

Most adolescents are emotionally confused. They are experiencing new feelings that they don't understand or know how to handle. All teenagers need to have a vent for these new emotions, including anger; they need to be heard and understood by their parents.

Still, you must distinguish between appropriate and inappropriate expressions of anger. Decide as a couple what you will accept as suitable expressions of anger and how you will punish unsuitable expressions of anger. For example, it should be clear that anytime a child expressing anger begins to harm another child or adult, the anger is inappropriate. In addition, we will not accept words of anger that bring harm or damage to a parent or tear someone down. These are sinful expressions of anger and need to be addressed with a child.

When the child is appropriately expressing anger, you can affirm her by saying, "I know you are upset and disagree with me, but I need to ask you to obey anyway." We have tried to model appropriate anger for the kids and we have role-played tense situations.

For parents and children to maintain good relationships, lines of communication must remain open. Train your kids to express all their emotions in appropriate ways so that bitterness doesn't build toward you. Don't let the sun go down on your wrath, or on theirs.

¹¹The LORD said:

"Surely it will be well with your
        remnant;
Surely I will cause the enemy to
        intercede with you
In the time of adversity and in the
        time of affliction.
¹² Can anyone break iron,
        The northern iron and the bronze?
¹³ Your wealth and your treasures
        I will give as plunder without price,
Because of all your sins,
        Throughout your territories.
¹⁴ And I will make *you* cross over with^a
        your enemies
Into a land *which* you do not know;
For a fire is kindled in My anger,
Which shall burn upon you."

¹⁵ O LORD, You know;
        Remember me and visit me,
And take vengeance for me on my
        persecutors.
In Your enduring patience, do not
        take me away.
Know that for Your sake I have
        suffered rebuke.
¹⁶ Your words were found, and I ate them,
And Your word was to me the joy
        and rejoicing of my heart;
For I am called by Your name,
O LORD God of hosts.
¹⁷ I did not sit in the assembly of the
        mockers,
Nor did I rejoice;
I sat alone because of Your hand,
For You have filled me with
        indignation.
¹⁸ Why is my pain perpetual
And my wound incurable,
Which refuses to be healed?
Will You surely be to me like an
        unreliable stream,
As waters *that* fail?

The LORD Reassures Jeremiah

¹⁹Therefore thus says the LORD:

"If you return,
Then I will bring you back;
You shall stand before Me;

If you take out the precious from the
        vile,
You shall be as My mouth.
Let them return to you,
But you must not return to them.
²⁰ And I will make you to this people a
        fortified bronze wall;
And they will fight against you,
But they shall not prevail against you;
For I *am* with you to save you
And deliver you," says the LORD.
²¹ "I will deliver you from the hand of
        the wicked,
And I will redeem you from the grip
        of the terrible."

Jeremiah's Life-Style and Message

16 The word of the LORD also came to
me, saying, ²"You shall not take a
wife, nor shall you have sons or daughters
in this place." ³For thus says the LORD concerning the sons and daughters who are
born in this place, and concerning their
mothers who bore them and their fathers
who begot them in this land: ⁴"They shall
die gruesome deaths; they shall not be
lamented nor shall they be buried, *but* they
shall be like refuse on the face of the earth.
They shall be consumed by the sword and
by famine, and their corpses shall be meat
for the birds of heaven and for the beasts
of the earth."

⁵For thus says the LORD: "Do not enter
the house of mourning, nor go to lament or
bemoan them; for I have taken away My
peace from this people," says the LORD, "lovingkindness and mercies. ⁶Both the great
and the small shall die in this land. They
shall not be buried; neither shall men lament
for them, cut themselves, nor make themselves bald for them. ⁷Nor shall *men* break
bread in mourning for them, to comfort
them for the dead; nor shall *men* give them
the cup of consolation to drink for their
father or their mother. ⁸Also you shall not
go into the house of feasting to sit with
them, to eat and drink."

⁹For thus says the LORD of hosts, the
God of Israel: "Behold, I will cause to cease
from this place, before your eyes and in
your days, the voice of mirth and the voice
of gladness, the voice of the bridegroom
and the voice of the bride.

15:14 ^aFollowing Masoretic Text and Vulgate;
Septuagint, Syriac, and Targum read *cause you to
serve* (compare 17:4).

Where Do You Turn in Times of Trouble?

AS SECULARISM AND HUMANISM continue to gain traction in our culture, we are increasingly bombarded with messages of positive thinking, of our ability to "do" and "accomplish," and with our ability to solve all our problems. *Just think positively*, the message goes, *and have faith in yourself!*

While we have written about the importance of building good self-esteem, we understand that good self-esteem doesn't mean putting our faith in our own abilities rather than in God. Jeremiah warned Israel against just that kind of self-sufficiency, "Thus says the LORD: 'Cursed is the man who trusts in man and makes flesh his strength, whose heart departs from the LORD'" (17:5). Contrast that warning with the promise two verses later which reads, "Blessed is the man who trusts in the LORD, and whose hope is the LORD."

This is an amazing warning/promise combination. It tells us that during the troubled times in our marriages and in our homes—and they will come!—we had better make sure we're not relying on our own talents and abilities. Instead, we need to consciously put our trust and our confidence completely in the God who created marriages and families in the first place.

---

¹⁰"And it shall be, when you show this people all these words, and they say to you, 'Why has the LORD pronounced all this great disaster against us? Or what *is* our iniquity? Or what *is* our sin that we have committed against the LORD our God?' ¹¹then you shall say to them, 'Because your fathers have forsaken Me,' says the LORD; 'they have walked after other gods and have served them and worshiped them, and have forsaken Me and not kept My law.

¹²And you have done worse than your fathers, for behold, each one follows the dictates of his own evil heart, so that no one listens to Me. ¹³Therefore I will cast you out of this land into a land that you do not know, neither you nor your fathers; and there you shall serve other gods day and night, where I will not show you favor.'

God Will Restore Israel

¹⁴"Therefore behold, the days are coming," says the LORD, "that it shall no more be said, 'The LORD lives who brought up the children of Israel from the land of Egypt,' ¹⁵but, 'The LORD lives who brought up the children of Israel from the land of the north and from all the lands where He had driven them.' For I will bring them back into their land which I gave to their fathers.

¹⁶"Behold, I will send for many fishermen," says the LORD, "and they shall fish them; and afterward I will send for many hunters, and they shall hunt them from every mountain and every hill, and out of the holes of the rocks. ¹⁷For My eyes *are* on all their ways; they are not hidden from My face, nor is their iniquity hidden from My eyes. ¹⁸And first I will repay double for their iniquity and their sin, because they have defiled My land; they have filled My inheritance with the carcasses of their detestable and abominable idols."

¹⁹   O LORD, my strength and my
            fortress,
      My refuge in the day of affliction,
      The Gentiles shall come to You
      From the ends of the earth and say,
      "Surely our fathers have inherited
            lies,
      Worthlessness and unprofitable
            things."

²⁰   Will a man make gods for himself,
      Which *are* not gods?

²¹   "Therefore behold, I will this once
            cause them to know,
      I will cause them to know
      My hand and My might;
      And they shall know that My name
      is the LORD.

Judah's Sin and Punishment

17 "The sin of Judah *is* written with
  a pen of iron;
With the point of a diamond *it is*
  engraved
On the tablet of their heart,
And on the horns of your altars,
2 While their children remember
Their altars and their wooden images[a]
By the green trees on the high hills.
3 O My mountain in the field,
I will give as plunder your wealth, all
  your treasures,
And your high places of sin within
  all your borders.
4 And you, even yourself,
Shall let go of your heritage which I
  gave you;
And I will cause you to serve your
  enemies
In the land which you do not know;
For you have kindled a fire in My
  anger *which* shall burn forever."

5 Thus says the LORD:

"Cursed *is* the man who trusts in man
And makes flesh his strength,
Whose heart departs from the LORD.
6 For he shall be like a shrub in the
  desert,
And shall not see when good comes,
But shall inhabit the parched places
  in the wilderness,
In a salt land *which is* not inhabited.

7 "Blessed *is* the man who trusts in the
  LORD,
And whose hope is the LORD.
8 For he shall be like a tree planted by
  the waters,
Which spreads out its roots by the
  river,
And will not fear[a] when heat comes;
But its leaf will be green,
And will not be anxious in the year
  of drought,
Nor will cease from yielding fruit.

9 "The heart *is* deceitful above all *things,*
And desperately wicked;
Who can know it?

BIBLICAL INSIGHTS • 17:9

Cherubic Faces, Deceitful Hearts

THE PROPHET JEREMIAH paints an ugly picture of what really lies at the core of every human being, "The heart is deceitful above all things, and desperately wicked; who can know it?" (17:9).

That unfortunate truth not only applies to us as parents, but also to our preteens and teens. A tendency toward lying and other types of deception—cheating in school, breaking promises, fudging on the truth—usually surfaces during adolescence. A child developing more complex thinking abilities has a better set of tools to use in being deceitful. Teenagers also have more freedom and independence than they enjoyed before, which means more opportunity to make choices they might want to hide. Peers also say things like, "Nobody will ever know," or "You don't have to tell your parents."

As we train our children, we sometimes look into their sweet, little faces and forget what we are really up against: a deceitful human heart. We should know that is true, but our tendency is to forget the condition of their hearts.

God once identified seven things He really hates (Prov. 6:16–19), and two of them concern deceit—"a lying tongue" and "a false witness who utters lies." If God took the time to make this list, then we parents had better do a good job of training and disciplining our children away from His hated seven!

If you have a child that has a bent toward lying, ask God to give you wisdom in knowing how to catch him in his lies. Pray for wise ways to bring about the painful consequences to your child's life so that he can learn now that deceit is truly dangerous.

10 I, the LORD, search the heart,
I test the mind,
Even to give every man according to
  his ways,
According to the fruit of his doings.

17:2 [a]Hebrew *Asherim,* Canaanite deities
17:8 [a]Qere and Targum read *see.*

11 "*As* a partridge that broods but does
     not hatch,
    So is he who gets riches, but not by
       right;
    It will leave him in the midst of his
       days,
    And at his end he will be a fool."

12 A glorious high throne from the
      beginning
    Is the place of our sanctuary.
13 O LORD, the hope of Israel,
    All who forsake You shall be ashamed.

    "Those who depart from Me
    Shall be written in the earth,
    Because they have forsaken
       the LORD,
    The fountain of living waters."

Jeremiah Prays for Deliverance

14 Heal me, O LORD, and I shall be
      healed;
    Save me, and I shall be saved,
    For You *are* my praise.
15 Indeed they say to me,
    "Where *is* the word of the LORD?
    Let it come now!"
16 As for me, I have not hurried away
       from *being* a shepherd *who*
       follows You,
    Nor have I desired the woeful day;
    You know what came out of my lips;
    It was right there before You.
17 Do not be a terror to me;
    You *are* my hope in the day of doom.
18 Let them be ashamed who persecute
       me,
    But do not let me be put to shame;
    Let them be dismayed,
    But do not let me be dismayed;
    Bring on them the day of doom,
    And destroy them with double
       destruction!

Hallow the Sabbath Day

19 Thus the LORD said to me: "Go and
stand in the gate of the children of the people, by which the kings of Judah come in
and by which they go out, and in all the
gates of Jerusalem; 20 and say to them, 'Hear
the word of the LORD, you kings of Judah,
and all Judah, and all the inhabitants of
Jerusalem, who enter by these gates.
21 Thus says the LORD: "Take heed to yourselves, and bear no burden on the Sabbath
day, nor bring *it* in by the gates of
Jerusalem; 22 nor carry a burden out of
your houses on the Sabbath day, nor do
any work, but hallow the Sabbath day, as I
commanded your fathers. 23 But they did
not obey nor incline their ear, but made
their neck stiff, that they might not hear
nor receive instruction.

24 "And it shall be, if you heed Me carefully," says the LORD, "to bring no burden
through the gates of this city on the
Sabbath day, but hallow the Sabbath day, to
do no work in it, 25 then shall enter the gates
of this city kings and princes sitting on the
throne of David, riding in chariots and on
horses, they and their princes, accompanied
by the men of Judah and the inhabitants of
Jerusalem; and this city shall remain forever. 26 And they shall come from the cities of
Judah and from the places around
Jerusalem, from the land of Benjamin and
from the lowland, from the mountains and
from the South, bringing burnt offerings
and sacrifices, grain offerings and incense,
bringing sacrifices of praise to the house
of the LORD.

27 "But if you will not heed Me to hallow
the Sabbath day, such as not carrying a
burden when entering the gates of
Jerusalem on the Sabbath day, then I will
kindle a fire in its gates, and it shall devour
the palaces of Jerusalem, and it shall not
be quenched." ' "

The Potter and the Clay

18 The word which came to Jeremiah
from the LORD, saying: 2 "Arise and
go down to the potter's house, and there I
will cause you to hear My words." 3 Then I
went down to the potter's house, and there
he was, making something at the wheel.
4 And the vessel that he made of clay was
marred in the hand of the potter; so he
made it again into another vessel, as it
seemed good to the potter to make.

5 Then the word of the LORD came to
me, saying: 6 "O house of Israel, can I not
do with you as this potter?" says the LORD.
"Look, as the clay *is* in the potter's hand, so
are you in My hand, O house of Israel!

⁷The instant I speak concerning a nation and concerning a kingdom, to pluck up, to pull down, and to destroy *it,* ⁸if that nation against whom I have spoken turns from its evil, I will relent of the disaster that I thought to bring upon it. ⁹And the instant I speak concerning a nation and concerning a kingdom, to build and to plant *it,* ¹⁰if it does evil in My sight so that it does not obey My voice, then I will relent concerning the good with which I said I would benefit it.

¹¹"Now therefore, speak to the men of Judah and to the inhabitants of Jerusalem, saying, 'Thus says the LORD: "Behold, I am fashioning a disaster and devising a plan against you. Return now every one from his evil way, and make your ways and your doings good." ' "

God's Warning Rejected

¹²And they said, "That is hopeless! So we will walk according to our own plans, and we will every one obey the dictates of his evil heart."

¹³Therefore thus says the LORD:

"Ask now among the Gentiles,
  Who has heard such things?
  The virgin of Israel has done a very
    horrible thing.
¹⁴ Will *a man* leave the snow water of
    Lebanon,
  Which comes from the rock of the
    field?
  Will the cold flowing waters be
    forsaken for strange waters?
¹⁵ "Because My people have forgotten Me,
  They have burned incense to
    worthless idols.
  And they have caused themselves to
    stumble in their ways,
  From the ancient paths,
  To walk in pathways and not on a
    highway,
¹⁶ To make their land desolate *and* a
    perpetual hissing;
  Everyone who passes by it will be
    astonished
  And shake his head.

---

¹⁷ I will scatter them as with an east
    wind before the enemy;
  I will show themᵃ the back and not
    the face
  In the day of their calamity."

Jeremiah Persecuted

¹⁸Then they said, "Come and let us devise plans against Jeremiah; for the law shall not perish from the priest, nor counsel from the wise, nor the word from the prophet. Come and let us attack him with the tongue, and let us not give heed to any of his words."

¹⁹ Give heed to me, O LORD,
  And listen to the voice of those who
    contend with me!
²⁰ Shall evil be repaid for good?
  For they have dug a pit for my life.
  Remember that I stood before You
  To speak good for them,
  To turn away Your wrath from them.
²¹ Therefore deliver up their children to
    the famine,
  And pour out their *blood*
  By the force of the sword;
  Let their wives *become* widows
  And bereaved of their children.
  Let their men be put to death,
  Their young men *be* slain
  By the sword in battle.
²² Let a cry be heard from their houses,
  When You bring a troop suddenly
    upon them;
  For they have dug a pit to take me,
  And hidden snares for my feet.
²³ Yet, LORD, You know all their counsel
  Which is against me, to slay *me.*
  Provide no atonement for their
    iniquity,
  Nor blot out their sin from Your sight;
  But let them be overthrown before
    You.
  Deal *thus* with them
  In the time of Your anger.

The Sign of the Broken Flask

19 Thus says the LORD: "Go and get a potter's earthen flask, and *take* some of the elders of the people and some of the elders of the priests. ²And go out to the Valley of the Son of Hinnom, which *is* by the entry of the Potsherd Gate; and proclaim there the words that I will tell you, [3]and say, 'Hear the word of the LORD, O kings of Judah and inhabitants of Jerusalem. Thus says the LORD of hosts, the God of Israel: "Behold, I will bring such a catastrophe on this place, that whoever hears of it, his ears will tingle.

[4]"Because they have forsaken Me and made this an alien place, because they have burned incense in it to other gods whom neither they, their fathers, nor the kings of Judah have known, and have filled this place with the blood of the innocents [5](they have also built the high places of Baal, to burn their sons with fire *for* burnt offerings to Baal, which I did not command or speak, nor did it come into My mind), [6]therefore behold, the days are coming," says the LORD, "that this place shall no more be called Tophet or the Valley of the Son of Hinnom, but the Valley of Slaughter. [7]And I will make void the counsel of Judah and Jerusalem in this place, and I will cause them to fall by the sword before their enemies and by the hands of those who seek their lives; their corpses I will give as meat for the birds of the heaven and for the beasts of the earth. [8]I will make this city desolate and a hissing; everyone who passes by it will be astonished and hiss because of all its plagues.

[9]And I will cause them to eat the flesh of their sons and the flesh of their daughters, and everyone shall eat the flesh of his friend in the siege and in the desperation with which their enemies and those who seek their lives shall drive them to despair."'

[10]"Then you shall break the flask in the sight of the men who go with you, [11]and say to them, 'Thus says the LORD of hosts: "Even so I will break this people and this city, as *one* breaks a potter's vessel, which cannot be made whole again; and they shall bury *them* in Tophet till *there is* no place to bury. [12]Thus I will do to this place," says the LORD, "and to its inhabitants, and make this city like Tophet. [13]And the houses of Jerusalem and the houses of the kings of Judah shall be defiled like the place of Tophet, because of all the houses on whose roofs they have burned incense to all the host of heaven, and poured out drink offerings to other gods."'"

[14]Then Jeremiah came from Tophet, where the LORD had sent him to prophesy; and he stood in the court of the Lord's house and said to all the people, [15]"Thus says the LORD of hosts, the God of Israel: 'Behold, I will bring on this city and on all her towns all the doom that I have pronounced against it, because they have stiffened their necks that they might not hear My words.'"

The Word of God to Pashhur

20 Now Pashhur the son of Immer, the priest who *was* also chief governor in the house of the LORD, heard that Jeremiah prophesied these things. ²Then Pashhur struck Jeremiah the prophet, and put him in the stocks that *were* in the high gate of Benjamin, which *was* by the house of the LORD.

³And it happened on the next day that Pashhur brought Jeremiah out of the stocks. Then Jeremiah said to him, "The LORD has not called your name Pashhur, but Magor-Missabib.ᵃ ⁴For thus says the LORD: 'Behold, I will make you a terror to yourself and to all your friends; and they shall fall by the sword of their enemies, and your eyes shall see *it*. I will give all Judah into the hand of the king of Babylon, and he shall carry them captive to Babylon and slay them with the sword. ⁵Moreover I will deliver all the wealth of this city, all its produce, and all its precious things; all the treasures of the kings of Judah I will give into the hand of their enemies, who will plunder them, seize them, and carry them to Babylon. ⁶And you, Pashhur, and all who dwell in your house, shall go into captivity. You shall go to Babylon, and there you shall die, and be buried there, you and all your friends, to whom you have prophesied lies.'"

Jeremiah's Unpopular Ministry

7 O LORD, You induced me, and I was
    persuaded;
  You are stronger than I, and have
    prevailed.
  I am in derision daily;
  Everyone mocks me.
8 For when I spoke, I cried out;
  I shouted, "Violence and plunder!"
  Because the word of the LORD was
    made to me
  A reproach and a derision daily.
9 Then I said, "I will not make mention
    of Him,
  Nor speak anymore in His name."
  But *His word* was in my heart like a
    burning fire

  Shut up in my bones;
  I was weary of holding *it* back,
  And I could not.
10 For I heard many mocking:
  "Fear on every side!"
  "Report," *they say,* "and we will report
    it!"
  All my acquaintances watched for
    my stumbling, *saying,*
  "Perhaps he can be induced;
  Then we will prevail against him,
  And we will take our revenge on
    him."

11 But the LORD *is* with me as a mighty,
    awesome One.
  Therefore my persecutors will
    stumble, and will not prevail.
  They will be greatly ashamed, for
    they will not prosper.
  Their everlasting confusion will
    never be forgotten.
12 But, O LORD of hosts,
  You who test the righteous,
  And see the mind and heart,
  Let me see Your vengeance on them;
  For I have pleaded my cause before
    You.

13 Sing to the LORD! Praise the LORD!
  For He has delivered the life of the
    poor
  From the hand of evildoers.

14 Cursed *be* the day in which I was
    born!
  Let the day not be blessed in which
    my mother bore me!
15 Let the man *be* cursed
  Who brought news to my father,
    saying,
  "A male child has been born to you!"
  Making him very glad.
16 And let that man be like the cities
  Which the LORD overthrew, and did
    not relent;
  Let him hear the cry in the morning
  And the shouting at noon,
17 Because he did not kill me from the
    womb,
  That my mother might have been my
    grave,
  And her womb always enlarged *with*
    me.

20:3 ᵃLiterally *Fear on Every Side*

18   Why did I come forth from the
       womb to see labor and sorrow,
     That my days should be consumed
       with shame?

Jerusalem's Doom Is Sealed

21 The word which came to Jeremiah from the LORD when King Zedekiah sent to him Pashhur the son of Melchiah, and Zephaniah the son of Maaseiah, the priest, saying, ²"Please inquire of the LORD for us, for Nebuchadnezzar[a] king of Babylon makes war against us. Perhaps the LORD will deal with us according to all His wonderful works, that *the king* may go away from us."

³Then Jeremiah said to them, "Thus you shall say to Zedekiah, ⁴'Thus says the LORD God of Israel: "Behold, I will turn back the weapons of war that *are* in your hands, with which you fight against the king of Babylon and the Chaldeans[a] who besiege you outside the walls; and I will assemble them in the midst of this city. ⁵I Myself will fight against you with an outstretched hand and with a strong arm, even in anger and fury and great wrath. ⁶I will strike the inhabitants of this city, both man and beast; they shall die of a great pestilence. ⁷And afterward," says the LORD, "I will deliver Zedekiah king of Judah, his servants and the people, and such as are left in this city from the pestilence and the sword and the famine, into the hand of Nebuchadnezzar king of Babylon, into the hand of their enemies, and into the hand of those who seek their life; and he shall strike them with the edge of the sword. He shall not spare them, or have pity or mercy."'

⁸"Now you shall say to this people, 'Thus says the LORD: "Behold, I set before you the way of life and the way of death. ⁹He who remains in this city shall die by the sword, by famine, and by pestilence; but he who goes out and defects to the Chaldeans who besiege you, he shall live, and his life shall be as a prize to him. ¹⁰For I have set My face against this city for adversity and not for good," says the LORD. "It shall be given into the hand of the king of Babylon, and he shall burn it with fire."'

Message to the House of David

¹¹"And concerning the house of the king of Judah, *say,* 'Hear the word of the LORD, ¹²O house of David! Thus says the LORD:

"Execute judgment in the morning;
    And deliver *him who is* plundered
    Out of the hand of the oppressor,
Lest My fury go forth like fire
    And burn so that no one can quench *it,*
Because of the evil of your doings.

13   "Behold, I *am* against you, O
       inhabitant of the valley,
     And rock of the plain," says the LORD,
   "Who say, 'Who shall come down
       against us?
     Or who shall enter our dwellings?'
14   But I will punish you according to
       the fruit of your doings," says
       the LORD;
   "I will kindle a fire in its forest,
     And it shall devour all things around
       it."'"

22 Thus says the LORD: "Go down to the house of the king of Judah, and there speak this word, ²and say, 'Hear the word of the LORD, O king of Judah, you who sit on the throne of David, you and your servants and your people who enter these gates! ³Thus says the LORD: "Execute judgment and righteousness, and deliver the plundered out of the hand of the oppressor. Do no wrong and do no violence to the stranger, the fatherless, or the widow, nor shed innocent blood in this place. ⁴For if you indeed do this thing, then shall enter the gates of this house, riding on horses and in chariots, accompanied by servants and people, kings who sit on the throne of David. ⁵But if you will not hear these words, I swear by Myself," says the LORD, "that this house shall become a desolation."'"

⁶For thus says the LORD to the house of the king of Judah:

"You *are* Gilead to Me,
    The head of Lebanon;

21:2 ᵃHebrew *Nebuchadrezzar,* and so elsewhere
21:4 ᵃOr *Babylonians*

Yet I surely will make you a
   wilderness,
Cities *which* are not inhabited.
7 I will prepare destroyers against you,
   Everyone with his weapons;
They shall cut down your choice
   cedars
And cast *them* into the fire.

8 And many nations will pass by this city; and everyone will say to his neighbor, 'Why has the LORD done so to this great city?' 9 Then they will answer, 'Because they have forsaken the covenant of the LORD their God, and worshiped other gods and served them.' "

10 Weep not for the dead, nor bemoan
   him;
Weep bitterly for him who goes
   away,
For he shall return no more,
Nor see his native country.

Message to the Sons of Josiah

11 For thus says the LORD concerning Shallum[a] the son of Josiah, king of Judah, who reigned instead of Josiah his father, who went from this place: "He shall not return here anymore, 12 but he shall die in the place where they have led him captive, and shall see this land no more.

13 "Woe to him who builds his house by
   unrighteousness
And his chambers by injustice,
Who uses his neighbor's service
   without wages
And gives him nothing for his work,
14 Who says, 'I will build myself a wide
   house with spacious chambers,
And cut out windows for it,
Paneling *it* with cedar
And painting *it* with vermilion.'
15 "Shall you reign because you enclose
   yourself in cedar?
Did not your father eat and drink,
And do justice and righteousness?
Then *it was* well with him.
16 He judged the cause of the poor and
   needy;
Then *it was* well.

Was not this knowing Me?" says the
   LORD.
17 "Yet your eyes and your heart *are* for
   nothing but your covetousness,
For shedding innocent blood,
And practicing oppression and
   violence."

18 Therefore thus says the LORD concerning Jehoiakim the son of Josiah, king of Judah:

"They shall not lament for him,
Saying, 'Alas, my brother!' or 'Alas,
   my sister!'
They shall not lament for him,
Saying, 'Alas, master!' or 'Alas, his
   glory!'
19 He shall be buried with the burial of
   a donkey,
Dragged and cast out beyond the
   gates of Jerusalem.

20 "Go up to Lebanon, and cry out,
And lift up your voice in Bashan;
Cry from Abarim,
For all your lovers are destroyed.
21 I spoke to you in your prosperity,
But you said, 'I will not hear.'
This *has been* your manner from
   your youth,
That you did not obey My voice.
22 The wind shall eat up all your rulers,
And your lovers shall go into
   captivity;
Surely then you will be ashamed and
   humiliated
For all your wickedness.
23 O inhabitant of Lebanon,
Making your nest in the cedars,
How gracious will you be when
   pangs come upon you,
Like the pain of a woman in labor?

INTIMATE MOMENTS

Pick up his favorite dish from his favorite restaurant and serve it to him on your best china.

22:11 [a] Also called *Jehoahaz*

Message to Coniah

24"As I live," says the LORD, "though Coniah[a] the son of Jehoiakim, king of Judah, were the signet on My right hand, yet I would pluck you off; 25and I will give you into the hand of those who seek your life, and into the hand *of those* whose face you fear—the hand of Nebuchadnezzar king of Babylon and the hand of the Chaldeans. 26So I will cast you out, and your mother who bore you, into another country where you were not born; and there you shall die. 27But to the land to which they desire to return, there they shall not return.

28   "Is this man Coniah a despised,
            broken idol—
        A vessel in which *is* no pleasure?
        Why are they cast out, he and his
            descendants,
        And cast into a land which they do
            not know?
29   O earth, earth, earth,
        Hear the word of the LORD!
30   Thus says the LORD:
    'Write this man down as childless,
        A man *who* shall not prosper in his
            days;
        For none of his descendants shall
            prosper,
        Sitting on the throne of David,
        And ruling anymore in Judah.'"

The Branch of Righteousness

23 "Woe to the shepherds who destroy and scatter the sheep of My pasture!" says the LORD. 2Therefore thus says the LORD God of Israel against the shepherds who feed My people: "You have scattered My flock, driven them away, and not attended to them. Behold, I will attend to you for the evil of your doings," says the LORD. 3"But I will gather the remnant of My flock out of all countries where I have driven them, and bring them back to their folds; and they shall be fruitful and increase. 4I will set up shepherds over them who will feed them; and they shall fear no more, nor be dismayed, nor shall they be lacking," says the LORD.

5   "Behold, *the* days are coming," says
        the LORD,

    "That I will raise to David a Branch
        of righteousness;
    A King shall reign and prosper,
    And execute judgment and
        righteousness in the earth.
6   In His days Judah will be saved,
    And Israel will dwell safely;
    Now this *is* His name by which He
        will be called:

THE LORD OUR RIGHTEOUSNESS.[a]

7"Therefore, behold, *the* days are coming," says the LORD, "that they shall no longer say, 'As the LORD lives who brought up the children of Israel from the land of Egypt,' 8but, 'As the LORD lives who brought up and led the descendants of the house of Israel from the north country and from all the countries where I had driven them.' And they shall dwell in their own land."

False Prophets and Empty Oracles

9   My heart within me is broken
    Because of the prophets;
    All my bones shake.
    I am like a drunken man,
    And like a man whom wine has
        overcome,
    Because of the LORD,
    And because of His holy words.
10   For the land is full of adulterers;
    For because of a curse the land
        mourns.
    The pleasant places of the
        wilderness are dried up.
    Their course of life is evil,
    And their might *is* not right.

11   "For both prophet and priest are
        profane;
    Yes, in My house I have found their
        wickedness," says the LORD.
12   "Therefore their way shall be to them
    Like slippery *ways;*
    In the darkness they shall be driven
        on
    And fall in them;
    For I will bring disaster on them,
    The year of their punishment," says
        the LORD.

22:24 [a]Also called *Jeconiah* and *Jehoiachin*
23:6 [a]Hebrew *YHWH Tsidkenu*

13 "And I have seen folly in the prophets
    of Samaria:
   They prophesied by Baal
   And caused My people Israel to err.
14 Also I have seen a horrible thing in
    the prophets of Jerusalem:
   They commit adultery and walk in lies;
   They also strengthen the hands of
    evildoers,
   So that no one turns back from his
    wickedness.
   All of them are like Sodom to Me,
   And her inhabitants like Gomorrah.

15 "Therefore thus says the LORD of
hosts concerning the prophets:

   'Behold, I will feed them with
    wormwood,
   And make them drink the water of
    gall;
   For from the prophets of Jerusalem
   Profaneness has gone out into all the
    land.' "

16 Thus says the LORD of hosts:

   "Do not listen to the words of the
    prophets who prophesy to you.
   They make you worthless;
   They speak a vision of their own
    heart,
   Not from the mouth of the LORD.
17 They continually say to those who
    despise Me,
   ‘ The LORD has said, "You shall
    have peace" ';
   And to everyone who walks
    according to the dictates of his
    own heart, they say,
   ‘No evil shall come upon you.' "

18 For who has stood in the counsel of
    the LORD,
   And has perceived and heard His
    word?
   Who has marked His word and
    heard it?
19 Behold, a whirlwind of the LORD has
    gone forth in fury—
   A violent whirlwind!
   It will fall violently on the head of
    the wicked.
20 The anger of the LORD will not turn
    back
   Until He has executed and performed
    the thoughts of His heart.
   In the latter days you will
    understand it perfectly.

PARENTING MATTERS

Q: What's the best approach to discipline my young child?

Children aged two to five years old are in the "intense training" stage. During these early years, you will notice your children becoming more defiant—more temper tantrums, hitting, biting, whining, even lying and stealing.

When these unacceptable behaviors occur, deal with them effectively and clearly, because you are establishing what is right and what is wrong within your family. These are often hard years, particularly for moms, because you may feel like the cycle is never-ending—that you're teaching the same lessons over and over again.

At this age, children start to become independent and they realize they have their own will. Plenty of toddlers control their entire family. If you find yourself in this situation, take steps to stop the children from dominating you. If you don't, you'll really pay the price when your child is a teenager.

Sit down with your spouse and make a list for the children of what they can and can't do; what actions require discipline and which you can let go. You will help your kids by drawing up very clear boundaries for them.

Also, go on the offensive. Remind your kids about what you do and do not expect. This will help your kids do what's right.

21   "I have not sent these prophets, yet
        they ran.
       I have not spoken to them, yet they
        prophesied.
22   But if they had stood in My counsel,
        And had caused My people to hear
         My words,
       Then they would have turned them
        from their evil way
       And from the evil of their doings.

23   "Am I a God near at hand," says the
        LORD,
       "And not a God afar off?
24   Can anyone hide himself in secret
        places,
        So I shall not see him?" says the
         LORD;
       "Do I not fill heaven and earth?" says
        the LORD.

25"I have heard what the prophets have
said who prophesy lies in My name, saying, 'I have dreamed, I have dreamed!'
26How long will *this* be in the heart of the
prophets who prophesy lies? Indeed *they
are* prophets of the deceit of their own
heart, 27who try to make My people forget
My name by their dreams which everyone
tells his neighbor, as their fathers forgot
My name for Baal.

28   "The prophet who has a dream, let
        him tell a dream;
       And he who has My word, let him
        speak My word faithfully.
       What *is* the chaff to the wheat?"
        says the LORD.
29   "Is not My word like a fire?" says the
        LORD,
       "And like a hammer *that* breaks the
        rock in pieces?

30"Therefore behold, I *am* against the
prophets," says the LORD, "who steal My
words every one from his neighbor.
31Behold, I *am* against the prophets," says
the LORD, "who use their tongues and say,
'He says.' 32Behold, I *am* against those who
prophesy false dreams," says the LORD,
"and tell them, and cause My people to err
by their lies and by their recklessness. Yet
I did not send them or command them;
therefore they shall not profit this people
at all," says the LORD.

33"So when these people or the prophet
or the priest ask you, saying, 'What is the
oracle of the LORD?' you shall then say to
them, 'What oracle?'a I will even forsake
you," says the LORD. 34"And *as for* the
prophet and the priest and the people who
say, 'The oracle of the LORD!' I will even
punish that man and his house. 35Thus
every one of you shall say to his neighbor,
and every one to his brother, 'What has the
LORD answered?' and, 'What has the LORD
spoken?' 36And the oracle of the LORD you
shall mention no more. For every man's
word will be his oracle, for you have perverted the words of the living God, the
LORD of hosts, our God. 37Thus you shall
say to the prophet, 'What has the LORD
answered you?' and, 'What has the LORD
spoken?' 38But since you say, 'The oracle of
the LORD!' therefore thus says the LORD:
'Because you say this word, "The oracle of
the LORD!" and I have sent to you, saying,
"Do not say, 'The oracle of the LORD!'"
39therefore behold, I, even I, will utterly forget you and forsake you, and the city that
I gave you and your fathers, and *will cast
you* out of My presence. 40And I will bring
an everlasting reproach upon you, and a
perpetual shame, which shall not be forgotten.'"

The Sign of Two Baskets of Figs

24 The LORD showed me, and there
were two baskets of figs set before
the temple of the LORD, after Nebuchadnezzar king of Babylon had carried away
captive Jeconiah the son of Jehoiakim,
king of Judah, and the princes of Judah
with the craftsmen and smiths, from
Jerusalem, and had brought them to
Babylon. 2One basket *had* very good figs,
like the figs *that are* first ripe; and the other
basket *had* very bad figs which could not
be eaten, they were so bad. 3Then the LORD
said to me, "What do you see, Jeremiah?"

And I said, "Figs, the good figs, very
good; and the bad, very bad, which cannot
be eaten, they are so bad."

4Again the word of the LORD came to
me, saying, 5"Thus says the LORD, the God

23:33 aSeptuagint, Targum, and Vulgate read 'You
are the burden.'

of Israel: 'Like these good figs, so will I acknowledge those who are carried away captive from Judah, whom I have sent out of this place for *their own* good, into the land of the Chaldeans. 6For I will set My eyes on them for good, and I will bring them back to this land; I will build them and not pull *them* down, and I will plant them and not pluck *them* up. 7Then I will give them a heart to know Me, that I *am* the LORD; and they shall be My people, and I will be their God, for they shall return to Me with their whole heart.

8'And as the bad figs which cannot be eaten, they are so bad'—surely thus says the LORD—'so will I give up Zedekiah the king of Judah, his princes, the residue of Jerusalem who remain in this land, and those who dwell in the land of Egypt. 9I will deliver them to trouble into all the kingdoms of the earth, for *their* harm, *to be* a reproach and a byword, a taunt and a curse, in all places where I shall drive them. 10And I will send the sword, the famine, and the pestilence among them, till they are consumed from the land that I gave to them and their fathers.'"

Seventy Years of Desolation

25 The word that came to Jeremiah concerning all the people of Judah, in the fourth year of Jehoiakim the son of Josiah, king of Judah (which *was* the first year of Nebuchadnezzar king of Babylon), 2which Jeremiah the prophet spoke to all the people of Judah and to all the inhabitants of Jerusalem, saying: 3"From the thirteenth year of Josiah the son of Amon, king of Judah, even to this day, this *is* the twenty-third year in which the word of the LORD has come to me; and I have spoken to you, rising early and speaking, but you have not listened. 4And the LORD has sent to you all His servants the prophets, rising early and sending *them,* but you have not listened nor inclined your ear to hear. 5They said, 'Repent now everyone of his evil way and his evil doings, and dwell in the land that the LORD has given to you and your fathers forever and ever. 6Do not go after other gods to serve them and worship them, and do not provoke Me to anger with the works of your hands; and I will

not harm you.' 7Yet you have not listened to Me," says the LORD, "that you might provoke Me to anger with the works of your hands to your own hurt.

8"Therefore thus says the LORD of hosts: 'Because you have not heard My words, 9behold, I will send and take all the families of the north,' says the LORD, 'and Nebuchadnezzar the king of Babylon, My servant, and will bring them against this land, against its inhabitants, and against these nations all around, and will utterly destroy them, and make them an astonishment, a hissing, and perpetual desolations. 10Moreover I will take from them the voice of mirth and the voice of gladness, the voice of the bridegroom and the voice of the bride, the sound of the millstones and the light of the lamp. 11And this whole land shall be a desolation *and* an astonishment, and these nations shall serve the king of Babylon seventy years.

12"Then it will come to pass, when seventy years are completed, *that* I will punish the king of Babylon and that nation, the land of the Chaldeans, for their iniquity,' says the LORD; 'and I will make it a perpetual desolation. 13So I will bring on that land all My words which I have pronounced against it, all that is written in this book, which Jeremiah has prophesied concerning all the nations. 14(For many nations and great kings shall be served by them also; and I will repay them according to their deeds and according to the works of their own hands.)'"

Judgment on the Nations

15For thus says the LORD God of Israel to me: "Take this wine cup of fury from My hand, and cause all the nations, to whom I send you, to drink it. 16And they will drink and stagger and go mad because of the sword that I will send among them."

17Then I took the cup from the LORD's hand, and made all the nations drink, to whom the LORD had sent me: 18Jerusalem and the cities of Judah, its kings and its princes, to make them a desolation, an astonishment, a hissing, and a curse, as *it is* this day; 19Pharaoh king of Egypt, his servants, his princes, and all his people; 20all the mixed multitude, all the kings of the land of Uz, all the kings of the land of the Philistines (namely, Ashkelon, Gaza, Ekron, and the remnant of Ashdod); 21Edom, Moab, and the people of Ammon; 22all the kings of Tymre, all the kings of Sidon, and the kings of the coastlands which *are* across the sea; 23Dedan, Tema, Buz, and all *who are* in the farthest corners; 24all the kings of Arabia and all the kings of the mixed multitude who dwell in the desert; 25all the kings of Zimri, all the kings of Elam, and all the kings of the Medes; 26all the kings of the north, far and near, one with another; and all the kingdoms of the world which *are* on the face of the earth. Also the king of Sheshacha shall drink after them.

27"Therefore you shall say to them, 'Thus says the LORD of hosts, the God of Israel: "Drink, be drunk, and vomit! Fall and rise no more, because of the sword which I will send among you."' 28And it shall be, if they refuse to take the cup from your hand to drink, then you shall say to them, 'Thus says the LORD of hosts: "You shall certainly drink! 29For behold, I begin to bring calamity on the city which is called by My name, and should you be utterly unpunished? You shall not be unpunished, for I will call for a sword on all the inhabitants of the earth," says the LORD of hosts.'

30"Therefore prophesy against them all these words, and say to them:

'The LORD will roar from on high,
  And utter His voice from His holy
    habitation;
He will roar mightily against His fold.
He will give a shout, as those who
  tread *the grapes,*
Against all the inhabitants of the
  earth.
31 A noise will come to the ends of the
    earth—
  For the LORD has a controversy with
    the nations;
  He will plead His case with all flesh.
  He will give those *who are* wicked to
    the sword,' says the LORD."

32Thus says the LORD of hosts:

"Behold, disaster shall go forth
  From nation to nation,
And a great whirlwind shall be
  raised up
From the farthest parts of the earth.

33"And at that day the slain of the LORD shall be from *one* end of the earth even to the *other* end of the earth. They shall not

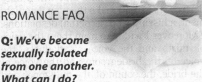

ROMANCE FAQ

Q: *We've become sexually isolated from one another. What can I do?*

Sexual isolation occurs when two people withdraw and no longer pursue meeting one another's needs. Perhaps the wife has found responding difficult and the husband has become angry and bitter. Resentment replaces growth. Ultimately the union that God designed as the celebration of oneness erodes into sexual and emotional isolation.

If you have an unresponsive mate:

• Consider that he or she may be going through a particularly stressful time, which could be caused by pressures at work, the birth of a child, an illness, loss of job, etc.

• Bitterness, worry or fear can also cause a lack of sexual response. You may want to ask your mate:

Is there anything I have done or am doing to inhibit our enjoyment of sex?

Is there any problem or conflict between us that needs to be resolved?

Is there anything in your background that is hard to talk about? Could you share it with me so I could try to help?

• Make a list of the things that would really please your mate and then begin to do them.

• Set aside time for frequent getaways. Barbara and I try to get away for at least two consecutive nights, two or three times a year.

25:26 aA code word for Babylon (compare 51:41)

be lamented, or gathered, or buried; they shall become refuse on the ground.

34 "Wail, shepherds, and cry!
   Roll about *in the ashes,*
   You leaders of the flock!
   For the days of your slaughter and
      your dispersions are fulfilled;
   You shall fall like a precious vessel.
35 And the shepherds will have no way
      to flee,
   Nor the leaders of the flock to escape.
36 A voice of the cry of the shepherds,
   And a wailing of the leaders to the
      flock *will be heard.*
   For the LORD has plundered their
      pasture,
37 And the peaceful dwellings are cut
      down
   Because of the fierce anger of the
      LORD.
38 He has left His lair like the lion;
   For their land is desolate
   Because of the fierceness of the
      Oppressor,
   And because of His fierce anger."

Jeremiah Saved from Death

26 In the beginning of the reign of Jehoiakim the son of Josiah, king of Judah, this word came from the LORD, saying, 2"Thus says the LORD: 'Stand in the court of the LORD's house, and speak to all the cities of Judah, which come to worship *in* the LORD's house, all the words that I command you to speak to them. Do not diminish a word. 3Perhaps everyone will listen and turn from his evil way, that I may relent concerning the calamity which I purpose to bring on them because of the evil of their doings.' 4And you shall say to them, 'Thus says the LORD: "If you will not listen to Me, to walk in My law which I have set before you, 5to heed the words of My servants the prophets whom I sent to you, both rising up early and sending *them* (but you have not heeded), 6then I will make this house like Shiloh, and will make this city a curse to all the nations of the earth."'"

7So the priests and the prophets and all the people heard Jeremiah speaking these words in the house of the LORD. 8Now it happened, when Jeremiah had made an end of speaking all that the LORD had commanded *him* to speak to all the people, that the priests and the prophets and all the people seized him, saying, "You will surely die! 9Why have you prophesied in the name of the LORD, saying, 'This house shall be like Shiloh, and this city shall be desolate, without an inhabitant'?" And all the people were gathered against Jeremiah in the house of the LORD.

10When the princes of Judah heard these things, they came up from the king's house to the house of the LORD and sat down in the entry of the New Gate of the LORD's *house.* 11And the priests and the prophets spoke to the princes and all the people, saying, "This man deserves to die! For he has prophesied against this city, as you have heard with your ears."

12Then Jeremiah spoke to all the princes and all the people, saying: "The LORD sent me to prophesy against this house and against this city with all the words that you have heard. 13Now therefore, amend your ways and your doings, and obey the voice of the LORD your God; then the LORD will relent concerning the doom that He has pronounced against you. 14As for me, here I am, in your hand; do with me as seems good and proper to you. 15But know for certain that if you put me to death, you will surely bring innocent blood on yourselves, on this city, and on its inhabitants; for truly the LORD has sent me to you to speak all these words in your hearing."

16So the princes and all the people said to the priests and the prophets, "This man does not deserve to die. For he has spoken to us in the name of the LORD our God."

17Then certain of the elders of the land rose up and spoke to all the assembly of the people, saying: 18"Micah of Moresheth prophesied in the days of Hezekiah king of Judah, and spoke to all the people of Judah, saying, 'Thus says the LORD of hosts:

   "Zion shall be plowed *like* a field,
   Jerusalem shall become heaps of
      ruins,
   And the mountain of the temple[a]
   Like the bare hills of the forest." '[b]

26:18 [a]Literally *house* [b]Compare Micah 3:12

¹⁹Did Hezekiah king of Judah and all Judah ever put him to death? Did he not fear the LORD and seek the LORD's favor? And the LORD relented concerning the doom which He had pronounced against them. But we are doing great evil against ourselves."

²⁰Now there was also a man who prophesied in the name of the LORD, Urijah the son of Shemaiah of Kirjath Jearim, who prophesied against this city and against this land according to all the words of Jeremiah. ²¹And when Jehoiakim the king, with all his mighty men and all the princes, heard his words, the king sought to put him to death; but when Urijah heard *it,* he was afraid and fled, and went to Egypt. ²²Then Jehoiakim the king sent men to Egypt: Elnathan the son of Achbor, and *other* men *who went* with him to Egypt. ²³And they brought Urijah from Egypt and brought him to Jehoiakim the king, who killed him with the sword and cast his dead body into the graves of the common people.

²⁴Nevertheless the hand of Ahikam the son of Shaphan was with Jeremiah, so that they should not give him into the hand of the people to put him to death.

Symbol of the Bonds and Yokes

27 In the beginning of the reign of Jehoiakim[a] the son of Josiah, king of Judah, this word came to Jeremiah from the LORD, saying,[b] ²"Thus says the LORD to me: 'Make for yourselves bonds and yokes, and put them on your neck, ³and send them to the king of Edom, the king of Moab, the king of the Ammonites, the king of Tyre, and the king of Sidon, by the hand of the messengers who come to Jerusalem to Zedekiah king of Judah. ⁴And command them to say to their masters, "Thus says the LORD of hosts, the God of Israel—thus you shall say to your masters: ⁵'I have made the earth, the man and the beast that *are* on the ground, by My great power and by My outstretched arm, and have given it to whom it seemed proper to Me. ⁶And now I have given all these lands into the hand of Nebuchadnezzar the king of Babylon, My servant; and the beasts of the field I have also given him to serve him. ⁷So all nations shall serve him and his son and his son's son, until the time of his land comes; and then many nations and great kings shall make him serve them. ⁸And it shall be, *that* the nation and kingdom which will not serve Nebuchadnezzar the king of Babylon, and which will not put its neck under the yoke of the king of Babylon, that nation I will punish,' says the LORD, 'with the sword, the famine, and the pestilence, until I have consumed them by his hand. ⁹Therefore do not listen to your prophets, your diviners, your dreamers, your soothsayers, or your sorcerers, who speak to you, saying, "You shall not serve the king of Babylon." ¹⁰For they prophesy a lie to you, to remove you far from your land; and I will drive you out, and you will perish. ¹¹But the nations that bring their necks under the yoke of the king of Babylon and serve him, I will let them remain in their own land,' says the LORD, 'and they shall till it and dwell in it.' " ' "

¹²I also spoke to Zedekiah king of Judah according to all these words, saying, "Bring your necks under the yoke of the king of Babylon, and serve him and his people, and live! ¹³Why will you die, you and your people, by the sword, by the famine, and by the pestilence, as the LORD has spoken against the nation that will not serve the king of Babylon? ¹⁴Therefore do not listen to the words of the prophets who speak to you, saying, 'You shall not serve the king of Babylon,' for they prophesy a lie to you; ¹⁵for I have not sent them," says the LORD, "yet they prophesy a lie in My name, that I may drive you out, and that you may perish, you and the prophets who prophesy to you."

¹⁶Also I spoke to the priests and to all this people, saying, "Thus says the LORD: 'Do not listen to the words of your prophets who prophesy to you, saying, "Behold, the vessels of the LORD's house will now shortly be brought back from Babylon"; for they

---

27:1 [a]Following Masoretic Text, Targum, and Vulgate; some Hebrew manuscripts, Arabic, and Syriac read *Zedekiah* (compare 27:3, 12; 28:1). [b]Septuagint omits verse 1.

prophesy a lie to you. ¹⁷Do not listen to them; serve the king of Babylon, and live! Why should this city be laid waste? ¹⁸But if they *are* prophets, and if the word of the LORD is with them, let them now make intercession to the LORD of hosts, that the vessels which are left in the house of the LORD, *in* the house of the king of Judah, and at Jerusalem, do not go to Babylon.'

¹⁹"For thus says the LORD of hosts concerning the pillars, concerning the Sea, concerning the carts, and concerning the remainder of the vessels that remain in this city, ²⁰which Nebuchadnezzar king of Babylon did not take, when he carried away captive Jeconiah the son of Jehoiakim, king of Judah, from Jerusalem to Babylon, and all the nobles of Judah and Jerusalem— ²¹yes, thus says the LORD of hosts, the God of Israel, concerning the vessels that remain in the house of the LORD, and in the house of the king of Judah and of Jerusalem: ²²'They shall be carried to Babylon, and there they shall be until the day that I visit them,' says the LORD. 'Then I will bring them up and restore them to this place.'"

Hananiah's Falsehood and Doom

28 And it happened in the same year, at the beginning of the reign of Zedekiah king of Judah, in the fourth year *and* in the fifth month, *that* Hananiah the son of Azur the prophet, who *was* from Gibeon, spoke to me in the house of the LORD in the presence of the priests and of all the people, saying, ²"Thus speaks the LORD of hosts, the God of Israel, saying: 'I have broken the yoke of the king of Babylon. ³Within two full years I will bring back to this place all the vessels of the LORD's house, that Nebuchadnezzar king of Babylon took away from this place and carried to Babylon. ⁴And I will bring back to this place Jeconiah the son of Jehoiakim, king of Judah, with all the captives of Judah who went to Babylon,' says the LORD, 'for I will break the yoke of the king of Babylon.'"

⁵Then the prophet Jeremiah spoke to the prophet Hananiah in the presence of the priests and in the presence of all the people who stood in the house of the LORD,

⁶and the prophet Jeremiah said, "Amen! The LORD do so; the LORD perform your words which you have prophesied, to bring back the vessels of the LORD's house and all who were carried away captive, from Babylon to this place. ⁷Nevertheless

INTIMATE MOMENTS

Take a Quiz

Sometimes we don't realize how often we do and say things that undermine our marriage commitment. Below I have put together a series of questions I'd like you to answer—a test, if you will, of your marital commitment:

- Do you ever threaten to leave your mate?
- Is your mate secure in your commitment to your marriage?
- Are you more committed to your mate than to your career?
- Are you more committed to your mate than to your children?
- Are you more committed to your mate than to your hobbies and favorite activities?
- Do you ever emotionally leave your mate by withdrawing for an extended period of time because of conflict?
- Do you mentally leave your mate by staying preoccupied with other things?
- Are you interested in meeting your mate's needs and actively doing what you can to meet them?
- Finally, how do you think your mate would answer each of these questions?

Questions like these can surface some important marital issues, from self-esteem issues to issues of time management and conflict resolution. I encourage you to take a quick commitment inventory by *really* answering these questions!

DEVOTIONS FOR COUPLES • 29:11
God's Plan for Our Good

Delays, diversions, and distractions. What do you think about them? How do you usually react to them? The truth is, we don't have to view interruptions as thieves who take away, but as divinely-ordered construction zones which God sets up in our lives.

I can imagine that if you're like me, you'd prefer a bypass, a smooth freeway with no stoplights or traffic jams. I want a map that shows me a way *around* the construction zone, not through it.

But guess where God wants me to go? Through a chuckhole-infested, gravel-covered construction zone—designed by God specifically for my character construction.

Over the past few years I've been through enough construction zones in my life that I've developed some convictions about these kinds of interruptions:

1. *God isn't looking at the clock, but at my character.* God is not so concerned about how these interruptions affect my schedule, even if I am busy doing His work. He wants His *will* for my life, not just my *work* for Him.

2. *He has liberally used interruptions to chip away at arrogance in my life.* I can tell I've got a problem with self-importance whenever I'm confronted with

an unscheduled problem and I think, *I don't need this! I shouldn't have to put up with this—not now!* Isn't it easy to arrogantly assume that we are above it all?

3. *Interruptions remind me I am not in control of my life.* Someone else is ordering my steps (see Prov. 16:9).

4. *A life without interruptions would become too predictable, even down-right boring.* God could have made it that way, of course. Only the dead have no interruptions. What if everything was 100 percent predictable?

So then, if we can't eliminate interruptions, what can you and I do?

When course-altering circumstances, whether they turn out to be trivial or monumental, bend our path, *you and I have the responsibility to respond rightly,* as God would have us respond. The Scripture teaches us how to handle God's construction zones for our lives, "In everything give thanks; for this is the will of God in Christ Jesus for you" (1 Thess. 5:18).

When we give thanks in all things, we affirm God's rightful place, that of the Sovereign Lord, the One Who orders our steps, the One Who knows the beginning and the end, and all that's sandwiched in between. Giving thanks in everything says, "God, You know what You're doing, and I trust You."

---

hear now this word that I speak in your hearing and in the hearing of all the people: 8The prophets who have been before me and before you of old prophesied against many countries and great kingdoms—of war and disaster and pestilence. 9As for the prophet who prophesies of peace, when the word of the prophet comes to pass, the prophet will be known *as* one whom the LORD has truly sent."

10Then Hananiah the prophet took the yoke off the prophet Jeremiah's neck and broke it. 11And Hananiah spoke in the presence of all the people, saying, "Thus says the LORD: 'Even so I will break the yoke of

Nebuchadnezzar king of Babylon from the neck of all nations within the space of two full years.'" And the prophet Jeremiah went his way.

12Now the word of the LORD came to Jeremiah, after Hananiah the prophet had broken the yoke from the neck of the prophet Jeremiah, saying, 13"Go and tell Hananiah, saying, 'Thus says the LORD: "You have broken the yokes of wood, but you have made in their place yokes of iron." 14For thus says the LORD of hosts, the God of Israel: "I have put a yoke of iron on the neck of all these nations, that they may serve Nebuchadnezzar king of

Babylon; and they shall serve him. I have given him the beasts of the field also." ' "

15Then the prophet Jeremiah said to Hananiah the prophet, "Hear now, Hananiah, the LORD has not sent you, but you make this people trust in a lie. 16Therefore thus says the LORD: 'Behold, I will cast you from the face of the earth. This year you shall die, because you have taught rebellion against the LORD.' "

17So Hananiah the prophet died the same year in the seventh month.

Jeremiah's Letter to the Captives

29 Now these *are* the words of the letter that Jeremiah the prophet sent from Jerusalem to the remainder of the elders who were carried away captive—to the priests, the prophets, and all the people whom Nebuchadnezzar had carried away captive from Jerusalem to Babylon. 2(This happened after Jeconiah the king, the queen mother, the eunuchs, the princes of Judah and Jerusalem, the craftsmen, and the smiths had departed from Jerusalem.) 3*The letter was sent* by the hand of Elasah the son of Shaphan, and Gemariah the son of Hilkiah, whom Zedekiah king of Judah sent to Babylon, to Nebuchadnezzar king of Babylon, saying,

4   Thus says the LORD of hosts, the God of Israel, to all who were carried away captive, whom I have caused to be carried away from Jerusalem to Babylon:

5   Build houses and dwell *in them;* plant gardens and eat their fruit. 6Take wives and beget sons and daughters; and take wives for your sons and give your daughters to husbands, so that they may bear sons and daughters—that you may be increased there, and not diminished. 7And seek the peace of the city where I have caused you to be carried away captive, and pray to the LORD for it; for in its peace you will have peace. 8For thus says the LORD of hosts, the God of Israel: Do not let your prophets and your diviners who are in your midst deceive you, nor listen to your dreams which you cause to be dreamed. 9For they prophesy falsely to you in My name; I have not sent them, says the LORD.

10   For thus says the LORD: After seventy years are completed at Babylon, I will visit you and perform My good word toward you, and cause you to return to this place. 11For I know the thoughts that I think toward you, says the LORD, thoughts of peace and not of evil, to give you a future and a hope. 12Then you will call upon Me and go and pray to Me, and I will listen to you. 13And you will seek Me and find *Me,* when you search for Me with all your heart. 14I will be found by you, says the LORD, and I will bring you back from your captivity; I will gather you from all the nations and from all the places where I have driven you, says the LORD, and I will bring you to the place from which I cause you to be carried away captive.

15   Because you have said, "The LORD has raised up prophets for us in Babylon"— 16therefore thus says the LORD concerning the king who sits on the throne of David, concerning all the people who dwell in this city, and concerning your brethren who have not gone out with you into captivity— 17thus says the LORD of hosts: Behold, I will send on them the sword, the famine, and the pestilence, and will make them like rotten figs that cannot be eaten, they are so bad. 18And I will pursue them with the sword, with famine, and with pestilence; and I will deliver them to trouble among all the kingdoms of the earth—to be a curse, an astonishment, a hissing, and a reproach among all the nations where I have driven them, 19because they have not heeded My words, says the LORD, which I sent to them by My servants the prophets, rising up early and sending *them;* neither would you heed, says the LORD.

BIBLICAL INSIGHTS • 29:11
Thoughts of Peace

GOD KNOWS WHAT HE IS DOING! Even when pain hits home, we can trust God to do what is best for us. Our problem is that we don't know His plan. We wonder how He could possibly cause this or that problem to work for our good.

But throughout Scripture, God hints that it can happen, even when we can't see how. So God says, "I know the thoughts that I think toward you, says the LORD, thoughts of peace and not of evil, to give you a future and a hope" (29:11).

There have been seasons in our lives when we have endured several trials. Barbara and I went through a time when she weathered major heart surgery, the removal of a benign lump in her breast, five debilitating sinus infections, sinus surgery, and just a general struggle with health issues. I have to admit that we grew weary that God would allow so many challenges into our lives!

Nevertheless, He has always brought good things out of the troubles. Our family has grown through the difficulties. Our struggle has enriched our ministry to other families who hurt.

I don't always understand the *why*, but I have come to trust God's plan. I know He will bring us into a magnificent future, even if at the moment I can't see His plan or purposes.

---

²⁰Therefore hear the word of the LORD, all you of the captivity, whom I have sent from Jerusalem to Babylon.

21 Thus says the LORD of hosts, the God of Israel, concerning Ahab the son of Kolaiah, and Zedekiah the son of Maaseiah, who prophesy a lie to you in My name: Behold, I will deliver them into the hand of Nebuchadnezzar king of Babylon,

and he shall slay them before your eyes. ²²And because of them a curse shall be taken up by all the captivity of Judah who *are* in Babylon, saying, "The LORD make you like Zedekiah and Ahab, whom the king of Babylon roasted in the fire"; ²³because they have done disgraceful things in Israel, have committed adultery with their neighbors' wives, and have spoken lying words in My name, which I have not commanded them. Indeed I know, and *am* a witness, says the LORD.

24 You shall also speak to Shemaiah the Nehelamite, saying, ²⁵Thus speaks the LORD of hosts, the God of Israel, saying: You have sent letters in your name to all the people who *are* at Jerusalem, to Zephaniah the son of Maaseiah the priest, and to all the priests, saying, ²⁶"The LORD has made you priest instead of Jehoiada the priest, so that there should be officers *in* the house of the LORD over every man *who* is demented and considers himself a prophet, that you should put him in prison and in the stocks. ²⁷Now therefore, why have you not rebuked Jeremiah of Anathoth who makes himself a prophet to you? ²⁸For he has sent to us *in* Babylon, saying, 'This *captivity is* long; build houses and dwell *in them,* and plant gardens and eat their fruit.'"

29 Now Zephaniah the priest read this letter in the hearing of Jeremiah the prophet. ³⁰Then the word of the LORD came to Jeremiah, saying: ³¹Send to all those in captivity, saying, Thus says the LORD concerning Shemaiah the Nehelamite: Because Shemaiah has prophesied to you, and I have not sent him, and he has caused you to trust in a lie— ³²therefore thus says the LORD: Behold, I will punish Shemaiah the Nehelamite and his family: he shall not have anyone to dwell among this people, nor shall he

see the good that I will do for My people, says the LORD, because he has taught rebellion against the LORD.

Restoration of Israel and Judah

30 The word that came to Jeremiah from the LORD, saying, 2"Thus speaks the LORD God of Israel, saying: 'Write in a book for yourself all the words that I have spoken to you. 3For behold, the days are coming,' says the LORD, 'that I will bring back from captivity My people Israel and Judah,' says the LORD. 'And I will cause them to return to the land that I gave to their fathers, and they shall possess it.'"

4Now these *are* the words that the LORD spoke concerning Israel and Judah.

5"For thus says the LORD:

'We have heard a voice of trembling,
Of fear, and not of peace.
6 Ask now, and see,
Whether a man is ever in labor with child?
So why do I see every man *with* his hands on his loins
Like a woman in labor,
And all faces turned pale?
7 Alas! For that day *is* great,
So that none *is* like it;
And it *is* the time of Jacob's trouble,
But he shall be saved out of it.

8 'For it shall come to pass in that day,'
Says the LORD of hosts,
'*That* I will break his yoke from your neck,
And will burst your bonds;
Foreigners shall no more enslave them.
9 But they shall serve the LORD their God,
And David their king,
Whom I will raise up for them.

10 'Therefore do not fear, O My servant Jacob,' says the LORD,
'Nor be dismayed, O Israel;
For behold, I will save you from afar,
And your seed from the land of their captivity.
Jacob shall return, have rest and be quiet,
And no one shall make *him* afraid.

11 For I *am* with you,' says the LORD, 'to save you;
Though I make a full end of all nations where I have scattered you,
Yet I will not make a complete end of you.
But I will correct you in justice,
And will not let you go altogether unpunished.'

12"For thus says the LORD:

'Your affliction *is* incurable,
Your wound *is* severe.
13 *There is* no one to plead your cause,
That you may be bound up;
You have no healing medicines.
14 All your lovers have forgotten you;
They do not seek you;
For I have wounded you with the wound of an enemy,
With the chastisement of a cruel one,
For the multitude of your iniquities,
Because your sins have increased.
15 Why do you cry about your affliction?
Your sorrow *is* incurable.
Because of the multitude of your iniquities,
Because your sins have increased,
I have done these things to you.

16 'Therefore all those who devour you shall be devoured;
And all your adversaries, every one of them, shall go into captivity;
Those who plunder you shall become plunder,
And all who prey upon you I will make a prey.
17 For I will restore health to you
And heal you of your wounds,' says the LORD,
'Because they called you an outcast *saying:*
"This *is* Zion;
No one seeks her."'

18"Thus says the LORD:

'Behold, I will bring back the captivity of Jacob's tents,
And have mercy on his dwelling places;

The city shall be built upon its own
    mound,
And the palace shall remain
    according to its own plan.
19 Then out of them shall proceed
    thanksgiving
And the voice of those who make
    merry;
I will multiply them, and they shall
    not diminish;
I will also glorify them, and they
    shall not be small.
20 Their children also shall be as before,
And their congregation shall be
    established before Me;
And I will punish all who oppress
    them.
21 Their nobles shall be from among
    them,
And their governor shall come from
    their midst;
Then I will cause him to draw near,
And he shall approach Me;
For who *is* this who pledged his
    heart to approach Me?' says the
    LORD.
22 'You shall be My people,
And I will be your God.'"

23 Behold, the whirlwind of the LORD
Goes forth with fury,
A continuing whirlwind;
It will fall violently on the head of
    the wicked.
24 The fierce anger of the LORD will not
    return until He has done it,
And until He has performed the
    intents of His heart.

In the latter days you will consider it.

The Remnant of Israel Saved

31 "At the same time," says the LORD,
"I will be the God of all the families
of Israel, and they shall be My people."
2 Thus says the LORD:

"The people who survived the sword
    Found grace in the wilderness—
Israel, when I went to give him rest."

3 The LORD has appeared of old to me,
    saying:
"Yes, I have loved you with an
    everlasting love;

Therefore with lovingkindness I have
    drawn you.
4 Again I will build you, and you shall
    be rebuilt,
O virgin of Israel!
You shall again be adorned with
    your tambourines,
And shall go forth in the dances of
    those who rejoice.
5 You shall yet plant vines on the
    mountains of Samaria;
The planters shall plant and eat
    them as ordinary food.
6 For there shall be a day
    When the watchmen will cry on
    Mount Ephraim,
'Arise, and let us go up *to* Zion,
To the LORD our God.'"

7 For thus says the LORD:

"Sing with gladness for Jacob,
And shout among the chief of the
    nations;
Proclaim, give praise, and say,
'O LORD, save Your people,
The remnant of Israel!'
8 Behold, I will bring them from the
    north country,
And gather them from the ends of
    the earth,
Among them the blind and the lame,
The woman with child
And the one who labors with child,
    together;
A great throng shall return there.
9 They shall come with weeping,
And with supplications I will lead
    them.
I will cause them to walk by the
    rivers of waters,
In a straight way in which they shall
    not stumble;
For I am a Father to Israel,
And Ephraim *is* My firstborn.

10 "Hear the word of the LORD, O
    nations,
And declare *it* in the isles afar off,
    and say,
'He who scattered Israel will gather
    him,
And keep him as a shepherd *does* his
    flock.'

11   For the LORD has redeemed Jacob,
        And ransomed him from the hand of
            one stronger than he.
12   Therefore they shall come and sing
            in the height of Zion,
        Streaming to the goodness of the
            LORD—
        For wheat and new wine and oil,
        For the young of the flock and the
            herd;
        Their souls shall be like a well-
            watered garden,
        And they shall sorrow no more at all.

13   "Then shall the virgin rejoice in the
            dance,
        And the young men and the old,
            together;
        For I will turn their mourning to joy,
        Will comfort them,
        And make them rejoice rather than
            sorrow.
14   I will satiate the soul of the priests
            with abundance,
        And My people shall be satisfied
            with My goodness, says the LORD."

Mercy on Ephraim

15Thus says the LORD:

        "A voice was heard in Ramah,
        Lamentation *and* bitter weeping,
        Rachel weeping for her children,
        Refusing to be comforted for her
            children,
        Because they *are* no more."

16Thus says the LORD:

        "Refrain your voice from weeping,
        And your eyes from tears;
        For your work shall be rewarded,
            says the LORD,
        And they shall come back from the
            land of the enemy.
17   There is hope in your future, says
            the LORD,
        That *your* children shall come back
            to their own border.

18   "I have surely heard Ephraim
            bemoaning himself:
        'You have chastised me, and I was
            chastised,
        Like an untrained bull;

        Restore me, and I will return,
        For You *are* the LORD my God.
19   Surely, after my turning, I repented;
        And after I was instructed, I struck
            myself on the thigh;
        I was ashamed, yes, even humiliated,
        Because I bore the reproach of my
            youth.'
20   *Is* Ephraim My dear son?
        Is he a pleasant child?
        For though I spoke against him,
        I earnestly remember him still;
        Therefore My heart yearns for him;
        I will surely have mercy on him, says
            the LORD.
21   "Set up signposts,
        Make landmarks;
        Set your heart toward the highway,
        The way in *which* you went.
        Turn back, O virgin of Israel,
        Turn back to these your cities.
22   How long will you gad about,
        O you backsliding daughter?
        For the LORD has created a new thing
            in the earth—
        A woman shall encompass a man."

Future Prosperity of Judah

23Thus says the LORD of hosts, the God
of Israel: "They shall again use this speech
in the land of Judah and in its cities, when
I bring back their captivity: 'The LORD
bless you, O home of justice, *and* mountain
of holiness!' 24And there shall dwell in
Judah itself, and in all its cities together,
farmers and those going out with flocks.
25For I have satiated the weary soul, and I
have replenished every sorrowful soul."

26After this I awoke and looked around,
and my sleep was sweet to me.

27"Behold, the days are coming, says the
LORD, that I will sow the house of Israel and
the house of Judah with the seed of man
and the seed of beast. 28And it shall come to
pass, *that* as I have watched over them to
pluck up, to break down, to throw down, to
destroy, and to afflict, so I will watch over
them to build and to plant, says the LORD.
29In those days they shall say no more:

        'The fathers have eaten sour grapes,
        And the children's teeth are set on
            edge.'

Three Dollars Worth of God

GOD IS SERIOUS about us getting to know Him. Jeremiah looked to a bright, future day when *all* of his countrymen would know God deeply, "from the least of them to the greatest of them" (31:34).

How well do *you* know God? Have you settled for a casual relationship with Him, or are you pursuing a deep, vibrant walk with Christ? Do the following words, penned by Wilbur Reese, describe you? "I would like to buy three dollars worth of God, please. Not enough to explode my soul or disturb my sleep, but just enough of Him to equal a cup of warm milk or a snooze in the sunshine . . . I want ecstasy, not transformation. I want the warmth of the womb, not a new birth. I want a pound of the Eternal in a paper sack, please. I would like to buy three dollars worth of God, please."

The church is only as great as its concept of God. Likewise your life is dependent upon your knowledge, experience, and trust in God. If you sense that your Christian experience is not what it should be, chances are that you are not spending time cultivating a growing relationship with the God who gave you life.

Perhaps it's time you bought more than three dollars worth of God?

---

³⁰But every one shall die for his own iniquity; every man who eats the sour grapes, his teeth shall be set on edge.

A New Covenant

³¹"Behold, the days are coming, says the LORD, when I will make a new covenant with the house of Israel and with the house of Judah— ³²not according to the covenant that I made with their fathers in the day *that* I took them by the hand to lead them out of the land of Egypt, My covenant which they broke, though I was a husband to them,ᵃ says the LORD. ³³But

this *is* the covenant that I will make with the house of Israel after those days, says the LORD: I will put My law in their minds, and write it on their hearts; and I will be their God, and they shall be My people. ³⁴No more shall every man teach his neighbor, and every man his brother, saying, 'Know the LORD,' for they all shall know Me, from the least of them to the greatest of them, says the LORD. For I will forgive their iniquity, and their sin I will remember no more."

35   Thus says the LORD,
         Who gives the sun for a light
             by day,
         The ordinances of the moon and
             the stars for a light by night,
         Who disturbs the sea,
         And its waves roar
         (The LORD of hosts *is* His name):

36   "If those ordinances depart
         From before Me, says the LORD,
         Then the seed of Israel shall also
             cease
         From being a nation before Me
             forever."

³⁷Thus says the LORD:

         "If heaven above can be measured,
         And the foundations of the earth
             searched out beneath,
         I will also cast off all the seed of
             Israel
         For all that they have done, says
             the LORD.

³⁸"Behold, the days are coming, says the LORD, that the city shall be built for the LORD from the Tower of Hananel to the Corner Gate. ³⁹The surveyor's line shall again extend straight forward over the hill Gareb; then it shall turn toward Goath. ⁴⁰And the whole valley of the dead bodies and of the ashes, and all the fields as far as the Brook Kidron, to the corner of the Horse Gate toward the east, *shall be* holy to the LORD. It shall not be plucked up or thrown down anymore forever."

31:32 ᵃFollowing Masoretic Text, Targum, and Vulgate; Septuagint and Syriac read *and I turned away from them.*

Jeremiah Buys a Field

32 The word that came to Jeremiah from the LORD in the tenth year of Zedekiah king of Judah, which was the eighteenth year of Nebuchadnezzar. ²For then the king of Babylon's army besieged Jerusalem, and Jeremiah the prophet was shut up in the court of the prison, which *was in* the king of Judah's house. ³For Zedekiah king of Judah had shut him up, saying, "Why do you prophesy and say, 'Thus says the LORD: "Behold, I will give this city into the hand of the king of Babylon, and he shall take it; ⁴and Zedekiah king of Judah shall not escape from the hand of the Chaldeans, but shall surely be delivered into the hand of the king of Babylon, and shall speak with him face to face,ᵃ and see him eye to eye; ⁵then he shall lead Zedekiah to Babylon, and there he shall be until I visit him," says the LORD; "though you fight with the Chaldeans, you shall not succeed"'?"

⁶And Jeremiah said, "The word of the LORD came to me, saying, ⁷'Behold, Hanamel the son of Shallum your uncle will come to you, saying, "Buy my field which *is* in Anathoth, for the right of redemption *is* yours to buy *it*."' ⁸Then Hanamel my uncle's son came to me in the court of the prison according to the word of the LORD, and said to me, 'Please buy my field that *is* in Anathoth, which *is* in the country of Benjamin; for the right of inheritance *is* yours, and the redemption yours; buy *it* for yourself.' Then I knew that this was the word of the LORD. ⁹So I bought the field from Hanamel, the son of my uncle who *was* in Anathoth, and weighed *out to* him the money—seventeen shekels of silver. ¹⁰And I signed the deed and sealed *it,* took witnesses, and weighed the money on the scales. ¹¹So I took the purchase deed, *both* that which was sealed *according* to the law and custom, and that which was open; ¹²and I gave the purchase deed to Baruch the son of Neriah, son of Mahseiah, in the presence of Hanamel my uncle's *son,* and in the presence of the witnesses who signed the purchase deed, before all the Jews who sat in the court of the prison.

¹³"Then I charged Baruch before them, saying, ¹⁴'Thus says the LORD of hosts, the God of Israel: "Take these deeds, both this purchase deed which is sealed and this deed which is open, and put them in an earthen vessel, that they may last many days." ¹⁵For thus says the LORD of hosts, the God of Israel: "Houses and fields and vineyards shall be possessed again in this land."'

Jeremiah Prays for Understanding

¹⁶"Now when I had delivered the purchase deed to Baruch the son of Neriah, I prayed to the LORD, saying: ¹⁷'Ah, Lord GOD! Behold, You have made the heavens and the earth by Your great power and outstretched arm. There is nothing too hard for You. ¹⁸*You* show lovingkindness to thousands, and repay the iniquity of the fathers into the bosom of their children after them—the Great, the Mighty God, whose name *is* the LORD of hosts. ¹⁹*You are* great in counsel and mighty in work, for Your eyes *are* open to all the ways of the sons of men, to give everyone according to his ways and according to the fruit of his doings. ²⁰You have set signs and wonders in the land of Egypt, to this day, and in Israel and among *other* men; and You have made Yourself a name, as it is this day. ²¹You have brought Your people Israel out of the land of Egypt with signs and wonders, with a strong hand and an outstretched arm, and with great terror; ²²You have given them this land, of which You swore to their fathers to give them—"a land flowing with milk and honey."ᵃ ²³And they came in and took possession of it, but they have not obeyed Your voice or walked in Your law. They have done nothing of all that You commanded them to do; therefore You have caused all this calamity to come upon them.

²⁴'Look, the siege mounds! They have come to the city to take it; and the city has been given into the hand of the Chaldeans who fight against it, because of the sword and famine and pestilence. What You have spoken has happened; there You see *it!* ²⁵And You have said to me, O Lord GOD,

---

32:4 ᵃLiterally *mouth to mouth* **32:22** ᵃExodus 3:8

BIBLICAL INSIGHTS • 32:39–41
Discovering God's Will

JEREMIAH MINISTERED during dark times in Israel's history. He spoke many messages of God's wrath and coming judgment, but he also spoke messages of God's comfort and love and reward for those who feared Him and remained close to Him, "I will give them one heart and one way, that they may fear Me forever, for the good of them and their children after them. And I will make an everlasting covenant with them, that I will not turn away from doing them good; but I will put My fear in their hearts so that they will not depart from Me. Yes, I will rejoice over them to do them good, and I will assuredly plant them in this land, with all My heart and with all My soul" (32:39–41).

If we fear God, we will remain in His presence—and that is what motivates us to obey Him and listen to what He has to say. That is how we can know His will for our lives, for our marriages, and for our families.

Do you want to know God's will for your life? If so, you first need to know that the fear of the Lord is the beginning of knowing His will.

"Buy the field for money, and take witnesses"!—yet the city has been given into the hand of the Chaldeans.'"

God's Assurance of the People's Return

26Then the word of the LORD came to Jeremiah, saying, 27"Behold, I *am* the LORD, the God of all flesh. Is there anything too hard for Me? 28Therefore thus says the LORD: 'Behold, I will give this city into the hand of the Chaldeans, into the hand of Nebuchadnezzar king of Babylon, and he shall take it. 29And the Chaldeans who fight against this city shall come and set fire to this city and burn it, with the houses on whose roofs they have offered incense to Baal and poured out drink offerings to

other gods, to provoke Me to anger; 30because the children of Israel and the children of Judah have done only evil before Me from their youth. For the children of Israel have provoked Me only to anger with the work of their hands,' says the LORD. 31'For this city has been to Me *a provocation of* My anger and My fury from the day that they built it, even to this day; so I will remove it from before My face 32because of all the evil of the children of Israel and the children of Judah, which they have done to provoke Me to anger— they, their kings, their princes, their priests, their prophets, the men of Judah, and the inhabitants of Jerusalem. 33And they have turned to Me the back, and not the face; though I taught them, rising up early and teaching *them,* yet they have not listened to receive instruction. 34But they set their abominations in the house which is called by My name, to defile it. 35And they built the high places of Baal which *are* in the Valley of the Son of Hinnom, to cause their sons and their daughters to pass through *the fire* to Molech, which I did not command them, nor did it come into My mind that they should do this abomination, to cause Judah to sin.'

36"Now therefore, thus says the LORD, the God of Israel, concerning this city of which you say, 'It shall be delivered into the hand of the king of Babylon by the sword, by the famine, and by the pestilence: 37Behold, I will gather them out of all countries where I have driven them in My anger, in My fury, and in great wrath; I will bring them back to this place, and I will cause them to dwell safely. 38They shall be My people, and I will be their God; 39then I will give them one heart and one way, that they may fear Me forever, for the good of them and their children after them. 40And I will make an everlasting covenant with them, that I will not turn away from doing them good; but I will put My fear in their hearts so that they will not depart from Me. 41Yes, I will rejoice over them to do them good, and I will assuredly plant them in this land, with all My heart and with all My soul.'

42"For thus says the LORD: 'Just as I have brought all this great calamity on this people, so I will bring on them all the good that I have promised them. 43And fields will be bought in this land of which you say, "It *is* desolate, without man or beast; it has been given into the hand of the Chaldeans." 44Men will buy fields for money, sign deeds and seal *them,* and take witnesses, in the land of Benjamin, in the places around Jerusalem, in the cities of Judah, in the cities of the mountains, in the cities of the lowland, and in the cities of the South; for I will cause their captives to return,' says the LORD."

Excellence of the Restored Nation

33 Moreover the word of the LORD came to Jeremiah a second time, while he was still shut up in the court of the prison, saying, 2"Thus says the LORD who made it, the LORD who formed it to establish it (the LORD *is* His name): 3'Call to Me, and I will answer you, and show you great and mighty things, which you do not know.'

4"For thus says the LORD, the God of Israel, concerning the houses of this city and the houses of the kings of Judah, which have been pulled down *to fortify*a against the siege mounds and the sword: 5'They come to fight with the Chaldeans, but *only* to fill their placesa with the dead bodies of men whom I will slay in My anger and My fury, all for whose wickedness I have hidden My face from this city. 6Behold, I will bring it health and healing; I will heal them and reveal to them the abundance of peace and truth. 7And I will cause the captives of Judah and the captives of Israel to return, and will rebuild those places as at the first. 8I will cleanse them from all their iniquity by which they have sinned against Me, and I will pardon all their iniquities by which they have sinned and by which they have transgressed against Me. 9Then it shall be to Me a name of joy, a praise, and an honor before all nations of the earth, who shall hear all the good that I do to them; they shall fear and tremble for all the goodness and all the prosperity that I provide for it.'

10"Thus says the LORD: 'Again there shall be heard in this place—of which you say, "It *is* desolate, without man and without beast"—in the cities of Judah, in the streets of Jerusalem that are desolate, without man and without inhabitant and without beast, 11the voice of joy and the voice of gladness, the voice of the bridegroom and the voice of the bride, the voice of those who will say:

"Praise the LORD of hosts,
  For the LORD *is* good,
  For His mercy *endures* forever"—

and of those *who will* bring the sacrifice of praise into the house of the LORD. For I will cause the captives of the land to return as at the first,' says the LORD.

12"Thus says the LORD of hosts: 'In this place which is desolate, without man and without beast, and in all its cities, there shall again be a dwelling place of shepherds causing *their* flocks to lie down. 13In the cities of the mountains, in the cities of the lowland, in the cities of the South, in the land of Benjamin, in the places around Jerusalem, and in the cities of Judah, the flocks shall again pass under the hands of him who counts *them,*' says the LORD.

14"Behold, the days are coming,' says the LORD, 'that I will perform that good thing which I have promised to the house of Israel and to the house of Judah:

15 'In those days and at that time
    I will cause to grow up to David
    A Branch of righteousness;
    He shall execute judgment and
      righteousness in the earth.
16 In those days Judah will be saved,
    And Jerusalem will dwell safely.
    And this *is the name* by which she
      will be called:

THE LORD OUR RIGHTEOUSNESS.'a

17"For thus says the LORD: 'David shall never lack a man to sit on the throne of the house of Israel; 18nor shall the priests, the Levites, lack a man to offer burnt offerings before Me, to kindle grain offerings, and to sacrifice continually.'"

33:4 aCompare Isaiah 22:10 33:5 aCompare
2 Kings 23:14 33:16 aCompare 23:5, 6

The Permanence of God's Covenant

¹⁹And the word of the LORD came to Jeremiah, saying, ²⁰"Thus says the LORD: 'If you can break My covenant with the day and My covenant with the night, so that there will not be day and night in their season, ²¹then My covenant may also be broken with David My servant, so that he shall not have a son to reign on his throne, and with the Levites, the priests, My ministers. ²²As the host of heaven cannot be numbered, nor the sand of the sea measured, so will I multiply the descendants of David My servant and the Levites who minister to Me.'"

²³Moreover the word of the LORD came to Jeremiah, saying, ²⁴"Have you not considered what these people have spoken, saying, 'The two families which the LORD has chosen, He has also cast them off'? Thus they have despised My people, as if they should no more be a nation before them.

²⁵"Thus says the LORD: 'If My covenant *is* not with day and night, *and if* I have not appointed the ordinances of heaven and earth, ²⁶then I will cast away the descendants of Jacob and David My servant, *so* that I will not take *any* of his descendants *to be* rulers over the descendants of Abraham, Isaac, and Jacob. For I will cause their captives to return, and will have mercy on them.'"

Zedekiah Warned by God

34 The word which came to Jeremiah from the LORD, when Nebuchadnezzar king of Babylon and all his army, all the kingdoms of the earth under his dominion, and all the people, fought against Jerusalem and all its cities, saying, ²"Thus says the LORD, the God of Israel: 'Go and speak to Zedekiah king of Judah and tell him, "Thus says the LORD: 'Behold, I will give this city into the hand of the king of Babylon, and he shall burn it with fire. ³And you shall not escape from his hand, but shall surely be taken and delivered into his hand; your eyes shall see the eyes of the king of Babylon, he shall speak with you face to face,ᵃ and you shall go to Babylon.'"' ⁴Yet hear the word of the LORD, O Zedekiah king of Judah! Thus says the LORD concerning you: 'You shall not die by the sword. ⁵You shall die in peace; as in the ceremonies of your fathers, the former kings who were before you, so they shall burn *incense* for you and lament for you, *saying,* "Alas, lord!" For I have pronounced the word, says the LORD.'"

⁶Then Jeremiah the prophet spoke all these words to Zedekiah king of Judah in Jerusalem, ⁷when the king of Babylon's army fought against Jerusalem and all the cities of Judah that were left, against Lachish and Azekah; for *only* these fortified cities remained of the cities of Judah.

Treacherous Treatment of Slaves

⁸*This is* the word that came to Jeremiah from the LORD, after King Zedekiah had made a covenant with all the people who *were* at Jerusalem to proclaim liberty to them: ⁹that every man should set free his male and female slave—a Hebrew man or woman—that no one should keep a Jewish brother in bondage. ¹⁰Now when all the princes and all the people, who had entered into the covenant, heard that everyone should set free his male and female slaves, that no one should keep them in bondage anymore, they obeyed and let *them* go. ¹¹But afterward they changed their minds and made the male and female slaves return, whom they had set free, and brought them into subjection as male and female slaves.

¹²Therefore the word of the LORD came to Jeremiah from the LORD, saying, ¹³"Thus says the LORD, the God of Israel: 'I made a covenant with your fathers in the day that I brought them out of the land of Egypt, out of the house of bondage, saying, ¹⁴"At the end of seven years let every man set free his Hebrew brother, who has been sold to him; and when he has served you six years, you shall let him go free from you." But your fathers did not obey Me nor incline their ear. ¹⁵Then you recently turned and did what was right in My sight—every man proclaiming liberty to his neighbor; and you made a covenant before Me in the house which is called by My name. ¹⁶Then

34:3 ᵃLiterally *mouth to mouth*

you turned around and profaned My name, and every one of you brought back his male and female slaves, whom you had set at liberty, at their pleasure, and brought them back into subjection, to be your male and female slaves.'

17"Therefore thus says the LORD: 'You have not obeyed Me in proclaiming liberty, every one to his brother and every one to his neighbor. Behold, I proclaim liberty to you,' says the LORD—'to the sword, to pestilence, and to famine! And I will deliver you to trouble among all the kingdoms of the earth. 18And I will give the men who have transgressed My covenant, who have not performed the words of the covenant which they made before Me, when they cut the calf in two and passed between the parts of it— 19the princes of Judah, the princes of Jerusalem, the eunuchs, the priests, and all the people of the land who passed between the parts of the calf— 20I will give them into the hand of their enemies and into the hand of those who seek their life. Their dead bodies shall be for meat for the birds of the heaven and the beasts of the earth. 21And I will give Zedekiah king of Judah and his princes into the hand of their enemies, into the hand of those who seek their life, and into the hand of the king of Babylon's army which has gone back from you. 22Behold, I will command,' says the LORD, 'and cause them to return to this city. They will fight against it and take it and burn it with fire; and I will make the cities of Judah a desolation without inhabitant.'"

The Obedient Rechabites

35 The word which came to Jeremiah from the LORD in the days of Jehoiakim the son of Josiah, king of Judah, saying, 2"Go to the house of the Rechabites, speak to them, and bring them into the house of the LORD, into one of the chambers, and give them wine to drink."

3Then I took Jaazaniah the son of Jeremiah, the son of Habazziniah, his brothers and all his sons, and the whole house of the Rechabites, 4and I brought them into the house of the LORD, into the chamber of the sons of Hanan the son of Igdaliah, a man of God, which was by the chamber of the princes, above the chamber of Maaseiah the son of Shallum, the keeper of the door. 5Then I set before the sons of the house of the Rechabites bowls full of wine, and cups; and I said to them, "Drink wine."

6But they said, "We will drink no wine, for Jonadab the son of Rechab, our father, commanded us, saying, 'You shall drink no wine, you nor your sons, forever. 7You shall not build a house, sow seed, plant a vineyard, nor have *any of these;* but all your days you shall dwell in tents, that you may live many days in the land where you are sojourners.' 8Thus we have obeyed the voice of Jonadab the son of Rechab, our father, in all that he charged us, to drink no wine all our days, we, our wives, our sons, or our daughters, 9nor to build ourselves houses to dwell in; nor do we have vineyard, field, or seed. 10But we have dwelt in tents, and have obeyed and done according to all that Jonadab our father commanded us. 11But it came to pass, when Nebuchadnezzar king of Babylon came up into the land, that we said, 'Come, let us go to Jerusalem for fear of the army of the Chaldeans and for fear of the army of the Syrians.' So we dwell at Jerusalem."

INTIMATE MOMENTS

Look in her eyes and just listen.

12Then came the word of the LORD to Jeremiah, saying, 13"Thus says the LORD of hosts, the God of Israel: 'Go and tell the men of Judah and the inhabitants of Jerusalem, "Will you not receive instruction to obey My words?" says the LORD. 14"The words of Jonadab the son of Rechab, which he commanded his sons, not to drink wine, are performed; for to this day they drink none, and obey their father's commandment. But although I have spoken to you, rising early and speaking, you did not obey Me. 15I have also sent to you all My servants the prophets, rising up early and sending *them,* saying, 'Turn now everyone from his evil way, amend your doings, and do not go after other gods to serve them; then you will dwell in the land which I have given you and your fathers.' But you have not inclined your ear, nor obeyed Me. [16]Surely the sons of Jonadab the son of Rechab have performed the commandment of their father, which he commanded them, but this people has not obeyed Me."'

[17]"Therefore thus says the LORD God of hosts, the God of Israel: 'Behold, I will bring on Judah and on all the inhabitants of Jerusalem all the doom that I have pronounced against them; because I have spoken to them but they have not heard, and I have called to them but they have not answered.'"

[18]And Jeremiah said to the house of the Rechabites, "Thus says the LORD of hosts, the God of Israel: 'Because you have obeyed the commandment of Jonadab your father, and kept all his precepts and done according to all that he commanded you, [19]therefore thus says the LORD of hosts, the God of Israel: "Jonadab the son of Rechab shall not lack a man to stand before Me forever."'"

The Scroll Read in the Temple

36 Now it came to pass in the fourth year of Jehoiakim the son of Josiah, king of Judah, *that* this word came to Jeremiah from the LORD, saying: [2]"Take a scroll of a book and write on it all the words that I have spoken to you against Israel, against Judah, and against all the nations, from the day I spoke to you, from the days of Josiah even to this day. [3]It may be that the house of Judah will hear all the adversities which I purpose to bring upon them, that everyone may turn from his evil way, that I may forgive their iniquity and their sin."

[4]Then Jeremiah called Baruch the son of Neriah; and Baruch wrote on a scroll of a book, at the instruction of Jeremiah,[a] all the words of the LORD which He had spoken to him. [5]And Jeremiah commanded Baruch, saying, "I *am* confined, I cannot go into the house of the LORD. [6]You go, therefore, and read from the scroll which you have written at my instruction,[a] the words of the LORD, in the hearing of the people in the LORD's

house on the day of fasting. And you shall also read them in the hearing of all Judah who come from their cities. [7]It may be that they will present their supplication before the LORD, and everyone will turn from his evil way. For great *is* the anger and the fury that the LORD has pronounced against this people." [8]And Baruch the son of Neriah did according to all that Jeremiah the prophet commanded him, reading from the book the words of the LORD in the LORD's house.

[9]Now it came to pass in the fifth year of Jehoiakim the son of Josiah, king of Judah, in the ninth month, *that* they proclaimed a fast before the LORD to all the people in Jerusalem, and to all the people who came from the cities of Judah to Jerusalem. [10]Then Baruch read from the book the words of Jeremiah in the house of the LORD, in the chamber of Gemariah the son of Shaphan the scribe, in the upper court at the entry of the New Gate of the LORD's house, in the hearing of all the people.

The Scroll Read in the Palace

[11]When Michaiah the son of Gemariah, the son of Shaphan, heard all the words of the LORD from the book, [12]he then went down to the king's house, into the scribe's chamber; and there all the princes were sitting—Elishama the scribe, Delaiah the son of Shemaiah, Elnathan the son of Achbor, Gemariah the son of Shaphan, Zedekiah the son of Hananiah, and all the princes. [13]Then Michaiah declared to them all the words that he had heard when Baruch read the book in the hearing of the people. [14]Therefore all the princes sent Jehudi the son of Nethaniah, the son of Shelemiah, the son of Cushi, to Baruch, saying, "Take in your hand the scroll from which you have read in the hearing of the people, and come." So Baruch the son of Neriah took the scroll in his hand and came to them. [15]And they said to him, "Sit down now, and read it in our hearing." So Baruch read *it* in their hearing.

[16]Now it happened, when they had heard all the words, that they looked in fear from one to another, and said to

36:4 [a]Literally *from Jeremiah's mouth*
36:6 [a]Literally *from my mouth*

Baruch, "We will surely tell the king of all these words." ¹⁷And they asked Baruch, saying, "Tell us now, how did you write all these words—at his instruction?"ᵃ

¹⁸So Baruch answered them, "He proclaimed with his mouth all these words to me, and I wrote *them* with ink in the book."

¹⁹Then the princes said to Baruch, "Go and hide, you and Jeremiah; and let no one know where you are."

The King Destroys Jeremiah's Scroll

²⁰And they went to the king, into the court; but they stored the scroll in the chamber of Elishama the scribe, and told all the words in the hearing of the king. ²¹So the king sent Jehudi to bring the scroll, and he took it from Elishama the scribe's chamber. And Jehudi read it in the hearing of the king and in the hearing of all the princes who stood beside the king. ²²Now the king was sitting in the winter house in the ninth month, with *a fire* burning on the hearth before him. ²³And it happened, when Jehudi had read three or four columns, *that the king* cut it with the scribe's knife and cast *it* into the fire that *was* on the hearth, until all the scroll was consumed in the fire that *was* on the hearth. ²⁴Yet they were not afraid, nor did they tear their garments, the king

nor any of his servants who heard all these words. ²⁵Nevertheless Elnathan, Delaiah, and Gemariah implored the king not to burn the scroll; but he would not listen to them. ²⁶And the king commanded Jerahmeel the king'sᵃ son, Seraiah the son of Azriel, and Shelemiah the son of Abdeel, to seize Baruch the scribe and Jeremiah the prophet, but the LORD hid them.

Jeremiah Rewrites the Scroll

²⁷Now after the king had burned the scroll with the words which Baruch had written at the instruction of Jeremiah,ᵃ the word of the LORD came to Jeremiah, saying: ²⁸"Take yet another scroll, and write on it all the former words that were in the first scroll which Jehoiakim the king of Judah has burned. ²⁹And you shall say to Jehoiakim king of Judah, 'Thus says the LORD: "You have burned this scroll, saying, 'Why have you written in it that the king of Babylon will certainly come and destroy this land, and cause man and beast to cease from here?'" ³⁰Therefore thus says the LORD concerning Jehoiakim king of Judah: "He shall have no one to sit on the throne of David, and his dead body shall be cast out to the heat of the day and the frost of the night. ³¹I will punish him, his family, and his servants for their iniquity; and I will bring on them, on the inhabitants of Jerusalem, and on the men of Judah all

---

36:17 ᵃLiterally *with his mouth* **36:26** ᵃHebrew *Hammelech* **36:27** ᵃLiterally *from Jeremiah's mouth*

Shun Verbal Dust-Offs

Ryne Duren, former pitcher for the New York Yankees, liked to intimidate batters. He became known as the patron saint of the psych-out. He knew how to mentally harass opposing batters, dusting them off with an assortment of wildly launched pitches.

Unfortunately, a similar thing can happen in our homes, although instead of a baseball, we launch hurtful, intimidating words that inflict fear, pain, and guilt. Too late we learn what the wise man meant when he said, "Death and life are in the power of the tongue" (Prov. 18:21).

Even though you may be very skillful with the quick retort, what do you gain when you fire off such verbal volleys? The same scripture that speaks of the tongue's destructive power also warns that those who exercise that power will have to eat whatever diseased fruit they plant. Often, that fruit is resentment, discord, and revenge. The dust-off experts not only hurt others; they poison their own relationships.

What can you do to decrease the inclination to attack each other with hurtful words? Since Jesus Christ is "the Word" (John 1:1), pray that your speech in every aspect of home life will reflect His role as Prince of Peace and Mediator.

the doom that I have pronounced against them; but they did not heed." ' "

32Then Jeremiah took another scroll and gave it to Baruch the scribe, the son of Neriah, who wrote on it at the instruction of Jeremiah[a] all the words of the book which Jehoiakim king of Judah had burned in the fire. And besides, there were added to them many similar words.

Zedekiah's Vain Hope

37 Now King Zedekiah the son of Josiah reigned instead of Coniah the son of Jehoiakim, whom Nebuchadnezzar king of Babylon made king in the land of Judah. 2But neither he nor his servants nor the people of the land gave heed to the words of the LORD which He spoke by the prophet Jeremiah.

3And Zedekiah the king sent Jehucal the son of Shelemiah, and Zephaniah the son of Maaseiah, the priest, to the prophet Jeremiah, saying, "Pray now to the LORD our God for us." 4Now Jeremiah was coming and going among the people, for they had not yet put him in prison. 5Then Pharaoh's army came up from Egypt; and when the Chaldeans who were besieging Jerusalem heard news of them, they departed from Jerusalem.

6Then the word of the LORD came to the prophet Jeremiah, saying, 7"Thus says the LORD, the God of Israel, 'Thus you shall say to the king of Judah, who sent you to Me to inquire of Me: "Behold, Pharaoh's army which has come up to help you will return to Egypt, to their own land. 8And the Chaldeans shall come back and fight against this city, and take it and burn it with fire." ' 9Thus says the LORD: 'Do not deceive yourselves, saying, "The Chaldeans will surely depart from us," for they will not depart. 10For though you had defeated the whole army of the Chaldeans who fight against you, and there remained only wounded men among them, they would rise up, every man in his tent, and burn the city with fire.' "

Jeremiah Imprisoned

11And it happened, when the army of the Chaldeans left the siege of Jerusalem for fear of Pharaoh's army, 12that Jeremiah

went out of Jerusalem to go into the land of Benjamin to claim his property there among the people. 13And when he was in the Gate of Benjamin, a captain of the guard was there whose name was Irijah the son of Shelemiah, the son of Hananiah; and he seized Jeremiah the prophet, saying, "You are defecting to the Chaldeans!"

14Then Jeremiah said, "False! I am not defecting to the Chaldeans." But he did not listen to him.

So Irijah seized Jeremiah and brought him to the princes. 15Therefore the princes were angry with Jeremiah, and they struck him and put him in prison in the house of Jonathan the scribe. For they had made that the prison.

16When Jeremiah entered the dungeon and the cells, and Jeremiah had remained there many days, 17then Zedekiah the king sent and took him out. The king asked him secretly in his house, and said, "Is there any word from the LORD?"

And Jeremiah said, "There is." Then he said, "You shall be delivered into the hand of the king of Babylon!"

18Moreover Jeremiah said to King Zedekiah, "What offense have I committed against you, against your servants, or against this people, that you have put me in prison? 19Where now are your prophets who prophesied to you, saying, 'The king of Babylon will not come against you or against this land'? 20Therefore please hear now, O my lord the king. Please, let my petition be accepted before you, and do not make me return to the house of Jonathan the scribe, lest I die there."

21Then Zedekiah the king commanded that they should commit Jeremiah to the court of the prison, and that they should give him daily a piece of bread from the bakers' street, until all the bread in the city was gone. Thus Jeremiah remained in the court of the prison.

Jeremiah in the Dungeon

38 Now Shephatiah the son of Mattan, Gedaliah the son of Pashhur, Jucal[a] the son of Shelemiah, and Pashhur the son

36:32 [a]Literally from Jeremiah's mouth
38:1 [a]Same as Jehucal (compare 37:3)

DEVOTIONS FOR COUPLES • 38:6
Handle Adversity as a Team

Hardships, troubles, and difficulties elbow their way into every marriage. No married couple, no matter how godly, can expect to get through life without having at some point to swim in some very deep and turbulent waters. It's just part of life.

So how do you handle this? First, realize that God allows difficulties in our lives for many reasons. I'm not saying He *causes* all difficulties, but He does allow them. The presence of difficulties does not mean something is wrong with your marriage.

Trials do not bring neutral results. They either drive people together or apart. The natural tendency is to go through a difficulty alone and not share it as a couple. The following are some principles we've learned:

•*Give your mate time and the freedom to process trials differently from the way you do.* Men need to avoid typical, non-compassionate responses such as: "Snap out of it, dear. Everything is going to be fine." A wife needs to resist thinking that because her husband isn't expecting the same emotions she is expressing, he must not really care. Men and women process suffering differently, so don't try to make your spouse react like you do.

•*Realize that the temptation is to become self-focused and to withdraw from each other.* Since it is very difficult for another person to carry your burden, there is a natural tendency to desire to pull away. As a result, you end up thinking the other person doesn't understand, and the resulting emotional pain makes you want to pull back to safety.

•*Respond to trials by embracing God's perspective of suffering as a couple.* The spouses who learn the art of facing storms together can develop a sweet and robust spiritual oneness. As we struggled with our trials, Barbara and I had to learn how to respond to trials by faith, "In everything give thanks" (1 Thess. 5:18).

•*Remember that your mate is never your enemy.* Your struggle is not against your spouse. Resist the urge to punish or think that he or she is the problem. Your spouse is your intimate ally, a fellow burden bearer who is there to encourage you as you go through a difficult time.

•*If the burden or suffering persists, seek outside help.* If you feel you are slipping off into a deep ditch, find godly counsel by calling your mentoring couple, your pastor, or a biblical counselor to gain outside perspective.

Suffering is common to all marriages, but how you respond to it will determine whether your marriage flourishes or flounders.

---

of Malchiah heard the words that Jeremiah had spoken to all the people, saying, 2"Thus says the LORD: 'He who remains in this city shall die by the sword, by famine, and by pestilence; but he who goes over to the Chaldeans shall live; his life shall be as a prize to him, and he shall live.'a 3Thus says the LORD: 'This city shall surely be given into the hand of the king of Babylon's army, which shall take it.'"

4Therefore the princes said to the king, "Please, let this man be put to death, for thus he weakens the hands of the men of war who remain in this city, and the hands of all the people, by speaking such words to them. For this man does not seek the welfare of this people, but their harm."

5Then Zedekiah the king said, "Look, he *is* in your hand. For the king can *do* nothing against you." 6So they took Jeremiah and cast him into the dungeon of Malchiah the king'sa son, which *was* in the court of the prison, and they let Jeremiah down with ropes. And in the dungeon *there was* no water, but mire. So Jeremiah sank in the mire.

38:2 aCompare 21:9　38:6 aHebrew *Hammelech*

7Now Ebed-Melech the Ethiopian, one of the eunuchs, who was in the king's house, heard that they had put Jeremiah in the dungeon. When the king was sitting at the Gate of Benjamin, 8Ebed-Melech went out of the king's house and spoke to the king, saying: 9"My lord the king, these men have done evil in all that they have done to Jeremiah the prophet, whom they have cast into the dungeon, and he is likely to die from hunger in the place where he is. For *there is* no more bread in the city." 10Then the king commanded Ebed-Melech the Ethiopian, saying, "Take from here thirty men with you, and lift Jeremiah the prophet out of the dungeon before he dies." 11So Ebed-Melech took the men with him and went into the house of the king under the treasury, and took from there old clothes and old rags, and let them down by ropes into the dungeon to Jeremiah. 12Then Ebed-Melech the Ethiopian said to Jeremiah, "Please put these old clothes and rags under your armpits, under the ropes." And Jeremiah did so. 13So they pulled Jeremiah up with ropes and lifted him out of the dungeon. And Jeremiah remained in the court of the prison.

Zedekiah's Fears and Jeremiah's Advice

14Then Zedekiah the king sent and had Jeremiah the prophet brought to him at the third entrance of the house of the LORD. And the king said to Jeremiah, "I will ask you something. Hide nothing from me."

15Jeremiah said to Zedekiah, "If I declare *it* to you, will you not surely put me to death? And if I give you advice, you will not listen to me."

16So Zedekiah the king swore secretly to Jeremiah, saying, "*As* the LORD lives, who made our very souls, I will not put you to death, nor will I give you into the hand of these men who seek your life."

17Then Jeremiah said to Zedekiah, "Thus says the LORD, the God of hosts, the God of Israel: 'If you surely surrender to the king of Babylon's princes, then your soul shall live; this city shall not be burned with fire, and you and your house shall live. 18But if you do not surrender to the king of Babylon's princes, then this city shall be given into the hand of the Chaldeans; they shall burn it with fire, and you shall not escape from their hand.'"

19And Zedekiah the king said to Jeremiah, "I am afraid of the Jews who have defected to the Chaldeans, lest they deliver me into their hand, and they abuse me."

20But Jeremiah said, "They shall not deliver *you*. Please, obey the voice of the LORD which I speak to you. So it shall be well with you, and your soul shall live. 21But if you refuse to surrender, this *is* the word that the LORD has shown me: 22'Now behold, all the women who are left in the king of Judah's house *shall be* surrendered to the king of Babylon's princes, and those *women* shall say:

"Your close friends have set upon you
And prevailed against you;
Your feet have sunk in the mire,
And they have turned away again."

23'So they shall surrender all your wives and children to the Chaldeans. You shall not escape from their hand, but shall be taken by the hand of the king of Babylon. And you shall cause this city to be burned with fire.'"

24Then Zedekiah said to Jeremiah, "Let no one know of these words, and you shall not die. 25But if the princes hear that I have talked with you, and they come to you and say to you, 'Declare to us now what you have said to the king, and also what the king said to you; do not hide *it* from us, and we will not put you to death,' 26then you shall say to them, 'I presented my request before the king, that he would not make me return to Jonathan's house to die there.'"

27Then all the princes came to Jeremiah and asked him. And he told them according to all these words that the king had commanded. So they stopped speaking with him, for the conversation had not been heard. 28Now Jeremiah remained in the court of the prison until the day that Jerusalem was taken. And he was *there* when Jerusalem was taken.

The Fall of Jerusalem

39 In the ninth year of Zedekiah king of Judah, in the tenth month, Nebuchadnezzar king of Babylon and all his army came against Jerusalem, and besieged it. ²In the eleventh year of Zedekiah, in the fourth month, on the ninth *day* of the month, the city was penetrated.

³Then all the princes of the king of Babylon came in and sat in the Middle Gate: Nergal-Sharezer, Samgar-Nebo, Sarsechim, Rabsaris,ª Nergal-Sarezer, Rabmag,ᵇ with the rest of the princes of the king of Babylon.

⁴So it was, when Zedekiah the king of Judah and all the men of war saw them, that they fled and went out of the city by night, by way of the king's garden, by the gate between the two walls. And he went out by way of the plain.ª ⁵But the Chaldean army pursued them and overtook Zedekiah in the plains of Jericho. And when they had captured him, they brought him up to Nebuchadnezzar king of Babylon, to Riblah in the land of Hamath, where he pronounced judgment on him. ⁶Then the king of Babylon killed the sons of Zedekiah before his eyes in Riblah; the king of Babylon also killed all the nobles of Judah. ⁷Moreover he put out Zedekiah's eyes, and bound him with bronze fetters to carry him off to Babylon. ⁸And the Chaldeans burned the king's house and the houses of the people with fire, and broke down the walls of Jerusalem. ⁹Then Nebuzaradan the captain of the guard carried away captive to Babylon the remnant of the people who remained in the city and those who defected to him, with the rest of the people who remained. ¹⁰But Nebuzaradan the captain of the guard left in the land of Judah the poor people, who had nothing, and gave them vineyards and fields at the same time.

Jeremiah Goes Free

¹¹Now Nebuchadnezzar king of Babylon gave charge concerning Jeremiah to Nebuzaradan the captain of the guard, saying, ¹²"Take him and look after him, and do him no harm; but do to him just as he says to you." ¹³So Nebuzaradan the captain of the guard sent Nebushasban, Rabsaris, Nergal-Sharezer, Rabmag, and all the king of Babylon's chief officers; ¹⁴then they sent *someone* to take Jeremiah from the court of the prison, and committed him to Gedaliah the son of Ahikam, the son of Shaphan, that he should take him home. So he dwelt among the people.

¹⁵Meanwhile the word of the LORD had come to Jeremiah while he was shut up in the court of the prison, saying, ¹⁶"Go and speak to Ebed-Melech the Ethiopian, saying, 'Thus says the LORD of hosts, the God of Israel: "Behold, I will bring My words upon this city for adversity and not for good, and they shall be *performed* in that day before you. ¹⁷But I will deliver you in that day," says the LORD, "and you shall not be given into the hand of the men of whom you *are* afraid. ¹⁸For I will surely deliver you, and you shall not fall by the sword; but your life shall be as a prize to you, because you have put your trust in Me," says the LORD.'"

INTIMATE MOMENTS

Spend time together in the kitchen making his favorite dinner, cookies, or dessert.

Jeremiah with Gedaliah the Governor

40 The word that came to Jeremiah from the LORD after Nebuzaradan the captain of the guard had let him go from Ramah, when he had taken him bound in chains among all who were carried away captive from Jerusalem and Judah, who were carried away captive to Babylon.

²And the captain of the guard took Jeremiah and said to him: "The LORD your God has pronounced this doom on this place. ³Now the LORD has brought *it,* and has done just as He said. Because you *people* have sinned against the LORD, and not obeyed His voice, therefore this thing has come upon you. ⁴And now look, I free you this day from the chains that *were* on your hand. If it seems good to you to come with me to Babylon, come, and I will look after you. But if it seems wrong for you to come

---

39:3 ªA title, probably *Chief Officer;* also verse 13 ᵇA title, probably *Troop Commander;* also verse 13
39:4 ªOr *the Arabah,* that is, the Jordan Valley

with me to Babylon, remain here. See, all the land *is* before you; wherever it seems good and convenient for you to go, go there."

⁵Now while Jeremiah had not yet gone back, *Nebuzaradan said,* "Go back to Gedaliah the son of Ahikam, the son of Shaphan, whom the king of Babylon has made governor over the cities of Judah, and dwell with him among the people. Or go wherever it seems convenient for you to go." So the captain of the guard gave him rations and a gift and let him go. ⁶Then Jeremiah went to Gedaliah the son of Ahikam, to Mizpah, and dwelt with him among the people who were left in the land.

⁷And when all the captains of the armies who *were* in the fields, they and their men, heard that the king of Babylon had made Gedaliah the son of Ahikam governor in the land, and had committed to him men, women, children, and the poorest of the land who had not been carried away captive to Babylon, ⁸then they came to Gedaliah at Mizpah—Ishmael the son of Nethaniah, Johanan and Jonathan the sons of Kareah, Seraiah the son of Tanhumeth, the sons of Ephai the Netophathite, and Jezaniah[a] the son of a Maachathite, they and their men. ⁹And Gedaliah the son of Ahikam, the son of Shaphan, took an oath before them and their men, saying, "Do not be afraid to serve the Chaldeans. Dwell in the land and serve the king of Babylon, and it shall be well with you. ¹⁰As for me, I will indeed dwell at Mizpah and serve the Chaldeans who come to us. But you, gather wine and summer fruit and oil, put *them* in your vessels, and dwell in your cities that you have taken." ¹¹Likewise, when all the Jews who *were* in Moab, among the Ammonites, in Edom, and who *were* in all the countries, heard that the king of Babylon had left a remnant of Judah, and that he had set over them Gedaliah the son of Ahikam, the son of Shaphan, ¹²then all the Jews returned out of all places where they had been driven, and came to the land of Judah, to Gedaliah at Mizpah, and gathered wine and summer fruit in abundance.

¹³Moreover Johanan the son of Kareah and all the captains of the forces that *were* in the fields came to Gedaliah at Mizpah, ¹⁴and said to him, "Do you certainly know that Baalis the king of the Ammonites has sent Ishmael the son of Nethaniah to murder you?" But Gedaliah the son of Ahikam did not believe them.

¹⁵Then Johanan the son of Kareah spoke secretly to Gedaliah in Mizpah, saying, "Let me go, please, and I will kill Ishmael the son of Nethaniah, and no one will know *it*. Why should he murder you, so that all the Jews who are gathered to you would be scattered, and the remnant in Judah perish?"

¹⁶But Gedaliah the son of Ahikam said to Johanan the son of Kareah, "You shall not do this thing, for you speak falsely concerning Ishmael."

Insurrection Against Gedaliah

41 Now it came to pass in the seventh month *that* Ishmael the son of Nethaniah, the son of Elishama, of the royal family and of the officers of the king, came with ten men to Gedaliah the son of Ahikam, at Mizpah. And there they ate bread together in Mizpah. ²Then Ishmael the son of Nethaniah, and the ten men who were with him, arose and struck Gedaliah the son of Ahikam, the son of Shaphan, with the sword, and killed him whom the king of Babylon had made governor over the land. ³Ishmael also struck down all the Jews who were with him, *that is,* with Gedaliah at Mizpah, and the Chaldeans who were found there, the men of war.

⁴And it happened, on the second day after he had killed Gedaliah, when as yet no one knew *it*, ⁵that certain men came from Shechem, from Shiloh, and from Samaria, eighty men with their beards shaved and their clothes torn, having cut themselves, with offerings and incense in their hand, to bring *them* to the house of the LORD. ⁶Now Ishmael the son of Nethaniah went out from Mizpah to meet them, weeping as he went along; and it happened as he met them that he said to them, "Come to Gedaliah the son of Ahikam!" ⁷So it was, when they came into the midst of the city, that Ishmael the son of Nethaniah killed them *and cast them* into the midst of a pit, he and the men who were with him. ⁸But

---

40:8 [a]Spelled *Jaazaniah* in 2 Kings 25:23

ten men were found among them who said to Ishmael, "Do not kill us, for we have treasures of wheat, barley, oil, and honey in the field." So he desisted and did not kill them among their brethren. ⁹Now the pit into which Ishmael had cast all the dead bodies of the men whom he had slain, because of Gedaliah, *was* the same one Asa the king had made for fear of Baasha king of Israel. Ishmael the son of Nethaniah filled it with *the* slain. ¹⁰Then Ishmael carried away captive all the rest of the people who *were* in Mizpah, the king's daughters and all the people who remained in Mizpah, whom Nebuzaradan the captain of the guard had committed to Gedaliah the son of Ahikam. And Ishmael the son of Nethaniah carried them away captive and departed to go over to the Ammonites.

¹¹But when Johanan the son of Kareah and all the captains of the forces that *were* with him heard of all the evil that Ishmael the son of Nethaniah had done, ¹²they took all the men and went to fight with Ishmael the son of Nethaniah; and they found him by the great pool that *is* in Gibeon. ¹³So it was, when all the people who *were* with Ishmael saw Johanan the son of Kareah, and all the captains of the forces who *were* with him, that they were glad. ¹⁴Then all the people whom Ishmael had carried away captive from Mizpah turned around and came back, and went to Johanan the son of Kareah. ¹⁵But Ishmael the son of Nethaniah escaped from Johanan with eight men and went to the Ammonites.

¹⁶Then Johanan the son of Kareah, and all the captains of the forces that were with him, took from Mizpah all the rest of the people whom he had recovered from Ishmael the son of Nethaniah after he had murdered Gedaliah the son of Ahikam— the mighty men of war and the women and the children and the eunuchs, whom he had brought back from Gibeon. ¹⁷And they departed and dwelt in the habitation of Chimham, which is near Bethlehem, as they went on their way to Egypt, ¹⁸because of the Chaldeans; for they were afraid of them, because Ishmael the son of Nethaniah had murdered Gedaliah the son of Ahikam, whom the king of Babylon had made governor in the land.

The Flight to Egypt Forbidden

42 Now all the captains of the forces, Johanan the son of Kareah, Jezaniah the son of Hoshaiah, and all the people, from the least to the greatest, came near ²and said to Jeremiah the prophet, "Please, let our petition be acceptable to you, and pray for us to the LORD your God, for all this remnant (since we are left *but* a few of many, as you can see), ³that the LORD your God may show us the way in which we should walk and the thing we should do."

⁴Then Jeremiah the prophet said to them, "I have heard. Indeed, I will pray to the LORD your God according to your words, and it shall be, *that* whatever the LORD answers you, I will declare *it* to you. I will keep nothing back from you."

⁵So they said to Jeremiah, "Let the LORD be a true and faithful witness between us, if we do not do according to everything which the LORD your God sends us by you. ⁶Whether *it is* pleasing or displeasing, we will obey the voice of the LORD our God to whom we send you, that it may be well with us when we obey the voice of the LORD our God."

⁷And it happened after ten days that the word of the LORD came to Jeremiah. ⁸Then he called Johanan the son of Kareah, all the captains of the forces which *were* with him, and all the people from the least even to the greatest, ⁹and said to them, "Thus says the LORD, the God of Israel, to whom you sent me to present your petition before Him: ¹⁰'If you will still remain in this land, then I will build you and not pull *you* down, and I will plant you and not pluck *you* up. For I relent concerning the disaster that I have brought upon you. ¹¹Do not be afraid of the king of Babylon, of whom you are afraid; do not be afraid of him,' says the LORD, 'for I *am* with you, to save you and deliver you from his hand. ¹²And I will show you mercy, that he may have mercy on you and cause you to return to your own land.'

¹³"But if you say, 'We will not dwell in this land,' disobeying the voice of the LORD your God, ¹⁴saying, 'No, but we will go to the land of Egypt where we shall see no war, nor hear the sound of the trumpet,

nor be hungry for bread, and there we will dwell'— ¹⁵Then hear now the word of the LORD, O remnant of Judah! Thus says the LORD of hosts, the God of Israel: 'If you wholly set your faces to enter Egypt, and go to dwell there, ¹⁶then it shall be *that* the sword which you feared shall overtake you there in the land of Egypt; the famine of which you were afraid shall follow close after you there *in* Egypt; and there you shall die. ¹⁷So shall it be with all the men who set their faces to go to Egypt to dwell there. They shall die by the sword, by famine, and by pestilence. And none of them shall remain or escape from the disaster that I will bring upon them.'

¹⁸"For thus says the LORD of hosts, the God of Israel: 'As My anger and My fury have been poured out on the inhabitants of Jerusalem, so will My fury be poured out on you when you enter Egypt. And you shall be an oath, an astonishment, a curse, and a reproach; and you shall see this place no more.'

¹⁹"The LORD has said concerning you, O remnant of Judah, 'Do not go to Egypt!' Know certainly that I have admonished you this day. ²⁰For you were hypocrites in your hearts when you sent me to the LORD your God, saying, 'Pray for us to the LORD our God, and according to all that the LORD your God says, so declare to us and we will do *it*.' ²¹And I have this day declared *it* to you, but you have not obeyed the voice of the LORD your God, or anything which He has sent you by me. ²²Now therefore, know certainly that you shall die by the sword, by famine, and by pestilence in the place where you desire to go to dwell."

Jeremiah Taken to Egypt

43 Now it happened, when Jeremiah had stopped speaking to all the people all the words of the LORD their God, for which the LORD their God had sent him to them, all these words, ²that Azariah the son of Hoshaiah, Johanan the son of Kareah, and all the proud men spoke, saying to Jeremiah, "You speak falsely! The LORD our God has not sent you to say, 'Do not go to Egypt to dwell there.' ³But Baruch the son of Neriah has set you against us, to deliver us into the hand of the Chaldeans, that they may put us to death or carry us away captive to Babylon." ⁴So Johanan the son of Kareah, all the captains of the forces, and all the people would not obey the voice of the LORD, to remain in the land of Judah. ⁵But Johanan the son of Kareah and all the captains of the forces took all the remnant of Judah who had returned to dwell in the land of Judah, from all nations

---

PARENTING MATTERS

Q: What's the best way to discipline my older child?

A lot of repetition takes place in the discipline process during the preadolescent years. Spanking gradually decreases; five- and six-year-olds get far more spankings than seven- and eight-year-olds.

At this time, become a good student of your child and evaluate other forms of discipline. For example, we have a chore box—a highly productive form of discipline—for the kid who has tried to get away with doing as little as possible. The outside of the box says, "For those to care enough to do the very least." Inside the box you find cards listing twenty-five to thirty of the most unpleasant chores Barbara does around the house. We have the child open the box, close her eyes, reach in, and draw out a card.

When our kids started griping and complaining frequently, we found a jar and put some coins in it. Each time a child complained, we took a coin out of the jar. We then informed our children that they could keep whatever was left in the jar at the end of thirty days, but if they went through all the coins in the jar, we would start taking from each child's allowance. Thus, the jar is both a reward and a penalty.

where they had been driven— ⁶men, women, children, the king's daughters, and every person whom Nebuzaradan the captain of the guard had left with Gedaliah the son of Ahikam, the son of Shaphan, and Jeremiah the prophet and Baruch the son of Neriah. ⁷So they went to the land of Egypt, for they did not obey the voice of the LORD. And they went as far as Tahpanhes.

⁸Then the word of the LORD came to Jeremiah in Tahpanhes, saying, ⁹"Take large stones in your hand, and hide them in the sight of the men of Judah, in the clay in the brick courtyard which *is* at the entrance to Pharaoh's house in Tahpanhes; ¹⁰and say to them, 'Thus says the LORD of hosts, the God of Israel: "Behold, I will send and bring Nebuchadnezzar the king of Babylon, My servant, and will set his throne above these stones that I have hidden. And he will spread his royal pavilion over them. ¹¹When he comes, he shall strike the land of Egypt *and deliver* to death *those appointed* for death, and to captivity *those appointed* for captivity, and to the sword *those appointed* for the sword. ¹²I will kindle a fire in the houses of the gods of Egypt, and he shall burn them and carry them away captive. And he shall array himself with the land of Egypt, as a shepherd puts on his garment, and he shall go out from there in peace. ¹³He shall also break the *sacred* pillars of Beth Shemesh^a that *are* in the land of Egypt; and the houses of the gods of the Egyptians he shall burn with fire." ' "

Israelites Will Be Punished in Egypt

44 The word that came to Jeremiah concerning all the Jews who dwell in the land of Egypt, who dwell at Migdol, at Tahpanhes, at Noph,^a and in the country of Pathros, saying, ²"Thus says the LORD of hosts, the God of Israel: 'You have seen all the calamity that I have brought on Jerusalem and on all the cities of Judah; and behold, this day they *are* a desolation, and no one dwells in them, ³because of

their wickedness which they have committed to provoke Me to anger, in that they went to burn incense *and* to serve other gods whom they did not know, they nor you nor your fathers. ⁴However I have sent to you all My servants the prophets, rising early and sending *them,* saying, "Oh, do not do this abominable thing that I hate!" ⁵But they did not listen or incline their ear to turn from their wickedness, to burn no incense to other gods. ⁶So My fury and My anger were poured out and kindled in the cities of Judah and in the streets of Jerusalem; and they are wasted *and* desolate, as it is this day.'

⁷"Now therefore, thus says the LORD, the God of hosts, the God of Israel: 'Why do you commit *this* great evil against yourselves, to cut off from you man and woman, child and infant, out of Judah, leaving none to remain, ⁸in that you provoke Me to wrath with the works of your hands, burning incense to other gods in the land of Egypt where you have gone to dwell, that you may cut yourselves off and be a curse and a reproach among all the nations of the earth? ⁹Have you forgotten the wickedness of your fathers, the wickedness of the kings of Judah, the wickedness of their wives, your own wickedness, and the wickedness of your wives, which they committed in the land of Judah and in the streets of Jerusalem? ¹⁰They have not been humbled, to this day, nor have they feared; they have not walked in My law or in My statutes that I set before you and your fathers.'

¹¹"Therefore thus says the LORD of hosts, the God of Israel: 'Behold, I will set My face against you for catastrophe and for cutting off all Judah. ¹²And I will take the remnant of Judah who have set their faces to go into the land of Egypt to dwell there, and they shall all be consumed *and* fall in the land of Egypt. They shall be consumed by the sword *and* by famine. They shall die, from the least to the greatest, by the sword and by famine; and they shall be an oath, an astonishment, a curse and a reproach! ¹³For I will punish those who dwell in the land of Egypt, as I have punished Jerusalem, by the sword, by famine, and by pestilence, ¹⁴so that none of

---

43:12 ^aFollowing Masoretic Text and Targum; Septuagint, Syriac, and Vulgate read *He.*
43:13 ^aLiterally *House of the Sun,* ancient On; later called Heliopolis **44:1** ^aThat is, ancient Memphis

the remnant of Judah who have gone into the land of Egypt to dwell there shall escape or survive, lest they return to the land of Judah, to which they desire to return and dwell. For none shall return except those who escape.'"

15Then all the men who knew that their wives had burned incense to other gods, with all the women who stood by, a great multitude, and all the people who dwelt in the land of Egypt, in Pathros, answered Jeremiah, saying: 16"*As for* the word that you have spoken to us in the name of the LORD, we will not listen to you! 17But we will certainly do whatever has gone out of our own mouth, to burn incense to the queen of heaven and pour out drink offerings to her, as we have done, we and our fathers, our kings and our princes, in the cities of Judah and in the streets of Jerusalem. For *then* we had plenty of food, were well-off, and saw no trouble. 18But since we stopped burning incense to the queen of heaven and pouring out drink offerings to her, we have lacked everything and have been consumed by the sword and by famine."

19*The women also said*, "And when we burned incense to the queen of heaven and poured out drink offerings to her, did we make cakes for her, to worship her, and pour out drink offerings to her without our husbands' *permission?*"

20Then Jeremiah spoke to all the people—the men, the women, and all the people who had given him *that* answer—saying: 21"The incense that you burned in the cities of Judah and in the streets of Jerusalem, you and your fathers, your kings and your princes, and the people of the land, did not the LORD remember them, and did it *not* come into His mind? 22So the LORD could no longer bear *it*, because of the evil of your doings *and* because of the abominations which you committed. Therefore your land is a desolation, an astonishment, a curse, and without an inhabitant, as *it is* this day. 23Because you have burned incense and because you have sinned against the LORD, and have not obeyed the voice of the LORD or walked in His law, in His statutes or in His testimonies, therefore this calamity has happened to you, as *at* this day."

24Moreover Jeremiah said to all the people and to all the women, "Hear the word of the LORD, all Judah who *are* in the land of Egypt! 25Thus says the LORD of hosts, the God of Israel, saying: 'You and your wives have spoken with your mouths and fulfilled with your hands, saying, "We will surely keep our vows that we have made, to burn incense to the queen of heaven and pour out drink offerings to her." You will surely keep your vows and perform your vows!' 26Therefore hear the word of the LORD, all Judah who dwell in the land of Egypt: 'Behold, I have sworn by My great name,' says the LORD, 'that My name shall no more be named in the mouth of any man of Judah in all the land of Egypt, saying, "The Lord GOD lives." 27Behold, I will watch over them for adversity and not for good. And all the men of Judah who *are* in the land of Egypt shall be consumed by the sword and by famine, until there is an end to them. 28Yet a small number who escape the sword shall return from the land of Egypt to the land of Judah; and all the remnant of Judah, who have gone to the land of Egypt to dwell there, shall know whose words will stand, Mine or theirs. 29And this *shall be* a sign to you,' says the LORD, 'that I will punish you in this place, that you may know that My words will surely stand against you for adversity.'

30"Thus says the LORD: 'Behold, I will give Pharaoh Hophra king of Egypt into the hand of his enemies and into the hand of those who seek his life, as I gave Zedekiah king of Judah into the hand of Nebuchadnezzar king of Babylon, his enemy who sought his life.'"

Assurance to Baruch

45 The word that Jeremiah the prophet spoke to Baruch the son of Neriah, when he had written these words in a book at the instruction of Jeremiah,[a] in the fourth year of Jehoiakim the son of Josiah, king of Judah, saying, 2"Thus says the LORD, the God of Israel, to you, O Baruch: 3'You said, "Woe is me now! For the LORD has added grief to my sorrow. I fainted in my sighing, and I find no rest."'

45:1 [a]Literally *from Jeremiah's mouth*

4"Thus you shall say to him, 'Thus says the LORD: "Behold, what I have built I will break down, and what I have planted I will pluck up, that is, this whole land. 5And do you seek great things for yourself? Do not seek *them;* for behold, I will bring adversity on all flesh," says the LORD. "But I will give your life to you as a prize in all places, wherever you go."'"

Judgment on Egypt

46 The word of the LORD which came to Jeremiah the prophet against the nations. 2Against Egypt.

Concerning the army of Pharaoh Necho, king of Egypt, which was by the River Euphrates in Carchemish, and which Nebuchadnezzar king of Babylon defeated in the fourth year of Jehoiakim the son of Josiah, king of Judah:

3 "Order the buckler and shield,
   And draw near to battle!
4 Harness the horses,
   And mount up, you horsemen!
   Stand forth with *your* helmets,
   Polish the spears,
   Put on the armor!
5 Why have I seen them dismayed *and* turned back?
   Their mighty ones are beaten down;
   They have speedily fled,
   And did not look back,
   For fear *was* all around," says the LORD.
6 "Do not let the swift flee away,
   Nor the mighty man escape;
   They will stumble and fall
   Toward the north, by the River Euphrates.

7 "Who *is* this coming up like a flood,
   Whose waters move like the rivers?
8 Egypt rises up like a flood,
   And *its* waters move like the rivers;
   And he says, 'I will go up *and* cover the earth,
   I will destroy the city and its inhabitants.'
9 Come up, O horses, and rage, O chariots!
   And let the mighty men come forth:
   The Ethiopians and the Libyans who handle the shield,
   And the Lydians who handle *and* bend the bow.

10 For this *is* the day of the Lord GOD of hosts,
   A day of vengeance,
   That He may avenge Himself on His adversaries.
   The sword shall devour;
   It shall be satiated and made drunk with their blood;
   For the Lord GOD of hosts has a sacrifice
   In the north country by the River Euphrates.

ROMANCE FAQ

Q: *How do I balance being a mother with my first calling as wife?*

FamilyLife conducted a survey of more than ten thousand couples, asking them to name the culprits that robbed their marriages of romance. The most commonly mentioned factors were children, stress, fatigue, busyness, misplaced priorities, anger, and unresolved conflict.

In the Bible we find an appropriate name for these romance robbers. The bride of King Solomon said to him, "Catch us the foxes, the little foxes that spoil the vines, for our vines have tender grapes" (Song 2:15).

In those days, a wise gardener would protect his vineyard from foxes. The nocturnal bandits would sneak in during the dead of the night and eat the most tender parts of the vine, rendering them fruitless and useless.

The vineyard is like your marriage. The foxes are the things that sneak up on you and snatch the fruit of passion before it can bloom. Drop your guard, and they'll reduce the vineyard of your marriage to a barren, lifeless place where romance shrivels on the vine.

At all costs, protect your marriage! That must remain first on your priority list. Children are a gift from God, but your spouse must take precedence. Never let him feel as though he's second in your life.

¹¹ "Go up to Gilead and take balm,
　O virgin, the daughter of Egypt;
　In vain you will use many medicines;
　You shall not be cured.
¹² The nations have heard of your
　　shame,
　And your cry has filled the land;
　For the mighty man has stumbled
　　against the mighty;
　They both have fallen together."

Babylonia Will Strike Egypt

¹³The word that the LORD spoke to Jeremiah the prophet, how Nebuchadnezzar king of Babylon would come *and* strike the land of Egypt.

¹⁴ "Declare in Egypt, and proclaim in
　　Migdol;
　Proclaim in Noph^a and in Tahpanhes;
　Say, 'Stand fast and prepare
　　yourselves,
　For the sword devours all around you.'
¹⁵ Why are your valiant *men* swept
　　away?
　They did not stand
　Because the LORD drove them away.
¹⁶ He made many fall;
　Yes, one fell upon another.
　And they said, 'Arise!
　Let us go back to our own people
　And to the land of our nativity
　From the oppressing sword.'
¹⁷ They cried there,
　'Pharaoh, king of Egypt, *is but* a
　　noise.
　He has passed by the appointed time!'

¹⁸ "*As* I live," says the King,
　Whose name *is* the LORD of hosts,
　"Surely as Tabor *is* among the
　　mountains
　And as Carmel by the sea, *so* he shall
　　come.
¹⁹ O you daughter dwelling in Egypt,
　Prepare yourself to go into captivity!
　For Noph^a shall be waste and
　　desolate, without inhabitant.

²⁰ "Egypt *is* a very pretty heifer,
　But destruction comes, it comes from
　　the north.
²¹ Also her mercenaries are in her
　　midst like fat bulls;

For they also are turned back,
　They have fled away together.
　They did not stand,
　For the day of their calamity had
　　come upon them,
　The time of their punishment.
²² Her noise shall go like a serpent,
　For they shall march with an army
　And come against her with axes,
　Like those who chop wood.

²³ "They shall cut down her forest," says
　　the LORD,
　"Though it cannot be searched,
　Because they *are* innumerable,
　And more numerous than
　　grasshoppers.
²⁴ The daughter of Egypt shall be
　　ashamed;
　She shall be delivered into the hand
　Of the people of the north."

²⁵The LORD of hosts, the God of Israel, says: "Behold, I will bring punishment on Amon^a of No,^b and Pharaoh and Egypt, with their gods and their kings—Pharaoh and those who trust in him. ²⁶And I will deliver them into the hand of those who seek their lives, into the hand of Nebuchadnezzar king of Babylon and the hand of his servants. Afterward it shall be inhabited as in the days of old," says the LORD.

God Will Preserve Israel

²⁷ "But do not fear, O My servant Jacob,
　And do not be dismayed, O Israel!
　For behold, I will save you from afar,
　And your offspring from the land of
　　their captivity;
　Jacob shall return, have rest and be
　　at ease;
　No one shall make *him* afraid.
²⁸ Do not fear, O Jacob My servant,"
　　says the LORD,
　"For I *am* with you;
　For I will make a complete end of all
　　the nations
　To which I have driven you,
　But I will not make a complete end of
　　you.

46:14 ^aThat is, ancient Memphis
46:19 ^aThat is, ancient Memphis
46:25 ^aA sun god ^bThat is, ancient Thebes

I will rightly correct you,
For I will not leave you wholly
unpunished."

Judgment on Philistia

47 The word of the LORD that came to Jeremiah the prophet against the Philistines, before Pharaoh attacked Gaza. [2]Thus says the LORD:

"Behold, waters rise out of the north,
And shall be an overflowing flood;
They shall overflow the land and
all that is in it,
The city and those who dwell
within;
Then the men shall cry,
And all the inhabitants of the land
shall wail.
[3] At the noise of the stamping hooves
of his strong horses,
At the rushing of his chariots,
At the rumbling of his wheels,
The fathers will not look back for
their children,
Lacking courage,
[4] Because of the day that comes to
plunder all the Philistines,
To cut off from Tymre and Sidon
every helper who remains;
For the LORD shall plunder the
Philistines,
The remnant of the country of
Caphtor.
[5] Baldness has come upon Gaza,
Ashkelon is cut off
With the remnant of their valley.
How long will you cut yourself?

[6] "O you sword of the LORD,
How long until you are quiet?
Put yourself up into your scabbard,
Rest and be still!
[7] How can it be quiet,
Seeing the LORD has given it a
charge
Against Ashkelon and against
the seashore?
There He has appointed it."

Judgment on Moab

48 Against Moab.
Thus says the LORD of hosts,
the God of Israel:

"Woe to Nebo!
For it is plundered,
Kirjathaim is shamed *and* taken;
The high stronghold[a] is shamed and
dismayed—
[2] No more praise of Moab.
In Heshbon they have devised evil
against her:
'Come, and let us cut her off as a
nation.'
You also shall be cut down, O Madmen![a]
The sword shall pursue you;
[3] A voice of crying *shall be* from
Horonaim:
'Plundering and great destruction!'

[4] "Moab is destroyed;
Her little ones have caused a cry to
be heard;[a]
[5] For in the Ascent of Luhith they
ascend with continual weeping;
For in the descent of Horonaim the
enemies have heard a cry of
destruction.

[6] "Flee, save your lives!
And be like the juniper[a] in the
wilderness.
[7] For because you have trusted in your
works and your treasures,
You also shall be taken.
And Chemosh shall go forth into
captivity,
His priests and his princes together.
[8] And the plunderer shall come
against every city;
No one shall escape.
The valley also shall perish,
And the plain shall be destroyed,
As the LORD has spoken.

[9] "Give wings to Moab,
That she may flee and get away;
For her cities shall be desolate,
Without any to dwell in them.
[10] Cursed *is* he who does the work of
the LORD deceitfully,
And cursed *is* he who keeps back his
sword from blood.

48:1 [a]Hebrew *Misgab* 48:2 [a]A city of Moab
48:4 [a]Following Masoretic Text, Targum, and
Vulgate; Septuagint reads *Proclaim it in Zoar.*
48:6 [a]Or *Aroer,* a city of Moab

11 "Moab has been at ease from his[a] youth;
     He has settled on his dregs,
     And has not been emptied from
          vessel to vessel,
     Nor has he gone into captivity.
     Therefore his taste remained in him,
     And his scent has not changed.

12 "Therefore behold, the days are
          coming," says the LORD,
     "That I shall send him wine-workers
     Who will tip him over
     And empty his vessels
     And break the bottles.

13   Moab shall be ashamed of Chemosh,
     As the house of Israel was ashamed
          of Bethel, their confidence.

14 "How can you say, 'We are mighty
     And strong men for the war'?

15   Moab is plundered and gone up from
          her cities;
     Her chosen young men have gone
          down to the slaughter," says the
          King,
     Whose name is the LORD of hosts.

16 "The calamity of Moab is near at hand,
     And his affliction comes quickly.

17   Bemoan him, all you who are around
          him;
     And all you who know his name,
     Say, 'How the strong staff is broken,
     The beautiful rod!'

18 "O daughter inhabiting Dibon,
     Come down from your glory,
     And sit in thirst;
     For the plunderer of Moab has come
          against you,
     He has destroyed your strongholds.

19   O inhabitant of Aroer,
     Stand by the way and watch;
     Ask him who flees
     And her who escapes;
     Say, 'What has happened?'

20   Moab is shamed, for he is broken
          down.
     Wail and cry!
     Tell it in Arnon, that Moab is
          plundered.

21 "And judgment has come on the plain
          country:
     On Holon and Jahzah and Mephaath,

22   On Dibon and Nebo and Beth
          Diblathaim,

23   On Kirjathaim and Beth Gamul and
          Beth Meon,

24   On Kerioth and Bozrah,
     On all the cities of the land of Moab,
          Far or near.

25   The horn of Moab is cut off,
     And his arm is broken," says the
          LORD.

26 "Make him drunk,
     Because he exalted himself against
          the LORD.
     Moab shall wallow in his vomit,
     And he shall also be in derision.

27   For was not Israel a derision to you?
     Was he found among thieves?
     For whenever you speak of him,
     You shake your head in scorn.

28   You who dwell in Moab,
     Leave the cities and dwell in the
          rock,
     And be like the dove which makes
          her nest
     In the sides of the cave's mouth.

29 "We have heard the pride of Moab
     (He is exceedingly proud),
     Of his loftiness and arrogance and
          pride,
     And of the haughtiness of his
          heart."

30 "I know his wrath," says the LORD,
     "But it is not right;
     His lies have made nothing right.

31   Therefore I will wail for Moab,
     And I will cry out for all Moab;
     I[a] will mourn for the men of Kir
          Heres.

32   O vine of Sibmah! I will weep for
          you with the weeping of Jazer.
     Your plants have gone over the sea,
     They reach to the sea of Jazer.
     The plunderer has fallen on your
          summer fruit and your vintage.

33   Joy and gladness are taken
     From the plentiful field
     And from the land of Moab;

48:11 [a]The Hebrew uses masculine and feminine pronouns interchangeably in this chapter.
48:31 [a]Following Dead Sea Scrolls, Septuagint, and
Vulgate; Masoretic Text reads He.

I have caused wine to fail from the
    winepresses;
No one will tread with joyous
    shouting—
Not joyous shouting!

34 "From the cry of Heshbon to Elealeh
    and to Jahaz
They have uttered their voice,
From Zoar to Horonaim,
Like a three-year-old heifer;ᵃ
For the waters of Nimrim also shall
    be desolate.

35 "Moreover," says the LORD,
"I will cause to cease in Moab
The one who offers *sacrifices* in the
    high places
And burns incense to his gods.
36 Therefore My heart shall wail like
    flutes for Moab,
And like flutes My heart shall wail
For the men of Kir Heres.
Therefore the riches they have
    acquired have perished.

37 "For every head *shall be* bald, and
    every beard clipped;
On all the hands *shall be* cuts, and on
    the loins sackcloth—
38 A general lamentation
On all the housetops of Moab,
And in its streets;
For I have broken Moab like a vessel
    in which *is* no pleasure," says the
    LORD.
39 "They shall wail:
'How she is broken down!
How Moab has turned her back with
    shame!'
So Moab shall be a derision
And a dismay to all those about her."

40For thus says the LORD:

"Behold, one shall fly like an eagle,
And spread his wings over Moab.
41 Kerioth is taken,
And the strongholds are surprised;
The mighty men's hearts in Moab on
    that day shall be

Like the heart of a woman in birth
    pangs.
42 And Moab shall be destroyed as a
    people,
Because he exalted *himself* against
    the LORD.
43 Fear and the pit and the snare *shall
    be* upon you,
O inhabitant of Moab," says the
    LORD.
44 "He who flees from the fear shall fall
    into the pit,
And he who gets out of the pit shall
    be caught in the snare.
For upon Moab, upon it I will bring
The year of their punishment," says
    the LORD.

45 "Those who fled stood under the
    shadow of Heshbon
Because of exhaustion.
But a fire shall come out of Heshbon,
A flame from the midst of Sihon,
And shall devour the brow of
    Moab,
The crown of the head of the
    sons of tumult.
46 Woe to you, O Moab!
The people of Chemosh perish;
For your sons have been taken
    captive,
And your daughters captive.

47 "Yet I will bring back the captives of
    Moab
In the latter days," says the LORD.

Thus far *is* the judgment of Moab.

Judgment on Ammon

49 Against the Ammonites.
Thus says the LORD:

"Has Israel no sons?
Has he no heir?
Why *then* does Milcomᵃ inherit Gad,
And his people dwell in its cities?
2 Therefore behold, the days are
    coming," says the LORD,
"That I will cause to be heard an
    alarm of war
In Rabbah of the Ammonites;
It shall be a desolate mound,
And her villages shall be burned
    with fire.

48:34 ᵃOr *The Third Eglath,* an unknown city
(compare Isaiah 15:5) 49:1 ᵃHebrew *Malcam,* literally
their king, a god of the Ammonites; also called
Molech (compare verse 3)

Then Israel shall take possession of
   his inheritance," says the LORD.

3 "Wail, O Heshbon, for Ai is plundered!
   Cry, you daughters of Rabbah,
   Gird yourselves with sackcloth!
   Lament and run to and fro by the
     walls;
   For Milcom shall go into captivity
   With his priests and his princes
     together.
4 Why do you boast in the valleys,
   Your flowing valley, O backsliding
     daughter?
   Who trusted in her treasures, *saying,*
   ' Who will come against me?'
5 Behold, I will bring fear upon you,"
   Says the Lord GOD of hosts,
   "From all those who are around you;
   You shall be driven out, everyone
     headlong,
   And no one will gather those who
     wander off.
6 But afterward I will bring back
   The captives of the people of
     Ammon," says the LORD.

**INTIMATE
MOMENTS**

Turn your bedroom into a romantic getaway; rose petals, scented candles, and
soft music.

Judgment on Edom

7Against Edom.
Thus says the LORD of hosts:

  "*Is* wisdom no more in Teman?
   Has counsel perished from the
     prudent?
   Has their wisdom vanished?
8 Flee, turn back, dwell in the depths,
   O inhabitants of Dedan!
   For I will bring the calamity of Esau
     upon him,
   The time *that* I will punish him.
9 If grape-gatherers came to you,

   Would they not leave *some* gleaning
     grapes?
   If thieves by night,
   Would they not destroy until they
     have enough?
10 But I have made Esau bare;
   I have uncovered his secret places,[a]
   And he shall not be able to hide
     himself.
   His descendants are plundered,
   His brethren and his neighbors,
   And he *is* no more.
11 Leave your fatherless children,
   I will preserve *them* alive;
   And let your widows trust in Me."

12For thus says the LORD: "Behold, those
whose judgment *was* not to drink of the
cup have assuredly drunk. And *are* you the
one who will altogether go unpunished?
You shall not go unpunished, but you shall
surely drink *of it.* 13For I have sworn by
Myself," says the LORD, "that Bozrah shall
become a desolation, a reproach, a waste,
and a curse. And all its cities shall be perpetual wastes."

14 I have heard a message from the LORD,
   And an ambassador has been sent to
     the nations:
   "Gather together, come against her,
   And rise up to battle!

15 "For indeed, I will make you small
     among nations,
   Despised among men.
16 Your fierceness has deceived you,
   The pride of your heart,
   O you who dwell in the clefts of the
     rock,
   Who hold the height of the hill!
   Though you make your nest as high
     as the eagle,
   I will bring you down from there,"
     says the LORD.[a]

17 "Edom also shall be an astonishment;
   Everyone who goes by it will be
     astonished
   And will hiss at all its plagues.
18 As in the overthrow of Sodom and
     Gomorrah

49:10 [a]Compare Obadiah 5, 6
49:16 [a]Compare Obadiah 3, 4

And their neighbors," says the LORD,
"No one shall remain there,
  Nor shall a son of man dwell in it.

19 "Behold, he shall come up like a lion
      from the floodplain[a] of the Jordan
    Against the dwelling place of the
      strong;
    But I will suddenly make him run
      away from her.
    And who is a chosen *man that* I may
      appoint over her?
    For who is like Me?
    Who will arraign Me?
    And who is that shepherd
    Who will withstand Me?"

20 Therefore hear the counsel of the
      LORD that He has taken against
      Edom,
    And His purposes that He has
      proposed against the inhabitants
      of Teman:
    Surely the least of the flock shall
      draw them out;
    Surely He shall make their dwelling
      places desolate with them.
21 The earth shakes at the noise of
      their fall;
    At the cry its noise is heard at the
      Red Sea.
22 Behold, He shall come up and fly like
      the eagle,
    And spread His wings over Bozrah;
    The heart of the mighty men of
      Edom in that day shall be
    Like the heart of a woman in birth
      pangs.

Judgment on Damascus

23 Against Damascus.

  "Hamath and Arpad are shamed,
    For they have heard bad news.
    They are fainthearted;
  There is trouble on the sea;
    It cannot be quiet.
24 Damascus has grown feeble;
    She turns to flee,
    And fear has seized *her.*
    Anguish and sorrows have taken her
      like a woman in labor.

25 Why is the city of praise not
      deserted, the city of My joy?
26 Therefore her young men shall fall in
      her streets,
    And all the men of war shall be cut
      off in that day," says the LORD of
      hosts.
27 "I will kindle a fire in the wall of
      Damascus,
    And it shall consume the palaces of
      Ben-Hadad."[a]

Judgment on Kedar and Hazor

28 Against Kedar and against the kingdoms of Hazor, which Nebuchadnezzar
king of Babylon shall strike.
    Thus says the LORD:

  "Arise, go up to Kedar,
    And devastate the men of the East!
29 Their tents and their flocks they
      shall take away.
    They shall take for themselves their
      curtains,
    All their vessels and their camels;
    And they shall cry out to them,
  'Fear *is* on every side!'

30 "Flee, get far away! Dwell in the
      depths,
    O inhabitants of Hazor!" says the
      LORD.
  "For Nebuchadnezzar king of
      Babylon has taken counsel
      against you,
    And has conceived a plan against
      you.

31 "Arise, go up to the wealthy nation
      that dwells securely," says the
      LORD,
  "Which has neither gates nor bars,
    Dwelling alone.
32 Their camels shall be for booty,
    And the multitude of their cattle for
      plunder.
    I will scatter to all winds those in the
      farthest corners,
    And I will bring their calamity from
      all its sides," says the LORD.
33 "Hazor shall be a dwelling for jackals,
      a desolation forever;
    No one shall reside there,
    Nor son of man dwell in it."

49:19 [a]Or *thicket* **49:27** [a]Compare Amos 1:4

Judgment on Elam

³⁴The word of the LORD that came to Jeremiah the prophet against Elam, in the beginning of the reign of Zedekiah king of Judah, saying, ³⁵"Thus says the LORD of hosts:

' Behold, I will break the bow of Elam,
   The foremost of their might.
³⁶ Against Elam I will bring the four winds
   From the four quarters of heaven,
   And scatter them toward all those winds;
   There shall be no nations where the outcasts of Elam will not go.
³⁷ For I will cause Elam to be dismayed before their enemies
   And before those who seek their life.
   I will bring disaster upon them,
   My fierce anger,' says the LORD;
' And I will send the sword after them
   Until I have consumed them.
³⁸ I will set My throne in Elam,
   And will destroy from there the king and the princes,' says the LORD.

³⁹ 'But it shall come to pass in the latter days:
   I will bring back the captives of Elam,' says the LORD."

Judgment on Babylon and Babylonia

50 The word that the LORD spoke against Babylon *and* against the land of the Chaldeans by Jeremiah the prophet.

² "Declare among the nations,
   Proclaim, and set up a standard;
   Proclaim—do not conceal *it*—
   Say, 'Babylon is taken, Bel is shamed.
   Merodachᵃ is broken in pieces;
   Her idols are humiliated,
   Her images are broken in pieces.'
³ For out of the north a nation comes up against her,
   Which shall make her land desolate,
   And no one shall dwell therein.
   They shall move, they shall depart,
   Both man and beast.

⁴ "In those days and in that time," says the LORD,

"The children of Israel shall come,
   They and the children of Judah together;
   With continual weeping they shall come,
   And seek the LORD their God.
⁵ They shall ask the way to Zion,
   With their faces toward it, *saying,*
' Come and let us join ourselves to the LORD
   In a perpetual covenant
   That will not be forgotten.'

⁶ "My people have been lost sheep.
   Their shepherds have led them astray;
   They have turned them away *on* the mountains.
   They have gone from mountain to hill;
   They have forgotten their resting place.
⁷ All who found them have devoured them;
   And their adversaries said, 'We have not offended,
   Because they have sinned against the LORD, the habitation of justice,
   The LORD, the hope of their fathers.'

⁸ "Move from the midst of Babylon,
   Go out of the land of the Chaldeans;
   And be like the rams before the flocks.
⁹ For behold, I will raise and cause to come up against Babylon
   An assembly of great nations from the north country,
   And they shall array themselves against her;
   From there she shall be captured.
   Their arrows *shall be* like *those* of an expert warrior;ᵃ
   None shall return in vain.
¹⁰ And Chaldea shall become plunder;
   All who plunder her shall be satisfied," says the LORD.

¹¹ "Because you were glad, because you rejoiced,

50:2 ᵃA Babylonian god; sometimes spelled *Marduk*
50:9 ᵃFollowing some Hebrew manuscripts, Septuagint, and Syriac; Masoretic Text, Targum, and Vulgate read *a warrior who makes childless.*

You destroyers of My heritage,
Because you have grown fat like a
   heifer threshing grain,
And you bellow like bulls,
12 Your mother shall be deeply ashamed;
She who bore you shall be ashamed.
Behold, the least of the nations *shall*
   be a wilderness,
A dry land and a desert.
13 Because of the wrath of the LORD
She shall not be inhabited,
But she shall be wholly desolate.
Everyone who goes by Babylon shall
   be horrified
And hiss at all her plagues.

14 "Put yourselves in array against
    Babylon all around,
All you who bend the bow;
Shoot at her, spare no arrows,
For she has sinned against the LORD.
15 Shout against her all around;
She has given her hand,
Her foundations have fallen,
Her walls are thrown down;
For it *is* the vengeance of the LORD.
Take vengeance on her.
As she has done, so do to her.
16 Cut off the sower from Babylon,
And him who handles the sickle at
   harvest time.
For fear of the oppressing sword
Everyone shall turn to his own people,
And everyone shall flee to his own
   land.

17 "Israel *is* like scattered sheep;
The lions have driven *him* away.
First the king of Assyria devoured
   him;
Now at last this Nebuchadnezzar
   king of Babylon has broken his
   bones."

18 Therefore thus says the LORD of
hosts, the God of Israel:

"Behold, I will punish the king of
   Babylon and his land,
As I have punished the king of
   Assyria.
19 But I will bring back Israel to his
   home,
And he shall feed on Carmel and
   Bashan;

BIBLICAL INSIGHTS • 50:20
Drop Your Grudges

SOMEONE ONCE ASKED, "Did you know that the longer you carry a grudge, the heavier it gets?" Refusing to forgive those who wrong us can be a wearying weight on the soul.

On the other hand, when we choose to forgive, we shed a huge burden that simply doesn't need to weigh us down. It can make us absolutely lighthearted to put down the heavy burden of a grudge. God calls us to do what He Himself does, to be willing to pardon those who hurt us (50:20).

So what can you do to keep from carrying grudges?

For one thing, clarify your inner occupation. Do you want to make judging others your spiritual career path? Be on guard against a spirit of self-righteousness. Jesus said, "Judge not, that you be not judged" (Matt. 7:1), indicating that those who insist on playing the judge, themselves get judged. Call it the boomerang effect.

Judging, just like taking vengeance, belongs to God, not to us: "'Vengeance is Mine, I will repay,' says the Lord" (Rom. 12:19). Since God makes the rules, He is the only true Judge. People who wrong others are offending God at the same time. So lay down your grudge and let go of your desire to see justice done. Relieve yourself of the responsibility that actually belongs only to God.

His soul shall be satisfied on Mount
   Ephraim and Gilead.
20 In those days and in that time," says
   the LORD,
"The iniquity of Israel shall be
   sought, but *there shall be* none;
And the sins of Judah, but they shall
   not be found;
For I will pardon those whom I
   preserve.

21 "Go up against the land of Merathaim,
    against it,
  And against the inhabitants of Pekod.
  Waste and utterly destroy them,"
    says the LORD,
  "And do according to all that I have
    commanded you.
22 A sound of battle *is* in the land,
  And of great destruction.
23 How the hammer of the whole earth
    has been cut apart and broken!
  How Babylon has become a
    desolation among the nations!
24 I have laid a snare for you;
  You have indeed been trapped, O
    Babylon,
  And you were not aware;
  You have been found and also caught,
  Because you have contended against
    the LORD.
25 The LORD has opened His armory,
  And has brought out the weapons of
    His indignation;
  For this *is* the work of the Lord GOD
    of hosts
  In the land of the Chaldeans.
26 Come against her from the farthest
    border;
  Open her storehouses;
  Cast her up as heaps of ruins,
  And destroy her utterly;
  Let nothing of her be left.
27 Slay all her bulls,
  Let them go down to the slaughter.
  Woe to them!
  For their day has come, the time of
    their punishment.
28 The voice of those who flee and
    escape from the land of Babylon
  Declares in Zion the vengeance of
    the LORD our God,
  The vengeance of His temple.

29 "Call together the archers against
    Babylon.
  All you who bend the bow, encamp
    against it all around;
  Let none of them escape.ᵃ
  Repay her according to her work;
  According to all she has done, do to
    her;
  For she has been proud against the
    LORD,

  Against the Holy One of Israel.
30 Therefore her young men shall fall in
    the streets,
  And all her men of war shall be cut
    off in that day," says the LORD.
31 "Behold, I *am* against you,
  O most haughty one!" says the Lord
    GOD of hosts;
  "For your day has come,
  The time *that* I will punish you.ᵃ
32 The most proud shall stumble and fall,
  And no one will raise him up;
  I will kindle a fire in his cities,
  And it will devour all around him."

33 Thus says the LORD of hosts:

  "The children of Israel *were* oppressed,
  Along with the children of Judah;
  All who took them captive have held
    them fast;
  They have refused to let them go.
34 Their Redeemer *is* strong;
  The LORD of hosts *is* His name.
  He will thoroughly plead their case,
  That He may give rest to the land,
  And disquiet the inhabitants of
    Babylon.

35 "A sword *is* against the Chaldeans,"
    says the LORD,
  "Against the inhabitants of Babylon,
  And against her princes and her wise
    men.
36 A sword *is* against the soothsayers,
    and they will be fools.
  A sword *is* against her mighty men,
    and they will be dismayed.
37 A sword *is* against their horses,
  Against their chariots,
  And against all the mixed peoples
    who *are* in her midst;
  And they will become like women.
  A sword *is* against her treasures, and
    they will be robbed.
38 A droughtᵃ *is* against her waters, and
    they will be dried up.
  For it *is* the land of carved images,

50:29 ᵃQere, some Hebrew manuscripts, Septuagint, and Targum add *to her*. **50:31** ᵃFollowing Masoretic Text and Targum; Septuagint and Vulgate read *The time of your punishment*. **50:38** ᵃFollowing Masoretic Text, Targum, and Vulgate; Syriac reads *sword*; Septuagint omits *A drought is*.

And they are insane with *their* idols.

39 "Therefore the wild desert beasts
       shall dwell *there* with the jackals,
   And the ostriches shall dwell in it.
   It shall be inhabited no more forever,
   Nor shall it be dwelt in from
       generation to generation.
40 As God overthrew Sodom and
       Gomorrah
   And their neighbors," says the LORD,
   "*So* no one shall reside there,
   Nor son of man dwell in it.

41 "Behold, a people shall come from the
       north,
   And a great nation and many kings
   Shall be raised up from the ends of
       the earth.
42 They shall hold the bow and the lance;
   They *are* cruel and shall not show
       mercy.
   Their voice shall roar like the sea;
   They shall ride on horses,
   Set in array, like a man for the battle,
   Against you, O daughter of Babylon.

43 "The king of Babylon has heard the
       report about them,
   And his hands grow feeble;
   Anguish has taken hold of him,
   Pangs as of a woman in childbirth.

44 "Behold, he shall come up like a lion
       from the floodplain[a] of the Jordan
   Against the dwelling place of the
       strong;
   But I will make them suddenly run
       away from her.
   And who *is* a chosen *man that* I may
       appoint over her?
   For who *is* like Me?
   Who will arraign Me?
   And who *is* that shepherd
   Who will withstand Me?"

45 Therefore hear the counsel of the
       LORD that He has taken against
       Babylon,
   And His purposes that He has
       proposed against the land of the
       Chaldeans:

Surely the least of the flock shall
    draw them out;
Surely He will make their dwelling
    place desolate with them.
46 At the noise of the taking of Babylon
   The earth trembles,
   And the cry is heard among the
       nations.

The Utter Destruction of Babylon

51
Thus says the LORD:

"Behold, I will raise up against Babylon,
   Against those who dwell in Leb
       Kamai,[a]
   A destroying wind.
2 And I will send winnowers to
       Babylon,
   Who shall winnow her and empty
       her land.
   For in the day of doom
   They shall be against her all around.
3 Against *her* let the archer bend his
       bow,
   And lift himself up against *her* in his
       armor.
   Do not spare her young men;
   Utterly destroy all her army.
4 Thus the slain shall fall in the land
       of the Chaldeans,
   And *those* thrust through in her
       streets.
5 For Israel is not forsaken, nor Judah,
   By his God, the LORD of hosts,
   Though their land was filled with sin
       against the Holy One of Israel."

6 Flee from the midst of Babylon,
   And every one save his life!
   Do not be cut off in her iniquity,
   For this *is* the time of the LORD's
       vengeance;
   He shall recompense her.
7 Babylon *was* a golden cup in the
       LORD's hand,
   That made all the earth drunk.
   The nations drank her wine;
   Therefore the nations are deranged.
8 Babylon has suddenly fallen and
       been destroyed.
   Wail for her!
   Take balm for her pain;
   Perhaps she may be healed.

50:44 [a]Or *thicket* **51:1** [a]A code word for Chaldea
(Babylonia); may be translated *The Midst of Those
Who Rise Up Against Me*

9 We would have healed Babylon,
But she is not healed.
Forsake her, and let us go everyone
to his own country;
For her judgment reaches to heaven
and is lifted up to the skies.

10 The LORD has revealed our
righteousness.
Come and let us declare in Zion the
work of the LORD our God.

11 Make the arrows bright!
Gather the shields!
The LORD has raised up the spirit of
the kings of the Medes.
For His plan is against Babylon to
destroy it,
Because it is the vengeance of
the LORD,
The vengeance for His temple.

12 Set up the standard on the walls of
Babylon;
Make the guard strong,
Set up the watchmen,
Prepare the ambushes.
For the LORD has both devised and
done
What He spoke against the
inhabitants of Babylon.

13 O you who dwell by many waters,
Abundant in treasures,
Your end has come,
The measure of your covetousness.

14 The LORD of hosts has sworn by
Himself:
"Surely I will fill you with men, as
with locusts,
And they shall lift up a shout against
you."

15 He has made the earth by His
power;
He has established the world by
His wisdom,
And stretched out the heaven by His
understanding.

16 When He utters His voice—
There is a multitude of waters in the
heavens:
"He causes the vapors to ascend from
the ends of the earth;
He makes lightnings for the rain;
He brings the wind out of His
treasuries."a

17 Everyone is dull-hearted, without
knowledge;
Every metalsmith is put to shame by
the carved image;
For his molded image is falsehood,
And there is no breath in them.

18 They are futile, a work of errors;
In the time of their punishment they
shall perish.

19 The Portion of Jacob is not like them,
For He is the Maker of all things;
And Israel is the tribe of His
inheritance.
The LORD of hosts is His name.

20 "You are My battle-ax and weapons of
war:
For with you I will break the nation
in pieces;
With you I will destroy kingdoms;

21 With you I will break in pieces the
horse and its rider;
With you I will break in pieces the
chariot and its rider;

22 With you also I will break in pieces
man and woman;
With you I will break in pieces old
and young;
With you I will break in pieces the
young man and the maiden;

23 With you also I will break in pieces
the shepherd and his flock;
With you I will break in pieces the
farmer and his yoke of oxen;
And with you I will break in pieces
governors and rulers.

24 "And I will repay Babylon
And all the inhabitants of Chaldea
For all the evil they have done
In Zion in your sight," says the LORD.

25 "Behold, I am against you, O
destroying mountain,
Who destroys all the earth," says
the LORD.
"And I will stretch out My hand
against you,
Roll you down from the rocks,
And make you a burnt mountain.

26 They shall not take from you a stone
for a corner

51:16 aPsalm 135:7

Nor a stone for a foundation,
But you shall be desolate forever,"
    says the LORD.

27 Set up a banner in the land,
    Blow the trumpet among the nations!
    Prepare the nations against her,
    Call the kingdoms together against
        her:
    Ararat, Minni, and Ashkenaz.
    Appoint a general against her;
    Cause the horses to come up like the
        bristling locusts.
28 Prepare against her the nations,
    With the kings of the Medes,
    Its governors and all its rulers,
    All the land of his dominion.
29 And the land will tremble and sorrow;
    For every purpose of the LORD shall
        be performed against Babylon,
    To make the land of Babylon a
        desolation without inhabitant.
30 The mighty men of Babylon have
        ceased fighting,
    They have remained in their
        strongholds;
    Their might has failed,
    They became *like* women;
    They have burned her dwelling
        places,
    The bars of her *gate* are broken.
31 One runner will run to meet another,
    And one messenger to meet another,
    To show the king of Babylon that his
        city is taken on *all* sides;
32 The passages are blocked,
    The reeds they have burned with fire,
    And the men of war are terrified.

33For thus says the LORD of hosts, the
God of Israel:

    "The daughter of Babylon *is* like a
        threshing floor
    When it is time to thresh her;
    Yet a little while
    And the time of her harvest will
        come."

34 "Nebuchadnezzar the king of Babylon
    Has devoured me, he has crushed me;
    He has made me an empty vessel,

He has swallowed me up like a
    monster;
He has filled his stomach with my
    delicacies,
He has spit me out.
35 Let the violence *done* to me and my
        flesh *be* upon Babylon,"
    The inhabitant of Zion will say;
    "And my blood be upon the
        inhabitants of Chaldea!"
    Jerusalem will say.

36Therefore thus says the LORD:

    "Behold, I will plead your case and
        take vengeance for you.
    I will dry up her sea and make her
        springs dry.
37 Babylon shall become a heap,
    A dwelling place for jackals,
    An astonishment and a hissing,
    Without an inhabitant.
38 They shall roar together like lions,
    They shall growl like lions' whelps.
39 In their excitement I will prepare
        their feasts;
    I will make them drunk,
    That they may rejoice,
    And sleep a perpetual sleep
    And not awake," says the LORD.
40 "I will bring them down
    Like lambs to the slaughter,
    Like rams with male goats.

41 "Oh, how Sheshach[a] is taken!
    Oh, how the praise of the whole
        earth is seized!
    How Babylon has become desolate
        among the nations!
42 The sea has come up over Babylon;
    She is covered with the multitude of
        its waves.
43 Her cities are a desolation,
    A dry land and a wilderness,
    A land where no one dwells,
    Through which no son of man passes.
44 I will punish Bel in Babylon,
    And I will bring out of his mouth
        what he has swallowed;
    And the nations shall not stream to
        him anymore.
    Yes, the wall of Babylon shall fall.

45 "My people, go out of the midst of
        her!

51:41 [a]A code word for Babylon (compare
Jeremiah 25:26)

And let everyone deliver himself
from the fierce anger of the LORD.

46 And lest your heart faint,
And you fear for the rumor that *will
be* heard in the land
(A rumor will come *one* year,
And after that, in *another* year
A rumor *will come,*
And violence in the land,
Ruler against ruler),

47 Therefore behold, the days are
coming
That I will bring judgment on the
carved images of Babylon;
Her whole land shall be ashamed,
And all her slain shall fall in her
midst.

48 Then the heavens and the earth and
all that *is* in them
Shall sing joyously over Babylon;
For the plunderers shall come to her
from the north," says the LORD.

49 As Babylon *has caused* the slain of
Israel to fall,
So at Babylon the slain of all the
earth shall fall.

50 You who have escaped the sword,
Get away! Do not stand still!
Remember the LORD afar off,
And let Jerusalem come to your mind.

INTIMATE MOMENTS

Arrange for a babysitter and then whisk
your wife away on a special day filled
with fun things she enjoys.

51 We are ashamed because we have
heard reproach.
Shame has covered our faces,
For strangers have come into the
sanctuaries of the LORD's house.

52 "Therefore behold, the days are
coming," says the LORD,
"That I will bring judgment on her
carved images,

And throughout all her land the
wounded shall groan.

53 Though Babylon were to mount up
to heaven,
And though she were to fortify the
height of her strength,
Yet from Me plunderers would come
to her," says the LORD.

54 The sound of a cry *comes* from
Babylon,
And great destruction from the land
of the Chaldeans,

55 Because the LORD is plundering
Babylon
And silencing her loud voice,
Though her waves roar like great
waters,
And the noise of their voice is
uttered,

56 Because the plunderer comes against
her, against Babylon,
And her mighty men are taken.
Every one of their bows is broken;
For the LORD *is* the God of
recompense,
He will surely repay.

57 "And I will make drunk
Her princes and wise men,
Her governors, her deputies, and her
mighty men.
And they shall sleep a perpetual
sleep
And not awake," says the King,
Whose name *is* the LORD of hosts.

58 Thus says the LORD of hosts:

"The broad walls of Babylon shall be
utterly broken,
And her high gates shall be burned
with fire;
The people will labor in vain,
And the nations, because of the fire;
And they shall be weary."

Jeremiah's Command to Seraiah

59 The word which Jeremiah the prophet
commanded Seraiah the son of Neriah, the
son of Mahseiah, when he went with
Zedekiah the king of Judah to Babylon in
the fourth year of his reign. And Seraiah
was the quartermaster. 60 So Jeremiah wrote
in a book all the evil that would come upon

Babylon, all these words that are written against Babylon. [61]And Jeremiah said to Seraiah, "When you arrive in Babylon and see it, and read all these words, [62]then you shall say, 'O LORD, You have spoken against this place to cut it off, so that none shall remain in it, neither man nor beast, but it shall be desolate forever.' [63]Now it shall be, when you have finished reading this book, *that* you shall tie a stone to it and throw it out into the Euphrates. [64]Then you shall say, 'Thus Babylon shall sink and not rise from the catastrophe that I will bring upon her. And they shall be weary.'"

Thus far *are* the words of Jeremiah.

The Fall of Jerusalem Reviewed

52 Zedekiah *was* twenty-one years old when he became king, and he reigned eleven years in Jerusalem. His mother's name *was* Hamutal the daughter of Jeremiah of Libnah. [2]He also did evil in the sight of the LORD, according to all that Jehoiakim had done. [3]For because of the anger of the LORD *this* happened in Jerusalem and Judah, till He finally cast them out from His presence. Then Zedekiah rebelled against the king of Babylon.

[4]Now it came to pass in the ninth year of his reign, in the tenth month, on the tenth *day* of the month, *that* Nebuchadnezzar king of Babylon and all his army came against Jerusalem and encamped against it; and *they* built a siege wall against it all around. [5]So the city was besieged until the eleventh year of King Zedekiah. [6]By the fourth month, on the ninth day of the month, the famine had become so severe in the city that there was no food for the people of the land. [7]Then the city *wall* was broken through, and all the men of war fled and went out of the city at night by way of the gate between the two walls, which *was* by the king's garden, even though the Chaldeans *were* near the city all around. And they went by way of the plain.[a]

[8]But the army of the Chaldeans pursued the king, and they overtook Zedekiah in the plains of Jericho. All his army was scattered from him. [9]So they took the king

and brought him up to the king of Babylon at Riblah in the land of Hamath, and he pronounced judgment on him. [10]Then the king of Babylon killed the sons of Zedekiah before his eyes. And he killed all the princes of Judah in Riblah. [11]He also put out the eyes of Zedekiah; and the king of Babylon bound him in bronze fetters, took him to Babylon, and put him in prison till the day of his death.

The Temple and City Plundered and Burned

[12]Now in the fifth month, on the tenth *day* of the month (which *was* the nineteenth year of King Nebuchadnezzar king of Babylon), Nebuzaradan, the captain of the guard, *who* served the king of Babylon, came to Jerusalem. [13]He burned the house of the LORD and the king's house; all the houses of Jerusalem, that is, all the houses of the great, he burned with fire. [14]And all the army of the Chaldeans who *were* with the captain of the guard broke down all the walls of Jerusalem all around. [15]Then Nebuzaradan the captain of the guard carried away captive *some* of the poor people, the rest of the people who remained in the city, the defectors who had deserted to the king of Babylon, and the rest of the craftsmen. [16]But Nebuzaradan the captain of the guard left *some* of the poor of the land as vinedressers and farmers.

[17]The bronze pillars that *were* in the house of the LORD, and the carts and the bronze Sea that *were* in the house of the LORD, the Chaldeans broke in pieces, and carried all their bronze to Babylon. [18]They also took away the pots, the shovels, the trimmers, the bowls, the spoons, and all the bronze utensils with which the *priests* ministered. [19]The basins, the firepans, the bowls, the pots, the lampstands, the spoons, and the cups, whatever *was* solid gold and whatever *was* solid silver, the captain of the guard took away. [20]The two pillars, one Sea, the twelve bronze bulls which *were* under *it, and* the carts, which King Solomon had made for the house of the LORD—the bronze of all these articles was beyond measure. [21]Now *concerning* the pillars: the height of one pillar *was* eighteen cubits, a measuring line of twelve

---

52:7 [a]Or *the Arabah,* that is, the Jordan Valley

cubits could measure its circumference, and its thickness *was* four fingers; *it was* hollow. ²²A capital of bronze *was* on it; and the height of one capital *was* five cubits, with a network and pomegranates all around the capital, all of bronze. The second pillar, with pomegranates was the same. ²³There were ninety-six pomegranates on the sides; all the pomegranates, all around on the network, *were* one hundred.

The People Taken Captive to Babylonia

²⁴The captain of the guard took Seraiah the chief priest, Zephaniah the second priest, and the three doorkeepers. ²⁵He also took out of the city an officer who had charge of the men of war, seven men of the king's close associates who were found in the city, the principal scribe of the army who mustered the people of the land, and sixty men of the people of the land who were found in the midst of the city. ²⁶And Nebuzaradan the captain of the guard took these and brought them to the king of Babylon at Riblah. ²⁷Then the king of Babylon struck them and put them to death at Riblah in the land of Hamath. Thus Judah was carried away captive from its own land.

²⁸These *are* the people whom Nebuchadnezzar carried away captive: in the seventh year, three thousand and twenty-three Jews; ²⁹in the eighteenth year of Nebuchadnezzar he carried away captive from Jerusalem eight hundred and thirty-two persons; ³⁰in the twenty-third year of Nebuchadnezzar, Nebuzaradan the captain of the guard carried away captive of the Jews seven hundred and forty-five persons. All the persons *were* four thousand six hundred.

Jehoiachin Released from Prison

³¹Now it came to pass in the thirty-seventh year of the captivity of Jehoiachin king of Judah, in the twelfth month, on the twenty-fifth *day* of the month, *that* Evil-Merodach[a] king of Babylon, in the *first* year of his reign, lifted up the head of Jehoiachin king of Judah and brought him out of prison. ³²And he spoke kindly to him and gave him a more prominent seat than those of the kings who *were* with him in Babylon. ³³So Jehoiachin changed from his prison garments, and he ate bread regularly before the *king* all the days of his life. ³⁴And as for his provisions, there was a regular ration given him by the king of Babylon, a portion for each day until the day of his death, all the days of his life.

52:31 ᵃOr *Awil-Marduk*

LAMENTATIONS

THE LATE BIBLE TEACHER J. VERNON MCGEE called the Book of Lamentations, "the wailing wall of the Bible ... a hymn of heartbreak . . . a symphony of sorrow." It contains an eyewitness account of the fall of Jerusalem in 586 BC. The book never names the eyewitness, but traditional and biblical evidence points to the prophet Jeremiah. If he is indeed the author, this book is written near the end of his life, as he sees the terrible fulfillment of all the ominous warnings he so faithfully delivered to his spiritually wandering people.

Even though God's hardhearted people ignored Jeremiah's message, the prophet still weeps at the fall of the holy city and at the suffering of God's chosen nation. Some find it incongruous that the same prophet who spoke so forcefully about God's coming judgment would also weep so bitterly and express such compassion for God's hurting children. But we see the same pattern in the life of Jesus, who spoke hard words of judgment to the Pharisees, yet who also wept over the doomed city of Jerusalem. Our Lord models for us the combination of boldness and tenderness that every follower of Christ should exhibit, under the control of God's Spirit.

The Book of Lamentations opens with a powerful metaphor. It pictures the nation of Israel as an abandoned, grieving widow; the fall of Jerusalem is like the death of her husband. What follows are a series of five poems of lament, dirges that describe the grief the prophet experiences at the horrifying fall of the once-great city of God.

Perhaps the best-known passage in Lamentations is found in 3:22–25, on which the hymn "Great Is Thy Faithfulness" is based. In the midst of grief, the prophet reminds God's people of their Lord's faithfulness, of His steadfast love and of His mercies that are "new every morning" (v. 23). In our own sorrows, we can find comfort for our hearts in remembering, "'The LORD is my portion,' says my soul, 'Therefore I hope in Him!' The LORD is good to those who wait for Him, to the soul who seeks Him" (3:24, 25).

Jerusalem in Affliction

1 How lonely sits the city
That was full of people!
How like a widow is she,
Who *was* great among the nations!
The princess among the provinces
Has become a slave!

2 She weeps bitterly in the night,
Her tears *are* on her cheeks;
Among all her lovers
She has none to comfort *her.*
All her friends have dealt
    treacherously with her;
They have become her enemies.

3 Judah has gone into captivity,
Under affliction and hard servitude;
She dwells among the nations,
She finds no rest;
All her persecutors overtake her in
    dire straits.

4 The roads to Zion mourn
Because no one comes to the set
    feasts.
All her gates are desolate;
Her priests sigh,
Her virgins are afflicted,
And she *is* in bitterness.

5 Her adversaries have become the
    master,
Her enemies prosper;
For the LORD has afflicted her
Because of the multitude of her
    transgressions.
Her children have gone into captivity
    before the enemy.

6 And from the daughter of Zion
All her splendor has departed.
Her princes have become like deer
That find no pasture,
That flee without strength
Before the pursuer.

7 In the days of her affliction and
    roaming,
Jerusalem remembers all her
    pleasant things
That she had in the days of old.
When her people fell into the hand of
    the enemy,
With no one to help her,

The adversaries saw her
And mocked at her downfall.[a]

8 Jerusalem has sinned gravely,
Therefore she has become vile.[a]
All who honored her despise her
Because they have seen her
    nakedness;
Yes, she sighs and turns away.

9 Her uncleanness *is* in her skirts;
She did not consider her destiny;
Therefore her collapse was awesome;
She had no comforter.
"O LORD, behold my affliction,
For *the* enemy is exalted!"

10 The adversary has spread his hand
Over all her pleasant things;
For she has seen the nations enter
    her sanctuary,
Those whom You commanded
Not to enter Your assembly.

11 All her people sigh,
They seek bread;
They have given their valuables for
    food to restore life.
"See, O LORD, and consider,
For I am scorned."

12 "*Is it* nothing to you, all you who pass
    by?
Behold and see
If there is any sorrow like my sorrow,
Which has been brought on me,
Which the LORD has inflicted
In the day of His fierce anger.

13 "From above He has sent fire into my
    bones,
And it overpowered them;
He has spread a net for my feet
And turned me back;
He has made me desolate
And faint all the day.

14 "The yoke of my transgressions was
    bound;[a]
They were woven together by His
    hands,
And thrust upon my neck.

1:7 [a]Vulgate reads *her Sabbaths.*
1:8 [a]Septuagint and Vulgate read *moved* or *removed.*
1:14 [a]Following Masoretic Text and Targum;
Septuagint, Syriac, and Vulgate read *watched over.*

He made my strength fail;
The Lord delivered me into the
   hands of *those whom* I am not
   able to withstand.

15 "The Lord has trampled underfoot all
   my mighty *men* in my midst;
He has called an assembly against me
To crush my young men;
The Lord trampled *as* in a winepress
The virgin daughter of Judah.

16 "For these *things* I weep;
My eye, my eye overflows with
   water;
Because the comforter, who should
   restore my life,
Is far from me.
My children are desolate
Because the enemy prevailed."

17 Zion spreads out her hands,
But no one comforts her;
The LORD has commanded
   concerning Jacob
That those around him *become* his
   adversaries;
Jerusalem has become an unclean
   thing among them.

18 "The LORD is righteous,
For I rebelled against His
   commandment.
Hear now, all peoples,
And behold my sorrow;
My virgins and my young men
Have gone into captivity.

19 "I called for my lovers,
But they deceived me;
My priests and my elders
Breathed their last in the city,
While they sought food
To restore their life.

20 "See, O LORD, that I *am* in distress;
My soul is troubled;
My heart is overturned within me,
For I have been very rebellious.
Outside the sword bereaves,
At home *it is* like death.

21 "They have heard that I sigh,
But no one comforts me.
All my enemies have heard of my
   trouble;

They are glad that You have done *it*.
Bring on the day You have announced,
That they may become like me.

22 "Let all their wickedness come before
   You,
And do to them as You have done to
   me
For all my transgressions;
For my sighs *are* many,
And my heart *is* faint."

INTIMATE MOMENTS

Tell her you would marry her all over
again.

God's Anger with Jerusalem

2 How the Lord has covered the
   daughter of Zion
With a cloud in His anger!
He cast down from heaven to the
   earth
The beauty of Israel,
And did not remember His footstool
In the day of His anger.

2 The Lord has swallowed up and has
   not pitied
All the dwelling places of Jacob.
He has thrown down in His wrath
The strongholds of the daughter of
   Judah;
He has brought *them* down to the
   ground;
He has profaned the kingdom and its
   princes.

3 He has cut off in fierce anger
Every horn of Israel;
He has drawn back His right hand
From before the enemy.
He has blazed against Jacob like a
   flaming fire
Devouring all around.

4 Standing like an enemy, He has bent
   His bow;
With His right hand, like an
   adversary,

He has slain all *who were* pleasing to
His eye;
On the tent of the daughter of Zion,
He has poured out His fury like fire.

5   The Lord was like an enemy.
He has swallowed up Israel,
He has swallowed up all her palaces;
He has destroyed her strongholds,
And has increased mourning and
lamentation
In the daughter of Judah.

6   He has done violence to His
tabernacle,
As if it were a garden;
He has destroyed His place of
assembly;
The LORD has caused
The appointed feasts and Sabbaths
to be forgotten in Zion.
In His burning indignation He has
spurned the king and the priest.

7   The Lord has spurned His altar,
He has abandoned His sanctuary;
He has given up the walls of her
palaces
Into the hand of the enemy.
They have made a noise in the house
of the LORD
As on the day of a set feast.

8   The LORD has purposed to destroy
The wall of the daughter of Zion.
He has stretched out a line;
He has not withdrawn His hand from
destroying;
Therefore He has caused the rampart
and wall to lament;
They languished together.

9   Her gates have sunk into the ground;
He has destroyed and broken her bars.
Her king and her princes *are* among
the nations;
The Law *is* no *more,*
And her prophets find no vision from
the LORD.

10 The elders of the daughter of Zion
Sit on the ground *and* keep silence;
They throw dust on their heads
And gird themselves with sackcloth.
The virgins of Jerusalem
Bow their heads to the ground.

11 My eyes fail with tears,
My heart is troubled;
My bile is poured on the ground
Because of the destruction of the
daughter of my people,
Because the children and the infants
Faint in the streets of the city.

12 They say to their mothers,
"Where *is* grain and wine?"
As they swoon like the wounded
In the streets of the city,
As their life is poured out
In their mothers' bosom.

13 How shall I console you?
To what shall I liken you,
O daughter of Jerusalem?
What shall I compare with you, that
I may comfort you,
O virgin daughter of Zion?
For your ruin *is* spread wide as the
sea;
Who can heal you?

14 Your prophets have seen for you
False and deceptive visions;
They have not uncovered your
iniquity,
To bring back your captives,
But have envisioned for you false
prophecies and delusions.

15 All who pass by clap *their* hands at
you;
They hiss and shake their heads
At the daughter of Jerusalem:
"*Is* this the city that is called
'The perfection of beauty,
The joy of the whole earth'?"

16 All your enemies have opened their
mouth against you;
They hiss and gnash *their* teeth.
They say, "We have swallowed *her* up!
Surely this *is* the day we have waited
for;
We have found *it,* we have seen *it!* "

17 The LORD has done what He
purposed;
He has fulfilled His word
Which He commanded in days of
old.
He has thrown down and has not
pitied,

And He has caused an enemy to
    rejoice over you;
He has exalted the horn of your
    adversaries.

18 Their heart cried out to the Lord,
"O wall of the daughter of Zion,
Let tears run down like a river day
    and night;
Give yourself no relief;
Give your eyes no rest.

19 "Arise, cry out in the night,
At the beginning of the watches;
Pour out your heart like water before
    the face of the Lord.
Lift your hands toward Him
For the life of your young children,
Who faint from hunger at the head
    of every street."

20 "See, O LORD, and consider!
To whom have You done this?
Should the women eat their offspring,
The children they have cuddled?a
Should the priest and prophet be slain
In the sanctuary of the Lord?

21 "Young and old lie
On the ground in the streets;
My virgins and my young men
Have fallen by the sword;
You have slain *them* in the day of
    Your anger,
You have slaughtered *and* not pitied.

22 "You have invited as to a feast day
The terrors that surround me.
In the day of the LORD's anger
There was no refugee or survivor.
Those whom I have borne and
    brought up
My enemies have destroyed."

The Prophet's Anguish and Hope

3 I *am* the man *who* has seen affliction
    by the rod of His wrath.
2 He has led me and made *me* walk
In darkness and not *in* light.
3 Surely He has turned His hand
    against me
Time and time again throughout the
    day.

4 He has aged my flesh and my skin,
And broken my bones.
5 He has besieged me
And surrounded *me* with bitterness
    and woe.
6 He has set me in dark places
Like the dead of long ago.

7 He has hedged me in so that I cannot
    get out;
He has made my chain heavy.
8 Even when I cry and shout,
He shuts out my prayer.
9 He has blocked my ways with hewn
    stone;
He has made my paths crooked.

10 He *has been* to me a bear lying in
    wait,
Like a lion in ambush.
11 He has turned aside my ways and
    torn me in pieces;
He has made me desolate.
12 He has bent His bow
And set me up as a target for the
    arrow.

13 He has caused the arrows of His
    quiver
To pierce my loins.a
14 I have become the ridicule of all my
    people—
Their taunting song all the day.
15 He has filled me with bitterness,
He has made me drink wormwood.

16 He has also broken my teeth with
    gravel,
And covered me with ashes.
17 You have moved my soul far from
    peace;
I have forgotten prosperity.
18 And I said, "My strength and my
    hope
Have perished from the LORD."

19 Remember my affliction and roaming,
The wormwood and the gall.
20 My soul still remembers
And sinks within me.
21 This I recall to my mind,
Therefore I have hope.

22 *Through* the LORD's mercies we are
    not consumed,
Because His compassions fail not.

2:20 aVulgate reads *a span long.*
3:13 aLiterally *kidneys*

Self-Denial Is Also for Kids

AFTER THE FALL of the once-great city of Jerusalem, the prophet Jeremiah wrote, "It is good for a man to bear the yoke in his youth" (3:27). I believe this verse implies that it is good for our children to learn to bear some burdens, to deny themselves, and to pay some price for the overall good of the family. Jeremiah declares to us moms and dads that, from time to time, it is good to remind ourselves that our children should learn self-denial and responsibility in the family.

It's not good to always cater to our kids' every whim. We do them no good by giving them everything they want. Jeremiah would remind us that the lack of self-control and the desire for pleasure lie at the root of Jerusalem's destruction. Our kids need to learn how to deny themselves and, at times, to do without, because suffering for the sake of Jesus and self-denial are central to following Christ.

Here's the question we need to ask ourselves: Do we want our children to be genuine disciples of Christ? Or would we prefer that they merely feel comfortable and happy and have everything they want in life?

---

23   *They are* new every morning;
Great *is* Your faithfulness.

24   "The LORD *is* my portion," says my
soul,
"Therefore I hope in Him!"

25   The LORD *is* good to those who wait
for Him,
To the soul *who* seeks Him.

26   *It is* good that *one* should hope and
wait quietly
For the salvation of the LORD.

27   *It is* good for a man to bear
The yoke in his youth.

28   Let him sit alone and keep silent,
Because *God* has laid *it* on him;

29   Let him put his mouth in the dust—
There may yet be hope.

30   Let him give *his* cheek to the one
who strikes him,
And be full of reproach.

31   For the Lord will not cast off forever.

32   Though He causes grief,
Yet He will show compassion
According to the multitude of His
mercies.

33   For He does not afflict willingly,
Nor grieve the children of men.

34   To crush under one's feet
All the prisoners of the earth,

35   To turn aside the justice *due* a man
Before the face of the Most High,

36   Or subvert a man in his cause—
The Lord does not approve.

37   Who *is* he *who* speaks and it comes
to pass,
When the Lord has not commanded *it?*

38   *Is it* not from the mouth of the Most
High
That woe and well-being proceed?

39   Why should a living man complain,
A man for the punishment of his sins?

40   Let us search out and examine our
ways,
And turn back to the LORD;

41   Let us lift our hearts and hands
To God in heaven.

42   We have transgressed and rebelled;
You have not pardoned.

43   You have covered *Yourself* with
anger
And pursued us;
You have slain *and* not pitied.

44   You have covered Yourself with a
cloud,
That prayer should not pass through.

45   You have made us an offscouring
and refuse
In the midst of the peoples.

46   All our enemies
Have opened their mouths against us.

47   Fear and a snare have come upon us,
Desolation and destruction.

48   My eyes overflow with rivers of water
For the destruction of the daughter
of my people.

49 My eyes flow and do not cease,
   Without interruption,
50 Till the LORD from heaven
   Looks down and sees.
51 My eyes bring suffering to my soul
   Because of all the daughters of my
      city.

52 My enemies without cause
   Hunted me down like a bird.
53 They silenced[a] my life in the pit
   And threw stones at me.
54 The waters flowed over my head;
   I said, "I am cut off!"

55 I called on Your name, O LORD,
   From the lowest pit.
56 You have heard my voice:
   "Do not hide Your ear
   From my sighing, from my cry for
      help."
57 You drew near on the day I called on
      You,
   And said, "Do not fear!"

58 O Lord, You have pleaded the case
      for my soul;
   You have redeemed my life.
59 O LORD, You have seen how I am
      wronged;
   Judge my case.
60 You have seen all their vengeance,
   All their schemes against me.

61 You have heard their reproach, O
      LORD,
   All their schemes against me,
62 The lips of my enemies
   And their whispering against me all
      the day.
63 Look at their sitting down and their
      rising up;
   I am their taunting song.

64 Repay them, O LORD,
   According to the work of their
      hands.
65 Give them a veiled[a] heart;
   Your curse be upon them!
66 In Your anger,
   Pursue and destroy them
   From under the heavens of the LORD.

3:53 [a]Septuagint reads *put to death.* **3:65** [a]A Jewish
tradition reads *sorrow of.* **4:7** [a]Or *nobles*

The Degradation of Zion

4 How the gold has become dim!
   How changed the fine gold!
   The stones of the sanctuary are
      scattered
   At the head of every street.

2 The precious sons of Zion,
   Valuable as fine gold,
   How they are regarded as clay pots,
   The work of the hands of the potter!

3 Even the jackals present their breasts
   To nurse their young;
   But the daughter of my people *is*
      cruel,
   Like ostriches in the wilderness.

4 The tongue of the infant clings
   To the roof of its mouth for thirst;
   The young children ask for bread,
   But no one breaks *it* for them.

5 Those who ate delicacies
   Are desolate in the streets;
   Those who were brought up in scarlet
   Embrace ash heaps.

6 The punishment of the iniquity of
      the daughter of my people
   Is greater than the punishment of
      the sin of Sodom,
   Which was overthrown in a moment,
   With no hand to help her!

7 Her Nazirites[a] were brighter than
      snow
   And whiter than milk;
   They were more ruddy in body than
      rubies,
   Like sapphire in their appearance.

8 *Now* their appearance is blacker than
      soot;
   They go unrecognized in the streets;
   Their skin clings to their bones,
   It has become as dry as wood.

9 *Those* slain by the sword are better off
   Than *those* who die of hunger;
   For these pine away,
   Stricken *for lack* of the fruits of the
      field.

10 The hands of the compassionate
      women
   Have cooked their own children;

They became food for them
In the destruction of the daughter of
my people.

11 The LORD has fulfilled His fury,
He has poured out His fierce anger.
He kindled a fire in Zion,
And it has devoured its foundations.

12 The kings of the earth,
And all inhabitants of the world,
Would not have believed
That the adversary and the enemy
Could enter the gates of Jerusalem—

13 Because of the sins of her prophets
And the iniquities of her priests,
Who shed in her midst
The blood of the just.

14 They wandered blind in the streets;
They have defiled themselves with
blood,
So that no one would touch their
garments.

**INTIMATE
MOMENTS**

You are never too old to flirt. Flirt with
the man you married.

15 They cried out to them,
"Go away, unclean!
Go away, go away,
Do not touch us!"
When they fled and wandered,
Those among the nations said,
"They shall no longer dwell *here.*"

16 The face[a] of the LORD scattered
them;
He no longer regards them.
The people do not respect the
priests
Nor show favor to the elders.

17 Still our eyes failed us,
Watching vainly for our help;
In our watching we watched
For a nation *that* could not save *us.*

18 They tracked our steps
So that we could not walk in our
streets.
Our end was near;
Our days were over,
For our end had come.

19 Our pursuers were swifter
Than the eagles of the heavens.
They pursued us on the mountains
And lay in wait for us in the
wilderness.

20 The breath of our nostrils, the
anointed of the LORD,
Was caught in their pits,
Of whom we said, "Under his shadow
We shall live among the nations."

21 Rejoice and be glad, O daughter of
Edom,
You who dwell in the land of Uz!
The cup shall also pass over to you
And you shall become drunk and
make yourself naked.

22 *The punishment of* your iniquity is
accomplished,
O daughter of Zion;
He will no longer send you into
captivity.
He will punish your iniquity,
O daughter of Edom;
He will uncover your sins!

A Prayer for Restoration

5 Remember, O LORD, what has come
upon us;
Look, and behold our reproach!
2 Our inheritance has been turned over
to aliens,
And our houses to foreigners.
3 We have become orphans and waifs,
Our mothers *are* like widows.

4 We pay for the water we drink,
And our wood comes at a price.
5 *They* pursue at our heels;[a]
We labor *and* have no rest.
6 We have given our hand *to* the
Egyptians
And the Assyrians, to be satisfied
with bread.

4:16 [a]Targum reads *anger.* 5:5 [a]Literally *necks*

7 Our fathers sinned *and are* no more,
But we bear their iniquities.

8 Servants rule over us;
There is none to deliver *us* from their
hand.

9 We get our bread *at the risk* of our
lives,
Because of the sword in the
wilderness.

10 Our skin is hot as an oven,
Because of the fever of famine.

11 They ravished the women in Zion,
The maidens in the cities of Judah.

12 Princes were hung up by their hands,
And elders were not respected.

13 Young men ground at the millstones;
Boys staggered under *loads of* wood.

14 The elders have ceased *gathering at*
the gate,
And the young men from their music.

15 The joy of our heart has ceased;
Our dance has turned into mourning.

16 The crown has fallen *from* our head.
Woe to us, for we have sinned!

17 Because of this our heart is faint;
Because of these *things* our eyes
grow dim;

18 Because of Mount Zion which is
desolate,
With foxes walking about on it.

19 You, O LORD, remain forever;
Your throne from generation to
generation.

20 Why do You forget us forever,
And forsake us for so long a time?

21 Turn us back to You, O LORD, and we
will be restored;
Renew our days as of old,

22 Unless You have utterly rejected us,
And are very angry with us!

EZEKIEL

WHEN BABYLONIAN INVADERS CAPTURED JERUSALEM in 597 BC, they took 10,000 captives back to their homeland. One of those Hebrew captives was a priest who, in exile, became a prophet. We know him as Ezekiel.

Many of God's people believed that the Lord would never allow Jerusalem to fall to an invading army. They believed the city offered divine protection, no matter how they lived or what gods they worshipped. When that idea proved false, the exiles in Babylon had many questions, among them, "How can we continue to serve and worship God in a foreign land?" (see Psalm 137), and "Did the fall of Jerusalem mean that God has been defeated by a more powerful pagan god?"

Ezekiel gave a clear and uncompromising message to his fellow exiles. The disobedience of God's people, despite His kindness and patience, had triggered these disastrous consequences. Ezekiel reinforces the central themes of God's sovereignty and holiness. More than sixty times in his book, he says that certain events will occur so that "you may know that I am the LORD."

Chapters 1—24 contain prophecies about the destruction of Jerusalem. Chapters 25—32 describe retribution on enemy nations, with a brief hint at God's restoration of Israel. In chapter 33 the prophet again calls for Israel to repent, providing specific instructions from God. Finally, chapters 34—48 provide God's people with hope that God will once again restore the nation. These final chapters provide very specific instructions for rebuilding the temple and the holy city.

Very little is known about Ezekiel. We do know that he was married and that his wife, called the desire of his eyes (24:16), died while in captivity (24:18). God instructed the prophet to use her death as a picture for His people of the final siege of Jerusalem.

A proverb found in Ezekiel should serve as a warning for every generation of parents, "The fathers have eaten sour grapes, and the children's teeth are set on edge" (18:2). Our choices don't affect us alone; they also affect our legacy. Ezekiel's prophecy shows clearly how the disobedience of one generation led to the long captivity of that generation's children.

Ezekiel's Vision of God

1 Now it came to pass in the thirtieth year, in the fourth *month,* on the fifth *day* of the month, as I *was* among the captives by the River Chebar, *that* the heavens were opened and I saw visions[a] of God. ²On the fifth *day* of the month, which *was* in the fifth year of King Jehoiachin's captivity, ³the word of the LORD came expressly to Ezekiel the priest, the son of Buzi, in the land of the Chaldeans[a] by the River Chebar; and the hand of the LORD was upon him there.

⁴Then I looked, and behold, a whirlwind was coming out of the north, a great cloud with raging fire engulfing itself; and brightness *was* all around it and radiating out of its midst like the color of amber, out of the midst of the fire. ⁵Also from within it *came* the likeness of four living creatures. And this *was* their appearance: they had the likeness of a man. ⁶Each one had four faces, and each one had four wings. ⁷Their legs *were* straight, and the soles of their feet *were* like the soles of calves' feet. They sparkled like the color of burnished bronze. ⁸The hands of a man *were* under their wings on their four sides; and each of the four had faces and wings. ⁹Their wings touched one another. *The creatures* did not turn when they went, but each one went straight forward.

¹⁰As for the likeness of their faces, *each* had the face of a man; each of the four had the face of a lion on the right side, each of the four had the face of an ox on the left side, and each of the four had the face of an eagle. ¹¹Thus *were* their faces. Their wings stretched upward; two *wings* of each one touched one another, and two covered their bodies. ¹²And each one went straight forward; they went wherever the spirit wanted to go, and they did not turn when they went.

¹³As for the likeness of the living creatures, their appearance *was* like burning coals of fire, like the appearance of torches going back and forth among the living creatures. The fire was bright, and out of the fire went lightning. ¹⁴And the living creatures ran back and forth, in appearance like a flash of lightning.

¹⁵Now as I looked at the living creatures, behold, a wheel *was* on the earth beside each living creature with its four faces. ¹⁶The appearance of the wheels and their workings *was* like the color of beryl, and all four had the same likeness. The appearance of their workings *was,* as it were, a wheel in the middle of a wheel. ¹⁷When they moved, they went toward any one of four directions; they did not turn aside when they went. ¹⁸As for their rims, they were so high they were awesome; and their rims *were* full of eyes, all around the four of them. ¹⁹When the living creatures went, the wheels went beside them; and when the living creatures were lifted up from the earth, the wheels were lifted up. ²⁰Wherever the spirit wanted to go, they went, *because* there the spirit went; and the wheels were lifted together with them, for the spirit of the living creatures[a] *was* in the wheels. ²¹When those went, *these* went; when those stood, *these* stood; and when those were lifted up from the earth, the wheels were lifted up together with them, for the spirit of the living creatures[a] *was* in the wheels.

²²The likeness of the firmament above the heads of the living creatures[a] *was* like the color of an awesome crystal, stretched out over their heads. ²³And under the firmament their wings *spread out* straight, one toward another. Each one had two which covered one side, and each one had two which covered the other side of the body. ²⁴When they went, I heard the noise of their wings, like the noise of many waters, like the voice of the Almighty, a tumult like the noise of an army; and when they stood still, they let down their wings. ²⁵A voice came from above the firmament that *was* over their heads; whenever they stood, they let down their wings.

²⁶And above the firmament over their heads *was* the likeness of a throne, in

---

1:1 [a]Following Masoretic Text, Septuagint, and Vulgate; Syriac and Targum read *a vision.*
1:3 [a]Or *Babylonians,* and so elsewhere in this book
1:20 [a]Literally *living creature;* Septuagint and Vulgate read *spirit of life;* Targum reads *creatures.*
1:21 [a]Literally *living creature;* Septuagint and Vulgate read *spirit of life;* Targum reads *creatures.*
1:22 [a]Following Septuagint, Targum, and Vulgate; Masoretic Text reads *living creature.*

Is There a Man in the House?

GOD CREATED MEN TO BE REAL MEN—and He insists that they act like it. So He told a quivering Ezekiel, "stand on your feet, and I will speak to you" (2:1).

Too many young men today do not know what it means to be a man. They have experienced neither a father's discipline and instruction nor his tender care and nurture. They have no role model of how a real man acts and relates to the opposite sex.

If that describes you, what can you do? First, pray that you will be a real man in the biblical sense—a man who humbly and sacrificially leads and loves your family.

Second, shape your definition and conviction of what a real man is from the Bible, not from the confused culture around you.

Third, find a godly mentor who will take a couple of years and coach you in what it means to be a man. If you want to be a man, spend time with *real men*.

And finally, provide your sons with a clear understanding of their masculine identity. Help them become men who honor their commitments, persevere, and serve their families.

I have found Robert Lewis's definition of biblical masculinity helpful. He says a real man rejects passivity, accepts responsibility, leads courageously, and expects God's greater reward. It's a great definition to learn and to pass on to your sons.

In what areas do you need to grow as a man? Pray that God will help you and your wife to understand manhood as God would have you grasp it—and then communicate this and live it out before your children.

appearance like a sapphire stone; on the likeness of the throne *was* a likeness with the appearance of a man high above it. ²⁷Also from the appearance of His waist and upward I saw, as it were, the color of amber with the appearance of fire all around within it; and from the appearance of His waist and downward I saw, as it were, the appearance of fire with brightness all around. ²⁸Like the appearance of a rainbow in a cloud on a rainy day, so *was* the appearance of the brightness all around it. This *was* the appearance of the likeness of the glory of the LORD.

Ezekiel Sent to Rebellious Israel

So when I saw *it,* I fell on my face, and I heard a voice of One speaking.

2 And He said to me, "Son of man, stand on your feet, and I will speak to you." ²Then the Spirit entered me when He spoke to me, and set me on my feet; and I heard Him who spoke to me. ³And He said to me: "Son of man, I am sending you to the children of Israel, to a rebellious nation that has rebelled against Me; they and their fathers have transgressed against Me to this very day. ⁴For *they are* impudent and stubborn children. I am sending you to them, and you shall say to them, 'Thus says the Lord GOD.' ⁵As for them, whether they hear or whether they refuse—for they *are* a rebellious house—yet they will know that a prophet has been among them.

⁶"And you, son of man, do not be afraid of them nor be afraid of their words, though briers and thorns *are* with you and you dwell among scorpions; do not be afraid of their words or dismayed by their looks, though they *are* a rebellious house. ⁷You shall speak My words to them, whether they hear or whether they refuse, for they *are* rebellious. ⁸But you, son of man, hear what I say to you. Do not be rebellious like that rebellious house; open your mouth and eat what I give you."

⁹Now when I looked, there was a hand stretched out to me; and behold, a scroll of a book *was* in it. ¹⁰Then He spread it before me; and *there was* writing on the inside and on the outside, and written on it *were* lamentations and mourning and woe.

3 Moreover He said to me, "Son of man, eat what you find; eat this scroll, and go, speak to the house of Israel." ²So I opened my mouth, and He caused me to eat that scroll.

³And He said to me, "Son of man, feed your belly, and fill your stomach with this scroll that I give you." So I ate, and it was in my mouth like honey in sweetness.

⁴Then He said to me: "Son of man, go to the house of Israel and speak with My words to them. ⁵For you *are* not sent to a people of unfamiliar speech and of hard language, *but* to the house of Israel, ⁶not to many people of unfamiliar speech and of hard language, whose words you cannot understand. Surely, had I sent you to them, they would have listened to you. ⁷But the house of Israel will not listen to you, because they will not listen to Me; for all the house of Israel *are* impudent and hard-hearted. ⁸Behold, I have made your face strong against their faces, and your forehead strong against their foreheads. ⁹Like adamant stone, harder than flint, I have made your forehead; do not be afraid of them, nor be dismayed at their looks, though they *are* a rebellious house."

¹⁰Moreover He said to me: "Son of man, receive into your heart all My words that I speak to you, and hear with your ears. ¹¹And go, get to the captives, to the children of your people, and speak to them and tell them, 'Thus says the Lord GOD,' whether they hear, or whether they refuse."

¹²Then the Spirit lifted me up, and I heard behind me a great thunderous voice: "Blessed *is* the glory of the LORD from His place!" ¹³*I* also *heard* the noise of the wings of the living creatures that touched one another, and the noise of the wheels beside them, and a great thunderous noise. ¹⁴So the Spirit lifted me up and took me away, and I went in bitterness, in the heat of my spirit; but the hand of the LORD was strong upon me. ¹⁵Then I came to the captives at Tel Abib, who dwelt by the River Chebar; and I sat where they sat, and remained there astonished among them seven days.

Ezekiel Is a Watchman

¹⁶Now it came to pass at the end of seven days that the word of the LORD came to me, saying, ¹⁷"Son of man, I have made you a watchman for the house of Israel; therefore hear a word from My mouth, and give them warning from Me: ¹⁸When I say to the wicked, 'You shall surely die,' and

BIBLICAL INSIGHTS • 2:6

Beware the Snare of Fear

FEAR IS A SNARE. A trap. It can paralyze and discourage us, intimidating us into feeling inferior. Fear operates like a magnifying glass, making small objects and circumstances seem giant and insurmountable.

The next time you feel afraid, consider it God's warning light to respond with faith. Fear and faith cannot exist simultaneously!

I believe too many Christians suffer from the "What If Syndrome." They struggle to make decisions because they continually worry, "What if . . . ?" This is exactly how the devil wants you to think.

You see, if Satan can line the interior of your soul with fear, it becomes an impenetrable coating that rips your focus off God. When God saw fear rising in the heart of Ezekiel, He said, "Do not be afraid of them nor be afraid of their words, though briers and thorns are with you and you dwell among scorpions; do not be afraid of their words or dismayed by their looks, though they are a rebellious house" (2:6).

God's Word says, "Whoever trusts in the LORD shall be safe" (Prov. 29:25). Although Satan may win a few battles on this earth, remember that, in the end, the victory belongs to God.

you give him no warning, nor speak to warn the wicked from his wicked way, to save his life, that same wicked *man* shall die in his iniquity; but his blood I will require at your hand. ¹⁹Yet, if you warn the wicked, and he does not turn from his wickedness, nor from his wicked way, he shall die in his iniquity; but you have delivered your soul.

²⁰"Again, when a righteous *man* turns from his righteousness and commits iniquity, and I lay a stumbling block before him, he shall die; because you did not give him warning, he shall die in his sin, and

Why We Preach the Good News

DID YOU KNOW that evangelism has always been a priority with God? It's true. And if you don't believe me, then just read Ezekiel 3:18, 19. That text makes it clear that even in Old Testament days, God wanted the good news to get out.

I can think of three reasons why we who follow Christ should make evangelism *our* priority.

First, *without Christ, all human beings are lost and without hope.* I never taught any of our six children how to steal a cookie, yet they all figured it out—it comes from their fallen nature.

Second, *I feel compelled to share Christ with others because I remember the reality of hell.* While hell is not en vogue today, the place of eternal judgment is more real than the room you are in right now. People who do not know Christ will spend eternity there. Hell *does* exist, and all those who die without Christ will go there.

Third, *the Good News is the very reason for which Christ came to earth.* Christ came "to seek and to save that which was lost" (Luke 19:10). Since He is the Master and we are His slaves, shouldn't we be about the Master's business?

Who do you know that needs to hear the Good News about Jesus Christ right now? Begin to pray for the courage and the settings to share your faith with them.

---

his righteousness which he has done shall not be remembered; but his blood I will require at your hand. ²¹Nevertheless if you warn the righteous *man* that the righteous should not sin, and he does not sin, he shall surely live because he took warning; also you will have delivered your soul."

²²Then the hand of the LORD was upon me there, and He said to me, "Arise, go out into the plain, and there I shall talk with you."

²³So I arose and went out into the plain, and behold, the glory of the LORD stood there, like the glory which I saw by the River Chebar; and I fell on my face. ²⁴Then the Spirit entered me and set me on my feet, and spoke with me and said to me: "Go, shut yourself inside your house. ²⁵And you, O son of man, surely they will put ropes on you and bind you with them, so that you cannot go out among them. ²⁶I will make your tongue cling to the roof of your mouth, so that you shall be mute and not be one to rebuke them, for they *are* a rebellious house. ²⁷But when I speak with you, I will open your mouth, and you shall say to them, 'Thus says the Lord GOD.' He who hears, let him hear; and he who refuses, let him refuse; for they *are* a rebellious house.

The Siege of Jerusalem Portrayed

4 "You also, son of man, take a clay tablet and lay it before you, and portray on it a city, Jerusalem. ²Lay siege against it, build a siege wall against it, and heap up a mound against it; set camps against it also, and place battering rams against it all around. ³Moreover take for yourself an iron plate, and set it *as* an iron wall between you and the city. Set your face against it, and it shall be besieged, and you shall lay siege against it. This *will be* a sign to the house of Israel.

⁴"Lie also on your left side, and lay the iniquity of the house of Israel upon it. *According* to the number of the days that you lie on it, you shall bear their iniquity. ⁵For I have laid on you the years of their iniquity, according to the number of the days, three hundred and ninety days; so you shall bear the iniquity of the house of Israel. ⁶And when you have completed them, lie again on your right side; then you shall bear the iniquity of the house of Judah forty days. I have laid on you a day for each year.

⁷"Therefore you shall set your face toward the siege of Jerusalem; your arm *shall be* uncovered, and you shall prophesy against it. ⁸And surely I will restrain you so that you cannot turn from one side to another till you have ended the days of your siege.

⁹"Also take for yourself wheat, barley, beans, lentils, millet, and spelt; put them into one vessel, and make bread of them for yourself. *During* the number of days that you lie on your side, three hundred and ninety days, you shall eat it. ¹⁰And your food which you eat *shall be* by weight, twenty shekels a day; from time to time you shall eat it. ¹¹You shall also drink water by measure, one-sixth of a hin; from time to time you shall drink. ¹²And you shall eat it *as* barley cakes; and bake it using fuel of human waste in their sight."

¹³Then the LORD said, "So shall the children of Israel eat their defiled bread among the Gentiles, where I will drive them."

¹⁴So I said, "Ah, Lord GOD! Indeed I have never defiled myself from my youth till now; I have never eaten what died of itself or was torn by beasts, nor has abominable flesh ever come into my mouth."

¹⁵Then He said to me, "See, I am giving you cow dung instead of human waste, and you shall prepare your bread over it."

¹⁶Moreover He said to me, "Son of man, surely I will cut off the supply of bread in Jerusalem; they shall eat bread by weight and with anxiety, and shall drink water by measure and with dread, ¹⁷that they may lack bread and water, and be dismayed with one another, and waste away because of their iniquity.

A Sword Against Jerusalem

5 "And you, son of man, take a sharp sword, take it as a barber's razor, and pass *it* over your head and your beard; then take scales to weigh and divide the *hair.* ²You shall burn with fire one-third in the midst of the city, when the days of the siege are finished; then you shall take one-third and strike around *it* with the sword, and one-third you shall scatter in the wind: I will draw out a sword after them. ³You shall also take a small number of them and bind them in the edge of your *garment.* ⁴Then take some of them again and throw them into the midst of the fire, and burn them in the fire. From there a fire will go out into all the house of Israel.

⁵"Thus says the Lord GOD: 'This *is* Jerusalem; I have set her in the midst of the nations and the countries all around her. ⁶She has rebelled against My judgments by doing wickedness more than the nations, and against My statutes more than the countries that *are* all around her; for they have refused My judgments, and they have not walked in My statutes.' ⁷Therefore thus says the Lord GOD: 'Because you have multiplied *disobedience* more than the nations that *are* all around you, have not walked in My statutes nor kept My judgments, nor even doneª according to the judgments of the nations that *are* all around you'— ⁸therefore thus says the Lord GOD: 'Indeed I, even I, *am* against you and will execute judgments in your midst in the sight of the nations. ⁹And I will do among you what I have never done, and the like of which I will never do again, because of all your abominations. ¹⁰Therefore fathers shall eat *their* sons in your midst, and sons shall eat their fathers; and I will execute judgments among you, and all of you who remain I will scatter to all the winds.

INTIMATE MOMENTS

Don't be a turkey this Thanksgiving—help your wife in the kitchen! And don't forget to tell her why you're thankful for her.

¹¹'Therefore, *as* I live,' says the Lord GOD, 'surely, because you have defiled My sanctuary with all your detestable things and with all your abominations, therefore I will also diminish *you;* My eye will not spare, nor will I have any pity. ¹²One-third of you shall die of the pestilence, and be consumed with famine in your midst; and one-third shall fall by the sword all around you; and I will scatter another third to all the winds, and I will draw out a sword after them. ¹³Thus shall My anger be spent, and I will cause My fury to rest upon them, and

5:7 ªFollowing Masoretic Text, Septuagint, Targum, and Vulgate; many Hebrew manuscripts and Syriac read *but have done* (compare 11:12).

I will be avenged; and they shall know that I, the LORD, have spoken *it* in My zeal, when I have spent My fury upon them. ¹⁴Moreover I will make you a waste and a reproach among the nations that *are* all around you, in the sight of all who pass by.

¹⁵"So it^a shall be a reproach, a taunt, a lesson, and an astonishment to the nations that *are* all around you, when I execute judgments among you in anger and in fury and in furious rebukes. I, the LORD, have

---

---

spoken. ¹⁶When I send against them the terrible arrows of famine which shall be for destruction, which I will send to destroy you, I will increase the famine upon you and cut off your supply of bread. ¹⁷So I will send against you famine and wild beasts, and they will bereave you. Pestilence and blood shall pass through you, and I will bring the sword against you. I, the LORD, have spoken.'"

Judgment on Idolatrous Israel

6 Now the word of the LORD came to me, saying: ²"Son of man, set your face toward the mountains of Israel, and prophesy against them, ³and say, 'O mountains of Israel, hear the word of the Lord GOD! Thus says the Lord GOD to the mountains, to the hills, to the ravines, and to the valleys: "Indeed I, *even* I, will bring a sword against you, and I will destroy your high places. ⁴Then your altars shall be desolate, your incense altars shall be broken, and I will cast down your slain *men* before your idols. ⁵And I will lay the corpses of the children of Israel before their idols, and I will scatter your bones all around your altars. ⁶In all your dwelling places the cities shall be laid waste, and the high places shall be desolate, so that your altars may be laid waste and made desolate, your idols may be broken and made to cease, your incense altars may be cut down, and your works may be abolished. ⁷The slain shall fall in your midst, and you shall know that I *am* the LORD.

⁸"Yet I will leave a remnant, so that you may have *some* who escape the sword among the nations, when you are scattered through the countries. ⁹Then those of you who escape will remember Me among the nations where they are carried captive, because I was crushed by their adulterous heart which has departed from Me, and by their eyes which play the harlot after their idols; they will loathe themselves for the evils which they committed in all their abominations. ¹⁰And they shall know that I *am* the LORD; I have not said in vain that I would bring this calamity upon them."

5:15 ^{a}Septuagint, Syriac, Targum, and Vulgate read *you.*

¹¹'Thus says the Lord GOD: "Pound your fists and stamp your feet, and say, 'Alas, for all the evil abominations of the house of Israel! For they shall fall by the sword, by famine, and by pestilence. ¹²He who is far off shall die by the pestilence, he who is near shall fall by the sword, and he who remains and is besieged shall die by the famine. Thus will I spend My fury upon them. ¹³Then you shall know that I *am* the LORD, when their slain are among their idols all around their altars, on every high hill, on all the mountaintops, under every green tree, and under every thick oak, wherever they offered sweet incense to all their idols. ¹⁴So I will stretch out My hand against them and make the land desolate, yes, more desolate than the wilderness toward Diblah, in all their dwelling places. Then they shall know that I *am* the LORD.'"'"

Judgment on Israel Is Near

7 Moreover the word of the LORD came to me, saying, ²"And you, son of man, thus says the Lord GOD to the land of Israel:

'An end! The end has come upon the four corners of the land.
³ Now the end *has come* upon you,
And I will send My anger against you;
I will judge you according to your ways,
And I will repay you for all your abominations.
⁴ My eye will not spare you,
Nor will I have pity;
But I will repay your ways,
And your abominations will be in your midst;
Then you shall know that I *am* the LORD!'

⁵"Thus says the Lord GOD:

'A disaster, a singular disaster;
Behold, it has come!
⁶ An end has come,
The end has come;
It has dawned for you;
Behold, it has come!
⁷ Doom has come to you, you who dwell in the land;
The time has come,

A day of trouble *is* near,
And not of rejoicing in the mountains.
⁸ Now upon you I will soon pour out My fury,
And spend My anger upon you;
I will judge you according to your ways,
And I will repay you for all your abominations.

⁹ 'My eye will not spare,
Nor will I have pity;
I will repay you according to your ways,
And your abominations will be in your midst.
Then you shall know that I *am* the LORD who strikes.

¹⁰ 'Behold, the day!
Behold, it has come!
Doom has gone out;
The rod has blossomed,
Pride has budded.
¹¹ Violence has risen up into a rod of wickedness;
None of them *shall remain*,
None of their multitude,
None of them;
Nor *shall there be* wailing for them.
¹² The time has come,
The day draws near.

'Let not the buyer rejoice,
Nor the seller mourn,
For wrath *is* on their whole multitude.
¹³ For the seller shall not return to what has been sold,
Though he may still be alive;
For the vision concerns the whole multitude,
And it shall not turn back;
No one will strengthen himself
Who lives in iniquity.

¹⁴ 'They have blown the trumpet and made everyone ready,
But no one goes to battle;
For My wrath *is* on all their multitude.
¹⁵ The sword *is* outside,
And the pestilence and famine within.

Whoever *is* in the field
Will die by the sword;
And whoever *is* in the city,
Famine and pestilence will devour
    him.

16 'Those who survive will escape and
        be on the mountains
    Like doves of the valleys,
    All of them mourning,
    Each for his iniquity.
17 Every hand will be feeble,
    And every knee will be *as* weak *as*
        water.
18 They will also be girded with
        sackcloth;
    Horror will cover them;
    Shame *will be* on every face,
    Baldness on all their heads.

19 'They will throw their silver into the
        streets,
    And their gold will be like refuse;
    Their silver and their gold will not be
        able to deliver them
    In the day of the wrath of the LORD;
    They will not satisfy their souls,
    Nor fill their stomachs,
    Because it became their stumbling
        block of iniquity.
20 'As for the beauty of his ornaments,
    He set it in majesty;

But they made from it
The images of their abominations—
Their detestable things;
Therefore I have made it
Like refuse to them.

21 I will give it as plunder
    Into the hands of strangers,
    And to the wicked of the earth as
        spoil;
    And they shall defile it.
22 I will turn My face from them,
    And they will defile My secret place;
    For robbers shall enter it and defile it.

23 'Make a chain,
    For the land is filled with crimes of
        blood,
    And the city is full of violence.
24 Therefore I will bring the worst of
        the Gentiles,
    And they will possess their houses;
    I will cause the pomp of the strong
        to cease,
    And their holy places shall be
        defiled.
25 Destruction comes;
    They will seek peace, but *there shall
        be* none.
26 Disaster will come upon disaster,
    And rumor will be upon rumor.
    Then they will seek a vision from a
        prophet;

PARENTING MATTERS

Q: *What should I do with a child who misbehaves at someone else's house or at a party or in the supermarket?*

When our kids were young, I talked to them even before we walked in the door. I would say, "We're going grocery shopping, and I am not going to buy you candy and gum. But if you are good and you allow me to do the grocery shopping, then I will do something fun for you. We'll go to the park or we'll go for a walk or there will be some kind of reward."

They didn't always comply, of course. Plenty of times they disobeyed or ran around the corners to the next aisle so that I couldn't find them! Be prepared as a parent to drop your grocery shopping or quit your errands, pick up your child, and go out to the car to administer discipline. At times I took my kids home and returned to the store later, as inconvenient as it may have been.

And when your child cries in the middle of the store—because he *will* test you—be sure you follow through with your word. I promise you, that little guy's eyes are firmly fixed on Mom or Dad to see, "Is my message getting through? Am I winning?" If they see the slightest hint of weakness, they'll go for the jugular!

But the law will perish from the
    priest,
And counsel from the elders.

27 'The king will mourn,
    The prince will be clothed with
        desolation,
    And the hands of the common
        people will tremble.
    I will do to them according to their
        way,
    And according to what they deserve
        I will judge them;
    Then they shall know that I *am* the
        LORD!'"

Abominations in the Temple

8 And it came to pass in the sixth year,
in the sixth *month,* on the fifth *day* of
the month, as I sat in my house with the
elders of Judah sitting before me, that the
hand of the Lord GOD fell upon me there.
²Then I looked, and there was a likeness,
like the appearance of fire—from the
appearance of His waist and downward,
fire; and from His waist and upward, like
the appearance of brightness, like the
color of amber. ³He stretched out the form
of a hand, and took me by a lock of my
hair; and the Spirit lifted me up between
earth and heaven, and brought me in
visions of God to Jerusalem, to the door of
the north gate of the inner *court,* where
the seat of the image of jealousy *was,*
which provokes to jealousy. ⁴And behold,
the glory of the God of Israel *was* there,
like the vision that I saw in the plain.

⁵Then He said to me, "Son of man, lift
your eyes now toward the north." So I lifted my eyes toward the north, and there,
north of the altar gate, was this image of
jealousy in the entrance.

⁶Furthermore He said to me, "Son of
man, do you see what they are doing, the
great abominations that the house of
Israel commits here, to make Me go far
away from My sanctuary? Now turn
again, you will see greater abominations."
⁷So He brought me to the door of the court;
and when I looked, there was a hole in the
wall. ⁸Then He said to me, "Son of man,
dig into the wall"; and when I dug into the
wall, there was a door.

⁹And He said to me, "Go in, and see the
wicked abominations which they are doing
there." ¹⁰So I went in and saw, and there—
every sort of creeping thing, abominable
beasts, and all the idols of the house of
Israel, portrayed all around on the walls.
¹¹And there stood before them seventy men
of the elders of the house of Israel, and in
their midst stood Jaazaniah the son of
Shaphan. Each man had a censer in his
hand, and a thick cloud of incense went up.
¹²Then He said to me, "Son of man, have
you seen what the elders of the house of
Israel do in the dark, every man in the room
of his idols? For they say, 'The LORD does
not see us, the LORD has forsaken the land.'"

¹³And He said to me, "Turn again, *and*
you will see greater abominations that
they are doing." ¹⁴So He brought me to the
door of the north gate of the LORD's house;
and to my dismay, women were sitting
there weeping for Tammuz.

¹⁵Then He said to me, "Have you seen
this, O son of man? Turn again, you will
see greater abominations than these." ¹⁶So
He brought me into the inner court of the
LORD's house; and there, at the door of the
temple of the LORD, between the porch and
the altar, *were* about twenty-five men with
their backs toward the temple of the LORD
and their faces toward the east, and they
were worshiping the sun toward the east.

¹⁷And He said to me, "Have you seen
this, O son of man? Is it a trivial thing to
the house of Judah to commit the abominations which they commit here? For they
have filled the land with violence; then
they have returned to provoke Me to anger.
Indeed they put the branch to their nose.
¹⁸Therefore I also will act in fury. My eye
will not spare nor will I have pity; and
though they cry in My ears with a loud
voice, I will not hear them."

The Wicked Are Slain

9 Then He called out in my hearing with
a loud voice, saying, "Let those who
have charge over the city draw near, each
with a deadly weapon in his hand." ²And
suddenly six men came from the direction
of the upper gate, which faces north, each
with his battle-ax in his hand. One man
among them *was* clothed with linen and

had a writer's inkhorn at his side. They went in and stood beside the bronze altar.

3Now the glory of the God of Israel had gone up from the cherub, where it had been, to the threshold of the temple.a And He called to the man clothed with linen, who *had* the writer's inkhorn at his side; 4and the LORD said to him, "Go through the midst of the city, through the midst of Jerusalem, and put a mark on the foreheads of the men who sigh and cry over all the abominations that are done within it."

5To the others He said in my hearing, "Go after him through the city and kill; do not let your eye spare, nor have any pity. 6Utterly slay old *and* young men, maidens and little children and women; but do not come near anyone on whom *is* the mark; and begin at My sanctuary." So they began with the elders who *were* before the temple. 7Then He said to them, "Defile the temple, and fill the courts with the slain. Go out!" And they went out and killed in the city.

INTIMATE MOMENTS

Sit down with your husband and listen to him. Ask him how you can help fulfill the dreams he has for his life.

8So it was, that while they were killing them, I was left *alone;* and I fell on my face and cried out, and said, "Ah, Lord GOD! Will You destroy all the remnant of Israel in pouring out Your fury on Jerusalem?"

9Then He said to me, "The iniquity of the house of Israel and Judah *is* exceedingly great, and the land is full of bloodshed, and the city full of perversity; for they say, 'The LORD has forsaken the land, and the LORD does not see!' 10And as for Me also, My eye will neither spare, nor will I have pity, *but* I will recompense their deeds on their own head."

11Just then, the man clothed with linen, who *had* the inkhorn at his side, reported back and said, "I have done as You commanded me."

The Glory Departs from the Temple

10 And I looked, and there in the firmament that was above the head of the cherubim, there appeared something like a sapphire stone, having the appearance of the likeness of a throne. 2Then He spoke to the man clothed with linen, and said, "Go in among the wheels, under the cherub, fill your hands with coals of fire from among the cherubim, and scatter *them* over the city." And he went in as I watched.

3Now the cherubim were standing on the south side of the templea when the man went in, and the cloud filled the inner court. 4Then the glory of the LORD went up from the cherub, *and paused* over the threshold of the temple; and the house was filled with the cloud, and the court was full of the brightness of the LORD's glory. 5And the sound of the wings of the cherubim was heard *even* in the outer court, like the voice of Almighty God when He speaks.

6Then it happened, when He commanded the man clothed in linen, saying, "Take fire from among the wheels, from among the cherubim," that he went in and stood beside the wheels. 7And the cherub stretched out his hand from among the cherubim to the fire that *was* among the cherubim, and took *some of it* and put *it* into the hands of the *man* clothed with linen, who took *it* and went out. 8The cherubim appeared to have the form of a man's hand under their wings.

9And when I looked, there were four wheels by the cherubim, one wheel by one cherub and another wheel by each other cherub; the wheels appeared *to have* the color of a beryl stone. 10As for their appearance, all four looked alike—as it were, a wheel in the middle of a wheel. 11When they went, they went toward *any of* their four directions; they did not turn aside when they went, but followed in the direction the head was facing. They did not turn aside when they went. 12And their whole body, with their back, their hands, their wings, and the wheels that the four had, *were* full of eyes all around. 13As for the wheels, they were called in my hearing, "Wheel."

9:3 aLiterally *house*
10:3 aLiterally *house,* also in verses 4 and 18

¹⁴Each one had four faces: the first face *was* the face of a cherub, the second face the face of a man, the third the face of a lion, and the fourth the face of an eagle. ¹⁵And the cherubim were lifted up. This *was* the living creature I saw by the River Chebar. ¹⁶When the cherubim went, the wheels went beside them; and when the cherubim lifted their wings to mount up from the earth, the same wheels also did not turn from beside them. ¹⁷When *the cherubim*^a stood still, *the wheels* stood still, and when *one*^b was lifted up, *the other*^c lifted itself up, for the spirit of the living creature *was* in them.

¹⁸Then the glory of the LORD departed from the threshold of the temple and stood over the cherubim. ¹⁹And the cherubim lifted their wings and mounted up from the earth in my sight. When they went out, the wheels *were* beside them; and they stood at the door of the east gate of the LORD's house, and the glory of the God of Israel *was* above them.

²⁰This *is* the living creature I saw under the God of Israel by the River Chebar, and I knew they *were* cherubim. ²¹Each one had four faces and each one four wings, and the likeness of the hands of a man *was* under their wings. ²²And the likeness of their faces *was* the same *as* the faces which I had seen by the River Chebar, their appearance and their persons. They each went straight forward.

Judgment on Wicked Counselors

11 Then the Spirit lifted me up and brought me to the East Gate of the LORD's house, which faces eastward; and there at the door of the gate were twenty-five men, among whom I saw Jaazaniah the son of Azzur, and Pelatiah the son of Benaiah, princes of the people. ²And He said to me: "Son of man, these *are* the men who devise iniquity and give wicked counsel in this city, ³who say, 'The time *is* not near to build houses; this *city is* the caldron, and we *are* the meat.' ⁴Therefore prophesy against them, prophesy, O son of man!"

⁵Then the Spirit of the LORD fell upon me, and said to me, "Speak! 'Thus says the LORD: "Thus you have said, O house of Israel; for I know the things that come into your mind. ⁶You have multiplied your slain in this city, and you have filled its streets with the slain." ⁷Therefore thus says the Lord GOD: "Your slain whom you have laid in its midst, they *are* the meat, and this *city is* the caldron; but I shall bring you out of the midst of it. ⁸You have feared the sword; and I will bring a sword upon you," says the Lord GOD. ⁹"And I will bring you out of

ROMANCE FAQ

Q: *What can I do when my marriage doesn't meet my expectations?*

When Barbara and I first got married, for dinner I expected meat and mounds of mashed potatoes with butter cascading down the sides. Alas, it was not to be! Barbara leans toward exotic tuna casseroles and lots of other things I could not begin to identify, and my expectation soon went up in a puff of smoke.

The truth is, each partner brings a certain set of expectations into a marriage. When these expectations don't get met, the drought of disillusionment can dry up the dialogue in the streams of your conversation. Don't let it happen to you!

Marriage provides a relationship where two people can hammer out *realistic* expectations. Remember, no mate will ever fulfill all of your desires in marriage. Only One is capable of that, and in His wisdom He has reserved that blessed experience for heaven.

For help here on earth, ask some probing questions. What expectations of your mate did you bring to your marriage? Which ones got met? Which ones didn't? How reasonable are they? What expectations does your spouse have of you? If you haven't ever done so, why not consider sitting down and communicating your mutual expectations to each other? It might be a real eye-opening experience.

its midst, and deliver you into the hands of strangers, and execute judgments on you. [10]You shall fall by the sword. I will judge you at the border of Israel. Then you shall know that I *am* the LORD. [11]This *city* shall not be your caldron, nor shall you be the meat in its midst. I will judge you at the border of Israel. [12]And you shall know that I *am* the LORD; for you have not walked in My statutes nor executed My judgments, but have done according to the customs of the Gentiles which *are* all around you." '"

[13]Now it happened, while I was prophesying, that Pelatiah the son of Benaiah died. Then I fell on my face and cried with a loud voice, and said, "Ah, Lord GOD! Will You make a complete end of the remnant of Israel?"

God Will Restore Israel

[14]Again the word of the LORD came to me, saying, [15]"Son of man, your brethren, your relatives, your countrymen, and all the house of Israel in its entirety, *are* those about whom the inhabitants of Jerusalem have said, 'Get far away from the LORD; this land has been given to us as a possession.' [16]Therefore say, 'Thus says the Lord GOD: "Although I have cast them far off among the Gentiles, and although I have scattered them among the countries, yet I shall be a little sanctuary for them in the countries where they have gone." ' [17]Therefore say, 'Thus says the Lord GOD: "I will gather you from the peoples, assemble you from the countries where you have been scattered, and I will give you the land of Israel." ' [18]And they will go there, and they will take away all its detestable things and all its abominations from there. [19]Then I will give them one heart, and I will put a new spirit within them,[a] and take the stony heart out

11:19 [a]Literally *you*

PARENTING MATTERS

Q: How can we teach our children to show they are sorry for something wrong they've done?

I think most kids want to please Mom and Dad; they regret doing something wrong. When you teach them to express sorrow, they'll eventually begin to feel remorse as well. Heart-felt sorrow is a character trait that is built into a child through your training. So from the time they begin to talk, children need to learn the words, "I'm sorry. I was wrong. Will you please forgive me?" You can't force the right attitude; that's something that has to come from within.

We need to realize we are training our children's consciences. They need to understand how they have hurt someone. Sometimes we move to forgiveness and reconciliation too quickly. Children are naturally selfish, and we need to show them how their unacceptable words or actions make others feel.

When a child hits his brother or excludes his sister, for example, you need to allow those siblings to express their feelings. Then quiz the child who committed the offense and ask, "Do you understand? Tell me how it made your sister feel when you treated her that way." As much as possible, take them into the experience and feelings of the other person.

And teach them to apologize specifically for what they did. If they say a general, "I'm sorry," then they haven't really acknowledged what they did.

We also need to help our children see their actions as not just an offense against a brother or sister, but also an offense before God. Teach your children passages like Ephesians 4:32, "And be kind to one another, tenderhearted, forgiving one another, even as God in Christ forgave you."

of their flesh, and give them a heart of flesh, ²⁰that they may walk in My statutes and keep My judgments and do them; and they shall be My people, and I will be their God. ²¹But *as for those* whose hearts follow the desire for their detestable things and their abominations, I will recompense their deeds on their own heads," says the Lord GOD.

²²So the cherubim lifted up their wings, with the wheels beside them, and the glory of the God of Israel *was* high above them. ²³And the glory of the LORD went up from the midst of the city and stood on the mountain, which *is* on the east side of the city.

²⁴Then the Spirit took me up and brought me in a vision by the Spirit of God into Chaldea,ᵃ to those in captivity. And the vision that I had seen went up from me. ²⁵So I spoke to those in captivity of all the things the LORD had shown me.

Judah's Captivity Portrayed

12 Now the word of the LORD came to me, saying: ²"Son of man, you dwell in the midst of a rebellious house, which has eyes to see but does not see, and ears to hear but does not hear; for they *are* a rebellious house.

³"Therefore, son of man, prepare your belongings for captivity, and go into captivity by day in their sight. You shall go from your place into captivity to another place in their sight. It may be that they will consider, though they *are* a rebellious house. ⁴By day you shall bring out your belongings in their sight, as though going into captivity; and at evening you shall go in their sight, like those who go into captivity. ⁵Dig through the wall in their sight, and carry *your belongings* out through it. ⁶In their sight you shall bear *them* on *your* shoulders *and* carry *them* out at twilight; you shall cover your face, so that you cannot see the ground, for I have made you a sign to the house of Israel."

⁷So I did as I was commanded. I brought out my belongings by day, as though going into captivity, and at evening I dug through the wall with my hand. I brought *them* out at twilight, *and* I bore *them* on *my* shoulder in their sight.

⁸And in the morning the word of the LORD came to me, saying, ⁹"Son of man, has not the house of Israel, the rebellious house, said to you, 'What are you doing?' ¹⁰Say to them, 'Thus says the Lord GOD: "This burden *concerns* the prince in Jerusalem and all the house of Israel who are among them."' ¹¹Say, 'I *am* a sign to you. As I have done, so shall it be done to them; they shall be carried away into captivity.' ¹²And the prince who *is* among them shall bear *his belongings* on *his* shoulder at twilight and go out. They shall dig through the wall to carry *them* out through it. He shall cover his face, so that he cannot see the ground with *his* eyes. ¹³I will also spread My net over him, and he shall be caught in My snare. I will bring him to Babylon, *to* the land of the Chaldeans; yet he shall not see it, though he shall die there. ¹⁴I will scatter to every wind all who *are* around him to help him, and all his troops; and I will draw out the sword after them.

¹⁵"Then they shall know that I *am* the LORD, when I scatter them among the nations and disperse them throughout the countries. ¹⁶But I will spare a few of their men from the sword, from famine, and from pestilence, that they may declare all their abominations among the Gentiles wherever they go. Then they shall know that I *am* the LORD."

Judgment Not Postponed

¹⁷Moreover the word of the LORD came to me, saying, ¹⁸"Son of man, eat your bread with quaking, and drink your water with trembling and anxiety. ¹⁹And say to the people of the land, 'Thus says the Lord GOD to the inhabitants of Jerusalem *and* to the land of Israel: "They shall eat their bread with anxiety, and drink their water with dread, so that her land may be emptied of all who are in it, because of the violence of all those who dwell in it. ²⁰Then the cities that are inhabited shall be laid waste, and the land shall become desolate; and you shall know that I *am* the LORD."'"

²¹And the word of the LORD came to me, saying, ²²"Son of man, what *is* this proverb *that* you *people* have about the land of

---

11:24 ᵃOr *Babylon,* and so elsewhere in this book

Israel, which says, 'The days are prolonged, and every vision fails'? ²³Tell them therefore, 'Thus says the Lord GOD: "I will lay this proverb to rest, and they shall no more use it as a proverb in Israel." But say to them, "The days are at hand, and the fulfillment of every vision. ²⁴For no more shall there be any false vision or flattering divination within the house of Israel. ²⁵For I *am* the LORD. I speak, and the word which I speak will come to pass; it will no more be postponed; for in your days, O rebellious house, I will say the word and perform it," says the Lord GOD.'"

²⁶Again the word of the LORD came to me, saying, ²⁷"Son of man, look, the house of Israel is saying, 'The vision that he sees *is* for many days *from now,* and he prophesies of times far off.' ²⁸Therefore say to them, 'Thus says the Lord GOD: "None of My words will be postponed any more, but the word which I speak will be done," says the Lord GOD.'"

INTIMATE MOMENTS

Put your wife to bed ... tuck her in ... tell her a story (make it a romantic story).

Woe to Foolish Prophets

13 And the word of the LORD came to me, saying, ²"Son of man, prophesy against the prophets of Israel who prophesy, and say to those who prophesy out of their own heart, 'Hear the word of the LORD!'"

³Thus says the Lord GOD: "Woe to the foolish prophets, who follow their own spirit and have seen nothing! ⁴O Israel, your prophets are like foxes in the deserts. ⁵You have not gone up into the gaps to build a wall for the house of Israel to stand in battle on the day of the LORD. ⁶They have envisioned futility and false divination, saying, 'Thus says the LORD!' But the LORD has not sent them; yet they

hope that the word may be confirmed. ⁷Have you not seen a futile vision, and have you not spoken false divination? You say, 'The LORD says,' but I have not spoken."

⁸Therefore thus says the Lord GOD: "Because you have spoken nonsense and envisioned lies, therefore I *am* indeed against you," says the Lord GOD. ⁹"My hand will be against the prophets who envision futility and who divine lies; they shall not be in the assembly of My people, nor be written in the record of the house of Israel, nor shall they enter into the land of Israel. Then you shall know that I *am* the Lord GOD.

¹⁰"Because, indeed, because they have seduced My people, saying, 'Peace!' when *there is* no peace—and one builds a wall, and they plaster it with untempered *mortar*— ¹¹say to those who plaster *it* with untempered *mortar,* that it will fall. There will be flooding rain, and you, O great hailstones, shall fall; and a stormy wind shall tear *it* down. ¹²Surely, when the wall has fallen, will it not be said to you, 'Where *is* the mortar with which you plastered *it?'"

¹³Therefore thus says the Lord GOD: "I will cause a stormy wind to break forth in My fury; and there shall be a flooding rain in My anger, and great hailstones in fury to consume *it.* ¹⁴So I will break down the wall you have plastered with untempered *mortar,* and bring it down to the ground, so that its foundation will be uncovered; it will fall, and you shall be consumed in the midst of it. Then you shall know that I *am* the LORD.

¹⁵"Thus will I accomplish My wrath on the wall and on those who have plastered it with untempered *mortar;* and I will say to you, 'The wall *is* no *more,* nor those who plastered it, ¹⁶*that is,* the prophets of Israel who prophesy concerning Jerusalem, and who see visions of peace for her when *there is* no peace,'" says the Lord GOD.

¹⁷"Likewise, son of man, set your face against the daughters of your people, who prophesy out of their own heart; prophesy against them, ¹⁸and say, 'Thus says the Lord GOD: "Woe to the *women* who sew *magic* charms on their sleevesᵃ and make

---

13:18 ᵃLiterally *over all the joints of My hands;* Vulgate reads *under every elbow;* Septuagint and Targum read *on all elbows of the hands.*

veils for the heads of people of every height to hunt souls! Will you hunt the souls of My people, and keep yourselves alive? [19]And will you profane Me among My people for handfuls of barley and for pieces of bread, killing people who should not die, and keeping people alive who should not live, by your lying to My people who listen to lies?"

[20]"Therefore thus says the Lord GOD: "Behold, I *am* against your *magic* charms by which you hunt souls there like birds. I will tear them from your arms, and let the souls go, the souls you hunt like birds. [21]I will also tear off your veils and deliver My people out of your hand, and they shall no longer be as prey in your hand. Then you shall know that I *am* the LORD.

[22]"Because with lies you have made the heart of the righteous sad, whom I have not made sad; and you have strengthened the hands of the wicked, so that he does not turn from his wicked way to save his life. [23]Therefore you shall no longer envision futility nor practice divination; for I will deliver My people out of your hand, and you shall know that I *am* the LORD."'"

Idolatry Will Be Punished

14 Now some of the elders of Israel came to me and sat before me. [2]And the word of the LORD came to me, saying, [3]"Son of man, these men have set up their idols in their hearts, and put before them that which causes them to stumble into iniquity. Should I let Myself be inquired of at all by them?

[4]"Therefore speak to them, and say to them, 'Thus says the Lord GOD: "Everyone of the house of Israel who sets up his idols in his heart, and puts before him what causes him to stumble into iniquity, and then comes to the prophet, I the LORD will answer him who comes, according to the multitude of his idols, [5]that I may seize the house of Israel by their heart, because they are all estranged from Me by their idols."'

[6]"Therefore say to the house of Israel, 'Thus says the Lord GOD: "Repent, turn away from your idols, and turn your faces away from all your abominations. [7]For anyone of the house of Israel, or of the strangers who dwell in Israel, who separates himself from Me and sets up his idols in his heart and puts before him what causes him to stumble into iniquity, then comes to a prophet to inquire of him concerning Me, I the LORD will answer him by Myself. [8]I will set My face against that man and make him a sign and a proverb, and I will cut him off from the midst of

ROMANCE FAQ

Q: *How can I best protect my wife?*

People use locks, burglar and fire alarms, and lighting systems to protect their most valuable possessions. I commend you for your desire to protect your wife! When you invest in protecting her, you make a statement about her great value to you.

Certainly, you already protect your wife physically. You discourage her going out at night if it seems dangerous. You encourage her to lock the car when she goes shopping. And you provide the kind of security she needs at home for the times you are away.

But are you protecting her from other muggers in her life, such as:

- Over scheduling her time?
- Her own unrealistic goals or expectations, which set her up for failure?
- Burnout at work? At home?
- The children, who would take advantage of her weaknesses that they know so well?

Obviously, you can't protect your wife from every pressure, worry, fear, or loss. But you *can* do your best to anticipate many of these problems before they occur, and to establish a solid security system for her protection. In addition, you might ask your wife about how you can protect her in different areas, especially those listed above.

My people. Then you shall know that I *am* the LORD.

9"And if the prophet is induced to speak anything, I the LORD have induced that prophet, and I will stretch out My hand against him and destroy him from among My people Israel. 10And they shall bear their iniquity; the punishment of the prophet shall be the same as the punishment of the one who inquired, 11that the house of Israel may no longer stray from Me, nor be profaned anymore with all their transgressions, but that they may be My people and I may be their God," says the Lord GOD.'"

Judgment on Persistent Unfaithfulness

12The word of the LORD came again to me, saying: 13"Son of man, when a land sins against Me by persistent unfaithfulness, I will stretch out My hand against it; I will cut off its supply of bread, send famine on it, and cut off man and beast from it. 14Even *if* these three men, Noah, Daniel, and Job, were in it, they would deliver *only* themselves by their righteousness," says the Lord GOD.

15"If I cause wild beasts to pass through the land, and they empty it, and make it so desolate that no man may pass through because of the beasts, 16*even though* these three men *were* in it, *as* I live," says the Lord GOD, "they would deliver neither sons nor daughters; only they would be delivered, and the land would be desolate.

17"Or *if* I bring a sword on that land, and say, 'Sword, go through the land,' and I cut off man and beast from it, 18even *though* these three men *were* in it, *as* I live," says the Lord GOD, "they would deliver neither sons nor daughters, but only they themselves would be delivered.

19"Or *if* I send a pestilence into that land and pour out My fury on it in blood, and cut off from it man and beast, 20even *though* Noah, Daniel, and Job *were* in it, *as* I live," says the Lord GOD, "they would deliver neither son nor daughter; they would deliver *only* themselves by their righteousness."

21For thus says the Lord GOD: "How much more it shall be when I send My four

severe judgments on Jerusalem—the sword and famine and wild beasts and pestilence—to cut off man and beast from it? 22Yet behold, there shall be left in it a remnant who will be brought out, *both* sons and daughters; surely they will come out to you, and you will see their ways and their doings. Then you will be comforted concerning the disaster that I have brought upon Jerusalem, all that I have brought upon it. 23And they will comfort you, when you see their ways and their doings; and you shall know that I have done nothing without cause that I have done in it," says the Lord GOD.

The Outcast Vine

15 Then the word of the LORD came to me, saying: 2"Son of man, how is the wood of the vine *better* than any other wood, the vine branch which is among the trees of the forest? 3Is wood taken from it to make any object? Or can *men* make a peg from it to hang any vessel on? 4Instead, it is thrown into the fire for fuel; the fire devours both ends of it, and its middle is burned. Is it useful for *any* work? 5Indeed, when it was whole, no object could be made from it. How much less will it be useful for *any* work when the fire has devoured it, and it is burned?

6"Therefore thus says the Lord GOD: 'Like the wood of the vine among the trees of the forest, which I have given to the fire for fuel, so I will give up the inhabitants of Jerusalem; 7and I will set My face against them. They will go out from *one* fire, but *another* fire shall devour them. Then you shall know that I *am* the LORD, when I set My face against them. 8Thus I will make the land desolate, because they have persisted in unfaithfulness,' says the Lord GOD."

God's Love for Jerusalem

16 Again the word of the LORD came to me, saying, 2"Son of man, cause Jerusalem to know her abominations, 3and say, 'Thus says the Lord GOD to Jerusalem: "Your birth and your nativity *are* from the land of Canaan; your father *was* an Amorite and your mother a Hittite. 4As for

DEVOTIONS FOR COUPLES • 16:8
Never Threaten to Leave

Several years ago, God gave us the wonderful privilege of helping a couple resurrect a marriage that seemed beyond hope. Their real commitment to Christ and to each other caused them to grow steadily in their relationship, bringing dramatic changes to their home.

But one day the wife came to us, discouraged once more about her marriage. Apparently she and her husband had reached an impasse. Each time they argued about the problem, the husband threatened to leave, a tactic from the past. He saturated their relationship with the fear that maybe he would follow through this time.

We often tell people that one of the Ten Commandments of marriage should be *Never threaten to leave*. As in so many areas of the Christian life, God gave us a memorable example to follow. Over and over in Scripture He tells us that He loves us, that He's committed to us, that He will never leave us nor forsake us. In Ezekiel He says it like this, "I spread My wing over you and covered your nakedness. Yes, I swore an oath to you and entered into a covenant with you, and you became Mine" (16:8).

Speak such loving, reassuring words to your mate. Regularly repeat your commitment, describe your love, and offer potent word pictures of your determination to stick together, regardless of what comes.

And when some problem does arise—and it will!—use the incident as yet another opportunity to reassure your spouse (even in the heat of battle) that your commitment to the marriage and to the relationship remains firm, solid, and secure. If God can tell us, "I will not leave you nor forsake you" (Josh. 1:5), then we can follow His model and speak words of faithfulness, commitment, and devotion into the lives of our mates.

Also, tell your mate that you'd choose to marry him or her again. When I've said this to Barbara, she has sometimes responded with, "Really?" At those times she's really saying, "I don't feel very lovable right now. In fact, I don't like myself. Are you sure you still like me?" She needs me to reinforce my love for her.

Why not write a letter that tells your spouse you would marry him or her all over again? Then read your note to your spouse and thank God for giving you your mate, no matter what problems you may face. Finish by reaffirming your marriage covenant with God together in prayer.

---

your nativity, on the day you were born your navel cord was not cut, nor were you washed in water to cleanse *you;* you were not rubbed with salt nor wrapped in swaddling cloths. 5No eye pitied you, to do any of these things for you, to have compassion on you; but you were thrown out into the open field, when you yourself were loathed on the day you were born.

6"And when I passed by you and saw you struggling in your own blood, I said to you in your blood, 'Live!' Yes, I said to you in your blood, 'Live!' 7I made you thrive like a plant in the field; and you grew, matured, and became very beautiful. *Your* breasts were formed, your hair grew, but you *were* naked and bare.

8"When I passed by you again and looked upon you, indeed your time *was* the time of love; so I spread My wing over you and covered your nakedness. Yes, I swore an oath to you and entered into a covenant with you, and you became Mine," says the Lord God.

9"Then I washed you in water; yes, I thoroughly washed off your blood, and I anointed you with oil. 10I clothed you in embroidered cloth and gave you sandals of badger skin; I clothed you with fine linen and covered you with silk. 11I adorned you with ornaments, put bracelets on your wrists, and a chain on your neck. 12And I put a jewel in your nose, earrings in your ears, and a beautiful crown on your head.

¹³Thus you were adorned with gold and silver, and your clothing *was of* fine linen, silk, and embroidered cloth. You ate *pastry of* fine flour, honey, and oil. You were exceedingly beautiful, and succeeded to royalty. ¹⁴Your fame went out among the nations because of your beauty, for it *was* perfect through My splendor which I had bestowed on you," says the Lord GOD.

Jerusalem's Harlotry

¹⁵"But you trusted in your own beauty, played the harlot because of your fame, and poured out your harlotry on everyone passing by who *would have* it. ¹⁶You took some of your garments and adorned multicolored high places for yourself, and played the harlot on them. *Such* things should not happen, nor be. ¹⁷You have also taken your beautiful jewelry from My gold and My silver, which I had given you, and made for yourself male images and played the harlot with them. ¹⁸You took your embroidered garments and covered them, and you set My oil and My incense before them. ¹⁹Also My food which I gave you—the pastry of fine flour, oil, and honey *which* I fed you—you set it before them as sweet incense; and *so* it was," says the Lord GOD.

²⁰"Moreover you took your sons and your daughters, whom you bore to Me, and these you sacrificed to them to be devoured. *Were* your *acts* of harlotry a small matter, ²¹that you have slain My children and offered them up to them by causing them to pass through *the fire?* ²²And in all your abominations and acts of harlotry you did not remember the days of your youth, when you were naked and bare, struggling in your blood.

²³"Then it was so, after all your wickedness—'Woe, woe to you!' says the Lord GOD— ²⁴*that* you also built for yourself a shrine, and made a high place for yourself in every street. ²⁵You built your high places at the head of every road, and made your beauty to be abhorred. You offered yourself to everyone who passed by, and multiplied your acts of harlotry. ²⁶You also committed harlotry with the Egyptians, your very fleshly neighbors, and increased your acts of harlotry to provoke Me to anger.

²⁷"Behold, therefore, I stretched out My hand against you, diminished your allotment, and gave you up to the will of those who hate you, the daughters of the Philistines, who were ashamed of your lewd behavior. ²⁸You also played the harlot with the Assyrians, because you were insatiable; indeed you played the harlot with them and still were not satisfied. ²⁹Moreover you multiplied your acts of harlotry as far as the land of the trader, Chaldea; and even then you were not satisfied.

³⁰"How degenerate is your heart!" says the Lord GOD, "seeing you do all these *things,* the deeds of a brazen harlot.

Jerusalem's Adultery

³¹"You erected your shrine at the head of every road, and built your high place in every street. Yet you were not like a harlot, because you scorned payment. ³²*You are* an adulterous wife, *who* takes strangers instead of her husband. ³³Men make payment to all harlots, but you made your payments to all your lovers, and hired them to come to you from all around for your harlotry. ³⁴You are the opposite of *other* women in your harlotry, because no one solicited you to be a harlot. In that you gave payment but no payment was given you, therefore you are the opposite."

Jerusalem's Lovers Will Abuse Her

³⁵'Now then, O harlot, hear the word of the LORD! ³⁶Thus says the Lord GOD: "Because your filthiness was poured out and your nakedness uncovered in your harlotry with your lovers, and with all your abominable idols, and because of the blood of your children which you gave to them, ³⁷surely, therefore, I will gather all your lovers with whom you took pleasure, all those you loved, *and* all those you hated; I will gather them from all around against you and will uncover your nakedness to them, that they may see all your nakedness. ³⁸And I will judge you as women who break wedlock or shed blood are judged; I will bring blood upon you in fury and jealousy. ³⁹I will also give you into their hand, and they shall throw down your shrines and break down your high places. They shall also strip you of your

clothes, take your beautiful jewelry, and leave you naked and bare.

⁴⁰"They shall also bring up an assembly against you, and they shall stone you with stones and thrust you through with their swords. ⁴¹They shall burn your houses with fire, and execute judgments on you in the sight of many women; and I will make you cease playing the harlot, and you shall no longer hire lovers. ⁴²So I will lay to rest My fury toward you, and My jealousy shall depart from you. I will be quiet, and be angry no more. ⁴³Because you did not remember the days of your youth, but agitated Meᵃ with all these *things,* surely I will also recompense your deeds on *your own* head," says the Lord GOD. "And you shall not commit lewdness in addition to all your abominations.

More Wicked than Samaria and Sodom

⁴⁴"Indeed everyone who quotes proverbs will use *this* proverb against you: 'Like mother, like daughter!' ⁴⁵You *are* your mother's daughter, loathing husband and children; and you *are* the sister of your sisters, who loathed their husbands and children; your mother *was* a Hittite and your father an Amorite.

⁴⁶"Your elder sister *is* Samaria, who dwells with her daughters to the north of you; and your younger sister, who dwells to the south of you, *is* Sodom and her daughters. ⁴⁷You did not walk in their ways nor act according to their abominations; but, as *if that were* too little, you became more corrupt than they in all your ways.

⁴⁸"*As* I live," says the Lord GOD, "neither your sister Sodom nor her daughters have done as you and your daughters have done. ⁴⁹Look, this was the iniquity of your sister Sodom: She and her daughter had pride, fullness of food, and abundance of idleness; neither did she strengthen the hand of the poor and needy. ⁵⁰And they were haughty and committed abomination

before Me; therefore I took them away as I saw *fit.*ᵃ

⁵¹"Samaria did not commit half of your sins; but you have multiplied your abominations more than they, and have justified your sisters by all the abominations which you have done. ⁵²You who judged your sisters, bear your own shame also, because the sins which you committed were more abominable than theirs; they are more righteous than you. Yes, be disgraced also, and bear your own shame, because you justified your sisters.

⁵³"When I bring back their captives, the captives of Sodom and her daughters, and the captives of Samaria and her daughters, then *I will also bring back* the captives of your captivity among them, ⁵⁴that you may bear your own shame and be disgraced by all that you did when you comforted them. ⁵⁵When your sisters, Sodom and her daughters, return to their former state, and Samaria and her daughters return to their former state, then you and your daughters will return to your former state. ⁵⁶For your sister Sodom was not a byword in your mouth in the days of your pride, ⁵⁷before your wickedness was uncovered. It was like the time of the reproach of the daughters of Syriaᵃ and all *those* around her, and of the daughters of the Philistines, who despise you everywhere. ⁵⁸You have paid for your lewdness and your abominations," says the LORD. ⁵⁹For thus says the Lord GOD: "I will deal with you as you have done, who despised the oath by breaking the covenant.

An Everlasting Covenant

⁶⁰"Nevertheless I will remember My covenant with you in the days of your youth, and I will establish an everlasting covenant with you. ⁶¹Then you will remember your ways and be ashamed, when you receive your older and your younger sisters; for I will give them to you for daughters, but not because of My covenant with you. ⁶²And I will establish My covenant with you. Then you shall know that I *am* the LORD, ⁶³that you may remember and be ashamed, and never open your mouth anymore because of your shame, when I provide you an atonement for all you have done," says the Lord GOD.'"

16:43 ᵃFollowing Septuagint, Syriac, Targum, and Vulgate; Masoretic Text reads *were agitated with Me.*
16:50 ᵃVulgate reads *you saw;* Septuagint reads *he saw;* Targum reads *as was revealed to Me.*
16:57 ᵃFollowing Masoretic Text, Septuagint, Targum, and Vulgate; many Hebrew manuscripts and Syriac read *Edom.*

The Eagles and the Vine

17 And the word of the LORD came to me, saying, [2]"Son of man, pose a riddle, and speak a parable to the house of Israel, [3]and say, 'Thus says the Lord GOD:

"A great eagle with large wings and
    long pinions,
Full of feathers of various colors,
Came to Lebanon
And took from the cedar the highest
    branch.
[4] He cropped off its topmost young
    twig
And carried it to a land of trade;
He set it in a city of merchants.
[5] Then he took some of the seed of
    the land
And planted it in a fertile field;
He placed *it* by abundant waters
And set it like a willow tree.
[6] And it grew and became a spreading
    vine of low stature;
Its branches turned toward him,
But its roots were under it.
So it became a vine,
Brought forth branches,
And put forth shoots.

[7] "But there was another[a] great eagle
    with large wings and many
    feathers;
And behold, this vine bent its roots
    toward him,
And stretched its branches toward
    him,
From the garden terrace where it had
    been planted,
That he might water it.
[8] It was planted in good soil by many
    waters,
To bring forth branches, bear fruit,
And become a majestic vine.'"

[9]"Say, 'Thus says the Lord GOD:

"Will it thrive?
Will he not pull up its roots,
Cut off its fruit,
And leave it to wither?
All of its spring leaves will wither,
And no great power or many people
Will be needed to pluck it up by its
    roots.

[10]   Behold, *it is* planted,
    Will it thrive?
    Will it not utterly wither when the
        east wind touches it?
    It will wither in the garden terrace
        where it grew.""'"

[11]Moreover the word of the LORD came to me, saying, [12]"Say now to the rebellious house: 'Do you not know what these *things mean?*' Tell *them,* 'Indeed the king of Babylon went to Jerusalem and took its king and princes, and led them with him to Babylon. [13]And he took the king's offspring, made a covenant with him, and put him under oath. He also took away the mighty of the land, [14]that the kingdom might be brought low and not lift itself up, *but* that by keeping his covenant it might stand. [15]But he rebelled against him by sending his ambassadors to Egypt, that they might give him horses and many people. Will he prosper? Will he who does such *things* escape? Can he break a covenant and still be delivered?

[16]'*As* I live,' says the Lord GOD, 'surely in the place *where* the king *dwells* who made him king, whose oath he despised and whose covenant he broke—with him in the midst of Babylon he shall die. [17]Nor will Pharaoh with *his* mighty army and great company do anything in the war, when they heap up a siege mound and build a wall to cut off many persons. [18]Since he despised the oath by breaking the covenant, and in fact gave his hand and still did all these *things,* he shall not escape.'"

[19]Therefore thus says the Lord GOD: "*As* I live, surely My oath which he despised, and My covenant which he broke, I will recompense on his own head. [20]I will spread My net over him, and he shall be taken in My snare. I will bring him to Babylon and try him there for the treason which he committed against Me. [21]All his fugitives[a] with all his troops shall fall by the sword, and those who remain shall be scattered to every wind; and you shall know that I, the LORD, have spoken."

17:7 [a]Following Septuagint, Syriac, and Vulgate; Masoretic Text and Targum read *one.* **17:21** [a]Following Masoretic Text and Vulgate; many Hebrew manuscripts and Syriac read *choice men;* Targum reads *mighty men;* Septuagint omits *All his fugitives.*

Israel Exalted at Last

²²Thus says the Lord GOD: "I will take also *one* of the highest branches of the high cedar and set *it* out. I will crop off from the topmost of its young twigs a tender one, and will plant *it* on a high and prominent mountain. ²³On the mountain height of Israel I will plant it; and it will bring forth boughs, and bear fruit, and be a majestic cedar. Under it will dwell birds of every sort; in the shadow of its branches they will dwell. ²⁴And all the trees of the field shall know that I, the LORD, have brought down the high tree and exalted the low tree, dried up the green tree and made the dry tree flourish; I, the LORD, have spoken and have done *it*."

A False Proverb Refuted

18 The word of the LORD came to me again, saying, ²"What do you mean when you use this proverb concerning the land of Israel, saying:

' The fathers have eaten sour grapes,
  And the children's teeth are set on
     edge'?

³"*As* I live," says the Lord GOD, "you shall no longer use this proverb in Israel.

⁴ "Behold, all souls are Mine;
  The soul of the father
  As well as the soul of the son is Mine;
  The soul who sins shall die.

5 But if a man is just
  And does what is lawful and right;
6 If he has not eaten on the mountains,
  Nor lifted up his eyes to the idols of
     the house of Israel,
  Nor defiled his neighbor's wife,
  Nor approached a woman during her
     impurity;
7 If he has not oppressed anyone,
  But has restored to the debtor his
     pledge;
  Has robbed no one by violence,
  But has given his bread to the
     hungry
  And covered the naked with
     clothing;
8 If he has not exacted usury
  Nor taken any increase,
  But has withdrawn his hand from
     iniquity
  And executed true judgment
     between man and man;
9 *If* he has walked in My statutes
  And kept My judgments faithfully—
  He *is* just;
  He shall surely live!"
  Says the Lord GOD.

10 "If he begets a son *who is* a robber
   Or a shedder of blood,
   Who does any of these *things*
11 And does none of those *duties*,
   But has eaten on the mountains
   Or defiled his neighbor's wife;

Make Sure You're Real

Over the years, we have learned that selfish people don't last long in relationships. Since we want our union to last, we have found that we need to be authentic, to be real, and to admit when we're wrong. Being real simply means admitting the truth, embracing it, and living by it. It means doing away with false fronts and silly masks.

In addition, we have come to realize that we are not very good listeners. Yet how can a couple be real if neither mate asks a question or listens carefully to the answer? How can a spouse feel valued if there is no genuine communication taking place?

The world cries out for people who live in *real* families, who represent a God who has given them something *real*—something better than the airbrushed images of *Better Homes and Gardens*.

How do you deal with household chaos? Do you put on a happy face and quote verses of Scripture, or do you deal with life in a real way, depending on God for real help? Pray that your family members will learn and grow as they move toward God's ideal for them, and that they will be real with one another.

12 If he has oppressed the poor and
    needy,
Robbed by violence,
Not restored the pledge,
Lifted his eyes to the idols,
Or committed abomination;
13 If he has exacted usury
Or taken increase—
Shall he then live?
He shall not live!
If he has done any of these
    abominations,
He shall surely die;
His blood shall be upon him.

14 "*If,* however, he begets a son
Who sees all the sins which his
    father has done,
And considers but does not do
    likewise;
15 *Who* has not eaten on the mountains,
Nor lifted his eyes to the idols of the
    house of Israel,
Nor defiled his neighbor's wife;
16 Has not oppressed anyone,
Nor withheld a pledge,
Nor robbed by violence,
But has given his bread to the hungry
And covered the naked with clothing;
17 *Who* has withdrawn his hand from
    the poor[a]
And not received usury or increase,
But has executed My judgments
And walked in My statutes—
He shall not die for the iniquity of
    his father;
He shall surely live!

18 "*As for* his father,
Because he cruelly oppressed,
Robbed his brother by violence,
And did what *is* not good among his
    people,
Behold, he shall die for his iniquity.

Turn and Live

19 "Yet you say, 'Why should the son not bear the guilt of the father?' Because the son has done what is lawful and right, and has kept all My statutes and observed them, he shall surely live. 20 The soul who sins shall die. The son shall not bear the guilt of the father, nor the father bear the guilt of the son. The righteousness of the righteous shall be upon himself, and the wickedness of the wicked shall be upon himself.

21 "But if a wicked man turns from all his sins which he has committed, keeps all My statutes, and does what is lawful and right, he shall surely live; he shall not die. 22 None of the transgressions which he has committed shall be remembered against him; because of the righteousness which he has done, he shall live. 23 Do I have any pleasure at all that the wicked should die?" says the Lord GOD, "*and* not that he should turn from his ways and live?

24 "But when a righteous man turns away from his righteousness and commits iniquity, and does according to all the abominations that the wicked *man* does, shall he live? All the righteousness which he has done shall not be remembered; because of the unfaithfulness of which he is guilty and the sin which he has committed, because of them he shall die.

25 "Yet you say, 'The way of the Lord is not fair.' Hear now, O house of Israel, is it not My way which is fair, and your ways which are not fair? 26 When a righteous *man* turns away from his righteousness, commits iniquity, and dies in it, it is because of the iniquity which he has done that he dies. 27 Again, when a wicked *man* turns away from the wickedness which he committed, and does what is lawful and right, he preserves himself alive. 28 Because he considers and turns away from all the transgressions which he committed, he shall surely live; he shall not die. 29 Yet the house of Israel says, 'The way of the Lord is not fair.' O house of Israel, is it not My ways which are fair, and your ways which are not fair?

30 "Therefore I will judge you, O house of Israel, every one according to his ways," says the Lord GOD. "Repent, and turn from all your transgressions, so that iniquity will not be your ruin. 31 Cast away from you all the transgressions which you have committed, and get yourselves a new heart and a new spirit. For why should you die, O house of Israel? 32 For I have no pleasure in the death of one who dies," says the Lord GOD. "Therefore turn and live!"

18:17 [a] Following Masoretic Text, Targum, and Vulgate; Septuagint reads *iniquity* (compare verse 8).

Israel Degraded

19 "Moreover take up a lamentation for the princes of Israel, ²and say:

' What *is* your mother? A lioness:
   She lay down among the lions;
Among the young lions she
      nourished her cubs.
³ She brought up one of her cubs,
   And he became a young lion;
He learned to catch prey,
   And he devoured men.
⁴ The nations also heard of him;
   He was trapped in their pit,
And they brought him with chains to
      the land of Egypt.

⁵ 'When she saw that she waited, *that*
      her hope was lost,
She took another of her cubs *and*
      made him a young lion.
⁶ He roved among the lions,
   And became a young lion;
He learned to catch prey;
   He devoured men.
⁷ He knew their desolate places,ᵃ
   And laid waste their cities;
The land with its fullness was
      desolated
By the noise of his roaring.
⁸ Then the nations set against him
      from the provinces on every side,
And spread their net over him;
   He was trapped in their pit.
⁹ They put him in a cage with chains,
   And brought him to the king of
      Babylon;
They brought him in nets,
   That his voice should no longer be
      heard on the mountains of Israel.

¹⁰ 'Your mother *was* like a vine in your
      bloodline,ᵃ
Planted by the waters,
   Fruitful and full of branches
Because of many waters.
¹¹ She had strong branches for scepters
      of rulers.

She towered in stature above the
      thick branches,
And was seen in her height amid the
      dense foliage.
¹² But she was plucked up in fury,
   She was cast down to the ground,
And the east wind dried her fruit.
Her strong branches were broken
      and withered;
   The fire consumed them.
¹³ And now she *is* planted in the
      wilderness,
In a dry and thirsty land.
¹⁴ Fire has come out from a rod of her
      branches
And devoured her fruit,
So that she has no strong branch— a
      scepter for ruling.'"

This *is* a lamentation, and has become a lamentation.

The Rebellions of Israel

20 It came to pass in the seventh year, in the fifth *month,* on the tenth *day* of the month, *that* certain of the elders of Israel came to inquire of the LORD, and sat before me. ²Then the word of the LORD came to me, saying, ³"Son of man, speak to the elders of Israel, and say to them, 'Thus says the Lord GOD: "Have you come to inquire of Me? *As* I live," says the Lord GOD, "I will not be inquired of by you."' ⁴Will you judge them, son of man, will you judge *them?* Then make known to them the abominations of their fathers.

⁵"Say to them, 'Thus says the Lord GOD: "On the day when I chose Israel and raised My hand in an oath to the descendants of the house of Jacob, and made Myself known to them in the land of Egypt, I raised My hand in an oath to them, saying, 'I *am* the LORD your God.' ⁶On that day I raised My hand in an oath to them, to bring them out of the land of Egypt into a land that I had searched out for them, 'flowing with milk and honey,'ᵃ the glory of all lands. ⁷Then I said to them, 'Each of you, throw away the abominations which are before his eyes, and do not defile yourselves with the idols of Egypt. I *am* the LORD your God.' ⁸But they rebelled against Me and would not obey Me. They did not

---

19:7 ᵃSeptuagint reads *He stood in insolence;* Targum reads *He destroyed its palaces;* Vulgate reads *He learned to make widows.* **19:10** ᵃLiterally *blood,* following Masoretic Text, Syriac, and Vulgate; Septuagint reads *like a flower on a pomegranate tree;* Targum reads *in your likeness.* **20:6** ᵃExodus 3:8

all cast away the abominations which were before their eyes, nor did they forsake the idols of Egypt. Then I said, 'I will pour out My fury on them and fulfill My anger against them in the midst of the land of Egypt.' ⁹But I acted for My name's sake, that it should not be profaned before the Gentiles among whom they *were,* in whose sight I had made Myself known to them, to bring them out of the land of Egypt.

¹⁰"Therefore I made them go out of the land of Egypt and brought them into the wilderness. ¹¹And I gave them My statutes and showed them My judgments, 'which, *if* a man does, he shall live by them.'ª ¹²Moreover I also gave them My Sabbaths, to be a sign between them and Me, that they might know that I *am* the LORD who sanctifies them. ¹³Yet the house of Israel rebelled against Me in the wilderness; they did not walk in My statutes; they despised My judgments, 'which, *if* a man does, he shall live by them';ª and they greatly defiled My Sabbaths. Then I said I would pour out My fury on them in the wilderness, to consume them. ¹⁴But I acted for My name's sake, that it should not be profaned before the Gentiles, in whose sight I had brought them out. ¹⁵So I also raised My hand in an oath to them in the wilderness, that I would not bring them into the land which I had given *them,* 'flowing with milk and honey,'ª the glory of all lands, ¹⁶because they despised My judgments and did not walk in My statutes, but profaned My Sabbaths; for their heart went after their idols. ¹⁷Nevertheless My eye spared them from destruction. I did not make an end of them in the wilderness.

¹⁸"But I said to their children in the wilderness, 'Do not walk in the statutes of your fathers, nor observe their judgments, nor defile yourselves with their idols. ¹⁹I *am* the LORD your God: Walk in My statutes, keep My judgments, and do them; ²⁰hallow My Sabbaths, and they will be a sign between Me and you, that you may know that I *am* the LORD your God.'

20:11 ªLeviticus 18:5   **20:13** ªLeviticus 18:5
20:15 ªExodus 3:8

| PARENTING MATTERS | **Q: *How should we handle our children when they test our authority?*** |

Most people have heard the expression, "Exactly what part of the word 'no' don't you understand?"

When our children were still at home, Barbara and I often got bombarded by our half-dozen banditos who wanted to persuade us to say yes when we had already said no. If they didn't get their way the first time, they'd come back and try a second, third, and even fourth pass. What is there about the word *no* that they didn't understand? Barbara and I came up with a couple of answers.

First, it's a child's nature to press issues, ignore, defy, rebel, challenge, resist, or just flat out disobey. Even the Minnesota Crime Commission has said, "Every baby starts life as a little savage. He is completely selfish and self-centered ... All children ... are born delinquents." Children *will* test you, and it's your responsibility to discipline them.

Second, we parents have trained them that way. Our children are better students of us than we are of them! They can spot flaws and manipulate our weaknesses to their advantage. If they discover they can wear you down with their requests, they'll do it.

We need to prayerfully pause and become students of ourselves, asking whether we are strong parents, or easily manipulated tools in this universal conspiracy of children.

²¹"Notwithstanding, the children rebelled against Me; they did not walk in My statutes, and were not careful to observe My judgments, 'which, *if* a man does, he shall live by them';ᵃ but they profaned My Sabbaths. Then I said I would pour out My fury on them and fulfill My anger against them in the wilderness. ²²Nevertheless I withdrew My hand and acted for My name's sake, that it should not be profaned in the sight of the Gentiles, in whose sight I had brought them out. ²³Also I raised My hand in an oath to those in the wilderness, that I would scatter them among the Gentiles and disperse them throughout the countries, ²⁴because they had not executed My judgments, but had despised My statutes, profaned My Sabbaths, and their eyes were fixed on their fathers' idols.

²⁵"Therefore I also gave them up to statutes *that were* not good, and judgments by which they could not live; ²⁶and I pronounced them unclean because of their ritual gifts, in that they caused all their firstborn to pass through *the fire,* that I might make them desolate and that they might know that I am the LORD." '

²⁷"Therefore, son of man, speak to the house of Israel, and say to them, 'Thus says the Lord GOD: "In this too your fathers have blasphemed Me, by being unfaithful to Me. ²⁸When I brought them into the land *concerning* which I had raised My hand in an oath to give them, and they saw all the high hills and all the thick trees, there they offered their sacrifices and provoked Me with their offerings. There they also sent up their sweet aroma and poured out their drink offerings. ²⁹Then I said to them, 'What *is* this high place to which you go?' So its name is called Bamahᵃ to this day." ' ³⁰Therefore say to the house of Israel, 'Thus says the Lord GOD: "Are you defiling yourselves in the manner of your fathers, and committing harlotry according to their abominations? ³¹For when you offer your gifts and make your sons pass through the fire, you defile yourselves with all your idols, even to this day. So shall I be inquired of by

you, O house of Israel? *As* I live," says the Lord GOD, "I will not be inquired of by you. ³²What you have in your mind shall never be, when you say, 'We will be like the Gentiles, like the families in other countries, serving wood and stone.'

God Will Restore Israel

³³"*As* I live," says the Lord GOD, "surely with a mighty hand, with an outstretched arm, and with fury poured out, I will rule over you. ³⁴I will bring you out from the peoples and gather you out of the countries where you are scattered, with a mighty hand, with an outstretched arm, and with fury poured out. ³⁵And I will bring you into the wilderness of the peoples, and there I will plead My case with you face to face. ³⁶Just as I pleaded My case with your fathers in the wilderness of the land of Egypt, so I will plead My case with you," says the Lord GOD.

³⁷"I will make you pass under the rod, and I will bring you into the bond of the covenant; ³⁸I will purge the rebels from among you, and those who transgress against Me; I will bring them out of the country where they dwell, but they shall not enter the land of Israel. Then you will know that I *am* the LORD.

³⁹"As for you, O house of Israel," thus says the Lord GOD: "Go, serve every one of you his idols—and hereafter—if you will not obey Me; but profane My holy name no more with your gifts and your idols. ⁴⁰For on My holy mountain, on the mountain height of Israel," says the Lord GOD, "there all the house of Israel, all of them in the land, shall serve Me; there I will accept them, and there I will require your offerings and the firstfruits of your sacrifices, together with all your holy things. ⁴¹I will accept you as a sweet aroma when I bring you out from the peoples and gather you out of the countries where you have been scattered; and I will be hallowed in you before the Gentiles. ⁴²Then you shall know that I *am* the LORD, when I bring you into the land of Israel, into the country *for* which I raised My hand in an oath to give to your fathers. ⁴³And there you shall remember your ways and all your doings with which you were defiled; and you shall

loathe yourselves in your own sight because of all the evils that you have committed. ⁴⁴Then you shall know that I *am* the LORD, when I have dealt with you for My name's sake, not according to your wicked ways nor according to your corrupt doings, O house of Israel," says the Lord GOD.'"

Fire in the Forest

⁴⁵Furthermore the word of the LORD came to me, saying, ⁴⁶"Son of man, set your face toward the south; preach against the south and prophesy against the forest land, the South,ᵃ ⁴⁷and say to the forest of the South, 'Hear the word of the LORD! Thus says the Lord GOD: "Behold, I will kindle a fire in you, and it shall devour every green tree and every dry tree in you; the blazing flame shall not be quenched, and all faces from the south to the north shall be scorched by it. ⁴⁸All flesh shall see that I, the LORD, have kindled it; it shall not be quenched."'"

⁴⁹Then I said, "Ah, Lord GOD! They say of me, 'Does he not speak parables?'"

Babylon, the Sword of God

21 And the word of the LORD came to me, saying, ²"Son of man, set your face toward Jerusalem, preach against the holy places, and prophesy against the land of Israel; ³and say to the land of Israel, 'Thus says the LORD: "Behold, I *am* against you, and I will draw My sword out of its sheath and cut off both righteous and wicked from you. ⁴Because I will cut off both righteous and wicked from you, therefore My sword shall go out of its sheath against all flesh from south *to* north, ⁵that all flesh may know that I, the LORD, have drawn My sword out of its sheath; it shall not return anymore."' ⁶Sigh therefore, son of man, with a breaking heart, and sigh with bitterness before their eyes. ⁷And it shall be when they say to you, 'Why are you sighing?' that you shall answer, 'Because of the news; when it comes, every heart will melt, all hands will be feeble, every spirit will faint, and all knees will be weak *as* water. Behold, it is coming and shall be brought to pass,' says the Lord GOD."

⁸Again the word of the LORD came to me, saying, ⁹"Son of man, prophesy and say, 'Thus says the LORD!' Say:

'A sword, a sword is sharpened
And also polished!
10   Sharpened to make a dreadful
        slaughter;
        Polished to flash like lightning!
        Should we then make mirth?
        It despises the scepter of My son,
        As it does all wood.
11   And He has given it to be polished,
        That it may be handled;
        This sword is sharpened, and it is
        polished
        To be given into the hand of the
        slayer.'

12   "Cry and wail, son of man;
        For it will be against My people,
        Against all the princes of Israel.
        Terrors including the sword will be
        against My people;
        Therefore strike *your* thigh.

13   "Because *it is* a testing,
        And what if *the sword* despises even
        the scepter?
        The scepter shall be no *more*,"

says the Lord GOD.

14   "You therefore, son of man, prophesy,
        And strike *your* hands together.
        The third time let the sword do
        double *damage.*
        It *is* the sword *that* slays,
        The sword that slays the great *men,*
        That enters their private chambers.
15   I have set the point of the sword
        against all their gates,
        That the heart may melt and many
        may stumble.
        Ah! *It is* made bright;
        It is grasped for slaughter:

16   "Swords at the ready!
        Thrust right!
        Set your blade!
        Thrust left—
        Wherever your edge is ordered!

17   "I also will beat My fists together,
        And I will cause My fury to rest;
        I, the LORD, have spoken."

20:46 ᵃHebrew *Negev*

[18]The word of the Lord came to me again, saying: [19]"And son of man, appoint for yourself two ways for the sword of the king of Babylon to go; both of them shall go from the same land. Make a sign; put *it* at the head of the road to the city. [20]Appoint a road for the sword to go to Rabbah of the Ammonites, and to Judah, into fortified Jerusalem. [21]For the king of Babylon stands at the parting of the road, at the fork of the two roads, to use divination: he shakes the arrows, he consults the images, he looks at the liver. [22]In his right hand is the divination for Jerusalem: to set up battering rams, to call for a slaughter, to lift the voice with shouting, to set battering rams against the gates, to heap up a *siege* mound, and to build a wall. [23]And it will be to them like a false divination in the eyes of those who have sworn oaths with them; but he will bring their iniquity to remembrance, that they may be taken.

[24]"Therefore thus says the Lord God: 'Because you have made your iniquity to be remembered, in that your transgressions are uncovered, so that in all your doings your sins appear—because you have come to remembrance, you shall be taken in hand.

[25]'Now to you, O profane, wicked prince of Israel, whose day has come, whose iniquity *shall* end, [26]thus says the Lord God:

"Remove the turban, and take off the
　　crown;
Nothing *shall remain* the same.
Exalt the humble, and humble the
　　exalted.
[27]Overthrown, overthrown,
I will make it overthrown!
It shall be no *longer,*
Until He comes whose right it is,
And I will give it *to Him.*"'

A Sword Against the Ammonites

[28]"And you, son of man, prophesy and say, 'Thus says the Lord God concerning the Ammonites and concerning their reproach,' and say:

'A sword, a sword *is* drawn,
Polished for slaughter,
For consuming, for flashing—

[29]While they see false visions for you,
While they divine a lie to you,
To bring you on the necks of the
　　wicked, the slain
Whose day has come,
Whose iniquity *shall* end.

[30]'Return *it* to its sheath.
I will judge you
In the place where you were created,
In the land of your nativity.
[31]I will pour out My indignation on you;
I will blow against you with the fire
　　of My wrath,
And deliver you into the hands of
　　brutal men *who are* skillful to
　　destroy.
[32]You shall be fuel for the fire;
Your blood shall be in the midst of
　　the land.
You shall not be remembered,
For I the Lord have spoken.'"

Sins of Jerusalem

22 Moreover the word of the Lord came to me, saying, [2]"Now, son of man, will you judge, will you judge the bloody city? Yes, show her all her abominations! [3]Then say, 'Thus says the Lord God: "The city sheds blood in her own midst, that her time may come; and she makes idols within herself to defile herself. [4]You have become guilty by the blood which you have shed, and have defiled yourself with the idols which you have made. You have caused your days to draw near, and have come to *the end of* your years; therefore I have made you a reproach to the nations, and a mockery to all countries. [5]*Those* near and *those* far from you will mock you as infamous *and* full of tumult.

[6]"Look, the princes of Israel: each one has used his power to shed blood in you. [7]In you they have made light of father and mother; in your midst they have oppressed the stranger; in you they have mistreated the fatherless and the widow. [8]You have despised My holy things and profaned My Sabbaths. [9]In you are men who slander to cause bloodshed; in you are those who eat on the mountains; in your midst they commit lewdness. [10]In you men uncover their fathers' nakedness; in you they violate

The Forgotten Commandment

DURING THE EARLY 1970'S, I worked with teenagers in a ministry in Boulder, Colorado. I titled one of my favorite messages, "How to Raise Your Parents," but my real challenge to these teens was to obey God's commandment, "Honor your father and your mother" (Ex. 20:12).

My message touched a raw nerve. Many teens had such difficult relationships with their parents that this command presented a challenge of immense proportions.

Years later in the 1980s, I taught a summer class to graduate students preparing for vocational ministry. The lecture called "Honoring Your Parents" surprisingly sparked the greatest response. Every summer, dozens of students who had difficult relationships with their parents left that class in tears, motivated to better honor their parents. One young man handed me a note describing how he waited too long to honor his dad. His father died of a heart attack two hours before the young man could say, "Dad, I love you."

Even by Ezekiel's time, people had so neglected this commandment that they actually "made light of father and mother" (22:7)—a sin that helped pave the road to exile. Today we could even call it "The Forgotten Commandment."

Don't let this be true in your life! Find ways to honor your mom and dad. God's promise to a culture that honors parents is "that it may be well with you and you may live long on the earth" (Eph. 6:3).

women who are set apart during their impurity. ¹¹One commits abomination with his neighbor's wife; another lewdly defiles his daughter-in-law; and another in you violates his sister, his father's daughter. ¹²In you they take bribes to shed blood; you take usury and increase; you have made profit from your neighbors by extortion, and have forgotten Me," says the Lord GOD.

¹³"Behold, therefore, I beat My fists at the dishonest profit which you have made, and at the bloodshed which has been in your midst. ¹⁴Can your heart endure, or can your hands remain strong, in the days when I shall deal with you? I, the LORD, have spoken, and will do *it*. ¹⁵I will scatter you among the nations, disperse you throughout the countries, and remove your filthiness completely from you. ¹⁶You shall defile yourself in the sight of the nations; then you shall know that I *am* the LORD."'"

Israel in the Furnace

¹⁷The word of the LORD came to me, saying, ¹⁸"Son of man, the house of Israel has become dross to Me; they *are* all bronze, tin, iron, and lead, in the midst of a furnace; they have become dross from silver. ¹⁹Therefore thus says the Lord GOD: 'Because you have all become dross, therefore behold, I will gather you into the midst of Jerusalem. ²⁰*As men* gather silver, bronze, iron, lead, and tin into the midst of a furnace, to blow fire on it, to melt *it;* so I will gather *you* in My anger and in My fury, and I will leave *you there* and melt you. ²¹Yes, I will gather you and blow on you with the fire of My wrath, and you shall be melted in its midst. ²²As silver is melted in the midst of a furnace, so shall you be melted in its midst; then you shall know that I, the LORD, have poured out My fury on you.'"

Israel's Wicked Leaders

²³And the word of the LORD came to me, saying, ²⁴"Son of man, say to her: 'You *are* a land that is not cleansed[a] or rained on in the day of indignation.' ²⁵The conspiracy of her prophets[a] in her midst is like a roaring lion tearing the prey; they have devoured people; they have taken treasure and precious things; they have made many widows in her midst. ²⁶Her priests have violated My law and profaned My holy things; they have not distinguished between the holy and unholy, nor have

22:24 [a]Following Masoretic Text, Syriac, and Vulgate; Septuagint reads *showered upon.*
22:25 [a]Following Masoretic Text and Vulgate; Septuagint reads *princes;* Targum reads *scribes.*

they made known *the difference* between the unclean and the clean; and they have hidden their eyes from My Sabbaths, so that I am profaned among them. ²⁷Her princes in her midst *are* like wolves tearing the prey, to shed blood, to destroy people, and to get dishonest gain. ²⁸Her prophets plastered them with untempered *mortar,* seeing false visions, and divining lies for them, saying, 'Thus says the Lord GOD,' when the LORD had not spoken. ²⁹The people of the land have used oppressions, committed robbery, and mistreated the poor and needy; and they wrongfully oppress the stranger. ³⁰So I sought for a man among them who would make a wall, and stand in the gap before Me on behalf of the land, that I should not destroy it; but I found no one. ³¹Therefore I have poured out My indignation on them; I have consumed them with the fire of My wrath; and I have recompensed their deeds on their own heads," says the Lord GOD.

Two Harlot Sisters

23 The word of the LORD came again to me, saying:

2   "Son of man, there were two women,
     The daughters of one mother.
3   They committed harlotry in Egypt,
     They committed harlotry in their
       youth;
     Their breasts were there embraced,
     Their virgin bosom was there
       pressed.
4   Their names: Oholah^a the elder and
       Oholibah^b her sister;
     They were Mine,
     And they bore sons and daughters.
     As for their names,
     Samaria *is* Oholah, and Jerusalem *is*
       Oholibah.

The Older Sister, Samaria

5   "Oholah played the harlot even
       though she was Mine;
     And she lusted for her lovers, the
       neighboring Assyrians,
6   *Who were* clothed in purple,

     Captains and rulers,
     All of them desirable young men,
     Horsemen riding on horses.
7   Thus she committed her harlotry
       with them,
     All of them choice men of Assyria;
     And with all for whom she lusted,
     With all their idols, she defiled
       herself.
8   She has never given up her harlotry
       brought from Egypt,
     For in her youth they had lain with
       her,
     Pressed her virgin bosom,
     And poured out their immorality
       upon her.

9   "Therefore I have delivered her
     Into the hand of her lovers,
     Into the hand of the Assyrians,
     For whom she lusted.
10   They uncovered her nakedness,
     Took away her sons and daughters,
     And slew her with the sword;
     She became a byword among women,
     For they had executed judgment on
       her.

The Younger Sister, Jerusalem

¹¹"Now although her sister Oholibah saw *this,* she became more corrupt in her lust than she, and in her harlotry more corrupt than her sister's harlotry.

12   "She lusted for the neighboring
       Assyrians,
     Captains and rulers,
     Clothed most gorgeously,
     Horsemen riding on horses,
     All of them desirable young men.
13   Then I saw that she was defiled;
     Both *took* the same way.
14   But she increased her harlotry;
     She looked at men portrayed on the
       wall,
     Images of Chaldeans portrayed in
       vermilion,
15   Girded with belts around their
       waists,
     Flowing turbans on their heads,
     All of them looking like captains,
     In the manner of the Babylonians of
       Chaldea,
     The land of their nativity.

23:4 ^a Literally *Her Own Tabernacle* ^b Literally *My Tabernacle Is in Her*

16   As soon as her eyes saw them,
She lusted for them
And sent messengers to them in
   Chaldea.

17   "Then the Babylonians came to her,
   into the bed of love,
And they defiled her with their
   immorality;
So she was defiled by them, and
   alienated herself from them.

18   She revealed her harlotry and
   uncovered her nakedness.
Then I alienated Myself from her,
As I had alienated Myself from her
   sister.

19   "Yet she multiplied her harlotry
In calling to remembrance the days
   of her youth,
When she had played the harlot in
   the land of Egypt.

20   For she lusted for her paramours,
Whose flesh *is like* the flesh of
   donkeys,
And whose issue *is like* the issue of
   horses.

21   Thus you called to remembrance the
   lewdness of your youth,
When the Egyptians pressed your
   bosom
Because of your youthful breasts.

Judgment on Jerusalem

22 "Therefore, Oholibah, thus says the
Lord GOD:

'Behold, I will stir up your lovers
   against you,
From whom you have alienated
   yourself,
And I will bring them against you
   from every side:

23   The Babylonians,
All the Chaldeans,
Pekod, Shoa, Koa,
All the Assyrians with them,
All of them desirable young men,
Governors and rulers,
Captains and men of renown,
All of them riding on horses.

24   And they shall come against you
With chariots, wagons, and war-
   horses,
With a horde of people.

They shall array against you
Buckler, shield, and helmet all
   around.

'I will delegate judgment to them,
And they shall judge you according
   to their judgments.

25   I will set My jealousy against you,
And they shall deal furiously with
   you;
They shall remove your nose and
   your ears,
And your remnant shall fall by the
   sword;
They shall take your sons and your
   daughters,
And your remnant shall be devoured
   by fire.

26   They shall also strip you of your
   clothes
And take away your beautiful
   jewelry.

27   'Thus I will make you cease your
   lewdness and your harlotry
Brought from the land of Egypt,
So that you will not lift your eyes to
   them,
Nor remember Egypt anymore.'

28"For thus says the Lord GOD: 'Surely I
will deliver you into the hand of those you
hate, into the hand *of those* from whom
you alienated yourself. 29They will deal
hatefully with you, take away all you have
worked for, and leave you naked and bare.
The nakedness of your harlotry shall be
uncovered, both your lewdness and your
harlotry. 30I will do these *things* to you
because you have gone as a harlot after the
Gentiles, because you have become defiled
by their idols. 31You have walked in the
way of your sister; therefore I will put her
cup in your hand.'

32"Thus says the Lord GOD:

'You shall drink of your sister's cup,
The deep and wide one;
You shall be laughed to scorn
And held in derision;
It contains much.

33   You will be filled with drunkenness
   and sorrow,
The cup of horror and desolation,
The cup of your sister Samaria.

34 You shall drink and drain it,
You shall break its shards,
And tear at your own breasts;
For I have spoken,'
Says the Lord GOD.

35"Therefore thus says the Lord GOD:

'Because you have forgotten Me and
cast Me behind your back,
Therefore you shall bear the *penalty*
Of your lewdness and your harlotry.'"

Both Sisters Judged

36The LORD also said to me: "Son of man, will you judge Oholah and Oholibah? Then declare to them their abominations. 37For they have committed adultery, and blood *is* on their hands. They have committed adultery with their idols, and even *sacrificed* their sons whom they bore to Me, passing them through *the fire,* to devour *them.* 38Moreover they have done this to Me: They have defiled My sanctuary on the same day and profaned My Sabbaths. 39For after they had slain their children for their idols, on the same day they came into My sanctuary to profane it; and indeed thus they have done in the midst of My house.

40"Furthermore you sent for men to come from afar, to whom a messenger *was* sent; and there they came. And you washed yourself for them, painted your eyes, and adorned yourself with ornaments. 41You sat on a stately couch, with a table prepared before it, on which you had set My incense and My oil. 42The sound of a carefree multitude *was* with her, and Sabeans *were* brought from the wilderness with men of the common sort, who put bracelets on their wrists and beautiful crowns on their heads. 43Then I said concerning *her who had grown* old in adulteries, 'Will they commit harlotry with her now, and she *with them?'* 44Yet they went in to her, as men go in to a woman who plays the harlot; thus they went in to Oholah and Oholibah, the lewd women. 45But righteous men will judge them after the manner of adulteresses, and after the manner of women who shed blood, because they *are* adulteresses, and blood *is* on their hands.

46"For thus says the Lord GOD: 'Bring up an assembly against them, give them up to trouble and plunder. 47The assembly shall stone them with stones and execute them with their swords; they shall slay their sons and their daughters, and burn their houses with fire. 48Thus I will cause lewdness to cease from the land, that all women may be taught not to practice your lewdness. 49They shall repay you for your lewdness, and you shall pay for your idolatrous sins. Then you shall know that I *am* the Lord GOD.'"

ROMANCE FAQ

Q: Is it wise to tell my spouse that I really need him/her?

Spouses who frequently and specifically verbalize their need for one another cement true partnerships. Yet somewhere between the wedding aisle and the fifth anniversary, a thief often makes off with such mutual admissions. How ironic that marriage, the ultimate admission of one person's need for another, would end up being an accomplice to the thief!

Think back to those early days of romance and intrigue. She made you laugh. He made you feel secure and stable. She brought warmth into a room. His touch transformed a drab apartment into a home. You knew you needed your mate because he or she:

- stopped to smell the roses that you didn't even notice were growing
- made art and museums come alive
- was organized and you weren't
- shared openly and honestly about emotions, whereas you locked up your feelings
- listened when you really needed someone to hear you

But perhaps most importantly, you needed to feel valued and important, and here was another person who authentically admitted he or she needed to spend the rest of his or her life with you.

Recapture those days! You can't afford not to.

Symbol of the Cooking Pot

24 Again, in the ninth year, in the tenth month, on the tenth *day* of the month, the word of the LORD came to me, saying, 2"Son of man, write down the name of the day, this very day—the king of Babylon started his siege against Jerusalem this very day. 3And utter a parable to the rebellious house, and say to them, 'Thus says the Lord GOD:

"Put on a pot, set *it* on,
    And also pour water into it.
4   Gather pieces *of meat* in it,
    Every good piece,
    The thigh and the shoulder.
    Fill *it* with choice cuts;
5   Take the choice of the flock.
    Also pile *fuel* bones under it,
    Make it boil well,
    And let the cuts simmer in it."

6'Therefore thus says the Lord GOD:

"Woe to the bloody city,
    To the pot whose scum *is* in it,
    And whose scum is not gone
        from it!
    Bring it out piece by piece,
    On which no lot has fallen.
7   For her blood is in her midst;
    She set it on top of a rock;
    She did not pour it on the ground,
    To cover it with dust.
8   That it may raise up fury and take
        vengeance,
    I have set her blood on top of a rock,
    That it may not be covered."

9'Therefore thus says the Lord GOD:

"Woe to the bloody city!
    I too will make the pyre great.
10 Heap on the wood,
    Kindle the fire;
    Cook the meat well,
    Mix in the spices,
    And let the cuts be burned up.
11 "Then set the pot empty on the coals,
    That it may become hot and its
        bronze may burn,
    That its filthiness may be melted
        in it,
    That its scum may be consumed.

12 She has grown weary with lies,
    And her great scum has not gone
        from her.
    Let her scum *be* in the fire!
13 In your filthiness *is* lewdness.
    Because I have cleansed you, and
        you were not cleansed,
    You will not be cleansed of your
        filthiness anymore,
    Till I have caused My fury to rest
        upon you.
14 I, the LORD, have spoken *it;*
    It shall come to pass, and I will do *it;*
    I will not hold back,
    Nor will I spare,
    Nor will I relent;
    According to your ways
    And according to your deeds
    They[a] will judge you,"
    Says the Lord GOD.'"

The Prophet's Wife Dies

15Also the word of the LORD came to me, saying, 16"Son of man, behold, I take away from you the desire of your eyes with one stroke; yet you shall neither mourn nor weep, nor shall your tears run down. 17Sigh in silence, make no mourning for the dead; bind your turban on your head, and put your sandals on your feet; do not cover *your* lips, and do not eat man's bread *of sorrow.*"

18So I spoke to the people in the morning, and at evening my wife died; and the next morning I did as I was commanded.

19And the people said to me, "Will you not tell us what these *things signify* to us, that you behave so?"

20Then I answered them, "The word of the LORD came to me, saying, 21'Speak to the house of Israel, "Thus says the Lord GOD: 'Behold, I will profane My sanctuary, your arrogant boast, the desire of your eyes, the delight of your soul; and your sons and daughters whom you left behind shall fall by the sword. 22And you shall do as I have done; you shall not cover *your* lips nor eat man's bread *of sorrow.* 23Your turbans shall be on your heads and your sandals on your feet; you shall neither

---

24:14 [a]Septuagint, Syriac, Targum, and Vulgate read *I.*

mourn nor weep, but you shall pine away in your iniquities and mourn with one another. ²⁴Thus Ezekiel is a sign to you; according to all that he has done you shall do; and when this comes, you shall know that I *am* the Lord GOD.'"

²⁵'And you, son of man—*will it* not *be* in the day when I take from them their stronghold, their joy and their glory, the desire of their eyes, and that on which they set their minds, their sons and their daughters: ²⁶*that* on that day one who escapes will come to you to let *you* hear *it* with *your* ears? ²⁷On that day your mouth will be opened to him who has escaped; you shall speak and no longer be mute. Thus you will be a sign to them, and they shall know that I *am* the LORD.'"

Proclamation Against Ammon

25 The word of the LORD came to me, saying, ²"Son of man, set your face against the Ammonites, and prophesy against them. ³Say to the Ammonites, 'Hear the word of the Lord GOD! Thus says the Lord GOD: "Because you said, 'Aha!' against My sanctuary when it was profaned, and against the land of Israel when it was desolate, and against the house of Judah when they went into captivity, ⁴indeed, therefore, I will deliver you as a possession to the men of the East, and they shall set their encampments among you and make their dwellings among you; they shall eat your fruit, and they shall drink your milk. ⁵And I will make Rabbah a stable for camels and Ammon a resting place for flocks. Then you shall know that I *am* the LORD."

⁶'For thus says the Lord GOD: "Because you clapped *your* hands, stamped your feet, and rejoiced in heart with all your disdain for the land of Israel, ⁷indeed, therefore, I will stretch out My hand against you, and give you as plunder to the nations; I will cut you off from the peoples, and I will cause you to perish from the countries; I will destroy you, and you shall know that I *am* the LORD."

Proclamation Against Moab

⁸Thus says the Lord GOD: "Because Moab and Seir say, 'Look! The house of Judah *is* like all the nations,' ⁹therefore, behold, I will clear the territory of Moab of cities, of the cities on its frontier, the glory of the country, Beth Jeshimoth, Baal Meon, and Kirjathaim. ¹⁰To the men of the East I will give it as a possession, together with the Ammonites, that the Ammonites may not be remembered among the nations. ¹¹And I will execute judgments upon Moab, and they shall know that I *am* the LORD."

Proclamation Against Edom

¹²Thus says the Lord GOD: "Because of what Edom did against the house of Judah by taking vengeance, and has greatly offended by avenging itself on them," ¹³therefore thus says the Lord GOD: "I will also stretch out My hand against Edom, cut off man and beast from it, and make it desolate from Teman; Dedan shall fall by the sword. ¹⁴I will lay My vengeance on Edom by the hand of My people Israel, that they may do in Edom according to My anger and according to My fury; and they shall know My vengeance," says the Lord GOD.

Proclamation Against Philistia

¹⁵'Thus says the Lord GOD: "Because the Philistines dealt vengefully and took vengeance with a spiteful heart, to destroy because of the old hatred," ¹⁶therefore thus says the Lord GOD: "I will stretch out My hand against the Philistines, and I will cut off the Cherethites and destroy the remnant of the seacoast. ¹⁷I will execute great vengeance on them with furious rebukes; and they shall know that I *am* the LORD, when I lay My vengeance upon them."'"

Proclamation Against Tyre

26 And it came to pass in the eleventh year, on the first *day* of the month, *that* the word of the LORD came to me, saying, ²"Son of man, because Tyre has said against Jerusalem, 'Aha! She is broken who *was* the gateway of the peoples; now she is turned over to me; I shall be filled; she is laid waste.'

³"Therefore thus says the Lord GOD: 'Behold, I *am* against you, O Tyre, and will cause many nations to come up against you, as the sea causes its waves to come up. ⁴And they shall destroy the walls of

Tyre and break down her towers; I will also scrape her dust from her, and make her like the top of a rock. ⁵It shall be *a place for* spreading nets in the midst of the sea, for I have spoken,' says the Lord GOD; 'it shall become plunder for the nations. ⁶Also her daughter *villages* which *are* in the fields shall be slain by the sword. Then they shall know that I am the LORD.'

INTIMATE MOMENTS

Reminisce about your favorite dating memories. Plan together to reproduce his or her favorite one.

⁷"For thus says the Lord GOD: 'Behold, I will bring against Tyre from the north Nebuchadnezzarᵃ king of Babylon, king of kings, with horses, with chariots, and with horsemen, and an army with many people. ⁸He will slay with the sword your daughter *villages* in the fields; he will heap up a siege mound against you, build a wall against you, and raise a defense against you. ⁹He will direct his battering rams against your walls, and with his axes he will break down your towers. ¹⁰Because of the abundance of his horses, their dust will cover you; your walls will shake at the noise of the horsemen, the wagons, and the chariots, when he enters your gates, as men enter a city that has been breached. ¹¹With the hooves of his horses he will trample all your streets; he will slay your people by the sword, and your strong pillars will fall to the ground. ¹²They will plunder your riches and pillage your merchandise; they will break down your walls and destroy your pleasant houses; they will lay your stones, your timber, and your soil in the midst of the water. ¹³I will put an end to the sound of your songs, and the sound of your harps shall be heard no more. ¹⁴I will make you like the top of a rock; you shall be *a place for* spreading nets, and you shall never be rebuilt, for I the LORD have spoken,' says the Lord GOD.

¹⁵"Thus says the Lord GOD to Tyre: 'Will the coastlands not shake at the sound of your fall, when the wounded cry, when slaughter is made in the midst of you? ¹⁶Then all the princes of the sea will come down from their thrones, lay aside their robes, and take off their embroidered garments; they will clothe themselves with trembling; they will sit on the ground, tremble *every* moment, and be astonished at you. ¹⁷And they will take up a lamentation for you, and say to you:

> "How you have perished,
>   O one inhabited by seafaring men,
>   O renowned city,
>   Who was strong at sea,
>   She and her inhabitants,
>   Who caused their terror *to be* on all
>   her inhabitants!
> 18 Now the coastlands tremble on the
>   day of your fall;
>   Yes, the coastlands by the sea are
>   troubled at your departure."'

¹⁹"For thus says the Lord GOD: 'When I make you a desolate city, like cities that are not inhabited, when I bring the deep upon you, and great waters cover you, ²⁰then I will bring you down with those who descend into the Pit, to the people of old, and I will make you dwell in the lowest part of the earth, in places desolate from antiquity, with those who go down to the Pit, so that you may never be inhabited; and I shall establish glory in the land of the living. ²¹I will make you a terror, and you *shall be* no *more;* though you are sought for, you will never be found again,' says the Lord GOD."

Lamentation for Tyre

27 The word of the LORD came again to me, saying, ²"Now, son of man, take up a lamentation for Tyre, ³and say to Tyre, 'You who are situated at the entrance of the sea, merchant of the peoples on many coastlands, thus says the Lord GOD:

> "O Tyre, you have said,
> ' I *am* perfect in beauty.'

26:7 ᵃHebrew *Nebuchadrezzar,* and so elsewhere in this book

⁴ Your borders *are* in the midst of the
  seas.
 Your builders have perfected your
  beauty.
⁵ They made all *your* planks of fir
  trees from Senir;
 They took a cedar from Lebanon to
  make you a mast.
⁶ *Of* oaks from Bashan they made
  your oars;
 The company of Ashurites have
  inlaid your planks
 With ivory from the coasts of Cyprus.ᵃ
⁷ Fine embroidered linen from Egypt
  was what you spread for your sail;
 Blue and purple from the coasts of
  Elishah was what covered you.

⁸ "Inhabitants of Sidon and Arvad were
  your oarsmen;
 Your wise men, O Tyre, were in you;
 They became your pilots.
⁹ Elders of Gebal and its wise men
 Were in you to caulk your seams;
 All the ships of the sea
 And their oarsmen were in you
 To market your merchandise.

¹⁰ "Those from Persia, Lydia,ᵃ and Libyaᵇ
 Were in your army as men of war;
 They hung shield and helmet in you;
 They gave splendor to you.
¹¹ Men of Arvad with your army *were*
  on your walls *all* around,
 And the men of Gammad were in
  your towers;
 They hung their shields on your
  walls *all* around;
 They made your beauty perfect.

¹²"Tarshish *was* your merchant because
of your many luxury goods. They gave
you silver, iron, tin, and lead for your
goods. ¹³Javan, Tubal, and Meshech *were*
your traders. They bartered human lives
and vessels of bronze for your merchandise. ¹⁴Those from the house of Togarmah
traded for your wares with horses, steeds,
and mules. ¹⁵The men of Dedan *were* your
traders; many isles *were* the market of
your hand. They brought you ivory tusks
and ebony as payment. ¹⁶Syria *was* your

merchant because of the abundance of
goods you made. They gave you for your
wares emeralds, purple, embroidery, fine
linen, corals, and rubies. ¹⁷Judah and the
land of Israel *were* your traders. They traded for your merchandise wheat of Minnith,
millet, honey, oil, and balm. ¹⁸Damascus
was your merchant because of the abundance of goods you made, because of your
many luxury items, with the wine of
Helbon and with white wool. ¹⁹Dan and
Javan paid for your wares, traversing back
and forth. Wrought iron, cassia, and cane
were among your merchandise. ²⁰Dedan
was your merchant in saddlecloths for riding. ²¹Arabia and all the princes of Kedar
were your regular merchants. They traded
with you in lambs, rams, and goats. ²²The
merchants of Sheba and Raamah *were*
your merchants. They traded for your
wares the choicest spices, all kinds of precious stones, and gold. ²³Haran, Canneh,
Eden, the merchants of Sheba, Assyria,
and Chilmad *were* your merchants. ²⁴These
were your merchants in choice items—in
purple clothes, in embroidered garments,
in chests of multicolored apparel, in stur-
dy woven cords, which were in your marketplace.

²⁵ "The ships of Tarshish were carriers
  of your merchandise.
 You were filled and very glorious in
  the midst of the seas.
²⁶ Your oarsmen brought you into
  many waters,
 But the east wind broke you in the
  midst of the seas.

²⁷ "Your riches, wares, and merchandise,
 Your mariners and pilots,
 Your caulkers and merchandisers,
 All your men of war who *are* in you,
 And the entire company which *is* in
  your midst,
 Will fall into the midst of the seas on
  the day of your ruin.
²⁸ The common-land will shake at the
  sound of the cry of your pilots.

²⁹ "All who handle the oar,
 The mariners,
 All the pilots of the sea
 Will come down from their ships *and*
  stand on the shore.

27:6 ᵃHebrew *Kittim*, western lands, especially
Cyprus **27:10** ᵃHebrew *Lud* ᵇHebrew *Put*

30 They will make their voice heard
because of you;
They will cry bitterly and cast dust
on their heads;
They will roll about in ashes;
31 They will shave themselves
completely bald because of you,
Gird themselves with sackcloth,
And weep for you
With bitterness of heart *and* bitter
wailing.
32 In their wailing for you
They will take up a lamentation,
And lament for you:
‘ What *city is* like Tyre,
Destroyed in the midst of the sea?
33 ‘When your wares went out by sea,
You satisfied many people;
You enriched the kings of the earth
With your many luxury goods and
your merchandise.
34 But you are broken by the seas in the
depths of the waters;
Your merchandise and the entire
company will fall in your midst.
35 All the inhabitants of the isles will
be astonished at you;
Their kings will be greatly afraid,
And *their* countenance will be
troubled.
36 The merchants among the peoples
will hiss at you;
You will become a horror, and *be* no
more forever.’ ”’ ”

Proclamation Against the King of Tyre

28 The word of the LORD came to me
again, saying, [2]“Son of man, say to
the prince of Tyre, ‘Thus says the Lord
GOD:

“Because your heart *is* lifted up,
And you say, ‘I *am* a god,
I sit *in* the seat of gods,
In the midst of the seas,’
Yet you *are* a man, and not a god,
Though you set your heart as the
heart of a god
3 (Behold, you *are* wiser than Daniel!
There is no secret that can be hidden
from you!
4 With your wisdom and your
understanding

You have gained riches for yourself,
And gathered gold and silver into
your treasuries;
5 By your great wisdom in trade you
have increased your riches,
And your heart is lifted up because
of your riches),”

[6]‘Therefore thus says the Lord GOD:

“Because you have set your heart as
the heart of a god,
7 Behold, therefore, I will bring
strangers against you,
The most terrible of the nations;
And they shall draw their swords
against the beauty of your
wisdom,
And defile your splendor.
8 They shall throw you down into the
Pit,
And you shall die the death of the
slain
In the midst of the seas.

9 “Will you still say before him who
slays you,
‘I *am* a god’?
But you *shall be* a man, and not a god,
In the hand of him who slays you.
10 You shall die the death of the
uncircumcised
By the hand of aliens;
For I have spoken,” says the Lord
GOD.’ ”

Lamentation for the King of Tyre

[11]Moreover the word of the LORD came
to me, saying, [12]“Son of man, take up a
lamentation for the king of Tyre, and say
to him, ‘Thus says the Lord GOD:

“You *were* the seal of perfection,
Full of wisdom and perfect in
beauty.
13 You were in Eden, the garden of
God;
Every precious stone *was* your
covering:
The sardius, topaz, and diamond,
Beryl, onyx, and jasper,
Sapphire, turquoise, and emerald
with gold.
The workmanship of your timbrels
and pipes

Was prepared for you on the day you
    were created.

14 "You *were* the anointed cherub who
    covers;
I established you;
You were on the holy mountain of
    God;
You walked back and forth in the
    midst of fiery stones.
15 You *were* perfect in your ways from
    the day you were created,
Till iniquity was found in you.

16 "By the abundance of your trading
You became filled with violence
    within,
And you sinned;
Therefore I cast you as a profane
    thing
Out of the mountain of God;
And I destroyed you, O covering
    cherub,
From the midst of the fiery stones.

17 "Your heart was lifted up because of
    your beauty;
You corrupted your wisdom for the
    sake of your splendor;
I cast you to the ground,
I laid you before kings,
That they might gaze at you.

18 "You defiled your sanctuaries
By the multitude of your iniquities,
By the iniquity of your trading;
Therefore I brought fire from your
    midst;
It devoured you,
And I turned you to ashes upon the
    earth
In the sight of all who saw you.

19 All who knew you among the
    peoples are astonished at you;
You have become a horror,
And *shall be* no more forever." ' "

Proclamation Against Sidon

20Then the word of the LORD came to
me, saying, 21"Son of man, set your face
toward Sidon, and prophesy against her,
22and say, 'Thus says the Lord GOD:

"Behold, I *am* against you, O Sidon;
I will be glorified in your midst;

BIBLICAL INSIGHTS • 28:12–17
Satan's Lies to Families

EVER SINCE THE DEVIL GOT KICKED OUT of
heaven, he's been breathing out lies and
violence (28:12–17). Consider four lies
Satan continually tells us:

1. *You're a failure.* Satan wants you to
believe that your faults are too big to
be covered by God's grace. God
would have you reply, "There is therefore now no condemnation to those
who are in Christ Jesus" (Rom. 8:1).

2. *You don't deserve to be unhappy.* Satan
attempts to convince you that if you
just get out from under this relationship or family pressure you'll be
happy. God's Word replies, "The
statutes of the LORD are right, rejoicing the heart" (Ps. 19:8).

3. *Nobody will find out.* You may think
nobody will ever discover that little
sin promising instant satisfaction, but
God's Word says, "Be sure your sin will
find you out" (Num. 32:23).

4. *If I had _____ , I'd be happier.* Satan
wants you to focus on what others
have. God's Word says, "Be content
with such things as you have. For He
Himself has said, 'I will never leave
you nor forsake you'" (Heb. 13:5).

If we refuse to believe Satan's lies, we
render him powerless. Resist him by
remembering the truth of God's Word!
And don't believe his lies.

And they shall know that I *am* the
    LORD,
When I execute judgments in her
    and am hallowed in her.
23 For I will send pestilence upon her,
And blood in her streets;
The wounded shall be judged in her
    midst
By the sword against her on every
    side;
Then they shall know that I *am* the
    LORD.

24"And there shall no longer be a pricking brier or a painful thorn for the house of Israel from among all *who are* around them, who despise them. Then they shall know that I *am* the Lord GOD."

Israel's Future Blessing

25Thus says the Lord GOD: "When I have gathered the house of Israel from the peoples among whom they are scattered, and am hallowed in them in the sight of the Gentiles, then they will dwell in their own land which I gave to My servant Jacob. 26And they will dwell safely there, build houses, and plant vineyards; yes, they will dwell securely, when I execute judgments on all those around them who despise them. Then they shall know that I *am* the LORD their God."'"

Proclamation Against Egypt

29 In the tenth year, in the tenth *month,* on the twelfth *day* of the month, the word of the LORD came to me, saying, 2"Son of man, set your face against Pharaoh king of Egypt, and prophesy against him, and against all Egypt. 3Speak, and say, 'Thus says the Lord GOD:

"Behold, I *am* against you,
O Pharaoh king of Egypt,
O great monster who lies in the
    midst of his rivers,
Who has said, 'My River[a] *is* my own;
I have made *it* for myself.'
4 But I will put hooks in your jaws,
And cause the fish of your rivers to
    stick to your scales;
I will bring you up out of the midst
    of your rivers,
And all the fish in your rivers will
    stick to your scales.
5 I will leave you in the wilderness,
You and all the fish of your rivers;
You shall fall on the open field;
You shall not be picked up or
    gathered.[a]
I have given you as food
To the beasts of the field
And to the birds of the heavens.

6 "Then all the inhabitants of Egypt
Shall know that I *am* the LORD,

Because they have been a staff of
    reed to the house of Israel.
7 When they took hold of you with the
    hand,
You broke and tore all their
    shoulders;[a]
When they leaned on you,
You broke and made all their backs
    quiver."

8Therefore thus says the Lord GOD: "Surely I will bring a sword upon you and cut off from you man and beast. 9And the land of Egypt shall become desolate and waste; then they will know that I *am* the LORD, because he said, 'The River *is* mine, and I have made *it.*' 10Indeed, therefore, I *am* against you and against your rivers, and I will make the land of Egypt utterly waste and desolate, from Migdol[a] *to* Syene, as far as the border of Ethiopia. 11Neither foot of man shall pass through it nor foot of beast pass through it, and it shall be uninhabited forty years. 12I will make the land of Egypt desolate in the midst of the countries *that are* desolate; and among the cities *that are* laid waste, her cities shall be desolate forty years; and I will scatter the Egyptians among the nations and disperse them throughout the countries."

13Yet, thus says the Lord GOD: "At the end of forty years I will gather the Egyptians from the peoples among whom they were scattered. 14I will bring back the captives of Egypt and cause them to return to the land of Pathros, to the land of their origin, and there they shall be a lowly kingdom. 15It shall be the lowliest of kingdoms; it shall never again exalt itself above the nations, for I will diminish them so that they will not rule over the nations anymore. 16No longer shall it be the confidence of the house of Israel, but will remind them of *their* iniquity when they turned to follow them. Then they shall know that I *am* the Lord GOD."'"

29:3 [a]That is, the Nile **29:5** [a]Following Masoretic Text, Septuagint, and Vulgate; some Hebrew manuscripts and Targum read *buried.* **29:7** [a]Following Masoretic Text and Vulgate; Septuagint and Syriac read *hand.* **29:10** [a]Or *tower*

Babylonia Will Plunder Egypt

[17]And it came to pass in the twenty-seventh year, in the first *month,* on the first *day* of the month, *that* the word of the LORD came to me, saying, [18]"Son of man, Nebuchadnezzar king of Babylon caused his army to labor strenuously against Tyre; every head *was* made bald, and every shoulder rubbed raw; yet neither he nor his army received wages from Tyre, for the labor which they expended on it. [19]Therefore thus says the Lord GOD: 'Surely I will give the land of Egypt to Nebuchadnezzar king of Babylon; he shall take away her wealth, carry off her spoil, and remove her pillage; and that will be the wages for his army. [20]I have given him the land of Egypt *for* his labor, because they worked for Me,' says the Lord GOD.

[21]'In that day I will cause the horn of the house of Israel to spring forth, and I will open your mouth to speak in their midst. Then they shall know that I *am* the LORD.'"

Egypt and Her Allies Will Fall

30 The word of the LORD came to me again, saying, [2]"Son of man, prophesy and say, 'Thus says the Lord GOD:

"Wail, 'Woe to the day!'
[3]　For the day *is* near,
　　Even the day of the LORD *is* near;
　　It will be a day of clouds, the time of the Gentiles.
[4]　The sword shall come upon Egypt,
　　And great anguish shall be in Ethiopia,
　　When the slain fall in Egypt,
　　And they take away her wealth,
　　And her foundations are broken down.

[5]"Ethiopia, Libya,[a] Lydia,[b] all the mingled people, Chub, and the men of the lands who are allied, shall fall with them by the sword."

[6]'Thus says the LORD:

"Those who uphold Egypt shall fall,
　And the pride of her power shall come down.

From Migdol *to* Syene
Those within her shall fall by the sword,"
Says the Lord GOD.

[7]　"They shall be desolate in the midst of the desolate countries,
　　And her cities shall be in the midst of the cities *that are* laid waste.
[8]　Then they will know that I *am* the LORD,
　　When I have set a fire in Egypt
　　And all her helpers are destroyed.
[9]　On that day messengers shall go forth from Me in ships
　　To make the careless Ethiopians afraid,
　　And great anguish shall come upon them,
　　As on the day of Egypt;
　　For indeed it is coming!"

INTIMATE MOMENTS

Make a stop on your way home from work and pick up that special treat your wife loves.

Keep a running list of his favorite things, clothes sizes, and gift ideas.

[10]'Thus says the Lord GOD:

"I will also make a multitude of Egypt to cease
　By the hand of Nebuchadnezzar king of Babylon.
[11]　He and his people with him, the most terrible of the nations,
　　Shall be brought to destroy the land;
　　They shall draw their swords against Egypt,
　　And fill the land with the slain.
[12]　I will make the rivers dry,
　　And sell the land into the hand of the wicked;
　　I will make the land waste, and all that is in it,
　　By the hand of aliens.
　　I, the LORD, have spoken."

30:5 [a]Hebrew *Put* [b]Hebrew *Lud*

¹³'Thus says the Lord God:

"I will also destroy the idols,
    And cause the images to cease from
        Noph;ª
    There shall no longer be princes from
        the land of Egypt;
    I will put fear in the land of Egypt.
¹⁴   I will make Pathros desolate,
    Set fire to Zoan,
    And execute judgments in No.ª
¹⁵   I will pour My fury on Sin,ª the
        strength of Egypt;
        I will cut off the multitude of No,
¹⁶   And set a fire in Egypt;
    Sin shall have great pain,
    No shall be split open,
    And Noph *shall be in* distress daily.
¹⁷   The young men of Avenª and Pi
        Beseth shall fall by the sword,
    And these *cities* shall go into
        captivity.
¹⁸   At Tehaphnehesª the day shall also
        be darkened,ᵇ
    When I break the yokes of Egypt
        there.
    And her arrogant strength shall
        cease in her;
    As for her, a cloud shall cover her,
    And her daughters shall go into
        captivity.
¹⁹   Thus I will execute judgments on
        Egypt,
    Then they shall know that I *am* the
        Lord.'"

Proclamation Against Pharaoh

²⁰And it came to pass in the eleventh
year, in the first *month,* on the seventh *day*
of the month, *that* the word of the Lord
came to me, saying, ²¹"Son of man, I have
broken the arm of Pharaoh king of Egypt;
and see, it has not been bandaged for healing, nor a splint put on to bind it, to make
it strong enough to hold a sword. ²²Therefore thus says the Lord God: 'Surely I *am*
against Pharaoh king of Egypt, and will
break his arms, both the strong one and
the one that was broken; and I will make
the sword fall out of his hand. ²³I will scatter the Egyptians among the nations, and
disperse them throughout the countries. ²⁴I
will strengthen the arms of the king of

Babylon and put My sword in his hand;
but I will break Pharaoh's arms, and he
will groan before him with the groanings
of a mortally wounded *man.* ²⁵Thus I will
strengthen the arms of the king of Babylon, but the arms of Pharaoh shall fall
down; they shall know that I *am* the Lord,
when I put My sword into the hand of the
king of Babylon and he stretches it out
against the land of Egypt. ²⁶I will scatter
the Egyptians among the nations and disperse them throughout the countries. Then
they shall know that I *am* the Lord.'"

Egypt Cut Down Like a Great Tree

31 Now it came to pass in the eleventh
year, in the third *month,* on the first
day of the month, *that* the word of the
Lord came to me, saying, ²"Son of man,
say to Pharaoh king of Egypt and to his
multitude:

' Whom are you like in your greatness?
³   Indeed Assyria *was* a cedar in
        Lebanon,
    With fine branches that shaded the
        forest,
    And of high stature;
    And its top was among the thick
        boughs.
⁴   The waters made it grow;
    Underground waters gave it height,
    With their rivers running around the
        place where it was planted,
    And sent out rivulets to all the trees
        of the field.

⁵   'Therefore its height was exalted
        above all the trees of the field;
    Its boughs were multiplied,
    And its branches became long
        because of the abundance of water,
    As it sent them out.
⁶   All the birds of the heavens made
        their nests in its boughs;
    Under its branches all the beasts of
        the field brought forth their young;

30:13 ªThat is, ancient Memphis 30:14 ªThat is,
ancient Thebes 30:15 ªThat is, ancient Pelusium
30:17 ªThat is, ancient On (Heliopolis)
30:18 ªSpelled *Tahpanhes* in Jeremiah 43:7 and elsewhere ᵇFollowing many Hebrew manuscripts,
Bomberg, Septuagint, Syriac, Targum, and Vulgate;
Masoretic Text reads *refrained.*

DEVOTIONS FOR COUPLES · 31:9
Dealing with Envy

Barbara and I wanted our children to grow up realizing God won't give each of them the same share of earthly benefits. But we also wanted them to know He will *always* deal with them in perfect judgment and according to His righteous character. Unfortunately, our limited perspective leads us to compare what we *think* we deserve with what others *appear* to get. The invariable result is ENVY.

Jesus offers a parable in Matthew 20:1–16 that could be titled, "Life isn't fair—but the Master IS!" The parable describes a landowner who hires laborers for his vineyard. Early in the morning he hires a few men for a fair day's wage. Throughout the day, the landowner hires additional laborers, promising to pay each one "whatever is right" (v. 4). They agree to his terms and go to work.

Later that evening, he pays each laborer. He begins by paying the ones who had last joined the workforce. Although they labored only a short time, he pays each one the full day's wage. The men who had worked throughout the scorching heat complain, "That's not fair!" The landowner replies that he has paid them just what he promised, and then says, "Is it not lawful for me to do what I wish with my own

things? Or is your eye evil [read, *envious*] because I am good?" (v. 15).

I find at least three principles here that will help us face situations that seem unfair.

First, *remember what you really deserve.* Every good thing we experience in life comes to us as a result of God's grace. In the parable, the men who worked all day thought they deserved a bonus. They thought the landowner owed them a little extra, even though he had promised them no such thing.

Second, *envy begins when we compare ourselves with others.* We get into trouble when we covet what others have. The laborers saw too much! Their eyes betrayed them, as can our own. Can you look clearly at what others have and be glad they have it? How do you handle the news of a friend remodeling her house? Or the promotion of an associate at work? Envy can cause spiritual cataracts and ultimately blindness!

Third, *we must trust that the Master knows what He is doing.* God, the Sovereign Ruler of the universe, alone controls and rules over all. And not only does He know what He is doing, but He also loves us!

No, life isn't fair. But I know God is fair, and He *can* be trusted.

And in its shadow all great nations
   made their home.

7 'Thus it was beautiful in greatness
      and in the length of its branches,
   Because its roots reached to
      abundant waters.

8 The cedars in the garden of God
      could not hide it;
   The fir trees were not like its boughs,
   And the chestnut[a] trees were not like
      its branches;
   No tree in the garden of God was
      like it in beauty.

9 I made it beautiful with a multitude
      of branches,
   So that all the trees of Eden envied
      it,
   That *were* in the garden of God.'

10 "Therefore thus says the Lord GOD: 'Because you have increased in height, and it set its top among the thick boughs, and its heart was lifted up in its height, [11]therefore I will deliver it into the hand of the mighty one of the nations, and he shall surely deal with it; I have driven it out for its wickedness. [12]And aliens, the most terrible of the nations, have cut it down and left it; its branches have fallen on the

31:8 [a]Hebrew *armon*

mountains and in all the valleys; its boughs lie broken by all the rivers of the land; and all the peoples of the earth have gone from under its shadow and left it.

13 'On its ruin will remain all the birds
     of the heavens,
     And all the beasts of the field will
       come to its branches—

14So that no trees by the waters may ever again exalt themselves for their height, nor set their tops among the thick boughs, that no tree which drinks water may ever be high enough to reach up to them.

     ' For they have all been delivered to
       death,
     To the depths of the earth,
     Among the children of men who go
       down to the Pit.'

INTIMATE MOMENTS

Have fun foolin' around on April Fool's Day. Share an umbrella, roll up your jeans, and splash in the puddles.

15"Thus says the Lord GOD: 'In the day when it went down to hell, I caused mourning. I covered the deep because of it. I restrained its rivers, and the great waters were held back. I caused Lebanon to mourn for it, and all the trees of the field wilted because of it. 16I made the nations shake at the sound of its fall, when I cast it down to hell together with those who descend into the Pit; and all the trees of Eden, the choice and best of Lebanon, all that drink water, were comforted in the depths of the earth. 17They also went down to hell with it, with those slain by the sword; and those who were its strong arm dwelt in its shadows among the nations.

18"To which of the trees in Eden will you then be likened in glory and greatness? Yet you shall be brought down with the trees of Eden to the depths of the earth; you shall lie in the midst of the

uncircumcised, with those slain by the sword. This is Pharaoh and all his multitude,' says the Lord GOD."

Lamentation for Pharaoh and Egypt

32 And it came to pass in the twelfth year, in the twelfth month, on the first day of the month, that the word of the LORD came to me, saying, 2"Son of man, take up a lamentation for Pharaoh king of Egypt, and say to him:

'You are like a young lion among the
     nations,
And you are like a monster in the
     seas,
Bursting forth in your rivers,
Troubling the waters with your feet,
And fouling their rivers.'

3"Thus says the Lord GOD:

'I will therefore spread My net over
     you with a company of many
     people,
And they will draw you up in My net.
4   Then I will leave you on the land;
     I will cast you out on the open fields,
     And cause to settle on you all the
       birds of the heavens.
     And with you I will fill the beasts of
       the whole earth.
5   I will lay your flesh on the mountains,
     And fill the valleys with your
       carcass.

6   'I will also water the land with the
       flow of your blood,
     Even to the mountains;
     And the riverbeds will be full of you.
7   When I put out your light,
     I will cover the heavens, and make
       its stars dark;
     I will cover the sun with a cloud,
     And the moon shall not give her
       light.
8   All the bright lights of the heavens I
       will make dark over you,
     And bring darkness upon your land,'
     Says the Lord GOD.

9"I will also trouble the hearts of many peoples, when I bring your destruction among the nations, into the countries which you have not known. 10Yes, I will make many peoples astonished at you, and their kings shall be horribly afraid of you when I brandish My sword before them; and they shall tremble *every* moment, every man for his own life, in the day of your fall.'

¹¹"For thus says the Lord GOD: 'The sword of the king of Babylon shall come upon you. ¹²By the swords of the mighty warriors, all of them the most terrible of the nations, I will cause your multitude to fall.

' They shall plunder the pomp of
　　Egypt,
　And all its multitude shall be
　　destroyed.
¹³　Also I will destroy all its animals
　From beside its great waters;
　The foot of man shall muddy them
　　no more,
　Nor shall the hooves of animals
　　muddy them.
¹⁴　Then I will make their waters clear,
　And make their rivers run like oil,'
　Says the Lord GOD.

¹⁵　'When I make the land of Egypt
　　desolate,
　And the country is destitute of all
　　that once filled it,
　When I strike all who dwell in it,
　Then they shall know that I *am* the
　　LORD.

¹⁶　'This *is* the lamentation
　With which they shall lament her;
　The daughters of the nations shall
　　lament her;
　They shall lament for her, for Egypt,
　And for all her multitude,'
　Says the Lord GOD."

Egypt and Others Consigned to the Pit

¹⁷It came to pass also in the twelfth year, on the fifteenth *day* of the month, *that* the word of the LORD came to me, saying:

¹⁸　"Son of man, wail over the multitude
　　of Egypt,
　And cast them down to the depths of
　　the earth,
　Her and the daughters of the famous
　　nations,
　With those who go down to the Pit:

¹⁹　'Whom do you surpass in beauty?
　Go down, be placed with the
　　uncircumcised.'

²⁰　"They shall fall in the midst of *those*
　　slain by the sword;
　She is delivered to the sword,
　Drawing her and all her multitudes.
²¹　The strong among the mighty
　Shall speak to him out of the midst
　　of hell
　With those who help him:
　'They have gone down,
　They lie with the uncircumcised,
　　slain by the sword.'

²²　"Assyria *is* there, and all her
　　company,
　With their graves all around her,
　All of them slain, fallen by the sword.
²³　Her graves are set in the recesses of
　　the Pit,
　And her company is all around her
　　grave,
　All of them slain, fallen by the sword,
　Who caused terror in the land of the
　　living.

²⁴　"There *is* Elam and all her multitude,
　All around her grave,
　All of them slain, fallen by the
　　sword,
　Who have gone down uncircumcised
　　to the lower parts of the earth,
　Who caused their terror in the land
　　of the living;
　Now they bear their shame with
　　those who go down to the Pit.
²⁵　They have set her bed in the midst of
　　the slain,
　With all her multitude,
　With her graves all around it,
　All of them uncircumcised, slain by
　　the sword;
　Though their terror was caused
　In the land of the living,
　Yet they bear their shame
　With those who go down to the Pit;
　It was put in the midst of the slain.

²⁶　"There *are* Meshech and Tubal and all
　　their multitudes,
　With all their graves around it,
　All of them uncircumcised, slain by
　　the sword,

Though they caused their terror in
the land of the living.
27 They do not lie with the mighty
Who are fallen of the uncircumcised,
Who have gone down to hell with
their weapons of war;
They have laid their swords under
their heads,
But their iniquities will be on their
bones,
Because of the terror of the mighty
in the land of the living.
28 Yes, you shall be broken in the midst
of the uncircumcised,
And lie with *those* slain by the sword.

29 "There *is* Edom,
Her kings and all her princes,
Who despite their might
Are laid beside *those* slain by the
sword;
They shall lie with the uncircumcised,
And with those who go down to the
Pit.
30 There *are* the princes of the north,
All of them, and all the Sidonians,
Who have gone down with the slain
In shame at the terror which they
caused by their might;
They lie uncircumcised with *those*
slain by the sword,
And bear their shame with those
who go down to the Pit.

31 "Pharaoh will see them
And be comforted over all his
multitude,
Pharaoh and all his army,
Slain by the sword,"
Says the Lord GOD.

32 "For I have caused My terror in the
land of the living;
And he shall be placed in the midst
of the uncircumcised
With *those* slain by the sword,
Pharaoh and all his multitude,"
Says the Lord GOD.

The Watchman and His Message

33 Again the word of the LORD came to
me, saying, 2"Son of man, speak to
the children of your people, and say to
them: 'When I bring the sword upon a land,
and the people of the land take a man from
their territory and make him their watchman, 3when he sees the sword coming upon
the land, if he blows the trumpet and warns
the people, 4then whoever hears the sound of
the trumpet and does not take warning, if
the sword comes and takes him away, his
blood shall be on his *own* head. 5He heard
the sound of the trumpet, but did not take
warning; his blood shall be upon himself.
But he who takes warning will save his life.
6But if the watchman sees the sword coming and does not blow the trumpet, and the
people are not warned, and the sword comes
and takes *any* person from among them, he
is taken away in his iniquity; but his blood I
will require at the watchman's hand.'

7"So you, son of man: I have made you
a watchman for the house of Israel; therefore you shall hear a word from My mouth
and warn them for Me. 8When I say to the
wicked, 'O wicked *man,* you shall surely
die!' and you do not speak to warn the
wicked from his way, that wicked *man*
shall die in his iniquity; but his blood I will
require at your hand. 9Nevertheless if you
warn the wicked to turn from his way, and
he does not turn from his way, he shall die
in his iniquity; but you have delivered your
soul.

10"Therefore you, O son of man, say to
the house of Israel: 'Thus you say, "If our
transgressions and our sins *lie* upon us,
and we pine away in them, how can we
then live?" ' 11Say to them: '*As* I live,' says
the Lord GOD, 'I have no pleasure in the
death of the wicked, but that the wicked
turn from his way and live. Turn, turn
from your evil ways! For why should you
die, O house of Israel?'

The Fairness of God's Judgment

12"Therefore you, O son of man, say to
the children of your people: 'The righteousness of the righteous man shall not
deliver him in the day of his transgression; as for the wickedness of the wicked,
he shall not fall because of it in the day
that he turns from his wickedness; nor
shall the righteous be able to live because
of *his righteousness* in the day that he
sins.' 13When I say to the righteous *that* he
shall surely live, but he trusts in his own

righteousness and commits iniquity, none of his righteous works shall be remembered; but because of the iniquity that he has committed, he shall die. ¹⁴Again, when I say to the wicked, 'You shall surely die,' if he turns from his sin and does what is lawful and right, ¹⁵*if* the wicked restores the pledge, gives back what he has stolen, and walks in the statutes of life without committing iniquity, he shall surely live; he shall not die. ¹⁶None of his sins which he has committed shall be remembered against him; he has done what is lawful and right; he shall surely live.

¹⁷"Yet the children of your people say, 'The way of the Lord is not fair.' But it is their way which is not fair! ¹⁸When the righteous turns from his righteousness and commits iniquity, he shall die because of it. ¹⁹But when the wicked turns from his wickedness and does what is lawful and right, he shall live because of it. ²⁰Yet you say, 'The way of the Lord is not fair.' O house of Israel, I will judge every one of you according to his own ways."

The Fall of Jerusalem

²¹And it came to pass in the twelfth year of our captivity, in the tenth *month,* on the fifth *day* of the month, *that* one who had escaped from Jerusalem came to me and said, "The city has been captured!"

²²Now the hand of the LORD had been upon me the evening before the man came who had escaped. And He had opened my mouth; so when he came to me in the morning, my mouth was opened, and I was no longer mute.

The Cause of Judah's Ruin

²³Then the word of the LORD came to me, saying: ²⁴"Son of man, they who inhabit those ruins in the land of Israel are saying, 'Abraham was only one, and he inherited the land. But we *are* many; the land has been given to us as a possession.'
²⁵"Therefore say to them, 'Thus says the Lord GOD: "You eat *meat* with blood, you lift up your eyes toward your idols, and shed blood. Should you then possess the land?
²⁶You rely on your sword, you commit abominations, and you defile one another's wives. Should you then possess the land?"'

²⁷"Say thus to them, 'Thus says the Lord GOD: "*As* I live, surely those who *are* in the ruins shall fall by the sword, and the one who *is* in the open field I will give to the beasts to be devoured, and those who *are* in the strongholds and caves shall die of the pestilence. ²⁸For I will make the land most desolate, her arrogant strength shall cease, and the mountains of Israel shall be so desolate that no one will pass through. ²⁹Then they shall know that I *am* the LORD, when I have made the land most desolate because of all their abominations which they have committed."'

Hearing and Not Doing

³⁰"As for you, son of man, the children of your people are talking about you beside the walls and in the doors of the houses; and they speak to one another, everyone saying to his brother, 'Please come and hear what the word is that comes from the LORD.' ³¹So they come to you as people do, they sit before you *as* My people, and they hear your words, but they do not do them; for with their mouth they show much love, *but* their hearts pursue their *own* gain. ³²Indeed you *are* to them as a very lovely song of one who has a pleasant voice and can play well on an instrument; for they hear your words, but they do not do them. ³³And when this comes to pass—surely it will come—then they will know that a prophet has been among them."

Irresponsible Shepherds

34 And the word of the LORD came to me, saying, ²"Son of man, prophesy against the shepherds of Israel, prophesy and say to them, 'Thus says the Lord GOD to the shepherds: "Woe to the shepherds of Israel who feed themselves! Should not the shepherds feed the flocks? ³You eat the fat and clothe yourselves with the wool; you slaughter the fatlings, *but* you do not feed the flock. ⁴The weak you have not strengthened, nor have you healed those who were sick, nor bound up the broken, nor brought back what was driven away, nor sought what was lost; but with force and cruelty you have ruled them. ⁵So they were scattered because *there was* no shepherd; and they became food for all the

Accept Your Role as Shepherd

It's time that parents started considering themselves the shepherds of their families. Hey, if David could be called the shepherd of Israel (2 Sam. 5:2), and pastors the shepherds of their congregations (1 Pet. 5:2), then why not start thinking of yourself as the shepherd of your family? I think the times in which we live almost demand it.

One major responsibility of a shepherd is to protect his sheep from predators. Perhaps at no time in history have we more needed parents who would make it a priority to protect their families. Predators of every stripe and pattern are on the loose, and our children need us to shepherd them well because when we don't, here's what happens: "They were scattered because there was no shepherd; and they became food for all the beasts of the field when they were scattered" (34:5). Just look up. Countless "beasts of the field" want to make a lunch of your children!

To begin, guard your children from two of the major negative influencers in their lives: media and peers. Know what they are watching (pornography on the internet? Movies full of sex and violence?). And pay attention to whom they are spending time with. Shepherd them well!

To be a successful shepherd you will need to be alert to the beasts that are circling your sheep and to proactively protect them.

beasts of the field when they were scattered. 6My sheep wandered through all the mountains, and on every high hill; yes, My flock was scattered over the whole face of the earth, and no one was seeking or searching *for them.*"

7"Therefore, you shepherds, hear the word of the LORD: 8"*As* I live," says the Lord GOD, "surely because My flock became a prey, and My flock became food for every

beast of the field, because *there was* no shepherd, nor did My shepherds search for My flock, but the shepherds fed themselves and did not feed My flock"— 9therefore, O shepherds, hear the word of the LORD! 10Thus says the Lord GOD: "Behold, I *am* against the shepherds, and I will require My flock at their hand; I will cause them to cease feeding the sheep, and the shepherds shall feed themselves no more; for I will deliver My flock from their mouths, that they may no longer be food for them."

God, the True Shepherd

11"For thus says the Lord GOD: "Indeed I Myself will search for My sheep and seek them out. 12As a shepherd seeks out his flock on the day he is among his scattered sheep, so will I seek out My sheep and deliver them from all the places where they were scattered on a cloudy and dark day. 13And I will bring them out from the peoples and gather them from the countries, and will bring them to their own land; I will feed them on the mountains of Israel, in the valleys and in all the inhabited places of the country. 14I will feed them in good pasture, and their fold shall be on the high mountains of Israel. There they shall lie down in a good fold and feed in rich pasture on the mountains of Israel. 15I will feed My flock, and I will make them lie down," says the Lord GOD. 16"I will seek what was lost and bring back what was driven away, bind up the broken and strengthen what was sick; but I will destroy the fat and the strong, and feed them in judgment."

17'And *as for* you, O My flock, thus says the Lord GOD: "Behold, I shall judge between sheep and sheep, between rams and goats. 18*Is it* too little for you to have eaten up the good pasture, that you must tread down with your feet the residue of your pasture—and to have drunk of the clear waters, that you must foul the residue with your feet? 19And *as for* My flock, they eat what you have trampled with your feet, and they drink what you have fouled with your feet."

20"Therefore thus says the Lord GOD to them: "Behold, I Myself will judge between the fat and the lean sheep

²¹Because you have pushed with side and shoulder, butted all the weak ones with your horns, and scattered them abroad, ²²therefore I will save My flock, and they shall no longer be a prey; and I will judge between sheep and sheep. ²³I will establish one shepherd over them, and he shall feed them—My servant David. He shall feed them and be their shepherd. ²⁴And I, the LORD, will be their God, and My servant David a prince among them; I, the LORD, have spoken.

²⁵"I will make a covenant of peace with them, and cause wild beasts to cease from the land; and they will dwell safely in the wilderness and sleep in the woods. ²⁶I will make them and the places all around My hill a blessing; and I will cause showers to come down in their season; there shall be showers of blessing. ²⁷Then the trees of the field shall yield their fruit, and the earth shall yield her increase. They shall be safe in their land; and they shall know that I *am* the LORD, when I have broken the bands of their yoke and delivered them from the hand of those who enslaved them. ²⁸And they shall no longer be a prey for the nations, nor shall beasts of the land devour them; but they shall dwell safely, and no one shall make *them* afraid. ²⁹I will raise up for them a garden of renown, and they shall no longer be consumed with hunger in the land, nor bear the shame of the Gentiles anymore. ³⁰Thus they shall know that I, the LORD their God, *am* with them, and they, the house of Israel, *are* My people," says the Lord GOD.' "

³¹"You are My flock, the flock of My pasture; you *are* men, *and* I *am* your God," says the Lord GOD.

Judgment on Mount Seir

35 Moreover the word of the LORD came to me, saying, ²"Son of man, set your face against Mount Seir and prophesy against it, ³and say to it, 'Thus says the Lord GOD:

"Behold, O Mount Seir, I *am* against you;
I will stretch out My hand against you,
And make you most desolate;

⁴ I shall lay your cities waste,
And you shall be desolate.
Then you shall know that I *am* the LORD.

⁵"Because you have had an ancient hatred, and have shed *the blood of* the children of Israel by the power of the sword at the time of their calamity, when their iniquity *came to an* end, ⁶therefore, *as* I live," says the Lord GOD, "I will prepare you for blood, and blood shall pursue you; since you have not hated blood, therefore blood shall pursue you. ⁷Thus I will make Mount Seir most desolate, and cut off from it the one who leaves and the one who returns. ⁸And I will fill its mountains with the slain; on your hills and in your valleys and in all your ravines those who are slain by the sword shall fall. ⁹I will make you perpetually desolate, and your cities shall be uninhabited; then you shall know that I *am* the LORD.

¹⁰"Because you have said, 'These two nations and these two countries shall be mine, and we will possess them,' although the LORD was there, ¹¹therefore, *as* I live," says the Lord GOD, "I will do according to your anger and according to the envy which you showed in your hatred against them; and I will make Myself known among them when I judge you. ¹²Then you shall know that I *am* the LORD. I have heard all your blasphemies which you have spoken against the mountains of Israel, saying, 'They are desolate; they are given to us to consume.' ¹³Thus with your mouth you have boasted against Me and multiplied your words against Me; I have heard *them*."

¹⁴'Thus says the Lord GOD: "The whole earth will rejoice when I make you desolate. ¹⁵As you rejoiced because the inheritance of the house of Israel was desolate, so I will do to you; you shall be desolate, O Mount Seir, as well as all of Edom—all of it! Then they shall know that I *am* the LORD." '

Blessing on Israel

36 "And you, son of man, prophesy to the mountains of Israel, and say, 'O mountains of Israel, hear the word of the

LORD! ²Thus says the Lord GOD: "Because the enemy has said of you, 'Aha! The ancient heights have become our possession,'"' ³therefore prophesy, and say, 'Thus says the Lord GOD: "Because they made *you* desolate and swallowed you up on every side, so that you became the possession of the rest of the nations, and you are taken up by the lips of talkers and slandered by the people"— ⁴therefore, O mountains of Israel, hear the word of the Lord GOD! Thus says the Lord GOD to the mountains, the hills, the rivers, the valleys, the desolate wastes, and the cities that have been forsaken, which became plunder and mockery to the rest of the nations all around— ⁵therefore thus says the Lord GOD: "Surely I have spoken in My burning jealousy against the rest of the nations and against all Edom, who gave My land to themselves as a possession, with wholehearted joy *and* spiteful minds, in order to plunder its open country."'

⁶"Therefore prophesy concerning the land of Israel, and say to the mountains, the hills, the rivers, and the valleys, 'Thus says the Lord GOD: "Behold, I have spoken in My jealousy and My fury, because you have borne the shame of the nations."' ⁷Therefore thus says the Lord GOD: "I have raised My hand in an oath that surely the nations that *are* around you shall bear their own shame. ⁸But you, O mountains of Israel, you shall shoot forth your branches and yield your fruit to My people Israel, for they are about to come. ⁹For indeed I *am* for you, and I will turn to you, and you shall be tilled and sown. ¹⁰I will multiply men upon you, all the house of Israel, all of it; and the cities shall be inhabited and the ruins rebuilt. ¹¹I will multiply upon you man and beast; and they shall increase and bear young; I will make you inhabited as in former times, and do better *for you* than at your beginnings. Then you shall know that I *am* the LORD. ¹²Yes, I will cause men to walk on you, My people Israel; they shall take possession of you, and you shall be their inheritance; no more shall you bereave them *of children."*

¹³'Thus says the Lord GOD: "Because they say to you, 'You devour men and bereave your nation *of children,'* ¹⁴therefore you shall devour men no more, nor bereave your nation anymore," says the Lord GOD. ¹⁵"Nor will I let you hear the taunts of the nations anymore, nor bear the reproach of the peoples anymore, nor shall you cause your nation to stumble anymore," says the Lord GOD.'"

The Renewal of Israel

¹⁶Moreover the word of the LORD came to me, saying: ¹⁷"Son of man, when the house of Israel dwelt in their own land, they defiled it by their own ways and deeds; to Me their way was like the uncleanness of a woman in her customary impurity. ¹⁸Therefore I poured out My fury on them for the blood they had shed on the land, and for their idols *with which* they had defiled it. ¹⁹So I scattered them among the nations, and they were dispersed throughout the countries; I judged them according to their ways and their deeds. ²⁰When they came to the nations, wherever they went, they profaned My holy name—when they said of them, 'These *are* the people of the LORD, *and* yet they have gone out of His land.' ²¹But I had concern for My holy name, which the house of Israel had profaned among the nations wherever they went.

²²"Therefore say to the house of Israel, 'Thus says the Lord GOD: "I do not do *this* for your sake, O house of Israel, but for My holy name's sake, which you have profaned among the nations wherever you went. ²³And I will sanctify My great name, which has been profaned among the nations, which you have profaned in their midst; and the nations shall know that I *am* the LORD," says the Lord GOD, "when I am hallowed in you before their eyes. ²⁴For I will take you from among the nations, gather you out of all countries, and bring you into your own land. ²⁵Then I will sprinkle clean water on you, and you shall be clean; I will cleanse you from all your filthiness and from all your idols. ²⁶I will give you a new heart and put a new spirit within you; I will take the heart of stone out of your flesh and give you a heart of flesh. ²⁷I will put My Spirit within you and cause you to walk in My statutes, and you will keep My judgments and do *them*. ²⁸Then you shall dwell in the land that I

gave to your fathers; you shall be My people, and I will be your God. ²⁹I will deliver you from all your uncleannesses. I will call for the grain and multiply it, and bring no famine upon you. ³⁰And I will multiply the fruit of your trees and the increase of your fields, so that you need never again bear the reproach of famine among the nations. ³¹Then you will remember your evil ways and your deeds that *were* not good; and you will loathe yourselves in your own sight, for your iniquities and your abominations. ³²Not for your sake do I do *this*," says the Lord GOD, "let it be known to you. Be ashamed and confounded for your own ways, O house of Israel!"

³³'Thus says the Lord GOD: "On the day that I cleanse you from all your iniquities, I will also enable *you* to dwell in the cities, and the ruins shall be rebuilt. ³⁴The desolate land shall be tilled instead of lying desolate in the sight of all who pass by. ³⁵So they will say, 'This land that was desolate has become like the garden of Eden; and the wasted, desolate, and ruined cities *are now* fortified *and* inhabited.' ³⁶Then the nations which are left all around you shall know that I, the LORD, have rebuilt the ruined places *and* planted what was desolate. I, the LORD, have spoken *it*, and I will do *it*."

³⁷'Thus says the Lord GOD: "I will also let the house of Israel inquire of Me to do this for them: I will increase their men like a flock. ³⁸Like a flock *offered as* holy *sacrifices*, like the flock at Jerusalem on its feast days, so shall the ruined cities be filled with flocks of men. Then they shall know that I *am* the LORD."'"

The Dry Bones Live

37 The hand of the LORD came upon me and brought me out in the Spirit of the LORD, and set me down in the midst of the valley; and it *was* full of bones. ²Then He caused me to pass by them all around, and behold, *there were* very many in the open valley; and indeed *they were* very dry. ³And He said to me, "Son of man, can these bones live?"

So I answered, "O Lord GOD, You know."

⁴Again He said to me, "Prophesy to these bones, and say to them, 'O dry bones, hear the word of the LORD! ⁵Thus says the

BIBLICAL INSIGHTS • 37:11

Let Jesus Heal Your Broken Heart

ARE YOU BROKENHEARTED over a child, a relationship with a family member, or some unpleasant incident between you and another person? These heartbreaks and sorrows are a part of life. I have faced many of them and almost always found myself without any word for them. But when we give Christ authority over our days, we discover that He has the authority, the power, and the wisdom to make our lives so much better than they would ever be without Him. He wants us to give Him our hurts and sorrows.

Will you take your broken heart with you to the grave and end up hopeless? Or will you take your broken heart to Christ and let the Great Physician heal you on His authority? Remember, Jesus is the incarnation of the God who said, "I will open your graves and cause you to come up from your graves ... I will put My Spirit in you, and you shall live" (37:12, 14).

Apart from Christ, we are dead in our trespasses and sins (Eph. 2:1), just like the dry bones in Ezekiel's vision. But Jesus came that we might have life, and have it more abundantly (John 10:10). If you have never experienced the abundant life that Christ came to give us, ask Him to breathe new life into your dry bones!

Lord GOD to these bones: "Surely I will cause breath to enter into you, and you shall live. ⁶I will put sinews on you and bring flesh upon you, cover you with skin and put breath in you; and you shall live. Then you shall know that I *am* the LORD."'"

⁷So I prophesied as I was commanded; and as I prophesied, there was a noise, and suddenly a rattling; and the bones came together, bone to bone. ⁸Indeed, as I looked, the sinews and the flesh came upon them, and the skin covered them over; but *there was* no breath in them.

⁹Also He said to me, "Prophesy to the breath, prophesy, son of man, and say to

the breath, 'Thus says the Lord GOD: "Come from the four winds, O breath, and breathe on these slain, that they may live."'" [10]So I prophesied as He commanded me, and breath came into them, and they lived, and stood upon their feet, an exceedingly great army.

[11]Then He said to me, "Son of man, these bones are the whole house of Israel. They indeed say, 'Our bones are dry, our hope is lost, and we ourselves are cut off!' [12]Therefore prophesy and say to them, 'Thus says the Lord GOD: "Behold, O My people, I will open your graves and cause you to come up from your graves, and bring you into the land of Israel. [13]Then you shall know that I *am* the LORD, when I have opened your graves, O My people, and brought you up from your graves. [14]I will put My Spirit in you, and you shall live, and I will place you in your own land. Then you shall know that I, the LORD, have spoken *it* and performed *it,*" says the LORD.'"

One Kingdom, One King

[15]Again the word of the LORD came to me, saying, [16]"As for you, son of man, take a stick for yourself and write on it: 'For Judah and for the children of Israel, his companions.' Then take another stick and write on it, 'For Joseph, the stick of Ephraim, and *for* all the house of Israel, his companions.' [17]Then join them one to another for yourself into one stick, and they will become one in your hand.

[18]"And when the children of your people speak to you, saying, 'Will you not show us what you *mean* by these?'— [19]say to them, 'Thus says the Lord GOD: "Surely I will take the stick of Joseph, which *is* in the hand of Ephraim, and the tribes of Israel, his companions; and I will join them with it, with the stick of Judah, and make them one stick, and they will be one in My hand."' [20]And the sticks on which you write will be in your hand before their eyes.

[21]"Then say to them, 'Thus says the Lord GOD: "Surely I will take the children of Israel from among the nations, wherever they have gone, and will gather them from every side and bring them into their own land; [22]and I will make them one nation in the land, on the mountains of Israel; and one king shall be king over them all; they shall no longer be two nations, nor shall they ever be divided into two kingdoms again. [23]They shall not defile themselves anymore with their idols, nor with their detestable things, nor with any of their transgressions; but I will deliver them from all their dwelling places in which they have sinned, and will cleanse them. Then they shall be My people, and I will be their God.

[24]"David My servant *shall be* king over them, and they shall all have one shepherd; they shall also walk in My judgments and observe My statutes, and do them. [25]Then they shall dwell in the land that I have given to Jacob My servant, where your fathers dwelt; and they shall dwell there, they, their children, and their children's children, forever; and My servant David *shall be* their prince forever. [26]Moreover I will make a covenant of peace with them, and it shall be an everlasting covenant with them; I will establish them and multiply them, and I will set My sanctuary in their midst forevermore. [27]My tabernacle also shall be with them; indeed I will be their God, and they shall be My people. [28]The nations also will know that I, the LORD, sanctify Israel, when My sanctuary is in their midst forevermore."'"

Gog and Allies Attack Israel

38 Now the word of the LORD came to me, saying, [2]"Son of man, set your face against Gog, of the land of Magog, the prince of Rosh,[a] Meshech, and Tubal, and prophesy against him, [3]and say, 'Thus says the Lord GOD: "Behold, I *am* against you, O Gog, the prince of Rosh, Meshech, and Tubal. [4]I will turn you around, put hooks into your jaws, and lead you out, with all your army, horses, and horsemen, all splendidly clothed, a great company *with* bucklers and shields, all of them handling swords. [5]Persia, Ethiopia,[a] and Libya[b] are with them, all of them *with* shield and helmet; [6]Gomer and all its troops; the house of Togarmah *from* the far north and all its troops—many people *are* with you.

[7]"Prepare yourself and be ready, you and all your companies that are gathered

---

38:2 [a]Targum, Vulgate, and Aquila read *chief prince of* (also verse 3). **38:5** [a]Hebrew *Cush* [b]Hebrew *Put*

about you; and be a guard for them. ⁸After many days you will be visited. In the latter years you will come into the land of *those brought back from the sword and gathered from many people on the mountains of Israel, which had long been desolate; they were brought out of the nations, and now all of them dwell safely. ⁹You will ascend, coming like a storm, covering the land like a cloud, you and all your troops and many peoples with you."

¹⁰"Thus says the Lord GOD: "On that day it shall come to pass *that* thoughts will arise in your mind, and you will make an evil plan: ¹¹You will say, 'I will go up against a land of unwalled villages; I will go to a peaceful people, who dwell safely, all of them dwelling without walls, and having neither bars nor gates'— ¹²to take plunder and to take booty, to stretch out your hand against the waste places *that are again* inhabited, and against a people gathered from the nations, who have acquired livestock and goods, who dwell in the midst of the land. ¹³Sheba, Dedan, the merchants of Tarshish, and all their young lions will say to you, 'Have you come to take plunder? Have you gathered your army to take booty, to carry away silver and gold, to take away livestock and goods, to take great plunder?'"'

¹⁴"Therefore, son of man, prophesy and say to Gog, 'Thus says the Lord GOD: "On that day when My people Israel dwell safely, will you not know *it?* ¹⁵Then you will come from your place out of the far north, you and many peoples with you, all of them riding on horses, a great company and a mighty army. ¹⁶You will come up against My people Israel like a cloud, to cover the land. It will be in the latter days that I will bring you against My land, so that the nations may know Me, when I am hallowed in you, O Gog, before their eyes."

¹⁷Thus says the Lord GOD: "Are *you* he of whom I have spoken in former days by My servants the prophets of Israel, who prophesied for years in those days that I would bring you against them?

Judgment on Gog

¹⁸"And it will come to pass at the same time, when Gog comes against the land of Israel," says the Lord GOD, "*that* My fury will show in My face. ¹⁹For in My jealousy *and* in the fire of My wrath I have spoken: 'Surely in that day there shall be a great earthquake in the land of Israel, ²⁰so that the fish of the sea, the birds of the heavens, the beasts of the field, all creeping things that creep on the earth, and all men who *are* on the face of the earth shall shake at My presence. The mountains shall be thrown down, the steep places shall fall, and every wall shall fall to the ground.' ²¹I will call for a sword against Gog throughout all My mountains," says the Lord GOD. "Every man's sword will be against his brother. ²²And I will bring him to judgment with pestilence and bloodshed; I will rain down on him, on his troops, and on the many peoples who *are* with him, flooding rain, great hailstones, fire, and brimstone. ²³Thus I will magnify Myself and sanctify Myself, and I will be known in the eyes of many nations. Then they shall know that I *am* the LORD."'

Gog's Armies Destroyed

39 "And you, son of man, prophesy against Gog, and say, 'Thus says the Lord GOD: "Behold, I *am* against you, O Gog, the prince of Rosh,ᵃ Meshech, and Tubal; ²and I will turn you around and lead you on, bringing you up from the far north, and bring you against the mountains of Israel. ³Then I will knock the bow out of your left hand, and cause the arrows to fall out of your right hand. ⁴You shall fall upon the mountains of Israel, you and all your troops and the peoples who *are* with you; I will give you to birds of prey of every sort and *to* the beasts of the field to be devoured. ⁵You shall fall on the open field; for I have spoken," says the Lord GOD. ⁶"And I will send fire on Magog and on those who live in security in the coastlands. Then they shall know that I *am* the LORD. ⁷So I will make My holy name known in the midst of My people Israel, and I will not *let them* profane My holy name anymore. Then the nations shall know that *I am* the LORD, the Holy One in Israel. ⁸Surely it is coming, and it shall be done," says the Lord GOD. "This *is* the day of which I have spoken.

39:1 ᵃTargum, Vulgate and Aquila read *chief prince of*

9"Then those who dwell in the cities of Israel will go out and set on fire and burn the weapons, both the shields and bucklers, the bows and arrows, the javelins and spears; and they will make fires with them for seven years. 10They will not take wood from the field nor cut down *any* from the forests, because they will make fires with the weapons; and they will plunder those who plundered them, and pillage those who pillaged them," says the Lord GOD.

The Burial of Gog

11"It will come to pass in that day *that* I will give Gog a burial place there in Israel, the valley of those who pass by east of the sea; and it will obstruct travelers, because there they will bury Gog and all his multitude. Therefore they will call *it* the Valley of Hamon Gog.ᵃ 12For seven months the house of Israel will be burying them, in order to cleanse the land. 13Indeed all the people of the land will be burying, and they will gain renown for it on the day that I am glorified," says the Lord GOD. 14"They will set apart men regularly employed, with the help of a search party,ᵃ to pass through the land and bury those bodies remaining on the ground, in order to cleanse it. At the end of seven months they will make a search. 15The search party will pass through the land; and *when anyone* sees a man's bone, he shall set up a marker by it, till the buriers have buried it in the Valley of Hamon Gog. 16*The* name of *the* city *will* also *be* Hamonah. Thus they shall cleanse the land."'

A Triumphant Festival

17"And as for you, son of man, thus says the Lord GOD, 'Speak to every sort of bird and to every beast of the field:

"Assemble yourselves and come;
Gather together from all sides to My
   sacrificial meal
Which I am sacrificing for you,
A great sacrificial meal on the
   mountains of Israel,
That you may eat flesh and drink
   blood.
18 You shall eat the flesh of the mighty,
Drink the blood of the princes of the
   earth,

Of rams and lambs,
Of goats and bulls,
All of them fatlings of Bashan.
19 You shall eat fat till you are full,
And drink blood till you are drunk,
At My sacrificial meal
Which I am sacrificing for you.
20 You shall be filled at My table
With horses and riders,
With mighty men
And with all the men of war," says
   the Lord GOD.

Israel Restored to the Land

21"I will set My glory among the nations; all the nations shall see My judgment which I have executed, and My hand which I have laid on them. 22So the house of Israel shall know that I *am* the LORD their God from that day forward. 23The Gentiles shall know that the house of Israel went into captivity for their iniquity; because they were unfaithful to Me, therefore I hid My face from them. I gave them into the hand of their enemies, and they all fell by the sword. 24According to their uncleanness and according to their transgressions I have dealt with them, and hidden My face from them."'

25"Therefore thus says the Lord GOD: 'Now I will bring back the captives of Jacob, and have mercy on the whole house of Israel; and I will be jealous for My holy name— 26after they have borne their shame, and all their unfaithfulness in which they were unfaithful to Me, when they dwelt safely in their *own* land and no one made *them* afraid. 27When I have brought them back from the peoples and gathered them out of their enemies' lands, and I am hallowed in them in the sight of many nations, 28then they shall know that I *am* the LORD their God, who sent them into captivity among the nations, but also brought them back to their land, and left none of them captive any longer. 29And I will not hide My face from them anymore; for I shall have poured out My Spirit on the house of Israel,' says the Lord GOD."

39:11 ᵃLiterally *The Multitude of Gog*
39:14 ᵃLiterally *those who pass through*

A New City, a New Temple

40 In the twenty-fifth year of our captivity, at the beginning of the year, on the tenth *day* of the month, in the fourteenth year after the city was captured, on the very same day the hand of the LORD was upon me; and He took me there. ²In the visions of God He took me into the land of Israel and set me on a very high mountain; on it toward the south *was* something like the structure of a city. ³He took me there, and behold, *there was* a man whose appearance *was* like the appearance of bronze. He had a line of flax and a measuring rod in his hand, and he stood in the gateway.

⁴And the man said to me, "Son of man, look with your eyes and hear with your ears, and fix your mind on everything I show you; for you *were* brought here so that I might show *them* to you. Declare to the house of Israel everything you see." ⁵Now there was a wall all around the outside of the temple.ᵃ In the man's hand was a measuring rod six cubits *long, each being a* cubit and a handbreadth; and he measured the width of the wall structure, one rod; and the height, one rod.

The Eastern Gateway of the Temple

⁶Then he went to the gateway which faced east; and he went up its stairs and measured the threshold of the gateway, *which was* one rod wide, and the other threshold *was* one rod wide. ⁷Each gate chamber *was* one rod long and one rod wide; between the gate chambers *was a space of* five cubits; and the threshold of the gateway by the vestibule of the inside gate *was* one rod. ⁸He also measured the vestibule of the inside gate, one rod. ⁹Then he measured the vestibule of the gateway, eight cubits; and the gateposts, two cubits. The vestibule of the gate *was* on the inside. ¹⁰In the eastern gateway *were* three gate chambers on one side and three on the other; the three *were* all the same size; also the gateposts were of the same size on this side and that side. ¹¹He measured the width of the entrance to the gateway, ten cubits; *and* the length of the gate, thirteen cubits. ¹²*There was* a

40:5 ᵃLiterally *house,* and so elsewhere in this book

BIBLICAL INSIGHTS • 40:3
God's Measuring Rod

"THE STRENGTH OF A NATION," said Abraham Lincoln, "lies in the homes of its people." In other words, the state of the union is determined by the state of the marriage union—the condition of our nation's marriages, families, and homes.

But by what yardstick can we accurately measure how our homes are doing? Ezekiel once saw a vision of an angel taking measurements of Jerusalem, symbolically giving God's estimation of the city (40:1—44:3). *That* is the kind of measure we need to apply to our homes and our nation—what does God think?

And what do we see as we use the divine measuring rod? We see that for every two marriages that begin this year there will be one marriage that will end in divorce. We see the birth rate declining, while juvenile delinquency, sexual perversion, and promiscuity continue to skyrocket.

Why is this happening? It's taking place because *the state of the union is determined by the state of the marriage union.*

Are we destined as a nation to follow in the footsteps of all other cultures throughout history that have fallen because of such a moral decline? Our only hope is to rebuild the walls of both the home and the nation according to God's measuring rod. And the rebuilding process begins in each of our families as we start to know, apply, experience, embrace, and ultimately proclaim God's truth about what makes strong, healthy marriages and families.

space in front of the gate chambers, one cubit *on this side* and one cubit on that side; the gate chambers *were* six cubits on this side and six cubits on that side. ¹³Then he measured the gateway from the roof of *one* gate chamber to the roof of the other; the width *was* twenty-five cubits, as door faces door. ¹⁴He measured the gateposts, sixty cubits high, and the court all around the gateway *extended* to the gatepost. [15]*From* the front of the entrance gate to the front of the vestibule of the inner gate *was* fifty cubits. [16]*There were* beveled window *frames* in the gate chambers and in their intervening archways on the inside of the gateway all around, and likewise in the vestibules. *There were* windows all around on the inside. And on each gatepost *were* palm trees.

The Outer Court

[17]Then he brought me into the outer court; and *there were* chambers and a pavement made all around the court; thirty chambers faced the pavement. [18]The pavement was by the side of the gateways, corresponding to the length of the gateways; *this was* the lower pavement. [19]Then he measured the width from the front of the lower gateway to the front of the inner court exterior, one hundred cubits toward the east and the north.

The Northern Gateway

[20]On the outer court was also a gateway facing north, and he measured its length and its width. [21]Its gate chambers, three on this side and three on that side, its gateposts and its archways, had the same measurements as the first gate; its length *was* fifty cubits and its width twenty-five cubits. [22]Its windows and those of its archways, and also its palm trees, *had* the same measurements as the gateway facing east; it was ascended by seven steps, and its archway *was* in front of it. [23]A gate of the inner court was opposite the northern gateway, just as the eastern *gateway;* and he measured from gateway to gateway, one hundred cubits.

The Southern Gateway

[24]After that he brought me toward the south, and there a gateway was facing south; and he measured its gateposts and archways according to these same measurements. [25]*There were* windows in it and in its archways all around like those windows; its length *was* fifty cubits and its width twenty-five cubits. [26]Seven steps led up to it, and its archway *was* in front of them; and it had palm trees on its gateposts, one on this

side and one on that side. [27]*There was* also a gateway on the inner court, facing south; and he measured from gateway to gateway toward the south, one hundred cubits.

Gateways of the Inner Court

[28]Then he brought me to the inner court through the southern gateway; he measured the southern gateway according to these same measurements. [29]Also its gate chambers, its gateposts, and its archways *were* according to these same measurements; *there were* windows in it and in its archways all around; *it was* fifty cubits long and twenty-five cubits wide. [30]*There were* archways all around, twenty-five cubits long and five cubits wide. [31]Its archways faced the outer court, palm trees *were* on its gateposts, and going up to it *were* eight steps.

[32]And he brought me into the inner court facing east; he measured the gateway according to these same measurements. [33]Also its gate chambers, its gateposts, and its archways *were* according to these same measurements; and *there were* windows in it and in its archways all around; *it was* fifty cubits long and twenty-five cubits wide. [34]Its archways faced the outer court, and palm trees *were* on its gateposts on this side and on that side; and going up to it *were* eight steps.

[35]Then he brought me to the north gateway and measured *it* according to these same measurements— [36]also its gate chambers, its gateposts, and its archways. It had windows all around; its length *was* fifty cubits and its width twenty-five cubits. [37]Its gateposts faced the outer court, palm trees *were* on its gateposts on this side and on that side, and going up to it *were* eight steps.

Where Sacrifices Were Prepared

[38]*There was* a chamber and its entrance by the gateposts of the gateway, where they washed the burnt offering. [39]In the vestibule of the gateway *were* two tables on this side and two tables on that side, on which to slay the burnt offering, the sin offering, and the trespass offering. [40]At the outer side of the *vestibule,* as one goes up to the entrance of the northern gateway, *were* two tables; and on the other side of the *vestibule* of the gateway *were* two

tables. ⁴¹Four tables *were* on this side and four tables on that side, by the side of the gateway, eight tables on which they slaughtered *the sacrifices.* ⁴²*There were* also four tables of hewn stone for the burnt offering, one cubit and a half long, one cubit and a half wide, and one cubit high; on these they laid the instruments with which they slaughtered the burnt offering and the sacrifice. ⁴³Inside *were* hooks, a handbreadth wide, fastened all around; and the flesh of the sacrifices *was* on the tables.

Chambers for Singers and Priests

⁴⁴Outside the inner gate *were* the chambers for the singers in the inner court, one facing south at the side of the northern gateway, and the other facing north at the side of the southern^a gateway. ⁴⁵Then he said to me, "This chamber which faces south *is* for the priests who have charge of the temple. ⁴⁶The chamber which faces north *is* for the priests who have charge of the altar; these *are* the sons of Zadok, from the sons of Levi, who come near the LORD to minister to Him."

Dimensions of the Inner Court and Vestibule

⁴⁷And he measured the court, one hundred cubits long and one hundred cubits wide, foursquare. The altar *was* in front of the temple. ⁴⁸Then he brought me to the vestibule of the temple and measured the doorposts of the vestibule, five cubits on this side and five cubits on that side; and the width of the gateway was three cubits on this side and three cubits on that side. ⁴⁹The length of the vestibule *was* twenty cubits, and the width eleven cubits; and by the steps which led up to it *there were* pillars by the doorposts, one on this side and another on that side.

Dimensions of the Sanctuary

41 Then he brought me into the sanctuary^a and measured the doorposts, six cubits wide on one side and six cubits wide on the other side—the width of the tabernacle. ²The width of the entryway *was* ten cubits, and the side walls of the entrance *were* five cubits on this side and five cubits on the other side; and he measured its length, forty cubits, and its width, twenty cubits.

³Also he went inside and measured the doorposts, two cubits; and the entrance, six cubits *high;* and the width of the entrance, seven cubits. ⁴He measured the length, twenty cubits; and the width, twenty cubits, beyond the sanctuary; and he said to me, "This *is* the Most Holy *Place.*"

The Side Chambers on the Wall

⁵Next, he measured the wall of the temple, six cubits. The width of each side

---

40:44 ^aFollowing Septuagint; Masoretic Text and Vulgate read *eastern.* **41:1** ^aHebrew *heykal,* here the main room of the temple, sometimes called the *holy place* (compare Exodus 26:33)

chamber all around the temple *was* four cubits on every side. [6]The side chambers *were* in three stories, one above the other, thirty chambers in each story; they rested on ledges which *were* for the side chambers all around, that they might be supported, but not fastened to the wall of the temple. [7]As one went up from story to story, the side chambers became wider all around, because their supporting ledges in the wall of the temple ascended like steps; therefore the width of the structure increased as one went up *from* the lowest *story* to the highest by way of the middle one. [8]I also saw an elevation all around the temple; it was the foundation of the side chambers, a full rod, *that is,* six cubits *high.* [9]The thickness of the outer wall of the side chambers *was* five cubits, and so also the remaining terrace by the place of the side chambers of the temple. [10]And between *it and the wall* chambers was a width of twenty cubits all around the temple on every side. [11]The doors of the side chambers opened on the terrace, one door toward the north and another toward the south; and the width of the terrace *was* five cubits all around.

The Building at the Western End

[12]The building that faced the separating courtyard at its western end *was* seventy cubits wide; the wall of the building *was* five cubits thick all around, and its length ninety cubits.

Dimensions and Design of the Temple Area

[13]So he measured the temple, one hundred cubits long; and the separating courtyard with the building and its walls *was* one hundred cubits long; [14]also the width of the eastern face of the temple, including the separating courtyard, *was* one hundred cubits. [15]He measured the length of the building behind it, facing the separating courtyard, with its galleries on the one side and on the other side, one hundred cubits, as well as the inner temple and the porches of the court, [16]their doorposts and the beveled window frames. And the galleries all around their three stories opposite the threshold were paneled with wood from the ground to the windows—the windows

were covered— [17]from the space above the door, even to the inner room,[a] as well as outside, and on every wall all around, inside and outside, by measure.

[18]And *it was* made with cherubim and palm trees, a palm tree between cherub and cherub. *Each* cherub had two faces, [19]so that the face of a man *was* toward a palm tree on one side, and the face of a young lion toward a palm tree on the other side; thus *it was* made throughout the temple all around. [20]From the floor to the space above the door, and on the wall of the sanctuary, cherubim and palm trees *were* carved.

[21]The doorposts of the temple *were* square, *as was* the front of the sanctuary; their appearance was similar. [22]The altar *was* of wood, three cubits high, and its length two cubits. Its corners, its length, and its sides *were* of wood; and he said to me, "This *is* the table that *is* before the LORD."

[23]The temple and the sanctuary had two doors. [24]The doors had two panels *apiece,* two folding panels: two *panels* for one door and two panels for the other *door.* [25]Cherubim and palm trees *were* carved on the doors of the temple just as they *were* carved on the walls. A wooden canopy *was* on the front of the vestibule outside. [26]*There were* beveled window *frames* and palm trees on one side and on the other, on the sides of the vestibule—also on the side chambers of the temple and on the canopies.

The Chambers for the Priests

42 Then he brought me out into the outer court, by the way toward the north; and he brought me into the chamber which *was* opposite the separating courtyard, and which *was* opposite the building toward the north. [2]Facing the length, *which was* one hundred cubits (the width was fifty cubits), was the north door. [3]Opposite the inner court of twenty *cubits,* and opposite the pavement of the outer court, *was* gallery against gallery in three *stories.* [4]In front of the chambers, toward the inside, *was* a walk ten cubits wide, at a distance of one cubit; and their doors faced north. [5]Now the upper chambers *were* shorter,

41:17 [a]Literally *house,* here *the Most Holy Place*

because the galleries took away *space* from them more than from the lower and middle stories of the building. [6]For they *were* in three *stories* and did not have pillars like the pillars of the courts; therefore *the upper level* was shortened more than the lower and middle levels from the ground up. [7]And a wall which *was* outside ran parallel to the chambers, at the front of the chambers, toward the outer court; its length *was* fifty cubits. [8]The length of the chambers toward the outer court *was* fifty cubits, whereas that facing the temple *was* one hundred cubits. [9]At the lower chambers *was* the entrance on the east side, as one goes into them from the outer court.

[10]Also *there were* chambers in the thickness of the wall of the court toward the east, opposite the separating courtyard and opposite the building. [11]*There was* a walk in front of them also, and their appearance *was* like the chambers which *were* toward the north; they *were* as long and as wide as the others, and all their exits and entrances *were* according to plan. [12]And corresponding to the doors of the chambers that *were* facing south, as one enters them, *there was* a door in front of the walk, the way directly in front of the wall toward the east.

[13]Then he said to me, "The north chambers *and* the south chambers, which *are* opposite the separating courtyard, *are* the holy chambers where the priests who approach the LORD shall eat the most holy offerings. There they shall lay the most holy offerings—the grain offering, the sin offering, and the trespass offering—for the place *is* holy. [14]When the priests enter them, they shall not go out of the holy *chamber* into the outer court; but there they shall leave their garments in which they minister, for they *are* holy. They shall put on other garments; then they may approach *that* which *is* for the people."

Outer Dimensions of the Temple

[15]Now when he had finished measuring the inner temple, he brought me out through the gateway that faces toward the east, and measured it all around. [16]He measured the east side with the measuring rod,[a] five hundred rods by the measuring rod all around. [17]He measured the north side, five hundred rods by the measuring rod all around. [18]He measured the south side, five hundred rods by the measuring rod. [19]He came around to the west side *and* measured five hundred rods by the measuring rod. [20]He measured it on the four sides; it had a wall all around, five hundred *cubits* long and five hundred wide, to separate the holy areas from the common.

The Temple, the LORD's Dwelling Place

43 Afterward he brought me to the gate, the gate that faces toward the east. [2]And behold, the glory of the God of Israel came from the way of the east. His voice *was* like the sound of many waters; and the earth shone with His glory. [3]*It was* like the appearance of the vision which I saw—like the vision which I saw when I[a] came to destroy the city. The visions *were* like the vision which I saw by the River Chebar; and I fell on my face. [4]And the glory of the LORD came into the temple by way of the gate which faces toward the east. [5]The Spirit lifted me up and brought me into the inner court; and behold, the glory of the LORD filled the temple.

[6]Then I heard *Him* speaking to me from the temple, while a man stood beside me. [7]And He said to me, "Son of man, *this is* the place of My throne and the place of the soles of My feet, where I will dwell in the midst of the children of Israel forever. No more shall the house of Israel defile My holy name, they nor their kings, by their harlotry or with the carcasses of their kings on their high places. [8]When they set their threshold by My threshold, and their doorpost by My doorpost, with a wall between them and Me, they defiled My holy name by the abominations which they committed; therefore I have consumed them in My anger. [9]Now let them put their harlotry and the carcasses of their kings far away from Me, and I will dwell in their midst forever.

[10]"Son of man, describe the temple to the house of Israel, that they may be ashamed of their iniquities; and let them measure the pattern. [11]And if they are ashamed of all that they have done, make

---

42:16 [a]Compare 40:5 43:3 [a]Some Hebrew manuscripts and Vulgate read *He.*

known to them the design of the temple and its arrangement, its exits and its entrances, its entire design and all its ordinances, all its forms and all its laws. Write *it* down in their sight, so that they may keep its whole design and all its ordinances, and perform them. ¹²This *is* the law of the temple: The whole area surrounding the mountaintop *is* most holy. Behold, this *is* the law of the temple.

Dimensions of the Altar

¹³"These are the measurements of the altar in cubits (the cubit *is* one cubit and a handbreadth): the base one cubit high and one cubit wide, with a rim all around its edge of one span. This *is* the height of the altar: ¹⁴from the base on the ground to the lower ledge, two cubits; the width of the ledge, one cubit; from the smaller ledge to the larger ledge, four cubits; and the width of the ledge, *one* cubit. ¹⁵The altar hearth *is* four cubits high, with four horns extending upward from the hearth. ¹⁶The altar hearth *is* twelve *cubits* long, twelve wide, square at its four corners; ¹⁷the ledge, fourteen *cubits* long and fourteen wide on its four sides, with a rim of half a cubit around it; its base, one cubit all around; and its steps face toward the east."

Consecrating the Altar

¹⁸And He said to me, "Son of man, thus says the Lord GOD: 'These *are* the ordinances for the altar on the day when it is made, for sacrificing burnt offerings on it, and for sprinkling blood on it. ¹⁹You shall give a young bull for a sin offering to the priests, the Levites, who are of the seed of Zadok, who approach Me to minister to Me,' says the Lord GOD. ²⁰You shall take some of its blood and put *it* on the four horns of the altar, on the four corners of the ledge, and on the rim around it; thus you shall cleanse it and make atonement for it. ²¹Then you shall also take the bull of the sin offering, and burn it in the appointed place of the temple, outside the sanctuary. ²²On the second day you shall offer a kid of the goats without blemish for a sin offering; and they shall cleanse the altar, as they cleansed *it* with the bull. ²³When you have finished cleansing *it,* you shall offer a young bull without blemish, and a ram from the flock without blemish. ²⁴When you offer them before the LORD, the priests shall throw salt on them, and they will offer them up *as* a burnt offering to the LORD. ²⁵Every day for seven days you shall prepare a goat *for* a sin offering; they shall

---

PARENTING MATTERS

Q: How can we most effectively communicate with our children the truths of sin and God's forgiveness?

Many parents think their children are too young to understand the gospel. Yet, many children understand faith at an early age—our own six children made professions of faith in Christ before the age of six.

Even the deepest of books of the Bible like Romans can be brought to life for a child. For example, kids learn of their mistakes within a family. They see their own tendencies to be selfish, to disobey, and to sin as they live under our roofs. You can explain a verse such as Romans 3:23 to them by using their selfishness as an example of what it means to "fall short of the glory of God."

Or take the concept of forgiveness. From a very early age, Barbara and I taught our children that when they disobeyed us or hurt a brother or sister, they needed to go and ask that person for forgiveness. They learned the process of forgiveness within the family, and we referred to those experiences when we explained to them God's forgiveness and having "peace with God" (Rom. 5:1).

The family is a divine incubator for teaching spiritual truths. We need to use it when teaching our children the fundamentals of faith.

also prepare a young bull and a ram from the flock, both without blemish. ²⁶Seven days they shall make atonement for the altar and purify it, and so consecrate *it*. ²⁷When these days are over it shall be, on the eighth day and thereafter, that the priests shall offer your burnt offerings and your peace offerings on the altar; and I will accept you,' says the Lord GOD."

The East Gate and the Prince

44 Then He brought me back to the outer gate of the sanctuary which faces toward the east, but it *was* shut. ²And the LORD said to me, "This gate shall be shut; it shall not be opened, and no man shall enter by it, because the LORD God of Israel has entered by it; therefore it shall be shut. ³*As for* the prince, *because* he *is* the prince, he may sit in it to eat bread before the LORD; he shall enter by way of the vestibule of the gateway, and go out the same way."

Those Admitted to the Temple

⁴Also He brought me by way of the north gate to the front of the temple; so I looked, and behold, the glory of the LORD filled the house of the LORD; and I fell on my face. ⁵And the LORD said to me, "Son of man, mark well, see with your eyes and hear with your ears, all that I say to you concerning all the ordinances of the house of the LORD and all its laws. Mark well who may enter the house and all who go out from the sanctuary.

⁶"Now say to the rebellious, to the house of Israel, 'Thus says the Lord GOD: "O house of Israel, let Us have no more of all your abominations. ⁷When you brought in foreigners, uncircumcised in heart and uncircumcised in flesh, to be in My sanctuary to defile it—My house—and when you offered My food, the fat and the blood, then they broke My covenant because of all your abominations. ⁸And you have not kept charge of My holy things, but you have set *others* to keep charge of My sanctuary for you." ⁹Thus says the Lord GOD: "No foreigner, uncircumcised in heart or uncircumcised in flesh, shall enter My sanctuary, including any foreigner who *is* among the children of Israel.

Laws Governing Priests

¹⁰"And the Levites who went far from Me, when Israel went astray, who strayed away from Me after their idols, they shall bear their iniquity. ¹¹Yet they shall be ministers in My sanctuary, *as* gatekeepers of the house and ministers of the house; they shall slay the burnt offering and the sacrifice for the people, and they shall stand before them to minister to them. ¹²Because they ministered to them before their idols and caused the house of Israel to fall into iniquity, therefore I have raised My hand in an oath against them," says the Lord GOD, "that they shall bear their iniquity. ¹³And they shall not come near Me to minister to Me as priest, nor come near any of My holy things, nor into the Most Holy

BIBLICAL INSIGHTS • 44:15

You Can Make a Difference

GOD WANTS YOUR FAMILY to be a light in a dark world. And make no mistake—an ordinary family really can have a tremendous impact on our world (see Ezek. 44:15).

In the early days of World War II, a large Allied army found itself trapped in the channel port of Dunkirk. Hitler's tank forces, only miles away, were ready to smash forward. Britain's Royal Navy lacked the ships to mount a rescue. But then, as William Manchester describes in his book, *The Last Lion*, "A strange fleet appeared: trawlers and tugs, scows and fishing sloops, lifeboats and pleasure craft, smacks and coasters . . . even the London Fire Brigade's fire-float Massey Shaw—all of them manned by civilian volunteers: English fathers, sailing to rescue England's exhausted, bleeding sons."

This ragtag civilian armada brought 338,682 men safely to the shores of England. Common people had made the difference.

Today, our nation's marriages and children face their own Dunkirk. And I wonder, *Will there be enough common people willing to set sail to rescue this generation of exhausted, bleeding children of divorce and broken families?*

The task may seem massive given the state of marriage and families in our culture. But like the common people who rescued the soldiers at Dunkirk, we can do our part by reaching out to those in our neighborhoods and our workplaces with the hope of the gospel and the wisdom of God's Word.

Place; but they shall bear their shame and their abominations which they have committed. [14]Nevertheless I will make them keep charge of the temple, for all its work, and for all that has to be done in it.

[15]"But the priests, the Levites, the sons of Zadok, who kept charge of My sanctuary when the children of Israel went astray from Me, they shall come near Me to minister to Me; and they shall stand before Me to offer to Me the fat and the blood," says the Lord GOD. [16]"They shall enter My sanctuary, and they shall come near My table to minister to Me, and they shall keep My charge. [17]And it shall be, whenever they enter the gates of the inner court, that they shall put on linen garments; no wool shall come upon them while they minister within the gates of the inner court or within the house. [18]They shall have linen turbans on their heads and linen trousers on their bodies; they shall not clothe themselves with *anything that causes* sweat. [19]When they go out to the outer court, to the outer court to the people, they shall take off their garments in which they have ministered, leave them in the holy chambers, and put on other garments; and in their holy garments they shall not sanctify the people.

[20]"They shall neither shave their heads, nor let their hair grow long, but they shall keep their hair well trimmed. [21]No priest shall drink wine when he enters the inner court. [22]They shall not take as wife a widow or a divorced woman, but take virgins of the descendants of the house of Israel, or widows of priests.

[23]"And they shall teach My people *the difference* between the holy and the unholy, and cause them to discern between the unclean and the clean. [24]In controversy they shall stand as judges, *and* judge it according to My judgments. They shall keep My laws and My statutes in all My appointed meetings, and they shall hallow My Sabbaths.

[25]"They shall not defile *themselves* by coming near a dead person. Only for father or mother, for son or daughter, for brother or unmarried sister may they defile themselves. [26]After he is cleansed, they shall count seven days for him. [27]And on the day that he goes to the sanctuary to minister in the sanctuary, he must offer his sin offering in the inner court," says the Lord GOD.

[28]"It shall be, in regard to their inheritance, *that* I *am* their inheritance. You shall give them no possession in Israel, for I *am* their possession. [29]They shall eat the grain offering, the sin offering, and the trespass offering; every dedicated thing in Israel

shall be theirs. [30]The best of all firstfruits of any kind, and every sacrifice of any kind from all your sacrifices, shall be the priest's; also you shall give to the priest the first of your ground meal, to cause a blessing to rest on your house. [31]The priests shall not eat anything, bird or beast, that died naturally or was torn *by wild beasts*.

The Holy District

45 "Moreover, when you divide the land by lot into inheritance, you shall set apart a district for the LORD, a holy section of the land; its length *shall be* twenty-five thousand *cubits,* and the width ten thousand. It *shall be* holy throughout its territory all around. [2]Of this there shall be a square plot for the sanctuary, five hundred by five hundred *rods,* with fifty cubits around it for an open space. [3]So this is the district you shall measure: twenty-five thousand *cubits* long and ten thousand wide; in it shall be the sanctuary, the Most Holy *Place.* [4]It shall be a holy *section* of the land, belonging to the priests, the ministers of the sanctuary, who come near to minister to the LORD; it shall be a place for their houses and a holy place for the sanctuary. [5]*An area* twenty-five thousand *cubits* long and ten thousand wide shall belong to the Levites, the ministers of the

45:5 [a]Following Masoretic Text, Targum, and Vulgate; Septuagint reads *a possession, cities of dwelling*.

temple; they shall have twenty chambers as a possession.[a]

Properties of the City and the Prince

[6]"You shall appoint as the property of the city *an area* five thousand *cubits* wide and twenty-five thousand long, adjacent to the district of the holy *section;* it shall belong to the whole house of Israel.

[7]"The prince shall have *a section* on one side and the other of the holy district and the city's property; and bordering on the holy district and the city's property, extending westward on the west side and eastward on the east side, the length *shall be* side by side with one of the *tribal* portions, from the west border to the east border. [8]The land shall be his possession in Israel; and My princes shall no more oppress My people, but they shall give *the rest of* the land to the house of Israel, according to their tribes."

Laws Governing the Prince

[9]Thus says the Lord GOD: "Enough, O princes of Israel! Remove violence and plundering, execute justice and righteousness, and stop dispossessing My people," says the Lord GOD. [10]"You shall have honest scales, an honest ephah, and an honest bath. [11]The ephah and the bath shall be of the same measure, so that the bath contains one-tenth of a homer, and the ephah one-tenth of a homer; their measure shall

---

ROMANTIC QUOTES AND NOTES
The Parable of the Porcupines

Have you heard the story of the two porcupines freezing in the winter cold? Shivering in the frigid air, the two porcupines moved closer together to share body heat. But when their sharp spines and quills pricked each other, they moved apart, victims once more of the bitter cold. Soon they felt they must come together once again or freeze to death. But their quills caused too much pain, and once again they parted.

Does the parable of the porcupines remind you at all of anything going on under your own roof? Family members can also suffer from the cold of isolation, and often they learn the pain of drawing close to someone with sharp quills. We desperately need to learn how to live with the barbs that are part of coming together in oneness!

The fact is, intimacy extracts a price. The closer I get to Barbara, the more she becomes aware of who I really am. The more transparent we become, the greater the possibility that she will reject me. But if both of us are committed to each other despite our quills—if we are willing, as Jesus said, to lose our lives instead of saving them—then intimacy awaits us.

be according to the homer. ¹²The shekel *shall be* twenty gerahs; twenty shekels, twenty-five shekels, *and* fifteen shekels shall be your mina.

¹³"This *is* the offering which you shall offer: you shall give one-sixth of an ephah from a homer of wheat, and one-sixth of an ephah from a homer of barley. ¹⁴The ordinance concerning oil, the bath of oil, *is* one-tenth of a bath from a kor. *A kor is* a homer or ten baths, for ten baths *are* a homer. ¹⁵And one lamb shall be given from a flock of two hundred, from the rich pastures of Israel. These shall be for grain offerings, burnt offerings, and peace offerings, to make atonement for them," says the Lord GOD. ¹⁶"All the people of the land shall give this offering for the prince in Israel. ¹⁷Then it shall be the prince's part *to give* burnt offerings, grain offerings, and drink offerings, at the feasts, the New Moons, the Sabbaths, and at all the appointed seasons of the house of Israel. He shall prepare the sin offering, the grain offering, the burnt offering, and the peace offerings to make atonement for the house of Israel."

Keeping the Feasts

¹⁸'Thus says the Lord GOD: "In the first *month,* on the first *day* of the month, you shall take a young bull without blemish and cleanse the sanctuary. ¹⁹The priest shall take some of the blood of the sin offering and put *it* on the doorposts of the temple, on the four corners of the ledge of the altar, and on the gateposts of the gate of the inner court. ²⁰And so you shall do on the seventh *day* of the month for everyone who has sinned unintentionally or in ignorance. Thus you shall make atonement for the temple.

²¹"In the first *month,* on the fourteenth day of the month, you shall observe the Passover, a feast of seven days; unleavened bread shall be eaten. ²²And on that day the prince shall prepare for himself and for all the people of the land a bull *for* a sin offering. ²³On the seven days of the feast he shall prepare a burnt offering to the LORD, seven bulls and seven rams without blemish, daily for seven days, and a kid of the goats daily *for* a sin offering. ²⁴And he shall prepare a grain offering of one ephah for each bull and one ephah for each ram, together with a hin of oil for each ephah.

²⁵"In the seventh *month,* on the fifteenth day of the month, at the feast, he shall do likewise for seven days, according to the sin offering, the burnt offering, the grain offering, and the oil."

The Manner of Worship

46 'Thus says the Lord GOD: "The gateway of the inner court that faces toward the east shall be shut the six working days; but on the Sabbath it shall be opened, and on the day of the New Moon it shall be opened. ²The prince shall enter by way of the vestibule of the gateway from the outside, and stand by the gatepost. The priests shall prepare his burnt offering and his peace offerings. He shall worship at the threshold of the gate. Then he shall go out, but the gate shall not be shut until evening. ³Likewise the people of the land shall worship at the entrance to this gateway before the LORD on the Sabbaths and the New Moons. ⁴The burnt offering that the prince offers to the LORD on the Sabbath day *shall be* six lambs without blemish, and a ram without blemish; ⁵and the grain offering *shall be one* ephah for a ram, and the grain offering for the lambs, as much as he wants to give, as well as a hin of oil with every ephah. ⁶On the day of the New Moon *it shall be* a young bull without blemish, six lambs, and a ram; they shall be without blemish. ⁷He shall prepare a grain offering of an ephah for a bull, an ephah for a ram, as much as he wants to give for the lambs, and a hin of oil with every ephah. ⁸When the prince enters, he shall go in by way of the vestibule of the gateway, and go out the same way.

⁹"But when the people of the land come before the LORD on the appointed feast days, whoever enters by way of the north gate to worship shall go out by way of the south gate; and whoever enters by way of the south gate shall go out by way of the north gate. He shall not return by way of the gate through which he came, but shall go out through the opposite gate. ¹⁰The prince shall then be in their midst. When they go in, he shall go in; and when they go out, he shall go out. ¹¹At the festivals and

the appointed feast days the grain offering shall be an ephah for a bull, an ephah for a ram, as much as he wants to give for the lambs, and a hin of oil with every ephah. [12]"Now when the prince makes a voluntary burnt offering or voluntary peace offering to the Lord, the gate that faces toward the east shall then be opened for him; and he shall prepare his burnt offering and his peace offerings as he did on the Sabbath day. Then he shall go out, and after he goes out the gate shall be shut.

[13]"You shall daily make a burnt offering to the Lord *of* a lamb of the first year without blemish; you shall prepare it every morning. [14]And you shall prepare a grain offering with it every morning, a sixth of an ephah, and a third of a hin of oil to moisten the fine flour. This grain offering is a perpetual ordinance, to be made regularly to the Lord. [15]Thus they shall prepare the lamb, the grain offering, and the oil, *as* a regular burnt offering every morning."

The Prince and Inheritance Laws

[16]'Thus says the Lord God: "If the prince gives a gift *of some* of his inheritance to any of his sons, it shall belong to his sons; it is their possession by inheritance. [17]But if he gives a gift of some of his inheritance to one of his servants, it shall be his until the year of liberty, after which it shall return to the prince. But his inheritance shall belong to his sons; it shall become theirs. [18]Moreover the prince shall not take any of the people's inheritance by evicting them from their property; he shall provide an inheritance for his sons from his own property, so that none of My people may be scattered from his property.' "

How the Offerings Were Prepared

[19]Now he brought me through the entrance, which *was* at the side of the gate, into the holy chambers of the priests which face toward the north; and there a place *was* situated at their extreme western end. [20]And he said to me, "This *is* the place where the priests shall boil the trespass offering and the sin offering, *and* where they shall bake the grain offering, so that they do not bring *them* out into the outer court to sanctify the people."

[21]Then he brought me out into the outer court and caused me to pass by the four corners of the court; and in fact, in every corner of the court *there was another* court. [22]In the four corners of the court *were* enclosed courts, forty *cubits* long and thirty wide; all four corners *were* the same size. [23]*There was* a row *of building stones* all around in them, all around the four of them; and cooking hearths were made under the rows of stones all around. [24]And he said to me, "These *are* the kitchens where the ministers of the temple shall boil the sacrifices of the people."

The Healing Waters and Trees

47 Then he brought me back to the door of the temple; and there was water, flowing from under the threshold of the temple toward the east, for the front of the temple faced east; the water was flowing from under the right side of the temple, south of the altar. [2]He brought me out by way of the north gate, and led me around on the outside to the outer gateway that faces east; and there was water, running out on the right side.

[3]And when the man went out to the east with the line in his hand, he measured one thousand cubits, and he brought me through the waters; the water *came up to my* ankles. [4]Again he measured one thousand and brought me through the waters; the water *came up to my* knees. Again he measured one thousand and brought me through; the water *came up to my* waist. [5]Again he measured one thousand, *and it was* a river that I could not cross; for the water was too deep, water in which one must swim, a river that could not be crossed. [6]He said to me, "Son of man, have you seen *this?*" Then he brought me and returned me to the bank of the river.

[7]When I returned, there, along the bank of the river, *were* very many trees on one side and the other. [8]Then he said to me: "This water flows toward the eastern region, goes down into the valley, and enters the sea. *When it* reaches the sea, *its* waters are healed. [9]And it shall be *that* every living thing that moves, wherever the rivers go, will live. There will be a very great multitude of fish, because these

waters go there; for they will be healed, and everything will live wherever the river goes. [10]It shall be *that* fishermen will stand by it from En Gedi to En Eglaim; they will be *places* for spreading their nets. Their fish will be of the same kinds as the fish of the Great Sea, exceedingly many. [11]But its swamps and marshes will not be healed; they will be given over to salt. [12]Along the bank of the river, on this side and that, will grow all *kinds of* trees used for food; their leaves will not wither, and their fruit will not fail. They will bear fruit every month, because their water flows from the sanctuary. Their fruit will be for food, and their leaves for medicine."

Borders of the Land

[13]Thus says the Lord GOD: "These *are* the borders by which you shall divide the land as an inheritance among the twelve tribes of Israel. Joseph *shall have two* portions. [14]You shall inherit it equally with one another; for I raised My hand in an oath to give it to your fathers, and this land shall fall to you as your inheritance.

[15]"This *shall be* the border of the land on the north: from the Great Sea, *by* the road to Hethlon, as one goes to Zedad, [16]Hamath, Berothah, Sibraim (which *is* between the border of Damascus and the border of Hamath), to Hazar Hatticon (which *is* on the border of Hauran). [17]Thus the boundary shall be from the Sea to Hazar Enan, the border of Damascus; and as for the north, northward, it is the border of Hamath. *This is* the north side.

[18]"On the east side you shall mark out the border from between Hauran and Damascus, and between Gilead and the land of Israel, along the Jordan, and along the eastern side of the sea. *This is* the east side.

[19]"The south side, toward the South,[a] *shall be* from Tamar to the waters of Meribah by Kadesh, along the brook to the Great Sea. *This is* the south side, toward the South.

[20]"The west side *shall be* the Great Sea, from the *southern* boundary until one comes to a point opposite Hamath. This *is* the west side.

[21]"Thus you shall divide this land among yourselves according to the tribes

of Israel. [22]It shall be that you will divide it by lot as an inheritance for yourselves, and for the strangers who dwell among you and who bear children among you. They shall be to you as native-born among the children of Israel; they shall have an inheritance with you among the tribes of Israel. [23]And it shall be *that* in whatever tribe the stranger dwells, there you shall give *him* his inheritance," says the Lord GOD.

Division of the Land

48 "Now these *are* the names of the tribes: From the northern border along the road to Hethlon at the entrance of Hamath, to Hazar Enan, the border of Damascus northward, in the direction of Hamath, *there shall be* one *section for* Dan from its east to its west side; [2]by the border of Dan, from the east side to the west, one *section for* Asher; [3]by the border of Asher, from the east side to the west, one *section for* Naphtali; [4]by the border of Naphtali, from the east side to the west, one *section for* Manasseh; [5]by the border of Manasseh, from the east side to the west, one *section for* Ephraim; [6]by the border of Ephraim, from the east side to the west, one *section for* Reuben; [7]by the border of Reuben, from the east side to the west, one *section for* Judah; [8]by the border of Judah, from the east side to the west, shall be the district which you shall set apart, twenty-five thousand *cubits* in width, and *in* length the same as one of the *other* portions, from the east side to the west, with the sanctuary in the center.

[9]"The district that you shall set apart for the LORD *shall be* twenty-five thousand *cubits* in length and ten thousand in width. [10]To these—to the priests—the holy district shall belong: on the north twenty-five thousand *cubits in length,* on the west ten thousand in width, on the east ten thousand in width, and on the south twenty-five thousand in length. The sanctuary of the LORD shall be in the center. [11]*It shall be* for the priests of the sons of Zadok, who are sanctified, who have kept My charge, who did not go astray when the children of Israel went astray, as the Levites went

47:19 [a]Hebrew *Negev*

astray. ¹²And *this* district of land that is set apart shall be to them a thing most holy by the border of the Levites.

¹³"Opposite the border of the priests, the Levites *shall have an area* twenty-five thousand *cubits* in length and ten thousand in width; its entire length *shall be* twenty-five thousand and its width ten thousand. ¹⁴And they shall not sell or exchange any of it; they may not alienate this best *part* of the land, for *it is* holy to the LORD.

¹⁵"The five thousand *cubits* in width that remain, along the edge of the twenty-five thousand, shall be for general use by the city, for dwellings and common-land; and the city shall be in the center. ¹⁶These *shall be* its measurements: the north side four thousand five hundred *cubits,* the south side four thousand five hundred, the east side four thousand five hundred, and the west side four thousand five hundred. ¹⁷The common-land of the city shall be: to the north two hundred and fifty *cubits,* to the south two hundred and fifty, to the east two hundred and fifty, and to the west two hundred and fifty. ¹⁸The rest of the length, alongside the district of the holy *section, shall be* ten thousand *cubits* to the east and ten thousand to the west. It shall be adjacent to the district of the holy *section,* and its produce shall be food for the workers of the city. ¹⁹The workers of the city, from all the tribes of Israel, shall cultivate it. ²⁰The entire district *shall be* twenty-five thousand *cubits* by twenty-five thousand *cubits,* foursquare. You shall set apart the holy district with the property of the city.

²¹"The rest *shall belong* to the prince, on one side and on the other of the holy district and of the city's property, next to the twenty-five thousand *cubits* of the *holy* district as far as the eastern border, and westward next to the twenty-five thousand as far as the western border, adjacent to the *tribal* portions; *it shall belong* to the prince. It shall be the holy district, and the sanctuary of the temple *shall be* in the center. ²²Moreover, apart from the possession of the Levites and the possession of the city *which are* in the midst of what *belongs* to the prince, *the area* between the border of Judah and the border of Benjamin shall belong to the prince.

BIBLICAL INSIGHTS • 48:11

Faithful in the Small Stuff

TOO OFTEN TODAY we seem to want *much more* by doing *very little.* We want the tip without the toil, the gain without the grind, the sweets without the sweat, the prize without the pain, and the perks without the perseverance. Duty, diligence, hard work, and attention to details have become rare commodities, whether it be at home, at work, or at church.

But God notices! He watches for faithfulness in the small things, because He intends to reward it. The family of a little-known Old Testament priest illustrates the point. While the nation of Israel chased after all the wrong things, this faithful family did its duty in the temple, and God promised to give a magnificent reward to "the priests of the sons of Zadok, who are sanctified, who have kept My charge, who did not go astray when the children of Israel went astray, as the Levites went astray" (48:11).

Every one of us is passionately pursuing something. It may be one more dollar at work. It may be recognition from our peers or the attention of others. It may be more enjoyment in life. Or are we people who seek first the kingdom of God and His righteousness (Matt. 6:33)? When our priorities are right and we are faithful in the small things, only then will we experience the blessing of God in our lives.

²³"As for the rest of the tribes, from the east side to the west, Benjamin *shall have* one *section;* ²⁴by the border of Benjamin, from the east side to the west, Simeon *shall have* one *section;* ²⁵by the border of Simeon, from the east side to the west, Issachar *shall have* one *section;* ²⁶by the border of Issachar, from the east side to the west, Zebulun *shall have* one *section;* ²⁷by the border of Zebulun, from the east side to the west, Gad *shall have* one *section;* ²⁸by the border of Gad, on the south side, toward

the South,[a] the border shall be from Tamar *to* the waters of Meribah *by* Kadesh, along the brook to the Great Sea. [29]This *is* the land which you shall divide by lot as an inheritance among the tribes of Israel, and these *are* their portions," says the Lord GOD.

The Gates of the City and Its Name

[30]"These *are* the exits of the city. On the north side, measuring four thousand five hundred *cubits* [31](the gates of the city *shall be* named after the tribes of Israel), the three gates northward: one gate for Reuben, one gate for Judah, and one gate for Levi; [32]on the east side, four thousand five hundred *cubits,* three gates: one gate for Joseph, one gate for Benjamin, and one gate for Dan; [33]on the south side, measuring four thousand five hundred *cubits,* three gates: one gate for Simeon, one gate for Issachar, and one gate for Zebulun; [34]on the west side, four thousand five hundred *cubits* with their three gates: one gate for Gad, one gate for Asher, and one gate for Naphtali. [35]All the way around *shall be* eighteen thousand *cubits;* and the name of the city from *that* day *shall be:* THE LORD IS THERE."[a]

48:28 [a]Hebrew *Negev*
48:35 [a]Hebrew *YHWH Shammah*

DANIEL

ALTHOUGH THE BOOK OF DANIEL CONTAINS some of the Bible's most familiar stories, many people who know the stories have no idea where Daniel fits into Israel's history.

Daniel was a contemporary of Ezekiel. As a teenager, Daniel was kidnapped (somewhere between 605—536 BC) from his noble family in Judea and taken to Babylon to serve the king. Eventually he became a trusted advisor to both King Nebuchadnezzar and to King Cyrus.

The Book of Daniel differs from the Old Testament's other prophetic books. It contains a style of literature known as apocalyptic—visions that use highly figurative language to describe coming world events. These portions of Daniel resemble the style of writing found in the New Testament Book of Revelation. It may help some readers to know that even Daniel didn't understand some of his own prophecies (12:8)!

Chapters 1—6 describe God's care of His faithful followers in Babylon. This first section of the book contains the famous stories of the three Hebrew men thrown into the fiery furnace and of Daniel in the lions' den. Chapters 7—12 describe Daniel's visions and tell of coming events in world history. Rather than focusing on some of the prophetic mysteries of Daniel, I believe we should concentrate on Daniel's life of godly obedience. That's where we'll find the greatest spiritual benefit.

Sinclair Ferguson notes, "What impresses the reader above everything else . . . is how God-centered Daniel is and how God-centered is his view of the political stage on which he plays his part. A genuinely God-centered worldview is something to which we are little accustomed today . . . . There is something thrilling about the 'diary' of a 'chief of staff' (Dan. 2:48) whose perspective on life is so biblical."

Many children in Sunday school have sung the chorus:

Dare to be a Daniel
Dare to stand alone
Dare to have a purpose firm
Dare to make it known

Indeed, the book of Daniel is a thrilling book for families to read and study together! And the God-centered prophet is a stunning role model for today's young men and women.

Daniel and His Friends Obey God

1 In the third year of the reign of Jehoiakim king of Judah, Nebuchadnezzar king of Babylon came to Jerusalem and besieged it. ²And the Lord gave Jehoiakim king of Judah into his hand, with some of the articles of the house of God, which he carried into the land of Shinar to the house of his god; and he brought the articles into the treasure house of his god.

³Then the king instructed Ashpenaz, the master of his eunuchs, to bring some of the children of Israel and some of the king's descendants and some of the nobles, ⁴young men in whom *there was* no blemish, but good-looking, gifted in all wisdom, possessing knowledge and quick to understand, who *had* ability to serve in the king's palace, and whom they might teach the language and literature of the Chaldeans. ⁵And the king appointed for them a daily provision of the king's delicacies and of the wine which he drank, and three years of training for them, so that at the end of *that time* they might serve before the king. ⁶Now from among those of the sons of Judah were Daniel, Hananiah, Mishael, and Azariah. ⁷To them the chief of the eunuchs gave names: he gave Daniel *the name* Belteshazzar; to Hananiah, Shadrach; to Mishael, Meshach; and to Azariah, Abed-Nego.

⁸But Daniel purposed in his heart that he would not defile himself with the portion of the king's delicacies, nor with the wine which he drank; therefore he requested of the chief of the eunuchs that he might not defile himself. ⁹Now God had brought Daniel into the favor and goodwill of the chief of the eunuchs. ¹⁰And the chief of the eunuchs said to Daniel, "I fear my lord the king, who has appointed your food and drink. For why should he see your faces looking worse than the young men who *are* your age? Then you would endanger my head before the king."

¹¹So Daniel said to the steward[a] whom the chief of the eunuchs had set over Daniel, Hananiah, Mishael, and Azariah, ¹²"Please test your servants for ten days, and let them give us vegetables to eat and water to drink. ¹³Then let our appearance be examined before you, and the appearance of the young men who eat the portion of the king's delicacies; and as you see fit, *so* deal with your servants." ¹⁴So he consented with them in this matter, and tested them ten days.

¹⁵And at the end of ten days their features appeared better and fatter in flesh than all the young men who ate the portion of the king's delicacies. ¹⁶Thus the steward took away their portion of delicacies and the wine that they were to drink, and gave them vegetables.

¹⁷As for these four young men, God gave them knowledge and skill in all literature and wisdom; and Daniel had understanding in all visions and dreams.

¹⁸Now at the end of the days, when the king had said that they should be brought in, the chief of the eunuchs brought them in before Nebuchadnezzar. ¹⁹Then the king interviewed[a] them, and among them all none was found like Daniel, Hananiah, Mishael, and Azariah; therefore they served before the king. ²⁰And in all matters of wisdom *and* understanding about which the king examined them, he found them ten times better than all the magicians *and* astrologers who *were* in all his realm. ²¹Thus Daniel continued until the first year of King Cyrus.

Nebuchadnezzar's Dream

2 Now in the second year of Nebuchadnezzar's reign, Nebuchadnezzar had dreams; and his spirit was *so* troubled that his sleep left him. ²Then the king gave the command to call the magicians, the astrologers, the sorcerers, and the Chaldeans to

INTIMATE MOMENTS

Drop by your husband's workplace unexpectedly and whisk him away for lunch.

1:11 ᵃHebrew *Melzar,* also in verse 16
1:19 ᵃLiterally *talked with them*

tell the king his dreams. So they came and stood before the king. ³And the king said to them, "I have had a dream, and my spirit is anxious to know the dream."

⁴Then the Chaldeans spoke to the king in Aramaic,ᵃ "O king, live forever! Tell your servants the dream, and we will give the interpretation."

⁵The king answered and said to the Chaldeans, "My decision is firm: if you do not make known the dream to me, and its interpretation, you shall be cut in pieces, and your houses shall be made an ash heap. ⁶However, if you tell the dream and its interpretation, you shall receive from me gifts, rewards, and great honor. Therefore tell me the dream and its interpretation."

⁷They answered again and said, "Let the king tell his servants the dream, and we will give its interpretation."

⁸The king answered and said, "I know for certain that you would gain time, because you see that my decision is firm: ⁹if you do not make known the dream to me, *there is only* one decree for you! For you have agreed to speak lying and corrupt words before me till the time has changed. Therefore tell me the dream, and I shall know that you can give me its interpretation."

¹⁰The Chaldeans answered the king, and said, "There is not a man on earth who can tell the king's matter; therefore no king, lord, or ruler has *ever* asked such things of any magician, astrologer, or Chaldean. ¹¹*It is* a difficult thing that the king requests, and there is no other who can tell it to the king except the gods, whose dwelling is not with flesh."

¹²For this reason the king was angry and very furious, and gave the command to destroy all the wise *men* of Babylon. ¹³So the decree went out, and they began killing the wise *men;* and they sought Daniel and his companions, to kill *them.*

God Reveals Nebuchadnezzar's Dream

¹⁴Then with counsel and wisdom Daniel answered Arioch, the captain of the king's guard, who had gone out to kill the wise

BIBLICAL INSIGHTS • 1:8

Shape Your Child's Convictions

THE BIBLE TELLS US ABOUT a prophet of God named Daniel who knew what he believed and what he stood for, "But Daniel purposed in his heart that he would not defile himself with the portion of the king's delicacies, nor with the wine which he drank" (1:8).

That verse alone illustrates what it means to have biblical convictions, something each of us desperately needs in today's corrupt and ungodly world. Every parent needs strong convictions, along with the wisdom to know how to instill them in their children.

Notice that Daniel had made up his mind in advance. He decided what he would do *before* he faced the temptation. For that reason, he models for us how to make sure we can avoid falling into the traps the devil and this world have laid for us.

Just deciding as we go or playing it by ear simply isn't going to cut it. We have the responsibility, even the privilege, of settling our convictions ahead of time so that when we come face to face with some temptation, we will be able to say, "No!" And we have the responsibility to teach our children to do the very same thing. Challenge your children to determine what they believe about the four M's:

- Morality and the opposite sex
- Morality and the same sex
- Movies, videos, and internet surfing
- Music

You, and they, will be glad you gave them a challenge to decide in advance what they will do with each of these issues.

---

men of Babylon; ¹⁵he answered and said to Arioch the king's captain, "Why is the decree from the king so urgent?" Then Arioch made the decision known to Daniel.

¹⁶So Daniel went in and asked the king to give him time, that he might tell the

2:4 ᵃThe original language of Daniel 2:4b through 7:28 is Aramaic.

king the interpretation. [17]Then Daniel went to his house, and made the decision known to Hananiah, Mishael, and Azariah, his companions, [18]that they might seek mercies from the God of heaven concerning this secret, so that Daniel and his companions might not perish with the rest of the wise *men* of Babylon. [19]Then the secret was revealed to Daniel in a night vision. So Daniel blessed the God of heaven.

[20]Daniel answered and said:

"Blessed be the name of God forever
  and ever,
For wisdom and might are His.
[21] And He changes the times and the
     seasons;
  He removes kings and raises up
     kings;
  He gives wisdom to the wise
  And knowledge to those who have
     understanding.
[22] He reveals deep and secret things;
  He knows what *is* in the darkness,
  And light dwells with Him.
[23] "I thank You and praise You,
  O God of my fathers;
  You have given me wisdom and
     might,
  And have now made known to me
     what we asked of You,
  For You have made known to us the
     king's demand."

Daniel Explains the Dream

[24]Therefore Daniel went to Arioch, whom the king had appointed to destroy the wise *men* of Babylon. He went and said thus to him: "Do not destroy the wise *men* of Babylon; take me before the king, and I will tell the king the interpretation."

[25]Then Arioch quickly brought Daniel before the king, and said thus to him, "I have found a man of the captives[a] of Judah, who will make known to the king the interpretation."

[26]The king answered and said to Daniel, whose name *was* Belteshazzar, "Are you able to make known to me the dream which I have seen, and its interpretation?"

[27]Daniel answered in the presence of the king, and said, "The secret which the king has demanded, the wise *men,* the astrologers, the magicians, and the soothsayers cannot declare to the king. [28]But there is a God in heaven who reveals secrets, and He has made known to King Nebuchadnezzar what will be in the latter days. Your dream, and the visions of your head upon your bed, were these: [29]As for you, O king, thoughts came *to* your *mind while* on your bed, *about* what would come to pass after this; and He who reveals secrets has made known to you what will be. [30]But as for me, this secret has not been revealed to me because I have more wisdom than anyone living, but for *our* sakes who make known the interpretation to the king, and that you may know the thoughts of your heart.

[31]"You, O king, were watching; and behold, a great image! This great image, whose splendor *was* excellent, stood before you; and its form *was* awesome. [32]This image's head *was* of fine gold, its chest and arms of silver, its belly and thighs[a] of bronze, [33]its legs of iron, its feet partly of iron and partly of clay.[a] [34]You watched while a stone was cut out without hands, which struck the image on its feet of iron and clay, and broke them in pieces. [35]Then the iron, the clay, the bronze, the silver, and the gold were crushed together, and became like chaff from the summer threshing floors; the wind carried them away so that no trace of them was found. And the stone that struck the image became a great mountain and filled the whole earth.

[36]"This *is* the dream. Now we will tell the interpretation of it before the king. [37]You, O king, *are* a king of kings. For the God of heaven has given you a kingdom, power, strength, and glory; [38]and wherever the children of men dwell, or the beasts of the field and the birds of the heaven, He has given *them* into your hand, and has made you ruler over them all—you *are* this head of gold. [39]But after you shall arise another kingdom inferior to yours; then another, a third kingdom of bronze, which shall rule over all the earth. [40]And the fourth kingdom shall be as strong as iron,

---

2:25 [a]Literally *of the sons of the captivity*
2:32 [a]Or *sides* **2:33** [a]Or *baked clay,* and so in verses 34, 35, and 42

inasmuch as iron breaks in pieces and shatters everything; and like iron that crushes, *that kingdom* will break in pieces and crush all the others. [41]Whereas you saw the feet and toes, partly of potter's clay and partly of iron, the kingdom shall be divided; yet the strength of the iron shall be in it, just as you saw the iron mixed with ceramic clay. [42]And *as* the toes of the feet *were* partly of iron and partly of clay, *so* the kingdom shall be partly strong and partly fragile. [43]As you saw iron mixed with ceramic clay, they will mingle with the seed of men; but they will not adhere to one another, just as iron does not mix with clay. [44]And in the days of these kings the God of heaven will set up a kingdom which shall never be destroyed; and the kingdom shall not be left to other people; it shall break in pieces and consume all these kingdoms, and it shall stand forever. [45]Inasmuch as you saw that the stone was cut out of the mountain without hands, and that it broke in pieces the iron, the bronze, the clay, the silver, and the gold—the great God has made known to the king what will come to pass after this. The dream is certain, and its interpretation is sure."

Daniel and His Friends Promoted

[46]Then King Nebuchadnezzar fell on his face, prostrate before Daniel, and commanded that they should present an offering and incense to him. [47]The king answered Daniel, and said, "Truly your God *is* the God of gods, the Lord of kings, and a revealer of secrets, since you could reveal this secret." [48]Then the king promoted Daniel and gave him many great gifts; and he made him ruler over the whole province of Babylon, and chief administrator over all the wise *men* of Babylon. [49]Also Daniel petitioned the king, and he set Shadrach, Meshach, and Abed-Nego over the affairs of the province of Babylon; but Daniel *sat* in the gate[a] of the king.

The Image of Gold

3 Nebuchadnezzar the king made an image of gold, whose height *was* sixty cubits *and* its width six cubits. He set it up

in the plain of Dura, in the province of Babylon. [2]And King Nebuchadnezzar sent *word* to gather together the satraps, the administrators, the governors, the counselors, the treasurers, the judges, the magistrates, and all the officials of the provinces, to come to the dedication of the image which King Nebuchadnezzar had set up. [3]So the satraps, the administrators, the governors, the counselors, the treasurers, the judges, the magistrates, and all the officials of the provinces gathered together for the dedication of the image that King Nebuchadnezzar had set up; and they stood before the image that Nebuchadnezzar had set up. [4]Then a herald cried aloud: "To you it is commanded, O peoples, nations, and languages, [5]*that* at the time you hear the sound of the horn, flute, harp, lyre, *and* psaltery, in symphony with all kinds of music, you shall fall down and worship the gold image that King Nebuchadnezzar has set up; [6]and whoever does not fall down and worship shall be cast immediately into the midst of a burning fiery furnace."

[7]So at that time, when all the people heard the sound of the horn, flute, harp, *and* lyre, in symphony with all kinds of music, all the people, nations, and languages fell down *and* worshiped the gold image which King Nebuchadnezzar had set up.

Daniel's Friends Disobey the King

[8]Therefore at that time certain Chaldeans came forward and accused the Jews. [9]They spoke and said to King Nebuchadnezzar, "O king, live forever! [10]You, O king, have made a decree that everyone who hears the sound of the horn, flute, harp, lyre, *and* psaltery, in symphony with all kinds of music, shall fall down and worship the gold image; [11]and whoever does not fall down and worship shall be cast into the midst of a burning fiery furnace. [12]There are certain Jews whom you have set over the affairs of the province of Babylon: Shadrach, Meshach, and Abed-Nego; these men, O king, have not paid due regard to you. They do not serve your gods or worship the gold image which you have set up."

[13]Then Nebuchadnezzar, in rage and fury, gave the command to bring Shadrach,

2:49 [a]That is, the king's court

Take a Stand

SOME TIME AGO Barbara and I chaperoned a junior high dance where, in a dark part of the dance floor, a number of students were using some questionable dance moves.

When I eased my way back toward the students in question, I felt shocked and embarrassed at what I saw. It looked as though about two dozen kids were having intercourse with their clothes on.

Now I faced a dilemma: Should I intervene? Do I wait for someone official to step in? I finally took action when two boys and a girl began a particularly vulgar move. I walked up to them, tapped the boys on the shoulder and said, "You've gone too far. This is indecent. Knock it off!" As they backed away from the girl, I looked her in the eyes and scolded her, "You shouldn't let boys treat you that way. It's immodest and vulgar. They are robbing you of your dignity as a young woman!"

I regret only that it took me so long to act. I'm grateful for courageous believers like the three boys described in Daniel 3, who not only refused to go along with a vile activity, but who also had the guts to tell the king exactly why. Courage begets courage. It's uncomfortable to kindly but firmly call others to do what's right. But when you do, others begin to step up. And that's how a culture is transformed, one courageous act at a time.

Meshach, and Abed-Nego. So they brought these men before the king. [14]Nebuchadnezzar spoke, saying to them, "*Is it* true, Shadrach, Meshach, and Abed-Nego, *that* you do not serve my gods or worship the gold image which I have set up? [15]Now if you are ready at the time you hear the sound of the horn, flute, harp, lyre, *and* psaltery, in symphony with all kinds of music, and you fall down and worship the image which I have made, *good!* But if you do not worship, you shall be cast immediately into the midst of a burning fiery furnace. And who *is* the god who will deliver you from my hands?"

[16]Shadrach, Meshach, and Abed-Nego answered and said to the king, "O Nebuchadnezzar, we have no need to answer you in this matter. [17]If that *is the case,* our God whom we serve is able to deliver us from the burning fiery furnace, and He will deliver *us* from your hand, O king. [18]But if not, let it be known to you, O king, that we do not serve your gods, nor will we worship the gold image which you have set up."

Saved in Fiery Trial

[19]Then Nebuchadnezzar was full of fury, and the expression on his face changed toward Shadrach, Meshach, and Abed-Nego. He spoke and commanded that they heat the furnace seven times more than it was usually heated. [20]And he commanded certain mighty men of valor who *were* in his army to bind Shadrach, Meshach, and Abed-Nego, *and* cast *them* into the burning fiery furnace. [21]Then these men were bound in their coats, their trousers, their turbans, and their *other* garments, and were cast into the midst of the burning fiery furnace. [22]Therefore, because the king's command was urgent, and the furnace exceedingly hot, the flame of the fire killed those men who took up Shadrach, Meshach, and Abed-Nego. [23]And these three men, Shadrach, Meshach, and Abed-Nego, fell down bound into the midst of the burning fiery furnace.

[24]Then King Nebuchadnezzar was astonished; and he rose in haste *and* spoke, saying to his counselors, "Did we not cast three men bound into the midst of the fire?"

They answered and said to the king, "True, O king."

[25]"Look!" he answered, "I see four men loose, walking in the midst of the fire; and they are not hurt, and the form of the fourth is like the Son of God."[a]

Nebuchadnezzar Praises God

[26]Then Nebuchadnezzar went near the mouth of the burning fiery furnace *and*

3:25 [a]Or *a son of the gods*

spoke, saying, "Shadrach, Meshach, and Abed-Nego, servants of the Most High God, come out, and come *here*." Then Shadrach, Meshach, and Abed-Nego came from the midst of the fire. 27And the satraps, administrators, governors, and the king's counselors gathered together, and they saw these men on whose bodies the fire had no power; the hair of their head was not singed nor were their garments affected, and the smell of fire was not on them.

28Nebuchadnezzar spoke, saying, "Blessed be the God of Shadrach, Meshach, and Abed-Nego, who sent His Angel[a] and delivered His servants who trusted in Him, and they have frustrated the king's word, and yielded their bodies, that they should not serve nor worship any god except their own God! 29Therefore I make a decree that any people, nation, or language which speaks anything amiss against the God of Shadrach, Meshach, and Abed-Nego shall be cut in pieces, and their houses shall be made an ash heap; because there is no other God who can deliver like this."

30Then the king promoted Shadrach, Meshach, and Abed-Nego in the province of Babylon.

Nebuchadnezzar's Second Dream

4 Nebuchadnezzar the king,

To all peoples, nations, and languages that dwell in all the earth:

Peace be multiplied to you.

2 I thought it good to declare the signs and wonders that the Most High God has worked for me.

3 How great *are* His signs,
   And how mighty His wonders!
   His kingdom *is* an everlasting kingdom,
   And His dominion *is* from generation to generation.

4 I, Nebuchadnezzar, was at rest in my house, and flourishing in my palace. 5I saw a dream which made me afraid, and the thoughts on my bed and the visions of my head troubled

me. 6Therefore I issued a decree to bring in all the wise *men* of Babylon before me, that they might make known to me the interpretation of the dream. 7Then the magicians, the astrologers, the Chaldeans, and the soothsayers came in, and I told them the dream; but they did not make known to me its interpretation. 8But at last Daniel came before me (his name *is* Belteshazzar, according to the name of my god; in him *is* the

---

ROMANCE FAQ

Q: How can we confront one another without being judgmental or condemning?

Perhaps the greatest roadblock to loving confrontation is the well-known plank in our eyes. Such handicapped vision inevitably distorts our relationships.

Here are five tips Barbara and I have found useful in keeping judgment out of confrontation:

1. Check your motivation. Are you bringing this up to help or to hurt? Pray about it. When we take the situation to God and He shines His light on us, we usually see our motivation for what it is.

2. Check your attitude. Loving confrontation says, "I care about you." Don't hop on your bulldozer and bury your mate.

3. Check the circumstance. Pick a suitable time, location, and setting. Don't confront your mate the moment he or she walks in the door after a hard day's work, at mealtime, or in front of others.

4. Check for other pressures. Be sensitive to the situation of others. What's the context of their lives?

5. Be ready to take it as well as dish it out. Confrontation can boomerang; there may be some issues in your life that need to be addressed too. If you expect others to listen, to understand, to hear you out and to accept your point of view, then be ready to do the same.

3:28 [a]Or *angel*

Spirit of the Holy God), and I told the dream before him, *saying:*
9 "Belteshazzar, chief of the magicians, because I know that the Spirit of the Holy God *is* in you, and no secret troubles you, explain to me the visions of my dream that I have seen, and its interpretation.

10 "These *were* the visions of my head *while* on my bed:

I was looking, and behold,
A tree in the midst of the earth,
And its height was great.
11 The tree grew and became strong;
Its height reached to the heavens,
And it could be seen to the ends of all the earth.
12 Its leaves *were* lovely,
Its fruit abundant,
And in it *was* food for all.
The beasts of the field found shade under it,
The birds of the heavens dwelt in its branches,
And all flesh was fed from it.

13 "I saw in the visions of my head *while* on my bed, and there was a watcher, a holy one, coming down from heaven. 14He cried aloud and said thus:

'Chop down the tree and cut off its branches,
Strip off its leaves and scatter its fruit.
Let the beasts get out from under it,
And the birds from its branches.
15 Nevertheless leave the stump and roots in the earth,
Bound with a band of iron and bronze,
In the tender grass of the field.
Let it be wet with the dew of heaven,
And *let* him graze with the beasts
On the grass of the earth.
16 Let his heart be changed from *that of* a man,
Let him be given the heart of a beast,
And let seven timesª pass over him.

17 'This decision *is* by the decree of the watchers,

And the sentence by the word of the holy ones,
In order that the living may know
That the Most High rules in the kingdom of men,
Gives it to whomever He will,
And sets over it the lowest of men.'

18 "This dream I, King Nebuchadnezzar, have seen. Now you, Belteshazzar, declare its interpretation, since all the wise *men* of my kingdom are not able to make known to me the interpretation; but you *are* able, for the Spirit of the Holy God *is* in you."

Daniel Explains the Second Dream

19 Then Daniel, whose name *was* Belteshazzar, was astonished for a time, and his thoughts troubled him. *So* the king spoke, and said, "Belteshazzar, do not let the dream or its interpretation trouble you."

Belteshazzar answered and said, "My lord, *may* the dream concern those who hate you, and its interpretation concern your enemies!

20 "The tree that you saw, which grew and became strong, whose height reached to the heavens and which *could be* seen by all the earth, 21whose leaves *were* lovely and its fruit abundant, in which *was* food for all, under which the beasts of the field dwelt, and in whose branches the birds of the heaven had their home— 22it *is* you, O king, who have grown and become strong; for your greatness has grown and reaches to the heavens, and your dominion to the end of the earth.

23 "And inasmuch as the king saw a watcher, a holy one, coming down from heaven and saying, 'Chop down the tree and destroy it, but leave its stump and roots in the earth, *bound* with a band of iron and bronze in the tender grass of the field; let it be wet with the dew of heaven, and let

---

4:16 ªPossibly *seven years,* and so in verses 23, 25, and 32

him graze with the beasts of the field, till seven times pass over him'; ²⁴this is the interpretation, O king, and this is the decree of the Most High, which has come upon my lord the king: ²⁵They shall drive you from men, your dwelling shall be with the beasts of the field, and they shall make you eat grass like oxen. They shall wet you with the dew of heaven, and seven times shall pass over you, till you know that the Most High rules in the kingdom of men, and gives it to whomever He chooses.

²⁶ "And inasmuch as they gave the command to leave the stump *and* roots of the tree, your kingdom shall be assured to you, after you come to know that Heaven rules. ²⁷Therefore, O king, let my advice be acceptable to you; break off your sins by *being* righteous, and your iniquities by showing mercy to *the* poor. Perhaps there may be a lengthening of your prosperity."

Nebuchadnezzar's Humiliation

²⁸ All *this* came upon King Nebuchadnezzar. ²⁹At the end of the twelve months he was walking about the royal palace of Babylon. ³⁰The king spoke, saying, "Is not this great Babylon, that I have built for a royal dwelling by my mighty power and for the honor of my majesty?"

³¹ While the word *was still* in the king's mouth, a voice fell from heaven: "King Nebuchadnezzar, to you it is spoken: the kingdom has departed from you! ³²And they shall drive you from men, and your dwelling *shall be* with the beasts of the field. They shall make you eat grass like oxen; and seven times shall pass over you, until you know that the Most High rules in the kingdom of men, and gives it to whomever He chooses."

³³ That very hour the word was fulfilled concerning Nebuchadnezzar;

he was driven from men and ate grass like oxen; his body was wet with the dew of heaven till his hair had grown like eagles' *feathers* and his nails like birds' *claws.*

Nebuchadnezzar Praises God

³⁴ And at the end of the time[a] I, Nebuchadnezzar, lifted my eyes to heaven, and my understanding returned to me; and I blessed the Most High and praised and honored Him who lives forever:

For His dominion *is* an everlasting dominion,
And His kingdom *is* from generation to generation.
³⁵ All the inhabitants of the earth *are* reputed as nothing;
He does according to His will in the army of heaven
And *among* the inhabitants of the earth.
No one can restrain His hand
Or say to Him, "What have You done?"

³⁶ At the same time my reason returned to me, and for the glory of my kingdom, my honor and splendor returned to me. My counselors and nobles resorted to me, I was restored to my kingdom, and excellent majesty was added to me. ³⁷Now I, Nebuchadnezzar, praise and extol and honor the King of heaven, all of whose works *are* truth, and His ways justice. And those who walk in pride He is able to put down.

Belshazzar's Feast

5 Belshazzar the king made a great feast for a thousand of his lords, and drank wine in the presence of the thousand. ²While he tasted the wine, Belshazzar gave the command to bring the gold and silver vessels which his father Nebuchadnezzar had taken from the temple which *had been* in Jerusalem, that the king and his lords, his wives, and his concubines might drink from them. ³Then they brought the gold vessels that had been taken from the temple of the house of God which *had been* in

---

4:34 ªLiterally *days*

Jerusalem; and the king and his lords, his wives, and his concubines drank from them. 4They drank wine, and praised the gods of gold and silver, bronze and iron, wood and stone.

5In the same hour the fingers of a man's hand appeared and wrote opposite the lampstand on the plaster of the wall of the king's palace; and the king saw the part of the hand that wrote. 6Then the king's countenance changed, and his thoughts troubled him, so that the joints of his hips were loosened and his knees knocked against each other. 7The king cried aloud to bring in the astrologers, the Chaldeans, and the soothsayers. The king spoke, saying to the wise *men* of Babylon, "Whoever reads this writing, and tells me its interpretation, shall be clothed with purple and *have* a chain of gold around his neck; and he shall be the third ruler in the kingdom." 8Now all the king's wise *men* came, but they could not read the writing, or make known to the king its interpretation. 9Then King Belshazzar was greatly troubled, his countenance was changed, and his lords were astonished.

10The queen, because of the words of the king and his lords, came to the banquet hall. The queen spoke, saying, "O king, live forever! Do not let your thoughts trouble you, nor let your countenance change. 11There is a man in your kingdom in whom *is* the Spirit of the Holy God. And in the days of your father, light and understanding and wisdom, like the wisdom of the gods, were found in him; and King Nebuchadnezzar your father—your father the king—made him chief of the magicians, astrologers, Chaldeans, *and* soothsayers. 12Inasmuch as an excellent spirit, knowledge, understanding, interpreting dreams, solving riddles, and explaining enigmasª were found in this Daniel, whom the king named Belteshazzar, now let Daniel be called, and he will give the interpretation."

The Writing on the Wall Explained

13Then Daniel was brought in before the king. The king spoke, and said to Daniel, "*Are* you that Daniel who is one of the captivesª from Judah, whom my father the king brought from Judah? 14I have heard of you, that the Spirit of God *is* in you, and *that* light and understanding and excellent wisdom are found in you. 15Now the wise *men,* the astrologers, have been brought in before me, that they should read this writing and make known to me its interpretation, but they could not give the interpretation of the thing. 16And I have heard of you, that you can give interpretations and explain enigmas. Now if you can read the writing and make known to me its interpretation, you shall be clothed with purple and *have* a chain of gold around your neck, and shall be the third ruler in the kingdom."

17Then Daniel answered, and said before the king, "Let your gifts be for yourself, and give your rewards to another; yet I will read the writing to the king, and make known to him the interpretation. 18O king, the Most High God gave Nebuchadnezzar your father a kingdom and majesty, glory and honor. 19And because of the majesty that He gave him, all peoples, nations, and languages trembled and feared before him. Whomever he wished, he executed; whomever he wished, he kept alive; whomever he wished, he set up; and

---

5:12 ªLiterally *untying knots,* and so in verse 16
5:13 ªLiterally *of the sons of the captivity*

whomever he wished, he put down. ²⁰But when his heart was lifted up, and his spirit was hardened in pride, he was deposed from his kingly throne, and they took his glory from him. ²¹Then he was driven from the sons of men, his heart was made like the beasts, and his dwelling *was* with the wild donkeys. They fed him with grass like oxen, and his body was wet with the dew of heaven, till he knew that the Most High God rules in the kingdom of men, and appoints over it whomever He chooses.

²²"But you his son, Belshazzar, have not humbled your heart, although you knew all this. ²³And you have lifted yourself up against the Lord of heaven. They have brought the vessels of His house before you, and you and your lords, your wives and your concubines, have drunk wine from them. And you have praised the gods of silver and gold, bronze and iron, wood and stone, which do not see or hear or know; and the God who *holds* your breath in His hand and owns all your ways, you have not glorified. ²⁴Then the fingersᵃ of the hand were sent from Him, and this writing was written.

²⁵"And this is the inscription that was written:

MENE,ᵃ MENE, TEKEL,ᵇ UPHARSIN.ᶜ

²⁶This *is* the interpretation of *each* word. Mᴇɴᴇ: God has numbered your kingdom, and finished it; ²⁷Tᴇᴋᴇʟ: You have been weighed in the balances, and found wanting; ²⁸Pᴇʀᴇs: Your kingdom has been divided, and given to the Medes and Persians."ᵃ ²⁹Then Belshazzar gave the command, and they clothed Daniel with purple and *put* a chain of gold around his neck, and made a proclamation concerning him that he should be the third ruler in the kingdom.

Belshazzar's Fall

³⁰That very night Belshazzar, king of the Chaldeans, was slain. ³¹And Darius the Mede received the kingdom, *being* about sixty-two years old.

5:24 ᵃLiterally *palm* **5:25** ᵃLiterally *a mina* (50 shekels) from the verb "to number" ᵇLiterally *a shekel* from the verb "to weigh" ᶜLiterally *and half-shekels* from the verb "to divide" **5:28** ᵃAramaic *Paras,* consonant with *Peres*

The Plot Against Daniel

6 It pleased Darius to set over the kingdom one hundred and twenty satraps, to be over the whole kingdom; ²and over these, three governors, of whom Daniel *was* one, that the satraps might give account to them, so that the king would suffer no loss. ³Then this Daniel distinguished himself above the governors and satraps, because an excellent spirit *was* in him; and the king gave thought to setting him over the whole realm. ⁴So the governors and satraps sought to find *some* charge against Daniel concerning the kingdom; but they could find no charge or fault, because he *was* faithful; nor was there any error or fault found in him. ⁵Then these men said, "We shall not find any charge against this Daniel unless we find *it* against him concerning the law of his God."

⁶So these governors and satraps thronged before the king, and said thus to him: "King Darius, live forever! ⁷All the governors of the kingdom, the administrators and satraps, the counselors and advisors, have consulted together to establish a royal statute and to make a firm decree, that whoever petitions any god or man for thirty days, except you, O king, shall be cast into the den of lions. ⁸Now, O king, establish the decree and sign the writing, so that it cannot be changed, according to the law of the Medes and Persians, which does not alter." ⁹Therefore King Darius signed the written decree.

Daniel in the Lions' Den

¹⁰Now when Daniel knew that the writing was signed, he went home. And in his upper room, with his windows open toward Jerusalem, he knelt down on his knees three times that day, and prayed and gave thanks before his God, as was his custom since early days.

¹¹Then these men assembled and found Daniel praying and making supplication before his God. ¹²And they went before the king, and spoke concerning the king's decree: "Have you not signed a decree that every man who petitions any god or man within thirty days, except you, O king, shall be cast into the den of lions?"

BIBLICAL INSIGHTS • 6:4

The Character of the Committed

IF PEOPLE TRIED TO FIND grounds for charging you with corruption, would they succeed? Can you be trusted to do what you know is right? Are you reliable?

It was said of Daniel, "So the governors and satraps sought to find some charge against Daniel concerning the kingdom; but they could find no charge or fault, because he was faithful; nor was there any error or fault found in him" (6:4).

Daniel was a man of character, and character says quietly, yet convincingly, "I do what is right, even when no one is around to see. You can count on me—at any cost!" To get a sense of whether others consider you a person of character, answer the following questions:

- Do people constantly have to remind you to get things done?
- Is your word a premium seal that secures the deal?
- Do you return phone calls?
- Do your children believe you when you promise to do something?
- If you promise you'll be home, do you call if you're going to be late?

Imagine the impact Christians would have on society if we replaced compromise and unfaithfulness with dependability, consistency and obedience toward God! Perhaps we could raise an army of young Daniels.

The king answered and said, "The thing *is* true, according to the law of the Medes and Persians, which does not alter."

[13]So they answered and said before the king, "That Daniel, who is one of the captives[a] from Judah, does not show due regard for you, O king, or for the decree that you have signed, but makes his petition three times a day."

[14]And the king, when he heard *these* words, was greatly displeased with himself,

and set *his* heart on Daniel to deliver him; and he labored till the going down of the sun to deliver him. [15]Then these men approached the king, and said to the king, "Know, O king, that *it is* the law of the Medes and Persians that no decree or statute which the king establishes may be changed."

[16]So the king gave the command, and they brought Daniel and cast *him* into the den of lions. *But* the king spoke, saying to Daniel, "Your God, whom you serve continually, He will deliver you." [17]Then a stone was brought and laid on the mouth of the den, and the king sealed it with his own signet ring and with the signets of his lords, that the purpose concerning Daniel might not be changed.

Daniel Saved from the Lions

[18]Now the king went to his palace and spent the night fasting; and no musicians[a] were brought before him. Also his sleep went from him. [19]Then the king arose very early in the morning and went in haste to the den of lions. [20]And when he came to the den, he cried out with a lamenting voice to Daniel. The king spoke, saying to Daniel, "Daniel, servant of the living God, has your God, whom you serve continually, been able to deliver you from the lions?"

[21]Then Daniel said to the king, "O king, live forever! [22]My God sent His angel and shut the lions' mouths, so that they have not hurt me, because I was found innocent before Him; and also, O king, I have done no wrong before you."

[23]Now the king was exceedingly glad for him, and commanded that they should take Daniel up out of the den. So Daniel was taken up out of the den, and no injury whatever was found on him, because he believed in his God.

Darius Honors God

[24]And the king gave the command, and they brought those men who had accused Daniel, and they cast *them* into the den of lions—them, their children, and their wives; and the lions overpowered them,

---

6:13 [a]Literally *of the sons of the captivity*
6:18 [a]Exact meaning unknown

and broke all their bones in pieces before they ever came to the bottom of the den.

25Then King Darius wrote:

> To all peoples, nations, and
> languages that dwell in all the earth:
>
> Peace be multiplied to you.

26 I make a decree that in every
dominion of my kingdom *men must*
tremble and fear before the God of
Daniel.

> For He *is* the living God,
> And steadfast forever;
> His kingdom *is the one* which shall
>   not be destroyed,
> And His dominion *shall endure* to the
>   end.

27 He delivers and rescues,
And He works signs and wonders
In heaven and on earth,
Who has delivered Daniel from the
    power of the lions.

28So this Daniel prospered in the reign of Darius and in the reign of Cyrus the Persian.

Vision of the Four Beasts

7 In the first year of Belshazzar king of Babylon, Daniel had a dream and visions of his head *while* on his bed. Then he wrote down the dream, telling the main facts.a

2Daniel spoke, saying, "I saw in my vision by night, and behold, the four winds of heaven were stirring up the Great Sea. 3And four great beasts came up from the sea, each different from the other. 4The first *was* like a lion, and had eagle's wings. I watched till its wings were plucked off; and it was lifted up from the earth and made to stand on two feet like a man, and a man's heart was given to it.

5"And suddenly another beast, a second, like a bear. It was raised up on one side, and *had* three ribs in its mouth between its teeth. And they said thus to it: 'Arise, devour much flesh!'

6"After this I looked, and there was another, like a leopard, which had on its

back four wings of a bird. The beast also had four heads, and dominion was given to it.

7"After this I saw in the night visions, and behold, a fourth beast, dreadful and terrible, exceedingly strong. It had huge iron teeth; it was devouring, breaking in pieces, and trampling the residue with its feet. It *was* different from all the beasts that *were* before it, and it had ten horns. 8I was considering the horns, and there was another horn, a little one, coming up among them, before whom three of the first horns were plucked out by the roots. And there, in this horn, *were* eyes like the eyes of a man, and a mouth speaking pompous words.

Vision of the Ancient of Days

9   "I watched till thrones were put in
        place,
    And the Ancient of Days was seated;
    His garment *was* white as snow,
    And the hair of His head *was* like
        pure wool.
    His throne *was* a fiery flame,
    Its wheels a burning fire;
10   A fiery stream issued
    And came forth from before Him.
    A thousand thousands ministered to
        Him;
    Ten thousand times ten thousand
        stood before Him.
    The courta was seated,
    And the books were opened.

11"I watched then because of the sound of the pompous words which the horn was speaking; I watched till the beast was slain, and its body destroyed and given to the burning flame. 12As for the rest of the beasts, they had their dominion taken away, yet their lives were prolonged for a season and a time.

13   "I was watching in the night visions,
    And behold, *One* like the Son of
        Man,
    Coming with the clouds of heaven!
    He came to the Ancient of Days,
    And they brought Him near before
        Him.
14   Then to Him was given dominion
        and glory and a kingdom,

7:1 aLiterally *the head* (or *chief*) *of the words*
7:10 aOr *judgment*

That all peoples, nations, and
    languages should serve Him.
His dominion *is* an everlasting
    dominion,
Which shall not pass away,
And His kingdom *the one*
Which shall not be destroyed.

Daniel's Visions Interpreted

15"I, Daniel, was grieved in my spirit within *my* body, and the visions of my head troubled me. 16I came near to one of those who stood by, and asked him the truth of all this. So he told me and made known to me the interpretation of these things: 17"Those great beasts, which are four, *are* four kings[a] *which* arise out of the earth. 18But the saints of the Most High shall receive the kingdom, and possess the kingdom forever, even forever and ever.'

19"Then I wished to know the truth about the fourth beast, which was different from all the others, exceedingly dreadful, *with* its teeth of iron and its nails of bronze, *which* devoured, broke in pieces, and trampled the residue with its feet; 20and the ten horns that *were* on its head, and the other *horn* which came up, before which three fell, namely, that horn which

had eyes and a mouth which spoke pompous words, whose appearance *was* greater than his fellows.

21"I was watching; and the same horn was making war against the saints, and prevailing against them, 22until the Ancient of Days came, and a judgment was made *in favor* of the saints of the Most High, and the time came for the saints to possess the kingdom.

23"Thus he said:

'The fourth beast shall be
A fourth kingdom on earth,
Which shall be different from all
    other kingdoms,
And shall devour the whole earth,
Trample it and break it in pieces.
24 The ten horns *are* ten kings
Who shall arise from this kingdom.
And another shall rise after them;
He shall be different from the first
    ones,
And shall subdue three kings.
25 He shall speak *pompous* words
    against the Most High,

7:17 [a]Representing their kingdoms (compare verse 23)

PARENTING MATTERS

Q: *How do we overcome cultural and personal barriers to teaching our children a godly view of sex?*

May I suggest three barriers we must dismantle if our children are to traverse a landscape infested with traps, temptations, and tests?

Barrier One: Your own ambivalent feelings about sex. Many parents never received solid sex education as children, so they don't know how to teach their own kids. Many others grew up in an era that promoted free love, yet learned it was neither free nor love.

Barrier Two: A shallow relationship with your child. Good relationships demand intimacy, risk and courage. Some parents instinctively sense they have not built strong relationships with their children, so when the time comes to broach this subject, they feel uncomfortable. But I believe God wants us to use these discussions with our children to move our relationship to a deeper, more intimate level.

Barrier Three: Fear. I've heard parents say, "Well, I could *never* talk to my kid about *that*." Many have told me they fear their children asking, "Were you a virgin when you married?" But you don't have to be an expert to talk to your kids about sex. Just walk in there, empowered by God, to represent His perspective of this sacred area of life. It's a great privilege! And it's your responsibility.

Shall persecute[a] the saints of the
　　Most High,
And shall intend to change times and
　　law.
Then *the saints* shall be given into
　　his hand
For a time and times and half a time.

26 'But the court shall be seated,
　　And they shall take away his
　　　　dominion,
　　To consume and destroy *it* forever.
27 　Then the kingdom and dominion,
　　And the greatness of the kingdoms
　　　　under the whole heaven,
　　Shall be given to the people, the
　　　　saints of the Most High.
　　His kingdom *is* an everlasting
　　　　kingdom,
　　And all dominions shall serve and
　　　　obey Him.'

28"This *is* the end of the account.[a] As
for me, Daniel, my thoughts greatly troubled me, and my countenance changed;
but I kept the matter in my heart."

Vision of a Ram and a Goat

8 In the third year of the reign of King
　　Belshazzar a vision appeared *to* me—
to me, Daniel—after the one that appeared
to me the first time. 2I saw in the vision,
and it so happened while I was looking,
that I *was* in Shushan, the citadel, which *is*
in the province of Elam; and I saw in the
vision that I was by the River Ulai. 3Then
I lifted my eyes and saw, and there, standing beside the river, was a ram which had
two horns, and the two horns *were* high;
but one *was* higher than the other, and the
higher *one* came up last. 4I saw the ram
pushing westward, northward, and southward, so that no animal could withstand
him; nor *was there any* that could deliver
from his hand, but he did according to his
will and became great.

5And as I was considering, suddenly a
male goat came from the west, across the
surface of the whole earth, without touching the ground; and the goat *had* a notable
horn between his eyes. 6Then he came to

the ram that had two horns, which I had
seen standing beside the river, and ran at
him with furious power. 7And I saw him
confronting the ram; he was moved with
rage against him, attacked the ram, and
broke his two horns. There was no power
in the ram to withstand him, but he cast
him down to the ground and trampled him;
and there was no one that could deliver the
ram from his hand.

8Therefore the male goat grew very
great; but when he became strong, the
large horn was broken, and in place of it
four notable ones came up toward the four
winds of heaven. 9And out of one of them
came a little horn which grew exceedingly
great toward the south, toward the east,
and toward the Glorious *Land*. 10And it
grew up to the host of heaven; and it cast
down *some* of the host and *some* of the
stars to the ground, and trampled them.
11He even exalted *himself* as high as the
Prince of the host; and by him the daily
sacrifices were taken away, and the place of
His sanctuary was cast down. 12Because of
transgression, an army was given over *to
the horn* to oppose the daily *sacrifices;* and
he cast truth down to the ground. He did
all this and prospered.

13Then I heard a holy one speaking; and
another holy one said to that certain *one*
who was speaking, "How long *will* the vision
be, concerning the daily *sacrifices* and the
transgression of desolation, the giving of
both the sanctuary and the host to be trampled underfoot?"

14And he said to me, "For two thousand
three hundred days;[a] then the sanctuary
shall be cleansed."

Gabriel Interprets the Vision

15Then it happened, when I, Daniel,
had seen the vision and was seeking the

**INTIMATE
MOMENTS**

If your wife is a collector of figurines, tea
cups, etc., buy her something that adds
to her collection.

7:25 [a]Literally *wear out* 7:28 [a]Literally *the word*
8:14 [a]Literally *evening-mornings*

DEVOTIONS FOR COUPLES • 9:5
Out of a Dark Corner

If you and your mate do not put the past behind you, then your past will continue to cast its shadow into your present and future. Specifically, if you want to help your mate develop confidence and a healthy self-image, you will have to talk about negative or hurtful things your in-laws may have said or done that left their marks on your spouse. The following are some tips for helping your mate in this area.

First, begin to work with your spouse to get the problem fully out in the open. Talk about how your own parents treated you, and then ask your mate to share his or her experiences. Be patient. Talking about these things can be very painful.

Second, help your mate understand his or her parents. Proverbs 24:3 reads, "Through wisdom a house is built, and by understanding it is established." Understanding is essential in your mate's relationship with his or her parents. Talk together about your mate's parents and seek to put their lives in proper perspective.

Third, remind your mate that God's grace and power are greater than any parents' mistakes. No matter how poor a person's home life may have been, God delights in resurrecting a damaged self-image and restoring dignity to that wounded person. Point your mate toward Christ and the hope He offers by verbally drawing attention to Jesus and expressing your confidence and belief in the greatness of God. Recall any shared instances when God showed Himself strong.

Fourth, help your mate determine how to respond to his or her parents. None of us controls how we were treated as a child, but we do have control over how we will relate to our parents today. Point out some positive things about your in-laws' parenting and how you are the benefactor of those good traits. This is important even if your mate's parents are no longer living.

Fifth, help your mate experience all that God has for you by clipping any ties of inappropriate dependence. Genesis 2:24 makes clear we are to leave our parents, which means we are no longer remain dependent on them for money, for an undue amount of emotional support, or for acceptance.

Sixth, encourage your mate to make the choice to forgive his or her parents—completely. To forgive someone means to give up the right to punish them. Patiently and gently urge your mate to deal with the past constructively, to put away punishing emotions and replace them with an attitude of love and understanding.

---

meaning, that suddenly there stood before me one having the appearance of a man. ¹⁶And I heard a man's voice between *the banks of* the Ulai, who called, and said, "Gabriel, make this *man* understand the vision." ¹⁷So he came near where I stood, and when he came I was afraid and fell on my face; but he said to me, "Understand, son of man, that the vision *refers* to the time of the end."

¹⁸Now, as he was speaking with me, I was in a deep sleep with my face to the ground; but he touched me, and stood me upright. ¹⁹And he said, "Look, I am making known to you what shall happen in the latter time of the indignation; for at the appointed time the end *shall be.* ²⁰The ram which you saw, having the two horns—*they are* the kings of Media and Persia. ²¹And the male goat *is* the kingdomᵃ of Greece. The large horn that *is* between its eyes *is* the first king. ²²As for the broken *horn* and the four that stood up in its place, four kingdoms shall arise out of that nation, but not with its power.

²³ "And in the latter time of their
     kingdom,
When the transgressors have
     reached their fullness,
A king shall arise,
Having fierce features,
Who understands sinister schemes.

8:21 ᵃLiterally *king,* representing his kingdom (compare 7:17, 23)

24   His power shall be mighty, but not
          by his own power;
        He shall destroy fearfully,
        And shall prosper and thrive;
        He shall destroy the mighty, and *also*
          the holy people.

25   "Through his cunning
        He shall cause deceit to prosper
          under his rule;[a]
        And he shall exalt *himself* in his
          heart.
        He shall destroy many in *their*
          prosperity.
        He shall even rise against the Prince
          of princes;
        But he shall be broken without
          human means.[b]

26   "And the vision of the evenings and
          mornings
        Which was told is true;
        Therefore seal up the vision,
        For *it refers* to many days *in the
          future.*"

²⁷And I, Daniel, fainted and was sick for
days; afterward I arose and went about the
king's business. I was astonished by the
vision, but no one understood it.

Daniel's Prayer for the People

9 In the first year of Darius the son of
  Ahasuerus, of the lineage of the
Medes, who was made king over the realm
of the Chaldeans— ²in the first year of his
reign I, Daniel, understood by the books
the number of the years *specified* by the
word of the LORD through Jeremiah the
prophet, that He would accomplish seventy
years in the desolations of Jerusalem.

³Then I set my face toward the Lord
God to make request by prayer and supplications, with fasting, sackcloth, and ashes.
⁴And I prayed to the LORD my God, and
made confession, and said, "O Lord, great
and awesome God, who keeps His covenant
and mercy with those who love Him, and
with those who keep His commandments,
⁵we have sinned and committed iniquity,
we have done wickedly and rebelled, even
by departing from Your precepts and Your

judgments. ⁶Neither have we heeded Your
servants the prophets, who spoke in Your
name to our kings and our princes, to our
fathers and all the people of the land. ⁷O
Lord, righteousness *belongs* to You, but to
us shame of face, as *it is* this day—to the
men of Judah, to the inhabitants of
Jerusalem and all Israel, those near and
those far off in all the countries to which
You have driven them, because of the
unfaithfulness which they have committed
against You.

⁸"O Lord, to us *belongs* shame of face,
to our kings, our princes, and our fathers,
because we have sinned against You. ⁹To
the Lord our God *belong* mercy and forgiveness, though we have rebelled against
Him. ¹⁰We have not obeyed the voice of the
LORD our God, to walk in His laws, which
He set before us by His servants the
prophets. ¹¹Yes, all Israel has transgressed
Your law, and has departed so as not to
obey Your voice; therefore the curse and
the oath written in the Law of Moses the
servant of God have been poured out on
us, because we have sinned against Him.
¹²And He has confirmed His words, which
He spoke against us and against our
judges who judged us, by bringing upon
us a great disaster; for under the whole
heaven such has never been done as what
has been done to Jerusalem.

¹³"As *it is* written in the Law of Moses,
all this disaster has come upon us; yet we
have not made our prayer before the LORD
our God, that we might turn from our iniquities and understand Your truth.
¹⁴Therefore the LORD has kept the disaster
in mind, and brought it upon us; for the
LORD our God *is* righteous in all the works
which He does, though we have not obeyed
His voice. ¹⁵And now, O Lord our God, who
brought Your people out of the land of
Egypt with a mighty hand, and made
Yourself a name, as *it is* this day—we
have sinned, we have done wickedly!

¹⁶"O Lord, according to all Your righteousness, I pray, let Your anger and Your
fury be turned away from Your city
Jerusalem, Your holy mountain; because
for our sins, and for the iniquities of our
fathers, Jerusalem and Your people *are* a
reproach to all *those* around us. ¹⁷Now

8:25 [a]Literally *hand* [b]Literally *hand*

therefore, our God, hear the prayer of Your servant, and his supplications, and for the Lord's sake cause Your face to shine on Your sanctuary, which is desolate. ¹⁸O my God, incline Your ear and hear; open Your eyes and see our desolations, and the city which is called by Your name; for we do not present our supplications before You because of our righteous deeds, but because of Your great mercies. ¹⁹O Lord, hear! O Lord, forgive! O Lord, listen and act! Do not delay for Your own sake, my God, for Your city and Your people are called by Your name."

The Seventy-Weeks Prophecy

²⁰Now while I *was* speaking, praying, and confessing my sin and the sin of my people Israel, and presenting my supplication before the LORD my God for the holy mountain of my God, ²¹yes, while I *was* speaking in prayer, the man Gabriel, whom I had seen in the vision at the beginning, being caused to fly swiftly, reached me about the time of the evening offering. ²²And he informed *me,* and talked with me, and said, "O Daniel, I have now come forth to give you skill to understand. ²³At the beginning of your supplications the command went out, and I have come to tell *you,* for you *are* greatly beloved; therefore consider the matter, and understand the vision:

24 "Seventy weeksᵃ are determined
    For your people and for your holy
        city,
    To finish the transgression,
    To make an end ofᵇ sins,
    To make reconciliation for iniquity,
    To bring in everlasting
        righteousness,
    To seal up vision and prophecy,
    And to anoint the Most Holy.

25 "Know therefore and understand,
    That from the going forth of the
        command
    To restore and build Jerusalem
    Until Messiah the Prince,
    There shall be seven weeks and
        sixty-two weeks;
    The streetᵃ shall be built again, and
        the wall,ᵇ
    Even in troublesome times.

26 "And after the sixty-two weeks
    Messiah shall be cut off, but not for
        Himself;
    And the people of the prince who is
        to come
    Shall destroy the city and the
        sanctuary.
    The end of it *shall be* with a flood,
    And till the end of the war
        desolations are determined.

27 Then he shall confirm a covenant
        with many for one week;
    But in the middle of the week
    He shall bring an end to sacrifice and
        offering.
    And on the wing of abominations
        shall be one who makes
        desolate,
    Even until the consummation, which
        is determined,
    Is poured out on the desolate."

Vision of the Glorious Man

10 In the third year of Cyrus king of Persia a message was revealed to Daniel, whose name was called Belteshazzar. The message *was* true, but the appointed time *was* long;ᵃ and he understood the message, and had understanding of the vision. ²In those days I, Daniel, was mourning three full weeks. ³I ate no pleasant food, no meat or wine came into my mouth, nor did I anoint myself at all, till three whole weeks were fulfilled.

⁴Now on the twenty-fourth day of the first month, as I was by the side of the great river, that *is,* the Tigris,ᵃ ⁵I lifted my eyes and looked, and behold, a certain man clothed in linen, whose waist *was* girded with gold of Uphaz! ⁶His body *was* like beryl, his face like the appearance of lightning, his eyes like torches of fire, his arms and feet like burnished bronze in color, and the sound of his words like the voice of a multitude.

⁷And I, Daniel, alone saw the vision, for the men who were with me did not see the vision; but a great terror fell upon them, so

---

9:24 ᵃLiterally *sevens,* and so throughout the chapter ᵇFollowing Qere, Septuagint, Syriac, and Vulgate; Kethib and Theodotion read *To seal up.*
9:25 ᵃOr *open square* ᵇOr *moat* **10:1** ᵃOr *and of great conflict* **10:4** ᵃHebrew *Hiddekel*

that they fled to hide themselves. 8Therefore I was left alone when I saw this great vision, and no strength remained in me; for my vigor was turned to frailty in me, and I retained no strength. 9Yet I heard the sound of his words; and while I heard the sound of his words I was in a deep sleep on my face, with my face to the ground.

Prophecies Concerning Persia and Greece

10Suddenly, a hand touched me, which made me tremble on my knees and *on* the palms of my hands. 11And he said to me, "O Daniel, man greatly beloved, understand the words that I speak to you, and stand upright, for I have now been sent to you." While he was speaking this word to me, I stood trembling.

12Then he said to me, "Do not fear, Daniel, for from the first day that you set your heart to understand, and to humble yourself before your God, your words were heard; and I have come because of your words. 13But the prince of the kingdom of Persia withstood me twenty-one days; and behold, Michael, one of the chief princes, came to help me, for I had been left alone there with the kings of Persia.

14Now I have come to make you understand what will happen to your people in the latter days, for the vision *refers* to *many* days yet *to come*."

15When he had spoken such words to me, I turned my face toward the ground and became speechless. 16And suddenly, *one* having the likeness of the sons[a] of men touched my lips; then I opened my mouth and spoke, saying to him who stood before me, "My lord, because of the vision my sorrows have overwhelmed me, and I have retained no strength. 17For how can this servant of my lord talk with you, my lord? As for me, no strength remains in me now, nor is any breath left in me."

18Then again, *the one* having the likeness of a man touched me and strengthened me. 19And he said, "O man greatly beloved, fear not! Peace *be* to you; be strong, yes, be strong!"

So when he spoke to me I was strengthened, and said, "Let my lord speak, for you have strengthened me."

20Then he said, "Do you know why I have come to you? And now I must return to fight with the prince of Persia; and when I have gone forth, indeed the prince of Greece will come. 21But I will tell you what is noted in the Scripture of Truth. (No one upholds me against these, except Michael your prince.

10:16 [a]Theodotion and Vulgate read *the son;* Septuagint reads *a hand.*

Time to Grow Up

It dawned on me one day, in the middle of a petty argument with Barbara, that it was time for me to grow up. I had to stop acting like one of the kids. I suddenly realized that if I were going to be a man, I couldn't go on acting like a child. And so, just as Paul said, I determined to put away childish things (1 Cor. 13:11).

Some of the unhappiest husband-wife relationships I know of are those in which one or both spouses have never grown up. They continue to act in petty, hurtful, and faultfinding ways. They still speak rashly and rudely, with little regard for how their words may hurt the other. They still think life revolves around them, and have trouble taking responsibility for their actions and choices. They refuse to admit they ever do anything wrong. They blame, ridicule, and find ways to get back at their spouses.

In other words, they speak, think, and reason as children.

Think of any tense times you've had with your mate recently. Can you detect in your own attitude any of the above descriptions of childishness? And if so, what will it take for you to grow up? Ultimately, it is our relationship with Christ and time spent in prayer, reading God's Word, and in relationships with other godly people that move us from being childish to being mature.

11 "Also in the first year of Darius the Mede, I, *even* I, stood up to confirm and strengthen him.) ²And now I will tell you the truth: Behold, three more kings will arise in Persia, and the fourth shall be far richer than *them* all; by his strength, through his riches, he shall stir up all against the realm of Greece. ³Then a mighty king shall arise, who shall rule with great dominion, and do according to his will. ⁴And when he has arisen, his kingdom shall be broken up and divided toward the four winds of heaven, but not among his posterity nor according to his dominion with which he ruled; for his kingdom shall be uprooted, even for others besides these.

Warring Kings of North and South

⁵"Also the king of the South shall become strong, as well as *one* of his princes; and he shall gain power over him and have dominion. His dominion *shall be* a great dominion. ⁶And at the end of *some* years they shall join forces, for the daughter of the king of the South shall go to the king of the North to make an agreement; but she shall not retain the power of her authority,ᵃ and neither he nor his authorityᵇ shall stand; but she shall be given up, with those who brought her, and with him who begot her, and with him who strengthened her in *those* times. ⁷But from a branch of her roots *one* shall arise in his place, who shall come with an army, enter the fortress of the king of the North, and deal with them and prevail. ⁸And he shall also carry their gods captive to Egypt, with their princesᵃ *and* their precious articles of silver and gold; and he shall continue *more* years than the king of the North.

⁹"Also *the king of the North* shall come to the kingdom of the king of the South, but shall return to his own land. ¹⁰However his sons shall stir up strife, and assemble a multitude of great forces; and *one* shall certainly come and overwhelm and pass through; then he shall return to his fortress and stir up strife.

¹¹"And the king of the South shall be moved with rage, and go out and fight with him, with the king of the North, who shall muster a great multitude; but the multitude shall be given into the hand of his *enemy.* ¹²When he has taken away the multitude, his heart will be lifted up; and he will cast down tens of thousands, but he will not prevail. ¹³For the king of the North will return and muster a multitude greater than the former, and shall certainly come at the end of some years with a great army and much equipment.

¹⁴"Now in those times many shall rise up against the king of the South. Also, violent menᵃ of your people shall exalt themselves in fulfillment of the vision, but they shall fall. ¹⁵So the king of the North shall come and build a siege mound, and take a fortified city; and the forcesᵃ of the South shall not withstand *him.* Even his choice troops *shall have* no strength to resist. ¹⁶But he who comes against him shall do according to his own will, and no one shall stand against him. He shall stand in the Glorious Land with destruction in his power.ᵃ

¹⁷"He shall also set his face to enter with the strength of his whole kingdom, and upright onesᵃ with him; thus shall he do. And he shall give him the daughter of women to destroy it; but she shall not stand *with him,* or be for him. ¹⁸After this he shall turn his face to the coastlands, and shall take many. But a ruler shall bring the reproach against them to an end; and with the reproach removed, he shall turn back on him. ¹⁹Then he shall turn his face toward the fortress of his own land; but he shall stumble and fall, and not be found.

²⁰"There shall arise in his place one who imposes taxes *on* the glorious kingdom; but within a few days he shall be destroyed, but not in anger or in battle. ²¹And in his place shall arise a vile person, to whom they will not give the honor of royalty; but he shall come in peaceably, and seize the kingdom by intrigue. ²²With the forceᵃ of a flood they shall be swept away from before him and be broken, and

---

11:6 ᵃLiterally *arm* ᵇLiterally *arm* **11:8** ᵃOr *molded images* **11:14** ᵃOr *robbers,* literally *sons of breakage* **11:15** ᵃLiterally *arms* **11:16** ᵃLiterally *hand* **11:17** ᵃOr *bring equitable terms* **11:22** ᵃLiterally *arms*

also the prince of the covenant. 23And after the league *is made* with him he shall act deceitfully, for he shall come up and become strong with a small *number of* people. 24He shall enter peaceably, even into the richest places of the province; and he shall do *what* his fathers have not done, nor his forefathers: he shall disperse among them the plunder, spoil, and riches; and he shall devise his plans against the strongholds, but *only* for a time.

25"He shall stir up his power and his courage against the king of the South with a great army. And the king of the South shall be stirred up to battle with a very great and mighty army; but he shall not stand, for they shall devise plans against him. 26Yes, those who eat of the portion of his delicacies shall destroy him; his army shall be swept away, and many shall fall down slain. 27Both these kings' hearts *shall be* bent on evil, and they shall speak lies at the same table; but it shall not prosper, for the end *will* still *be* at the appointed time. 28While returning to his land with great riches, his heart shall be *moved* against the holy covenant; so he shall do *damage* and return to his own land.

The Northern King's Blasphemies

29"At the appointed time he shall return and go toward the south; but it shall not be like the former or the latter. 30For ships from Cyprusa shall come against him; therefore he shall be grieved, and return in rage against the holy covenant, and do *damage.*

"So he shall return and show regard for those who forsake the holy covenant. 31And forcesa shall be mustered by him, and they shall defile the sanctuary fortress; then they shall take away the daily *sacrifices,* and place *there* the abomination of desolation. 32Those who do wickedly against the covenant he shall corrupt with flattery; but the people who know their God shall be strong, and carry out *great exploits.* 33And those of the people who understand shall instruct many; yet *for many* days they shall fall by sword

Be All There

MORE THAN ANYTHING, our children need us to take action and become more involved in their lives. They need more than just our time; they need our full attention.

They need our hearts knitted to theirs as they make their choices and hammer out their convictions. They need us to help them think about the clothing they wear, the types of people they date, and the peer pressure they face.

In order to be a parent worthy of honor, we can't just be there; we have to be *all* there.

That's a special challenge for fathers. Too many of us are consumed with our careers, preoccupied with our toys, and addicted to our hobbies. Real men with real character *act*; they take responsibility head on. They may not do it perfectly, but they tackle issues and battlefronts courageously. Daniel 11:32 describes them well, "But the people who know their God shall be strong, and caarry out great exploits."

Take the time to think of at least two things you can do during the coming week to get more involved in the lives of your children. And pray that God will help you to be all there at home with your spouse and children.

and flame, by captivity and plundering. 34Now when they fall, they shall be aided with a little help; but many shall join with them by intrigue. 35And *some* of those of understanding shall fall, to refine them, purify *them,* and make *them* white, *until* the time of the end; because *it is* still for the appointed time.

36"Then the king shall do according to his own will: he shall exalt and magnify himself above every god, shall speak blasphemies against the God of gods, and shall prosper till the wrath has been accomplished; for what has been determined shall be done. 37He shall regard neither the Goda of his fathers nor the desire of women, nor regard any god; for he shall

---

11:30 aHebrew *Kittim,* western lands, especially Cyprus 11:31 aLiterally *arms*
11:37 aOr *gods*

exalt himself above *them* all. ³⁸But in their place he shall honor a god of fortresses; and a god which his fathers did not know he shall honor with gold and silver, with precious stones and pleasant things. ³⁹Thus he shall act against the strongest fortresses with a foreign god, which he shall acknowledge, *and* advance *its* glory; and he shall cause them to rule over many, and divide the land for gain.

The Northern King's Conquests

⁴⁰"At the time of the end the king of the South shall attack him; and the king of the North shall come against him like a whirlwind, with chariots, horsemen, and with many ships; and he shall enter the countries, overwhelm *them,* and pass through. ⁴¹He shall also enter the Glorious Land, and many *countries* shall be overthrown; but these shall escape from his hand: Edom, Moab, and the prominent people of Ammon. ⁴²He shall stretch out his hand against the countries, and the land of Egypt shall not escape. ⁴³He shall have power over the treasures of gold and silver, and over all the precious things of Egypt; also the Libyans and Ethiopians *shall follow* at his heels. ⁴⁴But news from the east and the north shall trouble him; therefore he shall go out with great fury to destroy and annihilate many. ⁴⁵And he shall plant the tents of his palace between the seas and the glorious holy mountain; yet he shall come to his end, and no one will help him.

Prophecy of the End Time

12 "At that time Michael shall stand up,
The great prince who stands *watch*
    over the sons of your people;
And there shall be a time of trouble,
Such as never was since there was a
    nation,

Even to that time.
And at that time your people shall be
    delivered,
Every one who is found written in
    the book.
2   And many of those who sleep in the
        dust of the earth shall awake,
Some to everlasting life,
Some to shame *and* everlasting
    contempt.
3   Those who are wise shall shine
Like the brightness of the firmament,
And those who turn many to
    righteousness
Like the stars forever and ever.

⁴"But you, Daniel, shut up the words, and seal the book until the time of the end; many shall run to and fro, and knowledge shall increase."

⁵Then I, Daniel, looked; and there stood two others, one on this riverbank and the other on that riverbank. ⁶And *one* said to the man clothed in linen, who *was* above the waters of the river, "How long shall the fulfillment of these wonders *be?*"

⁷Then I heard the man clothed in linen, who *was* above the waters of the river, when he held up his right hand and his left hand to heaven, and swore by Him who lives forever, that *it shall be* for a time, times, and half *a time;* and when the power of the holy people has been completely shattered, all these *things* shall be finished.

⁸Although I heard, I did not understand. Then I said, "My lord, what *shall be* the end of these *things?*"

⁹And he said, "Go *your way,* Daniel, for the words *are* closed up and sealed till the time of the end. ¹⁰Many shall be purified, made white, and refined, but the wicked shall do wickedly; and none of the wicked shall understand, but the wise shall understand.

¹¹"And from the time *that* the daily *sacrifice* is taken away, and the abomination of desolation is set up, *there shall be* one thousand two hundred and ninety days. ¹²Blessed *is* he who waits, and comes to the one thousand three hundred and thirty-five days.

¹³"But you, go *your way* till the end; for you shall rest, and will arise to your inheritance at the end of the days."

INTIMATE MOMENTS

On a small piece of paper, write a short note of encouragement and slip it into his pants pocket. He'll find it later when he's fishing for change.

HOSEA

THE BOOK OF HOSEA BEGINS the last section of the Old Testament, known as the Minor Prophets. Unfortunately, most contemporary Christians ignore these books. To get the most benefit from reading them, we need to gain some understanding of their historical context.

Hosea lived and spoke about events taking place in the northern kingdom of Israel (sometimes called Ephraim) during the eighth century BC. Hosea prophesied during a time of political instability, following the death of Jereboam II in 746 BC. In addition to the relative anarchy, Israel also faced a growing threat from the Assyrians, who ultimately invaded and destroyed Israel in 722 BC.

Many Israelites of Hosea's day mixed Baal worship with the worship of Yahweh. As with many pagan religions, the worship of Baal included the practice of temple prostitution. Worshipers would visit their pagan shrines to engage in sexual relations, believing that by doing so, the gods would be pleased and would grant them continued fertility.

Into this spiritual and political cesspool, God called Hosea to be both a messenger and a living example of God's covenant faithfulness. God directed Hosea to marry a woman named Gomer, who soon became unfaithful. Her life provides a stark picture of the spiritual unfaithfulness of Israel. The marriage of Hosea and Gomer presents a powerful illustration of marital perseverance in the midst of very difficult circumstances. It memorably declares how much God loves His children, even when they act unfaithfully.

When God directs Hosea to "take yourself a wife of harlotry" (1:2), He is speaking prophetically. As Gomer becomes increasingly unfaithful sexually, God calls on Hosea to remain faithful to her; eventually, God instructs him to buy her back out of prostitution so that once again she might become his wife.

Hosea's example of covenant-keeping love, even in the face of blatant adultery, gives us a model of selfless, sacrificial love in marriage. While a spouse married to an unrepentant serial adulterer like Gomer has biblical warrant to pursue divorce (Matt. 19:9), Hosea's example provides us with a compelling demonstration of the humble love described in 1 Corinthians 13:4–7.

1 The word of the LORD that came to
Hosea the son of Beeri, in the days of
Uzziah, Jotham, Ahaz, *and* Hezekiah, kings
of Judah, and in the days of Jeroboam the
son of Joash, king of Israel.

The Family of Hosea

2When the LORD began to speak by Hosea,
the LORD said to Hosea:

"Go, take yourself a wife of harlotry
And children of harlotry,
For the land has committed great
harlotry
By *departing* from the LORD."

3So he went and took Gomer the daughter
of Diblaim, and she conceived and bore
him a son. 4Then the LORD said to him:

"Call his name Jezreel,
For in a little *while*
I will avenge the bloodshed of Jezreel
on the house of Jehu,
And bring an end to the kingdom of
the house of Israel.
5   It shall come to pass in that day
That I will break the bow of Israel in
the Valley of Jezreel."

6And she conceived again and bore a
daughter. Then *God* said to him:

"Call her name Lo-Ruhamah,a
For I will no longer have mercy on
the house of Israel,
But I will utterly take them away.b
7   Yet I will have mercy on the house of
Judah,
Will save them by the LORD their God,
And will not save them by bow,
Nor by sword or battle,
By horses or horsemen."

8Now when she had weaned Lo-Ruhamah, she conceived and bore a son. 9Then
God said:

"Call his name Lo-Ammi,a
For you *are* not My people,
And I will not be your *God.*

The Restoration of Israel

10   "Yet the number of the children of
Israel
Shall be as the sand of the sea,

Which cannot be measured or
numbered.
And it shall come to pass
In the place where it was said to
them,
'You *are* not My people,'a
There it shall be said to them,
'*You are* sons of the living God.'
11   Then the children of Judah and the
children of Israel
Shall be gathered together,
And appoint for themselves one
head;
And they shall come up out of the
land,
For great *will be* the day of Jezreel!
2 Say to your brethren, 'My people,'a
And to your sisters, 'Mercyb *is shown.*'

God's Unfaithful People

2   "Bring charges against your mother,
bring charges;
For she *is* not My wife, nor *am* I her
Husband!
Let her put away her harlotries from
her sight,
And her adulteries from between her
breasts;
3   Lest I strip her naked
And expose her, as in the day she
was born,
And make her like a wilderness,
And set her like a dry land,
And slay her with thirst.

4   "I will not have mercy on her children,
For they *are* the children of harlotry.
5   For their mother has played the
harlot;
She who conceived them has
behaved shamefully.
For she said, 'I will go after my lovers,
Who give *me* my bread and my water,
My wool and my linen,
My oil and my drink.'

6   "Therefore, behold,
I will hedge up your way with
thorns,

1:6 aLiterally *No-Mercy* bOr *That I may forgive them
at all* 1:9 aLiterally *Not-My-People*
1:10 aHebrew *lo-ammi* (compare verse 9)
2:1 aHebrew *Ammi* (compare 1:9, 10) bHebrew
Ruhamah (compare 1:6)

And wall her in,
So that she cannot find her paths.
7 She will chase her lovers,
But not overtake them;
Yes, she will seek them, but not find
them.
Then she will say,
'I will go and return to my first
husband,
For then *it was* better for me than now.'
8 For she did not know
That I gave her grain, new wine, and
oil,
And multiplied her silver and gold—
Which they prepared for Baal.

9 "Therefore I will return and take away
My grain in its time
And My new wine in its season,
And will take back My wool and My
linen,
Given to cover her nakedness.
10 Now I will uncover her lewdness in
the sight of her lovers,
And no one shall deliver her from
My hand.
11 I will also cause all her mirth to cease,
Her feast days,
Her New Moons,
Her Sabbaths—
All her appointed feasts.

12 "And I will destroy her vines and her
fig trees,
Of which she has said,
'These *are* my wages that my lovers
have given me.'
So I will make them a forest,
And the beasts of the field shall eat
them.
13 I will punish her
For the days of the Baals to which
she burned incense.
She decked herself with her earrings
and jewelry,
And went after her lovers;
But Me she forgot," says the LORD.

God's Mercy on His People

14 "Therefore, behold, I will allure her,
Will bring her into the wilderness,
And speak comfort to her.
15 I will give her her vineyards from
there,

BIBLICAL INSIGHTS • 2:5
Make an Investment

DO YOU SOMETIMES FEEL as though your wife is not excited about your sexual advances? If so, I advise you to step back and consider how much of an investment you've been making into her relational bank account.

Did you know that your wife's heart can be a lot like a bank account, where you make deposits and withdrawals? Far too often, I fear, we men can make withdrawal after withdrawal and disregard making deposits or investments. That makes a woman vulnerable. Read what the unfaithful harlot of Hosea 2:5 said about her reasons for committing adultery, "I will go after my lovers, who give me my bread and my water, my wool and my linen, my oil and my drink." Every wife needs you to invest into her life *security, acceptance,* and an *emotional connection*.

When you withhold a meaningful relationship—in other words, when you neglect her need for conversation with you, her desire to see you plugged into family life, her thirst to hear words of affirmation from you—she finds it difficult to give herself totally to you. But when you invest liberally into her life, you model the kindness and graciousness of God. That demonstration of love allows a wife to feel safe, accepted, and connected to her husband, and to respond to his love with her own love. Why not take a moment and ask her which of the three needs I mentioned earlier (security, acceptance, and emotional connection) are her greatest right now, and ask her what she needs you to do to make a few deposits?

And the Valley of Achor as a door of
hope;
She shall sing there,
As in the days of her youth,
As in the day when she came up
from the land of Egypt.

16 "And it shall be, in that day,"
Says the LORD,
"*That* you will call Me 'My Husband,'ᵃ
And no longer call Me
'My Master,'ᵇ

17 For I will take from her mouth the
names of the Baals,
And they shall be remembered by
their name no more.

18 In that day I will make a covenant
for them
With the beasts of the field,
With the birds of the air,
And *with* the creeping things of the
ground.
Bow and sword of battle I will
shatter from the earth,
To make them lie down safely.

19 "I will betroth you to Me forever;
Yes, I will betroth you to Me
In righteousness and justice,
In lovingkindness and mercy;

20 I will betroth you to Me in
faithfulness,
And you shall know the LORD.

21 "It shall come to pass in that day
That I will answer," says the LORD;
"I will answer the heavens,
And they shall answer the earth.

22 The earth shall answer
With grain,
With new wine,
And with oil;
They shall answer Jezreel.ᵃ

23 Then I will sow her for Myself in the
earth,
And I will have mercy on *her who
had* not obtained mercy;ᵃ
Then I will say to *those who were* not
My people,ᵇ
'You *are* My people!'
And they shall say, '*You are* my God!' "

Israel Will Return to God

3 Then the LORD said to me, "Go again,
love a woman *who is* loved by a loverᵃ
and is committing adultery, just like the
love of the LORD for the children of Israel,
who look to other gods and love *the* raisin
cakes *of the pagans.*"

2So I bought her for myself for fifteen
shekels of silver, and one and one-half

homers of barley. 3And I said to her, "You
shall stay with me many days; you shall
not play the harlot, nor shall you have a
man—so, too, *will* I *be* toward you."

4For the children of Israel shall abide
many days without king or prince, without
sacrifice or *sacred* pillar, without ephod or
teraphim. 5Afterward the children of Israel
shall return and seek the LORD their God
and David their king. They shall fear the
LORD and His goodness in the latter days.

God's Charge Against Israel

4 Hear the word of the LORD,
You children of Israel,
For the LORD *brings* a charge against
the inhabitants of the land:

"There is no truth or mercy
Or knowledge of God in
the land.

2 *By* swearing and lying,
Killing and stealing and committing
adultery,
They break all restraint,
With bloodshed upon bloodshed.

3 Therefore the land will mourn;
And everyone who dwells there will
waste away
With the beasts of the field
And the birds of the air;
Even the fish of the sea will be taken
away.

4 "Now let no man contend, or rebuke
another;
For your people *are* like those who
contend with the priest.

5 Therefore you shall stumble in the
day;
The prophet also shall stumble with
you in the night;
And I will destroy your mother.

6 My people are destroyed for lack of
knowledge.
Because you have rejected
knowledge,
I also will reject you from being
priest for Me;

2:16 ᵃHebrew *Ishi* ᵇHebrew *Baali*
2:22 ᵃLiterally *God Will Sow*
2:23 ᵃHebrew *lo-ruhamah* ᵇHebrew *lo-ammi*
3:1 ᵃLiterally *friend* or *husband*

Because you have forgotten the law
    of your God,
I also will forget your children.

7 "The more they increased,
    The more they sinned against Me;
I will change[a] their glory[b] into
    shame.
8 They eat up the sin of My people;
    They set their heart on their iniquity.
9 And it shall be: like people, like priest.
    So I will punish them for their ways,
    And reward them for their deeds.
10 For they shall eat, but not have
    enough;
They shall commit harlotry, but not
    increase;
Because they have ceased obeying
    the LORD.

The Idolatry of Israel

11 "Harlotry, wine, and new wine enslave
    the heart.
12 My people ask counsel from their
    wooden *idols,*
And their staff informs them.
For the spirit of harlotry has caused
    them to stray,
And they have played the harlot
    against their God.
13 They offer sacrifices on the
    mountaintops,
And burn incense on the hills,
Under oaks, poplars, and terebinths,
Because their shade *is* good.
Therefore your daughters commit
    harlotry,
And your brides commit adultery.

14 "I will not punish your daughters
    when they commit harlotry,
Nor your brides when they commit
    adultery;
For *the men* themselves go apart
    with harlots,
And offer sacrifices with a ritual
    harlot.[a]

Therefore people *who* do not
    understand will be trampled.
15 "Though you, Israel, play the harlot,
    Let not Judah offend.
Do not come up to Gilgal,
Nor go up to Beth Aven,
Nor swear an oath, *saying,* 'As the
    LORD lives'—

16 "For Israel is stubborn
    Like a stubborn calf;
Now the LORD will let them forage
    Like a lamb in open country.

17 "Ephraim *is* joined to idols,
    Let him alone.
18 Their drink is rebellion,
    They commit harlotry continually.
Her rulers dearly[a] love dishonor.
19 The wind has wrapped her up in its
    wings,
And they shall be ashamed because
    of their sacrifices.

Impending Judgment on Israel and Judah

5 "Hear this, O priests!
    Take heed, O house of Israel!
Give ear, O house of the king!
For yours *is* the judgment,
Because you have been a snare to
    Mizpah
And a net spread on Tabor.
2 The revolters are deeply involved in
    slaughter,
Though I rebuke them all.
3 I know Ephraim,
And Israel is not hidden
    from Me;
For now, O Ephraim, you commit
    harlotry;
Israel is defiled.

4:7 [a]Following Masoretic Text, Septuagint, and
Vulgate; scribal tradition, Syriac, and Targum read
They will change. [b]Following Masoretic Text,
Septuagint, Syriac, Targum, and Vulgate; scribal tradition reads *My glory.* 4:14 [a]Compare Deuteronomy
23:18 4:18 [a]Hebrew is difficult; a Jewish tradition
reads *Her rulers shamefully love, 'Give!'*

INTIMATE MOMENTS

Go with him to his favorite store and let
him treat himself to something he'd really
like. Don't try to talk him into something
else or criticize his choice; just let him have
fun. And *you* have some fun with him!

4 "They do not direct their deeds
    Toward turning to their God,
    For the spirit of harlotry is in their
        midst,
    And they do not know the LORD.
5 The pride of Israel testifies to his
        face;
    Therefore Israel and Ephraim
        stumble in their iniquity;
    Judah also stumbles with them.

6 "With their flocks and herds
    They shall go to seek the LORD,
    But they will not find *Him*;
    He has withdrawn Himself from them.
7 They have dealt treacherously with
        the LORD,
    For they have begotten pagan
        children.
    Now a New Moon shall devour them
        and their heritage.

8 "Blow the ram's horn in Gibeah,
    The trumpet in Ramah!
    Cry aloud *at* Beth Aven,
    '*Look* behind you, O Benjamin!'
9 Ephraim shall be desolate in the day
        of rebuke;
    Among the tribes of Israel I make
        known what is sure.

10 "The princes of Judah are like those
        who remove a landmark;
    I will pour out My wrath on them
        like water.
11 Ephraim is oppressed *and* broken in
        judgment,
    Because he willingly walked by
        human precept.
12 Therefore I *will be* to Ephraim like a
        moth,
    And to the house of Judah like
        rottenness.

PARENTING MATTERS

Q: *How should I respond if I find pornography in my son's room or on his computer?*

Don't be like the mother who did nothing. "Boys will be boys," she sighed.

If your child is not present when you find the material, first show it to your spouse. Decide who should talk with the child. Then lay out a game plan that gives your child a chance to tell the truth. Pray that God will guide you and give you the right words to say as you speak heart-to-heart with your teen.

If you find the material when your child is present, begin dealing with it right on the spot. If your spouse is at home, do this together. Sit down and talk to your child and discuss with him why he is looking at it. Help him understand that the way God designed him as a young man is good and that the world uses the wiring of young men to trap them into something that is very unhealthy and damaging. Then review with him what God's Word has to say about why pornography is wrong and destructive.

Make him aware of the dangers of pornography. Some people are as prone to a compulsive need for pornography as others are to alcohol or drugs. A little look can lead to a *lot* of looks and later in marriage he may find it difficult to be satisfied with his wife, who is not air-brushed to near perfection.

Finally, ask him if will be more accountable to you than he has been in the past. Regularly ask him hard questions. Install internet filters on your computers and make sure computers are in open rooms, like a living room or the den, not behind closed doors in a bedroom. You may want to consider installing a program that gives you a snapshot of all the screens your children are looking at. If your child has his own room, consider taking the door off its hinges. It's *that* serious.

13 "When Ephraim saw his sickness,
     And Judah *saw* his wound,
     Then Ephraim went to Assyria
     And sent to King Jareb;
     Yet he cannot cure you,
     Nor heal you of your wound.
14 For I *will be* like a lion to Ephraim,
     And like a young lion to the house of
          Judah.
     I, *even* I, will tear *them* and go away;
     I will take *them* away, and no one
          shall rescue.
15 I will return again to My place
     Till they acknowledge their offense.
     Then they will seek My face;
     In their affliction they will earnestly
          seek Me."

A Call to Repentance

6 Come, and let us return to the LORD;
     For He has torn, but He will heal us;
     He has stricken, but He will bind us
          up.
2 After two days He will revive us;
     On the third day He will raise
          us up,
     That we may live in His sight.
3 Let us know,
     Let us pursue the knowledge of the
          LORD.
     His going forth is established as the
          morning;
     He will come to us like the rain,
     Like the latter *and* former rain to the
          earth.

Impenitence of Israel and Judah

4 "O Ephraim, what shall I do to you?
     O Judah, what shall I do to you?
     For your faithfulness is like a
          morning cloud,
     And like the early dew it goes away.
5 Therefore I have hewn *them* by the
          prophets,
     I have slain them by the words of
          My mouth;
     And your judgments *are like* light
          that goes forth.
6 For I desire mercy and not sacrifice,

     And the knowledge of God more
          than burnt offerings.
7 "But like men[a] they transgressed the
          covenant;
     There they dealt treacherously with
          Me.
8 Gilead *is* a city of evildoers
     And defiled with blood.
9 As bands of robbers lie in wait for a
          man,
     So the company of priests murder on
          the way to Shechem;
     Surely they commit lewdness.
10 I have seen a horrible thing in the
          house of Israel:
     There *is* the harlotry of Ephraim;
     Israel is defiled.
11 Also, O Judah, a harvest is appointed
          for you,
     When I return the captives of My
          people.

7 "When I would have healed Israel,
     Then the iniquity of Ephraim was
          uncovered,
     And the wickedness of Samaria.
     For they have committed fraud;
     A thief comes in;
     A band of robbers takes spoil
          outside.
2 They do not consider in their hearts
     That I remember all their
          wickedness;
     Now their own deeds have
          surrounded them;
     They are before My face.
3 They make a king glad with their
          wickedness,
     And princes with their lies.

4 "They *are* all adulterers.
     Like an oven heated by a baker—
     He ceases stirring *the fire* after
          kneading the dough,
     Until it is leavened.
5 In the day of our king
     Princes have made *him* sick,
          inflamed with wine;
     He stretched out his hand with
          scoffers.
6 They prepare their heart like an
          oven,
     While they lie in wait;
     Their baker[a] sleeps all night;

6:7 [a]Or *like Adam*   **7:6** [a]Following Masoretic Text
and Vulgate; Syriac and Targum read *Their anger;*
Septuagint reads *Ephraim.*

In the morning it burns like a
   flaming fire.
7   They are all hot, like an oven,
   And have devoured their judges;
   All their kings have fallen.
   None among them calls upon Me.

8   "Ephraim has mixed himself among
      the peoples;
   Ephraim is a cake unturned.
9   Aliens have devoured his strength,
   But he does not know *it;*
   Yes, gray hairs are here and there on
      him,
   Yet he does not know *it.*
10   And the pride of Israel testifies to
      his face,
   But they do not return to the LORD
      their God,
   Nor seek Him for all this.

Futile Reliance on the Nations

11   "Ephraim also is like a silly dove,
      without sense—
   They call to Egypt,
   They go to Assyria.
12   Wherever they go, I will spread My
      net on them;
   I will bring them down like birds of
      the air;
   I will chastise them
   According to what their
      congregation has heard.
13   "Woe to them, for they have fled from
      Me!
   Destruction to them,
   Because they have transgressed
      against Me!
   Though I redeemed them,
   Yet they have spoken lies against
      Me.
14   They did not cry out to Me with
      their heart
   When they wailed upon their beds.

   "They assemble together for[a] grain
      and new wine,
   They rebel against Me;[b]
15   Though I disciplined *and*
      strengthened their arms,
   Yet they devise evil against Me;
16   They return, *but* not to the Most
      High;[a]

They are like a treacherous bow.
Their princes shall fall by the sword
For the cursings of their tongue.
This *shall be* their derision in the
   land of Egypt.

The Apostasy of Israel

8   "*Set* the trumpet[a] to your mouth!
   He shall come like an eagle against
      the house of the LORD,
   Because they have transgressed My
      covenant
   And rebelled against My law.
2   Israel will cry to Me,
   'My God, we know You!'
3   Israel has rejected the good;
   The enemy will pursue him.

4   "They set up kings, but not by Me;
   They made princes, but I did not
      acknowledge *them.*
   From their silver and gold
   They made idols for themselves—
   That they might be cut off.
5   Your calf is rejected, O Samaria!
   My anger is aroused against them—
   How long until they attain to
      innocence?
6   For from Israel *is* even this:
   A workman made it, and it *is* not God;
   But the calf of Samaria shall be
      broken to pieces.

7   "They sow the wind,
   And reap the whirlwind.
   The stalk has no bud;
   It shall never produce meal.
   If it should produce,
   Aliens would swallow it up.
8   Israel is swallowed up;
   Now they are among the Gentiles
   Like a vessel in which *is* no pleasure.
9   For they have gone up to Assyria,
   Like a wild donkey alone by itself;
   Ephraim has hired lovers.
10   Yes, though they have hired among
      the nations,

7:14 [a]Following Masoretic Text and Targum; Vulgate
reads *thought upon;* Septuagint reads *slashed themselves for* (compare 1 Kings 18:28). [b]Following
Masoretic Text, Syriac, and Targum; Septuagint
omits *They rebel against Me;* Vulgate reads *They
departed from Me.* **7:16** [a]Or *upward*
8:1 [a]Hebrew *shophar,* ram's horn

Now I will gather them;
And they shall sorrow a little,[a]
Because of the burden[b] of the king
of princes.

11 "Because Ephraim has made many
altars for sin,
They have become for him altars for
sinning.
12 I have written for him the great
things of My law,
But they were considered a strange
thing.
13 *For* the sacrifices of My offerings
they sacrifice flesh and eat *it,*
But the LORD does not accept them.
Now He will remember their iniquity
and punish their sins.
They shall return to Egypt.

14 "For Israel has forgotten his Maker,
And has built temples;[a]
Judah also has multiplied fortified
cities;
But I will send fire upon his cities,
And it shall devour his palaces."

Judgment of Israel's Sin

9 Do not rejoice, O Israel, with joy
like *other* peoples,
For you have played the harlot
against your God.
You have made love *for* hire on every
threshing floor.
2 The threshing floor and the
winepress
Shall not feed them,
And the new wine shall fail in her.
3 They shall not dwell in the LORD's
land,
But Ephraim shall return to Egypt,
And shall eat unclean *things* in
Assyria.
4 They shall not offer wine *offerings* to
the LORD,
Nor shall their sacrifices be pleasing
to Him.
It shall be like bread of mourners to
them;
All who eat it shall be defiled.

For their bread *shall be* for their *own*
life;
It shall not come into the house of
the LORD.

5 What will you do in the appointed
day,
And in the day of the feast of the
LORD?
6 For indeed they are gone because of
destruction.
Egypt shall gather them up;
Memphis shall bury them.
Nettles shall possess their valuables
of silver;
Thorns *shall be* in their tents.

7 The days of punishment have
come;
The days of recompense have come.
Israel knows!
The prophet *is* a fool,
The spiritual man *is* insane,
Because of the greatness of your
iniquity and great enmity.
8 The watchman of Ephraim *is* with
my God;
But the prophet *is* a fowler's[a] snare in
all his ways—
Enmity in the house of his God.
9 They are deeply corrupted,
As in the days of Gibeah.
He will remember their iniquity;
He will punish their sins.

10 "I found Israel
Like grapes in the wilderness;
I saw your fathers
As the firstfruits on the fig tree in its
first season.
But they went to Baal Peor,
And separated themselves *to that*
shame;
They became an abomination like the
thing they loved.

8:10 [a]Or *begin to diminish* [b]Or *oracle*
8:14 [a]Or *palaces*
9:8 [a]That is, one who catches birds in a trap or snare

INTIMATE MOMENTS

Tell your wife you love her every morning
and every night.

11 *As for* Ephraim, their glory shall fly
        away like a bird—
    No birth, no pregnancy, and no
        conception!
12 Though they bring up their children,
    Yet I will bereave them to the last
        man.
    Yes, woe to them when I depart from
        them!
13 Just as I saw Ephraim like Tyre,
        planted in a pleasant place,
    So Ephraim will bring out his
        children to the murderer."

14 Give them, O LORD—
    What will You give?
    Give them a miscarrying womb
    And dry breasts!

15 "All their wickedness *is* in Gilgal,
    For there I hated them.
    Because of the evil of their deeds
    I will drive them from My house;
    I will love them no more.
    All their princes *are* rebellious.
16 Ephraim is stricken,
    Their root is dried up;
    They shall bear no fruit.
    Yes, were they to bear children,
    I would kill the darlings of their
        womb."

17 My God will cast them away,
    Because they did not obey Him;
    And they shall be wanderers among
        the nations.

Israel's Sin and Captivity

10 Israel empties *his* vine;
    He brings forth fruit for himself.
    According to the multitude of his
        fruit
    He has increased the altars;
    According to the bounty of his land
    They have embellished *his sacred*
        pillars.
2   Their heart is divided;
    Now they are held guilty.
    He will break down their altars;
    He will ruin their *sacred* pillars.

3   For now they say,
    "We have no king,
    Because we did not fear the LORD.
    And as for a king, what would he do
        for us?"
4   They have spoken words,
    Swearing falsely in making a
        covenant.
    Thus judgment springs up like
        hemlock in the furrows of the
        field.

ROMANTIC QUOTES AND NOTES
Connect with Her Soul

Today's media constantly bombard men with the idea that great sex is all about the right techniques or finding a partner with whom they are sexually compatible. We live in an age in which some view sex as a recreational activity, like playing tennis. Just find a willing partner, follow what's outlined in the magazine article, and great sex is guaranteed.

It's a lie. Passionate romance is the *by-product* of a real relationship between a husband and wife who have committed themselves to each other for a lifetime.

The secret to real romance isn't found in sex manuals. It's found in a husband learning *how* and *what* to sow in the garden of his wife's heart. When a man sows the seeds of respect, kind words, acts of tenderness, and thoughtfulness, he is demonstrating Christ-like love for his wife. As God said through Hosea, "Sow for yourselves righteousness, reap in mercy" (10:12).

On the other hand, if a husband fails to cultivate this relationship—or if he sows seeds of criticism, neglect, or rage—then sex becomes little more than a cold, physical act in which his wife feels used and unloved.

God hard-wired a woman to desire a real relationship. Just as your wife has the power to affirm you sexually, so you have tremendous power to provide her with the relationship she longs for: namely, a connectedness to your very heart and soul.

5 The inhabitants of Samaria fear
Because of the calf[a] of Beth Aven.
For its people mourn for it,
And its priests shriek for it—
Because its glory has departed from it.

6 *The idol* also shall be carried to
Assyria
As a present for King Jareb.
Ephraim shall receive shame,
And Israel shall be ashamed of his
own counsel.

7 *As for* Samaria, her king is cut off
Like a twig on the water.

8 Also the high places of Aven, the sin
of Israel,
Shall be destroyed.
The thorn and thistle shall grow on
their altars;
They shall say to the mountains,
"Cover us!"
And to the hills, "Fall on us!"

9 "O Israel, you have sinned from the
days of Gibeah;
There they stood.
The battle in Gibeah against the
children of iniquity[a]
Did not overtake them.

10 When *it is* My desire, I will chasten
them.
Peoples shall be gathered against
them
When I bind them for their two
transgressions.[a]

11 Ephraim *is* a trained heifer
That loves to thresh *grain;*
But I harnessed her fair neck,
I will make Ephraim pull *a plow.*
Judah shall plow;
Jacob shall break his clods."

12 Sow for yourselves righteousness;
Reap in mercy;

Break up your fallow ground,
For *it is* time to seek the LORD,
Till He comes and rains
righteousness on you.

13 You have plowed wickedness;
You have reaped iniquity.
You have eaten the fruit of lies,
Because you trusted in your own way,
In the multitude of your mighty
men.

14 Therefore tumult shall arise among
your people,
And all your fortresses shall be
plundered
As Shalman plundered Beth Arbel in
the day of battle—
A mother dashed in pieces upon *her*
children.

15 Thus it shall be done to you, O
Bethel,
Because of your great wickedness.
At dawn the king of Israel
Shall be cut off utterly.

God's Continuing Love for Israel

11 "When Israel *was* a child,
I loved him,
And out of Egypt I called My son.

2 *As* they called them,[a]
So they went from them;[b]
They sacrificed to the Baals,
And burned incense to carved
images.

3 "I taught Ephraim to walk,
Taking them by their arms;[a]
But they did not know that I healed
them.

4 I drew them with gentle cords,[a]
With bands of love,
And I was to them as those who take
the yoke from their neck.[b]
I stooped *and* fed them.

5 "He shall not return to the land of
Egypt;
But the Assyrian shall be his king,
Because they refused to repent.

6 And the sword shall slash in his
cities,
Devour his districts,
And consume *them,*
Because of their own counsels.

10:5 [a]Literally *calves* **10:9** [a]So read many Hebrew
manuscripts, Septuagint, and Vulgate; Masoretic Text
reads *unruliness.* **10:10** [a]Or *in their two habitations*
11:2 [a]Following Masoretic Text and Vulgate;
Septuagint reads *Just as I called them;* Targum interprets as *I sent prophets to a thousand of them.*
[b]Following Masoretic Text, Targum, and Vulgate;
Septuagint reads *from My face.*
11:3 [a]Some Hebrew manuscripts, Septuagint, Syriac,
and Vulgate read *My arms.*
11:4 [a]Literally *cords of a man* [b]Literally *jaws*

7   My people are bent on backsliding
       from Me.
     Though they call to the Most High,ᵃ
     None at all exalt *Him.*

8   "How can I give you up, Ephraim?
     How can I hand you over, Israel?
     How can I make you like Admah?
     How can I set you like Zeboiim?
     My heart churns within Me;
     My sympathy is stirred.

9   I will not execute the fierceness of
       My anger;
     I will not again destroy Ephraim.
     For I *am* God, and not man,
     The Holy One in your midst;
     And I will not come with terror.ᵃ

10   "They shall walk after the LORD.
     He will roar like a lion.
     When He roars,
     Then *His* sons shall come trembling
       from the west;

11   They shall come trembling like a
       bird from Egypt,
     Like a dove from the land of Assyria.
     And I will let them dwell in their
       houses,"
     Says the LORD.

God's Charge Against Ephraim

12   "Ephraim has encircled Me with lies,
     And the house of Israel with deceit;
     But Judah still walks with God,
     Even with the Holy Oneᵃ *who is*
       faithful.

12 "Ephraim feeds on the wind,
     And pursues the east wind;
     He daily increases lies and
       desolation.
     Also they make a covenant with the
       Assyrians,
     And oil is carried to Egypt.

INTIMATE MOMENTS

The next time you're sitting with your wife in church, reach out and put your arm around her.

---

2   "The LORD also *brings* a charge
       against Judah,
     And will punish Jacob according to
       his ways;
     According to his deeds He will
       recompense him.

3   He took his brother by the heel in the
       womb,
     And in his strength he struggled
       with God.ᵃ

4   Yes, he struggled with the Angel and
       prevailed;
     He wept, and sought favor
       from Him.
     He found Him *in* Bethel,
     And there He spoke to us—

5   That is, the LORD God of hosts.
     The LORD *is* His memorable name.

6   So you, by *the help of* your God,
       return;
     Observe mercy and justice,
     And wait on your God continually.

7   "A cunning Canaanite!
     Deceitful scales *are* in his hand;
     He loves to oppress.

8   And Ephraim said,
     'Surely I have become rich,
     I have found wealth for myself;
     In all my labors
     They shall find in me no iniquity
       that *is* sin.'

9   "But I *am* the LORD your God,
     Ever since the land of Egypt;
     I will again make you dwell in tents,
     As in the days of the appointed
       feast.

10   I have also spoken by the prophets,
     And have multiplied visions;
     I have given symbols through the
       witness of the prophets."

11   Though Gilead *has* idols—
     Surely they are vanity—
     Though they sacrifice bulls in Gilgal,
     Indeed their altars *shall be* heaps in
       the furrows of the field.

12   Jacob fled to the country of Syria;
     Israel served for a spouse,
     And for a wife he tended *sheep.*

11:7 ᵃOr *upward* **11:9** ᵃOr *I will not enter a city*
11:12 ᵃOr *holy ones* **12:3** ᵃCompare Genesis 32:28

13 By a prophet the LORD brought Israel
     out of Egypt,
   And by a prophet he was preserved.
14 Ephraim provoked *Him* to anger
     most bitterly;
   Therefore his Lord will leave the
     guilt of his bloodshed upon him,
   And return his reproach upon him.

Relentless Judgment on Israel

13 When Ephraim spoke, trembling,
   He exalted *himself* in Israel;
   But when he offended through Baal
     worship, he died.
2 Now they sin more and more,
   And have made for themselves
     molded images,
   Idols of their silver, according to
     their skill;
   All of it *is* the work of craftsmen.
   They say of them,
   "Let the men who sacrifice[a] kiss the
     calves!"
3 Therefore they shall be like the
     morning cloud
   And like the early dew that passes
     away,
   Like chaff blown off from a
     threshing floor
   And like smoke from a chimney.

4 "Yet I *am* the LORD your God
   Ever since the land of Egypt,
   And you shall know no God but Me;
   For *there is* no savior besides Me.
5 I knew you in the wilderness,
   In the land of great drought.
6 When they had pasture, they were
     filled;
   They were filled and their heart was
     exalted;
   Therefore they forgot Me.

7 "So I will be to them like a lion;
   Like a leopard by the road I will lurk;
8 I will meet them like a bear deprived
     of her cubs;

I will tear open their rib cage,
And there I will devour them like a
  lion.
The wild beast shall tear them.

9 "O Israel, you are destroyed,[a]
   But your help[b] *is* from Me.
10 I will be your King;[a]
   Where *is any other,*
   That he may save you in all your
     cities?
   And your judges to whom you said,
   'Give me a king and princes'?
11 I gave you a king in My anger,
   And took *him* away in My wrath.

12 "The iniquity of Ephraim *is* bound up;
   His sin *is* stored up.
13 The sorrows of a woman in
     childbirth shall come upon him.
   He *is* an unwise son,
   For he should not stay long where
     children are born.

14 "I will ransom them from the power of
     the grave;[a]
   I will redeem them from death.
   O Death, I will be your plagues![b]
   O Grave,[c] I will be your destruction![d]
   Pity is hidden from My eyes."

15 Though he is fruitful among *his*
     brethren,
   An east wind shall come;
   The wind of the LORD shall come up
     from the wilderness.
   Then his spring shall become dry,
   And his fountain shall be dried up.
   He shall plunder the treasury of
     every desirable prize.
16 Samaria is held guilty,[a]
   For she has rebelled against her God.
   They shall fall by the sword,
   Their infants shall be dashed in
     pieces,
   And their women with child ripped
     open.

Israel Restored at Last

14 O Israel, return to the LORD your
     God,
   For you have stumbled because of
     your iniquity;
2 Take words with you,
   And return to the LORD.

13:2 [a]Or *those who offer human sacrifice*
13:9 [a]Literally *it* or *he destroyed you* [b]Literally *in your help* 13:10 [a]Septuagint, Syriac, Targum, and Vulgate read *Where is your king?*
13:14 [a]Or *Sheol* [b]Septuagint reads *where is your punishment?* [c]Or *Sheol* [d]Septuagint reads *where is your sting?* 13:16 [a]Septuagint reads *shall be disfigured*

BIBLICAL INSIGHTS · 14

Rebuilding after an Affair

JUST AS HOSEA LOVED GOMER despite her unfaithfulness, God continues to reach out to wayward Israel. In Hosea 14, He pledges, "I will heal their backsliding, I will love them freely" (v. 4). God's unconditional love for His people despite unfaithfulness has applications not only to our relationship with Him, but also to the marriage relationship. No matter what one spouse does to the other, restoration is possible.

The first thing a couple in this situation must realize is that they need a pastor, counselor, or mature Christian providing guidance and direction as they seek to restore their marriage. It's like a car stuck in a muddy ditch. If only one wheel is in the ditch, you probably can get it out on your own if the ground is flat. But if all four wheels are in that ditch, you will need a wrecker to come pull that car out. A marriage recovering from adultery is like that car with all four wheels stuck.

With the help of a godly counselor, a couple must work through at least three stages to restore their relationship. The first step is *confession*. The person who committed the transgression must come clean and fully understand and acknowledge the agony, grief, and hurt he or she caused.

At the same time—and this will be very difficult—the person who has been sinned against in this situation needs to acknowledge how he or she contributed to the deterioration of their marriage. As Pastor Dave Carder, who has counseled many couples in this situation, says, "If you want to develop or have an influence in the new marriage that you're going to have together, you've got to acknowledge what each of you did wrong in the old marriage."

Next, *forgiveness must occur*. The person who committed the adultery must not take the attitude of demanding this forgiveness or blaming the spouse if forgiveness does not come quickly or easily. But the marriage will not move forward until that forgiveness does come.

Finally, *trust must be rebuilt*. There must be a change of pattern, a change of behavior that gives the betrayed spouse hope and confidence. It may take a long time for trust to develop, but there are many couples today who can testify that even after an affair, a fully renewed and revived marriage relationship is possible.

Say to Him,
"Take away all iniquity;
Receive *us* graciously,
For we will offer the sacrifices[a] of
　our lips.
3 Assyria shall not save us,
We will not ride on horses,
Nor will we say anymore to the work
　of our hands, 'You are our gods.'
For in You the fatherless finds
　mercy."

4 "I will heal their backsliding,
I will love them freely,
For My anger has turned away from
him.

5 I will be like the dew to Israel;
He shall grow like the lily,
And lengthen his roots like Lebanon.
6 His branches shall spread;
His beauty shall be like an olive tree,
And his fragrance like Lebanon.
7 Those who dwell under his shadow
　shall return;
They shall be revived *like* grain,
And grow like a vine.
Their scent[a] *shall be* like the wine of
　Lebanon.

14:2 [a]Literally *bull calves;* Septuagint reads *fruit.*
14:7 [a]Literally *remembrance*

8 "Ephraim *shall say,* 'What have I
       to do anymore with idols?'
I have heard and observed him.
I *am* like a green cypress tree;
Your fruit is found in Me."
9 Who *is* wise?

Let him understand these things.
Who is prudent?
Let him know them.
For the ways of the LORD *are* right;
The righteous walk in them,
But transgressors stumble in them.

JOEL

INTRODUCTION

WE KNOW VERY LITTLE ABOUT THE PROPHET JOEL, and very few details in his book give any indication about the period in which he lived and ministered. Because he never mentions Assyria, Babylon, or Persia, some Bible scholars believe that the prophet lived sometime between 840 and 800 BC. Others place his ministry following the return from Babylon, in the late sixth century BC. But the timing of Joel's ministry has no effect on his timeless message.

A time of significant hardship had gripped Judah. An enormous swarm of locusts, coupled with a severe drought, had crippled the nation's food supply. The people looked to God, wondering if He had turned His back on them. Through Joel, God showed the Israelites that their hearts had drifted far from Him. They had replaced genuine spiritual devotion with merely going through the motions.

Joel says the awful natural disaster merely foreshadows "the day of the LORD," a phrase used by many prophets to describe either a coming day of chastisement from God or the time when Jesus comes at the end of the age to judge the world. The prophet calls on the nation to cry out to God in its time of trouble and to repent in anticipation of the coming "day of the LORD."

The first section of the book describes the current crisis (1:1–20). The second section illustrates the even more terrible day that is coming (2:1–17). The third section offers words of consolation and comfort to those who repent and who turn to God and follow Him (2:18—3:21).

Families and nations *will* face times of hardship. We may not experience swarms of locusts, but in our day we have seen hurricanes, tsunamis, earthquakes, and other natural disasters that have caused even non-religious people to wonder about God's providential care. Families also go through times of personal crisis when they wonder why God has allowed their painful circumstances.

Joel reminds us that during these difficult times, we should reexamine our hearts, repent, turn back to God, and trust Him to be with us and to care for us in the midst of our trial.

1

The word of the LORD that came to Joel the son of Pethuel.

The Land Laid Waste

2 Hear this, you elders,
And give ear, all you inhabitants of
    the land!
Has *anything like* this happened in
    your days,
Or even in the days of your fathers?
3 Tell your children about it,
Let your children *tell* their children,
And their children another
    generation.

4 What the chewing locust[a] left, the
    swarming locust has eaten;
What the swarming locust left, the
    crawling locust has eaten;
And what the crawling locust left,
    the consuming locust has eaten.

5 Awake, you drunkards, and weep;
And wail, all you drinkers of wine,
Because of the new wine,
For it has been cut off from your
    mouth.
6 For a nation has come up against My
    land,
Strong, and without number;
His teeth *are* the teeth of a lion,
And he has the fangs of a
    fierce lion.
7 He has laid waste My vine,
And ruined My fig tree;
He has stripped it bare and thrown *it*
    away;
Its branches are made white.

8 Lament like a virgin girded with
    sackcloth
For the husband of her youth.
9 The grain offering and the drink
    offering
Have been cut off from the house of
    the LORD;
The priests mourn, who minister to
    the LORD.
10 The field is wasted,
The land mourns;
For the grain is ruined,

The new wine is dried up,
The oil fails.

11 Be ashamed, you farmers,
Wail, you vinedressers,
For the wheat and the barley;
Because the harvest of the field has
    perished.
12 The vine has dried up,
And the fig tree has withered;
The pomegranate tree,
The palm tree also,
And the apple tree—
All the trees of the field are
    withered;
Surely joy has withered away from
    the sons of men.

Mourning for the Land

13 Gird yourselves and lament, you
    priests;
Wail, you who minister before the
    altar;
Come, lie all night in sackcloth,
You who minister to my God;
For the grain offering and the drink
    offering
Are withheld from the house of your
    God.
14 Consecrate a fast,
Call a sacred assembly;
Gather the elders
And all the inhabitants of the land
Into the house of the LORD your God,
And cry out to the LORD.

15 Alas for the day!
For the day of the LORD *is* at hand;
It shall come as destruction from the
    Almighty.
16 Is not the food cut off before our
    eyes,
Joy and gladness from the house of
    our God?
17 The seed shrivels under the clods,
Storehouses are in shambles;
Barns are broken down,
For the grain has withered.
18 How the animals groan!
The herds of cattle are restless,
Because they have no pasture;
Even the flocks of sheep suffer
    punishment.[a]

1:4 [a]Exact identity of these locusts is unknown.
1:18 [a]Septuagint and Vulgate read *are made desolate.*

19 O LORD, to You I cry out;
For fire has devoured the open
    pastures,
And a flame has burned all the trees
    of the field.
20 The beasts of the field also cry out
    to You,
For the water brooks are dried up,
And fire has devoured the open
    pastures.

The Day of the LORD

2 Blow the trumpet in Zion,
And sound an alarm in My holy
    mountain!
Let all the inhabitants of the land
    tremble;
For the day of the LORD is coming,
For it is at hand:
2 A day of darkness and gloominess,
A day of clouds and thick darkness,
Like the morning *clouds* spread over
    the mountains.
A people *come,* great and strong,
The like of whom has never been;
Nor will there ever be any *such* after
    them,
Even for many successive generations.

3 A fire devours before them,
And behind them a flame burns;
The land *is* like the Garden of Eden
    before them,
And behind them a desolate
    wilderness;
Surely nothing shall escape them.
4 Their appearance is like the
    appearance of horses;
And like swift steeds, so they run.
5 With a noise like chariots
Over mountaintops they leap,
Like the noise of a flaming fire that
    devours the stubble,

Like a strong people set in battle
    array.
6 Before them the people writhe in
    pain;
All faces are drained of color.ᵃ
7 They run like mighty men,
They climb the wall like men of war;
Every one marches in formation,
And they do not break ranks.
8 They do not push one another;
Every one marches in his own
    column.ᵃ
Though they lunge between the
    weapons,
They are not cut down.ᵇ
9 They run to and fro in the city,
They run on the wall;
They climb into the houses,
They enter at the windows like a
    thief.

10 The earth quakes before them,
The heavens tremble;
The sun and moon grow dark,
And the stars diminish their
    brightness.
11 The LORD gives voice before His
    army,
For His camp is very great;
For strong *is the One* who executes
    His word.
For the day of the LORD *is* great and
    very terrible;
Who can endure it?

A Call to Repentance

12 "Now, therefore," says the LORD,
"Turn to Me with all your heart,
With fasting, with weeping, and with
    mourning."
13 So rend your heart, and not your
    garments;
Return to the LORD your God,
For He *is* gracious and merciful,
Slow to anger, and of great kindness;
And He relents from doing harm.
14 Who knows *if* He will turn and
    relent,
And leave a blessing behind Him—

INTIMATE MOMENTS

Find a used bookstore or check online
for a collectible copy of his favorite book.

2:6 ᵃSeptuagint, Targum, and Vulgate read *gather blackness.* **2:8** ᵃLiterally *his own highway* ᵇThat is, they are not halted by losses

A grain offering and a drink offering
For the LORD your God?

15 Blow the trumpet in Zion,
Consecrate a fast,
Call a sacred assembly;
16 Gather the people,
Sanctify the congregation,
Assemble the elders,
Gather the children and nursing
babes;
Let the bridegroom go out from his
chamber,
And the bride from her dressing
room.
17 Let the priests, who minister to the
LORD,
Weep between the porch and the
altar;
Let them say, "Spare Your people, O
LORD,
And do not give Your heritage to
reproach,
That the nations should rule over
them.
Why should they say among the
peoples,
'Where *is* their God?'"

The Land Refreshed

18 Then the LORD will be zealous for
His land,
And pity His people.
19 The LORD will answer and say to His
people,
"Behold, I will send you grain and
new wine and oil,
And you will be satisfied by them;
I will no longer make you a reproach
among the nations.

20 "But I will remove far from you the
northern *army,*
And will drive him away into a
barren and desolate land,
With his face toward the eastern sea
And his back toward the western
sea;
His stench will come up,
And his foul odor will rise,
Because he has done monstrous
things."

BIBLICAL INSIGHTS • 2:8, 9

Proclaim a Solemn Assembly

AN INVASION devastated ancient Judah, leaving the people pillaged, plundered, and vulnerable. The prophet Joel likened the invasion to that of an army, a ruinous force of swarming locusts.

We, too, have been invaded by a cloud of locusts. Most Christian families feel overrun by evil, "They run to and fro in the city, they run on the wall; they climb into the houses, they enter at the windows like a thief" (2:9).

Like Judah, we have been laid waste. And the prophet's solution for them still works for the church, "Consecrate a fast, call a sacred assembly; gather . . . . all the inhabitants into the house of the LORD your God, and cry out to the LORD!" (1:14).

It's time to declare a solemn assembly and cry out for God to exterminate the locusts in our land and our homes. For more than symbolic reasons, I suggest that churches think about using Father's Day for such an assembly. Perhaps God will withdraw His judgment and grant us favor in battle. Perhaps God will bring healing to the walking-wounded generation of divorce and restore the years the locusts have eaten (2:20–25).

21 Fear not, O land;
Be glad and rejoice,
For the LORD has done marvelous
things!
22 Do not be afraid, you beasts of the
field;
For the open pastures are springing
up,
And the tree bears its fruit;
The fig tree and the vine yield their
strength.
23 Be glad then, you children of Zion,
And rejoice in the LORD your God;
For He has given you the former rain
faithfully,[a]

2:23 [a]Or *the teacher of righteousness*

And He will cause the rain to come
   down for you—
The former rain,
And the latter rain in the first *month*.
24 The threshing floors shall be full of
   wheat,
And the vats shall overflow with
   new wine and oil.

25 "So I will restore to you the years that
   the swarming locust has eaten,
The crawling locust,
The consuming locust,
And the chewing locust,[a]
My great army which I sent among
   you.
26 You shall eat in plenty and be
   satisfied,
And praise the name of the LORD
   your God,
Who has dealt wondrously with you;
And My people shall never be put to
   shame.
27 Then you shall know that I *am* in the
   midst of Israel:
I *am* the LORD your God
And there is no other.
My people shall never be put to shame.

INTIMATE MOMENTS

The next time you and your wife have to
be apart, leave a note for her to open
each day.

God's Spirit Poured Out

28 "And it shall come to pass afterward
   That I will pour out My Spirit on all
     flesh;
Your sons and your daughters shall
     prophesy,
Your old men shall dream dreams,
Your young men shall see visions.
29 And also on *My* menservants and on
   My maidservants
I will pour out My Spirit in those
   days.

30 "And I will show wonders in the
   heavens and in the earth:
Blood and fire and pillars of smoke.
31 The sun shall be turned into
   darkness,
And the moon into blood,
Before the coming of the great and
   awesome day of the LORD.
32 And it shall come to pass
That whoever calls on the name of
   the LORD
Shall be saved.
For in Mount Zion and in Jerusalem
   there shall be deliverance,
As the LORD has said,
Among the remnant whom the LORD
   calls.

God Judges the Nations

3 "For behold, in those days and at
   that time,
When I bring back the captives of
   Judah and Jerusalem,
2 I will also gather all nations,
And bring them down to the Valley
   of Jehoshaphat;
And I will enter into judgment with
   them there
On account of My people, My
   heritage Israel,
Whom they have scattered among
   the nations;
They have also divided up My land.
3 They have cast lots for My people,
Have given a boy *as payment* for a
   harlot,
And sold a girl for wine, that they
   may drink.

4 "Indeed, what have you to do with Me,
O Tyre and Sidon, and all the coasts
   of Philistia?
Will you retaliate against Me?
But if you retaliate against Me,
Swiftly and speedily I will return
   your retaliation upon your own
   head;
5 Because you have taken My silver
   and My gold,
And have carried into your temples
   My prized possessions.

2:25 [a]Compare 1:4

6 Also the people of Judah and the
  people of Jerusalem
 You have sold to the Greeks,
 That you may remove them far from
  their borders.

7 "Behold, I will raise them
 Out of the place to which you have
  sold them,
 And will return your retaliation upon
  your own head.
8 I will sell your sons and your
  daughters
 Into the hand of the people of Judah,
 And they will sell them to the
  Sabeans,[a]
 To a people far off;
 For the LORD has spoken."

9 Proclaim this among the nations:
 "Prepare for war!
 Wake up the mighty men,
 Let all the men of war draw near,
 Let them come up.
10 Beat your plowshares into swords
 And your pruning hooks into spears;
 Let the weak say, 'I am strong.'"
11 Assemble and come, all you nations,
 And gather together all around.
 Cause Your mighty ones to go down
  there, O LORD.

12 "Let the nations be wakened, and
  come up to the Valley of
  Jehoshaphat;
 For there I will sit to judge all the
  surrounding nations.
13 Put in the sickle, for the harvest is
  ripe.
 Come, go down;
 For the winepress is full,
 The vats overflow—
 For their wickedness is great."

14 Multitudes, multitudes in the valley
  of decision!
 For the day of the LORD is near in the
  valley of decision.
15 The sun and moon will grow dark,
 And the stars will diminish their
  brightness.
16 The LORD also will roar from Zion,
 And utter His voice from Jerusalem;
 The heavens and earth will shake;
 But the LORD will be a shelter for His
  people,
 And the strength of the children of
  Israel.

17 "So you shall know that I am the
  LORD your God,
 Dwelling in Zion My holy mountain.
 Then Jerusalem shall be holy,
 And no aliens shall ever pass
  through her again."

God Blesses His People

18 And it will come to pass in that day
 That the mountains shall drip with
  new wine,
 The hills shall flow with milk,
 And all the brooks of Judah shall be
  flooded with water;
 A fountain shall flow from the house
  of the LORD
 And water the Valley of Acacias.

19 "Egypt shall be a desolation,
 And Edom a desolate wilderness,
 Because of violence against the
  people of Judah,
 For they have shed innocent blood in
  their land.
20 But Judah shall abide forever,
 And Jerusalem from generation to
  generation.
21 For I will acquit them of the guilt of
  bloodshed, whom I had not
  acquitted;
 For the LORD dwells in Zion."

3:8 [a]Literally *Shebaites* (compare Isaiah 60:6 and
Ezekiel 27:22)

AMOS

THE PROPHET AMOS lived about 750 years before the birth of Jesus, during the days of Jonah, Hosea, Micah, and Isaiah. He lived in the southern kingdom, about ten miles south of Jerusalem, in the town of Tekoa. He was a sheep breeder (1:1) and tended sycamore fruit (7:14).

Although he lived in the southern kingdom, he prophesied to the northern kingdom, which at the time enjoyed peace and prosperity. Yet it had begun a steep moral and spiritual decline, so Amos made the trek from Tekoa to Bethel, a journey of a little more than twenty miles, to deliver his oracles. The high priest of Bethel promptly drove him out of town.

Amos's message has two dominant themes: the lack of true worship and the absence of social justice. Amos called on the Israelites to express real love for God through genuine worship, and to show their love for others by caring for the needs of the poor. Amos promised the judgment of God on the people of the northern kingdom if they continued their unrighteous and unjust ways. Perhaps the best-known verse from Amos is, "But let justice run down like water, and righteousness like a mighty stream" (5:24).

Amos delivered his prophetic message "two years before the earthquake" (1:1). We know nothing else about that earthquake, but it must have been a warning from God sent to shake up the people. They apparently ignored the warning and within three decades, God sent the Assyrians to invade the northern kingdom and destroy it. Its people never recovered.

The Book of Amos speaks to families in any affluent culture. We must always beware that we do not put our trust in wealth and so forget to wholeheartedly worship the One who has blessed us. And we must ask how we can care for those who are in need—the widow, the orphan and the poor. As families, we should look for tangible ways to express our concern. As parents, we must be sure to raise children who are generous, kind, and compassionate to those in need.

1

The words of Amos, who was among the sheepbreeders[a] of Tekoa, which he saw concerning Israel in the days of Uzziah king of Judah, and in the days of Jeroboam the son of Joash, king of Israel, two years before the earthquake.

2 And he said:

> "The LORD roars from Zion,
> And utters His voice from Jerusalem;
> The pastures of the shepherds mourn,
> And the top of Carmel withers."

Judgment on the Nations

3 Thus says the LORD:

> "For three transgressions of Damascus, and for four,
> I will not turn away its *punishment*,
> Because they have threshed Gilead with implements of iron.

4 But I will send a fire into the house of Hazael,
> Which shall devour the palaces of Ben-Hadad.

5 I will also break the *gate* bar of Damascus,
> And cut off the inhabitant from the Valley of Aven,
> And the one who holds the scepter from Beth Eden.
> The people of Syria shall go captive to Kir,"
> Says the LORD.

6 Thus says the LORD:

> "For three transgressions of Gaza, and for four,
> I will not turn away its *punishment*,
> Because they took captive the whole captivity
> To deliver *them* up to Edom.

7 But I will send a fire upon the wall of Gaza,
> Which shall devour its palaces.

8 I will cut off the inhabitant from Ashdod,
> And the one who holds the scepter from Ashkelon;
> I will turn My hand against Ekron,

And the remnant of the Philistines shall perish,"
> Says the Lord GOD.

9 Thus says the LORD:

> "For three transgressions of Tyre, and for four,
> I will not turn away its *punishment*,
> Because they delivered up the whole captivity to Edom,
> And did not remember the covenant of brotherhood.

10 But I will send a fire upon the wall of Tyre,
> Which shall devour its palaces."

11 Thus says the LORD:

> "For three transgressions of Edom, and for four,
> I will not turn away its *punishment*,
> Because he pursued his brother with the sword,
> And cast off all pity;
> His anger tore perpetually,
> And he kept his wrath forever.

12 But I will send a fire upon Teman,
> Which shall devour the palaces of Bozrah."

INTIMATE MOMENTS

Buy him that CD, DVD, book, or video game he's had his eye on.

13 Thus says the LORD:

> "For three transgressions of the people of Ammon, and for four,
> I will not turn away its *punishment*,
> Because they ripped open the women with child in Gilead,
> That they might enlarge their territory.

14 But I will kindle a fire in the wall of Rabbah,
> And it shall devour its palaces,
> Amid shouting in the day of battle,
> And a tempest in the day of the whirlwind.

1:1 [a]Compare 2 Kings 3:4

15 Their king shall go into captivity,
   He and his princes together,"
   Says the LORD.

2 Thus says the LORD:

"For three transgressions of Moab,
   and for four,
I will not turn away its *punishment,*
Because he burned the bones of the
   king of Edom to lime.
2 But I will send a fire upon Moab,
   And it shall devour the palaces of
      Kerioth;
   Moab shall die with tumult,
   With shouting *and* trumpet sound.
3 And I will cut off the judge from its
      midst,
   And slay all its princes with him,"
   Says the LORD.

INTIMATE MOMENTS

Make a list of all the things your sweet-heart does for you that you probably take for granted. Thank her for each one.

Judgment on Judah

4 Thus says the LORD:

"For three transgressions of Judah,
   and for four,
I will not turn away its *punishment,*
Because they have despised the law
   of the LORD,
And have not kept His
   commandments.
Their lies lead them astray,
Lies which their fathers followed.
5 But I will send a fire upon Judah,
   And it shall devour the palaces of
      Jerusalem."

Judgment on Israel

6 Thus says the LORD:

"For three transgressions of Israel,
   and for four,
I will not turn away its *punishment,*

Because they sell the righteous for
   silver,
And the poor for a pair of sandals.
7 They pant after[a] the dust of the
   earth *which is* on the head of the
      poor,
And pervert the way of the humble.
A man and his father go in to the
   same girl,
To defile My holy name.
8 They lie down by every altar on
   clothes taken in pledge,
And drink the wine of the
   condemned *in* the house of their
      god.

9 "Yet *it was* I *who* destroyed the
      Amorite before them,
Whose height *was* like the height of
   the cedars,
And he *was as* strong as the oaks;
Yet I destroyed his fruit above
And his roots beneath.
10 Also *it was* I *who* brought you up
   from the land of Egypt,
And led you forty years through the
   wilderness,
To possess the land of the Amorite.
11 I raised up some of your sons as
   prophets,
And some of your young men as
   Nazirites.
Is it not so, O you children of Israel?"
   Says the LORD.
12 "But you gave the Nazirites wine to
   drink,
And commanded the prophets saying,
   'Do not prophesy!'

13 "Behold, I am weighed down by you,
   As a cart full of sheaves is weighed
      down.
14 Therefore flight shall perish from the
   swift,
The strong shall not strengthen his
   power,
Nor shall the mighty deliver himself;
15 He shall not stand who handles the
   bow,
The swift of foot shall not escape,
Nor shall he who rides a horse
   deliver himself.

2:7 ªOr *trample on*

¹⁶ The most courageous men of might
Shall flee naked in that day,"
Says the LORD.

Authority of the Prophet's Message

3 Hear this word that the LORD has spoken against you, O children of Israel, against the whole family which I brought up from the land of Egypt, saying:

² "You only have I known of all the
families of the earth;
Therefore I will punish you for all
your iniquities."

³ Can two walk together, unless they
are agreed?

⁴ Will a lion roar in the forest, when he
has no prey?
Will a young lion cry out of his den,
if he has caught nothing?

⁵ Will a bird fall into a snare on the
earth, where there is no trap for
it?
Will a snare spring up from the
earth, if it has caught nothing at
all?

⁶ If a trumpet is blown in a city, will
not the people be afraid?
If there is calamity in a city, will not
the LORD have done *it?*

⁷ Surely the Lord GOD does nothing,
Unless He reveals His secret to His
servants the prophets.

⁸ A lion has roared!
Who will not fear?
The Lord GOD has spoken!
Who can but prophesy?

Punishment of Israel's Sins

⁹ "Proclaim in the palaces at Ashdod,^a
And in the palaces in the land of
Egypt, and say:
'Assemble on the mountains of
Samaria;
See great tumults in her midst,
And the oppressed within her.

¹⁰ For they do not know to do right,'
Says the LORD,

'Who store up violence and robbery
in their palaces.'"

¹¹Therefore thus says the Lord GOD:

"An adversary *shall be* all around the
land;
He shall sap your strength from you,
And your palaces shall be
plundered."

¹²Thus says the LORD:

"As a shepherd takes from the mouth
of a lion
Two legs or a piece of an ear,
So shall the children of Israel be
taken out
Who dwell in Samaria—
In the corner of a bed and on the
edge^a of a couch!

¹³ Hear and testify against the house of
Jacob,"
Says the Lord GOD, the God of hosts,

¹⁴ "That in the day I punish Israel for
their transgressions,
I will also visit *destruction* on the
altars of Bethel;
And the horns of the altar shall be
cut off
And fall to the ground.

¹⁵ I will destroy the winter house along
with the summer house;
The houses of ivory shall perish,
And the great houses shall have an
end,"
Says the LORD.

4 Hear this word, you cows of Bashan,
who *are* on the mountain of
Samaria,
Who oppress the poor,
Who crush the needy,
Who say to your husbands,^a "Bring
wine, let us drink!"

² The Lord GOD has sworn by His
holiness:

"Behold, the days shall come upon you
When He will take you away with
fishhooks,
And your posterity with fishhooks.

³ You will go out *through* broken *walls,*
Each one straight ahead of her,
And you will be cast into Harmon,"
Says the LORD.

3:9 ^aFollowing Masoretic Text; Septuagint reads
Assyria. **3:12** ^aThe Hebrew is uncertain.
4:1 ^aLiterally *their lords* or *their masters*

4 "Come to Bethel and transgress,
    At Gilgal multiply transgression;
    Bring your sacrifices every morning,
    Your tithes every three days.[a]
5 Offer a sacrifice of thanksgiving
        with leaven,
    Proclaim *and* announce the freewill
        offerings;
    For this you love,
    You children of Israel!"
    Says the Lord GOD.

Israel Did Not Accept Correction

6 "Also I gave you cleanness of teeth in
        all your cities.
    And lack of bread in all your places;
    Yet you have not returned to Me,"
    Says the LORD.

7 "I also withheld rain from you,
    When *there were* still three months
        to the harvest.
    I made it rain on one city,
    I withheld rain from another city.
    One part was rained upon,
    And where it did not rain the part
        withered.
8 So two *or* three cities wandered to
        another city to drink water,
    But they were not satisfied;
    Yet you have not returned to Me,"
    Says the LORD.

9 "I blasted you with blight and mildew.
    When your gardens increased,
    Your vineyards,
    Your fig trees,
    And your olive trees,
    The locust devoured *them;*
    Yet you have not returned to Me,"
    Says the LORD.

10 "I sent among you a plague after the
        manner of Egypt;
    Your young men I killed with a
        sword,
    Along with your captive horses;
    I made the stench of your camps
        come up into your nostrils;
    Yet you have not returned to Me,"
    Says the LORD.

11 "I overthrew *some* of you,
    As God overthrew Sodom and
        Gomorrah,

And you were like a firebrand
    plucked from the burning;
Yet you have not returned to Me,"
Says the LORD.

12 "Therefore thus will I do to you,
        O Israel;
    Because I will do this to you,
    Prepare to meet your God, O Israel!"

13 For behold,
    He who forms mountains,
    And creates the wind,
    Who declares to man what his[a]
        thought *is,*
    And makes the morning darkness,
    Who treads the high places of the
        earth—
    The LORD God of hosts *is* His name.

A Lament for Israel

5 Hear this word which I take up against
    you, a lamentation, O house of Israel:

2   The virgin of Israel has fallen;
    She will rise no more.
    She lies forsaken on her land;
    There is no one to raise her up.

3For thus says the Lord GOD:

    "The city that goes out by a thousand
    Shall have a hundred left,
    And that which goes out by a hundred
    Shall have ten left to the house of
        Israel."

A Call to Repentance

4For thus says the LORD to the house of
Israel:

    "Seek Me and live;
5   But do not seek Bethel,
    Nor enter Gilgal,
    Nor pass over to Beersheba;
    For Gilgal shall surely go into
        captivity,
    And Bethel shall come to nothing.
6   Seek the LORD and live,
    Lest He break out like fire *in* the
        house of Joseph,
    And devour *it,*
    With no one to quench *it* in Bethel—

4:4 aOr *years* (compare Deuteronomy 14:28)
4:13 aOr *His*

7 You who turn justice to wormwood,
  And lay righteousness to rest in the earth!"

8 He made the Pleiades and Orion;
  He turns the shadow of death into morning
  And makes the day dark as night;
  He calls for the waters of the sea
  And pours them out on the face of the earth;
  The LORD *is* His name.

9 He rains ruin upon the strong,
  So that fury comes upon the fortress.

10 They hate the one who rebukes in the gate,
   And they abhor the one who speaks uprightly.

11 Therefore, because you tread down the poor
   And take grain taxes from him,
   Though you have built houses of hewn stone,
   Yet you shall not dwell in them;
   You have planted pleasant vineyards,
   But you shall not drink wine from them.

12 For I know your manifold transgressions
   And your mighty sins:
   Afflicting the just *and* taking bribes;
   Diverting the poor *from justice* at the gate.

13 Therefore the prudent keep silent at that time,
   For it *is* an evil time.

14 Seek good and not evil,
   That you may live;
   So the LORD God of hosts will be with you,
   As you have spoken.

15 Hate evil, love good;
   Establish justice in the gate.
   It may be that the LORD God of hosts
   Will be gracious to the remnant of Joseph.

The Day of the LORD

16 Therefore the LORD God of hosts, the Lord, says this:

  " *There shall be* wailing in all streets,
  And they shall say in all the highways,

  'Alas! Alas!'
  They shall call the farmer to mourning,
  And skillful lamenters to wailing.

17 In all vineyards *there shall be* wailing,
   For I will pass through you,"
   Says the LORD.

18 Woe to you who desire the day of the LORD!
   For what good *is* the day of the LORD to you?
   It *will be* darkness, and not light.

19 It *will be* as though a man fled from a lion,
   And a bear met him!
   Or *as though* he went into the house,
   Leaned his hand on the wall,
   And a serpent bit him!

20 *Is* not the day of the LORD darkness, and not light?
   Is it not very dark, with no brightness in it?

21 "I hate, I despise your feast days,
    And I do not savor your sacred
        assemblies.
22 Though you offer Me burnt offerings
        and your grain offerings,
    I will not accept *them,*
    Nor will I regard your fattened peace
        offerings.
23 Take away from Me the noise of
        your songs,
    For I will not hear the melody of
        your stringed instruments.
24 But let justice run down like water,
    And righteousness like a mighty
        stream.

25 "Did you offer Me sacrifices and
        offerings
    In the wilderness forty years, O
        house of Israel?
26 You also carried Sikkuth[a] your king[b]
    And Chiun,[c] your idols,
    The star of your gods,
    Which you made for yourselves.
27 Therefore I will send you into
        captivity beyond Damascus,"
    Says the LORD, whose name *is* the
        God of hosts.

Warnings to Zion and Samaria

6 Woe to you *who are* at ease in Zion,
    And trust in Mount Samaria,
    Notable persons in the chief nation,
    To whom the house of Israel comes!
2 Go over to Calneh and see;
    And from there go to Hamath the
        great;
    Then go down to Gath of the
        Philistines.
    Are you better than these kingdoms?
    Or is their territory greater than
        your territory?

3 *Woe to* you who put far off the day
        of doom,
    Who cause the seat of violence to
        come near;
4 Who lie on beds of ivory,
    Stretch out on your couches,
    Eat lambs from the flock
    And calves from the midst of
        the stall;
5 Who sing idly to the sound of
        stringed instruments,

    And invent for yourselves musical
        instruments like David;
6 Who drink wine from bowls,
    And anoint yourselves with the best
        ointments,
    But are not grieved for the affliction
        of Joseph.
7 Therefore they shall now go captive
        as the first of the captives,
    And those who recline at banquets
        shall be removed.

8 The Lord GOD has sworn by Himself,
    The LORD God of hosts says:
"I abhor the pride of Jacob,
    And hate his palaces;
    Therefore I will deliver up
        the city
    And all that is in it."

9 Then it shall come to pass, that if ten
men remain in one house, they shall die.
10 And when a relative *of the dead,* with
one who will burn *the bodies,* picks up the
bodies[a] to take them out of the house, he
will say to one inside the house, "*Are there*
any more with you?"
    Then someone will say, "None."
    And he will say, "Hold your tongue! For
we dare not mention the name of the LORD."

11 For behold, the LORD gives a
        command:
    He will break the great house into
        bits,
    And the little house into pieces.

12 Do horses run on rocks?
    Does *one* plow *there* with oxen?
    Yet you have turned justice into gall,
    And the fruit of righteousness into
        wormwood,
13 You who rejoice over Lo Debar,[a]
    Who say, "Have we not taken
        Karnaim[b] for ourselves
    By our own strength?"

14 "But, behold, I will raise up a nation
        against you,
    O house of Israel,"
    Says the LORD God of hosts;

5:26 [a]A pagan deity [b]Septuagint and Vulgate read
tabernacle of Moloch. [c]A pagan deity
6:10 [a]Literally *bones* 6:13 [a]Literally *Nothing*
[b]Literally *Horns,* symbol of strength

"And they will afflict you from the
entrance of Hamath
To the Valley of the Arabah."

Vision of the Locusts

7 Thus the Lord GOD showed me:
Behold, He formed locust swarms at
the beginning of the late crop; indeed *it
was* the late crop after the king's mowings.
²And so it was, when they had finished
eating the grass of the land, that I said:

"O Lord GOD, forgive, I pray!
Oh, that Jacob may stand,
For he *is* small!"

³ So the LORD relented concerning this.
"It shall not be," said the LORD.

Vision of the Fire

⁴Thus the Lord GOD showed me: Behold,
the Lord GOD called for conflict by fire, and
it consumed the great deep and devoured
the territory. ⁵Then I said:

"O Lord GOD, cease, I pray!
Oh, that Jacob may stand,
For he *is* small!"

⁶ So the LORD relented concerning this.
"This also shall not be," said the Lord
GOD.

Vision of the Plumb Line

⁷Thus He showed me: Behold, the Lord
stood on a wall *made* with a plumb line,
with a plumb line in His hand. ⁸And the
LORD said to me, "Amos, what do you see?"
And I said, "A plumb line."
Then the Lord said:

"Behold, I am setting a plumb line
In the midst of My people Israel;
I will not pass by them anymore.

⁹ The high places of Isaac shall be
desolate,
And the sanctuaries of Israel shall
be laid waste.
I will rise with the sword against the
house of Jeroboam."

Amaziah's Complaint

¹⁰Then Amaziah the priest of Bethel
sent to Jeroboam king of Israel, saying,

"Amos has conspired against you in the
midst of the house of Israel. The land is
not able to bear all his words. ¹¹For thus
Amos has said:

'Jeroboam shall die by the sword,
And Israel shall surely be led away
captive
From their own land.'"

¹²Then Amaziah said to Amos:

"Go, you seer!
Flee to the land of Judah.
There eat bread,
And there prophesy.
¹³ But never again prophesy at Bethel,
For it *is* the king's sanctuary,
And it *is* the royal residence."

¹⁴Then Amos answered, and said to
Amaziah:

"I *was* no prophet,
Nor *was* I a son of a prophet,
But I *was* a sheepbreeder[a]
And a tender of sycamore fruit.
¹⁵ Then the LORD took me as I followed
the flock,
And the LORD said to me,
'Go, prophesy to My people Israel.'
¹⁶ Now therefore, hear the word of the
LORD:
You say, 'Do not prophesy against
Israel,
And do not spout against the house
of Isaac.'

¹⁷"Therefore thus says the LORD:

'Your wife shall be a harlot in the city;
Your sons and daughters shall fall
by the sword;
Your land shall be divided by *survey*
line;
You shall die in a defiled land;

INTIMATE MOMENTS

Compliment your husband in front of
others. You may be the only one in his
life who's doing it!

7:14 ªCompare 2 Kings 3:4

And Israel shall surely be led away
     captive
From his own land.'"

Vision of the Summer Fruit

8 Thus the Lord GOD showed me: Behold,
a basket of summer fruit. [2]And He said,
"Amos, what do you see?"
     So I said, "A basket of summer fruit."
Then the LORD said to me:

"The end has come upon My people
     Israel;
I will not pass by them anymore.
3   And the songs of the temple
     Shall be wailing in that day,"
Says the Lord GOD—
"Many dead bodies everywhere,
     They shall be thrown out in silence."

4   Hear this, you who swallow up[a] the
          needy,
     And make the poor of the land fail,

[5]Saying:

"When will the New Moon be past,
     That we may sell grain?
And the Sabbath,
     That we may trade wheat?
Making the ephah small and the
          shekel large,
Falsifying the scales by deceit,
6   That we may buy the poor for silver,
And the needy for a pair of
          sandals—
     Even sell the bad wheat?"

7   The LORD has sworn by the pride of
          Jacob:
"Surely I will never forget any of their
          works.
8   Shall the land not tremble for this,
     And everyone mourn who dwells in
          it?
All of it shall swell like the River,[a]
Heave and subside
Like the River of Egypt.

9   "And it shall come to pass in that
          day," says the Lord GOD,
"That I will make the sun go down at
          noon,
     And I will darken the earth in broad
          daylight;
10   I will turn your feasts into mourning,
     And all your songs into lamentation;
I will bring sackcloth on every waist,
     And baldness on every head;
I will make it like mourning for an
          only *son,*
     And its end like a bitter day.

8:4 [a]Or *trample on* (compare 2:7)
8:8 [a]That is, the Nile; some Hebrew manuscripts,
Septuagint, Syriac, Targum, and Vulgate read *River;*
Masoretic Text reads *the light.*

As in the Days of Old

The institution of marriage has fallen on hard times, but nothing says it has to stay that way. Our God loves to restore, renew, and repair, and He can do for our marriages what He promised the nation of Israel, "I will raise up the tabernacle of David, which has fallen down, and repair its damages; I will raise up its ruins, and rebuild it as in the days of old" (9:11).

Does your own marriage need some repair? If so, God can begin even today to rebuild it "as in the days of old." In fact, He wants to partner with you in this very task.

Too many marriages begin to unravel when one spouse mentally entertains the possibility of divorce. We must reject the notion of divorce as a solution. Barbara and I have been married since 1972, and we have had our share of illness, tragedy, and disagreements. But the word *divorce* has never passed through our lips.

May I challenge you to make the same commitment? Pledge to each other that you will never, ever, ever, use the *D* word in your marriage. Replace it with the *C* word—commitment. Tell your spouse, "Regardless of our challenges, I am committed to you until death."

Rebuilding your marriage begins with the commitment to fulfill your vows by staying married, no matter what. Your children's marriages, your legacy, and the strength of the church depend upon it.

11 "Behold, the days are coming," says
the Lord GOD,
"That I will send a famine on the
land,
Not a famine of bread,
Nor a thirst for water,
But of hearing the words of the
LORD.

12 They shall wander from sea to sea,
And from north to east;
They shall run to and fro, seeking
the word of the LORD,
But shall not find *it*.

13 "In that day the fair virgins
And strong young men
Shall faint from thirst.

14 Those who swear by the sin[a] of
Samaria,
Who say,
'As your god lives, O Dan!'
And, 'As the way of Beersheba lives!'
They shall fall and never rise again."

The Destruction of Israel

9 I saw the Lord standing by the altar,
and He said:

"Strike the doorposts, that the
thresholds may shake,
And break them on the heads of
them all.
I will slay the last of them with the
sword.
He who flees from them shall not get
away,
And he who escapes from them shall
not be delivered.

2 "Though they dig into hell,[a]
From there My hand shall take them;
Though they climb up to heaven,
From there I will bring them down;

3 And though they hide themselves on
top of Carmel,
From there I will search and take
them;
Though they hide from My sight at
the bottom of the sea,
From there I will command the
serpent, and it shall bite them;

4 Though they go into captivity before
their enemies,
From there I will command the
sword,
And it shall slay them.
I will set My eyes on them for harm
and not for good."

5 The Lord GOD of hosts,
He who touches the earth and it
melts,
And all who dwell there mourn;
All of it shall swell like the River,[a]
And subside like the River of Egypt.

6 He who builds His layers in the sky,
And has founded His strata in the
earth;
Who calls for the waters of the sea,
And pours them out on the face of
the earth—
The LORD *is* His name.

7 "*Are* you not like the people of
Ethiopia to Me,
O children of Israel?" says the LORD.
"Did I not bring up Israel from the
land of Egypt,
The Philistines from Caphtor,
And the Syrians from Kir?

8 "Behold, the eyes of the Lord GOD *are*
on the sinful kingdom,
And I will destroy it from the face of
the earth;
Yet I will not utterly destroy the
house of Jacob,"
Says the LORD.

9 "For surely I will command,
And will sift the house of Israel
among all nations,
As *grain* is sifted in a sieve;
Yet not the smallest grain shall fall
to the ground.

10 All the sinners of My people shall
die by the sword,
Who say, 'The calamity shall not
overtake nor confront us.'

Israel Will Be Restored

11 "On that day I will raise up
The tabernacle[a] of David, which has
fallen down,
And repair its damages;

8:14 [a]Or *Ashima,* a Syrian goddess   **9:2** [a]Or *Sheol*
9:5 [a]That is, the Nile   **9:11** [a]Literally *booth,* figure of
a deposed dynasty

I will raise up its ruins,
And rebuild it as in the days of old;

12 That they may possess the remnant
of Edom,[a]
And all the Gentiles who are called
by My name,"
Says the LORD who does this thing.

13 "Behold, the days are coming," says
the LORD,
"When the plowman shall overtake
the reaper,
And the treader of grapes him who
sows seed;
The mountains shall drip with sweet
wine,
And all the hills shall flow *with it.*

14 I will bring back the captives of My
people Israel;
They shall build the waste cities and
inhabit *them;*
They shall plant vineyards and drink
wine from them;
They shall also make gardens and
eat fruit from them.

15 I will plant them in their land,
And no longer shall they be pulled
up
From the land I have given them,"
Says the LORD your God.

9:12 [a]Septuagint reads *mankind.*

OBADIAH

THE 21 VERSES that make up the Book of Obadiah make it the shortest book in the Bible. Scholars have often scratched their heads about this short book, since so much about it is unknown.

The Old Testament mentions more than a dozen Obadiahs, and none of them is the obvious author of this book. We are not sure where or when Obadiah lived, although his repeated references to Judah and Jerusalem would indicate that he probably lived in the southern kingdom some time after Solomon but before the end of the Babylonian captivity. That narrows things down to a period of more than 400 years!

What is clear is that Obadiah longed to see God vindicate Himself and triumph over the enemy armies of Edom. The Edomites, descendents of Esau, lived in a mountainous region southeast of Jerusalem and the Dead Sea. They had a long-standing feud with the Israelites, and the Edomites often joined with other tribes in the region—the Moabites and the Ammonites, for example—to attack Israel.

The book can be divided into two main sections. The first fourteen verses make up the primary section and reflect Obadiah's desire that God would show His power and defeat His enemies. Obadiah is not as concerned with his own comfort or safety, or even with his own wellbeing, as he is with the God of Israel vindicating Himself and receiving the glory He deserves.

The second section (vv. 15–21) begins with the prophet pointing to the day when God will bring judgment and establish Himself as King of all nations. Obadiah looks forward to that day when "the kingdom shall be the LORD's" (v. 21).

Obadiah's inspired cry for God to bring judgment upon His enemies and to vindicate Himself was motivated by a jealous desire for God's glory. In our own lives, we should seek to cultivate a heart of compassion, kindness and love for our enemies, while maintaining a passion for God's kingdom to spread throughout the earth and for Jesus to make the enemies of God His footstool (see Ps. 110:1).

The Coming Judgment on Edom

The vision of Obadiah.

Thus says the Lord God concerning
Edom
(We have heard a report from the
Lord,
And a messenger has been sent
among the nations, *saying,*
"Arise, and let us rise up against her
for battle"):

2 "Behold, I will make you small among
the nations;
You shall be greatly despised.
3 The pride of your heart has deceived
you,
You who dwell in the clefts of the
rock,
Whose habitation is high;
You who say in your heart, 'Who will
bring me down to the ground?'
4 Though you ascend *as* high as the
eagle,
And though you set your nest among
the stars,
From there I will bring you down,"
says the Lord.

5 "If thieves had come to you,
If robbers by night—
Oh, how you will be cut off!—
Would they not have stolen till they
had enough?
If grape-gatherers had come to you,
Would they not have left *some*
gleanings?
6 "Oh, how Esau shall be searched out!
How his hidden treasures shall be
sought after!
7 All the men in your confederacy
Shall force you to the border;
The men at peace with you

Shall deceive you *and* prevail against
you.
Those who eat your bread shall lay a
trap[a] for you.
No one is aware of it.

8 "Will I not in that day," says the Lord,
"Even destroy the wise *men* from
Edom,
And understanding from the
mountains of Esau?
9 Then your mighty men, O Teman,
shall be dismayed,
To the end that everyone from the
mountains of Esau
May be cut off by slaughter.

Edom Mistreated His Brother

10 "For violence against your brother
Jacob,
Shame shall cover you,
And you shall be cut off forever.
11 In the day that you stood on the
other side—
In the day that strangers carried
captive his forces,
When foreigners entered
his gates
And cast lots for Jerusalem—
Even you *were* as one of them.
12 "But you should not have gazed on
the day of your brother
In the day of his captivity;[a]
Nor should you have rejoiced over
the children of Judah
In the day of their destruction;
Nor should you have spoken proudly
In the day of distress.
13 You should not have entered the gate
of My people
In the day of their calamity.
Indeed, you should not have gazed
on their affliction
In the day of their calamity,
Nor laid *hands* on their substance
In the day of their calamity.
14 You should not have stood at the
crossroads
To cut off those among them who
escaped;

**INTIMATE
MOMENTS**

Good manners and chivalry are romantic.

---

7 [a]Or *wound,* or *plot* 12 [a]Literally *on the day he
became a foreigner*

Nor should you have delivered up
    those among them who remained
In the day of distress.

15 "For the day of the LORD upon all the
    nations *is* near;
    As you have done, it shall be done to
      you;
    Your reprisal shall return upon your
      own head.
16 For as you drank on My holy
      mountain,
    So shall all the nations drink
      continually;
    Yes, they shall drink, and swallow,
    And they shall be as though they
      had never been.

Israel's Final Triumph

17 "But on Mount Zion there shall be
      deliverance,
    And there shall be holiness;
    The house of Jacob shall possess
      their possessions.
18 The house of Jacob shall be a fire,
    And the house of Joseph a flame;
    But the house of Esau *shall be*
      stubble;
    They shall kindle them and devour
      them,
    And no survivor shall *remain* of the
      house of Esau,"
    For the LORD has spoken.

19 The South[a] shall possess the
      mountains of Esau,
    And the Lowland shall possess
      Philistia.
    They shall possess the fields of
      Ephraim
    And the fields of Samaria.
    Benjamin *shall possess* Gilead.
20 And the captives of this host of the
      children of Israel
    Shall possess the land of the
      Canaanites
    As far as Zarephath.
    The captives of Jerusalem who are in
      Sepharad

BIBLICAL INSIGHTS • 15

A TRUE LEADER OF HIS FAMILY knows that there are times when he must remind his wife and children that there is hope. The prophet Obadiah knew the power of this as well. In verses 15–21 he reminds and promises the nation of Israel that God would indeed rule with justice. He keeps hope alive by reassuring them that God would exert His power and punish injustice.

Likewise, during a season of challenges, a family needs to know that there is a future. It has been said humans can live for 40 days without food, a few days without water, and a few minutes without air, but a human can't live without hope.

As the spiritual leader of your family, take note of the following ways to bring hope to your family:

• *The Scriptures*—reading the Bible to your family brings perspective to a discouraged heart. The Word of God is sure and certain in its promises.

• *Prayer*—crying out to the King who rules sovereignly brings hope. Leading your family in a prayer meeting after dinner can allow them to express their anguish to God and ask Him for help.

• *Spiritual milestones*—remembering and making a list of what God has done in the past can also produce hope.

Obadiah used just a few words to create hope. Make it your aim to use words wisely to remind your family of the truth about God and your circumstances. Hope can grow in the human heart that is focused on God and the truth about Him.

    Shall possess the cities of the South.[a]
21 Then saviors[a] shall come to Mount
      Zion
    To judge the mountains of Esau,
    And the kingdom shall be the LORD's.

---

19 [a]Hebrew *Negev* **20** [a]Hebrew *Negev* **21** [a]Or *deliverers*

JONAH

IMAGINE THAT YOU LIVED back in the year 1942 and received the following assignment from God, "Go to the leaders of the Nazi party in Germany and tell them that God sent you to say that their evil has come up before Him." How would you respond?

That is something like the prophetic mission God gave Jonah, a contemporary of Amos who lived in the northern kingdom in the middle of the eighth century BC. Israel's neighbors to the north, the Assyrians, had not yet established themselves as a major military power. Yet within fifty years, Assyrian armies would invade the northern kingdom, bringing it to an end.

The Assyrians had earned a reputation for wickedness and cruelty. And it appears Jonah had no interest in seeing God deal kindly with this pagan nation. So when God called him to visit Nineveh, the capital city of Assyria, the prophet ran the other way!

The book describes how Jonah runs from God's call, gets caught in a great storm on board a ship, is tossed overboard, and is swallowed alive by a great fish, spending three days in the beast's belly. Eventually he reaches Nineveh, where he fulfills his mission. Yet to his surprise—and dismay—the people of Nineveh repent, and God spares them, which leads to Jonah's sulking about God's kindness toward pagans.

Jonah has at least two important themes for couples and families:

First, we see God's love and grace being poured out beyond Israel to other nations—a foreshadowing of our own age. Jesus calls us as His followers to take part in making disciples of all nations. Pastor John Piper says there are only three groups when it comes to world missions: those who go; those who send; and those who are disobedient! Which group are you in?

Second, we see a clear example of God's sovereign control over all the events in our lives and the wisdom of obeying Him and teaching our children to do the same. All of us must recognize the tendency of our own hearts to wander. Let's learn from the reluctant prophet that real life and joy are found in obedience.

Jonah's Disobedience

1 Now the word of the LORD came to Jonah the son of Amittai, saying, [2]"Arise, go to Nineveh, that great city, and cry out against it; for their wickedness has come up before Me." [3]But Jonah arose to flee to Tarshish from the presence of the LORD. He went down to Joppa, and found a ship going to Tarshish; so he paid the fare, and went down into it, to go with them to Tarshish from the presence of the LORD.

The Storm at Sea

[4]But the LORD sent out a great wind on the sea, and there was a mighty tempest on the sea, so that the ship was about to be broken up.

[5]Then the mariners were afraid; and every man cried out to his god, and threw the cargo that *was* in the ship into the sea, to lighten the load.[a] But Jonah had gone down into the lowest parts of the ship, had lain down, and was fast asleep.

[6]So the captain came to him, and said to him, "What do you mean, sleeper? Arise, call on your God; perhaps your God will consider us, so that we may not perish."

[7]And they said to one another, "Come, let us cast lots, that we may know for whose cause this trouble *has come* upon us." So they cast lots, and the lot fell on Jonah. [8]Then they said to him, "Please tell us! For whose cause *is* this trouble upon us? What is your occupation? And where do you come from? What is your country? And of what people are you?"

[9]So he said to them, "I *am* a Hebrew; and I fear the LORD, the God of heaven, who made the sea and the dry *land*."

Jonah Thrown into the Sea

[10]Then the men were exceedingly afraid, and said to him, "Why have you done this?" For the men knew that he fled from the presence of the LORD, because he had told them. [11]Then they said to him, "What shall we do to you that the sea may be calm for us?"—for the sea was growing more tempestuous.

1:5 [a]Literally *from upon them*

BIBLICAL INSIGHTS • 1:1–3

Find and Follow Your Mission

WHILE GOD WANTS US TO HAVE a sense of mission for our lives and families, how do we determine what He wants us to do?

1. Pray—ask God to so burden your heart with someone or something that you can't let it go. This process may take several months. Sometimes I think God wants to see if we're really serious! But He will make it clear what He wants you to do.

2. Look back over the tapestry of your life. Do any threads show up repeatedly? God may have been preparing you for just this moment.

3. Begin to take your idea to just a few friends, beginning with your mate and family. Be careful here! Sometimes the Christian community can feel threatened with a genuine burden from the Lord. If someone has no vision for his own life or ministry, he can start to feel guilty when he hears about someone else's vision.

4. Count the cost—and then do something about it.

5. Remember that it is in your best interest to obey God. Jonah ran from God's assignment and wound up tossed overboard and in the belly of a giant fish! There is blessing that comes from obedience to God, and there is often chastening that comes when we disobey.

We are all called by God to be part of what's called the Great Commission, going into all the world to share God's good news for mankind and to make disciples of all nations (Matt. 28:19, 20). What are you and your family doing to share that good news with others?

[12]And he said to them, "Pick me up and throw me into the sea; then the sea will become calm for you. For I know that this great tempest *is* because of me."

[13]Nevertheless the men rowed hard to return to land, but they could not, for the sea continued to grow more tempestuous against them. [14]Therefore they cried out to

the LORD and said, "We pray, O LORD, please do not let us perish for this man's life, and do not charge us with innocent blood; for You, O LORD, have done as it pleased You." ¹⁵So they picked up Jonah and threw him into the sea, and the sea ceased from its raging. ¹⁶Then the men feared the LORD exceedingly, and offered a sacrifice to the LORD and took vows.

Jonah's Prayer and Deliverance

¹⁷Now the LORD had prepared a great fish to swallow Jonah. And Jonah was in the belly of the fish three days and three nights.

2 Then Jonah prayed to the LORD his God from the fish's belly. ²And he said:

"I cried out to the LORD because of my
    affliction,
And He answered me.

"Out of the belly of Sheol I cried,
    And You heard my voice.
³ For You cast me into the deep,
    Into the heart of the seas,
And the floods surrounded me;
All Your billows and Your waves
    passed over me.

⁴ Then I said, 'I have been cast out of
    Your sight;
Yet I will look again toward Your
    holy temple.'
⁵ The waters surrounded me, *even* to
    my soul;
The deep closed around me;
Weeds were wrapped around my
    head.
⁶ I went down to the moorings of the
    mountains;
The earth with its bars *closed* behind
    me forever;
Yet You have brought up my life
    from the pit,
O LORD, my God.

⁷ "When my soul fainted within me,
I remembered the LORD;
And my prayer went *up* to You,
Into Your holy temple.

⁸ "Those who regard worthless
    idols
Forsake their own Mercy.
⁹ But I will sacrifice to You
With the voice of thanksgiving;
I will pay what I have vowed.
Salvation *is* of the LORD."

PARENTING MATTERS

Q: *How do we strike a balance between teaching the value of working hard and learning to be still?*

There's certainly nothing wrong with an active life, so long as you maintain the right perspective. Idleness is just as bad as being too busy. Solomon warned, "Because of laziness the building decays, and through idleness of hands the house leaks" (Eccl. 10:18).

But the opposite problem, frenzy, creates a disturbance in our minds and souls that makes it hard for us to "Be still, and know that I am God" (Ps. 46:10). When God instructed a great fish to swallow Jonah, we suspect the Lord wanted to make sure Jonah had no choice but to be still for a little while.

Do you know how to be still? Does your child? We fear many Christian teens will not be able to hear God speak to them because they've not learned to rest and to listen. They are addicted to activity and constant external stimuli.

You need to set the course for your preadolescent child while you still have control of his or her schedule, knowing there is a time just around the corner when the activity monster will barge through your front door and begin to eat your time and resources. We encourage you to formulate a mission statement of activities that will set boundaries for the wellbeing of everyone in your family.

¹⁰So the LORD spoke to the fish, and it vomited Jonah onto dry *land.*

Jonah Preaches at Nineveh

3 Now the word of the LORD came to Jonah the second time, saying, ²"Arise, go to Nineveh, that great city, and preach to it the message that I tell you." ³So Jonah arose and went to Nineveh, according to the word of the LORD. Now Nineveh was an exceedingly great city, a three-day journeyª *in extent.* ⁴And Jonah began to enter the city on the first day's walk. Then he cried out and said, "Yet forty days, and Nineveh shall be overthrown!"

The People of Nineveh Believe

⁵So the people of Nineveh believed God, proclaimed a fast, and put on sackcloth, from the greatest to the least of them. ⁶Then word came to the king of Nineveh; and he arose from his throne and laid aside his robe, covered *himself* with sackcloth and sat in ashes. ⁷And he caused *it* to be proclaimed and published throughout Nineveh by the decree of the king and his nobles, saying,

Let neither man nor beast, herd nor flock, taste anything; do not let them eat, or drink water. ⁸But let man and beast be covered with sackcloth, and cry mightily to God; yes, let every one turn from his evil way and from the violence that is in his hands. ⁹Who can tell *if* God will turn and relent, and turn away from His fierce anger, so that we may not perish?

¹⁰Then God saw their works, that they turned from their evil way; and God relented from the disaster that He had said He would bring upon them, and He did not do it.

Jonah's Anger and God's Kindness

4 But it displeased Jonah exceedingly, and he became angry. ²So he prayed to the LORD, and said, "Ah, LORD, was not this what I said when I was still in my country?

Therefore I fled previously to Tarshish; for I know that You *are* a gracious and merciful God, slow to anger and abundant in lovingkindness, One who relents from doing harm. ³Therefore now, O LORD, please take my life from me, for *it is* better for me to die than to live!"

⁴Then the LORD said, "*Is it* right for you to be angry?"

⁵So Jonah went out of the city and sat on the east side of the city. There he made himself a shelter and sat under it in the shade, till he might see what would become of the city. ⁶And the LORD God prepared a plantª and made it come up over Jonah, that it might be shade for his head to deliver him from his misery. So Jonah was very grateful for the plant. ⁷But as morning dawned the next day God prepared a worm, and it *so* damaged the plant that it withered. ⁸And it happened, when the sun arose, that God prepared a vehement east wind; and the sun beat on Jonah's head, so that he grew faint. Then he wished death for himself, and said, "*It is* better for me to die than to live."

⁹Then God said to Jonah, "*Is it* right for you to be angry about the plant?"

And he said, "*It is* right for me to be angry, even to death!"

¹⁰But the LORD said, "You have had pity on the plant for which you have not labored, nor made it grow, which came up in a night and perished in a night. ¹¹And should I not pity Nineveh, that great city, in which are more than one hundred and twenty thousand persons who cannot discern between their right hand and their left—and much livestock?"

INTIMATE MOMENTS

Buy your guy a leather-bound journal and write inspirational and romantic quotes, thoughts, and love notes for him. As you journey through life together, continue adding new thoughts that affirm your love and respect for him.

3:3 ªExact meaning unknown
4:6 ªHebrew *kikayon,* exact identity unknown

MICAH

THE PROPHET MICAH, a contemporary of Isaiah, lived in the southern kingdom from about 735–690 BC. He had grown up in the foothills around Jerusalem, in the town of Moresheth (1:1, 14), near the Judea/Philistia border, near the Philistine city of Gath. Although he came from farm country, God raised up this farm boy to powerfully and clearly speak His word to the civil and religious leaders of Jerusalem.

The book is a collection of three oracles. Chapters 1 and 2 make up the first message, chapters 3—5 the second, and the last two chapters record the third message. Each message begins with Micah calling the people to hear (1:2; 3:1; 6:1). What follows in each is a warning about God's righteous judgment on the disobedient and the wicked. Each oracle concludes with words of hope and encouragement to the faithful remnant of Israel, that God will keep His covenant and will save all those who call to Him. Micah also contains the famous prophecy that declared where the Messiah would be born, in Bethlehem (5:2).

Spiritual malaise in Judah had risen to a crescendo during Micah's day. People openly practiced idolatry while maintaining an empty ceremonial worship of God. Whenever foreign armies threatened the people, they formed alliances with pagan nations in violation of God's Word, instead of crying out to the Lord for His protection. And they consistently failed as a nation to care for the poor and the outcast. One of the two best-known verses from Micah is 6:8, "He has shown you, O man, what is good; and what does the LORD require of you but to do justly, to love mercy, and to walk humbly with your God?"

That single verse from Micah foreshadows Jesus' instruction when He summed up all of the Old Testament teaching in two commands: love God and our neighbors (Matt. 22:37–40). As individuals and families, we must learn to walk in the power of the Holy Spirit so that we deal fairly with others, show mercy to all, and walk through life in humble dependence upon God's grace.

1 The word of the LORD that came to Micah of Moresheth in the days of Jotham, Ahaz, *and* Hezekiah, kings of Judah, which he saw concerning Samaria and Jerusalem.

The Coming Judgment on Israel

2 Hear, all you peoples!
Listen, O earth, and all that is in it!
Let the Lord GOD be a witness
    against you,
The Lord from His holy temple.

3 For behold, the LORD is coming out of
    His place;
He will come down
And tread on the high places of the
    earth.
4 The mountains will melt under Him,
And the valleys will split
Like wax before the fire,
Like waters poured down a steep
    place.
5 All this is for the transgression of
    Jacob
And for the sins of the house of
    Israel.
What *is* the transgression of Jacob?
Is it not Samaria?
And what *are* the high places of
    Judah?
Are they not Jerusalem?

6 "Therefore I will make Samaria a
    heap of ruins in the field,
Places for planting a vineyard;
I will pour down her stones into the
    valley,
And I will uncover her foundations.
7 All her carved images shall be
    beaten to pieces,
And all her pay as a harlot shall be
    burned with the fire;
All her idols I will lay desolate,
For she gathered *it* from the pay of a
    harlot,
And they shall return to the pay of a
    harlot."

Mourning for Israel and Judah

8 Therefore I will wail and howl,
I will go stripped and naked;
I will make a wailing like the jackals
And a mourning like the ostriches,
9 For her wounds *are* incurable.
For it has come to Judah;
It has come to the gate of My
    people—
To Jerusalem.

10 Tell *it* not in Gath,
Weep not at all;
In Beth Aphrah[a]
Roll yourself in the dust.
11 Pass by in naked shame, you
    inhabitant of Shaphir;
The inhabitant of Zaanan[a] does not
    go out.
Beth Ezel mourns;
Its place to stand is taken away from
    you.
12 For the inhabitant of Maroth pined[a]
    for good,
But disaster came down from the
    LORD
To the gate of Jerusalem.
13 O inhabitant of Lachish,
Harness the chariot to the swift steeds
(She *was* the beginning of sin to the
    daughter of Zion),
For the transgressions of Israel were
    found in you.
14 Therefore you shall give presents to
    Moresheth Gath;[a]
The houses of Achzib[b] *shall be* a lie
    to the kings of Israel.
15 I will yet bring an heir to you, O
    inhabitant of Mareshah;[a]
The glory of Israel shall come to
    Adullam.
16 Make yourself bald and cut off your
    hair,
Because of your precious children;
Enlarge your baldness like an eagle,
For they shall go from you into
    captivity.

Woe to Evildoers

2 Woe to those who devise iniquity,
And work out evil on their beds!
At morning light they practice it,

1:10 [a]Literally *House of Dust*   1:11 [a]Literally *Going Out*   1:12 [a]Literally *was sick*   1:14 [a]Literally *Possession of Gath*   [b]Literally *Lie*   1:15 [a]Literally *Inheritance*

Because it is in the power of their
  hand.
2 They covet fields and take *them* by
    violence,
  Also houses, and seize *them*.
  So they oppress a man and his
    house,
  A man and his inheritance.

3Therefore thus says the LORD:

  "Behold, against this family I am
    devising disaster,
  From which you cannot remove your
    necks;

Nor shall you walk haughtily,
  For this *is* an evil time.
4 In that day *one* shall take up a
    proverb against you,
  And lament with a bitter
    lamentation, saying:
  'We are utterly destroyed!
  He has changed the heritage of my
    people;
  How He has removed *it* from me!
  To a turncoat He has divided our
    fields.'"

5 Therefore you will have no one to
    determine boundariesª by lot
  In the assembly of the LORD.

Lying Prophets

6 "Do not prattle," *you say to those* who
    prophesy.
  So they shall not prophesy to you;ª
  They shall not return insult for
    insult.ᵇ
7 *You who are* named the house of
    Jacob:
  "Is the Spirit of the LORD restricted?
  Are these His doings?
  Do not My words do good
  To him who walks uprightly?

8 "Lately My people have risen up as an
    enemy—
  You pull off the robe with the garment
  From those who trust *you*, as they
    pass by,
  Like men returned from war.
9 The women of My people you cast
    out
  From their pleasant houses;
  From their children
  You have taken away My glory
    forever.

10 "Arise and depart,
  For this *is* not *your* rest;
  Because it is defiled, it shall destroy,
  Yes, with utter destruction.
11 If a man should walk in a false spirit
  And speak a lie, *saying,*
  'I will prophesy to you of wine and
    drink,'

ROMANCE FAQ

**Q: How can we
resolve our disagreements
before they escalate?**

When you have a conflict with your
spouse, focus on the issue at hand. Here
are some ways to keep your focus clear:

Stick to one issue. Don't save up a
series of complaints and let your mate
have it all at once. A good warning sign is
finding yourself saying, "And another
thing …"

*Focus on behavior rather than charac-
ter.* Confrontation must not turn into character assassination! If you need to talk
about sticking to a budget, discuss available finances and necessary expenses,
instead of calling your mate a spendthrift.
Avoid attacking the person, and remember to use *I* language. Say, "I think we can
keep from going in the hole each month
by _____," not "You always drain us dry
before the end of the month!"

*Focus on the facts rather than judging
motives.* Suppose your spouse forgot to
tell you what time some function would
end. Say, "I worry about you when you
aren't here when I expect you," not "You
just don't care about anyone but yourself!"

*Above all, keep your focus on under-
standing each other, rather than who is
winning or losing.* Listen carefully to
what the other person says. See if some
other issue is really at work.

2:5 ªLiterally *one casting a surveyor's line*
2:6 ªLiterally *to these* ᵇVulgate reads *He shall not
take shame.*

Even he would be the prattler of this
people.

Israel Restored

12 "I will surely assemble all of you, O
Jacob,
I will surely gather the remnant of
Israel;
I will put them together like sheep of
the fold,[a]
Like a flock in the midst of their
pasture;
They shall make a loud noise
because of *so many* people.
13 The one who breaks open will come
up before them;
They will break out,
Pass through the gate,
And go out by it;
Their king will pass before them,
With the LORD at their head."

Wicked Rulers and Prophets

3 And I said:

"Hear now, O heads of Jacob,
And you rulers of the house of
Israel:
Is it not for you to know justice?
2 You who hate good and love evil;
Who strip the skin from My people,[a]
And the flesh from their bones;
3 Who also eat the flesh of My people,
Flay their skin from them,
Break their bones,
And chop *them* in pieces
Like *meat* for the pot,
Like flesh in the caldron."

4 Then they will cry to the LORD,
But He will not hear them;
He will even hide His face from them
at that time,
Because they have been evil in their
deeds.

5 Thus says the LORD concerning the
prophets
Who make my people stray;
Who chant "Peace"
While they chew with their teeth,

But who prepare war against him
Who puts nothing into their mouths:
6 "Therefore you shall have night
without vision,
And you shall have darkness without
divination;
The sun shall go down on the
prophets,
And the day shall be dark for them.
7 So the seers shall be ashamed,
And the diviners abashed;
Indeed they shall all cover their lips;
For *there is* no answer from God."

8 But truly I am full of power by the
Spirit of the LORD,
And of justice and might,
To declare to Jacob his transgression
And to Israel his sin.
9 Now hear this,
You heads of the house of Jacob
And rulers of the house of Israel,
Who abhor justice
And pervert all equity,
10 Who build up Zion with bloodshed
And Jerusalem with iniquity:
11 Her heads judge for a bribe,
Her priests teach for pay,
And her prophets divine for money.
Yet they lean on the LORD, and say,
"Is not the LORD among us?
No harm can come upon us."
12 Therefore because of you
Zion shall be plowed *like* a field,
Jerusalem shall become heaps of
ruins,
And the mountain of the temple[a]
Like the bare hills of the forest.

The LORD's Reign in Zion

4 Now it shall come to pass in the
latter days
That the mountain of the LORD's
house
Shall be established on the top of the
mountains,
And shall be exalted above the hills;
And peoples shall flow to it.
2 Many nations shall come and say,
"Come, and let us go up to the
mountain of the LORD,
To the house of the God of Jacob;
He will teach us His ways,

2:12 [a]Hebrew *Bozrah* **3:2** [a]Literally *them*
3:12 [a]Literally *house*

And we shall walk in His paths."
For out of Zion the law shall go
forth,
And the word of the LORD from
Jerusalem.
3   He shall judge between many
peoples,
And rebuke strong nations afar off;
They shall beat their swords into
plowshares,
And their spears into pruning hooks;
Nation shall not lift up sword against
nation,
Neither shall they learn war
anymore.[a]

4   But everyone shall sit under his vine
and under his fig tree,
And no one shall make *them* afraid;
For the mouth of the LORD of hosts
has spoken.
5   For all people walk each in the name
of his god,
But we will walk in the name of the
LORD our God
Forever and ever.

Zion's Future Triumph

6   "In that day," says the LORD,
"I will assemble the lame,
I will gather the outcast
And those whom I have afflicted;
7   I will make the lame a remnant,
And the outcast a strong nation;
So the LORD will reign over them in
Mount Zion
From now on, even forever.
8   And you, O tower of the flock,
The stronghold of the daughter of
Zion,
To you shall it come,
Even the former dominion shall
come,
The kingdom of the daughter of
Jerusalem."

9   Now why do you cry aloud?
Is there no king in your midst?
Has your counselor perished?
For pangs have seized you like a
woman in labor.
10   Be in pain, and labor to bring forth,
O daughter of Zion,
Like a woman in birth pangs.

For now you shall go forth from the
city,
You shall dwell in the field,
And to Babylon you shall go.
There you shall be delivered;
There the LORD will redeem you
From the hand of your enemies.

11   Now also many nations have
gathered against you,
Who say, "Let her be defiled,
And let our eye look upon Zion."
12   But they do not know the thoughts
of the LORD,
Nor do they understand His counsel;
For He will gather them like sheaves
to the threshing floor.

13   "Arise and thresh, O daughter of
Zion;
For I will make your horn iron,
And I will make your hooves bronze;
You shall beat in pieces many
peoples;
I will consecrate their gain to the
LORD,
And their substance to the Lord of
the whole earth."

5   Now gather yourself in troops,
O daughter of troops;
He has laid siege against us;
They will strike the judge of Israel
with a rod on the cheek.

The Coming Messiah

2   "But you, Bethlehem Ephrathah,
Though you are little among the
thousands of Judah,
Yet out of you shall come forth
to Me
The One to be Ruler in Israel,
Whose goings forth *are* from of old,
From everlasting."

3   Therefore He shall give them up,
Until the time *that* she who is in
labor has given birth;
Then the remnant of His brethren
Shall return to the children of Israel.
4   And He shall stand and feed *His
flock*
In the strength of the LORD,

4:3 [a] Compare Isaiah 2:2–4

In the majesty of the name of the
LORD His God;
And they shall abide,
For now He shall be great
To the ends of the earth;
5 And this *One* shall be peace.

Judgment on Israel's Enemies

When the Assyrian comes into our
land,
And when he treads in our palaces,
Then we will raise against him
Seven shepherds and eight princely
men.
6 They shall waste with the sword the
land of Assyria,
And the land of Nimrod at its
entrances;
Thus He shall deliver *us* from the
Assyrian,
When he comes into our land
And when he treads within our
borders.

7 Then the remnant of Jacob
Shall be in the midst of many peoples,
Like dew from the LORD,
Like showers on the grass,
That tarry for no man
Nor wait for the sons of men.
8 And the remnant of Jacob
Shall be among the Gentiles,
In the midst of many peoples,
Like a lion among the beasts of the
forest,
Like a young lion among flocks of
sheep,
Who, if he passes through,
Both treads down and tears in pieces,
And none can deliver.
9 Your hand shall be lifted against
your adversaries,
And all your enemies shall be cut off.

10 "And it shall be in that day," says the
LORD,
"That I will cut off your horses from
your midst
And destroy your chariots.
11 I will cut off the cities of your land
And throw down all your
strongholds.

12 I will cut off sorceries from your
hand,
And you shall have no soothsayers.
13 Your carved images I will also cut
off,
And your sacred pillars from your
midst;
You shall no more worship the work
of your hands;
14 I will pluck your wooden images[a]
from your midst;
Thus I will destroy your cities.
15 And I will execute vengeance in
anger and fury
On the nations that have not heard."[a]

**INTIMATE
MOMENTS**

Prepare for special events: Maintain current e-mail addresses and cell phone numbers of your husband's friends. You may want to throw him a surprise birthday party or plan a celebration when he accomplishes something significant.

God Pleads with Israel

6 Hear now what the LORD says:

"Arise, plead your case before the
mountains,
And let the hills hear your voice.
2 Hear, O you mountains, the LORD's
complaint,
And you strong foundations of the
earth;
For the LORD has a complaint against
His people,
And He will contend with Israel.

3 "O My people, what have I done to
you?
And how have I wearied you?
Testify against Me.
4 For I brought you up from the land
of Egypt,
I redeemed you from the house of
bondage;
And I sent before you Moses, Aaron,
and Miriam.

5:14 [a]Hebrew *Asherim*, Canaanite deities
5:15 [a]Or *obeyed*

5   O My people, remember now
What Balak king of Moab counseled,
And what Balaam the son of Beor
     answered him,
From Acacia Grove[a] to Gilgal,
That you may know the
     righteousness of the LORD."

6   With what shall I come before the
     LORD,
And bow myself before the High
     God?
Shall I come before Him with burnt
     offerings,
With calves a year old?
7   Will the LORD be pleased with
     thousands of rams,
Ten thousand rivers of oil?
Shall I give my firstborn *for* my
     transgression,
The fruit of my body *for* the sin of
     my soul?

8   He has shown you, O man, what *is*
     good;
And what does the LORD require of
     you
But to do justly,
To love mercy,
And to walk humbly with your God?

Punishment of Israel's Injustice

9   The LORD's voice cries to the city—
Wisdom shall see Your name:

"Hear the rod!
Who has appointed it?
10   Are there yet the treasures of
     wickedness
In the house of the wicked,
And the short measure *that is* an
     abomination?
11   Shall I count pure *those* with the
     wicked scales,
And with the bag of deceitful
     weights?
12   For her rich men are full of violence,
Her inhabitants have spoken lies,
And their tongue is deceitful in their
     mouth.

13   "Therefore I will also make *you* sick
     by striking you,
By making *you* desolate because of
     your sins.

14   You shall eat, but not be satisfied;
Hunger[a] *shall be* in your midst.
You may carry *some* away,[b] but shall
     not save *them;*
And what you do rescue I will give
     over to the sword.

15   "You shall sow, but not reap;
You shall tread the olives, but not
     anoint yourselves with oil;
And *make* sweet wine, but not drink
     wine.
16   For the statutes of Omri are kept;
All the works of Ahab's house *are
     done;*
And you walk in their counsels,
That I may make you a
     desolation,
And your inhabitants a hissing.
Therefore you shall bear the
     reproach of My people."[a]

Sorrow for Israel's Sins

7   Woe is me!
For I am like those who gather
     summer fruits,
Like those who glean vintage
     grapes;
There is no cluster to eat
Of the first-ripe fruit *which* my soul
     desires.
2   The faithful *man* has perished from
     the earth,
And *there is* no one upright among
     men.
They all lie in wait for blood;
Every man hunts his brother with a
     net.

3   That they may successfully do evil
     with both hands—
The prince asks *for gifts,*
The judge *seeks* a bribe,
And the great *man* utters his evil
     desire;
So they scheme together.
4   The best of them *is* like a brier;
The most upright *is sharper* than a
     thorn hedge;

6:5 [a]Hebrew *Shittim* (compare Numbers 25:1; Joshua
2:1; 3:1)   **6:14** [a]Or *Emptiness* or *Humiliation*   [b]Targum
and Vulgate read *You shall take hold.*   **6:16** [a]Following
Masoretic Text, Targum, and Vulgate; Septuagint
reads *of nations.*

The day of your watchman and your
punishment comes;
Now shall be their perplexity.

5   Do not trust in a friend;
Do not put your confidence in a
companion;
Guard the doors of your mouth
From her who lies in your bosom.
6   For son dishonors father,
Daughter rises against her mother,
Daughter-in-law against her mother-
in-law;
A man's enemies *are* the men of his
own household.
7   Therefore I will look to the LORD;
I will wait for the God of my
salvation;
My God will hear me.

Israel's Confession and Comfort

8   Do not rejoice over me, my enemy;
When I fall, I will arise;
When I sit in darkness,
The LORD *will be* a light to me.
9   I will bear the indignation of the
LORD,
Because I have sinned against Him,
Until He pleads my case
And executes justice for me.
He will bring me forth to the light;
I will see His righteousness.
10 Then *she who is* my enemy will see,
And shame will cover her who said
to me,
"Where is the LORD your God?"
My eyes will see her;
Now she will be trampled down
Like mud in the streets.

11 *In* the day when your walls are to be
built,
In that day the decree shall go far
and wide.[a]
12 *In* that day they[a] shall come to you
From Assyria and the fortified
cities,[b]
From the fortress[c] to the River,[d]
From sea to sea,

BIBLICAL INSIGHTS • 7:19

Accept Your Mate Unconditionally

IF YOU ACCEPT YOUR MATE only in part,
you can love him or her only in part. That's
why unconditionally accepting your
mate is so important.

While serving aboard a gunboat in
Vietnam, Dave Roever was holding a
phosphorus grenade some six inches
from his face when a sniper's bullet ignited the explosive. The first time he saw
himself after the explosion, he says he
saw a monster, not a human being. "I was
alone in the way the souls in hell must
feel alone," he wrote.

When he returned to the states, he
feared how his young bride Brenda
would react. He had just watched a wife
tell another burn victim that she wanted
a divorce. But when Brenda walked in,
she kissed him on what was left of his
face, smiled, and said, "Welcome home,
Davey! I love you."

That's what marriage is all about.
Marriage is another person being committed enough to you to accept the real
you, scars and all. It means two people
working together to heal their deepest
wounds. It means following the example
of God in our marriage, "He will again
have compassion on us, and will subdue
our iniquities. You will cast all our sins
into the depths of the sea" (7:19).

And mountain *to* mountain.
13 Yet the land shall be desolate
Because of those who dwell in it,
And for the fruit of their deeds.

God Will Forgive Israel

14 Shepherd Your people with Your
staff,
The flock of Your heritage,
Who dwell solitarily *in* a woodland,
In the midst of Carmel;
Let them feed *in* Bashan and Gilead,
As in days of old.

7:11 [a]Or *the boundary shall be extended*
7:12 [a]Literally *he,* collective of the captives [b]Hebrew
arey mazor, possibly *cities of Egypt* [c]Hebrew *mazor,*
possibly *Egypt* [d]That is, the Euphrates

15 "As in the days when you came out of
       the land of Egypt,
     I will show them[a] wonders."

16 The nations shall see and be
       ashamed of all their might;
     They shall put *their* hand over *their*
       mouth;
     Their ears shall be deaf.
17 They shall lick the dust like a
       serpent;
     They shall crawl from their holes like
       snakes of the earth.
     They shall be afraid of the LORD our
       God,
     And shall fear because of You.
18 Who *is* a God like You,
     Pardoning iniquity

And passing over the transgression
     of the remnant of His heritage?

He does not retain His anger forever,
     Because He delights *in* mercy.
19 He will again have compassion on
       us,
     And will subdue our iniquities.

You will cast all our[a] sins
     Into the depths of the sea.
20 You will give truth to Jacob
     And mercy to Abraham,
     Which You have sworn to our
       fathers
     From days of old.

7:15 [a]Literally *him,* collective for the captives
7:19 [a]Literally *their*

NAHUM

WHEN GOD SENT JONAH TO WARN the people of Nineveh to repent of their wickedness, the Assyrians were just beginning to emerge as the dominant military and political power in the Middle East. A century later, the Assyrian empire had spread throughout the region, as far south as Egypt. Their capital city had become a mighty fortress considered impenetrable, with 100-foot high walls and a moat around the city 150 feet wide and 60 feet deep.

The Assyrians seemed invincible.

During their century of Middle Eastern domination, the Assyrians gained a reputation as one of the wickedest empires of the ancient world. God had used the Assyrians as an instrument of judgment against Israel in 722 BC, but He would not ignore their idolatry and cruelty. He raised up Nahum to announce to His people that the invincible Assyrians were about to see their empire broken at the hands of the Babylonians and the Medes.

We know very little about the prophet Nahum. Scholars have debated the location of his hometown Elkosh. But the book is not about Nahum; as with most of the minor prophets, this book records God's message as delivered through him.

Old Testament scholar Dr. Walter Keiser says the book is "about God's almighty rule over all peoples, nations and cultures. It is another affirmation that, since God created all persons in His image, a person cannot treat others inhumanely and hope to escape God's punishment. It also affirms that the law of God is based on His nature and personal character; therefore, holiness, righteousness, and justice are expected of all rulers, potentates, and nations, regardless of whether they believe in the Living God."

When our children wonder why God would allow a Stalin, a Hitler, a Mao, a Pol Pot, an Osama Bin Laden, or any other wicked leader to persist in his evil, we can remind them of the message of the Book of Nahum. We may not know when judgment will come, but we can be sure that "God is not mocked; for whatever a man sows, that he will also reap" (Gal. 6:7).

1 The burden[a] against Nineveh. The book of the vision of Nahum the Elkoshite.

God's Wrath on His Enemies

2 God *is* jealous, and the LORD avenges;
The LORD avenges and *is* furious.
The LORD will take vengeance on His adversaries,
And He reserves *wrath* for His enemies;

3 The LORD *is* slow to anger and great in power,
And will not at all acquit *the wicked*.

The LORD has His way
In the whirlwind and in the storm,
And the clouds *are* the dust of His feet.

4 He rebukes the sea and makes it dry,
And dries up all the rivers.
Bashan and Carmel wither,
And the flower of Lebanon wilts.

5 The mountains quake before Him,
The hills melt,
And the earth heaves[a] at His presence,
Yes, the world and all who dwell in it.

6 Who can stand before His indignation?
And who can endure the fierceness of His anger?
His fury is poured out like fire,
And the rocks are thrown down by Him.

7 The LORD *is* good,
A stronghold in the day of trouble;
And He knows those who trust in Him.

8 But with an overflowing flood
He will make an utter end of its place,
And darkness will pursue His enemies.

9 What do you conspire against the LORD?
He will make an utter end *of it*.
Affliction will not rise up a second time.

10 For while tangled *like* thorns,
And while drunken *like* drunkards,
They shall be devoured like stubble fully dried.

11 From you comes forth *one*
Who plots evil against the LORD,
A wicked counselor.

12 Thus says the LORD:

"Though *they are* safe, and likewise many,
Yet in this manner they will be cut down
When he passes through.
Though I have afflicted you,
I will afflict you no more;

13 For now I will break off his yoke from you,
And burst your bonds apart."

14 The LORD has given a command concerning you:
"Your name shall be perpetuated no longer.
Out of the house of your gods
I will cut off the carved image and the molded image.
I will dig your grave,
For you are vile."

15 Behold, on the mountains
The feet of him who brings good tidings,
Who proclaims peace!
O Judah, keep your appointed feasts,
Perform your vows.
For the wicked one shall no more pass through you;
He is utterly cut off.

The Destruction of Nineveh

2 He who scatters[a] has come up before your face.
Man the fort!
Watch the road!
Strengthen *your* flanks!
Fortify *your* power mightily.

2 For the LORD will restore the excellence of Jacob
Like the excellence of Israel,
For the emptiers have emptied them out
And ruined their vine branches.

1:1 [a]Or *oracle* **1:5** [a]Targum reads *burns*.
2:1 [a]Vulgate reads *He who destroys*.

3   The shields of his mighty men *are*
      made red,
    The valiant men *are* in scarlet.
    The chariots *come* with flaming
      torches
    In the day of his preparation,
    And the spears are brandished.[a]
4   The chariots rage in the streets,
    They jostle one another in the broad
      roads;
    They seem like torches,
    They run like lightning.

5   He remembers his nobles;
    They stumble in their walk;
    They make haste to her walls,
    And the defense is prepared.
6   The gates of the rivers are opened,
    And the palace is dissolved.
7   It is decreed:[a]
    She shall be led away captive,
    She shall be brought up;
    And her maidservants shall lead *her*
      as with the voice of doves,
    Beating their breasts.

8   Though Nineveh of old *was* like a
      pool of water,
    Now they flee away.
    "Halt! Halt!" *they cry;*
    But no one turns back.
9   Take spoil of silver!
    Take spoil of gold!
    There is no end of treasure,
    Or wealth of every desirable prize.
10 She is empty, desolate, and waste!
    The heart melts, and the knees
      shake;
    Much pain *is* in every side,
    And all their faces are drained of
      color.[a]

11 Where *is* the dwelling of the lions,
    And the feeding place of the young
      lions,
    Where the lion walked, the lioness
      and lion's cub,
    And no one made *them* afraid?
12 The lion tore in pieces enough for his
      cubs,
    Killed for his lionesses,
    Filled his caves with prey,
    And his dens with flesh.

13 "Behold, I *am* against you," says the
    LORD of hosts, "I will burn your[a] chariots
    in smoke, and the sword shall devour your

2:3 [a]Literally *the cypresses are shaken;* Septuagint
and Syriac read *the horses rush about;* Vulgate reads
the drivers are stupefied. **2:7** [a]Hebrew *Huzzab*
2:10 [a]Compare Joel 2:6 **2:13** [a]Literally *her*

Drop the Skipping Stones

Did you know that God's first purpose for marriage is for couples to mirror His image? To mirror God means to reflect Him, to magnify, exalt, and glorify Him. A successful marriage between two committed Christians not only honors God, but it also provides a tangible model of God's love to a world that desperately needs to see who He is.

Because we're created in the image of God, people who wouldn't otherwise know what God is like should be able to look at us and get a glimpse of Him. And people are never more like God than when they love one another and remain committed to each other, despite their flaws.

But what happens if you toss a stone into that perfect reflection? My good friend and colleague Dave Sunde told me he once visited a lake on a clear, still day. He watched a boy skip a small stone across the placid water, and immediately the perfect reflection of the mountains got distorted.

God's image, His reflection, gets distorted in us when a husband or wife allows sin to enter his or her life or relationship. Since your marriage represents God, protect it at all costs from the skipping stones, the sins that will distort His image.

Are you and your spouse fulfilling this high, noble calling of mirroring God to a lost world? There is no question in our minds that this is the ultimate assignment for a married couple. Not only will your children see what God is like in your marriage, but the world will as well.

young lions; I will cut off your prey from
the earth, and the voice of your messengers shall be heard no more."

The Woe of Nineveh

3 Woe to the bloody city!
It *is* all full of lies *and* robbery.
Its victim never departs.

2 The noise of a whip
And the noise of rattling wheels,
Of galloping horses,
Of clattering chariots!

3 Horsemen charge with bright sword
    and glittering spear.
There is a multitude of slain,
A great number of bodies,
Countless corpses—
They stumble over the corpses—

4 Because of the multitude of
    harlotries of the seductive harlot,
The mistress of sorceries,
Who sells nations through her
    harlotries,
And families through her
    sorceries.

5 "Behold, I *am* against you," says the
    LORD of hosts;
"I will lift your skirts over your face,
I will show the nations your
    nakedness,
And the kingdoms your shame.

6 I will cast abominable filth upon you,
Make you vile,
And make you a spectacle.

7 It shall come to pass *that* all who
    look upon you
Will flee from you, and say,
' Nineveh is laid waste!
Who will bemoan her?'
Where shall I seek comforters for
    you?"

8 Are you better than No Amon[a]
That was situated by the River,[b]
That had the waters around her,
Whose rampart *was* the sea,
Whose wall *was* the sea?

9 Ethiopia and Egypt *were* her
    strength,
And *it was* boundless;
Put and Lubim were your[a] helpers.

10 Yet she *was* carried away,
She went into captivity;

Her young children also were dashed
    to pieces
At the head of every street;
They cast lots for her honorable men,
And all her great men were bound in
    chains.

11 You also will be drunk;
You will be hidden;
You also will seek refuge from the
    enemy.

12 All your strongholds *are* fig trees
    with ripened figs:
If they are shaken,
They fall into the mouth of the eater.

13 Surely, your people in your midst *are*
    women!
The gates of your land are wide
    open for your enemies;
Fire shall devour the bars of your
    gates.

14 Draw your water for the siege!
Fortify your strongholds!
Go into the clay and tread the
    mortar!
Make strong the brick kiln!

15 There the fire will devour you,
The sword will cut you off;
It will eat you up like a locust.

Make yourself many—like the
    locust!
Make yourself many— like the
    swarming locusts!

16 You have multiplied your merchants
    more than the stars of heaven.
The locust plunders and flies away.

17 Your commanders *are* like *swarming*
    locusts,
And your generals like great
    grasshoppers,
Which camp in the hedges on a cold
    day;
When the sun rises they flee away,
And the place where they *are* is not
    known.

18 Your shepherds slumber, O king of
    Assyria;

3:8 [a]That is, ancient Thebes; Targum and Vulgate
read *populous Alexandria.* [b]Literally *rivers,* that is,
the Nile and the surrounding canals
3:9 [a]Septuagint reads *her.*

Your nobles rest *in the dust.*
Your people are scattered on the
      mountains,
And no one gathers them.
19 Your injury *has* no healing,

Your wound is severe.
All who hear news of you
Will clap *their* hands over you,
For upon whom has not your
      wickedness passed continually?

HABAKKUK

WE KNOW VERY LITTLE about the prophet Habakkuk, but the reference to the Chaldeans (1:6) suggests that the book may have been written around the time of the fall of Assyria (612 BC). Yet the circumstances, the setting, and the time in which Habakkuk lived are not important. The issues he addresses in this book are timeless.

For ages people have wondered about the existence of evil in a world under God's control. "If God is all-knowing, all-powerful and all-loving," they ask, "then why did He allow _____?" Some people have tried to resolve the issue by putting limits on God's knowledge or His power. Some have found the tension unbearable and so have rejected the very existence of God.

Like the Book of Job, the Book of Habakkuk revolves around how we are to respond to God in the face of tragedy or evil. The prophet calls on his audience to rejoice in God, even when the world around them is crumbling (3:17–19). But how can we do that?

Habakkuk's answer is found in 2:4, a phrase repeated three times in the New Testament (Rom. 1:17; Gal. 3:11; Heb. 10:38). "The just," he says, "shall live by his faith."

God calls us to live each day as a faith journey. The challenges and trials we face are the calisthenics that give our faith muscles the spiritual workout we need so that we can "be strong in the Lord and in the power of His might" (Eph. 6:10).

You may be facing personal trials, like a difficult marriage, a prodigal child, a health issue or a financial crisis, or you may simply be facing the strain of living in a culture crumbling under the weight of sin, injustice and unrighteousness. Whatever the case, the Book of Habakkuk offers you hope and encouragement as you discover that what the English preacher C. H. Spurgeon said is true, "God is too good to be unkind, He is too wise to be confused. If I cannot trace His hand, I can always trust His heart."

Learning that you can depend on the trustworthiness of God is the first step to learning to live by faith.

1

The burden[a] which the prophet Habakkuk saw.

The Prophet's Question

2 O LORD, how long shall I cry,
   And You will not hear?
   Even cry out to You, "Violence!"
   And You will not save.
3 Why do You show me iniquity,
   And cause *me* to see trouble?
   For plundering and violence *are*
      before me;
   There is strife, and contention arises.
4 Therefore the law is powerless,
   And justice never goes forth.
   For the wicked surround the
      righteous;
   Therefore perverse judgment
      proceeds.

The LORD's Reply

5 "Look among the nations and
      watch—
   Be utterly astounded!
   For *I will* work a work in your days
   Which you would not believe, though
      it were told *you.*
6 For indeed I am raising up the
      Chaldeans,
   A bitter and hasty nation
   Which marches through the breadth
      of the earth,
   To possess dwelling places *that are*
      not theirs.
7 They are terrible and dreadful;
   Their judgment and their dignity
      proceed from themselves.
8 Their horses also are swifter than
      leopards,
   And more fierce than evening
      wolves.
   Their chargers charge ahead;
   Their cavalry comes from afar;
   They fly as the eagle *that* hastens to
      eat.
9 "They all come for violence;
   Their faces are set *like* the east wind.
   They gather captives like sand.
10 They scoff at kings,
   And princes are scorned by them.

They deride every stronghold,
   For they heap up earthen *mounds*
      and seize it.
11 Then *his* mind[a] changes, and he
      transgresses;
   He commits offense,
   Ascribing this power to his god."

The Prophet's Second Question

12 Are You not from everlasting,
   O LORD my God, my Holy One?
   We shall not die.
   O LORD, You have appointed them for
      judgment;
   O Rock, You have marked them for
      correction.
13 *You are* of purer eyes than to behold
      evil,
   And cannot look on wickedness.
   Why do You look on those who deal
      treacherously,
   And hold Your tongue when the
      wicked devours
   A *person* more righteous than he?
14 *Why* do You make men like fish of
      the sea,
   Like creeping things *that have* no
      ruler over them?
15 They take up all of them with a
      hook,
   They catch them in their net,
   And gather them in their dragnet.
   Therefore they rejoice and are glad.
16 Therefore they sacrifice to their net,
   And burn incense to their dragnet;
   Because by them their share *is*
      sumptuous
   And their food plentiful.
17 Shall they therefore empty their net,
   And continue to slay nations without
      pity?

2

I will stand my watch
And set myself on the rampart,
And watch to see what He will say
   to me,
And what I will answer when I am
   corrected.

The Just Live by Faith

2Then the LORD answered me and said:

"Write the vision
And make *it* plain on tablets,

1:1 [a]Or *oracle*   1:11 [a]Literally *spirit* or *wind*

That he may run who reads it.
3 For the vision *is* yet for an appointed
    time;
But at the end it will speak, and it
    will not lie.
Though it tarries, wait for it;
Because it will surely come,
It will not tarry.

4 "Behold the proud,
    His soul is not upright in him;
But the just shall live by his faith.

**INTIMATE
MOMENTS**

Hire a handy man to fix things around
the house. Use the time you saved your
hubby to do something fun together.

Woe to the Wicked

5 "Indeed, because he transgresses by
    wine,
He is a proud man,
And he does not stay at home.
Because he enlarges his desire as
    hell,[a]
And he *is* like death, and cannot be
    satisfied,
He gathers to himself all nations
And heaps up for himself all
    peoples.

6 "Will not all these take up a proverb
    against him,
And a taunting riddle against him,
    and say,
' Woe to him who increases
What is not his—how long?
And to him who loads himself with
    many pledges'?[a]
7 Will not your creditors[a] rise up
    suddenly?
Will they not awaken who oppress
    you?
And you will become their booty.
8 Because you have plundered many
    nations,
All the remnant of the people shall
    plunder you,

Because of men's blood
And the violence of the land *and* the
    city,
And of all who dwell in it.

9 "Woe to him who covets evil gain for
    his house,
That he may set his nest on high,
That he may be delivered from the
    power of disaster!
10 You give shameful counsel to your
    house,
Cutting off many peoples,
And sin *against* your soul.
11 For the stone will cry out from the
    wall,
And the beam from the timbers will
    answer it.

12 "Woe to him who builds a town with
    bloodshed,
Who establishes a city by iniquity!
13 Behold, *is it* not of the LORD of hosts
That the peoples labor to feed the
    fire,[a]
And nations weary themselves in
    vain?
14 For the earth will be filled
With the knowledge of the glory of
    the LORD,
As the waters cover the sea.

15 "Woe to him who gives drink to his
    neighbor,
Pressing[a] *him to* your bottle,
Even to make *him* drunk,
That you may look on his nakedness!
16 You are filled with shame instead of
    glory.
You also—drink!
And be exposed as uncircumcised![a]
The cup of the LORD's right hand *will
    be* turned against you,
And utter shame will be on your glory.
17 For the violence *done to* Lebanon
    will cover you,
And the plunder of beasts *which*
    made them afraid,

2:5 [a]Or *Sheol* **2:6** [a]Syriac and Vulgate read *thick clay.*
2:7 [a]Literally *those who bite you* **2:13** [a]Literally *for
what satisfies fire,* that is, for what is of no lasting
value **2:15** [a]Literally *Attaching* or *Joining*
2:16 [a]Dead Sea Scrolls and Septuagint read *And
reel!;* Syriac and Vulgate read *And fall fast asleep!*

Because of men's blood
And the violence of the land *and* the
  city,
And of all who dwell in it.

18 "What profit is the image, that its
      maker should carve it,
  The molded image, a teacher of lies,
  That the maker of its mold should
    trust in it,
  To make mute idols?
19 Woe to him who says to wood,
    'Awake!'
  To silent stone, 'Arise! It shall teach!'
  Behold, it is overlaid with gold and
    silver,
  Yet in it there is no breath at all.

20 "But the LORD is in His holy temple.
  Let all the earth keep silence before
    Him."

The Prophet's Prayer

3 A prayer of Habakkuk the prophet, on
  Shigionoth.[a]

2   O LORD, I have heard Your speech
      and was afraid;
  O LORD, revive Your work in the
    midst of the years!
  In the midst of the years make *it*
    known;
  In wrath remember mercy.

3   God came from Teman,
  The Holy One from Mount Paran.
                                          Selah

  His glory covered the heavens,
  And the earth was full of His praise.
4 *His* brightness was like the light;
  He had rays *flashing* from His hand,
  And there His power *was* hidden.
5 Before Him went pestilence,
  And fever followed at His feet.

6 He stood and measured the earth;
  He looked and startled the nations.
  And the everlasting mountains were
    scattered,
  The perpetual hills bowed.
  His ways *are* everlasting.
7 I saw the tents of Cushan in
    affliction;

3:1 [a]Exact meaning unknown

BIBLICAL INSIGHTS • 3:17, 18

Worship God, Not Comfort

I DON'T KNOW ANYONE who enjoys suffering, but I do know many who have benefited from the growth that occurs through it. Are you worshiping God in the midst of your pain, or are you seeking comfort by trying to escape it? When suffering comes, move through the pain to the God who allowed it to come. We must learn the lesson taught by Habakkuk, "Though the fig tree may not blossom, nor fruit be on the vines; though the labor of the olive may fail, and the fields yield no food; though the flock may be cut off from the fold, and there be no herd in the stalls—yet I will rejoice in the LORD, I will joy in the God of my salvation" (3:17, 18).

Barbara and I have given thanks for short paychecks, for health issues, for misunderstandings and unmet expectations, for a teenage boy with muscular dystrophy, for the loss of friendships due to the call of God, the list goes on. Pain has pressed us against our Savior and reminded us that we are not in control.

We worship God through music, prayer, God's Word, and service to others in communion with our brothers and sisters in Christ. But we should also worship God even in the midst of suffering.

The real issue is whether you will respond with faith when you face a challenging season in your lives, marriage, and family. The prophet Habakkuk exhorts followers of Christ to live by faith. The Bible gives us many ways of exhibiting our faith: giving thanks in everything (1 Thess. 5:18), counting it as joy when we encounter trials (James 1:2), trusting that all things work together for good (Rom. 8:28). The apostle Paul instructs us in 2 Corinthians 5:7, "For we walk by faith, not by sight."

Will you walk by faith and teach your children to do the same?

The curtains of the land of Midian
    trembled.

8   O LORD, were *You* displeased with
      the rivers,
     Was Your anger against the rivers,
     Was Your wrath against the sea,
     That You rode on Your horses,
     Your chariots of salvation?
9   Your bow was made quite ready;
     Oaths were sworn over *Your* arrows.ᵃ
                        Selah

You divided the earth with rivers.
10   The mountains saw You *and*
      trembled;
     The overflowing of the water passed
      by.
     The deep uttered its voice,
     And lifted its hands on high.
11   The sun and moon stood still in their
      habitation;
     At the light of Your arrows they went,
     At the shining of Your glittering
      spear.

12   You marched through the land in
      indignation;
     You trampled the nations in anger.
13   You went forth for the salvation of
      Your people,
     For salvation with Your Anointed.
     You struck the head from the house
      of the wicked,
     By laying bare from foundation to
      neck.   Selah

**INTIMATE
MOMENTS**

Wash her car. Be sure to vacuum it, too.

14   You thrust through with his own
      arrows
     The head of his villages.
     They came out like a whirlwind to
      scatter me;
     Their rejoicing was like feasting on
      the poor in secret.
15   You walked through the sea with
      Your horses,
     Through the heap of great waters.

16   When I heard, my body trembled;
     My lips quivered at *the* voice;
     Rottenness entered my bones;
     And I trembled in myself,
     That I might rest in the day of
      trouble.
     When he comes up to the people,
     He will invade them with
      his troops.

A Hymn of Faith

17   Though the fig tree may not
      blossom,
     Nor fruit be on the vines;
     Though the labor of the olive may
      fail,
     And the fields yield no food;
     Though the flock may be cut off
      from the fold,
     And there be no herd in the stalls—
18   Yet I will rejoice in the LORD,
     I will joy in the God of my salvation.

19   The LORD Godᵃ is my strength;
     He will make my feet like deer's *feet,*
     And He will make me walk on my
      high hills.

To the Chief Musician. With my stringed
instruments.

3:9 ᵃLiterally *rods* or *tribes* (compare verse 14)
3:19 ᵃHebrew *YHWH Adonai*

ZEPHANIAH

THE PROPHET ZEPHANIAH was the great, great-grandson of King Hezekiah. His parents selected a name for their son that reflected their own confidence in God's care for His people. *Zephaniah* means "God hides" or "God protects." He was a contemporary of Jeremiah whose message, like that of the better-known prophet, also called for spiritual reform.

More than any other prophet, Zephaniah spoke about the coming "day of the LORD." He foresaw the divine judgment that would come on Judah if the nation did not turn from its idolatry and wickedness. He also looked ahead to the final "day of the LORD" when God promised to bring ultimate judgment upon the ungodly and restore His obedient people to a place of staggering blessing.

While much of this book centers on the phrase "the day of the LORD," Zephaniah's exhortation for his fellow Jews is found in 2:3, where the prophet says, "Seek the LORD, all you meek of the earth, who have upheld His justice. Seek righteousness, seek humility. It may be that you will be hidden in the day of the LORD's anger." That verse gives couples and families a great summary of how we can live in a way that honors the Lord.

Finally, it is interesting to note that Zephaniah ministered during a dark period of Judah's history when no written copies of the book of the Law were known to exist. So it was exclusively the prophets who spoke God's Word to the king, providing him with spiritual guidance. Zephaniah's royal blood may have gained him the ear of King Josiah of Judah, who likely was a teenager at the time. We can only speculate how the prophet's preaching may have influenced the young king to bring his aggressive spiritual reforms to Judah.

In a similar way, we may never fully understand the powerful influence our own words and lives can have on a younger generation. We may be the only Word of God these young people ever see! We must never forget or downplay the influence we have in the lives of our own children.

1 The word of the LORD which came to Zephaniah the son of Cushi, the son of Gedaliah, the son of Amariah, the son of Hezekiah, in the days of Josiah the son of Amon, king of Judah.

The Great Day of the LORD

2 "I will utterly consume everything
From the face of the land,"
Says the LORD;
3 "I will consume man and beast;
I will consume the birds of the
heavens,
The fish of the sea,
And the stumbling blocks[a] along
with the wicked.
I will cut off man from the face of
the land,"
Says the LORD.

4 "I will stretch out My hand against
Judah,
And against all the inhabitants of
Jerusalem.
I will cut off every trace of Baal
from this place,
The names of the idolatrous priests[a]
with the *pagan* priests—
5 Those who worship the host of
heaven on the housetops;
Those who worship and swear *oaths*
by the LORD,
But who *also* swear by Milcom;[a]
6 Those who have turned back from
following the LORD,
And have not sought the LORD, nor
inquired of Him."

7 Be silent in the presence of the Lord
GOD;
For the day of the LORD *is* at hand,
For the LORD has prepared a sacrifice;
He has invited[a] His guests.

8 "And it shall be,
In the day of the LORD's sacrifice,
That I will punish the princes and
the king's children,
And all such as are clothed with
foreign apparel.
9 In the same day I will punish
All those who leap over the
threshold,[a]
Who fill their masters' houses with
violence and deceit.

10 "And there shall be on that day," says
the LORD,
"The sound of a mournful cry from
the Fish Gate,
A wailing from the Second Quarter,
And a loud crashing from the hills.
11 Wail, you inhabitants of Maktesh![a]
For all the merchant people are cut
down;
All those who handle money are cut
off.

12 "And it shall come to pass at that
time
That I will search Jerusalem with
lamps,
And punish the men
Who are settled in complacency,[a]
Who say in their heart,
'The LORD will not do good,
Nor will He do evil.'
13 Therefore their goods shall become
booty,
And their houses a desolation;
They shall build houses, but not
inhabit *them;*
They shall plant vineyards, but not
drink their wine."

14 The great day of the LORD *is* near;
It is near and hastens quickly.
The noise of the day of the LORD is
bitter;
There the mighty men shall cry out.
15 That day *is* a day of wrath,
A day of trouble and distress,

**INTIMATE
MOMENTS**

Men are stimulated by sight—take a personal interest in your appearance.

1:3 [a]Figurative of idols **1:4** [a]Hebrew *chemarim*
1:5 [a]Or *Malcam,* an Ammonite god, also called
Molech (compare Leviticus 18:21) **1:7** [a]Literally *set
apart, consecrated* **1:9** [a]Compare 1 Samuel 5:5
1:11 [a]Literally *Mortar,* a market district of Jerusalem
1:12 [a]Literally *on their lees,* that is, settled like the
dregs of wine

A day of devastation and desolation,
A day of darkness and gloominess,
A day of clouds and thick darkness,
16 A day of trumpet and alarm
Against the fortified cities
And against the high towers.

17 "I will bring distress upon men,
And they shall walk like blind men,
Because they have sinned against the
LORD;
Their blood shall be poured out like
dust,
And their flesh like refuse."

18 Neither their silver nor their gold
Shall be able to deliver them
In the day of the LORD's wrath;
But the whole land shall be devoured
By the fire of His jealousy,
For He will make speedy riddance
Of all those who dwell in
the land.

A Call to Repentance

2 Gather yourselves together, yes,
gather together,
O undesirable[a] nation,
2 Before the decree is issued,
Or the day passes like chaff,

Before the LORD's fierce anger comes
upon you,
Before the day of the LORD's anger
comes upon you!
3 Seek the LORD, all you meek of the
earth,
Who have upheld His justice.
Seek righteousness, seek humility.
It may be that you will be hidden
In the day of the LORD's anger.

Judgment on Nations

4 For Gaza shall be forsaken,
And Ashkelon desolate;
They shall drive out Ashdod at
noonday,
And Ekron shall be uprooted.
5 Woe to the inhabitants of the seacoast,
The nation of the Cherethites!
The word of the LORD *is* against you,
O Canaan, land of the Philistines:
"I will destroy you;
So there shall be no inhabitant."

6 The seacoast shall be pastures,
With shelters[a] for shepherds and
folds for flocks.
7 The coast shall be for the remnant of
the house of Judah;
They shall feed *their* flocks there;
In the houses of Ashkelon they shall
lie down at evening.

2:1 [a]Or *shameless* 2:6 [a]Literally *excavations,* either
underground huts or cisterns

ROMANTIC QUOTES AND NOTES
The Danger of Complacency

Pastor and author Chuck Swindoll asks a great question, "Are there any termites in your troth?" In other words, is anything eating away at the foundation of your marriage? Have you done your best to make it divorce-proof?

One of those termites out to destroy your home could be complacency. How many ministers, missionaries, and laymen have fallen into affairs and divorce after allowing romantic complacency to settle into their marriages? God hates complacency. So He says through Zephaniah, "I will search Jerusalem with lamps, and punish the men who are settled in complacency" (1:12). First Corinthians 10:12 offers a formidable warning to the one who thinks this infestation of termites can't reach into his marriage, "Therefore let him who thinks he stands take heed lest he fall."

We need to resurrect the true meaning of commitment. In this age of *lite* beer, *lite* syrup, and *lite* salad dressing, it's no wonder we exhibit *lite* commitment, too. But for a Christian, commitment is a sacred vow to God. It's two people who hang in there during the best and worst of times and won't quit. It's a husband and wife who work through problems rather than walking out and enjoying the sweet bond of intimacy that comes as a result of persevering.

For the LORD their God will intervene
    for them,
And return their captives.

8   "I have heard the reproach of Moab,
    And the insults of the people of
       Ammon,
    With which they have reproached
       My people,
    And made arrogant threats against
       their borders.
9   Therefore, as I live,"
    Says the LORD of hosts, the God of
       Israel,
    "Surely Moab shall be like Sodom,
    And the people of Ammon like
       Gomorrah—
    Overrun with weeds and saltpits,
    And a perpetual desolation.
    The residue of My people shall
       plunder them,
    And the remnant of My people shall
       possess them."

10 This they shall have for their pride,
    Because they have reproached and
       made arrogant threats
    Against the people of the LORD of
       hosts.
11 The LORD *will be* awesome to them,
    For He will reduce to nothing all the
       gods of the earth;
    People shall worship Him,
    Each one from his place,
    Indeed all the shores of the nations.

12 "You Ethiopians also,
    You shall be slain by My sword."

13 And He will stretch out His hand
       against the north,
    Destroy Assyria,
    And make Nineveh a desolation,
    As dry as the wilderness.

14 The herds shall lie down in her midst,
    Every beast of the nation.
    Both the pelican and the bittern
    Shall lodge on the capitals *of* her
       pillars;
    Their voice shall sing in the
       windows;
    Desolation *shall be* at the threshold;
    For He will lay bare the cedar work.
15 This is the rejoicing city
    That dwelt securely,
    That said in her heart,
    "I *am it,* and *there is* none besides
       me."
    How has she become a desolation,
    A place for beasts to lie down!
    Everyone who passes by her
    Shall hiss and shake his fist.

The Wickedness of Jerusalem

3 Woe to her who is rebellious
    and polluted,
    To the oppressing city!
2 She has not obeyed *His* voice,
    She has not received correction;
    She has not trusted in the LORD,
    She has not drawn near to her God.

3 Her princes in her midst *are* roaring
       lions;
    Her judges *are* evening wolves
    That leave not a bone till morning.
4 Her prophets are insolent,
       treacherous people;
    Her priests have polluted the
       sanctuary,
    They have done violence to the law.
5 The LORD *is* righteous in her midst,
    He will do no unrighteousness.
    Every morning He brings His justice
       to light;
    He never fails,
    But the unjust knows no shame.

6 "I have cut off nations,
    Their fortresses are devastated;
    I have made their streets desolate,
    With none passing by.
    Their cities are destroyed;
    There is no one, no inhabitant.
7 I said, 'Surely you will fear Me,
    You will receive instruction'—
    So that her dwelling would not be cut
       off,

**INTIMATE
MOMENTS**

Take some time out of your busy schedule
to cook your wife a meal. Serve the meal
by candlelight using your wedding china.

Despite everything for which I
    punished her.
But they rose early and corrupted all
    their deeds.

A Faithful Remnant

8 "Therefore wait for Me," says the
    LORD,
    "Until the day I rise up for plunder;[a]
    My determination *is* to gather the
      nations
    To My assembly of kingdoms,
    To pour on them My indignation,
    All My fierce anger;
    All the earth shall be devoured
    With the fire of My jealousy.

9 "For then I will restore to the peoples
      a pure language,
    That they all may call on the name
      of the LORD,
    To serve Him with one accord.

10 From beyond the rivers of Ethiopia
    My worshipers,
    The daughter of My dispersed ones,
    Shall bring My offering.

11 In that day you shall not be shamed
      for any of your deeds
    In which you transgress against Me;
    For then I will take away from your
      midst
    Those who rejoice in your pride,
    And you shall no longer be haughty
    In My holy mountain.

12 I will leave in your midst
    A meek and humble people,
    And they shall trust in the name of
      the LORD.

13 The remnant of Israel shall do no
      unrighteousness
    And speak no lies,
    Nor shall a deceitful tongue be found
      in their mouth;
    For they shall feed *their* flocks and
      lie down,
    And no one shall make *them* afraid."

Joy in God's Faithfulness

14 Sing, O daughter of Zion!
    Shout, O Israel!

3:8 [a]Septuagint and Syriac read *for witness;* Targum
reads *for the day of My revelation for judgment;* Vulgate
reads *for the day of My resurrection that is to come.*

BIBLICAL INSIGHTS • 3:9
Call on the Lord

NO HUMAN RELATIONSHIP endures more hiding and hurling than marriage. Within this most intimate of human associations two people seek to know one another and be known. How tragic that many people marry to stop being lonely but soon find themselves lonelier than they were as singles.

We hide from one another by withdrawing and trying to hurt the other person with silence. And we hurl at one another when we use our words in hurtful ways that bring our spouses pain. Hiding and hurling don't create oneness; they give birth to isolation.

Perhaps 95 percent of all marriages suffer from isolation, and few people in marriage realize how desperately alone they really are. Often a husband and wife begin drifting apart so slowly that they hardly recognize the slide. Then, after a few years of hiding and poor communication, they realize their love has grown stale.

How do you avoid this drift to isolation?

I believe the most important thing you can do as a couple is to pray regularly together. When in the pure language of prayer you "call on the name of the LORD, to serve Him with one accord" (3:9), amazing things can happen. Barbara and I began this spiritual discipline shortly after we married in 1972, and it's done more for our marriage than any other spiritual discipline that we've practiced. Because of our commitment to end each day in prayer, there have been times when we have had to resolve our differences, build bridges of understanding, and forgive each other, so that we could pray together.

What are your tendencies when you've been hurt? To hide? To hurl? Why not replace the isolation that results from either with a time of praying together daily? I promise you that you will experience oneness on a whole new level.

Be glad and rejoice with all *your*
   heart,
O daughter of Jerusalem!
15 The LORD has taken away your
      judgments,
He has cast out your enemy.
The King of Israel, the LORD, *is* in
      your midst;
You shall see[a] disaster no more.

16 In that day it shall be said to
      Jerusalem:
 "Do not fear;
Zion, let not your hands be weak.
17 The LORD your God in your midst,
The Mighty One, will save;
He will rejoice over you with
      gladness,
He will quiet *you* with His love,
He will rejoice over you with
      singing."

18 "I will gather those who sorrow over
      the appointed assembly,

Who are among you,
To whom its reproach *is* a burden.
19 Behold, at that time
I will deal with all who afflict you;
I will save the lame,
And gather those who were driven
      out;
I will appoint them for praise and
      fame
In every land where they were put to
      shame.
20 At that time I will bring you back,
Even at the time I gather you;
For I will give you fame and praise
Among all the peoples of the earth,
When I return your captives before
      your eyes,"
Says the LORD.

3:15 [a]Some Hebrew manuscripts, Septuagint,
and Bomberg read *see;* Masoretic Text and Vulgate
read *fear.*

HAGGAI

MANY READERS THROUGHOUT HISTORY have wondered how the 38 verses that make up the little Book of Haggai have any relevance for God's people today. Stop for a moment and think: Have you ever heard any sermons preached from Haggai? Can you think of any Bible verses you know from Haggai? To many, the prophet's message about the rebuilding of the temple following the Babylonian captivity seems historically interesting but otherwise unimportant.

But if that's all you see when you read Haggai, you will miss how his message still informs and directs our lives today. For example, God worked powerfully through John Knox, the Scottish reformer, to bring renewal and revival to Scotland in the 1500's through a series of messages he preached based on the Book of Haggai.

Haggai's ministry lasted for five months in 520 BC. He and his contemporary, Zechariah, spoke to the same issues. Haggai did not focus on the themes addressed by many of the prophets who preceded him—injustice, idolatry, wickedness. Instead, he confronted the spiritual apathy of the people of Judah in their worship of God. The fact that the people lived in "paneled houses" while the temple lay in ruins (1:3) clearly revealed their misplaced priorities. Haggai saw the temple as the dwelling place of God, and the rebuilding of God's house reflected the prophet's desire for the Lord to dwell in the midst of His people.

He also looked ahead to the time when the Messiah, the "Desire of All Nations," would come to "fill this temple with glory" (2:7). And the "'glory of this latter temple shall be greater than the former,' says the LORD of hosts. 'And in this place I will give peace,' says the LORD of hosts" (2:9).

Haggai invites us to reexamine our spiritual priorities and to ask ourselves as families whether we are guided by a kingdom agenda or our own self-centered interests. Are we investing our time, our talents, and our treasure to serve God, or to serve ourselves? Keep *that* question in mind as you read the book of Haggai.

The Command to Build God's House

1 In the second year of King Darius, in the sixth month, on the first day of the month, the word of the LORD came by Haggai the prophet to Zerubbabel the son of Shealtiel, governor of Judah, and to Joshua the son of Jehozadak, the high priest, saying, ²"Thus speaks the LORD of hosts, saying: 'This people says, "The time has not come, the time that the LORD's house should be built."'"

³Then the word of the LORD came by Haggai the prophet, saying, ⁴"*Is it* time for you yourselves to dwell in your paneled houses, and this temple[a] *to lie* in ruins?" ⁵Now therefore, thus says the LORD of hosts: "Consider your ways!

6   "You have sown much, and bring in little;
    You eat, but do not have enough;
    You drink, but you are not filled with drink;
    You clothe yourselves, but no one is warm;
    And he who earns wages,
    Earns wages *to put* into a bag with holes."

INTIMATE MOMENTS

Tell your wife you'd like to start eating healthier so that you'll both be around to enjoy each other longer.

⁷Thus says the LORD of hosts: "Consider your ways! ⁸Go up to the mountains and bring wood and build the temple, that I may take pleasure in it and be glorified," says the LORD. ⁹"*You* looked for much, but indeed *it came to* little; and when you brought it home, I blew it away. Why?" says the LORD of hosts. "Because of My house that *is in* ruins, while every one of you runs to his own house. ¹⁰Therefore the heavens above you withhold the dew, and the earth withholds its fruit. ¹¹For I called

for a drought on the land and the mountains, on the grain and the new wine and the oil, on whatever the ground brings forth, on men and livestock, and on all the labor of *your* hands."

The People's Obedience

¹²Then Zerubbabel the son of Shealtiel, and Joshua the son of Jehozadak, the high priest, with all the remnant of the people, obeyed the voice of the LORD their God, and the words of Haggai the prophet, as the LORD their God had sent him; and the people feared the presence of the LORD. ¹³Then Haggai, the LORD's messenger, spoke the LORD's message to the people, saying, "I *am* with you, says the LORD." ¹⁴So the LORD stirred up the spirit of Zerubbabel the son of Shealtiel, governor of Judah, and the spirit of Joshua the son of Jehozadak, the high priest, and the spirit of all the remnant of the people; and they came and worked on the house of the LORD of hosts, their God, ¹⁵on the twenty-fourth day of the sixth month, in the second year of King Darius.

The Coming Glory of God's House

2 In the seventh *month,* on the twenty-first of the month, the word of the LORD came by Haggai the prophet, saying: ²"Speak now to Zerubbabel the son of Shealtiel, governor of Judah, and to Joshua the son of Jehozadak, the high priest, and to the remnant of the people, saying: ³'Who is left among you who saw this temple[a] in its former glory? And how do you see it now? In comparison with it, *is this* not in your eyes as nothing? ⁴Yet now be strong, Zerubbabel,' says the LORD; 'and be strong, Joshua, son of Jehozadak, the high priest; and be strong, all you people of the land,' says the LORD, 'and work; for I *am* with you,' says the LORD of hosts. ⁵'*According to* the word that I covenanted with you when you came out of Egypt, so My Spirit remains among you; do not fear!'

⁶"For thus says the LORD of hosts: 'Once more (it *is* a little while) I will shake heaven and earth, the sea and dry land; ⁷and I

1:4 ªLiterally *house,* and so in verse 8
2:3 ªLiterally *house,* and so in verses 7 and 9

will shake all nations, and they shall come to the Desire of All Nations,[a] and I will fill this temple with glory,' says the LORD of hosts. 8'The silver *is* Mine, and the gold *is* Mine,' says the LORD of hosts. 9'The glory of this latter temple shall be greater than the former,' says the LORD of hosts. 'And in this place I will give peace,' says the LORD of hosts."

The People Are Defiled

10On the twenty-fourth *day* of the ninth *month,* in the second year of Darius, the word of the LORD came by Haggai the prophet, saying, 11"Thus says the LORD of hosts: 'Now, ask the priests *concerning the law,* saying, 12"If one carries holy meat in the fold of his garment, and with the edge he touches bread or stew, wine or oil, or any food, will it become holy?"'"

Then the priests answered and said, "No."

13And Haggai said, "If *one who is* unclean *because* of a dead body touches any of these, will it be unclean?"

So the priests answered and said, "It shall be unclean."

14Then Haggai answered and said, " 'So is this people, and so is this nation before Me,' says the LORD, 'and so is every work of their hands; and what they offer there is unclean.

Promised Blessing

15'And now, carefully consider from this day forward: from before stone was laid

upon stone in the temple of the LORD— 16since those *days,* when *one* came to a heap of twenty ephahs, there were *but* ten; when *one* came to the wine vat to draw out fifty baths from the press, there were *but* twenty. 17I struck you with blight and mildew and hail in all the labors of your hands; yet you did not *turn* to Me,' says the LORD. 18'Consider now from this day forward, from the twenty-fourth day of the ninth month, from the day that the foundation of the LORD's temple was laid—consider it: 19Is the seed still in the barn? As yet the vine, the fig tree, the pomegranate, and the olive tree have not yielded *fruit. But* from this day I will bless *you.*' "

Zerubbabel Chosen as a Signet

20And again the word of the LORD came to Haggai on the twenty-fourth day of the month, saying, 21"Speak to Zerubbabel, governor of Judah, saying:

'I will shake heaven and earth.
22 I will overthrow the throne of
     kingdoms;
I will destroy the strength of the
     Gentile kingdoms.
I will overthrow the chariots
And those who ride in them;
The horses and their riders shall
     come down,
Every one by the sword of his
     brother.

23'In that day,' says the LORD of hosts, 'I will take you, Zerubbabel My servant, the son of Shealtiel,' says the LORD, 'and will make you like a signet *ring;* for I have chosen you,' says the LORD of hosts."

2:7 [a]Or *the desire of all nations*

ZECHARIAH

WHEN MANY PEOPLE HEAR THE WORD *REPENT*, they think of a wild-eyed preacher standing on a street corner with a sandwich board warning people that the world is coming to an end. But this term ought to have a regular place in our vocabulary as Christians.

To repent simply means to change your mind and so to alter how you live. It means you think and act differently than before. To repent means to *turn away* from sinful patterns and practices and to *turn to* God in order to live righteously in the power of the Holy Spirit. Repentance lies at the heart of Zechariah's message, which he brought to the people of Judah in the sixth century BC.

Zechariah appears to have come from a godly family. He mentions his grandfather, Iddo, and Nehemiah 12:4 and 16 identify a man by that name as a priest. If the two Iddos were the same man, then Zechariah also would have been a Levite, and so would join Jeremiah and Ezekiel in the dual role of prophet and priest.

Zechariah wrote the first eight chapters of his book in 520 BC, about the same time Haggai was calling Judah to rebuild the temple. Chapters 9—14 came much later, probably around 480–470 BC. His book is the longest of the twelve Minor Prophets, and the New Testament has more than seventy quotations from or allusions to the book.

The first six verses of Zechariah contain a powerful word from God for husbands and wives who did not grow up in Christian families. When we plant a stake in the ground and return to the Lord as a family, God promises that He will return to us (1:3). What a wonderful promise from a God who forgives and restores!

The book also suggests that Zechariah's father may have died when Zechariah was still young, and so the prophet may have stepped into his priestly and prophetic roles at an early age. We need to remember as we raise our own children that God can work powerfully in their lives while they are still young.

A Call to Repentance

1 In the eighth month of the second year of Darius, the word of the LORD came to Zechariah the son of Berechiah, the son of Iddo the prophet, saying, [2]"The LORD has been very angry with your fathers. [3]Therefore say to them, 'Thus says the LORD of hosts: "Return to Me," says the LORD of hosts, "and I will return to you," says the LORD of hosts. [4]"Do not be like your fathers, to whom the former prophets preached, saying, 'Thus says the LORD of hosts: "Turn now from your evil ways and your evil deeds."' But they did not hear nor heed Me," says the LORD.

[5]   "Your fathers, where *are* they?
     And the prophets, do they live
       forever?
[6]   Yet surely My words and My
       statutes,
     Which I commanded My servants
       the prophets,
     Did they not overtake your fathers?

  "So they returned and said:

    'Just as the LORD of hosts determined
      to do to us,
    According to our ways and
      according to our deeds,
    So He has dealt with us.'"'"

Vision of the Horses

[7]On the twenty-fourth day of the eleventh month, which is the month Shebat, in the second year of Darius, the word of the LORD came to Zechariah the son of Berechiah, the son of Iddo the prophet: [8]I saw by night, and behold, a man riding on a red horse, and it stood among the myrtle trees in the hollow; and behind him *were* horses: red, sorrel, and white. [9]Then I said, "My lord, what *are* these?" So the angel who talked with me said to me, "I will show you what they *are*."

[10]And the man who stood among the myrtle trees answered and said, "These *are the ones* whom the LORD has sent to walk to and fro throughout the earth."

[11]So they answered the Angel of the LORD, who stood among the myrtle trees, and said, "We have walked to and fro throughout the earth, and behold, all the earth is resting quietly."

The LORD Will Comfort Zion

[12]Then the Angel of the LORD answered and said, "O LORD of hosts, how long will You not have mercy on Jerusalem and on the cities of Judah, against which You were angry these seventy years?"

[13]And the LORD answered the angel who talked to me, *with* good *and* comforting words. [14]So the angel who spoke with me said to me, "Proclaim, saying, 'Thus says the LORD of hosts:

    "I am zealous for Jerusalem
      And for Zion with great zeal.
[15] I am exceedingly angry with the
      nations at ease;
    For I was a little angry,
    And they helped—*but* with evil
      intent."

[16]'Therefore thus says the LORD:

    "I am returning to Jerusalem with
      mercy;
    My house shall be built in it," says
      the LORD of hosts,

INTIMATE MOMENTS
The Eyes Have It

Husbands, listen to the observation of a single professional man from the Northeast who seldom has trouble finding a date, "When I am with a woman—whether I am talking to her, dancing with her, or eating with her, I make as much eye contact as possible. Not in a creepy way, but in a way that communicates, 'I am paying attention to you and am genuinely interested in being here with you.' Essentially, you want to convey that you have eyes only for her, no pun intended. Nothing makes a woman feel more insecure than a guy with whose eyes are darting around the room. I find women respond to this and really open up." A husband ought to do no less with his wife!

Is There a Minister in the House?

IS THERE A MINISTER AT YOUR HOUSE?

When I suggest to fathers that they are to be ministers to their families, they tend to shy away, thinking they have to be accomplished theologians who pray eloquently before meals. But that's not what being a family minister is all about. Maybe it would help to think of yourself as a "Joshua," "a brand plucked from the fire" and given "rich robes" by God almighty to allow you to minister as you should (3:2,4).

By being there and making your family a priority, you'll find plenty of opportunities to minister to your children by showing them what's really important. We need to learn how to take advantage of the teachable moments when our children are open to spiritual truth.

Years ago I was cuddled up having a conversation with my daughter Ashley on the lower bunk at bedtime. When her younger brother Benjamin heard us talking, he asked, "Dad, tomorrow would you tell me how to invite Jesus into my heart?" The next day, I had the privilege of leading him in a prayer as he made a profession of faith.

I couldn't know at that time whether Benjamin had made a true, life-changing commitment to Christ. But the fact was that when he was interested, I was there to be a minister in our house.

> "And a *surveyor's* line shall be
> stretched out over Jerusalem." '

17"Again proclaim, saying, 'Thus says the Lord of hosts:

> "My cities shall again spread out
> through prosperity;
> The Lord will again comfort Zion,
> And will again choose Jerusalem." ' "

Vision of the Horns

18Then I raised my eyes and looked, and there *were* four horns. 19And I said to the angel who talked with me, "What *are* these?"

So he answered me, "These *are* the horns that have scattered Judah, Israel, and Jerusalem."

20Then the Lord showed me four craftsmen. 21And I said, "What are these coming to do?"

So he said, "These *are* the horns that scattered Judah, so that no one could lift up his head; but the craftsmenᵃ are coming to terrify them, to cast out the horns of the nations that lifted up *their* horn against the land of Judah to scatter it."

Vision of the Measuring Line

2 Then I raised my eyes and looked, and behold, a man with a measuring line in his hand. 2So I said, "Where are you going?"

And he said to me, "To measure Jerusalem, to see what *is* its width and what *is* its length."

3And there *was* the angel who talked with me, going out; and another angel was coming out to meet him, 4who said to him, "Run, speak to this young man, saying: 'Jerusalem shall be inhabited *as* towns without walls, because of the multitude of men and livestock in it. 5For I,' says the Lord, 'will be a wall of fire all around her, and I will be the glory in her midst.' "

Future Joy of Zion and Many Nations

6"Up, up! Flee from the land of the north," says the Lord; "for I have spread you abroad like the four winds of heaven," says the Lord. 7"Up, Zion! Escape, you who dwell with the daughter of Babylon."

8For thus says the Lord of hosts: "He sent Me after glory, to the nations which plunder you; for he who touches you touches the apple of His eye. 9For surely I will shake My hand against them, and they shall become spoil for their servants. Then you will know that the Lord of hosts has sent Me.

10"Sing and rejoice, O daughter of Zion! For behold, I am coming and I will dwell in your midst," says the Lord. 11"Many nations shall be joined to the Lord in that day, and they shall become My people. And

---

1:21 ªLiterally *these*

I will dwell in your midst. Then you will know that the LORD of hosts has sent Me to you. ¹²And the LORD will take possession of Judah as His inheritance in the Holy Land, and will again choose Jerusalem. ¹³Be silent, all flesh, before the LORD, for He is aroused from His holy habitation!"

Vision of the High Priest

3 Then he showed me Joshua the high priest standing before the Angel of the LORD, and Satan standing at his right hand to oppose him. ²And the LORD said to Satan, "The LORD rebuke you, Satan! The LORD who has chosen Jerusalem rebuke you! *Is* this not a brand plucked from the fire?"

³Now Joshua was clothed with filthy garments, and was standing before the Angel. ⁴Then He answered and spoke to those who stood before Him, saying, "Take away the filthy garments from him." And to him He said, "See, I have removed your iniquity from you, and I will clothe you with rich robes."

⁵And I said, "Let them put a clean turban on his head."

So they put a clean turban on his head, and they put the clothes on him. And the Angel of the LORD stood by.

The Coming Branch

⁶Then the Angel of the LORD admonished Joshua, saying, ⁷"Thus says the LORD of hosts:

'If you will walk in My ways,
And if you will keep My command,
Then you shall also judge My house,
And likewise have charge of My
     courts;
I will give you places to walk
Among these who stand here.

8   'Hear, O Joshua, the high priest,
You and your companions who sit
     before you,
For they are a wondrous sign;
For behold, I am bringing forth My
     Servant the BRANCH.
9   For behold, the stone
That I have laid before Joshua:

Upon the stone *are* seven eyes.
Behold, I will engrave its inscription,'
Says the LORD of hosts,
'And I will remove the iniquity of
     that land in one day.
10 In that day,' says the LORD of hosts,
'Everyone will invite his neighbor
Under his vine and under his fig tree.'"

Vision of the Lampstand and Olive Trees

4 Now the angel who talked with me came back and wakened me, as a man who is wakened out of his sleep. ²And he said to me, "What do you see?"

So I said, "I am looking, and there *is* a lampstand of solid gold with a bowl on top of it, and on the *stand* seven lamps with seven pipes to the seven lamps. ³Two olive trees *are* by it, one at the right of the bowl and the other at its left." ⁴So I answered and spoke to the angel who talked with me, saying, "What *are* these, my lord?"

⁵Then the angel who talked with me answered and said to me, "Do you not know what these are?"

And I said, "No, my lord."

⁶So he answered and said to me:

"This *is* the word of the LORD to
     Zerubbabel:
'Not by might nor by power, but by
     My Spirit,'
Says the LORD of hosts.
7   'Who *are* you, O great mountain?
Before Zerubbabel *you shall become* a
     plain!
And he shall bring forth the
     capstone
With shouts of "Grace, grace to it!"'"

⁸Moreover the word of the LORD came to me, saying:

9   "The hands of Zerubbabel
Have laid the foundation of this
     temple;ᵃ
His hands shall also finish *it*.
Then you will know
That the LORD of hosts has sent Me
     to you.
10 For who has despised the day of
     small things?
For these seven rejoice to see

4:9 ᵃLiterally *house*

The plumb line in the hand of
  Zerubbabel.
They are the eyes of the LORD,
Which scan to and fro throughout
  the whole earth."

¹¹Then I answered and said to him, "What *are* these two olive trees—at the right of the lampstand and at its left?" ¹²And I further answered and said to him, "What *are these* two olive branches that *drip* into the receptaclesᵃ of the two gold pipes from which the golden *oil* drains?"

¹³Then he answered me and said, "Do you not know what these *are?*"

And I said, "No, my lord."

¹⁴So he said, "These *are* the two anointed ones, who stand beside the Lord of the whole earth."

ROMANCE FAQ

Q: How can we best build a strong marriage?

Genesis 2:24 presents four guidelines for building a strong and godly marriage. These are not multiple choice; all four are required for success.

1. *Leave.* That is, establish independence from your childhood home. It's amazing how many people fail to do this. They may look very adult and act very sophisticated, but really, they've never cut the apron strings. Counselor Dr. Dan Allender says that 90 percent of all marriage problems can be traced back to a failure to leave father and mother.

2. *Cleave.* That is, form a permanent bond with your mate. When God joins two people together, it is for keeps. "'Til death do us part" is more than a cliché; it's a vow we make that expresses our covenant commitment to each other.

3. *Be physically intimate.* That is, become one flesh in sexual intercourse. Physical intimacy comes *after* the walls of commitment have totally surrounded and secured the relationship.

4. *Become transparent.* That is, work toward the kind of emotional intimacy in which you and your mate can be totally open and unashamed with each other. Marriage becomes a true joy when you feel bathed in the warmth of knowing that another person totally accepts you.

Evaluate and grade yourselves as a couple on the four components of building a marriage. Where are you winning? Where do you need to work? Then pray that God would give you success as a couple in each of these four areas of your relationship.

Vision of the Flying Scroll

5 Then I turned and raised my eyes, and saw there a flying scroll.

²And he said to me, "What do you see?"

So I answered, "I see a flying scroll. Its length *is* twenty cubits and its width ten cubits."

³Then he said to me, "This *is* the curse that goes out over the face of the whole earth: 'Every thief shall be expelled,' according *to* this side of *the scroll;* and, 'Every perjurer shall be expelled,' according *to* that side of it."

⁴   "I will send out *the curse,*" says the
          LORD of hosts;
    "It shall enter the house of the thief
    And the house of the one who
          swears falsely by My name.
    It shall remain in the midst of his
          house
    And consume it, with its timber and
          stones."

Vision of the Woman in a Basket

⁵Then the angel who talked with me came out and said to me, "Lift your eyes now, and see what this *is* that goes forth."

⁶So I asked, "What *is* it?" And he said, "It *is* a basketᵃ that is going forth."

He also said, "This *is* their resemblance throughout the earth: ⁷Here *is* a lead disc lifted up, and this *is* a woman sitting inside the basket"; ⁸then he said, "This *is* Wickedness!" And he thrust her down into the basket, and threw the lead coverᵃ over its mouth. ⁹Then I raised my eyes and looked, and there *were* two women, coming with the

4:12 ᵃLiterally *into the hands of* **5:6** ᵃHebrew *ephah,* a measuring container, and so elsewhere **5:8** ᵃLiterally *stone*

wind in their wings; for they had wings like the wings of a stork, and they lifted up the basket between earth and heaven.

¹⁰So I said to the angel who talked with me, "Where are they carrying the basket?"

¹¹And he said to me, "To build a house for it in the land of Shinar;ᵃ when it is ready, *the basket* will be set there on its base."

Vision of the Four Chariots

6 Then I turned and raised my eyes and looked, and behold, four chariots *were* coming from between two mountains, and the mountains *were* mountains of bronze. ²With the first chariot *were* red horses, with the second chariot black horses, ³with the third chariot white horses, and with the fourth chariot dappled horses—strong *steeds*. ⁴Then I answered and said to the angel who talked with me, "What *are* these, my lord?"

5:11 ᵃThat is, Babylon

⁵And the angel answered and said to me, "These *are* four spirits of heaven, who go out from *their* station before the Lord of all the earth. ⁶The one with the black horses is going to the north country, the white are going after them, and the dappled are going toward the south country." ⁷Then the strong *steeds* went out, eager to go, that they might walk to and fro throughout the earth. And He said, "Go, walk to and fro throughout the earth." So they walked to and fro throughout the earth. ⁸And He called to me, and spoke to me, saying, "See, those who go toward the north country have given rest to My Spirit in the north country."

The Command to Crown Joshua

⁹Then the word of the LORD came to me, saying: ¹⁰"Receive *the gift* from the captives—from Heldai, Tobijah, and Jedaiah, who have come from Babylon—and go the same day and enter the house of Josiah the

---

| PARENTING MATTERS | **Q: How can we be encouraged as parents during times of discouragement?** |

One day the devil held a public auction. As prospective buyers assembled, they noticed Satan selling his tools of worry, fear, lust, greed, and selfishness. But off to one side, standing all alone, was one well-worn tool labeled, "Not for sale."

"I can spare my other tools," Satan explained, "but this is the most useful implement that I have. With it I can work my way deep into hearts otherwise inaccessible. It is the tool of discouragement."

What tools do we need to overcome discouragement?

First, *truthfulness*. God is not fooled by our lofty prayers for the missionaries in Africa when deep inside we're hurting. Be honest with yourself and God about your disappointment.

Second, *pray about it*. Are you discouraged about a child who rarely reaches your expectations? You need to turn to the Lord, asking Him for wisdom as a parent and asking Him to do a spiritual work in your child's life.

Third, *find the source of your discouragement*. Sometimes it's a goal not attained, yet again. Or the problem may be a child's cutting remark. Or you feel alone. Identifying the source can help you address root issues instead of symptoms.

Fourth, with a heart of faith, *look beyond your circumstances and your emotions to a God who will renew you, day by day*. Equip your child to live by faith by training him with the truth about who God is and what His purposes are.

Remember: God uses hardship to perfect your faith (see Rom. 5:1–10). If you're discouraged, remember that it is the enemy of your soul who wants you to be disheartened and defeated.

son of Zephaniah. [11]Take the silver and gold, make an elaborate crown, and set *it* on the head of Joshua the son of Jehozadak, the high priest. [12]Then speak to him, saying, 'Thus says the LORD of hosts, saying:

> "Behold, the Man whose name *is* the
> 　BRANCH!
> From His place He shall branch out,
> And He shall build the temple of the
> 　LORD;
[13]> Yes, He shall build the temple of the
> 　LORD.
> He shall bear the glory,
> And shall sit and rule on His throne;
> So He shall be a priest on His throne,
> And the counsel of peace shall be
> 　between them both."'

[14]"Now the elaborate crown shall be for a memorial in the temple of the LORD for Helem,[a] Tobijah, Jedaiah, and Hen the son of Zephaniah. [15]Even those from afar shall come and build the temple of the LORD. Then you shall know that the LORD of hosts has sent Me to you. And *this* shall come to pass if you diligently obey the voice of the LORD your God."

Obedience Better than Fasting

7 Now in the fourth year of King Darius it came to pass *that* the word of the LORD came to Zechariah, on the fourth *day* of the ninth month, Chislev, [2]when *the people*[a] sent Sherezer,[b] with Regem-Melech and his men, *to* the house of God,[c] to pray before the LORD, [3]*and* to ask the priests who *were* in the house of the LORD of hosts, and the prophets, saying, "Should I weep in the fifth month and fast as I have done for so many years?"

[4]Then the word of the LORD of hosts came to me, saying, [5]"Say to all the people of the land, and to the priests: 'When you fasted and mourned in the fifth and seventh *months* during those seventy years, did you really fast for Me—for Me? [6]When you eat and when you drink, do you not eat and drink *for yourselves?* [7]*Should you* not *have obeyed* the words which the LORD proclaimed through the former prophets when Jerusalem and the cities around it were inhabited and prosperous, and the South[a] and the Lowland were inhabited?'"

Disobedience Resulted in Captivity

[8]Then the word of the LORD came to Zechariah, saying, [9]"Thus says the LORD of hosts:

> 'Execute true justice,
> Show mercy and compassion
> Everyone to his brother.
[10]> Do not oppress the widow or the
> 　fatherless,
> The alien or the poor.
> Let none of you plan evil in his heart
> Against his brother.'

[11]But they refused to heed, shrugged their shoulders, and stopped their ears so that they could not hear. [12]Yes, they made their hearts like flint, refusing to hear the law and the words which the LORD of hosts had sent by His Spirit through the former prophets. Thus great wrath came from the LORD of hosts. [13]Therefore it happened, *that* just as He proclaimed and they would not hear, so they called out and I would not listen," says the LORD of hosts. [14]"But I scattered them with a whirlwind among all the nations which they had not known. Thus the land became desolate after them, so that no one passed through or returned; for they made the pleasant land desolate."

Jerusalem, Holy City of the Future

8 Again the word of the LORD of hosts came, saying, [2]"Thus says the LORD of hosts:

> 'I am zealous for Zion with great zeal;
> With great fervor I am zealous for
> 　her.'

[3]"Thus says the LORD:

> 'I will return to Zion,
> And dwell in the midst of Jerusalem.
> Jerusalem shall be called the City of
> 　Truth,
> The Mountain of the LORD of hosts,
> The Holy Mountain.'

[4]"Thus says the LORD of hosts:

6:14 [a]Following Masoretic Text, Targum, and Vulgate; Syriac reads *for Heldai* (compare verse 10); Septuagint reads *for the patient ones.* **7:2** [a]Literally *they* (compare verse 5) [b]Or *Sar-Ezer* [c]Hebrew *Bethel* **7:7** [a]Hebrew *Negev*

'Old men and old women shall again
    sit
In the streets of Jerusalem,
Each one with his staff in
    his hand
Because of great age.
5 The streets of the city
Shall be full of boys and girls
Playing in its streets.'

6 "Thus says the LORD of hosts:

'If it is marvelous in the eyes of the
    remnant of this people in these
    days,
Will it also be marvelous in My
    eyes?'
Says the LORD of hosts.

7 "Thus says the LORD of hosts:

'Behold, I will save My people from
    the land of the east
And from the land of the west;
8 I will bring them *back,*
And they shall dwell in the midst of
    Jerusalem.
They shall be My people
And I will be their God,
In truth and righteousness.'

9 "Thus says the LORD of hosts:

'Let your hands be strong,
You who have been hearing in these
    days
These words by the mouth of the
    prophets,
Who *spoke* in the day the foundation
    was laid
For the house of the LORD of
    hosts,
That the temple might be built.
10 For before these days
There were no wages for man nor
    any hire for beast;
There was no peace from the enemy
    for whoever went out or came in;
For I set all men, everyone, against
    his neighbor.

11 But now I *will* not *treat* the remnant of
this people as in the former days,' says the
LORD of hosts.

12 'For the seed *shall be* prosperous,
The vine shall give its fruit,

BIBLICAL INSIGHTS · 8:16
A Guide in the War Zone

ON TOP OF ALL THE CHALLENGES of parenting, there's something far more sinister taking place: We're in a spiritual war. The paths we walk, and the trails our children must walk, are dangerous, littered with traps set by a spiritual enemy that we can't see, an enemy who wants to destroy the souls of our children before they become adults.

Here's how Zechariah saw the situation centuries ago, "For the idols speak delusion; the diviners envision lies, and tell false dreams; they comfort in vain. Therefore the people wend their way like sheep; they are in trouble because there is no shepherd" (10:2).

You are the shepherd your children need. In the years while your child is at home, you can help him successfully navigate the war zone. Often you'll need to go first, showing step by step the way around Satan's deadly snares. Attempting to be God's shepherd is hard work, with long hours and no guarantees. But there are plenty of rewards!

Nothing can compare to the joy of seeing a child grow up to walk in the truth. Nothing is as exhilarating as watching your children bravely walk through the war zone, advancing the banner of Jesus Christ.

The ground shall give her increase,
And the heavens shall give their
    dew—
I will cause the remnant of this
    people
To possess all these.
13 And it shall come to pass
That just as you were a curse among
    the nations,
O house of Judah and house of Israel,
So I will save you, and you shall be a
    blessing.
Do not fear,
Let your hands be strong.'

14"For thus says the LORD of hosts:

'Just as I determined to punish you
When your fathers provoked Me to
    wrath,'
Says the LORD of hosts,
'And I would not relent,
15 So again in these days
    I am determined to do good
    To Jerusalem and to the house of
        Judah.
    Do not fear.
16 These *are* the things you shall do:
    Speak each man the truth to his
        neighbor;
    Give judgment in your gates for
        truth, justice, and peace;
17 Let none of you think evil in your[a]
        heart against your neighbor;
    And do not love a false oath.
    For all these *are things* that I hate,'
    Says the LORD."

18Then the word of the LORD of hosts
came to me, saying, 19"Thus says the LORD
of hosts:

'The fast of the fourth *month,*
The fast of the fifth,
The fast of the seventh,
And the fast of the tenth,
Shall be joy and gladness and
    cheerful feasts
For the house of Judah.
Therefore love truth and peace.'

20"Thus says the LORD of hosts:

'Peoples shall yet come,
Inhabitants of many cities;
21 The inhabitants of one *city* shall go
        to another, saying,
    "Let us continue to go and pray before
        the LORD,
    And seek the LORD of hosts.
    I myself will go also."
22 Yes, many peoples and strong nations
    Shall come to seek the LORD of hosts
        in Jerusalem,
    And to pray before the LORD.'

23"Thus says the LORD of hosts: 'In
those days ten men from every language of
the nations shall grasp the sleeve of a
Jewish man, saying, "Let us go with you,
for we have heard *that* God *is* with you."'"

Israel Defended Against Enemies

9 The burden[a] of the word of the LORD
    Against the land of Hadrach,
    And Damascus its resting place
    (For the eyes of men
    And all the tribes of Israel
    Are on the LORD);
2   Also *against* Hamath, *which* borders
        on it,
    And *against* Tyre and Sidon, though
        they are very wise.

3   For Tyre built herself a tower,
    Heaped up silver like the dust,
    And gold like the mire of the streets.
4   Behold, the Lord will cast her out;
    He will destroy her power in the sea,
    And she will be devoured by fire.

5   Ashkelon shall see *it* and fear;
    Gaza also shall be very sorrowful;
    And Ekron, for He dried up her
        expectation.
    The king shall perish from Gaza,
    And Ashkelon shall not be inhabited.

6   "A mixed race shall settle in Ashdod,
    And I will cut off the pride of the
        Philistines.
7   I will take away the blood from his
        mouth,
    And the abominations from between
        his teeth.
    But he who remains, even he *shall be*
        for our God,
    And shall be like a leader in Judah,
    And Ekron like a Jebusite.
8   I will camp around My house
    Because of the army,
    Because of him who passes by and
        him who returns.
    No more shall an oppressor pass
        through them,
    For now I have seen with My eyes.

The Coming King

9   "Rejoice greatly, O daughter of Zion!
    Shout, O daughter of Jerusalem!
    Behold, your King is coming to you;
    He *is* just and having salvation,
    Lowly and riding on a donkey,
    A colt, the foal of a donkey.

8:17 [a]Literally *his* 9:1 [a]Or *oracle*

10 I will cut off the chariot from
Ephraim
And the horse from Jerusalem;
The battle bow shall be cut off.
He shall speak peace to the nations;
His dominion *shall be* 'from sea to
sea,
And from the River to the ends of
the earth.'ᵃ

God Will Save His People

11 "As for you also,
Because of the blood of your
covenant,
I will set your prisoners free from the
waterless pit.
12 Return to the stronghold,
You prisoners of hope.
Even today I declare
That I will restore double to you.
13 For I have bent Judah, My *bow,*
Fitted the bow with Ephraim,
And raised up your sons, O Zion,
Against your sons, O Greece,
And made you like the sword of a
mighty man."

14 Then the LORD will be seen over
them,
And His arrow will go forth like
lightning.
The Lord GOD will blow the trumpet,
And go with whirlwinds from the
south.
15 The LORD of hosts will defend them;
They shall devour and subdue with
slingstones.
They shall drink *and* roar as if with
wine;
They shall be filled *with blood* like
basins,
Like the corners of the altar.
16 The LORD their God will save them in
that day,
As the flock of His people.
For they *shall be like* the jewels of a
crown,
Lifted like a banner over His land—
17 For how great is itsᵃ goodness
And how great itsᵇ beauty!

Grain shall make the young men
thrive,
And new wine the young women.

Restoration of Judah and Israel

10 Ask the LORD for rain
In the time of the latter rain.ᵃ
The LORD will make flashing clouds;
He will give them showers of rain,
Grass in the field for everyone.

2 For the idolsᵃ speak delusion;
The diviners envision lies,
And tell false dreams;
They comfort in vain.
Therefore *the people* wend their way
like sheep;
They are in trouble because *there is*
no shepherd.

3 "My anger is kindled against the
shepherds,
And I will punish the goatherds.
For the LORD of hosts will visit His
flock,
The house of Judah,
And will make them as His royal
horse in the battle.
4 From him comes the cornerstone,
From him the tent peg,
From him the battle bow,
From him every rulerᵃ together.
5 They shall be like mighty men,
Who tread down *their enemies*
In the mire of the streets in the
battle.
They shall fight because the LORD is
with them,
And the riders on horses shall be put
to shame.

6 "I will strengthen the house
of Judah,
And I will save the house of Joseph.
I will bring them back,
Because I have mercy on them.
They shall be as though I had not
cast them aside;
For I *am* the LORD their God,
And I will hear them.
7 *Those of* Ephraim shall be like a
mighty man,
And their heart shall rejoice as if
with wine.

9:10 ᵃPsalm 72:8 9:17 ᵃOr *His* ᵇOr *His*
10:1 ᵃThat is, spring rain 10:2 ᵃHebrew *teraphim*
10:4 ᵃOr *despot*

Yes, their children shall see *it* and be
glad;
Their heart shall rejoice in
the LORD.

8   I will whistle for them and gather
them,
For I will redeem them;
And they shall increase as they once
increased.

9   "I will sow them among the peoples,
And they shall remember Me in far
countries;
They shall live, together with their
children,
And they shall return.

10   I will also bring them back from the
land of Egypt,
And gather them from Assyria.
I will bring them into the land of
Gilead and Lebanon,
Until no *more room* is found for
them.

11   He shall pass through the sea with
affliction,
And strike the waves of the sea:
All the depths of the River[a] shall dry
up.
Then the pride of Assyria shall be
brought down,
And the scepter of Egypt shall
depart.

12   "So I will strengthen them in the
LORD,
And they shall walk up and down in
His name,"
Says the LORD.

Desolation of Israel

11 Open your doors, O Lebanon,
That fire may devour your cedars.
2   Wail, O cypress, for the cedar has
fallen,
Because the mighty *trees* are ruined.
Wail, O oaks of Bashan,
For the thick forest has come down.
3   *There is* the sound of wailing
shepherds!
For their glory is in ruins.
There is the sound of roaring lions!
For the pride[a] of the Jordan is in
ruins.

Prophecy of the Shepherds

4Thus says the LORD my God, "Feed the
flock for slaughter, 5whose owners slaughter them and feel no guilt; those who sell them say, 'Blessed be the LORD, for I am rich'; and their shepherds do not pity them. 6For I will no longer pity the inhabitants of the land," says the LORD. "But indeed I will give everyone into his neighbor's hand and into the hand of his king. They shall attack the land, and I will not deliver *them* from their hand."

7So I fed the flock for slaughter, in particular the poor of the flock.[a] I took for myself two staffs: the one I called Beauty,[b] and the other I called Bonds;[c] and I fed the flock. 8I dismissed the three shepherds in one month. My soul loathed them, and their soul also abhorred me. 9Then I said, "I will not feed you. Let what is dying die, and what is perishing perish. Let those that are left eat each other's flesh." 10And I took my staff, Beauty, and cut it in two, that I might break the covenant which I had made with all the peoples. 11So it was broken on that day. Thus the poor[a] of the flock, who were watching me, knew that it *was* the word of the LORD. 12Then I said to them, "If it is agreeable to you, give *me* my wages; and if not, refrain." So they weighed out for my wages thirty *pieces* of silver.

13And the LORD said to me, "Throw it to the potter"—that princely price they set on me. So I took the thirty *pieces* of silver and threw them into the house of the LORD for the potter. 14Then I cut in two my other staff, Bonds, that I might break the brotherhood between Judah and Israel.

15And the LORD said to me, "Next, take for yourself the implements of a foolish shepherd. 16For indeed I will raise up a shepherd in the land *who* will not care for those who are cut off, nor seek the young, nor heal those that are broken, nor feed those that still stand. But he will eat the flesh of the fat and tear their hooves in pieces.

10:11 [a]That is, the Nile 11:3 [a]Or *floodplain, thicket*
11:7 [a]Following Masoretic Text, Targum, and
Vulgate; Septuagint reads *for the Canaanites*. [b]Or
Grace, and so in verse 10 [c]Or *Unity,* and so in verse 14
11:11 [a]Following Masoretic Text, Targum, and
Vulgate; Septuagint reads *the Canaanites.*

[17] "Woe to the worthless shepherd,
   Who leaves the flock!
A sword *shall be* against his arm
And against his right eye;
   His arm shall completely wither,
   And his right eye shall be totally
      blinded."

The Coming Deliverance of Judah

12 The burden[a] of the word of the LORD against Israel. Thus says the LORD, who stretches out the heavens, lays the foundation of the earth, and forms the spirit of man within him: [2]"Behold, I will make Jerusalem a cup of drunkenness to all the surrounding peoples, when they lay siege against Judah and Jerusalem. [3]And it shall happen in that day that I will make Jerusalem a very heavy stone for all peoples; all who would heave it away will surely be cut in pieces, though all nations of the earth are gathered against it. [4]In that day," says the LORD, "I will strike every horse with confusion, and its rider with madness; I will open My eyes on the house of Judah, and will strike every horse of the peoples with blindness. [5]And the governors of Judah shall say in their heart, 'The inhabitants of Jerusalem *are* my strength in the LORD of hosts, their God.' [6]In that day I will make the governors of Judah like a firepan in the woodpile, and like a fiery torch in the sheaves; they shall devour all the surrounding peoples on the right hand and on the left, but Jerusalem shall be inhabited again in her own place—Jerusalem.

[7]"The LORD will save the tents of Judah first, so that the glory of the house of David and the glory of the inhabitants of Jerusalem shall not become greater than that of Judah. [8]In that day the LORD will defend the inhabitants of Jerusalem; the one who is feeble among them in that day shall be like David, and the house of David *shall be* like God, like the Angel of the LORD before them. [9]It shall be in that day *that* I will seek to destroy all the nations that come against Jerusalem.

Mourning for the Pierced One

[10]"And I will pour on the house of David and on the inhabitants of Jerusalem the Spirit of grace and supplication; then they will look on Me whom they pierced. Yes, they will mourn for Him as one mourns for *his* only *son,* and grieve for Him as one grieves for a firstborn. [11]In that day there shall be a great mourning in Jerusalem, like the mourning at Hadad Rimmon in the plain of Megiddo.[a] [12]And the land shall mourn, every family by itself: the family of the house of David by itself, and their wives by themselves; the family of the house of Nathan by itself, and their wives by themselves; [13]the family of the house of Levi by itself, and their wives by themselves; the family of Shimei by itself, and their wives by themselves; [14]all the families that remain, every family by itself, and their wives by themselves.

Idolatry Cut Off

13 "In that day a fountain shall be opened for the house of David and for the inhabitants of Jerusalem, for sin and for uncleanness.

[2]"It shall be in that day," says the LORD of hosts, "*that* I will cut off the names of the idols from the land, and they shall no longer be remembered. I will also cause the prophets and the unclean spirit to depart from the land. [3]It shall come to pass *that* if anyone still prophesies, then his father and mother who begot him will say to him, 'You shall not live, because you have spoken lies in the name of the LORD.' And his father and mother who begot him shall thrust him through when he prophesies.

[4]"And it shall be in that day *that* every prophet will be ashamed of his vision when he prophesies; they will not wear a robe of coarse hair to deceive. [5]But he will say, 'I *am* no prophet, I *am* a farmer; for a man taught me to keep cattle from my youth.' [6]And *one* will say to him, 'What are these wounds between your arms?'[a] Then he will answer, '*Those* with which I was wounded in the house of my friends.'

The Shepherd Savior

[7]   "Awake, O sword, against My
         Shepherd,

12:1 [a]Or *oracle*   12:11 [a]Hebrew *Megiddon*
13:6 [a]Or *hands*

Against the Man who is My
    Companion,"
Says the LORD of hosts.
"Strike the Shepherd,
    And the sheep will be scattered;
    Then I will turn My hand against the
        little ones.
8   And it shall come to pass in all the
        land,"
    Says the LORD,
    "*That* two-thirds in it shall be cut off
        and die,
    But *one*-third shall be left in it:
9   I will bring the *one*-third through the
        fire,
    Will refine them as silver is refined,
    And test them as gold is tested.
    They will call on My name,
    And I will answer them.
    I will say, 'This *is* My people';
    And each one will say, 'The LORD *is*
        my God.'"

The Day of the LORD

14 Behold, the day of the LORD is
        coming,
    And your spoil will be divided in
        your midst.
2   For I will gather all the nations to
        battle against Jerusalem;
    The city shall be taken,

The houses rifled,
And the women ravished.
Half of the city shall go into
    captivity,
But the remnant of the people shall
    not be cut off from the city.

3   Then the LORD will go forth
    And fight against those nations,
    As He fights in the day of battle.
4   And in that day His feet will stand
        on the Mount of Olives,
    Which faces Jerusalem on the east.
    And the Mount of Olives shall be
        split in two,
    From east to west,
    Making a very large valley;
    Half of the mountain shall move
        toward the north
    And half of it toward the south.

5   Then you shall flee *through* My
        mountain valley,
    For the mountain valley shall reach
        to Azal.
    Yes, you shall flee
    As you fled from the earthquake
    In the days of Uzziah king
        of Judah.

14:5 ªOr *you;* Septuagint, Targum, and Vulgate
read *Him.*

ROMANTIC QUOTES AND NOTES
The Leader Serves

Some men have a difficult time understanding that biblical leadership in the home begins with a man cultivating a servant's heart. Even though Jesus was Lord, He said, "The Son of Man did not come to be served, but to serve" (Matt. 20:28).

God calls us as husbands to lead our homes, but part of our leadership consists of serving our wives. So, as your wife's servant, can you name:

• Her top three needs?
• What worries her?
• What circumstances quickly empty her emotional gas tank?

Finally, ask your wife questions about what she is feeling, and then listen to her. Making the effort to know specifics about her background, her favorite things, and her dreams all communicate to her, "I want to *know* you. I want to be your *soul mate.*" I have yet to meet a woman who resented the loving service of a husband who took the time to communicate *that!*

Husbands, let me challenge you to lead, to love, and to serve. Take the time to rate yourself from one to five in all three categories: leading, loving, and serving. Pray that you will have the courage to lead, the sensitivity to love, and the humility to serve your wife.

Thus the LORD my God will come,
And all the saints with You.[a]

6 It shall come to pass in that day
That there will be no light;
The lights will diminish.
7 It shall be one day
Which is known to the LORD—
Neither day nor night.
But at evening time it shall
happen
That it will be light.

8 And in that day it shall be
That living waters shall flow from
Jerusalem,
Half of them toward the eastern
sea
And half of them toward the
western sea;
In both summer and winter it shall
occur.
9 And the LORD shall be King over all
the earth.
In that day it shall be—
"The LORD *is* one,"[a]
And His name one.

10All the land shall be turned into a
plain from Geba to Rimmon south of
Jerusalem. *Jerusalem*[a] shall be raised up
and inhabited in her place from Benjamin's
Gate to the place of the First Gate and the
Corner Gate, and *from* the Tower of
Hananel to the king's winepresses.

11 *The people* shall dwell in it;
And no longer shall there be utter
destruction,
But Jerusalem shall be safely
inhabited.

12And this shall be the plague with which
the LORD will strike all the people who
fought against Jerusalem:

Their flesh shall dissolve while they
stand on their feet,
Their eyes shall dissolve in their
sockets,

And their tongues shall dissolve in
their mouths.

13 It shall come to pass in that day
That a great panic from the LORD
will be among them.
Everyone will seize the hand of his
neighbor,
And raise his hand against his
neighbor's hand;
14 Judah also will fight at Jerusalem.
And the wealth of all the
surrounding nations
Shall be gathered together:
Gold, silver, and apparel in great
abundance.

15 Such also shall be the plague
On the horse *and* the mule,
On the camel and the donkey,
And on all the cattle that will be in
those camps.
So *shall* this plague *be*.

The Nations Worship the King

16And it shall come to pass *that* everyone who is left of all the nations which
came against Jerusalem shall go up from
year to year to worship the King, the LORD of
hosts, and to keep the Feast of Tabernacles.
17And it shall be *that* whichever of the families of the earth do not come up to
Jerusalem to worship the King, the LORD of
hosts, on them there will be no rain. 18If the
family of Egypt will not come up and enter
in, they *shall have* no *rain;* they shall receive
the plague with which the LORD strikes the
nations who do not come up to keep the
Feast of Tabernacles. 19This shall be the
punishment of Egypt and the punishment
of all the nations that do not come up to
keep the Feast of Tabernacles.

20In that day "HOLINESS TO THE
LORD" shall be *engraved* on the bells of
the horses. The pots in the LORD's house
shall be like the bowls before the altar.
21Yes, every pot in Jerusalem and Judah
shall be holiness to the LORD of hosts.[a]
Everyone who sacrifices shall come and
take them and cook in them. In that day
there shall no longer be a Canaanite in the
house of the LORD of hosts.

14:9 [a]Compare Deuteronomy 6:4   14:10 [a]Literally *She*
14:21 [a]Or *on every pot . . . shall be (engraved)*
"HOLINESS TO THE LORD OF HOSTS"

MALACHI

HAVE YOU EVER NOTICED that people rarely ask, "Why me?" when something good happens to them? But when they face adversity, they very often go to God with that question.

In this final book of the Old Testament, the prophet Malachi rebukes his kinsmen for taking God's kindness and love for granted. He calls them out for expecting God's blessing, despite the many ways they disobey His commandments.

By Malachi's day, the priesthood has become corrupt. The Jews have been withholding their tithes and offerings. Wealthy evildoers have been using their riches to escape justice. Malachi warns God's people not to presume that their status as the covenant people of God will somehow insulate them from the consequences of divine judgment. It won't!

Malachi rebukes the people for marrying pagans (2:11), a practice that always led to national idolatry. He also sternly addresses husbands who "deal treacherously" with their wives (2:14), by violating the covenant of marriage through polygamy, adultery, violence and abuse, and divorce. Malachi makes it clear that these practices are inconsistent with godliness. Although the Scripture elsewhere makes allowances for divorce in certain circumstances (see Matt. 19:3–12; 1 Cor. 7), here God states clearly, "that He hates divorce" (2:16). His perfect plan for married couples is for one man and one woman to live together in a loving and lifetime covenant relationship.

The final words of this book, the final message of the Old Testament, provide God's people with a reason for hope, as well as a warning. The prophet points to the second coming of Elijah, whom he says "will turn the hearts of the fathers to the children, and the hearts of the children to their fathers, lest I come and strike the earth with a curse" (4:6). And after more than 400 years without a prophet in Israel, John the Baptist came "in the spirit and power of Elijah" to announce the arrival of the Messiah and the kingdom of God (Luke 1:17). Jesus' sinless life, and His death, burial, and resurrection make it possible for us to live in a reconciled relationship with God and in loving relationships with each other.

1 The burden[a] of the word of the LORD to Israel by Malachi.

Israel Beloved of God

2 "I have loved you," says the LORD.
"Yet you say, 'In what way have You
    loved us?'
  Was not Esau Jacob's brother?"
Says the LORD.
"Yet Jacob I have loved;
3 But Esau I have hated,
  And laid waste his mountains and
    his heritage
  For the jackals of the wilderness."

4 Even though Edom has said,
"We have been impoverished,
  But we will return and build the
    desolate places,"

Thus says the LORD of hosts:

"They may build, but I will throw
    down;
  They shall be called the Territory of
    Wickedness,
  And the people against whom the
    LORD will have indignation
    forever.
5 Your eyes shall see,
  And you shall say,
  'The LORD is magnified beyond the
    border of Israel.'

Polluted Offerings

6 "A son honors *his* father,
  And a servant *his* master.
  If then I am the Father,
  Where *is* My honor?
  And if I *am* a Master,
  Where *is* My reverence?
  Says the LORD of hosts
  To you priests who despise My
    name.
  Yet you say, 'In what way have we
    despised Your name?'

7 "You offer defiled food on My altar,
  But say,
  'In what way have we defiled You?'
  By saying,

'The table of the LORD is
    contemptible.'
8 And when you offer the blind as a
    sacrifice,
  Is it not evil?
  And when you offer the lame and
    sick,
  Is it not evil?
  Offer it then to your governor!
  Would he be pleased with you?
  Would he accept you favorably?"
  Says the LORD of hosts.

INTIMATE MOMENTS

Plan a romantic birthday surprise. Book the honeymoon suite at your favorite hotel, and buy him a special gift.

9 "But now entreat God's favor,
  That He may be gracious to us.
  While this is being *done* by your
    hands,
  Will He accept you favorably?"
  Says the LORD of hosts.
10 "Who *is there* even among you who
    would shut the doors,
  So that you would not kindle fire *on*
    My altar in vain?
  I have no pleasure in you,"
  Says the LORD of hosts,
  "Nor will I accept an offering from
    your hands.
11 For from the rising of the sun, even
    to its going down,
  My name *shall be* great among the
    Gentiles;
  In every place incense *shall be* offered
    to My name,
  And a pure offering;
  For My name shall be great among
    the nations,"
  Says the LORD of hosts.

12 "But you profane it,
  In that you say,
  'The table of the LORD[a] is defiled;
  And its fruit, its food, *is*
    contemptible.'

1:1 [a]Or *oracle* **1:12** [a]Following Bomberg; Masoretic
Text reads *Lord.*

13 You also say,
'Oh, what a weariness!'
And you sneer at it,"
Says the LORD of hosts.
"And you bring the stolen, the lame,
and the sick;
Thus you bring an offering!
Should I accept this from your
hand?"
Says the LORD.
14 "But cursed *be* the deceiver
Who has in his flock a male,
And takes a vow,
But sacrifices to the Lord what is
blemished—
For I *am* a great King,"
Says the LORD of hosts,
"And My name *is to be* feared among
the nations.

Corrupt Priests

2 "And now, O priests, this
commandment is for you.
2 If you will not hear,
And if you will not take *it* to heart,
To give glory to My name,"
Says the LORD of hosts,
"I will send a curse upon you,
And I will curse your blessings.
Yes, I have cursed them already,
Because you do not take *it* to heart.

3 "Behold, I will rebuke your
descendants
And spread refuse on your faces,
The refuse of your solemn feasts;
And *one* will take you away with it.
4 Then you shall know that I have sent
this commandment to you,

PARENTING MATTERS

Q: How can we deal with a son/daughter who has gone beyond typical rebellion and has become a prodigal?

Keep loving. No matter how broken and totally alienated your child may be, you will always be Dad or Mom. You have the unique opportunity to love him or her without strings. This is a powerful tool!

Pray and wait expectantly. God is fully capable of grabbing your child's attention. The Great Shepherd pursues His lost sheep. Ask, and keep on asking (Matt. 7:7, 8).

Connect. Find ways to connect. Even in the face of angry words and cold body language, you can speak kind, encouraging words and give hugs and tender touches.

Establish boundaries. Do not accept abusive, destructive behavior. What will be the basic requirements for anyone living under your family's roof? These rules must be carefully thought through and clearly communicated to your prodigal. Your child needs to know that serious consequences will result from crossing boundaries.

Get help. Don't attempt to deal with a prodigal alone. You need prayer and emotional support from friends, spiritual wisdom, the counsel of the leaders (elders or deacons) of your church, and perhaps even professional advice. If your child is dangerously out of control or has run away, you may need to call the police. Don't let shame, pride, or anything else keep you from getting help.

Finally, it is important to be reminded that your children are not robots. They must make their own decisions, right or wrong. They must hammer out their faith and trust in Jesus Christ, just like you did. The challenge is giving them room to make their own decisions and not controlling their lives as they grow up. Remember the passage in Psalm 127, "Like arrows in the hand of a warrior, so are the children of one's youth" (v. 4). Mom, Dad, you and I must aim them at the right target and let go. I can assure you that this is one of the finest arts any person ever learns.

That My covenant with Levi may
continue,"
Says the LORD of hosts.
5 "My covenant was with him, *one* of
life and peace,
And I gave them to him *that he
might* fear *Me;*
So he feared Me
And was reverent before My name.
6 The law of truth[a] was in his mouth,
And injustice was not found on his
lips.
He walked with Me in peace and
equity,
And turned many away from
iniquity.

7 "For the lips of a priest should keep
knowledge,
And *people* should seek the law from
his mouth;
For he is the messenger of the LORD
of hosts.
8 But you have departed from the way;
You have caused many to stumble at
the law.
You have corrupted the covenant of
Levi,"
Says the LORD of hosts.
9 "Therefore I also have made you
contemptible and base
Before all the people,
Because you have not kept My ways
But have shown partiality in the
law."

Treachery of Infidelity

10 Have we not all one Father?
Has not one God created us?
Why do we deal treacherously with
one another
By profaning the covenant of the
fathers?
11 Judah has dealt treacherously,
And an abomination has been
committed in Israel and in
Jerusalem,
For Judah has profaned
The LORD's holy *institution* which He
loves:

BIBLICAL INSIGHTS • 2:15, 16

Keep the Vision Alive

Despite the current cultural pessimism about marriage, most people long for a married love that lasts. And this is exactly what the church has to offer—a plan from the very Creator of marriage on how to make love endure "so long as we both shall live."

The problem is that the vision of a life-long, satisfying marriage doesn't hold up for many hopeful couples. How can the Christian community keep this vision alive? I think a significant part of the answer rests with the restoration of a high view of the marriage commitment. It is time for churches to step forward and become guardians, protectors, and enforcers of the marriage covenant.

But that is not enough.

We must also speak the truth about divorce. God spoke clearly in Malachi 2:16 when He said He "hates divorce." Divorce breaks the sacred promise between two people and God Himself, and it also interferes with the propagation of godly offspring (2:15).

My generation is the most divorced group in the history of our nation. It's time we told the truth about divorce. Divorce is bad for a person. It's bad for a child. Bad for a family. Bad for a church. And bad for a nation.

Make it your assignment to be pro-marriage and pro-commitment in your church. As followers of Christ, we need to be known by what we are for, not just what we are against.

He has married the daughter of a
foreign god.
12 May the LORD cut off from the tents
of Jacob
The man who does this, being awake
and aware,[a]
Yet who brings an offering to the
LORD of hosts!

2:6 [a]Or *true instruction*
2:12 [a]Talmud and Vulgate read *teacher and student.*

13 And this is the second thing you do:
   You cover the altar of the LORD with
        tears,
   With weeping and crying;
   So He does not regard the offering
        anymore,
   Nor receive *it* with goodwill from
        your hands.
14 Yet you say, "For what reason?"
   Because the LORD has been witness
   Between you and the wife of your
        youth,
   With whom you have dealt
        treacherously;
   Yet she is your companion
   And your wife by covenant.
15 But did He not make *them* one,
   Having a remnant of the Spirit?
   And why one?
   He seeks godly offspring.
   Therefore take heed to your spirit,
   And let none deal treacherously with
        the wife of his youth.

**INTIMATE
MOMENTS**

Instead of feeling frustrated when he forgets to put the toilet seat down—thank
him when he remembers.

16 "For the LORD God of Israel says
   That He hates divorce,
   For it covers one's garment with
        violence,"
   Says the LORD of hosts.
   "Therefore take heed to your spirit,
   That you do not deal
        treacherously."

17 You have wearied the LORD with
        your words;
   Yet you say,
   "In what way have we wearied *Him?*"
   In that you say,
   "Everyone who does evil
   Is good in the sight of the LORD,
   And He delights in them,"
   Or, "Where *is* the God of justice?"

The Coming Messenger

3 "Behold, I send My messenger,
   And he will prepare the way
        before Me.
   And the Lord, whom you seek,
   Will suddenly come to His temple,
   Even the Messenger of the covenant,
   In whom you delight.
   Behold, He is coming,"
   Says the LORD of hosts.

2 "But who can endure the day of His
        coming?
   And who can stand when He
        appears?
   For He *is* like a refiner's fire
   And like launderers' soap.
3 He will sit as a refiner and a purifier
        of silver;
   He will purify the sons of Levi,
   And purge them as gold and silver,
   That they may offer to the LORD
   An offering in righteousness.

4 "Then the offering of Judah and
        Jerusalem
   Will be pleasant to the LORD,
   As in the days of old,
   As in former years.
5 And I will come near you for
        judgment;
   I will be a swift witness
   Against sorcerers,
   Against adulterers,
   Against perjurers,
   Against those who exploit wage
        earners and widows and orphans,
   And against those who turn away an
        alien—
   Because they do not fear Me,"
   Says the LORD of hosts.

6 "For I *am* the LORD, I do not change;
   Therefore you are not consumed, O
        sons of Jacob.
7 Yet from the days of your fathers
   You have gone away from My
        ordinances
   And have not kept *them.*
   Return to Me, and I will return to
        you,"
   Says the LORD of hosts.
   "But you said,
   'In what way shall we return?'

DEVOTIONS FOR COUPLES • 3:8
A Biblical Approach to Spending

Since the handling of finances consistently ranks among the top five causes of marital friction, as a couple you must gain the self-discipline to control spending and keep needs, wants, and desires in their proper relationship.

Needs: "And having food and clothing, with these we shall be content" (1 Tim. 6:8). Needs are the purchases necessary to provide your basic requirements, such as food, clothing, lodging, and medical care. Commit your needs to the Lord, obey His Word, follow His principles, and watch Him provide for your family's needs.

Wants: "Do not let your adornment be merely outward—arranging the hair, wearing gold, or putting on fine apparel—rather let it be the hidden person of the heart, with the incorruptible beauty of a gentle and quiet spirit, which is very precious in the sight of God" (1 Pet. 3:3, 4). Having material wants is not wrong; in fact, it is quite natural. The trouble comes from wanting too much, wanting it too soon, and being unhappy if we can't have all we want.

Desires: According to God's plan, we can purchase the things we desire from our surplus funds after all our obligations have been met. But we should be aware that our desires can lead us away from God. "Do not love the world or the things in the world. If anyone loves the world, the love of the Father is not in him. For all that is in the world—the lust of the flesh, the lust of the eyes, and the pride of life—is not of the Father, but is of the world" (1 John 2:15, 16).

While it is important to set a budget, before you do that you must first recognize that God owns it all. He doesn't just own ten percent. He is the giver of money and all possessions. He is interested in how you are a steward of the other ninety percent. There are division of income that help us evaluate how we are doing with what God has given us.

1. The first part needs to be given to God's work. God said through the prophet Malachi, "Will a man rob God? Yet you have robbed Me! But you say, 'In what way have we robbed You?' In tithes and offerings" (3:8).

2. Then come taxes: Jesus Himself said that it is right for us to pay our taxes (see Matt. 22:21; Rom. 13:6, 7).

3. The portion available after tithe and taxes is Net Spendable Income. From this you meet your family needs, such as housing, food, medical, and so on (see 1 Tim. 5:8).

4. Then, fulfill your commitments from past overspending. God says to pay your debts (see Ps. 37:21).

5. Faithful management will yield a surplus. From this surplus you can respond to the needs of others (see 2 Cor. 8:14).

Once our income has been wisely allocated, the Holy Spirit will guide you in how to steward what is left for your enjoyment and to help others. But don't forget that the stuff we accumulate in this life won't last forever, whereas our eternal investments are imperishable (Matt. 6:17–19).

Do Not Rob God

8 "Will a man rob God?
      Yet you have robbed Me!
      But you say,
   ' In what way have we robbed You?'
      In tithes and offerings.
9   You are cursed with a curse,
      For you have robbed Me,
      Even this whole nation.
10   Bring all the tithes into the storehouse,
      That there may be food in My house,
      And try Me now in this,"
      Says the LORD of hosts,
   "If I will not open for you the
         windows of heaven
      And pour out for you *such* blessing
      That *there will* not *be room* enough
         to receive it.

11   "And I will rebuke the devourer for
         your sakes,
      So that he will not destroy the fruit
         of your ground,

Nor shall the vine fail to bear fruit
    for you in the field,"
Says the LORD of hosts;

12 And all nations will call you blessed,
    For you will be a delightful land,"
Says the LORD of hosts.

The People Complain Harshly

13 "Your words have been harsh against
    Me,"
    Says the LORD,
"Yet you say,
    'What have we spoken against You?'

14 You have said,
    'It is useless to serve God;
    What profit *is it* that we have kept
      His ordinance,
    And that we have walked as
      mourners
    Before the LORD of hosts?

15 So now we call the proud blessed,
    For those who do wickedness are
      raised up;
    They even tempt God and go free.'"

A Book of Remembrance

16 Then those who feared the LORD
    spoke to one another,
    And the LORD listened and heard *them;*
    So a book of remembrance was
      written before Him
    For those who fear the LORD
    And who meditate on His name.

17 "They shall be Mine," says the LORD
    of hosts,
"On the day that I make them My
    jewels.[a]
    And I will spare them
    As a man spares his own son who
      serves him."

18 Then you shall again discern

Between the righteous and the wicked,
Between one who serves God
And one who does not serve Him.

The Great Day of God

4 "For behold, the day is coming,
    Burning like an oven,
    And all the proud, yes, all who do
      wickedly will be stubble.
    And the day which is coming shall
      burn them up,"
Says the LORD of hosts,
"That will leave them neither root nor
    branch.

2 But to you who fear My name
    The Sun of Righteousness shall arise
    With healing in His wings;
    And you shall go out
    And grow fat like stall-fed calves.

3 You shall trample the wicked,
    For they shall be ashes under the
      soles of your feet
    On the day that I do *this,*"
Says the LORD of hosts.

4 "Remember the Law of Moses, My
    servant,
    Which I commanded him in Horeb
      for all Israel,
    With the statutes and judgments.

5 Behold, I will send you Elijah the
    prophet
    Before the coming of the great and
      dreadful day of the LORD.

6 And he will turn
    The hearts of the fathers to the
      children,
    And the hearts of the children to
      their fathers,
    Lest I come and strike the earth with
      a curse."

3:17 [a]Literally *special treasure*

ROMANTIC QUOTES AND NOTES
Commitment, the Fortifying Wall

There is nothing like commitment to create the safety for romance to grow. Your marriage covenant is the wall that protects and fortifies your relationship so that you can experience love for a lifetime. If you haven't done it in the past couple of years, find a way to renew your vows with one another. Consider having a little vow renewal service in front of your children and asking them to assist you as well as observe. This is one of the best gifts a couple can give their children ... committed love for a lifetime.

NEW TESTAMENT

MATTHEW

MATTHEW IS THE FIRST OF FOUR BIOGRAPHIES of Jesus found in the New Testament. The book is named for its author, Matthew (also known as Levi), a tax collector from Galilee who became one of Jesus' original twelve disciples. Matthew was Jewish, and he wrote his Gospel to a Jewish audience to show conclusively that Jesus was the promised Messiah and therefore the rightful heir to David's throne as the King of the Jews.

Matthew begins his book by tracing Jesus' family tree from Abraham (the father of the nation) through David (the king from whom the Messiah was to descend) to Joseph, the husband of Mary and the adoptive father of Jesus. His account of Jesus' life includes details about His birth, well-known teaching from the Sermon on the Mount (chapters 5—7), including the Beatitudes (5:1–11) and the Lord's Prayer (6:9–13), familiar parables, more than twenty accounts of miracles, and reports about Jesus' crucifixion and resurrection.

Matthew quotes or alludes to the Old Testament 129 times, much more than any other Gospel writer. He is the only Bible writer to use the phrase, "that which was spoken," to refer to the Old Testament. The phrase, "the kingdom of heaven" appears in Matthew and nowhere else in the Bible.

About 60 percent of this Gospel recounts lessons Jesus taught His followers; some of this instruction touches on marriage and family issues. Only Matthew includes Jesus' full teaching on marriage and divorce (19:3–12). Matthew also records Jesus' teaching on the value and worth of children (18:3–5) and how following Him can and will divide family members (10:21).

Matthew also includes Jesus' summation of the entire teaching of the Old Testament. In what we know as the Great Commandment, Jesus said, "'You shall love the Lord your God with all your heart, with all your soul, and with all your mind.' This is the first and great commandment. And the second is like it: 'You shall love your neighbor as yourself.' On these two commandments hang all the Law and the Prophets" (22:37–40). This command to love your neighbor as yourself begins at home in our marriages and families.

Matthew's Gospel ends with a charge from Jesus that has become known as the Great Commission (28:19, 20), which calls each one of us to tell others about Jesus and to help them grow spiritually. As individuals and as families, we need to make sure our mission in life has this priority at its center.

The Genealogy of Jesus Christ

1 The book of the genealogy of Jesus Christ, the Son of David, the Son of Abraham:

²Abraham begot Isaac, Isaac begot Jacob, and Jacob begot Judah and his brothers. ³Judah begot Perez and Zerah by Tamar, Perez begot Hezron, and Hezron begot Ram. ⁴Ram begot Amminadab, Amminadab begot Nahshon, and Nahshon begot Salmon. ⁵Salmon begot Boaz by Rahab, Boaz begot Obed by Ruth, Obed begot Jesse, ⁶and Jesse begot David the king.

David the king begot Solomon by her *who had been the wife*ᵃ of Uriah. ⁷Solomon begot Rehoboam, Rehoboam begot Abijah, and Abijah begot Asa.ᵃ ⁸Asa begot Jehoshaphat, Jehoshaphat begot Joram, and Joram begot Uzziah. ⁹Uzziah begot Jotham, Jotham begot Ahaz, and Ahaz begot Hezekiah. ¹⁰Hezekiah begot Manasseh, Manasseh begot Amon,ᵃ and Amon begot Josiah. ¹¹Josiah begot Jeconiah and his brothers about the time they were carried away to Babylon.

¹²And after they were brought to Babylon, Jeconiah begot Shealtiel, and Shealtiel begot Zerubbabel. ¹³Zerubbabel begot Abiud, Abiud begot Eliakim, and Eliakim begot Azor. ¹⁴Azor begot Zadok, Zadok begot Achim, and Achim begot Eliud. ¹⁵Eliud begot Eleazar, Eleazar begot Matthan, and Matthan begot Jacob. ¹⁶And Jacob begot Joseph the husband of Mary, of whom was born Jesus who is called Christ.

¹⁷So all the generations from Abraham to David *are* fourteen generations, from David until the captivity in Babylon *are* fourteen generations, and from the captivity in Babylon until the Christ *are* fourteen generations.

Christ Born of Mary

¹⁸Now the birth of Jesus Christ was as follows: After His mother Mary was betrothed to Joseph, before they came together, she was found with child of the Holy Spirit. ¹⁹Then Joseph her husband, being a just *man,* and not wanting to make her a public example, was minded to put her away secretly. ²⁰But while he thought about these things, behold, an angel of the Lord appeared to him in a dream, saying, "Joseph, son of David, do not be afraid to take to you Mary your wife, for that which is conceived in her is of the Holy Spirit. ²¹And she will bring forth a Son, and you shall call His name JESUS, for He will save His people from their sins."

²²So all this was done that it might be fulfilled which was spoken by the Lord through the prophet, saying: ²³"Behold, the virgin shall be with child, and bear a Son, and they shall call His name Immanuel,"ᵃ which is translated, "God with us."

²⁴Then Joseph, being aroused from sleep, did as the angel of the Lord commanded him and took to him his wife, ²⁵and did not know her till she had brought forth her firstborn Son.ᵃ And he called His name JESUS.

Wise Men from the East

2 Now after Jesus was born in Bethlehem of Judea in the days of Herod the king, behold, wise men from the East came to Jerusalem, ²saying, "Where is He who has been born King of the Jews? For we have seen His star in the East and have come to worship Him."

³When Herod the king heard *this,* he was troubled, and all Jerusalem with him. ⁴And when he had gathered all the chief priests and scribes of the people together, he inquired of them where the Christ was to be born.

⁵So they said to him, "In Bethlehem of Judea, for thus it is written by the prophet:

⁶ 'But you, Bethlehem, in the land of
      Judah,
    Are not the least among the rulers of
      Judah;
    For out of you shall come a Ruler
    Who will shepherd My people
      Israel.' "ᵃ

⁷Then Herod, when he had secretly called the wise men, determined from them what time the star appeared. ⁸And he sent them to

---

1:6 ᵃWords in italic type have been added for clarity. They are not found in the original Greek.
1:7 ᵃNU-Text reads *Asaph.* **1:10** ᵃNU-Text reads *Amos.* **1:23** ᵃIsaiah 7:14. Words in oblique type in the New Testament are quoted from the Old Testament.
1:25 ᵃNU-Text reads *a Son.* **2:6** ᵃMicah 5:2

Bethlehem and said, "Go and search carefully for the young Child, and when you have found *Him,* bring back word to me, that I may come and worship Him also."

⁹When they heard the king, they departed; and behold, the star which they had seen in the East went before them, till it came and stood over where the young Child was. ¹⁰When they saw the star, they rejoiced with exceedingly great joy. ¹¹And when they had come into the house, they saw the young Child with Mary His mother, and fell down and worshiped Him. And when they had opened their treasures, they presented gifts to Him: gold, frankincense, and myrrh.

¹²Then, being divinely warned in a dream that they should not return to Herod, they departed for their own country another way.

The Flight into Egypt

¹³Now when they had departed, behold, an angel of the Lord appeared to Joseph in a dream, saying, "Arise, take the young Child and His mother, flee to Egypt, and stay there until I bring you word; for Herod will seek the young Child to destroy Him."

¹⁴When he arose, he took the young Child and His mother by night and departed for Egypt, ¹⁵and was there until the death of Herod, that it might be fulfilled which was spoken by the Lord through the prophet, saying, *"Out of Egypt I called My Son."*ᵃ

Massacre of the Innocents

¹⁶Then Herod, when he saw that he was deceived by the wise men, was exceedingly angry; and he sent forth and put to death all the male children who were in Bethlehem and in all its districts, from two years old and under, according to the time which he had determined from the wise men. ¹⁷Then was fulfilled what was spoken by Jeremiah the prophet, saying:

¹⁸ *"A voice was heard in Ramah,*
    Lamentation, weeping, and great
        mourning,
    Rachel weeping for her children,
    Refusing to be comforted,
    *Because they are no more."*ᵃ

The Home in Nazareth

¹⁹Now when Herod was dead, behold, an angel of the Lord appeared in a dream to Joseph in Egypt, ²⁰saying, "Arise, take the young Child and His mother, and go to the land of Israel, for those who sought the young Child's life are dead." ²¹Then he arose, took the young Child and His mother, and came into the land of Israel.

²²But when he heard that Archelaus was reigning over Judea instead of his father Herod, he was afraid to go there. And being warned by God in a dream, he turned aside into the region of Galilee. ²³And he came and dwelt in a city called Nazareth, that it might be fulfilled which was spoken by the prophets, "He shall be called a Nazarene."

INTIMATE MOMENTS

You probably already know what it is, but if not, find out your lover's least favorite chore—and do it for her for a month.

John the Baptist Prepares the Way

3 In those days John the Baptist came preaching in the wilderness of Judea, ²and saying, "Repent, for the kingdom of heaven is at hand!" ³For this is he who was spoken of by the prophet Isaiah, saying:

  "The voice of one crying in the
    wilderness:
  'Prepare the way of the LORD;
    *Make His paths straight.'"*ᵃ

⁴Now John himself was clothed in camel's hair, with a leather belt around his waist; and his food was locusts and wild honey. ⁵Then Jerusalem, all Judea, and all the region around the Jordan went out to him ⁶and were baptized by him in the Jordan, confessing their sins.

⁷But when he saw many of the Pharisees and Sadducees coming to his baptism, he said to them, "Brood of vipers! Who warned you to flee from the wrath to come?

2:15 ᵃHosea 11:1 **2:18** ᵃJeremiah 31:15
3:3 ᵃIsaiah 40:3

BIBLICAL INSIGHTS • 4:1–11

God's Word: Our Weapon of Choice

ONE OF THE MOST IMPORTANT messages we can take from the biblical account of the temptation of Jesus (4:1–11) is the importance of knowing God's Word and putting it to use when temptation comes knocking at our doors.

Jesus had spent His entire life learning and internalizing the Word of God, and when the Spirit led Him into the wilderness to be tempted by the devil (and they were very real temptations), He was able to answer each one of them with, "It is written …" He had studied and meditated for so long on the truths of God's Word, that they had become a part of Him.

Even in the best of marriages, we can be tempted toward straying—if not physically, then mentally and emotionally. The best way to fight these temptations is to memorize Scripture and have it ready when temptations present themselves.

Memorize verses such as, "Flee also youthful lusts; but pursue righteousness, faith, love, peace with those who call on the Lord out of a pure heart" (2 Tim. 2:22). That way, when you are tempted by lust, the Holy Spirit will bring to your mind those verses that you have committed to memory, and He will remind you of the truth so that you can flee.

---

⁸Therefore bear fruits worthy of repentance, ⁹and do not think to say to yourselves, 'We have Abraham as *our* father.' For I say to you that God is able to raise up children to Abraham from these stones. ¹⁰And even now the ax is laid to the root of the trees. Therefore every tree which does not bear good fruit is cut down and thrown into the fire. ¹¹I indeed baptize you with water unto repentance, but He who is coming after me is mightier than I, whose sandals I am not worthy to carry. He will baptize you with the Holy Spirit and fire.ª ¹²His winnowing fan *is* in His hand, and He will thoroughly clean out His threshing floor, and gather His wheat into the barn; but He will burn up the chaff with unquenchable fire."

John Baptizes Jesus

¹³Then Jesus came from Galilee to John at the Jordan to be baptized by him. ¹⁴And John *tried to* prevent Him, saying, "I need to be baptized by You, and are You coming to me?"

¹⁵But Jesus answered and said to him, "Permit *it to be so* now, for thus it is fitting for us to fulfill all righteousness." Then he allowed Him.

¹⁶When He had been baptized, Jesus came up immediately from the water; and behold, the heavens were opened to Him, and Heª saw the Spirit of God descending like a dove and alighting upon Him. ¹⁷And suddenly a voice *came* from heaven, saying, "This is My beloved Son, in whom I am well pleased."

Satan Tempts Jesus

4 Then Jesus was led up by the Spirit into the wilderness to be tempted by the devil. ²And when He had fasted forty days and forty nights, afterward He was hungry. ³Now when the tempter came to Him, he said, "If You are the Son of God, command that these stones become bread."

⁴But He answered and said, "It is written, '*Man shall not live by bread alone, but by every word that proceeds from the mouth of God.*' "ª

⁵Then the devil took Him up into the holy city, set Him on the pinnacle of the temple, ⁶and said to Him, "If You are the Son of God, throw Yourself down. For it is written:

'*He shall give His angels charge over you,*'

and,

'*In their hands they shall bear you up, Lest you dash your foot against a stone.*' "ª

⁷Jesus said to him, "It is written again, '*You shall not tempt the LORD your God.*' "ª

3:11 ªM-Text omits *and fire.* **3:16** ªOr *he*
4:4 ªDeuteronomy 8:3 **4:6** ªPsalm 91:11, 12
4:7 ªDeuteronomy 6:16

⁸Again, the devil took Him up on an exceedingly high mountain, and showed Him all the kingdoms of the world and their glory. ⁹And he said to Him, "All these things I will give You if You will fall down and worship me."

¹⁰Then Jesus said to him, "Away with you,ᵃ Satan! For it is written, 'You shall worship the LORD your God, and Him only you shall serve.' "ᵇ

¹¹Then the devil left Him, and behold, angels came and ministered to Him.

Jesus Begins His Galilean Ministry

¹²Now when Jesus heard that John had been put in prison, He departed to Galilee. ¹³And leaving Nazareth, He came and dwelt in Capernaum, which is by the sea, in the regions of Zebulun and Naphtali, ¹⁴that it might be fulfilled which was spoken by Isaiah the prophet, saying:

¹⁵ "The land of Zebulun and the land of Naphtali,
   By the way of the sea, beyond the Jordan,
   Galilee of the Gentiles:
¹⁶   The people who sat in darkness have seen a great light,
   And upon those who sat in the region and shadow of death Light has dawned."ᵃ

¹⁷From that time Jesus began to preach and to say, "Repent, for the kingdom of heaven is at hand."

Four Fishermen Called as Disciples

¹⁸And Jesus, walking by the Sea of Galilee, saw two brothers, Simon called Peter, and Andrew his brother, casting a net into the sea; for they were fishermen. ¹⁹Then He said to them, "Follow Me, and I will make you fishers of men." ²⁰They immediately left their nets and followed Him.

²¹Going on from there, He saw two other brothers, James the son of Zebedee, and John his brother, in the boat with Zebedee their father, mending their nets. He called them, ²²and immediately they left the boat and their father, and followed Him.

Jesus Heals a Great Multitude

²³And Jesus went about all Galilee, teaching in their synagogues, preaching the gospel of the kingdom, and healing all kinds of sickness and all kinds of disease among the people. ²⁴Then His fame went throughout all Syria; and they brought to Him all sick people who were afflicted with various diseases and torments, and those who were demon-possessed, epileptics, and paralytics; and He healed them. ²⁵Great multitudes followed Him—from Galilee, and from Decapolis, Jerusalem, Judea, and beyond the Jordan.

INTIMATE MOMENTS

Keep your romance closet well stocked with candles, greeting cards, massage oil, bubble bath, chocolates, etc.

The Beatitudes

5 And seeing the multitudes, He went up on a mountain, and when He was seated His disciples came to Him. ²Then He opened His mouth and taught them, saying:

³   "Blessed are the poor in spirit,
   For theirs is the kingdom of heaven.
⁴   Blessed are those who mourn,
   For they shall be comforted.
⁵   Blessed are the meek,
   For they shall inherit the earth.
⁶   Blessed are those who hunger and thirst for righteousness,
   For they shall be filled.
⁷   Blessed are the merciful,
   For they shall obtain mercy.
⁸   Blessed are the pure in heart,
   For they shall see God.
⁹   Blessed are the peacemakers,
   For they shall be called sons of God.
¹⁰   Blessed are those who are persecuted for righteousness' sake,
   For theirs is the kingdom of heaven.

4:10 ᵃM-Text reads Get behind Me. ᵇDeuteronomy 6:13 **4:16** ᵃIsaiah 9:1, 2

¹¹"Blessed are you when they revile and persecute you, and say all kinds of evil against you falsely for My sake. ¹²Rejoice and be exceedingly glad, for great *is* your reward in heaven, for so they persecuted the prophets who were before you.

Believers Are Salt and Light

¹³"You are the salt of the earth; but if the salt loses its flavor, how shall it be seasoned? It is then good for nothing but to be thrown out and trampled underfoot by men.

¹⁴"You are the light of the world. A city that is set on a hill cannot be hidden. ¹⁵Nor do they light a lamp and put it under a basket, but on a lampstand, and it gives light to all *who are* in the house. ¹⁶Let your light so shine before men, that they may see your good works and glorify your Father in heaven.

Christ Fulfills the Law

¹⁷"Do not think that I came to destroy the Law or the Prophets. I did not come to destroy but to fulfill. ¹⁸For assuredly, I say to you, till heaven and earth pass away, one jot or one tittle will by no means pass from the law till all is fulfilled. ¹⁹Whoever therefore breaks one of the least of these commandments, and teaches men so, shall be called least in the kingdom of heaven; but whoever does and teaches *them,* he shall be called great in the kingdom of heaven. ²⁰For I say to you, that unless your righteousness exceeds *the righteousness* of the scribes and Pharisees, you will by no means enter the kingdom of heaven.

Murder Begins in the Heart

²¹"You have heard that it was said to those of old, '*You shall not murder,*[a] and whoever murders will be in danger of the judgment.' ²²But I say to you that whoever is angry with his brother without a cause[a] shall be in danger of the judgment. And whoever says to his brother, 'Raca!' shall be in danger of the council. But whoever says, 'You fool!' shall be in danger of hell fire. ²³Therefore if you bring your gift to the altar, and there remember that your brother has something against you, ²⁴leave your gift there before the altar, and go your way. First be reconciled to your brother,

and then come and offer your gift. ²⁵Agree with your adversary quickly, while you are on the way with him, lest your adversary deliver you to the judge, the judge hand you over to the officer, and you be thrown into prison. ²⁶Assuredly, I say to you, you will by no means get out of there till you have paid the last penny.

Adultery in the Heart

²⁷"You have heard that it was said to those of old,[a] '*You shall not commit adultery.*'[b] ²⁸But I say to you that whoever looks at a woman to lust for her has already committed adultery with her in his heart. ²⁹If your right eye causes you to sin, pluck it out and cast *it* from you; for it is more profitable for you that one of your members perish, than for your whole body to be cast into hell. ³⁰And if your right hand causes you to sin, cut it off and cast *it* from you; for it is more profitable for you that one of your members perish, than for your whole body to be cast into hell.

Marriage Is Sacred and Binding

³¹"Furthermore it has been said, 'Whoever divorces his wife, let him give her a certificate of divorce.' ³²But I say to you that whoever divorces his wife for any reason except sexual immorality[a] causes her to commit adultery; and whoever marries a woman who is divorced commits adultery.

Jesus Forbids Oaths

³³"Again you have heard that it was said to those of old, 'You shall not swear falsely, but shall perform your oaths to the Lord.' ³⁴But I say to you, do not swear at all: neither by heaven, for it is God's throne; ³⁵nor by the earth, for it is His footstool; nor by Jerusalem, for it is the city of the great King. ³⁶Nor shall you swear by your head, because you cannot make one hair white or black. ³⁷But let your 'Yes' be 'Yes,' and your 'No,' 'No.' For whatever is more than these is from the evil one.

5:21 [a]Exodus 20:13; Deuteronomy 5:17
5:22 [a]NU-Text omits *without a cause.*
5:27 [a]NU-Text and M-Text omit *to those of old.*
[b]Exodus 20:14; Deuteronomy 5:18 **5:32** [a]Or *fornication*

DEVOTIONS FOR COUPLES • 6:9–13
Pray Together as a Couple

A follower of Jesus once said to Him, "Lord, teach us to pray" (Luke 11:1). Jesus' answer became known as the Lord's Prayer (Matt. 6:9–13), and it can provide us with a model of how can pray together as a couple. It is easy to understand and will also be easy to incorporate into your own experience as you and your mate begin to cultivate the spiritual habit of praying together.

Our Father who is in heaven, hallowed be Your name. Begin your prayer by acknowledging God's place of authority over your lives. He is mighty and holy—that's what *hallowed* means. Remember as you pray, that you are praying to a pure, righteous, spotless God who calls Himself holy.

Your kingdom come. Your will be done on earth as it is in heaven. These phrases declare what and who is most important in the grand scheme of life. When God directs us to do something, we are to do it as quickly and as wholeheartedly as the angels in heaven do what He directs them to do.

Give us this day our daily bread. As you pray, keep in mind that it is God who provides for His children. Bread represents everything we need in a given day—food and drink, work, relationships, everything.

And forgive us our debts, as we forgive our debtors. Forgiveness is at the core of God's heart. He was willing to sacrifice His only Son so that we could be completely cleansed and forgiven of our sins. In a similar way, He wants us to be proactive in forgiving one another.

And do not lead us into temptation, but deliver us from the evil one. God wants us to obey Him. He wants us to depend on Him and to choose good instead of evil.

For Yours is the kingdom and the power and the glory forever. Amen. This sentence repeats a sincere affirmation that life is about God and what He wants for our lives.

Many Christians pray the Lord's Prayer word-for-word. Other believers use it as a guide. *How* you use it is your choice. If either of you is uncomfortable praying aloud, simply reciting the Lord's Prayer together may be a wonderful way to start the daily prayer habit.

Get together with your spouse and discuss any discomfort you may have about praying aloud in front of others. Also ask yourselves, "What can each of us do to raise our comfort level of praying aloud together?"

Go the Second Mile

[38]"You have heard that it was said, *'An eye for an eye and a tooth for a tooth.'*[a] [39]But I tell you not to resist an evil person. But whoever slaps you on your right cheek, turn the other to him also. [40]If anyone wants to sue you and take away your tunic, let him have *your* cloak also. [41]And whoever compels you to go one mile, go with him two. [42]Give to him who asks you, and from him who wants to borrow from you do not turn away.

Love Your Enemies

[43]"You have heard that it was said, *'You shall love your neighbor*[a] and hate your enemy.' [44]But I say to you, love your enemies, bless those who curse you, do good to those who hate you, and pray for those who spitefully use you and persecute you,[a] [45]that you may be sons of your Father in heaven; for He makes His sun rise on the evil and on the good, and sends rain on the just and on the unjust. [46]For if you love those who love you, what reward have you? Do not even the tax collectors do the same? [47]And if you greet your brethren[a] only, what do you do more *than others?* Do not even the tax collectors[b] do so? [48]Therefore you shall be perfect, just as your Father in heaven is perfect.

5:38 [a]Exodus 21:24; Leviticus 24:20; Deuteronomy 19:21 **5:43** [a]Compare Leviticus 19:18 **5:44** [a]NU-Text omits three clauses from this verse, leaving, *"But I say to you, love your enemies and pray for those who persecute you."* **5:47** [a]M-Text reads *friends.* [b]NU-Text reads *Gentiles.*

Do Good to Please God

6 "Take heed that you do not do your charitable deeds before men, to be seen by them. Otherwise you have no reward from your Father in heaven. ²Therefore, when you do a charitable deed, do not sound a trumpet before you as the hypocrites do in the synagogues and in the streets, that they may have glory from men. Assuredly, I say to you, they have their reward. ³But when you do a charitable deed, do not let your left hand know what your right hand is doing, ⁴that your charitable deed may be in secret; and your Father who sees in secret will Himself reward you openly.ᵃ

The Model Prayer

⁵"And when you pray, you shall not be like the hypocrites. For they love to pray standing in the synagogues and on the corners of the streets, that they may be seen by men. Assuredly, I say to you, they have their reward. ⁶But you, when you pray, go into your room, and when you have shut your door, pray to your Father who *is* in the secret *place;* and your Father who sees in secret will reward you openly.ᵃ ⁷And when you pray, do not use vain repetitions as the heathen *do.* For they think that they will be heard for their many words.

6:4 ᵃNU-Text omits *openly.* **6:6** ᵃNU-Text omits *openly.*
6:13 ᵃNU-Text omits *For Yours* through *Amen.*

⁸"Therefore do not be like them. For your Father knows the things you have need of before you ask Him. ⁹In this manner, therefore, pray:

Our Father in heaven,
Hallowed be Your name.
10 Your kingdom come.
Your will be done
On earth as *it is* in heaven.
11 Give us this day our daily bread.
12 And forgive us our debts,
As we forgive our debtors.
13 And do not lead us into temptation,
But deliver us from the evil one.
For Yours is the kingdom and the
power and the glory forever.
Amen.ᵃ

¹⁴"For if you forgive men their trespasses, your heavenly Father will also forgive you. ¹⁵But if you do not forgive men their trespasses, neither will your Father forgive your trespasses.

Fasting to Be Seen Only by God

¹⁶"Moreover, when you fast, do not be like the hypocrites, with a sad countenance. For they disfigure their faces that they may appear to men to be fasting. Assuredly, I say to you, they have their reward. ¹⁷But you, when you fast, anoint your head and wash your face, ¹⁸so that you do not appear to men to be fasting, but

---

ROMANTIC QUOTES AND NOTES
Resolving Conflict Requires Forgiveness

No matter how hard two people try to love and please each other, they will fail. With failure comes hurt. And the only ultimate relief for hurt is the soothing salve of forgiveness.

The key to maintaining an open, intimate, and happy marriage is to ask for and grant forgiveness quickly. And the ability to do that is tied to each individual's relationship with God.

About the process of forgiveness, Jesus said, "For if you forgive men their trespasses, your heavenly Father will also forgive you. But if you do not forgive men their trespasses, neither will your Father forgive your trespasses" (Matt. 6:14, 15). The instruction is clear: God insists that we are to be forgivers—and marriage, probably more than any other relationship, presents frequent opportunities for practice.

Forgiving means giving up resentment and the desire to punish. By an act of your will, you let the other person off the hook. And as a Christian, you don't do so under duress, scratching and screaming in protest. Rather, you do it with a gentle spirit and love, as Paul urged, "Be kind to one another, tenderhearted, forgiving one another, even as God in Christ forgave you" (Eph. 4:32).

to your Father who *is* in the secret *place;* and your Father who sees in secret will reward you openly.[a]

Lay Up Treasures in Heaven

19"Do not lay up for yourselves treasures on earth, where moth and rust destroy and where thieves break in and steal; 20but lay up for yourselves treasures in heaven, where neither moth nor rust destroys and where thieves do not break in and steal. 21For where your treasure is, there your heart will be also.

The Lamp of the Body

22"The lamp of the body is the eye. If therefore your eye is good, your whole body will be full of light. 23But if your eye is bad, your whole body will be full of darkness. If therefore the light that is in you is darkness, how great *is* that darkness!

You Cannot Serve God and Riches

24"No one can serve two masters; for either he will hate the one and love the other, or else he will be loyal to the one and despise the other. You cannot serve God and mammon.

Do Not Worry

25"Therefore I say to you, do not worry about your life, what you will eat or what you will drink; nor about your body, what you will put on. Is not life more than food and the body more than clothing? 26Look at the birds of the air, for they neither sow nor reap nor gather into barns; yet your heavenly Father feeds them. Are you not of more value than they? 27Which of you by worrying can add one cubit to his stature? 28So why do you worry about clothing? Consider the lilies of the field, how they grow: they neither toil nor spin; 29and yet I say to you that even Solomon in all his glory was not arrayed like one of these. 30Now if God so clothes the grass of the field, which today is, and tomorrow is thrown into the oven, *will He* not much more *clothe* you, O you of little faith?

6:18 aNU-Text and M-Text omit *openly.*

BIBLICAL INSIGHTS • 6:19
Embrace Contentment

YOU'VE PROBABLY HEARD the saying, "He who has the most toys wins."

Says who? On the contrary, Jesus warns us, "Do not lay up for yourselves treasures on earth, where moth and rust destroy and where thieves break in and steal" (6:19). Do we own our stuff, or does it own us? Too often, it's the latter. That's why Jesus says, "For where your treasure is, there your heart will be also" (6:21).

So how do you and your mate keep from embracing the grand illusion that you should have it all? Barbara and I have done that by learning to cultivate a heart of contentment and rejecting the desire to acquire.

Contrary to the pied pipers of the American Dream Syndrome, enough is never enough. Learning the secret of contentment defuses the pressure to constantly acquire. Solomon, who had enough money to buy everything he wanted, write, "Then I looked on all the works that my hands had done and on the labor in which I had toiled; and indeed all was vanity and grasping for the wind. There was no profit under the sun" (Eccl. 2:11). No matter how hard we work or how much stuff we have, we will never reach the point of having enough.

True contentment arises from a spirit of thankfulness. It is a courageous choice to walk by faith and thank God for what you have—*and* for what you don't have.

31"Therefore do not worry, saying, 'What shall we eat?' or 'What shall we drink?' or 'What shall we wear?' 32For after all these things the Gentiles seek. For your heavenly Father knows that you need all these things. 33But seek first the kingdom of God and His righteousness, and all these things shall be added to you. 34Therefore do not worry about tomorrow, for tomorrow will worry about its own things. Sufficient for the day *is* its own trouble.

Do Not Judge

7 "Judge not, that you be not judged. ²For with what judgment you judge, you will be judged; and with the measure you use, it will be measured back to you. ³And why do you look at the speck in your brother's eye, but do not consider the plank in your own eye? ⁴Or how can you say to your brother, 'Let me remove the speck from your eye'; and look, a plank *is* in your own eye? ⁵Hypocrite! First remove the plank from your own eye, and then you will see clearly to remove the speck from your brother's eye.

⁶"Do not give what is holy to the dogs; nor cast your pearls before swine, lest they trample them under their feet, and turn and tear you in pieces.

Keep Asking, Seeking, Knocking

⁷"Ask, and it will be given to you; seek, and you will find; knock, and it will be opened to you. ⁸For everyone who asks receives, and he who seeks finds, and to him who knocks it will be opened. ⁹Or what man is there among you who, if his son asks for bread, will give him a stone? ¹⁰Or if he asks for a fish, will he give him a serpent? ¹¹If you then, being evil, know how to give good gifts to your children, how much more will your Father who is in heaven give good things to those who ask Him! ¹²Therefore, whatever you want men to do to you, do also to them, for this is the Law and the Prophets.

The Narrow Way

¹³"Enter by the narrow gate; for wide *is* the gate and broad *is* the way that leads to destruction, and there are many who go in by it. ¹⁴Becauseᵃ narrow *is* the gate and difficult *is* the way which leads to life, and there are few who find it.

You Will Know Them by Their Fruits

¹⁵"Beware of false prophets, who come to you in sheep's clothing, but inwardly they are ravenous wolves. ¹⁶You will know them by their fruits. Do men gather grapes from thornbushes or figs from thistles? ¹⁷Even so, every good tree bears good fruit, but a bad tree bears bad fruit. ¹⁸A good tree cannot bear bad fruit, nor *can* a bad tree bear good fruit. ¹⁹Every tree that does not bear good fruit is cut down and thrown into the fire. ²⁰Therefore by their fruits you will know them.

I Never Knew You

²¹"Not everyone who says to Me, 'Lord, Lord,' shall enter the kingdom of heaven,

---

7:14 ᵃNU-Text and M-Text read *How . . . !*

ROMANTIC QUOTES AND NOTES
Let's Fix Ourselves First

Couples would find marriage much more enjoyable and blessed if each partner would concern themselves more with smoothing out their own rough spots than with smoothing out those of their spouse.

Jesus addressed this very thing when He said, "Why do you look at the speck in your brother's eye, but do not consider the plank in your own eye? .... First remove the plank from your own eye, and then you will see clearly to remove the speck from your brother's eye" (Matt. 7:3, 5).

That's truly advice made for marriage! Sadly, too many couples expend far too much  time trying to correct each other and not nearly enough time (if any) trying to change themselves for the better. The result is absolutely predictable: frustration, anger, and bitterness—all of which can be poison to any human relationship, including marriage.

Jesus insists that if we're going to try to correct others and point out their annoying flaws, then we had better be willing to make sure we get the planks out of our own eyes first. That's good advice for all your interpersonal relationships—but especially excellent for your relationship with your spouse.

but he who does the will of My Father in heaven. ²²Many will say to Me in that day, 'Lord, Lord, have we not prophesied in Your name, cast out demons in Your name, and done many wonders in Your name?' ²³And then I will declare to them, 'I never knew you; depart from Me, you who practice lawlessness!'

Build on the Rock

²⁴"Therefore whoever hears these sayings of Mine, and does them, I will liken him to a wise man who built his house on the rock: ²⁵and the rain descended, the floods came, and the winds blew and beat on that house; and it did not fall, for it was founded on the rock.

²⁶"But everyone who hears these sayings of Mine, and does not do them, will be like a foolish man who built his house on the sand: ²⁷and the rain descended, the floods came, and the winds blew and beat on that house; and it fell. And great was its fall."

²⁸And so it was, when Jesus had ended these sayings, that the people were astonished at His teaching, ²⁹for He taught them as one having authority, and not as the scribes.

Jesus Cleanses a Leper

8 When He had come down from the mountain, great multitudes followed Him. ²And behold, a leper came and worshiped Him, saying, "Lord, if You are willing, You can make me clean."

³Then Jesus put out *His* hand and touched him, saying, "I am willing; be cleansed." Immediately his leprosy was cleansed.

⁴And Jesus said to him, "See that you tell no one; but go your way, show yourself to the priest, and offer the gift that Moses commanded, as a testimony to them."

Jesus Heals a Centurion's Servant

⁵Now when Jesus had entered Capernaum, a centurion came to Him, pleading with Him, ⁶saying, "Lord, my servant is lying at home paralyzed, dreadfully tormented."

⁷And Jesus said to him, "I will come and heal him."

YOUNG PEOPLE VENTURING toward marriage need to ask themselves a crucial question: "How do we go about being truly prepared for life as a married couple?" Jesus answered that question in Matthew 7:24, 25, suggesting that anything God has ordained—including marriage—must be built on His Word. Listen to His counsel, "Therefore whoever hears these sayings of Mine, and does them, I will liken him to a wise man who built his house on the rock: and the rain descended, the floods came, and the winds blew and beat on that house; and it did not fall, for it was founded on the rock."

All couples—new ones and those who have been married for some time—must know God's plan for their marriage and must be willing to build their relationships on the truth of the Lord's written Word, the Bible.

That marriage license that you get on the day of the wedding ceremony doesn't constitute a marriage! It only gives you the right to *begin* building a marriage, to *begin* to make that relationship work. If you follow God's blueprints together as a couple, your home will be able to survive the storms of life. And if you don't follow the blueprint of God's Word, you'll have a *very* different experience (see Matt. 7:26, 27).

⁸The centurion answered and said, "Lord, I am not worthy that You should come under my roof. But only speak a word, and my servant will be healed. ⁹For I also am a man under authority, having soldiers under me. And I say to this *one*, 'Go,' and he goes; and to another, 'Come,' and he comes; and to my servant, 'Do this,' and he does *it*."

¹⁰When Jesus heard *it*, He marveled, and said to those who followed, "Assuredly, I say to you, I have not found such great faith, not even in Israel! ¹¹And I say to you that many will come from east and west,

and sit down with Abraham, Isaac, and Jacob in the kingdom of heaven. ¹²But the sons of the kingdom will be cast out into outer darkness. There will be weeping and gnashing of teeth." ¹³Then Jesus said to the centurion, "Go your way; and as you have believed, *so* let it be done for you." And his servant was healed that same hour.

Peter's Mother-in-Law Healed

¹⁴Now when Jesus had come into Peter's house, He saw his wife's mother lying sick with a fever. ¹⁵So He touched her hand, and the fever left her. And she arose and served them.ᵃ

Many Healed in the Evening

¹⁶When evening had come, they brought to Him many who were demon-possessed. And He cast out the spirits with a word, and healed all who were sick, ¹⁷that it might be fulfilled which was spoken by Isaiah the prophet, saying:

> "He Himself took our infirmities
> And bore our sicknesses."ᵃ

The Cost of Discipleship

¹⁸And when Jesus saw great multitudes about Him, He gave a command to depart to the other side. ¹⁹Then a certain scribe came and said to Him, "Teacher, I will follow You wherever You go."

²⁰And Jesus said to him, "Foxes have holes and birds of the air *have* nests, but the Son of Man has nowhere to lay *His* head."

²¹Then another of His disciples said to Him, "Lord, let me first go and bury my father."

²²But Jesus said to him, "Follow Me, and let the dead bury their own dead."

Wind and Wave Obey Jesus

²³Now when He got into a boat, His disciples followed Him. ²⁴And suddenly a great tempest arose on the sea, so that the boat was covered with the waves. But He was asleep. ²⁵Then His disciples came to *Him* and awoke Him, saying, "Lord, save us! We are perishing!"

²⁶But He said to them, "Why are you fearful, O you of little faith?" Then He arose and rebuked the winds and the sea,

and there was a great calm. ²⁷So the men marveled, saying, "Who can this be, that even the winds and the sea obey Him?"

Two Demon-Possessed Men Healed

²⁸When He had come to the other side, to the country of the Gergesenes,ᵃ there met Him two demon-possessed *men*, coming out of the tombs, exceedingly fierce, so that no one could pass that way. ²⁹And suddenly they cried out, saying, "What have we to do with You, Jesus, You Son of God? Have You come here to torment us before the time?"

³⁰Now a good way off from them there was a herd of many swine feeding. ³¹So the demons begged Him, saying, "If You cast us out, permit us to go awayᵃ into the herd of swine."

³²And He said to them, "Go." So when they had come out, they went into the herd of swine. And suddenly the whole herd of swine ran violently down the steep place into the sea, and perished in the water.

³³Then those who kept *them* fled; and they went away into the city and told everything, including what *had happened* to the demon-possessed *men*. ³⁴And behold, the whole city came out to meet Jesus. And when they saw Him, they begged *Him* to depart from their region.

Jesus Forgives and Heals a Paralytic

9 So He got into a boat, crossed over, and came to His own city. ²Then behold, they brought to Him a paralytic lying on a bed. When Jesus saw their faith, He said to the paralytic, "Son, be of good cheer; your sins are forgiven you."

³And at once some of the scribes said within themselves, "This Man blasphemes!"

⁴But Jesus, knowing their thoughts, said, "Why do you think evil in your hearts? ⁵For which is easier, to say, 'Your sins are forgiven you,' or to say, 'Arise and walk'? ⁶But that you may know that the Son of Man has power on earth to forgive sins"—then He said to the paralytic, "Arise, take up your bed, and go to your

---

8:15 ᵃNU-Text and M-Text read *Him*. **8:17** ᵃIsaiah 53:4 **8:28** ᵃNU-Text reads *Gadarenes*. **8:31** ᵃNU-Text reads *send us*.

house." ⁷And he arose and departed to his house.

⁸Now when the multitudes saw *it,* they marveledᵃ and glorified God, who had given such power to men.

Matthew the Tax Collector

⁹As Jesus passed on from there, He saw a man named Matthew sitting at the tax office. And He said to him, "Follow Me." So he arose and followed Him.

¹⁰Now it happened, as Jesus sat at the table in the house, *that* behold, many tax collectors and sinners came and sat down with Him and His disciples. ¹¹And when the Pharisees saw *it,* they said to His disciples, "Why does your Teacher eat with tax collectors and sinners?"

¹²When Jesus heard *that,* He said to them, "Those who are well have no need of a physician, but those who are sick. ¹³But go and learn what *this* means: *'I desire mercy and not sacrifice.'*ᵃ For I did not come to call the righteous, but sinners, to repentance."ᵇ

Jesus Is Questioned About Fasting

¹⁴Then the disciples of John came to Him, saying, "Why do we and the Pharisees fast often,ᵃ but Your disciples do not fast?"

¹⁵And Jesus said to them, "Can the friends of the bridegroom mourn as long as the bridegroom is with them? But the days will come when the bridegroom will be taken away from them, and then they will fast. ¹⁶No one puts a piece of unshrunk cloth on an old garment; for the patch pulls away from the garment, and the tear is made worse. ¹⁷Nor do they put new wine into old wineskins, or else the wineskins break, the wine is spilled, and the wineskins are ruined. But they put new wine into new wineskins, and both are preserved."

A Girl Restored to Life and a Woman Healed

¹⁸While He spoke these things to them, behold, a ruler came and worshiped Him,

---

BIBLICAL INSIGHTS • 9:36

Demonstrate Compassion

JESUS WAS A VERY COMPASSIONATE man. Often in the Gospels you see some description of Him like the following: "But when He saw the multitudes, He was moved with compassion for them, because they were weary and scattered, like sheep having no shepherd" (9:36).

I wish those words always described me, but they don't. In fact, I struggle as much as anyone with demonstrating compassion. I have learned, however, that one way to follow Jesus in demonstrating compassion is to speak a timely word about Jesus to those who need Him most. There is a real art to turning a conversation to spiritual things, and doing so in a compelling and compassionate way.

More and more I *want* to share the Good News because it is the very reason that Jesus Christ came to the planet Earth in the first place. Jesus didn't go to the cross just so we could have happy homes. He came "to seek and to save that which was lost" (Luke 19:10).

Look around you. The army of God needs fresh, compassionate troops who are willing to go to the front lines. The hour couldn't be more urgent. And your family is an important part of the solution. Prayerfully consider who God has placed in your life, who needs to hear of God's love and forgiveness through Jesus Christ. Then take some steps to reach out in an appropriate way.

---

saying, "My daughter has just died, but come and lay Your hand on her and she will live." ¹⁹So Jesus arose and followed him, and so *did* His disciples.

²⁰And suddenly, a woman who had a flow of blood for twelve years came from behind and touched the hem of His garment. ²¹For she said to herself, "If only I may touch His garment, I shall be made well." ²²But Jesus turned around, and when He saw her He said, "Be of good cheer, daughter; your faith

---

9:8 ᵃNU-Text reads *were afraid.* **9:13** ᵃHosea 6:6
ᵇNU-Text omits *to repentance.* **9:14** ᵃNU-Text
brackets *often* as disputed.

has made you well." And the woman was made well from that hour.

23When Jesus came into the ruler's house, and saw the flute players and the noisy crowd wailing, 24He said to them, "Make room, for the girl is not dead, but sleeping." And they ridiculed Him. 25But when the crowd was put outside, He went in and took her by the hand, and the girl arose. 26And the report of this went out into all that land.

Two Blind Men Healed

27When Jesus departed from there, two blind men followed Him, crying out and saying, "Son of David, have mercy on us!" 28And when He had come into the house, the blind men came to Him. And Jesus said to them, "Do you believe that I am able to do this?"

They said to Him, "Yes, Lord."

29Then He touched their eyes, saying, "According to your faith let it be to you." 30And their eyes were opened. And Jesus sternly warned them, saying, "See *that* no one knows *it*." 31But when they had departed, they spread the news about Him in all that country.

A Mute Man Speaks

32As they went out, behold, they brought to Him a man, mute and demon-possessed. 33And when the demon was cast out, the mute spoke. And the multitudes marveled, saying, "It was never seen like this in Israel!"

34But the Pharisees said, "He casts out demons by the ruler of the demons."

The Compassion of Jesus

35Then Jesus went about all the cities and villages, teaching in their synagogues, preaching the gospel of the kingdom, and healing every sickness and every disease among the people.a 36But when He saw the multitudes, He was moved with compassion for them, because they were wearya and scattered, like sheep having no shepherd. 37Then He said to His disciples, "The harvest truly *is* plentiful, but the laborers *are* few. 38Therefore pray the Lord of the harvest to send out laborers into His harvest."

The Twelve Apostles

10 And when He had called His twelve disciples to *Him,* He gave them power *over* unclean spirits, to cast them out, and to heal all kinds of sickness and all kinds of disease. 2Now the names of the twelve apostles are these: first, Simon, who is called Peter, and Andrew his brother; James the *son* of Zebedee, and John his brother; 3Philip and Bartholomew; Thomas and Matthew the tax collector; James the *son* of Alphaeus, and Lebbaeus, whose surname wasa Thaddaeus; 4Simon the Cananite,a and Judas Iscariot, who also betrayed Him.

Sending Out the Twelve

5These twelve Jesus sent out and commanded them, saying: "Do not go into the way of the Gentiles, and do not enter a city of the Samaritans. 6But go rather to the lost sheep of the house of Israel. 7And as you go, preach, saying, 'The kingdom of heaven is at hand.' 8Heal the sick, cleanse the lepers, raise the dead,a cast out demons. Freely you have received, freely give. 9Provide neither gold nor silver nor copper in your money belts, 10nor bag for *your* journey, nor two tunics, nor sandals, nor staffs; for a worker is worthy of his food.

11"Now whatever city or town you enter, inquire who in it is worthy, and stay there till you go out. 12And when you go into a household, greet it. 13If the household is worthy, let your peace come upon it. But if it is not worthy, let your peace return to you. 14And whoever will not receive you nor hear your words, when you depart from that house or city, shake off the dust from your feet. 15Assuredly, I say to you, it will be more tolerable for the land of Sodom and Gomorrah in the day of judgment than for that city!

Persecutions Are Coming

16"Behold, I send you out as sheep in the midst of wolves. Therefore be wise as

---

9:35 aNU-Text omits *among the people.*
9:36 aNU-Text and M-Text read *harassed.*
10:3 aNU-Text omits *Lebbaeus, whose surname was.*
10:4 aNU-Text reads *Cananaean.* **10:8** aNU-Text reads *raise the dead, cleanse the lepers;* M-Text omits *raise the dead.*

serpents and harmless as doves. ¹⁷But beware of men, for they will deliver you up to councils and scourge you in their synagogues. ¹⁸You will be brought before governors and kings for My sake, as a testimony to them and to the Gentiles. ¹⁹But when they deliver you up, do not worry about how or what you should speak. For it will be given to you in that hour what you should speak; ²⁰for it is not you who speak, but the Spirit of your Father who speaks in you.

²¹"Now brother will deliver up brother to death, and a father *his* child; and children will rise up against parents and cause them to be put to death. ²²And you will be hated by all for My name's sake. But he who endures to the end will be saved. ²³When they persecute you in this city, flee to another. For assuredly, I say to you, you will not have gone through the cities of Israel before the Son of Man comes.

²⁴"A disciple is not above *his* teacher, nor a servant above his master. ²⁵It is enough for a disciple that he be like his teacher, and a servant like his master. If they have called the master of the house Beelzebub,ᵃ how much more *will they call* those of his household! ²⁶Therefore do not fear them. For there is nothing covered that will not be revealed, and hidden that will not be known.

Jesus Teaches the Fear of God

²⁷"Whatever I tell you in the dark, speak in the light; and what you hear in the ear, preach on the housetops. ²⁸And do not fear those who kill the body but cannot kill the soul. But rather fear Him who is able to destroy both soul and body in hell. ²⁹Are not two sparrows sold for a copper coin? And not one of them falls to the ground apart from your Father's will. ³⁰But the very hairs of your head are all numbered. ³¹Do not fear therefore; you are of more value than many sparrows.

Confess Christ Before Men

³²"Therefore whoever confesses Me before men, him I will also confess before My Father who is in heaven. ³³But whoever

denies Me before men, him I will also deny before My Father who is in heaven.

Christ Brings Division

³⁴"Do not think that I came to bring peace on earth. I did not come to bring peace but a sword. ³⁵For I have come to *'set a man against his father, a daughter against her mother, and a daughter-in-law against her mother-in-law';* ³⁶and *'a man's enemies will be those of his own household.'*ᵃ ³⁷He who loves father or mother more than Me is not worthy of Me. And he who loves son or daughter more than Me is not worthy of Me. ³⁸And he who does not take his cross and follow after Me is not worthy of Me. ³⁹He who finds his life will lose it, and he who loses his life for My sake will find it.

A Cup of Cold Water

⁴⁰"He who receives you receives Me, and he who receives Me receives Him who sent Me. ⁴¹He who receives a prophet in the name of a prophet shall receive a prophet's reward. And he who receives a righteous man in the name of a righteous man shall receive a righteous man's reward. ⁴²And whoever gives one of these little ones only a cup of cold *water* in the name of a disciple, assuredly, I say to you, he shall by no means lose his reward."

John the Baptist Sends Messengers to Jesus

11 Now it came to pass, when Jesus finished commanding His twelve disciples, that He departed from there to teach and to preach in their cities.

²And when John had heard in prison about the works of Christ, he sent two ofᵃ his disciples ³and said to Him, "Are You the Coming One, or do we look for another?"

⁴Jesus answered and said to them, "Go and tell John the things which you hear and see: ⁵*The* blind see and *the* lame walk; *the* lepers are cleansed and *the* deaf hear; *the* dead are raised up and *the* poor have the gospel preached to them. ⁶And blessed is he who is not offended because of Me."

⁷As they departed, Jesus began to say to the multitudes concerning John: "What did you go out into the wilderness to see?

10:25 ᵃNU-Text and M-Text read *Beelzebul.* **10:36** ᵃMicah 7:6 **11:2** ᵃNU-Text reads *by* for *two of.*

A reed shaken by the wind? [8]But what did you go out to see? A man clothed in soft garments? Indeed, those who wear soft *clothing* are in kings' houses. [9]But what did you go out to see? A prophet? Yes, I say to you, and more than a prophet. [10]For this is *he* of whom it is written:

'Behold, I send My messenger before
 Your face,
Who will prepare Your way before
 You.'[a]

[11]"Assuredly, I say to you, among those born of women there has not risen one greater than John the Baptist; but he who is least in the kingdom of heaven is greater than he. [12]And from the days of John the Baptist until now the kingdom of heaven suffers violence, and the violent take it by force. [13]For all the prophets and the law prophesied until John. [14]And if you are willing to receive *it*, he is Elijah who is to come. [15]He who has ears to hear, let him hear!

[16]"But to what shall I liken this generation? It is like children sitting in the marketplaces and calling to their companions, [17]and saying:

'We played the flute for you,
 And you did not dance;
We mourned to you,
 And you did not lament.'

[18]For John came neither eating nor drinking, and they say, 'He has a demon.' [19]The Son of Man came eating and drinking, and they say, 'Look, a glutton and a winebibber, a friend of tax collectors and sinners!' But wisdom is justified by her children."[a]

Woe to the Impenitent Cities

[20]Then He began to rebuke the cities in which most of His mighty works had been done, because they did not repent: [21]"Woe to you, Chorazin! Woe to you, Bethsaida! For if the mighty works which were done in you had been done in Tyre and Sidon, they would have repented long ago in sackcloth and ashes. [22]But I say to you, it will be more tolerable for Tyre and Sidon

---

11:10 [a]Malachi 3:1 11:19 [a]NU-Text reads *works*.

PARENTING MATTERS

Q: *How can I help my children stay pure—truly innocent—in the sexual area?*

First, remember that your relationship with your child is the bridge into his or her life. The enemy wants to cut you off from your teenagers; then he can isolate them and convince them of anything.

Second, give your preteens and teens some limits that will challenge them. Barbara and I challenged our children to not kiss a member of the opposite sex until the wedding kiss. They didn't all embrace that challenge, but we believe that by setting a high standard, we helped them maintain sexual purity in their dating relationships.

In addition, we tried to help them set standards that aided them in responding to other temptations. We cannot insulate our children from the world, but we can encourage them to avoid viewing television shows and movies that feature sexual content.

Finally, ask your teenager to become accountable to you. Accountability means staying involved in your teenager's life by asking some tough questions.

As you hold up high standards, be sure to explain some of the reasons God commanded us to abstain from sexual immorality: freedom from guilt and emotional scars, freedom from sexually transmitted diseases and unwanted pregnancies, and preservation of a gift that can be given only to one person—the gift of purity. God has our best in mind!

BIBLICAL INSIGHTS • 11:28–30
The Benefit of Stress

PRESSURE. WE ALL WORK UNDER IT. We are driven by it. We try to escape it. We take vitamins for it. We feel it in our chests. Our stomachs churn. Our palms get sweaty. And all of us get squeezed by it.

Two questions confront us: *How do we live with stress?* And *Is pressure always bad?*

The fact is, many of us want less pressure from the things that are *good* for us to bear. There *can* be positive effects from pressure. It is not pressure, but our response to pressure, that determines pressure's effect on us.

Isn't that what we need to seek God for? We should pray, "Change the pressure rating and broaden my shoulders. Strengthen me, Lord, so I can handle that which has come into my life."

He will! He promised, "Come to Me, all you who labor and are heavy laden, and I will give you rest. Take My yoke upon you and learn from Me, for I am gentle and lowly in heart, and you will find rest for your souls. For My yoke is easy and My burden is light" (11:28–30).

You may be experiencing stress because you are carrying burdens you should be bringing to Jesus and leaving with Him (1 Pet. 5:7). Or God may have brought certain kinds of pressure into your life to help you grow and become more like Jesus (Is. 48:10; James 1:2–4). When the pressure mounts in your life, be sure to cast your cares on Jesus and ask Him for strength to bear up under the load.

Hudson Taylor, the great missionary to China, summarizes, "It matters not how great the pressure is, only where the pressure lies. As long as the pressure doesn't come between me and my Savior, but presses me to Him, then the greater the pressure, the greater my dependence upon Him."

---

in the day of judgment than for you. ²³And you, Capernaum, who are exalted to heaven, will be[a] brought down to Hades; for if the mighty works which were done in you had been done in Sodom, it would have remained until this day. ²⁴But I say to you that it shall be more tolerable for the land of Sodom in the day of judgment than for you."

Jesus Gives True Rest

²⁵At that time Jesus answered and said, "I thank You, Father, Lord of heaven and earth, that You have hidden these things from *the* wise and prudent and have revealed them to babes. ²⁶Even so, Father, for so it seemed good in Your sight. ²⁷All things have been delivered to Me by My Father, and no one knows the Son except the Father. Nor does anyone know the Father except the Son, and *the one* to whom the Son wills to reveal *Him.* ²⁸Come to Me, all *you* who labor and are heavy laden, and I will give you rest. ²⁹Take My yoke upon you and learn from Me, for I am gentle and lowly in heart, and you will find rest for your souls. ³⁰For My yoke *is* easy and My burden is light."

Jesus Is Lord of the Sabbath

12 At that time Jesus went through the grainfields on the Sabbath. And His disciples were hungry, and began to pluck heads of grain and to eat. ²And when the Pharisees saw *it,* they said to Him, "Look, Your disciples are doing what is not lawful to do on the Sabbath!"

³But He said to them, "Have you not read what David did when he was hungry, he and those who were with him: ⁴how he entered the house of God and ate the showbread which was not lawful for him to eat, nor for those who were with him, but only for the priests? ⁵Or have you not read in

---

11:23 [a]NU-Text reads *will you be exalted to heaven? No, you will be.*

the law that on the Sabbath the priests in the temple profane the Sabbath, and are blameless? ⁶Yet I say to you that in this place there is *One* greater than the temple. ⁷But if you had known what *this* means, '*I desire mercy and not sacrifice*,'ᵃ you would not have condemned the guiltless. ⁸For the Son of Man is Lord evenᵃ of the Sabbath."

Healing on the Sabbath

⁹Now when He had departed from there, He went into their synagogue. ¹⁰And behold, there was a man who had a withered hand. And they asked Him, saying, "Is it lawful to heal on the Sabbath?"—that they might accuse Him.

¹¹Then He said to them, "What man is there among you who has one sheep, and if it falls into a pit on the Sabbath, will not lay hold of it and lift *it* out? ¹²Of how much more value then is a man than a sheep? Therefore it is lawful to do good on the Sabbath." ¹³Then He said to the man, "Stretch out your hand." And he stretched *it* out, and it was restored as whole as the other. ¹⁴Then the Pharisees went out and plotted against Him, how they might destroy Him.

Behold, My Servant

¹⁵But when Jesus knew *it,* He withdrew from there. And great multitudesᵃ followed Him, and He healed them all. ¹⁶Yet He warned them not to make Him known, ¹⁷that it might be fulfilled which was spoken by Isaiah the prophet, saying:

18   "*Behold! My Servant whom I have chosen,*
       My Beloved in whom My soul is well pleased!
       I will put My Spirit upon Him,
       And He will declare justice to the Gentiles.
19   *He will not quarrel nor cry out,*
       Nor will anyone hear His voice in the streets.
20   *A bruised reed He will not break,*
       And smoking flax He will not quench,
       Till He sends forth justice to victory;
21   *And in His name Gentiles will trust.*"ᵃ

A House Divided Cannot Stand

²²Then one was brought to Him who was demon-possessed, blind and mute; and He healed him, so that the blind andᵃ mute man both spoke and saw. ²³And all the multitudes were amazed and said, "Could this be the Son of David?"

²⁴Now when the Pharisees heard *it* they said, "This *fellow* does not cast out demons except by Beelzebub,ᵃ the ruler of the demons."

²⁵But Jesus knew their thoughts, and said to them: "Every kingdom divided against itself is brought to desolation, and every city or house divided against itself will not stand. ²⁶If Satan casts out Satan, he is divided against himself. How then will his kingdom stand? ²⁷And if I cast out demons by Beelzebub, by whom do your sons cast *them* out? Therefore they shall be your judges. ²⁸But if I cast out demons by the Spirit of God, surely the kingdom of God has come upon you. ²⁹Or how can one enter a strong man's house and plunder his goods, unless he first binds the strong man? And then he will plunder his house. ³⁰He who is not with Me is against Me, and he who does not gather with Me scatters abroad.

The Unpardonable Sin

³¹"Therefore I say to you, every sin and blasphemy will be forgiven men, but the blasphemy *against* the Spirit will not be forgiven men. ³²Anyone who speaks a word against the Son of Man, it will be forgiven him; but whoever speaks against the Holy Spirit, it will not be forgiven him, either in this age or in the *age* to come.

A Tree Known by Its Fruit

³³"Either make the tree good and its fruit good, or else make the tree bad and its fruit bad; for a tree is known by *its* fruit. ³⁴Brood of vipers! How can you, being evil, speak good things? For out of the abundance of the heart the mouth speaks. ³⁵A good man out of the good treasure of his

---

12:7 ᵃHosea 6:6 **12:8** ᵃNU-Text and M-Text omit *even.* **12:15** ᵃNU-Text brackets *multitudes* as disputed. **12:21** ᵃIsaiah 42:1–4 **12:22** ᵃNU-Text omits *blind and.* **12:24** ᵃNU-Text and M-Text read *Beelzebul.*

heart[a] brings forth good things, and an evil man out of the evil treasure brings forth evil things. 36But I say to you that for every idle word men may speak, they will give account of it in the day of judgment. 37For by your words you will be justified, and by your words you will be condemned."

The Scribes and Pharisees Ask for a Sign

38Then some of the scribes and Pharisees answered, saying, "Teacher, we want to see a sign from You."

39But He answered and said to them, "An evil and adulterous generation seeks after a sign, and no sign will be given to it except the sign of the prophet Jonah. 40For as Jonah was three days and three nights in the belly of the great fish, so will the Son of Man be three days and three nights in the heart of the earth. 41The men of Nineveh will rise up in the judgment with this generation and condemn it, because they repented at the preaching of Jonah; and indeed a greater than Jonah is here. 42The queen of the South will rise up in the judgment with this generation and condemn it, for she came from the ends of the earth to hear the wisdom of Solomon; and indeed a greater than Solomon is here.

An Unclean Spirit Returns

43"When an unclean spirit goes out of a man, he goes through dry places, seeking rest, and finds none. 44Then he says, 'I will return to my house from which I came.' And when he comes, he finds it empty, swept, and put in order. 45Then he goes and takes with him seven other spirits more wicked than himself, and they enter and dwell there; and the last state of that man is worse than the first. So shall it also be with this wicked generation."

Jesus' Mother and Brothers Send for Him

46While He was still talking to the multitudes, behold, His mother and brothers stood outside, seeking to speak with Him. 47Then one said to Him, "Look, Your mother and Your brothers are standing outside, seeking to speak with You."

48But He answered and said to the one who told Him, "Who is My mother and who are My brothers?" 49And He stretched out His hand toward His disciples and said, "Here are My mother and My brothers! 50For whoever does the will of My Father in heaven is My brother and sister and mother."

The Parable of the Sower

13 On the same day Jesus went out of the house and sat by the sea. 2And great multitudes were gathered together to Him, so that He got into a boat and sat; and the whole multitude stood on the shore.

3Then He spoke many things to them in parables, saying: "Behold, a sower went out to sow. 4And as he sowed, some seed fell by the wayside; and the birds came and devoured them. 5Some fell on stony places, where they did not have much earth; and they immediately sprang up because they had no depth of earth. 6But when the sun was up they were scorched, and because they had no root they withered away. 7And some fell among thorns, and the thorns sprang up and choked them. 8But others fell on good ground and yielded a crop: some a hundredfold, some sixty, some thirty. 9He who has ears to hear, let him hear!"

The Purpose of Parables

10And the disciples came and said to Him, "Why do You speak to them in parables?"

11He answered and said to them, "Because it has been given to you to know the mysteries of the kingdom of heaven, but to them it has not been given. 12For whoever has, to him more will be given, and he will have abundance; but whoever

INTIMATE MOMENTS

Make memories on Memorial Day. Purchase a disposable camera and then fill it up with snapshots of you and your spouse—together. You might need to ask others to take the pictures.

12:35 [a]NU-Text and M-Text omit of his heart.

does not have, even what he has will be taken away from him. 13Therefore I speak to them in parables, because seeing they do not see, and hearing they do not hear, nor do they understand. 14And in them the prophecy of Isaiah is fulfilled, which says:

'Hearing you will hear and shall not
 understand,
And seeing you will see and not
 perceive;
15 For the hearts of this people have
 grown dull.
Their ears are hard of hearing,
And their eyes they have closed,
Lest they should see with their eyes
 and hear with their ears,
Lest they should understand with
 their hearts and turn,
So that I should^a heal them.'^b

16But blessed are your eyes for they see, and your ears for they hear; 17for assuredly, I say to you that many prophets and righteous men desired to see what you see, and did not see it, and to hear what you hear, and did not hear it.

The Parable of the Sower Explained

18"Therefore hear the parable of the sower: 19When anyone hears the word of the kingdom, and does not understand it, then the wicked one comes and snatches away what was sown in his heart. This is he who received seed by the wayside. 20But he who received the seed on stony places, this is he who hears the word and immediately receives it with joy; 21yet he has no root in himself, but endures only for a while. For when tribulation or persecution arises because of the word, immediately he stumbles. 22Now he who received seed among the thorns is he who hears the word, and the cares of this world and the deceitfulness of riches choke the word, and he becomes unfruitful. 23But he who received seed on the good ground is he who hears the word and understands it, who indeed bears fruit and produces: some a hundredfold, some sixty, some thirty."

The Parable of the Wheat and the Tares

24Another parable He put forth to them, saying: "The kingdom of heaven is like a man who sowed good seed in his field; 25but while men slept, his enemy came and sowed tares among the wheat and went his way. 26But when the grain had sprouted and produced a crop, then the tares also appeared. 27So the servants of the owner came and said to him, 'Sir, did you not sow good seed in your field? How then does it have tares?' 28He said to them, 'An enemy has done this.' The servants said to him, 'Do you want us then to go and gather them up?' 29But he said, 'No, lest while you gather up the tares you also uproot the wheat with them. 30Let both grow together until the harvest, and at the time of harvest I will say to the reapers, "First gather together the tares and bind them in bundles to burn them, but gather the wheat into my barn." ' "

The Parable of the Mustard Seed

31Another parable He put forth to them, saying: "The kingdom of heaven is like a mustard seed, which a man took and sowed in his field, 32which indeed is the least of all the seeds; but when it is grown it is greater than the herbs and becomes a tree, so that the birds of the air come and nest in its branches."

The Parable of the Leaven

33Another parable He spoke to them: "The kingdom of heaven is like leaven, which a woman took and hid in three measures^a of meal till it was all leavened."

Prophecy and the Parables

34All these things Jesus spoke to the multitude in parables; and without a parable He did not speak to them, 35that it might be fulfilled which was spoken by the prophet, saying:

"I will open My mouth in parables;
I will utter things kept secret from
 the foundation of the world."^a

The Parable of the Tares Explained

36Then Jesus sent the multitude away and went into the house. And His disciples

---

13:15 ^aNU-Text and M-Text read would. ^bIsaiah 6:9, 10 13:33 ^aGreek sata, approximately two pecks in all 13:35 ^aPsalm 78:2

came to Him, saying, "Explain to us the parable of the tares of the field."

[37]He answered and said to them: "He who sows the good seed is the Son of Man. [38]The field is the world, the good seeds are the sons of the kingdom, but the tares are the sons of the wicked *one*. [39]The enemy who sowed them is the devil, the harvest is the end of the age, and the reapers are the angels. [40]Therefore as the tares are gathered and burned in the fire, so it will be at the end of this age. [41]The Son of Man will send out His angels, and they will gather out of His kingdom all things that offend, and those who practice lawlessness, [42]and will cast them into the furnace of fire. There will be wailing and gnashing of teeth. [43]Then the righteous will shine forth as the sun in the kingdom of their Father. He who has ears to hear, let him hear!

The Parable of the Hidden Treasure

[44]"Again, the kingdom of heaven is like treasure hidden in a field, which a man found and hid; and for joy over it he goes and sells all that he has and buys that field.

The Parable of the Pearl of Great Price

[45]"Again, the kingdom of heaven is like a merchant seeking beautiful pearls, [46]who, when he had found one pearl of great price, went and sold all that he had and bought it.

The Parable of the Dragnet

[47]"Again, the kingdom of heaven is like a dragnet that was cast into the sea and gathered some of every kind, [48]which, when it was full, they drew to shore; and they sat down and gathered the good into vessels, but threw the bad away. [49]So it will be at the end of the age. The angels will come forth, separate the wicked from among the just, [50]and cast them into the furnace of fire. There will be wailing and gnashing of teeth."

[51]Jesus said to them,[a] "Have you understood all these things?"

They said to Him, "Yes, Lord."[b]

[52]Then He said to them, "Therefore every scribe instructed concerning[a] the kingdom of heaven is like a householder who brings out of his treasure *things* new and old."

Jesus Rejected at Nazareth

[53]Now it came to pass, when Jesus had finished these parables, that He departed from there. [54]When He had come to His own country, He taught them in their synagogue, so that they were astonished and said, "Where did this *Man* get this wisdom and *these* mighty works? [55]Is this not the carpenter's son? Is not His mother called Mary? And His brothers James, Joses,[a] Simon, and Judas? [56]And His sisters, are they not all with us? Where then did this *Man* get all these things?" [57]So they were offended at Him.

But Jesus said to them, "A prophet is not without honor except in his own country and in his own house." [58]Now He did not do many mighty works there because of their unbelief.

John the Baptist Beheaded

14 At that time Herod the tetrarch heard the report about Jesus [2]and said to his servants, "This is John the Baptist; he is risen from the dead, and therefore these powers are at work in him." [3]For Herod had laid hold of John and bound him, and put *him* in prison for the sake of Herodias, his brother Philip's wife. [4]Because John had said to him, "It is not lawful for you to have her." [5]And although he wanted to put him to death, he feared the multitude, because they counted him as a prophet.

[6]But when Herod's birthday was celebrated, the daughter of Herodias danced before them and pleased Herod. [7]Therefore he promised with an oath to give her whatever she might ask.

[8]So she, having been prompted by her mother, said, "Give me John the Baptist's head here on a platter."

[9]And the king was sorry; nevertheless, because of the oaths and because of those who sat with him, he commanded *it* to be given to *her*. [10]So he sent and had John beheaded in prison. [11]And his head was brought on a platter and given to the girl,

---

13:51 [a]NU-Text omits *Jesus said to them.* [b]NU-Text omits *Lord.* **13:52** [a]Or *for* **13:55** [a]NU-Text reads *Joseph.*

and she brought *it* to her mother. [12]Then his disciples came and took away the body and buried it, and went and told Jesus.

Feeding the Five Thousand

[13]When Jesus heard *it,* He departed from there by boat to a deserted place by Himself. But when the multitudes heard it, they followed Him on foot from the cities. [14]And when Jesus went out He saw a great multitude; and He was moved with compassion for them, and healed their sick. [15]When it was evening, His disciples came to Him, saying, "This is a deserted place, and the hour is already late. Send the multitudes away, that they may go into the villages and buy themselves food."

[16]But Jesus said to them, "They do not need to go away. You give them something to eat."

[17]And they said to Him, "We have here only five loaves and two fish."

[18]He said, "Bring them here to Me." [19]Then He commanded the multitudes to sit down on the grass. And He took the five loaves and the two fish, and looking up to heaven, He blessed and broke and gave the loaves to the disciples; and the disciples gave to the multitudes. [20]So they all ate and were filled, and they took up twelve baskets full of the fragments that remained. [21]Now those who had eaten were about five thousand men, besides women and children.

Jesus Walks on the Sea

[22]Immediately Jesus made His disciples get into the boat and go before Him to the other side, while He sent the multitudes away. [23]And when He had sent the multitudes away, He went up on the mountain by Himself to pray. Now when evening came, He was alone there. [24]But the boat was now in the middle of the sea,[a] tossed by the waves, for the wind was contrary.

[25]Now in the fourth watch of the night Jesus went to them, walking on the sea. [26]And when the disciples saw Him walking on the sea, they were troubled, saying, "It is a ghost!" And they cried out for fear.

[27]But immediately Jesus spoke to them, saying, "Be of good cheer! It is I; do not be afraid."

[28]And Peter answered Him and said, "Lord, if it is You, command me to come to You on the water."

[29]So He said, "Come." And when Peter had come down out of the boat, he walked on the water to go to Jesus. [30]But when he saw that the wind *was* boisterous,[a] he was afraid; and beginning to sink he cried out, saying, "Lord, save me!"

[31]And immediately Jesus stretched out *His* hand and caught him, and said to him,

---

ROMANCE FAQ

Q: How can we best prepare for difficulties in our marriage?

Families fail to respond properly to adversity in two major ways. First, they fail to anticipate trials and problems. When Jesus spoke of building our lives on a sure foundation (7:25), He assumed that rains will come and winds will blow. As I read recently, "The man whose problems are all behind him is probably a school bus driver."

Second, when troubles do hit, many couples have no plan for dealing with the pain, so they turn against one another. One gentleman in the military once explained to me, "In the Green Berets we train over and over, and then over and over again. We repeat some exercises until we are sick of them, but our instructors know what they are doing. They want us so prepared and finely trained that when trials and difficulties come on the battlefield, we will be able to fall back upon that which has become second nature to us. We learn to respond by reflex action."

We need the same regular discipline of spiritual training to fine-tune our own reflexes. If we wait until a crisis hits and only then turn to the Scriptures, then we won't be as prepared—and we'll be more vulnerable to the enemy..

14:24 [a]NU-Text reads *many furlongs away from the land.* **14:30** [a]NU-Text brackets *that* and *boisterous* as disputed.

"O you of little faith, why did you doubt?" [32]And when they got into the boat, the wind ceased.

[33]Then those who were in the boat came and[a] worshiped Him, saying, "Truly You are the Son of God."

Many Touch Him and Are Made Well

[34]When they had crossed over, they came to the land of[a] Gennesaret. [35]And when the men of that place recognized Him, they sent out into all that surrounding region, brought to Him all who were sick, [36]and begged Him that they might only touch the hem of His garment. And as many as touched *it* were made perfectly well.

Defilement Comes from Within

15 Then the scribes and Pharisees who were from Jerusalem came to Jesus, saying, [2]"Why do Your disciples transgress the tradition of the elders? For they do not wash their hands when they eat bread."

[3]He answered and said to them, "Why do you also transgress the commandment of God because of your tradition? [4]For God commanded, saying, *'Honor your father and your mother'*;[a] and, *'He who curses father or mother, let him be put to death.'*[b] [5]But you say, 'Whoever says to his father or mother, "Whatever profit you might have received from me *is* a gift *to* God"—* [6]then he need not honor his father or mother.'[a] Thus you have made the commandment[b] of God of no effect by your tradition. [7]Hypocrites! Well did Isaiah prophesy about you, saying:

[8]   *'These people draw near to Me with
          their mouth,
        And*[a] *honor Me with their lips,
        But their heart is far from Me.*
[9]   *And in vain they worship Me,
        Teaching as doctrines the
          commandments of men.' "*[a]

[10]When He had called the multitude to *Himself,* He said to them, "Hear and under-

stand: [11]Not what goes into the mouth defiles a man; but what comes out of the mouth, this defiles a man."

[12]Then His disciples came and said to Him, "Do You know that the Pharisees were offended when they heard this saying?"

[13]But He answered and said, "Every plant which My heavenly Father has not planted will be uprooted. [14]Let them alone. They are blind leaders of the blind. And if the blind leads the blind, both will fall into a ditch."

[15]Then Peter answered and said to Him, "Explain this parable to us."

[16]So Jesus said, "Are you also still without understanding? [17]Do you not yet understand that whatever enters the mouth goes into the stomach and is eliminated? [18]But those things which proceed out of the mouth come from the heart, and they defile a man. [19]For out of the heart proceed evil thoughts, murders, adulteries, fornications, thefts, false witness, blasphemies. [20]These are *the things* which defile a man, but to eat with unwashed hands does not defile a man."

A Gentile Shows Her Faith

[21]Then Jesus went out from there and departed to the region of Tyre and Sidon. [22]And behold, a woman of Canaan came from that region and cried out to Him, saying, "Have mercy on me, O Lord, Son of David! My daughter is severely demon-possessed."

[23]But He answered her not a word.

And His disciples came and urged Him, saying, "Send her away, for she cries out after us."

[24]But He answered and said, "I was not sent except to the lost sheep of the house of Israel."

[25]Then she came and worshiped Him, saying, "Lord, help me!"

[26]But He answered and said, "It is not good to take the children's bread and throw *it* to the little dogs."

[27]And she said, "Yes, Lord, yet even the little dogs eat the crumbs which fall from their masters' table."

[28]Then Jesus answered and said to her, "O woman, great *is* your faith! Let it be to

---

14:33 [a]NU-Text omits *came and.* 14:34 [a]NU-Text reads *came to land at.* 15:4 [a]Exodus 20:12; Deuteronomy 5:16 [b]Exodus 21:17 15:6 [a]NU-Text omits *or mother.* [b]NU-Text reads *word.* 15:8 [a]NU-Text omits *draw near to Me with their mouth, And.* 15:9 [a]Isaiah 29:13

you as you desire." And her daughter was healed from that very hour.

Jesus Heals Great Multitudes

29Jesus departed from there, skirted the Sea of Galilee, and went up on the mountain and sat down there. 30Then great multitudes came to Him, having with them *the* lame, blind, mute, maimed, and many others; and they laid them down at Jesus' feet, and He healed them. 31So the multitude marveled when they saw *the* mute speaking, *the* maimed made whole, *the* lame walking, and *the* blind seeing; and they glorified the God of Israel.

Feeding the Four Thousand

32Now Jesus called His disciples to *Himself* and said, "I have compassion on the multitude, because they have now continued with Me three days and have nothing to eat. And I do not want to send them away hungry, lest they faint on the way."

33Then His disciples said to Him, "Where could we get enough bread in the wilderness to fill such a great multitude?"

34Jesus said to them, "How many loaves do you have?"

And they said, "Seven, and a few little fish."

35So He commanded the multitude to sit down on the ground. 36And He took the seven loaves and the fish and gave thanks, broke *them* and gave *them* to His disciples; and the disciples *gave* to the multitude. 37So they all ate and were filled, and they took up seven large baskets full of the fragments that were left. 38Now those who ate were four thousand men, besides women and children. 39And He sent away the multitude, got into the boat, and came to the region of Magdala.ᵃ

The Pharisees and Sadducees Seek a Sign

16 Then the Pharisees and Sadducees came, and testing Him asked that He would show them a sign from heaven. 2He answered and said to them, "When it is evening you say, '*It will be* fair weather, for the sky is red'; 3and in the morning, '*It will be* foul weather today, for the sky is red and threatening.' Hypocrites!ᵃ You know how to discern the face of the sky, but you cannot *discern* the signs of the times. 4A wicked and adulterous generation seeks after a sign, and no sign shall be given to it

---

15:39 ᵃNU-Text reads *Magadan*. **16:3** ᵃNU-Text omits *Hypocrites*.

PARENTING MATTERS

Q: How can we best encourage our son/daughter to serve others?

One of the best cures for a me-centered attitude is to give ourselves to others. Jesus modeled this Himself, "And whoever desires to be first among you, let him be your slave—just as the Son of Man did not come to be served, but to serve, and to give His life a ransom for many" (Matt. 20:27, 28).

Be on the lookout for situations where you can help your preadolescent or young teen shift from a selfish focus to the needs of others.

We know a mom who regularly took her son and daughter to a nursing home, just to get them to think of others. Later on, during the height of his teenage turmoil, her son came home from school one day discouraged and announced that he was going to the nursing home to minister to a resident there. A couple of hours later he returned home, fresh and encouraged, because his mom had taught him to give.

Bottom line: Real life is about serving others, whether in our relationship to Christ or with our brothers or sisters. We are training the next generation how to walk humbly with God and to reach out to others with a servant spirit.

except the sign of the prophet[a] Jonah." And He left them and departed.

The Leaven of the Pharisees and Sadducees

[5]Now when His disciples had come to the other side, they had forgotten to take bread. [6]Then Jesus said to them, "Take heed and beware of the leaven of the Pharisees and the Sadducees."

[7]And they reasoned among themselves, saying, "*It is* because we have taken no bread."

[8]But Jesus, being aware of *it,* said to them, "O you of little faith, why do you reason among yourselves because you have brought no bread?[a] [9]Do you not yet understand, or remember the five loaves of the five thousand and how many baskets you took up? [10]Nor the seven loaves of the four thousand and how many large baskets you took up? [11]How is it you do not understand that I did not speak to you concerning bread?—*but* to beware of the leaven of the Pharisees and Sadducees." [12]Then they understood that He did not tell *them* to beware of the leaven of bread, but of the doctrine of the Pharisees and Sadducees.

Peter Confesses Jesus as the Christ

[13]When Jesus came into the region of Caesarea Philippi, He asked His disciples, saying, "Who do men say that I, the Son of Man, am?"

[14]So they said, "Some *say* John the Baptist, some Elijah, and others Jeremiah or one of the prophets."

[15]He said to them, "But who do you say that I am?"

[16]Simon Peter answered and said, "You are the Christ, the Son of the living God."

[17]Jesus answered and said to him, "Blessed are you, Simon Bar-Jonah, for flesh and blood has not revealed *this* to you, but My Father who is in heaven. [18]And I also say to you that you are Peter, and on this rock I will build My church, and the gates of Hades shall not prevail against it. [19]And I will give you the keys of the kingdom of heaven, and whatever you bind on earth will be bound in heaven, and whatever you loose on earth will be loosed[a] in heaven."

[20]Then He commanded His disciples that they should tell no one that He was Jesus the Christ.

INTIMATE MOMENTS

Husbands, see if you can get any ideas from a thirty-something professional man from Boston: "One thing women always comment on is that I'm a spontaneous, take-charge kind of guy, and they really like that. If I'm out on a first date and a woman mentions how she used to go bowling a lot when she was a kid, I'll say, 'So let's go bowling right after we finish our dessert.' Or if it's winter and the mood strikes, I'll drive a date to the beach, just to look at the water. I think women like a man who isn't afraid to act on impulse and do things that really make you enjoy life."

Jesus Predicts His Death and Resurrection

[21]From that time Jesus began to show to His disciples that He must go to Jerusalem, and suffer many things from the elders and chief priests and scribes, and be killed, and be raised the third day.

[22]Then Peter took Him aside and began to rebuke Him, saying, "Far be it from You, Lord; this shall not happen to You!"

[23]But He turned and said to Peter, "Get behind Me, Satan! You are an offense to Me, for you are not mindful of the things of God, but the things of men."

Take Up the Cross and Follow Him

[24]Then Jesus said to His disciples, "If anyone desires to come after Me, let him deny himself, and take up his cross, and follow Me. [25]For whoever desires to save his life will lose it, but whoever loses his life for My sake will find it. [26]For what profit is it to a man if he gains the whole world, and loses his own soul? Or what

16:4 [a]NU-Text omits *the prophet.* **16:8** [a]NU-Text reads *you have no bread.* **16:19** [a]Or *will have been bound . . . will have been loosed*

will a man give in exchange for his soul? ²⁷For the Son of Man will come in the glory of His Father with His angels, and then He will reward each according to his works.

Jesus Transfigured on the Mount

²⁸Assuredly, I say to you, there are some standing here who shall not taste death till they see the Son of Man coming in His kingdom."

ROMANCE FAQ

Q: *What exactly does a submissive wife look like?*

I try to challenge women today to think of the word *submission* in other terms. The word does not mean, as some think, being a slave or allowing yourself to get walked on or abused. Instead, submission will more often involve things like supporting your husband, believing in him, giving him respect. Those words help describe what submission really means.

My role as a wife is to support my husband. I am to believe in him, respect him, and help him (see Gen. 2: 18, 20). I want to help Dennis become all that God intends for him to be. That doesn't mean, of course, that he's not also helping me to become all God intends me to be! We do that for each other. But my primary role is to be a helper, to believe in him and to support him in what he believes God is calling him to do.

When we first started talking about joining with others to launch a ministry to married couples and families, I was free to voice my concerns and express my opinions. Once the decision was made (in this case, a decision we both believed was God's will for us), my assignment was to respect, support, and encourage Dennis as he gave leadership to the ministry. He has told me many times that my believing in him gave him courage. When we wives demonstrate respect for our husbands, we make it easier for them to do what God has called them to do.

17 Now after six days Jesus took Peter, James, and John his brother, led them up on a high mountain by themselves; ²and He was transfigured before them. His face shone like the sun, and His clothes became as white as the light. ³And behold, Moses and Elijah appeared to them, talking with Him. ⁴Then Peter answered and said to Jesus, "Lord, it is good for us to be here; if You wish, let usᵃ make here three tabernacles: one for You, one for Moses, and one for Elijah."

⁵While he was still speaking, behold, a bright cloud overshadowed them; and suddenly a voice came out of the cloud, saying, "This is My beloved Son, in whom I am well pleased. Hear Him!" ⁶And when the disciples heard *it*, they fell on their faces and were greatly afraid. ⁷But Jesus came and touched them and said, "Arise, and do not be afraid." ⁸When they had lifted up their eyes, they saw no one but Jesus only.

⁹Now as they came down from the mountain, Jesus commanded them, saying, "Tell the vision to no one until the Son of Man is risen from the dead."

¹⁰And His disciples asked Him, saying, "Why then do the scribes say that Elijah must come first?"

¹¹Jesus answered and said to them, "Indeed, Elijah is coming firstᵃ and will restore all things. ¹²But I say to you that Elijah has come already, and they did not know him but did to him whatever they wished. Likewise the Son of Man is also about to suffer at their hands." ¹³Then the disciples understood that He spoke to them of John the Baptist.

A Boy Is Healed

¹⁴And when they had come to the multitude, a man came to Him, kneeling down to Him and saying, ¹⁵"Lord, have mercy on my son, for he is an epilepticᵃ and suffers severely; for he often falls into the fire and often into the water. ¹⁶So I brought him to Your disciples, but they could not cure him."

¹⁷Then Jesus answered and said, "O faithless and perverse generation, how long shall I be with you? How long shall I

17:4 ᵃNU-Text reads *I will.* **17:11** ᵃNU-Text omits *first.* **17:15** ᵃLiterally *moonstruck*

bear with you? Bring him here to Me." [18]And Jesus rebuked the demon, and it came out of him; and the child was cured from that very hour.

[19]Then the disciples came to Jesus privately and said, "Why could we not cast it out?"

[20]So Jesus said to them, "Because of your unbelief;[a] for assuredly, I say to you, if you have faith as a mustard seed, you will say to this mountain, 'Move from here to there,' and it will move; and nothing will be impossible for you. [21]However, this kind does not go out except by prayer and fasting."[a]

Jesus Again Predicts His Death and Resurrection

[22]Now while they were staying[a] in Galilee, Jesus said to them, "The Son of Man is about to be betrayed into the hands of men, [23]and they will kill Him, and the third day He will be raised up." And they were exceedingly sorrowful.

Peter and His Master Pay Their Taxes

[24]When they had come to Capernaum,[a] those who received the *temple* tax came to Peter and said, "Does your Teacher not pay the *temple* tax?"

[25]He said, "Yes."

And when he had come into the house, Jesus anticipated him, saying, "What do you think, Simon? From whom do the kings of the earth take customs or taxes, from their sons or from strangers?"

[26]Peter said to Him, "From strangers."

Jesus said to him, "Then the sons are free. [27]Nevertheless, lest we offend them, go to the sea, cast in a hook, and take the fish that comes up first. And when you have opened its mouth, you will find a piece of money;[a] take that and give it to them for Me and you."

Who Is the Greatest?

18 At that time the disciples came to Jesus, saying, "Who then is greatest in the kingdom of heaven?"

[2]Then Jesus called a little child to Him, set him in the midst of them, [3]and said, "Assuredly, I say to you, unless you are converted and become as little children, you will by no means enter the kingdom of heaven. [4]Therefore whoever humbles himself as this little child is the greatest in the kingdom of heaven. [5]Whoever receives one little child like this in My name receives Me.

Jesus Warns of Offenses

[6]"Whoever causes one of these little ones who believe in Me to sin, it would be better for him if a millstone were hung around his neck, and he were drowned in the depth of the sea. [7]Woe to the world because of offenses! For offenses must come, but woe to that man by whom the offense comes!

[8]"If your hand or foot causes you to sin, cut it off and cast *it* from you. It is better for you to enter into life lame or maimed, rather than having two hands or two feet, to be cast into the everlasting fire. [9]And if your eye causes you to sin, pluck it out and cast *it* from you. It is better for you to enter into life with one eye, rather than having two eyes, to be cast into hell fire.

The Parable of the Lost Sheep

[10]"Take heed that you do not despise one of these little ones, for I say to you that in heaven their angels always see the face of My Father who is in heaven. [11]For the Son of Man has come to save that which was lost.[a]

[12]"What do you think? If a man has a hundred sheep, and one of them goes astray, does he not leave the ninety-nine and go to the mountains to seek the one that is straying? [13]And if he should find it, assuredly, I say to you, he rejoices more over that *sheep* than over the ninety-nine that did not go astray. [14]Even so it is not the will of your Father who is in heaven that one of these little ones should perish.

Dealing with a Sinning Brother

[15]"Moreover if your brother sins against you, go and tell him his fault between you and him alone. If he hears you, you have gained your brother. [16]But if he will not hear, take with you one or two more, that 'by

---

17:20 [a]NU-Text reads *little faith.* 17:21 [a]NU-Text omits this verse. 17:22 [a]NU-Text reads *gathering together.* 17:24 [a]NU-Text reads *Capharnaum* (here and elsewhere). 17:27 [a]Greek *stater,* the exact amount to pay the temple tax (didrachma) for two 18:11 [a]NU-Text omits this verse.

DEVOTIONS FOR COUPLES • 19:3–9
A Reason for Divorce?

In our culture many people see divorce as a positive solution to a troubled marriage. But we also see a culture full of people who have been devastated by divorce. One woman who wrote me said, "Our divorce has been the most painful, horrid, ulcer-producing, agonizing event you can imagine . . . I wish I could put on this piece of paper, for all the world to see, a picture of what divorce feels like. Maybe my picture would stop people before it's too late."

From this evidence alone it should not be surprising that God declares, in Malachi 2:16, that He "hates divorce." Marriage was meant to be a special covenant between a man, a woman, and their God, and divorce tears this apart.

It's true that Jesus talks about exception clauses for divorce in Matthew 19. He says, "Moses, because of the hardness of your hearts, permitted you to divorce your wives, but from the beginning it was not so. And I say to you, whoever divorces his wife, except for sexual immorality, and marries another, commits adultery; and whoever marries her who is divorced commits adultery" (vv. 8, 9).

The Bible also addresses the issue of divorce in passages like Matthew 5:32, 33, and in 1 Corinthians 7:15–17. However a person interprets these passages, one thing is clear: God never ordained or created divorce. Humans did. God allowed for divorce because of the hardness of man's sinful heart.

Most Bible teachers believe there are a couple of circumstances in which God releases someone from the lifelong covenant of marriage:

- In the case of a spouse's consistent, unrepentant immorality
- When an unbelieving spouse deserts a believer

Most pastors and Christian leaders will discourage divorce even in these situations, but ultimately will not discourage it when all other options have been considered and exhausted. Divorce in these situations should be the last alternative—never the first choice in even a difficult set of circumstances.

What's really sad, however, is that *most couples seeking a divorce today do so for unbiblical reasons.* They cite reasons such as poor communication, incompatibility, financial problems, lack of commitment to the relationship, changes in priorities. In short, when marriage isn't working, a common solution is to get out.

At one Weekend to Remember™ marriage conference where I spoke, I heard from numerous couples about the problems they faced in their marriages. One wife with five children under the age of 10 wanted out of her marriage because of an insensitive husband. I was left with the impression that though he definitely had some things to learn, this was a marriage that could be repaired. I looked them both in the eyes and pleaded, "Give one another a chance. Take God at his Word. Don't get a divorce!"

Throughout the weekend I was struck again by how many couples are hurting today. But I also realized many of today's divorces do not have to happen. Couples need help and hope to have a successful marriage. And their only hope is found in a relationship with Jesus Christ and the message of this book, the Bible.

---

the mouth of two or three witnesses every word may be established.'a 17And if he refuses to hear them, tell it to the church. But if he refuses even to hear the church, let him be to you like a heathen and a tax collector.

18"Assuredly, I say to you, whatever you bind on earth will be bound in heaven, and whatever you loose on earth will be loosed in heaven.

19"Again I saya to you that if two of you agree on earth concerning anything that they ask, it will be done for them by My

18:16 aDeuteronomy 19:15 18:19 aNU-Text and M-Text read *Again, assuredly, I say.*

Father in heaven. ²⁰For where two or three are gathered together in My name, I am there in the midst of them."

The Parable of the Unforgiving Servant

²¹Then Peter came to Him and said, "Lord, how often shall my brother sin against me, and I forgive him? Up to seven times?"

²²Jesus said to him, "I do not say to you, up to seven times, but up to seventy times seven. ²³Therefore the kingdom of heaven is like a certain king who wanted to settle accounts with his servants. ²⁴And when he had begun to settle accounts, one was brought to him who owed him ten thousand talents. ²⁵But as he was not able to pay, his master commanded that he be sold, with his wife and children and all that he had, and that payment be made. ²⁶The servant therefore fell down before him, saying, 'Master, have patience with me, and I will pay you all.' ²⁷Then the master of that servant was moved with compassion, released him, and forgave him the debt.

²⁸"But that servant went out and found one of his fellow servants who owed him a hundred denarii; and he laid hands on him and took *him* by the throat, saying, 'Pay me what you owe!' ²⁹So his fellow servant fell down at his feet[a] and begged him, saying, 'Have patience with me, and I will pay you all.'[b] ³⁰And he would not, but went and threw him into prison till he should pay the debt. ³¹So when his fellow servants saw what had been done, they were very grieved, and came and told their master all that had been done. ³²Then his master, after he had called him, said to him, 'You wicked servant! I forgave you all that debt because you begged me. ³³Should you not also have had compassion on your fellow servant, just as I had pity on you?' ³⁴And his master was angry, and delivered him to the torturers until he should pay all that was due to him.

³⁵"So My heavenly Father also will do to you if each of you, from his heart, does not forgive his brother his trespasses."[a]

Marriage and Divorce

19 Now it came to pass, when Jesus had finished these sayings, *that* He departed from Galilee and came to the region of Judea beyond the Jordan. ²And great multitudes followed Him, and He healed them there.

³The Pharisees also came to Him, testing Him, and saying to Him, "Is it lawful for a man to divorce his wife for *just* any reason?"

⁴And He answered and said to them, "Have you not read that He who made[a] *them* at the beginning 'made them male and female,'[b] ⁵and said, 'For this reason a man shall leave his father and mother and be joined to his wife, and the two shall become one flesh'? [a] ⁶So then, they are no longer two but one flesh. Therefore what God has joined together, let not man separate."

⁷They said to Him, "Why then did Moses command to give a certificate of divorce, and to put her away?"

⁸He said to them, "Moses, because of the hardness of your hearts, permitted you to divorce your wives, but from the beginning it was not so. ⁹And I say to you, whoever divorces his wife, except for sexual immorality,[a] and marries another, commits adultery; and whoever marries her who is divorced commits adultery."

¹⁰His disciples said to Him, "If such is the case of the man with *his* wife, it is better not to marry."

Jesus Teaches on Celibacy

¹¹But He said to them, "All cannot accept this saying, but only *those* to whom it has been given: ¹²For there are eunuchs who were born thus from *their* mother's womb, and there are eunuchs who were made eunuchs by men, and there are eunuchs who have made themselves eunuchs for the kingdom of heaven's sake. He who is able to accept *it,* let him accept *it.*"

Jesus Blesses Little Children

¹³Then little children were brought to Him that He might put *His* hands on them and pray, but the disciples rebuked them. ¹⁴But Jesus said, "Let the little children come

---

18:29 [a]NU-Text omits *at his feet.* [b]NU-Text and M-Text omit *all.* **18:35** [a]NU-Text omits *his trespasses.* **19:4** [a]NU-Text reads *created.* [b]Genesis 1:27; 5:2 **19:5** [a]Genesis 2:24 **19:9** [a]Or *fornication*

BIBLICAL INSIGHTS • 19:6

One Flesh

JESUS' DISCIPLES WANTED TO TALK about divorce; Jesus wanted to talk about marriage. So He directed their attention back to the very beginning, "Have you not read that He who made them at the beginning 'made them male and female,' and said, 'For this reason a man shall leave his father and mother and be joined to his wife, and the two shall become one flesh'!? So then, they are no longer two but one flesh" (19:4–6).

If we do not leave our parents correctly, we will be like a couple I knew who unwisely remained financially dependent on the wife's family. The situation robbed the husband of the opportunity and responsibility to lead his family. How? The wife kept looking to her dad to bail them out of their poor financial choices. Her husband never learned how to grow up, face his responsibility to make correct choices for his family, and live with the consequences of his decisions. As he lost his self-respect as a man, his wife's respect for him eroded as well.

Continuing to remain emotionally dependent on a parent can be equally destructive. This dependence will hinder the super glue-like bonding that must occur between husband and wife.

Let me encourage you to go on a date as a couple and talk about both of you and your relationships with your parents. Have you truly left them? Have you shifted your loyalty fully to your spouse? Financially? Emotionally? Relationally? If you haven't, it would be a good idea to seek guidance from a wise, godly friend or counselor to talk about the best way to do this while still honoring your parents.

---

to Me, and do not forbid them; for of such is the kingdom of heaven." ¹⁵And He laid *His* hands on them and departed from there.

Jesus Counsels the Rich Young Ruler

¹⁶Now behold, one came and said to Him, "Good[a] Teacher, what good thing shall I do that I may have eternal life?"

¹⁷So He said to him, "Why do you call Me good?[a] No one *is* good but One, *that is,* God.[b] But if you want to enter into life, keep the commandments."

¹⁸He said to Him, "Which ones?"

Jesus said, "'*You shall not murder,' 'You shall not commit adultery,' 'You shall not steal,' 'You shall not bear false witness,'* ¹⁹'*Honor your father and your mother,'*[a] and, '*You shall love your neighbor as yourself.'*"[b]

²⁰The young man said to Him, "All these things I have kept from my youth.[a] What do I still lack?"

²¹Jesus said to him, "If you want to be perfect, go, sell what you have and give to the poor, and you will have treasure in heaven; and come, follow Me."

²²But when the young man heard that saying, he went away sorrowful, for he had great possessions.

With God All Things Are Possible

²³Then Jesus said to His disciples, "Assuredly, I say to you that it is hard for a rich man to enter the kingdom of heaven. ²⁴And again I say to you, it is easier for a camel to go through the eye of a needle than for a rich man to enter the kingdom of God."

²⁵When His disciples heard *it,* they were greatly astonished, saying, "Who then can be saved?"

²⁶But Jesus looked at *them* and said to them, "With men this is impossible, but with God all things are possible."

²⁷Then Peter answered and said to Him, "See, we have left all and followed You. Therefore what shall we have?"

19:16 [a]NU-Text omits *Good.* **19:17** [a]NU-Text reads *Why do you ask Me about what is good?* [b]NU-Text reads *There is One who is good.* **19:19** [a]Exodus 20:12–16; Deuteronomy 5:16–20 [b]Leviticus 19:18 **19:20** [a]NU-Text omits *from my youth.*

²⁸So Jesus said to them, "Assuredly I say to you, that in the regeneration, when the Son of Man sits on the throne of His glory, you who have followed Me will also sit on twelve thrones, judging the twelve tribes of Israel. ²⁹And everyone who has left houses or brothers or sisters or father or mother or wife[a] or children or lands, for My name's sake, shall receive a hundredfold, and inherit eternal life. ³⁰But many who are first will be last, and the last first.

The Parable of the Workers in the Vineyard

20 "For the kingdom of heaven is like a landowner who went out early in the morning to hire laborers for his vineyard. ²Now when he had agreed with the laborers for a denarius a day, he sent them into his vineyard. ³And he went out about the third hour and saw others standing idle in the marketplace, ⁴and said to them, 'You also go into the vineyard, and whatever is right I will give you.' So they went. ⁵Again he went out about the sixth and the ninth hour, and did likewise. ⁶And about the eleventh hour he went out and found others standing idle,[a] and said to them, 'Why have you been standing here idle all day?' ⁷They said to him, 'Because no one hired us.' He said to them, 'You also go into the vineyard, and whatever is right you will receive.'[a]

⁸"So when evening had come, the owner of the vineyard said to his steward, 'Call the laborers and give them *their* wages, beginning with the last to the first.' ⁹And when those came who *were hired* about the eleventh hour, they each received a denarius. ¹⁰But when the first came, they supposed that they would receive more; and they likewise received each a denarius. ¹¹And when they had received *it,* they complained against the landowner, ¹²saying, 'These last *men* have worked *only* one hour, and you made them equal to us who have borne the burden and the heat of the day.' ¹³But he answered one of them and said, 'Friend, I am doing you no wrong. Did you not agree with me for a denarius?

¹⁴Take *what is* yours and go your way. I wish to give to this last man *the same* as to you. ¹⁵Is it not lawful for me to do what I wish with my own things? Or is your eye evil because I am good?' ¹⁶So the last will be first, and the first last. For many are called, but few chosen."[a]

Jesus a Third Time Predicts His Death and Resurrection

¹⁷Now Jesus, going up to Jerusalem, took the twelve disciples aside on the road and said to them, ¹⁸"Behold, we are going

---

ROMANCE FAQ

Q: *My spouse is simply impossible. What can I do?*

When I hear of couples divorcing because of "irreconcilable differences," I think of Jesus' comment about the difficulty rich people face in cultivating a genuine, loving relationship of dependency on God, "With men this is impossible, but with God all things are possible" (19:26).

In a similar way, when a marriage looks doomed from a human perspective, that's when couples need to turn to God. If the almighty God can create the universe out of nothing; if He can part the Red Sea; if He can reconcile you to Him by the sacrifice of His Son—then why is it impossible for Him to heal a broken marriage?

You may be facing "irreconcilable differences" in your marriage, or perhaps in a relationship with another person at work, at church or in your neighborhood. If so, you need to remember that you aren't alone in this situation. God is more than big enough to enable you to overcome any of these seemingly insurmountable differences.

What situations are you facing that seem impossible to you? Ask God to help you believe that *nothing* is impossible with Him. Commit to praying with your mate that God would move in your lives as only He can.

19:29 [a]NU-Text omits *or wife.* **20:6** [a]NU-Text omits *idle.* **20:7** [a]NU-Text omits the last clause of this verse. **20:16** [a]NU-Text omits the last sentence of this verse.

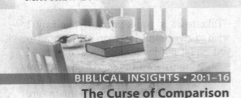

BIBLICAL INSIGHTS • 20:1–16

The Curse of Comparison

LIKE IT OR NOT, WE LIVE IN A CULTURE of comparison in which everyone assumes their rights and their entitlements. And such an atmosphere makes the culture's soil fertile for envy.

Do you ever struggle with envy? Envy can germinate in our souls when we decide to plant unwise seeds of comparison. It all starts with a prolonged look at what someone else has achieved or received, comparing what we have with what others appear to have. Generally, we can find a way to compare ourselves unfavorably with them—and when we do, envy inevitably takes root. When our limited perspective leads us to compare what we think we deserve with what others appear to receive, we become just like the grumblers of Jesus' parable in Matthew 20.

A Christian should avoid comparison at all costs. Don't plant the seed. Don't nurse it by watering and feeding it. Instead, learn what the employees in the parable did on that hot day. Our heavenly Master is just and good in all His judgments. And because He can be trusted, we can learn to be content in circumstances that by all outward appearances seem downright unfair.

Ultimately, the choice for each of us is whether we truly believe that God is in control and that He knows what He's doing. Be careful not to fall into the trap of comparison with others, but instead, learn to cultivate a heart of gratitude for the many ways God has blessed you. Ask God to give you a grateful heart as a couple and then pass that perspective on to your children.

up to Jerusalem, and the Son of Man will be betrayed to the chief priests and to the scribes; and they will condemn Him to death, ¹⁹and deliver Him to the Gentiles to mock and to scourge and to crucify. And the third day He will rise again."

Greatness Is Serving

²⁰Then the mother of Zebedee's sons came to Him with her sons, kneeling down and asking something from Him.

²¹And He said to her, "What do you wish?"

She said to Him, "Grant that these two sons of mine may sit, one on Your right hand and the other on the left, in Your kingdom."

²²But Jesus answered and said, "You do not know what you ask. Are you able to drink the cup that I am about to drink, and be baptized with the baptism that I am baptized with?"[a]

They said to Him, "We are able."

²³So He said to them, "You will indeed drink My cup, and be baptized with the baptism that I am baptized with;[a] but to sit on My right hand and on My left is not Mine to give, but *it is for those* for whom it is prepared by My Father."

²⁴And when the ten heard *it,* they were greatly displeased with the two brothers. ²⁵But Jesus called them to *Himself* and said, "You know that the rulers of the Gentiles lord it over them, and those who are great exercise authority over them. ²⁶Yet it shall not be so among you; but whoever desires to become great among you, let him be your servant. ²⁷And whoever desires to be first among you, let him be your slave— ²⁸just as the Son of Man did not come to be served, but to serve, and to give His life a ransom for many."

Two Blind Men Receive Their Sight

²⁹Now as they went out of Jericho, a great multitude followed Him. ³⁰And behold, two blind men sitting by the road, when they heard that Jesus was passing by, cried out, saying, "Have mercy on us, O Lord, Son of David!"

³¹Then the multitude warned them that they should be quiet; but they cried out all the more, saying, "Have mercy on us, O Lord, Son of David!"

³²So Jesus stood still and called them, and said, "What do you want Me to do for you?"

20:22 ªNU-Text omits *and be baptized with the baptism that I am baptized with.* **20:23** ªNU-Text omits *and be baptized with the baptism that I am baptized with.*

³³They said to Him, "Lord, that our eyes may be opened." ³⁴So Jesus had compassion and touched their eyes. And immediately their eyes received sight, and they followed Him.

The Triumphal Entry

21 Now when they drew near Jerusalem, and came to Bethphage,ᵃ at the Mount of Olives, then Jesus sent two disciples, ²saying to them, "Go into the village opposite you, and immediately you will find a donkey tied, and a colt with her. Loose *them* and bring *them* to Me. ³And if anyone says anything to you, you shall say, 'The Lord has need of them,' and immediately he will send them."

⁴Allᵃ this was done that it might be fulfilled which was spoken by the prophet, saying:

5   "*Tell the daughter of Zion,*
        'Behold, your King is coming to you,
        Lowly, and sitting on a donkey,
        A colt, the foal of a donkey.'"ᵃ

⁶So the disciples went and did as Jesus commanded them. ⁷They brought the donkey and the colt, laid their clothes on them, and set *Him*ᵃ on them. ⁸And a very great multitude spread their clothes on the road; others cut down branches from the trees and spread *them* on the road. ⁹Then the multitudes who went before and those who followed cried out, saying:

    "Hosanna to the Son of David!
    'Blessed is He who comes in the name
        of the LORD!'ᵃ
    Hosanna in the highest!"

¹⁰And when He had come into Jerusalem, all the city was moved, saying, "Who is this?"

¹¹So the multitudes said, "This is Jesus, the prophet from Nazareth of Galilee."

Jesus Cleanses the Temple

¹²Then Jesus went into the temple of Godᵃ and drove out all those who bought and sold in the temple, and overturned the tables of the money changers and the seats of those who sold doves. ¹³And He said to them, "It is written, '*My house shall be called a house of prayer,*'ᵃ but you have made it a '*den of thieves.*'"ᵇ

¹⁴Then *the* blind and *the* lame came to Him in the temple, and He healed them. ¹⁵But when the chief priests and scribes saw the wonderful things that He did, and the children crying out in the temple and saying, "Hosanna to the Son of David!" they were indignant ¹⁶and said to Him, "Do You hear what these are saying?"

And Jesus said to them, "Yes. Have you never read,

    '*Out of the mouth of babes and*
        nursing infants
        You have perfected praise'?"ᵃ

¹⁷Then He left them and went out of the city to Bethany, and He lodged there.

The Fig Tree Withered

¹⁸Now in the morning, as He returned to the city, He was hungry. ¹⁹And seeing a fig tree by the road, He came to it and found nothing on it but leaves, and said to it, "Let no fruit grow on you ever again." Immediately the fig tree withered away.

The Lesson of the Withered Fig Tree

²⁰And when the disciples saw *it,* they marveled, saying, "How did the fig tree wither away so soon?"

²¹So Jesus answered and said to them, "Assuredly, I say to you, if you have faith and do not doubt, you will not only do what was done to the fig tree, but also if you say to this mountain, 'Be removed and be cast into the sea,' it will be done. ²²And whatever things you ask in prayer, believing, you will receive."

Jesus' Authority Questioned

²³Now when He came into the temple, the chief priests and the elders of the people confronted Him as He was teaching, and said, "By what authority are You doing these things? And who gave You this authority?"

²⁴But Jesus answered and said to them, "I also will ask you one thing, which if you

---

21:1 ᵃM-Text reads *Bethsphage.* **21:4** ᵃNU-Text omits *All.* **21:5** ᵃZechariah 9:9 **21:7** ᵃNU-Text reads *and He sat.* **21:9** ᵃPsalm 118:26 **21:12** ᵃNU-Text omits *of God.* **21:13** ᵃIsaiah 56:7 ᵇJeremiah 7:11 **21:16** ᵃPsalm 8:2

tell Me, I likewise will tell you by what authority I do these things: 25The baptism of John—where was it from? From heaven or from men?"

And they reasoned among themselves, saying, "If we say, 'From heaven,' He will say to us, 'Why then did you not believe him?' 26But if we say, 'From men,' we fear the multitude, for all count John as a prophet." 27So they answered Jesus and said, "We do not know."

And He said to them, "Neither will I tell you by what authority I do these things.

The Parable of the Two Sons

28"But what do you think? A man had two sons, and he came to the first and said, 'Son, go, work today in my vineyard.' 29He answered and said, 'I will not,' but afterward he regretted it and went. 30Then he came to the second and said likewise. And he answered and said, 'I *go*, sir,' but he did not go. 31Which of the two did the will of *his* father?"

They said to Him, "The first."

Jesus said to them, "Assuredly, I say to you that tax collectors and harlots enter the kingdom of God before you. 32For John came to you in the way of righteousness, and you did not believe him; but tax collectors and harlots believed him; and when you saw *it,* you did not afterward relent and believe him.

The Parable of the Wicked Vinedressers

33"Hear another parable: There was a certain landowner who planted a vineyard and set a hedge around it, dug a winepress in it and built a tower. And he leased it to vinedressers and went into a far country. 34Now when vintage-time drew near, he sent his servants to the vinedressers, that they might receive its fruit. 35And the vinedressers took his servants, beat one, killed one, and stoned another. 36Again he sent other servants, more than the first, and they did likewise to them. 37Then last of all he sent his son to them, saying, 'They will respect my son.' 38But when the vinedressers saw the son, they said among themselves, 'This is the heir. Come, let us kill him and seize his inheritance.' 39So they took him and cast *him* out of the vineyard and killed *him*.

40"Therefore, when the owner of the vineyard comes, what will he do to those vinedressers?"

41They said to Him, "He will destroy those wicked men miserably, and lease *his* vineyard to other vinedressers who will render to him the fruits in their seasons."

42Jesus said to them, "Have you never read in the Scriptures:

> 'The stone which the builders rejected
> Has become the chief cornerstone.
> This was the LORD's doing,
> And it is marvelous in our eyes' ?a

43"Therefore I say to you, the kingdom of God will be taken from you and given to a nation bearing the fruits of it. 44And whoever falls on this stone will be broken; but on whomever it falls, it will grind him to powder."

45Now when the chief priests and Pharisees heard His parables, they perceived that He was speaking of them. 46But when they sought to lay hands on Him, they feared the multitudes, because they took Him for a prophet.

The Parable of the Wedding Feast

22 And Jesus answered and spoke to them again by parables and said: 2"The kingdom of heaven is like a certain king who arranged a marriage for his son, 3and sent out his servants to call those who were invited to the wedding; and they were not willing to come. 4Again, he sent out other servants, saying, 'Tell those who are invited, "See, I have prepared my dinner; my oxen and fatted cattle *are* killed, and all things *are* ready. Come to the wedding." ' 5But they made light of it and went their ways, one to his own farm, another to his business. 6And the rest seized his servants, treated *them* spitefully, and killed *them*. 7But when the king heard *about it,* he was furious. And he sent out his armies, destroyed those murderers, and burned up their city. 8Then he said to his servants, 'The wedding is ready, but those who were invited were not worthy. 9Therefore go into the highways, and as many as you find, invite to the wedding.' 10So those servants

21:42 aPsalm 118:22, 23

went out into the highways and gathered together all whom they found, both bad and good. And the wedding *hall* was filled with guests.

11"But when the king came in to see the guests, he saw a man there who did not have on a wedding garment. 12So he said to him, 'Friend, how did you come in here without a wedding garment?' And he was speechless. 13Then the king said to the servants, 'Bind him hand and foot, take him away, anda cast *him* into outer darkness; there will be weeping and gnashing of teeth.'

14"For many are called, but few *are* chosen."

The Pharisees: Is It Lawful to Pay Taxes to Caesar?

15Then the Pharisees went and plotted how they might entangle Him in *His* talk. 16And they sent to Him their disciples with the Herodians, saying, "Teacher, we know that You are true, and teach the way of God in truth; nor do You care about anyone, for You do not regard the person of men. 17Tell us, therefore, what do You think? Is it lawful to pay taxes to Caesar, or not?"

18But Jesus perceived their wickedness, and said, "Why do you test Me, *you* hypocrites? 19Show Me the tax money."

So they brought Him a denarius.

20And He said to them, "Whose image and inscription *is* this?"

21They said to Him, "Caesar's."

And He said to them, "Render therefore to Caesar the things that are Caesar's, and to God the things that are God's." 22When they had heard *these words,* they marveled, and left Him and went their way.

The Sadducees: What About the Resurrection?

23The same day the Sadducees, who say there is no resurrection, came to Him and asked Him, 24saying: "Teacher, Moses said that if a man dies, having no children, his brother shall marry his wife and raise up

offspring for his brother. 25Now there were with us seven brothers. The first died after he had married, and having no offspring, left his wife to his brother. 26Likewise the second also, and the third, even to the seventh. 27Last of all the woman died also. 28Therefore, in the resurrection, whose wife of the seven will she be? For they all had her."

29Jesus answered and said to them, "You are mistaken, not knowing the Scriptures nor the power of God. 30For in the resurrection they neither marry nor are given in marriage, but are like angels of Goda in heaven. 31But concerning the resurrection of the dead, have you not read what was spoken to you by God, saying, 32*I am the God of Abraham, the God of Isaac, and the God of Jacob'* ?a God is not the God of the dead, but of the living." 33And when the multitudes heard *this,* they were astonished at His teaching.

The Scribes: Which Is the First Commandment of All?

34But when the Pharisees heard that He had silenced the Sadducees, they gathered together. 35Then one of them, a lawyer, asked *Him a question,* testing Him, and saying, 36"Teacher, which *is* the great commandment in the law?"

37Jesus said to him, " '*You shall love the* LORD *your God with all your heart, with all your soul, and with all your mind.'*a 38This is *the* first and great commandment. 39And *the* second *is* like it: '*You shall love your neighbor as yourself.'*a 40On these two commandments hang all the Law and the Prophets."

Jesus: How Can David Call His Descendant Lord?

41While the Pharisees were gathered together, Jesus asked them, 42saying, "What do you think about the Christ? Whose Son is He?"

They said to Him, "*The Son* of David."

43He said to them, "How then does David in the Spirit call Him '*Lord*,' saying:

44   '*The* LORD *said to my Lord,*
    "*Sit at My right hand,*
    Till I make Your enemies Your
        *footstool"' ?*a

22:13 aNU-Text omits *take him away, and.*
22:30 aNU-Text omits *of God.* 22:32 aExodus 3:6, 15 22:37 aDeuteronomy 6:5 22:39 aLeviticus 19:18
22:44 aPsalm 110:1

45If David then calls Him *'Lord,'* how is He his Son?" 46And no one was able to answer Him a word, nor from that day on did anyone dare question Him anymore.

Woe to the Scribes and Pharisees

23 Then Jesus spoke to the multitudes and to His disciples, 2saying: "The scribes and the Pharisees sit in Moses' seat. 3Therefore whatever they tell you to observe,a *that* observe and do, but do not do according to their works; for they say, and do not do. 4For they bind heavy burdens, hard to bear, and lay *them* on men's shoulders; but they *themselves* will not move them with one of their fingers. 5But all their works they do to be seen by men. They make their phylacteries broad and enlarge the borders of their garments. 6They love the best places at feasts, the best seats in the synagogues, 7greetings in the marketplaces, and to be called by men, 'Rabbi, Rabbi.' 8But you, do not be called 'Rabbi'; for One is your Teacher, the Christ,a and you are all brethren. 9Do not call anyone on earth your father; for One is your Father, He who is in heaven. 10And do not be called teachers; for One is your Teacher, the Christ. 11But he who is greatest among you shall be your servant. 12And whoever exalts himself will be humbled, and he who humbles himself will be exalted.

13"But woe to you, scribes and Pharisees, hypocrites! For you shut up the kingdom of heaven against men; for you neither go in *yourselves,* nor do you allow those who are entering to go in. 14Woe to you, scribes and Pharisees, hypocrites! For you devour widows' houses, and for a pretense make long prayers. Therefore you will receive greater condemnation.a

15"Woe to you, scribes and Pharisees, hypocrites! For you travel land and sea to win one proselyte, and when he is won, you make him twice as much a son of hell as yourselves.

16"Woe to you, blind guides, who say, 'Whoever swears by the temple, it is nothing; but whoever swears by the gold of the temple, he is obliged *to perform it.'* 17Fools and blind! For which is greater, the gold or the temple that sanctifiesa the gold? 18And,

'Whoever swears by the altar, it is nothing; but whoever swears by the gift that is on it, he is obliged *to perform it.'* 19Fools and blind! For which is greater, the gift or the altar that sanctifies the gift? 20Therefore he who swears by the altar, swears by it and by all things on it. 21He who swears by the temple, swears by it and by Him who dwellsa in it. 22And he who swears by heaven, swears by the throne of God and by Him who sits on it.

23"Woe to you, scribes and Pharisees, hypocrites! For you pay tithe of mint and anise and cummin, and have neglected the weightier *matters* of the law: justice and mercy and faith. These you ought to have done, without leaving the others undone. 24Blind guides, who strain out a gnat and swallow a camel!

25"Woe to you, scribes and Pharisees, hypocrites! For you cleanse the outside of the cup and dish, but inside they are full of extortion and self-indulgence.a 26Blind Pharisee, first cleanse the inside of the cup and dish, that the outside of them may be clean also.

27"Woe to you, scribes and Pharisees, hypocrites! For you are like whitewashed tombs which indeed appear beautiful outwardly, but inside are full of dead *men's* bones and all uncleanness. 28Even so you also outwardly appear righteous to men, but inside you are full of hypocrisy and lawlessness.

29"Woe to you, scribes and Pharisees, hypocrites! Because you build the tombs of the prophets and adorn the monuments of the righteous, 30and say, 'If we had lived in the days of our fathers, we would not have been partakers with them in the blood of the prophets.'

31"Therefore you are witnesses against yourselves that you are sons of those who murdered the prophets. 32Fill up, then, the measure of your fathers' *guilt.* 33Serpents, brood of vipers! How can you escape the condemnation of hell? 34Therefore, indeed, I send you prophets, wise men, and scribes:

23:3 aNU-Text omits *to observe.* **23:8** aNU-Text omits *the Christ.* **23:14** aNU-Text omits this verse. **23:17** aNU-Text reads *sanctified.* **23:21** aM-Text reads *dwelt.* **23:25** aM-Text reads *unrighteousness.*

some of them you will kill and crucify, and *some* of them you will scourge in your synagogues and persecute from city to city, [35]that on you may come all the righteous blood shed on the earth, from the blood of righteous Abel to the blood of Zechariah, son of Berechiah, whom you murdered between the temple and the altar. [36]Assuredly, I say to you, all these things will come upon this generation.

Jesus Laments over Jerusalem

[37]"O Jerusalem, Jerusalem, the one who kills the prophets and stones those who are sent to her! How often I wanted to gather your children together, as a hen gathers her chicks under *her* wings, but you were not willing! [38]See! Your house is left to you desolate; [39]for I say to you, you shall see Me no more till you say, '*Blessed is He who comes in the name of the LORD!*' "[a]

Jesus Predicts the Destruction of the Temple

24 Then Jesus went out and departed from the temple, and His disciples came up to show Him the buildings of the temple. [2]And Jesus said to them, "Do you not see all *these* things? Assuredly, I say to you, not *one* stone shall be left here upon another, that shall not be thrown down."

The Signs of the Times and the End of the Age

[3]Now as He sat on the Mount of Olives, the disciples came to Him privately, saying, "Tell us, when will these things be? And what *will be* the sign of Your coming, and of the end of the age?"

[4]And Jesus answered and said to them: "Take heed that no one deceives you. [5]For many will come in My name, saying, 'I am the Christ,' and will deceive many. [6]And you will hear of wars and rumors of wars. See that you are not troubled; for all[a] *these things* must come to pass, but the end is not yet. [7]For nation will rise against nation, and kingdom against kingdom. And there will be famines, pestilences,[a] and earthquakes

in various places. [8]All these *are* the beginning of sorrows.

[9]"Then they will deliver you up to tribulation and kill you, and you will be hated by all nations for My name's sake. [10]And then many will be offended, will betray one another, and will hate one another. [11]Then many false prophets will rise up and deceive many. [12]And because lawlessness will abound, the love of many will grow cold. [13]But he who endures to the end shall be saved. [14]And this gospel of the kingdom will be preached in all the world as a witness to all the nations, and then the end will come.

The Great Tribulation

[15]"Therefore when you see the '*abomination of desolation,*'[a] spoken of by Daniel the prophet, standing in the holy place" (whoever reads, let him understand), [16]"then let those who are in Judea flee to the mountains. [17]Let him who is on the housetop not go down to take anything out of his house. [18]And let him who is in the field not go back to get his clothes. [19]But woe to those who are pregnant and to those who are nursing babies in those days! [20]And pray that your flight may not be in winter or on the Sabbath. [21]For then there will be great tribulation, such as has not been since the beginning of the world until this time, no, nor ever shall be. [22]And unless those days were shortened, no flesh would be saved; but for the elect's sake those days will be shortened.

[23]"Then if anyone says to you, 'Look, here *is* the Christ!' or 'There!' do not believe *it*. [24]For false christs and false prophets will rise and show great signs and wonders to deceive, if possible, even the elect. [25]See, I have told you beforehand.

[26]"Therefore if they say to you, 'Look, He is in the desert!' do not go out; *or* 'Look, *He is* in the inner rooms!' do not believe *it*. [27]For as the lightning comes from the east and flashes to the west, so also will the coming of the Son of Man be. [28]For wherever the carcass is, there the eagles will be gathered together.

The Coming of the Son of Man

[29]"Immediately after the tribulation of those days the sun will be darkened, and

---

23:39 [a]Psalm 118:26 **24:6** [a]NU-Text omits *all.* **24:7** [a]NU-Text omits *pestilences.* **24:15** [a]Daniel 11:31; 12:11

the moon will not give its light; the stars will fall from heaven, and the powers of the heavens will be shaken. [30]Then the sign of the Son of Man will appear in heaven, and then all the tribes of the earth will mourn, and they will see the Son of Man coming on the clouds of heaven with power and great glory. [31]And He will send His angels with a great sound of a trumpet, and they will gather together His elect from the four winds, from one end of heaven to the other.

The Parable of the Fig Tree

[32]"Now learn this parable from the fig tree: When its branch has already become tender and puts forth leaves, you know that summer *is* near. [33]So you also, when you see all these things, know that it[a] is near—at the doors! [34]Assuredly, I say to you, this generation will by no means pass away till all these things take place. [35]Heaven and earth will pass away, but My words will by no means pass away.

No One Knows the Day or Hour

[36]"But of that day and hour no one knows, not even the angels of heaven,[a] but My Father only. [37]But as the days of Noah *were*, so also will the coming of the Son of Man be. [38]For as in the days before the flood, they were eating and drinking, marrying and giving in marriage, until the day that Noah entered the ark, [39]and did not know until the flood came and took them all away, so also will the coming of the Son of Man be. [40]Then two *men* will be in the field: one will be taken and the other left. [41]Two *women will be* grinding at the mill: one will be taken and the other left. [42]Watch therefore, for you do not know what hour[a] your Lord is coming. [43]But know this, that if the master of the house had known what hour the thief would come, he would have watched and not allowed his house to be broken into. [44]Therefore you also be ready, for the Son of Man is coming at an hour you do not expect.

The Faithful Servant and the Evil Servant

[45]"Who then is a faithful and wise servant, whom his master made ruler over his household, to give them food in due season? [46]Blessed *is* that servant whom his master, when he comes, will find so doing. [47]Assuredly, I say to you that he will make him ruler over all his goods. [48]But if that evil servant says in his heart, 'My master is delaying his coming,' [a] [49]and begins to

---

24:33 [a]Or *He* **24:36** [a]NU-Text adds *nor the Son.* **24:42** [a]NU-Text reads *day.* **24:48** [a]NU-Text omits *his coming.*

ROMANTIC QUOTES AND NOTES
Help Your Mate Inventory His/Her Talents

Jesus once told His disciples what we know as the "Parable of the Talents" (Matt. 25:14–30), in which a master gave each of his three servants a certain sum of money. The master rewards the servants who faithfully use the resources he gave them, but he takes away the talent from the one who buried it.

Your assignment is to go on a talent search. You can help your mate discover his or her abilities and gifts, unique areas of spiritual capability, listed in Romans 12 and 1 Corinthians 12. With increased confidence, he or she can be a more faithful servant and use the talents that God has given him or her to further God's kingdom.

As you assess your mate's talents, both of you will probably feel the need for outside help. Ask friends who know your mate well to give their opinions. Ask your pastor or another mature Christian for ideas.

Encourage your mate to be faithful in what you both already know he or she does well. Beware of adding too many expectations or building them too high! Your mate doesn't have to do everything all at once. Your loved one can spend a lifetime investing those talents for the good of mankind and as an expression of gratitude for what Christ has done for us.

beat *his* fellow servants, and to eat and drink with the drunkards, ⁵⁰the master of that servant will come on a day when he is not looking for *him* and at an hour that he is not aware of, ⁵¹and will cut him in two and appoint *him* his portion with the hypocrites. There shall be weeping and gnashing of teeth.

The Parable of the Wise and Foolish Virgins

25 "Then the kingdom of heaven shall be likened to ten virgins who took their lamps and went out to meet the bridegroom. ²Now five of them were wise, and five *were* foolish. ³Those who *were* foolish took their lamps and took no oil with them, ⁴but the wise took oil in their vessels with their lamps. ⁵But while the bridegroom was delayed, they all slumbered and slept.

⁶"And at midnight a cry was *heard:* 'Behold, the bridegroom is coming;ª go out to meet him!' ⁷Then all those virgins arose and trimmed their lamps. ⁸And the foolish said to the wise, 'Give us *some* of your oil, for our lamps are going out.' ⁹But the wise answered, saying, 'No, lest there should not be enough for us and you; but go rather to those who sell, and buy for yourselves.' ¹⁰And while they went to buy, the bridegroom came, and those who were ready went in with him to the wedding; and the door was shut.

¹¹"Afterward the other virgins came also, saying, 'Lord, Lord, open to us!' ¹²But he answered and said, 'Assuredly, I say to you, I do not know you.'

¹³"Watch therefore, for you know neither the day nor the hourª in which the Son of Man is coming.

The Parable of the Talents

¹⁴"For *the kingdom of heaven is* like a man traveling to a far country, *who* called his own servants and delivered his goods to them. ¹⁵And to one he gave five talents, to another two, and to another one, to each according to his own ability; and immediately he went on a journey. ¹⁶Then he who had received the five talents went and traded with them, and made another five talents. ¹⁷And likewise he who *had received* two gained two more also. ¹⁸But he who had received one went and dug in the ground, and hid his lord's money. ¹⁹After a long time the lord of those servants came and settled accounts with them.

²⁰"So he who had received five talents came and brought five other talents, saying, 'Lord, you delivered to me five talents; look, I have gained five more talents besides them.' ²¹His lord said to him, 'Well *done,* good and faithful servant; you were faithful over a few things, I will make you ruler over many things. Enter into the joy of your lord.' ²²He also who had received two talents came and said, 'Lord, you delivered to me two talents; look, I have gained two more talents besides them.' ²³His lord said to him, 'Well *done,* good and faithful servant; you have been faithful over a few things, I will make you ruler over many things. Enter into the joy of your lord.'

²⁴"Then he who had received the one talent came and said, 'Lord, I knew you to be a hard man, reaping where you have not sown, and gathering where you have not scattered seed. ²⁵And I was afraid, and went and hid your talent in the ground. Look, *there* you have *what is* yours.'

²⁶"But his lord answered and said to him, 'You wicked and lazy servant, you knew that I reap where I have not sown, and gather where I have not scattered seed. ²⁷So you ought to have deposited my money with the bankers, and at my coming I would have received back my own with interest. ²⁸So take the talent from him, and give *it* to him who has ten talents.

²⁹'For to everyone who has, more will be given, and he will have abundance; but from him who does not have, even what he has will be taken away. ³⁰And cast the unprofitable servant into the outer darkness. There will be weeping and gnashing of teeth.'

The Son of Man Will Judge the Nations

³¹"When the Son of Man comes in His glory, and all the holyª angels with Him, then He will sit on the throne of His glory. ³²All the nations will be gathered before Him, and He will separate them one from another, as a shepherd divides *his* sheep

---

25:6 ªNU-Text omits *is coming.* **25:13** ªNU-Text omits the rest of this verse. **25:31** ªNU-Text omits *holy.*

BIBLICAL INSIGHTS • 25:21

Teach Them the Value of Excellence

WHEN YOUR CHILDREN LISTEN TO YOU speak or watch you work, do they get the idea that believers in Jesus Christ should strive for excellence in everything they do? Do they see you working wholeheartedly for the Lord, and not for men? We believe this should be one of our primary tasks, to use both our words and our actions to encourage our children toward a life of excellence.

Of course, we do not mean attaining perfection or applying identical standards to every child. Rather, we propose that within their God-given capabilities every child be challenged to rise above the crowd, to seek higher standards of achievement, and to become all that God has gifted him or her to be.

This was a real challenge, especially during the years when we had four teenagers living in our home. There's always tension between understanding a child's talent and ability and stretching them to attainable goals. Many times Barbara and I would pray and ask God if we were too lenient, and on other occasions we'd ask Him if we were too tough. In every situation, it was our dependence upon God that helped us decide and trust Him with both the process and the results.

Training children to step above mediocrity also helps them reject mediocrity in their relationships with God. Jesus pointed to a coming day when God will say to His diligent children, "Well done, good and faithful servant; you were faithful over a few things, I will make you ruler over many things" (25:21).

It is our job as parents to teach our children to be trustworthy, to fulfill their commitments, and to do a good job even when nobody is looking. In the end, they need to learn to do their work "heartily, as to the Lord" (Col. 3:23).

---

from the goats. ³³And He will set the sheep on His right hand, but the goats on the left. ³⁴Then the King will say to those on His right hand, 'Come, you blessed of My Father, inherit the kingdom prepared for you from the foundation of the world: ³⁵for I was hungry and you gave Me food; I was thirsty and you gave Me drink; I was a stranger and you took Me in; ³⁶I *was* naked and you clothed Me; I was sick and you visited Me; I was in prison and you came to Me.'

³⁷"Then the righteous will answer Him, saying, 'Lord, when did we see You hungry and feed *You*, or thirsty and give *You* drink? ³⁸When did we see You a stranger and take *You* in, or naked and clothe *You?* ³⁹Or when did we see You sick, or in prison, and come to You?' ⁴⁰And the King will answer and say to them, 'Assuredly, I say to you, inasmuch as you did *it* to one of the least of these My brethren, you did *it* to Me.'

⁴¹"Then He will also say to those on the left hand, 'Depart from Me, you cursed, into the everlasting fire prepared for the devil and his angels: ⁴²for I was hungry and you gave Me no food; I was thirsty and you gave Me no drink; ⁴³I was a stranger and you did not take Me in, naked and you did not clothe Me, sick and in prison and you did not visit Me.'

⁴⁴"Then they also will answer Him,ᵃ saying, 'Lord, when did we see You hungry or thirsty or a stranger or naked or sick or in prison, and did not minister to You?' ⁴⁵Then He will answer them, saying, 'Assuredly, I say to you, inasmuch as you did not do *it* to one of the least of these, you did not do *it* to Me.' ⁴⁶And these will go away into everlasting punishment, but the righteous into eternal life."

25:44 ᵃNU-Text and M-Text omit *Him.*

The Plot to Kill Jesus

26 Now it came to pass, when Jesus had finished all these sayings, *that* He said to His disciples, 2"You know that after two days is the Passover, and the Son of Man will be delivered up to be crucified."

3Then the chief priests, the scribes,a and the elders of the people assembled at the palace of the high priest, who was called Caiaphas, 4and plotted to take Jesus by trickery and kill *Him.* 5But they said, "Not during the feast, lest there be an uproar among the people."

The Anointing at Bethany

6And when Jesus was in Bethany at the house of Simon the leper, 7a woman came to Him having an alabaster flask of very costly fragrant oil, and she poured *it* on His head as He sat *at the table.* 8But when His disciples saw *it,* they were indignant, saying, "Why this waste? 9For this fragrant oil might have been sold for much and given to *the* poor."

10But when Jesus was aware of *it,* He said to them, "Why do you trouble the woman? For she has done a good work for Me. 11For you have the poor with you always, but Me you do not have always. 12For in pouring this fragrant oil on My body, she did *it* for My burial. 13Assuredly, I say to you, wherever this gospel is preached in the whole world, what this woman has done will also be told as a memorial to her."

Judas Agrees to Betray Jesus

14Then one of the twelve, called Judas Iscariot, went to the chief priests 15and said, "What are you willing to give me if I deliver Him to you?" And they counted out to him thirty pieces of silver. 16So from that time he sought opportunity to betray Him.

Jesus Celebrates Passover with His Disciples

17Now on the first *day of the Feast* of the Unleavened Bread the disciples came to Jesus, saying to Him, "Where do You want us to prepare for You to eat the Passover?"

18And He said, "Go into the city to a certain man, and say to him, 'The Teacher says, "My time is at hand; I will keep the Passover at your house with My disciples."'"

19So the disciples did as Jesus had directed them; and they prepared the Passover.

20When evening had come, He sat down with the twelve. 21Now as they were eating, He said, "Assuredly, I say to you, one of you will betray Me."

22And they were exceedingly sorrowful, and each of them began to say to Him, "Lord, is it I?"

23He answered and said, "He who dipped *his* hand with Me in the dish will betray Me. 24The Son of Man indeed goes just as it is written of Him, but woe to that man by whom the Son of Man is betrayed! It would have been good for that man if he had not been born."

25Then Judas, who was betraying Him, answered and said, "Rabbi, is it I?"

He said to him, "You have said it."

Jesus Institutes the Lord's Supper

26And as they were eating, Jesus took bread, blesseda and broke *it,* and gave *it* to the disciples and said, "Take, eat; this is My body."

27Then He took the cup, and gave thanks, and gave *it* to them, saying, "Drink from it, all of you. 28For this is My blood of the newa covenant, which is shed for many for the remission of sins. 29But I say to you, I will not drink of this fruit of the vine from now on until that day when I drink it new with you in My Father's kingdom."

30And when they had sung a hymn, they went out to the Mount of Olives.

Jesus Predicts Peter's Denial

31Then Jesus said to them, "All of you will be made to stumble because of Me this night, for it is written:

'I will strike the Shepherd,
And the sheep of the flock will be
    scattered.'a

32But after I have been raised, I will go before you to Galilee."

33Peter answered and said to Him, "Even if all are made to stumble because of You, I will never be made to stumble."

26:3 aNU-Text omits *the scribes.* **26:26** aM-Text reads *gave thanks for.* **26:28** aNU-Text omits *new.* **26:31** aZechariah 13:7

[34]Jesus said to him, "Assuredly, I say to you that this night, before the rooster crows, you will deny Me three times."

[35]Peter said to Him, "Even if I have to die with You, I will not deny You!"

And so said all the disciples.

The Prayer in the Garden

[36]Then Jesus came with them to a place called Gethsemane, and said to the disciples, "Sit here while I go and pray over there." [37]And He took with Him Peter and the two sons of Zebedee, and He began to be sorrowful and deeply distressed. [38]Then He said to them, "My soul is exceedingly sorrowful, even to death. Stay here and watch with Me."

[39]He went a little farther and fell on His face, and prayed, saying, "O My Father, if it is possible, let this cup pass from Me; nevertheless, not as I will, but as You *will*."

[40]Then He came to the disciples and found them sleeping, and said to Peter, "What! Could you not watch with Me one hour? [41]Watch and pray, lest you enter into temptation. The spirit indeed *is* willing, but the flesh *is* weak."

[42]Again, a second time, He went away and prayed, saying, "O My Father, if this cup cannot pass away from Me unless[a] I drink it, Your will be done." [43]And He came and found them asleep again, for their eyes were heavy.

[44]So He left them, went away again, and prayed the third time, saying the same words. [45]Then He came to His disciples and said to them, "Are *you* still sleeping and resting? Behold, the hour is at hand, and the Son of Man is being betrayed into the hands of sinners. [46]Rise, let us be going. See, My betrayer is at hand."

Betrayal and Arrest in Gethsemane

[47]And while He was still speaking, behold, Judas, one of the twelve, with a great multitude with swords and clubs, came from the chief priests and elders of the people. [48]Now His betrayer had given them a sign, saying, "Whomever I kiss, He is the One; seize Him." [49]Immediately he went up to Jesus and said, "Greetings, Rabbi!" and kissed Him.

[50]But Jesus said to him, "Friend, why have you come?"

Then they came and laid hands on Jesus and took Him. [51]And suddenly, one of those *who were* with Jesus stretched out *his* hand and drew his sword, struck the servant of the high priest, and cut off his ear.

[52]But Jesus said to him, "Put your sword in its place, for all who take the sword will perish[a] by the sword. [53]Or do you think that I cannot now pray to My Father, and He will provide Me with more than twelve legions of angels? [54]How then could the Scriptures be fulfilled, that it must happen thus?"

[55]In that hour Jesus said to the multitudes, "Have you come out, as against a robber, with swords and clubs to take Me? I sat daily with you, teaching in the temple, and you did not seize Me. [56]But all this was done that the Scriptures of the prophets might be fulfilled."

Then all the disciples forsook Him and fled.

Jesus Faces the Sanhedrin

[57]And those who had laid hold of Jesus led *Him* away to Caiaphas the high priest, where the scribes and the elders were assembled. [58]But Peter followed Him at a distance to the high priest's courtyard. And he went in and sat with the servants to see the end.

[59]Now the chief priests, the elders,[a] and all the council sought false testimony against Jesus to put Him to death, [60]but found none. Even though many false witnesses came forward, they found none.[a] But at last two false witnesses[b] came forward [61]and said, "This *fellow* said, 'I am able to destroy the temple of God and to build it in three days.'"

[62]And the high priest arose and said to Him, "Do You answer nothing? What *is it* these men testify against You?" [63]But Jesus kept silent. And the high priest answered and said to Him, "I put You under oath by

26:42 [a]NU-Text reads *if this may not pass away unless.* **26:52** [a]M-Text reads *die.* **26:59** [a]NU-Text omits *the elders.* **26:60** [a]NU-Text puts a comma after *but found none,* does not capitalize *Even,* and omits *they found none.* [b]NU-Text omits *false witnesses.*

the living God: Tell us if You are the Christ, the Son of God!"

64Jesus said to him, "*It is as* you said. Nevertheless, I say to you, hereafter you will see the Son of Man sitting at the right hand of the Power, and coming on the clouds of heaven."

65Then the high priest tore his clothes, saying, "He has spoken blasphemy! What further need do we have of witnesses? Look, now you have heard His blasphemy! 66What do you think?"

They answered and said, "He is deserving of death."

67Then they spat in His face and beat Him; and others struck *Him* with the palms of their hands, 68saying, "Prophesy to us, Christ! Who is the one who struck You?"

Peter Denies Jesus, and Weeps Bitterly

69Now Peter sat outside in the courtyard. And a servant girl came to him, saying, "You also were with Jesus of Galilee."

70But he denied it before *them* all, saying, "I do not know what you are saying."

71And when he had gone out to the gateway, another *girl* saw him and said to those *who were* there, "This *fellow* also was with Jesus of Nazareth."

72But again he denied with an oath, "I do not know the Man!"

73And a little later those who stood by came up and said to Peter, "Surely you also are *one* of them, for your speech betrays you."

74Then he began to curse and swear, *saying,* "I do not know the Man!"

Immediately a rooster crowed. 75And Peter remembered the word of Jesus who had said to him, "Before the rooster crows, you will deny Me three times." So he went out and wept bitterly.

Jesus Handed Over to Pontius Pilate

27 When morning came, all the chief priests and elders of the people plotted against Jesus to put Him to death. 2And when they had bound Him, they led Him away and delivered Him to Pontius[a] Pilate the governor.

Judas Hangs Himself

3Then Judas, His betrayer, seeing that He had been condemned, was remorseful and brought back the thirty pieces of silver to the chief priests and elders, 4saying, "I have sinned by betraying innocent blood."

And they said, "What *is that* to us? You see *to it!*"

5Then he threw down the pieces of silver in the temple and departed, and went and hanged himself.

6But the chief priests took the silver pieces and said, "It is not lawful to put them into the treasury, because they are the price of blood." 7And they consulted together and bought with them the potter's field, to bury strangers in. 8Therefore that field has been called the Field of Blood to this day.

9Then was fulfilled what was spoken by Jeremiah the prophet, saying, *"And they took the thirty pieces of silver, the value of Him who was priced,* whom they of the children of Israel priced, 10*and gave them for the potter's field, as the LORD directed me."*[a]

Jesus Faces Pilate

11Now Jesus stood before the governor. And the governor asked Him, saying, "Are You the King of the Jews?"

Jesus said to him, "*It is as* you say." 12And while He was being accused by the chief priests and elders, He answered nothing.

13Then Pilate said to Him, "Do You not hear how many things they testify against You?" 14But He answered him not one word, so that the governor marveled greatly.

Taking the Place of Barabbas

15Now at the feast the governor was accustomed to releasing to the multitude one prisoner whom they wished. 16And at that time they had a notorious prisoner called Barabbas.[a] 17Therefore, when they had gathered together, Pilate said to them, "Whom do you want me to release to you? Barabbas, or Jesus who is called Christ?" 18For he knew that they had handed Him over because of envy.

19While he was sitting on the judgment seat, his wife sent to him, saying, "Have

---

27:2 [a]NU-Text omits *Pontius.*   27:10 [a]Jeremiah 32:6–9   27:16 [a]NU-Text reads *Jesus Barabbas.*

BIBLICAL INSIGHTS • 28:19

Parents Are Disciple Makers

PARENTS FULFILL MANY IMPORTANT roles for their children: cook, innkeeper, medic, taxi driver, coach—it's a long list! But one role often gets overlooked or misunderstood, disciple maker.

Do you see yourself as a trainer of disciples? If not, here's why you should. You have been called to "make disciples of all the nations" (28:19), and your number one responsibility in making disciples is to your family. Fathers, in fact, are specifically directed to "bring [your children] up in the training and admonition of the Lord" (Eph. 6:4).

Children learn everything important about life from their parents. And they learn more from what they see us model than from what they hear us tell them. Does that sober you like it sobers us? From his first moments, your little tyke has marvelous radar that never stops picking up data from the big people roaming through his life, answering questions like, *How do people talk to one another? How is love expressed? How do people get attention? Who does what around this place? Am I important?*

Whether we like it or not, our words and actions are observed, evaluated, and stored by these remarkable little people placed in our care. That is why the Bible teaches us to instruct our children in the faith (see Deut. 6:9), and to "walk worthy of the calling with which you were called, with all lowliness and gentleness, with longsuffering, bearing with one another in love" (Eph. 4:1, 2).

I believe the family remains the most effective Great Commission Training Center on the planet. Throughout history, God has used families to train, shape, and launch generations for His work around the globe.

---

nothing to do with that just Man, for I have suffered many things today in a dream because of Him."

20But the chief priests and elders persuaded the multitudes that they should ask for Barabbas and destroy Jesus. 21The governor answered and said to them, "Which of the two do you want me to release to you?"

They said, "Barabbas!"

22Pilate said to them, "What then shall I do with Jesus who is called Christ?"

They all said to him, "Let Him be crucified!"

23Then the governor said, "Why, what evil has He done?"

But they cried out all the more, saying, "Let Him be crucified!"

24When Pilate saw that he could not prevail at all, but rather *that* a tumult was rising, he took water and washed *his* hands before the multitude, saying, "I am innocent of the blood of this just Person.[a] You see *to it.*"

25And all the people answered and said, "His blood *be* on us and on our children."

26Then he released Barabbas to them; and when he had scourged Jesus, he delivered *Him* to be crucified.

The Soldiers Mock Jesus

27Then the soldiers of the governor took Jesus into the Praetorium and gathered the whole garrison around Him. 28And they stripped Him and put a scarlet robe on Him. 29When they had twisted a crown of thorns, they put *it* on His head, and a reed in His right hand. And they bowed the knee before Him and mocked Him, saying, "Hail, King of the Jews!" 30Then they spat on Him, and took the reed and struck Him on the head. 31And when they had mocked Him, they took the robe off Him, put His *own* clothes on Him, and led Him away to be crucified.

27:24 [a]NU-Text omits *just.*

The King on a Cross

³²Now as they came out, they found a man of Cyrene, Simon by name. Him they compelled to bear His cross. ³³And when they had come to a place called Golgotha, that is to say, Place of a Skull, ³⁴they gave Him sourᵃ wine mingled with gall to drink. But when He had tasted *it,* He would not drink.

³⁵Then they crucified Him, and divided His garments, casting lots,ᵃ that it might be fulfilled which was spoken by the prophet:

"*They divided My garments among them,*
And for My clothing they cast lots."ᵇ

³⁶Sitting down, they kept watch over Him there. ³⁷And they put up over His head the accusation written against Him:

27:34 ᵃNU-Text omits *sour.* **27:35** ᵃNU-Text and M-Text omit the rest of this verse. ᵇPsalm 22:18 **27:41** ᵃM-Text reads *with the scribes, the Pharisees, and the elders.* **27:42** ᵃNU-Text reads *He is the King of Israel!* ᵇNU-Text and M-Text read *we will believe in Him.*

THIS IS JESUS THE KING OF
THE JEWS.

³⁸Then two robbers were crucified with Him, one on the right and another on the left.

³⁹And those who passed by blasphemed Him, wagging their heads ⁴⁰and saying, "You who destroy the temple and build *it* in three days, save Yourself! If You are the Son of God, come down from the cross."

⁴¹Likewise the chief priests also, mocking with the scribes and elders,ᵃ said, ⁴²"He saved others; Himself He cannot save. If He is the King of Israel,ᵃ let Him now come down from the cross, and we will believe Him.ᵇ ⁴³He trusted in God; let Him deliver Him now if He will have Him; for He said, 'I am the Son of God.'"

⁴⁴Even the robbers who were crucified with Him reviled Him with the same thing.

Jesus Dies on the Cross

⁴⁵Now from the sixth hour until the ninth hour there was darkness over all the land. ⁴⁶And about the ninth hour Jesus cried out with a loud voice, saying, "Eli,

---

PARENTING MATTERS

Q: How do we raise our kids with a taste for the Great Commission?

Do you realize that your most important disciples are your own children? I especially wish more mothers had this vision. The enemy is trying to get moms to devalue their positions so they won't raise the next generation to go to the world and have an impact for Christ.

If you want to raise your children with a sense of mission, then begin when they are young by talking to them of God's plan. Help them reach out to their peers.

Is one of your children strong-willed? Then she is the kind who will storm a country for Christ; he will be the one who never quits until he impacts his sphere of influence.

Pray for your children's mates with them.

Teach them they are pilgrims with a purpose in this world, not wanderers.

Give them biographies of missionaries to read.

Finally, give them the freedom to allow God to work in their lives. The biggest deterrent is to missions today is parents who want their kids to make money and "be successful!"

When Jesus Christ went to the cross, He passed the torch of the Great Commission to His followers. Our responsibility is to lead our children to Christ and to give them a sense of mission, passing the torch to reach the next generation.

DEVOTIONS FOR COUPLES • 28:19
Set Values, Bear Fruit

At one point in our marriage, Barbara and I had a conversation in which we found ourselves asking some very vexing questions:

- *What kind of family is God calling us to be?*
- *What does He want us uniquely to do?*
- *Where do we fit into the Great Commission?* (Matt. 28:19, 20)
- *How might God use our marriage to advance His work?*

As we wrestled with these questions, we discovered that we had never really hammered out our family's values *together*. We had never asked ourselves, "Where must we succeed? Where are we unwilling to fail?" We needed to look ten, twenty, even fifty years down the road and consider where we wanted to absolutely, positively win. That realization led us to our first courageous choice.

It can be yours, too.

Choose to spell out your family values together and use them to guide your future commitments of time, energy, money, and aspirations. What do you believe God has uniquely gifted you and called you to do? What kind of choices will most effectively enable you to carry out that calling? If you believe, for example, that God has called you to minister somehow to the Latino population of your community, would it make sense to spend a couple of years studying Russian? Probably not.

It takes courage to decide and define your values in this out-of-control, cookie-cutter, you-can-have-it-all, permissive culture. The simple fact is, we can't. We can't have it all, know it all, or do it all. Many of our fondest activities, longed-for purchases, and long-held aspirations must be left in the dust if we are to fulfill the mission God gives to us. It always comes down to the cold, hard fact of our human limitations and the knowledge that we have been designed to fulfill a specific purpose in God's good plan. So again, what's yours?

We discovered that understanding and embracing our own set of values based upon Scripture takes the pressure off. We don't need to worry about how others are living. We don't have to waste energy looking over our shoulders. We can focus on God's direction for *our* lives.

The apostle Paul wrote that we are God's "workmanship, created in Christ Jesus for good works, which God prepared beforehand that we should walk in them" (Eph. 2:10). By understanding how God has made us—our skills and abilities, our individual personalities and passions, and our values—we can begin to see which good works God has called us to and how we can fulfill His purposes for our lives.

Eli, lama sabachthani?" that is, *"My God, My God, why have You forsaken Me?"*[a]

47Some of those who stood there, when they heard *that,* said, "This Man is calling for Elijah!" 48Immediately one of them ran and took a sponge, filled *it* with sour wine and put *it* on a reed, and offered it to Him to drink.

49The rest said, "Let Him alone; let us see if Elijah will come to save Him."

50And Jesus cried out again with a loud voice, and yielded up His spirit.

51Then, behold, the veil of the temple was torn in two from top to bottom; and the earth quaked, and the rocks were split, 52and the graves were opened; and many bodies of the saints who had fallen asleep were raised; 53and coming out of the graves after His resurrection, they went into the holy city and appeared to many.

54So when the centurion and those with him, who were guarding Jesus, saw the earthquake and the things that had happened, they feared greatly, saying, "Truly this was the Son of God!"

55And many women who followed Jesus from Galilee, ministering to Him, were there

27:46 aPsalm 22:1

looking on from afar, [56]among whom were Mary Magdalene, Mary the mother of James and Joses,[a] and the mother of Zebedee's sons.

Jesus Buried in Joseph's Tomb

[57]Now when evening had come, there came a rich man from Arimathea, named Joseph, who himself had also become a disciple of Jesus. [58]This man went to Pilate and asked for the body of Jesus. Then Pilate commanded the body to be given to him. [59]When Joseph had taken the body, he wrapped it in a clean linen cloth, [60]and laid it in his new tomb which he had hewn out of the rock; and he rolled a large stone against the door of the tomb, and departed. [61]And Mary Magdalene was there, and the other Mary, sitting opposite the tomb.

Pilate Sets a Guard

[62]On the next day, which followed the Day of Preparation, the chief priests and Pharisees gathered together to Pilate, [63]saying, "Sir, we remember, while He was still alive, how that deceiver said, 'After three days I will rise.' [64]Therefore command that the tomb be made secure until the third day, lest His disciples come by night[a] and steal Him *away,* and say to the people, 'He has risen from the dead.' So the last deception will be worse than the first."

[65]Pilate said to them, "You have a guard; go your way, make *it* as secure as you know how." [66]So they went and made the tomb secure, sealing the stone and setting the guard.

He Is Risen

28 Now after the Sabbath, as the first *day* of the week began to dawn, Mary Magdalene and the other Mary came to see the tomb. [2]And behold, there was a great earthquake; for an angel of the Lord descended from heaven, and came and rolled back the stone from the door,[a] and sat on it. [3]His countenance was like lightning, and his clothing as white as snow. [4]And the guards shook for fear of him, and became like dead *men.*

[5]But the angel answered and said to the women, "Do not be afraid, for I know that you seek Jesus who was crucified. [6]He is not here; for He is risen, as He said. Come, see the place where the Lord lay. [7]And go quickly and tell His disciples that He is risen from the dead, and indeed He is

---

ROMANCE FAQ

Q: How can we choose a church that will help us grow together?

Spiritual value is the number one factor in choosing a church. No church will be perfect, but this checklist of questions will help you consider key areas.

_____ Do you agree with the church theologically? So long as you have no significant reservations, you should be able to join that church.

_____ Is the church alive spiritually, and are both of you fed spiritually from the Scriptures? You need a church that believes in the authority of Scripture and the power of the Holy Spirit and that equips you to fulfill your major commitments—marriage, family, work, finances, your mission, etc.

_____ Does the worship engage you and draw your heart to God? Its services should help you enter God's presence in heartfelt worship.

_____ Is it a church where you can experience true Christian community? You need a group of like-minded couples or a group led by an older mentor who will challenge you to grow spiritually.

_____ Does the church hold its members accountable to obey Scripture? A Bible-believing church will expect its people to seek to be like Christ.

_____ Does the church have an outreach mentality? How active is the church in evangelism? In helping the poor and needy? In supporting missions at home and abroad? All of these are good signs of a healthy, vibrant church.

27:56 [a]NU-Text reads *Joseph.* **27:64** [a]NU-Text omits *by night.* **28:2** [a]NU-Text omits *from the door.*

going before you into Galilee; there you will see Him. Behold, I have told you."

[8]So they went out quickly from the tomb with fear and great joy, and ran to bring His disciples word.

The Women Worship the Risen Lord

[9]And as they went to tell His disciples,[a] behold, Jesus met them, saying, "Rejoice!" So they came and held Him by the feet and worshiped Him. [10]Then Jesus said to them, "Do not be afraid. Go *and* tell My brethren to go to Galilee, and there they will see Me."

The Soldiers Are Bribed

[11]Now while they were going, behold, some of the guard came into the city and reported to the chief priests all the things that had happened. [12]When they had assembled with the elders and consulted together, they gave a large sum of money to the soldiers, [13]saying, "Tell them, 'His disciples came at night and stole Him *away* while we slept.' [14]And if this comes to the governor's ears, we will appease him and make you secure." [15]So they took the money and did as they were instructed; and this saying is commonly reported among the Jews until this day.

The Great Commission

[16]Then the eleven disciples went away into Galilee, to the mountain which Jesus had appointed for them. [17]When they saw Him, they worshiped Him; but some doubted.

[18]And Jesus came and spoke to them, saying, "All authority has been given to Me in heaven and on earth. [19]Go therefore[a] and make disciples of all the nations, baptizing them in the name of the Father and of the Son and of the Holy Spirit, [20]teaching them to observe all things that I have commanded you; and lo, I am with you always, *even* to the end of the age." Amen.[a]

28:9 [a]NU-Text omits the first clause of this verse. **28:19** [a]M-Text omits *therefore.* **28:20** [a]NU-Text omits *Amen.*

MARK

THIS ACCOUNT OF THE LIFE OF JESUS comes from the pen of John Mark, a disciple of Jesus who accompanied his cousin Barnabas and the apostle Paul on some early missionary journeys described in the book of Acts. As far as we know, he was not an eyewitness to the ministry of Jesus. Tradition says he gathered most of his information from Peter. Most scholars believe his book was the first of the four Gospels to be written.

John Mark paints a picture of Jesus as the suffering servant of the Lord. He focuses more on the *events* of Jesus' life than on His teaching ministry. Because he likely had a Roman audience in mind, Mark leaves out many things other Gospel writers include, such as the genealogy of Jesus, how His life fulfilled certain prophecies, and references to Jewish law and customs. Mark skips any account of the birth of Jesus and begins his story with Jesus' public ministry.

Mark also devotes much of his Gospel to the last week of Jesus' life. In Mark 8, Jesus points His followers to the cross, while in chapter 11, Mark begins to provide readers with details regarding Jesus' final days. Mark wants to make sure his readers understand that Jesus came to give His life as payment for our sin.

In one key passage (10:43–45), Jesus contrasts His ministry with the way the rulers of the Gentiles lord their power over their subjects. He instructs His followers to take a different approach, "Whoever desires to become great among you shall be your servant. And whoever of you desires to be first shall be slave of all. For even the Son of Man did not come to be served, but to serve, and to give His life a ransom for many."

This passage has a clear application to Christian homes. God calls husbands to lead their wives and their families, not in the lording-over style of the Gentiles, but instead as servant-leaders who give themselves up for their wives and their children. In this they follow the example of Jesus Himself.

John the Baptist Prepares the Way

1 The beginning of the gospel of Jesus Christ, the Son of God. [2]As it is written in the Prophets:[a]

"*Behold, I send My messenger before
    Your face,
Who will prepare Your way before
    You.*" [b]

[3] "*The voice of one crying in the
    wilderness:
'Prepare the way of the* LORD;
Make His paths straight.'"[a]

[4]John came baptizing in the wilderness and preaching a baptism of repentance for the remission of sins. [5]Then all the land of Judea, and those from Jerusalem, went out to him and were all baptized by him in the Jordan River, confessing their sins.

[6]Now John was clothed with camel's hair and with a leather belt around his waist, and he ate locusts and wild honey. [7]And he preached, saying, "There comes One after me who is mightier than I, whose sandal strap I am not worthy to stoop down and loose. [8]I indeed baptized you with water, but He will baptize you with the Holy Spirit."

John Baptizes Jesus

[9]It came to pass in those days *that* Jesus came from Nazareth of Galilee, and was baptized by John in the Jordan. [10]And immediately, coming up from[a] the water, He saw the heavens parting and the Spirit descending upon Him like a dove. [11]Then a voice came from heaven, "You are My beloved Son, in whom I am well pleased."

Satan Tempts Jesus

[12]Immediately the Spirit drove Him into the wilderness. [13]And He was there in the wilderness forty days, tempted by Satan, and was with the wild beasts; and the angels ministered to Him.

Jesus Begins His Galilean Ministry

[14]Now after John was put in prison, Jesus came to Galilee, preaching the gospel of the kingdom[a] of God, [15]and saying, "The time is fulfilled, and the kingdom of God is at hand. Repent, and believe in the gospel."

Four Fishermen Called as Disciples

[16]And as He walked by the Sea of Galilee, He saw Simon and Andrew his brother casting a net into the sea; for they were fishermen. [17]Then Jesus said to them, "Follow Me, and I will make you become fishers of men." [18]They immediately left their nets and followed Him.

[19]When He had gone a little farther from there, He saw James the *son* of Zebedee, and John his brother, who also *were* in the boat mending their nets. [20]And immediately He called them, and they left their father Zebedee in the boat with the hired servants, and went after Him.

Jesus Casts Out an Unclean Spirit

[21]Then they went into Capernaum, and immediately on the Sabbath He entered the synagogue and taught. [22]And they were astonished at His teaching, for He taught them as one having authority, and not as the scribes.

[23]Now there was a man in their synagogue with an unclean spirit. And he cried out, [24]saying, "Let *us* alone! What have we to do with You, Jesus of Nazareth? Did You come to destroy us? I know who You are— the Holy One of God!"

[25]But Jesus rebuked him, saying, "Be quiet, and come out of him!" [26]And when the unclean spirit had convulsed him and cried out with a loud voice, he came out of him. [27]Then they were all amazed, so that they questioned among themselves, saying, "What is this? What new doctrine *is* this? For with authority[a] He commands even the unclean spirits, and they obey Him." [28]And immediately His fame spread throughout all the region around Galilee.

Peter's Mother-in-Law Healed

[29]Now as soon as they had come out of the synagogue, they entered the house of Simon and Andrew, with James and John. [30]But Simon's wife's mother lay sick with a fever, and they told Him about her at once.

1:2 [a]NU-Text reads *Isaiah the prophet.* [b]Malachi 3:1
1:3 [a]Isaiah 40:3 **1:10** [a]NU-Text reads *out of.*
1:14 [a]NU-Text omits *of the kingdom.*
1:27 [a]NU-Text reads *What is this? A new doctrine with authority.*

³¹So He came and took her by the hand and lifted her up, and immediately the fever left her. And she served them.

Many Healed After Sabbath Sunset

³²At evening, when the sun had set, they brought to Him all who were sick and those who were demon-possessed. ³³And the whole city was gathered together at the door. ³⁴Then He healed many who were sick with various diseases, and cast out many demons; and He did not allow the demons to speak, because they knew Him.

Preaching in Galilee

³⁵Now in the morning, having risen a long while before daylight, He went out and departed to a solitary place; and there He prayed. ³⁶And Simon and those *who were* with Him searched for Him. ³⁷When they found Him, they said to Him, "Everyone is looking for You."

³⁸But He said to them, "Let us go into the next towns, that I may preach there also, because for this purpose I have come forth."

³⁹And He was preaching in their synagogues throughout all Galilee, and casting out demons.

Jesus Cleanses a Leper

⁴⁰Now a leper came to Him, imploring Him, kneeling down to Him and saying to Him, "If You are willing, You can make me clean."

⁴¹Then Jesus, moved with compassion, stretched out *His* hand and touched him, and said to him, "I am willing; be cleansed." ⁴²As soon as He had spoken, immediately the leprosy left him, and he was cleansed. ⁴³And He strictly warned him and sent him away at once, ⁴⁴and said to him, "See that you say nothing to anyone; but go your way, show yourself to the priest, and offer for your cleansing those things which Moses commanded, as a testimony to them."

⁴⁵However, he went out and began to proclaim *it* freely, and to spread the matter, so that Jesus could no longer openly enter the city, but was outside in deserted places; and they came to Him from every direction.

2:2 ᵃNU-Text omits *Immediately.*

BIBLICAL INSIGHTS • 1:18

Living under the Authority of Jesus

JESUS LIVED, taught, and led with authority. We see a good picture of this as we read what happened when He called Simon and Andrew to follow Him. They didn't take a few days to figure out what it would cost them to follow Jesus, or to ask their father if it was okay for them to go. No, "They immediately left their nets and followed Him" (1:18). They *heard* the voice of Jesus and acted.

Peter and Andrew dropped everything and followed Jesus that day for one reason: He had authority to call them—the same authority He still has today.

One of the main reasons we don't see more people leaving their nets and following Christ is that we in the church—and this includes Christian marriages and families—have not presented Jesus Christ in all of His splendor and authority. When people start to see Jesus in all His majesty, they will respond much as Simon and Andrew did.

Jesus calls each of us as individuals, as couples, and as families to become "fishers of men" (1:17), and it is only when we obey His calling that we will see our households effectively influence our neighborhoods and our towns for Christ.

Jesus Forgives and Heals a Paralytic

2 And again He entered Capernaum after *some* days, and it was heard that He was in the house. ²Immediatelyᵃ many gathered together, so that there was no longer room to receive *them,* not even near the door. And He preached the word to them. ³Then they came to Him, bringing a paralytic who was carried by four *men.* ⁴And when they could not come near Him because of the crowd, they uncovered the roof where He was. So when they had broken through, they let down the bed on which the paralytic was lying.

5When Jesus saw their faith, He said to the paralytic, "Son, your sins are forgiven you."

6And some of the scribes were sitting there and reasoning in their hearts, 7"Why does this *Man* speak blasphemies like this? Who can forgive sins but God alone?"

8But immediately, when Jesus perceived in His spirit that they reasoned thus within themselves, He said to them, "Why do you reason about these things in your hearts? 9Which is easier, to say to the paralytic, '*Your* sins are forgiven you,' or to say, 'Arise, take up your bed and walk'? 10But that you may know that the Son of Man has power on earth to forgive sins"—He said to the paralytic, 11"I say to you, arise, take up your bed, and go to your house." 12Immediately he arose, took up the bed, and went out in the presence of them all, so that all were amazed and glorified God, saying, "We never saw *anything* like this!"

Matthew the Tax Collector

13Then He went out again by the sea; and all the multitude came to Him, and He taught them. 14As He passed by, He saw Levi the *son* of Alphaeus sitting at the tax office. And He said to him, "Follow Me." So he arose and followed Him.

15Now it happened, as He was dining in *Levi's* house, that many tax collectors and sinners also sat together with Jesus and His disciples; for there were many, and they followed Him. 16And when the scribes anda Pharisees saw Him eating with the tax collectors and sinners, they said to His disciples, "How *is it* that He eats and drinks with tax collectors and sinners?"

17When Jesus heard *it,* He said to them, "Those who are well have no need of a physician, but those who are sick. I did not come to call *the* righteous, but sinners, to repentance."a

Jesus Is Questioned About Fasting

18The disciples of John and of the Pharisees were fasting. Then they came and said to Him, "Why do the disciples of John and of the Pharisees fast, but Your disciples do not fast?"

19And Jesus said to them, "Can the friends of the bridegroom fast while the bridegroom is with them? As long as they have the bridegroom with them they cannot fast. 20But the days will come when the bridegroom will be taken away from them, and then they will fast in those days. 21No one sews a piece of unshrunk cloth on an old garment; or else the new piece pulls away from the old, and the tear is made worse. 22And no one puts new wine into old wineskins; or else the new wine bursts

2:16 aNU-Text reads *of the.*
2:17 aNU-Text omits *to repentance.*

Get Alone with God

The best thing about reading the Bible, especially the four Gospels, is that we can examine the words and deeds of Jesus Christ, looking to apply to our own lives the divine lessons that we learn there.

Early in the Gospel of Mark, for example, we read how Jesus handled the stress and pressure that came while He ministered to hundreds of needy people who crossed His path, "Now in the morning, having risen a long while before daylight, He went out and departed to a solitary place; and there He prayed" (1:35).

Being a spouse and a parent carries many inherent pressures and stresses, and many individuals find it easy to make alone time with God the first casualty of a busy day. But if Jesus, who probably handled more stresses, pressures, and people before breakfast than any of us handle in a week, made the time to get alone and pray, then we have no excuse for not doing the same thing. If He did it, we should, too.

We are big advocates of couples praying together, but as important as that is, it is just as important for husbands and wives to find their own time to be *absolutely alone* with God.

the wineskins, the wine is spilled, and the wineskins are ruined. But new wine must be put into new wineskins."

Jesus Is Lord of the Sabbath

23Now it happened that He went through the grainfields on the Sabbath; and as they went His disciples began to pluck the heads of grain. 24And the Pharisees said to Him, "Look, why do they do what is not lawful on the Sabbath?"

25But He said to them, "Have you never read what David did when he was in need and hungry, he and those with him: 26how he went into the house of God *in the days* of Abiathar the high priest, and ate the showbread, which is not lawful to eat except for the priests, and also gave some to those who were with him?"

27And He said to them, "The Sabbath was made for man, and not man for the Sabbath. 28Therefore the Son of Man is also Lord of the Sabbath."

Healing on the Sabbath

3 And He entered the synagogue again, and a man was there who had a withered hand. 2So they watched Him closely, whether He would heal him on the Sabbath, so that they might accuse Him. 3And He said to the man who had the withered hand, "Step forward." 4Then He said to them, "Is it lawful on the Sabbath to do good or to do evil, to save life or to kill?" But they kept silent. 5And when He had looked around at them with anger, being grieved by the hardness of their hearts, He said to the man, "Stretch out your hand." And he stretched *it* out, and his hand was restored as whole as the other.a 6Then the Pharisees went out and immediately plotted with the Herodians against Him, how they might destroy Him.

A Great Multitude Follows Jesus

7But Jesus withdrew with His disciples to the sea. And a great multitude from Galilee followed Him, and from Judea 8and Jerusalem and Idumea and beyond the Jordan; and those from Tyre and Sidon, a great multitude, when they heard how many things He was doing, came to Him. 9So He told His disciples that a small boat should be kept ready for Him because of the multitude, lest they should crush Him. 10For He healed many, so that as many as had afflictions pressed about Him to touch Him. 11And the unclean spirits, whenever they saw Him, fell down before Him and cried out, saying, "You are the Son of God." 12But He sternly warned them that they should not make Him known.

The Twelve Apostles

13And He went up on the mountain and called to *Him* those He Himself wanted. And they came to Him. 14Then He appointed twelve,a that they might be with Him

INTIMATE MOMENTS

Get Specific

A young single actor from California has noticed that giving genuine compliments on a date goes a long way toward igniting the fires of romance. Husbands, take note of what he said ...we *can* learn something from Hollywood, "I've found that women love getting compliments on their appearance. I always pick one aspect of how she looks and comment on why I think it's fantastic. I try to be specific so she feels it's genuine and not just an attempt to score points. Instead of saying something general like, 'You look nice', I might say, 'I really like your earrings; that shade of blue matches your eyes' or 'I love those boots; they make your legs look incredible.' Women are amazed that I pay that kind of attention and they're always appreciative."

What is something specific you can say to your wife today to let her know you're paying attention and that you appreciate her? What qualities first attracted you to her? Perhaps it's time to look her in the eyes and remind her of why you love her.

3:5 aNU-Text omits *as whole as the other.*
3:14 aNU-Text adds *whom He also named apostles.*

and that He might send them out to preach, [15]and to have power to heal sicknesses and[a] to cast out demons: [16]Simon,[a] to whom He gave the name Peter; [17]James the *son* of Zebedee and John the brother of James, to whom He gave the name Boanerges, that is, "Sons of Thunder"; [18]Andrew, Philip, Bartholomew, Matthew, Thomas, James the *son* of Alphaeus, Thaddaeus, Simon the Cananite; [19]and Judas Iscariot, who also betrayed Him. And they went into a house.

A House Divided Cannot Stand

[20]Then the multitude came together again, so that they could not so much as eat bread. [21]But when His own people heard *about this,* they went out to lay hold of Him, for they said, "He is out of His mind."

[22]And the scribes who came down from Jerusalem said, "He has Beelzebub," and, "By the ruler of the demons He casts out demons."

[23]So He called them to *Himself* and said to them in parables: "How can Satan cast out Satan? [24]If a kingdom is divided against itself, that kingdom cannot stand. [25]And if a house is divided against itself, that house cannot stand. [26]And if Satan has risen up against himself, and is divided, he cannot stand, but has an end. [27]No one can enter a strong man's house and plunder his goods, unless he first binds the strong man. And then he will plunder his house.

The Unpardonable Sin

[28]"Assuredly, I say to you, all sins will be forgiven the sons of men, and whatever blasphemies they may utter; [29]but he who blasphemes against the Holy Spirit never has forgiveness, but is subject to eternal condemnation"— [30]because they said, "He has an unclean spirit."

Jesus' Mother and Brothers Send for Him

[31]Then His brothers and His mother came, and standing outside they sent to Him, calling Him. [32]And a multitude was sitting around Him; and they said to Him, "Look, Your mother and Your brothers[a] are outside seeking You."

[33]But He answered them, saying, "Who is My mother, or My brothers?" [34]And He looked around in a circle at those who sat about Him, and said, "Here are My mother and My brothers! [35]For whoever does the will of God is My brother and My sister and mother."

The Parable of the Sower

4 And again He began to teach by the sea. And a great multitude was gathered to Him, so that He got into a boat and sat *in it* on the sea; and the whole multitude was on the land facing the sea. [2]Then He taught them many things by parables, and said to them in His teaching:

[3]"Listen! Behold, a sower went out to sow. [4]And it happened, as he sowed, *that* some *seed* fell by the wayside; and the birds of the air[a] came and devoured it. [5]Some fell on stony ground, where it did not have much earth; and immediately it sprang up because it had no depth of earth. [6]But when the sun was up it was scorched, and because it had no root it withered away. [7]And some *seed* fell among thorns; and the thorns grew up and choked it, and it yielded no crop. [8]But other *seed* fell on good ground and yielded a crop that sprang up, increased and produced: some thirtyfold, some sixty, and some a hundred."

[9]And He said to them,[a] "He who has ears to hear, let him hear!"

The Purpose of Parables

[10]But when He was alone, those around Him with the twelve asked Him about the parable. [11]And He said to them, "To you it has been given to know the mystery of the kingdom of God; but to those who are outside, all things come in parables, [12]so that

'Seeing they may see and not perceive,
And hearing they may hear and not understand;
Lest they should turn,
And their sins be forgiven them.' "[a]

3:15 [a]NU-Text omits *to heal sicknesses and.*
3:16 [a]NU-Text reads *and He appointed the twelve: Simon. . . .* **3:32** [a]NU-Text and M-Text add *and Your sisters.* **4:4** [a]NU-Text and M-Text omit *of the air.*
4:9 [a]NU-Text and M-Text omit *to them.*
4:12 [a]Isaiah 6:9, 10

The Parable of the Sower Explained

13And He said to them, "Do you not understand this parable? How then will you understand all the parables? 14The sower sows the word. 15And these are the ones by the wayside where the word is sown. When they hear, Satan comes immediately and takes away the word that was sown in their hearts. 16These likewise are the ones sown on stony ground who, when they hear the word, immediately receive it with gladness; 17and they have no root in themselves, and so endure only for a time. Afterward, when tribulation or persecution arises for the word's sake, immediately they stumble. 18Now these are the ones sown among thorns; *they are* the ones who hear the word, 19and the cares of this world, the deceitfulness of riches, and the desires for other things entering in choke the word, and it becomes unfruitful. 20But these are the ones sown on good ground, those who hear the word, accept *it,* and bear fruit: some thirtyfold, some sixty, and some a hundred."

Light Under a Basket

21Also He said to them, "Is a lamp brought to be put under a basket or under a bed? Is it not to be set on a lampstand? 22For there is nothing hidden which will not be revealed, nor has anything been kept secret but that it should come to light. 23If anyone has ears to hear, let him hear." 24Then He said to them, "Take heed what you hear. With the same measure you use, it will be measured to you; and to you who hear, more will be given. 25For whoever has, to him more will be given; but whoever does not have, even what he has will be taken away from him."

The Parable of the Growing Seed

26And He said, "The kingdom of God is as if a man should scatter seed on the ground, 27and should sleep by night and rise by day, and the seed should sprout and grow, he himself does not know how. 28For the earth yields crops by itself: first the blade, then the head, after that the full grain in the head. 29But when the grain ripens, immediately he puts in the sickle, because the harvest has come."

The Parable of the Mustard Seed

30Then He said, "To what shall we liken the kingdom of God? Or with what parable shall we picture it? 31*It is* like a mustard seed which, when it is sown on the ground, is smaller than all the seeds on earth; 32but when it is sown, it grows up and becomes greater than all herbs, and shoots out large

---

ROMANCE FAQ

Q: How can I address the distractions that seem to be hurting my marriage?

It may help to consider the parable of the soils found in Mark 4. Christ said there that spiritual fruitfulness or barrenness depends upon the condition of the soil that receives the seed of God's Word.

In the parable, Jesus warned of the choking influence of thorns—pesky, prickly weeds that squeeze the life out of fruit-producing seedlings. Jesus explained that these are the worries of the world, the anxieties of this age.

Worry or anxiety means "to be drawn in different directions" or "to be distracted." What distracts you? What pulls you in a direction you know is unfruitful? For me, it can be busyness, a full schedule of good things that crowds out the best—like time in the morning spent in prayer and the Scripture. I can be distracted by urgent things that I could put off for just a few minutes.

Some people get distracted about what others think about them, preoccupied with pleasing others and gaining their approval. Still others get pulled by their insecurities, trying to find significance in achieving and performing.

Good marriages and families don't grow naturally; weeds do. That's why it's so important that we listen to the words of the Master Gardener, Jesus Christ. What are some of the weeds that are growing in your marriage garden? How can you begin uprooting them today?

branches, so that the birds of the air may nest under its shade."

Jesus' Use of Parables

³³And with many such parables He spoke the word to them as they were able to hear *it.* ³⁴But without a parable He did not speak to them. And when they were alone, He explained all things to His disciples.

Wind and Wave Obey Jesus

³⁵On the same day, when evening had come, He said to them, "Let us cross over to the other side." ³⁶Now when they had left the multitude, they took Him along in the boat as He was. And other little boats were also with Him. ³⁷And a great windstorm arose, and the waves beat into the boat, so that it was already filling. ³⁸But He was in the stern, asleep on a pillow. And they awoke Him and said to Him, "Teacher, do You not care that we are perishing?"

³⁹Then He arose and rebuked the wind, and said to the sea, "Peace, be still!" And the wind ceased and there was a great calm. ⁴⁰But He said to them, "Why are you so fearful? How *is it* that you have no faith?"ᵃ ⁴¹And they feared exceedingly, and said to one another, "Who can this be, that even the wind and the sea obey Him!"

A Demon-Possessed Man Healed

5 Then they came to the other side of the sea, to the country of the Gadarenes.ᵃ ²And when He had come out of the boat, immediately there met Him out of the

tombs a man with an unclean spirit, ³who had *his* dwelling among the tombs; and no one could bind him,ᵃ not even with chains, ⁴because he had often been bound with shackles and chains. And the chains had been pulled apart by him, and the shackles broken in pieces; neither could anyone tame him. ⁵And always, night and day, he was in the mountains and in the tombs, crying out and cutting himself with stones.

⁶When he saw Jesus from afar, he ran and worshiped Him. ⁷And he cried out with a loud voice and said, "What have I to do with You, Jesus, Son of the Most High God? I implore You by God that You do not torment me."

⁸For He said to him, "Come out of the man, unclean spirit!" ⁹Then He asked him, "What *is* your name?"

And he answered, saying, "My name *is* Legion; for we are many." ¹⁰Also he begged Him earnestly that He would not send them out of the country.

¹¹Now a large herd of swine was feeding there near the mountains. ¹²So all the demons begged Him, saying, "Send us to the swine, that we may enter them." ¹³And at once Jesusᵃ gave them permission. Then the unclean spirits went out and entered the swine (there were about two thousand); and the herd ran violently down the steep place into the sea, and drowned in the sea.

¹⁴So those who fed the swine fled, and they told *it* in the city and in the country. And they went out to see what it was that had happened. ¹⁵Then they came to Jesus, and saw the one *who had been* demon-possessed and had the legion, sitting and clothed and in his right mind. And they were afraid. ¹⁶And those who saw it told them how it happened to him *who had been* demon-possessed, and about the swine. ¹⁷Then they began to plead with Him to depart from their region.

¹⁸And when He got into the boat, he who had been demon-possessed begged Him that he might be with Him. ¹⁹However, Jesus did not permit him, but said to him, "Go home to your friends, and tell them

INTIMATE MOMENTS

October 19ᵗʰ is Sweetest Day. You might ask your husband's mother to list his favorite candies from childhood. Purchase those nostalgic goodies as a special gift *for your sweetie.*

Husbands, consider taking your sweetie on a sweet date that treats her to her favorite sweets.

4:40 ᵃNU-Text reads *Have you still no faith?*
5:1 ᵃNU-Text reads *Gerasenes.* **5:3** ᵃNU-Text adds *anymore.* **5:13** ᵃNU-Text reads *And He gave.*

what great things the Lord has done for you, and how He has had compassion on you." [20]And he departed and began to proclaim in Decapolis all that Jesus had done for him; and all marveled.

A Girl Restored to Life and a Woman Healed

[21]Now when Jesus had crossed over again by boat to the other side, a great multitude gathered to Him; and He was by the sea. [22]And behold, one of the rulers of the synagogue came, Jairus by name. And when he saw Him, he fell at His feet [23]and begged Him earnestly, saying, "My little daughter lies at the point of death. Come and lay Your hands on her, that she may be healed, and she will live." [24]So *Jesus* went with him, and a great multitude followed Him and thronged Him.

[25]Now a certain woman had a flow of blood for twelve years, [26]and had suffered many things from many physicians. She had spent all that she had and was no better, but rather grew worse. [27]When she heard about Jesus, she came behind *Him* in the crowd and touched His garment. [28]For she said, "If only I may touch His clothes, I shall be made well."

[29]Immediately the fountain of her blood was dried up, and she felt in *her* body that she was healed of the affliction. [30]And Jesus, immediately knowing in Himself that power had gone out of Him, turned around in the crowd and said, "Who touched My clothes?"

[31]But His disciples said to Him, "You see the multitude thronging You, and You say, 'Who touched Me?'"

[32]And He looked around to see her who had done this thing. [33]But the woman, fearing and trembling, knowing what had happened to her, came and fell down before Him and told Him the whole truth. [34]And He said to her, "Daughter, your faith has made you well. Go in peace, and be healed of your affliction."

[35]While He was still speaking, *some* came from the ruler of the synagogue's *house* who said, "Your daughter is dead. Why trouble the Teacher any further?"

[36]As soon as Jesus heard the word that was spoken, He said to the ruler of the synagogue, "Do not be afraid; only believe." [37]And He permitted no one to follow Him except Peter, James, and John the brother of James. [38]Then He came to the house of the ruler of the synagogue, and saw a tumult and those who wept and

ROMANCE FAQ

Q: *How can I most effectively grow toward spiritual maturity?*

If you want to see some significant spiritual growth, finding an accountability partner may be the most important step you could take.

First, *determine your needs.* What two or three things seem to entangle you more than anything else? Is it finances? Lustful thoughts? Misplaced priorities? Poor decision making? Overeating? Not spending enough time with the Lord?

Second, *select a mature Christian (of the same gender) who would have the courage to speak the truth and ask you tough questions.* Don't choose someone who would fear your rejection, or someone who has a weakness in the same area, or someone you feel you can manipulate or control. Select a person who will speak the truth in love.

Third, *ask this person to keep you accountable.* You might say, "Terry, I have a problem and I really need your help. I need you to lovingly hold my feet to the fire, but not be judgmental. I really need to get victory over this."

Finally, *regularly meet with this person to set measurable goals and to allow him to ask how you're doing.* Agree to a list of questions, "Frank, have you written out a budget yet? Why not? When will you do it?" And here's a powerful one, "Have you lied to me at all today?"

If we are going to grow on a regular basis, all of us need others in our lives who will stimulate us not to fall back into unproductive habits, but make the kinds of decisions that will create lasting, vibrant spiritual growth in our lives.

wailed loudly. ³⁹When He came in, He said to them, "Why make this commotion and weep? The child is not dead, but sleeping." ⁴⁰And they ridiculed Him. But when He had put them all outside, He took the father and the mother of the child, and those *who were* with Him, and entered where the child was lying. ⁴¹Then He took the child by the hand, and said to her, "Talitha, cumi," which is translated, "Little girl, I say to you, arise." ⁴²Immediately the girl arose and walked, for she was twelve years *of age*. And they were overcome with great amazement. ⁴³But He commanded them strictly that no one should know it, and said that *something* should be given her to eat.

Jesus Rejected at Nazareth

6 Then He went out from there and came to His own country, and His disciples followed Him. ²And when the Sabbath had come, He began to teach in the synagogue. And many hearing *Him* were astonished, saying, "Where *did* this Man *get* these things? And what wisdom *is* this which is given to Him, that such mighty works are performed by His hands! ³Is this not the carpenter, the Son of Mary, and brother of James, Joses, Judas, and Simon? And are not His sisters here with us?" So they were offended at Him.

⁴But Jesus said to them, "A prophet is not without honor except in his own country, among his own relatives, and in his own house." ⁵Now He could do no mighty work there, except that He laid His hands on a few sick people and healed *them*. ⁶And He marveled because of their unbelief. Then He went about the villages in a circuit, teaching.

Sending Out the Twelve

⁷And He called the twelve to *Himself*, and began to send them out two *by* two, and gave them power over unclean spirits. ⁸He commanded them to take nothing for the journey except a staff—no bag, no bread, no copper in *their* money belts— ⁹but to wear sandals, and not to put on two tunics.

¹⁰Also He said to them, "In whatever place you enter a house, stay there till you depart from that place. ¹¹And whoeverᵃ will not receive you nor hear you, when you depart from there, shake off the dust under your feet as a testimony against them.ᵇ Assuredly, I say to you, it will be more tolerable for Sodom and Gomorrah in the day of judgment than for that city!"

¹²So they went out and preached that *people* should repent. ¹³And they cast out many demons, and anointed with oil many who were sick, and healed *them*.

John the Baptist Beheaded

¹⁴Now King Herod heard *of Him,* for His name had become well known. And he said, "John the Baptist is risen from the dead, and therefore these powers are at work in him."

¹⁵Others said, "It is Elijah."

And others said, "It is the Prophet, orᵃ like one of the prophets."

¹⁶But when Herod heard, he said, "This is John, whom I beheaded; he has been raised from the dead!" ¹⁷For Herod himself had sent and laid hold of John, and bound him in prison for the sake of Herodias, his brother Philip's wife; for he had married her. ¹⁸Because John had said to Herod, "It is not lawful for you to have your brother's wife."

¹⁹Therefore Herodias held it against him and wanted to kill him, but she could not; ²⁰for Herod feared John, knowing that he *was* a just and holy man, and he protected him. And when he heard him, he did many things, and heard him gladly.

²¹Then an opportune day came when Herod on his birthday gave a feast for his nobles, the high officers, and the chief *men* of Galilee. ²²And when Herodias' daughter herself came in and danced, and pleased Herod and those who sat with him, the king said to the girl, "Ask me whatever you want, and I will give *it* to you." ²³He also swore to her, "Whatever you ask me, I will give you, up to half my kingdom."

²⁴So she went out and said to her mother, "What shall I ask?"

And she said, "The head of John the Baptist!"

²⁵Immediately she came in with haste to the king and asked, saying, "I want you to

---

6:11 ᵃNU-Text reads *whatever place*. ᵇNU-Text omits the rest of this verse.
6:15 ᵃNU-Text and M-Text omit *or.*

give me at once the head of John the Baptist on a platter."

26And the king was exceedingly sorry; *yet,* because of the oaths and because of those who sat with him, he did not want to refuse her. 27Immediately the king sent an executioner and commanded his head to be brought. And he went and beheaded him in prison, 28brought his head on a platter, and gave it to the girl; and the girl gave it to her mother. 29When his disciples heard *of it,* they came and took away his corpse and laid it in a tomb.

Feeding the Five Thousand

30Then the apostles gathered to Jesus and told Him all things, both what they had done and what they had taught. 31And He said to them, "Come aside by yourselves to a deserted place and rest a while." For there were many coming and going, and they did not even have time to eat. 32So they departed to a deserted place in the boat by themselves.

33But the multitudes[a] saw them departing, and many knew Him and ran there on foot from all the cities. They arrived before them and came together to Him. 34And Jesus, when He came out, saw a great multitude and was moved with compassion for them, because they were like sheep not having a shepherd. So He began to teach them many things. 35When the day was now far spent, His disciples came to Him and said, "This is a deserted place, and already the hour *is* late. 36Send them away, that they may go into the surrounding country and villages and buy themselves bread;[a] for they have nothing to eat."

37But He answered and said to them, "You give them something to eat."

And they said to Him, "Shall we go and buy two hundred denarii worth of bread and give them *something* to eat?"

38But He said to them, "How many loaves do you have? Go and see."

And when they found out they said, "Five, and two fish."

39Then He commanded them to make them all sit down in groups on the green grass. 40So they sat down in ranks, in hundreds and in fifties. 41And when He had taken the five loaves and the two fish, He looked up to heaven, blessed and broke the loaves, and gave *them* to His disciples to set before them; and the two fish He divided among *them* all. 42So they all ate and were filled. 43And they took up twelve baskets full of fragments and of the fish. 44Now those who had eaten the loaves were about[a] five thousand men.

Jesus Walks on the Sea

45Immediately He made His disciples get into the boat and go before Him to the other side, to Bethsaida, while He sent the multitude away. 46And when He had sent them away, He departed to the mountain to pray. 47Now when evening came, the boat was in the middle of the sea; and He *was* alone on the land. 48Then He saw them straining at rowing, for the wind was against them. Now about the fourth watch of the night He came to them, walking on the sea, and would have passed them by. 49And when they saw Him walking on the sea, they supposed it was a ghost, and cried out; 50for they all saw Him and were troubled. But immediately He talked with them and said to them, "Be of good cheer! It is I; do not be afraid." 51Then He went up into the boat to them, and the wind ceased. And they were greatly amazed in themselves beyond measure, and marveled. 52For they had not understood about the loaves, because their heart was hardened.

Many Touch Him and Are Made Well

53When they had crossed over, they came to the land of Gennesaret and anchored there. 54And when they came out of the boat, immediately the people recognized Him, 55ran through that whole surrounding region, and began to carry about on beds those who were sick to wherever they heard He was. 56Wherever He entered, into villages, cities, or the country, they laid the sick in the marketplaces, and begged Him that they might just touch the hem of His garment. And as many as touched Him were made well.

6:33 [a]NU-Text and M-Text read *they.* **6:36** [a]NU-Text reads *something to eat* and omits the rest of this verse. **6:44** [a]NU-Text and M-Text omit *about.*

Defilement Comes from Within

7 Then the Pharisees and some of the scribes came together to Him, having come from Jerusalem. 2Now when[a] they saw some of His disciples eat bread with defiled, that is, with unwashed hands, they found fault. 3For the Pharisees and all the Jews do not eat unless they wash *their* hands in a special way, holding the tradition of the elders. 4*When they come* from the marketplace, they do not eat unless they wash. And there are many other things which they have received and hold, *like* the washing of cups, pitchers, copper vessels, and couches.

5Then the Pharisees and scribes asked Him, "Why do Your disciples not walk according to the tradition of the elders, but eat bread with unwashed hands?"

6He answered and said to them, "Well did Isaiah prophesy of you hypocrites, as it is written:

'This people honors Me with their
      lips,
   But their heart is far from Me.
7   And in vain they worship Me,
      Teaching as doctrines the
         commandments of men.'[a]

8For laying aside the commandment of God, you hold the tradition of men[a]—the washing of pitchers and cups, and many other such things you do."

9He said to them, "*All too* well you reject the commandment of God, that you may keep your tradition. 10For Moses said, 'Honor your father and your mother';[a] and, 'He who curses father or mother, let him be put to death.'[b]11But you say, 'If a man says to his father or mother, "Whatever profit you might have received from me *is* Corban"—' (that is, a gift *to God*), 12then you no longer let him do anything for his father or his mother, 13making the word of God of no effect through your tradition which you have handed down. And many such things you do."

14When He had called all the multitude to *Himself,* He said to them, "Hear Me, everyone, and understand: 15There is nothing that enters a man from outside which can defile him; but the things which come out of him, those are the things that defile a man. 16If anyone has ears to hear, let him hear!"[a]

17When He had entered a house away from the crowd, His disciples asked Him concerning the parable. 18So He said to them, "Are you thus without understanding also? Do you not perceive that whatever enters a man from outside cannot defile him, 19because it does not enter his heart but his stomach, and is eliminated, *thus* purifying all foods?"[a] 20And He said, "What comes out of a man, that defiles a man. 21For from within, out of the heart of men, proceed evil thoughts, adulteries, fornications, murders, 22thefts, covetousness, wickedness, deceit, lewdness, an evil eye, blasphemy, pride, foolishness. 23All these evil things come from within and defile a man."

A Gentile Shows Her Faith

24From there He arose and went to the region of Tyre and Sidon.[a] And He entered a house and wanted no one to know *it,* but He could not be hidden. 25For a woman whose young daughter had an unclean spirit heard about Him, and she came and fell at His feet. 26The woman was a Greek, a Syro-Phoenician by birth, and she kept asking Him to cast the demon out of her daughter. 27But Jesus said to her, "Let the children be filled first, for it is not good to take the children's bread and throw *it* to the little dogs."

**INTIMATE
MOMENTS**

Take her on a date to a bookstore. Tell her you'd like to find a book on marriage that you can read together.

7:2 [a]NU-Text omits *when* and *they found fault.*
7:7 [a]Isaiah 29:13 7:8 [a]NU-Text omits the rest of this verse. 7:10 [a]Exodus 20:12; Deuteronomy 5:16 [a]Exodus 21:17 7:16 [a]NU-Text omits this verse.
7:19 [a]NU-Text ends quotation with *eliminated,* setting off the final clause as Mark's comment that Jesus has declared all foods clean.
7:24 [a]NU-Text omits *and Sidon.*

²⁸And she answered and said to Him, "Yes, Lord, yet even the little dogs under the table eat from the children's crumbs."

²⁹Then He said to her, "For this saying go your way; the demon has gone out of your daughter."

³⁰And when she had come to her house, she found the demon gone out, and her daughter lying on the bed.

Jesus Heals a Deaf-Mute

³¹Again, departing from the region of Tyre and Sidon, He came through the midst of the region of Decapolis to the Sea of Galilee. ³²Then they brought to Him one who was deaf and had an impediment in his speech, and they begged Him to put His hand on him. ³³And He took him aside from the multitude, and put His fingers in his ears, and He spat and touched his tongue. ³⁴Then, looking up to heaven, He sighed, and said to him, "Ephphatha," that is, "Be opened."

³⁵Immediately his ears were opened, and the impediment of his tongue was loosed, and he spoke plainly. ³⁶Then He commanded them that they should tell no one; but the more He commanded them, the more widely they proclaimed *it*. ³⁷And they were astonished beyond measure, saying, "He has done all things well. He makes both the deaf to hear and the mute to speak."

Feeding the Four Thousand

8 In those days, the multitude being very great and having nothing to eat, Jesus called His disciples *to Him* and said to them, ²"I have compassion on the multitude, because they have now continued with Me three days and have nothing to eat. ³And if I send them away hungry to their own houses, they will faint on the way; for some of them have come from afar."

⁴Then His disciples answered Him, "How can one satisfy these people with bread here in the wilderness?"

⁵He asked them, "How many loaves do you have?"

PARENTING MATTERS

Q: How old does a child have to be before he or she can place saving faith in Jesus Christ?

The great English preacher C. H. Spurgeon said, "A child who knowingly sins can savingly believe."

Many great church leaders became Christians when they were very young. Polycarp, a first-century church leader, walked with God for eighty-six years before he died at the age of ninety-five. Isaac Watts, the great hymn writer, came to saving faith in Christ at nine years of age.

I was six when I began to feel my need for forgiveness. I grew up in a church with a pastor who preached about heaven and hell. I recall becoming so aware of my sin that I was afraid I'd die in my sleep and spend an eternity in hell. So one Sunday I told my mom that I wanted to give my life to Christ. She didn't hinder me from making my commitment public.

That was more than fifty years ago. And thanks to my parents' faithful instruction, I can look back on that commitment as the most important decision in my life.

If your child shows an interest in spiritual things or wants to pray to become a Christian, encourage them to ask God to forgive her sins and give her a new heart. That spiritual interest may be very real even when your child is young.

Have your children expressed a desire to receive Christ? Ask God to give you wisdom and clarity in teaching your children about God's forgiveness through faith in His Son, Jesus Christ and His transforming work in the lives of His followers.

And they said, "Seven."

⁶So He commanded the multitude to sit down on the ground. And He took the seven loaves and gave thanks, broke *them* and gave *them* to His disciples to set before *them;* and they set *them* before the multitude. ⁷They also had a few small fish; and having blessed them, He said to set them also before *them.* ⁸So they ate and were filled, and they took up seven large baskets of leftover fragments. ⁹Now those who had eaten were about four thousand. And He sent them away, ¹⁰immediately got into the boat with His disciples, and came to the region of Dalmanutha.

The Pharisees Seek a Sign

¹¹Then the Pharisees came out and began to dispute with Him, seeking from Him a sign from heaven, testing Him. ¹²But He sighed deeply in His spirit, and said, "Why does this generation seek a sign? Assuredly, I say to you, no sign shall be given to this generation."

Beware of the Leaven of the Pharisees and Herod

¹³And He left them, and getting into the boat again, departed to the other side. ¹⁴Now the disciples[a] had forgotten to take bread, and they did not have more than one loaf with them in the boat. ¹⁵Then He charged them, saying, "Take heed, beware of the leaven of the Pharisees and the leaven of Herod." ¹⁶And they reasoned among themselves, saying, "*It is* because we have no bread." ¹⁷But Jesus, being aware of *it,* said to them, "Why do you reason because you have no bread? Do you not yet perceive nor understand? Is your heart still[a] hardened? ¹⁸Having eyes, do you not see? And having ears, do you not hear? And do you not remember? ¹⁹When I broke the five loaves for the five thousand, how many baskets full of fragments did you take up?"

They said to Him, "Twelve."

²⁰"Also, when I broke the seven for the *four thousand,* how many large baskets full of fragments did you take up?"

And they said, "Seven."

²¹So He said to them, "How *is it* you do not understand?"

A Blind Man Healed at Bethsaida

²²Then He came to Bethsaida; and they brought a blind man to Him, and begged Him to touch him. ²³So He took the blind man by the hand and led him out of the town. And when He had spit on his eyes and put His hands on him, He asked him if he saw anything.

²⁴And he looked up and said, "I see men like trees, walking."

²⁵Then He put *His* hands on his eyes again and made him look up. And he was restored and saw everyone clearly. ²⁶Then He sent him away to his house, saying, "Neither go into the town, nor tell anyone in the town."[a]

Peter Confesses Jesus as the Christ

²⁷Now Jesus and His disciples went out to the towns of Caesarea Philippi; and on the road He asked His disciples, saying to them, "Who do men say that I am?"

²⁸So they answered, "John the Baptist; but some *say,* Elijah; and others, one of the prophets."

²⁹He said to them, "But who do you say that I am?"

Peter answered and said to Him, "You are the Christ."

³⁰Then He strictly warned them that they should tell no one about Him.

Jesus Predicts His Death and Resurrection

³¹And He began to teach them that the Son of Man must suffer many things, and be rejected by the elders and chief priests and scribes, and be killed, and after three days rise again. ³²He spoke this word openly. Then Peter took Him aside and began to rebuke Him. ³³But when He had turned around and looked at His disciples, He rebuked Peter, saying, "Get behind Me, Satan! For you are not mindful of the things of God, but the things of men."

Take Up the Cross and Follow Him

³⁴When He had called the people to *Himself,* with His disciples also, He said to

---

8:14 [a]NU-Text and M-Text read *they.*
8:17 [a]NU-Text omits *still.*
8:26 [a]NU-Text reads *"Do not even go into the town."*

them, "Whoever desires to come after Me, let him deny himself, and take up his cross, and follow Me. [35]For whoever desires to save his life will lose it, but whoever loses his life for My sake and the gospel's will save it. [36]For what will it profit a man if he gains the whole world, and loses his own soul? [37]Or what will a man give in exchange for his soul? [38]For whoever is ashamed of Me and My words in this adulterous and sinful generation, of him the Son of Man also will be ashamed when He comes in the glory of His Father with the holy angels."

Jesus Transfigured on the Mount

9 And He said to them, "Assuredly, I say to you that there are some standing here who will not taste death till they see the kingdom of God present with power."

[2]Now after six days Jesus took Peter, James, and John, and led them up on a high mountain apart by themselves; and He was transfigured before them. [3]His clothes became shining, exceedingly white, like snow, such as no launderer on earth can whiten them. [4]And Elijah appeared to them with Moses, and they were talking with Jesus. [5]Then Peter answered and said to Jesus, "Rabbi, it is good for us to be here; and let us make three tabernacles: one for You, one for Moses, and one for Elijah"— [6]because he did not know what to say, for they were greatly afraid.

[7]And a cloud came and overshadowed them; and a voice came out of the cloud, saying, "This is My beloved Son. Hear Him!" [8]Suddenly, when they had looked around, they saw no one anymore, but only Jesus with themselves.

[9]Now as they came down from the mountain, He commanded them that they should tell no one the things they had seen, till the Son of Man had risen from the dead. [10]So they kept this word to themselves, questioning what the rising from the dead meant.

[11]And they asked Him, saying, "Why do the scribes say that Elijah must come first?"

[12]Then He answered and told them, "Indeed, Elijah is coming first and restores all things. And how is it written concerning the Son of Man, that He must suffer many things and be treated with contempt? [13]But I say to you that Elijah has also come, and they did to him whatever they wished, as it is written of him."

A Boy Is Healed

[14]And when He came to the disciples, He saw a great multitude around them, and scribes disputing with them. [15]Immediately, when they saw Him, all the people were greatly amazed, and running to *Him*, greeted Him. [16]And He asked the scribes, "What are you discussing with them?"

[17]Then one of the crowd answered and said, "Teacher, I brought You my son, who has a mute spirit. [18]And wherever it seizes him, it throws him down; he foams at the mouth, gnashes his teeth, and becomes rigid. So I spoke to Your disciples, that they should cast it out, but they could not."

[19]He answered him and said, "O faithless generation, how long shall I be with you? How long shall I bear with you? Bring him to Me." [20]Then they brought him to Him. And when he saw Him, immediately the spirit convulsed him, and he fell on the ground and wallowed, foaming at the mouth.

[21]So He asked his father, "How long has this been happening to him?"

And he said, "From childhood. [22]And often he has thrown him both into the fire and into the water to destroy him. But if You can do anything, have compassion on us and help us."

[23]Jesus said to him, "If you can believe,[a] all things *are* possible to him who believes."

[24]Immediately the father of the child cried out and said with tears, "Lord, I believe; help my unbelief!"

[25]When Jesus saw that the people came running together, He rebuked the unclean spirit, saying to it, "Deaf and dumb spirit, I command you, come out of him and enter him no more!" [26]Then *the spirit* cried out, convulsed him greatly, and came out of him. And he became as one dead, so that many said, "He is dead." [27]But Jesus took him by the hand and lifted him up, and he arose.

9:23 [a]NU-Text reads "'If *You can!' All things. . . .'"

²⁸And when He had come into the house, His disciples asked Him privately, "Why could we not cast it out?"

²⁹So He said to them, "This kind can come out by nothing but prayer and fasting."^a

Jesus Again Predicts His Death and Resurrection

³⁰Then they departed from there and passed through Galilee, and He did not want anyone to know *it.* ³¹For He taught His disciples and said to them, "The Son of Man is being betrayed into the hands of men, and they will kill Him. And after He is killed, He will rise the third day." ³²But they did not understand this saying, and were afraid to ask Him.

Who Is the Greatest?

³³Then He came to Capernaum. And when He was in the house He asked them, "What was it you disputed among yourselves on the road?" ³⁴But they kept silent, for on the road they had disputed among themselves who *would be the* greatest. ³⁵And He sat down, called the twelve, and said to them, "If anyone desires to be first, he shall be last of all and servant of all." ³⁶Then He took a little child and set him in the midst of them. And when He had taken him in His arms, He said to them, ³⁷"Whoever receives one of these little children in My name receives Me; and whoever receives Me, receives not Me but Him who sent Me."

Jesus Forbids Sectarianism

³⁸Now John answered Him, saying, "Teacher, we saw someone who does not follow us casting out demons in Your name, and we forbade him because he does not follow us."

³⁹But Jesus said, "Do not forbid him, for no one who works a miracle in My name can soon afterward speak evil of Me. ⁴⁰For he who is not against us is on our^a side. ⁴¹For whoever gives you a cup of water to drink in My name, because you belong to Christ, assuredly, I say to you, he will by *no means* lose his reward.

Jesus Warns of Offenses

⁴²"But whoever causes one of these little ones who believe in Me to stumble, it would be better for him if a millstone were hung around his neck, and he were thrown into the sea. ⁴³If your hand causes you to sin, cut it off. It is better for you to enter into life maimed, rather than having two hands, to go to hell, into the fire that shall never be quenched— ⁴⁴where

> *'Their worm does not die*
> *And the fire is not quenched.'*^a

⁴⁵And if your foot causes you to sin, cut it off. It is better for you to enter life lame, rather than having two feet, to be cast into hell, into the fire that shall never be quenched— ⁴⁶where

> *'Their worm does not die*
> *And the fire is not quenched.'*^a

⁴⁷And if your eye causes you to sin, pluck it out. It is better for you to enter the kingdom of God with one eye, rather than having two eyes, to be cast into hell fire— ⁴⁸where

> *'Their worm does not die*
> *And the fire is not quenched.'*^a

Tasteless Salt Is Worthless

⁴⁹"For everyone will be seasoned with fire,^a and every sacrifice will be seasoned with salt. ⁵⁰Salt *is* good, but if the salt loses its flavor, how will you season it? Have salt in yourselves, and have peace with one another."

Marriage and Divorce

10 Then He arose from there and came to the region of Judea by the other side of the Jordan. And multitudes gathered to Him again, and as He was accustomed, He taught them again.

²The Pharisees came and asked Him, "Is it lawful for a man to divorce *his* wife?" testing Him.

³And He answered and said to them, "What did Moses command you?"

⁴They said, "Moses permitted *a man* to write a certificate of divorce, and to dismiss *her.*"

9:29 ^aNU-Text omits *and fasting.* **9:40** ^aM-Text reads *against you is on your side.* **9:44** ^aNU-Text omits this verse. **9:46** ^aNU-Text omits the last clause of verse 45 and all of verse 46. **9:48** ^aIsaiah 66:24 **9:49** ^aNU-Text omits the rest of this verse.

DEVOTIONS FOR COUPLES • 10:7, 8
Five Guidelines for Building a Strong Marriage

As Jesus recalls the melodrama of God's presentation of Eve to Adam, He says, "But from the beginning of creation, God 'made them male and female.' 'For this reason a man shall leave his father and mother and be joined to his wife, and the two shall become one flesh" (10:6–8). This passage presents five guidelines for building a strong and godly marriage, which I find myself returning to again and again. There are principles in Scripture that are the biblical basics. This is one of those mandates that must use the rabbinical method of teaching: repetition!

1. *Leave.* The Hebrew word for *leave* quoted by Jesus here literally means "forsake dependence on." Many married couples have never stopped depending on their parents or on those who raised them. To leave doesn't mean to cut all ties, but to establish your independence from your households of origin. You have formed a new family unit; you're not merely an extension of someone else's family.

2. *Cleave.* To cleave means that you make a commitment to your spouse that you will always stick together, until death or the Lord's coming separates you. Such a commitment is the missing ingredient in many of today's marriages. In God's original plan, there were no escape hatches, no prenuptial agreements, no bailout clauses. Cleaving means you burn your bridges and make a lifelong commitment to love your spouse. No matter what.

3. *Be physically intimate.* Notice the progression: leave, cleave, and then one flesh. There is no room in God's plan for couples to try one another out before the marriage to see whether they are sexually compatible. That is a lie of this world, not the truth of God's Word. God designed sexual intercourse to seal the deal between a husband and wife, not to give unmarried couples an opportunity to fornicate.

4. *Become transparent.* The Genesis account says Adam and Eve were "both naked, the man and his wife, and were not ashamed" (Gen. 2:25). They felt no fear or rejection, but instead felt total acceptance from each other. Barbara knows that I accept and love her, just as she accepts and loves me. This enables both of us to be transparent, to be ourselves with each other.

5. *Fulfill your responsibilities.* The final part of God's plan calls for fulfilling your responsibilities. I believe that because we have been deceived into making some incorrect assumptions about what God intended, the discussion of roles in marriage has produced a lot of heat and very little light.

The dictionary says a role is "the part played by an actor." In marriage, however, we don't act. According to the Bible, husbands have clear responsibilities to sacrificially love and lead their wives, while wives have clear responsibilities to respect and support their husbands. When we fulfill those responsibilities, it makes for oneness and intimacy in marriage.

Perhaps a good application for your marriage would be for you to take each of these five and rate yourself and yours spouse on a ten-point scale. Be gracious as you rate your spouse, but be truthful. Then get together and discuss your conclusions. Pick one area for yourself that you want to work on in the days ahead.

When a couple learns how to practice these five biblical blueprints on a daily basis, they begin to experience marriage as God intended it.

---

[5]And Jesus answered and said to them, "Because of the hardness of your heart he wrote you this precept. [6]But from the beginning of the creation, God 'made them male and female.'[a] [7]For this reason a man shall leave his father and mother and be joined to his wife, [8]and the two shall become one flesh';[a] so then they are no longer two, but one flesh. [9]Therefore what God has joined together, let not man separate."

10:6 [a]Genesis 1:27; 5:2   **10:8** [a]Genesis 2:24

Keep Your Vows

Breaking a covenant made before God is one of the most treacherous sins possible. When it's a marriage vow, it betrays a sacred promise made to another person and defies the living God. Jesus tells us, "Therefore what God has joined together, let not man separate" (10:9).

When we make a vow, when we enter into the covenant of marriage, we no longer are in a place of asking *whether* we should keep it; now we are in a place of asking *how* we should keep it. "When you make a vow to God," says Ecclesiastes 5:4, "do not delay to pay it; for He has no pleasure in fools."

We need to ask, "How do we make this work? What must we do to make our marriage the kind of union God wants it to be? How can we make sure we are truly committed to one another and not just going through the motions?"

God established marriage, and He calls each of us who have entered into this covenant relationship to fulfill its most holy calling by treating it as a sacred covenant, not just between two people, but also between two people and a holy God.

---

¹⁰In the house His disciples also asked Him again about the same *matter.* ¹¹So He said to them, "Whoever divorces his wife and marries another commits adultery against her. ¹²And if a woman divorces her husband and marries another, she commits adultery."

Jesus Blesses Little Children

¹³Then they brought little children to Him, that He might touch them; but the disciples rebuked those who brought *them.* ¹⁴But when Jesus saw *it,* He was greatly displeased and said to them, "Let the little children come to Me, and do not forbid them; for of such is the kingdom of God. ¹⁵Assuredly, I say to you, whoever does not

receive the kingdom of God as a little child will by no means enter it." ¹⁶And He took them up in His arms, laid *His* hands on them, and blessed them.

Jesus Counsels the Rich Young Ruler

¹⁷Now as He was going out on the road, one came running, knelt before Him, and asked Him, "Good Teacher, what shall I do that I may inherit eternal life?"

¹⁸So Jesus said to him, "Why do you call Me good? No one *is* good but One, *that is,* God. ¹⁹You know the commandments: 'Do not commit adultery,' 'Do not murder,' 'Do not steal,' 'Do not bear false witness,' 'Do not defraud,' 'Honor your father and your mother.' "[a]

²⁰And he answered and said to Him, "Teacher, all these things I have kept from my youth."

²¹Then Jesus, looking at him, loved him, and said to him, "One thing you lack: Go your way, sell whatever you have and give to the poor, and you will have treasure in heaven; and come, take up the cross, and follow Me."

²²But he was sad at this word, and went away sorrowful, for he had great possessions.

With God All Things Are Possible

²³Then Jesus looked around and said to His disciples, "How hard it is for those who have riches to enter the kingdom of God!" ²⁴And the disciples were astonished at His words. But Jesus answered again and said to them, "Children, how hard it is for those who trust in riches[a] to enter the kingdom of God! ²⁵It is easier for a camel to go through the eye of a needle than for a rich man to enter the kingdom of God."

²⁶And they were greatly astonished, saying among themselves, "Who then can be saved?"

²⁷But Jesus looked at them and said, "With men *it is* impossible, but not with God; for with God all things are possible."

²⁸Then Peter began to say to Him, "See, we have left all and followed You."

10:19 [a]Exodus 20:12–16; Deuteronomy 5:16–20
10:24 [a]NU-Text omits *for those who trust in riches.*

²⁹So Jesus answered and said, "Assuredly, I say to you, there is no one who has left house or brothers or sisters or father or mother or wife[a] or children or lands, for My sake and the gospel's, ³⁰who shall not receive a hundredfold now in this time—houses and brothers and sisters and mothers and children and lands, with persecutions—and in the age to come, eternal life. ³¹But many *who are* first will be last, and the last first."

Jesus a Third Time Predicts His Death and Resurrection

³²Now they were on the road, going up to Jerusalem, and Jesus was going before them; and they were amazed. And as they followed they were afraid. Then He took the twelve aside again and began to tell them the things that would happen to Him: ³³"Behold, we are going up to Jerusalem, and the Son of Man will be betrayed to the chief priests and to the scribes; and they will condemn Him to death and deliver Him to the Gentiles; ³⁴and they will mock Him, and scourge Him, and spit on Him, and kill Him. And the third day He will rise again."

10:29 [a]NU-Text omits *or wife.*

Greatness Is Serving

³⁵Then James and John, the sons of Zebedee, came to Him, saying, "Teacher, we want You to do for us whatever we ask."

³⁶And He said to them, "What do you want Me to do for you?"

³⁷They said to Him, "Grant us that we may sit, one on Your right hand and the other on Your left, in Your glory."

³⁸But Jesus said to them, "You do not know what you ask. Are you able to drink the cup that I drink, and be baptized with the baptism that I am baptized with?"

³⁹They said to Him, "We are able."

So Jesus said to them, "You will indeed drink the cup that I drink, and with the baptism I am baptized with you will be baptized; ⁴⁰but to sit on My right hand and on My left is not Mine to give, but *it is for those* for whom it is prepared."

⁴¹And when the ten heard *it,* they began to be greatly displeased with James and John. ⁴²But Jesus called them to *Himself* and said to them, "You know that those who are considered rulers over the Gentiles lord it over them, and their great ones exercise authority over them. ⁴³Yet it shall not be so among you; but whoever

---

PARENTING MATTERS

Q: *How do we help our children understand the meaning behind Good Friday and Easter?*

Children and Easter—new life and new beginnings. What better time to share the gospel with your children? Here are the basics:

1. Teach your children who God is and how He loves them. They need to know what sets Him apart from humans:

- God is holy and perfect. People, however, are not perfect.

- God is just and always fair. We are not just in all our decisions.

- God is love and desires a relationship with us. We are not always motivated out of love for another.

2. Instruct your children that their sins must be forgiven (see Rom. 6:23). Many parents feel uncomfortable talking about hell. While God is patient, He is not tolerant. His justice calls for an atonement (a payment, a penalty) for human sin. Our children must have some understanding that their sins can keep them out of heaven. Their sins *must* be paid for, and that is what Jesus Christ did for us on the cross.

3. Train your children to receive God's forgiveness through faith in Jesus Christ (see Eph. 2:8, 9). Faith involves repenting from sin, turning to God in faith, and trusting Jesus Christ to be Savior and Lord.

BIBLICAL INSIGHTS • 10:17–22

What Do You Love?

What is the object of your affections? Power? Recognition? Hobbies?

Not too long ago, I visited an unbelievable house. As I walked around, for just a moment, I thought, *I could have had a house like this.*

Life is more than possessions. A house is not what life is all about!

The fascinating thing about my momentary envy of my friend's home is that we live in a beautiful home tucked away in the woods, overlooking a lake. A sunset view. Tranquility. God has provided a setting more than adequate for our needs. But I've found that no matter what I have or how much I've accomplished, I can always find someone close by who has more or has done it better.

The world seeks to seduce us into a love affair with its trinkets, but we must love God and be preoccupied with pleasing Him alone. Jesus' words to the rich young ruler in Mark 10 call us out of comparison and into the accountability we have with God, "Sell whatever you have and give it to the poor, and you will have treasure in heaven; and come, take up the cross, and follow Me" (v. 21). Mark says in the next verse that the young man "was sad at this word, and went away sorrowful, for he had great possessions."

Nearly all of us in America can identify with the rich young ruler. Most of us are wealthy compared to the vast majority of the world. We need to heed the warning of Jesus not to let riches seduce us and miss *real* life with Him in the process.

---

desires to become great among you shall be your servant. 44And whoever of you desires to be first shall be slave of all. 45For even the Son of Man did not come to be served, but to serve, and to give His life a ransom for many."

Jesus Heals Blind Bartimaeus

46Now they came to Jericho. As He went out of Jericho with His disciples and a great multitude, blind Bartimaeus, the son of Timaeus, sat by the road begging. 47And when he heard that it was Jesus of Nazareth, he began to cry out and say, "Jesus, Son of David, have mercy on me!"

48Then many warned him to be quiet; but he cried out all the more, "Son of David, have mercy on me!"

49So Jesus stood still and commanded him to be called.

Then they called the blind man, saying to him, "Be of good cheer. Rise, He is calling you."

50And throwing aside his garment, he rose and came to Jesus.

51So Jesus answered and said to him, "What do you want Me to do for you?"

The blind man said to Him, "Rabboni, that I may receive my sight."

52Then Jesus said to him, "Go your way; your faith has made you well." And immediately he received his sight and followed Jesus on the road.

The Triumphal Entry

11 Now when they drew near Jerusalem, to Bethphagea and Bethany, at the Mount of Olives, He sent two of His disciples; 2and He said to them, "Go into the village opposite you; and as soon as you have entered it you will find a colt tied, on which no one has sat. Loose it and bring *it.* 3And if anyone says to you, 'Why are you doing this?' say, 'The Lord has need of it,' and immediately he will send it here."

4So they went their way, and found thea colt tied by the door outside on the street, and they loosed it. 5But some of those who stood there said to them, "What are you doing, loosing the colt?"

6And they spoke to them just as Jesus had commanded. So they let them go. 7Then they brought the colt to Jesus and threw their clothes on it, and He sat on it. 8And many spread their clothes on the road, and others cut down leafy branches from the trees and spread *them* on the

11:1 aM-Text reads *Bethsphage.*
11:4 aNU-Text and M-Text read *a.*

road. ⁹Then those who went before and those who followed cried out, saying:

> "Hosanna!
> 'Blessed is He who comes in the name of the Lord!'ᵃ
>
> ¹⁰ Blessed is the kingdom of our father David
> That comes in the name of the Lord!ᵃ
> Hosanna in the highest!"

¹¹And Jesus went into Jerusalem and into the temple. So when He had looked around at all things, as the hour was already late, He went out to Bethany with the twelve.

The Fig Tree Withered

¹²Now the next day, when they had come out from Bethany, He was hungry. ¹³And seeing from afar a fig tree having leaves, He went to see if perhaps He would find something on it. When He came to it, He found nothing but leaves, for it was not the season for figs. ¹⁴In response Jesus said to it, "Let no one eat fruit from you ever again."

And His disciples heard it.

Jesus Cleanses the Temple

¹⁵So they came to Jerusalem. Then Jesus went into the temple and began to drive out those who bought and sold in the temple, and overturned the tables of the money changers and the seats of those who sold doves. ¹⁶And He would not allow anyone to carry wares through the temple. ¹⁷Then He taught, saying to them, "Is it not written, 'My house shall be called a house of prayer for all nations'?ᵃ But you have made it a 'den of thieves.'"ᵇ

¹⁸And the scribes and chief priests heard it and sought how they might destroy Him; for they feared Him, because all the people were astonished at His teaching. ¹⁹When evening had come, He went out of the city.

The Lesson of the Withered Fig Tree

²⁰Now in the morning, as they passed by, they saw the fig tree dried up from the roots. ²¹And Peter, remembering, said to Him, "Rabbi, look! The fig tree which You cursed has withered away."

²²So Jesus answered and said to them, "Have faith in God. ²³For assuredly, I say to you, whoever says to this mountain, 'Be removed and be cast into the sea,' and does not doubt in his heart, but believes that those things he says will be done, he will have whatever he says. ²⁴Therefore I say to you, whatever things you ask when you pray, believe that you receive them, and you will have them.

11:9 ᵃPsalm 118:26 **11:10** ᵃNU-Text omits *in the name of the Lord.* **11:17** ᵃIsaiah 56:7 ᵇJeremiah 7:11

ROMANTIC QUOTES AND NOTES
The One Flesh Challenge

As a wife, I believe the Bible calls me to commit to my husband in a mutually fulfilling sexual relationship, to truly become one flesh with him. That means I need to understand his needs and desires.

My husband's sexual needs should be higher on my priority list than menus, housework, projects, activities—even the children. A friend told me something that I think puts the sexual dimension of a man in a biblical perspective. A man can send his clothes to the laundry, eat all of his meals out, find companionship with friends, be

accepted and respected at work, be listened to by a counselor, and in all those things be in the will of God. But if he meets his sexual needs with someone other than his wife, it is sin.

I believe many wives don't understand how important the act of becoming one is to their husbands. We make time for the PTA, church work, and helping a child with homework, but how often do we set aside time to be together sexually?

One of the most spiritual acts you could do as a wife today would be to put the kids to bed early and invite your husband into the bedroom.

BIBLICAL INSIGHTS • 11:15

Use Anger Wisely

EVERY FAMILY NEEDS a plentiful supply of good anger. Note the emphasis on *good*!

I mean that when anger comes—and it will, inevitably—we should recognize it, understand its cause, and deal with it properly. We shouldn't stuff it inside, like a sleeping bag tightly packed into a knapsack. And we shouldn't spew it like molten, hot lava on those closest to us.

In basic terms, anger is an emotional alarm that sounds a warning when something goes wrong. Only a fool would hear a smoke alarm clanging in the middle of the night and stay in bed to enjoy the interesting tones of the alarm! No, the wise man gets out of bed to see what's wrong. Anger is usually a secondary emotion. Something else has occurred that results in our being angry. Usually it's disappointment or hurt when our expectations go unmet. Some express that disappointment in anger. Others stuff it.

Unfortunately, most individuals and families don't know how to keep good anger from fermenting into spoiled anger. And then, when a family has an adolescent or two, the anger issue can take on new, more explosive, dimensions.

Anger isn't always sinful—and if you don't believe that, just read Mark's account of Jesus cleansing the temple (11:15–18). Scripture frequently describes God exhibiting a righteous anger against human rebellion. The Bible instructs us, "'Be angry and do not sin': do not let the sun go down on your wrath, nor give place to the devil" (Eph. 4:26, 27). When the anger alarm goes off in your heart, make sure it doesn't spill out in ways that damage or destroy relationships. And when you do become sinfully angry with your spouse or family member, be quick to confess and to seek forgiveness.

Remember, "If it is possible, as much as depends on you, live peaceably with all men" (Rom. 12:18).

Forgiveness and Prayer

25"And whenever you stand praying, if you have anything against anyone, forgive him, that your Father in heaven may also forgive you your trespasses. 26But if you do not forgive, neither will your Father in heaven forgive your trespasses."a

Jesus' Authority Questioned

27Then they came again to Jerusalem. And as He was walking in the temple, the chief priests, the scribes, and the elders came to Him. 28And they said to Him, "By what authority are You doing these things? And who gave You this authority to do these things?"

29But Jesus answered and said to them, "I also will ask you one question; then answer Me, and I will tell you by what authority I do these things: 30The baptism of John—was it from heaven or from men? Answer Me."

31And they reasoned among themselves, saying, "If we say, 'From heaven,' He will say, 'Why then did you not believe him?' 32But if we say, 'From men'"—they feared the people, for all counted John to have been a prophet indeed. 33So they answered and said to Jesus, "We do not know."

And Jesus answered and said to them, "Neither will I tell you by what authority I do these things."

The Parable of the Wicked Vinedressers

12 Then He began to speak to them in parables: "A man planted a vineyard and set a hedge around *it*, dug *a place for* the wine vat and built a tower. And he leased it to vinedressers and went into a far country. 2Now at vintage-time he sent a servant to the vinedressers, that he might receive some of the fruit of the vineyard from the vinedressers. 3And they took *him* and beat him and sent *him* away empty-handed. 4Again he sent them another servant, and at him they threw stones,a wounded *him* in the head, and sent *him* away shamefully treated. 5And again he sent another, and him they killed; and many others, beating some and killing some.

11:26 aNU-Text omits this verse.
12:4 aNU-Text omits *and at him they threw stones.*

⁶Therefore still having one son, his beloved, he also sent him to them last, saying, 'They will respect my son.' ⁷But those vinedressers said among themselves, 'This is the heir. Come, let us kill him, and the inheritance will be ours.' ⁸So they took him and killed *him* and cast *him* out of the vineyard.

⁹"Therefore what will the owner of the vineyard do? He will come and destroy the vinedressers, and give the vineyard to others. ¹⁰Have you not even read this Scripture:

'The stone which the builders rejected
Has become the chief cornerstone.
¹¹ This was the LORD's doing,
And it is marvelous in our eyes'? "ᵃ

¹²And they sought to lay hands on Him, but feared the multitude, for they knew He had spoken the parable against them. So they left Him and went away.

The Pharisees: Is It Lawful to Pay Taxes to Caesar?

¹³Then they sent to Him some of the Pharisees and the Herodians, to catch Him in *His* words. ¹⁴When they had come, they said to Him, "Teacher, we know that You are true, and care about no one; for You do not regard the person of men, but teach the way of God in truth. Is it lawful to pay taxes to Caesar, or not? ¹⁵Shall we pay, or shall we not pay?"

But He, knowing their hypocrisy, said to them, "Why do you test Me? Bring Me a denarius that I may see *it.*" ¹⁶So they brought *it.*

And He said to them, "Whose image and inscription *is* this?" They said to Him, "Caesar's."

¹⁷And Jesus answered and said to them, "Render to Caesar the things that are Caesar's, and to God the things that are God's."

And they marveled at Him.

The Sadducees: What About the Resurrection?

¹⁸Then *some* Sadducees, who say there is no resurrection, came to Him; and they asked Him, saying: ¹⁹"Teacher, Moses wrote to us that if a man's brother dies,

BIBLICAL INSIGHTS • 11:25
Don't Fail to Forgive

FAILURES AT HOME COME in all sizes, shapes, and weights.

There are the small ones: breaking a piece of china, spilling ketchup on a new shirt, ripping your jeans, stepping on your wife's foot (with golf shoes), failing to carry out the garbage.

There are the heavier, medium-sized packages that hurt a little deeper: shouting at the kids (for the fourth time in one day), habitually promising something to your kids and then going back on your promise. Or just being selfish in general, not truly serving your spouse and family.

Then there are the cumbersome and heaviest that leave us feeling crushed under the weight: divorce, unfaithfulness, an estranged relationship, a rebellious teenager, physical or verbal abuse, failing to lead your wife and children spiritually.

How can families deal with big and little failures?

The Scriptures teach us to forgive. Forgiveness is not optional in the Christian life! Jesus said, "And whenever you stand praying, if you have anything against anyone, forgive him, that your Father in heaven may also forgive you your trespasses" (11:25). We are commanded to forgive because we've been forgiven.

Forgiveness lies at the heart of Christianity. Your marriage, and mine, must be the union of two people who are totally unwilling for *anything* to come between them. Is there anything you need to ask your spouse to forgive you for today? Or are you holding onto an offense that needs to be released by granting forgiveness to your mate?

Regardless of the size or shape of what's been done, don't allow another day to pass without making things right.

and leaves *his* wife behind, and leaves no children, his brother should take his wife and raise up offspring for his brother.

12:11 ᵃPsalm 118:22, 23

²⁰Now there were seven brothers. The first took a wife; and dying, he left no offspring. ²¹And the second took her, and he died; nor did he leave any offspring. And the third likewise. ²²So the seven had her and left no offspring. Last of all the woman died also. ²³Therefore, in the resurrection, when they rise, whose wife will she be? For all seven had her as wife."

²⁴Jesus answered and said to them, "Are you not therefore mistaken, because you do not know the Scriptures nor the power of God? ²⁵For when they rise from the dead, they neither marry nor are given in marriage, but are like angels in heaven. ²⁶But concerning the dead, that they rise, have you not read in the book of Moses, in the *burning* bush *passage,* how God spoke to him, saying, *'I am the God of Abraham, the God of Isaac, and the God of Jacob'* ?ᵃ ²⁷He is not the God of the dead, but the God of the living. You are therefore greatly mistaken."

INTIMATE MOMENTS

On Thanksgiving Day, give him a handwritten letter with the reasons you are thankful that he is in your life.

The Scribes: Which Is the First Commandment of All?

²⁸Then one of the scribes came, and having heard them reasoning together, perceivingᵃ that He had answered them well, asked Him, "Which is the first commandment of all?"

²⁹Jesus answered him, "The first of all the commandments *is:* '*Hear, O Israel, the* LORD *our God, the* LORD *is one. ³⁰And you shall love the* LORD *your God with all your heart, with all your soul, with all your mind, and with all your strength.'*ᵃ This *is* the first commandment.ᵇ ³¹And the second, like *it, is* this: '*You shall love your neighbor as yourself.'*ᵃ There is no other commandment greater than these."

³²So the scribe said to Him, "Well *said,*

Teacher. You have spoken the truth, for there is one God, and there is no other but He. ³³And to love Him with all the heart, with all the understanding, with all the soul,ᵃ and with all the strength, and to love one's neighbor as oneself, is more than all the whole burnt offerings and sacrifices."

³⁴Now when Jesus saw that he answered wisely, He said to him, "You are not far from the kingdom of God."

But after that no one dared question Him.

Jesus: How Can David Call His Descendant Lord?

³⁵Then Jesus answered and said, while He taught in the temple, "How *is it* that the scribes say that the Christ is the Son of David? ³⁶For David himself said by the Holy Spirit:

'The LORD said to my Lord,
"Sit at My right hand,
Till I make Your enemies Your
    footstool." 'ᵃ

³⁷Therefore David himself calls Him '*Lord*'; how is He *then* his Son?"

And the common people heard Him gladly.

Beware of the Scribes

³⁸Then He said to them in His teaching, "Beware of the scribes, who desire to go around in long robes, *love* greetings in the marketplaces, ³⁹the best seats in the synagogues, and the best places at feasts, ⁴⁰who devour widows' houses, and for a pretense make long prayers. These will receive greater condemnation."

The Widow's Two Mites

⁴¹Now Jesus sat opposite the treasury and saw how the people put money into the treasury. And many *who were* rich put in much. ⁴²Then one poor widow came and threw in two mites,ᵃ which make a quadrans. ⁴³So He called His disciples to *Himself*

12:26 ᵃExodus 3:6, 15   **12:28** ᵃNU-Text reads *seeing.*   **12:30** ᵃDeuteronomy 6:4, 5   ᵇNU-Text omits this sentence.   **12:31** ᵃLeviticus 19:18   **12:33** ᵃNU-Text omits *with all the soul.*   **12:36** ᵃPsalm 110:1   **12:42** ᵃGreek *lepta,* very small copper coins worth a fraction of a penny

and said to them, "Assuredly, I say to you that this poor widow has put in more than all those who have given to the treasury; [44]for they all put in out of their abundance, but she out of her poverty put in all that she had, her whole livelihood."

Jesus Predicts the Destruction of the Temple

13 Then as He went out of the temple, one of His disciples said to Him, "Teacher, see what manner of stones and what buildings *are here!*"

[2]And Jesus answered and said to him, "Do you see these great buildings? Not *one* stone shall be left upon another, that shall not be thrown down."

The Signs of the Times and the End of the Age

[3]Now as He sat on the Mount of Olives opposite the temple, Peter, James, John, and Andrew asked Him privately, [4]"Tell us, when will these things be? And what *will be* the sign when all these things will be fulfilled?"

[5]And Jesus, answering them, began to say: "Take heed that no one deceives you. [6]For many will come in My name, saying, 'I am *He,*' and will deceive many. [7]But when you hear of wars and rumors of wars, do not be troubled; for *such things* must happen, but the end *is* not yet. [8]For nation will rise against nation, and kingdom against kingdom. And there will be earthquakes in various places, and there will be famines and troubles.[a] These *are* the beginnings of sorrows.

[9]"But watch out for yourselves, for they will deliver you up to councils, and you will be beaten in the synagogues. You will be brought[a] before rulers and kings for My sake, for a testimony to them. [10]And the gospel must first be preached to all the nations. [11]But when they arrest *you* and deliver you up, do not worry beforehand, or premeditate[a] what you will speak. But whatever is given you in that hour, speak that; for it is not you who speak, but the Holy Spirit. [12]Now brother will betray brother to death, and a father *his* child; and children will rise up against parents and cause them to be put to death. [13]And you will be hated by all for My name's sake. But he who endures to the end shall be saved.

The Great Tribulation

[14]"So when you see the '*abomination of desolation,*'[a] spoken of by Daniel the prophet,[b] standing where it ought not" (let the reader understand), "then let those who are in Judea flee to the mountains. [15]Let him who is on the housetop not go down into the house, nor enter to take anything out of his house. [16]And let him who is in the field not go back to get his clothes. [17]But woe to those who are pregnant and to those who are nursing babies in those days! [18]And pray that your flight may not be in winter. [19]For *in* those days there will be tribulation, such as has not been since the beginning of the creation which God created until this time, nor ever shall be. [20]And unless the Lord had shortened those days, no flesh would be saved; but for the elect's sake, whom He chose, He shortened the days.

[21]"Then if anyone says to you, 'Look, here *is* the Christ!' or, 'Look, *He is* there!' do not believe it. [22]For false christs and false prophets will rise and show signs and wonders to deceive, if possible, even the elect. [23]But take heed; see, I have told you all things beforehand.

The Coming of the Son of Man

[24]"But in those days, after that tribulation, the sun will be darkened, and the moon will not give its light; [25]the stars of heaven will fall, and the powers in the heavens will be shaken. [26]Then they will see the Son of Man coming in the clouds with great power and glory. [27]And then He will send His angels, and gather together His elect from the four winds, from the farthest part of earth to the farthest part of heaven.

The Parable of the Fig Tree

[28]"Now learn this parable from the fig tree: When its branch has already become tender, and puts forth leaves, you know that summer is near. [29]So you also, when

---

13:8 [a]NU-Text omits *and troubles.* **13:9** [a]NU-Text and M-Text read *will stand.* **13:11** [a]NU-Text omits *or premeditate.* **13:14** [a]Daniel 11:31; 12:11 [b]NU-Text omits *spoken of by Daniel the prophet.*

you see these things happening, know that it[a] is near—at the doors! [30]Assuredly, I say to you, this generation will by no means pass away till all these things take place. [31]Heaven and earth will pass away, but My words will by no means pass away.

No One Knows the Day or Hour

[32]"But of that day and hour no one knows, not even the angels in heaven, nor the Son, but only the Father. [33]Take heed, watch and pray; for you do not know when the time is. [34]*It is* like a man going to a far country, who left his house and gave authority to his servants, and to each his work, and commanded the doorkeeper to watch. [35]Watch therefore, for you do not know when the master of the house is coming—in the evening, at midnight, at the crowing of the rooster, or in the morning— [36]lest, coming suddenly, he find you sleeping. [37]And what I say to you, I say to all: Watch!"

The Plot to Kill Jesus

14 After two days it was the Passover and *the Feast* of Unleavened Bread. And the chief priests and the scribes sought how they might take Him by trickery and put *Him* to death. [2]But they said, "Not during the feast, lest there be an uproar of the people."

The Anointing at Bethany

[3]And being in Bethany at the house of Simon the leper, as He sat at the table, a woman came having an alabaster flask of very costly oil of spikenard. Then she broke the flask and poured *it* on His head. [4]But there were some who were indignant among themselves, and said, "Why was this fragrant oil wasted? [5]For it might have been sold for more than three hundred denarii and given to the poor." And they criticized her sharply.

[6]But Jesus said, "Let her alone. Why do you trouble her? She has done a good work for Me. [7]For you have the poor with you always, and whenever you wish you may do them good; but Me you do not have always. [8]She has done what she could. She has come beforehand to anoint My body for burial. [9]Assuredly, I say to you, wherever this gospel is preached in the whole world, what this woman has done will also be told as a memorial to her."

Judas Agrees to Betray Jesus

[10]Then Judas Iscariot, one of the twelve, went to the chief priests to betray Him to them. [11]And when they heard *it,* they were glad, and promised to give him money. So he sought how he might conveniently betray Him.

Jesus Celebrates the Passover with His Disciples

[12]Now on the first day of Unleavened Bread, when they killed the Passover *lamb,* His disciples said to Him, "Where do You want us to go and prepare, that You may eat the Passover?"

[13]And He sent out two of His disciples and said to them, "Go into the city, and a man will meet you carrying a pitcher of water; follow him. [14]Wherever he goes in, say to the master of the house, 'The Teacher says, "Where is the guest room in which I may eat the Passover with My disciples?"' [15]Then he will show you a large upper room, furnished *and* prepared; there make ready for us."

[16]So His disciples went out, and came into the city, and found it just as He had said to them; and they prepared the Passover.

[17]In the evening He came with the twelve. [18]Now as they sat and ate, Jesus said, "Assuredly, I say to you, one of you who eats with Me will betray Me."

[19]And they began to be sorrowful, and to say to Him one by one, "*Is* it I?" And another *said, "Is* it I?"[a]

[20]He answered and said to them, "*It is* one of the twelve, who dips with Me in the dish. [21]The Son of Man indeed goes just as it is written of Him, but woe to that man by whom the Son of Man is betrayed! It would have been good for that man if he had never been born."

Jesus Institutes the Lord's Supper

[22]And as they were eating, Jesus took bread, blessed and broke *it,* and gave *it* to them and said, "Take, eat;[a] this is My body."

13:29 [a]Or *He* **14:19** [a]NU-Text omits this sentence. **14:22** [a]NU-Text omits *eat.*

²³Then He took the cup, and when He had given thanks He gave *it* to them, and they all drank from it. ²⁴And He said to them, "This is My blood of the new[a] covenant, which is shed for many. ²⁵Assuredly, I say to you, I will no longer drink of the fruit of the vine until that day when I drink it new in the kingdom of God."

²⁶And when they had sung a hymn, they went out to the Mount of Olives.

Jesus Predicts Peter's Denial

²⁷Then Jesus said to them, "All of you will be made to stumble because of Me this night,[a] for it is written:

'I will strike the Shepherd,
And the sheep will be scattered.'[b]

²⁸"But after I have been raised, I will go before you to Galilee."

²⁹Peter said to Him, "Even if all are made to stumble, yet I *will* not *be.*"

³⁰Jesus said to him, "Assuredly, I say to you that today, *even* this night, before the rooster crows twice, you will deny Me three times."

³¹But he spoke more vehemently, "If I have to die with You, I will not deny You!"

And they all said likewise.

The Prayer in the Garden

³²Then they came to a place which was named Gethsemane; and He said to His disciples, "Sit here while I pray." ³³And He took Peter, James, and John with Him, and He began to be troubled and deeply distressed. ³⁴Then He said to them, "My soul is exceedingly sorrowful, *even* to death. Stay here and watch."

³⁵He went a little farther, and fell on the ground, and prayed that if it were possible, the hour might pass from Him. ³⁶And He said, "Abba, Father, all things *are* possible for You. Take this cup away from Me; nevertheless, not what I will, but what You *will.*"

³⁷Then He came and found them sleeping, and said to Peter, "Simon, are you sleeping? Could you not watch one hour? ³⁸Watch and pray, lest you enter into temptation.

The spirit indeed *is* willing, but the flesh *is* weak."

³⁹Again He went away and prayed, and spoke the same words. ⁴⁰And when He returned, He found them asleep again, for their eyes were heavy; and they did not know what to answer Him.

⁴¹Then He came the third time and said to them, "Are you still sleeping and resting? It is enough! The hour has come; behold, the Son of Man is being betrayed into the hands of sinners. ⁴²Rise, let us be going. See, My betrayer is at hand."

Betrayal and Arrest in Gethsemane

⁴³And immediately, while He was still speaking, Judas, one of the twelve, with a great multitude with swords and clubs, came from the chief priests and the scribes and the elders. ⁴⁴Now His betrayer had given them a signal, saying, "Whomever I kiss, He is the One; seize Him and lead *Him* away safely."

⁴⁵As soon as he had come, immediately he went up to Him and said to Him, "Rabbi, Rabbi!" and kissed Him.

⁴⁶Then they laid their hands on Him and took Him. ⁴⁷And one of those who stood by drew his sword and struck the servant of the high priest, and cut off his ear.

⁴⁸Then Jesus answered and said to them, "Have you come out, as against a robber, with swords and clubs to take Me? ⁴⁹I was daily with you in the temple teaching, and you did not seize Me. But the Scriptures must be fulfilled."

⁵⁰Then they all forsook Him and fled.

A Young Man Flees Naked

⁵¹Now a certain young man followed Him, having a linen cloth thrown around *his* naked *body.* And the young men laid hold of him, ⁵²and he left the linen cloth and fled from them naked.

Jesus Faces the Sanhedrin

⁵³And they led Jesus away to the high priest; and with him were assembled all the chief priests, the elders, and the scribes. ⁵⁴But Peter followed Him at a distance, right into the courtyard of the high priest. And he sat with the servants and warmed himself at the fire.

14:24 [a]NU-Text omits *new.* **14:27** [a]NU-Text omits *because of Me this night.* [b]Zechariah 13:7

⁵⁵Now the chief priests and all the council sought testimony against Jesus to put Him to death, but found none. ⁵⁶For many bore false witness against Him, but their testimonies did not agree.

⁵⁷Then some rose up and bore false witness against Him, saying, ⁵⁸"We heard Him say, 'I will destroy this temple made with hands, and within three days I will build another made without hands.'" ⁵⁹But not even then did their testimony agree.

⁶⁰And the high priest stood up in the midst and asked Jesus, saying, "Do You answer nothing? What *is it* these men testify against You?" ⁶¹But He kept silent and answered nothing.

Again the high priest asked Him, saying to Him, "Are You the Christ, the Son of the Blessed?"

⁶²Jesus said, "I am. And you will see the Son of Man sitting at the right hand of the Power, and coming with the clouds of heaven."

⁶³Then the high priest tore his clothes and said, "What further need do we have of witnesses? ⁶⁴You have heard the blasphemy! What do you think?"

And they all condemned Him to be deserving of death.

⁶⁵Then some began to spit on Him, and to blindfold Him, and to beat Him, and to say to Him, "Prophesy!" And the officers struck Him with the palms of their hands.ᵃ

Peter Denies Jesus, and Weeps

⁶⁶Now as Peter was below in the courtyard, one of the servant girls of the high priest came. ⁶⁷And when she saw Peter warming himself, she looked at him and said, "You also were with Jesus of Nazareth."

⁶⁸But he denied it, saying, "I neither know nor understand what you are saying." And he went out on the porch, and a rooster crowed.

⁶⁹And the servant girl saw him again, and began to say to those who stood by, "This is *one* of them." ⁷⁰But he denied it again.

And a little later those who stood by said to Peter again, "Surely you are *one* of them; for you are a Galilean, and your speech shows *it*."ᵃ

⁷¹Then he began to curse and swear, "I do not know this Man of whom you speak!"

⁷²A second time *the* rooster crowed. Then Peter called to mind the word that Jesus had said to him, "Before the rooster crows twice, you will deny Me three times." And when he thought about it, he wept.

Jesus Faces Pilate

15 Immediately, in the morning, the chief priests held a consultation with the elders and scribes and the whole council; and they bound Jesus, led *Him* away, and delivered *Him* to Pilate. ²Then Pilate asked Him, "Are You the King of the Jews?"

He answered and said to him, "*It is as* you say."

³And the chief priests accused Him of many things, but He answered nothing. ⁴Then Pilate asked Him again, saying, "Do You answer nothing? See how many things they testify against You!"ᵃ ⁵But Jesus still answered nothing, so that Pilate marveled.

Taking the Place of Barabbas

⁶Now at the feast he was accustomed to releasing one prisoner to them, whomever they requested. ⁷And there was one named Barabbas, *who was* chained with his fellow rebels; they had committed murder in the rebellion. ⁸Then the multitude, crying aloud,ᵃ began to ask *him to do* just as he had always done for them. ⁹But Pilate answered them, saying, "Do you want me to release to you the King of the Jews?" ¹⁰For he knew that the chief priests had handed Him over because of envy.

¹¹But the chief priests stirred up the crowd, so that he should rather release Barabbas to them. ¹²Pilate answered and said to them again, "What then do you want me to do *with Him* whom you call the King of the Jews?"

¹³So they cried out again, "Crucify Him!"

¹⁴Then Pilate said to them, "Why, what evil has He done?"

But they cried out all the more, "Crucify Him!"

14:65 ᵃNU-Text reads *received Him with slaps.*
14:70 ᵃNU-Text omits *and your speech shows it.*
15:4 ᵃNU-Text reads *of which they accuse You.*
15:8 ᵃNU-Text reads *going up.*

[15]So Pilate, wanting to gratify the crowd, released Barabbas to them; and he delivered Jesus, after he had scourged *Him,* to be crucified.

The Soldiers Mock Jesus

[16]Then the soldiers led Him away into the hall called Praetorium, and they called together the whole garrison. [17]And they clothed Him with purple; and they twisted a crown of thorns, put it on His *head,* [18]and began to salute Him, "Hail, King of the Jews!" [19]Then they struck Him on the head with a reed and spat on Him; and bowing the knee, they worshiped Him. [20]And when they had mocked Him, they took the purple off Him, put His own clothes on Him, and led Him out to crucify Him.

The King on a Cross

[21]Then they compelled a certain man, Simon a Cyrenian, the father of Alexander and Rufus, as he was coming out of the country and passing by, to bear His cross. [22]And they brought Him to the place Golgotha, which is translated, Place of a Skull. [23]Then they gave Him wine mingled with myrrh to drink, but He did not take *it.* [24]And when they crucified Him, they divided His garments, casting lots for them *to determine* what every man should take.

[25]Now it was the third hour, and they crucified Him. [26]And the inscription of His accusation was written above:

THE KING OF THE JEWS.

[27]With Him they also crucified two robbers, one on His right and the other on His left. [28]So the Scripture was fulfilled[a] which says, *"And He was numbered with the transgressors."*[b]

[29]And those who passed by blasphemed Him, wagging their heads and saying, "Aha! *You* who destroy the temple and build *it* in three days, [30]save Yourself, and come down from the cross!"

[31]Likewise the chief priests also, mocking among themselves with the scribes, said, "He saved others; Himself He cannot save. [32]Let the Christ, the King of Israel, descend now from the cross, that we may see and believe."[a]

Even those who were crucified with Him reviled Him.

Jesus Dies on the Cross

[33]Now when the sixth hour had come, there was darkness over the whole land until the ninth hour. [34]And at the ninth hour Jesus cried out with a loud voice, saying, "Eloi, Eloi, lama sabachthani?" which is translated, *"My God, My God, why have You forsaken Me?"*[a]

[35]Some of those who stood by, when they heard *that,* said, "Look, He is calling for Elijah!" [36]Then someone ran and filled a sponge full of sour wine, put *it* on a reed, and offered *it* to Him to drink, saying, "Let Him alone; let us see if Elijah will come to take Him down."

[37]And Jesus cried out with a loud voice, and breathed His last.

[38]Then the veil of the temple was torn in two from top to bottom. [39]So when the centurion, who stood opposite Him, saw that He cried out like this and breathed His last,[a] he said, "Truly this Man was the Son of God!"

[40]There were also women looking on from afar, among whom were Mary Magdalene, Mary the mother of James the Less and of Joses, and Salome, [41]who also followed Him and ministered to Him when He was in Galilee, and many other women who came up with Him to Jerusalem.

Jesus Buried in Joseph's Tomb

[42]Now when evening had come, because it was the Preparation Day, that is, the day before the Sabbath, [43]Joseph of Arimathea, a prominent council member, who was himself waiting for the kingdom of God, coming and taking courage, went in to Pilate and asked for the body of Jesus. [44]Pilate marveled that He was already dead; and summoning the centurion, he asked him if He had been dead for some time. [45]So when he found out from the centurion, he granted the body to Joseph. [46]Then he bought fine linen, took Him down, and wrapped Him in the linen. And he laid Him

---

15:28 [a]Isaiah 53:12 [b]NU-Text omits this verse.
15:32 [a]M-Text reads *believe Him.* 15:34 [a]Psalm 22:1
15:39 [a]NU-Text reads *that He thus breathed His last.*

in a tomb which had been hewn out of the rock, and rolled a stone against the door of the tomb. ⁴⁷And Mary Magdalene and Mary *the mother* of Joses observed where He was laid.

He Is Risen

16 Now when the Sabbath was past, Mary Magdalene, Mary *the mother* of James, and Salome bought spices, that they might come and anoint Him. ²Very early in the morning, on the first *day* of the week, they came to the tomb when the sun had risen. ³And they said among themselves, "Who will roll away the stone from the door of the tomb for us?" ⁴But when they looked up, they saw that the stone had been rolled away—for it was very large. ⁵And entering the tomb, they saw a young man clothed in a long white robe sitting on the right side; and they were alarmed.

⁶But he said to them, "Do not be alarmed. You seek Jesus of Nazareth, who was crucified. He is risen! He is not here. See the place where they laid Him. ⁷But go, tell His disciples—and Peter—that He is going before you into Galilee; there you will see Him, as He said to you."

⁸So they went out quicklyᵃ and fled from the tomb, for they trembled and were amazed. And they said nothing to anyone, for they were afraid.

Mary Magdalene Sees the Risen Lord

⁹Now when *He* rose early on the first *day* of the week, He appeared first to Mary Magdalene, out of whom He had cast seven demons. ¹⁰She went and told those who had been with Him, as they mourned and wept. ¹¹And when they heard that He was alive and had been seen by her, they did not believe.

Jesus Appears to Two Disciples

¹²After that, He appeared in another form to two of them as they walked and went into the country. ¹³And they went and told *it* to the rest, *but* they did not believe them either.

The Great Commission

¹⁴Later He appeared to the eleven as they sat at the table; and He rebuked their unbelief and hardness of heart, because they did not believe those who had seen Him after He had risen. ¹⁵And He said to them, "Go into all the world and preach the gospel to every creature. ¹⁶He who believes and is baptized will be saved; but he who does not believe will be condemned. ¹⁷And these signs will follow those who believe: In My name they will cast out demons; they will speak with new tongues; ¹⁸they will take up serpents; and if they drink anything deadly, it will by no means hurt them; they will lay hands on the sick, and they will recover."

Christ Ascends to God's Right Hand

¹⁹So then, after the Lord had spoken to them, He was received up into heaven, and sat down at the right hand of God. ²⁰And they went out and preached everywhere, the Lord working with *them* and confirming the word through the accompanying signs. Amen.ᵃ

INTIMATE MOMENTS

Find the book your wife is reading and leave some encouraging note in it every 20 pages or so.

16:8 ᵃNU-Text and M-Text omit *quickly.*
16:18 ᵃNU-Text reads *and in their hands they will.*
16:20 ᵃVerses 9–20 are bracketed in NU-Text as not original. They are lacking in Codex Sinaiticus and Codex Vaticanus, although nearly all other manuscripts of Mark contain them.

LUKE

THE THIRD SCRIPTURAL BIOGRAPHY OF JESUS was written by a Gentile physician, missionary, historian and evangelist named Luke. Luke is also the author of the book of Acts, which describes the spread of Christianity in the first century A.D. Together, his two books make up about twenty percent of the New Testament.

Many leaders in the early church believed that Paul was talking about Luke in 2 Corinthians 8:18, when the apostle mentioned "the brother whose praise is in the gospel throughout all the churches." What a wonderful thing to be famous for, the ministry of the gospel!

Although Luke was not an eyewitness to the life of Jesus, he traveled on several missionary journeys with Paul and other apostles, from whom he learned the details of the life of Jesus. He very likely also spoke with Mary, the mother of Jesus, who would have provided him with insider information about the birth of her Son. He may have also had access to Mark's Gospel.

Luke writes to a non-Jewish audience and so presents Jesus in His full humanity as "the Son of Man." He wants his fellow Gentiles to know that the gospel message is for the whole world, including them. He repeatedly relates stories about Gentiles, Samaritans, women, children, tax collectors, sinners, and others often regarded in Israel as outcasts. Darrell Bock says that Luke's Gospel "explains how Jew and Gentile could end up as equals in a community planted by God, even though that community's roots were originally grounded in a promise to Israel."

Luke gives special emphasis to the ministry of the Holy Spirit. The Holy Spirit moves in power upon John the Baptist (1:15), Mary (1:35), Elizabeth (1:41), Zechariah (1:67), Simeon (2:25), Jesus (3:16; 4:1; 10:21), and us (12:12). Dr. Bill Bright used to refer to the Holy Spirit as the "forgotten member of the Trinity," an error we should never make. Pay special attention as you read through Luke to the ministry of the Spirit, keeping in mind that this same Spirit who raised Jesus from the dead is alive in you today! He *is* the power that equips you to love, lead, and serve your spouse and family.

Dedication to Theophilus

1 Inasmuch as many have taken in hand to set in order a narrative of those things which have been fulfilled[a] among us, [2]just as those who from the beginning were eyewitnesses and ministers of the word delivered them to us, [3]it seemed good to me also, having had perfect understanding of all things from the very first, to write to you an orderly account, most excellent Theophilus, [4]that you may know the certainty of those things in which you were instructed.

John's Birth Announced to Zacharias

[5]There was in the days of Herod, the king of Judea, a certain priest named Zacharias, of the division of Abijah. His wife *was* of the daughters of Aaron, and her name *was* Elizabeth. [6]And they were both righteous before God, walking in all the commandments and ordinances of the Lord blameless. [7]But they had no child, because Elizabeth was barren, and they were both well advanced in years.

[8]So it was, that while he was serving as priest before God in the order of his division, [9]according to the custom of the priesthood, his lot fell to burn incense when he went into the temple of the Lord. [10]And the whole multitude of the people was praying outside at the hour of incense. [11]Then an angel of the Lord appeared to him, standing on the right side of the altar of incense. [12]And when Zacharias saw *him,* he was troubled, and fear fell upon him.

[13]But the angel said to him, "Do not be afraid, Zacharias, for your prayer is heard; and your wife Elizabeth will bear you a son, and you shall call his name John. [14]And you will have joy and gladness, and many will rejoice at his birth. [15]For he will be great in the sight of the Lord, and shall drink neither wine nor strong drink. He will also be filled with the Holy Spirit, even from his mother's womb. [16]And he will turn many of the children of Israel to the Lord their God. [17]He will also go before Him in the spirit and power of Elijah, *'to turn the hearts of the fathers to the children,'*[a] and the disobedient to the wisdom of the just, to make ready a people prepared for the Lord."

[18]And Zacharias said to the angel, "How shall I know this? For I am an old man, and my wife is well advanced in years."

[19]And the angel answered and said to him, "I am Gabriel, who stands in the presence of God, and was sent to speak to you and bring you these glad tidings. [20]But behold, you will be mute and not able to speak until the day these things take place, because you did not believe my words which will be fulfilled in their own time."

[21]And the people waited for Zacharias, and marveled that he lingered so long in the temple. [22]But when he came out, he could not speak to them; and they perceived that he had seen a vision in the temple, for he beckoned to them and remained speechless.

[23]So it was, as soon as the days of his service were completed, that he departed to his own house. [24]Now after those days his wife Elizabeth conceived; and she hid herself five months, saying, [25]"Thus the Lord has dealt with me, in the days when He looked on *me,* to take away my reproach among people."

Christ's Birth Announced to Mary

[26]Now in the sixth month the angel Gabriel was sent by God to a city of Galilee named Nazareth, [27]to a virgin betrothed to a man whose name was Joseph, of the house of David. The virgin's name *was* Mary. [28]And having come in, the angel said to her, "Rejoice, highly favored *one,* the Lord *is* with you; blessed *are* you among women!"[a]

[29]But when she saw *him,*[a] she was troubled at his saying, and considered what manner of greeting this was. [30]Then the angel said to her, "Do not be afraid, Mary, for you have found favor with God. [31]And behold, you will conceive in your womb and bring forth a Son, and shall call His name JESUS. [32]He will be great, and will be called the Son of the Highest; and the Lord God will give Him the throne of His father David. [33]And He will reign over the house of Jacob forever, and of His kingdom there will be no end."

1:1 [a]Or *are most surely believed* **1:17** [a]Malachi 4:5, 6
1:28 [a]NU-Text omits *blessed are you among women.*
1:29 [a]NU-Text omits *when she saw him.*

³⁴Then Mary said to the angel, "How can this be, since I do not know a man?"

³⁵And the angel answered and said to her, "*The* Holy Spirit will come upon you, and the power of the Highest will overshadow you; therefore, also, that Holy One who is to be born will be called the Son of God. ³⁶Now indeed, Elizabeth your relative has also conceived a son in her old age; and this is now the sixth month for her who was called barren. ³⁷For with God nothing will be impossible."

³⁸Then Mary said, "Behold the maidservant of the Lord! Let it be to me according to your word." And the angel departed from her.

Mary Visits Elizabeth

³⁹Now Mary arose in those days and went into the hill country with haste, to a city of Judah, ⁴⁰and entered the house of Zacharias and greeted Elizabeth. ⁴¹And it happened, when Elizabeth heard the greeting of Mary, that the babe leaped in her womb; and Elizabeth was filled with the Holy Spirit. ⁴²Then she spoke out with a loud voice and said, "Blessed *are* you among women, and blessed *is* the fruit of your womb! ⁴³But why *is* this *granted* to me, that the mother of my Lord should come to me? ⁴⁴For indeed, as soon as the voice of your greeting sounded in my ears, the babe leaped in my womb for joy. ⁴⁵Blessed *is* she who believed, for there will be a fulfillment of those things which were told her from the Lord."

The Song of Mary

⁴⁶And Mary said:

"My soul magnifies the Lord,
⁴⁷   And my spirit has rejoiced in God
          my Savior.
⁴⁸   For He has regarded the lowly state
          of His maidservant;
       For behold, henceforth all
          generations will call me blessed.
⁴⁹   For He who is mighty has done great
          things for me,
       And holy *is* His name.
⁵⁰   And His mercy *is* on those who fear
          Him
       From generation to generation.

⁵¹   He has shown strength with His arm;
       He has scattered *the* proud in the
          imagination of their hearts.
⁵²   He has put down the mighty from
          their thrones,
       And exalted *the* lowly.
⁵³   He has filled *the* hungry with good
          things,
       And *the* rich He has sent away empty.
⁵⁴   He has helped His servant Israel,
       In remembrance of *His* mercy,
⁵⁵   As He spoke to our fathers,
       To Abraham and to his seed forever."

⁵⁶And Mary remained with her about three months, and returned to her house.

Birth of John the Baptist

⁵⁷Now Elizabeth's full time came for her to be delivered, and she brought forth a son. ⁵⁸When her neighbors and relatives heard how the Lord had shown great mercy to her, they rejoiced with her.

Circumcision of John the Baptist

⁵⁹So it was, on the eighth day, that they came to circumcise the child; and they would have called him by the name of his father, Zacharias. ⁶⁰His mother answered and said, "No; he shall be called John."

⁶¹But they said to her, "There is no one among your relatives who is called by this name." ⁶²So they made signs to his father—what he would have him called. ⁶³And he asked for a writing tablet, and wrote, saying, "His name is John." So they all marveled. ⁶⁴Immediately his mouth was opened and his tongue *loosed,* and he spoke, praising God. ⁶⁵Then fear came on all who dwelt around them; and all these sayings were discussed throughout all the hill country of Judea. ⁶⁶And all those who heard *them* kept *them* in their hearts, saying, "What kind of child will this be?" And the hand of the Lord was with him.

Zacharias' Prophecy

⁶⁷Now his father Zacharias was filled with the Holy Spirit, and prophesied, saying:

⁶⁸   "Blessed *is* the Lord God of Israel,
       For He has visited and redeemed His
          people,

69 And has raised up a horn of
salvation for us
In the house of His servant David,
70 As He spoke by the mouth of His
holy prophets,
Who *have been* since the world
began,
71 That we should be saved from our
enemies
And from the hand of all who hate
us,
72 To perform the mercy *promised* to
our fathers
And to remember His holy
covenant,
73 The oath which He swore to our
father Abraham:
74 To grant us that we,
Being delivered from the hand of our
enemies,
Might serve Him without fear,
75 In holiness and righteousness before
Him all the days of our life.

76 "And you, child, will be called the
prophet of the Highest;
For you will go before the face of the
Lord to prepare His ways,
77 To give knowledge of salvation to
His people
By the remission of their sins,
78 Through the tender mercy of our
God,
With which the Dayspring from on
high has visited[a] us;

79 To give light to those who sit in
darkness and the shadow of
death,
To guide our feet into the way of
peace."

80So the child grew and became strong
in spirit, and was in the deserts till the day
of his manifestation to Israel.

Christ Born of Mary

2 And it came to pass in those days *that* a
decree went out from Caesar Augustus
that all the world should be registered.
2This census first took place while
Quirinius was governing Syria. 3So all went
to be registered, everyone to his own city.
4Joseph also went up from Galilee, out of
the city of Nazareth, into Judea, to the city
of David, which is called Bethlehem,
because he was of the house and lineage of
David, 5to be registered with Mary, his
betrothed wife,[a] who was with child. 6So it
was, that while they were there, the days
were completed for her to be delivered.
7And she brought forth her firstborn Son,
and wrapped Him in swaddling cloths, and
laid Him in a manger, because there was no
room for them in the inn.

Glory in the Highest

8Now there were in the same country
shepherds living out in the fields, keeping

1:78 aNU-Text reads *shall visit.*
2:5 aNU-Text omits *wife.*

The Case for the Tender Man

In the early 1990's, a book came out whose title no doubt puzzled many men, pastor
and author Stu Weber's *Tender Warrior*. Stu, a former Green Beret, tried to show his
readers that real men could also have a soft side.

Still, I wonder how many men look at the apostle Paul"s words, "And be kind to one
another, tenderhearted" (Eph. 4:32), and think, *That doesn't apply to me.*

From an early age, many men are taught not to cry, to hide feelings, not to be tender toward their wives and children. But our nation has a real need for husbands and
fathers who will love and lead their families, who are not afraid to be tender.

Fathers need to be tender. Their hearts need to be knitted to their
wife's soul and their children's souls. Real men can be gentle men.

When did you last tell your wife you loved her? How about your
children? Ask your spouse and your children what tender love looks
like from their perspective. Ask God to develop your heart so you
will be able to communicate the tender side of love to your wife
and children.

watch over their flock by night. ⁹And behold,ᵃ an angel of the Lord stood before them, and the glory of the Lord shone around them, and they were greatly afraid. ¹⁰Then the angel said to them, "Do not be afraid, for behold, I bring you good tidings of great joy which will be to all people. ¹¹For there is born to you this day in the city of David a Savior, who is Christ the Lord. ¹²And this *will be* the sign to you: You will find a Babe wrapped in swaddling cloths, lying in a manger."

¹³And suddenly there was with the angel a multitude of the heavenly host praising God and saying:

¹⁴ "Glory to God in the highest,
And on earth peace, goodwill toward men!"ᵃ

¹⁵So it was, when the angels had gone away from them into heaven, that the shepherds said to one another, "Let us now go to Bethlehem and see this thing that has come to pass, which the Lord has made known to us." ¹⁶And they came with haste and found Mary and Joseph, and the Babe lying in a manger. ¹⁷Now when they had seen *Him,* they made widelyᵃ known the saying which was told them concerning this Child. ¹⁸And all those who heard *it* marveled at those things which were told them by the shepherds. ¹⁹But Mary kept all these things and pondered *them* in her heart. ²⁰Then the shepherds returned, glorifying and praising God for all the things that they had heard and seen, as it was told them.

Circumcision of Jesus

²¹And when eight days were completed for the circumcision of the Child,ᵃ His name was called JESUS, the name given by the angel before He was conceived in the womb.

Jesus Presented in the Temple

²²Now when the days of her purification according to the law of Moses were completed, they brought Him to Jerusalem to present *Him* to the Lord ²³(as it is written in the law of the Lord, *"Every male who opens the womb shall be called holy to the LORD"*),ᵃ ²⁴and to offer a sacrifice according to what is said in the law of the Lord, *"A pair of turtledoves or two young pigeons."*ᵃ

Simeon Sees God's Salvation

²⁵And behold, there was a man in Jerusalem whose name *was* Simeon, and this man *was* just and devout, waiting for the Consolation of Israel, and the Holy Spirit was upon him. ²⁶And it had been revealed to him by the Holy Spirit that he would not see death before he had seen the Lord's Christ. ²⁷So he came by the Spirit into the temple. And when the parents brought in the Child Jesus, to do for Him according to the custom of the law, ²⁸he took Him up in his arms and blessed God and said:

²⁹ "Lord, now You are letting Your
servant depart in peace,
According to Your word;
³⁰ For my eyes have seen Your
salvation
³¹ Which You have prepared before the
face of all peoples,
³² A light to *bring* revelation to the
Gentiles,
And the glory of Your people Israel."

³³And Joseph and His motherᵃ marveled at those things which were spoken of Him. ³⁴Then Simeon blessed them, and said to Mary His mother, "Behold, this *Child* is destined for the fall and rising of many in Israel, and for a sign which will be spoken against ³⁵(yes, a sword will pierce through your own soul also), that the thoughts of many hearts may be revealed."

Anna Bears Witness to the Redeemer

³⁶Now there was one, Anna, a prophetess, the daughter of Phanuel, of the tribe of Asher. She was of a great age, and had lived with a husband seven years from her virginity; ³⁷and this woman *was* a widow of about eighty-four years,ᵃ who did not depart from the temple, but served *God* with fastings and prayers night and day. ³⁸And coming in that instant she gave

---

2:9 ᵃNU-Text omits *behold.*
2:14 ᵃNU-Text reads *toward men of goodwill.*
2:17 ᵃNU-Text omits *widely.* 2:21 ᵃNU-Text reads *for His circumcision.* 2:23 ᵃExodus 13:2, 12, 15
2:24 ᵃLeviticus 12:8 2:33 ᵃNU-Text reads *And His father and mother.* 2:37 ᵃNU-Text reads *a widow until she was eighty-four.*

thanks to the Lord,[a] and spoke of Him to all those who looked for redemption in Jerusalem.

The Family Returns to Nazareth

[39]So when they had performed all things according to the law of the Lord,

---

ROMANCE FAQ

Q: What best communicates love to a woman?

Some time ago we surveyed 800 people at our Weekend To Remember ® marriage conferences. Here is our top 10 list, in reverse order, of what communicates romantic love to women.

10. *Holding hands.* This simple act communicates closeness.

9. *Massage.* Women often enjoy massages—with no strings attached!

8. *Acts of service and sacrifice.* When a husband denies himself, he tells his wife he cares about her and wants to make her feel special.

7. *A kiss.* I suspect women would rank kissing higher if they didn't know from experience that their husbands usually don't want to stop with a kiss.

6. *Taking a walk together.* Walks together allow her to take a break from daily distractions and focus on the relationship.

5. *Written notes, letters or cards.* Something this thoughtful reminds a wife what a wonderful husband she has.

4. *Going out on a date.* A date means time away, with no kids, just the two of you.

3. *Having special meals together.* Put the kids to bed early and have a quiet candlelight dinner at home.

2. *Touch.* This means hugging, cuddling, and caressing—*without* expectation of a later payoff.

1. *Flowers.* Flowers say, "You are special to me."

---

they returned to Galilee, to their *own* city, Nazareth. [40]And the Child grew and became strong in spirit,[a] filled with wisdom; and the grace of God was upon Him.

The Boy Jesus Amazes the Scholars

[41]His parents went to Jerusalem every year at the Feast of the Passover. [42]And when He was twelve years old, they went up to Jerusalem according to the custom of the feast. [43]When they had finished the days, as they returned, the Boy Jesus lingered behind in Jerusalem. And Joseph and His mother[a] did not know *it;* [44]but supposing Him to have been in the company, they went a day's journey, and sought Him among *their* relatives and acquaintances. [45]So when they did not find Him, they returned to Jerusalem, seeking Him. [46]Now so it was *that* after three days they found Him in the temple, sitting in the midst of the teachers, both listening to them and asking them questions. [47]And all who heard Him were astonished at His understanding and answers. [48]So when they saw Him, they were amazed; and His mother said to Him, "Son, why have You done this to us? Look, Your father and I have sought You anxiously."

[49]And He said to them, "Why did you seek Me? Did you not know that I must be about My Father's business?" [50]But they did not understand the statement which He spoke to them.

Jesus Advances in Wisdom and Favor

[51]Then He went down with them and came to Nazareth, and was subject to them, but His mother kept all these things in her heart. [52]And Jesus increased in wisdom and stature, and in favor with God and men.

John the Baptist Prepares the Way

3 Now in the fifteenth year of the reign of Tiberius Caesar, Pontius Pilate being governor of Judea, Herod being tetrarch of Galilee, his brother Philip tetrarch of Iturea and the region of Trachonitis, and Lysanias tetrarch of Abilene, [2]while Annas and

---

2:38 [a]NU-Text reads *to God.* **2:40** [a]NU-Text omits *in spirit.* **2:43** [a]NU-Text reads *And His parents.*

Caiaphas were high priests,[a] the word of God came to John the son of Zacharias in the wilderness. [3]And he went into all the region around the Jordan, preaching a baptism of repentance for the remission of sins, [4]as it is written in the book of the words of Isaiah the prophet, saying:

> "The voice of one crying in the wilderness:
> 'Prepare the way of the LORD;
> Make His paths straight.
> [5] Every valley shall be filled
> And every mountain and hill brought low;
> The crooked places shall be made straight
> And the rough ways smooth;
> [6] And all flesh shall see the salvation of God.' "[a]

John Preaches to the People

[7]Then he said to the multitudes that came out to be baptized by him, "Brood of vipers! Who warned you to flee from the wrath to come? [8]Therefore bear fruits worthy of repentance, and do not begin to say to yourselves, 'We have Abraham as *our* father.' For I say to you that God is able to raise up children to Abraham from these stones. [9]And even now the ax is laid to the root of the trees. Therefore every tree which does not bear good fruit is cut down and thrown into the fire."

[10]So the people asked him, saying, "What shall we do then?"

[11]He answered and said to them, "He who has two tunics, let him give to him who has none; and he who has food, let him do likewise."

[12]Then tax collectors also came to be baptized, and said to him, "Teacher, what shall we do?"

[13]And he said to them, "Collect no more than what is appointed for you."

[14]Likewise the soldiers asked him, saying, "And what shall we do?"

So he said to them, "Do not intimidate anyone or accuse falsely, and be content with your wages."

[15]Now as the people were in expectation, and all reasoned in their hearts about John, whether he was the Christ *or* not, [16]John answered, saying to all, "I indeed baptize you with water; but One mightier than I is coming, whose sandal strap I am not worthy to loose. He will baptize you with the Holy Spirit and fire. [17]His winnowing fan *is* in His hand, and He will thoroughly clean out His threshing floor, and gather the wheat into His barn; but the chaff He will burn with unquenchable fire."

[18]And with many other exhortations he preached to the people. [19]But Herod the tetrarch, being rebuked by him concerning Herodias, his brother Philip's wife,[a] and for all the evils which Herod had done, [20]also added this, above all, that he shut John up in prison.

John Baptizes Jesus

[21]When all the people were baptized, it came to pass that Jesus also was baptized; and while He prayed, the heaven was opened. [22]And the Holy Spirit descended in bodily form like a dove upon Him, and a voice came from heaven which said, "You are My beloved Son; in You I am well pleased."

The Genealogy of Jesus Christ

[23]Now Jesus Himself began *His ministry at* about thirty years of age, being (as was supposed) *the* son of Joseph, *the son* of Heli, [24]*the son* of Matthat,[a] *the son* of Levi, *the son* of Melchi, *the son* of Janna, *the son* of Joseph, [25]*the son* of Mattathiah, *the son* of Amos, *the son* of Nahum, *the son* of Esli, *the son* of Naggai, [26]*the son* of Maath, *the son* of Mattathiah, *the son* of Semei, *the son* of Joseph, *the son* of Judah, [27]*the son* of Joannas, *the son* of Rhesa, *the son* of Zerubbabel, *the son* of Shealtiel, *the son* of Neri, [28]*the son* of Melchi, *the son* of Addi, *the son* of Cosam, *the son* of Elmodam, *the son* of Er, [29]*the son* of Jose, *the son* of Eliezer, *the son* of Jorim, *the son* of Matthat, *the son* of Levi, [30]*the son* of

---

3:2 [a]NU-Text and M-Text read *in the high priesthood of Annas and Caiaphas.* **3:6** [a]Isaiah 40:3–5 **3:19** [a]NU-Text reads *his brother's wife.* **3:24** [a]This and several other names in the genealogy are spelled somewhat differently in the NU-Text. Since the New King James Version uses the Old Testament spelling for persons mentioned in the New Testament, these variations, which come from the Greek, have not been footnoted.

Simeon, *the son* of Judah, *the son* of Joseph, *the son* of Jonan, *the son* of Eliakim, 31*the son* of Melea, *the son* of Menan, *the son* of Mattathah, *the son* of Nathan, *the son* of David, 32*the son* of Jesse, *the son* of Obed, *the son* of Boaz, *the son* of Salmon, *the son* of Nahshon, 33*the son* of Amminadab, *the son* of Ram, *the son* of Hezron, *the son* of Perez, *the son* of Judah, 34*the son* of Jacob, *the son* of Isaac, *the son* of Abraham, *the son* of Terah, *the son* of Nahor, 35*the son* of Serug, *the son* of Reu, *the son* of Peleg, *the son* of Eber, *the son* of Shelah, 36*the son* of Cainan, *the son* of Arphaxad, *the son* of Shem, *the son* of Noah, *the son* of Lamech, 37*the son* of Methuselah, *the son* of Enoch, *the son* of Jared, *the son* of Mahalalel, *the son* of Cainan, 38*the son* of Enosh, *the son* of Seth, *the son* of Adam, *the son* of God.

Satan Tempts Jesus

4 Then Jesus, being filled with the Holy Spirit, returned from the Jordan and was led by the Spirit into[a] the wilderness, 2being tempted for forty days by the devil. And in those days He ate nothing, and afterward, when they had ended, He was hungry.

3And the devil said to Him, "If You are the Son of God, command this stone to become bread."

4But Jesus answered him, saying,[a] "It is written, '*Man shall not live by bread alone, but by every word of God.*' "[b]

5Then the devil, taking Him up on a high mountain, showed Him[a] all the kingdoms of the world in a moment of time. 6And the devil said to Him, "All this authority I will give You, and their glory; for *this* has been delivered to me, and I give it to whomever I wish. 7Therefore, if You will worship before me, all will be Yours."

8And Jesus answered and said to him, "Get behind Me, Satan![a] For[b] it is written, '*You shall worship the LORD your God, and Him only you shall serve.*' "[c]

9Then he brought Him to Jerusalem, set Him on the pinnacle of the temple, and said to Him, "If You are the Son of God, throw Yourself down from here. 10For it is written:

'*He shall give His angels charge over you,*
    To keep you,'

11and,

'*In their hands they shall bear you up,*
    Lest you dash your foot against a stone.' "[a]

12And Jesus answered and said to him, "It has been said, '*You shall not tempt the LORD your God.*' "[a]

13Now when the devil had ended every temptation, he departed from Him until an opportune time.

Jesus Begins His Galilean Ministry

14Then Jesus returned in the power of the Spirit to Galilee, and news of Him went out through all the surrounding region. 15And He taught in their synagogues, being glorified by all.

Jesus Rejected at Nazareth

16So He came to Nazareth, where He had been brought up. And as His custom was, He went into the synagogue on the Sabbath day, and stood up to read. 17And He was handed the book of the prophet Isaiah. And when He had opened the book, He found the place where it was written:

18   "*The Spirit of the LORD is upon Me,*
        Because He has anointed Me
        To preach the gospel to the poor;
        He has sent Me to heal the brokenhearted,[a]
        To proclaim liberty to the captives

INTIMATE MOMENTS

On occasion, wear his favorite perfume—even if it is not your favorite.

4:1 [a]NU-Text reads *in.* **4:4** [a]Deuteronomy 8:3 [b]NU-Text omits *but by every word of God.* **4:5** [a]NU-Text reads *And taking Him up, he showed Him.*
4:8 [a]NU-Text omits *Get behind Me, Satan.* [b]NU-Text and M-Text omit *For.* [c]Deuteronomy 6:13
4:11 [a]Psalm 91:11, 12 **4:12** [a]Deuteronomy 6:16
4:18 [a]NU-Text omits *to heal the brokenhearted.*

> And recovery of sight to the blind,
> To set at liberty those who are
>   oppressed;
> 19 To proclaim the acceptable year of
>   the LORD."[a]

BIBLICAL INSIGHTS • 4:18

Healing for a Broken Heart

THERE ARE THREE THINGS we need to know about broken hearts.

First, everyone experiences them.

Second, they need to be overcome if you want healthy relationships with your spouse and children and other loved ones.

Third, Jesus Christ has the authority to heal even the most shattered of hearts.

As Jesus read from the writings of the prophet Isaiah, He spoke of Himself, "The Spirit of the Lord is upon Me, because He has anointed Me to preach the gospel to the poor; He has sent Me to heal the brokenhearted" (Luke 4:18).

In nearly four decades of ministry around the world, we have met many people with broken hearts. People from dozens of nations who need healing, forgiveness, and cleansing because of something they've done or something that has been done to them. These people cannot be healed through the words or actions of any mere man or woman. To these people, Jesus, the Great Physician, would say, "Give me your hurts and your sorrows, and I will heal them."

If you are brokenhearted over something in your past, something your spouse has done or said to you, or over the words or deeds of one of your children, take those things to Jesus, who declared that God "has sent Me to heal the brokenhearted." Why not take a few moments right now to ask the Great Physician to take your heart as it is and begin to do His healing work?

20Then He closed the book, and gave *it* back to the attendant and sat down. And the eyes of all who were in the synagogue were fixed on Him. 21And He began to say to them, "Today this Scripture is fulfilled in your hearing." 22So all bore witness to Him, and marveled at the gracious words which proceeded out of His mouth. And they said, "Is this not Joseph's son?"

23He said to them, "You will surely say this proverb to Me, 'Physician, heal yourself! Whatever we have heard done in Capernaum,[a] do also here in Your country.'" 24Then He said, "Assuredly, I say to you, no prophet is accepted in his own country. 25But I tell you truly, many widows were in Israel in the days of Elijah, when the heaven was shut up three years and six months, and there was a great famine throughout all the land; 26but to none of them was Elijah sent except to Zarephath,[a] *in the region* of Sidon, to a woman *who was* a widow. 27And many lepers were in Israel in the time of Elisha the prophet, and none of them was cleansed except Naaman the Syrian."

28So all those in the synagogue, when they heard these things, were filled with wrath, 29and rose up and thrust Him out of the city; and they led Him to the brow of the hill on which their city was built, that they might throw Him down over the cliff. 30Then passing through the midst of them, He went His way.

Jesus Casts Out an Unclean Spirit

31Then He went down to Capernaum, a city of Galilee, and was teaching them on the Sabbaths. 32And they were astonished at His teaching, for His word was with authority. 33Now in the synagogue there was a man who had a spirit of an unclean demon. And he cried out with a loud voice, 34saying, "Let *us* alone! What have we to do with You, Jesus of Nazareth? Did You come to destroy us? I know who You are—the Holy One of God!"

35But Jesus rebuked him, saying, "Be quiet, and come out of him!" And when the demon had thrown him in *their* midst, it came out of him and did not hurt him. 36Then they were all amazed and spoke

---

4:19 [a]Isaiah 61:1, 2   4:23 [a]Here and elsewhere the NU-Text spelling is *Capharnaum.*
4:26 [a]Greek *Sarepta*

among themselves, saying, "What a word this *is!* For with authority and power He commands the unclean spirits, and they come out." ³⁷And the report about Him went out into every place in the surrounding region.

Peter's Mother-in-Law Healed

³⁸Now He arose from the synagogue and entered Simon's house. But Simon's wife's mother was sick with a high fever, and they made request of Him concerning her. ³⁹So He stood over her and rebuked the fever, and it left her. And immediately she arose and served them.

Many Healed After Sabbath Sunset

⁴⁰When the sun was setting, all those who had any that were sick with various diseases brought them to Him; and He laid His hands on every one of them and healed them. ⁴¹And demons also came out of many, crying out and saying, "You are the Christ,ᵃ the Son of God!"

And He, rebuking *them,* did not allow them to speak, for they knew that He was the Christ.

Jesus Preaches in Galilee

⁴²Now when it was day, He departed and went into a deserted place. And the crowd sought Him and came to Him, and tried to keep Him from leaving them; ⁴³but He said to them, "I must preach the kingdom of God to the other cities also, because for this purpose I have been sent." ⁴⁴And He was preaching in the synagogues of Galilee.ᵃ

Four Fishermen Called as Disciples

5 So it was, as the multitude pressed about Him to hear the word of God, that He stood by the Lake of Gennesaret, ²and saw two boats standing by the lake; but the fishermen had gone from them and were washing *their* nets. ³Then He got into one of the boats, which was Simon's, and asked him to put out a little from the land. And He sat down and taught the multitudes from the boat.

⁴When He had stopped speaking, He said to Simon, "Launch out into the deep and let down your nets for a catch."

⁵But Simon answered and said to Him, "Master, we have toiled all night and caught nothing; nevertheless at Your word I will let down the net." ⁶And when they had done this, they caught a great number of fish, and their net was breaking. ⁷So they signaled to *their* partners in the other boat to come and help them. And they came and filled both the boats, so that they began to sink. ⁸When Simon Peter saw *it,* he fell down at Jesus' knees, saying, "Depart from me, for I am a sinful man, O Lord!" ⁹For he and all who were with him were astonished at the catch of fish which they had taken; ¹⁰and so also *were* James and John, the sons of Zebedee, who were partners with Simon. And Jesus said to Simon, "Do not be afraid. From now on you will catch men." ¹¹So when they had brought their boats to land, they forsook all and followed Him.

Jesus Cleanses a Leper

¹²And it happened when He was in a certain city, that behold, a man who was full of leprosy saw Jesus; and he fell on *his* face and implored Him, saying, "Lord, if You are willing, You can make me clean."

¹³Then He put out *His* hand and touched him, saying, "I am willing; be cleansed." Immediately the leprosy left him. ¹⁴And He charged him to tell no one, "But go and show yourself to the priest, and make an offering for your cleansing, as a testimony to them, just as Moses commanded."

¹⁵However, the report went around concerning Him all the more; and great multitudes came together to hear, and to be healed by Him of their infirmities. ¹⁶So He Himself *often* withdrew into the wilderness and prayed.

Jesus Forgives and Heals a Paralytic

¹⁷Now it happened on a certain day, as He was teaching, that there were Pharisees and teachers of the law sitting by, who had come out of every town of Galilee, Judea, and Jerusalem. And the power of the Lord was *present* to heal them.ᵃ ¹⁸Then behold, men brought on a bed a man who was

---

4:41 ᵃNU-Text omits *the Christ.* 4:44 ᵃNU-Text reads *Judea.* 5:17 ᵃNU-Text reads *present with Him to heal.*

paralyzed, whom they sought to bring in and lay before Him. [19]And when they could not find how they might bring him in, because of the crowd, they went up on the housetop and let him down with *his* bed through the tiling into the midst before Jesus.

[20]When He saw their faith, He said to him, "Man, your sins are forgiven you."

[21]And the scribes and the Pharisees began to reason, saying, "Who is this who speaks blasphemies? Who can forgive sins but God alone?"

[22]But when Jesus perceived their thoughts, He answered and said to them, "Why are you reasoning in your hearts? [23]Which is easier, to say, 'Your sins are forgiven you,' or to say, 'Rise up and walk'? [24]But that you may know that the Son of Man has power on earth to forgive sins"— He said to the man who was paralyzed, "I say to you, arise, take up your bed, and go to your house."

[25]Immediately he rose up before them, took up what he had been lying on, and departed to his own house, glorifying God. [26]And they were all amazed, and they glorified God and were filled with fear, saying, "We have seen strange things today!"

Matthew the Tax Collector

[27]After these things He went out and saw a tax collector named Levi, sitting at the tax office. And He said to him, "Follow Me." [28]So he left all, rose up, and followed Him.

[29]Then Levi gave Him a great feast in his own house. And there were a great number of tax collectors and others who sat down with them. [30]And their scribes and the Pharisees[a] complained against His disciples, saying, "Why do You eat and drink with tax collectors and sinners?"

[31]Jesus answered and said to them, "Those who are well have no need of a physician, but those who are sick. [32]I have not come to call *the* righteous, but sinners, to repentance."

Jesus Is Questioned About Fasting

[33]Then they said to Him, "Why do[a] the disciples of John fast often and make prayers, and likewise those of the Pharisees, but Yours eat and drink?"

[34]And He said to them, "Can you make the friends of the bridegroom fast while the bridegroom is with them? [35]But the days will come when the bridegroom will be taken away from them; then they will fast in those days."

[36]Then He spoke a parable to them: "No one puts a piece from a new garment on an old one;[a] otherwise the new makes a tear, and also the piece that was *taken* out of the new does not match the old. [37]And no one puts new wine into old wineskins; or else the new wine will burst the wineskins and be spilled, and the wineskins will be ruined. [38]But new wine must be put into new wineskins, and both are preserved.[a] [39]And no one, having drunk old *wine,* immediately[a] desires new; for he says, 'The old is better.'"[b]

Jesus Is Lord of the Sabbath

6 Now it happened on the second Sabbath after the first[a] that He went through the grainfields. And His disciples plucked the heads of grain and ate *them,* rubbing *them* in *their* hands. [2]And some of the Pharisees said to them, "Why are you doing what is not lawful to do on the Sabbath?"

[3]But Jesus answering them said, "Have you not even read this, what David did when he was hungry, he and those who were with him: [4]how he went into the house of God, took and ate the showbread, and also gave some to those with him, which is not lawful for any but the priests to eat?" [5]And He said to them, "The Son of Man is also Lord of the Sabbath."

Healing on the Sabbath

[6]Now it happened on another Sabbath, also, that He entered the synagogue and taught. And a man was there whose right hand was withered. [7]So the scribes and Pharisees watched Him closely, whether He would heal on the Sabbath, that they might find an accusation against Him. [8]But He

---

5:30 [a]NU-Text reads *But the Pharisees and their scribes.* **5:33** [a]NU-Text omits *Why do,* making the verse a statement. **5:36** [a]NU-Text reads *No one tears a piece from a new garment and puts it on an old one.* **5:38** [a]NU-Text omits *and both are preserved.* **5:39** [a]NU-Text omits *immediately.* [b]NU-Text reads *good.* **6:1** [a]NU-Text reads *on a Sabbath.*

BIBLICAL INSIGHTS • 6:38
The Law of Giving

CHRISTIANITY IS FULL of apparent paradoxes, including one that Jesus teaches us in Luke 6:38, "Give, and it will be given to you: good measure, pressed down, shaken together, running over will be put into your bosom. For with the same measure that you use, it will be measured back to you."

Somehow a transfer takes place so that, when we give, we are enriched. This Law of Giving applies to many areas of life, but it is especially relevant to our self-worth and confidence. One woman wrote us in a letter, "I have realized that in giving of myself, I am actually getting in return a spouse who feels good about himself, which then makes me feel good about myself."

Perhaps you feel tired of giving. You may be thinking, *You don't know my mate. I don't want to give this time.* I can understand a little—what spouse hasn't had his or her moments? But acting on negative feelings will not build your marriage; it will only tear down what you've already built.

Even if you feel you've given for years without reward, please don't give up. Your mate needs you more than you realize. Continue to give, and see how God honors your faithfulness.

knew their thoughts, and said to the man who had the withered hand, "Arise and stand here." And he arose and stood. ⁹Then Jesus said to them, "I will ask you one thing: Is it lawful on the Sabbath to do good or to do evil, to save life or to destroy?"ᵃ ¹⁰And when He had looked around at them all, He said to the man,ᵃ "Stretch out your hand." And he did so, and his hand was restored as whole as the other.ᵇ ¹¹But they were filled with rage, and discussed with one another what they might do to Jesus.

The Twelve Apostles

¹²Now it came to pass in those days that He went out to the mountain to pray, and continued all night in prayer to God. ¹³And when it was day, He called His disciples to *Himself;* and from them He chose twelve whom He also named apostles: ¹⁴Simon, whom He also named Peter, and Andrew his brother; James and John; Philip and Bartholomew; ¹⁵Matthew and Thomas; James the *son* of Alphaeus, and Simon called the Zealot; ¹⁶Judas *the son* of James, and Judas Iscariot who also became a traitor.

Jesus Heals a Great Multitude

¹⁷And He came down with them and stood on a level place with a crowd of His disciples and a great multitude of people from all Judea and Jerusalem, and from the seacoast of Tyre and Sidon, who came to hear Him and be healed of their diseases, ¹⁸as well as those who were tormented with unclean spirits. And they were healed. ¹⁹And the whole multitude sought to touch Him, for power went out from Him and healed *them* all.

The Beatitudes

²⁰Then He lifted up His eyes toward His disciples, and said:

"Blessed *are you* poor,
　For yours is the kingdom of God.
²¹ Blessed *are you* who hunger now,
　For you shall be filled.
Blessed *are you* who weep now,
　For you shall laugh.
²² Blessed are you when men hate you,
　And when they exclude you,
　And revile *you,* and cast out your
　　name as evil,
　For the Son of Man's sake.
²³ Rejoice in that day and leap for joy!
　For indeed your reward *is* great in
　　heaven,
　For in like manner their fathers
　　did to the prophets.

Jesus Pronounces Woes

²⁴ "But woe to you who are rich,
　For you have received your
　　consolation.

6:9 ᵃM-Text reads *to kill.*　6:10 ᵃNU-Text and M-Text read *to him.*　ᵇNU-Text omits *as whole as the other.*

25 Woe to you who are full,
    For you shall hunger.
  Woe to you who laugh now,
    For you shall mourn and weep.
26 Woe to you[a] when all[b] men speak
      well of you,
    For so did their fathers to the
      false prophets.

Love Your Enemies

27"But I say to you who hear: Love your enemies, do good to those who hate you, 28bless those who curse you, and pray for those who spitefully use you. 29To him who strikes you on the *one* cheek, offer the other also. And from him who takes away your cloak, do not withhold *your* tunic either. 30Give to everyone who asks of you. And from him who takes away your goods do not ask *them* back. 31And just as you want men to do to you, you also do to them likewise.

32"But if you love those who love you, what credit is that to you? For even sinners love those who love them. 33And if you do good to those who do good to you, what credit is that to you? For even sinners do the same. 34And if you lend *to those* from whom you hope to receive back, what credit is that to you? For even sinners lend to sinners to receive as much back. 35But love your enemies, do good, and lend, hoping for nothing in return; and your reward will be great, and you will be sons of the Most High. For He is kind to the unthankful and evil. 36Therefore be merciful, just as your Father also is merciful.

Do Not Judge

37"Judge not, and you shall not be judged. Condemn not, and you shall not be condemned. Forgive, and you will be forgiven. 38Give, and it will be given to you: good measure, pressed down, shaken together, and running over will be put into your bosom. For with the same measure that you use, it will be measured back to you."

39And He spoke a parable to them: "Can the blind lead the blind? Will they not both fall into the ditch? 40A disciple is not above

BIBLICAL INSIGHTS • 6:46
Are You a Fake?

SOME PEOPLE are excellent fakes. Publicly, they may do an abundance of Christian deeds, use the right Christian clichés, and quote the right Christian publications. But privately, their lives are charades. They aren't listening to God. They don't even particularly care what He says.

Their lives are mockeries.

Sometimes we fake the Christian life in a dangerously similar way. We say we are followers of Christ, but we don't obey Him day-to-day. Preoccupied with self and wanting our own way, we ignore God and only pretend to be spiritual. Instead of having Christ's character imprinted on our lives, we go our own way, and our Christianity becomes a forgery. Jesus has a word for us, "Why do you call Me, 'Lord, Lord,' and not do the things which I say?" (6:46).

If someone accused you of being a fake Christian, what evidence could you present to prove otherwise? What about your life, in word and in deed, shows the people around you that you are an authentic Christian?

Jesus said that every tree is known by its own fruit (6:44). As you examine your own life, do you see the fruit of the Spirit (Gal. 5:22, 23)? Or is your life characterized by other things? Do you call Jesus "Lord," and then ignore His commands? Search your own heart to see if you truly love Christ and want to serve Him with your life. If the answer is yes, ask Him to transform your life by the Holy Spirit through the power of His Word.

his teacher, but everyone who is perfectly trained will be like his teacher. 41And why do you look at the speck in your brother's eye, but do not perceive the plank in your own eye? 42Or how can you say to your brother, 'Brother, let me remove the speck that *is* in your eye,' when you yourself do not see the plank that *is* in your own eye? Hypocrite! First remove the plank from

6:26 aNU-Text and M-Text omit *to you.* bM-Text omits *all.*

your own eye, and then you will see clearly to remove the speck that is in your brother's eye.

A Tree Is Known by Its Fruit

43"For a good tree does not bear bad fruit, nor does a bad tree bear good fruit. 44For every tree is known by its own fruit. For *men* do not gather figs from thorns, nor do they gather grapes from a bramble bush. 45A good man out of the good treasure of his heart brings forth good; and an evil man out of the evil treasure of his heart[a] brings forth evil. For out of the abundance of the heart his mouth speaks.

Build on the Rock

46"But why do you call Me 'Lord, Lord,' and not do the things which I say? 47Whoever comes to Me, and hears My sayings and does them, I will show you whom he is like: 48He is like a man building a house, who dug deep and laid the foundation on the rock. And when the flood arose, the stream beat vehemently against that house, and could not shake it, for it was founded on the rock.[a] 49But he who heard and did nothing is like a man who built a house on the earth without a foundation, against which the stream beat vehemently; and immediately it fell.[a] And the ruin of that house was great."

Jesus Heals a Centurion's Servant

7 Now when He concluded all His sayings in the hearing of the people, He entered Capernaum. 2And a certain centurion's servant, who was dear to him, was sick and ready to die. 3So when he heard about Jesus, he sent elders of the Jews to Him, pleading with Him to come and heal his servant. 4And when they came to Jesus, they begged Him earnestly, saying that the one for whom He should do this was deserving, 5"for he loves our nation, and has built us a synagogue."

6Then Jesus went with them. And when He was already not far from the house, the centurion sent friends to Him, saying to Him, "Lord, do not trouble Yourself, for I am not worthy that You should enter under my roof. 7Therefore I did not even think myself worthy to come to You. But

say the word, and my servant will be healed. 8For I also am a man placed under authority, having soldiers under me. And I say to one, 'Go,' and he goes; and to another, 'Come,' and he comes; and to my servant, 'Do this,' and he does *it*."

9When Jesus heard these things, He marveled at him, and turned around and said to the crowd that followed Him, "I say to you, I have not found such great faith, not even in Israel!" 10And those who were sent, returning to the house, found the servant well who had been sick.[a]

Jesus Raises the Son of the Widow of Nain

11Now it happened, the day after, *that* He went into a city called Nain; and many of His disciples went with Him, and a large crowd. 12And when He came near the gate of the city, behold, a dead man was being carried out, the only son of his mother; and she was a widow. And a large crowd from the city was with her. 13When the Lord saw her, He had compassion on her and said to her, "Do not weep." 14Then He came and touched the open coffin, and those who carried *him* stood still. And He said, "Young man, I say to you, arise." 15So he who was dead sat up and began to speak. And He presented him to his mother.

16Then fear came upon all, and they glorified God, saying, "A great prophet has risen up among us"; and, "God has visited His people." 17And this report about Him went throughout all Judea and all the surrounding region.

John the Baptist Sends Messengers to Jesus

18Then the disciples of John reported to him concerning all these things. 19And John, calling two of his disciples to *him*, sent *them* to Jesus,[a] saying, "Are You the Coming One, or do we look for another?"

20When the men had come to Him, they said, "John the Baptist has sent us to You, saying, 'Are You the Coming One, or do we

---

6:45 [a]NU-Text omits *treasure of his heart.*
6:48 [a]NU-Text reads *for it was well built.*
6:49 [a]NU-Text reads *collapsed.* **7:10** [a]NU-Text omits *who had been sick.* **7:19** [a]NU-Text reads *the Lord.*

look for another?'" [21]And that very hour He cured many of infirmities, afflictions, and evil spirits; and to many blind He gave sight.

[22]Jesus answered and said to them, "Go and tell John the things you have seen and heard: that *the* blind see, *the* lame walk, *the* lepers are cleansed, *the* deaf hear, *the* dead are raised, *the* poor have the gospel preached to them. [23]And blessed is *he* who is not offended because of Me."

[24]When the messengers of John had departed, He began to speak to the multitudes concerning John: "What did you go out into the wilderness to see? A reed shaken by the wind? [25]But what did you go out to see? A man clothed in soft garments? Indeed those who are gorgeously appareled and live in luxury are in kings' courts. [26]But what did you go out to see? A prophet? Yes, I say to you, and more than a prophet. [27]This is *he* of whom it is written:

'Behold, I send My messenger before
    Your face,
Who will prepare Your way before
    You.'[a]

[28]For I say to you, among those born of women there is not a greater prophet than John the Baptist;[a] but he who is least in the kingdom of God is greater than he."

[29]And when all the people heard *Him,* even the tax collectors justified God, having been baptized with the baptism of John. [30]But the Pharisees and lawyers rejected the will of God for themselves, not having been baptized by him.

[31]And the Lord said,[a] "To what then shall I liken the men of this generation, and what are they like? [32]They are like children sitting in the marketplace and calling to one another, saying:

'We played the flute for you,
    And you did not dance;
We mourned to you,
    And you did not weep.'

[33]For John the Baptist came neither eating bread nor drinking wine, and you say, 'He has a demon.' [34]The Son of Man has come

eating and drinking, and you say, 'Look, a glutton and a winebibber, a friend of tax collectors and sinners!' [35]But wisdom is justified by all her children."

A Sinful Woman Forgiven

[36]Then one of the Pharisees asked Him to eat with him. And He went to the Pharisee's house, and sat down to eat. [37]And behold, a woman in the city who was a sinner, when she knew that *Jesus* sat at the table in the Pharisee's house, brought an alabaster flask of fragrant oil, [38]and stood at His feet behind *Him* weeping; and she began to wash His feet with her tears, and wiped *them* with the hair of her head; and she kissed His feet and anointed *them* with the fragrant oil. [39]Now when the Pharisee who had invited Him saw *this,* he spoke to himself, saying, "This Man, if He were a prophet, would know who and what manner of woman *this is* who is touching Him, for she is a sinner."

[40]And Jesus answered and said to him, "Simon, I have something to say to you."

So he said, "Teacher, say it."

[41]"There was a certain creditor who had two debtors. One owed five hundred denarii, and the other fifty. [42]And when they had nothing with which to repay, he freely forgave them both. Tell Me, therefore, which of them will love him more?"

[43]Simon answered and said, "I suppose the *one* whom he forgave more."

And He said to him, "You have rightly judged." [44]Then He turned to the woman and said to Simon, "Do you see this woman? I entered your house; you gave Me no water for My feet, but she has washed My feet with her tears and wiped *them* with the hair of her head. [45]You gave Me no kiss, but this woman has not ceased to kiss My feet since the time I came in. [46]You did not anoint My head with oil, but this woman has anointed My feet with fragrant oil. [47]Therefore I say to you, her sins, which *are* many, are forgiven, for she loved much. But to whom little is forgiven, *the same* loves little."

[48]Then He said to her, "Your sins are forgiven."

[49]And those who sat at the table with Him began to say to themselves, "Who is this who even forgives sins?"

7:27 [a]Malachi 3:1
7:28 [a]NU-Text reads *there is none greater than John.*
7:31 [a]NU-Text and M-Text omit *And the Lord said.*

DEVOTIONS FOR COUPLES • 8:4–15
Watch Out for Weeds

All dedicated followers of Jesus want to bring delight to the heart of their Master. But did you know that spiritual fruitfulness depends in part upon the type of soil that receives the seed of God's Word?

Jesus warned of three kinds of pesky weeds that can squeeze the life out of fruit-producing seedlings (8:4–15). As you read the following, ask yourself, "Do I see any of these noxious plants growing in the garden of my own home?"

1. The Weed of Worry. Jesus first warned about the worries of the world and the anxieties of this age. This kind of weed pulls you in more than one direction. It distracts you with concerns both great and small. By so doing, it removes your focus from Christ and places it on events or circumstances mostly beyond your control.

What kinds of things tend to worry you? When do you normally feel most anxious? What sorts of weeds distract you from the central concern of loving and obeying God? Is fretting about something causing you to lose sleep and lose your perspective?

During a time of intense challenges, I was worrying, and a friend sensed my need for perspective. He sent me the following excerpt from Oswald Chambers's *My Utmost for His Highest*, "Resting in the Lord does not depend on external circumstances at all, but on your relationship to God Himself . . . . Fretting springs from a determination to get our own way . . . . Deliberately tell God that you will not fret about that thing. All our fret and worry is caused by calculating without God." His words were exactly what I needed to uproot the undesirable weed of worry.

2. The Weed of Deceitful Riches. Maybe you're thinking, *Hey, I'd rather take my chances with handling riches and whatever deceit comes with it than be poor! Wealth isn't so bad*. No, it's not; but wealth *is* a deceptive weed that can take over your life and choke out your responsiveness to God. Scripture warns, "But those who desire to be rich fall into temptation and a snare, and into many foolish and harmful lusts which drown men in destruction and perdition. For the love of money is the root of all kinds of evil, for which some have strayed from the faith in their greediness, and pierced themselves through with many sorrows" (1 Tim. 6:9, 10).

To measure the deceit of wealth in your life, answer the following question: Would you be willing to give up the safety of your job to invest your life in full-time vocational ministry? If not, it may be that riches own you, rather than your owning them. It may be time to reevaluate your life and pull some weeds.

3. The Weed of Desire. Some of these weeds are easily spotted, like sexual lust, an addiction to pornography, or perversions. But other cravings aren't so easily identifiable: success, food, clothing, jewelry, car, job, salary, a hobby or sport, or even the location or kind of house we live in. Any desire that drives us, controls our thinking, or preoccupies our minds, can be a weed that hinders spiritual growth. Even a good thing, like our marriage or our family, can become a snare if we care more about it than we do about God and His purposes for our lives.

One good way to spot this weed is to check your conversations. What most excites you? What comes up most in your discussions? What preoccupies your thoughts?

You want your life to be the kind of good, fertile soil in which the message of the gospel can take root. The result will be a life that is filled with fruitfulness. Make sure you're doing what you can do to keep the soil of your heart free from worry, the love of money, or unholy desires.

⁵⁰Then He said to the woman, "Your faith has saved you. Go in peace."

Many Women Minister to Jesus

8 Now it came to pass, afterward, that He went through every city and village, preaching and bringing the glad tidings of the kingdom of God. And the twelve *were* with Him, ²and certain women who had been healed of evil spirits and infirmities— Mary called Magdalene, out of whom had come seven demons, ³and Joanna the wife of Chuza, Herod's steward, and Susanna, and many others who provided for Him[a] from their substance.

The Parable of the Sower

⁴And when a great multitude had gathered, and they had come to Him from every city, He spoke by a parable: ⁵"A sower went out to sow his seed. And as he sowed, some fell by the wayside; and it was trampled down, and the birds of the air devoured it. ⁶Some fell on rock; and as soon as it sprang up, it withered away because it lacked moisture. ⁷And some fell among thorns, and the thorns sprang up with it and choked it. ⁸But others fell on good ground, sprang up, and yielded a crop a hundredfold." When He had said these things He cried, "He who has ears to hear, let him hear!"

The Purpose of Parables

⁹Then His disciples asked Him, saying, "What does this parable mean?"
¹⁰And He said, "To you it has been given to know the mysteries of the kingdom of God, but to the rest *it is given* in parables, that

> 'Seeing they may not see,
> And hearing they may not
>   understand.'[a]

The Parable of the Sower Explained

¹¹"Now the parable is this: The seed is the word of God. ¹²Those by the wayside are the ones who hear; then the devil comes and takes away the word out of their hearts, lest they should believe and be saved. ¹³But the ones on the rock *are those*

who, when they hear, receive the word with joy; and these have no root, who believe for a while and in time of temptation fall away. ¹⁴Now the ones *that* fell among thorns are those who, when they have heard, go out and are choked with cares, riches, and pleasures of life, and bring no fruit to maturity. ¹⁵But the ones *that* fell on the good ground are those who, having heard the word with a noble and good heart, keep *it* and bear fruit with patience.

The Parable of the Revealed Light

¹⁶"No one, when he has lit a lamp, covers it with a vessel or puts *it* under a bed, but sets *it* on a lampstand, that those who enter may see the light. ¹⁷For nothing is secret that will not be revealed, nor *any-thing* hidden that will not be known and come to light. ¹⁸Therefore take heed how you hear. For whoever has, to him *more* will be given; and whoever does not have, even what he seems to have will be taken from him."

Jesus' Mother and Brothers Come to Him

¹⁹Then His mother and brothers came to Him, and could not approach Him because of the crowd. ²⁰And it was told Him *by some,* who said, "Your mother and Your brothers are standing outside, desiring to see You."
²¹But He answered and said to them, "My mother and My brothers are these who hear the word of God and do it."

Wind and Wave Obey Jesus

²²Now it happened, on a certain day, that He got into a boat with His disciples. And He said to them, "Let us cross over to the other side of the lake." And they launched out. ²³But as they sailed He fell asleep. And a windstorm came down on the lake, and they were filling *with water,* and were in jeopardy. ²⁴And they came to Him and awoke Him, saying, "Master, Master, we are perishing!"
Then He arose and rebuked the wind and the raging of the water. And they ceased, and there was a calm. ²⁵But He said to them, "Where is your faith?"
And they were afraid, and marveled, saying to one another, "Who can this be?

8:3 [a]NU-Text and M-Text read *them.*   **8:10** [a]Isaiah 6:9

When Reality Hits Home

MANY NEW CHRISTIANS begin their new lives at an emotional high. They feel overwhelmed by God's forgiveness and grace, excited at seeing Him work in their lives, and delighted by the love they feel from their new family in Christ. They get involved in a local church and are aware of the power of God working through them.

Then, inevitably, they begin to come to grips with massive doses of reality. Perhaps a trusted Christian friend betrays them. Maybe a person they've grown to respect spiritually is caught in a compromise. Or they become so disillusioned that they can't see greater change in their lives in a key area. And they begin to learn, *Christians are full of faults, just like anyone else.*

Many Christians today respond to this reality by choosing the path of self-protection. Some withdraw from relationships because they reason, "I'll get hurt by people. Why try?" Others move from church to church, never settling down, trying to find the perfect group of people. And some become angry at the hypocrisy they see and lash out at the community of faith. When any of these paths are followed, it's easy to end up cynical and isolated. You miss the joy that comes when you determine to persevere and trust God with how He handles what's going on in the church.

As a new believer, you may have started off running in your walk with Christ. But the Christian life is not a sprint. It's a marathon. Only when you allow God to work through you, even after struggling through tough relationships, will you see the fruit that comes through perseverance, "But the ones that fell on the good ground are those who, having heard the word with a noble and good heart, keep it and bear fruit with patience" (8:15).

For He commands even the winds and water, and they obey Him!"

A Demon-Possessed Man Healed

26Then they sailed to the country of the Gadarenes,a which is opposite Galilee. 27And when He stepped out on the land, there met Him a certain man from the city who had demons for a long time. And he wore no clothes,a nor did he live in a house but in the tombs. 28When he saw Jesus, he cried out, fell down before Him, and with a loud voice said, "What have I to do with You, Jesus, Son of the Most High God? I beg You, do not torment me!" 29For He had commanded the unclean spirit to come out of the man. For it had often seized him, and he was kept under guard, bound with chains and shackles; and he broke the bonds and was driven by the demon into the wilderness.

30Jesus asked him, saying, "What is your name?"

And he said, "Legion," because many demons had entered him. 31And they begged Him that He would not command them to go out into the abyss.

32Now a herd of many swine was feeding there on the mountain. So they begged Him that He would permit them to enter them. And He permitted them. 33Then the demons went out of the man and entered the swine, and the herd ran violently down the steep place into the lake and drowned.

34When those who fed *them* saw what had happened, they fled and told *it* in the city and in the country. 35Then they went out to see what had happened, and came to Jesus, and found the man from whom the demons had departed, sitting at the feet of Jesus, clothed and in his right mind. And they were afraid. 36They also who had seen *it* told them by what means he who had been demon-possessed was healed. 37Then the whole multitude of the surrounding region of the Gadarenesa asked Him to depart from them, for they were seized with great fear. And He got into the boat and returned.

8:26 aNU-Text reads *Gerasenes.* 8:27 aNU-Text reads *who had demons and for a long time wore no clothes.* 8:37 aNU-Text reads *Gerasenes.*

Resist Crowded Loneliness

WITH THE WORLD'S POPULATION racing toward seven billion, it may seem strange that many observers see loneliness as society's number one problem. One author I know describes this phenomenon as "crowded loneliness."

Although families can provide a natural antidote for loneliness, we all know they don't always work that way. Individual needs for belonging are often ignored, and loneliness looms. Here are some symptoms of relationships that are drifting toward isolation:

• Some topics are declared "off-limits" for discussion.

• Television, small talk, or silence are substituted for meaningful conversation.

• Never-ending silence overwhelms time spent with each other.

• Activities are allowed to crowd time together.

• A wife immerses herself in the children (or the husband in his work) in order to avoid intimacy.

• Couples refuse to confront each other on important issues and cover them up for the sake of peace at any price.

Jesus lived in a tiny, crowded portion of Palestine. Yet even in the midst of a mob, all jostling each other, He took note of a lonely woman's personal touch (8:45, 46). In the middle of the crowd and all the activity, Jesus was aware of this woman's deepest needs, and He responded to it.

Your family can be the same kind of place, where each family member can experience both the security of togetherness and the meeting of individual needs. One of Satan's greatest strategies is to isolate people. Don't let him destroy your marriage or family with this strategy. Instead, ask God to allow you and your spouse to experience the oneness that comes from having Jesus Christ as the builder of your marriage.

38Now the man from whom the demons had departed begged Him that he might be with Him. But Jesus sent him away, saying, 39"Return to your own house, and tell what great things God has done for you." And he went his way and proclaimed throughout the whole city what great things Jesus had done for him.

A Girl Restored to Life and a Woman Healed

40So it was, when Jesus returned, that the multitude welcomed Him, for they were all waiting for Him. 41And behold, there came a man named Jairus, and he was a ruler of the synagogue. And he fell down at Jesus' feet and begged Him to come to his house, 42for he had an only daughter about twelve years of age, and she was dying.

But as He went, the multitudes thronged Him. 43Now a woman, having a flow of blood for twelve years, who had spent all her livelihood on physicians and could not be healed by any, 44came from behind and touched the border of His garment. And immediately her flow of blood stopped.

45And Jesus said, "Who touched Me?"

When all denied it, Peter and those with him[a] said, "Master, the multitudes throng and press You, and You say, 'Who touched Me?'"[b]

46But Jesus said, "Somebody touched Me, for I perceived power going out from Me." 47Now when the woman saw that she was not hidden, she came trembling; and falling down before Him, she declared to Him in the presence of all the people the

---

8:45 [a]NU-Text omits *and those with him*. [b]NU-Text omits *and You say, 'Who touched Me?'*

reason she had touched Him and how she was healed immediately.

[48]And He said to her, "Daughter, be of good cheer;[a] your faith has made you well. Go in peace."

[49]While He was still speaking, someone came from the ruler of the synagogue's *house,* saying to him, "Your daughter is dead. Do not trouble the Teacher."[a]

[50]But when Jesus heard *it,* He answered him, saying, "Do not be afraid; only believe, and she will be made well."

[51]When He came into the house, He permitted no one to go in[a] except Peter, James, and John,[b] and the father and mother of the girl. [52]Now all wept and mourned for her; but He said, "Do not weep; she is not dead, but sleeping." [53]And they ridiculed Him, knowing that she was dead.

[54]But He put them all outside,[a] took her by the hand and called, saying, "Little girl, arise." [55]Then her spirit returned, and she arose immediately. And He commanded that she be given *something* to eat. [56]And her parents were astonished, but He charged them to tell no one what had happened.

Sending Out the Twelve

9 Then He called His twelve disciples together and gave them power and authority over all demons, and to cure diseases. [2]He sent them to preach the kingdom of God and to heal the sick. [3]And He said to them, "Take nothing for the journey, neither staffs nor bag nor bread nor money; and do not have two tunics apiece.

[4]"Whatever house you enter, stay there, and from there depart. [5]And whoever will not receive you, when you go out of that city, shake off the very dust from your feet as a testimony against them."

[6]So they departed and went through the towns, preaching the gospel and healing everywhere.

Herod Seeks to See Jesus

[7]Now Herod the tetrarch heard of all that was done by Him; and he was perplexed, because it was said by some that John had risen from the dead, [8]and by some that Elijah had appeared, and by others that one of the old prophets had risen again. [9]Herod said, "John I have beheaded, but who is this of whom I hear such things?" So he sought to see Him.

Feeding the Five Thousand

[10]And the apostles, when they had returned, told Him all that they had done. Then He took them and went aside privately into a deserted place belonging to the city called Bethsaida. [11]But when the multitudes knew *it,* they followed Him; and He received them and spoke to them about the kingdom of God, and healed those who had need of healing. [12]When the day began to wear away, the twelve came and said to Him, "Send the multitude away, that they may go into the surrounding towns and country, and lodge and get provisions; for we are in a deserted place here."

[13]But He said to them, "You give them something to eat."

And they said, "We have no more than five loaves and two fish, unless we go and buy food for all these people." [14]For there were about five thousand men.

Then He said to His disciples, "Make them sit down in groups of fifty." [15]And they did so, and made them all sit down.

[16]Then He took the five loaves and the two fish, and looking up to heaven, He blessed and broke them, and gave *them* to the disciples to set before the multitude. [17]So they all ate and were filled, and twelve baskets of the leftover fragments were taken up by them.

Peter Confesses Jesus as the Christ

[18]And it happened, as He was alone praying, *that* His disciples joined Him, and He asked them, saying, "Who do the crowds say that I am?"

[19]So they answered and said, "John the Baptist, but some *say* Elijah; and others *say* that one of the old prophets has risen again."

[20]He said to them, "But who do you say that I am?"

Peter answered and said, "The Christ of God."

8:48 [a]NU-Text omits *be of good cheer.* 8:49 [a]NU-Text adds *anymore.* 8:51 [a]NU-Text adds *with Him.* [b]NU-Text and M-Text read *Peter, John, and James.* 8:54 [a]NU-Text omits *put them all outside.*

Jesus Predicts His Death and Resurrection

21And He strictly warned and commanded them to tell this to no one, 22saying, "The Son of Man must suffer many things, and be rejected by the elders and chief priests and scribes, and be killed, and be raised the third day."

Take Up the Cross and Follow Him

23Then He said to *them* all, "If anyone desires to come after Me, let him deny himself, and take up his cross daily,a and follow Me. 24For whoever desires to save his life will lose it, but whoever loses his life for My sake will save it. 25For what profit is it to a man if he gains the whole world, and is himself destroyed or lost? 26For whoever is ashamed of Me and My words, of him the Son of Man will be ashamed when He comes in His *own* glory, and *in His* Father's, and of the holy angels. 27But I tell you truly, there are some standing here who shall not taste death till they see the kingdom of God."

Jesus Transfigured on the Mount

28Now it came to pass, about eight days after these sayings, that He took Peter, John, and James and went up on the mountain to pray. 29As He prayed, the appearance of His face was altered, and His robe *became* white *and* glistening. 30And behold, two men talked with Him, who were Moses and Elijah, 31who appeared in glory and spoke of His decease which He was about to accomplish at Jerusalem. 32But Peter and those with him were heavy with sleep; and when they were fully awake, they saw His glory and the two men who stood with Him. 33Then it happened, as they were parting from Him, *that* Peter said to Jesus, "Master, it is good for us to be here; and let us make three tabernacles: one for You, one for Moses, and one for Elijah"—not knowing what he said.

34While he was saying this, a cloud came and overshadowed them; and they were fearful as they entered the cloud. 35And a voice came out of the cloud, saying, "This is

My beloved Son.a Hear Him!" 36When the voice had ceased, Jesus was found alone. But they kept quiet, and told no one in those days any of the things they had seen.

A Boy Is Healed

37Now it happened on the next day, when they had come down from the mountain, that a great multitude met Him. 38Suddenly a man from the multitude cried out, saying, "Teacher, I implore You, look on my son, for he is my only child. 39And behold, a spirit seizes him, and he suddenly cries out; it convulses him so that he foams *at the mouth;* and it departs from him with great difficulty, bruising him. 40So I implored Your disciples to cast it out, but they could not."

41Then Jesus answered and said, "O faithless and perverse generation, how long shall I be with you and bear with you? Bring your son here." 42And as he was still coming, the demon threw him down and convulsed *him.* Then Jesus rebuked the unclean spirit, healed the child, and gave him back to his father.

Jesus Again Predicts His Death

43And they were all amazed at the majesty of God.

But while everyone marveled at all the things which Jesus did, He said to His disciples, 44"Let these words sink down into your ears, for the Son of Man is about to be betrayed into the hands of men." 45But they did not understand this saying, and it was hidden from them so that they did not perceive it; and they were afraid to ask Him about this saying.

Who Is the Greatest?

46Then a dispute arose among them as to which of them would be greatest. 47And Jesus, perceiving the thought of their heart, took a little child and set him by Him, 48and said to them, "Whoever receives this little child in My name receives Me; and whoever receives Me receives Him who sent Me. For he who is least among you all will be great."

Jesus Forbids Sectarianism

49Now John answered and said, "Master, we saw someone casting out demons in

9:23 aM-Text omits *daily.* **9:35** aNU-Text reads *This is My Son, the Chosen One.*

Your name, and we forbade him because he does not follow with us."

⁵⁰But Jesus said to him, "Do not forbid *him,* for he who is not against us[a] is on our[b] side."

A Samaritan Village Rejects the Savior

⁵¹Now it came to pass, when the time had come for Him to be received up, that He steadfastly set His face to go to Jerusalem, ⁵²and sent messengers before His face. And as they went, they entered a village of the Samaritans, to prepare for Him. ⁵³But they did not receive Him, because His face was *set* for the journey to Jerusalem. ⁵⁴And when His disciples James and John saw *this,* they said, "Lord, do You want us to command fire to come down from heaven and consume them, just as Elijah did?"[a]

⁵⁵But He turned and rebuked them,[a] and said, "You do not know what manner of spirit you are of. ⁵⁶For the Son of Man did not come to destroy men's lives but to save *them.*"[a] And they went to another village.

The Cost of Discipleship

⁵⁷Now it happened as they journeyed on the road, *that* someone said to Him, "Lord, I will follow You wherever You go."

⁵⁸And Jesus said to him, "Foxes have holes and birds of the air *have* nests, but the Son of Man has nowhere to lay *His* head."

⁵⁹Then He said to another, "Follow Me."

But he said, "Lord, let me first go and bury my father."

⁶⁰Jesus said to him, "Let the dead bury their own dead, but you go and preach the kingdom of God."

⁶¹And another also said, "Lord, I will follow You, but let me first go *and* bid them farewell who are at my house."

⁶²But Jesus said to him, "No one, having put his hand to the plow, and looking back, is fit for the kingdom of God."

The Seventy Sent Out

10 After these things the Lord appointed seventy others also,[a] and sent them two by two before His face into every city and place where He Himself was about to go. ²Then He said to them, "The harvest truly *is* great, but the laborers *are* few; therefore pray the Lord of the harvest to send out laborers into His harvest. ³Go your way; behold, I send you out as lambs among wolves. ⁴Carry neither money bag, knapsack, nor sandals; and greet no one along the road. ⁵But whatever house you enter, first say, 'Peace to this house.' ⁶And if a son of peace is there, your peace will rest on it; if not, it will return to you. ⁷And remain in the same house, eating and drinking such things as they give, for the laborer is worthy of his wages. Do not go from house to house. ⁸Whatever city you enter, and they receive you, eat such things as are set before you. ⁹And heal the sick there, and say to them, 'The kingdom of God has come near to you.' ¹⁰But whatever city you enter, and they do not receive you, go out into its streets and say, ¹¹'The very dust of your city which clings to us[a] we wipe off against you. Nevertheless know this, that the kingdom of God has come near you.' ¹²But[a] I say to you that it will be more tolerable in that Day for Sodom than for that city.

Woe to the Impenitent Cities

¹³"Woe to you, Chorazin! Woe to you, Bethsaida! For if the mighty works which were done in you had been done in Tyre and Sidon, they would have repented long ago, sitting in sackcloth and ashes. ¹⁴But it will be more tolerable for Tyre and Sidon at the judgment than for you. ¹⁵And you, Capernaum, who are exalted to heaven, will be brought down to Hades.[a] ¹⁶He who hears you hears Me, he who rejects you rejects Me, and he who rejects Me rejects Him who sent Me."

The Seventy Return with Joy

¹⁷Then the seventy[a] returned with joy, saying, "Lord, even the demons are subject to us in Your name."

9:50 [a]NU-Text reads *you.* [b]NU-Text reads *your.*
9:54 [a]NU-Text omits *just as Elijah did.*
9:55 [a]NU-Text omits the rest of this verse.
9:56 [a]NU-Text omits the first sentence of this verse.
10:1 [a]NU-Text reads *seventy-two others.*
10:11 [a]NU-Text reads *our feet.* **10:12** [a]NU-Text and M-Text omit *But.* **10:15** [a]NU-Text reads *will you be exalted to heaven? You will be thrust down to Hades!*
10:17 [a]NU-Text reads *seventy-two.*

Allow Christ to Rule All

FOR SEVERAL YEARS as a young man, I allowed God access only to small portions of my life. I went to church, talked about God. But honestly, my heart was far from Him. I'm grateful for a number of events that occurred in my life that resulted in spiritual growth. One such event occurred when I came across a booklet called *My Heart, Christ's Home* that challenged me to give Jesus Christ full control of my life

The booklet compared the different parts of our lives to rooms in a home. some were open and Christ had complete access to everything in that room. Other rooms, however, had doors that were shut and bolted, declaring to the God of the universe, "This room is off-limits! This room is *mine*!" The changes that began to occur in my life as I began to allow Christ access to every room in heart were liberating.

What about the rooms in your heart? May I challenge you to reflect on His presence in the rooms of your own heart?

Is Christ welcome in *every* room of your heart? Jesus says, "You shall love the Lord your God with *all* your heart, with *all* your soul, with *all* your strength, and with *all* your mind" (10:27, emphasis added).

Allow Christ to rule the room where you keep your ego. When Jesus isn't allowed in, husbands and wives bicker; children become too competitive and selfish; and everyone is too proud to confess sins.

Open to Christ the room of expectations. With Christ excluded, this room can become filled with longings and unmet hopes—some of which are unrealistic, some of which we've never even expressed.

Let Christ into the room of relationships with your parents. Too many adult children have not fully obeyed the Scripture to "leave and cleave" (Gen. 2:24). Closing off this room to Christ results in inappropriate relationships between adult children and their parents.

Are there any other secret rooms that remain hidden from Him? Rooms that really need to be cleaned out? Lust, an addiction to pornography, a relationship that you already know is wrong? Open those doors and let Him in.

When Christ steps into these rooms, He does so with love, forgiveness, and grace. He takes the shame and wipes it clean. He takes the compromises and sets things right. He can be trusted as no house cleaner you've ever had.

Are there any rooms that you need to give Him complete, unhindered access to right now? Just do it.

[18]And He said to them, "I saw Satan fall like lightning from heaven. [19]Behold, I give you the authority to trample on serpents and scorpions, and over all the power of the enemy, and nothing shall by any means hurt you. [20]Nevertheless do not rejoice in this, that the spirits are subject to you, but rather[a] rejoice because your names are written in heaven."

Jesus Rejoices in the Spirit

[21]In that hour Jesus rejoiced in the Spirit and said, "I thank You, Father, Lord of heaven and earth, that You have hidden these things from *the* wise and prudent and revealed them to babes. Even so, Father, for so it seemed good in Your sight. [22]All[a] things have been delivered to Me by My Father, and no one knows who the Son is except the Father, and who the Father is except the Son, and *the one* to whom the Son wills to reveal *Him*."

10:20 [a]NU-Text and M-Text omit *rather*.
10:22 [a]M-Text reads *And turning to the disciples He said, "All . . .*

23Then He turned to *His* disciples and said privately, "Blessed *are* the eyes which see the things you see; 24for I tell you that many prophets and kings have desired to see what you see, and have not seen *it,* and to hear what you hear, and have not heard *it.*"

The Parable of the Good Samaritan

25And behold, a certain lawyer stood up and tested Him, saying, "Teacher, what shall I do to inherit eternal life?"

26He said to him, "What is written in the law? What is your reading *of it?*"

27So he answered and said, "'*You shall love the* LORD *your God with all your heart, with all your soul, with all your strength, and with all your mind,*'a and '*your neighbor as yourself.*'"b

28And He said to him, "You have answered rightly; do this and you will live."

29But he, wanting to justify himself, said to Jesus, "And who is my neighbor?"

30Then Jesus answered and said: "A certain *man* went down from Jerusalem to Jericho, and fell among thieves, who stripped him of his clothing, wounded *him,* and departed, leaving *him* half dead. 31Now by chance a certain priest came down that road. And when he saw him, he passed by on the other side. 32Likewise a Levite, when he arrived at the place, came and looked, and passed by on the other side. 33But a certain Samaritan, as he journeyed, came where he was. And when he saw him, he had compassion. 34So he went to *him* and bandaged his wounds, pouring on oil and wine; and he set him on his own animal, brought him to an inn, and took care of him. 35On the next day, when he departed,a he took out two denarii, gave *them* to the innkeeper, and said to him, 'Take care of him; and whatever more you spend, when I come again, I will repay you.' 36So which of these three do you think was neighbor to him who fell among the thieves?"

37And he said, "He who showed mercy on him."

Then Jesus said to him, "Go and do likewise."

Mary and Martha Worship and Serve

38Now it happened as they went that He entered a certain village; and a certain woman named Martha welcomed Him into her house. 39And she had a sister called Mary, who also sat at Jesus'a feet and heard His word. 40But Martha was distracted with much serving, and she approached Him and said, "Lord, do You not care that my sister has left me to serve alone? Therefore tell her to help me."

41And Jesusa answered and said to her, "Martha, Martha, you are worried and troubled about many things. 42But one thing is needed, and Mary has chosen that good part, which will not be taken away from her."

The Model Prayer

11 Now it came to pass, as He was praying in a certain place, when He ceased, *that* one of His disciples said to Him, "Lord, teach us to pray, as John also taught his disciples."

2So He said to them, "When you pray, say:

Our Father in heaven,a
Hallowed be Your name.
Your kingdom come.b
Your will be done
On earth as *it is* in heaven.
3   Give us day by day our daily bread.
4   And forgive us our sins,
For we also forgive everyone who is
        indebted to us.
And do not lead us into temptation,
But deliver us from the evil one."a

A Friend Comes at Midnight

5And He said to them, "Which of you shall have a friend, and go to him at midnight and say to him, 'Friend, lend me three loaves; 6for a friend of mine has come to me on his journey, and I have nothing to set before him'; 7and he will answer from within and say, 'Do not trouble me; the door is now shut, and my children are with me in bed; I cannot rise and give to you'? 8I say to you, though he will

---

10:27 aDeuteronomy 6:5 bLeviticus 19:18
10:35 aNU-Text omits *when he departed.*
10:39 aNU-Text reads *the Lord's.* 10:41 aNU-Text reads *the Lord.* 11:2 aNU-Text omits *Our* and *in heaven.* bNU-Text omits the rest of this verse.
11:4 aNU-Text omits *But deliver us from the evil one.*

not rise and give to him because he is his friend, yet because of his persistence he will rise and give him as many as he needs.

Keep Asking, Seeking, Knocking

9"So I say to you, ask, and it will be given to you; seek, and you will find; knock, and it will be opened to you. 10For everyone who asks receives, and he who seeks finds, and to him who knocks it will be opened. 11If a son asks for breada from any father among you, will he give him a stone? Or if *he asks* for a fish, will he give him a serpent instead of a fish? 12Or if he asks for an egg, will he offer him a scorpion? 13If you then, being evil, know how to give good gifts to your children, how much more will *your* heavenly Father give the Holy Spirit to those who ask Him!"

11:11 aNU-Text omits the words from *bread* through *for* in the next sentence.
11:15 aNU-Text and M-Text read *Beelzebul.*

A House Divided Cannot Stand

14And He was casting out a demon, and it was mute. So it was, when the demon had gone out, that the mute spoke; and the multitudes marveled. 15But some of them said, "He casts out demons by Beelzebub,a the ruler of the demons."

16Others, testing *Him,* sought from Him a sign from heaven. 17But He, knowing their thoughts, said to them: "Every kingdom divided against itself is brought to desolation, and a house *divided* against a house falls. 18If Satan also is divided against himself, how will his kingdom stand? Because you say I cast out demons by Beelzebub. 19And if I cast out demons by Beelzebub, by whom do your sons cast *them* out? Therefore they will be your judges. 20But if I cast out demons with the finger of God, surely the kingdom of God has come upon you. 21When a strong man, fully armed, guards his own palace, his

---

PARENTING MATTERS

Q: How can we teach our children to be sexually pure?

One week in my sixth-grade Sunday school class, I asked the 23 girls and 19 boys how far they intended to go physically before marriage. Here's how they answered:

	Boys	Girls
Holding hands, occasional hug	1	1
Occasional light kissing	6	7
Passionate kissing, close hugging	9	15
Passionate petting, touching in Private places	2	0
All the way	1	0

The results simply stunned me. These were kids from Christian homes who attend a solid, innovative, Bible-teaching church! If this was how far they intended to go before puberty fully hit, then how will they act when their raging hormones really course through the bloodstream?

Sex education is much more than talking to our kids about biological functions. It really involves character training and the biblical shaping of convictions. Our children must be able to handle one of the most powerful forces in life, the sex drive, and to do that they must learn how to make godly choices. And they need you, mom and dad, to help them.

How far do you want your children to go sexually before they marry? Help them decide in advance where their boundaries ought to be. Have the conversation with your children before they reach puberty. Ask God to give you wisdom and courage in protecting the innocence of your children.

goods are in peace. 22But when a stronger than he comes upon him and overcomes him, he takes from him all his armor in which he trusted, and divides his spoils. 23He who is not with Me is against Me, and he who does not gather with Me scatters.

An Unclean Spirit Returns

24"When an unclean spirit goes out of a man, he goes through dry places, seeking rest; and finding none, he says, 'I will return to my house from which I came.' 25And when he comes, he finds it swept and put in order. 26Then he goes and takes with him seven other spirits more wicked than himself, and they enter and dwell there; and the last state of that man is worse than the first."

Keeping the Word

27And it happened, as He spoke these things, that a certain woman from the crowd raised her voice and said to Him, "Blessed is the womb that bore You, and the breasts which nursed You!"

28But He said, "More than that, blessed are those who hear the word of God and keep it!"

Seeking a Sign

29And while the crowds were thickly gathered together, He began to say, "This is an evil generation. It seeks a sign, and no sign will be given to it except the sign of Jonah the prophet.a 30For as Jonah became a sign to the Ninevites, so also the Son of Man will be to this generation. 31The queen of the South will rise up in the judgment with the men of this generation and condemn them, for she came from the ends of the earth to hear the wisdom of Solomon; and indeed a greater than Solomon is here. 32The men of Nineveh will rise up in the judgment with this generation and condemn it, for they repented at the preaching of Jonah; and indeed a greater than Jonah is here.

The Lamp of the Body

33"No one, when he has lit a lamp, puts it in a secret place or under a basket, but on a lampstand, that those who come in may see the light. 34The lamp of the body

is the eye. Therefore, when your eye is good, your whole body also is full of light. But when your eye is bad, your body also is full of darkness. 35Therefore take heed that the light which is in you is not darkness. 36If then your whole body is full of light, having no part dark, the whole body will be full of light, as when the bright shining of a lamp gives you light."

Woe to the Pharisees and Lawyers

37And as He spoke, a certain Pharisee asked Him to dine with him. So He went in and sat down to eat. 38When the Pharisee saw it, he marveled that He had not first washed before dinner.

39Then the Lord said to him, "Now you Pharisees make the outside of the cup and dish clean, but your inward part is full of greed and wickedness. 40Foolish ones! Did not He who made the outside make the inside also? 41But rather give alms of such things as you have; then indeed all things are clean to you.

42"But woe to you Pharisees! For you tithe mint and rue and all manner of herbs, and pass by justice and the love of God. These you ought to have done, without leaving the others undone. 43Woe to you Pharisees! For you love the best seats in the synagogues and greetings in the marketplaces. 44Woe to you, scribes and Pharisees, hypocrites!a For you are like graves which are not seen, and the men who walk over them are not aware of them."

45Then one of the lawyers answered and said to Him, "Teacher, by saying these things You reproach us also."

46And He said, "Woe to you also, lawyers! For you load men with burdens hard to bear, and you yourselves do not touch the burdens with one of your fingers. 47Woe to you! For you build the tombs of the prophets, and your fathers killed them. 48In fact, you bear witness that you approve the deeds of your fathers; for they indeed killed them, and you build their tombs. 49Therefore the wisdom of God also said, 'I will send them prophets and apostles, and some of them they will kill

11:29 aNU-Text omits the prophet. **11:44** aNU-Text omits scribes and Pharisees, hypocrites.

and persecute,' ⁵⁰that the blood of all the prophets which was shed from the foundation of the world may be required of this generation, ⁵¹from the blood of Abel to the blood of Zechariah who perished between the altar and the temple. Yes, I say to you, it shall be required of this generation.

⁵²"Woe to you lawyers! For you have taken away the key of knowledge. You did not enter in yourselves, and those who were entering in you hindered."

⁵³And as He said these things to them,ᵃ the scribes and the Pharisees began to assail *Him* vehemently, and to cross-examine Him about many things, ⁵⁴lying in wait for Him, and seeking to catch Him in something He might say, that they might accuse Him.ᵃ

Beware of Hypocrisy

12 In the meantime, when an innumerable multitude of people had gathered together, so that they trampled one another, He began to say to His disciples first *of all,* "Beware of the leaven of the Pharisees, which is hypocrisy. ²For there is nothing covered that will not be revealed, nor hidden that will not be known. ³Therefore whatever you have spoken in the dark will be heard in the light, and what you have spoken in the ear in inner rooms will be proclaimed on the housetops.

Jesus Teaches the Fear of God

⁴"And I say to you, My friends, do not be afraid of those who kill the body, and after that have no more that they can do. ⁵But I will show you whom you should fear: Fear Him who, after He has killed, has power to cast into hell; yes, I say to you, fear Him!

⁶"Are not five sparrows sold for two copper coins?ᵃ And not one of them is forgotten before God. ⁷But the very hairs of your head are all numbered. Do not fear therefore; you are of more value than many sparrows.

Confess Christ Before Men

⁸"Also I say to you, whoever confesses Me before men, him the Son of Man also will confess before the angels of God. ⁹But he who denies Me before men will be denied before the angels of God.

¹⁰"And anyone who speaks a word against the Son of Man, it will be forgiven him; but to him who blasphemes against the Holy Spirit, it will not be forgiven.

¹¹"Now when they bring you to the synagogues and magistrates and authorities, do not worry about how or what you should answer, or what you should say. ¹²For the Holy Spirit will teach you in that very hour what you ought to say."

The Parable of the Rich Fool

¹³Then one from the crowd said to Him, "Teacher, tell my brother to divide the inheritance with me."

¹⁴But He said to him, "Man, who made Me a judge or an arbitrator over you?" ¹⁵And He said to them, "Take heed and beware of covetousness,ᵃ for one's life does not consist in the abundance of the things he possesses."

INTIMATE MOMENTS
Spice Up the Season

No doubt in past Christmas seasons you've heard some version of the old standby, "The Twelve Days of Christmas." No doubt you've also heard someone do a parody of the song, whether in an advertisement or strictly for comedy. Well, for your mate this year, try your own hand at spicing up the "Twelve Days of Christmas."

Each day from December 25 through January 5, create small, personal gifts (notes, cookies, cards, yourself—use your imagination!) for him or her only. On January 6, buy a King Cake (or better yet, make your own) to close out the Christmas season. Get your spouse anticipating what you're going to unveil each day!

11:53 ᵃNU-Text reads *And when He left there.*
11:54 ᵃNU-Text omits *and seeking* and *that they might accuse Him.*
12:6 ᵃGreek *assarion,* a coin of very small value
12:15 ᵃNU-Text reads *all covetousness.*

16Then He spoke a parable to them, saying: "The ground of a certain rich man yielded plentifully. 17And he thought within himself, saying, 'What shall I do, since I have no room to store my crops?' 18So he said, 'I will do this: I will pull down my barns and build greater, and there I will store all my crops and my goods. 19And I will say to my soul, "Soul, you have many goods laid up for many years; take your ease; eat, drink, *and* be merry."' 20But God said to him, 'Fool! This night your soul will be required of you; then whose will those things be which you have provided?'

21"So *is* he who lays up treasure for himself, and is not rich toward God."

Do Not Worry

22Then He said to His disciples, "Therefore I say to you, do not worry about your life, what you will eat; nor about the body, what you will put on. 23Life is more than food, and the body *is more* than clothing. 24Consider the ravens, for they neither sow nor reap, which have neither storehouse nor barn; and God feeds them. Of how much more value are you than the birds? 25And which of you by worrying can add one cubit to his stature? 26If you then are not able to do *the* least, why are you anxious for the rest? 27Consider the lilies, how they grow: they neither toil nor spin; and yet I say to you, even Solomon in all his glory was not arrayed like one of these. 28If then God so clothes the grass, which today is in the field and tomorrow is thrown into the oven, how much more *will He clothe* you, O *you* of little faith?

29"And do not seek what you should eat or what you should drink, nor have an anxious mind. 30For all these things the nations of the world seek after, and your Father knows that you need these things. 31But seek the kingdom of God, and all these thingsa shall be added to you.

32"Do not fear, little flock, for it is your Father's good pleasure to give you the kingdom. 33Sell what you have and give alms; provide yourselves money bags which do not grow old, a treasure in the heavens that does not fail, where no thief approaches nor moth destroys. 34For where your treasure is, there your heart will be also.

The Faithful Servant and the Evil Servant

35"Let your waist be girded and *your* lamps burning; 36and you yourselves be like men who wait for their master, when he will return from the wedding, that when he comes and knocks they may open to him immediately. 37Blessed *are* those servants whom the master, when he comes, will find watching. Assuredly, I say to you that he will gird himself and have them sit down *to eat,* and will come and serve them. 38And if he should come in the second watch, or come in the third watch, and find *them* so, blessed are those servants. 39But know this, that if the master of the house had known what hour the thief would come, he would have watched anda not allowed his house to be broken into. 40Therefore you also be ready, for the Son of Man is coming at an hour you do not expect."

41Then Peter said to Him, "Lord, do You speak this parable *only* to us, or to all *people?*"

42And the Lord said, "Who then is that faithful and wise steward, whom *his* master will make ruler over his household, to give *them their* portion of food in due season? 43Blessed *is* that servant whom his master will find so doing when he comes. 44Truly, I say to you that he will make him ruler over all that he has. 45But if that servant says in his heart, 'My master is delaying his coming,' and begins to beat the male and female servants, and to eat and drink and be drunk, 46the master of that servant will come on a day when he is not looking for *him,* and at an hour when he is not aware, and will cut him in two and appoint *him* his portion with the unbelievers. 47And that servant who knew his master's will, and did not prepare *himself* or do according to his will, shall be beaten with many *stripes.* 48But he who did not know, yet committed things deserving of stripes, shall be beaten with few. For everyone to

---

12:31 aNU-Text reads *His kingdom, and these things.*
12:39 aNU-Text reads *he would not have allowed.*

whom much is given, from him much will be required; and to whom much has been committed, of him they will ask the more.

Christ Brings Division

[49]"I came to send fire on the earth, and how I wish it were already kindled! [50]But I have a baptism to be baptized with, and how distressed I am till it is accomplished! [51]Do *you* suppose that I came to give peace on earth? I tell you, not at all, but rather division. [52]For from now on five in one house will be divided: three against two, and two against three. [53]Father will be divided against son and son against father, mother against daughter and daughter against mother, mother-in-law against her daughter-in-law and daughter-in-law against her mother-in-law."

Discern the Time

[54]Then He also said to the multitudes, "Whenever you see a cloud rising out of the west, immediately you say, 'A shower is coming'; and so it is. [55]And when *you see* the south wind blow, you say, 'There will be hot weather'; and there is. [56]Hypocrites! You can discern the face of the sky and of the earth, but how *is it* you do not discern this time?

Make Peace with Your Adversary

[57]"Yes, and why, even of yourselves, do you not judge what is right? [58]When you go with your adversary to the magistrate, make every effort along the way to settle with him, lest he drag you to the judge, the judge deliver you to the officer, and the officer throw you into prison. [59]I tell you, you shall not depart from there till you have paid the very last mite."

Repent or Perish

13 There were present at that season some who told Him about the Galileans whose blood Pilate had mingled with their sacrifices. [2]And Jesus answered and said to them, "Do you suppose that these Galileans were worse sinners than all *other* Galileans, because they suffered such things? [3]I tell you, no; but unless you repent you will all likewise perish. [4]Or those eighteen on whom the tower in Siloam fell and killed them, do you think

that they were worse sinners than all *other* men who dwelt in Jerusalem? [5]I tell you, no; but unless you repent you will all likewise perish."

The Parable of the Barren Fig Tree

[6]He also spoke this parable: "A certain *man* had a fig tree planted in his vineyard, and he came seeking fruit on it and found none. [7]Then he said to the keeper of his

---

ROMANCE FAQ

Q: What in a man communicates romance to a woman?

What does it take to become the romantic man of your wife's dreams?

- A romantic man engages his wife in a living and growing relationship, without losing sight that physical intimacy is an important part of that relationship.
- A romantic man commits to learning nonsexual ways to love his lover while nurturing in her the freedom to be sexually responsive.
- A romantic man can kiss, hug, touch, and cuddle without a sexual agenda.
- A romantic man does not pressure his wife into having sex, nor does he retreat from the pursuit of sexual oneness.
- A romantic man connects to his wife's world, supports, listens, and shares his heart, without applying sexual pressure, while remaining confidently aware that sexual intimacy is vital to the survival of his marriage.
- A romantic man will do all of these things, even when his spouse is sexually unresponsive.

You can learn to speak your wife's language of romantic love and still be fully a man, whose sexual desires are blessed by God and were created for His purposes. Remember, there is no shame, no condemnation, and no apology for fully being a man.

vineyard, 'Look, for three years I have come seeking fruit on this fig tree and find none. Cut it down; why does it use up the ground?' ⁸But he answered and said to him, 'Sir, let it alone this year also, until I dig around it and fertilize *it.* ⁹And if it bears fruit, *well.* But if not, after that[a] you can cut it down.' "

A Spirit of Infirmity

¹⁰Now He was teaching in one of the synagogues on the Sabbath. ¹¹And behold, there was a woman who had a spirit of infirmity eighteen years, and was bent over and could in no way raise *herself* up. ¹²But when Jesus saw her, He called *her* to *Him* and said to her, "Woman, you are loosed from your infirmity." ¹³And He laid *His* hands on her, and immediately she was made straight, and glorified God.

¹⁴But the ruler of the synagogue answered with indignation, because Jesus had healed on the Sabbath; and he said to the crowd, "There are six days on which men ought to work; therefore come and be healed on them, and not on the Sabbath day."

¹⁵The Lord then answered him and said, "Hypocrite![a] Does not each one of you on the Sabbath loose his ox or donkey from the stall, and lead *it* away to water it? ¹⁶So ought not this woman, being a daughter of Abraham, whom Satan has bound—think of it—for eighteen years, be loosed from this bond on the Sabbath?" ¹⁷And when He said these things, all His adversaries were put to shame; and all the multitude rejoiced for all the glorious things that were done by Him.

The Parable of the Mustard Seed

¹⁸Then He said, "What is the kingdom of God like? And to what shall I compare it? ¹⁹It is like a mustard seed, which a man took and put in his garden; and it grew and became a large[a] tree, and the birds of the air nested in its branches."

The Parable of the Leaven

²⁰And again He said, "To what shall I liken the kingdom of God? ²¹It is like leaven, which a woman took and hid in three measures[a] of meal till it was all leavened."

The Narrow Way

²²And He went through the cities and villages, teaching, and journeying toward Jerusalem. ²³Then one said to Him, "Lord, are there few who are saved?"

And He said to them, ²⁴"Strive to enter through the narrow gate, for many, I say to you, will seek to enter and will not be able. ²⁵When once the Master of the house has risen up and shut the door, and you begin to stand outside and knock at the door, saying, 'Lord, Lord, open for us,' and He will answer and say to you, 'I do not know you, where you are from,' ²⁶then you will begin to say, 'We ate and drank in Your presence, and You taught in our streets.' ²⁷But He will say, 'I tell you I do not know you, where you are from. Depart from Me, all you workers of iniquity.' ²⁸There will be weeping and gnashing of teeth, when you see Abraham and Isaac and Jacob and all the prophets in the kingdom of God, and yourselves thrust out. ²⁹They will come from the east and the west, from the north and the south, and sit down in the kingdom of God. ³⁰And indeed there are last who will be first, and there are first who will be last."

³¹On that very day[a] some Pharisees came, saying to Him, "Get out and depart from here, for Herod wants to kill You."

³²And He said to them, "Go, tell that fox, 'Behold, I cast out demons and perform cures today and tomorrow, and the third *day* I shall be perfected.' ³³Nevertheless I must journey today, tomorrow, and the *day* following; for it cannot be that a prophet should perish outside of Jerusalem.

Jesus Laments over Jerusalem

³⁴"O Jerusalem, Jerusalem, the one who kills the prophets and stones those who are sent to her! How often I wanted to gather your children together, as a hen *gathers* her brood under *her* wings, but you were not willing! ³⁵See! Your house is left to you

---

13:9 [a]NU-Text reads *And if it bears fruit after that, well. But if not, you can cut it down.*
13:15 [a]NU-Text and M-Text read *Hypocrites.*
13:19 [a]NU-Text omits *large.*
13:21 [a]Greek *sata,* approximately two pecks in all
13:31 [a]NU-Text reads *In that very hour.*

desolate; and assuredly,[a] I say to you, you shall not see Me until *the time* comes when you say, '*Blessed is He who comes in the name of the Lord!*'"[b]

A Man with Dropsy Healed on the Sabbath

14 Now it happened, as He went into the house of one of the rulers of the Pharisees to eat bread on the Sabbath, that they watched Him closely. 2And behold, there was a certain man before Him who had dropsy. 3And Jesus, answering, spoke

---

13:35 [a]NU-Text and M-Text omit *assuredly*. [b]Psalm 118:26 14:3 [a]NU-Text adds *or not*. 14:5 [a]NU-Text and M-Text read *son*.

---

to the lawyers and Pharisees, saying, "Is it lawful to heal on the Sabbath?"[a]

4But they kept silent. And He took *him* and healed him, and let him go. 5Then He answered them, saying, "Which of you, having a donkey[a] or an ox that has fallen into a pit, will not immediately pull him out on the Sabbath day?" 6And they could not answer Him regarding these things.

Take the Lowly Place

7So He told a parable to those who were invited, when He noted how they chose the best places, saying to them: 8"When you are invited by anyone to a wedding feast, do not sit down in the best place, lest one more honorable than you be invited by

---

PARENTING MATTERS	**Q: How can we manage what our children see on television or on the internet?**

I suggest taking TV and the internet in moderation. Here are some tips we try to follow in our family:

Instruct the kids to ask you for permission to watch TV or go online. Don't let them treat it as a given. Don't let them watch TV or go online randomly because they are bored, but determine what you want them to see.

Make TV and the computer off-limits in at least these two rooms: the room where you eat your meals, and their bedroom. We had a rule that there could be no TV's or computers in rooms that weren't public (rooms where a teenager could hide and view things that he or she shouldn't).

Agree on the number of hours and the programs that can be watched during the week and on weekends and the number of hours they can be online each day. Especially when they are young, you can provide them with a list of acceptable programs and websites.

Don't let your children watch a movie unless you know what's in it. Read online reviews of movies to get clues about the level of unacceptable language, sex and violence.

Don't let your children surf the web without some kind of filter. Find a software that can keep your children from stumbling into someplace dangerous online.

Watch specific TV programs for a specific purpose. Once, when I plopped down to watch nothing in particular, Barbara said, "There's nothing on worth watching. Spend time with *me*!" We turned the TV off and the conversation on.

In the early '80s, a Michigan State University study reported that one-third of four- and five-year-olds in the U.S. would give up their relationships with their dads in favor of TV. I believe God wants us to harness these helpful tools while we stay alert to the potential dangers involved. Don't let TV or the internet take the place of real relationships in your home.

him; [9]and he who invited you and him come and say to you, 'Give place to this man,' and then you begin with shame to take the lowest place. [10]But when you are invited, go and sit down in the lowest place, so that when he who invited you comes he may say to you, 'Friend, go up higher.' Then you will have glory in the presence of those who sit at the table with you. [11]For whoever exalts himself will be humbled, and he who humbles himself will be exalted."

[12]Then He also said to him who invited Him, "When you give a dinner or a supper, do not ask your friends, your brothers, your relatives, nor rich neighbors, lest they also invite you back, and you be repaid. [13]But when you give a feast, invite *the* poor, *the* maimed, *the* lame, *the* blind. [14]And you will be blessed, because they cannot repay you; for you shall be repaid at the resurrection of the just."

The Parable of the Great Supper

[15]Now when one of those who sat at the table with Him heard these things, he said to Him, "Blessed *is* he who shall eat bread[a] in the kingdom of God!"

[16]Then He said to him, "A certain man gave a great supper and invited many, [17]and sent his servant at supper time to say to those who were invited, 'Come, for all things are now ready.' [18]But they all with one *accord* began to make excuses. The first said to him, 'I have bought a piece of ground, and I must go and see it. I ask you to have me excused.' [19]And another said, 'I have bought five yoke of oxen, and I am going to test them. I ask you to have me excused.' [20]Still another said, 'I have married a wife, and therefore I cannot come.' [21]So that servant came and reported these things to his master. Then the master of the house, being angry, said to his servant, 'Go out quickly into the streets and lanes of the city, and bring in here *the* poor and *the* maimed and *the* lame and *the* blind.' [22]And the servant said, 'Master, it is done as you commanded, and still there is room.' [23]Then the master said to the servant, 'Go out into the highways and hedges, and compel *them* to come in, that my house may be filled. [24]For I say to you that none

of those men who were invited shall taste my supper.'"

Leaving All to Follow Christ

[25]Now great multitudes went with Him. And He turned and said to them, [26]"If anyone comes to Me and does not hate his father and mother, wife and children, brothers and sisters, yes, and his own life also, he cannot be My disciple. [27]And whoever does not bear his cross and come after Me cannot be My disciple. [28]For which of you, intending to build a tower, does not sit down first and count the cost, whether he has *enough* to finish *it*— [29]lest, after he has laid the foundation, and is not able to finish, all who see *it* begin to mock him, [30]saying, 'This man began to build and was not able to finish'? [31]Or what king, going to make war against another king, does not sit down first and consider whether he is able with ten thousand to meet him who comes against him with twenty thousand? [32]Or else, while the other is still a great way off, he sends a delegation and asks conditions of peace. [33]So likewise, whoever of you does not forsake all that he has cannot be My disciple.

Tasteless Salt Is Worthless

[34]"Salt *is* good; but if the salt has lost its flavor, how shall it be seasoned? [35]It is neither fit for the land nor for the dunghill, *but* men throw it out. He who has ears to hear, let him hear!"

The Parable of the Lost Sheep

15 Then all the tax collectors and the sinners drew near to Him to hear Him. [2]And the Pharisees and scribes complained, saying, "This Man receives sinners and eats with them." [3]So He spoke this parable to them, saying:

[4]"What man of you, having a hundred sheep, if he loses one of them, does not leave the ninety-nine in the wilderness, and go after the one which is lost until he finds it? [5]And when he has found *it*, he lays *it* on his shoulders, rejoicing. [6]And when he comes home, he calls together *his* friends and neighbors, saying to them, 'Rejoice

---

14:15 [a]M-Text reads *dinner*.

with me, for I have found my sheep which was lost!' [7]I say to you that likewise there will be more joy in heaven over one sinner who repents than over ninety-nine just persons who need no repentance.

The Parable of the Lost Coin

[8]"Or what woman, having ten silver coins,[a] if she loses one coin, does not light a lamp, sweep the house, and search carefully until she finds it? [9]And when she has found it, she calls her friends and neighbors together, saying, 'Rejoice with me, for I have found the piece which I lost!' [10]Likewise, I say to you, there is joy in the presence of the angels of God over one sinner who repents."

The Parable of the Lost Son

[11]Then He said: "A certain man had two sons. [12]And the younger of them said to his father, 'Father, give me the portion of goods that falls to me.' So he divided to them his livelihood. [13]And not many days after, the younger son gathered all together, journeyed to a far country, and there wasted his possessions with prodigal living. [14]But when he had spent all, there arose a severe famine in that land, and he began to be in want. [15]Then he went and joined himself to a citizen of that country, and he sent him into his fields to feed swine. [16]And he would gladly have filled his stomach with the pods that the swine ate, and no one gave him anything.

[17]"But when he came to himself, he said, 'How many of my father's hired servants have bread enough and to spare, and I perish with hunger! [18]I will arise and go to my father, and will say to him, "Father, I have sinned against heaven and before you, [19]and I am no longer worthy to be called your son. Make me like one of your hired servants."'

[20]"And he arose and came to his father. But when he was still a great way off, his father saw him and had compassion, and ran and fell on his neck and kissed him. [21]And the son said to him, 'Father, I have sinned against heaven and in your sight,

and am no longer worthy to be called your son.'

[22]"But the father said to his servants, 'Bring[a] out the best robe and put it on him, and put a ring on his hand and sandals on his feet. [23]And bring the fatted calf here and kill it, and let us eat and be merry; [24]for this my son was dead and is alive again; he was lost and is found.' And they began to be merry.

[25]"Now his older son was in the field. And as he came and drew near to the house, he heard music and dancing. [26]So he called one of the servants and asked what these things meant. [27]And he said to him, 'Your brother has come, and because he has received him safe and sound, your father has killed the fatted calf.'

[28]"But he was angry and would not go in. Therefore his father came out and pleaded with him. [29]So he answered and said to his father, 'Lo, these many years I have been serving you; I never transgressed your commandment at any time; and yet you never gave me a young goat, that I might make merry with my friends. [30]But as soon as this son of yours came, who has devoured your livelihood with harlots, you killed the fatted calf for him.'

[31]"And he said to him, 'Son, you are always with me, and all that I have is yours. [32]It was right that we should make merry and be glad, for your brother was dead and is alive again, and was lost and is found.'"

The Parable of the Unjust Steward

16 He also said to His disciples: "There was a certain rich man who had a steward, and an accusation was brought to him that this man was wasting his goods. [2]So he called him and said to him, 'What is

INTIMATE MOMENTS

Create your own little free cuddles coupon book. Every time she wants to cuddle, she turns in a coupon (with no expiration date).

15:8 [a]Greek drachma, a valuable coin often worn in a ten-piece garland by married women
15:22 [a]NU-Text reads Quickly bring.

BIBLICAL INSIGHTS • 16:11

Faithful in the Little Things

PEOPLE TODAY increasingly seem to feel they deserve perks such as, "I deserve a promotion (without earning it)," or "I deserve the prestige and responsibility (without having to pay the price)." Many are on a *career* path, but few seem to be on a *character* path.

With this kind of mindset, some have allowed their character to be sacrificed on the altar of ambition. Yet Jesus clearly taught, "If you have not been faithful in the unrighteous mammon, who will commit to your trust the true riches?" (16:11). In other words, if we don't prove faithful in little things (unrighteous mammon), why would God entrust us with big things (true riches)?

Today our pictures are reading in nearly an instant, our oatmeal is ready to eat in sixty seconds, our laundry is finished in sixty minutes, and our houses can be built in sixty days. We are used to getting what we want instantly. We aren't used to working patiently, or waiting on anything—even a hamburger.

Of course, if all we want is a hamburger, then I suppose that's okay. But if we want more than that, if we want the true riches described by Jesus, then we had better learn to persevere. And that means being faithful in the little things.

What are the little things that you need to focus on being faithful in, especially in your marriage and family?

---

this I hear about you? Give an account of your stewardship, for you can no longer be steward.'

³"Then the steward said within himself, 'What shall I do? For my master is taking the stewardship away from me. I cannot dig; I am ashamed to beg. ⁴I have resolved what to do, that when I am put out of the stewardship, they may receive me into their houses.'

⁵"So he called every one of his master's debtors to *him,* and said to the first, 'How much do you owe my master?' ⁶And he said, 'A hundred measuresª of oil.' So he said to him, 'Take your bill, and sit down quickly and write fifty.' ⁷Then he said to another, 'And how much do you owe?' So he said, 'A hundred measuresª of wheat.' And he said to him, 'Take your bill, and write eighty.' ⁸So the master commended the unjust steward because he had dealt shrewdly. For the sons of this world are more shrewd in their generation than the sons of light.

⁹"And I say to you, make friends for yourselves by unrighteous mammon, that when you fail,ª they may receive you into an everlasting home. ¹⁰He who *is* faithful in *what is* least is faithful also in much; and he who is unjust in *what is* least is unjust also in much. ¹¹Therefore if you have not been faithful in the unrighteous mammon, who will commit to your trust the true *riches?* ¹²And if you have not been faithful in what is another man's, who will give you what is your own?

¹³"No servant can serve two masters; for either he will hate the one and love the other, or else he will be loyal to the one and despise the other. You cannot serve God and mammon."

The Law, the Prophets, and the Kingdom

¹⁴Now the Pharisees, who were lovers of money, also heard all these things, and they derided Him. ¹⁵And He said to them, "You are those who justify yourselves before men, but God knows your hearts. For what is highly esteemed among men is an abomination in the sight of God.

¹⁶"The law and the prophets *were* until John. Since that time the kingdom of God has been preached, and everyone is pressing into it. ¹⁷And it is easier for heaven and earth to pass away than for one tittle of the law to fail.

¹⁸"Whoever divorces his wife and marries another commits adultery; and whoever

---

16:6 ªGreek *batos,* eight or nine gallons each (Old Testament *bath*) **16:7** ªGreek *koros,* ten or twelve bushels each (Old Testament *kor*) **16:9** ªNU-Text reads *it fails.*

marries her who is divorced from *her* husband commits adultery.

The Rich Man and Lazarus

19"There was a certain rich man who was clothed in purple and fine linen and fared sumptuously every day. 20But there was a certain beggar named Lazarus, full of sores, who was laid at his gate, 21desiring to be fed with the crumbs which fell[a] from the rich man's table. Moreover the dogs came and licked his sores. 22So it was that the beggar died, and was carried by the angels to Abraham's bosom. The rich man also died and was buried. 23And being in torments in Hades, he lifted up his eyes and saw Abraham afar off, and Lazarus in his bosom.

24"Then he cried and said, 'Father Abraham, have mercy on me, and send Lazarus that he may dip the tip of his finger in water and cool my tongue; for I am tormented in this flame.' 25But Abraham said, 'Son, remember that in your lifetime you received your good things, and likewise Lazarus evil things; but now he is comforted and you are tormented. 26And besides all this, between us and you there is a great gulf fixed, so that those who want to pass from here to you cannot, nor can those from there pass to us.'

27"Then he said, 'I beg you therefore, father, that you would send him to my father's house, 28for I have five brothers, that he may testify to them, lest they also come to this place of torment.' 29Abraham said to him, 'They have Moses and the prophets; let them hear them.' 30And he said, 'No, father Abraham; but if one goes to them from the dead, they will repent.' 31But he said to him, 'If they do not hear Moses and the prophets, neither will they be persuaded though one rise from the dead.'"

Jesus Warns of Offenses

17 Then He said to the disciples, "It is impossible that no offenses should come, but woe *to him* through whom they

BIBLICAL INSIGHTS • 17:3, 4

The Seventy Times Seven Club

AS DIFFICULT AS IT IS to ask for forgiveness, it can be equally hard to grant forgiveness when you have been wronged. But if you won't forgive until your spouse asks you for forgiveness, then your conflict may go on far longer than either of you want it to.

I often advise married couples to take out a joint membership in the Seventy Times Seven Club. Christ formed that club when Peter asked him how many times we are to forgive one another. Peter wondered if seven times would be enough. Christ answered, "Up to seventy times seven" (Matt. 18:21, 22; see also Luke 17:4).

In other words, *forgive an infinite number of times*. By an act of your will, put away resentment and the desire to punish your spouse.

You can tell if you have forgiven your mate by asking one question, "Have I given up my desire to punish my mate?" When you lay that desire aside and no longer seek revenge, you free your spouse (and yourself) from the bonds of anger. An ancient proverb says, "The man who opts for revenge should dig two graves; he will go in one of them."

Every marriage operates either on the basis of giving insult for insult or blessing for insult (see 1 Pet. 3:9–12). Choose the latter through membership in the Seventy Times Seven Club. If you do, you can expect a blessing in return.

do come! 2It would be better for him if a millstone were hung around his neck, and he were thrown into the sea, than that he should offend one of these little ones. 3Take heed to yourselves. If your brother sins against you,[a] rebuke him; and if he repents, forgive him. 4And if he sins against you seven times in a day, and seven times in a day returns to you,[a] saying, 'I repent,' you shall forgive him."

16:21 [a]NU-Text reads *with what fell.*
17:3 [a]NU-Text omits *against you.*
17:4 [a]M-Text omits *to you.*

Faith and Duty

⁵And the apostles said to the Lord, "Increase our faith."

⁶So the Lord said, "If you have faith as a mustard seed, you can say to this mulberry tree, 'Be pulled up by the roots and be planted in the sea,' and it would obey you. ⁷And which of you, having a servant plowing or tending sheep, will say to him when he has come in from the field, 'Come at once and sit down to eat'? ⁸But will he not rather say to him, 'Prepare something for my supper, and gird yourself and serve me till I have eaten and drunk, and afterward you will eat and drink'? ⁹Does he thank that servant because he did the things that were commanded him? I think not.ᵃ ¹⁰So likewise you, when you have done all those things which you are commanded, say, 'We are unprofitable servants. We have done what was our duty to do.'"

Ten Lepers Cleansed

¹¹Now it happened as He went to Jerusalem that He passed through the midst of Samaria and Galilee. ¹²Then as He entered a certain village, there met Him ten men who were lepers, who stood afar off. ¹³And they lifted up *their* voices and said, "Jesus, Master, have mercy on us!"

¹⁴So when He saw *them,* He said to them, "Go, show yourselves to the priests." And so it was that as they went, they were cleansed.

¹⁵And one of them, when he saw that he was healed, returned, and with a loud voice glorified God, ¹⁶and fell down on *his* face at His feet, giving Him thanks. And he was a Samaritan.

¹⁷So Jesus answered and said, "Were there not ten cleansed? But where *are* the nine? ¹⁸Were there not any found who returned to give glory to God except this foreigner?" ¹⁹And He said to him, "Arise, go your way. Your faith has made you well."

The Coming of the Kingdom

²⁰Now when He was asked by the Pharisees when the kingdom of God would come, He answered them and said, "The kingdom of God does not come with observation; ²¹nor will they say, 'See here!' or 'See there!'ᵃ For indeed, the kingdom of God is within you."

²²Then He said to the disciples, "The days will come when you will desire to see one of the days of the Son of Man, and you will not see *it.* ²³And they will say to you, 'Look here!' or 'Look there!'ᵃ Do not go after *them* or follow *them.* ²⁴For as the lightning that flashes out of one *part* under heaven shines to the other *part* under heaven, so also the Son of Man will be in His day. ²⁵But first He must suffer many things and be rejected by this generation. ²⁶And as it was in the days of Noah, so it will be also in the days of the Son of Man: ²⁷They ate, they drank, they married wives, they were given in marriage, until the day that Noah entered the ark, and the flood came and destroyed them all. ²⁸Likewise as it was also in the days of Lot: They ate, they drank, they bought, they sold, they planted, they built; ²⁹but on the day that Lot went out of Sodom it rained fire and brimstone from heaven and destroyed *them* all. ³⁰Even so will it be in the day when the Son of Man is revealed.

³¹"In that day, he who is on the housetop, and his goods *are* in the house, let him not come down to take them away. And likewise the one who is in the field, let him not turn back. ³²Remember Lot's wife. ³³Whoever seeks to save his life will lose it, and whoever loses his life will preserve it. ³⁴I tell you, in that night there will be two *men* in one bed: the one will be taken and the other will be left. ³⁵Two *women* will be

INTIMATE MOMENTS

Be a student of your husband. Know his likes and dislikes, his strengths and weaknesses, and fears. Keep a journal and see how much more you can learn about him this year than you knew last year.

17:9 ᵃNU-Text ends verse with *commanded;* M-Text omits *him.* **17:21** ᵃNU-Text reverses *here* and *there.* **17:23** ᵃNU-Text reverses *here* and *there.*

grinding together: the one will be taken and the other left. ³⁶Two *men* will be in the field: the one will be taken and the other left."ᵃ

³⁷And they answered and said to Him, "Where, Lord?"

So He said to them, "Wherever the body is, there the eagles will be gathered together."

The Parable of the Persistent Widow

18 Then He spoke a parable to them, that men always ought to pray and not lose heart, ²saying: "There was in a certain city a judge who did not fear God nor regard man. ³Now there was a widow in that city; and she came to him, saying, 'Get justice for me from my adversary.' ⁴And he would not for a while; but afterward he said within himself, 'Though I do not fear God nor regard man, ⁵yet because this widow troubles me I will avenge her, lest by her continual coming she weary me.'"

⁶Then the Lord said, "Hear what the unjust judge said. ⁷And shall God not avenge His own elect who cry out day and night to Him, though He bears long with them? ⁸I tell you that He will avenge them speedily. Nevertheless, when the Son of Man comes, will He really find faith on the earth?"

The Parable of the Pharisee and the Tax Collector

⁹Also He spoke this parable to some who trusted in themselves that they were righteous, and despised others: ¹⁰"Two men went up to the temple to pray, one a Pharisee and the other a tax collector. ¹¹The Pharisee stood and prayed thus with himself, 'God, I thank You that I am not like other men—extortioners, unjust, adulterers, or even as this tax collector. ¹²I fast twice a week; I give tithes of all that I possess.' ¹³And the tax collector, standing afar off, would not so much as raise *his* eyes to heaven, but beat his breast, saying, 'God, be merciful to me a sinner!' ¹⁴I tell you, this man went down to his house justified *rather* than the other; for everyone who exalts himself will be humbled, and he who humbles himself will be exalted."

17:36 ᵃNU-Text and M-Text omit verse 36.

BIBLICAL INSIGHTS • 18:1–8

Don't Give Up on Prayer

NEVER HESITATE to bring every concern, dream, or desire you have for your child to God in prayer. In difficult cases, the temptation may come to give up, but Jesus taught us "that men always ought to pray and not lose heart" (18:1).

Two of the best times to pray with your child are on the way to school (if you drive him or her) and at bedtime. When our children were still in school, we would pray every morning in the car about the things that were most important to them—tests, friends, teachers, activities. As the car topped the hill right before the school building, we always concluded with the same request, "And Lord, we ask that You would keep Ashley, Benjamin, Samuel, Rebecca, Deborah, and Laura from harm, evil, and temptation this day. I pray that they would experience You at work in their lives and be used by You to influence others for Your Kingdom and your purposes. Amen." When our children were old enough to drive themselves to school, we changed tactics and prayed with them just before they left.

Bedtime prayers can be more personal and less hectic. Pray for each child's future mate, relationships, activities, challenges, temptations, and heart for God. Don't assume that even a teenager is too big for you to kneel beside the bed and stroke his face and pray! After you pray, give your teens a kiss on the cheeks and tell them you love them and are proud of them.

Jesus Blesses Little Children

¹⁵Then they also brought infants to Him that He might touch them; but when the disciples saw *it,* they rebuked them. ¹⁶But Jesus called them to *Him* and said, "Let the little children come to Me, and do not forbid them; for of such is the kingdom of

God. [17]Assuredly, I say to you, whoever does not receive the kingdom of God as a little child will by no means enter it."

Jesus Counsels the Rich Young Ruler

[18]Now a certain ruler asked Him, saying, "Good Teacher, what shall I do to inherit eternal life?"

[19]So Jesus said to him, "Why do you call Me good? No one *is* good but One, *that is,* God. [20]You know the commandments: *'Do not commit adultery,' 'Do not murder,' 'Do not steal,' 'Do not bear false witness,' 'Honor your father and your mother.' "*[a]

[21]And he said, "All these things I have kept from my youth."

[22]So when Jesus heard these things, He said to him, "You still lack one thing. Sell all that you have and distribute to the poor, and you will have treasure in heaven; and come, follow Me."

[23]But when he heard this, he became very sorrowful, for he was very rich.

With God All Things Are Possible

[24]And when Jesus saw that he became very sorrowful, He said, "How hard it is for those who have riches to enter the kingdom of God! [25]For it is easier for a camel to go through the eye of a needle than for a rich man to enter the kingdom of God."

[26]And those who heard it said, "Who then can be saved?"

[27]But He said, "The things which are impossible with men are possible with God."

[28]Then Peter said, "See, we have left all[a] and followed You."

[29]So He said to them, "Assuredly, I say to you, there is no one who has left house or parents or brothers or wife or children, for the sake of the kingdom of God, [30]who shall not receive many times more in this present time, and in the age to come eternal life."

Jesus a Third Time Predicts His Death and Resurrection

[31]Then He took the twelve aside and said to them, "Behold, we are going up to Jerusalem, and all things that are written by the prophets concerning the Son of Man will be accomplished. [32]For He will be

delivered to the Gentiles and will be mocked and insulted and spit upon. [33]They will scourge *Him* and kill Him. And the third day He will rise again."

[34]But they understood none of these things; this saying was hidden from them, and they did not know the things which were spoken.

A Blind Man Receives His Sight

[35]Then it happened, as He was coming near Jericho, that a certain blind man sat by the road begging. [36]And hearing a multitude passing by, he asked what it meant. [37]So they told him that Jesus of Nazareth was passing by. [38]And he cried out, saying, "Jesus, Son of David, have mercy on me!"

[39]Then those who went before warned him that he should be quiet; but he cried out all the more, "Son of David, have mercy on me!"

[40]So Jesus stood still and commanded him to be brought to Him. And when he had come near, He asked him, [41]saying, "What do you want Me to do for you?"

He said, "Lord, that I may receive my sight."

[42]Then Jesus said to him, "Receive your sight; your faith has made you well." [43]And immediately he received his sight, and followed Him, glorifying God. And all the people, when they saw *it,* gave praise to God.

Jesus Comes to Zacchaeus' House

19 Then *Jesus* entered and passed through Jericho. [2]Now behold, *there was* a man named Zacchaeus who was a chief tax collector, and he was rich. [3]And he sought to see who Jesus was, but could not because of the crowd, for he was of short stature. [4]So he ran ahead and climbed up into a sycamore tree to see Him, for He was going to pass that *way.* [5]And when Jesus came to the place, He looked up and saw him,[a] and said to him, "Zacchaeus, make haste and come down, for today I must stay at your house." [6]So he made haste and came down, and received Him joyfully. [7]But when they saw *it,* they all complained, saying,

---

18:20 [a]Exodus 20:12–16; Deuteronomy 5:16–20
18:28 [a]NU-Text reads *our own.*
19:5 [a]NU-Text omits *and saw him.*

"He has gone to be a guest with a man who is a sinner."

⁸Then Zacchaeus stood and said to the Lord, "Look, Lord, I give half of my goods to the poor; and if I have taken anything from anyone by false accusation, I restore fourfold."

⁹And Jesus said to him, "Today salvation has come to this house, because he also is a son of Abraham; ¹⁰for the Son of Man has come to seek and to save that which was lost."

The Parable of the Minas

¹¹Now as they heard these things, He spoke another parable, because He was near Jerusalem and because they thought the kingdom of God would appear immediately. ¹²Therefore He said: "A certain nobleman went into a far country to receive for himself a kingdom and to return. ¹³So he called ten of his servants, delivered to them ten minas,ᵃ and said to them, 'Do business till I come.' ¹⁴But his citizens hated him, and sent a delegation after him, saying, 'We will not have this *man* to reign over us.'

¹⁵"And so it was that when he returned, having received the kingdom, he then commanded these servants, to whom he had given the money, to be called to him, that he might know how much every man had gained by trading. ¹⁶Then came the first, saying, 'Master, your mina has earned ten minas.' ¹⁷And he said to him, 'Well *done*, good servant; because you were faithful in a very little, have authority over ten cities.' ¹⁸And the second came, saying, 'Master, your mina has earned five minas.' ¹⁹Likewise he said to him, 'You also be over five cities.'

²⁰"Then another came, saying, 'Master, here is your mina, which I have kept put away in a handkerchief. ²¹For I feared you, because you are an austere man. You collect what you did not deposit, and reap what you did not sow.' ²²And he said to him, 'Out of your own mouth I will judge you, *you* wicked servant. You knew that I was an austere man, collecting what I did not deposit and reaping what I did not sow. ²³Why then did you not put my money in the bank, that at my coming I might have collected it with interest?'

²⁴"And he said to those who stood by, 'Take the mina from him, and give *it* to him who has ten minas.' ²⁵(But they said to him, 'Master, he has ten minas.') ²⁶'For I

ROMANCE FAQ

Q: When should we pursue professional marriage counseling?

Occasionally, outside help may be necessary in order to help your mate get beyond a particular problem. Dr. Frank Minirth says that the following half-dozen observations may mean that you should encourage your mate to seek a biblically trained counselor:

1. Physical Symptoms: An abrupt weight gain or loss, frequent headaches, complaints of poor physical health, or a loss of sleep or appetite.

2. Mental Symptoms: Observed mental anxiety, sadness of appearance, a confused state of mind, or prolonged or frequently repeated depression.

3. Frequent Complaints of Emotional Pain: Anyone suffering emotionally through a recent traumatic experience or who continues to have difficulty with an emotional problem from the past.

4. Impaired Basic Functioning: A mate having a difficult time coping at work, socially, or at home with the most basic responsibilities.

5. Dependence upon Drugs or Alcohol: Severe feelings of insignificance frequently result in chemical dependence, perhaps accompanied by thoughts of suicide.

6. Irresponsible Behavior: Inconsistent or immoral behavior.

If, over a period of time, you feel that the problem is much larger than your capability to help resolve it, then you should seek the advice of a trusted pastor or counselor who points people to the Scriptures and to Christ.

19:13 ᵃThe *mina* (Greek *mna,* Hebrew *minah*) was worth about three months' salary.

say to you, that to everyone who has will be given; and from him who does not have, even what he has will be taken away from him. ²⁷But bring here those enemies of mine, who did not want me to reign over them, and slay *them* before me.' "

The Triumphal Entry

²⁸When He had said this, He went on ahead, going up to Jerusalem. ²⁹And it came to pass, when He drew near to Bethphage[a] and Bethany, at the mountain called Olivet, *that* He sent two of His disciples, ³⁰saying, "Go into the village opposite *you,* where as you enter you will find a colt tied, on which no one has ever sat. Loose it and bring *it here.* ³¹And if anyone asks you, 'Why are you loosing *it?* thus you shall say to him, 'Because the Lord has need of it.' "

³²So those who were sent went their way and found *it* just as He had said to them. ³³But as they were loosing the colt, the owners of it said to them, "Why are you loosing the colt?"

³⁴And they said, "The Lord has need of him." ³⁵Then they brought him to Jesus. And they threw their own clothes on the colt, and they set Jesus on him. ³⁶And as He went, *many* spread their clothes on the road.

³⁷Then, as He was now drawing near the descent of the Mount of Olives, the whole multitude of the disciples began to rejoice and praise God with a loud voice for all the mighty works they had seen, ³⁸saying:

" 'Blessed is the King who comes in the name of the LORD!'[a]
Peace in heaven and glory in the highest!"

³⁹And some of the Pharisees called to Him from the crowd, "Teacher, rebuke Your disciples."

⁴⁰But He answered and said to them, "I tell you that if these should keep silent, the stones would immediately cry out."

Jesus Weeps over Jerusalem

⁴¹Now as He drew near, He saw the city and wept over it, ⁴²saying, "If you had known, even you, especially in this your day, the things *that make* for your peace! But now they are hidden from your eyes. ⁴³For days will come upon you when your enemies will build an embankment around you, surround you and close you in on every side, ⁴⁴and level you, and your children within you, to the ground; and they will not leave in you one stone upon another, because you did not know the time of your visitation."

Jesus Cleanses the Temple

⁴⁵Then He went into the temple and began to drive out those who bought and sold in it,[a] ⁴⁶saying to them, "It is written, 'My house is[a] a house of prayer,'[b] but you have made it a 'den of thieves.' "[c]

⁴⁷And He was teaching daily in the temple. But the chief priests, the scribes, and the leaders of the people sought to destroy Him, ⁴⁸and were unable to do anything; for all the people were very attentive to hear Him.

Jesus' Authority Questioned

20 Now it happened on one of those days, as He taught the people in the temple and preached the gospel, *that* the chief priests and the scribes, together with the elders, confronted *Him* ²and spoke to Him, saying, "Tell us, by what authority are You doing these things? Or who is he who gave You this authority?"

³But He answered and said to them, "I also will ask you one thing, and answer Me: ⁴The baptism of John—was it from heaven or from men?"

⁵And they reasoned among themselves, saying, "If we say, 'From heaven,' He will say, 'Why then[a] did you not believe him?' ⁶But if we say, 'From men,' all the people will stone us, for they are persuaded that John was a prophet." ⁷So they answered that they did not know where *it was* from.

⁸And Jesus said to them, "Neither will I tell you by what authority I do these things."

The Parable of the Wicked Vinedressers

⁹Then He began to tell the people this parable: "A certain man planted a vineyard, leased it to vinedressers, and went into a

---

19:29 [a]M-Text reads *Bethsphage.*   19:38 [a]Psalm 118:26   19:45 [a]NU-Text reads *those who were selling.* 19:46 [a]NU-Text reads *shall be.*   [b]Isaiah 56:7 [c]Jeremiah 7:11   20:5 [a]NU-Text and M-Text omit *then.*

far country for a long time. ¹⁰Now at vintage-time he sent a servant to the vinedressers, that they might give him some of the fruit of the vineyard. But the vinedressers beat him and sent *him* away empty-handed. ¹¹Again he sent another servant; and they beat him also, treated *him* shamefully, and sent *him* away empty-handed. ¹²And again he sent a third; and they wounded him also and cast *him* out.

¹³"Then the owner of the vineyard said, 'What shall I do? I will send my beloved son. Probably they will respect *him* when they see him.' ¹⁴But when the vinedressers saw him, they reasoned among themselves, saying, 'This is the heir. Come, let us kill him, that the inheritance may be ours.' ¹⁵So they cast him out of the vineyard and killed *him*. Therefore what will the owner of the vineyard do to them? ¹⁶He will come and destroy those vinedressers and give the vineyard to others."

And when they heard *it* they said, "Certainly not!"

¹⁷Then He looked at them and said, "What then is this that is written:

'The stone which the builders rejected
Has become the chief cornerstone'?ᵃ

¹⁸Whoever falls on that stone will be broken; but on whomever it falls, it will grind him to powder."

¹⁹And the chief priests and the scribes that very hour sought to lay hands on Him, but they feared the peopleᵃ—for they knew He had spoken this parable against them.

The Pharisees: Is It Lawful to Pay Taxes to Caesar?

²⁰So they watched *Him,* and sent spies who pretended to be righteous, that they might seize on His words, in order to deliver Him to the power and the authority of the governor. ²¹Then they asked Him, saying, "Teacher, we know that You say and teach rightly, and You do not show personal favoritism, but teach the way of God in truth: ²²Is it lawful for us to pay taxes to Caesar or not?"

²³But He perceived their craftiness, and said to them, "Why do you test Me?ᵃ ²⁴Show Me a denarius. Whose image and inscription does it have?"

They answered and said, "Caesar's."

20:17 ᵃPsalm 118:22
20:19 ᵃM-Text reads *but they were afraid.*
20:23 ᵃNU-Text omits *Why do you test Me?*

PARENTING MATTERS

Q: Is there a time when I should stop hugging and kissing my children?

As a child grows up and develops physically into a young woman or man, a concern may grow in you about how much physical affection you should give to your child of the opposite sex. The tendency is to think he or she is grown and doesn't need such affection.

Don't stop lavishing your children with physical affection! They need those hugs and kisses more than ever. A mom hugging her son and a dad hugging his daughter will send the message, "You are a young man (or a young woman) who is worthy of attention and affection from someone of the opposite sex." How many times have you heard young women say that they sought affection from boys because they never received it from their fathers? Don't make that mistake with your child!

Pursue a relationship with each of your children that includes appropriate touch. You know, if the apostle Paul can say to his friends at the church in Philippi, "God is my witness, how greatly I long for you all with the affection of Jesus Christ," (Phil. 1:8), then I think we parents can safely show some appropriate physical affection to our own children.

25And He said to them, "Render therefore to Caesar the things that are Caesar's, and to God the things that are God's."

26But they could not catch Him in His words in the presence of the people. And they marveled at His answer and kept silent.

The Sadducees: What About the Resurrection?

27Then some of the Sadducees, who deny that there is a resurrection, came to *Him* and asked Him, 28saying: "Teacher, Moses wrote to us *that* if a man's brother dies, having a wife, and he dies without children, his brother should take his wife and raise up offspring for his brother. 29Now there were seven brothers. And the first took a wife, and died without children. 30And the seconda took her as wife, and he died childless. 31Then the third took her, and in like manner the seven also; and they left no children,a and died. 32Last of all the woman died also. 33Therefore, in the resurrection, whose wife does she become? For all seven had her as wife."

34Jesus answered and said to them, "The sons of this age marry and are given in marriage. 35But those who are counted worthy to attain that age, and the resurrection from the dead, neither marry nor are given in marriage; 36nor can they die anymore, for they are equal to the angels and are sons of God, being sons of the resurrection. 37But even Moses showed in the *burning* bush *passage* that the dead are raised, when he called the Lord 'the God of Abraham, the God of Isaac, and the God of Jacob.'a 38For He is not the God of the dead but of the living, for all live to Him."

39Then some of the scribes answered and said, "Teacher, You have spoken well." 40But after that they dared not question Him anymore.

Jesus: How Can David Call His Descendant Lord?

41And He said to them, "How can they say that the Christ is the Son of David? 42Now David himself said in the Book of Psalms:

'The LORD said to my Lord,
  "Sit at My right hand,
43   Till I make Your enemies Your
      footstool."'a

44Therefore David calls Him 'Lord'; how is He then his Son?"

Beware of the Scribes

45Then, in the hearing of all the people, He said to His disciples, 46"Beware of the scribes, who desire to go around in long robes, love greetings in the marketplaces, the best seats in the synagogues, and the best places at feasts, 47who devour widows' houses, and for a pretense make long prayers. These will receive greater condemnation."

The Widow's Two Mites

21 And He looked up and saw the rich putting their gifts into the treasury, 2and He saw also a certain poor widow putting in two mites. 3So He said, "Truly I say to you that this poor widow has put in more than all; 4for all these out of their abundance have put in offerings for God,a but she out of her poverty put in all the livelihood that she had."

Jesus Predicts the Destruction of the Temple

5Then, as some spoke of the temple, how it was adorned with beautiful stones and donations, He said, 6"These things which you see—the days will come in which not *one* stone shall be left upon another that shall not be thrown down."

The Signs of the Times and the End of the Age

7So they asked Him, saying, "Teacher, but when will these things be? And what sign *will there be* when these things are about to take place?"

8And He said: "Take heed that you not be deceived. For many will come in My name, saying, 'I am *He*,' and, 'The time has

---

20:30 aNU-Text ends verse 30 here. **20:31** aNU-Text and M-Text read *the seven also left no children.*
20:37 aExodus 3:6, 15 **20:43** aPsalm 110:1
21:4 aNU-Text omits *for God.*

drawn near.' Therefore[a] do not go after them. [9]But when you hear of wars and commotions, do not be terrified; for these things must come to pass first, but the end *will* not *come* immediately."

[10]Then He said to them, "Nation will rise against nation, and kingdom against kingdom. [11]And there will be great earthquakes in various places, and famines and pestilences; and there will be fearful sights and great signs from heaven. [12]But before all these things, they will lay their hands on you and persecute *you,* delivering *you* up to the synagogues and prisons. You will be brought before kings and rulers for My name's sake. [13]But it will turn out for you as an occasion for testimony. [14]Therefore settle *it* in your hearts not to meditate beforehand on what you will answer; [15]for I will give you a mouth and wisdom which all your adversaries will not be able to contradict or resist. [16]You will be betrayed even by parents and brothers, relatives and friends; and they will put *some* of you to death. [17]And you will be hated by all for My name's sake. [18]But not a hair of your head shall be lost. [19]By your patience possess your souls.

The Destruction of Jerusalem

[20]"But when you see Jerusalem surrounded by armies, then know that its desolation is near. [21]Then let those who are in Judea flee to the mountains, let those who are in the midst of her depart, and let not those who are in the country enter her. [22]For these are the days of vengeance, that all things which are written may be fulfilled. [23]But woe to those who are pregnant and to those who are nursing babies in those days! For there will be great distress in the land and wrath upon this people. [24]And they will fall by the edge of the sword, and be led away captive into all nations. And Jerusalem will be trampled by Gentiles until the times of the Gentiles are fulfilled.

The Coming of the Son of Man

[25]"And there will be signs in the sun, in the moon, and in the stars; and on the earth distress of nations, with perplexity,

the sea and the waves roaring; [26]men's hearts failing them from fear and the expectation of those things which are coming on the earth, for the powers of the heavens will be shaken. [27]Then they will see the Son of Man coming in a cloud with power and great glory. [28]Now when these things begin to happen, look up and lift up your heads, because your redemption draws near."

The Parable of the Fig Tree

[29]Then He spoke to them a parable: "Look at the fig tree, and all the trees. [30]When they are already budding, you see and know for yourselves that summer is now near. [31]So you also, when you see these things happening, know that the kingdom of God is near. [32]Assuredly, I say to you, this generation will by no means pass away till all things take place. [33]Heaven and earth will pass away, but My words will by no means pass away.

The Importance of Watching

[34]"But take heed to yourselves, lest your hearts be weighed down with carousing, drunkenness, and cares of this life, and that Day come on you unexpectedly. [35]For it will come as a snare on all those who dwell on the face of the whole earth. [36]Watch therefore, and pray always that you may be counted worthy[a] to escape all these things that will come to pass, and to stand before the Son of Man."

[37]And in the daytime He was teaching in the temple, but at night He went out and stayed on the mountain called Olivet. [38]Then early in the morning all the people came to Him in the temple to hear Him.

The Plot to Kill Jesus

22 Now the Feast of Unleavened Bread drew near, which is called Passover. [2]And the chief priests and the scribes sought how they might kill Him, for they feared the people.

[3]Then Satan entered Judas, surnamed Iscariot, who was numbered among the twelve. [4]So he went his way and conferred with the chief priests and captains, how he might betray Him to them. [5]And they were glad, and agreed to give him money. [6]So he promised and sought opportunity to betray

---

21:8 [a]NU-Text omits *Therefore.*
21:36 [a]NU-Text reads *may have strength.*

Him to them in the absence of the multitude.

Jesus and His Disciples Prepare the Passover

[7]Then came the Day of Unleavened Bread, when the Passover must be killed. [8]And He sent Peter and John, saying, "Go and prepare the Passover for us, that we may eat."

[9]So they said to Him, "Where do You want us to prepare?"

[10]And He said to them, "Behold, when you have entered the city, a man will meet you carrying a pitcher of water; follow him into the house which he enters. [11]Then you shall say to the master of the house, 'The Teacher says to you, "Where is the guest room where I may eat the Passover with My disciples?" ' [12]Then he will show you a large, furnished upper room; there make ready."

[13]So they went and found it just as He had said to them, and they prepared the Passover.

Jesus Institutes the Lord's Supper

[14]When the hour had come, He sat down, and the twelve[a] apostles with Him.

[15]Then He said to them, "With *fervent* desire I have desired to eat this Passover with you before I suffer; [16]for I say to you, I will no longer eat of it until it is fulfilled in the kingdom of God."

[17]Then He took the cup, and gave thanks, and said, "Take this and divide *it* among yourselves; [18]for I say to you,[a] I will not drink of the fruit of the vine until the kingdom of God comes."

[19]And He took bread, gave thanks and broke *it,* and gave *it* to them, saying, "This is My body which is given for you; do this in remembrance of Me."

[20]Likewise He also *took* the cup after supper, saying, "This cup *is* the new covenant in My blood, which is shed for you. [21]But behold, the hand of My betrayer *is* with Me on the table. [22]And truly the Son of Man goes as it has been determined, but woe to that man by whom He is betrayed!"

[23]Then they began to question among themselves, which of them it was who would do this thing.

22:14 [a]NU-Text omits *twelve.*
22:18 [a]NU-Text adds *from now on.*

ROMANTIC QUOTES AND NOTES
Rise and Pray

If we are to stand up to the temptations coming our way, we must become more aware of Satan's tactics. The world certainly isn't going to issue warnings!

I've never seen a video rental store, for example, that placed warnings above certain movies: "Caution: This film could create an addiction to pornography, cause infidelity and violence, and result in the loss of your family."

I'm especially vulnerable to the enemy's schemes at certain times:

• *When I am alone.* Like most people, I'm most tempted when I'm away on a trip, apart from those who know me.

• *When I'm with someone willing to be a part of Satan's scheme.* The enemy likes to throw me in with people who tempt me to gossip, or to go with the crowd, to be a people pleaser. "Evil company corrupts good habits" (1 Cor. 15:33).

• *When I am tired.* When I am exhausted, I become susceptible to foolish thoughts about God, myself, and others. I need to retreat periodically to allow God to replenish my strength.

• *When I think I can justify my actions.* I am constantly amazed at my ability to rationalize wrong choices.

A friend who found help at Alcoholics Anonymous shared with me the acronym H.A.L.T. He said that alcoholics are taught to be on guard against temptation especially when they are Hungry, Angry, Lonely, or Tired. All of us yield to sin when our flesh is weak. We need to be spiritually on guard. I've found it's never a bad time to take Jesus' command, "Rise and pray" (Luke 22:46).

The Disciples Argue About Greatness

24Now there was also a dispute among them, as to which of them should be considered the greatest. 25And He said to them, "The kings of the Gentiles exercise lordship over them, and those who exercise authority over them are called 'benefactors.' 26But not so *among* you; on the contrary, he who is greatest among you, let him be as the younger, and he who governs as he who serves. 27For who *is* greater, he who sits at the table, or he who serves? *Is* it not he who sits at the table? Yet I am among you as the One who serves.

28"But you are those who have continued with Me in My trials. 29And I bestow upon you a kingdom, just as My Father bestowed *one* upon Me, 30that you may eat and drink at My table in My kingdom, and sit on thrones judging the twelve tribes of Israel."

Jesus Predicts Peter's Denial

31And the Lord said,a "Simon, Simon! Indeed, Satan has asked for you, that he may sift *you* as wheat. 32But I have prayed for you, that your faith should not fail; and when you have returned to *Me,* strengthen your brethren."

33But he said to Him, "Lord, I am ready to go with You, both to prison and to death."

34Then He said, "I tell you, Peter, the rooster shall not crow this day before you will deny three times that you know Me."

Supplies for the Road

35And He said to them, "When I sent you without money bag, knapsack, and sandals, did you lack anything?"

So they said, "Nothing."

36Then He said to them, "But now, he who has a money bag, let him take *it,* and likewise a knapsack; and he who has no sword, let him sell his garment and buy one. 37For I say to you that this which is written must still be accomplished in Me: 'And He was numbered with the transgressors.'a For the things concerning Me have an end."

38So they said, "Lord, look, here *are* two swords."

And He said to them, "It is enough."

The Prayer in the Garden

39Coming out, He went to the Mount of Olives, as He was accustomed, and His disciples also followed Him. 40When He came to the place, He said to them, "Pray that you may not enter into temptation."

41And He was withdrawn from them about a stone's throw, and He knelt down and prayed, 42saying, "Father, if it is Your will, take this cup away from Me; nevertheless not My will, but Yours, be done." 43Then an angel appeared to Him from heaven, strengthening Him. 44And being in agony, He prayed more earnestly. Then His sweat became like great drops of blood falling down to the ground.a

45When He rose up from prayer, and had come to His disciples, He found them sleeping from sorrow. 46Then He said to them, "Why do you sleep? Rise and pray, lest you enter into temptation."

Betrayal and Arrest in Gethsemane

47And while He was still speaking, behold, a multitude; and he who was called Judas, one of the twelve, went before them and drew near to Jesus to kiss Him. 48But Jesus said to him, "Judas, are you betraying the Son of Man with a kiss?"

49When those around Him saw what was going to happen, they said to Him, "Lord, shall we strike with the sword?" 50And one of them struck the servant of the high priest and cut off his right ear.

51But Jesus answered and said, "Permit even this." And He touched his ear and healed him.

52Then Jesus said to the chief priests, captains of the temple, and the elders who had come to Him, "Have you come out, as against a robber, with swords and clubs? 53When I was with you daily in the temple, you did not try to seize Me. But this is your hour, and the power of darkness."

Peter Denies Jesus, and Weeps Bitterly

54Having arrested Him, they led *Him* and brought Him into the high priest's house. But Peter followed at a distance.

22:31 aNU-Text omits *And the Lord said.*
22:37 aIsaiah 53:12 **22:44** aNU-Text brackets verses 43 and 44 as not in the original text.

55Now when they had kindled a fire in the midst of the courtyard and sat down together, Peter sat among them. 56And a certain servant girl, seeing him as he sat by the fire, looked intently at him and said, "This man was also with Him."

57But he denied Him,a saying, "Woman, I do not know Him."

58And after a little while another saw him and said, "You also are of them."

But Peter said, "Man, I am not!"

59Then after about an hour had passed, another confidently affirmed, saying, "Surely this *fellow* also was with Him, for he is a Galilean."

60But Peter said, "Man, I do not know what you are saying!"

Immediately, while he was still speaking, the roostera crowed. 61And the Lord turned and looked at Peter. Then Peter remembered the word of the Lord, how He had said to him, "Before the rooster crows,a you will deny Me three times." 62So Peter went out and wept bitterly.

Jesus Mocked and Beaten

63Now the men who held Jesus mocked Him and beat Him. 64And having blindfolded Him, they struck Him on the face and asked Him,a saying, "Prophesy! Who is the one who struck You?" 65And many other things they blasphemously spoke against Him.

Jesus Faces the Sanhedrin

66As soon as it was day, the elders of the people, both chief priests and scribes, came together and led Him into their council, saying, 67"If You are the Christ, tell us."

But He said to them, "If I tell you, you will by no means believe. 68And if I also ask *you,* you will by no means answer Me or let *Me* go.a 69Hereafter the Son of Man will sit on the right hand of the power of God."

70Then they all said, "Are You then the Son of God?"

So He said to them, "You *rightly* say that I am."

71And they said, "What further testimony do we need? For we have heard it ourselves from His own mouth."

Jesus Handed Over to Pontius Pilate

23 Then the whole multitude of them arose and led Him to Pilate. 2And they began to accuse Him, saying, "We found this *fellow* perverting thea nation, and forbidding to pay taxes to Caesar, saying that He Himself is Christ, a King."

3Then Pilate asked Him, saying, "Are You the King of the Jews?"

He answered him and said, "*It is as* you say."

4So Pilate said to the chief priests and the crowd, "I find no fault in this Man."

5But they were the more fierce, saying, "He stirs up the people, teaching throughout all Judea, beginning from Galilee to this place."

Jesus Faces Herod

6When Pilate heard of Galilee,a he asked if the Man were a Galilean. 7And as soon as he knew that He belonged to Herod's jurisdiction, he sent Him to Herod, who was also in Jerusalem at that time. 8Now when Herod saw Jesus, he was exceedingly glad; for he had desired for a long *time* to see Him, because he had heard many things about Him, and he hoped to see some miracle done by Him. 9Then he questioned Him with many words, but He answered him nothing. 10And the chief priests and scribes stood and vehemently accused Him. 11Then Herod, with his men of war, treated Him with contempt and mocked *Him,* arrayed Him in a gorgeous robe, and sent Him back to Pilate. 12That very day Pilate and Herod became friends with each other, for previously they had been at enmity with each other.

Taking the Place of Barabbas

13Then Pilate, when he had called together the chief priests, the rulers, and the people, 14said to them, "You have brought this Man to me, as one who misleads the people. And indeed, having examined *Him* in your

---

22:57 aNU-Text reads *denied it.* **22:60** aNU-Text and M-Text read *a rooster.* **22:61** aNU-Text adds *today.* **22:64** aNU-Text reads *And having blindfolded Him, they asked Him.* **22:68** aNU-Text omits *also* and *Me or let Me go.* **23:2** aNU-Text reads *our.* **23:6** aNU-Text omits *of Galilee.*

presence, I have found no fault in this Man concerning those things of which you accuse Him; [15]no, neither did Herod, for I sent you back to him;[a] and indeed nothing deserving of death has been done by Him. [16]I will therefore chastise Him and release *Him*" [17](for it was necessary for him to release one to them at the feast).[a]

[18]And they all cried out at once, saying, "Away with this *Man,* and release to us Barabbas"— [19]who had been thrown into prison for a certain rebellion made in the city, and for murder.

[20]Pilate, therefore, wishing to release Jesus, again called out to them. [21]But they shouted, saying, "Crucify *Him,* crucify Him!"

[22]Then he said to them the third time, "Why, what evil has He done? I have found no reason for death in Him. I will therefore chastise Him and let *Him* go."

[23]But they were insistent, demanding with loud voices that He be crucified. And the voices of these men and of the chief priests prevailed.[a] [24]So Pilate gave sentence that it should be as they requested. [25]And he released to them[a] the one they requested, who for rebellion and murder had been thrown into prison; but he delivered Jesus to their will.

The King on a Cross

[26]Now as they led Him away, they laid hold of a certain man, Simon a Cyrenian, who was coming from the country, and on him they laid the cross that he might bear *it* after Jesus.

[27]And a great multitude of the people followed Him, and women who also mourned and lamented Him. [28]But Jesus, turning to them, said, "Daughters of Jerusalem, do not weep for Me, but weep for yourselves and for your children. [29]For

indeed the days are coming in which they will say, 'Blessed *are* the barren, wombs that never bore, and breasts which never nursed!' [30]Then they will begin 'to say to the mountains, "Fall on us!" and to the hills, "Cover us!"' [a] [31]For if they do these things in the green wood, what will be done in the dry?"

[32]There were also two others, criminals, led with Him to be put to death. [33]And when they had come to the place called Calvary, there they crucified Him, and the criminals, one on the right hand and the other on the left. [34]Then Jesus said, "Father, forgive them, for they do not know what they do."[a]

And they divided His garments and cast lots. [35]And the people stood looking on. But even the rulers with them sneered, saying, "He saved others; let Him save Himself if He is the Christ, the chosen of God."

[36]The soldiers also mocked Him, coming and offering Him sour wine, [37]and saying, "If You are the King of the Jews, save Yourself."

[38]And an inscription also was written over Him in letters of Greek, Latin, and Hebrew:[a]

THIS IS THE KING OF THE JEWS.

[39]Then one of the criminals who were hanged blasphemed Him, saying, "If You are the Christ,[a] save Yourself and us."

[40]But the other, answering, rebuked him, saying, "Do you not even fear God, seeing you are under the same condemnation? [41]And we indeed justly, for we receive the due reward of our deeds; but this Man has done nothing wrong." [42]Then he said to Jesus, "Lord,[a] remember me when You come into Your kingdom."

[43]And Jesus said to him, "Assuredly, I say to you, today you will be with Me in Paradise."

Jesus Dies on the Cross

[44]Now it was[a] about the sixth hour, and there was darkness over all the earth until the ninth hour. [45]Then the sun was darkened,[a] and the veil of the temple was torn in two. [46]And when Jesus had cried out with a loud voice, He said, "Father, 'into Your hands I commit My spirit.' "[a] Having said this, He breathed His last.

23:15 [a]NU-Text reads *for he sent Him back to us.*
23:17 [a]NU-Text omits verse 17.   23:23 [a]NU-Text omits *and of the chief priests.*   23:25 [a]NU-Text and M-Text omit *to them.*   23:30 [a]Hosea 10:8
23:34 [a]NU-Text brackets the first sentence as a later addition.   23:38 [a]NU-Text omits *written* and *in letters of Greek, Latin, and Hebrew.*   23:39 [a]NU-Text reads *Are You not the Christ?*   23:42 [a]NU-Text reads *And he said, "Jesus, remember me.*   23:44 [a]NU-Text adds *already.*   23:45 [a]NU-Text reads *obscured.*
23:46 [a]Psalm 31:5

DEVOTIONS FOR COUPLES • 23:34
Prayerfully Apply the Oil of Forgiveness

No one will ever label me the consummate handyman. When Barbara's Saturday morning honey-do list has items like "stop the clunking sound in the dryer" or "fix the drip in the shower nozzle," I'd rather go hunting. But when contraptions are squeaking, squawking, and sticking, I usually rely on one handy tool to save the day—the amazing lubricating spray.

When it comes to squeaks in the martial relationship, forgiveness is a bit like what's in that familiar blue-and-yellow can. Mixing forgiveness with the habit of praying together is one way to reduce friction and make a marriage run more smoothly. As one wife put it, "How can you remain angry at someone who is praying blessings over you daily and asking forgiveness for wrongs committed?"

Praying together daily gives couples the perfect opportunity to speak the two most powerful statements in the healing of relationships: "Will you forgive me?" and "Yes, I will forgive you."

Because we know that incorrect ideas can make forgiveness seem like swimming upstream, we would like to clearly state that:

- forgiveness does not mean excusing sin
- forgiveness does not mean that you will forget the offender's sin
- forgiveness does not require denying or stuffing your feelings
- forgiveness does not always lead to instant reconciliation

Understanding even a few basics about how to forgive others is an important steppingstone toward relational and personal healing.

Forgiveness *embraces the offender*. By forgiving those who hurt Him the most, Christ modeled forgiveness at its best.

Forgiveness *is proactive*. On the cross, Jesus said, "Father, forgive them, for they do not know what they do" (Luke 23:34). To be like Jesus, we must also forgive others even before they ask for it.

Forgiveness *surrenders the right to get even*. As we have stated repeatedly in this Bible, the essence of forgiveness in a marriage is letting go of your right to punish and see justice done. A forgiving spouse ceases to demand restitution for hurt feelings and wounded pride.

The other night, before we prayed together, one of us turned to the other and said, "Sweetheart, before we pray together, there's something I need to ask forgiveness for." After some dialogue, the words, "I forgive you" were spoken. Praying together after such a time has a sweet, tender side, because we both know that He first forgave us.

Forgiving your mate will sometimes be hard, but when that happens, meditate a little on what Christ did for you.

---

⁴⁷So when the centurion saw what had happened, he glorified God, saying, "Certainly this was a righteous Man!"

⁴⁸And the whole crowd who came together to that sight, seeing what had been done, beat their breasts and returned. ⁴⁹But all His acquaintances, and the women who followed Him from Galilee, stood at a distance, watching these things.

Jesus Buried in Joseph's Tomb

⁵⁰Now behold, *there was* a man named Joseph, a council member, a good and just man. ⁵¹He had not consented to their decision and deed. *He was* from Arimathea, a city of the Jews, who himself was also waiting^a for the kingdom of God. ⁵²This man went to Pilate and asked for the body of Jesus. ⁵³Then he took it down, wrapped it in linen, and laid it in a tomb *that was* hewn out of the rock, where no one had ever lain before. ⁵⁴That day was the Preparation, and the Sabbath drew near.

23:51 ªNU-Text reads *who was waiting*

⁵⁵And the women who had come with Him from Galilee followed after, and they observed the tomb and how His body was laid. ⁵⁶Then they returned and prepared spices and fragrant oils. And they rested on the Sabbath according to the commandment.

He Is Risen

24 Now on the first *day* of the week, very early in the morning, they, and certain *other women* with them,ᵃ came to the tomb bringing the spices which they had prepared. ²But they found the stone rolled away from the tomb. ³Then they went in and did not find the body of the Lord Jesus. ⁴And it happened, as they were greatlyᵃ perplexed about this, that behold, two men stood by them in shining garments. ⁵Then, as they were afraid and bowed *their* faces to the earth, they said to them, "Why do you seek the living among the dead? ⁶He is not here, but is risen! Remember how He spoke to you when He was still in Galilee, ⁷saying, 'The Son of Man must be delivered into the hands of sinful men, and be crucified, and the third day rise again.'"

⁸And they remembered His words. ⁹Then they returned from the tomb and told all these things to the eleven and to all the rest. ¹⁰It was Mary Magdalene, Joanna, Mary *the mother* of James, and the other *women* with them, who told these things to the apostles. ¹¹And their words seemed to them like idle tales, and they did not believe them. ¹²But Peter arose and ran to the tomb; and stooping down, he saw the linen cloths lyingᵃ by themselves; and he departed, marveling to himself at what had happened.

The Road to Emmaus

¹³Now behold, two of them were traveling that same day to a village called Emmaus, which was seven milesᵃ from Jerusalem. ¹⁴And they talked together of all these things which had happened. ¹⁵So it was, while they conversed and reasoned, that Jesus Himself drew near and went with them. ¹⁶But their eyes were restrained, so that they did not know Him.

¹⁷And He said to them, "What kind of conversation *is* this that you have with one another as you walk and are sad?"ᵃ

24:1 ᵃNU-Text omits *and certain other women with them.* 24:4 ᵃNU-Text omits *greatly.* 24:12 ᵃNU-Text omits *lying* 24:13 ᵃLiterally *sixty stadia* 24:17 ᵃNU-Text reads *as you walk? And they stood still, looking sad.*

ROMANTIC QUOTES AND NOTES
Where Our Hope Lies

I came across a fascinating list of questions lately that all have the same answer. Can you guess what it is?

• What gives a widow courage as she stands beside a fresh grave?
• What is the ultimate hope of the cripple, the amputee, the abused or the burn victim?
• How can parents of a brain-damaged or physically handicapped child keep from living their lives totally and completely depressed?
• Where do the thoughts of a young couple go when they finally recover from the terrible grief of losing their baby?

• When a family receives the tragic news that a dad was killed in a plane crash or a son overdosed on drugs, what single truth becomes its whole focus?
• What is the final answer to pain, mourning, senility, insanity, terminal diseases, sudden calamities, and fatal accidents?

The answer to each of these questions is: *the hope God gives us because of the bodily resurrection of Jesus Christ.* The pivotal point in all of human history is the resurrection of Christ. The one thing that separates Christianity from other religions is that *God conquered death.* Since Jesus Christ has defeated death, He can offer eternal life to all who believe in Him!

He is risen! Yes, Christ is risen indeed!

¹⁸Then the one whose name was Cleopas answered and said to Him, "Are You the only stranger in Jerusalem, and have You not known the things which happened there in these days?"

¹⁹And He said to them, "What things?"

So they said to Him, "The things concerning Jesus of Nazareth, who was a Prophet mighty in deed and word before God and all the people, ²⁰and how the chief priests and our rulers delivered Him to be condemned to death, and crucified Him. ²¹But we were hoping that it was He who was going to redeem Israel. Indeed, besides all this, today is the third day since these things happened. ²²Yes, and certain women of our company, who arrived at the tomb early, astonished us. ²³When they did not find His body, they came saying that they had also seen a vision of angels who said He was alive. ²⁴And certain of those *who were* with us went to the tomb and found *it* just as the women had said; but Him they did not see."

²⁵Then He said to them, "O foolish ones, and slow of heart to believe in all that the prophets have spoken! ²⁶Ought not the Christ to have suffered these things and to enter into His glory?" ²⁷And beginning at Moses and all the Prophets, He expounded to them in all the Scriptures the things concerning Himself.

The Disciples' Eyes Opened

²⁸Then they drew near to the village where they were going, and He indicated that He would have gone farther. ²⁹But they constrained Him, saying, "Abide with us, for it is toward evening, and the day is far spent." And He went in to stay with them.

³⁰Now it came to pass, as He sat at the table with them, that He took bread, blessed and broke *it,* and gave it to them. ³¹Then their eyes were opened and they knew Him; and He vanished from their sight.

³²And they said to one another, "Did not our heart burn within us while He talked with us on the road, and while He opened the Scriptures to us?" ³³So they rose up that very hour and returned to Jerusalem, and found the eleven and those *who were*

with them gathered together, ³⁴saying, "The Lord is risen indeed, and has appeared to Simon!" ³⁵And they told about the things *that had happened* on the road, and how He was known to them in the breaking of bread.

Jesus Appears to His Disciples

³⁶Now as they said these things, Jesus Himself stood in the midst of them, and said to them, "Peace to you." ³⁷But they were terrified and frightened, and supposed they had seen a spirit. ³⁸And He said to them, "Why are you troubled? And why do doubts arise in your hearts? ³⁹Behold My hands and My feet, that it is I Myself. Handle Me and see, for a spirit does not have flesh and bones as you see I have."

⁴⁰When He had said this, He showed them His hands and His feet.ᵃ ⁴¹But while they still did not believe for joy, and marveled, He said to them, "Have you any food here?" ⁴²So they gave Him a piece of a broiled fish and some honeycomb.ᵃ ⁴³And He took *it* and ate in their presence.

The Scriptures Opened

⁴⁴Then He said to them, "These *are* the words which I spoke to you while I was still with you, that all things must be fulfilled which were written in the Law of Moses and *the* Prophets and *the* Psalms concerning Me." ⁴⁵And He opened their understanding, that they might comprehend the Scriptures.

⁴⁶Then He said to them, "Thus it is written, and thus it was necessary for the Christ to suffer and to riseᵃ from the dead the third day, ⁴⁷and that repentance and remission of sins should be preached in His name to all nations, beginning at Jerusalem. ⁴⁸And you are witnesses of these things. ⁴⁹Behold, I send the Promise of My Father upon you; but tarry in the city of Jerusalemᵃ until you are endued with power from on high."

24:40 ᵃSome printed New Testaments omit this verse. It is found in nearly all Greek manuscripts.
24:42 ᵃNU-Text omits *and some honeycomb.*
24:46 ᵃNU-Text reads *written, that the Christ should suffer and rise.* **24:49** ᵃNU-Text omits *of Jerusalem.*

The Ascension

⁵⁰And He led them out as far as Bethany, and He lifted up His hands and blessed them. ⁵¹Now it came to pass, while He blessed them, that He was parted from them and carried up into heaven. ⁵²And they worshiped Him, and returned to Jerusalem with great joy, ⁵³and were continually in the temple praising and[a] blessing God. Amen.[b]

24:53 [a]NU-Text omits *praising and.* [b]NU-Text omits *Amen.*

JOHN

THE BIBLE'S FINAL BIOGRAPHICAL ACCOUNT of Jesus is very different from the first three. The apostle John, one of the original twelve disciples, wants his readers to understand that Jesus is God in human flesh. This is clear from the very first chapter, where John uses the term "the Word" (which he identifies as God in v. 1) to describe Jesus becoming flesh and dwelling among us (1:14).

John's Gospel focuses on the identity of Jesus—from John the Baptist's declaration that Jesus is "The Lamb of God who takes away the sins of the world" (1:29), to the seven "I am" statements of Jesus ("I am the bread of life," 6:35, 48; "I am the light of the world," 8:12; 9:5; "I am the door," 10:7, 9; "I am the good shepherd," 10:11, 14; "I am the resurrection and the life," 11:25; "I am the way, the truth, and the life," 14:6; "I am the true vine," 15:1–5). In one confrontation with Jewish leaders, Jesus declares, "Before Abraham was, I AM" (8:58), using the very covenant name of God.

The Gospel of John emphasizes that we find new life in knowing Jesus. It contains the best-known and most quoted verse in all of Scripture, John 3:16, "For God so loved the world that He gave His only begotten Son, that whoever believes in Him should not perish but have everlasting life." Jesus makes this simple, clear presentation of the gospel to the Jewish leader Nicodemus after telling him that he must be "born again" in order to see the kingdom of God. Jesus tells His disciples that He came to give them life, that they "may have it more abundantly" (10:10). John explains that he wrote his Gospel "that you may believe that Jesus is the Christ, the Son of God, and that believing you may have life in His name" (20:31).

One key passage in John's Gospel has been significant in our spiritual growth. In chapter 15, John recounts Jesus' teaching on the importance of abiding in Him so that our lives bear much spiritual fruit (vv. 1–10). Abiding in Jesus means that we draw our meaning, purpose, and even our life from our relationship with Him. Without Him, we can do nothing (15:5). For our marriages and our families to be all that God wants them to be, we *must* learn how to abide in Jesus.

The Gospel of John was written to encourage our faith in Jesus Christ and finding life in Him. Many people recommend that those who are seeking God read this book first because it is designed to introduce people to the Savior. This is the book that helps all of us believe. Read it and grow in faith and knowledge of the King of kings and Lord of lords.

The Eternal Word

1 In the beginning was the Word, and the Word was with God, and the Word was God. [2]He was in the beginning with God. [3]All things were made through Him, and without Him nothing was made that was made. [4]In Him was life, and the life was the light of men. [5]And the light shines in the darkness, and the darkness did not comprehend[a] it.

John's Witness: The True Light

[6]There was a man sent from God, whose name *was* John. [7]This man came for a witness, to bear witness of the Light, that all through him might believe. [8]He was not that Light, but *was sent* to bear witness of that Light. [9]That was the true Light which gives light to every man coming into the world.[a]

[10]He was in the world, and the world was made through Him, and the world did not know Him. [11]He came to His own,[a] and His own[b] did not receive Him. [12]But as many as received Him, to them He gave the right to become children of God, to those who believe in His name: [13]who were born, not of blood, nor of the will of the flesh, nor of the will of man, but of God.

The Word Becomes Flesh

[14]And the Word became flesh and dwelt among us, and we beheld His glory, the glory as of the only begotten of the Father, full of grace and truth.

[15]John bore witness of Him and cried out, saying, "This was He of whom I said, 'He who comes after me is preferred before me, for He was before me.'"

[16]And[a] of His fullness we have all received, and grace for grace. [17]For the law was given through Moses, *but* grace and truth came through Jesus Christ. [18]No one has seen God at any time. The only begotten Son,[a] who is in the bosom of the Father, He has declared *Him.*

A Voice in the Wilderness

[19]Now this is the testimony of John, when the Jews sent priests and Levites from Jerusalem to ask him, "Who are you?"

[20]He confessed, and did not deny, but confessed, "I am not the Christ."

[21]And they asked him, "What then? Are you Elijah?"

He said, "I am not."

"Are you the Prophet?"

And he answered, "No."

[22]Then they said to him, "Who are you, that we may give an answer to those who sent us? What do you say about yourself?"

[23]He said: "I *am*

'The voice of one crying in the
     wilderness:
"Make straight the way of the LORD,"'[a]

as the prophet Isaiah said."

[24]Now those who were sent were from the Pharisees. [25]And they asked him, saying, "Why then do you baptize if you are not the Christ, nor Elijah, nor the Prophet?"

[26]John answered them, saying, "I baptize with water, but there stands One among you whom you do not know. [27]It is He who, coming after me, is preferred before me, whose sandal strap I am not worthy to loose."

[28]These things were done in Bethabara[a] beyond the Jordan, where John was baptizing.

The Lamb of God

[29]The next day John saw Jesus coming toward him, and said, "Behold! The Lamb of God who takes away the sin of the world!

INTIMATE MOMENTS

Men view romance differently from women. Ask your husband to describe what's romantic to him. Don't be surprised when his ideas sound very different from yours! Then consider sharing with him what you think is romantic.

1:5 [a]Or *overcome* **1:9** [a]Or *That was the true Light which, coming into the world, gives light to every man.*
1:11 [a]That is, His own things or domain [b]That is, His own people **1:16** [a]NU-Text reads *For.*
1:18 [a]NU-Text reads *only begotten God.*
1:23 [a]Isaiah 40:3 **1:28** [a]NU-Text and M-Text read *Bethany.*

[30]This is He of whom I said, 'After me comes a Man who is preferred before me, for He was before me.' [31]I did not know Him; but that He should be revealed to Israel, therefore I came baptizing with water."

[32]And John bore witness, saying, "I saw the Spirit descending from heaven like a dove, and He remained upon Him. [33]I did not know Him, but He who sent me to baptize with water said to me, 'Upon whom you see the Spirit descending, and remaining on Him, this is He who baptizes with the Holy Spirit.' [34]And I have seen and testified that this is the Son of God."

The First Disciples

[35]Again, the next day, John stood with two of his disciples. [36]And looking at Jesus as He walked, he said, "Behold the Lamb of God!"

[37]The two disciples heard him speak, and they followed Jesus. [38]Then Jesus turned, and seeing them following, said to them, "What do you seek?"

They said to Him, "Rabbi" (which is to say, when translated, Teacher), "where are You staying?"

[39]He said to them, "Come and see." They came and saw where He was staying, and remained with Him that day (now it was about the tenth hour).

[40]One of the two who heard John *speak,* and followed Him, was Andrew, Simon Peter's brother. [41]He first found his own brother Simon, and said to him, "We have found the Messiah" (which is translated, the Christ). [42]And he brought him to Jesus.

Now when Jesus looked at him, He said, "You are Simon the son of Jonah.[a] You shall be called Cephas" (which is translated, A Stone).

Philip and Nathanael

[43]The following day Jesus wanted to go to Galilee, and He found Philip and said to him, "Follow Me." [44]Now Philip was from Bethsaida, the city of Andrew and Peter. [45]Philip found Nathanael and said to him, "We have found Him of whom Moses in the law, and also the prophets, wrote— Jesus of Nazareth, the son of Joseph." [46]And Nathanael said to him, "Can anything good come out of Nazareth?"

Philip said to him, "Come and see."

[47]Jesus saw Nathanael coming toward Him, and said of him, "Behold, an Israelite indeed, in whom is no deceit!"

[48]Nathanael said to Him, "How do You know me?"

Jesus answered and said to him, "Before Philip called you, when you were under the fig tree, I saw you."

[49]Nathanael answered and said to Him, "Rabbi, You are the Son of God! You are the King of Israel!"

[50]Jesus answered and said to him, "Because I said to you, 'I saw you under the fig tree,' do you believe? You will see greater things than these." [51]And He said to him, "Most assuredly, I say to you, hereafter[a] you shall see heaven open, and the angels of God ascending and descending upon the Son of Man."

Water Turned to Wine

2 On the third day there was a wedding in Cana of Galilee, and the mother of Jesus was there. [2]Now both Jesus and His disciples were invited to the wedding. [3]And when they ran out of wine, the mother of Jesus said to Him, "They have no wine."

[4]Jesus said to her, "Woman, what does your concern have to do with Me? My hour has not yet come."

[5]His mother said to the servants, "Whatever He says to you, do *it.*"

[6]Now there were set there six waterpots of stone, according to the manner of purification of the Jews, containing twenty or thirty gallons apiece. [7]Jesus said to them, "Fill the waterpots with water." And they filled them up to the brim. [8]And He said to them, "Draw *some* out now, and take *it* to the master of the feast." And they took *it.* [9]When the master of the feast had tasted the water that was made wine, and did not know where it came from (but the servants who had drawn the water knew), the master of the feast called the bridegroom. [10]And he said to him, "Every man at the beginning sets out the good wine, and when the *guests* have well

---

1:42 [a]NU-Text reads *John.*
1:51 [a]NU-Text omits *hereafter.*

drunk, then the inferior. You have kept the good wine until now!"

[11]This beginning of signs Jesus did in Cana of Galilee, and manifested His glory; and His disciples believed in Him.

[12]After this He went down to Capernaum, He, His mother, His brothers, and His disciples; and they did not stay there many days.

Jesus Cleanses the Temple

[13]Now the Passover of the Jews was at hand, and Jesus went up to Jerusalem. [14]And He found in the temple those who sold oxen and sheep and doves, and the money changers doing business. [15]When He had made a whip of cords, He drove them all out of the temple, with the sheep and the oxen, and poured out the changers' money and overturned the tables. [16]And He said to those who sold doves, "Take these things away! Do not make My Father's house a house of merchandise!" [17]Then His disciples remembered that it was written, "Zeal for Your house has eaten[a] Me up."[b]

[18]So the Jews answered and said to Him, "What sign do You show to us, since You do these things?"

[19]Jesus answered and said to them, "Destroy this temple, and in three days I will raise it up."

[20]Then the Jews said, "It has taken forty-six years to build this temple, and will You raise it up in three days?" [21]But He was speaking of the temple of His body. [22]Therefore, when He had risen from the dead, His disciples remembered that He had said this to them;[a] and they believed the Scripture and the word which Jesus had said.

The Discerner of Hearts

[23]Now when He was in Jerusalem at the Passover, during the feast, many believed in His name when they saw the signs which He did. [24]But Jesus did not commit Himself to them, because He knew all men, [25]and had no need that anyone should testify of man, for He knew what was in man.

2:17 [a]NU-Text and M-Text read will eat.　[b]Psalm 69:9
2:22 [a]NU-Text and M-Text omit to them.

The New Birth

3 There was a man of the Pharisees named Nicodemus, a ruler of the Jews. [2]This man came to Jesus by night and said to Him, "Rabbi, we know that You are a teacher come from God; for no one can do these signs that You do unless God is with him."

[3]Jesus answered and said to him, "Most assuredly, I say to you, unless one is born again, he cannot see the kingdom of God."

[4]Nicodemus said to Him, "How can a man be born when he is old? Can he enter a second time into his mother's womb and be born?"

ROMANCE FAQ

Q: How can I best see my mate as a gift from God?

A good place to start is by asking how Adam received Eve. The way many read the familiar Genesis account, Adam's response seems ho-hum, "This is now bone of my bones and flesh of my flesh; she shall be called Woman, because she was taken out of Man" (Gen. 2:23). But I like The Living Bible paraphrase, "This is it!" In other words, Adam got so excited he was beside himself.

Of course, Eve looked pretty good to Adam. That's why he said, "This is bone of my bone and flesh of my flesh." She definitely looked better to him than all the animals he had just named. But there is a cornerstone principle for marriage here that we mustn't miss: Adam had faith in God's integrity.

Eve had done nothing to earn Adam's response. Adam knew only one thing about Eve: She was a gift from the God he knew intimately. Adam simply accepted her because God made her for him, and he knew that God could be trusted.

In the same way, God wants us to receive the spouse He has custom-made for us. He can still be trusted. Will you receive your spouse as God's gift for you?

⁵Jesus answered, "Most assuredly, I say to you, unless one is born of water and the Spirit, he cannot enter the kingdom of God. ⁶That which is born of the flesh is flesh, and that which is born of the Spirit is spirit. ⁷Do not marvel that I said to you, 'You must be born again.' ⁸The wind blows where it wishes, and you hear the sound of it, but cannot tell where it comes from and where it goes. So is everyone who is born of the Spirit."

⁹Nicodemus answered and said to Him, "How can these things be?"

¹⁰Jesus answered and said to him, "Are you the teacher of Israel, and do not know these things? ¹¹Most assuredly, I say to you, We speak what We know and testify what We have seen, and you do not receive Our witness. ¹²If I have told you earthly things and you do not believe, how will you believe if I tell you heavenly things? ¹³No one has ascended to heaven but He who came down from heaven, *that is,* the Son of Man who is in heaven.ᵃ ¹⁴And as Moses lifted up the serpent in the wilderness, even so must the Son of Man be lifted up, ¹⁵that whoever believes in Him should not perish butᵃ have eternal life. ¹⁶For God so loved the world that He gave His only begotten Son, that whoever believes in Him should not perish but have everlasting life. ¹⁷For God did not send His Son into the world to condemn the world, but that the world through Him might be saved.

¹⁸"He who believes in Him is not condemned; but he who does not believe is condemned already, because he has not believed in the name of the only begotten Son of God. ¹⁹And this is the condemnation, that the light has come into the world, and men loved darkness rather than light, because their deeds were evil. ²⁰For everyone practicing evil hates the light and does not come to the light, lest his deeds should be exposed. ²¹But he who does the truth comes to the light, that his deeds may be clearly seen, that they have been done in God."

John the Baptist Exalts Christ

²²After these things Jesus and His disciples came into the land of Judea, and there He remained with them and baptized. ²³Now John also was baptizing in Aenon near Salim, because there was much water there. And they came and were baptized. ²⁴For John had not yet been thrown into prison.

3:13 ᵃNU-Text omits *who is in heaven.*
3:15 ᵃNU-Text omits *not perish but.*

PARENTING MATTERS

Q: *How can we best speak words of encouragement to our kids?*

Years ago when speaking to a group of several hundred singles, I asked, "How many of you grew up in homes where you were told you were great, where your parents expressed how proud they were of you?" Perhaps a dozen raised their hands. The rest of these young adults remembered words of criticism from their parents far more than they remembered any encouragement.

If you want your mate to live a godly life, or if you would like to see your children grow up to love the Lord and walk with Him, then you need to make encouragement a part of your daily vocabulary.

All of us have an encouragement meter that runs near empty at times. In fact, has anybody ever been encouraged *too* much? Have you ever felt *overly* appreciated?

I have a challenge for you. Spend some time thinking of five good things about each member of your family. Now, commit to finding time to encourage each family member in these areas during the next week. Spend more time encouraging than criticizing.

Be warned, though; do not wait for somebody to praise you! As someone once said, "You can sometimes catch a terrible chill waiting for someone else to cover you with glory."

25Then there arose a dispute between *some* of John's disciples and the Jews about purification. 26And they came to John and said to him, "Rabbi, He who was with you beyond the Jordan, to whom you have testified—behold, He is baptizing, and all are coming to Him!"

27John answered and said, "A man can receive nothing unless it has been given to him from heaven. 28You yourselves bear me witness, that I said, 'I am not the Christ,' but, 'I have been sent before Him.' 29He who has the bride is the bridegroom; but the friend of the bridegroom, who stands and hears him, rejoices greatly because of the bridegroom's voice. Therefore this joy of mine is fulfilled. 30He must increase, but I *must* decrease. 31He who comes from above is above all; he who is of the earth is earthly and speaks of the earth. He who comes from heaven is above all. 32And what He has seen and heard, that He testifies; and no one receives His testimony. 33He who has received His testimony has certified that God is true. 34For He whom God has sent speaks the words of God, for God does not give the Spirit by measure. 35The Father loves the Son, and has given all things into His hand. 36He who believes in the Son has everlasting life; and he who does not believe the Son shall not see life, but the wrath of God abides on him."

A Samaritan Woman Meets Her Messiah

4 Therefore, when the Lord knew that the Pharisees had heard that Jesus made and baptized more disciples than John 2(though Jesus Himself did not baptize, but His disciples), 3He left Judea and departed again to Galilee. 4But He needed to go through Samaria.

5So He came to a city of Samaria which is called Sychar, near the plot of ground that Jacob gave to his son Joseph. 6Now Jacob's well was there. Jesus therefore, being wearied from *His* journey, sat thus by the well. It was about the sixth hour.

7A woman of Samaria came to draw water. Jesus said to her, "Give Me a drink." 8For His disciples had gone away into the city to buy food.

9Then the woman of Samaria said to Him, "How is it that You, being a Jew, ask a drink from me, a Samaritan woman?" For Jews have no dealings with Samaritans.

10Jesus answered and said to her, "If you knew the gift of God, and who it is who says to you, 'Give Me a drink,' you would have asked Him, and He would have given you living water."

11The woman said to Him, "Sir, You have nothing to draw with, and the well is deep. Where then do You get that living water? 12Are You greater than our father Jacob, who gave us the well, and drank from it himself, as well as his sons and his livestock?"

INTIMATE MOMENTS

On those chilly mornings, go out and warm up her car. Now, *that's* romantic!

13Jesus answered and said to her, "Whoever drinks of this water will thirst again, 14but whoever drinks of the water that I shall give him will never thirst. But the water that I shall give him will become in him a fountain of water springing up into everlasting life."

15The woman said to Him, "Sir, give me this water, that I may not thirst, nor come here to draw."

16Jesus said to her, "Go, call your husband, and come here."

17The woman answered and said, "I have no husband."

Jesus said to her, "You have well said, 'I have no husband,' 18for you have had five husbands, and the one whom you now have is not your husband; in that you spoke truly."

19The woman said to Him, "Sir, I perceive that You are a prophet. 20Our fathers worshiped on this mountain, and you *Jews* say that in Jerusalem is the place where one ought to worship."

21Jesus said to her, "Woman, believe Me, the hour is coming when you will neither on this mountain, nor in Jerusalem, worship the Father. ²²You worship what you do not know; we know what we worship, for salvation is of the Jews. ²³But the hour is coming, and now is, when the true worshipers will worship the Father in spirit and truth; for the Father is seeking such to worship Him. ²⁴God *is* Spirit, and those who worship Him must worship in spirit and truth."

²⁵The woman said to Him, "I know that Messiah is coming" (who is called Christ). "When He comes, He will tell us all things."

²⁶Jesus said to her, "I who speak to you am *He*."

The Whitened Harvest

²⁷And at this *point* His disciples came, and they marveled that He talked with a woman; yet no one said, "What do You seek?" or, "Why are You talking with her?"

²⁸The woman then left her waterpot, went her way into the city, and said to the men, ²⁹"Come, see a Man who told me all things that I ever did. Could this be the Christ?" ³⁰Then they went out of the city and came to Him.

³¹In the meantime His disciples urged Him, saying, "Rabbi, eat."

³²But He said to them, "I have food to eat of which you do not know."

³³Therefore the disciples said to one another, "Has anyone brought Him *anything* to eat?"

³⁴Jesus said to them, "My food is to do the will of Him who sent Me, and to finish His work. ³⁵Do you not say, 'There are still four months and *then* comes the harvest'? Behold, I say to you, lift up your eyes and look at the fields, for they are already white for harvest! ³⁶And he who reaps receives wages, and gathers fruit for eternal life, that both he who sows and he who reaps may rejoice together. ³⁷For in this the saying is true: 'One sows and another reaps.' ³⁸I sent you to reap that for which you have not labored; others have labored, and you have entered into their labors."

The Savior of the World

³⁹And many of the Samaritans of that city believed in Him because of the word of the woman who testified, "He told me all that I *ever* did." ⁴⁰So when the Samaritans had come to Him, they urged Him to stay with them; and He stayed there two days. ⁴¹And many more believed because of His own word.

⁴²Then they said to the woman, "Now we believe, not because of what you said, for we ourselves have heard *Him* and we know that this is indeed the Christ,ᵃ the Savior of the world."

Welcome at Galilee

⁴³Now after the two days He departed from there and went to Galilee. ⁴⁴For Jesus Himself testified that a prophet has no honor in his own country. ⁴⁵So when He came to Galilee, the Galileans received Him, having seen all the things He did in Jerusalem at the feast; for they also had gone to the feast.

A Nobleman's Son Healed

⁴⁶So Jesus came again to Cana of Galilee where He had made the water wine. And there was a certain nobleman whose son was sick at Capernaum. ⁴⁷When he heard that Jesus had come out of Judea into Galilee, he went to Him and implored Him to come down and heal his son, for he was at the point of death. ⁴⁸Then Jesus said to him, "Unless you *people* see signs and wonders, you will by no means believe."

⁴⁹The nobleman said to Him, "Sir, come down before my child dies!"

⁵⁰Jesus said to him, "Go your way; your son lives." So the man believed the word that Jesus spoke to him, and he went his way. ⁵¹And as he was now going down, his servants met him and told *him,* saying, "Your son lives!"

⁵²Then he inquired of them the hour when he got better. And they said to him, "Yesterday at the seventh hour the fever left him." ⁵³So the father knew that *it was* at the same hour in which Jesus said to him, "Your son lives." And he himself believed, and his whole household.

⁵⁴This again *is* the second sign Jesus did when He had come out of Judea into Galilee.

4:42 ᵃNU-Text omits *the Christ*.

A Man Healed at the Pool of Bethesda

5 After this there was a feast of the Jews, and Jesus went up to Jerusalem. ²Now there is in Jerusalem by the Sheep *Gate* a pool, which is called in Hebrew, Bethesda,ᵃ having five porches. ³In these lay a great multitude of sick people, blind, lame, paralyzed, waiting for the moving of the water. ⁴For an angel went down at a certain time into the pool and stirred up the water; then whoever stepped in first, after the stirring of the water, was made well of whatever disease he had.ᵃ ⁵Now a certain man was there who had an infirmity thirty-eight years. ⁶When Jesus saw him lying there, and knew that he already had been *in that condition* a long time, He said to him, "Do you want to be made well?"

⁷The sick man answered Him, "Sir, I have no man to put me into the pool when the water is stirred up; but while I am coming, another steps down before me."

⁸Jesus said to him, "Rise, take up your bed and walk." ⁹And immediately the man was made well, took up his bed, and walked.

And that day was the Sabbath. ¹⁰The Jews therefore said to him who was cured, "It is the Sabbath; it is not lawful for you to carry your bed."

¹¹He answered them, "He who made me well said to me, 'Take up your bed and walk.'"

¹²Then they asked him, "Who is the Man who said to you, 'Take up your bed and walk'?" ¹³But the one who was healed did not know who it was, for Jesus had withdrawn, a multitude being in *that* place. ¹⁴Afterward Jesus found him in the temple, and said to him, "See, you have been made well. Sin no more, lest a worse thing come upon you."

¹⁵The man departed and told the Jews that it was Jesus who had made him well.

Honor the Father and the Son

¹⁶For this reason the Jews persecuted Jesus, and sought to kill Him,ᵃ because He had done these things on the Sabbath.

¹⁷But Jesus answered them, "My Father has been working until now, and I have been working."

¹⁸Therefore the Jews sought all the more to kill Him, because He not only broke the Sabbath, but also said that God was His Father, making Himself equal with God. ¹⁹Then Jesus answered and said to them, "Most assuredly, I say to you, the Son can do nothing of Himself, but what He sees the Father do; for whatever He does, the Son also does in like manner. ²⁰For the Father loves the Son, and shows Him all things that He Himself does; and He will show Him greater works than these, that you may marvel. ²¹For as the Father raises the dead and gives life to *them,* even so the Son gives life to whom He will. ²²For the Father judges no one, but has committed all judgment to the Son, ²³that all should honor the Son just as they honor the Father. He who does not honor the Son does not honor the Father who sent Him.

Life and Judgment Are Through the Son

²⁴"Most assuredly, I say to you, he who hears My word and believes in Him who sent Me has everlasting life, and shall not come into judgment, but has passed from death into life. ²⁵Most assuredly, I say to you, the hour is coming, and now is, when the dead will hear the voice of the Son of God; and those who hear will live. ²⁶For as the Father has life in Himself, so He has granted the Son to have life in Himself, ²⁷and has given Him authority to execute judgment also, because He is the Son of Man. ²⁸Do not marvel at this; for the hour is coming in which all who are in the graves will hear His voice ²⁹and come forth—those who have done good, to the resurrection of life, and those who have done evil, to the resurrection of condemnation. ³⁰I can of Myself do nothing. As I hear, I judge; and My judgment is righteous, because I do not seek My own will but the will of the Father who sent Me.

The Fourfold Witness

³¹"If I bear witness of Myself, My witness is not true. ³²There is another who bears witness of Me, and I know that the

5:2 ᵃNU-Text reads *Bethzatha.*
5:4 ᵃNU-Text omits *waiting for the moving of the water* at the end of verse 3, and all of verse 4.
5:16 ᵃNU-Text omits *and sought to kill Him.*

witness which He witnesses of Me is true. ³³You have sent to John, and he has borne witness to the truth. ³⁴Yet I do not receive testimony from man, but I say these things that you may be saved. ³⁵He was the burning and shining lamp, and you were willing for a time to rejoice in his light. ³⁶But I have a greater witness than John's; for the works which the Father has given Me to finish—the very works that I do—bear witness of Me, that the Father has sent Me. ³⁷And the Father Himself, who sent Me, has testified of Me. You have neither heard His voice at any time, nor seen His form. ³⁸But you do not have His word abiding in you, because whom He sent, Him you do not believe. ³⁹You search the Scriptures, for in them you think you have eternal life; and these are they which testify of Me. ⁴⁰But you are not willing to come to Me that you may have life.

⁴¹"I do not receive honor from men. ⁴²But I know you, that you do not have the love of God in you. ⁴³I have come in My Father's name, and you do not receive Me; if another comes in his own name, him you will receive. ⁴⁴How can you believe, who receive honor from one another, and do not seek the honor that *comes* from the only God? ⁴⁵Do not think that I shall accuse you to the Father; there is *one* who accuses you—Moses, in whom you trust. ⁴⁶For if you believed Moses, you would believe Me; for he wrote about Me. ⁴⁷But if you do not believe his writings, how will you believe My words?"

INTIMATE MOMENTS

Pray for your husband every day.

Feeding the Five Thousand

6 After these things Jesus went over the Sea of Galilee, which is *the Sea* of Tiberias. ²Then a great multitude followed Him, because they saw His signs which He performed on those who were diseased.

³And Jesus went up on the mountain, and there He sat with His disciples.

⁴Now the Passover, a feast of the Jews, was near. ⁵Then Jesus lifted up *His* eyes, and seeing a great multitude coming toward Him, He said to Philip, "Where shall we buy bread, that these may eat?" ⁶But this He said to test him, for He Himself knew what He would do.

⁷Philip answered Him, "Two hundred denarii worth of bread is not sufficient for them, that every one of them may have a little."

⁸One of His disciples, Andrew, Simon Peter's brother, said to Him, ⁹"There is a lad here who has five barley loaves and two small fish, but what are they among so many?"

¹⁰Then Jesus said, "Make the people sit down." Now there was much grass in the place. So the men sat down, in number about five thousand. ¹¹And Jesus took the loaves, and when He had given thanks He distributed *them* to the disciples, and the disciplesª to those sitting down; and likewise of the fish, as much as they wanted. ¹²So when they were filled, He said to His disciples, "Gather up the fragments that remain, so that nothing is lost." ¹³Therefore they gathered *them* up, and filled twelve baskets with the fragments of the five barley loaves which were left over by those who had eaten. ¹⁴Then those men, when they had seen the sign that Jesus did, said, "This is truly the Prophet who is to come into the world."

Jesus Walks on the Sea

¹⁵Therefore when Jesus perceived that they were about to come and take Him by force to make Him king, He departed again to the mountain by Himself alone.

¹⁶Now when evening came, His disciples went down to the sea, ¹⁷got into the boat, and went over the sea toward Capernaum. And it was already dark, and Jesus had not come to them. ¹⁸Then the sea arose because a great wind was blowing. ¹⁹So when they had rowed about three or four miles,ª they saw Jesus walking on the

6:11 ªNU-Text omits *to the disciples, and the disciples.*
6:19 ªLiterally *twenty-five or thirty stadia*

sea and drawing near the boat; and they were afraid. [20]But He said to them, "It is I; do not be afraid." [21]Then they willingly received Him into the boat, and immediately the boat was at the land where they were going.

The Bread from Heaven

[22]On the following day, when the people who were standing on the other side of the sea saw that there was no other boat there, except that one which His disciples had entered,[a] and that Jesus had not entered the boat with His disciples, but His disciples had gone away alone— [23]however, other boats came from Tiberias, near the place where they ate bread after the Lord had given thanks— [24]when the people therefore saw that Jesus was not there, nor His disciples, they also got into boats and came to Capernaum, seeking Jesus. [25]And when they found Him on the other side of the sea, they said to Him, "Rabbi, when did You come here?"

[26]Jesus answered them and said, "Most assuredly, I say to you, you seek Me, not because you saw the signs, but because you ate of the loaves and were filled. [27]Do not labor for the food which perishes, but for the food which endures to everlasting life, which the Son of Man will give you, because God the Father has set His seal on Him."

[28]Then they said to Him, "What shall we do, that we may work the works of God?"

[29]Jesus answered and said to them, "This is the work of God, that you believe in Him whom He sent."

[30]Therefore they said to Him, "What sign will You perform then, that we may see it and believe You? What work will You do? [31]Our fathers ate the manna in the desert; as it is written, 'He gave them bread from heaven to eat.' "[a]

[32]Then Jesus said to them, "Most assuredly, I say to you, Moses did not give you the bread from heaven, but My Father gives you the true bread from heaven. [33]For the bread of God is He who comes down from heaven and gives life to the world."

[34]Then they said to Him, "Lord, give us this bread always."

[35]And Jesus said to them, "I am the bread of life. He who comes to Me shall never hunger, and he who believes in Me shall never thirst. [36]But I said to you that you have seen Me and yet do not believe. [37]All that the Father gives Me will come to Me, and the one who comes to Me I will by no means cast out. [38]For I have come down from heaven, not to do My own will, but the will of Him who sent Me. [39]This is the will of the Father who sent Me, that of all He has given Me I should lose nothing, but should raise it up at the last day. [40]And this is the will of Him who sent Me, that everyone who sees the Son and believes in Him may have everlasting life; and I will raise him up at the last day."

Rejected by His Own

[41]The Jews then complained about Him, because He said, "I am the bread which came down from heaven." [42]And they said, "Is not this Jesus, the son of Joseph, whose father and mother we know? How is it then that He says, 'I have come down from heaven'?"

[43]Jesus therefore answered and said to them, "Do not murmur among yourselves. [44]No one can come to Me unless the Father who sent Me draws him; and I will raise him up at the last day. [45]It is written in the prophets, 'And they shall all be taught by God.'[a] Therefore everyone who has heard and learned[b] from the Father comes to Me. [46]Not that anyone has seen the Father, except He who is from God; He has seen the Father. [47]Most assuredly, I say to you, he who believes in Me[a] has everlasting life. [48]I am the bread of life. [49]Your fathers ate the manna in the wilderness, and are dead. [50]This is the bread which comes down from heaven, that one may eat of it and not die. [51]I am the living bread which came down from heaven. If anyone eats of this bread, he will live forever; and the bread that I shall give is My flesh, which I shall give for the life of the world."

[52]The Jews therefore quarreled among themselves, saying, "How can this Man give us His flesh to eat?"

6:22 [a]NU-Text omits *that* and *which His disciples had entered.* **6:31** [a]Exodus 16:4; Nehemiah 9:15; Psalm 78:24 **6:45** [a]Isaiah 54:13 [b]M-Text reads *hears and has learned.* **6:47** [a]NU-Text omits *in Me.*

⁵³Then Jesus said to them, "Most assuredly, I say to you, unless you eat the flesh of the Son of Man and drink His blood, you have no life in you. ⁵⁴Whoever eats My flesh and drinks My blood has eternal life, and I will raise him up at the last day. ⁵⁵For My flesh is food indeed,ᵃ and My blood is drink indeed. ⁵⁶He who eats My flesh and drinks My blood abides in Me, and I in him. ⁵⁷As the living Father sent Me, and I live because of the Father, so he who feeds on Me will live because of Me. ⁵⁸This is the bread which came down from heaven—not as your fathers ate the manna, and are dead. He who eats this bread will live forever."

⁵⁹These things He said in the synagogue as He taught in Capernaum.

Many Disciples Turn Away

⁶⁰Therefore many of His disciples, when they heard *this,* said, "This is a hard saying; who can understand it?"

⁶¹When Jesus knew in Himself that His disciples complained about this, He said to them, "Does this offend you? ⁶²*What* then if you should see the Son of Man ascend where He was before? ⁶³It is the Spirit who gives life; the flesh profits nothing. The words that I speak to you are spirit, and *they* are life. ⁶⁴But there are some of you who do not believe." For Jesus knew from the beginning who they were who did not believe, and who would betray Him. ⁶⁵And He said, "Therefore I have said to you that no one can come to Me unless it has been granted to him by My Father."

⁶⁶From that *time* many of His disciples went back and walked with Him no more. ⁶⁷Then Jesus said to the twelve, "Do you also want to go away?"

⁶⁸But Simon Peter answered Him, "Lord, to whom shall we go? You have the words of eternal life. ⁶⁹Also we have come to believe and know that You are the Christ, the Son of the living God."ᵃ

⁷⁰Jesus answered them, "Did I not choose you, the twelve, and one of you is a devil?" ⁷¹He spoke of Judas Iscariot, *the son* of Simon, for it was he who would betray Him, being one of the twelve.

Jesus' Brothers Disbelieve

7 After these things Jesus walked in Galilee; for He did not want to walk in Judea, because the Jewsᵃ sought to kill Him. ²Now the Jews' Feast of Tabernacles was at hand. ³His brothers therefore said to Him, "Depart from here and go into Judea, that Your disciples also may see the works that You are doing. ⁴For no one does anything in secret while he himself seeks to be known openly. If You do these things, show Yourself to the world." ⁵For even His brothers did not believe in Him.

⁶Then Jesus said to them, "My time has not yet come, but your time is always ready. ⁷The world cannot hate you, but it hates Me because I testify of it that its works are evil. ⁸You go up to this feast. I am not yetᵃ going up to this feast, for My time has not yet fully come." ⁹When He had said these things to them, He remained in Galilee.

The Heavenly Scholar

¹⁰But when His brothers had gone up, then He also went up to the feast, not openly, but as it were in secret. ¹¹Then the Jews sought Him at the feast, and said, "Where is He?" ¹²And there was much complaining among the people concerning Him. Some said, "He is good"; others said, "No, on the contrary, He deceives the people." ¹³However, no one spoke openly of Him for fear of the Jews.

¹⁴Now about the middle of the feast Jesus went up into the temple and taught. ¹⁵And the Jews marveled, saying, "How does this Man know letters, having never studied?"

¹⁶Jesusᵃ answered them and said, "My doctrine is not Mine, but His who sent Me. ¹⁷If anyone wills to do His will, he shall know concerning the doctrine, whether it is from God or *whether* I speak on My own *authority.* ¹⁸He who speaks from himself seeks his own glory; but He who seeks the glory of the One who sent Him is true, and no unrighteousness is in Him. ¹⁹Did not

---

6:55 ᵃNU-Text reads *true food* and *true drink.*
6:69 ᵃNU-Text reads *You are the Holy One of God.*
7:1 ᵃThat is, the ruling authorities **7:8** ᵃNU-Text omits *yet.* **7:16** ᵃNU-Text and M-Text read *So Jesus.*

Moses give you the law, yet none of you keeps the law? Why do you seek to kill Me?"

20The people answered and said, "You have a demon. Who is seeking to kill You?"

21Jesus answered and said to them, "I did one work, and you all marvel. 22Moses therefore gave you circumcision (not that it is from Moses, but from the fathers), and you circumcise a man on the Sabbath. 23If a man receives circumcision on the Sabbath, so that the law of Moses should not be broken, are you angry with Me because I made a man completely well on the Sabbath? 24Do not judge according to appearance, but judge with righteous judgment."

Could This Be the Christ?

25Now some of them from Jerusalem said, "Is this not He whom they seek to kill? 26But look! He speaks boldly, and they say nothing to Him. Do the rulers know indeed that this is trulya the Christ? 27However, we know where this Man is from; but when the Christ comes, no one knows where He is from."

28Then Jesus cried out, as He taught in the temple, saying, "You both know Me, and you know where I am from; and I have not come of Myself, but He who sent Me is true, whom you do not know. 29Buta I know Him, for I am from Him, and He sent Me."

30Therefore they sought to take Him; but no one laid a hand on Him, because His hour had not yet come. 31And many of the people believed in Him, and said, "When the Christ comes, will He do more signs than these which this *Man* has done?"

Jesus and the Religious Leaders

32The Pharisees heard the crowd murmuring these things concerning Him, and the Pharisees and the chief priests sent officers to take Him. 33Then Jesus said to them,a "I shall be with you a little while longer, and *then* I go to Him who sent Me. 34You will seek Me and not find *Me,* and where I am you cannot come."

35Then the Jews said among themselves, "Where does He intend to go that we shall not find Him? Does He intend to go to the Dispersion among the Greeks and teach the Greeks? 36What is this thing that He said, 'You will seek Me and not find Me, and where I am you cannot come'?"

The Promise of the Holy Spirit

37On the last day, that great *day* of the feast, Jesus stood and cried out, saying, "If anyone thirsts, let him come to Me and drink. 38He who believes in Me, as the Scripture has said, out of his heart will flow rivers of living water." 39But this He spoke concerning the Spirit, whom those believinga in Him would receive; for the Holyb Spirit was not yet *given,* because Jesus was not yet glorified.

Who Is He?

40Thereforea manya from the crowd, when they heard this saying, said, "Truly this is the Prophet." 41Others said, "This is the Christ."

But some said, "Will the Christ come out of Galilee? 42Has not the Scripture said that the Christ comes from the seed of David and from the town of Bethlehem, where David was?" 43So there was a division among the people because of Him. 44Now some of them wanted to take Him, but no one laid hands on Him.

Rejected by the Authorities

45Then the officers came to the chief priests and Pharisees, who said to them, "Why have you not brought Him?"

46The officers answered, "No man ever spoke like this Man!"

47Then the Pharisees answered them, "Are you also deceived? 48Have any of the rulers or the Pharisees believed in Him? 49But this crowd that does not know the law is accursed."

50Nicodemus (he who came to Jesus by night,a being one of them) said to them, 51"Does our law judge a man before it hears him and knows what he is doing?"

52They answered and said to him, "Are you also from Galilee? Search and look, for no prophet has arisena out of Galilee."

7:26 aNU-Text omits *truly.* 7:29 aNU-Text and M-Text omit *But.* 7:33 aNU-Text and M-Text omit *to them.* 7:39 aNU-Text reads *who believed.* bNU-Text omits Holy. 7:40 aNU-Text reads *some.* 7:50 aNU-Text reads *before.* 7:52 aNU-Text reads *is to rise.*

An Adulteress Faces the Light of the World

[53]And everyone went to his *own* house.[a]

8 But Jesus went to the Mount of Olives. [2]Now early[a] in the morning He came again into the temple, and all the people came to Him; and He sat down and taught them. [3]Then the scribes and Pharisees brought to Him a woman caught in adultery. And when they had set her in the midst, [4]they said to Him, "Teacher, this woman was caught[a] in adultery, in the very act. [5]Now Moses, in the law, commanded[a] us that such should be stoned.[b] But what do You say?"[c] [6]This they said, testing Him, that they might have *something* of which to accuse Him. But Jesus stooped down and wrote on the ground with *His* finger, as though He did not hear.[a]

[7]So when they continued asking Him, He raised Himself up[a] and said to them, "He who is without sin among you, let him throw a stone at her first." [8]And again He stooped down and wrote on the ground. [9]Then those who heard *it,* being convicted by *their* conscience,[a] went out one by one, beginning with the oldest *even* to the last. And Jesus was left alone, and the woman standing in the midst. [10]When Jesus had raised Himself up and saw no one but the woman, He said to her,[a] "Woman, where are those accusers of yours?[b] Has no one condemned you?"

[11]She said, "No one, Lord."

And Jesus said to her, "Neither do I condemn you; go and[a] sin no more."

[12]Then Jesus spoke to them again, saying, "I am the light of the world. He who follows Me shall not walk in darkness, but have the light of life."

Jesus Defends His Self-Witness

[13]The Pharisees therefore said to Him, "You bear witness of Yourself; Your witness is not true."

[14]Jesus answered and said to them, "Even if I bear witness of Myself, My witness is true, for I know where I came from and where I am going; but you do not know where I come from and where I am going. [15]You judge according to the flesh; I judge no one. [16]And yet if I do judge, My judgment is true; for I am not alone, but I *am* with the Father who sent Me. [17]It is also written in your law that the testimony of two men is true. [18]I am One who bears witness of Myself, and the Father who sent Me bears witness of Me."

[19]Then they said to Him, "Where is Your Father?"

Jesus answered, "You know neither Me nor My Father. If you had known Me, you would have known My Father also."

[20]These words Jesus spoke in the treasury, as He taught in the temple; and no one laid hands on Him, for His hour had not yet come.

Jesus Predicts His Departure

[21]Then Jesus said to them again, "I am going away, and you will seek Me, and will die in your sin. Where I go you cannot come."

[22]So the Jews said, "Will He kill Himself, because He says, 'Where I go you cannot come'?"

[23]And He said to them, "You are from beneath; I am from above. You are of this world; I am not of this world. [24]Therefore I said to you that you will die in your sins; for if you do not believe that I am *He,* you will die in your sins."

[25]Then they said to Him, "Who are You?"

And Jesus said to them, "Just what I have been saying to you from the beginning. [26]I have many things to say and to judge concerning you, but He who sent Me is true; and I speak to the world those things which I heard from Him."

[27]They did not understand that He spoke to them of the Father.

7:53 [a]The words *And everyone* through *sin no more* (8:11) are bracketed by NU-Text as not original. They are present in over 900 manuscripts.
8:2 [a]M-Text reads *very early.* 8:4 [a]M-Text reads *we found this woman.* 8:5 [a]M-Text reads *in our law Moses commanded.* [b]NU-Text and M-Text read *to stone such.* [c]M-Text adds *about her.*
8:6 [a]NU-Text and M-Text omit *as though He did not hear.* 8:7 [a]M-Text reads *He looked up.*
8:9 [a]NU-Text and M-Text omit *being convicted by their conscience.* 8:10 [a]NU-Text omits *and saw no one but the woman;* M-Text reads *He saw her and said.* [b]NU-Text and M-Text omit *of yours.*
8:11 [a]NU-Text and M-Text add *from now on.*

²⁸Then Jesus said to them, "When you lift up the Son of Man, then you will know that I am *He,* and *that* I do nothing of Myself; but as My Father taught Me, I speak these things. ²⁹And He who sent Me is with Me. The Father has not left Me alone, for I always do those things that please Him." ³⁰As He spoke these words, many believed in Him.

The Truth Shall Make You Free

³¹Then Jesus said to those Jews who believed Him, "If you abide in My word, you are My disciples indeed. ³²And you shall know the truth, and the truth shall make you free."

³³They answered Him, "We are Abraham's descendants, and have never been in bondage to anyone. How *can* You say, 'You will be made free'?"

³⁴Jesus answered them, "Most assuredly, I say to you, whoever commits sin is a slave of sin. ³⁵And a slave does not abide in the house forever, *but* a son abides forever. ³⁶Therefore if the Son makes you free, you shall be free indeed.

Abraham's Seed and Satan's

³⁷"I know that you are Abraham's descendants, but you seek to kill Me, because My word has no place in you. ³⁸I speak what I have seen with My Father, and you do what you have seen withᵃ your father."

³⁹They answered and said to Him, "Abraham is our father."

Jesus said to them, "If you were Abraham's children, you would do the works of Abraham. ⁴⁰But now you seek to kill Me, a Man who has told you the truth which I heard from God. Abraham did not do this. ⁴¹You do the deeds of your father."

Then they said to Him, "We were not born of fornication; we have one Father—God."

⁴²Jesus said to them, "If God were your Father, you would love Me, for I proceeded forth and came from God; nor have I come of Myself, but He sent Me. ⁴³Why do you not understand My speech? Because you are not able to listen to My word. ⁴⁴You are

of *your* father the devil, and the desires of your father you want to do. He was a murderer from the beginning, and does not stand in the truth, because there is no truth in him. When he speaks a lie, he speaks from his own *resources,* for he is a liar and the father of it. ⁴⁵But because I tell the truth, you do not believe Me. ⁴⁶Which of you convicts Me of sin? And if I tell the truth, why do you not believe Me? ⁴⁷He who is of God hears God's words; therefore you do not hear, because you are not of God."

BIBLICAL INSIGHTS • 8:32

Do You Need to Change Course?

LIKE A SEA CAPTAIN WHO, after a storm, finds that his ship isn't headed where he thought it was, we may need to change course when confronted with the truth. Christ famously said, "The truth shall make you free" (8:32), but as Herbert Agar wrote in *A Time for Greatness,* "The truth that makes men free is for the most part the truth which men prefer not to hear."

What is the Bible to you? A collection of nice stories? The foundation of a conservative worldview? Or is it God's Word, "living and powerful, and sharper than any two-edged sword" (Heb. 4:12)? Is it your source of wisdom and truth about life? Does anything keep you from obeying God's Word in every area of your life—your business, your marriage, your family? Have you been avoiding some truth, or been unwilling to confront a particular area of your relationship? Do you need to adjust your course?

When you spend time reading and applying God's Word, you get your true bearings. Since its eternal truth doesn't change, you need to adjust your life to walk in that truth. As you do so, pray that God's Word will be your guide and your rock in establishing your personal convictions and beliefs, plus your family values and priorities.

8:38 ᵃNU-Text reads *heard from.*

Before Abraham Was, I AM

48Then the Jews answered and said to Him, "Do we not say rightly that You are a Samaritan and have a demon?"

49Jesus answered, "I do not have a demon; but I honor My Father, and you dishonor Me. 50And I do not seek My *own* glory; there is One who seeks and judges. 51Most assuredly, I say to you, if anyone keeps My word he shall never see death."

52Then the Jews said to Him, "Now we know that You have a demon! Abraham is dead, and the prophets; and You say, 'If anyone keeps My word he shall never taste death.' 53Are You greater than our father Abraham, who is dead? And the prophets are dead. Who do You make Yourself out to be?"

54Jesus answered, "If I honor Myself, My honor is nothing. It is My Father who honors Me, of whom you say that He is youra God. 55Yet you have not known Him, but I know Him. And if I say, 'I do not know Him,' I shall be a liar like you; but I do know Him and keep His word. 56Your father Abraham rejoiced to see My day, and he saw *it* and was glad."

57Then the Jews said to Him, "You are not yet fifty years old, and have You seen Abraham?"

58Jesus said to them, "Most assuredly, I say to you, before Abraham was, I AM."

59Then they took up stones to throw at Him; but Jesus hid Himself and went out of the temple,a going through the midst of them, and so passed by.

A Man Born Blind Receives Sight

9 Now as *Jesus* passed by, He saw a man who was blind from birth. 2And His disciples asked Him, saying, "Rabbi, who sinned, this man or his parents, that he was born blind?"

3Jesus answered, "Neither this man nor his parents sinned, but that the works of God should be revealed in him. 4Ia must work the works of Him who sent Me while it is day; *the* night is coming when no one can work. 5As long as I am in the world, I am the light of the world."

6When He had said these things, He spat on the ground and made clay with the saliva; and He anointed the eyes of the blind man with the clay. 7And He said to him, "Go, wash in the pool of Siloam" (which is translated, Sent). So he went and washed, and came back seeing.

8Therefore the neighbors and those who previously had seen that he was blinda said, "Is not this he who sat and begged?"

8:54 aNU-Text and M-Text read *our.*
8:59 aNU-Text omits the rest of this verse.
9:4 aNU-Text reads *We.*
9:8 aNU-Text reads *a beggar.*

ROMANTIC QUOTES AND NOTES
The Marital Gift of Perspective

There is great freedom in knowing what is the truth and what isn't. Jesus said, "You shall know the truth, and the truth shall make you free" (John 8:32). As partners in the pilgrimage of life, married people have the responsibility and the privilege to speak the truth to one another in order to help balance each other's perspectives.

Understanding the truth of God's sovereign rule brings an eternal perspective to everything in life, including your successes and, perhaps even more importantly, your mistakes. The promise of Romans 8:28, "All things work together for good to those who love God," beautifully illustrates His absolute supremacy. These words offer comfort, reminding us that nothing is wasted in His economy. God can use even our mistakes and failures.

Encourage your mate to believe God and, as a couple, ask Him to use your failures for good—your good, your children's good, and His good.

Remind your mate that most failures are not as big as they appear in our minds. All of us need the help of others to see the overall picture, the *bigger* picture. Momentary mistakes are not that monumental when seen against the backdrop of a person's entire life and against the backdrop of God's sovereignty.

⁹Some said, "This is he." Others *said,* "He is like him."ᵃ

He said, "I am *he.*"

¹⁰Therefore they said to him, "How were your eyes opened?"

¹¹He answered and said, "A Man called Jesus made clay and anointed my eyes and said to me, 'Go to the pool ofᵃ Siloam and wash.' So I went and washed, and I received sight."

¹²Then they said to him, "Where is He?" He said, "I do not know."

The Pharisees Excommunicate the Healed Man

¹³They brought him who formerly was blind to the Pharisees. ¹⁴Now it was a Sabbath when Jesus made the clay and opened his eyes. ¹⁵Then the Pharisees also asked him again how he had received his sight. He said to them, "He put clay on my eyes, and I washed, and I see."

¹⁶Therefore some of the Pharisees said, "This Man is not from God, because He does not keep the Sabbath."

Others said, "How can a man who is a sinner do such signs?" And there was a division among them.

¹⁷They said to the blind man again, "What do you say about Him because He opened your eyes?"

He said, "He is a prophet."

¹⁸But the Jews did not believe concerning him, that he had been blind and received his sight, until they called the parents of him who had received his sight. ¹⁹And they asked them, saying, "Is this your son, who you say was born blind? How then does he now see?"

²⁰His parents answered them and said, "We know that this is our son, and that he was born blind; ²¹but by what means he now sees we do not know, or who opened his eyes we do not know. He is of age; ask him. He will speak for himself." ²²His parents said these *things* because they feared the Jews, for the Jews had agreed already that if anyone confessed *that* He *was* Christ, he would be put out of the synagogue.

²³Therefore his parents said, "He is of age; ask him."

²⁴So they again called the man who was blind, and said to him, "Give God the glory! We know that this Man is a sinner."

²⁵He answered and said, "Whether He is a sinner *or not* I do not know. One thing I know: that though I was blind, now I see."

²⁶Then they said to him again, "What did He do to you? How did He open your eyes?"

²⁷He answered them, "I told you already, and you did not listen. Why do you want to hear *it* again? Do you also want to become His disciples?"

²⁸Then they reviled him and said, "You are His disciple, but we are Moses' disciples. ²⁹We know that God spoke to Moses; *as for* this *fellow,* we do not know where He is from."

³⁰The man answered and said to them, "Why, this is a marvelous thing, that you do not know where He is from; yet He has opened my eyes! ³¹Now we know that God does not hear sinners; but if anyone is a worshiper of God and does His will, He hears him. ³²Since the world began it has been unheard of that anyone opened the eyes of one who was born blind. ³³If this Man were not from God, He could do nothing."

³⁴They answered and said to him, "You were completely born in sins, and are you teaching us?" And they cast him out.

True Vision and True Blindness

³⁵Jesus heard that they had cast him out; and when He had found him, He said to him, "Do you believe in the Son of God?"ᵃ

³⁶He answered and said, "Who is He, Lord, that I may believe in Him?"

³⁷And Jesus said to him, "You have both seen Him and it is He who is talking with you."

³⁸Then he said, "Lord, I believe!" And he worshiped Him.

³⁹And Jesus said, "For judgment I have come into this world, that those who do not see may see, and that those who see may be made blind."

⁴⁰Then *some* of the Pharisees who were with Him heard these words, and said to Him, "Are we blind also?"

9:9 ᵃNU-Text reads *"No, but he is like him."*
9:11 ᵃNU-Text omits *the pool of.*
9:35 ᵃNU-Text reads *Son of Man.*

⁴¹Jesus said to them, "If you were blind, you would have no sin; but now you say, 'We see.' Therefore your sin remains.

Jesus the True Shepherd

10 "Most assuredly, I say to you, he who does not enter the sheepfold by the door, but climbs up some other way, the same is a thief and a robber. ²But he who enters by the door is the shepherd of the sheep. ³To him the doorkeeper opens, and the sheep hear his voice; and he calls his own sheep by name and leads them out. ⁴And when he brings out his own sheep, he goes before them; and the sheep follow him, for they know his voice. ⁵Yet they will by no means follow a stranger, but will flee from him, for they do not know the voice of strangers." ⁶Jesus used this illustration, but they did not understand the things which He spoke to them.

INTIMATE MOMENTS
Ask Good Questions

A 33-year-old graduate student from the nation's heartland has some good advice for husbands who want to rekindle the romance in their marriages. He says, "Most people love talking about themselves, so when I first meet a woman I'm interested in, I'll ask questions so that she's doing most of the talking. Not only does it make her happy, but it's a great way to get to know her—everyone wins! I usually ask about her childhood first: Where did she grow up? Did she like it? What did her parents do? And then I'll ask questions about her present job, apartment and her goals for the future. Women are drawn to me because it's clear I'm not just drawn to them for their looks."

What are some questions you could ask your spouse today? Make sure you set aside a block of time for a mini-date and get ready to listen!

Jesus the Good Shepherd

⁷Then Jesus said to them again, "Most assuredly, I say to you, I am the door of the sheep. ⁸All who *ever* came before Meᵃ are thieves and robbers, but the sheep did not hear them. ⁹I am the door. If anyone enters by Me, he will be saved, and will go in and out and find pasture. ¹⁰The thief does not come except to steal, and to kill, and to destroy. I have come that they may have life, and that they may have *it* more abundantly.

¹¹"I am the good shepherd. The good shepherd gives His life for the sheep. ¹²But a hireling, *he who is* not the shepherd, one who does not own the sheep, sees the wolf coming and leaves the sheep and flees; and the wolf catches the sheep and scatters them. ¹³The hireling flees because he is a hireling and does not care about the sheep. ¹⁴I am the good shepherd; and I know My *sheep,* and am known by My own. ¹⁵As the Father knows Me, even so I know the Father; and I lay down My life for the sheep. ¹⁶And other sheep I have which are not of this fold; them also I must bring, and they will hear My voice; and there will be one flock *and* one shepherd.

¹⁷"Therefore My Father loves Me, because I lay down My life that I may take it again. ¹⁸No one takes it from Me, but I lay it down of Myself. I have power to lay it down, and I have power to take it again. This command I have received from My Father."

¹⁹Therefore there was a division again among the Jews because of these sayings. ²⁰And many of them said, "He has a demon and is mad. Why do you listen to Him?" ²¹Others said, "These are not the words of one who has a demon. Can a demon open the eyes of the blind?"

The Shepherd Knows His Sheep

²²Now it was the Feast of Dedication in Jerusalem, and it was winter. ²³And Jesus walked in the temple, in Solomon's porch. ²⁴Then the Jews surrounded Him and said to Him, "How long do You keep us in doubt? If You are the Christ, tell us plainly." ²⁵Jesus answered them, "I told you, and you do not believe. The works that I do in

10:8 ᵃM-Text omits *before Me.*

My Father's name, they bear witness of Me. [26]But you do not believe, because you are not of My sheep, as I said to you.[a] [27]My sheep hear My voice, and I know them, and they follow Me. [28]And I give them eternal life, and they shall never perish; neither shall anyone snatch them out of My hand. [29]My Father, who has given *them* to Me, is greater than all; and no one is able to snatch *them* out of My Father's hand. [30]I and *My* Father are one."

Renewed Efforts to Stone Jesus

[31]Then the Jews took up stones again to stone Him. [32]Jesus answered them, "Many good works I have shown you from My Father. For which of those works do you stone Me?"

[33]The Jews answered Him, saying, "For a good work we do not stone You, but for blasphemy, and because You, being a Man, make Yourself God."

[34]Jesus answered them, "Is it not written in your law, '*I said, "You are gods"* '?[a] [35]If He called them gods, to whom the word of God came (and the Scripture cannot be broken), [36]do you say of Him whom the Father sanctified and sent into the world, 'You are blaspheming,' because I said, 'I am the Son of God'? [37]If I do not do the works of My Father, do not believe Me; [38]but if I do, though you do not believe Me, believe the works, that you may know and believe[a] that the Father *is* in Me, and I in Him." [39]Therefore they sought again to seize Him, but He escaped out of their hand.

The Believers Beyond Jordan

[40]And He went away again beyond the Jordan to the place where John was baptizing at first, and there He stayed. [41]Then many came to Him and said, "John performed no sign, but all the things that John spoke about this Man were true." [42]And many believed in Him there.

The Death of Lazarus

11 Now a certain *man* was sick, Lazarus of Bethany, the town of Mary and her sister Martha. [2]It was *that* Mary who

anointed the Lord with fragrant oil and wiped His feet with her hair, whose brother Lazarus was sick. [3]Therefore the sisters sent to Him, saying, "Lord, behold, he whom You love is sick."

[4]When Jesus heard *that,* He said, "This sickness is not unto death, but for the glory of God, that the Son of God may be glorified through it."

[5]Now Jesus loved Martha and her sister and Lazarus. [6]So, when He heard that he

ROMANCE FAQ

Q: *What are the duties and responsibilities in a wife's job description?*

When we were first married, an older woman in our church mentored Barbara— a wonderful experience. She needed an older woman to come beside her and affirm what she was doing. Encouragement from someone who had been in her shoes meant more than anything I could say.

Now, after many years of marriage, Barbara would say that a wife's role in marriage can be summed up in three words: love, support, and respect.

Titus 2:4 instructs older women to train the younger women to "love their husbands." Initially that's an easy job, because most of us get married while we're in love. After the feelings fade, though, we have to remember that love is a commitment.

Second, wives are to support their husbands. To submit to your husband's leadership (Eph. 5:22) is to support his leadership. It means being an encouraging, believing wife who allows her husband to lead the family. It doesn't mean being a doormat. You should share your opinions, your thoughts and feelings, and make decisions together.

Finally, a wife must respect her husband. Ephesians 5:33 commands, "Let the wife see that she respects her husband." Even if you feel your husband is not worthy of respect, you honor God when you respect him.

10:26 [a]NU-Text omits *as I said to you.*
10:34 [a]Psalm 82:6   **10:38** [a]NU-Text reads *understand.*

was sick, He stayed two more days in the place where He was. [7]Then after this He said to *the* disciples, "Let us go to Judea again."

[8]*The* disciples said to Him, "Rabbi, lately the Jews sought to stone You, and are You going there again?"

[9]Jesus answered, "Are there not twelve hours in the day? If anyone walks in the day, he does not stumble, because he sees the light of this world. [10]But if one walks in the night, he stumbles, because the light is not in him." [11]These things He said, and after that He said to them, "Our friend Lazarus sleeps, but I go that I may wake him up."

[12]Then His disciples said, "Lord, if he sleeps he will get well." [13]However, Jesus spoke of his death, but they thought that He was speaking about taking rest in sleep.

[14]Then Jesus said to them plainly, "Lazarus is dead. [15]And I am glad for your sakes that I was not there, that you may believe. Nevertheless let us go to him."

[16]Then Thomas, who is called the Twin, said to his fellow disciples, "Let us also go, that we may die with Him."

I Am the Resurrection and the Life

[17]So when Jesus came, He found that he had already been in the tomb four days. [18]Now Bethany was near Jerusalem, about two miles[a] away. [19]And many of the Jews had joined the women around Martha and Mary, to comfort them concerning their brother.

[20]Now Martha, as soon as she heard that Jesus was coming, went and met Him, but Mary was sitting in the house. [21]Now Martha said to Jesus, "Lord, if You had been here, my brother would not have died. [22]But even now I know that whatever You ask of God, God will give You."

[23]Jesus said to her, "Your brother will rise again."

[24]Martha said to Him, "I know that he will rise again in the resurrection at the last day."

[25]Jesus said to her, "I am the resurrection and the life. He who believes in Me, though he may die, he shall live. [26]And whoever lives and believes in Me shall never die. Do you believe this?"

[27]She said to Him, "Yes, Lord, I believe that You are the Christ, the Son of God, who is to come into the world."

Jesus and Death, the Last Enemy

[28]And when she had said these things, she went her way and secretly called Mary her sister, saying, "The Teacher has come and is calling for you." [29]As soon as she heard *that,* she arose quickly and came to Him. [30]Now Jesus had not yet come into the town, but was[a] in the place where Martha met Him. [31]Then the Jews who were with her in the house, and comforting her, when they saw that Mary rose up quickly and went out, followed her, saying, "She is going to the tomb to weep there."[a]

[32]Then, when Mary came where Jesus was, and saw Him, she fell down at His feet, saying to Him, "Lord, if You had been here, my brother would not have died."

[33]Therefore, when Jesus saw her weeping, and the Jews who came with her weeping, He groaned in the spirit and was troubled. [34]And He said, "Where have you laid him?"

They said to Him, "Lord, come and see."

[35]Jesus wept. [36]Then the Jews said, "See how He loved him!"

[37]And some of them said, "Could not this Man, who opened the eyes of the blind, also have kept this man from dying?"

Lazarus Raised from the Dead

[38]Then Jesus, again groaning in Himself, came to the tomb. It was a cave, and a stone lay against it. [39]Jesus said, "Take away the stone."

Martha, the sister of him who was dead, said to Him, "Lord, by this time there is a stench, for he has been *dead* four days."

[40]Jesus said to her, "Did I not say to you that if you would believe you would see the glory of God?" [41]Then they took away the stone *from the place* where the dead man was lying.[a] And Jesus lifted up *His*

11:18 [a]Literally *fifteen stadia*   **11:30** [a]NU-Text adds *still.*   **11:31** [a]NU-Text reads *supposing that she was going to the tomb to weep there.*   **11:41** [a]NU-Text omits *from the place where the dead man was lying*

eyes and said, "Father, I thank You that You have heard Me. [42]And I know that You always hear Me, but because of the people who are standing by I said *this,* that they may believe that You sent Me." [43]Now when He had said these things, He cried with a loud voice, "Lazarus, come forth!" [44]And he who had died came out bound hand and foot with graveclothes, and his face was wrapped with a cloth. Jesus said to them, "Loose him, and let him go."

The Plot to Kill Jesus

[45]Then many of the Jews who had come to Mary, and had seen the things Jesus did, believed in Him. [46]But some of them went away to the Pharisees and told them the things Jesus did. [47]Then the chief priests and the Pharisees gathered a council and said, "What shall we do? For this Man works many signs. [48]If we let Him alone like this, everyone will believe in Him, and the Romans will come and take away both our place and nation."

[49]And one of them, Caiaphas, being high priest that year, said to them, "You know nothing at all, [50]nor do you consider that it is expedient for us[a] that one man should die for the people, and not that the whole nation should perish." [51]Now this he did not say on his own *authority;* but being high priest that year he prophesied that Jesus would die for the nation, [52]and not for that nation only, but also that He would gather together in one the children of God who were scattered abroad.

[53]Then, from that day on, they plotted to put Him to death. [54]Therefore Jesus no longer walked openly among the Jews, but went from there into the country near the wilderness, to a city called Ephraim, and there remained with His disciples.

[55]And the Passover of the Jews was near, and many went from the country up to Jerusalem before the Passover, to purify themselves. [56]Then they sought Jesus, and spoke among themselves as they stood in the temple, "What do you think—that He will

not come to the feast?" [57]Now both the chief priests and the Pharisees had given a command, that if anyone knew where He was, he should report *it,* that they might seize Him.

The Anointing at Bethany

12 Then, six days before the Passover, Jesus came to Bethany, where Lazarus was who had been dead,[a] whom He had raised from the dead. [2]There they made Him a supper; and Martha served, but Lazarus was one of those who sat at the table with Him. [3]Then Mary took a pound of very costly oil of spikenard, anointed the feet of Jesus, and wiped His feet with her hair. And the house was filled with the fragrance of the oil.

[4]But one of His disciples, Judas Iscariot, Simon's *son,* who would betray Him, said, [5]"Why was this fragrant oil not sold for three hundred denarii[a] and given to the poor?" [6]This he said, not that he cared for the poor, but because he was a thief, and had the money box; and he used to take what was put in it.

[7]But Jesus said, "Let her alone; she has kept[a] this for the day of My burial. [8]For the poor you have with you always, but Me you do not have always."

The Plot to Kill Lazarus

[9]Now a great many of the Jews knew that He was there; and they came, not for Jesus' sake only, but that they might also see Lazarus, whom He had raised from the dead. [10]But the chief priests plotted to put Lazarus to death also, [11]because on account of him many of the Jews went away and believed in Jesus.

The Triumphal Entry

[12]The next day a great multitude that had come to the feast, when they heard that Jesus was coming to Jerusalem, [13]took branches of palm trees and went out to meet Him, and cried out:

"Hosanna!
'Blessed is He who comes in the name of the LORD!'[a]
The King of Israel!"

[14]Then Jesus, when He had found a young donkey, sat on it; as it is written:

11:50 [a]NU-Text reads *you.* **12:1** [a]NU-Text omits *who had been dead.* **12:5** [a]About one year's wages for a worker **12:7** [a]NU-Text reads *that she may keep.* **12:13** [a]Psalm 118:26

15 *"Fear not, daughter of Zion;*
    Behold, your King is coming,
    *Sitting on a donkey's colt."*a

16His disciples did not understand these things at first; but when Jesus was glorified, then they remembered that these things were written about Him and *that* they had done these things to Him.

17Therefore the people, who were with Him when He called Lazarus out of his tomb and raised him from the dead, bore witness. 18For this reason the people also met Him, because they heard that He had done this sign. 19The Pharisees therefore said among themselves, "You see that you are accomplishing nothing. Look, the world has gone after Him!"

The Fruitful Grain of Wheat

20Now there were certain Greeks among those who came up to worship at the feast. 21Then they came to Philip, who was from Bethsaida of Galilee, and asked him, saying, "Sir, we wish to see Jesus."

22Philip came and told Andrew, and in turn Andrew and Philip told Jesus.

23But Jesus answered them, saying, "The hour has come that the Son of Man should be glorified. 24Most assuredly, I say to you, unless a grain of wheat falls into the ground and dies, it remains alone; but if it dies, it produces much grain. 25He who loves his life will lose it, and he who hates his life in this world will keep it for eternal life. 26If anyone serves Me, let him follow Me; and where I am, there My servant will be also. If anyone serves Me, him *My* Father will honor.

Jesus Predicts His Death on the Cross

27"Now My soul is troubled, and what shall I say? 'Father, save Me from this hour'? But for this purpose I came to this hour. 28Father, glorify Your name."

Then a voice came from heaven, *saying,* "I have both glorified *it* and will glorify *it* again."

29Therefore the people who stood by and heard *it* said that it had thundered. Others said, "An angel has spoken to Him."

30Jesus answered and said, "This voice did not come because of Me, but for your sake. 31Now is the judgment of this world; now the ruler of this world will be cast out. 32And I, if I am lifted up from the earth, will draw all *peoples* to Myself." 33This He said, signifying by what death He would die.

34The people answered Him, "We have heard from the law that the Christ remains forever; and how *can* You say, 'The Son of Man must be lifted up'? Who is this Son of Man?"

35Then Jesus said to them, "A little while longer the light is with you. Walk while you have the light, lest darkness overtake you; he who walks in darkness does not know where he is going. 36While you have the light, believe in the light, that you may become sons of light." These things Jesus spoke, and departed, and was hidden from them.

Who Has Believed Our Report?

37But although He had done so many signs before them, they did not believe in Him, 38that the word of Isaiah the prophet might be fulfilled, which he spoke:

"Lord, who has believed our report?
    And to whom has the arm of the
        *LORD been revealed?"*a

39Therefore they could not believe, because Isaiah said again:

40 *"He has blinded their eyes and*
        hardened their hearts,
    Lest they should see with their eyes,
    Lest they should understand with
        their hearts and turn,
    *So that I should heal them."*a

41These things Isaiah said whena he saw His glory and spoke of Him.

Walk in the Light

42Nevertheless even among the rulers many believed in Him, but because of the Pharisees they did not confess *Him,* lest they should be put out of the synagogue; 43for they loved the praise of men more than the praise of God.

44Then Jesus cried out and said, "He who believes in Me, believes not in Me but

---

12:15 aZechariah 9:9 12:38 aIsaiah 53:1
12:40 aIsaiah 6:10 12:41 aNU-Text reads *because.*

in Him who sent Me. ⁴⁵And he who sees Me sees Him who sent Me. ⁴⁶I have come *as* a light into the world, that whoever believes in Me should not abide in darkness. ⁴⁷And if anyone hears My words and does not believe,ᵃ I do not judge him; for I did not come to judge the world but to save the world. ⁴⁸He who rejects Me, and does not receive My words, has that which judges him—the word that I have spoken will judge him in the last day. ⁴⁹For I have not spoken on My own *authority;* but the Father who sent Me gave Me a command, what I should say and what I should speak. ⁵⁰And I know that His command is everlasting life. Therefore, whatever I speak, just as the Father has told Me, so I speak."

Jesus Washes the Disciples' Feet

13 Now before the Feast of the Passover, when Jesus knew that His hour had come that He should depart from this world to the Father, having loved His own who were in the world, He loved them to the end.

²And supper being ended,ᵃ the devil having already put it into the heart of Judas Iscariot, Simon's *son,* to betray Him, ³Jesus, knowing that the Father had given all things into His hands, and that He had come from God and was going to God, ⁴rose from supper and laid aside His garments, took a towel and girded Himself. ⁵After that, He poured water into a basin and began to wash the disciples' feet, and to wipe *them* with the towel with which He was girded. ⁶Then He came to Simon Peter. And *Peter* said to Him, "Lord, are You washing my feet?"

⁷Jesus answered and said to him, "What I am doing you do not understand now, but you will know after this."

⁸Peter said to Him, "You shall never wash my feet!"

Jesus answered him, "If I do not wash you, you have no part with Me."

⁹Simon Peter said to Him, "Lord, not my feet only, but also *my* hands and *my* head!"

¹⁰Jesus said to him, "He who is bathed needs only to wash *his* feet, but is completely

BIBLICAL INSIGHTS • 13:1–17
Loving Through Serving

JESUS CHRIST did not just talk about serving; He demonstrated it (John 13:1–17). He is our model for servant leadership, and that includes our leadership in the home.

A husband is not his wife's master. His leadership must follow the example set by Christ, the Head of the church, who took on the very nature of a servant when He was made in human likeness (Phil. 2:7). Simply said, a husband must love and lead, like the Savior did, by serving.

One of the best ways to serve your wife is to understand her needs and try to meet them. Do you know your wife's top three needs? If she is a young mother, she has a certain set of basic needs. If you are in an empty nest, your wife has a different set of needs. What worries her? What troubles her? What kind of pressures does she feel? Learn the answers to questions like that, and then do what you can to reduce her worries, her troubles, and her pressures.

What do you know about your wife's hopes and dreams? I'll bet she has plenty—do you know what they are?

Are you cultivating her gifts? If she has a knack for decorating, do you help her develop that? Are you helping her grow into the woman that God made her to be?

This is your God-given assignment as a husband.

The Bible instructs husbands to live with their wives in an understanding way (1 Pet. 3:7). Part of how we serve our wives is by understanding their needs and finding ways to help meet those needs. How are you serving your wife as you lead your home?

Why not take your next date night and ask your wife how you are doing in this area? Ask her how you can do a better job of knowing and meeting her needs? Then begin to quietly go about the process of doing just that.

DEVOTIONS FOR COUPLES • 13:1
Honor Your Wife

After watching the marriages of numerous Christian leaders disintegrate, I have come to some conclusions. One is that there is no such thing as a marriage blowout—only slow, small leaks. Like a tire that gradually loses air without the driver noticing, these marriages were allowed to slowly go flat. If someone did check the air pressure in their marriages, he or she did nothing to return them to acceptable, safe levels.

Every marriage is susceptible to leaks; yours and mine are no exceptions. The world lures my wife with glittery, false promises of imitation fulfillment and phony significance. If I fail to honor her and esteem her as a woman of distinction, it's just a matter of time before she will begin to wear down and be tempted to look elsewhere for worth.

Consider a few proven techniques to honor and invest in your wife:

Learn the art of putting her on a pedestal. Demonstrate how much you value her by treating her with respect, tenderness, and the highest esteem.

Recognize her accomplishments. Frequently I look into Barbara's eyes and verbally express my wonder at all she does. She wears many hats and is an amazingly hard worker. At other times, I stand back in awe of the woman of character she has become. Her steady walk with God is a constant stream of ministry to me. And I make sure she knows how much respect I have for her.

Speak to her with respect. I work hard to honor Barbara with my tongue. I'm not always as successful as I'd like, but I know that honor begins with a proper attitude. "Out of the abundance of the heart the mouth speaks," Jesus said (Matt. 12:34), so I work to develop a respectful heart attitude toward my wife—and I insist that our children do the same.

Honor your wife by extending common courtesies. You may think that these little amenities were worthwhile only during courtship, but actually they are great ways to demonstrate respect and distinction over the long haul. Common courtesy is at the heart of servanthood; it says, "My life for yours." It bows before another to show esteem and dignity.

How is the air pressure in your marriage? Any tire leaks? A patch required? In what two specific ways can you honor your wife this week? Pray that you would discern slow leaks in your marriage before they cause serious problems, and that your mate would feel honored in her critical role as wife and mother.

clean; and you are clean, but not all of you." [11]For He knew who would betray Him; therefore He said, "You are not all clean."

[12]So when He had washed their feet, taken His garments, and sat down again, He said to them, "Do you know what I have done to you? [13]You call Me Teacher and Lord, and you say well, for *so* I am. [14]If I then, *your* Lord and Teacher, have washed your feet, you also ought to wash one another's feet. [15]For I have given you an example, that you should do as I have done to you. [16]Most assuredly, I say to you, a servant is not greater than his master; nor is he who is sent greater than he who sent him. [17]If you know these things, blessed are you if you do them.

Jesus Identifies His Betrayer

[18]"I do not speak concerning all of you. I know whom I have chosen; but that the Scripture may be fulfilled, '*He who eats bread with Me*[a] *has lifted up his heel against Me.*'[b] [19]Now I tell you before it comes, that when it does come to pass, you may believe that I am *He.* [20]Most assuredly, I say to you, he who receives whomever I send receives Me; and he who receives Me receives Him who sent Me."

[21]When Jesus had said these things, He was troubled in spirit, and testified and said, "Most assuredly, I say to you, one of you will betray Me." [22]Then the disciples

13:18 [a]NU-Text reads *My bread.* [b]Psalm 41:9

looked at one another, perplexed about whom He spoke.

²³Now there was leaning on Jesus' bosom one of His disciples, whom Jesus loved. ²⁴Simon Peter therefore motioned to him to ask who it was of whom He spoke.

²⁵Then, leaning back^a on Jesus' breast, he said to Him, "Lord, who is it?"

²⁶Jesus answered, "It is he to whom I shall give a piece of bread when I have dipped *it*." And having dipped the bread, He gave *it* to Judas Iscariot, *the son* of Simon. ²⁷Now after the piece of bread, Satan entered him. Then Jesus said to him, "What you do, do quickly." ²⁸But no one at the table knew for what reason He said this to him. ²⁹For some thought, because Judas had the money box, that Jesus had said to him, "Buy *those things* we need for the feast," or that he should give something to the poor.

³⁰Having received the piece of bread, he then went out immediately. And it was night.

The New Commandment

³¹So, when he had gone out, Jesus said, "Now the Son of Man is glorified, and God is glorified in Him. ³²If God is glorified in Him, God will also glorify Him in Himself, and glorify Him immediately. ³³Little children, I shall be with you a little while longer. You will seek Me; and as I said to the Jews, 'Where I am going, you cannot come,' so now I say to you. ³⁴A new commandment I give to you, that you love one another; as I have loved you, that you also love one another. ³⁵By this all will know that you are My disciples, if you have love for one another."

Jesus Predicts Peter's Denial

³⁶Simon Peter said to Him, "Lord, where are You going?"

Jesus answered him, "Where I am going you cannot follow Me now, but you shall follow Me afterward."

³⁷Peter said to Him, "Lord, why can I not follow You now? I will lay down my life for Your sake."

³⁸Jesus answered him, "Will you lay down your life for My sake? Most assuredly, I say to you, the rooster shall not crow till you have denied Me three times.

The Way, the Truth, and the Life

14 "Let not your heart be troubled; you believe in God, believe also in Me. ²In My Father's house are many mansions;^a if *it were* not *so,* I would have told you. I go to prepare a place for you.^b ³And if I go and prepare a place for you, I will come again and receive you to Myself; that where I am, *there* you may be also. ⁴And where I go you know, and the way you know."

⁵Thomas said to Him, "Lord, we do not know where You are going, and how can we know the way?"

⁶Jesus said to him, "I am the way, the truth, and the life. No one comes to the Father except through Me.

INTIMATE MOMENTS

Over coffee, ask your wife, "What are the three most romantic times we've had together?" Write them down and make plans to do them again.

The Father Revealed

⁷"If you had known Me, you would have known My Father also; and from now on you know Him and have seen Him."

⁸Philip said to Him, "Lord, show us the Father, and it is sufficient for us."

⁹Jesus said to him, "Have I been with you so long, and yet you have not known Me, Philip? He who has seen Me has seen the Father; so how can you say, 'Show us the Father'? ¹⁰Do you not believe that I am in the Father, and the Father in Me? The words that I speak to you I do not speak on My own *authority;* but the Father who dwells in Me does the works. ¹¹Believe Me that I *am* in the Father and the Father in Me, or else believe Me for the sake of the works themselves.

13:25 ^aNU-Text and M-Text add *thus.*
14:2 ^aLiterally *dwellings* ^bNU-Text adds a word which would cause the text to read either *if it were not so, would I have told you that I go to prepare a place for you?* or *if it were not so I would have told you; for I go to prepare a place for you.*

BIBLICAL INSIGHTS • 14:16
Rely on Your Helper

MOST CHRISTIANS AGREE that the Holy Spirit is the Third Person of the Trinity. When I was a little boy growing up in a church that used only the King James Version, we referred to Him as the Holy Ghost. And for a long time I could imagine only something like the cartoon character, Casper the Friendly Ghost, floating through walls like a puff of smoke. The Holy Ghost was not someone that I could relate to as a boy. I am glad today that He is referred to as the Holy Spirit.

For years I referred to the Holy Ghost as an "it." But the Holy Spirit Jesus describes is a person, sent not only to glorify Christ, but also to be our Counselor, Advisor, Advocate, Defender, Director and Guide. Speaking of the Holy Spirit, Jesus said, "And I will pray the Father, and He will give you another Helper, that He may abide with you forever" (14:16).

If you are interested in living the abundant life Jesus promised, then rightly relating to the Holy Spirit is vital. Just think of all the sermons you've heard on the Christian life. Think of all the books you've read about marriage. If you try in your own power to obey God and follow all that advice, you may have short-term success, but over time you will fail . . . period. It's impossible. You need God's power which is available to you as you yield moment by moment to the Holy Spirit, who was sent to us by Christ to empower us to live the Christian life.

The Answered Prayer

12"Most assuredly, I say to you, he who believes in Me, the works that I do he will do also; and greater *works* than these he will do, because I go to My Father. 13And whatever you ask in My name, that I will do, that the Father may be glorified in the Son. 14If you ask[a] anything in My name, I will do *it*.

Jesus Promises Another Helper

15"If you love Me, keep[a] My commandments. 16And I will pray the Father, and He will give you another Helper, that He may abide with you forever— 17the Spirit of truth, whom the world cannot receive, because it neither sees Him nor knows Him; but you know Him, for He dwells with you and will be in you. 18I will not leave you orphans; I will come to you.

Indwelling of the Father and the Son

19"A little while longer and the world will see Me no more, but you will see Me. Because I live, you will live also. 20At that day you will know that I *am* in My Father, and you in Me, and I in you. 21He who has My commandments and keeps them, it is he who loves Me. And he who loves Me will be loved by My Father, and I will love him, and manifest Myself to him."

22Judas (not Iscariot) said to Him, "Lord, how is it that You will manifest Yourself to us, and not to the world?"

23Jesus answered and said to him, "If anyone loves Me, he will keep My word; and My Father will love him, and We will come to him and make Our home with him. 24He who does not love Me does not keep My words; and the word which you hear is not Mine but the Father's who sent Me.

The Gift of His Peace

25"These things I have spoken to you while being present with you. 26But the Helper, the Holy Spirit, whom the Father will send in My name, He will teach you all things, and bring to your remembrance all things that I said to you. 27Peace I leave with you, My peace I give to you; not as the world gives do I give to you. Let not your heart be troubled, neither let it be afraid. 28You have heard Me say to you, 'I am going away and coming *back* to you.' If you loved Me, you would rejoice because I said,[a] 'I am going to the Father,' for My Father is greater than I.

29"And now I have told you before it comes, that when it does come to pass, you may believe. 30I will no longer talk much

---

14:14 [a]NU-Text adds *Me*. 14:15 [a]NU-Text reads *you will keep*. 14:28 [a]NU-Text omits *I said*.

with you, for the ruler of this world is coming, and he has nothing in Me. [31]But that the world may know that I love the Father, and as the Father gave Me commandment, so I do. Arise, let us go from here.

The True Vine

15 "I am the true vine, and My Father is the vinedresser. [2]Every branch in Me that does not bear fruit He takes away;[a] and every *branch* that bears fruit He prunes, that it may bear more fruit. [3]You are already clean because of the word which I have spoken to you. [4]Abide in Me, and I in you. As the branch cannot bear fruit of itself, unless it abides in the vine, neither can you, unless you abide in Me.

[5]"I am the vine, you *are* the branches. He who abides in Me, and I in him, bears much fruit; for without Me you can do nothing. [6]If anyone does not abide in Me, he is cast out as a branch and is withered; and they gather them and throw *them* into the fire, and they are burned. [7]If you abide in Me, and My words abide in you, you will[a] ask what you desire, and it shall be done for you. [8]By this My Father is glorified, that you bear much fruit; so you will be My disciples.

15:2 [a]Or *lifts up* 15:7 [a]NU-Text omits *you will.*

Love and Joy Perfected

[9]"As the Father loved Me, I also have loved you; abide in My love. [10]If you keep My commandments, you will abide in My love, just as I have kept My Father's commandments and abide in His love.

[11]"These things I have spoken to you, that My joy may remain in you, and *that* your joy may be full. [12]This is My commandment, that you love one another as I have loved you. [13]Greater love has no one than this, than to lay down one's life for his friends. [14]You are My friends if you do whatever I command you. [15]No longer do I call you servants, for a servant does not know what his master is doing; but I have called you friends, for all things that I heard from My Father I have made known to you. [16]You did not choose Me, but I chose you and appointed you that you should go and bear fruit, and *that* your fruit should remain, that whatever you ask the Father in My name He may give you. [17]These things I command you, that you love one another.

The World's Hatred

[18]"If the world hates you, you know that it hated Me before *it hated* you. [19]If you were of the world, the world would love its own. Yet because you are not of the world, but I chose you out of the world, therefore the world hates you. [20]Remember the word

Suffering Precedes Fruitfulness

Would you like your marriage to blossom and grow and become a great blessing to everyone your relationship touches? If so, then you need to learn something about pruning.

Jesus made it very clear that one prerequisite of bearing fruit in the Christian life is the painful process of pruning, in which the Father cuts away what is useless or hinders us from bearing fruit. He said, "Every branch that bears fruit He prunes, that it may bear more fruit" (15:2). Just as there are laws of nature, like gravity, so it is in the spiritual realm: Pruning precedes fruit bearing. God lovingly orders events, circumstances, and relationships to help us become more like Jesus Christ.

Personal godliness is God's primary goal for each of us. And while His pruning can seem severe—even too painful to bear—it is necessary, for without that pruning, we will bear little fruit.

One of the great privileges of marriage is that we do not have to go through these pruning periods alone. Through marriage, God has provided you a partner with whom you can share the pain of the pruning process. If your mate is in the midst of a season of pruning, you can come alongside and gently remind him or her of the hope of becoming more Christ-like through the suffering.

DEVOTIONS FOR COUPLES • 15:12
Three Big Little Words

I used to think the most difficult words to utter were "I love you."

I remember the first time I told my mom and dad "I love you." I was a typical unexpressive, ungrateful teenager, but on the day I left home for college, I looked my parents in the eyes and said those three little words (with excruciating pain).

Then there was the first time I told Barbara that I loved her. My heart jumped wildly and my adrenaline was the only thing flowing faster than the beads of sweat on my forehead. I remember wondering how young couples in love could survive the experience!

Telling another person, "I love you," represents risk and vulnerability. Yet however difficult these words of love may be to say, three other words are even more arduous to express: "I need you."

Consider the number of people to whom you have expressed your love: your mate, children, parents, extended family, and possibly a few select friends.

Now think of those to whom you have said, "I need you." A much smaller number, isn't it? Most of us have difficulty admitting need.

But why?

It's because admitting need means we depend upon another. It means we are less than complete. When the apostle Paul admitted he had no one but Timothy who could meet a particular need in his life (see Phil 2:20), he was making himself vulnerable, admitting his dependence on one beloved person.

It's interesting that in Genesis 2:18, Adam had to be told he had a need. God said, "It is not good for the man to be alone." And even after that authoritative statement, Adam probably had to name several thousand creatures to finally get the point: *He needed someone!* He needed a wife.

Today is no different. God often has to show us how much we need our mates and our children. And when He does, let's not be afraid to admit it!

Take a few moments today and focus on each person in your family. What does each person bring to your home? In what ways do you need each other? Take a risk and interact with your spouse and children on the various ways you need them. Then ask the Lord to give you and your clan a humble, grateful spirit, as you recognize and learn to appreciate the interconnectedness of your family—a connection that God Himself designed.

---

that I said to you, 'A servant is not greater than his master.' If they persecuted Me, they will also persecute you. If they kept My word, they will keep yours also. [21]But all these things they will do to you for My name's sake, because they do not know Him who sent Me. [22]If I had not come and spoken to them, they would have no sin, but now they have no excuse for their sin. [23]He who hates Me hates My Father also. [24]If I had not done among them the works which no one else did, they would have no sin; but now they have seen and also hated both Me and My Father. [25]But *this happened* that the word might be fulfilled which is written in their law, '*They hated Me without a cause.*'[a]

The Coming Rejection

[26]"But when the Helper comes, whom I shall send to you from the Father, the Spirit of truth who proceeds from the Father, He will testify of Me. [27]And you also will bear witness, because you have been with Me from the beginning.

16 "These things I have spoken to you, that you should not be made to stumble. [2]They will put you out of the synagogues; yes, the time is coming that whoever kills you will think that he offers God service. [3]And these things they will do to you[a] because they have not known the

15:25 [a]Psalm 69:4   16:3 [a]NU-Text and M-Text omit *to you.*

Father nor Me. ⁴But these things I have told you, that when the^a time comes, you may remember that I told you of them.

"And these things I did not say to you at the beginning, because I was with you.

The Work of the Holy Spirit

⁵"But now I go away to Him who sent Me, and none of you asks Me, 'Where are You going?' ⁶But because I have said these things to you, sorrow has filled your heart. ⁷Nevertheless I tell you the truth. It is to your advantage that I go away; for if I do not go away, the Helper will not come to you; but if I depart, I will send Him to you. ⁸And when He has come, He will convict the world of sin, and of righteousness, and of judgment: ⁹of sin, because they do not believe in Me; ¹⁰of righteousness, because I go to My Father and you see Me no more; ¹¹of judgment, because the ruler of this world is judged.

¹²"I still have many things to say to you, but you cannot bear *them* now. ¹³However, when He, the Spirit of truth, has come, He will guide you into all truth; for He will not speak on His own *authority*, but whatever He hears He will speak; and He will tell you things to come. ¹⁴He will glorify Me, for He will take of what is Mine and declare *it* to you. ¹⁵All things that the Father has are Mine. Therefore I said that He will take of Mine and declare *it* to you.^a

Sorrow Will Turn to Joy

¹⁶"A little while, and you will not see Me; and again a little while, and you will see Me, because I go to the Father."

¹⁷Then *some* of His disciples said among themselves, "What is this that He says to us, 'A little while, and you will not see Me; and again a little while, and you will see Me'; and, 'because I go to the Father'?" ¹⁸They said therefore, "What is this that He says, 'A little while'? We do not know what He is saying."

¹⁹Now Jesus knew that they desired to ask Him, and He said to them, "Are you inquiring among yourselves about what I said, 'A little while, and you will not see

---

BIBLICAL INSIGHTS • 15:20

Prepare Your Kids for Persecution

PROTECTION IS A BIG part of loving our children. We want to do all we can to protect, defend, shelter, and guard them. It's only natural.

But genuine love is a lot bigger than mere protection. Yes, there are times when our kids may need to borrow our faith and lean on our hope. But they don't always need us to rescue them. In fact, the thing we want to fix for them may be the very thing God wants to use to build character and faith into their lives—the only things that will last after we are gone.

As we love our children, we must also remember that Jesus clearly said, "If they persecuted Me, they will also persecute you. If they kept My word, they will keep yours also'" (15:20).

In the midst of the sufferings and trials that come because of genuine faith in Christ, our children need our constant love and encouragement. But they do *not* always need us to rescue them. In fact, many times these are great teaching opportunities, designed by God to instruct them, building their faith. They need to learn for themselves that God is faithful, even in the midst of persecution. We do them no favors by trying to build an impenetrable shield around them.

As parents, watching our children struggle and suffer is difficult (after raising six children, we know!). But when we remember that trials are tools in God's hand to help us grow (James 1:2–4), we can back off and allow God to do His work in our children's lives. Ultimately, our children must take our instruction and make it their own.

Me; and again a little while, and you will see Me'? ²⁰Most assuredly, I say to you that you will weep and lament, but the world will rejoice; and you will be sorrowful, but your sorrow will be turned into joy. ²¹A woman, when she is in labor, has sorrow

---

16:4 ^aNU-Text reads *their*. **16:15** ^aNU-Text and M-Text read *He takes of Mine and will declare it to you.*

BIBLICAL INSIGHTS · 16:33

Facing the Traps of Life

THIS WORLD IS FULL of traps that can ensnare and seriously harm our children. Part of our job as parents is to educate them about those traps, but also to assure them that Jesus promises to help them safely navigate around every satanic ambush.

Jesus told His disciples about the many traps and pitfalls they would surely face in life, "These things I have spoken to you, that in Me you may have peace. In the world you will have tribulation; but be of good cheer, I have overcome the world" (16:33). Yes, there is tribulation; but there is also peace, because Jesus has overcome the world and the prince of this world, Satan.

Preparing our children to face the traps of this world is a demanding challenge, but we do not need to feel fearful or intimidated. We must remember what the psalmist wrote about avoiding traps, "I will say of the LORD, 'He is my refuge and my fortress; my God, in Him I will trust.' Surely He shall deliver you from the snare of the fowler and from the perilous pestilence" (Ps. 91:2, 3).

The snares that the enemy has laid for our children are real, but so is God's promise to deliver them as we obey His Word. We instruct, warn, and guide, but God is the one who protects and delivers our children from danger. May God's favor be upon you as you guide your children through the traps of adolescence. And may He keep them from evil and use them for His purposes.

---

because her hour has come; but as soon as she has given birth to the child, she no longer remembers the anguish, for joy that a human being has been born into the world. ²²Therefore you now have sorrow; but I will see you again and your heart will rejoice, and your joy no one will take from you.

²³"And in that day you will ask Me nothing. Most assuredly, I say to you, whatever

you ask the Father in My name He will give you. ²⁴Until now you have asked nothing in My name. Ask, and you will receive, that your joy may be full.

Jesus Christ Has Overcome the World

²⁵"These things I have spoken to you in figurative language; but the time is coming when I will no longer speak to you in figurative language, but I will tell you plainly about the Father. ²⁶In that day you will ask in My name, and I do not say to you that I shall pray the Father for you; ²⁷for the Father Himself loves you, because you have loved Me, and have believed that I came forth from God. ²⁸I came forth from the Father and have come into the world. Again, I leave the world and go to the Father."

²⁹His disciples said to Him, "See, now You are speaking plainly, and using no figure of speech! ³⁰Now we are sure that You know all things, and have no need that anyone should question You. By this we believe that You came forth from God."

³¹Jesus answered them, "Do you now believe? ³²Indeed the hour is coming, yes, has now come, that you will be scattered, each to his own, and will leave Me alone. And yet I am not alone, because the Father is with Me. ³³These things I have spoken to you, that in Me you may have peace. In the world you will[a] have tribulation; but be of good cheer, I have overcome the world."

Jesus Prays for Himself

17 Jesus spoke these words, lifted up His eyes to heaven, and said: "Father, the hour has come. Glorify Your Son, that Your Son also may glorify You, ²as You have given Him authority over all flesh, that He should[a] give eternal life to as many as You have given Him. ³And this is eternal life, that they may know You, the only true God, and Jesus Christ whom You have sent. ⁴I have glorified You on the earth. I have finished the work which You have given Me to do. ⁵And now, O Father, glorify Me together with Yourself, with the glory which I had with You before the world was.

16:33 ªNU-Text and M-Text omit *will*.
17:2 ªM-Text reads *shall*.

Jesus Prays for His Disciples

6"I have manifested Your name to the men whom You have given Me out of the world. They were Yours, You gave them to Me, and they have kept Your word. 7Now they have known that all things which You have given Me are from You. 8For I have given to them the words which You have given Me; and they have received *them,* and have known surely that I came forth from You; and they have believed that You sent Me.

9"I pray for them. I do not pray for the world but for those whom You have given Me, for they are Yours. 10And all Mine are Yours, and Yours are Mine, and I am glorified in them. 11Now I am no longer in the world, but these are in the world, and I come to You. Holy Father, keep through Your name those whom You have given Me,ᵃ that they may be one as We *are.* 12While I was with them in the world,ᵃ I kept them in Your name. Those whom You gave Me I have kept;ᵇ and none of them is

lost except the son of perdition, that the Scripture might be fulfilled. 13But now I come to You, and these things I speak in the world, that they may have My joy fulfilled in themselves. 14I have given them Your word; and the world has hated them because they are not of the world, just as I am not of the world. 15I do not pray that You should take them out of the world, but that You should keep them from the evil one. 16They are not of the world, just as I am not of the world. 17Sanctify them by Your truth. Your word is truth. 18As You sent Me into the world, I also have sent them into the world. 19And for their sakes I sanctify Myself, that they also may be sanctified by the truth.

Jesus Prays for All Believers

20"I do not pray for these alone, but also for those who willᵃ believe in Me through their word; 21that they all may be one, as You, Father, *are* in Me, and I in You; that they also may be one in Us, that the world may believe that You sent Me. 22And the glory which You gave Me I have given them, that they may be one just as We are one: 23I in them, and You in Me; that they may be made perfect in one, and that the world may know that You have sent Me, and have loved them as You have loved Me.

17:11 ᵃNU-Text and M-Text read *keep them through Your name which You have given Me.*
17:12 ᵃNU-Text omits *in the world.* ᵇNU-Text reads *in Your name which You gave Me. And I guarded them;* (or *it;*). **17:20** ᵃNU-Text and M-Text omit *will.*

ROMANTIC QUOTES AND NOTES
Keep Your Vows—In Spite of _____

Modern society still suffers from the sickness of the "Me Generation," which has contaminated the covenant of marriage. The selfish, Me-Gen person says, in effect, "When marriage serves my purposes, I'm on board. When it ceases to make me happy, when it's too much effort, when the unexpected shows up and creates pressure, then I'm out of here." Some leave physically and move out, while others leave emotionally and withdraw.

Your vows mean your commitment will endure. When the pressure becomes relentless, white-hot and intense, when the cultural voices around you entice you to look out for yourself and quit your marriage, your vows should scream, "DON'T!"

The fact that we will not quit, that we will be there for one another, even when the unexpected happens, actually helps to mitigate the pressure between us. Besides, why are we so surprised when trouble comes our way? Jesus actually *promised* we would experience problems. "In the world," He said, "you *will* have tribulation" (italics added). Then in the next breath, He quickly pointed out, "But be of good cheer, I have overcome the world" (16:33).

Expect the unexpected: suffering, trials, difficulty. But don't give up! Jesus will be there in the midst of your troubles. And you can be there for one another, too. The covenant of marriage creates security and safety for a husband and a wife in the midst of the storms. That's one of the blessings of the covenant commitment of marriage.

A Prayer for Unity

MUCH OF JESUS' INSTRUCTION deals with bringing peace and harmony where conflict and dissension exists. He came to remove the barriers between God and us; He is our perfect peacemaker with God. He taught His disciples to break down barriers in relationships. He taught them to forgive each other. Love was the banner of His earthly ministry.

John 17 records the Savior's highpriestly prayer, offered near the end of His life. "I do not pray for these alone," He said, "but also for those also who will believe in Me through their word; that they all may be one" (17:20, 21).

Why did Jesus focus on unity and oneness at this crucial point? Could it be that the strongest demonstration of the Holy Spirit's power in our lives might be imperfect Christians living with one another? Could it also be that this unity, demonstrated in a marriage, is one of the most powerful statements of the love of God on the planet?

Communication is to a relationship what electricity is to a home. Just as electricity brings light and power to a home, communication carries the power to bring relationships to life and sustain them. It is vital to maintaining any healthy relationship. That can happen if you have a meal each day when your whole family sits down together, with the phones, iPods, and TV's all turned off. That can happen as you pray together at the end of the day with your mate and with each of your children. That can happen as you take a walk and talk with a troubled teen who just needs you to be there. That can happen as you call your parents weekly to see how they are doing.

The main thing is to take responsibility for doing your part to honor Jesus' prayer that "you all may be one."

24"Father, I desire that they also whom You gave Me may be with Me where I am, that they may behold My glory which You have given Me; for You loved Me before the foundation of the world. 25O righteous Father! The world has not known You, but I have known You; and these have known that You sent Me. 26And I have declared to them Your name, and will declare *it,* that the love with which You loved Me may be in them, and I in them."

Betrayal and Arrest in Gethsemane

18 When Jesus had spoken these words, He went out with His disciples over the Brook Kidron, where there was a garden, which He and His disciples entered. 2And Judas, who betrayed Him, also knew the place; for Jesus often met there with His disciples. 3Then Judas, having received a detachment *of troops,* and officers from the chief priests and Pharisees, came there with lanterns, torches, and weapons. 4Jesus therefore, knowing all things that would come upon Him, went forward and said to them, "Whom are you seeking?"

5They answered Him, "Jesus of Nazareth."

Jesus said to them, "I am *He.*" And Judas, who betrayed Him, also stood with them. 6Now when He said to them, "I am *He,*" they drew back and fell to the ground.

7Then He asked them again, "Whom are you seeking?"

And they said, "Jesus of Nazareth."

8Jesus answered, "I have told you that I am *He.* Therefore, if you seek Me, let these go their way," 9that the saying might be fulfilled which He spoke, "Of those whom You gave Me I have lost none."

10Then Simon Peter, having a sword, drew it and struck the high priest's servant, and cut off his right ear. The servant's name was Malchus.

11So Jesus said to Peter, "Put your sword into the sheath. Shall I not drink the cup which My Father has given Me?"

Before the High Priest

12Then the detachment *of troops* and the captain and the officers of the Jews arrested Jesus and bound Him. 13And they led Him away to Annas first, for he was the father-in-law of Caiaphas who was high priest that year. ¹⁴Now it was Caiaphas who advised the Jews that it was expedient that one man should die for the people.

Peter Denies Jesus

¹⁵And Simon Peter followed Jesus, and so *did* another^a disciple. Now that disciple was known to the high priest, and went with Jesus into the courtyard of the high priest. ¹⁶But Peter stood at the door outside. Then the other disciple, who was known to the high priest, went out and spoke to her who kept the door, and

18:15 ^aM-Text reads *the other.*

brought Peter in. ¹⁷Then the servant girl who kept the door said to Peter, "You are not also *one* of this Man's disciples, are you?"

He said, "I am not."

¹⁸Now the servants and officers who had made a fire of coals stood there, for it was cold, and they warmed themselves. And Peter stood with them and warmed himself.

Jesus Questioned by the High Priest

¹⁹The high priest then asked Jesus about His disciples and His doctrine.

²⁰Jesus answered him, "I spoke openly to the world. I always taught in synagogues and in the temple, where the Jews always

---

| PARENTING MATTERS | **Q: How can we overcome some of the negative emotions associated with parenthood?** |

I recently traveled to Seattle to observe two focus groups composed of young Christian parents raising younger kids. These parents expressed five primary feelings about raising children:

Fear. They talked of their fears of guiding their sons and daughters through adolescence, of not being able to communicate with their children while going through these turbulent years. They feared their kids would turn out to be just like them in ways they didn't like.

Guilt. They felt guilty over their mistakes and failures. They wondered if they were ruining their kids. They regretted things they had said and had done.

Frustration. They felt frustrated and even angry when their kids didn't obey them. They felt they had to explain everything too many times.

Self-doubt. Were they doing it all wrong? Were their expectations too high or too low? Should they just let the underwear lie on the floor?

Discouragement. They saw their own weaknesses—and their parents' weaknesses—emerging in their children. Many came from broken homes and had no idea what being a parent required. They felt they lacked skills to raise their children right.

None of us are perfect parents. We all make mistakes as we raise our children. That's why prayer needs to be our number one priority as our children are growing. Only God is able to cover our mistakes by His grace and give us the wisdom and strength to raise truly great children. If you want to fulfill your responsibility as a parent, I'd suggest three things: First, get in this Book. Take a look at how God parents us. He *is* the perfect parent. Second, find a mentor to give you a little training and coaching. Get together once a month for a year or two. You'll never regret doing this. And finally, pray together as a couple. "Unless the Lord builds the house, they labor in vain who build it (Ps. 127:1).

meet,ᵃ and in secret I have said nothing. 21Why do you ask Me? Ask those who have heard Me what I said to them. Indeed they know what I said."

22And when He had said these things, one of the officers who stood by struck Jesus with the palm of his hand, saying, "Do You answer the high priest like that?"

23Jesus answered him, "If I have spoken evil, bear witness of the evil; but if well, why do you strike Me?"

24Then Annas sent Him bound to Caiaphas the high priest.

Peter Denies Twice More

25Now Simon Peter stood and warmed himself. Therefore they said to him, "You are not also *one* of His disciples, are you?"

He denied *it* and said, "I am not!"

26One of the servants of the high priest, a relative *of him* whose ear Peter cut off, said, "Did I not see you in the garden with Him?" 27Peter then denied again; and immediately a rooster crowed.

In Pilate's Court

28Then they led Jesus from Caiaphas to the Praetorium, and it was early morning. But they themselves did not go into the Praetorium, lest they should be defiled, but that they might eat the Passover. 29Pilate then went out to them and said, "What accusation do you bring against this Man?"

30They answered and said to him, "If He were not an evildoer, we would not have delivered Him up to you."

31Then Pilate said to them, "You take Him and judge Him according to your law."

Therefore the Jews said to him, "It is not lawful for us to put anyone to death," 32that the saying of Jesus might be fulfilled which He spoke, signifying by what death He would die.

33Then Pilate entered the Praetorium again, called Jesus, and said to Him, "Are You the King of the Jews?"

34Jesus answered him, "Are you speaking for yourself about this, or did others tell you this concerning Me?"

35Pilate answered, "Am I a Jew? Your own nation and the chief priests have delivered You to me. What have You done?"

36Jesus answered, "My kingdom is not of this world. If My kingdom were of this world, My servants would fight, so that I should not be delivered to the Jews; but now My kingdom is not from here."

37Pilate therefore said to Him, "Are You a king then?"

Jesus answered, "You say *rightly* that I am a king. For this cause I was born, and for this cause I have come into the world, that I should bear witness to the truth. Everyone who is of the truth hears My voice."

38Pilate said to Him, "What is truth?" And when he had said this, he went out again to the Jews, and said to them, "I find no fault in Him at all.

Taking the Place of Barabbas

39"But you have a custom that I should release someone to you at the Passover. Do you therefore want me to release to you the King of the Jews?"

40Then they all cried again, saying, "Not this Man, but Barabbas!" Now Barabbas was a robber.

The Soldiers Mock Jesus

19 So then Pilate took Jesus and scourged *Him.* 2And the soldiers twisted a crown of thorns and put *it* on His head, and they put on Him a purple robe. 3Then they said,ᵃ "Hail, King of the Jews!" And they struck Him with their hands.

4Pilate then went out again, and said to them, "Behold, I am bringing Him out to you, that you may know that I find no fault in Him."

Pilate's Decision

5Then Jesus came out, wearing the crown of thorns and the purple robe. And *Pilate* said to them, "Behold the Man!"

6Therefore, when the chief priests and officers saw Him, they cried out, saying, "Crucify *Him,* crucify *Him!*"

Pilate said to them, "You take Him and crucify *Him,* for I find no fault in Him."

7The Jews answered him, "We have a law, and according to ourᵃ law He ought to

---

18:20 ᵃNU-Text reads *where all the Jews meet.*
19:3 ᵃNU-Text reads *And they came up to Him and said.* 19:7 ᵃNU-Text reads *the law.*

die, because He made Himself the Son of God."

[8]Therefore, when Pilate heard that saying, he was the more afraid, [9]and went again into the Praetorium, and said to Jesus, "Where are You from?" But Jesus gave him no answer.

[10]Then Pilate said to Him, "Are You not speaking to me? Do You not know that I have power to crucify You, and power to release You?"

[11]Jesus answered, "You could have no power at all against Me unless it had been given you from above. Therefore the one who delivered Me to you has the greater sin."

[12]From then on Pilate sought to release Him, but the Jews cried out, saying, "If you let this Man go, you are not Caesar's friend. Whoever makes himself a king speaks against Caesar."

[13]When Pilate therefore heard that saying, he brought Jesus out and sat down in the judgment seat in a place that is called *The* Pavement, but in Hebrew, Gabbatha. [14]Now it was the Preparation Day of the Passover, and about the sixth hour. And he said to the Jews, "Behold your King!"

[15]But they cried out, "Away with *Him,* away with *Him!* Crucify Him!"

Pilate said to them, "Shall I crucify your King?"

The chief priests answered, "We have no king but Caesar!"

[16]Then he delivered Him to them to be crucified. Then they took Jesus and led *Him* away.[a]

The King on a Cross

[17]And He, bearing His cross, went out to a place called *the Place* of a Skull, which is called in Hebrew, Golgotha, [18]where they crucified Him, and two others with Him, one on either side, and Jesus in the center. [19]Now Pilate wrote a title and put *it* on the cross. And the writing was:

JESUS OF NAZARETH,
THE KING OF THE JEWS.

[20]Then many of the Jews read this title, for the place where Jesus was crucified was near the city; and it was written in Hebrew, Greek, *and* Latin.

[21]Therefore the chief priests of the Jews said to Pilate, "Do not write, 'The King of the Jews,' but, 'He said, "I am the King of the Jews." ' "

[22]Pilate answered, "What I have written, I have written."

[23]Then the soldiers, when they had crucified Jesus, took His garments and made four parts, to each soldier a part, and also the tunic. Now the tunic was without seam, woven from the top in one piece. [24]They said therefore among themselves, "Let us not tear it, but cast lots for it, whose it shall be," that the Scripture might be fulfilled which says:

"*They divided My garments among them,*
And for My clothing they cast lots."[a]

Therefore the soldiers did these things.

Behold Your Mother

[25]Now there stood by the cross of Jesus His mother, and His mother's sister, Mary the *wife* of Clopas, and Mary Magdalene. [26]When Jesus therefore saw His mother, and the disciple whom He loved standing by, He said to His mother, "Woman, behold your son!" [27]Then He said to the disciple, "Behold your mother!" And from that hour that disciple took her to his own *home.*

It Is Finished

[28]After this, Jesus, knowing[a] that all things were now accomplished, that the Scripture might be fulfilled, said, "I thirst!" [29]Now a vessel full of sour wine was sitting there; and they filled a sponge with sour wine, put *it* on hyssop, and put *it* to His mouth. [30]So when Jesus had received the sour wine, He said, "It is finished!" And bowing His head, He gave up His spirit.

INTIMATE MOMENTS

Late one night grab a blanket and your wife and head outdoors. Find a nice spot to lie back and look at the stars together.

19:16 [a]NU-Text omits *and led Him away.*
19:24 [a]Psalm 22:18 **19:28** [a]M-Text reads *seeing.*

Jesus' Side Is Pierced

31Therefore, because it was the Preparation *Day,* that the bodies should not remain on the cross on the Sabbath (for that Sabbath was a high day), the Jews asked Pilate that their legs might be broken, and *that* they might be taken away. 32Then the soldiers came and broke the legs of the first and of the other who was crucified with Him. 33But when they came to Jesus and saw that He was already dead, they did not break His legs. 34But one of the soldiers pierced His side with a spear, and immediately blood and water came out. 35And he who has seen has testified, and his testimony is true; and he knows that he is telling the truth, so that you may believe. 36For these things were done that the Scripture should be fulfilled, *"Not one of His bones shall be broken."*a 37And again another Scripture says, *"They shall look on Him whom they pierced."*a

Jesus Buried in Joseph's Tomb

38After this, Joseph of Arimathea, being a disciple of Jesus, but secretly, for fear of the Jews, asked Pilate that he might take away the body of Jesus; and Pilate gave *him* permission. So he came and took the body of Jesus. 39And Nicodemus, who at first came to Jesus by night, also came, bringing a mixture of myrrh and aloes, about a hundred pounds. 40Then they took the body of Jesus, and bound it in strips of linen with the spices, as the custom of the Jews is to bury. 41Now in the place where He was crucified there was a garden, and in the garden a new tomb in which no one had yet been laid. 42So there they laid Jesus, because of the Jews' Preparation *Day,* for the tomb was nearby.

The Empty Tomb

20 Now the first *day* of the week Mary Magdalene went to the tomb early, while it was still dark, and saw *that* the stone had been taken away from the tomb. 2Then she ran and came to Simon Peter, and to the other disciple, whom Jesus loved, and said to them, "They have taken away the Lord out of the tomb, and we do not know where they have laid Him."

3Peter therefore went out, and the other disciple, and were going to the tomb. 4So they both ran together, and the other disciple outran Peter and came to the tomb first. 5And he, stooping down and looking in, saw the linen cloths lying *there;* yet he did not go in. 6Then Simon Peter came, following him, and went into the tomb; and he saw the linen cloths lying *there,* 7and the handkerchief that had been around His head, not lying with the linen cloths, but folded together in a place by itself. 8Then the other disciple, who came to the tomb first, went in also; and he saw and believed. 9For as yet they did not know the Scripture, that He must rise again from the dead. 10Then the disciples went away again to their own homes.

Mary Magdalene Sees the Risen Lord

11But Mary stood outside by the tomb weeping, and as she wept she stooped down *and looked* into the tomb. 12And she saw two angels in white sitting, one at the head and the other at the feet, where the body of Jesus had lain. 13Then they said to her, "Woman, why are you weeping?"

She said to them, "Because they have taken away my Lord, and I do not know where they have laid Him."

14Now when she had said this, she turned around and saw Jesus standing *there,* and did not know that it was Jesus. 15Jesus said to her, "Woman, why are you weeping? Whom are you seeking?"

She, supposing Him to be the gardener, said to Him, "Sir, if You have carried Him away, tell me where You have laid Him, and I will take Him away."

16Jesus said to her, "Mary!"

She turned and said to Him,a "Rabboni!" (which is to say, Teacher).

17Jesus said to her, "Do not cling to Me, for I have not yet ascended to My Father; but go to My brethren and say to them, 'I am ascending to My Father and your Father, and *to* My God and your God.'"

18Mary Magdalene came and told the disciples that she had seen the Lord,a and *that* He had spoken these things to her.

19:36 aExodus 12:46; Numbers 9:12; Psalm 34:20
19:37 aZechariah 12:10 **20:16** aNU-Text adds *in Hebrew.* **20:18** aNU-Text reads *disciples, "I have seen the Lord," . . .*

The Apostles Commissioned

¹⁹Then, the same day at evening, being the first *day* of the week, when the doors were shut where the disciples were assembled,ᵃ for fear of the Jews, Jesus came and stood in the midst, and said to them, "Peace *be* with you." ²⁰When He had said this, He showed them *His* hands and His side. Then the disciples were glad when they saw the Lord.

²¹So Jesus said to them again, "Peace to you! As the Father has sent Me, I also send you." ²²And when He had said this, He breathed on *them,* and said to them, "Receive the Holy Spirit. ²³If you forgive the sins of any, they are forgiven them; if you retain the *sins* of any, they are retained."

Seeing and Believing

²⁴Now Thomas, called the Twin, one of the twelve, was not with them when Jesus came. ²⁵The other disciples therefore said to him, "We have seen the Lord."

So he said to them, "Unless I see in His hands the print of the nails, and put my finger into the print of the nails, and put my hand into His side, I will not believe."

²⁶And after eight days His disciples were again inside, and Thomas with them. Jesus came, the doors being shut, and stood in the midst, and said, "Peace to you!" ²⁷Then He said to Thomas, "Reach your finger here, and look at My hands; and reach your hand *here,* and put *it* into My side. Do not be unbelieving, but believing."

²⁸And Thomas answered and said to Him, "My Lord and my God!"

²⁹Jesus said to him, "Thomas,ᵃ because you have seen Me, you have believed. Blessed *are* those who have not seen and *yet* have believed."

That You May Believe

³⁰And truly Jesus did many other signs in the presence of His disciples, which are not written in this book; ³¹but these are written that you may believe that Jesus is the Christ, the Son of God, and that believing you may have life in His name.

Breakfast by the Sea

21 After these things Jesus showed Himself again to the disciples at the Sea of Tiberias, and in this way He showed *Himself:* ²Simon Peter, Thomas called the Twin, Nathanael of Cana in Galilee, the *sons* of Zebedee, and two others of His disciples were together. ³Simon Peter said to them, "I am going fishing."

They said to him, "We are going with you also." They went out and immediatelyᵃ got into the boat, and that night they caught nothing. ⁴But when the morning had now come, Jesus stood on the shore; yet the disciples did not know that it was Jesus. ⁵Then Jesus said to them, "Children, have you any food?"

They answered Him, "No."

⁶And He said to them, "Cast the net on the right side of the boat, and you will find *some.*" So they cast, and now they were not able to draw it in because of the multitude of fish.

⁷Therefore that disciple whom Jesus loved said to Peter, "It is the Lord!" Now when Simon Peter heard that it was the Lord, he put on *his* outer garment (for he had removed it), and plunged into the sea. ⁸But the other disciples came in the little boat (for they were not far from land, but about two hundred cubits), dragging the net with fish. ⁹Then, as soon as they had come to land, they saw a fire of coals there, and fish laid on it, and bread. ¹⁰Jesus said to them, "Bring some of the fish which you have just caught."

¹¹Simon Peter went up and dragged the net to land, full of large fish, one hundred and fifty-three; and although there were so many, the net was not broken. ¹²Jesus said to them, "Come *and* eat breakfast." Yet none of the disciples dared ask Him, "Who are You?"—knowing that it was the Lord. ¹³Jesus then came and took the bread and gave it to them, and likewise the fish.

¹⁴This *is* now the third time Jesus showed Himself to His disciples after He was raised from the dead.

Jesus Restores Peter

¹⁵So when they had eaten breakfast, Jesus said to Simon Peter, "Simon, *son* of Jonah,ᵃ do you love Me more than these?"

20:19 ᵃNU-Text omits *assembled.* **20:29** ᵃNU-Text and M-Text omit *Thomas.* **21:3** ᵃNU-Text omits *immediately.* **21:15** ᵃNU-Text reads *John.*

BIBLICAL INSIGHTS • 20:29

Believing Without Seeing

A BUSINESS SLOGAN recently grabbed my attention. A Christian optometrist named his practice, "Seeing Is Believing." When I read that, my mind raced back to my junior college days.

I was a normal twenty-year-old in the midst of the tumultuous sixties. I had no purpose. My life was chock-full of compromise and perplexing questions I couldn't answer. Just like Thomas (20:25), I was full of doubts. I had many questions:

Is the Bible really God's Word?

Why does God allow suffering and injustice?

What is the purpose of life?

Eventually, I began to honestly seek what God had to say—but one question haunted me: *Must I really see it to believe it?* In the fall of 1968, God loved me out of my unbelief, in part through the words of Tom Skinner, an African-American speaker who came to our campus, "I spent a long time trying to come to grips with my doubts, when suddenly I realized I had better come to grips with what I

believe. I have since moved from the agony of questions that I cannot answer, to the reality of answers that I cannot escape ... and it's a great relief."

Although I still had unanswered questions, ultimately, I realized I needed to focus on the *answers* I couldn't escape. The great preacher D.L. Moody was once asked while he was enjoying a dinner of fresh fish whether he had any doubts or questions about his faith. Moody responded by opening his Bible and showing the questioner page after page that had question marks on them. He then pointed at the fish dinner before him and said, "Just as I don't allow the bones in this fish to get in the way of my enjoyment of this meal, so neither do I allow the questions I have about my faith keep me from believing and trusting in God!"

Like D. L. Moody, I still experience moments of doubt. And I too have a few questions that I cannot answer. But my confidence in God and His Word has grown as I have walked with the Savior.

He said to Him, "Yes, Lord; You know that I love You."

He said to him, "Feed My lambs."

[16]He said to him again a second time, "Simon, *son* of Jonah,[a] do you love Me?"

He said to Him, "Yes, Lord; You know that I love You."

He said to him, "Tend My sheep."

[17]He said to him the third time, "Simon, *son* of Jonah,[a] do you love Me?" Peter was grieved because He said to him the third time, "Do you love Me?"

And he said to Him, "Lord, You know all things; You know that I love You."

Jesus said to him, "Feed My sheep. [18]Most assuredly, I say to you, when you were younger, you girded yourself and walked where you wished; but when you are old, you will stretch out your hands,

and another will gird you and carry *you* where you do not wish." [19]This He spoke, signifying by what death he would glorify God. And when He had spoken this, He said to him, "Follow Me."

The Beloved Disciple and His Book

[20]Then Peter, turning around, saw the disciple whom Jesus loved following, who also had leaned on His breast at the supper, and said, "Lord, who is the one who betrays You?" [21]Peter, seeing him, said to Jesus, "But Lord, what *about* this man?"

21:16 [a]NU-Text reads *John.*
21:17 [a]NU-Text reads *John.*

²²Jesus said to him, "If I will that he remain till I come, what *is that* to you? You follow Me."

²³Then this saying went out among the brethren that this disciple would not die. Yet Jesus did not say to him that he would not die, but, "If I will that he remain till I come, what *is that* to you?"

²⁴This is the disciple who testifies of these things, and wrote these things; and we know that his testimony is true.

²⁵And there are also many other things that Jesus did, which if they were written one by one, I suppose that even the world itself could not contain the books that would be written. Amen.

ACTS

INTRODUCTION

THIS SEQUEL TO THE GOSPEL OF LUKE gives us a history of God's work through the ministry of the first-century church. We see how God's Holy Spirit empowered, directed and led the early followers of Jesus, and how the church grew numerically and in influence.

While Luke's account of the spread of Christianity includes information about many people, two men play central roles in the Book of Acts. Peter is the dominant figure in chapters 1—12, while Paul is the key individual in chapters 13—28.

A key theme in Acts is the spread of Christianity beyond the nation of Israel. In the Old Testament, God's people looked ahead to the coming of the Messiah who would reclaim the throne of David and reestablish the nation of Israel as the center of God's plan for all men. But Jesus introduced a very different kingdom than the expected one, a kingdom that includes *all* people—Jew and Gentile alike. He first called it the "church" in Matthew 16:18, and the book of Acts describes the birth and growth of Jesus' church. Luke shows how the followers of Jesus preached about Jesus to various audiences, and records that most Jews rejected the claim made by Jesus' followers that He was the Messiah. At the same time, many Gentiles heard the gospel for the first time and wholeheartedly believed in Jesus.

Acts clearly shows us that Jesus' followers took seriously His Great Commission as described in Matthew 28:19, 20, and fully intended to make disciples of all nations. But how could they accomplish such a daunting task? The answer is given in the opening verses of Acts, in which Jesus promises that the Holy Spirit would come upon His followers and empower them to be His witnesses in Jerusalem, Judea, Samaria and to the ends of the earth (1:8). After the coming of the Holy Spirit at Pentecost to indwell each member of Jesus' church, others soon describe these on-fire followers of Jesus as people "who have turned the world upside down" (17:6). We can learn much from their example as we seek to fulfill our own role in God's Great Commission.

Prologue

1 The former account I made, O Theophilus, of all that Jesus began both to do and teach, ²until the day in which He was taken up, after He through the Holy Spirit had given commandments to the apostles whom He had chosen, ³to whom He also presented Himself alive after His suffering by many infallible proofs, being seen by them during forty days and speaking of the things pertaining to the kingdom of God.

The Holy Spirit Promised

⁴And being assembled together with *them,* He commanded them not to depart from Jerusalem, but to wait for the Promise of the Father, "which," *He said,* "you have heard from Me; ⁵for John truly baptized with water, but you shall be baptized with the Holy Spirit not many days from now." ⁶Therefore, when they had come together, they asked Him, saying, "Lord, will You at this time restore the kingdom to Israel?" ⁷And He said to them, "It is not for you to know times or seasons which the Father has put in His own authority. ⁸But you shall receive power when the Holy Spirit has come upon you; and you shall be witnesses to Meᵃ in Jerusalem, and in all Judea and Samaria, and to the end of the earth."

Jesus Ascends to Heaven

⁹Now when He had spoken these things, while they watched, He was taken up, and a cloud received Him out of their sight. ¹⁰And while they looked steadfastly toward heaven as He went up, behold, two men stood by them in white apparel, ¹¹who also said, "Men of Galilee, why do you stand gazing up into heaven? This *same* Jesus, who was taken up from you into heaven, will so come in like manner as you saw Him go into heaven."

The Upper Room Prayer Meeting

¹²Then they returned to Jerusalem from the mount called Olivet, which is near Jerusalem, a Sabbath day's journey. ¹³And when they had entered, they went up into the upper room where they were staying: Peter, James, John, and Andrew; Philip and Thomas; Bartholomew and Matthew; James *the son* of Alphaeus and Simon the Zealot; and Judas *the son* of James. ¹⁴These all continued with one accord in prayer and supplication,ᵃ with the women and Mary the mother of Jesus, and with His brothers.

INTIMATE MOMENTS

Take an afternoon off and catch a matinee. Sit in the back row.

Matthias Chosen

¹⁵And in those days Peter stood up in the midst of the disciplesᵃ (altogether the number of names was about a hundred and twenty), and said, ¹⁶"Men *and* brethren, this Scripture had to be fulfilled, which the Holy Spirit spoke before by the mouth of David concerning Judas, who became a guide to those who arrested Jesus; ¹⁷for he was numbered with us and obtained a part in this ministry."

¹⁸(Now this man purchased a field with the wages of iniquity; and falling headlong, he burst open in the middle and all his entrails gushed out. ¹⁹And it became known to all those dwelling in Jerusalem; so that field is called in their own language, Akel Dama, that is, Field of Blood.)

²⁰"For it is written in the Book of Psalms:

> 'Let his dwelling place be desolate,
> And let no one live in it';ᵃ

and,

> 'Letᵇ another take his office.'ᶜ

²¹"Therefore, of these men who have accompanied us all the time that the Lord Jesus went in and out among us, ²²beginning from the baptism of John to that day when He was taken up from us, one of these must become a witness with us of His resurrection."

1:8 ᵃNU-Text reads *My witnesses.* **1:14** ᵃNU-Text omits *and supplication.* **1:15** ᵃNU-Text reads *brethren.* **1:20** ᵃPsalm 69:25 ᵇPsalm 109:8 ᶜGreek *episkopen,* position of overseer

23And they proposed two: Joseph called Barsabas, who was surnamed Justus, and Matthias. 24And they prayed and said, "You, O Lord, who know the hearts of all, show which of these two You have chosen 25to take part in this ministry and apostleship from which Judas by transgression fell, that he might go to his own place." 26And they cast their lots, and the lot fell on Matthias. And he was numbered with the eleven apostles.

Coming of the Holy Spirit

2 When the Day of Pentecost had fully come, they were all with one accorda in one place. 2And suddenly there came a sound from heaven, as of a rushing mighty wind, and it filled the whole house where they were sitting. 3Then there appeared to them divided tongues, as of fire, and *one* sat upon each of them. 4And they were all filled with the Holy Spirit and began to speak with other tongues, as the Spirit gave them utterance.

The Crowd's Response

5And there were dwelling in Jerusalem Jews, devout men, from every nation under heaven. 6And when this sound occurred, the multitude came together, and were confused, because everyone heard them speak in his own language. 7Then they were all amazed and marveled, saying to one another, "Look, are not all these who speak Galileans? 8And how *is it that* we hear, each in our own language in which we were born? 9Parthians and Medes and Elamites, those dwelling in Mesopotamia, Judea and Cappadocia, Pontus and Asia, 10Phrygia and Pamphylia, Egypt and the parts of Libya adjoining Cyrene, visitors from Rome, both Jews and proselytes, 11Cretans and Arabs—we hear them speaking in our own tongues the wonderful works of God." 12So they were all amazed and perplexed, saying to one another, "Whatever could this mean?"

13Others mocking said, "They are full of new wine."

Peter's Sermon

14But Peter, standing up with the eleven, raised his voice and said to them, "Men of Judea and all who dwell in Jerusalem, let this be known to you, and heed my words. 15For these are not drunk, as you suppose, since it is *only* the third hour of the day. 16But this is what was spoken by the prophet Joel:

17 '*And it shall come to pass in the last days, says God,*
That I will pour out of My Spirit on all flesh;
Your sons and your daughters shall prophesy,
Your young men shall see visions,
Your old men shall dream dreams.
18 *And on My menservants and on My maidservants*
I will pour out My Spirit in those days;
And they shall prophesy.
19 *I will show wonders in heaven above*
And signs in the earth beneath:
Blood and fire and vapor of smoke.
20 *The sun shall be turned into darkness,*
And the moon into blood,
Before the coming of the great and awesome day of the LORD.
21 *And it shall come to pass*
That whoever calls on the name of the LORD
Shall be saved.'a

22"Men of Israel, hear these words: Jesus of Nazareth, a Man attested by God to you by miracles, wonders, and signs which God did through Him in your midst, as you yourselves also know— 23Him, being delivered by the determined purpose and foreknowledge of God, you have takena by lawless hands, have crucified, and put to death; 24whom God raised up, having loosed the pains of death, because it was not possible that He should be held by it. 25For David says concerning Him:

'*I foresaw the LORD always before my face,*
For He is at my right hand, that I may not be shaken.
26 *Therefore my heart rejoiced, and my tongue was glad;*

2:1 aNU-Text reads *together.* 2:21 aJoel 2:28–32
2:23 aNU-Text omits *have taken.*

Moreover my flesh also will rest in
hope.
27 For You will not leave my soul in
Hades,
Nor will You allow Your Holy One to
see corruption.
28 You have made known to me the
ways of life;
You will make me full of joy in Your
presence.'ᵃ

²⁹"Men *and* brethren, let *me* speak freely
to you of the patriarch David, that he is
both dead and buried, and his tomb is with
us to this day. ³⁰Therefore, being a prophet,
and knowing that God had sworn with an
oath to him that of the fruit of his body,
according to the flesh, He would raise up
the Christ to sit on his throne,ᵃ ³¹he, foreseeing this, spoke concerning the resurrection of the Christ, that His soul was not left
in Hades, nor did His flesh see corruption.
³²This Jesus God has raised up, of which
we are all witnesses. ³³Therefore being
exalted to the right hand of God, and having received from the Father the promise of
the Holy Spirit, He poured out this which
you now see and hear.

³⁴"For David did not ascend into the
heavens, but he says himself:

'The Lord said to my Lord,
"Sit at My right hand,
35 Till I make Your enemies Your
footstool." 'ᵃ

³⁶"Therefore let all the house of Israel
know assuredly that God has made this
Jesus, whom you crucified, both Lord and
Christ."

³⁷Now when they heard *this,* they were
cut to the heart, and said to Peter and the
rest of the apostles, "Men *and* brethren,
what shall we do?"

³⁸Then Peter said to them, "Repent, and
let every one of you be baptized in the
name of Jesus Christ for the remission of
sins; and you shall receive the gift of the
Holy Spirit. ³⁹For the promise is to you and

BIBLICAL INSIGHTS • 2:42–47

Send Your Roots Deep

A FEW YEARS AGO I was working in my
office when the sky suddenly became
dark. The trees began to bend, rain started moving horizontally, and a siren went
off. We got word that a tornado was coming right up the street.

I dashed out and joined all our office
staff, already underneath a concrete stair-
well, and prayed. We stayed there for about
five minutes until we got the all-clear. It
turned out that the tornado bounced right
over our office, touched down fifty feet
away, and uprooted several massive pine
trees. One tree lying across the road must
have been over a hundred years old.

But about fifty feet away stood a tall
oak tree, with only a few limbs broken off.

I learned afterward that pine trees have
a shallow root system, leaving them susceptible to strong winds. But the root systems of oak trees go deep into the soil.

To the degree that you obey God, as
the early believers did, who "continued
steadfastly in the apostles' doctrine and
fellowship, in the breaking of bread, and
in prayers" (2:42), you dig your roots
down deep, which gives you the strength
to withstand storms.

The storms will come. How deep are
your roots? Psalm 1 says that the man
whose delight is in the law of the Lord
and who meditates on His law day and
night "shall be like a tree planted by the
rivers of water" (vv. 2, 3). In other words,
he is like a tree with deep roots. As you
spend time in God's Word today, you will
be preparing yourself to stand strong
when the storm clouds rise.

to your children, and to all who are afar off,
as many as the Lord our God will call."

A Vital Church Grows

⁴⁰And with many other words he testified and exhorted them, saying, "Be saved

---

2:28 ᵃPsalm 16:8–11 2:30 ᵃNU-Text omits *according
to the flesh, He would raise up the Christ* and completes the verse with *He would seat one on his throne.*
2:35 ᵃPsalm 110:1

from this perverse generation." [41]Then those who gladly[a] received his word were baptized; and that day about three thousand souls were added *to them.* [42]And they continued steadfastly in the apostles' doctrine and fellowship, in the breaking of bread, and in prayers. [43]Then fear came upon every soul, and many wonders and signs were done through the apostles. [44]Now all who believed were together, and had all things in common, [45]and sold their possessions and goods, and divided them among all, as anyone had need.

[46]So continuing daily with one accord in the temple, and breaking bread from house to house, they ate their food with gladness and simplicity of heart, [47]praising God and having favor with all the people. And the Lord added to the church[a] daily those who were being saved.

A Lame Man Healed

3 Now Peter and John went up together to the temple at the hour of prayer, the ninth *hour.* [2]And a certain man lame from his mother's womb was carried, whom they laid daily at the gate of the temple which is called Beautiful, to ask alms from those who entered the temple; [3]who, seeing Peter and John about to go into the temple, asked for alms. [4]And fixing his eyes on him, with

John, Peter said, "Look at us." [5]So he gave them his attention, expecting to receive something from them. [6]Then Peter said, "Silver and gold I do not have, but what I do have I give you: In the name of Jesus Christ of Nazareth, rise up and walk." [7]And he took him by the right hand and lifted *him* up, and immediately his feet and ankle bones received strength. [8]So he, leaping up, stood and walked and entered the temple with them—walking, leaping, and praising God. [9]And all the people saw him walking and praising God. [10]Then they knew that it was he who sat begging alms at the Beautiful Gate of the temple; and they were filled with wonder and amazement at what had happened to him.

Preaching in Solomon's Portico

[11]Now as the lame man who was healed held on to Peter and John, all the people ran together to them in the porch which is called Solomon's, greatly amazed. [12]So when Peter saw *it,* he responded to the people: "Men of Israel, why do you marvel at this? Or why look so intently at us, as though by our own power or godliness we had made this man walk? [13]The God of Abraham, Isaac, and Jacob, the God of our

2:41 [a]NU-Text omits *gladly.*
2:47 [a]NU-Text omits *to the church.*

ROMANTIC QUOTES AND NOTES
Times of Refreshing

John Wesley, the founder of Methodism, was talking with General James Oglethorpe when the general remarked, "I never forgive." Wesley replied, "Then I hope, sir, that you never sin." In other words, if you can't forgive others, then why should you expect God to forgive you?

The truth is, there has never been a husband on planet earth who did not sin. Nor has a wife who never sinned ever made an appearance on this world. Since all of us have sinned, all of us need forgiveness.

And really, why should it be so tough for us to ask our mates for forgiveness? Why should it be so hard for us to grant forgiveness to a mate who has hurt us? Don't we realize the healing power of forgiveness? Listen to how the apostle Peter put it, "Repent therefore and be converted, that your sins may be blotted out, so that times of refreshing may come from the presence of the Lord" (Acts 3:19).

Although Peter had in mind God's eternal forgiveness, the forgiveness we extend to each other in marriage also makes it possible for "times of refreshing" to sweep into our homes "from the presence of the Lord." Do you need to seek forgiveness from your mate? Or do you need to grant forgiveness for an offense? Don't allow bitterness, resentment, or anger to grow. Instead, "be kind to one another, tenderhearted, forgiving one another, even as God in Christ forgave you" (Eph. 4:32).

fathers, glorified His Servant Jesus, whom you delivered up and denied in the presence of Pilate, when he was determined to let *Him* go. ¹⁴But you denied the Holy One and the Just, and asked for a murderer to be granted to you, ¹⁵and killed the Prince of life, whom God raised from the dead, of which we are witnesses. ¹⁶And His name, through faith in His name, has made this man strong, whom you see and know. Yes, the faith which *comes* through Him has given him this perfect soundness in the presence of you all.

¹⁷"Yet now, brethren, I know that you did *it* in ignorance, as *did* also your rulers. ¹⁸But those things which God foretold by the mouth of all His prophets, that the Christ would suffer, He has thus fulfilled. ¹⁹Repent therefore and be converted, that your sins may be blotted out, so that times of refreshing may come from the presence of the Lord, ²⁰and that He may send Jesus Christ, who was preached to you before,ᵃ ²¹whom heaven must receive until the times of restoration of all things, which God has spoken by the mouth of all His holy prophets since the world began. ²²For Moses truly said to the fathers, *'The LORD your God will raise up for you a Prophet like me from your brethren. Him you shall hear in all things, whatever He says to you.* ²³*And it shall be that every soul who will not hear that Prophet shall be utterly destroyed from among the people.'*ᵃ ²⁴Yes, and all the prophets, from Samuel and those who follow, as many as have spoken, have also foretoldᵃ these days. ²⁵You are sons of the prophets, and of the covenant which God made with our fathers, saying to Abraham, *'And in your seed all the families of the earth shall be blessed.'*ᵃ ²⁶To you first, God, having raised up His Servant Jesus, sent Him to bless you, in turning away every one *of you* from your iniquities."

Peter and John Arrested

4 Now as they spoke to the people, the priests, the captain of the temple, and the Sadducees came upon them, ²being

BIBLICAL INSIGHTS • 4:7

The Prayer of the Helpless Parent

NO ONE HAS a perfect marriage. No one raises perfect kids. No one is the perfect parent. No one does it all.

Barbara and I have discovered a secret, though, and it's the greatest one of all: *God helps parents raise their kids.* He delights when we admit our weaknesses because that's when He gives us wisdom and power. He loves the prayer of the helpless parent.

When I go jogging, I like to pray for my family as I run. Often I cry out to the Lord, "Unless You build this house, it isn't going to work. You know the parents here. You know the children. Lord, you gave them to us, so help us be successful in raising them."

Ask God for help in building your home. Pray that you might keep your marriage holy and pure. Ask Him, by His power and through His name (4:7), to give you wisdom, strong and resilient commitments, pure romance, and vital relationships.

I believe God stands ready to intervene in your child's life when you cry out to Him. Ask Him to get your child's attention when he or she seems to be ignoring you. Plead with Him to build convictions where you can't. Ask Him to build your home. God loves the prayer of the helpless parent.

greatly disturbed that they taught the people and preached in Jesus the resurrection from the dead. ³And they laid hands on them, and put *them* in custody until the next day, for it was already evening. ⁴However, many of those who heard the word believed; and the number of the men came to be about five thousand.

Addressing the Sanhedrin

⁵And it came to pass, on the next day, that their rulers, elders, and scribes, ⁶as well as Annas the high priest, Caiaphas, John, and Alexander, and as many as were

BIBLICAL INSIGHTS • 4:12
Follow Him Alone

WHEN WE SEE JESUS for who He really is, no possession, no worldly honor or success can compare with the King of kings.

So why doesn't everyone follow Him? John 6 records that after Christ made some difficult and challenging statements, "many of His disciples went back and walked with Him no more" (v. 66). So Jesus said to the remaining twelve, "Do you also want to go away?" (v. 67). Peter gave a profound reply: "Lord, to whom shall we go? You have the words of eternal life" (v. 68). Peter saw no one else worthy of following.

Nor did Peter's opinion change in the subsequent weeks, months and years. After Jesus rose from the grave and the Holy Spirit came to dwell in the church at Pentecost, Peter stood up in front of the Jewish religious leaders and declared, "Nor is there salvation in any other, for there is no other name under heaven given among men by which we must be saved" (Acts 4:12).

The longer I live the Christian life, the more I see that *nothing matters more than Jesus Christ and His Word*. In recent days I've asked Him to re-infuse my life with the conviction that He alone is worth following. I have been following Christ since 1968, and I have absolutely no regrets. Because He is alive, He can and does bring purpose to my life. He instructs me. He corrects me. He forgives me. He guides me. He comforts me. He disciplines me. He loves me. He prays for me. And He is coming back for me.

It doesn't get any better than that.

a good deed *done* to a helpless man, by what means he has been made well, [10]let it be known to you all, and to all the people of Israel, that by the name of Jesus Christ of Nazareth, whom you crucified, whom God raised from the dead, by Him this man stands here before you whole. [11]This is the '*stone which was rejected by you builders, which has become the chief cornerstone.*'[a] [12]Nor is there salvation in any other, for there is no other name under heaven given among men by which we must be saved."

The Name of Jesus Forbidden

[13]Now when they saw the boldness of Peter and John, and perceived that they were uneducated and untrained men, they marveled. And they realized that they had been with Jesus. [14]And seeing the man who had been healed standing with them, they could say nothing against it. [15]But when they had commanded them to go aside out of the council, they conferred among themselves, [16]saying, "What shall we do to these men? For, indeed, that a notable miracle has been done through them *is* evident to all who dwell in Jerusalem, and we cannot deny *it.* [17]But so that it spreads no further among the people, let us severely threaten them, that from now on they speak to no man in this name."

[18]So they called them and commanded them not to speak at all nor teach in the name of Jesus. [19]But Peter and John answered and said to them, "Whether it is right in the sight of God to listen to you more than to God, you judge. [20]For we cannot but speak the things which we have seen and heard." [21]So when they had further threatened them, they let them go, finding no way of punishing them, because of the people, since they all glorified God for what had been done. [22]For the man was over forty years old on whom this miracle of healing had been performed.

Prayer for Boldness

[23]And being let go, they went to their own *companions* and reported all that the chief priests and elders had said to them. [24]So when they heard that, they raised

of the family of the high priest, were gathered together at Jerusalem. [7]And when they had set them in the midst, they asked, "By what power or by what name have you done this?"

[8]Then Peter, filled with the Holy Spirit, said to them, "Rulers of the people and elders of Israel: [9]If we this day are judged for

4:11 [a]Psalm 118:22

their voice to God with one accord and said: "Lord, You *are* God, who made heaven and earth and the sea, and all that is in them, 25who by the mouth of Your servant Davida have said:

'Why did the nations rage,
And the people plot vain things?
26   The kings of the earth took their
        stand,
And the rulers were gathered together
Against the LORD and against His
    Christ.'a

27"For truly against Your holy Servant Jesus, whom You anointed, both Herod and Pontius Pilate, with the Gentiles and the people of Israel, were gathered together 28to do whatever Your hand and Your purpose determined before to be done. 29Now, Lord, look on their threats, and grant to Your servants that with all boldness they may speak Your word, 30by stretching out Your hand to heal, and that signs and wonders may be done through the name of Your holy Servant Jesus."

31And when they had prayed, the place where they were assembled together was shaken; and they were all filled with the Holy Spirit, and they spoke the word of God with boldness.

Sharing in All Things

32Now the multitude of those who believed were of one heart and one soul; neither did anyone say that any of the things he possessed was his own, but they had all things in common. 33And with great power the apostles gave witness to the resurrection of the Lord Jesus. And great grace was upon them all. 34Nor was there anyone among them who lacked; for all who were possessors of lands or houses sold them, and brought the proceeds of the things that were sold, 35and laid *them* at the apostles' feet; and they distributed to each as anyone had need.

36And Joses,a who was also named Barnabas by the apostles (which is translated Son of Encouragement), a Levite of

BIBLICAL INSIGHTS • 5
Would It Make a Difference?

DO YOU THINK Ananias and Sapphira had children? If they did, what sort of heritage do you think this foolish couple left to their orphans?

Their sad story (Acts 5:1–11) makes me wonder—if we could see how our sin affected our descendants, would it make a difference in the way we live today?

One of our ministry staff members is committed to breaking the chains of his past. When speaking to individuals considering vocational Christian ministry, he always says, "I grew up in a broken home and I don't want to end up like my father. He lived his life for himself, and in the end, at his funeral, only ten people showed up. I want a *packed* funeral, full of lives my life has impacted. I want to leave a legacy that will outlast me."

I'll be honest with you. The thought of my kids falling prey to the sin in the same areas that I am tempted has bolstered my obedience to God. I'm reminded of the piercing statement by C. H. Spurgeon, "Sin would have fewer takers if its consequences occurred immediately."

In the case of Ananias and Sapphira, the consequences did occur immediately. But what of the consequences to the next generation? Are there patterns of sin in your own life that you need to confess to God and turn from? For your own spiritual health, and for the sake of your children, make a fresh commitment to holiness in your life today.

the country of Cyprus, 37having land, sold *it,* and brought the money and laid *it* at the apostles' feet.

Lying to the Holy Spirit

5 But a certain man named Ananias, with Sapphira his wife, sold a possession. 2And he kept back *part* of the proceeds, his wife also being aware *of it,* and brought a certain part and laid *it* at the

4:25 aNU-Text reads *who through the Holy Spirit, by the mouth of our father, Your servant David.*
4:26 aPsalm 2:1, 2   4:36 aNU-Text reads *Joseph.*

apostles' feet. ³But Peter said, "Ananias, why has Satan filled your heart to lie to the Holy Spirit and keep back *part* of the price of the land for yourself? ⁴While it remained, was it not your own? And after it was sold, was it not in your own control? Why have you conceived this thing in your heart? You have not lied to men but to God."

⁵Then Ananias, hearing these words, fell down and breathed his last. So great fear came upon all those who heard these things. ⁶And the young men arose and wrapped him up, carried *him* out, and buried *him*.

⁷Now it was about three hours later when his wife came in, not knowing what had happened. ⁸And Peter answered her, "Tell me whether you sold the land for so much?"

She said, "Yes, for so much."

⁹Then Peter said to her, "How is it that you have agreed together to test the Spirit of the Lord? Look, the feet of those who have buried your husband *are* at the door, and they will carry you out." ¹⁰Then immediately she fell down at his feet and breathed her last. And the young men came in and found her dead, and carrying *her* out, buried *her* by her husband. ¹¹So great fear came upon all the church and upon all who heard these things.

Continuing Power in the Church

¹²And through the hands of the apostles many signs and wonders were done among the people. And they were all with one accord in Solomon's Porch. ¹³Yet none of the rest dared join them, but the people esteemed them highly. ¹⁴And believers were increasingly added to the Lord, multitudes of both men and women, ¹⁵so that they brought the sick out into the streets and laid *them* on beds and couches, that at least the shadow of Peter passing by might fall on some of them. ¹⁶Also a multitude gathered from the surrounding cities to Jerusalem, bringing sick people and those who were tormented by unclean spirits, and they were all healed.

Imprisoned Apostles Freed

¹⁷Then the high priest rose up, and all those who *were* with him (which is the sect of the Sadducees), and they were filled with indignation, ¹⁸and laid their hands on the apostles and put them in the common prison. ¹⁹But at night an angel of the Lord opened the prison doors and brought them out, and said, ²⁰"Go, stand in the temple and speak to the people all the words of this life."

²¹And when they heard *that,* they entered the temple early in the morning and taught. But the high priest and those with him came and called the council together, with all the elders of the children of Israel, and sent to the prison to have them brought.

Apostles on Trial Again

²²But when the officers came and did not find them in the prison, they returned and reported, ²³saying, "Indeed we found the prison shut securely, and the guards standing outsideª before the doors; but when we opened them, we found no one inside!" ²⁴Now when the high priest,ª the captain of the temple, and the chief priests heard these things, they wondered what the outcome would be. ²⁵So one came and told them, saying,ª "Look, the men whom you put in prison are standing in the temple and teaching the people!"

²⁶Then the captain went with the officers and brought them without violence, for they feared the people, lest they should be stoned. ²⁷And when they had brought them, they set *them* before the council. And the high priest asked them, ²⁸saying, "Did we not strictly command you not to teach in this name? And look, you have filled Jerusalem with your doctrine, and intend to bring this Man's blood on us!"

²⁹But Peter and the *other* apostles answered and said: "We ought to obey God rather than men. ³⁰The God of our fathers raised up Jesus whom you murdered by hanging on a tree. ³¹Him God has exalted to His right hand *to be* Prince and Savior, to give repentance to Israel and forgiveness of sins. ³²And we are His witnesses to these things, and *so* also *is* the Holy Spirit whom God has given to those who obey Him."

5:23 ªNU-Text and M-Text omit *outside.*
5:24 ªNU-Text omits *the high priest.*
5:25 ªNU-Text and M-Text omit *saying*

Gamaliel's Advice

³³When they heard *this,* they were furious and plotted to kill them. ³⁴Then one in the council stood up, a Pharisee named Gamaliel, a teacher of the law held in respect by all the people, and commanded them to put the apostles outside for a little while. ³⁵And he said to them: "Men of Israel, take heed to yourselves what you intend to do regarding these men. ³⁶For some time ago Theudas rose up, claiming to be somebody. A number of men, about four hundred, joined him. He was slain, and all who obeyed him were scattered and came to nothing. ³⁷After this man, Judas of Galilee rose up in the days of the census, and drew away many people after him. He also perished, and all who obeyed him were dispersed. ³⁸And now I say to you, keep away from these men and let them alone; for if this plan or this work is of men, it will come to nothing; ³⁹but if it is of God, you cannot overthrow it—lest you even be found to fight against God."

⁴⁰And they agreed with him, and when they had called for the apostles and beaten *them,* they commanded that they should not speak in the name of Jesus, and let them go. ⁴¹So they departed from the presence of the council, rejoicing that they were counted worthy to suffer shame for His[a] name. ⁴²And daily in the temple, and in every house, they did not cease teaching and preaching Jesus *as* the Christ.

Seven Chosen to Serve

6 Now in those days, when *the number of* the disciples was multiplying, there arose a complaint against the Hebrews by the Hellenists,[a] because their widows were neglected in the daily distribution. ²Then the twelve summoned the multitude of the disciples and said, "It is not desirable that we should leave the word of God and serve tables. ³Therefore, brethren, seek out from among you seven men of *good* reputation, full of the Holy Spirit and wisdom, whom we may appoint over this business; ⁴but we will give ourselves continually to prayer and to the ministry of the word."

⁵And the saying pleased the whole multitude. And they chose Stephen, a man full of faith and the Holy Spirit, and Philip, Prochorus, Nicanor, Timon, Parmenas, and Nicolas, a proselyte from Antioch, ⁶whom they set before the apostles; and when they had prayed, they laid hands on them.

⁷Then the word of God spread, and the number of the disciples multiplied greatly

---

ROMANCE FAQ

Q: *What are some symptoms of isolation in marriage, and what can we do to combat them?*

Although most people get married hoping to find intimacy, the "I do" at the wedding ceremony too often changes to "No, I won't," and signs of isolation soon begin to appear:

No Trespassing. Many think Paul and Michelle have a model marriage, but over the years they have become alienated from one another because of an unsatisfying sex life. Too proud to seek counsel, they no longer discuss the subject. They have declared that area off-limits.

The ticking clock. Ben and Mary's marriage of thirty-five years has withstood time, but silence has now crept into their relationship. They don't know how to talk to each other because for so many years they focused on their children. Any relationship they once had is replaced by silence.

The crowded calendar. Steve and Angela are both aggressive professionals, but ever since they started their family, gone are the walks and late-night talks they used to enjoy. Now they live for the weekends. Neither has energy for romance.

Are there any areas in your own marriage that have been declared off-limits? It's time to take the barriers down and talk about them. Resist blame and defensiveness. Ask God to help you understand your spouse's perspective. If you find you need help talking through these issues, get it. And if you have no issues, give thanks to God that you don't!

5:41 [a]NU-Text reads *the name;* M-Text reads *the name of Jesus.* **6:1** [a]That is, Greek-speaking Jews in Jerusalem, and a great many of the priests were obedient to the faith.

Stephen Accused of Blasphemy

8And Stephen, full of faith[a] and power, did great wonders and signs among the people. 9Then there arose some from what is called the Synagogue of the Freedmen (Cyrenians, Alexandrians, and those from Cilicia and Asia), disputing with Stephen. 10And they were not able to resist the wisdom and the Spirit by which he spoke. 11Then they secretly induced men to say, "We have heard him speak blasphemous words against Moses and God." 12And they stirred up the people, the elders, and the scribes; and they came upon *him,* seized him, and brought *him* to the council. 13They also set up false witnesses who said, "This man does not cease to speak blasphemous[a] words against this holy place and the law; 14for we have heard him say that this Jesus of Nazareth will destroy this place and change the customs which Moses delivered to us." 15And all who sat in the council, looking steadfastly at him, saw his face as the face of an angel.

Stephen's Address: The Call of Abraham

7 Then the high priest said, "Are these things so?"

2And he said, "Brethren and fathers, listen: The God of glory appeared to our father Abraham when he was in Mesopotamia, before he dwelt in Haran, 3and said to him, 'Get out of your country and from your relatives, and come to a land that I will show you.'[a] 4Then he came out of the land of the Chaldeans and dwelt in Haran. And from there, when his father was dead, He moved him to this land in which you now dwell. 5And *God* gave him no inheritance in it, not even *enough* to set his foot on. But even when *Abraham* had no child, He promised to give it to him for a possession, and to his descendants after him. 6But God spoke in this way: that his descendants would dwell in a foreign land, and that they would bring them into bondage and oppress *them* four hundred years. 7'And the nation to whom they will be in bondage I will judge,'[a] said God, 'and after that they shall come out and serve Me

in this place.'[b] 8Then He gave him the covenant of circumcision; and so *Abraham* begot Isaac and circumcised him on the eighth day; and Isaac *begot* Jacob, and Jacob *begot* the twelve patriarchs.

The Patriarchs in Egypt

9"And the patriarchs, becoming envious, sold Joseph into Egypt. But God was with him 10and delivered him out of all his troubles, and gave him favor and wisdom in the presence of Pharaoh, king of Egypt; and he made him governor over Egypt and all his house. 11Now a famine and great trouble came over all the land of Egypt and Canaan, and our fathers found no sustenance. 12But when Jacob heard that there was grain in Egypt, he sent out our fathers first. 13And the second *time* Joseph was made known to his brothers, and Joseph's family became known to the Pharaoh. 14Then Joseph sent and called his father Jacob and all his relatives to *him,* seventy-five[a] people. 15So Jacob went down to Egypt; and he died, he and our fathers. 16And they were carried back to Shechem and laid in the tomb that Abraham bought for a sum of money from the sons of Hamor, *the father* of Shechem.

God Delivers Israel by Moses

17"But when the time of the promise drew near which God had sworn to Abraham, the people grew and multiplied in Egypt 18till another king arose who did not know Joseph. 19This man dealt treacherously with our people, and oppressed our forefathers, making them expose their babies, so that they might not live. 20At this time Moses was born, and was well pleasing to God; and he was brought up in his father's house for three months. 21But when he was set out, Pharaoh's daughter took him away and brought him up as her own son. 22And Moses was learned in all the wisdom of the Egyptians, and was mighty in words and deeds.

23"Now when he was forty years old, it came into his heart to visit his brethren,

---

6:8 [a]NU-Text reads *grace.* **6:13** [a]NU-Text omits *blasphemous.* **7:3** [a]Genesis 12:1 **7:7** [a]Genesis 15:14 [b]Exodus 3:12 **7:14** [a]Or *seventy* (compare Exodus 1:5)

the children of Israel. 24And seeing one of *them* suffer wrong, he defended and avenged him who was oppressed, and struck down the Egyptian. 25For he supposed that his brethren would have understood that God would deliver them by his hand, but they did not understand. 26And the next day he appeared to *two of* them as they were fighting, and *tried to* reconcile them, saying, 'Men, you are brethren; why do you wrong one another?' 27But he who did his neighbor wrong pushed him away, saying, '*Who made you a ruler and a judge over us? 28Do you want to kill me as you did the Egyptian yesterday?*'a 29Then, at this saying, Moses fled and became a dweller in the land of Midian, where he had two sons.

30"And when forty years had passed, an Angel of the Lorda appeared to him in a flame of fire in a bush, in the wilderness of Mount Sinai. 31When Moses saw *it*, he marveled at the sight; and as he drew near to observe, the voice of the Lord came to him, 32saying, '*I am the God of your fathers— the God of Abraham, the God of Isaac, and the God of Jacob.*'a And Moses trembled and dared not look. 33'*Then the Lord said to him, "Take your sandals off your feet, for the place where you stand is holy ground. 34I have surely seen the oppression of My people who are in Egypt; I have heard their groaning and have come down to deliver them. And now come, I will send you to Egypt."*'a

35"This Moses whom they rejected, saying, '*Who made you a ruler and a judge?*'a is the one God sent *to be* a ruler and a deliverer by the hand of the Angel who appeared to him in the bush. 36He brought them out, after he had shown wonders and signs in the land of Egypt, and in the Red Sea, and in the wilderness forty years.

Israel Rebels Against God

37"This is that Moses who said to the children of Israel,a '*The Lord your God will raise up for you a Prophet like me from your brethren. Him you shall hear.*'b

38"This is he who was in the congregation in the wilderness with the Angel who spoke to him on Mount Sinai, and *with* our fathers, the one who received the living oracles to give to us, 39whom our fathers would not obey, but rejected. And in their hearts they turned back to Egypt, 40saying to Aaron, '*Make us gods to go before us; as*

7:28 aExodus 2:14 7:30 aNU-Text omits *of the Lord.*
7:32 aExodus 3:6, 15 7:34 aExodus 3:5, 7, 8, 10
7:35 aExodus 2:14 7:37 aDeuteronomy 18:15 bNU-Text and M-Text omit *Him you shall hear.*

PARENTING MATTERS	**Q: *What role should Dad play with our daughter, and Mom with our son, in teaching our children about sex?***

Many dads feel tempted to avoid this topic because girls often push their dads out of their lives as they move toward adolescence. I felt it was better for Barbara to go over the basic facts about human reproduction with our girls. But I have had plenty of conversations with our daughters about protecting their purity and establishing moral boundaries. A father needs to be involved in discussions about sexual feelings and character issues, and in helping a young girl understand what's going on inside a young man's mind and body.

With sons, it is important for a mother to validate the things dad says, and to encourage a boy in his process of growing up. These are such difficult years for a boy! He is usually around women all the time, from mom at home to the teachers at school.

Encourage your son to be a servant-leader as a man. Be sure to praise him any time he does anything kind or sacrificial for someone else. Tell him that someday his wife will need him to help bring in the groceries. Encourage him to open the door for his sisters. And thank him for his manly help any time he gives it.

for this Moses who brought us out of the land of Egypt, we do not know what has become of him.'a 41And they made a calf in those days, offered sacrifices to the idol, and rejoiced in the works of their own hands. 42Then God turned and gave them up to worship the host of heaven, as it is written in the book of the Prophets:

'Did you offer Me slaughtered
    animals and sacrifices during
    forty years in the wilderness,
O house of Israel?
43 You also took up the tabernacle of
    Moloch,
And the star of your god Remphan,
Images which you made to worship;
And I will carry you away beyond
    Babylon.'a

God's True Tabernacle

44"Our fathers had the tabernacle of witness in the wilderness, as He appointed, instructing Moses to make it according to the pattern that he had seen, 45which our fathers, having received it in turn, also brought with Joshua into the land possessed by the Gentiles, whom God drove out before the face of our fathers until the days of David, 46who found favor before God and asked to find a dwelling for the God of Jacob. 47But Solomon built Him a house.

48"However, the Most High does not dwell in temples made with hands, as the prophet says:

49 'Heaven is My throne,
    And earth is My footstool.
    What house will you build for Me?
        says the LORD,
    Or what is the place of My rest?
50 Has My hand not made all these
        things?'a

Israel Resists the Holy Spirit

51"You stiff-necked and uncircumcised in heart and ears! You always resist the Holy Spirit; as your fathers did, so do you. 52Which of the prophets did your fathers not persecute? And they killed those who foretold the coming of the Just One, of whom you now have become the betrayers and murderers, 53who have received the law by the direction of angels and have not kept it."

Stephen the Martyr

54When they heard these things they were cut to the heart, and they gnashed at him with their teeth. 55But he, being full of the Holy Spirit, gazed into heaven and saw the glory of God, and Jesus standing at the right hand of God, 56and said, "Look! I see the heavens opened and the Son of Man standing at the right hand of God!"

57Then they cried out with a loud voice, stopped their ears, and ran at him with one accord; 58and they cast him out of the city and stoned him. And the witnesses laid down their clothes at the feet of a young man named Saul. 59And they stoned Stephen as he was calling on God and saying, "Lord Jesus, receive my spirit." 60Then he knelt down and cried out with a loud voice, "Lord, do not charge them with this sin." And when he had said this, he fell asleep.

Saul Persecutes the Church

8 Now Saul was consenting to his death. At that time a great persecution arose against the church which was at Jerusalem; and they were all scattered throughout the regions of Judea and Samaria, except the apostles. 2And devout men carried Stephen to his burial, and made great lamentation over him.

3As for Saul, he made havoc of the church, entering every house, and dragging off men and women, committing them to prison.

Christ Is Preached in Samaria

4Therefore those who were scattered went everywhere preaching the word. 5Then Philip went down to thea city of Samaria and preached Christ to them. 6And the multitudes with one accord heeded the things spoken by Philip, hearing and seeing the miracles which he did. 7For unclean spirits, crying with a loud voice, came out of many who were possessed; and many who were paralyzed and lame

7:40 aExodus 32:1, 23 7:43 aAmos 5:25–27
7:50 aIsaiah 66:1, 2 8:5 aOr a

were healed. ⁸And there was great joy in that city.

The Sorcerer's Profession of Faith

⁹But there was a certain man called Simon, who previously practiced sorcery in the city and astonished the people of Samaria, claiming that he was someone great, ¹⁰to whom they all gave heed, from the least to the greatest, saying, "This man is the great power of God." ¹¹And they heeded him because he had astonished them with his sorceries for a long time. ¹²But when they believed Philip as he preached the things concerning the kingdom of God and the name of Jesus Christ, both men and women were baptized. ¹³Then Simon himself also believed; and when he was baptized he continued with Philip, and was amazed, seeing the miracles and signs which were done.

The Sorcerer's Sin

¹⁴Now when the apostles who were at Jerusalem heard that Samaria had received the word of God, they sent Peter and John to them, ¹⁵who, when they had come down, prayed for them that they might receive the Holy Spirit. ¹⁶For as yet He had fallen upon none of them. They had only been baptized in the name of the Lord Jesus. ¹⁷Then they laid hands on them, and they received the Holy Spirit.

¹⁸And when Simon saw that through the laying on of the apostles' hands the Holy Spirit was given, he offered them money, ¹⁹saying, "Give me this power also, that anyone on whom I lay hands may receive the Holy Spirit."

²⁰But Peter said to him, "Your money perish with you, because you thought that the gift of God could be purchased with money! ²¹You have neither part nor portion in this matter, for your heart is not right in the sight of God. ²²Repent therefore of this your wickedness, and pray God if perhaps the thought of your heart may be forgiven you. ²³For I see that you are poisoned by bitterness and bound by iniquity."

²⁴Then Simon answered and said, "Pray to the Lord for me, that none of the things which you have spoken may come upon me."

BIBLICAL INSIGHTS • 8:1

The Best and Worst of Times

SOMEONE ONCE SAID, "Life is like licking honey off a thorn." Charles Dickens captured this thought when he wrote, "It was the best of times, it was the worst of times." Life can be both sweet and sour, simultaneously.

Many years ago, after a period of personal difficulty, Barbara and I learned she was pregnant . . . again. The news meant that in God's sovereign and loving will, we'd have six children, ages ten and under. The best of times?

Shortly afterward, Barbara walked into our bedroom and fell on the bed, complaining of a rapid heartbeat. As we sped to the hospital, a hundred thoughts flashed through my mind. Would I soon be saying good-bye to the woman I loved, and be left alone to raise five children? The worst of times?

No! Not for a Christian. For tribulations produce hope (Rom. 5:2). The very persecution that caused untold suffering among Jerusalem's Christians, for example, also helped to spread the Good News throughout the Roman world (Acts 8:1).

Fascinating, isn't it, how quickly our lives can be reduced to a simple faith in God? I've wondered on more than one occasion if God doesn't shake His head at how slow we are to realize *we are not in control!* Whatever the circumstances you are facing today, the best of times or the worst of times, God is working all things for our good and for His glory.

²⁵So when they had testified and preached the word of the Lord, they returned to Jerusalem, preaching the gospel in many villages of the Samaritans.

Christ Is Preached to an Ethiopian

²⁶Now an angel of the Lord spoke to Philip, saying, "Arise and go toward the south along the road which goes down from Jerusalem to Gaza." This is desert.

27So he arose and went. And behold, a man of Ethiopia, a eunuch of great authority under Candace the queen of the Ethiopians, who had charge of all her treasury, and had come to Jerusalem to worship, 28was returning. And sitting in his chariot, he was reading Isaiah the prophet. 29Then the Spirit said to Philip, "Go near and overtake this chariot."

30So Philip ran to him, and heard him reading the prophet Isaiah, and said, "Do you understand what you are reading?"

31And he said, "How can I, unless someone guides me?" And he asked Philip to come up and sit with him. 32The place in the Scripture which he read was this:

"*He was led as a sheep to the slaughter;*
And as a lamb before its shearer is
silent,
So He opened not His mouth.
33 *In His humiliation His justice was*
taken away,
And who will declare His generation?
For His life is taken from the earth."a

34So the eunuch answered Philip and said, "I ask you, of whom does the prophet say this, of himself or of some other man?" 35Then Philip opened his mouth, and beginning at this Scripture, preached Jesus to him. 36Now as they went down the road, they came to some water. And the eunuch said, "See, *here is* water. What hinders me from being baptized?"

37Then Philip said, "If you believe with all your heart, you may."

And he answered and said, "I believe that Jesus Christ is the Son of God."a

38So he commanded the chariot to stand still. And both Philip and the eunuch went down into the water, and he baptized him. 39Now when they came up out of the water, the Spirit of the Lord caught Philip away, so that the eunuch saw him no more; and he went on his way rejoicing. 40But Philip was found at Azotus. And passing through, he preached in all the cities till he came to Caesarea.

The Damascus Road: Saul Converted

9 Then Saul, still breathing threats and murder against the disciples of the Lord, went to the high priest 2and asked

letters from him to the synagogues of Damascus, so that if he found any who were of the Way, whether men or women, he might bring them bound to Jerusalem.

3As he journeyed he came near Damascus, and suddenly a light shone around him from heaven. 4Then he fell to the ground, and heard a voice saying to him, "Saul, Saul, why are you persecuting Me?"

5And he said, "Who are You, Lord?"

Then the Lord said, "I am Jesus, whom you are persecuting.a It *is* hard for you to kick against the goads."

6So he, trembling and astonished, said, "Lord, what do You want me to do?"

Then the Lord *said* to him, "Arise and go into the city, and you will be told what you must do."

7And the men who journeyed with him stood speechless, hearing a voice but seeing no one. 8Then Saul arose from the ground, and when his eyes were opened he saw no one. But they led him by the hand and brought *him* into Damascus. 9And he was three days without sight, and neither ate nor drank.

Ananias Baptizes Saul

10Now there was a certain disciple at Damascus named Ananias; and to him the Lord said in a vision, "Ananias."

And he said, "Here I am, Lord."

11So the Lord *said* to him, "Arise and go to the street called Straight, and inquire at the house of Judas for *one* called Saul of Tarsus, for behold, he is praying. 12And in a vision he has seen a man named Ananias coming in and putting *his* hand on him, so that he might receive his sight."

13Then Ananias answered, "Lord, I have heard from many about this man, how much harm he has done to Your saints in Jerusalem. 14And here he has authority from the chief priests to bind all who call on Your name."

15But the Lord said to him, "Go, for he is a chosen vessel of Mine to bear My name before Gentiles, kings, and the children of

8:33 aIsaiah 53:7, 8 **8:37** aNU-Text and M-Text omit this verse. It is found in Western texts, including the Latin tradition. **9:5** aNU-Text and M-Text omit the last sentence of verse 5 and begin verse 6 with *But arise and go.*

Israel. ¹⁶For I will show him how many things he must suffer for My name's sake."

¹⁷And Ananias went his way and entered the house; and laying his hands on him he said, "Brother Saul, the Lord Jesus,ᵃ who appeared to you on the road as you came, has sent me that you may receive your sight and be filled with the Holy Spirit." ¹⁸Immediately there fell from his eyes *something* like scales, and he received his sight at once; and he arose and was baptized. ¹⁹So when he had received food, he was strengthened. Then Saul spent some days with the disciples at Damascus.

Saul Preaches Christ

²⁰Immediately he preached the Christᵃ in the synagogues, that He is the Son of God. ²¹Then all who heard were amazed, and said, "Is this not he who destroyed those who called on this name in Jerusalem, and has come here for that purpose, so that he might bring them bound to the chief priests?"

²²But Saul increased all the more in strength, and confounded the Jews who dwelt in Damascus, proving that this *Jesus* is the Christ.

Saul Escapes Death

²³Now after many days were past, the Jews plotted to kill him. ²⁴But their plot became known to Saul. And they watched the gates day and night, to kill him. ²⁵Then the disciples took him by night and let *him* down through the wall in a large basket.

Saul at Jerusalem

²⁶And when Saul had come to Jerusalem, he tried to join the disciples; but they were all afraid of him, and did not believe that he was a disciple. ²⁷But Barnabas took him and brought *him* to the apostles. And he declared to them how he had seen the Lord on the road, and that He had spoken to him, and how he had preached boldly at Damascus in the name of Jesus. ²⁸So he was with them at Jerusalem, coming in and going out. ²⁹And he spoke boldly in the name of the Lord Jesus and disputed against the

Hellenists, but they attempted to kill him. ³⁰When the brethren found out, they brought him down to Caesarea and sent him out to Tarsus.

The Church Prospers

³¹Then the churchesᵃ throughout all Judea, Galilee, and Samaria had peace and were edified. And walking in the fear of the Lord and in the comfort of the Holy Spirit, they were multiplied.

Aeneas Healed

³²Now it came to pass, as Peter went through all *parts of the country,* that he also came down to the saints who dwelt in Lydda. ³³There he found a certain man named Aeneas, who had been bedridden eight years and was paralyzed. ³⁴And Peter said to him, "Aeneas, Jesus the Christ

INTIMATE MOMENTS
Take a Creative Challenge

A single New York marketing strategist has some helpful advice for any husband looking for ways to spice up his love life with his wife. "I always try to take a girl on a really *different* first date—one that will show her that I'm a spontaneous, up-for-anything person. I shy away from the typical dinner or movie and instead choose something that's different and cool, yet still within her comfort zone. I can't say it's always cheap or easy, but I like the creative challenge of coming up with something memorable and romantic. I've arranged for a private, at-home cooking lesson with a chef from one of my favorite restaurants, scheduled a rooftop massage for two and even once took a girl on a helicopter ride over the city. I want her to feel like she'll always have fun if she continues to see me."

When was the last time you did something spontaneous or creative with your spouse? Find a fresh and fun way to communicate your love this week.

9:17 ᵃM-Text omits *Jesus.* **9:20** ᵃNU-Text reads *Jesus.*
9:31 ᵃNU-Text reads *church . . . was edified.*

heals you. Arise and make your bed." Then he arose immediately. ³⁵So all who dwelt at Lydda and Sharon saw him and turned to the Lord.

Dorcas Restored to Life

³⁶At Joppa there was a certain disciple named Tabitha, which is translated Dorcas. This woman was full of good works and charitable deeds which she did. ³⁷But it happened in those days that she

ROMANCE FAQ

Q: How can we encourage uplifting language in our home?

Instead of smelling up the place with unwholesome talk, Paul says we should speak only that which is helpful and uplifting, according to the needs of those who listen (Eph. 4:29).

For example, Barbara would often feel emotionally empty after orchestrating trips to the dentist, doctor, lessons and meetings, plus all the draining conflicts that take place in a family of eight. She certainly didn't need me to criticize her for what she hadn't done! She needed me to be on her team, cheering her on and expressing appreciation for juggling all that she was doing for the kids, the ministry, and me.

Occasionally we'd use the dinner table to have a Praise Mom Party. Each of us would take turns expressing appreciation and encouragement. Our teenage boys would brag, "I like Mom because she cooks good food and a lot of it!" Our youngest would chirp, "I like Mom because she's pretty." Another would say, "I like Mom because she helps me with my homework." Without exception, when we'd finished our praise party, Barbara's countenance had brightened and her shoulders had straightened.

How about having some words with a positive aroma at your house tonight? Pick a family member and share what you most appreciate about him or her.

became sick and died. When they had washed her, they laid *her* in an upper room. ³⁸And since Lydda was near Joppa, and the disciples had heard that Peter was there, they sent two men to him, imploring *him* not to delay in coming to them. ³⁹Then Peter arose and went with them. When he had come, they brought *him* to the upper room. And all the widows stood by him weeping, showing the tunics and garments which Dorcas had made while she was with them. ⁴⁰But Peter put them all out, and knelt down and prayed. And turning to the body he said, "Tabitha, arise." And she opened her eyes, and when she saw Peter she sat up. ⁴¹Then he gave her *his* hand and lifted her up; and when he had called the saints and widows, he presented her alive. ⁴²And it became known throughout all Joppa, and many believed on the Lord. ⁴³So it was that he stayed many days in Joppa with Simon, a tanner.

Cornelius Sends a Delegation

10 There was a certain man in Caesarea called Cornelius, a centurion of what was called the Italian Regiment, ²a devout *man* and one who feared God with all his household, who gave alms generously to the people, and prayed to God always. ³About the ninth hour of the day he saw clearly in a vision an angel of God coming in and saying to him, "Cornelius!"

⁴And when he observed him, he was afraid, and said, "What is it, lord?"

So he said to him, "Your prayers and your alms have come up for a memorial before God. ⁵Now send men to Joppa, and send for Simon whose surname is Peter. ⁶He is lodging with Simon, a tanner, whose house is by the sea.ᵃ He will tell you what you must do." ⁷And when the angel who spoke to him had departed, Cornelius called two of his household servants and a devout soldier from among those who waited on him continually. ⁸So when he had explained all *these* things to them, he sent them to Joppa.

10:6 ᵃNU-Text and M-Text omit the last sentence of this verse.

Peter's Vision

9The next day, as they went on their journey and drew near the city, Peter went up on the housetop to pray, about the sixth hour. 10Then he became very hungry and wanted to eat; but while they made ready, he fell into a trance 11and saw heaven opened and an object like a great sheet bound at the four corners, descending to him and let down to the earth. 12In it were all kinds of four-footed animals of the earth, wild beasts, creeping things, and birds of the air. 13And a voice came to him, "Rise, Peter; kill and eat."

14But Peter said, "Not so, Lord! For I have never eaten anything common or unclean."

15And a voice *spoke* to him again the second time, "What God has cleansed you must not call common." 16This was done three times. And the object was taken up into heaven again.

Summoned to Caesarea

17Now while Peter wondered within himself what this vision which he had seen meant, behold, the men who had been sent from Cornelius had made inquiry for Simon's house, and stood before the gate. 18And they called and asked whether Simon, whose surname was Peter, was lodging there.

19While Peter thought about the vision, the Spirit said to him, "Behold, three men are seeking you. 20Arise therefore, go down and go with them, doubting nothing; for I have sent them."

21Then Peter went down to the men who had been sent to him from Cornelius,a and said, "Yes, I am he whom you seek. For what reason have you come?"

22And they said, "Cornelius *the* centurion, a just man, one who fears God and has a good reputation among all the nation of the Jews, was divinely instructed by a holy angel to summon you to his house, and to hear words from you." 23Then he invited them in and lodged *them*.

On the next day Peter went away with them, and some brethren from Joppa accompanied him.

Peter Meets Cornelius

24And the following day they entered Caesarea. Now Cornelius was waiting for them, and had called together his relatives and close friends. 25As Peter was coming in, Cornelius met him and fell down at his feet and worshiped *him*. 26But Peter lifted him up, saying, "Stand up; I myself am also a man." 27And as he talked with him, he went in and found many who had come together. 28Then he said to them, "You know how unlawful it is for a Jewish man to keep company with or go to one of another nation. But God has shown me that I should not call any man common or unclean. 29Therefore I came without objection as soon as I was sent for. I ask, then, for what reason have you sent for me?"

30So Cornelius said, "Four days ago I was fasting until this hour; and at the ninth houra I prayed in my house, and behold, a man stood before me in bright clothing, 31and said, 'Cornelius, your prayer has been heard, and your alms are remembered in the sight of God. 32Send therefore to Joppa and call Simon here, whose surname is Peter. He is lodging in the house of Simon, a tanner, by the sea.a When he comes, he will speak to you.' 33So I sent to you immediately, and you have done well to come. Now therefore, we are all present before God, to hear all the things commanded you by God."

Preaching to Cornelius' Household

34Then Peter opened *his* mouth and said: "In truth I perceive that God shows no partiality. 35But in every nation whoever fears Him and works righteousness is accepted by Him. 36The word which *God* sent to the children of Israel, preaching peace through Jesus Christ—He is Lord of all— 37that word you know, which was proclaimed throughout all Judea, and began from Galilee after the baptism which John preached: 38how God anointed Jesus of Nazareth with the Holy Spirit and with power, who went about doing good and healing all who were oppressed by the devil, for God was with Him. 39And we are witnesses of all things which He did both in the land of the Jews and in Jerusalem,

---

10:21 aNU-Text and M-Text omit *who had been sent to him from Cornelius.* 10:30 aNU-Text reads *Four days ago to this hour, at the ninth hour.* 10:32 aNU-Text omits the last sentence of this verse.

whom theyª killed by hanging on a tree. ⁴⁰Him God raised up on the third day, and showed Him openly, ⁴¹not to all the people, but to witnesses chosen before by God, *even* to us who ate and drank with Him after He arose from the dead. ⁴²And He commanded us to preach to the people, and to testify that it is He who was ordained by God *to be* Judge of the living and the dead. ⁴³To Him all the prophets witness that, through His name, whoever believes in Him will receive remission of sins."

The Holy Spirit Falls on the Gentiles

⁴⁴While Peter was still speaking these words, the Holy Spirit fell upon all those who heard the word. ⁴⁵And those of the circumcision who believed were astonished, as many as came with Peter, because the gift of the Holy Spirit had been poured out on the Gentiles also. ⁴⁶For they heard them speak with tongues and magnify God.

Then Peter answered, ⁴⁷"Can anyone forbid water, that these should not be baptized who have received the Holy Spirit just as we *have?*" ⁴⁸And he commanded them to be baptized in the name of the Lord. Then they asked him to stay a few days.

Peter Defends God's Grace

11 Now the apostles and brethren who were in Judea heard that the Gentiles had also received the word of God. ²And when Peter came up to Jerusalem, those of the circumcision contended with him, ³saying, "You went in to uncircumcised men and ate with them!"

⁴But Peter explained *it* to them in order from the beginning, saying: ⁵"I was in the city of Joppa praying; and in a trance I saw a vision, an object descending like a great sheet, let down from heaven by four corners; and it came to me. ⁶When I observed it intently and considered, I saw four-footed animals of the earth, wild beasts, creeping things, and birds of the air. ⁷And I heard a voice saying to me, 'Rise, Peter; kill and eat.' ⁸But I said, 'Not so, Lord! For nothing common or unclean has at any time entered my mouth.' ⁹But the voice answered me again from heaven, 'What God has cleansed you must not call common.' ¹⁰Now this was done three times, and all were drawn up again into heaven. ¹¹At that very moment, three men stood before the house where I

10:39 ªNU-Text and M-Text add *also.*

PARENTING MATTERS

Q: *How can we convince our daughter not to wear clothing that we think makes her look trashy?*

It's safe to assume that many of today's clothing designers do not share your biblical convictions! Your job as parents is to set some boundaries and guidelines that can guide your children even before they enter the teenage years.

We have sought to build a number of convictions within our children on this issue. Perhaps the most important is the conviction that their appearance and dress should not emphasize their body, but their heart's loyalty to Christ. Another conviction is this: When in doubt, modesty is the best policy.

We believe it's time for a modesty revolution. Modesty in clothing is a critical issue for girls. Boys really do pay more attention (and not in a good way) to a more enticing appearance. That might momentarily feel more enjoyable for girls, but often they don't fully realize the values they are portraying and what type of boys they're wooing.

The earlier our young women begin learning modesty, the better. It is very hard for teenage girls to start covering up if they've not been trained in modesty from an early age, especially when they are living in a culture that encourages females to flaunt their bodies. So start early!

was, having been sent to me from Caesarea. [12]Then the Spirit told me to go with them, doubting nothing. Moreover these six brethren accompanied me, and we entered the man's house. [13]And he told us how he had seen an angel standing in his house, who said to him, 'Send men to Joppa, and call for Simon whose surname is Peter, [14]who will tell you words by which you and all your household will be saved.' [15]And as I began to speak, the Holy Spirit fell upon them, as upon us at the beginning. [16]Then I remembered the word of the Lord, how He said, 'John indeed baptized with water, but you shall be baptized with the Holy Spirit.' [17]If therefore God gave them the same gift as *He gave* us when we believed on the Lord Jesus Christ, who was I that I could withstand God?"

[18]When they heard these things they became silent; and they glorified God, saying, "Then God has also granted to the Gentiles repentance to life."

Barnabas and Saul at Antioch

[19]Now those who were scattered after the persecution that arose over Stephen traveled as far as Phoenicia, Cyprus, and Antioch, preaching the word to no one but the Jews only. [20]But some of them were men from Cyprus and Cyrene, who, when they had come to Antioch, spoke to the Hellenists, preaching the Lord Jesus. [21]And the hand of the Lord was with them, and a great number believed and turned to the Lord.

[22]Then news of these things came to the ears of the church in Jerusalem, and they sent out Barnabas to go as far as Antioch. [23]When he came and had seen the grace of God, he was glad, and encouraged them all that with purpose of heart they should continue with the Lord. [24]For he was a good man, full of the Holy Spirit and of faith. And a great many people were added to the Lord.

[25]Then Barnabas departed for Tarsus to seek Saul. [26]And when he had found him, he brought him to Antioch. So it was that for a whole year they assembled with the church and taught a great many people. And the disciples were first called Christians in Antioch.

Relief to Judea

[27]And in these days prophets came from Jerusalem to Antioch. [28]Then one of them, named Agabus, stood up and showed by the Spirit that there was going to be a great famine throughout all the world, which also happened in the days of Claudius Caesar. [29]Then the disciples, each according to his ability, determined to send relief to the brethren dwelling in Judea. [30]This they also did, and sent it to the elders by the hands of Barnabas and Saul.

Herod's Violence to the Church

12 Now about that time Herod the king stretched out *his* hand to harass some from the church. [2]Then he killed James the brother of John with the sword. [3]And because he saw that it pleased the Jews, he proceeded further to seize Peter also. Now it was *during* the Days of Unleavened Bread. [4]So when he had arrested him, he put *him* in prison, and delivered *him* to four squads of soldiers to keep him, intending to bring him before the people after Passover.

Peter Freed from Prison

[5]Peter was therefore kept in prison, but constant[a] prayer was offered to God for him by the church. [6]And when Herod was about to bring him out, that night Peter was sleeping, bound with two chains between two soldiers; and the guards before the door were keeping the prison. [7]Now behold, an angel of the Lord stood by *him,* and a light shone in the prison; and he struck Peter on the side and raised him up, saying, "Arise quickly!" And his chains fell off *his* hands. [8]Then the angel said to him, "Gird yourself and tie on your sandals"; and so he did. And he said to him, "Put on your garment and follow me." [9]So he went out and followed him, and did not know that what was done by the angel was real, but thought he was seeing a vision. [10]When they were past the first and the second guard posts, they came to the iron gate that leads to the city, which opened to them of its own accord; and they went out and went down one street, and immediately the angel departed from him.

12:5 [a]NU-Text reads *constantly* (or *earnestly*).

¹¹And when Peter had come to himself, he said, "Now I know for certain that the Lord has sent His angel, and has delivered me from the hand of Herod and *from* all the expectation of the Jewish people."

¹²So, when he had considered *this,* he came to the house of Mary, the mother of John whose surname was Mark, where many were gathered together praying. ¹³And as Peter knocked at the door of the gate, a girl named Rhoda came to answer. ¹⁴When she recognized Peter's voice, because of *her* gladness she did not open the gate, but ran in and announced that Peter stood before the gate. ¹⁵But they said to her, "You are beside yourself!" Yet she kept insisting that it was so. So they said, "It is his angel."

¹⁶Now Peter continued knocking; and when they opened *the door* and saw him, they were astonished. ¹⁷But motioning to them with his hand to keep silent, he declared to them how the Lord had brought him out of the prison. And he said, "Go, tell these things to James and to the brethren." And he departed and went to another place.

¹⁸Then, as soon as it was day, there was no small stir among the soldiers about what had become of Peter. ¹⁹But when Herod had searched for him and not found him, he examined the guards and commanded that *they* should be put to death.

And he went down from Judea to Caesarea, and stayed *there.*

Herod's Violent Death

²⁰Now Herod had been very angry with the people of Tyre and Sidon; but they came to him with one accord, and having made Blastus the king's personal aide their friend, they asked for peace, because their country was supplied with food by the king's *country.* ²¹So on a set day Herod, arrayed in royal apparel, sat on his throne and gave an oration to them. ²²And the people kept shouting, "The voice of a god and not of a man!" ²³Then immediately an angel of the Lord struck him, because he did not give glory to God. And he was eaten by worms and died.

²⁴But the word of God grew and multiplied.

Barnabas and Saul Appointed

²⁵And Barnabas and Saul returned from[a] Jerusalem when they had fulfilled *their* ministry, and they also took with them John whose surname was Mark.

13 Now in the church that was at Antioch there were certain prophets and teachers: Barnabas, Simeon who was called Niger, Lucius of Cyrene, Manaen who had been brought up with Herod the tetrarch, and Saul. ²As they ministered to the Lord and fasted, the Holy Spirit said, "Now separate to Me Barnabas and Saul for the work to which I have called them." ³Then, having fasted and prayed, and laid hands on them, they sent *them* away.

Preaching in Cyprus

⁴So, being sent out by the Holy Spirit, they went down to Seleucia, and from there they sailed to Cyprus. ⁵And when they arrived in Salamis, they preached the word of God in the synagogues of the Jews. They also had John as *their* assistant.

⁶Now when they had gone through the island[a] to Paphos, they found a certain sorcerer, a false prophet, a Jew whose name *was* Bar-Jesus, ⁷who was with the proconsul, Sergius Paulus, an intelligent man. This man called for Barnabas and Saul and sought to hear the word of God. ⁸But Elymas the sorcerer (for so his name is translated) withstood them, seeking to turn the proconsul away from the faith. ⁹Then Saul, who also *is called* Paul, filled with the Holy Spirit, looked intently at him ¹⁰and said, "O full of all deceit and all fraud, *you* son of the devil, *you* enemy of all righteousness, will you not cease perverting the straight ways of the Lord? ¹¹And now, indeed, the hand of the Lord *is* upon you, and you shall be blind, not seeing the sun for a time."

And immediately a dark mist fell on him, and he went around seeking someone to lead him by the hand. ¹²Then the proconsul believed, when he saw what had been done, being astonished at the teaching of the Lord.

12:25 aNU-Text and M-Text read *to.*
13:6 aNU-Text reads *the whole island.*

At Antioch in Pisidia

¹³Now when Paul and his party set sail from Paphos, they came to Perga in Pamphylia; and John, departing from them, returned to Jerusalem. ¹⁴But when they departed from Perga, they came to Antioch in Pisidia, and went into the synagogue on the Sabbath day and sat down. ¹⁵And after the reading of the Law and the Prophets, the rulers of the synagogue sent to them, saying, "Men *and* brethren, if you have any word of exhortation for the people, say on."

¹⁶Then Paul stood up, and motioning with *his* hand said, "Men of Israel, and you who fear God, listen: ¹⁷The God of this people Israelᵃ chose our fathers, and exalted the people when they dwelt as strangers in the land of Egypt, and with an uplifted arm He brought them out of it. ¹⁸Now for a time of about forty years He put up with their ways in the wilderness. ¹⁹And when He had destroyed seven nations in the land of Canaan, He distributed their land to them by allotment.

²⁰"After that He gave *them* judges for about four hundred and fifty years, until Samuel the prophet. ²¹And afterward they asked for a king; so God gave them Saul the son of Kish, a man of the tribe of Benjamin, for forty years. ²²And when He had removed him, He raised up for them David as king, to whom also He gave testimony and said, '*I have found David*ᵃ *the son* of Jesse, *a man after My own heart, who will do all My will.*'ᵇ ²³From this man's seed, according to *the* promise, God raised up for Israel a Savior—Jesus—ᵃ ²⁴after John had first preached, before His coming, the baptism of repentance to all the people of Israel. ²⁵And as John was finishing his course, he said, 'Who do you think I am? I am not *He.* But behold, there comes One after me, the sandals of whose feet I am not worthy to loose.'

²⁶"Men *and* brethren, sons of the family of Abraham, and those among you who fear God, to you the word of this salvation

has been sent. ²⁷For those who dwell in Jerusalem, and their rulers, because they did not know Him, nor even the voices of the Prophets which are read every Sabbath, have fulfilled *them* in condemning *Him.* ²⁸And though they found no cause for death *in Him,* they asked Pilate that He should be put to death. ²⁹Now when they had fulfilled all that was written concerning Him, they took *Him* down from the tree and laid *Him* in a tomb. ³⁰But God raised Him from the dead. ³¹He was seen for many days by those who came up with Him from Galilee to Jerusalem, who are His witnesses to the people. ³²And we declare to you glad tidings—that promise which was made to the fathers. ³³God has fulfilled this for us their children, in that He has raised up Jesus. As it is also written in the second Psalm:

> '*You are My Son,*
> *Today I have begotten You.*'ᵃ

³⁴And that He raised Him from the dead, no more to return to corruption, He has spoken thus:

> '*I will give you the sure mercies of David.*'ᵃ

³⁵Therefore He also says in another *Psalm:*

> '*You will not allow Your Holy One to see corruption.*'ᵃ

³⁶"For David, after he had served his own generation by the will of God, fell asleep, was buried with his fathers, and saw corruption; ³⁷but He whom God raised up saw no corruption. ³⁸Therefore let it be known to you, brethren, that through this Man is preached to you the forgiveness of sins; ³⁹and by Him everyone who believes is justified from all things from which you could not be justified by the law of Moses. ⁴⁰Beware therefore, lest what has been spoken in the prophets come upon you:

⁴¹ > '*Behold, you despisers,*
> *Marvel and perish!*
> *For I work a work in your days,*
> *A work which you will by no means believe,*
> *Though one were to declare it to you.*' "ᵃ

13:17 ᵃM-Text omits *Israel.* **13:22** ᵃPsalm 89:20 ᵇ1
Samuel 13:14 **13:23** ᵃM-Text reads *for Israel salvation.*
13:33 ᵃPsalm 2:7 **13:34** ᵃIsaiah 55:3
13:35 ᵃPsalm 16:10 **13:41** ᵃHabakkuk 1:5

BIBLICAL INSIGHTS • 13:49

We Are Part of the Solution

THE ARMY OF GOD needs fresh troops. The enemy is real. The message is powerful. The hour couldn't be more urgent. And God wants to use you and your family to do just what He did in the book of Acts, "And the word of the Lord was being spread throughout all the region" (13:49).

"So what do I do?" you ask. How can my spouse and I be a part of what God is doing? Here are a few ideas. Together, we will make a difference.

1. Hold an evangelistic dinner party at your home for a few couples.

2. Host a Good News Club for children in your neighborhood.

3. Purchase a bundle of *The Four Spiritual Laws* booklets. Leave some on your desk for people to pick up and read. Put some in your pocket or purse. Share them or give them away as you do your errands.

4. Show your children how to share their faith and invite a neighborhood child to go to church.

5. Host an evangelistic coffee a couple of weeks before Christmas for your neighborhood or friends.

6. Share Christ with the next person you sit next to on a plane, bus or train.

7. Host a HomeBuilders Bible study with three or four couples who need to know Christ.

The mission of the church hasn't changed in over 2,000 years. We're still called to help spread the gospel to all people. Make your home the springboard for sharing the greatest news the world has ever heard!

Blessing and Conflict at Antioch

⁴²So when the Jews went out of the synagogue,ᵃ the Gentiles begged that these words might be preached to them the next Sabbath. ⁴³Now when the congregation had broken up, many of the Jews and devout proselytes followed Paul and Barnabas, who, speaking to them, persuaded them to continue in the grace of God.

⁴⁴On the next Sabbath almost the whole city came together to hear the word of God. ⁴⁵But when the Jews saw the multitudes, they were filled with envy; and contradicting and blaspheming, they opposed the things spoken by Paul. ⁴⁶Then Paul and Barnabas grew bold and said, "It was necessary that the word of God should be spoken to you first; but since you reject it, and judge yourselves unworthy of everlasting life, behold, we turn to the Gentiles. ⁴⁷For so the Lord has commanded us:

'I have set you as a light to the
    Gentiles,
That you should be for salvation to
    the ends of the earth.' "ᵃ

⁴⁸Now when the Gentiles heard this, they were glad and glorified the word of the Lord. And as many as had been appointed to eternal life believed.

⁴⁹And the word of the Lord was being spread throughout all the region. ⁵⁰But the Jews stirred up the devout and prominent women and the chief men of the city, raised up persecution against Paul and Barnabas, and expelled them from their region. ⁵¹But they shook off the dust from their feet against them, and came to Iconium. ⁵²And the disciples were filled with joy and with the Holy Spirit.

At Iconium

14 Now it happened in Iconium that they went together to the synagogue of the Jews, and so spoke that a great multitude both of the Jews and of the Greeks believed. ²But the unbelieving Jews stirred up the Gentiles and poisoned their minds against the brethren. ³Therefore they stayed there a long time, speaking boldly in the Lord, who was bearing witness to the word of His grace, granting signs and wonders to be done by their hands.

⁴But the multitude of the city was divided: part sided with the Jews, and part

13:42 ᵃOr *And when they went out of the synagogue of the Jews;* NU-Text reads *And when they went out, they begged.* 13:47 ᵃIsaiah 49:6

with the apostles. ⁵And when a violent attempt was made by both the Gentiles and Jews, with their rulers, to abuse and stone them, ⁶they became aware of it and fled to Lystra and Derbe, cities of Lycaonia, and to the surrounding region. ⁷And they were preaching the gospel there.

Idolatry at Lystra

⁸And in Lystra a certain man without strength in his feet was sitting, a cripple from his mother's womb, who had never walked. ⁹*This* man heard Paul speaking. Paul, observing him intently and seeing that he had faith to be healed, ¹⁰said with a loud voice, "Stand up straight on your feet!" And he leaped and walked. ¹¹Now when the people saw what Paul had done, they raised their voices, saying in the Lycaonian *language,* "The gods have come down to us in the likeness of men!" ¹²And Barnabas they called Zeus, and Paul, Hermes, because he was the chief speaker. ¹³Then the priest of Zeus, whose temple was in front of their city, brought oxen and garlands to the gates, intending to sacrifice with the multitudes.

¹⁴But when the apostles Barnabas and Paul heard this, they tore their clothes and ran in among the multitude, crying out ¹⁵and saying, "Men, why are you doing these things? We also are men with the same nature as you, and preach to you that you should turn from these useless things to the living God, who made the heaven, the earth, the sea, and all things that are in them, ¹⁶who in bygone generations allowed all nations to walk in their own ways. ¹⁷Nevertheless He did not leave Himself without witness, in that He did good, gave us rain from heaven and fruitful seasons, filling our hearts with food and gladness." ¹⁸And with these sayings they could scarcely restrain the multitudes from sacrificing to them.

Stoning, Escape to Derbe

¹⁹Then Jews from Antioch and Iconium came there; and having persuaded the multitudes, they stoned Paul *and* dragged *him* out of the city, supposing him to be dead. ²⁰However, when the disciples gathered around him, he rose up and went into the city. And the next day he departed with Barnabas to Derbe.

Strengthening the Converts

²¹And when they had preached the gospel to that city and made many disciples, they returned to Lystra, Iconium, and Antioch, ²²strengthening the souls of the disciples, exhorting *them* to continue in the faith, and *saying,* "We must through many tribulations enter the kingdom of God." ²³So when they had appointed elders in every church, and prayed with fasting, they commended them to the Lord in whom they had believed. ²⁴And after they had passed through Pisidia, they came to Pamphylia. ²⁵Now when they had preached the word in Perga, they went down to Attalia. ²⁶From there they sailed to Antioch, where they had been commended to the grace of God for the work which they had completed.

²⁷Now when they had come and gathered the church together, they reported all that God had done with them, and that He had opened the door of faith to the Gentiles. ²⁸So they stayed there a long time with the disciples.

Conflict over Circumcision

15 And certain *men* came down from Judea and taught the brethren, "Unless you are circumcised according to the custom of Moses, you cannot be saved." ²Therefore, when Paul and Barnabas had no small dissension and dispute with them, they determined that Paul and Barnabas and certain others of them should go up to Jerusalem, to the apostles and elders, about this question.

³So, being sent on their way by the church, they passed through Phoenicia and Samaria, describing the conversion of the Gentiles; and they caused great joy to all the brethren. ⁴And when they had come to Jerusalem, they were received by the

INTIMATE MOMENTS

Make your own holiday! Take this opportunity to create a holiday that is special and unique to the two of you.

church and the apostles and the elders; and they reported all things that God had done with them. ⁵But some of the sect of the Pharisees who believed rose up, saying, "It is necessary to circumcise them, and to command *them* to keep the law of Moses."

The Jerusalem Council

⁶Now the apostles and elders came together to consider this matter. ⁷And when there had been much dispute, Peter rose up *and* said to them: "Men *and* brethren, you know that a good while ago God chose among us, that by my mouth the Gentiles should hear the word of the gospel and believe. ⁸So God, who knows the heart, acknowledged them by giving them the Holy Spirit, just as *He did* to us, ⁹and made no distinction between us and them, purifying their hearts by faith. ¹⁰Now therefore, why do you test God by putting a yoke on the neck of the disciples which neither our fathers nor we were able to bear? ¹¹But we believe that through the grace of the Lord Jesus Christ[a] we shall be saved in the same manner as they."

¹²Then all the multitude kept silent and listened to Barnabas and Paul declaring how many miracles and wonders God had worked through them among the Gentiles. ¹³And after they had become silent, James answered, saying, "Men *and* brethren, listen to me: ¹⁴Simon has declared how God at the first visited the Gentiles to take out of them a people for His name. ¹⁵And with this the words of the prophets agree, just as it is written:

16 'After this I will return
     And will rebuild the tabernacle of
        David, which has fallen down;
     I will rebuild its ruins,
     And I will set it up;
17   So that the rest of mankind may
        seek the LORD,
     Even all the Gentiles who are called
        by My name,
     Says the LORD who does all these
        things.'[a]

¹⁸"Known to God from eternity are all His works.[a] ¹⁹Therefore I judge that we should not trouble those from among the Gentiles who are turning to God, ²⁰but that

we write to them to abstain from things polluted by idols, *from* sexual immorality,[a] *from* things strangled, and *from* blood. ²¹For Moses has had throughout many generations those who preach him in every city, being read in the synagogues every Sabbath."

The Jerusalem Decree

²²Then it pleased the apostles and elders, with the whole church, to send chosen men of their own company to Antioch with Paul and Barnabas, *namely,* Judas who was also named Barsabas,[a] and Silas, leading men among the brethren.

²³They wrote this, *letter* by them:

> The apostles, the elders, and the
> brethren,
>
> To the brethren who are of the
> Gentiles in Antioch, Syria, and
> Cilicia:
>
> Greetings.

24   Since we have heard that some who
     went out from us have troubled you
     with words, unsettling your souls,
     saying, "*You must* be circumcised
     and keep the law"[a]—to whom we
     gave no *such* commandment—²⁵it
     seemed good to us, being assembled
     with one accord, to send chosen men
     to you with our beloved Barnabas
     and Paul, ²⁶men who have risked
     their lives for the name of our Lord
     Jesus Christ. ²⁷We have therefore sent
     Judas and Silas, who will also report
     the same things by word of mouth.
     ²⁸For it seemed good to the Holy
     Spirit, and to us, to lay upon you no
     greater burden than these necessary
     things: ²⁹that you abstain from
     things offered to idols, from blood,
     from things strangled, and from
     sexual immorality.[a] If you keep

15:11 [a]NU-Text and M-Text omit *Christ.*
15:17 [a]Amos 9:11, 12 **15:18** [a]NU-Text (combining with verse 17) reads *Says the Lord, who makes these things known from eternity (of old).*
15:20 [a]Or *fornication* **15:22** [a]NU-Text and M-Text read *Barsabbas.* **15:24** [a]NU-Text omits *saying,* "*You must be circumcised and keep the law.*"
15:29 [a]Or *fornication*

yourselves from these, you will do well.

Farewell.

Continuing Ministry in Syria

[30]So when they were sent off, they came to Antioch; and when they had gathered the multitude together, they delivered the letter. [31]When they had read it, they rejoiced over its encouragement. [32]Now Judas and Silas, themselves being prophets also, exhorted and strengthened the brethren with many words. [33]And after they had stayed *there* for a time, they were sent back with greetings from the brethren to the apostles.[a]

[34]However, it seemed good to Silas to remain there.[a] [35]Paul and Barnabas also remained in Antioch, teaching and preaching the word of the Lord, with many others also.

Division over John Mark

[36]Then after some days Paul said to Barnabas, "Let us now go back and visit our brethren in every city where we have preached the word of the Lord, *and see* how they are doing." [37]Now Barnabas was determined to take with them John called Mark. [38]But Paul insisted that they should not take with them the one who had departed from them in Pamphylia, and had not gone with them to the work. [39]Then the contention became so sharp that they parted from one another. And so Barnabas took Mark and sailed to Cyprus; [40]but Paul chose Silas and departed, being commended by the brethren to the grace of God. [41]And he went through Syria and Cilicia, strengthening the churches.

Timothy Joins Paul and Silas

16 Then he came to Derbe and Lystra. And behold, a certain disciple was there, named Timothy, *the* son of a certain Jewish woman who believed, but his father *was* Greek. [2]He was well spoken of by the brethren who were at Lystra and Iconium. [3]Paul wanted to have him go on with him. And he took *him* and circumcised him because of the Jews who were in that region, for they all knew that his father was Greek. [4]And as they went through the cities, they delivered to them the decrees to keep, which were determined by the apostles and elders at Jerusalem. [5]So the churches were strengthened in the faith, and increased in number daily.

ROMANCE FAQ

Q: What does the Bible mean when it says, "Marriage is honorable among all, and the bed undefiled" (Heb. 13:4)?

It means that you should make your marriage bed a priority. Regular sexual expression in marriage is not only honorable, it's meant to bring you together as a team.

And yet, exhaustion is the great zapper of passion. Our already-tired blood is further thinned by a feverish pace and packed schedules. The result? We have little time and energy to share, give, or receive.

Fatigue does not fuel passion!

Some couples could go their own independent way indefinitely, denying their need of one another. But God gave us sex as a drive to merge, to force us out of our isolation. So Paul writes, "Do not deprive one another except with consent for a time, that you may give yourselves to fasting and prayer; and come together again so that Satan does not tempt you because of your lack of self-control" (1 Cor. 7:5).

Am I suggesting that you should write *sex* down on your calendar? I'll let you decide that one! But some who read this don't need a tablespoon of Geritol—they just need to say NO to some good things and go to bed early—say about 8:00 P.M. or so.

Instead of trying to kindle romance when both of you are wiped out, see if turning in early from time to time doesn't awaken some of the passion that's been asleep in your marriage.

15:33 [a]NU-Text reads *to those who had sent them.*
15:34 [a]NU-Text and M-Text omit this verse.

The Macedonian Call

⁶Now when they had gone through Phrygia and the region of Galatia, they were forbidden by the Holy Spirit to preach the word in Asia. ⁷After they had come to Mysia, they tried to go into Bithynia, but the Spiritᵃ did not permit them. ⁸So passing by Mysia, they came down to Troas. ⁹And a vision appeared to Paul in the night. A man of Macedonia stood and pleaded with him, saying, "Come over to Macedonia and help us." ¹⁰Now after he had seen the vision, immediately we sought to go to Macedonia, concluding that the Lord had called us to preach the gospel to them.

Lydia Baptized at Philippi

¹¹Therefore, sailing from Troas, we ran a straight course to Samothrace, and the next *day* came to Neapolis, ¹²and from there to Philippi, which is the foremost city of that part of Macedonia, a colony. And we were staying in that city for some days. ¹³And on the Sabbath day we went out of the city to the riverside, where prayer was customarily made; and we sat down and spoke to the women who met *there.* ¹⁴Now a certain woman named Lydia heard *us.*

She was a seller of purple from the city of Thyatira, who worshiped God. The Lord opened her heart to heed the things spoken by Paul. ¹⁵And when she and her household were baptized, she begged *us,* saying, "If you have judged me to be faithful to the Lord, come to my house and stay." So she persuaded us.

Paul and Silas Imprisoned

¹⁶Now it happened, as we went to prayer, that a certain slave girl possessed with a spirit of divination met us, who brought her masters much profit by fortune-telling. ¹⁷This girl followed Paul and us, and cried out, saying, "These men are the servants of the Most High God, who proclaim to us the way of salvation." ¹⁸And this she did for many days.

But Paul, greatly annoyed, turned and said to the spirit, "I command you in the name of Jesus Christ to come out of her." And he came out that very hour. ¹⁹But when her masters saw that their hope of profit was gone, they seized Paul and Silas and dragged *them* into the marketplace to the authorities.

16:7 ᵃNU-Text adds *of Jesus.*

PARENTING MATTERS

Q: *What should we do about ear piercing—for girls and for boys?*

We allowed our girls to get their ears pierced when they reached the sixth grade. At that point, they could wear only silver balls in their ears. They had to wait until they were thirteen for the fancier hoops, hearts, and pearls.

More than once our girls have asked, "Can we get out ears double-pierced or triple-pierced?" I have responded, "When you are on your own, you can do whatever you want. You can punch holes all over the place. But as long as you are living at home, no."

How about pierced ears for boys? This was never an issue with our sons, but probably we would have said, "If you want to get them pierced, you can do that when you get in college. But not as long as you are at home."

If either had asked why, we would have said, "We've decided that you'll have to wait a little longer and be on your own before you are allowed to deface your body."

Prayerfully decide which fads are truly sinful and which are just appearance choices. Where are you going to draw the line? Where are you willing to negotiate? A good bottom line: The appearance must be modest and God-honoring.

²⁰And they brought them to the magistrates, and said, "These men, being Jews, exceedingly trouble our city; ²¹and they teach customs which are not lawful for us, being Romans, to receive or observe." ²²Then the multitude rose up together against them; and the magistrates tore off their clothes and commanded *them* to be beaten with rods. ²³And when they had laid many stripes on them, they threw *them* into prison, commanding the jailer to keep them securely. ²⁴Having received such a charge, he put them into the inner prison and fastened their feet in the stocks.

The Philippian Jailer Saved

²⁵But at midnight Paul and Silas were praying and singing hymns to God, and the prisoners were listening to them. ²⁶Suddenly there was a great earthquake, so that the foundations of the prison were shaken; and immediately all the doors were opened and everyone's chains were loosed. ²⁷And the keeper of the prison, awaking from sleep and seeing the prison doors open, supposing the prisoners had fled, drew his sword and was about to kill himself. ²⁸But Paul called with a loud voice, saying, "Do yourself no harm, for we are all here."

²⁹Then he called for a light, ran in, and fell down trembling before Paul and Silas. ³⁰And he brought them out and said, "Sirs, what must I do to be saved?"

³¹So they said, "Believe on the Lord Jesus Christ, and you will be saved, you and your household." ³²Then they spoke the word of the Lord to him and to all who were in his house. ³³And he took them the same hour of the night and washed *their* stripes. And immediately he and all his *family* were baptized. ³⁴Now when he had brought them into his house, he set food before them; and he rejoiced, having believed in God with all his household.

Paul Refuses to Depart Secretly

³⁵And when it was day, the magistrates sent the officers, saying, "Let those men go."

³⁶So the keeper of the prison reported these words to Paul, saying, "The magistrates have sent to let you go. Now therefore depart, and go in peace."

³⁷But Paul said to them, "They have beaten us openly, uncondemned Romans, *and* have thrown *us* into prison. And now do they put us out secretly? No indeed! Let them come themselves and get us out."

³⁸And the officers told these words to the magistrates, and they were afraid when they heard that they were Romans. ³⁹Then they came and pleaded with them and brought *them* out, and asked *them* to depart from the city. ⁴⁰So they went out of the prison and entered *the house of* Lydia; and when they had seen the brethren, they encouraged them and departed.

Preaching Christ at Thessalonica

17 Now when they had passed through Amphipolis and Apollonia, they came to Thessalonica, where there was a synagogue of the Jews. ²Then Paul, as his custom was, went in to them, and for three Sabbaths reasoned with them from the Scriptures, ³explaining and demonstrating that the Christ had to suffer and rise again from the dead, and *saying,* "This Jesus whom I preach to you is the Christ." ⁴And some of them were persuaded; and a great multitude of the devout Greeks, and not a few of the leading women, joined Paul and Silas.

Assault on Jason's House

⁵But the Jews who were not persuaded,ᵃ becoming envious,ᵃ took some of the evil men from the marketplace, and gathering a mob, set all the city in an uproar and attacked the house of Jason, and sought to bring them out to the people. ⁶But when they did not find them, they dragged Jason and some brethren to the rulers of the city, crying out, "These who have turned the world upside down have come here too. ⁷Jason has harbored them, and these are all acting contrary to the decrees of Caesar, saying there is another king—Jesus." ⁸And they troubled the crowd and the rulers of the city when they heard these things. ⁹So when they had taken security from Jason and the rest, they let them go.

17:5 ᵃNU-Text omits *who were not persuaded;* M-Text omits *becoming envious.*

Ministering at Berea

[10]Then the brethren immediately sent Paul and Silas away by night to Berea. When they arrived, they went into the synagogue of the Jews. [11]These were more fair-minded than those in Thessalonica, in that they received the word with all readiness, and searched the Scriptures daily *to find out* whether these things were so. [12]Therefore many of them believed, and also not a few of the Greeks, prominent women as well as men. [13]But when the Jews from Thessalonica learned that the word of God was preached by Paul at Berea, they came there also and stirred up the crowds. [14]Then immediately the brethren sent Paul away, to go to the sea; but both Silas and Timothy remained there. [15]So those who conducted Paul brought him to Athens; and receiving a command for Silas and Timothy to come to him with all speed, they departed.

The Philosophers at Athens

[16]Now while Paul waited for them at Athens, his spirit was provoked within him when he saw that the city was given over to idols. [17]Therefore he reasoned in the synagogue with the Jews and with the *Gentile* worshipers, and in the marketplace daily with those who happened to be there. [18]Then[a] certain Epicurean and Stoic philosophers encountered him. And some said, "What does this babbler want to say?"

Others said, "He seems to be a proclaimer of foreign gods," because he preached to them Jesus and the resurrection. [19]And they took him and brought him to the Areopagus, saying, "May we know what this new doctrine *is* of which you speak? [20]For you are bringing some strange things to our ears. Therefore we want to know what these things mean." [21]For all the Athenians and the foreigners who were there spent their time in nothing else but either to tell or to hear some new thing.

Addressing the Areopagus

[22]Then Paul stood in the midst of the Areopagus and said, "Men of Athens, I perceive that in all things you are very religious; [23]for as I was passing through and considering the objects of your worship, I even found an altar with this inscription:

TO THE UNKNOWN GOD.

Therefore, the One whom you worship without knowing, Him I proclaim to you: [24]God, who made the world and everything in it, since He is Lord of heaven and earth, does not dwell in temples made with hands. [25]Nor is He worshiped with men's hands, as though He needed anything, since He gives to all life, breath, and all things. [26]And He has made from one blood[a] every nation of men to dwell on all the face of the earth, and has determined their preappointed times and the boundaries of their dwellings, [27]so that they should seek the Lord, in the hope that they might grope for Him and find Him, though He is not far from each one of us; [28]for in Him we live and move and have our being, as also some of your own poets have said, 'For we are also His offspring.' [29]Therefore, since we are the offspring of God, we ought not to think that the Divine Nature is like gold or silver or stone, something shaped by art and man's devising. [30]Truly, these times of ignorance God overlooked, but now commands all men everywhere to repent, [31]because He has appointed a day on which He will judge the world in righteousness by the Man whom He has ordained. He has given assurance of this to all by raising Him from the dead."

[32]And when they heard of the resurrection of the dead, some mocked, while others said, "We will hear you again on this *matter.*" [33]So Paul departed from among them. [34]However, some men joined him and believed, among them Dionysius the Areopagite, a woman named Damaris, and others with them.

Ministering at Corinth

18 After these things Paul departed from Athens and went to Corinth. [2]And he found a certain Jew named Aquila, born in Pontus, who had recently come from Italy with his wife Priscilla (because Claudius had commanded all the Jews to depart from Rome); and he came to

---

17:18 [a]NU-Text and M-Text add *also.*
17:26 [a]NU-Text omits *blood.*

them. ³So, because he was of the same trade, he stayed with them and worked; for by occupation they were tentmakers. ⁴And he reasoned in the synagogue every Sabbath, and persuaded both Jews and Greeks.

⁵When Silas and Timothy had come from Macedonia, Paul was compelled by the Spirit, and testified to the Jews *that* Jesus *is* the Christ. ⁶But when they opposed him and blasphemed, he shook *his* garments and said to them, "Your blood *be* upon your *own* heads; I *am* clean. From now on I will go to the Gentiles." ⁷And he departed from there and entered the house of a certain *man* named Justus,ᵃ *one* who worshiped God, whose house was next door to the synagogue. ⁸Then Crispus, the ruler of the synagogue, believed on the Lord with all his household. And many of the Corinthians, hearing, believed and were baptized.

⁹Now the Lord spoke to Paul in the night by a vision, "Do not be afraid, but speak, and do not keep silent; ¹⁰for I am with you, and no one will attack you to hurt you; for I have many people in this city." ¹¹And he continued *there* a year and six months, teaching the word of God among them.

¹²When Gallio was proconsul of Achaia, the Jews with one accord rose up against Paul and brought him to the judgment seat, ¹³saying, "This *fellow* persuades men to worship God contrary to the law."

¹⁴And when Paul was about to open *his* mouth, Gallio said to the Jews, "If it were a matter of wrongdoing or wicked crimes, O Jews, there would be reason why I should bear with you. ¹⁵But if it is a question of words and names and your own law, look *to it* yourselves; for I do not want to be a judge of such *matters*." ¹⁶And he drove them from the judgment seat. ¹⁷Then all the Greeksᵃ took Sosthenes, the ruler of the synagogue, and beat *him* before the judgment seat. But Gallio took no notice of these things.

Paul Returns to Antioch

¹⁸So Paul still remained a good while. Then he took leave of the brethren and sailed for Syria, and Priscilla and Aquila *were* with him. He had *his* hair cut off at Cenchrea, for he had taken a vow. ¹⁹And he came to Ephesus, and left them there; but he himself entered the synagogue and reasoned with the Jews. ²⁰When they asked *him* to stay a longer time with them, he did not consent, ²¹but took leave of them, saying, "I must by all means keep this coming feast in Jerusalem;ᵃ but I will return again to you, God willing." And he sailed from Ephesus.

18:7 ᵃNU-Text reads *Titius Justus.* **18:17** ᵃNU-Text reads *they all.* **18:21** ᵃNU-Text omits *I must* through *Jerusalem.*

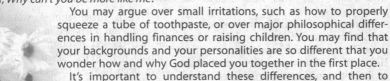

ROMANTIC QUOTES AND NOTES
Accept the Gift of Differentness

One big reason for conflict in marriage is that opposites attract. It may seem strange, but that's part of the reason you married whom you did. Your spouse added variety, spice, and difference to your life. You enjoyed the fresh perspective, the new way of doing things, the unfamiliar patterns of thought or the quirky habits. You found these things strangely alluring. Perhaps they made you laugh.

But after being married for a while—sometimes a *short* while—the attractions can become repellents. What you used to see as cute, you now consider annoying. And you wonder, *Why can't you be more like me?*

You may argue over small irritations, such as how to properly squeeze a tube of toothpaste, or over major philosophical differences in handling finances or raising children. You may find that your backgrounds and your personalities are so different that you wonder how and why God placed you together in the first place.

It's important to understand these differences, and then to accept and adjust to them. Just as Adam accepted God's gift of Eve, so you are called to accept His gift to you. God gave you a spouse who completes you in ways you haven't even learned!

²²And when he had landed at Caesarea, and gone up and greeted the church, he went down to Antioch. ²³After he had spent some time *there,* he departed and went over the region of Galatia and Phrygia in order, strengthening all the disciples.

Ministry of Apollos

²⁴Now a certain Jew named Apollos, born at Alexandria, an eloquent man *and* mighty in the Scriptures, came to Ephesus. ²⁵This man had been instructed in the way of the Lord; and being fervent in spirit, he spoke and taught accurately the things of the Lord, though he knew only the baptism of John. ²⁶So he began to speak boldly in the synagogue. When Aquila and Priscilla heard him, they took him aside and explained to him the way of God more accurately. ²⁷And when he desired to cross to Achaia, the brethren wrote, exhorting the disciples to receive him; and when he arrived, he greatly helped those who had believed through grace; ²⁸for he vigorously refuted the Jews publicly, showing from the Scriptures that Jesus is the Christ.

Paul at Ephesus

19 And it happened, while Apollos was at Corinth, that Paul, having passed through the upper regions, came to Ephesus. And finding some disciples ²he said to them, "Did you receive the Holy Spirit when you believed?"

So they said to him, "We have not so much as heard whether there is a Holy Spirit."

³And he said to them, "Into what then were you baptized?"

So they said, "Into John's baptism."

⁴Then Paul said, "John indeed baptized with a baptism of repentance, saying to the people that they should believe on Him who would come after him, that is, on Christ Jesus."

⁵When they heard *this,* they were baptized in the name of the Lord Jesus. ⁶And when Paul had laid hands on them, the Holy Spirit came upon them, and they spoke with tongues and prophesied. ⁷Now the men were about twelve in all.

⁸And he went into the synagogue and spoke boldly for three months, reasoning

and persuading concerning the things of the kingdom of God. ⁹But when some were hardened and did not believe, but spoke evil of the Way before the multitude, he departed from them and withdrew the disciples, reasoning daily in the school of Tyrannus. ¹⁰And this continued for two years, so that all who dwelt in Asia heard the word of the Lord Jesus, both Jews and Greeks.

Miracles Glorify Christ

¹¹Now God worked unusual miracles by the hands of Paul, ¹²so that even handkerchiefs or aprons were brought from his body to the sick, and the diseases left them and the evil spirits went out of them. ¹³Then some of the itinerant Jewish exorcists took it upon themselves to call the name of the Lord Jesus over those who had evil spirits, saying, "We[a] exorcise you by the Jesus whom Paul preaches." ¹⁴Also there were seven sons of Sceva, a Jewish chief priest, who did so.

¹⁵And the evil spirit answered and said, "Jesus I know, and Paul I know; but who are you?"

¹⁶Then the man in whom the evil spirit was leaped on them, overpowered[a] them, and prevailed against them,[b] so that they fled out of that house naked and wounded. ¹⁷This became known both to all Jews and Greeks dwelling in Ephesus; and fear fell on them all, and the name of the Lord Jesus was magnified. ¹⁸And many who had believed came confessing and telling their deeds. ¹⁹Also, many of those who had practiced magic brought their books together and burned *them* in the sight of all. And they counted up the value of them, and *it* totaled fifty thousand *pieces* of silver. ²⁰So the word of the Lord grew mightily and prevailed.

The Riot at Ephesus

²¹When these things were accomplished, Paul purposed in the Spirit, when he had passed through Macedonia and Achaia, to go to Jerusalem, saying, "After I have been there, I must also see Rome." ²²So he sent into Macedonia two of those

19:13 [a]NU-Text reads *I.* **19:16** [a]M-Text reads *and they overpowered.* [b]NU-Text reads *both of them.*

who ministered to him, Timothy and Erastus, but he himself stayed in Asia for a time.

23And about that time there arose a great commotion about the Way. 24For a certain man named Demetrius, a silversmith, who made silver shrines of Diana,a brought no small profit to the craftsmen. 25He called them together with the workers of similar occupation, and said: "Men, you know that we have our prosperity by this trade. 26Moreover you see and hear that not only at Ephesus, but throughout almost all Asia, this Paul has persuaded and turned away many people, saying that they are not gods which are made with hands. 27So not only is this trade of ours in danger of falling into disrepute, but also the temple of the great goddess Diana may be despised and her magnificence destroyed,a whom all Asia and the world worship."

28Now when they heard *this,* they were full of wrath and cried out, saying, "Great *is* Diana of the Ephesians!" 29So the whole city was filled with confusion, and rushed into the theater with one accord, having seized Gaius and Aristarchus, Macedonians, Paul's travel companions. 30And when Paul wanted to go in to the people, the disciples would not allow him. 31Then some of the officials of Asia, who were his friends, sent to him pleading that he would not venture into the theater. 32Some therefore cried one thing and some another, for the assembly was confused, and most of them did not know why they had come together. 33And they drew Alexander out of the multitude, the Jews putting him forward. And Alexander motioned with his hand, and wanted to make his defense to the people. 34But when they found out that he was a Jew, all with one voice cried out for about two hours, "Great *is* Diana of the Ephesians!"

35And when the city clerk had quieted the crowd, he said: "Men of Ephesus, what man is there who does not know that the city of the Ephesians is temple guardian of the great goddess Diana, and of the *image*

which fell down from Zeus? 36Therefore, since these things cannot be denied, you ought to be quiet and do nothing rashly. 37For you have brought these men here who are neither robbers of temples nor blasphemers of youra goddess. 38Therefore, if Demetrius and his fellow craftsmen have a case against anyone, the courts are open and there are proconsuls. Let them bring charges against one another. 39But if you have any other inquiry to make, it shall be determined in the lawful assembly. 40For we are in danger of being called in question for today's uproar, there being no reason which we may give to account for this disorderly gathering." 41And when he had said these things, he dismissed the assembly.

Journeys in Greece

20 After the uproar had ceased, Paul called the disciples to *himself,* embraced *them,* and departed to go to Macedonia. 2Now when he had gone over that region and encouraged them with many words, he came to Greece 3and stayed three months. And when the Jews plotted against him as he was about to sail to Syria, he decided to return through Macedonia. 4And Sopater of Berea accompanied him to Asia—also Aristarchus and Secundus of the Thessalonians, and Gaius of Derbe, and Timothy, and Tychicus and Trophimus of Asia. 5These men, going ahead, waited for us at Troas. 6But we sailed away from Philippi after the Days of Unleavened Bread, and in five days joined them at Troas, where we stayed seven days.

Ministering at Troas

7Now on the first *day* of the week, when the disciples came together to break bread, Paul, ready to depart the next day, spoke to them and continued his message until midnight. 8There were many lamps in the upper room where theya were gathered together. 9And in a window sat a certain young man named Eutychus, who was sinking into a deep sleep. He was overcome by sleep; and as Paul continued speaking, he fell down from the third story and was taken up dead. 10But Paul went down, fell on him, and embracing *him* said, "Do not trouble yourselves, for his life is in

BIBLICAL INSIGHTS • 20:24

Good and Stressful

THERE IS NO SUCH THING as a pressure-free life. Perhaps in heaven we'll feel no pressure, only total peace and contentment. But here and now we have responsibilities, and responsibilities create pressure and stress.

Pressures generally come from two directions: what others expect of us and what we expect of ourselves. It is so easy to let yourself be driven by the agendas of other people! Their voices form a deafening chorus, incessantly telling us what we ought to do. The apostle Paul heard such voices, but he had an inner settledness that enabled him to affirm, "But none of these things move me; nor do I count my life dear to myself, so that I may finish my race with joy" (Acts 20:24).

Like Paul, we can allow the pressures of life to point us to Jesus Christ and draw upon His strength. What J. Hudson Taylor, the veteran missionary to China, said bears repeating, "It matters not how great the pressure is, only where the pressure lies. As long as the pressure does not come between me and my Savior, but presses me to Him, then the greater the pressure, the greater my dependence upon Him."

If the pressures of life are keeping you from running your race with joy, bring them to Jesus. He has promised rest for all who are "heavy laden" (Matt. 11:28).

him." ¹¹Now when he had come up, had broken bread and eaten, and talked a long while, even till daybreak, he departed. ¹²And they brought the young man in alive, and they were not a little comforted.

From Troas to Miletus

¹³Then we went ahead to the ship and sailed to Assos, there intending to take Paul on board; for so he had given orders, intending himself to go on foot. ¹⁴And when he met us at Assos, we took him on board and came to Mitylene. ¹⁵We sailed from there, and the next *day* came opposite Chios. The following *day* we arrived at Samos and stayed at Trogyllium. The next *day* we came to Miletus. ¹⁶For Paul had decided to sail past Ephesus, so that he would not have to spend time in Asia; for he was hurrying to be at Jerusalem, if possible, on the Day of Pentecost.

The Ephesian Elders Exhorted

¹⁷From Miletus he sent to Ephesus and called for the elders of the church. ¹⁸And when they had come to him, he said to them: "You know, from the first day that I came to Asia, in what manner I always lived among you, ¹⁹serving the Lord with all humility, with many tears and trials which happened to me by the plotting of the Jews; ²⁰how I kept back nothing that was helpful, but proclaimed it to you, and taught you publicly and from house to house, ²¹testifying to Jews, and also to Greeks, repentance toward God and faith toward our Lord Jesus Christ. ²²And see, now I go bound in the spirit to Jerusalem, not knowing the things that will happen to me there, ²³except that the Holy Spirit testifies in every city, saying that chains and tribulations await me. ²⁴But none of these things move me; nor do I count my life dear to myself,ᵃ so that I may finish my race with joy, and the ministry which I received from the Lord Jesus, to testify to the gospel of the grace of God.

²⁵"And indeed, now I know that you all, among whom I have gone preaching the kingdom of God, will see my face no more. ²⁶Therefore I testify to you this day that I *am* innocent of the blood of all *men.* ²⁷For I have not shunned to declare to you the whole counsel of God. ²⁸Therefore take heed to yourselves and to all the flock, among which the Holy Spirit has made you overseers, to shepherd the church of Godᵃ which He purchased with His own blood. ²⁹For I know this, that after my departure savage wolves will come in among you, not sparing the flock. ³⁰Also

20:24 ᵃNU-Text reads *But I do not count my life of any value or dear to myself.* **20:28** ᵃM-Text reads *of the Lord and God.*

DEVOTIONS FOR COUPLES · 20:37
Your Mate's Mirror

When your mate looks into your face, what does he or she see? Acceptance or rejection? Affirmation or ridicule? Joy or disappointment?

Whether you realize it or not, you are a mirror to your mate. The amount of confidence your spouse feels in dealing with people and life is in many ways enormously influenced by your acceptance or rejection. When your mate sees confidence and pride and satisfaction reflected in your eyes, there's no telling what positive things will come. But when he or she sees doubt, disgust, or condemnation there ... well, something very different is likely to happen.

Your mate's self-image is central to just about everything he or she is and does. It will either hinder or enhance his or her ability to learn, make decisions, take risks and resolve conflicts with you and others. Your spouse's self-image will work either as a restraint or as a refueling point. He or she needs your genuine encouragement—don't ever doubt that!

I remember watching a PBS special in which Daniel Boorstein, then the Librarian of Congress, brought out a little blue box that contained the contents of Abraham Lincoln's pockets on the night he was assassinated. Among the contents were several news clippings applauding Lincoln's leadership and great deeds. It's easy to forget that when Lincoln lived, millions hated him. But he needed encouragement, just like everyone else.

Including your spouse.

Individuals who have a low self-concept often view life through the eyes of fear. In fact, the fear of rejection is one of the most powerful forces that motivates and controls people. If you want to strengthen your mate's self-image, then begin to recognize that the fear of rejection is your enemy.

What fears help to govern how your mate reacts in different situations? Discuss with one another how rejection and acceptance have had an impact in your life. But be assured of this: Fear will begin to dissolve in your mate under a steady stream of authentic love.

Love is the most powerful agent for change in the universe, because love casts out fear (1 John 4:18). Perfect love—God's love—is more powerful than the fear of rejection. Pray that God would use each of you to cast out fear through your love for one another. And never forget that the kind of love that accepts and embraces another, even in his or her weaknesses, will win the power struggle against fear *every time*.

---

from among yourselves men will rise up, speaking perverse things, to draw away the disciples after themselves. [31]Therefore watch, and remember that for three years I did not cease to warn everyone night and day with tears.

[32]"So now, brethren, I commend you to God and to the word of His grace, which is able to build you up and give you an inheritance among all those who are sanctified. [33]I have coveted no one's silver or gold or apparel. [34]Yes,[a] you yourselves know that these hands have provided for my necessities, and for those who were with me. [35]I have shown you in every way, by laboring like this, that you must support the weak. And remember the words of the Lord Jesus, that He said, 'It is more blessed to give than to receive.'"

[36]And when he had said these things, he knelt down and prayed with them all. [37]Then they all wept freely, and fell on Paul's neck and kissed him, [38]sorrowing most of all for the words which he spoke, that they would see his face no more. And they accompanied him to the ship.

Warnings on the Journey to Jerusalem

21 Now it came to pass, that when we had departed from them and set sail, running a straight course we came to Cos, the following *day* to Rhodes, and from

---

20:34 [a]NU-Text and M-Text omit *Yes.*

there to Patara. ²And finding a ship sailing over to Phoenicia, we went aboard and set sail. ³When we had sighted Cyprus, we passed it on the left, sailed to Syria, and landed at Tyre; for there the ship was to unload her cargo. ⁴And finding disciples,ᵃ we stayed there seven days. They told Paul through the Spirit not to go up to Jerusalem. ⁵When we had come to the end of those days, we departed and went on our way; and they all accompanied us, with wives and children, till *we were* out of the city. And we knelt down on the shore and prayed. ⁶When we had taken our leave of one another, we boarded the ship, and they returned home.

⁷And when we had finished *our* voyage from Tyre, we came to Ptolemais, greeted the brethren, and stayed with them one day. ⁸On the next *day* we who were Paul's companionsᵃ departed and came to Caesarea, and entered the house of Philip the evangelist, who was *one* of the seven, and stayed with him. ⁹Now this man had four virgin daughters who prophesied. ¹⁰And as we stayed many days, a certain prophet named Agabus came down from Judea. ¹¹When he had come to us, he took Paul's belt, bound his *own* hands and feet, and said, "Thus says the Holy Spirit, 'So shall the Jews at Jerusalem bind the man who owns this belt, and deliver *him* into the hands of the Gentiles.'"

¹²Now when we heard these things, both we and those from that place pleaded with him not to go up to Jerusalem. ¹³Then Paul answered, "What do you mean by weeping and breaking my heart? For I am ready not only to be bound, but also to die at Jerusalem for the name of the Lord Jesus." ¹⁴So when he would not be persuaded, we ceased, saying, "The will of the Lord be done."

Paul Urged to Make Peace

¹⁵And after those days we packed and went up to Jerusalem. ¹⁶Also some of the disciples from Caesarea went with us and brought with them a certain Mnason of Cyprus, an early disciple, with whom we were to lodge.

¹⁷And when we had come to Jerusalem, the brethren received us gladly. ¹⁸On the following *day* Paul went in with us to James, and all the elders were present. ¹⁹When he had greeted them, he told in detail those things which God had done among the Gentiles through his ministry. ²⁰And when they heard *it,* they glorified the Lord. And they said to him, "You see, brother, how many myriads of Jews there are who have believed, and they are all zealous for the law; ²¹but they have been informed about you that you teach all the Jews who are among the Gentiles to forsake Moses, saying that they ought not to circumcise *their* children nor to walk according to the customs. ²²What then? The assembly must certainly meet, for they willᵃ hear that you have come. ²³Therefore do what we tell you: We have four men who have taken a vow. ²⁴Take them and be purified with them, and pay their expenses so that they may shave *their* heads, and that all may know that those things of which they were informed concerning you are nothing, but *that* you yourself also walk orderly and keep the law. ²⁵But concerning the Gentiles who believe, we have written *and* decided that they should observe no such thing, except ᵃ that they should keep themselves from *things* offered to idols, from blood, from things strangled, and from sexual immorality."

Arrested in the Temple

²⁶Then Paul took the men, and the next day, having been purified with them, entered the temple to announce the expiration of the days of purification, at which time an offering should be made for each one of them.

²⁷Now when the seven days were almost ended, the Jews from Asia, seeing him in the temple, stirred up the whole crowd and laid hands on him, ²⁸crying out, "Men of Israel, help! This is the man who teaches all *men* everywhere against the people, the law, and this place; and furthermore he also brought Greeks into the temple and has defiled this holy place." ²⁹(For

---

21:4 ᵃNU-Text reads *the disciples.* 21:8 ᵃNU-Text omits *who were Paul's companions.* 21:22 ᵃNU-Text reads *What then is to be done? They will certainly.* 21:25 ᵃNU-Text omits *that they should observe no such thing, except.*

they had previously[a] seen Trophimus the Ephesian with him in the city, whom they supposed that Paul had brought into the temple.)

30And all the city was disturbed; and the people ran together, seized Paul, and dragged him out of the temple; and immediately the doors were shut. 31Now as they were seeking to kill him, news came to the commander of the garrison that all Jerusalem was in an uproar. 32He immediately took soldiers and centurions, and ran down to them. And when they saw the commander and the soldiers, they stopped beating Paul. 33Then the commander came near and took him, and commanded *him* to be bound with two chains; and he asked who he was and what he had done. 34And some among the multitude cried one thing and some another.

So when he could not ascertain the truth because of the tumult, he commanded him to be taken into the barracks. 35When he reached the stairs, he had to be carried by the soldiers because of the violence of the mob. 36For the multitude of the people followed after, crying out, "Away with him!"

Addressing the Jerusalem Mob

37Then as Paul was about to be led into the barracks, he said to the commander, "May I speak to you?"

He replied, "Can you speak Greek? 38Are you not the Egyptian who some time ago stirred up a rebellion and led the four thousand assassins out into the wilderness?"

39But Paul said, "I am a Jew from Tarsus, in Cilicia, a citizen of no mean city; and I implore you, permit me to speak to the people."

40So when he had given him permission, Paul stood on the stairs and motioned with his hand to the people. And when there was a great silence, he spoke to *them* in the Hebrew language, saying,

22 "Brethren and fathers, hear my defense before you now." 2And when they heard that he spoke to them in the Hebrew language, they kept all the more silent.

Then he said: 3"I am indeed a Jew, born in Tarsus of Cilicia, but brought up in this city at the feet of Gamaliel, taught according to the strictness of our fathers' law, and was zealous toward God as you all are today. 4I persecuted this Way to the death, binding and delivering into prisons both men and women, 5as also the high priest bears me witness, and all the council of the elders, from whom I also received letters to the brethren, and went to Damascus to bring in chains even those who were there in Jerusalem to be punished.

6"Now it happened, as I journeyed and came near Damascus at about noon, suddenly a great light from heaven shone around me. 7And I fell to the ground and heard a voice saying to me, 'Saul, Saul, why are you persecuting Me?' 8So I answered, 'Who are You, Lord?' And He said to me, 'I am Jesus of Nazareth, whom you are persecuting.'

9"And those who were with me indeed saw the light and were afraid,[a] but they did not hear the voice of Him who spoke to me. 10So I said, 'What shall I do, Lord?' And the Lord said to me, 'Arise and go into Damascus, and there you will be told all things which are appointed for you to do.' 11And since I could not see for the glory of that light, being led by the hand of those who were with me, I came into Damascus.

12"Then a certain Ananias, a devout man according to the law, having a good testimony with all the Jews who dwelt *there,* 13came to me; and he stood and said to me, 'Brother Saul, receive your sight.' And at that same hour I looked up at him. 14Then he said, 'The God of our fathers has chosen you that you should know His will, and see the Just One, and hear the voice of His mouth. 15For you will be His witness to all men of what you have seen and heard. 16And now why are you waiting? Arise and be baptized, and wash away your sins, calling on the name of the Lord.'

17"Now it happened, when I returned to Jerusalem and was praying in the temple, that I was in a trance 18and saw Him saying to me, 'Make haste and get out of Jerusalem quickly, for they will not receive your testimony concerning Me.' 19So I said, 'Lord, they know that in every synagogue

21:29 [a]M-Text omits *previously.* 22:9 [a]NU-Text omits *and were afraid.*

I imprisoned and beat those who believe on You. [20]And when the blood of Your martyr Stephen was shed, I also was standing by consenting to his death,[a] and guarding the clothes of those who were killing him.' [21]Then He said to me, 'Depart, for I will send you far from here to the Gentiles.'"

Paul's Roman Citizenship

[22]And they listened to him until this word, and *then* they raised their voices and said, "Away with such a *fellow* from the earth, for he is not fit to live!" [23]Then, as they cried out and tore off *their* clothes and threw dust into the air, [24]the commander ordered him to be brought into the barracks, and said that he should be examined under scourging, so that he might know why they shouted so against him. [25]And as they bound him with thongs, Paul said to the centurion who stood by, "Is it lawful for you to scourge a man who is a Roman, and uncondemned?"

[26]When the centurion heard *that*, he went and told the commander, saying, "Take care what you do, for this man is a Roman."

[27]Then the commander came and said to him, "Tell me, are you a Roman?"

He said, "Yes."

[28]The commander answered, "With a large sum I obtained this citizenship."

And Paul said, "But I was born *a citizen*."

[29]Then immediately those who were about to examine him withdrew from him; and the commander was also afraid after he found out that he was a Roman, and because he had bound him.

The Sanhedrin Divided

[30]The next day, because he wanted to know for certain why he was accused by the Jews, he released him from *his* bonds, and commanded the chief priests and all their council to appear, and brought Paul down and set him before them.

23 Then Paul, looking earnestly at the council, said, "Men *and* brethren, I have lived in all good conscience before God until this day." [2]And the high priest Ananias commanded those who stood by him to strike him on the mouth. [3]Then Paul said to him, "God will strike you, *you* whitewashed wall! For you sit to judge me according to the law, and do you command me to be struck contrary to the law?"

[4]And those who stood by said, "Do you revile God's high priest?"

[5]Then Paul said, "I did not know, brethren, that he was the high priest; for it is written, '*You shall not speak evil of a ruler of your people.*'"[a]

[6]But when Paul perceived that one part were Sadducees and the other Pharisees, he cried out in the council, "Men *and* brethren, I am a Pharisee, the son of a Pharisee;

22:20 [a]NU-Text omits *to his death.*
23:5 [a]Exodus 22:28

ROMANTIC QUOTES AND NOTES
Make Sure You Know Him

After Elvis Presley died, newspapers told of people who had almost made him the god of their lives. One young man in Florida altered his face to look like Elvis. "Presley has been my idol since I was five years old," he said. "I have every record he has cut twice over, pictures by the thousands, even two leaves from a tree from the mansion in Memphis."

But the tragic words of the interview fell flat as the young man confessed, "I never got close to him. I never saw him. I never knew him."

Now, that's one thing to say about Elivs, but how many of us have a relationship with God like this? We don't get close to God. We never see Him. We don't really know Him. We simply admire Him from afar. This is the ultimate tragedy of life: to live and miss God.

God has better plans for you than that! It can be said of you, as it was of Paul, "God . . . has chosen you that you should know His will, and see the Just One, and hear the voice of His mouth" (Acts 22:14).

On Judgment Day, make sure you don't have to confess to God, "I'm sorry that I never got close to You. I never knew You deeply. I guess I was just too busy."

concerning the hope and resurrection of the dead I am being judged!"

7And when he had said this, a dissension arose between the Pharisees and the Sadducees; and the assembly was divided. 8For Sadducees say that there is no resurrection—and no angel or spirit; but the Pharisees confess both. 9Then there arose a loud outcry. And the scribes of the Pharisees' party arose and protested, saying, "We find no evil in this man; but if a spirit or an angel has spoken to him, let us not fight against God."a

10Now when there arose a great dissension, the commander, fearing lest Paul might be pulled to pieces by them, commanded the soldiers to go down and take him by force from among them, and bring him into the barracks.

The Plot Against Paul

11But the following night the Lord stood by him and said, "Be of good cheer, Paul; for as you have testified for Me in Jerusalem, so you must also bear witness at Rome."

12And when it was day, some of the Jews banded together and bound themselves under an oath, saying that they would neither eat nor drink till they had killed Paul. 13Now there were more than forty who had formed this conspiracy. 14They came to the chief priests and elders, and said, "We have bound ourselves under a great oath that we will eat nothing until we have killed Paul. 15Now you, therefore, together with the council, suggest to the commander that he be brought down to you tomorrow,a as though you were going to make further inquiries concerning him; but we are ready to kill him before he comes near."

16So when Paul's sister's son heard of their ambush, he went and entered the barracks and told Paul. 17Then Paul called one of the centurions to him and said, "Take this young man to the commander, for he has something to tell him." 18So he took him and brought him to the commander and said, "Paul the prisoner called me to

him and asked me to bring this young man to you. He has something to say to you."

19Then the commander took him by the hand, went aside, and asked privately, "What is it that you have to tell me?" 20And he said, "The Jews have agreed to ask that you bring Paul down to the council tomorrow, as though they were going to inquire more fully about him. 21But do not yield to them, for more than forty of them lie in wait for him, men who have bound themselves by an oath that they will neither eat nor drink till they have killed him; and now they are ready, waiting for the promise from you."

22So the commander let the young man depart, and commanded him, "Tell no one that you have revealed these things to me."

Sent to Felix

23And he called for two centurions, saying, "Prepare two hundred soldiers, seventy horsemen, and two hundred spearmen to go to Caesarea at the third hour of the night; 24and provide mounts to set Paul on, and bring him safely to Felix the governor." 25He wrote a letter in the following manner:

26 Claudius Lysias,

To the most excellent governor Felix:

Greetings.

27 This man was seized by the Jews and was about to be killed by them. Coming with the troops I rescued him, having learned that he was a Roman. 28And when I wanted to know the reason they accused him, I brought him before their council. 29I found out that he was accused concerning questions of their law, but had nothing charged against him deserving of death or chains. 30And when it was told me that the Jews lay in wait for the man,a I sent him immediately to you, and also commanded his accusers to state before you the charges against him.

Farewell.

31Then the soldiers, as they were commanded, took Paul and brought him by night to Antipatris. 32The next day they

BIBLICAL INSIGHTS • 24:16

The Benefits of a Clean Conscience

ONE THING WE WANT to be on guard against—as individuals, as spouses, or as leaders of our families—is doing things that will numb our conscience. God gave us a conscience so that we could know when some sin or offense lies between God and ourselves or between ourselves and another person—our spouses, our children, our neighbors, our friends. I like what the apostle Paul said (and hope to model his habit in my own life), "I myself always strive to have a conscience without offense toward God and men" (Acts 24:16).

I have learned that a dirty conscience—one that holds onto sin, one that nurses a grudge, one that's filled with guilt—will weigh you down like concrete-filled galoshes. You will not be able to move forward in your relationship with God, with your spouse, with your children, or with others. You'll remain stuck.

When God nudges you in your conscience to deal with some issue that's put a wedge between you and Him or you and others, by all means, get to work on it. Is there something you need to clear up between you and the Lord or between you and another person? If so, do it *now*. Don't wait!

left the horsemen to go on with him, and returned to the barracks. ³³When they came to Caesarea and had delivered the letter to the governor, they also presented Paul to him. ³⁴And when the governor had read *it*, he asked what province he was from. And when he understood that *he was* from Cilicia, ³⁵he said, "I will hear you when your accusers also have come." And he commanded him to be kept in Herod's Praetorium.

Accused of Sedition

24 Now after five days Ananias the high priest came down with the elders and a certain orator *named* Tertullus. These gave evidence to the governor against Paul.

²And when he was called upon, Tertullus began his accusation, saying: "Seeing that through you we enjoy great peace, and prosperity is being brought to this nation by your foresight, ³we accept *it* always and in all places, most noble Felix, with all thankfulness. ⁴Nevertheless, not to be tedious to you any further, I beg you to hear, by your courtesy, a few words from us. ⁵For we have found this man a plague, a creator of dissension among all the Jews throughout the world, and a ringleader of the sect of the Nazarenes. ⁶He even tried to profane the temple, and we seized him,ᵃ and wanted to judge him according to our law. ⁷But the commander Lysias came by and with great violence took *him* out of our hands, ⁸commanding his accusers to come to you. By examining him yourself you may ascertain all these things of which we accuse him." ⁹And the Jews also assented,ᵃ maintaining that these things were so.

The Defense Before Felix

¹⁰Then Paul, after the governor had nodded to him to speak, answered: "Inasmuch as I know that you have been for many years a judge of this nation, I do the more cheerfully answer for myself, ¹¹because you may ascertain that it is no more than twelve days since I went up to Jerusalem to worship. ¹²And they neither found me in the temple disputing with anyone nor inciting the crowd, either in the synagogues or in the city. ¹³Nor can they prove the things of which they now accuse me. ¹⁴But this I confess to you, that according to the Way which they call a sect, so I worship the God of my fathers, believing all things which are written in the Law and in the Prophets. ¹⁵I have hope in God, which they themselves also accept, that there will be a resurrection of *the* dead,ᵃ both of *the* just and *the* unjust. ¹⁶This *being* so, I myself always strive to have a conscience without offense toward God and men.

¹⁷"Now after many years I came to bring alms and offerings to my nation, ¹⁸in

24:6 ᵃNU-Text ends the sentence here and omits the rest of verse 6, all of verse 7, and the first clause of verse 8. 24:9 ᵃNU-Text and M-Text read *joined the attack.* 24:15 ᵃNU-Text omits *of the dead.*

the midst of which some Jews from Asia found me purified in the temple, neither with a mob nor with tumult. [19]They ought to have been here before you to object if they had anything against me. [20]Or else let those who are here themselves say if they found any wrongdoing[a] in me while I stood before the council, [21]unless *it is* for this one statement which I cried out, standing among them, 'Concerning the resurrection of the dead I am being judged by you this day.'"

Felix Procrastinates

[22]But when Felix heard these things, having more accurate knowledge of *the* Way, he adjourned the proceedings and said, "When Lysias the commander comes down, I will make a decision on your case." [23]So he commanded the centurion to keep Paul and to let *him* have liberty, and told him not to forbid any of his friends to provide for or visit him.

[24]And after some days, when Felix came with his wife Drusilla, who was Jewish, he sent for Paul and heard him concerning the faith in Christ. [25]Now as he reasoned about righteousness, self-control, and the judgment to come, Felix was afraid and answered, "Go away for now; when I have a convenient time I will call for you." [26]Meanwhile he also hoped that money would be given him by Paul, that he might release him.[a] Therefore he sent for him more often and conversed with him.

[27]But after two years Porcius Festus succeeded Felix; and Felix, wanting to do the Jews a favor, left Paul bound.

Paul Appeals to Caesar

25 Now when Festus had come to the province, after three days he went up from Caesarea to Jerusalem. [2]Then the high priest[a] and the chief men of the Jews informed him against Paul; and they petitioned him, [3]asking a favor against him, that he would summon him to Jerusalem— while *they* lay in ambush along the road to kill him. [4]But Festus answered that Paul should be kept at Caesarea, and that he himself was going *there* shortly. [5]"Therefore," he said, "let those who have authority among you go down with *me* and accuse this man, to see if there is any fault in him."

[6]And when he had remained among them more than ten days, he went down to Caesarea. And the next day, sitting on the judgment seat, he commanded Paul to be brought. [7]When he had come, the Jews who had come down from Jerusalem stood about and laid many serious complaints against Paul, which they could not prove, [8]while he answered for himself, "Neither against the law of the Jews, nor against the temple, nor against Caesar have I offended in anything at all."

[9]But Festus, wanting to do the Jews a favor, answered Paul and said, "Are you willing to go up to Jerusalem and there be judged before me concerning these things?"

[10]So Paul said, "I stand at Caesar's judgment seat, where I ought to be judged. To the Jews I have done no wrong, as you very well know. [11]For if I am an offender, or have committed anything deserving of death, I do not object to dying; but if there is nothing in these things of which these men accuse me, no one can deliver me to them. I appeal to Caesar."

[12]Then Festus, when he had conferred with the council, answered, "You have appealed to Caesar? To Caesar you shall go!"

Paul Before Agrippa

[13]And after some days King Agrippa and Bernice came to Caesarea to greet Festus. [14]When they had been there many days, Festus laid Paul's case before the king, saying: "There is a certain man left a prisoner by Felix, [15]about whom the chief priests and the elders of the Jews informed *me*, when I was in Jerusalem, asking for a judgment against him. [16]To them I answered, 'It is not the custom of the Romans to deliver any man to destruction[a] before the accused meets the accusers face to face, and has opportunity to answer for himself concerning the charge against him.' [17]Therefore when they had come together, without any delay, the next day I sat on the judgment seat and commanded

24:20 [a]NU-Text and M-Text read *say what wrongdoing they found.* 24:26 [a]NU-Text omits *that he might release him.* 25:2 [a]NU-Text reads *chief priests.* 25:16 [a]NU-Text omits *to destruction,* although it is implied.

the man to be brought in. 18When the accusers stood up, they brought no accusation against him of such things as I supposed, 19but had some questions against him about their own religion and about a certain Jesus, who had died, whom Paul affirmed to be alive. 20And because I was uncertain of such questions, I asked whether he was willing to go to Jerusalem and there be judged concerning these matters. 21But when Paul appealed to be reserved for the decision of Augustus, I commanded him to be kept till I could send him to Caesar."

22Then Agrippa said to Festus, "I also would like to hear the man myself."

"Tomorrow," he said, "you shall hear him."

23So the next day, when Agrippa and Bernice had come with great pomp, and had entered the auditorium with the commanders and the prominent men of the city, at Festus' command Paul was brought in. 24And Festus said: "King Agrippa and all the men who are here present with us, you see this man about whom the whole assembly of the Jews petitioned me, both at Jerusalem and here, crying out that he was not fit to live any longer. 25But when I found that he had committed nothing deserving of death, and that he himself had appealed to Augustus, I decided to send him. 26I have nothing certain to write to my lord concerning him. Therefore I have brought him out before you, and especially before you, King Agrippa, so that after the examination has taken place I may have something to write. 27For it seems to me unreasonable to send a prisoner and not to specify the charges against him."

Paul's Early Life

26 Then Agrippa said to Paul, "You are permitted to speak for yourself."

So Paul stretched out his hand and answered for himself: 2"I think myself happy, King Agrippa, because today I shall answer for myself before you concerning all the things of which I am accused by the Jews, 3especially because you are expert in all customs and questions which have to do with the Jews. Therefore I beg you to hear me patiently.

4"My manner of life from my youth, which was spent from the beginning among my own nation at Jerusalem, all the Jews know. 5They knew me from the first, if they were willing to testify, that according to the strictest sect of our religion I lived a Pharisee. 6And now I stand and am judged for the hope of the promise made by God to our fathers. 7To this *promise* our twelve tribes, earnestly serving God night and day, hope to attain. For this hope's sake, King Agrippa, I am accused by the Jews. 8Why should it be thought incredible by you that God raises the dead?

9"Indeed, I myself thought I must do many things contrary to the name of Jesus of Nazareth. 10This I also did in Jerusalem, and many of the saints I shut up in prison, having received authority from the chief priests; and when they were put to death, I cast my vote against *them*. 11And I punished *them* often in every synagogue and compelled *them* to blaspheme; and being exceedingly enraged against them, I persecuted *them* even to foreign cities.

Paul Recounts His Conversion

12"While thus occupied, as I journeyed to Damascus with authority and commission from the chief priests, 13at midday, O king, along the road I saw a light from heaven, brighter than the sun, shining around me and those who journeyed with me. 14And when we all had fallen to the ground, I heard a voice speaking to me and saying in the Hebrew language, 'Saul, Saul, why are you persecuting Me? *It is* hard for you to kick against the goads.' 15So I said, 'Who are You, Lord?' And He said, 'I am Jesus, whom you are persecuting. 16But rise and stand on your feet; for I have appeared to you for this purpose, to make you a minister and a witness both of the things which you have seen and of the things which I will yet reveal to you. 17I will deliver you from the *Jewish* people, as well as *from* the Gentiles, to whom I nowª send you, 18to open their eyes, *in order* to turn *them* from darkness to light, and *from* the power of Satan to God, that they may receive forgiveness of

---

26:17 ªNU-Text and M-Text omit *now.*

sins and an inheritance among those who are sanctified by faith in Me.'

Paul's Post-Conversion Life

¹⁹"Therefore, King Agrippa, I was not disobedient to the heavenly vision, ²⁰but declared first to those in Damascus and in Jerusalem, and throughout all the region of Judea, and *then* to the Gentiles, that they should repent, turn to God, and do works befitting repentance. ²¹For these reasons the Jews seized me in the temple and tried to kill *me*. ²²Therefore, having obtained help from God, to this day I stand, witnessing both to small and great, saying no other things than those which the prophets and Moses said would come— ²³that the Christ would suffer, that He would be the first to rise from the dead, and would proclaim light to the *Jewish* people and to the Gentiles."

Agrippa Parries Paul's Challenge

²⁴Now as he thus made his defense, Festus said with a loud voice, "Paul, you are beside yourself! Much learning is driving you mad!"

²⁵But he said, "I am not mad, most noble Festus, but speak the words of truth and reason. ²⁶For the king, before whom I also speak freely, knows these things; for I am convinced that none of these things escapes his attention, since this thing was not done in a corner. ²⁷King Agrippa, do you believe the prophets? I know that you do believe."

²⁸Then Agrippa said to Paul, "You almost persuade me to become a Christian."

²⁹And Paul said, "I would to God that not only you, but also all who hear me today, might become both almost and altogether such as I am, except for these chains."

³⁰When he had said these things, the king stood up, as well as the governor and Bernice and those who sat with them; ³¹and when they had gone aside, they talked among themselves, saying, "This man is doing nothing deserving of death or chains."

³²Then Agrippa said to Festus, "This man might have been set free if he had not appealed to Caesar."

BIBLICAL INSIGHTS • 26:20
Don't Believe the Lie

YEARS AGO I HAD A CONVERSATION with a friend who had been married three times and I knew was seeing a marriage counselor now in his fourth marriage. "How's your marriage going?" I asked.

"Not too well," he admitted. "I've decided to get a divorce." Then he made a big mistake. "What do you think?" he asked.

"I think that's ridiculous," I replied, and then exhorted him to work at it, to refuse to give up. "You can make this marriage work if you really want to," I said.

But he didn't want to hear it. "I just don't think that God ever intended for me to be this unhappy," he said.

I saw it as a perfect example of someone being conformed to the world rather than to Christ. He claimed to be a Christian, but he had not allowed God to transform his life. He was embracing the world's philosophy: You deserve to be happy. You can have it all. I'm sure he wouldn't like Paul's summary of his life message, that people "should repent, turn to God, and do works befitting repentance" (Acts 26:20).

Another man, who had just seen his troubled marriage resurrected, heard about this conversation. "He's believing the lie," he said. "He thinks that the most important thing is to feel good. But what *really* feels good is working through the problems."

This culture is filled with messages that will destroy your marriage and family, but none more lethal than that you deserve to feel good, to be happy. We need to talk less about what we deserve and more about our duties to the one we have chosen by establishing a marriage covenant.

The Voyage to Rome Begins

27 And when it was decided that we should sail to Italy, they delivered Paul and some other prisoners to *one* named Julius, a centurion of the Augustan

DEVOTIONS FOR COUPLES • 27:15
Whatever Happened to Simplicity?

Rare is the family that doesn't grapple with friction caused by the complexity of life in the twenty-first century. In the last one hundred years, a strong cultural storm has swept the family far from its moorings of commitment and stability. Consider just a few of these changes.

During the 1800s, life was fairly simple. Most people lived on farms, working eighty-hour weeks to grow their own food and make most of their own clothes and furnishings.

Today, most Americans live in cities. We are urban and mobile. We turn to technology instead of agriculture to meet our needs. With more choices and more people, life becomes more complex.

Families one hundred years ago learned to function as a team, because survival was at stake. Their interdependence fused them together.

Today, we don't have the same need to work as a team. We can seek individual careers, education, hobbies, and entertainment. These interests inevitably conflict with each other at some points, causing friction.

All this complexity captures our attention, just as the storm captured the attention of the Roman soldiers who were taking the apostle Paul to Rome (27:15). When the hardened soldiers on his doomed ship followed his instructions, they found life; but when they allowed their fear to shift their focus to the storm, they endangered themselves. Only when they listened to Paul's words and acted on his counsel, did they all make it through the storm and save their very lives. Focus was the key. Listen to God through Paul? Or allow the howling storm to distract their attention and set them on a disastrous course?

There is no way to return to life as it was one hundred years ago. But we can exercise some control over complexities that cause friction in our own time. We can fix our eyes on Jesus. We can eliminate options that distract our attention from Him. We can organize the smaller commitments of life around our primary commitment to Him. And we can practice the most powerful word in the English vocabulary: "No!"

On a scale of 1 (poor) to 10 (great), how would you rate your family's ability to tolerate different interests and commitments? Should some be curtailed? Eliminated? Altered somehow? Then pray that your family will be able to see the need to knife through the complexities of modern living and instead organize your family life around Jesus Christ.

Regiment. ²So, entering a ship of Adramyttium, we put to sea, meaning to sail along the coasts of Asia. Aristarchus, a Macedonian of Thessalonica, was with us. ³And the next *day* we landed at Sidon. And Julius treated Paul kindly and gave *him* liberty to go to his friends and receive care. ⁴When we had put to sea from there, we sailed under *the shelter of* Cyprus, because the winds were contrary. ⁵And when we had sailed over the sea which is off Cilicia and Pamphylia, we came to Myra, *a city* of Lycia. ⁶There the centurion found an Alexandrian ship sailing to Italy, and he put us on board.

⁷When we had sailed slowly many days, and arrived with difficulty off Cnidus, the wind not permitting us to proceed, we sailed under *the shelter of* Crete off Salmone. ⁸Passing it with difficulty, we came to a place called Fair Havens, near the city *of* Lasea.

Paul's Warning Ignored

⁹Now when much time had been spent, and sailing was now dangerous because the Fast was already over, Paul advised them, ¹⁰saying, "Men, I perceive that this voyage will end with disaster and much loss, not only of the cargo and ship, but

also our lives." [11]Nevertheless the centurion was more persuaded by the helmsman and the owner of the ship than by the things spoken by Paul. [12]And because the harbor was not suitable to winter in, the majority advised to set sail from there also, if by any means they could reach Phoenix, a harbor of Crete opening toward the southwest and northwest, *and* winter *there*.

In the Tempest

[13]When the south wind blew softly, supposing that they had obtained *their* desire, putting out to sea, they sailed close by Crete. [14]But not long after, a tempestuous head wind arose, called Euroclydon.[a] [15]So when the ship was caught, and could not head into the wind, we let *her* drive. [16]And running under *the shelter of* an island called Clauda,[a] we secured the skiff with difficulty. [17]When they had taken it on board, they used cables to undergird the ship; and fearing lest they should run aground on the Syrtis[a] *Sands*, they struck sail and so were driven. [18]And because we were exceedingly tempest-tossed, the next *day* they lightened the ship. [19]On the third *day* we threw the ship's tackle overboard with our own hands. [20]Now when neither sun nor stars appeared for many days, and no small tempest beat on *us*, all hope that we would be saved was finally given up.

[21]But after long abstinence from food, then Paul stood in the midst of them and said, "Men, you should have listened to me, and not have sailed from Crete and incurred this disaster and loss. [22]And now I urge you to take heart, for there will be no loss of life among you, but only of the ship. [23]For there stood by me this night an angel of the God to whom I belong and whom I serve, [24]saying, 'Do not be afraid, Paul; you must be brought before Caesar; and indeed God has granted you all those who sail with you.' [25]Therefore take heart, men, for I believe God that it will be just as it was told me. [26]However, we must run aground on a certain island."

[27]Now when the fourteenth night had come, as we were driven up and down in the Adriatic *Sea*, about midnight the sailors sensed that they were drawing near some land. [28]And they took soundings and found *it* to be twenty fathoms; and when they had gone a little farther, they took soundings again and found *it* to be fifteen fathoms. [29]Then, fearing lest we should run aground on the rocks, they dropped four anchors from the stern, and prayed for day to come. [30]And as the sailors were seeking to escape from the ship, when they had let down the skiff into the sea, under pretense of putting out anchors from the prow, [31]Paul said to the centurion and the soldiers, "Unless these men stay in the ship, you cannot be saved." [32]Then the soldiers cut away the ropes of the skiff and let it fall off.

[33]And as day was about to dawn, Paul implored *them* all to take food, saying, "Today is the fourteenth day you have waited and continued without food, and eaten nothing. [34]Therefore I urge you to take nourishment, for this is for your survival, since not a hair will fall from the head of any of you." [35]And when he had said these things, he took bread and gave thanks to God in the presence of them all; and when he had broken *it* he began to eat. [36]Then they were all encouraged, and also took food themselves. [37]And in all we were two hundred and seventy-six persons on the ship. [38]So when they had eaten enough, they lightened the ship and threw out the wheat into the sea.

Shipwrecked on Malta

[39]When it was day, they did not recognize the land; but they observed a bay with a beach, onto which they planned to run the ship if possible. [40]And they let go the anchors and left *them* in the sea, meanwhile loosing the rudder ropes; and they hoisted the mainsail to the wind and made for shore. [41]But striking a place where two seas met, they ran the ship aground; and the prow stuck fast and remained immovable, but the stern was being broken up by the violence of the waves.

[42]And the soldiers' plan was to kill the prisoners, lest any of them should swim away and escape. [43]But the centurion, wanting to save Paul, kept them from *their*

27:14 [a]NU-Text reads *Euraquilon*. 27:16 [a]NU-Text reads *Cauda*. 27:17 [a]M-Text reads *Syrtes*.

purpose, and commanded that those who could swim should jump *overboard* first and get to land, [44]and the rest, some on boards and some on *parts* of the ship. And so it was that they all escaped safely to land.

Paul's Ministry on Malta

28 Now when they had escaped, they then found out that the island was called Malta. [2]And the natives showed us unusual kindness; for they kindled a fire and made us all welcome, because of the rain that was falling and because of the cold. [3]But when Paul had gathered a bundle of sticks and laid *them* on the fire, a viper came out because of the heat, and fastened on his hand. [4]So when the natives saw the creature hanging from his hand, they said to one another, "No doubt this man is a murderer, whom, though he has escaped the sea, yet justice does not allow to live." [5]But he shook off the creature into the fire and suffered no harm. [6]However, they were expecting that he would swell up or suddenly fall down dead. But after they had looked for a long time and saw no harm come to him, they changed their minds and said that he was a god.

[7]In that region there was an estate of the leading citizen of the island, whose name was Publius, who received us and entertained us courteously for three days. [8]And it happened that the father of Publius lay sick of a fever and dysentery. Paul went in to him and prayed, and he laid his hands on him and healed him. [9]So when this was done, the rest of those on the island who had diseases also came and were healed. [10]They also honored us in many ways; and when we departed, they provided such things as were necessary.

Arrival at Rome

[11]After three months we sailed in an Alexandrian ship whose figurehead was the Twin Brothers, which had wintered at the island. [12]And landing at Syracuse, we stayed three days. [13]From there we circled round and reached Rhegium. And after one day the south wind blew; and the next day we came to Puteoli, [14]where we found brethren, and were invited to stay with them seven days. And so we went toward Rome. [15]And from there, when the brethren heard about us, they came to meet us as far as Appii Forum and Three Inns. When Paul saw them, he thanked God and took courage.

[16]Now when we came to Rome, the centurion delivered the prisoners to the captain of the guard; but Paul was permitted to dwell by himself with the soldier who guarded him.

Paul's Ministry at Rome

[17]And it came to pass after three days that Paul called the leaders of the Jews together. So when they had come together, he said to them: "Men *and* brethren, though I have done nothing against our people or the customs of our fathers, yet I was delivered as a prisoner from Jerusalem into the hands of the Romans, [18]who, when they had examined me, wanted to let *me* go, because there was no cause for putting me to death. [19]But when the Jews[a] spoke against *it*, I was compelled to appeal to Caesar, not that I had anything of which to accuse my nation. [20]For this reason therefore I have called for you, to see *you* and speak with *you*, because for the hope of Israel I am bound with this chain."

[21]Then they said to him, "We neither received letters from Judea concerning you, nor have any of the brethren who came reported or spoken any evil of you. [22]But we desire to hear from you what you think; for concerning this sect, we know that it is spoken against everywhere."

[23]So when they had appointed him a day, many came to him at *his* lodging, to whom he explained and solemnly testified of the kingdom of God, persuading them concerning Jesus from both the Law of Moses and the Prophets, from morning till evening. [24]And some were persuaded by the things which were spoken, and some disbelieved. [25]So when they did not agree among themselves, they departed after Paul had said one word: "The Holy Spirit spoke rightly through Isaiah the prophet to our[a] fathers, [26]saying,

28:19 [a]That is, the ruling authorities
28:25 [a]NU-Text reads *your.*

'Go to this people and say:
"Hearing you will hear, and shall not
understand;
And seeing you will see, and not
perceive;
27 For the hearts of this people have
grown dull.
Their ears are hard of hearing,
And their eyes they have closed,
Lest they should see with their eyes
and hear with their ears,

Lest they should understand with
their hearts and turn,
So that I should heal them." ' a

28"Therefore let it be known to you that
the salvation of God has been sent to the
Gentiles, and they will hear it!" 29And when
he had said these words, the Jews departed
and had a great dispute among themselves.a

30Then Paul dwelt two whole years in
his own rented house, and received all who
came to him, 31preaching the kingdom of
God and teaching the things which concern the Lord Jesus Christ with all confidence, no one forbidding him.

28:27 aIsaiah 6:9, 10
28:29 aNU-Text omits this verse.

ROMANS

ONE SUMMER DURING MY COLLEGE YEARS, God used a Bible study of the Book of Romans to transform my life and wake me up spiritually. I'm not alone in having been powerfully impacted by this remarkable portion of Scripture. Men such as Augustine, Martin Luther, John Calvin and John Wesley all have pointed to this letter from the apostle Paul as pivotal in their lives.

It's not hard to see why. Perhaps no other book in the Bible so carefully and clearly lays out God's great plan for bringing sinful, rebellious people back into a loving relationship with Him through faith in the risen Christ. Paul says the gospel of Christ is "the power of God to salvation for everyone who believes" (1:16).

The first eight chapters of Romans provide a systematic look at how God has taken the initiative to restore the relationship with Him destroyed by humankind's rebellion. Paul shows how the death of Christ pays the price for our sin, and how, through our union with Christ, God begins to change us and make us more like Christ.

Like many believers throughout history, we have often found great comfort in the last verses of Romans 8, in which Paul tells us that the Holy Spirit prays on our behalf when we feel too grieved to pray ourselves (8:26). There we learn that God is providentially orchestrating all that we experience for our good and for His glory (8:28). We may face tribulations or persecution or any number of trials, but we find hope in the promise that God is for us (8:31), and that nothing can separate us from the love of God, which is in Christ Jesus our Lord (8:39).

Chapters 9—11 outline God's future plan for the Jewish people, who for the most part have continued to reject Jesus as the Messiah. The last five chapters of Romans give specific instruction for how we ought to live as followers of Christ. Married couples would benefit greatly from reading together Romans 12:9–21, and then asking themselves if they are displaying this kind of supernatural love in their relationship.

Greeting

1 Paul, a bondservant of Jesus Christ, called *to be* an apostle, separated to the gospel of God [2]which He promised before through His prophets in the Holy Scriptures, [3]concerning His Son Jesus Christ our Lord, who was born of the seed of David according to the flesh, [4]*and* declared *to be* the Son of God with power according to the Spirit of holiness, by the resurrection from the dead. [5]Through Him we have received grace and apostleship for obedience to the faith among all nations for His name, [6]among whom you also are the called of Jesus Christ;

[7]To all who are in Rome, beloved of God, called *to be* saints:

Grace to you and peace from God our Father and the Lord Jesus Christ.

Desire to Visit Rome

[8]First, I thank my God through Jesus Christ for you all, that your faith is spoken of throughout the whole world. [9]For God is my witness, whom I serve with my spirit in the gospel of His Son, that without ceasing I make mention of you always in my prayers, [10]making request if, by some means, now at last I may find a way in the will of God to come to you. [11]For I long to see you, that I may impart to you some spiritual gift, so that you may be established— [12]that is, that I may be encouraged together with you by the mutual faith both of you and me.

[13]Now I do not want you to be unaware, brethren, that I often planned to come to you (but was hindered until now), that I might have some fruit among you also, just as among the other Gentiles. [14]I am a debtor both to Greeks and to barbarians, both to wise and to unwise. [15]So, as much as is in me, *I am* ready to preach the gospel to you who are in Rome also.

The Just Live by Faith

[16]For I am not ashamed of the gospel of Christ,[a] for it is the power of God to salvation for everyone who believes, for the Jew first and also for the Greek. [17]For in it the righteousness of God is revealed from faith to faith; as it is written, *"The just shall live by faith."*[a]

God's Wrath on Unrighteousness

[18]For the wrath of God is revealed from heaven against all ungodliness and unrighteousness of men, who suppress the truth in unrighteousness, [19]because what may be known of God is manifest in them, for God has shown *it* to them. [20]For since the creation of the world His invisible *attributes* are clearly seen, being understood by the things that are made, *even* His eternal power and Godhead, so that they are without excuse, [21]because, although they knew God, they did not glorify *Him* as God, nor were thankful, but became futile in their thoughts, and their foolish hearts were darkened. [22]Professing to be wise, they became fools, [23]and changed the glory of the incorruptible God into an image made like corruptible man—and birds and four-footed animals and creeping things.

[24]Therefore God also gave them up to uncleanness, in the lusts of their hearts, to dishonor their bodies among themselves, [25]who exchanged the truth of God for the lie, and worshiped and served the creature rather than the Creator, who is blessed forever. Amen.

[26]For this reason God gave them up to vile passions. For even their women exchanged the natural use for what is against nature. [27]Likewise also the men, leaving the natural use of the woman, burned in their lust for one another, men with men committing what is shameful, and receiving in themselves the penalty of their error which was due.

[28]And even as they did not like to retain God in *their* knowledge, God gave them over to a debased mind, to do those things which are not fitting; [29]being filled with all unrighteousness, sexual immorality,[a] wickedness, covetousness, maliciousness; full of envy, murder, strife, deceit, evil-mindedness; *they are* whisperers, [30]backbiters, haters of God, violent, proud, boasters, inventors of evil things, disobedient to

---

1:16 [a]NU-Text omits *of Christ*. **1:17** [a]Habakkuk 2:4
1:29 [a]NU-Text omits *sexual immorality*.

parents, 31undiscerning, untrustworthy, unloving, unforgiving,a unmerciful; 32who, knowing the righteous judgment of God, that those who practice such things are deserving of death, not only do the same but also approve of those who practice them.

INTIMATE MOMENTS

To strengthen your marriage, make plans to attend a Weekend to Remember® seminar. For a schedule of events, visit www.familylife.com.

God's Righteous Judgment

2 Therefore you are inexcusable, O man, whoever you are who judge, for in whatever you judge another you condemn yourself; for you who judge practice the same things. 2But we know that the judgment of God is according to truth against those who practice such things. 3And do you think this, O man, you who judge those practicing such things, and doing the same, that you will escape the judgment of God? 4Or do you despise the riches of His goodness, forbearance, and longsuffering, not knowing that the goodness of God leads you to repentance? 5But in accordance with your hardness and your impenitent heart you are treasuring up for yourself wrath in the day of wrath and revelation of the righteous judgment of God, 6who *will render to each one according to his deeds*:a 7eternal life to those who by patient continuance in doing good seek for glory, honor, and immortality; 8but to those who are self-seeking and do not obey the truth, but obey unrighteousness—indignation and wrath, 9tribulation and anguish, on every soul of man who does evil, of the Jew first and also of the Greek; 10but glory, honor, and peace to everyone who works what is good, to the Jew first and also to the Greek. 11For there is no partiality with God.

12For as many as have sinned without law will also perish without law, and as many as have sinned in the law will be judged by the law 13(for not the hearers of the law *are* just in the sight of God, but the doers of the law will be justified; 14for when Gentiles, who do not have the law, by nature do the things in the law, these, although not having the law, are a law to themselves, 15who show the work of the law written in their hearts, their conscience also bearing witness, and between themselves *their* thoughts accusing or else excusing *them*) 16in the day when God will judge the secrets of men by Jesus Christ, according to my gospel.

The Jews Guilty as the Gentiles

17Indeeda you are called a Jew, and rest on the law, and make your boast in God, 18and know *His* will, and approve the things that are excellent, being instructed out of the law, 19and are confident that you yourself are a guide to the blind, a light to those who are in darkness, 20an instructor of the foolish, a teacher of babes, having the form of knowledge and truth in the law. 21You, therefore, who teach another, do you not teach yourself? You who preach that a man should not steal, do you steal? 22You who say, "Do not commit adultery," do you commit adultery? You who abhor idols, do you rob temples? 23You who make your boast in the law, do you dishonor God through breaking the law? 24For *"the name of God is blasphemed among the Gentiles because of you,"*a as it is written.

Circumcision of No Avail

25For circumcision is indeed profitable if you keep the law; but if you are a breaker of the law, your circumcision has become uncircumcision. 26Therefore, if an uncircumcised man keeps the righteous requirements of the law, will not his uncircumcision be counted as circumcision? 27And will not the physically uncircumcised, if he fulfills the law, judge you who, *even* with *your* written *code* and circumcision,

---

1:31 aNU-Text omits *unforgiving.* 2:6 aPsalm 62:12; Proverbs 24:12 2:17 aNU-Text reads *But if.* 2:24 aIsaiah 52:5; Ezekiel 36:22

are a transgressor of the law? 28For he is not a Jew who *is one* outwardly, nor *is* circumcision that which *is* outward in the flesh; 29but *he is* a Jew who *is one* inwardly; and circumcision *is that* of the heart, in the Spirit, not in the letter; whose praise *is* not from men but from God.

God's Judgment Defended

3 What advantage then has the Jew, or what *is* the profit of circumcision? 2Much in every way! Chiefly because to them were committed the oracles of God. 3For what if some did not believe? Will their unbelief make the faithfulness of God without effect? 4Certainly not! Indeed, let God be true but every man a liar. As it is written:

"That You may be justified in Your
    words,
And may overcome when You are
    judged."a

5But if our unrighteousness demonstrates the righteousness of God, what shall we say? *Is* God unjust who inflicts wrath? (I speak as a man.) 6Certainly not! For then how will God judge the world? 7For if the truth of God has increased through my lie to His glory, why am I also still judged as a sinner? 8And *why* not *say,* "Let us do evil that good may come"?—as we are slanderously reported and as some affirm that we say. Their condemnation is just.

All Have Sinned

9What then? Are we better *than they?* Not at all. For we have previously charged both Jews and Greeks that they are all under sin. 10As it is written:

"There is none righteous, no, not one;
11   There is none who understands;
    There is none who seeks after God.
12   They have all turned aside;
    They have together become
        unprofitable;

There is none who does good, no, not
    one."a
13   "Their throat is an open tomb;
    With their tongues they have
        practiced deceit";a
    "The poison of asps is under their
        lips";b
14   "Whose mouth is full of cursing and
        bitterness."a
15   "Their feet are swift to shed blood;
16   Destruction and misery are in their
        ways;
17   And the way of peace they have not
        known."a
18   "There is no fear of God before their
        eyes."a

19Now we know that whatever the law says, it says to those who are under the law, that every mouth may be stopped, and all the world may become guilty before God. 20Therefore by the deeds of the law no flesh will be justified in His sight, for by the law *is* the knowledge of sin.

God's Righteousness Through Faith

21But now the righteousness of God apart from the law is revealed, being witnessed by the Law and the Prophets, 22even the righteousness of God, through faith in Jesus Christ, to all and on alla who believe. For there is no difference; 23for all have sinned and fall short of the glory of God, 24being justified freely by His grace through the redemption that is in Christ Jesus, 25whom God set forth *as* a propitiation by His blood, through faith, to demonstrate His righteousness, because in His forbearance God had passed over the sins that were previously committed, 26to demonstrate at the present time His righteousness, that He might be just and the justifier of the one who has faith in Jesus.

Boasting Excluded

27Where *is* boasting then? It is excluded. By what law? Of works? No, but by the law of faith. 28Therefore we conclude that a man is justified by faith apart from the deeds of the law. 29Or *is* He the God of the Jews only? *Is* He not also the God of the Gentiles? Yes, of the Gentiles also, 30since *there is* one God who will justify the

---

3:4 aPsalm 51:4 3:12 aPsalms 14:1–3; 53:1–3;
Ecclesiastes 7:20 3:13 aPsalm 5:9 bPsalm 140:3
3:14 aPsalm 10:7 3:17 aIsaiah 59:7, 8
3:18 aPsalm 36:1 3:22 aNU-Text omits *and on all.*

circumcised by faith and the uncircumcised through faith. ³¹Do we then make void the law through faith? Certainly not! On the contrary, we establish the law.

Abraham Justified by Faith

4 What then shall we say that Abraham our father has found according to the flesh?ᵃ ²For if Abraham was justified by works, he has *something* to boast about, but not before God. ³For what does the Scripture say? *"Abraham believed God, and it was accounted to him for righteousness."*ᵃ ⁴Now to him who works, the wages are not counted as grace but as debt.

David Celebrates the Same Truth

⁵But to him who does not work but believes on Him who justifies the ungodly, his faith is accounted for righteousness, ⁶just as David also describes the blessedness of the man to whom God imputes righteousness apart from works:

7   *"Blessed are those whose lawless
        deeds are forgiven,
    And whose sins are covered;*
8   *Blessed is the man to whom the* LORD
        *shall not impute sin."*ᵃ

Abraham Justified Before Circumcision

⁹*Does* this blessedness then *come* upon the circumcised *only,* or upon the uncircumcised also? For we say that faith was accounted to Abraham for righteousness. ¹⁰How then was it accounted? While he was circumcised, or uncircumcised? Not while circumcised, but while uncircumcised. ¹¹And he received the sign of circumcision, a seal of the righteousness of the faith which *he had while still* uncircumcised, that he might be the father of all those who believe, though they are uncircumcised, that righteousness might be imputed to them also, ¹²and the father of circumcision to those who not only *are* of the circumcision, but who also walk in the steps of the faith which our father Abraham *had while still* uncircumcised.

The Promise Granted Through Faith

¹³For the promise that he would be the heir of the world *was* not to Abraham or to

his seed through the law, but through the righteousness of faith. ¹⁴For if those who are of the law *are* heirs, faith is made void and the promise made of no effect, ¹⁵because the law brings about wrath; for where there is no law *there is* no transgression.

¹⁶Therefore *it is* of faith that *it might be* according to grace, so that the promise might be sure to all the seed, not only to those who are of the law, but also to those who are of the faith of Abraham, who is the father of us all ¹⁷(as it is written, *"I have made you a father of many nations"*ᵃ) in the presence of Him whom he believed—God, who gives life to the dead and calls those things which do not exist as though they did; ¹⁸who, contrary to hope, in hope believed, so that he became the father of many nations, according to what was spoken, *"So shall your descendants be."*ᵃ ¹⁹And not being weak in faith, he did not consider his own body, already dead (since he was about a hundred years old), and the deadness of Sarah's womb. ²⁰He did not waver at the promise of God through unbelief, but was strengthened in faith, giving glory to God, ²¹and being fully convinced that what He had promised He was also able to perform. ²²And therefore *"it was accounted to him for righteousness."*ᵃ

²³Now it was not written for his sake alone that it was imputed to him, ²⁴but also for us. It shall be imputed to us who believe in Him who raised up Jesus our Lord from the dead, ²⁵who was delivered up because of our offenses, and was raised because of our justification.

Faith Triumphs in Trouble

5 Therefore, having been justified by faith, we haveᵃ peace with God through our Lord Jesus Christ, ²through whom also we have access by faith into this grace in which we stand, and rejoice in hope of the glory of God. ³And not only *that,* but we also glory in tribulations, knowing that tribulation produces perseverance; ⁴and

---

4:1 ᵃOr *Abraham our (fore)father according to the flesh has found?* 4:3 ᵃGenesis 15:6 4:8 ᵃPsalm 32:1, 2 4:17 ᵃGenesis 17:5 4:18 ᵃGenesis 15:5 4:22 ᵃGenesis 15:6 5:1 ᵃAnother ancient reading is, *let us have peace.*

perseverance, character; and character, hope. ⁵Now hope does not disappoint, because the love of God has been poured out in our hearts by the Holy Spirit who was given to us.

Christ in Our Place

⁶For when we were still without strength, in due time Christ died for the ungodly. ⁷For scarcely for a righteous man will one die; yet perhaps for a good man someone would even dare to die. ⁸But God demonstrates His own love toward us, in that while we were still sinners, Christ died for us. ⁹Much more then, having now been justified by His blood, we shall be saved from wrath through Him. ¹⁰For if when we were enemies we were reconciled to God through the death of His Son, much more, having been reconciled, we shall be saved by His life. ¹¹And not only *that,* but we also rejoice in God through our Lord Jesus Christ, through whom we have now received the reconciliation.

Death in Adam, Life in Christ

¹²Therefore, just as through one man sin entered the world, and death through sin, and thus death spread to all men, because all sinned— ¹³(For until the law sin was in the world, but sin is not imputed when there is no law. ¹⁴Nevertheless death reigned from Adam to Moses, even over those who had not sinned according to the likeness of the transgression of Adam, who is a type of Him who was to come. ¹⁵But the free gift *is* not like the offense. For if by the one man's offense many died, much more the grace of God and the gift by the grace of the one Man, Jesus Christ, abounded to many. ¹⁶And the gift *is* not like *that which came* through the one who sinned. For the judgment *which came* from one *offense resulted* in condemnation, but the free gift *which came* from many offenses *resulted* in justification. ¹⁷For if by the one man's offense death reigned through the one, much more those who receive abundance of grace and of the gift of righteousness will reign in life through the One, Jesus Christ.)

¹⁸Therefore, as through one man's offense *judgment came* to all men, resulting in condemnation, even so through one Man's righteous act *the free gift came* to all men, resulting in justification of life. ¹⁹For as by one man's disobedience many were made sinners, so also by one Man's obedience many will be made righteous.

²⁰Moreover the law entered that the offense might abound. But where sin abounded, grace abounded much more,

---

ROMANCE FAQ

Q: *How can I show my mate my true devotion for him/her?*

Few of us over the age of 35 will forget those long gasoline lines that occurred during the oil crisis of 1973–74. Naturally, some greedy people wanted to cut in line to get ahead of others. Newspapers carried stories about everything from profanity and lawsuits to stabbings and shootings, as people fought for their places in line to get gas.

One woman cut in front of a motorbike. The biker slowly got off his bike, took off his helmet and glasses, and proceeded to let the air out of all four of her tires while she sat helplessly caught in the line! But the most creative stunt I read about was the young man who retaliated against an offender by unscrewing the man's gas cap, replacing it with his own locking gas cap, and driving off—with the key in his pocket!

Selfishness is possibly the most dangerous threat to oneness that any marriage can face. When "We're Number One!" becomes not just a cheer at a football game, but a personal motto, a marriage is in trouble.

The apostle Paul's counsel, therefore, becomes a prescription for marital oneness, "In honor giving preference to one another" (Rom. 12:10). Marriage provides the opportunity to live for someone besides yourself. And nothing is more romantic than communicating to your spouse how special he or she is to you. How can you honor your spouse today?

²¹so that as sin reigned in death, even so grace might reign through righteousness to eternal life through Jesus Christ our Lord.

INTIMATE MOMENTS

Circle a day on the calendar and take your wife on a mystery date. As the day gets closer leave her clues: what to wear, when to be ready, etc. But keep it a surprise!

Dead to Sin, Alive to God

6 What shall we say then? Shall we continue in sin that grace may abound? ²Certainly not! How shall we who died to sin live any longer in it? ³Or do you not know that as many of us as were baptized into Christ Jesus were baptized into His death? ⁴Therefore we were buried with Him through baptism into death, that just as Christ was raised from the dead by the glory of the Father, even so we also should walk in newness of life.

⁵For if we have been united together in the likeness of His death, certainly we also shall be *in the likeness* of *His* resurrection, ⁶knowing this, that our old man was crucified with *Him,* that the body of sin might be done away with, that we should no longer be slaves of sin. ⁷For he who has died has been freed from sin. ⁸Now if we died with Christ, we believe that we shall also live with Him, ⁹knowing that Christ, having been raised from the dead, dies no more. Death no longer has dominion over Him. ¹⁰For *the death* that He died, He died to sin once for all; but *the life* that He lives, He lives to God. ¹¹Likewise you also, reckon yourselves to be dead indeed to sin, but alive to God in Christ Jesus our Lord.

¹²Therefore do not let sin reign in your mortal body, that you should obey it in its lusts. ¹³And do not present your members *as* instruments of unrighteousness to sin, but present yourselves to God as being alive from the dead, and your members *as* instruments of righteousness to God. ¹⁴For sin shall not have dominion over you, for you are not under law but under grace.

From Slaves of Sin to Slaves of God

¹⁵What then? Shall we sin because we are not under law but under grace? Certainly not! ¹⁶Do you not know that to whom you present yourselves slaves to obey, you are that one's slaves whom you obey, whether of sin *leading* to death, or of obedience *leading* to righteousness? ¹⁷But God be thanked that *though* you were slaves of sin, yet you obeyed from the heart that form of doctrine to which you were delivered. ¹⁸And having been set free from sin, you became slaves of righteousness. ¹⁹I speak in human *terms* because of the weakness of your flesh. For just as you presented your members *as* slaves of uncleanness, and of lawlessness *leading* to *more* lawlessness, so now present your members *as* slaves *of* righteousness for holiness.

²⁰For when you were slaves of sin, you were free in regard to righteousness. ²¹What fruit did you have then in the things of which you are now ashamed? For the end of those things *is* death. ²²But now having been set free from sin, and having become slaves of God, you have your fruit to holiness, and the end, everlasting life. ²³For the wages of sin *is* death, but the gift of God *is* eternal life in Christ Jesus our Lord.

Freed from the Law

7 Or do you not know, brethren (for I speak to those who know the law), that the law has dominion over a man as long as he lives? ²For the woman who has a husband is bound by the law to *her* husband as long as he lives. But if the husband dies, she is released from the law of *her* husband. ³So then if, while *her* husband lives, she marries another man, she will be called an adulteress; but if her husband dies, she is free from that law, so that she is no adulteress, though she has married another man. ⁴Therefore, my brethren, you also have become dead to the law through the body of Christ, that you may be married to another—to Him who was raised from the

dead, that we should bear fruit to God. [5]For when we were in the flesh, the sinful passions which were aroused by the law were at work in our members to bear fruit to death. [6]But now we have been delivered from the law, having died to what we were held by, so that we should serve in the newness of the Spirit and not *in* the oldness of the letter.

Sin's Advantage in the Law

[7]What shall we say then? *Is* the law sin? Certainly not! On the contrary, I would not have known sin except through the law. For I would not have known covetousness unless the law had said, *"You shall not covet."*[a] [8]But sin, taking opportunity by the commandment, produced in me all *manner of* evil desire. For apart from the law sin *was* dead. [9]I was alive once without the law, but when the commandment came, sin revived and I died. [10]And the commandment, which *was* to *bring* life, I found to *bring* death. [11]For sin, taking occasion by the commandment, deceived me, and by it killed *me.* [12]Therefore the law *is* holy, and the commandment holy and just and good.

Law Cannot Save from Sin

[13]Has then what is good become death to me? Certainly not! But sin, that it might appear sin, was producing death in me through what is good, so that sin through the commandment might become exceedingly sinful. [14]For we know that the law is spiritual, but I am carnal, sold under sin. [15]For what I am doing, I do not understand. For what I will to do, that I do not practice; but what I hate, that I do. [16]If, then, I do what I will not to do, I agree with the law that *it is* good. [17]But now, *it is* no longer I who do it, but sin that dwells in me. [18]For I know that in me (that is, in my flesh) nothing good dwells; for to will is present with me, but *how* to perform what is good I do not find. [19]For the good that I will *to do,* I do not do; but the evil I will not *to do,* that I practice. [20]Now if I do what I will not *to do,* it is no longer I who do it, but sin that dwells in me.

Embracing Forgiveness

IT IS IMPORTANT TO KNOW that if you or your mate has confessed to God some past failures, they are completely forgiven. The Bible unequivocally declares, "There is therefore now no condemnation to those who are in Christ Jesus" (Rom. 8:1).

Nevertheless, some believers find it hard to grasp that Christ took *all* the punishment they deserve. Even though Jesus *did* pay the *total* price for *all* our sins, many of us still feel shame, and so constantly replay mental images of past mistakes. The guilt can seem overpowering, especially when we see the long-term results of our selfish choices.

Let me encourage you to play a key role in nudging your spouse toward embracing God's forgiveness. You and your spouse may want to consider memorizing Romans 8:1 together. You have the great privilege of reminding your mate of what God has done for us—no matter what we have done.

I recall one occasion early in our marriage when I was struggling with feeling shame because of some earlier mistakes. Barbara was the one who reminded me of the truth, and who exhorted me to believe it. In fact, she firmly said to me, "Are you saying that God lied when He said 'there is no condemnation to those who are in Christ Jesus'?" She went on to encourage me to believe the truth and not to deny it.

As Paul says in his letter to the Philippians, "One thing I do, forgetting those things which are behind and reaching forward to those things which are ahead, I press toward the goal for the prize of the upward call of God in Christ Jesus" (Phil. 3:13, 14). Leave the past in the past, and choose to believe what God's Word says is true, instead of believing your feelings!

7:7 [a]Exodus 20:17; Deuteronomy 5:21

BIBLICAL INSIGHTS • 8:6–8

Obey God, Not Your Appetites

THERE IS A WAR GOING ON inside us every day. Our flesh and our carnal appetites do battle throughout the day against our desire to honor and serve God. Jesus made reference to this battle when, in the Garden of Gethsemane, He instructed His disciples to watch and pray, and then added, "The spirit indeed is willing, but the flesh is weak" (Matt. 26:41).

Here's how Paul characterized the battle, "For to be carnally minded is death, but to be spiritually minded is life and peace. Because the carnal mind is enmity against God; for it is not subject to the law of God, nor indeed can be. So then, those who are in the flesh cannot please God" (Rom. 8:6–8). Do you find yourself being carnally minded (being selfish, giving into sinful desires) in your marriage? When we are in the flesh, it is impossible for our lives to please God. Instead, we need to train ourselves to be spiritually minded, always asking ourselves if our actions, attitudes, and words are pleasing to Christ.

Obedience to God demands two main things. First, it demands the courage to say no to self, no to carnal appetites, no to lusts of the flesh, no to what's easy, and yes to carrying the cross. Second, it demands faithfulness, a plodding endurance to obey God, to His call, and to that for which He calls you to suffer. Only by yielding to the cross can you obey God, not your appetites.

21I find then a law, that evil is present with me, the one who wills to do good. 22For I delight in the law of God according to the inward man. 23But I see another law in my members, warring against the law of my mind, and bringing me into captivity to the law of sin which is in my members. 24O wretched man that I am! Who will deliver me from this body of death? 25I thank God—through Jesus Christ our Lord!

So then, with the mind I myself serve the law of God, but with the flesh the law of sin.

Free from Indwelling Sin

8 *There* is therefore now no condemnation to those who are in Christ Jesus,[a] who do not walk according to the flesh, but according to the Spirit. 2For the law of the Spirit of life in Christ Jesus has made me free from the law of sin and death. 3For what the law could not do in that it was weak through the flesh, God *did* by sending His own Son in the likeness of sinful flesh, on account of sin: He condemned sin in the flesh, 4that the righteous requirement of the law might be fulfilled in us who do not walk according to the flesh but according to the Spirit. 5For those who live according to the flesh set their minds on the things of the flesh, but those *who live* according to the Spirit, the things of the Spirit. 6For to be carnally minded *is* death, but to be spiritually minded *is* life and peace. 7Because the carnal mind *is* enmity against God; for it is not subject to the law of God, nor indeed can be. 8So then, those who are in the flesh cannot please God.

9But you are not in the flesh but in the Spirit, if indeed the Spirit of God dwells in you. Now if anyone does not have the Spirit of Christ, he is not His. 10And if Christ *is* in you, the body *is* dead because of sin, but the Spirit *is* life because of righteousness. 11But if the Spirit of Him who raised Jesus from the dead dwells in you, He who raised Christ from the dead will also give life to your mortal bodies through His Spirit who dwells in you.

Sonship Through the Spirit

12Therefore, brethren, we are debtors—not to the flesh, to live according to the flesh. 13For if you live according to the flesh you will die; but if by the Spirit you put to death the deeds of the body, you will live. 14For as many as are led by the Spirit of God, these are sons of God. 15For you did not receive the spirit of bondage again

---

8:1 [a]NU-Text omits the rest of this verse.

to fear, but you received the Spirit of adoption by whom we cry out, "Abba, Father." [16]The Spirit Himself bears witness with our spirit that we are children of God, [17]and if children, then heirs—heirs of God and joint heirs with Christ, if indeed we suffer with *Him,* that we may also be glorified together.

From Suffering to Glory

[18]For I consider that the sufferings of this present time are not worthy *to be compared* with the glory which shall be revealed in us. [19]For the earnest expectation of the creation eagerly waits for the revealing of the sons of God. [20]For the creation was subjected to futility, not willingly, but because of Him who subjected *it* in hope; [21]because the creation itself also will be delivered from the bondage of corruption into the glorious liberty of the children of God. [22]For we know that the whole creation groans and labors with birth pangs

8:26 [a]NU-Text omits *for us.*

together until now. [23]Not only *that,* but we also who have the firstfruits of the Spirit, even we ourselves groan within ourselves, eagerly waiting for the adoption, the redemption of our body. [24]For we were saved in this hope, but hope that is seen is not hope; for why does one still hope for what he sees? [25]But if we hope for what we do not see, we eagerly wait for *it* with perseverance.

[26]Likewise the Spirit also helps in our weaknesses. For we do not know what we should pray for as we ought, but the Spirit Himself makes intercession for us[a] with groanings which cannot be uttered. [27]Now He who searches the hearts knows what the mind of the Spirit *is,* because He makes intercession for the saints according to *the will of* God.

[28]And we know that all things work together for good to those who love God, to those who are the called according to *His* purpose. [29]For whom He foreknew, He also predestined *to be* conformed to the image of His Son, that He might be the

ROMANTIC QUOTES AND NOTES
The Key to Real Romance

Marriages go through different seasons. In some seasons, romantic love will flourish. In others, romance wanes. Seasons of disappointed love are inevitable, but they needn't be fatal. The apostle Paul reminds us, "All things work together for good to those who love God" (Rom. 8:28). Even in the midst of intense disappointment, God wants you and your spouse to discover the most important ingredient for a lasting, rich, and dynamic romance.

You can't know that kind of love, however, until you are willing to honestly confront your disappointments. For many couples, having an honest conversation about disappointments in marriage feels very risky. And it could that one foundational element is missing in your marriage. *Commitment.*

Commitment is choosing to take your spouse's hand and to *walk through* whatever reality God has allowed in your life, believing that you will find a deeper love and a healthier relationship than you had before. At other times, commitment is an inner resolve to keep going, a realigning of your thinking to conform to what you know to be true, despite your feelings.

I recently was invited to a couple's 50th wedding anniversary celebration. I wrote them a letter to thank them for standing strong during the storms of life—and they had a few. I expressed appreciation to them for turning their faces into the wind together as a couple, and modeling what true love really looks like.

God wants to take you on a lifelong journey to become what you were meant to be, to experience Him more and more, and to understand a hint of the relationship and unity God Himself knows within the Trinity. This intimacy is a vast mystery, but it makes marriage a spiritual journey and not merely a biological coupling.

firstborn among many brethren. ³⁰Moreover whom He predestined, these He also called; whom He called, these He also justified; and whom He justified, these He also glorified.

God's Everlasting Love

³¹What then shall we say to these things? If God *is* for us, who *can be* against us? ³²He who did not spare His own Son, but delivered Him up for us all, how shall He not with Him also freely give us all things? ³³Who shall bring a charge against God's elect? *It is* God who justifies. ³⁴Who *is* he who condemns? *It is* Christ who died, and furthermore is also risen, who is even at the right hand of God, who also makes intercession for us. ³⁵Who shall separate us from the love of Christ? *Shall* tribulation, or distress, or persecution, or famine, or nakedness, or peril, or sword? ³⁶As it is written:

> "For Your sake we are killed all day
>   long;
> We are accounted as sheep for the
>   slaughter."ᵃ

³⁷Yet in all these things we are more than conquerors through Him who loved us. ³⁸For I am persuaded that neither death nor life, nor angels nor principalities nor powers, nor things present nor things to come, ³⁹nor height nor depth, nor any other created thing, shall be able to separate us from the love of God which is in Christ Jesus our Lord.

Israel's Rejection of Christ

9 I tell the truth in Christ, I am not lying, my conscience also bearing me witness in the Holy Spirit, ²that I have great sorrow and continual grief in my heart. ³For I could wish that I myself were accursed from Christ for my brethren, my countrymenᵃ according to the flesh, ⁴who are Israelites, to whom *pertain* the adoption, the glory, the covenants, the giving of the law, the service *of God,* and the promises; ⁵of whom *are* the fathers and from whom, according to the flesh, Christ *came,* who is over all, *the* eternally blessed God. Amen.

Israel's Rejection and God's Purpose

⁶But it is not that the word of God has taken no effect. For they *are* not all Israel who *are* of Israel, ⁷nor *are they* all children because they are the seed of Abraham; but, *"In Isaac your seed shall be called."*ᵃ ⁸That is, those who *are* the children of the flesh, these *are* not the children of God; but the children of the promise are counted as the seed. ⁹For this *is* the word of promise: *"At this time I will come and Sarah shall have a son."*ᵃ

¹⁰And not only *this,* but when Rebecca also had conceived by one man, *even* by our father Isaac ¹¹(for *the children* not yet being born, nor having done any good or evil, that the purpose of God according to election might stand, not of works but of Him who calls), ¹²it was said to her, *"The older shall serve the younger."*ᵃ ¹³As it is written, *"Jacob I have loved, but Esau I have hated."*ᵃ

Israel's Rejection and God's Justice

¹⁴What shall we say then? *Is there* unrighteousness with God? Certainly not! ¹⁵For He says to Moses, *"I will have mercy on whomever I will have mercy, and I will have compassion on whomever I will have compassion."*ᵃ ¹⁶So then *it is* not of him who wills, nor of him who runs, but of God who shows mercy. ¹⁷For the Scripture says to the Pharaoh, *"For this very purpose I have raised you up, that I may show My power in you, and that My name may be declared in all the earth."*ᵃ ¹⁸Therefore He has mercy on whom He wills, and whom He wills He hardens.

¹⁹You will say to me then, "Why does He still find fault? For who has resisted His will?" ²⁰But indeed, O man, who are you to reply against God? Will the thing formed say to him who formed *it,* "Why have you made me like this?" ²¹Does not the potter have power over the clay, from the same lump to make one vessel for honor and another for dishonor?

²²*What* if God, wanting to show *His* wrath and to make His power known,

---

8:36 ᵃPsalm 44:22   **9:3** ᵃOr *relatives*
9:7 ᵃGenesis 21:12   **9:9** ᵃGenesis 18:10, 14
9:12 ᵃGenesis 25:23   **9:13** ᵃMalachi 1:2, 3
9:15 ᵃExodus 33:19   **9:17** ᵃExodus 9:16

endured with much longsuffering the vessels of wrath prepared for destruction, [23]and that He might make known the riches of His glory on the vessels of mercy, which He had prepared beforehand for glory, [24]even us whom He called, not of the Jews only, but also of the Gentiles?

[25]As He says also in Hosea:

"I will call them My people, who were
    not My people,
And her beloved, who was not
    beloved."[a]

[26] "And it shall come to pass in the place
        where it was said to them,
' You are not My people,'

There they shall be called sons of
    the living God."[a]

[27]Isaiah also cries out concerning Israel:[a]

"Though the number of the children
    of Israel be as the sand of the
    sea,
The remnant will be saved.
[28] For He will finish the work and cut it
    short in righteousness,
Because the LORD will make a short
    work upon the earth."[a]

[29]And as Isaiah said before:

"Unless the LORD of Sabaoth[a] had left
    us a seed,
We would have become like Sodom,
And we would have been made like
    Gomorrah."[b]

9:25 [a]Hosea 2:23 **9:26** [a]Hosea 1:10
9:27 [a]Isaiah 10:22, 23 **9:28** [a]NU-Text reads *For the LORD will finish the work and cut it short upon the earth.* **9:29** [a]Literally, in Hebrew, *Hosts* [b]Isaiah 1:9

PARENTING MATTERS	**Q: *What gender-specific sexual issues should we address with our children?***

A girl needs to dress modestly and appropriately—a difficult task in today's culture! She needs to learn how to sit correctly in a dress, and to be careful how she moves her body.

Also, a girl must be very cautious about how she touches a boy. Rubbing up against a boy, giving him a full hug, or even sitting too close, can all send the wrong signals. Your daughter may try to tell you that these things are no big deal, but she doesn't understand what her actions can stir up in a young man!

At the same time, I've wanted our sons to know that sexual conquests are not the measure of one's masculinity. Self-control and discipline are qualities of a real man. Treating a young lady with common courtesy, respect, and dignity—and learning how to love her—are the marks of a godly man.

I also talked with my sons as they were growing up about what was happening with their bodies, about pubic and facial hair, and how their voices would change. I talked about how their sex drives would become stronger, about erections and wet dreams. And we discussed masturbation and pornography.

If I could do one thing differently, I would have talked more with my sons about what was happening simultaneously with girls. Boys need to have insight into what is happening with a sister or the girl who sits next to them in their classrooms.

These times of transition present us parents with some great opportunities to drive a truckload of God's truth into their lives. Don't allow an uncomfortable feeling to rob you of some of the greatest conversation a father and son or a mother and daughter can ever have. And don't be afraid of having some of these same conversations with your opposite-sex child.

Present Condition of Israel

³⁰What shall we say then? That Gentiles, who did not pursue righteousness, have attained to righteousness, even the righteousness of faith; ³¹but Israel, pursuing the law of righteousness, has not attained to the law of righteousness.^a ³²Why? Because *they did* not *seek it* by faith, but as it were, by the works of the law.^a For they stumbled at that stumbling stone. ³³As it is written:

> "*Behold, I lay in Zion a stumbling*
> *stone and rock of offense,*
> *And whoever believes on Him will*
> *not be put to shame.*"^a

Israel Needs the Gospel

10 Brethren, my heart's desire and prayer to God for Israel^a is that they may be saved. ²For I bear them witness that they have a zeal for God, but not according to knowledge. ³For they being ignorant of God's righteousness, and seeking to establish their own righteousness, have not submitted to the righteousness of God. ⁴For Christ *is* the end of the law for righteousness to everyone who believes.

⁵For Moses writes about the righteousness which is of the law, "*The man who does those things shall live by them.*"^a ⁶But the righteousness of faith speaks in this way, "*Do not say in your heart, 'Who will ascend into heaven?' "*^a (that is, to bring Christ down *from above*) ⁷or, " '*Who will descend into the abyss?' "*^a (that is, to bring Christ up from the dead). ⁸But what does it say? "*The word is near you, in your mouth and in your heart*"^a (that is, the word of faith which we preach): ⁹that if you confess with your mouth the Lord Jesus and believe in your heart that God has raised Him from the dead, you will be saved. ¹⁰For with the heart one believes unto righteousness, and with the mouth confession is made unto salvation. ¹¹For the Scripture says, "*Whoever believes on Him will not be put to shame.*"^a ¹²For there is no distinction between Jew and Greek, for the same Lord over all is rich to all who call upon Him. ¹³For "*whoever calls on the name of the LORD shall be saved.*"^a

Israel Rejects the Gospel

¹⁴How then shall they call on Him in whom they have not believed? And how shall they believe in Him of whom they have not heard? And how shall they hear without a preacher? ¹⁵And how shall they preach unless they are sent? As it is written:

> "*How beautiful are the feet of those*
> *who preach the gospel of peace,*^a
> *Who bring glad tidings of good*
> *things!*"^b

¹⁶But they have not all obeyed the gospel. For Isaiah says, "*LORD, who has believed our report?*"^a ¹⁷So then faith *comes* by hearing, and hearing by the word of God.

¹⁸But I say, have they not heard? Yes indeed:

> "*Their sound has gone out to all the*
> *earth,*
> *And their words to the ends of the*
> *world.*"^a

¹⁹But I say, did Israel not know? First Moses says:

> "*I will provoke you to jealousy by*
> *those who are not a nation,*
> *I will move you to anger by a foolish*
> *nation.*"^a

²⁰But Isaiah is very bold and says:

> "*I was found by those who did not*
> *seek Me;*
> *I was made manifest to those who*
> *did not ask for Me.*"^a

²¹But to Israel he says:

> "*All day long I have stretched out My*
> *hands*
> *To a disobedient and contrary*
> *people.*"^a

9:31 ^aNU-Text omits *of righteousness.* **9:32** ^aNU-Text reads *by works.* **9:33** ^aIsaiah 8:14; 28:16
10:1 ^aNU-Text reads *them.* **10:5** ^aLeviticus 18:5
10:6 ^aDeuteronomy 30:12 **10:7** ^aDeuteronomy 30:13
10:8 ^aDeuteronomy 30:14 **10:11** ^aIsaiah 28:16
10:13 ^aJoel 2:32 **10:15** ^aNU-Text omits *preach the gospel of peace, Who.* ^bIsaiah 52:7; Nahum 1:15
10:16 ^aIsaiah 53:1 **10:18** ^aPsalm 19:4
10:19 ^aDeuteronomy 32:21 **10:20** ^aIsaiah 65:1
10:21 ^aIsaiah 65:2

Israel's Rejection Not Total

11 I say then, has God cast away His people? Certainly not! For I also am an Israelite, of the seed of Abraham, of the tribe of Benjamin. [2]God has not cast away His people whom He foreknew. Or do you not know what the Scripture says of Elijah, how he pleads with God against Israel, saying, [3]"LORD, they have killed Your prophets and torn down Your altars, and I alone am left, and they seek my life"?[a] [4]But what does the divine response say to him? "I have reserved for Myself seven thousand men who have not bowed the knee to Baal."[a] [5]Even so then, at this present time there is a remnant according to the election of grace. [6]And if by grace, then it is no longer of works; otherwise grace is no longer grace.[a] But if it is of works, it is no longer grace; otherwise work is no longer work.

[7]What then? Israel has not obtained what it seeks; but the elect have obtained it, and the rest were blinded. [8]Just as it is written:

"God has given them a spirit of stupor,
Eyes that they should not see
And ears that they should not hear,
To this very day."[a]

[9]And David says:

"Let their table become a snare and a trap,
A stumbling block and a recompense to them.
[10] Let their eyes be darkened, so that they do not see,
And bow down their back always."[a]

Israel's Rejection Not Final

[11]I say then, have they stumbled that they should fall? Certainly not! But through their fall, to provoke them to jealousy, salvation has come to the Gentiles. [12]Now if their fall is riches for the world, and their failure riches for the Gentiles, how much more their fullness!

[13]For I speak to you Gentiles; inasmuch as I am an apostle to the Gentiles, I magnify my ministry, [14]if by any means I may provoke to jealousy those who are my flesh and save some of them. [15]For if their being cast away is the reconciling of the world, what will their acceptance be but life from the dead?

[16]For if the firstfruit is holy, the lump is also holy; and if the root is holy, so are the branches. [17]And if some of the branches were broken off, and you, being a wild olive tree, were grafted in among them, and with them became a partaker of the root and fatness of the olive tree, [18]do not boast against the branches. But if you do boast, remember that you do not support the root, but the root supports you.

INTIMATE MOMENTS

Rent a convertible one weekend just for the fun of it. Drive her to her favorite places.

[19]You will say then, "Branches were broken off that I might be grafted in." [20]Well said. Because of unbelief they were broken off, and you stand by faith. Do not be haughty, but fear. [21]For if God did not spare the natural branches, He may not spare you either. [22]Therefore consider the goodness and severity of God: on those who fell, severity; but toward you, goodness,[a] if you continue in His goodness. Otherwise you also will be cut off. [23]And they also, if they do not continue in unbelief, will be grafted in, for God is able to graft them in again. [24]For if you were cut out of the olive tree which is wild by nature, and were grafted contrary to nature into a cultivated olive tree, how much more will these, who are natural branches, be grafted into their own olive tree?

[25]For I do not desire, brethren, that you should be ignorant of this mystery, lest you should be wise in your own opinion, that blindness in part has happened to

---

11:3 [a]1 Kings 19:10, 14   **11:4** [a]1 Kings 19:18
11:6 [a]NU-Text omits the rest of this verse.
11:8 [a]Deuteronomy 29:4; Isaiah 29:10   **11:10** [a]Psalm 69:22, 23   **11:22** [a]NU-Text adds of God.

BIBLICAL INSIGHTS • 12:18

Be Proactive in Conflict Resolution

THE LONGER I LIVE, the more I realize how difficult it is for many couples to live out the instruction of Romans 12:8, where the apostle Paul advises us, "If it is possible, as much as depends on you, live peaceably with all men." Living peaceably means pursuing peace. It means taking the initiative to resolve a difficult conflict rather than waiting for the other person to take the first step. God didn't command us to be at peace with all men—that nay not be achievable. But He did say, "As much as depends on you, live peaceably."

It means being proactive.

To pursue the resolution of a conflict means to set aside your own hurt, anger, and bitterness. It means refusing to lose heart. It means laying aside your desire to be proved right in whatever conflict you and your spouse are engaged in. It means valuing the relationship above the argument.

I challenge you to keep your relationships current. In other words, resolve that you will remain in solid fellowship with your spouse, as well as with your children, parents, coworkers, and friends. "As much as depends on you, live peaceably with all men."

Don't allow Satan to gain a victory by isolating you from someone you care about! Instead, reach out and make sure you resolve your conflicts in a way that helps to make your relationships all that God intends them to be.

Israel until the fullness of the Gentiles has come in. ²⁶And so all Israel will be saved,ᵃ as it is written:

" The Deliverer will come out of Zion,
    And He will turn away ungodliness
        from Jacob;
²⁷ For this is My covenant with them,
    When I take away their sins."ᵃ

²⁸Concerning the gospel *they are* enemies for your sake, but concerning the election *they are* beloved for the sake of the fathers. ²⁹For the gifts and the calling of God *are* irrevocable. ³⁰For as you were once disobedient to God, yet have now obtained mercy through their disobedience, ³¹even so these also have now been disobedient, that through the mercy shown you they also may obtain mercy. ³²For God has committed them all to disobedience, that He might have mercy on all.

³³Oh, the depth of the riches both of the wisdom and knowledge of God! How unsearchable *are* His judgments and His ways past finding out!

³⁴ "For who has known the mind of the
        LORD?
    Or who has become His counselor?"ᵃ
³⁵ "Or who has first given to Him
        And it shall be repaid to him?"ᵃ

³⁶For of Him and through Him and to Him *are* all things, to whom *be* glory forever. Amen.

Living Sacrifices to God

12 I beseech you therefore, brethren, by the mercies of God, that you present your bodies a living sacrifice, holy, acceptable to God, *which is* your reasonable service. ²And do not be conformed to this world, but be transformed by the renewing of your mind, that you may prove what *is* that good and acceptable and perfect will of God.

Serve God with Spiritual Gifts

³For I say, through the grace given to me, to everyone who is among you, not to think *of himself* more highly than he ought to think, but to think soberly, as God has dealt to each one a measure of faith. ⁴For as we have many members in one body, but all the members do not have the same function, ⁵so we, *being* many, are one body in Christ, and individually members of one another. ⁶Having then gifts differing according to the grace that is given to us, *let us use them:* if prophecy, *let us prophesy*

11:26 ᵃOr *delivered* **11:27** ᵃIsaiah 59:20, 21
11:34 ᵃIsaiah 40:13; Jeremiah 23:18 **11:35** ᵃJob 41:11

in proportion to our faith; [7]or ministry, *let us use it* in *our* ministering; he who teaches, in teaching; [8]he who exhorts, in exhortation; he who gives, with liberality; he who leads, with diligence; he who shows mercy, with cheerfulness.

Behave Like a Christian

[9]*Let* love *be* without hypocrisy. Abhor what is evil. Cling to what is good. [10]*Be* kindly affectionate to one another with brotherly love, in honor giving preference to one another; [11]not lagging in diligence, fervent in spirit, serving the Lord; [12]rejoicing in hope, patient in tribulation, continuing steadfastly in prayer; [13]distributing to the needs of the saints, given to hospitality.

[14]Bless those who persecute you; bless and do not curse. [15]Rejoice with those who rejoice, and weep with those who weep. [16]Be of the same mind toward one another. Do not set your mind on high things, but associate with the humble. Do not be wise in your own opinion.

[17]Repay no one evil for evil. Have regard for good things in the sight of all men. [18]If it is possible, as much as depends on you, live peaceably with all men. [19]Beloved, do not avenge yourselves, but *rather* give place to wrath; for it is written, *"Vengeance is Mine, I will repay,"*[a] says the Lord. [20]Therefore

> *"If your enemy is hungry, feed him;*
> *If he is thirsty, give him a drink;*
> *For in so doing you will heap coals of*
> *fire on his head."*[a]

[21]Do not be overcome by evil, but overcome evil with good.

Submit to Government

13 Let every soul be subject to the governing authorities. For there is no authority except from God, and the authorities that exist are appointed by God. [2]Therefore whoever resists the authority resists the ordinance of God, and those who resist will bring judgment on themselves. [3]For rulers are not a terror to good works, but to evil. Do you want to be unafraid of the authority? Do what is good, and you will have praise from the same. [4]For he is God's minister to you for good. But if you do evil, be afraid; for he does not bear the sword in vain; for he is God's minister, an avenger to *execute* wrath on him who practices evil. [5]Therefore *you* must be subject, not only because of wrath but also for conscience' sake. [6]For because of this you also pay taxes, for they are God's ministers attending continually to this very thing. [7]Render therefore to all their due: taxes to whom taxes *are due,* customs to whom customs, fear to whom fear, honor to whom honor.

Love Your Neighbor

[8]Owe no one anything except to love one another, for he who loves another has fulfilled the law. [9]For the commandments, *"You shall not commit adultery," "You shall not murder," "You shall not steal," "You shall not bear false witness,"*[a] *"You shall not covet,"*[a] and if *there is* any other commandment, are *all* summed up in this saying, namely, *"You shall love your neighbor as yourself."*[a] [10]Love does no harm to a neighbor; therefore love *is* the fulfillment of the law.

INTIMATE MOMENTS

Wives, shave your legs before you go to bed.

Put on Christ

[11]And *do* this, knowing the time, that now *it is* high time to awake out of sleep; for now our salvation *is* nearer than when we *first* believed. [12]The night is far spent, the day is at hand. Therefore let us cast off the works of darkness, and let us put on the armor of light. [13]Let us walk properly, as in the day, not in revelry and drunkenness, not in lewdness and lust, not in strife

---

12:19 [a]Deuteronomy 32:35 **12:20** [a]Proverbs 25:21, 22 **13:9** [a]NU-Text omits *"You shall not bear false witness."* [b]Exodus 20:13–15, 17; Deuteronomy 5:17–19, 21 [c]Leviticus 19:18

and envy. ¹⁴But put on the Lord Jesus Christ, and make no provision for the flesh, to *fulfill its* lusts.

The Law of Liberty

14 Receive one who is weak in the faith, *but* not to disputes over doubtful things. ²For one believes he may eat all things, but he who is weak eats *only* vegetables. ³Let not him who eats despise him who does not eat, and let not him who does not eat judge him who eats; for God has received him. ⁴Who are you to judge another's servant? To his own master he stands or falls. Indeed, he will be made to stand, for God is able to make him stand.

⁵One person esteems *one* day above another; another esteems every day *alike*. Let each be fully convinced in his own mind. ⁶He who observes the day, observes *it* to the Lord;^a and he who does not observe the day, to the Lord he does not observe *it*. He who eats, eats to the Lord, for he gives God thanks; and he who does not eat, to the Lord he does not eat, and gives God thanks. ⁷For none of us lives to himself, and no one dies to himself. ⁸For if we live, we live to the Lord; and if we die, we die to the Lord. Therefore, whether we live or die, we are the Lord's. ⁹For to this end Christ died and rose^a and lived again, that He might be Lord of both the dead and the living. ¹⁰But why do you judge your brother? Or why do you show contempt for your brother? For we shall all stand before the judgment seat of Christ.^a ¹¹For it is written:

"As I live, says the LORD,
  Every knee shall bow to Me,
  And every tongue shall confess to
    God."^a

¹²So then each of us shall give account of himself to God. ¹³Therefore let us not judge one another anymore, but rather resolve this, not to put a stumbling block or a cause to fall in *our* brother's way.

The Law of Love

¹⁴I know and am convinced by the Lord Jesus that *there is* nothing unclean of itself; but to him who considers anything to be unclean, to him *it is* unclean. ¹⁵Yet if your brother is grieved because of *your* food, you are no longer walking in love. Do not destroy with your food the one for whom Christ died. ¹⁶Therefore do not let your good be spoken of as evil; ¹⁷for the kingdom of God is not eating and drinking, but righteousness and peace and joy in the Holy Spirit. ¹⁸For he who serves Christ in these things^a *is* acceptable to God and approved by men.

¹⁹Therefore let us pursue the things *which make* for peace and the things by which one may edify another. ²⁰Do not destroy the work of God for the sake of food. All things indeed *are* pure, but *it is* evil for the man who eats with offense. ²¹*It is* good neither to eat meat nor drink wine nor *do anything* by which your brother stumbles or is offended or is made weak.^a ²²Do you have faith?^a Have *it* to yourself before God. Happy *is* he who does not condemn himself in what he approves. ²³But he who doubts is condemned if he eats, because *he does* not *eat* from faith; for whatever *is* not from faith is sin.^a

Bearing Others' Burdens

15 We then who are strong ought to bear with the scruples of the weak, and not to please ourselves. ²Let each of us please *his* neighbor for *his* good, leading to edification. ³For even Christ did not please Himself; but as it is written, *"The reproaches of those who reproached You fell on Me."*^a ⁴For whatever things were written before were written for our learning, that we through the patience and comfort of the Scriptures might have hope. ⁵Now may the God of patience and comfort grant you to be like-minded toward one another, according to Christ Jesus, ⁶that you may with one mind *and* one mouth glorify the God and Father of our Lord Jesus Christ.

14:6 ^aNU-Text omits the rest of this sentence. **14:9** ^aNU-Text omits *and rose*. **14:10** ^aNU-Text reads *of God*. **14:11** ^aIsaiah 45:23 **14:18** ^aNU-Text reads *this*. **14:21** ^aNU-Text omits *or is offended or is made weak*. **14:22** ^aNU-Text reads *The faith which you have—have*. **14:23** ^aM-Text puts Romans 16:25–27 here. **15:3** ^aPsalm 69:9

DEVOTIONS FOR COUPLES • 15:1–3
Focus on Pleasing Your Spouse

Pleasing your mate isn't merely some tactic that helps bring happiness to your marriage; it's also a command of Scripture. The apostle Paul wrote, "Let each of us please his neighbor for his good, leading to edification. For even Christ did not please Himself" (Rom. 15:2, 3).

Notice three key phrases here.

First, we should "not [just] please ourselves." God has not put us here merely to satisfy our own wants and needs. Nothing reveals selfishness more than a marriage and a family. You can't be selfish and have success in marriage at the same time. We are here to reflect Christ to the world, and we do that best by giving ourselves to others. There's no better place to be focused on others than in your marriage.

Second, "Let each of us please his neighbor for his good." Who is your closest neighbor? Your spouse! So the Bible says you are to please your spouse for his or her good. Think for a moment and establish a plan of action: What would truly bring good to your spouse? What would truly encourage him or her? Please him or her?

Finally, "For even Christ did not please Himself." What did Christ seek to do? He "humbled Himself and became obedient to the point of death, even the death of the cross" (Phil. 2:8). He died so that we might live! Following His example in marriage means that we must learn to die to self, deny selfish desires. Denying ourselves is at the heart of being a Christ-follower and of experiencing marriage as God intended it.

Paul comments in Philippians, "Let nothing be done through selfish ambition or conceit, but in lowliness of mind let each esteem others better than himself. Let each of you look out not only for his own interests, but also for the interests of others" (Phil. 2:3, 4). I am convinced that great marriages are rooted in self-denial. In a truly biblical, Christian marriage, both people are willing to give up their lives for one another in order to love their mates properly.

During the early years of my marriage, I remember looking in the rearview mirror of the car one Saturday as I pulled out to go fishing with several of our children. Barbara was standing on the porch, left with the two youngest kids in diapers while I went off to the lake with the older kids to have a good time. The image of her standing there by herself with two toddlers was etched in my mind.

While I was sitting in that boat, not catching anything, I continued to think about Barbara. *You know, I am pleasing myself, but I have not done a good job of pleasing her.* I realized I needed to give up some of my hobbies for a while in order to please her and reduce her burden.

But you know what happened? Once the youngest kids grew older and Barbara's burden began to lift, she began to encourage me to fish and hunt with the children. Now when I leave the house on one of these trips, I look in the rearview mirror and see her on that same porch, waving good-bye with a smile.

Are there ways you can humble yourself today, die to your own desires and seek to "please your neighbor," your spouse, for his or her own good? Your spouse won't be the only one who will be satisfied if you do. God will be pleased as well.

Glorify God Together

[7]Therefore receive one another, just as Christ also received us,[a] to the glory of God. [8]Now I say that Jesus Christ has become a servant to the circumcision for the truth of God, to confirm the promises *made* to the fathers, [9]and that the Gentiles might glorify God for *His* mercy, as it is written:

"*For this reason I will confess to You among the Gentiles,
And sing to Your name.*"[a]

15:7 [a]NU-Text and M-Text read *you.*
15:9 [a]2 Samuel 22:50; Psalm 18:49

BIBLICAL INSIGHTS • 15:23, 24
Communication or Isolation?

ISOLATION AND THE FAILURE TO communicate drain the life from relationships. Most people long for intimacy and fellowship, but without communication, these two essentials of a good relationship are impossible.

The apostle Paul was a single man, but he understood how vital communication is to any relationship. So he made a point to tell the Roman Christians of his "great desire these many years to come to you," and promised that "whenever I journey to Spain, I shall come to you" (Rom. 15:23, 24). He didn't want them to guess about his affection for them; he wanted them to hear it straight from his own heart.

Your marriage depends on your willingness to communicate. It is the only way you can cultivate the intimacy and fellowship God intends a husband and wife to share within a marriage.

Ask yourself if you can recall an example in your own family when a lack of communication created a problem. Then consider how you and your spouse could work together and take practical steps to improve your communication. Pray that the lines of communication be opened, and remain open, so that your relationship with God and with your spouse and children will flourish.

Spend an evening with your spouse discussing how each of you can better communicate with the other. It may be that one of you needs to talk less and listen more. The other may need to work at really disclosing what is going on in his or her life. A marriage with Christ at its center can be a safe place to learn how to communicate. And a family that has a great model of communication is the very best training ground for children to learn what true communication looks like.

[10]And again he says:

> "*Rejoice, O Gentiles, with His*
> *people!*"[a]

[11]And again:

> "*Praise the LORD, all you Gentiles!*
> *Laud Him, all you peoples!*"[a]

[12]And again, Isaiah says:

> "*There shall be a root of Jesse;*
> *And He who shall rise to reign over*
> *the Gentiles,*
> *In Him the Gentiles shall hope.*"[a]

[13]Now may the God of hope fill you with all joy and peace in believing, that you may abound in hope by the power of the Holy Spirit.

From Jerusalem to Illyricum

[14]Now I myself am confident concerning you, my brethren, that you also are full of goodness, filled with all knowledge, able also to admonish one another.[a] [15]Nevertheless, brethren, I have written more boldly to you on *some* points, as reminding you, because of the grace given to me by God, [16]that I might be a minister of Jesus Christ to the Gentiles, ministering the gospel of God, that the offering of the Gentiles might be acceptable, sanctified by the Holy Spirit. [17]Therefore I have reason to glory in Christ Jesus in the things *which pertain* to God. [18]For I will not dare to speak of any of those things which Christ has not accomplished through me, in word and deed, to make the Gentiles obedient— [19]in mighty signs and wonders, by the power of the Spirit of God, so that from Jerusalem and round about to Illyricum I have fully preached the gospel of Christ. [20]And so I have made it my aim to preach the gospel, not where Christ was named, lest I should build on another man's foundation, [21]but as it is written:

> "*To whom He was not announced,*
> *they shall see;*
> *And those who have not heard shall*
> *understand.*"[a]

15:10 [a]Deuteronomy 32:43 **15:11** [a]Psalm 117:1
15:12 [a]Isaiah 11:10 **15:14** [a]M-Text reads *others*.
15:21 [a]Isaiah 52:15

Plan to Visit Rome

22For this reason I also have been much hindered from coming to you. 23But now no longer having a place in these parts, and having a great desire these many years to come to you, 24whenever I journey to Spain, I shall come to you.a For I hope to see you on my journey, and to be helped on my way there by you, if first I may enjoy your *company* for a while. 25But now I am going to Jerusalem to minister to the saints. 26For it pleased those from Macedonia and Achaia to make a certain contribution for the poor among the saints who are in Jerusalem. 27It pleased them indeed, and they are their debtors. For if the Gentiles have been partakers of their spiritual things, their duty is also to minister to them in material things. 28Therefore, when I have performed this and have sealed to them this fruit, I shall go by way of you to Spain. 29But I know that when I come to you, I shall come in the fullness of the blessing of the gospela of Christ.

15:24 aNU-Text omits *I shall come to you* (and joins *Spain* with the next sentence). **15:29** aNU-Text omits *of the gospel.*

30Now I beg you, brethren, through the Lord Jesus Christ, and through the love of the Spirit, that you strive together with me in prayers to God for me, 31that I may be delivered from those in Judea who do not believe, and that my service for Jerusalem may be acceptable to the saints, 32that I may come to you with joy by the will of God, and may be refreshed together with you. 33Now the God of peace *be* with you all. Amen.

Sister Phoebe Commended

16 I commend to you Phoebe our sister, who is a servant of the church in Cenchrea, 2that you may receive her in the Lord in a manner worthy of the saints, and assist her in whatever business she has need of you; for indeed she has been a helper of many and of myself also.

Greeting Roman Saints

3Greet Priscilla and Aquila, my fellow workers in Christ Jesus, 4who risked their own necks for my life, to whom not only I give thanks, but also all the churches of the Gentiles. 5Likewise *greet* the church that is in their house.

ROMANTIC QUOTES AND NOTES
Family: The Grace Place

As Paul wraps up this book, he gives a concluding prayer that is appropriate for family relationships, "The grace of our Lord Jesus Christ be with you all. Amen" (16:24). I think Paul knew that we all need to know and experience the grace of Christ. And if there has ever been an institution that needed grace, it's the family.

In no other setting place is life lived so up close and personal than in marriage. The nature of this most intimate of relationships is to create expectations and to disappoint. We love one another and we hurt one another. Sometimes we wound our spouse without knowing it; other times we do it on purpose. Regardless of the intent or actions, when we do hurt one another, we need to give one another "the grace of our Lord Jesus Christ." What does grace look like in a marriage and a family?

Grace says you have failed me, but I will bless you.

Grace exhibits love when lashing out could be justified.

Grace creates relationships that are safe and where failure is not fatal.

Grace proves that a person can have value, even when he does not perform.

Grace forgives, forgets, perseveres, but it doesn't stop there, it finds a way to bless another person.

One of the greatest tragedies in life is to be married and never express or experience grace in your relationship. Make it your prayer as a couple that you will have a grace-based marriage and family. Ask God to teach what that means and how you can lavish the grace of our Lord Jesus Christ upon your spouse.

Greet my beloved Epaenetus, who is the firstfruits of Achaia[a] to Christ. 6Greet Mary, who labored much for us. 7Greet Andronicus and Junia, my countrymen and my fellow prisoners, who are of note among the apostles, who also were in Christ before me.

8Greet Amplias, my beloved in the Lord. 9Greet Urbanus, our fellow worker in Christ, and Stachys, my beloved. 10Greet Apelles, approved in Christ. Greet those who are of the *household* of Aristobulus. 11Greet Herodion, my countryman.[a] Greet those who are of the *household* of Narcissus who are in the Lord.

12Greet Tryphena and Tryphosa, who have labored in the Lord. Greet the beloved Persis, who labored much in the Lord. 13Greet Rufus, chosen in the Lord, and his mother and mine. 14Greet Asyncritus, Phlegon, Hermas, Patrobas, Hermes, and the brethren who are with them. 15Greet Philologus and Julia, Nereus and his sister, and Olympas, and all the saints who are with them.

16Greet one another with a holy kiss. The[a] churches of Christ greet you.

Avoid Divisive Persons

17Now I urge you, brethren, note those who cause divisions and offenses, contrary to the doctrine which you learned, and avoid them. 18For those who are such do not serve our Lord Jesus[a] Christ, but their own belly, and by smooth words and flattering speech deceive the hearts of the simple. 19For your obedience has become known to all. Therefore I am glad on your behalf; but I want you to be wise in what is good, and simple concerning evil. 20And the God of peace will crush Satan under your feet shortly.

The grace of our Lord Jesus Christ *be* with you. Amen.

Greetings from Paul's Friends

21Timothy, my fellow worker, and Lucius, Jason, and Sosipater, my countrymen, greet you.

22I, Tertius, who wrote *this* epistle, greet you in the Lord.

23Gaius, my host and *the host* of the whole church, greets you. Erastus, the treasurer of the city, greets you, and Quartus, a brother. 24The grace of our Lord Jesus Christ *be* with you all. Amen.[a]

Benediction

25Now to Him who is able to establish you according to my gospel and the preaching of Jesus Christ, according to the revelation of the mystery kept secret since the world began 26but now made manifest, and by the prophetic Scriptures made known to all nations, according to the commandment of the everlasting God, for obedience to the faith— 27to God, alone wise, *be* glory through Jesus Christ forever. Amen.[a]

16:5 [a]NU-Text reads *Asia*. **16:11** [a]Or *relative* **16:16** [a]NU-Text reads *All the churches*. **16:18** [a]NU-Text and M-Text omit *Jesus*. **16:24** [a]NU-Text omits this verse. **16:27** [a]M-Text puts Romans 16:25–27 after Romans 14:23.

1 CORINTHIANS

WHAT COMES TO MIND WHEN YOU THINK OF LAS VEGAS? A recent advertising campaign used the slogan, "What happens in Vegas, stays in Vegas." The campaign celebrates the idea that in Las Vegas, anything goes and no one tells.

In ancient times, the city of Corinth had a reputation much like that of Las Vegas. In the first century, the name of the city became virtually synonymous with carnality and debauchery. Located about 50 miles west of Athens in Southern Greece, Corinth was well-known for its temple of Aphrodite, where more than 1,000 priestesses (prostitutes) served worshipers. In addition to sexual sin, the Corinthian way of life included drunkenness, greed, and dishonesty.

This was the moral climate when the apostle Paul visited Corinth during his second missionary journey (Acts 18:1). He founded the church there and spent a year and a half ministering in the city before he moved on to Ephesus. Many Corinthian converts had lived very carnal lives prior to their conversion (6:9, 10), and after Paul left, many of these new Christians continued to indulge in some of their old immoral practices. When the leaders of the church wondered how to respond, they sought help from their former pastor, Paul, who wrote 1 Corinthians as his measured response.

Because Paul addresses sexual sin in his letter, 1 Corinthians has a lot to say about God's design for marriage. Paul specifically condemns incest (5:1–5), along with other forms of sexual immorality (6:9, 10). He provides the Corinthians with a godly perspective of the role of sex in marriage (7:1–5). In addition, he addresses singleness and widowhood (7:6, 7, 25–39), along with issues related to divorce and spousal desertion (7:8–16). Paul also makes a reference to the responsibility of men regarding spiritual leadership in marriage (11:1–3).

One of the best-known chapters of the Bible is found in 1 Corinthians 13. This entire chapter describes in beautiful and almost poetic terms the characteristics of godly love. Husbands and wives ought to read together 13:4–7 and ask themselves, "Am I displaying this kind of unselfish love toward my spouse?" All of us will find we have room to grow.

Greeting

1 Paul, called *to be* an apostle of Jesus Christ through the will of God, and Sosthenes *our* brother,

2To the church of God which is at Corinth, to those who are sanctified in Christ Jesus, called *to be* saints, with all who in every place call on the name of Jesus Christ our Lord, both theirs and ours:

3Grace to you and peace from God our Father and the Lord Jesus Christ.

Spiritual Gifts at Corinth

4I thank my God always concerning you for the grace of God which was given to you by Christ Jesus, 5that you were enriched in everything by Him in all utterance and all knowledge, 6even as the testimony of Christ was confirmed in you, 7so that you come short in no gift, eagerly waiting for the revelation of our Lord Jesus Christ, 8who will also confirm you to the end, *that you may be* blameless in the day of our Lord Jesus Christ. 9God *is* faithful, by whom you were called into the fellowship of His Son, Jesus Christ our Lord.

Sectarianism Is Sin

10Now I plead with you, brethren, by the name of our Lord Jesus Christ, that you all speak the same thing, and *that* there be no divisions among you, but *that* you be perfectly joined together in the same mind and in the same judgment. 11For it has been declared to me concerning you, my brethren, by those of Chloe's *household*, that there are contentions among you. 12Now I say this, that each of you says, "I am of Paul," or "I am of Apollos," or "I am of Cephas," or "I am of Christ." 13Is Christ divided? Was Paul crucified for you? Or were you baptized in the name of Paul?

14I thank God that I baptized none of you except Crispus and Gaius, 15lest anyone should say that I had baptized in my own name. 16Yes, I also baptized the household of Stephanas. Besides, I do not know whether I baptized any other. 17For Christ did not send me to baptize, but to preach the gospel, not with wisdom of words, lest the cross of Christ should be made of no effect.

Christ the Power and Wisdom of God

18For the message of the cross is foolishness to those who are perishing, but to us who are being saved it is the power of God. 19For it is written:

> "I will destroy the wisdom of the wise,
> And bring to nothing the understanding of the prudent."[a]

20Where *is* the wise? Where *is* the scribe? Where *is* the disputer of this age? Has not God made foolish the wisdom of this world? 21For since, in the wisdom of God, the world through wisdom did not know God, it pleased God through the foolishness of the message preached to save those who believe. 22For Jews request a sign, and Greeks seek after wisdom; 23but we preach Christ crucified, to the Jews a stumbling block and to the Greeks[a] foolishness, 24but to those who are called, both Jews and Greeks, Christ the power of God and the wisdom of God. 25Because the foolishness of God is wiser than men, and the weakness of God is stronger than men.

Glory Only in the Lord

26For you see your calling, brethren, that not many wise according to the flesh, not many mighty, not many noble, *are* called. 27But God has chosen the foolish things of the world to put to shame the wise, and God has chosen the weak things of the world to put to shame the things which are mighty; 28and the base things of the world and the things which are despised God has chosen, and the things

INTIMATE MOMENTS

Fill several Easter eggs with notes telling your husband why you love him. Nestle the eggs in a decorated basket.

1:19 [a]Isaiah 29:14   **1:23** [a]NU-Text reads *Gentiles*.

which are not, to bring to nothing the things that are, [29]that no flesh should glory in His presence. [30]But of Him you are in Christ Jesus, who became for us wisdom from God—and righteousness and sanctification and redemption— [31]that, as it is written, *"He who glories, let him glory in the LORD."*[a]

Christ Crucified

2 And I, brethren, when I came to you, did not come with excellence of speech or of wisdom declaring to you the testimony[a] of God. [2]For I determined not to know anything among you except Jesus Christ and Him crucified. [3]I was with you in weakness, in fear, and in much trembling. [4]And my speech and my preaching *were* not with persuasive words of human[a] wisdom, but in demonstration of the Spirit and of power, [5]that your faith should not be in the wisdom of men but in the power of God.

Spiritual Wisdom

[6]However, we speak wisdom among those who are mature, yet not the wisdom of this age, nor of the rulers of this age, who are coming to nothing. [7]But we speak the wisdom of God in a mystery, the hidden *wisdom* which God ordained before the ages for our glory, [8]which none of the rulers of this age knew; for had they known, they would not have crucified the Lord of glory.

[9]But as it is written:

"Eye has not seen, nor ear heard,
Nor have entered into the heart of
man
The things which God has prepared
for those who love Him."[a]

[10]But God has revealed *them* to us through His Spirit. For the Spirit searches all things, yes, the deep things of God. [11]For what man knows the things of a man except the spirit of the man which is in him? Even so no one knows the things of God except the Spirit of God. [12]Now we have received, not the spirit of the world,

but the Spirit who is from God, that we might know the things that have been freely given to us by God.

[13]These things we also speak, not in words which man's wisdom teaches but which the Holy[a] Spirit teaches, comparing spiritual things with spiritual. [14]But the natural man does not receive the things of the Spirit of God, for they are foolishness to him; nor can he know *them,* because they are spiritually discerned. [15]But he who is spiritual judges all things, yet he himself is *rightly* judged by no one. [16]For *"who has known the mind of the LORD that he may instruct Him?"*[a] But we have the mind of Christ.

Sectarianism Is Carnal

3 And I, brethren, could not speak to you as to spiritual *people* but as to carnal, as to babes in Christ. [2]I fed you with milk and not with solid food; for until now you were not able *to receive it,* and even now you are still not able; [3]for you are still carnal. For where *there are* envy, strife, and divisions among you, are you not carnal and behaving like *mere* men? [4]For when one says, "I am of Paul," and another, "I *am* of Apollos," are you not carnal?

Watering, Working, Warning

[5]Who then is Paul, and who *is* Apollos, but ministers through whom you believed, as the Lord gave to each one? [6]I planted, Apollos watered, but God gave the increase. [7]So then neither he who plants is anything, nor he who waters, but God who gives the increase. [8]Now he who plants and he who waters are one, and each one will receive his own reward according to his own labor.

[9]For we are God's fellow workers; you are God's field, *you are* God's building. [10]According to the grace of God which was given to me, as a wise master builder I have laid the foundation, and another builds on it. But let each one take heed how he builds on it. [11]For no other foundation can anyone lay than that which is laid, which is Jesus Christ. [12]Now if anyone builds on this foundation *with* gold, silver, precious stones, wood, hay, straw, [13]each one's work will become clear; for the Day

---

1:31 [a]Jeremiah 9:24 **2:1** [a]NU-Text reads *mystery.*
2:4 [a]NU-Text omits *human.* **2:9** [a]Isaiah 64:4
2:13 [a]NU-Text omits *Holy.* **2:16** [a]Isaiah 40:13

will declare it, because it will be revealed by fire; and the fire will test each one's work, of what sort it is. ¹⁴If anyone's work which he has built on *it* endures, he will receive a reward. ¹⁵If anyone's work is burned, he will suffer loss; but he himself will be saved, yet so as through fire.

ROMANCE FAQ

Q: How can we best make decisions in our marriage?

Barbara and I made a commitment early in our marriage to make all decisions together. Only if we come to an honest yet unshakable disagreement do I take the responsibility to make the final decision. But I can promise you, before I make that decision, I have *really* listened to what Barbara has had to say about the subject!

I mention this because many men use their headship as a sort of club to force their wives to submit. I don't think it's a mistake that Paul writes, "Neither is man independent of woman, nor is woman independent of man, in the Lord" (1 Cor. 11:11) We need each other in marriage, and when it comes to making decisions, we need the wisdom that comes from different ways of looking at issues.

I've learned that just because Barbara says something once, that doesn't mean that she thinks I've really heard her. Sometimes I need to hear her again and again to understand the emotional power behind her words. This is especially important when she disagrees with a decision I make because she will be ready to follow that decision only if she knows I understand her.

The reality is that paying careful attention to Barbara's concerns is important for me, even if it sometimes takes her a while to express them clearly. As husbands, we err in decision making when we don't genuinely take our wives' opinions into account. He is the wise man who does!

¹⁶Do you not know that you are the temple of God and *that* the Spirit of God dwells in you? ¹⁷If anyone defiles the temple of God, God will destroy him. For the temple of God is holy, which *temple* you are.

Avoid Worldly Wisdom

¹⁸Let no one deceive himself. If anyone among you seems to be wise in this age, let him become a fool that he may become wise. ¹⁹For the wisdom of this world is foolishness with God. For it is written, "*He catches the wise in their own craftiness*";ᵃ ²⁰and again, "*The LORD knows the thoughts of the wise, that they are futile.*"ᵃ ²¹Therefore let no one boast in men. For all things are yours: ²²whether Paul or Apollos or Cephas, or the world or life or death, or things present or things to come—all are yours. ²³And you *are* Christ's, and Christ *is* God's.

Stewards of the Mysteries of God

4 Let a man so consider us, as servants of Christ and stewards of the mysteries of God. ²Moreover it is required in stewards that one be found faithful. ³But with me it is a very small thing that I should be judged by you or by a human court.ᵃ In fact, I do not even judge myself. ⁴For I know of nothing against myself, yet I am not justified by this; but He who judges me is the Lord. ⁵Therefore judge nothing before the time, until the Lord comes, who will both bring to light the hidden things of darkness and reveal the counsels of the hearts. Then each one's praise will come from God.

Fools for Christ's Sake

⁶Now these things, brethren, I have figuratively transferred to myself and Apollos for your sakes, that you may learn in us not to think beyond what is written, that none of you may be puffed up on behalf of one against the other. ⁷For who makes you differ *from another?* And what do you have that you did not receive? Now if you did indeed receive *it,* why do you boast as if you had not received *it?*

3:19 ᵃJob 5:13 3:20 ᵃPsalm 94:11 4:3 ᵃLiterally *day*

[8]You are already full! You are already rich! You have reigned as kings without us—and indeed I could wish you did reign, that we also might reign with you! [9]For I think that God has displayed us, the apostles, last, as men condemned to death; for we have been made a spectacle to the world, both to angels and to men. [10]We *are* fools for Christ's sake, but you *are* wise in Christ! We *are* weak, but you *are* strong! You *are* distinguished, but we *are* dishonored! [11]To the present hour we both hunger and thirst, and we are poorly clothed, and beaten, and homeless. [12]And we labor, working with our own hands. Being reviled, we bless; being persecuted, we endure; [13]being defamed, we entreat. We have been made as the filth of the world, the offscouring of all things until now.

Paul's Paternal Care

[14]I do not write these things to shame you, but as my beloved children I warn *you.* [15]For though you might have ten thousand instructors in Christ, yet *you do* not *have* many fathers; for in Christ Jesus I have begotten you through the gospel. [16]Therefore I urge you, imitate me. [17]For this reason I have sent Timothy to you, who is my beloved and faithful son in the Lord, who will remind you of my ways in Christ, as I teach everywhere in every church.

[18]Now some are puffed up, as though I were not coming to you. [19]But I will come to you shortly, if the Lord wills, and I will know, not the word of those who are puffed up, but the power. [20]For the kingdom of God *is* not in word but in power. [21]What do you want? Shall I come to you with a rod, or in love and a spirit of gentleness?

Immorality Defiles the Church

5 It is actually reported *that there is* sexual immorality among you, and such sexual immorality as is not even named[a] among the Gentiles—that a man has his father's wife! [2]And you are puffed up, and

have not rather mourned, that he who has done this deed might be taken away from among you. [3]For I indeed, as absent in body but present in spirit, have already judged (as though I were present) him who has so done this deed. [4]In the name of our Lord Jesus Christ, when you are gathered together, along with my spirit, with the power of our Lord Jesus Christ, [5]deliver such a one to Satan for the destruction of the flesh, that his spirit may be saved in the day of the Lord Jesus.[a]

[6]Your glorying *is* not good. Do you not know that a little leaven leavens the whole lump? [7]Therefore purge out the old leaven, that you may be a new lump, since you truly are unleavened. For indeed Christ, our Passover, was sacrificed for us.[a] [8]Therefore let us keep the feast, not with old leaven, nor with the leaven of malice and wickedness, but with the unleavened *bread* of sincerity and truth.

INTIMATE MOMENTS

Surprise her with an unexpected gift. It doesn't have to be expensive—just something to let her know you were thinking of her.

Immorality Must Be Judged

[9]I wrote to you in my epistle not to keep company with sexually immoral people. [10]Yet *I* certainly *did* not *mean* with the sexually immoral people of this world, or with the covetous, or extortioners, or idolaters, since then you would need to go out of the world. [11]But now I have written to you not to keep company with anyone named a brother, who is sexually immoral, or covetous, or an idolater, or a reviler, or a drunkard, or an extortioner—not even to eat with such a person.

[12]For what *have* I *to do* with judging those also who are outside? Do you not judge those who are inside? [13]But those who are outside God judges. Therefore *"put away from yourselves the evil person."*[a]

5:1 [a]NU-Text omits *named.* **5:5** [a]NU-Text omits *Jesus.* **5:7** [a]NU-Text omits *for us.* **5:13** [a]Deuteronomy 17:7; 19:19; 22:21, 24; 24:7

Do Not Sue the Brethren

6 Dare any of you, having a matter against another, go to law before the unrighteous, and not before the saints? ²Do you not know that the saints will judge the world? And if the world will be judged by you, are you unworthy to judge the smallest matters? ³Do you not know that we shall judge angels? How much more, things that pertain to this life? ⁴If then you have judgments concerning things pertaining to this life, do you appoint those who are least esteemed by the church to judge? ⁵I say this to your shame. Is it so, that there is not a wise man among you, not even one, who will be able to judge between his brethren? ⁶But brother goes to law against brother, and that before unbelievers!

⁷Now therefore, it is already an utter failure for you that you go to law against one another. Why do you not rather accept wrong? Why do you not rather *let yourselves* be cheated? ⁸No, you yourselves do wrong and cheat, and *you do* these things *to your* brethren! ⁹Do you not know that the unrighteous will not inherit the kingdom of God? Do not be deceived. Neither fornicators, nor idolaters, nor adulterers, nor homosexuals,ᵃ nor sodomites, ¹⁰nor thieves, nor covetous, nor drunkards, nor revilers, nor extortioners will inherit the kingdom of God. ¹¹And such were some of you. But you were washed, but you were sanctified, but you were justified in the name of the Lord Jesus and by the Spirit of our God.

Glorify God in Body and Spirit

¹²All things are lawful for me, but all things are not helpful. All things are lawful for me, but I will not be brought under the power of any. ¹³Foods for the stomach and the stomach for foods, but God will destroy both it and them. Now the body *is* not for sexual immorality but for the Lord, and the Lord for the body. ¹⁴And God both raised up the Lord and will also raise us up by His power.

¹⁵Do you not know that your bodies are members of Christ? Shall I then take the members of Christ and make *them* members of a harlot? Certainly not! ¹⁶Or do you

not know that he who is joined to a harlot is one body *with her?* For "the two," He says, "shall become one flesh."ᵃ ¹⁷But he who is joined to the Lord is one spirit *with Him.*

¹⁸Flee sexual immorality. Every sin that a man does is outside the body, but he who commits sexual immorality sins against his own body. ¹⁹Or do you not know that your body is the temple of the Holy Spirit *who is* in you, whom you have from God, and you are not your own? ²⁰For you were bought at a price; therefore glorify God in your bodyᵃ and in your spirit, which are God's.

Principles of Marriage

7 Now concerning the things of which you wrote to me:

It is good for a man not to touch a woman. ²Nevertheless, because of sexual immorality, let each man have his own wife, and let each woman have her own husband. ³Let the husband render to his wife the affection due her, and likewise also the wife to her husband. ⁴The wife does not have authority over her own body, but the husband *does.* And likewise the husband does not have authority over his own body, but the wife *does.* ⁵Do not deprive one another except with consent for a time, that you may give yourselves to fasting and prayer; and come together again so that Satan does not tempt you because of your lack of self-control. ⁶But I say this as a concession, not as a commandment. ⁷For I wish that all men were even as I myself. But each one has his own gift from God, one in this manner and another in that.

⁸But I say to the unmarried and to the widows: It is good for them if they remain even as I am; ⁹but if they cannot exercise self-control, let them marry. For it is better to marry than to burn *with passion.*

Keep Your Marriage Vows

¹⁰Now to the married I command, *yet* not I but the Lord: A wife is not to depart from *her* husband. ¹¹But even if she does

---

6:9 ᵃThat is, catamites **6:16** ᵃGenesis 2:24
6:20 ᵃNU-Text ends the verse at *body.*

depart, let her remain unmarried or be reconciled to *her* husband. And a husband is not to divorce *his* wife.

¹²But to the rest I, not the Lord, say: If any brother has a wife who does not believe, and she is willing to live with him, let him not divorce her. ¹³And a woman who has a husband who does not believe, if he is willing to live with her, let her not divorce him. ¹⁴For the unbelieving husband is sanctified by the wife, and the unbelieving wife is sanctified by the husband; otherwise your children would be unclean, but now they are holy. ¹⁵But if the unbeliever departs, let him depart; a brother or a sister is not under bondage in such *cases.* But God has called us to peace. ¹⁶For how do you know, O wife, whether you will save *your* husband? Or how do you know, O husband, whether you will save *your* wife?

Live as You Are Called

¹⁷But as God has distributed to each one, as the Lord has called each one, so let him walk. And so I ordain in all the churches. ¹⁸Was anyone called while circumcised? Let him not become uncircumcised. Was anyone called while uncircumcised? Let him not be circumcised. ¹⁹Circumcision is nothing and uncircumcision is nothing, but keeping the commandments of God *is what matters.* ²⁰Let each one remain in the same calling in which he was called. ²¹Were you called *while* a slave? Do not be concerned about it; but if you can be made free, rather use *it.* ²²For he who is called in the Lord *while* a slave is the Lord's freedman. Likewise he who is called *while* free is Christ's slave. ²³You were bought at a price; do not become slaves of men. ²⁴Brethren, let each one remain with God in that *state* in which he was called.

To the Unmarried and Widows

²⁵Now concerning virgins: I have no commandment from the Lord; yet I give judgment as one whom the Lord in His mercy has made trustworthy. ²⁶I suppose therefore that this is good because of the present distress—that *it is* good for a man to remain as he is: ²⁷Are you bound to a wife? Do not seek to be loosed. Are you loosed from a wife? Do not seek a wife. ²⁸But even if you do marry, you have not sinned; and if a virgin marries, she has not sinned. Nevertheless such will have trouble in the flesh, but I would spare you.

²⁹But this I say, brethren, the time *is* short, so that from now on even those who have wives should be as though they had none, ³⁰those who weep as though they did not weep, those who rejoice as though they did not rejoice, those who buy as though

ROMANTIC QUOTES AND NOTES
A Spirit of Co-Ownership

A joint commitment to mutually satisfying sex requires that both of you honor the spirit of co-ownership described in Scripture.

The apostle Paul had this to say about sex within a marriage, "Let the husband render to his wife the affection due her, and likewise also the wife to her husband. The wife does not have authority over her own body, but the husband does. And likewise the husband does not have authority over his own body, but the wife does" (1 Cor. 7:3, 4).

Paul's advice is possibly even more practical today than it was when he wrote it. When either mate is deprived of sexual satisfaction, the temptations of our culture become overpowering.

If at all possible, schedule a long block of time (ideally a two-night stay), for special communication and sexual intimacy. Share your needs, fears, and questions. Treat each other with an attitude of understanding, sympathy, and forgiveness.

There are no cookie-cutter solutions for defeating isolation and achieving a fulfilling sexual relationship. Oneness can occur only as you remain teachable and willing to learn from and about the mate God has given you. Why not ask Him for fresh understanding? Then turn off the lights early tonight!

they did not possess, ³¹and those who use this world as not misusing *it*. For the form of this world is passing away.

³²But I want you to be without care. He who is unmarried cares for the things of the Lord—how he may please the Lord. ³³But he who is married cares about the things of the world—how he may please *his* wife. ³⁴There is^a a difference between a wife and a virgin. The unmarried woman cares about the things of the Lord, that she may be holy both in body and in spirit. But she who is married cares about the things of the world—how she may please *her* husband. ³⁵And this I say for your own profit, not that I may put a leash on you, but for what is proper, and that you may serve the Lord without distraction.

³⁶But if any man thinks he is behaving improperly toward his virgin, if she is past the flower of youth, and thus it must be, let him do what he wishes. He does not sin; let them marry. ³⁷Nevertheless he who stands steadfast in his heart, having no necessity, but has power over his own will, and has so determined in his heart that he will keep his virgin,^a does well. ³⁸So then he who gives her^a in marriage does well, but he who does not give *her* in marriage does better.

³⁹A wife is bound by law as long as her husband lives; but if her husband dies, she is at liberty to be married to whom she wishes, only in the Lord. ⁴⁰But she is happier if she remains as she is, according to my judgment—and I think I also have the Spirit of God.

Be Sensitive to Conscience

8 Now concerning things offered to idols: We know that we all have knowledge. Knowledge puffs up, but love edifies. ²And if anyone thinks that he knows anything, he knows nothing yet as he ought to know. ³But if anyone loves God, this one is known by Him.

⁴Therefore concerning the eating of things offered to idols, we know that an idol *is* nothing in the world, and that *there is* no other God but one. ⁵For even if there are so-called gods, whether in heaven or on earth (as there are many gods and many lords), ⁶yet for us *there is* one God, the Father, of whom *are* all things, and we for

Him; and one Lord Jesus Christ, through whom *are* all things, and through whom we *live*.

⁷However, *there is* not in everyone that knowledge; for some, with consciousness of the idol, until now eat *it* as a thing offered to an idol; and their conscience, being weak, is defiled. ⁸But food does not commend us to God; for neither if we eat are we the better, nor if we do not eat are we the worse.

⁹But beware lest somehow this liberty of yours become a stumbling block to those who are weak. ¹⁰For if anyone sees you who have knowledge eating in an idol's temple, will not the conscience of him who is weak be emboldened to eat those things offered to idols? ¹¹And because of your knowledge shall the weak brother perish, for whom Christ died? ¹²But when you thus sin against the brethren, and wound their weak conscience, you sin against Christ. ¹³Therefore, if food makes my brother stumble, I will never again eat meat, lest I make my brother stumble.

A Pattern of Self-Denial

9 Am I not an apostle? Am I not free? Have I not seen Jesus Christ our Lord? Are you not my work in the Lord? ²If I am not an apostle to others, yet doubtless I am to you. For you are the seal of my apostleship in the Lord.

³My defense to those who examine me is this: ⁴Do we have no right to eat and drink? ⁵Do we have no right to take along a believing wife, as *do* also the other apostles, the brothers of the Lord, and Cephas? ⁶Or *is it* only Barnabas and I *who* have no right to refrain from working? ⁷Who ever goes to war at his own expense? Who plants a vineyard and does not eat of its fruit? Or who tends a flock and does not drink of the milk of the flock?

⁸Do I say these things as a *mere* man? Or does not the law say the same also? ⁹For it is written in the law of Moses, "*You shall not muzzle an ox while it treads out the grain.*"^a Is it oxen God is concerned about?

7:34 ^aM-Text adds *also* **7:37** ^aOr *virgin daughter*
7:38 ^aNU-Text reads *his own virgin.*
9:9 ^aDeuteronomy 25:4

DEVOTIONS FOR COUPLES • 9:24–27
Run Your Own Race

Each of us, as individuals and as couples, is in a race. We're running a course of extremes. There's the summit of joy at the birth of a baby contrasted with the agony of the valley of the shadow of death. And there are miles of rugged terrain and climate changes in between.

Life is a race for every Christian. It is a race you and I must finish and win.

How are you running? Are you winning? Losing? Did you know that the omnipotent God of the universe given you the strategy for victory?

"Do you not know that those who run in a race all run, but one receives the prize? Run in such a way that you may obtain it. And everyone who competes for the prize is temperate in all things. Now they do it to obtain a perishable crown, but we for an imperishable crown. Therefore I run thus: not with uncertainty. Thus I fight: not as one who beats the air. But I discipline my body and bring it into subjection, lest, when I have preached to others, I myself should become disqualified" (1 Cor. 9:24–27).

So how do you run to win? Here are the apostle Paul's rules for the race:

1. *Self Control* (v. 25). The discipline of our desires forms the backbone of our character. Know what tempts you and avoid it. If you want to exhibit self-control, walk in the power of the Holy Spirit. He will produce that fruit in your life.

2. *Careful Aim* (v. 26). A runner intending to win must know where he is going. The finish line for the Christian is the person of Jesus Christ. Keep your eyes on Him. Know Him. Grow in your love for Him. Serve Him. Yield totally to Him. Make Him your aim.

3. *Sacrifice* (v. 27). The Christian life will cost you your life. You and I must die to ourselves, deny our rights. Anything, any prize, any relationship, anything of value *costs*. You may find that working through a problem in a relationship is harder than walking out. Doing the right thing isn't always the easiest option, but it's always the best option.

Any long-distance runner will tell you that finishing a race successfully often means pain. But they will also tell you that the pain is worth it! The same is true for us.

I've decided not to turn in my sneakers early. By God's grace, I'll wear 'em out!

How about you? Are you running for the prize?

---

¹⁰Or does He say *it* altogether for our sakes? For our sakes, no doubt, *this* is written, that he who plows should plow in hope, and he who threshes in hope should be partaker of his hope. ¹¹If we have sown spiritual things for you, *is it* a great thing if we reap your material things? ¹²If others are partakers of *this* right over you, *are* we not even more?

Nevertheless we have not used this right, but endure all things lest we hinder the gospel of Christ. ¹³Do you not know that those who minister the holy things eat *of the things* of the temple, and those who serve at the altar partake of *the offerings of* the altar? ¹⁴Even so the Lord has commanded that those who preach the gospel should live from the gospel.

¹⁵But I have used none of these things, nor have I written these things that it should be done so to me; for it *would be* better for me to die than that anyone should make my boasting void. ¹⁶For if I preach the gospel, I have nothing to boast of, for necessity is laid upon me; yes, woe is me if I do not preach the gospel! ¹⁷For if I do this willingly, I have a reward; but if against my will, I have been entrusted with a stewardship. ¹⁸What is my reward then? That when I preach the gospel, I may present the gospel of Christ[a] without charge, that I may not abuse my authority in the gospel.

9:18 [a]NU-Text omits *of Christ.*

God,[a] but under law toward Christ[b]), that I might win those *who are* without law; [22]to the weak I became as[a] weak, that I might win the weak. I have become all things to all *men,* that I might by all means save some. [23]Now this I do for the gospel's sake, that I may be partaker of it with *you.*

Striving for a Crown

[24]Do you not know that those who run in a race all run, but one receives the prize? Run in such a way that you may obtain *it.* [25]And everyone who competes *for the prize* is temperate in all things. Now they *do it* to obtain a perishable crown, but we *for* an imperishable *crown.* [26]Therefore I run thus: not with uncertainty. Thus I fight: not as *one who* beats the air. [27]But I discipline my body and bring *it* into subjection, lest, when I have preached to others, I myself should become disqualified.

Old Testament Examples

10 Moreover, brethren, I do not want you to be unaware that all our fathers were under the cloud, all passed through the sea, [2]all were baptized into Moses in the cloud and in the sea, [3]all ate the same spiritual food, [4]and all drank the same spiritual drink. For they drank of that spiritual Rock that followed them, and that Rock was Christ. [5]But with most of them God was not well pleased, for *their bodies* were scattered in the wilderness.

[6]Now these things became our examples, to the intent that we should not lust after evil things as they also lusted. [7]And do not become idolaters as *were* some of them. As it is written, *"The people sat down to eat and drink, and rose up to play."*[a] [8]Nor let us commit sexual immorality, as some of them did, and in one day twenty-three thousand fell; [9]nor let us tempt Christ, as some of them also tempted, and were destroyed by serpents; [10]nor complain, as some of them also complained, and were destroyed by the destroyer. [11]Now all[a] these things happened to

BIBLICAL INSIGHTS • 9:26, 27

Let Another In

THE MORE I HAVE WATCHED high-profile men fall prey to temptation and sexual immorality, the more I have purposed to lead a lifestyle of accountability. While I certainly have much to learn on the subject, I have resolved to be teachable, approachable, and most importantly, willing to hear what Barbara wants to say to me. I believe accountability starts at home.

The apostle Paul's words spur me on, "Therefore I run thus: not with uncertainty. Thus I fight: not as one who beats the air. But I discipline my body and bring it into subjection, lest, when I have preached to others, I myself should become disqualified" (1 Cor. 9:26, 27).

One of those disciplines for me is accountability. I rely on it to ensure that I stay away from anything that might disqualify me. True accountability involves letting another person into the interior of your life. You have the choice to submit to another human being for perspective, advice, or even to be taken to task for some wrong or questionable thing. Solomon says a wise man welcomes a helpful rebuke (Prov. 13:1).

Each of us must choose the right person to whom we can be accountable. It needs to be someone of the same sex, a good friend you respect, and someone who has your permission to speak the truth in love to you. Remember what Proverbs 27:6 says, "Faithful are the wounds of a friend."

Serving All Men

[19]For though I am free from all *men,* I have made myself a servant to all, that I might win the more; [20]and to the Jews I became as a Jew, that I might win Jews; to those *who are* under the law, as under the law,[a] that I might win those *who are* under the law; [21]to those *who are* without law, as without law (not being without law toward

---

9:20 [a]NU-Text adds *though not being myself under the law.* **9:21** [a]NU-Text reads *God's law.* [b]NU-Text reads *Christ's law.* **9:22** [a]NU-Text omits *as.* **10:7** [a]Exodus 32:6 **10:11** [a]NU-Text omits *all.*

them as examples, and they were written for our admonition, upon whom the ends of the ages have come.

[12]Therefore let him who thinks he stands take heed lest he fall. [13]No temptation has overtaken you except such as is common to man; but God *is* faithful, who will not allow you to be tempted beyond what you are able, but with the temptation will also make the way of escape, that you may be able to bear *it.*

Flee from Idolatry

[14]Therefore, my beloved, flee from idolatry. [15]I speak as to wise men; judge for yourselves what I say. [16]The cup of blessing which we bless, is it not the communion of the blood of Christ? The bread which we break, is it not the communion of the body of Christ? [17]For we, *though* many, are one bread *and* one body; for we all partake of that one bread.

[18]Observe Israel after the flesh: Are not those who eat of the sacrifices partakers of the altar? [19]What am I saying then? That an idol is anything, or what is offered to idols is anything? [20]Rather, that the things which the Gentiles sacrifice they sacrifice to demons and not to God, and I do not want you to have fellowship with demons. [21]You cannot drink the cup of the Lord and the cup of demons; you cannot partake of the Lord's table and of the table of demons. [22]Or do we provoke the Lord to jealousy? Are we stronger than He?

All to the Glory of God

[23]All things are lawful for me,[a] but not all things are helpful; all things are lawful for me,[b] but not all things edify. [24]Let no one seek his own, but each one the other's *well-being.*

[25]Eat whatever is sold in the meat market, asking no questions for conscience' sake; [26]for *"the earth is the LORD's, and all its fullness."*[a]

[27]If any of those who do not believe invites you *to dinner,* and you desire to go, eat whatever is set before you, asking no

question for conscience' sake. [28]But if anyone says to you, "This was offered to idols," do not eat it for the sake of the one who told you, and for conscience' sake;[a] for *"the earth is the LORD's, and all its fullness."*[b] [29]"Conscience," I say, not your own, but that of the other. For why is my liberty judged by another *man's* conscience? [30]But if I partake with thanks, why am I evil spoken of for *the food* over which I give thanks?

[31]Therefore, whether you eat or drink, or whatever you do, do all to the glory of God. [32]Give no offense, either to the Jews or to the Greeks or to the church of God, [33]just as I also please all *men* in all *things,* not seeking my own profit, but the *profit* of many, that they may be saved.

11 Imitate me, just as I also *imitate* Christ.

Head Coverings

[2]Now I praise you, brethren, that you remember me in all things and keep the traditions just as I delivered *them* to you. [3]But I want you to know that the head of every man is Christ, the head of woman *is* man, and the head of Christ *is* God. [4]Every man praying or prophesying, having *his* head covered, dishonors his head. [5]But every woman who prays or prophesies with *her* head uncovered dishonors her head, for that is one and the same as if her head were shaved. [6]For if a woman is not covered, let her also be shorn. But if it is shameful for a woman to be shorn or shaved, let her be covered. [7]For a man indeed ought not to cover *his* head, since he is the image and glory of God; but woman is the glory of man. [8]For man is not from woman, but woman from man. [9]Nor was man created for the woman, but woman for the man. [10]For this reason the woman ought to have *a symbol of* authority on *her* head, because of the angels. [11]Nevertheless, neither *is* man independent of woman, nor woman independent of man, in the Lord. [12]For as woman *came* from man, even so man also *comes* through woman; but all things are from God.

[13]Judge among yourselves. Is it proper for a woman to pray to God with her head uncovered? [14]Does not even nature itself

---

10:23 [a]NU-Text omits *for me.* [b]NU-Text omits *for me.* **10:26** [a]Psalm 24:1 **10:28** [a]NU-Text omits the rest of this verse. [b]Psalm 24:1

A Clear Structure for Marriage

THE SCRIPTURES PROVIDE a clear organizational structure for marriage, "But I want you to know that the head of every man is Christ, the head of woman is man, and the head of Christ is God" (1 Cor. 11:3).

Commentator William Hendriksen points out that God "placed ultimate responsibility with respect to the household on the shoulders of the husband ... The Lord has assigned the wife the duty of obeying her husband yet ... this obedience must be a voluntary submission on her part, and that only to her own husband."

The word *head* does not imply male dominance, where a man lords it over a woman and demands her total obedience. God's Word clearly states that we are all equally His children and of equal value and worth. As Galatians 3:28 tells us, "There is neither Jew nor Greek, there is neither slave nor free, there is neither male nor female; for you are all one in Christ Jesus." We are equal in worth and value, but according to the Scripture, we do have differing responsibilities within the marriage relationship.

Unfortunately, when a Christian husband does not treat his wife as a helpmate and a gift from God, a wife may be tempted to search for other ways to find significance and value, often outside of God's will.

Headship is a mix of God-given responsibility and authority. A husband bears the weight of leadership and decision making in a marriage. His leadership style must be one that demonstrates care for the needs of those allotted to his charge and a servant spirit. And as a husband he uniquely assumes responsibility for the impact of those decisions. He is responsible before God for his wife and family, not to control them, but to care for them and guide them.

teach you that if a man has long hair, it is a dishonor to him? [15]But if a woman has long hair, it is a glory to her; for *her* hair is given to her[a] for a covering. [16]But if anyone seems to be contentious, we have no such custom, nor *do* the churches of God.

Conduct at the Lord's Supper

[17]Now in giving these instructions I do not praise *you,* since you come together not for the better but for the worse. [18]For first of all, when you come together as a church, I hear that there are divisions among you, and in part I believe it. [19]For there must also be factions among you, that those who are approved may be recognized among you. [20]Therefore when you come together in one place, it is not to eat the Lord's Supper. [21]For in eating, each one takes his own supper ahead of *others;* and one is hungry and another is drunk. [22]What! Do you not have houses to eat and drink in? Or do you despise the church of God and shame those who have nothing? What shall I say to you? Shall I praise you in this? I do not praise *you.*

Institution of the Lord's Supper

[23]For I received from the Lord that which I also delivered to you: that the Lord Jesus on the *same* night in which He was betrayed took bread; [24]and when He had given thanks, He broke *it* and said, "Take, eat;[a] this is My body which is broken[b] for you; do this in remembrance of Me." [25]In the same manner *He* also *took* the cup after supper, saying, "This cup is the new covenant in My blood. This do, as often as you drink *it,* in remembrance of Me."

[26]For as often as you eat this bread and drink this cup, you proclaim the Lord's death till He comes.

Examine Yourself

[27]Therefore whoever eats this bread or drinks *this* cup of the Lord in an unworthy manner will be guilty of the body and blood[a] of the Lord. [28]But let a man examine himself, and so let him eat of the bread

---

11:15 [a]M-Text omits *to her.* **11:24** [a]NU-Text omits *Take, eat.* [b]NU-Text omits *broken.* **11:27** [a]NU-Text and M-Text read *the blood.*

and drink of the cup. ²⁹For he who eats and drinks in an unworthy manner[a] eats and drinks judgment to himself, not discerning the Lord's[b] body. ³⁰For this reason many *are* weak and sick among you, and many sleep. ³¹For if we would judge ourselves, we would not be judged. ³²But when we are judged, we are chastened by the Lord, that we may not be condemned with the world.

³³Therefore, my brethren, when you come together to eat, wait for one another. ³⁴But if anyone is hungry, let him eat at home, lest you come together for judgment. And the rest I will set in order when I come.

Spiritual Gifts: Unity in Diversity

12 Now concerning spiritual *gifts,* brethren, I do not want you to be ignorant: ²You know that[a] you were Gentiles, carried away to these dumb idols, however you were led. ³Therefore I make known to you that no one speaking by the Spirit of God calls Jesus accursed, and no one can say that Jesus is Lord except by the Holy Spirit.

⁴There are diversities of gifts, but the same Spirit. ⁵There are differences of ministries, but the same Lord. ⁶And there are diversities of activities, but it is the same God who works all in all. ⁷But the manifestation of the Spirit is given to each one for the profit *of all:* ⁸for to one is given the word of wisdom through the Spirit, to another the word of knowledge through the same Spirit, ⁹to another faith by the same Spirit, to another gifts of healings by the same[a] Spirit, ¹⁰to another the working of miracles, to another prophecy, to another discerning of spirits, to another *different* kinds of tongues, to another the interpretation of tongues. ¹¹But one and the same Spirit works all these things, distributing to each one individually as He wills.

Unity and Diversity in One Body

¹²For as the body is one and has many members, but all the members of that one body, being many, are one body, so also *is* Christ. ¹³For by one Spirit we were all baptized into one body—whether Jews or Greeks, whether slaves or free—and have all been made to drink into[a] one Spirit. ¹⁴For in fact the body is not one member but many.

¹⁵If the foot should say, "Because I am not a hand, I am not of the body," is it therefore not of the body? ¹⁶And if the ear should say, "Because I am not an eye, I am not of the body," is it therefore not of the body? ¹⁷If the whole body *were* an eye, where *would be* the hearing? If the whole *were* hearing, where *would be* the smelling? ¹⁸But now God has set the members, each one of them, in the body just as He pleased. ¹⁹And if they were all one member, where *would* the body *be?*

²⁰But now indeed *there are* many members, yet one body. ²¹And the eye cannot say to the hand, "I have no need of you"; nor again the head to the feet, "I have no need of you." ²²No, much rather, those members of the body which seem to be weaker are necessary. ²³And those *members* of the body which we think to be less honorable, on these we bestow greater honor; and our unpresentable *parts* have greater modesty, ²⁴but our presentable *parts* have no need. But God composed the body, having given greater honor to that *part* which lacks it, ²⁵that there should be no schism in the body, but *that* the members should have the same care for one another. ²⁶And if one member suffers, all the members suffer with *it;* or if one member is honored, all the members rejoice with *it.*

²⁷Now you are the body of Christ, and members individually. ²⁸And God has appointed these in the church: first apostles,

11:29 ᵃNU-Text omits *in an unworthy manner.* ᵇNU-Text omits *Lord's.* 12:2 ᵃNU-Text and M-Text add *when.* 12:9 ᵃNU-Text reads *one.* 12:13 ᵃNU-Text omits *into.*

INTIMATE MOMENTS

Father's Day is a great day to celebrate with your husband. Rent a convertible for the day and drive around with the top down.

Put Away Childishness

THE APOSTLE PAUL INSISTS that we all need to grow up, "When I was a child, I spoke as a child, I understood as a child, I thought as a child; but when I became a man, I put away childish things" (1 Cor. 13:11). Paul knew that kids will be kids; they will behave childishly. But he also makes it clear that as we grow, we must set aside childish behavior and become mature.

By nature, children are petty, hurtful, and fault-finding in relationships. They speak rashly, rudely, and selfishly, with little thought of how their words will affect others. Children think life revolves around *them*. They're self-centered. They think they are always right and others are always wrong, even when the evidence declares them guilty.

Paul challenges us to lay aside our childishness and finish the process of becoming adults. A part of maturing is the growing conviction that you are just as responsible for your marriage as your spouse is. Everyone on a team is equally responsible for their part in making the team successful. When you win, you all win; when you lose, you all lose.

Marriage has a way of bringing our selfish habits and immature attitudes to the surface of our lives. As we recognize this, we must put away childish things and grow up. Will you step away from childishness and step up toward mature love? As a couple, how can you each other grow toward maturity today?

second prophets, third teachers, after that miracles, then gifts of healings, helps, administrations, varieties of tongues. ²⁹*Are* all apostles? *Are* all prophets? *Are* all teachers? *Are* all workers of miracles? ³⁰Do all have gifts of healings? Do all speak with tongues? Do all interpret? ³¹But earnestly desire the best[a] gifts. And yet I show you a more excellent way.

The Greatest Gift

13 Though I speak with the tongues of men and of angels, but have not love, I have become sounding brass or a clanging cymbal. ²And though I have *the gift of* prophecy, and understand all mysteries and all knowledge, and though I have all faith, so that I could remove mountains, but have not love, I am nothing. ³And though I bestow all my goods to feed *the poor,* and though I give my body to be burned,[a] but have not love, it profits me nothing.

⁴Love suffers long *and* is kind; love does not envy; love does not parade itself, is not puffed up; ⁵does not behave rudely, does not seek its own, is not provoked, thinks no evil; ⁶does not rejoice in iniquity, but rejoices in the truth; ⁷bears all things, believes all things, hopes all things, endures all things.

⁸Love never fails. But whether *there are* prophecies, they will fail; whether *there are* tongues, they will cease; whether *there is* knowledge, it will vanish away. ⁹For we know in part and we prophesy in part. ¹⁰But when that which is perfect has come, then that which is in part will be done away. ¹¹When I was a child, I spoke as a child, I understood as a child, I thought as a child; but when I became a man, I put away childish things. ¹²For now we see in a mirror, dimly, but then face to face. Now I know in part, but then I shall know just as I also am known.

¹³And now abide faith, hope, love, these three; but the greatest of these *is* love.

Prophecy and Tongues

14 Pursue love, and desire spiritual *gifts,* but especially that you may prophesy. ²For he who speaks in a tongue does not speak to men but to God, for no one understands *him;* however, in the spirit he speaks mysteries. ³But he who prophesies speaks edification and exhortation and comfort to men. ⁴He who speaks in a tongue edifies himself, but he who prophesies edifies the church. ⁵I wish you all

12:31 ᵃNU-Text reads *greater.*
13:3 ᵃNU-Text reads *so I may boast.*

spoke with tongues, but even more that you prophesied; for[a] he who prophesies *is* greater than he who speaks with tongues, unless indeed he interprets, that the church may receive edification.

Tongues Must Be Interpreted

[6]But now, brethren, if I come to you speaking with tongues, what shall I profit you unless I speak to you either by revelation, by knowledge, by prophesying, or by teaching? [7]Even things without life, whether flute or harp, when they make a sound, unless they make a distinction in the sounds, how will it be known what is piped or played? [8]For if the trumpet makes an uncertain sound, who will prepare for battle? [9]So likewise you, unless you utter by the tongue words easy to understand, how will it be known what is spoken? For you will be speaking into the air. [10]There are, it may be, so many kinds of languages in the world, and none of them *is* without significance. [11]Therefore, if I do not know the meaning of the language, I shall be a foreigner to him who speaks, and he who speaks *will be* a foreigner to me. [12]Even so you, since you are zealous for spiritual *gifts, let it be* for the edification of the church *that* you seek to excel.

[13]Therefore let him who speaks in a tongue pray that he may interpret. [14]For if I pray in a tongue, my spirit prays, but my understanding is unfruitful. [15]What is *the conclusion* then? I will pray with the spirit, and I will also pray with the understanding. I will sing with the spirit, and I will also sing with the understanding. [16]Otherwise, if you bless with the spirit, how will he who occupies the place of the uninformed say "Amen" at your giving of thanks, since he does not understand what you say? [17]For you indeed give thanks well, but the other is not edified.

[18]I thank my God I speak with tongues more than you all; [19]yet in the church I would rather speak five words with my understanding, that I may teach others also, than ten thousand words in a tongue.

Tongues a Sign to Unbelievers

[20]Brethren, do not be children in understanding; however, in malice be babes, but in understanding be mature. [21]In the law it is written:

"With men of other tongues and other lips
I will speak to this people;
And yet, for all that, they will not hear Me,"[a]

says the Lord. [22]Therefore tongues are for a sign, not to those who believe but to unbelievers; but prophesying is not for unbelievers but for those who believe. [23]Therefore if the whole church comes together in one place, and all speak with tongues, and there come in *those who are* uninformed or unbelievers, will they not say that you are out of your mind? [24]But if all prophesy, and an unbeliever or an uninformed person comes in, he is convinced by all, he is convicted by all. [25]And thus[a] the secrets of his heart are revealed; and so, falling down on *his* face, he will worship God and report that God is truly among you.

Order in Church Meetings

[26]How is it then, brethren? Whenever you come together, each of you has a psalm, has a teaching, has a tongue, has a revelation, has an interpretation. Let all things be done for edification. [27]If anyone speaks in a tongue, *let there be* two or at the most three, *each* in turn, and let one interpret. [28]But if there is no interpreter, let him keep silent in church, and let him speak to himself and to God. [29]Let two or three prophets speak, and let the others judge. [30]But if *anything* is revealed to another who sits by, let the first keep silent. [31]For you can all prophesy one by one, that all may learn and all may be encouraged. [32]And the spirits of the prophets are subject to the prophets. [33]For God is not *the author* of confusion but of peace, as in all the churches of the saints.

[34]Let your[a] women keep silent in the churches, for they are not permitted to speak; but *they are* to be submissive, as the

14:5 [a]NU-Text reads *and.* 14:21 [a]Isaiah 28:11, 12
14:25 [a]NU-Text omits *And thus.*
14:34 [a]NU-Text omits *your.*

law also says. 35And if they want to learn something, let them ask their own husbands at home; for it is shameful for women to speak in church.

36Or did the word of God come *originally* from you? Or *was it* you only that it reached? 37If anyone thinks himself to be a prophet or spiritual, let him acknowledge that the things which I write to you are the commandments of the Lord. 38But if anyone is ignorant, let him be ignorant. a

39Therefore, brethren, desire earnestly to prophesy, and do not forbid to speak with tongues. 40Let all things be done decently and in order.

The Risen Christ, Faith's Reality

15 Moreover, brethren, I declare to you the gospel which I preached to you, which also you received and in which you stand, 2by which also you are saved, if you hold fast that word which I preached to you—unless you believed in vain.

3For I delivered to you first of all that which I also received: that Christ died for our sins according to the Scriptures, 4and that He was buried, and that He rose again the third day according to the Scriptures, 5and that He was seen by Cephas, then by the twelve. 6After that He was seen by over five hundred brethren at once, of whom the greater part remain to the present, but some have fallen asleep. 7After that He was seen by James, then by all the apostles. 8Then last of all He was seen by me also, as by one born out of due time.

9For I am the least of the apostles, who am not worthy to be called an apostle, because I persecuted the church of God. 10But by the grace of God I am what I am, and His grace toward me was not in vain; but I labored more abundantly than they all, yet not I, but the grace of God *which was* with me. 11Therefore, whether *it was* I or they, so we preach and so you believed.

The Risen Christ, Our Hope

12Now if Christ is preached that He has been raised from the dead, how do some

14:38 aNU-Text reads *if anyone does not recognize this, he is not recognized.*

PARENTING MATTERS

Q: *What should we tell our preteens about sex and about how to remain pure?*

We encourage parents to begin telling their children about some aspects of sex at an early age. By age ten, they should know the basics of how a child is created, and they should know about topics such as modest dress, obscene language, and the temptations they will face with media.

The preadolescent years are a key time to review all this information and talk about the issues and temptations they will soon face as teenagers—the emotional, physical, and relational changes, principles for dating, how to treat the opposite sex, and more.

One of the best things you can do is schedule a special father-son or mother-daughter weekend before your children enter adolescence. When I did this with each of our girls, I took some tapes and other resources to help initiate conversation about sexual development. The materials made it easier to begin talking.

One big topic for the weekend was how their bodies were about to change. Most girls begin menstruating between 11 and 13, but sometimes it happens earlier. If you have a nine- or ten-year-old daughter who begins developing physically, be sure to have this talk as soon as possible. Tens of thousands of parents have done this using a resource we helped develop called *Passport to Purity*. You can find out more about this resource at www.familylife.com.

among you say that there is no resurrection of the dead? [13]But if there is no resurrection of the dead, then Christ is not risen. [14]And if Christ is not risen, then our preaching *is* empty and your faith *is* also empty. [15]Yes, and we are found false witnesses of God, because we have testified of God that He raised up Christ, whom He did not raise up—if in fact the dead do not rise. [16]For if *the* dead do not rise, then Christ is not risen. [17]And if Christ is not risen, your faith *is* futile; you are still in your sins! [18]Then also those who have fallen asleep in Christ have perished. [19]If in this life only we have hope in Christ, we are of all men the most pitiable.

The Last Enemy Destroyed

[20]But now Christ is risen from the dead, *and* has become the firstfruits of those who have fallen asleep. [21]For since by man *came* death, by Man also *came* the resurrection of the dead. [22]For as in Adam all die, even so in Christ all shall be made alive. [23]But each one in his own order: Christ the firstfruits, afterward those *who are* Christ's at His coming. [24]Then *comes* the end, when He delivers the kingdom to God the Father, when He puts an end to all rule and all authority and power. [25]For He must reign till He has put all enemies under His feet. [26]The last enemy *that* will be destroyed *is* death. [27]For *"He has put all things under His feet."*[a] But when He says "all things are put under *Him,*" *it is* evident that He who put all things under Him is excepted. [28]Now when all things are made subject to Him, then the Son Himself will also be subject to Him who put all things under Him, that God may be all in all.

Effects of Denying the Resurrection

[29]Otherwise, what will they do who are baptized for the dead, if the dead do not rise at all? Why then are they baptized for the dead? [30]And why do we stand in jeopardy every hour? [31]I affirm, by the boasting in you which I have in Christ Jesus our Lord, I die daily. [32]If, in the manner of men, I have fought with beasts at Ephesus, what advantage *is it* to me? If *the* dead do not rise, *"Let us eat and drink, for tomorrow we die!"*[a]

[33]Do not be deceived: "Evil company corrupts good habits." [34]Awake to righteousness, and do not sin; for some do not have the knowledge of God. I speak *this* to your shame.

A Glorious Body

[35]But someone will say, "How are the dead raised up? And with what body do they come?" [36]Foolish one, what you sow is not made alive unless it dies. [37]And what you sow, you do not sow that body that shall be, but mere grain—perhaps wheat or some other *grain.* [38]But God gives it a body as He pleases, and to each seed its own body.

[39]All flesh *is* not the same flesh, but *there is* one *kind of* flesh[a] of men, another flesh of animals, another of fish, *and* another of birds.

[40]*There are* also celestial bodies and terrestrial bodies; but the glory of the celestial *is* one, and the *glory* of the terrestrial *is* another. [41]*There is* one glory of the sun, another glory of the moon, and another glory of the stars; for *one* star differs from *another* star in glory.

[42]So also *is* the resurrection of the dead. *The body* is sown in corruption, it is raised in incorruption. [43]It is sown in dishonor, it is raised in glory. It is sown in weakness, it is raised in power. [44]It is sown a natural body, it is raised a spiritual body. There is a natural body, and there is a spiritual body. [45]And so it is written, *"The first man Adam became a living being."*[a] The last Adam *became* a life-giving spirit.

[46]However, the spiritual is not first, but the natural, and afterward the spiritual. [47]The first man *was* of the earth, *made* of dust; the second Man *is* the Lord[a] from heaven. [48]As *was* the *man* of dust, so also *are* those *who are made* of dust; and as *is* the heavenly *Man,* so also *are* those *who are* heavenly. [49]And as we have borne the image of the *man* of dust, we shall also bear[a] the image of the heavenly *Man.*

15:27 [a]Psalm 8:6 **15:32** [a]Isaiah 22:13
15:39 [a]NU-Text and M-Text omit *of flesh.*
15:45 [a]Genesis 2:7 **15:47** [a]NU-Text omits *the Lord.*
15:49 [a]M-Text reads *let us also bear.*

Our Final Victory

[50]Now this I say, brethren, that flesh and blood cannot inherit the kingdom of God; nor does corruption inherit incorruption. [51]Behold, I tell you a mystery: We shall not all sleep, but we shall all be changed— [52]in a moment, in the twinkling of an eye, at the last trumpet. For the trumpet will sound, and the dead will be raised incorruptible, and we shall be changed. [53]For this corruptible must put on incorruption, and this mortal *must* put on immortality. [54]So when this corruptible has put on incorruption, and this mortal has put on immortality, then shall be brought to pass the saying that is written: *"Death is swallowed up in victory."*[a]

[55]   *"O Death, where is your sting?*[a]
     O Hades, where is your victory?"[b]

[56]The sting of death *is* sin, and the strength of sin *is* the law. [57]But thanks *be* to God, who gives us the victory through our Lord Jesus Christ.

[58]Therefore, my beloved brethren, be steadfast, immovable, always abounding in the work of the Lord, knowing that your labor is not in vain in the Lord.

Collection for the Saints

16 Now concerning the collection for the saints, as I have given orders to the churches of Galatia, so you must do also: [2]On the first *day* of the week let each one of you lay something aside, storing up as he may prosper, that there be no collections when I come. [3]And when I come, whomever you approve by *your* letters I will send to bear your gift to Jerusalem. [4]But if it is fitting that I go also, they will go with me.

Personal Plans

[5]Now I will come to you when I pass through Macedonia (for I am passing through Macedonia). [6]And it may be that I will remain, or even spend the winter with you, that you may send me on my journey, wherever I go. [7]For I do not wish to see you now on the way; but I hope to stay a while with you, if the Lord permits.

[8]But I will tarry in Ephesus until Pentecost. [9]For a great and effective door has opened to me, and *there are* many adversaries.

[10]And if Timothy comes, see that he may be with you without fear; for he does the work of the Lord, as I also *do*. [11]Therefore let no one despise him. But send him on his journey in peace, that he may come to me; for I am waiting for him with the brethren.

[12]Now concerning *our* brother Apollos, I strongly urged him to come to you with the brethren, but he was quite unwilling to come at this time; however, he will come when he has a convenient time.

Final Exhortations

[13]Watch, stand fast in the faith, be brave, be strong. [14]Let all *that* you *do* be done with love.

[15]I urge you, brethren—you know the household of Stephanas, that it is the firstfruits of Achaia, and *that* they have devoted themselves to the ministry of the saints— [16]that you also submit to such, and to everyone who works and labors with *us*.

[17]I am glad about the coming of Stephanas, Fortunatus, and Achaicus, for what was lacking on your part they supplied. [18]For they refreshed my spirit and yours. Therefore acknowledge such men.

Greetings and a Solemn Farewell

[19]The churches of Asia greet you. Aquila and Priscilla greet you heartily in the Lord, with the church that is in their house. [20]All the brethren greet you.

Greet one another with a holy kiss.

[21]The salutation with my own hand— Paul's.

[22]If anyone does not love the Lord Jesus Christ, let him be accursed.[a] O Lord, come![a]

[23]The grace of our Lord Jesus Christ *be* with you. [24]My love *be* with you all in Christ Jesus. Amen.

15:54 [a]Isaiah 25:8   **15:55** [a]Hosea 13:14   [b]NU-Text reads *O Death, where is your victory? O Death, where is your sting?*   **16:22** [a]Greek *anathema*   [b]Aramaic *Maranatha*

2 CORINTHIANS

THE APOSTLE PAUL founded the church in Corinth, ministered there for a year and half, and then faithfully corresponded with the church after he left. So you might think that the believers there would have displayed great affection for their founding pastor.

But while Paul was busy establishing a new church in Ephesus, he had to warn the members of his former church about continuing to fellowship with so-called Christians who lived in open sin. Although that letter no longer exists, Paul makes a reference to it in his first epistle to them (1 Cor. 5:9). Paul eventually made a return visit to Corinth, where he found his ministry under attack (2:5, 7:12). This visit prompted a third letter, often called "The Severe Letter," in which he rebukes the Corinthians and calls them to repentance (it, too, is lost to us).

So what we call 2 Corinthians is actually Paul's fourth letter to this church, written after Paul has received an encouraging report from Titus about the renewed spiritual condition of the people. He writes this time to reinforce his apostolic credentials and to urge his believing friends to continue to follow his teaching (1—7). He also strongly encourages them to provide financial support for the Jerusalem believers (8; 9). The final four chapters present a fresh warning to turn away from "false apostles" and contain a renewed defense of Paul's ministry.

One important theme in 2 Corinthians concerns our response to trials and hardships. Paul begins the letter by reminding us that suffering can have a redemptive purpose. We are to comfort one another with the comfort we have received from God. Later, Paul reminds his readers that trials in this life are a "light affliction, which is but for a moment, is working for us a far more exceeding and eternal weight of glory" (4:17). And toward the end of the letter, Paul describes the intense physical hardships he has endured in his ministry (11:23–28). Through it all, Paul says, "And He said to me, 'My grace is sufficient for you, for My strength is made perfect in weakness'" (12:9).

This letter brings to mind the words of Jesus, who told us to expect persecution, but who also said, "Be of good cheer, I have overcome the world" (John 16:33).

Greeting

1 Paul, an apostle of Jesus Christ by the will of God, and Timothy *our* brother,

To the church of God which is at Corinth, with all the saints who are in all Achaia:

²Grace to you and peace from God our Father and the Lord Jesus Christ.

Comfort in Suffering

³Blessed *be* the God and Father of our Lord Jesus Christ, the Father of mercies and God of all comfort, ⁴who comforts us in all our tribulation, that we may be able to comfort those who are in any trouble, with the comfort with which we ourselves are comforted by God. ⁵For as the sufferings of Christ abound in us, so our consolation also abounds through Christ. ⁶Now if we are afflicted, *it is* for your consolation and salvation, which is effective for enduring the same sufferings which we also suffer. Or if we are comforted, *it is* for your consolation and salvation. ⁷And our hope for you *is* steadfast, because we know that as you are partakers of the sufferings, so also *you will partake* of the consolation.

Delivered from Suffering

⁸For we do not want you to be ignorant, brethren, of our trouble which came to us in Asia: that we were burdened beyond measure, above strength, so that we despaired even of life. ⁹Yes, we had the sentence of death in ourselves, that we should not trust in ourselves, but in God who raises the dead, ¹⁰who delivered us from so great a death, and does[a] deliver us; in whom we trust that He will still deliver *us,* ¹¹you also helping together in prayer for us, that thanks may be given by many persons on our[a] behalf for the gift *granted* to us through many.

Paul's Sincerity

¹²For our boasting is this: the testimony of our conscience that we conducted ourselves in the world in simplicity and godly sincerity, not with fleshly wisdom but by the grace of God, and more abundantly toward you. ¹³For we are not writing any

other things to you than what you read or understand. Now I trust you will understand, even to the end ¹⁴(as also you have understood us in part), that we are your boast as you also *are* ours, in the day of the Lord Jesus.

Sparing the Church

¹⁵And in this confidence I intended to come to you before, that you might have a second benefit— ¹⁶to pass by way of you to Macedonia, to come again from Macedonia to you, and be helped by you on my way to Judea. ¹⁷Therefore, when I was planning this, did I do it lightly? Or the things I plan, do I plan according to the flesh, that with me there should be Yes, Yes, and No, No? ¹⁸But *as* God *is* faithful, our word to you was not Yes and No. ¹⁹For the Son of God, Jesus Christ, who was preached among you by us—by me, Silvanus, and Timothy—was not Yes and No, but in Him was Yes. ²⁰For all the promises of God in Him *are* Yes, and in Him Amen, to the glory of God through us. ²¹Now He who establishes us with you in Christ and has anointed us *is* God, ²²who also has sealed us and given us the Spirit in our hearts as a guarantee.

²³Moreover I call God as witness against my soul, that to spare you I came no more to Corinth. ²⁴Not that we have dominion over your faith, but are fellow workers for your joy; for by faith you stand.

2 But I determined this within myself, that I would not come again to you in sorrow. ²For if I make you sorrowful, then who is he who makes me glad but the one who is made sorrowful by me?

Forgive the Offender

³And I wrote this very thing to you, lest, when I came, I should have sorrow over those from whom I ought to have joy, having confidence in you all that my joy is *the joy* of you all. ⁴For out of much affliction and anguish of heart I wrote to you, with many tears, not that you should be grieved, but that you might know the love which I have so abundantly for you.

1:10 [a]NU-Text reads *shall.*
1:11 [a]M-Text reads *your behalf.*

⁵But if anyone has caused grief, he has not grieved me, but all of you to some extent—not to be too severe. ⁶This punishment which *was inflicted* by the majority *is* sufficient for such a man, ⁷so that, on the contrary, you *ought* rather to forgive and comfort *him,* lest perhaps such a one be swallowed up with too much sorrow. ⁸Therefore I urge you to reaffirm *your* love to him. ⁹For to this end I also wrote, that I might put you to the test, whether you are obedient in all things. ¹⁰Now whom you forgive anything, I also *forgive.* For if indeed I have forgiven anything, I have forgiven that oneᵃ for your sakes in the presence of Christ, ¹¹lest Satan should take advantage of us; for we are not ignorant of his devices.

Triumph in Christ

¹²Furthermore, when I came to Troas to *preach* Christ's gospel, and a door was opened to me by the Lord, ¹³I had no rest in my spirit, because I did not find Titus my brother; but taking my leave of them, I departed for Macedonia.

¹⁴Now thanks *be* to God who always leads us in triumph in Christ, and through us diffuses the fragrance of His knowledge in every place. ¹⁵For we are to God the fragrance of Christ among those who are being saved and among those who are perishing. ¹⁶To the one *we are* the aroma of death *leading* to death, and to the other the aroma of life *leading* to life. And who *is* sufficient for these things? ¹⁷For we are not, as so many,ᵃ peddling the word of God; but as of sincerity, but as from God, we speak in the sight of God in Christ.

Christ's Epistle

3 Do we begin again to commend ourselves? Or do we need, as some *others,* epistles of commendation to you or *letters* of commendation from you? ²You are our epistle written in our hearts, known and read by all men; ³clearly you are an epistle of Christ, ministered by us, written not with ink but by the Spirit of the living

Go for Transparency

MANY PEOPLE SPEND TREMENDOUS amounts of time and energy hiding their insecurities. They fear that if someone finds out who they really are, they will be rejected. Too many wives and husbands are afraid to be honest with each other.

The Scriptures, however, emphasize the importance of being open and vulnerable. Paul modeled transparency when he wrote to the Corinthians, many of whom were not exactly his admirers, "For out of much affliction and anguish of heart I wrote to you, with many tears, not that you should be grieved, but that you might know the love which I have so abundantly for you" (2 Cor. 2:4).

At the same time, Scripture warns about being *too* open and honest, "In the multitude of words sin is not lacking, but he who restrains his lips is wise" (Prov. 10:19). The familiar saying about words is false, "Sticks and stones can break my bones, but words can never hurt me." Words *can* hurt. The Bible also tells us, "There is one who speaks like the piercings of a sword, but the tongue of the wise promotes health" (Prov. 12:18).

Many couples could instantly improve their relationships by using gentle, encouraging words full of praise. While your communication as husband and wife should continue to grow in transparency, be careful that you speak the truth in love. Be wise about what you say and what you don't say.

God, not on tablets of stone but on tablets of flesh, *that is,* of the heart.

The Spirit, Not the Letter

⁴And we have such trust through Christ toward God. ⁵Not that we are sufficient of ourselves to think of anything as *being* from ourselves, but our sufficiency *is* from God, ⁶who also made us sufficient as ministers of the new covenant, not of the letter

---

2:10 ᵃNU-Text reads *For indeed, what I have forgiven, if I have forgiven anything, I did it.*
2:17 ᵃM-Text reads *the rest.*

DEVOTIONS FOR COUPLES • 2:11
Defeat the Enemy's Schemes

Our marriages are at ground zero of a very real spiritual war. That fact alone should compel us to join hands with our spouses and pray.

One of the key phrases of the Lord's Prayer is "deliver us from the evil one" (Matt. 6:13). Yes, evil is real and we must not be naive about the opposition we face. Paul was serious when he said, "Put on the whole armor of God, that you may be able to stand against the wiles of the devil" (Eph. 6:11). He gave this counsel "Lest Satan should take advantage of us; for we are not ignorant of his devices" (2 Cor. 2:11).

Fortunately, we possess a potent weapon against Satan and his schemes: praying together regularly. Because Satan understands the power unleashed when two become one and join forces to call upon God, he will strategize to keep you from praying together. He wants to divide you, isolate you from one another, and have you thinking unkind thoughts about your spouse.

Many followers of Christ underestimate the unseen battle that is being fought around them. If you are trying to live for Christ, if you are trying to honor God in your marriage and family, or if you are trying to raise children who will be God's messengers to their generation, then listen carefully: You *are* in a spiritual battle. Do not underestimate the wily enemy who wants to destroy you and your legacy.

We encourage you to be on guard against your spiritual adversary's schemes, especially when you are:

Alone and away from home. Temptation seems particularly tempting when no one else is looking.

Alone and at home. The lure of pornography on the internet is more enticing late at night when no one else in the house is awake.

Hanging out with the wrong company. If the enemy can't get us when we're alone, he may try to bring along the influence of someone already caught up in his web.

Fatigued. When we're worn out and weary, the enticements of the world can look very appealing.

Proud and arrogant. When we think life is going our way and that we don't need to pray, we can be sure that Satan has us in his sights.

So what is the answer? Stay alert, pray, and resist. Paul tells us to pray "always with all prayer and supplication in the Spirit ... with all perseverance and supplication for all the saints" (Eph. 6:18). And James gives us this command and promise, "Resist the devil and he will flee from you" (4:7).

To stay alert and resist Stan's evil schemes, faithfully pray together, communicate openly with each other about new challenges that arise, and help each other steer clear of situations that could make either of you more vulnerable to your spiritual adversary's schemes.

---

but of the Spirit;[a] for the letter kills, but the Spirit gives life.

Glory of the New Covenant

7But if the ministry of death, written *and* engraved on stones, was glorious, so that the children of Israel could not look steadily at the face of Moses because of the glory of his countenance, which *glory* was passing away, 8how will the ministry of the Spirit not be more glorious? 9For if the ministry of condemnation *had* glory, the ministry of righteousness exceeds much more in glory. 10For even what was made glorious had no glory in this respect, because of the glory that excels. 11For if what is passing away *was* glorious, what remains *is* much more glorious.

12Therefore, since we have such hope, we use great boldness of speech— 13unlike Moses, *who* put a veil over his face so that the children of Israel could not look steadily at the end of what was passing away. 14But

3:6 aOr *spirit*

their minds were blinded. For until this day the same veil remains unlifted in the reading of the Old Testament, because the *veil* is taken away in Christ. [15]But even to this day, when Moses is read, a veil lies on their heart. [16]Nevertheless when one turns to the Lord, the veil is taken away. [17]Now the Lord is the Spirit; and where the Spirit of the Lord *is,* there *is* liberty. [18]But we all, with unveiled face, beholding as in a mirror the glory of the Lord, are being transformed into the same image from glory to glory, just as by the Spirit of the Lord.

The Light of Christ's Gospel

4 Therefore, since we have this ministry, as we have received mercy, we do not lose heart. [2]But we have renounced the hidden things of shame, not walking in craftiness nor handling the word of God deceitfully, but by manifestation of the truth commending ourselves to every man's conscience in the sight of God. [3]But even if our gospel is veiled, it is veiled to those who are perishing, [4]whose minds the god of this age has blinded, who do not believe, lest the light of the gospel of the glory of Christ, who is the image of God, should shine on them. [5]For we do not preach ourselves, but Christ Jesus the Lord, and ourselves your bondservants for Jesus' sake. [6]For it is the God who commanded light to shine out of darkness, who has shone in our hearts to *give* the light of the knowledge of the glory of God in the face of Jesus Christ.

Cast Down but Unconquered

[7]But we have this treasure in earthen vessels, that the excellence of the power may be of God and not of us. [8]*We are* hard-pressed on every side, yet not crushed; *we are* perplexed, but not in despair; [9]persecuted, but not forsaken; struck down, but not destroyed— [10]always carrying about in the body the dying of the Lord Jesus, that the life of Jesus also may be manifested in our body. [11]For we who live are always delivered to death for Jesus' sake, that the life of Jesus also may be manifested in our mortal flesh. [12]So then death is working in us, but life in you.

[13]And since we have the same spirit of faith, according to what is written, *"I believed and therefore I spoke,"*[a] we also believe and therefore speak, [14]knowing that He who raised up the Lord Jesus will also raise us up with Jesus, and will present *us* with you. [15]For all things *are* for your sakes, that grace, having spread through the many, may cause thanksgiving to abound to the glory of God.

Seeing the Invisible

[16]Therefore we do not lose heart. Even though our outward man is perishing, yet the inward *man* is being renewed day by day. [17]For our light affliction, which is but for a moment, is working for us a far more exceeding *and* eternal weight of glory, [18]while we do not look at the things which are seen, but at the things which are not seen. For the things which are seen *are* temporary, but the things which are not seen *are* eternal.

INTIMATE MOMENTS

Go for a walk after dinner holding hands and ask her three questions:
　What happened today?
　What challenges are you facing that I can pray for?
　What are your dreams for the future after the children are gone?
　Just listen and tell her you heard her.

Assurance of the Resurrection

5 For we know that if our earthly house, *this* tent, is destroyed, we have a building from God, a house not made with hands, eternal in the heavens. [2]For in this we groan, earnestly desiring to be clothed with our habitation which is from heaven, [3]if indeed, having been clothed, we shall not be found naked. [4]For we who are in *this* tent groan, being burdened, not because we want to be unclothed, but further clothed, that mortality may be swallowed up by life. [5]Now He who has prepared us for this

very thing *is* God, who also has given us the Spirit as a guarantee.

6So *we are* always confident, knowing that while we are at home in the body we are absent from the Lord. 7For we walk by faith, not by sight. 8We are confident, yes, well pleased rather to be absent from the body and to be present with the Lord.

The Judgment Seat of Christ

9Therefore we make it our aim, whether present or absent, to be well pleasing to Him. 10For we must all appear before the judgment seat of Christ, that each one may receive the things *done* in the body, according to what he has done, whether good or bad. 11Knowing, therefore, the terror of the Lord, we persuade men; but we are well known to God, and I also trust are well known in your consciences.

Be Reconciled to God

12For we do not commend ourselves again to you, but give you opportunity to boast on our behalf, that you may have *an answer* for those who boast in appearance and not in heart. 13For if we are beside ourselves, *it is* for God; or if we are of sound mind, *it is* for you. 14For the love of Christ compels us, because we judge thus: that if One died for all, then all died; 15and He died for all, that those who live should live no longer for themselves, but for Him who died for them and rose again.

16Therefore, from now on, we regard no one according to the flesh. Even though we have known Christ according to the flesh, yet now we know *Him thus* no longer. 17Therefore, if anyone *is* in Christ, *he is* a new creation; old things have passed away; behold, all things have become new. 18Now all things *are* of God, who has reconciled us to Himself through Jesus Christ, and has given us the ministry of reconciliation, 19that is, that God was in Christ reconciling the world to Himself, not imputing their trespasses to them, and has committed to us the word of reconciliation.

20Now then, we are ambassadors for Christ, as though God were pleading through us: we implore *you* on Christ's behalf, be reconciled to God. 21For He made Him who knew no sin *to be* sin for us, that we might become the righteousness of God in Him.

Marks of the Ministry

6 We then, *as* workers together *with Him* also plead with *you* not to receive the grace of God in vain. 2For He says:

"*In an acceptable time I have heard you,
And in the day of salvation I have helped you.*"a

Behold, now *is* the accepted time; behold, now *is* the day of salvation.

3We give no offense in anything, that our ministry may not be blamed. 4But in all *things* we commend ourselves as ministers of God: in much patience, in tribulations, in needs, in distresses, 5in stripes, in imprisonments, in tumults, in labors, in sleeplessness, in fastings; 6by purity, by knowledge, by longsuffering, by kindness, by the Holy Spirit, by sincere love, 7by the word of truth, by the power of God, by the armor of righteousness on the right hand and on the left, 8by honor and dishonor, by evil report and good report; as deceivers, and *yet* true; 9as unknown, and *yet* well known; as dying, and behold we live; as chastened, and *yet* not killed; 10as sorrowful, yet always rejoicing; as poor, yet making many rich; as having nothing, and *yet* possessing all things.

Be Holy

11O Corinthians! We have spoken openly to you, our heart is wide open. 12You are not restricted by us, but you are restricted by your *own* affections. 13Now in return for the same (I speak as to children), you also be open.

14Do not be unequally yoked together with unbelievers. For what fellowship has righteousness with lawlessness? And what communion has light with darkness? 15And what accord has Christ with Belial? Or what part has a believer with an unbeliever? 16And what agreement has the temple

---

6:2 aIsaiah 49:8

of God with idols? For you[a] are the temple of the living God. As God has said:

> "I will dwell in them
> And walk among them.
> I will be their God,
> And they shall be My people."[b]

[17]Therefore

> "Come out from among them
> And be separate, says the Lord.
> Do not touch what is unclean,
> And I will receive you."[a]

[18] "I will be a Father to you,
> And you shall be My sons and
>   daughters,
> Says the LORD Almighty."[a]

7 Therefore, having these promises, beloved, let us cleanse ourselves from all filthiness of the flesh and spirit, perfecting holiness in the fear of God.

The Corinthians' Repentance

[2]Open *your hearts* to us. We have wronged no one, we have corrupted no one, we have cheated no one. [3]I do not say *this* to condemn; for I have said before that you are in our hearts, to die together and to live together. [4]Great *is* my boldness of speech toward you, great *is* my boasting on your behalf. I am filled with comfort. I am exceedingly joyful in all our tribulation.

[5]For indeed, when we came to Macedonia, our bodies had no rest, but we were troubled on every side. Outside *were* conflicts, inside *were* fears. [6]Nevertheless God, who comforts the downcast, comforted us by the coming of Titus, [7]and not only by his coming, but also by the consolation with which he was comforted in you, when he told us of your earnest desire, your mourning, your zeal for me, so that I rejoiced even more.

[8]For even if I made you sorry with my letter, I do not regret it; though I did regret it. For I perceive that the same epistle made you sorry, though only for a while. [9]Now I rejoice, not that you were made sorry, but that your sorrow led to repentance. For you

BIBLICAL INSIGHTS • 6:2

Seize the Moment

TEACHABLE MOMENTS provide us with opportunities to imprint God's values and pass on His agenda to the next generation. It's important to be alert to teachable moments, to listen carefully, to stop and respond immediately, and to gently share the truth when an opportune time arrives. If your child isn't ready for the truth you want to impart, your efforts will likely be in vain.

Paul writes, "'In an acceptabale time I have heard you, and in the day of salvation I have helped you.' Behold, now is the accepted time; behold, now is the day of salvation" (2 Cor. 6:2). The Greek word translated "the accepted time" is the term *kairos*, in distinction to *chronos*, which means linear time. God selected just the right time to bring salvation through Christ. And so He gives us *kairos* moments in the family, special times that we must seize before they pass.

Can you think of a time in your youth when you learned a spiritual lesson from an adult? I can. I can remember my dad's sixth-grade Sunday School class and my mom's Bible class. I don't recall what they said. I just recall that they taught me the Bible. They were committed to teaching God's truth to me as a young child.

What are the five most important truths you must teach your children? List them. What are a couple of Scriptures, or perhaps your favorite Scripture, that you want to pass on to your children? Pray that God will give you sensitivity to discern the right time and the wisdom to choose the right words at your children's *kairos* moments.

were made sorry in a godly manner, that you might suffer loss from us in nothing. [10]For godly sorrow produces repentance *leading* to salvation, not to be regretted; but the sorrow of the world produces death.

6:16 [a]NU-Text reads *we.* [b]Leviticus 26:12; Jeremiah 32:38; Ezekiel 37:27 6:17 [a]Isaiah 52:11; Ezekiel 20:34, 41 6:18 [a]2 Samuel 7:14

For observe this very thing, that you sorrowed in a godly manner: What diligence it produced in you, *what* clearing *of yourselves, what* indignation, *what* fear, *what* vehement desire, *what* zeal, *what* vindication! In all *things* you proved yourselves to be clear in this matter. ¹²Therefore, although I wrote to you, *I did* not *do it* for the sake of him who had done the wrong, nor for the sake of him who suffered wrong, but that our care for you in the sight of God might appear to you.

The Joy of Titus

¹³Therefore we have been comforted in your comfort. And we rejoiced exceedingly more for the joy of Titus, because his spirit has been refreshed by you all. ¹⁴For if in anything I have boasted to him about you, I am not ashamed. But as we spoke all things to you in truth, even so our boasting to Titus was found true. ¹⁵And his affections are greater for you as he remembers the obedience of you all, how with fear and trembling you received him. ¹⁶Therefore I rejoice that I have confidence in you in everything.

Excel in Giving

8 Moreover, brethren, we make known to you the grace of God bestowed on the churches of Macedonia: ²that in a great trial of affliction the abundance of their joy and their deep poverty abounded in the riches of their liberality. ³For I bear witness that according to *their* ability, yes, and beyond *their* ability, *they were* freely willing, ⁴imploring us with much urgency that we would receiveᵃ the gift and the fellowship of the ministering to the saints. ⁵And not *only* as we had hoped, but they first gave themselves to the Lord, and *then* to us by the will of God. ⁶So we urged Titus, that as he had begun, so he would also complete this grace in you as well. ⁷But as you abound in everything—in faith, in speech, in knowledge, in all diligence, and in your love for us—*see* that you abound in this grace also.

Christ Our Pattern

⁸I speak not by commandment, but I am testing the sincerity of your love by the diligence of others. ⁹For you know the grace of our Lord Jesus Christ, that though He was rich, yet for your sakes He became poor, that you through His poverty might become rich.

¹⁰And in this I give advice: It is to your advantage not only to be doing what you

---

ROMANCE FAQ

Q: What can I do when I feel overwhelmed in my marriage?

It's easy to feel overwhelmed. When we consider our responsibilities in marriage, family, work, church and extended family, feelings of inadequacy and hopelessness can rise suddenly and envelop us like a fog.

Yet you can keep from being overwhelmed by focusing on Christ, as Paul wrote, "Our sufficiency is from God" (2 Cor. 3:5). Jesus stands ready to guide you along the way. A great poem says:

Lord, I crawled across the barrenness to You with my empty cup
Uncertain of asking for any small drop of refreshment
If only I would have known You better, I would have come running with a bucket.

God wants us to know Him and to come to Him when we are weary. He has promised to give us rest when we trust Him. The Bible contains many wonderful principles and truths, but these principles will remain only stale dogma to you unless you put the person of Jesus Christ at the center of your life.

No matter how inadequate you feel, God is completely able to do what appears impossible. As Paul says, "I can do all things through Christ who strengthens me" (Phil. 4:13). Why not submit to Him today and ask Him to be your sufficiency and your strength?

8:4 ᵃNU-Text and M-Text omit *that we would receive,* thus changing text to *urgency for the favor and fellowship. . . .*

began and were desiring to do a year ago; [11]but now you also must complete the doing *of it;* that as *there was* a readiness to desire *it,* so *there* also *may be* a completion out of what *you* have. [12]For if there is first a willing mind, *it is* accepted according to what one has, *and* not according to what he does not have.

[13]For *I do* not *mean* that others should be eased and you burdened; [14]but by an equality, *that* now at this time your abundance *may supply* their lack, that their abundance also may *supply* your lack— that there may be equality. [15]As it is written, *"He who gathered much had nothing left over, and he who gathered little had no lack."*a

Collection for the Judean Saints

[16]But thanks *be* to God who putsa the same earnest care for you into the heart of Titus. [17]For he not only accepted the exhortation, but being more diligent, he went to you of his own accord. [18]And we have sent with him the brother whose praise *is* in the gospel throughout all the churches, [19]and

not only *that,* but who was also chosen by the churches to travel with us with this gift, which is administered by us to the glory of the Lord Himself and *to show* your ready mind, [20]avoiding this: that anyone should blame us in this lavish gift which is administered by us— [21]providing honorable things, not only in the sight of the Lord, but also in the sight of men.

[22]And we have sent with them our brother whom we have often proved diligent in many things, but now much more diligent, because of the great confidence which *we have* in you. [23]If *anyone inquires* about Titus, *he is* my partner and fellow worker concerning you. Or if our brethren *are inquired about, they are* messengers of the churches, the glory of Christ. [24]Therefore show to them, anda before the churches, the proof of your love and of our boasting on your behalf.

Administering the Gift

9 Now concerning the ministering to the saints, it is superfluous for me to write to you; [2]for I know your willingness, about which I boast of you to the Macedonians, that Achaia was ready a year ago; and your zeal has stirred up the majority. [3]Yet I

8:15 aExodus 16:18 **8:16** aNU-Text reads *has put.*
8:24 aNU-Text and M-Text omit *and.*

| PARENTING MATTERS | **Q: How do we carry on even though one of our children has become a prodigal?** |

1. Since problems with a prodigal develop over time, accept that the response and solution to those problems will take time as well. The Bible does not say how long the prodigal son remained in his rebellion. But it certainly was more than weeks or even months. Pray that resolution and reconciliation will come quickly, but prepare for a long haul, especially if your rebelling child is in the early teens.

2. Don't neglect the important relationships in your life—God, your spouse, your other children, and friends. We've watched in amazement as prodigals have polluted and disrupted every family relationship. They have a way of bringing out the worst in everyone. Cling to your spouse like glue.

3. Accept that a crisis with a child, and the pain that goes with it, means that everyone in the family is heading into a period of testing and growth. God uses difficulty to stretch and mold us, and the result is greater maturity. James 1:2–4 says, "Count it all joy when you fall into various trials, knowing that the testing of your faith produces patience. But let patience have its perfect work, that you may be perfect and complete, lacking nothing."

have sent the brethren, lest our boasting of you should be in vain in this respect, that, as I said, you may be ready; [4]lest if *some* Macedonians come with me and find you unprepared, we (not to mention you!) should be ashamed of this confident boasting.[a] [5]Therefore I thought it necessary to exhort the brethren to go to you ahead of time, and prepare your generous gift beforehand, which *you had* previously promised, that it may be ready as *a matter of* generosity and not as a grudging obligation.

The Cheerful Giver

[6]But this *I say:* He who sows sparingly will also reap sparingly, and he who sows bountifully will also reap bountifully. [7]*So let* each one *give* as he purposes in his heart, not grudgingly or of necessity; for God loves a cheerful giver. [8]And God *is* able to make all grace abound toward you, that you, always having all sufficiency in all *things,* may have an abundance for every good work. [9]As it is written:

"He has dispersed abroad,
    He has given to the poor;
    His righteousness endures forever."[a]

[10]Now may[a] He who supplies seed to the sower, and bread for food, supply and multiply the seed you have *sown* and increase the fruits of your righteousness, [11]while *you are* enriched in everything for all liberality, which causes thanksgiving through us to God. [12]For the administration of this service not only supplies the needs of the saints, but also is abounding through many thanksgivings to God, [13]while, through the proof of this ministry, they glorify God for the obedience of your confession to the gospel of Christ, and for *your* liberal sharing with them and all *men,* [14]and by their prayer for you, who long for you because of the exceeding grace of God in you. [15]Thanks *be* to God for His indescribable gift!

The Spiritual War

10 Now I, Paul, myself am pleading with you by the meekness and gentleness of Christ—who in presence *am* lowly among you, but being absent am bold toward you. [2]But I beg *you* that when

I am present I may not be bold with that confidence by which I intend to be bold against some, who think of us as if we walked according to the flesh. [3]For though we walk in the flesh, we do not war according to the flesh. [4]For the weapons of our warfare *are* not carnal but mighty in God for pulling down strongholds, [5]casting down arguments and every high thing that exalts itself against the knowledge of God, bringing every thought into captivity to the obedience of Christ, [6]and being ready to punish all disobedience when your obedience is fulfilled.

Reality of Paul's Authority

[7]Do you look at things according to the outward appearance? If anyone is convinced in himself that he is Christ's, let him again consider this in himself, that just as he *is* Christ's, even so we *are* Christ's.[a] [8]For even if I should boast somewhat more about our authority, which the Lord gave us[a] for edification and not for your destruction, I shall not be ashamed— [9]lest I seem to terrify you by letters. [10]"For *his* letters," they say, "*are* weighty and powerful, but *his* bodily presence *is* weak, and *his* speech contemptible." [11]Let such a person consider this, that what we are in word by letters when we are absent, such *we will* also *be* in deed when we are present.

Limits of Paul's Authority

[12]For we dare not class ourselves or compare ourselves with those who commend themselves. But they, measuring themselves by themselves, and comparing themselves among themselves, are not wise. [13]We, however, will not boast beyond measure, but within the limits of the sphere which God appointed us—a sphere which especially includes you. [14]For we are not overextending ourselves (as though *our authority* did not extend to you), for it was to you that we came with the gospel of Christ; [15]not boasting of things beyond measure, *that is,* in other men's labors, but

---

9:4 [a]NU-Text reads *this confidence.*   9:9 [a]Psalm 112:9
9:10 [a]NU-Text reads *Now He who supplies . . . will supply. . . .*   10:7 [a]NU-Text reads *even as we are.*
10:8 [a]NU-Text omits *us.*

having hope, *that* as your faith is increased, we shall be greatly enlarged by you in our sphere, [16]to preach the gospel in the *regions* beyond you, *and* not to boast in another man's sphere of accomplishment.

[17]But *"he who glories, let him glory in the Lord."*[a] [18]For not he who commends himself is approved, but whom the Lord commends.

Concern for Their Faithfulness

11 Oh, that you would bear with me in a little folly—and indeed you do bear with me. [2]For I am jealous for you with godly jealousy. For I have betrothed you to one husband, that I may present *you* as a chaste virgin to Christ. [3]But I fear, lest somehow, as the serpent deceived Eve by his craftiness, so your minds may be corrupted from the simplicity[a] that is in Christ. [4]For if he who comes preaches another Jesus whom we have not preached, or *if* you receive a different spirit which you have not received, or a different gospel which you have not accepted—you may well put up with it!

Paul and False Apostles

[5]For I consider that I am not at all inferior to the most eminent apostles. [6]Even though *I am* untrained in speech, yet *I am* not in knowledge. But we have been thoroughly manifested[a] among you in all things.

[7]Did I commit sin in humbling myself that you might be exalted, because I preached the gospel of God to you free of charge? [8]I robbed other churches, taking wages *from them* to minister to you. [9]And when I was present with you, and in need, I was a burden to no one, for what I lacked the brethren who came from Macedonia supplied. And in everything I kept myself from being burdensome to you, and so I will keep *myself.* [10]As the truth of Christ is in me, no one shall stop me from this boasting in the regions of Achaia. [11]Why? Because I do not love you? God knows!

[12]But what I do, I will also continue to do, that I may cut off the opportunity from those who desire an opportunity to be regarded just as we are in the things of which they boast. [13]For such *are* false apostles, deceitful workers, transforming themselves into apostles of Christ. [14]And no wonder! For Satan himself transforms himself into an angel of light. [15]Therefore *it is* no great thing if his ministers also transform themselves into ministers of righteousness, whose end will be according to their works.

Reluctant Boasting

[16]I say again, let no one think me a fool. If otherwise, at least receive me as a fool, that I also may boast a little. [17]What I speak, I speak not according to the Lord, but as it were, foolishly, in this confidence of boasting. [18]Seeing that many boast according to the flesh, I also will boast. [19]For you put up with fools gladly, since you *yourselves* are wise! [20]For you put up with it if one brings you into bondage, if one devours *you,* if one takes *from you,* if one exalts himself, if one strikes you on the face. [21]To *our* shame I say that we were too weak for that! But in whatever anyone is bold—I speak foolishly—I am bold also.

INTIMATE MOMENTS

Arrange for you and your spouse to take a day off—and then do something you enjoy together.

Suffering for Christ

[22]Are they Hebrews? So *am* I. Are they Israelites? So *am* I. Are they the seed of Abraham? So *am* I. [23]Are they ministers of Christ?—I speak as a fool—I *am* more: in labors more abundant, in stripes above measure, in prisons more frequently, in deaths often. [24]From the Jews five times I received forty *stripes* minus one. [25]Three times I was beaten with rods; once I was stoned; three times I was shipwrecked; a night and a day I have been in the deep; [26]in journeys often, *in* perils of waters, *in* perils of robbers, *in* perils of *my own*

10:17 [a]Jeremiah 9:24 **11:3** [a]NU-Text adds *and purity.*
11:6 [a]NU-Text omits *been.*

countrymen, *in* perils of the Gentiles, *in* perils in the city, *in* perils in the wilderness, *in* perils in the sea, *in* perils among false brethren; ²⁷in weariness and toil, in sleeplessness often, in hunger and thirst, in fastings often, in cold and nakedness— ²⁸besides the other things, what comes upon me daily: my deep concern for all the churches. ²⁹Who is weak, and I am not weak? Who is made to stumble, and I do not burn *with indignation?*

³⁰If I must boast, I will boast in the things which concern my infirmity. ³¹The God and Father of our Lord Jesus Christ, who is blessed forever, knows that I am not lying. ³²In Damascus the governor, under Aretas the king, was guarding the city of the Damascenes with a garrison, desiring to arrest me; ³³but I was let down in a basket through a window in the wall, and escaped from his hands.

The Vision of Paradise

12 It is doubtless^a not profitable for me to boast. I will come to visions and revelations of the Lord: ²I know a man in Christ who fourteen years ago—whether in the body I do not know, or whether out of the body I do not know, God knows— such a one was caught up to the third heaven. ³And I know such a man— whether in the body or out of the body I do not know, God knows— ⁴how he was caught up into Paradise and heard inexpressible words, which it is not lawful for a man to utter. ⁵Of such a one I will boast; yet of myself I will not boast, except in my infirmities. ⁶For though I might desire to boast, I will not be a fool; for I will speak the truth. But I refrain, lest anyone should think of me above what he sees me *to be* or hears from me.

The Thorn in the Flesh

⁷And lest I should be exalted above measure by the abundance of the revelations, a thorn in the flesh was given to me, a messenger of Satan to buffet me, lest I be exalted above measure. ⁸Concerning this thing I pleaded with the Lord three times that it might depart from me. ⁹And He said to me, "My grace is sufficient for you, for My strength is made perfect in weakness." Therefore most gladly I will rather boast in my infirmities, that the power of Christ may rest upon me. ¹⁰Therefore I take pleasure in infirmities, in reproaches, in needs, in persecutions, in distresses, for Christ's sake. For when I am weak, then I am strong.

Signs of an Apostle

¹¹I have become a fool in boasting;^a you have compelled me. For I ought to have

12:1 ^aNU-Text reads *necessary, though not profitable, to boast.* **12:11** ^aNU-Text omits *in boasting*

ROMANTIC QUOTES AND NOTES
Weak Enough for Grace

It's little wonder that we can have a hard time seeing God's will for our lives. His plan for us is much like a quilt, with an overall pattern made up of hundreds of pieces. Since we lack God's perspective, it shouldn't surprise us to wonder what this or that dark-colored piece is doing in the quilt.

Sometimes we find ourselves going through seasons in marriage that are like one of those pieces whose place in the larger pattern is hard to see. Even the most intimate couples find that it can take time to work through areas of disagreement. But becoming conformed to His will takes time; it's a process. Too often I forget that I'm only human. I often want (and expect) instant maturity. But God says, "My grace is sufficient for you, for My strength is made perfect in weakness" (2 Cor. 12:9). I have discovered that God's grace is designed for people just like me.

So, by faith I affirm that God is the Creative Designer of my life. When He looks at me, He sees an award-winning masterpiece. With that trust, I can rely on His plan, knowing that His grace gives me all I need to conform to His will when the pieces I see are not the pieces I would have chosen.

been commended by you; for in nothing was I behind the most eminent apostles, though I am nothing. ¹²Truly the signs of an apostle were accomplished among you with all perseverance, in signs and wonders and mighty deeds. ¹³For what is it in which you were inferior to other churches, except that I myself was not burdensome to you? Forgive me this wrong!

Love for the Church

¹⁴Now *for* the third time I am ready to come to you. And I will not be burdensome to you; for I do not seek yours, but you. For the children ought not to lay up for the parents, but the parents for the children. ¹⁵And I will very gladly spend and be spent for your souls; though the more abundantly I love you, the less I am loved. ¹⁶But be that *as it may,* I did not burden you. Nevertheless, being crafty, I caught you by cunning! ¹⁷Did I take advantage of you by any of those whom I sent to you? ¹⁸I urged Titus, and sent our brother with *him.* Did Titus take advantage of you? Did we not walk in the same spirit? Did *we* not *walk* in the same steps?

¹⁹Again, do you think[a] that we excuse ourselves to you? We speak before God in Christ. But *we do* all things, beloved, for your edification. ²⁰For I fear lest, when I come, I shall not find you such as I wish, and *that* I shall be found by you such as you do not wish; lest *there be* contentions, jealousies, outbursts of wrath, selfish ambitions, backbitings, whisperings, conceits, tumults; ²¹lest, when I come again, my God will humble me among you, and I shall mourn for many who have sinned before and have not repented of the uncleanness, fornication, and lewdness which they have practiced.

Coming with Authority

13 This *will be* the third *time* I am coming to you. *"By the mouth of two or three witnesses every word shall be established."*[a] ²I have told you before, and foretell as if I were present the second time, and now being absent I write[a] to those who have sinned before, and to all the rest, that if I come again I will not spare— ³since you seek a proof of Christ speaking in me, who is not weak toward you, but mighty in you. ⁴For though He was crucified in weakness, yet He lives by the power of God. For we also are weak in Him, but we shall live with Him by the power of God toward you.

⁵Examine yourselves *as to* whether you are in the faith. Test yourselves. Do you not know yourselves, that Jesus Christ is in you?—unless indeed you are disqualified. ⁶But I trust that you will know that we are not disqualified.

Paul Prefers Gentleness

⁷Now I[a] pray to God that you do no evil, not that we should appear approved, but that you should do what is honorable, though we may seem disqualified. ⁸For we can do nothing against the truth, but for the truth. ⁹For we are glad when we are weak and you are strong. And this also we pray, that you may be made complete. ¹⁰Therefore I write these things being absent, lest being present I should use sharpness, according to the authority which the Lord has given me for edification and not for destruction.

Greetings and Benediction

¹¹Finally, brethren, farewell. Become complete. Be of good comfort, be of one mind, live in peace; and the God of love and peace will be with you.

¹²Greet one another with a holy kiss.

¹³All the saints greet you.

¹⁴The grace of the Lord Jesus Christ, and the love of God, and the communion of the Holy Spirit *be* with you all. Amen.

12:19 [a]NU-Text reads *You have been thinking for a long time....* **13:1** [a]Deuteronomy 19:15 **13:2** [a]NU-Text omits *I write.* **13:7** [a]NU-Text reads *we.*

GALATIANS

IN ESSENCE, THE WORLD HAS ONLY TWO RELIGIONS. There is the religion of human achievement that says a man must do something for God to accept him; and there is Christianity, which says that no matter how hard a man tries, he can't please God.

The gospel declares that we can be accepted by God *only* because Jesus paid for our sin on the cross. It is only because of God's grace that anyone is saved.

That's the message the apostle Paul brought on his first missionary journey to the churches in the central part of Asia Minor. After he left, however, other teachers (known as Judaizers) came into the region and insisted the new converts had to add Jewish law-keeping to their faith in Christ for God to accept them. Paul wrote this letter to warn the Galatians that Christianity and Jewish law-keeping can't be mixed. Once any kind of human effort gets added to the grace of God for salvation, it becomes another gospel and is to be rejected (1:9).

Paul defends the idea of justification by grace through faith alone in the first four chapters of this book. The last two chapters show us what a life transformed by the grace of God looks like. Paul reminds his readers that their freedom in Christ is no excuse for self indulgence or sin, but for loving service to others (5:13). Paul contrasts the person controlled by his own selfish desires ("the flesh") with the person whose life is controlled by God's Spirit (5:19–26). Learning to walk in the Spirit is essential for couples to experience a healthy, harmonious, God-honoring marriage.

This letter also gives us instruction on how to restore someone who has fallen into sin (6:1, 2). Parents and spouses should regularly review these verses. We also find an important warning to take sin seriously, "Do not be deceived, God is not mocked; for whatever a man sows, that he will also reap" (6:7). Last, parents will need to remind one another of the charge in 6:9 not to grow weary as they raise their children. In due season, we will reap—if we do not lose heart.

Greeting

1 Paul, an apostle (not from men nor through man, but through Jesus Christ and God the Father who raised Him from the dead), [2]and all the brethren who are with me,

To the churches of Galatia:

[3]Grace to you and peace from God the Father and our Lord Jesus Christ, [4]who gave Himself for our sins, that He might deliver us from this present evil age, according to the will of our God and Father, [5]to whom *be* glory forever and ever. Amen.

Only One Gospel

[6]I marvel that you are turning away so soon from Him who called you in the grace of Christ, to a different gospel, [7]which is not another; but there are some who trouble you and want to pervert the gospel of Christ. [8]But even if we, or an angel from heaven, preach any other gospel to you than what we have preached to you, let him be accursed. [9]As we have said before, so now I say again, if anyone preaches any other gospel to you than what you have received, let him be accursed.

[10]For do I now persuade men, or God? Or do I seek to please men? For if I still pleased men, I would not be a bondservant of Christ.

Call to Apostleship

[11]But I make known to you, brethren, that the gospel which was preached by me is not according to man. [12]For I neither received it from man, nor was I taught *it,* but *it came* through the revelation of Jesus Christ.

[13]For you have heard of my former conduct in Judaism, how I persecuted the church of God beyond measure and *tried to* destroy it. [14]And I advanced in Judaism beyond many of my contemporaries in my own nation, being more exceedingly zealous for the traditions of my fathers.

[15]But when it pleased God, who separated me from my mother's womb and called *me* through His grace, [16]to reveal

His Son in me, that I might preach Him among the Gentiles, I did not immediately confer with flesh and blood, [17]nor did I go up to Jerusalem to those *who were* apostles before me; but I went to Arabia, and returned again to Damascus.

Contacts at Jerusalem

[18]Then after three years I went up to Jerusalem to see Peter,[a] and remained with him fifteen days. [19]But I saw none of the other apostles except James, the Lord's brother. [20](Now *concerning* the things which I write to you, indeed, before God, I do not lie.)

[21]Afterward I went into the regions of Syria and Cilicia. [22]And I was unknown by face to the churches of Judea which *were* in Christ. [23]But they were hearing only, "He who formerly persecuted us now preaches the faith which he once *tried to* destroy." [24]And they glorified God in me.

INTIMATE MOMENTS

On February 2, sleep in, have breakfast in bed, and watch the Groundhog Day prediction together. If the groundhog sees his shadow, unveil your six-week plan for staying warm.

Write down anniversaries, special days, sizes, etc.

Defending the Gospel

2 Then after fourteen years I went up again to Jerusalem with Barnabas, and also took Titus with *me.* [2]And I went up by revelation, and communicated to them that gospel which I preach among the Gentiles, but privately to those who were of reputation, lest by any means I might run, or had run, in vain. [3]Yet not even Titus who *was* with me, being a Greek, was compelled to be circumcised. [4]And *this occurred* because of false brethren secretly brought in (who came in by stealth to spy out our liberty which we have in Christ Jesus, that they might bring us into bondage), [5]to whom we did not yield submission even for an

---

1:18 [a]NU-Text reads *Cephas.*

hour, that the truth of the gospel might continue with you.

⁶But from those who seemed to be something—whatever they were, it makes no difference to me; God shows personal favoritism to no man—for those who seemed *to be something* added nothing to me. ⁷But on the contrary, when they saw that the gospel for the uncircumcised had been committed to me, as *the gospel* for the circumcised *was* to Peter ⁸(for He who worked effectively in Peter for the apostleship to the circumcised also worked effectively in me toward the Gentiles), ⁹and when James, Cephas, and John, who seemed to be pillars, perceived the grace that had been given to me, they gave me and Barnabas the right hand of fellowship, that we *should go* to the Gentiles and they to the circumcised. ¹⁰*They desired* only that we should remember the poor, the very thing which I also was eager to do.

INTIMATE MOMENTS

Play a board game or card game you both enjoy.

No Return to the Law

¹¹Now when Peterᵃ had come to Antioch, I withstood him to his face, because he was to be blamed; ¹²for before certain men came from James, he would eat with the Gentiles; but when they came, he withdrew and separated himself, fearing those who were of the circumcision. ¹³And the rest of the Jews also played the hypocrite with him, so that even Barnabas was carried away with their hypocrisy. ¹⁴But when I saw that they were not straightforward about the truth of the gospel, I said to Peter before *them* all, "If you, being a Jew, live in the manner of Gentiles and not as the Jews, why do youᵃ compel Gentiles to live as Jews?ᵇ ¹⁵We *who are* Jews by nature, and not sinners of the Gentiles, ¹⁶knowing that a man is

not justified by the works of the law but by faith in Jesus Christ, even we have believed in Christ Jesus, that we might be justified by faith in Christ and not by the works of the law; for by the works of the law no flesh shall be justified.

¹⁷"But if, while we seek to be justified by Christ, we ourselves also are found sinners, *is* Christ therefore a minister of sin? Certainly not! ¹⁸For if I build again those things which I destroyed, I make myself a transgressor. ¹⁹For I through the law died to the law that I might live to God. ²⁰I have been crucified with Christ; it is no longer I who live, but Christ lives in me; and the *life* which I now live in the flesh I live by faith in the Son of God, who loved me and gave Himself for me. ²¹I do not set aside the grace of God; for if righteousness *comes* through the law, then Christ died in vain."

Justification by Faith

3 O foolish Galatians! Who has bewitched you that you should not obey the truth,ᵃ before whose eyes Jesus Christ was clearly portrayed among youᵇ as crucified? ²This only I want to learn from you: Did you receive the Spirit by the works of the law, or by the hearing of faith? ³Are you so foolish? Having begun in the Spirit, are you now being made perfect by the flesh? ⁴Have you suffered so many things in vain—if indeed *it was* in vain?

⁵Therefore He who supplies the Spirit to you and works miracles among you, *does He do it* by the works of the law, or by the hearing of faith?— ⁶just as Abraham *"believed God, and it was accounted to him for righteousness."*ᵃ ⁷Therefore know that *only* those who are of faith are sons of Abraham. ⁸And the Scripture, foreseeing that God would justify the Gentiles by faith, preached the gospel to Abraham beforehand, *saying, "In you all the nations shall be blessed."*ᵃ ⁹So then those who *are* of faith are blessed with believing Abraham.

2:11 ᵃNU-Text reads *Cephas.* 2:14 ᵃNU-Text reads *how can you.* ᵇSome interpreters stop the quotation here. 3:1 ᵃNU-Text omits *that you should not obey the truth.* ᵇNU-Text omits *among you.* 3:6 ᵃGenesis 15:6 3:8 ᵃGenesis 12:3; 18:18; 22:18; 26:4; 28:14

The Law Brings a Curse

[10]For as many as are of the works of the law are under the curse; for it is written, *"Cursed is everyone who does not continue in all things which are written in the book of the law, to do them."*[a] [11]But that no one is justified by the law in the sight of God *is* evident, for *"the just shall live by faith."*[a] [12]Yet the law is not of faith, but *"the man who does them shall live by them."*[a]

[13]Christ has redeemed us from the curse of the law, having become a curse for us (for it is written, *"Cursed is everyone who hangs on a tree"*[a]), [14]that the blessing of Abraham might come upon the Gentiles in Christ Jesus, that we might receive the promise of the Spirit through faith.

The Changeless Promise

[15]Brethren, I speak in the manner of men: Though *it is* only a man's covenant, yet *if it is* confirmed, no one annuls or adds to it. [16]Now to Abraham and his Seed were the promises made. He does not say, "And to seeds," as of many, but as of one, *"And to your Seed,"*[a] who is Christ. [17]And this I say, *that* the law, which was four hundred and thirty years later, cannot annul the covenant that was confirmed before by God in Christ,[a] that it should make the promise of no effect. [18]For if the inheritance *is* of the law, *it is* no longer of promise; but God gave *it* to Abraham by promise.

Purpose of the Law

[19]What purpose then *does* the law serve? It was added because of transgressions, till the Seed should come to whom the promise was made; *and it was* appointed through angels by the hand of a mediator. [20]Now a mediator does not *mediate* for one *only,* but God is one.

[21]*Is* the law then against the promises of God? Certainly not! For if there had been a law given which could have given life, truly righteousness would have been by the law. [22]But the Scripture has confined all under sin, that the promise by faith in Jesus Christ might be given to those who believe. [23]But before faith came, we were kept under guard by the law, kept for the faith which would afterward be revealed. [24]Therefore the law was our tutor *to bring us* to Christ, that we might be justified by faith. [25]But after faith has come, we are no longer under a tutor.

Sons and Heirs

[26]For you are all sons of God through faith in Christ Jesus. [27]For as many of you as were baptized into Christ have put on Christ. [28]There is neither Jew nor Greek, there is neither slave nor free, there is neither male nor female; for you are all one in Christ Jesus. [29]And if you *are* Christ's, then you are Abraham's seed, and heirs according to the promise.

INTIMATE MOMENTS

Go to a local park or zoo. Spend some time reconnecting as a couple. Pack snacks and stay awhile.

4 Now I say *that* the heir, as long as he is a child, does not differ at all from a slave, though he is master of all, [2]but is under guardians and stewards until the time appointed by the father. [3]Even so we, when we were children, were in bondage under the elements of the world. [4]But when the fullness of the time had come, God sent forth His Son, born[a] of a woman, born under the law, [5]to redeem those who were under the law, that we might receive the adoption as sons.

[6]And because you are sons, God has sent forth the Spirit of His Son into your hearts, crying out, "Abba, Father!" [7]Therefore you are no longer a slave but a son, and if a son, then an heir of[a] God through Christ.

Fears for the Church

[8]But then, indeed, when you did not know God, you served those which by

---

3:10 [a]Deuteronomy 27:26　**3:11** [a]Habakkuk 2:4
3:12 [a]Leviticus 18:5　**3:13** [a]Deuteronomy 21:23
3:16 [a]Genesis 12:7; 13:15; 24:7　**3:17** [a]NU-Text omits *in Christ.*　**4:4** [a]Or *made*　**4:7** [a]NU-Text reads *through God* and omits *through Christ.*

nature are not gods. 9But now after you have known God, or rather are known by God, how *is it that* you turn again to the weak and beggarly elements, to which you desire again to be in bondage? 10You observe days and months and seasons and years. 11I am afraid for you, lest I have labored for you in vain.

12Brethren, I urge you to become like me, for I *became* like you. You have not injured me at all. 13You know that because of physical infirmity I preached the gospel to you at the first. 14And my trial which was in my flesh you did not despise or reject, but you received me as an angel of God, *even* as Christ Jesus. 15Whata then was the blessing you *enjoyed?* For I bear you witness that, if possible, you would have plucked out your own eyes and given them to me. 16Have I therefore become your enemy because I tell you the truth?

17They zealously court you, *but* for no good; yes, they want to exclude you, that you may be zealous for them. 18But it is good to be zealous in a good thing always, and not only when I am present with you. 19My little children, for whom I labor in birth again until Christ is formed in you, 20I would like to be present with you now and to change my tone; for I have doubts about you.

Two Covenants

21Tell me, you who desire to be under the law, do you not hear the law? 22For it is written that Abraham had two sons: the one by a bondwoman, the other by a freewoman. 23But he *who was* of the bondwoman was born according to the flesh, and he of the freewoman through promise, 24which things are symbolic. For these are thea two covenants: the one from Mount Sinai which gives birth to bondage, which is Hagar— 25for this Hagar is Mount Sinai in Arabia, and corresponds to Jerusalem which now is, and is in bondage with her children— 26but the Jerusalem above is free, which is the mother of us all. 27For it is written:

> "Rejoice, O barren,
> You who do not bear!
> Break forth and shout,
> You who are not in labor!
> For the desolate has many more
>   children
> Than she who has a husband."a

28Now we, brethren, as Isaac *was,* are children of promise. 29But, as he who was born according to the flesh then persecuted

---

4:15 aNU-Text reads *Where.* 4:24 aNU-Text and M-Text omit *the.* 4:27 aIsaiah 54:1

Choose Your Yoke

There are all kinds of yokes in life. There's the yoke of legalism (5:1), the yoke of a grudge, the yoke of resentment. We could describe all these yokes with one word: heavy.

Jesus has another kind of yoke. He used two words to describe His yoke: *easy* and *light* (Matt. 11:30).

I just came through a period of intense pressure in my life when at times the yoke was not easy and the load was not light. Life was tough and not very enjoyable. It didn't seem purposeful, and I found myself straining against a heavy yoke of worry, fear, and anxiety.

But you know what? I discovered I can't change the future by worrying about it. About the only thing my worry will do is change the inside of my stomach lining. And so I chose to take that heavy yoke off and place it to the side, and return to the *easy* and *light* yoke of Jesus.

So, what kind of yoke have you chosen for your marriage? Are you yoked up to Jesus Christ?

"How can I know?" you ask. You can answer that question by asking another one: Is your load easy and light, or is it heavy? If it's heavy, it's a yoke of your choosing. And if it's light, it's the Savior's yoke. As the Lord invites, "Take My yoke upon you and learn from me ... For My yoke is easy and My burden is light" (Matt. 11:29, 30).

him *who was born* according to the Spirit, even so *it is* now. [30]Nevertheless what does the Scripture say? *"Cast out the bond-woman and her son, for the son of the bondwoman shall not be heir with the son of the freewoman."*[a] [31]So then, brethren, we are not children of the bondwoman but of the free.

Christian Liberty

5 Stand fast therefore in the liberty by which Christ has made us free,[a] and do not be entangled again with a yoke of bondage. [2]Indeed I, Paul, say to you that if you become circumcised, Christ will profit you nothing. [3]And I testify again to every man who becomes circumcised that he is a debtor to keep the whole law. [4]You have become estranged from Christ, you who *attempt to* be justified by law; you have fallen from grace. [5]For we through the Spirit eagerly wait for the hope of right-eousness by faith. [6]For in Christ Jesus nei-ther circumcision nor uncircumcision avails anything, but faith working through love.

Love Fulfills the Law

[7]You ran well. Who hindered you from obeying the truth? [8]This persuasion does not *come* from Him who calls you. [9]A little leaven leavens the whole lump. [10]I have confidence in you, in the Lord, that you will have no other mind; but he who trou-bles you shall bear his judgment, whoever he is.

[11]And I, brethren, if I still preach cir-cumcision, why do I still suffer persecu-tion? Then the offense of the cross has ceased. [12]I could wish that those who trou-ble you would even cut themselves off!

[13]For you, brethren, have been called to liberty; only do not *use* liberty as an oppor-tunity for the flesh, but through love serve one another. [14]For all the law is fulfilled in one word, *even* in this: *"You shall love your neighbor as yourself."*[a] [15]But if you bite and devour one another, beware lest you be consumed by one another!

4:30 [a]Genesis 21:10 **5:1** [a]NU-Text reads *For freedom Christ has made us free; stand fast therefore.*
5:14 [a]Leviticus 19:18 **5:19** [a]NU-Text omits *adultery.*

BIBLICAL INSIGHTS • 5:16, 17
Bearing Fruit in a War Zone

MARRIAGE—and all of the Christian life, for that matter—will feel like pushing a dump truck up a hill if we try to live by just gritting our teeth, and we ignore the war going on between the Spirit and the flesh, "I say then: Walk in the Spirit, and you shall not fulfill the lust of the flesh. For the flesh lusts against the Spirit, and the Spirit against the flesh; and these are con-trary to one another, so that you do not do the things that you wish" (5:16, 17).

This constant war rages at the very core of every individual and affects all aspects of a relationship. You've experi-enced the internal battle, haven't you? One side of you wants to punish your mate, but the other side of you knows that you need to forgive. Or, because your selfishness is in conflict with the best interests of your spouse, criticizing and fault-finding seem easier than giving praise and encouragement.

If you attack the wickedness of the flesh by surrendering to and walking in the Spirit, your life will display the Spirit's delightful fruit: love, joy, peace, patience, kindness, goodness, faithfulness, gentle-ness, and self-control (5:22, 23). Take a moment and consider how a husband and wife can live together in an authentic way in the midst of the conflict between the flesh and the Spirit. Doesn't it make sense to yield to the Spirit and experience the benefits of this fruit together?

Walking in the Spirit

[16]I say then: Walk in the Spirit, and you shall not fulfill the lust of the flesh. [17]For the flesh lusts against the Spirit, and the Spirit against the flesh; and these are con-trary to one another, so that you do not do the things that you wish. [18]But if you are led by the Spirit, you are not under the law.

[19]Now the works of the flesh are evi-dent, which are: adultery,[a] fornication,

uncleanness, lewdness, [20]idolatry, sorcery, hatred, contentions, jealousies, outbursts of wrath, selfish ambitions, dissensions, heresies, [21]envy, murders,[a] drunkenness, revelries, and the like; of which I tell you beforehand, just as I also told *you* in time past, that those who practice such things will not inherit the kingdom of God.

[22]But the fruit of the Spirit is love, joy, peace, longsuffering, kindness, goodness, faithfulness, [23]gentleness, self-control. Against such there is no law. [24]And those *who are* Christ's have crucified the flesh with its passions and desires. [25]If we live in the Spirit, let us also walk in the Spirit. [26]Let us not become conceited, provoking one another, envying one another.

Bear and Share the Burdens

6 Brethren, if a man is overtaken in any trespass, you who *are* spiritual restore such a one in a spirit of gentleness, considering yourself lest you also be tempted. [2]Bear one another's burdens, and so fulfill the law of Christ. [3]For if anyone thinks himself to be something, when he is nothing, he deceives himself. [4]But let each one examine his own work, and then he will have rejoicing in himself alone, and not in another. [5]For each one shall bear his own load.

Be Generous and Do Good

[6]Let him who is taught the word share in all good things with him who teaches.

[7]Do not be deceived, God is not mocked; for whatever a man sows, that he will also reap. [8]For he who sows to his flesh will of the flesh reap corruption, but he who sows to the Spirit will of the Spirit reap everlasting life. [9]And let us not grow weary while doing good, for in due season we shall reap if we do not lose heart. [10]Therefore, as we have opportunity, let us do good to all, especially to those who are of the household of faith.

Glory Only in the Cross

[11]See with what large letters I have written to you with my own hand! [12]As many as desire to make a good showing in the flesh, these *would* compel you to be circumcised, only that they may not suffer persecution for the cross of Christ. [13]For not even those who are circumcised keep the law, but they desire to have you circumcised that they may boast in your flesh. [14]But God forbid that I should boast except in the cross of our Lord Jesus Christ, by whom[a] the world has been crucified to me, and I to the world. [15]For in Christ Jesus neither circumcision nor uncircumcision avails anything, but a new creation.

Blessing and a Plea

[16]And as many as walk according to this rule, peace and mercy *be* upon them, and upon the Israel of God.

[17]From now on let no one trouble me, for I bear in my body the marks of the Lord Jesus.

[18]Brethren, the grace of our Lord Jesus Christ *be* with your spirit. Amen.

5:21 [a]NU-Text omits *murders.*
6:14 [a]Or *by which* (the cross)

EPHESIANS

THE APOSTLE PAUL spent three years establishing a church in the city of Ephesus, an influential commercial and religious center in Asia Minor. When Paul's ministry began to grow, it created an uproar among the magicians and craftsmen who sold idols there, and Paul and his were companions eventually run out of town. Acts 20 records Paul's farewell speech to the elders of the Ephesian church.

Years later, Paul wrote this rich letter to the church he had founded, and his message speaks clearly to us today. The first half of the epistle (chapters 1—3) opens our eyes to God's wonderful work of grace—redeeming us, adopting us, sealing us with His Spirit, uniting us into one body, transforming us and empowering us to love and serve one another. The second half has no fewer than 35 commands for us to walk in a manner worthy of the great work God has done in us. Ephesians 2:10 brings both halves of the letter together, "For we are His workmanship, created in Christ Jesus for good works [chapters 1—3], which God prepared beforehand that we should walk in them [chapters 4—6]."

Ephesians contains perhaps the best-known passage on marriage in the Bible (5:22–31). Here we learn that a husband's primary responsibility is to sacrificially love his wife, as Christ loved the church. A wife's primary responsibility is to respect and honor her husband. God designed marriage to provide a picture of the holy relationship between Christ and His church.

Ephesians has much to say about healthy marriage and family relationships even beyond that pivotal passage. It instructs us to speak the truth in love to one another (4:25); to be on guard against sinful anger and not to allow conflicts to linger (4:26); to be careful how we speak to one another (4:29, 31); and to forgive each other (4:32). It warns us to be on guard against sexual sin (5:1–3) and to live under the influence and control of the Holy Spirit, something the Bible calls being "filled with the Spirit" (5:18). The last chapter of Ephesians instructs children to obey their parents (6:1–3) and warns fathers not to provoke their children to anger, but to train them in godly living (6:4). Chapter 6 also gives us a clear battle plan to withstand the schemes of the devil (6:10–18). Every person and married couple needs to understand that their relationships take place on a spiritual battlefield, not on a romantic balcony.

Greeting

1 Paul, an apostle of Jesus Christ by the will of God,

To the saints who are in Ephesus, and faithful in Christ Jesus:

2Grace to you and peace from God our Father and the Lord Jesus Christ.

Redemption in Christ

3Blessed *be* the God and Father of our Lord Jesus Christ, who has blessed us with every spiritual blessing in the heavenly *places* in Christ, 4just as He chose us in Him before the foundation of the world, that we should be holy and without blame before Him in love, 5having predestined us to adoption as sons by Jesus Christ to Himself, according to the good pleasure of His will, 6to the praise of the glory of His grace, by which He made us accepted in the Beloved.

7In Him we have redemption through His blood, the forgiveness of sins, according to the riches of His grace 8which He made to abound toward us in all wisdom and prudence, 9having made known to us the mystery of His will, according to His good pleasure which He purposed in Himself, 10that in the dispensation of the fullness of the times He might gather together in one all things in Christ, both[a] which are in heaven and which are on earth—in Him. 11In Him also we have obtained an inheritance, being predestined according to the purpose of Him who works all things according to the counsel of His will, 12that we who first trusted in Christ should be to the praise of His glory.

13In Him you also *trusted,* after you heard the word of truth, the gospel of your salvation; in whom also, having believed, you were sealed with the Holy Spirit of promise, 14who[a] is the guarantee of our inheritance until the redemption of the purchased possession, to the praise of His glory.

Prayer for Spiritual Wisdom

15Therefore I also, after I heard of your faith in the Lord Jesus and your love for all the saints, 16do not cease to give thanks for you, making mention of you in my prayers: 17that the God of our Lord Jesus Christ, the Father of glory, may give to you the spirit of wisdom and revelation in the knowledge of Him, 18the eyes of your understanding[a] being enlightened; that you may know what is the hope of His calling, what are the riches of the glory of His inheritance in the saints, 19and what *is* the exceeding greatness of His power toward us who believe, according to the working of His mighty power 20which He worked in Christ when He raised Him from the dead and seated *Him* at His right hand in the heavenly *places,* 21far above all principality and power and might and dominion, and every name that is named, not only in this age but also in that which is to come.

22And He put all *things* under His feet, and gave Him *to be* head over all *things* to the church, 23which is His body, the fullness of Him who fills all in all.

By Grace Through Faith

2 And you He *made alive,* who were dead in trespasses and sins, 2in which you once walked according to the course of this world, according to the prince of the power of the air, the spirit who now works in the sons of disobedience, 3among whom also we all once conducted ourselves in the lusts of our flesh, fulfilling the desires of the flesh and of the mind, and were by nature children of wrath, just as the others.

4But God, who is rich in mercy, because of His great love with which He loved us, 5even when we were dead in trespasses,

**INTIMATE
MOMENTS**

Celebrate summer by taking advantage of the longest day of the year. Start with breakfast in bed, treat her to lunch, then end the day with a summertime barbecue for two.

1:10 [a]NU-Text and M-Text omit *both.* **1:14** [a]NU-Text reads *which.* **1:18** [a]NU-Text and M-Text read *hearts.*

made us alive together with Christ (by grace you have been saved), [6]and raised *us* up together, and made *us* sit together in the heavenly *places* in Christ Jesus, [7]that in the ages to come He might show the exceeding riches of His grace in *His* kindness toward us in Christ Jesus. [8]For by grace you have been saved through faith, and that not of yourselves; *it is* the gift of God, [9]not of works, lest anyone should boast. [10]For we are His workmanship, created in Christ Jesus for good works, which God prepared beforehand that we should walk in them.

Brought Near by His Blood

[11]Therefore remember that you, once Gentiles in the flesh—who are called Uncircumcision by what is called the Circumcision made in the flesh by hands—[12]that at that time you were without Christ, being aliens from the commonwealth of Israel and strangers from the covenants of promise, having no hope and without God in the world. [13]But now in Christ Jesus you who once were far off have been brought near by the blood of Christ.

Christ Our Peace

[14]For He Himself is our peace, who has made both one, and has broken down the middle wall of separation, [15]having abolished in His flesh the enmity, *that is,* the law of commandments *contained* in ordinances, so as to create in Himself one new man *from* the two, *thus* making peace, [16]and that He might reconcile them both to God in one body through the cross, thereby putting to death the enmity. [17]And He came and preached peace to you who were afar off and to those who were near. [18]For through Him we both have access by one Spirit to the Father.

Christ Our Cornerstone

[19]Now, therefore, you are no longer strangers and foreigners, but fellow citizens with the saints and members of the household of God, [20]having been built on the foundation of the apostles and prophets, Jesus Christ Himself being the chief corner*stone,* [21]in whom the whole building, being fitted together, grows into a holy temple in the Lord, [22]in whom you

---

ROMANTIC QUOTES AND NOTES
Who Is Your Enemy?

Ms. magazine once declared, "Marriage is the only war where you sleep with the enemy."

I would rather picture the world as the true battlefield and your marriage as God's smallest battle formation for *winning* the war. Every married couple needs to understand a crucial biblical principle: Your mate is not your enemy. Paul says, "For we do not wrestle against flesh and blood" (Eph. 6:12).

Picture your marriage as two people joined together in a foxhole, cooperating in battle against a common enemy. Take a good look at your own foxhole. Are you fighting the enemy or each other? As a friend of ours told me, "I was so busy standing up in the foxhole, duking it out with my husband, that I had no time to be involved in fighting against the real enemy."

Keep in mind that whenever you declare war on your mate, ultimately you are opposing God Himself. You are rejecting the person He has provided to complete you and to meet your needs.

Here's a practical test to discover if you view your mate as an enemy or as a fellow soldier. Do you focus on the negative in your mate, or on the positive?

Our real enemy, the devil, loves to deceive us and convince us that our spouse is our enemy. His goal is to divide us, oppose each other, and set our focus on waging war against our spouse. The next time you find yourself in conflict, say to your mate, "You are not my enemy." Then begin to turn your focus on the strategies of the one who wants to destroy your oneness in marriage.

also are being built together for a dwelling place of God in the Spirit.

The Mystery Revealed

3 For this reason I, Paul, the prisoner of Christ Jesus for you Gentiles— [2]if indeed you have heard of the dispensation of the grace of God which was given to me for you, [3]how that by revelation He made known to me the mystery (as I have briefly written already, [4]by which, when you read, you may understand my knowledge in the mystery of Christ), [5]which in other ages was not made known to the sons of men, as it has now been revealed by the Spirit to His holy apostles and prophets: [6]that the Gentiles should be fellow heirs, of the same body, and partakers of His promise in Christ through the gospel, [7]of which I became a minister according to the gift of the grace of God given to me by the effective working of His power.

Purpose of the Mystery

[8]To me, who am less than the least of all the saints, this grace was given, that I should preach among the Gentiles the unsearchable riches of Christ, [9]and to make all see what is the fellowship[a] of the mystery, which from the beginning of the ages has been hidden in God who created all things through Jesus Christ;[b] [10]to the intent that now the manifold wisdom of God might be made known by the church to the principalities and powers in the heavenly places, [11]according to the eternal purpose which He accomplished in Christ Jesus our Lord, [12]in whom we have boldness and access with confidence through faith in Him. [13]Therefore I ask that you do not lose heart at my tribulations for you, which is your glory.

Appreciation of the Mystery

[14]For this reason I bow my knees to the Father of our Lord Jesus Christ,[a] [15]from whom the whole family in heaven and earth is named, [16]that He would grant you, according to the riches of His glory, to be strengthened with might through His Spirit in the inner man, [17]that Christ may dwell in your hearts through faith; that you, being rooted and grounded in love,

[18]may be able to comprehend with all the saints what is the width and length and depth and height— [19]to know the love of Christ which passes knowledge; that you may be filled with all the fullness of God.

[20]Now to Him who is able to do exceedingly abundantly above all that we ask or think, according to the power that works in us, [21]to Him be glory in the church by Christ Jesus to all generations, forever and ever. Amen.

Walk in Unity

4 I, therefore, the prisoner of the Lord, beseech you to walk worthy of the calling with which you were called, [2]with all lowliness and gentleness, with longsuffering, bearing with one another in love, [3]endeavoring to keep the unity of the Spirit in the bond of peace. [4]There is one body and one Spirit, just as you were called in one hope of your calling; [5]one Lord, one faith, one baptism; [6]one God and Father of all, who is above all, and through all, and in you[a] all.

Spiritual Gifts

[7]But to each one of us grace was given according to the measure of Christ's gift. [8]Therefore He says:

> "When He ascended on high,
> He led captivity captive,
> And gave gifts to men."[a]

[9](Now this, "He ascended"—what does it mean but that He also first[a] descended into the lower parts of the earth? [10]He who descended is also the One who ascended far above all the heavens, that He might fill all things.)

[11]And He Himself gave some to be apostles, some prophets, some evangelists, and some pastors and teachers, [12]for the equipping of the saints for the work of ministry, for the edifying of the body of Christ, [13]till we all come to the unity of the faith and of the knowledge of the Son of God, to a perfect man, to the measure of

---

3:9 [a]NU-Text and M-Text read stewardship (dispensation). [b]NU-Text omits through Jesus Christ.
3:14 [a]NU-Text omits of our Lord Jesus Christ.
4:6 [a]NU-Text omits you; M-Text reads us.
4:8 [a]Psalm 68:18 4:9 [a]NU-Text omits first.

the stature of the fullness of Christ; [14]that we should no longer be children, tossed to and fro and carried about with every wind of doctrine, by the trickery of men, in the cunning craftiness of deceitful plotting, [15]but, speaking the truth in love, may grow up in all things into Him who is the head— Christ— [16]from whom the whole body, joined and knit together by what every joint supplies, according to the effective working by which every part does its share, causes growth of the body for the edifying of itself in love.

The New Man

[17]This I say, therefore, and testify in the Lord, that you should no longer walk as the rest of[a] the Gentiles walk, in the futility of their mind, [18]having their understanding darkened, being alienated from the life of God, because of the ignorance that is in them, because of the blindness of their heart; [19]who, being past feeling, have given themselves over to lewdness, to work all uncleanness with greediness.

[20]But you have not so learned Christ, [21]if indeed you have heard Him and have been taught by Him, as the truth is in Jesus: [22]that you put off, concerning your former conduct, the old man which grows corrupt according to the deceitful lusts, [23]and be renewed in the spirit of your mind, [24]and that you put on the new man which was created according to God, in true righteousness and holiness.

Do Not Grieve the Spirit

[25]Therefore, putting away lying, *"Let each one of you speak truth with his neighbor,"*[a] for we are members of one another. [26]*"Be angry, and do not sin":*[a] do not let the sun go down on your wrath, [27]nor give place to the devil. [28]Let him who stole steal no longer, but rather let him labor, working with *his* hands what is good, that he may have something to give him who has need. [29]Let no corrupt word proceed out of your mouth, but what is good for necessary edification, that it may impart grace to the hearers. [30]And do not

grieve the Holy Spirit of God, by whom you were sealed for the day of redemption. [31]Let all bitterness, wrath, anger, clamor, and evil speaking be put away from you, with all malice. [32]And be kind to one another, tenderhearted, forgiving one another, even as God in Christ forgave you.

Walk in Love

5 Therefore be imitators of God as dear children. [2]And walk in love, as Christ also has loved us and given Himself for us,

ROMANCE FAQ

Q: What is the husband's role in marriage?

Today you can find all kinds of books that will be only too willing to give you all sorts of answers, but when you carefully analyze the biblical record, you arrive at a clear definition: The husband's role is servant-leader. God says the husband is to bear the weight of responsibility for leadership in his home.

Paul summarized well the man's position in Ephesians 5:25, "Husbands, love your wives, just as Christ also loved the church and gave Himself up for her." Just how did Christ love the church?

With self-denial: Jesus Christ stepped out of eternity into time and laid aside the privileges of deity. He denied himself, even to the point of death. Servant-leaders deny themselves for the good of their families.

With sacrificial action: Christ gave His life for those whom He loved. Husbands are called, daily, to give up their desires and die to self.

With a servant's heart: Jesus continually set aside his own desires to serve others. In the same way, husbands should surrender their own agendas—and their hobbies— to serve their wives and meet their needs.

By pointing to Christ's servant-leadership, Paul gave a radically new definition of leadership. What wife would not want to be loved like this?

4:17 [a]NU-Text omits *the rest of.* **4:25** [a]Zechariah 8:16 **4:26** [a]Psalm 4:4

Love Your Wife Unconditionally

YOUR UNCONDITIONAL ACCEPTANCE of your wife is not based upon her performance, but on her worth as God's gift to you. Ephesians 5:25 exhorts, "Husbands, love your wives, just as Christ also loved the church and gave Himself up for her."

If you want to love your wife unconditionally, regularly fill her emotional tank. One of the best ways to do that is to affirm her frequently. Let her know verbally that you value her, respect her, and love her. I have discovered that with Barbara I simply cannot do this enough. This doesn't mean she's needy. It simply means that she needs to be reminded frequently of my love for her.

While there is no question that words communicate love, so do actions. Become adept at both! As the apostle John wrote, "Let us not love in word or tongue, but in deed and in truth" (1 John 3:18). Sacrificial action is one of the missing ingredients in male leadership of the home.

When did you last give up something for your wife, something you genuinely valued, like your golf game, a fishing trip, or your hobby? Sometimes you need to give up something you enjoy so your wife can have a break, and so she can see your genuine love for her. There will also be times when you need to sacrifice something for a season or even permanently for her. It may seem like you are giving your life away, but in reality, you will be investing in your life when you love your wife. Are you not one flesh?

Our model for this kind of sacrificial, unconditional love is Jesus, who gave Himself for us. God demonstrated His love for us by sending His Son to die in our place. What is one way you can die to self this week to demonstrate your love for your wife? What should you consider giving up for a season to make a statement of love to your beloved?

an offering and a sacrifice to God for a sweet-smelling aroma.

³But fornication and all uncleanness or covetousness, let it not even be named among you, as is fitting for saints; ⁴neither filthiness, nor foolish talking, nor coarse jesting, which are not fitting, but rather giving of thanks. ⁵For this you know,ᵃ that no fornicator, unclean person, nor covetous man, who is an idolater, has any inheritance in the kingdom of Christ and God. ⁶Let no one deceive you with empty words, for because of these things the wrath of God comes upon the sons of disobedience. ⁷Therefore do not be partakers with them.

Walk in Light

⁸For you were once darkness, but now *you are* light in the Lord. Walk as children of light ⁹(for the fruit of the Spiritᵃ *is* in all goodness, righteousness, and truth), ¹⁰finding out what is acceptable to the Lord. ¹¹And have no fellowship with the unfruitful works of darkness, but rather expose *them*. ¹²For it is shameful even to speak of those things which are done by them in secret. ¹³But all things that are exposed are made manifest by the light, for whatever makes manifest is light. ¹⁴Therefore He says:

"Awake, you who sleep,
  Arise from the dead,
  And Christ will give you light."

Walk in Wisdom

¹⁵See then that you walk circumspectly, not as fools but as wise, ¹⁶redeeming the time, because the days are evil. ¹⁷Therefore do not be unwise, but understand what the will of the Lord *is*. ¹⁸And do not be drunk with wine, in which is dissipation; but be filled with the Spirit, ¹⁹speaking to one another in psalms and hymns and spiritual songs, singing and making melody in your heart to the Lord, ²⁰giving thanks always for all things to God the Father in the name of our Lord Jesus Christ, ²¹submitting to one another in the fear of God.ᵃ

5:5 ᵃNU-Text reads *For know this.* **5:9** ᵃNU-Text reads *light.* **5:21** ᵃNU-Text reads *Christ.*

DEVOTIONS FOR COUPLES • 5:25–29
Develop Her Gifts and Horizons

The Bible instructs Christian husbands to look out for their wives and encourage them in their spiritual growth and development. Consider the familiar passage in Ephesians 5:25–29, especially verses 28 and 29, "So husbands ought to love their own wives as their own bodies; he who loves his wife loves himself. For no one ever hated his own flesh, but nourishes and cherishes it, just as the Lord does the church."

Notice the words describing what husbands are to do for their wives: *love, nourish, and cherish.* All three activities are a big part of building into a wife's life and developing her self-confidence. If you're a Christian husband:

1. Help your wife grow as a Christian. Do you encourage spiritual growth in your wife? It's the smartest thing you could possibly do. When your wife grows in her relationship with God, not only does she triumph at life, but *you* benefit as well. Help her to grow spiritually by praying regularly for her and with her. It *will* encourage her. You can also take time to regularly interact over God's Word and its application to your lives and family. Encourage your wife to employ her spiritual gifts in service to others outside your home, if she has time. Be her greatest cheerleader.

2. Help her develop her talents. Take part in your wife's life by nurturing the development of her dormant talents. Like fruit seeds never planted in fertile soil, your wife's gifts may need your care and attention in order to germinate. If you have already done this, you know how she responds to this personalized focus. She feels that you value her and are helping her to expand her life and utilize her gifts so that she might be even more productive.

3. Help her develop new horizons. Most of us fail to anticipate major change points in the lives of our wives, such as the birth of a child, children's teen years, menopause, and the empty nest. When your children leave home, your wife will suddenly have enormous chunks of time and attention to devote to other worthwhile causes. It is a wise man who doesn't wait for this to happen, but who takes proactive steps two or three years in advance of children leaving home and begins to help his wife find her new niche.

Barbara is continuing to fashion a vision for her life that we both believe will be very satisfying to her. Why not assist your wife in uncovering a vision that will be meaningful to her? By helping her to keep her horizons clear and focused, you will encourage her growth and development.

Marriage—Christ and the Church

22Wives, submit to your own husbands, as to the Lord. 23For the husband is head of the wife, as also Christ is head of the church; and He is the Savior of the body. 24Therefore, just as the church is subject to Christ, so *let* the wives *be* to their own husbands in everything.

25Husbands, love your wives, just as Christ also loved the church and gave Himself for her, 26that He might sanctify and cleanse her with the washing of water by the word, 27that He might present her to Himself a glorious church, not having spot or wrinkle or any such thing, but that she should be holy and without blemish. 28So husbands ought to love their own wives as their own bodies; he who loves his wife loves himself. 29For no one ever hated his own flesh, but nourishes and cherishes it, just as the Lord *does* the church. 30For we are members of His body,a of His flesh and of His bones. 31*"For this reason a man shall leave his father and mother and be joined to his wife, and the two shall become one flesh."*a 32This is a great mystery, but I speak concerning Christ and the church.

5:30 aNU-Text omits the rest of this verse.
5:31 aGenesis 2:24

Respect Him

AN IMPORTANT PART of God's instruction to wives is found in Ephesians 5:33, "Let the wife see that she respects her husband." Why does God focus so strongly on this quality of respect? Why didn't He select other positive and necessary traits, such as kindness, sympathy, and forgiveness? Why not emphasize love?

I believe that God, as the designer of men, knew that our husbands would be built up as we respect them. When a wife respects her husband, he feels it, receives support from it, and is strengthened by it. A man needs respect like a woman needs love.

Your husband wants and needs to make a contribution through his life that he believes is worthy of another's respect. He needs to know that you feel he is important. Without your respect, he finds it hard to respect himself. You are his mirror. When you express your respect, he feels valuable and esteemed.

Prayerfully consider how you can demonstrate respect to him in tangible, practical ways. Is there an attitude you need to change? An action that would say to him, "You *are* my man and I really *do* respect you"? Begin to pray that God will show you how you can be an agent of love and respect to your husband.

33Nevertheless let each one of you in particular so love his own wife as himself, and let the wife *see* that she respects *her* husband.

Children and Parents

6 Children, obey your parents in the Lord, for this is right. 2"*Honor your father and mother,*" which is the first commandment with promise: 3"*that it may be well with you and you may live long on the earth.*"a

4And you, fathers, do not provoke your children to wrath, but bring them up in the training and admonition of the Lord.

Bondservants and Masters

5Bondservants, be obedient to those who are your masters according to the flesh, with fear and trembling, in sincerity of heart, as to Christ; 6not with eyeservice, as men-pleasers, but as bondservants of Christ, doing the will of God from the heart, 7with goodwill doing service, as to the Lord, and not to men, 8knowing that whatever good anyone does, he will receive the same from the Lord, whether *he is* a slave or free.

9And you, masters, do the same things to them, giving up threatening, knowing that your own Master alsoa is in heaven, and there is no partiality with Him.

The Whole Armor of God

10Finally, my brethren, be strong in the Lord and in the power of His might. 11Put on the whole armor of God, that you may be able to stand against the wiles of the devil. 12For we do not wrestle against flesh and blood, but against principalities, against powers, against the rulers of the darkness of this age,a against spiritual *hosts* of wickedness in the heavenly *places.* 13Therefore take up the whole armor of God, that you may be able to withstand in the evil day, and having done all, to stand.

14Stand therefore, having girded your waist with truth, having put on the breastplate of righteousness, 15and having shod your feet with the preparation of the gospel of peace; 16above all, taking the shield of faith with which you will be able to quench all the fiery darts of the wicked one. 17And take the helmet of salvation, and the sword of the Spirit, which is the word of God; 18praying always with all prayer and supplication in the Spirit, being watchful to this end with all perseverance and supplication for all the saints— 19and for me, that utterance may be given to me, that I may open my mouth boldly to make known the mystery of the gospel, 20for which I am an ambassador in chains; that in it I may speak boldly, as I ought to speak.

6:3 aDeuteronomy 5:16 **6:9** aNU-Text reads *He who is both their Master and yours.* **6:12** aNU-Text reads *rulers of this darkness.*

A Gracious Greeting

²¹But that you also may know my affairs *and* how I am doing, Tychicus, a beloved brother and faithful minister in the Lord, will make all things known to you; ²²whom I have sent to you for this very purpose, that you may know our affairs, and *that* he may comfort your hearts.

²³Peace to the brethren, and love with faith, from God the Father and the Lord Jesus Christ. ²⁴Grace *be* with all those who love our Lord Jesus Christ in sincerity. Amen.

PHILIPPIANS

CONSIDER THE BOOK OF PHILIPPIANS an extended thank you note sent by the apostle Paul to the church he founded in Philippi on his second missionary journey. This is one of four biblical letters that Paul wrote while he was in prison in Rome (the others are Ephesians, Colossians and Philemon). The church at Philippi had sent a man named Epaphroditus to deliver money its members had collected for Paul to care for his needs. The apostle's great love for this little church shines through in this short letter.

Philippians has been called the "Epistle of Joy"—remarkable, considering that Paul was in prison as he wrote. The former Chaplain of the U.S. Senate, Dr. Lloyd John Ogilvie, has said, "Joy is the missing ingredient in contemporary Christianity." And the great British pastor C.H. Spurgeon once said, "I will not glorify God simply by working hard. To truly bring Him honor, I must labor with a cheerful spirit. Therefore, I must not only serve my family each day, but I must serve them with joy."

In addition to joy, Paul speaks about many other issues families face in the Book of Philippians. We read about the priority of oneness in relationships (2:1, 2) and the critical importance of esteeming others better than ourselves (2:3–11). Paul challenges us to forget the baggage of our past and to press on toward the goal of knowing Christ (3:13, 14) with confidence that God, "who has begun a good work in you will complete it" (1:6). We discover that God can use even the hardships of life to glorify Himself and bless us (1:12).

We learn that the key to dealing with anxiety is to rejoice in all things and "in everything by prayer and supplication, with thanksgiving, let your requests be made known to God" (4:6). We hear instruction on being careful about what we allow ourselves to think about, and to focus on things that are noble, just and pure (4:8). Paul talks about how he learned to be content in every circumstance, as he realized that God would supply his needs.

This is God's formula for real peace.

Greeting

1 Paul and Timothy, bondservants of Jesus Christ,

To all the saints in Christ Jesus who are in Philippi, with the bishops[a] and deacons:

²Grace to you and peace from God our Father and the Lord Jesus Christ.

Thankfulness and Prayer

³I thank my God upon every remembrance of you, ⁴always in every prayer of mine making request for you all with joy, ⁵for your fellowship in the gospel from the first day until now, ⁶being confident of this very thing, that He who has begun a good work in you will complete *it* until the day of Jesus Christ; ⁷just as it is right for me to think this of you all, because I have you in my heart, inasmuch as both in my chains and in the defense and confirmation of the gospel, you all are partakers with me of grace. ⁸For God is my witness, how greatly I long for you all with the affection of Jesus Christ.

⁹And this I pray, that your love may abound still more and more in knowledge and all discernment, ¹⁰that you may approve the things that are excellent, that you may be sincere and without offense till the day of Christ, ¹¹being filled with the fruits of righteousness which *are* by Jesus Christ, to the glory and praise of God.

Christ Is Preached

¹²But I want you to know, brethren, that the things *which happened* to me have actually turned out for the furtherance of the gospel, ¹³so that it has become evident to the whole palace guard, and to all the rest, that my chains are in Christ; ¹⁴and most of the brethren in the Lord, having become confident by my chains, are much more bold to speak the word without fear.

¹⁵Some indeed preach Christ even from envy and strife, and some also from goodwill: ¹⁶The former[a] preach Christ from selfish ambition, not sincerely, supposing to add affliction to my chains; ¹⁷but the latter out of love, knowing that I am appointed for the defense of the gospel. ¹⁸What then? Only *that* in every way, whether in pretense or in truth, Christ is preached; and in this I rejoice, yes, and will rejoice.

To Live Is Christ

¹⁹For I know that this will turn out for my deliverance through your prayer and the supply of the Spirit of Jesus Christ, ²⁰according to my earnest expectation and hope that in nothing I shall be ashamed, but with all boldness, as always, so now also Christ will be magnified in my body, whether by life or by death. ²¹For to me, to live *is* Christ, and to die *is* gain. ²²But if *I* live on in the flesh, this *will mean* fruit from *my* labor; yet what I shall choose I cannot tell. ²³For[a] I am hard-pressed between the two, having a desire to depart and be with Christ, *which is* far better. ²⁴Nevertheless to remain in the flesh *is* more needful for you. ²⁵And being confident of this, I know that I shall remain and continue with you all for your progress and joy of faith, ²⁶that your rejoicing for me may be more abundant in Jesus Christ by my coming to you again.

INTIMATE MOMENTS

As the days begin to turn chilly, take your "pumpkin" to the pumpkin patch. Let her choose a few to accent your front door. Bring along a thermos of hot apple cider to share.

Striving and Suffering for Christ

²⁷Only let your conduct be worthy of the gospel of Christ, so that whether I come and see you or am absent, I may hear of your affairs, that you stand fast in one spirit, with one mind striving together for the faith of the gospel, ²⁸and not in any way terrified by your adversaries, which is to them a proof of perdition, but to you of salvation,[a] and that from God. ²⁹For to you it has been granted on behalf of Christ, not

---

1:1 ᵃLiterally *overseers* **1:16** ᵃNU-Text reverses the contents of verses 16 and 17. **1:23** ᵃNU-Text and M-Text read *But.* **1:28** ᵃNU-Text reads *of your salvation.*

only to believe in Him, but also to suffer for His sake, ³⁰having the same conflict which you saw in me and now hear *is* in me.

Unity Through Humility

2 Therefore if *there is* any consolation in Christ, if any comfort of love, if any fellowship of the Spirit, if any affection and mercy, ²fulfill my joy by being like-minded, having the same love, *being* of one accord, of one mind. ³*Let* nothing *be done* through selfish ambition or conceit, but in lowliness of mind let each esteem others better than himself. ⁴Let each of you look out not only for his own interests, but also for the interests of others.

The Humbled and Exalted Christ

⁵Let this mind be in you which was also in Christ Jesus, ⁶who, being in the form of God, did not consider it robbery to be equal with God, ⁷but made Himself of no reputation, taking the form of a bondservant, *and* coming in the likeness of men. ⁸And being found in appearance as a man, He humbled Himself and became obedient to *the point of* death, even the death of the cross. ⁹Therefore God also has highly exalted Him and given Him the name which is above every name, ¹⁰that at the name of Jesus every knee should bow, of those in heaven, and of those on earth, and of those under the earth, ¹¹and *that* every tongue should confess that Jesus Christ *is* Lord, to the glory of God the Father.

Light Bearers

¹²Therefore, my beloved, as you have always obeyed, not as in my presence only, but now much more in my absence, work out your own salvation with fear and trembling; ¹³for it is God who works in you both to will and to do for *His* good pleasure.

¹⁴Do all things without complaining and disputing, ¹⁵that you may become blameless and harmless, children of God without fault in the midst of a crooked and perverse generation, among whom you shine as lights in the world, ¹⁶holding fast the word of life, so that I may rejoice in the day of Christ that I have not run in vain or labored in vain.

¹⁷Yes, and if I am being poured out *as a drink offering* on the sacrifice and service of your faith, I am glad and rejoice with you all. ¹⁸For the same reason you also be glad and rejoice with me.

Timothy Commended

¹⁹But I trust in the Lord Jesus to send Timothy to you shortly, that I also may be encouraged when I know your state. ²⁰For I have no one like-minded, who will sincerely care for your state. ²¹For all seek their

own, not the things which are of Christ Jesus. [22]But you know his proven character, that as a son with *his* father he served with me in the gospel. [23]Therefore I hope to send him at once, as soon as I see how it goes with me. [24]But I trust in the Lord that I myself shall also come shortly.

Epaphroditus Praised

[25]Yet I considered it necessary to send to you Epaphroditus, my brother, fellow worker, and fellow soldier, but your messenger and the one who ministered to my need; [26]since he was longing for you all, and was distressed because you had heard that he was sick. [27]For indeed he was sick almost unto death; but God had mercy on him, and not only on him but on me also, lest I should have sorrow upon sorrow. [28]Therefore I sent him the more eagerly, that when you see him again you may rejoice, and I may be less sorrowful. [29]Receive him therefore in the Lord with all gladness, and hold such men in esteem; [30]because for the work of Christ he came close to death, not regarding his life, to supply what was lacking in your service toward me.

All for Christ

3 Finally, my brethren, rejoice in the Lord. For me to write the same things to you *is* not tedious, but for you *it is* safe.

[2]Beware of dogs, beware of evil workers, beware of the mutilation! [3]For we are the circumcision, who worship God in the Spirit,[a] rejoice in Christ Jesus, and have no confidence in the flesh, [4]though I also might have confidence in the flesh. If anyone else thinks he may have confidence in the flesh, I more so: [5]circumcised the eighth day, of the stock of Israel, *of* the tribe of Benjamin, a Hebrew of the Hebrews; concerning the law, a Pharisee; [6]concerning zeal, persecuting the church; concerning the righteousness which is in the law, blameless.

[7]But what things were gain to me, these I have counted loss for Christ. [8]Yet indeed I also count all things loss for the excellence of the knowledge of Christ Jesus my Lord, for whom I have suffered the loss of all things, and count them as rubbish, that I may gain Christ [9]and be found in Him, not having my own righteousness, which *is* from the law, but that which *is* through faith in Christ, the righteousness which is from God by faith; [10]that I may know Him and the power of His resurrection, and the

---

ROMANCE FAQ

Q: *Lately, my spouse seems unconvinced of my love. What can I do?*

As the years go by, you and your spouse see each other in a variety of situations. You see both achievements and failures. You raise a family, you experience ups and downs in your career, and you struggle through problems with relatives. You develop godly disciplines and, perhaps, some bad habits. You encounter health problems; you gain weight; your hair turns gray.

And through all that, as your mate grows to know you more than any other person on earth (and vice versa), it's easy to begin thinking, *I know you say you're committed to me, but are you glad you are committed to me? Would you do this again? You say you love me, but do you really?*

Many marriages fail because one or both partners begin to doubt each other's commitment over the years. If you sense your spouse wondering about your love, it may be that you have neglected expressing or demonstrating your commitment. The problem isn't with something you've done. It's with what you've left undone.

Try this. Look through the Book of Philippians and note all the positive phrases Paul uses to talk about his friends (such as "making request for you all with joy" or "I have you in my heart"). Use them as a model to speak to your spouse, and see what happens.

3:3 [a]NU-Text and M-Text read *who worship in the Spirit of God.*

BIBLICAL INSIGHTS • 4:6, 7

A Great Trade-Off

MANY THINGS CAN PUT STRESS on a marriage, and one of the chief culprits is anxiety: worry about money, worry about the kids, worry about in-laws, the list goes on and on. When we start worrying about things, it puts us in bad spirits all the way around, and that is never good for any relationship.

But the apostle Paul has an antidote for worry, "Be anxious for nothing, but in everything by prayer and supplication, with thanksgiving, let your requests be made known to God" (Phil. 4:6).

We can take this promise literally in every sense. Paul tells us to worry about nothing. And in this case, nothing *really* means nothing! Instead of worrying over your life situations, Paul tells each of us, take them to God in prayer, making sure to tell Him what we need and then thanking Him in advance for His answer.

There's a great trade-off in this passage, too. Paul tells us that if we take our concerns to God in prayer, we get to rest in and enjoy his peace, which "surpasses all understanding" (4:7).

One of my mom's favorite nicknames for me was "Worry-wart." I was constantly doing things that resulted in her worrying. It's true that all moms worry, but I think my mom struggled (and for good reason) with worrying about me. When I became a parent, myself, I finally understood. It's so easy to be anxious about our children. I'm glad that I committed this passage to memory and began to practice the spiritual disciplines of which it speaks.

Headaches, upset stomach, marital and family strife in exchange for perfect peace? Sounds like a great deal! So if there are things you are worrying about today, follow Paul's instruction to pray with thanksgiving and to "let your requests be made known to God." You *will* experience the "peace of God" which indeed surpasses all understanding. That's a nice trade: worry for God's peace!

---

fellowship of His sufferings, being conformed to His death, [11]if, by any means, I may attain to the resurrection from the dead.

Pressing Toward the Goal

[12]Not that I have already attained, or am already perfected; but I press on, that I may lay hold of that for which Christ Jesus has also laid hold of me. [13]Brethren, I do not count myself to have apprehended; but one thing I *do*, forgetting those things which are behind and reaching forward to those things which are ahead, [14]I press toward the goal for the prize of the upward call of God in Christ Jesus.

[15]Therefore let us, as many as are mature, have this mind; and if in anything you think otherwise, God will reveal even this to you. [16]Nevertheless, to *the degree* that we have already attained, let us walk by the same rule,[a] let us be of the same mind.

Our Citizenship in Heaven

[17]Brethren, join in following my example, and note those who so walk, as you have us for a pattern. [18]For many walk, of whom I have told you often, and now tell you even weeping, *that they are* the enemies of the cross of Christ: [19]whose end *is* destruction, whose god *is their* belly, and *whose* glory *is* in their shame—who set their mind on earthly things. [20]For our citizenship is in heaven, from which we also eagerly wait for the Savior, the Lord Jesus Christ, [21]who will transform our lowly body that it may be conformed to His glorious body, according to the working by which He is able even to subdue all things to Himself.

3:16 [a]NU-Text omits *rule* and the rest of the verse.

4 Therefore, my beloved and longed-for brethren, my joy and crown, so stand fast in the Lord, beloved.

Be United, Joyful, and in Prayer

²I implore Euodia and I implore Syntyche to be of the same mind in the Lord. ³And[a] I urge you also, true companion, help these women who labored with me in the gospel, with Clement also, and the rest of my fellow workers, whose names *are* in the Book of Life.

⁴Rejoice in the Lord always. Again I will say, rejoice!

⁵Let your gentleness be known to all men. The Lord *is* at hand.

⁶Be anxious for nothing, but in everything by prayer and supplication, with thanksgiving, let your requests be made known to God; ⁷and the peace of God, which surpasses all understanding, will guard your hearts and minds through Christ Jesus.

Meditate on These Things

⁸Finally, brethren, whatever things are true, whatever things *are* noble, whatever things *are* just, whatever things *are* pure, whatever things *are* lovely, whatever things *are* of good report, if *there is* any virtue and if *there is* anything praiseworthy—meditate on these things. ⁹The things which you learned and received and heard and saw in me, these do, and the God of peace will be with you.

4:3 aNU-Text and M-Text read *Yes.*
4:13 aNU-Text reads *Him who.*
4:23 aNU-Text reads *your spirit.*

Philippian Generosity

¹⁰But I rejoiced in the Lord greatly that now at last your care for me has flourished again; though you surely did care, but you lacked opportunity. ¹¹Not that I speak in regard to need, for I have learned in whatever state I am, to be content: ¹²I know how to be abased, and I know how to abound. Everywhere and in all things I have learned both to be full and to be hungry, both to abound and to suffer need. ¹³I can do all things through Christ[a] who strengthens me.

¹⁴Nevertheless you have done well that you shared in my distress. ¹⁵Now you Philippians know also that in the beginning of the gospel, when I departed from Macedonia, no church shared with me concerning giving and receiving but you only. ¹⁶For even in Thessalonica you sent *aid* once and again for my necessities. ¹⁷Not that I seek the gift, but I seek the fruit that abounds to your account. ¹⁸Indeed I have all and abound. I am full, having received from Epaphroditus the things *sent* from you, a sweet-smelling aroma, an acceptable sacrifice, well pleasing to God. ¹⁹And my God shall supply all your need according to His riches in glory by Christ Jesus. ²⁰Now to our God and Father *be* glory forever and ever. Amen.

Greeting and Blessing

²¹Greet every saint in Christ Jesus. The brethren who are with me greet you. ²²All the saints greet you, but especially those who are of Caesar's household.

²³The grace of our Lord Jesus Christ be with you all.[a] Amen.

COLOSSIANS

PAUL WROTE THIS LETTER to a church he didn't start and probably never visited. It's most likely that the Colossian church was started by some of the men and women who became Christians while Paul ministered in Ephesus. This letter reflects his intimate, if not firsthand, love for that church and its people.

As with the Book of Ephesians, Colossians divides neatly into two halves. The first two chapters lay a theological foundation for the practical instruction of the last two chapters. Colossians proclaims the exalted Christ, the image of the invisible God in whom the fullness of God dwells (1:15–19). At the church we attend, Barbara and I spent more than a decade teaching a sixth grade Sunday school class. We made Colossians 1:18 the centerpiece of the class, teaching these eleven- and twelve-year-olds that Jesus must have preeminence, first place, in everything.

Much of what Paul writes in the first half of Colossians is aimed at addressing false teaching about the deity of Christ. The church was being seduced away from Christ by "philosophy and empty deceit, according to the tradition of men, according to the basic principles of the world, and not according to Christ" (2:8). In addition, legalism, what Paul calls "self-imposed religion" (2:23), had led some to put their confidence in their works and not in Christ. In both cases, Paul tells the Colossians to keep their focus on Christ and the gospel of grace, "As you therefore received Christ Jesus as Lord, so walk in Him" (2:6).

Three verses in the third chapter (3:18–21) provide brief, basic instructions for the Christian home. Wives learn they are to submit to their husbands; men are to love their wives and guard against bitterness; children are to please the Lord by obeying their parents; and fathers are to avoid provoking and discouraging their children. Fulfilling these commands requires that we first put to death the patterns of our sinful flesh and instead "put on the new man" so our lives will overflow with kindness, compassion, humility, patience, gentleness, forgiveness and love (3:5–14).

These attributes should abound in every Christian home. Do they in yours?

Greeting

1 Paul, an apostle of Jesus Christ by the will of God, and Timothy our brother,

²To the saints and faithful brethren in Christ *who are* in Colosse:

Grace to you and peace from God our Father and the Lord Jesus Christ.ᵃ

Their Faith in Christ

³We give thanks to the God and Father of our Lord Jesus Christ, praying always for you, ⁴since we heard of your faith in Christ Jesus and of your love for all the saints; ⁵because of the hope which is laid up for you in heaven, of which you heard before in the word of the truth of the gospel, ⁶which has come to you, as *it has* also in all the world, and is bringing forth fruit,ᵃ as *it is* also among you since the day you heard and knew the grace of God in truth; ⁷as you also learned from Epaphras, our dear fellow servant, who is a faithful minister of Christ on your behalf, ⁸who also declared to us your love in the Spirit.

Preeminence of Christ

⁹For this reason we also, since the day we heard it, do not cease to pray for you, and to ask that you may be filled with the knowledge of His will in all wisdom and spiritual understanding; ¹⁰that you may walk worthy of the Lord, fully pleasing *Him,* being fruitful in every good work and increasing in the knowledge of God; ¹¹strengthened with all might, according to His glorious power, for all patience and longsuffering with joy; ¹²giving thanks to the Father who has qualified us to be partakers of the inheritance of the saints in the light. ¹³He has delivered us from the power of darkness and conveyed *us* into the kingdom of the Son of His love, ¹⁴in whom we have redemption through His blood,ᵃ the forgiveness of sins.

¹⁵He is the image of the invisible God, the firstborn over all creation. ¹⁶For by Him all things were created that are in heaven and that are on earth, visible and

BIBLICAL INSIGHTS • 1:28, 29
Family-Initiated Revival

GOD CALLS US TO PRAY for spiritual revival in our world, and the foundation for that revival is laid when husbands and wives, fathers and mothers, do the things within the home that keep everyone centered on Christ and the gospel.

The apostle Paul wrote, "Him [Jesus] we preach, warning every man and teaching every man in all wisdom, that we may present every man perfect in Christ Jesus. To this end I also labor, striving according to His working which works in me mightily" (Col. 1:28, 29).

Paul is talking here about a proclamation of Christ that comes not from a book and not just from words, but through a transformed life. That proclamation must come first from each of us as individuals, then from us as married couples, and then from our families.

That requires leading spiritually, maybe for the first time. It means asking our spouses and children to forgive us when we err. It means repenting and asking God to make us the servant-leaders we are called to be. And it means knowing that the church isn't going to do those things for us; we have to take the initiative to make sure that our own families can be presented "perfect in Christ Jesus."

May God grant you abundant favor as you lead your wife and family spiritually.

invisible, whether thrones or dominions or principalities or powers. All things were created through Him and for Him. ¹⁷And He is before all things, and in Him all things consist. ¹⁸And He is the head of the body, the church, who is the beginning, the firstborn from the dead, that in all things He may have the preeminence.

Reconciled in Christ

¹⁹For it pleased *the Father that* in Him all the fullness should dwell, ²⁰and by Him to reconcile all things to Himself, by Him,

---

1:2 ᵃNU-Text omits *and the Lord Jesus Christ.*
1:6 ᵃNU-Text and M-Text add *and growing.*
1:14 ᵃNU-Text and M-Text omit *through His blood.*

whether things on earth or things in heaven, having made peace through the blood of His cross.

21And you, who once were alienated and enemies in your mind by wicked works, yet now He has reconciled 22in the body of His flesh through death, to present you holy, and blameless, and above reproach in His sight— 23if indeed you continue in the faith, grounded and steadfast, and are not moved away from the hope of the gospel which you heard, which was preached to every creature under heaven, of which I, Paul, became a minister.

INTIMATE MOMENTS

Take a class together. Find a topic, hobby, or sport you both want to learn more about—and sign up!

Sacrificial Service for Christ

24I now rejoice in my sufferings for you, and fill up in my flesh what is lacking in the afflictions of Christ, for the sake of His body, which is the church, 25of which I became a minister according to the stewardship from God which was given to me for you, to fulfill the word of God, 26the mystery which has been hidden from ages and from generations, but now has been revealed to His saints. 27To them God willed to make known what are the riches of the glory of this mystery among the Gentiles: which[a] is Christ in you, the hope of glory. 28Him we preach, warning every man and teaching every man in all wisdom, that we may present every man perfect in Christ Jesus. 29To this *end* I also labor, striving according to His working which works in me mightily.

Not Philosophy but Christ

2 For I want you to know what a great conflict I have for you and those in Laodicea, and *for* as many as have not seen my face in the flesh, 2that their hearts may be encouraged, being knit together in love, and *attaining* to all riches of the full assurance of understanding, to the knowledge of the mystery of God, both of the Father and[a] of Christ, 3in whom are hidden all the treasures of wisdom and knowledge.

4Now this I say lest anyone should deceive you with persuasive words. 5For though I am absent in the flesh, yet I am with you in spirit, rejoicing to see your *good* order and the steadfastness of your faith in Christ.

6As you therefore have received Christ Jesus the Lord, so walk in Him, 7rooted and built up in Him and established in the faith, as you have been taught, abounding in it[a] with thanksgiving.

8Beware lest anyone cheat you through philosophy and empty deceit, according to the tradition of men, according to the basic principles of the world, and not according to Christ. 9For in Him dwells all the fullness of the Godhead bodily; 10and you are complete in Him, who is the head of all principality and power.

Not Legalism but Christ

11In Him you were also circumcised with the circumcision made without hands, by putting off the body of the sins[a] of the flesh, by the circumcision of Christ, 12buried with Him in baptism, in which you also were raised with *Him* through faith in the working of God, who raised Him from the dead. 13And you, being dead in your trespasses and the uncircumcision of your flesh, He has made alive together with Him, having forgiven you all trespasses, 14having wiped out the handwriting of requirements that was against us, which was contrary to us. And He has taken it out of the way, having nailed it to the cross. 15Having disarmed principalities and powers, He made a public spectacle of them, triumphing over them in it.

16So let no one judge you in food or in drink, or regarding a festival or a new moon or sabbaths, 17which are a shadow of things to come, but the substance is of Christ. 18Let no one cheat you of your reward, taking delight in *false* humility and

1:27 [a]M-Text reads *who.* 2:2 [a]NU-Text omits *both of the Father and.* 2:7 [a]NU-Text omits *in it.*
2:11 [a]NU-Text omits *of the sins.*

worship of angels, intruding into those things which he has not[a] seen, vainly puffed up by his fleshly mind, 19and not holding fast to the Head, from whom all the body, nourished and knit together by joints and ligaments, grows with the increase *that is* from God.

20Therefore,[a] if you died with Christ from the basic principles of the world, why, as *though* living in the world, do you subject yourselves to regulations— 21"Do not touch, do not taste, do not handle," 22which all concern things which perish with the using—according to the commandments and doctrines of men? 23These things indeed have an appearance of wisdom in self-imposed religion, *false* humility, and neglect of the body, *but are* of no value against the indulgence of the flesh.

Not Carnality but Christ

3 If then you were raised with Christ, seek those things which are above, where Christ is, sitting at the right hand of God. 2Set your mind on things above, not on things on the earth. 3For you died, and your life is hidden with Christ in God. 4When Christ *who is* our life appears, then you also will appear with Him in glory.

2:18[a]NU-Text omits *not.*
2:20[a]NU-Text and M-Text omit *Therefore.*

PARENTING MATTERS

Q: *How can we keep from provoking our child to anger or exasperating him/her?*

The apostle Paul highlighted the role we play in training our children to stay out of the unresolved anger trap. Speaking straightforwardly to dads, he said, "And you, fathers, do not provoke your children to wrath, but bring them up in the training and admonition of the Lord" (Eph. 6:4). In Colossians Paul wrote, "Fathers, do not provoke your children, lest they become discouraged" (3:21).

From our experience with teens and our work with families, we've established a list of the things parents do to provoke anger in their children. Here are our top five:

1. *An authoritarian, dictatorial style of relating.* Attempting to enforce parental rules without a relationship of love, affection, and fun times together.

2. *A critical spirit.* Parents who consistently tear down their teens with a sarcastic or demeaning tone of voice.

3. *Outright neglect of a child.* Abandonment of a child emotionally, relationally or even physically will wound a child.

4. *Inconsistent parenting.* Kids aren't clearly told the family's boundaries, limits, and rules.

5. *A parent who rejects or withdraws from a relationship with his or her child.*

The emotional tone of your family is critically important. Crawl inside your child's perspective. As you look at yourself as a parent, are there areas where you may be provoking your child's anger? And in those areas in which you have failed, claim God's grace and forgiveness in prayer right now. You do not have to live under the weight of shame for your past mistakes. If you know the Savior as your Lord and Master, you *are* forgiven. If your children are nearing adulthood or are already adults, you may need to take one additional step. Go to them and admit your wrong and ask them to forgive you. The healing that takes place will be real in your life as well as theirs, if they forgive you.

⁵Therefore put to death your members which are on the earth: fornication, uncleanness, passion, evil desire, and covetousness, which is idolatry. ⁶Because of these things the wrath of God is coming upon the sons of disobedience, ⁷in which you yourselves once walked when you lived in them.

⁸But now you yourselves are to put off all these: anger, wrath, malice, blasphemy, filthy language out of your mouth. ⁹Do not lie to one another, since you have put off the old man with his deeds, ¹⁰and have put on the new *man* who is renewed in knowledge according to the image of Him who created him, ¹¹where there is neither Greek nor Jew, circumcised nor uncircumcised, barbarian, Scythian, slave *nor* free, but Christ *is* all and in all.

INTIMATE MOMENTS

Make an effort to keep yourself healthy and physically fit.

Character of the New Man

¹²Therefore, as *the* elect of God, holy and beloved, put on tender mercies, kindness, humility, meekness, longsuffering; ¹³bearing with one another, and forgiving one another, if anyone has a complaint against another; even as Christ forgave you, so you also *must do.* ¹⁴But above all these things put on love, which is the bond of perfection. ¹⁵And let the peace of God rule in your hearts, to which also you were called in one body; and be thankful. ¹⁶Let the word of Christ dwell in you richly in all wisdom, teaching and admonishing one another in psalms and hymns and spiritual songs, singing with grace in your hearts to the Lord. ¹⁷And whatever you do in word or deed, *do* all in the name of the Lord Jesus, giving thanks to God the Father through Him.

The Christian Home

¹⁸Wives, submit to your own husbands, as is fitting in the Lord.

¹⁹Husbands, love your wives and do not be bitter toward them.

²⁰Children, obey your parents in all things, for this is well pleasing to the Lord.

²¹Fathers, do not provoke your children, lest they become discouraged.

²²Bondservants, obey in all things your masters according to the flesh, not with eyeservice, as men-pleasers, but in sincerity of heart, fearing God. ²³And whatever you do, do it heartily, as to the Lord and not to men, ²⁴knowing that from the Lord you will receive the reward of the inheritance; forᵃ you serve the Lord Christ. ²⁵But he who does wrong will be repaid for what he has done, and there is no partiality.

4 Masters, give your bondservants what is just and fair, knowing that you also have a Master in heaven.

Christian Graces

²Continue earnestly in prayer, being vigilant in it with thanksgiving; ³meanwhile praying also for us, that God would open to us a door for the word, to speak the mystery of Christ, for which I am also in chains, ⁴that I may make it manifest, as I ought to speak.

⁵Walk in wisdom toward those *who are* outside, redeeming the time. ⁶*Let* your speech always *be* with grace, seasoned with salt, that you may know how you ought to answer each one.

Final Greetings

⁷Tychicus, a beloved brother, faithful minister, and fellow servant in the Lord, will tell you all the news about me. ⁸I am sending him to you for this very purpose, that heᵃ may know your circumstances and comfort your hearts, ⁹with Onesimus, a faithful and beloved brother, who is *one* of you. They will make known to you all things which *are happening* here.

¹⁰Aristarchus my fellow prisoner greets you, with Mark the cousin of Barnabas (about whom you received instructions: if he comes to you, welcome him), ¹¹and Jesus who is called Justus. These *are my* only fellow workers for the kingdom of God who

---

3:24 ᵃNU-Text omits *for.* **4:8** ᵃNU-Text reads *you may know our circumstances and he may.*

are of the circumcision; they have proved to be a comfort to me.

¹²Epaphras, who is *one* of you, a bond-servant of Christ, greets you, always laboring fervently for you in prayers, that you may stand perfect and complete[a] in all the will of God. ¹³For I bear him witness that he has a great zeal[a] for you, and those who are in Laodicea, and those in Hierapolis. ¹⁴Luke the beloved physician and Demas greet you. ¹⁵Greet the brethren who are in Laodicea, and Nymphas and the church that *is* in his[a] house.

Closing Exhortations and Blessing

¹⁶Now when this epistle is read among you, see that it is read also in the church of the Laodiceans, and that you likewise read the *epistle* from Laodicea. ¹⁷And say to Archippus, "Take heed to the ministry which you have received in the Lord, that you may fulfill it."

¹⁸This salutation by my own hand—Paul. Remember my chains. Grace *be* with you. Amen.

4:12 [a]NU-Text reads *fully assured.* **4:13** [a]NU-Text reads *concern.* **4:15** [a]NU-Text reads *Nympha . . . her house.*

1 THESSALONIANS

BEFORE YOU READ 1 THESSALONIANS, remind yourself of Acts 17:1–9, the brief account of Paul's first visit to Thessalonica, where Paul apparently had a very short ministry. When some of his new converts were accused of "acting contrary to the decrees of Caesar, saying there is another king—Jesus" (Acts 17:7), Paul and his companions had to flee the city to protect their safety.

Some weeks later, Paul wondered if the church had taken root or faded away. So he sent Timothy to find out how the church was doing. He received a mixed report. While the church was standing strong and held Paul in high esteem, doctrinal divisions and cultural temptations—especially sexual ones—presented an ongoing problem. Timothy found confusion in the church regarding the return of Christ and whether deceased loved ones had somehow missed eternal life. Paul addressed those issues in this letter.

You may want to pay particular attention to a few significant themes found in 1 Thessalonians:

- Paul reminds the church how he modeled godliness and tender love (2:1–12). He points to the kind of gentle concern a mother has for a nursing child (2:7) and the kind of faithful instruction a father provides for his children (2:11). We need to demonstrate the truth of the gospel in front of our children by how we live.
- Paul calls the church to sexual purity in a sexually immoral culture (4:1–8)—a much needed word today, especially with the easy availability of pornography.
- Paul carefully describes the events surrounding the return of Christ (4:16) and the "day of the Lord" (5:2). The return of Christ should provide comfort for all those who know Him.
- A series of brief exhortations at the end of the letter (4:12–22) provide helpful instruction for interpersonal relationships and for our own walks with Christ. One major exhortation is to give thanks in everything (4:18). During times of suffering we have to learn how to give thanks *by faith*—not because of what we see, but because we know God is good and that He is in control.

This book is unique in that it mixes instruction for a practical walk with Christ in the present with a view of the future. Each chapter is loaded with truths that will equip us to love and build our families, but each chapter also concludes with our hope—that Jesus is coming back for us and has a much better place prepared for us. Read the last few verses in each of these brief five chapters, and be encouraged by "what is our hope, our joy, our crown of rejoicing? Is it not even you in the presence of our Lord Jesus Christ at His coming?" (2:19).

Greeting

1 Paul, Silvanus, and Timothy,

To the church of the Thessalonians in God the Father and the Lord Jesus Christ:

Grace to you and peace from God our Father and the Lord Jesus Christ.[a]

Their Good Example

²We give thanks to God always for you all, making mention of you in our prayers, ³remembering without ceasing your work of faith, labor of love, and patience of hope in our Lord Jesus Christ in the sight of our God and Father, ⁴knowing, beloved brethren, your election by God. ⁵For our gospel did not come to you in word only, but also in power, and in the Holy Spirit and in much assurance, as you know what kind of men we were among you for your sake.

⁶And you became followers of us and of the Lord, having received the word in much affliction, with joy of the Holy Spirit, ⁷so that you became examples to all in Macedonia and Achaia who believe. ⁸For from you the word of the Lord has sounded forth, not only in Macedonia and Achaia, but also in every place. Your faith toward God has gone out, so that we do not need to say anything. ⁹For they themselves declare concerning us what manner of entry we had to you, and how you turned to God from idols to serve the living and true God, ¹⁰and to wait for His Son from heaven, whom He raised from the dead, *even* Jesus who delivers us from the wrath to come.

Paul's Conduct

2 For you yourselves know, brethren, that our coming to you was not in vain. ²But even[a] after we had suffered before and were spitefully treated at Philippi, as you know, we were bold in our God to speak to you the gospel of God in much conflict. ³For our exhortation *did* not *come* from error or uncleanness, nor *was it* in deceit.

⁴But as we have been approved by God to be entrusted with the gospel, even so we speak, not as pleasing men, but God who tests our hearts. ⁵For neither at any time did we use flattering words, as you know, nor a cloak for covetousness—God *is* witness. ⁶Nor did we seek glory from men, either from you or from others, when we might have made demands as apostles of Christ. ⁷But we were gentle among you, just as a nursing *mother* cherishes her own children. ⁸So, affectionately longing for you, we were well pleased to impart to you not only the gospel of God, but also our own lives, because you had become dear to us. ⁹For you remember, brethren, our labor and toil; for laboring night and day, that we might not be a burden to any of you, we preached to you the gospel of God.

¹⁰You *are* witnesses, and God *also,* how devoutly and justly and blamelessly we behaved ourselves among you who believe; ¹¹as you know how we exhorted, and comforted, and charged[a] every one of you, as a father *does* his own children, ¹²that you would walk worthy of God who calls you into His own kingdom and glory.

INTIMATE MOMENTS

If your lives are crazy busy, schedule some special time for romance on your calendars. Use little red heart stickers to mark the days.

Their Conversion

¹³For this reason we also thank God without ceasing, because when you received the word of God which you heard from us, you welcomed *it* not *as* the word of men, but as it is in truth, the word of God, which also effectively works in you who believe. ¹⁴For you, brethren, became imitators of the churches of God which are in Judea in Christ Jesus. For you also suffered the same things from your own countrymen, just as they *did* from the Judeans, ¹⁵who killed both the Lord Jesus and their own prophets, and have persecuted us; and they do not please God and are contrary to all men, ¹⁶forbidding us to

---

1:1 [a]NU-Text omits *from God our Father and the Lord Jesus Christ.* **2:2** [a]NU-Text and M-Text omit *even.* **2:11** [a]NU-Text and M-Text read *implored.*

speak to the Gentiles that they may be saved, so as always to fill up *the measure of* their sins; but wrath has come upon them to the uttermost.

Longing to See Them

17But we, brethren, having been taken away from you for a short time in presence, not in heart, endeavored more eagerly to see your face with great desire. 18Therefore we wanted to come to you—even I, Paul, time and again—but Satan hindered us. 19For what *is* our hope, or joy, or crown of rejoicing? *Is it* not even you in the presence of our Lord Jesus Christ at His coming? 20For you are our glory and joy.

Concern for Their Faith

3 Therefore, when we could no longer endure it, we thought it good to be left in Athens alone, 2and sent Timothy, our brother and minister of God, and our fellow laborer in the gospel of Christ, to establish you and encourage you concerning your faith, 3that no one should be shaken by these afflictions; for you yourselves know that we are appointed to this. 4For, in fact, we told you before when we were with you that we would suffer tribulation, just as it happened, and you know. 5For this reason, when I could no longer endure it, I sent to know your faith, lest by some means the tempter had tempted you, and our labor might be in vain.

Encouraged by Timothy

6But now that Timothy has come to us from you, and brought us good news of your faith and love, and that you always have good remembrance of us, greatly desiring to see us, as we also *to see* you— 7therefore, brethren, in all our affliction and distress we were comforted concerning you by your faith. 8For now we live, if you stand fast in the Lord. 9For what thanks can we render to God for you, for all the joy with which we rejoice for your sake before our God, 10night and day praying exceedingly that we may see your face and perfect what is lacking in your faith?

Prayer for the Church

11Now may our God and Father Himself, and our Lord Jesus Christ, direct our way to you. 12And may the Lord make you increase and abound in love to one another and to all, just as we *do* to you, 13so that He may establish your hearts blameless in holiness before our God and Father at the coming of our Lord Jesus Christ with all His saints.

Plea for Purity

4 Finally then, brethren, we urge and exhort in the Lord Jesus that you should abound more and more, just as you received from us how you ought to walk and to please God; 2for you know what

ROMANTIC QUOTES AND NOTES
A Holy Kiss

We wives often do not really understand that our husbands' identities as men are vitally linked to their sexuality. Sometimes we judge our husbands' sexual needs by our own.

Many wives have told me that they feel offended because their husbands are such sexual creatures, but this attitude communicates rejection to a man. To ignore his sexual needs, to resist his initiation of sex, or merely to tolerate his advances, is to tear at the heart of his self-esteem.

George Gilder said in *Men and Marriage*, "The truth is, the typical man worries a lot. He worries about his sexual performance, his wife's enjoyment, and his ability to satisfy her. A man who feels like a failure in the marriage bed will seldom have the deep, abiding self-respect for which he longs."

To please your husband sexually is to build his sense of value as a man. Reassure your husband verbally of your unconditional acceptance of him, especially if he feels insecure in this area. Tell him that you like his body and that his imperfections and mistakes don't matter to you. His confidence will grow as you respond to him and let him know that you find him desirable.

commandments we gave you through the Lord Jesus.

³For this is the will of God, your sanctification: that you should abstain from sexual immorality; ⁴that each of you should know how to possess his own vessel in sanctification and honor, ⁵not in passion of lust, like the Gentiles who do not know God; ⁶that no one should take advantage of and defraud his brother in this matter, because the Lord *is* the avenger of all such, as we also forewarned you and testified. ⁷For God did not call us to uncleanness, but in holiness. ⁸Therefore he who rejects *this* does not reject man, but God, who has also givenᵃ us His Holy Spirit.

A Brotherly and Orderly Life

⁹But concerning brotherly love you have no need that I should write to you, for you yourselves are taught by God to love one another; ¹⁰and indeed you do so toward all the brethren who are in all Macedonia. But we urge you, brethren, that you increase more and more; ¹¹that you also aspire to lead a quiet life, to mind your own business, and to work with your own hands, as we commanded you, ¹²that you may walk properly toward those who are outside, and *that* you may lack nothing.

The Comfort of Christ's Coming

¹³But I do not want you to be ignorant, brethren, concerning those who have fallen asleep, lest you sorrow as others who have no hope. ¹⁴For if we believe that Jesus died and rose again, even so God will bring with Him those who sleep in Jesus.ᵃ

¹⁵For this we say to you by the word of the Lord, that we who are alive *and* remain until the coming of the Lord will by no means precede those who are asleep. ¹⁶For the Lord Himself will descend from heaven with a shout, with the voice of an archangel, and with the trumpet of God. And the dead in Christ will rise first. ¹⁷Then we who are alive *and* remain shall be caught up together with them in the clouds to meet the Lord in the air. And thus we shall always be with the Lord.

4:8 ᵃNU-Text reads *who also gives.*
4:14 ᵃOr *those who through Jesus sleep*

BIBLICAL INSIGHTS • 5:24

Difficulties Lead to Maturity

I KNOW THAT GOD will equip me to do whatever He has planned for me. I believe the Word, "He who calls you is faithful, who will also do it" (1 Thess. 5:24).

Yet I often forget I am human (though I am acutely aware of my humanity and often wonder if there is *any* of the divine!). I want instant maturity. I don't consciously think of Christianity as a magical fairy tale life, like Cinderella; but in my finite ability to understand and perceive reality, I want the magic wand. I would love a "bibbity bobbity boo" formula of escape when life gets tough. Just a wave of the wand and poof, it's gone!

Perhaps that's why I sometimes find prayer difficult. It's *not* a magic formula. I am a restricted, limited human being, communicating with an infinite, all-wise, all-knowing God, and a great chasm of difference yawns between us. Although Jesus Christ has bridged the gap, given me His Holy Spirit to intercede for me, and positionally seated me with Him in the heavenlies, I am still confined to a frail body and a finite mind.

It's good for me to remember these lessons. Difficulties afford me the opportunity to know Him better and become more conformed to Christ. The great English preacher C. H. Spurgeon said, "God get his finest warriors out of the highlands of affliction." Perhaps He is grooming you for a strategic and noble assignment in the kingdom battle. Stand firm. Be faithful. And love the King.

¹⁸Therefore comfort one another with these words.

The Day of the Lord

5 But concerning the times and the seasons, brethren, you have no need that I should write to you. ²For you yourselves know perfectly that the day of the Lord so comes as a thief in the night. ³For when

they say, "Peace and safety!" then sudden destruction comes upon them, as labor pains upon a pregnant woman. And they shall not escape. [4]But you, brethren, are not in darkness, so that this Day should overtake you as a thief. [5]You are all sons of light and sons of the day. We are not of the night nor of darkness. [6]Therefore let us not sleep, as others *do,* but let us watch and be sober. [7]For those who sleep, sleep at night, and those who get drunk are drunk at night. [8]But let us who are of the day be sober, putting on the breastplate of faith and love, and *as* a helmet the hope of salvation. [9]For God did not appoint us to wrath, but to obtain salvation through our Lord Jesus Christ, [10]who died for us, that whether we wake or sleep, we should live together with Him.

[11]Therefore comfort each other and edify one another, just as you also are doing.

Various Exhortations

[12]And we urge you, brethren, to recognize those who labor among you, and are over you in the Lord and admonish you, [13]and to esteem them very highly in love for their work's sake. Be at peace among yourselves.

[14]Now we exhort you, brethren, warn those who are unruly, comfort the fainthearted, uphold the weak, be patient with all. [15]See that no one renders evil for evil to anyone, but always pursue what is good both for yourselves and for all.

[16]Rejoice always, [17]pray without ceasing, [18]in everything give thanks; for this is the will of God in Christ Jesus for you.

[19]Do not quench the Spirit. [20]Do not despise prophecies. [21]Test all things; hold fast what is good. [22]Abstain from every form of evil.

Blessing and Admonition

[23]Now may the God of peace Himself sanctify you completely; and may your whole spirit, soul, and body be preserved blameless at the coming of our Lord Jesus Christ. [24]He who calls you *is* faithful, who also will do *it.*

[25]Brethren, pray for us.

[26]Greet all the brethren with a holy kiss.

[27]I charge you by the Lord that this epistle be read to all the holy[a] brethren.

[28]The grace of our Lord Jesus Christ *be* with you. Amen.

5:27 [a]NU-Text omits *holy.*

2 THESSALONIANS

THE APOSTLE PAUL touched on the issue of Jesus' glorious return in his first letter to the Thessalonians (4:16—5:11), but a continuing misunderstanding of that future event led to controversy and false teaching in the church. Paul wrote this second letter to his Thessalonian friends to provide further instruction about the return of Christ and to correct the errors that had troubled the confused members of this young church.

By the time Paul wrote them, religious persecution had descended upon the Thessalonians, and many in the church felt discouraged and disheartened. Some false teachers misread the hard times and suggested that "the day of the Lord" had already taken place, causing great confusion in the church. Some had quit working, convinced that Jesus would appear any day. Paul designed his letter to comfort the faithful, correct the false teaching, and confront those who had quit their jobs and so had become a financial burden on others.

How does the fact of Jesus' second coming affect your marriage and your family? During our college years, many young Christians expressed an earnest anticipation for the soon return of Christ. We lived with the mindset that the end was near and that "today could be the day when Jesus comes back!" Our conviction about the nearness of the end times gave us a sense of great urgency about fulfilling the Great Commission of Matthew 28:19, 20.

Today, as the sense of expectation of Christ's soon return has faded, much of that former urgency has evaporated. As a result, many Christians seem little motivated to share their faith or to make disciples. Yet what John said about the return of Christ remains as true as ever, "We know that when He is revealed, we shall be like Him, for we shall see Him as He is. And everyone who has this hope in Him purifies himself, just as He is pure" (1 John 3:2, 3).

As you read 2 Thessalonians, realize that Jesus *is* coming back. We don't know when, but we ought to live each day with the understanding that *this might be the day!*

Greeting

1 Paul, Silvanus, and Timothy,

To the church of the Thessalonians in God our Father and the Lord Jesus Christ:

²Grace to you and peace from God our Father and the Lord Jesus Christ.

INTIMATE MOMENTS

Be resolute in romancing your love all year long. Choose your favorite ideas and enter them into your day planner, January through December.

God's Final Judgment and Glory

³We are bound to thank God always for you, brethren, as it is fitting, because your faith grows exceedingly, and the love of every one of you all abounds toward each other, ⁴so that we ourselves boast of you among the churches of God for your patience and faith in all your persecutions and tribulations that you endure, ⁵*which is* manifest evidence of the righteous judgment of God, that you may be counted worthy of the kingdom of God, for which you also suffer; ⁶since *it is* a righteous thing with God to repay with tribulation those who trouble you, ⁷and to *give* you who are troubled rest with us when the Lord Jesus is revealed from heaven with His mighty angels, ⁸in flaming fire taking vengeance on those who do not know God, and on those who do not obey the gospel of our Lord Jesus Christ. ⁹These shall be punished with everlasting destruction from the presence of the Lord and from the glory of His power, ¹⁰when He comes, in that Day, to be glorified in His saints and to be admired among all those who believe,ᵃ because our testimony among you was believed.

¹¹Therefore we also pray always for you that our God would count you worthy of *this* calling, and fulfill all the good pleasure of *His* goodness and the work of faith with power, ¹²that the name of our Lord

Jesus Christ may be glorified in you, and you in Him, according to the grace of our God and the Lord Jesus Christ.

The Great Apostasy

2 Now, brethren, concerning the coming of our Lord Jesus Christ and our gathering together to Him, we ask you, ²not to be soon shaken in mind or troubled, either by spirit or by word or by letter, as if from us, as though the day of Christᵃ had come. ³Let no one deceive you by any means; for *that Day will not come* unless the falling away comes first, and the man of sinᵃ is revealed, the son of perdition, ⁴who opposes and exalts himself above all that is called God or that is worshiped, so that he sits as Godᵃ in the temple of God, showing himself that he is God.

⁵Do you not remember that when I was still with you I told you these things? ⁶And now you know what is restraining, that he may be revealed in his own time. ⁷For the mystery of lawlessness is already at work; only Heᵃ who now restrains *will do so* until Heᵇ is taken out of the way. ⁸And then the lawless one will be revealed, whom the Lord will consume with the breath of His mouth and destroy with the brightness of His coming. ⁹The coming of the *lawless one* is according to the working of Satan, with all power, signs, and lying wonders, ¹⁰and with all unrighteous deception among those who perish, because they did not receive the love of the truth, that they might be saved. ¹¹And for this reason God will send them strong delusion, that they should believe the lie, ¹²that they all may be condemned who did not believe the truth but had pleasure in unrighteousness.

Stand Fast

¹³But we are bound to give thanks to God always for you, brethren beloved by the Lord, because God from the beginning chose you for salvation through sanctification by the Spirit and belief in the truth, ¹⁴to which He called you by our gospel, for

---

1:10 ᵃNU-Text and M-Text read *have believed.*
2:2 ᵃNU-Text reads *the Lord.* **2:3** ᵃNU-Text reads *lawlessness.* **2:4** ᵃNU-Text omits *as God.*
2:7 ᵃOr *he* ᵇOr *he*

the obtaining of the glory of our Lord Jesus Christ. 15Therefore, brethren, stand fast and hold the traditions which you were taught, whether by word or our epistle.

16Now may our Lord Jesus Christ Himself, and our God and Father, who has loved us and given *us* everlasting consolation and good hope by grace, 17comfort your hearts and establish you in every good word and work.

Pray for Us

3 Finally, brethren, pray for us, that the word of the Lord may run *swiftly* and be glorified, just as *it is* with you, 2and that we may be delivered from unreasonable and wicked men; for not all have faith.

3But the Lord is faithful, who will establish you and guard *you* from the evil one. 4And we have confidence in the Lord concerning you, both that you do and will do the things we command you.

5Now may the Lord direct your hearts into the love of God and into the patience of Christ.

Warning Against Idleness

6But we command you, brethren, in the name of our Lord Jesus Christ, that you withdraw from every brother who walks disorderly and not according to the tradition which hea received from us. 7For you

---

3:6 aNU-Text and M-Text read *they.*

yourselves know how you ought to follow us, for we were not disorderly among you; 8nor did we eat anyone's bread free of charge, but worked with labor and toil night and day, that we might not be a burden to any of you, 9not because we do not have authority, but to make ourselves an example of how you should follow us.

10For even when we were with you, we commanded you this: If anyone will not work, neither shall he eat. 11For we hear that there are some who walk among you in a disorderly manner, not working at all, but are busybodies. 12Now those who are such we command and exhort through our Lord Jesus Christ that they work in quietness and eat their own bread.

13But *as for* you, brethren, do not grow weary *in* doing good. 14And if anyone does not obey our word in this epistle, note that person and do not keep company with him, that he may be ashamed. 15Yet do not count *him* as an enemy, but admonish *him* as a brother.

Benediction

16Now may the Lord of peace Himself give you peace always in every way. The Lord *be* with you all.

17The salutation of Paul with my own hand, which is a sign in every epistle; so I write.

18The grace of our Lord Jesus Christ *be* with you all. Amen.

1 TIMOTHY

FOR MANY YEARS, a mature apostle Paul and a young Timothy traveled together as co-laborers in the ministry of the gospel. They had a very close relationship; Paul referred to Timothy as his "true son in the faith" (1:2). After Timothy became the pastor of the church in Ephesus, Paul wrote this first letter to his protégé to encourage and instruct him in his new pastoral duties.

In recent years, controversy has arisen about Paul's instruction in this letter regarding the role of women in the church (2:9–15). On one side of the dispute are the egalitarians, who believe no distinctions in role exist between men and women in marriage and in the church. On the other side are the complementarians—like me—who insist that while men and women have equal value and identical worth before God, and so share equally in the church's mission to make disciples, God has specifically called men to bear the load of providing spiritual authority and carrying out the regular teaching ministry of the church. In fact, Paul insists that one requirement for a man to serve as a spiritual overseer (or elder) is that he is the husband of one wife. Being a faithful, covenant-keeping husband is a mark of a spiritually mature man.

Paul also speaks in this letter about the need for the church to care for its widows (5:3–16). He insists that men, as the heads of their households, have a divine responsibility to provide for the physical needs of their families.

In my own Bible, I have highlighted one passage in 1 Timothy that addresses those who are "rich in this present age" (6:17). Today, that would include virtually everyone in America! God's Word warns us about being haughty or proud, and encourages us to trust in Him instead of our wealth, to be rich in good works, and to be ready to give and willing to share (6:17–19). We should teach our children that it is both a privilege and a responsibility to give, first to our local church, and then, as God enables us, to ministries and missionaries dedicated to advancing the work of the kingdom.

Greeting

1 Paul, an apostle of Jesus Christ, by the commandment of God our Savior and the Lord Jesus Christ, our hope,

2To Timothy, a true son in the faith:

Grace, mercy, *and* peace from God our Father and Jesus Christ our Lord.

No Other Doctrine

3As I urged you when I went into Macedonia—remain in Ephesus that you may charge some that they teach no other doctrine, 4nor give heed to fables and endless genealogies, which cause disputes rather than godly edification which is in faith. 5Now the purpose of the commandment is love from a pure heart, *from* a good conscience, and *from* sincere faith, 6from which some, having strayed, have turned aside to idle talk, 7desiring to be teachers of the law, understanding neither what they say nor the things which they affirm.

8But we know that the law *is* good if one uses it lawfully, 9knowing this: that the law is not made for a righteous person, but for *the* lawless and insubordinate, for *the* ungodly and for sinners, for *the* unholy and profane, for murderers of fathers and murderers of mothers, for manslayers, 10for fornicators, for sodomites, for kidnappers, for liars, for perjurers, and if there is any other thing that is contrary to sound doctrine, 11according to the glorious gospel of the blessed God which was committed to my trust.

Glory to God for His Grace

12And I thank Christ Jesus our Lord who has enabled me, because He counted me faithful, putting *me* into the ministry, 13although I was formerly a blasphemer, a persecutor, and an insolent man; but I obtained mercy because I did *it* ignorantly in unbelief. 14And the grace of our Lord was exceedingly abundant, with faith and love which are in Christ Jesus. 15This *is* a faithful saying and worthy of all acceptance, that Christ Jesus came into the world to save sinners, of whom I am chief.

16However, for this reason I obtained mercy, that in me first Jesus Christ might show all longsuffering, as a pattern to those who are going to believe on Him for everlasting life. 17Now to the King eternal, immortal, invisible, to God who alone is wise,a *be* honor and glory forever and ever. Amen.

Fight the Good Fight

18This charge I commit to you, son Timothy, according to the prophecies previously made concerning you, that by them you may wage the good warfare, 19having faith and a good conscience, which some having rejected, concerning the faith have suffered shipwreck, 20of whom are Hymenaeus and Alexander, whom I delivered to Satan that they may learn not to blaspheme.

INTIMATE MOMENTS

Seek to resolve misunderstandings and conflict before you go to sleep each night.

Pray for All Men

2 Therefore I exhort first of all that supplications, prayers, intercessions, *and* giving of thanks be made for all men, 2for kings and all who are in authority, that we may lead a quiet and peaceable life in all godliness and reverence. 3For this *is* good and acceptable in the sight of God our Savior, 4who desires all men to be saved and to come to the knowledge of the truth. 5For *there is* one God and one Mediator between God and men, *the* Man Christ Jesus, 6who gave Himself a ransom for all, to be testified in due time, 7for which I was appointed a preacher and an apostle—I am speaking the truth in Christa *and* not lying—a teacher of the Gentiles in faith and truth.

Men and Women in the Church

8I desire therefore that the men pray everywhere, lifting up holy hands, without wrath and doubting; 9in like manner also, that the women adorn themselves in modest apparel, with propriety and moderation,

---

1:17 aNU-Text reads *to the only God.*
2:7 aNU-Text omits *in Christ.*

not with braided hair or gold or pearls or costly clothing, ¹⁰but, which is proper for women professing godliness, with good works. ¹¹Let a woman learn in silence with all submission. ¹²And I do not permit a woman to teach or to have authority over a man, but to be in silence. ¹³For Adam was formed first, then Eve. ¹⁴And Adam was not deceived, but the woman being deceived, fell into transgression. ¹⁵Nevertheless she will be saved in childbearing if they continue in faith, love, and holiness, with self-control.

Qualifications of Overseers

3 This *is* a faithful saying: If a man desires the position of a bishop,ᵃ he desires a good work. ²A bishop then must be blameless, the husband of one wife, temperate, sober-minded, of good behavior, hospitable, able to teach; ³not given to wine, not violent, not greedy for money,ᵃ but gentle, not quarrelsome, not covetous; ⁴one who rules his own house well, having *his* children in submission with all reverence ⁵(for if a man does not know how to rule his own house, how will he take care of the church of God?); ⁶not a novice, lest being puffed up with pride he fall into the *same* condemnation as the devil. ⁷Moreover he

must have a good testimony among those who are outside, lest he fall into reproach and the snare of the devil.

Qualifications of Deacons

⁸Likewise deacons *must be* reverent, not double-tongued, not given to much wine, not greedy for money, ⁹holding the mystery of the faith with a pure conscience. ¹⁰But let these also first be tested; then let them serve as deacons, being *found* blameless. ¹¹Likewise, *their* wives *must be* reverent, not slanderers, temperate, faithful in all things. ¹²Let deacons be the husbands of one wife, ruling *their* children and their own houses well. ¹³For those who have served well as deacons obtain for themselves a good standing and great boldness in the faith which is in Christ Jesus.

The Great Mystery

¹⁴These things I write to you, though I hope to come to you shortly; ¹⁵but if I am delayed, *I write* so that you may know how you ought to conduct yourself in the house of God, which is the church of the living

---

3:1 ᵃLiterally *overseer*
3:3 ᵃNU-Text omits *not greedy for money.*

PARENTING MATTERS

Q: *What kind of man has God called me to be as the leader of my home?*

The apostle Paul required that an overseer in the early church manage his household well (1 Tim. 3:2, 4). My dad was that kind of leader—a man of quiet authority, who always had time for us.

What kind of memories will your children have of you? Will they remember a father who spent time with them, played with them, laughed with them? Or will they think of you as someone preoccupied with work, unfinished projects, or a hobby?

What would happen if you switched the energy you give to your job with the energy you give to your home and family? What would happen to work? What would happen to your home?

I realize this may be an unfair question, because many men have to work long hours away from home. But too many fathers give almost all their energy to their jobs and leave none for their families.

I have a friend who has a 3x5-inch card on his desk that reads, "Leave some for home." He realizes that without this daily reminder, he'd go home with no energy most of the time.

We need fathers determined to save the energy to succeed at home, regardless of the cost. We'll need that energy if we're going to manage our households well.

God, the pillar and ground of the truth. [16]And without controversy great is the mystery of godliness:

> God[a] was manifested in the flesh,
> Justified in the Spirit,
> Seen by angels,
> Preached among the Gentiles,
> Believed on in the world,
> Received up in glory.

The Great Apostasy

4 Now the Spirit expressly says that in latter times some will depart from the faith, giving heed to deceiving spirits and doctrines of demons, [2]speaking lies in hypocrisy, having their own conscience seared with a hot iron, [3]forbidding to marry, *and commanding* to abstain from foods which God created to be received with thanksgiving by those who believe and know the truth. [4]For every creature of God *is* good, and nothing is to be refused if it is received with thanksgiving; [5]for it is sanctified by the word of God and prayer.

A Good Servant of Jesus Christ

[6]If you instruct the brethren in these things, you will be a good minister of Jesus Christ, nourished in the words of faith and of the good doctrine which you have carefully followed. [7]But reject profane and old wives' fables, and exercise yourself toward godliness. [8]For bodily exercise profits a little, but godliness is profitable for all things, having promise of the life that now is and of that which is to come. [9]This *is* a faithful saying and worthy of all acceptance. [10]For to this *end* we both labor and suffer reproach,[a] because we trust in the living God, who is *the* Savior of all men, especially of those who believe. [11]These things command and teach.

Take Heed to Your Ministry

[12]Let no one despise your youth, but be an example to the believers in word, in conduct, in love, in spirit,[a] in faith, in purity. [13]Till I come, give attention to reading, to exhortation, to doctrine. [14]Do not neglect the gift that is in you, which was given to you by prophecy with the laying on of the hands of the eldership. [15]Meditate on these things; give yourself entirely to them, that your progress may be evident to all. [16]Take heed to yourself and to the doctrine. Continue in them, for in doing this you will save both yourself and those who hear you.

3:16 [a]NU-Text reads *Who.* **4:10** [a]NU-Text reads *we labor and strive.* **4:12** [a]NU-Text omits *in spirit.*

Slay the Phantom

American forces during World War II had a phantom military outfit, a group called the Twenty-third Headquarters Special Troops. With careful staging and show-business theatrics, they impersonated real troops and created an illusion of military strength to strategically fool the Germans.

Many husbands and wives have such phantoms lurking in their minds—an unreal mental image that they think they need to battle. No one can see these phantoms except the individuals who conjure them up, but they seem real.

You probably have a mental picture of how you should act as a husband or wife. And chances are this image is so perfect, so idyllic, that it is completely unattainable. Yet, every day you judge your performance by this phantom! And since you cannot match those standards, your self-confidence suffers.

Phantoms can derail marriages.

Do you have unrealistic expectations of yourself? Are you aware of your mate having such a phantom? What's the difference between healthy goals for personal growth and an illusion or unattainable self-image? Pray that God will enable you to be happy with the person He made you to be, and to find a healthy balance between who you are and your personal goals for growth.

BIBLICAL INSIGHTS • 5:8

Serving through Providing

HUSBANDS WHO LOVE THEIR WIVES in a way that pleases the heart of God will willingly and even eagerly serve them. And a great biblical way for a husband to serve his wife is to provide for her.

This provision first involves assuming responsibility for meeting the material needs of the family. The apostle Paul writes, "But if anyone does not provide for his own, and especially for those of his household, he has denied the faith, and is worse than an unbeliever" (1 Tim. 5:8). Maybe you can quote thirty Bible verses a minute, but if you fail to provide for your household, Paul calls you "worse than an unbeliever."

Providing for your wife also means taking the initiative to help meet her spiritual needs. You do this by modeling godly character, by praying with her, by spending time together in God's Word, and by looking for ways to encourage her to grow spiritually.

To be a leader, a lover, and a servant is to assume responsibility to care for the gift God has given you—your wife. Give up your life for hers, and at the Judgment Seat of Christ, He will say, "Well done, good and faithful servant" (Matt. 25:21).

Treatment of Church Members

5 Do not rebuke an older man, but exhort *him* as a father, younger men as brothers, ²older women as mothers, younger women as sisters, with all purity.

Honor True Widows

³Honor widows who are really widows. ⁴But if any widow has children or grandchildren, let them first learn to show piety at home and to repay their parents; for this is good and[a] acceptable before God. ⁵Now she who is really a widow, and left alone, trusts in God and continues in supplications and prayers night and day. ⁶But she who lives in pleasure is dead while she lives. ⁷And these things command, that they may be blameless. ⁸But if anyone does not provide for his own, and especially for those of his household, he has denied the faith and is worse than an unbeliever.

⁹Do not let a widow under sixty years old be taken into the number, *and not unless* she has been the wife of one man, ¹⁰well reported for good works: if she has brought up children, if she has lodged strangers, if she has washed the saints' feet, if she has relieved the afflicted, if she has diligently followed every good work.

¹¹But refuse *the* younger widows; for when they have begun to grow wanton against Christ, they desire to marry, ¹²having condemnation because they have cast off their first faith. ¹³And besides they learn *to be* idle, wandering about from house to house, and not only idle but also gossips and busybodies, saying things which they ought not. ¹⁴Therefore I desire that *the* younger *widows* marry, bear children, manage the house, give no opportunity to the adversary to speak reproachfully. ¹⁵For some have already turned aside after Satan. ¹⁶If any believing man or[a] woman has widows, let them relieve them, and do not let the church be burdened, that it may relieve those who are really widows.

Honor the Elders

¹⁷Let the elders who rule well be counted worthy of double honor, especially those who labor in the word and doctrine. ¹⁸For the Scripture says, *"You shall not muzzle an ox while it treads out the grain,"*[a] and, "The laborer *is* worthy of his wages."[b] ¹⁹Do not receive an accusation against an elder except from two or three witnesses. ²⁰Those who are sinning rebuke in the presence of all, that the rest also may fear.

²¹I charge *you* before God and the Lord Jesus Christ and the elect angels that you observe these things without prejudice, doing nothing with partiality. ²²Do not lay hands on anyone hastily, nor share in other people's sins; keep yourself pure.

5:4 [a]NU-Text and M-Text omit *good and.*   **5:16** [a]NU-Text omits *man or.*   **5:18** [a]Deuteronomy 25:4   [b]Luke 10:7

²³No longer drink only water, but use a little wine for your stomach's sake and your frequent infirmities.

²⁴Some men's sins are clearly evident, preceding *them* to judgment, but those of some *men* follow later. ²⁵Likewise, the good works *of some* are clearly evident, and those that are otherwise cannot be hidden.

Honor Masters

6 Let as many bondservants as are under the yoke count their own masters worthy of all honor, so that the name of God and *His* doctrine may not be blasphemed. ²And those who have believing masters, let them not despise *them* because they are brethren, but rather serve *them* because those who are benefited are believers and beloved. Teach and exhort these things.

Error and Greed

³If anyone teaches otherwise and does not consent to wholesome words, *even* the words of our Lord Jesus Christ, and to the doctrine which accords with godliness, ⁴he is proud, knowing nothing, but is obsessed with disputes and arguments over words, from which come envy, strife, reviling, evil suspicions, ⁵useless wranglings^a of men of corrupt minds and destitute of the truth, who suppose that godliness is a *means of* gain. From such withdraw yourself.^a

⁶Now godliness with contentment is great gain. ⁷For we brought nothing into *this* world, *and it is* certain^a we can carry nothing out. ⁸And having food and clothing, with these we shall be content. ⁹But those who desire to be rich fall into temptation and a snare, and *into* many foolish and harmful lusts which drown men in destruction and perdition. ¹⁰For the love of money is a root of all *kinds of* evil, for which some have strayed from the faith in their greediness, and pierced themselves through with many sorrows.

6:5 ^aNU-Text and M-Text read *constant friction.*
^bNU-Text omits this sentence.
6:7 ^aNU-Text omits *and it is certain.*

The Good Confession

¹¹But you, O man of God, flee these things and pursue righteousness, godliness, faith, love, patience, gentleness. ¹²Fight the good fight of faith, lay hold on eternal life, to which you were also called and have confessed the good confession in the presence of many witnesses. ¹³I urge you in the sight of God who gives life to all things, and *before* Christ Jesus who witnessed the good confession before Pontius Pilate, ¹⁴that you keep *this* commandment without spot, blameless until our Lord Jesus Christ's appearing, ¹⁵which He will manifest in His own time, *He who is* the blessed and only Potentate, the King of kings and Lord of lords, ¹⁶who alone has immortality, dwelling in unapproachable light, whom no man has seen or can see, to whom *be* honor and everlasting power. Amen.

INTIMATE MOMENTS

March 17 is St. Patrick's Day. Celebrate it by leaving your wife a note that says, "I'm lucky to have you by my side."

Instructions to the Rich

¹⁷Command those who are rich in this present age not to be haughty, nor to trust in uncertain riches but in the living God, who gives us richly all things to enjoy. ¹⁸*Let them* do good, that they be rich in good works, ready to give, willing to share, ¹⁹storing up for themselves a good foundation for the time to come, that they may lay hold on eternal life.

Guard the Faith

²⁰O Timothy! Guard what was committed to your trust, avoiding the profane *and* idle babblings and contradictions of what is falsely called knowledge— ²¹by professing it some have strayed concerning the faith.

Grace *be* with you. Amen.

2 TIMOTHY

THIS IS PROBABLY THE LAST LETTER the apostle Paul ever wrote. He penned the letter from prison in Rome, expecting that in a very short while he would be executed for his faith. At the time, Timothy was serving as the pastor of the church Paul founded in Ephesus. The apostle wrote to his protégé to provide encouragement and counsel as the young man carried out his pastoral duties.

The reality of suffering permeates this letter. Paul wants Timothy to know that trials and hardships are a normal part of life for the faithful follower of Jesus, so it should surprise no one that real suffering has overtaken the apostle in prison. Paul acknowledges that Timothy also faces persecution and attacks, albeit of a different kind, in his own ministry. Paul exhorts Timothy to persevere, to stand firm, and to faithfully serve Christ, even in the face of discouragement and difficulties.

This letter gives us some insight into the home where Timothy grew up. While Timothy's father was a Greek, his mother and grandmother were Jewish, and the latter pair regularly taught a young Timothy the Jewish Scriptures (1:5, 3:15). We're not sure when or how Timothy and his mother became Christians, but it may have been during Paul's first visit to their hometown of Lystra (Acts 14:8–20). When Paul later returned to Lystra, Timothy and his mother were both identified as followers of Jesus (Acts 16:1).

Because Paul refers to Timothy in his letters as his "son in the faith," we presume that Timothy first heard the gospel from Paul and was converted through the apostle's ministry. But as Paul makes clear, it was the faithful biblical instruction from Timothy's mother and grandmother, beginning when Timothy was still a boy (3:15), that prepared him to respond enthusiastically to the gospel message.

This letter makes it clear that a believing parent's responsibility is to instruct his or her children in the Christian faith. While the church and other organizations can help teach our children the truths of Scripture, the primary responsibility for this always remains with us parents.

Greeting

1 Paul, an apostle of Jesus Christ[a] by the will of God, according to the promise of life which is in Christ Jesus,

²To Timothy, a beloved son:

Grace, mercy, *and* peace from God the Father and Christ Jesus our Lord.

Timothy's Faith and Heritage

³I thank God, whom I serve with a pure conscience, as *my* forefathers *did,* as without ceasing I remember you in my prayers night and day, ⁴greatly desiring to see you, being mindful of your tears, that I may be filled with joy, ⁵when I call to remembrance the genuine faith that is in you, which dwelt first in your grandmother Lois and your mother Eunice, and I am persuaded is in you also. ⁶Therefore I remind you to stir up the gift of God which is in you through the laying on of my hands. ⁷For God has not given us a spirit of fear, but of power and of love and of a sound mind.

Not Ashamed of the Gospel

⁸Therefore do not be ashamed of the testimony of our Lord, nor of me His prisoner, but share with me in the sufferings for the gospel according to the power of God, ⁹who has saved us and called *us* with a holy calling, not according to our works, but according to His own purpose and grace which was given to us in Christ Jesus before time began, ¹⁰but has now been revealed by the appearing of our Savior Jesus Christ, *who* has abolished death and brought life and immortality to light through the gospel, ¹¹to which I was appointed a preacher, an apostle, and a teacher of the Gentiles.[a] ¹²For this reason I also suffer these things; nevertheless I am not ashamed, for I know whom I have believed and am persuaded that He is able to keep what I have committed to Him until that Day.

Be Loyal to the Faith

¹³Hold fast the pattern of sound words which you have heard from me, in faith

BIBLICAL INSIGHTS • 1:7
How to Overcome Fear

THE ANTIDOTE FOR THE FEAR that can come your way as a spouse or as a parent is to appropriate God's power over your circumstances. The apostle Paul writes, "For God has not given us a spirit of fear, but of power and of love and of a sound mind" (2 Tim. 1:7).

In order to overcome fear, first remember who lives in you as a believer in Jesus Christ—the Holy Spirit. You may not always feel as though He lives within you, but the Bible promises you that He does. And because God's Spirit lives within you, all the fullness of God lives in you.

When you, your spouse, or other members of your family encounter fear, you should first step back and realize whose you are and what you have because of the presence of the Holy Spirit within you.

Then recall that He gives you the power and love you need to overcome your fear and your circumstances. When you do that, a "sound mind" will replace fear. God will supply you with the courage you need to move out and do the things He calls you to do as a father or mother, husband or wife.

What fear are you struggling with right now? Is your spouse struggling with fears? Why not take an inventory of those issues that are troubling you concerning the future and bring them all to God in prayer together as a couple, or even as a family?

and love which are in Christ Jesus. ¹⁴That good thing which was committed to you, keep by the Holy Spirit who dwells in us.

¹⁵This you know, that all those in Asia have turned away from me, among whom are Phygellus and Hermogenes. ¹⁶The Lord grant mercy to the household of Onesiphorus, for he often refreshed me, and was not ashamed of my chain; ¹⁷but when he arrived in Rome, he sought me out very zealously and found *me.* ¹⁸The Lord grant to him

1:1 ᵃNU-Text and M-Text read *Christ Jesus.*
1:11 ᵃNU-Text omits *of the Gentiles.*

that he may find mercy from the Lord in that Day—and you know very well how many ways he ministered *to me*[a] at Ephesus.

Be Strong in Grace

2 You therefore, my son, be strong in the grace that is in Christ Jesus. ²And the things that you have heard from me among many witnesses, commit these to faithful men who will be able to teach others also. ³You therefore must endure[a] hardship as a good soldier of Jesus Christ. ⁴No one engaged in warfare entangles himself with the affairs of *this* life, that he may please him who enlisted him as a soldier. ⁵And also if anyone competes in athletics, he is not crowned unless he competes according to the rules. ⁶The hardworking farmer must be first to partake of the crops. ⁷Consider what I say, and may[a] the Lord give you understanding in all things.

⁸Remember that Jesus Christ, of the seed of David, was raised from the dead according to my gospel, ⁹for which I suffer trouble as an evildoer, *even* to the point of chains; but the word of God is not chained. ¹⁰Therefore I endure all things for the sake of the elect, that they also may obtain the salvation which is in Christ Jesus with eternal glory.

¹¹*This is* a faithful saying:

For if we died with *Him,*
　We shall also live with *Him.*
¹²　If we endure,
　We shall also reign with *Him.*
If we deny *Him,*
　He also will deny us.

13　If we are faithless,
　He remains faithful;
　He cannot deny Himself.

Approved and Disapproved Workers

¹⁴Remind *them* of these things, charging *them* before the Lord not to strive about words to no profit, to the ruin of the hearers. ¹⁵Be diligent to present yourself approved to God, a worker who does not need to be ashamed, rightly dividing the word of truth. ¹⁶But shun profane *and* idle babblings, for they will increase to more ungodliness. ¹⁷And their message will spread like cancer. Hymenaeus and Philetus are of this sort, ¹⁸who have strayed concerning the truth, saying that the resurrection is already past; and they overthrow the faith of some. ¹⁹Nevertheless the solid foundation of God stands, having this seal: "The Lord knows those who are His," and, "Let everyone who names the name of Christ[a] depart from iniquity."

²⁰But in a great house there are not only vessels of gold and silver, but also of wood and clay, some for honor and some for dishonor. ²¹Therefore if anyone cleanses himself from the latter, he will be a vessel for honor, sanctified and useful for the Master, prepared for every good work. ²²Flee also youthful lusts; but pursue righteousness, faith, love, peace with those who call on the Lord out of a pure heart. ²³But avoid foolish and ignorant disputes, knowing that they generate strife. ²⁴And a servant of the Lord must not quarrel but be gentle to all, able to teach, patient, ²⁵in humility correcting those who are in opposition, if God perhaps will grant them repentance, so that they may know the truth, ²⁶and *that* they may come to their senses *and escape* the snare of the devil, having been taken captive by him to *do* his will.

Perilous Times and Perilous Men

3 But know this, that in the last days perilous times will come: ²For men will be lovers of themselves, lovers of money,

INTIMATE MOMENTS

This Fourth of July, light up your own fireworks in the night sky. Add glow-in-the-dark stars to your bedroom ceiling, and snuggle under your own private starry sky.

1:18 [a]*To me* is from the Vulgate and a few Greek manuscripts. **2:3** [a]NU-Text reads *You must share.* **2:7** [a]NU-Text reads *the Lord will give you.* **2:19** [a]NU-Text and M-Text read *the Lord.*

boasters, proud, blasphemers, disobedient to parents, unthankful, unholy, ³unloving, unforgiving, slanderers, without self-control, brutal, despisers of good, ⁴traitors, headstrong, haughty, lovers of pleasure rather than lovers of God, ⁵having a form of godliness but denying its power. And from such people turn away! ⁶For of this sort are those who creep into households and make captives of gullible women loaded down with sins, led away by various lusts, ⁷always learning and never able to come to the knowledge of the truth. ⁸Now as Jannes and Jambres resisted Moses, so do these also resist the truth: men of corrupt minds, disapproved concerning the faith; ⁹but they will progress no further, for their folly will be manifest to all, as theirs also was.

The Man of God and the Word of God

¹⁰But you have carefully followed my doctrine, manner of life, purpose, faith, longsuffering, love, perseverance, ¹¹persecutions, afflictions, which happened to me at Antioch, at Iconium, at Lystra—what persecutions I endured. And out of *them* all the Lord delivered me. ¹²Yes, and all who desire to live godly in Christ Jesus will suffer persecution. ¹³But evil men and impostors will grow worse and worse, deceiving and being deceived. ¹⁴But you must continue in the things which you have learned and been assured of, knowing from whom you have learned *them,* ¹⁵and that from childhood you have known the Holy Scriptures, which are able to make you wise for salvation through faith which is in Christ Jesus.

¹⁶All Scripture *is* given by inspiration of God, and *is* profitable for doctrine, for reproof, for correction, for instruction in righteousness, ¹⁷that the man of God may be complete, thoroughly equipped for every good work.

Preach the Word

4 I charge *you* therefore before God and the Lord Jesus Christ, who will judge

Learn to Communicate Openly

By God's grace, we can grow in our ability to be vulnerable and transparent with those we love. Author John Powell describes this process in his excellent book, *Why Am I Afraid to Tell You Who I Am?* He lists five levels of communication.

Most people start at *level five*—clichés. We might call this "elevator talk" ("Have a nice day.") in which you speak, but share nothing.

Level four involves sharing facts. You are willing to report what you know, but still you share nothing of yourself.

At *level three*, people reveal opinions, their ideas, judgments and viewpoints. At this level, you start to come out of your shell and reveal a little of who you are. At the same time, you're ready to retreat in the face of disagreement or rejection.

At *level two* you begin to share emotions. You let the other person know just what you feel. Again, this is risky and you must be careful not to hurt one another, but it is an essential step if you're going to move toward a deeper relationship.

Level one is transparency—being completely open with each other, sharing the real you, from the heart. This level of communication requires a large amount of trust and commitment.

We spend most of our lives communicating with others at the safest levels of communication. In marriage, however, we ought to be getting beneath the surface. When was the last time you and your spouse had a truly transparent conversation? What do you need to do to go deeper in your communication with each other?

Take some time on your next date night to review these five levels and rate yourselves and one another on how well you are doing in each of the five. Then begin to talk. Talk about how you can deepen your love for each other by becoming more intimate and transparent with each other.

the living and the dead at[a] His appearing and His kingdom: [2]Preach the word! Be ready in season *and* out of season. Convince, rebuke, exhort, with all longsuffering and teaching. [3]For the time will come when they will not endure sound doctrine, but according to their own desires, *because* they have itching ears, they will heap up for themselves teachers; [4]and they will turn *their* ears away from the truth, and be turned aside to fables. [5]But you be watchful in all things, endure afflictions, do the work of an evangelist, fulfill your ministry.

Paul's Valedictory

[6]For I am already being poured out as a drink offering, and the time of my departure is at hand. [7]I have fought the good fight, I have finished the race, I have kept the faith. [8]Finally, there is laid up for me the crown of righteousness, which the Lord, the righteous Judge, will give to me on that Day, and not to me only but also to all who have loved His appearing.

The Abandoned Apostle

[9]Be diligent to come to me quickly; [10]for Demas has forsaken me, having loved this present world, and has departed for Thessalonica—Crescens for Galatia, Titus for Dalmatia. [11]Only Luke is with me. Get Mark and bring him with you, for he is useful to me for ministry. [12]And Tychicus I have sent to Ephesus. [13]Bring the cloak that I left with Carpus at Troas when you come—and the books, especially the parchments.

[14]Alexander the coppersmith did me much harm. May the Lord repay him according to his works. [15]You also must beware of him, for he has greatly resisted our words.

[16]At my first defense no one stood with me, but all forsook me. May it not be charged against them.

The Lord Is Faithful

[17]But the Lord stood with me and strengthened me, so that the message might be preached fully through me, and *that* all the Gentiles might hear. Also I was delivered out of the mouth of the lion. [18]And the Lord will deliver me from every evil work and preserve *me* for His heavenly kingdom. To Him *be* glory forever and ever. Amen!

Come Before Winter

[19]Greet Prisca and Aquila, and the household of Onesiphorus. [20]Erastus stayed in Corinth, but Trophimus I have left in Miletus sick.

[21]Do your utmost to come before winter. Eubulus greets you, as well as Pudens, Linus, Claudia, and all the brethren.

Farewell

[22]The Lord Jesus Christ[a] be with your spirit. Grace be with you. Amen.

4:1 [a]NU-Text omits *therefore* and reads *and by* for *at*.
4:22 [a]NU-Text omits *Jesus Christ*.

TITUS

THE BOOK OF TITUS was probably written about the same time as Paul's first letter to Timothy, and it addresses some of the same themes. Titus served as pastor of the church on the island of Crete, whose citizens had a reputation for laziness and lying (1:12, 13).

Paul stresses the way in which our character and our conduct should "adorn the doctrine of God our Savior in all things" (2:10). Sound doctrine will always express itself in godly behavior and works of kindness and compassion. Paul tells Titus that God's grace has brought salvation to all men so that we may deny ungodliness and worldly lusts, and may live soberly, righteously and godly in this present age (2:11, 12). We must remember that how we live as husbands and wives and as parents can either cause people to respect God and His Word, or discredit the gospel. We should be very careful to cultivate the kind of life that will make our message attractive.

Sometimes we hear about the "Titus 2 Mandate" for women. This refers to Paul's instructions to older women about how they are to mentor the younger women in the church. They are to "admonish the young women to love their husbands, to love their children, to be discreet, chaste, homemakers, good, obedient to their own husbands, that the word of God may not be blasphemed" (2:4, 5). This passage clearly trumpets the priority of the marriage relationship and the home for women. While it does not teach that a woman cannot work outside the home (as some have mandated), it clearly does teach that love for her husband, her children, and care of her home should be her top priorities. Like her husband, she needs to realize that no amount of success in the marketplace can compensate for failure at home. A mother does have a unique responsibility to care for her children, as only a mom can do.

Many young husbands and wives would love to have an older couple step into their lives and share their wisdom and their life experiences. As you read Titus 2, ask God to bring to mind a young man or young woman who might benefit from hearing about your life experiences. Call the person and suggest that you get together for lunch sometime soon.

Greeting

1 Paul, a bondservant of God and an apostle of Jesus Christ, according to the faith of God's elect and the acknowledgment of the truth which accords with godliness, [2]in hope of eternal life which God, who cannot lie, promised before time began, [3]but has in due time manifested His word through preaching, which was committed to me according to the commandment of God our Savior;

[4]To Titus, a true son in *our* common faith:

Grace, mercy, *and* peace from God the Father and the Lord Jesus Christ[a] our Savior.

Qualified Elders

[5]For this reason I left you in Crete, that you should set in order the things that are lacking, and appoint elders in every city as I commanded you— [6]if a man is blameless, the husband of one wife, having faithful children not accused of dissipation or insubordination. [7]For a bishop[a] must be blameless, as a steward of God, not self-willed, not quick-tempered, not given to wine, not violent, not greedy for money, [8]but hospitable, a lover of what is good, sober-minded, just, holy, self-controlled, [9]holding fast the faithful word as he has been taught, that he may be able, by sound doctrine, both to exhort and convict those who contradict.

The Elders' Task

[10]For there are many insubordinate, both idle talkers and deceivers, especially those of the circumcision, [11]whose mouths must be stopped, who subvert whole households, teaching things which they ought not, for the sake of dishonest gain. [12]One of them, a prophet of their own, said, "Cretans *are* always liars, evil beasts, lazy gluttons." [13]This testimony is true. Therefore rebuke them sharply, that they may be sound in the faith, [14]not giving heed to Jewish fables and commandments of men who turn from the truth. [15]To the pure all things are pure, but to those who are defiled and unbelieving nothing is pure; but even their mind and conscience are defiled. [16]They profess to know God, but in works they deny *Him,* being abominable, disobedient, and disqualified for every good work.

Qualities of a Sound Church

2 But as for you, speak the things which are proper for sound doctrine: [2]that the older men be sober, reverent, temperate, sound in faith, in love, in patience; [3]the older women likewise, that they be reverent in behavior, not slanderers, not given to much wine, teachers of good things— [4]that they admonish the young women to love their husbands, to love their children, [5]*to be*

1:4 [a]NU-Text reads *and Christ Jesus.*
1:7 [a]Literally *overseer*

The Many Faces of Respect

Every husband needs a wife who respects him (see Eph. 5:33). That means she regards him, honors him, prefers him and esteems him.

One way to respect your husband is to consider and understand the weight of his responsibilities as a servant-leader in the home. It is easy to look at your husband and see what is wrong instead of right. As someone once said, "Faults are like the headlights of your car; those of others seem more glaring."

One way to communicate respect to your husband is to accept his schedule. For example, in past years I had to learn to be content with packing up and leaving for most of the summer for Dennis's teaching assignments, conferences, and meetings. We also had to learn how to live a great deal of time out of a suitcase and traveling in a car with six children.

When it would get to be too much, I'd tell Dennis, and we'd make adjustments. Yes, my husband's schedule is important to me. I choose to be a part of what he does, to watch and help, to be a part of his work, and to be available to him. And I know that by choosing to support Dennis in these ways, I am showing him great respect.

discreet, chaste, homemakers, good, obedient to their own husbands, that the word of God may not be blasphemed.

⁶Likewise, exhort the young men to be sober-minded, ⁷in all things showing yourself *to be* a pattern of good works; in doctrine *showing* integrity, reverence, incorruptibility,ᵃ ⁸sound speech that cannot be condemned, that one who is an opponent may be ashamed, having nothing evil to say of you.ᵃ

⁹*Exhort* bondservants to be obedient to their own masters, to be well pleasing in all *things,* not answering back, ¹⁰not pilfering, but showing all good fidelity, that they may adorn the doctrine of God our Savior in all things.

Trained by Saving Grace

¹¹For the grace of God that brings salvation has appeared to all men, ¹²teaching us that, denying ungodliness and worldly lusts, we should live soberly, righteously, and godly in the present age, ¹³looking for the blessed hope and glorious appearing of our great God and Savior Jesus Christ, ¹⁴who gave Himself for us, that He might redeem us from every lawless deed and purify for Himself *His* own special people, zealous for good works.

¹⁵Speak these things, exhort, and rebuke with all authority. Let no one despise you.

Graces of the Heirs of Grace

3 Remind them to be subject to rulers and authorities, to obey, to be ready for every good work, ²to speak evil of no one, to be peaceable, gentle, showing all humility to all men. ³For we ourselves were also once foolish, disobedient, deceived, serving various lusts and pleasures, living in malice and envy, hateful and hating one another. ⁴But when the kindness and the love of God our Savior toward man appeared, ⁵not by works of righteousness which we have done, but according to His mercy He saved us, through the washing of regeneration and renewing of the Holy Spirit, ⁶whom He poured out on us abundantly through Jesus Christ our Savior, ⁷that having been

BIBLICAL INSIGHTS • 2:4
Love Your Husband

TITUS 2:4 INSTRUCTS WIVES "to love their husbands." That means your husband needs unconditional acceptance. In other words, accept your husband just as he is—imperfect.

Love also means being committed to a mutually fulfilling sexual relationship. I realize there is a whole lot more to love than sex, but this is part of fulfilling God's command to love our husbands. Therefore, we must look at love from their perspective, not just our own.

Surveys show that sex is one of a man's most important needs—if not the most important. When a wife resists intimacy, is uninterested, or is only passively interested, her husband may feel rejection. This can cut at his self-image, tear at him to the very center of his being, and create isolation.

My husband's sexual needs should be more important and higher on my priority list than menus, housework, projects, activities, and even the children. I do not need to think about sex all day, every day, but I do need to find ways to remember my husband and his needs. I must save some of my energy for him. Maintaining that focus helps me defeat isolation in our marriage.

justified by His grace we should become heirs according to the hope of eternal life.

⁸This is a faithful saying, and these things I want you to affirm constantly, that those who have believed in God should be careful to maintain good works. These things are good and profitable to men.

Avoid Dissension

⁹But avoid foolish disputes, genealogies, contentions, and strivings about the law; for they are unprofitable and useless. ¹⁰Reject a divisive man after the first and second admonition, ¹¹knowing that such a person is warped and sinning, being self-condemned.

2:7 ᵃNU-Text omits *incorruptibility.*
2:8 ᵃNU-Text and M-Text read *us.*

INTIMATE MOMENTS

On Christmas Eve, give your little Mrs. Claus a basket full of bubble bath supplies, and then get the water ready for her.

Final Messages

¹²When I send Artemas to you, or Tychicus, be diligent to come to me at Nicopolis, for I have decided to spend the winter there. ¹³Send Zenas the lawyer and Apollos on their journey with haste, that they may lack nothing. ¹⁴And let our *people* also learn to maintain good works, to *meet* urgent needs, that they may not be unfruitful.

Farewell

¹⁵All who *are* with me greet you. Greet those who love us in the faith.

Grace *be* with you all. Amen.

PHILEMON

THIS LETTER BY THE APOSTLE PAUL is so short that some have called it a postcard. It was written to a beloved friend and co-worker on behalf of a runaway slave who had repented and become a follower of Jesus. At the time of its writing, Paul was under house arrest in Rome, while the slave in question, Onesimus, was in the same city, hiding out after running away from his master, Philemon. Onesimus may have also stolen some money from his master (v.18).

Somehow Onesimus had come into contact with Paul in Rome, and the apostle led the runaway slave to Christ (v.10). Onesimus became a close companion who cared for Paul's needs. But Paul knew Onesimus had broken Roman law and had defrauded his master, so he sent Onesimus back to Philemon in Colossae. This letter is Paul's passionate and wise appeal to his dear friend to show compassion and mercy to this repentant slave, now a treasured brother in Christ.

In the ancient world, slaves served in a variety of roles—teachers, financial stewards, even doctors. Because slaves were considered their master's property, many slave owners mistreated and abused them. Paul chose to address the issue of slavery, not by condemning it as a social evil, but by showing the equal value and worth of both masters and slaves in Christ. He called all followers of Christ—slaves and masters alike—to show kindness, compassion, mercy, and sincere love for one another (v. 16).

Although Paul never uses the word *forgiveness* in this letter, his tender, tactful, and gentle appeal to Philemon was written to encourage this believing master to respond to his runaway slave with grace and a generous spirit.

Many times in marriage we will be called upon to show the same kind of generous grace. Ruth Bell Graham, the wife of Billy Graham, was once quoted as saying, "A happy marriage is the union of two forgivers." As you read through this short letter, ask yourself if you are quick to forgive your spouse and eager to restore your relationship in a spirit of humility, grace, and tenderness.

Greeting

Paul, a prisoner of Christ Jesus, and Timothy *our* brother,

To Philemon our beloved *friend* and fellow laborer, [2]to the beloved[a] Apphia, Archippus our fellow soldier, and to the church in your house:

[3]Grace to you and peace from God our Father and the Lord Jesus Christ.

Philemon's Love and Faith

[4]I thank my God, making mention of you always in my prayers, [5]hearing of your love and faith which you have toward the Lord Jesus and toward all the saints, [6]that the sharing of your faith may become effective by the acknowledgment of every good thing which is in you[a] in Christ Jesus. [7]For we have[a] great joy[b] and consolation in your love, because the hearts of the saints have been refreshed by you, brother.

The Plea for Onesimus

[8]Therefore, though I might be very bold in Christ to command you what is fitting, [9]yet for love's sake I rather appeal *to you*— being such a one as Paul, the aged, and now also a prisoner of Jesus Christ— [10]I appeal to you for my son Onesimus, whom I have begotten *while* in my chains, [11]who once was unprofitable to you, but now is profitable to you and to me.

[12]I am sending him back.[a] You therefore receive him, that is, my own heart, [13]whom I wished to keep with me, that on your behalf he might minister to me in my chains for the gospel. [14]But without your consent I wanted to do nothing, that your good deed might not be by compulsion, as it were, but voluntary.

[15]For perhaps he departed for a while for this *purpose,* that you might receive him forever, [16]no longer as a slave but more than a slave—a beloved brother, especially to me but how much more to you, both in the flesh and in the Lord.

Philemon's Obedience Encouraged

[17]If then you count me as a partner, receive him as *you would* me. [18]But if he has

---

2 [a]NU-Text reads *to our sister Apphia.*
6 [a]NU-Text and M-Text read *us.*
7 [a]NU-Text reads *had.* [b]M-Text reads *thanksgiving.*
12 [a]NU-Text reads *back to you in person, that is, my own heart.*

The Peacemaker and the Prizefighter

One reason people have conflict in marriage is that opposites attract. One typical such pairing is the peacemaker and the prizefighter.

The peacemaker would rather hide than fight. The peacemaker says, "Let's forget it. It isn't worth the hassle." The prizefighter, meanwhile, says, "Put on your gloves and let's duke it out!"

One husband I know came from a long line of prizefighters. He grew up watching his family having spirited discussions. The beauty of it was that they could discuss issues, argue vehemently, and then hang up their gloves, hug, and make up afterwards.

But his wife came from a long line of peacemakers who swept everything under the rug. They avoided confrontations. That rug in their home had to look like a mountain!

So what kind of a marriage did these two have? He was chasing her around trying to get her to put on the gloves, and she was searching for a place to hide. Unfortunately, their daughter landed between them, trying desperately to bring her parents together.

There's a lot at stake in the way you and your mate handle your conflicts! It's not just the intimacy in your marriage that's on the line, but the lives of impressionable sons and daughters as well. Train your children in the basics of conflict resolution. They need to know how two imperfect people resolve their differences with each other. It's likely that some day they will be married, and they *will* need this skill for the rest of their lives.

wronged you or owes anything, put that on my account. ¹⁹I, Paul, am writing with my own hand. I will repay—not to mention to you that you owe me even your own self besides. ²⁰Yes, brother, let me have joy from you in the Lord; refresh my heart in the Lord.

²¹Having confidence in your obedience, I write to you, knowing that you will do even more than I say. ²²But, meanwhile, also prepare a guest room for me, for I trust that through your prayers I shall be granted to you.

Farewell

²³Epaphras, my fellow prisoner in Christ Jesus, greets you, ²⁴as do Mark, Aristarchus, Demas, Luke, my fellow laborers.

²⁵The grace of our Lord Jesus Christ be with your spirit. Amen.

INTIMATE MOMENTS

On the third Saturday in October, buy your sweetheart a few fall treats for Sweetest Day: popcorn balls, caramel apples, and candy corn, to name a few. Or if those aren't her favorites, buy her chocolate!

HEBREWS

JESUS ONCE INSISTED that He did not come to abolish the Old Testament law or the teaching of the prophets, but to fulfill them (Matt. 5:17, 18). The Book of Hebrews helps us understand how He completely and specifically fulfilled what God had promised in the Old Testament.

We don't know who wrote the Book of Hebrews, since the book itself doesn't say. The author had a broad knowledge of the Old Testament, particularly of the book of Leviticus and the work of the priests. He wrote to converted Jews who were familiar with many aspects of the ceremonial law and were living outside of the Holy Land. He wanted his readers to see that Jesus fulfilled the promises of God and that His sacrifice made obsolete the imperfect sacrificial system. Some of what he wrote was addressed specifically to people who were not following Christ, even though they seemed persuaded that Jesus was the Messiah.

Hebrews 11, often called "The Faith Hall of Fame," shows how the great men and women of the Old Testament had one thing in common: They believed God's Word and then acted on their conviction. If we want our lives to please God—and if we want our marriages and our families to please Him—then we must begin by proving through our actions that we genuinely believe in Him. That's what it means to have faith, and "without faith, it is impossible to please Him" (11:6).

A couple of passages in Hebrews address marriage and family issues. Hebrews 13:4 gives married couples great freedom to experience sexual enjoyment, but also reminds readers that any kind of intimate sexual activity outside of marriage dishonors God. The writer of Hebrews also uses the example of a human father, correcting and disciplining his children in love to illustrate how a loving God may bring measured amounts of pain into our lives to discipline us (12:5–11). The illustration points out our need to instruct, correct, and discipline our own children, as Proverbs 13:24 teaches, "He who spares his rod hates his son, but he who loves him disciplines him promptly."

God's Supreme Revelation

1 God, who at various times and in various ways spoke in time past to the fathers by the prophets, ²has in these last days spoken to us by *His* Son, whom He has appointed heir of all things, through whom also He made the worlds; ³who being the brightness of *His* glory and the express image of His person, and upholding all things by the word of His power, when He had by Himself[a] purged our[a] sins, sat down at the right hand of the Majesty on high, ⁴having become so much better than the angels, as He has by inheritance obtained a more excellent name than they.

The Son Exalted Above Angels

⁵For to which of the angels did He ever say:

"*You are My Son,*
Today I have begotten You"?[a]

And again:

"*I will be to Him a Father,*
And He shall be to Me a Son"?[a]

⁶But when He again brings the firstborn into the world, He says:

"*Let all the angels of God worship Him.*"[a]

⁷And of the angels He says:

"*Who makes His angels spirits*
And His ministers a flame of fire."[a]

⁸But to the Son *He says:*

"*Your throne, O God, is forever and*
ever;
A scepter of righteousness is the
scepter of Your kingdom.
⁹   *You have loved righteousness and*
hated lawlessness;
Therefore God, Your God, has
anointed You
With the oil of gladness more than
Your companions."[a]

1:3 [a]NU-Text omits *by Himself.* [b]NU-Text omits *our.*
1:5 [a]Psalm 2:7 [b]2 Samuel 7:14 **1:6** [a]Deuteronomy 32:43 (Septuagint, Dead Sea Scrolls); Psalm 97:7
1:7 [a]Psalm 104:4 **1:9** [a]Psalm 45:6, 7 **1:12** [a]Psalm 102:25–27 **1:13** [a]Psalm 110:1

¹⁰And:

"*You, LORD, in the beginning laid the*
foundation of the earth,
And the heavens are the work of
Your hands.
¹¹   *They will perish, but You remain;*
And they will all grow old like a
garment;
¹²   *Like a cloak You will fold them up,*
And they will be changed.
But You are the same,
And Your years will not fail."[a]

¹³But to which of the angels has He ever said:

"*Sit at My right hand,*
Till I make Your enemies Your
footstool"?[a]

¹⁴Are they not all ministering spirits sent forth to minister for those who will inherit salvation?

INTIMATE MOMENTS

Initiate daily prayer with your spouse. This one spiritual discipline has transformed millions of marriages. Make a commitment, and then begin to pray together every day. Begin by giving thanks for your spouse and your family, then pray about both of your worries and challenges. Ask your spouse to pray about a challenge you are facing.

Do Not Neglect Salvation

2 Therefore we must give the more earnest heed to the things we have heard, lest we drift away. ²For if the word spoken through angels proved steadfast, and every transgression and disobedience received a just reward, ³how shall we escape if we neglect so great a salvation, which at the first began to be spoken by the Lord, and was confirmed to us by those who heard *Him,* ⁴God also bearing witness both with signs and wonders, with various miracles, and gifts of the Holy Spirit, according to His own will?

The Son Made Lower than Angels

⁵For He has not put the world to come, of which we speak, in subjection to angels. ⁶But one testified in a certain place, saying:

"What is man that You are mindful of
  him,
  Or the son of man that You take care
  of him?
⁷ You have made him a little lower
  than the angels;
  You have crowned him with glory
  and honor,ᵃ
  And set him over the works of Your
  hands.
⁸ You have put all things in subjection
  under his feet."ᵃ

For in that He put all in subjection under him, He left nothing *that is* not put under him. But now we do not yet see all things put under him. ⁹But we see Jesus, who was made a little lower than the angels, for the suffering of death crowned with glory and honor, that He, by the grace of God, might taste death for everyone.

INTIMATE MOMENTS

Write, "I'm crazy about you, honey. You're the best!" or another personal message on a yellow sticky note. Attach it to his bathroom mirror.

Bringing Many Sons to Glory

¹⁰For it was fitting for Him, for whom *are* all things and by whom *are* all things, in bringing many sons to glory, to make the captain of their salvation perfect through sufferings. ¹¹For both He who sanctifies and those who are being sanctified *are* all of one, for which reason He is not ashamed to call them brethren, ¹²saying:

"I will declare Your name to My
  brethren;
  In the midst of the assembly I will
  sing praise to You."ᵃ

¹³And again:

"I will put My trust in Him."ᵃ

And again:

"Here am I and the children whom
  God has given Me."ᵇ

¹⁴Inasmuch then as the children have partaken of flesh and blood, He Himself likewise shared in the same, that through death He might destroy him who had the power of death, that is, the devil, ¹⁵and release those who through fear of death were all their lifetime subject to bondage. ¹⁶For indeed He does not give aid to angels, but He does give aid to the seed of Abraham. ¹⁷Therefore, in all things He had to be made like *His* brethren, that He might be a merciful and faithful High Priest in things *pertaining* to God, to make propitiation for the sins of the people. ¹⁸For in that He Himself has suffered, being tempted, He is able to aid those who are tempted.

The Son Was Faithful

3 Therefore, holy brethren, partakers of the heavenly calling, consider the Apostle and High Priest of our confession, Christ Jesus, ²who was faithful to Him who appointed Him, as Moses also *was faithful* in all His house. ³For this One has been counted worthy of more glory than Moses, inasmuch as He who built the house has more honor than the house. ⁴For every house is built by someone, but He who built all things *is* God. ⁵And Moses indeed *was* faithful in all His house as a servant, for a testimony of those things which would be spoken *afterward,* ⁶but Christ as a Son over His own house, whose house we are if we hold fast the confidence and the rejoicing of the hope firm to the end.ᵃ

Be Faithful

⁷Therefore, as the Holy Spirit says:

"Today, if you will hear His voice,
⁸   Do not harden your hearts as in
  the rebellion,

2:7 ᵃNU-Text and M-Text omit the rest of verse 7.
2:8 ᵃPsalm 8:4–6 **2:12** ᵃPsalm 22:22
2:13 ᵃ2 Samuel 22:3; Isaiah 8:17 ᵇIsaiah 8:18
3:6 ᵃNU-Text omits *firm to the end.*

In the day of trial in the wilderness,
9 Where your fathers tested Me, tried
   Me,
   And saw My works forty years.
10 Therefore I was angry with that
   generation,
   And said, 'They always go astray in
   their heart,
   And they have not known My ways.'
11 So I swore in My wrath,
   'They shall not enter My rest.'"ᵃ

¹²Beware, brethren, lest there be in any
of you an evil heart of unbelief in departing from the living God; ¹³but exhort one
another daily, while it is called *"Today,"*
lest any of you be hardened through the
deceitfulness of sin. ¹⁴For we have become
partakers of Christ if we hold the beginning of our confidence steadfast to the
end, ¹⁵while it is said:

   *"Today, if you will hear His voice,
      Do not harden your hearts as in the
      rebellion."*ᵃ

Failure of the Wilderness Wanderers

¹⁶For who, having heard, rebelled?
Indeed, *was it* not all who came out of
Egypt, *led* by Moses? ¹⁷Now with whom
was He angry forty years? *Was it* not with
those who sinned, whose corpses fell in the
wilderness? ¹⁸And to whom did He swear
that they would not enter His rest, but to
those who did not obey? ¹⁹So we see that
they could not enter in because of unbelief.

The Promise of Rest

4 Therefore, since a promise remains of
entering His rest, let us fear lest any of
you seem to have come short of it. ²For
indeed the gospel was preached to us as
well as to them; but the word which they
heard did not profit them,ᵃ not being
mixed with faith in those who heard *it.*
³For we who have believed do enter that
rest, as He has said:

   *"So I swore in My wrath,
      'They shall not enter My rest,'"*ᵃ

BIBLICAL INSIGHTS • 3:19
Believe That God Can

FAR TOO MANY PEOPLE today feel impotent to make a difference in their own
homes, much less in their communities.
The battlefront is so vast and the problems
so overwhelming that many have determined that redeeming our nation is
impossible. National polls consistently
show that Americans are pessimistic about
our country's future, and I believe this pessimism leads to a feeling of powerlessness.

Such pessimism betrays a lack of faith
in the power of God. A follower of Christ
controlled by unbelief will almost never
see God work in and through his life.
Unbelief caused nearly an entire generation of Israelites to perish in the wilderness. As the writer of Hebrews says, "So
we see that they could not enter in
because of unbelief" (3:19). They simply
didn't believe God could overcome the
giants they saw in their way.

Unbelief begins with dangerous
assumptions and concludes that the
problem is too big for God, that God
doesn't want to act on our behalf, and
that we might as well eat, drink, and be
merry, for tomorrow we die (1 Cor. 15:32).
Unbelief is the parent that gives birth to
a mundane Christian life that knows little
of the supernatural working of God. The
ultimate waste is a life of mediocrity.

Don't give in to it! Learn to take small
steps of faith by choosing to believe God's
Word and acting on that belief, whether
you feel like it or not. Keep in mind the
words of Martin Luther, "Feelings come
and feelings go, and feelings are deceiving; my warrant is the Word of God,
naught else is worth believing."

3:11 ᵃPsalm 95:7–11 **3:15** ᵃPsalm 95:7, 8
4:2 ᵃNU-Text and M-Text read *profit them, since they
were not united by faith with those who heeded it.*
4:3 ᵃPsalm 95:11 **4:4** ᵃGenesis 2:2 **4:5** ᵃPsalm 95:11

although the works were finished from the
foundation of the world. ⁴For He has spoken in a certain place of the seventh *day* in
this way: *"And God rested on the seventh
day from all His works"*;ᵃ ⁵and again in
this *place:* *"They shall not enter My rest."*ᵃ

⁶Since therefore it remains that some *must* enter it, and those to whom it was first preached did not enter because of disobedience, ⁷again He designates a certain day, saying in David, *"Today,"* after such a long time, as it has been said:

> *"Today, if you will hear His voice,*
> *Do not harden your hearts."*ᵃ

⁸For if Joshua had given them rest, then He would not afterward have spoken of another day. ⁹There remains therefore a rest for the people of God. ¹⁰For he who has entered His rest has himself also ceased from his works as God *did* from His.

INTIMATE MOMENTS

Call her from work and say, "I've been thinking of how good I have it with you in my life. Thanks for all that you are as a woman and all that you do for me and our family."

The Word Discovers Our Condition

¹¹Let us therefore be diligent to enter that rest, lest anyone fall according to the same example of disobedience. ¹²For the word of God *is* living and powerful, and sharper than any two-edged sword, piercing even to the division of soul and spirit, and of joints and marrow, and is a discerner of the thoughts and intents of the heart. ¹³And there is no creature hidden from His sight, but all things *are* naked and open to the eyes of Him to whom we *must give* account.

Our Compassionate High Priest

¹⁴Seeing then that we have a great High Priest who has passed through the heavens, Jesus the Son of God, let us hold fast *our* confession. ¹⁵For we do not have a High Priest who cannot sympathize with our weaknesses, but was in all *points* tempted as *we are, yet* without sin. ¹⁶Let us therefore come boldly to the throne of grace, that we may obtain mercy and find grace to help in time of need.

Qualifications for High Priesthood

5 For every high priest taken from among men is appointed for men in things *pertaining* to God, that he may offer both gifts and sacrifices for sins. ²He can have compassion on those who are ignorant and going astray, since he himself is also subject to weakness. ³Because of this he is required as for the people, so also for himself, to offer *sacrifices* for sins. ⁴And no man takes this honor to himself, but he who is called by God, just as Aaron *was.*

A Priest Forever

⁵So also Christ did not glorify Himself to become High Priest, but *it was* He who said to Him:

> *"You are My Son,*
> *Today I have begotten You."*ᵃ

⁶As He also says in another *place:*

> *"You are a priest forever*
> *According to the order of*
> *Melchizedek";*ᵃ

⁷who, in the days of His flesh, when He had offered up prayers and supplications, with vehement cries and tears to Him who was able to save Him from death, and was heard because of His godly fear, ⁸though He was a Son, *yet* He learned obedience by the things which He suffered. ⁹And having been perfected, He became the author of eternal salvation to all who obey Him, ¹⁰called by God as High Priest *"according to the order of Melchizedek,"* ¹¹of whom we have much to say, and hard to explain, since you have become dull of hearing.

Spiritual Immaturity

¹²For though by this time you ought to be teachers, you need *someone* to teach you again the first principles of the oracles of God; and you have come to need milk and not solid food. ¹³For everyone who partakes *only* of milk *is* unskilled in the word of righteousness, for he is a babe. ¹⁴But solid food belongs to those who are of full age, *that is,* those who by reason of use

4:7 ᵃPsalm 95:7, 8 5:5 ᵃPsalm 2:7 5:6 ᵃPsalm 110:4

have their senses exercised to discern both good and evil.

The Peril of Not Progressing

6 Therefore, leaving the discussion of the elementary *principles* of Christ, let us go on to perfection, not laying again the foundation of repentance from dead works and of faith toward God, ²of the doctrine of baptisms, of laying on of hands, of resurrection of the dead, and of eternal judgment. ³And this we willᵃ do if God permits.

⁴For *it is* impossible for those who were once enlightened, and have tasted the heavenly gift, and have become partakers of the Holy Spirit, ⁵and have tasted the good word of God and the powers of the age to come, ⁶if they fall away,ᵃ to renew them again to repentance, since they crucify again for themselves the Son of God, and put *Him* to an open shame.

⁷For the earth which drinks in the rain that often comes upon it, and bears herbs useful for those by whom it is cultivated, receives blessing from God; ⁸but if it bears thorns and briers, *it is* rejected and near to being cursed, whose end *is* to be burned.

A Better Estimate

⁹But, beloved, we are confident of better things concerning you, yes, things that accompany salvation, though we speak in this manner. ¹⁰For God *is* not unjust to forget your work and labor ofᵃ love which you have shown toward His name, *in that* you have ministered to the saints, and do minister. ¹¹And we desire that each one of you show the same diligence to the full assurance of hope until the end, ¹²that you do not become sluggish, but imitate those who through faith and patience inherit the promises.

God's Infallible Purpose in Christ

¹³For when God made a promise to Abraham, because He could swear by no one greater, He swore by Himself, ¹⁴saying, *"Surely blessing I will bless you, and multiplying I will multiply you."*ᵃ ¹⁵And so, after he had patiently endured, he obtained

the promise. ¹⁶For men indeed swear by the greater, and an oath for confirmation *is* for them an end of all dispute. ¹⁷Thus God, determining to show more abundantly to the heirs of promise the immutability of His counsel, confirmed *it* by an oath, ¹⁸that by two immutable things, in which it *is* impossible for God to lie, we mightᵃ have strong consolation, who have fled for refuge to lay hold of the hope set before *us*.

¹⁹This *hope* we have as an anchor of the soul, both sure and steadfast, and which enters the *Presence* behind the veil, ²⁰where the forerunner has entered for us, *even* Jesus, having become High Priest forever according to the order of Melchizedek.

The King of Righteousness

7 For this Melchizedek, king of Salem, priest of the Most High God, who met Abraham returning from the slaughter of the kings and blessed him, ²to whom also Abraham gave a tenth part of all, first being translated "king of righteousness," and then also king of Salem, meaning "king of peace," ³without father, without mother, without genealogy, having neither beginning of days nor end of life, but made like the Son of God, remains a priest continually.

⁴Now consider how great this man *was*, to whom even the patriarch Abraham gave a tenth of the spoils. ⁵And indeed those who are of the sons of Levi, who receive the priesthood, have a commandment to receive tithes from the people according to the law, that is, from their brethren, though they have come from the loins of Abraham; ⁶but he whose genealogy is not derived from them received tithes from Abraham and blessed him who had the promises. ⁷Now beyond all contradiction the lesser is blessed by the better. ⁸Here mortal men receive tithes, but there he *receives them*, of whom it is witnessed that he lives. ⁹Even Levi, who receives tithes, paid tithes through Abraham, so to speak, ¹⁰for he was still in the loins of his father when Melchizedek met him.

Need for a New Priesthood

¹¹Therefore, if perfection were through the Levitical priesthood (for under it the people received the law), what further need

---

6:3 ᵃM-Text reads *let us do.* 6:6 ᵃOr *and have fallen away* 6:10 ᵃNU-Text omits *labor of.* 6:14 ᵃGenesis 22:17 6:18 ᵃM-Text omits *might.*

was there that another priest should rise according to the order of Melchizedek, and not be called according to the order of Aaron? [12]For the priesthood being changed, of necessity there is also a change of the law. [13]For He of whom these things are spoken belongs to another tribe, from which no man has officiated at the altar.

[14]For *it is* evident that our Lord arose from Judah, of which tribe Moses spoke nothing concerning priesthood.[a] [15]And it is yet far more evident if, in the likeness of Melchizedek, there arises another priest [16]who has come, not according to the law of a fleshly commandment, but according to the power of an endless life. [17]For He testifies:[a]

> "*You are a priest forever*
>   *According to the order of*
>   *Melchizedek.*"[a]

[18]For on the one hand there is an annulling of the former commandment because of its weakness and unprofitableness, [19]for the law made nothing perfect; on the other hand, *there is the* bringing in of a better hope, through which we draw near to God.

Greatness of the New Priest

[20]And inasmuch as *He was* not *made priest* without an oath [21](for they have become priests without an oath, but He with an oath by Him who said to Him:

> "*The LORD has sworn*
>   *And will not relent,*
>   '*You are a priest forever*[a]
>   *According to the order of*
>   *Melchizedek*'"),[b]

[22]by so much more Jesus has become a surety of a better covenant.

[23]Also there were many priests, because they were prevented by death from continuing. [24]But He, because He continues forever, has an unchangeable priesthood. [25]Therefore He is also able to save to the uttermost those who come to God through Him, since He always lives to make intercession for them.

[26]For such a High Priest was fitting for us, *who is* holy, harmless, undefiled, separate from sinners, and has become higher

than the heavens; [27]who does not need daily, as those high priests, to offer up sacrifices, first for His own sins and then for the people's, for this He did once for all when He offered up Himself. [28]For the law appoints as high priests men who have weakness, but the word of the oath, which came after the law, *appoints* the Son who has been perfected forever.

The New Priestly Service

8 Now *this is* the main point of the things we are saying: We have such a High Priest, who is seated at the right hand of the throne of the Majesty in the heavens, [2]a Minister of the sanctuary and of the true tabernacle which the Lord erected, and not man.

[3]For every high priest is appointed to offer both gifts and sacrifices. Therefore *it is* necessary that this One also have something to offer. [4]For if He were on earth, He would not be a priest, since there are priests who offer the gifts according to the law; [5]who serve the copy and shadow of the heavenly things, as Moses was divinely instructed when he was about to make the tabernacle. For He said, "*See that you make all things according to the pattern shown you on the mountain.*"[a] [6]But now He has obtained a more excellent ministry, inasmuch as He is also Mediator of a better covenant, which was established on better promises.

A New Covenant

[7]For if that first *covenant* had been faultless, then no place would have been sought for a second. [8]Because finding fault with them, He says: "*Behold, the days are coming, says the LORD, when I will make a new covenant with the house of Israel and with the house of Judah—* [9]*not according to the covenant that I made with their fathers in the day when I took them by the hand to lead them out of the land of Egypt; because they did not continue in My covenant, and I disregarded them, says the LORD.* [10]*For this is the covenant that I will make with the house of Israel after*

7:14 [a]NU-Text reads *priests.*   7:17 [a]NU-Text reads *it is testified.*   [b]Psalm 110:4   7:21 [a]NU-Text ends the quotation here.   [b]Psalm 110:4   8:5 [a]Exodus 25:40

those days, says the LORD: I will put My laws in their mind and write them on their hearts; and I will be their God, and they shall be My people. ¹¹None of them shall teach his neighbor, and none his brother, saying, 'Know the LORD,' for all shall know Me, from the least of them to the greatest of them. ¹²For I will be merciful to their unrighteousness, and their sins and their lawless deedsᵃ I will remember no more."ᵇ

¹³In that He says, "A new covenant," He has made the first obsolete. Now what is becoming obsolete and growing old is ready to vanish away.

The Earthly Sanctuary

9 Then indeed, even the first *covenant* had ordinances of divine service and the earthly sanctuary. ²For a tabernacle was prepared: the first *part,* in which *was* the lampstand, the table, and the showbread, which is called the sanctuary; ³and behind the second veil, the part of the tabernacle which is called the Holiest of All, ⁴which had the golden censer and the ark of the covenant overlaid on all sides with gold, in which *were* the golden pot that had the manna, Aaron's rod that budded, and the tablets of the covenant; ⁵and above it were the cherubim of glory overshadowing the mercy seat. Of these things we cannot now speak in detail.

Limitations of the Earthly Service

⁶Now when these things had been thus prepared, the priests always went into the first part of the tabernacle, performing the services. ⁷But into the second part the high priest *went* alone once a year, not without blood, which he offered for himself and *for* the people's sins *committed* in ignorance; ⁸the Holy Spirit indicating this, that the way into the Holiest of All was not yet made manifest while the first tabernacle was still standing. ⁹It *was* symbolic for the present time in which both gifts and sacrifices are offered which cannot make him who performed the service perfect in regard to the conscience— ¹⁰concerned

only with foods and drinks, various washings, and fleshly ordinances imposed until the time of reformation.

The Heavenly Sanctuary

¹¹But Christ came *as* High Priest of the good things to come,ᵃ with the greater and more perfect tabernacle not made with hands, that is, not of this creation. ¹²Not with the blood of goats and calves, but with His own blood He entered the Most Holy Place once for all, having obtained eternal redemption. ¹³For if the blood of bulls and goats and the ashes of a heifer, sprinkling the unclean, sanctifies for the purifying of the flesh, ¹⁴how much more shall the blood of Christ, who through the eternal Spirit offered Himself without spot to God, cleanse your conscience from dead works to serve the living God? ¹⁵And for this reason He is the Mediator of the new covenant, by means of death, for the redemption of the transgressions under the first covenant, that those who are called may receive the promise of the eternal inheritance.

The Mediator's Death Necessary

¹⁶For where there *is* a testament, there must also of necessity be the death of the testator. ¹⁷For a testament *is* in force after men are dead, since it has no power at all while the testator lives. ¹⁸Therefore not even the first *covenant* was dedicated without blood. ¹⁹For when Moses had spoken every precept to all the people according to the law, he took the blood of calves and goats, with water, scarlet wool, and hyssop, and sprinkled both the book itself and all the people, ²⁰saying, "This is the blood of the covenant which God has commanded you."ᵃ ²¹Then likewise he sprinkled with blood both the tabernacle and all the vessels of the ministry. ²²And according to the law almost all things are purified with blood, and without shedding of blood there is no remission.

Greatness of Christ's Sacrifice

²³Therefore *it was* necessary that the copies of the things in the heavens should be purified with these, but the heavenly things themselves with better sacrifices

---

8:12 ᵃNU-Text omits *and their lawless deeds.* ᵇJeremiah 31:31–34 9:11 ᵃNU-Text reads *that have come.* 9:20 ᵃExodus 24:8

than these. [24]For Christ has not entered the holy places made with hands, *which are* copies of the true, but into heaven itself, now to appear in the presence of God for us; [25]not that He should offer Himself often, as the high priest enters the Most Holy Place every year with blood of another— [26]He then would have had to suffer often since the foundation of the world; but now, once at the end of the ages, He has appeared to put away sin by the sacrifice of Himself. [27]And as it is appointed for men to die once, but after this the judgment, [28]so Christ was offered once to bear the sins of many. To those who eagerly wait for Him He will appear a second time, apart from sin, for salvation.

Animal Sacrifices Insufficient

10 For the law, having a shadow of the good things to come, *and* not the very image of the things, can never with these same sacrifices, which they offer continually year by year, make those who approach perfect. [2]For then would they not have ceased to be offered? For the worshipers, once purified, would have had no more consciousness of sins. [3]But in those *sacrifices there is* a reminder of sins every year. [4]For *it is* not possible that the blood of bulls and goats could take away sins.

Christ's Death Fulfills God's Will

[5]Therefore, when He came into the world, He said:

"*Sacrifice and offering You did not desire,*
     But a body You have prepared for Me.
[6]   *In burnt offerings and sacrifices for sin*
     You had no pleasure.
[7]   *Then I said, 'Behold, I have come—*
     In the volume of the book it is written of Me—
     To do Your will, O God.'"[a]

[8]Previously saying, "*Sacrifice and offering, burnt offerings, and offerings for sin You did not desire, nor had pleasure in them*" (which are offered according to the law), [9]then He said, "*Behold, I have come to do Your will, O God.*"[a] He takes away the first that He may establish the second. [10]By that will we have been sanctified through the offering of the body of Jesus Christ once *for all.*

Christ's Death Perfects the Sanctified

[11]And every priest stands ministering daily and offering repeatedly the same sacrifices, which can never take away sins. [12]But this Man, after He had offered one sacrifice for sins forever, sat down at the right hand of God, [13]from that time waiting till His enemies are made His footstool. [14]For by one offering He has perfected forever those who are being sanctified.

[15]But the Holy Spirit also witnesses to us; for after He had said before,

[16]"*This is the covenant that I will make with them after those days, says the LORD: I will put My laws into their hearts, and in their minds I will write them,*"[a] [17]*then He adds, "Their sins and their lawless deeds I will remember no more.*"[a] [18]Now where there is remission of these, *there is* no longer an offering for sin.

Hold Fast Your Confession

[19]Therefore, brethren, having boldness to enter the Holiest by the blood of Jesus, [20]by a new and living way which He consecrated for us, through the veil, that is, His flesh, [21]and *having* a High Priest over the house of God, [22]let us draw near with a true heart in full assurance of faith, having our hearts sprinkled from an evil conscience and our bodies washed with pure water. [23]Let us hold fast the confession of *our* hope without wavering, for He who promised *is* faithful. [24]And let us consider one another in order to stir up love and good works, [25]not forsaking the assembling of ourselves together, as *is* the manner of some, but exhorting *one another,* and so much the more as you see the Day approaching.

The Just Live by Faith

[26]For if we sin willfully after we have received the knowledge of the truth, there no longer remains a sacrifice for sins, [27]but

---

10:7 [a]Psalm 40:6–8   **10:9** [a]NU-Text and M-Text omit *O God.*   **10:16** [a]Jeremiah 31:33   **10:17** [a]Jeremiah 31:34

a certain fearful expectation of judgment, and fiery indignation which will devour the adversaries. [28]Anyone who has rejected Moses' law dies without mercy on *the testimony of* two or three witnesses. [29]Of how much worse punishment, do you suppose, will he be thought worthy who has trampled the Son of God underfoot, counted the blood of the covenant by which he was sanctified a common thing, and insulted the Spirit of grace? [30]For we know Him who said, *"Vengeance is Mine, I will repay,"*[a] says the Lord.[a] And again, *"The LORD will judge His people."*[a] [31]It is a fearful thing to fall into the hands of the living God.

[32]But recall the former days in which, after you were illuminated, you endured a great struggle with sufferings: [33]partly while you were made a spectacle both by reproaches and tribulations, and partly while you became companions of those who were so treated; [34]for you had compassion on me[a] in my chains, and joyfully accepted the plundering of your goods, knowing that you have a better and an enduring possession for yourselves in heaven.[b] [35]Therefore do not cast away your confidence, which has great reward. [36]For you have need of endurance, so that after you have done the will of God, you may receive the promise:

[37]   *"For yet a little while,
        And He[a] who is coming will come
            and will not tarry.*
[38]   *Now the[a] just shall live by faith;
        But if anyone draws back,
        My soul has no pleasure in him."*[a]

[39]But we are not of those who draw back to perdition, but of those who believe to the saving of the soul.

By Faith We Understand

11 Now faith is the substance of things hoped for, the evidence of things not seen. [2]For by it the elders obtained a *good* testimony.

10:30 [a]Deuteronomy 32:35 [b]NU-Text omits *says the Lord.* [c]Deuteronomy 32:36 **10:34** [a]NU-Text reads *the prisoners* instead of *me in my chains.* [b]NU-Text omits *in heaven.* **10:37** [a]Or *that which* **10:38** [a]NU-Text reads *My just one.* [b]Habakkuk 2:3, 4

PARENTING MATTERS

Q: *How can I teach my family the value of church?*

Although church attendance remains quite high in America, many younger people have bought into the idea that regular involvement in a local church is an optional part of their Christian life. Of course, God can be worshiped anywhere and at any time, but God has made us part of His living body. Others need us as much as we need them, and such dynamic relationships typically occur in a local church.

The writer of Hebrews explains the importance of active engagement with other believers, "Let us hold fast the confession of our hope without wavering, for He who promised is faithful. And let us consider one another in order to stir up love and good works, not forsaking the assembling of ourselves together, as is the manner of some, but exhorting one another; and so much the more as you see Day approaching" (10:23–25).

Caution: Do not assume your children understand their need for a church. This is a generation that is growing up in church, but when they become adults they are leaving the church. Train them and discuss with them *why* they need a church now and why they'll need to be a connected part of the church in the future.

Trust me: You *need* a family of families. You need that family now, and you'll need that family later. If you follow Jesus Christ, you are already connected to the body of Christ—the church. Active involvement in a local church provides not only spiritual nourishment, but also strength and support that will help you honor your marriage covenant and build a godly family.

Give the Good Word

GOD SPENDS A LOT OF TIME in His Word encouraging His children to encourage others. Have you ever noticed that? As the writer to the Hebrews says, "Let us consider one another in order to stir up love and good works" (10:24).

In this context, the word *consider* means ponder, think, and evaluate how to stimulate someone to express their love for others through good deeds. We need to recover this lost art in the Christian world. When was the last time you pondered how to encourage someone—even your spouse or children—toward good works?

Being a true leader in your home means that you have a shepherd's heart that encourages your loved ones to do what is right and good in the sight of God. It means you don't spend your time chiding, criticizing, or becoming frustrated with your loved ones.

Yes, there will be times when confrontation and verbal correction will be needed; but far more frequently, God calls you to selflessly *encourage* those who are closest to you, to be and do what God wants them to be and do.

Everybody needs encouragement! Likewise, almost everyone will respond better to encouraging words than to constant badgering and criticism. Make it your aim to consider how you can stir others to love and good deeds with your words—words of believe, words that instill courage, words that lift up out of difficult circumstances, and words that comfort those who despair.

3By faith we understand that the worlds were framed by the word of God, so that the things which are seen were not made of things which are visible.

Faith at the Dawn of History

4By faith Abel offered to God a more excellent sacrifice than Cain, through which he obtained witness that he was righteous, God testifying of his gifts; and through it he being dead still speaks.

5By faith Enoch was taken away so that he did not see death, *"and was not found, because God had taken him";*a for before he was taken he had this testimony, that he pleased God. 6But without faith *it is* impossible to please *Him,* for he who comes to God must believe that He is, and *that* He is a rewarder of those who diligently seek Him.

7By faith Noah, being divinely warned of things not yet seen, moved with godly fear, prepared an ark for the saving of his household, by which he condemned the world and became heir of the righteousness which is according to faith.

Faithful Abraham

8By faith Abraham obeyed when he was called to go out to the place which he would receive as an inheritance. And he went out, not knowing where he was going. 9By faith he dwelt in the land of promise as *in* a foreign country, dwelling in tents with Isaac and Jacob, the heirs with him of the same promise; 10for he waited for the city which has foundations, whose builder and maker *is* God.

11By faith Sarah herself also received strength to conceive seed, and she bore a childa when she was past the age, because she judged Him faithful who had promised. 12Therefore from one man, and him as good as dead, were born *as many* as the stars of the sky in multitude—innumerable as the sand which is by the seashore.

The Heavenly Hope

13These all died in faith, not having received the promises, but having seen them afar off were assured of them,a embraced *them* and confessed that they were strangers and pilgrims on the earth. 14For those who say such things declare plainly that they seek a homeland. 15And truly if they had called to mind that *country* from which they had come out, they would have had opportunity to return. 16But now they desire a better,

---

11:5 aGenesis 5:24 **11:11** aNU-Text omits *she bore a child.* **11:13** aNU-Text and M-Text omit *were assured of them.*

that is, a heavenly *country.* Therefore God is not ashamed to be called their God, for He has prepared a city for them.

The Faith of the Patriarchs

[17]By faith Abraham, when he was tested, offered up Isaac, and he who had received the promises offered up his only begotten *son,* [18]of whom it was said, *"In Isaac your seed shall be called,"*[a] [19]concluding that God *was* able to raise *him* up, even from the dead, from which he also received him in a figurative sense.

[20]By faith Isaac blessed Jacob and Esau concerning things to come.

[21]By faith Jacob, when he was dying, blessed each of the sons of Joseph, and worshiped, *leaning* on the top of his staff.

[22]By faith Joseph, when he was dying, made mention of the departure of the children of Israel, and gave instructions concerning his bones.

The Faith of Moses

[23]By faith Moses, when he was born, was hidden three months by his parents, because they saw *he was* a beautiful child; and they were not afraid of the king's command.

11:18 aGenesis 21:12
11:26 aNU-Text and M-Text read *of.*

[24]By faith Moses, when he became of age, refused to be called the son of Pharaoh's daughter, [25]choosing rather to suffer affliction with the people of God than to enjoy the passing pleasures of sin, [26]esteeming the reproach of Christ greater riches than the treasures in[a] Egypt; for he looked to the reward.

[27]By faith he forsook Egypt, not fearing the wrath of the king; for he endured as seeing Him who is invisible. [28]By faith he kept the Passover and the sprinkling of blood, lest he who destroyed the firstborn should touch them.

[29]By faith they passed through the Red Sea as by dry *land, whereas* the Egyptians, attempting to do so, were drowned.

By Faith They Overcame

[30]By faith the walls of Jericho fell down after they were encircled for seven days. [31]By faith the harlot Rahab did not perish with those who did not believe, when she had received the spies with peace.

[32]And what more shall I say? For the time would fail me to tell of Gideon and Barak and Samson and Jephthah, also *of* David and Samuel and the prophets: [33]who through faith subdued kingdoms, worked righteousness, obtained promises, stopped the mouths of lions, [34]quenched the violence

---

ROMANTIC QUOTES AND NOTES
Faith Makes a Marriage Work

Faith is an invisible but active ingredient in every spiritually growing marriage. It's the catalyst that causes you to implement biblical principles into your relationship, trusting God to use your obedience to build oneness.

Many people, however, would find it difficult to give a true biblical definition of faith. Some people use the word almost as a substitute for belief, as in, "I am part of the Christian faith, while my neighbor is part of the Muslim faith."

I like the definition of faith provided by my friend Ney Bailey in her book, *Faith Is Not a Feeling,* "Faith is taking God at His word. . . . God's Word is truer than anything I feel. God's Word is truer than anything I experience. God's Word is truer than any circumstances I will ever face. God's Word is truer than anything in the world." That's what the writer of Hebrews means when he describes faith as "the substance of things hoped for, the evidence of things not seen" (11:1).

The object of our faith is God and His Word. You must place your trust in what God has said. But if you don't know what He has said in His Word, how can you believe? That's why Paul tells the Romans, "Faith comes by hearing, and hearing by the word of God" (Rom. 10:17).

What are you trusting God for that only He can do in your marriage? Ask God to increase your faith and enable you to grow closer to Him and to each other.

Losing Weight and Avoiding Potholes

HEBREWS 12:1 CONTAINS a fabulous word picture designed to keep us running strong in the race of life. It describes current believers running a crucial race, with thousands of saints who already have gone on to their reward cheering them on from heaven.

Those men and women are cheering for *us* to finish our race successfully!

To finish this race successfully, we have some choices to make. We don't have to make perfect choices every time, but there are some crucial choices we must make correctly every time. Those choices are:

•to lay aside the things that weigh us down

•to give up the sin that trips us up.

This word picture suggests a runner stripping off excess pounds and clothing in order to run faster, and that same runner avoiding potholes on the course.

The application to marriage is clear: Marriage can be difficult enough without those unneeded—and avoidable— encumbrances and potholes. We need to train ourselves to get rid of the extra weight we don't need and to avoid the things that can trip us up.

What's that extra weight in your life? What are the things that consistently trip you up? Here's our list of those things that have weighed us down from time to time:

•Schedules that had no margin, no room for the unexpected

•Miscommunication in the midst of pressurized situations

•Not believing the best about each other's motives

•Differing approaches to a problem, discipline of a young child, or just our approaches to life. Differences aren't wrong, they're just different.

•Failure to anticipate certain seasons of the year, like Christmas, the end of school in May, and all the activities in between.

Your list will undoubtedly be different. The key is to talk about those matters that weigh you down or trip you up. And decide what you are going to do about each of them. Listen carefully, and you can hear a great cloud of witnesses cheering you on, "Leave them both behind!"

The crowd roars, "Leave them both behind!"

---

of fire, escaped the edge of the sword, out of weakness were made strong, became valiant in battle, turned to flight the armies of the aliens. ³⁵Women received their dead raised to life again.

Others were tortured, not accepting deliverance, that they might obtain a better resurrection. ³⁶Still others had trial of mockings and scourgings, yes, and of chains and imprisonment. ³⁷They were stoned, they were sawn in two, were tempted,ᵃ were slain with the sword. They wandered about in sheepskins and goatskins, being destitute, afflicted, tormented— ³⁸of whom the world was not worthy. They

wandered in deserts and mountains, *in* dens and caves of the earth.

³⁹And all these, having obtained a good testimony through faith, did not receive the promise, ⁴⁰God having provided something better for us, that they should not be made perfect apart from us.

The Race of Faith

12 Therefore we also, since we are surrounded by so great a cloud of witnesses, let us lay aside every weight, and the sin which so easily ensnares *us,* and let

11:37 ᵃNU-Text omits *were tempted.*

us run with endurance the race that is set before us, [2]looking unto Jesus, the author and finisher of *our* faith, who for the joy that was set before Him endured the cross, despising the shame, and has sat down at the right hand of the throne of God.

The Discipline of God

[3]For consider Him who endured such hostility from sinners against Himself, lest you become weary and discouraged in your souls. [4]You have not yet resisted to bloodshed, striving against sin. [5]And you have forgotten the exhortation which speaks to you as to sons:

> "My son, do not despise the
>   chastening of the LORD,
> Nor be discouraged when you are
>   rebuked by Him;
> [6] For whom the LORD loves He
>   chastens,
> And scourges every son whom He
>   receives."[a]

[7]If[a] you endure chastening, God deals with you as with sons; for what son is there whom a father does not chasten? [8]But if you are without chastening, of which all have become partakers, then you are illegitimate and not sons. [9]Furthermore, we have

---

12:6 [a]Proverbs 3:11, 12 12:7 [a]NU-Text and M-Text read *It is for discipline that you endure; God . . . .*

had human fathers who corrected *us,* and we paid *them* respect. Shall we not much more readily be in subjection to the Father of spirits and live? [10]For they indeed for a few days chastened *us* as seemed *best* to them, but He for *our* profit, that *we* may be partakers of His holiness. [11]Now no chastening seems to be joyful for the present, but painful; nevertheless, afterward it yields the peaceable fruit of righteousness to those who have been trained by it.

Renew Your Spiritual Vitality

[12]Therefore strengthen the hands which hang down, and the feeble knees, [13]and make straight paths for your feet, so that what is lame may not be dislocated, but rather be healed.

[14]Pursue peace with all *people,* and holiness, without which no one will see the Lord: [15]looking carefully lest anyone fall short of the grace of God; lest any root of bitterness springing up cause trouble, and by this many become defiled; [16]lest there *be* any fornicator or profane person like Esau, who for one morsel of food sold his birthright. [17]For you know that afterward, when he wanted to inherit the blessing, he was rejected, for he found no place for repentance, though he sought it diligently with tears.

Marriage: Both Romantic and Redemptive

God could have made marriage to be as predictable as gravity. He could have enabled Barbara and me to kick it into neutral so that we could coast for fifty years. But He didn't.

God created marriage to be both romantic and redemptive.

God aims to rid us of selfishness. He uses difficulties in marriage to melt away the dross in our lives, or as the writer of Hebrews puts it, God chastens us "for our profit, that we may be partakers of His holiness. Now no chastening seems to be joyful for the present, but painful; nevertheless, afterward it yields the peaceable fruit of righteousness to those who have been trained by it" (12:10, 11).

Once the illusion of the low maintenance marriage has been stripped away, every man is faced with a crossroads. He must decide whether he's willing to put aside his own desires and commit to loving his wife, no matter what—and so enjoy the fruits of that investment—or he can take the path of least resistance, which ultimately leads to isolation or divorce.

The romance you desire will never occur unless you commit to cherish your wife. Begin by caring for her and her needs. Then, gently address the harder issues. A great marriage takes time and effort to grow, but the rewards are well worth the investment.

DEVOTIONS FOR COUPLES • 12:14, 15
How to Cut out Bitterness

Do you ever struggle with angry or vengeful feelings? If you're married, I'm sure you do! That's the human way.

It is not, however, God's way. And it's also not the way to a strong, vibrant, and growing marriage. God tells us in no uncertain terms to rid ourselves of the bitterness that often accompanies some kind of hurt. And He gives us instructions about how to do that.

First, *cut down any bitterness growing in your life and dig it up—roots and all.* Hebrews 12:15 warns us not to let a "root of bitterness" spring up. A root is the result of a seed that has been nourished and cultivated. Dig up those bitter roots and eradicate them from your life by confessing them one by one to God (see 1 John 1:5–10). God promises forgiveness to all who confess their sin. After restoring your relationship with God, it may be appropriate to go to the person with whom you have been angry and seek his or her forgiveness.

Second, *make the crucial choice to forgive.* Forgiving someone doesn't necessarily mean we forget what they did to us, either immediately or even completely, but it does mean we no longer hold a private grudge that desires to punish, or to see them punished. Understand that the choice to punish another with bitterness will boomerang on you. Baseball player Satchel Paige said it well, "What goes around, comes around." Forgiveness, on the other hand, says, "I will give up my right to punish you for how you have wronged me."

Third, *experience peace by resolving conflicts as they occur.* "Do not let the sun go down on your wrath," Paul counsels (Eph. 4:26). Which would you rather face—the short-term, emotional pain of asking another to forgive you for your anger, or carrying the cancerous feelings of bitterness for a lifetime? It's your choice. No person really enjoys harboring a poisonous grudge against another, but our pride many times keeps us from going to others and confessing our error.

God commands us to "pursue peace with all people" (Heb. 12:14), and He also gives us some practical ways to foster better relationships, "Repay no one evil for evil. . . If it is possible, as much as depends on you, live peaceably with all men. Beloved, do not avenge yourselves. . . Do not be overcome by evil, but overcome evil with good" (Rom. 12:17–21).

The Glorious Company

18For you have not come to the mountain that[a] may be touched and that burned with fire, and to blackness and darkness[a] and tempest, 19and the sound of a trumpet and the voice of words, so that those who heard *it* begged that the word should not be spoken to them anymore. 20(For they could not endure what was commanded: *"And if so much as a beast touches the mountain, it shall be stoned[a] or shot with an arrow."*[b] 21And so terrifying was the sight *that* Moses said, *"I am exceedingly afraid and trembling."*[a])

22But you have come to Mount Zion and to the city of the living God, the heavenly Jerusalem, to an innumerable company of angels, 23to the general assembly and church of the firstborn *who are* registered in heaven, to God the Judge of all, to the spirits of just men made perfect, 24to Jesus the Mediator of the new covenant, and to the blood of sprinkling that speaks better things than *that of* Abel.

Hear the Heavenly Voice

25See that you do not refuse Him who speaks. For if they did not escape who refused Him who spoke on earth, much more *shall we not escape* if we turn away from Him who *speaks* from heaven, 26whose voice then shook the earth; but now He has

---

12:18 [a]NU-Text reads *to that which.* [b]NU-Text reads *gloom.* 12:20 [a]NU-Text and M-Text omit the rest of this verse. [b]Exodus 19:12, 13 12:21 [a]Deuteronomy 9:19

promised, saying, *"Yet once more I shake*[a] *not only the earth, but also heaven."*[a] [27]Now this, *"Yet once more,"* indicates the removal of those things that are being shaken, as of things that are made, that the things which cannot be shaken may remain.

[28]Therefore, since we are receiving a kingdom which cannot be shaken, let us have grace, by which we may[a] serve God acceptably with reverence and godly fear. [29]For our God *is* a consuming fire.

Concluding Moral Directions

13 Let brotherly love continue. [2]Do not forget to entertain strangers, for by so *doing* some have unwittingly entertained angels. [3]Remember the prisoners as if chained with them—those who are mistreated—since you yourselves are in the body also.

[4]Marriage *is* honorable among all, and the bed undefiled; but fornicators and adulterers God will judge.

[5]*Let your* conduct *be* without covetousness; *be* content with such things as you have. For He Himself has said, *"I will never leave you nor forsake you."*[a] [6]So we may boldly say:

> *"The LORD is my helper;*
> *I will not fear.*
> *What can man do to me?"*[a]

Concluding Religious Directions

[7]Remember those who rule over you, who have spoken the word of God to you, whose faith follow, considering the outcome of *their* conduct. [8]Jesus Christ *is* the same yesterday, today, and forever. [9]Do not be carried about[a] with various and strange doctrines. For *it is* good that the heart be established by grace, not with foods which have not profited those who have been occupied with them.

[10]We have an altar from which those who serve the tabernacle have no right to eat. [11]For the bodies of those animals, whose blood is brought into the sanctuary by the high priest for sin, are burned outside the camp. [12]Therefore Jesus also, that He might sanctify the people with His own blood, suffered outside the gate. [13]Therefore let us go forth to Him, outside the camp, bearing His reproach. [14]For here we have no continuing city, but we seek the one to come. [15]Therefore by Him let us continually offer the sacrifice of praise to God, that is, the fruit of *our* lips, giving thanks to His name. [16]But do not forget to do good and to share, for with such sacrifices God is well pleased.

[17]Obey those who rule over you, and be submissive, for they watch out for your souls, as those who must give account. Let them do so with joy and not with grief, for that would be unprofitable for you.

Prayer Requested

[18]Pray for us; for we are confident that we have a good conscience, in all things desiring to live honorably. [19]But I especially urge *you* to do this, that I may be restored to you the sooner.

Benediction, Final Exhortation, Farewell

[20]Now may the God of peace who brought up our Lord Jesus from the dead, that great Shepherd of the sheep, through the blood of the everlasting covenant, [21]make you complete in every good work to do His will, working in you[a] what is well pleasing in His sight, through Jesus Christ, to whom *be* glory forever and ever. Amen.

[22]And I appeal to you, brethren, bear with the word of exhortation, for I have written to you in few words. [23]Know that *our* brother Timothy has been set free, with whom I shall see you if he comes shortly. [24]Greet all those who rule over you, and all the saints. Those from Italy greet you. [25]Grace *be* with you all. Amen.

12:26 [a]NU-Text reads *will shake.* [b]Haggai 2:6
12:28 [a]M-Text omits *may.* **13:5** [a]Deuteronomy 31:6, 8; Joshua 1:5 **13:6** [a]Psalm 118:6 **13:9** [a]NU-Text and M-Text read *away.* **13:21** [a]NU-Text and M-Text read *us.*

JAMES

THIS VERY PRACTICAL LETTER, written by the half brother of Jesus, is addressed to Jewish Christians living outside of Palestine. James has a lot to say about how we demonstrate genuine faith in God through a life of obedience. It's not enough merely to *say* we have faith; genuine faith always reveals itself in godly living.

James teaches that real faith bears up under trials (1:2–4). Real faith understands how temptation works, and resists it (1:12–14). Real faith obeys God's Word and cares for the weakest and most vulnerable (1:27). Real faith does not play favorites (2:1–12). Real faith reveals itself through acts of mercy, compassion, and obedience (2:13–26). Real faith controls the tongue (1:19, 3:1–11). Real faith leads to wisdom, displayed through godly character (3:12–18). Real faith looks forward to the return of Christ and purposes to live righteously and kindly toward others while waiting for the day of the Lord (5:7–20).

James reminds us that God uses trials and suffering for our good and for His glory (1:2–4). For that reason, we should not be surprised when we go through seasons of suffering in our marriage or in our family; it simply means that God is at work. As parents, we can find comfort in the promise that when we lack wisdom in raising our children, we can ask God to guide us (1:5), and that He will use His Word, His Holy Spirit, and the counsel of godly men and women to direct us.

While James does not speak directly to the relationship between a husband and a wife, this book has much to say to couples. For example, one key to loving marital communication is found in this counsel, "Be swift to hear, slow to speak, slow to wrath" (1:19). James issues important warnings about the need to control our tongues and about the disastrous relational consequences of uncontrolled speech (3:2–12). Finally, James unmasks the source of strife and conflict in relationships—"the desires for pleasure that war in your members" (4:1)—as well as the antidote, humility (4:6, 10).

Although the Book of James is not a marriage and family book, it could be subtitled "Real Faith, Real Family Life." It really is a great book for the issues you and I are facing in our marriages and families.

Greeting to the Twelve Tribes

1 James, a bondservant of God and of the Lord Jesus Christ,

To the twelve tribes which are scattered abroad:

Greetings.

Profiting from Trials

²My brethren, count it all joy when you fall into various trials, ³knowing that the testing of your faith produces patience. ⁴But let patience have *its* perfect work, that you may be perfect and complete, lacking nothing. ⁵If any of you lacks wisdom, let him ask of God, who gives to all liberally and without reproach, and it will be given to him. ⁶But let him ask in faith, with no doubting, for he who doubts is like a wave of the sea driven and tossed by the wind. ⁷For let not that man suppose that he will receive anything from the Lord; ⁸*he is* a double-minded man, unstable in all his ways.

The Perspective of Rich and Poor

⁹Let the lowly brother glory in his exaltation, ¹⁰but the rich in his humiliation, because as a flower of the field he will pass away. ¹¹For no sooner has the sun risen with a burning heat than it withers the grass; its flower falls, and its beautiful appearance perishes. So the rich man also will fade away in his pursuits.

Loving God Under Trials

¹²Blessed *is* the man who endures temptation; for when he has been approved, he will receive the crown of life which the Lord has promised to those who love Him. ¹³Let no one say when he is tempted, "I am tempted by God"; for God cannot be tempted by evil, nor does He Himself tempt anyone. ¹⁴But each one is tempted when he is drawn away by his own desires and enticed. ¹⁵Then, when desire has conceived, it gives birth to sin; and sin, when it is full-grown, brings forth death.

¹⁶Do not be deceived, my beloved brethren. ¹⁷Every good gift and every perfect gift is from above, and comes down from the Father of lights, with whom there

1:19 ªNU-Text reads *Know this* or *This you know.*

BIBLICAL INSIGHTS • 1:14, 15

Control Your Thoughts

EVEN IN THE BEST OF MARRIAGES, there are moments when one or both partners finds themselves attracted to someone other than their spouses, and can even tempted to act on that attraction.

Some people have felt tremendous guilt over these kinds of thoughts, but the Bible tells us that it is not a sin to be tempted or even to feel attracted to someone other than one's spouse. Sin occurs when we *act* on that temptation, either in deed or in thought. "But each one is tempted when he is drawn away by his own desires and enticed. Then, when desire has conceived, it gives birth to sin; and sin, when it is full-grown, brings forth death" (1:14, 15).

That is a strong warning, isn't it? It tells us that the result of acting on temptation isn't pleasure or long-term satisfaction. Rather, it's death—meaning full-blown destruction. That means destruction in your relationships—your relationship with your spouse *and* your relationship with God.

Nothing good comes from entertaining sinful thoughts and fantasies. That is why it's so important to control your thought life. It will keep you from all sorts of sins, including sin of adultery.

is no variation or shadow of turning. ¹⁸Of His own will He brought us forth by the word of truth, that we might be a kind of firstfruits of His creatures.

Qualities Needed in Trials

¹⁹So then,ª my beloved brethren, let every man be swift to hear, slow to speak, slow to wrath; ²⁰for the wrath of man does not produce the righteousness of God.

Doers—Not Hearers Only

²¹Therefore lay aside all filthiness and overflow of wickedness, and receive with meekness the implanted word, which is able to save your souls.

²²But be doers of the word, and not hearers only, deceiving yourselves. ²³For if anyone is a hearer of the word and not a doer, he is like a man observing his natural face in a mirror; ²⁴for he observes himself, goes away, and immediately forgets what kind of man he was. ²⁵But he who looks into the perfect law of liberty and continues *in it,* and is not a forgetful hearer but a doer of the work, this one will be blessed in what he does.

²⁶If anyone among you[a] thinks he is religious, and does not bridle his tongue but deceives his own heart, this one's religion *is* useless. ²⁷Pure and undefiled religion before God and the Father is this: to visit orphans and widows in their trouble, *and* to keep oneself unspotted from the world.

Beware of Personal Favoritism

2 My brethren, do not hold the faith of our Lord Jesus Christ, *the Lord* of glory, with partiality. ²For if there should come into your assembly a man with gold rings, in fine apparel, and there should also come in a poor man in filthy clothes, ³and you pay attention to the one wearing the fine clothes and say to him, "You sit here in a good place," and say to the poor man, "You stand there," or, "Sit here at my footstool," ⁴have you not shown partiality among yourselves, and become judges with evil thoughts?

⁵Listen, my beloved brethren: Has God not chosen the poor of this world *to be* rich in faith and heirs of the kingdom which He promised to those who love Him? ⁶But you have dishonored the poor man. Do not the rich oppress you and drag you into the courts? ⁷Do they not blaspheme that noble name by which you are called?

⁸If you really fulfill *the* royal law according to the Scripture, "*You shall love your neighbor as yourself,*"[a] you do well; ⁹but if you show partiality, you commit sin, and are convicted by the law as transgressors. ¹⁰For whoever shall keep the whole law, and yet stumble in one *point,* he is guilty of all. ¹¹For He who said, "*Do not commit adultery,*"[a] also said, "*Do not murder.*"[b] Now if you do not commit adultery, but you do murder, you have become a transgressor of the law. ¹²So speak and so do as those who will be judged by the law of liberty. ¹³For judgment is without mercy to the one who has shown no mercy. Mercy triumphs over judgment.

Faith Without Works Is Dead

¹⁴What *does it* profit, my brethren, if someone says he has faith but does not

1:26 ªNU-Text omits *among you.* 2:8 ªLeviticus 19:18 2:11 ªExodus 20:14; Deuteronomy 5:18 ᵇExodus 20:13; Deuteronomy 5:17

What Does It Profit?

While we certainly need to do everything in our power to strengthen our own marriages, as believers in Christ, we can't stop with that. We need to fight for marriages other than our own.

James says, "If a brother or sister is naked and destitute of daily food, and one of you says to them, 'Depart in peace, be warmed and filled,' but you do not give them the things which are needed for the body, what does it profit?" (2:15, 16).

A growing number of Christians, upon hearing of the hurt and anguish of their friends, do not reach for their Bibles, but instead, hastily offer a parachute and say, "Bail out!" Or they simply sit by, saying and doing nothing.

James would ask, "What does it profit?"

Instead, we have to "give them the things which are needed." You and I have to go to the guy who just left his family and urge him to keep his covenant and to reconcile his relationship with his wife. And that woman in our Sunday School class? She can't simply leave her husband for this other guy and think things will be business as usual.

Plead, beg, and pray with them. If necessary, lovingly confront them. And get them some help. We are "members of one another" (Eph. 4:25), and that compels us to speak the truth to one another.

have works? Can faith save him? [15]If a brother or sister is naked and destitute of daily food, [16]and one of you says to them, "Depart in peace, be warmed and filled," but you do not give them the things which are needed for the body, what *does it* profit? [17]Thus also faith by itself, if it does not have works, is dead.

[18]But someone will say, "You have faith, and I have works." Show me your faith without your[a] works, and I will show you my faith by my[b] works. [19]You believe that there is one God. You do well. Even the demons believe—and tremble! [20]But do you want to know, O foolish man, that faith without works is dead?[a] [21]Was not Abraham our father justified by works when he offered Isaac his son on the altar? [22]Do you see that faith was working together with his works, and by works faith was made perfect? [23]And the Scripture was fulfilled which says, *"Abraham believed God, and it was accounted to him for righteousness."*[a] And he was called the friend of God. [24]You see then that a man is justified by works, and not by faith only.

[25]Likewise, was not Rahab the harlot also justified by works when she received the messengers and sent *them* out another way? [26]For as the body without the spirit is dead, so faith without works is dead also.

The Untamable Tongue

3 My brethren, let not many of you become teachers, knowing that we shall receive a stricter judgment. [2]For we all stumble in many things. If anyone does not stumble in word, he *is* a perfect man, able also to bridle the whole body. [3]Indeed,[a] we put bits in horses' mouths that they may obey us, and we turn their whole body. [4]Look also at ships: although they are so large and are driven by fierce winds, they are turned by a very small rudder wherever the pilot desires. [5]Even so the tongue is a little member and boasts great things.

See how great a forest a little fire kindles! [6]And the tongue *is* a fire, a world of

iniquity. The tongue is so set among our members that it defiles the whole body, and sets on fire the course of nature; and it is set on fire by hell. [7]For every kind of beast and bird, of reptile and creature of the sea, is tamed and has been tamed by mankind. [8]But no man can tame the tongue. *It is* an unruly evil, full of deadly poison. [9]With it we bless our God and Father, and with it we curse men, who have been made in the similitude of God. [10]Out of the same mouth proceed blessing and cursing. My brethren, these things ought not to be so. [11]Does a spring send forth fresh *water* and bitter from the same opening? [12]Can a fig tree, my brethren, bear olives, or a grapevine bear figs? Thus no spring yields both salt water and fresh.[a]

INTIMATE MOMENTS

Go to bed at the same time with her for a week; just talk or read a book and share the quietness together. Or play a card game that you used to play when you dated or were just married.

Heavenly Versus Demonic Wisdom

[13]Who *is* wise and understanding among you? Let him show by good conduct *that* his works *are done* in the meekness of wisdom. [14]But if you have bitter envy and self-seeking in your hearts, do not boast and lie against the truth. [15]This wisdom does not descend from above, but *is* earthly, sensual, demonic. [16]For where envy and self-seeking *exist,* confusion and every evil thing *are* there. [17]But the wisdom that is from above is first pure, then peaceable, gentle, willing to yield, full of mercy and good fruits, without partiality and without hypocrisy. [18]Now the fruit of righteousness is sown in peace by those who make peace.

Pride Promotes Strife

4 Where do wars and fights *come* from among you? Do *they* not *come* from your *desires for* pleasure that war in your members? [2]You lust and do not have. You

---

2:18 [a]NU-Text omits *your.* [b]NU-Text omits *my.*
2:20 [a]NU-Text reads *useless.* **2:23** [a]Genesis 15:6
3:3 [a]NU-Text reads *Now if.* **3:12** [a]NU-Text reads *Neither can a salty spring produce fresh water.*

murder and covet and cannot obtain. You fight and war. Yet[a] you do not have because you do not ask. ³You ask and do not receive, because you ask amiss, that you may spend *it* on your pleasures. ⁴Adulterers and[a] adulteresses! Do you not know that friendship with the world is enmity with God? Whoever therefore wants to be a friend of the world makes himself an enemy of God. ⁵Or do you think that the Scripture says in vain, "The Spirit who dwells in us yearns jealously"?

⁶But He gives more grace. Therefore He says:

"God resists the proud,
But gives grace to the humble."[a]

Humility Cures Worldliness

⁷Therefore submit to God. Resist the devil and he will flee from you. ⁸Draw near to God and He will draw near to you. Cleanse *your* hands, *you* sinners; and purify *your* hearts, *you* double-minded. ⁹Lament and mourn and weep! Let your laughter be turned to mourning and *your* joy to gloom. ¹⁰Humble yourselves in the sight of the Lord, and He will lift you up.

Do Not Judge a Brother

¹¹Do not speak evil of one another, brethren. He who speaks evil of a brother and judges his brother, speaks evil of the law and judges the law. But if you judge the law, you are not a doer of the law but a judge. ¹²There is one Lawgiver,[a] who is able to save and to destroy. Who[a] are you to judge another?[b]

Do Not Boast About Tomorrow

¹³Come now, you who say, "Today or tomorrow we will[a] go to such and such a city, spend a year there, buy and sell, and make a profit"; ¹⁴whereas you do not know what *will happen* tomorrow. For what *is* your life? It is even a vapor that appears for a little time and then vanishes away. ¹⁵Instead you *ought* to say, "If the Lord wills, we shall live and do this or that." ¹⁶But now you boast in your arrogance. All such boasting is evil.

¹⁷Therefore, to him who knows to do good and does not do *it,* to him it is sin.

Rich Oppressors Will Be Judged

5 Come now, *you* rich, weep and howl for your miseries that are coming upon *you!* ²Your riches are corrupted, and your garments are moth-eaten. ³Your gold and silver are corroded, and their corrosion will be a witness against you and will eat your flesh like fire. You have heaped up treasure in the last days. ⁴Indeed the wages of the laborers who mowed your fields, which you kept back by fraud, cry out; and the cries of the reapers have reached the ears of the Lord of Sabaoth.[a] ⁵You have lived on the earth in pleasure and luxury; you have fattened your hearts as[a] in a day of slaughter. ⁶You have condemned, you have murdered the just; he does not resist you.

Be Patient and Persevering

⁷Therefore be patient, brethren, until the coming of the Lord. See *how* the farmer waits for the precious fruit of the earth, waiting patiently for it until it receives the early and latter rain. ⁸You also be patient. Establish your hearts, for the coming of the Lord is at hand.

⁹Do not grumble against one another, brethren, lest you be condemned.[a] Behold, the Judge is standing at the door! ¹⁰My brethren, take the prophets, who spoke in the name of the Lord, as an example of suffering and patience. ¹¹Indeed we count them blessed who endure. You have heard of the perseverance of Job and seen the end *intended by* the Lord—that the Lord is very compassionate and merciful.

¹²But above all, my brethren, do not swear, either by heaven or by earth or with any other oath. But let your "Yes" be "Yes," and *your* "No," "No," lest you fall into judgment.[a]

Meeting Specific Needs

¹³Is anyone among you suffering? Let him pray. Is anyone cheerful? Let him sing

---

4:2 [a]NU-Text and M-Text omit *Yet.* 4:4 [a]NU-Text omits *Adulterers and.* 4:6 [a]Proverbs 3:34 4:12 [a]NU-Text adds *and Judge.* [b]NU-Text and M-Text read *But who.* [c]NU-Text reads *a neighbor.* 4:13 [a]M-Text reads *let us.* 5:4 [a]Literally, in Hebrew, *Hosts* 5:5 [a]NU-Text omits *as.* 5:9 [a]NU-Text and M-Text read *judged.* 5:12 [a]M-Text reads *hypocrisy.*

psalms. [14]Is anyone among you sick? Let him call for the elders of the church, and let them pray over him, anointing him with oil in the name of the Lord. [15]And the prayer of faith will save the sick, and the Lord will raise him up. And if he has committed sins, he will be forgiven. [16]Confess *your* trespasses[a] to one another, and pray for one another, that you may be healed. The effective, fervent prayer of a righteous man avails much. [17]Elijah was a man with a nature like ours, and he prayed earnestly that it would not rain; and it did not rain on the land for three years and six months. [18]And he prayed again, and the heaven gave rain, and the earth produced its fruit.

Bring Back the Erring One

[19]Brethren, if anyone among you wanders from the truth, and someone turns him back, [20]let him know that he who turns a sinner from the error of his way will save a soul[a] from death and cover a multitude of sins.

5:16 [a]NU-Text reads *Therefore confess your sins.*
5:20 [a]NU-Text reads *his soul.*

1 PETER

JESUS HAD TOLD HIS DISCIPLES TO EXPECT PERSECUTION and suffering, "In the world," He said, "you will have tribulation" (John 16:33). He also said believers would be hated for His name's sake (Luke 21:17). One apostle who clearly heard Jesus' words was Peter, who later experienced the persecution Jesus had predicted. He writes this letter to teach believers how to live faithfully in the midst of tribulation without losing hope or becoming bitter. The key, he says, is to trust the Lord and to look forward to His second coming.

What makes it possible for us to persevere in the midst of suffering? Peter points to a living hope, the firm conviction that God knows what He's doing and that, despite our circumstances, He remains in control. Peter had firsthand knowledge of this living hope. He had suffered through the loss of hope that came after the arrest and crucifixion of the man he felt sure was the Messiah. Yet God brought his hope alive again when Peter saw the empty tomb and spoke to the resurrected Christ.

We, too, can find hope in the midst of trials and suffering, since the same power that raised Christ from the dead lives in us!

One of the Bible's best-known passages on marriage is found in 1 Peter 3:1–7, in which Peter instructs wives married to unbelieving husbands to cultivate "the incorruptible beauty of a gentle and a quiet spirit" (3:4) so that their conduct and the evidence of God's grace in their lives might influence their husbands (3:1). The apostle teaches husbands to honor their wives and to live with them in an understanding way; in fact, failure in this area can hinder a husband's prayers (3:7). In the same context, Peter teaches couples to cultivate an attitude of harmony, kindness, compassion and tenderness toward one another, and not to return evil for evil, but to return a blessing instead (3:8–12). In doing so, they follow the example of Jesus, "who, when He was reviled, did not revile in return; when He suffered, He did not threaten, but committed Himself to Him who judges righteously" (2:23).

Greeting to the Elect Pilgrims

1 Peter, an apostle of Jesus Christ,

To the pilgrims of the Dispersion in Pontus, Galatia, Cappadocia, Asia, and Bithynia, ²elect according to the foreknowledge of God the Father, in sanctification of the Spirit, for obedience and sprinkling of the blood of Jesus Christ:

Grace to you and peace be multiplied.

A Heavenly Inheritance

³Blessed *be* the God and Father of our Lord Jesus Christ, who according to His abundant mercy has begotten us again to a living hope through the resurrection of Jesus Christ from the dead, ⁴to an inheritance incorruptible and undefiled and that does not fade away, reserved in heaven for you, ⁵who are kept by the power of God through faith for salvation ready to be revealed in the last time.

⁶In this you greatly rejoice, though now for a little while, if need be, you have been grieved by various trials, ⁷that the genuineness of your faith, *being* much more precious than gold that perishes, though it is tested by fire, may be found to praise, honor, and glory at the revelation of Jesus Christ, ⁸whom having not seenᵃ you love.

Though now you do not see *Him,* yet believing, you rejoice with joy inexpressible and full of glory, ⁹receiving the end of your faith—the salvation of *your* souls.

¹⁰Of this salvation the prophets have inquired and searched carefully, who prophesied of the grace *that would come* to you, ¹¹searching what, or what manner of time, the Spirit of Christ who was in them was indicating when He testified beforehand the sufferings of Christ and the glories that would follow. ¹²To them it was revealed that, not to themselves, but to usᵃ they were ministering the things which now have been reported to you through those who have preached the gospel to you by the Holy Spirit sent from heaven—things which angels desire to look into.

Living Before God Our Father

¹³Therefore gird up the loins of your mind, be sober, and rest *your* hope fully upon the grace that is to be brought to you at the revelation of Jesus Christ; ¹⁴as obedient children, not conforming yourselves to the former lusts, *as* in your ignorance; ¹⁵but as He who called you *is* holy, you also be holy in all *your* conduct, ¹⁶because it is written, *"Be holy, for I am holy."*ᵃ

¹⁷And if you call on the Father, who without partiality judges according to each one's work, conduct yourselves throughout the time of your stay *here* in fear; ¹⁸knowing that you were not redeemed with corruptible

1:8 ªM-Text reads *known.* 1:12 ªNU-Text and M-Text read *you.* 1:16 ªLeviticus 11:44, 45; 19:2; 20:7

Marital Conflicts Test Our Faith

As difficult as it is to work through conflict in marriage, we can claim God's promises as we do so. Not only does God bless our efforts based on His Word, but He also tells us He has an ultimate purpose for our trials, even the most trying ones.

The apostle Peter tells us, "In this you greatly rejoice, though now for a little while, if need be, you have been grieved by various trials, that the genuineness of your faith, being much more precious than gold that perishes, though it is tested by fire, may be found to praise, honor, and glory at the revelation of Jesus Christ" (1 Pet. 1:6, 7).

God wants to use our conflicts to test our faith, to produce endurance, to refine us, and to bring glory to Himself. This process isn't easy! It can be like a fire hot enough to melt gold, and it's natural to feel grieved in such heated incidents. Yet note the results. When you pass the test, your faith is "much more precious than gold"!

This is the great hope that God gives us, that we can approach our conflicts as opportunities to strengthen our faith and to glorify God. You honor Him in the process when you walk by faith together through the fire.

things, *like* silver or gold, from your aimless conduct *received* by tradition from your fathers, ¹⁹but with the precious blood of Christ, as of a lamb without blemish and without spot. ²⁰He indeed was foreordained before the foundation of the world, but was manifest in these last times for you ²¹who through Him believe in God, who raised Him from the dead and gave Him glory, so that your faith and hope are in God.

INTIMATE MOMENTS

While she studies her face in the mirror, come up behind her and gently kiss the back of her neck. Say, "God broke the mold after He made you. You are so beautiful."

The Enduring Word

²²Since you have purified your souls in obeying the truth through the Spirit[a] in sincere love of the brethren, love one another fervently with a pure heart, ²³having been born again, not of corruptible seed but incorruptible, through the word of God which lives and abides forever,[a] ²⁴because

"*All flesh is as grass,*
And all the glory of man[a] as the
flower of the grass.
The grass withers,
And its flower falls away,
²⁵ *But the word of the LORD endures*
forever."[a]

Now this is the word which by the gospel was preached to you.

2 Therefore, laying aside all malice, all deceit, hypocrisy, envy, and all evil speaking, ²as newborn babes, desire the pure milk of the word, that you may grow thereby,[a] ³if indeed you have tasted that the Lord *is* gracious.

The Chosen Stone and His Chosen People

⁴Coming to Him *as to* a living stone, rejected indeed by men, but chosen by God *and* precious, ⁵you also, as living stones,

are being built up a spiritual house, a holy priesthood, to offer up spiritual sacrifices acceptable to God through Jesus Christ. ⁶Therefore it is also contained in the Scripture,

"*Behold, I lay in Zion*
A chief cornerstone, elect, precious,
And he who believes on Him will by
no means be put to shame."[a]

⁷Therefore, to you who believe, *He is* precious; but to those who are disobedient,[a]

"*The stone which the builders rejected*
Has become the chief cornerstone,"[b]

⁸and

"*A stone of stumbling*
And a rock of offense."[a]

They stumble, being disobedient to the word, to which they also were appointed.

⁹But you *are* a chosen generation, a royal priesthood, a holy nation, His own special people, that you may proclaim the praises of Him who called you out of darkness into His marvelous light; ¹⁰who once *were* not a people but *are* now the people of God, who had not obtained mercy but now have obtained mercy.

Living Before the World

¹¹Beloved, I beg *you* as sojourners and pilgrims, abstain from fleshly lusts which war against the soul, ¹²having your conduct honorable among the Gentiles, that when they speak against you as evildoers, they may, by *your* good works which they observe, glorify God in the day of visitation.

Submission to Government

¹³Therefore submit yourselves to every ordinance of man for the Lord's sake, whether to the king as supreme, ¹⁴or to governors, as to those who are sent by him for the punishment of evildoers and *for the* praise of those who do good. ¹⁵For this is the will of God, that by doing good you

---

1:22 [a]NU-Text omits *through the Spirit.* **1:23** [a]NU-Text omits *forever.* **1:24** [a]NU-Text reads *all its glory.* **1:25** [a]Isaiah 40:6–8 **2:2** [a]NU-Text adds *up to salvation.* **2:6** [a]Isaiah 28:16 **2:7** [a]NU-Text reads *to those who disbelieve.* [b]Psalm 118:22 **2:8** [a]Isaiah 8:14

may put to silence the ignorance of foolish men— [16]as free, yet not using liberty as a cloak for vice, but as bondservants of God. [17]Honor all *people*. Love the brotherhood. Fear God. Honor the king.

Submission to Masters

[18]Servants, *be* submissive to *your* masters with all fear, not only to the good and gentle, but also to the harsh. [19]For this *is* commendable, if because of conscience toward God one endures grief, suffering wrongfully. [20]For what credit *is it* if, when you are beaten for your faults, you take it patiently? But when you do good and suffer, if you take it patiently, this *is* commendable before God. [21]For to this you were called, because Christ also suffered for us,[a] leaving us[b] an example, that you should follow His steps:

[22] "*Who committed no sin,*
   Nor was deceit found in His mouth";[a]

[23]who, when He was reviled, did not revile in return; when He suffered, He did not threaten, but committed *Himself* to Him who judges righteously; [24]who Himself bore our sins in His own body on the tree, that we, having died to sins, might live for righteousness—by whose stripes you were healed. [25]For you were like sheep going astray, but have now returned to the Shepherd and Overseer[a] of your souls.

Submission to Husbands

3 Wives, likewise, *be* submissive to your own husbands, that even if some do not obey the word, they, without a word, may be won by the conduct of their wives, [2]when they observe your chaste conduct *accompanied* by fear. [3]Do not let your adornment be *merely* outward—arranging the hair, wearing gold, or putting on *fine* apparel— [4]rather *let it be* the hidden person of the heart, with the incorruptible *beauty* of a gentle and quiet spirit, which is very precious in the sight of God. [5]For in this manner, in former times, the holy women who trusted in God also adorned themselves, being submissive to their own husbands, [6]as

BIBLICAL INSIGHTS • 3:7

Treat Your Wife as a Fully Participating Partner

THE BUSINESS WORLD has all kinds of partnerships: silent partners, financial partners, equal partners, controlling partners, minority partners, and more. But in marriage, God intended for us to have only one kind: a fully participating partnership.

The apostle Peter sets forth the concept of mutual partnership when he instructs men to treat their wives as "heirs together of the grace of life" (3:7). Although a wife's function and role differ from that of her husband, she has an equal inheritance as a child of God. There are no inferiors or superiors in marriage.

Husband, when you recognize your wife as a fully participating partner in your life and marriage, you build her esteem. If you exclude her from your life, you devalue her worth as a person and her identity suffers. Without realizing it, you send her an unmistakably clear signal that says, "I don't need you. I can live my life without you."

But God designed your wife specifically for you. Maximize and utilize her fits and abilities to their fullest. Not only will she benefit, but you will also.

It's difficult for some husbands to express their need for their wives. They somehow believe that doing so shows weakness. But when you express that need, she *feels* needed because you become vulnerable and dependent upon her, and she *experiences* her importance in your life. If you haven't done so recently, tell her three ways that you need her and appreciate her before you go to sleep tonight.

Sarah obeyed Abraham, calling him lord, whose daughters you are if you do good and are not afraid with any terror.

A Word to Husbands

[7]Husbands, likewise, dwell with *them* with understanding, giving honor to the wife, as to the weaker vessel, and as *being*

heirs together of the grace of life, that your prayers may not be hindered.

Called to Blessing

8Finally, all *of you be* of one mind, having compassion for one another; love as brothers, *be* tenderhearted, *be* courteous;[a] 9not returning evil for evil or reviling for reviling, but on the contrary blessing, knowing that you were called to this, that you may inherit a blessing. 10For

"He who would love life
And see good days,
Let him refrain his tongue from evil,
And his lips from speaking deceit.
11   Let him turn away from evil and do
good;
Let him seek peace and pursue it.
12   For the eyes of the LORD are on the
righteous,
And His ears are open to their
prayers;
But the face of the LORD is against
those who do evil."[a]

INTIMATE MOMENTS

Write him a short love letter in which you list several ways that he has blessed you this year.

Suffering for Right and Wrong

13And who *is* he who will harm you if you become followers of what is good? 14But even if you should suffer for righteousness' sake, *you are* blessed. *"And do not be afraid of their threats, nor be troubled."*[a] 15But sanctify the Lord God[a] in your hearts, and always *be* ready to *give* a defense to everyone who asks you a reason for the hope that is in you, with meekness and fear; 16having a good conscience, that when they defame you as evildoers, those who revile your good conduct in Christ may be ashamed. 17For *it is* better, if it is the will of God, to suffer for doing good than for doing evil.

Christ's Suffering and Ours

18For Christ also suffered once for sins, the just for the unjust, that He might bring us[a] to God, being put to death in the flesh but made alive by the Spirit, 19by whom also He went and preached to the spirits in prison, 20who formerly were disobedient, when once the Divine longsuffering waited[a] in the days of Noah, while *the* ark was being prepared, in which a few, that is, eight souls, were saved through water. 21There is also an antitype which now saves us—baptism (not the removal of the filth of the flesh, but the answer of a good conscience toward God), through the resurrection of Jesus Christ, 22who has gone into heaven and is at the right hand of God, angels and authorities and powers having been made subject to Him.

4 Therefore, since Christ suffered for us[a] in the flesh, arm yourselves also with the same mind, for he who has suffered in the flesh has ceased from sin, 2that he no longer should live the rest of *his* time in the flesh for the lusts of men, but for the will of God. 3For we *have spent* enough of our past lifetime[a] in doing the will of the Gentiles—when we walked in lewdness, lusts, drunkenness, revelries, drinking parties, and abominable idolatries. 4In regard to these, they think it strange that you do not run with *them* in the same flood of dissipation, speaking evil of *you.* 5They will give an account to Him who is ready to judge the living and the dead. 6For this reason the gospel was preached also to those who are dead, that they might be judged according to men in the flesh, but live according to God in the spirit.

Serving for God's Glory

7But the end of all things is at hand; therefore be serious and watchful in your prayers. 8And above all things have fervent love for one another, for *"love will cover a multitude of sins."*[a] 9*Be* hospitable to one another without grumbling. 10As each one

---

3:8 [a]NU-Text reads *humble.* 3:12 [a]Psalm 34:12–16 3:14 [a]Isaiah 8:12 3:15 [a]NU-Text reads *Christ as Lord.* 3:18 [a]NU-Text and M-Text read *you.* 3:20 [a]NU-Text and M-Text read *when the longsuffering of God waited patiently.* 4:1 [a]NU-Text omits *for us.* 4:3 [a]NU-Text reads *time.* 4:8 [a]Proverbs 10:12

has received a gift, minister it to one another, as good stewards of the manifold grace of God. [11]If anyone speaks, *let him speak* as the oracles of God. If anyone ministers, *let him do it* as with the ability which God supplies, that in all things God may be glorified through Jesus Christ, to whom belong the glory and the dominion forever and ever. Amen.

Suffering for God's Glory

[12]Beloved, do not think it strange concerning the fiery trial which is to try you, as though some strange thing happened to you; [13]but rejoice to the extent that you partake of Christ's sufferings, that when His glory is revealed, you may also be glad with exceeding joy. [14]If you are reproached for the name of Christ, blessed *are you*, for the Spirit of glory and of God rests upon you.[a] On their part He is blasphemed, but on your part He is glorified. [15]But let none of you suffer as a murderer, a thief, an evildoer, or as a busybody in other people's matters. [16]Yet if *anyone suffers* as a Christian, let him not be ashamed, but let him glorify God in this matter.[a]

[17]For the time *has come* for judgment to begin at the house of God; and if *it begins* with us first, what will *be* the end of those who do not obey the gospel of God? [18]Now

> "If the righteous one is scarcely
> saved,
> Where will the ungodly and the
> sinner appear?"[a]

[19]Therefore let those who suffer according to the will of God commit their souls *to Him* in doing good, as to a faithful Creator.

Shepherd the Flock

5 The elders who are among you I exhort, I who am a fellow elder and a witness of the sufferings of Christ, and also a partaker of the glory that will be revealed: [2]Shepherd the flock of God which is among you, serving as overseers, not by compulsion but willingly,[a] not for

dishonest gain but eagerly; [3]nor as being lords over those entrusted to you, but being examples to the flock; [4]and when the Chief Shepherd appears, you will receive the crown of glory that does not fade away.

Submit to God, Resist the Devil

[5]Likewise you younger people, submit yourselves to *your* elders. Yes, all of *you* be submissive to one another, and be clothed with humility, for

> "God resists the proud,
> But gives grace to the humble."[a]

[6]Therefore humble yourselves under the mighty hand of God, that He may exalt you in due time, [7]casting all your care upon Him, for He cares for you.

ROMANCE FAQ

Q: *How can I best deal with my unresponsive spouse?*

This is definitely one of the most challenging problems facing many couples today. You need to know you are not alone.

To begin, decide on the important issues you need to address. Some of us can get a burr under our saddles and attempt to fix an area of our relationship that may not be a critical issue. Then we nag too much and cause our mates to become uninterested or embittered. Nagging is like being nibbled to death by a duck!

Then pray about it. God loves the prayers of a helpless spouse! Ask God to give you wisdom and show you how to get your mate's attention in this situation. Or ask God to get your spouse's attention. Most importantly, pray that God will touch your mate so that he or she will develop a heart to walk closely with Him.

Next, find out what motivates your spouse. Find out what communicates love, and then speak words of love in your spouse's language. This may mean stepping out of your comfort zone to show a love that your spouse will understand but may be different than how you want love shown to you.

4:14 [a]NU-Text omits the rest of this verse.
4:16 [a]NU-Text reads *name.* 4:18 [a]Proverbs 11:31
5:2 [a]NU-Text adds *according to God.*
5:5 [a]Proverbs 3:34

⁸Be sober, be vigilant; because^a your adversary the devil walks about like a roaring lion, seeking whom he may devour. ⁹Resist him, steadfast in the faith, knowing that the same sufferings are experienced by your brotherhood in the world. ¹⁰But may^a the God of all grace,

INTIMATE MOMENTS

Evict Leno and Letterman from your bedroom. Cart off the TV and when she asks what you're doing, tell her you'd like to start making a habit of listening to *her* rather then a couple of middle-aged men in pancake makeup.

who called us^a to His eternal glory by Christ Jesus, after you have suffered a while, perfect, establish, strengthen, and settle *you.* ¹¹To Him *be* the glory and the dominion forever and ever. Amen.

Farewell and Peace

¹²By Silvanus, our faithful brother as I consider him, I have written to you briefly, exhorting and testifying that this is the true grace of God in which you stand.

¹³She who is in Babylon, elect together with *you,* greets you; and *so does* Mark my son. ¹⁴Greet one another with a kiss of love.

Peace to you all who are in Christ Jesus. Amen.

5:8 ^aNU-Text and M-Text omit *because.*
5:10 ^aNU-Text reads *But the God of all grace . . . will perfect, establish, strengthen, and settle you.* ^bNU-Text and M-Text read *you.*

2 PETER

A PERSON'S LAST WORDS often carry a great freight of meaning. Queen Elisabeth I of England is supposed to have said, just before she died in 1603, "All my possessions for a moment in time." George Washington said, "I die hard, but I am not afraid to go." Woodrow Wilson said simply, "I am ready." Perhaps my favorite last words come from a French grammarian, Dominique Bouhours, who died in 1702. He is reported to have said, "I am about to—or I am going to—die: either expression is correct."

The apostle Peter writes this second letter just before his execution as a martyr for Jesus. He dictates these words, among his last, to his travel companion, Sylvanus, warning the people of God about the dangers of false teachers, who peddle corrupt doctrine and who live morally bankrupt lives. Peter tells believers they must remain anchored in the truth of Scripture and in the knowledge of the living God, so they will be ready for any false teachers who show up.

Peter wrote this letter around AD 66 or 67 to the churches spread throughout the region we know as Asia Minor, many of the same churches Jesus would address 25 to 30 years later in Revelation 2—3. Sadly, it appears that most of these churches failed to take Peter's letter to heart. They allowed false teachers to infiltrate their ranks, and these greedy charlatans exploited the people for their own advantage. As a result, the churches gradually grew apart from God and became increasingly ungodly in their behavior.

Believers in every age must guard against false teaching. Some of it will come from people outside the church who don't hold a Christian worldview, while some of it will come from pastors or from others who claim to be Christians. So what is the best antidote for toxic teaching? It's the book you're reading—the Bible. We all need to regularly read the Bible, listen to biblical preaching, spend time meditating on God's Word, and memorize Scripture. History shows that counterfeit teaching has very little appeal to those who know and love the genuine article.

Greeting the Faithful

1 Simon Peter, a bondservant and apostle of Jesus Christ,

To those who have obtained like precious faith with us by the righteousness of our God and Savior Jesus Christ:

²Grace and peace be multiplied to you in the knowledge of God and of Jesus our Lord, ³as His divine power has given to us all things that *pertain* to life and godliness, through the knowledge of Him who called us by glory and virtue, ⁴by which have been given to us exceedingly great and precious promises, that through these you may be partakers of the divine nature, having escaped the corruption *that is* in the world through lust.

INTIMATE MOMENTS

Each day this month, leave her a Hershey's kiss where she'll be sure to find it. Ask her to save the little paper flags in a jar and redeem them for actual kisses.

Fruitful Growth in the Faith

⁵But also for this very reason, giving all diligence, add to your faith virtue, to virtue knowledge, ⁶to knowledge self-control, to self-control perseverance, to perseverance godliness, ⁷to godliness brotherly kindness, and to brotherly kindness love. ⁸For if these things are yours and abound, *you* will be neither barren nor unfruitful in the knowledge of our Lord Jesus Christ. ⁹For he who lacks these things is shortsighted, even to blindness, and has forgotten that he was cleansed from his old sins.

¹⁰Therefore, brethren, be even more diligent to make your call and election sure, for if you do these things you will never stumble; ¹¹for so an entrance will be supplied to you abundantly into the everlasting kingdom of our Lord and Savior Jesus Christ.

Peter's Approaching Death

¹²For this reason I will not be negligent to remind you always of these things, though you know and are established in the present truth. ¹³Yes, I think it is right, as long as I am in this tent, to stir you up by reminding *you,* ¹⁴knowing that shortly I *must* put off my tent, just as our Lord Jesus Christ showed me. ¹⁵Moreover I will be careful to ensure that you always have a reminder of these things after my decease.

The Trustworthy Prophetic Word

¹⁶For we did not follow cunningly devised fables when we made known to you the power and coming of our Lord Jesus Christ, but were eyewitnesses of His majesty. ¹⁷For He received from God the Father honor and glory when such a voice came to Him from the Excellent Glory: "This is My beloved Son, in whom I am well pleased." ¹⁸And we heard this voice which came from heaven when we were with Him on the holy mountain.

¹⁹And so we have the prophetic word confirmed,ᵃ which you do well to heed as a light that shines in a dark place, until the day dawns and the morning star rises in your hearts; ²⁰knowing this first, that no prophecy of Scripture is of any private interpretation,ᵃ ²¹for prophecy never came by the will of man, but holy men of Godᵃ spoke *as they were* moved by the Holy Spirit.

Destructive Doctrines

2 But there were also false prophets among the people, even as there will be false teachers among you, who will secretly bring in destructive heresies, even denying the Lord who bought them, *and* bring on themselves swift destruction. ²And many will follow their destructive ways, because of whom the way of truth will be blasphemed. ³By covetousness they will exploit you with deceptive words; for a long time their judgment has not been idle, and their destruction doesᵃ not slumber.

1:19 ᵃOr *We also have the more sure prophetic word.* **1:20** ᵃOr *origin* **1:21** ᵃNU-Text reads *but men spoke from God.* **2:3** ᵃM-Text reads *will not.*

Doom of False Teachers

⁴For if God did not spare the angels who sinned, but cast *them* down to hell and delivered *them* into chains of darkness, to be reserved for judgment; ⁵and did not spare the ancient world, but saved Noah, *one of* eight *people,* a preacher of righteousness, bringing in the flood on the world of the ungodly; ⁶and turning the cities of Sodom and Gomorrah into ashes, condemned *them* to destruction, making *them* an example to those who afterward would live ungodly; ⁷and delivered righteous Lot, *who was* oppressed by the filthy conduct of the wicked ⁸(for that righteous man, dwelling among them, tormented *his* righteous soul from day to day by seeing and hearing *their* lawless deeds)— ⁹*then* the Lord knows how to deliver the godly out of temptations and to reserve the unjust under punishment for the day of judgment, ¹⁰and especially those who walk according to the flesh in the lust of uncleanness and despise authority. *They are* presumptuous, self-willed. They are not afraid to speak evil of dignitaries, ¹¹whereas angels, who are greater in power and might, do not bring a reviling accusation against them before the Lord.

Depravity of False Teachers

¹²But these, like natural brute beasts made to be caught and destroyed, speak evil of the things they do not understand, and will utterly perish in their own corruption, ¹³*and* will receive the wages of unrighteousness, *as* those who count it pleasure to carouse in the daytime. *They are* spots and blemishes, carousing in their own deceptions while they feast with you, ¹⁴having eyes full of adultery and that cannot cease from sin, enticing unstable souls. They have a heart trained in covetous practices, *and are* accursed children. ¹⁵They have forsaken the right way and gone astray, following the way of Balaam

the *son* of Beor, who loved the wages of unrighteousness; ¹⁶but he was rebuked for his iniquity: a dumb donkey speaking with a man's voice restrained the madness of the prophet.

¹⁷These are wells without water, clouds[a] carried by a tempest, for whom is reserved the blackness of darkness forever.[a]

Deceptions of False Teachers

¹⁸For when they speak great swelling *words* of emptiness, they allure through the lusts of the flesh, through lewdness, the ones who have actually escaped[a] from those who live in error. ¹⁹While they promise them liberty, they themselves are slaves of corruption; for by whom a person is overcome, by him also he is brought into bondage. ²⁰For if, after they have escaped the pollutions of the world through the knowledge of the Lord and Savior Jesus Christ, they are again entangled in them and overcome, the latter end is worse for them than the beginning. ²¹For it would have been better for them not to have known the way of righteousness, than having known *it,* to turn from the holy commandment delivered to them. ²²But it has happened to them according to the true proverb: *"A dog returns to his own vomit,"*[a] and, *"a sow, having washed, to her wallowing in the mire."*

God's Promise Is Not Slack

3 Beloved, I now write to you this second epistle (in *both of* which I stir up your pure minds by way of reminder), ²that you may be mindful of the words which were spoken before by the holy prophets, and of the commandment of us,[a] the apostles of the Lord and Savior, ³knowing this first: that scoffers will come in the last days, walking according to their own lusts, ⁴and saying, "Where is the promise of His coming? For since the fathers fell asleep, all things continue as *they were* from the beginning of creation." ⁵For this they willfully forget: that by the word of God the heavens were of old, and the earth standing out of water and in the water, ⁶by which the world *that* then existed perished, being flooded with water. ⁷But the heavens and the earth *which* are now preserved by the

---

2:17 ᵃNU-Text reads *and mists.* ᵇNU-Text omits *forever.* **2:18** ᵃNU-Text reads *are barely escaping.* **2:22** ᵃProverbs 26:11 **3:2** ᵃNU-Text and M-Text read *commandment of the apostles of your Lord and Savior* or *commandment of your apostles of the Lord and Savior.*

BIBLICAL INSIGHTS • 3:14

When Peace Seems Elusive

AT 6:45 A.M. I WALKED into Barbara's hospital room and found her peacefully asleep. At least she was resting. I sure couldn't.

The IV hooked up to her arm told me this was for *real*. The doctor told me my wife faced a lengthy surgery. Barbara and I had traveled to Oklahoma City to correct a problem that on four occasions had caused her heart to race at more than 300 beats per minute. It was life threatening every time.

As I sat there that morning, waiting for the end of the procedure, a horde of fears crashed through my mind. I felt so helpless, knowing that I could do nothing but pray.

At 1:00 P.M., a receptionist told me that, even though Barbara's heart had raced a few times, everything was fine. But I suspected more was going on than she was telling me! Over 15 hours after the surgery, I found out I was right. The doctor, perhaps the leading cardiologist in the world on this procedure, told me

afterwards that Barbara's procedure was among the worst he'd ever tackled.

It was certainly among the worst days of my life. All day long peace was elusive. It would come and then the muggers of worry, doubt, and anxiety would work me over, only to have me once again ask God to quiet my soul. It was a long day, but God was faithful even when I wasn't.

In such times it's difficult to follow Peter's counsel, "Be diligent to be found by Him in peace" (3:14). My fear made peace elusive, but it finally came when I got alone, read the Psalms and prayed. Yes, I could trust God.

Although the surgery was years ago, I can still recall very clearly the fear and anxiety I felt then. I can also still recall the comfort and peace God gave me when I turned to Him with my worries. While it's tough to know God's peace during suspense-filled times, it can be done—with God's help.

---

same word, are reserved for fire until the day of judgment and perdition of ungodly men.

[8]But, beloved, do not forget this one thing, that with the Lord one day *is* as a thousand years, and a thousand years as one day. [9]The Lord is not slack concerning *His* promise, as some count slackness, but is longsuffering toward us,[a] not willing that any should perish but that all should come to repentance.

The Day of the Lord

[10]But the day of the Lord will come as a thief in the night, in which the heavens will pass away with a great noise, and the elements will melt with fervent heat; both the earth and the works that are in it will be burned up.[a] [11]Therefore, since all these things will be dissolved, what manner *of persons* ought you to be in holy conduct

and godliness, [12]looking for and hastening the coming of the day of God, because of which the heavens will be dissolved, being on fire, and the elements will melt with fervent heat? [13]Nevertheless we, according to His promise, look for new heavens and a new earth in which righteousness dwells.

Be Steadfast

[14]Therefore, beloved, looking forward to these things, be diligent to be found by Him in peace, without spot and blameless; [15]and consider *that* the longsuffering of our Lord *is* salvation—as also our beloved brother Paul, according to the wisdom given to him, has written to you, [16]as also in all his epistles, speaking in them of these things, in which are some things hard to understand, which untaught and unstable *people*

3:9 [a]NU-Text reads *you.*
3:10 [a]NU-Text reads *laid bare* (literally *found*).

twist to their own destruction, as *they do* also the rest of the Scriptures.

¹⁷You therefore, beloved, since you know *this* beforehand, beware lest you also fall from your own steadfastness, being led away with the error of the wicked; ¹⁸but grow in the grace and knowledge of our Lord and Savior Jesus Christ.

To Him *be* the glory both now and forever. Amen.

1 JOHN

LEGENDARY COLLEGE BASKETBALL COACH John Wooden, who led the UCLA Bruins basketball team to ten national championships in the 1960s and 1970s, used to begin every season the same way—by teaching his players how to put on their socks and lace up their sneakers. Coach Wooden was a strong believer in the fundamentals, and his methods paid off!

This letter from the apostle John is about the fundamentals of the Christian faith.

John, the younger of the two "Sons of Zebedee" mentioned in the Gospels, was likely the last apostolic eyewitness to Jesus still living when he wrote this letter. As Christianity spread throughout the Roman Empire, right alongside came a variety of false teachers who distorted the message of the gospel. John wrote this letter to provide his readers with two clear fundamentals that distinguish authentic Christianity from its many counterfeits. A genuine follower of Christ has a correct view of the identity of Jesus and a transformed life characterized by supernatural love.

In his Gospel, John refers to himself as the "disciple whom Jesus loved" (John 13:23; 21:7, 20). John thought a lot about love, and so we shouldn't be surprised to find that God's love for us and our love for each other are core themes in all of John's writings.

How we love one another in marriage is one way we demonstrate that we are truly children of God (4:7, 8). It is God's transforming love for us that enables us to love God and to love each other unselfishly (4:19).

Making a commitment to love, honor and cherish one person for a lifetime involves taking a step of faith. And that can be a frightening thing! What if the person changes? What if hard times come? What about illness or financial challenges or problems with children?

When Barbara and I got married, we chose to have 1 John 4:18 engraved on the inside of her wedding band. It says, "There is no fear in love, but perfect love casts out fear." As you read 1 John, ask yourself if the love you show one another in your own marriage is the kind of love described by the apostle John in this letter.

What Was Heard, Seen, and Touched

1 That which was from the beginning, which we have heard, which we have seen with our eyes, which we have looked upon, and our hands have handled, concerning the Word of life— ²the life was manifested, and we have seen, and bear witness, and declare to you that eternal life which was with the Father and was manifested to us— ³that which we have seen and heard we declare to you, that you also may have fellowship with us; and truly our fellowship *is* with the Father and with His Son Jesus Christ. ⁴And these things we write to you that your[a] joy may be full.

Fellowship with Him and One Another

⁵This is the message which we have heard from Him and declare to you, that God is light and in Him is no darkness at all. ⁶If we say that we have fellowship with Him, and walk in darkness, we lie and do not practice the truth. ⁷But if we walk in the light as He is in the light, we have fellowship with one another, and the blood of Jesus Christ His Son cleanses us from all sin.

⁸If we say that we have no sin, we deceive ourselves, and the truth is not in us. ⁹If we confess our sins, He is faithful and just to forgive us *our* sins and to cleanse us from all unrighteousness. ¹⁰If we say that we have not sinned, we make Him a liar, and His word is not in us.

2 My little children, these things I write to you, so that you may not sin. And if anyone sins, we have an Advocate with the Father, Jesus Christ the righteous. ²And He Himself is the propitiation for our sins, and not for ours only but also for the whole world.

The Test of Knowing Him

³Now by this we know that we know Him, if we keep His commandments. ⁴He who says, "I know Him," and does not keep His commandments, is a liar, and the truth is not in him. ⁵But whoever keeps His word, truly the love of God is perfected in him. By this we know that we are in Him.

⁶He who says he abides in Him ought himself also to walk just as He walked.

⁷Brethren,[a] I write no new commandment to you, but an old commandment which you have had from the beginning. The old commandment is the word which you heard from the beginning.[b] ⁸Again, a new commandment I write to you, which thing is true in Him and in you, because the darkness is passing away, and the true light is already shining.

⁹He who says he is in the light, and hates his brother, is in darkness until now. ¹⁰He who loves his brother abides in the light, and there is no cause for stumbling in him. ¹¹But he who hates his brother is in darkness and walks in darkness, and does not know where he is going, because the darkness has blinded his eyes.

INTIMATE MOMENTS

Take her car to the gas station, fill the tank, vacuum the floor mats, and clean the windows. When you park it at the house, leave a note on the dash with just a heart and the words, "Thinking of you."

Their Spiritual State

12 I write to you, little children,
   Because your sins are forgiven
   you for His name's sake.
13 I write to you, fathers,
   Because you have known Him
   who is from the beginning.
   I write to you, young men,
   Because you have overcome the
   wicked one.
   I write to you, little children,
   Because you have known the
   Father.
14 I have written to you, fathers,
   Because you have known Him
   who is from the beginning.
   I have written to you, young men,
   Because you are strong, and the
   word of God abides in you,
   And you have overcome the
   wicked one.

1:4 ᵃNU-Text and M-Text read *our*. 2:7 ᵃNU-Text reads *Beloved*. ᵇNU-Text omits *from the beginning*.

Do Not Love the World

¹⁵Do not love the world or the things in the world. If anyone loves the world, the love of the Father is not in him. ¹⁶For all that *is* in the world—the lust of the flesh, the lust of the eyes, and the pride of life— is not of the Father but is of the world. ¹⁷And the world is passing away, and the lust of it; but he who does the will of God abides forever.

Deceptions of the Last Hour

¹⁸Little children, it is the last hour; and as you have heard that the[a] Antichrist is coming, even now many antichrists have come, by which we know that it is the last hour. ¹⁹They went out from us, but they were not of us; for if they had been of us, they would have continued with us; but *they went out* that they might be made manifest, that none of them were of us. ²⁰But you have an anointing from the Holy One, and you know all things.[a] ²¹I have not written to you because you do not know the truth, but because you know it, and that no lie is of the truth. ²²Who is a liar but he who denies that Jesus is the Christ? He is antichrist who denies the Father and the Son. ²³Whoever denies the Son does not have the Father either; he who acknowledges the Son has the Father also.

Let Truth Abide in You

²⁴Therefore let that abide in you which you heard from the beginning. If what you heard from the beginning abides in you, you also will abide in the Son and in the Father. ²⁵And this is the promise that He has promised us—eternal life.

²⁶These things I have written to you concerning those who *try to* deceive you. ²⁷But the anointing which you have received from Him abides in you, and you do not need that anyone teach you; but as the same anointing teaches you concerning all things, and is true, and is not a lie, and just as it has taught you, you will[a] abide in Him.

The Children of God

²⁸And now, little children, abide in Him, that when[a] He appears, we may have confidence and not be ashamed before Him at His coming. ²⁹If you know that He is righteous,

---

2:18 [a]NU-Text omits *the*. 2:20 [a]NU-Text reads *you all know.* 2:27 [a]NU-Text reads *you abide.* 2:28 [a]NU-Text reads *if.*

ROMANCE FAQ

Q: In what areas should a husband and wife be accountable to one another?

Marriage is a perfect arena for accountability. As you and your mate face continuing pressures and stress, it's best to handle life in a duet, not a solo. Two can always see more clearly than one. Your mate can detect blind spots that you may not be able to see.

Here are three key areas where Barbara and I practice accountability in our own marriage:

Schedules. We try to help each other make good decisions by monitoring each other's workload and schedule. When somebody invites me to speak, I say, "I can't give you an answer now. My wife and I have agreed that I don't take any speaking engagements without talking with her." And so we talk about it, and Barbara helps me say no if that's the wisest choice.

Money and values. We constantly check our personal values. What is really important to each of us? Why are we doing what we are doing? Where do we dare not lose?

Fidelity. Couples should communicate regularly and openly about potential problems in the area of fidelity. For example, if one of you feels like a relationship between your spouse and someone of the opposite sex is getting a little too friendly, it is good to bring that out in the open. If you can't resolve the issue, ask a pastor or counselor to help you.

All of these areas of discussion occur because of the safety of our commitment to each other and ultimately our submission to Jesus Christ.

you know that everyone who practices righteousness is born of Him.

3 Behold what manner of love the Father has bestowed on us, that we should be called children of God!ᵃ Therefore the world does not know us,ᵇ because it did not know Him. ²Beloved, now we are children of God; and it has not yet been revealed what we shall be, but we know that when He is revealed, we shall be like Him, for we shall see Him as He is. ³And everyone who has this hope in Him purifies himself, just as He is pure.

Sin and the Child of God

⁴Whoever commits sin also commits lawlessness, and sin is lawlessness. ⁵And you know that He was manifested to take away our sins, and in Him there is no sin. ⁶Whoever abides in Him does not sin. Whoever sins has neither seen Him nor known Him.

⁷Little children, let no one deceive you. He who practices righteousness is righteous, just as He is righteous. ⁸He who sins is of the devil, for the devil has sinned from the beginning. For this purpose the Son of God was manifested, that He might destroy the works of the devil. ⁹Whoever has been born of God does not sin, for His seed remains in him; and he cannot sin, because he has been born of God.

The Imperative of Love

¹⁰In this the children of God and the children of the devil are manifest: Whoever does not practice righteousness is not of God, nor *is* he who does not love his brother. ¹¹For this is the message that you heard from the beginning, that we should love one another, ¹²not as Cain *who* was of the wicked one and murdered his brother. And why did he murder him? Because his works were evil and his brother's righteous.

¹³Do not marvel, my brethren, if the world hates you. ¹⁴We know that we have passed from death to life, because we love the brethren. He who does not love *his* brotherᵃ abides in death. ¹⁵Whoever hates his brother is a murderer, and you know that no murderer has eternal life abiding in him.

The Outworking of Love

¹⁶By this we know love, because He laid down His life for us. And we also ought to lay down *our* lives for the brethren. ¹⁷But whoever has this world's goods, and sees his brother in need, and shuts up his heart from him, how does the love of God abide in him?

¹⁸My little children, let us not love in word or in tongue, but in deed and in truth. ¹⁹And by this we knowᵃ that we are of the truth, and shall assure our hearts before Him. ²⁰For if our heart condemns us, God is greater than our heart, and knows all things. ²¹Beloved, if our heart does not condemn us, we have confidence toward God. ²²And whatever we ask we receive from Him, because we keep His commandments and do those things that are pleasing in His sight. ²³And this is His commandment: that we should believe on the name of His Son Jesus Christ and love one another, as He gave usᵃ commandment.

The Spirit of Truth and the Spirit of Error

²⁴Now he who keeps His commandments abides in Him, and He in him. And by this we know that He abides in us, by the Spirit whom He has given us.

4 Beloved, do not believe every spirit, but test the spirits, whether they are of God; because many false prophets have gone out into the world. ²By this you know the Spirit of God: Every spirit that confesses that Jesus Christ has come in the flesh is of God, ³and every spirit that does not confess thatᵃ Jesus Christ has come in the flesh is not of God. And this is the *spirit* of the Antichrist, which you have heard was coming, and is now already in the world.

⁴You are of God, little children, and have overcome them, because He who is in you is greater than he who is in the world. ⁵They are of the world. Therefore they speak *as* of the world, and the world hears them. ⁶We are of God. He who knows God hears us; he who is not of God does not hear us. By this we know the spirit of truth and the spirit of error.

3:1 ᵃNU-Text adds *And we are.* ᵇM-Text reads *you.* **3:14** ᵃNU-Text omits *his brother.* **3:19** ᵃNU-Text reads *we shall know.* **3:23** ᵃM-Text omits *us.* **4:3** ᵃNU-Text omits *that* and *Christ has come in the flesh.*

DEVOTIONS FOR COUPLES • 4:18
Love Creates an Open Atmosphere

Inside Barbara's wedding band is the inscription, "1 John 4:18." That verse says, "There is no fear in love; but perfect love casts out fear, because fear involves torment." We both know we are totally committed in our love for each other, and we can be open to each other without fear. Transparency begins with a firm commitment to creating an atmosphere in which it is safe to be totally open.

Because I tend to be the more open one in our marriage, I work at expressing the message engraved in Barbara's wedding ring. One problem has often plagued us—my behavior of talking too much when we go out to dinner with other couples. Because I'm the gregarious, life-of-the-party type, I'll pick up a lagging conversation by asking a good question. All I'm trying to do is to better get to know the other people and keep the evening alive and interesting. But I frequently err by not allowing time for someone like Barbara, who is not as aggressive as I am, to enter the conversation.

Early in our marriage, we would drive home after a dinner party and I would say, "Goodness, sweetheart, we were with those people for several hours, and you didn't say two or three words all evening."

"Well," Barbara would reply, "you didn't give me a chance."

We would usually drive the next few blocks in silence and I would apologize for not including her. Later I would ask what she thought of one of the people at the party. Barbara would then make profound observations about what had taken place that evening and what had been said.

On another occasion we had to make a decision about our daughter's gymnastics involvement. I maintained that we should move her out of gymnastics, but Barbara hesitated. As Barbara recalls, "I knew intuitively Dennis was probably right, but I wasn't ready to make that decision yet. I loved watching Rebecca perform. She was built for gymnastics and she loved it. I also was concerned because I didn't want her to grow up and resent us for forcing her to quit. I needed to share with Dennis how I felt. It just took me time to come to where I felt like I had adequately expressed that." On this occasion, I did not do what she needed me to do, allow her to fully express her opinion (many times) and listen carefully to her perspective. It paid off. Even though she didn't agree with my decision, I had honored her in the process and she felt valued, appreciated, and included.

Barbara has keen insights and perceptions about people, and I've learned to rely on her insights, even though I may have to wait a while before she's ready to share them.

Ultimately, Barbara knows that it's safe for her to share her feelings, her opinions, and all that she's thinking because of our commitment to each other. Beyond that, we have worked to cultivate a climate of respect in which we value and appreciate each other's strengths and ideas.

Knowing God Through Love

7Beloved, let us love one another, for love is of God; and everyone who loves is born of God and knows God. 8He who does not love does not know God, for God is love. 9In this the love of God was manifested toward us, that God has sent His only begotten Son into the world, that we might live through Him. 10In this is love, not that we loved God, but that He loved us and sent His Son *to be* the propitiation for our sins. 11Beloved, if God so loved us, we also ought to love one another.

Seeing God Through Love

12No one has seen God at any time. If we love one another, God abides in us, and His love has been perfected in us. 13By this we know that we abide in Him, and He in us, because He has given us of His Spirit. 14And we have seen and testify that the Father has sent the Son *as* Savior of the world. ¹⁵Whoever confesses that Jesus is the Son of God, God abides in him, and he in God. ¹⁶And we have known and believed the love that God has for us. God is love, and he who abides in love abides in God, and God in him.

The Consummation of Love

¹⁷Love has been perfected among us in this: that we may have boldness in the day of judgment; because as He is, so are we in this world. ¹⁸There is no fear in love; but perfect love casts out fear, because fear involves torment. But he who fears has not been made perfect in love. ¹⁹We love Himª because He first loved us.

Obedience by Faith

²⁰If someone says, "I love God," and hates his brother, he is a liar; for he who does not love his brother whom he has seen, how canª he love God whom he has not seen? ²¹And this commandment we have from Him: that he who loves God *must* love his brother also.

5 Whoever believes that Jesus is the Christ is born of God, and everyone who loves Him who begot also loves him who is begotten of Him. ²By this we know that we love the children of God, when we love God and keep His commandments. ³For this is the love of God, that we keep His commandments. And His commandments are not burdensome. ⁴For whatever is born of God overcomes the world. And this is the victory that has overcome the world—ourª faith. ⁵Who is he who overcomes the world, but he who believes that Jesus is the Son of God?

The Certainty of God's Witness

⁶This is He who came by water and blood—Jesus Christ; not only by water, but by water and blood. And it is the Spirit who bears witness, because the Spirit is truth. ⁷For there are three that bear witness in heaven: the Father, the Word, and

BIBLICAL INSIGHTS • 5:19
The Spiritual Safari

HAVE YOU TAKEN A SPIRITUAL safari into lion country?

Lion country is territory temporarily controlled by the devil. It is the daily domain of the ruler of this world. The apostle John comments on the whereabouts of lion country when he says, "We know that we are of God, and the whole world lies under the sway of the wicked one" (1 John 5:19).

Yet many Christians are unaware that enemy territory even exists. Peter warns, "Be sober, be vigilant; because your adversary the devil walks about like a roaring lion, seeking whom he may devour" (1 Pet. 5:8).

Lions in Africa prey on weak, unsuspecting animals, and those struggling behind the protection of the herd. Likewise, the devil prowls about, seeking to devour those with weak convictions. Christians who aren't in regular community with other believers find themselves isolated and defenseless—delicious prey for the crafty deceiver.

Instead of being prey, we must become aggressive soldiers recapturing land for Christ. Far too many followers of Christ never get into lion country. They are not on the offensive; they do not seek to be soldiers engaged in enemy territory. The goal of our battle is to confine the enemy to limited spheres of influence, just as the lions of Africa are limited to the confines of game preserves. When Christ returns, He will lock up the enemy forever (Rev. 20:10).

the Holy Spirit; and these three are one. ⁸And there are three that bear witness on earth:ª the Spirit, the water, and the blood; and these three agree as one.

⁹If we receive the witness of men, the witness of God is greater; for this is the

---

4:19ªNU-Text omits *Him.* **4:20**ªNU-Text reads *he cannot.* **5:4**ªM-Text reads *your.* **5:8**ªNU-Text and M-Text omit the words from *in heaven* (verse 7) through *on earth* (verse 8). Only four or five very late manuscripts contain these words in Greek.

witness of God which[a] He has testified of His Son. [10]He who believes in the Son of God has the witness in himself; he who does not believe God has made Him a liar, because he has not believed the testimony that God has given of His Son. [11]And this is the testimony: that God has given us eternal life, and this life is in His Son. [12]He who has the Son has life; he who does not have the Son of God does not have life. [13]These things I have written to you who believe in the name of the Son of God, that you may know that you have eternal life,[a] and that you may *continue to* believe in the name of the Son of God.

Confidence and Compassion in Prayer

[14]Now this is the confidence that we have in Him, that if we ask anything according to His will, He hears us. [15]And if we know that He hears us, whatever we ask, we know that we have the petitions that we have asked of Him.

[16]If anyone sees his brother sinning a sin *which does* not *lead* to death, he will ask, and He will give him life for those who commit sin not *leading* to death. There is sin *leading* to death. I do not say that he should pray about that. [17]All unrighteousness is sin, and there is sin not *leading* to death.

Knowing the True—Rejecting the False

[18]We know that whoever is born of God does not sin; but he who has been born of God keeps himself,[a] and the wicked one does not touch him.

[19]We know that we are of God, and the whole world lies *under the sway of* the wicked one.

[20]And we know that the Son of God has come and has given us an understanding, that we may know Him who is true; and we are in Him who is true, in His Son Jesus Christ. This is the true God and eternal life.

[21]Little children, keep yourselves from idols. Amen.

5:9 [a]NU-Text reads *God, that.* **5:13** [a]NU-Text omits the rest of this verse. **5:18** [a]NU-Text reads *him.*

2 JOHN

JOHN DIRECTS THE 13 VERSES that make up his brief letter to "the elect lady and her children" (v. 1). He also includes a final greeting from "the children of your elect sister" (v. 13). A debate over whether the apostle was writing to a specific woman and her children, or whether his letter uses poetic language to describe a church and its membership, has raged among Bible teachers for many years.

But there is no dispute about the main theme of this letter.

This is a brief, passionate plea for believers in Christ to hold fast to truth, in particular, to the truth about the incarnation of Jesus, and not to be fooled by those who would teach otherwise. In addition, John reminds the lady to faithfully obey the commandment "which we have had from the beginning: that we love one another" (v. 5). John makes it crystal clear that love and truth belong together.

In our day, some church leaders have suggested that if someone has to make a choice between accepting a heretic and creating division within the church, we should choose heresy every time. Second John makes it clear that when heresy involves error relating to essential elements of the faith, we *must* be divided, "Do not receive him into your house nor greet him" (v.10). Love and grace should "cover a multitude of sins" (1 Pet. 4:8), but love should *never* cover up or ignore false teaching on essential biblical issues.

Greeting the Elect Lady

The Elder,

To the elect lady and her children, whom I love in truth, and not only I, but also all those who have known the truth, [2]because of the truth which abides in us and will be with us forever:

[3]Grace, mercy, *and* peace will be with you[a] from God the Father and from the Lord Jesus Christ, the Son of the Father, in truth and love.

Walk in Christ's Commandments

[4]I rejoiced greatly that I have found *some* of your children walking in truth, as we received commandment from the Father. [5]And now I plead with you, lady, not as though I wrote a new commandment to you, but that which we have had

INTIMATE MOMENTS

Put down the newspaper or turn off the computer, and say, "Why don't we go for a walk and talk? I'd love to hear about your day."

from the beginning: that we love one another. [6]This is love, that we walk according to His commandments. This is the commandment, that as you have heard from the beginning, you should walk in it.

Beware of Antichrist Deceivers

[7]For many deceivers have gone out into the world who do not confess Jesus Christ *as* coming in the flesh. This is a deceiver and an antichrist. [8]Look to yourselves, that we[a] do not lose those things we worked for, but *that* we[b] may receive a full reward.

[9]Whoever transgresses[a] and does not abide in the doctrine of Christ does not have God. He who abides in the doctrine of Christ has both the Father and the Son. [10]If anyone comes to you and does not bring this doctrine, do not receive him into your house nor greet him; [11]for he who greets him shares in his evil deeds.

John's Farewell Greeting

[12]Having many things to write to you, I did not wish *to do so* with paper and ink; but I hope to come to you and speak face to face, that our joy may be full.

[13]The children of your elect sister greet you. Amen.

---

3 [a]NU-Text and M-Text read *us.*
8 [a]NU-Text reads *you.* [b]NU-Text reads *you.*
9 [a]NU-Text reads *goes ahead.*

3 JOHN

THIS FINAL LETTER IS THE MOST PERSONAL of the three epistles written by "that disciple whom Jesus loved" (John 21:7). The apostle John addresses his letter to a man named Gaius, a common name in the Roman world. We know nothing about this particular Gaius (other than what we can learn by reading his mail!). It appears he was a well-respected member of a church either John had visited or where the apostle had served as a pastor.

John emphasizes the importance of hospitality and caring for those in ministry. He commends Gaius for how he and others in the church had demonstrated their love for missionaries who had visited them. John is pleased that the church sent them "on their journey in a manner worthy of God" (v. 6). In our own day, we ought to imitate the example of Gaius when we have the opportunity to show kindness and hospitality to those working fulltime to fulfill the Great Commission.

One of our favorite verses as parents has always been 3 John 4, where the apostle expresses his great joy in hearing that his children are walking in truth. The context makes it clear that John has his spiritual children in mind—those who have grown spiritually as a result of his ministry.

As parents, our greatest joy comes when we hear that our sons and daughters are walking in a way that honors and glorifies God. Whatever successes they may achieve in life will matter little if their lives get spiritually off track. Children ultimately have to decide for themselves to follow Christ, and no parenting recipe can ensure perfect, spiritually-minded children. But we ought to make sure that, above all else, we focus on our children's spiritual development, so that one day we might be able to echo John's words that our own children "walk in truth."

Greeting to Gaius

The Elder,

To the beloved Gaius, whom I love in truth:

2Beloved, I pray that you may prosper in all things and be in health, just as your soul prospers. 3For I rejoiced greatly when brethren came and testified of the truth *that is* in you, just as you walk in the truth. 4I have no greater joy than to hear that my children walk in truth.a

Gaius Commended for Generosity

5Beloved, you do faithfully whatever you do for the brethren anda for strangers, 6who have borne witness of your love before the church. *If* you send them forward on their journey in a manner worthy of God, you will do well, 7because they went forth for His name's sake, taking nothing from the Gentiles. 8We therefore ought to receivea such, that we may become fellow workers for the truth.

Diotrephes and Demetrius

9I wrote to the church, but Diotrephes, who loves to have the preeminence among them, does not receive us. 10Therefore, if I come, I will call to mind his deeds which he does, prating against us with malicious words. And not content with that, he himself does not receive the brethren, and forbids those who wish to, putting *them* out of the church.

11Beloved, do not imitate what is evil, but what is good. He who does good is of God, buta he who does evil has not seen God.

12Demetrius has a *good* testimony from all, and from the truth itself. And we also bear witness, and you know that our testimony is true.

Farewell Greeting

13I had many things to write, but I do not wish to write to you with pen and ink; 14but I hope to see you shortly, and we shall speak face to face.

Peace to you. Our friends greet you. Greet the friends by name.

---

4 aNU-Text reads *the truth.* 5 aNU-Text adds *especially.* 8 aNU-Text reads *support.* 11 aNU-Text and M-Text omit *but.*

INTIMATE MOMENTS

Say, "Thank you," after every meal she serves. Then help her clear the table or offer to do the dishes with her.

JUDE

MANY SIMILARITIES EXIST between the Book of 2 Peter and this brief letter from one of the four half brothers of Jesus. It would appear that Jude had read Peter's letter, since he quotes from 2 Peter 3:3 and encourages his readers to "remember the words which were spoken before by the apostles" (v.17). Whereas Peter wrote to warn Gentile converts about false teachers, Jude raised the same concerns for an audience of Jewish Christians.

Jude instructs his readers to keep themselves in the love of God (v. 21) and to "contend earnestly for the faith" (v. 3). So how do we reconcile this advice with other biblical passages that warn us against being quarrelsome or contentious (see Prov. 26:21; Titus 3:2)? In a culture increasingly hostile to the Christian faith, we will face situations where we are called upon to defend our faith. When we do, we should keep these twin truths in mind: Even while we contend vigorously, we must also be careful never to become argumentative or uncharitable toward those with whom we disagree.

Jude exposes the false teachers of his day, who mouthed foolish and empty words (vv. 12, 13). Their character and way of life invalidated their message (vv. 8, 16–19). People whose lives are marked by sexual impurity, disrespect for rightly appointed authorities, grumbling, complaining and mocking, and using flattery for their own ends, give evidence that they don't really know God. So we should never look to them for spiritual guidance or counsel!

Jude ends his letter with a wonderful doxology, an expression of praise and thanksgiving to the One who is able to keep us from stumbling and who will one day present us blameless before God the Father. On our own we are not blameless, of course. All have sinned (Rom. 3:23). But because of Jesus' sinless life and sacrificial death on our behalf, we can stand before God forgiven and wrapped in His righteousness. No wonder Jude says that all glory, majesty, dominion and power belong to Jesus, both now and forever (v. 25)!

Greeting to the Called

Jude, a bondservant of Jesus Christ, and brother of James,

To those who are called, sanctified[a] by God the Father, and preserved in Jesus Christ:

[2]Mercy, peace, and love be multiplied to you.

Contend for the Faith

[3]Beloved, while I was very diligent to write to you concerning our common salvation, I found it necessary to write to you exhorting you to contend earnestly for the faith which was once for all delivered to the saints. [4]For certain men have crept in unnoticed, who long ago were marked out for this condemnation, ungodly men, who turn the grace of our God into lewdness and deny the only Lord God[a] and our Lord Jesus Christ.

INTIMATE MOMENTS

If you overhear him engaged in a difficult situation on the phone or with a child, pray for him, and then compliment the way he handled the conversation.

Old and New Apostates

[5]But I want to remind you, though you once knew this, that the Lord, having saved the people out of the land of Egypt, afterward destroyed those who did not believe. [6]And the angels who did not keep their proper domain, but left their own abode, He has reserved in everlasting chains under darkness for the judgment of the great day; [7]as Sodom and Gomorrah, and the cities around them in a similar manner to these, having given themselves over to sexual immorality and gone after strange flesh, are set forth as an example, suffering the vengeance of eternal fire.

[8]Likewise also these dreamers defile the flesh, reject authority, and speak evil of dignitaries. [9]Yet Michael the archangel, in contending with the devil, when he disputed about the body of Moses, dared not bring against him a reviling accusation, but said, "The Lord rebuke you!" [10]But these speak evil of whatever they do not know; and whatever they know naturally, like brute beasts, in these things they corrupt themselves. [11]Woe to them! For they have gone in the way of Cain, have run greedily in the error of Balaam for profit, and perished in the rebellion of Korah.

Apostates Depraved and Doomed

[12]These are spots in your love feasts, while they feast with you without fear, serving *only* themselves. *They are* clouds without water, carried about[a] by the winds; late autumn trees without fruit, twice dead, pulled up by the roots; [13]raging waves of the sea, foaming up their own shame; wandering stars for whom is reserved the blackness of darkness forever.

[14]Now Enoch, the seventh from Adam, prophesied about these men also, saying, "Behold, the Lord comes with ten thousands of His saints, [15]to execute judgment on all, to convict all who are ungodly among them of all their ungodly deeds which they have committed in an ungodly way, and of all the harsh things which ungodly sinners have spoken against Him."

Apostates Predicted

[16]These are grumblers, complainers, walking according to their own lusts; and they mouth great swelling *words,* flattering people to gain advantage. [17]But you, beloved, remember the words which were spoken before by the apostles of our Lord Jesus Christ: [18]how they told you that there would be mockers in the last time who would walk according to their own ungodly lusts. [19]These are sensual persons, who cause divisions, not having the Spirit.

Maintain Your Life with God

[20]But you, beloved, building yourselves up on your most holy faith, praying in the Holy Spirit, [21]keep yourselves in the love of

1 [a]NU-Text reads *beloved.*   4 [a]NU-Text omits *God.*
12 [a]NU-Text and M-Text read *along.*

God, looking for the mercy of our Lord Jesus Christ unto eternal life.

²²And on some have compassion, making a distinction;ᵃ ²³but others save with fear, pulling *them* out of the fire,ᵃ hating even the garment defiled by the flesh.

---

22 ᵃNU-Text reads *who are doubting* (or *making distinctions*). **23** ᵃNU-Text adds *and on some have mercy with fear* and omits *with fear* in first clause. **24** ᵃM-Text reads *them.* **25** ᵃNU-Text reads *To the only God our Savior.* ᵇNU-Text omits *Who . . . is wise* and adds *Through Jesus Christ our Lord.* ᶜNU-Text adds *Before all time.*

Glory to God

24 Now to Him who is able to keep youᵃ
       from stumbling,
   And to present *you* faultless
   Before the presence of His glory
       with exceeding joy,

25 To God our Savior,ᵃ
   Who alone is wise,ᵇ
   Be glory and majesty,
   Dominion and power,ᶜ
   Both now and forever.
   Amen.

REVELATION

PERHAPS NO BOOK IN THE BIBLE has so confounded readers as the Book of Revelation. John wrote it near the end of his life, as a prisoner living in isolation on the Greek island of Patmos.

John identifies this letter both as a revelation (1:1) and as a prophecy (1:3). While books of prophecy may involve details of coming events, most prophetic writing involves a strong call for God's people to obey Him and for all men to repent of their sins and turn to Him as their Lord and King.

The book begins with John's vision of Jesus, who appears as the exalted Prophet, Priest and King to announce the coming day of the Lord. Chapters 2 and 3 offer messages to seven ancient churches, both commending them for their faithfulness and challenging them to remain strong in the face of increasing persecution. Most of the book (chapters 4—22) describes God's judgment of the earth, although Bible teachers disagree widely about the timing of the events that are depicted.

Whatever events are in view, the book of Revelation declares that God has the right to judge the earth and that His justice will prevail. The faithful will be vindicated, while the wicked will perish. At the center of the book is Jesus, pictured as the glorified Son of Man (1:12–16); the Lion of Judah (5:5); the worthy Lamb (5:8–13); the Son who will rule over all (12:5); the Bridegroom (19:7–9); and the conquering King of kings and Lord of lords (19:16).

The image of Jesus as the bridegroom receiving His bride at the marriage supper of the Lamb (19:7) offers a powerful reminder that marriage is a living picture of God's love for His people (Eph. 5:22–31). The Bible begins with a wedding (Gen. 2:24) and it ends with this picture of God ratifying His everlasting covenant of love with His bride. The marriage supper is the culmination of God's faithful love for us, and our anticipation of that glorious day should stir in us a powerful desire to be a pure and faithful bride while we wait for the wedding day.

Introduction and Benediction

1 The Revelation of Jesus Christ, which God gave Him to show His servants—things which must shortly take place. And He sent and signified *it* by His angel to His servant John, ²who bore witness to the word of God, and to the testimony of Jesus Christ, to all things that he saw. ³Blessed *is* he who reads and those who hear the words of this prophecy, and keep those things which are written in it; for the time *is* near.

Greeting the Seven Churches

⁴John, to the seven churches which are in Asia:

Grace to you and peace from Him who is and who was and who is to come, and from the seven Spirits who are before His throne, ⁵and from Jesus Christ, the faithful witness, the firstborn from the dead, and the ruler over the kings of the earth.

To Him who loved us and washedᵃ us from our sins in His own blood, ⁶and has

---

1:5 ᵃNU-Text reads *loves us and freed;* M-Text reads *loves us and washed.* **1:6** ᵃNU-Text and M-Text read *a kingdom.* **1:8** ᵃNU-Text and M-Text omit *the Beginning and the End.* ᵇNU-Text and M-Text add *God.* **1:9** ᵃNU-Text and M-Text omit *both.* **1:11** ᵃNU-Text and M-Text omit *I am* through third *and.* ᵇNU-Text and M-Text omit *which are in Asia.*

---

made us kingsᵃ and priests to His God and Father, to Him *be* glory and dominion forever and ever. Amen.

⁷Behold, He is coming with clouds, and every eye will see Him, even they who pierced Him. And all the tribes of the earth will mourn because of Him. Even so, Amen.

⁸"I am the Alpha and the Omega, *the* Beginning and *the* End,"ᵃ says the Lord,ᵇ "who is and who was and who is to come, the Almighty."

Vision of the Son of Man

⁹I, John, bothᵃ your brother and companion in the tribulation and kingdom and patience of Jesus Christ, was on the island that is called Patmos for the word of God and for the testimony of Jesus Christ. ¹⁰I was in the Spirit on the Lord's Day, and I heard behind me a loud voice, as of a trumpet, ¹¹saying, "I am the Alpha and the Omega, the First and the Last,"ᵃ and, "What you see, write in a book and send *it* to the seven churches which are in Asia:ᵇ to Ephesus, to Smyrna, to Pergamos, to Thyatira, to Sardis, to Philadelphia, and to Laodicea."

¹²Then I turned to see the voice that spoke with me. And having turned I saw seven golden lampstands, ¹³and in the midst

---

ROMANTIC QUOTES AND NOTES
Applying the I-Solution

A veteran member of the Billy Graham Crusade team once told me that loneliness is the number one issue Graham addressed when he spoke. Even when surrounded by thousands or even millions of people, many of us feel alone, detached. We all yearn for intimacy.

Yet Satan finds ways to leave married couples and other family members feeling isolated from one another. He does so in many ways, and the impact of his tactics cannot be understated.

Isolation makes suffering unbearable. Your heart can grow cold and indifferent to things of ultimate importance. Isolation can make you vulnerable, bringing a loss of perspective about self, life, and others. Isolation can cause you to conjure up wild fantasies about your mate's thoughts, plans or motivations. You may even contemplate taking your life.

The solution to isolation is the I-Solution. *I* must take responsibility for my part in relationships. *I* must ask for forgiveness when I've hurt someone and he or she wants to hide from me.

The difficulty with applying the I-Solution, of course, is that first word: *I.* The I-Solution also involves dying to self, giving up anger and pride, and the right to revenge. That's the key to defeating this enemy of intimacy.

BIBLICAL INSIGHTS • 2:10

Paying the Price

WHO WOULDN'T WANT the spiritual impact of John? He helped shape the first-century church. He journeyed to other countries, preached alongside the other apostles, entrusted his life to faithful men who lived within a spear tip of death—we're talking *gain*, real gain.

But we're also talking pain, major league pain. John spent time in prison. He was exiled to a barren rock, threatened with execution, betrayed by people in his church, and helpless to do anything as his compatriots in the faith were killed, one by one.

He illustrates the truth that no discipline means no growth.

And so he could write, "Do not fear any of those things which you are about to suffer. Indeed, the devil is about to throw some of you into prison, that you may be tested, and you will have tribulation ten days. Be faithful until death, and I [Jesus] will give you the crown of life" (Rev. 2:10).

When some believers read a text like that, they worry about having the guts to "be faithful until death." But you don't need that kind of faith right now. Today, you need the kind of faith that submits to discipline. That must come first. And if God should direct you down difficult paths in the days ahead, He will give you in that hour the grace you need to persevere.

---

of the seven lampstands *One* like the Son of Man, clothed with a garment down to the feet and girded about the chest with a golden band. ¹⁴His head and hair *were* white like wool, as white as snow, and His eyes like a flame of fire; ¹⁵His feet *were* like fine brass, as if refined in a furnace, and His voice as the sound of many waters; ¹⁶He had in His right hand seven stars, out of His mouth went a sharp two-edged sword, and His countenance *was* like the sun shining in its strength. ¹⁷And when I saw Him, I fell at His feet as dead. But He laid His right hand on me, saying to me,[a] "Do not be afraid; I am the First and the Last. ¹⁸I *am* He who lives, and was dead, and behold, I am alive forevermore. Amen. And I have the keys of Hades and of Death. ¹⁹Write[a] the things which you have seen, and the things which are, and the things which will take place after this. ²⁰The mystery of the seven stars which you saw in My right hand, and the seven golden lampstands: The seven stars are the angels of the seven churches, and the seven lampstands which you saw[a] are the seven churches.

The Loveless Church

2 "To the angel of the church of Ephesus write,

'These things says He who holds the seven stars in His right hand, who walks in the midst of the seven golden lampstands: ²"I know your works, your labor, your patience, and that you cannot bear those who are evil. And you have tested those who say they are apostles and are not, and have found them liars; ³and you have persevered and have patience, and have labored for My name's sake and have not become weary. ⁴Nevertheless I have *this* against you, that you have left your first love. ⁵Remember therefore from where you have fallen; repent and do the first works, or else I will come to you quickly and remove your lampstand from its place—unless you repent. ⁶But this you have, that you hate the deeds of the Nicolaitans, which I also hate.

⁷"He who has an ear, let him hear what the Spirit says to the churches. To him who overcomes I will give to eat from the tree of life, which is in the midst of the Paradise of God."'

The Persecuted Church

⁸"And to the angel of the church in Smyrna write,

'These things says the First and the Last, who was dead, and came to life: ⁹"I know your works, tribulation, and poverty (but you are rich); and *I know* the blasphemy of those who say they are Jews and are not, but

---

1:17 [a]NU-Text and M-Text omit *to me*.
1:19 [a]NU-Text and M-Text read *Therefore, write*.
1:20 [a]NU-Text and M-Text omit *which you saw*.

DEVOTIONS FOR COUPLES • 2–3
A Classic Story of Love

The first three chapters of Revelation tell a love story for the ages about a bride and her Bridegroom. The Bridegroom, Jesus, delivered brutally honest report cards to seven churches (His bride) of the day. He bluntly told them where they were succeeding and where they were failing.

In chapter 2, Jesus gave the believers in Ephesus good marks for their work, their labor, and their patient perseverance for His name. But after commending them, He rebuked them, "I have this against you, that you have left your first love" (v. 4). Those first century followers of Christ had wandered away from the enthusiasm and joy of their early days of faith. They were all work and no relationship; they served God diligently, but they neglected their relationship with Him.

In other words, they lost sight of what being a follower of Jesus is all about—a relationship with Him.

The same thing happens over and over again in marriages. Because Christianity and marriage are both intimate, personal relationships, the comparison is appropriate. Couples experience new love with great enthusiasm and joy, like new believers in Christ. And they, too, soon get busy with the responsibilities of life and tend to drift away from their first love.

While we can't return to the original experience of new love and very little responsibility, we can rekindle the embers of the romantic love we used to enjoy. We can fan them into a warm flame of mature love that will sustain our marriages for a lifetime. How? Read the solution Jesus delivered to the Ephesians, "Remember therefore from where you have fallen; repent and do the first works" (2:5). The application for your marriage is the same: *remember, repent,* and *return to the first works.*

You must *remember* what you loved about your spouse, then you must *repent* from negative attitudes, and finally you must *return* to fanning the flames of the relationship as you did so willingly at first.

Where are you right now?

Do you need to go to the God of the universe and ask Him to help you to refocus? Perhaps as you pray, you could ask Him to enlarge your heart for your mate. Ask the Lord to help you recall the "things you did at first" that initially stirred your love for each other. And then ask Him to give you the ability to really please your mate; what's more, pray that these steps toward your first love would become mutual.

---

are a synagogue of Satan. [10]Do not fear any of those things which you are about to suffer. Indeed, the devil is about to throw *some* of you into prison, that you may be tested, and you will have tribulation ten days. Be faithful until death, and I will give you the crown of life.

[11]"He who has an ear, let him hear what the Spirit says to the churches. He who overcomes shall not be hurt by the second death." '

The Compromising Church

[12]"And to the angel of the church in Pergamos write,

2:15 [a]NU-Text and M-Text read *likewise* for *which thing I hate.*

'These things says He who has the sharp two-edged sword: [13]"I know your works, and where you dwell, where Satan's throne *is.* And you hold fast to My name, and did not deny My faith even in the days in which Antipas *was* My faithful martyr, who was killed among you, where Satan dwells. [14]But I have a few things against you, because you have there those who hold the doctrine of Balaam, who taught Balak to put a stumbling block before the children of Israel, to eat things sacrificed to idols, and to commit sexual immorality. [15]Thus you also have those who hold the doctrine of the Nicolaitans, which thing I hate.[a] [16]Repent, or else I will come to you quickly and will fight against them with the sword of My mouth.

[17]"He who has an ear, let him hear what the Spirit says to the churches. To him who overcomes I will give some of the hidden manna to eat. And I will give him a white stone, and on the stone a new name written which no one knows except him who receives *it*."'

The Corrupt Church

[18]"And to the angel of the church in Thyatira write,

'These things says the Son of God, who has eyes like a flame of fire, and His feet like fine brass: [19]"I know your works, love, service, faith,[a] and your patience; and *as* for your works, the last *are* more than the first. [20]Nevertheless I have a few things against you, because you allow[a] that woman[b] Jezebel, who calls herself a prophetess, to teach and seduce[c] My servants to commit sexual immorality and eat things sacrificed to idols. [21]And I gave her time to repent of her sexual immorality, and she did not repent.[a] [22]Indeed I will cast her into a sickbed, and those who commit adultery with her into great tribulation, unless they repent of their[a] deeds. [23]I will kill her children with death, and all the churches shall know that I am He who searches the minds and hearts. And I will give to each one of you according to your works.

[24]"Now to you I say, and[a] to the rest in Thyatira, as many as do not have this doctrine, who have not known the depths of Satan, as they say, I will[b] put on you no other burden. [25]But hold fast what you have till I come. [26]And he who overcomes, and keeps My works until the end, to him I will give power over the nations—

[27] 'He shall rule them with a rod of iron;
      They shall be dashed to pieces like
         the potter's vessels'[a]—

as I also have received from My Father; [28]and I will give him the morning star. [29]"He who has an ear, let him hear what the Spirit says to the churches."'

The Dead Church

3 "And to the angel of the church in Sardis write,

'These things says He who has the seven Spirits of God and the seven stars: "I know your works, that you have a name that you are alive, but you are dead. [2]Be watchful, and strengthen the things which remain, that are ready to die, for I have not found your works perfect before God.[a] [3]Remember therefore how you have received and heard; hold fast and repent. Therefore if you will not watch, I will come upon you as a thief, and you will not know what hour I will come upon you. [4]You[a] have a few names even in Sardis who have not defiled their garments; and they shall walk with Me in white, for they are worthy. [5]He who overcomes shall be clothed in white garments, and I will not blot out his name from the Book of Life; but I will confess his name before My Father and before His angels.

[6]"He who has an ear, let him hear what the Spirit says to the churches."'

The Faithful Church

[7]"And to the angel of the church in Philadelphia write,

'These things says He who is holy, He who is true, *"He who has the key of David, He who opens and no one shuts, and shuts and no one opens"*:[a] [8]"I know your works. See, I have set before you an open door, and no one can shut it;[a] for you have a little strength, have kept My word, and have not denied My name. [9]Indeed I will make *those* of the synagogue of Satan, who say they are Jews and are not, but lie—indeed I will make them come and worship before your feet, and to know that I have loved you. [10]Because you have kept My command to persevere, I also will keep you from the hour of trial which shall come upon the whole world, to test those who dwell on the earth. [11]Behold,[a] I am coming

---

2:19 [a]NU-Text and M-Text read *faith, service.*
2:20 [a]NU-Text and M-Text read *I have against you that you tolerate.* [b]M-Text reads *your wife Jezebel.* [c]NU-Text and M-Text read *and teaches and seduces.*
2:21 [a]NU-Text and M-Text read *time to repent, and she does not want to repent of her sexual immorality.*
2:22 [a]NU-Text and M-Text read *her.* **2:24** [a]NU-Text and M-Text omit *and.* [b]NU-Text and M-Text omit *will.*
2:27 [a]Psalm 2:9 **3:2** [a]NU-Text and M-Text read *My God.* **3:4** [a]NU-Text and M-Text read *Nevertheless you have a few names in Sardis.* **3:7** [a]Isaiah 22:22
3:8 [a]NU-Text and M-Text read *which no one can shut.*
3:11 [a]NU-Text and M-Text omit *Behold.*

BIBLICAL INSIGHTS • 3:20

A Model of Communication

WE OFTEN HEAR adults say things like, "I think I would have gotten along better with my mom and dad if we had just talked more."

Now that you're a parent, you have a chance to create a new model.

In Jesus, we have a great model of what it means to be available to our children. Our Lord said, "Behold, I stand at the door and knock. If anyone hears My voice and opens the door, I will come in to him and dine with him, and he with Me" (Rev. 3:20). This picture of a loving God eager to spend time in fellowship with those who hear His voice is a picture of how our children should perceive us.

A spiritually strong family is built on a foundation of relational concrete. Tell your children your values, expectations, goals, and dreams for them, your family, and yourself. Ask them about their worries and their own dreams and goals. Words by themselves don't communicate love—talking with your children in a way that shows deep interest and a strong desire to be involved in their lives does that. Even during their adolescence, when your teenagers may act like they

aren't interested in a conversation with you, keep pursuing and keep the lines of communication open,

Relationships between parent and child are built as we practically do the following:

• *Share memories.* Vacations, adventures, dates with your children, anything you do together builds a reservoir of experiences together.

• *Hang tough.* When they push back against your standards, values, or your authority, just keep on expressing love to them.

• *Live daily with them.* Pay attention to them. Talk with them and not just at them. Listen instead of preaching.

All of these are a part of the fabric of building a relationship with your child. Conversations can ultimately strengthen the trust and foundation of your relationship with your child. This loving conversation begins while your baby is still in the womb. It grows and matures throughout a child's development, so that when your child reaches adulthood, you can communicate like friendly peers.

---

quickly! Hold fast what you have, that no one may take your crown. ¹²He who overcomes, I will make him a pillar in the temple of My God, and he shall go out no more. I will write on him the name of My God and the name of the city of My God, the New Jerusalem, which comes down out of heaven from My God. And *I will write on him* My new name.

¹³"He who has an ear, let him hear what the Spirit says to the churches."'

The Lukewarm Church

¹⁴"And to the angel of the church of the Laodiceansᵃ write,

'These things says the Amen, the Faithful and True Witness, the Beginning of the creation of God: ¹⁵"I know your works, that you are neither cold nor hot. I could wish you were cold or hot. ¹⁶So then, because you are lukewarm, and neither cold nor hot,ᵃ I will vomit you out of My mouth. ¹⁷Because you say, 'I am rich, have become wealthy, and have need of nothing'—and do not know that you are wretched, miserable, poor, blind, and naked— ¹⁸I counsel you to buy from Me gold refined in the fire, that you may be rich; and white garments, that you may be clothed, *that* the shame of your nakedness may not be revealed; and anoint your eyes with eye salve, that you may see. ¹⁹As many as I love, I rebuke and

---

3:14 ᵃNU-Text and M-Text read *in Laodicea.*
3:16 ᵃNU-Text and M-Text read *hot nor cold.*

chasten. Therefore be zealous and repent. ²⁰Behold, I stand at the door and knock. If anyone hears My voice and opens the door, I will come in to him and dine with him, and he with Me. ²¹To him who overcomes I will grant to sit with Me on My throne, as I also overcame and sat down with My Father on His throne.

²²"He who has an ear, let him hear what the Spirit says to the churches." ' "

INTIMATE MOMENTS

Hug and kiss her *every morning* before leaving the house. Research indicates that marriages that practice this simple discipline are much healthier than those that don't. If she's sleeping, leave her a note, or gently kiss her forehead and whisper, "Have a wonderful day, sweetheart."

The Throne Room of Heaven

4 After these things I looked, and behold, a door *standing* open in heaven. And the first voice which I heard *was* like a trumpet speaking with me, saying, "Come up here, and I will show you things which must take place after this."

²Immediately I was in the Spirit; and behold, a throne set in heaven, and *One* sat on the throne. ³And He who sat there was ᵃ like a jasper and a sardius stone in appearance; and *there was* a rainbow around the throne, in appearance like an emerald. ⁴Around the throne *were* twenty-four thrones, and on the thrones I saw twenty-four elders sitting, clothed in white robes; and they had crowns ᵃ of gold on their heads. ⁵And from the throne proceeded lightnings, thunderings, and voices. ᵃ Seven lamps of fire *were* burning before the throne, which are the ᵇ seven Spirits of God.

⁶Before the throne *there was* ᵃ a sea of glass, like crystal. And in the midst of the throne, and around the throne, *were* four living creatures full of eyes in front and in back. ⁷The first living creature *was* like a

lion, the second living creature like a calf, the third living creature had a face like a man, and the fourth living creature *was* like a flying eagle. ⁸*The* four living creatures, each having six wings, were full of eyes around and within. And they do not rest day or night, saying:

> "Holy, holy, holy, ᵃ
> Lord God Almighty,
> Who was and is and is to come!"

⁹Whenever the living creatures give glory and honor and thanks to Him who sits on the throne, who lives forever and ever, ¹⁰the twenty-four elders fall down before Him who sits on the throne and worship Him who lives forever and ever, and cast their crowns before the throne, saying:

> 11 "You are worthy, O Lord, ᵃ
> To receive glory and honor and power;
> For You created all things,
> And by Your will they exist ᵃ and were created."

The Lamb Takes the Scroll

5 And I saw in the right *hand* of Him who sat on the throne a scroll written inside and on the back, sealed with seven seals. ²Then I saw a strong angel proclaiming with a loud voice, "Who is worthy to open the scroll and to loose its seals?" ³And no one in heaven or on the earth or under the earth was able to open the scroll, or to look at it.

⁴So I wept much, because no one was found worthy to open and read ᵃ the scroll, or to look at it. ⁵But one of the elders said to me, "Do not weep. Behold, the Lion of the tribe of Judah, the Root of David, has prevailed to open the scroll and to loose ᵃ its seven seals."

4:3 ᵃM-Text omits *And He who sat there was* (which makes the description in verse 3 modify the throne rather than God). 4:4 ᵃNU-Text and M-Text read *robes, with crowns.* 4:5 ᵃNU-Text and M-Text read *voices, and thunderings.* ᵇM-Text omits *the.* 4:6 ᵃNU-Text and M-Text add *something like.* 4:8 ᵃM-Text has *holy* nine times. 4:11 ᵃNU-Text and M-Text read *our Lord and God.* ᵇNU-Text and M-Text read *existed.* 5:4 ᵃNU-Text and M-Text omit *and read.* 5:5 ᵃNU-Text and M-Text omit *to loose.*

[6]And I looked, and behold,[a] in the midst of the throne and of the four living creatures, and in the midst of the elders, stood a Lamb as though it had been slain, having seven horns and seven eyes, which are the seven Spirits of God sent out into all the earth. [7]Then He came and took the scroll out of the right hand of Him who sat on the throne.

Worthy Is the Lamb

[8]Now when He had taken the scroll, the four living creatures and the twenty-four elders fell down before the Lamb, each having a harp, and golden bowls full of incense, which are the prayers of the saints. [9]And they sang a new song, saying:

"You are worthy to take the scroll,
And to open its seals;
For You were slain,
And have redeemed us to God by
    Your blood
Out of every tribe and tongue and
    people and nation,
[10] And have made us[a] kings[b] and
    priests to our God;
And we[c] shall reign on the earth."

[11]Then I looked, and I heard the voice of many angels around the throne, the living creatures, and the elders; and the number of them was ten thousand times ten thousand, and thousands of thousands, [12]saying with a loud voice:

"Worthy is the Lamb who was slain
To receive power and riches and
    wisdom,
And strength and honor and glory
    and blessing!"

[13]And every creature which is in heaven and on the earth and under the earth and such as are in the sea, and all that are in them, I heard saying:

"Blessing and honor and glory and
    power
Be to Him who sits on the throne,
And to the Lamb, forever and ever!"[a]

[14]Then the four living creatures said, "Amen!" And the twenty-four[a] elders fell down and worshiped Him who lives forever and ever.[b]

First Seal: The Conqueror

6 Now I saw when the Lamb opened one of the seals;[a] and I heard one of the four living creatures saying with a voice like thunder, "Come and see." [2]And I looked, and behold, a white horse. He who

---

ROMANCE FAQ

Q: How can others encourage us to improve our marriage?

First, make sure you are part of a growing body of believers through a local church. You need to be surrounded by people who will cheer you on and pray for you in the midst of days of struggle. As Proverbs 27:17 tells us, "As iron sharpens iron, so a man sharpens the countenance of his friend."

Second, find a godly woman or a godly man (someone of the same sex as you) who can become your friend, mentor and sounding board. You need someone who can give you wise advice, help you entrust yourself to God, and keep a balanced perspective during times when you may be tempted to become bitter.

Third, take a life inventory to see what you might need to do, give up, or deny that would help ensure the success of your marriage. Is anything competing with the attention God wants you to give your spouse? What action do you need to take? A friend or a mentor can help you think through the list and can hold you accountable to follow through.

Fourth, beware of criticizing your mate to your parents. Most in-laws have little tolerance for imperfections in the person who married their child. Be careful of running home to their listening ear. Instead, ask a few godly friends to pray for your spouse to respond spiritually to God.

5:6 [a]NU-Text and M-Text read *I saw in the midst . . . a Lamb standing.* **5:10** [a]NU-Text and M-Text read *them.* [b]NU-Text reads *a kingdom.* [c]NU-Text and M-Text read *they.* **5:13** [a]M-Text adds *Amen.* **5:14** [a]NU-Text and M-Text omit *twenty-four.* [b]NU-Text and M-Text omit *Him who lives forever and ever.* **6:1** [a]NU-Text and M-Text read *seven seals.*

sat on it had a bow; and a crown was given to him, and he went out conquering and to conquer.

Second Seal: Conflict on Earth

3When He opened the second seal, I heard the second living creature saying, "Come and see."ᵃ 4Another horse, fiery red, went out. And it was granted to the one who sat on it to take peace from the earth, and that *people* should kill one another; and there was given to him a great sword.

Third Seal: Scarcity on Earth

5When He opened the third seal, I heard the third living creature say, "Come and see." So I looked, and behold, a black horse, and he who sat on it had a pair of scales in his hand. 6And I heard a voice in the midst of the four living creatures saying, "A quartᵃ of wheat for a denarius,ᵇ and three quarts of barley for a denarius; and do not harm the oil and the wine."

Fourth Seal: Widespread Death on Earth

7When He opened the fourth seal, I heard the voice of the fourth living creature saying, "Come and see." 8So I looked, and behold, a pale horse. And the name of him who sat on it was Death, and Hades followed with him. And power was given to them over a fourth of the earth, to kill with sword, with hunger, with death, and by the beasts of the earth.

Fifth Seal: The Cry of the Martyrs

9When He opened the fifth seal, I saw under the altar the souls of those who had been slain for the word of God and for the testimony which they held. 10And they cried with a loud voice, saying, "How long, O Lord, holy and true, until You judge and avenge our blood on those who dwell on the earth?" 11Then a white robe was given to each of them; and *it* was said to them that they should rest a little while longer, until both *the number of* their fellow servants and their brethren, who would be killed as they *were,* was completed.

Sixth Seal: Cosmic Disturbances

12I looked when He opened the sixth seal, and behold,ᵃ there was a great earthquake; and the sun became black as sackcloth of hair, and the moonᵇ became like blood. 13And the stars of heaven fell to the earth, as a fig tree drops its late figs when it is shaken by a mighty wind. 14Then the sky receded as a scroll when it is rolled up, and every mountain and island was moved out of its place. 15And the kings of the earth, the great men, the rich men, the commanders,ᵃ the mighty men, every slave and every free man, hid themselves in the caves and in the rocks of the mountains, 16and said to the mountains and rocks, "Fall on us and hide us from the face of Him who sits on the throne and from the wrath of the Lamb! 17For the great day of His wrath has come, and who is able to stand?"

The Sealed of Israel

7 After these things I saw four angels standing at the four corners of the earth, holding the four winds of the earth, that the wind should not blow on the earth, on the sea, or on any tree. 2Then I saw another angel ascending from the east, having the seal of the living God. And he cried with a loud voice to the four angels to whom it was granted to harm the earth and the sea, 3saying, "Do not harm the earth, the sea, or the trees till we have sealed the servants of our God on their foreheads." 4And I heard the number of those who were sealed. One hundred *and* forty-four thousand of all the tribes of the children of Israel *were* sealed:

5   of the tribe of Judah twelve
       thousand *were* sealed;ᵃ
    of the tribe of Reuben twelve
       thousand *were* sealed;
    of the tribe of Gad twelve thousand
       were sealed;

6:3 ᵃNU-Text and M-Text omit *and see.* **6:6** ᵃGreek *choinix;* that is, approximately one quart ᵇThis was approximately one day's wage for a worker. **6:12** ᵃNU-Text and M-Text omit *behold.* ᵇNU-Text and M-Text read *the whole moon.* **6:15** ᵃNU-Text and M-Text read *the commanders, the rich men.* **7:5** ᵃIn NU-Text and M-Text *were sealed* is stated only in verses 5a and 8c; the words are understood in the remainder of the passage.

6 of the tribe of Asher twelve thousand *were* sealed;
of the tribe of Naphtali twelve thousand *were* sealed;
of the tribe of Manasseh twelve thousand *were* sealed;
7 of the tribe of Simeon twelve thousand *were* sealed;
of the tribe of Levi twelve thousand *were* sealed;
of the tribe of Issachar twelve thousand *were* sealed;
8 of the tribe of Zebulun twelve thousand *were* sealed;
of the tribe of Joseph twelve thousand *were* sealed;
of the tribe of Benjamin twelve thousand *were* sealed.

A Multitude from the Great Tribulation

9After these things I looked, and behold, a great multitude which no one could number, of all nations, tribes, peoples, and tongues, standing before the throne and before the Lamb, clothed with white robes, with palm branches in their hands, 10and crying out with a loud voice, saying, "Salvation *belongs* to our God who sits on the throne, and to the Lamb!" 11All the angels stood around the throne and the elders and the four living creatures, and fell on their faces before the throne and worshiped God, 12saying:

"Amen! Blessing and glory and wisdom,
Thanksgiving and honor and power and might,
Be to our God forever and ever. Amen."

13Then one of the elders answered, saying to me, "Who are these arrayed in white robes, and where did they come from?"

14And I said to him, "Sir,a you know."

So he said to me, "These are the ones who come out of the great tribulation, and washed their robes and made them white in the blood of the Lamb. 15Therefore they

are before the throne of God, and serve Him day and night in His temple. And He who sits on the throne will dwell among them. 16They shall neither hunger anymore nor thirst anymore; the sun shall not strike them, nor any heat; 17for the Lamb who is in the midst of the throne will shepherd them and lead them to living fountains of waters.a And God will wipe away every tear from their eyes."

Seventh Seal: Prelude to the Seven Trumpets

8 When He opened the seventh seal, there was silence in heaven for about half an hour. 2And I saw the seven angels who stand before God, and to them were given seven trumpets. 3Then another angel, having a golden censer, came and stood at the altar. He was given much incense, that he should offer *it* with the prayers of all the saints upon the golden altar which was before the throne. 4And the smoke of the incense, with the prayers of the saints, ascended before God from the angel's hand. 5Then the angel took the censer, filled it with fire from the altar, and threw *it* to the earth. And there were noises, thunderings, lightnings, and an earthquake.

6So the seven angels who had the seven trumpets prepared themselves to sound.

First Trumpet: Vegetation Struck

7The first angel sounded: And hail and fire followed, mingled with blood, and they were thrown to the earth.a And a third of the trees were burned up, and all green grass was burned up.

Second Trumpet: The Seas Struck

8Then the second angel sounded: And *something* like a great mountain burning with fire was thrown into the sea, and a third of the sea became blood. 9And a third of the living creatures in the sea died, and a third of the ships were destroyed.

Third Trumpet: The Waters Struck

10Then the third angel sounded: And a great star fell from heaven, burning like a torch, and it fell on a third of the rivers and on the springs of water. 11The name of the star is Wormwood. A third of the waters

---

7:14 aNU-Text and M-Text read *My lord.*
7:17 aNU-Text and M-Text read *to fountains of the waters of life.* 8:7 aNU-Text and M-Text add *and a third of the earth was burned up.*

became wormwood, and many men died from the water, because it was made bitter.

Fourth Trumpet: The Heavens Struck

¹²Then the fourth angel sounded: And a third of the sun was struck, a third of the moon, and a third of the stars, so that a third of them were darkened. A third of the day did not shine, and likewise the night.

¹³And I looked, and I heard an angel[a] flying through the midst of heaven, saying with a loud voice, "Woe, woe, woe to the inhabitants of the earth, because of the remaining blasts of the trumpet of the three angels who are about to sound!"

Fifth Trumpet: The Locusts from the Bottomless Pit

9 Then the fifth angel sounded: And I saw a star fallen from heaven to the earth. To him was given the key to the bottomless pit. ²And he opened the bottomless pit, and smoke arose out of the pit like the smoke of a great furnace. So the sun and the air were darkened because of the smoke of the pit. ³Then out of the smoke locusts came upon the earth. And to them was given power, as the scorpions of the earth have power. ⁴They were commanded not to harm the grass of the earth, or any green thing, or any tree, but only those men who do not have the seal of God on their foreheads. ⁵And they were not given *authority* to kill them, but to torment them *for* five months. Their torment *was* like the torment of a scorpion when it strikes a man. ⁶In those days men will seek death and will not find it; they will desire to die, and death will flee from them.

⁷The shape of the locusts was like horses prepared for battle. On their heads were crowns of something like gold, and their faces *were* like the faces of men. ⁸They had hair like women's hair, and their teeth were

8:13 ªNU-Text and M-Text read *eagle.*

PARENTING MATTERS

Q: *Is it appropriate to resolve conflict in front of younger children? Should we let them see us arguing and making up?*

I think it can be good for our children to see us disagree, so long as we keep it to a minimum and don't frighten them. Children can learn how to resolve conflict by watching us do it.

In our marriage, there have been moments where the kids suddenly realized, *Oh, my goodness—Mom and Dad are having an argument.* Barbara and I had to recognize that our children were fixed on us like radar units; we were their most secure reference points, and the foundation was looking shaky to them.

When the children saw us disagreeing, we took a time-out to reassure them. We would say, "Mom and Dad are having a disagreement. This happens in marriage. Marriage is between two people who sometimes differ, and your mom and I differ. However, we are still committed to each other, we love each other, and this is part of a healthy married relationship."

Barbara and I tried to make sure that most of our "intense fellowship" happened behind closed doors. Most of our true disagreements were resolved privately, but some of the smaller issues were handled in front of the children. If your argument crescendos to a yelling match, then that's *not* part of healthy love. Even in your disagreements, you should model Christ's love. If this is a regular part of how you relate to each other, seek a mentor couple, a pastor, or a counselor who can help you break the pattern.

Your kids need to see you working through a conflict, resolving it, and forgiving each other. They need to feel reassured by seeing the reconciliation as well as the argument.

like lions' *teeth*. ⁹And they had breastplates like breastplates of iron, and the sound of their wings *was* like the sound of chariots with many horses running into battle. ¹⁰They had tails like scorpions, and there were stings in their tails. Their power *was* to hurt men five months. ¹¹And they had as king over them the angel of the bottomless pit, whose name in Hebrew *is* Abaddon, but in Greek he has the name Apollyon.

¹²One woe is past. Behold, still two more woes are coming after these things.

Sixth Trumpet: The Angels from the Euphrates

¹³Then the sixth angel sounded: And I heard a voice from the four horns of the golden altar which is before God, ¹⁴saying to the sixth angel who had the trumpet, "Release the four angels who are bound at the great river Euphrates." ¹⁵So the four angels, who had been prepared for the hour and day and month and year, were released to kill a third of mankind. ¹⁶Now the number of the army of the horsemen *was* two hundred million; I heard the number of them. ¹⁷And thus I saw the horses in the vision: those who sat on them had breastplates of fiery red, hyacinth blue, and sulfur yellow; and the heads of the horses *were* like the heads of lions; and out of their mouths came fire, smoke, and brimstone. ¹⁸By these three *plagues* a third of mankind was killed—by the fire and the smoke and the brimstone which came out of their mouths. ¹⁹For their powerᵃ is in their mouth and in their tails; for their tails *are* like serpents, having heads; and with them they do harm.

²⁰But the rest of mankind, who were not killed by these plagues, did not repent of the works of their hands, that they should not worship demons, and idols of gold, silver, brass, stone, and wood, which can neither see nor hear nor walk. ²¹And they did not repent of their murders or their sorceriesᵃ or their sexual immorality or their thefts.

The Mighty Angel with the Little Book

10 I saw still another mighty angel coming down from heaven, clothed with a cloud. And a rainbow *was* on his head, his face *was* like the sun, and his feet like pillars of fire. ²He had a little book open in his hand. And he set his right foot on the sea and *his* left *foot* on the land, ³and cried with a loud voice, as *when* a lion roars. When he cried out, seven thunders uttered their voices. ⁴Now when the seven thunders uttered their voices,ᵃ I was about to write; but I heard a voice from heaven saying to me,ᵇ "Seal up the things which the seven thunders uttered, and do not write them."

⁵The angel whom I saw standing on the sea and on the land raised up his handᵃ to heaven ⁶and swore by Him who lives forever and ever, who created heaven and the things that are in it, the earth and the things that are in it, and the sea and the things that are in it, that there should be delay no longer, ⁷but in the days of the sounding of the seventh angel, when he is about to sound, the mystery of God would be finished, as He declared to His servants the prophets.

John Eats the Little Book

⁸Then the voice which I heard from heaven spoke to me again and said, "Go, take the little book which is open in the hand of the angel who stands on the sea and on the earth."

⁹So I went to the angel and said to him, "Give me the little book."

And he said to me, "Take and eat it; and it will make your stomach bitter, but it will be as sweet as honey in your mouth."

¹⁰Then I took the little book out of the angel's hand and ate it, and it was as sweet as honey in my mouth. But when I had

INTIMATE MOMENTS

Reach across the front seat of the car when you drive and hold his hand, even for a few moments. Allow your fingers to become entwined.

9:19 ᵃNU-Text and M-Text read *the power of the horses*. 9:21 ᵃNU-Text and M-Text read *drugs*. 10:4 ᵃNU-Text and M-Text read *sounded*. ᵇNU-Text and M-Text omit *to me*. 10:5 ᵃNU-Text and M-Text read *right hand*.

eaten it, my stomach became bitter. [11]And he[a] said to me, "You must prophesy again about many peoples, nations, tongues, and kings."

The Two Witnesses

11 Then I was given a reed like a measuring rod. And the angel stood,[a] saying, "Rise and measure the temple of God, the altar, and those who worship there. [2]But leave out the court which is outside the temple, and do not measure it, for it has been given to the Gentiles. And they will tread the holy city underfoot *for* forty-two months. [3]And I will give *power* to my two witnesses, and they will prophesy one thousand two hundred and sixty days, clothed in sackcloth."

[4]These are the two olive trees and the two lampstands standing before the God[a] of the earth. [5]And if anyone wants to harm them, fire proceeds from their mouth and devours their enemies. And if anyone wants to harm them, he must be killed in this manner. [6]These have power to shut heaven, so that no rain falls in the days of their prophecy; and they have power over waters to turn them to blood, and to strike the earth with all plagues, as often as they desire.

The Witnesses Killed

[7]When they finish their testimony, the beast that ascends out of the bottomless pit will make war against them, overcome them, and kill them. [8]And their dead bodies *will lie* in the street of the great city which spiritually is called Sodom and Egypt, where also our[a] Lord was crucified. [9]Then *those* from the peoples, tribes, tongues, and nations will see their dead bodies three-and-a-half days, and not allow[a] their dead bodies to be put into graves. [10]And those who dwell on the earth will rejoice over them, make merry, and send gifts to one another, because these two prophets tormented those who dwell on the earth.

The Witnesses Resurrected

[11]Now *after* the three-and-a-half days the breath of life from God entered them, and they stood on their feet, and great fear fell on those who saw them. [12]And they[a] heard a loud voice from heaven saying to them, "Come up here." And they ascended to heaven in a cloud, and their enemies saw them. [13]In the same hour there was a great earthquake, and a tenth of the city fell. In the earthquake seven thousand people were killed, and the rest were afraid and gave glory to the God of heaven.

[14]The second woe is past. Behold, the third woe is coming quickly.

Seventh Trumpet: The Kingdom Proclaimed

[15]Then the seventh angel sounded: And there were loud voices in heaven, saying, "The kingdoms[a] of this world have become *the kingdoms* of our Lord and of His Christ, and He shall reign forever and ever!" [16]And the twenty-four elders who sat before God on their thrones fell on their faces and worshiped God, [17]saying:

"We give You thanks, O Lord God
    Almighty,
The One who is and who was and
    who is to come,[a]
Because You have taken Your great
    power and reigned.
[18] The nations were angry, and Your
    wrath has come,
And the time of the dead, that they
    should be judged,
And that You should reward Your
    servants the prophets and the
    saints,
And those who fear Your name,
    small and great,
And should destroy those who
    destroy the earth."

[19]Then the temple of God was opened in heaven, and the ark of His covenant[a] was seen in His temple. And there were lightnings, noises, thunderings, an earthquake, and great hail.

10:11 [a]NU-Text and M-Text read *they.*
11:1 [a]NU-Text and M-Text omit *And the angel stood.*
11:4 [a]NU-Text and M-Text read *Lord.*
11:8 [a]NU-Text and M-Text read *their.*
11:9 [a]NU-Text and M-Text read *nations see . . . and will not allow.* 11:12 [a]M-Text reads *I.*
11:15 [a]NU-Text and M-Text read *kingdom . . . has become.* 11:17 [a]NU-Text and M-Text omit *and who is to come.* 11:19 [a]M-Text reads *the covenant of the Lord.*

The Woman, the Child, and the Dragon

12 Now a great sign appeared in heaven: a woman clothed with the sun, with the moon under her feet, and on her head a garland of twelve stars. ²Then being with child, she cried out in labor and in pain to give birth.

³And another sign appeared in heaven: behold, a great, fiery red dragon having seven heads and ten horns, and seven diadems on his heads. ⁴His tail drew a third of the stars of heaven and threw them to the earth. And the dragon stood before the woman who was ready to give birth, to devour her Child as soon as it was born. ⁵She bore a male Child who was to rule all nations with a rod of iron. And her Child was caught up to God and His throne. ⁶Then the woman fled into the wilderness, where she has a place prepared by God, that they should feed her there one thousand two hundred and sixty days.

Satan Thrown Out of Heaven

⁷And war broke out in heaven: Michael and his angels fought with the dragon; and the dragon and his angels fought, ⁸but they did not prevail, nor was a place found for them[a] in heaven any longer. ⁹So the great dragon was cast out, that serpent of old, called the Devil and Satan, who deceives the whole world; he was cast to the earth, and his angels were cast out with him.

¹⁰Then I heard a loud voice saying in heaven, "Now salvation, and strength, and the kingdom of our God, and the power of His Christ have come, for the accuser of our brethren, who accused them before our God day and night, has been cast down. ¹¹And they overcame him by the blood of the Lamb and by the word of their testimony, and they did not love their lives to the death. ¹²Therefore rejoice, O heavens, and you who dwell in them! Woe to the inhabitants of the earth and the sea! For the devil has come down to you, having great wrath, because he knows that he has a short time."

The Woman Persecuted

¹³Now when the dragon saw that he had been cast to the earth, he persecuted the

12:8 [a]M-Text reads *him*.

BIBLICAL INSIGHTS • 12:9
Satan's Tactics

FORMER HEAVYWEIGHT BOXING champion Joe Louis once described the secret of his success. Since he always studied each opponent thoroughly, he was rarely surprised and so could stay on the offensive.

I fear that too many Christians know too little about Satan's tactics. As a result, many live defensive, shell-shocked lifestyles. I'd like to help you stay on the offensive and win your family's encounters with the adversary by learning one of his primary strategies. One friend told me, "The only power that Satan has is in his lies and getting us to believe them." The apostle John calls our adversary " that serpent of old, called the Devil and Satan, who deceives the whole world" (Rev. 12:9).

I recall how in the early 1990's Saddam Hussein used lies to create fear and keep allied forces off balance before Operation Desert Storm. In the first 24 hours of the ground war, Baghdad radio reported that, "Allied troops are dropping like flies." I felt afraid, certain that he had killed thousands of our troops with chemical and biological weapons.

But it was a lie. In fact, US forces and allied troops were achieving overwhelming victory.

Satan's real power comes through his lies. When you refuse to believe him, you strip him of that power. Guide your family in believing the truth of God's Word instead of Satan's lies.

woman who gave birth to the male *Child*. ¹⁴But the woman was given two wings of a great eagle, that she might fly into the wilderness to her place, where she is nourished for a time and times and half a time, from the presence of the serpent. ¹⁵So the serpent spewed water out of his mouth like a flood after the woman, that he might cause her to be carried away by the flood.

[16]But the earth helped the woman, and the earth opened its mouth and swallowed up the flood which the dragon had spewed out of his mouth. [17]And the dragon was enraged with the woman, and he went to make war with the rest of her offspring, who keep the commandments of God and have the testimony of Jesus Christ.[a]

The Beast from the Sea

13 Then I[a] stood on the sand of the sea. And I saw a beast rising up out of the sea, having seven heads and ten horns,[b] and on his horns ten crowns, and on his heads a blasphemous name. [2]Now the beast which I saw was like a leopard, his feet were like *the feet of* a bear, and his mouth like the mouth of a lion. The dragon gave him his power, his throne, and great authority. [3]And I saw one of his heads as if it had been mortally wounded, and his deadly wound was healed. And all the world marveled and followed the beast. [4]So they worshiped the dragon who gave authority to the beast; and they worshiped the beast, saying, "Who *is* like the beast? Who is able to make war with him?"

[5]And he was given a mouth speaking great things and blasphemies, and he was given authority to continue[a] for forty-two months. [6]Then he opened his mouth in blasphemy against God, to blaspheme His name, His tabernacle, and those who dwell in heaven. [7]It was granted to him to make war with the saints and to overcome them. And authority was given him over every tribe,[a] tongue, and nation. [8]All who dwell on the earth will worship him, whose names have not been written in the Book of Life of the Lamb slain from the foundation of the world.

[9]If anyone has an ear, let him hear. [10]He who leads into captivity shall go into captivity; he who kills with the sword must be killed with the sword. Here is the patience and the faith of the saints.

The Beast from the Earth

[11]Then I saw another beast coming up out of the earth, and he had two horns like a lamb and spoke like a dragon. [12]And he exercises all the authority of the first beast in his presence, and causes the earth and those who dwell in it to worship the first beast, whose deadly wound was healed.

12:17 [a]NU-Text and M-Text omit *Christ*. **13:1** [a]NU-Text reads *he*. [b]NU-Text and M-Text read *ten horns and seven heads*. **13:5** [a]M-Text reads *make war*. **13:7** [a]NU-Text and M-Text add *and people*.

ROMANTIC QUOTES AND NOTES
The Trouble with Temptation

Many people think it's a sin just to be tempted, but the fact is, being tempted is normal for a Christian, especially a growing one. Even Christ was tempted in that classic confrontation with the devil at the beginning of His ministry. Temptation is not the problem; *giving in* to temptation is the problem.

So how can you resist the roaring lion?

First, know your weaknesses. If temptation occurs when you are alone, then build in some safeguards. Ask your spouse to keep you honest and accountable by asking the hard questions.

Second, draw upon God's power to stand firm. The saints of Revelation overcame the devil's temptations "by the blood of the Lamb and by the word of their testimony" (Rev. 12:11).

Third, if you are toying with a temptation, realize that you might as well be handling a serpent. As I was writing this, I received a phone call from a man about to lose his marriage and job because he crossed the line. I wish you could have listened to the agony in his voice. There was despair, regret, and shame.

Let me encourage and exhort you to live a holy life and to resist the temptations that the devil sets before you! Live your life so that God is honored by all that you say and do. May your life, marriage, and family be vessels of honor for the glory of God.

[13]He performs great signs, so that he even makes fire come down from heaven on the earth in the sight of men. [14]And he deceives those[a] who dwell on the earth by those signs which he was granted to do in the sight of the beast, telling those who dwell on the earth to make an image to the beast who was wounded by the sword and lived. [15]He was granted *power* to give breath to the image of the beast, that the image of the beast should both speak and cause as many as would not worship the image of the beast to be killed. [16]He causes all, both small and great, rich and poor, free and slave, to receive a mark on their right hand or on their foreheads, [17]and that no one may buy or sell except one who has the mark or[a] the name of the beast, or the number of his name.

[18]Here is wisdom. Let him who has understanding calculate the number of the beast, for it is the number of a man: His number *is* 666.

The Lamb and the 144,000

14 Then I looked, and behold, a[a] Lamb standing on Mount Zion, and with Him one hundred *and* forty-four thousand, having[b] His Father's name written on their foreheads. [2]And I heard a voice from heaven, like the voice of many waters, and like the voice of loud thunder. And I heard the sound of harpists playing their harps. [3]They sang as it were a new song before the throne, before the four living creatures, and the elders; and no one could learn that song except the hundred *and* forty-four thousand who were redeemed from the earth. [4]These are the ones who were not defiled with women, for they are virgins. These are the ones who follow the Lamb wherever He goes. These were redeemed[a] from *among* men, *being* firstfruits to God and to the Lamb. [5]And in their mouth was found no

deceit,[a] for they are without fault before the throne of God.[b]

The Proclamations of Three Angels

[6]Then I saw another angel flying in the midst of heaven, having the everlasting gospel to preach to those who dwell on the earth—to every nation, tribe, tongue, and people— [7]saying with a loud voice, "Fear God and give glory to Him, for the hour of His judgment has come; and worship Him who made heaven and earth, the sea and springs of water."

INTIMATE MOMENTS

The next time you get a pair of tickets to a ball game, theater, or concert that she'd like to go to, make a sacrifice. Instead of going with a buddy, tuck them in her purse with a note saying, "You deserve a night off. Have fun with a girlfriend."

[8]And another angel followed, saying, "Babylon[a] is fallen, is fallen, that great city, because she has made all nations drink of the wine of the wrath of her fornication."

[9]Then a third angel followed them, saying with a loud voice, "If anyone worships the beast and his image, and receives *his* mark on his forehead or on his hand, [10]he himself shall also drink of the wine of the wrath of God, which is poured out full strength into the cup of His indignation. He shall be tormented with fire and brimstone in the presence of the holy angels and in the presence of the Lamb. [11]And the smoke of their torment ascends forever and ever; and they have no rest day or night, who worship the beast and his image, and whoever receives the mark of his name."

[12]Here is the patience of the saints; here *are* those[a] who keep the commandments of God and the faith of Jesus.

[13]Then I heard a voice from heaven saying to me,[a] "Write: 'Blessed *are* the dead who die in the Lord from now on.'"

"Yes," says the Spirit, "that they may rest from their labors, and their works follow them."

13:14 [a]M-Text reads *my own people*.
13:17 [a]NU-Text and M-Text omit *or*.
14:1 [a]NU-Text and M-Text read *the*. [b]NU-Text and M-Text add *His name and*. **14:4** [a]M-Text adds *by Jesus*. **14:5** [a]NU-Text and M-Text read *falsehood*. [b]NU-Text and M-Text omit *before the throne of God*. **14:8** [a]NU-Text reads *Babylon the great is fallen, is fallen, which has made*; M-Text reads *Babylon the great is fallen. She has made*. **14:12** [a]NU-Text and M-Text omit *here are those*. **14:13** [a]NU-Text and M-Text omit *to me*.

Reaping the Earth's Harvest

14Then I looked, and behold, a white cloud, and on the cloud sat *One* like the Son of Man, having on His head a golden crown, and in His hand a sharp sickle. 15And another angel came out of the temple, crying with a loud voice to Him who sat on the cloud, "Thrust in Your sickle and reap, for the time has come for You[a] to reap, for the harvest of the earth is ripe." 16So He who sat on the cloud thrust in His sickle on the earth, and the earth was reaped.

Reaping the Grapes of Wrath

17Then another angel came out of the temple which is in heaven, he also having a sharp sickle. 18And another angel came out from the altar, who had power over fire, and he cried with a loud cry to him who had the sharp sickle, saying, "Thrust in your sharp sickle and gather the clusters of the vine of the earth, for her grapes are fully ripe." 19So the angel thrust his sickle into the earth and gathered the vine of the earth, and threw *it* into the great winepress of the wrath of God. 20And the winepress was trampled outside the city, and blood came out of the winepress, up to the horses' bridles, for one thousand six hundred furlongs.

Prelude to the Bowl Judgments

15 Then I saw another sign in heaven, great and marvelous: seven angels having the seven last plagues, for in them the wrath of God is complete.

2And I saw *something* like a sea of glass mingled with fire, and those who have the victory over the beast, over his image and over his mark[a] *and* over the number of his name, standing on the sea of glass, having harps of God. 3They sing the song of Moses, the servant of God, and the song of the Lamb, saying:

"Great and marvelous *are* Your works,
 Lord God Almighty!
Just and true *are* Your ways,
 O King of the saints![a]
4 Who shall not fear You, O Lord, and
 glorify Your name?
For *You* alone *are* holy.

For all nations shall come and
 worship before You,
For Your judgments have been
 manifested."

5After these things I looked, and behold,[a] the temple of the tabernacle of the testimony in heaven was opened. 6And out of the temple came the seven angels having the seven plagues, clothed in pure bright linen, and having their chests girded with golden bands. 7Then one of the four living creatures gave to the seven angels seven golden bowls full of the wrath of God who lives forever and ever. 8The temple was filled with smoke from the glory of God and from His power, and no one was able to enter the temple till the seven plagues of the seven angels were completed.

16 Then I heard a loud voice from the temple saying to the seven angels, "Go and pour out the bowls[a] of the wrath of God on the earth."

First Bowl: Loathsome Sores

2So the first went and poured out his bowl upon the earth, and a foul and loathsome sore came upon the men who had the mark of the beast and those who worshiped his image.

Second Bowl: The Sea Turns to Blood

3Then the second angel poured out his bowl on the sea, and it became blood as of a dead *man;* and every living creature in the sea died.

Third Bowl: The Waters Turn to Blood

4Then the third angel poured out his bowl on the rivers and springs of water, and they became blood. 5And I heard the angel of the waters saying:

"You are righteous, O Lord,[a]
 The One who is and who was and
  who is to be,[b]
 Because You have judged these
  things.

14:15 [a]NU-Text and M-Text omit *for You.*
15:2 [a]NU-Text and M-Text omit *over his mark.*
15:3 [a]NU-Text and M-Text read *nations.*
15:5 [a]NU-Text and M-Text omit *behold.*
16:1 [a]NU-Text and M-Text read *seven bowls.*
16:5 [a]NU-Text and M-Text omit *O Lord.* [b]NU-Text and M-Text read *who was, the Holy One.*

6 For they have shed the blood of
    saints and prophets,
    And You have given them blood to
    drink.
    For[a] it is their just due."

7And I heard another from[a] the altar saying, "Even so, Lord God Almighty, true and righteous *are* Your judgments."

Fourth Bowl: Men Are Scorched

8Then the fourth angel poured out his bowl on the sun, and power was given to him to scorch men with fire. 9And men were scorched with great heat, and they blasphemed the name of God who has power over these plagues; and they did not repent and give Him glory.

Fifth Bowl: Darkness and Pain

10Then the fifth angel poured out his bowl on the throne of the beast, and his kingdom became full of darkness; and they gnawed their tongues because of the pain. 11They blasphemed the God of heaven because of their pains and their sores, and did not repent of their deeds.

Sixth Bowl: Euphrates Dried Up

12Then the sixth angel poured out his bowl on the great river Euphrates, and its water was dried up, so that the way of the kings from the east might be prepared. 13And I saw three unclean spirits like frogs *coming* out of the mouth of the dragon, out of the mouth of the beast, and out of the mouth of the false prophet. 14For they are spirits of demons, performing signs, *which* go out to the kings of the earth and[a] of the whole world, to gather them to the battle of that great day of God Almighty. 15"Behold, I am coming as a thief. Blessed *is* he who watches, and keeps his garments, lest he walk naked and they see his shame." 16And they gathered them together to the place called in Hebrew, Armageddon.[a]

16:6 [a]NU-Text and M-Text omit *For.*
16:7 [a]NU-Text and M-Text omit *another from.*
16:14 [a]NU-Text and M-Text omit *of the earth and.*
16:16 [a]M-Text reads *Megiddo.*

Seventh Bowl: The Earth Utterly Shaken

17Then the seventh angel poured out his bowl into the air, and a loud voice came out of the temple of heaven, from the throne, saying, "It is done!" 18And there were noises and thunderings and lightnings; and there was a great earthquake, such a mighty and great earthquake as had not occurred since men were on the earth. 19Now the great city was divided into three parts, and the cities of the nations fell. And great Babylon was remembered before God, to give her the cup of the wine of the fierceness of His wrath. 20Then

ROMANCE FAQ

Q: How can we deal with the failures in our marriage?

First, we have to be truthful about our sins. The Bible calls this *confession.* To confess a sin means we agree with God concerning the wrongness of that sin and then turn from it. We can't just keep on sinning and take lightly the impact of the wrong or hurtful decision we have made. Remember, it was our sin that put Jesus Christ on the cross in the first place. How can we (who say we love Him) continue to live for something that brought Him such terrible pain?

Second, the Scriptures teach that we must forgive those who hurt us. Forgiveness lies at the heart of Christianity, and that means forgiveness is not optional for a Christian. God commands us to forgive because He's forgiven us. To forgive others means we give up the right to punish the offender. We no longer hold the offenses against the person.

Are you usually quick to ask for forgiveness, and to extend it? Why is it often hard to forgive others who fail us? Has your spouse done anything for which you are still punishing him or her? Thank God for His willingness to forgive you, and then pray for a heart that is willing to forgive those who fail you.

every island fled away, and the mountains were not found. ²¹And great hail from heaven fell upon men, *each hailstone* about the weight of a talent. Men blasphemed God because of the plague of the hail, since that plague was exceedingly great.

The Scarlet Woman and the Scarlet Beast

17 Then one of the seven angels who had the seven bowls came and talked with me, saying to me,ᵃ "Come, I will show you the judgment of the great harlot who sits on many waters, ²with whom the kings of the earth committed fornication, and the inhabitants of the earth were made drunk with the wine of her fornication."

³So he carried me away in the Spirit into the wilderness. And I saw a woman sitting on a scarlet beast *which was* full of names of blasphemy, having seven heads and ten horns. ⁴The woman was arrayed in purple and scarlet, and adorned with gold and precious stones and pearls, having in her hand a golden cup full of abominations and the filthiness of her fornication.ᵃ ⁵And on her forehead a name *was* written:

MYSTERY, BABYLON THE GREAT,
THE MOTHER OF HARLOTS AND
OF THE ABOMINATIONS OF
THE EARTH.

⁶I saw the woman, drunk with the blood of the saints and with the blood of the martyrs of Jesus. And when I saw her, I marveled with great amazement.

The Meaning of the Woman and the Beast

⁷But the angel said to me, "Why did you marvel? I will tell you the mystery of the woman and of the beast that carries her, which has the seven heads and the ten horns. ⁸The beast that you saw was, and is not, and will ascend out of the bottomless pit and go to perdition. And those who dwell on the earth will marvel, whose names are not written in the Book of Life from the foundation of the world, when they see the beast that was, and is not, and yet is.ᵃ

⁹"Here *is* the mind which has wisdom: The seven heads are seven mountains on which the woman sits. ¹⁰There are also seven kings. Five have fallen, one is, *and* the other has not yet come. And when he comes, he must continue a short time. ¹¹The beast that was, and is not, is himself also the eighth, and is of the seven, and is going to perdition.

¹²"The ten horns which you saw are ten kings who have received no kingdom as yet, but they receive authority for one hour as kings with the beast. ¹³These are of one mind, and they will give their power and authority to the beast. ¹⁴These will make war with the Lamb, and the Lamb will overcome them, for He is Lord of lords and King of kings; and those *who are* with Him *are* called, chosen, and faithful."

¹⁵Then he said to me, "The waters which you saw, where the harlot sits, are peoples, multitudes, nations, and tongues. ¹⁶And the ten horns which you saw onᵃ the beast, these will hate the harlot, make her desolate and naked, eat her flesh and burn her with fire. ¹⁷For God has put it into their hearts to fulfill His purpose, to be of one mind, and to give their kingdom to the beast, until the words of God are fulfilled. ¹⁸And the woman whom you saw is that great city which reigns over the kings of the earth."

The Fall of Babylon the Great

18 After these things I saw another angel coming down from heaven, having great authority, and the earth was illuminated with his glory. ²And he cried

INTIMATE MOMENTS

Go an entire day without criticizing anything about him. Instead, try to notice him doing something that you really appreciate, and tell him how much you value him.

17:1 ᵃNU-Text and M-Text omit *to me.*
17:4 ᵃM-Text reads *the filthiness of the fornication of the earth.* 17:8 ᵃNU-Text and M-Text read *and shall be present.* 17:16 ᵃNU-Text and M-Text read *saw, and the beast.*

mightily[a] with a loud voice, saying, "Babylon the great is fallen, is fallen, and has become a dwelling place of demons, a prison for every foul spirit, and a cage for every unclean and hated bird! [3]For all the nations have drunk of the wine of the wrath of her fornication, the kings of the earth have committed fornication with her, and the merchants of the earth have become rich through the abundance of her luxury."

[4]And I heard another voice from heaven saying, "Come out of her, my people, lest you share in her sins, and lest you receive of her plagues. [5]For her sins have reached[a] to heaven, and God has remembered her iniquities. [6]Render to her just as she rendered to you,[a] and repay her double according to her works; in the cup which she has mixed, mix double for her. [7]In the measure that she glorified herself and lived luxuriously, in the same measure give her torment and sorrow; for she says in her heart, 'I sit as queen, and am no widow, and will not see sorrow.' [8]Therefore her plagues will come in one day—death and mourning and famine. And she will be utterly burned with fire, for strong is the Lord God who judges[a] her.

The World Mourns Babylon's Fall

[9]"The kings of the earth who committed fornication and lived luxuriously with her will weep and lament for her, when they see the smoke of her burning, [10]standing at a distance for fear of her torment, saying, 'Alas, alas, that great city Babylon, that mighty city! For in one hour your judgment has come.'

[11]"And the merchants of the earth will weep and mourn over her, for no one buys their merchandise anymore: [12]merchandise of gold and silver, precious stones and pearls, fine linen and purple, silk and scarlet, every kind of citron wood, every kind of object of ivory, every kind of object of most precious wood, bronze, iron, and marble; [13]and cinnamon and incense, fragrant oil and frankincense, wine and oil, fine flour and wheat, cattle and sheep, horses and chariots, and bodies and souls of men. [14]The fruit that your soul longed for has gone from you, and all the things which are rich and splendid have gone from you,[a] and you shall find them no more at all. [15]The merchants of these things, who became rich by her, will stand at a distance for fear of her torment, weeping and wailing, [16]and saying, 'Alas, alas, that great city that was clothed in fine linen, purple, and scarlet, and adorned with gold and precious stones and pearls! [17]For in one hour such great riches came to nothing.' Every shipmaster, all who travel by ship, sailors, and as many as trade on the sea, stood at a distance [18]and cried out when they saw the smoke of her burning, saying, 'What is like this great city?'

[19]"They threw dust on their heads and cried out, weeping and wailing, and saying, 'Alas, alas, that great city, in which all who had ships on the sea became rich by her wealth! For in one hour she is made desolate.'

[20]"Rejoice over her, O heaven, and you holy apostles[a] and prophets, for God has avenged you on her!"

Finality of Babylon's Fall

[21]Then a mighty angel took up a stone like a great millstone and threw it into the sea, saying, "Thus with violence the great city Babylon shall be thrown down, and shall not be found anymore. [22]The sound of harpists, musicians, flutists, and trumpeters shall not be heard in you anymore. No craftsman of any craft shall be found in you anymore, and the sound of a millstone shall not be heard in you anymore. [23]The light of a lamp shall not shine in you anymore, and the voice of bridegroom and bride shall not be heard in you anymore. For your merchants were the great men of the earth, for by your sorcery all the nations were deceived. [24]And in her was found the blood of prophets and saints, and of all who were slain on the earth."

18:2 [a]NU-Text and M-Text omit *mightily*.
18:5 [a]NU-Text and M-Text read *have been heaped up*.
18:6 [a]NU-Text and M-Text omit *to you*.
18:8 [a]NU-Text and M-Text read *has judged*.
18:14 [a]NU-Text and M-Text read *been lost to you*.
18:20 [a]NU-Text and M-Text read *saints and apostles*.

Heaven Exults over Babylon

19 After these things I heard[a] a loud voice of a great multitude in heaven, saying, "Alleluia! Salvation and glory and honor and power *belong* to the Lord[b] our God! ²For true and righteous *are* His judgments, because He has judged the great harlot who corrupted the earth with her fornication; and He has avenged on her the blood of His servants *shed* by her." ³Again they said, "Alleluia! Her smoke rises up forever and ever!" ⁴And the twenty-four elders and the four living creatures fell down and worshiped God who sat on the throne, saying, "Amen! Alleluia!" ⁵Then a voice came from the throne, saying, "Praise our God, all you His servants and those who fear Him, both[a] small and great!"

⁶And I heard, as it were, the voice of a great multitude, as the sound of many waters and as the sound of mighty thunderings, saying, "Alleluia! For the[a] Lord God Omnipotent reigns! ⁷Let us be glad and rejoice and give Him glory, for the marriage of the Lamb has come, and His wife has made herself ready." ⁸And to her it was granted to be arrayed in fine linen, clean and bright, for the fine linen is the righteous acts of the saints.

⁹Then he said to me, "Write: 'Blessed *are* those who are called to the marriage supper of the Lamb!' " And he said to me, "These are the true sayings of God." ¹⁰And I fell at his feet to worship him. But he said to me, "See *that you do* not *do that!* I am your fellow servant, and of your brethren who have the testimony of Jesus. Worship God! For the testimony of Jesus is the spirit of prophecy."

Christ on a White Horse

¹¹Now I saw heaven opened, and behold, a white horse. And He who sat on him *was* called Faithful and True, and in righteousness He judges and makes war. ¹²His eyes *were* like a flame of fire, and on His head *were* many crowns. He had[a] a name written that no one knew except Himself. ¹³He *was* clothed with a robe dipped in blood, and His name is called The Word of God. ¹⁴And the armies in heaven, clothed in fine linen, white and clean,[a] followed Him on white

horses. ¹⁵Now out of His mouth goes a sharp[a] sword, that with it He should strike the nations. And He Himself will rule them with a rod of iron. He Himself treads the winepress of the fierceness and wrath of Almighty God. ¹⁶And He has on *His* robe and on His thigh a name written:

KING OF KINGS AND LORD OF LORDS.

The Beast and His Armies Defeated

¹⁷Then I saw an angel standing in the sun; and he cried with a loud voice, saying to all the birds that fly in the midst of heaven, "Come and gather together for the supper of the great God,[a] ¹⁸that you may eat the flesh of kings, the flesh of captains, the flesh of mighty men, the flesh of horses and of those who sit on them, and the flesh of all *people,* free[a] and slave, both small and great."

¹⁹And I saw the beast, the kings of the earth, and their armies, gathered together to make war against Him who sat on the horse and against His army. ²⁰Then the beast was captured, and with him the false prophet who worked signs in his presence, by which he deceived those who received the mark of the beast and those who worshiped his image. These two were cast alive into the lake of fire burning with brimstone. ²¹And the rest were killed with the sword which proceeded from the mouth of Him who sat on the horse. And all the birds were filled with their flesh.

Satan Bound 1000 Years

20 Then I saw an angel coming down from heaven, having the key to the bottomless pit and a great chain in his hand. ²He laid hold of the dragon, that serpent of old, who is *the* Devil and Satan, and bound him for a thousand years; ³and he cast him into the bottomless pit, and shut him up, and set a seal on him, so that he should deceive

---

19:1 [a]NU-Text and M-Text add *something like.* [b]NU-Text and M-Text omit *the Lord.* **19:5** [a]NU-Text and M-Text omit *both.* **19:6** [a]NU-Text and M-Text read *our.* **19:12** [a]M-Text adds *names written, and.* **19:14** [a]NU-Text and M-Text read *pure white linen.* **19:15** [a]M-Text adds *two-edged.* **19:17** [a]NU-Text and M-Text read *the great supper of God.* **19:18** [a]NU-Text and M-Text read *both free.*

the nations no more till the thousand years were finished. But after these things he must be released for a little while.

The Saints Reign with Christ 1000 Years

⁴And I saw thrones, and they sat on them, and judgment was committed to them. Then *I saw* the souls of those who had been beheaded for their witness to Jesus and for the word of God, who had not worshiped the beast or his image, and had not received *his* mark on their foreheads or on their hands. And they lived and reigned with Christ for aᵃ thousand years. ⁵But the rest of the dead did not live again until the thousand years were finished. This *is* the first resurrection. ⁶Blessed and holy *is* he who has part in the first resurrection. Over such the second death has no power, but they shall be priests of God and of Christ, and shall reign with Him a thousand years.

Satanic Rebellion Crushed

⁷Now when the thousand years have expired, Satan will be released from his prison ⁸and will go out to deceive the nations which are in the four corners of the earth, Gog and Magog, to gather them together to battle, whose number *is* as the sand of the sea. ⁹They went up on the breadth of the earth and surrounded the camp of the saints and the beloved city. And fire came down from God out of heaven and devoured them. ¹⁰The devil, who deceived them, was cast into the lake of fire and brimstone whereᵃ the beast and the false prophet *are*. And they will be tormented day and night forever and ever.

The Great White Throne Judgment

¹¹Then I saw a great white throne and Him who sat on it, from whose face the earth and the heaven fled away. And there was found no place for them. ¹²And I saw the dead, small and great, standing before God,ᵃ and books were opened. And another book was opened, which is *the Book* of

---

20:4 ᵃM-Text reads *the.* 20:10 ᵃNU-Text and M-Text add *also.* 20:12 ᵃNU-Text and M-Text read *the throne.* 20:14 ᵃNU-Text and M-Text add *the lake of fire.*

BIBLICAL INSIGHTS • 20:11, 12

Jesus the Judge

ONLY ONE PERSON HAS FINAL authority over the judgment of humankind: Jesus Christ. Not only will Jesus open the books on our lives and judge us according to what is written in them, but He will also judge death itself as well as those who don't know Him. "Then I saw a great white throne and Him who sat on it, from whose face the earth and the heaven fled away. And there was found no place for them. And I saw the dead, small and great, standing before God, and books were opened. And another book was opened, which is the Book of Life. And the dead were judged according to their works, by the things which were written in the books" (Rev. 20:11, 12).

We know this describes Jesus, for He told us, "The Father judges no one, but has committed all judgment to the Son" (John 5:22). Knowing this should motivate us to make sure our top priority is taking the message of salvation through Jesus Christ to everyone possible. It should move us toward answering two questions:

1. What we will do with Jesus?

2. How can we best ask our friends, neighbors, and family members the same question?

The message of Revelation is that the Judge is coming; how then shall we live?

Life. And the dead were judged according to their works, by the things which were written in the books. ¹³The sea gave up the dead who were in it, and Death and Hades delivered up the dead who were in them. And they were judged, each one according to his works. ¹⁴Then Death and Hades were cast into the lake of fire. This is the second death.ᵃ ¹⁵And anyone not found written in the Book of Life was cast into the lake of fire.

All Things Made New

21 Now I saw a new heaven and a new earth, for the first heaven and the first earth had passed away. Also there was no more sea. ²Then I, John,ᵃ saw the holy city, New Jerusalem, coming down out of heaven from God, prepared as a bride adorned for her husband. ³And I heard a loud voice from heaven saying, "Behold, the tabernacle of God *is* with men, and He will dwell with them, and they shall be His people. God Himself will be with them *and be* their God. ⁴And God will wipe away every tear from their eyes; there shall be no more death, nor sorrow, nor crying. There shall be no more pain, for the former things have passed away."

⁵Then He who sat on the throne said, "Behold, I make all things new." And He said to me,ᵃ "Write, for these words are true and faithful."

⁶And He said to me, "It is done!ᵃ I am the Alpha and the Omega, the Beginning and the End. I will give of the fountain of the water of life freely to him who thirsts. ⁷He who overcomes shall inherit all things,ᵃ and I will be his God and he shall be My son. ⁸But the cowardly, unbelieving,ᵃ abominable, murderers, sexually immoral, sorcerers, idolaters, and all liars shall have their part in the lake which burns with fire and brimstone, which is the second death."

The New Jerusalem

⁹Then one of the seven angels who had the seven bowls filled with the seven last plagues came to meᵃ and talked with me, saying, "Come, I will show you the bride, the Lamb's wife."ᵇ ¹⁰And he carried me away in the Spirit to a great and high mountain, and showed me the great city, the holyᵃ Jerusalem, descending out of heaven from God, ¹¹having the glory of God. Her light *was* like a most precious stone, like a jasper stone, clear as crystal. ¹²Also she had a great and high wall with twelve gates, and twelve angels at the gates, and names written on them, which are *the names* of the twelve tribes of the children of Israel: ¹³three gates on the east, three gates on the north, three gates on the south, and three gates on the west.

¹⁴Now the wall of the city had twelve foundations, and on them were the namesᵃ of the twelve apostles of the Lamb. ¹⁵And he who talked with me had a gold reed to measure the city, its gates, and its wall. ¹⁶The city is laid out as a square; its length is as great as its breadth. And he measured the city with the reed: twelve thousand furlongs. Its length, breadth, and height are equal. ¹⁷Then he measured its wall: one hundred *and* forty-four cubits, *according* to the measure of a man, that is, of an angel. ¹⁸The construction of its wall was *of* jasper; and the city *was* pure gold, like clear glass. ¹⁹The foundations of the wall of the city *were* adorned with all kinds of precious stones: the first foundation *was* jasper, the second sapphire, the third chalcedony, the fourth emerald, ²⁰the fifth sardonyx, the sixth sardius, the seventh chrysolite, the eighth beryl, the ninth topaz, the tenth chrysoprase, the eleventh jacinth, and the twelfth amethyst. ²¹The twelve gates *were* twelve pearls: each individual gate was of one pearl. And the street of the city *was* pure gold, like transparent glass.

The Glory of the New Jerusalem

²²But I saw no temple in it, for the Lord God Almighty and the Lamb are its temple. ²³The city had no need of the sun or of the moon to shine in it,ᵃ for the gloryᵇ of God illuminated it. The Lamb *is* its light. ²⁴And the nations of those who are savedᵃ shall walk in its light, and the kings of the earth bring their glory and honor into it.ᵇ ²⁵Its gates shall not be shut at all by day (there shall be no night there). ²⁶And they shall bring the glory and the honor of the nations into it.ᵃ ²⁷But there shall by no means enter

21:2 ᵃNU-Text and M-Text omit *John*. 21:5 ᵃNU-Text and M-Text omit *to me*. 21:6 ᵃM-Text omits *It is done*. 21:7 ᵃM-Text reads *overcomes, I shall give him these things*. 21:8 ᵃM-Text adds *and sinners*. 21:9 ᵃNU-Text and M-Text omit *to me*. ᵇM-Text reads *I will show you the woman, the Lamb's bride*. 21:10 ᵃNU-Text and M-Text omit *the great* and read *the holy city, Jerusalem*. 21:14 ᵃNU-Text and M-Text read *twelve names*. 21:23 ᵃNU-Text and M-Text omit *in it*. ᵇM-Text reads *the very glory*. 21:24 ᵃNU-Text and M-Text omit *of those who are saved*. ᵇM-Text reads *the glory and honor of the nations to Him*. 21:26 ᵃM-Text adds *that they may enter in*.

it anything that defiles, or causes[a] an abomination or a lie, but only those who are written in the Lamb's Book of Life.

The River of Life

22 And he showed me a pure[a] river of water of life, clear as crystal, proceeding from the throne of God and of the Lamb. [2]In the middle of its street, and on either side of the river, *was* the tree of life, which bore twelve fruits, each *tree* yielding its fruit every month. The leaves of the tree *were* for the healing of the nations. [3]And there shall be no more curse, but the throne of God and of the Lamb shall be in it, and His servants shall serve Him. [4]They shall see His face, and His name *shall be* on their foreheads. [5]There shall be no night there: They need no lamp nor light of the sun, for the Lord God gives them light. And they shall reign forever and ever.

The Time Is Near

[6]Then he said to me, "These words *are* faithful and true." And the Lord God of the holy[a] prophets sent His angel to show His servants the things which must shortly take place.

[7]"Behold, I am coming quickly! Blessed *is* he who keeps the words of the prophecy of this book."

[8]Now I, John, saw and heard[a] these things. And when I heard and saw, I fell down to worship before the feet of the angel who showed me these things.

[9]Then he said to me, "See *that you do not do that.* For[a] I am your fellow servant, and of your brethren the prophets, and of those who keep the words of this book. Worship God." [10]And he said to me, "Do not seal the words of the prophecy of this book, for the time is at hand. [11]He who is unjust, let him be unjust still; he who is

---

BIBLICAL INSIGHTS • 20:13
One Way to Know God Better

NEAR THE VERY END OF THE BIBLE, we hear God saying, "I am the Alpha and the Omega, the Beginning and the End, the First and the Last" (Rev. 22:13). This divine self-description reminds us that one of the best ways we can get to know God better—how to fear Him and love Him and serve Him more deeply—is to learn and study His different names and titles as they appear in various parts of the Bible. It's a rich study, one where we can learn of His attributes and character just by reading how He refers to Himself.

Many books have been written on the subject, and they can be of great help. For example, there is the classic *The Pursuit of God* by A.W. Tozer (his all-time best seller) and *Knowing God* by J.I. Packer. I highly recommend both titles and suggest that they be read annually.

As you prayerfully read classic literature along with the Bible, you can begin to learn the many names of God in Scripture. When you do, you'll learn volumes about what His many names say about His character—His greatness, His majesty, His holiness, His omnipotence, His sovereignty, and His authority. And I promise, you'll come away from your study a changed person with a different perspective on your life, marriage, and family.

---

filthy, let him be filthy still; he who is righteous, let him be righteous[a] still; he who is holy, let him be holy still."

Jesus Testifies to the Churches

[12]"And behold, I am coming quickly, and My reward *is* with Me, to give to every one according to his work. [13]I am the Alpha and the Omega, *the* Beginning and *the* End, the First and the Last."[a]

[14]Blessed *are* those who do His commandments,[a] that they may have the right to the tree of life, and may enter through

---

21:27 [a]NU-Text and M-Text read *anything profane, nor one who causes.* 22:1 [a]NU-Text and M-Text omit *pure.* 22:6 [a]NU-Text and M-Text read *spirits of the prophets.* 22:8 [a]NU-Text and M-Text read *am the one who heard and saw.* 22:9 [a]NU-Text and M-Text omit *For.* 22:11 [a]NU-Text and M-Text read *do right.* 22:13 [a]NU-Text and M-Text read *the First and the Last, the Beginning and the End.* 22:14 [a]NU-Text reads *wash their robes.*

the gates into the city. [15]But[a] outside *are* dogs and sorcerers and sexually immoral and murderers and idolaters, and whoever loves and practices a lie.

[16]"I, Jesus, have sent My angel to testify to you these things in the churches. I am the Root and the Offspring of David, the Bright and Morning Star."

[17]And the Spirit and the bride say, "Come!" And let him who hears say, "Come!" And let him who thirsts come. Whoever desires, let him take the water of life freely.

A Warning

[18]For[a] I testify to everyone who hears the words of the prophecy of this book: If anyone adds to these things, God will add[b] to him the plagues that are written in this book; [19]and if anyone takes away from the words of the book of this prophecy, God shall take away[a] his part from the Book[b] of Life, from the holy city, and *from* the things which are written in this book.

I Am Coming Quickly

[20]He who testifies to these things says, "Surely I am coming quickly."

Amen. Even so, come, Lord Jesus!

[21]The grace of our Lord Jesus Christ *be* with you all.[a] Amen.

22:15 [a]NU-Text and M-Text omit *But.*
22:18 [a]NU-Text and M-Text omit *For.* [b]M-Text reads *may God add.* **22:19** [a]M-Text reads *may God take away.* [b]NU-Text and M-Text read *tree of life.*
22:21 [a]NU-Text reads *with all;* M-Text reads *with all the saints.*

30 DAYS WITH JESUS

Day – 1 John 1:1-51

The Perfect God-Man

Jesus is the Word, God the Son Himself, who has always existed with His heavenly Father—all light, not one bit of darkness, no shortcomings, no imperfections. Does that produce awe and wonder in you today? Do you believe in Him? Do you worship Him? Have you "received of His fullness" (1:16)? Take a minute to let the joy soak in!

Day 2 – Luke 2:1-52

The Greatest Gift Ever

What an event it was when the Son of God became a helpless baby in a poor family, so sinners could be saved! He actually became one of us! Can you share the happiness of Anna and Simeon, and like the angels, can you give glory to God in the highest (2:14) for giving the world the greatest gift anyone could ever imagine?

Day 3 – Mark 1:1-11

Strange But True

John the Baptist was God's messenger to prepare the way for Jesus. John was an eccentric, and he was not afraid to speak his mind. Although many people loved him, there were others who despised him. But John's eyes were on Jesus. His mission as Christ's forerunner was all that mattered to him. What matters to you?

Day 4 – Luke 4:1-44

That's Life

Temptation by Satan, rejection by so-called friends, a struggle with demons—these were just some normal events in the life of Jesus! Isn't it a comfort to know that living wasn't easy for the Son of God either? But He still had time to pay attention to those who were hurting and needed His love. Who could use some attention from you today?

Day 5 – John 3:1-36

Seek the Light

Light has come into the world (3:19). Are you one of the ones who seek the light, or do you hide from it? The light shows what flawed, imperfect sinners we are. "But he who believes in the Son has everlasting life" (3:36). With the cleansing Jesus gives us, we can have our fellowship with him restored, and then we can love being in His light.

Day 6 – Luke 5:1-39

New Wineskins Needed

Many were disgusted that Jesus cared more about lepers and tax collectors than He did about traditions. But Jesus came to love those who needed it, and that meant changing a few things. He brought a message that was "new wine" (5:37), and it needed to be put in a "new wineskin." What new wineskins are needed in your world?

Day 7 – John 4:1-54

Fields Are Ready to Harvest

Jesus was ready to move outside of man-made boundaries, like when He conversed with a Samaritan, and a woman at that! But there was a field of souls ready to be harvested, and this Samaritan woman wasn't shy about telling her people that she had met Jesus. Who do you know who needs to hear about the Messiah?

Day 8 – Luke 6:1-49

Expect the Unexpected

Jesus taught things that the world did not expect. People who seem not to be blessed are truly blessed, and vice versa; we are to love our enemies, not hate them; we should accept attacks, not resist them. The world's way of looking at things is often not anything like God's way. Whose way is your way?

Day 9 – Luke 7:1-50

Check the Evidence

Jesus reassured John the Baptist by pointing to the results of His ministry: Jesus healed the afflicted, even raised the dead—and on top of that, He forgave sins, something only God could do. These things were an offense to many. But those who were not offended, such as the woman at Jesus' feet (7:37-50), were blessed through faith!

Day 10 – Luke 8:1-56

The Heart We Bring to Him

Do you hear God's word with a good heart, one that's like the good ground in Jesus' parable of the sower (8:15)? Jairus and the woman with the flow of blood both had that kind of trusting faith, a focus on the Lord that would not be distracted. That's how Jesus wants us to come to Him. We won't be disappointed if we do.

Day 11 – Mark 8:1-38

Take Up Your Cross

Peter recognized that Jesus was the Messiah his people had been waiting for. But that took some adjusting. Jesus came not to conquer and reign (not yet anyway), but to suffer and die for sinners. He challenged His followers to "take up their cross" and follow Him (8:34). Can you stand to be humble and weak in the world's eyes like Jesus was?

Day 12 – Luke 10:1-42

The Unusual Neighbor

In the parable of the Good Samaritan, the true neighbor was the one who showed mercy to the one who needed it. In this case the neighbor was a Samaritan, who was not expected to care much for a man from Jerusalem. Is there somebody you know who needs a neighbor today? Maybe it's even somebody you don't usually associate with.

Day 13 – Matthew 5:1-48

Clean on the Inside

If we're going to be salt and light in the world like Jesus said (5:13-16), we need to make sure our hearts are right. Hatred in the heart is no better than murder. Lust in the heart is no better than adultery. A good life starts with love and purity in the heart. But that's not easy, is it? We really do need God's help to make us clean on the inside.

Day 14 – Matthew 6:1-34

Treasures That Last

Jesus said our treasures ought to be in heaven, not on earth (6:19, 20). One benefit to that is that we don't have to worry about our treasures there! Earthly riches and "security" can vanish in an instant. But heaven's treasures are eternal, something no one can ever take away. It's crazy to serve mammon (6:24), earthly riches that cannot last. Serve God!

Day 15 – Matthew 7:1-29

Walking in the Narrow Way

Obeying Jesus is like building on a solid foundation (7:24). That calls for wisdom and self-control. We need to identify the narrow way and walk in it (7:13). And we need to resist the urge to judge others (7:1), extending to them the same kind of grace God gave to us. That's the golden rule: doing to others what we want done to us (7:12).

Day 16 – Luke 14:1-35

Radical Discipleship

We have to be willing to let go of some things to follow Christ. Honor and recognition will have to go, since following Jesus means taking the lower place (14:7-11). We are also told to seek out those who have little (14:12-14). We might even have to give up precious family connections for Jesus' sake (14:26). That's radical discipleship!

Day 17 – Luke 15:1-32

Returning to the Father

The love of God the Father is shown in the extraordinary parable of the Lost Son. Even though one son stayed home while the other one left and wasted his money, the father had enough love for them both, and welcomed the spendthrift home when he repented and asked forgiveness. God loves us that much and more when we return to Him!

Day 18 – Luke 16:1-31

This World or the Next?

Where would you like your reward to be? In this world or the next? The rich man in Jesus' parable (16:19) had his reward in this life, but he ignored God's revelation of Himself in His word. Lazarus was poor in this world but had comfort in the next, where his blessings would last forever. Is your goal to pile up temporary riches or eternal ones?

Day 19 – John 8:1-59

Happy to Please the Father

Even though Jesus was Himself God, He insisted that He was only doing His Father's will (8:28, 29). Jesus was always a dependable and attentive Son, wishing only to please His Father. There is no indignity or shame in giving Christlike obedience to parents and others who have been placed in authority over us.

Day 20 – Luke 17:1-37

Thanks Be to God!

Do you remember to thank God for what He has given us? The blessings He gives are so plentiful it's easy to take them for granted. Of ten lepers cleansed by Jesus (17:14) only one went back to praise and adore the one who had helped him. Do you express your gratitude in worship, in prayer, and in conversation? Our Lord deserves our praise!

Day 21 – Luke 18:1-43

Your Inner Child

Humility is important in God's kingdom. The tax collector in Jesus' parable (18:9-14) was humble enough to realize that he, a sinner, had to rely totally on God's mercy. Jesus said anyone who comes to God must do so "as a little child" (18:17), simply trusting Him. As you get older, are you making sure you don't lose your inner child?

Day 22 – John 9:1-41

The Blind Man Saw

Jesus gave sight to a man who had been born blind, then the man boldly testified about the one who had healed him, even in the face of pressure from the Pharisees. In a way, the religious experts were blinder than the blind man was. Physically they might have had perfect vision, but spiritually they were in the dark. Pride will do that to you!

Day 23 – Luke 19:1-48

Jesus Wants to Change Lives

When Jesus went to Zacchaeus' house, it was a scandal. This fellow was a chief tax collector, which to the Jews was a miserable occupation. He wasn't a proper host for a respectable rabbi! Yet he showed true repentance and a changed life after meeting Jesus. It's all about what Jesus came to do: "to seek and to save that which was lost" (19:10).

Day 24 – Luke 20:1-47

Government Comes from God

Jesus' enemies tried to trap Him by getting Him to say that people shouldn't pay taxes (20:20-26). But Jesus said they should give the government its due. Authorities exist because God has determined it to be so, and all have their God-intended role. Of course we should refuse to sin, but beyond that we should obey authority. That honors God.

Day 25 – John 10:1-42

God's Sheep from Eternity

Jesus is the Good Shepherd, and we are His sheep. Isn't it great to realize that God knows us, and always has? If we have trusted in Christ to save us, it means we are among those whom God has chosen from eternity to be His very own, and we always will be. Nothing can ever separate us from God (10:28). Do you feel the power of that assurance?

Day 26 – John 11:1-57

The Heartbreak of Sin

The Bible's shortest verse (11:35) is a profound one. The death of Lazarus made Jesus weep. Death got started because of sin—an awful, ugly destroyer that breaks our hearts as we experience its sad effects—sickness, hatred, violence, death. Even though Jesus knew He could raise Lazarus, He wept over the sin that hurts people and spoils His creation.

Day 27 – Mark 13:1-37

Our Mission

As Jesus described the events leading up to His return, He said "the gospel must first be preached to all nations" (13:10).

Maybe you'd like to become a preacher, or maybe a missionary. But aren't you one now? You can help deliver the good news to your friends today. All believers are ambassadors for Christ. That's our mission as we wait for Him!

Day 28—Luke 22:1-71

The Unimportance of Importance

Right up until the time Jesus was turned over to be crucified, His disciples still argued about who of them was the greatest! Jesus told them that the greatest should be as the least, and "he who governs as he who serves" (22:26). Jesus was a true servant. When you're tempted to dwell on importance and respect, do you remember our humble Lord?

Day 29 – Matthew 27:1-66

Life Isn't Fair

The Son of God, the only perfect man who ever lived, was killed by a bunch of corrupt sinners. Life isn't fair. Maybe you think you've been treated unfairly, that you deserve better from the people around you. But you're not walking anywhere that Jesus hasn't already been. And in all that He endured, He never sinned; He just forgave!

Day 30 – Luke 24:1-53

The Most Extreme Love

The risen Jesus appeared to two of His followers on the road to Emmaus, and "He opened their understanding" about the Scriptures. Now that Jesus has risen and ascended to heaven, we can look back and see how the whole Bible points to Him. God always knew He would send His Son to save sinners. That's the most extreme kind of love there is!

INDEX TO BIBLICAL INSIGHTS, DEVOTIONS FOR COUPLES AND ROMANTIC QUOTES AND NOTES

Biblical Insights *(B)* and Devotions for Couples *(DC)* are listed with their corresponding scriptures; Romantic Quotes and Notes *(R)* are listed by page number.

INDEX TO PARENTING MATTERS

NOTES

NOTES

NOTES

NOTES

NOTES

NOTES

NOTES

NOTES

NOTES

NOTES

BRIGHT NOTES

DON QUIXOTE BY MIGUEL DE CERVANTES SAAVEDRA

Intelligent Education

INFLUENCE
PUBLISHERS

Nashville, Tennessee

BRIGHT NOTES: Don Quixote

www.BrightNotes.com

ISBN: 978-1-645423-40-9 (Paperback)

ISBN: 978-1-645423-41-6 (eBook)

Published in accordance with the U.S. Copyright Office Orphan Works and Mass Digitization report of the register of copyrights, June 2015.

Originally published by Monarch Press.

Gregor Roy; Ralph A. Ranald; John Jay Allen, 1965

2019 Edition published by Influence Publishers.

Interior design by Lapiz Digital Services. Cover Design by Thinkpen Designs.

Printed in the United States of America.

Library of Congress Cataloging-in-Publication Data forthcoming.

Names: Intelligent Education

Title: BRIGHT NOTES: Don Quixote

Subject: STU004000 STUDY AIDS / Book Notes

CONTENTS

INTRODUCTION TO MIGUEL DE CERVANTES SAAVEDRA

Miguel de Cervantes Saavedra was born in 1547 in Alcalá de Henares, a university town near Madrid, probably on September 29, the fourth of seven children of Rodrigo de Cervantes, an itinerant apothecary-surgeon of extremely limited means. We know almost nothing of the first twenty years of Cervantes' life. His father moved the family several times, and it is probable that Miguel studied as a boy with the Jesuits in Seville. In 1568 he is known to have studied in the City School of Madrid, where he was a favored pupil of Juan López de Hoyos, a Spanish disciple of Erasmus. Cervantes' first poems date from this period.

In 1569, Cervantes traveled to Italy, probably fleeing from the authorities, who had ordered the arrest of one Miguel de Cervantes in Madrid for his involvement in a duel, and condemned him in absentia to have his right hand cut off and to ten years of exile from the court.

In Italy, he served briefly in the entourage of Guilio Acquaviva, named cardinal in 1570, but soon joined the Spanish army in Naples, then under the Spanish crown. He fought in the historic naval battle of Lepanto, in 1571, where the Turkish fleet was defeated, and lost the use of his left hand as a result of one of several wounds. After a brief period of convalescence, he continued his military career, participating in the campaign of 1572–73 on the North Africa coast. The ship on which Miguel and his brother, Rodrigo, were returning to Spain in 1575 was captured by pirates, and the two were taken to Algiers as prisoners and held for ransom. Although Rodrigo was ransomed after two years, the sum demanded for Miguel's release was not raised until 1580, when, after five years of captivity and several heroic but unsuccessful attempts to escape, he was finally able to return to Spain.

Cervantes married Catalina de Salazar y Palacios in 1584 and published his first novel, *La Galatea*, in 1585. During the mid-1580s he wrote a number of plays, of which only two, *La Numantia* and *Pictures of Algiers*, have survived. For a number of years beginning in 1587 he held the post of commissary of the government, which involved him in the requisitioning of supplies for the armed forces. His tenure in this post was marked by a series of financial and other difficulties with higher authorities, resulting in his being jailed briefly in 1592, and again for three months in 1597, for irregularities in his accounts, owing on the latter occasion to the failure of a banker with whom he had deposited government money.

In 1604, Cervantes moved to Valladolid, and published in 1605 the first part of *Don Quixote*. Though the work was an immediate success, his own share of the profits did not significantly improve his marginal financial situation. When the Court moved from Valladolid back to Madrid in 1606, Cervantes also returned, and in 1613 his collection of twelve short stories, the *Exemplary Novels*, was published. In 1614 his verse eulogy of contemporary authors, *The Journey to Parnassus*, appeared followed in 1615 by the second part of *Don Quixote* and *Eight Comedies and Eight Interludes*. Miguel de Cervantes died on

April 22, 1616, and his last novel, *The Hardships of Persiles and Sigismunda*, was published posthumously in 1617.

HISTORICAL AND LITERARY BACKGROUND

Cervantes lived and wrote during what has since come to be called the Siglo de Oro - the Golden Century - a period spanning most of the 16th and 17th centuries, during which Spain achieved tremendous successes - political, military, literary, and artistic. The groundwork was laid for the ascendancy of this first of the modern nations which have successively taken the role of dominant power in Europe by the unification of the Crowns of Aragón and Castile through the marriage of Ferdinand and Isabella in 1469; by their successful completion, in 1492, of the Reconquest of Spain from the Moors, who had been pushed gradually further and further toward the straits of Gibraltar in the centuries since their initial holy war gained them almost the entire Iberian peninsula in 711; and by the discovery of America.

Charles V ascended to the throne in 1517, and, as king of Spain and Holy Roman Emperor, came to control a vast empire which included most of Italy, Germany, Holland, Belgium and Spain, parts of France, and nearly all of Central and South America.

Spanish Inquisition

But if Cervantes was born at the close of the period of imperial expansion, in a Spain which still looked outward on the world, open to all of the intellectual ferment of Renaissance Europe, his literary production came at a time when Spain had turned in upon herself, having failed to achieve the Catholic unity of

Europe which had been her ideal, and beset by foreign enemies from without, and by financial and economic instability from within. In the Spain of Philip II (1556–1598) and his successors, the works of Erasmus, who had been more popular in Spain than anywhere else in Europe, were banned by the Inquisition, and in 1559, Spain, which had founded a College for Spaniards in Bologna two centuries earlier, forbade any foreign study for her youth.

DEFEAT OF THE ARMADA

Cervantes' own life is intimately bound up with major events on both sides of the watershed of Spain's imperial destiny. He refers again and again in subsequent years to his participation in the great Spanish victory over the Turks at Lepanto in 1571, which he saw as "the greatest occasion which any age, past, present, or future, ever saw or can ever hope to see" (II, Prologue); yet only seventeen years later, after the long African captivity and his return, impoverished, to Spain, he was reduced to the unpleasant post of government agent, requisitioning supplies for the ill-fated "Invincible" Armada, whose defeat in 1588 marked the beginning of the nation's long and painful decline.

FROM RENAISSANCE TO BAROQUE PERIOD

This political and historical watershed between Spanish hegemony in Europe and decline and decadence has also its literary parallel, for if Cervantes was born and raised in the period of the full flowering of the Renaissance in Spain, he published his masterpiece in the early years of the Baroque period, in which the dominant elements of Renaissance style are intensified, exaggerated, twisted, parodied, and in general subjected to various kinds of extreme elaboration. If Renaissance literature in Spain is characterized by simplicity, clarity and elegance, as in the poetry of Garcilaso, for example, or the pastoral novels of Montemayor and Gil Polo, the characteristic productions of the Baroque are the brilliantly sensuous images of Góngora and the difficult Latinized **syntax** of his *Soledades* (1613), or the sharp and subtle word-play and hyperbolic **satire** of Quevedo's *Buscón* (1626). The two major tendencies of Baroque style, conceptismo and cultismo, exemplified in Quevedo and in Góngora, respectively, share a common ground of complexity, exaggeration, stylization, and consequent unreality, which can be related to a pervasive feeling of doubt, dissatisfaction, and disillusionment, whether reflected in savage **satire** and **parody**, or in elegant escapism. The transitoriness of earthly existence, the deceptions of appearances, the inevitability of death - these are all **themes** common to both of these great Baroque writers, bitter enemies though they were of one another.

Cervantes seems to have absorbed the deepest and most central aspects of both the Renaissance and the Baroque sensibilities: a kind of Renaissance balance and serenity which embraces the full range of troubling Baroque uncertainty. As a learned Oriental critic has written, "*Don Quixote* was written with the pen of doubt upon the paper of conviction.

DON QUIXOTE AS TRANSITIONAL WORK

As is the case with many literary masterpieces, *Don Quixote* represents the culmination of what had gone before, as a kind of compendium of all of the main lines of the development of fiction in 16th-century Spain, and provides at the same time the foundation for the subsequent development of the novel. *La Celestina* (1499–1502), Fernando de Rojas' novel in dialogue, can in turn be seen as the culmination of the Middle Ages and initiation of the Renaissance. In *La Celestina*, Rojas combined two central tendencies off Renaissance aesthetics - Neoplatonic idealism and the critical observation of reality. The rarified atmosphere in which the two noble lovers, Calixto and Melibea, live contrasts sharply with the crude reality of the go-between Celestina and the servants. Sixteenth-century fiction developed both of these lines in isolation, and not until their inspired fusion in *Don Quixote*, in 1605, were they brought together again.

The principal types of prose fiction in Spain during the hundred years before the publication of *Don Quixote* were the novels of chivalry and the pastoral novels, representing the ideal plane, and the picaresque, drawn from the direct critical observation of the most sordid aspects of contemporary Spanish life.

NOVELS OF CHIVALRY

The most widely read novels of the first half of the 16th century in Spain were the novels of chivalry. The progenitor of this literary vogue was Garci-Rodríguez de Montalvo's Amadis of Gaul (1508.) It was the exploits of Amadis which led Don Quixote to choose him over Roland as his model. Medieval in inspiration (Montalvo's Amadis is a reworking of 14th-century material), the novels of chivalry struck a responsive chord in Renaissance idealism. They narrate the extraordinary adventures of knights-errant, who perform fantastic deeds for the glory of their ladies, righting wrongs and protecting the innocent, in interminable peregrination through unknown lands. These novels are of course of central importance for the creation of *Don Quixote*, as the cause of Don Quixote's madness and the pattern for his existence as knight-errant.

PASTORAL NOVELS

A second type of poetic, idealizing novel began to flourish in Spain with the publication of *La Diana*, by Jorge de Montemayor, in 1559, and became as popular in the second half of the century as the novels of chivalry had been in the first, though written for a more limited, aristocratic public. The models for these novels were works of the Italian Renaissance: Petrarch (*Carmen Bucolicum*), Boccaccio (*Ninfale Fiesolano* and *Ameto*), and above all Sannazaro, whose *Arcadia* (1504) was translated into Spanish in 1547.

A mixture of prose and verse, the pastoral novel places courtiers disguised as shepherds in an idealized bucolic setting of green fields and crystal springs, embroiled in insoluble amorous mismatchings which are the subject of endless Neoplatonic rationalizations and lyrical laments. If the novels of chivalry involve constant action, the pastoral **genre** substitutes a constant analysis which paralyzes action. It is nevertheless unwise to dismiss out of hand what strikes us today as a totally conventional and artificial **genre**, for Cervantes, whose first attempt at fiction, *La Galatea* (1585) was a pastoral novel, noted well the advance in psychological penetration which the **genre** represented, and important **episodes** in Part I of *Don Quixote* have their roots in the pastoral.

PICARESQUE NOVELS

Neither the chivalric nor the pastoral, however, provided Cervantes with the fictional world - contemporary reality - the language - unaffected contemporary Spanish, including slang and proverbs - or the tone - pervasive **irony** - which he needed for *Don Quixote*. All of these were to be found in the picaresque, and indigenous Spanish creation which began with the anonymous *Lazarillo de Tormes* in 1554, and achieved its greatest public success in *Guzmán de Alfarache* (1599–1604), whose second part appeared only months before the first part of *Don Quixote*. The following are the principal characteristics of the genre:

1. autobiographical narration of the life of a picaro, who usually serves a succession of masters, which leads to

2. **satire** of different elements of society as seen through the eyes of the picaro, whose movements are restricted to

3. a socially and morally low plane, in a known geographical area. In order to survive in these circumstances, the picaro's efforts are directed toward

4. the satisfaction of the most elementary necessities of life; the picaro's antagonist is hunger.

5. Development of his own ingenuity and craftiness becomes essential for survival.

The picaro is an anti-hero, a "half-outsider" who looks at society with a jaundiced eye, the victim of his own weakness and society's cynicism and hypocrisy. In one of Lazarillo's masters, the squire, we can see one of the literary antecedents of *Don Quixote*. The proud but penniless squire, whose sense of his own importance far outstrips his own realistically appraised possibilities, is a pale fore-runner of the Manchegan knight, and Lazarillo pities the man for his folly, much as the reader of Cervantes pities the mad knight.

OTHER GENRES

Among the other, less important **genres** of the 16th century - the sentimental novel, the Moorish tale, and the Italian novella, or short story - the last of these is perhaps the most influential in Cervantes, both as inspiration for his *Exemplary Novels* (1613), and as a model for "The Tale of Foolish Curiosity," interpolated in Part I of *Don Quixote* (I, 33–35).

These, then, were the conditions of Spain and the literary traditions which produced the first - and still perhaps the greatest - modern novel.

CERVANTES' LITERARY CAREER

The evolution of Cervantes' novelistic technique has never been satisfactorily delineated by literary critics and historians. It has often perplexed critics to note that Cervantes' first work, *La Galatea* (1585), is an example of the highly artificial and imitative **genre** of the pastoral novel, and that he refers several times throughout the rest of his life to a "second part," in which he seems to have been interested even as he was writing *Don Quixote*. The curate finds a copy of *La Galatea* in the course of his scrutiny of *Don Quixote's* library, and concludes that "we must wait for the second part which he [Cervantes] promises," and in the Prologue to *Don Quixote* II, and even in the Dedication of his *Persiles*, he is still promising the reader this continuation of *La Galatea*. The problem for criticism is of course the reconciliation of this affection for the stylized and artificial pastoral in the author who created the modern realistic novel. It is in fact Cervantes himself who first points out the artificiality of the **genre**, in one of his exemplary novels, "The Colloquy of the Dogs," when Berganza brings up the discrepancy between the lives of real shepherds and those books "dreamed up and well written for the entertainment of idle folks, and not true at all." Two aspects of the pastoral novel may have attracted Cervantes. First, it constituted an established **genre** and therefore a logical vehicle for a writer's apprenticeship, and one which combined prose and verse, thus affording a place for the poetry which Cervantes very much wanted to write successfully. Second, it also afforded the opportunity for a degree of psychological penetration in the characters' introspective laments.

CERVANTES' INTEREST IN DELUSION

After publishing *La Galatea* at thirty-eight years of age, Cervantes published nothing further until 1605, when *Don Quixote* appeared. Yet, extraordinarily, this book, published when he was fifty-eight, was only the beginning of his real literary legacy. In 1613 his *Exemplary Novels* appeared, establishing Cervantes as the founder of the modern Spanish short story. Although the influence of the Italian novellieri can be seen in some of these stories, the best of the collection: "Rinconete and Cortadillo," "The Deceitful Marriage," "The Colloquy of the Dogs," are entirely original in content, conception and style. "Rinconete and Cortadillo" and "The Colloquy of the Dogs" each share some characteristics with the picaresque novel, though neither falls entirely within the **genre**. Another of the stories in this group, "The Man of Glass," reflects the interest in madness and delusion which is so important in the creation of *Don Quixote*. There are twelve stories in all, which critics tend to divide roughly in half, one group of realistic stories contrasting with another of romantic, Italianate tales.

In 1615 both *Don Quixote* II and *Eight Comedies and Eight Interludes* appeared. The eight plays, never produced, reveal

Cervantes' attempt to come to terms with the new conditions which Lope de Vega's outstanding talent and prolificness had imposed upon the theater. The plays in this volume are all of the Lopean, three-act, construction, as opposed to Cervantes' earlier predilection for four or five acts. They are quite overshadowed by the interludes published with them. These are brief, farcical pieces in prose or verse which were presented between the acts of full-length Golden Age plays, and Cervantes is the acknowledge master of the **genre**. His interludes are often presented even today.

AN UNRESOLVED DILEMMA

Cervantes' last prose work, *The Hardships of Persiles and Sigismunda*, published posthumously in 1617, presents another enigma for the critics. Why, after creating the modern realistic novel, did Cervantes turn again to a stylized and artificial **genre**, this time the so-called Byzantine novel of *Heliodorus*, a Greek author of the fourth century, A.D., whose work was popular in Spanish translation? Some critics, unable to accept this dramatic change or reversal of aesthetic orientation, have talked of the rapid onset of senility, or suggested that *Persiles* is a work written much earlier, and published in the wake of the fame of *Don Quixote*, but most have seen Cervantes' last work as an ambitious, though flawed, effort to write the prose **epic** which he had mentioned in *Don Quixote* (I, 47), in the symbolic adventures of his pair of idealized lovers. The most recent criticism has emphasized the unresolved dilemma which the book reflects between the canons of Aristotelian criticism and Cervantes' instinctive advocacy of unrestricted freedom for the creative writer, and the symbolic interpretation of the movement of the plot.

DON QUIXOTE

. . . .

Perhaps even more indicative of Cervantes' importance for the subsequent development of the novel as a **genre** than the consistent critical acclaim that his masterpiece has received, is the debt acknowledged to him by almost every major novelist of the past three hundred years. Lionel Trilling has said that "all prose fiction is a variation of *Don Quixote*." The novel prior to Cervantes, whether chivalric, pastoral or picaresque, had been episodic and linear. The novels of chivalry presented an interminable series of adventures, and the picaresque an equally arbitrary string of **episodes** linked only by the presence of the **protagonist**, unfinishable by its very nature as autobiographical narrative, as Ginés de Pasamonte reveals when he tells Don Quixote that he has written his own picaresque autobiography:

"And is it finished?" asked Don Quixote.

"How can it be finished," he answered, "if my life isn't over yet?"

The disguised courtiers of the pastoral are paralyzed by the circumstances of their impossible love affairs; in *La Diana* the author was obliged to resort to a magic potion for the resolution of the tangled love affairs, and it is precisely this aspect of the novel which Cervantes explicitly criticizes (I, 6). *Don Quixote* contrasts with all of these in the finality and conclusiveness of its ending, and in its effectiveness as an organic whole, with coherent development of the characters replacing an arbitrarily ordered series of episodes.

The paramount importance of *Don Quixote* was recognized by Fielding, who wrote *Joseph Andrews* "in imitation of the manner of Cervantes," by Smollet, who translated the novel, and by Sterne. In French literature, the parallel between *Don Quixote* and *Madame Bovary* has become classic, and Flaubert repeatedly indicates his admiration for Cervantes. Among the great Russian novelists, Dostoyevsky's *Idiot* bears an obvious relationship to *Don Quixote*, and Turgenev wrote one of the best-known essays on the novel, contrasting *Don Quixote* with *Hamlet*.

CERVANTES' INNOVATIONS

Interest has not diminished in the 20th century, and writers as different as Thomas Mann, Miguel de Unamuno, W. H. Auden, and J. L. Borges have paid tribute to Cervantes' masterpiece. Many of the central preoccupations of writers of modern fiction were first explored in depth by Cervantes: the **protagonist** as sympathetic anti-hero, who finds himself in opposition to the rest of the world, the ironic vision which stresses the disparity between heroic aspirations and human limitations, "magic" **realism**, the elaboration of character through self-revelation in action alone, unencumbered by commentary, and a concomitant ambiguity and authorial detachment, to mention only a few.

The central focus of interest, for novelists, psychologists, and philosophers, as well as for the ordinary reader, is not such abstractions as the ideal vs. the real, or the intrinsic value of chivalric idealism, but rather the masterful elaboration of the characters Don Quixote and Sancho, and the subtlety and complexity of their interrelationship as revealed in the dialogue. *Don Quixote* is above all a novel of character, not of action, and this is perhaps its primary legacy to modern fiction.

LAING AND CERVANTES

The Romantic interpretation mentioned above of Don Quixote as the exaltation of the idealistic knight in a futile confrontation with an unworthy environment is still very much alive, and in the world of *Dr. Strangelove* and *Catch-22*, where Western Civilization itself seems to have come unhinged, the figure of Don Quixote standing erect in solitary opposition to his world has a strange new appeal, as an illustration of R. D. Laing's point that schizophrenia could be a logical answer to an insane world. Perhaps these circumstances account for the fact that while contemporary Cervantine criticism has moved away from the Romantic view in an attempt to recapture Cervantes' own attitude toward his **protagonist**, the popular, re-creations of the novel which have proliferated in recent years have all been unabashedly romantic.

MAN OF LA MANCHA

The first of these recent adaptations was a television production called *I, Don Quixote*, produced in the late 1950s and starring Lee J. Cobb. This work seems to have been the basis for the hit Broadway musical of 1965, *Man of La Mancha*, by Dale

Wasserman, which was in turn made into a film with the same title, starring Peter O'Toole. Then in 1972 the BBC screened "The Adventures of Don Quixote," starring Rex Harrison, one of the most ambitious productions they have ever mounted. All of these productions reflect the conception which the Romantics had of the book, and thus all embody decisions on essential matters which Cervantes purposely left ambiguous, and all violate the text at significant points. Dulcinea is a character in these adaptations, although she never appears in the novel, either as Dulcinea or as Aldonza, the peasant girl, and they all distort the novel's ending, replacing Don Quixote's categorical renunciation of his chivalric fantasies with the re-kindling of his former ideals and aspiration at his dying moment.

But the novel itself refuses to submit to such simplistic solutions. Ortega y Gasset's questions about *Don Quixote* still stand:

Is Cervantes joking? And what is he making fun of?

COOVER ON CERVANTES

As a final indication of the relevance of *Don Quixote* for contemporary thought and fiction, even for those novelists who are straining to break the molds of fiction which Cervantes cast and which have yet to be transcended, here are the words of Robert Coover, contemporary novelist and short-story writer, in the "Dedicatoria y Prólogo a don Miguel de Cervantes Saavedra" to "Seven Exemplary Fictions," in his *Pricksongs and Descants: Fictions* (New York: Dutton and Co., 1969):

Your stories also exemplified the dual nature of all good narrative art: they struggled against the

unconscious mythic residue in human life and sought to synthesize the unsynthesizable, sallied forth against adolescent thought modes and art forms, and returned home with new complexities. In fact, your creation of a synthesis between poetic analogy and literal history (not to mention reality and illusion, sanity and madness, the erotic and the ludicrous, the visionary and the scatological) gave birth to the Novel - perhaps above all else your works were exemplars of a revolution in narrative fiction, a revolution which governs us - not unlike the way you found yourself abused by the conventions of the Romance - to this very day (p. 27).

DON QUIXOTE IN OTHER MEDIA

Don Quixote, as we have seen, has leaped from the printed page to the cinema, TV screen, and musical-comedy stage. The student interested in Cervantes' influence on artists in other media can also trace the *Don Quixote* **theme** in such diverse forms as painting, symphonic composition, opera, and ballet. For example, Cervantes must be credited with inspiring: one of the best water-color paintings of *Honoré Daumier* (1808–1879), "Don Quixote and Sancho Panza," which hangs in the Metropolitan Museum of Art in New York; the tone poem *Don Quixote* (1898) with which the composer Richard Strauss is said to have "reached his zenith as a musical realist"; a dozen operas on the same **theme**, most prominent of which is *Don Quichotte* (1910) by Jules Massenet; and most recently in dance. Rudolph Nureyev's film version of the Russian ballet, *Don Quixote*, which has received enthusiastic critical acclaim.

DON QUIXOTE

. . . .

PRELIMINARIES

The standard 17th-century preliminaries precede Chapter I: Terms of Sale, Royal Privilege, Certificate of Errors, Dedication (to the Duke of Béjar, patron of Cervantes at the time), the Prologue, and ten introductory poems.

Comment

The Prologue is unconventional, and reveals many basic features of Cervantes' art. In place of the usual prologue, we are given a treatment of the problem of writing a prologue, just as the novel itself is, to a significant extent, about the writing of a novel. Cervantes relates that he was meditating upon the difficulty of composing a prologue for *Don Quixote*, and was in fact on the point of not publishing the novel, when a friend came to visit and told him how to proceed, with a series of satiric thrusts at the pedantry of Lope de Vega and others of Cervantes' contemporaries. Cervantes presents the dialogue between himself and his friend as his prologue, thus revealing another essential element of his art, for dialogue is central to *Don Quixote*. By placing his friend's remarks at the center of the Prologue, Cervantes also achieves the kind of distance and detachment characteristic of the whole work, which is always presented through authorial intermediaries. Such a distance between Cervantes and his characters is alluded to early in the Prologue when Cervantes tells us that he is not Don Quixote's father, but his stepfather. There is also an **allusion** in the prologue to Don Quixote's having been conceived in jail, and many critics date the beginning of the composition from 1597, when Cervantes was in jail in Seville.

Finally, in the friend's remarks there is a very clear statement of Cervantes' purpose in writing Part I: "the entire work is an attack upon the books of chivalry." Don Quixote is of course much more than this, but the reader can scarcely afford to overlook such a clear and categorical statement, written after Part I had been completed.

The introductory poems are included to **parody** the usual prefatory verses in praise of the author and the work. Among them are poems by Amadis of Gaul and Belianis of Greece, two heroes of chivalric novels, to Don Quixote, and one by Babieca, the horse of the Spanish **epic** hero El Cid, to Don Quixote's horse Rocinante.

CHAPTER 1

The novel begins with a description of Alonso Quijano, a country gentleman from *La Mancha* of about fifty, and his household, and relates that he goes crazy from reading too many novels of chivalry. He decides to become a knight-errant like those whose exploits had so fascinated him in the novels, and takes great pains to name himself (Don Quixote de la Mancha), his horse, a bony nag (Rocinante), and his lady (Dulcinea del Toboso). The girl whom he makes mistress of his thoughts is a peasant girl named Aldonza Lorenzo whom he scarcely knows.

He carefully cleans a set of ancestral armor, and upon finding that his helmet is missing the visor, he constructs one of cardboard. When he tests his work with a blow and it falls apart, he rebuilds it, and, refusing to test it again, "he adopts it then and there as the finest helmet ever made."

Comment

The initial paragraphs of the novel are filled with details of Alonso Quijano's circumstances: the clothes he wore, the food he ate, etc... , which, though largely meaningless to a modern reader, gave Cervantes' contemporaries a very precise idea of what we would now call the socio-economic condition of the **protagonist**. This is very important for an understanding of Alonso Quijano's motivation in his bizarre undertaking. Alonso Quijano was a country gentleman of the lesser nobility - a hidalgo, a type which the contemporary reader had already met in the famous Lazarillo de Tormes, the first picaresque novel of which we have already spoken. Lazarillo's third master was just such a man, and had left his country home to seek his fortune at court. He was a man with a great sense of his own self-importance, who insisted upon being treated with the respect to which he felt his pretensions to nobility entitled him, though he was penniless and starving. Lazarillo pitied him because of the miserable existence to which his presumption condemned him. Alonso Quijano's assumption of the title of respect, Don, would have clearly indicated similar pretensions to 17th-century readers. Cervantes himself, by the way, never assumed the title Don for himself.

The author establishes early in the first chapter the idea that he is not writing a novel, but rather compiling a history derived from a number of conflicting sources. Thus, some say his name was Quijada, others Quesada, but "according to the most likely conjectures we are to understand that it was really Quejana."

Don Quixote's attitude toward his rebuilt visor gives the reader an important initial indication as to how he will react to adverse experience: he believes that the visor is sound, and does not put it to the test again.

CHAPTER 2

Don Quixote imagines how the story of his exploits will begin, and extemporizes a flowery **epic** beginning for his story. He then addresses an apostrophe to Dulcinea in the archaic language used by the knights of Amadis of Gaul and other chivalric novels. Another difference of opinion among several authors is recorded, as to which was the first adventure encountered by Don Quixote. He arrives at an inn, which he takes for a castle, and politely greets two prostitutes at the gate as if they were ladies, which indeed he takes them to be.

Comment

Don Quixote is shown to be a master of style, not only of the archaic style of the novels of chivalry, but also of contemporary high, rhetorical style. His principal motivation in sallying forth is explicitly shown to be the desire for fame, and the idea that his exploits must be recorded for posterity is central to that desire.

CHAPTER 3

Don Quixote convinces the innkeeper to knight him, and keeps vigil over his arms in the courtyard during the night which is to precede the ceremony. When a mule-driver pushes the armor away to get water from the well, Don Quixote deals him a fierce blow with his lance. Another driver gets the same treatment, and the innkeeper decides to go on with the ceremony and get Don Quixote on his way and out of his inn. With the assistance of the two prostitutes, who arm the new knight with sword and spurs, the innkeeper knights Don Quixote, and the new knight leaves the inn to seek adventure.

CHAPTER 4

On the road again, Don Quixote comes upon a farmer whipping a young lad, Andrés, tied to a tree. He frees the boy and demands that the farmer pay the boy the back wages due him. The farmer gives his word, and Don Quixote leaves, "very well satisfied with himself." As soon as he is out of sight, however, the farmer ties Andrés to the tree again and beats him severely, taunting him by mocking Don Quixote.

The knight next encounters a party of merchants on their way to Murcia. He demands that they swear that Dulcinea is the most beautiful girl in the world, and when one of the merchants asks to see a picture of her in order to have some basis for decision, Don Quixote asserts that the important thing is precisely that they affirm her supremacy without having seen her. The merchant again asks for some evidence, insulting Dulcinea in the process. Don Quixote immediately attacks. Rocinante stumbles and falls, and one of the lads with the merchants breaks the knight's lance and beats him severely with the pieces. Don Quixote has been so badly beaten that he can't get up, but still considers himself fortunate at having had a "chivalric" adventure.

Comment

The **irony** in the **episode** of the boy, Andrés, is very strongly stressed by Cervantes, and it is perhaps here that different readers of the novel begin to diverge in their reactions to the **protagonist**. Those who are moved by Don Quixote's sincere efforts to right the wrongs of the world are impressed by his actions, while those more affected by Cervantes' **irony** feel strongly the inadequacy of Quixote's intervention, his deliberate disregard for the circumstances, and his pompous self-satisfaction.

CHAPTER 5

A neighbor of Don Quixote's finds him still lying on the ground, reciting verses from chivalric **ballads** and confusing himself with two heroes, Valdovinos, and the Moor Abindarráez. The neighbor takes him home, where the local curate and the barber are discussing his disappearance with his niece and his housekeeper. He is immediately put to bed to recover.

CHAPTER 6

While Don Quixote sleeps, the curate goes through the books in his library to eliminate the cause of his madness. He examines a series of novels of chivalry, a few pastoral novels, and several Renaissance epics, consigning most to be burned in the courtyard in a mock inquisition.

Comment

The scrutiny of Don Quixote's library is a device for Cervantes to comment upon 16th-century literature and to elaborate upon his dissatisfaction with the novels of chivalry. Since Amadis of Gaul and Tirante el Blanco are both spared, it is clear that it is not the **genre** itself which Cervantes condemns, but rather the pretentious and clumsy style and the lack of verisimilitude which he feels characterize the majority of the works.

CHAPTER 7

The curate has the library door walled up, and Don Quixote is told that the enchanter Frestón has carried off the library with all its books. Don Quixote determines to sally forth again, and he enlists a peasant from the neighborhood, Sancho Panza, as his squire, promising him the governorship of an island when one should fall to him among the fruits of his chivalric victories. Sancho rides off with his new master, quite content with his prospects, though he has difficulty imagining his wife in the high social station that she will occupy if his expectations are fulfilled.

CHAPTER 8

The first adventure of this second sally is the famous battle with the windmills. Despite Sancho's assertion that the giants Don

Quixote says he is attacking are windmills, the knight attacks at full gallop and is thrown from Rocinante by the force of the encounter. He explains the disaster by affirming that the enchanter who made off with his library has turned the giants into windmills to rob him of the glory of defeating them.

Comment

We realize at this point that the priest's explanation for the disappearance of the library has afforded Don Quixote a useful device for maintaining his exalted fantasies of his now prowess in the face of defeat: an evil enchanter, opposed to Don Quixote's heroic exploits.

CHAPTER 8 (CONTINUED)

As the two **protagonists** ride on, they meet a party consisting of two friars, a coach, and its accompaniment. Don Quixote imagines that the whole entourage is escorting a captive princess, and immediately attacks. The friars flee, leaving behind a mule, but when Sancho proceeds to loot the saddlebags, the friars' servants take revenge upon the squire, beating him soundly and leaving him lying on the road.

Meanwhile, Don Quixote has approached the coach, and announces to the lady within that she is now free. One of her squires, however, a Biscayan who is riding a mule alongside the coach, tells Don Quixote to mind his own business and go on his way, and a battle ensues. At the **climax** of the fight, with both combatants ready to unleash terrible blows, Cervantes abruptly interrupts, saying that unfortunately at this point his source has given out.

Comment

With this interruption at the climactic point of the battle, Cervantes parodies the feigned dependence of the authors of chivalric novels upon their sources. The interruption also brings to a close the first of four parts into which Cervantes divided the *Don Quixote* of 1605.

CHAPTER 9

The chapter begins with Cervantes' discovery, in the market of Toledo, of a manuscript in Arabic containing more of the adventures of *Don Quixote* written by Cid Hamete Benengeli. This new text relates that Don Quixote defeated the "valorous Biscayan" and announced to the ladies in the coach that they were now free, and asked only that they present themselves before Dulcinea del Toboso. The ladies of course agree, though without the slightest intention of complying with the knight's wishes.

Comment

The introduction of Cid Hamete, henceforth Cervantes' only source, adds yet another factor to the distance which we have seen Cervantes create between himself and his characters, for Cid Hamete is a Moor (Benengeli means eggplant in Arabic), and as Cervantes remarks, it is characteristic of the Moors to be liars.

CHAPTER 10

Sancho picks himself up off the ground and asks Don Quixote to give him the island he had promised him as the fruits of the successful battle, and Don Quixote explains that this was not the sort of encounter which produces any tangible benefits. Don Quixote, who has a bad cut on one ear, laments not having the balm of Fierabras, which would effect a miraculous cure, and swears to win for himself a new helmet to replace his own, which was broken in the battle.

CHAPTER 11

Don Quixote and Sancho decide to spend the night with a group of goatherds nearby, and when he is invited to share their dinner, he magnanimously asks Sancho to sit and eat at his side, in the spirit of equality which he says chivalry fosters. Sancho refuses, saying he would rather eat alone, but Don Quixote forces him to sit and eat with him. The goatherds' acorns inspire Don Quixote to deliver a long speech on the Golden Age, that happy time when innocence and freedom were the rule, before the corrupting influence of "modern" civilization. The goatherds don't understand a word of what he has said, but one of them reciprocates by singing a rustic song.

Comment

The Golden Age speech is one of two major discourses by Don Quixote in Part I (1605) of the novel. It is highly rhetorical and conventional, having its sources in Ovid, Virgil, and the 16th-century Spanish author Fray Luis de Guevara. There is of course **irony** in Don Quixote's choice of audience: the goatherds, quite close to the shepherds of the Golden Age in occupation, don't understand a word. In his exemplary novel, "The Colloquy of the Dogs," Cervantes draws a similar contrast more explicitly between the reality of Spanish shepherds and the **conventions** of the pastoral novel.

CHAPTER 12-14

These three chapters relate an interpolated story: The goatherds relate the unrequited love of a young man, Grisóstomo, for a rich young girl, Marcela, who has chosen the life of a shepherdess, and rejects all romantic entanglements. Grisóstomo has died for love of Marcela, and the goatherds invite Don Quixote to accompany them to his funeral. The knight agrees, and on the way they meet two gentlemen who, realizing that he is crazy, question Don Quixote rather pointedly about Dulcinea's lineage and certain aspects of knight-errantry. The knight replies very defensively, and at that point they arrive at the lonely spot where Grisóstomo has left instructions for his friend Ambrosio to bury him.

One of Grisóstomo's poems is read over his grave, and Marcela makes a dramatic appearance to assert her innocence of the young man's death in a long monologue in the style of the pastoral novel. On finishing her speech, she disappears into the woods, and Don Quixote forbids anyone to follow her, as she has asked to be left alone. Chapter 14 concludes the second of the four parts into which Cervantes originally divided what is now called Part I (1605).

Comment

The encounter with the goatherds and Don Quixote's Golden Age speech have established another plane of idealized pastoral fiction behind the foreground of realistic narrative of the adventures of the knight. The goatherd's introductory narrative of the love of Grisóstomo for Marcela is a masterpiece of stylistic modulation from rustic speech to the rhetorical **conventions** of the pastoral **genre**, so subtly done that the reader scarcely realizes the transition between the two strikingly different modes. The theme of thwarted love will be picked up again in later interpolated stories of Part I.

CHAPTER 15

Don Quixote and Sancho leave the group of mourners at the funeral and stop to rest in the afternoon in a meadow, and Rocinante, attracted by some mares in a nearby field, is rebuffed by the mares and beaten by their drivers. Don Quixote rushes to his defense, and he and Sancho are severely beaten by the drivers. Sancho manages to get Don Quixote on his donkey's back, and leading Rocinante by the reins, they manage to make their way to a nearby inn, which Don Quixote again takes for a castle.

CHAPTER 16

The innkeeper's wife and a grotesquely ugly maidservant, Maritornes, bandage Don Quixote's and Sancho's wounds, which Sancho explains as the result of a fall. The knight and his squire bed down in a large room where a mule-driver is also sleeping, and when Maritornes slips quietly in the middle of the night to keep a date with the mule-driver, Don Quixote, imagining that she is the innkeeper's beautiful daughter, who, overcome with love for him, has come to sleep with him, seizes her arm and protests his inability to comply with what he thinks are her desires. When the mule-driver realizes what is happening, he begins to beat and trample Don Quixote. The innkeeper, hearing the noise, comes to see what is happening, and in the ensuing confusion, Sancho, in whose bed Maritornes has climbed to escape the wrath of her master, and Don Quixote, are both soundly beaten. A member of the local constabulary, awakened by the noise, enters the dark bedroom, and, touching the unconscious Don Quixote, shouts that there has been a murder. At that the innkeeper, Maritornes, and the mule-driver all scatter, and the constable goes for a lamp.

CHAPTER 17

Sancho and Don Quixote awaken, and, unable to move from the beatings they have received, are talking over the events of the night, when the constable returns with a lamp and asks Don Quixote how he feels. Don Quixote is offended at the form of address used by the constable, and insults him, so the man bashes him with the oil lamp and leaves. In the dark once more, both are now convinced that the inn (castle) is enchanted.

Don Quixote sends Sancho to the innkeeper for the ingredients to make the balm of Fierabras, mixes his brew, and drinks it. After being violently ill for a few moments, he sleeps for three hours, and awakes feeling marvelously restored, Sancho then tries the balm, but it produces an even more violent effect upon him, and he feels even worse afterward. Don Quixote's explanation is that since Sancho is not a knight-errant, the balm will apparently not work for him.

Feeling fit again, Don Quixote sallies forth from the inn, refusing to pay when the innkeeper asks for money for the night's lodgings, on the grounds that knights-errant are due such consideration in recompense for their arduous and beneficent profession. Unable to collect from Don Quixote, the innkeeper stops Sancho, and when he, too, refuses, several young rogues at the inn toss the squire in a blanket. The compassionate Maritornes gives Sancho a glass of wine to recover from the shock, and he rides out, quite happy at not having had to pay, but unaware that the innkeeper has taken his saddlebags in payment.

CHAPTER 18

Don Quixote explains to Sancho that he was unable to come to his aid because the enchanter had paralyzed him. Actually, Don Quixote found himself incapable of climbing over the fence to Sancho's rescue because he was so weak from the recent beatings.

The two then see two clouds of dust in the distance bearing down each upon the other. Don Quixote imagines that they are two armies and describes in great detail the knights and the colors of the opposing bands. He rushes to enter the fray, as Sancho shouts to him that a flock of sheep and another of goats are the cause of the dust, and Don Quixote is felled by stones from the slings of the shepherds who are enraged at his destruction of their flocks. Don Quixote is soundly beaten again and loses several teeth in the encounter.

CHAPTER 19

That same night the two encounter a funeral procession on a country road, and Don Quixote attacks and scatters the entourage. One of the men in the group lies pinned beneath his mule, and Don Quixote helps him up and on his way. Sancho, seeing his master's face by torchlight, thin and changed with the recent loss of teeth, refers to him as the Knight of the Mournful Countenance, and Don Quixote accepts the new name as inspired by the sage who is to record his exploits.

Comment

Although the translation of Sancho's new name for Don Quixote (El caballero de la triste figura) is usually Knight of the Sad,

Woeful, or Mournful Countenance, this is not really what was understood by the 17th-century Spanish reader. Shelton's early English translation of "Knight of the Ilfavored Face" is much closer to the original.

CHAPTER 20

Having appropriated the supplies of the funeral entourage as booty from the battle, Sancho is anxious to leave the scene of the crime, and leads Don Quixote into the woods in search of water. They soon hear the sound of a stream, but they can also hear the sound of heavy blows and the noise of chains. Sancho is terrified, and when Don Quixote insists on attacking, despite the darkness of the night, he pleads with him not to leave him alone. When Don Quixote persists in his determination, Sancho ties Rocinante's legs together while he is tightening the cinches, and manages to convince his master that Rocinante must be enchanted. He unties Rocinante just before dawn, and both ride toward the source of the mysterious sounds. After the initial shock of recognition, Don Quixote and Sancho both laugh upon seeing that the noise had been coming from six water-powered fulling hammers. But when Sancho begins to mock Don Quixote's pompous speech of the night before when he was about to attack, the latter becomes so angry that he deals his squire two heavy blows with his lance.

Comment

The reader should note that this is the first time that Sancho uses his master's delusions to gain his own ends. He, in effect, "enchants" Rocinante.

DON QUIXOTE

PART I: CHAPTERS 21–52

. . . .

CHAPTER 21

Having patched up their quarrel as they ride on, the two soon encounter a barber riding on a mule, with his basin on his head to keep off a light rain that has begun to fall. Don Quixote is convinced that the basin is the helmet of Mambrino, and attacks. The barber leaps from his mule and flees, leaving the basin behind. Don Quixote takes up the basin, and Sancho takes the barber's saddlebags and trades the donkey's trappings for those of his own.

As they renew their travels after the "battle," Sancho suggests that it would be a good idea to seek some emperor to serve, in order to attain more quickly the glory and the rewards which they seek. Don Quixote replies that he must first make a name for himself, and then proceeds to sketch the plot of a typical novel of chivalry, casting himself as the hero, culminating the story with his marriage to a princess and the marriage of Sancho to one of her ladies. Sancho listens to the story with mounting enthusiasm, and the chapter concludes with a discussion of how Sancho is to behave in his new role as gentleman.

Comment

In his elaboration of this chivalric fantasy, Don Quixote has forgotten for the moment about Dulcinea, and Sancho does not even seem to remember his wife, Teresa.

CHAPTER 22

The two then come upon a chain of galley slaves en route to the galleys. Don Quixote inquires of each the reasons for his misfortunes, and, though it is clear that they are, in fact, criminals, demands that their guards release them. The guards of course refuse, and are taken by surprise when Don Quixote attacks. With the help of the prisoners the guards are routed, and Don Quixote orders them to go in a group, carrying their chains, to El Toboso, to present themselves before Dulcinea. They refuse, and led by Ginés de Pasamonte, a rogue who was the most heavily chained and who has written his own picaresque biography, they stone Don Quixote and Sancho.

CHAPTER 23

Fearful that the guards may regroup and come after them, Sancho persuades Don Quixote to ride deep into the wilderness of the Sierra Morena mountains, and that night, in a passage which is inexplicably missing from the first edition of the novel, Sancho's donkey is stolen by Ginés de Pasamonte. As they ride on the following morning, they come upon a suitcase abandoned in the woods, from which Sancho extracts an album of poems and letters telling of an unhappy love affair, and more than a hundred gold crowns. Soon after, they catch a glimpse of a wild-looking young man running through the woods, and come upon a dead mule, still saddled. A shepherd whom they meet tells them that the young man entered the area about six months before and that at times he accepts food which they offer him, and at others, when his madness comes upon him, he attacks them and takes food by force. The chapter closes with the meeting of the two madmen, as Don Quixote embraces the young man "as if he had known him for a long time."

CHAPTER 24

The young man, whose name is Cardenio, begins to tell them the story of his misfortunes, at Don Quixote's request, but first stipulates that there be no interruptions in the course of his tale. He tells of the mutual love of himself and Luscinda, equal in wealth and nobility, and sweethearts since childhood. But his praise of Luscinda inflames a nobleman, Fernando, whom Cardenio has gone to serve in a nearby town, and Fernando sees her and falls in love. At this point in the story, Cardenio mentions having lent Luscinda a copy of Amadis of Gaul, and Don Quixote interrupts to praise her taste in books. The interruption breaks Cardenio's train of thought, his madness recurs, and he insults one of the noble characters of Amadis; Don Quixote defends her, Cardenio knocks him down with a rock, and then pummels Sancho and the goatherd, who come to his defense. Sancho ends up fighting with the goatherd over whose fault the whole thing was, and Don Quixote has to separate them. Cardenio, meanwhile, has disappeared into the woods.

CHAPTER 25

As they go on their way, Don Quixote tells Sancho that he has determined to do penance in the mountains, in imitation of Amadis, while Sancho carries a letter to Dulcinea. Here, for the first time, Don Quixote tells Sancho Dulcinea's real name, Aldonza Lorenzo, and the squire launches into rustic praise of her strength and stamina. Don Quixote admits that he has idealized her for his own purposes. He writes a flowery letter to Dulcinea in Cardenio's album in archaic chivalric language lamenting his absence from her, and another ceding Sancho three mules which he had promised him after Sancho's mount was stolen. Don Quixote then asks Sancho to stay and witness some of the mad deeds he will do during his penance, this time in imitation of Roland, crazed by Angelica's infidelity, but Sancho can only bear watching one somersault, and heads out of the mountains toward El Toboso.

Comment

At this point the reader begins to be aware that Don Quixote's madness is more complex than it had seemed. He is obviously conscious of some of the distortions of his chivalric fantasy, as he has shown in his discussion of Dulcinea with Sancho.

CHAPTER 26

The first part of the chapter is devoted to Don Quixote's soliloquy, in which he vacillates between imitating Amadis in sorrowful penance or Roland in crazed activity. He decides finally that Amadis will henceforth be his sole model, and carves verses in praise of Dulcinea on the trees around him.

Sancho, meanwhile, has by the next day reached the inn where he was tossed in a blanket, and, still doubtful as to whether he should risk going in, he meets the curate and the barber from home. Though he tries to avoid it, he finally tells them that he has left Don Quixote doing penance in Sierra Morena to deliver a letter to Dulcinea. At this point he realizes that he has forgotten the album with the two letters, but the curate assures him that he will take care of everything if Sancho will take them back to where Don Quixote awaits. The curate decides that he will dress as a damsel in distress, with the barber in a false beard as his squire, to ask Don Quixote for aid, as a ruse to take him home again.

CHAPTER 27

When they arrive near the place where Sancho left Don Quixote, they send Sancho ahead to announce their arrival, the curate and the barber having exchanged roles when the former decided it was really not proper for a priest to be dressed up like a woman. As they wait they hear a poetic lament nearby, and come upon Cardenio, who continues his story, relating that Fernando asked for Luscinda's hand, was accepted by her parents and married her. Cardenio, who had been sent out of town by Fernando's design, returned in time to witness their wedding, though hidden from view. As soon as she said "I do," Luscinda fainted, and Cardenio took advantage of the confusion to leave the house and ride into Sierra Morena, despairing of his future.

This concludes the third of the four parts of the original *Don Quixote* of 1605.

CHAPTER 28

Scarcely has Cardenio concluded his story when the sounds of another lament are heard, and the three discover a beautiful girl, dressed as a shepherd, washing her feet in a nearby stream. She then tells her story, another tale of an unhappy love affair. Her name is Dorotea, and she has been seduced under promise of marriage by the same Fernando who married Cardenio's Luscinda.

CHAPTER 29

Cardenio tells Dorotea who he is and vows to help her obtain justice from Fernando. Dorotea agrees to play the damsel in distress in the ruse to trick Don Quixote, and when Sancho returns she is introduced to him as the Princess Micomicona. They go to meet Don Quixote, and Dorotea, who is an avid reader of novels of chivalry, invents a tale of a giant who is keeping her from taking possession of her rightful throne. Don Quixote agrees to help her, and the chapter ends with a malicious reference by the curate to the galley slaves whom Don Quixote freed, as he had learned from the innkeeper. He says that the prisoners attacked and robbed him, and that whoever set them free must either be crazy, or as bad as they.

Comment

There is, of course, **irony** in the encounter between Don Quixote, acting the part of the crazed lover in Sierra Morena, and Dorotea, acting the part of the Princess Micomicona: A madman acting mad, and a damsel in distress playing a damsel in distress! Prior to the curate's mention of the galley slaves, Don Quixote's pride has been much inflated by Dorotea's inordinate praise of him, and he does not dare mention that it was he who set the prisoners free.

CHAPTER 30

Sancho reveals that his master was the one who freed the galley slaves, and Don Quixote is mortified. Dorotea tells the story of her lost kingdom, and reveals that the slayer of the giant will win her hand in marriage, and Sancho dances with glee at the prospect of winning his island. When Don Quixote tells Dorotea that he cannot marry her because of Dulcinea, Sancho is so disappointed he insults Don Quixote and even Dulcinea, and his master deals him two blows with his lance. Dorotea makes peace between them, however, and Don Quixote proceeds to interrogate Sancho about his errand to Dulcinea.

CHAPTER 31

As Don Quixote questions his squire about the circumstances of the interview with Dulcinea, Sancho invents a series of details of how the meeting might have taken place with the real Aldonza Lorenzo, and the knight manages to twist every vulgar detail to maintain his idealized vision of Dulcinea. Sancho says that Dulcinea requested that he come to see her, but Don Quixote decides he must first restore Dorotea's kingdom, and consoles Sancho by telling him that even though he does not marry her, he will reward him with the governorship he desires.

At this point Andrés, the lad whom Don Quixote found being whipped by his master, in Chapter 4, appears, and Don Quixote leads the boy before the group of travelers to give testimony to the beneficial activity of knights-errant like himself. When the boy relates the outcome of Don Quixote's intervention, he concludes by begging Don Quixote never to help him again, even if he finds him being skinned alive, and the knight is humiliated once more.

CHAPTER 32

The next day they arrive again at the inn of the blanket-tossing, Don Quixote goes immediately to bed, and when the curate explains to the innkeeper that Don Quixote has gone crazy from reading too many novels of chivalry, the man, his wife and daughter, and even Maritornes reveal themselves to be avid devotees of the **genre**, and that the novels are often read aloud to the assembled guests and laborers at the inn. He brings out a suitcase with several books in it, and as he discusses them with the curate, it is clear that he, too, believes the knights' exploits to be true. Among the books is a short story entitled "The Tale of Foolish Curiosity," which the curate proceeds to read aloud.

Comment

The introduction of the innkeeper who believes in the historical truth of the novels of chivalry offers a needed distinction between committed faith and simple belief. The curate chides him for his credulity, saying: "Please God you do not go lame on the same foot as your guest Don Quixote." The innkeeper's response is significant: "That I shall not. I could never be so mad as to turn knight-errant, for I am aware that the customs of those days when famous knights roamed the world no longer prevail today." The innkeeper is content to affirm the truth of the novels of chivalry; Don Quixote must witness to it.

CHAPTERS 33–35

These chapters consist of the "Tale of Foolish Curiosity," interrupted once at the beginning of Chapter 35 when Don Quixote slashes a pair of wineskins in the room where he is sleeping, thinking he has killed the malignant giant who stands in the way of Dorotea's accession to the throne. Sancho is so blinded by his desire for the governorship that he believes what Don Quixote tells him, saying that he saw the giant's head roll on the floor. As the author says, "Sancho awake was worse than his master asleep."

The "Tale of Foolish Curiosity" takes place in Florence, and tells of two inseparable friends, Anselmo and Lothario. Anselmo marries Camilla, and soon after, begs Lothario to attempt to seduce her, as a test of her fidelity. Lothario reluctantly accepts, and the story runs its logical course to the tragedy of Anselmo's death of grief, on his discovery that his friend and his bride are lovers.

Comment

This interpolated "exemplary novel," omitted by many readers of Don Quixote, is important in the reader's subtly changing attitude toward the **protagonist**. If Don Quixote has been consistently presented as a man of faith, Anselmo is the diametrically opposed man of a reason, who compulsively puts his wife's fidelity to the empirical test. As Lothario tells him, in trying to dissuade him, he is like the Moors, who cannot accept the truths of the Catholic faith without mathematical and tangible proofs. The reader should thus be aware that if Don Quixote's orientation toward existence is erroneous, the solution is not to be found in an opposite orientation of rational empiricism, which if pursued strictly leads to death. The story is also interesting in its deviation from the standard 17th-century concept of the demands of honor, since Anselmo, who by the code of honor consistently exemplified in the theater of the time should have killed Camilla and Lothario, forgives them on his deathbed recognizing that he has gone against nature in his pursuit of certainty. Lothario and Camilla die in the end, he in battle, and she of grief in a convent, but not at the hands of the wronged husband.

CHAPTER 36

At the close of the reading of the story, another group of travelers enters the inn, and in a dramatic scene of recognition, Dorotea and Cardenio are brought face to face with Fernando and Luscinda. We learn that the marriage between Luscinda and Fernando was never consummated, and Dorotea persuades Fernando to honor his obligation to her, thus leaving Luscinda free to marry Cardenio.

CHAPTERS 37–38

Fernando and Dorotea agree to continue with the deception of Don Quixote until they reach his village, and yet another pair of travelers arrives at the inn. The latest arrivals are a man dressed in the garb of a Christian recently freed from captivity by the Moors of North Africa, and his Moorish bride. When all are seated for dinner, Don Quixote, inspired by the fortuitous assembly of such an illustrious group, delivers the second of his major discourses from Part I: The Discourse on Arms and Letters. It is an eloquent speech, free of chivalric archaism and appropriate for and convincing to his listeners. He details the respective goals, hardships, and rewards of the careers of arms and of law, concluding that the profession of arms is superior. His eloquence causes those who are present to pity the fact that his madness has so disturbed such a fine mind.

Comment

Don Quixote's two major discourses, that on the Golden Age, in Chapter 11, and this one on Arms and Letters, serve more than one important function in the novel. The first, though eloquent, is conventional and inappropriate to its audience, while the second is much more original, though on a common **theme** of the time, and is praised by its hearers, thus deepening our admiration for and pity of the mad knight. Both also serve to set the theme for the surrounding context, the first being followed by the pastoral tale of Marcela and Grisóstomo and the second by the captive's tale, an example of the profession of arms, and by the subsequent appearance of the judge, who represents the profession of law.

CHAPTERS 39-41

The recently freed prisoner of the Moors, Ruy Pérez de Viedma, then relates his tale of capture by the Turks at Lepanto, captivity in Algiers, where he knew "a certain Saavedra," who is Cervantes himself, and of his luck in being favored by the daughter of a Moorish nobleman, a girl who had been converted to Christianity without her father's knowledge by a woman captive who worked in the household. After many vicissitudes, the couple make their escape, leaving her anguished father on the African beach.

Comment

The captive's tale contains a great amount of detail relating to Cervantes' own service in the army and captivity in Algiers.

CHAPTER 42

Yet another party of guests arrive at the inn, a judge and his daughter. The judge proves to be Ruy Pérez's brother, and the two are joyously reunited.

CHAPTER 43

A neighbor of the judge's, Luis, the son of a local nobleman, has fallen in love with the judge's daughter and followed them to the inn, disguised as a stable boy. He serenades the girl, Clara, at night, and she confesses to Dorotea who the boy is and the love she feels for him.

Don Quixote has decided to stand watch outside the inn all night, fearful of the danger to the collection of beauties within from evil-doers. Maritornes and the innkeeper's daughter decide to play a trick on him, and calling him from a hayloft near where he keeps his vigil, Maritornes asks for his hand, and ties it firmly to the stable door: Don Quixote has had to stand on Rocinante's saddle to reach the loft and when another group of travelers arrive, Rocinante, attracted by their mares, moves toward them leaving Don Quixote hanging by his wrist a few inches from the ground.

CHAPTER 44

Maritornes unties the rope and the knight falls to the ground, convinced again that evil enchanters are at work. The latest arrivals at the inn are servants of Luis' father, come to bring him home, and when they find him, the judge becomes aware of the boy's love for his daughter. It is clear that this pair of lovers, too, will end up happily married.

Meanwhile, two guests have attempted to leave the inn without paying, and the innkeeper is being badly beaten in an attempt to collect from them. Maritornes and the innkeeper's wife and daughter ask Don Quixote to help him, and in a nice piece of poetic justice, Don Quixote is unable to comply, first because he must ask Dorotea's permission, since he is temporarily in her service, and then, permission having been granted, because he notes that the combatants are not knights-errant. Eventually, however, he manages to convince them to stop fighting, and no sooner have things calmed down when the barber from whom Don Quixote took the helmet of Mambrino comes into the inn, and, recognizing the trappings of his mule on Sancho's donkey, begins to fight with him. Don Quixote separates them, and sends Sancho for the helmet to prove to the others that it is not a basin at all.

CHAPTER 45

When Sancho brings out the basin, the barber from Don Quixote's home town swears it is a helmet, and, to continue the joke,

Don Fernando takes a vote and announces that the trappings Sancho had taken from the barber's mule are indeed those of a thoroughbred horse. Others in the inn, however, including three Civil Guards who had just arrived, are not in on the joke, and disagree, so a fight ensues, and just as calm is once more restored, one of the Civil Guards, checking a description which he carries with him, recognizes Don Quixote as the man who freed the galley slaves, and grabs him by the neck.

CHAPTER 46

While Don Fernando separates Don Quixote and the Civil Guard, the curate explains his madness to the others, and their plan to take him home again, and pays the barber for the loss of his basin and the trappings of his mule. The curate then invents a new plan for getting Don Quixote home again without Dorotea, so that she and Don Fernando can go their way.

They contract an oxcart and build a cage on it, then appear in disguise in Don Quixote's bedroom after he is asleep, tie him up, and lock him in the cage. The barber delivers a chivalric prophecy, saying that the enchantment will be over when Don Quixote and Dulcinea are married.

CHAPTER 47

They then depart from the inn, with Sancho trying to persuade Don Quixote that it is all a hoax, to no avail. As they proceed, they are overtaken by a canon and his party, and when the curate explains the strange situation to the canon, the latter launches into a critique of the novels of chivalry, criticizing their lack of unity and verisimilitude, but noting that the genre, which he conceives as type of the **epic**, does have unexplored possibilities.

CHAPTER 48

The literary discussion continues, and after admitting that he had actually begun to write a proper novel of chivalry, the canon proceeds criticize the theater of the time with the same criteria, citing some successful, well-written plays as evidence that the claim that the public will not accept good plays is false. Among the plays he cites are some by L. de Argensola and Lope de Vega, and Cervantes' own Numantia. The curate agrees and continues the critique.

Meanwhile, Sancho perseveres in his attempt to undeceive Don Quixote as to his supposed enchantment, pointing out that he still needs to go to the bathroom, which would not be the case if he were truly enchanted.

Comment

Nearing the end of Part I, Cervantes has raised again, and in more detail, the literary questions which arose in Chapter 6, in the scrutiny of Don Quixote's library, and which were clearly basic to his original purpose in writing the novel. The discussion does not issue in a clear victory for the Aristotelian theorists, but as Alban Forcione has shown, leaves an unresolved dilemma between neo-classical theory and the creative freedom which Cervantes instinctively arrogates to himself as author.

CHAPTER 49

After another discussion, in which Don Quixote agrees to make a later attempt to escape from the cage, as Sancho advises, the canon approaches Don Quixote and gently remonstrates with him about his belief in the novels of chivalry. Don Quixote replies at length, mixing the Cid and other historical individuals with King Arthur and other chivalric characters, and the canon attempts to get him to distinguish between them.

CHAPTER 50

In reply, Don Quixote invents a chivalric **episode** of a knight who intrepidly plunges into a lake of boiling pitch, and finds below a crystal palace with a beautiful princess, as if to validate his argument by sheer imaginative power.

The group, now passing the siesta in a shady valley, is approached by a goatherd chasing a lost ewe, who joins them, and tells a story of his misfortunes in love.

CHAPTER 51

The goatherd, whose name is Eugenio, was in love with Leandra, but her head was turned by a flamboyant soldier named Vicente de la Roca. She ran off with him, but he soon abandoned her, robbing her of everything of value that she had taken along. Eugenio and a friend, who also loved Leandra, have retired from society to the wilds, in disillusionment.

CHAPTER 52

After a slur on Don Quixote's sanity, the goatherd and the knight begin to fight, Don Quixote having been allowed out of the cage to go to the bathroom. The curate and the canon are much amused by the fight, and the barber even helps the goatherd get on top of Don Quixote, but the sound of a trumpet stops the fight, and Don Quixote senses a new adventure in the offing. The inhabitants of a nearby village are carrying a statue of the Virgin in a procession through the fields, praying for rain, and Don Quixote commands them to free the captive lady. They begin to laugh, and Don Quixote attacks, but is received with blows, and left senseless on the ground. The knight is deposited in the cart again, on a pile of hay, and six days later they arrive in Don Quixote's village, taking him through the town plaza at Sunday noon, with the whole town crowding around him. Don Quixote is taken home and put to bed, and the author concludes by saying that the knight is said to have sallied forth again, this time taking part in the jousts at Saragossa, but that he can find no more written about his adventures. He does say that a lead box was found in the foundations of an old hermitage containing certain poems and **epitaphs** to Dulcinea, Sancho, Rocinante and Don Quixote, which he includes in closing.

Comment

The poems, ascribed to "the academicians of Argamasilla, a town in La Mancha," are in the same **burlesque** vein as those which precede Part I.

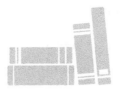

DON QUIXOTE

PRELIMINARIES

Terms of Sale, Certificate of Errors, three Approbations authorizing publication, Royal Privilege, the Dedication, to Pedro Fernández de Castro, Conde de Lemos, Cervantes' patron, and the "Prologue to the Reader."

Comment

Ten years had passed since the publication of Part I, and its success had been extraordinary. It had already been printed three times in Madrid, twice in Lisbon, twice in Valencia, twice in Brussels, and once in Milan, and had appeared in Shelton's English translation in London in 1612. It is interesting to note that in the approvals of José de Valdivielso and Márquez Torres direct reference is made to Cervantes' expressed intention of discrediting the novels of chivalry. Both reviewers laud this purpose and affirm that the author has been successful in his effort.

The Dedication contrasts sharply with its conventional counterpart in the *Don Quixote* of 1605. It is clever and original, and like the prologues of both parts, includes dialogue, this time between Cervantes and an imaginary emissary of the Emperor of China, who brings an offer of a position there as a University Rector, but no money. Cervantes elects to stay in Spain under the Duke's patronage, and promises to send him soon his last novel, *The Hardships of Persiles and Sigismunda*.

A year before the publication of Part II, in 1614, an apocryphal second part appeared, printed in Tarragona and written by one Alonso Fernández de Avellaneda. The author has never been identified, and it is likely that Cervantes himself did not know who really had written the book, though it seems that he felt himself to be the target of some veiled **satire** in Part I. In his prologue Cervantes limits himself to chiding Avellaneda for having derided him for being old and maimed, and to suggesting to the reader that, should he meet him, he tells Avellaneda two stories of madmen, one a man who took ridiculous pride in an absurd achievement, and another who took on more than he could handle.

CHAPTER 1

About a month after Don Quixote was brought home by the curate and the barber, as described at the close of Part I, the two come to visit him, having been advised by the niece and the housekeeper that he is recuperating and seems to be completely sane. The two friends are almost convinced of Don Quixote's sanity until the discussion touches on matters of state, and Don Quixote suggests that if the king were only to summon all the knights-errant of the realm, the Turks would be easily beaten, even if only one answered the call. To this, the barber replies with a tale of a madman, who having convinced the authorities that he was sane, revealed at the last moment that he was still insane. Don Quixote sees the point immediately, and furiously denounces the barber. The curate expresses his doubt as to the truth of the novels of chivalry, Don Quixote replies, and the talk veers off into details of individual chivalric characters.

CHAPTER 2

The arrival of Sancho terminates the discussion of chivalric novels, and when the knight and squire are left alone, Don Quixote eagerly inquires of Sancho what people are saying about him. Sancho frankly reveals that people think he is crazy and presumptuous, but that some note his bravery and courtesy, and others find him amusing. He adds that if Don Quixote really wants to know the full story of his reputation, he should talk with Sansón Carrasco, a bachelor of Salamanca, who has told Sancho that a book of the exploits of knight and squire has been published. The squire immediately goes out to bring the bachelor for a visit.

CHAPTER 3

After Sancho has left, Don Quixote reflects upon this latest development in his search for fame, astonished at the rapidity which his exploits have been recorded and published "since the blood of the enemies he had slain was not yet dry on the blade of his sword," and, ascribing the work to the arts of enchanters, he begins to worry about the fidelity of the account, especially as its author was apparently a Moor, "seeing that they are all of them cheats, forgers and schemers."

Carrasco arrives with Sancho, praising Don Quixote as a great knight-errant, and the three discuss Part I, reflecting certain criticism among the generally favorable comments with which the Bachelor says it has been received. Some have said that the author could have omitted some of the many beatings the knight received, and others thought the "Tale of Foolish Curiosity" extraneous to the novel.

Comment

The introduction of Part I as an element of Part II has several important consequences:

1. While in Part I Don Quixote's activities and attitudes were controlled by precedents in the novels of chivalry, the point of reference henceforth will be to a considerable extent his previous activities already published.

2. The contrast between Part I, the "biography" of Don Quixote, and Part II, the "real", "live" Don Quixote, makes the latter more seem real and immediate to the reader.

3. Up to this point, the demands of verisimilitude have been met consistently in the novel; perhaps the principal strain on the reader's credulity was the series

of coincidental encounters involved in the resolution of the Cardenio-Luscinda, Fernando-Dorotea intrigue. The problem now, however, is that Don Quixote's assumption must be correct: only an enchanter could have written this omniscient account of Don Quixote's activities of the previous month. The **irony** is, of course, that neither the reader nor the other characters in the book, who, like Sansón Carrasco, accept both the history and its **protagonist** as real, realize that this implies their acquiescence in the actual existence of enchanters. My experience has been that readers do not feel that verisimilitude has been violated.

CHAPTER 4

After a siesta, Sancho, Sansón Carrasco and Don Quixote continue the discussion of Part I; Sancho answers Sansón's questions as to the mix-up of the lost mule, in Part I, and how he spent the hundred crowns which he found in Cardenio's suitcase. Mention is made of the author's promise of a second part, and Sancho expresses his enthusiasm to be on the road again. Don Quixote asks Sansón to compose some verses to his lady, Dulcinea, and plans are laid for a third sally, in eight days. Sancho returns home to prepare for the journey.

CHAPTER 5

The chapter begins with a parenthetical remark indicating that the translator believes it to be apocryphal, since it seems to him that Sancho exceeds his possibilities in style and subtlety in his conversation with his wife, Teresa. The translator twice interrupts his text in the course of the chapter to reiterate his doubts.

Sancho tells his wife of his plans to accompany Don Quixote again, and a long discussion follows as to the wisdom of Sancho's intention to marry their daughter, Mari Sancha, to a nobleman, after he receives the island governorship which his master has promised him. Sancho eloquently defends his position, and Teresa, though without losing her misgivings about the gossip such a change of station will produce, bows to the will of her husband.

Comment

Despite the feigned misgivings of Cervantes' "translator," the author is careful to keep Sancho's style within the bounds of plausibility, thus causing the reader to defend the authenticity of Sancho's style while at the same time highlighting the squire's linguistic advances under the tutelage of his eloquent master. Sancho plays the role with Teresa that Don Quixote plays with him: he corrects her speech and generally treats her as an intellectual inferior.

CHAPTER 6

The niece and the housekeeper attempt to dissuade Don Quixote from making a third chivalric sally, and he lectures them on the virtues of knight-errantry, contrasting knights-errant with gentlemen of the court and reaffirming his intention to gain honor as a knight-errant. Sancho returns, and the two retire to the knight's room.

CHAPTER 7

As the two withdraw, the housekeeper hurries to Sansón Carrasco's house to beg him to intercede, and prevent the third sally. Sansón assures her that everything will be all right, and that he will visit her master soon.

Meanwhile, Sancho, at the insistence of Teresa, asks Don Quixote to give him a fixed wage. Finding no precedent in the novels of chivalry, Don Quixote refuses, saying that he will find someone else to accompany him. At that moment, Sansón appears, praising the knight's intention to sally forth again, and offering himself as squire. Don Quixote refuses to allow Sansón to interrupt his career, saying that he will find someone else for his squire, since Sancho does not deign to accompany him. Sancho, crushed by the equanimity with which Don Quixote has accepted his refusal to serve without salary, agrees with tears in his eyes to serve again on the same terms as before, and the two embrace and continue their plans to leave.

CHAPTER 8

Don Quixote and Sancho set out once again, this time on the road to El Toboso, and talk again of Sancho's pretended former visit with Dulcinea. Since Sancho persists in his vulgar and prosaic description of Dulcinea and her activities when he delivered Don Quixote's message, the knight assures him that she must have been enchanted. Sancho suggests to his master that they would achieve more glory if they were to work at being saints instead of following knight-errantry. Don Quixote asserts that chivalry is also a religious way. Night has already fallen when they arrived at El Toboso.

CHAPTER 9

As they enter the darkened village, Don Quixote tells Sancho to lead the way to Dulcinea's palace, and Sancho offers a number of excuses for being unable to find the house he is supposed to have visited, telling Don Quixote to lead the way. At this point the knight affirms that he has never seen Dulcinea, and has fallen in love with her solely because of her great reputation for beauty and discretion. Sancho finally persuades his master to await the day in a nearby wood, while he returns to announce Don Quixote's arrival to Dulcinea.

CHAPTER 10

Cid Hamete remarks that he would prefer to pass over the next **episode** in the story, as he is afraid he will not be believed, so extreme is the manifestation of Don Quixote's madness in what he is about to relate.

Sancho sets out again for El Toboso, and, sitting under a tree just out of sight of his master he ponders his dilemma, deciding finally to try to persuade his master that the first country wench he sees is Dulcinea, attributing the whole affair to enchanters. He soon sees three peasant girls approaching on mules, and brings his master out to see them, swearing that the party is Dulcinea and two of her ladies. Don Quixote sees only the reality of the three girls, but Sancho convinces him that he sees them in all their regal beauty. Don Quixote is finally convinced, and kneels before his lady. The girls, of course, feel they are being made fun of, turn their mules around, and flee. "Dulcinea" falls from her mount and when Don Quixote attempts to help her up, she leaps over the mule's hindquarters and gallops off.

Sancho and Don Quixote, the latter deeply disturb at the transformation of his lady, then set out for the jousts at Saragossa.

CHAPTER 11

On the road once again, the two meet a cart full of actors still in custom, traveling between two small towns to the next performance. Don Quixote challenges the driver, dressed as a devil, and demands that he tell them who they are and where they are going. The actor explains their costumes, and Don Quixote is mollified, but one of the actors frightens Rocinante, who gallops off and falls, unhorsing Don Quixote. When Sancho runs to help him up, the actor leaps on Sancho's donkey and rides off. Don Quixote re-mounts and prepares to rescue the donkey, but the actor has by this time tumbled off the beast, and it heads back to Sancho.

Sancho is finally able to dissuade his master from seeking revenge for the insult from the actors, who by now have formed a line and arm themselves with rocks, by pointing out that they are not knights-errant. When his master suggests that Sancho might want to avenge the insult to his mule himself, he declines.

CHAPTER 12

When they are settled for the night in a grove of trees, Don Quixote remarks on the **didactic** value of the theater, and points out to Sancho the analogy between the equality of the players when they have finished their roles and that of all men before God in death, and Sancho replies with a similar analogy he has heard between life and the game of chess. Don Quixote praises Sancho's perception, and the latter attributes it to his association with the knight.

Mention is made by Cervantes of the existence of a belief that Cid Hamete wrote some chapters dealing with the friendship between Rocinante and Sancho's donkey, but that they were eliminated in the interest of decorum.

At this point two other men are heard making camp in the dark nearby, and when the knight hears one of them boast that he has conquered Don Quixote and made him swear that his lady, Casildea de Vandalia, is the most beautiful woman in the world, he goes over to meet the mysterious knight-errant. Sancho and the other knight's squire retire some distance away, and the two knights sit down to talk.

CHAPTER 13

The author first records the conversation of the two squires. The squire of the "Knight of the Wood," as the newly-arrived knight is first called, comments upon the rigors of such a life, and tries to persuade Sancho to leave his master and go home, but Sancho affirms that he loves Don Quixote for his simplicity and good intentions, and is thus unable to leave him. The other man produces food and wine, and as the two eat and drink together, Sancho tells a story of two of his relatives who were famous winetasters. Finally, both men drop off to sleep.

CHAPTER 14

The Knight of the Wood relates his exploits for the glory of his lady, Casildea, and when he repeats his boast of having defeated

Don Quixote, the latter challenges him to combat, and they prepare to fight at dawn.

While the two squires are preparing their masters' steeds, the squire of the Knight of the Wood informs Sancho that they, too, must fight one another while their masters joust. Sancho is reluctant, because he sees no point to their fighting, but the other man goads him into accepting. When dawn breaks, Sancho sees to his dismay that the other squire has a huge, disproportionate and grotesque nose, covered with warts, and, terrified, he asks Don Quixote to help him climb a tree, "to better watch the knights' gallant encounter." While Don Quixote delays with Sancho, his opponent has turned and begun his charge, but seeing that Don Quixote is occupied, he reins in his broken-down nag. When Don Quixote rushes to the attack, the Knight of the Mirrors, as he is now called, because of the decoration of his armor, is unable to get his horse to move, and Don Quixote easily unhorses him.

When Don Quixote removes his unconscious opponent's helmet, he is amazed to see the face of Sansón Carrasco. He attributes this strange circumstances to the work of enchanters, and is only stopped from running him through with his sword by the pleas of his squire, who, having removed his false nose, reveals himself to be Tomé Cecial, an acquaintance of Sancho's. Sansón Carrasco regains consciousness and swears to the supremacy of Dulcinea over his lady, and Don Quixote and Sancho continue on their way.

CHAPTER 15

It is here explained that the encounter which turned out so badly for him was planned by Sansón Carrasco, together with the curate and the barber, as a means to force Don Quixote to return home, the conditions of combat having been that the loser would remain at the disposition of his victor. After the defeat, Tomé Cecial asks Sansón "'Who is the crazier: the one who is so because he cannot help it, or he who turns crazy of his own free will?'

'The difference between the two,' replied Sansón, 'lies in this: that the one who cannot help being crazy will be so always, whereas the one who is a madman by choice can leave off being one whenever he chooses.'" He vows to pursue Don Quixote, and says that his motivation henceforth will not be so charitable; he wants revenge.

CHAPTER 16

Sancho has difficulty accepting Don Quixote's assertion that the Knight of the Mirrors and his squire are not Sansón and Tomé, and a reference, by way of proof, to the transformation of Dulcinea into an ugly peasant girl, of course only increases Sancho's doubts.

As they proceed, they are overtaken by an elegant gentleman dressed in green, with whom Don Quixote strikes up a conversation. Upon learning that Don Quixote is a knight-errant, engaged, as he says, in "succoring widows, protecting damsels, and aiding the fallen, the orphans, and the young," the gentleman, Don Diego De Miranda, says how happy he is that such a man exists, especially since the book of his exploits, which Don Quixote has mentioned, will "cast into oblivion the innumerable stories of fictitious knights-errant with which the world is filled." The knight, of course, disagrees, but lets the matter rest in hopes of convincing Don Diego later on as to the historicity of the novels of chivalry. Don Diego then describes his own life: calm, decorous, charitable and unostentatious, and Sancho is so impressed that he dismounts and kisses his feet, saying that Don Diego is the first saint on horseback he has ever met. Don Diego is astonished, and remarks that Sancho is much nearer a saint than he, for his ingenuousness.

Don Diego mentions that he has a son who, to his regret, aspires to be a poet, and Don Quixote argues very cogently the son's case, so that Don Diego is quite perplexed by Don Quixote's alternation between reason and madness.

Comment

Don Diego, "the Man in the Green Overcoat," has become a focal point for disagreement as to the proper ethical stance toward Don Quixote. The "hard" critics, who see Don Quixote as vain and foolish, see Don Diego as a kind of ethical norm for the whole novel, while the "soft' critics, for whom Don Quixote is the hero of the book, see him as somewhat vain and prosaic.

CHAPTER 17

A cart approaches, flying royal flags, and Don Quixote calls for Sancho to bring his helmet. The squire, however, has gone some distance away to buy curds from a group of shepherds, and having no way to carry the curds, has deposited them in the helmet. Don Quixote claps it on his head, and discovers the curds as they begin running down all over his face and beard. Sancho blames the enchanters, and Don Quixote rides out to stop the cart, which contains two fierce and hungry caged lions being delivered as a present to the king.

The knight insists that the lion-keeper open the cages so that he may fight the lions, brushing aside the protest and admonitions of Don Diego and the others. When everyone else has retired a safe distance away, the keeper opens one of the cages. The lion stretches, yawns, and puts his head out the door of the cage, then "turned his back and presented his hind parts to Don Quixote and then very calmly and peaceably lay down." Don Quixote orders the keeper to stir him up with a stick, but this he refuses to do, since that would provoke the lion to attack him. He convinces the knight that he has vanquished the lion, and Don Quixote allows him to shut the cage, and signals the others to return, announcing that he wishes henceforth to take the title of Knight of the Lions.

Sensing Don Diego's thoughts, Don Quixote admits that his actions may seem insane, but defends himself by pointing out that it is better to err in matters of valor on the side of rashness than on that of cowardice, and Don Diego again marvels at the mixture of madness and reason which the knight displays.

CHAPTER 18

Don Quixote and Sancho spend the next four days as guests in Don Diego's house. Don Quixote eloquently elucidates to Don Diego's son, Lorenzo, his profession of knight-errantry, and praises the boy's poetry.

CHAPTER 19–21

These three chapters comprise the story of Quiteria, Camacho, and Basilio. On leaving Don Diego's house the knight meets a party of peasants and students and accompanies them to the wedding of Quiteria and the wealthy Camacho. Basilio and Quiteria had been sweethearts since childhood and there is considerable apprehension as to what Basilio may do at the wedding. On the way, the two students fight a duel, in which the one who has studied the art handily defeats the other, who relies on brute force.

The wedding is a lavish affair, with much food and pageantry, but before the ceremony, Basilio appears, wishes the couple happiness, draws his sword and runs himself through. Basilio refuses to make a last confession to the priest until Quiteria marries him, and since Camacho, like everyone else, assumes Basilio is dying, he agrees, expecting his own marriage to the girl to follow immediately on Basilio's death. As soon as the vows are said, however, Basilio leaps up and reveals that it has all been a trick with the sword. Camacho's first impulse is to avenge himself, but Don Quixote eloquently argues for Basilio's right to have Quiteria, and Camacho desists.

CHAPTER 22

Don Quixote and Sancho spend three pleasant days in the house of Basilio, who is grateful for Don Quixote's help, after which they set out, with a guide, for the Cave of Montesinos, which Don Quixote is determined to explore. The guide presents himself as a humanist author-scholar, and proves to be a credulous author of useless Tomés, made fun of by Sancho and indirectly criticized by Don Quixote.

Sancho and the "humanist" lower Don Quixote into the cave by a rope, and after half an hour they pull him up again.

He seems to be sound asleep, and after they have shaken him back to consciousness, he laments having been cut off from a delightful experience by being brought out of the cave.

CHAPTER 23

Don Quixote now relates his adventure in the cave. He had entered a recess in the side of the cave, and sat down to rest, when a profound sleep fell upon him. When he awoke, he found himself in a meadow, gazing upon a crystal palace. He was greeted by a venerable old man with a long white beard, who proved to be Montesinos himself, and who announced that he had long awaited Don Quixote's arrival. He led the knight before the recumbent Durandarte, and related the story of Durandarte's death at Roncesvalles, and his own compliance with the knight's last request that his heart be cut off and taken to his lady Belerma. He also related the fate of Durandarte's squire, transformed into a river. A rather grotesque Belerma appeared, carrying the mummified heart.

At this point, Sancho expresses doubt as to the veracity of his master's tale, especially as to his assertion that he has spent three days and nights in the cave. Don Quixote then tells of an encounter in the cave with Dulcinea in the enchanted state in which she appeared outside El Toboso, and Sancho's doubts are confirmed, since he was responsible for that particular transformation. Don Quixote relates that one of Dulcinea's ladies approached him for a loan for her, but that he had almost no money to give her. Sancho openly expresses his disbelief, but his master calmly asserts that he will tell him more details later which will surely convince him.

Comment

The **episode** of the Cave of Montesinos is of major importance in the development of Part II, and is one of the most interesting **episodes** in the entire novel.

1. It is marvelously perceptive and convincing as a presentation of a dream, mixing Don Quixote's deepest fears and aspirations with **allusions** to recent events, inconsequential details and non-sequiturs, grotesque description, and realistic description.

2. We are allowed to see Don Quixote's fantasy freely at work, untrammeled by the inconveniences for recalcitrant reality, and are disturbed to see that his lofty aspirations are undermined from within, by, in the words of Gerald Brenan, "a fundamental dryness and prosaicness in the mind of this man who has set himself up against the prosaic scheme of things."

CHAPTER 24

The chapter begins with a "marginal note" by Cid Hamete to the effect that he cannot believe Don Quixote's account of what happened in the cave, though he is sure that the knight would not lie, and could scarcely have invented so much nonsense in so short a time. He tells the reader that he must judge for himself, but adds that it has been reported that at the time of his death they say he admitted having invented the incident. The Humanist is astonished at Sancho's impudence in doubting his master, and delighted to pick up some useful information from Don Quixote's account for use in his books.

The three continue on their way, meeting briefly a man carrying a load of lances and halberds and a young man off to join the army, and soon arrive at an inn, which Sancho is pleased to see that his master takes to be an inn, and not a castle.

CHAPTER 25

Once installed in the inn, Don Quixote prevails upon the man whom they had met carrying the load of arms to tell him their purpose. It seems that two aldermen from a nearby town had made themselves ridiculous by braying like asses in search of a lost donkey, and the townspeople are now preparing to fight those of a neighboring village who had taunted them about the matter. As he finishes his tale, a man called Master Pedro, with a patch over one eye and a pet ape, enters the inn. Master Pedro has come to present a puppet show and to answer questions with the aid of his divining ape. The ape jumps upon his master's shoulder and chatters in his ear, and Master Pedro kneels before Don Quixote, praising him as the reviver of knight-errantry, and astounding all those present with this demonstration of the ape's divining faculty. Don Quixote anxiously inquires whether the events in the Cave of Montesinos really happened or if they were dreams, and Master Pedro says the ape's reply is that the events are partly true and partly false. Master Pedro then prepares his puppet show, the liberation of Melisendra by Don Gaiferos.

CHAPTER 26

Master Pedro presents his puppet show, in which he moves the puppets and a young boy narrates the action. It is the story of Don Gaiferos, who, scolded by the Emperor Charlemagne for allowing his wife Melisendra to languish in captivity under the Moors in Saragossa, rides alone into Spain and carries her back to France. In the course of the production, Don Quixote interrupts twice to lecture the boy for his extraneous comments and to complain of the lack of historical **realism** in the presentation. Then, suddenly, as the hero and heroine are riding desperately toward France, Don Quixote leaps up and attacks the little stage, to prevent the band of pursuing Moors from recapturing Melisendra. Many of the puppets are damaged or destroyed, and when Don Quixote realizes what he has done, he offers to pay for the damages, attributing his confusion to the work of enchanters.

Comment

This **episode** has been much discussed by critics in the twentieth century. It is, as Ortega y Gasset has pointed out, a fascinating revelation of the thin line which separates Don Quixote's madness from his sanity, since one minute he perceives the slightest breach of verisimilitude, and the next he loses all detachment and enters the action as if it were a part of life itself. George Haley has also expounded in some detail the extent to which the relationships between author, narrator, and audience in the puppet show parallel those same relationships in the novel as a whole.

DON QUIXOTE

. . . .

CHAPTER 27

It is now revealed by the author that Master Pedro was really Ginés de Pasamonte, leader of the galley slaves whom Don Quixote freed earlier (Part I, Chapter 22).

As Don Quixote and Sancho continue on their way to Saragossa, they come upon the massed formation of the townspeople of the offended village whose plight had been told to Don Quixote at the inn. The knight and Sancho ride into their midst, and Don Quixote speaks eloquently of the various justifications for taking up arms, in an attempt to dissuade them from doing battle with those of the neighboring town. Sancho interrupts, however, and in a misguided attempt to reinforce his master's argument, he demonstrates his own talent at braying. The villagers think they are being made fun of, and one of them knocks Sancho to the ground. When Don Quixote starts to avenge his fallen squire, the villagers begin to stone him, and load their crossbows. At this, Don Quixote turns and flees, forgetting Sancho and thinking only of his own safety.

Comment

The reader is astonished at this, the first, and only, manifestation of fear in *Don Quixote*, and the conviction grows that the knight is gradually losing his grip on the chivalric illusions which have sustained him so well. He is no longer mistaking inns for castles, he is ready to pay for damages he causes, and his replies to those who question the veracity of the novels of chivalry are increasingly weary and hopeless. One has the impression that fitful attempts, such as the **episode** of the lions, to reassert the vigor and conviction of the early adventures are his own semi-conscious efforts to regain the initiative in the struggle against recalcitrant reality.

CHAPTER 28

The villagers put Sancho back on his donkey and send him after his master. Sancho remonstrates with Don Quixote for having abandoned him, and talks again of returning home, but the knight makes him feel so ungrateful that even though he offers to pay him and let him go, Sancho agrees to ride on with him.

CHAPTER 29

Finding a small boat tied up at the bank of the Ebro river, Don Quixote senses an adventure, and he and Sancho set out in the boat, much against the squire's better judgment. The current carries them to the wheels of a flour mill down-river and the two are thrown into the water as the millers vainly attempt to keep the boat from breaking up in the wheels of the mill. The millers fish the two from the water, and Don Quixote, with a weary complaint as to his impotence in the face of the opposition of powerful enchanters, offers to pay for the damaged boat.

CHAPTER 30

As they ride on after this unfortunate adventure, Don Quixote and Sancho encounter two characters who figure very importantly in the remaining chapters: the duke and duchess. The initial encounter with the noble pair, who are hunting in the woods, begins badly for the knight, who falls to the ground as he dismounts to greet them, but the duke and duchess are delighted to meet them, having read the published first part of their adventures.

CHAPTER 31

They are taken with great ceremony to the country house, or "castle" of the duke and duchess, and "that was the first time that Don Quixote really and wholly believed himself to be a true knight-errant, and not a fanciful one, for here he was being treated in the very same manner as knights-errant in ages past."

Sancho has a brief altercation with Doña Rodriguez, one of the ladies-in-waiting, who is highly offended when the squire entrusts his donkey to her special care, and Don Quixote is infuriated by a harsh attack during dinner on the folly of his chivalric fantasies by an ecclesiastic in the duke's household.

Comment

The sojourn with the duke and duchess initiates an important phase of the development of Don Quixote:

1. The duke and duchess, like many of the characters in the succeeding chapters, have read Part I, and one consequence is that their relationship with him involves a great deal of manipulation of his activity, rather than a straightforward reaction, of astonishment, anger, etc... . to his strange behavior.

2. Don Quixote is involved increasingly in a more complex, controlled, urbane environment, which contrasts with the dusty roads and wayside inns of Part I. This new milieu makes new demands upon him and reveals new facets of his character.

3. The ecclesiastic, and the duke and duchess in their later development, as well as Sansón Carrasco, represent a different kind of opponent or antagonist for Don Quixote when contrasted with the curate and the canon of Part I. As the motives of Don Quixote's antagonists become more suspect and their stature diminishes, the knight is bound to rise in the reader's estimation.

CHAPTER 32

Don Quixote replies eloquently to the ecclesiastic's attack, and the man leaves in a huff, his irritation increased by the duke's announcement that he is conferring upon Sancho the government of an island in his realm.

When the meal is finished, four damsels appear with towels and a silver bowl, and proceed to wash Don Quixote's beard. So that the knight will not discover the jest, the duke insists that his beard be washed, too, and the girls obediently comply. Sancho is agreeably surprised by the strange practice, and the duchess assures him that he will get equal treatment, and sends him off to eat with her attendants.

The duke and duchess wish to hear about Dulcinea del Toboso, and Don Quixote tells them of her recent enchantment. When the duchess presses him as to the reality of Dulcinea, Don Quixote replies as follows: "God knows whether or not there is a Dulcinea in this world or if she is a fanciful creation. This is not one of those cases where you can prove a thing conclusively." He counters doubts as to her nobility with praise of her virtue and good works, and reveals that he believes that the enchanters have transformed her as a way of hurting him, since they cannot conquer him directly.

In the course of the conversation, Don Quixote affirms his affection for Sancho, and the doubts he has as to his performance as governor of the island, but remarks that he intends to give him a good deal of advice before he takes office.

At this point, Sancho bursts into the room, pursued by a number of servants who are attempting to scrub his beard with dish-water. The duchess orders them to leave him alone and invites Sancho to spend the afternoon with her and her ladies.

CHAPTER 33

The duchess opens her conversations with Sancho by asking how he dared invent the visit to Dulcinea on which he reported to Don Quixote in Chapter 31 of Part I. Sancho replies that he knows Don Quixote is crazy and easily deceived, and recounts in detail his "enchantment" of Dulcinea outside El Toboso, but defends his continued service with Don Quixote in the following terms: "We're from the same village, I've eaten his bread, I like him very much, he's generous to me ... , and above all, I'm loyal," and says that if they doubt his ability to govern the promised island, he can live without it.

The duchess promises that Sancho will be granted his governorship, but manages to convince Sancho that Dulcinea really is enchanted, and that the enchanters have simply led Sancho to believe that he was playing a hoax on his master. Sancho then decides that Don Quixote must have been telling the truth about his adventures in the Cave of Montesinos, and he relates to the duchess the details of that **episode**. With a parting expression of concern for the care of his donkey, Sancho retires from the chambers of the duchess.

CHAPTER 34

A few days later, the duke and duchess arrange a hunt, in which Don Quixote participates, and during which Sancho is so frightened at the approach of a wild hog that he climbs a tree and tears the new hunting outfit the duke had given him. Sancho complains that the hunt seems to him to be a dangerous waste of time, but the duke defends the sport as important preparation for war. When night has fallen, Sancho is terrified to hear sounds of battle all around them in the forest, and takes refuge behind the duchess' skirts at the approach of a series of heavy oxcarts driven by outlandish figures, accompanied by the sound of trumpets, drums, and artillery fire. The devil, seated upon one of the carts, announces that Montesinos will soon arrive with Dulcinea, bringing news of how her disenchantment is to be accomplished.

CHAPTER 35

At last a cart appears bearing a veiled Dulcinea and the enchanter Merlin, who recites from his throne a poem which reveals that to return Dulcinea to her original state, Sancho must voluntarily give himself 3,300 lashes. Sancho is, of course, indignant, failing, as he says, to see the connection between Dulcinea's enchantment and his backside, and is unmoved even when Dulcinea stands, removes her veil, revealing an extremely beautiful face, and gives him a good tongue-lashing for his insensitivity to her plight. Sancho replies that she is not very good at asking for favors, and that he does not intend to go through with it. The duke, however, makes Sancho's cooperation a condition for his governorship, and after stipulating that he can take his own time at whipping himself, he finally accepts, to Don Quixote's delight.

CHAPTER 36

The author reveals that the roles of Merlin and Dulcinea were played by the Duke's major-domo and a page, and that Don Quixote's hosts had another adventure planned for the knight and his squire. The next day, Sancho shows the duchess a letter that he has dictated to his wife, Teresa, in which he gives her the news of his governorship and remarks that he expects to make a lot of money. The duchess approves of the letter, but reproves Sancho for the interest he shows in making money. At this point an extravagant procession enters the garden, and the imminent arrival is announced of the countess Trifaldi, otherwise known as the Distressed Duenna, who has come to seek Don Quixote's aid.

CHAPTER 37

As they await the arrival of the countess, Sancho expresses his disdain for duennas in general, and Doña Rodriguez rises to their defense. The dispute is cut short by arrival of the countess, accompanied by a group of musicians playing a doleful lament.

CHAPTER 38

Twelve veiled duennas file at processional pace into the garden, accompanying the countess, whose face is also veiled in black. The lady, speaking in a rough, hoarse voice, throws herself at Don Quixote's feet, imploring his aid, and then beseeches Sancho to intercede with his master on her behalf. She then tells how she served as go-between in the love affair of Don Clavijo and the Princess Antonomasia of her native kingdom of Candaya. When the princess became pregnant a marriage was hastily arranged and performed by the Vicar. At this point Sancho urges the countess to hurry up and get to the end of her story.

CHAPTER 39

The countess continues, relating that the couple were married by the Vicar, and that Antonomasia's mother, Queen Maguncia, was so grieved at the news that she died. After they had buried her, the enchanter Malambruno, a cousin of the queen's appeared over her grave and punished the couple by transforming the princess into a brass ape, and Don Clavijo into a crocodile made of some unknown metal, with a pillar standing between them which proclaimed that they would not regain their original form until "the valiant Manchegan" should meet the giant in single combat. In punishment for the countess' part in the love affair, he caused the faces of all the palace duennas to become bearded, and at this point in her story, the countess and the twelve duennas accompanying her raise their veils and reveal that they are all, in fact, heavily bearded. The chapter closes with the Distressed Duenna's lament that they, who are universally despised anyway as duennas, are now doubly cursed.

CHAPTER 40

Don Quixote vows to meet Malambruno, and asks the countess what must be done. She replies that Malambruno has promised to send a flying wooden horse, called Clavileño, to bring the knight and his squire to meet him. Over Sancho's vehement objections, Don Quixote accepts the challenge and assures her that he and his squire will mount Clavileño.

CHAPTER 41

At the sight of the wooden horse, which is borne into the garden by four men dressed as savages, Sancho becomes frightened, and again refuses to ride with his master, but the duke makes the trip another condition for obtaining the governorship, and Sancho agrees to go. He indignantly rejects Don Quixote's suggestion that he gets in a few lashes toward the 3,300 necessary to disenchant Dulcinea, protesting that this is no time to strip the flesh off his backside, with such a rough trip ahead of them.

They mount Clavileño, with instructions to maneuver by means of a peg on the horse's neck, and allow themselves to be blindfolded as Malambruno has instructed. The group assembled around them shout their goodbyes, and with a set of bellows and some small brush fires they simulate the passage of Clavileño through the aerial region and the region of fire in the heavens. The countess and her ladies slip out of the garden, and the wooden horse, which was filled with detonating rockets, explodes, throwing knight and squire to the ground. The two pick themselves up, and are astonished to see everyone in the garden stretched out on the ground, as if unconscious. A parchment attached to a lance thrust into the ground, announces that Don Quixote has successfully completed the restoration of Antonomasia and Don Clavijo, and removed the beards from the palace duennas, simply by undertaking the adventure. The duke and the others in the garden pretend to return slowly to their senses, arise, and congratulate Don Quixote on his success.

Sancho says that during the flight he peeked out from under his blindfold and saw the earth as small as a grain of mustard, with the people on it a little larger than hazelnuts. When the duchess remarks on the odd proportions in his description, Sancho adds that he slid down from Clavileño and played for three-quarters of an hour with the seven goats of the constellation Pleiades, which are, he says, two of them green, two flesh-colored, two blue, and one a mixture. In a cryptic conclusion to the chapter, Don Quixote whispers in Sancho's ear: if you want us to believe what you saw in Heaven, then you must believe me when I tell you what I saw in the Cave of Montesinos. I need say no more."

CHAPTER 42

The next day, on learning that Sancho is soon to depart for his island. Don Quixote takes him aside to advise him as to his conduct of the governorship. The advice is sound, and eloquently put: Fear God, seek self-knowledge, follow virtue, take pride in your humble origins, educate and polish your wife, be compassionate, and not arbitrary, and temper justice with mercy.

Comment

The opening paragraph of Don Quixote's advice to Sancho reflects with masterful subtlety the mixed emotions with which the knight reacts to his squire's good fortune. He is happy for him, of course, but there is a note of envy and irritation in the face of Sancho's unmerited good fortune, while he, who has struggled so hard, has not found comparable rewards.

CHAPTER 43

As Don Quixote continues with more personal advice to Sancho as to his conduct and the care of his person, Cid Hamete remarks on the knight's eloquence, noting once more that Don Quixote is an eminently reasonable man in all matters except knight-errantry. Sancho is to keep himself neat and clean, keep the number of his servants within reasonable bounds, eat and drink temperately, foregoing the onions and garlic of his usual diet, and in general cultivate a measured and sober bearing.

Sancho listens carefully to the advice and receives it gratefully, but remarks that he will probably forget it, since he can't write it down, and he sprinkles his reply so liberally with the proverbs which have increasingly become his trademark, that Don Quixote despairs of any chance of his success in the governorship. Sancho replies that if his master does not feel that he is adequate to the job, he will resign, for he is quite conscious of his limitations. With this, Don Quixote admits that his squire has a naturally good disposition and the best of intentions, which are, after all, the most important qualifications.

CHAPTER 44

Cervantes remarks in a comically confusing aside that at this point in Cid Hamete's manuscript, the translator did not translate faithfully the text, which included the Moor's lament at having to limit himself to the adventures of Don Quixote and Sancho, excluding in Part II such interpolations as "The Tale of Foolish Curiosity", and "The Captive's Tale," in Part I, for fear they would not be fully appreciated. He asked therefore, to be praised, not for what he has written, but for what he has left unwritten.

Comment

Cervantes here reflects the seriousness with which he took the criticism of the interpolations in Part I, referred to in Chapter III of Part II.

Sancho sets out for his governorship with considerable pomp, remarking to Don Quixote as he leaves that the duke's majordomo, who heads his retinue, looks exactly like the Countess. Trifaldi. Don Quixote of course attributes the likeness to enchanters, but agrees that Sancho should keep a close eye on him.

As soon as Sancho has gone, Don Quixote begins to miss him, and, remarking to the duchess that though he misses his squire, his absence is not the chief cause of his melancholy, he retires to his room. As he undresses, his stocking tears, provoking an exclamation from Cid Hamete on the humiliation which poverty can bring to a poor nobleman.

Don Quixote hears voices outside his window, and, opening it, is astonished to hear a love song sung to him by Altisidora, a young lady in the duchess' entourage. Slamming the window shut, Don Quixote complains bitterly that every girl who sees him seems to fall in love with him, and vows to remain true to Dulcinea. He seems not to have noticed the obviously farcical nature of the song Altisidora sings to him.

CHAPTER 45

A mock-epic invocation to Apollo introduces the account of Sancho's governorship of the "island" Barataria, actually a small town in the duke's domain, and the next nine chapters, covering the duration of the governorship, alternate between the events at Barataria and the adventures of Don Quixote with the duke and duchess.

Sancho is received by his new constituency with great ceremony, and the villagers are somewhat taken aback by the strange aspect of their new governor, especially those who are not aware that it is a hoax. He is taken to the judge's chair, and three cases are presented to him for judgment.

The first case involves a tailor whose client refuses to pay for five tiny caps he had made for the man after being pressed to make the maximum use of cloth he had brought. Sancho sees that both are at fault and decrees that the client shall lose his cloth and the tailor his work, and that the caps shall be given away.

In the second case two old men dispute whether a debt of one to the other has been repaid. The alleged debtor hands his staff to the other man, and steps forward to swear that he has given back the money. His accuser accepts the oath, knowing him to be an honest man, and hands him back the staff, but as they leave, Sancho asks for the staff and gives it to the plaintiff, having realized that the defendant has hidden the money in it to be able to swear that he has given it back.

In the third and last case, a woman appears, lamenting the loss of her honor at the hands of a rich drover whom she has dragged into court with her. The man's version of what happened is that it was not rape, and that the woman was simply dissatisfied with what he paid her. Sancho orders the man to give her his leather purse with all his money in it, and the woman leaves with it, thanking the governor profusely.

As soon as she is gone, Sancho tells the man to go and take back his purse. The two return, struggling over the purse, and it is clear that the man cannot get it back from her. Sancho returns the purse to the drover, saying that she could easily have defended her body with half as much effort, and banishes her from Barataria.

CHAPTER 46

The morning after Altisidora's serenade, Don Quixote passes her in the halls of the palace, and she faints in the arms of a companion. Don Quixote asks that a lute be brought to his room that evening, and at eleven o'clock he begins a song at his window, advising Altisidora to busy herself with needlework and to avoid transient infatuations, reiterating his fidelity to Dulcinea. His song is interrupted by the din of a sackful of cats and bells which the duke and duchess had arranged to have lowered by rope to his balcony. One of several of the cats which had gotten into Don Quixote's room leaps at his face and sinks its claws so tenaciously that the duke, who has rushed to his room, has to tear it loose. Altisidora binds up his wounds, complaining of his disdain of her advances.

CHAPTER 47

Sancho has meanwhile passed a very frustrating day in office. Seated before a sumptuous banquet, he is dismayed to see one plate after another whisked away untouched at a sign from Doctor Pedro Recio, who, as he says, is employed to look after the governor's health. In utter exasperation, Sancho finally orders the doctor out, but at that moment a letter arrives from the duke, warning that the island is under threat of attack, and that there are certain individuals within the island who intend to kill him.

Fearful of poison, Sancho eats only some bread and grapes, and is unable to relax during the siesta, when an impertinent peasant intrudes with an absurd request for money from the governor for the wedding for his grotesque daughter and her fiance. Sancho angrily dismisses him.

CHAPTER 48

One night after the unfortunate encounter with the cats, Don Quixote receives a visit from Doña Rodriguez, at the outset of which each comically asks assurance of the other that there will not be assaults on his chastity. Doña Rodriguez reveals that her daughter is pregnant by the son of a rich peasant whom the duke is unwilling to alienate by seeking to force the son to marry the girl. The simple Doña Rodriguez has come to persuade Don Quixote to reclaim her daughter's honor by challenging the young man, and she reveals in passing some intimate inadequacies of Altisidora and of the duchess: Altisidora has bad breath, and the duchess owes her beauty, "first to God, and then to two issues which she has, one in each leg, through which are discharged all the evil humors of which the doctors say she is full."

At this point the door bursts open, toppling Doña Rodriguez's candle and plunging the room into darkness. The duenna is soundly spanked, and Don Quixote is pinched and scratched; the phantom figures silently depart, leaving Doña Rodriguez to whimper back to her quarter, and the knight to wonder at the perversity of the enchanter who plagues him.

CHAPTER 49

Sancho's ability so far in the governorship has so exceeded all expectation that the majordomo remarks that he is astonished to hear him "uttering so many wise maxims and observations, all of which is quite contrary to what was expected of your Grace's intelligence by those who sent us… . Each day new things are seen in this world, jests are turned into earnest and the jesters mocked."

On his evening rounds, Sancho encounters successively a gambler fighting with a disgruntled hanger-on, a young vagabond, and a frightened young girl who has dressed as a man to slip out of her father's house and escape his constant vigilance to see something of life in the town, and he deals sagely with all.

CHAPTER 50

It is revealed that Altisidora and the duchess had been listening at Don Quixote's door, and that it was they who had punished the two in the dark for their gossip.

The next day the duchess sends a page with Sancho's letter and one from herself to Sancho's wife Teresa, in which she addresses her as one friend to another and asks Teresa to send her two dozen acorns. She also sends a coral necklace with the letter as a present. Teresa and her daughter Sanchica are of course thrilled at the news of Sancho's governorship, and impressed by the handsome page in his fine livery and the lovely necklace, but the curate and the barber are unable to make head or tail of the affair, since the page affirms that Sancho is, in fact, a governor. He returns to the castle carrying Teresa's letters to the duchess and to Sancho.

CHAPTER 51

Doctor Pedro Recio has continued in office, and Sancho feels as if he were starving, but the next morning he begins hearing cases again. The first case involves the fate of a man who has violated the law governing the passage across a bridge joining two separate territories. The law is that anyone who crosses must swear as to where he is going, and why. If he swears truthfully, he is allowed to pass; if he lies he is hanged on a scaffold provided there for the purpose. The problem is that this particular man has sworn that he was going to the scaffold to be hanged. Seeing the logical impossibility, Sancho remembers his master's advice and decrees that the man may freely pass, tempering justice with mercy.

Impressed with Sancho's discretion, the majordomo arranges for Sancho to lunch well that day. A letter arrives for Sancho from Don Quixote, saying that he has heard that Sancho is governing very well, and giving him some more practical advice: Do not make too many laws, but see that those enacted are enforced; visit the jails, the plazas, and the markets; write to the duke. He mentions the affair with the cats, and that he may be involved in another matter which will earn him the duke's enmity, but that he will put his duty first.

Sancho answers immediately, noting how busy he is, and giving his master an account of his recent activities. He spends the rest of the afternoon drafting ordinances moderating the price of shoes, outlining the quality control of wines, instituting wage controls, banning lascivious songs and **ballads** of false miracles sung by blind beggars, and creating an officer in charge of weeding out fake cripples among the village's poor. "In brief, he ordered things so wisely that to this day his decrees are preserved in that town, under the title of The Constitutions of the Great Governor, Sancho Panza."

DON QUIXOTE

....

CHAPTER 52

A few days later, as Don Quixote is about to tell his hosts that he is leaving for Saragossa, the duke and duchess are astonished at the appearance of Doña Rodriguez and her daughter both dressed in black, to present formally their plea to Don Quixote for redress. He agrees to be their champion, and the duke accepts his challenge in the name of the young man who has wronged the girl and arranges for Don Quixote to meet him in single combat. The duke assigns the two women special quarters in the castle.

The page then arrives with Teresa's letters, which are read aloud and laughed over by all. In her letter to the duchess, Teresa thanks her for the necklace, expresses her determination to go to court and ride in a coach, to do justice to Sancho's new status, and mentions that she is sending some acorns, though this year's crop was very bad. The letter to Sancho gives news of the family and the town and of the year's crops.

CHAPTER 53

Cervantes introduces his account of the end of Sancho's governorship with a predominantly serious paragraph in which Cid Hamete reflects on the brevity of life in connection with Sancho's fortunes.

On the seventh night of his stay in Barataria, Sancho is roused from bed by the sounds of battle. His men burst into his room, strap him so tightly between two large shields that he cannot bend his knees, and thrust a lance in his hand. At his first attempt to walk he falls to the floor, encased in the shields like a helpless turtle, and as the simulated battle rages around him, one of the combatants even stands on top of him, shouting instructions to his comrades. The din of battle is succeeded by shouts of victory, and his men help him to his feet while talking of a celebration for the great victory to which he has led them.

Sancho denies having vanquished anyone, and asks for a drink of wine, and they untie the shields. Without saying a word, he slowly dresses, goes to the stable and leads his donkey out, saying that it is now clear to him that he was not born to be a governor, and that he wants to return to his life of old. He announces that he is going to see the duke, and will render to him directly an account of his term of office, and leaving those around him ashamed of their harsh joke, and impressed with his resolution, he sets out alone, with only a little bread and cheese, and feed for his donkey.

Comment

The scene of Sancho's departure from Barataria is very forceful and touching, and there is a sense in which the presentation of his brief governorship - mock-heroic preparation, essentially comic, though surprisingly laudable exercise of the new profession, change to a serious tone in anticipation of the **denouement**, confession of error based on pride, and repentance - parallels in its principal outlines the genesis, practice, and renunciation by Don Quixote of his chivalric mission, the final stage of which is thus foreshadowed.

CHAPTER 54

While preparations for the duel are underway at the castle, Sancho proceeds on his way there, meeting a group of foreign pilgrims on their way to Santiago. One of the groups proves to be an acquaintance from Sancho's village, a Moor who has returned to Spain in disguise to smuggle out his buried treasure, defying the edicts which had forced all the Moors into exile from Spain between 1609 and 1613.

The Moor, whose name is Ricote, praises the royal decision to exile the Moors, admitting that there were many false converts who jeopardized the Catholic faith, recounts his travels in exile, and offers Sancho two hundred crowns to help him recover his treasure. Sancho refuses, and the pilgrims continue on their way.

CHAPTER 55

Continuing on his way, Sancho turns off the road at nightfall to look for a place to sleep, and falls, donkey and all, into a deep pit whose walls are too steep to allow him to climb out. Bitterly remarking on his luck, and contrasting it with Don Quixote's delightful adventure in the cave of Montesinos, Sancho manages to make his way along an underground passage until finally he perceives light filtering down from above. Meanwhile, Don Quixote has ridden out to practice for the battle which awaits him, and, hearing cries for help, discovers Sancho still stranded in the pit below. With the aid of ropes, Sancho and his donkey are finally pulled to the surface, and he tells the duke of his decision to renounce the governorship.

CHAPTER 56

The day of the battle arrives, and as the ceremonies which precede the encounter between Don Quixote and his adversary are taking place, the duke's lackey, Tosilos, whom the duke has substituted for the real seducer, now fled to Flanders, catches sight of Doña Rodriguez's daughter. He falls instantly in love with her, and concedes the victory to Don Quixote, much to the duke's irritation. When he removes his helmet, Doña Rodriguez protests that it is the wrong man, but her daughter gladly accepts the offer of marriage. Sancho attributes the transformation to enchantment, and it is decided that the marriage will be postponed while the matter is investigated.

Comment

This is, of course, another case of the tables being turned on the tricksters. The reader should also note how the fortunes of Don Quixote and Sancho have independently varied during this phase of the novel. When Sancho was at the height of his success as governor, his master was suffering the humiliation of torn stockings and the shame and disfigurement of the episode of the cats - a pathetic reduction of the victory over the lions. Now, however, Sancho has fallen from his lofty position, recognizing the folly of his pride, and Don Quixote is victorious once again.

CHAPTER 57

Sancho and Don Quixote prepare to leave the duke and duchess, and the squire cries as he reads Teresa's letter, thinking of her dashed hopes. As they are leaving, Altisidora appears and recites a poem reproaching Don Quixote for his unresponsiveness and asking for the return of some kerchiefs and garters which she alleges he has. Sancho turns up the kerchiefs, and Altisidora remembers that she is wearing the garters, and the two are finally able to depart.

CHAPTER 58

As they set out, Don Quixote expresses his relief at their being on their own again with some remarks in praise of liberty, and Sancho reveals that the duke has given him two hundred crowns for the trip. They then encounter a group of men bearing four altar pieces with images of Saint George, Saint Martin, Saint James (San Diego Matamoros) and Saint Paul, and Don Quixote explains to Sancho who each of them is, alluding to their most famous exploits. He concludes by remarking that they all also followed the profession of arms. "The only difference between them and me is that they, being saints, waged a holy warfare, while I fight after the manner of men. They conquered Heaven by force of arms, for Heaven suffered violence; but, up to now, I do not know what I have won with all the hardships I have endured. However, if my lady Dulcinea were but free of those that she is suffering, it may be that my fortunes would improve, and with a sounder mind I should be able to tread a better path than the one I follow at present."

Comment

I have quoted this passage directly because of its obvious significance as the clearest indication of Don Quixote's intimate consciousness that something is wrong with his life. That phase of the knight's career which Unamuno has called the via crucis of Don Quixote, culminating in definitive defeat, is now beginning.

As they ride on, Sancho remarks that he cannot see what Altisidora found so irresistible about Don Quixote, since he is certainly not handsome. Don Quixote replies that if a man is chaste, straightforward, generous, and well-bred, and is not actually ugly, he may well be loved.

They suddenly come upon a group of people on an outing in the woods, dressed as shepherds and preparing to entertain themselves by reciting eclogues by Garcilaso and Camões. They have all read the first part of Don Quixote, and welcome the pair into their midst. After lunch, Don Quixote vows to sustain for two days the supremacy of beauty of the ladies in the party, excepting of course, Dulcinea, against the claims of all comers on the royal highway to Saragossa. He has no sooner taken up his position on the road, however, when he and Sancho and their mounts are trampled by a herd of bulls which sweeps down the road. They pick themselves up, and "with more shame than pleasure," they continue on their way.

CHAPTER 59

Don Quixote is deeply depressed as they ride on, and Sancho attempts to revive his sagging spirits, turning a deaf ear, nevertheless, to his master's pleas that he get on with the lashing which is to effect the disenchantment of Dulcinea.

They stop for the night at an inn, and when Don Quixote overhears his names in conversation in the next room, he calls to the men who are conversing and they enter his room and show him a copy of Avellaneda's apocryphal second part of Don Quixote. The knight leaves through the book and criticizes the insults in the prologue, an Aragonese tendency to omit articles, and a mistake as to Teresa's name. He consents to dine with the two gentlemen, and brings them up to date on his activities, refusing to look at Avellaneda's book again. When he mentions that he is on his way to Saragossa, one of the men remarks that Avellaneda has included an account of his participation in the jousts there. Don Quixote decides not to set foot in Saragossa, and thus demonstrate clearly the apocryphal nature of the book.

CHAPTER 60

Exasperated by Sancho's unwillingness to lash himself to accomplish the disenchantment of Dulcinea, Don Quixote awakens him one night while they are camped on the way to Barcelona and attempts to administer the lashes himself. They struggle, and Sancho pins his master to the ground, making him promise never again to try to whip him. The two then discover the bodies of several bandits hanging from some nearby trees, and find themselves surrounded by another band of robbers led by Roque Guinart, who has heard of Don Quixote and his adventures. No sooner has Roque arrived, giving orders to his men not to rob Don Quixote and Sancho, than a young woman named Claudia Jerónima rides up seeking Roque's aid. She tells of having shot her former fiance as he was on his way to marry another girl, and asks Roque for protection. He accompanies her to the scene of the crime, and with his dying breath, the fiance reveals that Claudia was mistaken, and that he remains faithful to her in death. The repentant girl arranges for Roque to take her to a convent to finish out her life as a nun. Roque's bandits hold up a stagecoach, and the bandit leader demonstrates both his generosity and the strict discipline with which he governs his men.

Comment

Roque Guinart is a historical figure whom Cervantes had praised in his interlude The Cave of Salamanca. He was a major figure in the politically oriented banditry which plagued Catalonia in the early 17th century.

CHAPTER 61

Roque accompanies Don Quixote part of the way and sends a messenger ahead to tell his friends in Barcelona that the knight and his squire will soon arrive. When the pair reach the coast at Barcelona, seeing the ocean for the first time, they are met with a great military display arranged by Roque's friends, but their triumphal entry into the city is marred by the malice of a group of boys who put burrs under the tails of Rocinante and Sancho's donkey, causing them to buck and throw their riders to the ground.

CHAPTER 62

The knight and his squire are guests in Barcelona of Don Antonio Moreno, a rich nobleman. Don Quixote is taken on a ride through the city, unaware of a sign on his back which says "This is Don Quixote de la Mancha." His pleasure at being recognized by all is mitigated by a harsh rebuke which he receives from a Castilian in the streets who tells him he is crazy and advises him to go home. At a dance in Don Antonio's home, the knight ends up sitting down exhausted on the dance floor, after a concerted attack on his chastity by two ladies who flirt and dance with him incessantly.

He is shown a bust on a pedestal purported by Don Antonio to be an enchanted head which answers questions. The answers come in reality through a channel into the head from the room below, but Don Quixote never discovers the truth, and reveals his continuing preoccupation with the adventure of the Cave of Montesinos by asking again if it was true or only a dream. The head responds, as did Master Pedro, that the **episode** had a little of everything, and in answer to further questions, it indicates that Dulcinea's enchantment will be undone in due time. We are told that the Inquisition later ordered the head destroyed, as it was an encouragement to superstition. The chapter closes with a visit by Don Quixote to a printing shop, where he disparages the practice of translating works from other romance languages into Spanish. Seeing that they are printing Avellaneda's Quixote, he leaves the shop in disgust.

CHAPTER 63

Don Quixote visits the galleys in the port, and Sancho, who is astounded at all the strange sights he sees there, is badly frightened when he is suddenly passed hand-over-hand down the banks of oarsmen on one of the ships. An alarm sounds abruptly, and in the subsequent skirmish with a Moorish frigate, two of the Spanish soldiers are killed and the Moorish vessel is captured.

When the captain of the captured ship is about to be executed, it is discovered that she is a beautiful young girl, and she narrates her adventures as a Spanish Moor converted to Christianity who has brought the ship to the coast with the intention of getting ashore to arrange the rescue of her Christian fiance, a captive in Algiers. From among the crowd of onlookers, a man steps forward to reveal that he is her father, Sancho's friend Ricote. The general in command pardons the girl, whose name is Ana Félix, and plans are made for the rescue of her fiance, Don Gregorio.

CHAPTER 64

Ana Félix is warmly received as a guest in Don Antonio's house, and Don Quixote offers to go himself to Africa and rescue Don Gregorio if the plan involving the aid of a Spanish renegade does not succeed. One morning while Don Quixote is riding on the beach in full armor, he is abruptly challenged by another man armed for battle who throws down an arrogant challenge to single combat over whose lady is the more beautiful, identifying himself as the Knight of the White Moon, and stipulating that if Don Quixote loses he must agree to retire to his village for one year. In a sober and measured reply, Don Quixote accepts the principal conditions of the duel, and the two knights rush headlong at one another. At the moment of impact, the Knight of the White Moon raises his lance, but Don Quixote is nevertheless thrown violently from Rocinante. Holding his lance at Don Quixote's throat the Knight of the White Moon threatens to run Quixote through if he does not acknowledge the supremacy of his lady. Don Quixote replies as follows: "Dulcinea del Toboso is the most beautiful woman in the world and I the most unhappy knight upon the face of the earth. It is not right that my weakness should serve to defraud the truth. Drive home your lance, O knight, and take my life since you already have deprived me of my honor."

The Knight of the White Moon refuses to take his life, however, and asks only that Don Quixote agree to retire to his village for a year, and this the defeated knight accepts. Sancho is brokenhearted, not knowing what to say or do. Don Quixote is carried back to town to recuperate, and Don Antonio follows the victor to find out who he is.

CHAPTER 65

Don Antonio discovers that Sansón Carrasco is the Knight of the White Moon, and reproaches him for what he has done, saying: "Do you not see that the benefit accomplished by restoring Don Quixote to his senses can never equal the pleasure others derive from his vagaries?" Sansón returns to Castile, and Don Quixote spends six days recovering from his fall, with Sancho attempting to dispel the melancholy into which his defeat has plunged him.

News is brought of the successful liberation of Don Gregorio, and Don Diego leaves for the court, to negotiate permission for the Moorish Ana Félix to remain in Spain, on the same day that Don Quixote and Sancho begin their sad journey home.

CHAPTER 66

Don Quixote laments anew as he passes the scene of his defeat, and Sancho urges resignation, citing his own reaction to the loss of the governorship. Don Quixote remarks that he cannot attribute his defeat to Fortune, for "each man is the architect of his own fortune. I was the architect of mine, but I did not observe the necessary prudence, and as a result my presumptuousness has brought me to a sorry end."

As they continue on their way, Sancho gives a tongue-in-cheek suggestion to a group of men who are trying to resolve a discrepancy in weight between two contestants in a foot race which dissolves the dispute into an offer of drinks for the knight and his squire at a nearby tavern, but Don Quixote declines.

They next meet the duke's lackey, Tosilos, who tells them that the duke had him beaten for having refused to meet Don Quixote in combat, and that Doña Rodriguez's daughter has entered a convent. Don Quixote is irritated with Sancho for refusing to agree that Tosilos is enchanted, and leaves the two alone to eat and drink together. During the conversation Sancho again admits that Don Quixote is crazy, and tells Tosilos of his master's recent defeat.

CHAPTER 67

Don Quixote sits down alone under a tree, preoccupied with thoughts of Dulcinea's disenchantment and of his forced retirement. When Sancho returns, his master announces that he has decided to live out his year of retirement in the role of a shepherd like those in the pastoral novels, calling himself the shepherd Quijotiz, and asks Sancho to join him. Sancho takes up the idea enthusiastically and they begin to plan their new existence, deciding to invite the curate, Sansón, and the barber to join them. As happens frequently in their dialogues, Sancho begins to pile up one proverb on another, and Don Quixote stops him, using a proverb himself in his rebuke to indicate that it is the lack of appropriateness of Sancho's proverbs to which he objects.

CHAPTER 68

It was their proximity to the place where they had previously encountered the feigned Arcadia which suggested the pastoral role to Don Quixote, and as they were before trampled by the herd of bulls, they are now overrun by a herd of pigs being driven to market. Don Quixote accepts this humiliation as a logical concomitant of his defeat. He spends the night lamenting his fate, and sings a sad song which he has composed. The following morning they are surrounded by about fifteen armed men who, to their astonishment, march them off to the castle of the duke and duchess.

CHAPTER 69

They are dragged into the castle courtyard, which is ablaze with torches, to confront an elaborate scene - the body of the beautiful Altisidora laid out on a bier in the center, the duke and duchess seated on a stage to one side, next to two kingly figures, with seats also provided for Don Quixote and Sancho. The two imposing figures prove to be Minos and Rhadamanthus, the mythological judges of Hell, and they reveal that to restore Altisidora to life Sancho must be slapped, pricked and pinched by six duennas. The squire quite naturally launches a vigorous protest, but finally submits, at Don Quixote's urging, though he draws the line when his master remarks that this would be a good time to give himself a few lashes for Dulcinea, while "the virtue in you is ripe." Altisidora gets up, as if awaking from a faint, and thanks Sancho, promising to give him six used chemises as a reward for bringing her back to life.

CHAPTER 70

Sancho and Don Quixote are accommodated for the night, and Cid Hamete reveals how the duke, through Sansón Carrasco, had kept apprised of the knight's activities and whereabouts, and was thus able to stage the elaborate **episode** of the resuscitation of Altisidora. The Moorish author remarks that "it is his personal opinion that the jesters were as crazy as their victims and that the duke and duchess were not two fingers' breadth removed from being fools when they went to so much trouble to make sport of the foolish." The following morning Altisidora visits the knight and his squire in their room, and Cervantes uses her brief account of what it was like at the gates of Hell, where she lay for two days after dying of love for Don Quixote, to poke fun at certain extravagances of contemporary fashions in clothing, and to disparage once again Avellaneda's Quixote, which the devils are using for a football. Don Quixote cuts short Altisidora's continued reproaches by affirming once again that he loves only Dulcinea, and the girl is so stung by his rebuff that for a moment she drops her pose and angrily admits that it has all been an act, and she couldn't care less for Don Quixote.

CHAPTER 71

Altisidora fails to give Sancho the chemises she had promised him, and as they ride out from the castle, Sancho laments the curse that his healing virtues have proved to be, contrasting his luck with that of the many doctors who get paid for killing people. To this, Don Quixote replies that he will gladly pay whatever price Sancho thinks just for the lashes necessary to disenchant Dulcinea. Sancho accepts the offer with alacrity, and that same evening he beings to lash himself. Don Quixote has remained a little distance away, and after six or eight lashes Sancho begins to lash the trees instead, as his master counts the blows.

Don Quixote forces Sancho to stop after more than a thousand lashes, lest he kill himself, and they lie down to sleep. They arrive the next day at an inn and are given a room decorated with crude leather hangings depicting the abduction of Helen of Troy and the desertion of Dido by Aeneas, which leads Sancho to remark that soon their own adventures will doubtless decorate every inn, tavern, and barbershop. They plan to go out in the woods again that evening so that Sancho can continue flogging himself amidst the trees which he says keep him company and help him bear the pain.

CHAPTER 72

While at the inn awaiting nightfall, Don Quixote chances to meet Don Álvaro Tarfe, a character from Avellaneda's apocryphal Quixote, and after conversing about the inaccuracy of Avellaneda's characterization of the knight and his squire, Don Álvaro signs a notarized statement to the effect that he had not previously met Don Quixote, who was not the man represented in Avellaneda's sequel. Don Quixote and Sancho spend that night in the woods as planned, and the following night Sancho finishes giving the trees the 3,300 lashes necessary to disenchant Dulcinea. The next day they come in sight of their village, and Sancho kneels and exclaims: "Open your eyes, O beloved homeland, and behold your son, Sancho Panza, returning to you. If he does not come back very rich, he comes well flogged. Open your arms and receive also your other son, Don Quixote, who returns vanquished by the arm of another but a victor over himself; and this, so I have been told, is the greatest victory that could be desired."

CHAPTER 73

As they enter the village, they hear two boys argue over a lost birdcage, and a rabbit pursued by a group of hunters takes refuge under Sancho's donkey. Don Quixote takes both incidents as bad omens for Dulcinea's future. Sancho goes off with Teresa, and Don Quixote tells the curate and Sansón Carrasco of his defeat and of his plans for a pastoral life during the year of enforced idleness. They agree wholeheartedly with his plans, but Don Quixote's niece and the housekeeper try to dissuade him.

CHAPTER 74

Don Quixote falls ill with a fever and despite the attempts of his friends to revive his spirits with talk of their prospective pastoral life, the doctor's diagnosis is that he is dying of melancholy. Awakening from a long sleep, Don Quixote suddenly thanks God for having returned him to sanity. Over the protests of Sancho and the others, who try desperately once again to interest him in their pastoral plans, Don Quixote denounces the novels of chivalry, asserting that he is no longer Don Quixote, but Alonso Quijano, once called for his mode of life "The Good." He asks that a scribe be summoned to draw up his will while the curate confesses him. His will specifies that Sancho is to keep the money he has been carrying for his master; and he asks Sancho to forgive him for having made him, too, seem mad. Sancho begs him not to let himself die, and Don Quixote replies with a proverb: "In last year's nests, there are no birds this year." The will next specifies that his estate will go to his niece, excepting certain monies for the housekeeper, but stipulates that the estate must go to charity should she marry any man who knows anything at all about novels of chivalry. The final item in the will instructs his executors, the curate and Sansón Carrasco, that should they meet the author of the false sequel to Don Quixote, they are to beg his pardon on the part of the deceased for having been responsible for his writing so much foolishness.

Don Quixote is semi-conscious for the next three days, and the household is in turmoil, though in spite of everything, "the niece continued to eat her meals, the housekeeper had her drink, and Sancho was in good spirits; for this business of inheriting property effaces or mitigates the sorrow which the heir ought to feel and causes him to forget."

At the end of that time he dies, and the novel closes with an epitaph written by Sansón Carrasco and with Cid Hamete's farewell to his pen, in which he warns against any further continuation of Don Quixote's adventures by other authors, saying: "For me alone Don Quixote was born and I for him; it was for him to act, for me to write, and we two are one ... " His final statement reiterates once again his purpose in writing the novel: "I have had no other purpose than to arouse the abhorrence of mankind toward those false and nonsensical stories to be met within the books of chivalry, which thanks to this tale of the genuine Don Quixote, are already tottering and without a doubt are doomed to fall."

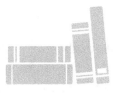

DON QUIXOTE

Question: What justification can be given for Cervantes' inclusion of the interpolated stories in Part I?

Answer: Cervantes himself reflects contemporary criticism of the inclusion of "The Tale of Foolish Curiosity" and "The Captive's Tale," in Part I, and indicates that he will avoid such digressions in Part II, restricting himself to **episodes** more intimately linked with the adventures of Don Quixote and Sancho (II, 44). Although a number of critics share this view, many have pointed out that these stories perform important functions in the novel. Anselmo, in "The Tale of Foolish Curiosity," represents another case of "madness," but one diametrically opposed to that of Don Quixote. If the knight is eminently a man of faith, who scorns empirical verification of the principles he lives by, Anselmo represents the opposite extreme of rational empiricism: everything, including his wife's chastity, must be proved or tested. Cervantes may be saying that neither of these extreme positions is viable. "The Captive's Tale" is thematically justified as an exemplification of the life of Arms extolled by Don Quixote in his Discourse on Arms and Learning, with the captive's brother the judge exemplifying

Learning. In any event, both stories have the effect of any "play within a play," that is, they enhance the illusion of reality of the main narrative, by establishing a plane of "literature" with respect to which the activities of Don Quixote represent "reality."

Question: Discuss the relationship of Don Quixote to the literary **genres** and **conventions** of Cervantes' time.

Answer: The principal kinds of prose fiction current in Cervantes' time were several: the Italian novella or short story, the novels of chivalry, the pastoral novel, and the picaresque. All of these were used by Cervantes in writing his masterpiece. "The Tale of Foolish Curiosity" is set in Italy, has Italian sources, and is written very much in the style of the Italian novella. The novels of chivalry are of course basic to Cervantes' creation, as the cause of Don Quixote's madness and the pattern for his existence as knight-errant. It is the contrast between his chivalric fantasies and the real, local, and contemporary world of the picaresque in which Don Quixote must live that provides the basic vehicle for Cervantes' expression. The elements of **irony** and **satire** which are central to the picaresque are also of prime importance in *Don Quixote*. The clear, simple style of Cervantes' narrative, and the importance of proverbs and slang also owe much to their development in the picaresque, while the altisonant and archaic style of Don Quixote's speech is based upon that of the novels of chivalry.

The pastoral novel, though less centrally important in *Don Quixote*, provides the style and content for the **episode** of Marcela and Grisóstomo. Cervantes' masterful assimilation of all these conventional **genres** makes *Don Quixote* one of the stylistically richest novels ever written.

Question: What is meant by the "Quixotization" of Sancho and the "Sanchification" of Don Quixote? Answer: These terms, first introduced by Salvador de Madariaga (see Bibliography), characterize the interpenetration between the two protagonists and the deep reciprocal effects they have on one another. Madariaga and others have challenged the traditional stereotyping of the knight and his squire as, respectively, the idealist and the realist, pointing out that they both are mixtures from the beginning (Sancho's ideal is the island), and stressing the importance in Part II of Sancho's increasing fantasy and his master's increasing **realism**. These changes are reflected in both attitudes and style, and are easily documented.

Question: What **episodes** would you select as among the most significant in the novel, and why?

Answer: Among those **episodes** to which critics of the novel have devoted most attention are the Cave of Montesinos (II, 23), Maese Pedro's puppet show (II, 26), and the "enchantment" of Dulcinea by Sancho (II, 10).

The **episode** of the Cave of Montesinos is of capital importance for a number of reasons. First, it is an amazingly perceptive re-creation of a dream, with its bizarre mixture of the most prosaic elements of ordinary reality, including bits and pieces of Don Quixote's recent experience, the knight's chivalric fantasies and wish-fulfillment, and the incongruous and grotesque elements so characteristic of dreams. It is also the only occasion when Don Quixote's mind is free from the constraints of everyday reality - that is, it is pure creation, and not transformation of some existing reality with which he is confronted. Finally, the ambiguity with which Cervantes has Cid Hamete Benengeli surround the adventure - he is unable to say whether or not Don Quixote made it all up - simply underlines the reader's overall uncertainty as to how far Don Quixote is conscious of his transformation of reality.

As George Haley (see Bibliography) has pointed out, Maese Pedro's Puppet Show re-creates in a specific **episode** all of the complex relations between the reader, the author, and his intermediaries, which exist in the novel as a whole. Other critics have pointed out how finely drawn in this **episode** is the line between Don Quixote's sanity and his madness, since he passes in an instant from a detached and critical appraisal of the implausibility of the show to active participation in its events, as if it were part of his reality.

Sancho's enchantment of Dulcinea has profound psychological consequences for Don Quixote, since Sancho is now using his master's fantasies to gain his own ends, and forcing him to play the game on Sancho's own terms. The disenchantment of his lady is a central preoccupation for Don Quixote throughout the rest of the novel, and when the Duke and Duchess contrive to make Sancho the agent of her disenchantment, Don Quixote's essential powerlessness is brought forcefully home to him, and this influences his subsequent return to sanity.

Question: What are some of the fundamental differences between Part I and Part II?

Answer: As indicated in the answer to the preceding question, the **episodes** in Part II have consistently aroused much more critical interest than those in Part I, because of their greater subtlety and complexity. The interpenetration between Sancho and Don Quixote, the telling intrusions of reality upon Don Quixote's formerly impregnable stronghold of chivalric fantasy, the introduction of characters who have already read of Don Quixote when they meet him - these are all facets which distinguish Part II from Part I. It has also been pointed out that Don Quixote's existence in Part II is much more social than his former life of isolated adventures on the road.

Question: Discuss Cervantes' possible motives in writing *Don Quixote*.

Answer: Critics have adduced evidence which suggests that Cervantes' original intent was to write a short, satirical piece containing roughly the material which now constitutes Chapters I-VIII of Part I. Certainly one cannot ignore the indications in the Prologue to Part I that the book "aims at no more than destroying the authority and influence which books of chivalry have in the world," echoed in the approbations to Part II, and reiterated in the final chapter of the book, but most readers have felt that once his project was underway, Cervantes realized the much more complex potential of his material, and that Part II represents a second major expansion of his consciousness of the possibilities that he had created in Part I. It is difficult to imagine a Cervantes unconscious of the implications of his work for the future of prose fiction, for an understanding of the limitations and inadequacy of any single perspective on reality, and for many of the other fascinating issues raised in the development of his masterpiece.

Question: What techniques and perspectives of the modern novel are initiated or developed by Cervantes?

Answer: Here again, the prospects are limitless. Lionel Trilling has said that "all prose fiction is a variation of *Don Quixote*." The **protagonist** as anti-hero, the centrality of character, the pervasive ironic perspective, the authorial detachment and dissociation, the persistent ambiguity, the interplay of stylistic levels, the relationship of literature to life, the perspectivism, the essential verisimilitude, the conflict between the real and the ideal, or reality and illusion - these and many other aspects of *Don Quixote*, some developed in part in the early picaresque, are all basic to the subsequent development of the modern novel.

Question: Discuss the bases for the humor of *Don Quixote*.

Answer: There are many levels of humor in the novel, from the subtleties of stylistic contrasts and clever puns through broad slapstick comedy, and on to the grotesque, but at the roots of much Cervantine humor there often lies some basic contrast or incongruity. Don Quixote's expectations over against recalcitrant reality, or, a variation, the knight over against his squire, lofty chivalric rhetoric over against the common and vulgar language of peasants and the slang of thieves - Cervantes exploits all of the possibilities of these confrontations, at times with the comic release of the explosive fulfillment of the reader's expectations, at others with a surprising twist which overturns one's convictions as to what the outcome of a particular misadventure will be.

Question: Discuss some of the more important secondary characters in *Don Quixote*.

Answer: Pero Pérez, the curate, and Maritornes, the serving-girl at Juan Palomeque's inn, are among the most interesting secondary characters from Part I, aside from the principals in the interpolated stories, and Sansón Carrasco, Don Diego de Miranda - the man in the Green Overcoat - and Ginés de Pasamonte - Maese Peter - are among those who stand out in Part II.

The curate is the instrument of Don Quixote's return home in Part I, and Sansón Carrasco is the agent in Part II, and a comparison of the two reveals something of the difference between the two Parts. The curate is clearly Cervantes' spokesman in literary matters, as evidenced in the examination of Don Quixote's library (I, 6) and the discussions with the canon of Toledo (I, 47–48). Sansón Carrasco is presented much less sympathetically, especially after his defeat by Don Quixote (II, 14) when his motive for seeking to defeat the knight has changed from pity to revenge.

Maritornes is a grotesque figure who is yet humanized by her charity toward Sancho after the blanket-tossing. Evidence of the attraction she holds for the reader is found in her fusion with the vague figure of Aldonza in incarnations of Dulcinea which appear in such derivative works as *Man of La Mancha*.

Don Diego de Miranda is the focus of a central critical disagreement on the interpretation of the novel. Those who tend to exalt Don Quixote as the hero as well as the **protagonist** of the work see Don Diego as somewhat vain and prosaic, while those who stress Cervantes' castigation of the knight see him as an ethical norm.

Ginés de Pasamonte, the galley-slave and author of his own picaresque autobiography in Part I, reappears in Part II disguised as Master Pedro, the illusionist who mounts the famous puppet show of the liberation of Melisendra.

DON QUIXOTE

AREAS FOR RESEARCH AND CRITICISM

. . . .

1. Cervantes' portrayal of contemporary Spanish society

2. An appraisal of English translations of *Don Quixote*

3. The incorporation of contemporary historical, cultural, and political events into *Don Quixote*

4. Autobiographical elements in *Don Quixote*

5. Literary theory in *Don Quixote* and its relation to Cervantes' practice

6. Time in *Don Quixote*

7. Authorial commentary in *Don Quixote*

8. Description in *Don Quixote*

9. The interpolated stories in Part I

10. *Man of La Mancha* and *Don Quixote*: comparison and contrast

DON QUIXOTE

The problem of the reader's attitude toward *Don Quixote* is perhaps unparalleled in the history of literature, both in duration and in extent. Cervantes' first public saw in *Don Quixote* only a book of entertainment, a **parody** of the novels of chivalry. The second stage seems to have been one of identification with Don Quixote in his folly. Motteux could say, in 1700, that "every man has something of Don Quixote in his Humour, some darling Dulcinea of his thoughts, that sets him very often upon mad adventures." Dr. Johnson remarked, in 1750, that "very few readers, amidst their mirth or pity can deny that they have admitted visions of the same kind ... When we pity him, we reflect on our own disappointments; and when we laugh, our hearts inform us that he is not more ridiculous than ourselves, except that he tells what we have only thought." At about the same time, other commentary in England indicates that the shift to the idealization of *Don Quixote* had already begun, In 1739, a friend of Pope's seemed to him "so very a child in true Simplicity of Heart, that I love him; as he loves Don Quixote, for the most Moral and Reasoning Madman in the world." In 1754, finally, Sarah Fielding could say: "To travel through a whole work only to laugh at the chief companion allotted us, is an unsupportable burthen. And we should imagine that the reading of that incomparable piece of humor left us by Cervantes, can give but little pleasure to those persons who can extract no other entertainment or emolument from it than laughing at Don Quixote's reveries, and sympathizing in the malicious joy of his tormentors ... That strong and beautiful representation of human nature, exhibited in Don Quixote's madness in one point, and extraordinary good sense in every other, is indeed very much thrown away on such readers as consider him only as the object of their mirth."

These notes of pity and admiration constitute the seeds of the Romantic interpretation of *Don Quixote* which was to dominate 19th-century criticism. Don Quixote is increasingly seen as the "knight of the faith" who embodies the spiritual force of human aspirations, being "superior in moral fiber to the people who flout him." This is perhaps still the popular view of the book, though 20th-century criticism has tended increasingly to return to earlier points of view which see the knight, in spite of his nobility, as the butt of Cervantes' satire.

The range of viewpoints has indeed been broad in this century. Cervantes has been seen as a reactionary (Cesare De Lollis), a non-conformist (Américo Castro), a relativist (Jean Cassou), a revolutionary (Pavel Novitsky, A. Gerchunoff), an Erasmian (Ludwig Pfandl), man of the Middle Ages (Mario Casella), Baroque man (Marcel Bataillon), counter-reformationist (Helmut Hatzfeld), and iconoclast (Arthur Efron). This enormous diversity of opinion testifies to the extreme complexity of *Don Quixote*, and to its propensity to suggest much more than it actually says. This situation obviously argues persuasively against attempting a judgment of the novel based upon anything less than a full and careful reading of the complete text.

Another aspect of 20th-century criticism has been its increasing tendency to examine the structure, narrative technique, and style of the novel as new methods of the analysis of fiction have been developed. These kinds of investigation have been aided by the publication of excellent critical editions by Francisco Rodríguez Marín and Rudolph Schevill.

Finally, it can be said, as Helmut Hatzfeld has pointed out, that the most recent criticism tends to emphasize the pitfalls of the Romantic identification of Cervantes with his **protagonist**, and to take seriously the implications of Cervantes' statement that he is the "stepfather" of Don Quixote, and not the father. (I, Prologue).

BIBLIOGRAPHY

Allen, John J. *Don Quixote: Hero or Fool?* Gainesville, Florida: University of Florida Press, 1969.

A study in narrative technique, attempting to indicate the bases for conflicting interpretations of the work and to elucidate Cervantes' ethical orientation of the reader.

Auden, W.H. See under Nelson.

Auerbach, Erich. See under Barbera.

Barbera, Raymond E., ed. *Cervantes: A Critical Trajectory.* Boston: Mirage Press, 1971.

A collection of translations of critical articles, including the following:

"*Hamlet* and *Don Quixote*," by Ivan Turgenev.

One of the classic essays in Quixote criticism. Turgenev sees the contrasting figures of *Hamlet* and *Don Quixote* as exemplars of two fundamental aspects of human nature: the rational skeptical, haughty, indecisive, aesthetically oriented and ultimately egocentric Hamlet, as opposed to the man of faith, commitment, altruism, and perseverance embodied in Don Quixote.

"The Enchanted Dulcinea," by Erich Auerbach.

An interpretation of the novel as "a comedy in which well-founded reality holds madness up to ridicule," based upon a detailed examination of Chapter 10, Part II, the "enchantment" of Dulcinea by Sancho.

The collection also includes articles by Coleridge, Heine, Unamuno (q.v.), Ortega y Gasset (q.v.), Pirandello, Mandariaga (q.v.), W. P. Ker, Mario Casella, Américo Castro (q.v.), Pedro Salinas, and Wyndham Lewis.

Benardete, M. J., and Angel Flores, eds. *The Anatomy of "Don Quixote." A Symposium.* Ithaca: The Dragon Press, 1932. (Reprinted in 1969 by Kennikat Press, Port Washington, N. Y.) A collection of translations of critical articles including the following:

"The Genesis," by Ramón Menéndez-Pidal.

The **exposition** of the thesis that Don Quixote's first sally, and thus the initial intent of the novel, is based upon an obscure anonymous dramatic interlude: *The Interlude of the Ballads*, written about 1597, and an examination of the direction and significance of Cervantes' subsequent change in intention.

"The Style," by Helmut Hatzfeld.

Stressing the rich stylistic variety of Don Quixote, Hatzfeld identifies central motifs and examines their embodiment in a series of dominant stylistic devices such as antithesis, contrary-to-fact conditional constructions, puns and word-play, and hyperbole. The article sketches the central points of the author's book "Don Quixote" als Wortkunstwerk.

The collection also includes articles by A. Morel-Fatio and Turgenev (q.v.).

- *Cervantes Across the Centuries*. New York: Dryden Press, 1947.

A collection of translation of critical articles, including the following:

"The Composition of *Don Quixote*," by Joaquín Casalduero.

A detailed **exposition** of Casalduero's thesis of the Baroque circular structure of *Don Quixote*, identifying leitmotifs and **themes** around which the book is organized, the article presents the central points of the author's book: Sentido y forma del "Quijote".

"Incarnation in *Don Quixote*," by Américo Castro.

Though Castro's profoundly provocative El pensamiento de Cervantes has not been translated into English, this combination of translations of two of his subsequent articles offers a sample of the thought of this very influential critic. Castro delineates the development of the principal characters in Cervantes' masterpiece as embodying individualizing responses to outside "incitements" which change both their goals and their conduct. He also stresses the "elusive" technique of Cervantes, with his many conscious omissions, and an "extremist" style which focuses on heights and depths, rather than a middle ground. Finally, he explores in detail the significance of the written word for Cervantes (the novels of chivalry, for *Don Quixote*), and affirms that, for Cervantes, "reality is always an aspect of the experience of the person who is living it."

"*Don Quixote* and *Moby Dick*," by Harry Levin.

After tracing the influence of *Don Quixote* in America, Mr. Levin explores the relationship of Melville's thought to that of Cervantes.

The collection also includes sixteen other articles, among them a series on Cervantes' influence in England, France, Germany and Russia.

Blanco Aguinaga, Carlos. See under Nelson.

Brenan, Gerald. "Cervantes," in *The Literature of the Spanish People*. New York: Meridian Books, 1957.

A central element in this essay is the examination and interpretation of the **episode** of the Cave of Montesinos (II, 23). Brenan also offers original insight into the nature of the relationship between Don Quixote and Sancho.

Casalduero, Joaquín. See under Benardete

Castro, Américo. See under Benardete

Efron, Arthur. *Don Quixote and the Dulcineated World*.

Austin: University of Texas Press, 1971.

Probably the most radical interpretation of *Don Quixote* ever, this book attempts to show that Cervantes not only "laughed Spain's chivalry away," as Byron claimed, but that he mounted an attack on marriage, chastity, and other ideals of his time. "Dulcineism means the living of life in accord with the prescribed ideals of the received culture." The hardest of the "hard" critics.

Girard, René. *Deceit, Desire and the Novel*, trans. Yvonne Freccero. Baltimore: The Johns Hopkins Press, 1965. Girard's concept of "triangular" or mediated" desire is proposed as central to understanding the fiction of Cervantes, Stendhal, Flaubert, and Dostoyevsky. The seeds of the study by Efron (q.v.) are here, since desire mediated artificially through some model (Amadis of Gaul, for *Don Quixote*) is shown by all these novelists, in Girard's view, to have replaced the direct, spontaneous desire which should rightly animate human activity.

Haley, George. "The Narrator in *Don Quixote*." Modern Language Notes 80 (1965), 145–65.

An illuminating **exposition** of the fundamental relationships between the author, his intermediaries Cid Hamete and the Moorish translator, and the characters, through an analysis of the analogous relationships in Master Pedro's puppet show (II, 22).

Hatzfeld, Helmut. See under Benardete.

Levin, Harry. See under Nelson

Madariaga, Salvador de. "Don Quixote." *An Introductory Essay in Psychology*. Oxford: Clarendon Press, 1935.

A small but important book which has suggested much that later critics have elaborated upon, especially the Sanchification of *Don Quixote*, and the Quixotization of Sancho.

Mandel, Oscar. "The Function of the Norm in *Don Quixote*." Modern Philology 55 (1958), 154–63.

The "Gentleman in the Green Overcoat" (II, 16) is proposed as an ethical norm for the novel, against which Don Quixote's deviations are to be measured and judged.

Mann, Thomas. See under Nelson.

Menéndez Pidal, Ramón. See under Benardete.

Nelson, Lowry, Jr., ed. *Cervantes*. Englewood Cliffs, N. J.:

Prentice Hall 1969.

A collection of critical articles including the following:

"The Example of Cervantes," by Harry Levin.

Professor Levin identifies the critical achievement of Cervantes in *Don Quixote* as the presentation of "the pattern of art embarrassed by confrontation with nature." **Parody**, explicitly criticizing a mode of literature [the chivalric novels], developed into **satire**, implicitly criticizing a way of life."

"Voyage with Don Quixote," by Thomas Mann.

The novelist's random comments on re-reading *Don Quixote* during a sea voyage. He deals in some detail with the adventure of the Lions ("the climax of the novel"), Camacho's wedding, the adventure of the Braying Aldermen, and the ending, which he finds unsatisfying. He sees the novel as a marvelous reflection of Cervantes' time, and an anticipation of the Romantic's fruitful thoughts about "the weird depths, the trick mirrors and false bottoms of artistic illusion."

"The Ironic Hero: Some Reflections on *Don Quixote*," by W. H. Auden.

In an essay in outline form, Auden characterizes Don Quixote as a Christian Saint, as distinguished from the **Epic** Hero and the Comic Hero.

"Cervantes and the Picaresque Mode: Notes on Two Kinds of Realism," by Carlos Blanco Aguinaga.p A convincing differentiation between the "objective" **realism** of Cervantes, open and prismatic, and the "dogmatic or disillusionist **realism**" of the picaresque, with its single, limited point of view which issues in a closed, **didactic** novel.

Ortega y Gasset, Jose. *Meditations on "Quixote"*, trans. Evelyn Rugg and Diego Marin. New York: W. W. Norton, 1961.

The Spanish philosopher wrote only the "Preliminary" and "First" of his projected "meditations." He discusses the fundamental differences between *Don Quixote* and the **epic**, the question of the nature of reality as posed by Cervantes, and other basic issues.

Predmore, Richard L. *The World of "Don Quixote"*. Cambridge, Mass.: Harvard University Press, 1967.

Contains chapters on the interplay between literature and life in *Don Quixote* and on the question of appearance versus reality. Predmore seeks to establish that Cervantes shows that although reality is often deceptive, the phenomenal world in which the characters live and move is rational and consistent.

_____ *Cervantes*. New York: Dodd, Mead, 1973.

A readable, magnificently illustrated biography which incorporates the essential contributions of all recent work on the life of Cervantes.

Riley, Edward C. *Cervantes' Theory of the Novel*. Oxford: Clarendon Press, 1962.

A major attempt to establish Cervantes' ideas on the novel through an examination of the critical comments of characters in his novels, of contemporary theorists such as the Aristotelian López Pinciano, and of Cervantes' own practice.

_____ "Three Versions of *Don Quixote*." *Modern Language Review* 68 (1973), 807–819.

Professor Riley's latest contribution to the study of Cervantes' novelistic technique is an examination of the interrelationships among Cid Hamete Benengeli's version of Don Quixote's activities ("historical"), the apocryphal Part II, by Avellaneda (spurious), and the flattering, romanticized account which Don Quixote believes is being written about him ("poetic"). These three "versions" are related to what other critics have called Cervantes' "perspectivism," that is, to his fictional exemplification of the fact that, in the words of Jorge Luis Borges, "historical truth ... is not what happened; it is what we judge has happened."

Russell, P. E. "Don Quixote as a Funny Book." *Modern Language Review* 64 (1969), 312–26.

A review of pre-romantic European reactions to *Don Quixote* and of the attitudes of Cervantes' contemporaries toward insanity, on the one hand, and toward humor and the comic in literature, on the other. Russell concludes that given the almost unanimous reception of the novel as a comic masterpiece in its first 200 years of existence, and the prevailing attitudes toward and characterizations of the madman, it is difficult not to accept at face value Cervantes' indications that *Don Quixote* is indeed the butt of his humor.

Schevill, Rodolfo. *Cervantes*. New York: Frederick Ungar, 1966. [First ed.: 1919]

A sound, readable biography.

Serrano Plaja, Arturo. *"Magic"* **realism** *in Cervantes: "Don Quixote" as seen through "Tom Sawyer" and "The Idiot,"* trans. Robert S. Rudder. Berkeley: University of California Press, 1970.

An exploration of the commonality between Myshkin, Dostoyevsky's "Idiot," who "takes everything seriously," Tom Sawyer, who lives a game, and Don Quixote, who shares something of both Myshkin's "pure soul" and Tom's role and game playing, and is, in a sense, the father of both.

Spitzer, Leo. "Linguistic Perspectivism in *Don Quixote*." In *Linguistics and Literary History*. Princeton: Princeton University Press, 1948.

Spitzer examines the great variety and instability of names in *Don Quixote*, and related phenomena, to substantiate what he sees as Cervantes' desire to highlight the different aspects under which a character may appear to others. Allied to this "perspectivism" of the novel is Cervantes' glorification of the author as a kind of God-like fixed point which comprehends all the partial perspectives of the participants in the fictional world.

Turgenev, Ivan. See under Barbera.

Unamuno, Miguel de. *Life of Don Quijote and Sancho According to Miguel de Cervantes Saavedra*. New York and London: 1927.

A chapter by chapter commentary in which Unamuno develops his concept of Don Quixote as the Knight of the Faith, whose stance toward the world must be emulated by those who would lead Spain to a renewal of its former greatness, coupled with a disdain for Cervantes, whom the author presents as inferior to his creation.

Van Doren, Mark. *Don Quixote's Profession*. New York: Columbia University Press, 1957.

Van Doren's thesis in this series of lectures is that Don Quixote's real profession is that of actor, not knight-errant. The author stresses, as does Serrano-Plaja (q.v.), the indications of Don Quixote's consciousness of his falsification of reality, and sees the question of what reality really is as central to the novel.

Willis, Raymond S., Jr. *The Phantom Chapters of the "Quixote"*. New York: Hispanic Institute, 1953.

A study of the chapter divisions of *Don Quixote* which proposes that Cervantes' technique is to deliberately overflow and obliterate his own arbitrary division into chapters to highlight the flow of life which he sees as violated by any serious attempt to force it into divisible chronological segments.